ATHLETICS
2013
THE INTERNATIONAL
TRACK AND FIELD ANNUAL

BY PETER MATTHEWS
ASSOCIATION OF
TRACK & FIELD STATISTICIANS

Published by SportsBooks Ltd

Copyright: SportsBooks Limited and Peter Matthews 2013

SportsBooks Limited
1 Evelyn Court
Malvern Road
Cheltenham
GL50 2JR
United Kingdom
Tel: 01242 256755
e-mail   randall@sportsbooks.ltd.uk
Website   www.sportsbooks.ltd.uk

This publication incorporates the ATFS Annual.

Photographs supplied by Mark Shearman, 22 Grovelands Road, Purley, Surrey, CR8 4LA.
Tel: 0208 660 0156: mark@athleticsimages.com

British Library Cataloguing in Publication Data

Athletics: the international track and
field annual – 2013
1. Athletics. Track & Field events –
Serials
1. International athletics annual (London)
796.4'2'05

ISBN 9781907524370

Cover design: Kath Grimshaw

Printed by TJ International

CONTENTS

INTRODUCTION

I HAVE BEEN a sports fan for 60 years, but surely there has never been a sporting year to match 2012. The glorious sporting moments of a generally dismal summer in northern Europe had included a magnificent Wimbledon final and a wondrous win by Bradley Wiggins in the Tour de France before the full splendour of the Olympic Games. These were followed by the Paralympic Games, which so captivated the hearts and minds of the British people, and then the most gripping television spectacle with the Ryder Cup as Europe's players come through in the singles after the inspired Ian Poulter has started the magic with his five successive birdies in the closing four-balls of the previous day. Then we had the majestic batting of new cricket captains Michael Clarke and Alistair Cook, the thrilling unbeaten run of possibly the great ever racehorse *Frankel*, Andy Murray, who went on to add the US Open title to his Wimbledon title, ending a 76-year drought for British tennis, and so much more for sports fans to revel in. Earlier, of course, we had even been stirred by the ever-present and dominant football, with a sensational end to the Football League season, not to mention the Champions' League final.

But above everything was the Olympics. With the splendid work of the London Organising Committee, led so brilliantly by its chairman the indefatigable Lord Coe, himself one of the world's greatest ever athletes. London 2012 showed a British people, who tend to be self-deprecating, just how wonderfully well we can organise major sporting events. The English weather, for once, was reasonably kind most of the time and quite apart from the continually exhilarating action, there was the truly wondrous joy and helpfulness of the volunteers, the Games makers. There was marvellous action in so many sports, and Britain did so exceptionally well, but athletics as ever was at the heart of the Games. It was just so exhilarating to walk amongst the happy people packing the Olympic Park every day. The first morning brought Jessica Ennis, whose beautiful face and body had been seen on a multitude of posters and whose every deed and aspiration featured in countless newspaper and magazine articles, into immediate action. And how she performed in the Olympic Stadium that was filled to capacity as it was for every session! The crowds were far from the most informed as so many athletics regulars were unable to get tickets (or to afford them in many cases!) but they supported the athletes of all nations so generously, reaching unsurpassed crescendos of noise and excitement for Britain's super Saturday of three gold medals and perhaps even more for the return eight days later of Mo Farah for his second gold medal. Never have I heard a national anthem sung with such fervour in an Olympic arena.

Now all that is history, but what bliss it was to be involved in London 2012, and how fitting that such a great Games should take centre stage in the year of the IAAF's Centenary. That was celebrated in Barcelona in November by a host of the greatest names of the sport. Now onward again as we settle into the four-year cycle leading up to Rio 2016, and, batteries recharged, look back to the past year and prepare for the challenges ahead, especially this year with the World Championships in Moscow. As can be seen from the lists in this Annual, new standards in depth were set in many athletics events in 2012 and it will be fascinating to see if and how these are maintained in the year ahead. ATHLETICS 2014 will tell you.

Peter Matthews

Information can be sent to me to 10 Madgeways Close, Great Amwell, Ware, Herts SG12 9RU, England.
Email: p.matthews@btinternet.com
Information or requests re sales, distribution, publication etc. to the publishers, SportsBooks Ltd.

ABBREVIATIONS

The following abbreviations have been used for meetings with, in parentheses, the first year that they were held.

AAU	(USA) Amateur Athletic Union Championships (1888) (later TAC)
Af-AsG	Afro-Asian Games (2003)
AfCh	African Championships (1979)
AfG	African Games (1965)
Af-J	African Junior Championships (1994)
AmCp	America's Cup (World Cup Trial) (1977)
APM	Adriaan Paulen Memorial, Hengelo
Aragón	Gran Premio Internacional de Atletismo Gobierno de Aragón, Zaragoza (2004)
AsiC	Asian Championships (1973)
AsiG	Asian Games (1951)
Asi-J	Asian Junior Championships (1990)
ASV	Weltklasse in Köln, ASV club meeting (1934)
Athl	Athletissima, Lausanne (1976)
Balk	Balkan Games (1929), C – Championships
Barr	(Cuba) Barrientos Memorial (1946)
BGP	Budapest Grand Prix (1978)
Bisl	Bislett Games, Oslo (1965) (Bergen 2004)
Bol G	Bolivar Games (1938)
BrGP	British Grand Prix
CAC	Central American and Caribbean Championships (1967)
CAG	Central American and Caribbean Games (1926)
CalR	California Relays (1942)
C.Asian	Central Asian Championships
CAU	Inter-counties, GBR (1934)
CISM	International Military Championships (1946)
CG	Commonwealth Games (1930)
C.Cup	Continental Cup (2010)
Déca	Décanation, Paris (C) (2005)
DL	Diamond League (2010)
DNG	DN Galan, Stockholm (1966)
Drake	Drake Relays (1910)
EAF	European Athletics Festival, Bydgoszcz (2001)
EAsG	East Asian Games (1993)
EC	European Championships (1934)
ECCp	European Clubs Cup (1975)
EChall	European Challenge (10,000m 1997, Throws 2001)
ECp	European Cup – track & field (1965), multi-events (1973)
EI	European Indoor Championships (1970, Games 1966-9)
EICp	European Indoor Cup (2003)
EJ	European Junior Championships (1970)
ET	European Team Championships (replaced European Cup, 2009)
EU23	European Under-23 Championships (1997) and European Under-23 Cup (1992-4)
FBK	Fanny Blankers-Koen Games, Hengelo (formerly APM) (1981)
FlaR	Florida Relays (1939)
FOT	(USA) Final Olympic Trials (1920)
Franc	Francophone Games (1989)
Gaz	Gaz de France meeting, FRA (was BNP) (1968)
GGala	Golden Gala, Roma (from 1980), Verona (1988), Pescara (1989), Bologna (1990)
GL	Golden League (1998-2009)
GNR	Great North Run – Newcastle to South Shields, GBR (1981)
GP	Grand Prix
GPF	IAAF Grand Prix Final (1985)
GS	Golden Spike, Ostrava (1969)
Gugl	Zipfer Gugl Grand Prix, Linz (1988)
GWG	Goodwill Games (1986)
Hanz	Hanzekovic Memorial, Zagreb
Herc	Herculis, Monte Carlo, Monaco (1987)
IAAF	International Association of Athletics Federations
IAC	IAC meeting (1968), formerly Coca-Cola
IAU	International Association of Ultrarunners
IbAm	Ibero-American Championships (1983)
ISTAF	Internationales Stadionfest, Berlin (1921)
Jenner	Bruce Jenner Classic, San Jose (1979)
Jerome	Harry Jerome Track Classic (1984)
Jordan	Payton Jordan U.S. Track & Field Open, Stanford (2004)
JUCO	Junior Colleges Championships, USA
KansR	Kansas Relays, Lawrence (1923)
Kuso	Janusz Kusocinski Memorial (1954)
Kuts	Vladimir Kuts Memorial ((1978))
LGP	London Grand Prix, Crystal Palace
MAI	Malmö Al Galan, Sweden (formerly Idag) (1958)
Mal	Malinowski Memorial, Poland
Mast	Masters pole vault, Grenoble (1987)
MedG	Mediterranean Games (1951)
Mill	Millrose Games, New York indoors (1908)
ModR	Modesto Relays
MSR	Mt. San Antonio College Relays (1959)
NA	Night of Athletics, Heusden (2000) formerly Hechtel
NACAC	North American, Central American & Caribbean Ch (2003)
NC	National Championships
NC-w	National Winter Championships
NCAA	National Collegiate Athletic Association Championships, USA (1921)
NCAA-r	NCAA Regional Championships (2003)
NCp	National Cup
Nebiolo	Memorial Primo Nebiolo, Torino (2000, originally 1963)
NG	National Games
Nik	Nikaïa, Nice (1976)
NM	Narodna Mladezhe, Sofia (1955)
N.Sch	National Schools
Nurmi	Paavo Nurmi Games (1957)
NYG	New York Games (1989)
OD	Olympischer Tag (Olympic Day)
Oda	Mikio Oda Memorial Meeting, Hiroshima
Odlozil	Josef Odlozil Memorial, Prague (1994)
OG	Olympic Games (1896)
OT	Olympic Trials
Owens	Jesse Owens Memorial (1981)
PAm	Pan American Games (1951)
PArab	Pan Arab Championships (1977) (G-Games 1953)
Pedro	Pedro's Cup, Poland (2005)
PennR	Pennsylvania Relays (1895)
PTS	Pravda Televízia Slovnaft, Bratislava (1957) (later GPB)

Pre	Steve Prefontaine Memorial (1976)
RdVin	Route du Vin Half Marathon, Luxembourg (1962)
RomIC	Romanian International Championships (1948)
RWC	Race Walking Challenge Final (2007)
SACh	South American Championships (1919)
SAsG	South Asian Games (1984)
SEAG	South East Asia Games (1959)
SEC	Southeast Conference Championships
SGP	IAAF Super Grand Prix
Slovn	Slovnaft, Bratislava (formerly PTS) (1990)
Spark	Sparkassen Cup, Stuttgart (indoor) (1987)
Spart	(URS) Spartakiad (1956)
Spitzen	Spitzen Leichtathletik Luzern (1987)
Stra	Stramilano Half marathon, Milan
Super	Super Meet, Japan (Tokyo, Shizuoka, Yokohama, Kawasaki)
Tsik	Athens Grand Prix Tsiklitiria (1998)
TexR	Texas Relays (1925)
USOF	US Olympic Festival
VD	Ivo Van Damme Memorial, Brussels (1977)
Veniz	Venizélia, Haniá, Crete (1936)
WAC	Western Athletic Conference Championships
WAF	World Athletics Finals (2003)
WCh	World Championships (1983)
WCM	World Challenge Meeting (2010)
WCp	World Cup – track & field (1977), marathon (1985) Walking – Lugano Trophy – men (1961), Eschborn Cup – women (1979)
WCT	World Championships Trial
WG	World Games, Helsinki (1961)
WI	World Indoor Championships (1987), World Indoor Games (1985)
WJ	World Junior Championships (1986)
WK	Weltklasse, Zürich (1962)
WMilG	World Military Games (or CISM) (1995)
WUG	World University Games (1923)
WY	World Youth Championships (1999)
Zat	Emil Zátopek Classic, Melbourne
Znam	Znamenskiy Brothers Memorial (1958)
-j, -y, -23	Junior, Youth or under-23

Dual and triangular matches are indicated by "v" (versus) followed by the name(s) of the opposition. Quadrangular and larger inter-nation matches are denoted by the number of nations and -N; viz 8-N designates an 8-nation meeting.

Events

CC	cross-country
Dec	decathlon
DT	discus
h	hurdles
Hep	heptathlon
HJ	high jump
HMar	half marathon
HT	hammer
JT	javelin
LJ	long jump
Mar	marathon
Pen	pentathlon
PV	pole vault
R	relay
SP	shot
St	steeplechase
TJ	triple jump
W	walk
Wt	weight

Miscellaneous abbreviations

+	Intermediate time in longer race
=	Tie (ex-aequo)
A	Made at an altitude of 1000m or higher
b	date of birth
D	Made in decathlon competition
dnf	did not finish
dnq	did not qualify
dns	did not start
exh	exhibition
h	heat
H	Made in heptathlon competition
hr	hour
i	indoors
kg	kilograms
km	kilometres
m	metres
M	mile
m/s	metres per second
mx	Made in mixed men's and women's race
nh	no height
O	Made in octathlon competition
P	Made in pentathlon competition
pb	personal best
Q	Made in qualifying round
qf	quarter final (or q in lists)
r	Race number in a series of races
sf	semi final (or s in lists)
w	wind assisted
WIR	world indoor record
WR	world record or best
y	yards
*	Converted time from yards to metres: For 200m: 220 yards less 0.11 second For 400m: 440 yards less 0.26 second For 110mh: 120yh plus 0.03 second

Countries

(IAAF membership reached 213 in 2008, back to 212 in 2011). IAAF and IOC abbreviations are now identical.

AFG	Afghanistan
AHO	Netherlands Antilles #
AIA	Anguilla
ALB	Albania
ALG	Algeria
AND	Andorra
ANG	Angola
ANT	Antigua & Barbuda
ARG	Argentina
ARM	Armenia
ARU	Aruba
ASA	American Samoa
AUS	Australia
AUT	Austria
AZE	Azerbaijan
BAH	Bahamas
BAN	Bangladash
BAR	Barbados
BDI	Burundi
BEL	Belgium
BEN	Benin
BER	Bermuda
BHU	Bhutan
BIH	Bosnia Herzegovina
BIZ	Belize
BLR	Belarus
BOL	Bolivia
BOT	Botswana
BRA	Brazil
BRN	Bahrain
BRU	Brunei
BUL	Bulgaria
BUR	Burkina Faso
CAF	Central African

	Republic
CAM	Cambodia
CAN	Canada
CAY	Cayman Islands
CGO	Congo
CHA	Chad
CHI	Chile
CHN	People's Republic of China
CIV	Côte d'Ivoire (Ivory Coast)
CMR	Cameroon
COD	Democratic Republic of Congo
COK	Cook Islands
COL	Colombia
COM	Comoros
CPV	Cape Verde Islands
CRC	Costa Rica
CRO	Croatia
CUB	Cuba
CUR	Curaçao
CYP	Cyprus
CZE	Czech Republic
DEN	Denmark
DJI	Djibouti
DMA	Dominica
DOM	Dominican Republic
ECU	Ecuador
EGY	Egypt
ENG	England
ERI	Eritrea
ESA	El Salvador
ESP	Spain
EST	Estonia
ETH	Ethiopia
FIJ	Fiji
FIN	Finland
FRA	France
FRG	Federal Republic of Germany (1948-90)
FSM	Micronesia
GAB	Gabon
GAM	The Gambia
GBR	United Kingdom of Great Britain & Northern Ireland
GBS	Guinea-Bissau
GDR	German Democratic Republic (1948-90)
GEO	Georgia
GEQ	Equatorial Guinea
GER	Germany (pre 1948 and from 1991)
GHA	Ghana
GIB	Gibraltar
GRE	Greece
GRN	Grenada
GUA	Guatemala
GUI	Guinea
GUM	Guam
GUY	Guyana
HAI	Haiti
HKG	Hong Kong, China
HON	Honduras
HUN	Hungary
INA	Indonesia
IND	India
IRI	Iran
IRL	Ireland
IRQ	Iraq
ISL	Iceland
ISR	Israel
ISV	US Virgin Islands
ITA	Italy
IVB	British Virgin Islands
JAM	Jamaica
JOR	Jordan
JPN	Japan
KAZ	Kazakhstan
KEN	Kenya
KGZ	Kyrgyzstan
KIR	Kiribati
KOR	Korea
KSA	Saudi Arabia
KUW	Kuwait
LAO	Laos
LAT	Latvia
LBA	Libya
LBR	Liberia
LCA	St Lucia
LES	Lesotho
LIB	Lebanon
LIE	Liechtenstein
LTU	Lithuania
LUX	Luxembourg
MAC	Macao
MAD	Madagascar
MAR	Morocco
MAS	Malaysia
MAW	Malawi
MDA	Moldova
MDV	Maldives
MEX	Mexico
MGL	Mongolia
MKD	Former Yugoslav Republic of Macedonia
MLI	Mali
MLT	Malta
MNE	Montenegro
MNT	Montserrat
MON	Monaco
MOZ	Mozambique
MRI	Mauritius
MSH	Marshall Islands
MTN	Mauritania
MYA	Myanmar
NAM	Namibia
NCA	Nicaragua
NED	Netherlands
NEP	Nepal
NFI	Norfolk Islands
NGR	Nigeria
NGU	Papua New Guinea
NI	Northern Ireland
NIG	Niger
NMA	Northern Marianas Islands
NOR	Norway
NRU	Nauru
NZL	New Zealand
OMA	Oman
PAK	Pakistan
PAN	Panama
PAR	Paraguay
PER	Peru
PHI	Philippines
PLE	Palestine
PLW	Palau
PNG	Papua New Guinea
POL	Poland
POR	Portugal
PRK	North Korea (DPR Korea)
PUR	Puerto Rico
PYF	French Polynesia
QAT	Qatar
ROU	Romania
RSA	South Africa
RUS	Russia
RWA	Rwanda
SAM	Samoa
SCG	Serbia & Montenegro (to 2006)
SCO	Scotland
SEN	Sénégal
SEY	Seychelles
SIN	Singapore
SKN	St Kitts & Nevis
SLE	Sierra Leone
SLO	Slovenia
SMR	San Marino
SOL	Solomon Islands
SOM	Somalia
SRB	Serbia
SRI	Sri Lanka
STP	São Tomé & Principé
SUD	Sudan
SUI	Switzerland
SUR	Surinam
SVK	Slovakia
SWE	Sweden
SWZ	Swaziland
SYR	Syria
TAN	Tanzania
TCH	Czechoslovakia (to 1991)
TGA	Tonga
THA	Thailand
TJK	Tadjikistan
TKM	Turkmenistan
TKS	Turks & Caicos Islands
TLS	East Timor
TOG	Togo
TPE	Taiwan (Chinese Taipei)
TRI	Trinidad & Tobago
TUN	Tunisia
TUR	Turkey
TUV	Tuvalu
UAE	United Arab Emirates
UGA	Uganda
UKR	Ukraine
URS	Soviet Union (to 1991)
URU	Uruguay
USA	United States
UZB	Uzbekistan
VAN	Vanuatu
VEN	Venezuela
VIE	Vietnam
VIN	St Vincent & the Grenadines
WAL	Wales
YEM	Republic of Yemen
YUG	Yugoslavia (to 2002)
ZAM	Zambia
ZIM	Zimbabwe

ceased to exist as a separate territory in 2010, and absorbed into the Netherlands.

ACKNOWLEDGEMENTS

ONEC AGAIN I would like to thak all those who have helped me to compile this Annual – whether in a major way or just with a few items of information. As they have throughout the 63-year history of the ATFS Annual, the annual world lists provide the essential core of the book and I have worked up these lists from original compilations by Richard Hymans for men and Mirko Jalava for women. I refer all who want to follow the results of the sport closely to Mirko's superb web site his superb web site www.tilastopaja.net. Milan Skocovsky again provided deep lists for juniors and I am indebted to Carlos Fernández for his expertise on the road lists and to Ray Herdt for the walks. I circulate draft lists to a number of ATFS experts and receive much valuable information from a worldwide circle of correspondents. is the expert for walks, and of the great Spanish group Miguel Villaseñor and Juan Mari Iriondo checked the biographies and obituaries with great care. Börre Lilloe provided much index data and Ken Nakamura checked distance lists. I am delighted that Bob Phillips and Roberto Quercetani have again provided articles.

Both for this annual and throughout the year with *Athletics International* Winfried Kramer helps with national records and widespread probing for results as do the area experts: *Africa*: Yves Pinaud, *Asia*: Heinrich Hubbeling, *Central and South America*: Eduardo Biscayart and Luis Vinker, and specialists: *Records* György Csiki, *Road racing*: Marty Post, *Ultrarunning* Andy Milroy, *Indoors* Ed Gordon, *Pole vault* Kenneth Lindqvist, *Multi events:* Hans van Kuijen.

Australia: Paul Jenes and David Tarbotton; *Austria*: Dr Karl Graf; *Belarus*: Dmitri Vorobyov; Belgium: André de Hooghe and Alain Monet; *Bulgaria*: Aleksandar Vangelov; *China*: Mirko Jalava; *Croatia*: Vladimir Mikulec; *Cuba*: Alfredo Sánchez; *Czech Republic*: Milan Skocovsky and Milan Urban; *Denmark*: Erik Laursen; *Dominican Republic*: Arisnel Rodríguez; *Estonia*: Erlend Teemägi and Enn Endjärv; *Finland*: Juhani Jalava, Mirko Jalava, Mikko Nieminen and Matti Hannus; *France*: Alain Bouillé, Patrice Bertignon, Patricia Doilin and José Guilloto; *Germany*: Sven Kuus and Klaus Amrhein; *Greece*: Thomas Konstas and Nikos Kriezis; *Hungary*: György Csiki; *India*: Ram. Murali Krishnan; *Ireland*: Pierce O'Callaghan; *Israel*: David Eiger; *Italy*: Raul Leoni and Enzo Rivas; *Japan*: Yoshimasa Noguchi, Akihiro Onishi and Ken Nakamura; *Latvia*: Andris Stagis; *Lithuania*: Stepas Misiunas; *Luxembourg*: Georges Klepper; *Montenegro*: Ivan Popovic; *New Zealand*: Murray McKinnon and Tony Hunt; *Norway*: Tore Johansen, Ole Petter Sandvig and Børre Lilloe; *Poland*: Zbigniew Jonik, Janusz Rozum and Tadeusz Wolejko; *Portugal:* Manuel Arons Carvalho; *Puerto Rico*: Pedro Anibal Diaz; *Romania*: Alexandru Boriga; *Russia*: Sergey Tikhonov and Rostislav Orlov; *Serbia*: Ozren Karamata and Olga Acic; *Slovakia*: Alfons Juck; *Slovenia*: Zdravko Peternelj; *South Africa:* Danie Cornelius and Riël Hauman; *Spain*: José Luis Hernández, Carles Baronet and the AEEA team; *Sweden*: Jonas Hedman and Peter Larsson; *Switzerland*: Alberto Bordoli and Antonin Hejda; *Trinidad:* Bernard Linley, *Turkey*: Nejat Kök, *Ukraine*: Yuriy Kostritsky and Valentin Krynin; *UK*: Tony Miller; *USA*: Tom Casacky, Garry Hill, Sieg Lindstrom, Marty Post, Jack Shepherd and Mike Kennedy, and *Track Newsletter*. Also various national federation lists and to those who post results or ranking lists to various web sites.

Also to Francisco Ascorbe, Marco Buccellato, Mark Butler, Ottavio Castellini (IAAF), José Maria García, Stan Greenberg, Christian Lenz, Alan Lindop, Rooney Magnusson (obituaries), Bill Mallon, Pino Mappa, Phil Minshull, Bob Phillips, Zdenek Procházka (hammer), Roberto Quercetani and Rob Whittingham.

My apologies to anybody whose name I may have missed or who have corresponded with other key ATFS personnel, but all help, however small is deeply appreciated.

Keep the results flowing

During the year Mel Watman and I publish marks to ATFS standards (150-200 deep on world lists) in *Athletics International*, of which there are over 35 issues per year by email. This serves as a base from which the lists in this book can be compiled, together with information from web sites and the major magazines such as *Track & Field News* (USA) with its email results spin-off *Track Newsletter* and *Leichtathletik* (Germany) and the newsletters with particular spheres of interest such as *Atletismo en España* by Francisco J Ascorbe and José Luis Hernández, and Luis Vinker's *South America Bulletin*.

In order to ensure that the record of 2013 is as complete as possible I urge results contribution worldwide to AI, and then in turn our lists in *Athletics 2014* will be as comprehensive as we can make them.

Peter Matthews

THE ASSOCIATION OF TRACK & FIELD STATISTICIANS

The ATFS was founded in Brussels (at the European Championships) in 1950 and ever since has built upon the work of such key founding members as Roberto Quercetani, Don Potts and Fulvio Regli to produce authoritative ranking lists in the International Athletics Annual and elsewhere.

Current Executive Committee

President: Paul Jenes AUS
Vice-President: A.Lennart Julin SWE

Treasurer: Tom Casacky USA
Secretary: Michael J McLaughlin AUS
Past Presidents: Rooney Magnusson SWE, Dr Roberto Quercetani ITA
Committee: Eduardo Biscayart ARG/USA, Riël Hauman RSA, Nejat Kök TUR, Bernard Linley TRI, Giuseppa Mappa ITA, Peter J Matthews GBR, Yoshimasa Noguchi JPN, Yves Pinaud FRA,

Website: www.afts.org

Internet – Websites

IAAF	www.iaaf.org
IAU	www.iau-ultramarathon.org
African AC	www.webcaa.org
Asian AA	www.athleticsasia.org
CAC Confederation.	www.cacacathletics.org
European AA	www.european-athletics.org
NACAC	www.athleticsnacac.org
Oceania AA	www.athletics-oceania.com
S. American Fed.	www.consudatle.org
WMRA	www.wmra.info
World Masters	www.world-masters-athletics.org
Marathon Majors	www.worldmarathonmajors.com
Africa	www.africathle.com
Algeria	www.faa-dz.org
Andorra	www.faa.ad
Argentina	www.cada-atletismo.org
Australia	www.athletics.com.au
Austria	www.oelv.at
Bahamas	www.bahamastrack.com
Bahrain	www.bahrainathletics.org
Belarus	www.bfla.eu
Belgium	www.val.be
Bermuda	www.btfa.bm
Bosnia Hercegovina	www.asbih.org
Brazil	www.cbat.org.br
Bulgaria	www.bfla.org
Canada	www.athletics.ca
Chile	www.fedachi.cl
China	www.athletics.org.cn
Colombia	www.fecodatle.org
Croatia	www.has.hr
Cyprus	www.koeas.org.cy
Czech Republic	www.atletika.cz
Denmark	www.dansk-atletik.dk
Dominican Republic	www.fedomatle.org
England	www.englandathletics.org
Estonia	www.ekjl.ee
Finland	www.sul.fi
France	www.athle.com
Germany	www.deutscher- leichtathletik-verband.de
	www.leichtathletik.de
Great Britain	www.uka.org.uk
deep statistics	www.topsinathletics.info
	www.thepowerof10.info
Greece	www.segas.gr
Hong Kong	www.hkaaa.com
Hungary	www.masz.hu
Iceland	www.fri.is
India	www.indianathletics.org
Indonesia	www.indonesia-athletics.org
Ireland	www.athleticsireland.ie
Israel	www.iaa.co.il
unofficial (in English)	http://eigers.tripod.com
Italy	www.fidal.it
Jamaica	www.trackandfieldja.com
Japan	www.jaaf.or.jp
Kazakhstan	www.kazathletics.kz

Kenya	www.athleticskenya.org.ke
Latvia	http://lat-athletics.lv
Lithuania	www.laf.lt
Luxembourg	www.fla.lu
Macedonia	www.afm.org.mk
Mexico	www.fmaa.mx
Moldova	www.fam.com.md/
Monaco	www.fma.mc
Montenegro	www.ascg.co.me
Morocco	www.moroccanathletics.com
Netherlands	www.atletiekunie.nl
New Zealand	www.athletics.org.nz
Northern Ireland	www.niathletics.org
Norway	www.friidrett.no
Peru	www.fepeatle.com
Poland	www.pzla.pl
Portugal	www.fpatletismo.pt
Puerto Rico	www.atletismofapur.com
Qatar	www.qatarathletics.com/en/
Romania	www.fra.ro
Russia	www.rusathletics.com
Scotland	www.scottishathletics.org.uk
	www.scotstats.com
Serbia	www.serbia-athletics.org.rs
Singapore	www.singaporeathletics.org.sg
Slovakia	www.atletikasvk.sk
Slovenia	www.atletska-zveza.si
South Africa	www.athletics.org.za
Spain	www.rfea.es
Sri Lanka	srilankaathletics.com/index.html
Sweden	www.friidrott.se
Switzerland	www.swiss-athletics.ch
Taiwan	www.cttfa.org.tw
Trinidad & Tobago	www.ttnaaa.org
Turkey	www.taf.org.tr
Ukraine	www.uaf.org.ua
Uruguay	www.atlecau.org.uy
USA	www.usatf.org (results) www.tfrrs.org
Venezuela	www.fva.cavillo.com.ve
Wales	www.welshathletics.org
	athleticsstatswales.webeden.co.uk

Other recommended sites for statistics and results

AIMS	www.aimsworldrunning.org
ARRS	www.arrs.net
British historical	www.gbrathletics.com
DGLD (German stats)	www.ladgld.de Marathons
French history etc.	http://cdm.athle.com
Marathons	www.marathonguide.com
Masters Track & Field	www.mastersathletics.net
Mirko Jalava	www.tilastopaja.com
NUTS/Track Stats	www.nuts.org.uk
Rankings etc	www.all-athletics.com
Runners World	www.runnersworld.com
Tracklion (NED/BEL)	sportslion.net/tracklione.html
Track & Field News	www.trackandfieldnews.com
Track in Sun	www.trackinsun.com
World junior news	www.wjan.org
Olympic Games	www.aafla.org
	www.sports-reference.com

DIARY OF 2012
by Peter Matthews

A chronological survey of highlights in major events in the world of track and field athletics.

See Championships or National sections for more details. OG = Olympic Games, DL = Samsung Diamond League, WCM = World Challenge Meeting.

January

6   **San Giorgio**, Italy. Edwin Soi and Mercy Cherono had victories in the 55th Campaccio International CC, the first IAAF Permit race of the year.

14   **Houston**, USA. The US Olympic Trials for the marathon were held on a fast, level course. The winners both set pbs and made their third Olympic teams: Meb Keflezighi 2:09:08 (his eighth 2:09 time) and Shalane Flanagan 2:25:38.

15   **Houston**, USA. On the same course as the US Trial races there were much faster times from Ethiopian winners Tariku Jifar 2:06:51 and Alemitu Abera 2:23:14.

15   **Seville**, Spain. Geoffrey Kipsang and Linet Masai overcame surprisingly rainy conditions to score victories in the sixth leg of the IAAF Cross Country Permit series, the 30th Cross International de Itálica. The following week Kipsang was beaten in the EA permit meeting at Elgóibar by Paul Tanui.

20   **Villeurbanne**, France. Holly Bleasdale set UK and Commonwealth pole vault records at 4.72, 4.80 and 4.87, the last also a world age-20 best.

27   **Chemnitz**, Germany. Rees Hoffa beat David Storl 21.87 to 20.75 in the shot at the 16th ERDGAS International.

27   **Dubai**, United Arab Emirates. 13th Standard Chartered Dubai Marathon. In ideal conditions Ayele Abshero ran the fastest ever time for a debut marathon, winning in 2:04:23 with Dino Sefer (previous best 2:10:33), Markos Geneti (2:06:35), and Jonathan Maiyo (2:12:45) breaking 2:05 to go to 4th, 8th, 9th and 12th equal on the world all-time list for standard courses. This was the first time four men have ever run under that time in a marathon apart from Boston last year, and the depth of performance was astonishing, as there were world records for 8 men under 2:06, 10 under 2:07, 13 under 2:08 and 15 under 2:09, with best ever times for places 3 to 17. There were the best ever times for places 3-9 in the women's race won for the second time by Aselefech Mergia, in a course and national

record 2:19:31 with Lucy Wangui Kabuu 2:19:34 for the second fastest ever women's debut and Mare Dibaba 2:19:52, who became at 22 the youngest ever sub-2:20 woman. These three went to 7th, 8th and 15th on the world all-time list with the next two Bezunesh Bekele 2:20:30 and Aberu Kebede 2:20:33 to 16th and 17th.

28   **Glasgow**, GBR. The Kelvin Hall hosted athletics for the last time with the annual Aviva International: GBR 56, Russia 53, Germany 53, Commonwealth Select 47, USA 41. Mo Farah clinched victory for the British team with a thrilling victory at 1500m over Augustine Choge.

28   **New York** (Madison Square Garden). US Open. Asafa Powell and Veronica Campbell-Brown were 50m winners in 5.64 and 6.08 and Lolo Jones the 50m in 6.78, the world's fastest times since 2005, 2000 and 2008 respectively.

February

4   **Arnstadt**, Germany. Anna Chicherova set a Russian indoor record of 2.06 at the 36th indoor "High Jump with Music" event.

4   **Boston (Roxbury)**, USA. New Balance GP, Reggie Lewis Track & Athletic Center. Jenn Suhr became the first US woman to pole vault 16 ft (50 years and 2 days after the first man to do so), with her 4.88 American record for second on the world all-time list. In her first track race since August 2010, Tirunesh Dibaba won the 2 miles in 9:21.60.

5   **Moscow**. Russian Winter meeting (IAAF Permit). Andrey Silnov high jumped 2.36 and Adam Kszczot 1:15.26 beat Yuriy Borzakovskiy 1:16.08 at 600m, national records for both. Valeriy Borchin won the 3000m walk in 18:16.54 with Vladimir Kanaykin and Sergey Bakulin also into the world all-time top 12.

6-7   **Moscow**, Russia. Yekaterina Bolshova won the Russian pentathlon title with 4896 points.

10   **Düsseldorf**, Germany. Thomas Longosiwa became the sixth man to break 13 min for 5000m indoors when winning in 12:58.67 from Isiah Koech 13:02.36 and Paul Koech 13:02.69 at the PSD Bank Meeting.

11   **Donetsk**, Ukraine. Winners at the Samsung Pole Vault Stars meeting were Renaud Lavillenie 5.82 (on count-back from Björn Otto) and Jirina Ptácníková 4.72.

11   **Fayetteville**, USA. USATF Classic. Jillian Camarena-Williams (19.89 shot) and Galen Rupp (8:09.72 2 miles) set American indoor records.

11   **New York (Armory)**, USA. The 105th Millrose Games, staged for the first time not at Madison Square Garden but on the 200m track at the New Balance Track & Field Center at the Armory included a US record by Bernard Lagat 13:07.15 for 5000m (thus swapping records with Rupp *above*).

11-12   **UK Indoor Championships**, Sheffield. Jessica Ennis won high jump (1.91) and 60m hurdles (7.95) and Dwain Chambers won his fifth successive 60m title with 6.58.

12   **Karlsruhe**, Germany. The 3000m produced the top four marks of the indoor season, Augustine Choge 7:29.94 winning from Edwin Soi 7:29.94, Yenew Alamirew 7:31.23 and Eliud Kipchoge 7:32.03, and another world best came from Genzebe Dibaba, 4:00.13 for 1500m.

14   **Liévin**, France. Adam Kszczot won the 800m in 1:44.96, a Polish record and third on the world indoor all-time list. Pamela Jelimo gave notice that she was back as she ran 1:59.10 for 800m, her best since 2008, behind Malika Akkaoui, Moroccan record 1:59.01.

16-19   **Ukrainian Indoor Championships**, Sumy. Nataliya Dobrynska scored 4880 points in the pentathlon.

17   **Ra's Al Khaymah**, United Arab Emirates. Strong southeasterly winds slowed times in the RAK Half Marathon, but Mary Keitany was again a brilliant winner, in 66:49. Dennis Kipruto Koech won the men's race in 60:40.

18   **Birmingham**, GBR. Aviva Grand Prix. Mo Farah broke the European record for 2 miles with 8:08.07 but was beaten by Eliud Kipchoge 8:07.39. Lerone Clarke won the 60m in 6.47 from Nesta Carter 6.49 and Asafa Powell 6.50, after Powell had tied the 2012 world-leading mark of 6.50 in his heat. Liu Xiang won the 60m hurdles in 7.41 to take 0.01 off his 2007 Asian record and was well clear of Dayron Robles 7.50 and Jessica Ennis won the women's race in a pb 7.87. There was also a world-leading time of 8:31.56 in the women's 3000m by Meseret Defar.

18   **Balkan Indoor Championships**, Istanbul, Turkey. Top mark was a 5.75 pole vault by Konstadínos Filippídis.

18   **Sydney**, Australia. Sally Pearson ran 12.66 for 100m hurdles, Henry Frayne long jumped 8.27 and Valerie Adams put the shot 20.67 at the Track Classic.

18-19   **Asian Indoor Championships**, Hangzhou, China. Mutaz Essa Barshim had set Asian indoor records at 2.26, 2.30 and 2.33 at Spala a week earlier and here went on to 2.34 and 2.37. Championship records were set in ten events.

18-19   **Russian Winter Walks Championships**, Sochi. As usual there was an excellent standard. Andrey Ruzavin 1:17:47 won the 20k from Sergey Morozov 1:17:52, and five men broke 2:30 for the 35k headed by Sergey Kirdyapkin 2:25:42 and Mikhail Ryzhov 2:25:59. Eight women were under 1:29 for 20k, with Elmira Alembekova winning in 1:25:27 from Yelena Lashmanova 1:26:39.

22-24   **Russian Indoor Championships**, Moscow. Ivan Ukhov beat Andrey Silnov on count-back as both cleared 2.34 in the high jump.

23   **Stockholm**, Sweden. XL Galen. Yelena Isinbayeva improved her three year-old world indoor pole vault record to 5.01 at her second attempt; this was her 28th world record in all. Yelena Chicherova won her sixth successive high jump competition of the season at 1.97 and came very close at 2.04.

25-26   **German Indoor Championships**, Karlsruhe. Björn Otto won the pole vault with 5.92 from Maite Mohr 5.87.

25-26   **US Indoor Championships**, Albuquerque. Chaunté Lowe broke the 13 year-old US indoor record for high jump with 2.02, and world-leading marks for the year were recorded by Trell Kimmons 60m 6.45, Dexter Faulk 60m hurdles 7.40, Will Claye triple jump 17.63, Tianna Madison 60m (equal) 7.02, Sanya Richards-Ross 400m 50.71, and Kristi Castlin 60m hurdles 7.84. Meet records were set by Amber Campbell, 24.78 weight, and Richards-Ross. Ashton Eaton beat Claye to take the long jump title with 8.06. Jill Camarena-Williams won her eighth US indoor shot title with 19.56 and Reese Hoffa was in top form with 21.75. Lowe and Galen Rupp (who was 3rd here at both 1500m and 3000m) won the 2012 Indoor Visa Championship Series titles with $25,000 cash prizes.

26   **Rome-Ostia**, Italy. Florence Kiplagat ran a superb 66:38 for half marathon in the 36th edition of this race. Three men went under the hour, headed by Philemon Limo 59:32, also a course record.

26   **San Juan,** Puerto Rico, Despite a strong headwind in the first third of the race, Vivian Cheruiyot ran 30:47 to win women's race in the 15th World's Best 10k.

26   **Tokyo**, Japan. Michael Kipyego won the sixth Tokyo Marathon in 2:07:37, as Haile Gebrselassie was only fourth, in 2:08:17. Atsede Habtamu set a new women's course record of 2:25:28. There were 34,656 finishers (27,336 men and 7320 women).

March

2-3 **Melbourne** Track Classic Australia. Sally Pearson won the 100m hurdles in 12.49 and David Rudisha opened for the year with a 1:44.33 win at 800m in the first IAAF World Challenge Meeting of 2012.

9-10 **NCAA Indoor Championships**, Nampa, Idaho. Florida won the men's title and Oregon the women's, both for the third successive year. Oregon were helped by the third successive pentathlon title by Brianne Theisen, whose 4536 was just 19 short of her recent collegiate record. Lawi Lalang won both 3000m (7:46.64) and 5000m (13:25.11).

9-11 14th **World Indoor Championships**, Istanbul, Turkey. World records in both the combined events competitions headed performances. Ashton Eaton added 77 points to his heptathlon mark with 6645, and Nataliya Dobrynska broke through 5000 with 5013 in beating Jessica Ennis 4965 for a Commonwealth record. There was one other championships record: Nery Brenes, 400m 45.11. Yelena Isinbayeva won her fourth WI title, 4.80 in the pole vault, and world best marks for the indoor season were set in eleven events in all. Best of these perhaps was Brittney Reese's 7.23 long jump. Mohamed Aman (800m) became the youngest ever world indoor champion at 18 years 60 days, while 39 year-old Yamilé Aldama produced a marvellous 14.82 to win the women's triple jump, her first global title.   Bernard Lagat won his third 3000m title, and at 37 was the oldest ever medallist at any event. The USA topped the medal table with 18 including 10 golds. *For leading results see Athletics 2012 p. 88-9.*

11 **Asian Walks Championships**, Nomi, Japan. Winners at 20k were Zhu Chundong 1:21:22 and Ding Huiqin 1:30:14.

11 **The Hague**, Netherlands. Five men ran 59:31 or better as Stephen Kibet ran the year's fastest half marathon, 58:45.

17-18 12th **European Cup Winter Throwing**, Bar, Montenegro. Excellent depth of performance was headed by Nadine Müller 68.89 (and 68.81) in the women's discus, and Sandra Perkovic won the U23 event with 67.19. Zalina Marghieva improved her Moldovan hammer record to 73.60 and beat Tatyana Lysenko 72.87, and Mario Fortes added 13cm to his Portuguese shot record with 21.02.

18 **African Cross-Country Championships**, Cape Town, South Africa. Clement Langat led Kenya to the men's team title and Joyce Chepkirui headed a Kenyan 1-2-3-4 in the women's race. Kenya won the men's U20 title and took the first three places in the women's U20 race, but lacked a fourth scorer so Ethiopia won the team title.

18 **Lugano**. Switzerland. Alex Schwazer, later discredited for failing a drugs test, recorded the year's fastest 20k time of 1:17:30, and was followed by Yohann Diniz 1:17:43 and Erick Barrondo 1:18:25. Women's winner was Tatyana Sibileva 1:28:03 and second placed Mirna Ortiz set a CAC record of 1:28:54.

18 **New York**, USA. A race record 15,331 runners (7455 men and 7876 women) contested the seventh annual New York City half marathon. Winners were Peter Kirui 59:39 and Firehiwot Dado 68:35.

23-24 **Copa Cuba**, Havana, Cuba. Yarelys Barrios won the national discus title with 68.03.

24 **Asian Cross-Country Championships**, Qingzhen, China. Bahrain won both men's and women's team titles and had individual winners in Alemu Bekele and Shitaye Eshete.

24 **Dudince**, Slovakia. Alex Schwazer followed his fast 20k with 3:40:58 for 50k to win at the 31st "Dudinska patdesiatka" meeting.

25 **Lisbon**, Portugal. Zersenay Tadese had a third successive half marathon win here in 59:34.

29-31 **Austin**, USA. 85th Texas Relays. Sanya Richards-Ross ran her fastest ever 100m, 10.89w/+2.9.

29-31 **Taicang**, China. Asian records were set by both winners in the IAAF Race Walking Challenge meeting. Wang Zhen was men's winner in 1:17:36 from Chen Ding 1:17:40 and Cai Zelin 1:18:47, and the Chinese 1-2-3-4 in the women's race was led by Liu Hong 1:25:46 from Lu Xiuzhi who set an Asian junior record of 1:27:01.

31 **Prague**, Czech Republic. Atsedu Tsegay, who had been second in 61:12 in Rabat in 2011 in his only previous half marathon, made an astonishing breakthrough by winning the 14th Hervis Prague Half Marathon in an Ethiopian record time of 58:47. Joyce Chepkirui also broke the course record with 67:03, a 2:01 improvement on her pb, and Lydia Cheromei was second in 67:26, seven seconds off her best.

April

1 **Berlin**, Germany. Dennis Kimetto, thought by some at the time to be a junior but actually 10 years older, won in 59:14 with Kenyans taking the top ten places, and a Kenyan women's 1-2-3 was headed by Philes Ongori 68:25.

3-8 **World Masters Indoor Championships**, Jyväskylä, Finland. Medal table leaders: FIN 105G, 103S, 104B; GER 59-57-57, GBR 40-43-35, FRA 35-21-19, RUS 27-24-21, USA 25-25-11.

10   Rotterdam Marathon, Netherlands. Yemane Adhane won in 2:04:48 by two seconds from Getu Feleke with Moses Mosop third in 2:05:03. The women's winner was Tiki Gelana in an Ethiopian record 2:18:58 from Valeria Straneo 2:23:44.

15   Paris, France. With East Africans taking the first 18 places, Stanley Biwott won in a pb 2:05:12 from Raji Assefa 2:06:24 and Sisay Jisa (on debut) 2:06:27. Women's winner was Tirfe Tsegaye 2:21:40. There were a record 32,980 finishers (26,626 men and 6354 women).

15   Vienna. Haile Gebrselassie ran 60:52 for half marathon in 60:52 but Paula Radcliffe given a head-start of 7:52 to match their pbs was very disappointed to run 72:03 in what probed to be her only race of 2012. Henry Sugut won the marathon in 2:06:58.

16   Boston Marathon, USA. Hot weather (21°C going up to 31°C) slowed times very considerably so that winners Wesley Korir and Sharon Cherop ran 2:12:40 and 2:31:50.

18-21   Kansas Relays, Lawrence, USA. Reese Hoffa beat Christian Cantwell 21.73 to 21.71 in the shot and Bershawn Jackson ran 400m hurdles in 48.20.

19-21   54th Mt SAC Relays, Walnut, California, USA. Walter Dix opened his season with 9.85w for 100m and Brittney Reese long jumped 7.12.

22   Virgin London Marathon, GBR. There was a Kenyan 1-2 in the men's race as Wilson Kipsang had a decisive victory in 2:04:44 from Martin Lel 2:06:51, a second ahead of Tsegaye Kedebe, and a 1-5 in the women's race won by Mary Keitany in an African record 2:18:37, for third on the all-time list, from Edna Kiplagat 2:19:50, Priscah Jeptoo 2:20:14 and Florence Kiplagat 2:20:57. There was a race record 36,705 finishers from 37,227 starters.

22   IAU World 100k Championships, Seregno, Italy. Giorgio Calcaterra 6:23:20 and Amy Sproston 7:34:08 won the individual titles, with Italy men's team and USA women's team champions.

26-28   103rd Drake Relays, Des Moines, USA. Despite windy and cool conditions Wallace Spearmon broke Michael Johnson's meet record with 20.02 for 200m.

26-28   118th Penn Relays, Philadelphia, USA. A three-day attendance of 112,416 included 49,810 for the final day when US teams won all six of the relays against "The World"; these included such top times as 3:00.15 for men's 4x400m and 42.19 and 3:21.18 for the women's 4x100 and 4x400.

28   Brest, Belarus. Oksana Menkova improved her four year-old national hammer record from 77.32 to 78.19.

29   Stanford, USA. Payton Jordan/ Cardinal Invitational. Sally Kipyego ran a virtually solo 5000m in 14:43.11 and there was excellent depth in the 10,000m races with best times from Cam Levins 27:27.96 and Betsy Saina 31:15.97.

May

5   Kingston, Jamaica (WCM). Usain Bolt took the 100m in 9.82 by a 2m margin over Michael Frater and Yohann Blake won the 200m with a very strong finish in 19.91 from Nickel Ashmeade 20.09. There were world-leading marks also in the women's 100m and 400m. Carmelita Jeter ran 10.81 followed by Kelly-Ann Baptiste 10.86, and Novlene Williams-Mills held off Sanya Richards-Ross, 49.99 to 50.11, with Christine Ohuruogu third in 50.93. Brigitte Foster-Hylton recaptured top form with 12.51 for 100m hurdles.

6   Berlin, Germany, Dennis Kimetto set a world record with 1:11:18 for a road 25km and second placed Wilfred Kigen 1:11:29 was also inside the old record.

6   Kawasaki, Japan. (WCM). Liu Xiang started his outdoor campaign with a 13.09 win at 110m hurdles, but the meeting was much affected by difficult conditions.

11   Doha, Qatar (DL). The opening Diamond League fixture was again of a very high quality and there were nine early season world-leading marks. These included 800m wins by Pamela Jelimo 1:56.94 and David Rudisha 1:43.10. Vivian Cheruiyot held off the desperate challenge of Meseret Defar to win the 3000m by 0.05 in 8:46.44, Silas Kiplagat won the 1500m in 3:29.63 from Asbel Kiprop 3:29.78, Paul Kipsiele Koech the steeplechase in 7:56.68, Augustine Choge the 3000m in 7:30.42, with double Olympic champion Kenenisa Bekele labouring home in seventh, LaShawn Merritt the 400m in 44.19, and Justin Gatlin shaded Asafa Powell 9.87 to 9.88 at 100m. Alyson Felix ran a 100m pb 10.92 to beat Veronica Campbell-Brown 10.94 and Shelly-Ann Fraser-Pryce 11.00.

12   Ponce, Puerto Rico (WCM). Home star Javier Culson had a clear win at 400m hurdles in 48.00 and Tianna Madison had a brilliant sprint double with pbs of 11.01 and 22.37.

12-13   IAAF World Race Walking Cup, Saransk, Russia. Russia uniquely won all five team titles and were especially dominant in the 50k, won by Sergey Kirdyapkin 3:38:08 from Igor Yerokhin 3:38:10, and the women's 20k, won by Yelena Lashmanova 1:27:38 from Olga Kaniskina 1:28:33. China's Wang Zhen won the 20k in 1:19:13 with Russians following as 2-3-5.

Hot weather slowed times a little. There were a record 471 contestants from 61 countries.

16 **Daegu**, Korea (WCM). Betty Heidler had a significant win in the hammer, 77.24 to 76.14, over Tatyana Lysenko, who had three of her four throws over 75m. Zhang Wenxiu was third with 75.68, just 4cm short of her Asian record. Aries Merritt beat David Oliver 13.21 to 13.22 in the Colorful meeting.

18 **Los Angeles (Eagle Rock)**, USA. Training companions Mo Farah 3:34.66 and Galen Rupp, pb 3:34.75 from previous best of 3:39.14, were 1-2 at 1500m and Farah then lined up for the 5000m less than a hour later, and, running in flats, won in 13:12.87.

19 **Halle**, Germany. Robert Harting won the discus with 70.31, his first ever 70m throw, and three other men exceeded 68m including 20 year-old Laurence Okoye, third with a British record 68.24. In very close competition Zhang Wenxiu 74.90 at hammer beat Anita Wlodarczyk by 2 cm and David Storl produced a last round 21.13 by beat Tomasz Majewski by 1cm in the shot.

19 **Shanghai**, China (DL). In torrential rain Veronica Campbell-Brown beat Carmelita Jeter, 22.50w to 22.62 in the women's 200m and Genzebe Dibaba broke 4 minutes for 1500m for the first time with 3:57.77 from Abeba Aregawi 3:59.23. The weather was better, however, when Liu Xiang ran an outstanding 110m hurdles in 12.97 to beat David Oliver 13.13 and Jason Richardson 13.16. Sandra Perkovic set a Croatian record of 68.24 on the final throw in the women's discus.

22 **Turnov**, Czech Republic. Ludvik Danek Memorial. Robert Harting improved his discus best to 70.66.

24-26 **NCAA Qualifying**, USA. Preliminary rounds for the NCAA Championships were held in Eastern and Western sections at Jacksonville and Austin. Sprints especially were excellent, with top marks at 200m in Jacksonville, 20.13 by Maurice Mitchell and 22.22 by Kimberlyn Duncan.

25 **Ostrava**, Czech Republic. 51st Golden Spike (WCM). Usain Bolt won the 100m into a 0.8m/s headwind in 10.04, his slowest ever time in a 100m final. World-leading marks were set by Barbora Spotáková, javelin 67.78, Renaud Lavillenie, pole vault 5.90, and Krisztián Pars, hammer 82.28. Betty Heidler threw a season's hammer best of 78.07 with 2nd placed Zhang Wenxiu throwing an Asian record 76.99.

26 **Brest**, Belarus. In his first meeting since the 2008 Olympic Games, Ivan Tikhon threw the hammer 82.81, the world's best of the year – but he did not appear again (with drugs doubts).

26-27 **European Clubs Cup**, Vila Real de Santo António, Portugal. Luch Moskva achieved their 16th successive win in the women's match, but were beaten into third behind Fiamme Galle of Italy and Playas de Castellón of Spain in the men's. New Cup records were set by Frank Casañas 67.74 discus, and by Tatyana Lysenko, 71.96 women's hammer.

26-27 **Götzis**, Austria. Jessica Ennis set three events pbs while adding 83 points to her heptathlon best with a Commonwealth and UK record 6906 in winning from Tatyana Chernova 6774. There were best ever marks for all places 13th to 22nd and 22 women exceeding 6000 points tied the record set here in 2008. The decathlon was much closer as just 13 points separated Hans Van Alphen and Eelco Sintnicolaas, who set Belgian (8519) and Dutch (8506) records respectively from previous bests of 8200 and 8436.

26-27 **Russian Team Championships**, Sochi. Top marks included a world-leading 53.87 from 400m hurdles by Irina Davydova, 7.03 long jump Olga Kucherenko, 67.00 discus Darya Pishchalnikova, and 17.53 triple jump by Lyukman Adams.

27 **Hengelo**, Netherlands. 30th Fanny Blankers-Koen Games (WCM). On a hot day Tariku Bekele won the Ethiopian 10,000m trial in 27:11.70 but Haile Gebrselassie had to settle for 7th in 27:20.39. Luguelin Santos (18) set a Dominican Republic 400m record of 44.45 and Nixon Chepseba ran 3:29.90 for 1500m.

27 **Rabat**, Morocco. 5th Mohammed VI meeting (WCM). Great depth in middle and long distance running included a breakthrough 9:16.14 at 3000m steeplechase by Hiwot Ayalew and a win at 5000m in a world-leading 12:59.28 by Vincent Chepkok. Top home result was the women's 5000m win by Meriem Selsouli in 14:45.91. The top two from the 2010 World Youth Championships 800m had a great race but the order was reversed as Mohammed Aman beat Leonard Kosencha by 0.02 in 1:43.58.

31 **Rome**, Italy. Golden Gala (DL). A crowd of nearly 60,000 in the Olympic Stadium saw seven world-leading marks, including 9.76 for 100m by Usain Bolt, well ahead of Asafa Powell 9.91. Paul Kipsiele Koech ran the third fastest ever 3000m steeplechase, 7:54.31, a record ninth time under 8 minutes by him, and in a classic women's 5000m in which Vivian Cheruiyot ran a 58.44 last lap to beat Meseret Defar by 0.03 in 14:35.62. Abeba Aregawi needed an Ethiopian record of 3:56.64 to beat Genzebe Dibaba 3:57.77 in the 1500m, Valerie Adams put the shot 21.03 and Barbora Spotáková increased her 2012 javelin best to 68.65.

June

1   **Eugene**, USA. 38th Prefontaine Classic (DL). With the wind just over the legal limit at +2.4, Liu Xiang tied the world's fastest ever 110m hurdles time of 12.87, winning from Aries Merritt 12.96 and Jason Richardson 13.11. Sixteen finishers in the Bowerman Mile ran 3:56.77 or faster, headed by Asbel Kiprop 3:49.40. The men's 10,000m, won by Wilson Kiprop 27:01.98 from Moses Masai and Bidan Karoki, was a Trial for Kenya's Olympic team, while Tirunesh Dibaba won the women's race in 30:24.39. Sanya Richards-Ross ran 49.39, her fastest 400m for three years, and Allyson Felix was also sharp, with 22.23 for 200m. Mo Farah won the 5000m in 12:56.98 from Isiah Koech 12:57.63 and Galen Rupp 12:58.90, and Milcah Chemos the women's steeplechase in 9:13.69 while best in the field were Christian Taylor, 17.62 TJ, and Reese Hoffa, 21.81 shot.

2-3   **Russian Multis Champs**, Cheboksary. Kristina Savitskaya made a massive improvement from 5989 to 6681 to win the heptathlon.

3   **Bydgoszcz**, Poland. 12th European Athletics Festival. Vanya Stambolova beat Natalya Antyukh at 400m hurdles, 54.08 to 54.50.

3   **European Cup 10,000m**, Bilbao, Spain. Polat Kemboi Arikan of Turkey (the former Paul Kemboi of Kenya), won on debut at the event in 27:56.28, a European U23 record and Sara Moreira won the women's race in 31:23.61, to repeat her 2011 win.

6-9   **NCAA Championships**, Des Moines, USA. Florida 50, won their first ever men's title form LSU 48 and Texas 40, and were helped by Tony McQuay winning the 400m in 44.58 and running 44.00 anchor leg on their 4x400m team's 3:00.10. Andrew Riley had a unique 100m/110h double and another double came from Cam Levins at 5000m and 10,000m, while Erik Kynard retained his high jump title with 2.34. Louisiana State won their 15th women's title in 26 years with 76 points from Oregon 62 and Texas A&M 38, but later LSU lost that title due to a positive drugs test by Semoy Hackett (3rd 100m, 5th 200m, 1st 4x100m). LSU's Kimberlyn Duncan ran 22.19 in her 200m semi but was slowed by a strong headwind to 22.86 for her win in the final. Brianne Theisen won the heptathlon (as she had in 2009-10) with 6440. *See USA section for winners.*

7   **Oslo**, Norway (DL). Exxon Mobil Bislett Games, Usain Bolt ran his ninth sub-9.80 for 100m with a 9.79 win from Asafa Powell 9.85. Sally Pearson matched her year's best of 12.49 for 100m hurdles and there were four more world-leading performances: 3:49.22 by Asbel Kiprop in the Dream Mile which had eight men under 3:51, 47.92 400m hurdles Javier Culson, 88.11 javelin Vitezslav Vesely, and 9:07.14 steeplechase Milcah Chemos. An Ethiopian clash at 5000m was won by Dejen Gebremeskel 12:58.92 from Hagos Gebrhiwet 12:58.99 and Imane Merga 12:59.77.

8   **Turin**, Italy. 13th Primo Nebiolo Memorial (EA Premium).

8-10   **Ibero-American Championships**, Barquisimeto, Venezuela. Brazil was the most successful nation and two South American records were set by their athletes: Andressa de Morais 64.21 in the women's discus and Lucimara da Silva, 6160 heptathlon.

8-10   **Japanese Championships**, Osaka. Koji Murofushi won his 18th successive national hammer title, while top mark was 48.41 for 400m hurdles by Takayuki Kishimoto.

9   **Istanbul**, Turkey. 65th Cezmi Or Memorial.

9   **New York (Randall's Island)**, USA. adidas GP (DL). David Rudisha was the star as he won the 800m in 1:41.74. In his first race since injury in July 2012, Tyson Gay had a fine win in the B 100m in 10.00 despite a 1.5m/s headwind. Later Yohan Blake won the A race in 9.90, but the wind had turned round to +0.7. Sanya Richards-Ross improved her 6 year-old 200m pb to 22.09 and Barbora Spotáková maintained her fine javelin form with her year's best of 68.72 but was beaten by Sunette Viljoen, who threw an African and Commonwealth record 69.35. Fantu Magiso celebrated her 20th birthday by lowering her recent Ethiopian 800m record from 1:57.56 to 1:57.48.   In the high jump Jesse Williams claimed victory on count back as both he and Robbie Grabarz cleared 2.36.

9   **Villeneuve d'Ascq**, France. 40 year-old Virgilijus Alekna had five discus throws over 68m headed by 69.04.

9-11   **Asian Junior Championships**, Colombo, Sri Lanka.

11   **Moscow Challenge**, Russia. Mariya Savinova won the women's 800m in 1:57.93.

11   **Prague**, Czech Republic. 17th Josef Odlozil Memorial. Top marks included Silke Spiegelburg, 4.76 pole vault, Zuzana Hejnová, 54.43 400mh, and Barbara Spotáková, javelin 65.88.

12   **Minsk**, Belarus. Olympic Champions Prizes. Oksana Menkova equalled her world-leading hammer mark of 78.18 from Yelena Matoshko who threw 76.56 with five throws over her previous best. Nadezhda Ostapchuk added 4cm to her national shot record with 21.13.

13   **Moscow**, Russia. Kuts Memorial. Svetlana Podosyonova, from a previous best of 4:07.26, won the 1500m in 3:59.61 followed by five more women under 4:02, including returning drug cheats Yelena Sobolova and Tatyana Tomashova, and Yekaterina Poistogova won the 800m in 1:57.93 with four more women under 2 minutes. Sergey Litvinov threw the hammer three times over 80m, topped by 80.98.

15-16 French Championships, Angers. Christophe Lemaitre won a sprint double with 9.94w and 20.31.

15-17 Polish Championships, Bydgoszcz. Tomasz Majewski won his tenth shot title in eleven years with 21.07 while Pavel Fajdek beat Szymon Ziólkowski for hammer title 80.32 to 78.25.

16-17 Belgian Championships, Brussels. Kevin Borlée improved his brother Jonathan's Belgian 400m record from 44.71 to 44.56 in the heats and almost matched that with 44.63 in the final. Meanwhile Jonathan improved his 200m best from 20.42 to 20.31.

16-17 German Championships, Wattenscheid. Betty Heidler won her eighth successive hammer title with 73.65 and Robert Harting his sixth at discus with 67.79. Sabine Mockenhaupt won an eleventh 5000m title.

16-17 Greek Championships, Athens. Top mark was a 14.71 triple jump by Athanasía Pérra, and Perikís Iakovákis (400mh) and Aléxandros Papadimitríou (HT) each won a record 15th Greek title.

17 Zhukovskiy, Russia. 54th Znamenskiy Memorial (WCM). Yekaterina Poistogova improved from 4:13.1i to win the 1500m in 4:00.11 and Tatyana Lysenko won the hammer with 75.48.

19-21 Russian Junior Championships, Cheboksary. Sergey Morgunov made a sensational improvement (from bests of 8.10/8.20w) to 8.35 to take the longest lasting world junior record (Randy Williams 8.34 to win the 1972 Olympic title).

21-23 Kenyan Olympic Trials, Nairobi. David Rudisha strode to 800m victory in 1:42.12, easily the best ever at high altitude, and Isiah Koech ran 13:09.80 and Thomas Longosiwa 13:11.48 in the 5000m, very fast times at 1675m altitude.

22-23 UK Championships, Birmingham. In cool, windy weather national records were set by Holly Bleasdale, pole vault 4.71, and Shara Proctor, long jump 6.95 to beat Bev Kinch's 29 year-old mark. Goldie Sayers won her tenth consecutive javelin title. Four Ethiopians made a guest appearances in the 10,000m and Kenenisa Bekele won in 27:02.59 from brother Tariku 27:03.24.

22- Jul 1 US Olympic Trials/Championships, Eugene. Several days were affected by rain, but Ashton Eaton overcame the elements to add 13 points to the world record for the decathlon with 9039 points (also 148 ahead of the old US record). A great meeting featured further world leads from LaShawn Merritt, 400m 44.12, Aries Merritt, 110mh 12.93, Christian Taylor, triple jump 17.62, Reese Hoffa, shot 22.00, Allyson Felix, 200m 21.69 for fourth all-time and the world's fastest since 1998, Sanya Richards-Ross, 400m 49.28, and Brittney Reese, long jump 7.15. Justin Gatlin beat Tyson Gay 9.80 to 9.86, and Carmelita Jeter beat Tianna Madison 10.92 to 10.96 in the 100m races. Winners in the Visa Championship Series were Eaton and Felix. Fifth successive US titles were won by Reese and by Nick Symmonds at 800m, and the one double winner was Galen Rupp at 5000m and 10,000m. An eight-day total watched at Eugene's historic Hayward Field, with a stadium record 22,602 on 28 June.

23 Klaipeda, Lithuania. Virgilijus Alekna set a world M40 discus record of 70.28.

23-24 Trinidad & Tobago Championships, Port of Spain. Keston Bledman 9.88 and Kelly-Ann Baptiste 10.98 won the 100m titles.

27-30 Canadian Championships, Calgary. Jessica Zelinka beat a top 100m hurdles field in 12.68 two days after she had won the heptathlon with 6599, her sixth national record.

27- Jul 1 African Championships, Porto Novo, Benin. Amantle Montsho won her fifth successive African Games or Championships title and improved her Botswana 400m record by 0.02 to 49.54. Further African Championships records were set in the men's 800m, Taoufik Makhloufi 1:43.88, 1500m, Caleb Ndiku 3:35.71, 10,000m, Kenneth Kipkemoi 27:19.74, and 110mh, Lehann Fourie 13.55 in his heat, and in the women's 1500m, Rabab Arafi, 4:05.80, long jump, Blessing Okagbare 6.96, Vivian Chukwuemeka, who improved her African record to 18.56 and 18.86 in winning her seventh African shot title (before losing this through a positive drugs test), and both Nigerian relay teams. Chris Harmse was just 50cm off his CBP with 77.22 for the hammer as he won his ninth African gold medal (second only to ten by Algerian hammer thrower Hakim Toumi 1984-98) and his silver medals in 2010 and 2011 give him the single event medal total record of eleven.

27- Jul 1 European Championships, Helsinki, Finland. Controversially advanced to biennial status, there were no championship records but three world-leading marks: by Irina Davidova, W 400m hurdles 53.77, and by the man and woman voted as Athletes of the Meeting: Renaud Lavillenie, pole vault 5.97, and Olga Saladuha, triple jump 14.99. Other impressive winners included men: Sergey Shubenkov, 110m hurdles 13.16 after 13.09 in his semi, Fabrizio Donato, triple jump 17.63w, David Storl, shot 21.58, Robert Harting, discus 68.30, Pascal Behrenbruch, decathlon 8558; women: Yelena Arzhakova, 800m 1:58.51, Sandra Perkovic, discus 67.62, and Vira Rebryk, javelin 66.86. After making all major finals from 1997, Nadine Kleinert at last won an outdoor shot gold.

28- Jul 1 **Jamaican Championships**, Kingston. Yohan Blake beat Usain Bolt in both 100m, 9.75 to 9.86, and 200m, 19.80 to 19.83. Asafa Powell 9.88 and Michael Frater 9.94 were also under 10 secs in the 100m, and Walter Weir was 3rd at 300m in 20.03, after 19.99 in his semi. Shelly-Ann Fraser-Pryce was also a great sprint doubler: 100m in a Commonwealth and CAC record 10.70 from Veronica Campbell-Brown 10.82, and the 200m in 22.10 from Sherone Simpson 22.37 and VCB 22.42.

July

3-4 **Russian Championships**, Cheboksary. Natalya Antyukh, 400m hurdles 53.40, and Anna Chicherova, high jump 2.03, set world-leading marks on the second day, followed by four more on the third day: Tatyana Lysenko, hammer 78.51, Darya Pishchalnikova, discus 70.69 (later disqualified), Antonina Krivoshapka, 400m 49.16 and Ivan Ukhov, high jump 2.39, as he headed Andrey Silnov 2.37 and Aleksandr Shustov 2.35. Triple jumper Tatyana Lebedeva returned to form with a 14.68 victory and in just her second year at the event Yekaterina Kostetskaya won the 1500m in 3:59.28 (after 1:57.46 and 1:58.83 for 3rd at 800m).

5 **Liège (Naimette-Xhovément)**; Belgium. Jonathan Borlée ran a Belgian record 31.87 for 300m.

6 **Saint-Denis**, France. Areva meeting (DL). David Rudisha starred with a brilliant 800m win in 1:41.54 and there was a record depth of times in the 5000m won by Dejen Gebremeskel in 12:46.81 from Hagos Gebrhiwet 12:47.53, with six men under 12:50 and 11 under 13 minutes (previous records 3 and 10 respectively). Times from 3rd (Isiah Koech, 12:48.64) to 13th were the quickest ever. Sally Pearson ran her third fastest ever 100m hurdle time of 12.40 and more world leads came from Javier Culson, 400m hurdles 47.78, and Meriem Alaoui Selsouli, 1500m 3:56.15 (although that was later lost to a drugs dq) heading five women under 4 minutes.

6-7 **Belarus Championships**, Grodno. Nadezhda Ostapchuk improved her national shot record to 21.39.

6-8 **NACAC (U23) Championships**, Irapuato, Mexico. High altitude made for fast sprint times.

7 **European Mountain Running Championships**, Denizil-Pamulkkale, Turkey. Ahmet Aslan won the men's race for the sixth successive year while Italy achieved their 17th men's team win in the 18 years of the event, Great Britain were women's team winners with Monika Fürholz individual champion.

7 **Heusden-Zolder**, Belgium. KBC Night of Athletics. The middle and long distance races provided the highlights as usual. The 800m winners were Abrahim Kipchirchir Rotich, in a Kenyan junior record 1:43 15, and Pamela Jelimo 1:56.76.

7 **Madrid**, Spain (WCM). Krisztián Pars won the hammer with 80.85 and there were new sub-10 men with Kemar Hyman (after a Cayman Island record 9.95 in his heat) winning in 9.95w from Kemar Bailey Cole 9.98.

7-8 **Italian Championships**, Bressanone. Daniele Greco beat Fabrizio Donato 17.67w to 17.52 at triple jump.

8 **Tomblaine**, France. Top mark was 20.97 in the shot by Valerie Adams.

10 **Sotteville-lès-Rouen**. Yelena Isinbayeva made her seasonal debut with a 4.75 pole vault win.

10-16 **World Junior Championships**, Barcelona, Spain. Although there was some swirling wind, conditions were generally excellent. The Egyptian-born Qatari Ashraf Amgad El-Seify (17) starred with a world junior 6kg hammer record of 85.57, and other championships records included men's 100m Adam Gemili 10.05, 800m Nijel Amos 1:43.79, 3000mSt Consesius Kipruto 8:06.10, junior 110mh Yordan O'Farril 13.18, 6kg shot Jacko Gill 22.20; and women: 200m Anthonique Strachan 22.53 (she also won the 100m), 400m Ashley Spencer 50.50, 1500m Faith Chepngetich Kipyegon 4:04.96, pole vault Angelica Bengtsson 4.50, and hammer Alexandra Tavernier 70.62. Gill and Bengtsson retained their titles from Moncton 2010. The US was easily the most successful nation with 20 medals, including 9 golds.

13-14 **London (Crystal Palace)**, GBR. Aviva London Grand Prix (DL). Hurdlers captured many of the headlines, as Aries Merritt 12.93 for 110m and Javier Culson 47.78 tied their best marks of the year, Kellie Wells beat Sally Pearson 12.57 to 12.59, and Perri Shakes-Drayton returned to form with a clear win over Irina Davydova 53.77 to 54.63 at 400m. Goldie Sayers broke her four year-old British record with 66.17 with Barbora Spotáková 2nd at 64.19, The Emsley Carr Mile was won by Silas Kiplagat 3:52.44.

17 **Luzern**, Switzerland. The 26th Spitzen

Leichtathletik meeting had lovely conditions and included a 200m breakthrough from 20.42 to 19.86 by Jason Young. Yohan Blake won the 100m in 9.85 and Virginia Crawford won a top-class women's 100m hurdles in 12.61.

18   **Minsk**, Belarus. There were further improvements to national records by Oksana Menkova hammer mark 78.69 and Nadezhda Ostapchuk shot 21.47 and 21.58.

20   **Herculis, Monaco** (DL). On a warm, windless evening, this was again a meeting of very high quality. Many athletes had excellent pre-Olympic performances but some, such as Yelena Isinbayeva (nh PV), Caster Semenya (9th 800m) and LaShawn Merritt (dnf 400m) did not. There were the best ever place times for 5th and 6th in the 1500m, in which the 1-2-3 set pbs: Asbel Kiprop 3:28.88, Nixon Chepseba 3:29.77 and Nick Willis 3:30.35 Oceania record. Consesius Kipruto ran the second best ever by a junior, 8:03.49, to beat Paul Koech in the 3000m steeplechase, with Evan Jager taking 10.59 secs off his pb with a North American record 8:06.81, and other Kenyans juniors excelled in the 800m, Abraham Rotich beating Leonard Kosencha 1:43.13 to 1:43.40. Aries Merritt ran his third successive 12.93 for 110m hurdles.

21   **Szczecin**, Poland. 58th Kusocinski Memorial. Steve Lewis won the pole vault with a British record 5.82 and home success included a women's hammer win by Anita Wlodarczyk 76.81.

August

3-12   **Olympic Games**, London. The Games were a huge success, the exhilarating atmosphere and superb organisation bringing great credit to all concerned. Capacity crowds flocked to all the athletics sessions. David Rudisha provided the highlight with his front-running 1:40.19 world record for 800m, leading all the finalists to the best ever place times, closely followed by super-star Usain Bolt, who completed another sprint treble, and was one of seven individual champions from Beijing to retain their titles with three 2004 winners regaining theirs. There were magnificent world records at both 4x100m relays – Jamaica 36.84 and the GDR 40.82, a sensational 0.55 off the 27 year-old GDR time. Triple British success on the second day was the nation's greatest ever with huge credit to Jessica Ennis for her smashing heptathlon victory after being "the face" of the Games and Mo Farah went to double distance success. The United States easily headed the medal and points table, with Allyson Felix and Sanya Richards-Ross winning three and two gold medals respectively, each taking their career total to tie the women's record of four. *See Championships section for reports and results.*

15   **Albi,** France. 8th DécaNation. 1. USA 66, 2. RUS 56, 3. GER 39, 4. FRA 38. Top mark was 9.81w by Justin Gatlin at 100m.

17   **Stockholm**, Sweden. 46th DN Galan (DL). Six of the eleven Olympic gold medallists who took part in this first post-Games major meeting won their events. The most impressive of these was Yuliya Zaripova, who improved her 3000m steeplechase best to 9:05.02, and she won one-carat diamonds to the value of $10,000 for setting a stadium record, as did Valerie Adams, shot 20.26, and Sandra Perkovic, discus 68.77. Isiah Koech improved to third on the world junior all-time list for 3000m with 7:30.43.

18-19   **Eberstadt**, Germany. Mutaz Essa Barshim equalled his Qatari record with 2.35 at the annual high jump meeting. Robbie Grabarz was second with 2.33. Women's winner Irina Gordeyeva added 2cm to her all-time and 5cm to her season's best with 2.04, clear of Svetlana Shkolina 2.00.

19   **Warsaw**, Poland. Skolimowska Memorial. Anna Wlodarczyk beat Tatyana Lysenko at hammer 76.70 to 73.95 to reverse the Olympic order.

20   **Budapest**, Hungary. 2nd István Gyulai Memorial Meeting. Three Olympic champions won: Christian Taylor, TJ 17.30, Krisztián Pars, HT 79.74, and Sanya Richards-Ross, 200m 22.70.

20   **Linz**, Austria, Gugl Games (EA Classic). Olympic champion Félix Sánchez won the 400m hurdles in 48.13.

23   **Lausanne**, Switzerland. Athletissima (DL). Usain Bolt and Yohan Blake ran separate races, but both won readily: Bolt the 200m in 19.58 from Churandy Martina who set a Dutch record of 19.85 and Nickel Ashmeade 19.94, with Wallace Spearmon running the fastest ever (20.02) for 6th place, and Blake the 100m in 9.69 from Tyson Gay 9.83 and Nesta Carter 9.95. Carmelita Jeter just beat Shelly-Ann Fraser-Pryce, 10.856 to 10.857. Mutaz Essa Barshim won a terrific high jump competition by equalling the Asian record at 2.39 as Ivan Ukhov was 2nd and Robbie Grabarz (equalling British record) 3rd, both at 2.37. The 2008 Olympic champion beat the 2012 one at women's 800m, Pamela Jelimo 1:57.59 from Mariya Savinova 1:58.10, but Aries Merritt false started in the 110m hurdles.

23-26   **Finnish Championships**, Lahti. Top performance was 87.79 at the javelin by Antti Ruuskanen. Ola-Pekka Karjalainen won his 15th successive hammer title with 73.21.

24-26   **Swedish Championships**, Gävle. Anna Söderberg won her 20th successive

Swedish title at the discus, improving her own record for any event.

25-26 Spanish Championships, Pamplona. Mario Pestano won his 12th successive Spanish discus title with 63.28 and Berta Castells her 10th with 68.35 at hammer.

26   Birmingham, GBR. Aviva Grand Prix (DL). Aries Merritt was back in prime form with a 12.95 win at 110m hurdles and Carmelita Jeter had a more clear-cut 100m win over Shelly-Ann Fraser-Pryce than at Lausanne, 10.81 to 10.90.

26   Dubnica nad Váhom, Slovakia. 10th Athletics Bridge meeting. Top marks came in the hammer from Krisztián Pars 79.84 and Betty Heidler 75.18.

30   Zürich, Switzerland. Weltklasse (DL). As in 2011 the meeting featured half the Diamond League finals and, as in 2011, David Rudisha lost his final race of the year 1:42.81 to 1:42.54 by Mohammed Aman, who edged past in the home straight. Aman also took the Diamond League title. Nickel Ashmeade took the honours at 200m as he ran a pb 19.85 behind Usain Bolt 19.66, and despite pouring rain Yohan Blake won the 100m in 9.76. The hot women's sprint rivalry continued as Shelly-Ann Fraser-Pryce beat Carmelita Jeter 10.83 to 10.97. Valerie Adams (shot 20.81) and Sandra Perkovic (discus 63.97) completed six wins in seven DL meetings. The shot competitions were again held the day before the main meeting at Zürich's main railway station.

September

1   Lille, France. Five men broke 60 minutes for the half marathon, all with pbs, led by Ezekiel Chebii 59:05.

1-2   Finland v Sweden, Gothenburg, Sweden were men's winners 220-187 and Finland women's 223-187 as Olla-Pekka Karjalainen (72.72) had his 13th successive hammer win in the annual Finnkampen.

2   28th WMRA World Mountain Running Championships, Tirana, Albania. A record 40 nations took part. Eritrea were men's and the USA women's team champions. Andrea Mayr had her fourth individual win.

4   Rovereto, Italy. Highlight of the 48th Palio Citta della Quercia meeting was a 400m run by Antonina Krivoshapka in 49.94.

4   Zagreb, Croatia. 62nd Boris Hanzekovic Memorial (WCM). Local star Sandra Perkovic won the discus with 65.79 and Allyson Felix ended the meeting by winning the 200m by 0.6 secs in 22.35. Rosemarie Whyte ran her season's fastest of 50.08 for a big win at 400m, and the young steeplechaser Jairus Kipchoge Birech led home five more Kenyans in 8:11.80.

Resse Hoffa capped a great shot series (five over 21.30) with 21.80 to beat Tomasz Majewski by 1.1m and record his fifth successive victory since the Olympic Games.

5   Aachen, Germany. Björn Otto became the 18th pole vaulter to clear 6m with 6.01, a German record and best mark of 2012.

7   Brussels, Belgium. 36th Van Damme Memorial (DL). The capacity crowd of 47,000 was treated to an astonishing feat when Aries Merritt skimmed over 110m hurdles in 12.80 to take 0.07 off Dayron Robles' world record. Usain Bolt won the 100m in 9.86 for the Diamond League title, but Yohan Blake recorded an even more impressive time with 19.54 for 200m. Three successive DL titles were confirmed for Paul Kipsiele Koech, who was third here in the steeplechase 8:04.01 behind Brimin Kipruto 8:03.11 and Consesius Kipruto 8:03.70, and for Kaliese Spencer, who won the 400m hurdles in 53.69. The great Brussels 10,000m tradition was maintained as Emmanuel Bett won in 26:51.16 from Vincent Chepkok 26:51.68, Kenneth Kipkemoi 26:52.65 and world junior champion Yigrem Demelash an Ethiopian junior record 26:57.56 as the first nine (seven Kenyans and two Ethiopians) ran pbs.

8-9   IAU World 24 Hours Championships, Katowice, Poland. Mike Morton won the men's race in a North American record 277.543km and Michaela Dimitraidu was women's winner as they went to third and fourth respectively on the world all-time lists.

9   Rieti, Italy (WCM). The 42nd edition of this meeting. Krisztián Pars, 79.22, and Anita Wlodarczyk, 74.52, won here to seal season's wins in the IAAF Hammer Challenges. Taoufik Makhloufi ran strongly to beat the highly promising junior Edwin Kiplagat Melly 1:43.74 to 1:43.81 at 800m.

12   Berlin, Germany. 71st ISTAF (WCM). Aries Merritt ran his seventh wind-legal sub-13 second time for 110mh in 2012, a meeting record 12.97, to equal the season's record set by Dayron Robles in 2008. Maintaining an even better record was Robert Harting whose discus win at 67.40 was his 33rd in succession, and another Olympic champion to win was Félix Sánchez, 400mh 48.89. This was again the best-attended one-day meeting of the year, with 55,565 spectators in the Olympic Stadium.

13-18 Tianjin, China. National Student Games. Asian walks records were set by Wang Zhen 39:30.38 for 10,000m and Liu Hong, 20:34.76 for 5000m.

14   IAAF Race Walking Challenge Final, Ordos, China. Chinese walkers won both 10km races and the overall series $30,000 prizes: Wang Zhen 39:27 and Liu Hong 43:18.

15-16 **Talence**, France. Decastar Multis. Hans Van Alphen, who won the decathlon with 8293 points, took the IAAF Combined Events Challenge for 2012, while the women's Challenge winner was Tatyana Chernova, although only 4th here with 6315 behind Lyudmyla Yosypenko 6401. Barbora Spotáková was sixth with a pb 5880 and set a world heptathlon best for the javelin with 60.90.

16 32nd **Great North Run, Newcastle to South Shields**, GBR. Wilson Kipsang unleashed a fantastic sprint to beat Micah Kogo by 1 second in 59:06, and Tirunesh Dibaba made a notable debut at half marathon by winning the women's race in 67:35, 6 secs ahead of Edna Kiplagat.

22 **5th Avenue Mile, New York**, USA. Winners were Matt Centrowitz 3:52.9 and Brenda Martinez 4:24.2.

22-25 **Chinese Championships**, Kunshan. Gong Lijiao won her sixth successive women's shot title with 19.87 and Zhang Wenxiu her seventh hammer title with 74.94.

23 **Amsterdam** to **Zaandam**, Netherlands. Leonard Patrick Komon won the 28th annual Dam tot Damloop 10 miles race in 44:46.

30 **Berlin Marathon**, Germany. Geoffrey Mutai won the 39th BMW Berlin marathon in 2:04:15 by just 1 second from Dennis Kimetto, won ran the fastest ever debut marathon. This win gave Mutai the World Marathon Majors title for 2011/12. Abere Kebede won the women's race in 2:20:30 from Tirfe Tsegaye 2:21:19.

October

7 **World Half Marathon Championships**, Kavarna, Bulgaria. Zersenay Tadese won his fourth IAAF World title at the half marathon (plus a fifth road title at 20k) to confirm his status as the supreme master of the event. He took the lead from just beyond 5k and despite the hot (up to 30°C) and humid conditions opened up a big lead from just beyond 6k. He won in 60:19 from Deressa Chimsa 60:51. Kenya who had 4-5-6 finishers won the team title. Meseret Hailu won the women's race by 1 second from compatriot Feysa Tadesse, leading Ethiopia to the team title.

7 **Chicago Marathon**, USA. Tsegaye Kebede broke the course record by nearly a minute with 2:04:28. Feyisa Lelisa was second in 2:04:52 and then there were outstanding debuts from Tilahun Regassa 2:05:27 and Samuel Kitwara 2:05:54. In the women's race Atsede Baysa 2:22:03 beat Rita Jeptoo by just a second. There were a record 37,455 finishers (20,688 men and 16,787 women).

21 **Amsterdam**, Netherlands. Both men's and women's course records were broken in the 37th edition of the TCS Amsterdam Marathon, an IAAF Silver Label road race. Wilson Chebet won in 2:05:41, 12 seconds faster than in his 2011 win, and Meseret Hailu improved her best from 2:27:15 to 2:21:09.

28 **Frankfurt-am-Main**, Germany. Patrick Makau put his frustration at not being selected for the Olympic Games behind him as he won in 2:06:08 from Deressa Chimsa 2:06:52. Despite cold weather two women broke the course record, marathon debutante Meselech Melkamu 2:21:01 and Georgina Rono 2:21:39 with Mamitu Daska, who had set the record at 2:21:59 in 2011, third in 2:23:52.

November

4 **New York City Marathon**, USA. The race was cancelled as a consequence of the damage caused by Hurricane Sandy.

18 **Nijmegen**, Netherlands. Tirunesh Dibaba stepped up in distance to 15k and won the women's Seven Hills race in 47:08.

18 **Yokohama**, Japan. Lydia Cheromei broke away from the lead pack at 15k in the 4th Yokohama Women's Marathon and, after covering the next 5k in 16:25 went on to take 49 secs off the course record with 2:23:07.

23 **Chiba**, Japan. The annual International Ekiden in which men and women run alternate legs of the 42.195k course was won by Kenya in 2:05:06, 10 seconds ahead of Japan.

24 **Barcelona**, Spain. The IAAF celebrated its centenary with a Gala at the Museu Nacional de'Art de Catalunya attended by scores of all-time greats of our sport. There was a marvellous exhibition of athletics memorabilia at the Museu Olimpic i de l'Esport Joan Antoni Samaranch, next to the Olympic Stadium.

December

2 **Fukuoka**, Japan. Joseph Gitau won the 66th Fukuoka International race in 2:06:58.

9 **European Cross-Country Championships**, Szentendre, Hungary. Senior men's winner Andrea Lalli became the first runner to complete the hat-trick of winning at junior, U23 and senior level and Fionnuala Britton became the first woman to defend her title. The British team was again the most successful with 10 medals (2 gold, 3 silver and 5 bronze). Sergiy Lebid maintained his amazing record of running in all 19 editions of this race, finishing 15th.

ATHLETES OF 2012
By Peter Matthews

Male Athlete of the Year

THE IAAF SHORT list of three for the title of World Male Athlete of the Year was Usain Bolt, David Rudisha and Aries Merritt. All set marvellous world records in 2012: Bolt anchoring the Jamaican team at 4x100m in the Olympic Games in London, Rudisha with a stupendous front-running display at 800m at the Games, and Merritt with the greatest-ever display of smooth fast 110mh hurdling in the Diamond League final in Brussels. All were great candidates and so, too, was the other world record breaker, Ashton Eaton, who scored 9039 points despite adverse conditions at the US Olympic Trials in Eugene and who went on to win the Olympic title, having earlier won the World Indoor heptathlon title with a world record score of 6645 points. Then there was Robert Harting, who for the second successive year was unbeaten in the discus (12 competitions). For sure his world-leading mark of 70.66 was a long way short of Jürgen Schult's world record of 74.08, but Harting has not gone chasing wind-friendly locations. And the Olympic 5000m and 10,000m champion Mo Farah was unbeaten in eight outdoor finals: 5 at 5000m and one 1 each at 1500m, 2 miles and 10,000m; he had however lost 4 of 5 indoors.

Although he did not meet his top rivals in other events the surprise Olympic javelin champion Keshorn Walcott was also unbeaten and Sergey Kirdyapkin won both his 50k walks: World Cup and Olympics. Krisztián Pars lost just one of his 15 hammer competitions.

None of the top three were unbeaten, but all had much more than their Olympic triumphs, Daniel Rudisha is my Male Athlete of the Year for the third successive year. Just as in 2011 he won all his races (six finals) but lost his last race of the year to the young Ethiopian Mohamed Aman, 1:42.53 to 1:42.81 at Zürich. His ability is such that many are expecting that he can become the first man to break 1:40 for 800m. Usain Bolt has been the super-star of the sport for several years and he remains hungry for success, Just because he has done it before, a superb sprint triple in London 2012, as in Beijing 2008 and Berlin 2009 and two golds in Daegu 2012, is no less of a magnificent feat, with a series of successes unprecedented in Olympic/World Championships history. And his growing rivalry with his hugely talented training companion Yohan Blake should give us plenty to enthuse over in future.

Aries Merritt had shown early promise in high school in Georgia, including 36.71 at 300m hurdles as well as 110mh success, and he consolidated that by winning the World Junior title in 2004. He improved from a best of 13.47 that year (when 4th at the NCAAs) to 13.38 and 13.34w in 2005. He then finished his college career at the University of Tennessee in 2006, forgoing his senior year to turn professional, with a brilliant unbeaten season in college competition and winning NCAA tiles indoors and out. He also took his personal best down to 13.12 when 5th at Lausanne in the world record race (12.88) of Liu Xiang. In 2007 he ran 13.09 in a win in Stockholm, but he did not improve further until 2012. He was successively 7th, 6th, 6th, 4th and 3rd at US Championships from 2005-09 and was 2nd in 2011, going on to place 5th equal at the World Championships. All good international-class form, but he left that behind with his super season in 2012 when, having changed from eight to seven strides to the first hurdle he ran nine sub-13 second times (including one wind-assisted), won the Olympic title by over a metre, and ended with that marvellous 12.80 in the Diamond League final in Brussels.

100 Metres

WITH HIS SECOND Olympic sprint treble Usain Bolt is firmly established as the greatest sprinter of all time. He started his 100m campaign in 2012 with four wins, including Dia-

Selections for World Top Ten

My selection of the top 10 athletes of 2010 together with the lists compiled by international experts polled by *Track & Field News* and those of *Athletics International* readers:

	PJM	TFN	AI
David Rudisha	1	1	1
Usain Bolt	2	3	2
Aries Merritt	3	4	3
Ashton Eaton	4	2	5
Mo Farah	5	5	4
Robert Harting	6	6	6
Yohan Blake	7	7	8
Kirani James	8	9	9
Renaud Lavillenie	9	10	7
Krisztián Pars	10	8	10

mond League wins in Rome 9.76 and Oslo 9.79. But he was beaten 9.75 to 9.86 by Yohan Blake at the Jamaican Championships. Any doubts about his supremacy were cast aside, however, at the Olympic Games as while Blake again ran 9.75 Bolt clocked 9.63. Without Blake, he ended his year with victory in the Diamond League final in Brussels in 9.86, for a season's record of seven sub-9.90 times, a number matched by Blake, who lost just that Olympic final in nine 100m competitions and went on to run a pb 9.69 in Lausanne. It was again a great year for 100m running with a record 64 wind-legal sub-10.00 times plus 11 with excess wind assistance (61 and 20 in 2011) and the 100th best man running 10.20 (previous record 10.20 in 2011), although 19 men under 10.00 compared to 20 in 2011. Despite temperate conditions in London there were the best ever times for places 3-7 in the Olympic final with Justin Gatlin, Tyson Gay, Ryan Bailey, Churandy Martina (who only had two other minor 100m races) and Richard Thompson all under 10 secs, and just the injured Asafa Powell missing out. Gatlin was 2-1 against Gay (returning after hip surgery in 2011), having also beaten him to take the US title with Bailey, Mike Rodgers and Darvis Patton following in sub-10 times. Powell ran three sub 9.90 times, including when 3rd in the Jamaican Champs, when Michael Frater, Kemar Bailey Cole and Nesta Carter were 4th to 6th. Carter then had a fine campaign in Europe, and was 2-0 v Thompson and 3-0 v Kim Collins, although beaten 3-2 by Bailey. Another Jamaican Nickel Ashmeade was 1-1 v Carter and ahead against Thompson, Rodgers and Frater. After winning the European title Christophe Lemaitre chose to concentrate on the 200m at the Games, but was 2-1 v Collins and 1-0 v Rodgers, who was 3-0 v Collins before his season was ended by a stress fracture in his foot in July. Just missing out on Olympic final places were Kestin Bledman, Dwain Chambers and Adam Gemili, who in just his second year of serious running was a brilliant winner of the World Junior title.

Trell Kimmons ran the fastest indoor 60m time with 6.45A to win the US title from Gatlin 6.47, but he was 4th at the World Indoors well behind Gatlin who won in 6.46 from Carter 6.54 and Chambers 6.60. Lerone Clarke 6.47 and Carter 6.49 at Birmingham ran the season's other 6.50 times.

Most times at 10.00/10.05 or faster: Blake 10/13, Gatlin 8+1w/9+1w, Bolt 7/9, R Bailey 6/10, Powell 6/8, Gay 5/9, Carter 4/8, Rodgers 2+2w/5+3w, Bledman 2+1w/5+1w, Ashmeade 2/5, Thompson 2/3, Martina 2/2, Frater 1/7, Bailey-Cole 1+1w/3+1w, Patton 1/3, Kemar Hyman 1+1w/2+1w, Travis Padgett 2w/1+2w, Lemaître 1w/2+2w, Collins 1w/3+1w, Walter Dix 1w/2+1w.

1. Bolt, 2. Blake, 3. Gatlin, 4. Gay, 5. R Bailey, 6. Powell, 7. Carter, 8. Ashmeade, 9. Frater, 10. Lemaitre

200 Metres

AS IN THE 100m Usain Bolt was beaten by Yohan Blake at the Jamaican Champs (19.80 to 19.83), but won the Olympic final in 19.32 (the equal fourth fastest ever), 0.12 ahead of Blake, and followed with wins in Lausanne 19.58 and Zürich (DL final) in 19.66. Blake also had wins in Kingston 19.91 and Brussels 19.54. With his surprise Olympic bronze Walter Weir was the third fastest at 19.84, 0.01 quicker than Churandy Martina and Nickel Ashmeade, who missed his Games chance after being 4th at the Jamaican Champs. Ashmeade was behind Weir there but overall beat him 4-1 in a fine campaign which included 2nd in Zürich. Jason Young, who improved from 20.53 in 2011 to 19.86, made it five Jamaicans in the top six in the rankings as he too (7th Jamaican Champs) beat Weir 4-1 but was 0-3 v Ashmeade. Weir, however, beat the US champion and Olympic 4th placer Wallace Spearmon 3-0. Martina and Christophe Lemaitre were 5th and 6th in the Olympic final, and 1-1 in their clashes. Martina was 2-2 v Weir, and was 2nd in Lausanne in 19.85, a race contested by most of the world élite, when he was followed by Ashmeade, Young, Weir, Spearmon and Marvin Anderson. Four top sprinters had just one race at 200m in 2012: Walter Dix 20.02, Justin Gatlin 20.11, LaShawn Merritt 20.16 and Tyson Gay 20.21, and some way after the top eight remaining ranking places were contested by Alex Quiñónez (Ibero-American champion and 7th OG), Marvin Anderson, and the US 2-3-4 Maurice Mitchell, Isiah Young and Calesio Newman. World 100th best was a new record at 20.57 (previous best 20.62 in 2011).

Most times at 20.30 or better: Weir 12, Spearmon 10+2w, Ashmeade 8, Martina 7, Bolt, Blake 6; J Young, Lemaitre 4

1. Bolt, 2. Blake, 3. Ashmeade, 4. Martina, 5. Young, 6. Weir, 7. Spearmon, 8. Lemaitre, 9. Anderson, 10. Mitchell

400 Metres

KIRANI JAMES FOLLOWED wins in the 2009 World Youths, 2010 World Juniors and 2011 Worlds Championships with a hugely impressive clear Olympic win in 43.94, becoming the tenth man ever to break 44 seconds – and still before his 20th birthday. He had a false start disqualification in Eugene but had five wins in his seven finals, his only loss being to Jonathan Borlée in Monaco. LaShawn Merritt was the fastest in pre-Olympic competition with 44.19 in Doha and 44.12 at the US Olympic Trials the fastest of his six successive wins, but then he pulled up injured in Monaco and was unable to get far in his heat at the Olympics. He had, however, three wins over Luguelín Santos, over a year younger than James, who won the World Junior title before taking Olympic silver and who went to third on the world all-time junior list with 44.45 at Hengelo. Santos was 2-2 against both the Borlée twins, of whom Kevin had the slight edge, 2-1 including 5th to 6th at the Olympics and as they finished 1 Kevin, 2 Jonathan in the Diamond League final in Brussels. Chris Brown, 4th OG, was 2-0 v Kevin Borlée and 2-1 against Demetrius Pinder, 7th OG. Lalonde Gordon broke through from 45.51 in 2011 to 44.52 for the Olympic bronze and he was 3rd in Brussels but without the depth of performance of the above. Australian champion Steven Solomon tied for the bronze at the World Juniors and after a series of mid-45 times broke through to 44.97 and 8th in 45.14 at the Olympics. The fastest non-qualifier at the Olympics was Bryshon Nellum, who had been 3rd at the US Trials. Tony McQuay, 2nd there also won the NCAA title and had better times than all the Americans bar Merritt. Jeremy Wariner ran consistently in the low 45s, but was far from his old world number one form and was 6th at the US Trials; he also lost his one clash against Angelo Taylor, who had a good win in Birmingham. Martyn Rooney, who after three early-season 44.9s was stuck in the mid-45s, and European champion Pavel Maslák were the best Europeans after the Borlées. The world 100th best equalled the all-time best of 45.78 from 2000.

Nery Brenes who had a best of 45.20 outdoors, headed the indoor lists with his World Indoor 45.11, which earned him the gold medal ahead of Pinder and Brown.

Most sub-45.00 times: James, Santos 7; K Borlée & J Borlée 6; Merritt, Pinder 5; McQuay 4, Brown, Gil Roberts, M Rooney 3

1. James, 2. Merritt, 3. Santos, 4. Brown.
5. K Borlée, 6. J Borlée, 7. Gordon, 8. McQuay,
9. Pinder, 10. Taylor

800 Metres

DAVID RUDISHA BUILT on his already exemplary reputation to rank top for the fifth time. His season led, after five earlier 800m wins, to that wonderful Olympic triumph when he front-ran to his third world record time of 1:40.91 (49.28 +51.19). Then, just as in 2011, he lost his last race to the precocious Mohamed Aman 1:42.53 to 1:42.81 in the Diamond League final in Zürich. This was the second of three successive post-Olympic wins by Aman, who had also had three wins in four indoor races including the World Indoor title and outdoors three wins and one second place (to Abubaker Kaki in Eugene) before being one of three juniors in the Olympic final. There Aman took 6th place in a great race which featured the best ever times for each of the places 1-8. And it was the other juniors who followed Rudisha home: Nijel Amos was 2nd and Timothy Kitum 3rd and these two had been

1-2 in the World Juniors, missed by Aman. The season's record for Amos was five wins and that second place, and he improved from a 2011 best of 1:47.28 to 1:46.21 in May and then an astonishing breakthrough to 1:43.11 in Mannheim, the second best ever by a junior. But both he and Kitum bettered the world junior record with 1:41.73 and 1:42.53 in London as Amos showed that he was not frightened in taking on Rudisha. The remaining Olympic places were taken by 4. Duane Solomon, 5. Nick Symmonds, 7. Kaki and 8. Andrew Osagie. Abraham Kipchirchir Rotich was 4th in the Kenyan Olympic Trials behind Rudisha, Kitum and Anthony Chemut, but had three big wins in the 1:43s, Liège, Heusden and Monaco, and was 2-0 v Solomon, 1-0 v Symmonds and 2-0 v Kaki. He was also 1-1 against another Kenyan (6th heat in their Trials) Leonard Kosencha, who actually had a 4-1 record v Kitum with major wins in Shanghai and Rome and a fine end-of-season run of 2nd Monaco, 3rd Zürich and 4th Berlin. Symmonds won the US title from Khadevis Robinson and Solomon, but Solomon beat Symmonds 2-1 as both these Americans were 2-1 v Kaki. Taoufik Makhloufi had four 800m wins and two second places; he beat Chemut to win the African title and finished with 2nd in Stockholm to Aman, ahead of Rotich and Solomon, and 1st in Rieti from Edwin Kiplagat Melly, the World Junior bronze medallist. Adam Kszczot beat Osagie 2-0, but like Chemut, went out in the semis at the Olympics. Osagie beat Kaki 3-1, but Kaki had three quicker times and was crucially a place ahead in London after being the one man to try to stay with Rudisha.

Most times sub-1:44.5: Rudisha, Aman 9; Rotich 5, Kitum, Kosencha, Symmonds, Kaki 4, Amos, Makhloufi, Solomon, Job Kinyor 3

1. Rudisha, 2. Amos, 3. Aman, 4. Kitum,
5. Rotich, 6. Kosencha, 7. Makhloufi,
8. Solomon, 9. Symmonds, 10. Kaki

1500 Metres

THIS WAS A tricky event to rank. Three Kenyans headed the world lists under 3:30: Asbel Kiprop and Nixon Chepseba at Monaco and Silas Kiplagat at Doha, but they came in 12th, 11th and 7th in a rather unsatisfactory Olympic final, with the last placer Kiprop injured at the time. Taoufik Makhloufi took the gold medal quite clearly from Leonel Manzano, Abdelaati Iguider, Matt Centrowitz and European champion Henrik Ingebrigtsen. It was a very different story, however in the Diamond League in which Olympic 6th Mekonnen Gebremedhin had one win and Kiprop and Kiplagat each had three wins. Kiplagat won the DL final in Brussels from Gebremedhin, Bethan Birgen, Centrowitz, Kiprop, Daniel K Komen, Chepseba, Makhloufi and Caleb Ndiku also under 3:50. Overall Kiplagat is best; he beat Kiprop 4-1 and

Chepseba 5-1 and had six wins in nine races; Kiprop, who twice ran sub-3:50 for the top two mile times of the year (Oslo and Eugene), was 2-1 v Makhloufi and 3-2 v Chepseba and Gebremedhin, who was 4-2 v Chepseba. Two more Kenyans, 4th and 5th in their Trials, came next on their sequence of marks, with Ndiku beating Birgen 5-3 (Ndiku better in first half of season and Birgen in second half) and these two 6-2 and 7-1 against Collins Cheboi, who was nonetheless good enough to beat Iguider 3-1. Nick Willis (9th OG) and Ayanleh Souleiman (2nd African Champs) just miss ranking places while Manzano was 10th-12th in all his five DL races. The world 100th best of 3:36.84 was a huge improvement on the previous record from 2011 of 3:37.77; indeed 124 men bettered that time.

Iguider beat Ilham Tanui Özbilen and Gebremedhin to win a slowly run World Indoor race.

Most times sub-3:34 or 3:51M: Birgen 7, Gebremedhin, Makhloufi, Chepseba 6; Kiprop, C Ndiku, Cheboi 5, Kiplagat 4, Komen, Benson Seurei 3

1. Kiplagat, 2. Kiprop, 3. Makhloufi,
4. Gebremedhin, 5. Chepseba, 6. Centrowitz,
7. Ndiku, 8. Birgen, 9. Cheboi, 10. Iguider

3000 Metres/2 Miles

THE YEAR'S FASTEST times were run indoors: Augustine Choge and Edwin Soi, both 7:29.94 at Karlsruhe with Yenew Alamirew and Eliud Kipchoge close behind. Choge was also fastest outdoors with 7:30.42 at Doha, followed by Kipchoge, Moses Kipsiro, Isiah Koech and Thomas Longosiwa, all under 7:34. The other fast outdoor race came at Stockholm, won by Koech in 7:30.43 from Caleb Ndiku 7:30.99, and Koech also won major races indoors in Stockholm and outdoors in Oslo. Kipchoge ran the year's fastest 2 miles with 8:07.39 indoors in Birmingham from Mo Farah 8:08.07 and Kipsiro 8:08.16 and Tariku Bekele 8:08.27. Bernard Lagat won the World Indoor 3000m in 7:41.44 from Choge, Soi, Farah and Dejen Gebremeskel.

5000 Metres

MO FARAH WON all his five 5000m races. Nobody could catch him either in a fast race, as in his 12:56.98 in Eugene or in slower ones, as in the Europeans 13:29.91 and Olympics 13:41.66. The ten fastest times of the year all came at Saint-Denis, won by Dejen Gebremeskel 12:46.81 from Hagos Gebrhiwet world junior record 12:48.64, Isiah Koech 12:48.64, Yenew Alamirew 12:48.77, Thomas Longosiwa 12:49.04 and John Kipkoech 12:49.50 with Tariku Bekele, Eliud Kipchoge, Kenenisa Bekele and Edwin Soi all under 12:56. Gebremeskel, Gebrhiwet and Imane Merga were also under 13 minutes in Oslo (with Tariku and Kenenisa Bekele just

outside) as were Koech and Galen Rupp in Eugene behind Farah, and Koech, Longosiwa and Bernard Lagat in Zürich. Gebremeskel was fourth in that last race, but takes second ranking with his silver at the Olympics, when he was followed by Longosiwa, Lagat, Koech, Abdelaati Iguider and Rupp. Kipkoech, T Bekele. Yigren Demelesh, Merga, Rupp and Alamirew were 5th to 10th in the Diamond League final in Zürich. A record 108 men beat 13:25 (99 in 2008).

Most times sub 13:06: Gebremeskel, I Koech, Longosiwa, T Bekele, K Bekele 3.

1. Farah, 2. Gebremeskel, 3. Koech,
4. Longosiwa, 5. Lagat, 6. Gebrhiwet,
7. Kipkoech, 8. T Bekele, 9. Rupp, 10. K Bekele

10,000 Metres

THE 10,000 METRES race at the Van Damme Memorial in Brussels once again provided a raft of fast times, indeed the top five of 2012. Emmanuel Bett won in 26:51.16 followed by Vincent Chepkok, Kenneth Kipkemoi and world junior champion Yigrem Demelash under 27 minutes and Leonard Komon and Mike Kigen just outside. The year's next fastest times came in Eugene, where the Kenyan Trial was held at the Prefontaine meeting and won by Wilson Kiprop in 27:01.98 from Moses Masai, Bidan Karoki, Bett, Geoffrey Kirui. Lucas Rotich and Eliud Kipchoge, and in Birmingham where the top Ethiopians were in action: Kenenisa Bekele winning in 27:02.59 from Tariku Bekele, Gebregzhiaber Gebremariam, Sileshi Sihine and Ugandan Moses Kipsiro, Another top-class race was at Hengelo where Tariku Bekele won from Leslisa Desisa (also a winner in Liège), Sihine and Gebremariam. The 34 fastest times of the year were run by 26 East Africans. When it came to the Olympic Games, however, East Africans filled places 3 to 8, beaten by the last kilometre (2:28.45) pace of Mo Farah (his one 10k of the year), and US champion Galen Rupp. Tariku and Kenenisa Bekele were 3rd and 4th, followed by Karoki, Zersenay Tadese, Teklemariam Medhin and Gebremariam. Of the other Kenyans Masai was 12th and Kiprop did not finish. Masai had won the Kenyan pre-trial race in Nairobi from Kipchoge and Rotich but Bett, Karoki and Kiprop were 8th, 9th and 10th, and Kipkemoi won the Kenyan Championship in 27:49.53, a fast high altitude time, and also the African title. The 2011 world champion Ibrahim Jeylan did not finish his one 10,000m race of 2012 and third-placer Imane Merga was 9th in Hengelo and 7th in Brussels. World 100th best of 28:06.74 was the second best ever.

1. Farah, 2. Rupp. 3. T Bekele, 4. K Bekele,
5. Karoki, 6. Masai, 7. Bett, 8. Kipkemoi,
9. Gebremariam, 10. Demelash

Half Marathon

THE CLASSIC 1 HOUR was beaten by 29 men in 2012, headed by Atsedu Tsegay 58:47 in Prague.

Down the list in 17th place is Zersenay Tadese with his 59:34 win at Lisbon but once again he showed his mastery of the distance as he won the World Championship in 60:19 well clear of Deressa Chimsa 60:51. Three men had two sub-1 hour times: Ezekiel Chebii, who won in Lille after 3rd in Berlin behind Dennis Kimetto and Wilson Kiprop, Kenneth Kipkemoi, 3rd in The Hague and 2nd in Valencia, and Bernard Koech, winner in Nice and 2nd in Lille. The year's second and third fastest times were run by the 1-2 in The Hague: 58:54 Stephen Kibet (6th Worlds) and 59:02 Jonathan Maiyo, and Wilson Kipsang won the Great North Run in 59:06 by a second from Micah Kogo.

Marathon

THERE WAS AGAIN unprecedented depth with 11 men under 2:05 compared to the previous record of 7, 23 under 2:06 (13), 43 under 2:07 (29), 79 under 2:08 (52), 123 under 2:09 (89), 174 under 2:10 (147) and 234 under 2:11 (217). There was, however, no clear-cut claim as the world's number 1. Geoffrey Mutai 2:04:15 and Dennis Kimetto 2:04:16 ran the year's fastest times in Berlin, but Mutai had not finished in Boston and Kimetto ran no other marathons. In much more difficult conditions Stephen Kiprotich won the Olympic title in 2:08:01, but his best time of the year, 2:07:50 for 3rd in Tokyo put him at 75th on the world list. The other Olympic medallists were Abel Kirui and Wilson Kipsang who had been 1st and 6th in London, and Kipsang went on to win in Honolulu. Other fast winners were Ayele Abshero, 1st in Dubai 2:04:23 but dnf OG, Tsegaye Kebede, 1st in Chicago 2:04:38 and 3rd London, and Yemane Adhane, 1st Rotterdam 2:04:48 and also 10th Dubai and dnf Frankfurt. The Dubai race, in which Dino Sefer and Markos Geneti completed an Ethiopian 1-2-3, had record place times for 3rd to 17th (2:09:22). Deresse Chimsa, 8th in Dubai, went on to 2:06 times for 1st in Prague and 2nd in Frankfurt. James Kwambai excelled in the two Seoul Marathons, 1st in 2:05:50 and 2nd in 2:06:03, but did not meet other top men, and Abdullah Dawit Shami, 7th in Dubai in 2:05.42, had another fast time with his Hamburg win in 2:05:58. Feyisa Lelisa, after 19th in London, was 2nd in Chicago in 2:04:52, but many of the top men had just one top mark with the cancellation of the New York marathon depriving many of a top-class race. Ethiopians and Kenyans filled the first 49 places in the world list for 2012; with 7 ETH and 3 KEN in the top 10 and 12 and 8 in the top 20, but the balance then swinging to Kenya with 17 KEN and 13 ETH in the top 30, 27 KEN and 24 ETH in the top 50, 59 KEN and 33 ETH in the top 100, and 111 KEN and 51 ETH in the top 200

> 1. Kebede, 2. Kiprotich, 3. Kipsang, 4. G Mutai,
> 5. Kirui, 6. Abshero, 7. Adhane, 8. Lelisa,
> 9. Chimsa, 10. Kimetto

3000 Metres Steeplechase

ONCE AGAIN IT was sad that Paul Kipsiele Koech was unable to run well at high altitude; he was 7th in the Kenyan Trials, won by Brimin Kipruto from Ezekiel Kemboi, Abel Mutai, Julius Birech, Richard Mateelong and Consesius Kipruto. All those men and 9th Hillary Yego and 10th Bernard Nganga were in the world top 15 in which there were 11 Kenyans. Koech, however, ran three of the year's fastest times, wins in Rome 7:54.31, Doha 7:56.58 and Saint-Denis 8:00.57, with a fourth Diamond League win in Lausanne for an overall season's record of five wins in eight races. Kemboi was 4th in Rome and won the Olympic gold medal easily enough (it would surely have been a very different and much faster race if Koech had been in the field), but just three races without any really fast times is not enough for top ranking. Mateelong ran the only other sub-8 munute time, 7:56.81 for 2nd in Doha, but after his Kenyan 5th place did not finish in Saint-Denis and was 7th in Monaco in his only other races. Another light racer was B Kipruto, but he had good results with 2nd in Saint-Denis and 1st in the DL final in Brussels, when followed by C Kipruto, Koech, Birech, Yego and Mutai, and was unlucky to fall in the Olympic final, finishing 5th. Mahiedine Mekhissi-Benabbad raced sparingly and did not better 8:10 (5th in Rome) but followed his European title with silver at the Olympics when Mutai and Roba Gari were 3rd and 4th. Evan Jager won the US title and took the North American record in just his fifth steeplechase with 8:06.81 when 3rd at Monaco before 6th at the Olympics. Birech had more sub-8:15 times than anyone else, and had win-loss advantage with 4-3 against the most promising world junior champion C Kipruto, 5-4 v Mutai and 2-1 v Mateelong. World 100th best of 8:31.2 was just 0.14 off the record.

Most times under 8:15: Birech 8, Koech, Mutai 7; C Kipruto, Gari, Nganga 4, B Kipruto, Yego, Brahim Taleb 3

> 1. Koech, 2. Kemboi, 3. B Kipruto, 4. Mutai,
> 5. Birech, 6. C Kipruto, 7. Mekhissi-Benabbad,
> 8. Gari, 9. Yego, 10. Jager

110 Metres Hurdles

ARIES MERRITT GAVE the most perfect display of sprint hurdling ever seen when he took 0.07 off the world record with his 12.80 in the DL final in Brussels. This was a marvelous climax to a season in which he won 9 of 13 finals as he was 4th in Shanghai behind Liu Xiang, David Oliver and Jason Richardson, and 2nd to Liu in Eugene, with false start disqualifications in NewYork and Lausanne. He had the season's seven fastest times with a record eight sub-13 (plus one wind-assisted), all between 12.92 and 12.97 before the 12.80. Richardson had 10 wins, 7 second places, including US, Olympic and

DL, and 3 third places. Liu started with wins in Kawasaki and then those two over Merrit before pulling out after winning his heat in the London Grand Prix and being unable through injury to complete his Olympic heat. While unable to match his previous form for much of the year David Oliver, 5th in the US Trials (3 Jeff Porter, 4 Antwon Hicks) was 3-1 against Olympic bronze medallist Hansie Parchment and 2-2 v the promising European champion Sergey Shubenkov (6th sf OG). Parchment improved to a new level with six sub-13.20 times and also impressed with 3rd in Brussels ahead of Shubenkov, Oliver and Lehann Fourie (7th OG). Ryan Wilson was 5th in the US Trials but beat Porter (4th sf OG) 5-3 and was 5-0 v Ryan Brathwaite (5th OG). Dayron Robles was injured when challenging for a medal in the Olympic final and was 2-2 against his compatriot Orlando Ortega (OG 6th), but 2-0 v Porter. Lawrence Clarke completes the Olympic finalists, but despite his splendid 4th there does not have the overall record to get to close to a ranking spot, and number two European was Garfield Darien, 2nd Europeans and 5th sf OG, who beat Clarke 2-1. Fourie was 3-1 v Porter, 2-1 v Wilson and 2-2 v Brathwaite, who was 0-3 down to Porter. Dexter Faulk is another who mixed it with the above and the United States remained the dominant nation with 31 men in the world top 100. 10th and 100th bests of 13.13 and 13.66 set new records.

Indoors Faulk topped the world rankings with 7.40A but Merritt was number one with wins at the US Champs and World Indoors when Liu Xiang took the silver.

Most times under 13.30: Merritt, Richardson 17+2w; Oliver 11+1w, Shubenkov 11, Parchment, Darien 6, Wilson 5+2w, Porter, Ortega 5; Faulk 4+2w, Fourie, Brathwaite 4, Liu 3+1w, Robles 3, Omo Osaghae 1+3w, Ronnie Ash 1+2w.

   1. Merritt, 2. Richardson, 3. Liu, 4. Oliver,
   5. Parchment, 6. Shubenkov, 7. Wilson,
   8. Ortega, 9. Robles, 10. Fourie

400 Metres Hurdles

FÉLIX SÁNCHEZ MADE a remarkable comeback to his best form with his fastest times for eight years to run 47.76 in his semi and then 47.63 to win the Olympic title. He had three other wins in his nine hurdles finals. But he was beaten 3-2 by Javier Culson who won all his six races, including four in the Diamond League, prior to Olympic bronze and 5th in the DL final in Zürich. That race was won by Angelo Taylor from Omar Cisneros, Jehue Gordon and Sánchez. Taylor also had a DL win in Shanghai but was beaten 4-2 by Michael Tinsley including when they were 1-2 at the US Olympic Trials (3 Kerron Clement, 4 Bershawn Jackson) and when 2nd and 5th at the Olympic Games. Brit-ish champion David Greene was disappointed to be 4th at the Olympics, unable to quite recapture his 2011 form; he was 2-2 v Sánchez and 2-0 v Taylor. Although he just missed the US Olympic team, Jackson was 3-1 v Olympic 6th placer Gordon and also 2-0 v Cisneros (3rd sf OG). Completing the Olympic final line-up, 7th and 8th, were Jamaican champion Leford Green and Clement, returning from hernia surgery. Just missing a ranking were Amaechi Morton, who won NCAA, Nigerian and African titles, but was disqualified in the semis at the Olympics, and US Trials 5th placer Justin Gaymon.

Most times under 48.60: Culson 9, Sánchez, Taylor 5; Tinsley, Greene 4; Jackson, Cisneros 3

   1. Culson, 2. Sánchez, 3, Tinsley, 4. Greene,
   5. Taylor, 6. Jackson, 7. Gordon, 8. Cisneros,
   9. Green, 10. Clement

High Jump

IVAN UKHOV PRODUCED the year's bests outdoors, 2.39 to win the Russian title and 2.38 to win Olympic gold. He had 3 wins in 7 events indoors and 5 in 9 outdoors, sealing top ranking with a win in the DL final at Zürich. Jesse Williams and Robbie Grabarz each had two DL wins. Williams lost form after 2.36 at New York and was 4th in the US Champs and 9= at the Olympics, but Grabarz, who had a pre-2012 best of 2.28, had a splendid year, winning the European title and with 11 competitions at 2.30 or better, leaping to 2.34 indoors and to tie the British record outdoors at 2.37 in a remarkable competition at Lausanne, when he was 3rd to Mutaz Essa Barshim, who set national records at 2.35, 2.37 and 2.39, with Ukhov second with 2.37. Grabarz was 3-3 v Ukhov outdoors after being 6= (with Williams) to Ukhov's 3rd at the World Indoors (with Barshim 9=), and tied with Barshim and Derek Drouin for the Olympic bronze. Erik Kynard, NCAA champion and 2nd US Champs, took the Olympic silver. Kynard was 2-0 v Barshim, who was 3-2 v Drouin (2nd NCAAs). The World indoor title was won by Dimítrios Hondrokoúkis, but his outdoor season ended when he failed a drugs test. Andrey Silnov was 2nd in the World Indoors and had a series of good marks indoors, headed by 2.36, 2.35 and 2.34, but apart from a magnificent 2.37 for 2nd in the Russian Champs did not clear higher than 2.28 outdoors. Similarly Aleksandr Shustov and Aleksey Dmitrik cleared 2.35 and 2.33 for 3-4 at the Russian Champs, but had generally better marks indoors. Jamie Nieto was 6th at the Olympics, but had marginally inferior marks than Trevor Barry (8th World Indoors, dnq 16= OG). Barry was 2-1 outdoors and 1-1 indoors v Dmitrik, but was behind Andriy Prot-senko (9=) at the Olympics.

Most competitions over 2.30m (outdoors/in): Barshim 8, Grabarz 7/4, Ukhov 6/7, Barshim 6/2, Williams 4/3, Drouin 4, Dmitrik 3/4,

Kynard 3/1, Barry 2/2, Sergey Mudrov, Andrey Protsenko 2/1; Shustov 1/6, Silnov 1/5.

1. Ukhov, 2. Grabarz, 3. Kynard, 4. Barshim, 5. Drouin (7), 6. Williams (6), 7. Silnov (5), 8. Protsenko (10), 9. Barry, 10. Dmitrik (9), - Shustov (8). (Including indoors).

Pole Vault

BJÖRN OTTO HEADED the world list with 6.01, and had a fine season with World Indoor and Olympic silver medals, but Renaud Lavillenie, who won both those major titles and the Europeans (with his season's best of 5.97), was very clearly the top man. He won 12 of his 15 outdoor competitions, including five DL events, and 5 of 6 indoors. Otto had indoor/outdoor win-loss records of 4-1/8-4 v Maite Mohr and 2/3/10-1 v Raphael Holzdeppe as the last came 3rd at both Europeans and Olympics and Mohr was 4th and 9=. Between these two Germans Mohr (3rd WI) was 3-0 up indoors and they went 4-4 outdoors. Mohr was national champion indoors and Otto outdoors. Dmitriy Starodubtsev (9th WI) was 4th at the Olympics followed by 5= Steve Lewis and Yevgeniy Lukyanenko, 7th Konstadínos Filippídis (5th Europeans) and 8th Jan Kudlicka (6th Europeans). Of these men Lewis (5= WI) had the best marks and was 4-2 out, 1-1 in v Holzdeppe and 3-3 out, 1-1 in v Filippídis (7th WI). Brad Walker joined Lavillenie and the three Germans in clearing 5.90 and he was US champion indoors and out, but his ranking suffered from no heights in three major events, Olympics, Zürich and Berlin and he was 0-4 v Lewis and 1-3 v Filippídis outdoors. He was best indoors with his 5.97A for the US title and 3rd at the World Indoors. There he beat Starodubtsev (7th), but outdoors was 2-2 and 1 tie aganst the Russian. Former top man Steve Hooker and 2011 world champion Pawel Wojciechowski struggled for form with bests of 5.72 and 5.62. Only eight men beat 5.80, the least since 1983.

Most competitions over 5.70m (outdoors/in): Otto 13/6, Lavillenie 12/5, Walker 8/5, Mohr 6/4, Holzdeppe 5/4, Lewis 5/3, Filippídis 3/5, Romain Mesnil 3/1, Karsten Dilla 2/3, Starodubtsev 2/2, Lukasz Michalski 1/2

1. Lavillenie, 2. Otto, 3. Holzdeppe (4), 4. Mohr (3). 5. Lewis, 6. Filippídis, 7. Starodubtsev (8), 8. Walker (7), 9. Lukyanenko (10), 10. Kudlicka (9). (Including indoors).

Long Jump

IT WAS A non-vintage year for long jumping and the world best of the year, 8.35 by Greg Rutherford and Sergey Morgunov (world junior record), was the worst since 1978. The world best had been over 8.60 every year from 1981 to 2000 and with a low of 8.43 in 2001 in the previous 33 years. Rutherford followed tying the British record at Chula Vista by taking the Olympic title and he was 2-1 against the Olympic silver medalist Mitchell Watt, who in turn was 2-1 against Aleksandr Menkov, who although only 11th at the Olympics had three Diamond League wins. Those included the final in Brussels when Khotso Mokoena was 2nd and world junior champion Morgunov (dnq 16 OG) third. Indoors Mauro da Silva was a surprise World champion with 8.28, winning from Henry Frayne (9th OG), Menkov and Will Claye, who later added to his triple jump silver with Olympic bronze at this event. Outdoors da Silva's best was 8.10 and he was 7th at the Olympics as ahead of him 4th to 6th were Michel Tornéus, Sebastian Bayer and Chris Tomlinson. Defending Olympic champion Irving Saladino returned from a left knee injury with a promising 8.16 win in Monaco but then did three no jumps in the Olympic qualifying. Marquise Goodwin was NCAA champion and beat Claye at the US Champs before 6th Monaco and 10th OG in his only European outings. Bayer was German champion indoors and out and was in top form at the Europeans, winning with 8.34 after 8.34w in qualifying with Tornéus 3rd; he was 2-2 v Tomlinson and 2-1 v Claye. Tomlinson was 2-1 v Claye, 4-2 v Mokoena (8th OG) and 2-0 v Goodwin. Four-time World Champion Dwight Phillips missed the year with a recurring Achilles problem.

Most competitions over 8.15m (outdoors/in): Rutherford, Menkov 5; Watt 4+1w, Mokoena 3, Goodwin 2+1w

1. Rutherford, 2. Watt, 3. Menkov, 4. Bayer, 5. Tomlinson, 6. Mokoena (7), 7. Claye (6), 8. Tornéus (10), 9. da Silva (8), 10. Goodwin (9).

Triple Jump

UNIVERSITY OF FLORIDA team-mates Christian Taylor and Will Claye shared the honours. Claye won World Indoor gold with 17.70 to Taylor's 17.63 and Taylor Olympic gold with 17.81 to Claye's 17.62. The story was the same at the US Champs with Claye winning indoors 17.63 to 17.21 and Taylor outdoors 17.63 to 17.55. Claye had the year's top two performances indoors and Taylor the top three outdoors. Fabrizio Donato, who had too often disappointed in the past, never making a World or Olympic final despite three attempts at each, came good this year with World Indoor 4th place, European gold and Olympic bronze before beating Taylor in the Diamond League final in Zürich. Lyukman Adams won World Indoor bronze and was joint third with Donato on the outdoor year list before 9th at the Olympics. Daniele Greco beat Donato to take the Italian title and was 5th WI and 4th OG, while Benjamin Compaoré was 6th in both these events (and 3rd in the DL final) and Alexis Copello 7th and 8th. Leevan Sands was 5th at the Olympics and had a Diamond League victory in Saint-Denis.

Former world champion Phillips Idowu started well with wins at Shanghai and Hengelo and 3rd at Eugene but was then injured with a dnq 14th at the Olympics in his only other competition. Tosin Oke won the African title and was 7th at the Olympics, while Copello beat Sheryf El-Sheryf, 2nd Europeans and dnq 13 OG, 3-1. Teddy Tamgho missed the whole year after his broken ankle in 2011 and 6-month ban from the French federation.

Most competitions over 17.15 (outdoors/in): Taylor 8/3, Donato 4/2, Claye 3/3, Greco 3/2, Sands 3, Compaoré 3, Arnie David Girat 2+1w

> 1. Taylor, 2. Claye, 3. Donato, 4. Greco,
> 5. Sands (6), 6. Adams (5), 7. Compaoré, 8.
> Idowu, 9. Oke, 10. Copello. (Including indoors).

Shot

TOMASZ MAJEWSKI WON the Olympic title by 3cm from David Storl, and Ryan Whiting won the World Indoor title by 12cm from Storl, but Reese Hoffa was the clear choice for top ranking. He was 4th at the World Indoors and 3rd at the Olympics but he beat Majewski 7-1 and Storl 2-1 outdoors, although 2-1 down indoors to them both. Majewski, 7-1 v Storl outdoors (2-2 in), was 3rd at the World Indoors, and other men to make both WI and OG finals were Maksim Sidorov, 5th and 11th, and Germán Lauro, 6th with South American records in both. Dylan Armstrong, a prolific competitor, was 9th at the World Indoors but beat Storl 4-1 outdoors. However, he was well behind with 20.93 for 5th at the Olympics compared to Storl 21.86, and Storl also showcd that he peaked brilliantly in major events with 21.58 to win the European title. The year's 22m throws were produced by Americans, Whiting (9th OG) 22.00 at the World Indoors and outdoors Christian Cantwell 22.31 and Hoffa 22.00. Armstrong was 4-4 v Whiting (0-1 indoors) and 4-2 v Cantwell outdoors. Whiting beat Cantwell 6-2 outdoors and 2-0 indoors, including when they were 2nd and 3rd at US Champs indoors and out, with Hoffa winning both. Adam Nelson was 4th in the indoor US Champs but managed only a 15th place outdoors. Justin Rodhe and Cory Martin were the next best on marks, with the former winning 3-0 in their clashes, and Artur Kolasinac (3rd Europeans and 7th OG) and Pavel Lyzhin (8th OG) just missed a ranking. There was a surge in the standard in depth as 100th best man threw 19.51, a new record and easily the best since the previous record of 19.48 in 1984.

Most competitions over 20.80 (outdoors/in): Majewski 16/7, Armstrong 14, Hoffa 13/6, Storl, Whiting 8/7; Sidorov 6/1, Cantwell 5/4, Rodhe 2/1

> 1. Hoffa, 2. Majewski, 3. Storl (4), 4, Armstrong
> (5), 5. Whiting (3), 6. Cantwell, 7. Sidorov, 8.
> Rodhe, 9. Martin, 10. Lauro. (including indoors).

Discus

ROBERT HARTING IS top for the fourth successive year, and, as in 2011, he was unbeaten. He won all 12 competitions, seven of them over 68m, and for the first time exceeded 70m, first 70.13 at Halle then 70.66 at Turnov three days later in May. Virgilijus Alekna, now aged 40, was the other 70m man. The positions of the first four at the Olympics stand up on win-loss as 2nd placed Ehsan Hadadi was 3-2 v 3rd placed Gerd Kanter and 3-1 v 4th placed Alekna, and Kanter was 6-2 v Alekna. Kanter, also 2nd to Harting at the Europeans, competed far more often than Hadadi and had three Diamond League wins to the Iranian's one. Others to gain a DL win were Piotr Malachowski (5th OG, beaten 6-1 by Alekna), Zoltán Kövágó (3rd Europeans before a drugs ban) and Harting. Win-loss also helps sort out the remaining men: Martin Wierig (6th OG) beat Frank Casañas (7th OG) and Laurence Okoye 3-2 and Erik Cadée 4-2, while Casañas was 5-4 v Okoye and 4-2 v Cadée. Okoye showed huge promise and improved his British record to 68.24; he had an excellent series of post-Olympic results, but disappointed with 11th at the Europeans and 12th at the Olympics. Cadée, 7-3 v Okoye, was also a little below his usual level with 11th and 10th in these big events. Mario Pestano, 4th Europeans and dnq 14th OG, was 5-3 v Casañas and 2-1 v Okoye, and Rutger Smith, 3rd Europeans and dnq 16th OG, was 4-3 v Okoye. Completing the Olympic finalists, Vikas Gowda was 8th, Benn Harradine 9th and Jorge Fernández 11th. 100th best of 60.94 was just 1cm off the record from 1984.

Most competitions over 65m: Kanter 17, Alekna 16, Harting14; Cadée 11, Malachowski 9, Casañas, Okoye 7; Hadadi, Wierig 6; Pestano, R Smith 4. dq: Kövágó 7.

> 1. Harting, 2. Kanter, 3. Hadadi, 4. Alekna,
> 5. Malachowski, 6. Wierig, 7. Casañas, 8. Cadée,
> 9. Pestano, 10. Okoye

Hammer

KRISZTIÁN PARS WAS very clearly the top hammer thrower of 2012; he lost only one of his 15 competitions and won European and Olympic titles, Pavel Fajdek was the one man to better him. 81.39 to 80.22 at Montreuil, but had no throws in failing to qualify at the Olympics. Pars had six of the top ten marks but not the best – which was an extraordinary 82.61 in his one competition since 2008 by Ivan Tikhon, who was, however, withdrawn from the Belarus OG team on suspicions of drugs abuse. The Olympic silver and bronze medallists competed only four times, Primoz Kozmus (after his short retirement), and twice, Koji Murofushi (as usual making his only other appearance at the Japanese Champs), while Fajdek, Sergey Litvinov and Kirill Ikonnikov (5th OG) followed Pars with the best series of marks. Fajdek was 1-2 against his Polish colleague Szymon Ziólkowski (3rd Europeans, 7th OG) and was also 2nd in the IAAF Hammer Throw Challenge with Oleksiy Sokryskyy 3rd, Lukás Melich 4th and Dilshod Nazarov (10th OG) 5th. Sokyrskyy (4th OG) was 4-3 v Fajdek and 5-2 v Ikonnikov, who won the Russian title from Igor Vinichenko. Litvinov, who otherwise had 8 wins, a second and a third, had no throws both in the Russian Champs and at the Znamenskiy Memorial. Aleksey Zagornyi was 2nd at the Europeans but dnq 22rd at the Olympics, while Melich fared badly at the Europeans but made up for that with OG 6th; he was 4-4 v Ziólkowski. Nicola Vizzoni did well in both major events, 5th Europeans and 8th OG. Pavel Krivitskiy and Andrey Vorontsov were over 80m in Minsk, but did not back big throws at home with good form outside Belarus. The Ukrainian champion Oleksandr Drygol set new world over-45 records with 76.55, 78.47 and 79.42 but was below 70m at the Olympics. News of a positive test for Ikonnikov means that he would lose his seventh ranking if confirmed, with the rest moving up. 100th best of 71.12 was the best since 2004.

Most competitions over 80m/78.50m: Pars 8/17, Fajdek 3/5, Litvinov 2/5, Ikonnikov 1/5, Krivitskiy 1/3, Melich 0/5, Sokyrskyy, Drygol 0/4

    1. Pars, 2. Sokryskyy, 3. Fajdek, 4. Litvinov,
    5. Kozmus, 6. Murofushi, (7. Ikonnikov),
    8. Melich, 9. Ziólkowski, 10. Nazarov, 11. Vizzoni

Javelin

ANDREAS THORKILDSEN HAD a poor season by his standards, as he was 4th at the Europeans and 6th at the Olympics and Matthias de Zordo, the 2011 number 2, was restricted by back and elbow problems to a handful of competitions and a best of 81.62. That left the way open for a new top man, but it was not always clear who that was. Vitezslav Vesely had the top marks of 88.34 and 88.11 and 9 wins in 14 competitions. He also had two Diamond League wins and was European champion, but he slipped a little to 4th at the Olympics and in the DL final in Zürich. Ahead of him on both occasions was Oleksandr Pyatnytsa (2nd OG, 3rd Zürich, but 5th Europeans) against whom he was 3-3. Tero Pitkämäki struggled for form early on, 11th at the Europeans and 5th at the Olympics, but won the DL final and had his best marks in wins at Stockholm 86.98 and in the match against Sweden with 86.86. Overall he beat both the other top Finns Antti Ruuskanen and Ari Mannio 6-3 and was 2-2 v Pyatnytsa but 2-5 to Vesely. Ruuskanen (3rd OG, 2nd Zürich) beat Mannio (3rd Euros, 11th OG) 5-2. The new star, however, was undoubtedly Keshorn Walcott, who at the age of 19 set five national records for Trinidad and Tobago from 78.94 up to 83.51 and 84.58 in London when his win was one of the greatest shocks in Olympic history. He won all his nine competitions, including CAC and World Junior titles, but only met any of the top men at the Olympics. Other Olympic finalists were 7th Spirídon Lebésis, 8th Tino Häber, 9th Stuart Farquhar, 10th Genki Dean and 12th African champion Julius Yego. Valeriy Iordan was an excellent 2nd at the European Champs but had inferior marks to others in consideration for ranking. Vadims Vasilevskis had a DL win at Eugene but was very inconsistent and nowhere near qualifying for either European or Olympic finals. The upshot is that only Vesely and Thorkildsen of the 2011 top ten rank again. Sergey Makarov threw 83.39 in February to make it 19 successive years over 82m, but tailed off thereafter.

Most competitions over 84m/82.50m: Vesely, Pyatnytsa 5/10; Ruuskanen 5/8, Pitkämäki 4/8, Thorkildsen 2/3, Dean, Vasilevskis 2/0, Ivan Zaytsev 1/3

    1. Vesely, 2. Pyatnytsa, 3. Pitkämäki, 4. Walcott,
    5, Ruuskanen. 6. Mannio, 7. Thorkildsen,
    8. Lebésis, 9. Farquhar, 10. Iordan

Decathlon

ASHTON EATON ADDED 23 points to Roman Sebrle's 11-year-old world record despite poor conditions in Eugene and after starting with world decathlon bests in both 100m (10.21) and long jump (8.23) cruised to the Olympic title; Trey Hardee was second on both occasions. After 5th at Götzis, Leonard Suárez took the Olympic bronze medal but the 4th placer Hans Van Alphen ranks third as he won at both Götzis and Talence and took the IAAF Combined Events Challenge. Eelco Sintnicolaas and Pascal Behrenbruch were 2nd and 3rd at Götzis, but while the former was then 11th at the Olympics and 4th at Talence, Behrenbruch won the European title in fine style with 8558 for third on the world list behind the two top Americans before 10th at the Olympics. He was third in the Challenge with Oleksiy Kasyanov (2nd Europeans, 7th OG, 2nd Talence) third. Other top Olympic placers were 5th Damian Warner (9th Götzis), 6th Rico Freimuth (4th Götzis), 8th Sergey Sviridov and 9th Willem Coertzen. Warner improved his pb by 335 points to 8442 in London.

Eaton improved his world record for the heptathlon to 6645 points at Istanbul in taking the World Indoor title by the huge margin of 574 points from Kasyanov, who earlier had the year's second highest score of 6237.

    1. Eaton, 2. Hardee, 3. Van Alphen, 4. Behrenbruch, 5. Suárez, 6. Freimuth, 7. Kasyanov,
    8. Warner, 9. Sviridov, 10. Sintnicolaas.

20 Kilometres Walk

CHEN DING WON the Olympic title (the first ever at the event for China) with Erick Barrondo

2nd, but top ranking goes to bronze medallist Wang Zhen, as he had won his other races – Taicang (in an Asian record 1:17:36) and the World Cup. Chen was 2nd and 9th in those races as well as 3rd at Husian, won by Cai Zeliin, later 3rd at Taicang and 4th Olympics (although only 35th at the World Cup). Barrondo had been 3rd at Lugano behind Alex Schwazer, whose 1:17:30 was the year's fastest but who fell foul of a drugs ban later, and Yohann Diniz (dnf Dudince in his other 20k race). Andrey Krivov was 2nd and Vladimir Kanaykin 3rd at the World Cup but these Russians were 37th and dnf at the Olympics as only Wang and Chen plus Eder Sánchez (8th WCp and 6th OG) managed top ten placings in both the top races. Georgio Rubino (22 WCp) and Jared Tallent were 4th and 5th at Taicang and Tallent also had good results with 2nd to Sánchez at Chihuahua and 7th at the Olympics. As usual there were fast times at the Russian Winter Championships with Andrey Ruzavin and Sergey Morozov under 1:18 and Krivov and Stanislav Yemelyanov just outside. Morozov and Ruzavin were 5th and 6th in the World Cup and 1st and 2nd in the Russian summer championships, but at the end of the year Morozov was disqualified and lost all his performances from 25 Feb 2011. Miguel Ángel López was 5th at the Olympics but only 44th at the World Cup. Matej Tóth did not contest those 20k races, but won all three of his 20k races.

The IAAF Race Walking Challenge was determined over 10k in Ordos, China. Wang Zhen was the winner from Cai Zelin, Chen Ding and Li Jianbo, with the Challenge 1-2-3 Wang, Chen and Jared Tallent (11th in this race).

1. Wang Zhen, 2. Chen Ding. 3. Cai Zelin,
4. Sánchez, 5. Barrondo, 6. Ruzavin, 7. Tallent,
8. Krivov, 9. Kanaykin, 10. Tóth

50 Kilometres Walk

SERGEY KIRDYAPKIN WON at both the World Cup and Olympic Games in sub 3:40 times and Igor Yerokhin, 2nd and 5th, also broke 3:40 in both, while Jared Tallent 3rd and 2nd, Si Tianfeng 4th and 3rd and Sergey Bakulin 5th and 6th also doubled up well. There were unprecedented standards at the Olympics as the first seven broke 3:40, including 4th Robert Heffernan (his only 50k of the year) and 7th Li Jianbo (1st Husian but dnf Taicang and World Cup). Then 8-10 were Matej Tóth, Lukasz Nowak and Koichiro Morioka. Nowak was another non-finisher at the World Cup but also 2nd at Dudince, a race won by the discredited Schwazer. Other times just outside 3:40 were recorded by Yuriy Andronov and Yuki Yamazakl in winning Russian and Japanese Championships. There were new records for the world's 10th and 100th best at 3:41:24 and 4:03:04.

1. Kirdyapkin, 2. Tallent, 3. Si, 4. Yerokhin,
5. Bakulin, 6. Heffernan, 7. Li Jianbo. 8. Tóth,
9. Nowak, 10. Morioka

Female Athlete of the Year

MY TOP CANDIDATES for woman athlete of the year were Allyson Felix and Jessica Ennis. After silver medals in 2004 and 2008 Felix won her Olympic title at 200 metres by a healthy 2m margin in 21.88 after earlier taking the US title in 21.69, the fastest time run by a woman since 1998. She was undefeated at 200m (four meetings) and was also 5th in the Olympic 100m before going on to add two more Olympic gold medals to her collection – running the second leg on the US team that smashed the world record at 4x100m and finally contributing a brilliant 48.1 second leg for the US team that won the 4x400m by a huge margin. Ennis had been the 'face' of the Games leading up to athletics events in the Olympic stadium. Her profile and attendant expectations could hardly have been higher, but how she delivered! The very first event of the opening morning session was the women's heptathlon 100m hurdles. This was Ennis's best event, but even such a relentless over-performer in major events could scarcely believe it as she reduced her personal best from 12.79 to 12.54, a British record and the best ever recorded in a heptathlon, also ranking fifth on the 2012 world list. She was a little below par in the high jump, but personal bests at 200m and javelin followed as she won the heptathlon gold medal by the huge margin of 306 points, Her score of 6955 points, for fifth on the world all-time list, was her second British and Commonwealth record of the year, having earlier won in Götzis (by 132 points from Tatyana Chernova, who had beaten her to the World title in 2011) with 6906. Ennis was also UK champion again at 100m hurdles and high jump.

Felix and Ennis were joined as Olympic champions who went through the year undefeated at their events by steeplechase winner Yuliya Zaripova, 10,000m winner Tirunesh Dibaba and Tiki Gelana at marathon, but they only had three, two and two competitions at their respective events. But also unbeaten, in 14 competitions in 2012 after 13 in 2011 was shot putter Valerie Adams, once, of course Nadezhda Ostapchuk was disqualified after finishing ahead at the Olympics. Losing just once during the year were Sanya Richards-Ross in eight finals at 400m, Sally Pearson in nine at 100m hurdles, Sandra Perkovic in 15 at discus and Yelena Lashmanova in three 20km walk races. Jenn Suhr won 12 times at pole vault and had two no heights.

As we come to the 30th anniversary of the longest lasting women's world record, the 1:53.28 for 800m by Jarmila Kratochvílová at Munich on 25 Jul 1983, the pace of record breaking has slowed so considerably that the only world records at standard events in 2012 were that wonderful time of 40.82 run by the US sprint relay team (breaking the 27 year-old GDR mark) and the 1:25:02 by Lashmanova at 20km walk, but that was not the best ever mark as it was inferior to marks set under unratifiable conditions.

100 Metres

SHELLY-ANN FRASER-PRYCE won only four of her nine 100m finals, but did so when it mattered most, retaining her Olympic title and at the DL final in Zürich. She set a CAC record of 10.70 in winning the Jamaican title and had the year's second best time of 10.75 in the Olympic final, in which there were best ever times for places 3-4 and 6-8. She was 3-3 against Carmelita Jeter, second in those big two races, who otherwise lost only to Tianna Madison (2nd to Jeter's 3rd in New York) and to Blessing Okagbare, who had a big win in the London GP. Veronica Campbell-Brown raced the 100m only five times, but was 2nd in the Jamaican Champs (3. Kerron Stewart, 4. Sherone Simpson) and 3rd at the Olympics. VCB also broke 11 seconds when 2nd to Allyson Felix in Doha (3. Fraser) and when 4th in Lausanne, behind Jeter, Fraser-Pryce and Kelly-Ann Baptiste. Madison, Felix and Baptiste finished 4-6 at the Olympics, with Murielle Ahouré and Okagbare 7th and 8th and these two were 2-1 and 4-0 respectively against Stewart. Jeter and Madison were the US 1-2 with Felix and Jeneba Tarmoh tying for third. Tarmoh contests the final ranking spot with Laverne Jones-Ferrette, with whom she was 1-1, and Gloria Asumnu (3rd African, 5th sf OG). Ivet Lalova won the European title and Ruddy Zang Milama the African, but they were only 6th and 7th in Olympic semis. The 100th best of 11.34 set a new record (11.36 in 2008 and 2011).

Campbell-Brown had won the World Indoor 60m title in the year's fastest time of 7.01 from Ahouré and Madison.

Most times under 11.00/11.10: Jeter 8/15, Fraser-Pryce 8/12, Madison 7/9, Campbell-Brown 6/8, Baptiste 5/7, Okagbare 4/7, Felix 3/6+1w. Stewart 2/5, Ahouré 1/5, English Gardner 0/3w

> 1. Fraser-Pryce, 2. Jeter, 3. Campbell-Brown, 4. Madison, 5. Felix, 6. Baptiste, 7. Okagbare, 8. Ahouré, 9. Stewart, 10. Tarmoh

200 Metres

AFTER TWO SILVER medals Allyson Felix at last won her Olympic 200m crown. She had an unbeaten season at the event and ran the year's two best times: 21.69 at the US Trials and 21.88

Selections for World Top Ten			
	PJM	TFN	AI
Jessica Ennis	1	2	2
Allyson Felix	2	3	1
Sally Pearson	3	4	3
Valerie Adams	4	1	5
Yuliya Zaripova	5	8	9
Sanya Richards-Ross	6	5	4
Shelley-Ann Fraser-Pryce	7	6	6
Tirunesh Dibaba	8	-	7
Barbora Spotáková	9	-	8
Yelena Lashmanova	10	-	-
Anna Chicherova	-	-	10
Sandra Perkovic	-	7	-
Tiki Gelena	-	9	-
Jenn Suhr	-	10	-

at the Olympics. The average winning margin for her four finals was 0.40. Most of the top women raced fairly sparingly at 200m, but produced high quality with three events at 200m for Olympic 2nd Shelly-Ann Fraser and five each for the 3rd, 4th and 5th: Carmelita Jeter, Veronica Campbell-Brown and Sanya Richards-Ross. Felix, Jeter and Richards-Ross were 1-2-3 at the US Olympic Trials with the 4th and 5th Kimberlyn Duncan (NCAA champion) and Jeneba Tarmoh also making the world list top ten. Tianna Madison was 6th but only had one other 200m race while Bianca Knight, 7th, had a successful campaign in Europe, and Charonda Williams, 4th in her Trials semi, was a prolific racer and went on to win the Diamond League title. She was 4-1 v Knight and had two individual DL victories as did Murielle Ahouré, Olympics 6th placer. Myriam Soumaré was 7th at the Olympics and ended by wining the DL final in Brussels. She had been third in the Europeans, won by Mariya Ryemyen, who was 4th in her Olympic semi, as Semoy Hackett, 8th, completed the Olympic final. The rankings were very close after the top five. Antonique Strachan was 5th in her Olympic semi, having looked superb in winning a World Junior 100m/200m double. The 100th best of 23.10 beat the previous record of 23.17 (2008) and 10th at 22.37 was the best since 1999.

Most times under 22.70: Jeter 8, Richards-Ross 7, Duncan 6+2w, Felix 6, Knight 5+1w, Campbell-Brown, Fraser-Pryce, Ahouré 5; Fedoriva 4, Tarmoh, Jones-Ferrette 3+1w; Soumaré, Hackett 3; Madison 2+1w.

> 1. Felix, 2. Fraser-Pryce, 3. Jeter, 4. Campbell-Brown, 5. Richards-Ross, 6. Duncan, 7. Tarmoh. 8. Ahouré, 9. Williams, 10. Knight.

400 Metres

SANYA RICHARDS-ROSS had a near perfect year, with just one loss, to Novlene Williams-Mills at Kingston in May, to four indoor (including the World Indoors) and seven outdoor wins. Her best time was 49.28 at the US Olympic

Trials. The Olympic finalists make up the top eight in the rankings, but I put African champion Amantle Montsho second as, although 4th in London, she had the best depth of times and beat silver medallist Christine Ohuruogu 3-2 and bronze medallist Deedee Trotter 4-1. Jamaican champion Williams-Mills (3-1 v Ohuruogu) was 5th and Antonina Krivoshapka 6th at the Games, with the latter having run the year's fastest time of 49.16 to win the Russian title and being 2-0 v Trotter and 3-0 v Olympic 7th Francena McCorory. The last beat Trotter 6-2 but crucially was behind her rival in both US Trials and Olympics. Rosemarie Whyte was 8th at the Olympics and the rankings are completed by the Russian Champs 2-3: Yuliya Gushchina, 49.28 then but 4th in her Olympic semi, and Tatyana Firova. Although not meeting the top women, Ashley Spencer had a brilliant unbeaten season at 400m, running 51.02 in her first major outdoor meeting and improving to 50.95 to win the NCAAs and to 50.50 to take the World Junior title. Tenth woman at 50.06 was the best since 2000 and before then since 1988.

Most times under 50.50: Montsho 10, Richards-Ross, Williams-Mills 8; Krivoshapka 7, McCorory 6, Ohuruogu, Trotter, Whyte, Gushchina 3.

1. Richards-Ross, 2. Montsho, 3. Williams-Mills,
4. Ohuruogu, 5. Krivoshapka, 6. Trotter,
7. McCorory, 8. Whyte, 9. Gushchina, 10. Firova.

800 Metres

MARIYA SAVINOVA RANKS top for the third successive year. Her season was not perfect but she won the Olympic title in consummate style in the year's fastest time of 1:56.19. Taking the silver medal was Caster Semenya, but she was poor in her two DL races, 8th in Rome and 9th in Monaco. The Russian champion Yekaterina Poistogova won bronze in a European U23 record 1:57.53, but a much better overall record was recorded by Olympic 4th Pamela Jelimo, who had the best depth of times and who beat Savinova 3-2. Undoubtedly the greatest breakthrough was that of Francine Niyonsaba, who in her first season won the African title and was 7th at the Olympics, before 2nd in Berlin and two major wins, in Brussels and Rieti. Her 1:56.59 in the Diamond League final in Brussels was the year's second fastest time and she beat Jelimo and Savinova. The rest of the Olympic finalists were 5th US champion Alysia Montaño, 6th European champion Yelena Arzhakova and 8th Janeth Jepkosgei. Unfortunately missing the Games through injury was Fantu Magiso, who ran three 1:57 times: 2nd to Jelimo in Doha, and wins in Rome and New York for 2-0 v Jepkosgei; she had been 4th in the World Indoors won by Jelimo. Yelena Kofanova, winner in Monaco and 4th in the Russian Champs, had a good set of times to take tenth ranking ahead of Yusneysi Santiusti. 10th best of 1:57.77 was the best since 1993 and 100th best of 2:01.46 is a new record, beating the old mark of 2:01.50 from back in 1984.

Most times under 1:59.5 (outdoors/in): Jelimo 10/1, Savinova, Kofanova 8; Niyonsaba, Montaño, Arzhakova 6; Jepkosgei 4, Semenya, Magiso, Santiusti 3.

1. Savinova, 2. Jelimo, 3. Niyonsaba,
4. Poistogova, 5. Montaño, 6. Magiso. 7. Semenya, 8. Arzhakova, 9. Jepkosgei, 10. Kofanova

1500 Metres

IT WAS EXTREMELY difficult ranking this event in 2011, and so it proved in 2012. As with the 2011 World Champs race, the Olympic final was a pretty unsatisfactory affair as it was run at such a very slow pace before Asli Cakir and Gamze Bulut burst away over the final lap in 57.9 and 58.2 respectively. The two Turks had also been 1-2 at the Europeans, but were otherwise seen little. Bulut had just two other 1500 races, two wins at home. Cakir had been 3rd in a competitive World Indoor final behind Genzebe Dibaba and Meriem Alaoui Selsouli, with Natalya Koreyvo fourth, and ran just one other 1500m race. That, however, was a 3:56.62 in Saint-Denis behind the year's fastest 3:56.15 by Selsouli, who is not ranked as she faces a drugs ban, with Abebe Aregawi 3rd in 3:58.59. Aregawi was the only woman to run more than once under 4 minutes, as she won in Rome in 3:56.54 and had been 2nd in Shanghai in 3:59.23 behind Dibaba 3:57.77, and after Olympic 5th was 3rd in Stockholm behind Maryam Jamal and Mimi Belete before ending the year with a win in the DL final in Zürich. Dibaba had looked brilliant with three indoor wins in 4:00-4:01 and she was also 2nd in Oslo to Aregawi, but then suffered injury and her only other race was 10th in her Olympic heat. Jamal had another big win in London and was 3rd at the Olympics, when other leading places were taken by Tatyana Tomashova 4th, Shannon Rowbury 6th, Koreyvo 7th and Lucia Klocová 8th. Ninth was Yekaterina Kostetskaya, who had won the Russian title from Yekaterina Martynova, Tomashova and Yelena Soboleva. Morgan Uceny beat Rowbury and Jennifer Simpson to take the US title, but as at the 2011 Worlds (and 2010 DL final) met with misfortune as she tripped and fell in the Olympic final, suffering injuries that ended her season. Koreyvo was 2-0 v Kenyan champion and Trials winner Hellen Obiri, who was 12th at the Olympics and beat Uceny 3-0. 115 women under 4:10 beat 2011's record and, after none in 2011, 11 women under 4 minutes was the most since the Chinese domination in 1993.

Most times under 4:04 (or 4:23.6 mile): Aregawi 6, Tomashova, Obiri 4, Dibaba, Jamal, Soboleva, Martynova 3

1. Cakir, 2. Aregawi, 3. Jamal (4), 4. Bulut (5),
5. G Dibaba (3), 6. Tomashova, 7. Rowbury,
8. Kostetskaya, 9. Soboleva, 10. Koreyvo.
(Including indoors).

3000 Metres/2 Miles

THE YEAR'S FASTEST time was run indoors in Birmingham, 8:31.56 by Meseret Defar in winning from Hellen Obiri and Gelete Burka. These three took the World Indoor medals, but in the order: Obiri, Defar, Burka with Sylvia Kibet a close fourth. Outdoors the fastest time was 8:34.47 by Mariem Alaoui Selsouli, who faces a drugs ban, ahead of Sally Kipyego in New York. There were four Diamond League races at the distance, resulting in one win for Vivian Cheruiyot and three for Mercy Cherono. Cheruiyot also won in Rieti and was 2nd in Birmingham to Cherono, who made it four wins in four 3000m races with a further win in Luzern. Kibet had three second places and a third in major outdoor races.

5000 Metres

THE FOUR FASTEST times were run at the Golden Gala in Rome, Vivian Cheruiyot beating Meseret Defar by 0.03 in 14:35.62, followed by Viola Kibiwott and Gelete Burka, with Veronica Nyaruai, Sylvia Kibet and Genet Ayalew completing seven women under 14:50. Cheruiyot went on to three more wins: Kenyan Trials (from Sally Kipyego, Kibiwott and Kibet), London and Brussels but was beaten by Defar at the Olympics. This was a slower race (Defar 15:04.25) and finishing 3rd to 6th were Tirunesh Dibaba, Kipyego, Burka and Kibiwott before the top Europeans Jo Pavey, Julia Bleasdale (4th Europeans) and Olga Golovkina (European champion). Mercy Cherono was 2nd in both London and Brussels after 11th in Rome, and further top placings in the DL final in Brussels were 3rd to 7th: Kibiwott, Burka, Kibet, world junior champion Buze Diriba and Kipyego. Dibaba beat Defar and Burka in New York, and Kipyego won in Stanford. It was not a vintage year in terms of times, as 16 women under 15 minutes was the least since 1999.

Most times under 15:05: Cheruiyot 5, Defar, Burka 4; Kipyego, Kibiwott, Nyaruai 3

1. Defar, 2, Cheruiyot, 3. T Dibaba, 4. Kipyego,
5. Kibiwott, 6. Burka, 7. M Cherono, 8. Kibet,
9. Nyaruai, 10. Diriba

10,000 Metres

THE TOP TEN in the world lists set their times either at the Olympic Games or in the Prefontaine Classic race in Eugene. The latter was won by Tirunesh Dibaba 30:24.39 from Florence Kiplagat, Belaynesh Oljira and Worknesh Kidane. Dibaba, who had missed most of 2011 with severe shin splints, then went even faster with her brilliant Olympic victory in 30:20.75 when she was followed home by Sally Kipyego, Viv-

ian Cheruiyot, Kidane, Oljira, Shitaye Eshete, Jo Pavey, Julia Bleasdale, Hitomi Niiya and Kayoko Fukushi. Kiplagat missed her chance of Olympic glory as she was 4th in the high-altitude Kenyan Championship race behind Cheruiyot, Joyce Chepkirui (dnf OG) and Kipyego. Pavey had been 2nd in the European Cup to Sara Moreira (14th OG) and in the European Champs to Dulce Félix. Niiya also had a good win in Kobe.

1. Dibaba, 2. Kipyego, 3. Cheruiyot, 4. Kidane,
5. Oljira, 6. Kiplagat, 7. Eshete, 8. Pavey,
9. Bleasdale, 10. Niiya

Half Marathon

FLORENCE KILPAGAT RAN the year's fastest time, 66:38 in the Rome-Ostia race, 11 seconds faster than Mary Keitany ran at Ra's Al Khaymah, where conditions were not as good as when she set the world record there in 2011. Meseret Hailu was a surprise winner of the World title as she ran 68:55 from a previous best of 71:18 (1st Egmond in January). Behind her in Kavarna came Feysa Tadesse (4th RAK), Pasalia Kipkoech and Lydia Cheromei. Kipkoech had a busy year as she won her five other half marathons, and was the only woman to run more than one sub 68:30 time as she did that three times. Tirunesh Dibaba made a notable debut at the distance as she won the Great North Run from Edna Kiplagat and Tiki Gelana.

Marathon

AS FOR THE men, there were again new records for the depth of marathon running with 6 women under 2:20 compared to the previous record of 3, 16 under 2:22 (8), 32 under 2:24 (25), 63 under 2:26 (58), 98 under 2:28 (99), and 145 under 2:30 (139). The year's fastest times came in Spring big city races: from Mary Keitany who won in London in 2:18:37 and from Tiki Gelana who won in Rotterdam in 2:18:58. Gelana went on to win the Olympic title by 5 seconds from Priscah Jeptoo (3rd London), the surprising Tatyana Arkhipova, who had earlier been 5th in Tokyo, and Keitany, the favourite, fourth. Edna Kiplagat, second in London, came only 20th. There were record times for place for positions from 18th in the Olympic race, with 29 women under 2:30 (previous best 21 in the 2011 London Marathon), 54 under 2:35 and 78 under 2:40. Aselefech Mergia repeated her 2011 win in Dubai as she, 2:19:31, and Lucy Kabuu 2:19:34 ran the year's third and fourth fastest times, while behind them there were best ever place times for 3rd (2:19:52 Mare Dibaba) to 9th (2:24:24). Kabuu followed with 5th in London and 3rd in Chicago, but Dibaba was 23rd at the Olympics. The next fastest race winners were Aberu Kebede, 2:20:30 in Berlin, Meselech Melkamu, 2:21:01 on debut in Frankfurt, and Meseret Hailu, 2:21:09 in Amsterdam and also

3rd in Prague. Kebede had earlier been 5th in Dubai and 6th in London and Atsede Baysa was 8th and 9th in these races before winning at Chicago in 2:22:03. Tirfi Tsegaye had two 2:21 times: winning in Paris in 2:21:40 and 2nd in Berlin in 2:21:19, and Lydia Cheromei, 6th in Dubai, won in Yokohama,

    1. Gelana, 2. P Jeptoo, 3. Keitany, 4. Kabuu,
    5. Kebede, 6. Baysa, 7. E Kiplagat, 8. Tsegaye,
    9. M Dibaba, 10. Cheromei

3000 Metres Steeplechase

YULIYA ZARIPOVA CONTESTED only three steeplechases, but won them all: Russian Championships, Olympics and at Stockholm and she ran the top two and ninth fastest times of the year in so doing, excelling with a brilliant front-running display in London. Olympic silver medallist Habiba Ghribi beat the 3rd and 4th placers Sofia Assefa and Milcah Chemos Cheywa 3-0. Chemos started the year in fine style with three DL wins, but fell in Stockholm and was only 9th in the final in Zürich after falling at a hurdle. Assefa thought she had overhauled Chemos to top the steeplechase ranking by winning that race comfortably, but her celebrations were cut short when she was disqualified for running inside the cones when approaching the final water jump, so Etenesh Diro gained that victory from Hiwot Ayalew, Hyvin Jepkemoi, Lydia Chepkurui and Ghribi. Ayalew and Diro were 5th and 6th at the Olympics, with Ayalew 2-1 up on win-loss. Mercy Njoroge won the Kenyan title and was 2nd in the Trials, but Chepkurui, 6th in the latter, was 4-2 ahead overall and Jepkemoi was 2nd and 5th in those races to make it four Kenyans in the top ten. Gülcan Mingir won the European title but ran only four times and was 10th in her Olympic heat. Next in the Europeans were 2nd Svitlana Schmidt, 3rd Antje Möldner-Schmidt, 4th Gesa Felicitas Krause and 5th Ancuta Bobocel with the two Germans best at the Olympics as they came in 7th and 8th. World record holder Gulnara Galkina won in Moscow and was 2nd in the Russian Champs, but did not finish in the Olympic final. The 100th best at 9:53.79 was the best ever, as might be expected for this developing event.

Most times under 9:30: Chemos, Assefa 7; Njoroge 6, Zaripova 5, Rotich 3.

    1. Zaripova, 2. Ghribi, 3. Chemos, 4. Assefa,
    5. Ayalew, 6. Diro, 7. Chepkurui, 8. Njoroge,
    9. Jepkemoi, 10. Möldner-Schmidt

100 Metres Hurdles

SALLY PEARSON MAINTAINED her brilliant sprint hurdling form of 2011 and again lost just once. That defeat came by just 0.02 to Kellie Wells at the London Grand Prix. Pearson was, however, pushed hard by Dawn Harper in a great Olympic final, winning 12.35 to 12.37, the year's fastest times with the world list next featuring two times by Pearson and two by Harper, who only lost one other outdoor hurdles race, to Jessica Ennis at Manchester (with one hurdle missing). Wells and Lolo Jones were 2-3 behind Harper in the US Olympic Trials (followed by Ginnie Crawford and Christina Manning) and 3-4 at the Olympics, while Crawford was next best, beating European champion and Olympic 5th placer Nevin Yanit in their one clash. Two women who exited in the semi-finals of the US Trials had the next best depth of times with Queen Harrison 4-0 up on Kristi Castlin, together with a group of Canadians. Jessica Zelinka (7th OG) won the Canadian title from Phylicia George (6th OG) and Nikita Holder. Priscilla Lopes-Schliep was only 5th in that race but overall was 8-5 v George and 1-1 v Zelinka. It should be noted that Ennis, apart from that win over Harper, beat Zelinka 12.54 to 12.65 in her brilliant Olympic heptathlon race and also took the British title as she beat Tiffany Porter 12.92 to 13.21. Brigitte Foster-Hylton started the year with a 12.51 for fourth on the world list and won the Jamaican title, but had the misfortune to fall in her heat at the Olympics; both she and Manning were 1-1 with Porter. The 100th best was a new record at 13.18 in 2011 and was improved further in 2012 to 13.11.

Pearson's one indoor event resulted in a clear win in the World Indoor 60m hurdles, 7.73, two metres clear of Porter and Alina Talay. Second and third fastest were Castlin, US champion at 7.84A, and Ennis, British champion at 7.87.

Most times at 12.70 or faster: Pearson 11, Wells 10+3w, Harper 9, Crawford 8, Zelinka 4, Foster-Hylton, Yanit 3; Porter 2+2w, Jones, Castlin, Manning 2+1w

    1. Pearson, 2. Harper, 3. Wells, 4. Jones,
    5. Crawford, 6. Yanit, 7. Harrison, 8. Castlin,
    9. Ennis, 10. Zelinka

400 Metres Hurdles

NATALYA ANTYUKH AND Lashinda Demus went to 5th and 7= on the world all-time list with the 52.70 and 52.77 that they ran in the Olympic final, well clear of Zuzana Hejnová, 3rd in 53.38. Antyukh had two more of the year's top five times and ranks top despite only winning two of her eight 400mh competitions, finishing 2nd to 7th in the other races and showing modest form in her three post-Olympic races. Demus won the US title and had three seconds and a sixth in her other races. Kaliese Spencer was 4th at the Olympics (as she had been at the Worlds in 2009 and 2011) but had the best depth of times and beat Antyukh 3-1 and Hejnová 4-1. She won her three post-Olympic races culminating with the DL final in Brussels, where Hejnová was third and second and fourth were athletes to have had an even more disappointing Olympics (3rd and 6th in their semis), Perri Shakes-Drayton and Melaine

Walker. Shakes-Drayton was 4-0 and Walker 1-1 against European champion Irina Davydova (5th semi OG). Georgeanne Moline and T'erea Brown were 2nd and 3rd in the US Trials and 5th and 6th at the Olympics, but the former had no other European races and Brown was 6th in her two DL races, London and Monaco. Vania Stambolova had a good set of times with five wins, including one each over Antyukh and Hejnová, and a second to Hejnová before failing to finish in her Olympic heat. Just missing ranking spots are the Olympics 7-8, Denisa Rosolová (also 2nd Europeans) and Joke Odumosu (also African champion) as 8th to 12th was very close. 100th best at 57.14 was a new record.

Most times under 54.0/55.0: Spencer 6/10, Hejnová 4/9, Antyukh 4/7, Shakes-Drayton 3/5, Demus 2/7, Davydova 2/5, Walker 1/7, Moline 1/5, Odumosu 0/7, Brown, Stambolova 0/6; Rosolová 0/5.

> 1. Antyukh, 2. Demus, 3. Spencer, 4. Hejnová,
> 5. Shakes-Drayton, 6. Moline, 7. Davydova,
> 8. Walker, 9. Stambolova, 10. Brown

High Jump

ANNA CHICHEROVA TOPPED the world lists both indoors, 2.06 at Arnstadt, and outdoors, 2.05 to win the Olympic title, and is clearly world number one. She won five of her indoor events, although only tying for silver with Ebba Jungmark and Antonietta Di Martino (who did not compete outdoors due to a knee injury) at the World Indoors, won by Chaunté Lowe, and won five of eight outdoors. Svetlana Shkolina improved from 2.00 to 2.01 at the Russian Championships and to 2.03 at the Olympic Games, where, however, she lost silver on count-back to Brigetta Barrett, NCAA champion indoors and out, who had a pre-season best of 1.96. Shkolina beat Chicherova at the Diamond League final. Lowe won four DL meetings but slipped to 6th at the Olympics; she was 2-1 v Barrett, including winning when both cleared 2.01 at the US Olympic Trials. Irena Gordeyeva went to second on the world list with a 2.04 win at Eberstadt, but her next best was 1.99 for third at the Russian Champs behind Chicherova and Shkolina and she was 10th at the Olympics with 1.93. Ruth Beitia (aged 33) and Tia Hellebaut (34) were 4th and 5th at the Olympics and 6th and 5th respectively at the World Indoors. After the top seven, the top women were Svetlana Radzivil (8th WI, 7th OG) and European medallists Tonje Angelsen, Olena Holosha and Emma Green-Tregaro (8th OG). Jungmark beat Green-Tregaro 5-0 indoors but lost 3-0 outdoors. Blanka Vlasic competed just once, no height at the World Indoors, but hopes to be back from injury in 2013.

Most competitions over 2.00/1.96m outdoors (+indoors): Shkolina 6/9, Chicherova 4+5i/6+5i, Lowe 3+1i/7+2i, Beitia 2/5, Barrett 2/2+1i, Gordeyeva 1/2+1i, Hellebaut 0/3+1i

> 1. Chicherova, 2. Shkolina, 3. Barrett (4),
> 4. Lowe (3), 5. Beitia, 6. Hellebaut, 7. Gordeyeva,
> 8. Radzivil, 9. Angelsen, 10. Green-Tregaro (-),
> Jungmark (10). (Including indoors)

Pole Vault

JENN SUHR NO HEIGHTED twice, but was otherwise unbeaten in 2012; she cleared 4.88 indoors and 4.83 outdoors. She missed the World Indoors with a sore Achilles but won Olympic gold and US titles indoors and out. The best jump of the year came however, with another world indoor record by Yelena Isinbayeva, 5.01 in Stockholm. She won all her four other indoor competitions, but outdoors won only one of three, 4.73 at Sotteville, while she took Olympic bronze at 4.70, 5cm behind Suhr and silver medallist Yarisley Silva. The last showed excellent consistency and was 4-1 outdoors v Olympic 4th-placer Silke Spiegelburg. At the World Indoors Vanessa Boslak and Holly Bleasdale were 2nd and 3rd (with Spiegelburg 4th and Lacy Janson 5th), but both were less good outdoors, 6= and 10th respectively at the Olympics. Jirina Ptácníková (WI 6th) tied for Olympic 6th and was European champion; she beat Martina Strutz (OG 5th) 5-1 outdoors and 1-0 indoors and was 2-1 with 1 tie v Fabiana Murer, who just missed qualifying for the Olympic final but was 3-1 v Lisa Ryzih (7th Europeans, 6= Olympics) and 3-2 v Bleasdale. Alana Boyd had six competitions at 4.60 or better, topped with 4.76, but fared less well in major clashes and was 11th at the Olympics. Injury cost Anna Rogowska most of the outdoor season and she no-heighted in the Olympic final, as did Russian champion Svetlana Feofanova in qualifying. Angelica Bengtsson was again the top junior and won the World Junior title a week after her best ever outdoor jump of 4.58. 100th best at 4.31 was a new record, after 4.30 in 2011.

Most competitions over 4.60m (outdoors/in): Suhr, Spiegelburg 7/4; Boyd 6, Ptácníková 5/2, Murer 4, Bleasdale 3/7, Isinbayeva 2/5, Silva 7, Anastasiya Savchenko 3, Rogowska 1/2.

> 1. Suhr, 2. Silva (3), 3. Spiegelburg (4),
> 4, Isinbayeva (2), 5. Ptácníková, 6. Murer (7),
> 7. Ryzih (8), 8. Bleasdale (6), 9. Boyd (-),
> 10. Strutz (9), - Boslak (10). (Including indoors)

Long Jump

ALTHOUGH SHE ONLY scraped into the Olympic final, and won with her only good jump there, plus several poor performances in other meetings, Brittney Reese had the longest jumps of the year: 7.23 to win the World Indoor title and outdoors 7.15 at the US Olympic Trials and 7.12 at both Mount SAC and Olympics. Seven other women jumped over 7 metres, two of them twice, Yelena Sokolova and Anastasiya Mironchik-Ivanova. Russian champion Sokolova had the most consistently top class season as she won 8 of 10 competitions outdoors, including at four Diamond League meetings and she was 2nd at the Olympics. Mironchik-Ivanova, after starting well with 7.08 in Minsk and 7.22w to win the BLR title, was beaten 4-1 by Shara Proctor, who with Janay DeLoach and Olga Kucherenko each had a DL win. DeLoach was 2nd at the World Indoors and 3rd at the Olympics, while Proctor was 3rd and 9th and Mironchik-Ivanova 5th and 7th. Ineta Radevica again showed her championships ability with 4th at the Olympics with 6.88, but 6.65 was her best at any other event. She was 6th at the Europeans, won by Éloyse Lesueur, who went on to 8th at the Olympics, a place ahead of Proctor, with Anna Nazarova and Lyudmila Kolchanova placing 5-6. Proctor was 2-1 v Lesueur, 4-1 v Mironchik-Ivanova and 3-1 v Kolchanova outdoors. Darya Klishina was 4th at the World Indoors, one of three indoor competitions over 6.80 and she jumped 6.93 outdoors but her form fell away. Blessing Okagbare jumped 6.97 and 6.96 to win Nigerian and African titles and, although a non-qualifier for the Olympic final, was 2nd in the DL final in Zürich behind Sokolova and ahead of Proctor, Kucherenko, Mironchik and Kolchanova (with DeLoach and Reese 8th and 9th). In both Russian and US Championships five women exceeded 6.80m. 10th best of 6.97 was the best since 1984 while 100th at 6.55 was the best ever.

Most competitions over 6.70m (outdoors/in): Sokolova 12/1, DeLoach 8+1w/4, Reese 7/4, Kucherenko 6+1w/3, Nazarova 6, Proctor 5/3, Mironchik- Ivanova 5/1, Whitney Gipson 3, Lesueur 2+2w, Klishina 2/4, Chelsea Hayes 2+1w, Veronika Shutkova 2/1.

    1. Reese, 2. Sokolova, 3. DeLoach, 4. Proctor,
    5. Kucherenko, 6. Lesueur, 7. Mironchik-Ivanova,
    8. Okagbare, 9. Radevica, 10. Nazarova.

Triple Jump

JUST FOUR CENTIMETRES separated the top three women in 2012 and each had 5 or 6 marks in the top 20 outdoor performances. Olga Saladuha jumped 14.99 to win the European title, Olga Rypakova 14.98 to win at the Olympics and Caterine Ibargüen had a best of 14.95A. Rypakova ranks top with four DL wins and win-loss of 2-1 against Ibargüen and 3-2 v Saladuha, the Olympic 2-3, who were 2-2 in their clashes. The next best jump of the year came indoors from Yamilé Aldama, who beat Rypakova 14.78 to 14.63 to take the World Indoor title, but who struggled with injuries and so was restricted to four outdoor competitions, although those included a fine 5th at the Olympics. A place ahead of her there was Hanna Knyazheva, who was 2-1 v Kimberley Williams (6th World Indoors and OG), who had four marks at 14.50 or better. Competing at the event for the first time since 2009, the great Tatyana Lebedeva won the Russian title with 14.68, but was 10th at the Olympics; she had,

however, a 3-2 advantage against Dana Veldáková (5th Europeans, 12th OG) and Viktoriya Valyukevich (8th OG). Veldáková was 2-1 out and 1-0 in v Valyukevich. The Cubans were less strong this year with their champion Dailenys Alcántara having the best marks; she was 2-2 v Yargeris Savigne, who was better at the Olympics 9th to dnq 16th and better indoors than out, including 4th at the World Indoors. Mabel Gay was 3rd at the World Indoors, but only had three outdoor competitions. The Greeks Athanasia Pérra 14.71 and Paraskeví Papahrístou 14.58/14.77w had big jumps but without the depth of performance to support those. Yana Borodina only had three outdoor competitions: two wins and then third at the Europeans, with Simone LaMantia, Veldáková, Niki Panétta and Pérra 4-7. Anna Krylova won the Russian title and was 6th at the Worlds indoors, on each occasion beating Valyukevich.

Most competitions over 14.40m (outdoors/in): Saladuha 9/2, Ibargüen 9, Rypakova 8/2, Williams 6, Aldama /3, Alcántara 3

    1. Rypakova, 2. Ibargüen, 3. Saladuha,
    4. Knyazheva (5), 5. Aldama (4), 6. Williams,
    7. Lebedeva (8), 8. Veldáková (9), 9. Valyukevich
    (-), 10. Alcántara (-), - Savigne (7), Krylova (10).
    (Including indoors).

Shot

VALERIE ADAMS IS top for the sixth time in seven years and extended her winning sequence to 30 by winning all her 14 competitions in 2012. She had, however, finished well behind Nadezhda Ostapchuk at the Olympics, 21.36 to 20.70 but then came news of Ostapchuk's disqualification due to a positive drugs test. Before then Ostapchuk had set Belarus records with 21.13, 21.32, 21.39 and 21.58, whereas Adams had a best of 21.11. The next best of 2012 was 20.48 at the Olympics by Yevgeniya Kolodko; she also won the Russian title with 20.15 and threw 20.22 at Adler but after the Games her form fell away, while Olympic bronze medallist Gong Lijiao, also three times over 20m, had a more consistent series of marks. Next on the world lists were Li Ling (4th Olympics) and Jill Camarena-Williams, who after three indoor and six outdoor meetings over 19.50 was injured and 15th dnq at the Olympics. She was, however, 5-1 outdoors (2-1 indoors) v Michelle Carter (5th OG). Nadine Kleinert at last won a major title, with the Europeans, but missed an Olympic final spot by one place; she had a better series of marks than Natalya Mikhnevich (11th OG), who beat her 3-0, and than Liu Xiangrong (6th OG and 2-2 v Kleinert, 2-1 v Christina Schwanitz). Mikhnevich was 4-2 v Irina Tarasova (8th OG, 2nd Europeans), but lost 4-0 to Schwanitz (10th OG, 5th Europeans). The World Indoor title was won by Adams from Ostapchuk, Carter, Camarena-Williams,

Kleinert, Liu, Kolodko and Tarasova. The 10th and 100th best at 19.60 and 16.82 were the best since 1994 and 1988 respectively.

Most competitions over 19m (outdoors/in): Adams 13/3, Gong 12, Camarena-Williams 8/5, Kleinert 8/4, Carter 5/4, Kolodko 5/3, Li, Tarasova 4; Mikhnevich 3, Schwanitz 1/3; Ostapchuk 6+2dq/3

> 1. Adams, 2. Kolodko, 3. Gong, 4. Li Ling (6),
> 5. Camarena-Williams (4), 6. Carter (5),
> 7. Kleinert, 8. Schwanitz, 9. Mikhnevich,
> 10. Liu Xiangrong. (Including indoors).

Discus

SANDRA PERKOVIC, after serving a 6-month ban in 2011, returned with a magnificent season as she won of her 13 of her 14 competitions including the Olympic and European titles and six of the seven Diamond League meetings. Her one loss was to Dani Samuels in Saint-Denis. Perkovic had nine of the top 20 marks of the year (to 66.85) and a winning margin at the Olympics of 1.55m over Darya Pishchalnikova, who had the two best throws of the year, 70.79 and 69.34 in Russia, but who was reported at the end of the year as having failed a drugs test (again). Nadine Müller was the most prolific competitor for marks in depth and was 2nd at the Europeans but she was 5th at the Olympics behind 3rd Li Yangfang and 4th Yarelys Barrios who were respectively 2-2 and 4-3 v Müller. US champion Stephanie Brown Trafton, who set an American record in Hawaii, completed the world list top six, who between them had the best 38 marks of the year, with Denia Caballero and Zaneta Glanc also exceeding 65m. Brown Trafton was 8th at the Olympics but beat 6th placer Mélina Robert-Michon 3-1 overall. Glanc was also 3-1 v Robert-Michon and was 1-1 v Krishna Poonia, who was Olympic 7th but did not have many contests against the world's best. Zinaida Sendriute and Samuels were 9th and 12th at the Olympics, but the Australian champion had a 2-1 win-loss advantage and Sendriute was 6-3 v Robert-Michon. Caballero had some big throws in Cuba, but like Glanc and Chinese champion Tan Jian was a long way from qualifying for the Olympic final, and European 3rd placer Nataliya Semenova, 2-3 v Robert-Michon, was another non-qualifier. 100th best at 56.86 was the best since 1996.

Most competitions over 63m: Müller 16, Perkovic 14, Li, Brown Trafton 12; Barrios 11, Pishchalnikova 10, Poonia 5, Glanc 4, Tan, Fischer, Caballero 3.

> 1. Perkovic, 2. (Pishchalnikova), 3. Li, 4. Barrios,
> 5. Müller, 6. Brown Trafton, 7. Glanc, 8. Poonia,
> 9. Samuels, 10. Sendriute, 11. Robert-Michon

Hammer

OKSANA MENKOVA HAD three of the top four performances of the year, all Belarus records. But she was 4m down on such form when 7th in the very high standard Olympic final. Tatyana Lysenko won the gold medal with four throws over 77m and Anita Wlodarczyk and Betty Heidler were also over 77m, followed by Zhang Wenxiu and Kathrin Klaas over 76m and Yipsi Moreno 7th. The Olympic top four plus Moreno all had 11 or more competitions over 72m, with Heidler on top for 75m plus competitions, as she had 9 to 5 by Lysenko and Wlodarczyk, 4 by Zhang, 3 by Menkova and 2 by Moreno and Klaas. Heidler won 11 of 14 competitions and was 4-1 v Lysenko (who won 6 of 14) and 2-2 v Wlodarczyk (who won 6 of 11) (that was the order of the top three in the IAAF Hammer Throw Challenge), but failed to qualify at the Europeans, won by Wlodarczyk from Martina Hrasnová, Anna Bulgakova and Klaas. Wlodarczyk was 4-1 v Lysenko and 3-1 v Moreno. Zalina Marghieva was 8th at both Europeans and Olympics and was 5th in the Challenge (4th Klaas, 6th Hrasnová). Gulfiya Khanafeyeva was fifth on the world list with 77.08 at the Znamenskiy Memorial and threw 76.04 for second at the Russian Champs, but her only two events outside Russia were dnq 16th at the Olympics and 7th in Berlin; she was, however 6-1 v Russian 3rd placer Mariya Bespalova (11th OG). The other Olympic finalists were 9th Stéphanie Falzon, 10th Joanna Fiodorow and 12th Sophie Hitchon. Continuing rising standards were shown with the world's 100th best of 65.78 compared to the previous record of 64.79 in 2011 and 11 women over 75m beat the previous record of 7 in 2006.

Most competitions over 72m: Lysenko, Moreno 14; Heidler 13, Wlodarczyk 12, Zhang 11, Klaas, Z Marghieva, Khanafeyeva 7; Menkova 6, Bespalova 5, Hrasnová, Fiodorow 4; Alena Matoshko, Bulgakova, Anna Skydan, Jenny Dahlgren, Jessica Cosby 3.

> 1. Heidler, 2. Wlodarczyk, 3. Lysenko, 4. Zhang,
> 5. Moreno, 6. Klaas, 7. Menkova,
> 8. Z Marghieva, 9. Fiodorow, 10. Khanafeyeva.

Javelin

BARBORA SPOTÁKOVÁ WAS very clearly the world number one, with four throws better than anyone else at the Olympics and six of the world's top ten performances. She had nine wins and four second places, one loss each to Mariya Abakumova (Doha) and Goldie Sayers (London) and two to Sunette Viljoen (African and Commonwealth record of 69.35 in New York and also in Berlin) and was over 64m in every competition except for 60.90 in the Talence heptathlon. The Germans Christina Obergföll and Linda Stahl took Olympic silver and bronze but 4th placer Viljoen ranks higher with a 3-2 record v Obergföll and three better marks. Russian champion Abakumova slipped to 10th at the Olympics, but was 3-1 v Stahl and 2-1 v Vira Rebryk and Sayers, whose injured elbow meant she was unable to throw properly at the Games. Rebryk beat Obergföll, Stahl, Sayers and Katharina Molitor for the European title, but was dnq 19th at the Olympics. Lu Huihui only once competed outside China, but that was when 5th at the Olympics, when she was followed by Molitor, Martina Ratej, Madara Palameika and Kathryn Mitchell. Ratej beat Sayers to win at the European Cup Winter Throwing. Just three days after her 17th birthday Sofi Flinck won the World Junior title with 61.10, a sensational improvement from her pre-meeting best of 54.85. 10th best of 64.91 amd 100th of 55.97 were records with the current javelin specification.

Most competitions over 62m: Spotáková, Obergföll 13; Viljoen, Abakumova 9; Stahl, Rebryk, Sayers, Lu 7; Molitor 5, Mitchell, Ratej 4, Kim Mickle 3.

1. Spotáková, 2. Viljoen, 3. Obergföll,
4, Abakumova, 5. Stahl, 6. Lu. 7. Rebryk,
8. Sayers, 9. Molitor, 10. Ratej

Heptathlon

JESSICA ENNIS WAS simply superb, setting British and Commonwealth records, 6906 at Götzis and 6955 at the Olympic Games, despite the huge pressure of being the face of the Games in the long build-up. Tatyana Chernova had the year's second best score 6774 for 2nd at Götzis and her Olympics 3rd and Talence 4th scores meant that she retained her IAAF World Combined Events Challenge crown. In that she was followed by Lyudmyla Yosypenko (3rd Götzis, 2nd Europeans, 4th OG, 1st Talence), and Antoinette Nana Djimou (12th, 1st, 6th and 2nd in those events). Olympic silver medallist Lilli Schwarzkopf, also 5th Götzis, did not finish at Talence so could not feature in the Challenge which needs three scores, but Austra Skujyte was fourth with a consistent series: 4th Götzis, 5th Olympics, 3rd Talence. The Olympics order pretty much determines the rest of the rankings as Jessica Zelinka (6th Götzis), Kristina Savitskaya (Russian champion with 6631 for 3rd on the world list), Laura Ikauniece (3rd Europeans), Anna Melnychenko and Brianne Theisen were 7th to 11th, although Theisen benefits from four scores over 6350 to move up two places. Nataliya Dobrynska, after the death of her husband, was 9th at Götzis and did not finish at the Olympics. Showing huge promise for the future were top junior Katarina Johnson-Thompson, World Junior champion at long jump, who improved Ennis's British junior record with 6007, 6248 and 6267 for 15th at the Olympics, and top youth Yorelis Rodríguez, who won the World Junior title with two more years as a junior, and had a best of 5994. 100th best at 5702 was the best since 1990.

The best indoor pentathlon scores were achieved at the World Indoors won with a world record score by 5013 by Dobrynska from Ennis, Commonwealth record 4965, as places 3-7 went to Skujyte, Karolina Tyminska, Chernova, Yekaterina Bolshova (who had the year's third best score of 4896 to win the Russian title) and Anna Melnychenko.

1. Ennis, 2, Chernova, 3. Schwarzkopf,
4. Yosypenko, 5. Skujyte, 6. Nana Djimou,
7. Zelinka, 8. Savitskaya, 9. Theisen,
10. Ikauniece

20 Kilometres Walk

YELENA LASHMANOVA AND Olga Kaniskina were 1-2 in the two big races, World Cup and Olympic Games. Other top combinations of those races came from the junior Lu Xiuzhi 4th and 6th, Anisya Kirdyapkina 6th and 5th, Beatriz Pascual 5th and 8th, Elisa Rigaudo 7th in both, Ana Cabacinha 9th in both, and Maria José Poves 3rd and 12th. The year's top three times were recorded in the Olympic race, with Lashmanova setting an official world record of 1:25:02 and Qieyang Shenjie 3rd. The last was only 15th in the World Cup but had been third at Taicang, where Liu Hong had set an Asian record of 1:25:46 and Lu was second. Liu also had a major win at La Coruña from Pascual, who won at Rio Maior. Elmira Alembekova had the year's fourth fastest time with 1:25:27 to win the Russian winter title from Lashmanova, but a dnf at the World Cup was her only other race. María Vasco (dnf World Cup, 10th Olympics) was 2-2 against compatriot Poves. The world list top ten comprised eight Russians and two Chinese women, Both 10th (1:27:08) and 100th (1:33:52) were new records.

Again the IAAF World Race Walking Challenge was decided in a one-off race at 10 kilometres after the women had qualified from 20k races. Liu Hong won in 43:18 from Cabecinha, Lu Xiuzhi, Pascual and Rigaudo.

1. Lashmanova, 2. Kaniskina, 3. Liu Hong,
4. Qieyang, 5. Kirdyapkina, 6. Lu Xiuzhi,
7. Rigaudo, 8. Pascual, 9. Cabecinha, 10. Vasco

European Athletics – Athlete of the Year Awards 2012

Men: Mo Farah GBR; (2. Renaud Lavillenie FRA, 3. Christophe Lemaitre, 4. Ivan Ukhov, 5. Robert Harting, 6. Tomasz Majewski, 7. Churandy Martina, 8. Krisztián Pars, 9. Kevin Borlée, 10. Greg Rutherford)
Women: Jessica Ennis GBR; (2. Anna Chicherova RUS, 3. Barbora Spotáková CZE, 4. Sandra Perkovic CRO, 5. Mariya Savinova RUS, 6. Ivet Lalova BUL, 7. Éloyse Leseuer FRA, 8. Natalya Antyukh RUS, 9. Dulce Félix POR, 10, Nevin Yanit TUR)
Rising Star Men: Pavel Maslák CZE; (2. Adam Gemili GBR, 3. Jimmy Vicaut FRA)
Rising Star Women: Angelica Bengtsson SWE; (2. Katarina Johnson-Thompson GBR, 3. Moa Hjelmer SWE).

CROSS-COUNTRY – NATIONAL CHAMPIONS 2012

	Men (long distance)	Women (long distance)
Algeria	Abdelhamid Moussaoui	Kenza Dahmani
Argentina	Ulises Sanguinetti	Sandar Amarillo
Australia (Aug)	James Nipperess	Celia Sulohearn
Austria	Günther Weidlinger	Anita Baierl
Belarus (Oct)	Sergey Platonov	Anastasiya Dashkevich
Belgium	Atelaw Bekele	Veerle Dejaeghere
Brazil	Gilberto Lopes	Tatiele de Carvalho
Bulgaria	Khristo Stefanov	Silvia Danekova
Canada (Nov)	Cameron Levins	Megan Brown
China	Dong Guojian	Hao Xiaofan
Colombia	Miguel Amador/Jefferson Peña	Angie Orjuela
Croatia (Nov)	Matea Matosevic	Dino Bosnjak
Cuba	Henry Jaen	Liuris M.Figueredo
Czech Republic	Milan Kocourek	Pavla Matyásová Schorná
Denmark	Abdi Hakim Ulad	Anna Holm Baumeister
England	Keith Gerrard	Gemma Steel
Estonia	Keio Kits	Evelyn Talts
Finland	Lewis Korir KEN	Sandra Eriksson
France	Benjamin Malaty	Laurane Picoche
Germany	Musa Roba-Kinkal	Eleni Gebrehiwot ETH
Greece	Konstadínos Poúlios	Konstadína Kefalá
Hungary (Nov)	Albert Minczér	Krisztina Papp
India	Suresh Kumar Patel	Lalita Babar
Ireland (Nov)	Joseph Sweeney	Ava Hutchinson
Israel	Yimer Getahun	Mary Elias
Italy	Gabriele De Nard	Silvia Weissteiner
Kenya	Bidan Karoki	Joyce Chepkirui
Latvia	Janis Girgensons	Polina Yelizarova
Lithuania (Autumn)	Marius Diliunas	Aleksandra Dulyba UKR
Luxembourg	Vincent Nothum	Tania Ley-Fransissi
Moldova (Oct)	Roman Prodius	Natalia Cherches
Morocco	El Hassan El Abbassi	Nadia Noujani
Netherlands (Nov)	Khalid Choukoud	Adrienne Herzog
New Zealand	Sam Wreford	Mikayla Nielsen
Northern Ireland	Joe McAllister	Breege Connolly
Norway (Sep)	Ørjan Grønnevig	Karoline B. Grøvdal
Poland	Tomasz Szymkowiak	Katarzyna Kowalska
Portugal	Manuel Damião	Dulce Félix
Romania	Nicolae Soare	Ancuta Bobocel
Russia	Andrey Leyman	Natalya Vlasova
(Sep)	Yuriy Chechun	Lyudmila Lebedeva
Scotland	Derek Hawkins	Freya Murray
Serbia	Mirko Petrovic	Amela Terzic
Slovakia (Nov)	Juraj Vitko	Katarina Beresová
Slovenia	Primoz Kobe	Sonja Roman
South Africa (Feb)	Elroy Galant	Dina Lebo Phalula
(Sep)	Elroy Galant	Nolene Conrad
Spain	Carles Castlllejo	Diana Martín
Sweden	Adid Bouafif	Isabellah Andersson
Switzerland	Philipp Bandi	Livia Burri
Trinidad & Tobago	Denzel Ramirez	Tonya Nero
UK (CAU)	Keith Gerrard	Gemma Steel
Ukraine (Mar)	Bogdan Semenovych	Oksana Simonova
(Oct)	Igor Heletiy	Olga Kotovska
USA	Bobby Mack	Sara Hall
Wales	Dewi Griffiths	Caryl Jones
Asian	Alemu Bekele BRN	Shitaye Eshete BRN
U20	Shoto Baba JPN	Miyuki Uehara JPN
Balkan	Bekir Karayel TUR	Ancuta Bobocel ROU
Central American	Santos Pirir GUA	Merlin Vinet GUA
European Clubs	Ayad Lamdassem ESP	Belaynesh Oljira ETH
Teams	Bikila ESP	Usküdar Belediyesi TUR
Gulf	Abdullah Al-Joud KSA	
NACAC	Cameron Levins CAN	Liz Costello USA
NCAA (Nov)	Kennedy Kithuka KEN	Betsy Saina KEN

Nordic (Nov)	Abdi Hakim Ulad DEN	Simone Glad DEN
Oceania	James Nipperess AUS	Celia Sullohern AUS
South American	Gilberto Lopes BRA	Tatiele de Carvalho BRA
Southern Africa	Lungisa Mdelwa RSA	Mpho Mabuza RSA
World Universities	Abdelmajed Touil ALG	Ancuta Bobocel ROU
Team	Japan	Japan
Short course winners	**Men**	**Women**
Austria	Andreas Vojta	
Belarus	Sergey Platonov	Irina Ananeko
Denmark	Jacob Hannibal	Simone Glad
Estonia	Keio Kits	Jekaterina Patjuk
Finland	Lewis Korir KEN	
France	Noureddine Smaïl	Claire Navez
Germany	Tobias Grobl	
Lithuania (Spring)	Arturas Meska	Evelina Usebaite
Norway	Johannes Alnes	Ingeborg Lind
Poland	Mateusz Demczyszak	Katarzyna Broniatowska
Portugal	Rui Silva	Salomé Rocha
Russia	Valentin Smirnov	Yekaterina Martynova
Scotland (Nov)	Mark Mitchell	Elspeth Curran
Slovakia	Jaroslav Szabo	
South Africa	Edwin Molepo	Teboga Masehla
Sweden	Adid Bouafif	Isabellah Andersson
Switzerland	Mario Bächtiger	Joëlle Flück
Ukraine	Oleksandr Zhulinskyy	
(Oct)	Roman Pasichnyk	Kateryna Stetsenko

Winners of EAA and IAAF Permit Cross-Country Races 2012

6 Jan	San Giorgio su Legnano (IAAF)	Edwin Soi KEN	Mercy Cherono KEN
7 Jan	Edinburgh (IAAF)	Ayad Lamdassem ESP	Fionnuala Britton IRL
15 Jan	Sevilla (IAAF)	Geoffrey Kipsang KEN	Lineth Masai KEN
21 Jan	Antrim (IAAF)	Mike Kigen KEN	Fionnuala Britton IRL
22 Jan	Elgóibar (EA)	Paul Tanui KEN	Wade Ayalew ETH
29 Jan	Belgrade (EA)	Mirko Petrovic SRB	Amela Terzic SRB
12 Feb	Chiba (IAAF)	Charles Ndirangu KEN	Susan Wairimu KEN
12 Feb	Diekirch (IAAF)	Japheth Korir KEN	Almensch Belete BEL
18 Feb	Nairobi (IAAF)	Bitan Karoki KEN	Joyce Chepkirui KEN
26 Feb	Albufeira (IAAF)	Kiprono Menjo KEN	Gorreti Jepkoech KEN
18 Mar	San Vittore Olana (IAAF)	Thomas Longosiwa KEN	Priscah Cherono KEN
11 Nov	Burgos (IAAF)	Imane Merga ETH	Hiyot Ayalew ETH
18 Nov	Soria (IAAF)	Emmanuel Bett KEN	Nazeret Weldu ERI
25 Nov	Leffinckroucke (EA)	Cornelius Kangogo BEL	Waganesh Mekasha ETH
25 Nov	Roeselare (EA)	Patrick Ereng BEL	Almensch Belete BEL
25 Nov	Tilburg (EA)	Tasama Dame ETH	Dulce Félix POR
16 Dec	Venta de Baños (EA)	Vincent Chepkok KEN	Mercy Cherono KEN

African Cross-Country Championships 2012

Senior Men (12k)
1. Clement Langat KEN 35:43
2. Teklemariam Medhin ERI 35:50
3. Atsedu Tsegay ETH 36:14
4. Timothy Kiptoo KEN 36:26
5. Vincent Chepkok KEN 36:27
6. Kidane Tadese ERI 36:42
7. Ayele Megerssa ETH 36:53
8. Abera Chane ETH 37:00
9. Robert Kajuga RWA 37:10
10. Timothy Toroitich UGA 37:21
Team: 1. KEN, 2. ERI, 3. ETH, 4. RWA, 5. RSA, 6. UGA
Junior Men (8k)
1. Muktar Edris ETH 23:30
2. Japheth Korir KEN 23:31
3. Justin Cheruiyot KEN 23:31
4. Hagos Gebrhiwot ETH 23:32
5. Cornelius Kangogo KEN 23:36
6. Yitayal Atnafu ETH 23:39
Team: 1. KEN, 2. ETH, 3. ERI, 4. UGA, 5. MAR, 6. BOT, 7. RSA
Senior Women (8k)
1. Joyce Chepkirui KEN 27:04
2. Margaret Muriuki KEN 27:05
3. Emily Chebet KEN 27:06
4. Esther Chemtai KEN 27:07
5. Belaynesh Oljira ETH 27:12
6. Abebech Afework ETH 27:37
7. Aberash Nesga ETH 27:47
8. Genet Yalew ETH 27:49
9. Afera Godfay ETH 27:57
10. Annet Negesa UGA 27:58
Team: 1. ERI, 2. ETH, 3. KEN, 4. RSA, 5. UGA
Junior Women (6k)
1. Faith Kipyegon KEN 19:32
2. Agnes Tirop KEN 19:34
3. Nancy Chepkwemoi KEN 19:37
4. Ruti Aga ETH 19:45
5. Alemitu Heroye ETH 19:55
6. Buze Diriba ETH 20:07
Team: 1. ETH, 2. ERI, 3. MAR, 4. RSA, (KEN had no fourth scorer).

European Cross-Country Championships 2012

Senior Men (9.88k)
1. Andrea Lalli ITA 30:01
2. Hassan Chahdi FRA 30:11
3. Daniele Meucci ITA 30:13
4. Thomas Farrell GBR 30:14
5. Carles Castillejo ESP 30:14
6. Ayad Lamdassem ESP 30:14
7. Kemboi Arikan TUR 30:21
8. Javier Guerra ESP 30:22
9. Bashir Abdi BEL 30:26
10. Steve Vernon GBR 30:28
11. Jonathan Taylor GBR 30:30
12. Milan Kocourek CZE 30:33
13. Andy Vernon GBR 30:33

14. Vedat Günen TUR 30:36
15. Sergiy Lebid UKR 30:36
84 of 92 finished
Teams: 1. ESP 35, 2. GBR 38, 3. ITA 63, 4. FRA 86, 5. UKR 119, 6. TUR 128, 7. IRL 131, 8. NED 149, 9. NOR 153, 10. DEN 184, 11. POR 188, 12. HUN 238, 13. AUT 262.
Under-23 Men (8.025k)
1. Henrik Ingebrigtsen NOR 24:30
2. Soufiane Bouchikhi BEL 24:40
3. James Wilkinson GBR 24:43
4. Jesper van der Wielen NED 24:46
5. Romain Collenot-Spiret FRA 24:50
6. Antonio Abadía ESP 24:57
7. Abdelaziz Merzoughi ESP 24:57
8. Hayle Ibrahimov AZE 24:59
94 of 99 finished
Teams: 1. FRA 50, 2. ESP 59, 3. GBR 80, 4. NOR 81, 5. ITA 124; 15 completed.
Junior Men (6,025k)
1. Szymon Kulka POL 18:43
2. Mitko Tsenov BUL 18:47
3. Kieran Clements GBR 18:57

4. Ferdinand Kvan Edman NOR 18:59
5. Djilali Bedrani FRA 18:59
114 of 116 finished.
Teams: 1. RUS 50, 2. FRA 51, 3. GBR 54, 4. POL 77, 5. TUR 102; 21 completed.
Senior Women (8.025k)
1. Fionnuala Britton IRL 27:45
2. Ana Dulce Félix POR 27:47
3. Adriënne Herzog NED 27:48
4. Alemensch Belete BEL 27:54
5. Laurane Picoche FRA 27:55
6. Sophie Duarte FRA 27:55
7. Nadia Ejjafini ITA 27:59
8. Linda Byrne IRL 28:17
9. Lisa Stublic CRO 28:18
10. Diana Martín ESP 28:19
11. Louise Damen GBR 28:22
12. Sara Moreira POR 28:26
13. Christine Bardelle FRA 28:27
14. Fatna Maraoui ITA 28:29
15. Caryl Jones GBR 28:29
54 of 54 finished
Teams: 1. IRL 52, 2. FRA 52, 3. GBR 60, 4. ESP 73, 5. ITA 82, 6.

POR 91, 7. BIH 207
Under-23 Women (6.025k)
1. Jessica Coulson GBR 20:40
2. Lyudmila Lebedeva RUS 20:49
3. Clémence Calvin FRA 20:52
4. Gulshat Fazlitdinova RUS 20:52
5. Lauren Howarth GBR 20:56
6. Corinna Harrer GER 21:04
7. Carla Salomé Rocha POR 21:05
8. Yekaterina Matyunina RUS 21:07
63 of 63 finished
Teams: 1. RUS 27, 2. GBR 33, 3. GER 84, 4. POR 105, 5. FRA 113, 9 completed.
Junior Women (4k)
1. Amela Terzic SRB 13:29
2. Emelia Gorecka GBR 13:37
3. Maya Rehberg GER 13:43
4. Marusa Mismas SLO 13:44
5. Annabel Mason GBR 13:47
94 of 94 finished
Teams: 1. GBR 28, 2. GER 106, 3. RUS 111, 4. ROU 116, 5. SWE 122, 15 completed.

2012 WORLD ROAD RACE REVIEW
By Marty Post

IT SEEMS THAT every year new distance running talent emerges from East Africa and 2012 was no exception. In February previously unknown Dennis Kipruto Koech was the victor at one of the world's top road races, the RAK Half-Marathon. Then in April he sped to a 59:14 at the Vattenfall Berliner Halbmarathon, not only winning but apparently setting a new world junior record as well. However when he returned to Berlin on May 6 for the Big 25 it was revealed his last name was actually Kimetto and that he was born in 1984. One thing that did not change was his immense talent, as his finish time of 1:11:18 obliterated the 25 kilometres world (and course) record by 32 seconds. Kimetto even beat the fastest time in history, a 1:11:37 by Haile Gebrselassie that was not ratified because of technical irregularities.

Zersenay Tadese, considered by many to be the greatest half-marathon runner in history, enhanced his reputation in 2012. In October the 30-year-old from Eritrea won the IAAF World Half-Marathon Championships in 1:00:19, crushing the field by 32 seconds. This was the fifth world half-marathon or road running title he has won since 2006. Tadese also won even more convincingly at one of the world's premier annual races, the Meia-Maratona Internacional de Lisboa EDP, reaching the finish in 59:34, a full seventy seconds before the runner-up; it was the third consecutive victory for him at this race.

Two men broke into sub-59 minutes territory for the half-marathon in 2012. Atsedu Tsegaye of Ethiopia posted the year's fastest time of 58:47 at Praha in March; he became the fourth fastest half-marathoner in history with the fifth fastest time. Three weeks earlier Kenyan Stephen Kibet of Kenya won at Den Haag in 58:54, elevating him to the seventh fastest man ever. Den Haag was one of three half-marathon races which produced five sub-one hour finishers, the others being at Berlin and Lille. East Africans flexed their strength as 26 different men – 21 Kenyans, 4 Ethiopians and 1 Eritrean – ran under sixty minutes.

Africans also dominated at other road distances. Geoffrey Mutai led the 2012 performance list at 10 kilometres, with a 27:28.2 at Boston in June. He was one of 15 Kenyans to break 28 minutes, with the other ten on the list comprising nine Ethiopians and one Moroccan.

The two fastest 15 kilometre times of 2012 came at the always-fast ABN-AMRO Zevenheuvelenloop 15k in Nijmegen. Nicholas Kipkemboi crushed world record-holder Leonard Patrick Komon by 17 seconds, with his extended time of 42:00.8 leaving him just a second away from becoming the fifth man to break 42 minutes. Twenty-six broke 43 minutes, including an American and Frenchman of African heritage with the rest consisting of

13 Kenyans, 9 Ethiopians, and two Eritreans. At other less frequently contested distances, Dejen Gebremeskel led the world in 2012 at 5 kilometres (13:11), Tilahun Regassa at 8 kilometres (22:16) and Komon at 10 miles (44:48).

The women's sub-67 minute half-marathon club welcomed its tenth member when Kenya's Florence Kiplagat won the Rome-Ostia race in 66:38, also the year's fastest time and seventh fastest all-time for all courses. Mary Keitany extended her own record for most lifetime sub-67 minute times to five with a 66:49 victory at the Ra's Al Khaymah half-marathon, 59 seconds off the world record she set there in 2011. More women's times were run under 68 minutes (15), 69 minutes (46) and 70 minutes (88) than in any previous year. Kenyans Pasalia Kipkoech Chepkorir and Lydia Cheromei both ran five sub-70s in 2012, the latter including two marathon splits.

The World's Best 10k in San Juan has been the site of many fast times, including Paula Radcliffe's 2003 world record (30:21). In 2012 Vivian Cheruiyot made one of her infrequent visits to the road and won there with the year's fastest time of 30:47. Three other Kenyans broke 31 minutes, Pasalia Kipkoech Chepkorir (30:57), Gladys Cherono (30:57) and Emily Chebet (30:58), and Kenyans produced 19 of the year's 20 fastest times.

Tirunesh Dibaba had the year's fastest time at 15 kilometres, 47:08, in winning the ABN-AMRO Zevenheuvelenloop race in Nijmegen, site of her 2009 world record 46:28. There were an additional ten performances under 48 minutes in 2012, although all occurred as splits en route to fast half-marathon finishes. As is often the case, the number one time for 20 kilometres was also a half-marathon split, as Mary Keitany posted a 63:12 in the R'as al Khaymah Half Marathon.

What doesn't happen so often is a year-leading time at 25 kilometres within a marathon, but Ethiopia's Tiki Gelana did just that with a 1:22:33 at Rotterdam; she ran the full distance in 2:18:58, the second fastest women's marathon in 2012. (Mary Keitany was more than a minute slower, 1:23:37 at the 25km marker in her 2:18:37 at the Virgin London Marathon, although she covered the distance between 15 and 40 kms in 1:21:19). Gelana also had the fastest 30 kilometres for 2012 with a 1:39:07 split at the ABN/AMRO Rotterdam Marathon.

Leaders at other distances included Tirunesh Dibaba, 15:01 at 5 kilometres, Cheruiyot (24:28 split) at 8 kilometres and Sylvia Kibet, 51:42 at 10 miles.

Leading Road Races 2012

Date	Race	Men	Women
8 Jan	Egmond aan Zee HMar	Dawit Wolde ETH 60:46	Meseret Hailu ETH 71:16
15 Jan	Houston HMar	Feyisa Lelisa ETH 59:22	Belaynesh Olijira ETH 68:26
29 Jan	Almeria HMar	Abdelhadi El Mouaziz MAR 63:24	Olha Ochal POL 72:47
29 Jan	Eldoret HMar	Edwin Kipyego KEN 62:31	*men only*
5 Feb	Granollers HMar	Carles Castillejo ESP 62:37	Beatrice Chepchumba KEN 72:42
5 Feb	Marugame HMar	Mathew Kisorio KEN 60:02	Tiki Gelana ETH 68:48
12 Feb	Schoorl 10km	Abdi Nageeye NED 28:55	Lornah Kiplagat NED 32:27
17 Feb	Ra's Al Khaymah HMar	Dennis Kimetto KEN 60:40	Mary Keitany KEN 66:49
19 Feb	Guadalajara HMar (A)	Julius Keter KEN 62:59	Genoveva Kigen KEN 73:16
19 Feb	Kumamoto 30km	Tsuyoshi Ugachi JPN 1:30:01	Yuka Hakoyama JPN 1:43:26
19 Feb	Ohme 30km	Hideaki Tamura JPN 1:33:26	Asami Kato JPN 1:43:55
19 Feb	Verona HMar	Kennedy Kipyeko KEN 62:37	Emily Chepkorir KEN 73:25
26 Feb	Barcelona HMar	Abel Kirui KEN 60:28	Lineth Chepkirui KEN 71:49
26 Feb	Rome-Ostia HMar	Philemon Limo KEN 59:32	Florence Kiplagat KEN 66:38
26 Feb	San Juan 10km	Sammy Kitwara KEN 28:02	Vivian Cheruiyot KEN 30:47
4 Mar	Alphen aan den Rijn 20km	Michael Mutai KEN 59:30	Ruth van der Meijden NED 71:16
4 Mar	Paris HMar	Stanley Biwott KEN 59:44	Pauline Njeri KEN 67:55
4 Mar	São Paulo HMar	Joseph Aperumoi KEN 61:38	Pasalia Chepkorir KEN 72:29
10 Mar	Laredo 10km	Carles Castillejo ESP 28:29	Marta Domínguez ESP 31:47
11 Mar	Bath HMar	Edwin Kiptoo KEN 62:01	Jane Muia KEN 71:19
11 Mar	Den Haag HMar	Stephen Kibet KEN 58:54	Josephine Chepkoech KEN 71:20
11 Mar	Jacksonville 15km NC	Mo Trafeh USA 43:23	Janet Cherobon-Bawcom USA 49:41
11 Mar	Stressa-Verbania HMar	Belaya Bedede ETH 60:59	Jemima Jelagat KEN 68:35
11 Mar	Taroudant 10km	Ahmed Baday MAR 27:56	Amare Mekasha ETH 31:47
17 Mar	Kerzers 15km	Geoffrey Ndungu KEN 43:47	Caroline Chepkwony KEN 49:43
18 Mar	New York City HMar	Peter Kirui KEN 59:39	Firehiwot Dado ETH 68:35
18 Mar	Yamaguchi HMar	Chihiro Miyawaki JPN 60:53	Tomomi Tanaka JPN 69:47
24 Mar	Mobile 10km	Shadrack Kosgei KEN 28:19	Janet Cherobon-Bawcom USA 32:41
25 Mar	Lisbon HMar	Zersenay Tadese ERI 59:34	Shalane Flanagan USA 68:52

Date	Event	Men	Women
25 Mar	Milano HMar	Yakob Jarso ETH 61:07	Valeria Straneo ITA 68:48
25 Mar	Tarsus HMar	Gebretsadik Abraha ETH 62:19	Atsede Baysa ETH 69:39
25 Mar	Venlo HMar	Urige Buta NOR 62:35	Sharon Tavengwa ZIM 71:25
31 Mar	Azkoitia HMar	Wakeyo Habtamu ETH 61:09	Eunice Jepkirui KEN 68:39
31 Mar	Charleston 10km	Solomon Deksisa ETH 29:37	Janet Cherobon-Bawcom USA 33:01
31 Mar	Praha HMar	Atsedu Tsegaye ETH 58:47	Joyce Chepkirui KEN 67:03
1 Apr	Berlin HMar	Dennis Kimetto KEN 59:14	Philes Ongori KEN 68:25
1 Apr	Brunssum 10km	Philip Yego KEN 27:50	Esther Chemtai KEN 31:33
1 Apr	Carlsbad 5km	Dejene Gebremeskel ETH 13:11	Tirunesh Dibaba ETH 15:01
1 Apr	Madrid HMar	Elind Kiili KEN 62:07	Jane Mwikali KEN 73:16
1 Apr	Poznan HMar	Solomon Kiptoo KEN 62:00	Lucy Macharia KEN 70:26
1 Apr	Rabat HMar	Julius Arile KEN 61:07	Waganesh Mekasha ETH 71:11
1 Apr	Reading HMar	Edwin Kipyego KEN 63:08	Alice Mogire KEN 71:01
1 Apr	Washington DC 10M	Allan Kiprono KEN 45:15	Jelliah Tinega KEN 54:02
7 Apr	New Orleans 10km	Solomon Deksisa ETH 28:14	Genoveva Jelagat Kigen KEN 32:19
7 Apr	Paderborn 10km	Mosinet Geremew ETH 27:53	Esther Chemtai KEN 31:36
7 Apr	Paderborn HMar	Philemon Rono KEN 60:58	Jacqueline Nytepi KEN 71:04
8 Apr	Ivry/Vitry-sur-Seine HMar	Justus Moranga KEN 61:07	Cynthia Jerotich KEN 70:06
9 Apr	Dongio 10km	Edwin Soi KEN 28:32	Eliana Patelli ITA 33:07
15 Apr	Boston 5km	Ben True USA 13:41	Werknesh Kidane ETH 15:12
15 Apr	Dublin 10km	Kenenisa Bekele ETH 27:47	Gemma Steel GBR 32:06
15 Apr	Wien HMar	Haile Gebrselassie ETH 60:52	Paula Radcliffe GBR 72:03
22 Apr	Hilversum 10km	Alfred Cherop KEN 28:38	Agnes Jepkosgei KEN 32:24
22 Apr	Toronto 10km	Reid Coolsaet CAN 28:36	Tarah Mackay-Korir CAN 32:07
29 Apr	Nice HMar	Bernard Koech KEN 59:57	Shone Imana ETH 71:11
29 Apr	Würzburg 10km	Jacob Kendagor KEN 28:21	Maryanne Wangari Wanjiru KEN 32:45
1 May	Marseille 10km	Titus Masai KEN 28:20	Shone Imana ETH 32:44
1 May	Puy-en-Velay 15km	Hafta Fikadu ETH 43:10	Sarah Chepchirchir KEN 49:28
6 May	Berlin 25km	Dennis Kimetto KEN 1:11:18 WR	Caroline Chepkwony KEN 1:22:56
6 May	Spokane 12km	Allan Kiprono KEN 34:29	Mamitu Daska ETH 38:26
6 May	Trieste HMar	Solomon Kirwa Yego KEN 62:46	Rosaria Console ITA 71:23
12 May	Bern 10M	Daniel Chebii KEN 46:15	Caroline Chepkwony KEN 54:38
12 May	Göteborg HMar	Victor Kipchirchir KEN 60:25	Hilda Kibet KEN 69:27
12 May	Grand Rapids 25km NC	Robert Letting USA 1:14:54	Janet Cherobon-Bawcom USA 1:24:36
12 May	New York 10km	Daniele Meucci ITA 28:28	Bekelech Bedada ETH 34:54
13 May	Den Haag 10km	Frederick Musyoki KEN 28:21	Lucy Macharia KEN 32:55
13 May	Sendai HMar	Johana Maina KEN 61:34	Asami Kato JPN 71:21
20 May	Gifu HMar	Martin Mathathi KEN 61:29	René Kalmer RSA 73:02
20 May	Jakarta 10km	Silas Kipruto KEN 29:20	Philes Ongori KEN 33:12
20 May	Manchester 10km	Haile Gebrselassie ETH 27:39	Linet Masai KEN 31:35
20 May	San Francisco 12km	Sammy Kitwara KEN 34:41	Mamitu Daska ETH 39:03
20 May	Santos 10km	Mark Korir KEN 28:01	Pasalia Kipkoech Chepkorir KEN 30:57
26 May	Ottawa 10km	Geoffrey Mutai KEN 27:42	Lindsey Scherf USA 33:13
27 May	Bangalore 10km	Geoffrey Kipsang KEN 28:00	Helah Kiprop KEN 32:22
27 May	Lisboa 5km	*women only*	Ana Dulce Félix POR 15:36
28 May	Boulder 10km (A)	Allan Kiprono KEN 29:54	Mamitu Daska ETH 33:06
28 May	London 10km	Mo Farah GBR 29:21	Mara Yamauchi GBR 32:53
2 Jun	Albany 5km	*women only*	Mamitu Daska ETH 15:20
3 Jun	Groesbeek 10km	Tebalu Zawude ETH 28:17	Helah Kiprop KEN 31:44
3 Jun	San Diego HMar (dh 84m)	Meb Keflezighi USA 63:11	Kim Smith NZL 68:37
3 Jun	Wien 5km	*women only*	Ana Dulce Félix POR 15:31
8 Jun	Oelde 10km	Leonard Lagat KEN 28:05	Tola Fate ETH 32:03
9 Jun	Ceské Budejovice HMar	Daniel Chebii KEN 59:49	Tadelech Bekele ETH 70:54
9 Jun	Green Bay 10km	Allan Kiprono KEN 29:04	Risper Gesabwa KEN 33:07
9 Jun	New York 10km	*women only*	Edna Kiplagat KEN 32:08
16 Jun	Duluth HMar NC	Abdi Abdirahman USA 62:46	Kara Goucher USA 69:46
16 Jun	Peoria 4M	Shadrack Kosgei KEN 18:01	Risper Gesabwa KEN 20:26
23 Jun	Languex 10km	Fikadu Haftu ETH 28:17	Christelle Daunay FRA 31:48
23 Jun	Olomouc HMar	Nicholas Kipkemboi KEN 61:46	Yebergual Meleje ETH 71:33
24 Jun	Boston 10km	Geoffrey Mutai KEN 27:29	Kim Smith NZL 31:36
24 Jun	Hamburg HMar	Jacob Kendagor KEN 62:20	Caroline Chepkwony KEN 73:27

30 Jun	Appingedam 10km	Philip Langat KEN 27:57	Yebergual Melese ETH 32:38
1 Jul	Sapporo HMar	Martin Mathathi KEN 61:35	Mai Ito JPN 70:52
4 Jul	Atlanta 10km	Peter Kirui KEN 27:37	Mamitu Daska ETH 32:22
4 Jul	Cedar Rapids 8km	Alene Emere ETH 23:04	Diane Nukuri-Johnson BDI 25:50
8 Jul	Iguazu HMar	Benjamin Mutai KEN 62:03	Pasalia Kipkoech Chepkorir KEN 68:20
8 Jul	London 10km	Edwin Kipyego KEN 27:49	Beata Naigambo NAM 33:58
8 Jul	Nairobi HMar	Victor Kipchirchir KEN 61:45	Grace Momanyi KEN 71:42
8 Jul	Utica 15km	Tilahun Regassa ETH 43:01	Mamitu Daska ETH 49:26
14 Jul	Kingsport 8km	Tilahun Regassa ETH 22:16	*elite men only*
28 Jul	Davenport 7M	Silas Kipruto KEN 32:31	Margaret Muriuki KEN 36:17
29 Jul	Bogotá HMar (A)	Peter Kirui KEN 62:26	Gladys Cherono KEN 73:27
4 Aug	Corribianco 9.9km/6.6km	Imane Merga ETH 28:13	Asmerawork Bekele ETH 21:41
4 Aug	Cape Elizabeth 10km	Stanley Biwott KEN 28:00	Margaret Muriuki KEN 31:52
12 Aug	Falmouth 7M	Stanley Biwott KEN 31:59	Margaret Muriuki KEN 36:54
18 Aug	Parkersburg HMar	Julius Kogo KEN 63:36	Asami Kato JPN 72:58
19 Aug	Rio de Janeiro HMar	Wilson Loyanae KEN 61:46	Pasalia Kipkoech Chepkorir KEN 67:17
25 Aug	Flint 10M	Julius Kogo KEN 46:45	Caroline Rotich KEN 53:43
26 Aug	Cape Town HMar NC	Stephen Mokoka RSA 60:57	René Kalmer RSA 74:40
1 Sep	Lille HMar	Ezekiel Chebii KEN 59:05	Flomena Chepchirchir KEN 68:06
2 Sep	Altötting HMar	Dickson Kirui KEN 63:49	Agnes Kirop KEN 68:38
2 Sep	Düsseldorf 10km	Frederick Ngeny KEN 28:13	Mary Maina KEN 32:34
2 Sep	Glasgow HMar	Joseph Birech KEN 63:14	Bezunesh Bekele ETH 1:09:09
2 Sep	Tilburg 10M/10km	Pius Kirop KEN 45:38	Gladys Cherono KEN 30:57
3 Sep	New Haven 20km NC	Matt Tegenkamp USA 58:30	Renee Metevier-Baillie USA 67:08
8 Sep	Praha 10km/5km	Henry Kiplagat KEN 27:51	Tadelech Bekele ETH 15:48
9 Sep	Hamburg 10km	Richard Mengich KEN 28:17	Cynthia Kosgei KEN 32:28
16 Sep	Castelbuono 10km	Tariku Bekele ETH 30:01	*elite men only*
16 Sep	Philadelphia HMar	Stanley Biwott KEN 60:03	Sharon Cherop KEN 67:21
16 Sep	Porto HMar	Benson Barus KEN 61:44	Alice Mogire KEN 70:23
16 Sep	Providence 5km NC	Ben True USA 13:52	Molly Huddle USA 15:30
16 Sep	South Shields HMar dh 30.5m)	Wilson Kipsang KEN 59:06	Tirunesh Dibaba ETH 67:35
16 Sep	Ústí nad Labem HMar	Henry Kiplagat KEN 61:26	Betelhem Moges ETH 71:51
16 Sep	Wachau HMar	Robert Langat KEN 61:05	Magdalene Mukunzi KEN 70:26
22 Sep	Zürich-Uster HMar	Jacob Kendagor KEN 61:15	Sabine Fischer SUI 73:19
23 Sep	Torino HMar	Nicholas Togom KEN 61:37	Hellen Jepkurgut KEN 72:28
23 Sep	Udine HMar	Robert Chomesin KEN 60:23	Georgina Rono KEN 67:58
23 Sep	Zaandam 10M	Leonard P Komon KEN 44:48	Sylvia Kibet KEN 51:42
29 Sep	Lynchburg 10M	Julius Kogo KEN 47:48	Hellen Jemutai KEN 55:51
30 Sep	Bristol HMar	Dominic Ondoro KEN 62:51	Emily Biwott KEN 71:22
30 Sep	Lisboa HMar	Martin Lel KEN 61:28	Priscah Jeptoo KEN 70:32
30 Sep	New Delhi HMar	Edwin Kipyego KEN 60:55	Wude Ayalew ETH 71:10
30 Sep	Paris-Versailles 16.3km	Zawude Tebalu ETH 47:01	Cynthia Jerotich KEN 54:58
30 Sep	Remich HMar	Richard Mengich KEN 60:48	Farida Chelagat KEN 70:36
30 Sep	Utrecht 10km	Charles Cheruiyot KEN 28:22	Miranda Boonstra NED 34:05
7 Oct	Boston HMar	Allan Kiprono KEN 61:44	Kim Smith NZL 70:57
7 Oct	Breda HMar	Philip Langat KEN 61:05	Monica Jepkoech KEN 70:21
7 Oct	Nancy HMar	Alfred Cherop KEN 61:58	Leonidah Mosop KEN 71:11
7 Oct	St. Paul 10M NC	Mo Trafeh USA 46:56	Janet Bawcom USA 53:43
8 Oct	Boston 10km	*women only*	Hellen Jemutai KEN 32:30
13 Oct	Trento 10km	Edwin Soi KEN 28:43	*men only*
14 Oct	Berlin 10km	Leonard P Komon KEN 27:46	Anna Hahner GER 33:50
14 Oct	Cardiff HMar	Andrew Lesuuda KEN 62:21	Susan Partridge GBR 71:10
14 Oct	Groningen 4M	Brimin Kipruto KEN 17:13	Viola Kibiwott KEN 19:31
14 Oct	Paris 20km	Ezechiel Nizigiyimana BDI 58:11	Cynthia Jerotich KEN 65:34
14 Oct	Pordenone HMar	Solomon Kirwa Yego KEN 61:34	Hellen Jepkurgat KEN 72:28
14 Oct	Rennes 10km/5km	Edwin Kipyego KEN 27:50	Buze Diriba ETH 15:14
21 Oct	Birmingham HMar	Micah Kogo KEN 60:17	Sara Moreira POR 72:49
21 Oct	Cremona HMar	Solomon Kirwa Yego KEN 61:37	Hellen Jepkurgat KEN 71:16
21 Oct	Reims HMar	Philemon Yator KEN 61:50	Woynishet Girma Tafa ETH 71:13
21 Oct	St. Denis HMar	Alfred Cherop KEN 62:51	Mary Wacera KEN 70:54
21 Oct	Valencia HMar	Joel Kimurer KEN 59:36	Alice Mogire KEN 69:57

Date	Event	Men's Winner	Women's Winner
27 Oct	Tulsa 15km	Julius Kogo KEN 44:36	Hellen Jemutai KEN 51:13
28 Oct	Arezzo HMar	Abere Chane ETH 61:11	Eunice Chebet KEN 74:47
28 Oct	Marseille-Casis 20km	Edwin Kipyego KEN 58:16	Mercy Kibarus KEN 67:58
28 Oct	Nairobi HMar (A)	Mathew Kiprotich KEN 62:18	Pasalia Kipkoech Chepkorir KEN 68:11
28 Oct	Portsmouth 10M	Stephen Mokoka RSA 46:40	Jo Pavey GBR 53:00
4 Nov	Morlaix 10km	Ezechiel Nizigiyimana BDI 28:24	Mercyline Ondieki KEN 32:58
11 Nov	Istanbul 15km	Biruk Demiye ETH 43:57	Seboka Seyfu ETH 48:38
11 Nov	Roanoke HMar	Julius Kogo KEN 63:34	Hellen Jemutai KEN 72:40
17 Nov	Bulle 8km/6km	Tsegaye Mekonnen ETH 23:08	Maryam Yusuf Jamal BRN 19:38
17 Nov	Phildelphia 8km	Isaac Korir KEN 22:29	Misiker Mekonnin ETH 25:46
18 Nov	Boulogne-Billancourt HMar	Tesfaalem Meharii ETH 61:07	Tigisti Kiros ETH 71:11
18 Nov	Nijmegen 15km	Nicholas Kipkemboi KEN 42:01	Tirunesh Dibaba ETH 47:08
18 Nov	Philadelphia HMar	Isaac Korir KEN 62:52	Misiker Mekonnin ETH 71:56
22 Nov	Manchester 4.75M	Aaron Braun USA 21:20	Delilah DiCrescenzo USA 24:34
22 Nov	San Jose 5km	Stephen Sambu KEN 13:28	Kim Conley USA 15:40
24 Nov	Basel 10km/7.8km	Abraham Tadesse ERI 27:06	Jane Muia KEN 25:49
25 Nov	Addis Ababa 10km (A)	Hagos Gebrhiwet ETH 28:37	Aberu Kebede ETH 33:27
25 Nov	Hyderabad 10km	Mosinet Geremew ETH 27:36	Yebergual Melese ETH 33:21
1 Dec	Genève 7.25km/4.78km	Jacob Kendagor KEN 20:52	Jane Muia KEN 15:35
2 Dec	Kosa 10M	Enock Omwamba KEN 46:25	*men only*
2 Dec	's-Heerenberg 15km	Geoffrey Mutai KEN 42:25	Atsede Baysa ETH 49:15
8 Dec	Sion 7.35km/5.25km	Tadesse Abraham ETH 20:04	Caroline Chepkwony KEN 16:28
16 Dec	Zürich 8.8km/6.3km	Patrick Ereng KEN 24:59	Cynthia Kosgei KEN 20:39
31 Dec	Bolzano 10.05km/5.05km	Imane Merga ETH 29:13	Sylvia Kibet KEN 16:22
31 Dec	Luanda 10km	Atsedu Tsegaye ETH 28:17	Priscah Jeptoo KEN 32:31
31 Dec	Madrid 10km	Tariku Bekele ETH 28:29	Gelete Burka ETH 30:53
31 Dec	New York 4M	Christian Thompson USA 18:49	Delilah DiCrescenzo USA 21:07
31 Dec	Peurbach 6.8km/5.1km	Leonard P Komon KEN 18:32	Amela Terzic SRB 16:03
31 Dec	São Paolo 15km	Edwin Kipsang Rotich KEN 44:04	Maurine Kipchumba KEN 51:42
31 Dec	Trier 8km/5km	Moses Kipsiro UGA 22:42	Corinna Harrer GER 16:06

2012 WORLD MARATHON REVIEW
By Marty Post

THE OLYMPIC GAMES marathon has often produced a surprise gold medallist and London 2012 was no exception. Kenyans had dominated the pre-Olympic world scene so much so that men who had just the year before produced the fastest time in history (2:03:02, Geoffrey Mutai) and a new world record (2:03:38, Patrick Makau) were left at home. In their stead was the current two-time world champion (Abel Kirui), the 2012 London Marathon champion (Wilson Kipsang) and the London Marathon course record-holder (Emmanuel Mutai). Kipsang tried to break open the race, running 14:11 between 10k and 15k, the fastest 5k split ever in Olympic marathon competition, but Kirui pulled back alongside. A third runner, Stephen Kiprotich of Uganda, maintained contact with the Kenyan duo, and with five kilometres to go made the decisive move which would take him to victory in 2:08:01. Kiprotich won only the second Ugandan gold medal ever as Kirui and Kipsang took the silver and bronze medals.

The second biggest surprise of the day was how many of the starting trio of Ethiopians finished: zero. After a down year in 2011, the Ethiopians began 2012 with a vengeance. At the Standard Chartered Dubai Marathon, Ayele Abshero crossed the finish in 2:04:23, then the sixth fastest time in history and a massive 87 seconds improvement over the previous best marathon debut on a record-quality course. Two more countrymen broke 2:05 – Dina Sefir (2:04:50) and Markos Geneti (2:04:54). And while Kenyan Jonathan Maiyo was fourth in 2:04:56, Ethiopians swept the rest of the top 13, all under 2:08. All-time best times were recorded for places three through 17. Abshero and Sefir were joined at the Olympics by Getu Feleke who ran a course record 2:04:50 to win at Rotterdam in April. In post-Olympic competition, countryman Kebede Balcha finally broke 2:05, taking the course record at the Bank of America Chicago Marathon down to 2:04:38.

The two fastest times of the year were turned in at the BMW Berlin Marathon on the last day of September. Despite a relatively slow start, leader Geoffrey Mutai passed through 35 kilometres in 1:42:30 (a 2:03:35 projected finish) but the pace slowed thereafter. Mutai crossed the finish in 2:04:15, with Kimetto on his heels, posting 2:04:16, a new fastest debut on a standard course. This race also determined the outcome of the 2011-12 World Marathon Majors series, with Mutai clinching the $500,000 first place award. Makau bypassed a defence of Berlin to compete a month later on another German course in Frankfurt, where in 2011 Wilson Kipsang ran the second fastest time in history, 2:03:42. Weather conditions weren't favourable for a world-record challenge, but Makau added another victory to his résumé in 2:06:05. Runner-up Deressa Chimsa (2:06:52) earned a place in history as the first man with three sub-2:07s in one year and fastest single-year marathon triple with a total time of 6:18:59 in three races.

Standards of performance took another beating in 2012. New records were set for numbers of sub-2:05s (11), sub 2:06s (24), sub-2:07s (51), sub-2:08s (92), sub-2:09s (153) and sub-2:10s (225).

A year before the women's Olympic Marathon few would have considered Tiki Gelana, with a 2:28:28 PR, as even a medal contender. Then in October 2011 she won the Amsterdam Marathon in 2:22:08 and at Rotterdam the following April she set an Ethiopian national record of 2:18:58. Many picked Mary Keitany, who had won London four months earlier in the year's fastest time of 2:18:37, as the Olympic favourite and she would eventually take the 2011-12 World Marathon Majors title, but it was Gelana's day as a sub-70 minutes second half spurred her on to the gold medal in an Olympic record 2:23:07. The depth of the field was extraordinary with a record 29 women under 2 hours 30 minutes and best times in history for places 18 through 97.

A number of fastest times for place, third through ninth, were run at the first major marathon of the year, at Dubai. Lucy Kabuu, one of an unprecedented trio of 2:19 runners there, had the second fastest debut ever (2:19:34) and set a record for the fastest one-year total time for three marathons of 7 hours 5 minutes 27 seconds.

As with the men, standards of performance in 2013 were unprecedented. There were a record number of marathon times under 2:20 (6), 2:21 (11), 2:22 (18), 2:23 (24), 2:24 (44), 2:25 (61), and 2:30 (211).

Finally the competition that attracted the most world-wide media attention in 2012 was for one that ultimately was never held: the New York City Marathon. Initially plans were to stay the course for the November 4 event despite widespread destruction to the metropolitan area caused by Superstorm Sandy, but with just over 40 hours to go until the start, the race was cancelled. Although the running community lost one of its signature events, in view of the circumstances the prevailing sentiment was that it was the right decision.

Winners of 2012 International Marathons

Date	City	Men's winner	Time	Women's winner	Time
7 Jan	Xiamen	Peter Kamais KEN	2:07:37	Ashu Kasim ETH	2:23:09
12 Jan	Tiberias	Patrick Tambwe FRA	2:07:30	Tinet Gidey ETH	2:40:08
15 Jan	Houston	Tariku Jifar ETH	2:06:51	Alemitu Abera ETH	2:23:14
15 Jan	Mumbai	Laban Moiben KEN	2:10:48	Netsanet Achamo ETH	2:26:12
27 Jan	Dubai	Ayele Abshero ETH	2:04:23	Aselefech Mergia ETH	2:19:31
29 Jan	Marrakech	Stephen Tum KEN	2:08:51	Soumia Labani MAR	2:34:56
29 Jan	Osaka	women only		Risa Shigetomo JPN	2:23:23
5 Feb	Beppu-Oita	Harun Njoroge KEN	2:09:38	Chiyuki Mochizuki JPN	2:43:12
5 Feb	Hong Kong	Dereje Abera ETH	2:11:27	Misiker Mekonnin ETH	2:30:12
26 Feb	Tokyo	Michael Kipyego KEN	2:07:37	Atsede Habtamu ETH	2:25:28
4 Mar	Otsu (Lake Biwa)	Samuel Ndungu KEN	2:07:04	men only	
4 Mar	Torreón (A)	Erick Monyeye Mose KEN	2:10:40	Marisol Romero MEX	2:31:15
11 Mar	Nagoya	women only		Albina Mayorova RUS	2:23:52
17 Mar	Chongqing	Cosmas Kemboi KEN	2:10:33	Wang Jiali CHN	2:22:41
18 Mar	Los Angeles (dh 122m)	Simon Njoroge KEN	2:12:12	Fatuma Sado ETH	2:25:39
18 Mar	Roma	Luka Kanda KEN	2:08:04	Hellen Kimutai KEN	2:31:11
18 Mar	Seoul	Wilson Loyanai KEN	2:05:37	Feysa Tadesse ETH	2:23:26
25 Mar	Barcelona	Julius Chepkwony KEN	2:11:14	Emily Samoei KEN	2:26:52
8 Apr	Daegu	David Kiyeng KEN	2:07:57	Alemitu Abera ETH	2:24:57
8 Apr	Pyongyang	Oleksandr Matviychuk UKR	2:12:54	Kim Mi-gyong PRK	2:30:41
8 Apr	Zhengzhou	Mathew Sigei KEN	2:12:39	He Yinli CHN	2:33:25
15 Apr	Brighton	Peter Some KEN	2:12:03	Svetlana Kovgan BLR	2:29:37
15 Apr	Debno	David Metto KEN	2:12:53	Olga Mazurenok BLR	2:33:56

Date	Venue	Men	Time	Women	Time
15 Apr	Milano	Daniel Kirwa Too KEN	2:08:39	Irene Jerotich KEN	2:31:07
15 Apr	Nagano	Francis Kibiwott KEN	2:09:05	Pauline Wangui KEN	2:34:22
15 Apr	Paris	Stanley Biwott KEN	2:05:12	Tirfe Tsegaye ETH	2:21:40
15 Apr	Rotterdam	Yemane Adhane ETH	2:04:48	Tiki Gelana ETH	2:18:58
15 Apr	Wien	Henry Sugut KEN	2:06:58	Fate Tola ETH	2:26:39
16 Apr	Boston (dh 136m)	Wesley Korir KEN	2:12:40	Sharon Cherop KEN	2:31:50
22 Apr	Beograd	James Barmasai KEN	2:16:01	Mary Ptikany KEN	2:42:48
22 Apr	Enschede	Ismael Chemtan KEN	2:09:09	Konstadína Kefalá GRE	2:41:01
22 Apr	Kraków	Peter Kariuki Wanjiru KEN	2:12:11	Lucia Kimani BIH	2:36:54
22 Apr	Linz	Josephat Keiyo KEN	2:11:18	Daneja Grandovec SLO	2:41:20
22 Apr	London	Wilson Kipsang KEN	2:04:44	Mary Keitany KEN	2:18:37
22 Apr	Madrid	Patrick Korir KEN	2:12:07	Margaret Agai KEN	2:32:23
22 Apr	Padova	Robert Kwambai KEN	2:09:14	Marily dos Santos BRA	2:31:55
22 Apr	Zürich	Franklin Chepkwony KEN	2:10:58	Worknesh Tola ETH	2:31:24
28 Apr	Gunsan	Sammy Korir KEN	2:11:29	Kim Sun-jung KOR	2:43:52
29 Apr	Düsseldorf	Seboka Tola ETH	2:08:27	Agnes Barsosio Jeruto KEN	2:25:49
29 Apr	Hamburg	Abdullah Dawit ETH	2:05:58	Netsanet Achamo ETH	2:24:12*
6 May	Hannover	Joseph Kiptum KEN	2:09:56	Natalya Puchkova RUS	2:30:17
6 May	Mainz	Silas Toek KEN	2:12:19	Tatyana Vilisova RUS	2:32:03
6 May	Pittsburgh	James Kirwa KEN	2:14:09	Malika Mejdoub MAR	2:39:31
6 May	Salzburg	Martin Kiprugut Kosgei KEN	2:16:36	Joan Rotich KEN	2:36:08
7 May	Belfast	Urga Negewo ETH	2:13:41	Alice Chelangat KEN	2:39:02
12 May	Dalian	Julius Kiplimo Maisei KEN	2:13:03	Wei Xiaojie CHN	2:29:46
13 May	Dongying	Philip Biwott KEN	2:12:51	Emmah Muthoni KEN	2:30:09
13 May	Lens	Jackson Kiprono KEN	2:10:35	Bizuayehu Ehite ETH	2:32:19
13 May	Mont-St-Michael	Abraham Girma ETH	2:11:51	Gadise Fita ETH	2:36:56
13 May	Praha	Deressa Chimsa ETH	2:06:25	Agnes Kiprop KEN	2:25:41
20 May	Riga	Titus Kurgat Kipkorir KEN	2:16:54	Iraida Aleksandrova RUS	2:37:38
26 May	Tianjin	Michael Tiony KEN	2:16:16	Naomi Jepngetich KEN	2:37:22
27 May	Ottawa	Laban Moiben KEN	2:09:13	Yeshi Esayias ETH	2:28:46
2 Jun	Stockholm	Methkal Abu Drais JOR	2:19:16	Derebe Godana ETH	2:40:19
3 Jun	San Diego (dh 86.5m)	Nixon Machichim KEN	2:10:03	Alevtina Ivanova RUS	2:27:44
10 Jun	Lanzhou (A)	Solomon Tsige ETH	2:15:18	Zhang Jingxia CHN	2:38:02
16 Jun	Duluth	Berhanu Girma ETH	2:12:25	Everlyne Lagat KEN	2:33:14
17 Jun	São Paolo	Solonei da Silva BRA	2:12:25	Elizabeth Rumokol KEN	2:31:31
24 Jun	Kuala Lumpur	Lilan Kennedy Kiprop KEN	2:14:46	Elizabeth Chemweno KEN	2:40:25
1 Jul	Gold Coast	Alemayehu Shumye ETH	2:10:35	Kaori Yoshida JPN	2:30:36
1 Jul	Ordos	Haile Haji Gemeda ETH	2:14:15	Winfridah Nyansikera KEN	2:39:00
1 Jul	St Petersburg	Hassane Ahouchar MAR	2:13:37	Vera Trubnikova RUS	2:35:34
8 Jul	Rio de Janeiro	Willy Kangogo KEN	2:15:01	Thabita Kibet KEN	2:34:41
26 Aug	Mombasa	Paul Theuri KEN	2:12:26	Hellen Mugo KEN	2:37:16
26 Aug	Sapporo	Yuki Kawauchi JPN	2:18:38	Yuri Yoshizumi KEN	2:39:07
2 Sep	Johannesburg (A)	Timothy Kibet KEN	2:17:33	Eunice Muchiri KEN	2:43:08
2 Sep	Mexico City (A)	Peter Lemayian KEN	2:15:53	Alene Amare ETH	2:39:50
2 Sep	Taiyuan	Berhanu Shiferaw ETH	2:08:58	Jiang Xiaoli CHN	2:34:50
9 Sep	Moscow	Fyodor Shutov RUS	2:12:09	Natalya Sokolova RUS	2:30:10
22 Sep	Hengshui	Hailu Mekonnen ETH	2:08:07	Etalemahu Kidane ETH	2:28:03
22 Sep	Yingkou	Andrew Kiprop KEN	2:13:18	Wei Xiaojie CHN	2:30:04
23 Sep	Karlsruhe	Samwel Maswai KEN	2:11:46	Joyce Kandie KEN	2:34:36
23 Sep	Odense	Luka Chelimo KEN	2:10:37	Emily Chepkorir KEN	2:34:48
30 Sep	Berlin	Geoffrey Mutai KEN	2:04:15	Aberu Kebede ETH	2:20:30
30 Sep	Warsaw	James Mutua KEN	2:15:02	Agnieszka Ciolek POL	2:34:15
7 Oct	Bregenz	Titus Kosgei KEN	2:14:25	Ednah Kimaiyo KEN	2:35:27
7 Oct	Bucharest	Felix Kangogo KEN	2:15:19	Almaz Negede ETH	2:38:09
7 Oct	Buenos Aires	Eric Nzioki KEN	2:12:05	Lucy Karimi KEN	2:41:38
7 Oct	Chicago	Tsegaye Kebede ETH	2:04:38	Atsede Baysa ETH	2:22:03
7 Oct	Kosice	Lawrence Kimaiyo KEN	2:07:01	Hellen Mugo KEN	2:29:59
7 Oct	St. Paul	Christopher Kipyego KEN	2:14:53	Jeanette Faber USA	2:32:37
7 Oct	Verona	Kiprotich Kirui KEN	2:11:34	Everline Atacha KEN	2:42:42

Date	Location	Men		Women	
13 Oct	Baltimore	Stephen Muange KEN	2:13:08	Elfheshe Yado ETH	2:38:46
14 Oct	Carpi (dh 82.7m)	Sisay Lemma ETH	2:11:58	Ivana Iozzia ITA	2:35:08
14 Oct	Eindhoven	Dickson Chumba KEN	2:05:46	Mekuria Aberume ETH	2:27:20
14 Oct	Graz	Peter Kariuki KEN	2:11:17	Esther Macharia KEN	2:40:03
14 Oct	Köln	Alfred Kering KEN	2:07:37	Helena Kirop KEN	2:25:34
14 Oct	Melbourne	Jonathan Chesoo KEN	2:12:35	Lauren Shelley AUS	2:36:29
14 Oct	Poznan	Edwin Yator KEN	2:16:16	Svetlana Kovgan BLR	2:35:08
14 Oct	Toronto	Sahle Warga ETH	2:10:36	Mary Davies NZL	2:28:57
21 Oct	Amsterdam	Wilson Chebet KEN	2:05:41	Meseret Hailu ETH	2:21:09
21 Oct	Gyeongju	Boniface Mbuvi KEN	2:08:39	Choi Bo-ra SKO	2:40:20
21 Oct	Reims	Mariki Kipchumba KEN	2:06:05	Zeytuna Arba ETH	2:38:45
28 Oct	Chunchon	David Kiyeng KEN	2:10:05	Park Yu-jin KOR	2:41:55
28 Oct	Frankfurt	Patrick Makau KEN	2:06:08	Meselech Melkamu ETH	2:21:01
28 Oct	Ljubljana	Berhanu Shiferaw ETH	2:09:40	Worknesh Tola ETH	2:30:45
28 Oct	Nairobi (A)	Wesley Kibet KEN	2:10:40	Salome Biwott KEN	2:26:41
28 Oct	Porto	Anthony Wairuri KEN	2:12:14	Abera Teklu ETH	2:39:51
28 Oct	Venezia	Philemon Kipsang KEN	2:17:00	Emebet Etea ETH	2:38:10
29 Oct	Dublin	Geoffrey Ndungu KEN	2:11:09	Magdalene Mukunzi KEN	2:30:46
4 Nov	Cannes	Eliud Magut KEN	2:10:31	Aregu Lechisa ETH	2:31:56
4 Nov	Guadalajara (A)	Hillary Kimaiyo KEN	2:16:24	Truphena Tarus KEN	2:39:25
4 Nov	Rennes	Lema Feyisa ETH	2:09:47	Tesga Gelaw ETH	2:37:15
4 Nov	Seoul	James Kwambai KEN	2:05:50	Choi Kyung-hee KOR	2:39:20
11 Nov	Athína	Raymond Bett KEN	2:11:35	Consolater Yadaa KEN	2:40:00
11 Nov	Beirut	Kedir Fekadu ETH	2:12:57	Saeda Kedir ETH	2:35:08
11 Nov	Istanbul	Stephen Chebogut KEN	2:11:05	Koren Jelela ETH	2:28:06
18 Nov	Guangzhou	Bekana Daba ETH	2:11:05	Mulu Seboka ETH	2:26:46
18 Nov	Yokohama	women only		Lydia Cheromei KEN	2:23:07
18 Nov	Torino	Patrick Terer KEN	2:10:34	Sharon Cherop KEN	2:23:57
18 Nov	Valencia	Luke Kanda KEN	2:08:14	Birhane Dibaba ETH	2:29:22
25 Nov	Beijing	Tariku Jifar ETH	2:09:39	Jia Chaofeng CHN	2:27:40
25 Nov	Firenze	Endeshaw Negesse ETH	2:09:59	Shuru Diriba ETH	2:30:08
25 Nov	La Rochelle	Ismael Chemtan KEN	2:09:12	Zerfe Boku ETH	2:32:59
25 Nov	Osaka	Ser-Od Bat Ochir MGL	2:11:52	Lidia Simon ROU	2:33:12
2 Dec	Fukuoka	Joseph Gitau KEN	2:06:58	men only	
2 Dec	Macau (c. 45km)	Haile Haja Gemeda ETH	2:23:56	Ehitu Kiros ETH	2:50:10
2 Dec	Sacramento (dh 105m)	Daniel Tapia USA	2:16:30	Alisha Williams USA	2:34:58
2 Dec	Shanghai	Sylvester Teimet KEN	2:09:01	Feysa Tadesse ETH	2:23:07
2 Dec	Singapore	Kennedy Kiptoo Lilan KEN	2:17:21	Irene Jerotich Kosgei KEN	2:37:54
9 Dec	Castellón	Simon Mukun KEN	2:11:32	Leah Jerotich KEN	2:42:14
9 Dec	Honolulu	Wilson Kipsang KEN	2:12:31	Valentina Galimova RUS	2:31:23
15 Dec	Danzhou	Mike Mutai KEN	2:13:54	Radiya Adlo ETH	2:39:45
16 Dec	Hofu	Yuki Kawauchi JPN	2:10:46	Emiko Hirao JPN	2:45:44
16 Dec	Kisumu (short?)	Daniel Kilimo KEN	2:14:26	Magdalene Chemjor KEN	2:31:32
16 Dec	Taipei	Josphat Jepkopol KEN	2:15:27	Caroline Kilel KEN	2:30:19

* Rael Kiyara Nguriatukei KEN, 2:23:47 disqualified, doping violation

A = altitude over 1000m; dh = net downhill >1m/km

The inexorable progress of World Marathon Running

100th best each year

Year	Men	Women						
1980	2:14:25	2:49:08	1991	2:13:13	2:35:40	2003	2:10:38	2:31:21
1981	2:14:24	2:45:46	1992	2:13:22	2:36:14	2004	2:11:13	2:31:53
1982	2:14:32	2:43:19	1993	2:12:50	2:35:04	2005	2:11:20	2:31:43
1983	2:14:24	2:38:52	1994	2:12:24	2:35:07	2006	2:10:54	2:31:08
1984	2:13:20	2:37:29	1995	2:12:32	2:34:25	2007	2:10:43	2:31:25
1985	2:13:39	2:38:17	1996	2:12:25	2:33:24	2008	2:10:22	2:29:53
1986	2:13:38	2:37:58	1997	2:12:03	2:33:38	2009	2:09:53	2:30:08
1987	2:13:34	2:37:06	1998	2:11:50	2:33:45	2010	2:09:31	2:29:36
1988	2:13:08	2:35:29	1999	2:11:26	2:33:05	2011	2:09:19!	2:28:32
1989	2:13:37	2:37:04	2000	2:11:24	2:32:25	2012	2:08:32	2:28:01
1990	2:13:30	2:36:48	2001	2:11:18	2:31:05			
			2002	2:11:08	2:31:29			

! No longer including Boston Marathon

Review of Ultrarunning 2012
by Andy Milroy

ALTHOUGH THE impact of Japanese and African runners on Ultrarunning has been assessed in this Summary over the years, one nation has not had the credit it deserves. US ultra teams in international competition have generally done markedly better than other US long distance running teams. Their performances in the 2012 World 100km at Seregno in Italy are a case in point; the women's team was first and the men second. This was no flash in the pan. The women's team won the 1995 World title with Ann Trason winning in a world record time, and since then have taken the world team title thrice more – in 2005 and 2008 and now 2012, The men have also won in 2011 and were second in 2007 and 2012. Bronze medals have been routine.

There are probably a number of reasons for the success of the US ultrarunners. They do not face the overwhelming competitive pressure of the Kenyan and Ethiopians as yet, although this also applies to other nations as well. At the marathon and sub-marathon Ethiopians and other Africans have dominated US distance running on the roads for years, but ultrarunners do not face that kind of fierce foreign competitive pressure. There is prize money in US ultras, but definitely not enough to attract the elite competitors from overseas. US ultrarunners are therefore used to winning, to having the freedom to go out and run hard, face problems and still win. Novice US ultrarunners can learn their craft in races not dominated by foreign runners, having role models of successful US runners winning races. Thus the US 100km team members have a positive background of success to draw upon when they enter the international scene.

The World 100km took place at Seregno in Italy. Giorgio Calcaterra took the title for the third time in 6:23:22 on home soil, well clear of the Swede Jonas Buud 6:28:58 with another Italian Alberico Di Cecco 6:40:32 third. With Calcaterra running the fastest time in the World 100km he is obviously the World No 1. The team title was won by Italy from the USA and France, while with the European 100km Championships held in conjunction Germany moved up to third.

With many of the fastest women's times for 2012 coming from the World 100km the World No 1 would appear to be Amy Sproston of the United States who won that race in 7:34:07 from Kaisa Berg SWE 7:35:21 and the Russian Irina Vishnevskaya 7:35:57. The United States also took the team gold ahead of Japan and Russia, and in the European Championship Berg took the title and Russia team gold from Italy and Germany.

There has been some strong performances at 24 hours this year Mike Morton USA ran 277.543km to win the World 24 hour Challenge well clear of Florian Reus of Germany 261.718km and Ludovic Dilmi FRA 257.819km. Morton's distance was a new US record by a sizeable margin and places him third on the all-time list. There had been stellar performances by women with new track and road world bests in 2011. This year Michaela Dimitriadu CZE ran a distance second only to Lizzy Hawker's world road best (244.232km) with Connie Gardner of the USA running a national record 240.385km for second. Third placed Emily Gelder of Britain ran 238.875km to rank second behind Lizzy Hawker on the British all-time lists. Earlier in the year Mikie Sakane of Japan had also set a new national road record with 243.381km. The pre-2012 world top ten for the road 24 hours has been substantially revised.

Without the usually strong 48 hour races of Surgères and Köln, standards in the event were depressed. Yiannis Kouros ran 371.500km on the track in Skövde in Sweden, with Wolfgang Schwerk ranked second with his split at Balatonfüred in Hungary (360.000km), and a Hungarian in the same race (Csaba Lajko) ranked third with 355.237km. Heather Foundling-Hawker's 48-hour split at Monaco of 315.948km was the best women's mark of the year, well clear of Jannet Lange NED 304.564km at Ronne in Denmark.

Frenchman Olivier Chaigne ran the greatest distance in the world for a 6-day race in 2012 with 881.509km at Antibes in France. Wolfgang Schwerk ran the second best mark of the year, 874.864km at Balatonfüred in Hungary, and in this race there were the best female marks of the year: Monica Barchetti ITA 723.227km and Krisztina Nagyne Bakucz HUN 712.171km.

In longer events Didier Sessegolo set a French 1000km record of 7 days 13:58:21 in the Monaco 8-day race and in the longest race on a certified course in the world – the 3100 miles race in New York – Australian Graham Cunningham not only won in 43 days 10:36:39, but also set the fastest 1000 mile mark of the year and a new Australian record - 1000 miles 13 days, 16 hours, 13 minutes and 22 seconds.

Points to point courses have a long and distinguished history. The Comrades Marathon from Pietermaritzburg to Durban (86.96km) was won by Ludwick Mamabolo RSA in 5:31:03, from fellow countryman Bongmusa Mthembu 5:32:40, Leboka Noto LES 5:33:07 and Marko Mambo ZIM 5:33:44. Unfortunately. Mamabolo then failed a doping test and at the time of writing the official results have yet to be declared. Yelena Nurgaliyeva of Russia predictably won the race for the seventh time in 6:07:12, but Britain's Ellie Greenwood provided forceful opposition, finishing in 6:08:24. A distant third was another Russian Marina Zhalybina (née Bychkova) in 6:30:54.

The Spartathlon from Athens to Sparta over 245.3km was won by Stefan "Stu" Thoms GER in 26:28:19 from Tetsuo Kiso JPN 26:36:23 and Markus Thalmann AUT 27:14:25. The first woman actually finished third overall – Lizzy Hawker GBR, who set a world 24 hour road best last year, ran 27:02:17, a course record, well ahead of Leonie van den Haak NED 28:42:36 and Szilvia Lubics HUN 29:45:56.

There were numerous ultra stage races in 2012, the longest was the Trans-Europe Footrace from Skagen in Denmark to Gibraltar. The race over 4175km/64 days was won by Henry Wehder GER in an elapsed time of 376:42:28 with Ria Buiten NED the first woman in 504:18:29.

Last year I commented on the sheer number of Japanese ultra races and competitors. To a degree in terms of the growing interest in Asia, this could well be the tip of the iceberg, but the sport is growing particularly in the Far East with ultra races in particularly TPE, HKG, IND, KOR, SIN, MGL and PHI. And there are races and competitors in the Middle East too.

Most Years in World Merit Rankings

Of those ranked in the top tens in 2012, the athletes to have had most years ranked (10 or more) and most years at number one (four or more, in brackets years including indoor form) are as follows:

Name	Event	Years	No.1
Men			
Virgilijus Alekna	DT	17	7
Ezekiel Kemboi	3000mSt	11	3
Paul Kipsiele Koech	3000mSt	11	3
Koji Murofushi	HT	11	3
Phillips Idowu	TJ	11	2 (1)
Christian Cantwell	SP	10	4 (3)
Liu Xiang	110mh	10	2 (3)
Reese Hoffa	SP	10	3
Asafa Powell	100m	10	2
Gerd Kanter	DT	10	1
Andreas Thorkildsen	JT	9	6
Usain Bolt	200m	9	5
(and 3 years no. 1 of 5 ranked at 100m)			
Kenenisa Bekele	10000m	8	6
Kenenisa Bekele	5000m	8	5
Félix Sánchez	400mh	8	4
David Rudisha	800m	6	5
Robert Harting	DT	6	4

Name	Event	Years	No.1
Women			
Nadine Kleinert	SP	15	0
Yamilé Aldam	TJ	13	0
Yelena Isinbayeva	PV	12	6
Tatyana Lebedeva	TJ	12	5 (6)
María Vasco	20kmW	11	0
Sanya Richards-Ross	400m	10	6
Valerie Adams	SP	10	6
Meseret Defar	5000m	10	3
Veronica Campbell-Brown	100m	10	2
Veronica Campbell-Brown	200m	9	4
Allyson Felix	200m	9	4
Tirunesh Dibaba	5000m	9	4
Betty Heidler	HT	9	4
Barbora Spotáková	JT	8	6
Maryam Jamal	1500m	7	5 (4)
Olga Kaniskina	20kmW	7	4
Tirunesh Dibaba	10000m	5	5
Brittney Reese	LJ	5	4

Notes from the Editor cont.

Shot put Olympic champion 1992 Svetlana Krivelyova loses all her results from 18 Aug 2004 to 18 Aug 2006 thus including a bronze medal at the 2004 Olympics and 4th at the 2005 Worlds. Hammer throw Olympic gold medalist Olga Kuzenkova has her results from 12 Aug 2005 to 11 Aug 2007 annulled, and that means she loses her gold medal from the 2005 Worlds and third place from the 2005 World Athletics Final. So Yipsi Moreno becomes the Helsinki world champion with Tatyana Lysenko and Manuéla Montebrun taking silver and bronze.

Meanwhile the Ukrainian athletics federation has annoucced the deletion of results from 18 Aug 2005 to 17 Aug 2006 for Yuriy Bilonog, so confirming the loss of his 2004 Olympic gold (see page 108), 4th at 2005 Worlds and 6th at 2006 Europeans.

Reluctant as one is to re-write history, it must he hoped that such retrospective bans will act as a substantial warning to athletes.

OLYMPIC GAMES 2012

August 3-12, London, GBR

THE GAMES OF the 30th Olympiad were a huge success. Any pre-Games scepticism was swept aside first by the great success of the construction of the venues, especially at the Olympic Park, and then by the execution of all the sporting events, the enthusiasm and helpfulness of the volunteers and the exhilaration of terrific sport … and the British success across the range of sports.

Topped by sensational world records from David Rudisha (front-running 1:40.91 for 800m) and both men's (Jamaica 36.84) and women's (USA 40.82, a staggering 0.55 off the 27 year-old GDR time) sprint relay teams, the athletics provided a feast of top quality action. There was often terrific depth of performances as even with temperate conditions the times for instance in the men's and women's 100m and 4x100m races were especially brilliant, as was the men's 800m on the fast, hard Mondo track. There were Olympic records in 11 events with world leading marks in 22. Yelena Lashmanova also set a world record for the women's 20k walk.

Up to 80,000 spectators packed the stadium for every session; surely never before have there been such crowds for morning sessions. And surely never such enthusiasm and joy permeating the crowds as the decibel counts reached their peak, of course, for the triple British triumph of the second day, the greatest in the history of British athletics, of Jessica Ennis, Mo Farah and Greg Rutherford, and for Farah's second gold on the final night. And then there was Usain Bolt in all his majesty contributing a unique repeat treble.

The United States easily headed the medal and points tables with more gold medals than at any Games since Atlanta 1996, most medals since Barcelona 1992 and more points than at any since Los Angeles 1984. Their men's successes were headed by Aries Merritt at 110mh hurdles and by Ashton Eaton at decathlon. Allyson Felix won the 200m in great style and added gold on both relays, including a brilliant 48.1 leg in the 4x400, where Sanya Richards-Ross, already 400m champion, anchored the team to a clear win; both women took their Olympic gold tally to four to match the all-time record. Russia was as usual the second most successful nation, followed by Kenya and Jamaica.

Host nation Britain moved up a little on the points basis. Jessica Ennis had been the face of the Games for years, and more than lived up to expectations with a superb women's heptathlon win while Farah went where no British athlete had been before in winning the 10,000m and the 5000m. Ethiopia moved up the points table a little boosted by the return of Tirunesh Dibaba, who showed she was back to her elegant best in retaining her 10,000m title, and China did far better than on home ground in Beijing. Belarus was easily the biggest loser, ending up with just three 7th places and one eighth after 65 points in 2008 and 59 in 2004 plus, of course, the disgrace of Ostapchuk who was disqualified after 'winning' the shot. Caribbean nations excelled with brilliant wins by Kirani James of Grenada at 400m and Félix Sánchez of the Dominican Republic at 400mh as well as the Jamaican successes.

Medals and Points Table

Points: 8 for 1st to 1 for 8th place. 70 nations placed athletes in top eight, 42 won medals, and 23 won gold.

Nation	G	S	B	Points	2008	2004
USA	9	13	7	304	207	233.5
RUS	8	5	5	178.5	200	192
KEN	2	4	5	112	136	67
JAM	4	4	4	107	120	78
GER	1	4	3	94	43.5	45
ETH	3	1	3	90	76	72
GBR	4	1	1	83.5	72	69.5
CHN	1	0	5	73	39	31
UKR	0	1	2	47	50	47.5
FRA	1	1	0	39	37	23.5
TRI	1	0	3	35	18	2
CZE	1	0	1	29	23	25
AUS	1	2	0	27	40	34
CUB	0	1	1	25	61	52
CAN	0	0	1	21.5	23	9.5
POL	1	1	0	21	43	47
TUR	1	1	0	20	16	7
BAH	1	0	0	19	22	29
BEL	0	0	0	19	19	6
RSA	0	1	0	17	14	24
DOM	1	1	0	15	0	8
ITA	0	0	1	15	20	27
JPN	0	0	1	13	12	39
NED	0	0	0	13	3	12
BOT	0	1	0	12	1	1
ESP	0	0	0	12	31.5	36.5
MAR	0	0	1	11	17	29
BRA	0	0	0	11	21	13

FIN (1B) 10; SLO (1S), BRN (1B), LTU, NGR 9; ALG, CRO, GRN, HUN, KAZ. NZL, UGA (all 1G) 8; COL, GUA, IRI, TUN (all 1S), BLR (65 pts in '08, 59 in 04), NOR 7; EST (1B), PUR (1B), LAT, SWE 6; QAT (1B) 5.5; CIV, ERI, IRL 5; BAR, GRE, MEX 4; ARG, IND 3; BDI, ECU, POR, SRB, SVK, SUD, UZB, VEN, ZIM 2; AUT, MDA 1.

Seven individual champions retained their titles: three men, Bolt (100 & 200), and Tomasz Majewski (shot), and four women: Shelly-Ann Fraser-Pryce (100m), Dibaba (10,000)m, Valerie Adams (shot) and Barbora Spotáková (javelin); and three 2004 winners regained them: Ezekiel Kemboi (3000mSt), Sánchez (400mh) and Meseret Defar (5000m). Thirteen Daegu 2011 world champions at individual events won here.

Several juniors excelled, with Keshorn Walcott causing the biggest shock, adding the Olympic crown to his World Junior gold in the javelin, and two other World Junior champions won silver medals: Luguelin Santos at 400m and Nijel Amos at 800m (in a world junior record 1:41.73). In that last race Timothy Kitum added Olympic bronze to WJ silver.

Jesús Ángel García ESP in the 50k walk and Dragutin Topic SRB in the high jump equalled the men's record by competing in a sixth Games.

As well as Ostapchuk, athletes disqualified during the Games were Syrian 400m hurdler Ghofrane Al-Mohammed and French 5000m runner Hassan Hirt, and there had also been a disturbing number of really top names withdrawn after positive tests just prior to the Games, such as Hungarian discus thrower Zoltán Kövágó, Italian walker Alex Schwazer and Belarus hammer thrower Ivan Tikhon (apparently due to re-tested samples from 2004 and 2005!).

Men

100 Metres   (prelim, h 4th, sf, F 5th 1.5)

1. Usain Bolt JAM	9.63*
2. Yohan Blake JAM	9.75
3. Justin Gatlin USA	9.79
4. Tyson Gay USA	9.80
5. Ryan Bailey USA	9.88
6. Churandy Martina NED	9.94
7. Richard Thompson TRI	9.98
8. Asafa Powell JAM	11.99

BOLT TOOK 0.06 off his Olympic record as he ran the second fastest ever time. He got a reasonable start (reaction time 0.165) but it was only at halfway that he began to draw clear. His final 40m were awesome as he left his nearest challenger, Blake, nearly a metre and a half behind with Gatlin edging Gay by inches for the bronze. The stellar field recorded the best ever times for 3rd to 7th places, all under 10 secs although Powell pulled up with a groin pull just after halfway. Bailey 9.88 and Gatlin 9.97 ran the fastest ever times for first round heats as Blake won in 10.00 and Bolt cruised through his in 10.08. Semi-finals were won by Gatlin 9.82, Bolt 9.87 and Blake 9.85 as all the finalists bar Thompson (10.02) broke 10 secs.

Keston Bledman with 10.04 tied the best ever legal-wind non-qualifying mark and Dwain Chambers ran 10.05 after 10.02 in his heat and World Junior champion Adam Gemili 10.05.

200 Metres   (h 7th, sf 8th, F 9th 0.4)

1. Usain Bolt JAM	19.32
2. Yohan Blake JAM	19.44
3. Warren Weir JAM	19.84
4. Wallace Spearmon USA	19.90
5. Churandy Martina NED	20.00
6. Christophe Lemaitre FRA	20.19
7. Alex Quiñónez ECU	20.57
8. Anaso Jobodwana RSA	20.69

IT WAS A clean sweep of the medals for Jamaica and Bolt became the first man to complete the 100/200m double twice. He tore through the first 100m in 10.0 (Blake 10.2) and his 19.32 was the joint fourth quickest ever and his seventh clocking inside 19.60. Blake's 19.44 for second was the fastest ever second place and he narrowed the gap as Bolt eased somewhat. Weir reduced his best from 19.99 to 19.84 for the bronze. Quiñónez, who was fastest in round one with a national record 20.28, became the first athlete from Ecuador, apart from walker Jefferson Pérez, to make an Olympic final. The semis were won by Blake 20.01 from Spearmon 20.02 and Lemaitre 20.03, Bolt 20.18 and Martina 20.17.

400 Metres   (h 4th, sf 5th, F 6th)

1. Kirani James GRN	43.94
2. Luguelín Santos DOM-J	44.46
3. Lalonde Gordon TRI	44.52
4. Chris Brown BAH	44.79
5. Kévin Borlée BEL	44.81
6. Jonathan Borlée BEL	44.83
7. Demetrius Pinder BAH	44.98
8. Steven Solomon AUS-J	45.14

JAMES, STILL ONLY 19, became the first non-American to crack 44 sec with a resounding Commonwealth record and world-leading mark of 43.94 for 9th on the world all-time list, improving his national record from his 2011 best of 44.36. After Pinder took an early lead in the final (100m 10.9), James pushed ahead to 200m in 21.3 and to a clear lead at 300m in 32.0 from Pinder 32.3, Santos and Brown 32.4, increasing his lead to win by 0.52 from 18 year-old Santos and the surprising Gordon taking bronze. Brown was fourth for the fourth time in a global final. The world leader LaShawn Merritt had to yield to his Achilles injury early in his heat, while J Borlée ran a Belgian record 44.43 with the next quickest of the round Pavel Maslák in a Czech record 44.91 and Pinder 44.92. The medallists were all semi-final winners: Gordon 44.58, James 44.59 and Santos 44.78, as all the qualifiers broke 45 secs. Amazingly no US runner made the final.

800 Metres (h 6th, sf 7th, F 9th)

1. David Rudisha KEN	1:40.91*
2. Nijel Amos BOT-J	1:41.73
3. Timothy Kitum KEN-J	1:42.53
4. Duane Solomon USA	1:42.82
5. Nick Symmonds USA	1:42.95
6. Mohammed Aman ETH-J	1:43.20
7. Abubaker Kaki SUD	1:43.32
8. Andrew Osagie GBR	1:43.77

RUDISHA PRODUCED ONE of the greatest runs in Olympic history, as, just as he had to win the 2011 world title, he led all the way. His 200m splits were 23.5, 49.28 and 1:14.30 before his slowest 200m of the race to end in his third world record of 1:40.91. Two juniors, Amos and Kitum, took the other medals, with a third Aman setting an Ethiopian record, and there were best ever marks for all places 1-8. Kaki was the one man who tried to stay close to Rudisha, a pace behind with 49.4 for 400m, but he cracked for a second half in 53.9 and he was the only finalist not to set a pb. After Kaki had run the fastest heat, 1:45.51, all the finalists broke 1:45 in the semis, won by Kaki 1:44.51, Rudisha 1:44.35 and Aman 1:44.34.

1500 Metres (h 3rd, sf 5th, F 7th)

1. Taoufik Makhloufi ALG	3:34.08
2. Leonel Manzano USA	3:34.79
3. Abdelaati Iguider MAR	3:35.13
4. Matt Centrowitz USA	3:35.17
5. Henrik Ingebrigtsen NOR	3:35.43
6. Mekonnen Gebremedhin ETH	3:35.44
7. Silas Kiplagat KEN	3:36.19
8. Ilham Tanui Özbilen TUR	3:36.72
9. Nick Willis NZL	3:36.94
10. Belal Mansoor Ali BRN	3:37.98
11. Nixon Chepseba KEN	3:39.04
12. Asbel Kiprop KEN	3:43.83

MAKHLOUFI WAS MUCH the fastest in the heats with 3:35.15, and after winning the first semi in a slow 3:42.24, surged away from the field in the final from 250m out, covering the 200m from 1200 to 1400m in 25.4. Manzano swept past four men in the straight to take second and Iguider also finished fast for the bronze. World champion Kiprop was clearly unfit following a hamstring injury and the other two Kenyans faded badly on the last lap after leading at 800m, Chepseba 1:58.63, and 1200m, Kiplagat 2:54.72. The second semi has been much faster then the first with Iguider winning in 3:33.99 and Andy Baddeley, 9th, leading the non-qualifiers with 3:36.03. Makhloufi was curiously entered also for the 800m but quickly dropped out of his heat – the day before the 1500m final – citing a knee problem. He was at first debarred from any future races at the Games for not providing a bona fide effort, but after a review of medical evidence (!) he was permitted to take his place in the 1500m final.

5000 Metres (h 8th, F 11th)

1. Mo Farah GBR	13:41.66
2. Dejen Gebremeskel ETH	13:41.98
3. Thomas Longosiwa KEN	13:42.36
4. Bernard Lagat USA	13:42.99
5. Isiah Koech KEN	13:43.83
6. Abdelaati Iguider MAR	13:44.19
7. Galen Rupp USA	13:45.04
8. Juan Luis Barrios MEX	13:45.30
9. Hayle Ibrahimov AZE	13:45.37
10. Lopez Lomong USA	13:48.19
11. Hagos Gebrhiwet ETH-J	13:49.59
12. Yenew Alamirew ETH	13:49.68
13. Mumin Gala DJI	13:50.26
14. Cameron Levins CAN	13:51.87
15. Moses Kipsiro UGA	13:52.25

SUPPORTED BY A deafening roar from the crowd, Farah moved into the lead with 700m left in a very slowly run final and became the seventh man to win the distance double at the same Games with a last lap of 52.94. His finish was last 100m 13.1, 200m 26.4, 800m 1:54.0, 1200m 2:56.1 and 1600m 3:57.0. Gebremeskel, who had led at 4k in 11:16.47 overtook Longosiwa just before the finish to settle the other medals. Farah had come back after his 10k victory despite the hard track being unhelpful for distance runners and finished a comfortable third in 13:26.00 in the first heat, won by Ibrahimov in 13:25.23; the second heat was faster as Gebremeskel won in 13:15.15, the fastest in Olympic history, with the first ten (to 13:21.21) all making the final.

10,000 Metres (4th)

1. Mo Farah GBR	27:30.42
2. Galen Rupp USA	27:30.90
3. Tariku Bekele ETH	27:31.43
4. Kenenisa Bekele ETH	27:32.44
5. Bidan Karoki Muchiri KEN	27:32.94
6. Zersenay Tadese ERI	27:33.51
7. Teklemariam Medhin ERI	27:34.76
8. Gebr. Gebremariam ETH	27:36.34
9. Polat Kemboi Arikan TUR	27:38.81
10. Moses Kipsiro UGA	27:39.22
11. Cameron Levins CAN	27:40.68
12. Moses Masai KEN	27:41.34
13. Dathan Ritzenhein USA	27:45.89
14. Robert Kajuga RWA	27:56.67
15. Nguse Tesfaldet ERI	27:56.78

FARAH BECAME THE first Briton – male or female – ever to win at any of the current Olympic distance running events, and he did so after the others had played into his hand by running the race at a pretty slow tempo, so that he could unleash his devastating finish. Halfway was reached in 14:05.79 after Tadese had done much of the leading. The seventh kilometre was run in 2:39.87 but then the pace slowed again to 2:42.91 and 2:46.48. With two laps remaining Tariku Bekele and Farah were just ahead of Rupp, and at the bell Farah was ahead, remaining in front throughout a pulsating last lap of 53.48. That final kilometre was covered in just 2:28.45, the second 5000m in 13:24.63. Rupp got past Bekele the younger for the silver with Kenenisa – bidding for a record third consecutive title – out of the medals.

Marathon (12th)

1. Stephen Kiprotich UGA	2:08:01
2. Abel Kirui KEN	2:08:27
3. Wilson Kipsang KEN	2:09:37
4. Meb Keflezighi USA	2:11:06
5. Marilson dos Santos BRA	2:11:10
6. Kentaro Nakamoto JPN	2:11:16
7. Cuthbert Nyasango ZIM	2:12:08
8. Paulo Paula BRA	2:12:17
9. Henryk Szost POL	2:12:28
10. Ruggero Pertile ITA	2:12:45
11. Viktor Röthlin SUI	2:12:48
12. Oleksandr Sitkovskyy UKR	2:12:56
13. Franck de Almeida BRA	2:13:35
14. Aleksey Reunkov RUS	2:13:49
15. Wirimai Juwawo ZIM	2:14:09

EAST AFRICA SWEPT the medals but it was unheralded Kiprotich from Uganda who took gold, the second ever for his nation at Olympic athletics, winning by a surprisingly big margin over two Kenyans. The race, on a four-lap course in Central London, started at 11 am and it was a warm, humid day. Such conditions and a twisty course slowed the times and 20 of the 105 starters did not finish. Kipsang made an early move and kicked in a 14:11 5k split from 10k to open up a 13 sec lead over Kirui and non-finisher Getu Feleke and remained ahead at halfway in 63:15, with six men following 16-17 secs back. By 25k Kipsang (15:01) had his lead reduced to 7 sec, the chasing group now down to three: Kirui, Kiprotich and Ayele Abshero, and he was caught at 26.6k. Abshero (dnf) was 36 sec behind the top trio at 30k (1:30:15). The pace slowed with 15:48 for the 5k to 35k and then the two Kenyans began to go away, but Kiprotich fought back and passed them with just over 3 miles to go, so that he led by 19 secs from Kirui at 40k (2:01:12).

3000m Steeplechase (h 3rd, F 5th)

1. Ezekiel Kemboi KEN	8:18.56
2. Mahiedine Mekhissi-Benabbad FRA	8:19.08
3. Abel Mutai KEN	8:19.73
4. Roba Gari ETH	8:20.00
5. Brimin Kipruto KEN	8:23.03
6. Evan Jager USA	8:23.87
7. Hamid Ezzine MAR	8:24.90
8. Donald Cabral USA	8:25.91
9. Tarik Langat Akdag TUR	8:27.64
10. Ion Luchianov MDA	8:28.15
11. Brahim Taleb MAR	8:32.40
12. Nahom Mesfin ETH	8:35.12
13. Yuri Floriani ITA	8:40.07
dq. Benjamin Kiplagat UGA	(?)
dnf. Jukka Keskisalo FIN	–

ALTHOUGH DEFENDING CHAMPION Kipruto fell on the sixth lap and had to settle for fifth, the Kenyan steeplechase dominance continued as Kemboi regained his title and Mutai took bronze. The final was a fairly unsatisfactory race, as in the absence of Paul Koech, who would surely have done so, nobody was prepared to push the pace. So the opening kilometres were run in 2:52.70 and 2:50.56, but it took just 2:35.30 for the third. Gari led at the bell but Kemboi flew down the back straight from 300m to go and, although Mekhissi-Benabbad (second as in Beijing) gave valiant chase, was able to showboat in his accustomed style, crossing the finishing line in lane eight! All but three of the finalists had run faster in the heats, with Mekhissi fastest (8:16.23).

110 Metres Hurdles (h 7th, sf, F 8th -0.3)

1. Aries Merritt USA	12.92
2. Jason Richardson USA	13.04
3. Hansle Parchment JAM	13.12
4. Lawrence Clarke GBR	13.39
5. Ryan Brathwaite BAR	13.40
6. Orlando Ortega CUB	13.43
7. Lehann Fourie RSA	13.53
dq. Dayron Robles CUB	(42.86)

MERRITT WAS EASILY the fastest in each round: 13.07 in his heat from Brathwaite 13.23, 12.94 (tying the fastest ever wind-legal qualifying time) in his semi, and then 12.92 in the final. That was just 0.01 from the Olympic record set in 2004 by Liu Xiang, who crashed into the first hurdle in his heat with the same Achilles tendon injury that had ruined his 2008 Olympic chances. The other semis were won by Richardson 13.13 and Robles 13.10. The last was a season's best for the defending champion and world record holder, who like Li was returning from injury, with only three pre-Olympic races in 2012, but in the final he sustained an injury while in third place mid-race. Richardson was a clear second and Parchment took bronze, running Jamaican records in semi (13.14) and final.

400 Metres Hurdles (h 3rd, sf 4th, F 6th)

1. Félix Sánchez DOM	47.63
2. Michael Tinsley USA	47.91
3. Javier Culson PUR	48.10
4. David Greene GBR	48.24
5. Angelo Taylor USA	48.25
6. Jehue Gordon TRI	48.86
7. Leford Green JAM	49.12
8. Kerron Clement USA	49.15

JUST A FEW weeks short of his 35th birthday, Sánchez ran his fastest time for eight years in winning his semi in 47.76 and went yet faster in the final as his 47.63 was exactly the same time as when he won in Athens 2004. He thus became the fourth man to win two Olympic

400mh titles. He was out well with favourite Culson and Taylor, the 2000 and 2008 champion, and powered into the lead ahead of Culson, finishing with a powerful home straight drive, as Tinsley came through for second after Culson hit hurdle seven. Culson 48.33 and Clement 48.48 were fastest in the heats and as well as Sánchez, three men broke 48 in the semis: Culson 47.93, Taylor 47.95 and Gordon 47.96, a national record. World champion Greene only made the final as a fastest loser in 48.19 while Omar Cisneros ran 48.23 for the fastest ever non-qualifying time.

High Jump   (Q 2.32 5th, F 7th)

1. Ivan Ukhov RUS	2.38
2. Erik Kynard USA	2.33
3= Mutaz Essa Barshim QAT	2.29
3= Derek Drouin CAN	2.29
3= Robbie Grabarz GBR	2.29
6. Jamie Nieto USA	2.29
7. Bogdan Bondarenko UKR	2.29
8. Michael Mason CAN	2.29
9= Wanner Miller COL	2.25
9= Andriy Protsenko UKR	2.25
9= Jesse Williams USA	2.25
12. Andrey Silnov RUS	2.25
13. Kyriakis Ioannou CYP	2.20
14. Mickaël Hanany FRA	2.20

UKHOV DOMINATED THE final with first-time clearances at 2.33, 2.36 and 2.38, but Kynard accompanied him as, after also clearing 2.33 first time, he had one failure at each of 2.36, 2.38 and 2.40. Only six men cleared 2.29 in qualifying with the rest going through with 2.26. That 2.29 also served as enough for medals with three men sharing bronze – all with clean cards to that height. There was then too big a jump to the next height of 2.33, at which all three medallists went very close.

Pole Vault   (Q 5.70m 8th, F 10th)

1. Renaud Lavillenie FRA	5.97*
2. Björn Otto GER	5.91
3. Raphael Holzdeppe GER	5.91
4. Dmitriy Starodubtsev RUS	5.75
5= Steven Lewis GBR	5.75
5= Yevgeniy Lukyanenko RUS	5.75
7. Konstadínos Filippídis GRE	5.65
8. Jan Kudlicka CZE	5.65
9= Romain Mesnil FRA	5.50
9= Malte Mohr GER	5.50
11. Lukasz Michalski POL	5.50
12. Igor Bychkov ESP	5.50
nh. Steve Hooker AUS	–
nh. Brad Walker USA	–

EVEN 5.50 WAS enough to make the final as the qualifying competition was held in difficult conditions, Lavillenie and Holzdeppe heading the list with 5.65 clearances. The 2011 World 1-2 Pawel Wojciechowski (nh) and Lázaro Borges (5.50) failed to make it. There was, however, an excellent standard in the final, with Lavillenie, after first-time successes at 5.65, 5.75 and 5.85 but a failure at 5.91, adding 1 cm to Hooker's Olympic record with his second attempt clearance at 5.97, after both Otto and Holzdeppe had gone over 5.91 on their first attempts. Former Olympic and World champions Hooker and Walker were unable to clear their opening height of 5.65.

Long Jump   (Q 8.10m 3rd, F 4th)

1. Greg Rutherford GBR	8.31/-0.4
2. Mitchell Watt AUS	8.16/-0.2
3. Will Claye USA	8.12/-0.2
4. Michel Tornéus SWE	8.11/-0.7
5. Sebastian Bayer GER	8.10/0.4
6. Chris Tomlinson GBR	8.07/0.2
7. Mauro da Silva BRA	8.01/-0.1
8. Khotso Mokoena RSA	7.93/-2.3
9. Henry Frayne AUS	7.85/-0.3
10. Marquise Goodwin USA	7.80/0.2
11. Aleksandr Menkov RUS	7.78/-0.9
12. Tyrone Smith BER	7.70/0.9

ONLY TWO MEN met the automatic qualifying standards: da Silva and Goodwin 8.11 with Menkov 8.09 and Rutherford 8.08 just outside, and Irving Saladino failing to register a jump. Good jumps were also rare in the final, with tricky wind conditions and there only 14 jumps at 8m or more. To the huge delight of home fans Rutherford was best able to cope as he took a second round lead with 8.22 and nobody could match that, while he stretched out to 8.31 in round four, in which there were three moves into second place: Bayer 8.10, Tornéus 8.11 and Claye 8.12. Then Watt took silver with his last two jumps of 8.13 and 8.16.

Triple Jump   (Q 17.10m 7th, F 9th)

1. Christian Taylor USA	17.81/0.6
2. Will Claye USA	17.62/0.6
3. Fabrizio Donato ITA	17.48/0.6
4. Daniele Greco ITA	17.34/0.9
5. Leevan Sands BAH	17.19/0.2
6. Benjamin Compaoré FRA	17.08/0.0
7. Tosin Oke NGR	16.95/0.7
8. Alexis Copello CUB	16.92/0.5
9. Lyukman Adams RUS	16.78/0.2
10. Dong Bin CHN	16.75/0.3
11. Samyr Laine HAI	16.65/0.8
12. Dmitriy Platnitskiy BLR	16.19/-0.7

AFTER QUALIFYING FOR the final only with his last effort of 16.87, Claye became the first man since Naoto Tajima in 1936 to win medals at both long jump and triple jump. After Donato had jumped 17.34 in round one, Claye led with a second round 17.54 but in the fourth round World champion Taylor, who had led the qualifiers with 17.21 and was previously fifth with a safe third round 17.15 after two no jumps, connected at last with a world-leading distance of 17.81. Claye gamely responded with 17.62, his best outdoor mark of the season, while Donato was brilliantly consistent with 17.44, 17.45 and 17.48 in rounds 2-4. The 2008 silver medallist Phillips Idowu, not recovered from injury, missed the final, 14th with 16.53.

Shot (Q 20.65m, F 3rd)

1.	Tomasz Majewski POL	21.89
2.	David Storl GER	21.86
3.	Reese Hoffa USA	21.23
4.	Christian Cantwell USA	21.19
5.	Dylan Armstrong CAN	20.93
6.	Germán Lauro ARG	20.84
7.	Asmir Kolasinac SRB	20.71
8.	Pavel Lyzhin BLR	20.69
9.	Ryan Whiting USA	20.64
10.	Dorian Scott JAM	20.61
11.	Maksim Sidorov RUS	20.41
12.	Chang Ming-Huang TPE	19.99

SIXTEEN MEN EXCEEDED 20m in qualifying, with Soslan Tsirikhov's 20.17 the best ever non-qualifying mark. The top qualifiers, Hoffa 21.36, Storl 21.15 and Majewski 21.03, took the medals but in reverse order. Majewski started the final with 21.19 but his lead was short-lived as World champion Storl opened with a formidable outdoor pb of 21.84. Majewski responded with a season's best of 21.72 in the second round ... only for Storl to improve to 21.86. Undaunted, Majewski – fired up to defend his Olympic crown – added 1cm to that with his third effort and added 21.72 and 21.89 with his last two efforts. Hoffa's third round 21.23 took bronze. There were the best ever marks for places 8-11 (and 12th in qualifying)

Discus (Q 65.00m 6th, F 7th)

1.	Robert Harting GER	68.27
2.	Ehsan Hadadi IRI	68.18
3.	Gerd Kanter EST	68.03
4.	Virgilijus Alekna LTU	67.38
5.	Piotr Malachowski POL	67.19
6.	Martin Wierig GER	65.85
7.	Frank Casañas ESP	65.56
8.	Vikas Gowda IND	64.79
9.	Benn Harradine AUS	63.59
10.	Erik Cadée NED	62.78
11.	Jorge Fernández CUB	62.02
12.	Lawrence Okoye GBR	61.03

JUST 24CM SEPARATED the medallists, but Harting was a most worthy champion with five throws over 66m and he was the first German Olympic champion at athletics since 2000. Hadadi took a first-round lead with 68.18 to which Harting responded with 67.79 and 40 year-old Alekna was third at 67.38. The medals were decided in round four as Kanter improved from 66.02 to 68.03 and Harting took over with 68.27. Top qualifying marks came from Kanter 66.39 and Harting 66.22, and

Apostolos Parellis, 13th, threw 63.48 for the best ever non-qualifying mark with a record 16 men over 63m and 19 men over 62m. As after his World Championships wins Harting celebrated by ripping off his short like the Incredible Hulk.

Hammer (Q 77.00m 3rd, F 5th)

1.	Krisztián Pars HUN	80.59
2.	Primoz Kozmus SLO	79.36
3.	Koji Murofushi JPN	78.71
4.	Oleksiy Sokyrskyy UKR	78.25
5.	Kirill Ikonnikov RUS	77.86
6.	Lukás Melich CZE	77.17
7.	Szymon Ziólkowski POL	77.10
8.	Nicola Vizzoni ITA	76.07
9.	Kibwe Johnson USA	74.95
10.	Dilshod Nazarov TJK	73.80
11.	Valeriy Svyatokho BLR	73.13
12.	Alex Smith GBR	72.87

PARS BECAME THE first Hungarian hammer champion and led the qualifiers (with 79.37) and the final from round one. He started with 79.14 and improved to 80.59 in the third round, with all six throws at 78.33 or better. Kozmus came closest with an opening 78.97 and 79.36 and 78.59 as his last two throws. That great competitor Murofushi, with just one competition (a modest 72.95) behind him in 2012, threw 78.48 in qualifying and had three over 78m topped by a third round 78.71 in the final to complete the same podium (but in a different order) as in Daegu 2011.

Javelin (Q 82.00m 8th, F 11th)

1.	Keshorn Walcott TRI-J	84.58
2.	Oleksandr Pyatnytsya UKR	84.51
3.	Antti Ruuskanen FIN	84.12
4.	Vitezslav Vesely CZE	83.34
5.	Tero Pitkämäki FIN	82.80
6.	Andreas Thorkildsen NOR	82.63
7.	Spirídon Lebésis GRE	81.91
8.	Tino Häber GER	81.21
9.	Stuart Farquhar NZL	80.22
10.	Genki Dean JPN	79.95
11.	Ari Mannio FIN	78.60
12.	Julius Yego KEN	77.15

WALCOTT'S WIN WAS one of the most surprising in Olympic athletics history. From 75.77 in October 2011 he had improved to successive national records of 78.94, 80.11 and 82.83 in 2012, before going even better with 83.51 and 84.58 (just 11cm short of the world junior record) in the first two rounds of the Olympic final. He became Trinidad's first Olympic champion since Hasely Crawford (100m) in 1976 and the first athlete to win World Junior and Olympic titles in an individual event in the same year. The favourite Vesely had led the qualifiers with 88.34 from the champion of 2004 and 2008 Thorkildsen 84.47, but neither could reach such form in the final and the other medals went to Pyatnytsa with a third round 84.51 and Ruuskanen with 84.12 in the fifth.

Decathlon (8th-9th)

1. Ashton Eaton USA		8869
2. Trey Hardee USA		8671
3. Leonel Suárez CUB		8523
4. Hans Van Alphen BEL		8447
5. Damian Warner CAN		8442
6. Rico Freimuth GER		8320
7. Oleksiy Kasyanov UKR		8283
8. Sergey Sviridov RUS		8219
9. Willem Coertzen RSA		8173
10. Pascal Behrenbruch GER		8126
11. Eelco Sintnicolaas NED		8034
12. Brent Newdick NZL		7988
13. Gonzalo Barroilhet CHI		7972
14. Yordaní García CUB		7956
15. Kevin Mayer FRA		7952

EATON LED FROM the start with his Olympic decathlon best of 10.35 for 100m and 8.03 long jump, and concentrated on winning rather than pushing to beat the world record he set in worse conditions in Eugene. His final score of 8869 was the eighth highest ever and he had a winning margin of 198 over double world champion Hardee, whose best result was a 13.54 to 13.56 win over Eaton in the 110mh and who was thrilled with a 66.65 javelin throw after elbow surgery. A close tussle for third was resolved by a superb 76.94 javelin throw by Suárez. Roman Sebrle withdrew after the 100m, but kept his Olympic record as Eaton needed 4:29.86 for 1600m to beat it but was content to run round in 4:33.29.

4 x 100m Relay (h 10th, F 11th)

1. JAM	36.84* WR	Carter 10.1, Frater 8.9, Blake 9.0, Bolt 8.8 (Bailey-Cole ran 4th leg in ht)
2. USA	37.04	Kimmons 10.2, Gatlin 8.9, Gay 9.0, Bailey 8.9 heat: Demps, Patton, Kimmons, Gatlin
3. TRI	38.12	Bledman, Burns, Callender, Thompson
4. FRA	38.16	Vicaut, Lemaitre, Pessonneaux, Pognon
5. JPN	38.35	Yamagata, Eriguchi, Takahira, Iizuka
6. NED	38.39	Mariano, Martina, Codrington, van Luijk
7. AUS	38.43	Alozie, Ntiamoah, McCabe, Ross
dq. CAN	(38.07)	Smellie, Smith, Connaughton, J Warner

A BRILLIANT WORLD record by the Jamaicans provided a fitting climax in the final event of the Games. The heats had presaged something very special as there were the fastest ever preliminary times: Jamaica won the first in 37.39 and the USA the second 37.38, for 0.02 off the North American record. The US ran 37.04 to tie the old world record in the final, but were still two metres down on Jamaica, whose team was identical to their record team from Daegu 2011 and almost the same as the 2008 Olympic champions – Blake and Bolt to finish instead of Bolt and Powell. Britain ran 37.93 in heat one but were disqualified as the last change was outside the zone and such was the standard that best ever times for places 6-8 (38.31, 38.37 and 38.61) were run in heat two.

4 x 400m Relay (h 9th, F 10th)

1. BAH	2:56.72	Brown 45.2, Pinder 43.3, Mathieu 44.25, Miller 44.01
2. USA	2:57.05	Nellum 45.1, Mance 43.7, McQuay 43.41, A Taylor 44.85 heat: Manteo Mitchell, Mance, McQuay, Nellum
3. TRI	2:59.40	L Gordon 44.6, Solomon 44.6, Allyene-Forte 45.51, Lendore 44.73
4. GBR	2:59.53	C Williams 45.1, J Green 44.9, D Greene 45.53, Rooney 44.09
5. RUS	3:00.09	Dyldin 45.3, Alekseyev 45.3, Krasnov 44.69, Trenikhin 44.83
6. BEL	3:01.83	K Borlée 45.3, Gillet 45.7, J Borlée 44.55, Bultheel 46.31
7. VEN	3:02.18	Ramírez 46.0, Aguilar 45.6, Bravo 45.11, Longart 45.76
8. RSA	3:03.46	de Jager 46.3, de Beer 45.2, van Zyl 46.27, Pistorius 45.69
dnf. CUB	–	Collazo 45.3e, Acea 44.3e, Ruíz dnf, Cisneros

THE USA HAD won 17 of 21 previous Olympic 4x400m races that they had contested, but had to yield to the Bahamas team, who took 0.03 off the CAC and Commonwealth record and won their nation's first ever Olympic men's title. For them Demetrius Pinder ran 43.3 on the second leg, while the next fastest leg was 43.41 by Tony McQuay on the third leg. Manteo Mitchell ran heroically as he broke his left fibula bone midrace in heat two but defied the pain to complete his stint (in 45.9!) and the USA qualified for the final inches behind Bahamas (both 2:58.87). Trinidad & Tobago set a national record of 3:00.38 in heat two and improved that to 2:59.40 in the final, just holding off Britain, for whom Martyn Rooney gained ground from sixth. South Africa were advanced to the final after being brought down by Kenya in their heat.

20 Kilometres Walk (4th)

1. Chen Ding CHN	1:18:46*
2. Erick Barrondo GUA	1:18:57
3. Wang Zhen CHN	1:19:25
4. Cai Zelin CHN	1:19:44
5. Miguel Ángel López ESP	1:19:49
6. Eder Sánchez MEX	1:19:52
7. Jared Tallent AUS	1:20:02

8. Bertrand Moulinet FRA	1:20:12	
9. Robert Heffernan IRL	1:20:18	
10. Irfan Kolothum Thodi IND	1:20:21	
11. João Vieira POR	1:20:41	
12. Denis Simanovich BLR	1:20:42	
13. Inaki Gomez CAN	1:20:58	
14. Erik Tysse NOR	1:21:00	
15. Alexándros Papamihaíl GRE	1:21:12	

CHEN BROKE Robert Korzeniowski's Olympic record of 1:18:59 by 13 sec and became the youngest ever walks gold medallist at one day short of his 20th birthday. No Chinese man had previously won an Olympic gold medal and now they placed 1-3-4. The decisive move came between 16 and 18k as Chen with a 7:35 split opened up a 6 sec lead over Valeriy Borchin, who collapsed at about 19k, and another Russian Vladimir Kanaykin was disqualified. Chen, who covered the first half in 40:08 and the second in 38:38, finished with a 7:31 2k lap. Silver medallist Barrondo was also inside the old Olympic record and he became the first Guatemalan to win any Olympic medal.

50 Kilometres Walk (11th)

1. Sergey Kirdyapkin RUS	3:35:59*
2. Jared Tallent AUS	3:36:53
3. Si Tianfeng CHN	3:37:16
4. Robert Heffernan IRL	3:37:54
5. Igor Yerokhin RUS	3:37:54
6. Sergey Bakulin RUS	3:38:55
7. Li Jianbo CHN	3:39:01
8. Matej Tóth SVK	3:41:24
9. Lukasz Nowak POL	3:42:47
10. Koichiro Morioka JPN	3:43:14
11. André Höhne GER	3:44:26
12. Bertrand Moulinet FRA	3:45:35
13. Park Chil-sung KOR	3:45:55
14. Ivan Trotskiy BLR	3:46:09
15. Jarkko Kinnunen FIN	3:46:25

UNPRECEDENTED STANDARDS meant that times for all the finishers from 3rd (to 51st) were the best ever. 51 of 63 men finished (8 disqualified). A record seven men broke 3:40 (previous best five), 25 were inside 3:50 and 40 finished under 4 hours! No fewer than 21 of those sub-4 men set pbs and six national records. The leaders passed 10k in 44:15 and 20k in 1:27:44. At 30k in 2:10:49 (43:05 third 10k) Bakulin and Erick Barrondo held a 5 sec lead over Yohann Diniz, Deakes and Yerokhin with Kirdyapkin and Tallent in hot pursuit. Then Kirdyapkin began to surge and led Si and Bakulin by 1 sec at 40k in 2:53:53 before going clear with 5k splits of 21:14 and 20:52 to take 1:10 off the Olympic record. Barrondo and Diniz were disqualified.

Women

100 Metres (prelim, h 3rd, sf, F 4th 1.5)

1. Shelly-Ann Fraser-Pryce JAM	10.75
2. Carmelita Jeter USA	10.78
3. Veronica Campbell-Brown JAM	10.81
4. Tianna Madison USA	10.85
5. Allyson Felix USA	10.89
6. Kelly-Ann Baptiste TRI	10.94
7. Murielle Ahouré CIV	11.00
8. Blessing Okagbare NGR	11.01

FRASER-PRYCE AGAIN showed her ability when it comes to the major event as she retained her title in 10.75, a time that only Flo Jo has ever surpassed in Olympic competition. Out well, she was shaded by Jeter just after halfway but came through to win with a brilliant dip finish. The standard was unprecedented with best ever times for places 3-4 and 6-8 and Kerron Stewart's semi-final 4th place in 11.04 was the best ever non-qualifying time. Six women, headed by Jeter 10.83, had broken 11 secs in the heats and six did so in the semis, won by Jeter 10.83 (from Campbell-Brown 10.89), Fraser-Pryce 10.85 (from Felix 10.94) and Okagbare 10.92 (from Madison 10.92).

200 Metres (h 6th, sf 7th, F 8th -1.0)

1. Allyson Felix USA	21.88
2. Shelly-Ann Fraser-Pryce JAM	22.09
3. Carmelita Jeter USA	22.14
4. Veronica Campbell-Brown JAM	22.38
5. Sanya Richards-Ross USA	22.39
6. Murielle Ahouré CIV	22.57
7. Myriam Soumaré FRA	22.63
8. Semoy Hackett TRI	22.87

AFTER TAKING THE silver medal behind Campbell-Brown at the previous two Games, Felix ran an excellent bend and pulled away in the home straight to add Olympic gold to her three world titles at 200m. Fraser-Pryce ran a pb 22.09 for silver and Jeter took bronze, fading a little after vying for the lead at halfway (11.0). Richards-Ross was fastest in both heats 22.48 and semis 22.30, with the other semis won by Felix 22.31 and Campbell-Brown 22.32.

400 Metres (h 3rd, sf 4th, F 5th)

1. Sanya Richards-Ross USA	49.55
2. Christine Ohuruogu GBR	49.70
3. Deedee Trotter USA	49.72
4. Amantle Montsho BOT	49.75
5. Novlene Williams-Mills JAM	50.11
6. Antonina Krivoshapka RUS	50.17
7. Francena McCorory USA	50.33
8. Rosemarie Whyte JAM	50.79

KRIVOSHAPKA HAD GONE out hard in her semi (11.8. 23.1 and 35.7) to 49.81 from Trotter 49.87 and Williams-Mills 49.91 and repeated the tactics in the final through 11.8, 23.2 and 35.8 before Richards-Ross (11.9, 23.7 and 36.0) came past and eased way for a well-deserved Olympic title at her third attempt. The other two Americans had been just ahead of R-R at 300m, but while McCorory faded Trotter held on well for bronze. Meanwhile Ohuruogu (36.2 at 300m and Montsho (36.3) finished hard so that the first four were separated by two metres at the finish. Montsho was fastest in the heats with 50.40 and the other semis were won by Richards-Ross 50.07 and Montsho 50.15.

800 Metres   (h 8th, sf 9th, F 11th)

1. Mariya Savinova RUS	1:56.19
2. Caster Semenya RSA	1:57.23
3. Yekaterina Poistogova RUS	1:57.53
4. Pamela Jelimo KEN	1:57.59
5. Alysia Montaño USA	1:57.93
6. Yelena Arzhakova RUS	1:59.21
7. Francine Niyonsaba BDI-J	1:59.63
8. Janeth Jepkosgei KEN	2:00.19

ELEVEN WOMEN BROKE 2 minutes in the semis with Halima Hachlaf missing out despite running 1:58.64 and easily the fastest was Semenya with 1:57.67, despite a pre-Games season's best of 1:59.18. Montaño (who had run 55.25 for the first 400m in her heat) ensured fast times in the final by ripping through 200m in 26.9 and 400m in 56.31. Then came Jepkosgei, Jelimo and Savinova while Semenya was at the back of the field. Jelimo struck from 300m out, was the leader at 600m in 1:25.89 and was still ahead entering the final straight but finished outside the medals as Savinova (1:26.6 at 600m), with her cool racing brain, overhauled Jelimo with around 80m to go and strode to victory in 1:56.19. Semenya (7th in 1:27.2 at 600m) moved through along the straight in her usual lumbering style to take second, 1.04 behind.

1500 Metres   (h 6th, sf 8th, F 10th)

1. Asli Cakir TUR	4:10.23
2. Gamze Bulut TUR	4:10.40
3. Maryam Jamal BRN	4:10.74
4. Tatyana Tomashova RUS	4:10.90
5. Abeba Aregawi ETH	4:11.03
6. Shannon Rowbury USA	4:11.26
7. Natalya Koreyvo BLR	4:11.58
8. Lucia Klocová SVK	4:12.64
9. Yekaterina Kostetskaya RUS	4:12.90
10. Lisa Dobriskey GBR	4:13.02
11. Laura Weightman GBR	4:15.60
12. Hellen Obiri KEN	4:16.57

EVEN MORE SO than at the 2011 World Champs, the final was a most unsatisfactory race as the early pace was so very slow. Bulut led through 68.85, 2:23.97 and 3:26.88 before the two Turks, Cakir and Bulut repeated their European Champs 1-2 with final laps in 57.9 and 58.2 respectively. Aregawi had been fastest in heats (4:04.55) and semis (4:01.03) and all the finalists had run 4:06.47 or better in the semis,

with Siham Hilali the fastest non-qualifier at 4:04.79 and the slowest of the 24 runners at 4:08.44.

5000 Metres   (h 7th, F 10th)

1. Meseret Defar ETH	15:04.25
2. Vivian Cheruiyot KEN	15:04.73
3. Tirunesh Dibaba ETH	15:05.15
4. Sally Kipyego KEN	15:05.79
5. Gelete Burka ETH	15:10.66
6. Viola Kibiwott KEN	15:11.59
7. Jo Pavey GBR	15:12.72
8. Julia Bleasdale GBR	15:14.55
9. Olga Golovkina RUS	15:17.88
10. Shitaye Eshete BRN	15:19.13
11. Molly Huddle USA	15:20.29
12. Tejitu Daba BRN	15:21.34
13. Yelena Nagovitsyna RUS	15:21.38
14. Julie Culley USA	15:28.22
15. Elena Romagnolo ITA	15:35.69

THIS WAS ANOTHER final in which a dawdling early pace was followed by an explosive finish. All the finalists had run faster in the heats, in which three women broke 15 minutes: Dibaba 14:58.48, Defar 14:58.70 and Kibiwott 14:59.31. Pavey led at 3k in 9:27.7 before Dibaba changed the tempo with 71.0 and 69.0 laps and Kibiwott led at 4k in 12:24.81. At the bell it was Dibaba from Defar and Cheruiyot, but Dibaba was outpaced not only by Defar but also by Cheruiyot. Clocking 60.20 for the last lap and 2:39.44 for the last kilometre, Defar (1st in 2004 and 3rd in 2008) triumphed by 3m. After the Ethiopians and Kenyans took 1-6, as in the 10,000m (in which both had set pbs) Pavey and Bleasdale were the first European finishers in 7th and 8th.

10,000 Metres   (3rd)

1. Tirunesh Dibaba ETH	30:20.75
2. Sally Kipyego KEN	30:26.37
3. Vivian Cheruiyot KEN	30:30.44
4. Worknesh Kidane ETH	30:39.38
5. Belaynesh Oljira ETH	30:45.56
6. Shitaye Eshete BRN	30:47.25
7. Jo Pavey GBR	30:53.20
8. Julia Bleasdale GBR	30:55.63
9. Hitomi Niiya JPN	30:59.19
10. Kayoko Fukushi JPN	31:10.35
11. Amy Hastings USA	31:10.69
12. Janet Bawcom USA	31:12.68
13. Lisa Uhl USA	31:12.80
14. Sara Moreira POR	31:16.44
15. Fionnuala Britton IRL	31:46.71

HAVING RACED AT 10,000m only twice since her Olympic win in 2008, Dibaba was back to her brilliant best as after a slowish first half of 15:32.06 (with the Japanese runners doing the early work), she sped through the second 5000m in 14:48.69, her final kilometre taking just 2:45.68. Dibaba pounced with 500m to go and she went on to win by over 30m from

Kipyego with Cheruiyot losing almost 10 sec to Dibaba on that last circuit. There were best ever times for 13th and 14th.

Marathon   (5th)

1. Tiki Gelana ETH	2:23:07*
2. Priscah Jeptoo KEN	2:23:12
3. Tatyana Arkhipova RUS	2:23:29
4. Mary Keitany KEN	2:23:56
5. Tetyana Gamera-Shmyrko UKR	2:24:32
6. Zhu Xiaolin CHN	2:24:48
7. Jéssica Augusto POR	2:25:11
8. Valeria Straneo ITA	2:25:27
9. Albina Mayorova RUS	2:25:38
10. Shalane Flanagan USA	2:25:51
11. Kara Goucher USA	2:26:07
12. Helalia Johannes NAM	2:26:09
13. Marisa Barros POR	2:26:13
14. Irina Mikitenko GER	2:26:44
15. Kimberley Smith NZL	2:26:59

THE RACE, WHICH started in The Mall and comprised one lap of 2.2 miles and three of 8 miles, was held mainly in rain, refreshing for the 118 runners if not for the huge crowds who lined the twisting course through the centre of London. The early pace was steady rather than fast with 5k splits of 17:20, 17:26, 17:24 and 17:16 leading to 73:13 at halfway with more than 20 runners packed within a couple of seconds. By 25k (16:57) three Kenyans and three Ethiopians had opened up a 4 sec gap over Flanagan, and in the next 5k stretch of 16:21 Aselefech Mergia dropped away, leaving Keitany, Jeptoo, Gelana, Edna Kiplagat and Mare Dibaba level at 30k in 1:42:44 with Arkhipova 9 sec behind. Arkhipova then came up to share the lead with Gelana at 35k (1:59:29), 1 sec ahead of Keitany and Jeptoo. The ultimate top four were together at 40k in 2:16:10 before Gelana found the speed to race to the finish. Despite the twisting course, new records for places were set from 18th with 29 women breaking 2:30 compared to the previous record of 21 in London 2011, and 54 under 2:35 and 78 under 2:40 compared to previous records of 36 and 55 set at the 2008 Olympics.

3000m Steeplechase   (h 4th, F 6th)

1. Yuliya Zaripova RUS	9:06.72
2. Habiba Ghribi TUN	9:08.37
3. Sofia Assefa ETH	9:09.84
4. Milcah Chemos Cheywa KEN	9:09.88
5. Hiwot Ayalew ETH	9:12.98
6. Etenesh Diro ETH	9:19.89
7. Antje Möldner-Schmidt GER	9:21.78
8. Gesa Felicitas Krause GER	9:23.52
9. Emma Coburn USA	9:23.54
10. Mercy Njoroge KEN	9:26.73
11. Clarisse Cruz POR	9:32.44
12. Marta Domínguez ESP	9:36.45
13. Polina Jelizarova LAT	9:38.56
14. Bridget Franek USA	9:45.51
dnf. Gulnara Galkina RUS	–

ZARIPOVA ADOPTED THE same tactics as at the 2011 World Champs: she led every inch of the way to gain a magnificent victory. She ran 3:06.24 for the first kilometre and 3:05.36 (6:11.60) for the second before really stepping up the tempo with a relentless final kilometre of 2:55.12; her final 9:07.72 was the world's quickest for four years. Chemos tried to challenge Zaripova on the penultimate lap, to no avail, and finished out of the medals as Ghribi placed second as she had in the 2011 Worlds, this time with a Tunisian record of 9:08.37 for 6th on the world all-time list, winning the first Olympic medal by a Tunisian woman, while Assefa improved to 9:09.84 for third. All but one of the finalists had beaten 9:30 in the heats, headed by Ayalew 9:24.01.

100 Metres Hurdles   (h 6th, sf, F 7th -0.2)

1. Sally Pearson AUS	12.35*
2. Dawn Harper USA	12.37
3. Kellie Wells USA	12.48
4. Lolo Jones USA	12.58
5. Nevin Yanit TUR	12.58
6. Phylicia George CAN	12.65
7. Jessica Zelinka CAN	12.69
8. Beate Schrott AUT	13.07

REVERSING THEIR ORDER from the Beijing 1-2, Pearson and Harper were this time separated by just 0.02, neither being sure who had won until the verdict went to Pearson, who had been fastest away with Wells as Harper came through fast over the last three hurdles and to the finish. Jones also finished well to edge Yanit, who equalled the Turkish record she had run in her semi. The favourite Pearson was fastest in both heats (12.57) and semis 12.39), with Harper 12.46 and Wells 12.51 the other semi-final winners.

400 Metres Hurdles   (h 5th, sf 6th, F 8th)

1. Natalya Antyukh RUS	52.70
2. Lashinda Demus USA	52.77
3. Zuzana Hejnová CZE	53.38
4. Kaliese Spencer JAM	53.66
5. Georganne Moline USA	53.92
6. T'Erea Brown USA	55.07
7. Denisa Rosolová CZE	55.27
8. Joke Odumosu NGR	55.31

ANTYUKH, BRONZE MEDALLIST at 400m in 2004, became the latest woman to make rapid progress from the flat to the hurdles over 400m as she was fastest in the prelims with 53.90 in her heat and 53.33 in her semi, before moving to 6th on the world all-time list with 52.70 in the final. She was a clear leader entering the final straight but Demus was closing with every stride and at the finish there was barely half a metre between them. Defending champion Melaine Walker was only 6th in her semi-final.

High Jump (Q 1.96 9th, F 11th)

1. Anna Chicherova RUS	2.05
2. Brigetta Barrett USA	2.03
3. Svetlana Shkolina RUS	2.03
4. Ruth Beitia ESP	2.00
5. Tia Hellebaut BEL	1.97
6. Chaunté Lowe USA	1.97
7. Svetlana Radzivil UZB	1.97
8. Emma Green Tregaro SWE	1.93
9. Mélanie Melfort FRA	1.93
10. Irina Gordeyeva RUS	1.93
11. Airine Palsyte LTU	1.89
12. Burcu Ayhan TUR	1.89

FOURTEEN WOMEN CLEARED 1.93 in qualifying, with Adonía Steryíou and Ariane Friedrich missing a final place on count-back.
In the final Lowe was a surprising casualty
at 2m, cleared by Shkolina, Chicherova and
Beitia at the first try and by Barrett at the
second. Chicherova maintained a perfect card
by clearing 2.03 at the first go, while Barrett
went over on her second try and Shkolina on
her final attempt, both adding 2cm to their
lifetime bests. Chicherova sealed gold by going
over 2.05 second time and, overjoyed by her
triumph, did not attempt higher.

Pole Vault (Q 4.60m 4th, F 6th)

1. Jennifer Suhr USA	4.75
2. Yarisley Silva CUB	4.75
3. Yelena Isinbayeva RUS	4.70
4. Silke Spiegelburg GER	4.65
5. Martina Strutz GER	4.55
6= Holly Bleasdale GBR	4.45
6= Jirina Ptácniková CZE	4.45
6= Lisa Ryzih GER	4.45
9. Becky Holliday USA	4.45
10. Vanessa Boslak FRA	4.30
11. Alana Boyd AUS	4.30
nh. Anna Rogowska POL	(4.45)

TWELVE WOMEN QUALIFIED for the final by
clearing 4.55 with Stélla-Iró Ledáki and Fabiana Murer being eliminated despite clearing
4.50. There was, however, a tricky cross-wind
and casualties included a no height for Svetlana
Feofanova who complained bitterly afterwards.
In the final it was cool and damp and the
wind again gusty, and only four went higher.
Suhr took the lead with first time successes
at 4.55 and 4.70, while Silva and Isinbayeva,
like Spiegelburg over 4.65 first time but with a
previous failure, also cleared 4.70 on their first
attempts. Spiegelburg failed once at 4.70 and
twice at 4.75. Jumping first, Suhr made 4.75 at
the second attempt, as did the dynamic Silva to
equal her CAC record, but both failed at 4.80,
while Isinbayeva failed twice at 4.75 and had to
settle for bronze when she missed with a final
attempt at 4.80.

Long Jump (Q 6.70m 7th, F 8th)

1. Brittney Reese USA	7.12/0.8
2. Yelena Sokolova RUS	7.07/0.5
3. Janay DeLoach USA	6.89/0.2
4. Ineta Radevica LAT	6.88/1.2
5. Anna Nazarova RUS	6.77/0.5
6. Lyudmila Kolchanova RUS	6.76/0.0
7. Anastasiya Mironchik-Ivanova BLR	6.72/0.0
8. Éloyse Lesueur FRA	6.67/-0.2
9. Shara Proctor GBR	6.55/0.2
10. Veronika Shutkova BLR	6.54/1.4
11. Ivana Spanovic SRB	6.35/0.9
dns. Karin Mey Melis TUR	–

REESE ONLY MANAGED 6.57 after two fouls
in qualifying, and only had two valid jumps in
the final, but her second round 7.12 was enough
for the gold (6.69 her other in the fifth). Sokolova's silver came from her second round 7.07 and
in contrast all her six jumps were at 6.79 or better. Radevica took a first round lead with 6.88
and that remained good for third place until in
the fifth round DeLoach added 1cm. Defending champion Maurren Maggi failed to reach
the final with 6.37, while Mey Melis was withdrawn from the final after news of a positive
drugs test. She had jumped 6.80 in qualifying,
behind Proctor 6.83 and DeLoach 6.81.

Triple Jump (Q 14.40m 3rd, F 5th)

1. Olga Rypakova KAZ	14.98/-0.4
2. Caterine Ibargüen COL	14.80/0.4
3. Olga Saladuha UKR	14.79/0.5
4. Hanna Knyazyeva UKR	14.56/-0.1
5. Yamilé Aldama GBR	14.48/-0.6
6. Kimberly Williams JAM	14.48/0.3
7. Trecia Smith JAM	14.35/-0.2
8. Viktoriya Valyukevich RUS	14.24/-0.7
9. Yargeris Savigne CUB	14.12/-0.2
10. Tatyana Lebedeva RUS	14.11/-0.7
11. Marija Sestak SLO	13.98/-0.7
12. Dana Veldáková SVK	11.92/-0.5

Rypakova led the qualifiers with 14.79 from
Williams 14.53, and in the final took a first
round lead with 14.54. That was passed in the
second round by Knyazyeva 14.56 and in the
third by Ibargüen 14.67. But then Rypakova
jumped 14.98. She backed that up with a fifth
round 14.89 and in the last round Saladuha
moved to second 14.79 only for Ibargüen to
respond with 14.80.

Shot (Q 18.90m, F 6th)

1. Valerie Adams NZL	20.70
2. Yevgeniya Kolodko RUS	20.48
3. Gong Lijiao CHN	20.22
4. Li Ling CHN	19.63
5. Michelle Carter USA	19.42
6. Liu Xiangrong CHN	19.18
7. Geisa Arcanjo BRA	19.02
8. Irina Tarasova RUS	19.00
9. Natalia Ducó CHI	18.80
10. Christina Schwanitz GER	18.47

11. Natalya Mikhnevich BLR   18.42
12. Cleopatra Borel TRI 18.36q reclassified as finalist
dq. Nadezhda Ostapchuk BLR   21.36

OSTAPCHUK v ADAMS was anticipated to be a keen contest, but the former led 20.76 to 20.40 in qualifying and had easily the best throws in the final, with 21.21, 21.36, 21.15, and 21.32 from rounds 2-5 while Adams started with 20.61, improving to 20.70 in round three. The Belarussian received the gold medal but then came the news that she had been tested the day before the event and again after 'winning' it; both samples indicated the presence of metenolone, classified as an anabolic agent, so she was disqualified. Kolodko was next best in qualifying 19.31 and with a pb 20.48 in the last round of the final to move up two places and overtake Gong, who had three throws over 20m.

Discus (Q 63.00m 3rd, F 4th)

1. Sandra Perkovic CRO		69.11
2? Darya Pishchalnikova RUS		67.56
3. Li Yanfeng CHN		67.22
4. Yarelys Barrios CUB		66.38
5. Nadine Müller GER		65.94
6. Mélina Robert-Michon FRA		63.98
7. Krishna Poonia IND		63.62
8. Stephanie Brown Trafton USA		63.01
9. Zinaida Sendriute LTU		61.68
10. Anna Rüh GER-J		61.36
11. Ma Xuejun CHN		61.02
12. Dani Samuels AUS		60.40

MÜLLER LED THE qualifiers with 65.94 and took a first round lead in the final with 65.71. She improved to 65.94 in the last round, but that was only good for fifth as in the second round Li took the lead with 67.22, followed by Barrios 66.38 and then Perkovic 68.11. The last became Croatia's first Olympic champion, improving by exactly a metre with a national record in the third round and Pishchalnikova came through from her opening 65.19 with 66.42 and 67.56 in rounds 4-5 – subject to possible drugs ban.

Hammer (Q 73.00m 8th, F 10th)

1. Tatyana Lysenko RUS		78.18*
2. Anita Wlodarczyk POL		77.60
3. Betty Heidler GER		77.12
4. Zhang Wenxiu CHN		76.34
5. Kathrin Klaas GER		76.05
6. Yipsi Moreno CUB		74.60
7. Oksana Menkova BLR		74.40
8. Zalina Marghieva MDA		74.06
9. Stéphanie Falzon FRA		73.06
10. Joanna Fiodorow POL		72.37
11. Mariya Bespalova RUS		71.13
12. Sophie Hitchon GBR		69.33

IMPROVING WOMEN'S HAMMER standards were shown with the best ever marks for 5th to 16th and from 20th onwards, as there were a record 12 women over 70m and 30 over 67m in the qualifying round. Amber Campbell was 13th with 69.93, the best ever non-qualifying mark, while Wlodarczyk's 75.68 was the best ever in a qualifying round. 74m was also exceeded by Zhang, Heidler, Lysenko and Klaas. In the first round of the final Wlodarczyk threw 75.01, followed by Lysenko, who added 1.22 to the Olympic record with 77.56. In round two Zhang 76.34 and Wlodarczyk went to 2-3 with 76.34 and 76.02, with Klaas throwing 76.05 in round 3. The eventual medallists excelled in round five: first Heidler 77.13 (although the distance was lost for a long while in the EDM system), then Wlodarczyk 77.10 and Lysenko 78.18. That was it except for Wlodarczyk seizing silver with a last round 77.60. There were best ever marks from 2nd to 10th and five women over 76m compared to a previous best of three.

Javelin (Q 62.00m 7th, F 9th)

1. Barbora Spotáková CZE		69.55
2. Christina Obergföll GER		65.16
3. Linda Stahl GER		64.91
4. Sunette Viljoen RSA		64.53
5. Lu Huihui CHN		63.70
6. Kathrina Molitor GER		62.89
7. Martina Ratej SLO		61.62
8. Madara Palameika LAT		60.73
9. Kathryn Mitchell AUS		59.46
10. Mariya Abakumova RUS		59.34
11. Asdis Hjálmsdóttir ISL		59.08
12. Elizabeth Gleadle CAN		58.78

QUALIFYING WAS LED by Spotáková 66.29, Obergföll 66.14 and Viljoen 65.92 as there were a record nine women over 62m and best ever marks for 7th to 9th. Goldie Sayers was unable to throw properly due to a right elbow injury and did not record a throw. Spotáková reached 66.90 in the very first throw of the final, and no one else got close, although she improved after two more 66m throws to a fourth round 69.55. Obergföll opened with 65.16 but had no more valid throws, while Viljoen's 64.53 opener held third until Stahl improved to 64.91 in the fourth round.

Heptathlon (29/30th)

1. Jessica Ennis GBR		6955
2. Lilli Schwarzkopf GER		6649
3. Tatyana Chernova RUS		6628
4. Lyudmila Yosypenko UKR		6618
5. Austra Skujyte LTU		6599
6. Antoinette Nana Djimou FRA		6576
7. Jessica Zelinka CAN		6480
8. Kristina Savitskaya RUS		6452
9. Laura Ikaunice LAT		6414
10. Hanna Melnychenko UKR		6392
11. Brianne Theisen CAN		6383
12. Dafne Schippers NED		6324
13. Nadine Broersen NED		6319
14. Jessica Samuelsson SWE		6300
15. Katarina Johnson-Thompson GBR		6267

ENNIS MORE THAN lived up to pre-Games pressure with a win in a Commonwealth record 6955 and a huge winning margin of 306 points. She started with a bang as she took 0.25 off her 100m hurdles best with a scintillating 12.54 (best ever in a heptathlon) and quick pbs were recorded behind her by Zelinka 12.65 and Fountain 12.70. Ennis was below par in the high jump with 1.86 but after an OK shot of 14.28 showed her wonderful ability to excel on the biggest occasion, ending the first day with a pb 22.83 for 200m. She stretched her overnight lead of 184 points over Skujyte (who jumped a pb 1.92 and set a world heptathlon shot best of 17.31) with a fine 6.48 long jump and a pb 47.49 pb javelin. Then Ennis went for it in the 800m, reaching 400m in 61.89, and to the huge and noisy crowd's delight she won the race in 2:08.65. Sofía Ifantídou threw 56.06, the best ever (new) javelin throw in a heptathlon. It took the 800m to sort out the other medals as Schwarzkopf (initially disqualified for leaving her lane too early) and Chernova came through from fifth and sixth after six events to second and third.

4 x 100m Relay (h 9th, F 10th)

1. USA	40.82* WR	Madison, Felix, B Knight, Jeter (Tarmoh and L Williams ran in heat)
2. JAM	41.41	Fraser-Pryce, Simpson, Campbell-Brown, Stewart (Henry-Robinson and Calvert ran in heat)
3. UKR	42.04	Povh, Stuy, Ryemyen, Bryzgina
4. NGR	42.64	Osayomi, Asumnu, Abinuwa, Okagbare
5. GER	42.67	Günther, Cibis, Pinto, Sailer
6. NED	42.70	Vassell, Schippers, Lubbers, Samuel
7. BRA	42.91	Silva, Krasucki, E dos Santos, R Santos
dnf. TRI	–	Ahye, Baptiste, Selvon, Hackett

THE USA TEAM ran 41.64 in their heat, just 0.04 off the Olympic record (next fastest Trinidad 42.31, Ukraine 42.36 and Jamaica 42.37) and had Jeter and Felix to bring in. So something special was promised for the final. And so it proved as the US gave a brilliant display of fast running and slick baton passing. The time was an almost unbelievable 40.82 ... one of the oldest of all world records (GDR 41.37 at Canberra in 1985) had been shattered by over half a second. Jamaica also brought in their top stars Fraser-Pryce and Campbell-Brown for the final and their 41.41 was a CAC and Commonwealth record. Ukraine set a national record for the bronze. New records were set for places 1-2 and 6-7.

4 x 400m Relay   (h 10th, F 11th)

1. USA	3:16.87	Trotter 50.3, Felix 48.1, McCorory 49.39, Richards-Ross 49.10 (Baker and Dixon ran in ht)
2. RUS	3:20.23	Gushchina 50.9, Krivoshapka 49.8, Firova 49.88, Antyukh 49.67 (Nazarova and Kapachinskaya ran in ht
3. JAM	3:20.95	Day 51.1, Whyte 50.1, S Williams 50.29, N Williams-Mills 49.46 (Lloyd ran in heat)
4. UKR	3:23.57	Logvynenko 51.0, Zemlyak 50.4, Yaroshchuk 51.56, Pygyda 50.63
5. GBR	3:24.76	Cox 52.8, McConnell 51.1, Shakes-Drayton 50.28, Ohuruogu 50.65
6. FRA	3:25.92	Anacharsis 52.1, Hurtis 51.8, Gayot 51.15, Guei 50.93
7. CZE	3:27.77	Rosolová 51.0, Bergrová 52.3, Bartonícková 52.62, Hejnová 50.92
dq. NGR	–	Omotosho 52.6e. Odumosu 51.2e, George 50.88, Abogunloko 51.76

WINNING BY THE widest margin since the GDR in 1976, the USA team produced the equal fifth quickest time ever with 3:16.87, the world's fastest for 19 years. Trotter, with 50.3, gave them a 6m lead that was stretched to 20m by a brilliant 48.1 leg by Felix. The US were fastest in the heats with 3:22.09 ahead of Russia 3:23.11.

20 Kilometres Walk (11th)

1. Yelena Lashmanova RUS	1:25:02*
2. Olga Kaniskina RUS	1:25:09
3. Qieyang Shenjie CHN	1:25:16
4. Liu Hong CHN	1:26:00
5. Anisya Kirdyapkina RUS	1:26:26
6. Lu Xiuzhi CHN	1:27:10
7. Elisa Rigaudo ITA	1:27:36
8. Beatriz Pascual ESP	1:27:56
9. Ana Cabecinha POR	1:28:03
10. María Vasco ESP	1:28:14
11. Masumi Fuchise JPN	1:28:41
12. Maria José Poves ESP	1:29:36
13. Olive Loughnane IRL	1:29:39
14. Eleonora Giorgi ITA	1:29:48
15. Inês Henriques POR	1:29:54

LASHMANOVA, AT 20 the youngest Olympic female walking champion, took six seconds off the official world record in beating Kaniskina who had been supreme at this event for five years and Qieyang who set a new Asian record. There were best ever times for places 2-3, 6-7, 10 and 15-18 with 15 women under 1:30 and 41 of the 55 finishers under 1:35. Kaniskina led at 10k in 42:33 from Liu 42:50, Kirdyapkina, Lashmanova, Qieyang and Lu all 43:16, and increased that lead to 22 sec at 12k and 33 sec at 14k, but then Lashmanova and Qieyang began to close, 24 sec down at 16k and 17 at 18k, before Lashmanova kicked home with 8:07 for the final lap compared to 8:31 by Kaniskina.

EUROPEAN CHAMPIONSHIPS 2012

June 27 – Jul 1, Helsinki, Finland

THIS WAS UNDOUBTEDLY a most enjoyable meeting, the 21st edition of an event that has always been, for all European athletes, the major event of the year in which it has been held. This, however, is no longer the case with the questionable decision of European Athletics (EA) to hold it in an Olympic year as well as in the middle year of each Olympiad. Despite the spin of EA (and their admirable determination to promote European athletics) this event is now devalued to some extent at least, and it remains to be seen how much that is the case in future years. EA President Hans-Jörg Wirz said, "I am happy to say that the response from our Member Federations and their athletes regarding this new format for the championships has been extremely positive." Well the facts were that some nations did indeed send near full-strength teams, but others including such important ones as Russia and Britain did not. There were also no new championship records.

It us interesting to analyse how many of the top three Europeans at the subsequent Olympic Games had competed at the Europeans. Male field eventers (including multis) led the way as 18 of 27 OG athletes as been in their events at the EC with 14 having won EC medals. Men's track figures were 15/30 (10 medals), women's track 17/30 (10) and women's field (&

heptathlon) 12/27 (8). So a total of 62 of the top three Europeans at the Olympics (from 114 in all, thus nearly half) had competed at the European Championships and 42 (68%) of them had won European medals. There was one instance of gold, silver and bronze being won by the same athletes at both events: Renaud Lavillenie, Björn Otto and Raphael Holzdeppe at pole vault.

The Championships were held without the marathons and walks and with a compressed five-day format. Lavillenie and Olga Saladuha (women's triple jump) were voted athletes of the meeting by the media. These two retained titles won in Barcelona 2010 with five others: Christophe Lemaitre 100m, Mo Farah 5000m, Mahiedine Mekhissi-Benabbad 3000mSC, and two more women: Nevan Yanit 100mh and Sandra Perkovic discus.

In all 18 nations won gold medals, 27 medals and 35 placed athletes in the top eight (respectively 11, 21 and 33 in 2010). Ukraine, Turkey, Netherlands and the Czech Republic made notable advances while Britain, Spain and Poland slipped considerably. Very sadly the host nation Finland with their great history and their ever enthusiastic and knowledgeable fans were rewarded with just one bronze medal (Ari Mannio in the javelin) and a sixth place for just two top eight places.

Medals and Points Table

Points: 8 for 1st to 1 for 8th place.

Nation	G	S	B	Points	2010
GER	6	6	4	198.5	153
RUS	5	4	6	153.5	263
UKR	4	7	6	142.5	95.5
FRA	5	4	5	139.5	183
GBR	3	3	1	94	167
TUR	4	2	1	70.5	41
CZE	3	1	1	67.5	39
ESP	1	1	2	63	104.5
NED	2	3	1	61	28
ITA	1	1	1	58.5	92
POL	1	0	3	54.5	97
BLR	0	2	3	46	56
NOR	1	1	2	38	27
POR	1	1	1	38	45
SWE	1	0	2	35	18
BEL	1	0	0	27	30
LAT	0	0	1	23	17
SRB	0	1	1	21	7
HUN	1	1	0	19	19
SVK	0	1	0	18.5	21
GRE	0	0	1	17	13
BUL	1	0	0	16	4
LTU	0	1	1	14	21

More points (medals): EST (1S), IRL 11; ROU 10.5; DEN (1S), FIN (1B), SUI 9; CRO (1G) 8; AUT 7; ISR 6; AZE 3; CYP, MDA 2

Men

100 Metres (h 27th, sf & F 28th -0.7)

1. Christophe Lemaître FRA	10.09	
2. Jimmy Vicaut FRA	10.12	
3. Jaysuma Saidy Ndure NOR	10.17	
4. Harry Aikines-Aryeetey GBR	10.31	
5. Sergiy Smelyk UKR	10.34	
dnf. Ronalds Arajs LAT	–	
dnf. Rytis Sakalauskas LTU	–	
dq. Simone Collio ITA	fs	

LEMAITRE RAN 10.14 in heat and semi before retaining his title, winning by only 0.03 from Vicaut, who led to 60m. Saidy Ndure, fastest in the semis with 10,13, was 3rd despite leg cramp.

200 Metres (h & sf 29th, F 30th -0.9)

1. Churandy Martina NED	20.42	
2. Patrick van Luijk NED	20.87	
3. Daniel Talbot GBR	20.95	
4. Jonathan Borlée BEL	20.99	
5. Nil de Oliveira SWE	21.11	
6. Chris Clarke GBR	21.26	
7. Diego Marani ITA	21.26	
8. Paul Hession IRL	21.27	

THE CLEAR FAVOURITE Martina won by

0.45 to tie the record winning margin and head the first Dutch 1-2 at any European Champs. A problem was the peculiar bends which were not circular and with straights of 96m rather than 84m, the arena having been adjusted to cater for football but with the proviso of not cutting into the stands; Likoúgos-Stéfanos Tsákonas was disqualified for a lane violation when winning his semi in what would have been a pb of 20.48.

400 Metres (h 27th, sf 28th, F 29th)

1. Pavel Maslák CZE   45.24
2. Marcell Deák Nagy HUN   45.52
3. Yannick Fonsat FRA   45.82
4. Donald Sanford ISR   45.91
5. Richard Buck GBR   45.92
6. Brian Gregan IRL   46.04
7. Marcin Marciniszyn POL   46.46
8. Marco Vistalli ITA   4:04.20

GREGAN WAS FASTEST in the heats with 45.63 and Maslák in the semis with 45.66. Eight athletes were disqualified in the heats and semis for straying out of their lanes on this difficult track (see above).

800 Metres (h 28th, sf 29th, F 31st)

1. Yuriy Borzakovskiy RUS   1:48.61
2. Andreas Bube DEN   1:48.69
3. Pierre-Ambroise Bosse FRA   1:48.83
4. Antonio M. Reina ESP   1:48.98
5. Jakub Holusa CZE   1:48.99
6. Robert Lathouwers NED   1:49.22
7. Jozef Repcik SVK   1:49.42
8. Thomas Roth NOR   1:49.54

GARETH WARBURTON (seeking an Olympic qualifying time) was fastest in the heats with 1:45.80 and Reina in the semis with 1:46.49. The final was slow with Bosse leading through 400m in 55.17 and 600m in 1:22.79. Borzakovskiy moved from 10m down at 100m to be poised in fourth place with 200m to go and then sprinted clear in his inimitable fashion.

1500 Metres (h 30th, F 1st)

1. Henrik Ingebrigtsen NOR   3:46.20
2. Florian Carvalho FRA   3:46.33
3. David Bustos ESP   3:46.45
4. Helio Gomes POR   3:46.50
5. Bartosz Nowicki POL   3:46.69
6. Ilham Tanui Özbilen TUR   3:46.85
7. Dmitrijs Jurkevics LAT   3:47.36
8. Goran Nava SRB   3:47.74

AN UNDISTINGUISHED RACE was won by 21 year-old Ingebrigtsen, whose sub-54 last lap carried him to the finish a metre ahead in the slowest winning time since 1950.

5000 Metres (27th)

1. Mohammed Farah GBR   13:29.91
2. Arne Gabius GER   13:31.83
3. Polat Kemboi Arikan TUR   13:32.63
4. Yohan Durand FRA   13:32.65
5. Daniele Meucci ITA   13:32.69
6. Hayle Ibrahimov AZE   13:36.05
7. Dennis Licht NED   13:37.99
8. Bashir Abdi BEL   13:39.01

FARAH BECAME THE first man in the Championships' 78-year history to retain the 5000m title. Predictably, he was in a class of his own on the last lap, covered in 53.69. Anatoliy Rybakov was 30m clear of the pack at 1000m in 2:42.45 and covered the second kilometre in 2:47.87 before being caught before 3000m, at which point Farah led in a pedestrian 8:17.50 (2:47.18) with 2:45.64 for the fourth kilometre before 2:26.76 for the last. Jesús España, who outkicked Farah for the title in 2006 and was second in 2010, finished 20th in 13:55.98.

10,000 Metres (30th)

1. Polat Kemboi Arikan TUR   28:22.27
2. Daniele Meucci ITA   28:22.73
3. Yevgeniy Rybakov RUS   28:22.95
4. Bashir Abdi BEL   28:23.72
5. Carles Castillejo ESP   28:24.51
6. Ayad Lamdassem ESP   28:26.46
7. Khalid Choukoud NED   28:26.82
8. Rui Pedro Silva POR   28:31.16

RUN IN POURING rain, the first half was 14:21.93 (Silva) and the second 14:00.34. Arikan (the former Kenyan Paul Kipkosgei Kemboi) ran 29.1 and 28.1 for a last lap in 57.22.

3000m Steeplechase (h 27th, F 29th)

1. Mahiedine Mekhissi-Benabbad FRA   8:33.23
2. Tarik Langat Akdag TUR   8:35.24
3. Víctor García ESP   8:35.87
4. Nordine Gezzar FRA   8:36.98
5. Abdelaziz Merzoughi ESP   8:38.58
6. Lukasz Parszczynski POL   8:38.76
7. Yuri Floriani ITA   8:39.22
8. Krystian Zalewski POL   8:39.35

THIS WAS WON in the slowest time since 1958, with kilometres of 2:59.48, 2:57.73 and 2:36.02, and all the 15 finalists had run faster in the heats, headed by Akdag (the former Kenyan, Patrick Langat) 8:27.31. García fell at the last barrier when some 15m clear of Akdag, but got back into the race remarkably quickly.

110m Hurdles (h 30th, sf, F 1st 0.5)

1. Sergey Shubenkov RUS   13.16
2. Garfield Darien FRA   13.20
3. Artur Noga POL   13.27
4. Alexander John GER   13.38
5. Emanuele Abate ITA   13.43
6. Gregory Sedoc NED   13.45
7. Philip Nossmy SWE   13.59
8. Konstadínos Douvalídis GRE   13.59

SHUBENKOV IMPRESSED WITH 13.28 in his heat and next day looked sensationally good as he clocked 13.09 into a 1.1m wind in his semi. Darien (2nd in 2010) also took 0.09 from his pb in the next semi with 13.15/-0.3. In the final Noga equalled the Polish record behind those two.

400m Hurdles (h 27th, sf 28th, F 29th)

1. Rhys Williams GBR	49.33
2. Emir Bekric SRB	49.49
3. Stanislav Melnykov UKR	49.69
4. Adrien Clemenceau FRA	49.70
5. Rasmus Mägi EST	50.01
6. Georg Fleischhauer GER	50.11
7. Nathan Woodward GBR	50.20
8. Periklís Iakovákis GRE	50.57

WILLIAMS MOVED UP from 3rd in 2006 and 2nd in 2010 but had the slowest winning time since 1969. Iakovákis, the 2006 champion, led into the final straight. Bekric had been fastest in the semis with a Serbian record 49.37. Brent LaRue, the former American now representing Slovenia, was disqualified (on the same day) in his heat of both this event and the flat 400m for running out of his lane!

High Jump (Q 2.28 27th, F 29th)

1. Robbie Grabarz GBR	2.31
2. Raivydas Stanys LTU	2.31
3. Mickaël Hanany FRA	2.28
4. Sergey Mudrov RUS	2.28
5. Gianmarco Tamberi ITA	2.24
6= Michal Kabelka SVK	2.24
6= Szymon Kiecana POL	2.24
8= Jaroslav Bába CZE	2.24
8= Mihai Donisan ROU	2.24

GRABARZ BECAME BRITAIN'S first European HJ champion since 1950, winning on countback from Stanys who added 3cm to his pb.

Pole Vault (Q 5.65m 30th, F 1st)

1. Renaud Lavillenie FRA	5.97
2. Björn Otto GER	5.92
3. Raphael Holzdeppe GER	5.77
4. Malte Mohr GER	5.77
5. Konstadínos Filippídis GRE	5.72
6. Jan Kudlicka CZE	5.60
7. Rasmus Jørgensen DEN	5.50
8= Maksym Mazuryk UKR	5.40
8= Claudio Michel Stecchi ITA	5.40

LAVILLENIE WON WITH first time clearances at 5.87, 5.92 and 5.97 while Otto made 5.92 on his second go and Holzdeppe beat Mohr by virtue of first to second attempt clearances of 5.77.

Long Jump (Q 8.15m 30th, F 1st)

1. Sebastian Bayer GER	8.34/0.3
2. Luis Felipe Méliz ESP	8.21/1.7
3. Michel Tornéus SWE	8.17/0.0
4. J.J.Jegede GBR	8.10w/2.4
5. Eusebio Cáceres ESP	8.06/0.4
6. Roni Ollikainen FIN	8.05/1.5
7. Marcos Chuva POR	7.92/0.5
8. Tomasz Jaszczuk POL	7.90/1.4

A RIDICULOUSLY AMBITIOUS qualifying standard of 8.15 was met by just one man, but Bayer jumped 8.34w with the next best 8.07 by Tornéus. At halfway in the final Méliz led with a second round 8.21 from the 8.17 opener of Tornéus. Bayer started with two long fouls,

then played safe with 8.03 from the edge of the board. He improved slightly to 8.09 in the fourth round with some 9cm to spare and then, hitting the board perfectly in the last two rounds, registered 8.33 and 8.34.

Triple Jump (Q 16.75m 28th, F 30th)

1. Fabrizio Donato ITA	17.63w/2.8
2. Sheryf El-Sheryf UKR	17.28w/2.2
3. Aleksey Tsapik BLR	16.97w/3.8
4. Aleksey Fyodorov RUS	16.83/1.3
5. Momchil Karailiev BUL	16.77w/2.1
6. Karol Hoffmann POL	16.74/1.5
7. Dmitriy Platnitskiy BLR	16.68/0.9
8. Yochai Halevi ISR	16.67/0.5

DONATO LED THE qualifiers with 17.17 from Hoffmann 17.09, and dominated the final as his first four jumps were 17.63w, 17.53/0.8, 17.49 and 17.17. El-Sheryf opened with 17.28w and backed that up with 16.99/0.5.

Shot (Q 20.30m 27th, F 29th)

1. David Storl GER	21.58
2. Rutger Smith NED	20.55
3. Asmir Kolasinac SRB	20.36
4. Hüseyin Atici TUR	20.24
5. Marco Fortes POR	20.24
6. Antonin Zalsky CZE	19.94
7. Borja Vivas ESP	19.81
8. Marco Schmidt GER	19.65

STORL HAD A winning margin of 1.03m, the widest since 1950). He opened with 21.19 and improved to 21.55 in the third round. Smith threw 20.55 in both qualifying (Storl 20.30) and final.

Discus (Q 66.00m 29th, F 30th)

1. Robert Harting GER	68.30
2. Gerd Kanter EST	66.53
3. Rutger Smith NED	64.02
4. Mario Pestano ESP	63.87
5. Frank Casañas ESP	63.60
6. Robert Urbanek POL	62.99
7. Gerhard Mayer AUT	62.85
8. Markus Munch GER	61.25
dq 3. Zoltán Kövágó HUN	66.42

ALTHOUGH THE AUTOMATIC qualifying standard was set at a ludicrous 66m, the preliminary round was of a remarkably high standard as eight men exceeded 64m, headed by Pestano 66.27, and a throw of 62.22 by Przemyslaw Czajkowki didn't make the 12-man final. Harting took the lead in the second round with 65.80 and improved to 68.30 on his fourth attempt. Kanter than threw his best in the fifth round and Kövágó, later to receive a 2-year drugs ban, who had opened with 65.45, in the last.

Hammer (Q 77.50m 28th, F 30th)

1. Krisztián Pars HUN	79.72
2. Aleksiy Zagorniy RUS	77.40
3. Szymon Ziólkowski POL	76.67
4. Valeriy Svyatokho BLR	75.83
5. Nicola Vizzoni ITA	75.13
6. Mattias Jons SWE	74.56

| 7. Markus Esser GER | 74.49 |
| 8. Jérôme Bortoluzzi FRA | 74.49 |

PARS HAD THE five best throws in the final after leading the qualifying with 78.09. He opened with 78.57, followed by 79.40, x, 79.72, 79.56 and 77.47.

Javelin (Q 83.00m 27th, F 28th)

1. Vitezslav Vesely CZE	83.72
2. Valeriy Iordan RUS	83.23
3. Ari Mannio FIN	82.63
4. Andreas Thorkildsen NOR	81.55
5. Oleksandr Pyaynytsya UKR	81.41
6. Igor Janik POL	81.21
7. Kim Amb SWE	79.03
8. Gabriel Wallin SWE	77.18

MANNIO LED THE qualifiers with 84.31, and that was better than anybody managed in the final, won by Vesely with his second round 83.72, backed up by 83.51 in the fifth. All the finalists from 3rd to 12th had thrown better in qualifying apart from Thorkildsen, who only just made it.

Decathlon (27th-28th)

1. Pascal Behrenbruch GER	8558
2. Oleksiy Kasyanov UKR	8321
3. Ilya Shkurenyov RUS	8219
4. Mihail Dudas SRB	8154
5. Gaël Quérin FRA	8098
6. Roman Sebrle CZE	8052
7. Norman Müller GER	8003
8. Adam Helcelet CZE	7998

KASYANOV LED AT the end of the first day with 4352 to Behrenbruch 4291, but the German had a much better second day and went on to win by 237 points with a pb 8558, including a pole vault best of 5.00.

4x100m Relay (h 30th, F 1st)

1. NED	38.34	Mariano, Martina, Codring ton, van Luijk; (ht: 3 Feller, 4 Codrington)
2. GER	38.44	Reus, Unger, Kosenkow, Jakubczyk; (ht: Jakubczyk, Unger, Kosenkow, Keller)
3. FRA	38.46	Pognon, Lemaitre, Pessonneaux, Biron; (ht: 1 Biron, 4 Vicaut)
4. RUS	38.67	
5. SUI	38.83	
6. POR	39.96	
dnf. CZE	–	
dnf. GBR	–	

BRITAIN WAS FASTEST with 38.98 in the heats, but on the first change in the final Christian Malcolm, slowing due to the change in angle of the bend, was unable to transfer the baton to Dwain Chambers, who went off in anticipation of a swifter arrival. The well-drilled Dutch team, in the outside lane, won in a national record 38.34 from Germany and France, who suffered from the absence of 100m silver medallist Vicaut.

4x400m Relay (h 30th, F 1st)

1. BEL	3:01.09	Gillet 46.5, J Borlée 44.3, Bouckaert 45.96, K Borlée 44.22
2. GBR	3:01.56	Levine 45.4, C Williams 44.8, Tobin 45.88, Buck 45.31
3. GER	3:01.77	Plass 46.0, Gaba 45.3, Krüger 45.66, Schneider 44.73
4. POL	3:02.37	5. CZE 3:02.72
6. FRA	3:03.04	7. UKR 3:04.56
		8. NED 3:05.68

OUTSTANDING RUNS BY the Borlée twins were the key to Belgium's win, and the next fastest was Pavel Maslák, a second leg 44.5 in helping the Czechs to a national record.

Women

100 Metres (h, sf 27th, F 28th -0.7)

1. Ivet Lalova BUL	11.28
2. Olesya Povh UKR	11.32
3. Lina Grincikaite LTU	11.32
4. Ezinne Okparaebo NOR	11.39
5. Olga Belkina RUS	11.42
6. Verena Sailer GER	11.42
7. Anne Cibis GER	11.54
8. Tatjana Pinto GER	11.62

LALOVA RAN 11.06/1.7 and Sailer 11.14/1.0 in the heats, and Povh 11.13 and Sailer 11.17 had a +2.0 wind in the semis, but times were slowed by a headwind in the final.

200 Metres (h, sf 29th, F 30th -1.3)

1. Mariya Ryemyen UKR	23.05
2. Hrystyna Stuy UKR	23.17
3. Myriam Soumaré FRA	23.21
4. Viktoriya Pyatachenko UKR	23.25
5. Dafne Schippers NED	23.53
6. Jamile Samuel NED	23.55
7. Eleni Artymata CYP	23.59
8. Johanna Danois FRA	23.61

UKRAINE TOOK THREE of the top four places. Ryemyen ran the fastest heat time of 22.77 and won her semi in 22.82 after Schippers had run 22.70 to win the first semi, but it was cool and damp and there was a headwind in the final, when Schippers was yet another athlete badly affected by the curious bends.

400 Metres (h 27th, sf 28th, F 29th)

1. Moa Hjelmer SWE	51.13
2. Kseniya Zadorina RUS	51.26
3. Ilona Usovich BLR	51.94
4. Olga Zemlyak UKR	52.01
5. Lee McConnell GBR	52.20
6. Libania Grenot ITA	52.57
7. Darya Prystupa UKR	53.03
8. Muriel Hurtis FRA	54.50

USOVICH WAS FASTEST in the heats with 51.98 and the first semi was won by Zadorina 51.35 from Hjelmer, who set a Swedish record 51.40. In the final Grenot led into the home straight, but faded badly leaving Zadorina in the lead before 22 year-old Hjelmer edged past and set another Swedish record of 51.11.

800 Metres (h 28th, F 29th)

1. Yelena Arzhakova RUS	1:58.51
2. Lynsey Sharp GBR	2:00.52
3. Irina Maracheva RUS	2:00.66
4. Marina Arzamasova BLR	2:01.02
5. Liliya Lobanova UKR	2:01.29
6. Lucia Klocová SVK	2:01.38
7. Jemma Simpson GBR	2:02.14
8. Natalija Piliusina LTU	2:06.59

MARACHEVA SET A very fast pace in the final with 57.29 at halfway and 1:27.34 at 600m, at which point Arzhakova and Arzamasova (fastest in the heats with 2:00.54) were in close attendance, before Arzhakova produced much the strongest finish and Sharp came from seventh to second in the straight for a pb.

1500 Metres (h 30th, F 1st)

1. Asli Cakir TUR	4:05.31
2. Gamze Bulut TUR	4:06.04
3. Anna Mishchenko UKR	4:07.74
4. Yekaterina Gorbunova RUS	4:08.63
5. Nuria Fernández ESP	4:08.80
6. Diana Sujew GER	4:09.28
7. Tereza Capková CZE	4:10.17
8. Kristina Khaleyeva RUS	4:10.26

AFTRE OPENING LAPS of 66.09 and 72.58 the Turks ran the third in 63.61 and Cakir raced to victory wth a final 400m in 57.91.

5000 Metres (28th)

1. Olga Golovkina RUS	15:11.70
2. Lyudmyla Kovalenko UKR	15:12.03
3. Sara Moreira POR	15:12.05
4. Julia Bleasdale GBR	15:12.77
5. Roxana Bârca ROU	15:13.40
6. Nadia Ejjafini ITA	15:16.54
7. Svetlana Kireyeva RUS	15:19.55
8. Almensch Belete BEL	15:22.15

BOTH GOLOVKINA ANd Kovalenko passed Moreira in the final straight. The kilometre splits were 3:04.31, 3:01.45, 3:10.98, 3:05.41 and 2:49.55.

10,000 Metres (1st)

1. Dulce Félix POR	31:44.75
2. Jo Pavey GBR	31:49.03
3. Olga Skrypak UKR	31:51.32
4. Fionnuala Britton IRL	32:05.54
5. Sabrina Mockenhaupt GER	32:16.55
6. Charlotte Purdue GBR	32:28.46
7. Ana Dias POR	32:35.82
8. Elena Romagnolo ITA	32:42.31

BRITTON LED FOR much of the first half to 5000m in 15:59.85 and Félix made the decisive move approaching 7000m. No one attempted to go with her and Pavey outkicked Skrypak for silver.

3000m Steeplechase (h 28th, F 30th)

1. Gulcan Mingir TUR	9:32.96
2. Svitlana Shmidt UKR	9:33.03
3. Antje Möldner-Schmidt GER	9:36.37
4. Gesa-Felicitas Krause GER	9:38.20
5. Ancuta Bobocel ROU	9:41.32
6. Polina Jelizarova LAT	9:41.38
7. Natalya Gorchakova RUS	9:42.98
8. Diana Martín ESP	9:45.36
dnf. Gulnara Galkina RUS	–

EVEN THOUGH SHE won by a narrow margin Mingir, who had been fastest in the heats with 9:32.39, always seemed in control; the kilometres were run in 3:14.53, 3:17.39 and 3:01.04.

100m Hurdles (h 29th, sf, F 30th -1.4)

1. Nevin Yanit TUR	12.81
2. Alina Talay BLR	12.91
3. Yekaterina Poplavskaya BLR	12.97
4. Beate Schrott AUT	12.98
5. Anne Zagré BEL	13.02
6. Marzia Caravelli ITA	13.11
7. Cindy Roleder GER	13.11
8. Micol Cattaneo ITA	13.16

YANIT BECAME THE third Turkish champion of the day, having been fastest in heats 12.78/0.3 and semis 12.92.

400m Hurdles (h 27th, sf 28th, F 29th)

1. Irina Davydova RUS	53.77
2. Denisa Rosolová CZE	54.24
3. Anna Yaroshchuk UKR	54.35
4. Zuzana Hejnová CZE	54.49
5. Yelena Churakova RUS	54.78
6. Élodie Ouédraogo BEL	55.95
7. Zuzana Bergrová CZE	56.26
8. Jessie Barr IRL	56.83

HEJNOVÁ WAS FASTEST in the heats with 55.24 and Davydova in the semis with 54.68, and the latter ran a most accomplished race to win the title in a pb. Rosolová also ran a pb for second in her first year at the event.

High Jump (Q 1.92 27th, F 28th)

1. Ruth Beitia ESP	1.97
2. Tonje Angelsen NOR	1.97
3= Irina Gordeyeva RUS	1.92
3= Emma Green Tregaro SWE	1.92
3= Olena Holosha UKR	1.92
6= Burcu Ayhan TUR	1.92
6= Mélanie Melfort FRA	1.92
8. Mirela Demireva BUL	1.92

ELEVEN WOMEN CLEARED 1.90 in qualifying and in the final both Beitia and Angelsen (pb) cleared 1.97 on their third attempt. Beitia had a clear card up to that point while Angelsen had one failure (at 1.89).

Pole Vault (Q 4.45m 28th, F 30th)

1. Jirina Ptácníková CZE	4.60*
2. Martina Strutz GER	4.60*
3. Nikolia Kiriakopoülou GRE	4.60*
4= Silke Spiegelburg GER	4.50
4= Anastasiya Savchenko RUS	4.50
6. Vanessa Boslak FRA	4.50
7. Lisa Ryzih GER	4.40
8. Aleksandra Kiryashova RUS	4.40

DESPITE WET AND windy conditions the three medallists cleared 4.60, clearing on their first, second and third attempts respectively. Eleven finalists qualified at 4.40, together with Ptácníkova who passed that but made 4.45.

Long Jump (Q 6.65m 27th, F 28th)

1. Éloyse Lesueur FRA	6.81/0.5
2. Olga Sudarova BLR	6.74/0.6
3. Margrethe Renstrøm NOR	6.67/1.2
4. Sosthene Moguenara GER	6.66/0.7
5. Karin Melis Mey TUR	6.63/0.8
6. Ineta Radevica LAT	6.55/-0.6
7. Irène Pusterla SUI	6.53/0.9
8. Melanie Bauschke GER	6.50/-0.1

LESUEUR, WHO HAD led the qualifying at 6.66 with Renstrøm and Mey, jumped 6.81 in the first round of the final, and the closest anyone including her came to that was Sudarova's fifth round 6.74.

Triple Jump (Q 14.20m 27th, F 29th)

1. Olga Saladuha UKR	14.99/0.2
2. Patricia Mamona POR	14.52/1.8
3. Yana Borodina RUS	14.36/0.7
4. Simona La Mantia ITA	14.25/2.0
5. Dana Veldáková SVK	14.24/2.0
6. Niki Panétta GRE	14.23/0.7
7. Athanasía Pérra GRE	14.23/2.0
8. Françoise Mbango FRA	14.19w/2.7

SALADUHA WAS A class apart with 14.77 in qualifying and the four best jumps of the final in which her series was 14.99 (15.09 from take-off), 14.84, x, 14.65, x, 14.89. Mamona set a Portuguese record in the first round.

Shot (Q 18.90m, F 6th)

1. Nadine Kleinert GER	19.18
2. Irina Tarasova RUS	18.91
3. Chiara Rosa ITA	18.47
4. Josephine Terlecki GER	18.33
5. Christina Schwanitz GER	18.25
6. Radoslava Mavrodieva BUL	18.14
7. Anita Márton HUN	17.93
8. Helena Engman SWE	17.64

IN HER 24th successive major championship final and having won eight medals (but 6/6/6/7 in previous Europeans) from 1997, Kleinert at last won a gold medal. She was best in qualifying with 18.65 and had the three best throws in the final with 19.15, 19.15 and 19.18 in rounds two to four.

Discus (Q 61.00m 30th, F 1st)

1. Sandra Perkovic CRO	67.62
2. Nadine Müller GER	65.41
3. Nataliya Semenova UKR	62.91
4. Anna Rüh GER-J	62.65
5. Julia Fischer GER	62.10
6. Mélina Robert-Michon FRA	60.41
7. Vera Cechlová CZE	60.08
8. Natalia Artic MDA	58.64

MÜLLER LED THE qualifiers with 64.49 and started well in the final with 63.53, 64.99 and 65.41, while Perkovic had two no throws before a brilliant 67.62.

Hammer (Q 71.00m 29th, F 1st)

1. Anna Wlodarczyk POL	74.29
2. Martina Hrasnová SVK	73.34
3. Anna Bulgakova RUS	71.47
4. Kathrin Klaas GER	70.44
5. Tugce Sahutoglu TUR	70.21
6. Stephanie Falzon FRA	68.03
7. Éva Orbán HUN	67.92
8. Zalina Marghieva MDA	67.92

PERHAPS THE BIGGEST shock of the Championships was Betty Heidler's failure to qualify – just 17th with 65.06. In the first round of the final Wlodarczyk threw 74.02 and improved in the fourth to 74.29 with three other throws over 73m, a distance otherwise reached only by Hrasnová in round two. Wlodarczyk 71.38 was the only woman over 70m in qualifying.

Javelin (Q 60.00m 27th, F 29th)

1. Vira Rebryk UKR	66.86
2. Christina Obergföll GER	65.12
3. Linda Stahl GER	63.69
4. Goldie Sayers GBR	63.01
5. Katharina Molitor GER	60.99
6. Sinta Ozolina-Kovale LAT	59.34
7. Tatjana Jelaca SRB	57.58
8. Madara Palameika LAT	56.82

OBERGFÖLL OPENED WITH 65.12 in the final and her own 64.55 was the closest anyone came in the first four rounds, but then Rebryk, who had led qualifying with 61.84, had 66.86 and 64.77 as her final two throws after lying third with 63.44.

Heptathlon (29/30th)

1. Antoinette Nana Djimou FRA	6544
2. Lyudmila Yosypenko UKR	6387
3. Laura Ikauniece LAT	6335
4. Aiga Grabuste LAT	6325
5. Yekaterina Bolshova RUS	6298
6. Jessica Samuelsson SWE	6262
7. Claudia Rath GER	6210
8. Eliska Klucinová CZE	6151

NANA DJIMOU GOT off to a great start by clocking the quickest hurdles time with a pb 13.11, and was second at the end of day one on 3739 points, 46 behind Yosypenko. Then she had pbs of LJ 6.42 and JT 55.82 to effectively seal her victory with a score that added 135 to her best. There were eleven women over 6000.

4x100m Relay (h 30th, F 1st)

1. GER	42.51	Günther, Cibis, Pinto, Sailer
2. NED	42.80	Vassell, Schippers, Lubbers, Samuel; (ht: Akihary and Dopheide ran in heat)
3. POL	43.06	Popowicz, Korczynska, Jeschke, Ptak
4. RUS	43.37	5. FRA 43.44
6. SUI	43.61	7. BLR 44.06
		dnf. UKR –

THE UKRAINIAN TEAM of Povh, Pogrebnyak, Ryemyen and Pyatachenko ran 42.70 in their heat, but failed to pass the baton on the first exchange in the final. Germany took advantage in 42.51 and an equally delighted Dutch squad finished second with a national record of 42.80, having, resting their top two sprinters, only got through to the final due to Britain's disqualification in their heat.

4x400m Relay (h 30th, F 1st)

1. UKR 3:25.07 Olishevska 52.6, Zemlyak 50.4, Pygyda 50.52, Logvy nenko 51.49 (Prystupa ran in heat)
2. FRA 3:25.49 Anacharsis 51.7, Guion Firmin 51.4, Gayot 51.35, Guei 50.91 (Diarra ran in heat)

3. CZE 3:26.02 Hejnová 52.2, Bergrová 52.0, Bartonícková 51.12, Rosolová 50.59
4. GBR 3:26.20
5. GER 3:27.81
6. RUS 3:28.36
7. ROU 3:29.80
8. POL 3:30.17

THE FASTEST SPLIT was run by Joanne Cuddihy, 50.1 for her second leg in the heat, but Ireland did not qualify. Next fastest were Zemlyak and Pygyda for the winning Ukraine team.

2012 CHAMPIONSHIPS

WORLD JUNIOR CHAMPIONSHIPS 2012

At Barcelona, Spain 10-15 July

The Olympic Stadium in Barcelona, with a current capacity of over 50,000 was pretty empty throughout the Championships, but any lack of atmosphere was more than compensated by superb conditions for top-class athletics. And the competitors responded so well that there were many who felt that these were the best ever World Juniors. Generally the temperature was very warm, around 25°C, but times were occasionally held back by headwinds, and the wind did tend to swirl around somewhat – with some rain at the end of the final evening session.

The brilliant 17-year-old Qatari hammer thrower Ashraf Amgad El-Seify was the stellar performer of the Championships with a marvellous world junior hammer record of 85.57m. Two athletes retained their titles from Moncton 2010: Jacko Gill at shot and Angelica Bengtsson at pole vault, and stepping up from winning World Youth titles in 2011 to win again here were Consesius Kipruto, Jacko Gill, Fedrick Dacres, Ajee Wilson and Faith Kipyegon, plus two from 2009, Bengtsson and Alessia Trost. The USA was easily the most successful nation, their points tally being 0.5 better than their previous record from Kingston 2002, and their 20 medals just one short of that year with the women tying a record 10 medals from 2006. Kenya followed with 13 medals.

Men

100 Metres (11) (0.1)
1. Adam Gemili GBR 10.05*
2. Aaron Ernest USA 10.17
3. Odean Skeen JAM 10.28
4. Tyreek Hill USA 10.29
5. Jazeel Murphy JAM 10.29
6. Chijindu Ujah GBR 10.39
7. Carlos Nascimento POR 10.41
8. Xie Zhenye CHN 10.49

200 Metres (13): (-0.4)
1, Delano Williams TKS 20.48
2. Aaron Ernest USA 20,53
3. Tyreek Hill USA 20.54
4. Karol Zalewski POL 20.54
5. Xie Zhenye CHN 20.66
6. David Bolarinwa GBR 20.69
7. Teray Smith BAH 20.99
8. Julian Forte JAM 21.00

400 Metres (12)
1. Luguelin Santos DOM 44.85
2. Arman Hall USA 45.39
3= Aldrich Bailey USA 45.52
3= Steven Solomon AUS 45.52
5. Machel Cedenio TRI-Y 46.17
6. Alfas Kishoyian KEN 46.19
7. Boniface Mweresa KEN 46.50
8. Nikita Uglov RUS 46.61

800 Metres (15)
1. Nijel Amos BOT 1:43.79*
2. Timothy Kitum KEN 1:44.56
3. Edwin Kiplagat Melly KEN-Y 1:44.79
4. Wesley Vázquez PUR 1:45.29
5. Mark English IRL 1:46.02
6. Brandon McBride CAN 1:46.07
7. Mohamed Belbachir ALG 1:46.70
8. Dennis Krüger GER 1:46.92

1500 Metres (12)
1. Hamza Driouche QAT 3:39.04
2. Hillary Ngetich KEN-Y 3:40.39
3. Abdelhadi Labâli MAR 3:40.60
4. Musyad Abid MAR-Y 3:41.73
5. Teklit Teweldebrhan ERI 3:42.63
6. Dominic Mutili KEN 3:42.79
7. Carlos Díaz CHI 3:44.02
8. Yenew Tebikew ETH-Y 3:44.06

5000 Metres (14)
1. Muktar Edris ETH 13:38.95
2. Abrar Osman Adem ERI 13:40.52

3. William Malel Sitonik KEN 13:40.52
4. Youness El Salhi MAR 13:41.69
5. Tsegaye Mekonnen ETH 13:44.43
6. Phillip Kipyego UGA-Y 13:45.52
7. Moses Kurong UGA 13:52.96
8. Moses Mukono KEN 13:56.60
10,000 Metres (10)
1. Yigrem Demelash ETH 28:16.07
2. Philemon Cheboi KEN 28:23.98
3. Geoffrey Kirui KEN 28:30.47
4. Kinde Atanaw ETH 28:53.02
5. Moses Kurong UGA 29:06.87
6. Kenta Murayama JPN 29:40.56
7. Ken Yokote JPN 29:41.81
8. Rahul Kumar Pal IND 29:42.15
3000m Steeplechase (15)
1. Consesius Kipruto KEN 8:06.10*
2. Gilbert Kirui KEN 8:19.94
3. Hicham Sigueni MAR 8:30.14
4. Jaouas Chemlal MAR 8:30.92
5. Bilal Tabti ALG 8:32.08
6. Weynay Ghebreselasie ERI 8:33.87
7. Meresa Kahsay ETH 8:36.13
8. Ahmed Mohammed Burhan KSA 8:36.14
99cm **110 Metres Hurdles** (12): (-1.0)
1. Yordan O'Farrill CUB 13.18*
2. Nicholas Hough AUS 13.27
3. Wilhem Belocian FRA-Y 13.29
4. James Gladman GBR 13.37
5. Jussi Kanervo FIN 13.62
6. Dondre Echols USA 13.71
7. Shin-ya Tanaka JPN 13.72
8. Chi Pengfei CHN 13.77
400 Metres Hurdles (13)
1. Eric Futch USA 50.24
2. Takahiro Matsumoto JPN 50.41
3. Ibrahim Mohammed Saleh KSA-Y 50.47
4. Javern Gallimore JAM 50.49
5. Felix Franz GER 50.80
6. Oskari Mörö FIN 50.80
7. Timofey Chalyy RUS 51.17
8. Mitja Lindic SLO 51.26
High Jump (13)
1. Andrey Churyla BLR 2.24
2. Falk Wendrich GER-Y 2.24
3. Ryan Ingraham BAH 2.24
4= Ilya Ivanyuk RUS 2.21
4= Dmitriy Kroyter ISR 2.21
6. Brandon Starc AUS 2.17
7. Milan Dissanayake SRI 2.17
8. Péter Bakosi HUN 2.13
Pole Vault (12)
1. Thiago da Silva BRA 5.55
2. Ivan Horvat CRO 5.55
3. Shawnacy Barber CAN 5.55
4. Didac Salas ESP 5.50
5. Robert Renner SLO 5.40
6. Melker Svärd Jakobsson SWE 5.35
7. Thibault Boisseau FRA 5.30
8. Nikita Kirillov 5.30
Long Jump (11)
1. Sergey Morgunov RUS 8.09/0.4
2. Andreas Trajkovski DEN 7.82/-0.4
3. Jarion Lawson USA 7.64/0.1
4. Huang Haibing CHN 7.64/0.4

5. Stephan Hartmann GER 7.54/0.3
6. Elliott Safo GBR 7.51/-0.4
7. Li Qing CHN-Y 7.49/0.9
8. Frederik Thomsen DEN 7.36/0.1
Triple Jump (13)
1. Pedro Pichardo CUB 16.79/-0.1
2. Artem Primak RUS 16.60/-0.2
3. Latario Collie-Minns BAH 16.37/0.8
4. Georgi Tsonov BUL 16.10w/2.9
5. Henrique da Silva BRA 16.04/1.2
6. Lasha Gulelauri GEO 16.00w/2.3
7. Fu Haitao CHN 15.93/1.2
8. Nikólaos Tsiókos GRE 15.91/1.4
6 kg **Shot** (11)
1. Jacko Gill NZL 22.20*
2. Krzysztof Brzozowski POL 21.78*
3. Damien Birkenhead AUS (20.01q)
4. Arttu Kangas FIN 19.85
5. Mesud Pezer BIH 19.83
6. Li Jun CHN 19.72
7. Bodo Göder GER 19.70
8. Alejandro Noguera ESP 19.55
1.75kg **Discus** (12)
1. Fedrick Dacres JAM 62.80
2. Wojciech Praczyk POL 62.75 (60.72q)
3. Gerhard de Beer RSA 61.57
4. Viktor Butenko RUS 61.48
5. Felipe Lorentzon BRA 61.18
6. Jordan Young CAN 60.44
7. Dalton Rowan USA 59.31
8. Nicholas Percy GBR 57.79
6 kg **Hammer** (14)
1. Ashraf Amgad El-Seify QAT-Y 85.97*
2. Bence Pásztor HUN-Y 76.74
3. Sukhrob Khodjayev UZB 76.16
4. Alexandros Poursanides CYP 76.05
5. Igor Buryi RUS 75.83
6. Ilmari Lahtinen FIN 75.26
7. Juho Saarikoski FIN 74.89
8. Valeriy Pronkin RUS 74.51
Javelin (13)
1. Keshorn Walcott TRI 78.64
2. Braian Toledo ARG 77.09
3. Morné Moolman RSA 76.29
4. Bernhard Seifert GER 75.84
5. Intars Isejevs LAT 74.12
6. Joni Karvinen FIN 70.90
7. Luke Cann AUS 70.15
8. William White AUS-Y 69.62
Junior **Decathlon** (10/11)
1. Gunnar Nixon USA 8018
2. Jake Stein AUS 7955
3. Tim Dekker NED 7815
4. Cedric Dubler AUS 7584
5. Karl-Robert Saluri EST 7583
6. Manuel González CUB 7513
7. Ruben Gado FRA 7498
8. Lukas Schmitz GER 7444
10,000 Metres Walk (13)
1. Eider Arévalo COL 40:09.74
2. Aleksandr Ivanov RUS 40:12.90
3. Su Guanyu CHN 40:16.87
4. Takumi Saito JPN 40:19.10
5. Alvaro Martín ESP 40:35.52
6. Jesús Vega MEX 41:05.39

7. Nils Brembach GER 41:19.12
8. Igor Lyashchenko UKR 41:21.60
4x100 Metres (14)
1. USA　(Hill, Bailey, Delaney, Ernest) 38.67
　　　　(Burrell and Hall ran in heat)
2. JAM　(Tracey, Skeen, Minzie, Murphy) 38.97
　　　　(Givans ran in heat)
3. JPN　(Oseto, Hashimoto, Cambridge, Kanamori)
　　　　39.02
4. POL　39.47
5. AUS　39.59
6. BAH　39.74
7. BRA　39.75
dnf. GBR
4x400 Metres (15)
1. USA　(Downing 46.1, Bailey 45.8, Okezie 46.40,
　　　　Hall 45.78) 3:03.99 (Futch ran in heat)
2. POL　(Zalewski, Smolen, Kusnierz, Dobek) 3:05.05
　　　　(Walczuk ran in heat)
3. TRI (　Guevara, Richards, Benjamin, Cedenio)
　　　　3:06.32
4. AUS　3:06.58
5. JAM　3:07.31
6. KSA　3:09.26
7. JPN　3:09.67
dq. ITA

Women

100 Metres (11): (1.7)
1. Anthonique Strachan BAH 11.20
2. Nimet Karakus TUR 11.36
3. Tamiris de Liz BRA-Y 11.45
4. Khamica Bingham CAN 11.46
5. Jennifer Madu USA 11.52
6. Sophie Papps GBR 11.54
7. Fani Chalas DOM 11.58
8. Ida Mayer GER 11.59
200 Metres (13): (0.2)
1. Anthonique Strachan BAH 22.53*
2. Olivia Ekponé USA 23.15
3. Dezerea Bryant USA 23.15
4. Desiree Henry GBR-Y 23.34
5. Janet Amponsah GHA 23.41
6. Imke Vervaet BEL 23.47
7. Dina Asher-Smith GBR-Y 23.50
8. Shericka Jackson JAM 23.53
400 Metres (13)
1. Ashley Spencer USA 50.50*
2. Kadecia Baird GUY-Y 51.04
3. Erika Rucker USA 51.10
4. Shaunae Miller BAH 51.78
5. Justine Palframan RSA 51.87
6. Bianca Razor ROU 52.20
7. Chris-Ann Gordon JAM 52.31
8. Olivia James JAM 52.68
800 Metres (12)
1. Ajee' Wilson USA 2:00.91
2. Jessica Judd GBR-Y 2:00.96
3. Manal El Bahraoui MAR 2:03.09
4. Aníta Hindriksdóttir ISL-Y 2:03.23
5. Sonja Mosler GER 2:04.07
6. Emily Dudgeon GBR 2:04.68
7. Anastasiya Tkachuk UKR 2:04.92
8. Winnie Nanyondo UGA 2:07.23
1500 Metres (15)
1. Faith Chepngetich Kipyegon KEN 4:04.96*

2. Amela Terzic SRB 4:07.59
3. Senbere Teferi ETH-Y 4:08.28
4. Nancy Chepkwemoi KEN 4:09.72
5. Jessica Judd GBR-Y 4:09.93
6. Mary Cain USA-Y 4:11.01
7. Alem Embaye ETH 4:12.92
8. Jennifer Walsh GBR 4:12.96
3000 Metres (10)
1. Mercy Chebwogen KEN-Y 9:08.88
2. Hiwot Gebrekidan ETH-Y 9:09.27
3. Emelia Gorecka GBR 9:09.43
4. Haftamnesh Tesfay ETH 9:10.02
5. Brillian Kipkoech KEN-Y 9:14.32
6. Aisling Cuffe USA 9:19.95
7. Rebekah Greene NZL 9:21.23
8. Miyuki Uehara JPN-J 9:21.81
5000 Metres (11)
1. Buze Diriba ETH 15:32.94
2. Ruti Aga ETH 15:32.95
3. Agnes Chebet Tirop KEN-Y 15:36.74
4. Catla Hatton USA 15:50.32
5. Caroline Kipkirui KEN 15:58.10
6. Alena Kudashkina RUS 16:05.64
7. Monica Florea ROU 16:08.07
8. Allie Woodward USA 16:08.29
3000m Steeplechase (11)
1. Daisy Chepkemei KEN-Y 9:47.22
2. Tejinesh Gebisa ETH-Y 9:50.51
3. Stella Rutto KEN-Y 9:50.58
4. Yevdokiya Bukina RUS 9:56.46
5. Brianna Nerud USA 10:00.72
6. Maya Rehburg GER 10:03.09
7. Oona Kettunen FIN 10:03.15
8. Elena Panaet ROU 10:19.34
100 Metres Hurdles (15): (-2.4)
1. Morgan Snow USA 13.38
2. Noemi Zbären SUI 13.43
3. Yekaterina Bleskina RUS 13.43
4. Franziska Hofmann GER 13.51
5. Michelle Jenneke AUS 13.54
6. Jenna Berghem FIN 13.56
7. Wang Dou CHN 13.58
dq. Dior Hall USA-Y
400 Metres Hurdles (14)
1. Janieve Russell JAM 56.62
2. Aurèlie Chaboudez FRA 57.14
3. Kaila Barber USA 57.63
4. Olena Kolesnychenko UKR 58.10
5. Kübra Sesli TUR 58.35
6. Vilde Svortevik NOR 58.45
7. Taylor Farquhar CAN 58.77
dnf. Shamier Little USA-Y
High Jump (15)
1. Alessia Trost ITA 1.91
2. Lissa Labiche SEY 1.88
3. Mariya Kuchina RUS 1.88
4. Alexandra Plaza GER 1.88
5. Dior Delophont FRA 1.85
6. Melina Brenner GER 1.85
7. Iryna Herashchenko UKR-Y 1.85
8. Jeanelle Scheper LCA 1.82
Pole Vault (14)
1. Angelica Bengtsson SWE 4.50*
2. Liz Parnov AUS 4.30
3. Roberta Bruni ITA 4.20
4= Anjuli Knäsche GER 4.15

Placing and Medal Table Leaders

Nat	G	S	B	Pts	Nat	G	S	B	Pts
USA	9	4	7	187.5	JPN	0	1	1	29
KEN	4	4	5	112	SWE	2	0	0	26
GER	2	4	0	94.5	UKR	0	0	0	26
RUS	2	3	3	84.5	FIN	0	0	0	25
GBR	2	1	2	71	NZL	1	0	0	24
ETH	3	3	1	70	CAN	0	0	1	22
CHN	0	2	2	64	HUN	0	2	0	18
AUS	0	3	2	59.5	ESP	1	0	0	18
JAM	2	2	1	59	TRI	1	0	1	18
POL	0	3	0	42	QAT	2	0	0	16
CUB	3	0	1	41	RSA	0	0	2	16
BRA	1	o	3	39	ITA	1	0	1	15
BAH	2	0	2	38	BLR	1	0	1	14
FRA	1	2	1	36	COL	1	0	1	14
MAR	0	0	3	33	ERI	0	1	0	14

In all athletes from 22 nations won gold, 43 won medals and 74 placed athletes in the top eight.

4= Kira Grünberg AUT 4.15
6. Emily Grove USA 4.15
7. Alissa Söderberg SWE 4.15
8. Xu Huiqin CHN 4.05
Long Jump (13)
1. Katarina Johnson-Thompson GBR 6.81w/2.5
2. Lena Malkus GER 6.80w/2.7
3. Jazmin Sawyers GBR 6.67/1.2
4. Chanice Porter JAM 6.58/0.7
5. Alina Rotaru ROU 6.52/1.6
6. Jéssica dos Reis BRA 6.51/1.6
7. Brooke Stratton AUS 6.42/0.1
8. Maryna Bekh UKR-Y 6.35/1.8
Triple Jump (12)
1. Ana Peleteiro ESP-Y 14.17/-1.0
2. Dovité Dzindzalietaité LTU 14.17/1.6
3. Liuba Zaldívar CUB 13.90/0.3
4. Hanna Aleksandrova UKR 13.48/1.5
5. Chen Mudan CHN 13.42/0.2
6. Ciarra Brewer USA 13.38/1.0
7. Yekaterina Sariyeva AZE-Y 13.33/0.2
8. Ottavia Cestonaro ITA 13.29/1.5
Shot (10)
1. Shanice Craft GER 17.15
2. Gao Yang CHN 16.57
3. Bian Ka CHN 16.48
4. Christina Hillman USA 16.27
5. Natalya Troneva RUS 16.18
6. Sophie McKinna GBR 15.98
7. Torie Owers USA 15.88
8. Emel Dereli TUR-Y 15.86
Discus (15)
1. Anna Rüh GER 62.38
2. Shanice Craft GER 60.42
3. Shelbi Vaughan USA 60.07
4. Siositina Hakeai NZL 56.17
5. Gu Siyu CHN 55.78
6. Subenrat Insaeng THA 54.47
7. Krisztina Váradi HUN 51.44
8. Alex Collatz USA 49.28
Hammer (12)
1. Alexandra Tavernier FRA 70.62*
2. Alexia Sedykh FRA 67.34
3. Alena Novogrodskaya BLR 67.13
4. Julia Ratcliffe NZL 67.00
5. Iliána Korosídou GRE-Y 63.32

6. Luo Na CHN 63.19
7. Eva Reinders NED 61.63
8. Réka Gyurátz HUN-Y 60.88
Javelin (11)
1. Sofi Flinck SWE-Y 61.40
2. Liu Shiying CHN 59.20
3. Marija Vucenovic SRB 57.12
4. Lismania Muñoz CUB 54.97
5. Karolina Boldysz POL 54.95
6. Ismaray Armentero CUB 54.54
7. Cnristin Hussong GER 53.20
8. Liveta Jasiunaité LTU 53.00
Heptathlon (12/13)
1. Yorgelis Rodríguez CUB-Y 5966
2. Xénia Krizsán HUN 5957
3. Tamara de Sousa BRA 5900
4. Sofia Linde SWE-Y 5872
5. Portia Bing NZL 5653
6. Lucia Mokrásová SVK 5610
7. Wang Qingling CHN 5598
8. Kendell Williams USA-Y 5578
10,000 Metres Walk (11)
1. Yekaterina Medvedeva RUS 45:41.74
2. Nadezhda Leontyeva RUS 45:43.64
3. Lorena Arenas COL 45:44.46
4. Lyudmyla Olyanovska UKR 45:53.50
5. Mao Yanxue CHN 46:10.60
6. Anezka Drahatová CZE 46:29.95
7. Alejandra Ortega MEX 47:03.42
8. Nozomi Yagi JPN 47:04.92
4x100 Metres (14)
1. USA (Snow, Bryant, Madu, Sanders) 43.89
    (Davis-White ran in heat)
2. GER (Burghardt, Mayer, Grompe, Maduka) 44.24
3. BRA (C de Souza, de Liz, da Rosa, dos Reis)
    44.29
4. POL 44.95
5. BEL 45.12
6. NED 45.22
dq, NGR, dnf. GBR
4x400 Metres (15)
1. USA (Rucker 52.7, Ekpone 52.7, Baisden 53.9,
    Spencer 50.7) 3:30.01
    (Reynolds and {Porter ran in heat)
2. JAM (Farquharson, James, Jackson, Russell)
    3:32.97 (Leith ran in heat)

3. RUS   (Glotova, Galitskaya, Koltachikhina, Renzhina) 3:36.42
4. UKR   3:37.02
5. GER   3:37.23
6. CAN   3:37.84
7. POL   3:37.90
8. AUS   3:38.84
9. RSA   3:40.31

IAAF Hammer Throw Challenge 2012

Final standings for 2012. top three meetings to score. Prize money from $30,000 for 1st to $500 for 12th.
Men: 1. Krisztián Pars HUN 242.35, 2. Pawel Fajdek 236.47, 3. Oleksiy Sokyrskyy 233.39, 4. Lukás Melich 227.44, 5. Dilshod Nazarov 224.97, 6. Mattias Jons 223.92, 7. Szymon Ziólkowski 223.44.
Women: 1. Betty Heidler 230.49, 2. Anita Wlodarczyk 223.13, 3. Tatyana Lysenko 222.05. 4. Kathrin Klaas GER 216.660, 5. Zalina Marghieva 215.07, 6. Martina Hrasnová 212.30, 7. Sultana Frizell 204.61.

IAAF World Half Marathon Championships 2012

At Kavarna, Bulgaria 7 October
Men
1. Zersenay Tadese ERI 60:19
2. Deressa Chimsa ETH 60:51
3. John Mwangangi KEN 61:01
4. Pius Kirop KEN 61:11
5. Stephen Kibet KEN 61:40
6. Eliud Kipchoge KEN 61:52
7. Jackson Kiprop UGA 62:05
8. Stephen Mokoka RSA 62:06
9. Tewelde Estifanos ERI 62:10
10. Kiflom Slum Weldemichael ERI 62:12
11. Belay Assefa ETH 62:17
12. Robert Kajuga RWA 62:22
13. Mulue Andom ERI 62:23
14. Giovani dos Santos BRA 62:32
15. Augustus Maiyo USA 62:33
78 of 86 finished
Teams: 1. KEN 3:03:52, 2. ERI 3:04:41, 3. ETH 3:05:43, 4. USA 3:09:56, 5. UGA 3:10:20, 6. RWA 3:12:34, 7. RSA 3:13:09, 8. FRA 3:13:49, 9. JPN 3:14:33, 10. AUS 3:15:52, 13 teams scored.
Women
1. Meseret Hailu ETH 68:55
2. Feysa Tadesse ETH 68:56
3. Pasalia Kipkoech KEN 69:04
4. Lydia Cheromei KEN 69:13
5. Emebet Etea ETH 70:01
6. Pauline Njeri Kahenya KEN 70:22
7. Gemma Steel GBR 71:09
8. Tomomi Tanaka JPN 71:09
9. Mai Ito JPN 71:25
10. Caryl Jones GBR 71:52
11. Sabrina Mockenhaupt GER 72:04
12. Asami Kato JPN 72:11
13. Maegan Krifchin USA 72:29
14. Lara Tamsett AUS 72:58
15. Yoko Miyauchi JPN 73:00
59 of 60 finished

Teams: 1. ETH 3:27:52, 2. KEN 3:28:39, 3. JPN 3:34:45, 4. GBR 3:36:56, 5. USA 3:40:40, 6. RSA 3:50:47, 7. MEX 3:51:45, 8. BRA 3:54:45, 9. BUL 4:11:05.

IAAF World Race Walking Cup 2012

At Saransk, Russia 12-13 May
Men – 20km (12 May)
1. Wang Zhen CHN 1:19:13
2. Andrey Krivov RUS 1:19:27
3. Vladimir Kanaykin RUS 1:19:43
4. Ruslan Dmytrenko UKR 1:20:17
5. Andrey Ruzavin RUS 1:20:37
6. Nazar Kovalenko UKR 1:20:38
7. Eder Sánchez MEX 1:20:58
8. Chen Ding CHN 1:21:05
9. Valeriy Borchin RUS 1:21:29
10. Zhao Qi CHN 1:21:46
11. Robert Heffernan IRL 1:21:51
12. Ivan Losev UKR 1:21:57
13. Iñaki Gómez CAN 1:21:58
14. Rafal Fedaczynski POL 1:21:55
15. Isamu Fujisawa JPN 1:22:05
drugs dq (5) Sergey Morozov RUS 1:20:26
105 of 123 finished
Teams: 1. RUS 10, 2. CHN 21, 3. UKR 24, 4. AUS 71, 5. IND 77, 6. JPN 81, 7. MEX 87, 8. COL 92, 9. ITA 109, 10. BLR 110, 11. ESP 121, 12. POL 136, 13. FRA 138, 14. BRA 154, 15. CAN 182, 16. ECU 192, 17. FIN 194, 18. RSA 204, 19. GBR 223, 20. USA 239.
Men – 50km (13 May)
1. Sergey Kirdyapkin RUS 3:38:08
2. Igor Yerokhin RUS 3:38:10
3. Jared Tallent AUS 3:40:32
4. Si Tianfeng CHN 3:43:05
5. Sergey Bakulin RUS 3:46:14
6. Christopher Linke GER 3:47:33
7. Jesús Ángel García ESP 3:48:15
8. Xu Faguang CHN 3:48:47
9. Marco De Luca ITA 3:49:50
10. Rafal Augustyn POL 3:49:53
11. Oleksiy Kazanin UKR 3:50:17
12. Horacio Nava MEX 3:51:23
13. Igor Hlavan UKR 3:51:24
14. Rafal Sikora POL 3:51:43
15. Colin Griffin IRL 3:52:55
74 of 110 finished
Teams: 1. RUS 8, 2. CHN 36, 3. UKR 40, 4. MEX 52, 5. ESP 80, 6. KOR 85, 7. ITA 91, 8. POR 121, 9. BLR 125, 10. IND 125, 11. KAZ 154

Women – 20km (12 May)
1. Yelena Lashmanova RUS 1:27:38
2. Olga Kaniskina RUS 1:28:33
3. María José Poves ESP 1:29:10
4. Lu Xiuzhi CHN 1:29:55
5. Beatriz Pascual ESP 1:30:46
6. Anisya Kirdyapkina RUS 1:31:00
7. Elisa Rigaudo ITA 1:31:25
8. Olive Loughnane IRL 1:31:32
9. Ana Cabacinha POR 1:31:42
10. Inês Henriques POR 1:31:43

IAAF World Combined Events Challenge 2012

Based on the sum of the best scores achieved in any three of the 13 designated competitions during the year.

Men Decathlon

1	Hans Van Alphen BEL	25,259	8519 Götzis	8447 Olympics	8293 Talence
2	Pascal Behrenbruch GER	25,117	8433 Götzis	8558 Europeans	8126 Olympics
3	Oleksiy Kasyanov UKR	24,822	8321 Europeans	8283 Olympics	8218 Talence
4	Eelco Sintnicolaas NED	24,481	8506 Götzis	8034 Olympics	7941 Talence
5	Dmitriy Karpov KAZ	24,271	8172 Desenzano	8173 Kladno	7926 Olympics
6	Adam Helcelet CZE	24,106	8044 Kladno	7998 Europeans	8064 Talence
7	Yordaní García CUB	24,022	8061 Götzis	8005 Ratingen	7956 Olympics
8	Ashley Bryant GBR	23,194	7689 Desenzano	7837 Götzis	7668 Europeans

Women Heptathlon

1	Tatyana Chernova RUS	19,717	6774 Götzis	6628 Olympics	6315 Talence
2	Lyudmyla Yosypenko UKR	19,520	6501 Götzis	6618 Olympics	6401 Talence
3	Antoinette Nana Djimou FRA	19,510	6544 Europeans	6576 Olympics	6390 Talence
4	Austra Skujyte LTU	19,408	6493 Götzis	6599 Olympics	6316 Talence
5	Laura Ikauniece LAT	19,031	6282 Götzis	6335 Europeans	6414 Olympics
6	Jessica Samuelsson SWE	18,790	6228 Götzis	6262 Europeans	6300 Olympics
7	Sharon Day USA	18,731	6156 Götzis	6343 US Champs	6232 Olympics
8	Eliska Klucinová CAE	18,543	6283 Kladno	6151 Europeans	6109 Olympics

Prize Money: 1st $30,000, 2nd $20,000, 3rd $15,000, 4th $10,000, 5th $8000, 6th $7000, 7th $6000, 8th $5000.

Note that, as usual, world's top heptathlete Jessica Ennis only competed in two heptathlons during the year. And similarly the top decathletes Ashton Eaton and Trey Hardee each competed in just two decathlons.

11. Júlia Takács ESP 1:32:05
12. Claudia Stef ROU 1:32:15
13. Olena Shumkina UKR 1:32:19
14. Eleonora Giorgi ITA 1:32:57
15. Qieyang Shenjie CHN 1:33:00
88 of 105 finished
Teams: 1. POR 13, 2. ESP 22, 3. CHN 32, 4. RUS 33, 5. JPN 53, 6. MEX 90, 7. ECU 106, 8. POL 110
Junior Men – 10km (12 May)
1. Eider Arévalo COL 41:17
2. Aleksandr Ivanov RUS 41:42
3. Jesús Vega MEX 41:56
4. Damir Baybikov RUS 42:11
5. Francesco Fortunato ITA 42:13
6. Yin Jiaxing CHN 42:18
63 of 67 finished
Teams: 1. RUS 6, 2. COL 10, 3. CHN 14, 4. MEX 14, 5. ITA 23, 6. BLR 31, 7. AUS 41, 8. UKR 42, 9. ESP 48, 10. ECU 57; 22 teams scored.
Junior Women – 10km (12 May)
1. Lorena Arenas COL 45:57
2. Alejandra Ortega MEX 46:00
3. Nadezhda Leontyeva RUS 46:02
4. Yekaterina Medvedeva RUS 46:18
5. Lyudmyla Olyanovska UKR 46:35
6. Kate Veale IRL 46:53
48 of 50 finished
Teams: 1. RUS 7, 12. CHN 15, 3. UKR 15, 4. MEX 17, 5. COL 18, 6. ESP 35, 7. ITA 36, 8. BLR 37, 9. AUS 51, 10. IRL 51; 17 teams scored
Prize Money: Individual: 1st $30,000, 2nd $15,000, 3rd $10,000, 4th $7000, 5th $5000, 6th $3000, Team: 1st $15,000, 2nd $12,000, 3rd $9,000, 4th $7500, 5th $6000, 6th $3000. Total: $367,500. No prize money for the Junior 10ks. 5 could start, 3 to score on senior teams.

IAAF World Race Walking Challenge 2012

Results of walks at 12 meetings in 2012 qualified. Walkers needed to compete at three or more of these to qualify and pre-final positions were based on the best positions from these races, with a sliding scale of points from the three categories. Prize money was awarded then in the finishing order of eligible walkers in the final 10k race at: 1st $30,000, 2nd $20,000, 3rd $14,000, 4th $9000, 5th $7000, 6th $6000, 7th $4500, 8th $4000, 9th $3000, 10th $2000, 11th $1000, 12th $500.

14 September, Ordos, China. Men 10k: 1. Wang Zhen CHN 39:27, 2. Cai Zelin CHN 39:44, 3. Chen Ding CHN 39:51, 4. Li Jianbo CHN 39:56, 5. Dane Bird-Smith AUS 40:32, 6. Hiroki Arai JPN 40:41, 7. Eder Sánchez MEX 40:50, 8. Miguel Ángel López ESP 41:01, 9. Luke Adams AUS 41:06, 10. Majej Tóth SVK 41:33, 11. Jarred Tallent AUS 42:29, dnf. Si Tianfeng CHN, **Women 10k**: 1. Liu Hong 43:18, 2. Ana Cabecinha POR 43:31, 3. Lu Xiuzhi CHN 43:37, 4. Beatriz Pascual ESP 43:54, 5. Elisa Rigaudo ITA 44:24, 6. Tatyana Korotkova RUS 44:52; 7. Claire Tallent AUS 45:29; 8. Inês Henriques POR 46:10; 9. Olive Loughnane IRL 46:57, dq, Qieyang Shenjie CHN.
Overall placings: 1. Wang Zhen 66, 2. Chen Ding 48, 3. Tallent 40, 4=. Cai Zelin & Sánchez 36, 6. Si Tianfeng 31, Women – 1. Liu Hong 56, 2=. Lu Xiuzhi & Pascual 44, 4. Cabecinha 34, 5, Tallent 30; 6, Henriques 28.

World Marathon Majors 2011-12

London, Boston, Berlin, Chicago and New York Marathons 2011 and 2012, plus Olympic Games and World Championships. The series expands to add Tokyo in 2013. Ecah champion is paid $500,000.

Final points, winners earn $500,000: **Men**: 1. Geoffrey Mutai KEN 75, 2. Tsegaye Kebede ETH 46, 3. Wesley Korir KEN 41, 4= Abel Kirui KEN, Moses Mosop KEN, Emmanuel Mutai KEN 40; 7= Wilson Kipsang KEN, Patrick Makau KEN 35, 9. Martin Lel KEN 30, 10= Stephen Kiprotich UGA, Feyisa Lelisa ETH 25. **Women**: 1. Mary Keitany KEN 65, 2. Edna Kiplagat KEN 50, 3= Sharon Cherop KEN, Liliya Shobukhova RUS 45, 5. Piscah Jeptoo KEN 40, 6= Firehiwot Dado ETH, Florence Kiplagat KEN 30, 8. Atsede Baysa ETH 28, 9= Tiki Gelana ETH, Aberu Kebede ETH, Caroline Kilel KEN 25.

18th African Championships 2012

At Porto Novo, Benin 27 June – 1 July

Men

100m	1. Simon Magakwe RSA 10.29
(-0.9)	2. Amr Ibrahim Mostafa Seoud EGY 10.34
	3. Hua Wilfred Koffi CIV 10.37
200m	1. Ben Youssef Meité CIV 20.62
(-1.4)	2. Amr Ibrahim Mostafa Seoud 20.76
	3. Noah Akwu NGR 20.83
400m	1. Isaac Makwala BOT 45.25
	2. Oscar Pistorius RSA 45.52
	3. Willem de Beer RSA 45.67
800m	1. Taoufik Makhloufi ALG 1:43.88*
	2. Anthony Chemut KEN 1:44.53
	3. André Olivier RSA 1:45.09
1500m	1. Caleb Ndiku KEN 3:35.71*
	2. Ayanleh Souleiman DJI 3:36.34
	3. James Magut KEN 3:36.35
5000m	1. Mark Kiptoo KEN 13:22.38
	2. Jonathan Maiyo KEN 13:22.89
	3. Timothy Kiptoo KEN 13:24.67
10,000m	1. Kenneth Kipkemoi KEN 27:19.74*
	2. Mark Kiptoo IND 27:20.77
	3. Lewis Mosoti KEN 27:22.54
3000mSt	1. Abel Mutai KEN 8:16.05
	2. Wilson Maraba KEN 8:16.96
	3. Benjamin Kiplagat UGA 8:18.73
110mh	1. Lehann Fourie RSA 13.60
(-1.1)	2. Selim Nurudeen NGR 13.68
	3. Lyès Mokdel ALG 13.73
400mh	1. Amaechi Morton NGR 49.32
	2. Mamadou Kasse Hann SEN 49.39
	3. Boniface Mucheru KEN 49.45
HJ	1. Kabelo Kgosiemang BOT 2.25
	2. Ali Mohamed Younes Idris SUD 2.15
	3. Mathew Sawe KEN 2.15
PV	1. Mouhcine Cheaouri MAR 5.10
	2. Samir El Mafhoum MAR 5.00
	3. Ruaan van Wyk RSA 4.90
LJ	1. Ndiss Kaba Badji SEN 8.04/0.1
	2. Zarck Visser RSA 7.98/1.7
	3. Ignisious Gaisah GHA 7.73/0.2
TJ	1. Tosin Oke NGR 16.98/1.2
	2. Issam Nima ALG 16.69/0.3
	3. Hugo Mamba CMR 16.34/0.6
SP	1. Burger Lambrechts RSA 19.51
	2. Orazio Cremona RSA 19.19
	3. Yasser Ibrahim EGY 18.78
DT	1. Victor Hogan RSA 61.80
	2. Yasser Ibrahim EGY 59.61
	3. Russel Tucker RSA 57.99
HT	1. Chris Harmse RSA 77.22
	2. Mohsen Anani EGY 74.31
	3. Mostafa Hicham Al-Gamal EGY 73.81
JT	1. Julius Yego KEN 76.68
	2. John Ampomah GHA 70.65
	3. Kenechukwu Ezeofor NGR 69.58
Dec	1. Ali Kamé MAD 7252
	2. Mourad Souissi ALG 7000
	3. Guillaume Thierry MRI 6955
4x100m	1. RSA (Dreyer, Mogakwe, Engel, Mpuang) 39.26
	2. NGR 39.34
	3. GHA 39.40
4x400m	1. NGR (Weigopwa, Morton, Onakoya, Salihu) 3:02.39
	2. RSA 3:04.01
	3. KEN 3:04.12
20kmW	1. David Kimutai KEN 1:32:06
	2. Kamahmed Ameur ALG 1:33:24

Women

100m	1. Ruddy Zang Milama GAB 11.16
(-0.8)	2. Blessing Okagbare NGR 11.18
	3. Gloria Asumnu NGR 11.28
200m	1. Gloria Asumnu NGR 22.93
(-0.7)	2. Lauretta Ozoh NGR 22.93
	3. Marie José Lou Gonerie CIV 23.44
400m	1. Amantle Montsho BOT 49.54
	2. Regina George NGR 51.11
	3. Amy Mbacké Thiam SEN 51.68
800m	1. Francine Niyonsaba BDI 1:59.11
	2. Eunice Sum KEN 1:59.13
	3. Malika Akkaoui MAR 1:59.90
1500m	1. Rabab Arrafi MAR 4:05.80*
	2. Mary Kuria KEN 4:06.22
	3. Margaret Muriuki KEN 4:06.50
5000m	1. Gladys Cherono KEN 15:40.04
	2. Veronica Nyaruai KEN 15:40.65
	3. Gotytom Gebreslase ETH 15:53.34
10,000m	1. Gladys Cherono KEN 32:41.40
	2. Priscah Cherono KEN 32:45.73
	3. Betsy Saina KEN 32:48.36
3000mSt	1. Mercy Njorege KEN 9:43.26
	2. Birtukan Adamu ETH 9:45.41
	3. Hyvin Jepkemoi KEN 9:45.95
100mh	1. Gnima Faye SEN 13.36
(-0.2)	2. Amina Ferguène ALG 13.56
	3. Uhunoma Osazuwa NGR 13.61
400mh	1. Joke Odumosu NGR 54.99
	2. Hayat Lambarki MAR 55.41
	3. Raasin McIntosh LBR 55.99
HJ	1. Lissa Labiche SEY 1.86
	2. Anika Smit RSA 1.86
	3. Ghizlane Siba MAR 1.75
PV	1. Syrine Balti TUN 3.80
	2. Juanita Stander RSA 3.50
	3. Dorra Mahfoudhi TUN 3.40

Medals and Points Table

Points: 8 for 1st to 1 for 8th.

Nation	Men			Women			Total			Total pts	
	G	S	B	G	S	B	G	S	B	Medals	total pts
RSA	6	4	4	0	6	4	6	10	8	24	285.5
KEN	5	5	6	4	4	3	9	9	9	27	247
NGR	3	2	2	7	4	3	10	6	5	21	233.5
ETH	0	0	0	0	1	2	0	1	2	3	114
GHA	0	1	2	1	1	0	1	2	2	5	89
CIV	1	0	1	0	1	3	1	1	4	6	66.5
EGY	0	4	2	0	0	0	0	4	2	6	66
MAR	1	1	0	1	1	3	2	2	3	7	64
ALG	1	2	2	1	1	0	2	3	2	7	61
SEN	1	1	0	2	0	2	3	1	2	6	56
BOT	2	0	0	1	1	0	3	1	0	4	51
TUN	1	0	0	1	1	2	2	1	2	5	47.5
BEN	0	0	0	0	0	0	0	0	0	0	31.5
UGA	1	0	0	1	0	0	1	0	1	2	27
CMR	0	0	0	0	0	1	0	0	1	1	27

More points (medals): LBR (1B) 22, BDI (1G) 20, MAD (1G) 16, MRI (1B) 14, SEY (1G) 13, TOG 12, BUR (1S) 10, SUD (1S), NIG, MLI 9; GAB (1G), NAM 8; DJI (1S), RWA 7; LBA, CGO 6; LES, ZIM 5, STP 3, MOZ 2, COM 37. 23 nations won medals (15 gold) and 37 placed athletes in the top 8.

LJ
1. Blessing Okagbare NGR 6.96*/1.7
2. Janice Josephs RSA 6.29/1.5
3. Lynique Prinsloo RSA 6.22/1.8

TJ
1. Sarah Nambawa UGA 13.90w/2.3
2. Charlene Potgieter RSA 13.90w/3.1
3. Jamaa Chaïk MAR 13.75/2.0

SP
1. Chinwe Okoro NGR 16.21
2. Omotayo Talabi NGR 15.63
3. Auriole Dongmo CMR 15.41
drugs dq (1), Vivian Chukwuemeka NGR 18.86

DT
1. Chinwe Okoro NGR 56.60
2. Elizna Naude RSA 55.88
3. Suzanne Kragbé CIV 54.56

HT
1. Amy Sène SEN 65.55
2. Laëtitia Bambara BUR 65.08
3. Sarah Bensaad TUN 60.75

JT
1. Margaret Simpson GHA 54.62
2. Justine Robbeson RSA 52.81
3. Gerlize de Klerk RSA 49.85

Hep
1. Yasmina Omrani ALG 5924
2. Gabriela Kouassi CIV 5481
3. Bianca Erwee RSA 5338

4x100m
1. NGR (Udoh, Asumnu, Osayomi, Ozoh) 43.21*
2. GHA 44.35
3. CIV 45.29

4x400m
1. NGR (Abinuwa, Omotso, Etim, Abogumloko) 3:28.77*
2. BOT 3:31.27
3. SEN 3:31.64

20kmW
1. Grace Wanjiru KEN 1:40:53
2. Olfa Lafi TUN 1:46:07
3. Aynalem Eshetu ETH 1:49:45

** Championships record*

African Multi-events Champs

At Bombous. Mauritius 13-14 April.
Dec: Ali Kamé 7409; **Women**: Hep: Margaret Simpson GHA 6184.

Asian Walks Champs 2012

At Nomi City, Japan 11 March
20km: 1. Zhu Chundong CHN 1:21:22, 2. Gurmeet Singh IND 1:21:31, 3. Byun Young-jun KOR 1:21:42; **Women 20k**m: 1, Ding Huiqin CHN 1:30:14, 2. Rei Inoue JPN 1:34:06. 3. Nguyen Thi Thanh Phuc VIE 1:35:13.

5th Asian Indoor Championships 2012

At Hangzhou, China 18-19 February
Men: **60m**: Reza Ghasemi IRI 6.68, **400m**: Reza Bouazar IRL 48.09, **800m**: Mohamed Al-Azimi KUW 1:47.37*, **1500m**: Mohamed Shahwaan KSA 3:57.84, **3000m**: Bilisuma Shugi BRN 7:43.88*, **60mh**: Jiang Fan CHN 7.74*, **HJ**: Moataz Essa Barshim QAT 2.37*, **PV**: Yang Yansheng CHN 5.50, **LJ**: Li Jinzhe CHN 7.98, **TJ**: Dong Bin CHN 17.01*, 2, Cao Shuo CHN 17.01*), **SP**: Zhang Jun CHN 19.78*, **Hep**: Dmitriy Karpov KAZ 5928*, **4x400m**: *not held*; **Women**: **60m**: Wei Yongli CHN 7.37 (Viktoriya Zyabkina KAZ 7.33* in sf), **400m**: Maryam Toosi IRI 53.85, **800m**: Zhao Jing CHN 2:04.15, **1500m**: Genzebe Shami BRN 4:15.85, **3000m**: Shitaye Eshete BRN 8:49.27*, **60mh**: Wu Shujiao CHN 8.24*, **HJ**: Zheng Xingjuan CHN 1.92, **PV**: Li Ling CHN 4.50*, **LJ**: Lu Minjia CHN 6.33, **TJ**: Xi Limei CHN 14.06, **SP**: Liu Xiangrong CHN 18.37*, **Pen**: Irina Karpova KAZ 4050, **4x400m**: CHN 3:40.34. **Medal Table Leaders**: CHN 14G-9S-10B, IRI 3-2-2, BRN 3-1-2, KAZ 2-3-2, QAT 1-2-0, KUW 1-1-1, KSA 1-0-0, JPN 0-2-3; 16 nations won medals.

66th Balkan Championships

At Eskisehir, Turkey 21-22 July
Men: 1. ROU 187, 2. TUR 180, 3. GRE 163, 4. BUL 158, 5. SRB 136, 6. MKD 87, 7. ALB 37, 8. BIH 22, 9. MDA 17, 10. MNE 15. **100m**: Darko Sarovic SRB

10.76, **200m**: Petar Kremenski BUL 20.99w, **400m**: Mehmet Güzel TUR 47.16, **800m**: Amel Tuka BIH 1:49.36, **1500m**: Andréas Dimitrákis GRE 4:03.89, **3000m**: Cihat Ulus TUR 8:30.77, **5000m**: Vedat Günen TUR 14:48.40, **3000mSt**: Hakan Duvar TUR 8:58.04, **110mh**: Milan Ristic SRB 13.95w, **400mh**: Spiridon Papadopoúlos GRE 51.43, **HJ**: Mihai Donisan ROU 2.27, **PV**: Bogdan Popa ROU 5.00, **LJ**: Adrian Vasile ROU 7.79, **TJ**: Dimítrios Tsiámis GRE 16.64w, **SP**: Hüseyin Atici TUR 19.87, **DT**: Sergiu Ursu ROU 59.51, **HT**: Fatih Eryildirim TUR 71.02, **JT**: Dejan Mileusnic BIH 75.23, **4x100m/4x400m**: GRE 40.34/3:10.53; **Women**: 1. ROU 184, 2. GRE 181, 3. TUR 178, 4. SRB 146, 5. BUL 138, 6. MKD 68, 7. BIH 56, 8. ALB 20, 9. MDA 10. **100m**: María Gátou GRE 11.49w, **200m**: Alina Panainte ROU 24.10, **400m**: Sanda Belgyan ROU 53.85, **800m**: Dorina Köröszi ROU 2:06.37, **1500m/3000m**: Amela Terzic SRB 4:24.06/9:24.79, **5000m**: Milena Rmandic SRB 17:13.06, **3000mSt**: Athína Koíni GRE 10:28.22, **100mh**: Nevin Yanit TUR 12.61, **400mh**: Sema Apak TUR 57.43, **HJ**: Burcu Ayhan TUR 1.90, **PV**: Loréla Mánou GRE 4.40, **LJ**: Emel Güngör TUR 6.34w, **TJ**: Gita Dodova BUL 13.44, **SP**: Anca Heltne ROU 16.40, **DT**: Hrisoúla Anagnostopoúlou GRE 56.82, **HT**: Ilana Korosídou GRE 62.20, **JT**: Aggelíki Tsiolakoúdi GRE 53.06, **4x100m**: TUR 45.61, **4x400m**: ROU 3:35.91.
Walks: At *Bucuresti, Romania 7 April.* **20km**: Predrag Filipovic SRB 1:28:50; **Women 20km**: Ana Rodean ROU 1:35:19.
Half Marathon: *At Kavarna, Bulgaria 1 Sep.* Vitalie Gheorghita MDA 1:10:48; Women: Sladjana Perunovic (Mne) 1:22:41.
Marathon: *At Belgrade, Serbia 21 Apr.* Ercan Musliu TUR 2:28:15.

Central American Walks Champs

At Cartago, CRC 24 March
20km: Anibal Paau GUA 1:26:13; **Women 10km**: Ilena Ocampo CRC 64:24.

Central American & Caribbean Junior Championships 2012

At San Salvador, El Salvador 20 June 1 July
Men: **100m**: Teray Smith BAR 10.58, **200m/400m**: Yoandys Lescay CUB 20.87/46.17, **800m/1500m**: Wesley Vázquez PUR 1:46.89/3:53.91, **5000m**: Víctor Montañez MEX 15:14.92, **10,000m**: Víctor Santana PUR 32:18.10, **3000mSt**: Néstor Mijangos GUA 9:50.88, **110mh-J**: Yordan O'Farrill CUB 13.27, **400mh**: Jarvarn Gallimore JAM 50.83, **HJ**: Kemar Jones BAR 1.90, **PV**: Víctor Castillero MEX 4.60, **LJ**: Clive Pullen JAM 7.20, **TJ**: Pedro Pichardo CUB 16.40, 6k **SP**: Ashinia Miller JAM 19.90*, 1.75kg **DT**: Fedrick Dacres JAM 59.99*, 6k **HT**: Diego Del Real MEX 73.96*, **JT**: Keshorn Walcott TRI 82.83*, J-**Dec**: Lindon Toussaint GRN 6455, **10,000mW**: Jesús Vega MEX 42:03.68, **4x100m/4x400m**: JAM 39.39*/3:08.94. **Women**: **100m/200m**: Fanny Chalas DOM 11.53/23.79, **400m**:

Olivia James JAM 53.89, **800m**: Desreen Montague JAM 2:06.43, **1500m/5000m**: Alexis Panisse DOM 4:36.33/17:55.67, **3000m/3000mSt**: Leila Mantilla PUR 10:09.50/11:11.91, **100mh**: Sade-Mariah Greenidge BAR 13.48, **400mh**: Kenesha Spann TRI 59.09, **HJ**: Jeannelle Scheper LCA 1.85, **PV**: Diamara Planell PUR 3.95, **LJ**: Tamara Myers BAH 6.02, **TJ**: Liuba Zaldívar CUB 13.78, **SP**: Racquel Williams BAH 13.54, **DT**: Tara-Sue Barnett JAM 49.62, **HT**: Yolanda González MEX 52.89, **JT**: Lismania Muñoz CUB 55.20*, **Hep**: Shavonte Bradshaw BAR 4365, **5000mW**: Alejandra Ortega MEX 23:21.71, **4x100m/4x400m**: JAM 44.51/3:37.31. **Medal table leaders** (U20 & U17): JAM 20G-15S-9B, MEX 11-6-2, TRI 8-6-9, PUR 7-10-7, CUB 7-4-1, BAR 6-6-6, BAH 5-10-13, DOM 5-2-4, BER 2-1-2, ESA 1-3-7, AIA 1-3-0, GUA 1-2-7.

European Winter Throwing Cup 2012

At Bar, Montenegro 17-18 March
Men: 1. RUS 4342, 2. ITA 4203, 3. EST 4010, 4. ROU 3983, 5. UKR 3976, 6. BIH 3309. **SP**: 1. Marco Fortes POR 20.02, 2. Asmir Kolasinac SRB 20.50, 3. Borja Vivas ESP 20.06; **DT**: 1. Erik Cadée NED 64.09, 2. Ercüment Olgundeniz TUR 63.59, 3. Rutger Smith NED 63.30; **HT**: 1. Kirill Ikonnikov RUS 75.95, 2. Sergey Kalomoyets BLR 75.15, 3. Kristóf Németh HUN 74.23; **JT**: 1. Fatih Avan TUR 81.09, 2. Dmitriy Tarabin RUS 79.94, 3. Risto Mätas EST 78.74; **U23**: 1. UKR 4018, 2. RUS 3995, 3. BLR 3758. **Women**: 1, RUS 4424, 2. FRA 4193, 3. GBR 4055, 4. UKR 4050, 5. ITA 4031, 6. ROU 3707, 7. BIH 3033; **SP**: 1. Nadezhda Ostapchuk BLR 20.29, 2. Nadine Kleinert GER 19.12, 3. Josephine Terlecki GER 18.59; **DT**: 1. Nadine Müller GER 68.89, 2. Darya Pishchalnikova RUS 63.86, 3. Mélina Robert-Michon FRA 63.03; **HT**: 1. Zalina Marghieva MDA 73.60, 2. Tatyana Lysenko RUS 72.87, 3. Stéphanie Falzon FRA 72.60; **JT**: 1. Martina Ratej SLO 63.59, 2. Goldie Sayers GBR 62.75, 3. Marina Maksimova RUS 60.33; **U23**: 1. UKR 3950, 2. GER 3815, 3. RUS 3732; **DT**: Sandra Perkovic CRO 67.19.

European Cup 10,000m 2012

At Bilbao, Spain 3 June
Men: 1. Polat Kemboi Arikan TUR 27:56.28, 2. Ayad Lamdassem ESP 28:04.22, 3. Carles Castillejo ESP 28:07.50; Team: 1. ESP 1:24:45.71, 2. POR 1:26:13.34, 3, FRA 1:26:33.60. **Women**: 1. Sara Moreira POR 31:23.61. 2. Jo Pavey GBR 31:32.22, 3. Christelle Daunay FRA 21:35.81; Team: 1. GBR 1:36:25.47, 2. ITA 1:36:40.13, 3. POR 1:36:51.26.

Ibero-American Championships 2012

At Barquisimeto, Venezuela 8-10 June
Men: **100m/200m**: Alex Quiñónez ECU 10.33/20.34, **400m**: Ânderson Henriques BRA 45.59, **800m**: Andy González CUB 1:46.91, **1500m**: Leandro Oliveira BRA 3:47.76, **3000m**: Víctor Aravena CHI 8:04.46, **5000m**: Marvin Blanco VEN 14:19.89, **3000mSt**: José Gregorio Peña VEN 8:37.67, **110mh**: Ignacio Morales CUB 13.54, **400mh**: Eric Alejandro PUR 49.36, **HJ**: Wanner

Miller COL 2.28, **PV**: Germán Chiaraviglio ARG 5.40, **LJ**: Georni Jaramillo VEN 8.02w, **TJ**: Yoandri Betanzos CUB 16.75w, **SP/DT**: Germán Lauro ARG 20.13/63.55, **HT**: Roberto Janet CUB 72.78, **JT**: Braian Toledo ARG 77.33, **Dec**: Luíz Alberto de Araújo BRA 7772, **20,000mW**: James Rendón COL 1:26:12.1, **4x100m**: BRA 38.95; **4x400m**: CUB 3:00.43. **Women**: **100m**: Rosângela Santos BRA 11.41, **200m**: Evelyn dos Santos BRA 22.99, **400m**: Daysurami Bonne CUB 52.27, **800m**: Rosibel García COL 2:03.00, **1500m**: Adriana Muñoz CUB 4:20.36, **3000m**: Tatiele de Carvalho BRA 9:20.07, **5000m**: Sandra López MEX 16:10.77, **3000mSt**: Yoni Ninahuamán PER 10:24.95, **100mh**: Eliecit Palacios COL 13.15, **400mh**: Lucimar Teodoro BRA 56.99, **HJ**: Romary Rifka MEX 1.89, **PV**: Dailis Caballero CUB 4.50, **LJ**: Eliane Martins BRA 6.55, **TJ**: Susana Costa POR 13.78, **SP**: Geisa Arcanjo BRA 18.84, **DT**: Andressa de Morais BRA 64.21, **HT**: Rosa Rodríguez VEN 71.76*, **JT**: Flor Denis Ruíz COL 58.21, **Hep**: Lucimara da Silva BRA 6160*, **10,000mW**: Arabelly Orjuela COL 46:21.88, **4x100m/4x400m**: BRA 43.90/3:28.56. **Medal table leaders**: BRA 14G-17S-13B, CUB 8-6-4, COL 6-3-5, VEN 4-4-2, ARG 4-3-2; 11 nations won gold, 17 won medals.

NACAC (U23) Championships 2012

At Irapuato, Mexico (1800mA) 6-8 July
Men: **100m**: Jason Rogers SKN 10.06, **200m**: Tremaine Harris CAN 20.22, **400m**: David Verburg USA 45.14, **800m**: Michael Preble USA 1:48.69, **1500m**: Kyle Merber USA 3:51.61, **5000m**: Andrew Bayer USA 15:13.01, **10,000m**: Gabe Proctor USA 30:46.85, **3000mSt**: Luis Gallegos MEX 9:22.75, **110mh**: Shane Brathwaite BAR 13.31, **400mh**: Jeffrey Gibson BAH 50.27, **HJ**: Edgar Rivera MEX 2.23, **PV**: Michael Woepse USA 5.40, **LJ**: Marquis Dendy USA 7.68, **TJ**: Chris Phipps USA 16.19, **SP**: Jacob Thormaehlen USA 19.86, **DT**: Traves Smikle JAM 62.11, **HT**: Jeremy Postin USA 68.32, **JT**: Tim Glover USA 78.28, **Dec**: Jack Szmansan USA 7061, **20,000mW**: Evan Dunfee CAN 1:26:15.32, **4x100m/4x400m**: USA 38.94/3:03.81; **Women**: **100m**: Aurieyall Scott USA 11.19, **200m**: Kimberlyn Duncan USA 22.72, **400m**: Rebecca Alexander USA 51.13, **800m**: Chanelle Price USA 2:04.48, **1500m**: Jordan Hasay USA 4:22.16, **5000m**: Karla Díaz MEX 16:54.83, **10,000m**: Sarah Callister USA 35:46.12, **3000mSt**: Alyssa Kulik USA 10:21.04, **100mh**: Brianna Rollins USA 12.60w, **400mh**: Cassandra Tate USA 55.62, **HJ**: Tynita Butts USA 1.82, **PV**: Mélanie Blouin CAN 4.36, **LJ**: Christabel Nettey CAN 6.18, **TJ**: Andrea Geubelle USA 13.14, **SP**: Brittany Smith USA 17.03, **DT**: Anna Jelmini USA 53.93, **HT**: Amanda Bingson USA 71.39, **JT**: Abigail Gómez MEX 56.89, **Hep**: Kiani Profit USA 5653, **10,000mW**: María Mena MEX 52:52.54, **4x100m/4x400m**: USA 43.58/3:28.64.

South American Marathon Champs

At Caracas, VEN 26 February
Men: José David Cardona COL 2:19:18; **Women**: Conçeicão Carvalho BRA 2:53:15.

South American Walks Champs

At Salinas, Ecuador 17-18 March
Men: **20km**: Caio Bonfim BRA 1:23:59; **50km**: Mário José dos Santos BRA 4:12:52; **Women 20km**: Arabelly Orjuela COL 1:34:41; **Junior**: **Men 10km**: Eider Arévalo COL 43:25, **Women 10km**: Lorena Arenas 45:17; **Youth**: **Men 10km**: Paolo Yurivilca PER 45:00, **Women 10km**: Karla Jaramillo ECU 24:49.

South American U23 Championships 2012

At São Paulo, Brazil 10-12 September
Men: **100m/200m**: Aldemir da Silva BRA 10.42/20.51*, **400m**: Pedro de Oliveira BRA 45.52*, **800m**: Tomás Squella CHI 1:48.06, **1500m**: Federico Bruno ARG 3:47.13; **5000m/10,000m**: Víctor Aravena CHI 14:16.25/30:31.93, **3000mSt**: Alexis Peña VEN 8:53.42, **110mh**: João de Oliveira BRA 14.14, **400mh**: Hederson Estefani BRA 51.02, **HJ**: Talles Silva BRA 2.21*, **PV**: Matheus da Silva BRA 5.05, **LJ**: Rebert Firmiano BRA 7.96w, **TJ**: Jonathan Silva BRA 16.19, **SP**: Darlan Romani BRA 19.93*, **DT**: Mauricio Ortega COL 53.94, **HT**: Allan Wolski BRA 63.20, **JT**: Braian Toledo ARG 78.49*, **Dec**: Guillermo Ruggeri ARG 7196, **20,000mW**: Caio Bonfim BRA 1:23:22.83*; **4x100m/4x400m**: BRA 40.10/3:07.44. **Women**: **100m**: Vanusa dos Santos BRA 11.72, **200m**: Nercelys Soto VEN 23.40, **400m**: Yenifer Padilla COL 53.12*, **800m**: Jéssica dos Santos BRA 2:07.42, **1500m**: Erika Lima BRA 4:26.29, **5000m**: Yoni Ninahuamán PER 16:50.21, **10,000m**: Florencia Borelli ARG 35:29.08, **3000mSt**: Zulema Arenas PER 10:14.52*, **100mh**: Nelsibeth Villalobos VEN 14.48, **400mh**: Déborah Rodríguez URU 57.63*, **HJ**: Kashani Ríos PAN 1.76, **PV**: Sara Pereira BRA 3.90, **LJ**: Jéssica dos Reis BRA 6.18, **TJ**: Giselle Landázury COL 13.31, **SP**: Geisa Arcanjo BRA 18.43*, **DT**: Andressa de Morais BRA 57.66*, **HT**: Zuleima Mina ECU 62.59, **JT**: Jucilene de Lima BRA 56.00, **Hep**: Vanesa Spínola BRA 5899*, **20,000mW**: Yeseida Carrillo COL 1:38:29.51*, **4x100m**: CHI 45.61, **4x400m**: BRA 3:41.16.
Medal Table: BRA 24G-14S-14B, COL 4-7-3, ARG 4-5-8, CHI 4-5-4, VEN 3-8-14, PER 2-3-3, ECU 1-1-2, URU 1-0-2, PAN 1-0-0, BOL 0-1-1, GUY 0-0-2, PAR 0-0-1.

21st South American Youth Championships 2012

At Ciudad de Mendoza, Argentina 26-28 October
Men: **100m/200m**: Arturo Deliser PAN 10.95/21.31, **400m**: William Landázury COL 48.88, **800m**: Jorge Collares URU 1:51.69, **1500m**: Eric Pomaski ARG 4:05.28, **3000m**: André do Rosário BRA 8:34.47, **2000m St**: Mateo Rossetto ARG 6:07.55, 0.914m **110mh**: João Gabriel Bento BRA 14.14, 0.84m **400mh**: Wilson Bello VEN 52.62, **HJ**: Yohan Chaverra COL 2.10*, **PV**: Matías Guerrero CHI 4.40, **LJ**: Gabriel Constantino BRA 7.35, **TJ**: Mateus Daniel de Sá BRA 15.26, 5kg **SP**: Felipe Leal BRA 18.23, 1.5kg **DT**: Giovanni Bonilla CHI 57.00, 5kg **HT**: Joaquín Gómez ARG 81.15 CR, 700g **JT**: Alesander Valencia COL 64.08, **Oct**: Jefferson Santos BRA 6141*, **Medley Relay**: BRA (Jonatan Rodrigues, Vitor Hugo dos Santos, Gabriel

dos Santos, Rafael Peres) 1:55.50, **10,000mW**: Brayan Fuentes COL 47:05.21. **Women: 100m**: Tamiris de Liz BRA 11.99, **200m**: Letícia de Souza BRA 24.30, **400m**: Zulley Torres COL 55.20, **800m**: Ana Karolyne Silva 2:12.60, **1500m**: Marguie Ryvera COL 4:37.58, **3000m**: Evelyn Escobar PER 10:09.88, **2000m St**: Zulema Arenas PER 6:40.28*, 0.76m **100mh**: Génesis Romero VEN 14.32, **400mh**: Briannill Cardonna VEN 61.49, **HJ**: Ana Paula de Oliveira BRA 1.76 CR, **PV**: Noelina Madarieta ARG 3.65, **LJ**: Gabriele dos Santos BRA 5.79, **TJ**: Ingrid Lira BRA 12.54, 3kg **SP/DT**: Izabella da Silva BRA 16.82*/47.19, 3kg **HT**: Ana María Vásquez PER 61.19*, 500g **JT**: Laura Paredes PAR 45.81*, **Hep**: Leonela Graciani ARG 5090, **Medley Relay**: VEN (Aries Sánchez, Jhoanmy Luque, Génesis Romero, Briannill Cardonna) 2:13.12, **5000m Walk**: Stefany Coronado BOL 25:16.33.

2nd West Asian Championships 2012

At Dubai, United Arab Emirates 12–15 December
Men: 100m: Barakat Al-Harthy OMA 10.39, **200m**: Reza Ghasemi IRI 21.04, **400m**: Ma'youf Hassan Ahmed UAE 46.99, **800m**: Karar Abdelzehra IRQ 1:51.40, **1500m**: Omar Awadh Al-Rashidi KUW 3:56.04, **5000m**: Qais Salim Al-Mahrooqi OMA 16:05.57, **10,000m/HMar**: Methgal Marouf Abu Drais JOR 33:18.45/67:38, **3000mSt**: Hossein Keyhani IRI 8:55.59, **110mh**: Abdulaziz Al-Mandeel KUW 13.68, **400mh**: Jamal Abdelnaser Omar QAT 51.87, **HJ**: Moataz Essa Barshim QAT 2.32, **PV**: Fahed Bader Al-Mershad KUW 4.90, **LJ**: Ali Reza Habibi IRI 7.38, **TJ**: Mohamed Abbas Abd. Darwish UAE 16.20, **SP**: Ahmed Abd.Hassan Gholoum KUW 18.97, **DT**: Mohamed Samimi IRI 62.36, **HT**: Ali Mohamed Al-Zankawi KUW 76.14, **JT**: Ammar Makki Al-Najm IRQ 69.31, **Dec**: Abdoljalil Toomaj IRI 6611, **20kW**: Mabrouk Saleh Nasser QAT 1:32:02, **4x100m**: IRI 40.26, **4x400**m: UAE 3:10.80, **Women: 100m**: Danah Hussein Abdulrazzak IRQ 11.91, **200m/400m**: Gretta Taslakian LIB 24.16/54.13, **800m/1500m**: Mariam Abdallah Mubarak (Betlhem Desalegn Belayneh) UAE 2;14.30/4:32.92, **5000m/10,000m**: Alia Mohamed Saeed UAE 16:20.62/34:23.72, **3000mSt**: Fatima Ghassan Rayya SYR 11:45.64, **100mh**: Buthayna Ayed Al-Yacoobi OMA 15.21, **400mh**: Mahlaghaa Khanbashi IRI 65.82, **HJ/Hep**: Sepideh Tavakoli IRI 1.70/4802, **PV**: Diana Al-Khawasnah JOR 3.00, **LJ/TJ**: Jawaher Zamani IRI 5.46/12.03, **SP/DT**: Leila Rajabi IRI 16.96/ 41.21, **HT**: Parinaz Ebrahimi IRI 44.64, **JT**: Amine Amiri IRI 42.97, **10kW**: Rania Othman SYR 61:31, **4x100**: LIB 49.01, **4x400m**: IRI 4:05.57.

26th IAU World 100km Championships 2012

At Seregno, Italy 22 April. Incorporated European Championships
Men: 1. Giorgio Calcaterra ITA 6:23:22, 2. Jonas Buud SWE 6:28:58, 3. Alberico Di Cecco ITA 6:40:32, 4. Asier Cuevas ESP 6:44:54, 5. David Riddle USA 6:45:19, 6. André Collet FRA 6:45:49, 7. Jon Olsen USA 6:48:51; Team: 1. ITA 20:06:41; 2. USA 20:23:09; 3. FRA 20:58:44; 4, GER 21:17:50; 5, NOR 21:22:35; **Women:** 1. Amy Sproston USA 7:34:07, 2. Kajsa Berg SWE (1 EUR) 7:35:21, 3. Irina Vishnevskaya RUS (2 EUR) 7:35:57, 4. Meghan Arbogast USA 7:41:52, 5. Pam Smith USA 7:43:04, 6. Judit Földing Nagy HUN (3 EUR) 7:43:55, 7. Mami Kudo JPN 7:48:05; **Team**: 1. USA 22:59:03, 2. JPN 23:44:02, 3. RUS (1 EUR) 24:02:28, 4. ITA (2 EUR) 24:53:14, 5. GER (3 EUR) 25:46:44.

IAU 24 Hour World Championships 2012

At Katowice, Poland 8-9 September. Incorporated European Championships.
Men: 1. Mike Morton USA 277.543k, 2. Florian Reus GER (1 EUR) 261.718, 3. Ludovic Dilmi FRA (2 EUR) 257.819, 4. Ryo Abiko JPN 255.487, 5. Piotr Sawicki POL (3 EUR) 254.093; **Team**: 1. GER 759.457, 2. FRA 756.710, 3. USA 754,.86, 4. POL (3 EUR) 741.267, 5. JPN 738.566. **Women**: 1. Michaela Dimitraidu CZE (1 EUR) 244.232, 2. Connie Gardner USA 240.385, 3. Emily Gelder GBR (2 EUR) 238.875, 4. Cécile Nissen FRA (3 EUR) 234.524, 5. Suzanna Bon USA 231.074; **Team**: 1. USA 694.620, 2. FRA (1 EUR) 666,503, 3. GBR (2 EUR) 666.461, 4. GER (3 EUR) 651.221, 5. SWE 649.297.

World Mountain Running Championships 2012

At Ponte Di Legno, Italy 2 September
Men 14.1k (1150m height difference): 1. Petro Mamu ERI 61:34, 2. Azeria Teklay ERI 62:47, 3. Andrey Safronov RUS 63:06; Team: 1. ERI 17, 2. ITA 31, 3. RUS 75; **Junior Men** 8.8k, 760m HD: Michael Cherop UGA 42:33; Team: UGA 13; **Women** 8.8k, 760m HD: 1. Andrea Mayr AUT (4th win) 46:35, 2. Valentina Bellotti ITA 47:04, 3. Morgan Aritola USA 47:26; Team: 1. USA 18, 2. ITA 29, 3. SUI 58; **Junior Women** 3.9k, 310m HD: Sevilay Eytemis TUR 20:14; Team: TUR 9.

European Mountain Racing Championships 2012

At Denizli-Pamukkale, Turkey 7 July
Men 12.2k (715m height difference): 1. Ahmet Arslan TUR (sixth successive win) 49:46, 2. Ercan Muslu TUR 49:47, 3. Ionat Zinca ROU 50:19; Team: 1. ITA 16, 2. TUR 19, 3. FRA 48, **Junior Men** 8.3k (480m HD): Ahmet Özrek TUR 35:18; Team: TUR 9. **Women** 8.3k (480m HD): 1. Monika Fürholz SUI 39:54, 2. Nadezhda Leshchinskaya RUS 40:03, 3. Pavla Schoma CZE 40:07; Team: 1. GBR 20, 2, ITA 20, 3. RUS 30. **Junior Women** 4.4k (240m HD): Annabel Mason GBR 20:25, Team: TUR 5.

IAAF DIAMOND LEAGUE

The IAAF's successor to the Golden League, the expanded and more globally widespread Diamond League, was launched in 2010 with 14 meetings spread across Asia, Europe, the Middle East and the USA. The total prize money was increased from $6.63 million (with a $50,000 bonus for any new world record) in 2010 to $8 million in 2011 and 2012 and winners of each Race received a Diamond Trophy (4 carats of diamonds) and a $40,000 cash prize.

SAMSUNG DIAMOND LEAGUE – winners 2012

D Doha May 11, **Sh** Shanghai May 19, **R** Rome May 31, **E** Eugene Jun 2, **O** Oslo Jun 7, **NY** New York Jun 9, **P** Paris Saint-Denis Jul 6, **CP** London (CP) Jul 13-14; **M** Monaco Jul 20, **St** Stockholm Aug 17, **L** Lausanne Aug 23, **Bi** Birmingham Aug 26; Finals at: **Z** Zürich Aug 30, **Br** Brussels Sep 7.

Men
100m: Asafa Powell Sh- 10.02; Usain Bolt R- 9.76, O- 9.79. Br- 9.86; Tyson Gay P- 9.99, CP- 10.03; Ryan Bailey St- 9.93

200m: Walter Dix D- 20.02; Wallace Spearmon E- 20.27; Churandy Martina NY- 19.94; Nickel Ashmeade M- 20.02, Bi- 20.12; Usain Bolt L- 19.58, Z- 19.56

400m: LaShawn Merrit D- 44.19, E- 44.91; Luguelin Santos NY- 45.14; Jacques Borlée M- 44.74; Kirani James L- 44.37; Angelo Taylor Bi- 44.93; Kevin Borlée Br- 44.75

800m: Leonard Kosencha Sh- 1:46.04; Abubaker Kaki E- 1:43.71; David Rudisha NY- 1:41.74, P- 1:41.54; Adam Kszczot POL CP- 1:44.49; Mohammed Aman St- 1:43.56, Z- 1:42.53

1500m/1M: Silas Kiplagat D- 3:29.63, L- 3:31.78, Br- 3:31.98 Asbel Kiprop E- 3:49.40M, O- 3:49.22, M- 3:28.88; Mekonnen Gebremedhin Bi- 3:34.80

3/5000m: Hagos Gebrehiwot Sh- 13:11.00; Mo Farah E- 12:56.98; Dejen Gebremeskel O- 12:58.92, P- 12:46.81; Mo Farah CP- 13:06.04; Isiah Koech St- 7:30.43, Z- 12:58.98

3000mSt: Paul K Koech D- 7:56.58, R- 7:54.31, P- 8:00.57, L-8:05.80; Consesius Kipruto M- 8:03.49; Jairus Birech Bi- 8:20.27; Brimin Kipruto Br- 8:03.11

110mh: Liu Xiang Sh- 12.97, E- 12.87w; Jason Richardson NY- 13.18, L- 13.08; Aries Merritt M- 12.93, Bi- 12.95, Br- 12.80

400mh: Angelo Taylor Sh- 48.98, Z- 48.29; Javier Culson R- 48.14, O- 47.92, P- 47.78, CP- 47.78; Michael Tinsley St- 48.50

HJ: Dimitríos Hondrokúkis D- 2.32, Robbie Grabarz R- 2.33, Bi- 2.32; Jesse Williams NY- 2.36, M- 2.33; Mutaz Essa Barshim L- 2.39, Ivan Ukhov Z- 2.31

PV: Yang Yansheng Sh- 5.65 ; Renaud Lavillenie R- 5.82, O- 5.82, P- 5.77, L- 5.80. Z- 5.70; Björn Otto CP- 5.74

LJ: Aleksandr Menkov D- 8.22, Bi- 8.18, Br- 8.29; Greg Rutherford R- 8.32; Mitchell Watt NY- 8.16, CP- 8.28; Irving Saladino M- 8.16

TJ: Phillips Idowu Sh- 17.24; Christian Taylor E- 17.62, CP- 17.41, St- 17.11; Lyukman Adams O- 17.09; Leevan Sands P- 17.23; Fabrizio Donato Z- 17.29

SP: Reese Hoffa Sh- 20.98, E- 21.81, CP- 21.34, St- 21.24, Z- 21.64; Tomasz Majewski O- 21.36; Dylan Armstrong P- 20.54

DT: Piotr Malachowski D- 67.53; Ehsan Hadadi IRI 66.73; Zoltán Kövágó 66.36; Gerd Kanter CP- 64.85, L- 65.79, Br- 66.84; Robert Harting Bi- 66.64

JT: Vitezslav Vesely Sh- 85.40, O- 88.11; Vadims Vasilevskis 84.65; Oleksandr Pyatnytsa P- 85.67, M- 82.85; Tero Pitkämäki St- 86.98, Z- 85.27

Women
100m: Allyson Felix D- 10.92; Murielle Ahouré Sh- 11.00; Shelly-Ann Fraser-Pryce NY- 10.92, Z- 10.83; Blessing Okagbare M- 10.96; Carmelita Jeter L- 10.86, Bi- 10.81

200m: Veronica Campbell-Brown Sh- 22.50; Allyson Felix E- 22.53; Murielle Ahouré O- 22.42, P- 22.55; Charonda Williams CP- 22.75, St- 22.82; Myriam Soumaré Br- 22.63

400m: Noelene Williams-Mills Sh- 50.00; Sanya Richards-Ross E- 49.39, St- 49.89, Z- 50.21; Amantle Montsho O- 49.68, P- 49.77; Christine Ohuruogu CP- 50.42

800m: Pamela Jelimo D- 1:56.94, L- 1:57.59; Fantu Magiso R- 1:57.56, NY- 1:57.48; Yelena Kofanova M- 1:58.41; Mariya Savinova Bi- 2:00.40; Francine Niyonsaba Br- 1:56.59

1500m: Genzebe Dibaba Sh- 3:57.77; Abeba Aregawi R- 3:56.54, O- 4:02.42, Z- 4:05.29; Asli Cakir P- 3:56.62 (Mariem Selsouli 3:56.15 drugs dq); Maryam Jamal CP- 4:06.78, St- 4:01.19

3/5000m: Vivian Cheruiyot D- 8:46.44, R- 14:35.62, Br- 14:46.01; Tirunesh Dibaba NY- 14:50.80; Mercy Cherono M- 8:38.51, L- 8:40.59, Bi- 8:41.21

3000mSt: Milcah Chemos Sh- 9:15.81, E- 9:13.69, O- 9:07.14; Habiba Ghribi P- 9:28.81; Anuta Bobocel CP- 9:27.24; Yuliya Zaripova St- 9:05.02; Etenesh Diro Z- 9:24.97

100mh: Brigitte Foster-Hylton D- 12.60; Dawn Harper R- 12.66, St- 12.65, Z- 12.59; Sally Pearson O- 12.49, P- 12.40; Kellie Wells CP- 12.57

400mh: Michele Walker D- 54.62; Kaliese Spencer R- 54.39, L- 53.49, Bi- 53.78, Br- 53.59; T'Erea Brown NY- 54.85; Zuzana Hejnová M- 54.12

HJ: Chaunté Lowe Sh- 1.92, O- 1.97, P- 1.97, CP- 2.00; Anna Chicherova E- 2.02, St- 2.00; Svetlana Shkolina Br- 2.00

PV: Anastasiya Savchenko D- 4.57; Fabiana Murer E- 4.63, NY- 4.77; Silke Spiegelburg M- 4.82, Br- 4.75; Yarisley Silva St- 4.70; Jennifer Suhr Bi- 4.65

LJ: Janay DeLoach Sh- 6.73; Shara Proctor E- 6.84; Olga Kucherenko O- 6.96w; Yelena Sokolova P- 6.70. St- 6.82, L- 6.89, Z- 6.92

TJ: Olga Rypakova D- 14.33, NY- 14.71, L- 14.68, Br- 14.72; Olga Saladuha R- 14.75, Bi- 14.40; Caterine Ibargüen M- 14.85

SP: Nadezhda Ostapchuk D- 20.53; Valerie Adams R- 21.03, NY- 20.60, St- 20.26, L- 20.95, Bi- 20.52, Z- 20.81

DT: Sandra Perkovic Sh- 68.24, E- 66.92, O- 64.89, M- 65.29, St- 68.77, Z- 63.97; Dani Samuels P- 61.81

JT: Mariya Abakumova D- 66.86; Barbora Spotáková R- 68.65, L- 67.19, Bi- 66.08, Br- 66.91; Sunette Viljoen NY- 69.35; Goldie Sayers CP- 66.17

FINAL PLACINGS 2012

Men: 100m: 1. Bolt 16, 2. Nesta Carter 8, 3. Bailey 6; **200m:** 1. Ashmeade 16, 2. Bolt 12, 3. Martina 12; **400m:** 1. K Borlée 10, 2. Santos 10, 3. J Borlée 9; **800m:** 1. Aman 14, 2. Rudisha 12, 3. Kosencha 6; **1500m:** 1. Kiplagat 16, 2. Kiprop 14, 3. Gebremedhin 13; **5000m:** 1. I Koech 15, 2. Gebremeskel 8, 3. Thomas Longosiwa 6; **3000mSt:** 1. Koech 20, 2. B Kipruto 10, 3. C Kipruto 8; **110mh:** 1. Merritt 18, 2. Richardson 18, 3. David Oliver 5; **400mh:** 1. Culson 16, 2. Taylor 13, 3. Tinsley 4; **HJ:** 1. Grabarz 17, 2. Williams 12, 3. Ukhov 12; **PV:** 1. Lavillenie 24, 2. Björn Otto 11, 3. Malte Mohr 6; **LJ:** 1. Menkov 17, 2. Khotso Mokoena 7, 3. Sergey Morgunov 4; **TJ:** 1. Taylor 19, 2. Donato 8, 3. Sheryf El-Sheryf 3; **SP:** 1. Hoffa 24, 2. Majewski 12, 3. Armstrong 10; **DT:** 1. Kanter 19, 2. Virgilijus Alekna 7, 3. Martin Wierig 4; **JT:** 1. Vesely 14, 2. Pitkämäki 12, 3. Pyatnytsya 11. **Women: 100m:** 1. Fraser-Pryce 19, 2. Jeter 13, 3. Felix 6; **200m:** 1. C Williams 12, 2. Soumaré 8, 3. Anneisha McLaughlin 6; **400m:** 1. Montsho 20, 2. Richards-Ross 16, 3. Ohuruogu 5; **800m:** 1. Jelimo 16, 2. Niyonsaba 10, 3. Savinova 9; **1500m:** 1. Aregawi 21, 2. Jamal 8, 3. Mercy Cherono 4; **5000m:** 1. Cheruiyot 18, 2. M Cherono 16, 3. Sylvia Kibet 5; **3000mSt:** 1. Chemos 12, 2. Diro 9, 3. Sofia Assefa 7; **100mh:** 1. Harper 16, 2. Wells 12, 3. Queen Harrison 4; **400H:** 1. Spencer 24, 2. Perri Shakes-Drayton 8, 3. Hejnová 7; **HJ:** 1. Lowe 17, 2. Chicherova 13, 3. Shkolina 12; **PV:** 1. Spiegelburg 16, 2. Murer 14, 3. Silva 12; **LJ:** 1. Sokolova 22, 2. Shara Proctor 8, 3. DeLoach 8; **TJ:** 1. Rypakova 24, 2. Saladuha 14, 3. Kimberly Williams 6; **SP:** 1. Adams 28, 2. Michelle Carter 9, 3. Cleopatra Borel 3; **DT:** 1. Perkovic 30, 2. Yarelys Barrios 6, 3. Nadine Müller 5; **JT:** 1. Spotáková 26, 2. Viljoen 11, 3. Abakumova 6.

The calendar for 2013 is: Doha 10 May, Shanghai 18 May, New York 25 May, Eugene 1 Jun, Rome 6 Jun, Oslo 13 June, Birmingham 30 Jun, Lausanne 4 Jul, Paris Saint-Denis 6 July, Monaco 19 July, London 26-27 Jul, Stockholm 23 Aug, Zürich 29 Aug, Brussels 6 Sep.

MAJOR MEETINGS 2012-2013

DL – Diamond League, WC – World Challenge, EAP European Premium Meeting (EAC Classic).

Diamond League, World Challenge and European Athletics Premium Meetings

2012 date	Meeting		2013 date	
3 Mar	WC	Telstra Melbourne Track Classic, AUS	6 Apr	WC
5 May	WC	Jamaica International, JAM	4 May	WC
6 May	WC	Golden Grand Prix, Kawasaki, JPN , 2013 in Tokyo	5 May	WC
11 May	DL	Qatar Super Grand Prix, Doha, QAT	Cancelled	
16 May	WC	Colorful Daegu, Korea	16 May	WC
12 May	WC	GP Brasil de Atletismo, Rio de Janeiro BRA, 2013 Belem	19 May	WC
12 May	WC	Ponce Grand Prix, PUR	18 May	WC
19 May	DL	Shanghai Golden Grand Prix, CHN	18 May	DL
		Bejing, CHN	21 May	WC
9 Jun	DL	adidas Grand Prix, New York (RI), USA	25 May	DL
2 Jun	DL	Prefontaine Classic, Eugene, Oregon, USA	1 Jun	DL
31 May	DL	Golden Gala, Rome, ITA	6 Jun	DL
3 Jun	EAP	European Athletics Festival, Bydgoszcz, POL	8 Jun	EAP
5 Jun	EAP	Montreuil-sous-Bois, FRA	3 Jun	EAC
27 May	WC	Fanny Blankers-Koen Games, Hengelo, NED	8 Jun	WC
27 May	Afr	Mohammed VI d'Athlétisme, Rabat, MAR	9 Jun	WC
8 Jun	EAP	Memorial Primo Nebiolo, Turin, ITA	9 Jun	EAP
11 Jun	EAP	Josef Odlozil Memorial, Prague, CZE	10 Jun	EAP
11 Jun	WC	Moscow Challenge, RUS	11 Jun	WC
–		Dakar, SEN	12 Jun	WC
7 Jun	DL	Bislett Games, Oslo, NOR	13 Jun	DL
21 Jul	EAP	Janusz Kusocinski Memorial, Szczecin, POL	15 Jun	EAC
4 Jul	EAP	Ville de Reims, FRA	26 Jun	EAP
25 May	WC	Golden Spike, Ostrava, CZE	27 Jun	WC
9 Jun	EAP	Meeting Lille Metropole, Villeneuve d'Ascq, FRA	Cancelled	
26 Aug	DL	British Grand Prix, Birmingham, GBR	30 Jun	DL
8 Jul	EAP	Meeting Stanislas, Nancy (Tomblaine), FRA	2 Jul	EAC
23 Aug	DL	Athletissima, Lausanne, SUI	4 Jul	DL
6 Jul	DL	Meeting AREVA Paris Saint-Denis, FRA	6 Jul	DL
7 Jul	EAP	KBC Night of Athletics, Heusden-Zolder, BEL	13 Jul	EAP
–		Atletismo Madrid, ESP	13 Jul	WC
20 Jul	DL	Herculis, Monaco, MON	19 Jul	DL
13/14 Jul	DL	Aviva London Grand Prix, (CP) 2012, (OS) 2013, GBR	26/27 Jul	DL
17 Aug	SGP	DN Galan, Stockholm, SWE	22 Aug	DL
18-19 Aug		Hochsprung-Meeting, Eberstadt, GER	23-25 Aug	EPM

20 Aug	EAC	Gugl Games, Linz, AUT	26 Aug	EPM
30 Aug	GL	Weltklasse, Zürich, SUI	29 Aug	DL
2 Sep	WC	ISTAF, Berlin, GER	1 Sep	WC
4 Sep	WC	Zagreb, CRO	3 Sep	WC
4 Sep	EAP	Palio Citta della Quercia, Rovereto, ITA	3 Sep	EAP
7 Sep	DL	Van Damme Memorial, Brussels, BEL	6 Sep	DL
9 Sep	WC	Rieti, ITA	8 Sep	WC

INDOORS

2012 date   Meeting   2013 date

IAAF and EAA – respective indoor permit meetings; US USATF series in USA.

2012 date		Meeting	2013 date	
		International Games, Reykjavik, ISL	19 Jan	EAA
28 Jan	IAAF	US Open, New York, USA	25/26 Jan	IAAF
28 Jan		GBR-USA-RUS-GER-Comm. Select, Glasgow, GBR	26 Jan	EAA
3/4 Feb		International Combined Events, Tallinn, EST	1/2 Feb	EAA
4 Feb	US	New Balance Indoor GP, Boston (Roxbury), USA	2 Feb	US
4 Feb	EAA	Samsunggalan, Göteborg, SWE	—	
12 Feb	IAAF	BW-Bank Meeting, Karlsruhe, GER	2 Feb	IAAF
5 Feb	IAAF	Russian Winter, Moscow, RUS	3 Feb	IAAF
8 Feb		Europa HJ Meeting, Banská Bystrica, CZE	6 Feb	EAA
12 Feb	EAA	Samsung Pole Vault Stars, Donetsk, UKR	9 Feb	EAA
18 Feb		Flanders Indoor, Gent, BEL	10 Feb	IAAF
8 Feb	EAA	Pedro's Cup, Bydgoszcz, POL	12 Feb	EAA
14 Feb	IAAF	Meeting du Pas de Calais, Liévin, FRA		
11 Feb		Millrose Games, New York (Armory), USA	16 Feb	US
18 Feb	IAAF	Aviva Indoor Grand Prix, Birmingham, GBR	16 Feb	IAAF
23 Feb	IAAF	XL-Galan, Stockholm, SWE	21 Feb	IAAF
10 Feb	EAA	International PSD Bank, Düsseldorf, GER	10 Feb	EAA
11 Feb	US	USATF Classic, Fayetteville, USSR		
25-26 Feb	US	USA Indoor Championships. Albuquerque	1-3 Mar	US

IAAF WORLD COMBINED EVENTS CHALLENGE 2012 & 2013

5/6 May	Multistars, Desenzano del Garda, ITA (Firenze 2013)	4/5 May
26/27 May	Hypo-Mehrkampf Meeting, Götzis, AUT	25/26 May
9/10 Jun	TNT-Fortuna Meeting, Kladno, CZE	8/9 Jun
14/15 Jun	Erdgas DLV Mehrkampf, Ratingen, GER	15/16 Jun
15/16 Sep	Decastars, Talence, FRA	14/15 Sep

Plus International Games and Championships

IAAF WORLD RACE WALKING CHALLENGE 2012 & 2013

3 Mar	Chihuahua MEX	23 Feb
30 Mar	Taicang, CHN	1 Mar
15 Apr	Rio Maior, POR	15 Apr
17 Jun	Coppa Città di Sesto San Giovanni, ITA	1 May
9 Jun*	Gran Premio Cantones de La Coruña, ESP	1 Jun
14 Sep	Challenge Final: Edros CHN tbc 2013	Sep

* Race Walking Challenge Final

AFRICA 2012 CAA Permit Meetings

Brazzaville CGO 10 Jun, Radès TUN 16 Jun, Tanger MAR 7 Jul

ASIAN AA Grands Prix

2012: Bangkok 6 May, Kanchanaburi 9 May, Nokomratsima 13 May (all THA)
2013: Bangkok THA 30 Apr, Colombo SRI 4 May, Chennai IND 8 May

EUROPEAN AA CLASSIC MEETINGS 2013

(with 2012 dates of these meetings first)
See also above for EAP Meetings 2012 that are EAC 2013.

Riga LAT 5 Jun/30 May, Dessau GER 25/31 May, Kalamáta GRE 2/1 Jun, Velenje SLO 14/4 Jun, Huelva ESP 7/12 Jun, Göteborg SWE 14/15 Jun, Turku FIN (Paavo Nurmi Games) 13/16 Jun, Cagliari ITA -/26 Jun, Sollentuna SWE 5 Jul/27 Jun, Zhukovskiy RUS (Znamenskiy Memorial) 17/30 Jun, Sotteville-lès-Rouen 10/8 Jul, Budapest HUN (István Gyulai Memorial) 20 Aug/10 Jul, Luzern SUI 17/17 Jul, Karlstad SWE 19/25 Jul, Dubnica nad Váhom SVK (Athletic Bridge) 26/24 Aug, Padua ITA 2/1 Sep.
2012 only: Istanbul TUR (Cezmi Or Memorial) 9 Jun

NORTH AMERICA Premium Meetings 2012–2013 dates

Baie Mahault, Guadeloupe 1/8 May, Victoria CAN 13/8 Jun, Toronto 11 Jul/11 Jun, Vancouver CAN (Harry Jerome International) 10 Jun/1 Jul, Edmonton CAN 16 Jun/-, Halifax CAN 8/17 July, Moncton CAN 5/20 Jul

SOUTH AMERICA APM/SGP 2012–2013 dates

Mar del Plata ARG 28/21 Apr, Belém BRA 6/5 May, Fortaleza BRA 9/8 May, Uberlândia BRA 13/15 May, São Paulo BRA 16/19 May

MAJOR INTERNATIONAL EVENTS 2013–2019

European Indoor Championships – Göteborg, Sweden (1-3 March)
European Cup Winter Throwing – Castellón, Spain (16-17) March)
IAAF World Cross Country Championships – Bydgoszcz, Poland (24 March)
European Cup of Race Walking – Dudince, Slovakia (19 May)
European Cup 10,000m – Pravets, Bulgaria (8 June)
European Team Championships – Gateshead, GBR & 3 others (22-23 June)
Mediterranean Games – Mersin, Turkey (26-29 June)
European Cup Combined Events (29-30 June)
Asian Championships – Chennai, India (?)
World University Games – Kazan, Russia (7-12 July)
IAAF World Youth Championships – Donetsk, Ukraine (10-14 July)
European U23 Championships – Tampere, Finland (11-14 July)
Central American & Caribbean Championships – Port of Spain, Trinidad (12-14 July)
European Youth OLympic Festival – Utrecht, Netherlands (14-19 July)
European Junior Championships – Rieti, Italy (18-21 July)
Pan-American Junior Championships – Medellín, Colombia (2-4 Aug)
IAAF World Championships – Moscow, Russia (10-18 Aug)
Francophone Games Nice, France (10-14 Sep)
European Cross Country Championships – Belgrade, Serbia (8 Dec)

2014

IAAF World Indoor Championships – Sopot, Poland (7-9 March)
IAAF World Half Marathon Championships – Copenhagen, Denmark (29 Mar)
IAAF World Race Walking Cup – Tiacang, China (5-6 May)
IAAF World Relays – Nassau, Bahamas (24-25 May)
European Team Championships – Braunschweid, GER
IAAF World Junior Championships – Eugene, USA (22-27 July)
Commonwealth Games – Glasgow, GBR (23 Jul – 3 Aug)
European Championships – Zürich, Switzerland (12-17 Aug)
Youth Olympic Games – Nanjing, China (16-28 August)
IAAF Continental Cup – Marrakech, Morocco (13-14 Sep)
Asian Games – Incheon, Korea (19 Sep–4 Oct)

2015

European Indoor Championships – Prague, Czech Republic (6-8 Mar)
IAAF World Cross Country Championships – Guiyang (A), China
IAAF World Relays – Nassau, Bahamas (May)
European Team Championships – Cheboksary, RUS
IAAF World Youth Championships – Cali (A), Colombia
Pan-American Junior Championships, Edmonton, Canada
Pan-American Games – Toronto, CAN (10-26 July)
All-Africa Games – Brazzaville, Congo
IAAF World Championships – Beijing, China (22-30 July)

2016

European Championships – Amsterdam, Netherlands

2017

IAAF World Championships – London, GBR (5-13 August)

2018

Commonwealth Games – Gold Coast, Australia (4-15 April)

EUROPEAN INDOOR CHAMPIONSHIPS 2013

At Paris (Bercy), 12-14 March

THE 32ND EDITION of these Championships (after four earlier 'European Indoor Games') was most enjoyable. Many top names passed the indoor season, but those here showed how championships provide really meaningful track and field action. Best of the ten world-leading performances was the 6.01 pole vault by Renaud Lavillenie for his third successive title... and he celebrated going higher than anyone other than Sergey Bukba at 6.07, only to see the red flag raised as the bar shifted off the pegs while staying up in the air. The best women's mark was the 14.88 triple jump by Olga Saladuha and Darya Klishina was back to her best with 7.01 in the long jump. Perri Shakes-Drayton had a triumphant final day, as she won the 400m in great style in 50.85 and came back to anchor the British 4x400m team to the one championship record of the meeting, 3:27.56.

Impressive sprinting depth was headed by the world-leading 60m marks of 6.48 by Jimmy Vicaut and James Dasoulu and, if short of the world best, six women ran 60m between 7.07 and 7.12 here. Sergey Shubenkov also went to the top of the world list with 7.49 for 60m hurdles, but was pushed hard with five more men under 7.60, and his compatriot Aleksandr Menkov long jumped 8.31, just ahead of Michel Tornéus who set Swedish records at 8.27 and 8.29. Then there was a huge triple jump of 17.70 by Daniele Greco and the sixth men's world lead came in the heptathlon as Eelco Sintnicolaas scored 6372 points, adding 31 to his Dutch record.

Athletes to retain their titles were Lavillenie, Adam Kszczot (800m), Darya Klishina (LJ) and Antoinette Nana Djimou (Pentathlon). Anna Rogowska narrowly failed to do so, as she was beaten in a jump-off by Holly Bleasdale in the women's pole vault. Ruth Beitia won the high jump with 1.99 for her fifth European Indoor medal and her first gold. Her compatriot Juan Carlos Higuero followed three previous medals at 1500m with silver at 3000m.

Russia, as usual, headed the medal table. They were followed by Britain, whose team did well with four golds and eight medals in all, although with a disgracefully small team. Fortunately other nations do not follow such a short-sighted policy and by contrast the Swedish team included many (most?) who would not have met British selection criteria, but who excelled with many pbs, some by large margins. France did well but Germany was surprisingly some way back in fourth place.

The Championships were, as one would expect, very well organised, and innovations included staging the qualifying rounds of the shot competitions in the Market Square of the adjoining Swedish Exhibition & Congress Centre, with all the medal presentations there.

MEN

60 Metres (2)
1. Jimmy Vicaut FRA — 6.48
2. James Dasaolo GBR — 6.48
3. Michael Tumi ITA — 6.52
4. Jaysuma Saidy Ndure NOR — 6.61
5. Odain Rose SWE — 6.62
6. Julian Reus GER — 6.62
7. Harry Aikines-Aryeetey GBR — 6.63
8. Emmanuel Biron FRA — 6.63

400 Metres (3)
1. Pavel Maslák CZE — 45.66
2. Nigel Levine GBR — 46.21
3. Pavel Trenikhin RUS — 46.70
4. Volodymyr Burakov UKR — 46.79
5. Michael Bingham GBR — 46.81
6. Richard Strachan GBR — 47.02

800 Metres (3)
1. Adam Kszczot POL — 1:48.69
2. Kevin López ESP — 1:49.31
3. Mukhtar Mohammed GBR — 1:49.60
4. Anis Ananenko BLR — 1:49.61
5. Taras Bybyk UKR — 1:50.38
6. Luis Alberto Marco ESP — 1:51.69

1500 Metres (3)
1. M. Mekhissi Benabbad FRA — 3:37.17
2. Ilham Tanui Özbilen TUR — 3:37.22
3. Simon Denissel FRA — 3:37.70
4. Marcin Lewandowski POL — 3:39.19
5. Arturo Casado ESP — 3:39.36
6. Hélio Gomes POR — 3:39.46
7. Bartosz Nowicki POL — 3:39.74
8. David Bustos ESP — 3:40.14

3000 Metres (2)
1. Hayle Ibrahimov AZE — 7:49.74
2. Juan Carlos Higuero ESP — 7:50.26
3. Ciarán O'Lionáird IRL — 7:50.40
4. Yoann Kowal FRA — 7:50.89
5. Florian Carvalho FRA — 7:53.23
6. Halil Akkas TUR — 7:54.89
7. Roberto Alaiz ESP — 7:55.12
8. Lander Tijgat BEL — 7:55.59

60 Metres Hurdles (1)
1. Sergey Shubenkov RUS — 7.49
2. Paolo Dal Molin ITA — 7.51
3. Pascal Martinot Lagarde FRA — 7.53
4. Balázs Baji HUN — 7.56
5. Erik Balnuweit GER — 7.58
6. Maksim Lynsha BLR — 7.58
7. Konstadínos Douvalídis GRE — 7.64
8. Konstantin Shabanov RUS — 7.66

High Jump (2)
1. Sergey Mudrov RUS — 2.35
2. Aleksey Dmitrik RUS — 2.33
3. Jaroslav Bába CZE — 2.31
4. Adónios Mástoras GRE — 2.29
5. Gianmarco Tamberi ITA — 2.29
6. Robbie Grabarz GBR — 2.23
7. Mickaël Hanany FRA — 2.23
8. Dmytro Demyanyuk UKR — 2.21

Pole Vault (3)
1. Renaud Lavillenie FRA — 6.01
2. Björn Otto GER — 5.76
3. Malte Mohr GER — 5.76
4. Konstadínos Filippídis GRE — 5.76
5. Jan Kudlicka CZE — 5.71
6= Steve Lewis GBR — 5.71
6= Robert Sobera POL — 5.71
8. Raphael Holzdeppe GER — 5.61

Long Jump (3)
1. Aleksandr Menkov RUS   8.31
2. Michel Tornéus SWE   8.29
3. Christian Reif GER   8.07
4. Eero Haapala FIN   8.05
5. Loúis Tsátoumas GRE   8.00
6. Tommi Evilä FIN   7.96
7. Chris Tomlinson GBR   7.95
8. Elvjs Misans LAT   7.68

Triple Jump (2)
1. Daniele Greco ITA   17.70
2. Ruslan Samitov RUS   17.30
3. Aleksey Fyodorov RUS   17.12
4. Viktor Kuznetsov UKR   17.02
5. Harold Correa FRA   16.92
6. Karl Taillepierre FRA   16.72
7. Zlatozar Atanasov BUL   16.57
8. Fabian Florant NED   16.55

Shot (1)
1. Asmir Kolasinac SRB   20.62
2. Hamza Alic BIH   20.34
3. Ladislav Prásil CZE   20.29
4. Ralf Bartels GER   20.16
5. Marco Fortes POR   20.02
6. Aleksandr Bulanov RUS   19.70
7. Marco Schmidt GER   19.63
8. Niklas Arrhenius SWE   19.17

Heptathlon (2/3)
1. Eelco Sintnicolaas NED   6372
2. Kevin Mayer FRA   6297
3. Mihail Dudas SRB   6099
4. Adam Helcelet CZE   6095
5. Ilya Shkurenyov RUS   6018
6. Fabian Rosenquist SWE   5979
7. Artyom Lukyanenko RUS   5953
8. Pelle Rietveld NED   5906

4 x 400 Metres Relay (3)
1. GBR   3:05.78
    M Bingham, R Buck,
    N Levine, R Strachan
2. RUS   3:06.96
    P Trenikhin, Y Trambo
    vetski, K Svechkar,
    V Krasnov
3. CZE   3:07.64
    D Nemecek, J Prorok,
    P Lichy, V Maslák
4. BEL 3:07.98, 5. SWE 3:09.42
dq. POL (3:07.53)

WOMEN

60 Metres (3)
1. Tezdzhan Naimova BUL   7.10
2. Mariya Ryemyen UKR   7.10
3. Myriam Soumaré FRA   7.11
4. Ivet Lalova BUL   7.12
5. Dafne Schippers NED   7.14
6. Asha Philip GBR   7.15
7. Ezinne Okparaebo NOR   7.16
8. Verena Sailer GER   7.16

400 Metres (3)
1. Perri Shakes-Drayton GBR   50.85
2. Eilidh Child GBR   51.45
3. Moa Hjelmer SWE   52.04
4. Zuzana Hejnová CZE   52.12
5. Denisa Rosolová CZE   52.71
6. Shana Cox GBR   53.15

800 Metres (3)
1. Nataliya Lupu UKR   2:00.26
2. Yelena Kotulskaya RUS   2:00.98
3. Marina Arzamasova BLR   2:01.21
4. Jennifer Meadows GBR   2:01.52
5. Olga Lyakhovaya UKR   2:02.12
6. Ciara Everard IRL   2:02.55

1500 Metres (2)
1. Abeba Aregawi SWE   4:04.47
2. Isabel Macías ESP   4:14.19
3. Katarzyna Broniatowska POL
        4:14.30
4. Natalya Koroyvo BLR   4:15.15
5. Svetlana Podosenova RUS
        4:16.32
6. Yelena Soboleva RUS   4:16.50
7. Giulia Viola ITA   4:16.83
8. Laura Muir GBR   4:18.39

3000 Metres (2)
1. Sara Moreira POR   8:58.50
2. Corinna Harrer GER   9:00.50
3. Fionnuala Britton IRL   9:00.54
4. Yelena Korobkina RUS   9:00.59
5. Almensch Belete BEL   9:03.89
6. Lauren Howarth GBR   9:04.04
7. Christine Bardelle FRA   9:08.62
8. Polina Jelizarova LAT   9:09.86

60 Metres Hurdles (1)
1. Nevin Yanit TUR   7.89
2. Alina Talay BLR   7.94
3. Veronica Borsi ITA   7.94
4. Derval O'Rourke IRL   7.95
5. Yuliya Kondakova RUS   7.99
6. Eline Berings BEL   8.08
7. Micol Cattaneo ITA   8.11
8. Nooralotta Neziri FIN   8.19

High Jump (3)
1. Ruth Beitia ESP   1.99
2. Ebba Jungmark SWE   1.96
3. Emma Green Tregaro SWE 1.96
4= Anna Iljustsenko EST   1.92
4= Alessia Trost ITA   1.92
6. Venelina Veneva-Mateeva BUL
        1.92
7. Mirela Demireva BUL   1.87
8. Tia Hellebaut BEL   1.87

Pole Vault (2)
1. Holly Bleasdale GBR   4.67
2. Anna Rogowska POL   4.67
3. Anzhelika Sidorova RUS   4.62
4. Jirina Svobodová CZE   4.62
5= Anastasiya Savchenko RUS
        4.37
5= Angelina Zhuk-Krasnova RUS
        4.37
7. Kristina Gadschiew GER   4.37
8. Katharina Bauer GER   4.22

Long Jump (2)
1. Darya Klishina RUS   7.01
2. Éloyse Lesueur FRA   6.90
3. Erica Jarder SWE   6.71
4. Shara Proctor GBR   6.69
5. Ivana Spanovic SRB   6.68
6. Olga Kucherenko RUS   6.62
7. Cornelia Deiac ROU   6.52
8. Anastasiya Mokhnyuk UKR 6.46

Triple Jump (3)
1. Olga Saladuha UKR   14.88
2. Irina Gumenyuk RUS   14.30
3. Simona La Mantia ITA   14.26
4. Veronika Mosina RUS   14.21
5. Patricia Sarrapio ESP   14.07
6. Yamilé Aldama GBR   13.95
7. Jenny Elbe GER   13.81
8. Patricia Mamona POR   13.72

Shot (3)
1. Christina Schwanitz GER   19.25
2. Yevgeniya Kolodko RUS   19.04
3. Alena Kopets BLR   18.85
4. Chiara Rosa ITA   18.37
5. Irina Tarasova RUS   18.31
6. Josephine Terlecki GER   18.16
7. Anca Heltne ROU   17.64
8. Ursula Ruíz ESP   17.22

Pentathlon (1)
1. Antoinette Nana Djimou Ida FRA
        4666
2. Yana Maksimova BLR   4658
3. Anna Melnychenko UKR   4608
4. Ramona Fransen NED   4571
5. Sofia Linde SWE-J   4531
6. Nafissatou Thiam BEL-J   4493
7. Julia Mächtig GER   4463
8. Alina Fyodorova UKR   4420

4 x 400 Metres Relay (3)
1. GBR   3:27.56*
        E Child, S Cox,
        C Ohuruogu,
        P Shakes-Drayton
2. RUS   3:28.18
        O Tovarnova,
        T Veshkurova,
        N Kotlyarova, K Zadorina
3. CZE   3:28.49
        D Rosolová, J Bartoníck
        ová, L Masná, Z Hejnová
4. FRA 3:28.71, 5. UKR 3:34.61, 6.
SWE 3:36.17

Leading Nations – Medals & Points

Nation	G	S	B	Points
RUS	4	7	3	144
GBR	4	3	1	98.5
FRA	4	2	3	90
GER	1	2	2	60
SWE	1	2	3	59
CZE	1	0	4	55
UKR	2	1	1	54
ITA	1	1	3	50.5
ESP	1	3	0	44
BLR	0	2	2	39
POL	1	1	1	30.5
BUL	1	0	0	20
IRL	0	0	2	20

15 nations won gold, 19 medals and 27 placed athletes in top 8.

WORLD CROSS COUNTRY CHAMPIONSHIPS 2013

At Bydgoszcz, Poland 24 March

EVEN THOUGH their senior teams were weaker than usual Kenya won three of the four individual titles and three of the four team awards. Ethiopia claimed the junior men's winner and had victorious teams in both men's races, their first wins since 2005 (senior) and 1998 (junior). The only other countries to win medals were Eritrea in the senior men's race and teams from USA, Morocco, Bahrain and Britain. Just 398 athletes (215 men and 183 women) from 41 countries competed. These were the lowest figures since the 1980s, while the percentage of European athletes at 25.8% was the lowest ever when the event has been held in Europe.

The only European countries to field teams in all four races were Britain, Spain and host nation Poland. France, Italy and Portugal had only partial representation, while Germany and Russia as well as all the Scandinavian countries did not send a single athlete. Japheth Korir was a surprise men's winner and at 19 was the youngest ever; he edged away from defending champion Imane Merga in the closing stages. Emily Chebet chased down Hiwot Ayalew, who had led by 50m at one point, in the last 200m, returning to top form as she regained the women's title that she had won in 2010. Hagos Gebrhiwet was a classy junior men's winner while Faith Kipyegon became just the third junior woman to retain her title. The course was challenging, twisting and hilly and with the temperature at -2-3°C, this was the coldest ever for the event.

Senior Men 11.148km

1. Japheth Korir KEN	32:45
2. Imane Merga ETH	32:51
3. Teklemariam Medhin ERI	32:54
4. Moses Kipsiro UGA	33:08
5. Timothy Toroitich UGA	33:09
6. Ben True USA	33:11
7. Goitom Kifle ERI	33:16
8. Collis Birmingham AUS	33:18
9. Feyisa Lilesa ETH	33:22
10. Chris Derrick USA	33:23
11. Rabah Aboud ALG	33:28
12. Hosea Macharinyang KEN	33:29
13. Abera Chane ETH	33:31
14. Tesfaye Abera ETH	33:35
15. Geoffrey Kirui KEN	33:38
16. Sergio Sánchez ESP	33:38
17. Ryan Vail USA	33:42
18. Abrar Osman ERI	33:42
19. Bobby Mack USA	33:49
20. Elroy Gelant RSA	33:53
21. Hicham Bouchicha ALG	33:54
22. Mohammed Ahmed CAN	33:56
23. Liam Adams AUS	34:07
24. Mosinet Geremew ETH	34:09
25. Geoffrey Kusuro UGA	34:09

96 of 102 finished

Team 4 to score, 15 teams completed

1. ETH	38	6. ALG	107
2. USA	52	7. AUS	116
3. KEN	54	8. ESP	127
4. ERI	75	9. CAN	140
5. UGA	76	10. POL	164

Junior Men's 7.488km

1. Hagos Gebrhiwet ETH	21:04
2. Leonard Barsoton KEN	21:08
3. Muktar Edris ETH	21:13
4. Tsegay Tuemay ERI	21:26
5. Conseslus Kipruto KEN	21:40
6. Birhan Nebebew ETH	21:42
7. Ghirmay Ghebreslassie ERI	21:50
8. Dawit Weldesilasie ERI	21:58
9. Ronald Kewmoi KEN	21:58
10. Michael Bett KEN	22:21
11. Moses Letoyie KEN	22:28
12. Mohammed Abid MAR	22:31

110 of 113 finished

Team 4 to score. 17 teams completed

1. ETH	23	6. ITA	164
2. KEN	26	7. UGA	170
3. MAR	65	8. AUS	171
4. USA	106	9. GBR	181
5. JPN	138	10. CAN	187

Senior Women's 7.488km

1. Emily Chebet KEN	24:24
2. Hiwot Ayalew ETH	24:27
3. Belaynesh Oljira ETH	24:33
4. Shitaye Eshete BRN	24:34
5. Margaret Muriuki KEN	24:39
6. Janet Kisa KEN	24:46
7. Viola Kibiwot KEN	24:46
8. Tejitu Daba BRN	24:55
9. Juliet Chekwel UGA	24:58
10. Irene Cheptai KEN	25:01
11. Beatrice Mutai KEN	25:05
12. Salima El Ouali Alami MAR	25:05
13. Neely Spence USA	25:08
14. Fionnuala Britton IRL	25:08
15. Genet Yalew ETH	25:10
16. Sophie Duarte FRA	25:17
17. Almensch Belete BEL	25:24
18. Kenza Dahmani ALG	25:26
19. Nazret Weldu ERI	25:27
20. Kareema Jasim BRN	25:27
21. Emily Infeld USA	25:27
22. Diana Martín ESP	25:29
23. Nadia Noujani MAR	25:30
24. Natasha Fraser CAN	25:30
25. Rachel Cliff CAN	25:30

96 of 97 finished

Team 4 to score. 15 teams completed

1. KEN	19	6. FRA	122
2. ETH	48	7. GBR	154
3. BRN	73	8. CAN	167
4. USA	90	9. ESP	183
5. IRL	115	10. UGA	188

Junior Women's 5.658km

1. Faith Kipyegon KEN	17:51
2. Agnes Tirop KEN	17:51
3. Alemitu Heroye ETH	17:57
4. Caroline Kipkirui KEN	18:09
5. Ruti Aga ETH	18:18
6. Sofiya Shemsu ETH	18:20
7. Rosefline Chepngetich KEN-Y	18:21
8. Sheila Keter KEN	18:21
9. Buze Diriba ETH	18:29
10. Alemitu Hawi ETH	18:35
11. Pauline Kamulu KEN	18:43
12. Gotytom Gebreslase ETH	18:44

86 of 86 finished

Team 4 to score, 14 teams completed

1. KEN	14	6. USA	105
2. ETH	23	7. POL	165
3. GBR	81	8. AUS	172
4. JPN	90	9. CAN	203
5. UGA	99	10. ALG	227

WORLD CHAMPIONSHIPS 2013

THE 14th IAAF World Championships will be staged in Moscow, Russia 10-18 2013.

Previous Championships

ATHLETICS EVENTS at the Olympic Games have had world championship status, but the first championships for athletics alone were staged in 1983. It should, however, be noted that separate World Championships were held for men's 50 kilometres walk in 1976 and for women's 3000m and 400m hurdles in 1980, as those events were not on the Olympic programme in those years.

Year	Venue	Athletes	Nations
1983	Helsinki, FIN	1572	153
1987	Rome, ITA	1741	157
1991	Tokyo, JPN	1551	164
1993	Stuttgart, GER	1624	187
1995	Göteborg, SWE	1804	191
1997	Athens, GRE	1882	198
1999	Sevilla, ESP	1821	201
2001	Edmonton, CAN	1677	189
2003	Saint-Denis, FRA	1679	198
2005	Helsinki, FIN	1688	189
2007	Osaka, JPN	1800	197
2009	Berlin GER	1895	200
2011	Daegu KOR	1742	199

World Championship Records

Men

Event	Mark	Athlete	Year
100m	9.58	Usain Bolt JAM	2009
200m	19.19	Usain Bolt JAM	2009
400m	43.18	Michael Johnson USA	1999
800m	1:43.06	Billy Konchellah KEN	1987
1500m	3:27.65	Hicham El Guerrouj MAR	1999
5000m	12:52.79	Eliud Kipchoge KEN	2003
10,000m	26:46.31	Kenenisa Bekele ETH	2009
Mar	2:06:54	Abel Kirui KEN	2009
3000mSt	8:00.43	Ezekiel Kemboi KEN	2009
110mh	12.91	Colin Jackson GBR	1993
400mh	47.18	Kevin Young USA	1993
HJ	2.40	Javier Sotomayor CUB	1993
PV	6.05	Dmitriy Markov AUS	2001
LJ	8.95	Mike Powell USA	1991
TJ	18.29	Jonathan Edwards GBR	1995
SP	22.23	Werner Günthör SUI	1987
DT	70.17	Virgilijus Alekna BLR	2005
HT	83.89	Ivan Tikhon BLR	2005
JT	92.80	Jan Zelezny CZE	2001
Dec	8902	Tomás Dvorák CZE	2001
4x100m	37.04	Jamaica	2011
4x400m	2:54.29	USA	1993
20kmW	1:17:21	Jefferson Pérez ECU	2003
50kmW	3:36:03	Rob. Korzeniowski POL	2003

Women

Event	Mark	Athlete	Year
100m	10.70	Marion Jones USA	1999
200m	21.74	Silke Gladisch GDR	1987
400m	47.99	Jarmila Kratochvílová TCH	1983
800m	1:54.68	Jarmila Kratochvílová TCH	1983
1500m	3:58.52	Tatyana Tomashova RUS	2003
3000m	8:28.71	Qu Yunxia CHN	1993
5000m	14:38.59	Tirunesh Dibaba ETH	2005
10,000m	30:04.18	Berhane Adere ETH	2003
Mar	2:20:57	Paula Radcliffe GBR	2005
3000mSt	9:06.57	Yekaterina Volkova RUS	2007
100mh	12.28	Sally Pearson AUS	2011
400mh	52.42	Melaine Walker JAM	2009
HJ	2.09	Stefka Kostadinova BUL	1987
PV	5.01	Yelena Isinbayeva RUS	2005
LJ	7.36	Jackie Joyner-Kersee USA	1987
TJ	15.50	Inessa Kravets UKR	1995
SP	21.24	Natalya Lisovskaya URS	1987
SP	21.24	Valerie Adams NZL	2011
DT	71.62	Martina Hellmann GDR	1987
HT	77.96	Anita Wlodarczyk POL	2009
JT	71.99	Marita Abakumova RUS	2011
Hep	7128	Jackie Joyner-Kersee USA	1987
4x100m	41.47	USA	1997
4x400m	3:16.71	USA	1993
20kmW	1:25:41	Olimpiada Ivanova RUS	2005

Winners of the most medals

14 Merlene Ottey JAM gold 4x100m 1991, 200m 1993 & 1995; silver 200m 1983, 100m 1993 & 1995, 4x100m 1995; bronze 4x100m 1983, 100m & 200m 1987 & 1991, 4x100m 1993, 200m 1997

10 Carl Lewis USA gold 100m, LJ & 4x100m 1983; 100m, LJ & 4x100m 1987, 100m & 4x100m 1991; silver LJ 1991; bronze 200m 1993

10 Allyson Felix USA gold 200m 2005, 2007 & 2009; 4x100m 2007 & 2011; 4x400m 2007, 2009 & 2011; silver 400m & bronze 200m 2011

9 Jearl Miles Clark USA gold 400m 1993, 4x400m 1993, 1995 & 2003; silver 4x400m 1991, 1997, 1999; bronze 400m 1995 & 1997

9 Veronica Campbell-Brown JAM gold 100m 2007, 200m 2011; silver 100m 2005, 2011; 200m 2007, 4x100m 2005, 2007 & 2011, 200m 2009

(8) Michael Johnson USA gold 200m 1991 & 1995, 400m 1993, 1995, 1997 & 1999, 4x400m 1993, 1995 (lost 1999 gold when team dq)

Winners of the most gold medals

8 Michael Johnson, Carl Lewis, Allyson Felix – above

6 Sergey Bubka PV 1983, 1987, 1991, 1993, 1995, 1997

5 Gail Devers, Marion Jones, Maurice Greene USA 1997-2001, Lars Riedel GER DT 1991-2001, Allen Johnson USA 1995-2003, Jeremy Wariner, Kenenisa Bekele ETH 2005-09, Usain Bolt 2007-11

Oldest world champions

Men 37y 258d V. Soldatenko USSR 50kW 1996

Women 40y 268d Ellina Zvereva BLR DT 2001

Oldest medallists

Men 40y 274d Troy Douglas NED 3rd 4x1 2003
40y 71d John Powell USA 2nd DT 1987
Women 40y 268d Ellina Zvereva BLR 1st DT 2001

Youngest gold medallists

Women 17y 248d Merlene Frazer JAM 4x100m
(ran in heat) 1991
Men 18y 177d Ismael Kirui KEN 10,000m 1993

Youngest medallists

M: 16y 305d Darrel Brown TRI 4x100m 2001
W: 15y 153d Sally Barsosio KEN 10,000m 1993

Most wins by event

Men	inc. all with 3 or more
100m	3 Carl Lewis USA 1983-87-91
	3 Maurice Greene USA 1997-99-2001
200m	2 Calvin Smith USA 1983, 1987
	2 Michael Johnson USA 1991-95
400m	4 Michael Johnson 1993-95-97-99
800m	3 Wilson Kipketer DEN 1995-97-99
1500m:	4 Hicham El Guerrouj MAR 1997-99-01-03
	3 Nourredine Morceli ALG 1991-93-95
5000m	2 Ismael Kirui KEN 1993-95
10,000m	4 Haile Gebrselasie ETH 1993-95-97-99
	4 Kenenisa Bekele ETH 2003-05-07-09
Mar	2 Abel Antón ESP 1997-9
	2 Jaouad Gharib MAR 2003-05
	2 Abel Kirui KEN 2009-11
3000mSt	3 Moses Kiptanui KEN 1991-93-95
110mh	4 Allen Johnson USA 1995-97-2001-03
	3 Greg Foster USA 1983-87-91
400mh	2 Edwin Moses 1983-87; Félix Sánchez
	DOM 2001-03; Kerron Clement USA 2007-09
HJ	2 Javier Sotomayor CUB 1993-97
PV	6 Sergey Bubka UKR 1983-87-91-93-95-97
LJ	4 Iván Pedroso CUB 1995-97-99-2001
	4 Dwght Phillips USA 2003-05-09-11
TJ	2 Jonathan Edwards GBR 1995-2001
SP	3 Werner Günthör SUI 1987-91-93
	3 John Godina USA 1995-97-2001
DT	5 Lars Riedel GER 1991-93-95-97-2001
HT	3 Ivan Tikhon BLR 2003-05-07
JT	3 Jan Zelezny CZE 1993-95-2001
Dec	3 Dan O'Brien USA 1991-93-95
	3 Tomás Dvorák CZE 1997-99-2001
4x100m	8 USA 1983-87-91-93-99-2001-03-07
4x400m	7 USA 1987-93-95-2005-07-09-11
20kmW	3 Jefferson Pérez ECU 2003-05-07
50kmW	3 Rob. Korzeniowski POL 1997-2001-03
Women	
100m	2 Marion Jones USA 1997-99
200m	3 Allyson Felix USA 2005-07-09
400m	2 Cathy Freeman AUS 1997-99
800m	3 Maria Mutola MOZ 1993-2001-03
1500m	2 Hassiba Boulmerka ALG 1991-95
	2 Tatyana Tomashova RUS 2003-05
	2 Maryam Jamal BRN 2007-09
5000m	2 Gabriela Szabo ROU 1997-99
	2 Tirunesh Dibaba ETH 2003-05
	2 Vivian Cheruiyot KEN 2009-11
10,000m	2 Tirunesh Dibaba ETH 2005-07
Mar	2 Catherine Ndereba KEN 2003-07
3000mSt	1 by four women
100mh	3 Gail Devers USA 1993-95-99
400mh	2 Nezha Bidouane MAR 1997-2001
HJ	2 Stefka Kostadinova BUL 1987-1995
	2 Hestrie Cloete RSA 2001-03
	2 Blanka Vlasic CRO 2007-09
PV	2 Stacy Dragila USA 1999-2001
	2 Yelena Isinbayeva RUS 2005-07
LJ	2 Jackie Joyner-Kersee USA 1987-91
	2 Heike Drechsler GDR/GER 1983-93
	2 Fiona May ITA 1995-2001
	2 Brittney Reese USA 2009-11
TJ	2 Tatyana Lebedeva RUS 2001-03
	2 Yargelis Savigne CUB 2007-09
SP	3 Astrid Kumbernuss GER 1995-97-99
	3 Valerie Adams NZL 2007-09-11
DT	3 Franka Dietzsch GER 1999-2005-07
HT	2 Yipsi Moreno CUB 2001-03
JT	2 Trine Hattestad NOR 1993-97
	2 Miréla Manjani GRE 1999-2003
	2 Osleidys Menéndez CUB 2001-05
Hep	3 Carolina Klüft SWE 2003-5-07
4x100m	5 USA 1995-97-2001-05-07
4x400m	5 USA 1993-95-2003-07-09
20kmW	3 Olga Kaniskina RUS 2007-09-11

Timetable and Qualifying Standards

NINE DAYS of competition are scheduled.
Dates of successive rounds (27 Aug - 4 Sep)

Event	Days	Qual. standards A	B
Men		A	B
100m	10*-10-11-11	10.15	10.21
200m	16-16-17	20.52	20.60
400m	11-12-13	45.28	45.60
800m	10-11-13	1:45.30	1:46.20
1500m	14-16-18	3:35.00	3:37.00
5000m	13-16	13:15.00	13:20.00
10,000m	10	27:40.00	28:05.00
Mar	17	2:17:00	
3000mSt	12-15	8:26.00	8:32.00
110mh	11-12-12	13.40	13.50
400mh	12-13-15	49.40	49.60
HJ	13-15	2.31	2.28
PV	10-12	5.70	5.60
LJ	14-16	8.25	8.10
TJ	16-18	17.20	16.85
SP	15-16	20.60	20.10
DT	12-13	66.00	64.00
HT	10-12	79.00	76.00
JT	15-17	83.50	81.00
Dec	10/11	8200	8000
4x100m	18-18	39.20	
4x400m	15-16	3:05.00	
20kmW	11	1:24:00	1:26:00
50kmW	14	4:02:00	4:16:00
Women			
100m	10*-11-12-12	11.28	11.36
200m	15-15-16	23.05	23.30
400m	10-11-12	51.55	52.35
800m	15-16-18	2:00.00	2:01.50
1500m	11-13-15	4:05.50	4:09.00
5000m	14-17	15:18.00	15:24.00

10,000m	11	31:45.00	32:05.00
Mar	10	2:43:00	
3000mSt	10-13	9:43.00	9:48.00
100mh	16-17-17	12.94	13.10
400mh	12-13-15	55.40	56.55
HJ	15-17	1.95	1.92
PV	11-13	4.60	4.50
LJ	10-11	6.75	6.65
TJ	13-15	14.40	14.20
SP	11-12	18.30	17.20
DT	10-11	62.00	59.50
HT	14-18	72.00	69.50
JT	16-18	62.00	60.00
Hep	12/13	6100	5950
4x100m	18-18	44.00	
4x400m	16-17	3:33.00	
20kmW	13	1:36:00	1:38:00

* Preliminary round

Each country can field a maximum of three athletes per event with the A standard, or two athletes with the A standard and one with the B standard, or one athlete with the B standard. Countries with no qualified athletes can enter one male or one female in one individual event except for the 10,000m, 3000mSC and Combined Events. As host nation, Russia is entitled to enter one athlete or relay team per event regardless of the entry standard except for Combined Events and field events. Area champions in all individual events, except for marathon, automatically qualify and will be considered as having achieved the A standard. Also credited with the A standard are the top 15 finishers in the senior men's and women's races at the 2013 World Cross Country Champs, top three in the 2012 IAAF Combined Events Challenge and top three in the 20k walk at the Race Walking Challenge Final. In the marathon a maximum of five athletes per country can start, but it should be noted that the World Marathon Cup has been discontinued. In addition to the above, the current World champion and the winner of the 2012 Diamond League (in the corresponding World Champs events) will be accepted as wild cards. Indoor marks for all field events and for races of 200m and longer will be accepted (except on oversized tracks). The qualification period is 1 Jan 2012 to 29 Jul 2013 for the 10,000m, marathon, walks, relays and Combined Events; 1 Oct 2012 to 29 Jul 2013 for all other events.

Most Appearances

Men

10 Jesús Ángel García ESP 1993-2011
9   four men

Women

11 Susana Feitor POR 1991-2011
10 Franka Dietzsch GER 1991-2009
9   five women

Oldest Competitor

47y 108d Merlene Ottey SLO 100m (1st round) 2007

WORLD YOUTH CHAMPIONSHIPS

The 8th IAAF World Youth (U18) Championships will be staged in Donetsk,Ukraine on 10-14 July 2013.

Previous Championships

Year	Venue	Athletes	Nations
1999	Bydgoszcz, POL	1055	131
2001	Edmonton, CAN	1262	159
2003	Sherbrooke, CAN	1013	153
2005	Marrakech, MAR	1250	177
2007	Ostrava, CZE	1217	150
2009	Bressanone, ITA	1284	167
2011	Villeneuve d'Ascq FRA	1322	166

World U18 Championship Records

Men

100m	10.31	Darrel Brown TRI	2001
200m	20.40	Usain Bolt JAM	2003
400m	45.24	Kirani James GRN	2009
800m	1:44.08	Leronard Kosencha KEN	2011
1500m	3:36.78	Isaac Songok KEN	2001
3000m	7:40.10	William Sitonik KEN	2011
2000mSt	5:24.69	Abel Kiprop KEN	2005
110mh *	13.18	Wayne Davis USA	2007
400mh *	49.01	William Wynne USA	2007
HJ	2.27	Huang Haiqiang CHN	2005
PV	5.26	Nico Weiler	2007
LJ	7.95/7.97w	Chris Noffke AUS	2005
TJ	16.63	Héctor Fuentes CUB	2005
SP 5kg	24.35	Jacko Gill NZL	2011
DT 1.5kg	70.67q	Mykyta Nesterenko UKR	2007
HT 5kg	82.30	Bence Pásztor HUN	2011
JT 700g	82.96	Reinhardt van Zyl RSA	2011
Octathlon	6491	Jake Stein AUS	2011
MedleyR	1:49.47	USA	2011
10000mW	40:51.31	Pavel Parshin RUS	2011

Women

100m	11.31	Jessica Onyepunuka USA	2003
200m	22.99	Aymée Martínez CUB	2005
400m	51.19	Nawal Al-Jack SUD	2005
800m	2:01.67	Cherono Koech KEN	2009
1500m	4:09.48	Faith Kipyegon KEN	2011
3000m	8:53.94	Mercy Cherono KEN	2007
2000mSt	6:11.83	Korahubish Itaa ETH	2009
100mh *	13.08	Adriana Lamalle FRA	1999
400mh	55.96	Ebony Collins USA	2005
HJ	1.92	Irina Kovalenko UKR	2003
PV	4.35	Vicky Parnov AUS	2007
LJ	6.47	Darya Klishina RUS	2007
TJ	13.86	Cristine Spîtaru ROU	2003
SP	16.87	Valerie Adams NZL	2001
DT	54.93	Ma Xuejun CHN	2001
HT	64.61	Bianca Perie ROU	2007
JT	59.74	Christin Hussong GER	2011
Hep	5875	Tatyana Chernova RUS	2005
4x100m	44.30	Jamaica	1999
MedleyR	2:03.42	Jamaica	2011
5000mW	20:28.05	Tatyana Kalmykova RUS	2007

* At Youth heights: 110mh 91.4cm, 400mh 84cm, W 100mh 84cm

OBITUARY 2012

See ATHLETICS 2012 for obituaries from early 2012: Gösta Arvidsson, Márta Báccskai, Margaret Bisereko, Torgeir Brandvold, John Hartfield, Frank Horwill, Laila Jensen, Kauko Jouppila, Miroslav Juza, Heikki Kyösola, Steven Lenart, Pavel Litovchenko, Vern McGrew, Bertie Messitt, Lutz Philipp, Fernando Rozo, István Rózsavölgyi, Gábor Tamás, Jo Zwaan.

Vitaliy ALISEVICH (Belarus) (b. 15 Jun 1967 Minsk) on 28 October. World Junior hammer champion in 1986, his pb of 82.16 was eighth in the world in 1988 and eleventh on the world all-time list. He was 9th at the European Champs in 1994 and BLR champion 1992 and 1994.

Annual progression at HT: 1983- 61.46, 1984- 62.94, 1985- 70.20, 1986- 73.22, 1987- 78.60, 1988- 82.16, 1989- 77.70, 1990- 77.52, 1991- 79.16, 1992- 80.00, 1993- 81.32, 1994- 80.68, 1995- 77.78, 1996- 76.74, 1997- 78.18, 1998- 76.63, 1999- 76.62, 2000- 75.10, 2001- 73.87, 2002- 73.55, 2003- 72.65.

He was married to Tatyana Alisevich, European Cup heptathlon winner in 2005 with pb 6173.

Samuel Aurelio **ANDERSON** Schweyer (Cuba) (b. 25 Sep 1929 Matanzas) on 18 August in Riverview, Florida, USA. At 110m hurdles he was 3rd in 1961 and 4th in 1955 (14.67A) at the Pan-American Games and was CAC Games champion in 1954 after 2nd in 1950, also competing (heats) at the 1952 Olympic Games. Pbs: 110mh Cuban record 14.2 (1951), 400mh 55.4 (1951). After graduating from the National Institute of Physical Education in Cuba, he attended the University of Illinois on a track scholarship and stayed in the United States. He had a tryout with the Chicago White Sox, but never played professional baseball.

Donald William James **ANTHONY** (GBR) (b. 6 Nov 1928 Watford) on 28 May. He had a hammer best of 58.14 (1956), was 4th in 1954 and 5th in 1958 at the Empire Games, and 12th at the 1956 Olympics. He was AAA champion in 1953 and Inter-Counties 1954-6; 13 UK internationals 1953-9. He was a lecturer at Manchester and Loughborough Universities before being head of the PE department at Avery Hill College in southeast London 1959-85. He became an AAA senior coach and frequently wrote about hammer throwing. He was a founder member of the Hammer Circle and had a long association with the Olympic Movement as a historian, writer and researcher. He was a founder of the English Volleyball Association in 1955 and was heavily involved with the sport from then, representing the sport on the British Olympic Association for 33 years. Awarded the MBE in 2011.

Veikko ARTMAN (Finland) (b. 22 May 1930 Helsinki) on 26 January in Helsinki. A legendary starter at athletics meetings for almost 50 years from 1948, in his white coat he was aptly known as "Startman", highlighted by the Worlds in 1983 and the Europeans in 1971 and 1994 in the Helsinki Olympic Stadium. He had a long career for the Finnish Federation as Starting Trainer from the mid-1960s to 2000.

Gösta Åke Wilhelm **ARVIDSSON** (Sweden) (b. 21 Aug 1925 Norra Åsarp). Six internationals, pb DT 48.43 (1951).

Anna-Lisa AUGUSTSSON (Sweden) (b. 29 Dec 1924 Sunne) on 22 September. In 1952 she was Swedish champion at 100m and 200m and ran in the heats of 100m and 4x100m at the Olympics Games. Eight internationals; pbs: 100m 12.1/11.9w, 200m 25.2 SWE record (all 1952).

Guy BAILLY (France) (b. 7 Dec 1932 Drancy) on 4 August in Beauvais. French champion at 50km walk 1970 and 100km walk 1970 and 1973. Pbs: 20kmW 1:38:20 (1964), 50kmW 4:27:14 (1970), 100kmW 9:53:47 (1972). 18 internationals 1963-73.

Jörg BALKE (Germany) (b. 23 Mar 1936 Berlin Spandau) on 5 March in Unna. In 1960 he ran a pb of 1:47.1 for 800m and was 4th in his semi-final at the Olympic Games. He was FRG indoor champion at 800m in 1962, 1964 and 1967, running a European indoor 800m best of 1:48.6 in 1965. Other pbs 400m 48.1 (1961), 1000m 2:21.6 (1965), 1500m 3:45.0 (1960). 14 internationals 1959-67. He married Rosi Klute, 800m 2:05.54 (1972), in 1972.

Algimantas BALTUSNIKAS (Lithuania) (b. 5 Sep 1934 Veziskiai) on 16 May in Kaunas. In 1948 Soviets deported his whole family to Siberia; he returned to Lithuania in 1956 but was never allowed to compete in Western countries. He was USSR discus champion in 1957, 1960 and 1961 and Lithuanian champion in 1959, 1961, 1963-4 and 1967. After a Lithuanian record 54.83 in 1957 he set USSR discus records at 56.58 in 1958 and 57.93 in 1961. He also set Lithuanian shot records with 16.63 and 16.73 (1958).

Annual progression: 1955- 44.10, 1956- 50.96, 1957- 54.83, 1958- 56.58, 1959- 53.97, 1960- 55.46, 1961- 57.93, 1962- 55.52, 1963- 56.60, 1964- 56.89, 1965- 55.85, 1966- 49.32, 1967- 54.60, 1968- 51.34, 1969- 49.42, 1970- 48.14, 1971- 48.62. Pbs: SP 16.73 (1958), HT 51.87 (1959).

Oscar BARLETTA (Italy) (b. 15 May 1917 Civitavecchia, Rome) on 2 February. After one international in 1941, he he ran pbs of 800m 1:57.2 and 1500m 3:57.8 in 1942, but was then stopped by WW II. He became a notable coach.

Johannes Hendrikus 'Jan' **BARNARD** (South Africa) (b. 21 Oct 1929 Lichenburg) on his 83rd birthday on 21 October. He first competed for South Africa at the 1954 Commonwealth Games, where he won the bronze medal in that dramatic race in which Jim Peters succumbed to heat exhaustion when well clear of the rest of the field. Two months earlier Barnard had won the SA trials race in a national record time of 2:25:31.8. He improved that record to 2:21:37.2 in 1956; both records set in Port Elizabeth. He did not finish the 1956 Olympic marathon but won the Commonwealth Games silver medal in 1958. South African champion at 6 miles and marathon in 1955-6 and 1958 and at cross-country in 1953,1955-6, 1961 and 1963, he set RSA records at 2M 9:20.2 (1955), 6M 30:23.4 (1955) and 30:07.3 (1956), 10,000m 30:58.7A (1956), 10M 51:40.4 (1955) and 1 Hour 18,655mA (1956). Other pb: 3M 14:16.5 (1953). He became a top coach,

Daniel BATMAN (Australia) (b. 20 Mar 1981 Melbourne) was killed in a car crash on 26 June in Humpty Doo, Northern Territory, southeast of Darwin. He won a gold medal on Australia's 4x100m team at the 1998 World Juniors, and competed at the 2000 Olympic Games (dnf heat 400m) and at the Worlds in 2003 (ht 400m) and 2005 (sf 200m and 5th 4x100m). He was 6th in the 2003 World Indoor 200m, was a 200m semi-finalist at the 2006 Commonwealth Games and Australian champion at 200m in 2005 and 2006. A direct descendant of John Batman, the founder of Melbourne, he married Nova Peris-Kneebone, the 1998 Commonwealth Games 200m champion. Pbs: 60m 6.77 (2005), 100m 10.19 & 10.14w (2005), 200m 20.44 (2005), 20.29w (2006); 400m 45.02 (2003), 800m 1:52.53 (2002).

Bernadette BURGER (née Hummel) (France) (b. 23 Jul 1938 Denting) on 2 February in Girmont. French champion at shot 1959 and 1961-2. Pbs: SP 14.25 (1962), DT 41.14 (1967). 7 internationals.

Milton Gray **CAMPBELL** (USA) (b. 9 Dec 1933 Plainfield, New Jersey) on 2 November in Gainesville, Georgia. While an 18 year-old high school student he won the 1952 Olympic silver medal in the decathlon in Helsinki (6975 points/6948 on the current tables). Four years later he won the gold medal in Melbourne with his best ever score of 7937 points (7565), then the second best of all-time. His best event was the high hurdles and in 1957 he improved the world indoor record for 60y hurdles to 7.0 (twice) and outdoors tied the world record for 120 yards

at 13.4. He won both AAU and NCAA titles at 120y hurdles in 1955 while at the University of Indiana, and was 4th in the US Olympic Trials at 110mh in 1956, just 0.01 behind Joel Shankle. He contested just five decathlons in his career, with second places in the AAU/Olympic Trials in 1952 (7055/6997) and 1956 (7559/7292) and an AAU win in 1953 with 7232/7040. Other pbs: 100y 9.6, 100m 10.5, 220ySt 20.7 (all 1953), and 400m 48.8, 1500m 4:50.6, HJ 1.90, PV 3.66, LJ 7.33, SP 14.75, DT 44.96, JT 57.08 (all 1956).

Beautifully built at 1.91m and 94kg, he also excelled at football, playing briefly for the Cleveland Browns in the NFL and for seven years for the Montreal Alouettes in the CFL, as well as swimming and judo. In 2001 he stood for a state senate seat as a Republican.

Carmen Yolanda **CAMPTON** (b. 24 Apr 1952) (de Vlieger) (Australia) on 4 December. She ran a pb 58.53 for 400m hurdles when 3rd at the Pacific Conference Games in 1977 and ran at 800m (sf) and 1500 (ht) at the 1978 Commonwealth Games. Other pbs: 400m 55.89, 800m 2:03.0, 1500m 4:18.5 (all 1978).

Leonard Walter **CARTER** (GBR) (b. 21 Nov 1942 Acton, London) in October. A member of Ruislip & Northwood AC (later Hillingdon) he won English Schools titles in 1959 and 1960. Then in his best year of 1961 he was AAA junior champion at 100y and 220y and CAU 220y champion and had five internationals for Britain, including a British record when he ran the first leg of the team that ran 40.1 for 4x100m v West Germany. In 1962 he was a quarter-finalist at both 100y and 220y and won a gold medal (second leg) for England at 4x110 yards at the Commonwealth Games in Perth. Pbs: 60y 6.4i (1960), 100y 9.6 (1961, equal European junior record), 100m 10.5 (1961), 220y 21.5/21.4w (1961).

Stanley Ernest Walter **COX** (GBR) (b. 15 Jul 1918 Wood Green, London) on 27 June in Felixstowe. A member of Southgate Harriers, he made the first of four British international appearances at 5000m in 1939 after 4th in the AAA 3 miles. After the War he won the AAA 6 miles and was 7th at 10,000m in the Olympics in 1948 before placing 2nd to Jim Peters in 2:34:34 on his debut in the 1951 Poly Marathon. A year later he was again 2nd in this race as both men smashed the previous world best, Peters 2:20:42.2, Cox 2:21:42. Both men failed to finish at the Olympic Games, but Cox was again 2nd in the Poly Marathons of 1953 (2:26:19) and 1954 (2:23:08) behind more world bests from Peters and also 2nd to Peters at Enschede 1953 (2:24:38), so he was the world's second fastest each year 1952-4. Like Peters, Cox collapsed from the heat at the 1954 Empire Games. He went on to 3rd in Enschede 1955 and 2nd in the Poly and AAAs in 1956. Other pbs: 1M 4:22.4 (1939), 2M 9:08.0 (1939), 3M 14:13.6

(1939), 5000m 15:02.2 (1946), 6M 29:53.2 (1953), 10,000m 31:08.4 (1948).

Jack Wells **DAVIS** (USA) (b. 11 Sep 1930 Amarillo, Texas) on 21 July in San Diego, California. Double Olympic silver medallist, he was ranked by *Track & Field News* as world number one in 1953-4 and 1956 and as number two in 1951-2 and 1955. In 1952 he was second to Harrison Dillard at the AAU, the Final US Trials and at the Olympic Games, and in 1956 he was beaten by Lee Calhoun 13.70 to 13.73 at the Olympics in Melbourne. He equalled the world record for 120y hurdles with 13.5 at Sanger on 9 June 1956 and improved it to 13.4 for 110mh in his heat at the 1956 AAUs. Then he ran an unratified 13.3 for 120yh at Bendigo, Australia on 17 Nov 1956. He won 37 consecutive high hurdles finals including being unbeaten in 1953 and 1954, and was NCAA champion for the University of Southern California each year 1951-3 (2nd 200m in 1952) and won the AAU 120yh in 1953 and 1954 and 200mh/220yh in 1951 and 1953-4. He also won the Pan-American Games 110mh in 1955. Other pbs 200m 21.1 (1952), 220yh straight 22.8 (1953) and turn 23.2 (1954), 400mh 53.7 (1956). LJ 7.25 (1949). He was later a real estate developer.

Annual progression (position on world list) at 110m/120yh: 1950- 14.6y (38=), 1951- 13.7y (2), 1952- 13.7 (1=), 1953- 13.6y (1), 1954- 13.6y (1), 1955- 13.8A/13.7Aw (1), 1956- 13.3y (1).

Martin John **DAYKIN** (GBR) (b. 14 Jun 1947 Norfolk) in Shropshire on 12 September. He competed for Gloucester AC and ran his best time for 100km of 6:35:05 when winning at Winschoten in 1980 (fastest in the world that year), but the course was not known to have been measured by calibrated bicycle. Next best was 6:43:51 for 2nd at Santander in 1984. Other pbs: 24 hours (track) 245.272k (1985), 100 miles 12:16:46 (1981), and marathon 2:24:24 (1982).

Robert Winston **'Bob' DAY** (USA) (b. 31 Oct 1944 Los Angeles) in Irvine, California on 15 March. In 1968 he won the AAU and Olympic Trials races at 5000m, but did not qualify from his heat at the Olympic Games. While at UCLA, he won the NCAA 1 mile in 1965. Pbs: 880y 1:50.3 (1964), 1500m 3:41.6 (1967), 1M 3:56.4 (1965), 3000m 7:56,0 (1967), 2M 8:33.0i (1966), 8:35.4 (1965); 3M 13:16.4 (1968), 5000m 13:40.2 (1968).

Francis James **'Jim' DELANEY** (USA) (b. 1 Mar 1921 Butte, Montana) on 2 April in Santa Rosa, California. After winning the AAU title in 1947 and 1948 (3rd 1943, 2nd 1946) and the Olympic Trials in 1948 with his pb of 16.81, he took the Olympic silver medal at shot. He went to Notre Dame University (4th-3rd-3rd NCAA 1941-3) and later competed for the Olympic Club in San Francisco.

Fredericus Arnoldus **'Frits' de RUIJTER** (Netherlands) (b. 5 Apr 1917 Rotterdam) on 20 March in Heemstede. He won national titles at 1500m (1937-42, 1944 and 1947-8), 800m (1946-7) and cross-country (1939 & 1942) and AAA titles in England at 880y 1947 and mile 1946 and 1948, and ran at the 1948 Olympics (heats 800m and 1500m). In all he set 17 Dutch records from 1935 with bests of 800m 1:51.8 (1947), 1000m 2:26.4 (1946) and 1500m 3:51.7 (1947). He became managing director of an international catering company and also worked as a sports journalist.

Ralf DRECOLL (Germany) (b.29 Sep 1944 Buxtehude) on 23 September. A high jumper, he was 6th for FRG at the 1964 Olympic Games and set national records at 2.10 and 2.11 in 1964 and 2.15 in 1967. Other pbs 100m 10.8 and LJ 6.77 (both 1964). 7 Internationals 1963-4.

Juan Carlos DYRZKA (Argentina) (b. 24 Mar 1941 Buenos Aires) on 26 June. A 400m hurdler, ranked 2nd in the world in 1963, he set four South American records from 51.2 in 1961, then 50.9 (1962), 50.2 (1963) and 49.82 in his heat at the 1968 Olympic Games in Mexico City (before 5th in his semi-final in 49.86). He was also a quarter-finalist at 400m (pb 46.85) in 1968 and had run in the heats at 400m, 110mh and 400mh in 1964. He was Pan American champion in 1963 and won 14 medals at South American Championships: 1st at 400mh in 1961, 1963, 1969 and 1971 plus 2nd in 1965 and 1967, and also 2nd at 400m in 1961 and 1963 and 3rd at 110mh in 1967 with five 4x400m relay medals (1 gold, 2 silver 2 bronze). In all he won 19 Argentine titles. Pb 110mh 14.4 (1962).

Édouard ESKÉNAZI (France) (b. 12 Aug 1947) on 7 June. An international technical official and vice president of the French Athletics Federation 1996-7 and 2001-08.

Anna Jeanette **FICK** (South Africa) (b. 5 May 1926) in January. A left-handed thrower, she set 15 SA discus records from 1950 to 48.39A in 1960, was 7th at the 1958 Commonwealth Games, and was national champion eight times: 1950 and 1955-61. She was a lecturer at the Pretoria Teachers Training College for many years and was married to Willie Herbst.

Paul FRIEDEN (Luxembourg) (b. 25 May 1925) on 25 July in Luxembourg. He competed at the Olympic Games in 1948 (3000mSt) and 1952 (5000m) and European Champs in 1950 (3000mSt), and won 24 national titles: 800m 1945, 1500m 1946-7, 1949, 1951 and 1953; 5000m 1952 and 1954-7; 10,000m 1955-8, CC 1951-9. He set Luxembourg records at 3000m: 5 to 8:26.4 (1955), and 5000m: 3 to 14:36.2 (1955). Pbs 1500m 3:56.4 (1957), 10,000m 31:14.8 (1955).

Keith Alvin Saint Hope **GARDNER** (Jamaica) (b. 6 Sep 1929) on 25 May in Livingstone, New Jersey, USA. He starred at the 1958 Empire Games in close rivalry with Tom Robinson BAH, whom he beat by 0.03 at 100y in 9.4 (9.66 on auto timing) and lost to by the same margin at 220y in 21.0w (21.11). He also retained his 120y hurdles title in 14.0w (14.20) and added 4x440y bronze on the Jamaican Team. He had been 6th at both relays and 9th at long jump in 1954. At the Olympic Games he went out in the heats at 100m and 110mh in 1956 and was 5th at 110mh and 3rd at 4x400m in 1960, and at the Pan-American Games was 2nd at 4x400m and 110mh in 1955. He was 2nd at 110mh and 3rd at long jump with gold at both relays in the CAC Games in 1954 before studying at the University of Nebraska, for whom he was 2nd in the 1958 NCAA 120yh. He set Jamaican records at 100y (above), 100m 10.3 (1958 three times), 220y straight 20.4 (1958), 110mh 13.8 (1958). Other pbs: 220y turn 21.0 (1958), 440y 46.6 (1958).

Hsns-Günter GEISTER (Germany) (b. 28 Sep 1928 Hamborn, Duisberg) on 16 May in Krefeld. FRG champion at 400m in 1951 (2nd 1950, 1952-4, 3rd 1948, 1955), he was 4th in his semi-final at the 1952 Olympics in his pb of 47.00 (46.7 hand time) and won a bronze medal at 4x400m. At the 1954 Europeans he won a 4x400m silver medal, but was disqualified in his semi-final at 400m. Other pbs: 100m 10.5 (1951), 200m 21.3 (1954), 19 internationals 1951-6.

Marcel GERDIL (France) (b. 24 Jan 1928 Annemasse) on 20 February in San Justo Desvern, Barcelona, Spain. Semi-finalist at 200m at the 1952 Olympic Games with pb 21.9 (1952).

Donald Cameron Easterbrook **GORRIE** (GBR) (b. 2 Apr 1933 Dehra-Dan, India) on 25 August. He was Scottish champion at 880y in 1955 and ran his pb of 1:50.8 in 1957 when he was president of Oxford University AC. He ran the 800m leg on the winning British medley relay team at the 1955 World University Games. Having been a schoolteacher, he was a member of first Edinburgh from 1971 and then Lothian Regional Councils, and a Member of Parliament for Edinburgh West before serving in the Scottish Parliament as a liberal democrat for Central Scotland from 1999 to 2007.

Henryk GRABOWSKI (Poland) (b. 19 Oct 1929 Czeladz, Katowice) in Czeladz on 3 March. He ranked in the world top ten for long jump each year 1955-8 and won the 1958 European bronze medal, having competed at the Olympic Games in 1952 (dnq) and 1956, when he was 10th after leading the qualifiers with 7.52 but being restricted by a minor leg injury to just 7.12 in the final. Polish champion 1952, 1956 and 1958, he improved the Polish national record eight times from 7.51 in 1952 to 7.81 in 1958.

Gerard GRAMSE (Poland) (b. 18 Aug 1944 Mrocza) on 8 November in Poznan. At 4x100m he won a silver medal at the 1971 Europeans and gold at the 1970 World University Games. Pbs: 100m 10.3 (1968), 200m 21.0 (1966).

William Earnest **'Bill' GREEN** (USA) (b. 1 May 1961 Pittsburgh) in Spokane, Washington on 4 March. In 1979 while at Cubberley Hill High School in Palo Alto he was 3rd in the AAU 400m in a high school record 45.51. Later that year he ran on the winning US team 4x400m at the World Cup. He went to USC and in 1980 he won the US Olympic Trials 400m, but was unable to compete in Moscow due to the Olympic boycott, and he was also 3rd in the AAU 400m in 1984. Pbs: 100y 9.56 (1979), 100m 10.25, 200m 20.53/20.51w, 400m 45.07/45.0A (all 1981).

Emma **Fay GUDSELL** (later STRIGLEY) (New Zealand) on 24 February in Wellington. She won the NZ 100y title in 1935 in 11.4 to tie her pb (1933).

Johnny Svein HAUGEN (Norway) (b. 13 Sep 1951) on 30 March. Norwegian champion at long jump 1974 and 1978 and 200m 1975 and 1977, he competed in eight internationals 1974-8. Pbs: 400mh 55.0 (1972), HJ 1.95 (1974), PV 3.60 (1970), LJ 7.77 (1977), TJ 14.96 (1974).

Kimitada HAYASE (Japan) (b. 5 Sep 1940 Aichi) on 7 May in Nagakute. He was eliminated in the heats of the 200m in 1960 and 200m and 400m in 1964 at the Olympic Games, and was Asian Games bronze medallist at 400m and 4x400m in 1962. He took the Japanese 400m record from 47.8 (1960) to 47.2 (1964). Other pbs: 100m 10.5 (1962), 200m 21.72 (1961).

Henry John **'Harry' HICKS** (GBR) (b. 6 Aug 1925 Barnet) on 25 April in Finchley, London. After 4th in the Poly Marathon in June 1956 in his pb of 2:22:37.2, he won the AAA Marathon six weeks later to earn selectiom for the Olympic Games, in which he was 15th in Melbourne. He also ran for Britain at 3 miles against France in 1951 after 3rd in the AAAs, and he was 16th in 1949 and 22nd in 1950 in the International Cross-country. Pbs: 2M 9:07.0 (1957), 3M 13:59.6 (1954), 6M 30:17.6 (1952). He ran for Hampstead Harriers and was President of the English CC Association in 1993.

Alice Jean **HODGE** née **ARDEN** (USA) (b. 23 Jul 1914 Philadelphia) on 29 February in Roscoe, New York. At high jump she was ninth equal at the 1936 Olympic Games, AAU champion in 1933 and indoors in 1934-5, and had a best of 1.61 to top the world list in 1935. She was national girls champion each year 1933-5 and 2nd in the AAU/Olympic Trials in 1936. She was a member of Olympic Women's Committee in 1952 and 1956. Her son Russ Hodge followed her as an Olympian when he was ninth in the decathlon in 1964 and set the decathlon world record at 8230 points (8220 on current tables) in 1966.

Annual progression (position on world list): 1933- 1.605 (2), 1934- 1.55 (11=), 1935- 1.61 (1), 1936- 1.56 (17=).

Hans Yngve **HÖGLUND** (Sweden) (b. 23 Jul 1952 Mölndal) on 4 October at Sätila. Eighth at the 1976 Olympic Games and Swedish champion each year 1974-6, he set Swedish shot records with 20.60 in 1973, 20.66 in 1974 and 21.33 in 1975. He was NCAA champion outdoors in 1973 and 1975 and indoors in 1973-5 while at the University of Texas El Paso. Pb DT 46.70 (1973).
Annual progression: 1970- 16.45, 1971- 17.66, 1972- 19.53, 1973- 20.60, 1974- 20.66, 1975- 21.33. 1976- 20.47, 1977- 20.02, 1978- 19.32, 1979- 16.93, 1980- 17.16, 1981- 16.18, 1982- 16.32, 1983- 16.43.

Anton IHRING (Slovakia) on 31 August at the age of 70. President of the Slovak Athletics Federation 1982-98.

Vladimir JANCEK (Slovakia) (b. 25 Sep 1947 Kezmarok) on 25 January in Kosice. He set the Czechoslovakian/SVK 100m record with 10.2 in 1968; 4 internationals 1968-9. Pb 200m 21.5 (1967).

Nils **Gustav JANSSON** (Sweden) (b. 5 Jan 1922 Brattfors, Värmland) on 11 April in Karlstad. He took the bronze medal at the 1952 Olympic Games in Helsinki in 2:26:07 and was 5th in the Europeans in 1954 with ten more appearances for Sweden. He was 2nd at Kosice in 1950 and 1954 and Swedish champion at marathon each year 1951-3 and at 25k 1950-3. He ran a faster 2:21:40 for 6th in Boston in 1955 but that was on a short course (41.1km). Pbs: 5000m 14:50.2, 10000m 29:51.2 (both 1952).

Mamadou Kimathi DaCosta **JOHNSON** (USA) (b. 29 Nov 1972 New York) on 29 April. He was the only Ivy Leaguer (Penn) to clear over 18ft in the pole vault, with pb 5.52 (1993).

Sten Jean '**Stein' JOHNSON** (Norway) (b. 20 Oct 1921 Bergen) on 28 April in Oslo. At discus he was 8th in 1948 and dnq 1952 at the Olympic Games and 5th in 1946 and 4th in 1950 at the Europeans. Pbs: HJ 1.90 (1949), LJ 6.68 (1950), SP 13.94 (1950), DT 50.33 (1952). He became a highly successful trainer at various sports, working in all for 12 national federations, most notably of the Norwegian national speed skating team, being the man behind their "skating revolution" in 1963. His aunt Sonia competed at swimming at the 1912 Olympic Games.

Henrik KALOCSAI (Hungary) (b. 28 Nov 1940 Budapest) on 22 May in Budapest. He set five Hungarian records at long jump from 7.78 in 1962 to 7.86 in 1970 and ten at triple jump from 15.78 in 1962 to 16.73 in 1967 and won 19 Hungarian titles: LJ 1960-3, 1965-7, 1969-71 and 1973; TJ 1962-3, 1965, 1967-8, 1970-1 and 1973; 45 internationals 1958-75. Olympic Games: 1964

dnq LJ & TJ, 1968 10th TJ; Europeans: 1962 6th LJ, 1966 3rd TJ, 1969 10th TJ, 1971 dnq LJ & TJ; World University Games: 1965: 1st TJ; European Indoors: 1966 6th TJ, 1967 2nd TJ, 1970 6th LJ, 1971 dnq LJ & 13th TJ. Other pbs: 100m 10.5 (1967), 200m 21.7 (1967).

Karl **Bertil KARLSSON** (Sweden) (b. 19 Sep 1919 Skogstibble) on 31 December in Uppsala. At the 1952 Olympic Games he was 13th at 10,000m and 9th in his heat at 5000m and at the 1950 Europeans he was 11th at 5000m. Swedish champion at 5000m 1950, 10,000m 1952 and 4km cross 1949. Pbs: 3000m 8:18.2 (1947), 5000m 14:31.4 (1947), 10,000m 30:10.0 (1951); three internationals.

Karl-Erik Viktor **KARLSSON** (Sweden) (b. 7 May 1922 Björnlunda) on 29 June. He ran 3:49.8 for 1500m when 4th in the 1950 Swedish Championships for 8th equal on the world list that year. Onr international. Other pbs: 1M 4:09.8 (1947), 3000m 8:24.4 (1952).

John KELLY (Ireland) (6 Dec 1929 Loughmore) on 13 November in Prescott, Arizona, USA. In 1968 heset an Irish 50km walk record of 4:24:22 and competed at the Olympic Games (dnf). He lived in Australia and New Zealand and competed in a wide range of sports, especially boxing, from 1949 before moving to America in 1959. He then took up marathon running and, in several inches of snow, won the Philadelphia Marathon in 2:37:23. Pb 20kW 1:32:30 (1967). In 1973 he earned a place in the *Guinness Book of Records* when he walked 120 miles in the notorious Death Valley Desert, California in the non-stop record time of 34 hours 9 minutes and 9 seconds.

George Ezekiel **KERR** (Jamaica) (b. 16 Oct 1937 Maryland, Hanover) on 15 June in St. Andrew. A great 400/800 runner, he competed at three Olympic Games – for Jamaica in 1956 (heat 400m and dq 4x400m) and 1964 (4th 800m and 4x400m), and for the West Indies Federation in 1960 when he won bronze medals at both 800m and 4x400m. He won five medals at the Commonwealth Games: bronze 4x400y in 1958 (sf 400m), gold at 440y and 4x440y and silver at 880y in 1962, and bronze at 880y (4th 4x440y) in 1966. He won triple gold (400m, 800m and 4x400m) at the Central American & Caribbean Games in 1966, and at the Pan-American Games was 1st at 400m and 4x400m and 2nd at 800m in 1959. He won the British West Indies titles at 400m in 1959 and at 800m in 1957 and 1959, and Jamaican 400m and 800m in 1959 and 1961. Following his mentor Herb McKenley, he studied at the University of Illinois and won the NCAA 800m/880y title in 1959 and 1960. *Track & Field News* world rankings: 400m/800m:1959- 2/3, 1960- 6/3, 1961- 8/3, 1962- 3/7, 1964- -/6, 1966- -/8. CAC records

440y 46.0 (1960), 880y 1:46.5 (1964), 1000m 2:22.5 (1960); and other pbs: 100m 10.5, 220y 21.6, 1500m 3:52.6 (1964).

Annual progression (position on world list): 1956- 47.7 (69=), 1957- 47.7 (76=), 1:50.5 (82=); 1958- 46.5* (5), 1:48.4* (20=); 1959- 46.0* (6=), 1:47.1* (4); 1960- 45.7* (6=), 1:46.4 (2); 1961- 46.3* (19=), 1:46.4 (1=); 1962- 45.9 (8=), 1:47.1* (5=), 1963- 47.0* (61=), 1:49.0* (54=); 1964- 46.1 (13=), 1:45.8* (4). * *conversions from 440y or 880y.*

Paul KERRY (USA) (b. 6 Apr 1945, Ardmore, Oklahoma) on 6 October. NCAA 120y hurdles champion for the University of Southern California in 1965. Pbs: 120yh 13.7 (1965), 110mh 13.7/13.94 (1968), 440yh 52.1. He taught and coached at Santa Monica High School 1969-96.

Anabella María von KESSELSTATT (Argentina) (b. 12 June 1969 Córdoba) in Buenos Aires on 7 June of a cardiac arrest. She set four national records at 400 metres hurdles 1991-3. At South American Championships she won the 400mh in 1993, was third at 100mh in 1991 and 1993; and at 4x100m was 3rd in 1991 and 2nd in 1993, and 2nd at 4x400m in 1993. She was 3rd in the Ibero-American heptathlon in 2002 and competed at 400mh (heat) in the 1993 Worlds. Pbs 100m 12.41 (2007), 11.8 (1991); 200m 24.75 (1992), 24.1 (1993); 300m 39.33 (2007), 39.1 (1994); 400m 54.73 (1994), 600m 1:31.9 (1994), 800m 2:10.9 (1994), 100mh 13.78 (1993), 300mh 41.3 (1994), 400mh 57.42/57.2 (1993), HJ 1.69 (2002), LJ 5.84/6.09w (2001), Hep 5237A (2002).

Joseph KIMANI Karanja (Kenya) (b. 1 Sep 1972 Nakuru) on 1 November of pneumonia. He had track bests of 1M 4:03.11, 3000m 7:44.97, 2M 8:30.78, 5000m 13:12.05 and 10,000m 27:28.07 all in 1995 and had outstanding success on the US road running circuit. This included world bests for 10k on a loop course 27:41 '95 and 27:20 '96 and on a slightly downhill course 27:04 '96, and 33:21 for 12k in 1997 Other road bests: 15k 42:40 '96, HMar 60:04 '98, Mar 2:25:32 '98.

Raymond KIRSTETTER (France) (b. 23 May 1919 Benfeld) on 2 July at Saint-Pierre dels Forcats. He set his discus pb and was French discus champion in1948; 6 internationals. 1948-52.

ISTVÁN KISS (Hungary) (b. 7 May 1940, Örkény), on 10 December in Budapest. He competed at the European Champs in 1962 (ht 5000m) and 1966 (7th 5000m) and was 3rd at 3000m at the 1966 European Indoor Games. Hungarian 5000m champion 1962; 11 internationals 1961-7 at 1500m and 5000m. Pbs: 800m 1:54.5 (1963), 1500m 3:44.9 (1966), 3000m 8:00.0 (1966), 5000m 13:42.15 (1965), 10,000m 29:04.0 (1967).

Dilbagh Singh KLER (Malaysia) (b. 14 Apr 1936 Kota Kinabalu, Sabah) on 18 October in Kota Kinabalu. A steeplechaser, he competed at the 1964 Olympics (heat), and was 11th in 1962 and 12th in 1966 at the Commonwealth Games (also heat 1M in 1962 and 19th 3M in 1966). At the Asian Games, competing for North Borneo in 1962 and Malaysia in 1966 and 1970, he was respectively 5th, 5th and 7th at the steeplechase, also 10th at 1500m in 1962. He also won one 5000m and three steeplechase tiles at SEAP Games. His Malaysian records included a best for 3000mSt of 9:16.0 (1971). His younger brother Balwant Singh Kler was the former Asian AA statistician.

Josephine KOHL-KRÜGER (Germany) (b. 23 Jun 1921 Hainstedt) on 27 April in Seligenstadt. She ran the first leg on the German 4x100m team that won the European title in 1938. Pb 100m 12.2 (1939).

Martin KUTMAN (Georgia/Estonia) (b. 12 Jul 1928 Abkhazia, Georgia) on 29 May in Tartu. He was the Georgian champion and record holder in the pole vault from 1949 to 1952 when he moved to Estonia and began his lecturing career at the University of Tartu; during his long career he coached athletes who set around 50 national records. He won three Estonian titles at pole vault between 1953 and 1958 and had a best of 4.10 (1953).

Mirko KUZMANOVIC (Serbia) (b. 8 Jan 1937) on 8 May in Belgrade. He competed (dnq) at pole vault in the 1962 Europeans and was Yugoslav champion and 2nd in the World University Games in 1959. Pb 4.40 (1960).

Tadeusz KWAPIEN (Poland) (b. 25 Feb 1923 Koscielisko) on 23 November in Zakopane. He was Polish champion at 1500m in 1949 and 5000m in 1950 before going to renown as a cross-country skier, winning 18 Polish titles and competing at the 1948, 1952 and 1956 Winter Olympics.

Hans Verner LAGESSON (Sweden) (b. 21 Aug 1940 Västerstad) on 22 October. Swedish javelin champion in 1961 with pb that year of 76.54; 12 internationals. He studied at Pacific Lutheran University.

Thorbjørn Arnold LARSEN (Norway) (b. 18 Feb 1942) on 20 August. Norwegian champion at marathon 1974 and 1977, international 1972-81. Pbs: 5000m 14:23.6 (1976), 10,000m 30:01.4 (1969), Marathon 2:18:03 (1978).

António LEITÃO (Portugal) (b. 22 July 1960) died on 18 March in Porto. After winning the bronze medal at the 1979 European Juniors, he improved at 5000m from 13:42.5 in 1981 to a Portuguese record 13:07.70 in 1982. He had posted several fast times but had little major success until the 1984 Olympic Games, when he ensured that the pace was fast in the final, and reaped his reward with a bronze medal. Also: Worlds 10th 1983, Europeans 5th 1986, heat 1982 and 1990. Portuguese champion at 5000m and 3000mSt in 1981, and records at 3000m 7:39.69 (1983) and 3000mSt 8:26.19 (1984). Other pbs: 800m 1:53.55 (1987), 1500m 3:38.2 (1982), 2000m 5:09.74 (1985), 2M 8:20.86 (1984), 10,000m 29:07.59 (1985). He ran eight times in the World Cross, with best placings of 20th junior (1978), 25th (1984) and 13th (1985) and team bronze in 1984.

Terje LILLESETH (Norway) (b. 10 Aug 1926) on 19 May. Norwegian champion at 1500m 1952-3, 16 internationals 1949-56. Pbs: 800m 1:52.5, 1500m 3:45.4, 1M 4:07.8, 3000m 8:25.8 (all 1956).

Bruce LONGDEN (GBR) (b. 6 Aug 1939 Sheffield) in July. BAAB National Coach 1976-84 and head coach for the Norwegian Athletic Federation 1984-8, returning to Britain as a BAF National Coach 1991-7. He coached Daley Thompson and Sally Gunnell to World and Olympic titles. His wife Susan (née Wright) was 12th in 1976 and 15th in 1980 at the 1976 Olympic Games, and set five UK records at pentathlon 1976-80 to 4402 points (1984 tables) and one at heptathlon, 5139 (1979).

Dr John LUCAS (USA; b. 24 Dec 1927 Boston), on 9 November. An Olympic historian and long-time Penn State University coach and professor, he attended every Olympics from 1960 to 2008; became an official IOC lecturer in 1992 and was awarded the Olympic Order by the IOC in 1996. He ran in the US Olympic Trials 10,000m in 1952.

Sune Ossian **LUNDGREN** (Sweden) (b. 5 Nov 1917 Lidingö) on 2 November. A pole vaulter, he made his only international in 1951, after 3rd in 1943 and 2nd in 1946 and 1949 at Swedish championships; pb 4.10 (1949)

Edward Finn **'Ted' McGLYNN** (Australia) (b. 29 Aug 1931) on 24 April. He ran the opening leg for the Australian 4x100m team at the 1956 Olympic Games in both heat and semi where they finished 4th in 40.72, just missing the final. Pbs: 100y 9.6 (1953), 100m 10.6 (1954), 220y 21.5 (1953).

Károly MAGYAR (Hungary) (b. 8 Aug 1945 Budapest) on 10 May in Budapest. Ran in seven internationals 1966-72 at 3000m steeplechase with heat at 1966 Europeans. Pbs: 5000m 14:02.4 (1972), 10.000m 29:40.6 (1971), 3000mSt 8:39.2 (1972).

George Frank **MATTOS** (USA) (b. 6 Oct 1929, Santa Cruz, California) in Oregon on 18 October. Ranked in the world top ten at pole vault seven times between 1949 and 1959, he was 9th in 1952 and 4th in 1956 at the Olympic Games after 3rd and 2nd respectively in the US Olympic Trials. He was US champion in 1953 plus 2nd in 1950 and 3rd in 1952 and 1957 (tied). He went to San Jose State University, tying for

2nd in the NCAAs in 1950-1. He spent three decades as a music teacher (played clarinet & saxophone in jazz bands). Pb 4.57 (1959, steel pole).

Annual progression (position on world list): 1944- 2.67, 1945- 3.39, 1946- 3.59, 1947- 3.96 (59=), 1948- 4.11 (30=), 1949- 4.27 (15), 1950- 4.39 (4=), 1951- 4.29 (12=), 1952- 4.47 (4), 1953- 4.47 (3=), 1954- 4.37 (14=). 1955- 4.35 (21), 1956- 4.53 (6), 1957- 4.49 (12), 1958- 4.49 (13=), 1959- 4.57 (10=), 1960- 4.49 (28=).

William Lee **'Willie' MAY** (USA) (b. 11 Nov 1936 Knoxville) on 28 March in Evanston, Illinois. He was silver medallist at 110m hurdles at the 1960 Olympic Games (beaten by just 0.01 sec. by Lee Calhoun) and at the 1963 Pan-American Games. In 1960 he was 2nd in the US Olympic Trials and 3rd in the AAU. For Indiana University he was 3rd in 1958 and 2nd in 1959 at 120yh and 3rd in 1958 at 220yh at NCAAs. Pbs: 110mh 13.4 (1960), 13.84 (1959); 200mh (turn) 22.9 (1959), 220ySt 22.9 (1957). He was at Evanston Township High School from 1967 and was a highly successful head boys track coach there from 1975 to 2006, and athletic director from 1983.

Annual progression (position on world list): 1957- 14.3y/14.2yw (32=), 1958- 14.0y/13.8yw (12=), 1959- 13.6 (2=), 1960- 13.4 (2), 1962- 14.4y/14.0yw (85=), 1963- 13.7y (4=), 1964- 14.0 (26=)/13.9yw.

Jacqueline MAZÉAS (France) (née Martin) (b. 10 Oct 1920 Denain) on 9 July at Darnétal near Rouen. At the discus she was the Olympic bronze medallist in 1948 with 40.47, French champion in 1946-7 and set three French records to 40.49 (1948); 3 internationals 1947-8, pb SP 11.16 (1946).

Albert Richmond **'Boo' MORCOM** (USA) (b. 1 May 1921, Braintree, Mass) on 3 October in Braintree, Massachusetts. Having served as an Army officer and paratrooper in the Pacific Theatre during World War II, he was US pole vault champion in 1945 (tie), 1947 and 1948 (tie) (indoors 1942 & 1949, 2nd 1947-8) and was 6th at the 1948 Olympics. He was also 2nd in the AAU high jump in 1942 and tied for the NCAA pole vault title for New Hampshire in 1947. After being third ranked in the world at 4.34 in 1947, he was equal first in 1948 at 4.47 (equal 4th on the world all-time list) and improved in 1949 to 4.49 indoors, second to Bob Richards on the world list. He started coaching in 1948 but in 1950 was recalled for duty in the Korean War where he served as an officer and jumpmaster in the Airborne Division; returning to coaching at the University of Pennsylvania 1952-87. He was coach to the US women's Olympic team at Melbourne in 1956. Later he became a prolific record setter in masters' athletics from 1966 when he converted to fibreglass poles, including 4.02i at age 60 in 1981. Other pbs: HJ 1.98 (1942), LJ 7.23 (1947).

Annual progression (position on world list): 1937- 2.95, 1938- 3.30, 1939- 3.85, 1940- 3.80, 1941- 4.16i/4.11 (19), 1942- 4.37i/4.29 (3=), 1943- 4.37i/4.26 (3), 1944- 3.96 (23=), 1945- 4.11 (8=), 1946- 4.22? (7), 1947- 4.34 (3=), 1948- 4.47 (1=), 1949- 4.49i (2); 1966- 3.96,1970- 3.96, 1971- 4.16, 1972- 4.19, 1973- 4.27, 1974- 4.11, 1975- 4.00i, 1976- 4.12, 1977- 4.04;... inc. 1981- 4.02i/3.96.

Sir John Oscar **MORETON** (GBR) (b. 28 Dec 1917 Oakham, Rutland) on 14 October. A close second to his Achilles Club colleague Godfrey Brown in the 1939 AAA Champs 880y (1:55.3), having clocked his fastest time of 1:54.4 just a few days earlier, he had his one international with 4th at 800m against Germany in Köln on 20 Aug 1939. Days later, war was declared and his promising athletics career came to an end at the age of 21. He won the Military Cross with the Royal Bucks Yeomanry in Burma. He joined the Colonial Office in 1948, serving in Kenya and Nigeria before being appointed Ambassador to Saigon at the height of the Vietnam War. His final appointment was as deputy to the Ambassador to the USA. He was still playing golf in his nineties. Awarded KCMG and KCVO.

Dr Peter Morgan **MULLINS** (Australia) (b. 9 July 1926 Bondi) on 14 April in Sydney. He was 6th in the decathlon at the 1948 Olympic Games with a Commonwealth record 6739 points (6334 on current table). He was Australian champion at high jump in 1949 and shot in 1950; pbs: 120yh 14.6 (1948), HJ 1.93, SP 13.71. A graduate of Washington State University in the USA, he excelled at many sports and played basketball for Canada in 1959. He became a 'legendary' basketball coach in two decades as head coach of the men's team at the University of British Columbia in Vancouver, Canada until retiring from that role in 1982 but continuing to coach track and field.

Terry L. **MUSIKA** (USA) (b. 20 Jan 1948 Coatesville) on 18 December at his home in Hunt Valley, Maryland. An accountant and international expert on intellectual property damages, he was a fine athlete while at Indiana University with bests for 440y: 46.0 to rank 28= on the world list in 1972, and 400mh: 50.4 for 27= in 1971.

Yves Ibrahim **NIARÉ** (France) (b. 20 Jul 1977 Saint-Maurice) was killed in a car crash on 5 December near Le Mans. He set three French records at shot from 20.21 (2007) to 20.72 (2008), first exceeding 18m in 1988, 19m in 2000 and 20m in 2006. Competing in 32 internationals 1999-2010, he won the European Indoor silver medal in 2009 and competed (dnq in all) at the Olympic Games in 2008, Worlds in 2007 and 2009, and Europeans in 2006. French champion 2000-05, 2007-10 and indoors 1999, 2001-02 and 2009. Other pbs: DT 63.44 (2007), HT 48.40 (2005). His father Namakoro Niaré had discus best of 62.48 (1972) and mother Martine Pouré 52.64 (1984).

Soini Mikael **NIKKINEN** (Finland) (b. 29 Jul 1923 Kiuruvesi) on 2 June in Nastola. On 24 Jun 1956 at Kuhmoinen, using an old-fashioned Finnish birch javelin he improved his pb by four metres to a short-lived world record 83.56 (bettered by Janusz Sidlo's 83.66 just six days later). Later in the season he lost his form so badly that, after 12th in 1948 and 8th in 1952, he was not selected for the Melbourne Olympic Games. He was third at the 1954 Europeans and won the Finnish title in 1952 (plus four silvers and three bronzes), with four wins in 15 dual matches in 1951-6. He actually was born 19.7.1923 (according to his mother).

Zolani NTONGANA (South Africa) (b. 7 Jul 1980) died on 3 May after being struck by a car in Khayelitsha, Cape Town the previous weekend. He ran his marathon best of 2:16:50 for 3rd in the 2012 national championships. He was 26th in the World Half Marathon in 2010. Pbs: 10km 28:46 (2006), HMar 62:23 (2009).

Jorun NYGAARD (Norway) (b. 6 May 1929 Lunner, Oppland) (née Askersrud, then Tangen 1952, Nygaard 1961) on 12 October in Lunner. She competed in 1952 at both Winter (12th 10km cross-country skiing) and Summer (heats of 100m and 80m hurdles) Olympic Games. At the European Championships she was 15th in 1954 and 17th in 1958 at pentathlon. Norwegian records : 80mh (10 to six at 11.8 1954-8), pentathlon (6 to 4081 (1954 tables) in 1957). Pb 100m 12.2 (1954).

James Stephen Omajuwa **'Jimmy' OMAGBEMI** (Nigeria) (b. 26 Nov 1930 Warri, Delta) on 12 November in Hooks, Texas, USA, where he had lived for several years. He won a silver medal at 4x110y after placing 5th at 100y at the British Empire Games in 1958. He competed at the Olympic Games in 1960 (heat 200m & 4x100) and 1964 (heat 4x100m) and was AAA 100y champion in England in 1958. Pbs: 100y 9.4 (= African record 1959), 100m 10.4 (NGR record 1958), 220y 21.4 (1960). He became a leading coach and was the father-in-law of Mary Onyali-Omagbemi. His son Victor ran at the 1991 World Champs and had bests of 100m 10.27 (1991), 10.26w (1993); 200m 20.70 (1992), 400m 46.47 (1993).

Reginald James **'Reggie' PEARMAN** (USA) (b, 23 May 1923 Manhattan, New York) on 8 June. The son of Ethiopian immigrants and 1.88m tall, he was 7th at 800m at the 1952 Olympic Games after 3rd at the US Olympic Trials, having failed to finish in the US Trials

800m final in 1948. He ran for the New York Pioneer Club and won AAU titles at 440y in 1957 and at 800m/880y in 1947 and 1952, and indoors at 600y in 1954. He was 2nd for New York University in the 1949 NCAA 880y and later earned a doctorate in educational administration from the University of Massachusetts before teaching at various universities, Pbs: 400m 46.7 (1952), 800m 1:49.7 (1953). A great relay runner, in August 1952 he ran on the US teams that set world records at the White City in London at 4x440y (3:08.8) and 4x880y (7:29.2, fastest leg (the 2nd) in 1:50.3 against the British Empire).

Jan PEREK (Czech Republic) (b. 21 Dec 1928 Zlín) on 26 May in Zlín. He set Czechoslovak records for javelin at 72.85 (1955) and 73.13 (1956) and had a best of 74.29 (1959). 19 internationals 1950-60; other pbs: 200m 21.7 (1950) and Dec 6401 (1950, on 1934 tables, 6152 on current tables).

Jean-Pierre PERROT (France) (b. 7 Mar 1952 Montbron) on 28 November in Annecy. Second in the European Junior 400mh in 1970 in 50.3, then 4th on the junior world all-time list, his career was cut short by a severe broken ankle injury in May 1971.

Chris PERRY (Australia) (b. 21 May 1959) on 5 October. Winner of the Stawell Gift race in 1982 as a professional, he competed in the 1986 Commonwealth Games 100m (semi-final) and had a pb of 10.34 (and 10.29w) that year. 2nd AUS 100m 1986-7.

Christina May **PERSIGHETTI** (GBR) (b. 6 Jul 1936 Shoeburyness, Essex) (née Cops, later Frost) on 31 October in Southend-on-Sea. She competed in eight internationals 1956-61 for Britain at long jump, including the 1960 Olympic Games, at which she was 19th. Her best result was a win with 5.93 against the USSR in 1957, and that year she was WAAA champion (2nd 1961 and indoors 1962, 3rd 1955-6). Pbs: 80mh 11.7 (1961), LJ 5.95 (1961), Pen 3807 (1954 tables) (1962).

Frank POOE (South Africa) (b. 2 Dec 1974 Vereeniging), formerly Rakosa, in Sebokeng on 22 April. He had marathon bests of 2:11:37 dh (3rd Boston) and 2:12:40 to win the SA title in 1999; he was also SA champion and 5th in the Commonwealth Games in 1998, and 3rd in the 1999 All-Africa Games. He was 4th and a member of the winning RSA team at the 1994 World Half Marathon. Other pbs: 10km 29:32, 1Hr 20,399m (1997), HMar 61:17 (1998).

Dmitry POLYAKOV (Ukraine), husband and coach of Olympic heptathlon champion Nataliya Dobrynska, on 25 March, aged 48. Originally a boxing coach, he started working with Dobrynska in 2007 and lived to see her set a world pentathlon record of 5013 to win the

World Indoor title on 9 Mar 2013. "My Istanbul win was for him," said Dobrynska.

Patrick Ralph **PORTER** (USA) (b. 21 May 1959 Wadena, Minnesota) was killed when a plane he was piloting went off a runway in Sedona, Arizona, and burst into flames on 27 July. He won a record eight US cross-country titles 1982-9 and was four times in the top ten at the World CC: 1983- 9th, 1984- 4th, 1986- 6th and 1987- 7th. On the track at 10,000m he competed twice in the Olympic Games – 15th in 1984 and heat in 1988 – and was the World University Games bronze medallist in 1987 and US champion in 1989; also 2nd at the 1985 World Cup. He went to Adams State College in Alamosa, Colorado. Pbs: 3000m 7:51.0 (1988), 2M 8:43.2i (1983), 5000m 13:33.91 (1988), 10,000m 27:46.80 (1988), 3000mSt 8:58.81 (1981). He married Trish King (1988 US Olympian at HJ, pb 1.96) on 15 Dec 1991.

Hannu POSTI (Finland) (b. 15 Jan 1926 Vehkalahti) on 13 June in Helsinki. The only Finnish track & field athlete to compete at both Summer and Winter Olympic Games, he was 8th in the 20k biathlon in Innsbruck 1964, also winning World silver in 1963. He was 5th in the European 5000m in 1950 and 14th in 1954, Finnish champion at 5000m 1952-3, 10,000m 1952-5, and cross country 1951-2 and 1954, and competed in 18 international dual matches 1950-7. Serving in the Finnish Army and Frontier Guard in 1943-73, he was also a leading coach. Pbs: 1500m 3:54.8 (1950), 3000m 8:14.8 (1952), 5000m 14:11.8 (1957), 10,000m 29:49.8 (1953).

Edmund POTRZEBOWSKI (Poland) (b. 16 Jun 1926 Chorzów) on 22 May in Vancouver, Canada. He ran at the 1952 Olympics (sf 800m, ht 1500m) and at both events at the 1954 Europeans. He was Polish champion at 800m 1953-4 and 1500m 1950 and 1952 and set Polish records at 800m 1:51.5 (1951), and 1:50.7 (1954). 1000m 2:27.2 (1952) and 2:25.6 (1954), and 1500m 3:53.0 (1952) and 3:48.4 (1954).

Nélson PRUDÊNCIO (Brazil) (b. 4 Apr 1944 Lins, São Paulo) on 23 November in São Carlos from lung cancer. A great triple jumper, he competed at three Olympic Games, winning the silver medal in 1968, bronze in 1972 and missing the final in 14th place in 1976. From a pre-Olympic best of 16.30, in a great clash at high altitude in Mexico City in 1968 he qualified with 16.46 and in the final jumped 16.33, 17.05 and 16.75 before he set a world record of 17.27 in the fifth round plus 17.15 in the last round, when Viktor Saneyev responded with 17.39 (both the world records had wind readings given at +2.0 as did Bob Beamon for his 8.90!). He produced a low altitude best of 17.05 for the bronze in Munich

1972. At Pan-American Games he won silver medals in 1967 and 1971 and was 4th in 1975 and he was South American and Brazilian champion in 1965, 1967, 1969 and 1971 (S.Am 2nd 1974-5). He was also Brazilian long jump champion in 1967. Other pbs: HJ 1.90, LJ 7.60. He became a Physical Education Professor and later a doctor; he was also a professor at the Universidade Federal de São Carlos and vice-president of the Brazilian Confederation.

Annual progression (position on world list): 1964- 14.77, 1965- 14.82, 1966- 16.18 (22), 1967- 16.30/16.45w (23), 1968- 17.27A (2), 1969- 16.34A (16), 1970- 16.29 (27=), 1971- 16.82A/16.33 (5), 1972- 17.05 (5), 1974- 16.33 (43=), 1975- 16.93 (7), 1976- 16.22 (68=).

Gérard RASQUIN (Luxembourg) (b. 30 Jul 1927 Paris, France) on 11 December in Luxembourg. He won the World Universities 400m in 1951, was 6th in the European 800m in 1954, and competed at the Olympic Games in 1952 (hts 400m & 4x400m)) and 1956 (hts 400m & 800m). He set national records for 400m three to 48.7 (1951) and 800m 1:50.4 (1953) and won 12 Luxembourg titles: 400m 1949-57, 800m 1953-4 and 1956. He was formerly a member of the ATFS.

Hans Werner Herbert **'Juan' RECCIUS** Ellwanger (Chile) (b. 9 Apr 1911 Valdivia) on 29 June in Valdivia at the age of 101. Having competed at triple jump at the 1936 Games in Berlin, he was the oldest living Olympian at any sport. He was South American champion in 1935 and set the Chilean record with 14.64 in 1932. His older brother Adolfo was the inaugural South American triple jump champion in 1920.

Pentti REKOLA (Finland) (b. 13 Mar 1934 Nakkila) at Tampere on 13 September. A fine all-round sprinter for Turku club Turun Toverit and a fireman, he competed in all 29 international matches for Finland 1956-62 with a total of 101 races (57 individual and 44 relays, inc. 27 times 4x400) to equal the all-time record of his club mate Voitto Hellsten. Rekola competed at 4x400m in the 1956 and 1960 Olympics and 1958 and 1962 Europeans. He won medals in all his 14 Finnish Champs finals, winning the 100m in 1956-8 and 1961, and a 200m/400m double in 1959 plus six silvers and two bronzes. Pbs: 100m 10.5 (1959, Finnish record that lasted 11 years), 200m 21.5 (1959), 400m 47.4 (1957). His son Harri was third in the Finnish long jump in 1983 with a pb 7.55.

Thomas Augustus **'Tom' ROBINSON** (Bahamas) (b. 16 Mar 1938 Nassau) on 25 November in Nassau. At age 17 he competed at the 1955 Pan-American Games and in 1956 he became the first Bahamian to compete at the Olympic Games (heats 100m & 200m).

He was 3rd at 100m and 4x100m at the West Indian Federation Games in 1957 and came to international prominence at the British Empire Games in Cardiff in 1958. There he was 2nd to Keith Gardner in the 100y in 9.6 (9.69) after equalling the Empire record with 9.5 in heat and semi-final, and beat Gardner in the 220y in 21.0w (21.08w) after 20.85w in his semi. He won further Empire/Commonwealth silver medals at 100y in 1962 (9.6) and 1966 (9.44) and also took part (at 4x100m) in 1970. He competed at four Olympic Games, making the final with 8th (after pulling a muscle) at 100m in 1964 and was CAC Games 100m champion in 1962. He also won the 100m at the West Indian Federation Games in 1958 and 1964. He was at the University of Michigan in the USA 1958-62 and there won nine Big Ten titles and was 5th in the NCAA 100y and 220y in 1960. He later studied at the University of Toronto. Other pbs: 60y 6.1i (1959), 100m 10.3 (1960), 10.38 (1964), 10.2w/10.22w (1964); 220y 20.9 (1960), 300m 35.0i (1964). He set a world indoor record for 220y at Chicago in 1959. The new National Stadium in Nassau, opened in 2012, was named in his honour.

Stewart ROGERSON (GBR) (b. 4 Feb 1962) on 18 December, having fought Non-Hodgkin lymphoma for 18 months. He had a hammer best of 70.30 (1988) and was 3rd in the UK champs in 1989. He was Inter-counties champion in 1987 and Northern in 1989, and threw for England v Norway in 1988.

Edwin H. **'Eddie' RYE** (New Zealand) in Napier on 17 May at the age of 90. He was NZ marathon champion in 1954 and 1957, pb 2:33:42 (1956).

Unni Svanhild SÆTHER (Norway) (b. 20 Oct 1932) (later Dahlstrøm) on 9 September. She was sixth in the pentathlon at the 1950 Europeans, Norwegian champion at 200m 1948, 80mh 1950, HJ & LJ 1953, triathlon 1949-50 and 1953, and set NOR records HJ 1.51 (1949), Pentathlon 2870 (1950).

Tenho Pietari **SALAKKA** (Finland) (b. 18 Jun 1934 Jääski, now part of Russia) on 11 February in Imatra. At the marathon he won Nordic titles in 1961 and 1965 and was Finnish champion in 1962 and 1965. He was 11th at the 1962 Europeans, 8th at Fukuoka later the same year, and 2nd at Boston in 1964. Pb 2.20.03 (1964).

Frank Dennis **SANDO** (GBR) (b. 14 Mar 1931 Maidstone) on 12 October. He competed in 11 internationals for Britain, all at 6M or 10,000m including 5th in 1952 (in British record 29:51.8) and 10th in 1956 at the Olympic Games and 3rd in 1954 at the Europeans (in his pb 29:27.6). For England he won bronze at 3 miles and silver at 6 miles at the Empire Games in 1954. He also set a British record with 8:25.6 for 3000m in 1952. A great cross-country runner, he was successively 9th, 2nd, 4th, 1st, 2nd=, 1st, 3rd, 2nd and 8th in the International Cross-country 1952-60 after being in the English National CC top ten each year, winning in 1957, 2nd in 1953 and 1958-9 and 3rd in 1954. Other pbs: 1M 4:12.0 (1954), 3000m 8:25.6 (1952), 2M 8:56.8 (1955), 3M 13:29.8 (1955), 5000m 14:10.6 (1956), 6M 28:14.2 (1956, 2nd to Ken Norris in AAAs). After gaining a degree in statistics from Birkbeck College, London he became a statistician in the Civil Service.

Rashid SHARAFETDINOV (Russia) (b. 10 Jul 1943 Ekhovo Ozero, Tatar ASSR) on 21 November. He had a fine race against Ian Stewart in taking the European 5000m silver medal in 1969 and two years later set a USSR 10,000m record of 27:56.25 (then 5th world all-time) in taking the European bronze medal. At the Olympic Games he went out in the heats at 5000m 1968 and 10,000m 1972. He won the World University Games 10,000m in 1970, was 2nd in the European Indoor 3000m in 1967, and USSR champion at 5000m 1968-9 and 1971, 10,000m 1970 and 1972 and cross-country 1968-71. Other USSR records: 3000m 7:50.6 (1972), 5000m 13:33.6 (1971); also pb 1500m 3:44.4 (1971).

Ragnar Lunde SKAUTVEDT (Norway) (b. 18 Nov 1936) on 24 February. A discus international 1962-9, he had pbs: SP 15.41 (1965), DT 54.78 (1963), HT 43.88 (1964), Dec 5905 (1962).

Tore **Ingemar SKYLDEBERG** (Sweden) (b. 17 May 1952 Borås) on 21 February. One international; pbs: 1500m 3:42.9 (1974), 3000m 7:55.8 (1977), 5000m 13:56.6 (1977).

Wlodzimierz SOKOLOWSKI (Poland) (b. 3 Sep 1940 Myszków) on 29 June in New York, USA. He competed in the 1964 Olympic Games at pole vault (no height in qualifying) and was 6th in 1966 and 5th in 1971 at the Europeans. Polish champion 1963-6 and 1971, he set seven Polish records from 4.69 in 1963 to 5.05 in 1967 and was the first Pole over 5m (and the 13th in the world, in 1964). Pb 5.13 (1971).

Annual progression: 1959- 3.21, 1960- 3.71. 1961- 3.80, 1962- 4.40, 1963- 4.70, 1964- 5.02, 1965- 4.90, 1966- 4.95i/4.90, 1967- 5.05, 1968- 5.00, 1969- 5.01, 1970- 4.81, 1971- 5.13, 1972- 5.10, 1973- 5.10i/4.90, 1981- 4.60, 1982- 4.11. 1983- 4.41, 1984- 4.27, 1985- 4.20.

Melville E. **SPENCE** (Jamaica) (b. 2 Jan 1936) on 28 October in Lauderhill, Florida. At the Pan-American Games he was 5th in 1955 and 4th in 1959 at 400m and 2nd in 1955 and, with his twin Malcolm, 1st in 1959 and 3rd in 1963 at 4x400m. At the CAC Games he was 4th at 400m and the twins ran on the winning relay team in 1962. He ran at the Olympic Games in 1956 (heats 200m & 400m) and 1964 (4th 4x400m) and at three Commonwealth Games: 1958 & 1966 (ht 440y), 1962 (6th 440, ht 880y, 1st 4x440y). Pbs: 400m 46.8 (1963), 880y 1:50.5 (1961).

Xenia STAD-DE JONG (Netherlands) (b. 4 Mar 1922 Semarang, Jawa Tengah, (now) Indonesia) (later van Bijleveld) on 3 April in Zoetermeer. Nicknamed 'Tom Thumb' due to her diminutive stature, she ran the first leg on the Dutch team that won the 4x100m at the 1948 Olympic Games, having been a semi-finalist in the 100m, and was a relay silver medallist (heat 100m) at the 1950 Europeans. Pbs: 100y 11.4 (1948), 100m 12.2 (1948), 200m 25.7 (1950).

Djordje STEFANOVIC (Serbia) (born 8 Nov 1921 Budapest, Hungary) on 30 July in Belgrade. He competed in the Olympic Games at 3000mSt in 1948 (heat) and was 10th in the European 10,000m in 1950. He set Yugoslav records at 3000m (2, 1948), 5000m (4, 1947-8), 10,000m (2, 1946-7) and 3000mSt (1948), and was Yugoslav champion at 5000m 1946-7, 3000mSt 1946, 1948, 1950 and 1953, and cross-country 1946-7 and 1949-51. Earlier he had been Hungarian junior champion at 3000m at track and cross-country in 1940. 22 internationals for Yugoslavia. Pbs: 1500m 3:58.6 (1947), 3000m 8:33.0 (1951), 5000m 14:44.8 (1950), 10,000m 30:39.4 (1952), 3000mSt 9:17.4 (1953).

Kosa STOJKOVIC (Serbia) (b. 13 Oct 1949, née Nikolic) on 17 July in Loznica. At discus she set Yugoslav records at 49.28 (1973) and 52.58 (1977) and was YUG champion in 1967, 1969, 1972 and 1975-80. Her younger son Vladimir is the goalkeeper of the Yugoslav national team.

Lena STUMPF (Germany) (b. 27 Apr 1924 Leer, Ostfriesland) on 6 February in Leer. At pentathlon she set an unratified world record of 447 points (4487 on 1954 tables) at Bremen on 23/24 July 1949, plus a German record of 459 (4427) in 1951, and was 4th at the 1954 European Championships. She was FRG champion at long jump in 1950 and 1954-5 and pentathlon 1948-9 and 1951. Pbs: 100m 12.0 (1951), 200m 25.7 (1951), 80mh 12.0 (1951), HJ 1.60 (1949), LJ 6.01 (1951), SP 12.87 (1948), DT 35.56 (1961), JT 42.60 (1949). 4 internationals 1953-5.

David TABAK (Israel) (b. 5 Aug 1927 Beit Oved) on 21 July. He ran at the 1952 Olympic Games (qf 100m and 200m) and set Israeli records of 10.6 and 21.8 that year that lasted 14 and 26 years respectively.

Donald Geoffrey **TAYLOR** (GBR) (b. 1 Jun 1936 Grimsby) on 5 July. Competing in three internationals for Britain in 1963, he set a British record for 10,000m with 28:52.4 (passing 6 miles in 28:00.0) in winning v West Germany at the White City on 23 August. Other pbs: 1500m 3:53.0 (1964), 1M 4:03.8 (1963), 3000m

7:58.2, 2M 8:43.2 (1963), 3M 13:27.4 (1963), 5000m 13:56.8 (1963), 10M 49:00.0 (1963), 3000mSt 9:07.2 (1961).

John Francis **TRELOAR** (Australia) (b. 10 Jan 1928 Sydney) on 23 July in Sydney. A world ranked sprinter 1947-52, he won the sprint treble, 100y, 220y and 4x110y, at the 1950 Empire Games in Auckland and, having been 4th in his semi-finals at both 100m and 200m in 1948, was 6th at 100m (dnf semi 200m) in 1952 at the Olympic Games. He was Australian champion at 100y in 1947-8 and 1950 and, at 220y in 1948, 1950 and 1952, and he tied the Australian record of 9.6 for 100y each year 1946-8 before running 9.5w and an estimated 9.5 in a handicap race in 1950. Other pbs: 100m 10.5 (1948), 220y 21.2 (1946-7 and 1950).

Irina Robertovna **TUROVA-BOCHKARYOVA** (b. 14 May 1935 Leningrad) on 8 February in Moskva. At the 1954 European Championships she won gold medals at 100m and 4x100m and silver at 200m and that year set her pbs of 11.6 (USSR record to top the world list) and 24.4. She ran at the Olympic Games in 1952 (qf 100m) and 1956 (4th 4x100m).

Dr **Leroy** Tashreau **WALKER** (USA) (b. 14 Jun 1918 Atlanta) on 23 April in Durham, NC. Coach at North Carolina Central University, he was chairman of the AAU men's track and field committee 1973-6 and the coordinator of coaching assignments for the AAU and TAC (forerunner to USATF) 1973-80. He coached track teams of five nations at Olympic Games 1960-72, before being head coach to the US Olympic track and field team in 1976. He was TAC president 1984-8 and later served as senior vice-president for sport of the Atlanta Committee for the Olympic Games. He also served as president (the first African-American to do so) of the U.S. Olympic Committee 1992-6. He received degrees from Benedict College and Columbia University and a PhD in biomechanics from New York University in 1957.

Stanislaw WASKIEWICZ (Poland) (b. 9 Mar 1947 Drewnica) on 28 September in Steamwood, Illinois, USA. He was a semi-finalist at 800m at the European Championships of 1969 and 1971 and won relay silver medals at the European Indoors, silver for medley relay in 1970 and bronze for 4 x 4 laps in 1972. Pb 800m 1:46.8 (1971).

Elles Charles **WEST** (South Africa) (b. 13 Oct 1924 Lahore, India [now in Pakistan]) on 17 July in California. He set four South African triple jump records in 1952-3 to 15.35A and was national champion at LJ and decathlon 1947 and TJ 1947-8 and 1952-3. Pb decathlon 6205A (current tables, 1948 on non-successive days). After Air Force service in the War, he

achieved an MA in anthropology at Stanford University and a doctorate in medicine at the University of Oregon in the USA. He was then appointed as an associate professor at Wichita State University, Kansas.

Jörg WISCHMEYER (Germany) (b. 16 Aug 1935 Dortmund) on 3 October at Korschenbroich. He competed in 15 internationals for FRG 1958-61, including at the 1960 Olympic Games and was national triple jump champion in 1959 and 1961. Pb 15.73 (FRG record, 1961)

John YARBROUGH (USA) (b. 16 Aug 1985) on 17 March in a car accident in Orlando, Florida. He had a 110m hurdles best of 13.36 in 2010, having been 4th at the NCAAs in 2006 when he was at the University of Mississippi. His older brother **Linnie** (pb 13.34 in 2007) was also in the car and was in a critical condition.

Died in early 2013

Hartmut BRIESENICK (GDR/Germany) (b. 7 Mar 1949 Luckenwalde) on 8 March in Berlin. He was European shot champion outdoors in 1971 and 1974 and indoors in 1970, 1971 and 1972 after 2nd in 1969. He won the Olympic bronze medal in 1976 and also won the European Junior title in 1968 (and bronze at discus) and at the European Cup in 1970 and 1973 and the World University Games in 1970. He was GDR champion outdoors in 1970-1 and 1973-4 and indoors 1969-72, and competed in 28 internationals for the GDR 1968-75. After five European Junior records from 17.61 to 18.71 in 1968, he set eight European records indoors from 19.58 (1969) to 20.67 (1972) and five European records outdoors from 20.69 (1971) to his pb of 21.67 (1973). He ranked successively 8-2-1-3-2-4-6 in the *Track & Field News* world rankings 1969-75. Pb DT 57.56 (1969). He married Ilona Slupianek (née Schoknecht) who won the 1980 Olympic and 1978 and 1982 European titles, also setting world records at 22.36 and 22.45 in 1980.

Petronella '**Nel**' **BÜCH** (de Vos) (Netherlands) (b. 6 Dec 1931 Amsterdam) on 5 February in Amsterdam . She ran on the Dutch 4x100m team that was 6th at the 1952 Olympic Games (and heat of the 100m). Pb 100m 12.1w (1953).

Charles Joseph **CAPOZZOLI** (USA) (b. 19 Jun 1931 College Point, New York) on 22 January. He was AAU 3 miles champion in 1953 and won the NCAA and IC4A cross-country titles in 1952. At the NCAAs he was 2nd in the 2 miles in 1951 and 1953 and at 5000m in 1952 for Georgetown University and was IC4A 2 miles champion in 1952-3. In 1952 he was 7th in his heat at 5000m at the Olympic Games before setting an American record of 13:51.8 for 3 miles in a notable victory in the USA v British Empire match in London. Other pbs: 1500m

3:51.6 (1953), 1M 4:07.8 (1953), 2M 8:55.3i (1953), 5000m 14:27.4 (1953). He became a salesman and settled in Dana Point, California.

Cummin Martin **CLANCY** (Ireland) (b. 9 Nov 1922 Glann, Oughterard, Galway) in Garden City, New York on 15 February. Irish discus champion in 1947-9 (and at shot in 1946), he competed at the 1948 Olympic Games and after an Irish record 46.49 (1949) had a pb of 49.35 (1951). He went to Villanova University and settled in the USA. where he established a very successful brokerage firm Clancy & Clancy in New York. His son Sean played as a linebacker in the NFL with the Miami Dolphins and St. Louis Cardinals.

Roger DUNKLEY (GBR) (b. 20 Jun 1935 Highgate, London) on 2 January in Kingston-upon-Thames. He set a British junior record for 1 mile at 4:12.8 in 1955 (then 0.8 outside the world junior best) and won the mile at the English Schools in 1952 (inters) and 1953 and AAA Juniors in 1953 and 1954. He was 2nd in the AAA 3 Miles in 1957. Shaftesbury H and Cambridge University. Pbs: 1500m 3:49.1 (1956), 1M 4:05.4 (1958), 2M 9:03.2 (1956), 3M 13:34.8 (1956), 5000m 14:11.4 (1956), 3000mSt 9:09.2 (1955).

Carl Allen John **'Jack' EMERY** (GBR) (b. 27 Dec 1913 Stoke-on-Trent) at his home in Cumbria n February. A graduate of Cambridge University, he was the 1938 International Cross Country champion after 2nd place in the National CC that year, and also enjoyed a fine track career with four GB internationals 1938-9. He was 2nd in the 1937 World Student Games 1500m, won the AAA 3 miles in 1938 and 1939 and was 4th in the 1938 European Champs 5000m. He set British records in 1938 at 3000m (8:29.6, which stood until 1950) and 2 miles (9:07.6, breaking Alf Shrubb's 1904 record; and also 9:03.4 for 2M in 1939– unbeaten until Chris Chataway in 1952). Other pbs: 880y 1:56.4 (1938), 1500m 3:53.3 (1938), 1M 4:13.8 (1937), 3M 14:08.0 (1939) and 5000m 14:40.4 (1939). A schoolmaster by profession, he competed successfully as a veteran up to the 1980s

Abderrahim GOUMRI (Morocco) (b. 21 May 1976 Safi) was killed in a car crash in Temara, a suburb of Rabat on 18 January. He was given a four-year drugs ban in 2012, losing all results from 17 August 2009. He took up the marathon in 2007, when he was 2nd in London in 2:07:44, and went on to a fine record in major races: New York 2nd 2007 & 2008 (4th dq 2010), Chicago 2nd dq 2009, London 3rd 2008, when he set a Moroccan record of 2:05:30, and 6th 2009. He had track pbs of: 1500m 3:39.80 (1998), 1M 4:02.46 (1999), 2000m 5:02.2 (2006), 3000m 7:32.36 (2001), 5000m 12:50.25 (2005), 10,000m 27:02.62 (2005) with a major championships

record: At 5000m: OG: '04- 13; WCh: '03- 10. At 10000m: WCh: '01- 16, '05- 8; AfCh: '02- 4. At 3000m: WI: '03- 9. His best placing at the World Cross was 7th in 2002, but he fared poorly in championships marathons: 20th OG 2008, dnf Worlds 2007, 2009 and 2011.

Noé HERNÁNDEZ Valentín (Mexico) (b. 15 Mar 1978 Chimalhuacán) of a heart attack on 16 January in Chimalhuacán, two weeks after being shot in the head in a bar. He won the Olympic bronze medal in 2000 at 20km walk – also dq Worlds 2001 and OG 2004, 4th Worlds 2003 and 2nd in the World Cup in 2002. He was CAC champion in 1999 and 2nd in the PanAm Cup in 2000. Pbs 20k 1:18:14 (2003), 50k 4:11:35 (2002).

Karl-Erik ISRAELSSON (Sweden) (b. 23 Aug 1929 Stockholm) on 10 January in Uppsala. He was 7th in the long jump at the Olympic Games in 1952. Swedish chanpion LJ 1951 and 110mh 1952. Pbs: 110mh 15/1/14.8w (1952), LJ 7.27 (1952), 7.33w (1950); Pen 3194 (1949), Dec 6497 (1950); 10 internationals.

Karl Gustaf **Lennart KARLSSON** (Sweden) (b. 30 Dec 1932 Ledberg near Linköping) on 16 January in Trollhättan. At 20km walk he was 4th at the 1958 Europeans and 14th at the 1960 Olympic Games. Pbs: 10,000m 46:19.4t (1958), 1:33:09.0t (1959). Swedish champion 10,000mW 1958, 20kmW 1959; 8 internationals.

Samson KIMOBWA (Kenya) (b. 15 Sep 1955) on 16 January in Nairobi. As a 21-year-old student at Washington State University, USA who had won the NCAA title a few weeks earlier and with a previous best of 28:10.3, he set a surprise world record for 10,000m with 27:30.47 at the World Games in Helsinki on 30 June 1977, taking 0.3 sec. off Dave Bedford's 1973 mark. He ran 27:37.28 in Stockholm four days later, but after that year never showed any top-class form; he was 11th at the Commonwealth Games in 1978. Other pbs: 3000m 7:47.8 (1977), 5000m 13:21.56 (1977).

Ann-Britt LEYMAN-OLSSON (Sweden) (b. 10 Jun 1922 Norum) on 5 January in Hisings Kärra. Olsson from 1949. She took the Olympic bronze medal at long jump in 1948 (also heats 200m), but was better known as a sprinter winning Swedish titles at 80m in 1941, 100m in 1942-4 and 1946-9, and 200m in 1942-7 and 1949 (best at LJ 3rd in 1946 and 1948). She set Swedish records at 100m from 12.3 in 1942 to 12.0 in 1948 and had pbs of 200m 25.8 (1946) and LJ 5.58 (1948, unratified at SWE record). At the 1946 European Champs she was 4th at 100m, 6th at 200m and 5th at 4x100m. Three internationals.

The Hon. Neville **'Teddy' McCOOK** (Jamaica) (b. 27 Apr 1939) in Kingston on 11 February. An IAAF Council member since 1999 and President of NACAC (North American, Central American & Caribbean AA, having been President of the Jamaica AAA 1984-96. IAAF President Lamine Diack said, "The systems he helped put in place in Jamaica laid the foundations and today continue to underpin the country's success at global championship level." He was awarded the Order of Jamaica in 2006.

Elaine MARTYN (later Wheeler) New Zealand) in Auckland on 9 February aged 101. Possibly the oldest living national champion, representing Canterbury she won the New Zealand women's 100 yards title in 1929 and that year NZ 100y records at 11.6 and 11.2 in 1929.

Paulo **Pietro MENNEA** (Italy) (b. 28 Jun 1952 Barletta) on 21 March in Rome. He won ten major championships gold medals in a sprint career rivalled at the time only by Don Quarrie. The 1980 Olympic 200m champion (when he beat Allan Wells by 0.02), Mennea competed in three further Olympic 200m finals, 3rd 1972, 4th 1976 and 7th 1984 and won bronze at 4x400m in 1980. He won European titles at 200m in 1974 (2nd 100m & 4x100m) and both 100m and 200m in 1978, after 6th at 200m and bronze at 4x100m in 1971. Further championships record: WCh: '83- 3/2R; EJ: '70- 5; WUG: '73- 3/1/3R, '75- 1/1, '79- 1/1R; WCp: '77- 4/2; ECp: '75- 2/1/3R, '77- (2), '79- 1/2, '83- 2/1R. At 400m/4x400mR: EI: '78- 1. Won Italian 100m (3): 1974, 1978, 1980; 200m (11): 1971-4, 1976-8, 1980, 1983-4

At high altitude in Mexico City in 1979 he ran a European record 10.01 for 100m and then won the World Universities 200m in 19.72, This was the longest lasting world record until Michael Johnson beat it twice in 1996. At 300m Mennea ran a world best of 32.23 at Rieti in 1979, after a hand timed 32.3 in 1975 and a world indoor best of 32.84 in 1978. He originally retired after 1980, when he became the oldest man ever to win an Olympic 200m title, but returned to top class three years later, and in 1984 became the first athlete to contest a track final at four Olympic Games. He retired again at the end of that year in protest against "the growing use of drugs by athletes", but came back again to compete at Seoul in 1988, but did not get beyond the heats of the 200m. He was notorious for running at the extreme edge of his lane, or on some notable occasions possibly over the line.

Trained as a lawyer, he was elected to the European Parliament as a Democrat in 1979, but failing to be re-elected for the second time in 2004.

Annual progress at 100m, 200m: 1969- 10.8; 1970- 10.5, 21.5; 1971- 10.2, 20.88/20.5w; 1972- 10.0, 20.30; 1973- 10.2, 20.56; 1974- 10.29, 20.53; 1975- 10.0/10.20, 20.1/20.23; 1976- 10.2/10.35, 20.1/20.23; 1977- 10.25, 20.11; 1978- 10.19/9.99w, 20.16; 1979- 10.01A/10.15, 19.72A/20.20; 1980- 10.19, 19.96; 1982- 20.68; 1983- 10.30, 20.22; 1984- 10.28, 20.07; 1987- 10.43, 20.68; 1988- 10.51/10.2/10.43w, 20.87. Other pbs: 60m 6.68i (1976), 400m 45.87 (1977).

Rita RIDLEY (Mrs Cleaver; née Lincoln) (GBR) (b. 4 Nov 1946 Hackney, London) on 12 February. At 1500m she won the 1970 Commonwealth Games title, and set UK records at the European Champs when 7th in 1969 (4:15.9) and 4th in 1971 (4:12.65). At 1500m or 1 mile she was WAAA champion in 1966-8 and 1970-1 and 2nd in 1969 and 3rd in 1973. She set four UK records at 1500m in all – also in her WAAA wins in 1970 (4:15.4) and 1971 (4:14.3), and two at 3000m, 9:59.6 in Dec 1968 and 9:22.6 in 1972. Other pbs: 800m 2:05.5 (1971), 1M 4:37.4 (1971), 3000m 9:13.6 (1973). She was also a prolific champion at cross-country, winning the English title 1969-72 and 1974 (2nd 1965 and 1973. In the IAAF World CC she was 4th in 1973 and 3rd in 1974 (leading England to team victory), after 2nd in 1967 and 1970, 3rd in 1972 and 10th in 1971 in the International CC. Her twin sister Iris Cook ran 2:05.8 for 800m and 4:45.7 for 1 mile (topping the UK year list) in 1968.

Alemayehu SHUMYE Tafare (Ethiopia) (b. 6 Apr 1988) was killed in a car crash on 11 January in Ethiopia. A consistent marathon runner, he made his debut at the event with three wins in 2008 and a best of 2:11:50 at Warsaw, and improved to his pb of 2:08:46 when 5th at Frankfurt in 2009. He had three more 2:09 times in 2011 and in 2012 had a best of 2:09:09 for 9th in Paris and won at Gold Coast in 2:10:35. Pb half marathon 62:16 (2011).

Éva SZIGETI-TÓTH (Hungary) (b. 12 Nov 1952 Budapest) on 30 January in Budapest. She competed at the 1980 Olympics (5th 4x400m – third leg – in a Hungarian record 3:27.86) and was a 400m semi-finalist at the 1976 European Indoor. Hungarian champion at 400m 1975-6; 12 internationals 1974-80. Pbs: 100m 12.66 (1978), 12.2 (1974); 200m 24.18 (1979), 400m 53.23 (1979), 52.9 (1975).

John Curtis **THOMAS** (USA) (b. 3 Mar 1941 Boston) on 15 January in Brockton, Massachusetts. In 1959 the 17 year-old Thomas shot to the top with six world indoor high jump bests from 2.11m to 2.16, including the first 7ft 2.13m jump under cover (at the Millrose Games in New York). He caught his left (take-off) foot in an elevator shaft, and the injury was so serious that he missed the outdoor season. However, in 1960 he added another four indoor bests, this time in excess of the outdoor world record of 2.16, taking the record from 2.17 to 2.20, and then outdoors set five world records from 2.17 to 2.23, the last two at the US Olympic Trials (actually the last was 7'3 7/8 = 2.2322, but rounded down to 7'3¾, and that was converted to 2.22 and ratified as that!). Then, however, he disappointed with third place at the Olympics at only 2.14 and for the rest of his career he remained one of the world's best but was overshadowed by Valeriy Brumel, behind whom he won the Olympic silver in 1964 when both cleared 2.18. AAU champion outdoors in 1960 and 1962 (2nd 1961, 3rd 1958 & 1964) and indoors seven times 1959-64 and 1966, NCAA winner for Boston University in 1960-1 and winner again of the Olympic Trials in 1964. He worked as a sales manager for the Bell Telephone Company. Other pbs: 120yh 14.5 (1962), LJ 7.24 (1962).

Annual progression (position on world list): 1956- 1.72, 1957- 1.95, 1958- 2.10 (4=), 1959- 2.165i (1), 1960- 2.23 (1), 1961- 2.215i/2.19 (2), 1962- 2.15 (5=), 1963- 2.185 (4), 1964- 2.20i/2.18 (3=), 1965- 2.08 58(=), 1966- 2.13i/2.09 (24=), 1967- 2.16i/2.14 (8=), 1968- 2.13i (33=).

Died in 2007: Pentti Otto Rikhard **SNELLMAN** (Finland) (b. 17 Feb 1926 Ulvila) on 14 Oct in Hendersonville, NC, USA. He was 9th at long jump at the 1952 Olympic Games, and had a pb of 7.45 (1956).

2008: Freidoune 'Fred' **SAHEBJAM** (Iran/France) (b. 4 Feb 1933 Nice) on 26 March. He set Iranian records with 10.7 for 100m and 21.7 for 200m in 1958 and was a member of the ATFS. He was a journalist, war correspondent and novelist, gaining international recognition for his 1990 novel *La Femme Lapidée*, which was the basis for the 2008 film *The Stoning of Soraya M*. His grandfather had been the Persian ambassador to Russia prior to 1917.

2010: Charles ELLIOTT (b. 8 Aug 1932 Birmingham)

Died in 2011

Corrections to ATHLETICS 2012: Clay GIBBS (b. 6 Jun 1929); Antony Patrick 'Tony' **WARD** (b. 18 July 1931 Torquay)

Nicole BESSO (née Langlade) (France) (b. 31 Jan 1946 Saint-Junien) on 27 September near Toulouse. French javelin champion 1977-8, pb 51.62 (1977), 17 internationals 1971-8.

Zdravko CERAJ (Croatia) (b. 4 Oct 1920 Bjelovar) on 6 October in Zagreb. He represented Yugoslavia in 26 internationals, including at the 1952 Olympic Games (heat 5000m) and at the 1950 Europeans (heat 1500m). He was Balkan champion at 5000m in 1953 and Yugoslav champion at 1500m 1946-52, 5000m 1953, 10,000m 1954 and 4.5k cross-country 1950. Pbs 1500m 3:50.6 (1951), 3000m 8:18.8 (1952), 5000m 14:26.2 (1952), 10,000m 31:14.8 (1954) with several Yugoslav records.

Otis **Roscoe COOK** Jr (b. 2 Mar 1939 El Centro, California) on 30 December in Alpharetta, Georgia. He tied the world records for 100y with 9.3 on 30 May 1959 at the California Relays in Modesto and indoors at 60y with four times of 6.0, two each in 1960 and 1961. His career was, however, blighted by a rare skin condition and his best placing in a national championship outdoors was 4th in the NCAA 100y in 1961. He graduated in physical education from the University of Oregon and gained a doctorate in education from the University of Massachusetts before his career as a teacher and then administrator with Los Angeles schools. Other pbs: 220y straight 21.0 (1956), LJ 7.26 (1957).

Domnitsa Lanitou **KAVOUNIDOU** (Greece) (b. 7 Apr 1914 Limassol, Cyprus) in Athens on 20 June at the age of 97. She was the first Greek woman to compete in athletics at the Olympic Games, doing so at 100m and 80mh (semi) in 1936 and competing again at 80mh in 1948. She won 41 national titles, including non-current events and relays and 25 at the main four: 100m 1931-7 and 1948; 80mh 1932-7 and 1948; HJ 1931-5 and 1937, LJ 1931-3 and 1935. Pbs (all Greek records, 31 in all at these events): 100m 12.4 (1936), 80mh 12.2 (1936), HJ 1.50 (1935), LJ 5.09 (1935).

Odd MÆHLUM (Norway) (b. 8 Oct 1921 Hamar) on 5 July in Hamar. At the javelin he was 4th at the 1946 Europeans and 5th at the 1948 Olympics. Norwegian champion 1946-9, 13 internationals 1946–51, pb 69.08 (1947). Later he coached 1956 Olympic champion Egil Danielsen. Mæhlum's son Terje had (old) javelin best of 75.48 (1973).

Paul SOINE (South Africa) (b. 19 Jun 1932 Krugersdorp) on 20 August in Port Alfred. He was South African champion at 880y in 1955 and 1956 and set national records for 880y with 1:52.2 in 1955 and 1:50.6 in 1956 and for 800m with 1:49.8 in 1957. pbs: 1500m 3:53.4 (1956), 1M 4:14.3 (1956). He was an electrical engineer.

Vladimir PRIKHODKO (France) (b. 1 Mar 1944 Paris) on 27 November in Concarneau. Russian father and Yugoslav mother. French hammer champion 1971-3 with national records 70.54 and 71.60 (1972) and pb 72.20 (1975) after a French junior record 53.54 in 1963. 25 internationals 1963-73.

DRUG BANS 2012

As announced by IAAF or national governing bodies. Suspension: L - life ban, y = years, m = months, W = warning and disqualification, P = pending hearing

Leading athletes

Men Name	Date	Ban
Andrei Alestar ROU	21 Jul	2y
Mazlum Aydemir TUR	7 Jul	2y
Larbi Bouraada ALG	15 Jun	2y
Bostjan Buc SLO		1y
Recep Celik TUR	12 May	2y
Ricardo Cunningham JAM		
Dementiy Cheparev RUS	18 Feb	2y
Mohamed El Hachimi MAR	26 May	6m
Róbert Fazekas HUN	16 Jun	8y
Yervásios Filippídis GRE	14 Jun	2y
Ivan Gertleyn RUS	15 Oct	P
Nour-eddine Gezzar FRA	17 Jun	10y
Hassan Hirt FRA		
Dimitríos Hondrokoúkis GRE		
Kirill Ikonnikov RUS	8 Oct	P
Ronald Rutto Kipchumba KEN	22 Apr	2y
Mathew Kisorio KEN	14 Jun	2y
Kripal Singh IND	21 Apr	
Rohit Kumar IND	23 Apr	2y
Damian Kusiak POL	15 Jun	2y
Cosmas Kyeva KEN	5 Feb	2y
Pascal Mancini SUI	30 Jan	2y
Luvo Manyonga RSA	20 Mar	18m
Tatyana Mineyeva RUS	17 Nov	2y
Kagishi Mumbane RSA	25 Feb	2y
Diego Palomeque COL	26 Jul	2y
Alex Schwazer ITA	30 Jul	4y
Kirpal Singh IND	21 Apr	2y
Yoel Tapia DOM	31 Mar	6m
Aleksandr Vashurkin RUS	14 Jul	2y

Women

Name	Date	Ban
Mariem Alaoui Selsouli MAR		P
Alina Antipova RUS	2 Mar	2y
Dimitra Arachoviti CYP	6 Mar	2y
Natalya Artic BLR	3 Jul	2y
Bimbo Miel Ayédou BEN	9 Mar	2y
Charmaine Barnard RSA	19 May	2y
Zahra Bouras ALG	5 Jun	2y
Lada Chernova RUS	29 Feb	L
Vivian Chukwuemeka NGR	21 Jun	L
Debbie Dunn USA	22 Jun	2y
Irina Eftimova BUL	16 May	2y
Semoy Hackett TRI	Jun	P
Genoveva Kigen KEN	28 May	2y
Rael Kiyara KEN	29 Apr	2y
Iríni Kokkinaríou GRE	–	4y
Marina Marghieva BLR	24 Jul	2y
Irina Meleshina RUS	7 Feb	2y
Elena Meuti ITA	22 Sep	5m
Karen Mey Melis TUR	27 Jun	2y
Ghofrane Mohammad SYR	4 Aug	2y
Yolanda Osana DOM	31 Mar	2y
Nadezhda Ostapchuk BLR		1y
Lauretta Ozoh NGR	11 Jul	2y
Darya Pishchalnikova RUS	20 May	P
Simret Restle-Apel GER	2 May	2y
Tânia Spindler BRA	26 Feb	W
Sun Lu CHN		P
Tshilofelo Thipe RSA	30 Jun	
Natalya Tsitsoryna BLR	3 Dec	2y
Yuliya Tutayeva RUS	27 Jun	2y
Maggie Vessey USA	4 Sep	W
Tameka Williams SKN		
Anna Wloka POL	28 Jan	6m
Fatima Yvelain FRA	20 May	2y

8y: Hassan Heidarpoort IRI (19 Jan); **3y**: Redha Megdoud ALG)16 May); **2y**: Emad Al-Amri KSA, Stéphane Berthe FRA (23 Jun), Mohammed Al Blooshy KUW (6 Mar), Nasser Al-Khaldi KSA, Bimbo Ayedou BEN, Deepak Choudhary IND (8 May), Marsida Dardha ALG (25 Jan), Litan Deb IND (21 Mar), Shardha-nand Dharmbir IND (13 Sep), Dharmvir Singh IND (4 Feb), Hayet Ferahtia ALG (26 May), Gai Laiyuan CHN (18 Apr), Supana Gosh IND (24 Jun), Suraj Gogai IND (21 Mar), Inderhjeet Singh IND (13 Mar), Thabiso Kekana RSA (20 Apr), Meryem Khali MAR (21 Dec),Sanhanara Khatun IND (23 Jun), Nixon Kiplagat KEN (4 Nov), Andre Koekemoer RSA (6 Mar), Handan Kocyigit Cavdar TUR (13 May), Pavel Kritskov RUS (8 Sep), Kulvinder Tanwar IND (8 Aug), Nitin Kumar IND (7 Aug), Lakavinder Singh IND (7 Aug), Adoro Lephethesang LES (3 Jun, Ilie Macovei ROU (30 Jun), Maria Maraviglia ARG (17 Dec), Juliana Moreira BRA (20 May), Vladimir Nikitin RUS (20 Jul), Sergey Nurgaliyev RUS (14 Jul), Ajibola Olawuyi NGR (16 May), Wieslaw Pietka POL (23 Aug), Prabhjit Singh IND (11 Sep), Anshu Rai IND (21 Apr), Arvinda Rathwa IND (15 Mar), Tilémahos Roútas GRE (15 Jun), Sandeep Singh IND (8 Aug), Rafula Sefamyetso RSA (20 Apr), Harvender Singh Dagar IND (23 Apr), Shakti Singh IND (26 Jun), Simranjeet Singh iND (14 Mar), Oleg Sysoletin RUS (21 Jul), Elaine Vieira BRA, Lokesh Yadav IND (14 Mar); **1y**: Elias Leal POR, W K Eashan SRI (11 Nov); **6m**: Ruan Claasen RSA (5 May), Piotr Lisek POL (15 Jun), Jorge Ortiz DOM (31 Mar); **5m**: Atanas Petrov BUL (2 Jun); **3m**: Yann Bruylandts BEL, Raphael Guillamet FRA (17 Jul), Jimmy Melfort FRA; **2m**: Nhan Cao FRA, Nicholas Macadam AUS (9 Aug); **W**: Guillaume Lecoq FRA, Zohar Zemiro ISR.

Add to Drugs Bans 2011

Men

Name	Date	Ban
Barakat Al-Harthi OMA	15 Dec	2y
Minás Alozíidis CYP	25 Jun	2y
Yahya Berrabeh MAR	23 Nov	4y
Victor Castillo VEN	25 Oct	4y
Sisay Ezkyas ETH	6 Nov	2y
Zoltán Kövágö HUN	11 Aug	2y
Pascal Mancini SUI	20 Nov	2y
Sergey Morozov RUS	25 Feb	L
Ali Abubaker Kamal QAT	15 Dec	2y
Femi Ogunode QAT	15 Dec	2y

Women

Name	Date	Ban
Alessandra Aguilar ESP	8 Dec	3m
Akkunjki Ashwini IND	27 Jun	2y
Aïcha Bani MAR	17 Jul	2y
Rose Cheshire KEN	4 Dec	1y
Inna Eftimova BUL	26 Aug	2y
Guan Yue CHN	19 Oct	2y
Sini Jose IND	12 Jun	2y
Mandeep Kaur IND	25 May	2y
Iríni Kokkinaríou GRE	27 Oct	4y

Lebogang Phalula RSA   27 Aug   2y*
Marielys Rojas VEN   27 Oct   2y
Simone da Silva BRA   3 Aug   5y
Nataliya Tobias UKR   23 Aug   2y
Antonina Yefremova UKR   23 Aug   2y
* one year suspended for exceptional circumstances (coach given a five-year ban).
8y: Pekka Viippo FIN (4 Sep); **2y**: Benek Abramiani GEO (11 Aug), R,S.M. Al Meqbali UAE (3 Apr), Henry Azike NGR (27 Apr), Luis Collazo PUR (6 Sep), Hemidah Mohamed El Saled EGY (25 Oct), Clarisse Hoarau FRA (15 Oct), Hsu Yu-Fang TPE (23 Oct), Nelson Korb BRA (21 Dec), Avin Kumar IND (19 Dec), Yunus Laselle MAS (16 Dec), Manish IND (11 Sep), Juna Murmu IND (25 May), Yerram Naidu IND (20 Dec), Tposin Ogedengbe NGR (7 Jul), Priyanka Panwar IND (27 Jun), Dorota Piskorowska POL (10 Apr), Alka Rani IND (11 Sep), Ranjana Roy IND (23 Jul), Vinita Sami IND (11 Sep), Alexander de los Santos URU (17 Dec), Shabeena IND (21 Dec), Tiana Mary Thomas IND (12 Jun), Ramesh Vignesh IND (28 Sep); **1y**: Reena Bittan IND (16 May); **9m**: Nicolas Chjarretier FRA (25 Sep); **8m**: Margarida Dionisio POR (16 Jul); **3m**: Frédéric Berland FRA (12 Jun). Joël Louise FRA (27 Nov).
Ornelas become the first athlete to be banned due to the IAAF's Athlete Biological Passport programme.

Add to Drugs Bans 2010: 4y: Ian Burns GBR (results annulled from 1 Oct); **2y**: Akish Antil IND (8 Aug), Eliud Cheptei KEN (5 Dec), Christian Hesch USA (27 Aug), Ranjita Mahanta IND (23 Apr), M Thavaraj IND (23 Apr), Sourab Vij IND (8 Aug)

Add to Drugs Bans 2009: 2y: Hanane Ouhaddou MAR (14 Aug)

From IAAF Athlete Biological Passport programme:

The Athlete Biological Passport involves measuring and monitoring an athlete's blood variables over time and establishes an individual longitudinal profile which can indicate the use of prohibited substances or prohibited methods.

Men
Abderrahim Goumri MAR (4-year ban to 14 Mar 2016) loses marks from 17 Aug 2009, inc. 2nd Chicago 2009 in 2:06:04, 1st Seoul marathon 2011.
Mikhail Lemayev RUS (2 year ban to 29 Jan 2015) loses marks from 20 Aug 2009.
Hélder Ornelas POR (4-year ban to 12 Jan 2016) loses marks from 8 Oct 2010.
Sergey Morozov RUS (Life) banned from 25 Feb 2011. Cancelled were his 12th in World Champs and 15th in European Cup at 20km in 2011 as well as his national titles in 2011 and 2012 and 5th World Cup 2012.
Women
Olga Abitova RUS (2-year ban to 10 Oct 2014) loses all performances from 10 Oct 2009.
Alemitu Bekele TUR (4-year ban to 14 Feb 2016) loses marks from 17 Aug 2009, inc. 13th World 5000m 2009, and in 2010: 5th World Indoor 2010, 1st European 5000m, 2nd Continental Cup 3000m.
Meryem Erdogan TUR (2-year ban to 14 Feb 2014) loses marks from 27 Jul 2010, inc. European 5000m 7th and 10,000m 5th 2010 and European U23 CC win in 2010.
Svetlana Klyuka RUS (2-year ban to 14 Feb 2014) loses marks from 15 Aug 2009, inc. at 800m: 2009 World semis, 2nd 2010 European Team, 8th 2010 European Champs in Barcelona, and in 2011 5th at DN Galan in Stockholm and 8th at Bislett Games in Oslo.
Tatyana Kotova RUS provisionally suspended as of 29 Jan 2013 after the anti-doping laboratory in Lausanne, re-analysed a sample taken at the 2005 World Champs and found she had tested positive for a prohibited substance. Kotova won a third consecutive World Champs silver medal and assuming her result (6.79) is annulled, the revised medallists are: 1, Tianna Madison USA 6.89; 2, Eunice Barber FRA 6.78w; 3, Yargelis Savigne CUB 6.69. Kotova went on to 3rd at the 2007 Worlds and to win the 2006 World Indoors. If her 2006 victory (7.00) is cancelled, the medallists would be: 1, Madison 6.80; 2, Naide Gomes POR 6.76; 3, Concepción Montaner ESP 6.76.
Tatyana Mineyeva RUS (2-year ban to 16 Nov 2014) loses marks from 12 Nov 2011.
Yuliya Rusanova RUS (2-year ban to 27 Jan 2015) loses marks from 3 Mar 2011, inc. 2nd European Indoor 800m and 8th World 800m in 2011 and 6th World Indoor 800m in 2012.
Olesya Syreva RUS (2-year ban to 1 Feb 2014) loses marks from 3 Mar 2011, inc. 2nd 2011 European Indoor 3000m.
Nailya Yulamanova RUS (2-year ban to 9 Feb 2014) loses marks from August 20, 2009. inc. European Champs marathon win in Barcelona, 8th in 2009 World Champs Marathon, 9th Boston, win in Shanghai 2010 and 5th in Amsterdam 2011.
Yevgeniya Zinurova RUS (2-year ban to 12 Sep 2013) loses marks from March 6, 2010, including 2011 European Indoor title.
In March 2013 the IAAF announced that there were adverse findings from their re-testing of samples from the **2005 World Championships** in Helsinki so that disciplinary proceedings were initiated for: Andrey Mikhnevich UKR (6 SP), Ivan Tikhon BLR (1 HT), Vadim Devyatovskiy BLR (2 HT), Tatyana Kotova RUS (2 W LJ), Nadezhda Ostapchuk BLR (1 W SP) and Olga Kuzenkova RUS (1 W HT).
After admitting to doping **Crystal Cox** (who had run in the heats) was stripped of her 2004 Olympic gold medal for 4x400m by the IOC, but they deferred a decision on whether to disqualify the US team (passing that to the IAAF).
World Anti-Doping Agency President, John Fahey, welcomed the decision of the IOC on December 5 to strip four athletes of their medals after samples taken at the **2004 Olympics** were re-analysed, although these decisions await confirmation They are: Yuriy Bilonog (UKR, 1 SP), Ivan Tikhon (BLR, 2 HT), Svetlana Krivelyova (RUS, 3 SP), and Irina Yatchenko (BLR, 3 DT). Bilonog and Krivelyova tested positive for oxandrolone, Tikhon and Yatchenko for methandienone. Irina Korzhanenko (RUS) had already forfeited the gold medal in the shot after a test revealed the use of stanozolol.
The revised medallists in the affected events would be: SP: 1, Nelson USA 21.16; 2, Olsen DEN 21.07; 3, Martínez ESP 20.84; HT: 1, Murofushi JPN 82.91; 2, Apak TUR 79.51; 3, Devyatovskiy BLR 78.82; W SP: 1, Cumbá CUB 19.59; 2, Kleinert GER 19.55; 3, Ostapchuk BLR 19.01 (currently banned); DT: 1, Sadova RUS 67.02; 2, Kelesidou GRE 66.68; 3, Cechlová CZE 66.08.
The **Kenyan Government** is to set up a committee to independently investigate allegations by a German TV programme of widespread doping in Kenya. Athletics Kenya chairman Isaiah Kiplagat has stated: "We are in negotiation with IAAF to open up a new laboratory in Nairobi. But for the time being, we only have one place in the entire continent, in South Africa."

WORLD LISTS 1963

! = world record   **MEN**

100 YARDS

9.1!	Bob Hayes USA	1s	St Louis	21 Jun
9.3	Dennis Richardson USA	1	Abilene	27 Mar
9.3	Gary Ray USA	1	Birmingham	18 May
9.3	Henry Carr USA	1	Tempe	25 May
9.3	Paul Drayton USA	1s	St Louis	21 Jun
9.2w	Odell Barry USA	1	Hillsdale	2 May
9.2w	John House USA	1	Van Nuys	11 May
9.2w	John Gilbert USA	2	St Louis	21 Jun

10th best 9.4, 100th 9.6

100 METRES

10.2	Arquimedes Herrera VEN	1h	São Paulo	27 Apr
	10.0Aw	1s	Calí	28 Jun
10.2	Andrzej Zielinski POL	1	Warszawa	1 Jun
10.2	Bob Hayes USA	1	Moskva	20 Jul
	9.9w	1	Walnut	27 Apr

10.3 29 men. 10th best 10.3, 100th 10.5

10.0w	Henry Carr USA	2	Walnut	27 Apr
10.0w	John Gilbert USA	3	Walnut	27 Apr
10.1w	Peter Wagner GER	1	Leipzig	16 May
10.1Aw	Joe Satow BRA	1h	Calí	28 Jun
10.1w	Enrique Figuerola CUB	1h	Praha	26 Jul

200 METRES (* 220y less 0.1 sec.)

20.2*!	Henry Carr USA	1	Tempe	23 Mar
20.4*!	Bob Hayes USA	1	Coral Gables	2 Mar
20.5*	Adolph Plummer USA	1	Compton	7 Jun
20.5A*	Larry Questad USA	2	Albuquerque	15 Jun

20.7 13 men. 10th best 20.7, 100th 21.2

20.3*w	Paul Drayton USA	1=	St Louis	22 Jun
20.5*w	John Moon USA	3	St Louis	22 Jun
20.5*w	Don Webster USA	4	St Louis	22 Jun

220 YARDS Straight Track (* 200m +0.1)

20.2	Bill Harvey USA	1	Logan	18 May
19.9w	Tim Russell USA	1	Long Beach	15 Mar
20.1w	Gerald Arline USA	1	Ft Lauderdale	27 Apr
20.1w*	John Moon USA	1	San Antonio	15 Jun

400 METRES (* 440y less 0.3 sec.)

44.6*!	Adolph Plummer USA	1	Tempe	25 May
45.3*	Ulis Williams USA	2	Tempe	25 May
45.4	Henry Carr USA	1	Hannover	31 Jul
45.7A*	Bob Tobler USA	1	Logan	18 May
45.7*	Rex Cawley USA	1s	Albuquerque	14 Jun
45.9*	Ron Freeman USA	3	Tempe	25 May

46.0* Ray Saddler USA, Charles Strong USA, Elzie Higginbottom USA

46.0 Jürgen Kalfelder, Manfred Kinder both FRG

10th best 46.0, 100th 47.3

800 METRES (* 880y less 0.7 sec.)

1:46.1*	Bill Crothers CAN	1	St Louis	22 Jun
1:46.4	Manfred Matuschewski GDR	1	Erfurt	39 Jul
1:46.6*	Jim Dupree USA	2	St Louis	22 Jun
1:46.8*	Noel Carroll IRL	1	Los Angeles	17 May
1:46.8*	Morgan Groth USA	3	St Louis	22 Jun
1:46.9*	Steve Haas USA	4	St Louis	22 Jun
1:47.1*	Kevin Hogan USA	2	Los Angeles	17 May
1:47.1*	John Boulter GBR	1	London (WC)	12 Jun

10th best 1:47.4, 100th 1:49.7

1000 METRES

2:17.9	Siegfried Valentin GDR	1	Potsdam	18 Jun
2:19.1	Michel Jazy FRA	1	Madrid	18 May
2:19.9	Jürgen May GDR	1	Erfurt	27 Sep

1500 METRES

3:37.8	Michel Jazy FRA	1	Colombes	28 Jul
3:38.7	Michel Bernard FRA	2	Colombes	28 Jul
3:38.9	Siegfried Valentin GDR	1	Varna	9 Oct
3:39.3+	Cary Weisiger USA	1	Compton	7 Jun
3:39.3	Jürgen May GDR	2	Varna	9 Oct
3:39.4+	Peter Snell NZL	2	Compton	7 Jun
3:39.8	Siegfried Herrmann GDR	3	Varna	9 Oc
3:40.5	Witold Baran POL	1	Bydgoszcz	12 May
3:41.0	Dyrol Burleson USA	1	Moskva	21 Jul

10th best 3:41.3, 100th 3:47.8

1 MILE

3:54.9	Peter Snell NZL	1	Modesto	25 May
3:55.5	Jim Beatty USA	2	Compton	7 Jun
3:55.6	Dyrol Burleson USA	3	Compton	7 Jun
3:56.7	Jim Grelle USA	2	Toronto	25 Jun
3:56.6	Cary Weisiger USA	5	Compton	7 Jun
3:56.9	Tom O'Hara USA	2	St Louis	22 Jun
3:56.9	Siegfried Valentin GDR	1	Potsdam	26 Jun
3:58.2	Michel Bernard FRA	1	Cambrai	8 Jull

10th best 3:59.1, 100th 4:07.4

3000 METRES

7:51.2	Siegfried Herrmann GDR	1	Bydgoszcz	16 Jun
7:55.4	Witold Baran POL	2	Bydgoszcz	16 Jun
7:55.6	Lech Boguszewicz POL	3	Bydgoszcz	16 Jun
7:56.4	Kazimierz Zimny POL	4	Bydgoszcz	16 Jun

2 MILES

8:29.6!	Michel Jazy FRA	1	Paris (C)	6 Jun
8:30.7i	Jim Beatty USA	1	Chicago	8 Mar
8:33.0	Albert Thomas AUS	1	Sydney	4 Dec
8:34.8	Michel Bernard FRA	1	Cambrai	31 Aug
8:35.0	Robert Bogey FRA	2	Paris (C)	6 Jun
8:35.2	Ron Clarke AUS	1	Melbourne	10 Dec

5000 METRES

13:41.2	Murray Halberg NZL	1	Manurewa	17 Jan
13:45.6	Gaston Roelants BEL	1	Torhout	9 Sep
13:46.2	Siegfried Herrmann GDR	1	Bucuresti	12 Oct
13:48.2	Yuriy Tyurin URS	1	Moskva	15 Aug
13:49.2	Sven-Olof Larsson SWE	1	Stockholm	9 Jul
13:49.2	Leonid Ivanov URS	2	Moskva	15 Aug
13:49.4	Valentin Samoylov URS	3	Moskva	15 Aug

10th best 13:50.1, 100th 14:5.0

3 Miles

13:15.5+	Murray Halberg NZL	1	Manurewa	17 Jan
13:20.8+	Neville Scott NZL	2	Manurewa	17 Jan

10,000 METRES

28:15.6!	Ron Clarke AUS	1	Melbourne	18 Dec
28:48,2	Robert Bogey FRA	1	Moskva	3 Jul
28:48.6	Leonid Ivanov URS	2	Moskva	3 Jul
28:52.4	Don Taylor GBR	1	London (WC)	23 Aug
28:55.8	Basil Heatley GBR	1	London (WC)	13 Sep
29:01.0	Mel Batty GBR	2	London (WC)	13 Sep

10th best 29:04.8, 100th 30:02.0

6 Miles

27:17.6!	Ron Clarke AUS	1	Melbourne	18 Dec
27:49.8	Ron Hill GBR	1	London (WC)	12 Jul
27:54.2	Jim Hogan IRL	2	London (WC)	12 Jul
27:57.0	Basil Heatley GBR	2	London (WC)	3 Aug
27:59.4	Ron Gomez GBR	3	London (WC)	12 Jul
28:00.0+	Don Taylor GBR	1	London (WC)	23 Aug
28:00.8	Buddy Edelen USA	4	London (WC)	12 Jul

MARATHON

2:14:28!	Buddy Edelen USA	1	Chiswick	15 Jun
2:14:43	Brian Kilby GBR	1	Port Talbot	6 Jul
2:15:15.8!	Toru Terasawa JPN	1	Beppu	17 Feb
2:15:39.4	Kazumi Watanabe JPN	2	Beppu	17 Feb
2:15:57	Haruo Otani JPN	3	Beppu	17 Feb
2:16:19.0	Kenji Kimihara JPN	4	Beppu	17 Feb
2:16:33.8	Hisakazu Sato JPN	5	Beppu	17 Feb
2:17:32	Hidekuni Hiroshma JPN	6	Beppu	17 Feb

10th best 2:17:45.2, 100th 2:25:25.2

3000m STEEPLECHASE

8:29.6!	Gaston Roelants BEL	1	Louvain	7 Sep
8:34.4	Eduard Osipov URS	1	Stockholm	6 Aug
8:34.8	Matvey Dmitriyev URS	1	Kyiv	7 Sep
8:35.0	József Macsar HUN	1	Budapest	2 Oct

8:35.4	Maurice Herriott GBR	2	Budapest	2 Oct
8:34.8	Kestutis Orentas URS	2	Kyiv	7 Sep
8:36.6	Nikolay Sokolov URS	2	Volgograd	29 Sep
8:37.6	Hermann Buhl GDR	2	Stockholm	6 Aug

10th best 8:39.4, 100th 8:57.0

110 METRES HURDLES (y = 120yh)

13.4y	Hayes Jones USA	1	St Louis	21 Jun
13.5y	Blaine Lindgren USA	2	St Louis	21 Jun
13.5y	Roy Hicks USA	3	St Louis	21 Jun
13.7y	Russ Rogers USA	1	Sioux Falls	1 Jun
13.7y	Willie May USA	1s	St Louis	21 Jun
13.8	Anatoliy Mikhailov URS	1	Moskva	20 Jul
13.8Ay	Steve Cortright USA	1h	Albuquerque	13 Jun

10th best 13.9, 100th 14.3

220 YARDS HURDLES Straight Track

22.7	James Liggins USA	1	Petersburg	6 Apr

400 METRES HURDLES (* 440y less 0.3 sec.)

49.3*A	Rex Cawley USA	1	Albuquerque	15 Jun
49.9	Helmut Janz FRG	1	Augsburg	11 Aug
50.0*A	Ron Whitney USA	2	Albuquerque	15 Jun
50.0	Ferdinand Haas FRG	2	Augsburg	11 Aug
50.1	Jim Allen USA	2	Hannover	1 Aug
50.2	Juan Dyrzka ARG	1	São Paulo	1 May
50.3*	Willie Atterberry USA	1	Los Angeles	31 May
50.4	Roberto Frinolli ITA	1	Bruxelles	25 Aug

10th best 50.5, 100th 52.5

HIGH JUMP

2.28!	Valeriy Brumel URS	1	Moskva	21 Jul
2.20	Ni Zhiqin CHN	1	Beijng	17 Aug
2.20	Tony Sneazwell AUS	1	Tokyo	14 Oct
2.18	John Thomas USA	1	Nashville	30 Mar
2.15	Viktor Bolshov URS	1	Leningrad	23 Mar
2.15	Gene Johnson USA	2	Moskva	21 Jul
2,145	Lew Hoyt USA	1	Los Angeles	23 Feb
2.14	Jo Faust USA	1	Los Angeles	16 Mar

10th best 2.13, 100th 2.045

POLE VAULT

5.20!	John Pennel USA	1	Coral Gables	24 Aug
5.10i!	Pentti Nikula FIN	1	Pijulahti	2 Feb
5.00		1	Pori	5 May
5.08!	Brian Sternberg USA	1	Compton	7 Jun
5.02	Ron Morris USA	1	Mikkeli	25 Aug
5.00	Yang Chuan-Kwang TPE	1	Bremerhaven	20 Jul
4.95	John Uelses USA	2	Warszawa	26 Jul
4.94A	Don Meyers USA	1	Fort Collins	25 May
4.93i	Dave Tork USA	1	Toronto	25 Jan

10th best 4.91, 100th 4.57

LONG JUMP

8.20/8.30w	Ralph Boston USA	2	Modesto	25 May
8.18i	Igor Ter-Ovanesyan URS	1	New York	1 Feb
8.15		1	Yerevan	29 Oct
8.04	Pentti Eskola FIN	1	Helsinki	4 Jul
8.15w		1	Kauhava	21 Jun
8.02	Darrell Horn USA	2	St Louis	21 Jun
7.97A/8.04Aw	Bill Miller USA	2	Albuquerque	13 Jun
7.91	Ali Brakchi ALG	1	Dakar	18 Apr
7.90	Leonid Barkhovskiy URS	4	Moskva	20 Jul

10th best 7.87, 100th 7.49

8.33w	Phil Shinnick USA	1	Modesto	25 May
8.10Aw	Cliton Mayfield USA	1	Albuquerque	13 Jun
7.98Aw	Paul Warfield USA	3	Albuquerque	13 Jun
7.96w	Józef Schmidt POL	1	Bydgoszcz	16 Jun
7.94w	Godfrey Moore USA	1	San Antono	15 Jun
7.93w	Charlie Mays USA	3	Sioux Falls	31 May

TRIPLE JUMP

16.99	Józef Schmidt POL	1	Bydgoszcz	25 Aug
16.60	Aleksandr Zolotaryev URS	1	Moskva	18 May
16.45	Vitold Kreyer URS	1	Moskva	2 Jul
16.39	Anatoliy Alyabyev URS	1	Kyiv	12 Jul
16.35	Hans-Jürgen Ruckborn GDR	1	Bydgoszcz	21 Sep
16.34	Oleg Fyedoseyev URS	2	Moskva	2 Jul
16.34	Vladimir Goryayev URS	1	Moskva	13 Aug

10th best 16.23, 100th 15.53

16.59w	Mahoney Samuels JAM	1	Fresno	11 May

SHOT

19.68i	Gary Gubner USA	1	Los Angeles	9 Feb
19.02		1	Albuquerque	15 Jun
19.43	Dallas Long USA	1	Los Angeles	5 Sep
19.42	Vilmos Varju HUN	1	Pecs	23 Jun
19.24	Alfred Sosgornik POL	1	Elblag	12 May
19.20	Dave Davis USA	1	Long Beach	15 Jun
19.11i	Parry O'Brien USA	1	San Francisco	15 Feb
19.10		1	Long Beach	14 Jul
18.88	Dave Steen CAN	2	Albuquerque	15 Jun

10th best 18.74, 100th 17.00

DISCUS

62.62!	Al Oerter USA	1	Walnut	27 Apr
62.37	Jay Silvester USA	1	Mainz	26 Jun
62.10	Rink Babka USA	1	Long Beach	4 May
61.68	Bob Humphreys USA	2	Long Beach	4 May
60.97	Ludvik Danek TCH	1	Praha	8 Sep
59.03	Jens Reimers FRG	1	Augsburg	16 Jun
58.95	Jirí Zemba TCH	2	Brno	29 Sep
58.88	Dave Weill USA	1	Berkeley	4 May

10th best 58.12, 100th 52.54

HAMMER

69.77	Heinrich Thun AUT	1	Leoben	15 Sep
69.06	Gyula Zsivótzky HUN	1	Budapest	14 Jul
68.78	Josef Matousek TCH	1	Praha	21 Jul
68.48	Hal Connolly USA	2	Wien	5 Oct
67.97	Gennadiy Kondrashov URS	1	Praha	27 Jul
67.91	Romuald Klim URS	1	Staiki	1 Aug
67.73	Takao Sugawara JPN	1	Hyvinkää	26 Jun
67.70	Guy Husson FRA	1	Troyes	29 Jun

10th best 67.20, 100th 59.12

JAVELIN

86.33	Pauli Nevala FIN	1	Helsinki	16 Jul
85.11	Vladimir Kuznyetsov URS	1	Baku	30 Oct
83.90	Terje Pedersen NOR	1	Oslo	12 Aug
83.65	Janis Lusis URS	1	Berlin	22 Jun
82.27	Janusz Sidlo POL	1	Leverkusen	17 Aug
82.19	Hermann Saloman FRG	1	Augsburg	11 Aug
81.48	Willy Rasmussen NOR	1	Oslo	14 Sep
81.46	Larry Stuart USA	1	Los Angeles	30 Mar

10th best 80.82, 100th 73.66

DECATHLON (1952 tables)

9121!	Yang Chuan-Kwang TPE	1	Walnut	28 Apr

8089 on 1964 tables, 8010 on 1984 tables

8085	Willi Holdorf FRG	1	Hannover	8 Sep
8061	Paul Herman USA	2	Walnut	28 Apr
7856	Werner Von Moltke FRG	1	Bad R'enhall	2 Jun
7854	Vasiliy Kuznetsov URS	1	Moskva	15 Aug
7852	Steve Pauly USA	1	Corvallis	29 Jun
7839	Anatoliy Ovsyenko URS	2	Moskva	15 Aug
7791	Hans-Joachim Walde FRG	2	Bad R'enhall	2 Jun

10th best 7654, 100th 6385

20 KILOMETRES WALK

1:28:03.8	Vladimir Senin RUS	1	Moskva	2 Jul
1:28:23.8	Gennadoy Solodov URS	2	Moskva	2 Jul
1:28:25.0	Abdon Pamich ITA	1	Milano	12 May
1:28:47.4	Boris Khrolovich URS	1	Minsk	9 Jul
1:29:31.6t	Vytautas Zurnia URS	1	Riga	15 Jun
1:29:46.6	Albert Kotov URS	2	Minsk	9 Jul

50 KILOMETRES WALK

4:10:46.8	Christophe Höhne GDR	1	Bad Saarow	27 Oct
4:10:48.2	Anatoliy Vedyakov URS	1	Moskva	14 Aug
4:13:01	Aleks. Shcherbina URS	2	Moskva	14 Aug
4:14:15	George Gulpecs URS	1	Riga	16 Jun
4:14:16	Kurt Sakowski GDR	2	Bad Saarow	27 Oc
4:14:24.2t	István Havasi HUN	1	Varese	12 Oct

4 x 100 METRES

39.6	USA	1	Warsawa	26 Jul
39.6	France	1	Chambéry	15 Sep
39.6	FR Germany	1	Kornwestheim	21 Sep
39.7	Great Britain	1	London (WC)	23 Aug
39.9	Poland	1	Moskva	14 Sep
39.9	Hungary	2	Budapest	2 Oct

4 x 400 METRES

3:02.8	USA	1	Hannover	1 Aug
3:03.5	FR Germany	2	Hannover	1 Aug
3:06.6	Great Britain	1	Volgograd	29 Sep
3:07.5	France	2	Enschede	14 Jul

WOMEN – 100 YARDS

10.5	Diane Bowering AUS	1	Adelaide	9 Feb
10.3w	Margaret Burvill AUS	1	Perth	30 Nov

10.5w Glennys Beasley, Dorothy Hyman, Marylin Black

100 METRES

11.3	Dorothy Hyman GBR	1	Budapest	2 Oct
11.4	Maria Itkina URS	1h	Riga	1 Jun
11.4	Elzbieta Szyroka POL	1	Bydgoszcz	15 Jun
11.4	Galina Popova URS	1	Leningrad	9 Jun
11.4	Barbara Sobotta POL	1h	Bydgoszcz	23 Aug
11.4	Hannelore Raepke GDR	1	Varna	5 Oct

11.5 four women, 10th best 11.5, 50th 11.8

11.4w	Irene Kirszenstein POL	1h	Bydgoszcz	15 Jun
11.4w	Tamara Burdinskaya URS	1	Minsk	31 Jul

200 METRES (* 220y less 0.1 sec.)

23.1*	Margaret Burvill AUS	1	Perth	12 Jan
23.2	Dorothy Hyman GBR	1	Budapest	3 Oct
23.4*	Joyce Bennett AUS	1	Brisbane	23 Mar
23.4	Galina Popova URS	1	Moskva	3 Jul
23.5	Maria Itkina URS	1	Berlin	22 Jun
23.5	Shin Keum-dan PRK	1	Pyongyang	Oct
23.6*	Betty Cuthbert AUS	2	Brisbane	23 Mar

23.8 five women, 10th best 23.8, 50th 24.3

23.6w	Elzbieta Szyroka POL	1	Bydgoszcz	16 Jun

400 METRES

51.4!	Shin Keum-dan PRK	1	Jakarta	12 Nov
53.0*!	Betty Cuthbert AUS	1	Brisbane	22 Mar
53.1*	Dixie Willis AUS	2	Brisbane	22 Ma
53.2	Maria Itkina URS	1	Kyiv	6 Sep
53.2	Joy Grieveson GBR	1	London (WC)	14 Sep
53.3	Ann Packer GBR	1	Volgograd	28 Sep
53.8+	Judy Amoore AUS	2	Melbourne	11 Mar
53.9*	Marise Chamberlain NZL	1	Dunedin	2 Mar

10th best 54.1, 50th 56.2, * 440y less 0.3 sec.

800 METRES

1:59.1!	Shin Keum-dan PRK	1	Jakarta	12 Nov
2:04.4*	Marise Chamberlain NZL	1	Dunedin	15 Feb
2:04.7*	Gerda Kraan NED	1	London (WC)	31 Aug
2:05.4*	Dixie Willis AUS	2	Sydney	16 Mar
2:05.4	Olga Kazi HUN	1	Budapest	3 Oct
2:06.0	Vyera Mukhanova URS	1	Moskva	15 Aug
2:06.1	Zoya Skobtsova URS	1	Volgograd	29 Sep

10th best 2:06.9, 50th 2:10.2. * 880y less 0.8 sec

1 MILE

4:57.0	Phyllis Perkins GBR	1	London (Ch)	8 Jun

80 METRES HURDLES

10.6	Pamela Kilborn AUS	1	Melbourne	12 Jan
	10.4w	1	Melbourne	3 Feb
10.6	Galina Grinvald URS	1	Leningrad	20 Jun
10.6	Nilia Kulkova URS	1	Kyiv	7 Sep
10.6	Rimma Koshelyeva URS	1	Odessa	22 Sep
10.6	Ikuko Yoda JPN	1s	Tokyo	13 Sep

10.7 Alla Chernisheva USR, Maria Piatkowska POL, Erika Fisch FRG, Zinaida Kryunova URS, Karin Balzer GDR
10th best 10.7, 50th 11.0

100 METRES HURDLES (2'6")

13.3	Nilia Kulkova URS	1	Moskva	14 Aug
13.4	Jutta Stock FRG	1	Kassel	14 Jul
13.3w	Mary Rand GBR	1	London (WC)	23 Aug

HIGH JUMP

1.88	Iolanda Balas ROM	1	Oradea	22 Jun
1.78	Cheng Feng-jung CHN	1	Nanking	26 Jun
1.75	Michele Mason AUS	1	Sydney	16 Mar
1.75	Robyn Woodhouse AUS	1	Okayama	2 Apr
1.75	Wu Fu-shan CHN	1	Beijing	19 May
1.75	Klara Pushkaryeva URS	1	Moskva	14 Sep
1.74	Taisia Chenchik URS	1	Odessa	22 Sep

10th best 1.73, 50th 1.67

LONG JUMP

6.60	Tatyana Shchelkanova URS	1	Kurayoshi	19 Oct
6.47	Vlasta Prikrylova URS	1	Hradec Králove	14 Jul
6.44	Mary Rand GBR	1	London (WC)	5 Aug
6.34	Cor Bakker NED	1	Den Haag	21 Jul
6.34	Willye White USA	1	Braunschweig	30 Jul
6.32	Helga Hoffmann FRG	1	Augsburg	9 Aug
6.31	Bärbel Gessler GDTR	1	Leipzig	5 Aug

10th best 6.23, 50th 6.00

SHOT

17.59	Tamara Press URS	1	Moskva	21 Jul
17.33	Renaye Garisch GDR	1	Bucuresti	12 Oct
17.30	Margarita Helmboldt GDR	1	Varna	19 Oct
17.06	Johanna Hübner GDR	1	Leipzig	16 Jun
16.75	Galina Zybina URS	2	Moskva	2 Jul
16.63	Judit Bognar HUN	1	Budapest	3 Oct
16.36	Zinaida Doynikova URS	2	Leningad	22 Jun
16.13	Lyudmila Zhdanova URS	3	Moskva	12 Aug

10th best 15.99, 50th 14.72

DISCUS

59.29!	Tamara Press URS	1	Moskva	18 May
55.88	Jirina Nemcová TCH	1	Hradec Králove	13 Jul
55.75	Ingrid Lotz GDR	1	Bucuresti	13 Oct
56.39	Doris Lorenz GDR	1	Varna	9 Oct
54.96	Albina Yelkina URS	1	Kapfenburg	10 Sep
54.99	Marie Simancová TCH	1	Praha	22 Aug
54.68	Lamara Tugushi URS	1	Tbilisi	11 Jun
54.60	Yevgeniya Kuznyetsova	1	Kyiv	1 Sep

10th best 53.93, 50th 48.57

JAVELIN

59.78!	Elvira Ozolina URS	1	Moskva	3 Jul
58.45	Marion Graefe GDR	1	Jena	31 Aug
56.47	Virve Poldsam URS	1	Tartu	27 Jul
55.76	Inge Schwalbe GDR	2	Jena	31 Aug
55.62	Yelena Gorchakova URS	1	Odessa	22 Sep
55.39	Anneliese Gerhards FRG	1	Hamm	15 Sep
54.64	Galina Visotskaya URS	1	Kyiv	15 Sep
54.36	Aldona Stanciute URS	1	Vilnius	10 May

10th best 53.37, 50th 49.80

PENTATHLON (1954 tables)

4863	Tatyana Shchelkanova URS	1	Moskva	15 Aug
4767	Jutta Heine FRG	1	Bad R'enhall	2 Jun
4737	Olga Kardash URS	1	Kyiv	3 Sep
4726	Mary Rand GBR	1	London (WC)	24 Aug
4684	Zinaida Kryunova URS	1	Kyiv	10 Sep
4672	Ingrid Becker FRG	2	Bad R'enhall	2 Jun
4668	Galina Bystrova URS	1	Gorkiy	11 Jul
4658	Maria Piatkowska POL	1	Kassel	6 Oct

10th best 4633, 100th best 4381

4 x 100 METRES

44.8	Great Britain	1	Volgograd	28 Sep
45.0	USSR	1	Moskva	20 Jul
45.2	USA	2	Moskva	20 Jul
45.3	GDR	2	Moskva	14 Sep
45.5	Poland	1	Kraków	8 Sep
45.5	Hungary	1	Budapest	2 Oct

THE 'PURE AND GENUINE' LOSES OUT TO THE 'SHOW AND SPECTACLE'

By Bob Phillips

THE TRACK EXPLOITS of Victor Jacquemin and Jacques Keijser do not figure at all prominently in any of the comprehensive histories of athletics. To be more precise, they do not figure at all. Nevertheless, these otherwise totally obscure runners share an interesting claim to remembrance as having both competed in the 1908 Olympics (with little success, it has to be said) and then won their events in the first ever international match to be staged between two countries – Holland versus Belgium at the VOC football ground in Rotterdam on Sunday, 2 July 1911. Jacquemin, still only 19 years of age, won the 400m for the Belgians while Keijser – who was born in Paris and was originally named Keyser – won the one mile for the Dutch.

Neither this neighbourly encounter involving nine events, nor further meetings between Belgium and France in Brussels on 1 September 1912 and between Hungary and Austria in Budapest a fortnight later, each consisting of 11 events, were glowing advertisements for the potentially keen competitiveness of such fixtures. Belgium won all but two events against the Dutch and lost all but two to the French. Hungary won eight against the Austrians and shared a ninth. Even less of a contest had been the meeting between New York Athletic Club and London Athletic Club at Manhattan Field in 1895, which fell not far short of USA v GB status, where the hosts won all 11 events. Yet this was a type of head-to-head contest which would become the abiding feature throughout every non-Olympic season until the 1980s, when the commercially-driven onset of World Championships and the Grand Prix circuit would sadly relegate them to an increasingly minor role, so that now only the annual Finland v Sweden match is a merit-worthy survivor.

None of the performances at those three pioneering fixtures between national teams were of any great consequence, save possibly a high jump of 1.82m by Baron Iván Wardener, of Hungary (had he been English he would surely have been known as the 'Bounding Baron' or the 'Leaping Lord'), but the most notable

of those pioneering winners in the fullness of time would be Charles Alexandre Casimir Poulenard at 400m for France. He had earned a 4x400m relay silver medal at the Stockholm Olympics seven weeks before and later became an accomplished coach, whose protegé, Jules Ladoumègue, would in 1930–31 be the first man to break 3min 50sec for 1500m and 4min 10sec for the mile. Keijser's winning mile time in Rotterdam had been a rather more pedestrian 4:41 3/5.

The French were particularly enthusiastic supporters of the head-to-head format throughout the 1920s and 1930s, averaging four such matches a season, with Great Britain and Germany as regular opponents – the former every year from 1921 to 1938 except when there was an Olympic Games – and Belgium, Finland, Hungary, Italy, Sweden and Switzerland figuring on occasions. There were even two fixtures taken on by the French team 'on tour' in Japan in 1928 and a triangular meeting with Japan and the USA in Paris a week after the 1936 Olympics had finished. The post-Olympic matches between the British Empire and the USA which had begun in 1920 could perhaps have been the most prestigious two-sided encounters of all, but the organisers whimsically based their schedule of events mainly on relays, including a 4xtwo-lap steeplechase which brought together some odd bedfellows; the winning Empire team of 1936 included but one genuine international-class steeplechaser, Tom Evenson, who was joined by, among others, the Olympic 400m hurdles silver-medallist, John Loaring. Some of the best performances by the Empire in the five such matches during the 1920s and 1930s even broke world records, but to no avail because they were multi-national teams, as in the 4x880 yards of 1932 and the 4x440 yards of 1936.

France was also in the forefront when it came to promoting women's matches and won all eight events against Belgium in Brussels on 28 August 1921. A further venture two months later, on 30 October, entailed the visit of an England team to Stade Pershing, in Paris, and it was the English who won, 52-38, marking the occasion with no less than four world records – the first for either sex ever to be set in an international match between two countries. The heroine of the day was Mary Lines, who had a hand in all four which formed part of the eclectic schedule: 100 yards in 11 4/5, 300m in 43 4/5, 4x110 yards relay in 51 4/5 and 4x220 yards relay in 1:53.0. The intrepid Miss Lines was a 27-year-old London tea-shop waitress who had never run a race prior to 1921.

The British men – as always 'perfidious Albion' – daringly added to their regular encounters with Germany and France occasional matches against Italy, Finland and Norway in the 1930s, but there was a certain degree of scepticism about the whole business, largely based on an indifference to, even a contempt for, the field events. In his preview of the 1933 fixture against Italy in Milan, the correspondent of *The Times* captured the mood of public disdain: 'To the average Englishman the Amateur Athletic Association may seem at fault in entangling Britain in international competitions in which they are neither proficient nor interested, but the answer is that if international athletic matches are wanted the field events must be included. The foreigners are set upon them ... 'throwing things about' can be attractive.' Predictably, Britain lost all five field events to the Italians, four of them by maximum scores, and therefore the match by 85 points to 62.

The earliest male world record to be set in a full-scale international match was Charles Hoff's pole vault of 4.12 for Norway against Denmark and Sweden in Copenhagen on 3 September 1922, though not too many other records followed in similar circumstances in that decade or the following one. A German quartet ran the first sub-41sec 4x100m relay (actually 40.8) against the French in 1928. Erik Wennström, of Sweden, set the first 14.4 for 110m hurdles against Norway in 1929. Frantisek Douda won the shot at 16.04 for Czechoslovakia against Austria in 1931 and then at 16.20 against Poland the next year. Luigi Beccali, Italy's reigning Olympic 1500m champion, ran the distance in 3:49.0 to beat the Empire Games mile champion, Reg Thomas, of Great Britain, by 4.6sec in that Milan match of 1933. Within a month of each other in 1934 world records were beaten twice in the same event: Harald Andersson, discus throws of 52.20 and 52.42 for Sweden against Norway in Oslo; then two Japanese, Masao Harada and Kenkichi Oshima, triple jumps of 15.75 and 15.82 respectively against the USA in Osaka, though their only opponent was a decathlete, Robert Clark, who managed merely 11.09!

The pre-war era ended desperately late in the day as the Great Britain team was overwhelmed 93.5 points to 42.5 in Cologne on 20 August 1939 and then beat a hasty retreat out of the country, as war was declared a fortnight later. Maybe over-anxious to make up for lost time, the British – with a team of athletes as ill-prepared as their army had been six years earlier – then agreed to a resumption of their fixtures with France in Paris on 2 September 1945 and lost by a similar margin, 73 to 29. Of the 12 events on the latter occasion, the only one which went to Britain was the 1500m, where Sydney Wooderson, still holder of the European title, repeated his successes against the French of 1935, 1937 and 1938. The Gallic 800m winner was delightfully named Robert Chef d'Hotel; most of the Britons could be said to have been merely waiting at table that afternoon. It took rather longer for the British to meet Germany again, and when they did so, in Berlin in 1953, they faced a team drawn entirely from the western side of the Iron Curtain. Such political strictures made no odds as the Germans won for the sixth time in seven meetings.

During that same year 24 matches were held in Europe, and Germany – to no one's great surprise – also beat in turn Italy, Holland, Switzerland, Yugoslavia, Greece and Turkey. It was just a pity that they did not meet the USSR, which country settled instead as a follow-up to their first Olympic appearance of the previous year on a less ambitious venture in Eastern Europe, meeting Hungary in Budapest and winning 121-91. Interestingly, at that early stage of their state-aided athletic development the two teams could raise only one world record-holder between them, and he was Leonid Shcherbakov, who a couple of months earlier had cleared 16.23 in the triple jump and settled for 16m exactly to beat the Hungarians by a very long way. The hosts had a consolation record of their own as József Kovács ran the third fastest 5000m ever, and the fastest in an international match, of 14:01.2.

Yet within five years the Soviet Union's athletics commissars had gained sufficiently in confidence to take on the most formidable opponent of all – the USA. The first of a series which would continue in various forms – outdoors, indoors, multi-events – until 1985 took place at the Lenin Stadium, in Moscow, on 27-28 July 1958 and was described by the foremost athletics expert of the era, Roberto Quercetani, as 'the dual meet of the century', though maybe it was the laconic appraisal of the decathlon winner, Rafer Johnson, beating the world record in the process, that it was 'Communism versus the Free World' that most neatly captured the essence and the popular appeal of these contests. Not the least attractions for the eager public in an era sated with potentially lethal Cold War confrontations were to be the irresistible photo opportunities presented by the likes of Brumel and Thomas, Boston and Ter-Ovanesyan, Johnson and Kuznyetsov as they cheerily fraternised after their events. The USA, further aided by a brilliant 400m/400m hurdles double for Glenn Davis, won this first men's match 126-109 but lost the women's 63-44, thus enabling the not-so-free World to claim an overall supremacy by two points. Within the next nine days the hard-working Americans also met Poland and Hungary, and in the fullness of time this sort of excessive demand made upon them by their AAU governing body would help lead to the decline of such fixtures.

But that is leaping too far ahead in history – at least for a paragraph or so – and the reality was that a vast array of dual (and sometimes triple) matches occupied the calendar by the 1960s. Taking 1963 as a convenient example, even if only because it is precisely 50 years ago, there were 97 men's matches recorded (56 senior and 19 junior, 12 walks, seven decathlon, two road and one indoors) and 40 women's (31 senior and six junior, two pentathlon, one indoors). The USA again met the USSR, narrowly winning 119-114 (men) and disastrously losing 75-28 (women), and then Poland, Germany and Great Britain in quick succession. Other humbler encounters surely provided the highlight of the season for many of their participants, though sometimes the outcome was decidedly one-sided, such as the United Arab Republic v Cyprus (128-71 men, 37-17 women) or the German Democratic Republic v Bulgaria (152-67 and 89-39 respectively), if on other occasions thrillingly close, most notably Belgium v Austria (107-105, men) and France v Holland (59-58, women).

The Anglo-German series, celebrating in London the 10th anniversary of its revival, resulted in a mutually satisfactory draw, Germany winning the men's match 109-101 and Great Britain the women's 73½-63½. The British saved their very best for the season's end, travelling to Volgograd – the exact whereabouts of which might have been a mystery to most of the team as the city had been known as Stalingrad until two years before – and astonishingly beating the Russian Federal Republic's men 113-97 and honourably losing to the women

64-55. Writing his autobiography almost 50 years later, Mike Fleet, who had won the 800m for Britain from his team-mate, Chris Carter, wittily recalled, 'I was surprised to learn from one of my Russian rivals that he had been in the army for five years and that his work was athletics! His specialisation had clearly not helped him against a fully employed Surrey schoolmaster and a Sussex policeman.'

Unfortunately, these sharp differences in athletic life-style helped to put an end to such worthwhile matches as this. Writing at length about the USA-USSR meetings in the *Journal of Sport* in 2001, the American academic, Joseph M. Turrini, concluded that the 'series devolved from the biggest non-Olympic track meet in the World – a meet of enormous political and athletic importance – into a meet of little significance and inferior quality.' What Turrini euphemistically described as 'the growth of financial opportunities' for athletes during the 1970s led to conflicts with officialdom and boycotts of the match by leading American competitors, and by 1985 when the last of the 'summit meetings' was held with full-scale professionalism now firmly in place it had faded so much in importance that only one sentence was devoted to it in the following year's ATFS AnnuaL That swansong match was actually a three-way affair also involving Japan, and the USA's men beat the USSR 114-104, helped by Carl Lewis winning the 100m and long jump and anchoring the 4x100 team, but the American women lost 117-50, taking only one of the 16 women's events, and that was at 3000m by Mary Knisely – could any reporter that day resist the temptation to pen the phrase 'Nicely does it'? There had been 19 matches in the 27-year series: the USA had won the men's 13-6, the USSR the women's 18-1. For those who revel in decidedly esoteric statistics, the total points scores were 3370.5 for the USSR and 3141.5 for the USA – they probably knew that in the White House and the Kremlin.

Actually, the two super-powers met again within a fortnight, but this was at the World Cup in Australia, won by the USA men and the GDR women, and it was this competition involving teams from a mixture of nations and continents, and inaugurated in 1977, plus the IAAF/Mobil Grand Prix annual series started up in 1985, bringing 16 major meetings together into a rationalised competitive structure, which had rendered two-a-side matches between nations irrelevant so far as most athletes were concerned. Then, of course, a highly successful first World Championships had been held two years before, and by the 1990s that would become a biennial fixture.

There was, though, still one anomaly, as the renowned Finnish sports writer, Matti Hannus, pointed out in that same 1986 issue of the ATFS Annual. 'Six Decades Of Passion' was how he summarised his article about the Finland–Sweden matches which had begun in 1925 – and which, remarkably, had never produced a single world record. 'Nowadays,' Hannus wrote, 'when show and spectacle seem to be the mainstreams of athletics, it is reassuring to see something so pure and genuine survive.' In 2012, even though there have still been no world records, and the sole significance outside Scandinavia of the 72nd match in the sequence was that it marked the modest farewell appearance of Carolina Klüft, the same heartfelt sentiments could still have been expressed. There was very nearly a perfect balance in the results – Sweden won the men's match 220-187 and Finland the women's 223-187. Maybe the continuing motivation for the Swedes is that the fixture is known throughout their land as 'Finnkamp' – the Finn Battle – and Sweden has not been at war in the proper military sense of the term for 199 years.

UPSETS THAT MADE HISTORY IN OLYMPIC ANNALS

By Roberto L Quercetani

AS EVERYBODY KNOWS, throughout the years the Olympic Games never ceased to grow in stature. Only ten nations were represented in the inaugural edition, that of 1896 in Athens. Exactly a century later (Atlanta 1996) they had grown to 197. Now they are 200-plus, and the larger the fields, the greater the likelihood of upsets. Without wishing to indulge in a ranking of the latter, we will just evoke three of the hottest ones.

The sprints usually belong to a set where pre-Games predictions are respected, more or less. Yet the case of Lindy Remigino is likely to be remembered as one apart. This American of Italian (Piedmontese) extraction really made the headlines at Helsinki in 1952. He won what is usually called 'the blue ribbon event', the 100 metres. His victory came as the result of a long series of close decisions, or lucky cards if you prefer. At the beginning of that season, he was regarded in the States merely as a good sprinter – one of many – with a fierce competitive spirit. At that stage there were at least three Americans who clearly outclassed him as 100m aces – Jim Golliday, the best of them all, was sidelined with a muscle injury on the eve of the Olympic Trials; Andy Stanfield, another injury-prone sprinter, decided to put all his eggs in the 200-metre basket; Art Bragg, winner of the 100 metres at the Trials, was stopped by an injury in one of the Olympic semi-finals. Remigino, a 21-year-old medium-size sprinter, went through the ordeal of the selection process almost unnoticed: fifth in the NCAA meeting in 10.8 (Golliday first in 10.4);

eliminated in a semi-final of the AAU meet; second in the all-important Olympic Trials race in 10.6 – the same time credited to three others who finished close behind him! In Helsinki he won Olympic gold in 10.4 – an unofficial automatic timing device saw him barely two hundredths of a second ahead of Herb McKenley of Jamaica, the runner-up. Be as it may, it must be conceded that Remigino was at his best at the right time. After all, even luck needs assistance (from man) in order to be effective ... The story has a worthy PS: a few days later, at Oslo, Remigino equalled the world record (10.2), alas with a wind just above the limit (2.08 m/s).

Tale no. 2 concerns a distance runner from Kenya, Amos Biwott, who won the 3000m steeplechase at the 1968 Olympics in Mexico City. Believe it or not, at the end of that (for him) memorable season, Biwott was no higher than ... 75th equal in the world year list with an unimpressive 8:44.8. That was chiefly due to the fact that most if not all his races that year were run in the rarefied atmosphere of high altitude venues, detrimental to long distance times. Yet he lost only once, to his countryman Benjamin Kogo in a pre-Olympic meeting. But he did vanquish Kogo and all others in the Olympic final. I may add that on the eve of those Games, the US magazine *Track & Field News* published predictions made by six international 'experts' (including yours truly). In the steeplechase only one of those prognosticators had Biwott as high as third and barely another had him sixth! Time-wise, Biwott's career best was 8:23.73, in a heat of the 1972 Olympics in

Munich (in the final he had to be content with sixth).

In terms of upsets, however, the most extraordinary case – at least in my opinion –was offered at the London Olympics last summer, when a 19-year-old boy from Trinidad & Tobago, Keshorn Walcott, won the javelin with 84.58, his best ever up to now. This was only the second time in Olympic history that a non-European had won this event (the first was in 1952, when Cyrus Young of USA won at Helsinki). Walcott really came from nowhere. If you look for his name in the 2011 World List, you'll find it in the ... 130th position, with 75.77. In fact, it was only in the spring of 2012 that he conquered the T&T record with 78.94. From then on he kept improving, with 80.11,

82.83 and finally 84.58 in the Olympics, as related above. He won the World Junior title in Barcelona, then beat the cream of Europe in the Olympics. None of the *Track & Field News* prognosticators had 'seen' him any higher than fourth.

Without wishing to detract from the rightful patriotic feelings of a country, we are ready to bet that few reporters and historians are likely to remember that the longest throw seen in the London Olympics was a powerful 88.34 by Vitezslav Vesely of the Czech Republic, made in the qualifying rounds (held three days earlier). In the final, under more difficult weather conditions, the Czech had to be content with 83.34 and fourth. But then, the right thing must occur at the right time.

Athletes at Other Sports

American Football

Robert Griffin III (USA) (b. 12 Feb 1990 Okinawa, Japan) was the world's third fastest junior at 400mh in 2008 with 49.22A to win the Big 12 title, having topped the world junior rankings with 49.56 as a youth in 2007. He then concentrated on American Football and won the Heisman Trophy as top college player with Baylor University in 2011. After being the second pick of the 2012 NFL draft he had a sensational season with Washington Redskins in the NFL in 2012, smashing the yards rushing record by a rookie quarterback with 748 and completing 66.4% of passes for 2902 yards gained.

Joining Griffin as a Pro Bowl selection for 2012 was **Jamaal Charles** (b. 27 Dec 1986) who had also been selected in 2010 (when he was in the first team All-Pro). Playing for the Kansas City Chiefs, he is the current NFL all-time leader in yards-per carry average among running backs at 5.79 (well ahead of the long-standing record of 5.2 by the legendary Jim Brown). As an athlete he won the 400m hurdles bronze medal at the 2003 World Youth Championships while at high school. At college at Texas he had a 100m best of 10.23 in 2006 and was 5th at 100m and 7th at 200m at the NCAAs.

Bobsleigh

Lolo Jones (USA), in a 2-woman bob with Elana Meyers, was on the US team that won the combined bobsled-skeleton mixed team event at the World Championships in 2013. Also at the se World Championships: 2-Man: 19th Craig Pickering GBR, 4-Man: 5th Joel Fearon GBR; Women 2M: 8th Aja Evans USA (SP 17.08i '10), 14th Gillian Cooke GBR (LJ 6.43i '08), 16th Jana Pittman AUS; Mixed team: 7th Cooke & Pickering GBR, 8th Evans USA.

Rugby Union

Carlin Isles (USA) (b. 21 Nov 1989) caused a stir with his speed when playing for the United States in the IRB World Sevens just a few months after taking up rugby. Earlier in 2012 he ran a pb of 10.13w for100m.

Trends in World Performances

Across the spectrum of athletics events standards in depth in 2012 were easily the best ever. Every year when I have finished work (in so far as one ever can!) on world lists for the International Annual I check 10th best, 100th best and base level standards (up to 200 deep) for all men's and women's events. Generally I have found, with the exception of big improvements in long distance running, that standards have remained fairly steady in recent years. But there were massive improvements overall in 2012. The men's 10th best levels were only a little higher, as 2012 was better than 2011 in 14 events to 9 with 1 tie, but for women 10th bests and both men's and women's 100th and base levels the count was massively in favour of 2012. See pages 528 and 529 for the details. Note that every 'record' was broken in both men's and women's half marathon and marathon and in the men's 50k walk and women's 20k walk. In all the total of athletes meeting my base level standards was 4464 for men and 4311 for women compared to the previous record figures of 3908 and 3782 respectively in 2011.

NOTES FROM THE EDITOR

Olympic Games – Legacy?

THE STAGING OF the Games of the XXXth Olympiad in London 2012 was a huge success, surely exceeding the highest expectations of most people. The organisation went so well, we had a real sport fest during the Games and the subsequent Paralympic Games, and the atmosphere throughout was simply exhilarating. But where now? The legacy aspects had been deemed vital in the lead up to the Games and one hopes that there will be many long lasting benefits and in particular that a generation of youngsters will have been inspired to take part in sport. But looking at athletics specifically, some seven months after the great days of August 2012, one can but see a rather dismal picture in Britain. I wrote about this subject in last year's annual but I make no apology for returning to it.

Firstly there is the long-running saga of the Olympic Stadium. Very sadly the original concept of having a stadium that could be downsized to a 25,000 or so capacity was discarded as the temptation to maximise the return meant that football was brought into the planning. For sure football is the only means by which 50,000 plus crowds could be attracted to a stadium for week after week, but the stadium is not constructed to suit the demands of a football crowd and reconstruction costs (including a roof and retractable seats over the athletics track, taking the capacity down to 54,000) are estimated at £150–190 million – even then can it really ever be suitable for both athletics and football? At the time of writing, while the government has said that the use of the stadium for athletics is guaranteed for 99 years there remains much uncertainty over its use although, as expected, West Ham United have, after protracted negotiations, signed a 99-year lease to use the stadium. It remains the case that there is highly unlikely to be much athletics there – perhaps just the annual Diamond League London Grand Prix meeting and the occasional major event, such as the 2017 World Championships, while the stadium will not satisfy football fans, many of whom will find themselves much further away from the action than they deem essential. Fortunately athletics will return to the track in 2013 – for the London Anniversary Games, by which this year's Diamond League meeting will be known, as work on reconstruction of the stadium will not have started by then.

Then there is the state of athletics in Britain. The sports paymasters have determined that success is judged by results at the highest level, and six athletics medals at the Olympic Games including four gold, was most satisfactory. One hopes that Jessica Ennis and Mo Farah, heading superb role models, will indeed inspire legions of new talent to step up. But such concentration on the (current) elite seems to be at the cost of lack of direction for development, to ensure a flow of such talent in years to come from the clubs that actually nurture young talent. The facts are that the number of regular competitors at senior level (ages 20–35) in track and field athletics (leaving aside the road runners) continues to decline steadily, so that there are surely fewer participants than at any time in the past half century or more and all too many of them compete far too little. While the governing bodies have, for years been very complacent over this, statistician Rob Whittingham has worked hard on assessing the true numbers involved. Over the page I have included his graph, with figures taken from UKA's Power of Ten website showing the number of athletes for each age who competed in 2012. This, quite dramatically, shows the way the number drops sharply from 4529 active 16-year-olds to 292 at age 30 and a levelling off from 34 onwards. If one looks for those who compete ten times or more (surely a fair test for real participation) then he shows that there are less than 2000 active athletes in the 20–35 age range. There are indeed far more competitive opportunities for young athletes than ever before and many take advantage of this, but the drop out rate in the late teenage years is huge. Even with the junior age group competitions, the governing bodies have been fiddling with the structure of the competitions against the advice of experts and the interests of the clubs and their athletes.

The concentration in Britain on the elite (even super-elite) is such that domestic competition for lower levels is being seriously ignored, even undermined, by the governing bodies. This is shown by the fact that all too many British runners choose to chase around the European continent to compete rather than support what could be much higher standard meetings at home. The number of top-quality meetings in Britain is now much less than it was in say the 1960s to 1980s and standards in such essential competitions for second-tier athletes as those run by the British Athletics League (BAL)

British T&F Athletes by Age

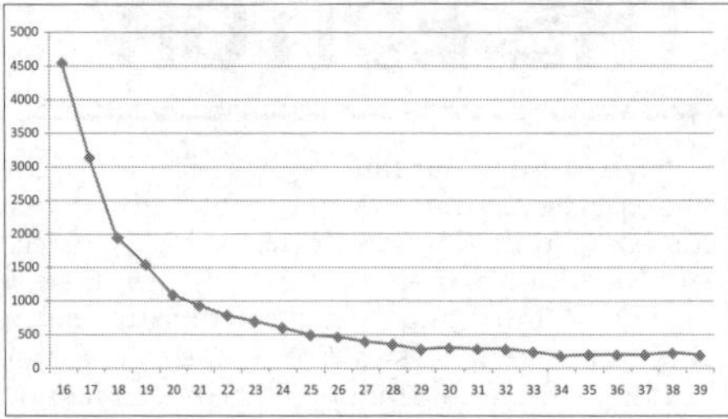

and the UK CAU (Inter-Counties) meeting are declining fast. Then, with the emphasis on selecting teams that include only athletes that are considered podium or top eight candidates, an increasing number of events at major meetings have become virtually off limits to the top British athletes. In the past, athletes in every event could aspire to represent Britain in the full internationals against other nations. The abandonment of such fixtures means that top athletes in many events have little or no such opportunities (perhaps just the European Team Championships). Britain will not be sending a team to this year's World University Games.

UK Athletics had marvellous sponsorship for many years from Aviva (formerly Norwich Union). That ended after the Olympics, and UK Athletics, having taken dealing with sponsorship in-house rather than using the expertise of FastTrack, announced that they were looking for some half a dozen new sponsors and expected to have them on board soon. The months have gone by and there has been nothing on this front. Indeed surely there is scope only for one major sponsor, concentrating on the marketing prize of name-association with the three or four major televised meetings (there used to be many more!).

The sport will surely have to manage on fewer resources than it has enjoyed in recent years, top executives and coaches (many foreign) are being very well paid and far too little is going to the grass roots. Meanwhile facilities are running down or. like the Don Valley stadium in Sheffield, being closed, and a top club, Belgrave Harriers, has had to withdraw from the BAL because of its inability to find a team manager. Volunteers to actually run most of the sport are indeed in short supply and the situation is worsening. As Dame Kelly Holmes said "We need to professionalise the grass roots." But that means directing resources away from administration and the super-elite towards the clubs and the mainstream of the sport.

I have written above about the state of the sport in Britain, but the picture may not be so different in other Western nations, and one has noted the demise (at least temporarily) of major meetings in France, Germany etc. It would be interesting to know whether the age profile in our chart varies substantially in other countries.

Championships Timetable

I COMMENTED ABOVE on the great success of the Olympic Games. But not everything was perfect! Luciano Barra, the vastly experienced Italian and international athletics administrator, drew attention to problems with the timetable for the Games and is even more critical of that drawn up for the World Championships in Moscow 2013.

He said: "(1) For the first time in Olympic history the 4x400 final was scheduled before the 4x100, both for men and women, and as the last event of the Games; (2) The custom that in all field events (except shot put) you should give one day rest between qualification and final was not respected; (3) The custom that in the 400m you give one day rest before the final was disregarded; (4) The long established custom of dividing the running events in 100–400–1500–10,000 in the first half of the schedule and 200–800-5000 in the second half was not generally respected. The consequence was that nobody could have doubled 1500 and 800." He continues: "I discovered that all four principles I outlined for London have been reaffirmed for Moscow and in some cases have been made significantly worse," pointing out that the gap between 20k and 50k walks has been reduced from seven days to two, that no one will now be able to double at 1500m and 5000m as the order of 800 and 1500 has been reversed, and that the 4x400 heats are scheduled prior to the 400 hurdles finals despite the fact that many hurdlers are used in the relays. The reversal of the men's 4x100 and 4x400m means that male sprinters (such as Usain Bolt) are pretty much prevented from running the 4x400 as well as the 200, but women (such as Allyson Felix) can do this. Of course it is the transcendent appeal of Usain Bolt has brought about the programme being completed by the 4x100 rather than the traditional 4x400, and the spectacular world record in this final event in London could be seen to have justified this move, but is it at a cost to the overall interests of the athletes?

World Cross-Country Championships

NOW HELD BIENNIALLY it is very sad to see that the World CC Championships continue to decline. Many top athletes did of course compete this year in Bydgoszcz, but all too many top distance runners did not, and the overall quality was far from the level of decades ago. We know that cross-country provides terrific preparation for distance runners facing track campaigns later in the year, but all too few in the Western world seem to listen to the advice of those who were brought up to realise this. The lessons of history are being lost. All credit to the Kenyans and Ethiopians who have dominated the Championships since they first entered teams in the 1980s and who have long placed great emphasis on getting their athletes together in training camps for an event that they take very seriously, But even they now "lose" many top stars to the lure of the big money available from marathon racing. But the collapse of distance running in so much of the Western world was demonstrated by the complete absence of any athletes from all too many European nations, including Germany, Russia and all the Scandinavian and Balkan nations, in Bydgoszcz. In all Europe provided just 25.8% of the entrants, its lowest ever and hugely less than in the early days of the event,

The lifestyle in so much of the developed world is the main factor behind the collapse of endurance running with so few provided to train hard enough and early enough. But the recent resurgence of distance running in the world's richest nation, the United States, was confirmed by an excellent showing in Bydgoszcz – so it can be done. Nonetheless one cannot be confident that the decline in the World Cross-country will be arrested. There were few takers to stage the next edition in 2015 and holding it in China is all too likely to result in a further decline in participants.

Walks out!

IT IS SAD to learn that there will be no race walking events at the Commonwealth Games in Glasgow 2014. The events remain, however, eligible for inclusion so there is every hope that they could be restored at the 2018 Gold Coast Games as race walking remains popular and well contested at a high standard in Australia, in contrast to its severe decline in Britain. The walking community has been incensed by this decision and I share their concern, for while numbers have been poor at recent Games, such a break from the traditional programme could be seen as the thin end of the wedge for other events as well and this is no way to encourage participation across the whole range of accepted events in our sport. There have been moves to cut out race walking before, as for instance when the 50k event was omitted from the 1976 Olympic programme and we had a separate World Championship, and at the Commonwealth Games there had been plans to cut the events from the 2010 programme in

New Delhi. But protest in the latter case was successful and the Games went ahead with walks; perhaps a campaign to reinstate the events for Glasgow could yet be successful?

Venues

It seems that we have kept changing our minds over the years as to the names of some US college locations. I strive for consistency; so do not want to change back again. Having settled on Stanford and Notre Dame (on US advice some years back) I am reluctant to change, as some would prefer, to Palo Alto and South Bend respectively although those major universities are located in those substantial towns. Also I use University Park rather than State College. But I do not think in any of these cases that there is any confusion as to the venue.

I do, however, want to elaborate on the venues for performances in many major cities that have multiple tracks. If most meetings are generally held at the major venue, such as Berlin, Budapest, Beijing than I am happy to use just that, but if there is possible doubt then I like to identify the actual track. And so, for instance, I use Berlin (Elstal), Boston (Roxbury), Paris (C) for Chartéty, etc. or for London I add (CP) for Crystal Palace, (He) for Hendon, (LV) for Lea Valley and for the new Olympic Stadium, which may or may not become the city's main venue, I have for now at least, added (OS). Anyway, I would like to receive more details for future lists, because there are many places just given the city/town name in our lists that could actually be at several locations.

Rewriting History

MORE ATHLETES HAVE been banned for drugs abuse over the past year than ever before – as can be seen by our lists on pages 107 and 108. The list includes many very big names in our sport and as we go to press further revelations mean extensive re-writing of past results as athletics continues its relentless war against the use of performance enhancing drugs with the IAAF and IOC re-examining samples stretching back eight years (unfortunately the maximum under the statute of limitations) as testing procedures become increasingly sophisticated. Russian athletes have been particularly culpable and after the previous mass exclusion of top women middle distance runners, the anti-doping commission of the All-Russian athletics federations (ARAF) confirmed two-year bans for three athletes. These are current athlete, 400m hurdler Yelena Churakova, and two retired athletes, for whom the bans are from the retesting process.

Cont. on page 51

Changes of Name and Allegiance

Transfer of Nationality/Allegiance

Name ___ From To ___ Noted ___ Eligible
Dates in final column indicate that athlete is not eligible to compete in international championships for new nation until later date. Underlined are changes from previous lists.

Men

Name	From	To	Noted	Eligible
Shadrack Biwott	KEN	USA	18.6.12	3.7.12
Azzeddine Boudjemaa	ALG	FRA	27.1.10	14.5.12
Boaz Cheboiywo	KEN	USA	5.4.12	2.5.12
Yordanis Durañona	CUB	DMA	2.1.12	
Ashraf Amgad El Seify	EGY	QAT	22.5.12	20.6.12
Tesfaye Eticha	ETH	SUI	5.12.11	2.4.12
Yordanis García	CUB	DMA	29.12.11	28.12.14
Ramil Guliyev	AZE	TUR	1.3.11	4.4.13
Ryan Haebe	USA	AUT	31.5.12	
Abdellah Haidane	MAR	ITA	1.3.12	23.5.12
Eusebio Haliti	ALB	ITA	20.7.12	3.10.12
Mark Johnson	USA	ISL	28.6.11	27.6.12
Abraham Kiprotich	KEN	FRA	22.6.10	14.5.12
Jackson Langat	KEN	USA	7.5.10	2.7.12
Brent LaRue	USA	SLO	13.7.11	12.3.12
Conor McCullough	USA	IRL	8.7.12	
Augustus Maiyo	KEN	USA	1.4.10	1.10.12
Yassine Mandour	MAR	FRA	26.5.08	7.12.12
Girma Gelan Mecheso	ETH	USA	5.7.11	22.5.12
Amaechi Morton	NGR	USA	24.6.12	22.8.12
Errol Nolan	USA	JAM	7.7.12	
Maksym Obrubanskyy	UKR	ITA	23.5.12	18.6.12
Brahian Peña	DOM	SUI	15.5.12	
Gian Piero Ragonesi	PER	ITA	2.1.13	
Justin Rodhe	USA	CAN	1.11.11	3.5.12
Maciej Rosiewicz	POL	GEO	8.11.11	5.4.12
Donald Sanford	USA	ISR	15.6.11	12.3.12
Konstantinos Stathelakos	GRE	CYP	23.3.12	15.5.12
Braion Taplin	USA	GRN	20.12.12	

Women

Name	From	To	Noted	Eligible
Abeba Aregawi	ETH	SWE	10.12.12	
Laëtitia Bambara	FRA	BUR	22.5.12	
Almensch Belete	ETH	BEL	15.6.12	22.6.12
Mathilde Boateng	FRA	GHA	2.5.12	13.7.12
Angela Cooper	USA	LBR	30.6.12	
Fawn Dorr	USA	CAN	1.1.12	20.6.12
Yordanys Durañona	CUB	DMA	29.12.11	28.12.14
Regina George	USA	NGR	27.6.12	
Jennifer Grossarth	USA	ITA	19.12.12	
Karen Harewood	GBR	BAR	19.4.12	2.5.12
Olga Kalendarova-Ochal	UKR	POL	21.9.11	2.4.12
Martha Komu Munytu	KEN	FRA	28.6.11	27.12.12
Françoise Mbango	CMR	FRA	16.9.10	16.4.12
Joanna Mills	IRL	GBR	16.1.13	11.7.15
Rosvitha Okou	FRA	CIV	27.6.12	10.7.12
Nuta Olaru	ROU	USA	22.11.11	20.6.12
Yasmina Omrani	FRA	ALG	28.3.12	2.7.12
Nina Serbezova-Mitkova	BUL	CYP	28.6.12	5.7.13
Omatoyo Talabi	USA	NGR		
Leila Traby	MAR	FRA	28.12.09	27.12.12

Further recent women's name changes

Original	Married name
Darya Akhmedova UZB	Reznichenko
Linda Allen AUS	Leverton
Alixe Auvray FRA	Guigon
Chantae Bayne USA	Watson
Olga Bludova KAZ	Safronova
Sarah Bowman USA	Brown
Chelsea Carrier USA	Eades
Candice Davis USA	Price
Janay DeLoach USA	Soukup
Urszula Domel POL	Gradzielewska
Yuliya Gavrilova KAZ	Rakhmanova
Özge Gürler TUR	Akin
Eunice Kales KEN	Kioko
Yekaterina Kayukova RUS	Chernenko
Yelena Kofanova RUS	Kotulskaya
Aleksandra Kuzina KAZ	Romanova
Margareta Matsko KAZ	Mukasheva
Anne Möllinger GER	Cibis
Ashley Muffet USA	Duncan
Freya Murray GBR	Ross
Jeccica Pixler USA	Tebo
Yekaterina Zavyalova RUS	Poistogova
Tina Polak POL	Matusinska
Dana Pounds USA	Lyon
Trecey Rew USA	Hoover
Vicky Robson CAN	Dressler
Olga Sergeyenko BLR	Sudarova
Sevim Sinmez TUR	Serbest
Olga Tereshkova KAZ	Tsykunova
Viktoriya Yakovtseva KAZ	Aksenova
Marion Wagner GER	Baumgärtner
Janet Wienand RSA	Lawless
Angelina Zhuk RUS	Krasnova

See also Recent Marriages on page 279 and lists on page 128 of ATHLETICS 2012 (and earlier Annuals)

Change of name and nationality

Men

		Noted	Eligible
Ivan Hryshyn UKR	Irfan Yirdirim TUR		
Patrick Langat KEN	Tarik Langat Akdag TUR	22.6.11	2.5.12

Women

		Noted	Eligible
Bethlem Desalegn ETH	Mariam Abdallah Mubarak UAE		
Teyba Naser ETH/BRN	Misiker Mekonnin Demissie ETH		
Adriana Pârtea ROM	Adriana Fisher USA	4.1.11	4.4.12

ATHLETICS BOOKS 2012–13
Reviewed by Peter Matthews

The Official History of the Women's AAA (1922-2012). 401 pages hardback, profusely illustrated. Mel Watman has followed his Official History of the AAA with this companion volume on women's athletics in Britain. He tells the story of the formation of the WAAA in 1922 and the determination of its pioneers to establish the sport in a man's world as they did so successfully, and later, with women an integral part of athletics, the excruciatingly long saga leading to the eventual merging of the AAA and WAAA in 1988. Throughout, covering a lot of ground with great skill, he details the successes of British women on the international stage and provides the highlights of each WAAA Championships meeting to 1987 and from then of the combined National Championships (AAA or AAA of England to 2006, UK from 2007). There are lists of all these national champions indoors and out plus WAAA/England age-group champions and England senior champions 2010-12 (although the separate UK Championships 1977-93 and 1997 are ignored). As in the AAA volume there are copious notes on the women's later achievements. Published by SportsBooks Ltd. £19.99. www.sportsbooks.ltd.uk.

Chris Brasher: The Man Who Made The London Marathon, by John Bryant. Hardback; 310 pages. Published by Aurum Press; £20, see www.aurumpress.co.uk. The fascinating story of the Olympic steeplechase champion of 1956, who went on to pioneer orienteering in Britain and found the London Marathon as well as forging a highly successful career as a businessman marketing sports shoes and walking boots and as a journalist and broadcaster.

The Official History of the Olympic Games and the IOC: Athens to London 1894-2012, by David Miller. Large format hardback; 719 pages. Published by Mainstream Publishing; £40; see www.mainstreampublishing.com. This massive work is the third edition of the definitive historic account of the Games and the International Olympic Committee by an author who has covered 22 Summer and Winter Olympic Games during his 56-year career as a journalist. Superbly illustrated, highlights of each Games from 1908 are prefaced by first-person reminiscences by a distinguished figure from that year. Updated after the 2012 Games in London.

Britain & The Olympics 1896–2010, by Bob Phillips. Paperback, 214 pages. Published by Carnegie Publishing Ltd; £12.99; www.carnegiepublishing.com. The editor of *Track Stats*, describes entertainingly and informatively the lives of Britain's Olympic champions – in all sports – and how they came to win their gold medals.

National Records for all Countries in the World by Winfried Kramer, Heinrich Hubbeling, Yves Pinaud and Steffen Stübe. A5 248pp. The 2012 edition of this valuable work has records for all events for each country and many territories (234 in all). New in this edition are records for Kosovo and various French overseas territories. 25 euros (cash only) from Winfried Kramer, Kohlrodweg 12, 66539 Neunkirchen-Kohlhof, Germany.

Weltrekorde und Weltrekordlerinnen – Kugelstoßen, Diskuswurf Frauen. A4 178pp, **Weltrekorde und Weltrekordlerinnen – Hammerwurf, Speerwurf Frauen**. A4 138pp. Manfred Holzhausen continues his series of splendidly detailed surveys (text in German, but masses of statistics) of world records and world record holders with these, first on women's shot and discus and second on hammer and javelin. There are results of all WR competitions with detailed career profiles (and many illustrations) of record breakers, tables of annual world bests and results of major championships contested by these record breakers. Each 15 euros in Europe from the author at Dresdener Str. 4, 41516 Grevenbroich, Germany. e-mail: manfred.holzhausen@gmx.de. Also contact him for the previous 12 men's and 8 women's books.

Stan Greenberg's Olympic Almanack. Paperback; 304 pages. Published by SportsBooks Ltd, £12.99; www.sportsbooks.ltd.uk. The author has updated his work (this is the eighth edition) to include the 2008 Summer and 2010 Winter Games and incorporated many revisions to previous results, in all too many cases due to retrospective doping disqualifications. It contains just about every fact that any Olympic enthusiast could possibly want to know, with athletics of course taking pride of place.

Aventuras en Las Pistas. By Luis Vinker, published by Ediciones Al Arco. 160p paperback. Written in Spanish, this book gives the story of the leading protagonists in Argentine athletics history from their first Olympic 'hero' triple jump silver medallist Luis Brunetto in 1924 to the present day. For details contact the author at luisvin@sinectis.com.ar.

Mulheres no Pódio. This 132-page large format book presents, in Portuguese, the history of Brazilian women's athletics. It has a fairly light text but is beautifully illustrated. Published by the Brazilian federation CBAt and CIAXA. Email contact: cbat@cbat.org.br

Heptathlon and Pentathlon – A Statistical Survey of British Women's Combined Events by Stuart Mazdon with help from Alan Lindop. A5 144pp. This, the 16th in the NUTS Historical Booklet Series, is a magnificent compilation, packed with information on the women's multi-events for Britain. A history of the events, including the formulae for the 1971 tables, is followed by UK progressive records (senior and junior). UK age bests, statistics over the years, merit rankings analysis (and the author's all-time view of the top women), and then the detailed all-time performers and performance lists for the various combinations of events indoors and out. There follows details of British athletes in international championships and matches and domestic championships results. Then we have 54 pages of biographies of 51 women including their complete multi-event career records and finally the best performances at individual events made in these competitions. There is also an 8-page picture section. Statistics are complete to 31 March 2012 with a 2012 update sent with all orders.

Price: £10 in UK, euro 16 or £13 in Europe, $25 or £15 for the rest of the world from Stuart Mazdon, 77 Forest Approach, Woodford Green, Essex IG8 9BU, UK – or from www.nuts.org.uk/heptathlon.htm with payment by PayPal or credit/debit card

Historical Dictionary of Track and Field by Peter Matthews. Hardback 320 pages. Published by Scarecrow Press Inc. in the USA. $85. After a selective chronology, covering several millennia but the past century and a half most densely, the introduction provides an overall view of the history and development of track and field. Then The Dictionary provides the detail, with entries on each track and field discipline, hundreds of top performers, and nations and organizations plus a variety of miscellaneous topics. Winners of all World and Olympic titles are listed in the Appendixes and there is an extensive bibliography initiated by Richard Hymans. See https://rowman.com/ISBN/9780810867819

Golden Century of IAAF Records – National Records 1912-2012 by Janusz Wasko, John Brant, György Csiki, Andrzej Socha. Due to be published in March/April this looks to be a most important statistical volume, a 458-page volume containing the evolution of national records for all the standard men's and women's events for all major nations. This updates the first edition, published in 2007, and adds top 30 records by nation after 1940, 1960, 1980, 1990, 2000 and 2010, and scores for nations. Contact at rwasko@onet.eu

ANNUALS

European Athletics Yearbook 2011-12. A5 568pp. From the European Athletic Association, Avenue Louis-Ruchonnet 18, CH-1003 Lausanne, Switzerland (25 euro in Europe, 30 euro elsewhere) – see www.European-athletics.org. Half the book contains reviews and results of EAA meetings in 2011 plus a wealth of other useful information, and half European lists: 100-deep for 2011 with 50-deep U23 and junior lists, 30-deep indoor lists and 50-deep all-time lists compiled as usual by Mirko Jalava. This annual was replaced for the 2012 season by two publications: **Athletics Review 2012**, a glossy 144-page A4 publication with many photographs and **Statistics Yearbook 2012**, a 448-page A5 book with the lists for 2012 as above.

Combined Events Annual 2012 by Hans van Kuijen. A5, 208pp. The 20th edition of this attractively produced annual, published in the year of the centenary of the decathlon, included top 200 men's decathlon and women's heptathlon lists for 2012 and all scores over 7550 and 5500 respectively with deep all-time world lists (to 8000 and 6000) plus indoor year and all-time lists. Also results of major events, records, profiles and complete career details for the world's top multi-eventers. In Europe: 30 euro or £30 sterling cash (no cheques). Outside Europe: US $50 cash or $70 cheques – from Hans van Kuijen, de Bergen 66, 5706 RZ Helmond, Netherlands. Email: j.kuijen4@upcmail.nl. Back numbers 2005-11: €15 each.

L'Athlétisme Africain/African Athletics 2012. A5, 152 pages. By Yves Pinaud. Published by Éditions Polymédias with support from the IAAF, the 31st edition in this splendid series has 100 deep men's and women's lists for Africa for 2011, with all-time lists, national championships and major meetings results. 20 euro, £18 or US $30 including postage from La Mémoire du Sport, 46 rue des Bordeaux, 94220 Charenton-le-pont, France. (Also available: booklist with very extensive list of athletics books and magazines for sale).

Asian Athletics 2011 Rankings. A5 96 pages. Heinrich Hubbeling continues his magnificent annual job of compiling Asian statistics. The booklet contains top 30s for 2011 for athletes from Asian nations, with continuation lists for countries other than China and Japan, indicating new national records, and full lists of Asian records. Euro 15/US $22 in cash or by International Money Order from the author, Haydnstrasse 8, 48691 Vreden, Germany. email hhubbeling@t-online.de. Copies also available for 1998, 2004-09 at €10/US $15 each.

Athlérama 2011. A5 688pp. The French Annual, edited by Patricia Doilin with a strong team of compilers, is again a superb reference book. Packed with information on French athletics – records, deep year lists for 2011, indexes, athlete profiles, results and all-time lists for all age groups. Extras include French top ten lists for 1911 and 1961. 28 euros from the FFA, 33 avenue Pierre de Coubertin, 7540 Paris Cedex 13, France. email Patricia.Doilin@athle.org

British Athletics 2013. A5 408 pages. The 55th NUTS Annual, edited by Rob Whittingham, Peter Matthews, and Tony Miller. Deep UK ranking lists for all age groups in 2011, top 12 merit rankings, all-time lists, results etc. £18 plus postage (£2 UK & Europe, £5 outside Europe); from Rob Whittingham, 7 Birch Green, Croft Manor, Glossop, Derbyshire SK13 8PR, UK. Cash or Sterling cheques.

Israeli Athletics Annual 2012/13. 240 x 170mm, 54pp, illustrated. By David Eiger. Records, championship results, 2012 top 20s and all-time lists, with profiles of leading Israeli athletes. 7 euro or US $10 from David Eiger, 10 Ezra Hozsofer Str, Herzliya 46 371, Israel. Back numbers also available.

Latvijas Vieglatletikas Gadagramata 2013. A5 560 pp. Comprehensive coverage of Latvian athletics for 2012, including records, results, athlete profiles and year and all-time lists with some colour photos, compiled by Andris Stagis. From the Latvian Athletic Association, Augsiela 1, Riga LV-1009, Latvia.

Annuaire FLA 2012. A4 204p. The Luxembourg Annual, edited by Georges Klepper, is again an extraordinarily comprehensive volume, with every possible detail for this nation– reviews, results, 2012 and all-time lists, plus many colour photographs. 15 euros locally, by post €18 in Luxembourg, €27 elsewhere to account no. LU32 1111 0200 0321 0000. See www.fla.lu.

Malaysian Athletics Annual Best Performances 2012 by Jad Adrian Washif. 82pp with 2012 Malaysian Rankings, All-Time Rankings, National Records, and results of major Malaysian meets in 2012. Contact the author (see below).

Athletics New Zealand 2011 Almanac. A5 158pp. Edited by Steve Hollings and Simon Holroyd. The second annual from Athletics NZ includes national ranking lists for 2011 up to 50 deep for seniors plus lists for juniors and youths, all-time top 20s, records for the various age groups and results of championships and other major events. See www.athletics.org.nz and go to "Shop".

Friidrott 2012. 170 x 240 mm 464pp, 255 pictures, hardback. Edited by Jonas Hedman, text in Swedish. A high quality production which covers world and Scandinavian athletics, including detailed championships and major events results with narrative, world outdoor top 50 year and all-time-lists, top 25 Scandinavian and Swedish year and all-time lists plus indoor top tens and record lists for World, Europe, Scandinavia and Sweden. 395 kronor from TextoGraf Förlag, Jonas Hedman, Springarvägen 14, 142 61 Trångsund, Sweden. See www.textograf.com.

Southeast Asia Athletics Annual 2011/12. A5, 123 pages. This pioneer publication contains results of major meetings, annual and all-time ranking lists, national records (outdoor & indoor) for all countries and athlete's profiles for the area. Price EUR 10 (SEA), EUR 15 (outside SEA) inc. shipping and handling fees. Payment in cash or cheque, bank transfers, credit card, debit card, Paypal, and western union to: Jad Adrian Washif, L7 - 12th College UPM, 43400 Serdang Selangor, Malaysia. See: www.adriansprints.com. Email: jad_adrianwashif@yahoo.com

Anuario Athlético Español 2011/2012. A5 242pp. Spanish rankings for 2012 (outdoors) plus indoors 2011/12 as well as lists of best marks each year from 1900 for all events and progressive records for various age groups. This is **bulletin no. 91** of the Spanish statistical group, the AEEA, (see later).

Anuario 2011/2012 – Pista Cubierta y Campo a Través. A5 446pp. Comprehensive details for the Spanish cross country and indoor seasons with lists and results, all-time lists, lists of previous champions and photographs. 14 euros plus postage (€3.75 in Spain, €12 elsewhere) from the RFEA.

2012 USA Track & Field Media Guide & FAST Annual; general editors: Jared Slinde and Tom Casacky. A5 782pp. The first 262 pages is the USATF Media Guide with detailed profiles of top US athletes plus Olympics details, published for the 18th year with the FAST Annual, of which this is the 34th edition, containing records, 50-deep US lists for 2011 and all-time, with 15-deep junior and college all-time lists. The massive final index section includes annual progressions and championships details for top American athletes. $25 post paid in the USA or $42 or 30 Euros airmail from Tom Casacky, PO Box 3122, Oak Brook, IL 60523, USA. Payment is easiest by PayPal (to tom@interis.com); also cash, postal money orders and Western Union transfers.

Yleisurheilu 2012. A5 672pp. The Finnish Yearbook, published by Suomen Urheilulitto

(Finnish Athletics) and compiled by Juhani and Mirko Jalava, contains every conceivable statistic for Finnish athletics (with results and deep year lists) in 2012 and also world indoor, outdoor and junior lists for the year as known at November. 19 euros plus 10 euros for postage and packaging. Orders by e-mail to juhani@tilastopaja.fi.

See also ATHLETICS 2012 for other national annuals. New editions covering 2012 can be expected.

Statistical Bulletins

Hammer Throw Stats History and News Bulletin No. 12. By Zdenek Procházka. The latest in this series features hammer lists all-time to 1948 and then top 100s for each Olympiad, so 1949-52,1953-6 etc. to 2009-12. These lists feature the best for other nations (to 50 deep) and also show all-time bests for all athletes listed. Also shown are winners of major championships and deep lists with bests at the Olympic Games and analyses of Olympic competition and an index of all competitors. Four bulletins (usually of between 54 -200 pages) will be published by email annually. Year price is 30 Euro or $40 (only e-mail version in PDF or Excel format) cash or by International Money from Zdeněk Procházka, Washingtonova 9, 11000 Praha 1, Czech Republic. email: atlet2003@volny.cz.

TRACK STATS. The NUTS quarterly bulletin, edited by Bob Phillips, includes a wealth of fascinating statistics and articles. A5, 68-80 pages. Annual subscription (4 issues) is £20 (UK), £25 (rest of Europe) or £28 (elsewhere); contact Liz Sissons, 9 Fairoak Lane, Chessington, Surrey KT9 2NS, UK.

2012 issues: April included profiles of British sprint stars of the 1920s, Jack London and Harry Edward, and walkers George Larner and Tebbs Lloyd Johnson. There was an intriguing article on the first (unofficial) Pan-American Games held in Dallas in 1937, at which Johnny Woodruff was timed at 1:47.8 for 1.52m short of 800m, and a list of all of Harold Abrahams' competitions between 1909 and 1920. **October:** 24 of its 68 pages contained reflections on the London Olympics. Among other features was the first part of a list of progressive UK all-comers' records (100y-2000m). **January 2013:** Packed with 'goodies' including Gordon Pirie 1953, careers of Peter Driver and Cliff Blair, complete results of Monte Carlo Women's International 1922, and fantasy all-time British 5000m and 10,000m races.

The Olympics 100 Years Ago. A4 86 pages. *Track Stats* Special, subtitled 'How Great Britain's athletes performed at Stockholm in 1912, by editor Bob Phillips with David Thurlow. This fine publication reviewed the British season with results from major meetings leading up to the Olympic Games, with details (including dates and places of birth and death, clubs and 2012 results) for the British team, then a list of all competitors in Stockholm and full results with reports on each Olympic athletics event. Additional articles include David Thurlow's relation of the experiences of 1500m gold medallist Arnold Strode-Jackson. £8 in UK £10 overseas from Don Turner, 40 Rosedale Road, Stoneleigh, Epsom, Surrey KT17 2JH, UK. Sterling cheques payable to NUTS.

Don Turner (donturner@btinternet.com) also has stocks of NUTS publications; including back various back issues of Track Stats from 1998.

Each £5: Event booklets (detailed statistics on UK athletes including results of championships and very detailed all-time lists, profiles etc.): UK women's hurdles (2004), Long Jump (2005), Shot Put (2006), Pole Vault (2008). Also 1930-39 UK men's ranking lists. And two recent publications: **Hammer** by Ian Tempest (2011), 88pp at £8 including postage, **Decathlon** (2011) 120pp by Alan Lindop at £9 including postage.

The **DGLD** – the **German** statistical group, Deutsche Gesellschaft für Leichtathletik-Dokumentation produces annual national ranking lists (**Deutsche Bestenliste**, 204 pages) for Germany and impressive bulletins of up to 292 pages, packed with historical articles and statistical compilations. Each issue (three per year) includes statistical profiles of athletes born 70, 75, 80, 85, 90 years ago etc. Membership, with free Deutsche Bestenliste – euro 55 per year. Contact Hans Waynberg, Liebigstrasse 9, 41464 Neuss, Germany; hans.waynberg@t-online.de. Website: www.leichtathletik-dgld.de

No. 62 – 208 pages – included an extensive survey of how German athletes qualified for the Olympic Games 1896-1964 with results of trials meetings/events, all-time lists for Saxony as at 1918, German women's record progressions and all-time lists 1900-45 for 50 to 1000m, and a 70-page compilation by athlete of all German 800m times sub 1:50.0. Plus a DGLD bulletin index 1990-2012. **No. 63** – 184 pages – included Olympic marathons 1908, 1912 and 1948; German yearly leaders for all events 1945-2011; Ranking of 214 nations and territories by their records. **No 64** – 292 pages – year lists for Saxony 1898-1918, all-time lists for East Prussia and Danzig at 1945, deep German women's all-time relay lists to 1945, analysis of German qualifiers for European Champs 1934-62, German Services Championships 1922-38, Index of FRG athletes 1949-90, and the complete career of Karin Balzer 1955-72.

The latest in the series of books published by the DGLD dealing with the history of 100 years of athletics in Germany, event-by-event – **100 Jahre Leichtathletik in Deutschland** is **100 m-Lauf**

Männer by Harry Themel. 464 pages. 25 euros from Hans Waynberg (as above). No cheques from outside Germany.

The **Spanish group, the AEEA** continues to produce magnificent publications. Membership (four bulletins per year) is 55 euros per year (€61 outside Europe) from AEEA secretary Ignacio Mansilla, C/Encinar del Rey, 18 - 28450 Collado Mediano, Madrid, Spain. email: ranking@rfea.es

The 25th anniversary of the founding of the Asociación Española de Estadisticos de Atletismo was celebrated in its **Bulletin No. 90.** In the first 88 pages there are details and illustrations of the history of the group with contents listings and index of all its bulletins and other publications 1987-2012. Then there was a 107-page section by Miguel Villaseñor: "European Championships Miscellaneous" with all manner of statistics from the Championships, such as best marks by place, biggest and smallest margins, medal sweeps, doubles, bests and firsts for each country, multiple medallists, families etc. Finally there are lists of Spanish relay marks for 1960.

IAAF Handbooks

Athletics Statistics Handbook for the **Games of the XXX Olympiad, London 2012**. Available for download (http://www.iaaf.org/mini/oly12/index.aspx) from the IAAF website. This 386-page book, edited by the redoubtable Mark Butler, was, as ever with these marvellous handbooks, a wonder of comprehensive detail.

IAAF Directory and Calendar 2012. A5, 324 pages. Essential reference with contact details for officials, organisations and national federations, plus calendar and lists of records and IAAF champions. $16. Also **Outdoor Handbook** (141 pp) $12, **Winter Handbook** (38pp) $10, **Competition Rules** (282pp) $10, **Directory of Athletes' Representatives 2011** (116 pp) $8.

Contact the IAAF (or see www.iaaf.org) for their extensive list of publications and videos for sale at 17 rue Princesse Florestine, BP 359, MC 98007, Monaco. Prices include postage by airmail. Email to: headquarters@iaaf.org. Payment by credit card (Visa, Mastercard or eurocard only), quoting name on card, number of card, expiry date, name and address and signature.

IAAF 1912-2012 10 Years of Athletics Excellence

This profusely illustrated, large format (430 pages, 35 x 25.5cm) commemorative book is a mighty tome indeed, published by the IAAF at its gala in Barcelona in November 2012. A most worthy celebration of the IAAF's Centenary it has text in English and French, edited by Mel Watman with Alain Billouin for the French adaptation. It is profusely illustrated with splendid photos from the Getty Images archive,

The scope of the book is shown by the contributors and their articles that cover the full range of athletics activities and events:

Lamine Diack – President's message

Roberto Quercetani – One hundred years of the IAAF

David Miller – a. The IAAF's five presidents, b. The end of amateurism

Dave Johnson – A history of IAAF rules

Sergey Bubka – 100 years of athletics development

Victor López – Development of coaches' education in athletics

Pierre Weiss – History of the IAAF's marketing strategy

Arne Ljungqvist – The relentless fight against doping

Maurice Nicholas & Mirko Jalava – An awakening for Asian athletics

Yves Pinaud – The stunning rise of Africa

Eduardo Biscayart – South America's great leap forward

Anne Roger – Europe remains at the heart of athletics

Parker Morse & Mel Watman – The new world brings new blood

Fletcher McEwen – Top athletes from "Down Under"

Mel Watman – a. The Stockholm Olympics of 1912, b. A dream of a decathlon, c. The greatest ever Olympics?

Richard Hymans – The world's fastest human

Alain Billouin – The mile – an everlasting legend

Peter Radford – Women's athletics – the road to recognition

Pat Butcher – a. The rise of African distance running, b. The kings and queens of the road

Mark Butler – a. Cross Country: an inter-continental journey, b. The jewel in the IAAF's crown (World Championships)

Paul Warburton – The most misunderstood discipline (walking)

Doug Gillon – a. The centuries-old pursuit of excellence, b. The inside story (indoor athletics)

Phil Minshull – Teenage talent takes the stage (World Junior and Youth Championships).

Amendments to ATHLETICS 2012

p.33 Athletes of 2011. 20km Walk: note Morozov drugs dq, so amend rankings to 9. Sánchez, 10. Krivov

p.59 World Champs. 20kmW: (12) Morozov drugs dq, so 12 Wang, 13 Tóth, 14 Sánchez, 15 João Vieira POR 1:23:36. p.60: W 800m: (8) Rusanova drugs dq

p.64 Women 4x100m: TRI (4th) dq (Hackett #)

p.77 Pan-American Games. Women HJ: Rojas drugs dq, so 2, Rifka and 3. Deirdre Mullen USA 1.84

p.79 Arab Games: Femi Ogunode & A A Kamal drugs dq, so winners: 100m: Barakat Al-Harthi OMA 10.38, 5000m: Soufiyan Bouqantar MAR 13:45.81, 3000mSt: Hamid Ezzine MAR 8:38.37.

p.91 Olympic Games medal table: USA 242 silver, Bulgaria 5-6-7 = 18, Mexico 5 silver

p.139 Australia: 2011 Champion

p.189 Japan, 2011 champions: 110mh: Yazawa 13.86

p.214 RUS champ 20kW: Andrey Krivov 1:20:47

p.260 World U18 record: 48.89 L.J.van Zyl RSA at Kingston 19 Jul 2002 over senior hurdles is superior to that by Wynne over 84cm hurdles

p.261/279 Delete World U20 half marathon 59:14 by Dennis Koech (born 1984), reinstate 59:16 Samuel Wanjiru KEN Rotterdam 11 Sep 2005

Records and All-time lists: some more amendments have been incorporated in this year's Annual.

2011 World Lists

Men: 100m: 10.04w Brown at Mucurapo

200m Jnr: 20.89 Stewart 11.6.93, Armstrong 26.2.94

400m: 45.51 Hewitt 18.6.89, 45.85 Offereins 12.3.86, Junior: 46.34A Kishoyan 12.10.94

800m: 1:46.06 Kemboi 12.12.93 and add to Juniors

3000m/5000m: Diego Estrada MEX to naturalised USA Autumn 2011; ran for Mexico at 2012 OG.

10,000m: 27:12.24 Rotich 12; **10km/HMar**: 27:50/59:27 Jonathan Maiyo 5.5.88; **HMar**: 61:11 Tum 12.6.86, 61:30A Dennis Kimetto 22.4.84 (so not -Y)

Mar: 2:08:35 Ngungu 11.3.87, 2:08:38 Nickson Kurgat (& 10k 28:20, HMar 61:43), 2:09:50 Dawit 16.7.84, top Junior was 2:06:07 Eric Ndiema (see main list)

110mh: 13.54 & 13.58 Brathwaite BAR; 13.85/13.76w Parks 28.7.89; Jnr: 13.90 Lathan 15.7.92, 14.09 Forde 13.3.92, 14.01w Masuno 24.5.93; **400mh**: 49.04 McFarlane 14.6.72

HJ: Three lines omitted following 2.36 Dmitrik 2.15/2, 2.19/1, 2.23/1, 2.27/1, 2.30/1, 2.32/1, 2.34/2, 2.36/2, 2.38/xxx; 2.35 (1) Huelva, 2 Jun: 2.13/1, 2.17/1, 2.20/1, 2.23/2, 2.26/1, 2.31/1, 2.35/3; 2.35 (2) WCh Daegu 1 Sep: 2.20/1, 2.25/1, 2.29/2, 2.32/2, 2.35/2, 2.37/xxx; 2.25 J Harris 18.9.91,

PV: Juniors 5.30 Art – also 5.33i 3B Villeurbanne 22 Jan

LJ: 8.23 Forbes 11.9.90, 7.80w Samaai 25.9.91

SP: 20.13 Bookout 16.3.83 19.82 DeChant 31.5.89, 19.65 Mesic; Best out: 18.30 Garrett 26 May

DT: Jnr 57.92 Shiri 21.5.93; **JT**: Jnr 73.50 Parker 27.6.92

4x400m: Delete 3:07.22 KSA

3000mW: while suspended: 11:14.63 Fernández

5000m/10,000mW: 19:49.62/41:34.0 Thorne 19.3.93

10,000mW: Jnr: 41:47.98 Kimura 5.2.93, 41:50.75 Wang 16.2.94; **20kmW**: Morozov marks to drugs dq: 1:19:18 on 12 Jun (and change position for 1:21:09 Ruzavin 2, 1:21:46 Filipchuk), and 1:20:08 and move up remaining NC-w places; 1:20:10 Kim Hyun-sub; while suspended: 1:22:17 Fernández; 100th best 1:23:41.

Women

100m: 11.34/11.18w Hayes 9.2.88 (& LJ 6.50/6.53w), 11.43/11.35w/1 Y Voronenkova b. 8.9.88 (& 200m 23.42/23.37i/23.10w, 400m 52.42)

200m: (32/11) to 22.55; 22.94 Montsho wind +2.9, different race from -0.6?; Indoors: delete 23.47 Wesh

400m: (31/9) to 50.46; **800m**: Drugs dq: 1:56.99 Rusanova, 1:58.03 Klyuka, thus change positions in RUS NC; Rusanova had best before drugs ban of 1:58.14i; 2:02.2 Yekaterina Poistogova RUS 1.3.91 1 Yekaterinburg 11 Jun, 2:03.41 Grace 24.10.88

1500m: To drugs dq: 4:02.73 Syreva (earlier 4:08.93i 1 Omsk 21 Jan), 4:05.14 Rusanova; **2000m/3000m/5000m/HMar**: 5:44.89i/8:49.99/15:22.10/70:18 Syreva to drugs dq; **10000m**: Juniors: delete 33:34.32 Bergnan as born 1.11.91

HMar: 69:45 Chelimo 12.7.89 (& 10k 32:04. 20k), 70:04 Macharia 7.12.87 (& 10k 32:39), 70:39 Jerotich Rono 18.12.89, 70:43 Cherono 12.5.83, 71:05 Pritz 7.4.88, 71:50 Kwambai 22.3.86 (10k 32:29), 74:03A Jepkurgat 21.4.89 so not junior.

Mar: 2:26:31 drugs dq Abitova (& 71:27+ HMar), 2:30:39 Yihunlish 22.10.81, 2:31:41 Girma 28.7.86 (& HMar 72:09)

400mh: 55.09 Nagehan Karadere

HJ: Drugs dq: 1.89 Rojas ¶ 26 Oct – replace in main lists by 1.85 1 Sep; **PV**: (46/11) to 4.70

LJ: 6.71i Voykina 1 Sankt Peterburg 5 Feb (6.55 to best out); **TJ**: 14.55 Panétta; **HT**: 62.24 Novogradskaya

JT: 58.61 Gromova 23.9.80; **5000mW**: delete 20:56.1+ Rigaudo, replace by 21:12.73 1 Firenze 4 Jun

10,000mW: 42:59.48t Lashmanova 9.4.92

20kW: 1:34:39 Herrera 20.12.88

Amendments to World Indoor Lists 2012

Men: 800m: 1:46.64# Kemboi 12.12.93; **3000m**: deleye 7:48.25 Levins (see 7:45.75); **HJ**: 2.31 Kabelka SVK, 2.27 J Harris 18.9.91, 2.26 Simón Siverio ESP 2.8.88 18 Feb; **LJ**: 8.12 Forbes 11.9.90

Women: 60m: 7.15 Freeman 20.4.92; **200m**: 23.24 Spencer J 8.6.93; **800m**: drugs dq 2:00.26 Rusanova; **1500m**: 4:07.72 Diana Sujew, 4:07.99 Elina Sujew; **60mh**: 8.06 Caravelli 28 Jun (delete 8.04); **LJ**: 6.61 Hayes 9.2.88; **TJ**: 14.47 Panétta; **Hep**: 4616 Maksimova & 4310 Netsvetayeva on 18 Feb

Amendments to Previous World Lists

2010: Inge Abitova all marks drugs dq: 10k, HMar, Mar IAAF World Race Walking Cup (p.72) Men 20k: Erik Tysse drugs dq from 4th, so move all the rest up a place, add 15 Rafal Augustyn POL 1:25:28. 1:24:05 Bakulin 7th (p.443)

1988: 2000m 5:00.7+, 3000m 7:40.92i & 2M 8:18.92i all by Bekana Daba ETH 29.7.88

1957: JT: 84.00 Danielsen was on 2 Oct (and meeting was an unauthorised one), 81.03 (not 80.90) Danielsen 8 Sep; 71.18 Røberg at Plassen 28 Aug (from 71.15)

With thanks to José María García, Ed Gordon, Juan Mari Iriondo, Jirí Ondrácek, Bernt Solaas

Some Changes in Medallists at Recent Championships

Olympic Games 2008: 1500m: 1, Asbel Kiprop KEN, 2. Nick Willis NZL, 3. Mehdi Baala FRA

World Indoor Championships 2010: 60m: 1. Veronica Campbell-Brown JAM, 2. Carmelita Jeter USA; 3= Sherri-Ann Brooks JAM, Ruddy Zang-Milama GAB; 4x400m: 1, USA, 2. RUS, 3. CZE

European Championships 2010: 5000m: 1. Elvan Abeylegesse TUR, 2. Sara Moreira, 3. Jéssica Augusto POR; 10,000m: 1. Elvan Abeylegesse TUR, 2. Jéssica Augusto POR; 3. Hilda Kibet NED; Marathon: 1. Anna Incerti ITA, 2. Tetyana Filonyuk UKR, 3. Isabellah Andersson SWE

European Indoors 2011: 800m: 1. Jennifer Meadows GBR, 2. Linda Marguet FRA, 3. Marilyn Okoro GBR 3000m: 2. Lidia Chojecka POL, 3. Layes Abdullayeva AZE

HALL OF FAME 2013

WE STARTED A Hall of Fame in ATHLETICS 2001. Each year we now add five new athletes – a mix of past and current stars, taking special consideration of athletes who have just retired. Current stars can only be included if they have already had at least ten years in international competition. Prior to this year 81 athletes have been included (there was a bumper selection in ATHLETICS 2003 following a survey of the best athletes for each event).

In 2012 the IAAF celebrated their centenary and introduced their Hall of Fame, initially comprising 24 athletes. Twenty of those were amongst our list of 81 and we are delighted to add their additional four to our list together with one further addition. This is Tirunesh Dibaba, who is still just 27 years of age, but she has now completed a decade in international competition, and surely has the finest record of any woman 10,000m runner.

Tirunesh DIBABA (Ethiopia) (b. 1 October 1985 Bekoji, Arsi region).

When she won the 5000m in 2003 Dibaba became, at 17 years 333 days, the youngest ever world champion at an individual event. She had set a world junior record of 14:39.94 in Oslo and earlier in the year she had won the World Junior cross-country title, after 5th in this race in 2001 and 2nd in 2002, when she was also 2nd in the World Junior 5000m.

In 2004 she set world junior records for 3000m indoors with 8:33.56 and 5000m outdoors in 14:30.88, Competing now as a senior, she was second in the World 4km cross-country and took the Olympic bronze medal at 5000m. She set a world indoor record with 14:32.93 for 5000m in 2005 and went on to win four world titles. After a World Cross-country double, she won both 5000m and 10,000m at the Worlds in Helsinki, a unique double by a woman at a global event. In both these races she ran sub-60 second last laps and the 10,000m was in only her second ever track race at the distance – in 30:24.02, having run 30:15.67 in June.

In 2006 she retained her World Cross 8km title but dropped out of the 4km race and outdoors improved her 5000m best to 14:30.40 and traded wins with compatriot Meseret Defar at the World Athletics Final, winning the 5000m but being outkicked in the 3000m, before winning the World Cup 3000m. In 2007 she set a world indoor record of 14:27.42 for 5000m and was runner-up in the World Cross before taking her third successive World 10,000m title on the track.

She again won the World Cross in 2008, and after winning the African 10,000m title ran a brilliant world record 14:11.15 for 5000m in Oslo. She later won a marvellous 5000m and 10,000m double at the Olympic Games – a feat achieved in contrasting ways. First she won the 10,000m in an African record 29:54.66, the second fastest ever by a woman, after an enthralling duel against Elvan Abeylegesse and then her prodigious finishing kick proved too much for her opponents in a 5000m that was run at a very slow pace until the final kilometre. She won the African title at 10,000m in 2010, but did not compete on the track in 2011 through injury. She returned, however, in 2012 to retain her Olympic title at 10,000m, taking the lead with 500m to go and romping clear to win by 30m in 30:20.75 (her ninth win in nine 10,000m track races). A week later she added bronze at 5000m.

Mildred 'Babe' DIDRIKSON (USA). (b. 26 June 1911 Port Arthur, Texas, d. 27 September 1956 Galveston, Texas.) Married professional wrestler George Zaharias. Named as the female athlete of the half-century by Associated Press in 1950, she has an outstanding claim to be the most versatile sportswoman ever. She won two gold medals (80m hurdles and javelin) and a silver (high jump) at the 1932 Olympics and set world records at those three very different events 1930-2. She was an All-American basketball player each year 1930-2 and set the world record for throwing the baseball 90.22m *296 ft*. Switching to golf she won the US Women's Amateur title in 1946 and the US Women's Open in 1948, 1950 and 1954. She also excelled at various other sports and was nicknamed 'Babe' after baseballer Babe Ruth for hitting 13 home runs in a game against boys.

Her world records set in 1932 lasted as US records for decades: 80m hurdles 11.7 not beaten until 1956; high jump 1.65m to 1948; javelin 40.80m to 1956. She also set a US long jump record of 5.69m in 1930 that lasted to 1953, and an unofficial world record for 100y of 11.0 in 1931. Her three-year championship career in track and field included AAU titles at 80m hurdles 1931-2, javelin 1930-2, long jump 1931, high jump and shot 1932.

After her Olympic success she toured in vaudeville and with her own basketball team, before achieving golfing success. Having been earning up to $1000 a week on an exhibition tour with Gene Sarazen she was declared a professional, but regained her amateur status by staying out of competition for three years. She turned pro again in 1948. After contracting cancer in 1953 she made a courageous return to win the 1954 US Open by a record 12 strokes, but eventually lost her battle against the disease and died in 1956.

Alberto JUANTORENA Danger (Cuba) (b. 21 November 1950 Santiago de Cuba). With the 400m and 800m double in 1976 he achieved a double unique in Olympic history; he set a world record of 1:43.50 at 800m and his 44.26 for 400m was then the fastest ever at low altitude. With his huge stride (he was 1.90m tall) it was felt that he had taken middle distance running into a new era, but he made only one improvement on these times. In 1977 he ran the 800m in 1:43.44 to win the World Student Games title and he won the 400m/800m double at the inaugural World Cup. In the latter he won an epic race against Mike Boit of Kenya, who had missed the 1976 Olympics.

He had been identified as a potential basketball star when 1.88m tall at age 14 and he went to a state basketball school. But his track talent was spotted and he was a semi-finalist at the 1972 Olympic Games; this was at 400m at which he won the World Student Games gold in 1973 and the Pan-American silver in 1975. A severe Achilles tendon injury prevented him from defending his Olympic 800m title in 1980 after he had placed fourth at 400m, and his career ended when he was carried off, screaming in agony and frustration after tripping over the kerb in a semi-final of the 800m at the 1983 World Championships.

He became the president of the Cuban athletics federation and council member of the IAAF.

Adhemar Ferreira da SILVA (Brazil) (b. 29 September 1927 São Paulo, d. 12 January 2001 São Paulo). He set five world records at triple jump from 16.00m in 1950 to 16.56 in 1955, the last at high altitude in Mexico City when winning the second of three Pan-American Games titles. Having opened his Olympic career with 11th place in 1948 he won Olympic gold in 1952 and 1956 and bowed out at the 1960 Games but, reportedly suffering from tuberculosis, could place only 14th. *See ATHLETICS 2012 for Obituary.*

WANG Junxia (China) (b. 9 January 1973 Jiahoe City, Jilin Province). The top star from Ma Junren's training group of Chinese women, she had a sensational year in 1993. Two weeks after running a world best Ekiden relay 5km split of 14:52 she ran 2:24:07 on her marathon début in Tianjin in April. She won both 3000m and 10,000m at the Chinese Championships and took the World 10,000m title with a last 3000m in 8:42.49. Even such feats were left far behind, however, at the Chinese National Games in September, when she ran 10,000m in 29:31.78, taking 41.96 sec off the world record on the 8th, was second to Qu Yunxia at 1500m in 3:51.92, inside the 13 year-old world record, on the 11th, and then set 3000m world records of 8:12.29 on the 12th and 8:06.11 on the 13th, compared to the 8:22.62 which had remained the world record since 1984. In her 10,000m record she ran the first half in 15:05.69 and the second half in 14:26.09 – yet the world record for 5000m was 14:37.33 by Ingrid Kristiansen! Wang ended the year by winning the World Marathon Cup in an easy 2:28:16 and taking the Asian 10,000m title in a very slow time.

Wang had emerged in 1992 with second to Paula Radcliffe in the World Junior Cross-country and first in the World Junior 10,000m. She won the Asian Games 10,000m in 1994 and Asian Championships 5000m and 10,000m in 1995. She left the controversial Ma while a hip injury, the legacy of his excessive training regime, curtailed her racing in 1994-5, but rejoined him in October 1995. However, she was with a new coach by the time of her ambitious Olympic double bid in 1996. That meant a 10,000m heat then a heat and final, which she won, at 5000m and then the 10,000m final. That proved just too tough and she took the silver medal behind Fernanda Ribeiro, her first loss in 14 10,000m track finals. Suffering from the pressures of her intensive training, she took a break in 1997, but although back in training by the end of the year did not reappear in competition. She has lived in Denver, USA with her second husband Huang Tianwen since 2008.

Retired in 2012–13

Men: Larry Achike GBR, James Adjetey-Nelson CAN, Eugenio Barrios ESP, Ben Challenger GBR, Walter Davis USA, Nathan Deakes AUS, Danny Ecker RUS, Tyrone Edgar GBR, Francisco Javier Fernández ESP, Atsushi Fujita JPN, Filmon Ghirmai GER, Christian Glatting GER, Dennis Goossens BEL, Jacob Hernandez USA, Yoshitaka Iwamizu JPN, Jukka Keskisalo FIN, Khalid Khannouchi USA, Felix Limo KEN, Tim Lobinger GER, Derek Miles USA, Juan Manuel Molina ESP, Tomo Morimoto JPN, Masato Naito JPN, Cédric Nabe SUI, Christian Olsson SWE, Satoshi Osaki JPN, Kevin Rans BEL, Andres Raja EST, Dayron Robles CUB, Scott Russell CAN, Stuart Stokes GBR, Bastian Swillims GER, Linus Thörnblad SWE, Kristof Van Malderen BEL, Jirí Vojtik CZE, Nils Winter GER

Women: Natasha Danvers GBR, Kate Dennison GBR, Élodie Ouédraogo BEL, Brigitte Foster-Hylton JAM, Yushiko Fujinaga JPN, Claudia Grunwald GER, Joanna Hayes USA, Tia Hellebaut BEL (after EI 2013), Jolanda Keizer NED, Carolina Klüft SWE, Olive Loughnane IRL, Tamsyn Manou AUS, Hanna Mariën BEL, Mayte Martínez ESP, Monika Pyrek POL, Iveta Radevica LAT, Naoko Sakamoto JPN, Kelly Sotherton GBR. Marion Wagner GER, Kim Wall GBR, Mara Yamauchi GBR

Jessica Ennis wins the Olympic heptathlon in front of her home crowd.

Aries Merritt had the greatest ever season of sprint hurdling, following Olympic gold with the world record of 12.80 in Brussels.

The US women's sprint relay team smashed the 27-year-old world record in London.

Ashton Eaton, multi-event superstar, set world indoors at indoor heptathlon and outdoors at decathlon before winning Olympic gold.

Yelena Lashmanova won the women's 20km walk title in world record time.

Keshorn Walcott, just 19 years old, caused the biggest Olympic upset as he took the javelin title.

Final of Olympic 100m final – Usain Bolt retaining his title.

Yuliya Zaripova was unbeaten at the steeplechase and gave a brilliant front-running display in London.

Krisztián Pars was clearly the world's top hammer thrower of the year.

Kirani James added 2012 Olympic gold to 2011 World gold at 400m.

Mo Farah outsprinted the top East Africans in the 5000m to win his second Olympic gold medal.

NATIONAL CHAMPIONS 2012
and BIOGRAPHIES OF LEADING ATHLETES
By Peter Matthews

THIS SECTION incorporates biographical profiles of 809 of the world's top athletes, 420 men and 389 women, listed by nation. Also listed are national champions at standard events in 2012 for the leading countries prominent in athletics (for which I have such details).

The athletes profiled have, as usual, changed quite considerably from the previous year , not only that all entries have been updated, but also that many newcomers have been included to replace those who have retired or faded a little from the spotlight. The choice of who to include is always invidious, but I have concentrated on those who are currently in the world's top 10-15 per event, those who have the best championship records and some up-and-coming athletes who I consider may make notable impact during the coming year.

Since this section was introduced in the 1985 Annual, biographies have been given for a total of 4272 different athletes (2436 men and 1836women).

The ever continuing high turnover in our sport is reflected in the fact that there are many newcomers to this section (151 in all, 89 men, 62 women), as well as 16 athletes (3 men, 13 women) reinstated from previous Annuals. So, as even bigger change than usual. The athletes to have had the longest continuous stretch herein are Haile Gebrselassie 20 years, and Jesús Ángel García and Nicoleta Grasu 19 years. Athletes who have retired have generally been omitted.

No doubt some of those dropped from this compilation will also again make their presence felt; the keen reader can look up their credentials in previous Annuals, and, of course, basic details may be in the athletes' index at the end of this book.

Athletes included in these biographies are identified in the index at the end of this Annual by * for those profiled in this section and by ^ for those who were included in previous Annuals.

The biographical information includes:

a) Name, date and place of birth, height (in metres), weight (in kilograms).

b) Previous name(s) for married women; club or university; occupation.

c) Major championships record – all placings in such events as the Olympic Games, World Championships, European Championships, Commonwealth Games, World Cup and Continental Cup; leading placings in finals of the World Indoor Championships, European or World Junior Championships, European Under-23 Championships and other Continental Championships; and first three to six in European Indoors or World University Games. European Cup/Team Champs and IAAF Grand Prix first three at each event or overall. World Athletics Final (WAF) and Diamond League series (DL) winners

d) National (outdoor) titles won or successes in other major events.

e) Records set: world, continental and national; indoor world records/bests (WIR/WIB).

f) Progression of best marks over the years at each athlete's main event(s).

g) Personal best performances at other events.

h) Other comments.

See Introduction to this Annual for lists of abbreviations used for events and championships.

Information given is as known at 3 April 2013 (to include performances at the World Cross-Country and European Indoor Championships and some other early indoor and outdoor events of 2013).

I am most grateful to various ATFS members who have helped check these details. Additional information or corrections would be welcomed for next year's Annual.

Peter Matthews

ALGERIA

Governing body: Fédération Algerienne d'Athlétisme, BP n°61, Dely-Ibrahim 160410, Alger. Founded 1963.

National Champions 2012: Men: 100m/200m: Sofiane Bouhada 10.77/21.32, 400m/400mh: Mohamed Ahmed Gouniber 47.19/50.69, 800m: Khaled Benmehdi 1:47.30, 1500m: Antar Zerg–uelaine 3:37.67, 5000m: Lyès Belkier 14:00.20, 10,000m: Nassim Drifel 30:34.33, HMar: Ahmed Dali 68:33, 3000mSt: Rabia Makhloufi 8:38.97, 110mh: Lyès Mokdel 13.64, HJ: Ahcène Ali Lahmar 2.04, PV: Youssef Cheradi 5.00, LJ: Hamza Chouikh 7.40, TJ: Issam Nima 16.34, SP: Mohamed Benzaaza 14.84, DT: Abdelmoumen Bourekba 46.62, HT: Ferhat Samcha 54.32, JT: Lyès Bellouze 58.60, Dec: Mourad Souissi 7518, 20kW: Yacine Makhfi 1:38:36; **Women**. 100m: Nadia Remaoune 12.17, 200m: Kheïra Bourahla 24.33, 400m: Narimène Ammara 56.31, 800m: Amel Zighem 2:10.69, 1500m/3000mSt: Amina Bettiche 4:34.23/9:57.46, 5000m/10,000m: Barkahoum Drissi 16:39.30/34:46.87, 100mh: Romaissa Belabiod 14.38, 400mh: Dihia Hadar 61.26, HJ: Sara Madouni 1.58, PV: Sonia Halliche 3.40, LJ: Khadidja Ammour 5.83, TJ: Baya Rahouli 13.35, SP/HT: Zouina Bouzebra 13.01/60.45, DT: Dalila Makhloufi 39.40, JT: Ouarda Benamrane 41.32, Hep: Katia Amokrane 4276, 20kW: Asma Boulechbek 2:07:07.

Taoufik MAKHLOUFI b. 29 Apr 1988 Souk Ahras 1.76m 70kg.
At (800m)/1500m: OG: '12- 1; WCh: '09/11- sf; AfG: '11- 1/3; AfCh: '10- h, '12- (1).
Progress at 800m, 1500m: 2008- 3:43.4, 2009- 1:49.40, 3:34.34; 2010- 1:48.39, 3:32.94; 2011- 1:46.32, 3:34.4; 2012- 1:43.71, 3:30.80.

ARGENTINA

Governing body: Confederación Argentina de Atletismo, 21 de Noviembre No. 207. 3260 Concepción del Uruguay, Entre Ríos. Founded 1954 (original governing body founded 1919).

National Championships first held in 1920 (men), 1939 (women). **2012 Champions: Men**: 100m: Lucas Semino 10.82, 200m/400m: Fabio Martínez 21.92/47.49, 800m: Franco Díaz 1:52.45, 1500m: Federico Bruno 3:56.90, 5000m: Javier Carriqueo 14:23.90, 10,000m/3000mSt: Mariano Mastromarino 30:36.58/8:45.60, HMar: Luis Molina 66:58, Mar: Nicolás Ternavasio 2:19:09, 110mh: Agustín Carrera 14.45, 400mh: José Ignacio Pignataro 52.05, HJ: Carlos Layoy 2.03, PV: Germán Chiaraviglio 5.35, LJ/TJ: Maximil–iano Díaz 7.53/15.95, SP/DT: Germán Lauro 20.24/59.89, HT: Juan Cerra 70.71, JT: Braian Toledo 77.21, Dec: Fernando Korniejczuk 6889, 10,000W: Carlos Noguera 48:46.63. **Women**: 100m: Emily Maher 12.40, 200m: Macarena Solis 25.52, 400m: María Ayelén Diogo 57.60,

800m/1500m: Evangelina Lujan Thomas 2:10.08/4:26.30, 5000m/10,000m: Nadia Rodríguez 16:21.90/33:50.17, HMar: Sandra Amarillo 76:34, Mar: María Gabriela Almada 2:53:29, 3000mSt: Florencia Borelli 10:51.09, 100mh: Noelina Madarieta 15.45, 400mh: Belén Adaluz Casetta 63.16, HJ: Mariana Rojas 1.65, PV: Daniela Inchausti 4.10, LJ: Josefina Loyza 5.90, TJ: Melisa Romero 11.69, SP: Noelia Sersen 14.24, DT: Rocío Comba 57.37, HT: Jennifer Dahlgren 72.79, JT: Bárbara López 51.53, Hep: Jéssica Torres 4376, 10,000W: Daiana Luján 53:05.98.

Germán LAURO b. 2 Apr 1984 Trenque Lauquen, Buenos Aires 1.85m 127kg. Ferro Carril Oeste.
At SP/(DT): OG: '08- dnq 32, '12- 6/dnq 37; WCh: '07/11- dnq 24/11; WI: '12- 6; PAm: '07- 5/4, '11- 3; SACh: '05-06-07-09-11: 4/1/1&1/1&1/1&1. Won IbAM SP & DT 2012; ARG SP 2005-12, DT 2007-12.
Ten Argentinian shot records 2006-12., two S.American indoor records 2012.
Progress at SP: 2001- 15.24, 2002- 15.14, 2003- 16.87, 2004- 17.79, 2005- 18.17, 2006- 19.78, 2007- 19.67, 2008- 19.88, 2009- 19.20, 2010- 20.43, 2011- 20.42, 2012- 20.84, 2013- 20.59. pb DT 63.55 '12.

Women

Jennifer DAHLGREN b. 21 Apr 1984 Buenos Aires 1.80m 115kg. Studied English teaching at the University of Georgia
At HT: OG: '04-08-12: dnq 22/29/nt; WCh: '05-07-09: dnq nm/24/17, '11- 10; WJ: '00- dnq 23, 02- 5; WY: '01- 4; PAm: '07- 3, '11- 6; SACh: '05-06-09-11: 1/1/3/1; CCp: '10- 5; Won SAm-J 2000, PAm-J 2003, NCAA 2006-07, IbAm 2010, ARG 2008-09, 2011-12.
14 South American hammer records 2004-10.
Progress at HT: 1999- 46.36, 2000- 56.68, 2001- 57.18, 2002- 59.48, 2003- 61.60, 2004- 66.12, 2005- 67.07, 2006- 72.01, 2007- 72.94, 2008- 66.38, 2009- 72.79, 2010- 73.74, 2011- 73.44, 2012- 72.79. pbs: SP 15.54i '04, 15.03 '03; DT 44.28 '03, Wt 24.04i '06 (S.Am rec).
Her mother Irene Fitzner competed at 100m at the 1972 Olympics and was 2nd in the South American 100m in 1971.

AUSTRALIA

Governing body: Athletics Australia, Suite 22, Fawkner Towers, 431 St.Kilda Rd, Melbourne, Victoria 3004. Founded 1897.

National Championships first held in 1893 (men) (Australasian until 1927), 1930 (women). **2012 Champions: Men**: 100m: Joshua Ross 10.23, 200m: Matt Davies 21.36 (Joseph Millar NZL 21.27), 400m: Steven Solomon 45.54, 800m: Johnny Rayner 1:48.10, 1500m: Jeff Riseley 3:47.78, 5000m: Harry Summers 14:03.84, 10,000m: Ben St Lawrence 28:35.92, HMar/Mar: Scott Westcott 64:47/2:15:59, 3000mSt: Peter

Nowill 8:44.47, 110mh: Mitch Tysoe 14.04 (Siddhanth Thingalaya IND 13.66), 400mh: Tristan Thomas 51.37, HJ: Nick Moroney 2.15, PV: Joel Pocklington 5.15, LJ: Scott Crowe 7.69 (Frédéric Erin FRA 7.70), TJ: Alwyn Jones 16.32, SP: Damien Birkenhead 18.14 (Emanuele Fuamatu SAM 18.62), DT: Benn Harradine 63.58, HT: Timothy Driesen 70.55, JT: Joshua Robinson 78.31, Dec: Jarrod Sims 7456 (Brent Newdick NZL 8057), 5000mW/20kW: Jared Tallent 19:08.83/1:23:01; 20kW: Dane Bird-Smith 1:23:28; 50kW: Luke Adams 3:57:24. **Women**: 100m/200m/Melissa Breen 11.41/23.30, 400m: Caitlin Sargent 53.21 (Joanna Cuddihy IRL 51.69), 800m: Tamsyn Manou 2:02.00, 1500m/5000m: Kaila McKnight 4:18.02/16:24.56, 10,000m: Lara Tamsett 33:03.84, HMar: Sinead Diver 76:00, Mar: Lauren Shelley 2:36:29, 3000mSt: Milly Clark 10:05.60, 100mh: Shannon McCann 13.48, 400mh: Jess Gulli 57.96, HJ: Ashleigh Reid 1.80 (Miyuki Fukumoto JPN 1.86), PV: Vicky Parnov 4.20, LJ: Kerrie Perkins 6.70w, TJ: Ellen Pettitt 13.66w, SP/DT: Dani Samuels 16.65/62.34, HT: Gabrielle Neighbour 66.20, JT: Kimberley Mickle 61.70, Hep: Megan Wheatley 5832, 5000mW/20kW: Claire Tallent 22:12.64/1:32:58/1:31:12.

Jarrod BANNISTER b. 3 Oct 1984 Townsville 1.90m 100kg. Athletics Essendon.
At JT: OG: '08- 6, '12- dnq 27; WCh: '07- dnq 22, '11- 7; CG: '06- 6, '10- 1; WJ: '02- 4; CCp: '10- 4. AUS champion 2007-08, 2010-11.
Australian javelin record 2008.
Progress at JT: 2002- 73.31, 2003- 68.34, 2005- 73.20, 2006- 78.06, 2007- 83.70, 2008- 89.02, 2010- 83.17, 2011- 82.25, 2012- 83.70.

Henry FRAYNE b. 14 Apr 1990 Adelaide 1.87m 72kg. Old Melbournians. Student.
At LJ/TJ: OG: '12- 9/dnq 17; WI: '11- 2. At TJ: WCh: '11- 9; WJ: '08- 5, Won AUS TJ 2010.
Oceania indoor long jump record 2012.
Progress at LJ, TJ: 2006- 7.01, 2007- 7.05, 15.55; 2008- 7.39, 16.58; 2009- 7.99, 16.62; 2010- 7.50w, 16.63; 2011- 7.98, 17.04; 2012- 8.27, 17.23/17.34w.
Cousin of 400m international Bruce Frayne (2nd 4x400m CG 1986).

Benn HARRADINE b. 14 Oct 1982 Newcastle, NSW 1.98m 115kg. Ringwood. Personal trainer.
At DT: OG: '08- dnq 31, '12- 9; WCh: '09- dnq 15, '11- 5; CG: '06- 8, '10- 1; CCp: '10- 2. AUS champion 2007-08, 2010-11.
Four Oceania discus records 2008-12.
Progress at DT: 2000- 51.50, 2001- 54.76, 2002- 57.78, 2003- 55.25, 2004- 57.68, 2005- 63.65, 2006- 60.70, 2007- 62.99, 2008- 66.37, 2009- 64.97, 2010- 66.45, 2011- 66.07, 2012- 67.53. pb SP 15.17 '05.

Steve HOOKER b. 16 Jul 1982 Melbourne 1.87m 85kg. Perth.
At PV: OG: '04- dnq 28=, '08- 1, '12- nh; WCh: '05-07-09-11: dnq 17=/9/1/dnq nh; CG: '06- 1,

'10- 1; WJ: '00- 4; WI: '08- 3, '10- 1; WCp: '06- 1, '10- 1. AUS champion 2008, 2010.
Three Oceania indoor records 2007-09, two Commonwealth indoor records 2009.
Progress at PV: 1999- 5.00, 2000- 5.20, 2001- 5.30, 2002- 5.25, 2003- 5.45, 2004- 5.65, 2005- 5.87, 2006- 5.96, 2007- 5.91, 2008- 6.00, 2009- 6.06i/5.95, 2010- 6.01i/5.95, 2011- 5.60, 2012- 5.72. pbs: 100m 10.82 '10, 10.6, 10.68w '05; 200m 21.1 '05, LJ 7.10 '05.
Suffering from an adductor injury, he took just one jump to qualify for the World final in 2009, amd then was able to take just two jumps in the final, but he cleared 5.90 for the gold. Played Australian Rules football before taking up pole vaulting. His father Bill was 6th CG 800m 1974, had pbs: 800m 1:45.36 '73, 400mh pb 50.6 '69, and his mother Erica (née Nixon) was 6th LJ, 4th Pen 1974 and 2nd LJ 1978 (in pb 6.58) at CG. Married Russian runner Yekaterina Kostetskaya in 2012.

Steve SOLOMON b. 16 May 1993 St. Leonards, New South Wales 1.86m 73kg. Randwick Botany H. Medical student at Stanford University, USA.
At 400m: OG: '12- 8; WJ: '12- 3=; AUS champion 2011-12.
Progress at 400m: 2009- 48.39, 2010- 46.44, 2011- 45.58, 2012- 44.97. pb 200m 21.25 '11.

Jared TALLENT b. 17 Oct 1984 Ballarat 1.78m 60kg. Ballarat YCW. Graduate of University of Canberra.
At 20kW(/50kW): OG: '08- 3/2, '12- 7/2; WCh: '05- 18, '07- dq, '09- 6/7, '11- 26/3; CG: '06- 3, '10- 1; WCp: '06-08-10-12: 14/10/(3)/(3). At 10,000mW: WJ: '02- 19; WY: '01- 7. Won AUS 5000mW 2012, 20kW 2008-11, 30kW 2004, 50kW 2007, 2009, 2011.
Commonwealth 5000m walk record 2009.
Progress at 20kW, 50kW: 2002- 1:40:21, 2003- 1:31:24, 2004- 1:27:02, 2005- 1:22:53, 2006- 1:21:36, 3:55:08; 2007- 1:21:25, 3:44:45, 2008- 1:19:41, 3:39:27; 2009- 1:19:42, 3:38:56; 2010- 1:19:15, 3:54:55; 2011- 1:19:57, 3:43:36; 2012- 1:20:02, 3:36:53. pbs: 3000mW 11:15.07 '09, 5000mW 18:41.83 '09, 10,000mW 40:41.5 '06, 10kW 38:29 '10, 30kW 2:11:36 '09, 35kW; 2:33:07 '09.
Won IAAF Walks Challenge 2008. Married Claire Woods on 30 Aug 2008, she has 20kW pb 1:28:53 '12, 2 CG '10.

Mitchell WATT b. 25 Mar 1988 Bendigo, Victoria 1.84m 83kg. QE2 Track Club. Studying law and commerce at University of Queensland.
At LJ: OG: '12- 2; WCh: '09- 3, '11- 2; WI: '10- 3. Won AUS 2011, DL 2011.
Oceania long jump record 2011.
Progress at LJ: 2001- 6.32, 2002- 6.98, 2008- 7.97, 2009- 8.43, 2010- 8.16, 2011- 8.54, 2012- 8.28. pb 100m 10.31 '11.
After playing Australian Rules football and rugby, he returned to athletics in 2008 and made rapid advance.

Women

Kimberley MICKLE b. 28 Dec 1984 Perth 1.69m 69kg. Deakin.
At JT: OG: '12- dnq 17; WCh: '09- dnq 15, '11- 6; CG: '06- 4, '10- 2; WJ: '02- 9; WY: '01- 1; WCp: '06- 5, '10- 3. AUS champion 2005-07, 2009-12.
Progress at JT: 1999- 45.13, 2000- 45.76, 2001- 51.83, 2002- 52.77, 2003- 48.03, 2004- 50.38, 2005- 58.16, 2006- 58.56, 2007- 59.36, 2008- 57.64, 2009- 63.49, 2010- 61.36, 2011- 63.82, 2012- 64.12.

Sally PEARSON b. 19 Sep 1986 Sydney 1.66m 60kg. née McLellan. Gold Coast Victory. Griffith University.
At (100m)/100mh: OG: '08- 2, '12- 1; WCh: '03- hR, '07- sf/sf, '09- 5, '11- 1; CG: '06- fell/dq/3R, '10- dq/1; WJ: '04- 3/4; WY: '03- 1; WCp: '06- 8/4, '10- 1. At 60mh: WI: '12- 1. AUS champion 100m & 100mh 2005-7, 2009, 2011; 200m 2011.
Records: Oceania 100mh (8) 2007-11, 60m 2009 & 60mh indoors (3) 2009-12; Commonwealth 100mh (2) 2011.
Progress at 100mh: 2003- 14.01, 2004- 13.30, 2005- 13.01, 2006- 12.95, 2007- 12.71, 2008- 12.53, 2009- 12.50, 2010- 12.57, 2011- 12.28, 2012- 12.35.
pbs: 60m 7.16 '11, 100m 11.14 '07, 150m 16.86 '10, 200m 23.02/22.66w '09, 300m 38.34 '09, 400m 53.86mx '11, 200mh 27.54 '06, 60mh 7.73i '12, 200mh 26.96 '09, 400mh 62.98 '07.
Married Kieran Pearson on 3 April 2010. IAAF female Athlete of the Year 2011.

Dani SAMUELS b. 26 May 1988 Fairfield, NSW 1.82m 82kg. Westfields, University of Western Sydney.
At DT/(SP): OG: '08- 9, '12- 12; WCh: '07- dnq 13, '09- 1, '11- 10; CG: '06- 3/12; WJ: '06- 1/7; WY: '05- 1/3; WCp: '06- 6; WUG: '07- 2, '09- 1; CCp: '10- 4. AUS champion SP 2006-07, 2009, 2012; DT 2005-11.
Progress at DT: 2001- 39.17, 2002- 45.52, 2003- 47.29, 2004- 52.21, 2005- 58.52, 2006- 60.63, 2007- 60.47, 2008- 62.95, 2009- 65.44, 2010- 65.84, 2011- 62.33, 2012- 63.97, 2013- 64.46. pbs: SP 16.82 '13, HT 45.39 '05.
Sisters Jamie and Casey played basketball for Australia.

AUSTRIA

Governing body: Österreichischer Leichtathletik Verband, 1040 Vienna, Prinz Eugenstrasse 12. Founded 1902.
National Championships first held in 1911 (men), 1918 (women). 2012 **Champions: Men**: Benjamin Grill 10.88, 200m/400m: Christian Smetana 22.05/47.87, 800m: Raphael Pallitsch 1:50.16, 1500m/10,000m: Andreas Vojta 3:42.22/30:47.40, 5000m: Brenton Rowe 14:38.73, HMar/3000mSt: Valentin Pfeil 66:51/9:11.54, Mar: Karl Aumayr 2:23:25, 110mh: Manuel Prazek 14.44, 400mh: Samuel Ajayi 54.47, HJ: Josep Kopic 2.01, PV: Paul Kilbertus 4.80, LJ: Manuel Leitner 7.49, TJ: Roman Schmied 15.39,

SP: Lukas Weiss-haidinger 18.47, DT: Gerhard Mayer 60.08, HT: Benjamin Siart 63.52, JT: Matthias Kaserer 68.62, Dec: Dominik Siedlaczek 6744, 20kW: Christian Siegele 1:40:47, 50kW: Dietmar Hirschmugl 5:29:10. **Women**: 100m: Petra Urbankova 11.85, 200m: Doris Röser 24.07, 400m: Ines Futterknecht 55.00, 800m/1500m: Pamela Märzendorfer 2:09.66/ 4:25.62, 5000m: Anita Baierl 16:45.20, 10,000m: Eva Hieblinger-Schütz 35:49.12, HMar: Bernadette Schuster 1:21:32, Mar: Karin Freitag 2:47:14, 3000mSt: Stefanie Huber 10:58.10, 100mh: Beate Schrott 13.05, 400mh: Verena Menapace 58.99, HJ: Monika Gollner 1.86, PV: Kira Grünberg 3.80, LJ/TJ: Michaela Egger 5.98/12.47, SP/DT: Veronika Watzek 14.12/53.73, HT: Julia Siart 56.49, JT: Elisabeth Pauer 51.84, Hep: Ivona Dadic 5552, 20kW: Kathrin Schulze 1:56:28.

Beate SCHROTT b. 15 Apr 1988 St. Pölten 1.77m 68kg. Union St. Pölten. Student.
At 100mh: OG: '12- 8; WCh: '11- sf; EC: '12- 4; EU23: '09- sf; EJ: '07- h, At LJ: WJ: '06- dnq 23. Won Austrian 100mh 2009-12.
Four Austrian 100mh records 2011-12.
Progress at 100mh: 2004- 15.55, 2005- 14.79, 2006- 14.34, 2007- 13.90, 2008- 13.72, 2009- 13.29, 2010- 13.55, 2011- 12.95, 2012- 12.82. pbs: 60m 7.61i '11, 200m 25.59 '07, 300m 38.34 '09, 60mh 8.02i '12, LJ 6.10 '06.

AZERBAIJAN

Hayle IBRAHIMOV b. 18 Jan 1990 Mek'ele, Tigray, Ethiopia 1.68m 58kg. Baku.
At 5000m: OG: '12- 9; EC: '10- 3, '12- 6; EJ: '09- 1 (1 10,000m). At 3000m: EI: '11- 2, '13- 1. Eur U23 CC: '12- 8.
AZE records: 3000m 2012, 5000m (4) 2010-12.
Progress at 5000m: 2009- 13:53.60, 2010- 13:32.98, 2011- 13:34.54, 2012- 13:11.54. pbs: 1500m 3:44.76 '10, 3000m 7:39.59 '11, 7:45.92 '12; 10,000m 30:03.57 '11. Was Haile Desta Hagos of Ethiopia.

BAHAMAS

Governing body: Bahamas Association of Athletics Associations, P.O.Box SS 5517, Nassau. Founded 1952.
National Champions 2012: Men: 100m: Derrick Atkins 10.38, 200m: Trevorvany Mackey 20.68 20.66, 400m: Demetrius Pinder 44.77, 800m: Wesley Neymour 1:52.36, 1500m/5000m: O'Neil Williams 3:55.96/15:07.06, 110mh: Shamar Sands 13.62, 400mh: Nathan Arnett 51.33, HJ: Trevor Barry 2.29, LJ: Raymond Higgs 7.86, TJ: Leevan Sands 17.04, SP/DT: Leslie Whyte 13.78/48.04, HT: Delros Inniss 42.92, JT: Tre Adderley 56.29. **Women**: 100m: Chandra Sturrup 11.53, 200m: Carmiesha Cox 23.43, 400m: Rashan Brown 52.41, 800m: Te'shon Adderley 2:06.96, 1500m/3000m: Hughnique Rolle 4:54.55/10:54.37, 100mh: Ivanique Kemp 13.48, 400mh: Pedrya Seymour 60.18, HJ: Saniel

Atkinson 1.79, LJ: Bianca Stuart 6.46, TJ: Keythra Richards 11.82, SP: Racquel Williams 14.17, DT: Juliana Duncanson 38.74, JT: Laverne Eve 49.05.

Trevor BARRY b. 14 Jun 1983 Nassau 1.90m 77kg. NoDak.
At HJ: OG: '12- dnq 16=; WCh: '09- dnq 17, '11- 3; CG: '10- 2; PAm: '07- 7; WI: '12- 8. Won CAC 2011, BAH 2004-06, 2009, 2012.
Progress at HJ: 2002- 2.14, 2004- 2.13, 2005- 2.20, 2006- 2.19, 2007- 2.26, 2008- 2.25A, 2009- 2.28, 2010- 2.29, 2011- 2.32, 2012- 2.31. pb LJ 7.78/7.82w '06.

Christopher BROWN b. 15 Oct 1978 Nassau 1.78m 68kg. Was at Norfolk State University.
At 400m/4x400mR: OG: '00- qf/3R, '04- sf, '08- 4/2R, '12- 4/1R; WCh: '01-03-05-07-09-11: h&1R/ sf&3R/4&2R/4&2R/5/sf; CG: '02- 7/3R, '06- 4; PAm: '07- 1/1R; PAm-J: '97- 2R; CAG: '98- 3R, '99- 1R, '03- 2/1R; WI: '06-08-10-12: 3/3/1/3; BAH champion 2002, 2004, 2007-09. At 800m: CG: '98- h.
Bahamas records 400m 2007 & 2008, 800m 1998. CAC & Commonwealth 4x400m record 2012.
Progress at 400m: 1997- 47.46, 1998- 46.44, 1999- 45.96, 2000- 45.08, 2001- 45.45, 2002- 45.11, 2003- 44.94A/45.16, 2004- 45.09, 2005- 44.48, 2006- 44.80, 2007- 44.45, 2008- 44.40, 2009- 44.81, 2010- 45.05, 2011- 44.79, 2012- 44.67. pbs: 200m 21.05 '03, 20.56w '06; 300m 32.4+ '12, 800m 1:49.54 '98.
Fourth at four global championships outdoors. Had fastest split (43.42 anchor leg) in 2005 World 4x400m.

Demetrius PINDER b. 13 Feb 1989 Grand Bahama 1.78m 70kg. Studied theatre at Texas A&M University, USA.
At 400m: OG: '12- 7/1R; WCh: '11- sf; WI: '12- 2; BAH champion 2010-12.
CAC & Commonwealth 4x400m record 2012.
Progress at 400m: 2006- 49.03, 2007- 47.48, 2008- 47.34, 2009- 48.21i, 2010- 44.93, 2011- 44.78, 2012- 44.77. pbs: 200m 20.23 '12, 300m 32.3+ '12.

Leevan SANDS b. 16 Aug 1981 Nassau 1.90m 75kg. Was at Auburn University, USA.
At TJ (LJ): OG: '04- dnq 27, '08- 3, '12- 5; WCh: '03- 3, '05- 4 (dnq), '07- dnq 21, '09- 4, '11- 7; CG: '02- 3; WJ: '98- dnq, '00- 5 (dnq 19); PAm: '99- 6, '07- 6; PAm-J: '99- 2 (1); GAG: '10- 1; won CAC LJ 2005, TJ 2003, 2008; CAm-J 1998, 2000; NCAA LJ 2003 & TJ 2004, BAH LJ 2003, TJ 2008-12.
Bahamas triple jump records 2002 & 2008.
Progress at TJ: 1998- 15.70, 1999- 16.00/16.02w, 2000- 16.22, 2001- 16.39, 2002- 17.50, 2003- 17.40, 2004- 17.41, 2005- 17.30/17.39w, 2006- 16.99i/17.10idq, 2007- 17.23/17.55w, 2008- 17.59, 2009- 17.32, 2010- 17.21, 2011- 17.21/17.39w, 2012- 17.23. pbs: 200m 21.84 '09, LJ 8.13 '05, 8.28w '03.
6-month suspension after testing positive for a banned stimulant, methamphetamine, in Feb 2006. His cousin **Shamar** Sands (b. 30 Apr 1985) holds BAH records for 110mh 13.38 '09 (&

13.32Aw '08) (sf WCh '09, 3 WJ '02, 1 CAC '08) and 60mh 7.49i '09.

Donald THOMAS b. 1 Jul 1984 Freeport 1.90m 75kg. Lindenwood University, USA.
At HJ: OG: '08/12- dnq 21=/30=; WCh: '07- 1, '09- dnq 15, '11- 11; CG: '06- 4, '10- 1; PAm: '07- 2; CAG: '06- 4=, '10- 1; CCp: '10- 2. Won WAF & NCAA indoors 2007, BAH 2007, 2010-11.
Progress at HJ: 2006- 2.24, 2007- 2.35, 2008- 2.28i/2.26, 2009- 2.30, 2010- 2.32, 2011- 2.32, 2012- 2.27.
A basketball player, he made a sensational start by clearing 2.22 indoors in January 2006 with no high jump training since he had jumped at school five years earlier. 19 months later he was world champion.

Women

Anthonique STRACHAN b. 22 Aug 1993 Nassau 1.68m 57kg. Going to Auburn University, USA.
At (100m)/200m: OG: '12- sf; WJ: '10- sf, '12- 1/1. Two CAC junior 200m records 2011-12.
Progress at 200m: 2009- 23.95, 2010- 23.66, 2011- 22.70, 2012- 22.53. Pbs: 100m 11.20 '12, 400m 54.48 '10. IAAF Female Rising Star Award 2012.

BAHRAIN

Governing body: Bahrain Athletics Association, PO Box 29269, Isa Twon-Manama. Founded 1974.

Belal Ali MANSOUR b. John Yego (KEN) 17 Oct 1983 or 17 Oct 1988 (accepted by IAAF) Kenya 1.70m 61kg.
At (800m)/1500m: OG: '08- sf/7, '12- 10; WCh: '05- 7/h, '07- h/11, '09- sf/9; WJ: '06- 7/3; WY: '05- 1; AsiG: '06- 2, '10- 7/3; AsiC: '11- 5; CCp: '10- (3). World CC: '05- 9J. Won Arab 800m 2009, W.Asian 800m & 1500m 2010.
Asian 1000m record 2007. World youth bests for 800m and 1500m (with 1988 birthdate).
Progress at 800m, 1500m: 2004- 1:46.8A, 2005- 1:44.34, 3:33.86; 2006- 1:45.27, 3:34.30; 2007- 1:44.02, 3:31.49; 2008- 1:45.95, 3:33.11; 2009- 1:45.26, 3:32.10; 2010- 1:44.80, 3:34.98; 2011- 1:47.22, 3:38.61; 2012- 1:45.78, 3:35.40. pbs: 1000m 2:15.23 '07, 1M 3:52.35 '07.

Women

Mimi BELETE b. 9 Jun 1988 Ethiopia 1.64m 62kg.
At 1500m/(5000m): OG: '12- sf; WCh: '09- sf, '11- 7; AsiG: '10- 3/1; AsiC: '09- 6; CCp: '10- 4; won W.Asian 2010.
Progress at 1500m: 2007- 4:13.55, 2008- 4:06.84, 2009- 4:04.36, 2010- 4:00.25, 2011- 4:03.13, 2012- 4:01.72. pbs: 800m 2:04.63 '10, 3000m 8:32.18 '10, 5000m 15:15.59 '10.
From Ethiopia, has lived in Belgium from 2005; BRN from 2009. Younger sister Almensch Belete BEL pbs 1500m 4:06.87 '10, 5000m 15:03.63 '11; 5 EI 3000m 2013.

Shitaye ESHETE Habtegebrei b. 21 May 1990 Ethiopia 1.59m 46kg.
At (5000m/)10,000m: OG: '12- 10/6; WCh: '11- 6; AsiG: '10- 3; AsiC: '11- 1; AfC: '09- (6); CCp: '10- (6). At 3000m: WI: '12- 5. World CC: '10-11-13: 11/12/4. Won Arab CC 2010, 2013; Asian CC 2012, Asian indoor 3000m 2012.
Three BRN 10,000m records 2010-12.
Progress at 10,000m: 2010- 31:53.27, 2011- 31:21.57, 2012- 30:47.25. pbs: 3000m 8:49.27i '12, 5000m 15:05.48 '12.

Maryam Yusuf **JAMAL** b. 16 Sep 1984 Alkesa, Arsi Province, Ethiopia 1.55m 44kg. Stade Lausanne, Switzerland.
At (800m)/1500m: OG: '08- 5, '12- 3; WCh: '05-07-09-11: 5/1/1/12; WI: '06- 3, '08- 2; AsiG: '06- 1/1, '10- 6/1; WCp: '06- 1. World CC: '09- 9, '11- 23; Won WAF 2005-08, Swiss CC 2003, P.Arab 800m, 1500m & 5000m 2005, Arab 4k CC 2006, Asian CC 2007, 2009.
Records: Two Asian 1M 2007, 2000m 2009, Bahrain 800m (3), 1500m (3), 2000m, 3000m (3), 5000m 2005-09. Asian indoor 1500m 2006 & 2008, 1M (4:24.71) 2010.
Progress at 800m, 1500m, 5000m: 2003- 4:18.12, 2004- 2:02.18, 4:07.78, 15:19.45mx; 2005- 1:59.69, 3:56.79, 14:51.68; 2006- 1:59.04, 3:56.18, 2007- 3:58.75, 15:20.28; 2008- 1:57.80, 3:59.79i/3:59.84; 2009- 1:59.98, 3:56.55; 2010- 1:59.89, 3:58.93; 2011- 4:00.33, 2012- 2:00.44, 4:01.19. pbs: 1M 4:17.75 '07, 2000m 5:31.88 '09, 3000m 8:28.87 '05, HMar 71:43 '04.
Has a record 16 sub-4 min 1500m times. Formerly Ethiopian Zenebech Kotu Tola, based in Switzerland, ran series of fast times after converting to Jamal of Bahrain in 2005. First Olympic medallist for Bahrain at any sport. Married to Mnashu Taye (now Tareq Yaqoob BRN).

BARBADOS

Governing body: Amateur Athletic Association of Barbados, P.O.Box 46, Bridgetown. Fd. 1947.
National Champions 2012: Men: 100m: Ramon Gitten 10.32, 200m/400m: Burkheart Ellis 20.96/46.61, 800m: Anthonio Mascoll 1:48.73, 1500m: Matthew Agard 4:09.38, 5000m: Jerome Blackett 16:23.19, 110mh: Ryan Brathwaite 13.39, 400mh: Kion Joseph 51.63, HJ: Henderson Dottin 2.15, LJ: Charles Greaves 7.09, TJ: Barry Batson 15.65, SP/DT: Michael Gibson 12.47/40.38, JT: Justin Cummins 69.14. **Women:** 100m/200m: Shakera Reece 11.49/23.58, 400m: Althea Maximillen 53.70, 800m: Sonia Gaskin 2:09.21, 100mh: Kierre Beckles 13.27, 400mh: Tia-Adana Belle 59.14, LJ: Akela Jones 6.35, TJ: Seidre Forde 12.01, SP: Samantha Alcide 10.51, DT: Leah Bannister 44.33, JT: Jenila Atherley 40.35.

Ryan BRATHWAITE b. 6 Aug 1988 Bridgetown 1.86m 75kg. Sociology graduate of the University of Mississippi.
At 110mh: OG: '08- sf, '12- 5; WCh: '07- sf, '09- 1, '11- h; WY: '05- 2; WJ: '06- h; PAm: '07- 4; CAG: '10- 1; PAm-J: '07- 3; won WAF 2009, CAC-J 2006, BAR 2008-09, 2011.
Seven Barbados 110mh records 2008-09
Progress at 110mh: 2005- 14.64, 2006- 14.14, 2007- 13.61, 2008- 13.38, 2009- 13.14/13.05w, 2010- 13.34/13.10w, 2011- 13.54, 2012- 13.23. pbs: 60m 7.02i '08, 55mh 7.18i '09, 60mh 7.61i '10.
First world medallist for Barbados in athletics. Younger brother Shane (b. 8 Feb 1990) has 110mh pb 13.31A/13.46 '12 and was world youth octathlon champion 2007.

BELARUS

Governing body: Belarus Athletic Federation, Kalinovskogo Street 111A, Minsk 220119. Founded 1991.
National Champions 2012: Men: 100m/200m: Aleksandr Linnik 10.68/21.27, 400m: Dmitriy Paluyan 47.75, 800m: Igor Davydov 1:47.36, 1500m: Aleksandr Borysyuk 3:40.38, 5000m: Sergey Chaberok 14:10.61, 10,000m: Maksim Pankratov 29:30.15, 3000mSt: Ilya Slavinskiy 8:51.09, 400mh: Nikita Yakovlev 50.35, HJ: Artyom Zaytsev 2.12, PV: Dmitriy Gashchuk 5.10, LJ: Vladimir Kobets 7.82, TJ: Dmitriy Platnitskiy 16.87w, SP: Pavel Lyzhin 20.26, DT: Dmitriy Sivakov 61.40, HT: Pavel Krivitskiy 77.81, JT: Vladimir Kozlov 82.86, Dec: Nikolay Shubenok 7900, 20kW: Ivan Trotskiy 1:28:55, 50kW: Andrey Stepanchuk 4:26:48.
Women: 100m: Yuliya Balykina 11.61, 200m/400m: Yelena Kievich 23.43/51.73, 800m: Tatyana Suprun 2:03.11, 1500m: Marina Arzamasova 4:20.28, 5000m/3000mSt: Irina Ananenko 16:43.45/ 10:03.54, 10,000m: Marina Domantsevich 34:03.23, 100mh: Kseniya Medvedeva 14.41, 400mh: Anastasiya Buldakova 57.81, HJ: Yana Maksimova 1.86, PV: Anastasiya Shvedova 4.50, LJ: Anastasiya Mirochik-Ivanova 7.22w, TJ: Tatyana Nogornaya 13.42w, SP: Nadezhda Ostapchuk 21.39, DT: Svetlana Serova 60.90, HT: Yelena Matoshko 73.76, JT: Tatyana Kholadovich 59.15, Hep: Yekaterina Netsvetayeva 5835, 20kW: Alina Matveyuk 1:46:58.

Pavel KRIVITSKIY b. 17 Apr 1984 Grodno 1.84m 115kg.
At HT: OG: '12- dnq 28; WCh: '09- 8, '11- 5; EC: '10- dnq 16, '12- 9; EU23: '05- 1; ET: '10- 1. Won BLR 2007, 2010-12.
Progress at HT: 2004- 72.05, 2005- 77.51, 2006- 78.62, 2007- 78.61, 2008- 80.02, 2009- 79.48, 2010- 80.44, 2011- 80.67, 2012- 80.25.

Pavel LYZHIN b. 24 Mar 1981 Voronok, Russia 1.89m 110kg. Mogilyov. Army.
At SP(/DT): OG: '04= dnq 17, '08- 5, '12- 8; WCh: '03-05-07-09-11: dnq 14/nt/20/6/dnq 16; EC: '02- dnq, '06- 10, '10- 7; WJ: '00- 4/7; EU23: '01- 8, '03- 1; EJ: '99- 4/2; WI: '10- 6; EI: '02- 6, '07- 2; WUG: '03- 2, '05- 5. BLR champion 2001, 2004, 2009, 2011-12.

Progress at SP: 1999- 17.98, 2000- 19.12, 2001- 20.12, 2002- 20.15, 2003- 20.86, 2004- 20.92, 2005- 20.38, 2006- 20.85, 2007- 20.82i/20.02, 2008- 20.98, 2009- 20.98, 2010- 21.21, 2011- 20.85, 2012- 20.69. pb DT 61.72 '07.

Andrey MIKHNEVICH b. 12 Jul 1976 Bobruysk 2.02m 140kg. Minsk.
At SP: OG: '00- 9, '04- 5, '08- 3, '12- dnq 17; WCh: '01-03-05-07-09-11: dq 10/1/6/3/7/3; EC: '98- dnq 17, '06- 2, '10- 1; WUG: '97- 6, '03- 1; WI: '99-04-06-08-10: 8/6/2/4/2; EI: '07- 5; CCp: '10- 3; ET: '11- 3. BLR champion 2000, 2005-08.
BLR shot records 2010 & 2011.
Progress at SP: 1992- 13.06, 1993- 15.02, 1994- 16.74, 1995- 17.36, 1996- 19.24, 1997- 19.57i/19.27, 1998- 20.07i/19.90, 1999- 20.52i/20.30, 2000- 20.48i/20.12, 2001- 20.92, 2003- 21.69, 2004- 21.23, 2005- 21.08, 2006- 21.60, 2007- 21.27, 2008- 22.00, 2009- 21.02, 2010- 22.09, 2011- 22.10, 2012- 20.90.
Two year drugs ban from positive test on 4 Aug 2001, when he lost 10th at the World Champs. Threw 21.66 four days after return from ban in August 2003, world title 2 weeks later. Married Natalya Khoroneko on 17 Mar 2007.

Yuriy SHAYUNOV b. 22 Oct 1987 Minsk 1.93m 105kg.
At HT: WCh: '09- dnq 26, '11- nt; EC: '10-12: dnq 20/17; WJ: '04- dnq 13, '06- 4; EU23: '07- 1, '09- 1; EJ: '05- 3; WUG: '09- 1. BLR champion 2009.
Progress at HT: 2007- 74.92, 2008- 77.32, 2009- 80.72, 2010- 78.73, 2011- 78.70, 2012- 79.00.

Valeriy SVYATOKHO b. 20 Jul 1981 Grodno 1.86m 112kg.
At HT: OG: '08- dnq 17, '12- 11; WCh: '11- dnq 23; EC: '10- 4, '12- 4; EU23: '03- 4; WUG: '05- 3.
Progress at HT: 1999- 60.73, 2001- 68.02, 2003- 72.42, 2004- 77.25, 2005- 76.31, 2006- 81.49, 2007- 76.13, 2008- 81.37, 2009- 74.86, 2010- 78.33, 2011- 78.02, 2012- 78.44.

Women

Oksana MENKOVA b. 28 Mar 1982 Krichev, Mogilev region 1.83m 91kg.
At HT: OG: '08- 1, '12- 7; WCh: '03/07/09- dnq 23/nt/13; EC: '02/06: dnq 27/23; EU23: 03- 2; EJ: '01- 5; WUG: '05- 5; ECp: '07- 2, '08- 1.
Five Belarus hammer records 2006-12.
Progress at HT: 1999- 47.87, 2000- 56.50, 2001- 59.24, 2002- 66.42, 2003- 67.58, 2004- 70.23, 2005- 70.15, 2006- 76.86, 2007- 73.94, 2008- 77.32, 2009- 76.32, 2010- 67.27, 2011- 67.78, 2012- 78.69.
Had a terrible record at major events and only 11th in qualifying, but took gold with Olympic record 76.34 in 2008. Gave birth to daughter on 25 Sep 2010.

Natalya MIKHNEVICH b. 25 May 1982 Nevinnomysk, Russia 1.80m 85kg. née Khoroneko.
At SP: OG: '04- 5, '08- 2, '12- 11; WCh: '05- 8, '09- 4, '11- 11; EC: '06- 1, '10- 2; WJ: '00- 3; WY: '99- 2; EJ: '01- 1; EU23: '03- 1; WI: '04-06-10: dnq 9/1/3;

WUG: '05- 1; WCp: '06- 4. Won WAF 2006, BLR 2001, 2004-06, 2011.
Progress at SP: 1999- 16.12, 2000- 16.58, 2001- 17.25, 2002- 17.20, 2003- 18.05, 2004- 20.04, 2005- 19.78, 2006- 20.17, 2008- 20.70, 2009- 20.03, 2010- 20.42i/19.80, 2011- 19.05, 2012- 19.77.
Married Andrey Mikhnevich on 17 Mar 2007, their son Ilya was born on 11 Aug 2007.

Anastasiya MIRONCHIK-IVANOVA b. 13 Apr 1989 Slutsk 1.71m 54kg. Minsk.
At LJ: OG: '12- 7; WCh: '09- 11, '11- 4; EC: '10- 6; WJ: '08- 2; WY: '05- 8; EU23: '09- 2, '11- 6; WI: '12- 5; EI: '11- 6. BLR champion 2007, 2010-12.
Progress at LJ: 2004- 5.90, 2005- 6.10/6.13w, 2007- 6.03i/5.89, 2008- 6.71, 2009- 6.65/6.76w, 2010- 6.84, 2011- 6.85/6.92w, 2012- 7.08/7.22w. pb TJ 14.29 '11.

Alina TALAY b. 14 May 1989 Orsha, Vitebsk 1.64m 54kg.
At 100mh: OG: '12- sf; EC: '10- h, '12- 2; WJ: '08- 4; EU23: '09- 3, '11- 1; won W.MilG 2011, BLR 2009-10. At 60mh: WI: '12- 3; EI: '11-5, '13- 2..
Progress at 100mh: 2007- 14.38/14.01w, 2008- 13/31, 2009- 13.07, 2010- 12.87, 2011- 12.91, 2012- 12.71. pbs: 60m 7.35i '13, 100m 11.48 '11, 200m 23.59 '11, 50mh 6.89i '11, 60mh 7.94i '13.

BELGIUM

Governing bodies: Ligue Royale Belge d'Athlétisme, Stade Roi Baudouin, avenue du Marathon 199B, 1020 Bruxelles (KBAB/LRBA). Vlaamse Atletiekliga (VAL); Ligue Belge Francophone d'Athlétisme (LBFA). Original governing body founded 1889.
National Championships first held in 1889 (women 1921). **2012 Champions: Men**: 100m: Julien Watrin 10.47, 200m: Jonathan Borlée 20.32, 400m: Kevin Borlée 44.63, 800m: Pierre Antoine Balhan 1:51.43, 1500m: Kristof van Malderen 3:45.67, 5000m: Mats Lunders 13:58.02, 10,000m: Michael Brandenbourg 29:26.22, HMar: Bourzak Lahcen 67:24, Mar: Bart Verschoren 2:30:11, 3000mSt: Krijn Van Koolwyk 8:48.90, 110mh: Adrien Deghelt 13.64, 400mh: Michaël Bultheel 49.60, HJ: Bram Ghuys 2.07, PV: Sébastien Hoffelt 5.10, LJ: Nicolas Stempnick 7.65, TJ: Leopold Kapeta 15.45, SP: Richard Reveyn 16.76; DT: Philip Milanov 55.44, HT: Nicolas Pierre 64.20, JT: Tom Goyvaerts 74.05, Dec: Niels Pittomvils 7597.
Women: 100m/100mh: Anne Zagré 11.42/12.92, 200m: Hanne Claes 23.33, 400m: Sofie Daelemans 55.26, 800m: Mariska Parewyck 2:10.50, 1500m: Veerle Dejaeghere 4:21.42, 5000m: Veerle Van Linden 16:16.36, 10,000m: Ferahiwat Gamachu 35:25.60, HMar/Mar: Els Rens 78:13/2:45:32; 3000mSt: Anne Sophie Marechal 10:27.89, 400mh: Axelle Dauwens 57.22, HJ: Hannelore Desmet 1.86, PV: Chloe Henry 4.20, LJ: Jesse Vercruysse 5,99, LJ: Linda Onana 13.14, SP: Catherine Timmermans 15.23,

DT: Veerle Blondeel 49.06, HT: Jolien Boumkwo 58.67, JT: Melissa Dupre 54.06, Hep: Nafissatou Thiam 5916.

Jonathan BORLÉE b. 22 Feb 1988 Woluwe-Saint Lambert 1.80m 70kg. Was at Florida State University.
At 400m: OG: '08- sf/5R, '12- 6; WCh: '11- 5; EC: '10- 7/3R; WJ: '06- 4; WY: '05- 5; EJ: '07- h; WI: '10- 2R; EI: '11- 3R. Won NCAA 2009, BEL 2006, 2011. At 200m: EC: '12- 4.
Four Belgian 400m records 2009-12, 300m 2012.
Progress at 400m: 2005- 47.50, 2006- 46.06, 2007- 47.85, 2008- 45.11, 2009- 44.78, 2010- 44.71, 2011- 44.78, 2012- 44.43. pbs: 60m 6.81i '07, 100m 10.78 '07, 200m 20.31 '12, 300m 31.87 '12, 600m 1:18.60i '11.
Twin brother of Kevin Borlée, their sister Olivia (b. 10 Apr 1986) has pbs 100m 11.39 '07, 200m 22.98 '06, 3 WCh '07, 2 OG '08 at 4x100mR. Younger brother Dylan 6 4x400m EJ 2011 Their father Jacques was an international 400m runner (45.4 '79), mother Edith Demartelaere had pbs 200m 23.89 and 400m 54.09 in 1984.

Kevin BORLÉE b. 22 Feb 1988 Woluwe-Saint Lambert 1.80m 71kg. WS. Was at Florida State University.
At 400m: OG: '08- sf/5R, '12- 5; WCh: '09- sf/4R, '11- 3; EC: '10- 1/3R; WJ: '06- sf; EI: '11- 3R; CCp: '10- 4/2R. At 200m: WY: '05- sf. Won BEL 200m 2009, 2011; 400m 2007.
Belgian 400m records 2008 and 2012.
Progress at 400m: 2005- 47.86, 2006- 46.63, 2007- 46.38, 2008- 44.88, 2009- 45.28, 2010- 45.01, 2011- 44.74, 2012- 44.56. pbs: 60m 7.03i '07, 100m 10.62 '07, 200m 20.72 '11, 300m 32.72i '13, 32.76 '08; 600m 1:15.65i '11.

Hans VAN ALPHEN b. 12 Jan 1982 Turnhout 1.91m 91kg. ZWAT
At Dec: OG: '08- dnf, '12- 4; WCh: '07- 11; EC: '10- 5. Won BEL Dec 2005.
Three Belgian decathlon records 2007-12.
Progress at Dec: 2002- 6840, 2004- 7054, 2005- 7064, 2006- 7411, 2007- 8047, 2008- 7634, 2009- 8070, 2010- 8091, 2011- 8200, 2012- 8519. pbs: 60m 7.08i '08, 100m 10.96 '12, 400m 48.25 '07, 1000m 2:37.06i '11, 1500m 4:17.51 '09, 60mh 8.19i '06, 110mh 14.55 '12, HJ 2.06 '12, PV 4.96 '12, LJ 7.64 '12, SP 15.68 '10, DT 51.89 '12, JT 67.59 '12, Hep 5938i '11.
Improved by 319 points to win at Götzis 2012; Won at Talence 2011 and 2012. Won IAAF Combined Events Challenge 2012.

Women

Svetlana BOLSHAKOVA b. 14 Oct 1984 Leningrad, USSR 1.74m 59kg. SPVI.
At TJ: OG: '12- dnq 12; WCh: '09- dnq 20; EC: '10- 3, '12- 9; WY: '01- 2; EJ: '03- 3; EU23: '05- 2; WI: '10- 8.
Four Belgian triple jump records 2009-10.
Progress at TJ: 2000- 12.93, 2001- 13.48, 2002- 13.55, 2003- 13.64i/13.43, 2004- 13.75, 2005- 14.11,

2006- 14.17, 2007- 14.28i, 2009- 14.27/14.46w, 2010- 14.55, 2011- 14.31i/13.70, 2012- 14.28. pb LJ 6.43i '07, 6.29 '09.
Married Stijn Stroobants (HJ 2.26 '09) on 26 Aug 2006. Belgian citizen from 13 Jul 2008.

Tia HELLEBAUT b. 16 Feb 1978 Antwerpen 1.82m 66kg. Atletica '84. Chemistry graduate.
At HJ: OG: '04- 12, '08- 1, '12- 5; WCh: '05- 6, '07- 14; EC: '06- 1, '10- 5; WI: '06- 6, '12- 5; EI: '07- 1, '13- 8; WCp: '06- 2. At Hep: WCh: '01- 14, '03- dnf; EJ: '97- 11; EU23: '99- 7. At Pen: WI: '04- 5, '08- 1. Won BEL HJ 2000, 2002-03, 2005; LJ 2006-08, Hep 1999-2000, 2002.
Belgian records: HJ (10) 2004-08, Hep 2006, Indoor HJ (7) 2006-07, Indoor LJ 2006 & 2007, Pen 2004 & 2007.
Progress at HJ, Hep: 1992- 1.56, 1993- 1.70, 1994- 1.73, 4731; 1995- 1.76, 5167; 1996- 1.78, 5104; 1997- 1.75+, 5197; 1998- 1.81, 5381; 1999- 1.87i/1.82, 5629; 2000- 1.89, 5646; 2001- 1.89i/1.87, 5859; 2002- 1.85, 5584; 2003- 1.91, 6019; 2004- 1.95, 5954; 2005- 1.93, 2006- 2.03, 6201; 2007- 2.05i/1.98, 2008- 2.05, 2010- 1.97, 2012- 1.97, 2013- 1.97i. pbs: 200m 24.65 '06, 800m 2:14.75 '06, 50mh 7.34i '04, 60mh 8.34i '07, 100mh 13.91 '05, LJ 6.42i/6.41 '07, TJ 12.54i '01, SP 13.85i '08, 13.10 '99; JT 44.37 '01, Pen 4877i '07.
A supreme big-event competitor: Belgian records at 2.01 and 2.03 to win EC gold 2006 and at 2.03 and 2.05 to win Olympic gold (first ever by a Belgian woman) in 2008, with indoor records at 2.01, 2.03, 2.05 to win EI 2007. Partner Win Van de Ven was BEL 110mh champion in 1990; son Vince born in June 2009 and daughter Saartje in February 2011.

BOTSWANA

Governing body: Botswana Athletics Association, PO Box 2399, Gaborone. Founded 1972.

Nijel AMOS b. 15 Mar 1994 Marobela 1.79m 60kg.
At 800m: OG: '12- 2; WJ: '12- 1.
World junior 800m and two Botswana 800m records 2012.
Progress at 800m: 2011- 1:47.28, 2012- 1:41.73. pbs: 400m 45.66A '13, 45.94 '12, 600m 1:15.0+ '12.

Women

Amantle MONTSHO b. 4 Jul 1983 Mabudutsa 1.73m 64kg.
At 400m: OG: '04- h, '08- 8, '12- 4; WCh: '05-07-09-11: h/sf/8/1; CG: '06- sf, '10- 1; AfG: '03-07-11: h/1/1; AfCh: '04-06-08-10-12: h/2/1/1/1; WI: '10- 4; CCp: '10- 1/3R. Won DL 2011-12.
Botswana records 100m 2011, 200m 2001-12, 400m 2003-12.
Progress at 400m: 2003- 55.03, 2004- 53.77, 2005- 52.59, 2006- 52.14, 2007- 50.90, 2008- 49.83A/50.54, 2009- 49.89, 2010- 49.89, 2011- 49.56, 2012- 49.54. pbs: 100m 11.60 '11, 200m 22.89 '12, 22.88w '11, 300m 36.33i '10 (African record).
First Botswana woman to win a major title.

BRAZIL

Governing body: Confederação Brasileira de Atletismo (CBAt), Avenida Rio Purus No. 103 - Conj. Vieiralves, Bairro N.Sra das Graças, Manaus, AM 69053-050. Founded 1914 (Confederação 1977).

National Championships first held in 1925. **2012 Champions: Men**: 100m: José Carlos Moreira 10.34, 200m: Bruno de Barros 20.37, 400m: Hederson Estefani 45.25, 800m: Kléberson Davide 1:46.03, 1500m: Fabiano Peçanha 3:46.31, 5000m: Rafael Novais 14:01.04, 10,000m: Damião de Spouza 28:51.31, 3000mSt: Gladson Barbosa 8:48.76, 110mh: Matheus Inocêncio 13.74, 400mh: Mahau Suguimati 49.24, HJ: Talles Silva 2.20, PV: Fábio da Silva 5.40, LJ: Mauro da Silva 7.97, TJ: Jadel Gregório 16.99, SP: Darlan Romani 19.42, DT: Ronald Julião 63.13, HT: Wágner Domingos 69.44, JT: João Martins 72.34, Dec: Luiz Alberto de Araújo 8276, 20kW: Caio Bonfim 1:21:36, 50kW: Mário José dos Santos 4:16:31. **Women**: 100m/200m: Rosângela Santos 11.28/22.92, 400m: Geisa Coutinho 51.46, 800m/1500m: Juliana dos Santos 2:05.20/4:20.84, 5000m/ 10,000m: Cruz da Silva 15:36.57/32:15.72, 3000mSt: Tatiane da Silva 10:25.04, 100mh: Maíla Machado 13.31, 400mh: Jaílma de Lima 56.16, HJ: Valdiléia Martins 1.84, PV: Karla da Silva 4.30, LJ: Eliane Martins 6.45, TJ: Keila Costa 14.18, SP: Geisa Arcanjo 18.08, DT: Andressa de Morais 58.80, HT: Josiane Soares 59.25, JT: Jucilene de Lima 57.85, Hep: Lucimara da Silva 6026, 20000mW: Érica de Sena 1:42:05.

Bruno de BARROS b. 7 Jan 1987 Maceió 1.78m 70kg. AD Criciuma.
At 200m/4x100mR: OG: '08- h, '12- sf; WCh: '11- 6; PAm: '11- 3/1R. Won BRA 100m 2011, 200m 2011-12.
Progress at 200m: 2006- 21.15, 2007- 21.05, 2008- 20.47, 2009- 20.48, 2011- 20.16, 2012- 20.37. pb 100m 10.16 '09, 10.1 '06.
Two year drugs ban 2009-11.

Marílson Gomes **dos SANTOS** b. 6 Aug 1977 Brasília, DF 1.74m 58kg. BM&F Atletismo.
At Mar: OG: '08- dnf, '12- 5; WCh: '05- 10, '09- 16. At 5000m(/10,000m): PAm: '03- 3/2, '07- (2), '11- (1); SAm: '03- 1; WJ: '96- dnq; WCp: '06- 5. At HMar: WCh: '07- 7, '08- 8; WUG: '97- 1, '99- 1. Won IbAm 5000m 2006, BRA 5000m 2003, 2007- 09; 10,000m 2003-04, 2006-11; SAm HMar 2011, CC 2008.
South American records 5000m 2006, 10,000m, 15km, 20km & HMar 2007, 30km 2010; two BRA 10,000m records 2006-07.
Progress at 5000m, 10,000m, Mar: 1995- 14:29.7, 30:19.05; 1996- 14:18.3, 29:52.5; 1997- 14:08.1, 29:30.41; 1998- 14:20.08, 29:12.05; 1999- 14:05.35, 28:54.9; 2000- 13:52.19, 28:39.87; 2001- 14:03.47, 29:02.89; 2002- 14:00.68, 28:34.59; 2003- 13:48.52, 28:22.58; 2004- 13:48.07, 28:21.38, 2:08:48; 2005- 13:40.8, 29:05.42, 2:13:40; 2006- 13:19.43, 27:48.49, 2:09:58; 2007- 13:22.11, 27:28.12, 2:08:37; 2008- 27:35.05, 2:08:43; 2009- 13:34.79, 27:58.83, 2:15:13; 2010- 13:34.92, 28:44.59; 2:08:46; 2011- 28:09:24, 2:06:34; 2012- 2:08:03. Road pbs: 15km 42:15 '07, 20km 56:32 '07, HMar 59:33 '07, 30km 1:29:23+ '10. Won New York City Marathon 2006 and 2008. Married to Juliana de Azevedo (3rd WJ 800m 2002. At 1500m: SACh: '03- 1, '06- 1 (1 4x400m); PAm: '05- 1; pbs 800m 2:01.35 '05, 1500m 4:11.39 '07).

Fábio GOMES da SILVA b. 4 Aug 1983 Campinas, São Paulo 1.78m 74kg. BM&F Atletismo.
At PV: OG: '08/12- dnq 21=/nh; WCh: '07- 10, '09- dnq, '11- 8; WJ: '02- 12; PAm: '07- 1. '11- 5; SACh: '05-06-07-09-11: 1/3/1/1/1. Won Ib-Am 2004; and SACh-j 2002; BRA 2005-07, 2009-12.
South American pole vault records 2007 & 2011, four indoors 2008-13.
Progress at PV: 1999- 4.75, 2000- 5.01, 2001- 5.16, 2002- 5.17, 2003- 5.25, 2004- 5.55, 2005- 5.50, 2006- 5.65, 2007- 5.77, 2008- 5.45, 2009- 5.55, 2010- 5.65, 2011- 5.80, 2012- 5.70, 2013- 5.70i.

Mauro Vinícius da SILVA b. 26 Dec 1986 Presidente Prudente 1.83m 69kg.
At LJ: OG: '08- dnq 26, '12- 7; WI: '11- 1. BRA champion 2010, 2012.
Progress at LJ: 2005- 7.35/7.73w, 2006- 7.61, 2007- 7.66, 2008- 8.10/8.20w?, 2009- 8.04i/7.94, 2010- 8.12, 2011- 8.27, 2012- 8.28i/8.11. pbs: 60m 6.76i '09, 100m 10.40 '07, 200m 21.02 '07.
Won World Indoor title with 8.23 but took off behind the board with 24cm to spare.

Women

Maurren Higa **MAGGI** b. 25 Jun 1976 São Carlos, São Paulo 1.78m 66kg. FC São Paulo.
At LJ (/100mh): OG: '00- dnq 25, '08- 1, '12- dnq 15; WCh: '99- 8/qf, '01- 7/h, '07- 6, '09- 7, '11- 11; PAm: '99- 1/2, '07- 1 (4 TJ), '11- 1; SACh: '97- 1/2, '99- 1/1, '01- 1/1, '06-07-11: 1/1/1; WUG: '99- 3, '01- 1/2/2R; WI: '03- 3, '08- 2. Won GP 2002, GWG 2001, IbAm 2000, 2002; SA-J 100mh 1994, BRA 100mh 1997-2000, LJ 1999-2002, 2006, 2008, 2011; TJ 2002.
South American (BRA) records: LJ 1 (3) 1999, 100mh 4 (6) 1999-2001, TJ 2002-03 (3); S.Am indoor LJ (4) 2003-08.
Progress at 100mh, LJ, TJ: 1994- 14.13, 5.86; 1995- 14.46/14.3w, 5.75/6.02w; 1996- 13.99, 6.47; 1997- 13.67/13.53w, 6.54; 1998- 13.60, 6.42; 1999- 12.86, 7.26A/6.79/6.81w, 2000- 6.93, 2001- 12.71, 6.94/6.98w, 13.60; 2002- 7.02/7.17w, 14.32; 2003- 7.06, 14.53; 2006- 6.84/6.86Aw, 14.02; 2007- 6.95, 14.44; 2008- 7.04, 2009- 6.90, 2010- 6.45, 2011- 6.94A/6.89, 2012- 6.85. pbs: 60mh 8.12i '00.
Won first Olympic medal by a Brazilian woman and first South American women's gold in 2008. Father intended to name her Maureen (after first wife of Ringo Starr), but name was misspelled on her birth certificate. Formerly a gymnast, made huge breakthrough in 1999

with her 7.26 LJ at the high altitude of Bogotá from a previous best of 6.79. Two year ban for positive drugs test 14 Jun 2003, later reversed by CBAt but not by IAAF. Formerly married to racing driver Antonio Pizzonia; their daughter Sophia was born in December 2004.

Fabiana de Almeida **MURER** b. 16 Mar 1981 Campinas, São Paulo 1.72m 64kg. BM&F Atletismo. Degree in physiotherapy.
At PV: OG: '08- 10=, '12- dnq 14; WCh: '05- dnq 15, '07- 6=, '09- 5, '11- 1; WJ: '98- dnq 14=, '00- 10; PAm: '99-07-11: 9/1/2; WI: '08- 3=, '10- 1; SACh: '99-01-05-06-07-09-11: 3/6/2/1/1/1/1; WCp: '06- 2, '10- 3. Won DL 2010, IbAm 2006, 2010; SAm-J 1998-2000, BRA 2005-07, 2010.
13 South American pole vault records, 15 indoors 2006-11, 29 BRA records 1998-2011.
Progress at PV: 1998- 3.66, 1999- 3.81, 2000- 3.90, 2001- 3.91, 2002- 3.70, 2003- 4.06, 2004- 4.25, 2005- 4.40, 2006- 4.66, 2007- 4.66i/4.65, 2008- 4.80, 2009- 4.82, 2010- 4.85, 2011- 4.85, 2012- 4.77. Married to coach Élson de Souza (pb 5.02 '89).

BULGARIA

Governing body: Bulgarian Athletics Federation, 75 bl. Vassil Levski, Sofia 1000. Founded 1924.
National Championships first held in 1926 (men), 1938 (women). **2012 Champions**: **Men**: 100m: Georgi Georgiev 10.32, 200m: Peter Kremenski 21.22, 400m: Krasimir Braykov 47.62, 800m: Radoslav Stefanov 1:53.09, 1500m: Sava Todorov 3:5.33, 5000m/3000mSt: Yolo Nikolov 14:32.37/8:45.71, 10,000m/HMar/Mar: Khristo Stefanov 31:03.34/71:39/2:33:02, 110mh: Martin Arnaudov 13.68, 400mh: Milan Volkanov 54.52, HJ: Angel Kararadev 2.20, PV: Zdravko Gourdev 4.25, LJ: Denis Eradiri 7.97w, TJ: Momchil Karailiev 16.93w, SP: Georgi Ivanov 20.33, DT: Rosen Karamfilov 56.26, HT: Zdravko Dimitrov 64.85, JT: Kolio Neshev 67.30, Dec: Ivan Minchev 6192, 20kW: Bozhidar Vasilev 1:47:04. **Women**: 100m/200m: Gabriela Laleva 11.56w/23.89, 400m/800m: Teodora Kolarova 53.69/2:02.80, 1500m: Monika Georgieva 4:39.30, 50000m/10,000m/HMar/ 3000mSt: Silvia Danekova 17:00.72/38:05.40/1:22:58/9:51.14, Mar: Milka Mikhaylova 3:06:34, 100mh: Elena Miteva 14.69, 400mh: Iva Dimova 61.30, HJ: Gergana Mincheva 1.60, PV: Anna Ivanova 3.65, LJ/TJ: Andriana Bânova 6.42w/14.03, SP: Marierta Koutsarova 14.45, DT: Grigoria Naneva 48.18, HT: Mikhaela Metodieva 47.23, JT: Denista Koleva 45.43, Hep: Alexandra Ribarova 3945, 20kW: Emanoela Yankova 2:19:07.

Women

Ivet LALOVA b. 18 May 1984 Sofia 1.68m 56kg. Levski Sofia, Panellínios GRE.
At 100m/(200m): OG: '04- 4/5, '08- sf/qf, '12- sf/sf; WCh: '07/09- qf, '11- 7/sf; EC: '10- h, "12- 1/sf;

WJ: '02- sf; WY: '01- h/sf; EJ: '03: 1/1; EI: '05- (1). At 60m: WI: '12- 8; EI: '13- 4. Won BUL 100m 2004-05, 200m 2004; Balkan 100m 2011.
Bulgarian 100m record 2004.
Progress at 100m, 200m: 1998- 13.0, 27.2; 1999- 12.71, 2000- 12.14, 25.24; 2001- 11.72, 24.03; 2002- 11.59, 24.4; 2003- 11.14, 22.87; 2004- 10.77, 22.51/22.36w; 2005- 11.03, 22.76; 2007- 11.26/11.15w, 23.00; 2008- 11.31/11.28w, 23.13; 2009- 11.48/11.24w, 23.60; 2010- 11.43, 23.71; 2011- 10.96, 22.66; 2012- 11.06/11.01w, 22.98. pbs: 50m 6.23i+ '12, 60m 7.12i '13.
Broke her leg in a collision with another athlete on 14 Jun 2005. Engaged to sprinter Simone Collio (Italy). Her father Miroslav Lalov had 100m best of 10.4 and was BUL 200m champion in 1966, her mother Liliya (née Petrunova) was also a sprinter.

Tezdzhan NAIMOVA b. 1 May 1987 Parvomay 1.66m 58kg. Lokomotiv 2004 Plovdiv.
At 100m/200m: OG: '08- h/-; WCh: '07- sf/sf; WJ: '04- -/sf, '06- 1/1; EJ: '05- 4/7. At 60m: EI: '07- 5, '13- 1. Won Balkan 100m & 200m 2007; BUL 100m 2006. 200m 2005, 2007.
Progress at 100m/200m: 2004- 11.85/11.78w, 24.33; 2005- 11.61/11.48w, 23.82; 2006- 11.23/11.11w, 2007- 11.04, 22.43; 2008- 11.43, 23.44; 2011- 11.42, 23.85; 2012- 11.26/11.0. pb 60m 7.10i '13.
Two-year drugs ban from 30 Sep 2008. Tezdzhan means 'fast soul'.

Vania STAMBOLOVA b. 28 Nov 1983 Varna 1.75m 53kg. Cehrno more Atletik Varna. Student at the Sports Academy of Sofia.
At 400m: EC: '06- 1; WI: '06-10-12: 2/3/4; EI: '11- 4; WCp: '06- 2. At 400mh: OG: '12- h; WCh: '05- h, '09- sf, '11- 6; EC: '10- 2; WUG: '09- 1; CCp: '10- 3. Won Balkan 400mh 2005, 400m & 400mh 2011; BUL 400m 2009, 400mh 2002, 2005-06.
Bulgarian Records: 400m (5) 2006, 400mh (2) 2006-10.
Progress at 400m. 400mh: 1998- 57.91, 64.34; 1999- 57.45, 63.53; 2000- 58.82, 62.72; 2001- 57.86, 61.38; 2002- 58.30, 61.11; 2005- 52.99, 56.29; 2006- 49.53, 54.55; 2009- 51.47, 55.14; 2010- 50.88, 53.82; 2011- 50.98, 53.68; 2012- 50.87, 54.04. pb 200m 22.81 '06, 22.7 '10; 300m 36.81i '12, 800m 2:02.03i '12.
Former footballer. Two-year drugs ban 2007-09.

Venelina VENEVA-MATEEVA b. 13 Jun 1974 Ruse 1.79m 61kg. Dunav Ruse.
At HJ: OG: '96-04-12: dnq 29=/15/20=, '00- 9=; WCh: '91-5-9-09-11: dnq 21=/14/14=/15/21, '01-03-05: 4/4/10; EC: '98-06-0-12: 5/2/dnq 22=/12; EJ: '91- 2; WI: '01- 3, '04- 7; EI: '00-05-07-11-13: 4/3/dq3/7=/6. BUL champion 1995, 2004, 2009-10; Balkan 2003.
Progress at HJ: 1987- 1.68, 1988- 1.80, 1989- 1.86, 1990- 1.93i/1.90, 1991- 1.91, 1992- 1.91, 1993- 1.89i/1.85, 1994- 1.90, 1995- 1.94, 1996- 1.94i/1.88, 1998- 2.03, 1999- 1.90, 2000- 2.01, 2001- 2.04,

2002- 2.02i, 2003- 2.01, 2004- 2.01, 2005- 1.98, 2006- 2.04, 2007- 1.96i/2.02idq, 2009- 1.95, 2010- 1.95, 2011- 1.98, 2012- 1.95. pbs: LJ 6.17 '90, TJ 12.51 '95.
Daughter Neapola born in 1997. World age-15 best of 1.93i in 1990. Two year drugs ban from positive test 24 Jan 2007.

BURUNDI

Francine NIYONSABA b. 5 May 1993 Nkanda Bweru, Ruyiqi 1.61m 56kg.
At 800m: OG: '12- 7; AfCh: '12- 1.
Five Burundi 800m records 2012.
Progress at 800m: 2012- 1:56.59. pb 600m 1:27.6 '12.

CANADA

Governing body: Athletics Canada, Suite B1-110, 2445 S-Laurent Drive, Ottawa, Ontario K1G 6C3. Formed as Canadian AAU in 1884.
National Championships first held in 1884 (men), 1925 (women). **2012 Champions: Men**: 100m: Justyn Warner 10.15, 200m: Tremaine Harrius 20.68, 400m: Philip Osei 46.29, 800m: Geoff Harris 1:46.49, 1500m: Nathan Brannen 3:49.22, 5000m: Cam Levins 14:34.82, 10,000m: Mohammed Ahmed 30:49.13, HMar: Eric Gillis 64:38, Mar: Réjean Chiasson 2:19:54, 3000mSt: Alex Genest 8:45.0, 110mh: Matthew Brisson 13.73, 400mh: Tait Nystuen 51.23, HJ: Derek Drouin 2.31, PV: Jason Wurster 5.25, LJ: Taylor Stewart 7.78w, TJ: Tacum Anderson-Richards 15.19, SP: Dylan Armstrong 21.29, DT: Tim Nedow 58.77, HT: James Steacy 72.22, JT: Curtis Moss 77.83, Dec: Damian Warner 8107, 10000W: Evan Dunfee 40:15.5, 20kW: Benjamin Thorne 1:21:55. **Women**: 100m: Phylicia George 11.30w, 200m: Crystal Emmanuel 23.27, 400m: Jenna Martin 51.53, 800m: Lemlem Ogbasilassie 2:07.37, 1500m: Malindi Elmore 4:13.58, 5000m: Sheila Reid 16:15.23, 10,000m: Leslie Sexton 35:18.97, HMar: Kate Bazeley 76:34, Mar: Lisa Avery 2:42:53, 3000mSt: Dana Buchanan 10:19.52, 100mh/Hep: Jessica Zelinka 12.68/6599, 400mh: Sarah Wells 55.71, HJ: Nicole Forrester 1.86, PV: Mélanie Blouin 4.35, LJ: Krysha Bayley 6.47w, TJ: Carolina Eberhardt 12.94w, SP/DT: Julie Labonté 17.51/54.02, HT: Heather Steacy 70.48, JT: Liz Gleadle 60.13, 10000W: Rachel Seaman 48:19.4, 20kW: Nicola Evangelista 1:37:32.

Dylan ARMSTRONG b. 15 Jan 1981 Kamloop, British Columbia 1.90m 125kg. Dylan BC Athletics. Was at University of Texas.
At SP: OG: '08- 4, '12- 5; WCh: '07- 9, '09- dnq 17, '11- 2; CG: '10- 1; WI: '10- 4; PAm: '07- 1, '11- 1; PAm-J: '99- 2 (1 HT, 3 DT); CCp: '10- 5. At HT: WCh: '01- dnq 31; WJ: '00- 2 (dnq DT). Won Canadian HT 2001-02, SP 2005-10, 2012; DL SP 2011.
Seven Canadian shot records 2008-11.

Progress at SP: 1999- 16.16, 2000- 16.30, 2001- 18.07, 2004- 19.55, 2005- 19.83, 2006- 20.62, 2007- 20.72, 2008- 21.04, 2009- 20.92, 2010- 21.58, 2011- 22.21, 2012- 21.50. pbs: DT 54.60 '00, HT 71.51 '03, Wt 22.78i '03.

Derek DROUIN b. 6 Mar 1990 Sarnia, Ontario 1.95m 80kg. Student of exercise science at Indiana University.
At HJ: OG: '12- 3=; WY: '07- 10. Canadian champion 2012.
Progress at HJ: 2007- 2.07, 2008- 2.11, 2009- 2.27, 2010- 2.28i/2.26, 2011- 2.33i/2.23, 2012- 2.31, 2013- 2.35i, 2013- 2.35i. pbs: 60mh 7.98i '12, 1000m 2:45.06i '13, 110mh 14.24'10, PV 4.15i '13. 3.65 '11; LJ 7.13i '13, 6.85 '11; Hep 5817i '13.

Damian WARNER b. 4 Nov 1989 London, Ontario 1.85m 83kg.
At Dec: OG: '12- 5; WCh: '11- 18. Canadian champion 2011-12.
Progress at Dec: 2010- 7449, 2011- 8102A/7832, 2012- 8442. pbs: 60m 6.74i '10, 100m 10.41A '11, 10.48 '12; 200m 21.80 '08, 400m 48.20 '12, 1500m 4:29.85 '12, 60mh 7.93i '12, 110mh 13.61 '12, HJ 2.06 '12, PV 4.80A '12, LJ 7.54 '12, TJ 14.75w '08, SP 13.74 '12, DT 45.90 '12, JT 62.77 '12.
Made 340 points improvement on pb when 5th at 2012 Olympics, setting six pbs.

Women

Perdita FELICIEN b. 29 Aug 1980 Oshawa, Ontario 1.65m 63kg. Phoenix TC. Studied kinesiology at University of Illinois, USA.
At 100mh: OG: '00- h, '04- dnf; WCh: '01-03-05-07-09-11: sf/1/sf/2/8/sf; PAm: '03- 2, '07- 2; CCp: '10- 3. At 60mh: WI: '04- 1, '10- 2. Won FrancG 2001, CAN 2000, 2002-07, 2009-11; NCAA 2002-03.
Canadian 100mh records 2003 & 2004.
Progress at 100mh: 1998- 13.69/13.47w, 1999- 13.69, 2000- 12.91, 2001- 12.73, 2002- 12.83/12.77w, 2003- 12.53, 2004- 12.46/12.45w, 2005- 12.58, 2006- 12.58, 2007- 12.49, 2009- 12.54, 2010- 12.58, 2011- 12.73, 2012- 12.93A/12.80w. pbs: 60m 7.37i '02, 100m 11.62 '01, 200m 24.21 '02, 50mh 6.80i '04, 60mh 7.75i '04.
Improved her best from 12.68 to 12.53 to win World 100mh in 2003 and from 7.90 to 7.75 to win World Indoor 60mh in 2004. Fell in 2004 Olympic final.

Sultana FRIZELL b. 24 Oct 1984 Perth, Ontario 1.83m 110kg. Was at University of Georgia.
At HT: OG: '08/12- dnq 33/26; WCh: '09- 10; CG: '10- 1; PAm: '07- 7, '11- 2; PAm-J: '03- 4; Canadian champion 2007-08, 2010.
Four Commonwealth hammer records 2009-12, North American 2012, seven Canadian 2008-12.
Progress at HT: 2002- 54.75, 2003- 57.95, 2004- 63.36, 2005- 66.42, 2006- 63.39, 2007- 67.92, 2008- 70.94, 2009- 72.07, 2010- 72.24, 2011- 71.46, 2012- 75.04. pbs: SP 15.82 '06, Wt 20.37i '05, JT 46.58 '04.

Phylicia GEORGE b. 16 Nov 1987 Toronto 1.78m 65kg. Was at University of Connecticut, USA.
At 100mh: OG: '12- 6; WCh: '11- 7. At 200m: WJ: 06- h.
Progress at 100mh: 2006- 14.53w, 2007- 14.44w, 2008- 13.71/13.62w, 2009- 13.74, 2010- 13.39, 2011- 12.73, 2012- 12.65. pbs: 60m 7.35i '12, 100m 11.25 '12, 200m 23.10 '11, 50mh 6.90i '12, 55mh 7.69i '10, 60mh 8.03i '12.

Brianne THEISEN b. 18 Dec 1988 Humboldt 1.80m 64kg. Sasketchewan. Student at University of Oregon
At Hep: OG: '12- 11; WCh: '09- 15; WJ: '06- 19. Won PAm-J 2007, NCAA 2009-10, 2012.
Progress at Hep: 2005- 5181, 2006- 5240, 2007- 5413, 2008- 5738, 2010- 6094, 2012- 6440. pbs: 200m 23.90 '12, 400m 53.72 '12, 800m 2:09.27 '12, 60mh 8.25i '12, 100mh 13.09A/13.30 '12, HJ 1.88i '12, 1.86 '10; LJ 6.32A/6.28 '12, SP 13.21 '12, JT 46.47 '12, Pen 4555i '12.

Jessica ZELINKA b. 3 Sep 1981 London, Ontario 1.72m 62kg. Calgary AB.
At Hep(/100mh): OG: '08- 5, '12- 7/7; WCh: '05- 11, '11- 9; CG: '06- 4, '10- 2; PAm: '07- 1; WJ: '00- 5/h. Won CAN Hep 2001, 2004-06, 2008, 2010, 2012; 100mh 2012.
Six Canadian heptathlon records 2006-12.
Progress at 100mh. Hep: 1996- 4700, 1997- 4586, 1998- 14.18/14.13w, 4859; 1999- 14.18, 5059; 2000- 13.81, 5583; 2001- 13.67, 5702; 2002- 5962, 2003- 13.52, 6031; 2004- 13.26/13.10w, 6296; 2005- 13.42/13.15w, 6137; 2006- 13.08, 6314; 2007- 13.25, 6343; 2008- 12.97, 6490; 2010- 13.19, 6204; 2011- 13.01, 6353; 2012- 12.65, 6599A/6480. 50m 6.56i '02, 60m 7.53i '04, 100m 12.10A '06, 200m 23.32 '12, 800m 2:07.95 '08, 60mh 8.19i '06, HJ 1.79 '07, LJ 6.19/6.23w '06, SP 14.97 '07, JT 46.60A '12, Pen 4386i '07

CHILE

Governing body: Federación Atlética de Chile, Calle Santo Toribio No 660, Ñuñoa, Santiago de Chile. Founded 1914.
National Champions 2012: Men: 100m/200m: Cristián Reyes 10.61/21.02, 400m: Pierre Sepúlveda 49.30, 800m: Iván López 1:51.04, 1500m: Mauricio Valdivia 3:56.33, 3000m/5000m: Víctor Aravena 8:09.23/14:24.38, 10,000m: Patricio Uribe 31:08.98, 3000mSt: Enzo Yáñez 9:12.0, 110mh: Víctor Arancibia 14.50, 400mh: Cristián Gutiérrez 52.36, HJ: Rodrigo Arriagada 1.95, PV: Felipe Fuentes 4.80, LJ: Daniel Pineda 8.08, TJ: Alejandro Horn 14.90, SP/DT: Nicolás Laso 16.16/50.59, HT: Roberto Sáez 66.50, JT: Pablo Koch Reyes 57.10, Dec: Matías Dallaserra 6677, 20000mW: Herry Gajardo 1:45:34.3. **Women**: 100m: Daniela Pavez 11.78, 200m: María Fernanda Mackenna 24.18, 400m/400mh: Javiera Errázuriz 56.23/60.80, 800m/1500m: Javiera Faletto 2:17.70/4:46.54, 3000m: Eliana Vásquez 10:45.61, 5000m:

Guisselle Álvarez 19:07.85, 10,000m: Bárbara González 43:21.10, 3000mSt: Yetsemin González 12:46, 100mh: Carolina Castillo 14.62, HJ: Florencia Vergara 1.70, LJ: Daniela Pávez 6.23, TJ: Valeria Sánchez 11.16, SP: Marcela Barrientos 12.90, DT: Karen Gallardo 55.94, HT: Leslie Torrejón 45.63, JT: María Paz Ríos 48.81, 20000mW: Bernardita Maldonado 2:16:08.1.

CHINA

Governing body: Athletic Association of the People's Republic of China, 2 Tiyuguan Road, Beijing 100763.
National Championships first held in 1910 (men), 1959 (women). **2012 Champions: Men**: 100m: Su Bingtian 10.21, 200m: Xie Zhenye 20.77, 400m: Chang Pengben 46.45, 800m: Teng Haining 1:47.91, 1500m: Teng Haining 3:42.88, 5000m: Tai Yunlong 13:59.92, 10,000m: Ren Longyun 28:44.76, Mar: Dong Guojian 2:15:03, 3000SC: Wang Yashuan 8:39.22, 110mh: Xie Wenjun 13.36, 400mh: Li Zhilong 50.25, HJ: Zheng Guowei 2.31, PV: Yang Tansheng 5.70, LJ: Wang Jianan 8.04, TJ: Cao Shuo 17.04, SP: Wang Guangfu 20.20, DT: Wu Jian 60.19, HT: Qi Dakai 70.59, JT: Zhao Qinggang 81.74, Dec: Qi Haifeng 7573. 20kW: Cai Zelin 1:19:42, 50kW: Li Jianbo 3:47:30. **Women**: 100m/200m: Wei Yongli 11.51/23.37, 400m: Chen Jingwen 52.80, 800m: Zhao Jing 2:01.46, 1500m: Sun Lu 4:12.16, 5000m: Fu Tinglian 15:47.82, 10,000m: Xiao Huimin 33:00.32, Mar: Wang Jiali 2:22:41, 3000SC: Jin Yuan 10:03.85, 100mh: Wu Shujiao 12.98, 400mh: Yang Qi 56.66, HJ: Zhang Xingjuan 1.92, PV: Li Ling 4.40, LJ: Xu Xiaoling 6.58, TJ: Wang Huiqin 14.02, SP: Gong Lijao 19.87, DT: Tan Jian 62.83, HT: Zhang Wenxiu 74.94, JT: Chang Chungeng 59.16, Hep: Wang Yunhan 5578, 20kW: Wang Shanshan 1:30:12.

CAI Zelin b. 11 Apr 1991 Dali, Yunnan 1.72m 55kg.
At 20kW: OG: '12- 4. At 10,000mW: WJ: '10- 2; WCp: '10- 2J. CHN 20kW champion 2012.
Progress at 20kW: 2010- 1:22:28, 2011- 1:21:07, 2012- 1:18:47. Pbs: 10,000W 38:59.98 '12, 30kmW 2:45:13 '09.

CHEN DING b. 5 Aug 1992 Dali, Yunnan 1.80m 62kg. Guangdong.
At 20kW: OG: '12- 1; WCp: '10- 5, '12- 8. At 10,000mW: WJ: '08- 2; WCp: '08- 2J.
World youth 10,000m walk record 2008
Progress at 20kW: 2008- 1:20:16, 2009- 1:21:21, 2010- 1:21:59, 2011- 1:18:52, 2012- 1:17:40. Pbs: 10kW 38:23 '10, 39:47.20t '08; 30kmW 2:12:16 '10.

CHU Yafei b. 5 Sep 1988 Haikou 1.72m 55kg. Inner Mongolia.
At 20kW: OG: '08- 10; WCh: '09- 13, '11- 11; WCp: '10- 2; AsiG: '10- 2; AsiC: '09- 2; WUG: '07- 1. 2nd RWC 2011.
At 10km road walk records: Asian junior (39:00) 2006, Asian (38:40) 2010.

Progress at 20kW: 2004- 1:27:23, 2005- 1:22:18, 2006- 1:18:44, 2007- 1:24:37, 2008- 1:21:04, 2009- 1:19:51, 2010- 1:21:11, 2011- 1:18:38, 2012- 1:24:48. Pbs: 10,000mW 39:22.47 '12, 37:57R '10; 30kW 2:14:46 '06.

LI Jianbo b. 14 Nov 1986 Qujing, Yunnan 1.76m 57kg.
At 50kW: OG: '12- 7; WCh: '11- 25; AsiC: '07- 3. At 20kW: WCh: '09- 12; Asi: '09- 1. Won CHN 50kW 2012.
Progress at 20kW, 50kW: 2003- 1:26:37, 4:03:08; 2004- 1:26:21, 2005- 1:19:34, 3:45:13; 2006- 1:19:38, 3:43:02; 2007- 1:23:23, 3:53:24; 2008- 1:20:47, 3:52:12; 2009- 1:19:10, 3:44:59; 2010- 1:21:08, 2011- 1:25:45, 3:43:38; 2012- 1:20:55, 3:39:01.

LIU Xiang b. 13 Jul 1983 Shanghai 1.89m 74kg.
At 110mh: OG: '04- 1, '08/12- h; WCh: '01-03-05-07-11: sf/3/2/1/2; WJ: '00- 4; WUG: '01- 1; AsiG: '02-06-10: 1/1/1; AsiC: '02-05-09: 1/1/1; WCp: '02- dnf, '06- 2. Won WAF 2006, CHN 2002, 2004-06; CHN NG 2005, E.Asian 2001, 2005, 2009. At 60mh: WI: '03-04-08-10-12: 3/2/1/7/2. World 110mh records 2004 & 2006, five Asian & CHN records 2002-06; World junior records 110mh 2002, indoors 50mh (6.53 and 6.52) & 60mh (7.61 and 7.55). Eight Asian indoor 60mh records 2002-12.
Progress at 110mh: 1999- 14.19, 2000- 13.75, 2001- 13.32, 2002- 13.12, 2003- 13.17, 2004- 12.91, 2005- 13.05, 2006- 12.88, 2007- 12.92, 2008- 13.18, 2009- 13.15, 2010- 13.09, 2011- 13.00, 2012- 12.97/12.87w. pbs: 200m 21.27 '02. 50mh 6.52i '02, 60mh 7.41i '12, HJ 2.04 '98.
With his brilliant Olympic 110mh win in 2004 he tied the world record of 12.91 and become the first Chinese man to win a global athletics gold medal. Took world record to 12.88 at Lausanne 2006. Set world age records 16 (13.94)-17-18 in 2000-02. Injured at 2008 and 2012 Olympics.

SI Tianfeng b. 17 Jun 1984 Xintai, Shandong 1.81m 67kg. Shandong
At 50kW: OG: '08- 17 '12- 3; WCh: '11- 4; AsiG '10- 1; WCp: '10- 4, '12- 4. Won CHN 2008.
Progress at 50kW: 2003- 3:59:23, 2004- 3:55:37, 2005- 3:42:55, 2006- 3:52:06, 2007- 3:58:27, 2008- 3:45:13, 2009- 3:44:15, 2010- 3:47:04, 2011- 3:38:48, 2012- 3:37:16. pb 20kW 1:20:05 '05, 30k 2:11:07 '12, 35k 2:32:16 '12.

WANG Hao b. 16 Aug 1989 Qiqihaer, Inner Mongolia 1.80m 65kg. Heilongjiang.
At 20kW: OG: '08- 4; WCh: '09- 2, '11- 12; WCp: '10- 1; AsiG: '10- 1; won CHN 2007, CHN NG 2009.
Progress at 20kW, 50kW: 2007- 1:21:20.69t, 2008- 1:19:47, 2009- 1:18:13, 3:41:55; 2010- 1:20:50, 2011- 1:21:03, 2012- 1:23:40. Pbs: 10,000mW 41:42.08 '07, 10kW 38:00 '10, 30kW 2:20:47 '07, 50kW 4:10:45 '12.

WANG Zhen b. 24 Aug 1991 Changzhou 1.80m 62kg. Heilongjiang.

At 20kW: OG: '12- 3; WCh: 11- 4; WCp: '12- 1; CHN champion 2011. Won World Race Walking Challenge Final 10k 2010, 2012 (2nd 2011).
Walks records: World junior 10k 2010, Asian 20k & 10,000m track 2012.
Progress at 20kW: 2008- 1:28:01, 2009- 1:22:10, 2010- 1:20:42, 2011- 1:18:30, 2012- 1:17:36. Pbs: 5000mW 20:16.04 '09, 10kW 37:44 '10, 38:30.38 '12; 30kmW 2:08:46 '08, 50kmW 3:53:00 '09.

Women

GONG Lijiao b. 24 Jan 1989 Luquan, Hebei Prov. 1.74m 110kg. Hebei.
At SP: OG: '08- 5, '12- 3; WCh: '07- 7, '09- 3, '11- 4; WI: '10- 8; AsiG: '10- 2; AsiC: '09- 1; CCp: '10- 3. Chinese champion 2007-12, NG 2009; Asian indoor 2008.
Progress at SP: 2005- 15.41i, 2006- 17.92, 2007- 19.13, 2008- 19.46, 2009- 20.35, 2010- 20.13, 2011- 20.11, 2012- 20.22. pb JT 53.94 '07.

LI Ling b. 7 Feb 1985 Shenyang, Liaoning Prov. 1.83m 84kg. Liaoning.
At SP: OG: '08- 14, '12- 4; WCh: '07- 4, '11- 6; AsiG: '06- 1, '10- 1; AsiC: '05- 3; AsJ: '04- 1; WCp: '06- 5. Chinese champion 2006.
Progress at SP: 2002- 15.45, 2003- 16.55, 2004- 17.34, 2005- 18.68, 2006- 19.05, 2007- 19.38, 2008- 18.86, 2009- 18.97, 2010- 19.94, 2011- 19.72, 2012- 19.95.

LI Yanfeng b. 15 May 1979 Qinggang, Heilongjiang 1.79m 90kg.
At DT: OG: '04- 9, '08- 7, '12- 3; WCh: '11- 1; AsiG: '10- 1; AsiC: '00-02-03-07: 3/2/1/2; WUG: '01- 2, '03- 2; WCp: '02- 4, '10- 1. Won E.Asian G & CHN NG 2009, CHN 2010-11.
Progress at DT: 1997- 56.68, 1998- 57.30, 1999- 63.67, 2000- 60.84, 2001- 61.77, 2002- 62.52, 2003- 61.87, 2004- 64.34, 2005- 61.61, 2007- 62.24, 2008- 63.79, 2009- 66.40, 2010- 66.18, 2011- 67.98, 2012- 67.84.

LIU Hong b. 12 May 1987 Anfu, Jiangxi Prov. 1.61m 48kg. Guangdong.
At 20kW: OG: '08- 4, '12- 4; WCh: '07- 19, '09- 3, '11- 2; WCp: '06- 6; AsiG: '06- 1, '10- 1; won CHN 2010-11, NG 2009. At 10,000mW: WJ: '06- 1; won World Race Walking Challenge Final 10k 2012 (2nd 2011).
Asian records 5000m & 20k walk 2012.
Progress at 20kW: 2004- 1:35:04, 2005- 1:29:39, 2006- 1:28:26, 2007- 1:29:41, 2008- 1:27:17, 2009- 1:28:11, 2010- 1:30:06, 2011- 1:27:17, 2012- 1:25:46. pbs: 3000mW 12:18.18 '05, 5000mW 20:34.76 '12, 10kW 42:30R '10, 43:16.68t '12.

LIU Xiangrong b. 6 Jun 1988 Nei Mongol 1.85m 119kg.
At SP: OG: '12- 6; WCh: '09- 10, '11- dnq 17; WI: '12- 6; AsiC: '07-09-11: 1/2/2; Won Asian Indoor 2012.
Progress at SP: 2006- 16.94, 2007- 18.58, 2008- 18.69, 2009- 18.69, 2010- 18.49, 2011- 18.74, 2012- 19.24. pb DT 47.77 '06.

LU Huihui b. 26 Jun 1989 Huwan, Henan 1.71m 68kg.
At JT: OG: '12- 5. Asian javelin record 2012.
Progress at JT: 2005- 49.62, 2006- 49.96, 2010- 55.35, 2011- 58.72, 2012- 64.95, 2013- 64:48.

LU Xiuzhi b. 26 Oct 1993 Chuzhou 1.56m 45kg.
At 20kW: OG: '12- 6; WCp: '12- 4; 3rd RWC 2012. Asian junior 20k walk record 2012.
Progress at 20kW: 2011- 1:29:50, 2012- 1:27:01. pb 10kW 43:16 '12.

MA Xuejun b. 26 Mar 1985 Shandong Prov. 1.85m 96kg. Shandong.
At DT: OG: '08- dnq 23, '12- 11; WCh: '07- 8, '09- 11, '11- dnq 14; AsiG: '06- 2; AsiCh: '09- 2, '11- 2; WJ: '02- 1, '04- 1; WY: '01- 1. Won Asi-J 2004, CHN 2006, 2009.
Progress at DT: 1999- 52.79, 2001- 58.65, 2002- 58.85, 2003- 60.20, 2004- 57.85, 2005- 61.87, 2006- 65.00, 2007- 62.57, 2008- 61.92, 2009- 63.63, 2010- 60.39, 2011- 63.93, 2012- 63.91.

QIEYANG Shenjie b. 11 Nov 1990 Haiyan, Qinghai Prov. 1.60m 50kg.
At 20kW: OG: '12- 3; WCh: '11- 5; WCp: '12- 15. Asian 20k walk record 2012.
Progress at 20kW: 2009- 1:35:54, 2010- 1:30:33, 2011- 1:28:04, 2012- 1:25:16. pbs: 5000mW 20:42.67 '12, 10kW 43:16 '12.
First athlete from Tibet to win an Olympic medal.

TAN Jian b. 20 Jan 1988 Chengdu 1.79m 80kg. Sichuan,
At DT: OG: '12- dnq; WCh: '11- 6; WJ: '06- 3. Chinese champion 2012.
Progress at DT: 2004- 56.00, 2005- 57.01, 2007- 56.99, 2008- 55.04, 2009- 57.40, 2010- 59.65, 2011- 63.72, 2012- 64.45.

ZHANG Wenxiu b. 22 Mar 1986 Dalian 1.82m 108kg. Army.
At HT: OG: '04- 7, '08- 3, '12- 5; WCh: '01-03-05-07-09-11: 11/dnq 14/5/3/5/3; WJ: '02- dnq 20; AsiG: '06- 1, '10- 1; AsiC: '05- 1, '09- 1; WCp: '06- 4, '10- 2. Won Asi-J 2002, CHN 2004, 2006-10, 2012; NG 2003, 2009.
Nine Asian hammer records 2001-12, world youth 2003, two world junior 2004-05.
Progress at HT: 2000- 60.30, 2001- 66.30, 2002- 67.13, 2003- 70.60, 2004- 72.42, 2005- 73.24, 2006- 74.15, 2007- 74.86, 2008- 74.32, 2009- 74.25, 2010- 73.83, 2011- 75.65, 2012- 75.72, 2012- 76.99.
World age bests at 15-16-18.

ZHOU Chunxiu b. 15 Nov 1978 Suzhou, Jiangsu Prov. 1.63m 44kg. Henan.
At Mar: OG: '04- 33, '08- 3; WCh: '05- 5, '07- 2, '09- 4; AsiG: '06- 1, '10- 1. World HMar: '04- 12. Won CHN HMar 2008, Mar 2003-05
Progress at 10,000m, Mar: 2000- 33:14.63, 2003- 32:13.96, 2:23:41; 2004- 33:03.04, 2:23:28; 2005- 31:09.03, 2:21:11; 2006- 32:42.46, 2:19:51; 2007- 32:44.13, 2:20:38; 2008- 32:21.13, 2:27:07; 2009- 31:59.93, 2:25:39; 2010- 2:25:00, 2011- 2:34:29,

2012- 2:23:42. pbs: 1500m 4:16.59 '98, 3000m 9:34.68 '00, 5000m 15:22.46 '03, HMar 68:59 '09, 30km 1:39:35 '08.
Seven marathon wins. Four sub 2:30 runs in 2005 (first woman to do so in one year), won Seoul in pb 2:23:24 and improved by 2:13 for 2nd in Beijing. Won Seoul 2006, London 2007.

ZHU Xiaolin b. 20 Feb 1984 Xiuyan, Liaoning Prov. 1.66m 50kg. Liaoning.
At Mar: OG: '08- 4, '10- 6; WCh: '07- 4, '09- 5, '11- 6; AsiG: '10- 2. Won Chinese 1500m 2006, Mar & CC 2007.
Progress at Mar: 2002- 2:23:57, 2004- 2:41:04, 2005- 2:32:27, 2006- 2:28:27, 2007- 2:26:08, 2008- 2:27:16, 2009- 2:26:08, 2010- 2:26:35, 2011- 2:26:28, 2012- 2:24:19. pbs: 800m 2:18.51 '06, 1500m 4:12.73 '05, 3000m 9:04.64i '02, 5000m 15:22.35 '05, 10,000m 31:53.96 '08, HMar 70:07 '10.
Marathon wins: Dalian 2002, 2005-06; Xiamen 2007.

COLOMBIA

Governing body: Federación Colombiana de Atletismo, Calle 27° No. 25-18, Apartado Aéreo 6024, Santafé de Bogotá. Founded 1937.
National Games Champions 2012: Men: 100m: Isidro Montoya 10.72, 200m: Daniel Grueso 21.08, 400m/800m: Rafith Rodríguez 46.38/1:47.34, 1500m: Iván Darío González 3:43.6, 5000m: José Mauricio González 14:05.61, 10,000m: William Naranjo 29:48.8, Mar: Juan Carlos Cardona 2:25:36, 3000mSt: Gerald Giraldo 8:52.36, 110mh/400mh: Paul César Villar 13.93/50.52, HJ: Wanner Miller 2.20, PV: Víctor Hugo Medina 5.00, LJ: Edwin Murillo 7.50, TJ: Jhon Freddy Murillo 16.37, SP: Eder Moreno 19.53, DT: Mauricio Ortega 55.00, HT: Jacobo de León 61.43, JT: Dayron Márquez 76.91, Dec: José Gregorio Lemus 7097, 20kW: Eider Arévalo 1:25:00, 50kW: Ferney Rojas 4:06:24.
Women: 100m: Eliecet Palacios 11.92, 200m: Merlin Palacios 23.93, 400m: Yenifer Padilla 53.78, 800m/1500m: Rosibel García 2:02.33/ 4:17.60, 5000m/10,000m: Carolina Tabares 16:29.69/34:37.62, Mar: Erika Abril 2:53:15, 3000mSt: Ángela Figueroa 10:39.83, 100mh: Lina Florez 12.95, 400mh: Yadira Moreno 59.20, HJ/LJ/TJ: Caterine Ibargüen 1.74/6.69/14.00, PV: Milena Agudelo 3.80, SP: Sandra Lemus 16.94, DT: Johana Martínez 52.84, HT: Johana Moreno 64.65, JT: Flor Denis Ruiz 56.28, Hep: Sandra Milena Denis 4785, 20kW: Lorena Arenas 1:36:33.

Luis Fernando LÓPEZ b. 3 Jun 1979 Pasto, Nariño 1.73m 60kg.
At 20kW: OG: '04- 24, '08- 9, '12- dq; WCh: '05-07-09-11: 12/22/5/3; PAm: '03-07-11: 4/dq/3; SACh: '08/09- 1; CAG: '06- 1; WCp: '10- 4. Won PAm Cup 2011.
Walk records: S.Am. 20,000m (1:20:53.6) 2009 and 10km 2010; Colombian 20km walk 2009.

Progress at 20kW: 2001- 1:26:31A, 2002- 1:26:47.6t, 2003- 1:25:09, 2004- 1:22:52, 2005- 1:20:26, 2006- 1:24:11, 2007- 1:24:22.7tA, 2008- 1:20:59, 2009- 1:20:03, 2010- 1:21:12, 2011- 1:20:38, 2012- 1:23:41. pb 10kW Rd 38:10 '10.
Won Colombia's first ever medal at the World Championships in 2011.

Women

Caterine IBARGÜEN b. 12 Feb 1984 Apartadó, Antioquia 1.81m 65kg. Studying nursing.
At TJ/(LJ): OG: '12- 2; WCh: '11- 3; WJ: '02: dnq 17; PAm: '11- 1/3; SACh: '03- 3/2, '05- 3/3, '06- 2/2, '07- (3), '09- 1, '11- 1/3; CAG: '02- 2, '06- (2), '10- 2. At HJ: OG: '04- dnq 28=; WCh: '09- dnq 28=; PAm: '07- 4; SACh: '99-05-06-07-09: 3/1/1/1/1; CAG: '02- 2, '06- 2. Won COL HJ 1999, 2001-03, 2005-12; LJ 2003-04, 2006-08, 2011-12; TJ 2002-05, 2007-12.
Records: South American triple jump (6) 2011, junior HJ 2004. Colombia HJ (7) 2002-05, LJ (7) 2004-11, TJ (14) 2004-11
Progress at TJ: 2001- 12.90, 2002- 13.38A, 2003- 13.23A, 2004- 13.64A, 2005- 13.66A, 2006- 13.91A/13.98Aw, 2007- 12.66A, 2008- 13.79A, 2009- 13.96A/13.93, 2010- 14.29, 2011- 14.99A/14.84, 2012- 14.95A/14.85. pbs: 200m 25.34 '08, 100mh 14.09 '11, HJ 1.93A '05, LJ 6.73A/6.87Aw/6.63/6.66w '12, SP 13.79 '10, JT 44.81 '09, Hep 5742 '09.
First Colombian woman to win a medal in world champs. She lives in Puerto Rico.

COSTA RICA

Governing body: Federación Costarricense de Atletismo, 1032-1007 San José. Founded 1960.

Nery BRENES b. 25 Sep 1985 Limón 1.74m 62kg. Student of political science.
At 400m: OG: '08- sf, '12- h; WCh: '05- h, '07/11- sf; PAm: '11- 1; CAG: '10- 1; WI: '08-10-12: 4/4/1; CCp: '10- 1R. Won IbAm 2010, C.Am 2011.
Six CRC 400m records 2005-11, 200m 2009.
Progress at 400m: 2004- 47.90A, 2005- 46.42, 2006- 47.57, 2007- 45.01, 2008- 44.94, 2009- 45.73A/45.92, 2010- 44.84, 2011- 44.65A/45.29, 2012- 45.11i/45.20. pb 200m 20.62 '12, 20.3 '08.
Improved pb by 0.99 to win his heat at 2007 World Champs. Won Costa Rica's first ever athletics gold medals at Pan-American Games in 2011 and World Indoors in 2012.

CROATIA

Governing body: Hrvatski Atletski Savez, Trg kralja Petra Svacica 17, 10000 Zagreb. Founded 1912.
National Champions 2012 Men: 100m: Goran Pekic 10.69, 200m: Hrvoje Udiljak 21.83, 400m: Mateo Rzjic 47.92, 800m: Jure Bozinovic 1:52.36, 1500m: Ante Pokrajcic 4:03.13, 3000m/5000m: Dino Bosnjak 8:29.73/15:07.96, 10,000m: Goran Grdenic 31:59.72, Mar: Goran Muric 2:45:43, 3000mSt: Zoran Zilic 9:42.99, 110mh: Andi Erega 15.18, 400mh: Milan Kotur 53.29, HJ: Tomislav Popek 2.05, PV: Ivan Horvat 5.40, LJ/TJ: Sanjin Simic 7.36/14.90, SP: Marin Premeru 20.45, DT: Martin Maric 64.28, HT: Andras Haklits 70.36, JT: Roko Zemunik 64.36, Dec: Daniel Bracko 4518, 20kmW: Zelimir Haubrih 1:55:58. **Women**: 100m: Sandra Parlov 12.01, 200m/400m: Anita Banovic 25.51/56.27, 800m: Vanja Perisic 2:07.86, 1500m: Sanda Kocis 4:49.80, 3000m/ 5000m/ 10,000m: Matea Matosevic 9:39.30/ 16:51.92/ 34:29.11, Mar: Marija Vrajic 2:56:30, 3000mSt: Nikolina Hrelec 10:49.46, 100mh: Ivana Loncarek 13.63, 400mh: Nikolina Horvat 58.49, HJ: Lucija Zubcic 1.73, PV: Petra Malkoc 3.75, LJ: Mirjana Gagic 5.93, TJ: Marija Babic 12.20, SP: Valentina Muzaric 16.31, DT: Sandra Perkovic 66.94, HT: Petra Jakeljic 51.80, JT: Sara Kolak 51.10, Hep: Lucija Cvitanovic 5240, 10kmW: Ljiljana Culibrk 60:50.

Women

Sandra PERKOVIC b. 21 Jun 1990 Zagreb 1.83m 80kg. Zagreb.
At DT(/SP): OG: '12- 1; WCh: '09- 9; EC: '10- 1, '12- 1; WJ: '06- dnq 21, '08- 3/dnq 13; WY: '07- 2/ dnq 13; EJ: '07- 2, '09- 1/5; CCp: '10- 2. Won DL DT 2012; CRO SP 2008-10, DT 2010, 2012.
Seven Croatian DT records 2009-12, two SP 2010-11.
Progress at DT: 2006- 50.11, 2007- 55.42, 2008- 55.89, 2009- 62.79, 2010- 66.93, 2011- 67.96/69.99dq, 2012- 69.11. pb SP 16.99i/16.40 '11.
First woman to win European and Olympic gold for Croatia. Six months drugs ban 2011.

Blanka VLASIC b. 8 Nov 1983 Split 1.92m 75kg. ASK Split.
At HJ: OG: '00- dnq 17, '04- 11, '08- 2; WCh: '01-03-05-07-09-11: 6/7/dnq 19=/1/1/2; EC: '02- 5=, '06- 4, 10- 1; WJ: '00- 1, '02- 1; WY: '99- 8; EU23: '03- 1; EJ: '01- 7; WI: '03-04-06-08-10: 4/3/2/1/1; EI: '07- 4, '09- 5=; CCp: '10- 1. Won DL 2010, WAF 2007-09, DL 2011, MedG 2001, CRO 2001-02, 2005.
Ten Croatian high jump records 2003-09.
Progress at HJ: 1998- 1.68, 1999- 1.80, 2000- 1.93, 2001- 1.95, 2002- 1.96, 2003- 2.01, 2004- 2.03, 2005- 1.95, 2006- 2.05i/2.03, 2007- 2.07, 2008- 2.06, 2009- 2.08, 2010- 2.06i/2.05, 2011- 2.03.
IAAF Woman Athlete of the Year 2010. Won 5/6 Golden League HJs in both 2007 and 2008. She has had 101 competitions at 2m or higher to the end of 2011 (and 169 jumps over 2m), including 42 successive Jul 2007- Feb 2009, but in 2008 lost on count-back both at Olympic Games (when she won first ever athletics medal for Croatia) and in the final Golden League meeting, thus losing her share of the Jackpot. She had 60 attempts at the world record 2007-10. Her father Josko set the Croatian decathlon record with 7659 (1983) and named his daughter after Casablanca, where he won Mediterranean Games title.

CUBA

Governing body: Federación Cubana de Atletismo, Calle 13 y C Vedado 601, Zona Postal 4, La Habana 10400. Founded 1922.

National Champions 2012: Men: 100m: Yadier Luis 10.44, 200m: Roberto Skyers 20.64, 400m: Williams Collazo 46.18, 800m: Jorge Félix Liranzo 1:51.79, 1500m: Andy González 3:47.70, 5000m: José Alberto Sánchez 14:47.38, 10,000m: Richer Pérez 31:05.4, Mar: Jorge Luis Suárez 2:23:19, 3000mSt:, 110mh: Dayron Capetillo 13.69, 400mh: Yosdany Marrero 51.54, HJ: Sergio Mestre 2.22, PV: Yankier Lara 5.20, LJ: Pedro Díaz 7.65, TJ: Ernesto Revé 17.13, SP: Carlos Véliz 20.50, DT: Jorge Fernández 64.14, HT: Roberto Janet 77.08, JT: Guillermo Martínez 82.72, Dec: Junior Díaz 7956, 20kW: Joel Vargas 1:25:59. **Women**: 100m/200m: Nelkys Casabona 11.43w/23.65, 400m: Diosmely Peña 54.26, 800m/1500m: Adriana Muñoz 2:08.10/4:26.51, 5000m: Milena Pérez 18:22.01, 10,000m: Dailín Belmonte 34:27.54, Mar: Yailén García 2:45:27, 100mh: Belkis Milanés 13.35, 400mh: Zurian Hechavarría 60.29, HJ: Lesyaní Mayor 1.79, PV: Yarisley Silva 4.40, LJ: Irisdaymi Herrera 6.35w, TJ: Dailenys Alcántara 14.41, SP: Misleydis González 18.51, DT: Yarelys Barrios 68.03, HT: Yipsi Moreno 73.50, JT: Yanet Cruz 62.75, Hep: Yasmiany Pedroso 5849.

Yoandris BETANZOS b. 15 Feb 1982 Ciego de Ávila 1.80m 81kg
At TJ: OG: '04- 4, '12- dnq 23; WCh: '03- 2, '05- 2, '07/09- dnq 20/17, '11- 11; WJ: '00- 2; WY: '99- 2; PAm: '03- 1, '07- 3, '11- 2 (1 4x400m); CAG: '06- 1; WUG: '01- 5; WI: '04-06-10: 3/3/2; Won WAF 2005-06, CAC 2005, PAm-J 2001, CUB 2002-06.
Progress at TJ: 1998- 14.96, 1999- 15.94/16.07w, 2000- 16.82, 2001- 16.84/16.86w, 2002- 17.29, 2003- 17.28, 2004- 17.53, 2005- 17.46, 2006- 17.63/17.67w, 2007- 17.12i/16.96/17.21w, 2008- 17.11i/17.03/17.23w, 2009- 17.65, 2010- 17.69i/17.22, 2011- 17.23A/17.18, 2012- 16.87. pbs: HJ 2.10, LJ 7.51i '11.

Lázaro BORGES b. 19 Jun 1986 La Habana 1.73m 70kg.
At TJ: OG: '08/12- dnq nh/16=; WCh: '11- 2; WI: '12- 5=; PAm: '07- nh, '11- 1; Won IbAm 2010, CAC 2008, Cuban 2005-07, 2009-10, 2013.
Pole vault records: two CAC 2011, 7 Cuban 2011, CAC indoor 2012.
Progress at TJ: 2002- 3.60, 2003- 4.25, 2004- 4.80, 2005- 5.10, 2006- 5.30, 2007- 5.50, 2008- 5.70, 2009- 5.65, 2010- 5.60, 2011- 5.90, 2012- 5.72i/5.60.
Breakthrough season in 2011. when he improved national record by 25 centimetres from six occasions, and became first Cuban ever to medal at PV in a World Championship, and first ever PV Cuban male gold at Pan-American Games.

Omar CISNEROS b. 19 Nov 1989 Camagüey 1.86m 80kg.
At 400mh: OG: '12- sf; WCh: '09/11- sf; PAmG: '11- 1/1R. Won IbAm 2010, Cuban 2009-10, 2013.
At 400m: PAm: '07- sf.
Three Cuban 400mh records 2010-11.
Progress at 400mh: 2007- 49.57, 2008- 50.1, 2009- 48.87, 2010- 48.21, 2011- 47.99A/49.26, 2012- 48.23. pbs: 200m 21.36 '07, 400m 45.47 '12.

Alexis COPELLO b. 12 Aug 1985 Santiago de Cuba 1.85m 80kg.
At TJ: OG: '08- dnq 13, '12- 8; WCh: '09- 3, '11- 4; WI: '12- 7; PAmG: '11- 1; CAG: '06- 2; CCp: '10- 2. Won IbAm 2010, CAC 2009, Cuban 2009, 2011.
Progress at TJ: 2002- 15.38, 2003- 16.34, 2004- 16.90, 2005- 16.95/17.09w, 2006- 17.38, 2007- 16.87/17.15w, 2008- 17.50, 2009- 17.65/17.69w, 2010- 17.55, 2011- 17.68A/17.47, 2012- 17.17. pb LJ 7.35 '04.
Elder brother Alexander decathlon pb 7359 '02.

Jorge FERNÁNDEZ b. 2 Dec 1987 Matanzas 1.90m 100kg. MTZ.
At DT: OG: '08- dnq 27, '12- 11; WCh: '11- 8; PAmG: '11- 1; WJ: '06- 5. Won CAC 2008-09, Cuban 2009-13.
Progress at DT: 2005- 53.69, 2006- 54.77, 2007- 57.57, 2008- 63.31, 2009- 63.92, 2010- 66.00, 2011- 65.89, 2012- 66.05. pb SP 16.93 '12.

Yordani GARCÍA b. 21 Nov 1988 San Luis, Pinar del Río 1.93m 88kg.
At Dec: OG: '08- 15, '12- 14; WCh: '07- 8, '09- 8, '11- dnf; PAm: '07- 2, '11- 3; WJ: '06- 2. At Oct: WY: '05- 1. At Hep: WI: '12- 7. Won Cuban Dec 2006-07, 2010; PV 2011.
Cuban & CAC junior decathlon record 2007. World youth octathlon record (6482) 2005.
Progress at Dec: 2005- 6765, 2006- 7879h, 2007- 8257, 2008- 7992, 2009- 8496, 2010- 8381h, 2011- 8397, 2012- 8061. pbs: 60m 6.89i '09, 100m 10.60 '09, 10.5dt '10, 400m 48.34 '09, 1000m 2:50.21i '12, 1500m 4:31.40 '11, 60mh 7.80i '10, 110mh 13.89 '09, HJ 2.10 '09, PV 4.90 '10, LJ 7.36 '09, SP 16.50 '09, DT 47.70 '08, JT 69.37 '09, Hep 5905i '09.

Arnie David GIRAT b. 26 Aug 1984 Santiago de Cuba 1.82m 72kg.
At TJ: OG: '04- dnq 17, '08- 4, '12- dnq 16; WCh: '03-05-07-09-11: 4/8/7/5/dnq 13; WJ: '02- 1, WY: '01- 2; WI: '08- 2. '10- 3. Won PAm-J 2003 (2 LJ), Ib-Am 2004, WAF 2009, Cuban 2010.
Progress at TJ: 2000- 15.23, 2001- 16.33, 2002- 16.84, 2003- 17.31, 2004- 17.12, 2005- 17.14, 2006- 16.97/17.06w, 2007- 17.39i/17.10/17.18w, 2008- 17.52, 2009- 17.62, 2010- 17.49, 2011- 17.29/17.42w, 2012- 17.17/17.34w. pb LJ 7.70 '02.
Father (also David, who preferred spelling Giralt, b. 26 Jun 1955) had LJ pbs 8.22/8.32w, was 3rd in the World Cup and 2nd at Pan-American Games in 1979. Younger sister **Suslaidy** (b. 19 Aug 1987) has LJ pb 6.61 '11 despite being a deaf-mute.

Guillermo MARTÍNEZ b. 28 Jun 1981 Camagüey 1.85m 100kg.
At JT: OG: '12- dnq 16; WCh: '05-07-09-11: 10/9/2/3; PAm: '07- 1, '11- 1; CAG: '06- 1. Won CAC 2009, 2011; IbAm 2010, Cuban 2004-07, 2009-13.
Cuban & CAC javelin records 2006 & 2011.
Progress at JT: 1999- 64.66, 2000- 70.82, 2001- 73.50, 2002- 75.90, 2003- 75.35, 2004- 81.45, 2005- 84.06, 2006- 87.17, 2007- 85.93, 2009- 86.41, 2010- 86.38, 2011- 87.20A, 2012- 82.72, 2013- 85.59.

Orlando ORTEGA b. 29 Jul 1991 La Habana 1.85m 70kg.
At 110mh: OG: '12- 6; WJ: '10- h; PAm: '11- 3. Cuban champion 2011.
Progress at 110mh: 2009- 14.11, 2010- 13.99, 2011- 13.29/13.1w, 2012- 13.09. pbs: 100m 10.62 '11, 400m 47.84 '09, 50mh 6.66+i '12, 60mh 7.54i '13.

Ernesto REVÉ b. 26 Feb 1992 Guantánamo 1.81m 65kg.
At TJ: WJ: '10- 2. Cuban champion 2012-13.
CAC junior triple jump record 2011.
Progress at TJ: 2006- 14.97, 2007- 15.22, 2008- 16.32, 2009- 16.56, 2010- 16.73, 2011- 17.40, 2012- 17.13, 2013- 17.46. pb LJ 7.00 '03.

Dayron ROBLES b. 19 Nov 1986 Guantánamo 1.91m 91kg.
At 110mh: OG: '08- 1, '12- dq; WCh: '05-07-09-11: sf/4/sf/dq(1); WJ: '04- 2, WY: '03- 6; CAG: '06- 1; PAm: '07- 1, '11- 1; WCp: '06- 3; won PAm-J 2005, WAF 2007, CAC 2009, Cuban 2006-07, DL 2011.
At 60mh: WI: '06- 2, '10- 1.
World 110mh record 2008, three Cuban & CAC 2006-08, CAC junior record 2005. Two CAC 60mh indoor records 2008.
Progress at 110mh: 2002- 15.01, 2003- 14.30, 2004- 13.75, 2005- 13.46/13.2/13.41w, 2006- 13.00, 2007- 12.92, 2008- 12.87, 2009- 13.04, 2010- 13.01, 2011- 13.00, 2012- 13.10. pbs: 100m 10.70 '06, 200m 21.85 '06, 50mh 6.39i '08, 60mh 7.33i '08.
Season's record 7 sub-13 second times in 2008. Disqualified for obstructing Liu Xiang after finishing first at 2011 Worlds. Pulled muscle in 2012 Olympic final.

Leonel SUÁREZ b. 1 Sep 1987 Holguín 1.81m 76kg.
At Dec: OG: '08- 3, '12- 3; WCh: '09- 2, '11- 3; PAm: '07- 4, '11- 1. CAC and Cuban champion 2009. At Hep: WI: '10- 7.
CAC decathlon record 2009, four Cuban records 2008-09.
Progress at Dec: 2005- 7267, 2006- 7357, 2007- 8156, 2008- 8527, 2009- 8654, 2010- 8328, 2011- 8501, 2012- 8523. pbs: 60m 7.11i '09, 100m 10.90 '08, 10.6w '06; 400m 47.65 '09, 1000m 2:36.12i '10, 1500m 4:16.70 '08, 60mh 7.90i '10, 110mh 14.12 '08, HJ 2.17 '08, PV 5.00 '09, LJ 7.52 '11, SP 15.20 '09, DT 47.32 '11, JT 77.47 '09, Hep 5964i '10.
Won at Talence 2010. Won IAAF Combined Events Challenge 2011.

Women

Yarelys BARRIOS b. 12 Jul 1983 Pinar del Río 1.72m 98kg.
At DT: OG: '08- 2, '12- 4; WCh: '07- 2, '09- 2, '11- 3; WJ: '02- 7; PAm: '07- 1, '11- 1; CAG: '06- 2; WUG: '07- 1; CCp: '10- 3. Won DL 2010-11, WAF 2008-09, CAC 2005, 2008-09; Cuban 2009-12.
Progress at DT: 1999- 44.45, 2000- 50.22, 2001- 48.92, 2002- 54.10, 2003- 58.37, 2004- 59.51, 2005- 60.61, 2006- 61.01, 2007- 63.90/66.68ex, 2008- 66.13, 2009- 65.86, 2010- 65.96, 2011- 66.40A, 2012- 68.03.

Mabel GAY b. 5 May 1983 Santiago de Cuba 1.85m 69kg.
At TJ: OG: '08- dnq 15; WCh: '03-05-09-11: 5/dnq 18/2/4; WJ: '02- 1; WY: '99- 1; PAm: '03-07-11: 1/3/3; PAm-J: '01- 1; CAG: '06- 1; WI: '04-10-12: 9/5/3; Won WAF 2009. CAC 2008, CAC-J 2002, IbAm 2002, Cuban 2003-04, 2006, 2013.
CAC junior TJ record 2002.
Progress at TJ: 1997- 13.00, 1998- 13.48, 1999- 13.82, 2000- 14.02, 2001- 14.05, 2002- 14.29, 2003- 14.52, 2004- 14.57i/14.20, 2005- 14.21/14.44w, 2006- 14.27, 2007- 14.66, 2008- 14.41A/14.39, 2009-14.64, 2010- 14.30i/14.06, 2011- 14.67, 2012- 14.40. pb LJ 6.28 '09.
World age 17 record in 1999.

Misleydis GONZÁLEZ b. 19 Jun 1978 Bayamo, Granma 1.78m 85kg.
At SP: OG: '04- 7, '08- 4, '12- dnq 20; WCh: '05-07-09-11: 10/11/8/dnq 16; PAm: '03-07-11: 1/4/1/1; CAG: '06- 2; WI: '04-08-10: 6/4/7; WUG: '05- 3; CCp: '10- 4 won CAC 2001, 2003, 2009; IbAm 2010, Cuban 2007, 2010-12.
Progress at SP: 1994- 12.41, 1995- 14.48, 1996- 15.80, 1997- 15.87, 1998- 15.76, 1999- 16.19, 2000- 17.55, 2001- 17.54, 2002- 17.79, 2003- 18.11, 2004- 18.73, 2005- 18.92, 2006- 19.10, 2007- 18.97, 2008- 19.50, 2009- 19.13, 2010- 19.22, 2011- 19.04, 2012- 18.62.

Yipsi MORENO b. 19 Nov 1980 Camagüey 1.71m 81kg.
At HT: OG: '00- 4, '04- 2, '08- 2, '12- 6; WCh: '99-01-03-05-07-11: 18/1/1/2/2/4; WJ: '98- 4; PAm: '99-03-07-11: 2/1/1/1; CAG: '06- 1; WUG: '01- 2; WCp: '02-06-10: 2/3/3. Won WAF 2003, 2005, 2007-08, PAm-J 1997, IbAm 2004, Cuban 2000-04, 2007, 2012-13.
World junior hammer record 1999, 22 CAC records 1999-2008.
Progress at HT: 1996- 53.94, 1997- 61.96, 1998- 61.00, 1999- 66.34, 2000- 69.36, 2001- 70.65, 2002- 71.47, 2003- 75.14, 2004- 75.18, 2005- 74.95, 2006- 74.69, 2007- 76.36, 2008- 76.62, 2010- 75.19, 2011- 75.62, 2012- 75.59.
Married to hammer thrower Abdel Murguía (pb 61.73 '02). Their son (Abdel Murguía Moreno) born in August 2009.

Yargeris SAVIGNE b. 13 Nov 1984 Niceto Pérez, Guantánamo 1.68m 59kg.

At (LJ)/TJ: OG: '08- dnq 17/5, '12- 9; WCh: '05-4/2, '07- 1, '09- 1, '11- 6; WJ: '02- (dnq); PAm: '03- (3), '07- 3/1, '11- 2; WI: '06- 6/5, '08- 1, '10- 2, '12- 4; CCp: '10- 2/3 Won DL 2010, WAF 2007, CAC TJ 2005, 2009 (LJ 2005,); IbAm 2010, Cuban TJ 2007, 2009, 2011 (LJ 2006-07).
Records: three Cuban TJ 2005-07, two CAC indoor 2008.
Progress at LJ, TJ: 1998- 12.13, 1999- 5.60, 12.65; 2000- 5.92, 12.70; 2001- 6.24, 13.03; 2002- 6.46, 2003- 6.63, 2004- 6.60A/6.52, 2005- 6.77/6.88w, 14.82; 2006- 6.67/6.81w, 14.91; 2007-6.79i/6.66/6.81w, 15.28; 2008- 6.77i/6.49, 15.20; 2009- 6.77, 15.00; 2010- 6.91, 15.09; 2011- 14.99, 2012- 6.30, 14.55i/14.35.

Yarisley SILVA b. 1 Jul 1987 Pinar del Rio 1.69m 68kg.
At TJ: OG: '08- dnq 27=, '12- 2; WCh: '11- 5; WI: '12- 7; WJ: '06- dnq; PAm: '07- 3, '11- 1; Won CAC 2009, Cuban 2004, 2006-07, 2009, 2012-13.
Pole vault records: 16 Cuban & CAC 2007-13 (9 in 2011), 7 CAC indoor 2012 & 2013 (4.78).
Progress at TJ: 2001- 2.50, 2002- 3.10, 2003- 3.70, 2004- 4.00, 2005- 4.10, 2006- 4.20, 2007- 4.30, 2008- 4.50, 2009- 4.50, 2010- 4.40, 2011-4.75A/4.70, 2012- 4.75, 2013- 4.81.

CYPRUS

Governing body: Amateur Athletic Association of Cyprus, Olympic House, 2025 Strovolos, Nicosia. Founded 1983. **National Champions 2012: Men**: 100m/200m: Panayiotis Ioannou 10.4/21.71, 800m: Kyriakos Antoniou 48.14, 800m/1500m: Christos Demetriou 1:53.66/3:54.15, 5000m/3000mSt: Charalambos Charal–ambous 15:38.51/9:38.78, 10,000m/HMar: Fivos Constantinou 32:47.57/73:37, Mar: Michael Keenan 2:41:20, 110mh: Milan Trajkovic 14.09, 400mh: Aris Xoufarides 52.59, HJ: Kyriakos Ioannou 2.30, PV: Nicandros Stylianou 4.90, LJ/TJ: Zacharias Arnos 7.52/16.10, SP: Georgios Arestis 18.83, DT: Apostolos Parellis 63.66, HT: Constantinos Stathelakos 71.89, JT: Ioannis Stephanou 61.34, Dec: Elvis Kryukov 6715. **Women**: 100m/200m: Eleni Artymata 11.54/23.18, 400m: Kalliopi Kountouri 58.01, 800m/1500m: Natalia Evangelidou 2:07.79/4:27.24, 5000m: Marilena Sophocleous 16:58.33, HMar/Mar: Panayiota Andreou 1:28:13/3:27:49, 3000mSt: Chrystalla Hadjipolydorou 11:35.23, 100mh: Polyxeni Herodotou 14.26, 400mh: Elena Stefanou 64.32, HJ: Leontia Kallenou 1.75, PV: Anna Fitidou 3.70, LJ: Nectaria Panayi 6.32, TJ: Nina Serbezova BUL 13.85, SP: Florentia Kappa 15.81, DT: Androniki Lada 51.52, HT: Paraskevi Theodorou 63.16, JT: Eleni Mavroude 48.99, , Hep: Rafaella Ioannou 4417

Kyriakos IOANNOU b. 26 Jul 1984 Limassol 1.93m 66kg. GS Olympia Limassol. Student of PE at University of Athens.
At HJ: OG: '04/08- dnq 18=/18, '12- 13; WCh:

'05- 10, '07- 3, '09- 2; CG: '06- 3; WJ: '02- dnq; WY: '01- dnq; EJ: '03- 6=; EU23: '05- 4; WI: '08- 3=, '10- 4; EI: '09- 2=; WUG: '07- 2. Won Med G 2005, 2009; Greek 2005, 2007, CYP 2004-05, 2009-12; EUR Small States 2005, 2009.
Nine Cyprus high jump records 2004-07.
Progress at HJ: 2001- 2.00, 2002- 2.15, 2003- 2.17, 2004- 2.28, 2005- 2.27, 2006- 2.30i/2.23, 2007-2.35, 2008- 2.32i/2.27, 2009- 2.32, 2010- 2.30, 2011- 2.33, 2012- 2.30.
First athlete from Cyprus to win a medal at Olympics or World Championships.

CZECH REPUBLIC

Governing body: Cesky atleticky svaz, Diskarská 100, 16900 Praha 6 -Strahov, PO Box 40. AAU of Bohemia founded in 1897.
National Championships first held in 1907 (Bohemia), 1919 (Czechoslovakia), 1993 CZE.
2012 Champions: **Men**: 100m: Lukás Milo 10.39, 200m: Pavel Maslák 20.60, 400m: Daniel Nemecek 46.36, 800m: Miroslav Burian 1:52.06, 1500m: Lukás Kourek 3:51.83, 5000m/Mar: Jan Kreisinger 14:28.41/2:16:26, 10,000m/3000mSt: Milan Kocourek 29:33.56/9:04.13, HMar: Vít Pavlista 67:05, 110mh: Petr Penáz 13.87, 400mh: Václav Barák 50.04, HJ: Jaroslav Bába 2.20, PV: Jan Kudlicka 5.45, LJ: Roman Novotny 8.05, TJ: Martin Vachata 15.46, SP: Ladislav Prásil 19.79, DT: Igor Gondor 59.51, HT: Lukas Melich 78.22, JT: Vitezslav Vesely 81.15, Dec: Marek Lukás 7448, 20kW: Karel Ketner 1:28:12, 50kW: Lukás Gdula 4:14:56. **Women**: 100m/200m: Katerina Cechová 11.32/23.45, 400m: Jitka Bartonicková 52.72, 800m: Sylva Skabrahová 2:08.29, 1500m: Tereza Capková 4:12.49, 5000m: Kvetoslava Pecková 16:51.86, 10,000m: Ivana Sekyrová 35:12.47; HMar/Mar: Petra Pastorová 78:18/2:39:42, 3000mSt: Michaela Drábková 10:42.72, 100mh: Lucie Skrobáková 13.40, 400mh: Denisa Rosolová 54.38, HJ: Romana Dubnova 1.82, PV: Monika Chlebíková 3.65, LJ: Eliska Klucinová 6.17, TJ: Lucie Májková 13.60, SP: Jana Kárníková 16.13, DT: Eliska Stanková 56.19, HT: Tereza Králová 68.19, JT: Barbora Spotáková 64.40, Hep: Markéta Malariková 5352, 20kW: Lucie Pelantová 1:34:36.

Jaroslav BÁBA b. 2 Sep 1984 Karviná 1.96m 82kg. Dukla Praha.
At HJ: OG: '04- 3, '08- 6, '12- dnq 21=; WCh: '03-05-07-09: 11/5=/8/5=; EC: '10- 5, '12- 8=; WJ: '02- 8; WY: '01- 10=; EU23: '05- 1; EJ: '03- 1; WI: '03-04-08: 9/3=/9; EI: '05-11-13: 4/2/3; ET: '09- 2, '11- 3=. Won CZE 2003, 2005, 2009-12.
Czech high jump record 2005.
Progress at HJ: 1997- 1.72i, 1998- 1.81i/1.75, 1999- 1.93i/1.92, 2000- 1.95, 2001- 2.16i/2.15, 2002- 2.27/2.28et, 2003- 2.32i/2.30, 2004- 2.34, 2005- 2.37i/2.36, 2006- 2.28i, 2007- 2.29, 2008-2.30i/2.29, 2009- 2.33, 2010- 2.28, 2011- 2.34i/2.32, 2012- 2.31i/2.28, 2013- 2.13i. pb TJ 15.43 '03.

Jan KUDLICKA b. 29 Apr 1988 Opava 1.83m 76kg. Dukla Praha.
At PV: OG: '08- 10, '12- 8; WCh: '09: dnq 23=, '11- 9; EC: '10- 10, '12- 6; WJ: '06- 5; WY: '05- 6; EU23: '09- 8; EI: '13- 5; Won CZE 2008, 2010-12.
Progress at PV: 2003- 4.21, 2004- 4.80, 2005- 5.09, 2006- 5.30, 2007- 5.61/5.62ex, 2008- 5.70, 2009- 5.62, 2010- 5.65, 2011- 5.81, 2012- 5.73, 2013- 5.77i. pbs: 60m 7.11i '07, HJ 2.05i/2.03 '07, LJ 7.55 '07, TJ 14.41 '07.

Pavel MASLÁK b. 21 Feb 1991 Havírov 1.76m 67kg. Dukla Praha.
At 400m: OG: '08- 10, '12- 8; EC: '12- 1; WY: '07- h; WI: '12- 5; EI: '13- 1/3R. At 200m: WJ: '10- 7; EU23: '11- 3; EJ: '09- 5. At 100m: WJ: '08- h. Won CZE 200m 2012, 400m 2011.
Czech records: 200m (2), 400m (3) 2012.
Progress at 400m: 2007- 48.30, 2008- 47.60, 2009- 47.44, 2010- 46.89, 2011- 47.43, 2012- 44.91. pbs: 60m 6.76i '10, 100m 10.43 '11, 200m 20.59 '12, 300m 32.35 '12, 500m 1:01.98 '12.
Won European Athletics Rising Star Award 2012.

Lukás MELICH b. 16 Sep 1980 Jilemnice, Liberecky kraj 1.86m 110kg. Dukla Praha.
At HT: OG: '12- sf; WCh: '05-09: dnq 14/14; WJ: '98- 10; EC: '06/12: dnq 16/28; EU23: '01- 11; EJ: '99- 5. CZE champion 2003, 2006-10, 2012.
Progress at HT: 1996- 52.02, 1997- 59.90, 1998- 64.64, 1999- 68.73, 2000- 69.08, 2001- 71.47, 2002- 70.82, 2003- 76.38, 2004- 76.22, 2005- 79.36, 2006- 77.91, 2007- 74.74, 2008- 76.97, 2009- 78.91, 2010- 73.24, 2011- 75.40, 2012- 79.44. pbs: DT 51.56 '03, Wt 24.75 '06.

Roman SEBRLE b. 26 Nov 1974 Lanskroun 1.86m 88kg. Dukla Praha. Soldier.
At Dec: OG: '00- 2, '04- 1, '08- 6. '12- dnf; WCh: '97-99-01-03-05-07-09-11: 9/dnf/10/2/2/1/11/14; EC: '98-02-06-12: 6/1/1/6; WUG: '97- 1; ECp: '97-8-9: 1/2/2. At Hep: WI: '99-01-03-04-06-08-10: 3/1/3/1/3/dnf/5; EI: '00-02-05-07-09-11: 2/1/1/1/3/3. At 110mh: ECp: '99- 6. At LJ: ECp: '05- 7. Won Czech Dec 1996, LJ 1998.
World decathlon record 2001, European indoor heptathlon record 2004.
Progress at Dec: 1991- 5187, 1992- 6541, 1993- 7066, 1994- 7153, 1995- 7642, 1996- 8210, 1997- 8380, 1998- 8589, 1999- 8527, 2000- 8757, 2001- 9026, 2002- 8800, 2003- 8807, 2004- 8893, 2005- 8534, 2006- 8526, 2007- 8697, 2008- 8241, 2009- 8348, 2010- dnf, 2011- 8109, 2012- 8097. pbs: 60m 6.87i '02, 100m 10.64 '01, 200m 21.74 '04, 400m 47.76 '09, 1000m 2:37.86i '01, 1500m 4:21.98 '01, 60mh 7.84i '02, 110mh 13.79 '99, 13.68w '01; HJ 2.15 '00, PV 5.20 '03, LJ 8.11 '01, SP 16.47 '07, DT 49.46 '09, JT 71.18 '07, Hep 6438i '04.
Married Eva Kasalová (b. 4 Dec 1976, pb 800m 2:02.79 '98), on 14 Oct 2000. At Götzis in 2001 he became the first decathlete to exceed 9000 points with the current scoring tables, setting five personal bests. Won again at Götzis 2002-

05 and at Talence in 2004-05, and he won IAAF Combined Events Challenge in 2002, 2004-05 and 2007. Has 21 decathlons over 8500 and 49 over 8000 (79 in all).

Vitezslav VESELY b. 27 Feb 1983 Hodonin 1.86m 92kg. Dukla Praha.
At JT: OG: '08- 12, '12- 4; WCh: '09- dnq 28, '11- 4; EC: '10- 9, '12- 1; WJ: '02- 9. Won DL 2012, CZE 2008, 2010-12.
Progress at JT: 2001- 66.18, 2002- 73.22, 2003- 66.95, 2004- 72.32, 2005- injured, 2006- 75.98, 2007- 79.45, 2008- 81.20, 2009- 80.35, 2010- 86.45, 2011- 84.11, 2012- 88.34.

Women

Zuzana HEJNOVÁ b. 19 Dec 1986 Liberec 1.70m 54kg. USK Praha.
At 400mh/4x400mR: OG: '08- 7, '12- 3; WCh: '05-07-09- sf, '11- 7; EC: '06- sf, '10- 4, 12- 4/3R; EU23: '07- 3; WJ: '02- 5, '04- 2; EJ: '03- 3, '05- 1; WY: '03- 1; WI: '10- 3R; ET: '09- 3, '11- 1. At 400m: EI: '13- 4/3R. At Pen: EI: '11- 7. Won CZE 400m 2006, 2009.
Nine Czech 400mh records 2005-11.
Progress at 400mh: 2002- 58.42, 2003- 57.54, 2004- 57.44, 2005- 55.89, 2006- 55.83, 2007- 55.04, 2008- 54.96, 2009- 54.90, 2010- 54.13, 2011- 53.29, 2012- 53.38. pbs: 200m 23.93 '12, 300m 37.49A '13, 400m 52.61 '09, 800m 2:07.99i '11, 60mh 8.25i '11, 100mh 13.36 '11, 13.18w '10; 300mh 38.91 '11 (world best), HJ 1.80i '11, 1.74 '04; LJ 5.96i '11, 5.76 '07, SP 12.11i '11, JT 36.11 '10, Pen 4453i '11.
Sister of Michaela Hejnová (b. 10 Apr 1980) pb Hep 6174w/6065 '04; OG: '04- 26; EC '02- 7; EU23: '01- 5; WJ: '98- 5; EJ: '97- 6/'99- 6 (100mh); WUG: '01- 5, '03- 3.

Eliska KLUCINOVÁ b. 14 Apr 1988 Prague 1.77m 69kg. USK Praha.
At Hep: OG: '12- 18; WCh: '09- 23; EC: '10- 7, '12- 8; WJ: '06- 8; WY: '05- 8; EU23: '09- 4, EJ: '07- 2. Won CZE LJ 2012, Hep 2008-09.
CZE heptathlon records 2010 and 2012
Progress at Hep: 2004- 5006, 2005- 5074, 2006- 5468, 2007- 5844, 2008- 5728, 2009- 6015, 2010- 6268, 2012- 6283. pbs: 200m 24.56 '12, 800m 2:12.82 '10, 60mh 8.67i '13, 100mh 14.01 '12, HJ 1.85 '12, LJ 6.30 '10, SP 14.49i/14.48 '10, JT 50.75 '10, Pen 4291i '11.

Denisa ROSOLOVÁ b. 21 Aug 1986 Karvina 1.75m 63kg. née Scerbová. USK Praha.
At 400m/4x400mR: WCh: '11- sf; EC: '10- 5; WI: '10- 3R, '12- 6; EI: '11- 1, '13- 5/3R; ET: '11- 2. At 400mh: OG: '12- 7; EC: '12- 2/3R. At LJ: OG: '04/08- dnq 25/20; WCh: '07- dnq 13; WJ: '04- 1; WY: '01- 10, '03- 2; EJ: '03- 4, '05- 1; EI: '07- 3. At Hep: OG: '08- dnf; EC: '06- dnf. Won CZE LJ 2004, 2007-08; 200m 2008, 2010-11; 400mh 2012.
Progress at 400m, 400mh: 2001- 57.26, 2002- 55.55, 2004- 60.09H, 2007- 54.05i, 2008- 53.61i, 2009- 55.63i, 2010- 50.85, 2011- 50.84, 2012- 52.07, 54.24. pbs: 60m 7.44i '11, 100m 11.61/11.32w '10,

200m 23.03 '10, 300m 36.94i/37.09 '10, 800m 2:11.70 '08, 60mh 8.20i '08, 100mh 13.32 '08, HJ 1.80i/1.77 '06, LJ 6.68 '04, TJ 13.10 '05, SP 12.48 '08, JT 35.12 '07, Pen 4632i '06, Hep 6104 '08.
Divorced from husband tennis player Lukas Rosol, who achieved top fame in 2012 by beating Rafael Nadal at Wimbledon.

Barbora SPOTÁKOVÁ b. 30 Jun 1981 Jablonec nad Nisou 1.82m 80kg. Dukla Praha.
At JT: OG: '04- dnq 23, '08- 1, '12- 1; WCh: '05-07-09-11: dnq 13/1/2/2; EC: '02- dnq 17, '06- 2, '10- 3; EU23: '03- 6; WUG: '03- 4, '05- 1; ET: '09- 2, '11- 3; won DL 2010, 2012; WAF 2006-08, Czech 2003, 2005-12. At Hep: WJ: '00- 4.
World javelin record 2008, two European records 2008, 11 Czech records 2006-08. World heptathlon javelin best (60.90) in 2012.
Progress at JT: 1996- 31.32, 1997- 37.28, 1998- 44.56, new: 1999- 41.69, 2000- 54.15, 2001- 51.97, 2002- 56.76, 2003- 56.65, 2004- 60.95, 2005- 65.74, 2006- 66.21, 2007- 67.12, 2008- 72.28, 2009- 68.23, 2010- 68.66, 2011- 71.58, 2012- 69.55. pbs: 200m 25.33/25.11w '00, 800m 2:18.29 '00, 60mh 8.68i '07, 100mh 13.99 '00, 400mh 62.68 '98, HJ 1.78 '00, LJ 5.65 '00, SP 14.53 '07, DT 36.80 '02, Hep 5880 '12, Dec 6749 '04.
Expecting a baby in 2013.

Jirina SVOBODOVÁ b. 20 May 1986 Plzen 1.75m 69kg. née Ptácníková. PSK Olymp Praha.
At PV: OG: '12- 6=; WCh: '09- dnq 16=, '11- 7; EC: '06- dnq 27, '10- 5, '12- 1; WJ: '02/04- nh; EJ: '03- 6, '05- 4; WY: '03- 5; WUG: '09- 1; WI: '12- 6; EI: '11- 4=, '13- 4; ET: '09- 5, '11- 3. CZE champion 2009-11.
Progress at PV: 2001- 3.20, 2002- 4.00, 2003- 4.02, 2004- 4.11i/3.90, 2005- 4.15, 2006- 4.27, 2007- 4.22i/4.00, 2008- 4.28, 2009- 4.55, 2010- 4.66, 2011- 4.65, 2012- 4.72, 2013- 4.64i. pb LJ 5.85 '10, 5.95i '11.
Married Petr Svoboda (1 EI 60mh 2011, CZE 110mh record 13.27 '10) on 19 Sep 2012.

DENMARK

Governing body: Dansk Athletik Forbund, Idraettens Hus, Brøndby Stadion 20, DK-2605 Brøndby. Founded 1907.
National Championships first held in 1894.
2012 Champions: **Men**: 100m: Frederik Thomsen 10.63, 200m/400m: Nick Ekelund-Arenander 21.38/47.41, 800m: Andreas Bube 1:56.51, 1500m: Andreas Bueno 3:56.32, 5000m: Jakob Hannibal 14:30.33, 10,000m: Abdi Hakim Ulad 29:53.67, HMar: Henrik Them Andersen 64:55, Mar: Martin Parkhøj 2:24:49, 3000mSt: Ole Hesselbjerg 9:32.97, 110mh/400mh: Christian Laugesen 14.64/52.32, HJ: Charles Kamau 2.03, PV: Mikkel M. Nielsen 5.25, LJ: Morten Jensen 7.64, TJ: Anders Møller 16.00, SP: Kim Christensen 19.76, DT: Emil Mikkelsen 50.13, HT: Torben Wolf 61.98, JT: Gert Skals 59.93, Dec: *not held*, 50kW: Peer Jensen 5:32:52.

Women: 100m: Anna Olsson 12.16, 200m/400mh: Sara Petersen 24.18/57.87, 400m: Stina Troest 56.92, 800m: Dagmar Olsen 2:13.51, 1500m: Maria Larsen 4:50.41, 5000m/10,000m: Sara Sig Møller 16:36.39/35:25.62, HMar: Anna Holm Baumeister 76:29, Mar: Lene Hjelmsø 2:45:17, 3000mSt: Simone Glad 10:29.74, 100mh: Mathilde Heltbech 14.28, HJ: Sandra Christensen 1.70, PV: Caroline Bonde Holm 4.25, LJ/TJ: Jessie Ipsen 6.04/12.67, SP: Trine Mulbjerg 16.04, DT: Maria Sløk Hansen 50.10, HT: Meiken Greve 59.34, JT: Marie Vestergaard 48.70, Hep: Tine Bach Ejlersen 5507, 3000mW/5000mW: *none*.

DOMINICAN REPUBLIC

Governing body: Federación Dominicana de Asociaciones de Atletismo. Avenida J.F. Kennedy, Centro Olímpico "Juan Pablo Duarte". Santo Domingo. Founded 1953.

Félix SÁNCHEZ b. 30 Aug 1977 New York, USA 1.78m 73kg. Was at University of Southern California.
At 400mh: OG: '00- sf, '04- 1, '08- h; WCh: '99-01-03-05-07-09-11: ht/1/1/dnf/2/8/4; PAm: '99- 4, '03- 1/3R, '07- 4/3R, '11- 3; CAG: '02- 1R, '10- 4; WCp: '02- 1R. Won NCAA 2000, GWG 2001, GP 2002 (3rd overall), WAF 2003.
Three CAC 400mh records 2001-03. DOM records: 400mh (11) 1997-2003, 400m (3) 2001-02.
Progress at 400mh: 1995- 51.33, 1996- 51.19, 1997- 50.01, 1998- 51.30, 1999- 48.60, 2000- 48.33, 2001- 47.38, 2002- 47.35, 2003- 47.25, 2004- 47.63, 2005- 48.24, 2006- 49.10, 2007- 48.01, 2008- 51.10, 2009- 48.34, 2010- 48.17, 2011- 48.74, 2012- 47.63. pbs: 100m 10.45 '05, 200m 20.87 '01, 400m 44.90 '01, 800m 1:49.36 '04, 200mSt 22.94 '10.
Born in New York and raised in California, he first competed for the Dominican Republic, where his parents were born, in 1999 after 6th in US 400mh. He took a share of the Golden League jackpot in 2002 and won 43 successive 400mh races (including 7 heats) from loss to Dai Tamesue on 2 Jul 2001 until dnf in Brussels on 3 Sep 2004. Ran his fastest time for eight years to regain Olympic title in 2012, the same time (47.63) with which he had won in 2004.

Luguelín SANTOS b. 12 Nov 1993 Bayaguana 1.73m 61kg. Universidad Interamericana de San Germán, Puerto Rico.
At 400m: OG: '12- 2; WJ: '10- 6, '12- 1; PAm: '11- 2/2R; YthOG: '10- 1.
Three DOM 400m records 2011-12.
Progress at 400m: 2009- 47.88, 2010- 46.19, 2011- 44.71A, 2012- 44.45. pbs: 200m 20.73 '12, 300m 32.4+/32.56 '12.

ERITREA

Governing body: Eritrean National Athletics Federation, PO Box 1117, Asmara. F'd 1992.

Teklemariam MEDHIN Weldeselassie b. 24 Jun 1989 Hazega 1.78m 57kg.

At (5000m/)10,000m: OG: '08- 32,'12- 7; WCh: '09- 15/12; WJ: '06- (12). World CC: 2006-07-08-09-10-11-13: 13J/14J/23/9/2/14/3. African CC: '12- 2.
Progress at 5000m, 10,000m: 2006- 14:13.9, 2008- 13:48.18, 27:46.50; 2009- 13:11.01, 27:58.89; 2010- 13:04.55, 28:50.63A; 2011- 13:16.53, 27:37.21; 2012- 13:17.25, 27:16.69. pbs: 3000m 7:48.6+ '11, Road 10M 47:11 '09.

Zersenay TADESE b. 8 Feb 1982 Adi Bana 1.60m 56kg. C.A. Adidas. Madrid, Spain.
At (5000m)/10,000m: OG: '04- 7/3, '08- 5, '12- 6; WCh: '03- (8), '05- 14/6, '07- 4, '09- 2, '11- 4; AfCh: '02- 6, AfG: '07- 1. World CC: 2002-03-04-05-06-07-08-09: 30/9/6/2/4/1/3/3; 20k: '06- 1; HMar: '02-03-07-08-09-10-12: 21/7/1/1/1/2/1.
Records: World 20km and half marathon 2010. Eritrean 3000m (2), 2M, 5000m (4), 10,000m (5) HMar (3) 2003-10.
Progress at 5000m, 10,000m, HMar: 2002- 13:48.79, 28:47.29, 63:05; 2003- 13:05.57, 28:42.79, 61:26; 2004- 13:13.74, 27:22.57; 2005- 13:12.23, 27:04.70, 59:05; 2006- 12:59.27, 26:37.25, 59:16; 2007- 27:00.30, 58:59; 2008- 27:05.11, 59:56; 2009- 13:07.02, 26:50.12, 59:35; 2010- 58:23, 2011- 12:59.32, 26:51.09, 58:30; 2012- 27:33.51, 59:34. pbs: 3000m 7:39.93 '05, 2M 8:19.34 '07, Road: 15km 41:27 '05, 10M 45:52 '07, 20km 55:21+ '10, Mar 2:10:41 '12.
Won Eritrea's first medal at Olympics in 2004 and World CC in 2005 and first gold in the World 20k in 2006 before four more at half marathon. Ran 59:05 for the fastest ever half marathon to win the Great North Run (slightly downhill overall) in 2005. Won Lisbon half marathon 2010-11 in two fastest ever times. Won a national road cycling title in 2001 before taking up athletics. His younger brother **Kidane** (b. 31 Aug 1987) has pbs 5000m 13:11.85 '10, 10,000m 27:06.16 '08; at 5000m/(10,000m): OG: '08- 10/12, WCh: '09- h/9; World CC: '12- 6.

ESTONIA

Governing body: Eesti Kergejôustikuliit, Maakri 23, Tallinn 10145. Founded 1920.
National Championships first held in 1917.
2012 Champions: **Men**: 100m/200m: Marek Niit 10.28w/21.48, 400m: Rasmus Mägi 46.63, 800m: Nikolai Vedehin 1:49.53, 1500m: Tiidrek Nurme 3:44.16, 5000m/3000mSt: Allar Lamp 14:17.26/9:17.77, 10,000m: Taivo Püi 30:25.10, HMar/Mar: Viljar Vallimäe 64:59/2:21:27, 110mh: Rauno Kirschbaum 14.56, 400mh: Aarne Nirk 52.57, HJ: Karl Lumi 2.10, PV/Dec: Hendrik Lepik 5.00/7662, LJ: Kaarel Jöeväli 7.45, TJ: Jaanus Suvi 15.20, SP: Raigo Toompuu 19.15, DT: Gerd Kanter 65.02, HT: Martin Lehemets 66.34, JT: Risto Mätas 80.50, 20000mW/50kW: Margus Luik 1:40:36.45/4:33:13. **Women**: 100m: Maarja Kalev 12.05, 200m: Laura-Maria Oja 25.19, 400m: Dane Must 56.58, 800m/1500m: Liina Tsernov 2:11.66/4:32.32, 5000m/HMar/3000mSt: Jekaterina Patjuk 16:44.61/77:33/10:25.88, 10,000m/Mar: Evelin Talts 35:51.69/2:45:02, 100mh/LJ: Grit Sadeiko 13.82/6.18, 400mh: Laura Maasik 63.36, HJ: Eleriin Haas 1.85, PV: Lembi Vaher 4.01, TJ: Triin Erme 12.71, SP: Kätlin Piirimäe 14.81, DT: Anu Teesaar 51.49, HT: Kati Ojaloo 56.28, JT: Raine Kuningas 52.21, Hep: Mari Klaup 5658, 10,000mW/20kW: Maarika Taukul 51:48.02/1:49:58.

Gerd KANTER b. 6 May 1979 Tallinn 1.96m 125kg. Tallinna SS Kalev. Business management graduate.
At DT: OG: '04- dnq 19, '08- 1, '12- 3; WCh: '03-05-07-09-11: dnq 25/2/1/3/2; EC: '02-06-10-12: 12/2/4/2; EU23: '01- 5; WUG: '05- 1. Won WAF 2007-08, DL 2012, Estonian 2004-09, 2011-12.
Five Estonian discus records 2004-06.
Progress at DT: 1998- 47.37, 1999- 49.65, 2000- 57.68, 2001- 60.47, 2002- 66.31, 2003- 67.13, 2004- 68.50, 2005- 70.10, 2006- 73.38, 2007- 72.02, 2008- 71.88, 2009- 71.64, 2010- 71.45, 2011- 67.99, 2012- 68.03. pb SP 17.31i '04, 16.11 '00.
Threw over 70m in four rounds at Helsingborg on 4 Sep 2006; a feat matched only by Virgilijus Alekna. Six successive seasons over 70m.

Women

Ksenija BALTA b. 1 Nov 1986 Minsk, Belarus 1.68m 53kg. Tallinna SS Kalev.
At LJ: OG: '08- dnq 27; WCh: '09- 8; EC: '06- dnq 26 (h 100m), '10- dnq 16 (h 200m); WI: '10- 4; EI: '09- 1. At Hep: EJ: '05- 3; ECp: '06- 3. Won EST 100m 2006-08, 200m 2008, LJ 2008, 2010; Hep 2005.
EST records: 100m, 200m 2006, LJ (4) 2006-10.
Progress at LJ: 2003- 5.79, 2004- 6.01, 2005- 6.46i/6.32, 2006- 6.80, 2007- 6.55i, 2008- 6.65/6.76w, 2009- 6.87i/6.79/6.85w, 2010- 6.87, 2011- 6.73i. pbs: 50m 6.35i '08, 60m 7.34i '10, 100m 11.47 '06, 11.43w '08; 200m 23.05 '06, 400m 54.79i '05, 800m 2:09.80 '05, 60mh 8.16i '10, 100mh 13.89 '05, 13.70w '06; HJ 1.74 '06, SP 11.94 '05, JT 37.60 '05, Pen 4105i '05, Hep 6180 '06.

Anna ILJUSTSENKO b. 12 Oct 1985 Sillamäe 1.68m 49kg. Orthodontist, graduate of dental medicine from University of Tartu. Tartu Ülikooli Akadeemiline SK.
At HJ: OG: '08/12- dnq 21/15=; WCh: '09 dnq 17=, '11- 12; EC: '06-10-12: dnq 20/11/dnq 15=; WJ: '04- dnq; EU23: '05-11, '07- dnq 13; EI: '13- 4=; WUG: 11- 3; Estonian champion 2005-11.
Eight Estonian high jump records 2008-11.
Progress at HJ: 2002- 1.80i, 2003- 1.77, 2004- 1.82, 2005- 1.85, 2006- 1.89, 2007- 1.85, 2008- 1.91, 2009- 1.93i/1.91, 2010- 1.95, 2011- 1.96, 2012- 1.93i/1.91, 2013- 1.94i.

ETHIOPIA

Governing body: Ethiopian Athletic Federation, Addis Ababa Stadium, PO Box

3241, Addis Ababa. Founded 1961. **2012 National Champions**: **Men**: 800m: Israel Aweke 1:46.5, 1500m: Abiyot Abnet 3:41.5, 5000m: Muktar Edris 14:04.0, 10,000m: Tebelu Zewde 29:09.0, 3000mSt: Legese Lamiso 8:56.8, 20kW: Chernet Mikoro 1:43:23. **Women**: 400m: Selam Abrhaley 54.4, 800m: Mantegbosh Melese 2:05.5, 1500m: Senbera Teferi 4:13.1, 5000m: Buze Diriba 16:14.7, 10,000m: Aberu Kebede 32:48.6, 3000mSt: Hiwot Ayalew 9:34.6, 20kW: Askale Gugsa 1:59:23.

Ayele ABSHERO b. 28 Dec 1990 Yeboda 1.67m 52kg.
At 5000m: Af-J: '09- 4. At Mar: OG: '12- dnf. World CC: '08- 2J, '09- 1J.
Progress at 10,000m, Mar: 2009- 27:54.29, 2011- 27:48.94, 2012- 2:04:23. pbs: 3000m 7:40.08 '10, 5000m 13:11.38 '09; Road: 15km 42:02 '10, 10M 45:33 '10, HMar 59:42 '11.
Second fastest ever debut marathon to win at Dubai in 2012. Elder brother Tessema has marathon pb 2:08:26 '08.

Yemane ADHANE Tsegay b. 8 Apr 1985.
At Mar: WCh: '09- 4.
Progress at Mar: 2008- 2:13:29, 2009- 2:06:30, 2010- 2:07:11, 2011- 2:10:24, 2012- 2:06:29. pbs: HMar 61:37 '10, 30km 1:27:40 '12.
Marathon wins: Macau 2008, Gongju 2009, Lake Biwa 2010, Taipei 2011, Rotterdam 2012.

Yenew ALAMIREW b. 27 May 1990 Tilili l.75m 57kg.
At 5000m: AfG: '11- 2. At 3000m: WI: '12- 9.
Progress at 5000m: 2010- 13:16.53, 2011- 13:00.46, 2012- 12:48.77. pbs: 1500m 3:35.09+ '11, 1M 3:50.43 '11, 3000m 7:27.26 '11, 10kmRd 29:26A '10.

Mohammed AMAN Geleto b. 10 Jan 1994 Asella 1.69m 55kg.
At 800m: OG: '12- 6; WCh: '11- 8; WY: '11- 2; WI: '12- 1; won DL 2012, Afr-J 800m 2011, Yth OG 1000m 2010.
Records: Ethiopian (5) 2011-12, world youth 800m 2011, world junior 600m indoor 2013 (1:15.60).
Progress at 800m: 2008- 1:50.29, 2009- 1:46.34, 2010- 1:48.5A, 2011- 1:43.37, 2012- 1:42.53. pbs: 600m 1:15.0+ '12, 1000m 2:19.54 '10, 1500m 3:43.52 '11, 1M 3:57.14 '11.
Was disqualified from taking the African Junior 800m gold in 2009 for being under-age (at 15). Youngest ever World Indoor champion at 18 years 60 days in 2012. Beat David Rudishsa in the latter's last races in both 2011 and 2012.

Kenenisa BEKELE b. 13 Jun 1982 near Bekoji, Arsi Province 1.62m 54kg.
At 5000m(/10,000m): OG: '04- 2/1, '08- 1/1, '12- (4); WCh: '03- 3/1, '05- (1), '07- (1), '09- 1/1; WJ: '00- 2; AfG: '03- 1; AfCh: '06- 1, '08- 1. At 3000m: WY: '99- 2; WI: '06- 1; WCp: '06- 2. World CC: '99- 9J, 4k: '01- 1J/2 4k, '02-03-04-05-06: all 1/1, '08- 1. Won WAF 3000m 2003, 2009; 5000m 2006.

World records: 5000m 2004, 10,000m 2004 & 2005, indoor 5000m (12:49.60) 2004, 2000m 2007, 2M 2008; World junior record 3000m 2001.
Progress at 5000m, 10,000m: 2000- 13:20.57, 2001- 13:13.33, 2002- 13:26.58, 2003- 12:52.26, 26:49.57; 2004- 12:37.35, 26:20.31; 2005- 12:40.18, 26:17.53; 2006- 12:48.09, 2007- 12:49.53, 26:46.19; 2008- 12:50.18, 26:25.97; 2009- 12:52.32, 26:46.31; 2011- 13:27e+, 26:43.16; 2012- 12:55.79, 27:02.59. pbs: 1000m 2:21.9+ '07, 1500m 3:32.35 '07, 1M 3:56.2+ '07, 2000m 4:49.99i '07, 4:58.40 '09, 3000m 7:25.79 '07, 2M 8:04.35i '08, 8:13.51 '07; Rd 15km 42:42 '01.
At cross-country has a record 20 (12 individual, 8 team) world gold medals from his record winning margin of 33 seconds for the World Juniors in 2001, a day after second in senior 4km. The only man to win both World senior races in the same year, he did this five times. Unbeaten in 27 races from Dec 2001 to March 2007 when he did not finish in the Worlds. After winning all his 12 10,000m track races including five major gold medals, from a brilliant debut win over Haile Gebrselassie at Hengelo in June 2003, he had two years out through injury and then dropped out of World 10,000 in 2011 before running the year's fastest time to win at Brussels. 17 successive wins at 5000m 2006-09. Shared Golden League jackpot in 2009. IAAF Athlete of the Year 2004-05.
His fiancée Alem Techale (b. 13.12.87, the 2003 World Youth 1500m champion) died of a heart attack on 4 Jan 2005. He married film actress Danawit Gebregziabher on 18 Nov 2007.

Tariku BEKELE b. 21 Jan 1987 near Bekoji 1.68m 52kg.
At 5000m: OG: '08- 6; WCh: '05- 7, '07- 5; WJ: '04- 3, '06- 1; AfG: '07- 3; AfCh: '08- 4, '10- 6. At 10,000m: OG: '12- 3. At 3000m: WY: '03- 2; WI: '06-08-10: 6/1/4; CCp: '10- 4; won WAF 3000m 2006. World CC: '05- 6J, '06- 3J.
World junior indoor 2M best 2006.
Progress at 5000m, 10,000m: 2004- 13:11.97, 2005- 12:59.03, 2006- 12:53.81, 2007- 13:01.60, 2008- 12:52.45, 2010- 12:53.97, 2011- 12:59.25, 2012- 12:54.13, 27:03.24. pbs: 1500m 3:37.26 '08, 2000m 5:00.1 '06, 3000m 7:28.70 '10, 2M 8:04.83 '07, Road: 15km 43:35 '11, 10M 46:33 '10.
Younger brother of Kenenisa Bekele.

Abreham CHERKOS Feleke b. 23 Sep 1989 Asella, Oromia reg. 1.60m 52kg.
At 5000m: OG: '08- 5; WCh: '07- 8; WJ: '06- 2, '08- 1; AfG: '07- 4. At 3000m: WY: '05- 1; WI: '08- 3.
World youth 3000m, 2M & 5000m records 2006, world junior indoor 3000m best (7:38.03) 2008.
Progress at 5000m, Mar: 2006- 12:54.19, 2007- 13:05.83, 2008- 12:57.56, 2009- 13:07.83i, 2010- 2:07:29, 2011- 2:06:13wdh, 2012- 2:12:46. pbs: 1500m 3:42.91 '05, 2000m 5:02.4 '06, 3000m 7:31.81 '09, 2M 8:16.07 '06, 10km 28:14 '11, HMar 61:42 '11.

4th Amsterdam on marathon debut 2010, 5th Boston 2011.

Deressa CHIMSA Edae b. 21 Nov 1986 Koreodo 1.75m 62kg.
World HMar: '12- 2. Won ETH HMar 2009.
Progress at Mar: 2008- 2:10:16, 2009- 2:07:54, 2010- 2:08:45, 2011- 2:07:39, 2012- 2:05:42. pbs: HMar 60:51 '12.
Marathon wins: Daegu 2010, Prague 2012.

Yigrem DEMELASH b. 28 Jan 1994 1.67m 52kg.
At 10,000m: WJ: '12- 1.
Progress at 50000m, 10,000m: 2012- 13:03.30, 26:57.56.

Lelisa DESISA Benti b. 14 Jan 1990 1.70m.
At 10,000m: Af-J: '99- 1. World HMar: '10- 7.
Progress at 10,000m, HMar, Mar: 2009- 28:46.74, 2010- 59:39; 2011- 59:30, 2012- 27:11.98, 62:50; 2013- 2:04:45. pbs: 5000m 13:22.91 '12, Road: 15km 42:25 '10, 10M 45:36 '11.
Brilliant marathon debut to win Dubai 2013.

Roba GARI Chebute b. 12 Apr 1982 Wera Jarso. Oromiya region 1.81m 60kg.
At 3000mSt: OG: '08- h, '12- 4; WCh: '07- 10, '09- 6, '11- 5; AfG: '07- 5, '11- 2; AfCh: '10- 3; CCp: '10- 2; ETH champion 2005, 2007, 2010.
Five Ethiopian 3000mSt records 2009-12.
Progress at 3000mSt: 2007- 8:15.05, 2008- 8:22.07, 2009- 8:11.32, 2010- 8:09.87, 2011- 8:10.03, 2012- 8:06.16. pbs: 3000m 7:42.12i '08, 7:43.38 '10; 5000m 13:33.17 '08, 2000mSt 5:19.96 '07.

Gebre-egziabher GEBREMARIAM b. 10 Sep 1984 Shere, Tigray region 1.78m 56kg.
At 10,000m (5000m): OG: '04- (4); WCh: '03- (6), '05- 15, '07- 6, '09- 10; WJ: '02- 1 (3); AfG: '03- 2, '07- 3; AfCh: '08- 1. At Mar: WCh: '11- dnf.
World CC: '02-03-04-05-06-08-09-10: 1J/3/2&2/ 9(4k)/13/17/1/10. Won ETH CC 2003 & 2009, 5000m 2005, 10,000m 2005., 2009; E.Afr 2004.
Progress at 5000m, 10,000m, Mar: 2001- 14:13.74A, 31:04.61A; 2002- 13:12.14, 27:25.61; 2003- 12:58.08, 28:03.03; 2004- 12:55.59, 26:53.73; 2005- 12:52.80, 27:11.57; 2006- 13:30.95, 27:03.95; 2007- 13:10.29, 26:52.33; 2008- 13:36.67, 27:20.65; 2009- 13:13.20, 27:44.04; 2010- 2:08:14, 2011- 2:04:53wdh/2:08:00, 2012- 13:33.2+, 27:03.58, 2:22:56. pbs: 3000m 7:39.48 '05, 2M 9:34.82i '06, HMar 60:25 '10, 3000mSt 8:57.7A '02.
Won New York 2010 on marathon debut, 3rd Boston 2011. Married Worknesh Kidane on 4 Feb 2006. She has 21 World CC medals, he has 16.

Mekonnen GEBREMEDHIN Woldegiorgis b. 11 Oct 1988 Addis Ababa 1.80m 64kg.
At 1500m: OG: '12- 6; WCh: '07-09-11: sf/h/7; WI: '08-10-12: 6/4/3; AfCh: '10- 3; CCp: '10- 2. At 800m: WJ: '06- sf.
Progress at 1500m: 2004- 3:47.1A, 2006- 3:41.00, 2007- 3:36.04, 2008- 3:35.68, 2009- 3:34.49, 2010- 3:31.57, 2011- 3:31.90, 2012- 3:31.45. pbs: 800m 1:46.63 '12, 1M 3:49.70 '11, 3000m 7:41.42 '11, 3000mSt 8:59.06 '12.

Dejen GEBREMESKEL b. 24 Nov 1989 Adiqrat, Tigray region 1.78m 53kg.
At 5000m: OG: '12- 2; WCh: '11- 3; WJ: '08- 3; Af-J: '07- 2. At 3000m: WI: '10- 10, '12- 5.
Progress at 5000m: 2007- 13:21.05, 2008- 13:08.96, 2009- 13:03.13, 2010- 12:53.56, 2011- 12:55.89, 2012- 12:46.81. pbs: 3000m 7:34.14i '12, 7:45.9+ '10; 10km Rd 27:45 '11.

Hagos GEBRHIWET Berhe b. 11 May 1994 Tsaedaenba 1.67m 65kg. Mesfen Engineering
At 5000m: OG: '12- 11;. At 3000m: WY: '11- 5. World CC: '13- 1J. African CC: '12- 4.
World junior records 5000m 2012, indoor 3000m 2013.
Progress at 5000m: 2011- 14:10.0A, 2012- 12:47.53. pbs: 3000m 7:32.87i '13, 7:45.11 '11; 10km Rd 27:57 dh '11.

Haile GEBRSELASSIE b. 18 Apr 1973 Arsi 1.64m 53kg.
At 10,000m (5000m): OG: '96- 1, '00- 1, '04- 5, '08- 6; WCh: '93- 1 (2), '95- 1, '97- 1, '99- 1, '01- 3, '03- 2; WJ: '92- 1 (1); AfG: '93- 3 (2). At 3000m: WI: '97- 1, '99- 1 (1 1500m), '03- 1. Won GP 3000m 1995, 1998. World CC: '91-2-3-4-5-6: 8J/2J/7/3/4/5; HMar: '01- 1; Rd Rly team: '94- 2.
World records 5000m (4) 1994-8, 10,000m (3) 1995-8, 20000m & 1Hr 2007; 10km road (27:02) 2002, 15km & 10M road 2005, 20km, HMar & 25km 2006, Marathon 2007 & 2008, 30km road 2009; Indoors 2000m 1998, 3000m (7:30.72 '96, 7:26.15 '98), 5000m (13:10.98 '96, 12:59.04 '97, 12:50.38 '99); World best 2M 1995 (8:07.46) & 1997, indoors 8:04.69 (2003). ETH records 1993-9: 1500m (3), 1M (1), 3000m (6), 5000m (6), 10,000m (3), marathon (5) 2002-08. World M35 bests 10,000m & Mar 2008.
Progress at 5000m, 10,000m, Mar: 1992- 13:36.06, 28:03.99; 1993- 13:03.17, 27:30.17; 1994- 12:56.96, 27:15.00; 1995- 12:44.39, 26:43.53; 1996- 12:52.70, 27:07.34; 1997- 12:41.86, 26:31.32; 1998- 12:39.36, 26:22.75; 1999- 12:49.64, 27:57.27; 2000- 12:57.95, 27:18.20; 2001- 27:54.41, 2002- 28:16.50, 2:06:35; 2003- 12:54.36, 26:29.22; 2004- 12:55.51, 26:41.58; 2005- 2:06:20, 2006- 2:05:56, 2007- 26:52.81, 2:04:26; 2008- 26:51.20, 2:03:59; 2009- 28:22.3+, 2:05:29, 2010- 2:06:09, 2011- dnf, 2012- 13:33.6+, 27:20.39, 2:08:17. pbs: 800m 1:49.35i '97, 1000m 2:20.3+i '98, 1500m 3:31.76i '98, 3:33.73 '99; 1M 3:52.39 '99, 2000m 4:52.86i '98, 4:56.1 '97; 3000m 7:25.09 '98, 2M 8:01.08 '97, 10M 45:23.80 '07, 20000m 56:25.98 '07, 1Hr 21285m '07; Road: 15km 41:22 '05, 10M 44:24 '05, 20km 55:48 '06, HMar 58:55 '06, 25km 1:11:37 '06, 30km 1:27:49 '09.
He set the first of his 27 world records (20 officially ratified) in Hengelo in 1994 at 5000m. From 1992 to 2004 he had 13 wins in 19 races at 10,000m, 26/28 at 3000m/2M, and 28/36 at 5000 including 16 successive 1996 to 2000. He has 12/14 wins at half marathon 2001-11, including the 2010 Great North Run. After missing the 2002 summer season through injury he set a

world 10km road record of 27:02 at Doha, Qatar in December for a reward of $1 million.

He had run c.2:48 for the marathon at the age of 15, but made his senior debut at the distance at London 2002, when he was third in 2:06:35 and won at Amsterdam in 2:06:20 in 2005. In 2006 he was 9th in London, then won the Berlin and Fukuoka marathons, but dnf London 2007. He smashed the world record with 2:04:26 to win the Berlin Marathon in 2007 and in 2008 he won in Dubai in 2:04:53 before another WR at Berlin – 2:03:59. He won again in Dubai and Berlin in 2009 and in Dubai 2010. IAAF Athlete of the Year 1998.
His brother Tekeye had marathon pb 2:11:45 '94 and was 13th in 1991 World Cup.

Markos GENETI b. 30 May 1984 Walega 1.75m 55kg.
At 5000m: WJ: '02- 2; AfG: '03- 4. At 3000m: WY: '01- 1; WI: '04- 3. At 1500m: WCh: '05- sf. World CC: '07- 15.
Progress at 5000m: 2001- 13:50.14, 2002- 13:28.83, 2003- 13:11.87, 2004- 13:17.57, 2005- 13:00.25, 2006- 13:13.98, 2007- 13:07.65, 2008- 13:08.22, 2009- 13:31.71i, 2010- 13:18.64i/13:21.99. At Mar: 2011- 2:06:35, 2012- 2:04:54. pbs: 1500m 3:33.83 '05, 1M 4:08.8 '10, 3000m 7:32.69i '07, 7:38.11 '05; 2M 8:08.39i '04, 8:19.61 '06, Road: 10km 29:38 '11, HMar 62:01 '11
Won in Los Angeles 2011 in sixth fastest ever debut marathon time. Third Dubai 2012.

Ibrahim JEYLAN Gashu b. 12 Jun 1989 1.68m 57kg. Muger Cement.
At 10,000m: WCh: '11- 1; WJ: '06- 1, '08- 3; AfG: '11- 1; AfCh: '08- 2. At 3000m: WY: '05- 2. World CC: '06- 5J, '08- 1J.
Two world youth 10,000m records 2006.
Progress at 5000m, 10,000m: 2006- 13:09.38, 27:02.81; 2007- 13:17.99, 27:50.53; 2008- 13:15.12, 27:13.85; 2009- 13:19.70, 27:22.19; 2010- 13:21.29, 27:12.43; 2011- 13:09.95, 27:09.02. pbs: 3000m 8:04.21 '05, 15km 43:38 '08.

Tsegaye KEBEDE Wordofa b. 15 Jan 1987 Gerar Ber 1.58m 50kg.
At Mar: OG: '08- 3; WCh: '09- 3.
Progress at Mar: 2007- 2:08:16, 2008- 2:06:10, 2009- 2:05:18, 2010- 2:05:19, 2011- 2:07:48, 2012- 2:04:38. pbs: Road: 10km 28:10 '08, HMar 59:35 '08.
Marathon wins: Addis Ababa 2007, Paris 2008, Fukuoka 2008-09, London 2010, Chicago 2012; 2nd London 2009 and Chicago 2010; 3rd New York 2011, London 2012. Won Great Ethiopian Run 2007, Great North Run 2008.

Abera KUMA Lema b. 31 Aug 1990 Ambo 1.60m 50kg.
At 5000m: WCh: '11- 5; Af-J: '09- 1. At 3000m: WY: '07- 5.
Progress at 5000m, 10,000m: 2009- 13:29.40, 2010- 13:07.83, 2011- 13:00.15, 27:22.54; 2012-

13:09.32, 27:18.39. pbs: 1500m 3:48.73 '09, 3000m 7:39.09i/7:40.85 '12, Rd 15km 42:01 '10, 10M 45:28 '11, HMar 60:19 '12.

Feyisa LILESA b. 1 Feb 1990 Addis Ababa 1.58m 50kg.
At Mar: WCh: '11- 3, World CC: 2008-09-10-11-13: 14J/12/25/17/9.
Progress at Mar: 2009- 2:09:12, 2010- 2:05:23, 2011- 2:10:32, 2012- 2:04:52. pbs: 5000m 13:34.80 '08, 10,000m 27:46.97 '08; Road: 15km 42:15+ '13, 20km 56:19+ '12, HMar 59:22 '12, 30km 1:28:58 '10.
Marathons won: Dublin 2009, Xiamen 2010. 3rd/2nd Chicago 2010/2012, 4th Rotterdam 2010 in then fastest ever by 20 year-old.

Deresse MEKONNEN Tsigu b. 20 Oct 1987 Sheno, Oromia reg. 1.75m 60kg.
At 1500m: OG: '08- sf; WCh: '07- h, '09- 2, '11- sf; WI: '08- 1, '10- 1; AfG: '07- 5, AfCh: '08- 4.
Ethiopian 1M records 2008 & 2009.
Progress at 1500m: 2007- 3:36.41, 2008- 3:33.71, 2009- 3:32.18, 2010- 3:33.10i/3:33.85, 2011- 3:32.90. pbs: 1000m 2:19.12i '11, 1M 3:48.95 '09, 3000m 7:32.93 '09, 5000m 13:07.75 '09.

Deribe MERGA Ejigu b. 26 Oct 1982 Nekemte 1.68m 52kg.
At Mar: OG: '08- 4; WCh: '09- dnf. World 20km Rd: '06- 6, HMar: '07- 4.
World 15km road record (=) 2009.
Progress at 10,000m, Mar: 2007- 27:02.62, 2:06:50; 2008- 2:06:38, 2009- 2:07:52, 2010- 2:08:39, 2011- 2:09:13. pbs: Road: 10km 27:31 '11, 15km 41:29 '09, 10M 44:53 '11, 20km 56:13 '07, HMar 59:15 '08, 30km 1:28:30 '08.
Marathon career: 2006- dnf Boston, 2007- 10th Paris 2:13:33, 2nd Fukuoka, 2008- 6th London, 4th OG; 2009- 1st Houston & Boston, 2010- 3rd Boston, 2011- 2nd Lake Biwa.

Imane MERGA Jida b. 15 Oct 1988 Tulu Bolo, Oromia region 1.74m 61kg. Defence.
At 5000m/(10,000m): WCh: '09- (4), '11- dq/3; AfCh: '10- 5; Af-J: '07- (3); CCp: '10- 5; won DL 2010-11, WAF 2009. World CC: '07-11-13: 7J/1/2
Progress at 5000m, 10,000m: 2007- 13:33.52, 30:12.03; 2008- 13:08.20, 27:33.53, 2009- 12:55.66, 27:15.94; 2010- 12:53.58; 2011- 12:54.21, 26:48.35; 2012- 12:59.77, 27:14.02. pbs: 3000m 7:45.8+ '10, HMar 59:56 '12.
Disqualified for running inside the kerb after finishing 3rd in World 5000m 2011.

Dino SEFIR Kemal b. 28 May 1988 Shoa 1.72m 59kg.
At 10,000m: AfG: '11- 4. At Mar: OG: '12- dnf. World CC: '09- 15, '11- 12.
Progress at Mar: 2010- 2:20:36, 2011- 2:10:33, 2012- 2:04:50, 2013- 2:09:13. pbs: 3000m 7:44.37 '09, 5000m 13:11.69 '08, 10,000m 28:23.40 '11; Road: 15km 43:57 '11, HMar 59:42 '11.
2nd Dubai Marathon 2012.

Berhanu SHIFERAW Tolcha b. 31 May 1993.
At 2000mSt: WY: '09- 5.

Progress at Mar: 2011- 2:09:11, 2012- 2:08:51, 2013- 2:04:48. pbs: HMar 61:41 '10, 2000mSt 5:37.32 '09, 3000mSt 8:36.02 '12.
Won Taiyuan and Ljubljana marathons 2012, fastest by 19 year-old when 2nd Dubai 2013.

Sileshi SIHINE b. 29 Jan 1983 Sheno 1.68m 58kg.
At (5000m)/10,000m: OG: '04- 2, '08- 2; WCh: '03- 3, '05- 2/2, '07- 2, '11- 8; WJ: '02- 2; AfG: '03- 1. World CC: '02-03-04-06-07-08: 6J/7/3/2 & 12 4k/16/15. World HMar: '05- 4. Won WAF 5000m 2004-05, Ethiopian 5000m 2003, 10,000m 2003-04, Af-AsG 10,000m 2003.
Progress at 5000m, 10,000m: 2002- 13:21.81, 27:26.12; 2003- 13:06.53, 26:58.76; 2004- 12:47.04, 26:39.69; 2005- 13:13.04, 26:57.27; 2006- 13:06.72i, 2007- 12:50.16, 26:48.73; 2008- 12:58.41, 26:50.53; 2009- 13:06.63, 2011- 12:57.86, 26:52.84; 2012- 13:01.39, 27:03.65. pbs: 2000m 5:01.2i+ '04, 5:02.2 '05; 3000m 7:29.92 '05, 2M 8:27.03i '06; Road: 15km 41:38 '04, HMar 61:14 '05.
Six major silver medals. Married Tirunesh Dibaba on 26 Oct 2008.

Tadesse TOLA b. 31 May 1993 1.78m 60kg.
At 10,000m: WCh: '07- 13; AfCh: '06- 5; AfG: '07- 2. World 20k: '06- 7; World CC: '06- 10J, '07- 7, '09- 17.
Progress at 10,000m, Mar: 2006- 28:15.16, 2007- 27:04.89, 2008- 27:15.17, 2009- 28:51.4A, 2:15:48; 2010- 2:06:31, 2011- 2:07:13, 2012- 2:05:10, 2013- 2:04:49. pbs: 3000m 7:43.70 '07, 5000m 13:18.82 '07, 10,000m 27:04.89 '07; Road: 15km 43:49 '08, 20km 57:27 '06, HMar 59:49 '10.

Women

Birtukan ADAMU b. 29 Apr 1992.
At 3000mSt: WCh: '11- 15; WJ: '10-2; AfG: '11- 3; AfCh: '12- 2, Af-J: '11- 1.
World junior 3000m steeplechase record 2011.
Progress at 3000mSt: 2010- 9:31.39, 2011- 9:20.37, 2012- 9:36.40. pbs: 1500m 4:24.91 '11, 3000m 8:58.73i '12.

Sofia ASSEFA Abebe b. 14 Nov 1987 Tenta District, south Wello 1.71m 58kg. Ethiopian Bank.
At 3000mSt: OG: '08- h, '12- 3; WCh: '09- 13, '11- 6; AfCh: '08- 4, '10- 2; CCp: '10- 3.
Ethiopian 3000mSt records 2011 and 2012.
Progress at 3000mSt: 2006- 10:17.48, 2007- 9:48.46, 2008- 9:31.58, 2009- 9:19.91, 2010- 9:20.72, 2011- 9:15.04, 2012- 9:09.00. pbs: 1000m 2:49.79 '07, 5000m 15:59.74 '07, 2000mSt 6:33.49 '07.

Hiwot AYALEW b. 6 Mar 1990 Gojam, Amhara 1.73m 51kg. Commercial Bank.
At 3000mSt: OG: '12- 5; AfG: '11- 2. World CC: '11- 11, '13- 2.
Progress at 3000mSt: 2011- 9:23.88, 2012- 9:09.61. pbs: 5000m 14:49.36 '12, 10km Rd 33:22A '11.

Wude AYALEW Yimer b. 4 Jul 1987 Sekela, Amhara region 1.50m 44kg.

At 10,000m: WCh: '09- 3; AfG: '11- 2; AfCh: '08- 3, '10- 4. At 5000m: WJ: '06- 5. World CC: '06-07-09-11: 5/10/5/6. Won ETH CC 2009.
Progress at 5000m, 10,000m: 2006- 14:57.23, 33:57.0; 2008- 15:07.65, 31:06.84; 2009- 14:38.44, 30:11.87; 2010- 15:02.47, 32:29.92A; 2011- 14:59.71, 31:24.09. pbs: 1500m 4:14.85 '07, 3000m 8:30.93 '09; Road: 10km 31:41+ '08, 15km 48:52 '11, HMar 67:58 '09.
Won Great Ethiopian Run 2008. Older sister of Hiyot Ayalew.

Atsede BAYSA Tesema **(or BAYISA)** b. 16 Apr 1987.
At Mar: WCh: '09- 27, '11- 14. At HMar: WCh: '07- 11; AfG: '07- 2.
Progress at Mar: 2006- 2:37:48, 2007- 2:29:08, 2008- 2:33:07, 2009- 2:24:42, 2010- 2:22:04, 2011- 2:23:50, 2012- 2:22:03. pbs: Road: 10km 33:14 '09, 15km 49:15 '12, HMar 67:33 '13.
Marathon wins: Istanbul 2007, Paris 2009-10, Xiamen 2010, Chicago 2012 (2nd 2010).

Bezunesh BEKELE Sertsu b. 29 Jan 1983 Addis Ababa 1.45m 38kg..
At Mar: WCh: '09- 16, '11- 4. At HMar: WCh: '07- 4. At 10,000m: AfCh: '06- 5. World CC: '02- 6J; '05- 10 (12 4k)
Progress at Mar: 2008- 2:23:09, 2009- 2:24:02, 2010- 2:23:17, 2011- 2:23:42, 2012- 2:20:30. pbs: 3000m 8:52.08 '06, 5000m 15:02.48 '06, 10,000m 31:10.68 '05; Road: 15km 47:36 '07, HMar 68:07 '07.
Won Dubai Marathon 2009 (2nd 2008, 4th 2010 & 2012), 2nd Berlin 2010. Married to Tessema Abshiro (Mar 2:08:26 '08).

Gelete BURKA Bati b. 15 Feb 1986 Kofele 1.65m 45kg.
At 1500m: OG: '08- h; WCh: '05- 8, '09- 10 (fell), '11- sf; WI: '08- 1, '10- 3; AfG: '07- 1; AfCh: '08- 1, '10- 2; CCp: '10- 7. At 3000m: WI: '12- 3. At 5000m: OG: '12- 5; WCh: '07- 10. World CC: '03-05-06-07-08-09: 3J/1J/1 4k/4/6/8. Won ETH 800m 2011, 1500m 2004-05, 2007; 5000m 2005, 4k CC 2006.
African records: 1M 2008, 200m 2009, indoor 1500m 2008, junior 1500m 2005. World youth 1M best (4:30.81) 2003.
Progress at 1500m, 5000m: 2003- 4:10.82, 16:23.8A, 2004- 4:06.10, 2005- 3:59.60, 14:51.47; 2006- 4:02.68, 14:40.92; 2007- 4:00.48, 14:31.20; 2008- 3:59.75i/4:00.44, 14:45.84; 2009- 3:58.79, 2010- 3:59.28, 2011- 4:03.28, 2012- 14:41.43. pbs: 800m 2:02.89 '10, 1M 4:18.23 '08, 2000m 5:30.19 '09, 3000m 8:25.92 '06; Rd: 10k 32:38+ '12, 15k 49:26 '12.
Married Taddele Gebrmehden in 2007.

Firehiwot DADO Tufa b. 9 Jan 1984 Arsi 1.65m.
Progress at Mar: 2008- 2:37:34, 2009- 2:27:08, 2010- 2:25:28, 2011- 2:23:15. pbs: Road: 10km 32:00+ '12, 15km 48:32+ '12, 20km 65:06+ '12, HMar 68:35 '12, 30km 1:40:45 '11.
Marathon wins: New York 2011, Rome 2009-11.

Mamitu DASKA Molisa b. 16 Oct 1983 Liteshoa 1.65m.
At HMar: AfrG: '11- 2. World CC: '09- 12, '10- 8. Progress at Mar: 2009- 2:26:38, 2010- 2:24:19, 2011- 2:21:59, 2012- 2:23:52. pbs: 10,000m 31:36.88 '09. Road: 20km 68:09 '10, HMar 68:07 '09, 30km 1:39:46 '11.
Marathon wins: Dubai 2010, Houston and Frankfurt 2011.

Bizunesh DEBA b. 8 Sep 1987.
Progress at Mar: 2009- 2:32:17, 2010- 2:27:24, 2011- 2:23:19, 2013- 2:24:26. pbs: 5000m 15:52.33 '04, Road: 10km 32:10 '10, HMar 69:53 '11.
Lives in Bronx, New York. Marathon wins: Sacramento 2009, San Diego 2010, Los Angeles & San Diego 2011. 2nd New York 2011, Houston 2013.

Meseret DEFAR b. 19 Nov 1983 Addis Ababa 1.55m 42kg.
At 5000m(/10,000m): OG: '04- 1, '08- 3, '12- 1; WCh: '03- h, '05- 2, '07- 1, '09- 3/5, '11- 3/dnf; WJ: '00- 2, '02- 1; AfG: '03- 1, '07- 1; AfCh: '00-06-08-10: 2/1/2/2; WCp: '06- 1. At 3000m: WJ: '02- 1; WY: '99- 2; WI: '03-04-06-08-10-12: 3/1/1/1/1/2; CCp: '10- 1. Won WAF 3000m 2004-09, 5000m 2005, 2008-09. World CC: '02- 13J.
Records: World 5000m 2006 & 2007, 2M 2007 (2); indoor 3000m 2007, 2M 2008 (9:10.50) & 2009 (9:06.26), 5000m 2009; African 5000m 2005, Ethiopian 3000m (2) 2006-07. World 5k road best 14:46 Carlsbad 2006.
Progress at 3000m, 5000m, 10,000m: 1999- 9:02.08, 33:54.9A; 2000- 8:59.90, 15:08.36; 2001- 8:52.47, 15:08.65; 2002- 8:40.28, 15:26.45; 2003- 8:38.31, 14:40.34; 2004- 8:33.44i/8:36.46, 14:44.81; 2005- 8:30.05i/8:33.57, 14:28.98; 2006- 8:24.66, 14:24.53; 2007- 8:23.72i/8:24.51, 14:16.63; 2008- 8:27.93i/8:34.53, 14:12.88; 2009- 8:26.99i/8:30.15, 14:24.37i/14:36.38, 29:59.20; 2010- 8:24.46i/8:36.09, 14:24.79i/14:38.87; 2011- 8:36.91i/8:50.36+, 14:29.52, 31:05.05; 2012- 8:31.56i/8:46.49, 14:35.85. pbs: 1500m 4:02.00 '10, 1M: 4:28.5ei '06, 4:33.07+ '07; 2000m 5:34.74i/5:38.0 '06, 2M 8:58.58 '07, HMar 67:25 '13.
Married to Teodros Hailu. IAAF woman athlete of the year 2007. Record nine WAF wins.

Genzebe DIBABA b. 8 Feb 1991 Bekoji. Muger Cement. 1.68m 52kg.
At 1500m: OG: '12- h; WI: '12- 1. At 5000m: WCh: '09 -8, '11- 8; WJ: '08- 2, '10- 1; Af-J: '09- 1. World CC: '07-08-09-10-11: 5J/1J/1J/11J/9. Won ETH 1500m 2010.
Ethiopian 1500m record 2012.
Progress at 1500m, 5000m: 2007- 15:53.46, 2008- 15:02.41, 2009- 14:55.52, 2010- 4:04.80i/4:06.10, 15:08.06; 2011- 4:05.90, 14:37.56; 2012- 3:57.77, 2013- 4:00.63i. pbs: 2000m 5:37.2i '13, 3000m 8:26.95i '13, 8:48.35 '10.
Younger sister of Ejegayehu (2 OG 10,000m 2004, 3 WCh 5000 & 10,000m 2005) and Tirunesh Dibaba.

Mare DIBABA Hurssa b. 20 Oct 1989 Sululta 1.60m 42kg.
At Mar: OG: '12- 23. At HMar: AfG: '11- 1. Won AZE 3000m and 5000m 2009.
AZE records (as Mare Ibrahimova) at 3000m and 5000m 2009.
Progress at HMar, Mar: 2008- 70:28, 2009- 68:45, 2010- 67:13, 2:25:27, 2011- 68:39, 2:23:25; 2012- 67:44, 2:19:52. pbs: 3000m 9:16.94 '09, 5000m 15:42.83 '09, Road: 10km 31:55+ '10, 15km 48:04+ '10, 10M 51:29+ '10, 20km 63:47+ '10.
She switched to Azerbaijan in December 2008 but back to Ethiopia as of 1 Feb 2010. Third Dubai Marathon 2012.

Tirunesh DIBABA b. 1 Oct 1985 Bekoji, Arsi region 1.60m 47kg.
At 5000m(/10,000m): OG: '04- 3, '08- 1/1, '12- 3/1; WCh: '03- 1, '05- 1/1, '07- (1); WJ: '02- 2; AfG: '03- 4; AfCh: '06- 2, '08- (1), '10- (1). At 3000m: WCp: '06- 1. World CC: '01-02-03-05-06-07-08-10: 5J/2J/1J/1/1/2/1/4; 4k: '04-05: 2/1. Won WAF 5000m 2006, ETH 4k CC & 5000m 2003. 8k CC 2005.
World records: 5000m 2008, indoor 5000m 2005 (14:32.93) & 2007, junior 5000m 2003-04, indoor 3000m & 5000m 2004, world road 5k best 14:51 '05, 15k 2009. African 10,000m record 2008.
Progress at 5000m: 2002- 14:49.90, 2003- 14:39.94, 2004- 14:30.88, 2005- 14:32.42, 30:15.67; 2006- 14:30.40, 2007- 14:27.42i/14:35.67, 31:55.41; 2008- 14:11.15, 29:54.66; 2009- 14:33.65, 2010- 14:34.07, 31:51.39A; 2012- 14:50.80, 30:20.75. pbs: 2000m 5:42.7 '05, 3000m 8:29.55 '06, 2M 9:12.23i '10, road 15k 46:28 '09, HMar 67:35 '12.
In 2003 she became, at 17 years 333 days, the youngest ever world champion at an individual event and in 2005 the first woman to win the 5000m/10,000m double (with last laps of 58.19 and 58.4) at a global event after earlier in the year winning both World CC titles. Now has women's record 21 World CC medals. Married Sileshi Sihine on 26 Oct 2008. Due to injuries, did not compete in 2011 until the final day of the year when she won a 10k road race in Madrid in 31:30. Then she retained the Olympic 10,000m title and won the Great North Run on half marathon debut in 2012. She has run nine 10,000m track races – and won them all.

Etenesh DIRO Neda b. 10 May 1991 Jeidu, Oromiya 1.69m 47kg..
At 3000mSt: OG: '12- 6.
Progress at 3000mSt: 2011- 9:49.18, 2012- 9:14.07. pbs: 3000 9:00.39 '11, 5000m 15:19.77 '12, Road: 10km 33:32A '11, 15km 51:21 '09, HMar 71:35 '10.

Sentayehu EJIGU b. 21 Jun 1985 Gojjam, Amhara region 1.60m 45kg.
At 1500m: WY: '01- 3. At 3000m: WI: '06- 4, '10- 3. At 5000m: OG: '04- 10; WCh: '09- 4, '11- 4; AfG: '03- 5; AfCh: '10- 3; CCp: '10- 2. World CC: '03- 6J, '09- 14.
Progress at 5000m: 2002- 14:53.99, 2003- 15:00.53,

2004- 14:35.18, 2005- 14:51.11, 2007- 15:27.84, 2008- 15:06.37, 2009- 14:40.00, 2010- 14:28.39, 2011- 14:31.66. pbs: 1500m 4:15.89 '01, 1M 4:40.43i '03, 2000m 5:41.6+i '10, 3000m 8:25.27i/8:28.41 '10; 2M 9:12.68i '10, 10km Rd 31:50 '11.
Won Houston Marathon 2009 & 2010, Boston 2010; 4th Chicago 2009.

Erba Tiki GELANA b. 22 Oct 1987 Bok'oji, Oromiya 1.65m 48kg.
At Mar: OG: '12- 1. ETH marathon record 2012.
Progress at Mar: 2009- 2:33:49, 2010- 2:28:28, 2011- 2:22:08, 2012- 2:18:58. pbs: 3000m 8:55.88 '08, 5000m 15:17.74 '08, 10,000m 31:27.80 '08; Road: 15k 48:09 '12, 20k 65:06+ '12, HMar 67:48 '12, 30km 1:40:45 '11.
Won Amsterdam Marathon 2011, Rotterdam 2012.

Kalkidan GEZAHEGNE b. 8 May 1991 Addis Ababa.
At 1500m: WCh: '09- 9, '11- 5; WJ: '08- 2; WI: '10- 1; Af-J: '09- 2. At 800m: AfCh: '08- h.
World junior indoor records 1500m & 1M 2010.
Progress at 1500m: 2008- 4:10.14, 2009- 4:02.98, 2010- 4:03.28i, 2011- 4:00.97. pbs: 800m 2:06.2 '08, 1M 4:24.10i '10, 4:37.76 '08; 3000m 8:47.37i '11, 8:38.61 '09.

Atsede HABTAMU Besuye b. 26 Oct 1987 Addis Ababa 1.62m 50kg.
World HMar: '07- 5, '08- 8.
Progress at HMar, Mar: 2007- 68:29, 2008- 69:37, 2009- 72:29, 2:24:47; 2010- 68:30, 2:25:35; 2011- 71:12+, 2:24:25; 2012- 2:25:28. pbs: Road: 10km 31:55+ '09, 15km 48:21+ '10, 20km 65:04+ '10, 30km 1:42:50 '09.
Won Berlin Marathon 2009, Eindhoven 2010, Daegu 2011, Tokyo 2012.

Meseret HAILU b. 12 Sep 1980.
World HMar: '12- 1.
Progress at Mar: 2009- 2:43:29, 2010- 2:30:42, 2011- 2:34:38, 2012- 2:21:09. pbs: HMar 68:55 '12, 30km 1:41:06 '12.
Won Amsterdam Marathon 2012.

Koren JELELA Yal b. 18 Jan 1987 Shewa 1.65m 50kg.
World CC: '07- 08-09: 19/14/30.
Progress at Mar: 2009- 2:28:41, 2010- 2:24:33, 2011- 2:22:43, 2012- 2:28:05. pbs: 3000m 9:11.64 '07, 5000m 15:51.81 '07, Road: 10km 32:17 '09, 15km 48:36A '11, HMar 68:39+ '11, 30km 1:38:33 '11.
Won Mumbai and Toronto Marathons 2011.

Aberu KEBEDE Shewaye b. 12 Sep 1989 Shoa 1.63m 50kg.
World HMar: '09- 3. World CC: '07- 16J. Won ETH 10,000m 2009.
Progress at 10,000m, Mar: 2009- 30:48.26, 2010- 32:17.74, 2:23:58; 2011- 2:24:34, 2012- 31:09.28, 2:20:30; 2013- 2:25:34. pbs: 5km Rd 15:13 '09, HMar 67:39 '09.
Won Rotterdam and Berlin marathons 2010

after 2nd Dubai on debut, won Berlin again in 2012 and Tokyo 2013.

Werknesh KIDANE b. 21 Nov 1981 Mayshie district, Tigray region 1.58m 42kg.
At 10,000m: OG: '04- 4, '12- 4; WCh: '03- 2, '05- 6; AfG: '03- 2; At 5000m: OG: '00- 7; WCh: '01- h; WJ: '98- 6; AfG: '99- 4. At 3000m: WI: '01- 9. World CC: '97-8-9-00-01-03-04-05-10: 13J/3J/ 1J/9J/1/3/3/9; 4k: '01-02-03-04-05: 5/2/2/4/2. Won ETH 10,000m 2003, 2005; 4k CC 2001-02, E.Afr 4k & 8k CC 2004.
Progress at 5000m, 10,000m: 1998- 15:50.10, 1999- 15:24.56, 2000- 14:47.40, 33:48.7A; 2001- 15:29.96, 31:43.41; 2002- 14:43.53, 2003- 14:33.04, 30:07.15; 2004- 14:38.05, 30:28.30; 2005- 15:01.6, 30:19.39; 2009- 31:19.00, 2011- 31:08.92, 2012- 15:04.65, 30:39.38. pbs: 1500m 4:17.0A '03, 3000m 8:36.39 '05, Road: 15km 47:37 '11, 10M 51:03 '11, HMar 67:28 '11, Mar 2:26:15dh/2:27:15 '11.
Has won women's record 21 team and individual medals at World CC. Married Gebre Gebremariam on 4 Feb 2006, sons Nathaniel born 2 May 2006, Muse born 2 Aug 2007.

Fantu MAGISO Manedo b. 9 Jun 1992 Hosana Lenchicho 1.78m 60kg.
At 800m: WCh: '11- sf; WI: '12- 4; AfG: '11- 2. At 400m/400mR: AfCh: '10- 2R; Af-J: '11- 1/3R (2 200m).
Ethiopian records: 200m (4) 2010-11, 400m 2011, 800m (4) 2011-12.
Progress at 800m: 2011- 1:59.17, 2012- 1:57.48. pbs: 200m 23.90A '11, 400m 52.09A, 52.23 '11.

Meselech MELKAMU b. 27 Apr 1985 Debre Markos, Amhara region 1.58m 47kg.
At 5000m(/10,000m): OG: '08- 8; WCh: '05- 4, '07- 6, '09- 5/2, '11- 5; AfG: '07- 2, '11- (dnf); AfCh: '06- 6, '08- 1, '10- (2); WJ: '04- 1. At 3000m: WI: '08- 2. World CC: '03-04-05-06-07-08-09-10- 11: 4J/1J/4 & 6/3 & 3/3/9/3/3/4 (17 medals). Won ETH 5000m 2004, 4k CC 2005, CC 2006-07. African 10,000m record 2009.
Progress at 5000m, 10,000m: 2003- 15:27.93, 2004- 15:00.02, 2005- 14:38.97, 2006- 14:37.44, 2007- 14:33.83, 2008- 14:38.78, 31:04.93; 2009- 14:34.17, 29:53.80; 2010- 14:31.91, 31:04.52; 2011- 14:39.44, 30:56.55. pbs: 1500m 4:07.52 '07, 1M 4:33.94 '03, 2000m 5:39.2i+, 5:46.3+ '07; 3000m 8:23.74i '07, 8:34.73 '05, Road: HMar 68:05 '13, 25k 1:23:23 '12, 30k 1:39:58 '12, Mar 2:21:01 '12.
Third fastest ever marathon debut to win at Frankfurt 2012.

Aselefech MERGIA b. 23 Jan 1985 Woliso 1.68m 45kg.
At Mar: OG: '12- 42; WCh: '09- 3, '11- dnf. HMar: WCh: '08- 2. World CC: '08- 16.
Ethiopian marathon record 2012.
Progress at HMar, Mar: 2006- 74:13, 2007- 74:50, 2008- 68:17, 2009- 67:48, 2:25:02; 2010- 67:22, 2:22:38; 2011- 67:21, 2:22:45; 2012- 69:42+, 2:19:31.

pbs: 1500m 4:14.85 '07, 3000m 8:54.42 '08; Road: 10km 31:25+ '08, 15km 47:53 '09, 20km 64:13 '09, 30km 1:41:52 '09.
2nd Paris Marathon 2009 on debut, 3rd London 2010, won Dubai 2011-12.

Belaynesh OLJIRA Jemane b. 8 Feb 1991 Welek'a, Amhara 1.65m 49kg.
At 10,000m: OG: '12- 5. World CC: '11- 10, "13- 3. Won ETH 10,000m 2011.
Ethiopian 1500m record 2012.
Progress at 10,000m, Mar: 2011- 31:17.80, 2012- 30:26.70, 2013- 2:25:01. pbs: 1500m 4:33.14 '12, 3000m 8:40.73 '10, 5000m 14:58.16 '10, Road: 15km 49:46 '10, HMar 67:27 '11.

Askale TAFA Magarsa b. 27 Sep 1984 Arsi Province.
At Mar: WCh: '07- 22.
Progress at Mar: 2005- 2:28:27, 2006- 2:27:57, 2007- 2:25:07, 2008- 2:21:31, 2010- 2:24:39, 2011- 2:25:24, 2012- 2:25:29. pbs: 10km 32:49 '08, 15km 49:18 '08, 20km 65:56 '08, HMar 69:37 '08, 25km 1:22:50 '08, 30km 1:39:36 '08.
Won marathons in Milan 2006, Dubai & Paris 2007; 2nd Berlin & 3rd Dubai 2008, 3rd Berlin 2005. Married to Debele Tola (Mar 2:21:31 '08).

Tirfe TSEGAYE Beyene b. 25 Nov 1984 Bokoji 1.65m 54kg.
World HMar: '09- 6.
Progress at Mar: 2008- 2:35:32, 2009- 2:28:16, 2010- 2:22:44, 2011- 2:24:12, 2012- 2:21:19, 2013- 2:23:23. pbs: HMar 67:42 '12.
Marathon wins: Porto 2008, Paris 2012, Dubai 2013; 2nd Shanghai 2009-11.

FINLAND

Governing body: Suomen Urheiluliitto, Radiokatu 20, SF-00240 Helsinki. Founded 1906.
National Championships first held in 1907 (men), 1913 (women). **2012 Champions: Men**: 100m: Visa Hongisto 10.54, 200m: Jonathan Åstrand 20.72, 400m: Christoffer Envall 48.13, 800m/1500m: Niclas Sandells 1:52.72/3:44.17, 5000m/10,000m/HMar/Mar: Lewis Korir KEN 13:55.80/28:59.75/65:22/2:13:36, 3000mSt: Joonas Harjamäki 8:58.94, 110mh: Jussi Kanervo 13.94, 400mh: Oskari Mörö 51.72, HJ: Osku Torro 2.16, PV: Eemeli Salomäki 5.50, LJ: Roni Ollikainen 7.91, TJ: Aleksi Tammentie 16.36w, SP: Tomas Söderlund 18.46, DT: Mikko Kyyrö 60.45, HT: Olli-Pekka Karjalainen 73.21, JT: Antti Ruuskanen 87.79, Dec: Sami Itani 7636, 20kW/30kW: Jarkko Kinnunen 1:26:17/2:08:49.
Women: 100m/200m: Hanna-Maari Latvala 11.74/23.38, 400m: Ella Räsänen 53.69, 800m: Karin Storbacka 2:06.09, 1500m/10,000m: Johanna Lehtinen 4:18.31/33:25.70, 5000m/ 3000mSt: Sandra Eriksson 16:16.04/9:57.72, HMar: Elina Lindgren 78:53, Mar: Johanna Kykyri 2:43:11, 100mh: Nooralotta Neziri 13.22, 400mh: Anniina Laitinen 58.30, HJ: Elina

Smolander 1.86, PV: Minna Nikkanen 4.30, LJ: Jaana Sieviläinen 6.23, TJ: Elina Torro 13.48, SP: Suvi Helin 15.01, DT: Tanja Komulainen 55.09, HT: Merja Korpela 67.43, JT: Oona Sormunen 59.14, Hep: Niina Kelo 5649, 10kW/20kW: Karolina Kaasalainen 46:58/1:38:10.

Olli-Pekka KARJALAINEN b. 7 Mar 1980 Töysä 1.94m 118kg. Töysän Veto. Political science student at University of Helsinki.
At HT: OG: '00/04- dnq 34/15, '08- 6; WCh: '99-01-03-05-07-09-11: 11/10/dnq 14/5/9/dnq 16/9; EC: '02-06-10-12: 8/2/10/11; WJ: '98- 1; EJ: '97- 3, '99- 1; EU23: '01- 2; ECp: '02- 1, '06- 3. Won WAF 2004, Finnish 1998-2012.
World junior hammer record 1999, three Finnish 2002-04.
Progress at HT: 1995- 48.26, 1996- 58.80, 1997- 69.84, 1998- 75.08, 1999- 78.33, 2000- 80.55, 2001- 80.54, 2002- 81.70, 2003- 80.20, 2004- 83.30, 2005- 79.81, 2006- 80.84, 2007- 78.35, 2008- 79.59, 2009- 78.70, 2010- 76.94, 2011- 76.60, 2012- 75.16.
Has 13 successive victories in annual match against Sweden.

Ari MANNIO b. 23 Jul 1987 Lehtimäki 1.85m 104kg. Lehtimäen Jyske.
At JT: OG: '12- 11; WCh: '11- dnq 14; EC: '12- 3; WJ: '04- 6, '06- 2; EU23: '07- 4, '09- 1; EJ: '05- 3; ET: '10- 3. Finnish champion 2011.
Progress at JT: 2004- 70.83, 2005- 76.40, 2006- 79.68, 2007- 80.31, 2008- 81.54, 2009- 85.70, 2010- 85.12. 2011- 85.12, 2012- 84.62.

Tero PITKÄMÄKI b. 19 Dec 1982 Ilmajoki 1.95m 92kg. Nurmon Urheilijat. Electrical engineer.
At JT: OG: '04- 8, '08- 3, '12- 5; WCh: '05-07-09-11: 4/1/5/dnq 17; EC: '06- 2, '10- 3, '12- 11; EU23: '03- 3; EJ: '01- 6; ECp: '06- 1. Won WAF 2005, 2007; Finnish 2004-07.
Progress at JT: 1999- 66.83, 2000- 73.75, 2001- 74.89, 2002- 77.24, 2003- 80.45, 2004- 84.64, 2005- 91.53, 2006- 91.11, 2007- 91.23, 2008- 87.70, 2009- 87.79, 2010- 86.92, 2011- 85.33, 2012- 86.98.

Antti RUUSKANEN b. 21 Feb 1984 Kokkola 1.89m 86kg. Pielaveden Sampo.
At JT: OG: '12- 3; WCh: '09- 6, '11- 9; EU23: '05- 2; EJ: '03- 3. Finnish chmpion 2012.
Progress at JT: 2002- 66.08, 2003- 72.87, 2004- 75.84, 2005- 79.75, 2006- 84.10, 2007- 82.71/87.88dh, 2008- 87.33, 2009- 85.39, 2010- 83.45, 2011- 82.29, 2012- 87.79.

Teemu WIRKKALA b. 21 Feb 1984 Pielavesi 1.87m 85kg. Toholammin Urheilijat.
At JT: OG: '08- 5; WCh: '07- 12, '09- 9; EC: '06- dnq 13, '10- 5, '12- dnq; WJ: '02- 7; EU23: '05- 6; EJ: '03- 1. Finnish champion 2009.
Progress at JT: 2001- 69.22, 2002- 74.56, 2003- 80.57, 2004- 80.87, 2005- 80.68, 2006- 82.82, 2007- 84.06, 2008- 84.10, 2009- 87.23, 2010- 86.53, 2011- 82.39, 2012- 83.73.

FRANCE

Governing body: Fédération Française d'Athlétisme, 33 avenue Pierre de Coubertin, 75640 Paris cedex 13. Founded 1920.

National Championships first held in 1888 (men), 1918 (women). **2012 Champions: Men**: 100m/200m: Christophe Lemaitre 9.94w/20.31, 400m: Yannick Fonsat 45.39, 800m: Pierre Ambroise Bosse 1:48.52, 1500m: Florian Carvalho 3:46.90, 5000m: Yohan Durand 13:51.81, 10,000m: Driss El Himer 29:19.19, HMar: Nicolas Fernandez 65:52, Mar: Stéphane Lefrand 2:18:01, 3000mSt: Mahiédine Mekhissi-Benabbad 8:27.80, 110mh: Garfield Darien 13.28, 400mh: Héni Kéchi 49.91, HJ: Mickaël Hanany 2.25, PV: Renaud Lavillenie 5.85, LJ: Frédéric Erin 8.01w, TJ: Harold Correa 16.74, SP: Tumatai Dauphin 19.23, DT: Lolassonn Djouhan 57.04, HT: Nicolas Figère 75.21, JT: Killian Durechou 75.06, Dec: Florian Geffrouais 8118, 10,000mW: Yohann Diniz 39:46.74, 20kW: Bertrand Moulinet 1:21:42, 50kW: Johan Augeron 4:06:55. **Women**: 100m/200m: Myriam Soumaré 11.21/22.74, 400m: Muriel Hurtis 52.17, 800m: Linda Marguet 2:03.79, 1500m: Hind Dehiba 4:18.60, 5000m: Christine Bardelle 15:48.38, HMar: Fatima Klilech-Fauvel 75:35, Mar: Aline Camboulives 2:38:49, 3000mSt: Claire Navez 9:51.62, 100mh: Alice Decaux 12.88, 400mh: Phara Anacharsis 55.97, HJ: Mélanie Melfort 1.91, PV: Vanessa Boslak 4.40, LJ: Eloyse Lesueur 6.45, TJ: Françoise Mbango 14.27, SP: Jessica Cérival 16.93, DT: Mélina Robert-Michon 60.57, HT: Stéphanie Falzon 70.57, JT: Matilde Andraud 56.34, Hep: Blandine Maisonnier 5858, 10,000mW: Anne-Gaëlle Retout 47:32.57, 20kW: Sylwia Korzeniowska 1:34:11.

Mehdi BAALA b. 17 Aug 1978 Strasbourg 1.83m 65kg. Lille Métropole Athlétisme.
At 1500m (800m): OG: '00- 4, '04- h, '08- 3; WCh: '01- 12, '03- 2, '05- sf (6), '07- dq sf, '09- 7, '11- 9; EC: '02- 1, '06- 1; WJ: '96- h; EU23: '99- 3; EJ: '97- 7; EI: '00- 3; WCp: '02- 3; ECp: '00-01-02-04-07-08: 1 (1)/2/1/1/1/1. Won FRA 800m 2001, 1500m 2002, 2005, 2009.
French records 800m 2002, 1000m (2) 2002-03, 1500m (2) 2003, 2000m 2005.
Progress at 800m, 1500m: 1994- 1:56.5, 4:08.1; 1995- 1:53.76, 3:48.74; 1996- 1:49.62, 3:43.50; 1997- 1:50.08, 3:45.34; 1998- 1:49.57, 3:41.86; 1999- 1:46.41, 3:34.83; 2000- 1:46.24, 3:32.05; 2001- 1:46.94, 3:31.97; 2002- 1:43.15, 3:32.03; 2003- 1:44.17, 3:28.98; 2004- 1:45.52, 3:31.25; 2005- 1:44.74, 3:30.80; 2006- 1:44.04, 3:32.01; 2007- 3:31.01, 2008- 3:32.00, 2009- 3:30.96, 2010- 3:34.59, 2011- 3:33.69, 2012- 3:39.42i. pbs: 1000m 2:13.96 '03, 1M 3:52.51i '09, 2000m 4:53.12 '05, 3000m 8:08.06i/8:23.69 '98.
Just one race in 2012. Married Hanane Sabri (ht WC 1500m '01, FRA champion 2001) in September 2000. His elder brother Samir won French marathon in 2002 and 2008.

Romain BARRAS b. 1 Aug 1980 Calais 1.94m 86kg. SO Calais.
At Dec: OG: '04- 13, '08- 5; WCh: '05-07-09-11: 7/7/12/11; EC: '06- 8, '10- 1; EU23: '01- 4; WUG: '01- 5, 03- 1; ECp: '03-06-08-10: 1/1/2/1; Won French 2005, 2011; MedG & Franc G 2005. At Hep: EI: '07- 6.
Progress at Dec: 1998- 6505, 1999- 7147, 2000- 7609, 2001- 7876, 2002- 7835, 2003- 8196, 2004- 8067, 2005- 8185, 2006- 8416w/8138, 2007- 8298, 2008- 8253, 2009- 8239, 2010- 8453, 2011- 8134. pbs: 60m 7.21i '07, 100m 11.02 '03, 10.89w '08; 400m 48.21 '06, 1000m 2:39.89i '06, 1500m 4:20.90 '09, 50mh 7.09i '04, 6.8i '03; 60mh 8.14i '01, 110mh 14.11 '08, HJ 2.04 '10, PV 5.05 '07, LJ 7.35 '05, SP 16.19 '10, DT 47.21 '04, JT 65.84 '05, Hep 5895i '06.
Won IAAF Combined Events Challenge 2010. Brother Guillaume has Dec pb 7523 '08, younger sister Diane Hep pb 5449 '11.

Benjamin COMPAORÉ b. 5 Aug 1987 Bar-le-Duc 1.89m 86kg. Strasbourg AA.
At TJ: OG: '12- 6; WCh: '11- 8; EWI: '12- 6; C: '10- 5; WJ: '06- 1; EJ: '05- 9.
Progress at TJ: 2003- 14.50, 2004- 15.48, 2005- 16.00/16.12w, 2006- 16.61, 2007- 16.62, 2008- 17.05, 2009- 16.98, 2010- 17.21/17.28w, 2011- 17.31, 2012- 17.17. pbs: 60m 7.13i '08, 100m 10.77 '12, 400m 48.69 '12, 1500m 4:44.43 '12, 110h 15.72 '12, HJ 1.98 '12, LJ 7.88 '08, Dec 6704 '12.

Garfield DARIEN b. 22 Dec 1987 Lyon 1.87m 76kg. EA Chambéry.
At 110mh: OG: '12- sf; WCh: '09- sf; EC: '10- 2, '12- 2; WJ: '04- 7; EJ: '05- 1; CCp: '10- 4; ET: '11- 2; FRA champion 2012. At 60mh: EI: '09- 6, '11- 2.
Progress at 110mh: 2004- 14.03/13.98w, 2005- 13.73, 2006- 13.94/13.92w, 2008- 13.50/13.43w, 2009- 13.36, 2010- 13.34, 2011- 13.37, 2012- 13.15. pbs: 200m 22.05 '06, 60mh 7.56i '11, HJ 1.83 '04. Father Daniel Darien had 110mh pb 13.76 '87.

Yohann DINIZ b. 1 Jan 1978 Epernay 1.85m 69kg. EFS Reims Athlétisme.
At 20kW: ECp: '07- 1; At 50kW: OG: '08- dnf, '12- dq; WCh: '05-07-09-11: dq/2/12/dq; EC: '06- 1, '10- 1; ECp: '05- 4. Won French 10,000mW 2010, 2012; 20kW 2007-09, 50kW 2005.
World record 50,000m track walk 2011. French records 5000mW (3) 2006-08, 20kW (3) 2005-12, 50kW 2006 & 2009, 1 Hr 2010.
Progress at 20kW, 50kW: 2001- 1:35:05.0t, 2002- 1:30:40, 2003- 1:26:54.99t, 2004- 1:24:25, 3:52:11.0t; 2005- 1:20:20, 3:45:17; 2006- 1:23:19, 3:41:39; 2007- 1:18:58, 3:44:22; 2008- 1:22:31, 2009- 1:22:50, 3:38:45; 2010- 1:20:23, 3:40:37; 2011- 3:35:27.2t, 2012- 1:17:43. pbs: 3000mW 10:52.44 '08, 5000mW 18:18.01 '08, 10,000mW 38:44.97 '11, 1HrW 15,395m '10.

Renaud LAVILLENIE b. 18 Sep 1986 Barbezieux-Saint-Hilaire 1.77m 69kg. Clermont Athl. Auvergne.

At PV: OG: '12- 1; WCh: '09- 3, '11- 3; WI: '12- 1; EC: '10- 1, '12- 1; EU23: '07- 10; EI: '09-11-13: 1/1/1; CCp: '10- 1; ET: '09-10: 1/1. Won DL 2010-12, French 2010, 2012.
French record (indoors) 2011.
Progress at 100m: 2002- 3.40, 2003- 4.30, 2004- 4.60, 2005- 4.81i/4.70, 2006- 5.25i/5.22, 2007- 5.58i/5.45, 2008- 5.81i/5.65, 2009- 6.01, 2010- 5.94, 2011- 6.03i/5.90, 2012- 5.97, 2013- 6.01i. pbs: 60m 7.23i '08, 60mh 8.41i '08, 100m 11.20 '11, 110mh 14.51 '10, HJ 1.89i '08, 1.87 '07; LJ 7.31 '10, Hep 5363i '08.
His brother Valentin (b. 16 Jul 1991) has PV pb 5.70i '13.

Christophe LEMAITRE b. 11 Jun 1990 Annecy 1.89m 74kg. AS Aix-les-Bains.
At 100m/(200m): OG: '12- (6); WCh: '09- qf, '11- 4/3/2R; EC: '10- 1/1/1R, '12- 1/3R; WJ: '08- (1); WY: '07- 4/5; EJ: '09- 1; CCp: '10- 1; ET: '10- 2, '11- 1/1. At 60m: EI: '11- 3. Won French 100m & 200m 2010-12.
French records 100m (7) 2010-11, 200m (2) 2010-11, European junior 100m 2009. U23 2010-11.
Progress at 100m, 200m: 2005- 11.46, 2006- 10.96, 2007- 10.53, 21.08; 2008- 10.26, 20.83; 2009- 10.04/10.03w, 20.68; 2010- 9.97, 20.16; 2011- 9.92, 19.80; 2012- 10.04/9.94w, 19.91. pb 60m 6.55i '10.
First Caucasian sub-10.00 100m runner and first to win sprint treble at European Champs.

Kevin MAYER b. 10 Feb 1992 Argenteuil 1.86m 77kg. EA Tain-Tournant..
At Dec: OG: '12- 15; EC: '12- dnf; WJ: '10- 1; EJ: '11- 1. At Oct: WY: '09- 1. At Hep: EI: '13- 2.
Progress at Dec: 2011- 7992, 2012- 8415. pbs: 60m 7.10i '13, 100m 11.10 '12, 400m 48.66 '11, 1000m 2:37.30i '13, 1500m 4:18.04 '12, 60mh 8.01i '13, 110mh 14.21 '12, HJ 2.10i '10, 2.09 '12; PV 5.20 '12, LJ 7.54i '13, 7.52 '11, SP 15.16i '13, 14.34 '12, DT 43.13 '12, JT 62.41 '12, Hep 6297i '13.

Mahiédine MEKHISSI-BENABBAD b. 15 Mar 1985 Reims 1.90m 75kg. EFS Reims.
At 3000mSt: OG: '08- 2, '12- 2; WCh: '07/09- h, '11- 3; EC: '10- 1, '12- 1; WJ: '04- h; EU23: '05- h, '07- 1; CCp: '10- 3; ECp: '07- 2, '08- 1; French champion 2008, 2012. At 1500m: WI: '10- 8; EI: '13- 1; WCp: '06- 7.
World best 2000m steeplechase 2010.
Progress at 3000mSt: 2003- 9:52.07, 2004- 9:01.01, 2005- 8:34.45, 2006- 8:28.25, 2007- 8:14.22, 2008- 8:08.95, 2009- 8:06.98, 2010- 8:02.52, 2011- 8:02.09, 2012- 8:10.90. pbs: 800m 1:53.61 '04, 1000m 2:17.14 '09, 1500m 3:33.86 '11, 2000m 5:00.17 '11, 3000m 7:44.98 '10, 5000m 14:32.9 '05, 2000mSt 5:10.68 '10.

Romain MESNIL b. 13 Jun 1977 Le Plessis Bouchard 1.88m 82kg. AC Paris Joinville. IT Engineer.
At PV: OG: '00-04-08-12: dnq 31/18/14=;/9= WCh: '99-01-03-07-09-11: nh/5/dnq/2/2/nh; EC: '02-06-10-12: dnq/2=/8/dnq; EU23: '99-1; WJ: '96- dnq 13=; WI: '99-01-03-04-12: 6=/3/7/7/8; EI: '09- 7; WCp: '06- 4; ECp: '03-04-06-07: 1/1/1/2. FRA champion 2000-03, 2008-09, 2011.
Progress at PV: 1993- 4.30, 1994- 4.65, 1995- 5.15, 1996- 5.30, 1997- 5.40, 1998- 5.80, 1999- 5.93, 2000- 5.75, 2001- 5.86i/5.85, 2002- 5.75, 2003- 5.95, 2004- 5.80, 2005- 5.75, 2006- 5.81, 2007- 5.86, 2008- 5.71, 2009- 5.85, 2010- 5.80, 2011- 5.80i/5.73, 2012- 5.72. pb Dec 5724 '98.
Former gymnast. Married to Karine Bénézech (PV 3.75i '99).

Bouabdellah 'Bob' TAHRI b. 20 Dec 1978 Metz 1.91m 68kg. Athlétisme Metz Métropole.
At 3000mSt: OG: '00- h, '04- 7, '08- 5; WCh: '99-01-03-05-07-09-11: 12/5/4/8/5/3/4; EC: '98-02-06-10: 10/4/3/2; WJ: '96- 7; WCp: '06- 3; ECp: '00-01-02-04: 1/1/1/1. At 5000m: EJ: '97- 1; CCp: '10- 3; ECp: '05- 2. At 3000m: WI: '01- 11; EI: '98-07-09: 8/2/2; ECp: '07- 1. World CC: '97- 22J, '04- 15 4k; Eur CC: '05- 4, '08- 6. Won FRA 1500m 2004, 2006; 3000mSt 1998, 2010-11.
Three European records 3000mSt 2003-09, indoor 5000m (13:11.13) 2010; best 2000mSt 2002 & 2009. World best 2000mSt 2010.
Progress at 3000mSt: 1996- 8:44.65, 1998- 8:19.75, 1999- 8:12.24, 2000- 8:16.14, 2001- 8:09.23, 2002- 8:10.83, 2003- 8:06.91, 2004- 8:14.26, 2005- 8:09.58, 2006- 8:09.53, 2007- 8:09.06, 2008- 8:12.72, 2009- 8:01.18, 2010- 8:03.72, 2011- 8:05.72. pbs: 800m 1:48.96 '01, 1000m 2:20.34 '05, 1500m 3:34.65 '09, 1M 3:52.95 '02, 2000m 4:57.58 '02, 3000m 7:33.18 '09, 5000m 13:12.29 '07, 10,000m 27:31.46 '11, 15km Rd 43:49 '12, HMar 66:12 '03, 2000mSt 5:13.47 '10. Missed 2012 season through injury.

Teddy TAMGHO b. 15 Jun 1989 Paris 1.87m 82kg. CA Montreuil.
At TJ: WCh: '09- 11; EC: '10- 3; WI: '10- 1; WJ: '08- 1; EJ: '07- 4; EI: '11- 1 (4 LJ); ET: '10- 3. Won DL 2010, French 2009-10.
Four World indoor triple jump records 2010 (17.90) & 2011, absolute French record 2009; three French (and Eur U23) records 2010.
Progress at TJ: 2004- 12.56, 2005- 14.89, 2006- 15.58, 2007- 16.53i/16.35/16.42w, 2008- 17.19/17.33w, 2009- 17.58i/17.11, 2010- 17.98, 2011- 17.92i/17.91. pbs: 60m 6.92i '06, 100m 10.60 '09, LJ 8.01i '11, 7.63 '07.
2011 season ended when broke ankle in warm-up for European U23s and also missed all of 2012 through injury.

Jimmy VICAUT b. 27 Feb 1992 Bondy 1.88m 83kg. Paris Avenir Athletic.
At 100m/4x100mR: OG: '12- sf; WCh: '11- 6/2R; EC: '10- 1R, '12- 2/3R; WJ: '10- 3; WY: '09- 7; EJ: '11- 1/1R. At 60m: EI: '13- 1.
Progress at 100m: 2005- 13.0, 2006- 12.50, 2007- 11.0, 2008- 10.75/10.69w, 2009- 10.56, 2010- 10.16, 2011- 10.07, 2012- 10.02. pbs: 60m 6.48i '12, 200m 20.58 '12.
His brother Willi was French U17 shot champion in 2012.

Women

Vanessa BOSLAK b. 11 Jun 1982 Lesquin 1.70m 57kg. Lagardère Paris Racing. Physiotherapist.
At PV: OG: '04- 6=, '08- 9, '12- 10; WCh: '05- 8, '07- 5; EC: '02-06-12: 11=/dnq 17=/6; WJ: '98- 6; '00- 3=; EU23: '03- 2; EJ: '01- 3; WI: '04-06-12: 5=/5/2; EI: '07- 6=; ECp: '01-02-04-06-07: 5/3/5/2/3; won Med G 2005, French 2001, 2003-05, 2007, 2012.
13 French pole vault records 2002-07.
Progress at PV: 1995- 3.25, 1996- 3.76, 1997- 3.90, 1998- 4.10, 1999- 4.15i/4.11, 2000- 4.32, 2001- 4.33i/4.30, 2002- 4.46, 2003- 4.50, 2004- 4.51, 2005- 4.60, 2006- 4.70, 2007- 4.70, 2008- 4.60i/4.55, 2011- 4.51i/4.30, 2012- 4.70i/4.55. pb JT 44.27 '99.

Stéphanie FALZON b. 7 Jan 1983 Bordeaux 1.70m 77kg. B. Sud Médoc Athlé.
At HT: OG: '12- 9; WCh: '07- dnq 16, '09- 9, '11- 12; EC: '06/10- dnq 15/17, '12- 6; WJ: '00- dnq 28, '02- 6; EU23: '03- dnq, '05- 8; EJ: '01- 8; French champion 2006, 2008, 2010, 2012.
Progress at HT: 2000- 53.71, 2001- 57.31, 2002- 59.98, 2003- 64.16, 2004- 65.21, 2005- 65.12, 2006- 68.84, 2007- 71.11, 2008- 73.40, 2009- 72.54, 2010- 73.40, 2011- 71.53, 2012- 73.06.

Eloyse LESUEUR b. 15 Jul 1988 Créteil 1.79m 65kg. Saint Denis Emotion.
At LJ: OG: '12- 8; WCh: '09- 11: dnq 18/26; WI: '08- 4; WY: '05- 2 (7 100m); EC: '12- 1; EU23: '09- 3; EJ: '07- 2; EI: '11- 4, '13- 2; ET: '10- 1, 11- 3. FRA champion 2010-12. At Hep: WJ: '06- dnf.
Progress at LJ: 2002- 5.72, 2003- 5.50, 2004- 5.68, 2005- 6.40, 2006- 6.30/6.47w, 2007- 6.47, 2008- 6.84i/6.50, 2009- 6.64/6.72w, 2010- 6.78, 2011- 6.91, 2012- 6.81/7.04w, 2013- 6.90i. pbs: 60m 7.34i '12, 100m 11.57 '06, 200m 24.11 '06, 800m 2:21.67 '06, 100mh 13.89 '06, HJ 1.75 '06, Hep 5370w/5320 '06.

Françoise MBANGO Etone b. 14 Apr 1976 Yaoundé 1.72m 63kg.
At TJ(/LJ): OG: '00- 10, '04- 1, '08- 1; WCh: '99- dnq 13, '01- 2, '03- 2; EC: '12- 8; CG: '98- 2/10, '02- 2, AfG: '99- 1/2; AfCh: '96-8-00-02-08: 3/2/2/1/1 (02- 1); WI: '03- 2, '04- 6; WCp: '02- 1/8. Won WAF 2004. FRA champion 1999, 2001-02.
Eleven African triple jump records 1999-2008, CMR records LJ from 1993, TJ from 1997.
Progress at TJ: 1994- 12.18, 1995- 11.92, 1996- 12.59, 1997- 13.75A, 1998- 14.02, 1999- 14.70A/14.65, 2000- 14.18, 2001- 14.65, 2002- 14.95, 2003- 15.05, 2004- 15.30, 2005- 14.07, 2008- 15.39, 2009- 13.83, 2012- 14.27/14.38w. pbs: 100m 12.00 '04, 11.5w '00, LJ 6.55A/6.43 '99, 6.68w '02.
First athlete from CMR to win Olympic, World and Commonwealth medals. Son Asma-Neils born in 2006. Suspended indefinitely by Cameroon's Athletics Federation in 2007 following her absence from the All Africa Games in Algiers and her withdrawal from the World Champs in Osaka. Returned, however, to compete at 2008 African Champs and went on to retain her Olympic title. Eligible to compete for France from 16 April 2012.

Mélanie MELFORT b. 8 Nov 1982 Hersbrück, Germany 1.82m 62kg. née Skotnik. Alsace Nord Athlétisme. Secretary.
At HJ: OG: '08- dnq 16=, '12- 9; WCh: '05-07-09-11: dnq 15=/7=/9/dnq 15; EC: 12- 6=; WJ: '00- 5; WY: '99- 5; EU23: '03- 5; EI: '07- 5=, '11- 4=; ECp: '05-07- 3/3. German champion 2003, French 2005, 2007-12.
French high jump record 2007.
Progress at HJ: 1995- 1.61, 1996- 1.65, 1997- 1.72, 1998- 1.72, 1999- 1.85, 2000- 1.86, 2001- 1.86, 2002- 1.88, 2003- 1.97i/1.91, 2004- 1.93i/1.90, 2005- 1.95, 2006- 1.93i/1.92, 2007- 1.97i/1.96, 2008- 1.95, 2009- 1.96i/1.93, 2010- 1.92i/1.89, 2011- 1.95, 2012- 1.93. pbs: 200m 25.22i/25.63w '10, 400m 56.34 '10.
French mother. Switched nationality from Germany to France with effect from 6 Mar 2005. Married coach Jimmy Melfort in 2009.

Antoinette NANA DJIMOU Ida b. 2 Aug 1985 Douala, Cameroon 1.74m 69kg. CA Montreuil.
At Hep: OG: '08- 18, '12- 6; WCh: '07- dnf, '09- 7, '11- 7; EC: '06-10-12: 21/dnf/1; WJ: '04- 4; EU23: '05- 5, '07- 7; ECp: '08- 2. At Pen: WI: '10- 5; EI: '09- 11-13: 3/1/1. Won French LJ 2008, Hep 2006-07.
CMR heptathlon record 2003, French indoor pentathlon record 2011.
Progress at Hep: 2003- 5360, 2004- 5649, 2005- 6089w/5792, 2006- 5981, 2007- 5982, 2008- 6204, 2009- 6323, 2010- 5994, 2011- 6409, 2012- 6576. pbs: 60m 7.51i '11, 100m 11.78 '08, 200m 24.36 '11, 800m 2:15.94 '12, 60mh 8.11i '10, 100mh 12.96 '12, HJ 1.84i '10, 1.83 '11; LJ 6.44i '09, 6.42 '12, 6.61w '08; SP 15.41i '13, 14.62 '12; JT 57.27 '12, Pen 4723i '11.
Came to France at age 14, naturalised French citizen in 2004. Three pbs when winning European gold in 2012.

Mélina ROBERT-MICHON b. 18 Jul 1979 Voiron 1.80m 85kg. Lyon Athlétisme
At DT: OG: '00/04- dnq 29/31, '08- 8, '12- 6; WCh: '01-03-07-09: dnq 20/11/11/8; EC: '98-02-06-12: dnq 29/12/dnq 17/6; WJ: '98- 2; EU23: '99-12, '01- 1; WUG: '01- 3; ECp: '00-01-02-03-04-06-07-08-09: 5/6/8/2/4/7/5/4/2. French champion 2000-09, 2011-12; MedG 2009.
Four French discus records 2000-02.
Progress at DT: 1997- 49.10, 1998- 59.27, 1999- 60.17, 2000- 63.19/63.61dh, 2001- 63.87, 2002- 65.78, 2003- 64.27, 2004- 64.54, 2005- 58.01, 2006- 59.89, 2007- 63.48, 2008- 62.21, 2009- 63.04, 2010- 56.52, 2011- 61.07, 2012- 63.98. pbs: SP 15.23 '07, HT 47.92 '02.
Daughter Elyssa born in 2010.

Myriam SOUMARÉ b. 29 Oct 1986 Paris 1.67m 57kg. AA Pays de France Athlé 95.

At 100m/(200m): OG: '12- sf/7; WCh: '09- qf, '11- sf/sf; EC: '10- 3/1/2R, '12- (3); EU23: '07- 3. At 4x400m: EJ: '05- 7. At 60m: WI: '10- 7; EI: '11- 7, '13- 3. Won FRA 100m 2009, 2012; 200m 2011-12. Progress at 100m: 2004- 24.66i, 2005- 12.07/11.98w, 24.05; 2006- 11.68, 23.78; 2007- 11.50/11.39w, 23.44; 2008- 11.43, 23.64/23.40w; 2009- 11.34, 23.34; 2010- 11.18/11.13w, 22.32; 2011- 11.17/11.12w, 22.71; 2012- 11.07, 22.56. pbs: 50m 6.22i '10, 55m 6.86i '13, 60m 7.07i '13, 400m 53.44'11, LJ 5.72 '07.
Astonishing breakthrough in final of European 200m 2010 when she improved pb from 23.01 to win in 22.32. Parents came from Mauritania.

GERMANY

Governing body: Deutscher Leichtathletik Verband (DLV), Alsfelder Str. 27, 64289 Darmstadt. Founded 1898.

National Championships first held in 1891.
2012 Champions: **Men**: 100m: Lucas Jakubczyk 10.16w, 200m: Julian Reus 20.58, 400m: Eric Krüger 46.15, 800m: Sören Ludolph 1:49.04, 1500m: Florian Orth 3:43.71, 5000m: Arne Gabius 13:51.78, 10,000m: Phillipp Pflieger 28:45.76, HMar: Stefan Koch 65:22, Mar: Jan Simon Hamann 2:19:46, 3000mSt: Benedikt Karus 8:42.81, 110mh: Alexander John 13.52, 400mh: Georg Fleischhauer 49.74, HJ: Elke Onnen 2.25, PV: Malte Mohr 5.82, LJ: Sebastian Bayer 7.91, TJ: Andreas Pohle 16.64, SP: David Storl 20.96, DT: Robert Harting 67.79, HT: Markus Esser 75.38, JT: Thomas Röhler 78.58, Dec: Kai Kazmirek 7924, 10,000mW: André Höhne 40:10.47, 20kW: Christopher Linke 1:20:55, 50kW: Carsten Schmidt 4:14:41. **Women**: 100m: Verena Sailer 11.22, 200m: Inna Weit 23.52, 400m: Esther Cremer 52.21, 800m: Anne Kesslering 2:04.60, 1500m: Corrinna Harrer 4:11.04, 5000m/10,000m: Sabrina Mockenhaupt 15:47.01/32:24.36, HMar: Simret Restle 72:59, Mar: Susanne Hahn 2:32:11, 3000mSt: Antje Möldner-Schmidt 9:42.42, 100mh: Carolin Nytra 12.74, 400mh: Tina Kron 57.36, HJ: Ariane Friedrich 1.86, PV: Silke Spiegelburg 4.70, LJ: Beatrice Marscheck 6.49, TJ: Jenny Elbe 14.06, SP: Nadine Kleinert 19.18, DT: Nadine Müller 66.47, HT: Betty Heidler 73.65, JT: Christina Obergfoll 65.86, Hep: Lira Biesenbach 5779, 5000mW/20kW: Sabine Krantz 21:01.73/1:33:02.

Ralf BARTELS b. 21 Feb 1978 Malchin 1.86m 138kg. SC Neubrandenburg. Soldier.
At SP: OG: '04- 8, '12- dnq 16; WCh: '01-03-05-07-09-11: dnq 17/5/3/7/3/10; EC: '02- 3, '06- 1, '10- 3; WJ: '96- 1; EU23: '99- 6; EJ: '95- 4, '97- 1; WI: '10- 3; EI: '09-11-13: 3/1/4; WCp: '02- 3, '06- 1; ECp: '04-05-06-10: 3/1/3/2. GER champion 2002-06, 2008-10.
Progress at SP: 1995- 17.63, 1996- 18.71, 1997- 18.35, 1998- 18.50, 1999- 18.95, 2000- 19.34, 2001- 20.30, 2002- 20.85, 2003- 20.67, 2004- 20.88, 2005-

21.36, 2006- 21.43i/21.13, 2007- 20.75, 2008- 20.60, 2009- 21.37, 2010- 21.44i/21.14, 2011- 21.16i/20.58, 2012- 20.40.

Sebastian BAYER b. 11 Jun 1986 Aachen 1.89m 79kg. Hamburger SV. Soldier.
At LJ: OG: '08- dnq 23, '12- 5; WCh: '09- dnq 19, '11- 8; EC: '06- dnq 20. '12- 1; WJ: '04- dnq 17; EJ: '05- 2; EI: '09- 1, '11- 1. German champion 2006, 2008-09, 2011-12.
Progress at LJ: 2000- 5.65, 2001- 6.14, 2002- 6.57, 2003- 7.27, 2004- 7.57, 2005- 7.82i/7.73, 2006- 7.95, 2007- 7.88i, 2008- 8.15, 2009- 8.71i/8.49, 2010- 8.06, 2011- 8.17, 2012- 8.34. pbs: 60m 6.80i '09, 100m 10.73 '09, HJ 1.83 '03.
Sensational improvement at 2009 European Indoors – from pb of 8.17 to 8.29 and then European record 8.71 with final jump.

Pascal BEHRENBRUCH b. 19 Jan 1985 Offenbach 1.96m 94kg. LG Eintracht Frankfurt.
At Dec: OG: '12- 10; WCh: '09- 6, '11- 7; EC: '06- 5, '12- 1; EJ: '03- 10; EU23: '07- 2.
Progress at Dec: 2005- 7842, 2006- 8209, 2007- 8239, 2008- 8242, 2009- 8439, 2010- 8202, 2011- 8232, 2012- 8558. pbs: 60m 7.08i '10, 100m 10.84 '07, 400m 48.48 '06, 1000m 2:53.39i '06, 1500m 4:24.16 '06, 60mh 8.10i '10, 110mh 14.02 '09, HJ 2.03 '08, PV 5.00 '12, LJ 7.21 '11, 7.32w '07, SP 16.89 '12, DT 51.31 '09, JT 71.40 '11, Hep 5604i '06.

Matthias de ZORDO b. 21 Feb 1988 Bad Kreuznach 1.90m 97kg. SC Magdeburg.
At JT: OG: '12- dnq; WCh: '11- 1; EC: '10- 2; EU23: '09- 8; EJ: '07- 1, CCp: '10- 3; ET: '10- 1. Won DL 2011, German 2010-11.
Progress at JT: 2006- 71.67, 2007- 78.67, 2008- 82.51, 2009- 80.15, 2010- 87.81, 2011- 88.36, 2012- 81.62.
Left-handed.thrower.

Markus ESSER b. 3 Feb 1980 Leverkusen 1.80m 105kg. TSV Bayer 04 Leverkusen. Army lieutenant.
At HT: OG: '00-04-08: dnq 35/11/9; WCh: '05-07-09-11: 4/8/6/4; EC: '02-06-10-12: dnq 29/4/dnq 19/7; WJ: '98- 12; EJ: '99- 3; EU23: '01- 7; ECp: '04-05-07-08-09-10-11: 2/3/2/3/3/3/1. German champion 2006-08, 2010-12.
Progress at HT: 1997- 64.78, 1998- 73.10, 1999- 70.29, 2000- 76.66, 2001- 75.69, 2002- 76.94, 2003- 78.13, 2004- 79.01, 2005- 80.00, 2006- 81.10, 2007- 80.68, 2008- 79.97, 2009- 79.43, 2010- 78.87, 2011- 79.69, 2012- 77.93.

Rico FREIMUTH b. 14 Mar 1988 Potsdam 1.96m 92kg. Hallesche LA-Freunde.
At Dec: OG: '12- 6; WCh: '11- dnf; EU23: 09- 10; EJ: '07- 3.
Progress at Dec: 2009- 7689, 2010- 7826, 2011- 8287, 2012- 8322. pbs: 60m 6.98i '12, 100m 10.62 '12, 10.50w '11; 200m 21.39 '12, 400m 47.51 '12, 1000m 2:48.22i '12, 1500m 4:35.77 '10, 60mh 8.06i '11, 110mh 13.79 '12, HJ 1.94 '10, PV 4.90 '12, LJ

The men's Olympic marathon with the Houses of Parliament as a backdrop.

Renaud Lavillenie was the supreme pole vaulter of 2012.

At her third attempt Sanya Richards-Ross at last won the Olympic 400m title.

Barbora Spotáková had four javelin throws better than any rival at the Olympics.

Tirunesh Dibaba returned to win the Olympic 10,000m title.

Natalya Antyukh (2nd right) won 400m hurdles gold after a decade of winning relay medals.

Jenn Suhr had a limited season but won the Olympic pole vault title.

Alberto Juantorena on his way to victory in the 1976 Olympics at 800m, leading Ivo Van Damme and a bearded Steve Ovett.

Wang Junxia wins the Olympic 5000m in 1996.

7.41 '10, 7.42w '11, SP 15.14 '12, DT 49.11 '12, JT 65.04 '11, Hep 5715i '12.

His father Uwe had decathlon best of 8794 (1984), and was 4th at 1983 Worlds and 1986 Europeans and twice winner at Götzis. Uwe and Rico are the highest scoring father-son combination. His uncle Jörg won the high jump bronze medal at the 1980 Olympic Games in a pb of 2.31.

Robert HARTING b. 18 Oct 1984 Cottbus 2.01m 126kg. SCC Berlin.
At DT: OG: 08- 4, '12- 1; WCh: '07- 2, '09- 1, '11- 1; ECh: '06- dnq 13, '10- 2, '12- 1; CCp: '10- 1; ECp: '07-08-09-10-11: 2/2/2/1/1; WJ: '02- dnq 13; EU23: '05- 1. German champion 2007-12.
Progress at DT: 2002- 54.25, 2003- 59.54, 2004- 64.05, 2005- 66.02, 2006- 65.22, 2007- 66.93, 2008- 68.65, 2009- 69.43, 2010- 69.69, 2011- 68.99, 2012- 70.66. pb SP 18.63 '07.
Unbeaten in 16 competitions 2011 and in 12 in 2021. Younger brother Christoph (b. 4 Oct 1990) has pb 62.12 '11.

Raphael HOLZDEPPE b. 28 Sep 1989 Kaiserslautern 1.78m 69kg. LAZ Zweibrücken.
At PV: OG: 08- 8, '12- 3; WCh: '11- dnq 20; EC '10- 9, '12- 3; WJ: '06- 5, '08- 1; EU23: '09- 1; EJ: '07- dnq; EI: '13- 8.
World junior pole vault record (=) 2008 (and indoors 5.68).
Progress at PV: 2002- 3.45, 2003- 4.25, 2004- 4.50, 2005- 5.00, 2006- 5.42, 2007- 5.50, 2008- 5.80, 2009- 5.65, 2010- 5.80, 2011- 5.72, 2012- 5.91, 2013- 5.82i.

Jan Felix KNOBEL b. 16 Jan 1989 Bad Homburg 1.92m 91kg. LG Eintracht Frankfurt. Architecture student.
At Dec: OG: '12- dnf; WCh: '11- 8; EU23: '11- 19; WJ: '06- 1. Won GER 2009. At Oct: WY: 05- 5.
Progress at Dec: 2009- 7758, 2010- dnf, 2011- 8288, 2012- 8228. pbs: 60m 7.18i '10, 100m 11.04 '12, 400m 48.89 '12, 1000m 2:49.22i '10, 1500m 4:43.12 '11, 60mh 8.27i '13, 110mh 14.60 '12, HJ 2.01 '11, PV 5.03 '12, LJ 7.30 '11, 7.32w '10, SP 16.06 '11, DT 49.60 '11, JT 72.99 '11, Hep 5778i '10.

Malte MOHR b. 24 Jul 1986 Bochum 1.92m 84kg. TV Wattenscheid.
At PV: OG: '12- 9=; WCh: '09- 14, '11- 5; EC: '10- dnq 17=, '121- 4; WI: '10- 2, '12- 4; EI: '11- 3, 13- 3; ET: '09- 2, '11- 2. German champion 2010-12.
Progress at PV: 2003- 4.81, 2004- 5.11i, 2005- 5.30, 2006- 5.71, 2007- 5.31, 2008- 5.76, 2009- 5.80, 2010- 5.90, 2011- 5.86i/5.85, 2012- 5.91, 2013- 5.81i.
His father (and coach) Wolfgang Mohr had a best of 5.41 in 1976 and his mother Gisela Derksen was a good junior multi-eventer.

Björn OTTO b. 16 Oct 1977 Frechen 1.91m 90kg. ASV Köln.
At PV: OG: '12- 2; WCh: '07- 5, '09- dnq 18=; EC: '12- 2; WI: '12- 2; EI: '00-05-07-11: 6/4/3/2; WUG: '99-01-03-05: 8/7/3=/1.

German pole vault record 2012.
Progress at PV: 1991- 3.20, 1992- 3.20, 1993- 4.10, 1994- 4.71, 1995- 5.00, 1996- 5.30i/5.20, 1997- 5.40, 1998- 5.52sq/5.40, 1999- 5.55/5.60ex, 2000- 5.65/5.71ex, 2001- 5.51/5.63ex, 2002- 5.63sq/5.60, 2003- 5.72i/5.70, 2004- 5.82i/5.70, 2005- 5.80, 2006- 5.85, 2007- 5.90, 2008- 5.70, 2009- 5.71, 2010- 5.60i/5.41, 2011- 5.75/5.80ex, 2012- 6.01, 2013- 5.90i. Two world over-35 records 2013.

Christian REIF b. 24 Oct 1984 Speyer 1.96m 84kg. LC Rehlingen. Sports student.
At LJ: OG: '12- dnq 13; WCh: '07- 9, '11- 7; EC: '10- 1; WI: '05- 5; EI: '13- 3; CCp: '10- 3. German champion 2010.
Progress at LJ: 2001- 7.15, 2002- 7.55, 2004- 7.83, 2005- 7.64i, 2006- 7.90, 2007- 8.19, 2008- 7.80, 2009- 8.18, 2010- 8.47, 2011- 8.26/8.38w, 2012- 8.26. pbs: 60m 6.86i '06, 100m 10.68 '06, 200m 21.90 '06.
Tied pb of 8.27 in qualifying, then 8.47 in final of Europeans 2010.

Raúl SPANK b. 13 Jul 1988 Dresden 1.90m 75kg. Dresdner SC. Economics student.
At HJ: OG: '08- 5; WCh: '09- 3=, '11- 9; WJ: '06- 5; WY: '05- 7; EJ: '07- 2; WI: '12- 9=; EI: '09- 7, '11- 8; ET: '11- 3+; German champion 2008, 2010-11.
Progress at HJ: 2003- 1.88, 2004- 2.02, 2005- 2.12, 2006- 2.23, 2007- 2.24, 2008- 2.32, 2009- 2.33, 2010- 2.30, 2011- 2.32, 2012- 2.32i/2.25. pbs: 200m 22.02i '08, 60mh 8.00i '12, LJ 7.36i '11, TJ 16.54i/16.44 '12.

David STORL b. 21 Jul 1990 Rochlitz 1.99m 115kg. LAC Erdgas Chemnitz. Federal police officer.
At SP: OG: '12- 2; WCh: '09- dnq 28. '11- 1; EC: '10- 5, '12- 1; WJ: '08- 1; WY: '07- 1; EU23: '11- 1; EJ: '09- 1; WI: '10- 7, '12- 2; EI: '11- 2; ET: '11- 1. German champion 2011-12.
World junior shot record and three with 6kg (to 22.73) 2009.
Progress at SP: 2008- 18.46, 2009- 20.43, 2010- 20.77, 2011- 21.78, 2012- 21.88i/21.86.

Martin WIERIG b. 10 Jun 1987 Neindorf 2.02m 108kg. SC Magdeburg. Federal police officer.
At DT: OG: '12- 6; WCh: '11- dnq 18; EC: '10- 7, '12- dnq 14; WJ: '04- 8, '06- 3; EU23: '07- 1, '09- 3; EJ: '05- 3 (dnq SP).
Progress at DT: 2005- 57.44, 2006- 57.37, 2007- 61.10, 2008- 63.09, 2009- 63.90, 2010- 64.93, 2011- 67.21, 2012- 68.33. pb SP 17.30 '11.

Women

Anna BATTKE b. 3 Jan 1985 Düsseldorf 1.73m 58kg. USC Mainz.
At PV: WCh: '09- 7=; EU23: '07- 3; EI: '09- 3; WI: '08- 8.
Progress at PV: 2004- 4.00, 2005- 4.20, 2006- 4.20, 2007- 4.56, 2008- 4.50i/4.40, 2009- 4.68, 2010- 4.60, 2011- 4.51i/4.50, 2012- 4.52i.
Twin sister Sara ran 200m pb 23.73 in heats of World Juniors 2004.

Ariane FRIEDRICH b. 10 Jan 1984 Nordhausen/Harz 1.79m 57kg. LG Eintracht Frankfurt.
At HJ: OG: '08- 7=, '12- dnq 14; WCh: '09- 3; EC: '10- 3; EU23: '05- 3; EJ: '03- 1; WI: '08- 8=; EI: '09- 1; ECp: 04-08-09-10: 3/1/1/3; WUG: '05-07-09: 3/2/1. German champion 2008-10, 2012.
German high jump record 2009.
Progress at HJ: 1998- 1.62, 1999- 1.68, 2000- 1.73, 2001- 1.81, 2002- 1.86, 2003- 1.88, 2004- 1.92, 2005- 1.90, 2006- 1.91, 2007- 1.94, 2008- 2.03, 2009- 2.06, 2010- 2.02, 2012- 1.93.
Missed the 2011 season after surgery to repair a ruptured Achilles tendon.

Kristina GADSCHIEW b. 3 Jul 1984 Vassilyev–ka, Kyrgyzstan 1.70m 62kg. LAZ Zweibrücken.
At PV: WCh: '09- 10, '11- 10=; WUG: '07- 2, '09- 3; WI: '10- 7; EI: '09-11-13: 5/3/7.
Progress at PV: 1999- 3.50, 2000- 3.65, 2001- 3.90i/3.70, 2005- 4.22, 2006- 4.35, 2007- 4.40, 2008- 4.52, 2009- 4.58, 2010- 4.60, 2011- 4.66i/4.60, 2012- 4.60, 2013- 4.55i.
Moved to Germany as a child.

Betty HEIDLER b. 14 Oct 1983 Berlin 1.75m 80kg. LG Eintracht Frankfurt. Federal police officer.
At HT: OG: '04- 4, '08- 9, '12- 3; WCh: '03-05-07-09-11: 11/dnq 29/1/2/2; EC: '06-10-12: 5/1/dnq 17; EU23: '03- 4, '05- 2; WJ: '00/02- dnq 19/17; EJ: '01- 9, WUG: '09- 1; CCp: '10- 4; ECp: '04-07-09-10-11: 3/1/2/1/1. Won WAF 2006, 2009; World HT challenge 2010-12, GER 2005-12.
World hammer record 2011, seven German records 2004-11.
Progress at HT: 1999- 42.07, 2000- 56.02, 2001- 60.54, 2002- 63.38, 2003- 70.42, 2004- 72.73, 2005- 72.19, 2006- 76.55, 2007- 75.77, 2008- 74.11, 2009- 77.12, 2010- 76.38, 2011- 79.42, 2012- 78.07.

Carolin HINGST b. 18 Sep 1980 Donauwörth 1.74m 60kg. USC Mainz.
At PV: OG: '04- dnq 22=, '08- 6; WCh: '01-03-05-07: 10/dnq 15=/10/dnq 17=; EC: '02- dnq 13=, '10- 11; EU23: '01- 3; WI: '04- dnq 9; EI: '05- 4; ECp: '05- 2; German champion 2004, 2008.
Progress at PV: 1999- 3.60, 2000- 4.01, 2001- 4.50, 2002- 4.50, 2003- 4.51, 2004- 4.66, 2005- 4.65i/4.50, 2006- 4.52, 2007- 4.70i/4.61, 2008- 4.65, 2009- 4.60i/4.53, 2010- 4.72, 2011- 4.65, 2012- 4.40. pbs: 100mh 14.54 '98, HJ 1.75 '98, LJ 5.81 '98.

Kathrin KLAAS b. 6 Feb 1984 Haiger 1.68m 72kg. LG Eintracht Frankfurt.
At HT: OG: '08- dnq 24, '12- 5; WCh: '05- dnq, '07- dnq 27, '09- 4, '11- 7; EC: '06-10-12: 6/dnq 15/4; EJ: '03-8, EU23: '05- 4; WUG: '09- 3.
Progress at HT: 2000- 44.24, 2001- 50.10, 2002- 57.74, 2003- 63.72, 2004- 68.01, 2005- 70.91, 2006- 71.67, 2007- 73.45, 2008- 70.39, 2009- 74.23, 2010- 74.53, 2011- 75.48, 2012- 76.05.

Nadine KLEINERT b. 20 Oct 1975 Magdeburg 1.90m 90kg. SC Magdeburg. Soldier.
At SP: OG: '00- 8, '04- 2, '08- 7, '12- dnq 13; WCh: '97- 99-01-03-05-07-09-11: 7/2/2/7/5/3/2/8; EC: '98-02-06-10-12: 6/6/6/7/1; WJ: '92- 12, '94- 6; EU23: '94- 3Cp, '97- 1; EJ: '93- 2; WI: '99-01-04-06-10-12: 5/4/3/2/5/5; EI: '96-98-00: 5/5/2; ECp: '99-01-04-05-09-11: 2/1/3/2/1/1. Won GP 1999. German champion 1998, 2000-01, 2005, 2008, 2010, 2012 (& 7 indoors).
Progress at SP: 1990- 13.85, 1991- 15.08, 1992- 16.32, 1993- 17.07, 1994- 17.44, 1995- 17.13, 1996- 18.37, 1997- 18.91, 1998- 19.22, 1999- 19.61, 2000- 19.81, 2001- 19.86, 2002- 19.24, 2003- 19.33i/19.14, 2004- 19.55, 2005- 20.06, 2006- 19.64i/19.15, 2007- 19.77, 2008- 19.89, 2009- 20.20, 2010- 19.64, 2011- 19.26, 2012- 19.67. pb DT 50.99 '01.
Made all 24 major World and European finals she contested from 1997 until missing Olympic final by one place in 2012.

Gesa Felicitas KRAUSE b. 3 Aug 1992 Ehringshausen 1.67m 50kg. LG Eintracht Frankfurt. Student.
At 3000mSt: OG: '12- 8; WCh: '11- 9; EC: '12- 4; WJ: '10- 4; EJ: '11- 1. At 2000mSt: WY: '09- 7.
European junior 3000mSt record 2011.
Progress at 3000mSt: 2010- 9:47.78, 2011- 9:32.74, 2012- 9:23.52. pbs: 800m 2:05.25 '11, 1000m 2:44.68 '10, 1500m 4:11.94 '12, 3000m 9:01.16i '12, 5km Rd 16:15 '11, 2000mSt 6:22.45 '11.

Irina MIKITENKO b. 23 Aug 1972 Bakanas, Kazakhstan 1.58m 49kg. née Volynskaya. TV Wattenscheid 01.
At 5000m: OG: '96- h, '00- 5, '04- 7; WCh: '99- 4, '01- 5, '03- h; ECp: '99-00: 2/2. At 10,000m: EC: '98- 8, '06- 9; WCp: '98- 5. At Mar: OG: '12- 14. 3rd GP 3000m 1999. World 4k CC: '00- 19. Won Central Asian 1500m 1995; German 10,000m 1998, 2006, 2008; 5000m 1999-2000, 2006.
W35 marathon best 2008, German records 3000m 2000, 5000m (3) 1999, marathon 2008.
Progress at 5000m, 10,000m, Mar: 1995- 15:47.85, 1996- 15:49.59, 1997- 15:48.29, 1998- 15:18.86, 32:10.61; 1999- 14:42.03, 31:38.68; 2000- 14:43.59; 2001- 14:53.00, 31:29.55; 2003- 14:56.64, 31:38.48; 2004- 14:55.43, 32:04.86; 2006- 15:28.00, 31:44.82; 2007- 32:42.95, 2:24:51; 2008- 31:57.71, 2:19:19; 2009- 2:22:11, 2010- 32:48.69, 2:26:40; 2011- 2:22:18, 2012- 2:24:53, 2013- 2:26:41. pbs: 800m 2:09.97 '98, 1500m 4:06.08 '01, 2000m 5:40.6 '01, 3000m 8:30.39 '00, Road: 10km 30:57 '08, HMar 68:51 '08, 25km 1:23:08 '08, 30km 1:39:36 '08.
Made fine marathon debut with 2nd Berlin 2007 and in 2008 won London in pb 2:24:14, improving by 4:55 when she won in Berlin. Won again in London and 2nd Chicago 2009. She won the Marathon Majors prize for 2007-08 and 2008-09. 2nd Berlin 2011. German parents; changed nationality from Kazakhstan to Germany in March 1998. Her husband Alexander had 5000m pb of 13:39.95 (1994); son Alexander, and daughter Vanessa (born in

July 2005). Her father-in-law Leonid Mikitenko won the 1966 European bronze medal at 10,000m with pbs 13.36.4 for 5000m, 28:12.4 at 10,000m.

Antje MÖLDNER-SCHMIDT b. 13 Jun 1984 Babelsberg 1.73m 56kg. SC Potsdam. Police officer.
At 3000mSt: OG: '08- h, '12- 7; WCh: '09- 9; EC: '12- 3; ECp: '09- 1. At 1500m: WJ: '02- h, EU23: '05- 3, EJ: '03- 6; EI: '05- 6. Won GER 1500m 2005, 2007; 3000mSt 2009, 2012.
GER records 3000mSt (5) 2000mSt (2) 2008-09.
Progress at 3000mSt: 2008- 9:29.86, 2009- 9:18.54, 2012- 9:21.78. pbs: 800m 2:04.34 '05, 1000m 2:48.36 '07, 1500m 4:08.81 '05, 2000m 5:47.66 '06, 3000m 9:00.74 '05, 5000m 16:05.82 '07, 2000mSt 6:15.90 '09. Unable to compete in 2010 due to a lymphoid cells disorder.

Katharina MOLITOR b. 8 Nov 1983 Bedurg, Erft 1.82m 76kg. TSV Bayer 04 Leverkusen.
At JT: OG: '08- 8; WCh: '11- 5, '12- 6; EC: '10- 4, '12- 5; EU23: '05- 2; WUG: '07- 6, '08- 4. German champion 2010.
Progress at JT: 2000- 42.94, 2001- 48.53, 2002- 49.01, 2003- 48.03, 2004- 50.04, 2005- 57.01, 2006- 57.58, 2007- 58.87, 2008- 61.74, 2009- 62.69, 2010- 64.53, 2011- 64.67, 2012- 63.20.
Played volleyball in the Bundesliga.

Nadine MÜLLER b. 21 Nov 1985 Leipzig 1.93m 90kg. Hallesche LA-Freunde. Federal police officer.
At DT: OG: '12- 5; WCh: '07- dnq 23, '09- 6, '11- 2; EC: '10- 8, '12- 2; WJ: '04- 3; EU23: '05- 10, '07- 8; EJ: '03- 2; ET: '10- 1. German champion 2010-12.
Progress at DT: 2000- 36.10, 2001- 46,27, 2002- 48.90, 2003- 53.44, 2004- 57.85, 2005- 59.35, 2006- 58.46, 2007- 62.93, 2008- 61.36, 2009- 63.46, 2010- 67.78, 2011- 66.99, 2012- 68.89.

Carolin NYTRA b. 26 Feb 1985 Hamburg 1.75m 62kg. MTG Mannheim. Sports management student.
At 100mh: OG: '08/12- sf; WCh: '09- sf; EC: '10- 3; WJ: '04- 6; EU23: '05- 6, '07- 6; ET: '10- 2. German champion 2008-10, 2012. At 60mh: EI: '11- 1.
Progress at 100mh: 2002- 13.91, 2003- 14.36, 2004- 13.54, 2005- 13.28, 2006- 13.32, 2007- 13.17, 2008- 12.82, 2009- 12.78, 2010- 12.57, 2012- 12.74. pbs: 60m 7.50i '10, 100m 11.96 '07, 60mh 7.80i '11. LJ 6.04i/5.89 '05.

Christina OBERGFÖLL b. 22 Aug 1981 Lahr (Baden) 1.75m 79kg. LG Offenburg.
At JT: OG: '04- dnq 15, '08- 3, '12- 2; WCh: '05-07-09-11: 2/2/5/4; EC: '06-10-12: 4/2/2; EU23: '01- 9, '03- 8; WJ: '00- 8; ECp: '07-09-10-11: 1/1/1/1. Won DL 2011, German 2007-08, 2011-12.
European javelin records 2005 & 2007.
Progress at JT: 1997- 49.20, 1998- 48.52, new: 1999- 50.57, 2000- 54.50, 2001- 56.83, 2002- 60.61, 2003- 57.40, 2004- 63.34, 2005- 70.03, 2006- 66.91, 2007- 70.20, 2008- 69.81, 2009- 68.59, 2010- 68.63, 2011- 69.57, 2012- 67.04.
Made a Great breakthrough at the 2005 World Champs to take her pb from 64.59 to a European record 70.03 and the silver medal.

Jennifer OESER b. 29 Nov 1983 Brunsbüttel 1.76m 65kg. TSV Bayer 04 Leverkusen. Federal police officer.
At Hep: OG: '08- 11, '12- 30 (dnf 1500m); WCh: '07- 7, '09- 2, '11- 3; EC: '06- 4, '10- 3; WJ: '02- 8; EU23: '03- 1. German champion 2006.
Progress at Hep: 2000- 5167, 2001- 5531, 2002- 5595, 2003- 5901, 2004- 5936, 2005- 5637, 2006- 6376, 2007- 6378, 2008- 6436, 2009- 6493, 2010- 6683, 2011- 6663, 2012- 6345. pbs: 200m 23.95 '11, 800m 2:10.39 '11, 60mh 8.56i '09, 100mh 13.14 '11, HJ 1.86 '06, LJ 6.68 '10, 6.70w '11; SP 14.29 '09, JT 51.30 '11, Pen 4423i '09.
Four pbs in EC Heptathlon bronze 2010.

Elisaveta 'Lisa' RYZIH b. 27 Sep 1988 Omsk, Russia 1.79m 58kg. Formerly Ryshich. ABC Ludwigshafen. Psychology student.
At PV: OG: '12- 6=; EC: '10- 3, '12- 7; WJ: '04- 1, '06- nh; WY: '03- 1; EU23: '09- 1; EJ: '07- 4; EI: '11- 7; CCp: '10- 2.
Progress at PV: 2002- 3.92, 2003- 4.10, 2004- 4.30, 2005- 4.15, 2006- 4.35, 2007- 4.35, 2008- 4.52i/4.50, 2009- 4.50, 2010- 4.65, 2011- 4.65i, 2012- 4.65. pb LJ 5.38w '06.
Set world age bests at 13 in 2002 and 15 in 2004. Her sister 'Nastja' was World Indoor champion in 1999 and set four world junior and five European junior PV records in 1996 to 4.15, and three German records in 1999 to 4.50i/4.44 and had a pb of 4.63 in 2006. Their family left Omsk in Siberia in 1992 to live in Ulm; mother Yekaterina Ryzhikh (née Yefimova b. 20 Jan 1959) had HJ pb 1.91i '85 and 1.89 '81, and father Vladimir is a pole vault coach.

Verena SAILER b. 16 Oct 1985 Illertissen 1.66m 57kg. MTG Mannheim
At 100m: OG: '08- 5R, '12- sf; WCh: '07- qf, '09- sf/3R; EC: '06- sf, '10- 1, '12- 6/1R; WJ: '04- 5; EU23: '05- 3, '07- 1; EJ: '03- 6; CCp: '10- 4; ECp: '07- 2. At 60m: EI: '09- 3, '13- 8. Won German 100m 2006-10, 2012.
Progress at 100m: 2001- 12.13, 2002- 11.88, 2003- 11.58, 2004- 11.49. 2005- 11.51, 2006- 11.43, 2007- 11.31, 2008- 11.28, 2009- 11.18/11.11w, 2010- 11.10/11.06w, 2011- 11.63/11.46w, 2012- 11.05. pbs: 60m 7.12i '13, 200m 24.01 '06.
Former gymnast.

Christina SCHWANITZ b. 24 Dec 1985 Dresden 1.80m 103kg. LV 90 Erzebirge. Soldier.
At SP: OG: '08- 11, '12- 10; WCh: '05- 9, '09- 12, '11- 12; EC: '12- 5; WJ: '04- 3; EU23: '05- 2; WI: '08- 6; EI: '11- 2, '13- 1; ECp: '08- 1. German champion 2011.
Progress at SP: 2001- 13.57, 2002- 14.26, 2003-

15.25, 2004- 16.98, 2005- 18.84, 2007- 17.06, 2008- 19.68i/19.31, 2009- 19.06, 2010- 18.28, 2011- 19.20, 2012- 19.15i/19.05, 2013- 19.79i. pb DT 47.27 '03.

Lilli SCHWARZKOPF b. 28 Aug 1983 Novo Pokrovka, Kyrgyzhstan 1.74m 65kg. LG Rhein-Wied. Student.
At Hep: OG: '08- 8, '12- 2; WCh: '05-07-09-11: 13/5/dnf/6; EC: '06- 3; WJ: '02- 5; EU23: '05- 2. German champion 2004.
Progress at Hep: 2001- 5079, 2002- 5597, 2003- 5735, 2004- 6161, 2005- 6146, 2006- 6420, 2007- 6439, 2008- 6536, 2009- 6355, 2010- 6386, 2011- 6370, 2012- 6649. pbs: 100m 12.22 '10, 200m 24.72 '11, 800m 2:09.63 '06, 60mh 8.46i '10, 100mh 13.26 '12, HJ 1.83 '07, LJ 6.35i/6.34 '07, SP 14.89 '11, JT 55.25 '09, Pen 4641i '08.
Has lived in Germany from age 7.

Silke SPIEGELBURG b. 17 Mar 1986 Georgsmarienhütte 1.73m 64kg. TSV Bayer 04 Leverkusen. Economics student.
At PV: OG: '04- 13, '08- 7, '12- 4; WCh: '07- nh, '09- 4, '11- 9; EC: '06-10-12: 6/2/4=; WJ: '02- 8; WY: '01- 1; EU23: '07- 4; EJ: '03- 1, '05- 1; WI: '06- 8, '12- 4; EI: '07-09-11: 5/2/2; ECp: '08-09-10-11: 3/3/2/2; Won WAF 2008, DL 2011, German 2005-10, 2012.
PV records: World junior 2005, German 2012.
Progress at PV: 1998- 2.75, 1999- 3.30, 2000- 3.75, 2001- 4.00, 2002- 4.20, 2003- 4.20i/4.15, 2004- 4.40, 2005- 4.48i/4.42, 2006- 4.56, 2007- 4.60, 2008- 4.70, 2009- 4.75i/4.70, 2010- 4.71, 2011- 4.76i/4.75, 2012- 4.82.
Brothers: Henrik PV pb 4.80, Christian (b. 15 Apr 1976) 5.51 '98; **Richard** (b. 12 Aug 1977) 5.85 '01; 6= WCh 01, 1 WUG 99.

Linda STAHL b. 2 Oct 1985 Steinheim 1.74m 72kg. TSV Bayer 04 Leverkusen. Medical student.
At JT: OG: '12- 3; WCh: '07- 8, '09- 6, '11- dns; EC: '10- 1, '12- 3; EU23: '07- 1; CCp: '10- 4.
Progress at JT: 2000- 42.94, 2001- 43.96, 2002- 47.23, 2003- 47.32, 2004- 50.11, 2005- 53.94, 2006- 57.17, 2007- 62.80, 2008- 66.06, 2009- 63.86, 2010- 66.81, 2011- 60.78, 2012- 64.91. pb SP 13.91i '06.

Martina STRUTZ b. 4 Nov 1981 Schwerin 1.60m 57kg. SC Neubrandenburg. Police officer.
At PV: OG: '12- 5; WCh: '11- 2; EC: '06- 5, '12- 2; WJ: '00- 5; EU23: '01- 4, '03- 9=; WCp: '06- 4. German champion 2011.
Two German pole vault records 2011.
Progress at PV: 1996- 3.30, 1997- 3.60i/3.50, 1998- 3.80, 1999- 4.10, 2000- 4.20, 2001- 4.42, 2002- 4.30, 2003- 4.20, 2004- 4.31, 2005- 4.40i/4.35, 2006- 4.50, 2007- 4.45, 2008- 4.52, 2009- 4.40, 2010- 4.30, 2011- 4.80, 2012- 4.81.

GHANA
Governing body: Ghana Athletics Association, National Sports Council, PO Box 1272, Accra. Founded 1944.

Women
Margaret Esi **SIMPSON** b. 31 Dec 1981 Kumase 1.62m 53kg.
At Hep: OG: '04- 9; WCh: '01-03-05-07-11: 13/dnf/3/dnf/14; CG: '02- 3, '10- dnf; WJ: '00- dnf; AfG: '03-07-11: 1/1/1; AfCh: '00-02-04-10-12: 5/1/1/1/1 (1 JT '12). Won Af-J 1999. At HJ: CCp: '10- 8.
African heptathlon record 2005, Ghana records at HJ, JT and eight heptathlon 1999-2004.
Progress at Hep: 1999- 5366, 2000- 5543, 2001- 5836, 2002- 6105w/6004, 2003- 6152, 2004- 6306, 2005- 6423, 2007- 6278, 2009- 5872, 2010- 6031A, 2011- 6270w/6183, 2012- 6245. pbs: 200m 24.38 '07, 800m 2:17.02 '05, 100mh 13.41 '05, HJ 1.85 '05, LJ 6.32 '05, SP 13.58 '12, JT 56.36 '05, Dec 6915 '07. Child born July 2006.

GREECE
Governing body: Hellenic Amateur Athletic Association (SEGAS), 137 Siggroú Avenue, 171 21 Nea Smirni, Athens. Founded 1897.
National Championships first held in 1896 (men), 1930 (women). **2012 Champions:** 100m: Hrístos Kalamarás 10.50, 200m: Likoúrgos-Stéfanos Tsákonas 20.55, 400m: Tilémahos Roútas 46.58, 800m/1500m: Andréas Dimitrákis 1:48.99/3:41.77, 5000m: Konstadínos Gelaoúzos 14:44.87, 10,000m: Hristóforos Meroúsis 30:51.78, HMar: Dimítrios Tsioúnis 74:17, Mar: Mihaíl Parmákis 2:21:56, 3000mSt: Efstáthios Mavridópoulos 9:10.08, 110mh: Konstadínos Douvalídis 13.47, 400mh: Periklís Iakovákis 49.19, HJ: Dimítrios Hondrokoúkis 2.25, PV: Konstadínos Filippídis 5.65, LJ: Dimítrios Diamantáras 8.09w, TJ: Dimítrios Tsiámis 16.63, SP: Mihaíl Stamatóyiannis 19.65, DT: Yeóryios Trémos 59.97, HT: Aléxandros Papadimitríou 69.85, JT: Spirídon Lebésis 82.25, Dec: Kiriákos Pilídis 6804, 20kW: Vasílios Hrisikós 1:35:58, 50kW: Yeóryios Kelepoúris 4:34:21. **Women:** 100m/200m: María Belibasáki 11.34/23.28, 400m: Agní Dervéni 53.69, 800m: Eléni Filándra 2:00.44, 1500m: Eléni Theodorakopoúlou 4:20.19, 5000m/3000mSt: Athiná Koíni 16:21.99/9:59,96, 10,000m: Ouranía Reboúli 34:33.63, HMar: Konstadína Stefanopoúlou 1:24:54, Mar: Magdaliní Gazéa 2:44:42, 100mh: Olibía Petsoúdi 13.53, 400mh: Hristína Hantzí-Neag 59.31, HJ: Adonía Steryíou 1.85, PV: Nikoléta Kiriakopoúlou 4.50, LJ: Paraskeví Papahrístou 6.60, TJ: Athanasía Pérra 14.71, SP: Hrisí Moisídou 15.49, DT: Hrisoúla Anagnosto-poúlou 55.86, HT: Iliána Korosídou 62.03, JT: Sávva Líka 58.56, Hep: Iríni Daniíl 4658, 20kW: Déspina Zapounídou 1:40:36.

Konstadínos BANIÓTIS b. 6 Nov 1986 Komotini, Rhodope 2.02m 80kg. PMS Olympiada Komotinis.
At HJ: OG: '08/12- dnq 37=/25=; WCh: '09/11- dnq 16/15=; EC: '10- 8, '12- dnq 16=; WI: '12- 4=;

EU23: '07- 12; EI: '09- 6, '11- 4. Greek champion 2008-11.
Progress at HJ: 2002- 1.98, 2003- 2.02, 2004- 1.90, 2005- 2.07, 2006- 2.17, 2007- 2.23, 2008- 2.27, 2009- 2.29i/2.28, 2010- 2.28, 2011- 2.32i/2.28, 2012- 2.31i/2.25, 2013- 2.30i.

Konstadínos FILIPÍDDIS b. 26 Nov 1986 Athens 1.90m 78kg. Panellínios YS Athens. Student of Economics at University of Athens.
At PV: OG: '12- 7; WCh: '05- dnq 14=, '09- dnq 17, '11- 6; EC: '06-10: dnq 26/21=, '12- 5; WJ: '04- 4; WY: '03- 4; EJ: '05- 2; WI: '10- 4=, '12- 7; EI: '13- 4; WUG: '05- 2; ET: '09/10- 4; Won MedG 2005; Greek champion 2005, 2009-12.
Eight Greek pole vault records 2005-12.
Progress at PV: 2001- 3.70, 2002- 4.80, 2003- 5.22, 2004- 5.50, 2005- 5.75, 2006- 5.55, 2007- 5.35i/5.30/5.40dq, 2009- 5.65, 2010- 5.70i/5.55, 2011- 5.75, 2012- 5.80, 2013- 5.83i.
Two-year drugs ban from positive test on 16 June 2007.

Loúis TSÁTOUMAS b. 12 Feb 1982 Messíni 1.87m 76kg. Olympiakós SF Piraeus.
At LJ: OG: '04-08-12: dnq 22/nj/dnq 29; WCh: '03- 12, '09- 11, '11- dnq 14; EC: '06- 8, '10- 6; WJ: '00- dnq 21; WY: '99- 4; EU23: '03- 1; EJ: '01- 1; WI: '06- 4, '12- 6; EI: '07- 2, '13- 5; WCp: '06- nj; ECp: '03-07-08-09: 1/1/1/3; Greek champion 2003-08, 2010-11(& 8 indoors).
Greek long jump record 2007.
Progress at LJ: 1996- 6.56, 1997- 7.07, 1998- 7.41/7.43w, 1999- 7.64, 2000- 7.52, 2001- 7.93/7.98w, 2002- 8.17, 2003- 8.34, 2004- 8.19/8.37w, 2005- 8.15i/8.14, 2006- 8.30, 2007- 8.66, 2008- 8.44, 2009- 8.21, 2010- 8.09/8.17w, 2011- 8.26, 2012- 8.05i/7.98, 2013- 8.08i. pb 200m 22.3 '98.
8.66 is best outdoors by European at sea-level.

Women

Nikoléta KIRIAKOPOÚLOU b. 21 Mar 1986 Athens 1.68m 57kg. AYES Kámiros Rhodes.
At PV: OG: '08/12- dnq 27=/19=; WCh: '09- dnq 19, '11- 8; EC: '10- dnq 13, '12- 3; WJ: '04- 6; EJ: '05- 7; EI: '11- 9. Balkan champion 2008, Med G 2009, Greek 2009, 2011-12.
Five Greek pole vault records 2010-11.
Progress at PV: 2001- 2.90, 2002- 3.10, 2003- 3.70, 2004- 4.00, 2005- 4.10, 2006- 3.60, 2007- 4.00i/3.90, 2008- 4.45, 2009- 4.50, 2010- 4.55, 2011- 4.71, 2012- 4.60, 2013- 4.60i.

Paraskeví 'Voula' PAPAHRÍSTOU b. 17 Apr 1989 Athens 1.70m 53kg. AEK.
At TJ: WCh: '09/11- dnq 29/16; EC: '12- 11; WJ: '08- 3; EU23: '09/11- 1. Won Greek LJ 2011-12, TJ 2009, 2011.
Progress at TJ: 2005- 12.75, 2006- 12.81/13.13w, 2007- 12.98i/12.92, 2008- 13.86i/13.79/13.94w, 2009- 14.47i/14.35, 2010- 13.94i/13.85, 2011- 14.72, 2012- 14.58/14.77w. pb LJ 6.60 '12.

GRENADA

Governing body: Grenada Athletic Assocation, PO Box 419, St George's. Founded 1924.

Rondell BARTHOLOMEW b. 7 Apr 1990 St Patrick 1.92m 79kg. South Plains College, USA.
At (200m)/400m: WCh: '11- 6; WJ: '08- sf.
Progress at 400m: 2008- 46.86, 2009- 45.58, 2010- 45.28, 2011- 44.65, 2012- 47.84. pbs: 100m 10.42A '11, 200m 20.95 '10, 20.48w '10; 600y 1:09.45i '10, 600m 1:18.10i '11, 800m 1:51.25 '11.

Kirani JAMES b. 1 Sep 1992 St George's 1.85m 74kg. Student at University of Alabama, USA
At (200m)/400m: OG: '12- 1; WCh: '11- 1; WJ: '08- 2, '10- 1; WY: '07- 2, '09- 1/1; ; WI: '12- 6. Won DL 2011, PAm-J 400m 2009, 200m 2011; NCAA 2010-11.
Records: CAC & Commonwealth 400m 2012, GRN 200m 2011, 400m (2) 2011-12; Indoor 400m: CAC & Commonwealth 2010 (45.24) & 2011, World Junior (44.80) 2011.
Progress at 400m: 2007- 46.96, 2008- 45.70, 2009- 45.24, 2010- 45.01, 2011- 44.36, 2012- 43.94. pbs: 200m 20.41A/20.53w '11, 20.76 '10; 300m: 32.0+ '12.
He set world age bests at 14 and 15. In 2011 he became the youngest ever World or Olympic champion at 400m and in 2012 the first Olympic medallist for Grenada at any sport. In January 2012 the 'Kirani James Boulevard' was opened in the Grenadan capital St.George. IAAF Rising Star award 2011.

GUATEMALA

Governing body: Federación Nacional de Atletismo, Palacio de los Deportes, 26 Calle 9-31, Zona 5, Ciudad de Guatemala. Fd 1896.

Erick BARRONDO b. 14 Jun 1991 Aldea Chiyuc, San Cristóbal Verapaz 1.72m 60kg.
At 20kW(/50kW): OG: '12- 2/dq; WCh: '11- 10; PAm: '11- 1. Won GUA 50kW 2012.
50k walk records: CAC 2013, GUA 2012.
Progress at 20kW, 50kW: 2011- 1:20:58, 2012- 1:18:25, 3:44:5; 2013- 3:41.09.
Won Guatemala's first Olympic medal at any sport in 2012.

HUNGARY

Governing body: Magyar Atlétikai Szövetség, 1146 Budapest, Istvánmezei út 1-3. Fd 1897.
National Championships first held in 1896 (men), 1932 (women). **2012 Champions. Men:** 100m: Miklós Szebeny 10.91, 200m: Tibor Kása 21.17, 400m: Marcell Deák Nagy 45.93, 800m: Péter Szemeti 1:48.96, 1500m: *none*, 5000m: Barnabás Bene 14:32.93, 10,000m: László Tóth 30:51.17, HMar/Mar Gábor Józsa 66:36/2:21:08, 3000mSt: Albert Minczér 8:54.43, 110mh: Balázs Baji 13.74, 400mh: Tibor Koroknai 51.60, HJ: Olivér Harsányi 2.15, PV: Márton Horváth 4.70, LJ: István Virovecz 7.66w, TJ: Stavros Georgiou

16.09, SP: Lajos Kürthy 19.95, DT: Gábor Máté 56.99, HT: Krisztián Pars 80.28, JT: Bence Papp 75.66, Dec: Attila Szabó 7545, 20kW: Máté Helebrandt 1:30:41, 50kW: Róbert Tubak 4:24:55. **Women**: 100m/200m: Éva Kaptur 11.71/23.71, 400m: Bianka Kéri 53.42, 800m: Boglárka Bozzay 2:06.13, 1500m/10,000m/HMar: Krisztina Papp 4:17.61/33:58.67/75:07, 5000m: Andrea Szeder–kényi-Takács 17:14.44, Mar: Timea Merényi 2:49:30, 3000mSt: LiviaTóth 10:36.17, 100mh: Sophie Jancsurák 14.08, 400mh: Nóra Zajovics 60.43, HJ: Barbara Szabó 1.86, PV: Daniella Szabó 4.00, LJ: Xénia Krizsán 6.03, TJ: Krisztina Hoffer 13.25, SP/DT: Anita Márton 16.79/52,64, HT: Cintia Gergelics 64.83, JT: Vanda Juhász 59.31, Hep: Xénia Krizsán 5890, 20kW: Edina Füsti 1:34:07.

Krisztián PARS b. 18 Feb 1982 Körmend 1.88m 113kg. Dobó SE.
At HT: OG: '04- 5, '08- 4, '12- 1; WCh: '05-07-09-11: 7/5/4/2; EC: '06- 6, '10- 3, '12- 1; WY: '99- 1; EJ: '01- 1; EU23: '03- 1. Won HUN 2005-12; World HT challenge 2011-12.
World junior records with 6kg hammer: 80.64 & 81.34 in 2001.
Progress at HT: 1998- 54.00, 1999- 61.92, 2000- 66.80, 2001- 73.09, 2002- 74.18, 2003- 78.81, 2004- 80.90, 2005- 80.03, 2006- 82.45, 2007- 81.40, 2008- 81.96, 2009- 81.43, 2010- 79.64, 2011- 81.89, 2012- 82.28. pbs: SP 15.60 '05, DT 53.80 '06.

ICELAND

Governing body: Frjálsíthróttasamband Islands, Engjavegur 6, IS-104 Reykjavik. Founded 1947.
National Championships first held in 1927.
2012 National champions: Men: 100m/200m: Trausti Stefánsson 10.92w/21.89, 400m: Trausti Stafánsson 48.31, 800m: Kristin Thór Kristinsson 1:55.15, 1500m/5000m: Thórarinn Uørn Thrándarson 4:07.21/15:15.01, 3000mSt: Arnar Pétursson 10:07.20, 110mh/HJ/PV: Einar Dadi Lárusson 14.64/2.05/4.62, 400mh: Sölvi Gudmundsson 56.95, LJ/TJ: Kristinn Torfason 7.39.14.08w, SP: Ódinn Björn Thorsteinsson 18.51, DT: Ingi Rúnar Kristinsson 40.10, HT: Bergur Ingi Pétursson 56.17, JT: Gudmundur Sverrison 72.11. **Women**: 100m/200m/LJ: Hafdís Sigurdar–dóttir 11.93/24.35/5.89, 400m: Stefania Valdimars–dóttir 57.35, 800m: Melkorka Embla Hjartardóttir 2:29.89, 1500m/3000m: Arndis Yr Hafthorsdóttir 4:49.53/10:16.46, 100mh/400mh/HJ: Fjóla Signy Hannesdóttir 14.47/59.62/1.66, PV: Sveinborg Danielsdóttir 3.02, TJ: Jóhanna Ingadóttir 10.96, SP: Sveinbjörg Zophaniasdóttir 12.63, DT: Jófridur Ísdís Skafladóttir 34.38, HT: Kristbjörg Ingvarsdóttir 52.36, JT: Ásdis Hjálmsdóttir 60.54.

INDIA

Governing body: Athletics Federation of India, WZ-72, Todapur Main Road, Dev Prakash Shastri Marg, New Delhi - 110012. Fd 1946.
National Championships first held as Indian Games in 1924. **2012 Champions: Men**: 100m: Murugiah Manikanda Raj 10.60, 200m Dharambir Singh 21.00, 400m: Arokia Rajiv 46.57, 800m/1500m: Sajeesh Joseph 1:51.93/3:46.69, 5000m: Rahul Kumar Pal 14:14.64, 10,000m: Inderjeet Patel 29:42.76, 3000mSt: Ramadas Ramchandran 8:53.06, 110mh: A.Suresh 14.21, 400mh: Joseph G. Abraham 50.87, HJ: Jithin C.Thomas 2.22, PV: K.P.Bimin 4.95, LJ: Kumaravel Prem Kumar 7.72, TJ: Renjith Maheswary 16.72, SP: Jasdeep Singh 18.14, DT/HT: Kamalpreet Singh 55.34/66.28, JT: Davinder Singh 75.09, Dec: Daya Ram 6690, 20kW: Babu Bhai Panocha 1:27:26. **Women**: 100m: Manisha Dhankar 11.77, 200m: Bebi Sumaya 24.91, 400m: M.R.Poovamma 53.79, 800m: Tintu Luka 2:04.69, 1500m: Simon Rajam Bindu 4:25.58, 5000m/10,000m: Suriya Loganathan 17:29.94/35:18.2, 3000mSt: Priyanka Singh Patel 10:51.66, 100mh: M.M.Anchu 14.40, 400mh: A.Papathi 60.33, HJ: Sahana Kumari 1.84, PV: Vakaharia Khyati 3.70, LJ/TJ: Shradha Ghule 6.36/13.17, SP: Pinki Dey 12.82, DT: Parmila 49.08, HT: Manju Bala Singh 58.46, JT: Annu Rani 49.58, Hep: Liksy Joseph 4933, 20kW: Khushbir Kaur 1:44:55.

Vikas GOWDA b. 5 Jul 1983 Mysore, Karnataka 2.06m 115kg. Was at University of North Carolina, USA.
At DT: OG: '04/08- 14/22, '12- 8; WCh: '05/07- dnq 14/17, '11- 7; CG: '06- 6, '10- 2; AsiG: '06- 6, '10- 3; AsiC: 05- 2, '11- 2. Won NCAA 2006.
Three Indian discus records 2005-12
Progress at DT: 2002- 55.28, 2003- 59.32, 2004- 64.35, 2005- 64.69, 2006- 61.76, 2007- 64.96, 2008- 64.83, 2010- 63.69, 2011- 64.91, 2012- 66.28. pb SP 19.62 '06.

Women

Krishna POONIA b. 5 May 1982 Agroha, Haryana 1.82m 80kg. Indian Railways.
At DT: OG: '08- dnq 24, '12- 7; WCh: '07/09- dnq 22/28; CG: '06- 5, '10- 1; AsiG: '06- 3, '10- 3; AsiC: 05-07-09-11: 3/3/3/4. Indian champion 2006-08.
Progress at DT: 2000- 53.66, 2003- 53.31, 2004- 57.19, 2005- 58.33, 2006- 61.53, 2007- 58.80, 2008- 63.41, 2009- 60.78, 2010- 63.69, 2011- 62.25, 2012- 64.76. Married to her coach Virender Poonia.

IRAN

Governing body: Amateur Athletic Federation of Islamic Republic of Iran, Shahid Keshvari Sports Complex, Razaneh Junibi St Mirdamad Ave, Tehran. Founded 1936.

Ehsan HADADI b. 21 Jan 1985 Ahvaz 1.93m 125kg.
At DT: OG: '08- dnq 17, '12- 2; WCh: '07- 7, '11- 3;

WJ: '04- 1; AsiG: '06- 1, '10- 1; AsiC: '03-05-07-09-11: 8/1/1/1/1; AsiJ: '04- 1; WCp: '06- 2, '10- 3. W.Asian champion 2005.
Eight Asian discus records 2005-08.
Progress at DT: 2002- 53.66, 2003- 54.40, 2004- 54.96, 2005- 65.25, 2006- 63.79, 2007- 67.95, 2008- 69.32, 2009- 66.19, 2010- 68.45, 2011- 66.08, 2012- 68.20. pb SP 17.82i '08, 16.00 '06.
First Iranian athlete fto win an Olympic medal.

IRELAND

Governing Body: The Athletic Association of Ireland (AAI), Unit 19, Northwood Court, Northwood Business Campus, Santry, Dublin 9. Founded in 1999. Original Irish AAA founded in 1885.
National Championships first held in 1873.
2012 Champions: **Men**: 100m: Paul Hession 10.37, 200m: Steven Colvert 20.78w, 400m: Brian Murphy 46.97, 800m: Dean Cronin 1:52.48, 1500m: Colin Costello 3:54.57, 5000: Mark Hanrahan 14:13.80, 10,000m: Brian Maher 30:17.07, HMar: Paul Pollock 64:16, Mar: Paul Pollock 2:16:30, 3000mSt: David Flynn 9:06.58, 110mh: Simon Taggart 14.27, 400mh: Thomas Barr 50.87, HJ: Simon Phelan 2.05, PV: David Donegan 4.70, LJ: Adam McMullen 7.47, TJ: Denis Finnegan 15.55, SP: Seán Breathnach 15.85, DT: Tomas Rauktys LTU 53.40, HT: Conor McCullough 72.51, JT: Matthew Martin 61.37, Dec: Michael Bowler 5992, 10,000mW: Colin Griffin 41:47.66, 20kW: Cian McManamon 1:37:37. **Women**: 100m: Amy Foster 11.60, 200m/400m: Joanne Cuddihy 23.15w/51.89, 800m: Siobhan Eviston 2:06.04, 1500m: Orla Drumm 4:19.55, 5000m/HMar/Mar: Maria McCambridge 16:02.52/75:24/2:35:28, 3000mSt: Michelle Finn 10:45.49, 100mh: Mairead Murphy 14.47, 400mh: Jessie Barr 57.33, HJ: Deirdre Ryan 1.80, PV: Tori Pena 4.35, LJ: Kelly Proper 6.33w, TJ: Mary McLoone 12.69, SP/DT: Claire Fitzgerald 14.39/49.48, HT: Cara Kennedy 56.22, JT: Anita Fitzgibbon 49.54, Hep: Julie Morrison 4187, 5000mW/20kW: Maeve Curley 24:41.07/1:52:23.

Robert HEFFERNAN b. 20 Feb 1978 Cork City 1.73m 55kg. Togher AC.
At 20kW/(50kW): OG: '00- 28, '04- dq, '08- 8, '12- 9/4; WCh: '01-05-07-09: 14/dq/6/15; EC: '02- 8, '10- 4/4; WCp: '08- 9, '12- 11; ECp: '07- 5, '09- 4. At 10,000mW: EJ: '97- 14; EU23: '99- 13. Won Irish 10,000mW 2001-02, 2004-5, 2007-11; 20kW 2000-02, 2004, 2009; 30kW 2008.
Four Irish 20kW records 2001-08, three 50kW 2010-12.
Progress at 20kW, 50kW: 1999- 1:26:45, 2000- 1:22:43, 2001- 1:21:11, 2002- 1:20:25, 2003- 1:23:03, 2004- 1:20:55, 2005- 1:24:20, 2006- 1:22:24, 2007- 1:20:15, 2008- 1:19:22, 2009- 1:22:09, 2010- 1:20:45, 3:45:30; 2011- 1:20:54, 3:49:28; 2012- 1:20:18, 3:37:54. pbs: 3000mW 11:10.02i '02, 11:27.6 '05;

5000mW 18:51.46i '08, 18:59.37 '07; 10,000mW 38:27.57 '08, 30kW 2:07:48 '11, 35kW 2:31:19 '00. Married to Marian Andrews (b. 16 Apr 1982, Irish 400m champion 2008-09).

Women

Fionnuala BRITTON b. 24 Sep 1984 Wicklow 1.58m 45kg. Kilcoole.
At 10,000m: OH: '12- 15 (h 5000m); EC: '12- 4. At 3000m: EI: '13- 3. At 3000mSt: OG: '08- h; WCh: '07- 12, '11- h; EC: '06- h, '10- 11; EU23: 05- 9. World CC: '13- 14. Eur CC: '07-09-10-11-12: 7/11/4/1/1. Won Irish 3000mSt 2008-9, CC 2007-08.
Progress at 10,000m, 3000mSt: 2004- 10:33.10, 2005- 10:06.26, 2006- 9:49.20, 2007- 9:41.36, 2008- 9:43.57, 2009- 9:54.10, 2010- 9:42.49, 2011- 9:37.60, 2012- 31:29.22. pbs: 1500m 4:13.96i '13, 4:18.03 '11; 3000m 8:54.37i '13, 8:55.01mx '12; 5000m 15:12.97 '12.

Derval O'ROURKE b. 28 May 1981 Cork 1.68m 57kg. Leevale. Graduate of University College Dublin; sports administrator for Dublin City University.
At 100mh: OG: '04/08- h, '12- sf; WCh: '03- h, '05/07/11- sf, '09- 4; EC: '02- h, '06- 2=, '10- 2; WJ: '00- sf; EU23: '01- 7, '03- 4; EJ: '99- sf; WUG: '05- 3; CCp: '10- 5; Irish champion 2001-02, 2004-08, 2010-11. At 60mh: WI: '06- 1; EI: '09-11-13: 3/4/4. Seven Irish 100mh records 2003-10.
Progress at 100mh: 1998- 14.29/13.88w, 1999- 13.82, 2000- 13.49, 2001- 13.57, 2002- 13.38, 2003- 12.96, 2004- 13.39, 2005- 13.00/12.95w, 2006- 12.72, 2007- 12.88, 2008- 12.90, 2009- 12.67, 2010- 12.65, 2011- 12.84, 2012- 12.91. pbs: 60m 7.59i '05, 100m 11.54 '05, 11.43w '07; 200m 23.71 '10, 50mh 6.80i '06, 60mh 7.84i '06.
Set six Irish records at 60mh from 8.02 to 7.84 to win World Indoor title in 2006.

ISRAEL

Governing body: Israeli Athletic Association, PO Box 24190, Tel Aviv 61241. Founded as Federation for Amateur Sport in Palestine 1931.
National Championships first held in 1935.
2012 Champions: **Men**: 100m/200m: Dmitriy Barskiy 10.44/21.43, 400m: Ruben Majola 47.51, 800m: Dustin Emrani 1:46.92, 1500m: Mokat Petna 3:48.39, 5000m/10,000m: Tasama Moogas 14:09.29/28:31.96, HMar: Wodage Zvadya 67:59, Mar: Zohar Zimro 2:15:06, 3000mSt: Itai Moggidi 9:08.49, 110mh: Maor Szeged 14.85, 400mh: Khai Cohen 54.20, HJ: Dmitriy Kroyter 2.17, PV: Udi Karni 4.87, LJ/TJ: Yochai Halevi 7.47/16.86w, SP/DT: Itamar Levi 17.34/53.94, HT: Viktor Zaginaiko 62.00, JT: Assa'el Arad 62.36, Dec: Roman Kogan 5401. **Women**: 100m/200m: Olga Lenskiy 11.63/24.07, 400m/800m: Shanie Landen 57.07/2:13.21, 1500m: Azawant Teka 4:35.92, 5000m/HMar: Ricki Salem 17:44.96/1:22:18, 10,000m: Mary

Elias 37:02.53, Mar: Svetlana Bakhmand 2:54:00. 3000mSt: Dana Levinn 11:32.94, 100mh: Irina Lenskiy 14.13, 400mh: Olga Dogadko-Bronstein (12th title) 62.99, HJ: Maayan Furman 1.77, PV: Jillian Schwartz 4.34, LJ/Hep: Tal Ben-Artzi 5.64/4838, TJ: Joy Konengisser 11.38w, SP/DT: Anastasia Muchkaev 16.42/54.98, HT: Yevgeniya Zabolotniy 59.42, JT: Dorit Naor 43.91 (15th title).

ITALY

Governing Body: Federazione Italiana di Atletica Leggera (FIDAL), Via Flaminia Nuova 830, 00191 Roma. Constituted 1926. First governing body formed 1896.
National Championships first held in 1897 (one event)/1906 (men), 1927 (women). **2012 Champions**: **Men**: 100m: Fabio Cerutti 10.43, 200m: Andrew Howe 20.76, 400m: Claudio Liccardello 46.15, 800m: Giordano Benedetti 1:48.68, 1500m: Christian Obrist 3:48.16, 5000m/HMar: Stefano La Rosa 14:01.49/62:15, 10,000m: Simone Gariboldi 29:14.41, Mar: Migidio Bourifa 2:20:45, 3000mSt: Matteo Villani 8:54.93, 110mh: Paolo Dal Molin 13.74, 400mh: José Bencosme de Leon 49.33, HJ: Gianmarco Tamberi 2.31, PV: Claudio Michel Stecchi 5.60, LJ: Fabrizio Schembri 7.67w, TJ: Daniele Greco 17.67w, SP: Paolo Dal Soglio 18.70, DT: Eduardo Albertazzi 60.50, HT: Lorenzo Povegliano 76.29, JT: Giacomo Puccini 76.42, Dec: William Frullani 7378, 10kW: Giorgio Rubino 39:17, 20kW/50kW: Federico Tontodonati 1:28:37/3:51:37. **Women**: 100m: Audrey Alloh 11.48, 200m: Libania Grenot 22.91, 400m: Maria Enrica Spacca 52.53, 800m: Marta Milani 2:05.21, 1500m: Elisa Cusma Piccione 4:18.04, 5000m: Silvia Weissteiner 15:50.15, 10,000m: Federica Dal Ri 33:20.70, HMar: Valeria Straneo 67:46, Mar: Ivana Iozzia 2:35:08, 3000mSt: Valentina Costanza 10:14.22, 100mh: Marzia Caravelli 13.15, 400mh: Manuela Gentili 55.87, HJ: Chiara Vitobello 1.89, PV: Anna Giordano Bruno 4.35, LJ: Tania Vicenzino 6.65w, TJ: Simona La Mantia 14.24w, SP: Chiara Rosa 18.30, DT: Tamara Apostolico 58.62, HT: Silvia Salis 70.18, JT: Zahra Bani 58.40, Hep: Elisa Trevisan 5574, 10kW: Eleonora Giorgi 45:19, 20kW: Federica Ferraro 1:37:43.

Fabrizio DONATO b. 14 Aug 1976 Latina 1.89m 82kg. Fiamme Gialle.
At TJ: OG: '00/04/08: dnq 25/21/21, '12- 3; WCh: '03/07-09: dnq 13/32/41, '11- 10; EC: '02-06-10-12: 4,/dnq 16/9/1; EJ: '95- 5; WI: '01-08-10-12: 6/4/5/4; EI: '00-02-09-11: 6/4/1/2; ECp: '00-02-03-04-06: 2/2/1/6/1. Won MedG 2001, Italian 2000, 2004, 2006-08, 2010-11.
Italian triple jump record 2000.
Progress at TJ: 1992- 12.88, 1993- 14.36, 1994- 15.27, 1995- 15.81, 1996- 16.35, 1997- 16.40A, 1998- 16.73, 1999- 16.66i/16.53w, 2000- 17.60, 2001-

17.05, 2002- 17.17, 2003- 17.16, 2004- 16.90, 2005- 16.65/16.68w, 2006- 17.33i/17.24, 2007- 16.97/17.06w, 2008- 17.27i/16.91/17.29w, 2009- 17.59i/15.81, 2010- 17.39i/17.08, 2011- 17.73i/17.17, 2012- 17.53/17.63w. pb LJ 8.03i '11, 8.00 '06.
Italian indoor record to win 2009 European Indoor title. Married Patrizia Spuri (400m 51.74 '98, 8 EC 98, 800m 1:59.96 '98) on 27 Sep 2003.

Daniele GRECO b. 1 Mar 1989 Nardó, Apulia 1.84m 75kg. Fiamme Oro, Padova.
At TJ: OG: '08- 4; WCh: '09: dnq 34; EC: '10-12: dnq 17/24; WJ: '08- 4; EU23: '09- 1; EJ: '07- 12; WI: '12: 5; EI: '13- 1. Won Italian 2012.
Progress at TJ: 2005- 15.01, 2006- 15.45, 2007- 15.58i/15.54, 2008- 16.41, 2009- 17.20, 2010- 16.95i/16.57, 2011- 16.89, 2012- 17.47/17.67w, 2013- 17.70i. pbs: 60m 6.75i '09, 100m 10.38 '08, 200m 21.17 '12, LJ 7.20 '09.
Engaged to Francesca Lanciano (b. 3 Apr 1994), 11 WY '11, 12 WJ '12, NJR 13.59 '12.

Giorgio RUBINO b. 15 Apr 1986 Roma 1.76m 55kg. Fiamme Gialle.
At 20kW: OG: '08- 18, '12- 42; WCh: '07- 5, '09- 4, '11- dq; EC: '06- 8, '10- 5; EU23: '07- dq; ECp: '09- 1, '11- 5. At 10,000mW: WJ: '04- 10; WY: '03- 4; EJ: '05- 3. Won ITA 10kW 2012, 20kW 2005.
Progress at 20kW: 2005- 1:23:58, 2006- 1:22:05, 2007- 1:21:17, 2008- 1:22:11, 2009- 1:19:37, 2010- 1:22:12, 2011- 1:20:44, 2012- 1:20:10. pbs: 5000mW 19:14.33i '08, 19:38.5 '06; 10,000mW 39:43.20 '11, 38:00R '10; 35kW 2:36:50 '09.

Nicola VIZZONI b. 4 Nov 1973 Pietrasanta, Lucca 1.93m 126kg. Fiamme Gialle.
At HT: OG: '00- 2, '04- 10, '08- dnq 13, '12- 8; WCh: '97- dnq 22, '99- 7, '01- 4, '03/05/07- dnq 15/25/17, '09- 9, '11- 8; EC: '98-02-06-10-12: dnq 17/dnq 13/9/2/5; WJ: '92- 5; EJ: '91- 8; WUG: '97- 5, '99- 5, '01- 1; WCp: '10- 4; ECp: '99-01-02-03-04-05-08-09-10: 4/2/7/5/3/4/2/1/2; EU23Cp: '92- 5. Won Med G 2009, ITA 1998, 2000-07, 2009-11.
Progress at HT: 1991- 66.62, 1992- 69.32, 1993- 70.76, 1994- 71.78, 1995- 74.48, 1996- 75.30, 1997- 77.10, 1998- 77.89, 1999- 79.59, 2000- 79.64, 2001- 80.50, 2002- 78.80, 2003- 77.69, 2004- 76.95, 2005- 74.82, 2006- 76.89, 2007- 78.21, 2008- 78.79, 2009- 79.74, 2010- 79.12, 2011- 80.29, 2012- 76.42.
Left-handed thrower. Engaged to Claudia Coslovich (ITA javelin record 65.30 '00).

Women

Antonietta DI MARTINO b. 1 Jun 1978 Cava de' Tirreni, Salerno 1.69m 58kg. Fiamme Gialle.
At HJ: OG: '08- 10=; WCh: '01-07-09-11: 12/2=/4/3; EC: '06- 10, '10- dnq 13=; WI: '06- 5, '12- 2=; EI: '07- 2, '11- 1; ECp: '01-02-05-08-09-10: 3=/7=/5/2=/3/1. Won MedG 2009, Italian 2000-01, 2006-08, 2010.
Three Italian high jump records 2007.

Progress at HJ: 1993- 1.63, 1994- 1.71, 1995- 1.69, 1996- 1.66, 1997- 1.78, 1998- 1.73, 1999- 1.63, 2000- 1.88, 2001- 1.98, 2002- 1.91, 2003- 1.96i/1.90, 2004- 1.86, 2005- 1.90, 2006- 1.96i/1.94, 2007- 2.03, 2008- 1.97, 2009- 2.00, 2010- 2.01, 2011- 2.04i/2.00, 2012- 1.95i. pbs: 200m 25.93 '00, 800m 2:24.21 '01, 60mh 8.94i '01, 100mh 14.11 '01, LJ 5.60 '01, SP 11.74 '01, JT 46.64 '01, Pen 3980i '01, Hep 5687w/5542 '01.

Has the record for the greatest ever height differential, 35cm, by a woman high jumper. Married Massimilliano Di Matteo in September 2009. Had surgery on her left knee in July 2012.

Libania GRENOT b. 12 Jul 1983 Santiago de Cuba 1.75m 65kg. Fiamme Galle.
At 400m: OG: '08/12- sf; WCh: '01- hR, '05- h, '09- sf; EC: '10- 4, '12- 6; WY: '99- 5; PAm: '03- 4; CCp: '10- 6/2R; ET: '10- 1. Won MedG 2009, CUB 2002-05, ITA 400m 2009-10, 200m 2012.
Four Italian 400m records 2008-09.
Progress at 400m: 1997- 56.2, 1998- 54.9, 1999- 53.87, 2000- 53.79, 2001- 52.91, 2002- 53.34A, 2003- 52.20, 2004- 51.68, 2005- 51.51, 2007- 54.21, 2008- 50.83, 2009- 50.30, 2010- 50.43, 2011- 52.17, 2012- 50.55. pbs: 200m 22.85 '12, 500m 1:08.26 '09.
Switched from Cuba to Italy after she married Silvio Scaffetti in 2006 and gained Italian citizenship on 18 Mar 2008.

Simone LA MANTIA b. 14 Apr 1983 Palermo 1.77m 65kg. Fiamme Gialle. Studied PE at Palermo University.
At TJ: OG: '04/12- dnq 17/18; WCh: '03/05/11- dnq 17/14/15; EC: '10- 2, "12- 4; WJ: '02- 8; EJ: '01- 10; EU23: '03- 2, '05- 1; WI: '04- 11, '06- dnq 16; EI: '05-11-13: 8/1/3; CCp: '10- 5; ET: '11- 2. ITA champion 2004-06, 2010-12; W.Mil G 2011.
Progress at TJ: 1998- 12.71, 1999- 12.03, 2000- 12.50, 2001- 13.51/13.63w, 2002- 13.33, 2003- 14.31, 2004- 14.49/14.71w, 2005- 14.69, 2006- 14.21, 2007- 13.89, 2008- 13.79, 2009- 13.79/13.83w, 2010- 14.56, 2011- 14.60i/14.43, 2012- 14.29. pb LJ 6.48 '05.
Her father Antonino La Mantia had 3000mSt pb 8:42.2 '74 and mother Monica Mutschlechner 800m 2:08.3 '77.

Elisa RIGAUDO b. 17 Jun 1980 Cuneo 1.68m 56kg. Fiamme Gialle.
At 20kW: OG: '04- 6, '08- 3, '12- 7; WCh: '03-05-07-09-11: 10/7/dnf/9/4; EC: '06- 3; EU23: '03- 1; WCp: '02-04-06-12: 16/5/10/7; ECp: '05-07: 3/4. At 5000mW: WJ: '98- 7; EJ: '99-6. Won MedG 20kW 2005, Italian 5000mW 2004, 2007; 20kW 2004-05, 2008.
Progress at 20kW: 1999- 1:42:40. 2000- 1:32:50, 2001- 1:29:54, 2002- 1:30:42, 2003- 1:30:34, 2004- 1:27:49, 2005- 1:29:26, 2006- 1:28:37, 2007- 1:29:15, 2008- 1:27:12, 2009- 1:29:04, 2011- 1:30:44, 2012- 1:27:36. pbs: 3000mW 11:57.00i '04, 12:28.92 '02; 5000mW 20:56.29 '02, 10kW 42:33 '09, 43:06.4t '04. Won IAAF Walks Challenge 2004. Daughter Elena born in September 2010.

Alessia TROST b. 8 Mar 1993 Pordenone 1.88m 66kg. Fiamme Gialle
At HJ: WJ: '12- 1; WY: '09- 10; EJ: '11- 4; EI: '13- 4=; YthOG: '10- 2.
Progress at HJ: 2003- 1.37, 2004- 1.55, 2005- 1.62, 2006- 1.68, 2008- 1.81, 2009- 1.89, 2010- 1.90, 2011- 1.87, 2012- 1.92, 2013- 2.00i. pbs: 100mh 15.5 '11, LJ 5.96 '10.

IVORY COAST

Governing Body: Fédération Ivoirienne d'Athlétisme, Abidjan. Founded 1960.

Murielle AHOURÉ b. 23 Aug 1987 Abidjan 1.67m 57kg. Graduated in criminal law from the University of Miami, USA
At 100m/200m: OG: '12- 7/6. At 60m: WI: '12- 2. Won NCAA Indoor 200m 2009.
Two African 60m indoor records 2013. Three CIV 100m records 2009-11, 200m 2012.
Progress at 100m: 2005- 11.96, 2006- 11.42, 23.33; 2007- 11.41/11.28w, 23.34; 2008- 11.45, 23.50; 2009- 11.09, 22.78; 2010- 11.41, 2011- 11.06, 2012- 10.99, 22.42. pbs: 60m 6.99i '13, 300m 38.09i '07, 400m 54.77 '08.

JAMAICA

Governing body: Jamaica Athletics Administrative Association, PO Box 272, Kingston 5. Founded 1932.
2012 Champions: **Men**: 100m/200m: Yohan Blake 9.75/19.80, 400m: Dane Hyett 44.83, 800m: Ricardo Cunningham 1:48.00, 1500m: Rayan Lawrence 3:52.58, 3000mSt: Kirk Brown 9:21.37, 110mh: Hansle Parchment 13.18, 400mh: Leford Green 48.88, HJ: Darrel Garwood 2.14, PV: K'Don Samuels 5.02, LJ: Damar Forbes 7.89, TJ: Wilbert Walker 15.94, SP: Dorian Scott 20.72, DT: Traves Smikle 67.12, HT: Caniggia Raynor 56.05, JT: Jeffrey King 60.35. **Women**: 100m/ 200m: Shelly-Ann Fraser 10.70/22.10, 400m: Novlene Williams-Mills 50.60, 800m: Kenia Sinclair 2:01.55, 3000mSt: Koreen Hinds 9:46.46, 100mh: Brigitte Foster-Hylton 12.68, 400mh: Melaine Walker 54.77, HJ: Sheree Francis 1.86, LJ: Todea-Kay Willis 6.37, TJ: Kimberly Williams 14.52, SP: Zara Northover 16.42, DT: Allison Randall 55.92, HT: Natalie Grant 57.39, JT: Kateema Riettie 52.51.

Marvin ANDERSON b. 12 May 1982 Trelawny 1.75m 69kg. Reebok. Was at University of Southern California.
At 200m/4x100mR: OG: '08- qf; WCh: '07- 6/2R, '11- h; PAm: '07- 2; WJ: '00- 6; won CAC-J 100 '00.
Progress at 200m: 2000- 20.84, 2001- 21.01, 2002- 21.39, 2003- 21.20, 2004- 20.84, 2005- 20.75/20.36w, 2006- 20.65; 2007- 20.06, 2008- 20.17, 2009- 20.15, 2010- 20.48, 2011- 20.27, 2012- 20.21. pbs: 100m 10.11 '08, 10.07dq '09, 10.03w '07, 400m 48.42 '11. 3-month drugs ban from positive test at Jamaican Champs 25 Jun 2009.

Nickel ASHMEADE b. 7 Apr 1990 Ocho Rios, Saint-Ann1.84m 87kg.
At 200m/4x100mR (100m): WCh: '11- 5; WJ: '08- 2/2R (2 4x400m); WY: '07- 3 (2, 3 MedR); won DL 2012, CAC 2009.
Progress at 100m, 200m: 2006- 10.60, 21.30; 2007- 10.39, 20.76; 2008- 10.34, 20.80/20.16w; 2009- 10.37/10.21w, 20.40; 2010- 10.39, 20.63; 2011- 9.96, 19.91; 2012- 9.93, 19.85. pbs: 60m 6.92i '09, 400m 47.19 '12.

Kemar BAILEY-COLE b. 10 Jan 1992 St. Catherine 1.93m 83kg. Racers TC.
At 100m/4x100mR (200m): OG: '12- res (1)R; WY: '09- sf/sf.
Progress at 100m: 2008- 10.85, 2009- 10.41/10.38w, 2010- 10.53, 2011- 10.28, 2012- 9.97. pbs 200m 20.83 '12.

Yohan BLAKE b. 26 Dec 1989 St. James 1.81m 79kg. Racers TC.
At 100m/4x100mR: OG: '12- 2/2/1R; WCh: '11- 1/1R; WJ: '06- 3/1R, '08- 4/2R; WY: '05- 7; PAm-J: '07- 2 (3 4x400m); won CAC-J 100m & 200m 2006; JAM 100m & 200m 2012.
World record 4x100m 2012.
Progress at 100m, 200m: 2005- 10.56, 22.10; 2006- 10.33, 20.92; 2007- 10.11, 20.62; 2008- 10.27/10.20w, 21.06; 2009- 10.07/9.93dq, 20.60; 2010- 9.89, 19.78; 2011- 9.82/9.80w, 19.26; 2012- 9.69, 19.44. pbs: 60m 6.75i '08, 400m 46.32 '13.
3-month drugs ban from positive test at Jamaican Champs 25 Jun 2009. Cut 200m pb from 20.60 to 19.78 in Monaco 2010 and then to 19.26 in Brussels 2011. Youngest ever World 100m champion at 21 in 2011.

Usain BOLT b. 21 Aug 1986 Sherwood Content, Trelawny 1.96m 88kg. Racers TC.
At (100m)/200m/4x100mR: OG: '04- h, '08- 1/1/1R; WCh: '05- 8, '07- 2/2R, '09- 1/1/1R, '11- dq/1/1R; WJ: 02- 1/2R/2R; WY: '01- sf, '03- 1; PAm-J: '03- 1/2R; WCp: '06- 2; won WAF 200m 2009, DL 100m 2012, CAC 200m 2005, JAM 100m 2008-09, 200m 2005, 2007-09.
World records: 100m (3), 200m (2), 4x100m (4) 2008-12, best low altitude 300m 2010, CAC records 100m (4) 2008-09, 200m (3) 2007-09, WJR 200m 2003 & 2004, World U18 200m record 2003.
Progress at 100m, 200m, 400m: 2000- 51.7; 2001- 21.73, 48.28; 2002- 20.58, 47.12; 2003- 20.13, 45.35; 2004- 19.93, 2005- 19.99, 2006- 19.88, 2007- 10.03, 19.75, 45.28; 2008- 9.69, 19.30, 46.94; 2009- 9.58, 19.19, 45.54; 2010- 9.82, 19.56, 45.87; 2011- 9.76, 19.40; 2012- 9.63, 19.32; 2013- 46.74. pbs: 60m 6.31+ '09, 100y 9.14+ '11, 150m 14.35 straight & 14.44+ turn '09 (world bests), 300m 30.97 '10 (world low altitude best).
Bolt was the sensational superstar of the 2008 Olympics when he won triple gold – all in world records – and in the year he won 8 of 9 100m races and all 5 at 200m. In 2009 he smashed both the 100m and 200m WRs at the World Champs and after two more golds at the 2011 Worlds (dq for false start at 100m) he repeated his Olympic treble in 2012. In 2002, after running 20.61 to win the CAC U17 200m title, he became the youngest ever male world junior champion at 15y 332d and set a world age best with 20.58, with further age records for 16 and 17 in 2003-04. Won IAAF 'Rising Star' award for men in 2002 and 2003 and male Athlete of the Year Award 2008-09, 2011-12. He has won 31 of his 34 100m finals 2007-11. He was appointed an Ambassador-at-Large for Jamaica.

Nesta CARTER b. 10 Nov 1985 Banana Ground 1.78m 70kg. MVP TC.
At 100m/4x100mR: OG: '08/12- 1R; WCh: '07- sf/2R, '11- 7/1R. At 200m: WJ: '04- sf/res (2)R. At 60m: WI: '10- 7, '12- 2.
Three world 4x100m records 2008-12.
Progress at 100m: 2004- 10.0/10.56/10.52w, 2005- 10.59, 2006- 10.20, 2007- 10.11, 2008- 9.98, 2009- 9.91, 2010- 9.78, 2011- 9.89, 2012- 9.95. pbs: 50m 5.67i '12, 60m 6.49i '12, 200m 20.25 '11, 400m 47.82 '09.

Lerone CLARKE b. 2 Oct 1981 Trelawny Parish 1.74m 66kg. Puma. Graduate of visual arts from Lincoln University, Missouri, USA.
At 100m/4x100mR: WCh: '05- 4R, '09- res1R; CG: '10- 1/2R; PAm: '11- 1; CAG: '06- 4/3R, '10- 3/2R.
CAC 60m indoor record 2012.
Progress at 100m: 2002- 10.50, 2003- 10.43/10.49w, 2004- 10.29/10.12w, 2005- 10.24, 2006- 10.28, 2007- 10.15, 2008- 10.30A, 2009- 9.99, 2010- 10.10/9.98w, 2011- 10.01A/10.05/9.90w, 2012- 9.99. pbs: 50m 5.63i '12, 55m 6.21i '08, 60m 6.47i '12, 100y 9.38+ '10, 200m 20.89 '10.

Michael FRATER b. 6 Oct 1982 Manchester 1.70m 67kg. Racers TC. Political science graduate of Texas Christian University.
At 100m/4x100mR: OG: '04- sf, '08- 6/1R, '12- 1R; WCh: '03- qf, '05- 2, '09- sf/1R, '11- sf/1R; CG: '02- sf, '06- sf/1R; PAm: '03- 1; WJ: '00- 5; PAm-J: '99- 2R. Won NCAA 100m 2004, JAM 100m 2006.
Three world 4x100m records 2008-12.
Progress at 100m: 1999- 10.73/10.47w, 2000- 10.46, 2001- 10.26, 2002- 10.21/10.05w, 2003- 10.13, 2004- 10.06, 2005- 10.03, 2006- 10.06, 2007- 10.03/9.95w, 2008- 9.97, 2009- 10.02, 2010- 9.98/9.94w, 2011- 9.88/9.86w, 2012- 9.94. pbs: 55m 5.74i '12, 60m 6.62i '12, 200m 20.63, 20.45w '02; 400m 49.13 '07.
Older brother Lindel was former Jamaican champion, pb 100m 10.07 '00, 9.9w '98.

Jermaine GONZALES b. 26 Nov 1984 St. Catherine 1.90m 72kg. Racers TC.
At 400m/4x400mR: OG: '04- hR, '12- h; WCh: '11- 4/3R; CG: '06- 3/3R; WJ: '02- 3/2R; WY: 01- 3. Jamaican 400m record 2010.

Progress at 400m: 2001- 47.51, 2002- 45.80, 2003- 46.15i/46.81, 2004- 45.41, 2005- 46.51, 2006- 44.85, 2007- 45.78, 2008- 46.32, 2009- 45.81, 2010- 44.40, 2011- 44.69, 2012- 45.18. pbs: 200m 20.79 '12, 300m 32.49 '10.

Leford GREEN b. 14 Nov 1986 St. Catherine 1.86m 79kg.
At 400mh: OG: '12- 7; WCh: '11- sf/3R; CAG: 10- 1; Won CAC 2011, JAM 2009-12. At 400m/4x400m: WCh: '07- 4R, '11- 2R; CAG: '06- sf/1R; PAm: '07- sf.
At 400m: 2004- 48.14, 2005- 46.68, 53.01; 2006- 45.82, 50.81; 2007- 45.71, 52.69; 2008- 45.56, 50.51; 2009- 46.19; 2010- 45.68, 48.47; 2011- 45.46, 49.03; 2012- 46.76, 48.61. pbs: 200m 20.61 '11, 20.41w '09; 600m 1:19.41i '12.

Hansle PARCHMENT b. 17 Jun 1990 Saint Thomas 1.96m 90kg. Student of psychology at University of the West Indies.
At 110mh: OG: '12- 3; CG: '10- 5; WY: '07- sf; WUG: '11- 1.Two Jamaican 110mh records 2012. Progress at 110mh: 2010- 13.71, 2011- 13.24, 2012- 13.12. Pb 400mh 53.74 '08.

Asafa POWELL b. 23 Nov 1982 St Catherine 1.90m 88kg. MVP. Studied sports medicine at Kingston University of Technology.
At 100m/4x100mR: OG: '04- 5 (dns 200), '08- 5/1R, '12- 8; WCh: '03- qf, '07- 3/2R, '09- 3/1R; CG: '02- sf/2R, '06- 1/1R; PAm-J: '01- 2R. Won JAM 100m 2003-05, 2007, 2011; 200m 2006, 2010; WAF 100m 2004, 2006-08; 200m 2004; DL 100m 2011, GL 2004.
Four world 100m records, five CAC & Commonwealth 2005-07, seven JAM 2004-7; WR 4x100m 2008. Two world bests 100y 2010.
Progress at 100m, 200m: 2001- 10.50, 2002- 10.12, 20.48; 2003- 10.02/9.9, 2004- 9.87, 20.06; 2005- 9.77, 2006- 9.77, 19.90; 2007- 9.74, 20.00; 2008- 9.72, 2009- 9.82, 2010- 9.82/9.72w, 19.97; 2011- 9.78, 20.55; 2012- 9.85. pbs: 50m 5.64i '12, 60m 6.42+ '09, 6.50i '12; 100y 9.07+ '10, 400m 45.94 '09.
Disqualified for false start in World quarters 2003 after fastest time (10.05) in heats. In 2004 he tied the record of nine sub-10 second times in a season and in 2005 he took the world record for 100m at Athens, tying that at Gateshead and Zürich in 2006, when he ran a record 12 sub-10 times and was world athlete of the year. Took record to 9.74 in Rieti 2007 and ran 15 sub-10 times in 2008, including seven sub-9.90 in succession after 5th place at Olympics. Now has record 80 sub-10 times (plus 7w). Withdrew from 2011 Worlds through injury. IAAF Athlete of the Year 2006. Elder brother Donovan (b. 31 Oct 1971): at 60m: 6.51i '96 (won US indoors '96, 6 WI '99; 100m 10.07/9.7 '95).

Andrew RILEY b. 9 Sep 1988 Saint Thomas 1.88m 80kg. Was at University of Illinois.
At 110mh: OG: '12- h; WCh: '11- sf. Jamaican champion 2011, won NCAA 100m 2012, 110mh 2010 & 2012.
Progress at 110mh: 2009- 13.74/13.61w, 2010- 13.45, 2011- 13.32, 2012- 13.19. Pbs: 60m 6.57i '12, 100m 10.02 '12, 200m 21.25w '12, 60mh 7.53i '12, HJ 2.10 '08.
First to win NCAA 100m & 110mh double 2012.

Dwight THOMAS b. 23 Sep 1980 Kingston 1.85m 82kg. adidas.
At 110mh: WCh: '09- 7, '11- dns. At 100m/4x-100mR: OG: '04- sf, '08- res 1R; WCh: '03- sf, '05- 5, '07- res 2R, '09- res 1R; CG: '02- 4=/2R; PAm: '99- 3R; WJ: '98- 3/1R. At 200m: OG: '00- qf/4R. At 60m: WI: '03- sf. At 60mh: WI: '04- 8. Won CAC-J 110mh 1998, PAm-J 100m & 200m 1999, Jamaican 100m & 200m 2002.
Jamaican 110mh records 2009 & 2011.
Progress at 100m, 110mh: 1998- 10.38, 14.40/13.86w; 1999- 10.37, 2000- 10.12, 2001- 10.19, 2002- 10.15, 13.74; 2003- 10.19, 2004- 10.12, 13.34; 2005- 10.00, 2006- 10.11, 2007- 10.15/10.07w, 14.25; 2008- 10.20/10.14w; 2009- 10.33, 13.16; 2010- 13.25/13.1w, 2011- 13.15, 2012- 13.36/13.17w. pbs: 55m 6.27i '01, 60m 6.61i '03, 200m 20.32 '07, 60mh 7.59i '04.

Warren WEIR b. 31 Oct 1989 Trelawny 1.78m 75kg. Racers TC.
At 200m: OG: '12- 3. At 110mh: WJ: '08- sf.
Progress at 200m: 2008- 22.26, 2009- 21.46w, 2010- 21.52, 2011- 20.43, 2012- 19.84. pbs: 100m 10.50 '09, 10.39w '10; 400m 46.23 '13, 110mh 13.65 '07, 13.45w '08; 400mh 53.28 '09.

Jason YOUNG b. 21 Mar 1991 1.80m 68kg. Racers TC.
At 200m: WUG: '11- 2.
Progress at 200m: 2007- 22.10, 2008- 21.61, 2009- 21.57, 2011- 20.53, 2012- 19.86. pb 100m 10.06 '12.

Women

Aleen BAILEY b. 25 Nov 1980 St Mary 1.70m 64g. Student at University of South Carolina.
At 100m/(200m)/4x100mR: OG: '04- 5/4/1R; WCh: '01- (h), '03- 6/qf, '05- sf/2R, '07- (6), '09- 8/1R; WJ: '96- 2R, '98- 3R; PAm: '07- (5)/1R; PAm-J: '97- 2R, '99- 1/1/2R; WCp: '06- 1R. At 60m: WI: '12- 7. Won NCAA 100m & 200m (and indoor 200m) 2003, Jamaican 100m & 200m 2001, 2003.
Progresion at 100m, 200m: 1995- 12.10, 1996- 11.67, 23.99; 1997- 11.60/11.55w, 23.65; 1998- 11.37, 23.96/23.16w, 1999- 11.41, 23.37; 2000- 11.47/11.38w, 23.45/22.86w; 2001- 11.14, 22.59; 2002- 11.33, 22.54; 2003- 11.07, 22.59; 2004- 11.04, 22.33; 2005- 11.07, 23.00/22.75w; 2006- 11.27, 23.70; 2007- 11.17, 22.60; 2008- 11.20, 22.85/22.82w; 2009- 11.07, 22.83; 2010- 11.19, 23.15; 2011- 11.15, 22.79; 2012- 11.04, 22.84/22.79w. pbs: 60m 7.18i '12, 400m 54.43 '07.
Her brother Capleton is a reggae star.

Schillonie CALVERT b. 27 Jul 1988 Saint-James. Racers TC. University of Technology.

At 100m/4x100R: OG: '12- res (2)R; WJ: '04- 7, '06- sf/3/3R; WY: '05- 3; PAm-J '05- 2, '07-1 (2 200m).
Progress at 100m: 2004- 11.44/11.33w, 2005- 11.40, 2006- 11.21, 2007- 11.35, 2008- 11.23, 2009- 11.19, 2010- 11.36, 2011- 11.05, 2012- 11.05. pbs: 200m 22.55 '11, 400m 53.50 '12.

Veronica CAMPBELL-BROWN b. 15 May 1982 Clarks Town, Trelawny 1.63m 61kg. Adidas. Was at University of Arkansas, USA.
At (100m)/200m/4x100mR: OG: '00- 2R, '04- 3/1/1R, '08- 1, '12- 3/4/2R; WCh: '05- 2/4/2R, '07- 1/2/2R, '09- 4/2, '11- 2/1/2R; CG: '02- (2)/2R, '06- 2; WJ: '98- (qf), '00- 1/1/2R; WY: '99- (1)/1R; PAm-J: '99- 2R. At 60m: WI: '10- 1, '12- 1. Won WAF 100m 2004-05, 200m 2004, CAC-J 100m 2000, JAM 100m 2002, 2004-05, 2007, 2011; 200m 2004-05, 2007-09, 2011.
CAC junior 100m record 2000.
Progress at 100m, 200m: 1999- 11.49, 23.73; 2000- 11.12/11.1, 22.87; 2001- 11.13/22.92; 2002- 11.00, 22.39; 2004- 10.91, 22.05; 2005- 10.85, 22.35/22.29w; 2006- 10.99, 22.51; 2007- 10.89, 22.34; 2008- 10.87/10.85w, 21.74; 2009- 10.89/10.81w, 22.29; 2010- 10.78, 21.98; 2011- 10.76, 22.22; 2012- 10.81, 22.32. pbs: 50m 6.08i '12, 60m 7.00i '10, 100y 9.91+ '11 (world best), 400m 52.24i '05, 52.25 '11.
In 2000 became the first woman to become World Junior champion at both 100m and 200m. Unbeaten at 200m in 28 finals (42 races in all) from 11 March 2000 to 22 July 2005 (lost to Allyson Felix). Married Omar Brown (1 CG 200m 2006) on 3 Nov 2007.

Shelly-Ann FRASER-PRYCE b. 27 Dec 1986 Kingston 1.60m 52kg. MVP. Graduate of the University of Technology. née Fraser. Married Jason Pryce on 7 Jan 2011.
At 100m/4x100mR: OG: '08- 1, '12- 1/2/2R; WCh: '07- res (2)R, '09- 1/1R. '11- 4/2R; won WAF 2008, DL 2012, JAM 100m 2009, 2012; 200m 2012. CAC and Commonwealth 100m records 2009 & 2012.
Progress at 100m, 200m: 2002- 11.8, 2003- 11.57, 2004- 11.72, 24.08; 2005- 11.72; 2006- 11.74, 24.8; 2007- 11.31/11.21w, 23.5; 2008- 10.78, 22.15; 2009- 10.73, 22.58; 2010- 10.82dq, 22.47dq; 2011- 10.95, 22.59/22.10w; 2012- 10.70, 22.09. pb 60m 7.04i '13. Huge improvement in 2008 and moved to joint third on world all-time list for 100m when winning 2009 world 100m title. 6-month ban for positive test for a non-performance enhancing drug on 23 May 2010.

Anneisha McLAUGHLIN b. 6 Jan 1986 Manchester 1.63m 54kg. University of Technology.
At 200m/4x100mR: WCh: '09- 5; WJ: '02- 2/1R, '04- 2/2R; WY: '03- 1 (2 MedR); WUG: '11- 1/3R; PAm-J: '03- 2/2R, '05- 1. At 400m/4x400mR: WJ: '00- 2R; WY: '01- 3 (2 MedR). Won CAC-J 400m 2000, 100m & 200m 2002' JAM 200m 2010.

Progress at 200m: 2000- 24.33w, 2001- 23.11, 2002- 22.94, 2003- 23.19, 2004- 23.21, 2005- 23.00, 2006- 23.47, 2007- 23.28/23.27w, 2008- 23.34, 2009- 22.55, 2010- 22.54, 2011- 22.54, 2012- 22.61. pbs: 100m 11.24 '12, 400m 51.89 '12.

Sherone SIMPSON b. 12 Aug 1984 Manchester, Jamaica 1.73m 58kg. MVP. Graduate of Kingston University of Technology.
At 100m/(200m)/4x100mR: OG: '04- 6/1R, '08- 2=/6, '12- (sf)/2R; WCh: '05- 6/2R, '11- (8)/2R; CG: '06- (1)/1R; WJ: '02- 1R; PAm-J: '03- 2/2R; WCp: '06- 1/1R. Won WAF 100m 2006, JAM 100m 2006, 2010; 200m 2006.
Progress at 100m, 200m: 2000- 12.54, 2001- 12.17, 25.01; 2002- 11.60, 24.21; 2003- 11.37/11.1, 23.60; 2004- 11.01, 22.70; 2005- 10.97, 22.54; 2006- 10.82, 22.00; 2007- 11.43, 22.76; 2008- 10.87, 22.11; 2009- 11.15/11.04w; 2010- 11.02, 22.65/22.64w; 2011- 11.00, 22.73; 2012- 11.01, 22.37. pbs: 400m 51.25 '08, 100mh 14.10 '02.

Kenia SINCLAIR b. 14 July 1980 St Catherine 1.67m 54kg. Was at Seton Hall University, USA.
At 800m: OG: '08- 6; WCh: '05/07/09- sf, '11- 7; CG: '06- 2; WI: '06- 2; CCp: '10- 2. Won JAM 800m 2005-09, 2011-12; 1500m 2006-07, 2011.
Five Jamaican 800m records 2005-06. CAC indoor 1000m record (2:38.62) 2010.
Progress at 800m: 2002- 2:05.26i/2:07.39, 2003- 2:03.21, 2005- 1:58.88, 2006- 1:57.88, 2007- 1:58.61, 2008- 1:58.24, 2009- 1:59.13, 2010- 1:58.16, 2011- 1-58.21, 2012- 2:01.55. pbs: 400m 56.84 '03, 600m 1:25.6+ '09, 1000m 2:37.37 '05, 1500m 4:05.56 '07, 1M 4:32.33i '05, 3000m 9:52.71i '02, 10kmRd 34:27 '11.   Based in Gainesville, Florida.

Kaliese SPENCER b. 6 May 1987 Westmoreland 1.73m 59kg. Was at University of Texas.
At 400mh/4x400mR: OG: '12- 4; WCh: '07- sf, '09- 4/res 2R, '11- 4; WJ: '06- 1/3R. Won DL 2010-12, JAM 400mh 2011.
Progress at 400mh: 2006- 55.11, 2007- 55.62, 2009- 53.56, 2010- 53.33, 2011- 52.79, 2012- 53.49. pbs: 200m 23.62 '12, 400m 50.55 '08, 800m 2:03.01 '11.

Kerron STEWART b. 16 Apr 1984 Kingston 1.75m 61kg. Adult education student at Auburn University, USA.
At 100m/(200m)/4x100mR: OG: '08- 2=/3, '12- sf/2R; WCh: '07- 7/2R, '09- 2/1R, '11- 6/5/2R; WJ: '02- 4/1R; WY: '01- 2/2R. Won NCAA 200m 2007, indoor 60m & 200m 2007; JAM 100m 2008.
Progress at 100m, 200m: 2000- 11.89, 24.09w; 2001- 11.70, 23.90; 2002- 11.46, 24.21; 2003- 11.34, 23.50; 2004- 11.40, 23.63i/23.66; 2005- 11.63, 23.77i/24.22/23.46w; 2006- 11.03, 22.65; 2007- 11.03, 22.41; 2008- 10.80, 21.99; 2009- 10.75, 22.42; 2010- 10.96, 22.57/22.34w; 2011- 10.87, 22.63.; 2012- 10.92, 22.70 pbs: 55m 6.71i '06, 60m 7.14i '07, 400m 52.08 '08.

Melaine WALKER b. 1 Jan 1983 Kingston 1.73m 58kg. MVP. Social work graduate of University of Texas, USA.

At 400mh/4x400mR: OG: '08- 1, '12- sf; WCh: '01-07-09-11: h/sf/1/2; CG: '02- 4; WJ: '00- 3/2R, '02- 2 (5 100mh); CAG: '06- 3/2R; Jamaican champion 2006-09, 2012; WAF 2008-09. At 200m: WJ: '98- 5/3 4x100R; WY: '99- 2.
Two CAC 400mh records 2008-09.
Progress at 400mh: 1999- 58.99, 2000- 56.96, 2001- 55.62, 2002- 55.84, 2003- 57.24, 2004- 56.62, 2005- 55.09, 2006- 54.87, 2007- 54.14, 2008- 52.64, 2009- 52.42, 2010- 55.33, 2011- 52.73, 2012- 53.74. pbs: 60m 7.40i '05, 100m 11.63 '99, 200m 23.46 '12, 400m 51.61 '08, 800m 2:11.96 '11, 60mh 8.05i '06, 100mh 12.75 '06.

Rosemarie WHYTE b. 8 Sep 1986 Trelawny 1.75m 66kg. Racers TC.
At 400m/4x400mR: OG: '08- 7/3R, '12- 8/3R; WCh: '09- 2R, '11- sf/2R. Won JAM 400m 2008.
Progress at 400m: 2002- 55.51, 2007- 53.47, 2008- 50.05, 2009- 51.55, 2010- 50.67, 2011- 49.84, 2012- 50.08. pbs: 100m 11.60/11.4 '06, 200m 22.74 '09, 100mh 14.27/14.2 '06, 400mh 59.89 '09, HJ 1.65 '06, LJ 6.35 '06, TJ 13.04 '06, JT 31.15 '06, Hep 5262 '06.

Kimberly WILLIAMS b. 3 Nov 1988 Saint Thomas 1.70m 61kg. Florida State University, USA.
At TJ: OG: '12- 6; WCh: '09/11 dnq 15/14; WJ: '06- dnq 15; WY: '05- dnq; WI: '12- 5. Won NCAA LJ & TJ 2009, JAM TJ 2010, 2012.
Progress at TJ: 2004- 12.53/12.65w, 2005- 12.63/13.09w, 2006- 13.18, 2007- 13.52, 2008- 13.82i/13.69/13.83w, 2009- 14.08/14.38w, 2010- 14.23, 2011- 14.25, 2012- 14.53. pbs: 100m 11.76 '12, 200m 24.55 '11, LJ 6.55i 11, 6.42/6.66w '09.

Novlene WILLIAMS-MILLS b. 26 Apr 1982 St Ann 1.70m 57kg. Studied recreation at University of Florida, USA.
At 400m/4x400mR: OG: '04- sf/2R, '08- sf/3R, '12- 5/3R; WCh: '05- 2R, '07- 3/2R, '09- 4/2R, '11- 8/2R; CG: '06- 3; PAm: '03- 6/2R; WI: '06- 5; WCp: '06- 3/1R. Won JAM 400m 2006-07, 2009-12.
Progress at 400m: 1999- 55.62, 2000- 53.90, 2001- 54.99, 2002- 52.05, 2003- 51.93, 2004- 50.59, 2005- 51.09, 2006- 49.63, 2007- 49.66, 2008- 50.11, 2009- 49.77, 2010- 50.04, 2011- 50.05, 2012- 49.78. pbs: 200m 23.25 '10, 500m 1:11.83i '03.
Married 2007. Younger sister Clora Williams (b. 26.11.83) joined her on JAM's 3rd place 4x400m team at 2010 WI; she has 400m pb 51.06 and won NCAA 2006.

Shericka WILLIAMS b. 17 Sep 1985 Black River, St. Elizabeth 1.70m 64kg. MVP. Kingston University of Technology.
At 400m/4x400mR: OG: '08- 2/3R, '12- 3R; WCh: '05- sf/2R, '07- sf/2R, '09- 2/2R, '11- 6/2R; CG: '06- 5; WCp: '06- 1R, '10- 4/1R; won JAM 400m 2005.
Progress at 200m, 400m: 2001- 24.74, 2003- 23.90, 55.44; 2004- 23.96/23.70w, 53.52; 2005- 23.08, 50.97; 2006- 22.55, 50.24; 2007- 23.32, 50.37; 2008- 22.50, 49.69; 2009- 22.57, 49.32; 2010- 23.25, 50.04; 2011- 23.49/23.16w, 50.45; 2012- 23.12, 50.34. pb 100m 11.34 '07, 800m 2:09.17 '07.

Nickiesha WILSON b. 28 Jul 1986 Kingston 1.73m 64kg. Racers TC. Was at Louisiana State University, USA.
At 400mh: OG: '08/12- sf/sf; WCh: '07- 4, '09/11- sf; CG: '10- 3; PAm: '07- 2; PAm-J: '05-1; CAG: '10- 1; CCp: '10- 1/1R; won NCAA 2008, CAC 2009, JAM 2010.
Progress at 100mh, 400mh: 2005- 13.98, 57.38; 2006- 13.64/13.44w, 56.77; 2007- 12.93, 53.97; 2008- 12.85/12.63w, 54.45; 2009- 12.79/12.72w, 54.89; 2010- 13.17, 54.52; 2011- 13.23, 55.57; 2012- 13.00, 55.50. pbs: 60m 7.55i '10, 200m 23.59i '08, 400m 53.66i '08, 54.88 '06; 60mh 8.01i '07, LJ 6.26 '11.

JAPAN

Governing body: Nippon Rikujo-Kyogi Renmei, 1-1-1 Jinnan, Shibuya-Ku, Tokyo 150-8050. Founded 1911.

National Championships first held in 1914 (men), 1925 (women). **2012 Champions**: **Men**: 100m: Masashi Eriguchi 10.29, 200m: Kei Takase 20.42, 400m: Yuzo Kanemaru 46.18, 800m: Masato Yokota 1:48.12, 1500m: Keisuke Tanaka 3:45.49, 5000m: Kazuya Deguchi 13:47.17, 10,000m: Yuki Sato 28:18.15, Mar: Arata Fujiwara 2:07:48, 3000mSt: Minato Yamashita 8:34.95, 110mh: Kenji Yahata 13.72, 400mh: Takayuki Kishimoto 48.41, HJ: Hiromi Takahari 2.20, PV: Seito Yamamoto 5.37, LJ: Daisuke Arakawa 7.78, TJ: Yuma Okabe 16.54, SP: Satoshi Hatase 17.91, DT: Yuji Tsutsumi 56.19, HT: Koji Murofushi 72.85, JT: Genki Dean 84.03, Dec: Keisuke Ushiro 8037, 20kW: Isamu Fujisawa 1:20:38, 50kW: Yuki Yamazaki 3:41:47. **Women**: 100m/200m: Chisato Fukushima 11.45/23.35, 400m: Mayu Sato 53.86, 800m: Ruriko Kubo 2:04.18, 1500m: Ayako Jinnouchi 4:16.42, 5000m: Hitomi Niiya 15:17.92, 10,000m: Mika Yoshikawa 31:28.71, Mar: Risa Shigetomo 2:23:23, 3000mSt: Yoshika Arai 9:55.93, 100mh: Ayako Kimura 13.25, 400mh: Satomi Kubokura 55.98, HJ: Azumi Maeda 1.80, PV: Tomomi Abiko 4.40, LJ: Saeko Okayama 6.55, TJ: Fumiyo Yoshida 12.98, SP: Yukiko Shirai 15.47, DT: Ai Shikimoto 52.74, HT: Masumi Aya 64.91, JT: Yuki Ebihara 62.36, Hep: Suzuka Akai 5451, 20kW: Kimi Otoshi 1:29:48.

Koichiro MORIOKA b. 2 Apr 1985 Isahaya, Nagasaki 1.83m 65kg.
At 20kW: OG: '08- 16; WCh: '05-07-09: 29/11/11; AsiG: '06- 3; AsiC: '07- 2; WUG: '05- 3, '07- 3. At 50kW: OG: '12- 10; WCh: '09- 19, '11- 6; AsiG: '10- 3. At 10,000mW: WJ: '04- 6. Won Asian 20kW 2008, JPN 20kW 2007, 2009-10, 50kW 2011.
Progress at 20kW, 50kW: 2004- 1:28:22, 2005- 1:22:52, 2006- 1:22:46, 2007- 1:21:30, 2008- 1:21:55, 3:55:40; 2009- 1:21:16, 3:49:12; 2010- 1:20:43, 3:47:41; 2011- 1:22:10, 3:44:45; 2012- 1:21:52, 3:43:14. pbs: 5000mW 19:13.77 '09, 10,000mW: 39:07.84 '10 (Asian record), 35kW 2:35:20 '12.

Yukifumi MURAKAMI b. 23 Dec 1979 Ueshima, Ehime 1.85m 90kg. Suzuki Motor, Was at Nihon University.
At JT: OG: '04/08/12- dnq 18/15/24; WCh: '05-07-11: dnq 27/21/15, '09- 3; WJ: '98- 3; AsiG: 02-06-10: 2/2/1; AsiC: '09- 1, '11- 1; Asi-J: '97- 2; JPN champion 2000-11.
Progress at JT: 19950 56.60, 1996- 68.00, 1997- 76.54, 1998- 73.62, 1999- 71.70, 2000- 78.57, 2001- 80.59, 2002- 78.77, 2003- 78.98, 2004- 81.71, 2005- 79.79, 2006- 78.54, 2007- 79.85, 2008- 79.71, 2009- 83.10, 2010- 83.15, 2011- 83.53, 2012- 83.95.

Koji MUROFUSHI b. 8 Oct 1974 Shizuoka 1.87m 100kg. Graduate of Chukyo University. Mizuno.
At HT: OG: '00- 9, '04- 1, '08- 5, '12- 3; WCh: '95-97-99-01-03-07-11: dnq/10/dnq 14/2/3/6/1; WJ: '92- 8; AsiG: '94- 2, '98- 1, '02- 1; AsiC: '93-5-8-02: 2/2/2/1; WCp: '02- 2 (9 DT), '06- 1. Won GWG 2001, GP 2002 (2nd 2000), WAF 2006, World HT challenge 2010, E.Asian 1997, 2001; Japanese 1995-2012.
18 Japanese hammer records 1998-2003, Asian records 2001 & 2003.
Progress at HT: 1991- 61.76, 1992- 66.30, 1993- 68.00, 1994- 69.54, 1995- 72.32, 1996- 73.82, 1997- 75.72, 1998- 78.57, 1999- 79.17, 2000- 81.08, 2001- 83.47, 2002- 83.33, 2003- 84.86, 2004- 83.15, 2005- 76.47, 8006- 82.01, 2007- 82.62, 2008- 81.87, 2009- 78.36, 2010- 80.99, 2011- 81.24, 2012- 78.71. pb DT 44.64 '96.
Won IAAF HT Challenge 2010. His father Shigenobu Murofushi won a record five Asian Games gold medals 1970-86 and held the Japanese hammer record with 75.96 (Los Angeles 1984) until Koji broke it for the first time on 26 Apr 1998. His mother was the 1968 European Junior javelin champion, Serafina Moritz (Romania). His sister **Yuka** (b. 11 Feb 77) holds Japanese records: DT 58.62 '07 and HT 67.77 '04; 6th WJ DT 1996.

Yuki YAMAZAKI b. 16 Jan 1984 Toyama 1.77m 65kg. Was at Juntendo University.
At (20kW)/50kW: OG: '04- 16, '08- 11/7, '12- dq; WCh: '05-07-09: 8/dnf/dq; WCp: '10- 6; AsiG: '02- dq/dq, '06- (4); AsiC: '03- (2), '07- 2. At 10,000mW: WJ: '00- 20, '02- 5; WY: '01- 4. Won JPN 20kW 2002, 50kW 2004-10, 2012.
Four Japanese 50k walk records 2006-09. World youth 5000m walk best 2001.
Progress at 50kW: 2004- 3:55:20, 2005- 3:50:40, 2006- 3:43:38, 2007- 3:47:40, 2008- 3:41:29, 2009- 3:40:12, 2010- 3:46:46, 2011- 3:44:03, 2012- 3:41:47. pbs: 5000mW 19:35.79 '01, 10,000mW 39:48.52 '08, 20kW 1:20:38 '03.

Women

Masumi FUCHISE b. 2 Sep 1986 Himegi, Hyogo pref. 1.60m 45kg.
At 20kW: OG: '12- 11; WCh: '07- 27, '09- 7, '11- dnf; AsiG: '10- 2; AsiC: '08-09-10: 3/1/1; WUG: '09- 2; Japanese champion 2007, 2009; Asian 2009-10.
Two Japanese 20km walk records 2007-09.
Progress at 20kW: 2006- 1:33:59, 2007- 1:29:36, 2008- 1:31:11. 2009- 1:28:03, 2010- 1:29:35, 2011- 1:31:51, 2012- 1:28:41, 2013- 1:30:27. pbs: 5000m run 16:59.86 '07, 5000mW 21:37.25 '09, 10kW 43:24.00t '11.

Kayoko FUKUSHI b. 25 Mar 1982 Itayanagi, Aiomori pref. 1.60m 45kg. Wacoal.
At 5000m/(10,000m): OG: '04- (26), '08- h/11, '12- h/10; WCh: '03- h/11, '05- 12/11, '07- 14/10, '09- (9); WJ: '00- 4; AsiG: '02- 2/2, '06- (1), '10- 5/4; WCp: '06- 3 (5 3000m). World 20km: '06- 6; CC: '02- 15, '06- 6. Won JPN 5000m 2002, 2004-07, 2010; 10,000m 2002-07, 2010.
World 15km record & Asian 20km & HMar records 2006, Japanese records: 3000m 2002, 5000m (4) 2002-05.
Progress at 5000m, 10,000m, Mar: 1998- 16:56.35, 1999- 16:38.69, 35:37.54; 2000- 15:29.70, 2001- 15:10.23, 31:42.05; 2002- 14:55.19, 30:51.81; 2003- 15:09.02, 31:10.57; 2004- 14:57.73, 31:05.68; 2005- 14:53.22, 31:03.75; 2006- 15:03.17, 30:57.90; 2007- 15:05.73, 32:13.58; 2008- 15:12.7, 31:01.14, 2:40:54; 2009- 15:23.44mx, 31:23.49; 2010- 15:17.86, 31:29.03; 2011- 30:54.29, 2:24:38; 2012- 15:09.31, 31:10.35. pbs: 3000m 8:44.40 '02, 15km 46:55 '06, 20km 63:41 '06, HMar 67:26 '06, 30km 1:41:25 '08.
Set Japanese junior records at 3000m, 5000m and 10,000m in 2001.

Hitomi NIIYA b. 26 Feb 1988 Soja, Okayama pref. 1.65m 44kg.
At (5000m)/10,000m: OG: '12- h/9; WCh: '11- (13); AsiC: '11- (2). At 3000m: WY: '05- 3. Won JPN 5000m 2012.
Progress at 10,000m: 2012- 30:59.19. pbs: 3000m 9:10.34 '05, 5000m 15:10.20 '12, HMar 71:41 '08, Mar 2:30:58 '09.

Mizuki NOGUCHI b. 3 Jul 1978 Kanagawa 1.50m 41kg. Globary.
At 10,000m: WCh: '01- 13. At Mar: OG: '04- 1; WCh: '03- 2. World HMar: '99-00-01-02: 2/4/4/9. Won Asian CC 1999, E.Asian HMar 2001, JPN Mar 2003.
Asian marathon record 2005. World road records 25km 1:22:12 & 30km 1:38:48 in 2005 Berlin Marathon.
Progress at 10,000m, Mar: 1999- 33:09.98, 2000- 32:05.23, 2001- 31:51.13, 2002- 31:50.18, 2:25:35; 2003- 31:59.28, 2:21:18; 2004- 31:21.03, 2:26:20, 2005- 31:44.29, 2:19:12; 2006- 31:50.13, 2007- 2:21:37, 2013- 2:24:05. pbs: 3000m 9:24.51 '98, 5000m 15:34.36 '99, Rd: 15km 48:11 '01, HMar 67:43 '06, 30km 1:39:09 '04.
Formerly excelling at half marathon, she won the Nagoya marathon on debut in 2002 and again at Osaka in January 2003, at the Olympics in 2004, in Berlin 2005 and Tokyo 2007. 3rd Nagoya 2013.

Yoshimi OZAKI b. 1 Jul 1981 Yamakita, Kanagawa Pref. 1.54m 41kg. Daiichi Seimei.
At Mar: OG: '12- 19; WCh: '09- 2, '11- 18; JPN champion 2008. At HMar: WCh: '07- 13, '09- 9. World CC: '06- 19.
Progress at 10,000m, Mar: 2004- 32:19.30, 2005- 31:47.23, 2006- 31:48.92, 2007- 32:13.95, 2008- 32:01.07, 2:23:30; 2009- 2:25:25, 2011- 2:23:56, 2012- 2:24:14. pbs: 1500m 4:20.78 '02, 3000m 9:13.09 '04, 5000m 15:28.55 '04, 15km 49:13 '08, 20km 65:57 '08, HMar 69:26 '07.
Second in 2:26:19 on marathon debut in Nagoya 2008, then won at Tokyo in 2:23:30. Won Yokohama Marathon 2011. Her older sister Akemi Ozaki has pb 2:27:23 '09.

KAZAKHSTAN

Governing body: Athletic Federation of the Republic of Kazakhstan, Abai Street 48, 480072 Almaty. Founded 1959.

2012 National Champions: Men: 100m: Grigoriy Volodin 10.65, 200m: Vyacheslav Muravyev 21.16, 400m: Sergey Zaykov 45.67, 800m: Alexandr Sysoyev 1:49.38, 1500m: Sergey Yershov 3:48.96, 5000m: Mikhail Krasilov 14:55.75, 10,000m: Hassan Gafarov TJK 32:53.9, 3000mSt: Ermek Arkhabayev 9:28.50, 110mh: Denis Semenov 14.13, 400mh: Artem Dyatlov UZB 49.78, HJ: Sergey Zassimovich 2.24, PV: Nikita Filippov 5.20, LJ: Yevgeniy Piskun 7.75, TJ: Roman Valiyev 17.20, SP: Ivan Ivanov 19.47, DT: Yevgeniy Labutov 52.28, HT: Sukhrob Khodjayev UZB 74.20, JT: Rostom Chincharauli GEO 67.64, Dec: Baurzhan Serikbayev 6677, 20000mW: Stanislav Borissov 1:39:11.8, **Women**: 100m: Olga Bludova 11.19, 200m: Anastasiya Tulapina 23.51, 400m: Marina Maslenko 52.26, 800m: Margarita Mukasheva 1:59.88, 1500m: Yelena Gofman 4:38.68, 5000m: Marina Vasilyeva 20:07.31, 10,000m: Gulzhanat Zhanatbek 40:33.8, 3000mSt: Yelena Gofman 10:47.48, 100mh: Nataliya Ivoninskaya 12.68, 400mh: Alexandra Kuzina 56.35, HJ: Anna Ustinova 1.85, PV: Olesya Yermolenko 3.85, LJ: Anastasiya Kudinova 6.39, TJ: Irina Ektova 14.17, SP: Yelena Smolyanova UZB 17.68, DT: Mariya Telushkina 43.12, HT: Diana Nusupbekova 48.12, JT: Asiya Rabayeva 41.38, Hep: Mariya Sozykina 5275.

Dmitriy KARPOV b. 23 Jul 1981 Karaganda 1.98m 94kg.
At Dec: OG: '04- 3, '08- dnf, '12- 18; WCh: '03-05-07-09-11: 3/dnf/3/21/21; WJ: '00- 4; AsiG: '02-06-10: 2/1/1; won E.Asian 2001. At Hep: WI: '04- 4, '08- 3; won Asian indoors 2012. At 110mh: AsiC: '02- 5. Won KAZ 200m 2003, Dec 1999.
Two Asian decathlon records 2004 (& four KAZ 2003-04), three indoor heptathlon 2004-08.
Progress at Dec: 1999- 7105, 2000- 7620, 2001- 7567, 2002- 7995, 2003- 8374, 2004- 8725, 2006- 8438, 2007- 8586, 2008- 8504, 2009- 8029, 2010- 8026, 2011- 8089, 2012- 8173. pbs: 60m 7.04i '04, 100m 10.69 '06, 10.50w '04; 200m 21.65 '03, 400m 46.81 '04, 1000m 2:42.34i '04, 1500m 4:32.34 '06, 60mh 7.79i '03, 110mh 13.93 '02, HJ 2.12 '03, PV 5.30 '08, LJ 8.05 '02, SP 16.95 '10, DT 52.80 '04, JT 60.31 '06, Hep 6229i '08.
Set national record of 8253 to win at Desenzano in 2003 from previous best of 7995. Then three pbs en route to World bronze and another KAZ record with 8374. In 2004 he was third at Götzis with 8512 and set three pbs in his 8725 for Olympic bronze. Did not compete in 2005 apart from two false starts in World Champs decathlon 100m, but won at Ratingen and Talence after 2nd Götzis in 2006 to win the IAAF Combined Events Challenge. Won at Götzis 2008.

Women

Marina AITOVA b. 13 Sep 1982 Karaganda 1.80m 60kg. née Korzhova.
At HJ: OG: '04- dnq 31=, '08- 10=, '12- dnq; WCh: '03-09-11: dnq 22=/13=/19=, '07- 7=; AsiG: '02- 2, '06- 1; AsiC: '00- 2, '02- 3, '11- 3; WJ: '00- 9=; WY: '99- 4; WI: '08- 5, '10- 7=; WUG: '07- 1; WCp: '06- 3. Won Asi-J 2001, Af-AsG & C.Asian G 2003, Asian indoor 2006, 2010; KAZ 2002-04, 2011.
Two Asian high jump records 2008-09.
Progress at HJ: 1999- 1.86, 2000- 1.90, 2001- 1.86i/1.85, 2002- 1.94, 2003- 1.89, 2004- 1.91i/1.89, 2005- 1.75, 2006- 1.95, 2007- 1.96, 2008- 1.97, 2009- 1.99, 2010- 1.94i, 2011- 1.94, 2012- 1.95. pb LJ 6.00 '01.

Olga RYPAKOVA b. 30 Nov 1984 Kamenogorsk 1.83m 62kg. née Alekseyeva.
At TJ/(LJ): OG: '08- 4 (dnq 29), '12- 1; WCh: '07-11, '09- 10, '11- 2; WJ: '00- (dnq 23); AsiG: '06- (3), '10- 1/2; AsiC: '07- 1/1, '09- 1; WI: '08-10-12: 4/1/2; WUG: '07- (1); WCp: '06- (8), '10- 1/3; won DL TJ 2012, Asian Indoor LJ & TJ 2009. At Hep: WJ: '02- 2; WY: '01- 4; AsiG: '06- 1; won C.Asian 2003. Won KAZ LJ 2005, 2008, 2011; TJ 2008, 2011; Hep 2006.
Four Asian TJ records 2008-10, five indoors 2008-10, seven KAZ records 2007-10.
Progress at LJ, TJ: 2000- 6.23, 2001- 6.00, 2002- 6.26, 2003- 6.34i/6.14, 2004- 6.53i, 2005- 6.60, 2006- 6.63, 2007- 6.85, 14.69; 2008- 6.52/6.58w, 15.11; 2009- 6.58i/6.42, 14.53/14.69w; 2010- 6.60, 15.25; 2011- 6.56, 14.96; 2012- 14.98. pbs: 200m 24.83 '02, 800m 2:20.12 '02, 60mh 8.67i '06, 100mh 14.02 '06, HJ 1.92 '06, SP 13.04 '06, JT 41.60 '03, Hep 6122 '06, Pen 4582i '06 (Asian rec).
Former heptathlete, concentrated on long jump after birth of daughter. Four KAZ and three Asian TJ records with successive jumps in Olympic final 2008, three Asian indoor records when won World Indoor gold in 2010.

KENYA

Governing body: Kenya Amateur Athletic Association, PO Box 46722, 00100 Nairobi. Founded 1951.

2012 National Champions: Men: 100m: Ibrahim Muya 10.38, 200m: Mike Nyangau 20.94, 400m: Vincent Mumo 46.10, 800m: Anthony Chemut 1:46.1, 1500m: Caleb Ndiku 3:33.85, 5000m: Geoffrey Kipsang 13:31.3, 10,000m: Kenneth Kipkemoi 27:49.53, 3000mSt: Abel Mutai 8:27.7, 110mh: Julius Bungei 14.1, 400mh: Boniface Tumuti 49.81, HJ: Mathew Sawe 2.14, LJ/TJ: Elijah Kimitei 8.09/16.66, SP/DT: David Limo 14.81/47.22, HT: Dennis Sakawa 55.20, JT: Julius Yego 77.06, 20kW: David Kimutai 1:23:36.
Women: 100m: Mildred Gamba UGA 11.85, 200m: Millicent Ndoro 24.05, 400m: Joyce Zakari 52.0, 800m: Eunice Sum 1:59.75, 1500m: Hellen Obiri 4:07.4, 5000m: Gladys Cherono 15:39.5, 10,000m: Vivian Cheruiyot 32:24.52, 3000mSt: Mercy Njorege 9:40.0, 100mh: Jentricks Nelima 14.59, 400mh: Maureen Maiyo 56.9, HJ: Cherotich Koech 1.70, PV: Caroline Cherotich 2.95, LJ/TJ: Regina Mulatya 5.89/12.38, SP: Priscilla Isiao 13.16, DT: Betty Chebet 42.31, HT: Linda Oseso 59.72, JT: Berry Chebet 48.06, 20kmW: Grace Wanjiru 1:37:45.

Emmanuel Kipkemei **BETT** b. 30 Mar 83 1.70m 55kg.
Progress at 10,000m: 2011- 26:51.95, 2012- 26:51.16. pb 5000m 13:08.35 '12, 15km 43:00+ '11, HMar 60:56 '12.

Josphat Kipkoech **BETT** b. 12 Jun 1990 Kericho 1.73m 60kg.
At 10,000m: WJ: '10- 1.
Progress at 5000m, 10,000m: 2008- 13:44.51, 27:30.85; 2009- 12:57.43, 28:21.51; 2010- 13:11.60, 28:05.46A; 2011- 13:11.29, 26:48.99; 2012- 13:32.20i, 27:39.65. pbs: 3000m 7:42.38 '09, HMar 61:01 '12.

Jairus Kipchoge **BIRECH** b. 14 Dec 1992 1.68m 54kg.
At 3000mSt: AfG: '11- 4; AfCh: '11- 2.
Progress at 3000mSt: 2010- 8:50.0A, 2011- 8:11.31, 2012- 8:03.43. pbs: 2000m 4:58.76 '11, 5000m 14:01.4A '12.

Bethwel BIRGEN b. 6 Aug 1988 Eldoret 1.78m 64kg.
Progress at 1500m: 2010- 3:35.60, 2011- 3:34.59, 2012- 3:31.00. pbs: 800m 1:48.32 '11, 1M 3:50.43 '12, 3000m 7:39.65 '10, 5000m 14:01.0A '12.

Stanley Kipleting **BIWOTT** b. 21 Apr 1986 1.76m 60kg.
World CC: '11- 1J.
Progress HMar, Mar: 2006- 214:265, 2007- 61:20, 2010- 2:09:41, 2011- 60:23, 2:07:03; 2012- 59:44, 2:05:12; 2013- 58:55. Road pbs: 10k 28:00 '12, 15k 42:13 '13, 20k 56:02 '13.
Marathon wins: São Paulo 2010, Chunchon 2011, Paris 2012.

Wilson Kwambai **CHEBET** b. 12 Jul 1985 Marakwet 1.74m 59kg.
World HMar: '09- 6.
Progress at HMar, Mar: 2005- 62:19, 2006- 62:38, 2007- 60:13, 2008- 59:33, 2009- 59:15, 2010- 60:31. 2:06:12; 2011- 2:05:27, 2012- 2:05:41. pbs: 5000m 13:38.4A '11, Road: 10km 27:33 '09, 15km 41:44 '09, 20km 57:33 '09.
Second fastest debut marathon for 2nd Amsterdam 2010; won Rotterdam 2011 and Amsterdam 2011-12. His elder brother Joseph Biwott has marathon pb 2:09:40 '11.

Collins CHEBOI b. 25 Sep 1987 1.75m 64kg.
At 1500m: AfG: '11- 2.
Progress at 1500m: 2007- 3:490A, 2009- 3:36.24, 2010- 3:34.17, 2011- 3:32.45, 2012- 3:32.08. pbs: 1M 3:51.44 '12, 2000m 5:00.30+ '12, 3000m 7:51.41 '10.

Elijah CHELIMO Kipterege b. 10 Mar 1984 1.75m 57kg.
At 3000mSt: AfG: '07- 4.
Progress at 3000mSt: 2005- 8:28.62, 2006- 8:34.1A, 2007- 8:16.28, 2008- 8:22.1, 2009- 8:10.63, 2010- 8:12.93, 2011- 8:14.22, 2012- 8:12.84. pbs: 1500m 3:43.96 '07, 3000m 8:02.00 '05, 5000m 14:00.45 '07, 2000mSt 5:23.68 '07, Rd 10km 28:59 '07.

Vincent Kiprop **CHEPKOK** b. 5 Jul 1988 Kapkitony, Keiyo district 1.74m 60kg.
At 5000m: WCh: '09- 9. World CC: '07- 2J, '11- 3. African CC: '12- 5.
Progress at 5000m, 10,000m: 2006- 13:17.57, 28:23.46; 2008- 13:06.41, 2009- 12:55.98, 2010- 12:51.45, 2011- 12:55.29, 2012- 12:59.28, 26:51.68. pbs: 1500m 3:40.47 '08, 3000m 7:30.15 '11. Rd 10km 28:11 '12.

Nixon Kiplimo **CHEPSEBA** b. 12 Dec 1990 Keiyo 1.85m 66kg.
At 1500m: OG: '12- 11; Af-J: '09- 2. Won DL 2011.
Progress at 1500m: 2009- 3:37.2A, 2010- 3:32.42, 2011- 3:30.94, 2012- 3:29.77. pbs: 800m 1:45.6A '12, 1000m 2:18.61 '09, 1M 3:53.36 '11, 3000m 7:37.64i '11.

Augustine Kiprono **CHOGE** b. 21 Jan 1987 Kipsigat, Nandi 1.62m 53kg.
At 5000m: CG: '06- 1; WJ: '04- 1. At 3000m: WY: '03- 1; WI: '10- 11, '12- 2. At 1500m: OG: '08- 9; WCh: '05- h, '09- 5. World CC: '03-05-06-08: 4J/1J/7 (4k)/12. Won E.African Youth 800m/1500m/3000m 2003, Junior 1500m 2004.
Records: World 4x1500m 2009, world youth 5000m 2004, world junior 3000m 2005.
Progress at 1500m, 5000m: 2003- 3:37.48, 13:20.08; 2004- 3:36.64, 12:57.01; 2005- 3:33.99, 12:53.66; 2006- 3:32.48, 12:56.41; 2007- 3:31.73, 2008- 3:31.57, 13:09.75; 2009- 3:29.47, 2010- 3:30.22, 13:04.64; 2011- 3:31.14, 13:21.24; 2012- 3:37.47, 13:15.50. pbs: 800m 1:44.86 '09, 1000m 2:17.79i '09, 1M 3:50.14 '10, 2000m 4:56.30i '07, 3000m 7:28.00i/7:28.76 '11, 10,000m 29:06.5A '02.

At 17 in 2004 he become youngest to break 13 minutes for 5000m.

Gideon GATHIMBA b. 9 Mar 1980 1.79m 64kg.
At 1500m: CG: '10- 5; AfG: '07- 4; AfCh: '08- 2; KEN champion 2008-09, World Military 2007. World 4x1500m record 2009.
Progress at 1500m: 2003- 3:44.3A, 2006- 3:38.2A, 2007- 3:38.7A, 2008- 3:33.63, 2009- 3:33.97, 2010- 3:34.75, 2011- 3:33.53, 2012- 3:33.83. pbs: 1M 3:50.24 '12, 2000m 5:00.51i, 5:01.69 '10; 3000m 7:39.70i '12, 7:40.10 '11.

Bidan KAROKI Muchiri b. 21 Aug 1990 Nyandarua 1.67m 65kg. S&B Foods, Japan.
At 10,000m: OG: 12- 5; AfG: '11- 2. Won Kenyan CC 2012.
Progress at 10,000m: 2010- 27:23.62, 2011- 27:13.67, 2012- 27:05.50. pbs: 1500m 3:50.91 '08, 3000m 7:49.38 '10, 5000m 13:15.76 '11.
Went to Japan in 2007.

Haron KEITANY b. 17 Dec 1983 Moi's Bridge, Eldoret 1.83m 70kg.
At 1500m: WCh: '09- sf (dns); WI: '10- 3; AfCh: '08- 1, won WAF 2008.
Progress at 1500m: 2005- 3:47.0A, 2006- 3:41.5A, 2007- 3:37.75, 2008- 3:32.06, 2009- 3:30.20, 2010- 3:35.69i/3:37.87, 2011- 3:31.86. pbs: 800m 1:49.86 '10, 1000m 2:16.76i '09, 1M 3:48.78 '09.
His father Paul Keitany was a Kenyan Armed Forces CC champion in the 1960s.

Ezekiel KEMBOI Cheboi b. 25 May 1982 Matira, near Kapsowar, Marakwet District 1.75m 62kg.
At 3000mSt: OG: '04- 1, '08- 7, '12- 1; WCh: '03-05-07-09-11: 2/2/2/1/1; CG: '02-06-10: 2/1/2; AfG: '03- 1, '07- 2; AfCh: '02- 4, '06- dq, '10- 2; Af-J: '01- 1. Won WAF 2009, Kenyan 2003, 2006-07.
Progress at 3000mSt: 2001- 8:23.66, 2002- 8:06.65, 2003- 8:02.49, 2004- 8:02.98, 2005- 8:09.04, 2006- 8:09.29, 2007- 8:05.50, 2008- 8:09.25, 2009- 7:58.85, 2010- 8:01.74, 2011- 7:55.76, 2012- 8:10.55. pbs: 1500m 3:40.8A '04, 3000m 7:44.24 '12, 5000m 13:50.61 '11, 10km Rd 28:38 '11.

Stephen Kipkosgei **KIBET** b. 9 Nov 1986.
At HMar: WCh: '12- 5.
Progress at HMar: 2009- 60:34, 2010- 60:09, 2011- 60:20, 2012- 58:54. road pbs: 10km 27:51+ '12, 15km 42:01+ '12, 20km 55:55+ '12, Mar 2:08:05 '12. Six successive half marathon wins 2009-12

Mike Kipruto **KIGEN** b. 15 Jan 1986 Keiyo district 1.70m 54kg.
At 5000m/(10,000m): AfCh: '06- 2/2; WCp: '06- 2. World CC: '06- 5. Won Kenyan 5000m 2006.
Progress at 5000m, 10,000m: 2005- 13:22.48, 2006- 12:58.58, 28:03.70; 2008- 13:09.84, 2009- 13:04.38, 2011- 13:11.65, 27:30.53; 2012- 13:21.55A, 27:03.49. pbs: 3000m 7:35.87 '06, 2M 8:20.09 '05, HMar 59:58 '12, Mar 2:08:24 '13.

Dennis Kipruto **KIMETTO** b. 22 Jan 1984.
World 25km road record 2012,

Progress at Mar: 2012- 2:04:16, 2013- 2:06:50. Road pbs: 10km 28:21 '12, 15km 42:46 '11, HMar 59:14 '12, 25km 1:11:18 12.
Second Berlin 2012 in fastest ever marathon debut after earlier major road wins at half marathon and 25k in Berlin in 2012. Won Tokyo Marathon 2013.

Eliud KIPCHOGE b. 5 Nov 1984 Kapsisiywa, Nandi 1.67m 52kg.
At 5000m: OG: '04- 3, '08- 2; WCh: '03-05-07-09-11: 1/4/2/5/8; CG: '10- 2. At 3000m: WI: '06- 3. World CC: '02-03-04-05: 5J/1J/4/5; HMar: '12- 6. Won WAF 5000m 2003, 3000m 2004, Kenyan CC 2005.
World junior 5000m record 2003. World road best 4M 17:10 '05.
Progress at 1500m, 5000m, 10,000m: 2002- 13:13.03, 2003- 3:36.17, 12:52.61; 2004- 3:33.20, 12:46.53; 2005- 3:33.80, 12:50.22; 2006- 3:36.25i, 12:54.94; 2007- 3:39.98, 12:50.38, 26:49.02; 2008- 13:02.06, 26:54.32; 2009- 12:56.46, 2010- 3:38.36, 12:51.21; 2011- 12:55.72i/12:59.01, 26:53.27; 2012- 12:55.34, 27:11.93. pbs: 1M 3:50.40 '04, 2000m 4:59.?+ '04, 3000m 7:27.66 '11, 2M 8:07.39i '12, 8:07.68 '05; 10km Rd 26:55dh '06, 27:34 '05; HMar 59:25 '12.
Kenyan Junior CC champion 2002-03, followed World Junior CC win by winning the World 5000m title, becoming at 18 years 298 days the second youngest world champion. Age 19 bests for 3000m & 5000m 2004. Ran 26:49.02 in 10,000m debut at Hengelo in 2007.

Kenneth Kiprop **KIPKEMOI** b. 5 Aug 1984 1.65m 52kg.
At 10,000m: AfCh: '12- 1. KEN champion 2012, Progress at 10,000m, HMar: 2009- 62:59A, 2011- 27:48.5A, 59:47; 2012- 26:52.65, 59:11. pbs: 3000m 7:49.28+ '11, 5000m 13:03.37 '12, 15km 43:22 '12.

John KIPKOECH b. 29 Dec 1991 1.60m 52kg.
At 5000m: WJ: '10- 2. World CC: '09- 9J.
Progress at 5000m: 2010- 13:26.03, 2012- 12:49.50. pb 3000m 7:32.72 '10.

Silas KIPLAGAT b. 20 Aug 1989 Siboh village, Marakwet 1.70m 57kg.
At 1500m: OG: '12- 7; WCh: '11- 2; CG: '10- 1; AfCh: '10- 4; WI: '12- 6. Won DL 2012, KEN 2011.
Progress at 1500m: 2009- 3:39.1A, 2010- 3:29.27, 2011- 3:30.47, 2012- 3:29.63. pbs: 800m 1:44.8A '12, 1M 3:49.39 '11, 3000m 7:39.94 '10, 10km Rd 28:00 '09.

Asbel Kipruto **KIPROP** b. 30 Jun 1989 Uasin Gishu, Eldoret. North Rift 1.86m 70kg.
At (800m)/1500m: OG: '08- 1, '12- 12; WCh: '07- 4, '09- sf/4, '11- 1; AfG: '07- 1; AfCh: '10- 1; CCp: '10- 6; Won DL 2010, Kenyan 2007, 2010. At 800m: AfCh: '08- 3. World CC: '07- 1J.
Progress at 800m, 1500m: 2007- 3:35.24, 2008- 1:44.71, 3:31.64; 2009- 1:43.17, 3:31.20; 2010- 1:43.45, 3:31.78; 2011- 1:43.15, 3:30.46; 2012- 1:45.91, 3:28.88. pbs: 1M 3:48.50 '09, 3000m

7:42.32 '07, 5000m 13:59.7A '10.
Father David Kebenei was a 1500m runner.

Wilson KIPROP b. 14 Apr 1987 Soi, Uasin Gishu 1.72m 62kg.
At 10,000m: OG: '12- dnf; AfCh: '10- 1. World HMar: '10- 1. Won KEN 10,000m 2010.
Progress at 10,000m, Mar: 2010- 27:26.93A, 2:09:09; 2011- 27:32.9A; 2012- 27:01.98. pbs: 5000m 13:30.13i '09, 13:45.38 '08; 1Hr 20756m '09; 15km Rd 43:50 '08, HMar 59:15 '12.

Brimin KIPRUTO b. 31 Jul 1985 Korkitony, Marakwet District 1.76m 54kg.
At 3000mSt: OG: '04- 2, '08- 1 '12- 5; WCh: '05-07-09-11: 3/1/7/2; CG: '10- 3; Af-J: '03- 2; KEN champion 2011. At 1500m: WJ: '04- 3. At 2000St: WY: '01- 2. World 4k CC: '06- 18.
Commonwealth & African 3000mSt record 2011. Progress at 3000mSt: 2002- 8:33.0A, 2003- 8:34.5A, 2004- 8:05.52, 2005- 8:04.22, 2006- 8:08.32, 2007- 8:02.89, 2008- 8:10.26, 2009- 8:03.17, 2010- 8:00.90, 2011- 7:53.64, 2012- 8:01.73. pbs: 1500m 3:35.23 '06, 2000m 4:58.76i '07, 3000m 7:39.07i '12, 7:47.33 '06; 5000m 13:58.82 '04, 2000mSt 5:36.81 '01.
First name is actually Firmin, but he has stayed with the clerical error of Brimin, written when he applied for a birth certificate in 2001.

Consesius KIPRUTO b. 8 Dec 1994 1.74m 55kg.
At 3000mSt: WJ: '12- 1. At 2000St: WY: '11- 1. World CC: '13- 5J.
Progress at 3000mSt: 2011- 8:27.30, 2012- 8:03.49. pbs: 1000m 2:19.85 '12, 3000m 7:44.09 '12, 2000mSt 5:28.65 '11.

Geoffrey Kamworer **KIPSANG** b. 28 Nov 1992 1.76m 60kg.
World CC: '11- 1J.
Progress at 10,000m, HMar, Mar: 2011- 27:06.35, 59:31; 2012- 59:26, 2:06:12; 2013- 58:54. pbs: 1500m 3:48.15 '10, 3000m 7:54.15 '10. 5000m 13:12:23 '11; Road: 15k 42:05 '12, 20k 56:02 '13.
3rd in Berlin 2012 on marathon debut. Won RAK half marathon 2013.

Wilson KIPSANG Kiprotich b. 15 Mar 1982 Keiyo district 1.82m 62kg.
At Mar: OG: '12- 3; HMar: WCh: '09- 4.
Progress at HMar, Mar: 2008- 59:16, 2009- 58:59, 2010- 60:04, 2:04:57; 2011- 60:49, 2:03:42; 2012- 59:06, 2:04:44. pbs: 5000m 13:55.7A '09, 10,000m 28:37.0A '07; Road: 10k 27:42 '09, 15k 41:51+ '11, 10M 44:59+ '11, 20k 56:10+ '12, 30k 1:29:12 '10.
At marathon: third in Paris in 2:07:13 on debut, and won Frankfurt for eighth all-time in 2010; won Lake Biwa and Frankfurt 2011, London and Honolulu 2012. Won Great North Run 2012

Eliud KIPTANUI b. 6 Jun 1989 Kaplelach, Uasin Gishu.
At Mar: WCh: '11- 6.
Progress at Mar: 2009- 2:12:17, 2010- 2:05:39, 2011- 2:09:08, 2012- 2:06:44. pbs: 3000m 8:04.57 '09, 30km Rd 1:29:26 '10; HMar 61:24 '11.

Won Safaricom Marathon in Kisimu in December 2009, then made a stunning improvement to win Prague Marathon in 2010; 3rd Seoul 2012.

Mark Kosgei **KIPTOO** b. 21 Jun 1976 Lugafri 1.75m 64kg. Kenyan Air Force.
At 5000m: CG: '10- 3; AfG: '07- 9; AfCh: '10- 3, '12- 1 (2 10,000m). World CC: '08- 14, '09- 7. Won W.Mil 5000m (2nd 10,000m) 2007, KEN 5000m 2008.
Progress at 5000m, 10,000m: 2007- 13:12.60, 28:22.62; 2008- 13:06.60, 27:14.67; 2009- 12:57.62, 2010- 12:53.46, 28:37.4A; 2011- 12:59.91, 26:54.64; 2012- 13:06.23, 27:18.22. pbs: 1500m 3:48.0A '05, 3000m 7:32.97 '09, 2M 8:29.96 '12, HMar 60:29 '11.

Bernard KIPYEGO Kiprop b. 16 Jul 1986 Kapkitony, Keiyo district 1.60m 50kg.
At 10,000m: WCh: '09- 5; Af-J: '03- 3. World CC: '05-07-08: 2J/3/10; HMar: '09- 2.
Progress at 10,000m, Mar: 2003- 29:29.09, 2004- 28:18.94, 2005- 27:04.45, 2006- 27:19.45, 2007- 26:59.51, 2008- 27:08.06, 2009- 27:18.47, 2010- 2:07:01, 2011- 2:06:29, 2012- 2:06:40, 2013- 2:07:53. pbs: 3000m 7:54.91 '05, 5000m 13:09.96 '05, Rd: 15km 42:34 '11, 10M 45:44 '11, HMar 59:10 '09.
Won in Berlin on half marathon debut in 59:34 in 2009, 5th Rotterdam on marathon debut 2010, 2nd Paris; 3rd Chicago 2011 and Tokyo 2013.

Michael Kipkorir **KIPYEGO** b. 2 Oct 1983 Kemeloi, Marakwet 1.68m 59kg.
At 3000mSt: WCh: '03- h; WJ: '02- 1; AfCh: '08- 2. At 3000m: WY: '99- 8; Af-J: '01- 2. World CC: '02-03-07: 12J/4 4k/6.
Progress at 3000mSt: 2001- 8:41.26, 2002- 8:22.90, 2003- 8:13.02, 2004- 8:23.14, 2005- 8:10.66, 2006- 8:14.99, 2007- 8:11.62, 2008- 8:09.05, 2009- 8:08.48, 2010- 8:16.46. At Mar: 2011- 2:06:48, 2012- 2:07:37, 2013- 2:06:58. pbs: 1500m 3:39.93 '05, 3000m 7:50.03 '09.
Won Tokyo Marathon 2012, 2nd 2013.

Abel KIRUI b. 4 Jun 1982 Bornet, Rift Valley 1.77m 62kg. Police.
At Mar: OG: '12- 3; WCh: '09- 1, '11- 1.
Progress at Mar: 2006- 2:15:22, 2007- 2:06:51, 2008- 2:07:38, 2009- 2:05:04, 2010- 2:08:04, 2011- 2:07:38, 2012- 2:07:56. pbs: 1500m 3:46.10 '05, 3000m 7:55.90 '06, 5000m 13:52.71 '05, 10,000m 28:16.86A '08; Road: 10km 27:59 '09, 15km 42:22 '07, 10M 46:40 '11, HMar 60:11 '07, 25km: 1:13:41 '08, 30km 1:28:25 '08.
Brilliantly retained World marathon title with halves of 65:07 and 62:31 and a fastest 5k split of 14:18. Won Vienna Marathon 2008, 2nd Berlin 2007, 3rd Rotterdam 2009. Uncle Mike Rotich has marathon pb 2:06:33 '03.

Peter Cheruiyot **KIRUI** b. 2 Jan 1988 Mt Elgon 1.82m 66kg.
At 10,000m: WCh: '11- 6; won KEN 2011.
Progress at 10,000m: 2011- 27:25.63. pbs: 1500m

3:44.20 '08, 3000m 7:45.79 '09, 5000m 13:15.90 '09, 15km Rd 42:48 '10, HMar 59:39 '12, 30km 1:27:37 '11.
Was pacemaker in Berlin Marathon 2101 and led at 30km at 1:27:37 but ineligible for world record as he did not finish race.

Alfred KIRWA YEGO b. 28 Nov 1986 Eldoret 1.75m 56kg. Cento Torri Pavia, Italy.
At 800m: OG: '08- 3; WCh: '05- h, '07- 1, '09- 2, '11- 7; WJ: '04- 2; AfCh: '06- 3, '10- 2. Won WAF 2008.
Progress at 800m, 1500m: 2004- 1:47.39, 3:37.95; 2005- 1:44.45, 3:50.14; 2006- 1:43.89, 3:38.55; 2007- 1:44.50, 2008- 1:44.01, 3:33.69; 2009- 1:42.67, 3:33.68; 2010- 1:43.97, 2011- 1:44.07, 2012- 1:44.49. pbs: 1000m 2:17.60 '10, 1M 3:55.18 '11.
Ran 24.6 last 200m to win 2007 World 800m.

Timothy KITUM b. 20 Nov 1994 Marakwet 1.72m 60kg.
At 800m: OG: '12- 3; WJ: '12- 2; WY: '11- 3.
Progress at 800m: 2011- 1:44.98, 2012- 1:42.53. pbs: 600m 1:14.4A '12, 1000m 2:17.96 '12.

Sammy Kiprop **KITWARA** b. 26 Nov 1986 Sagat village, Marakwet district 1.77m 54kg.
At 10,000m: Kenyan champion 2009. World HMar: '09- 10, '10- 3.
Progress at 10,000m, HMar, Mar: 2007- 28:11.6A, 2008- 28:12.26A, 60:54; 2009- 27:44.46A, 58:58; 2010- 28:32.77A, 59:34; 2011- 58:47, 2012- 2:05:54. pbs: 5000m 13:34.0A '08, Road: 10km 27:11 '10, 15km 41:54 '09, 10M 45:17 '08, 20km 57:42 '08.
4th Chicago on marathon debut 2012.

Isiah Kiplangat **KOECH** b. 19 Dec 1993 Kericho 1.78m 60kg.
At 5000m: OG: '12- 5; WCh: '11- 4; won DL 5000m, Kenyan 2011. At 3000m: WY: '09- 1. World CC: '10- 4J, '11- 10J.
World junior records indoors: 5000m 2011, 3000m 2011 & 2012.
Progress at 5000m, 10,000m: 2010- 13:07.70, 2011- 12:53.29i/12:54.18. 2012- 12:48.64, 27:17.03. pbs: 1500m 3:38.7A '12, 3000m 7:30.43 '12, 2M 8:14.16 '11, 10km Rd 27:33 '13.

Paul Kipsiele **KOECH** b. 10 Nov 1981 Cheplanget, Buret District 1.68m 57kg.
At 3000mSt: OG: '04- 3; WCh: '05- 7, '09- 4; AfG: '03- 2; AfCh: '06- 1; WCp: '06- 2; won DL 2010-12, WAF 2005-08. At 3000m: WI: 08- 2.
Progress at 3000mSt: 2001- 8:15.92, 2002- 8:05.44, 2003- 7:57.42, 2004- 7:59.65, 2005- 7:56.37, 2006- 7:59.94, 2007- 7:58.80, 2008- 8:00.57, 2009- 8:01.26, 2010- 8:02.07, 2011- 7:57.32, 2012- 7:54.31. pbs: 1500m 3:37.92 '07, 2000m 5:00.9+i '08, 3000m 7:32.78i '10, 7:33.93 '05; 2M 8:06.48i/8:13.31 '08, 5000m 13:02.69i 12, 13:05.18 '10.

Micah Kemboi **KOGO** b. 3 Jun 1986 Burnt Forest, Uasin Gishu 1.70m 60kg.
At 10,000m: OG: '08- 3; WCh: '09- 7.
World 10k road record (27:01) 2009.
Progress at 5000m, 10,000m: 2004- 14:02.99,

2005- 13:16.31, 2006- 13:00.07, 26:35.63; 2007- 13:10.68, 26:58.42; 2008- 13:03.71, 27:04.11; 2009- 13:01.30, 27:26.33; 2010- 13:07.62, 2011- 13:46.01, 27:50.50. pbs: 2000m 5:03.05 '06, 3000m 7:38.67 '07, 2M 8:20.88 '05; Road: 15k 41:51+ '11, 10M 44:59+ '11, 20k 56:10+ '12, HMar 59:07 '12.
Won Van Damme 10,000m in Brussels in 2006 for 6th world all-time.

Daniel Kipchirchir **KOMEN** b. 27 Nov 1984 Chemorgong, Kolbatek district 1.75m 60kg.
At 1500m: WCh: '05- h, '07/11- sf; WI: '06- 2, '08- 2; won WAF 2007. At 5000m: Af-J: '03- 2.
Progress at 1500m, 5000m: 2003- 13:49.20, 2004- 3:34.66, 13:16.26; 2005- 3:29.72, 2006- 3:29.02, 2007- 3:31.75, 2008- 3:31.49, 13:24.39; 2009- 3:34.86i, 2010- 3:32.16, 13:04.02; 2011- 3:32.47A, 13:20.80; 2012- 3:32.98, 13:09.90. pbs: 800m 1:47.3A '05, 1000m 2:16.9+ '06, 1M 3:48.28 '07, 3000m 7:31.41 '11.

Leonard Patrick **KOMON** b. 10 Jan 1988 Korungotuny Village, Mt. Eldon District 1.75m 52kg.
World CC: '06-07-08-09-10: 2J/4J/2/4/4.
World road records 10km and 15km 2010.
Progress at 5000m, 10,000m: 2006- 13:04.12, 2007- 13:04.79, 2008- 13:17.48, 26:57.08; 2009- 12:58.24, 28:02.24A; 2010- 12:59.15, 2011- 26:55.29, 2012- 27:01.58. pbs: 2000m 5:04.0+ '07, 3000m 7:33.27 '09, 2M 8:22.56 '07, road 10km 26:44 '10, 15km 41:13 '10, 10M 44:27 '11.

Japheth Kipyegon **KORIR** b. 30 Jun 1993 Sotik 1.68m 55kg.
At 5000m: 3rd Comm YthG 2008. World CC: 09-10-13: 5J/3J/1; Af-J CC: 11- 1, 12- 2 .
Progress at 5000m: 2008- 13:57.2A, 2010- 13:19.43, 2011- 13:17.18, 2012- 13:11.44i. pbs: 3000m 7:40.37 '12, 10k Rd 28:43 '12.
Became youngest ever senior men's world cross-country champion in 2013.

Leonard Kirwa **KOSENCHA** b. 21 Aug 1994 Trans Mara 1.76m 62kg.
At 800m: WY: 11- 1.
World youth 800m record 2011.
Progress at 800m: 2011- 1:44.08, 2012- 1:43.40.

James Kipsang **KWAMBAI** b. 28 Feb 1983 Marakwet East district 1.62m 52kg
Commonwealth marathon record 2009.
Progress at Mar: 2006- 2:10:20, 2007- 2:12:25, 2008- 2:05:36, 2009- 2:04:27, 2010- 2:11:31, 2011- 2:08:50, 2012- 2:05:50, 2013- 2:08:02. pbs: Road: 10km 28:17 '02, 20km 58:51 '08, HMar 59:09 '09, 30km 1:28:27 '08.
Won Brescia and Beijing marathons 2006, took 4:44 off pb when 2nd in Berlin 2008 and went to joint second all-time when 2nd in Rotterdam 2009. Won Joongang Seoul Marathon 2011 and 2012.

Boaz Kiplagat **LALANG** b. 8 Feb 1989 Marakwet 1.74m 62kg. Rend Lake College, USA.
At 800m: OG: '08- sf, CG: '10- 1; AfG: '11- 2; WI: '10- 2.

Progress at 800m: 2008- 1:44.68, 2009- 1:45.36, 2010- 1:42.95, 2011- 1:44.13, 2012- 1:44.83. pbs: 400m 47.60 '08, 1000m 2:14.83 '10, 1500m 3:35.80 '10, 1M 3:52.18 '10.
His younger brother **Lawi Lalang** (b. 15 Sep 1991) set pbs in 2012: 1M 3:55.09i, 5000m 13:08.28i US collegiate indoor record.

Martin Kiptolo **LEL** b. 29 Oct 1978 Kapsabet 1.71m 54kg.
At Mar: OG: '08- 5. World HMar: '03- 1.
African record 30km 2008.
Progress at Mar: 2002- 2:10:02, 2003- 2:10:30, 2004- 2:13:38, 2005- 2:07:26, 2006- 2:06:41, 2007- 2:07:41, 2008- 2:05:15, 2011- 2:05:45, 2012- 2:06:51. pbs: 10km 27:25 '06, 15km 42:41 '07, 10M 45:40 '07, HMar 59:30 '06, 30km 1:28:30 '08.
Exclusively a road runner. Marathons: dnf Prague and 2nd in Venice 2002, 3rd Boston 2003-04, 1st New York 2003 and 2007 and London 2005, 2007 and 2008 (2nd 2006 and 2011-12). He won the Marathon Majors prize for 2007-08. Won Great North Run 2007, 2009.

Thomas Pkemei **LONGOSIWA** b. 14 Jan 1982 West Pokot 1.75m 57kg. North Rift.
At 5000m: OG: '08- 12, '12- 3; WCh: '11- 6; AfG: '07- 6. World CC: '06- 13J (but dq after birthdate found to be 1982). Won Kenyan 5000m 2007.
Progress at 5000m: 2006- 13:35.3A, 2007- 12:51.95, 2008- 13:14.36, 2009- 13:03.43, 2010- 13:05.60, 2011- 12:56.08, 2012- 12:49.04. pbs: 2000m 5:01.6+ '10, 3000m 7:30.09 '09, 10,000m 28:11.3A '06.

Patrick MAKAU Musyoki b. 2 Mar 1985 Man–yanzwani, Tala Kangundo district 1.73m 57kg.
World HMar: '07- 2, '08- 2.
World 30km and marathon records 2011.
Progress at HMar, Mar: 2005- 62:00, 2006- 62:42, 2007- 58:56, 2008- 59:29, 2009- 58:52, 2:06:14; 2010- 59:51, 2:04:48; 2011- 2:03:38, 2012- 2:06:08. pbs: 3000m 7:54.50 '07, 5000m 13:42.84 '06. Road: 10km 27:27 '07, 15km 41:30 '09, 10M 45:41 '12, 20km 55:53 '07, 30km 1:27:38 '11.
Second fastest ever debut marathon when 4th Rotterdam 2009 and won there a year later in 2:04:48 for fourth world all-time. Won Berlin 2010 and 2011, Frankfurt 2012.

Moses Ndiema **MASAI** b. 1 Jun 1986 Kapsogom 1.72m 57kg.
At 10,000m: OG: '08- 4, '12- 12; WCh: '09- 3; WJ: '04- 10. World CC: '04-05-08: 16J/7J/5. Won Afr-J 5000 & 10,000m 2005, Kenyan CC 2006.
World junior marathon record 2005.
Progress at 5000m, 10,000m: 2004- 13:25.5+e, 27:07.29; 2005- 13:24.36, 28:08.6A; 2006- 13:13.28, 27:03.20; 2007- 13:08.81, 26:49.20; 2008- 12:50.55, 27:04.11; 2009- 13:06.16, 26:57.39; 2010- 13:02.45, 2011- 13:13.03, 27:10.05; 2012- 12:59.21. 27:02.25. pbs: 1500m 3:37.3A '08, 3000m 7:44.75 '09; Road: 15km 45:18 '09, 10M 45:16 '09, Mar 2:10:13 '05.
Marathon wins (while a junior) at Hannover

2004 and Essen 2005. His sister is **Linet Masai** (qv) and their younger brother **Dennis** won the World Junior 10,000m in pb 27:53.88 in 2010. His partner **Doris Changeiywo** was 4th in the 2008 World CC, 2nd CG 10,000m 2010.

Richard Kipkemboi **MATEELONG** b. 14 Oct 1983 Lenape, Narok District 1.79m 65g. Police.
At 3000mSt: OG: '08- 3; WCh: '07- 3, '09- 2, '11- 7; CG: '10- 1; AfCh: '04-08-10: 2/1/1; CCp: '10- 1. World CC: '10- 7. Won Kenyan CC 2007, 3000mSt 2009.
Progress at 3000mSt: 2004- 8:05.96, 2005- 8:10.97, 2006- 8:07.50, 2007- 8:06.66, 2008- 8:07.64, 2009- 8:00.89, 2010- 8:06.44, 2011- 8:07.41. pbs: 1500m 3:41.79 '05, 3000m 7:48.71 '05, 5000m 13:30.4A '06, 10,000m 28:18.4A '07.

Martin Irungu MATHATHI b. 25 Dec 1985 Nyahururu 1.67m 52kg. Suzuki, Japan.
At 10,000m: OG: '08- 7; WCh: '05- 5, '07- 3, '11- 5. World CC: '06- 3.
Progress at 5000m, 10,000m: 2003- 14:09.3A, 27:43.16; 2004- 13:03.84, 27:22.46; 2005- 13:05.99, 27:08.42; 2006- 13:05.55, 27:10.51; 2007- 13:22.13, 27:09.90; 2008- 13:46.87, 27:08.25; 2009- 13:11.46, 26:59.88; 2010- 13:10.94, 2011- 13:15.93, 27:23.85; 2012- 13:27.06, 27:35.16. pbs: 1500m 3:38.57 '06, Road: 10M 44:51 '04 (world junior best), 15km 42:14 '10, 20km 56:44 '10, HMar 58:56 '11.
Won Great North Run 2011.

Bernard Nganga **MBUGUA** b. 17 Jan 1985 1.70m 55kg.
Progress at 3000mSt: 2007- 8:43.0A, 2009- 8:17.94, 2010- 8:16.22, 2011- 8:05.88, 2012- 8:08.33. pbs: 1500m 3:43.68 '09, 5000m 13:49.19 '11, 2000mSt 5:25.70 '10.

Josphat Kiprono MENJO b. 20 Aug 1979 Kapsabet 1.68m 50kg.
At 5000m: AfG: '07- 2; AfCh: '06- 5, '08- 5. At 10,000m: WCh: '07- 8; won W.Mil G 2011.
Progress at 5000m, 10,000m: 2004- 13:48.7A, 2005- 13:14.38, 2006- 13:09.24, 27:29.45; 2007- 13:06.69, 27:04.61; 2008- 13:06.17, 27:09.37; 2010- 12:55.95, 26:56.74; 2011- 13:21.10, 27:55.81; 2012- 13:10.55. pbs: 1500m 3:38.40 '10, 1M 3:53.62 '10. 3000m 7:42.6+ '10, 2M 8:18.96 '07, HMar 61:42 '10.

Moses Cheruiyot **MOSOP** b. 17 Jul 1985 Kamasia, Marakwet 1.72m 57kg. Police officer.
At 10,000m: OG: '04- 7; WCh: '05- 3. World CC: '02-03-05-07-09: 10J/7J/18/2/11; HMar: '10- 10. Won KEN 10,000m 2006, CC 2009.
World records 25,000m and 30,000m 2011.
Progress at 5000m, 10,000m: 2002- 29:38.6A, 2003- 13:11.75, 27:13.66; 2004- 13:09.68, 27:30.66; 2005- 13:06.83, 27:08.96; 2006- 12:54.46, 27:17.00; 2007- 13:07.89, 26:49.55. At Mar: 2011- 2:03:06w dh/2:05:37, 2012- 2:05:03. pbs: 3000m 7:36.88 '06, 15km Rd 42:25+ '10, HMar 59:20 '10, 20000m 58:02.2 '11, 25000m 1:12:25.4 '11, 30000m 1:26:47.4 '11.

Second with fastest ever marathon debut at Boston and won Chicago 2011. 3rd Rotterdam 2012. Married to Florence Kiplagat (qv).

Josphat MUCHIRI Ndambiri b. 12 Feb 1985 1.71m 52kg. Komori, Japan.
At 10,000m: WCh: '07- 5.
Progress at 5000m, 10,000m, Mar: 2001- 13:54.65, 29:06.30; 2002- 13:36.77, 28:45.05; 2003- 13:36.14, 28:02.09; 2004- 13:27.53, 27:46.10; 2005- 13:05.33, 27:19.19; 2006- 13:09.39, 27:04.79; 2007- 13:18.49, 27:28.38; 2008- 13:23.11, 27:14.03; 2009- 13:11.46, 26:57.36; 2010- 13:09.19, 27:16.51; 2011- 13:12.77, 27:39.21, 2:07:36. pbs: 1500m 3:38.72 '04, 3000m 7:42.98 '06, HMar 61:07 '10.
Won at Fukuoka on marathon debut 2011.

Abel Kiprop **MUTAI** b. 2 Oct 1988 Nandi 1.87m 73kg.
At 3000mSt: OG: '12- 3; Af-J: '07- 1; Kenyan champion 2012. At 2000mSt: WY: '05- 1.
Progress at 3000mSt: 2006- 8:35.38, 2007- 8:29.76, 2009- 8:11.40, 2011- 8:21.02, 2012- 8:01.67. pbs: 3000m 8:05.16 '06, 5000m 14:07.80 '06, 2000mSt 5:24.69 '05.

Emmanuel Kipchirchir **MUTAI** b. 12 Oct 1984 Tulwet, Rift Valley 1.68m 54kg.
At Mar: OG: '12- 17; WCh: '09- 2.
Progress at Mar: 2007- 2:06:29, 2008- 2:06:15, 2009- 2:06:53, 2010- 2:06:23, 2011- 2:04:40, 2012- 2:08:01. pbs: 10,000m 28:21.14 '06, Road: 10km 27:51 '06, 15km 42:11 '10, 20km 56:44 '10, HMar 59:52 '11, 30km 1:28:30 '08.
Made marathon debut with 7th in Rotterdam in 2:13:06 in 2007, then won in Amsterdam. London: 4th 2008 & 2009, 2nd 2010, 1st 2011. 2nd New York 2010-11.

Geoffrey Kiprono **MUTAI** b. 7 Oct 1981 Koibatek District 1.83m 56kg. Policeman.
At 10,000m: AfCh: '10- 3. World CC: '11- 5. Won Kenyan CC 2011.
Progress at 10,000m, Mar: 2007- 2:12:50sh?, 2008- 28:01.74, 2:07:50; 2009- 2:07:01, 2010- 27:27.79A, 2:04:55; 2011- 2:03:02wdh/2:05:06, 2012- 28:23.0A, 2:04:15. pbs: 15km 42:12+ '13, 20km 56:02 '13, HMar 58:58 '13, 30km 1:28:52+ '10.
Marathons: Won Monte Carlo 2008, Eindhoven 2008 & 2009, Boston & New York 2011, Berlin 2012; 2nd Rotterdam and Berlin 2010. World Marathon Majors winner 2011/12.

Caleb Mwangangi **NDIKU** b. 9 Oct 1992 1.83m 68kg.
At 1500m: WJ: '10- 1; WY: '09- 2; AfG: '11- 1; AfCh: '12- 1; Kenyan champion 2012. World CC: '10- 1J.
Progress at 1500m: 2009- 3:38.2A, 2010- 3:37.30, 2011- 3:32.02, 2012- 3:32.39. pbs: 800m 1:52.6A '07, 1M 3:49.77 '11, 3000m 7:30.99 '12, 5000m 13:18.96 '10.

Jonathan Muia **NDIKU** b. 18 Sep 1991 1.70m 55kg. Team Hitachi Cable, Japan.
At 3000mSt: WJ: '08- 1, '10- 1; Af-J: '09- 1. At 2000mSt: WY: '07- 4.
Progress at 3000mSt: 2008- 8:17.28, 2009- 8:28.1A, 2010- 8:19.25A. 2011- 8:07.75, 2012- 8:17.88. pbs: 1500m 3:39.27 '10, 3000m 7:52.89 '09, 5000m 13:11.99 '09, 10,000m 27:37.72 '09, 2000mSt 5:37.30 '07.

Abraham Kipchirchir **ROTICH** b. 26 Jun 1993 1.81m 62kg.
Progress at 800m: 2010- 1:50.76A, 2011- 1:46.4A, 2012- 1:43.13. pb 1000m 2:17.08 '12

Lucas Kimeli **ROTICH** b. 16 Apr 1990 1.71m 57kg.
At 3000mSt: WY: '07- 2. World CC: '08- 3J, '10- 18.
Progress at 5000m, 10,000m: 2007- 29:12.5A, 2008- 13:15.54, 2009- 12:58.70, 28:15.0A; 2010- 12:55.06, 27:33.59; 2011- 13:00.02, 26:43.98; 2012- 13:09.58, 27:09.38. pbs: 1500m 3:43.64 '08, 3000m 7:35.57 '11, HMar 59:44 '11.

David Lekuta **RUDISHA** b. 17 Dec 1988 Kilgoris 1.89m 73kg. Masai.
At 800m: OG: '12- 1; WCh: '09- sf; WJ: '06- 1/4R; AfCh: '08- 1, '10- 1; Af-J: '07- 1; CCp: '10- 1. Won DL 2010-11, WAF 2009, Kenyan 2009-11.
Three world 800m records 2010-12, four African records 2009-10.
Progress at 800m: 2006- 1:46.3A, 2007- 1:44.15, 2008- 1:43.72, 2009- 1:42.01, 2010- 1:41.01, 2011- 1:41.33, 2012- 1:40.91. pbs: 400m 45.50 '10, 600m 1:14.28+ '11.
IAAF Male Athlete of the Year 2010, won 26 successive 800m finals 2009-11. His father Daniel won 4x400m silver medal at 1968 Olympics with 440y pb 45.5A '67.

Edwin Cheruiyot **SOI** b. 3 Mar 1986 Kericho 1.68m 53kg.
At 5000m: OG: '08- 3, '12- h; AfCh: '10- 1; CCp: '10- 4. At 3000m: WI: '08- 4, '12- 3; won WAF 3000m 2007, 5000m 2007-08. World CC: '06- 8 4k, '07- 9.
Progress at 5000m, 10,000m: 2002- 29:06.5A, 2004- 13:22.57, 2005- 13:10.78, 2006- 12:52.40, 27:14.83; 2007- 13:10.21, 2008- 13:06.22, 2009- 12:55.03, 2010- 12:58.91, 2011- 12:59.15, 2012- 12:55.99. pbs: 1500m 3:44.76 '05, 2000m 5:01.4+ '10, 3000m 7:27.55 '11, 2M 8:14.10 '11, 10km Rd 28:13 '08.

Paul Kipngetich **TANUI** b. 22 Dec 1990 Chesubeno village, Moio district 1.72m 54kg. Kyudenko Corporation, Japan.
At 10,000m: WCh: '11- 9. World CC: '09-10-11: 4J/8/2. Won Kenyan CC 2010.
Progress at 10,000m: 2009- 27:25.24, 2010- 27:17.61, 2011- 26:50.63, 2012- 27:27.56. pbs: 1500m 3:43.97 '10, 3000m 7:50.88 '11, 5000m 13:04.65 '11.

John Kimondo **THUO** b. 27 Nov 1985 Mailo Inya, Nyahururu 1.68m 53kg. Toyota, Japan.
World CC: '08- 18.
Progress at 10,000m: 2005- 29:47.6A, 2008- 27:31.61, 2009- 27:11.88, 2010- 27:15.73, 2011-

27:23.99, 2012- 27:32.72. pbs: 1500m 3:35.27 '07, 3000m 7:46.01 '11, 5000m 13:15.53 '11, 10M Rd 45:23 '09.

Hillary Kipsang **YEGO** b. 2 Apr 1992 1.78m 60kg.
At 2000mSt: WY: '09- 1.
Progress at 3000mSt: 2009- 8:46.8A, 2010- 8:19.50, 2011- 8:07.71, 2012- 8:11.83. pbs: 1500m 3:43.3 '10, 3000m 7:53.18 '10, 2000mSt 5:25.33 '09, 10km Rd 29:10 '11.

Women

Emily CHEBET Muge b. 18 Feb 1986 Bornet 1.57m 45kg.
At 10,000m: WCh: '07- 9; AfCh: '06- 3. World CC: '03-10-13: 5J/1/1.
Progress at 10,000m: 2006- 31:33.39, 2007- 32:31.21, 2010- 32:49.43A. 2011- 31:30.22. pbs: 1500m 4:18.75 '05, 3000m 8:53.46 '05; Road 10km 30:58 '12, HMar 72:00 '11. Has daughter Emily.

Milcah CHEMOS Cheywa b. 24 Feb 1986 Bugaa Village, Mt. Elgon district 1.63m 48kg. Police.
At 3000mSt: OG: '12- 4; WCh: '09- 3, '11- 3; CG: '10- 1; AfCh: '10- 1; CCp: '10- 2. Won DL 2010-12, KEN 2010-11.
Commonwealth & African 3000mSt record 2012. Progress at 3000mSt: 2009- 9:08.57, 2010- 9:11.71, 2011- 9:07.14. pbs: 800m 2:04.35A '11, 1500m 4:12.3A '09, 2000m 5:41.64 '09, 3000m 8:43.92 '09. Married to Alex Sang (pb 800m 1:46.84 '08). Started athletics seriously after birth of daughter Lavine Jemutai and in first season, 2008, was 4th in Kenyan 800m. Rapid progress from first steeplechase in April 2009.

Joyce CHEPKIRUI b. 20 Aug 1988.
At 10,000m: OG: '12- dnf. At 1500m: AfG: '11- 2; AfCh: '07- 5. At HMar: WCh: '10- 5. African CC: '12- 1. Won Kenyan CC 2012.
Progress at 10,000m, HMar: 2007- 75:11, 2009- 71:47, 2010- 69:25, 2011- 31:26.10, 69:04; 2012- 32:34.71A, 67:03. pbs: 1500m 4:08.80A '11, 3000mSt 10:26.7A '08; Road: 10km 30:38 '11.

Lidya Tum **CHEPKURUI** b. 23 Aug 1984.
At 3000mSt: AfG: '11- 4.
Progress at 3000mSt: 2011- 9:30.73, 2012- 9:14.98. pbs 1500m 4:14.97 '12.

Lydia CHEROMEI b. 11 May 1977 Baringo district 1.62m 47kg. Married Hosea Kogo (5000m 13:24.22 '97) in December 1996.
At 5000m: OG: '96- h, '00- 6; WCh: '97- 5; AfG: '95- 3; 2nd GP 1997. At 10,000m: OG: '92- h; WJ: '90- 3, '92- 4; AfG: '91- 2; AfCh: '92- 2, '93- 2 (8 3000m). At HMar: WCh: '04- 2, '12- 4. World CC: '91-2: 1J/3J, '97-00-01: 11/4/3. Won Kenyan 10,000m 1991-2, 5000m 1997, 2000.
Records: World junior 5000m 1995, African junior 3000m 1992, Kenyan 5000m 1995, 3000m 1997 and 2000.
Progress at 5000m, 10,000m: 1990- 16:56.7, 33:20.83; 1991- 33:07.7, 1992- 15:17.31, 31:41.09;

1993- 32:54.55, 1994- 36:29.0, 1995- 14:53.44, 1996- 15:18.34, 1997- 14:46.72, 2000- 14:47.35. At Mar: 2008- 2:25:57; 2009- 2:28:09, 2011- 2:22:34, 2012- 2:21:30. pbs: 1500m 4:09.32 '97, 2000m 5:38.9 '97, 3000m 8:29.14 '00, road 10km 31:57 '08, 15km 47:50 '11, HMar 67:26 '12, 30km 1:42:47 '08. Youngest ever world junior cross-country champion at 13 in 1991. World age bests for 3000m, 5000m and 10,000m at 13, 5000m at 15. Daughter Faith born 2005. Won at Amsterdam on marathon debut 2008, 2nd Dubai and won Prague 2011, won Yokohama 2012. Two year drugs ban 2005-07.

Mercy CHERONO b. 7 May 1991 Kericho 1.78m 59kg.
At 3000m/(5000m): WCh: '11- (5); WJ: '08- 1, '10- 1/2; WY: '07- 1; Af-J: '09- 1/2. World CC: '07-09-10: 23J/2J/1J. Won Afr CC 2011.
Progress at 5000m: 2007- 16:49.13A, 2009- 15:46.74A, 2010- 14:47.13, 2011- 14:35.13, 2012- 14:47.18. pbs: 1500m 4:02.31 '11, 2000m 5:35.65 '10, 3000m 8:38.51 '12, 10,000m 34:33.4A '06.

Priscah Jepleting **CHERONO** b. 27 Jun 1980 Nandi 1.60m 47kg. née Ngetich.
At 5000m: OG: '08- 11; WCh: '05- 7, '07- 3; WJ: '96- 8, '98- 7; AfCh: '04- 2. Kenyan champion 2004. At 10,000m: WCh: '11- 4; AfCh: '12- 2. World CC J/4k: '97-8-02-03-04-0: 2J/11J/18/11/4/2; 8k: '07-08-11: 7/7/5.
Progress at 5000m, 10,000m: 1996- 15:39.1A, 1998- 16:07.12, 1999- 16:24.4A, 2001- 16:42.4A, 2002- 15:41.13A, 2003- 15:35.7A, 2004- 14:54.24, 2005- 14:44.00, 2006- 14:35.30, 2007- 14:42.00, 2008- 14:45.12, 2011- 14:40.86, 30:56.43; 2012- 14:59.53, 32:38.29A. pbs: 800m 2:07.8A '99, 1500m 4:15.7A '00, 3000m 8:29.06 '07, 2M 9:14.09 '07 (Kenyan best); Road: 15km 48:24 '11, 10M 51:57 '11, HMar 68:35 '12.
Married Charles Cherono in December 2006; child in 2010.

Sharon Jemutai **CHEROP** b. 16 Mar 1984 Marakwet district 1.58m 44kg.
At Mar: WCh: '11- 3. At 10,000m: AfG: '99- 5. At 5000m: WJ: '00- 3. World CC: '02- 10J.
Progress at Mar: 2007- 2:38:45, 2008- 2:39:52, 2009- 2:33:53, 2010- 2:22:43, 2011- 2:22:42wdh/2:29:14, 2012- 2:22:39. pbs: 3000m 9:09.23 '04, 5000m 15:40.7A '00, 10,000m 32:03.0A '11, HMar 67:08 '11.
Won Toronto and Hamburg marathon 2010, 3rd Boston 2011.

Vivian CHERUIYOT b. 11 Sep 1983 Keiyo 1.55m 38kg.
At 5000m (/10,000m): OG: '00- 14, '08- 5, '12- 2/3; WCh: '07- 2, '09- 1, '11- 1/1; CG: '10- 1; WJ: '02- 3; AfG '99- 3; AfCh: '10- 1; CCp: '10- 1; won DL 2010. At 3000m: WY: '99- 3; WI: '10- 2. World CC: '98-9-00-01-02-04-06-07-11: 5J/2J/1J/4J/3J/8 4k/8 4k/8/1. Won DL 5000m 2011-12; KEN 1500m 2009, 5000m 2010-11, 10,000m 2011-12.

African 2000m record 2009, Commonwealth 5000m 2009 & 2011, indoor 3000m (8:30.53) 2009; Kenyan 5000m 2007 & 2011.
Progress at 5000m, 10,000m: 1999- 15:42.79A, 2000- 15:11.11, 2001- 15:59.4A, 2002- 15:49.7A, 2003- 15:44.8A, 2004- 15:13.26, 2006- 14:47.43, 2007- 14:22.51, 2008- 14:25.43, 2009- 14:37.01, 2010- 14:27.41, 2011- 14:20.87, 30:48.98; 2012- 14:35.62, 30:30.44. pbs: 1500m 4:06.6A '12, 2000m 5:31.52 '09, 3000m 8:28.66 '07, 2M 9:12.35i '10.
Laureus Sportswomen of the Year for 2011. Married Moses Kirui on 14 Apr 2012.

Irene JELAGAT b. 10 Dec 1988 Samutet, Nyanza 1.62m 45kg.
At 1500m: OG: '08- h; WCh: '09- h; CG: '10- 6; AfG: '11- 1; AfCh: '08- 5, '10- 4; WJ: '06- 1; WY: '05- dns; WI: '10- 5.
Progress at 1500m: 2005- 4:21.3A, 2006- 4:08.88, 2007- 4:10.27, 2008- 4:04.59, 2009- 4:03.62, 2010- 4:03.76, 2011- 4:02.59. pb 800m 2:02.99 '06.

Pamela JELIMO b. 5 Dec 1989 Kapsabet 1.75m 60kg.
At 800m: OG: '08- 1, '12- 4; WCh: '09- sf; WI: '12- 1; AfCh: '08- 1/2R. At 400m: Af-J: '07- 1 (7 200m). Won WAF 800m 2008, DL 2012, Kenyan 400m 2008.
Five world junior and four African & Commonwealth 800m records 2008. Kenyan 600m records 2008 & 2012.
Progress at 800m: 2007- c.2:14, 2008- 1:54.01, 2009- 1:59.49A, 2010- 2:01.52, 2011- 2:09.12, 2012- 1:56.76. pbs: 200m 24.68 '07, 400m 52.14A '12, 600m 1:23.36 '12, 1500m (4:07.11idq '12).
Set world junior records in just third and fourth major 800m finals. Won Golden League jackpot 2008, when in her first season of 800m running she won all 13 finals and three heats. Married Peter Kiprotich Murrey in November 2007.

Janeth JEPKOSGEI b. 13 Dec 1983 Kabirirsang, near Kapsabet 1.67m 47kg. North Rift.
At 800m: OG: '08- 2, '12- 8; WCh: '07- 1, '09- 2, '11- 3; CG: '06- 1; AfCh: '06- 1, '10- 2; WJ: '02- 1; WY: '99- h; WCp: '06- 2, '10- 1; won DL 2010, WAF 2007, KEN 2011.
Five Kenyan 800m records 2005-07.
Progress at 800m, 1500m: 1999- 2:11.0A, 2001- 2:06.21, 2002- 2:00.80, 2003- 2:03.05, 2004- 2:00.52, 4:11.91; 2005- 1:57.82, 4:15.77; 2006- 1:56.66, 4:15.43; 2007- 1:56.04, 4:14.70; 2008- 1:56.07, 4:08.48; 2009- 1:57.90, 4:13.87; 2010- 1:57.84, 4:04.17; 2011- 1:57.42, 4:02.32; 2012- 1:57.79, 4:07.34. pbs: 400m 54.06A '10, 600m 1:25.0+ '08, 1000m 2:37.98 '02, 1M 4:28.72 '08.
Brilliant front-running victory at 2007 Worlds.

Priscah JEPTOO b. 26 Jun 1984 Nandi, Rift Valley 1.65m 49kg.
At Mar: OG: '12- 2; WCh: '11- 2. At 10,000m: AfG: '99- 5. At 5000m: WJ: '00- 3. World CC: '02- 10J.
Progress at Mar: 2009- 2:30:40, 2010- 2:27:02, 2011- 2:22:55, 2012- 2:20:14. Road pbs: 15k 47:14+ '13, 20k 62:53 '13, HMar 66:11 '13.
Marathon wins: Porto 2009, Turin 2010, Paris 2011. 3rd London 2012. Married to Douglas Chepsiro, son born 20 Feb 2009.

Rita Sitienei **JEPTOO** b. 15 Feb 1981 Eldoret 1.65m 48kg.
At Mar: WCh: '05- 7, '07- 7; World 20k: '06- 3; HMar: '04- 14.
African record 20km road 2006.
Progress at Mar: 2004- 2:28:11, 2005- 2:24:22, 2006- 2:23:38, 2007- 2:32:03, 2008- 2:26:34, 2011- 2:25:44, 2012- 2:22:04. pbs: 3000m 9:38.13 '98, 5000m 15:56.90 '02, 10,000m 33:23.04A '05; Road: 10km 31:36 '08, 150km 47:13+ '13, 20km 63:11 '13, HMar 66:27 '11.
Marathon wins: Stockholm, Milan 2004, Boston 2006 (3rd 2008), Eldoret 2011; 2nd Chicago 2012.

Lucy Wangui KABUU b. 24 Mar 1984 Ichamara, Nyeri region 1.55m 41kg. Suzuki, Japan.
At (5000m)/10,000m: OG: '04- 9, '08- 7; CG: '06- 3/1; AfCh: '08- 4. World 4k CC: '05- 5.
Progress at 5000m, 10,000m, HMar: 2001- 15:45.04, 2002- 15:33.03, 32:54.70; 2003- 15:10.23, 31:06.20; 2004- 14:47.09, 31:05.90, 69:47; 2005- 15:00.20, 31:22.37; 2006- 14:56.09, 31:29.66; 2007- 14:57.55, 31:32.52; 2008- 14:33.49, 30:39.96; 2009- 16:50.3A, 2011- 67:04, 2013- 66:09. At Mar: 2012- 2:19:34. pbs: 1500m 4:08.6A '12, 3000m 8:46.15 '08. Road 15k 47:13+ 13, 20k 62:48 '13.
At the marathon set the pace in Osaka 2007, but at her first proper try was 2nd in 2:19:34 at Dubai 2012. 3rd Chicago 2012. Won Great North Run 2011, RAK half marathon 2013.

Mary Jepkosgei **KEITANY** b. 18 Jan 1982 Kisok, Kabarnet 1.68m 53kg.
At Mar: OG: '12- 4. World HMar: '07- 2, '09- 1.
Records: World 25km 2010, 10M, 20km, half marathon 2011. African and two Kenyan half marathon 2009. Kenyan marathon 2012.
Progress at HMar, Mar: 2000- 72:53, 2002- 73:01, 2003- 73:25, 2004- 71:32, 2005- 70:18, 2006- 69:06, 2007- 66:48, 2009- 66:36, 2010- 67:14, 2:29:01; 2011- 65:50, 2:19:19; 2012- 66:49, 2:18:37. pbs: 1500m 4:24.33 '99, 10,000m 32:18.07 '07; Road: 5k 15:25 '11, 10k 30:45 '11, 15k 46:40 '11, 10M 50:05 '11, 20k 62:36 '11, 25k 1:19:53 '10.
11 wins in 12 half marathons 2006-12. Marathons: 3rd New York 2010-11, won London 2011-12. Married to Charles Koech (pbs 10km 27:56 & HMar 61:27 '07), son Jared born in June 2008, expecting a second child in 2013.

Sylvia Chibiwott **KIBET** b. 28 Mar 1984 Kapchorwa, Keiyo district 1.57m 44kg. Kenya Police.
At 5000m: OG: '08- 4; WCh: '07- 4, '09- 2, '11- 2; CG: '10- 2; AfG: '07- 3; AfCh: '06- 3. At 3000m: WI: '08- 10-12: 4/4/4, won Afr-Y 1998. At 1500m: WY: '99-

2. World CC: '11- 13. Won KEN 5000m 2011.
Progress at 5000m, 10,000m: 2006- 15:02.54, 31:39.34; 2007- 14:57.37, 2008- 15:00.03, 2009- 14:37.77, 30:47.20; 2010- 14:31.91, 2011- 14:35.43, 2012- 14:46.73. pbs: 1500m 4:05.33i/4:07.87 '10, 3000m 8:37.48 '10, 2M 9:16.62 '07, Road: 15km 48:24 '12, 10M 51:42 '12, HMar 69:51 '09.
Did not compete in 2001-02. Married Erastus Limo in 2003, daughter Britney Jepkosgei born in 2004. Older sister is Hilda Kibet NED and cousin of Lornah Kiplagat NED.

Viola KIBIWOTT b. 22 Dec 1983 Keiyo 1.57m 45kg.
At 1500m: OG: '08- h; WCh: '07- 5, '09/11- sf; CG: '06- 7, '10- 7; WJ: '02- 1. World CC: '00-01-02-13: 3J/1J/1J/7. AfCC: '11- 2.
Progress at 1500m, 5000m: 2003- 15:32.87, 2004- 4:06.64, 2006- 4:08.74, 2007- 4:02.10, 2008- 4:04.17, 14:51.59; 2009- 4:02.70, 2010- 4:03.39, 14:48.57; 2011- 4:05.51, 14:34.86; 2012- 3:59.25, 14:39.53. pbs: 800m 2:04.7A '12, 2000m 5:42.57 '09, 3000m 8:40.14 '03, 2M 9:18.26 '07.

Edna Ngeringwony **KIPLAGAT** b. 15 Nov 1979 Eldoret 1.71m 54kg. Corporal in Kenyan Police.
At Mar: OG: '12- 20; WCh: '11- 1. At 3000m: WJ: '96- 2, '98- 3. World CC: '96-97-06: 5J/4J/13.
African record 30km 2008.
Progress at Mar: 2005- 2:50:20, 2010- 2:25:38, 2011- 2:20:46, 2012- 2:19:50. pbs: 3000m 8:53.06 '96, 5000m 15:57.3A '06, 10,000m 33:27.0A '07; Road: 5km 15:20 '10, 10km 31:18 '10, 15km 47:57 '10, 10M 54:56 '09, HMar 67:41 '12.
Won Los Angeles and New York Marathons 2010, 3rd/2nd London 2011/2012. Married to Gilbert Koech (10,000m 27:55.30 '01, 10km 27:32 '01, Mar 2:13:45 dh '05, 2:14:39 '09); two children.

Florence Jebet **KIPLAGAT** b. 27 Feb 1987 Kapkitony, Keiyo district 1.55m 42kg.
At 5000m: WJ: '06- 2. At 10,000m: WCh: '09- 12. World CC: '07- 5, '09- 1; HMar: '10- 1. Won Kenyan 1500m 2007, CC 2007 & 2009.
Kenyan 10,000m record 2009.
Progress at 5000m, 10,000m, Mar: 2006- 15:32.34, 2007- 14:40.74, 31:06.20; 2009- 14:40.14, 30:11.53; 2010- 14:52.64, 32:46.99A; 2011- 2:19:44, 2012- 30:24.85, 2:20:57. pb 1500m 4:09.0A '07, 3000m 8:40.72 '10, Road: 15km 47:43 '12, 20km 64:02 '10, HMar 66:38 '12, 30km 1:40:00 '11.
Won half marathon debut in Lille in 2010, followed a month later by World title. Did not finish in Boston on marathon debut in 2011, but then won in Berlin. Partner of Moses Mosop, daughter Aisha Chelagat born April 2008. Niece of William Kiplagat (Mar 2:06:50 '99, 8 WCh '07).

Sally Jepkosgei **KIPYEGO** b. 19 Dec 1985 Kapsowar, Marakwet district 1.68m 52kg. Was at Texas Tech University, USA.
At (5000m)/10,000m: OG: '12- 4/2; WCh: '11- 2. World CC: '01- 8J. Won record equalling nine

NCAA titles 5000m 2008, 10,000m 2007, CC 2006-08, indoor 3000m 2007, 5000m 2007-09.
Progress at 5000m, 10,000m: 2005- 16:34.90, 2006- 16:13.39, 2007- 15:19.72, 31:56.72; 2008- 15:11.88, 31:25.48; 2009- 15:09.03, 33:44.7A; 2010- 14:38.64, 2011- 14:30.42, 30:38.35; 2012- 14:43.11, 30:26.37. pbs: 800m 2:08.26 '08, 1500m 4:06.23 '11, 1M 4:27.19i/4:29.64 '09, 2000m 5:35.20 '09, 3000m 8:35.89 '12.
Married to Kevin Chelimo (5000m 13:14.57 '12). One of her eight brothers is Mike Kipyego (3000mSt 8:08.48).

Faith Chepngetich **KIPYEGON** b. 10 Jan 1994 Bornet 1.57m 42kg.
At 1500m: OG: '12- h; WJ: '11- 1; WY: '10- 1. World CC: '10-11-13: 4J/1J/1J, Won African Jnr CC 2012.
Progress at 1500m: 2010- 4:17.1A, 2011- 4:09.48, 2012- 4:03.82. pb 800m 2:03.9 '12.
Older sister is Beatrice Mutai (b. 19 Apr 1987) 11 World CC 2013.

Pauline Chemning **KORIKWIANG** b. 1 Mar 1988 Kaptabuk Village, West Pokot District 1.63m 39kg.
At 3000m: WJ: '06- 2; WY: '05- 2. At 5000m: AfG: '11- 3; Af-J: '03- 4, '07- 3. At 10,000m: AfCh: '10- 6. World CC: '05-06-09-11: 7J/1J/11/7.
Progress at 5000m, 10,000m: 2003- 16:58.26, 2004- 15:55.5A, 2005- 16:15.8A, 2006- 14:45.98, 2007- 15:59.61, 2008- 16:07.78, 2009- 14:50.08, 2010- 14:46.80, 31:06.29; 2011- 14:41.28, 31:59.5A; 2012- 32:19.32. pbs: 1500m 4:12.93+ '09, 2000m 5:36.11 '09, 3000m 8:41.11 '10.

Nancy Chebet **LANGAT** (or LAGAT) b. 22 Aug 1981 Eldoret 1.53m 49kg.
At (800m)/1500m: OG: '04- sf, '08- 1; WCh: '05- h, '09/1- sf; CG: '10- 1/1; AfCh: '04-08-10: 1/4/1; CCp: '10- 8; won DL 2010, WAF 2009, KEN 2010. At 800m: WJ: '96- 3, '98- 2, '00- 1; Af-J: '95/97- 1. World 4k CC: '05- 8.
Progress at 800m, 1500m: 1996- 2:03.10A, 4:22.93; 1997- 2:01.6A, 1998- 2:03.88A, 1999- 2:04.7A, 2000- 2:01.26, 4:23.78; 2001- 4:23.78, 2004- 2:05.63, 4:04.76; 2005- 2:02.51, 4:02.31; 2008- 2:05.84, 4:00.23; 2009- 1:59.17, 4:01.64; 2010- 1:57.75, 4:00.13; 2011- 2:02.8A, 4:03.66; 2012- 4:09.10. pbs: 1000m 2:45.5+ '08, 5000m 16:33.9A '08.
Married to Kenneth Cheruiyot (Mar 2:07:18 '01, 3 WCh HMar 1997 in pb 60:00). Sons Keith (b. 2002) and Klein (b. 2006).

Linet Chepkwemoi **MASAI** b. 5 Dec 1989 Kapsokwony, Mount Elgon district 1.70m 55kg.
At (5000m)/10,000m: OG: '08- 4; WCh: '09- 1, '11- 6/3; AfCh: '10- 3. World CC: '07-08-09-10-11: 1J/3/2/2/2. Won Kenyan 10,000m 2010, CC 2010-11. World junior record and Kenyan record at 10,000m 2008, World 10 miles road record 2009.
Progress at 5000m, 10,000m: 2007- 14:55.50, 2008- 14:47.14, 30:26.50; 2009- 14:34.36, 30:51.24; 2010- 14:31.14, 31:59.36A; 2011- 14:32.95, 30:53.59;

2012- 14:53.93. pbs: 1500m 4:12.26 '09, 2000m 5:33.43 '09, 3000m 8:38.97 '07. Road: 15km 47:21 '09, 10M 50:39 '09.
Younger sister of Moses (qv) and Dennis Masai.

Mercy Wanjiru **NJOROGE** b. 10 Jun 1986 Njabini, Nyandarua District 1.58m 46kg.
At 3000mSt: OG: '12- 10; WCh: '11- 4; CG: '10- 2; AfG: '07- 5; AfCh: '08- 5, '10- 4; WJ: '04- 4; Kenyan champion 2012. Won Afr-J 3000m & 3000mSt 2005. World CC: '05- 4J, '06- 12.
Progress at 3000mSt: 2004- 9:52.25, 2005- 9:50.63, 2007- 9:43.02, 2008- 9:42.99, 2010- 9:26.64, 2011- 9:16.94, 2012- 9:25.21. pbs: 1500m 4:19.08 '11, 3000m 8:39.70i '11, 8:48.16 '06; 5000m 15:17.03 '11, 10kmRd 33:52 '06.

Veronica Wanjiru **NYARUAI** b. 29 Oct 1989 Nyahururu 1.65m 43kg.
At 5000m: AfCh: '08- 5, '12- 2. At 1500m: AfG: '07- 2; WCh: '07- sf. At 3000m: WJ: '06- 1, WY: '05- 1. At 3000mSt: OG: '08- h. World CC: '05-06-07: 2J/2J/3J.
Progress at 5000m: 2004- 16:05.7A, 2005- 15:13.1A. 2006- 15:42.1A, 2007- 15:23.37, 2008- 15:05.38. 2012- 14:44.82. pbs: 1500m 4:08.22 '06, 3000m 8:40.81 '12, 3000mSt 9:37.11 '08. Road: 10km 32:32 '09, HMar 73:55 '11.

Hellen Onsando **OBIRI** b. 13 Dec 1989 Nyangusu, Kisii 1.55m 45kg.
At 1500m: OG: '12- 12; WCh: '11- 11 (fell). At 3000m: WI: '12- 1. Won Kenyan 1500m 2011-12.
Progress at 1500m: 2011- 4:02.42, 2012- 3:59.68. pbs: 800m 2:00.54 '11, 1000m 2:46.00i '12, 2000m 5:44.8+i '12, 3000m 8:35.35i '12, 5000m 16:15.1A '12.

Philes ONGORI b. 19 Jul 1986 Chironge, Kisii district 1.58m 47kg. Based in Sapporo, Japan.
At 10,000m: WCh: '07- 8. World HMar: '09- 2.
Progress at 5000m, 10,000m, Mar: 2003- 16:11.32, 2004- 15:08.3mx/15:25.50, 2005- 15:09.49, 32:30.83; 2006- 15:19.90, 31:18.85; 2007- 14:50.15, 31:39.11;2008-14:46.20mx/14:46.06,30:29.21mx /31:19.73; 2009- 15:12.15, 31:53.46; 2011- 2:24:20 pbs: 800m 2:05.56 '04, 1500m 4:11.90 '04, 3000m 8:47.88 '07, Road: 15k 47:38 '08, HMar 67:38 '09.
Won Japanese High School 3000m 2004. Won Rotterdam Marathon 2011 on debut.

Lydia Chebet **ROTICH** b. 8 Aug 1988 Kipkilot, Keiyo District 1.63m 42kg. Kenya Police traffic officer.
At 3000mSt: OG: '12- h; WCh: '11- 5; AfCh: 10- 3.
Progress at 3000mSt: 2007- 10:44.3A, 2008- 9:55.62, 2009- 9:26.51, 2010- 9:18.03, 2011- 9:19.20. 2012- 9:31.09. pb 5000m 16:22.1A '09.

KOREA

Governing body: Korea Athletics Federation, 10 Chamshil Dong, Songpa-Gu, Seoul. Founded 1945. **National Champions 2012: Men:** 100m: Kim Min-kyun 10.68, 200m: Lee Jae-ha 21.29w, 400m: Lee joon 47.62, 800m: Kyung Ku-hwang 1:51.81, 1500m: Shin Sang-min 3:44.40, 5000m: Yuk Kun-tae 14:26.64, 10,000m: Shin Hyun-su 31:06.31, 3000mSt: Kwon Jae-woo 9:09.05, 110mh: Kim Byung-jun 13.79, 400mh: Kim Dae-hong 50.36, HJ: Lee Sung 2.16, PV: Jim Min-sup 5.50, LJ: Kim Sang-su 7.87, TJ: Kim Dong-han 15.95, SP: Choi Tae-ho 17.49, DT: Choi Jong-bum 55.11, HT: Lee Yun-chul 71.12, JT: Jung Sang-jin 82.05, Dec: Kim Kun-woo 6164, 20kW: Kim Hyun-sub 1:24:59. **Women:** 100m/200m: Kim Min-ki 11.98/24.54, 400m: Woo Yu-jin 55.28, 800m: Huh Yeon-jung 2:09.44, 1500m: Lee Da-mi 4:25.65, 5000m: Kim Eun-yeong 16:39.48, 10,000m: Lim Kyung-hee 35:12.52, 3000mSt: Shim Mi-young 10:44.42, 100mh: Jung Hye-lim 13.30, 400mh: Choi Eun-ju 58.52, HJ: Noh Hye-sook 1.76, PV: Choi Yun-hee 4.20, LJ/TJ: Bae Chan-mi 6.35w/13.15, SP: Lee Mi-young 16.58, DT: Lee Yeon-kyung 51.06, HT: Kang Na-ru 61.29, JT: Kim Kyong-ae 53.70, Hep: Jung Yeon-jin 4537, 20kW: Jeon Yong-eun 1:42:31.

KIM Hyun-sub b. 31 May 1985 Sokcho 1.75m 53kg.
At 20kW: OG: '08- 23, '12- 17; WCh: '07-09-11/34/6; AsiG: '06- 2, '10- 3; WUG: '05-07-09: 2/6/5. Asian champion 2011, KOR 2005-06, 2008-12. At 1000m/10kmW: WJ: '04- 3; WCp: '04- 8.
Three Korean 20km road walk records 2008-11.
Progress at 20kW: 2004- 1:24:58, 2005- 1:22:15, 2006- 1:21:45, 2007- 1:20:54, 2008- 1:19:41, 2009- 1:22:00, 2010- 1:19:36, 2011- 1:19:31, 2012- 1:21:36. Pb 10,000mW 39:30.56 '09, 38:13R '10.

KUWAIT

Governing body: Kuwait Association of Athletic Federation, PO Box 5499, 13055 Safat, Kuwait. Founded 1957.

Ali **Mohammed AL-ZINKAWI** b. 27 Feb 1984 Kuwait City 1.86m 97kg.
At HT: OG: '04/08/12- dnq 30/18/18; WCh: '05/09/11- dnq 21/13/13, '07- 12; WJ: '02- 2; AsiG: '06- 2; AsiC: '03-05-07-11: 1/1/1/1; CCp: '10- 3. Pan-Arab champion 2004-05, 2007, 2009, 2011; West Asian 2005, 2010.
13 Kuwait hammer records 2004-09, Asian junior record 2003.
Progress at HT: 2001- 64.66, 2002- 66.88, 2003- 72.70, 2004- 76.54, 2005- 76.25, 2006- 76.97, 2007- 77.14, 2008- 77.25, 2009- 79.74, 2010- 78.40, 2011- 79.27, 2012- 75.28.
His father Mohamed Al-Zinkawi competed at 1976, 1980 and 1988 Olympics at shot, best 18.65 '81.

LATVIA

Governing body: Latvian Athletic Association, 1 Augsiela Str, Riga LV-1009. Founded 1921.
National Championships first held in 1920 (men), 1922 (women). **2012 Champions: Men:** 100m/200m: Janis Mezitis 10.54w/21.32w, 400m: Janis Baltuss 48.06, 800m: Oskars Bormanis 1:51.45, 1500m: Ugis Jocis 3:57.38,

3000m: Dmitrijs Jurkevics 7:54.83, 5000m: Janis Girgensons 14:43.57, HMar: Valerijs Zolnerovics 68:13, Mar: Aigars Fadejevs 2:35:45, 3000mSt: Alberts Blajs 9:45.23, 110mh: Maris Grenins 14.72w, 400mh: Vladislavs Prosmickis 53.43, HJ: Janis Vanags 2.10, PV: Mereks Arents 5.40, LJ: Elvijs Misans 7.81, TJ: Davis Kalnins 14.41, SP: Maris Urtans 19.19, DT: Oskars Vaisjuns 54.48, HT: Igors Sokolov 71.99, JT: Eriks Rags 76.49, Dec: Reinis Kregers 6925. **Women**: 100m: Laura Ikauniece 11.98w, 200m: Gunta Latiseva-Cudare 24.50, 400m/100mh/400mh: Inese Nagle 58.80/14.98/63.09, 800m/1500m: Valerija Linkevica 2:13.40/4:48.43, 3000m: Liene Püke 11:08.60, 5000m/HMar/3000mSt: Irina Stula-Pankoka 18:50.63/1:25:52/11:32.58, Mar/10,000mW: Anita Kazemaka 2:52:00/48:12.9, HJ: Jelena Fenuka 1.74, LJ: Krista Zubova 5.71w, TJ: Santa Matule 13.45, SP: Evelina Petunova 13.01, DT: Dace Steinerte 44.32, HT: Vaira Kumermane 50.64, JT: Sinta Ozolina-Kovale 59.60, Hep: Ilona Dramacokoka 4521.

Zigismunds SIRMAIS b. 6 May 1992 Riga 1.91m 90kg.
At JT: OG: '12- dnq; WCh: '11: dnq 32; EC: '12- dnq 23; WJ: '10- 7; EJ: '11- 1.
Two world junior javelin records 2011.
Progress at JT: 2009- 65.03, 2010- 82.27, 2011- 84.69, 2012- 84.06.
Sister Katrina Sirma (b. 31 Mar 1994) JT 51.69 '11.

Vadims VASILEVSKIS b. 5 Ja/n 1982 Riga 1.88m 101kg. Jekabpils.
At JT: OG: '04- 2, '08- 9, '12- dnq 37; WCh: '05- dnq 16, '07- 4, '09- 4, '11- dnq 25; EC: '02-06-10-12: dnq 16/4/dnq 23/dnq; WJ: '00- 8; EU23: '03- 7; EJ: '01- 7; WUG: '07- 1. Latvian champion 2008, 2011; WAF 2008.
Three Latvian javelin records 2006-07.
Progress at JT: 1998- 59.17, 1999- 63.82, 2000- 73.07, 2001- 73.25, 2002- 81.92, 2003- 77.81, 2004- 84.95, 2005- 81.30, 2006- 90.43, 2007- 90.73, 2008- 86.65, 2009- 90.71, 2010- 84.08, 2011- 88.22, 2012- 86.50.
Set personal bests in qualifying (84.43) and final at 2004 Olympics.

Women

Aiga GRABUSTE b. 24 Mar 1988 Rezekne 1.78m 67kg. Rezeknes BJSS.
At Hep: OG: '08- 19, '12- dnf; WCh: '07- 17, '09- 13, '11- 12; EC: '12- 4; WJ: '06- 9; WY: '05- 27; EJ: '07- 1; EU23: '09- 1. At Pen: WI: '10- 8; EI: '11- 10. Won LAT 100mh 2007-08, 2011; LJ 2011, SP 2010-11, Hep 2009, 2011.
Latvian heptathlon record 2011.
Progress at Hep: 2006- 5443, 2007- 6019, 2008- 6050, 2009- 6396, 2011- 6507(w)/6414, 2012- 6325. Pbs: 60m 7.82i '08, 100m 12.09 '12, 200m 24.42/24.35w '11, 400m 55.43 '11, 800m 2:12.90 '12, 60mh 8.48i '12, 100mh 13.46 '11, HJ 1.79i '11,

1.77 '07; LJ 6.65 '11, SP 14.81i '12, 14.56 '09; JT 48.67 '11, Pen 4463i '09.

Laura IKAUNIECE b. 31 May 1992 Jürmala 1.79m 60kg. Jürmalas SS.
At Hep: OG: '12- 9; EC: '12- 3; WJ: '10- 6; WY: '09- 2. Won LAT 100m 2012, 200m 2009, 100mh & HJ 2010.
Latvian heptathlon record 2012.
Progress at Hep: 2008- 5175, 2009- 5618, 2011- 6063, 2012- 6414. Pbs: 60m 7.65i '12, 200m 24.16 '12, 800m 2:12.13 '12, 60mh 8.44i '12, 100mh 13.53 '12, HJ 1.85i/1.83 '12, LJ 6.31 '12, SP 12.67 '12, JT 53.73 '12, Hep 4346i '09.
Mother Vineta Ikauniece set current Latvian records at 110m 11.34A '87, 200m 22.49A '87 and 400m 50.71 '88, and her father Aivars Ikaunieks had 110mh bests of 13.71A '87 and 13.4 '84.

Madara PALAMEIKA b. 18 Jun 1987 Valdemarpils 1.85m 76kg. Ventspils.
At JT: OG: '12- 8; WCh: '09: dnq 27, '11- 11; EC: '10- 8, '12- 8; WJ: '06- dnq 16; EU23: '07- 3, '09- 1; EJ: '05- dnq 17. Latvian champion 2009-11.
Latvian javelin record 2009.
Progress at JT: 2002- 42.31, 2003- 49.11, 2004- 51.50, 2005- 51.75, 2006- 54.19, 2007- 57.98, 2008- 53.45, 2009- 64.51, 2010- 62.02, 2011- 63.46, 2012- 62.74.

Ineta RADEVICA b. 13 Jul 1981 Kraslava 1.73m 56kg. Was at University of Nebraska.
At LJ/(TJ): OG: '04- dnq 13/20, '12- 4; WCh: '05- dnq 23, '11- 3; EC: '10- 1, '12- 6; WJ: '00- dnq 14; EU23: '03- 3/3; EJ: '99- dnq 19; WI: '06- 5, '08- 6; EI: '05- 5, '07- 8; CCp: '10- 4; won NCAA TJ 2003-04, LAT LJ 2000, 2005-06; TJ 2001.
Latvian long jump record 2010.
Progress at LJ, TJ: 1996- 5.39, 1997- 5.36, 10.85; 1998- 5.59, 11.78/11.86w; 1999- 5.90, 12.64; 2000- 6.33, 12.80; 2001- 6.12/6.14w, 13.14; 2002- 6.32i/6.26, 13.75; 2003- 6.70, 14.04; 2004- 6.53/6.60w, 14.12; 2005- 6.80, 2006- 6.59i/6.46/6.64w, 13.43; 2007- 6.67i/6.35, 13.30i; 2008- 6.66i/6.65/6.75w, 13.71; 2010- 6.92, 13.89/14.40w; 2011- 6.76, 13.89i; 2012- 6.88. pbs: 100m 12.23 '02, 100mh 15.00 '98, HJ 1.70 '99, Hep 4262 '98.
Improved LJ pb from 6.80 to 6.92 to win 2010 European title. Married to Russian ice hockey player Pyotr Schastlivy, their son Mark was born in 2009.

LITHUANIA

Governing body: Athletic Federation of Lithuania, Kareiviu 6, LT-09117 Vilnius. Founded 1921.
National Championships first held in 1921 (women 1922). **2012 Champions: Men**: 100m: Mantas Silkauskas 10.53, 200m: Zilvinas Adomavicius 21.84, 400m: Gediminas Kucinskas 48.79, 800m: Vitalij Kozlov 1:50.07, 1500m: Petras Gliebus 3:51.61, 5000m/10,000m: Martynas Stanys 14:48.21/30:49.81, HMar: Mindaugas Virsilas 71:13, Mar: Tomas Venckunas 2:26:55,

3000mSt: Andrius Juknevicius 9:24.93, 110mh: Rahib Mammadov AZE 14.43, 400mh: Silvestras Guogis 50.76, HJ: Seiranas Puscius 2.08, PV: Marek Arents LAT 5.20, LJ: Povilas Mykolaitis 7.85, TJ: Darius Aucyna 16.84, SP: Rimantas Martisauskas 18.44, DT: Virgilijus Alekna 67.93, HT: Tomas Juknevicius 64.19, JT: Nerijus Luckauskas 65.92, Dec: Benas Kentra 6812, 20kW: Marius Ziukas 1:23:54, 50kW: Tomas Gaidamavicius 4:06:48. **Women**: 100m: Lina Grincikaite 11.77, 200m/400m: Agne Serksniene 23.63/52.56, 800m: Egle Balciunaite 2:04.97, 1500m: Loreta Kancyte 4:41.80, 5000m: Valda Zusianaite 16:25.72, 10,000m/HMar: Milda Vilcinskaite 36:29.46/1:23:04, Mar: Modesta Kaminskiene 3:15:52, 3000mSt: Karina Onufrijeva 11:58.26, 100mh/LJ: Austra Skujyte 14.12/6.43w, 400mh: Egle Staisiunaite 57.39, HJ: Airine Palsyte 1.95, PV: Rolanda Demcenko 3.91, TJ: Jolanta Verseckaite 13.52, SP: Laura Gedminaité 13.53, DT: Zinaida Sendriute 61.56, HT: Sandra Miseikyte 46.00, JT: Lina Muze LAT 61.04, Hep: Sandra Raizgyté 4263, 10kW: Brigita Virbalyte 44:17, 20kW: Inga Mastianica 1:42:00.

Virgilijus ALEKNA b. 13 Feb 1972 Terpeikiai, Kupiskis 2.00m 130kg. Graduate of Lithuanian Academy of Physical Culture. Guard of the Lithuanian president 1995-2010, advisor to the Lithuanian Ministry of the Interior from 2011.. At DT: OG: '96-00-04-08-12: 5/1/1/3/4; WCh: '95-97-99-01-03-05-07-09-11: dnq 19/2/4/2/1/1/ 4/4/6; EC: '98-02-06-10: 3/2/1/5; WCp: '98- 1, '06- 1. Won WAF 2003, 2005-06, 2009; GP 2001 (2nd 1999); DL 2011. LTU champion 1998, 2000-05, 2008-09, 2011-12.
Four Lithuanian discus records 2000. World over-40 record 2012.
Progress at DT: 1990- 52.84, 1991- 57.16, 1992- 60.86, 1993- 62.84, 1994- 64.20, 1995- 62.78, 1996- 67.82, 1997- 67.70, 1998- 69.66A, 1999- 68.25, 2000- 73.88, 2001- 70.99, 2002- 66.90, 2003- 69.69, 2004- 70.97, 2005- 70.67, 2006- 71.08, 2007- 71.56, 2008- 71.25, 2009- 69.59, 2010- 65.33, 2011- 67.90, 2012- 70.28. pb SP: 19.99 '97.
His 72.35 and 73.88 at the 2000 LTU Championships were the second and third longest ever discus throws. His 70.17 to win the 2005 World title (coming from 2nd at 68.10 with the last throw) was the first ever 70m throw at a global championships. He has 20 competitions and 31 throws over 70m. 37 successive wins from August 2005 to 4th at Worlds August 2007.
Married on 4 Mar 2000 Kristina Sablovskyte (pb LJ 6.14 '96, TJ 12.90 '97, sister of Remigija Nazaroviene).

Women

Austra SKUJYTE b. 12 Aug 1979 Birzai 1.88m 80kg. Graduated in kinesiology from Kansas State University, USA. Masters degree from the Lithuanian Academy of Physical Culture.

At Hep: OG: '00- 12, '04- 2, '08- dnf, '12- 5; WCh: '01-03-05-07-11: 6/10/4/6/8; EC: '02- 4; WJ: '98- 6; EU23: '99- 6, '01- 3. At Pen: WI: '04-08-12: 3/5/3; EI: '07- 4, '11- 2. At SP: WCh: '09- dnq 17; EC: '10- 12, '12- 11 (dnq 13= HJ). Won NCAA 2001-02; LTU 100mh 2000, 2005, 2012; HJ 2005, LJ 2005, 2007, 2012; SP 2001-02, 2004-05, 2007, 2009-11; DT 2009; Hep 1997.
World decathlon record 2005.
Progress at Hep: 1997- 4930, 1998- 5606, 1999- 5724, 2000- 6104, 2001- 6150w, 2002- 6275, 2003- 6213, 2004- 6435, 2005- 6386, 2007- 6380, 2008- 6235, 2011- 6338, 2012- 6599. pbs: 100m 12.49 '05, 200m 24.82 '04, 24.79w '07; 400m 57.19 '05, 800m 2:15.92 '04, 1500m 5:15.86 '05, 60mh 8.57i '12, 100mh 13.96 '11, 13.83w '04; HJ 1.92 '12, PV 3.20 '06, LJ 6.39i '05, 6.34 '12, 6.43w '12; SP 17.86 '09, DT 53.89 '10, JT 52.63 '07, Pen 4802i '12, Dec 8358 '05. Set three pbs in 2004 Olympics, including two seconds off 800m best to secure silver. Returned to multi-events in 2011 after two years concentrating on shot.

LUXEMBOURG

Governing body: Fédération Luxembourgeoise d'Athlétisme, 3 Route d'Arlon, L-8009 Strassen, Luxembourg. Founded 1928.
2012 National Champions: Men: 100m/200m: Marc Debanck 11.33/22.40, 400m/400mh: Jacques Frisch 49.28/52.17, 800m/1500m: Christophe Bettgen 1:55.46/3:57.10, 5000m: Pol Mellina 15:05.91, 10,000m: David Karonei 30:57.10, HMar/Mar: Vincent Nothum 67:56/2:27:36, 3000mSt: Yannick Frantz 11:33.42, 110mh: Claude Godart 14.3, HJ: Sven Liefgen 1.93, PV: Sebastien Hoffelt 4.80, LJ: Yoann Bebon 6.78, TJ: Asmir Mirascic 13.80, SP/JT: Tun Wagner 13.44/62.44, DT: Steve Schneider 47.44, HT: Steve Tonizzo 48.47, Dec: Wesley Charlet 6005. **Women**: 100m/200m: Anaïs Bauer 12.28/ 25.11, 400m/800m: Charlene Mathias 57.22/ 2:17.25, 1500m: Martine Mellina 4:42.65, 3000m: Jessica Schaaf 10:43.06, 10,000m: Pascale Schmoetten 36:35.69, HMar: Annette Jaffke 1:23:56, Mar: Sandra Huberty 3:07:50, 3000mSt: Liz Weiler 12:16.19, 100m: Mandy Charlet 15.40, 400mh: Chantal Hayen 65.72, HJ: Noémie Pleimling 1.68, PV: Cathy Schmit 2.80, LJ: Laurence Jones 5.55, TJ: Nita Bokomba 11.06, SP: Isabeau Pleimling 12.16, DT/JT: Noémie Pleimling 36.27/44.86, HT: Mireille Tonizzo 42.44, Hep: Marie-Daphnée Ries 3592.

MEXICO

Governing body: Federación Mexicana de Atletismo, Anillo Periférico y Av. del Conscripto, 11200 México D.F. Founded 1933.
National Champions 2012: Men: 100m: Julian Tamez 10.50w, 200m: José Carlos Herrera 20.72, 400m: Orlando García 47.21, 800m: Cesar Daniel Belman 1:51.95, 1500m: Isaías Haro 3:55.36,

5000m: Aldo Vega 14:40.01, 10,000m: Erick Pérez 30:32.54, 3000mSt: Javier Luna 9:26.13, 110mh: Genaro Rodríguez 14.09, 400mh: Sergio Rios 51.15, HJ: Jorge Rouco 2.18, PV: Giovanni Lanaro 5.40, LJ: Luis Rivera 8.00, TJ: Alberto Álvarez 16.19, SP/DT: Mario Cota 17.91/57.42, HT: Diego del Real 62.75, JT: Juan José Méndez 74.73, Dec: Roman Garibay 7053, 20000mW: Omar Segura 1:26:14.72. **Women:** 100m/200m: Jessica Sánchez 11.74/23.53, 400m: Gabriela Medina 53.01, 800m: Cristina Guevara 2:07.70, 1500m: Anayelli Navarro 4:29.37, 5000m: Marisol Romero 16:33.00, 10,000m: Angélica Sánchez 35:33.75, 3000mSt: Sara Prieto 10:50.89, 100mh: Violeta Ávila 13.93, 400mh: Anicia Castro 58.15, HJ: Romary Rifka 1.90, PV: Cecilia Villar 3.70, LJ: Amancay González 6.11, TJ: Jacqueline Triana 13.27, SP: Cecilia Dzul 14.73, DT: Paulina Flores 46.63, HT: Sharon Ayala 57.72, JT: Abigail Gómez 53.61, Hep: Christa Ruíz 5283, 10,000mW: Rosalia Ortiz 47:13.96.

Jorge **Horacio NAVA** b. 20 Jan 1982 Chihuahua 1.75m 62kg.
At 50kW: OG: '08- 6, '12- 16; WCh: '05-07-09: 9/9/19; PAm: '07- 2, '11- 1; CAG: '10- 1; WCp: '06-08-10-12: 7/5/2/12. At 20kW: WCh: '11- 19. At 10,000mW: WY: '99- 5; PAm-J: '01- 2.
Progress at 50kW: 2005- 3:53:57, 2006- 3:48:22, 2007- 3:52:35, 2008- 3:45:21, 2009- 3:56:26, 2010- 3:54:16, 2011- 3:45:29, 2012- 3:46:59. pbs: 5000m 18:40.11 '09, 10,000mW 40:33.52 '04, 20kW 1:22:15 '11.

Éder SÁNCHEZ b. 21 May 1986 Toluca 1.76m 67kg. Mexican army sergeant.
At 20kW: OG: '08- 15, '12- 6; WCh: '05-07-09-11: 8/4/3/14; WCp: '08-10-12: 3/6/7; CAG: '06- 2, '10- 1; won MEX 2006. At 10,000mW: WJ: '02- 4; PAm-J: '03- 2; WCp: '04- 2J.
CAC 5000mW record 2009, junior 20kW 2005.
Progress at 20kW: 2005- 1:19:02, 2006- 1:23:24A, 2007- 1:20:08, 2008- 1:18:34, 2009- 1:19:22, 2010- 1:21:16, 2011- 1:19:36, 2012- 1:19:52. pbs: 3000mW 11:13.45 '09, 5000mW 18:40.11 '09, 10,000mW 40:46.29 '04, 10km Rd 38:31 '09, 50kW 3:53:19 '11. Won IAAF Race Walking Challenge 2009. Nephew of Rosario Sánchez (2nd PAm 20kW 1999 & 2003) and of Joel Sánchez (3rd OG 50kW 2000).

MOLDOVA

Governing Body: Federatia de Atletism din Republica Moldova. Founded 1991.

Zalina MARGHIEVA b. 5 Feb 1988 Osetia-Alaniya, Russia 1.74m 90kg. AS-CSPLN.
At HT: OG: '08- dnq 37, '12- 8; WCh: '09- dnq 26, '11- 8; EC: '10- 5; WJ: '06- 4; WY: '05- 7; EU23: '09- 1; EJ: '07- 5; WUG: '11- 1.
12 Moldovan hammer records 2005-12.
Progress at HT: 2005- 61.80, 2006- 65.50, 2007- 65.40, 2008- 70.22, 2009- 71.56, 2010- 71.50, 2011- 72.93, 2012- 74.47, 2013- 74.28.

Sister **Marina** (b. 28 Jun 1986) HT: 72.53 '09, five MDA records 2007-09, WCh: '11- dnq 17; EC: '10- 6, received a 3-year drugs ban from 24 July 2012. Brother **Sergiu** (b. 6 Nov 1992) HT 75.20 '12, 2 EJ '11.

MOROCCO

Governing Body: Fédération Royale Marocaine d'Athlétisme, Complex Sportif Prince Moulay Abdellah, PO Box 1778 R/P, Rabat. Fd. 1957.
2012 National Champions: Men: 100m: Khalid Idrissi Zougari 10.58, 200m: Abdelghani Zaghali 21.28, 400m: Abdelkarim Khoudri 46.60, 800m: Samir Jamaa 1:47.69; 1500m: Yassine Bensghir 3:35.64, 5000m: Anis Salmouni 13:54.81, 10,000m: El Abassi El Hassane 28:12.40, HMar: Khaled Sadden 62:29, 3000mSt: Hamid Ezzine 8:26.52, 110mh: El Mehdi El Mellouki 14.56, 400mh: Hassan Akabbou 52.02, HJ: Yassine Oulga 2.01 (Manirou Dembélé SEN 2.05), PV: Chéaouri Mouhcine 5.20, LJ: El Mehdi Kabbachi 7.68, TJ: Ihab El Hajri 15.34, SP: Mohamed Gharrous 16.25, DT: Kamal El Omrani El Idrissi 55.24, HT: Driss Barid 65.09, JT: El Hakour El Khatib 60.60, Dec: Lhoucine Ayad 5871, 5000mW: Ali Daghiri 21:16.58. **Women**: 100m/200m: Ghita El Kafi 11.90/24.44, 400m: Hayat Lambarki 53.81; 800m: Khadidja El Moussaoui 2:07.01, 1500m: Salima Elouali Alami 4:12.25, 5000m: Rkia Moukim 15:22.27, 10,000m: Fatima Zahra Ouhrisse 37:43.60, HMar: Malika Belfakih 73:08, 3000mSt: Hafida Benjilali 10:42.52, 100mh: Yamina Hajjaji 13.44, 400mh: Lamia Lhabz 56.80, HJ: Dounia Menni 1.61, PV: Nisrine Dinar 3.80, LJ: Yamina Hajjaji 6.34, TJ: Jihad Bakhechi 13.40, SP: Sara Chebbawi 11.60, DT/HT: Karima Chahine 44.56/52.39, JT: Nezha Merzak 41.28, Hep: Soukaine Zakour 4164, 5000mW: Nezha Ezzhani 25:35.08.

Hamid EZZINE b. 5 Dec 1983 Aït Ali 1.74m 60kg.
At 3000mSt: OG: '08- h. '12- 7; WCh: '05- h, '11- 9; AfCh: 04- 4, '06- 5.
Progress at 3000mSt: 2004- 8:25.10, 2005- 8:21.38, 2006- 8:19.37, 2007- 8:09.72, 2008- 8:13.20, 2011- 8:11.81, 2012- 8:16.93. pbs: 1500m 3:43.03 '12, 3000m 7:54.65 '11, 5000m 14:28.68 '02.
Two-year drugs ban 2009-11. Older brother Ali set MAR 300mSt record 8:03.57 '00; OG: '00- 3, '04- 8; WCh: '99- 3, '01- 2, '03- 10; WJ: '96- 3.

Jaouad GHARIB b. 22 May 1972 Khénifra 1.76m 60kg.
At Mar: OG: '04- 11, '08- 2; WCh: '03- 1, '05- 1. At 10,000m: WCh: '01- 11; AfCh: '02- 8. At 3000m: WI: '03- 11. World HMar: '01- 9, '02- 2; CC: '02- 10. Won MedG 10,000m 2001.
Moroccan marathon record 2009.
Progress at 5000m, 10,000m, Mar: 2001- 13:19.69, 27:29.51; 2002- 13:20.59, 28:02.09i/28:57.12; 2003- 2:08:31, 2004- 2:07:12, 2005- 2:07:49, 2006- 2:07:19,

2007- 2:07:54, 2008- 2:07:16, 2009- 2:05:27, 2010- 2:06:55, 2011- 2:08:26, 2012- 2:07:44. pbs: 3000m 7:39.22 '01, 2M 8:29.23i '02, 15km 43:08 '01, HMar 59:56 '04.

Began running at 22, made sudden emergence into top class in 2001. Sixth in 2:09:15 at Rotterdam 2003 on marathon debut and won world title in next marathon; London: 3rd 2004 & 2009-10, 2nd 2005, 4th 2007, 5th 2012, 6th 2011, 8th 2006. Won Fukuoka 2010 (3rd 2006), 2nd Chicago 2007, 3rd New York 2009.

Abdelaati IGUIDER b. 25 Mar 1987 Errachidia 1.70m 52kg.
At 1500m(/5000m): OG: '08- 5, '12- 3/6; WCh: '07- h, '09- 11, '11- 5; WJ: '04- 1, '06- 2; WI: '10- 2, '12- 1.
Progress at 1500m, 5000m: 2004- 3:35.53, 2005- 3:35.63, 2006- 3:32.68, 2007- 3:32.75, 2008- 3:31.88, 2009- 3:31.47, 2010- 3:34:25, 2011- 3:31.60, 2012- 3:33.99, 13:09.17. pbs: 800m 1:47.14 '07, 1000m 2:19.14 '07, 1M 3:51.78 '12, 3000m 7:34.92i '13, 7:41.95 '07.

Amine LAÂLOU b. 13 May 1982 Salé 1.78m 57kg.
At 800m(/1500m): OG: '04/08- sf; WCh: '03-05-07: h/sf/6, '09- 5/10, '11- (sf); WJ: '00- sf; WY: '99-h; WI: '04-10-12: 4/(5)/(9); AfCh: '02- h, '10- (2); AfJ: '01- 2; CCp: '10- (1); Won MAR 800m 2003, MedG 800m 2009, FrancG 800m & 1500m 2009, Arab 1500m 2009.
Moroccan 800m record 2006.
Progress at 800m, 1500m: 2000- 1:51.55, 2001- 1:49.94, 2002- 1:46.5, 2003- 1:45.20, 2004- 1:43.68, 2005- 1:44.22, 2006- 1:43.25, 2007- 1:43.94, 2008- 1:44.27, 2009- 1:43.36, 3:31.56; 2010- 1:43.71, 3:29.53; 2011- 1:45.11, 3:31.92; 2012- 1:45.28, 3:30.54. pbs: 400m 47.21 '04, 47.0 '03; 1000m 2:15.31 '11, 1M 3:50.22 '10.

Mohamed MOUSTAOUI b. 2 Apr 1985 Khouribga 1.74m 60kg.
At 1500m: OG: '08/12- sf; WCh: '07- sf, '09- 6, '11- 6; AfCh: '06- 5; WJ: '04- 4; AfJ: '03- 2; Arab champion 2007. World CC: '04- 14J, '05- 14 4k.
Progress at 1500m: 2003- 3:42.9, 2004- 3:37.44, 2005- 3:36.20, 2006- 3:32.51, 2007- 3:32.67, 2008- 3:32.06, 2009- 3:32.60, 2010- 3:36.92+, 2011- 3:31.84, 2012- 3:35.46. pbs: 800m 1:45.44 '09, 1000m 2:20.00i '08, 1M 3:50.08 '08, 2000m 5:00.98i '07, 3000m 7:43.08i '09, 7:43.99 '11; 2M 8:26.49i '05, 5000m 13:22.61 '05.

Women

Halima HACHLAF b. 6 Sep 1988 Boumia, Meknès-Tafilalet 1.68m 56kg.
At 800m: OG: '12- sf; WCh: '09/11- h; AfCh: '07- 2 (3 1500m), '08- 4; WJ: '04- 9, '06- sf; WY: '03- sf, '05- 4.
Progress at 800m: 2004- 2:06.06, 2005- 2:06.91, 2006- 2:05.75, 2007- 2:02.60, 2008- 2:04.05, 2009- 2:00.91, 2010- 1:58.40, 2011- 1:58.27, 2012- 1:58.84. pbs: 400m 54.96 '11, 600m 1:28.22 '07, 1500m 4:07.63 '12.

Older brother Abdelkader Hachlaf had pbs 1500m 3:33.59 '01, 3000mSt 8:08.76 '06.

Btissam Boucif **LAKHOUAD** b. 7 Dec 1980 Khouribga 1.70m 52kg.
At 1500m: OG: '08- 12, '12- h; WCh: '09- sf, '11- 4; AfCh: '10- 3 (4 800m); CCp: '10- dnf.
Moroccan 1500m records 2010 and 2012.
Progress at 1500m: 2004- 4:11.26, 2005- 4:18.01, 2006- 4:08.22, 2007- 4:03.4, 2008- 4:06.37, 2009- 4:03.23, 2010- 3:59.35, 2011- 4:01.09, 2012- 3:59.65. pbs: 800m 2:00.22 '12, 1000m 2:38.14i '12, 1M 4:25.35 '07, 3000m 9:08.02 '07, 10k Rd 33:22 '06.

NETHERLANDS

Governing body: Koninklijke Nederlandse Atletiek Unie (KNAU), Postbus 60100, NL-6800 JC Arnhem. Founded 1901.
National Championships first held in 1910 (men), 1921 (women). **2012 Champions: Men**: 100m: Churandy Martina 10.22, 200m: Jerrel Feller 20.76, 400m: Joeri Moerman 46.61, 800m: Robert Lathouwers 1:52.90, 1500m: Wouter Ploeger 3:51.71, 5000m: Abdi Nageeye 14:25.83, 10,000m: Khalid Choukoud 28:59.94, HMar/ Mar: Patrick Stitzinger 63:28/2:16:51, 3000mSt: Simon Vroemen 8:51.67, 110mh: Kopen Smet 13.97, 400mh: Thomas Kortbeek 50.97, HJ: Douwe Amels 2.18, PV: Nils Mulder 5.35, LJ: Marus Kranendonk 7.53, TJ: Erwin Slokker 14,85, SP: Erik van Vreumingen 19.35, DT: Erik Cadée 63.14, HT: Vincent Onos 65.55, JT: Bjorn Blommerde 73.60, Dec: Harald Bust 7418.
Women: 100m/LJ: Dafne Schippers 11.38/6.54, 200m: Jamile Samuel 23.15, 400m: Nicky van Leuveren 54.27, 800m: Sanne Verstegen 2:04.61, 1500m: Maureen Koster 4:20.91, 5000m: Lesley van Miert 16:31.75, 10,000m: Stefanie Bouma 36:04.39, HMar: Andrea Deelstra 73:47, Mar: Miranda Boonstra 2:28:18, 100mh: Rosina Hodde 13.53, 3000mSt: Helen Hofstede 10:08.00, 100mh: Sharona Bakker 13.32, 400mh: Bianca Baak 58.73. HJ: Sietske Noorman 1.87, PV: Rianna Galiart 4.25, TJ: Maruska Eduarda 12.50, SP: Melissa Boekelman 17.00, DT: Monique Jansen 59.27, HT: Eva Reinders 60.65, JT: Eveklien Dekkers 53.43, Hep: Myrte Goor 5405.

Erik CADÉE b. 15 Feb 1984 s'Hertogenbosch 2.01m 120kg. Prins Hendrik, Vught.
At DT: OG: '12- 10; WCh: '07-09-11: dnq 23/19/19; EC: '10- nt, '12- 10; WJ: '02- dnq 22; EU23: '05- 5; EJ: '03- 1; EYth: '01- 2. Dutch champion 2010, 2012.
Progress at DT: 2002- 50.63, 2003- 54.05, 2004- 56.59, 2005- 60.27, 2006- 61.36, 2007- 62.68, 2008- 61.75, 2009- 65.61, 2010- 66.20, 2011- 66.95, 2012- 67.30. pb SP 18.99i, 17.70 '09.

Churandy MARTINA b. 3 Jul 1984 Willemstad, Curaçao 1.80m 68kg. Nike. Studied civil engineering at University of Texas at El Paso, USA.

At 100m/(200m): OG: '04- qf, '08- 4/dq, '12- 6/5; WCh: '03- h, '05- qf, '07- 5/5, '09- qf, '11- sf/sf; WJ: '00- h/h, '02- qf; WY: '99- sf; EC: '12- (1)/1R; PAm: '03- sf, '07- 1; CAG: '06- 1/1R, '10- 1/1/3R; CCp: '10- (2)/1R. Won PAm-J 2003; NED 100m 2011-12, 200m 2011.

Records: AHO 100m (8) 2004-08, 200m (6) 2005-10, 400m 2007; NED 100m (2) 2011-12, 200m (2)2012.

Progress at 100m, 200m: 2000- 10.73, 21.73; 2001- 10.64A, 21.55; 2002- 10.30, 20.81; 2003- 10.29/10.26w, 20.71; 2004- 10.13, 20.75; 2005- 10.13/9.93Aw, 20.32/20.31w; 2006- 10.04A/ 10.06/9.76Aw/9.99w, 20.27A; 2007- 10.06, 20.20; 2008- 9.93, 20.11; 2009- 9.97, 20.76; 2010- 10.03A/10.07/9.92w, 20.08; 2011- 10.10, 20.38; 2012- 9.91, 19.85. pbs: 60m 6.58i '10, 400m 46.13A '07.

At 2008 Olympics set three national records at 100m and one at 200m before crossing line in second place in final in 19.82 only to be disqualified for running out of his lane. Competed for Netherlands Antilles until 2010.

Eelco SINTNICOLAAS b. 7 Apr 1987 Dordrecht 1.86m 81kg. AV '34 (Apeldoorn). Economics student.

At Dec: OG: '12- 11; WCh: '09- dnf, '11- 5; EC: '10- 2; WJ: '06- 8; EU23: '09- 1; EJ: '05- 14. At Hep: EI: '11- 4, '13- 1.

Dutch decathlon record 2012,

Progress at Dec: 2007- 7466, 2008- 7507w, 2009- 8112, 2010- 8436, 2011- 8304, 2012- 8506. pbs: 60m 6.88i '13, 100m 10.71 '10, 10.69w '08; 200m 21.62 '10, 400m 47.88 '10, 1000m 2:37.42i '06, 1500m 4:22.29 '11, 60mh 7.88i '13, 110mh 14.10 '12, 400mh 51.59 '10, HJ 2.08i '13, 2.00 '12; PV 5.52i '11, 5.45 '10; LJ 7.65i, 7.59, 7.76w '09, SP 14.46i/14.31 '11, DT 43.18 '12, JT 63.59 '12, Hep 6372i '13.

Set six pbs in improving pb by 277 points for European silver 2010.

Rutger SMITH b. 9 Jul 1981 Groningen 1.97m 130kg. Groningen Atletiek.

At SP (/DT): OG: '04- dnq 14/16, '08- 9/7, '12- dnq 14/16; WCh: '03- dnq 25/15, '05- 2, '07- 4/3, '11- (dnq 15); EC: '02- 8. '06- 4/7, '12- 2/3; WJ: '00- 1/3; EU23: '03- 3/1; EJ: '99- 1/1; WI: '03-08- 12: dnq 10/5/7; EI: '05- 2; ECp: '04- 2/2. Won NED SP 2000, 2002-08; DT 2002-08, 2011.

Three Dutch shot records 2005-06.

Progress at SP, DT: 1998- 15.23, 51.18; 1999- 18.27, 53.81; 2000- 19.48, 58.74; 2001- 18.92i/18.21, 59.96; 2002- 20.39, 64.69; 2003- 20.52, 62.70; 2004- 20.94, 63.79; 2005- 21.41, 65.51; 2006- 21.62, 64.60; 2007- 21.19, 67.63; 2008- 20.89i/20.80, 66.85, 2011- 19.95i, 67.77; 2012- 20.56i/20.55, 66.97.

First athlete to win World Championships medals in shot and discus.

Women

Dafne SCHIPPERS b. 15 Jun 1992 Utrecht 1.79m 68kg. Hellas.

At Hep: OG: '12- 12; WJ: '10- 1; EJ: '09- 4, '11- 1. At 200m/4x100mR: WCh: '11- sf; EC: 5/2R; WJ: '10- 3R. At 60m: EI: '13- 5. Won NED 100m 2011-12, LJ 2012.   Dutch 200m record 2011.

Progress at Hep: 2009- 5507, 2010- 5967, 2011- 6172, 2012- 6360. pbs: 60m 7.14i '13, 100m 11.19. 11.13w '11; 150m 16.96 '11 200m 22.69 '11, 800m 2:15.52 '12, 60mh 8.18i '12, 100mh 13.27 '11, HJ 1.80 '12, LJ 6.54 '12, SP 14.19 '11, JT 41.80 '11.

NEW ZEALAND

Governing body: Athletics New Zealand, Auckland.

National Championships first held in 1887 (men), 1926 (women). **2012 Champions: Men**: 100m/200m: Joseph Millar 10.36/21.74, 400m: Alex Jordan 46.83, 800m: Brad Mathas 1:51.50, 1500m: Julian Matthews 3:54.37, 3000m: Malcolm Hicks 8:07.94, 5000m: Nick Willis 13:54.29, 10,000m: Stephen Lett 30:36.35, HMar: Oska Inkster-Baynes 69:13, Mar: Tony Payne 2:31:07, 3000mSt: Brent Tingay 9:18.67, 110mh/LJ: Brent Newdick 14.58/7.17, 400mh: James Mortimer 50.83, HJ: William Crayford 2.12, PV: Brent Newdick & Nicholas Southgate 4.85, TJ: Todd Swanson 14.76w, SP: Tom Walsh 17.92, DT: Marshall Hall 52.47, HT: Philip Jensen (18th title) 60.65, JT: Stuart Farquhar 79.37, Dec: Nicholas Gerrard 6884, 3000mW/20kW: Scott Nelson 13:04.52/1:39:47, 50kW: Graeme Jones 5:11:58. **Women**: 100m/200m: Monique Williams 11.95/24.50, 400m: Kristie Baillie 53.71, 800m: Angela Smit 2:04.50, 1500m: Nikki Hamblin 4:19.63, 3000m: Camille Buscomb 9:29.60, 5000m: Hannah Newbould 16:26.37, 10,000m: Sally Gibbs 34:45.21, HMar: Lisa Robertson 76:53, Mar: Alex Williams 2:41:28, 3000mSt: Fiona Crombie 10:29.06, 100mh: Andrea Miller 13.49, 400mh: Tracey Hale 60.69, HJ: Elizabeth Lamb 1.82, PV: Lucy McGall 3.43, LJ/Hep: Sarah Cowley 5.74/5905w, TJ: Nneka Okpala 12.78, SP/DT: Siositina Hakeai 13.47/49.70, HT: Julia Ratcliffe 59.92, JT: Tori Peeters 45.59, 3000mW/20kW: Roseanne Robinson 14:08.01/1:45:49.

Stuart FARQUHAR b. 15 Mar 1982 Te Aroha, Waikato 1.86m 98kg. Hamilton City Hawkes.

At SP: OG: '04/08- dnq 25/20, '12- 9; WCh: '07- 09: dnq 19/14, 11: 11; CG: '06- 7, '10- 2; WJ: '00- dnq 26; WCp: '06- 6. Won NZ 2000, 2003-13.

Progress at JT: 1998- 66.50, 1999- , 2000- 72.22, 2001- 69.25, 2002- 78.51, 2003- 76.41, 2004- 79.68, 2005- 72.14, 2006- 81.70, 2007- 78.08, 2008- 83.23, 2009- 80.16, 2010- 85.35, 2011- 84.21, 2012- 86.31.

Jacko GILL b. 20 Dec 1994 Auckland 1.90m 115kg. Takapuna.

At SP: WJ: '10- 1, '12- 1; WY: '11- 1, YthOG: '10- 2. Five World youth shot records 5kg 23.86 '10, 24.35 and 24.45 '11; 6kg (4) 21.34 to 22.31, 7.26kg (3) in 2011. Three NZL records 2011.

Progress at SP: 2010- 18.57, 2011- 20.38, 2012- 20.05.

World age 15 and 16 bests for 5kg, 6kg and 7.26kg shot. His father Walter was NZ champion at SP 1987 & 1989, DT 1975, pbs 16.57 '86 & 53.78 (1975); his mother Nerida (née Morris) DT pb 51.32 and was NZ champion in 1990.

Nick WILLIS b. 25 Apr 1983 Lower Hutt 1.83m 68kg. Economics graduate of University of Michigan, USA.
At 1500m: OG: '04- sf, '08- 2, '12- 9; WCh: '05- sf, '07- 10, '11- 12; CG: '06-1, '10- 3; WJ: '02- 4; WI: '08- dq; WCp: '06- 3. Won NCAA indoor 2005, NZ 1500m 2006, 3000m 2013, 5000m 2011-12. Four NZ 1500m records 2005-12. Oceania 1500m record 2012 and indoors (3:35.80) 2010.
Progress at 1500m: 2001- 3:43.54, 2002- 3:42.69, 2003- 3:36.58, 2004- 3:32.64, 2005- 3:32.38, 2006- 3:32.17, 2007- 3:35.85, 2008- 3:33.51, 2009- 3:38.85i, 2010- 3:35.17, 2011- 3:31.79, 2012- 3:30.35. pbs: 800m 1:45.54 '04, 1000m 2:16.58 '12, 1M 3:50.66 '08, 3000m 7:44.90i '04, 7:45.97 '05; 5000m 13:27.54 '05.
His brother Steve (b. 25 Apr 1975) had pbs: 1500m 3:40.29 '99, 1M 3:59.04 '00.

Women

Valerie ADAMS b. 6 Oct 1984 Rotorua 1.93m 123kg. Auckland City.
At SP: OG: '04- 8, '08- 1, '12- 1; WCh: '03-05-07-09-11: 5/3/1/1/1; CG: '02-06-10: 2/1/1; WJ: '02- 1; WY: '99- 10, '01- 1; WI: '04-08-10-12: dnq 10/1/2/1; WCp: '02- 6, '06- 1, '10- 1. Won WAF 2008-09, DL 2011-12, NZL SP 2001-11, 2013; DT 2004, HT 2003.
Nine Oceania & Commonwealth shot records 2005-11, 22 NZ 2002-11, 8 OCE indoor 2004-12.
Progress at SP: 1999- 14.83, 2000- 15.72, 2001- 17.08, 2002- 18.40, 2003- 18.93, 2004- 19.29, 2005- 19.87, 2006- 20.20, 2007- 20.54, 2008- 20.56, 2009- 21.07, 2010- 20.86, 2011- 21.24, 2012- 21.11. pbs: DT 58.12 '04, HT 58.75 '02.
Matched her age with metres at the shot from 14 to 18 and missed that at 19 by only two months. 28 successive shot wins from September 2007 to World Indoor silver in March 2010, and another 30 from August 2010 to the end of 2012. Her father came from England and her mother from Tonga. Married New Caledonia thrower Bertrand Vili (SP 17.81 '02, DT 63.66 '09, 4 ECp '07 for France) in November 2004 (now separated).

Kimberley SMITH b. 19 Nov 1981 Papakura 1.66m 49kg. Social science graduate of Providence College.
At 5000m: OG: '04- h; WUG: '05- 1; WCp: '06- 4. At 10,000m: OG: '08- 9; WCh: '05- 15, '07- 5, '09- 8. At 3000m: WI: '08- 6. At Mar: OG: '12- 15. World CC: '05- 12, '09- 13; HMar: '09- 7. Won NCAA 5000m and indoor 3000m & 5000m 2004; NZ 5000m 2002, 2006, 2008; CC 2002.
Oceania records: 3000m 2007, 5000m & 10,000m 2008; indoor 1M 2008, 3000m 2007, 5000m 2005

& 2009. NZ records 5000m (3) 2005-07, 10,000m (3) 2005-08, HMar (4) 2009-11, Mar 2010.
Progress at 5000m, 10,000m, Mar: 2002- 16:30.10, 2003- 15:47.92, 2004- 15:09.72, 33:45.81; 2005- 14:50.46i/15:05.68, 31:21.00, 2006- 14:56.58, 2007- 14:49.41, 31:20.63; 2008- 14:45.93, 30:35.54; 2009- 14:39.89i/14:52.49, 31:21.42; 2010- 2:25:21, 2011- 15:14.02, 2:25:46; 2012- 2:26:59. pbs: 1500m 4:11.25 '04, 1M 4:24.14i '04, 3000m 8:35.31 '07, 2M 9:13.94i '08, Rd: 15km 47:37 '11, 10M 53:10 '10, 20km 63:38+ '11, HMar 67:11 '11.
Did not finish on marathon debut in New York 2008. Married Pat Tarpy on 1 Sep 2012.

NIGERIA

Governing body: The Athletic Federation of Nigeria, P.O.Box 18793, Garki, Abuja. F'd 1944.
2012 National Champions: **Men**: 100m/200m: Obinna Metu 10.11/20.91, 400m: Abiola Oniakoya 46.29, 800m: Isaku Mohammed 1:52.47, 1500m: Hamajan Soudi 3:54.38, 5000m/3000mSt: Ishmael Sadjo 14:33.19/9:14.84, 10,000m: Tokbe Giwete 34:09.26, Mar: Stephen Jurbe 3:06.71, 110mh: Samuel Okon 13.78, 400mh: Amaechi Morton 50.31, HJ: Obiora Arnze 2.10, PV: Lekan Soetan 3.60, LJ: Stanley Ggagbeke 8.20, TJ: Tosin Oke 17.23, SP/DT/JT: Kenechukwu Ezeofor 16.53/52.30/68.44, HT: Ibrahim Bada 5307, Dec: Lukmen Oguntade 5938, 20000mW: Kazeem Adeyemi 1:44:09.70. **Women**: 100m/LJ: Blessing Okagbare 11.12/6.97, 200m: Laretta Ozoh 22.73, 400m: Regina Jacobs 51.17, 800m: Philomena Ihekandu 2:08.65, 1500m: Abiyi David 4:43.01, 5000m/10,000m: Pam Deborah 17:38.97/37:58.21, HMar: Vivian Ashuli 1:22:42, 100mh: Seun Adigun 13.13w, 400mh: Ajoke Odumosu 55.08, HJ: Doreen Amata 1.86, TJ: Blessing Ibrahim 13.73, SP: Omotayo Talabi 15.46 (drugs dq Vivian Chukwuemeka 18.18), DT: Ibhag–uezesie Uwaje 36.26, HT: Feyisaso Daramola 55.75, JT: Patience Okoro 42.04, 20000mW: Asedo Queenley 1:49:49.23.

Tosin OKE b. 1 Oct 1980 London, UK 1.78m 77kg. Woodford Green, UK. Chemistry graduate of Manchester University.
At TJ: OG: '12- 7; WCh: '09/11- dnq 16/16; EC: '02- nj; CG: '02- 5, '10- 1; AfG: '11- 1; AfCh: '10- 1, '12- 1; EJ: '99- 1; CCp: '10- 6. ECp: '03- 4. Won UK 2007, NGR 2009-10, 2012.
Progress at TJ: 1997- 14.07, 1998- 15.16/15.62w, 1999- 16.57, 2000- 16.04/16.37w, 2001- 16.08i/15.72, 2002- 16.65, 2003- 16.61i/16.59, 2004- 16.49/16.75w, 2005- 16.12/16.30w, 2006- 16.33/16.50w, 2007- 16.86, 2008- 16.47/16.63w, 2009- 16.87, 2010- 17.22A/17.16, 2011- 17.21, 2012- 17.23. pb LJ 7.31 '05.
Switched allegiance from Britain to Nigeria (parents) from 10 Feb 2009.

Women

Doreen AMATA b. 6 May 1988. Lagos 1.85m

55kg. Was at Lagos State University.
At HJ: OG: '08/12- dnq 16=/17; WCh: '09- dnq 27, '11- 8=; AfG: '07- 1, '11- 1; AfCh: '12- 4. Won Nigerian 2007-09, 2011.
Three Nigerian high jump records 2009-11.
Progress at HJ: 2005- 1.70, 2006- 1.70, 2007- 1.89, 2008- 1.95, 2009- 1.90, 2011- 1.95, 2012- 1.90.

Ajoke ODUMOSU b. 27 Oct 1987 Lagos 1.68m 59kg. Was at University of South Alabama, USA.
At 400mh: OG: '12- 8; WCh: '07-09-11: h/sf/sf; CG: '10- 1; AfG: '07- 3, '11- 1; AfCh: '08- 1,'10- 2 ; WJ: '06- 5/2R; CCp: '10- 2. Won Af-J 2003, Nigerian 2009-12. At 400m: OG: '08- sf.
Four Nigerian 400mh records 2009-12.
Progress at 400mh: 2003- 60.03, 2004- 57.33, 2006- 56.09, 2007- 55.37, 2008- 55.92A, 2009- 54.80, 2010- 54.59, 2011- 56.23, 2012- 54.40. pbs: 100m 11.71 '09, 200m 23.42 '10, 400m 51.39 '08, 50.46dt '07.

Blessing OKAGBARE b. 9 Oct 1988 Sapele 1.80m 60kg. Student at University of Texas at El Paso, USA.
At LJ/(100m): OG: '08- 3, '12- dnq 17/8; WCh: '11- dnq 18/5; AfG: '07- 2 (4 TJ), '11- 1; AfCh: '10- 1/1/1R, '12- 1/1; WJ: '06- 16 (dnq 17 TJ); CCp: '10- 6/3/3R; Won Nigerian 100m 2009-12, LJ 2008-09, 2011-12; TJ 2008; NCAA 100m & LJ 2010.
Nigerian & African junior TJ record 2007.
Progress at 100m, LJ: 2004- 5.85 irreg, 2006- 6.16, 2007- 6.51, 2008- 6.91, 2009- 11.16, 6.73/6.90w; 2010- 11.00/10.98w/10.7Aw, 6.88; 2011- 11.08/11.01w, 6.78/6.84w; 2012- 10.92, 6.97. pbs: 60m 7.18i '10, 200m 22.63 '12, 300m 37.04 '13, TJ 14.13 '07.

NORWAY

Governing body: Norges Friidrettsforbund, Serviceboks 1, Ullevaal Stadium, 0840 Oslo. Founded 1896.

National Championships first held in 1896 (men), 1947 (women, walks 1937). **2012 Champions**: **Men**: 100m: Philip Bjørnå Berntsen 10.82, 200m: Jaysuma Saidy Ndure 20.91, 400m/800m: Thomas Roth 47.93/1:51.35, 1500m: Henrik Ingebrigtsen 3:43.07, 5000m: Hans Kristian Fløystad 14:20.29, 10,000m: Håkon Brox 30:22.35, HMar: Trond Arne Rugland 67:55, Mar: Øystein Sylta 2:25:42, 3000mSt: Tom Erling Kårbø 9:05.29, 110mh: Vladimir Vukicevic 13.96, 400mh: Øyvind Kjerpeset 51.67, HJ: Kristoffer Nilsen 2.15, PV: Per Magne Florvaag 4.90, LJ: Vetle Utsi Onstad 7.26, TJ: Sindre Almsengen 15.34, SP: Stian Andersen 18.77, DT: Gaute Myklebust 57.51, HT: Eivind Henriksen 71.83, JT: Størk Avelsgård Lien 72.67, Dec: Martin Roe 7384, 5000mW: ErikTysse 19:08.89, 10kW/20kW: Trond Nymark 42:09/1:28:59, 50kW: Håvard Haukenes 3:56:38.
Women: 100m: Ezinne Okparaebo 11.70,

200m/400m: Line Kloster 24.22/53.71, 800m: Martine Eikemo Borge 2:11.64, 1500m: Frida Berge 4:25.39, 5000m: Karoline Bjerkeli Grøvdal 15:36.18, 10,000m: Tone Hjalmarsen 33:09.25, HMar: Anne Jorunn Hodne 1:20:11, Mar: Marthe Katrine Myhre 2:44:43, 3000mSt: Veronika Brennhovd Blom 10:45.77, 100mh: Tale Ørving 14.36, 400mh: Vilde Svortevik 61.62, HJ: Tonje Angelsen 1.90, PV: Cathrine Larsåsen 4.05, LJ: Isabelle Pedersen 6.00, TJ: Inger Anne Frøysedal 13.71, SP: Kristin Sundsteigen 14.46, DT: Grete Etholm 54.01, HT: Mona Holm 62.34, JT: Tove Beate Dahle 50.18, Hep: Silje Laupstad 3726, 3000mW/10kW: Merete Helgheim 14:00.09/50:29.

Henrik INGEBRIGTSEN b. 24 Feb 1991 Stavanger 1.80m 69kg. Sandnes IL
At 1500m: OG: '12- 5; ECh: '10- h, '12- 1; WJ: '10- h; EU23: '11- h; EJ: '09- h; won NOR 1500m 2010, 2012. Eur U23 CC: '12- 1.
Norwegian records at 1500m & 1M 2012.
Progress at 1500m: 2004- 4:30.63, 2005- 4:22.48, 2006- 4:04.15, 2007- 3:54.08, 2008- 3:50.63, 2009- 3:44.53, 2010- 3:38.61, 2011- 3:39.50, 2012- 3:35.43. pbs: 800m 1:48.60 '12, 1M 3:54.28 '12, 3000m 7:58.15 '10, 2000mSt 5:41.03 '09, 3000mSt 8:52.56 '09.
Younger brother Filip was 10th at 1500m in the 2012 World Juniors.

Jaysuma SAIDY NDURE b. 1 Jan 1984 Bakau, The Gambia 1.92m 72kg. IL i BUL, Oslo.
At (100m)/200m: OG: '04- qf/qf, '08- qf/sf, '12- h/sf; WCh: '03- h, '05- sf, '09- (sf), '11- sf/4; EC: '10- 6/5, '12- (3); CG: '02- qf, '06- sf; WJ: '02- h; AfG: '03- h/sf; AfCh: '04- 3/6; CCp: '10- dnf. At 60m: EI: '13- 4. Won WAF 200m 2007, Norwegian 100m 2007-08, 2011; 200m 2007, 2010, 2012.
Records: Gambian 100m & 200m 2001-06, Norwegian 100m (6) 2007-11, 200m 2007.
Progress at 100m, 200m: 2001- 10.66, 21.27; 2002- 10.73/10.59w, 21.20; 2003- 10.52/10.51w, 21.18; 2004- 10.26, 20.69; 2005- 10.31/10.18w, 20.51/20.14w, 2006- 10.27, 20.47; 2007- 10.06, 19.89; 2008- 10.01, 20.45; 2009- 10.10/10.07w, 20.55; 2010- 10.00/9.98w, 20.29; 2011- 9.99, 19.95; 2012- 10.13, 20.34. pbs: 60m 6.55i '08, 300m 33.76 '09, 400m 48.71 '09.
Having lived in Oslo from 2001, became a Norwegian citizen in November 2006.

Andreas THORKILDSEN b. 1 Apr 1982 Kristiansand 1.88m 90kg. Kristiansands IF.
At JT: OG: '04- 1, '08- 1, '12- 6; WCh: '01-03-05-07-09-11: dnq 26/11/2/2/1/2; EC: '02-06-10-12: dnq 15/1/1/4; WJ: '00- 2; EU23: '03- 4; EJ: '99- 7, '01- 2; EY: '97- 1; CCp: '10- 1; ET: '10- 1. Won DL 2010, WAF 2006, 2009; NOR 2001-06, 2009-11.
World junior javelin record 2001, seven Norwegian records 2005-06.
Progress at JT: 1996- 53.82, 1998- 61.57, 1999- 72.11, 2000- 77.48, 2001- 83.87, 2002- 83.43, 2003- 85.72, 2004- 86.50, 2005- 89.60, 2006- 91.59, 2007-

89.51, 2008- 90.57, 2009- 91.28, 2010- 90.37, 2011-
90.61, 2012- 84.72. pbs: SP 9.96 '01, DT 38.02 '01.
His mother Bente Amundsen was a Norwegian
champion at 100mh (pb 14.6), father Tomm was
a junior international with bests of 100m 10.9
and javelin 71.64.

Women

Tonje ANGELSEN b. 17 Jan 1990 Trondheim
1.79m 62kg. Trondheim Friidrett.
At HJ: OG: '12- dnq 28; WCh: '11- dnq 23; EC:
'10- dnq 20, '12- 2; WJ: '06-08: dnq 22/28; EJ: '09-
dnq 17; EU23: '11- 4. NOR champion 2011-12.
Progress at HJ: 2005- 1.75, 2006- 1.82, 2007- 1.76,
2008- 1.80, 2009- 1.84, 2010- 1.89, 2011- 1.92, 2012-
1.97. pbs: 100mh 15.55 '06, LJ 5.87 '06, JT 42.90
'06, Hep 5074 '06.

PANAMA

Governing body: Federación Panameña de
Atletismo, Apartado 0860-00684, Villa Lucre,
Ciudad de Panamá. Founded 1945.

Irving SALADINO b. 23 Jan 1983 Ciudad de
Colón 1.83m 70kg. Studied electrical engineering at University of São Paulo.
At LJ: OG: '04- dnq 36, '08- 1, '12- dnq; WCh:
'05-07-09-11: 6/1/nj/dnq 22; WJ: '02- dnq; PAm:
'07- 1; CAG: '06- 1; SACh: '03- 3; WI: '06- 2; WCp:
'06- 1; won WAF & IbAm 2006, AmG 2013, SAm
U23 2004.
Three South American LJ records 2006-08,
indoors (7) 2006-08, 12 Panama 2002-08.
Progress at LJ: 2001- 7.11, 2002- 7.51A/7.39, 2003-
7.46, 2004- 8.12A/7.79, 2005- 8.29/8.51w, 2006-
8.56/8.65w, 2007- 8.57, 2008- 8.73, 2009- 8.63,
2010- 8.30/8.46w, 2011- 8.40, 2012- 8.16. pbs:
100m 10.4 '04, TJ 14.47 '04.
Set South American indoor record in qualifying and four more in final of WI 2006 for the
first medal ever for Panama at World
Championships. Clear world number one in
2006, winning 15/16 outdoors and in 2007
when he won all nine competitions, 21 successive wins to June 2008.

POLAND

Governing body: Polski Zwiazek Lekkiej
Atletyki (PZLA), ul. Myslowicka 4, 01-612
Warszawa. Founded 1919.
National Championships first held in 1920
(men), 1922 (women). **2012 Champions: Men**:
100m: Dariusz Kuc 10.20, 200m: Kamil Krynski
20.57, 400m: Piotr Wiaderek 45.46, 800m: Adam
Kszczot 1:46.53, 1500m: Bartosz Nowicki
3:38.93, 5000m: Radoslaw Kleczek 14:23.36,
10,000m: Lukasz Parszczynski 28:54.33, HMar:
Arkadiusz Gardzielewski 64:04, Mar: Yared
Shegumo 2:15:19, 3000mSt: Lukasz Parszczynski
8:26.55, 110mh: Artur Noga 13.38, 400mh:
Marek Plawgo 49.96, HJ: Szymon Kiecana 2.28,
PV: Lukasz Michalski 5.60, LJ: Tomasz Jaszczuk

8.05, TJ: Karol Hoffmann 16.98, SP: Tomasz
Majewski 21.07, DT: Piotr Malachowski 66.89,
HT: Pawel Fajdek 80.32, JT: Igor Janik 81.31, Dec:
Pawel Wiesiolek 7342, 20kW: Grzegorz Sudol
1:24:27, 50kW: Lukasz Nowak 3:44:24. **Women**:
100m: Daria Korczynska 11.39, 200m: Marika
Popowicz 23.18, 400m: Agata Bednarek 52.41,
800m: Angelika Cichocka 2:01.71, 1500m:
Renata Plis 4:06.96, 5000m/10,000m: Wioletta
Frankiewicz 15:50.70/34:06.38, HMar: Alek-
sandra Jawor 74:36, Mar: Agnieszka Ciolek
2:34:15, 3000mSt: Katarzyna Kowalska 9:49.34,
100mh: Urszula Bhebhe 13.34, 400mh: Anna
Jesien 55.74, HJ: Izabela Mikolajczyk 1.89, PV:
Monika Pyrek 4.45, LJ: Teresa Dobija 6.65, TJ:
Malgorzata Trybanska 13.88 SP: Paulina Guba
17.47, DT: Joanna Wisniewska 61.92, HT: Anna
Wlodarczyk 74.71, JT: Magdalena Czenska
57.22, Hep: Izabela Mikolajczyk 5968, 20kW:
Paulina Buziak 1:36:10.

Pawel FAJDEK b. 4 Jun 1989 Swiebodzice
1.86m 120kg. KS Agros Zamosc.
At HT: OG: '12- dnq; WCh: '11- 11; WJ: '08- 4;
EU23: '09- 8, '11- 1; WUG: '11- 1; ET: '11- 2. Polish
champion 2012
Progress at HT: 2008- 64.58, 2009- 72.36, 2010-
76.07, 2011- 78.54, 2012- 81.39.

Igor JANIK b. 18 Jan 1983 Gdynia 2.00m 108kg.
AZS AWFIS Gdansk. PE student.
At JT: OG: 08/12- dnq 16/19; WCh: '07- 7, '09/11-
dnq 31/13; WJ: '02- 1; EC: '12- 6; EU23: '03- 2,
'05- 1; EJ: '01- 6; WUG: '03-05-07-09-11:
1/5/2/4/3; ECp: '06-07-08-09: 3/3/3/3. Polish
champion 2007-08, 2010, 2012.
Progress at JT: 2001- 72.08, 2002- 78.90, 2003-
82.54, 2004- 74.49, 2005- 77.25, 2006- 82.86, 2007-
83.38, 2008- 84.76, 2009- 83.52, 2010- 80.83, 2011-
82.81, 2012- 82.37.

Adam KSZCZOT b. 2 Sep 1989 Opoczno 1.78m
68kg. RKS Lódz. Studied organisation and
management.
At 800m: OG: '12- sf; WCh: '09- sf, '11- 6; EC:
'10- 3; WJ: '08- 4; EU23: '09/11- 1; EJ: '07- 3; WI:
'10- 3, '11- 4; EI: '09-11-13: 4/1/1; ET: '11- 1. Polish
champion 2009-10, 2012.
Polish 1000m record 2011.
Progress at 800m: 2005- 1:59.57, 2006- 1:51.09,
2007- 1:48.10, 2008- 1:47.16, 2009- 1:45.72, 2010-
1:45.07, 2011- 1:43.30, 2012- 1:43.83. pbs: 400m
46.51 '11, 600m 1:14.55 '10, 1000m 2:16.99 '11,
1500m 3:46.53 '10.

Marcin LEWANDOWSKI b. 13 Jun 1987
Szczecin 1.79m 64kg. SL WKS Zawisza
Bydgoszcz. PE student.
At 800m: OG: '08/12- sf; WCh: '09- 8, '11- 4; EC:
'10- 1; WJ: '06- 4; EU23: '07- 1, '09- 2; EI: '09- 6,
'11- 2; CCp: '10- 2; ECp: '08- 2, '10- 3; won World
Military 2011. At 1500m: EJ: '05- 7; EI: '13- 4.
Won Polish 800m 2011, 1500m 2008, 2010.
Polish 1000m record 2011.

Progress at 800m: 2004- 1:51.73, 2005- 1:48.86, 2006- 1:46.69, 2007- 1:45.52, 2008- 1:45.84, 2009- 1:43.84, 2010- 1:44.10, 2011- 1:44.53, 2012- 1:44.34. pbs: 400m 47.76 '09, 600m 1:15.77 '10, 1000m 2:15.76 '11, 1500m 3:37.76i '12, 3:40.38 '10. Coached by brother Tomasz (1:51.00 '03).

Tomasz MAJEWSKI b. 30 Aug 1981 Nasielsk 2.04m 142kg. AZS-AWF Warszawa. Graduated in politics from Cardinal Wyszynski University. At SP: OG: '04- dnq 18, '08- 1, '12- 1; WCh: '05-07-09-11: 9/5/2/9; EC: '06- 8, '10- 2; EU23: '03- 4; WI: '04-06-08-10-12: 4/7/3/5/3; EI: '09- 1; WUG: '03- 5, '05- 1; CCp: '10- 2; ECp: '07-08-09-10-11: 3/2/1/1/2. Won WAF 2008, Polish 2002-05, 2007-12.
Polish shot record 2009.
Progress at SP: 1998- 12.91, 1999- 15.77, 2000- 17.77, 2001- 18.34, 2002- 19.33, 2003- 20.09, 2004- 20.83i/20.52, 2005- 20.64, 2006- 20.66, 2007- 20.87, 2008- 21.51, 2009- 21.95, 2010- 21.44, 2011- 21.60, 2012- 21.89. pb DT 51.79 '07.
Improved pb every year of his career to 2009. Went from 20.97 to 21.04 in qualifying and 21.21 and 21.51 in final to win Olympic gold in 2008.

Piotr MALACHOWSKI b. 7 Jun 1983 Zuromin 1.93m 130kg. Slask Wroclaw. Army corporal. At DT: OG: '08- 2, '12- 5; WCh: '07- 12, '09- 2, '11- 9; EC: '06- 6, '10- 1; WJ: '02- 6; EU23: '03- 9, '05- 2; EJ: '01- 5; CCp: '10- 4; ECp: '06-07-08-09-10-11: 1/1/3/1/2/3. Won DL 2010, POL 2005-10, 2012.
Eight Polish discus records 2006-10.
Progress at DT: 2000- 52.04, 2001- 54.19, 2002- 56.84, 2003- 57.83, 2004- 62.04, 2005- 64.74, 2006- 66.21, 2007- 66.61, 2008- 68.65, 2009- 69.15, 2010- 69.83, 2011- 68.49, 2012- 68.94.

Lukasz MICHALSKI b. 2 Aug 1988 Bydgoszcz 1.90m 85kg. SL WKS Zawisza Bydgoszcz. Studied medicine.
At PV: OG: '12- 11; WCh: '09- dnq 22=, '11- 4; EC: '10- 7; WJ: '06- 8; WY: '05- 4; EU23: '09- 5; EJ: '07- 3; WUG: '11- 1; WI: '10- 9; EI: '09- 6; ET: '09- 3; Polish champion 2010, 2011 (tie), 2012.
Progress at PV: 2004- 4.80, 2005- 5.25, 2006- 5.30, 2007- 5.50, 2008- 5.51, 2009- 5.71, 2010- 5.80, 2011- 5.85, 2012- 5.72. pb LJ 6.95 '08.

Lukasz NOWAK b. 18 Dec 1988 Poznan 1.94m 77kg. AZS Poznan.
At 50kW: OG: '12- 9; EC: '10- 8. At 20kW: EU23: '09- 13. Won POL 50kW 2012.
Progress at 50kW: 2009- 3:58:57, 2010- 3:50:30, 2011- 3:46:40, 2012- 3:42:47. pbs: 3000mW 11:41.30 '11; 5000mW 19:24.57 '11; 10kW 41:01 '11; 20kW 1:21:12 '12; 30kW 2:13:51 '12; 35kW 2:35:55 '12.

Grzegorz SUDOL b. 28 Aug 1978 Nowa Deba 1.75m 64kg. AZS-AWF Kraków. PE graduate.
At 50kW: OG: '04- 7, '08- 9; WCh: '03-05-07-09-11: dq/dq/21/4/dnf; EC: '02- 10, '06- 10, '10- 2. At 20kW: OG: '12- 24. At 10,000mW: WJ: '96- 7, EJ: '97- 10. Won POL 20kW 2008-09, 2012; 50kW

2002, 2007-08.
Unratified Polish 30,000m record 2011.
Progress at 50kW: 2002- 3:50:37, 2003- 3:55:40, 2004- 3:49:09, 2006- 3:50:24, 2007- 3:55:22, 2008- 3:45:47, 2009- 3:42:34, 2010- 3:42:24, 2012- 3:46:01. pbs: 3000mW 11:21.90 '12, 5000mW 18:55.01i '05, 19:06.07 '12; 10kW 39:01 '05, 20kW 1:20:50 '10, 30kW 2:11:12.0t '11, 35kW 2:35:34 '10.
Three times Polish 50k champion – each event held in different countries (CZE, AUT, SVK).

Pawel WOJCIECHOWSKI b. 6 Jun 1989 Bydgoszcz 1.90m 85kg. SL WKS Zawisza Bydgoszcz. PE student.
At PV: OG: '12- dnq; WCh: '11- 1; WJ: '08- 2; EU23: '11- 1; EJ: '07- dnq 16; EI: '11- 4. Won W. Military 2011.
Polish pole vault record 2011.
Progress at PV: 2001- 2.50, 2002- 2.70, 2003- 3.10, 2004- 3.50, 2005- 4.10, 2006- 4.70, 2007- 5.00, 2008- 5.51, 2009- 5.40i/5.22, 2010- 5.60, 2011- 5.91, 2012- 5.62.

Szymon ZIÓLKOWSKI b. 1 Jul 1976 Poznan 1.92m 120kg. OS AZS Poznan.
At HT: OG: '96-00-04-08-12: 10/1/dnq 13/7/7; WCh: '95-99-01-05-07-09-11: dnq 22/dnq 23/1/3/7/2/7; EC: '98-02-06-10-12: 5/dnq 15/5/5/3; WJ: '94- 1; EJ: '93- 7, '95- 1; EU23: '97- 2; ECp: '96-99-01-04-05-06-07-08-09: 2/2/1/1/1/1/1/1/2. Polish champion 1996-7, 1999-2002, 2004-09, 2011.
Six Polish hammer records 2000-01.
Progress at HT: 1991- 55.96, 1992- 63.84, 1993- 67.34, 1994- 72.48, 1995- 75.42, 1996- 79.52, 1997- 79.14, 1998- 79.58, 1999- 79.01, 2000- 81.42, 2001- 83.38, 2002- 79.78, 2003- 76.97, 2004- 79.41, 2005- 79.35, 2006- 82.31, 2007- 80.70, 2008- 79.55, 2009- 79.30, 2010- 77.99, 2011- 79.02, 2012- 78.51. pbs: SP 15.25 '95, DT 49.58 '00.
His sister Michalina (b. 1983) was second in the 2000 Polish U18 Championships, pb 58.33 '04. Married javelin thrower (50.90 '98 (old), 50.64 '99) Joanna Domagala in December 2000 and after divorce Iwona Dorobisz (100m 11.47 '09) in 2008.

Women

Joanna FIODOROW b. 4 Mar 1989 Augustów 1.69m 89kg. AZS Poznań.
At HT: OG: '12- 10; WCh: '11- dnq 21; WJ: '08- dnq 19; EU23: '09- 4, '11- 2.
Progress at HT: 2005- 40.96, 2006- 50.18, 2007- 55.93, 2008- 61.22, 2009- 62.80, 2010- 64.66, 2011- 70.06, 2012- 74.18. pbs: SP 12.87 '10, JT 35.56 '09.

Zaneta GLANC b. 11 Mar 1983 Poznan 1.86m 95kg. OS AZS Poznan. Studied sociology.
At DT: OG: '08/12- dnq nt/24; WCh: '09- 4, '11- 4; EC: '10- dnq 13; EJ: '05- dnq; WUG: '09- 2, '11- 1; ET: '11- 3. Won POL 2009.
Progress at DT: 2003- 47.03, 2004- 51.30, 2005- 56.15, 2006- 56.00, 2007- 59.36, 2008- 61.42, 2009- 63.96, 2010- 62.16, 2011- 63.99, 2012- 65.34.

Anna ROGOWSKA b. 21 May 1981 Gdynia 1.71m 57kg. SKLA Sopot. PE student.
At PV: OG: '04- 3, '08- 10=, '12- nh; WCh: '03-05-07-09-11: 7/6=/8/1/10=; EC: '02- 7=; EU23: '03- 3; WI: '03-04-06-08-10: 6=/7/2/6/3; EI: '05-07-11-13: 2/3/1/1; ECp: '05-08-10-11: 1/2/3/1. Polish champion 2009, 2011.
Nine Polish pole vault records 2004-05, indoors (2) 2010-11.
Progress at PV: 1997- 2.60, 1998- 2.90, 1999- 3.40, 2000- 3.60, 2001- 3.90, 2002- 4.40, 2003- 4.47i/4.45, 2004- 4.71, 2005- 4.83, 2006- 4.80i/4.70, 2007- 4.72i/4.60, 2008- 4.66, 2009- 4.80, 2010- 4.81i/4.71, 2011- 4.85i/4.75, 2012- 4.71i/4.70, 2013- 4.67i.
Coached by husband Jacek Torlinski, PV 4.85 '97.

Karolina TYMINSKA b. 4 Oct 1984 Swiebodzin 1.75m 69kg. SKLA Sopot.
At Hep: OG: '08- 7, '12- dnf; WCh: '07- 15, '09- dnf, '11- 4; EC: '06- dnf (dnq LJ), '10- 5; EU23: '05- dnf (LJ dnq 17); ECp: '06-'09: 2/3. At Pen: WI: '08-10-12: 6/6/4; EI: '05-07-09-11: 8/7/5/4. Won POL 100mh 2011, Hep 2006-07, 2011.
Progress at Hep: 2002- 5147, 2004- 5787, 2005- 6026, 2006- 6402, 2007- 6200, 2008- 6428, 2009- 6191, 2010- 6230, 2011- 6544, 2012- dnf. pbs: 60m 7.61i '09, 100m 12.15 '05, 200m 23.32 '06, 800m 2:05.21 '11, 60mh 8.34i '10, 100mh 13.12 '11, HJ 1.78 '11, LJ 6.63 '08, SP 15.11i/14.82 '08, JT 41.32 '11, Pen 4769i '08.

Anita WLODARCZYK b. 8 Aug 1985 Rawicz 1.78m 95kg. RKS Skra Warszawa. PE student.
At HT: OG: '08- 6, '12- 2; WCh: '09- 1, '11- 5; EC: '10- 3, '12- 1; EU23: '07- 9; ET: '09- 1. Polish champion 2009, 2011-12.
Two world hammer records, three Polish records 2009-10.
Progress at HT: 2003- 43.24, 2004- 54.74, 2005- 60.51, 2006- 65.53, 2007- 69.07, 2008- 72.80, 2009- 77.96, 2010- 78.30, 2011- 75.33, 2012- 77.60. pbs: SP 13.25 '06, DT 52.26 '08.

PORTUGAL

Governing body: Federação Portuguesa de Atletismo, Largo da Lagoa, 1799-538 Linda-a-Velha. Founded in 1921.
National Championships first held in 1910 (men), 1937 (women). **2012 Champions: Men**: 100m: Carlos Nascimento 10.19w, 200m: David Lima 20.82w, 400m: André Marques 48.18, 800m/1500m: Miguel Moreira 1:50.92/3:55.41, 5000m: Bruno Albuquerque 14:14.62, 10,000m: José Rocha 28:37.95, Mar: Bruno Fraga 2:19:02, 3000mSt: Alberto Paulo 8:38.39, 110mh: João Almeida 13.47, 400mh: Jorge Paula 50.43, HJ: Roman Gully 2.08, PV: Edi Maia 5.28, LJ: Marcos Chuva 7.88w, TJ: Marcos Caldeira 15.87w, SP: Marco Fortes 19.62, DT: Jorge Grave 57.56, HT: Dário Manso 69.81, JT: Tiago Aperta 73.09, Dec: Tiago Marto 7272, 10,000mW/50kW: João Vieira 41:40.73/3:45:17, 20kW: Sérgio Vieira 1:25:24.

Women: 100m: Eva Vital 11.82w, 200m: Tânia Duarte 24.39w, 400m: Carolina Duarte 54.55, 800m: Micaela Lopes 2:11.07, 1500m: Sara Moreira 4:13.01, 5000m: Ana Ferreira 16:07.09, 10,000m: Ana Dias 32:13.62, Mar: Anabela Tavares 2:45:44, 3000mSt: Clarisse Cruz 10:29.47, 100mh: Andreia Felisberto 13.40w, 400mh: Vera Barbosa 56.76, HJ: Liliana Viana 1.82, PV: Maria Eleonor Tavares 4.30, LJ: Marta Godinho Costa 6.09w, TJ: Patricia Mamona 14.42w, SP/DT: Irina Rodrigues 14.00/57.06, HT: Vânia Silva 61.59, JT: Sílvia Cruz 50.60, Hep: Cláudia Rodrigues 4987w, 10,000mW/20kW: Ana Cabecinha 43:37.91/1:29:53.

Nelson ÉVORA b. 20 Apr 1984 Abidjan, Côte d'Ivoire 1.81m 64kg. Sport Lisboa e Benfica.
At (LJ/)TJ: OG: '04- dnq 40, '08- 1; WCh: '05-07-09-11: dnq 14/1/2/5; EC: '06- 6/4; WJ: '02- dnq 18/6; EU23: '05- 3; EJ: '03- 1/1; WUG: '09- 1, '11- 1; WI: '06- 6, '08- 3; EI: '07- 5; ECp: '09- 2/1; Won WAF TJ 2008, POR LJ 2006-07, TJ 2003-04, 2006-07, 2009-11.
Six Portuguese triple jump records 2006-07, Cape Verde LJ & TJ records 2001-02.
Progress at TJ: 1999- 14.35, 2000- 14.93i, 2001- 16.15, 2002- 15.87, 2003- 16.43, 2004- 16.85i/16.04, 2005- 16.89, 2006- 17.23, 2007- 17.74, 2008- 17.67, 2009- 17.66/17.82w, 2010- 16.36, 2011- 17.35. pbs: HJ 2.07i '05, 1.98 '99; LJ 8.10 '07.
Portugal's first male world champion in 2007. He suffered a serious injury in right tibia (in same place where he had an operation in February 2010) in January 2012 and missed season. Father from Cape Verde, mother from Côte d'Ivoire, relocating to Portugal when he was five. He switched nationality in 2002. Sister Dorothé (b. 28 May 1991) 400m pb 55.19 '12.

Marco FORTES b. 26 Sep 1982 Lisboa 1.89m 139kg. Sport Lisboa e Benfica.
At SP: OG: '08/12: dnq 38/15; WCh: '09- dnq 18, '11- 6; EC: '10- dnq 13, '12-5; WJ: '00- dnq 18 (dnq DT); EU23: '03- 12; EJ: '01- 3; EI: '11- 8, '13- 5; Won IbAm 2010, POR SP 2002-12 (& 10 indoor), DT 2009, 2011
Five Portuguese shot records 2008-12.
Progress at SP: 2000- 17.31, 2001- 18.02, 2002- 18.76, 2003- 18.57, 2004- 18.19, 2005- 17.89, 2006- 18.74, 2007- 19.18, 2008- 20.13, 2009- 20.52, 2010- 20.69, 2011- 20.89, 2012- 21.02. pb DT 58.32 '09.

Women

Jéssica AUGUSTO b. 8 Nov 1981 Paris, France 1.65m 46kg. Nike.
At Mar: OG: '12- 7. At 3000mSt: OG: '08- h (h 5000); WCh: '09- 11. At 5000m/(10,000m): WCh: '05- h, '07- 15, '11- (10); EC: '10- 3/2; EU23: '03- dnf; WUG: '07- 1; CCp: '10- 7. At 3000m (1500m): WJ: '00- 8; EU23: '01- (10); EJ: '99- 6 (12); WI: '08- 8, '10- 7; EI: '09- 10. World CC: '07- 12, '10- 21; Eur

CC: '98-99-00-02-04-05-06-07-08-09-10: 12J/8J/ 1J/16/18/30/9/11/2/4/1. Won POR 1500m 2007, 2011; 5000m 2006, IbAm 3000m 2004, 2006, 2010. Two Portuguese 3000m steeplechase records 2008-10, European indoor 2M best 2010.
Progress at 5000m, 10,000m, Mar, 3000mSt: 2003- 15:51.63, 2004- 15:15.76, 2005- 15:20.45, 2006- 15:37.55, 2007- 14:56.39, 2008- 15:19.67, 9:22.50; 2009- 9:25.25, 2010- 14:37.07, 31:19.15, 9:18.54; 2011- 15:19.60, 32:06.68, 2:24:33; 2012- 2:24:59. pbs: 800m 2:07.97i '02, 1500m 4:07.89i/4:08.32 '10, 1M 4:32.58i '09, 4:42.15 '99, 2000m 5:45.6i '09, 3000m 8:41.53 '07, 2M 9:19.39i '10, 9:22.89 '07; road 15km 48:40 '08, 10M 53:15 '08, HMar 69:08 '09. Won Great North Run 2009.

Ana CABECINHA b. 29 Apr 1984 Beja 1.68m 52kg. CO Pechão.
At 20kW: OG: '08- 8, '12- 9; WCh: '11- 7; EC: '10- 8; EU23: '05- 4; WCp '08-10-12: 11/8/9. At 5000mW: WY: '01- 10. At 10,000mW: WJ: '02- 12; EJ: '03- 3; won IbAm 2006, 2010; 2nd RWC 2012; POR 10,000mW 2005, 2008, 2010, 2012, 20kW 2012-13. POR records 10,000m and 20km walk 2008.
Progress at 20kW: 2004- 1:37:39, 2005- 1:34:13, 2006- 1:31:02, 2007- 1:32:46, 2008- 1:27:46, 2009- 1:33:05, 2010- 1:31:14, 2011- 1:31:08, 2012- 1:28:03. pbs: 3000mW 12:21.56i '13, 12:31.86 '12; 5000mW 21:46.34 '11, 21:21R '12; 10,000mW 43:08.17 '08; running 1500m 4:31.73 '07. 5000m 17:57.34 '12.

Naide GOMES b. 20 Nov 1979 São Tomé, São Tomé e Principe 1.81m 70kg. Sporting Clube de Portugal.
At LJ/(Hep): OG: '04- (13), '08- dnq 31; WCh: '05- dnq 17/7, '07- 4, '09- 4, '11- 10; EC: '02- 10/18, '06- 2, '10- 2; AfrG: '99- (5); WUG: '05- 2; WI: '06-08-10: 3/1/2; EI: '05-07-11: 1/1/2; WCp: '06- 2, '10- 5; ECp: '09- 1. At Pen: WI: '03- 5, '04- 1; EI: '02- 2. At 100mh: OG: '00- h. Won WAF LJ 2008, POR Hep 2001, 100mh 2004-05, HJ 2002, LJ 2002, 2004, 2006-11.
Portuguese records LJ (9) 2002-08 Heptathlon (3) 2002-05, indoor HJ & Pen 2004, LJ 2005-08.
Progress at LJ, Hep: 1996- 5.60, 1997- 5.63, 4578; 1998- 5.80, 1999- 5.81, 4964; 2000- 6.15, 5671; 2001- 6.36, 5606w; 2002- 6.57, 6160; 2003- 6.53, 6120; 2004- 6.51, 6151; 2005- 6.72, 6230; 2006- 6.82/6.84w, 2007- 7.01, 2008- 7.12, 2009- 6.99, 2010- 6.92, 2011- 6.79i/6.76/6.78w, 2012- 6.43. pbs: 60m 7.84i '04, 200m 24.87 '05, 400m 57.91i '05, 800m 2:16.31 '05, 60mh 8.39i '05, 100mh 13.50 '05, HJ 1.88i '04, 1.86 '02; TJ 11.73 '99, SP 15.08i/14.71 '04, JT 42.86 '00, Pen 4759i '04.
Changed nationality from São Tome e Principe (for whom she set 30 national records – at 100mh, HJ, LJ, TJ. SP, JT & Hep) to Portugal in 2001. Set pbs at HJ (Portuguese record) and SP en route to WI gold in 2004. Full name is Enezenaide do Rosario da Vera Cruz Gomes.

Inês HENRIQUES b 1 May 1980 Santarém

1.56m 48kg. CN Rio Maior.
At 20kW: OG: '04- 25, '12- 15; WCh: '01-05-07-09-11: dq/27/7/11/10; EC: '02-06-10: 15/12/9; EU23: '01- 10; WCp: '06-10-12: 13/3/10; ECp: '07- 7; Won POR 10,000mW 2006, 2009, 2011; 20kmW 2009, 2011. At 5000mW: EJ: '99- 12.
Progress at 20kW: 2000- 1:41:09, 2001- 1:34:49, 2002- 1:34:46.5t, 2003- 1:36:03, 2004- 1:31:23.7t, 2005- 1:33:24, 2006- 1:30:28, 2007- 1:30:24, 2008- 1:31:06, 2009- 1:30:34, 2010- 1:29:36, 2011- 1:30:29, 2012- 1:29:54. pbs: 3000mW 12:28.70i '11, 12:38.75 '07; 5000mW 21:38.05 '10, 10,000mW 43:22.05 '08, 43:09R '10.

Sara MOREIRA b. 17 Oct 1985 Santo Tirso 1.68m 51kg. Maratona.
At (5000m)/3000mSt: WCh: '07- 13, '09- 10/h, '11- dq; EC: '10- (2), '12- (3); EU23: '07- 3; WUG: '07- 4, '09- 1/1, '11- (2); ET: '11- 2. At 3000m: WI: '10- 5; EI: '09- 2, '13- 1; CCp: '10- 6. At 1500m: EI: '11- 7. At 10,000m: OG: '12- 14; ECp: '10-11-12: 3/1/1. Eur CC: '09-10-12: 10/9/12. Won POR 1500m 2010, 2012; 3000mSt 2007-09, 2011. POR 3000mSt record 2008.
Progress at 5000m, 10,000m, 3000mSt: 2005- 10:27.72, 2007- 9:42.47, 2008- 9:34.30; 2009- 14:58.11, 9:28.64; 2010- 14:54.71, 31:26.55; 2011- 15:11.97, 31:39.11, 9:35.11; 2012- 15:08.33, 31:16.44. pbs: 1500m 4:07.11 '10, 3000m 8:42.69 '10, 2M 9:47.99i '10, 15kmRd 48:48 '13, HMar 70:08 '10.
Married to Pedro Ribeiro, 3000mSt 8:32.20 '06, POR champion 2010.

Vera SANTOS b. 3 Dec 1981 Santarém 1.64m 57kg. Sporting Clube de Portugal.
At 20kW: OG: '08- 9, '12- 49; WCh: '03-05-07-09: 15/15/11/5; EC: '02- 17, '06- 8, '10- 6; EU23: '01- 12, '03- 2; WUG: '05- 2; WCp '08- 3, '10- 2; ECp: '05- 7. At 10,000mW: WJ: '00- 5. Won POR 20kW 2005, 2010.
Progress at 20kW: 2000- 1:39:20.5t, 2001- 1:35:51, 2002- 1:34:46.6t, 2003- 1:32:43, 2004- 1:33:00, 2005- 1:31:30, 2006- 1:30:41, 2007- 1:32:53, 2008- 1:28:14, 2009- 1:29:27, 2010- 1:28:29, 2011- 1:29:55, 2012- 1:32:48. pbs: 3000mW 12:17.59 '10, 5000mW 21:01.43 '10, 10,000mW 43:52.73 '10.

PUERTO RICO

Governing body: Federación de Atletismo Amateur de Puerto Rico, 90, Ave. Río Hondo, Bayamón, PR 00961-3113. Founded 1947.
National Champions 2012: Men: 100m: Hector de Leon 10.62 200m: Miguel Lopez 21.26, 400m: Juan Vega 47.44, 800m: Eric Estrada 1:53.22, 1500m: Edgardo Martínez 4:02.05, 3000mSt: Miguel Cartagena 9:14.16, 110mh: Héctor Cotto 14.06, 400mh: Ramfis Vega 51.75, HJ: Luis Joel Castro 2.02, PV: Alexander Castillo 5.05, LJ: Michael Williams 7.48, TJ: Juriel Rivera 14.45, SP: Orestes Ortiz 15.29, DT: Alfredo Romero 52.70, HT: Christian Vargas 59.95, JT: Kenny Mendez 63.74. **Women**: 100m: Ginoska Cancel 11.76, 200m: Beatriz Cruz 24.19, 400m: Grace

Claxton 55.68, 800m: Marangeli Lugo 2:15.16, 1500m: Angelin Figueroa 4:41.51, 100mh: Litzy Vázquez 13.86, 400mh: Klerian Etanislao 62.07, PV: Alexandra Gonzalez 4.00, LJ: Nelsi Bernardi 5.88, TJ: Maria Reyes 11.51, SP: Sormarie Colon 14.13, DT: Ashley Arroyo Pérez 50.43, HT: Taiara Negron 47.96, JT: Coralys Ortiz 52.87.

Javier CULSON b. 25 Jul 1984 Ponce 1.98m 79kg.
At 400mh: OG: '08- sf, '12- 1; WCh: '07- sf, '09- 2, '11- 2; PAm: '07- 6; CAG: '06- 5, '10- 2; PAm-J: '03- 3; WUG: '07- 3; CCp: '10- 2; won DL 2012, IbAm 2006, CAC 2009.
Seven Puerto Rican 400mh records 2007-10.
Progress at 400mh: 2002- 50.47, 2003- 51.10, 2004- 50.77, 2005- 50.62, 2006- 49.48, 2007- 49.07, 2008- 48.87, 2009- 48.09, 2010- 47.72. 2011- 48.32, 2012- 47.78. pbs: 200m 21.64w '07, 400m 45.99 '12, 800m 1:49.97 '11, 110mh 13.84 '07.

QATAR

Governing body: Qatar Association of Athletics Federation, PO Box 8139, Doha. Founded 1963.

Mutaz Essa BARSHIM Ahmed b. 24 Jun 1991 Doha 1.92m 70kg. Team Aspire.
At HJ: OG: '12- 3=' WCh: '11- 7; WJ: '10- 1; AsiG: '10- 1; AsiC: '11- 1; WI: '12- 9=; won Asian indoors 2012; Asi-J 2010, W.Mil G & Pan-Arab 2011.
Tied Asian high jump record 2012 and indoors 2013, 13 Qatar records 2010-12.
Progress at HJ: 2008- 2.07, 2009- 2.14, 2010- 2.31, 2011- 2.35, 2012- 2.39, 2013- 2.37i.
Qatari father, Sudanese mother. Younger brother Muamer Aissa Barshim has pb 2.20 (2012).

ROMANIA

Governing body: Federatia Romana de Atletism, 2 Primo Nebiolo Str, 011349 Bucuresti. Founded 1912.
National Championships first held in 1914 (men), 1925 (women). **2012 Champions: Men**: 2100m/200m: Marian Câmpeanu 10.48/21.21, 400m: Sorin Vatamanu 46.99, 800m: Cristian Vorovenci 1:49.19, 1500m: Raul Botezan 3:52.87, 5000m/10,000m: Nicolae Soare 14:43.21/30:23.27, HMar: Marius Ionescu 64:58, Mar: Ilie Corneschi 2:36:02, 3000mSt: Alexandru Ghinea 8:58.88, 110mh: Cornel Bananau 14.35, 400mh: Attila Nagy 51.19, HJ: Mihai Donisan 2.27, PV: Bogdan Popa 4.60, LJ: Adrian Vasile 7.77, TJ: Adrian Daianu 16.45, SP: Laurentiu Popa 18.23, DT: Sergiu Ursu 60.10, HT: Andrei Alestar 68.80, JT: Levente Bartha 69.89, Dec: Ionut Feniuc 6722, 20kW: Marius Cocioran 1:27:36/1:30:17, 50kW: Ciprian Deac 4:25:16. **Women**: 100m: Andreea Ograzeanu 11.29w, 200m/400mh: Angela Morosanu 23.21/56.15, 400m/800m: Elena Lavric 52.11/2:01.93, 1500m: Ioana Doaga 4:09.19, 5000m: Roxana Bârca 15:45.10, 10,000m: Mihaela Prundus 35:40.40, HMar: Cristiana Frumuz 73:39, Mar: Paula Todoran 2:48:20, 3000mSt: Ancuta Bobocel 9:31.95, 100mh: Beatrice Puiu 13.53, HJ: Georgiana Zârcan 1.85, PV: Lavinia Scurtu 3.50, LJ: Ciornelia Deiac 6.54, TJ: Cristina Bujin 14.25w, SP: Anca Heltne 17.12, DT: Nicoleta Grasu 61.79 (17th title), HT: Bianca Perie 69.14, JT: Maria Negoita 54.35, Hep: Judit Nagy 5973, 20kW: Ana Rodean 1:34:53/1:36:20.

Marian OPREA b. 6 Jun 1982 Pitesti 1.90m 80kg. Rapid Bucuresti & Dinamo Bucuresti. Sports teacher.
At TJ: OG: '04- 2, '08- 5; WCh: '01- dnq 13, '03- dnq 17, '05- 3, '11- dnq 15; EC: '02-06-10-12: dnq 14/3/2.dnq 21; WJ: '00- 1; WY: '99- 4; EU23: '03- 2; EJ: '99- 3, '01- 1; WI: '03-04-06: 8/5/4; EI: '02- 2, '11- 3; WUG: '01- 2; WCp: '06- 3, '10- 1. ROU champion 2001, 2003-08; Balkan 2001-03.
Romanian TJ records 2003 and 2005.
Progress at TJ: 1997- 14.37, 1998- 14.78, 1999- 15.98, 2000- 16.49, 2001- 17.11/17.13w, 2002- 17.29i/17.11/17.39w, 2003- 17.63, 2004- 17.55, 2005- 17.81, 2006- 17.74i/17.56, 2007- 17.32, 2008- 17.28, 2010- 17.51, 2011- 17.62i/17.19, 2012- 16.97i/16.56/16.68w. pb LJ 7.73 '05, 8.06w '11.
Silver medal in 2004 was best ever Olympic placing by a Romanian male. Major surgery on his left knee in October 2008 meant that he did not compete in 2009.

Women

Cristina-Ioana **BUJIN** b. 12 Apr 1988 Constanta 1.71m 52kg. Farul Constanta. Student
At (LJ)/TJ: WCh: '09- 7; WJ: '04- dnq/10, '06- 6; WY: '03- (5), '05- 3; EU23: '09- 2; EJ: '05- dnq/2, '07- 3; WUG: '11- 3; EI: '11- 5. ROU champion 2009, 2012.
Progress at TJ: 2004- 13.46, 2005- 13.72, 2006- 14.06i/13.68, 2007- 13.99i/13.57, 2008- 14.07i/13.94, 2009- 14.42, 2010- 13.62, 2011- 14.30, 2012- 14.14i/14.13/14.25w. pb LJ 6.38 '09.

Lenuta-Nicoleta **GRASU** b. 11 Sep 1971 Secuieni 1.76m 88kg. née Gradinaru. Administration officer. Dinamo Bucuresti.
At DT: OG: '92-96-00-04-08-12: dnq 13/7/dnq 19/6/12/dnq 14; WCh: '93-95-97-99-01-05-07-09-11: 7/dnq 18/10/3/2/5/3/3/8; EC: '94-98-06-10: 4/3/3/2; WJ: '90- 6; WUG: '97- 3, '99- 1; WCp: '98- 2, '10- 6; ECp: '97-9-00-01-02-05-06: 4/2/1/3/2/4/3; EU23Cp: '92- 1. Won Balkan 1992, 1997-9; ROU 1992-3, 1995-7, 1999-2002, 2004-06, 2008-12. 3rd GP 1996.
Progress at DT: 1985- 36.02, 1986- 43.56, 1987- 50.82, 1988- 51.06, 1989- 52.54, 1990- 56.02, 1991- 59.90, 1992- 65.66, 1993- 65.16, 1994- 64.40, 1995- 64.62, 1996- 65.26, 1997- 64.68, 1998- 67.80, 1999- 68.80, 2000- 68.70, 2001- 68.31, 2002- 64.90, 2004- 64.92, 2005- 64.89, 2006- 65.21, 2007- 65.60, 2008- 66.51, 2009- 65.20, 2010- 63.78, 2011- 62.62, 2012- 61.86. pb SP 15.00i '92, 14.56 '91.
Married her coach Costel Grasu (b. 5 Jul 1967) DT pb 67.08 '92; 4 OG 1992.

Angela MOROSANU b. 26 Jul 1986 Iasi 1.78m 57kg. Dinamo Bucuresti & Enka SC, TUR.
At (200m)/400mh: OG: '08- sf, '12- h; WCh: '09- 8; EC: '06- 8/sf, '10- 5, '12- sf; WJ: '04- 8; EU23: '07- 1; ECp: '06- 2/4. At 100m: ECp: '05- 5. At 400m: EJ: '05- 1 (3 200m); WI: '04- 3R, '08- 5; EI: '07- 4. Won ROU 100m 2005-06, 200m 2003-06, 2012; 400m 2005-07, 400mh 2009-10, 2012.
Progress at 400mh: 2004- 58.30, 2005- 59.28, 2006- 55.37, 2007- 54.40, 2008- 56.07, 2009- 53.95, 2010- 54.58, 2011- 58.05, 2012- 54.81. pbs: 60m 7.30i '05, 100m 11.47 '05, 200m 22.91 '06, 400m 51.93i '07, 52.48 '05; 60mh 8.11i '12.

Bianca-Florentina **PERIE** b. 1 Jun 1990 Roman, Neamt district 1.70m 70kg. S.C.M. Bacau. Student.
At HT: OG: '08/12- dnq 18/22; WCh: '07/09- dnq 26/19, '11- 6; EC: '10-4, '12- 11; WJ: '06/08- 1; WY: '05/07- 1; EU23: '11- 1; EJ: '07/09- 1; WUG: '11- 3; ROU champion 2009-12.
Progress at HT: 2003- 47.14, 2004- 57.67, 2005- 65.13, 2006- 67.38, 2007- 67.24, 2008- 69.59, 2009- 69.63, 2010- 73.52, 2011- 72.04, 2012- 70.05. pb SP 13.04i '07.
World age 14 best of 65.13 in 2005. Her younger sister Roxana won the bronze medal in the 2011 World Youth hammer.

Esthera PETRE b. 13 May 1990 Bucuresti 1.75m 60kg.
At HJ: OG: '12- dnq 20=; WCh: '11: dnq 14; WJ: '06- dnq 14, '08- 6; WY: '07- 5; WI: '12- 7; EU23: '11- 1; EJ: '07- 9, '09- 5. ROU champion 2009, 2011-12.
Progress at HJ: 2000- 1.80, 2001- 1.81, 2002- 1.83, 2003- 1.86, 2004- 1.88, 2005- 1.94, 2006- 1.90, 2007- 1.94, 2008- 1.93, 2009- 1.88, 2010- 1.85, 2011- 1.98, 2012- 1.94i/1.85.
Improved from 1.92 to 1.98 to win 2011 European U23 title.

RUSSIA

Governing body: All-Russia Athletic Federation, Luzhnetskaya Nab. 8, Moscow 119992. Founded 1911.
National Championships first held 1908, USSR women from 1922. **2012 Champions: Men**: 100m: Mikhail Idrisov 10.39, 200m: Konstantin Petryashov 20.73w, 400m: Maksim Dyldin 45.01, 800m: Ivan Nesterov 1:48.05, 1500m: Yegor Nikolayev 3:39.25, 5000m: Andrey Safronov 13:30.30, 10,000m: Yevgeniy Rybakov 28:35.95; HMar: Andrey Leyman 63:49, Mar: Fyodor Shutov 2:12:09, 3000mSt: Nikolay Chavkin 8:26.38, 110mh: Konstantin Shabanov 13.57, 400mh: Vyacheslav Sakayev 49.59, HJ: Ivan Ukhov 2.39, PV: Sergey Kucheryanu 5.72, LJ: Aleksandr Menkov 8.24, TJ: Lyukman Adams 17.06, SP: Maksim Sidorov 21.51, DT: Bogdan Pishchal–nikov 65.64, HT: Kirill Ikonnikov 80.71, JT: Ilya Korotkov 79.61, Dec: Sergey Sviridov 8088, 20kW: Andrey Ruzavin 1:20:49, 50kW: Yuriy Andronov 3:40:46. **Women**: 100m:

Yelizaveta Savlinis 11.40, 200m: Aleksandra Fedoriva 22.19, 400m: Antonina Krivoshapka 49.16, 800m: Yekaterina Poistogova 1:56.95, 1500m: Yekaterina Kostetskaya 3:59.28, 5000m: Yuliya Vasilyeva 15:20.41, 10,000m: Yelizaveta Grechishnikova 31:07.88, HMar: Irina Premitina 72:34, Mar: Natalya Sokolova 2:30:10, 3000mSt: Yuliya Zaripova 9:09.99, 100mh: Tatyana Dektyareva 12.81, 400mh: Natalya Antyukh 53.40, HJ: Anna Chicherova 2.03, PV: Svetlana Feofanova 4.55, LJ: Yelena Sokolova 7.06, TJ: Tatyana Lebedeva 14.68, SP: Yevgeniya Kolodko 19.33, DT: Vera Ganeyeva 64.20, HT: Tatyana Lysenko 78.51, JT: Mariya Abakumova 64.41, Hep: Kristina Savitskaya 6681, 20kW: Anisya Kirdyapkina 1:27:43. Clubs abbreviations: Dyn – Dynamo, TU – Trade Union sports society, VS – Army, YR – Yunest Rossii.

Lyukman ADAMS b. 24 Sep 1988 St. Petersburg 1.94m 87kg.
At TJ: OG: '12- 9; EC: '10- 6; EJ: '07- 1; WI: '12- 3. Russian champion 2012.
Progress at TJ: 2005- 15.97, 2006- 15.16, 2007- 16.75, 2008- 16.86i/16.78, 2009- 16.22i/16.20, 2010- 17.17/17.21w, 2011- 17.32i/15.60, 2012- 17.53. pb LJ 7.47i '05, 7.42 '07.

Yuriy ANDRONOV b. 6 Nov 1971 Samara 1.80m 68kg. Samara VS.
At 50kW: OG: '04- 9; WCh: '09- dnf; EC: '02-06-10: dq/3/10; WCp: '04- 3, '06- 3; ECp: '05-09: 3/3; RUS champion 2010, 2012.
World M40 50k walk reord 2012,
Progress at 50kW: 1991- 4:06:49, 1993- 3:59:28, 1994- 3:52:30, 1995- 3:57:54, 1996- 3:47:04, 1997- 3:54:52, 1999- 3:50:34, 2001- 3:52:57, 2002- 3:42:06, 2003- 3:48:26, 2004- 3:46:49, 2005- 3:42:34, 2006- 3:42:38, 2007- 3:42:55, 2009- 3:49:09, 2010- 3:54:22, 2011- 3:42:25, 2012- 3:40:46. pbs: 5000mW 19:09.7i '02, 20kW: 1:22:42.0t '02, 30kW 2:07:23 '04, 35kW 2:28:01 '03.

Sergey BAKULIN b. 13 Nov 1986 Insar, Mordoviya. 1.69m 58kg. Mordoviya VS.
At 20kW: EC: '06- 5; EU23: '07- 3; WCp: '06- 6, '10- 7; WUG: '09- 1. At 50kW: OG: '12- 6; WCh: '11- 1; EC: '10- 3; WCop: '12- 5; ECp: '09- 4; Russian champion 2011.
Progress at 20kW, 50kW: 2006- 1:19:54, 2007- 1:19:14, 2008- 1:18:18, 3:52:38; 2010- 1:24:05, 3:43:26; 2011- 3:38:46, 2012- 3:38:55. pbs: 5000mW 18:26.82i '12, 10kW: 39:03 '06, 35kW 2:24:25 '09.

Valeriy BORCHIN b. 11 Sep 1986 Povodimovo, Mordoviya 1.78m 63kg. Saransk VS.
At 20kW: OG: '08- 1, '12- dnf; WCh: '07- dnf, '09- 1, '11- 1; EC: '06- 2; EU23: '07- 1; WCp: '08- 2, '12- 9; Russian champion 2006.
Progress at 20kW: 2006- 1:20:00, 2007- 1:18:56, 2008- 1:17:55, 2009- 1:17:38, 2011- 1:18:55, 2012- 1:21:29. pbs: 3000mW 18:11.8i '10, 5000mW 18:16.54 '12, 10kW: 38:42 '11.
Served one year drugs ban 2005-06.

Yuriy BORZAKOVSKIY b. 12 Apr 1981 Kratovo, Moskva reg. 1.82m 72kg. Moskva Dyn. At 800m/4x400mR: OG: '00-04-08-12: 6/1/sf/sf; WCh: '03-05-07-09-11: 2/2/3/4/3; EC: '02- 2R, '12- 1; EJ: '99- 1; WI: '01- 1, '06- 3; EI: '00- 1, '09- 1; ECp: '99-02-10: 1/1/1; 2nd GP 2001. At 400m: EC: '02- sf; EU23: '01- 1; At 1500m: ECp: '03- 3. Won Russian 800m 2004, 2009-11; 1500m 2005, 2007-08.
Records: Two world junior indoor 800m 2000, European Junior 800m (2) & 1000m 2000; Russian: 800m (4) 2001, 1000m 2008.
Progress at 800m: 1997- 1:52.8i/1:53.69, 1998- 1:47.71, 1999- 1:46.13, 2000- 1:44.33, 2001- 1:42.47, 2002- 1:44.20, 2003- 1:43.68, 2004- 1:43.92, 2005- 1:44.18, 2006- 1:43.42, 2007- 1:44:38, 2008- 1:42.79, 2009- 1:43.58, 2010- 1:44.65, 2011- 1:43.99, 2012- 1:45.09. pbs: 200m 22.56 '99, 400m 45.84 '00, 600m 1:16.02i '10, 1000m 2:15.50 '08, 1500m 3:40.28 '05, 3000m 8:32 '99.
He typically leaves himself a tremendous amount to do on the second lap of his 800m races but Olympic success in 2004 came from a remarkably even-paced race.

Aleksey DMITRIK b. 12 Apr 1984 Slantsy. Leningrad reg, 1.91m 69kg. St Petersburg YR. At HJ: WCh: '11- 2; EC: '10- 7; WJ: '02- 14; WY: '01- 1; EJ: '03- 2; EU23: '05- 6; EI: '09- 2=, '13- 2; ECp: '05- 1, '11- 2. Russian champion 2011.
Progress at HJ: 2000- 2.08, 2001- 2.23, 2002- 2.26, 2003- 2.28, 2004- 2.30, 2005- 2.34i/2.30, 2006- 2.28, 2007- 2.30, 2008- 2.33i/2.27, 2009- 2.33, 2010- 2.32i/2.31, 2011- 2.36, 2012- 2.35i/2.33, 2013- 2.36i.
Mother Yelana was a 1.75m high jumper.

Kirill IKONNIKOV b. 5 Mar 1984 Leningrad 1.86m 115kg.
At HT: OG: '08- dnq 19, '12- 5; WCh: '11- 6; WJ: '02- 5; EJ: '03- 4. Russian champion 2011-12.
Progress at HT: 2003- 68.09, 2004- 71.32, 2005- 70.30, 2006- 70.26, 2007- 78.03, 2008- 79.20, 2009- 75.40, 2010- 77.73, 2011- 79.04, 2012- 80.71.

Vladimir KANAYKIN b. 21 Mar 1985 Atyur–yevo, Mordoviya 1.70m 65kg. Saransk VS.
At 20kW: OG: '12- dq; WCh: '11- 2; ECp: '11- 6. At 50kW: WCh: '05- dq, '07- dnf; EC: '06- 9; WCp: '08- dq(2), '12- 3; ECp: '07- 1; Won RWC 30kW 2007, RUS 20km 2007, 50km 2005-06. At 10,000mW: WJ: '02- 1, '04- 2; WY: '01- 1.
World record 20km walk 2007, three world bests 30km & 35km walk 2004-06 (each to win Russian winter 35k).
Progress at 20kW, 50kW: 2003- 1:21:23, 2004- 1:22:00, 3:40:40; 2005- 1:21:11, 3:40:40; 2006- 1:21:20, 3:45:57; 2007- 1:17:16, 3:40:57; 2008- 1:16:53dq, 3:36:55dq; 2010- 1:22:23. 2011- 1:19:14, 2012- 1:19:43. pbs: 5000mW 18:17.13i '12, 20:20.26 '03; 10,000mW: 40:58.48 '04, 10kW: 38:16 '04, 30kW 2:01:13 '06, 35kW 2:21:31 '06.
Disqualified when well clear of field in 2004 at World Cup junior 10km. 2-year drugs ban after positive EPO test 20 Apr 2008.

Sergey KIRDYAPKIN b. 18 Jun 1980 Insar, Mordoviya Rep. 1.78m 67kg. Saransk VS. At 50kW: OG: '08- dnf, '12- 1; WCh: '05-07-09-11: 1/dnf/1/dnf; EC: '10- dnf; WCp: '08- 6, '12- 1; ECp: '05- 2. Won RUS 50kW 2009.
Progress at 50kW: 2001- 4:08:16, 2002- 3:52:19, 2004- 3:43:20, 2005- 3:38:08, 2006- 4:23:27, 2008- 3:48:29, 2009- 3:38:35, 2012- 3:35:59. pbs: 5000mW 19:28.35i '13, 10kW 40:23 '10, 20kW 1:23:57 '11, 30kW 2:05:06 '03, 35kW 2:25:42 '12.
Married to Anisya Kirdyapkina (qv).

Andrey KRIVOV b. 14 Nov 1985 Komsomolsky, Mordovia 1.85m 72kg. Mordovia. Sports student.
At 20kW: OG: '12- 37; WCh: '09- 17; EC: '10- 6; EU23: '07- 2; WCp: '08-10-12: 5/3/2; ECp: '11- 8; WUG: '11- 1. Russian champion 2009, 2011.
Progress at 20kW: 2005- 1:22:21, 2007- 1:20:12, 2008- 1:19:06, 2009- 1:19:55, 2010- 1:22:20, 2011- 1:20:16, 2012- 1:18:25. pbs: 10,000mW: 40:35.2 '05, 35kW 2:29:44 '06.

Sergey LITVINOV b. 27 Jan 1986 Rostov-on-Don, Russia 1.85m 105kg.
At HT: WCh: '09- 5, '11- dnq 15; WJ: '04- 9; EU23: '07- 11; EJ: '05- 9. German champion 2009.
Progress at HT: 2004- 60.00, 2005- 73.98, 2006- 66.46, 2007- 74.80, 2008- 75.35, 2009- 77.88, 2010- 78.98, 2011- 78.90, 2012- 80.98.
Switched from Belarus to Germany 15 Jul 2008, but for 2011 had moved to Russia. His father Sergey Litvinov (USSR) set three world records at hammer 1980-3 with a pb of 86.04 '86; he was Olympic champion 1988 (2nd 1980) and World champion 1983 and 1987. His mother was born in Germany.

Aleksandr MENKOV b. 7 Dec 1990 Krasnoyarsk 1.78m 74kg. Krasnoyarsk VS.
At LJ: OG: '12- 11; WCh: '09- dnq 32, '11- 6; WI: '12- 3; EU23: '11- 1; EJ: '09- 1; EI: '13- 1; ET: '11- 1. Won DL 2012, Russian 2012.
Progress at LJ: 2008- 6.98, 2009- 8.16, 2010- 8.10, 2011- 8.28, 2012- 8.29, 2013- 8.31i. pbs: HJ 2.15 '10, TJ 15.20 '09.

Sergey MORGUNOV b. 9 Feb 1993 Shakhty, Rostov 1.78m 70kg..
At LJ: OG: '12- dnq 16; WJ: '12- 1; EJ: '11- 1. World junior long jump record 2012.
Progress at LJ: 2010- 7.66, 2011- 8.10/8.18w, 2012- 8.35.

Sergey MUDROV b. 8 Sep 1990 1.88m 79kg. Luch Moskva Reg
At HJ: WJ: '08- 4; WY: '07- 2; EU23: '11- 2; EJ: '09- 1; EI: '13- 1; WUG: '11- 1.
Progress at HJ: 2006- 2.10, 2007- 2.22, 2008- 2.18, 2009- 2.25, 2010- 2.30i/2.27, 2011- 2.30, 2012- 2.31, 2013- 2.35i.

Denis NIZHEGORODOV b. 26 Jul 1980 Saransk 1.80m 61kg. Saransk VS.
At 50kW: OG: '04- 2, '08- 3; WCh: '03-07-09-11: 5/4/dnf/2; EC: '06- dq; WCp: '06- 1, '08- 1; ECp: '09- 1,

'11- 1; Russian champion 2003-04, 2007. At 20kW: EU23: '01- 5; WUG: '01- 4; ECp: '00- 17, '01- 7. World record 50km walk 2008, best (no drugs test) 2004.
Progress at 20kW, 50kW: 2000- 1:21:47, 2001- 1:18:20; 2003- 1:23:23, 3:38:23; 2004- 3:35:29, 2005- dnf, 2006- 1:22:45, 3:38:02; 2007- 3:40:53, 2008- 3:34:14, 2009- 3:42:47, 2011- 3:42:45. pbs: 5000mW 18:58.81i '12, 30kW 2:05:08 '06, 35kW 2:24:50 '06.

Bogdan PISHCHALNIKOV b. 26 Aug 1982 Krasnodar 1.96m 120kg. Moskva Dyn.
At DT: OG: '08- 6, '12- dnq 15; WCh: '05/07- dnq 18/18, '09- 7; EC: '06/10: dnq 16/16; EU23: '03- 3; WCp: '06- 7; ET: '10- 3. Russian champion 2005, 2007-12.
Progress at DT: 1999- 42.71, 2000- 50.36, 2001- 52.86, 2002- 56.97, 2003- 57.08, 2004- 60.89, 2005- 64.08, 2006- 64.19, 2007- 64.95, 2008- 65.88, 2009- 65.58, 2010- 67.23, 2011- 62.40, 2012- 65.96. pb SP 16.58 '03.
Brother of Darya Pishchalnikova (b. 19 Jul 1985), 2006 European discus champion who received a two-year drugs ban from 10 Apr 2007. Married to Olga Ivanova (SP 19.48 '08).

Andrey RUZAVIN b. 28 Mar 1986 1.75m 70kg. Mordoviya
At 20kW: WCp: '12- 5; WUG: '09- 2; Russian champion 2008, 2012. At 10,000m/10kW: WJ: '04- 1; EJ: '05- 1; WCp: '04- 6J; ECp: '05- 1J.
Progress at 20kW: 2004- 1:25:48, 2005- 1:21:51, 2006- 1:24:24, 2007- 1:20:07, 2009- 1:21:08, 2010- 1:21:01, 2011- 1:21:09, 2012- 1:17:47. pbs: 10,000mW 38:48.03 '08, 10kW 38:17 '09, 35kW 2:25:19 '09.

Ruslan SAMITOV b. 11 Jul 1991 1.87m 77kg. Tatarstan.
At TJ: EC: '12: dnq 15; EJ: '09- 4; EI: '13- 2.
Progress at TJ: 2008- 15.09, 2009- 16.02, 2010- 16.51i/16.42, 2011- 16.90, 2012- 17.25, 2013- 17.30i.

Sergey SHUBENKOV b. 4 Oct 1990 Barnaul, Altay Kray 1.90m 75kg.
At 110mh: OG: '12- sf; WCh: '11- h; EC: '12- 1; EU23: '11- 1; EJ: '09- 2. At 60mh: EI: '13- 1.
FourRussian 110mh records 2012.
Progress at 110mh: 2010- 13.54, 2011- 13.46, 2012- 13.09. pb 60mh 7.49i '13.
Mother Natalya Shubenkova had heptathlon pb 6859 '04; and 4th 1988 OG and 3rd 1986 EC.

Aleksandr SHUSTOV b. 29 Jun 1984 Kara–ganda, Kazakhstan 1.99m 85kg. Moskva VS.
At HJ: OG: '12- dnq 15; WCh: '11- 8; EC: '10- 1; EU23: '05- 12; WUG: '07- 1; EI: '09- 4=, '11- 3; ET: '09-10: 3/1. Russian champion 2010.
Progress at HJ: 2002- 2.10, 2003- 2.11, 2004- 2.15, 2005- 2.23, 2006- 2.28, 2007- 2.31, 2008- 2.30, 2009- 2.32i, 2010- 2.33, 2011- 2.36, 2012- 2.35. pbs: LJ 7.18i '12, Hep 4564i '12.
Married to Yekaterina Kondratyeva (200m 22.64 '04, 2 WUG '03, 6 EC '06).

Maksim SIDOROV b. 13 May 1986 Moskva 1.90m 126kg. Moskva Reg. Dyn.

At SP: OG: '12- 11; WCh: '09/11- dnq 31/15; EU23: '07- 8; EJ: '05- 3; WUG: '07- 1; WI: '12- 5; EI: '11- 3. Russian champion 2009, 2011-12.
Progress at SP: 2006- 18.52, 2007- 20.01, 2008- 19.98, 2009- 20.92, 2010- 20.50, 2011- 21.45, 2012- 21.51. pb DT 50.71 '06.

Andrey SILNOV b. 9 Sep 1984 Shakhty, Rostov region 1.98m 83kg. Moskva Reg. VS.
At HJ: OG: '08- 1, '12- 12; WCh: '07- 11=; EC: '06- 1; EU23: '05- 9; WI: '12- 2; WCp: '06- 2; ECp: '06- 1, '08- 1. Won WAF 2008, Russian 2006.
Progress at HJ: 2002- 2.10, 2003- 2.10, 2004- 2.15, 2005- 2.28, 2006- 2.37, 2007- 2.36i/2.30, 2008- 2.38, 2009- 2.21, 2010- 2.33, 2011- 2.36, 2012- 2.37.

Dmitriy STARODUBTSEV b. 3 Jan 1986 Chelyabinsk region 1.91m 79kg. Moskva TU.
At PV: OG: '08- 5, '10- 4; WCh: '11- 12=; EC: '06- dnq 21=, '10- nh; WJ: '04- 1; WY: '03- 2; EU23: '07- 4; EJ: '05- 1; WI: '10- 6=, '12- 9; EI: '07- 6; WUG: '07- 3; WCp: '06- 9. Won RUS 2010.
Progress at PV: 2003- 5.10, 2004- 5.50, 2005- 5.50, 2006- 5.65i/5.61, 2007- 5.70, 2008- 5.75, 2009- 5.70, 2010- 5.70i/5.65, 2011- 5.90i/5.72, 2012- 5.80i/5.75. pb Dec 7412 '07.

Sergey SVIRIDOV b. 20 Oct 1990 Yekaterinburg 1.92m 85kg. Moskva YU.
At Dec: OG: '12- 8; EJ: '09- 15. Russian champion 2012.
Progress at Dec: 2010- 7449, 2011- 8102A/7832, 2012- 8442. pbs: 60m 6.98i '12, 100m 10.78 '12, 400m 48.28 '12, 1000m 2:43.52i '12, 1500m 4:25.15 '12, 60mh 8.26i '12, 110mh 14.83 '12, HJ 2.04i '13, 1.99 '12; PV 4.60 '12, LJ 7.55i '13, 7.52 '12; SP 15.03 '12, DT 50.02 '12, JT 69.00 '12, Hep 5855i '12.

Dmitriy TARABIN b. 29 Oct 1991 Berlin, Germany 1.76m 85kg.
At JT: WCh: '11- 10; WJ: '09- 3; EU23: '11- 3; EJ: '09- dnq 13.
Progress at JT: 2007- 55.18, 2008- 67.39, 2009- 69.63, 2010- 77.65, 2011- 85.10, 2012- 82.75.
Switched from Moldova to Russia 9 June 2010. To marry Mariya Abakumova in October 2012.

Ivan UKHOV b. 29 Mar 1986 Chelyabinsk 1.92m 67kg. Sverdlovsk TU.
At HJ: OG: '12- 1; WCh: '09- 10, '11- 5=; EC: '06- 12=, '10- 2; WJ: '04- dnq 13; EJ: '05- 1; WUG: '05- 4; WI: '10- 1, '12- 3; EI: '09- 1, '11- 1. Won DL 2010, Russian 2009, 2012.
Progress at HJ: 2004- 2.15, 2005- 2.30, 2006- 2.37i/2.33, 2007- 2.39i/2.20, 2008- 2.36i/2.30, 2009- 2.40i/2.35, 2010- 2.38i/2.36, 2011- 2.38i/2.34, 2012- 2.39.   Former discus thrower.

Stanislav YEMELYANOV b. 23 Oct 1990 Pavlovo, Nizhni Novgorod Reg. 1.75m 62kg. Mordoviya VS. Law student.
At 20kmW: WCh: '11- 5; EC: '10- 1; ECp: '11- 1; RUS champion 2010. At 10,000mW: WJ: '08- 1; WY: '07- 1; EJ: '09- 1; ECp: '09- 1J.
World junior 10k walk record 2009.
Progress at 20kW: 2010- 1:19:43, 2011- 1:19:33,

2012- 1:18:29. pbs: 10kW 38:28 '09, 39:35.01t '08; 30kW 2:24:25 '09.

Igor YEROKHIN b. 4 Sep 1985 Saransk 1.66m 56kg.
At 20kmW: WCh: '07- dq; EU23: '05- 1; ECp: '07- 3, At 50kW: OG: '12- 5; WCh: '11- dq; WCp: '11- 2; ECp: '11- 2; Russian champion 2008.
Progress at 20kW, 50kW: 2005- 1:20:16, 2006- 1:19:32, 2007- 1:19:21, 2008- 3:38.08, 2011- 3:49:05, 2012- 3:37:54. pbs: 10,000mW: 38:54.07 '06, 30kW 2:05:50 '07, 35kW 2:26:36 '11.
Two year drugs ban 2008-10.

Aleksey ZAGORNYI b. 31 May 1978 Yaroslavl 1.97m 130kg. Luch Moskva.
At HT: OG: '00-12: dnq 22/23; WCh: '03/07- dnq 22/25, '09- 3; EC: '02- 11, '12- 2; EJ: '97- 5; EU23: '99- 7; WUG: '01- 4. Russian champion 2007, 2009.
Progress at HT: 1994- 59.90, 1995- 71.00, 1996- 71.94, 1997- 71.30, 1998- 77.03, 1999- 77.20, 2000- 79.68, 2001- 80.80, 2002- 83.43, 2003- 80.13, 2004- 78.79, 2005- 80.81, 2006- 78.18, 2007- 79.12, 2008- 81.39, 2009- 80.10, 2010- 78.22, 2011- 81.73, 2012- 78.40.

Women

Mariya ABAKUMOVA b. 15 Jan 1986 Stavropol 1.78m 85kg. Krasnodar VS.
At JT: OG: '08- 2, '12- 10; WCh: '07- 09-11: 7/3/1; EC: '10- 5; WJ: '04- dnq 25; WY: '03- 4; EU23: '07- 6; EJ: '05- 1; CCp: '10- 1; ECp: '08-09-10: 2/3/3. Won WAF 2009, Russian 2008, 2011-12.
European javelin record 2008, four Russian 2008-11.
Progress at JT: 2002- 51.81, 2003- 51.41, 2004- 58.26, 2005- 59.53, 2006- 60.12, 2007- 64.28, 2008- 70.78, 2009- 68.92, 2010- 68.89, 2011- 71.99, 2012- 66.86, 2013- 69.34.
To marry Dmitriy Tarabin (qv) in October 2012

Elmira ALEMBEKOVA b. 30 Jun 1990 Saransk. Mordoviya.
At 10,000m/10kmW: WJ: '08- 2; EJ: '09- 1; WCp: '08- 3J, At 5000mW: WY: '05- 2.
Progress at 20kW: 2010- 1:35:53, 2011- 1:27:35, 2012- 1:25:27. pbs: 10,000mW: 43:45.26 '08.

Natalya ANTYUKH b. 26 Jun 1981 Leningrad 1.82m 73kg. Moskva VS.
At 400m/4x400mR: OG: '04- 3/1R; WCh: '05- sf/1R, '07- 6, '11- 3/3R; EC: '02- 2R; WI: '03-04- 06: 1R/GR/1R; EI: '02- 1, '07- 2R, '09- 4/1R; WCp: '02- 3R; ECp: '01- 3/1R, '05- 1/1R, '06- 1R. At 200m: ECp: '04- 2. At 400mh: OG: '12- 1/2R; WCh: '09- 6/res 3R, '11- 3/3R; EC: '10- 1; CCp: '10- 4; ET: '10- 1&1R, '11- 2. Won Russian 400m 2007, 400mh 2010-12.
Progress at 400m: 2000- 54.79, 2001- 51.19, 2002- 51.17i/51.24, 2003- 51.73i/52.28, 2004- 49.85, 2005- 50.67, 2006- 50.37i/50.47, 2007- 49.93, 2008- 51.19, 2009- 50.90, 2011- 50.73, 2012- 51.27. At 400mh: 1996- 60.11, 1997- 59.75, 1998- 59.94, 2000- 58.30, 2009- 54.11, 2010- 52.92, 2011- 53.75, 2012- 52.70. pbs: 200m 22.73 '12, 300m 36.0+ '04.

Tatyana ARKHIPOVA b. 8 Apr 1983 Chebok– sary 1.60m 53kg. née Petrova. Moskva VS.
At Mar: OG: '12- 3. At 3000mSt: OG: '08- 4; WCh: '07- 2; EC: '06- 2; WCp: '06- 5. At 3000m/5000m: WJ: '02- 4/6. At 5000m/10,000m: EU23: '05- 2/1. Eur CC: '01- 19J, '02- 4J.
World best indoor 3000mSt 9:07.00 '06.
Progress at 10,000m, Mar, 3000mSt: 2003- 10:05.70, 2004- 32:37.88, 2:36:44; 2005- 32:17.49, 2:31:03; 2006- 9:22.82, 2007- 9:09.19, 2008- 9:12.33, 2009- 2:25:53, 10:00.36; 2011- 32:18.88, 2:25:01; 2012- 2:23:29. pbs: 1500m 4:23.95i '02, 3000m 8:44.13 '06, 5000m 15:46.58 '03, 10km Rd 32:10 '07. Won Los Angeles marathon 2009. Expecting a baby in 2013.

Yelena ARZHAKOVA b. 8 Sep 1989 Barnaul, Altay region 1.70m 56kg. Moskva SC.
At (800m)/1500m: OG: '12- (6); EC: '12- (1); EU23: '11- 1/1; WI: '12- 7; EI: '11- 1; WUG: '11- 4. At 3000mSt: WJ: '06- h. Won RUS 800m 2012.
Progress at 800m, 1500m: 2006- 4:23.79, 2009- 4:26.17, 2010- 4:08.05; 2011- 1:58.77, 4:07.69; 2012- 1:57.67, 4:00.82. pbs: 400m 54.05 '12, 600m 1:26.9+ '12, 1000m 2:35.21i '11, 2000m 5:48.85i '12, 3000m 9:21.71 '10, 3000mSt 9:49.05 '11.

Anna AVDEYEVA b. 6 Apr 1985 Orenburg 1.71m 100kg. Mordovia VS.
At SP: OG: '12- dnq 24; WCh: '07- dnq 14, '09- 5, '11- 7; EC: '10- 3; WJ: '02- 8, '04- 2; EJ: '03- 1; EU23: '03- 6, '05- 3; WI: '10- 4; EI: '09- 6, '11- 1; ET: '10- 1, '11- 2; Russian champion 2009-10.
Progress at SP: 2001- 13.58, 2002- 15.83, 2003- 16.91, 2004- 17.13, 2005- 17.39, 2006- 18.45, 2007- 19.11, 2008- 19.10, 2009- 20.07, 2010- 19.47i/19.39, 2011- 19.54, 2012- 19.54.

Mariya BESPALOVA b. 21 May 1986 Leningrad 1.83m 85kg. Mordovia VS.
At HT: OG: '12- 11; WJ: '04- dnq; WY: '03- 2.
Progress at HT: 2002- 52.62, 2003- 58.47, 2004- 59.72, 2005- 61.73, 2006- 62.58, 2007- 63.50, 2008- 67.08, 2009- 69.02, 2010- 64.92, 2011- 71.93, 2012- 76.72. pb DT 44.19 '06.

Yekaterina BOLSHOVA b. 4 Feb 1988 St. Peterburg 1.78m 66kg. St. Petersburg.
At Hep: EC: '12- 5. At Pen: WI: '12- 6. At HJ: WY: '05- 8.
Progress at Hep: 2007- 5297, 2008- 4940, 2009- 5590, 2010- 5738, 2011- 5050, 2012- 6466. pbs: 200m 24.17 '12, 800m 2:10.10 '12, 60mh 8.14i '12, 100mh 13.50 '12, HJ 1.92i/1.91 '12, LJ 6.52i/6.45 '12, SP 13.98 '12, JT 40.47 '12, Pen 4896i '12.

Anna BULGAKOVA b. 17 Jan 1988 Stavropol 1.73m 90kg. Stavropol VS.
At HT: OG: '08- dnq 20; EC: '12- 3; WJ: '04- 4, '06- 2; WY: '05- 2; EJ: '07- 4.
Progress at HT: 2003- 57.24, 2004- 63.83, 2005- 64.43, 2006- 67.79, 2007- 68.49, 2008- 73.79, 2010- 66.29, 2011- 69.10, 2012- 74.02. pb DT 44.19 '06.

Tatyana CHERNOVA b. 29 Jan 1988 Krasnodar 1.90m 70kg. Krasnodar VS.
At Hep: OG: '08- 3, '12- 3; WCh: '07- dnf, '09- 8,

'11- 1; EC: '10- 4; WJ: '06- 1; WY: '05- 1. At Pen: WI: '08-10-12: 7/3/5.
Progress at Hep: 2006- 6227, 2007- 6768w, 2008- 6618, 2009- 6386, 2010- 6572, 2011- 6880, 2012- 6774. pbs: 200m 23.49 '12, 23.32w '11; 800m 2:06.50 '08, 60mh 8.02i '12, 100mh 13.32 '11, 13.04w '07, 400mh 56.14 '07, HJ 1.87 '07, LJ 6.82 '11, SP 14.54i '10, 14.17 '11, JT 54.49 '06, Pen 4855i '10.
Won at Talence 2010-11 and IAAF Combined Events Challenge 2010-12 Her mother Lyudmila (née Zenina) won a 4x400m Olympic gold medal (ran in heats) for 4x400m in 1980, pbs: 200m 22.9 '82, 400m 50.91 '83.

Anna CHICHEROVA b. 22 Jul 1982 Yerevan, Armenia 1.80m 57kg. Moskva VS. Physical culture graduate.
At HJ: OG: '04- 6, '08- 3, '12- 1; WCh: '03-05-07-09-11: 6/4/2=/2/1; EC: '06- 7=; WJ: '00- 4; WY: '99- 1; EJ: '01- 2; WUG: '05- 1; WI: '03-04-12: 3/2/2=; EI: '05- 1, '07- 5=; ECp: '06- 3. Russian champion 2004, 2007-09, 2011-12.
Progress at HJ: 1998- 1.80, 1999- 1.89, 2000- 1.90, 2001- 1.92, 2002- 2.00i/1.89, 2003- 2.04i/2.00, 2004- 2.04i/1.98, 2005- 2.01i/1.99, 2006- 1.96i/1.95, 2007- 2.03, 2008- 2.04, 2009- 2.02, 2011- 2.07, 2012- 2.06i/2.05.
Moved with family to Russia at the beginning of the 1990s. Married to Gennadiy Chernoval KAZ, pbs 100m 10.18, 200m 20.44 (both 2002), 2 WUG 100m & 200m 2001, 2 AsiG 2002 2002; their daughter Nika born on 7 Sep 2010.

Irina DAVYDOVA b. 27 May 1988 Vladimir region 1.70m 58kg. Moskva SC.
At 400mh: OG: '12- sf; EC: '12- 1; EU23: '09-5; WUG: '11- 2.
Progress at 400mh: 2006- 60.27, 2007- 58.55, 2008- 58.62, 2009- 56.14, 2010- 55.74, 2011- 55.48, 2012- 53.77. pbs: 200m 24.53i '11, 400m 51.94i '12, 53.12 '11; 500m 1:10.54i '12.

Tatyana DEKTYAREVA b. 5 Aug 1981 Yekaterinburg 1.74m 60kg. Finpromko.
At 100mh: OG: '08- h, '12- sf; WCh: '09- h, '11- 5; EC: '10- 6; ET: '10- 1, '11- 1; Russian champion 2011-12. At 60mh: WI: '10- 8.
Progress at 100mh: 2004- 13.98, 2005- 13.36/13.30w, 2006- 13.04, 2007- 13.30/13.10w, 2008- 12.84/12.81w, 2009- 12.96, 2010- 12.68, 2011- 12.76, 2012- 12.75. pbs: 60m 7.42i '08, 100m 11.76 '08, 200m 23.59 '06, 300m 37.93i '06, 800m 2:05.87 '04, 60mh 7.94i '10.

Aleksandra FEDORIVA b. 13 Sep 1988 Moskva 1.75m 60kg. SC Luch Moskva. Student of advertising at Moscow University of Humanitarian Studies.
At 400m/4x400m: WI: '12- 2/3R. At 200m/4x-100mR: OG: '08- sf/1R, '12- sf; EC: '10- 3; EU23: '09- 1; CCp: '10- 1; ECp: '10- 1R, '11- 3/2R. At 100m: WCh: '11- sf; ET: '11- 3. At 100mh: WJ: '06- 4; WY: '05- sf; EJ: '07- 1. Won RUS 200m 2011-12.

Progress at 200m: 2007- 23.29, 2008- 22.56, 2009- 22.97, 2010- 22.41, 2011- 23.17, 2012- 22.19. pbs: 60m 7.24i '10, 100m 11.28, 11.09w '11; 300m 36.54i '12, 400m 51.18i '12, 60mh 7.91i '10, 100mh 12.90 '08.
Her mother Lyudmila Belova/Fedoriva had 400m best 50.63 '84, father Andrey Fedoriv 200m 3rd EC and best 20.53 '86; ran at five Worlds and two Olympics. Married Aleksandr Shpayer (RUS 60m indoor champion 6.63 '11) in 2012; Expecting a baby in 2013.

Svetlana FEOFANOVA b. 16 Jul 1980 Moskva 1.64m 53kg. Moskva TU.
At PV: OG: '00- dnq, '04- 2, '08- 3, '12- dnq; WCh: '01-03-07-11: 2/1/3/3; EC: '02- 1, '06- 4, '10- 1; WI: '01-03-04-06-08-10: 2=/1/3/3/5/2; EI: '02- 1, '07- 1; WCp: '02- 2, '10- 1; ECp: '00-01-02-10: 1/1/1/1; 2nd GP 2001. Won RUS 2001, 2006, 2008, 2011-12.
Pole vault records: World 2004, 9 European 2001-04, 11 Russian 2000-04, 9 world indoor 2002-04 (4.71-4.85), 13 European indoor 2001-04.
Progress at PV: 1998- 3.90, 1999- 4.10, 2000- 4.50, 2001- 4.75, 2002- 4.78, 2003- 4.80i/4.75, 2004- 4.88, 2005- 4.70i, 2006- 4.70, 2007- 4.82, 2008- 4.75, 2009- 4.70, 2010- 4.80i/4.75, 2011- 4.75, 2012- 4.65.
Was a top gymnast, winning Russian titles at youth, junior and U23 level at asymmetric bars and floor exercises. Set five indoor world records in a month in 2002.

Tatyana FIROVA b. 10 Oct 1982 Sarov, Nizhegorodskaya region 1.78m 68kg. Moskva Reg. Dyn.
At 400m/4x400m: OG: '04- res 1R, 08- 6/2R, '12- 2R; WCh: '05- res 1R, '09- 3R; EC: '06- res 1R, '10- 1/1R; EU23: '03- 3/1R; EJ: '01- 1; WI: '10- 2/2R; WUG: '03- 1; CCp: '10- 3/2R; ECp: '03- 1R.
Progress at 400m: 2000- 53.69, 2001- 52.94, 2002- 53.72, 2003- 51.43, 2004- 50.44, 2005- 50.41, 2006- 50.08, 2007- 50.98, 2008- 50.11, 2009- 50.59, 2010- 49.89, 2011- 50.84, 2012- 49.72. pbs: 200m 23.27 '11, 500m 1:09.41i '08, 600m 1:25.23i '08.

Gulnara GALKINA b. 9 Jul 1978 Naberezhnye Chelny, Tatarstan 1.75m 55kg. née Samitova. Naberezhnye Chelny Dyn.
At 3000mSt (5000m): OG: '04- (6), '08- 1 (12), '12- dnf; WCh: '03- (7), '07- 7, '09- 4; ECp: '03-08-11: 1/1/1. At 1500m: WI: '04- 3. At 3000m: ECp: '04-07-09: 1/1/1. Eur CC: '08- 12. Won WAF 3000mSt 2008, RUS 1500m 2004, 5000m 2003-04, 3000mSt 2003, 2008.
Three world and five Russian records 3000m steeplechase 2003-08.
Progress at 5000m, 3000mSt: 2003- 14:54.38, 9:08.33; 2004- 14:53.70, 9:01.59; 2006- 9:53.83, 2007- 9:11.68, 2008- 14:33.13, 8:58.81; 2009- 9:11.09, 2011- 16:06.09, 9:29.75; 2012- 15:39.97, 9:24.60. pbs: 800m 2:00.29 '09, 1000m 2:35.91i '04, 1500m 4:01.29 '04, 1M 4:20.23 '07, 2000m 5:31.03 '07, 3000m 8:41.72i '04, 8:42.96 '08; 10k Rd 32:43 '12.

Great breakthrough in 2003, starting with world indoor 3000mSt best of 9:29.54. Married Anton Galkin (400m 44.83 '04) in 2004. Daughter Alina born 24 Jun 2010.

Irina GORDEYEVA b. 9 Oct 1986 Leningrad 1.85m 55kg. Yunost Rossii.
At HJ: OG: '12- 10; EC: '10- dnq 13=, '12- 3=; WJ: '04- 9; WY: '03- 7=; EJ: '05- 4; EI: '09- 5=.
Progress at HJ: 2001- 1.75, 2002- 1.82, 2003- 1.84, 2004- 1.88, 2005- 1.88, 2006- 1.88, 2007- 1.87i/1.83, 2008- 1.95, 2009- 2.02, 2010- 1.97, 2011- 1.94, 2012- 2.04.

Irina GUMENYUK b. 6 Jan 1988. St.Petersburg.
At TJ: EJ: '07- 9; EI: '13- 2.
Progress at TJ: 2006- 13.06, 2007- 13.52, 2008- 13.65, 2009- 13.49i, 2010- 13.33, 2011- 14.14, 2012- 14.24i/14.03, 2013- 14.48i. pb LJ 6.38 '11.

Yuliya GUSHCHINA b. 4 Mar 1983 Novo–cherkask 1.75m 63kg. Moskva reg. VS.
At 200m(/100m)/4x100mR: OG: '08- 1R, '12- sf/2R; WCh: '05- 6, '07- 5R, '09/11- sf; EC: '06- 2/5/1R, '10- 4R; EU23: '03- 5; WCp: '06- 4/5/1R; ECp: '05-06-07-10-11: 1R/(1)&1R/1R/1R/2R. At 400m/4x400mR: OG: '08- 4/2R; WI: '06-08-12: GR/1R/3R; ECp: '05/07/08- 1R. Won RUS 100m 2011, 200m 2005, 2009; 400m 2008.
World indoor records 4x200m 2005, 4x400m 2006.
Progress at 200m, 400m: 1997- 25.96, 1998- 25.32, 1999- 58.18, 2000- 25.01, 55.85; 2001- 24.24, 55.91; 2002- 23.92/23.88w, 53.26; 2003- 23.58, 51.94; 2004- 23.06, 2005- 22.53, 53.81i; 2006- 22.69/22.52w, 51.26i; 2007- 22.75, 2008- 22.58, 50.01; 2009- 22.63, 51.06; 2010- 22.80/22.79w, 52.04i; 2011- 22.88/22.69w, 52.18; 2012- 22.95, 49.28. pbs: 60m 7.24i '07, 7.2i '03; 100m 11.13 '06, 300m 36.93i '10.
Married Ivan Buzolin (400m 46.24 '08, 2R EI '07) on 12 Sep 2010.

Yelena ISINBAYEVA b. 3 Jun 1982 Volgograd 1.74m 66kg. Volgograd Dyn.
At PV: OG: '00- dnq, '04- 1, '08- 1, '12- 3; WCh: '03-05-07-09-11: 3/1/1/nh/6; EC: '02- 2, '06- 1; WJ: '98- 9, '00- 1, WY: '99- 1; EU23: '03- 1; EJ: '99- 5, '01- 1; WI: '01-03-04-06-08-10-12: 7/2/1/1/1/4/1; EI: '05- 1; WCp: '06- 1. Won WAF 2004-07, 2009; Russian 2002.
15 outdoor world pole vault records 2003-09, 13 indoor 2004-12 (inc. 3 absolute WR), world junior indoor records 2000 and 2001.
Progress at PV: 1997- 3.30, 1998- 4.00, 1999- 4.20, 2000- 4.45i/4.40, 2001- 4.47i/4.46, 2002- 4.60/4.65ex, 2003- 4.82, 2004- 4.92, 2005- 5.01, 2006- 4.91, 2007- 4.93i/4.91, 2008- 5.05, 2009- 5.06, 2010- 4.85i, 2011- 4.85i/4.76, 2012- 5.01i/4.75.
Former gymnast. World age bests at 17-18-19 in 2000-02, world titles as Youth, junior and senior. World indoor records in all four competitions 2005 and a further five outdoors in 2005. These included the first 5m vault by a woman (at the London GP) followed by 5.01 to win the World title by 41 cm. Shared Golden League jackpot in 2007 and 2009. Passed 2010 summer season. IAAF female Athlete of the Year 2004-05 & 2008.

Olga KANISKINA b. 19 Jan 1985 Napolnaya Tavla, Mordoviya 1.60m 43kg. Saransk VS. Mathematics student at University of Mordovia.
At 20kW: OG: '08- 1, '12- 2; WCh: '07-09-11: 1/1/1; EC: '06- 2, '10- 1; WCp: '06-08-12: 5/1/2; EU23: '05- 2; ECp: '07- 2; won RWC 2011.
Progress at 20kW: 2005- 1:29:25, 2006- 1:26:02, 2007- 1:26:47, 2008- 1:25:11, 2009- 1:24:56, 2010- 1:27:44, 2011- 1:28:35, 2012- 1:25:09. pbs: 3000mW 12:23.5 '05, 5000mW 20:38.2 '05, 10kW 41:42R '09. Eight successive 20km walk wins 2007-09 and 11 wins in 12 races 2008-11.

Anastasiya KAPACHINSKAYA b. 21 Nov 1979 Moskva 1.76m 65kg. Luch Moskva.
At 200m/4x400mR: OG: '12- res(2)R; WCh: '03- 1, '11- 3/3R; EC: '10- 4/1R; WI: '03- 2, '04- dq (1); ECp: '03- 1. At 400m: OG: '08- 5/2R; WCh: '01- sf/3R, '03- 2R, '09- 7/3R; EC: '02- 5/2R. Won Russian 200m 2008, 400m 2011.
Progress at 200m, 400m: 1999- 23.85, 2000- 23.66, 53.32; 2001- 23.24i/22.6, 50.97; 2002- 23.41, 51.39; 2003- 22.38, 50.59; 2004- 22.71i, 2006- 22.80, 51.16; 2007- 23.73, 52.14; 2008- 22.48, 50.02; 2009- 22.92, 49.97; 2010- 22.47, 50.16; 2011- 22.55, 49.35; 2012- 50.37. pbs: 100m 11.79 '99, 300m 36.61 '02, 800m 2:09.75i '07.
She served a 2-year drugs ban after finishing first in the World Indoor 200m in 2004.

Gulfiya KHANAFEYEVA b. 4 Jun 1982 Chelyabinsk 1.73m 84kg. Moskva TU.
At HT: OG: '12- dnq 16; WCh: '07- dq(10); EC: '06- 2; EU23: '03- 3; EJ: '01- 10; WUG: '03- 2; ECp: '05- 3. Russian champion 2006.
World hammer record 2006.
Progress at HT: 1998- 51.10, 1999- 53.80, 2000- 57.20, 2001- 61.10, 2002- 62.19/64.50dq, 2003- 68.92, 2004- 72.71, 2005- 70.76, 2006- 77.26, 2007- 72.10/77.36dq, 2008- 75.07dq, 2011- 71.11, 2012- 77.08.
She had a 3-month ban in 2002 after testing positive for a stimulant and 2 year drugs ban from 9 May 2007.

Anisya KIRDYAPKINA b. 23 Oct 1989 Saransk, Mordoviya 1.65m 51kg. née Kornikova. Mordovia TU.
At 20kmW: OG: '12- 5; WCh: '09- 4. '11- 3; EC: '10- 2; WCp: '10- 6, '12- 6; ECp: '09- 2, '11- 2; RUS champion 2010, 2012. At 10,000mW: EJ: '07- 1; ECp: '07- 1J.
World junior 20km walk best 2008.
Progress at 20kW: 2007- 1:28:00, 2008- 1:25:30, 2009- 1:25:26, 2010- 1:25:11, 2011- 1:25:09, 2012- 1:26:26. 2013- 1:25:59. pbs: 3000mW 11:44.10i '12, 5000mW 21:06.3 '06, 10,000mW 43:27.30 '06, 42:04R '11.

Married to Sergey Kirdyapkin (qv).

Aleksandra KIRYASHOVA b. 21 Aug 1985 Leningrad 1.66m 53kg. Luch Moskva.
At PV: WCh: '09- 9; EC: '12- 8; WJ: '04- nh; WY: '01- 2; EU23: '07- 1; EJ: '03- 3; WUG: '07- 1, '11- 1; EI: '09- 4, '11- 6.
Progress at PV: 2000- 3.70, 2001- 4.00, 2002- 4.21, 2003- 4.21i/4.15, 2004- 4.25i/4.20, 2005- 4.30, 2006- 4.30i/4.20, 2007- 4.50, 2008- 4.50, 2009- 4.65, 2010- 4.65i/4.54, 2011- 4.65, 2012- 4.58.

Darya KLISHINA b. 15 Jan 1991 Tver 1.80m 57kg. Moskva. Model.
At LJ: WCh: '11- 7; WY: '07- 1; EU23: '11- 1; EJ: '09- 1; WI: '10- 5, '12- 4; EI: '11- 1, '13- 1, ET: '11- 1.
Progress at LJ: 2005- 5.83, 2006- 6.33/6.47w, 2007- 6.49, 2008- 6.52i/6.20, 2009- 6.80, 2010- 7.03, 2011- 7.05, 2012- 6.93, 2013- 7.01i.

Lyudmila KOLCHANOVA b. 1 Oct 1979 Sharya, Kostroma 1.75m 60kg. Kostroma TU.
At LJ: OG: '12- 6; WCh: '07- 2; EC: '06- 1, '10- 5; WUG: '05- 1; EI: '05- 5; WCp: '06- 1; ECp: '08- 1.
Russian champion 2007, 2010.
Progress at LJ: 2000- 6.20, 2001- 6.12i/6.07, 2002- 6.32, 2003- 6.09i/6.07, 2004- 6.54, 2005- 6.79, 2006- 7.11, 2007- 7.21, 2008- 7.04, 2009- 6.72, 2010- 7.01, 2011- 6.84/7.06w, 2012- 6.87. pbs: HJ 1.82 ?, TJ 13.88 '04.
Having been a high jumper, she played basketball before returning to athletics in 2000.

Yevgeniya KOLODKO b. 2 Jul 1990 Neryungi, Yakutia 1.84m 94kg.
At SP: OG: '12- 2; WCh: '11- 5; WI: '12- 7; EU23: '11- 1; EJ: '09- 9; EI: '13- 2. RUS champion 2012.
Progress at SP: 2007- 14.26, 2008- 15.04i/14.87, 2009- 15.38, 2010- 16.73, 2011- 19.78, 2012- 20.48.

Mariya KONOVALOVA b. 14 Aug 1974 Angarsk 1.78m 62kg. née Pantyukhova. Moskva VS.
At 10,000m: OG: '08- 5; WCh: '09- 11. At 5000m: WCh: '95- 6, '99- 7, '07- 11; EC: '10- 4. At 3000m: WI: '95- 12; EI: '96- 5. Eur CC: '05-06-08: 10/2/4. Won RUS 5000m 2009-10.
Progress at 5000m, 10,000m, Mar: 1995- 15:01.23, 1997- 16:10.4/32:53.69; 1998- 15:13.22, 1999- 14:58.60, 2000- 15:49.04, 2007- 15:02.96, 2008- 14:38.09, 30:35.84; 2009- 14:42.06, 30:31.03; 2010- 14:49.68, 2:23:50; 2011- 2:25:18, 2012- 15:27.54, 2:25:38. pbs: 1500m 4:05.10 '98, 2000m 5:38.98i '10, 3000m 8:30.18 '99, 15km 49:58+ '10, HMar 69:56 '12, 30km 1:41:18+ '10.

Yekaterina KOSTETSKAYA b. 31 Dec 1986 St Petersburg 1.68m 53kg. Yunost Rossli. Was at Texas State University, USA.
At 800m: OG: '08- sf; WCh: '11- 5; WUG: '07- 2; ET: '09- 2. At 1500m: OG: '12- 9. At 400mh: WJ: '04- 1; WY: '03- 2; EJ: '03- 1, '05- 2/1R. Won RUS 1500m 2012.
Progress at 400mh, 800m, 1500m: 2000- 50.48, 2001- 55.26, 2002- 2:10.36, 59.68; 2003- 2:05.95, 57.52; 2004- 2:11.8i, 55.55; 2005- 55.89, 2006-

56.75, 2007- 1:59.52, 2008- 1:56.67, 2009- 1:59.31, 2010- 2:01.19, 2011- 1:57.19, 4:01.77; 2012- 1:57.46, 3:59.28. pbs: 200m 24.51i '05, 400m 53.72i '05, 53.75 '07; 60mh 8.71i '05, 100mh 13.67 '05, TJ 12.18 '05.
Mother Olga Dvirna was European 1500m champion 1982 (pb 3:54.23 '82), father Aleksandr Kostetskiy 800m pb 1:45.17 '84. She married Australian pole vaulter Steve Hooker in 2012 and is expecting a baby in June 2013.

Yelena KOTULSKAYA b. 8 Aug 1988 1.74m 61kg. née Kofanova. Moskva.
At 800m: WCh: '09- sf; WI: '12- 5; EU23: '09- 1; EJ: '07- h; EI: '13- 2; WUG: '11- 2.
World indoor 4x800m record 2010 & 2011.
Progress at 800m: 2003- 2:13.11, 2005- 2:08.61, 2006- 2:05.82i, 2007- 2:02.66, 2008- 2:01.80, 2009- 1:58.60, 2010- 1:58.50, 2011- 1:58.04, 2012- 1:57.77. pbs: 400m 53.19 '09, 500m 1:13.23i '06, 600m 1:26.38i '11, 1000m 2:37.58i '12, 1500m 4:15.49 '09.

Antonina KRIVOSHAPKA b. 21 Jul 1987 Volgograd 1.68m 60kg. Rostov-na-Donu VS.
At 400m/4x400m: OG: '12- 6/2R; WCh: '09- 3/3R, '11- 5/3R; EC: '10- 3/1R; WJ: '04- h; WY: '03- 2; EI: '09- 1/1R; CCp: '10- 2R. Won RUS 2009, 2012.
Progress at 400m: 2002- 54.35, 2003- 53.09, 2004- 53.67, 2005- 55.03i/55.63, 2006- 55.40i, 2007- 52.32, 2008- 51.24, 2009- 49.29, 2010- 50.10, 2011- 49.92, 2012- 49.16. pbs: 200m 23.03 '12, 300m 36.38i '09.

Anna KRYLOVA b. 3 Oct 1985. née Kuropatkina. Luch Moskva.
At TJ: WCh: '11- 7; WI: '12- 6; EU23: '07- 4.
Progress at TJ: 2001- 12.85, 2002- 12.75, 2003- 12.86, 2004- 13.34/13.62w, 2005- 13.25, 2006- 14.13, 2007- 14.20, 2008- 13.84i/13.32, 2009- 14.14i/13.27, 2010- 14.02i/13.69/13.77w, 2011- 14.35, 2012- 14.40. pb LJ 6.45 '06.
Cousin of Denis Kapustin, TJ 1 EC 94, 3 OG 00.

Olga KUCHERENKO b. 5 Nov 1985 Sidory, Volgograd region 1.72m 59kg. Lokomotiv Penza.
At LJ: WCh: '09- 5, '11- 2; EC: '10- 3; EU23: '07- 12; EI: '09-3, '13- 6; ET: '09-10: 2/2.
Progress at LJ: 2002- 6.08, 2004- 6.30, 2005- 6.34, 2006- 6.72/6.80w, 2007- 6.41/6.70w, 2008- 6.87i/6.70, 2009- 6.91, 2010- 7.13, 2011- 6.86, 2012- 7.03, 2013- 7.00i.

Mariya KUCHINA b. 14 Jan 1993 Prokhladny, Kabradino-Balkar 1.82m 60kg. Moskovskaya.
At HJ: WJ: '12- 3; WY: '09- 2; EJ: '11- 1.
World junior indoor high jump record 2011.
Progress at HJ: 2009- 1.87, 2010- 1.91, 2011- 1.97i/1.95, 2012- 1.96i/1.89.

Olga KURBAN b. 16 Dec 1987 Irkutsk 1.73m 63kg. Irkutsk TU.
At Hep: OG: '08- 13. '12- 20; WCh: '07- 19; EU23: '09- 2; WUG: '11- 1; Russian champion 2008, 2011. At Pen: EI: '09- 4.

Progress at Hep: 2005- 5330, 2006- 5675, 2007- 6185, 2008- 6559, 2009- 6205, 2011- 6151, 2012- 6528. pbs: 200m 23.67 '12, 800m 2:11.38 '12, 60mh 8.31i '09, 100mh 13.29 '08, HJ 1.86i '12, 1.85 '11; PV 3.80i '06, 3.60 '05; LJ 6.51 '08, SP 14.78 '12, JT 49.23 '08, Pen 4792i '12.
Had a baby in 2010.

Yelena LASHMANOVA b. 9 Apr 1992 Saransk 1.70m 48kg. Biology student at Mordovia State University.
At 20kmW: OG: '12- 1; WCp: '12- 1. At 10000mW: WJ: '10- 1; EJ: '11- 1; ECp: '11- 1J. At 5000mW: WY: '09- 1.
Official world 20km walk record 2012, world junior 10,000m walk record 2011.
Progress at 20kW: 2012- 1:25:02, 2013- 1:25:49. pbs: 5000mW 20:44.37i '10, 10000mW 42:59.48 '11.
Best ever debut at 20k walk (1:26:30 in 2012).

Lyudmila LITVINOVA b. 8 Jun 1985 Lipetsk 1.77m 60kg. Moskva VS.
At 400m/4x400m: OG: 08- 2R; WCh: '07- 4R, '09- sf/3R, '11- 3R; EU23: '07- 1/1R; ECp: '08- 1R, '09- 2/1R.
Progress at 400m: 2001- 55.59, 2004- 53.84, 2005- 54.36, 2006- 51.99, 2007- 51.25, 2008- 50.62, 2009- 50.27, 2011- 50.92, 2012- 50.61. pb 200m 22.82 '09.
Married Russian team physio Aleksey Kosenkov in August 2009.

Tatyana LYSENKO b. 9 Oct 1983 Bataisk, Rostov region 1.86m 81kg. Bataisk VS.
At HT: OG: '04- dnq 19, '12- 1; WCh: '05- 3, '09- 6, '11- 1; EC: '06- 1, '10- 2; EU23: '03- 5; WUG: '03- 5; WCp: '06- 2, '10- 1; ECp: '06-07-10-11: 1/ dq1/2/2. Won RUS 2005, 2009-12.
Three world hammer records, eight Russian records 2005-12.
Progress at HT: 2000- 49.08, 2001- 55.73, 2002- 61.85, 2003- 67.19, 2004- 71.54, 2005- 77.06, 2006- 77.80, 2007- 77.30/78.61dq, 2009- 76.41, 2010- 76.03, 2011- 77.13, 2012- 78.51.
Two-year drugs ban after positive test on 9 May 2007.

Yekaterina MARTYNOVA b. 6 Aug 1986 Bryansk 1.72m 59kg. Sverdlovsk Dyn.
At 1500m: OG: '12- h; WCh: '11- sf; EJ: '05- 2; EI: '11- 3; ET: '11- 2. At 800m: WJ: '04- sf; WY: '03- 4; EU23: '07- 7. Won Russian 1500m 2011.
Progress at 1500m: 2004- 4:24.71i, 2005- 4:15.46, 2006- 4:15.09, 2007- 4:15.81, 2008- 4:03.68i/4:05.06, 2009- 4:05.40, 2010- 4:09.46, 2011- 4:01.68, 2012- 3:59.49. pbs: 400m 55.97i '08, 56.59 '06; 800m 1:59.17 '11, 1000m 2:37.63i '08.

Anna NAZAROVA b. 3 Feb 1986 St. Petersburg 1.72m 58kg.
At LJ: OG: '12- 5; WJ: '04- dnq; EJ: '05- 3; EU23: '07- 1; WUG: '11- 1; WI: '10- 6.
Progress at LJ: 2003- 6.00/6.12w, 2004- 6.48, 2005- 6.50i/6.31, 2006- 6.66, 2007- 6.81, 2008- 6.71/6.75w, 2009- 6.60, 2010- 6.75i/6.54, 2011- 6.89i/6.88, 2012- 7.11. pb TJ 13.80i '07, 13.39 '10.

Natalya NAZAROVA b. 26 May 1979 Moskva 1.68m 57kg. Luch Moskva.
At 400m/4x400mR: OG: '00- sf/res (3)R, '04- 8/1R, '12- res (2)R; WCh: '99- 6/1R, '03- 4/2R, '07- 4R, '09- res 3R; EC: '02- 2R, '10- 1resR; WJ: '98- 1/2R; WI: '99-03-04-06-08-10: 1R,/1&1R /1&1R/4&1R/2&1R/2R; EI: '00- 2; EJ: '97- 7; WUG: '05- 1; WCp: '02- 3R; ECp: '99- 1R. Won RUS 1999-2000, 2003-04.
World indoor 4x400m world records 1999 & 2004.
Progress at 400m: 1995- 55.79, 1996- 54.59, 1997- 52.94, 1998- 51.50, 1999- 50.48, 2000- 50.10, 2002- 51.15, 2003- 49.78, 2004- 49.65, 2005- 51.31, 2006- 49.98i/51.09, 2007- 50.52, 2008- 51.10i/51.60, 2009- 50.56, 2010- 50.88, 2012- 50.00. pbs: 100m 11.57 '99, 200m 23.01/22.9 '99, 300m 36.3+ '03, 500m 1:07.36i '04 (world best), 600m 1:26.35i '00.
Plays violin and piano. Record nine World Indoor medals.

Anna OMAROVA b. 3 Oct 1981 Pyatigorsk 1.80m 108kg. née Tolokina. Moskva VS. Economics student.
At SP: OG: '08- 6; WCh: '07- 9, '11- 10; WJ: 00- 5; WI: '08- 8; EI: '07- 6, '09- 4; ECp: '07- 1, '08- 2. Russian champion 2007.
Progress at SP: 1997- 12.98, 1998- 15.88i/14.18, 1999- 13.45, 2000- 16.12, 2001- 17.13, 2003- 17.28, 2004- 17.12, 2005- 17.04i/16.70, 2006- 18.40, 2007- 19.69, 2008- 19.29, 2009- 18.53, 2010- 19.00i/18.72, 2011- 19.23, 2012- 18.80. pb DT 51.62 '07.
Daughter Aminat born in 2002.

Darya PISHCHALNIKOVA b. 19 Jul 1985 Astrakhan 1.88m 125kg. Saransk VS
At DT: OG: '12- 2dq?; WCh: '07- dq(2), '11- 11; EC: '06- 1; WJ: '02- 8, '04- 2; WY: '01- 2; EU23: '05- 2, '07- dq(2); EJ: '03- 3; EY: '01- 1; WCp: '06- 4; ECp: '06- 2, '07- dq (2), '11- 2. Russian champion 2011.
Progress at DT: 2000- 50.48, 2001- 55.26,) 2002- 56.24, 2003- 54.80, 2004- 58.26, 2005- 60.62, 2006- 65.55, 2007- 63.13/65.78dq, 2008- 67.28dq, 2011- 63.91, 2012- 64.56/70.69dq. pb SP 14.55 '12.
Her 70.69 at the 2012 Russian Champs was the longest by a woman since 2002. 2-year drugs bans to 2011 and stripped of her 2007 World silver medal. Ban also pending for positive test in 2012 which may cost her Olympic silver medal and Russian title. Sister of Bogdan Pishchalnikov (qv). Their father Vitaliy had DT pb 67.76 '84 and mother Tatyana DT pb 61.62 '84.

Yekaterina POISTOGOVA b. 1 Mar 1991 Nizhny Novgorod 1.75m 65kg. née Zavyalova.
At 800m: OG: '12- 3; WJ: '08- sf, '10- 8; WY: '07- sf; EJ: '09- 3 (10 1500m). Wobn RUS 2012.
Progress at 800m, 1500m: 2007- 2:06.96, 2008- 2:04.96, 2009- 2:02.11, 4:18.82; 2010- 2:04.33, 4:27.68; 2011- 2:02.2, 4:17.9; 2012- 1:57.53, 4:00.11. pbs: 600 1:26.6+ '12, 1000m 2:36.97i '13.

Anastasiya POTAPOVA b. 6 Sep 1985 Volgo-

grad 1.78m 61kg. née Taranova. Volgograd VS.
At TJ: WJ: '04- 1; EJ: '03- 1, EU23: '05- 5, '07- 3;
WI: '10- 4; EI: '09- 1.
Progress at TJ: 2002- 13.18, 2003- 13.93, 2004-
14.11, 2005- 14.20, 2006- 14.04i/13.90, 2007- 14.24,
2008- 14.36, 2009- 14.68i/14.40, 2010- 14.44i, 2011-
14.00/14.13w, 2012- 14.23i/14.20. pb LJ 6.71i '09,
6.52 '08.

Anastasiya SAVCHENKO b. 15 Nov 1989
1.75m 65kg. Luch Moskva.
At PV: OG: '12- dnq 26-; EC: '12- 4; EU23: '09- 8,
'11- 6; EI: '13- 5=.
Progress at PV: 2005- 3.80, 2006- 3.80i/3.70,
2007- 3.90, 2008- 4.20i/4.10, 2009- 4.30i/4.20,
2010- 4.30, 2011- 4.40, 2012- 4.60, 2013- 4.71i.

Mariya SAVINOVA b. 13 Aug 1985 Chelyabinsk
1.72m 60kg. Sverdlovsk Dyn.
At 800m: OG: '12- 1; WCh: '09- 5, '11- 1; EC: '10-
1; WI: '10- 1; EI: '09- 1; CCp: '10- 3; ET: '11- 1. Won
Russian 800m 2009, 2011.
World indoor 4x800m record 2008.
Progress at 800m: 2002- 2:09.68, 2003- 2:08.38,
2004- 2:07.43, 2005- 2:07.03, 2006- 2:05.91, 2007-
2:00.78, 2008- 2:01.07, 2009- 1:57.90, 2010- 1:57.56,
2011- 1:55.87, 2012- 1:56.19. pbs: 400m 51.43 '12,
600m 1:26.11i '09, 1:26.6+ '12; 1000m 2:34.56i '09,
1500m 4:08.2i, 4:10.25 '10.
Married Aleksey Farnosov (1500m 3:41.69i '11)
on 10 Sep 2010.

Kristina SAVITSKAYA b. 10 Jun 1991
Krasnoyarsk 1.80m 72kg. Student at the
Krasnoyarsk Academy of Summer Sports.
At Hep: OG: '12- 8; WY: '07- 16; EU23: '11- 7, EJ:
'09- 6; Russian champion 2012.
Progress at Hep: 2009- 5642, 2011- 5989, 2012-
6681. pbs: 200m 24.46 '12, 800m 2:12.27 '12,
60mh 8.37i '12, 100mh 13.37 '12, HJ 1.88 '12, LJ
6.65 '12, SP 15.27 '12, JT 46.83 '12, Pen 4590i '12.

Svetlana SHKOLINA b. 9 Mar 1986 Yartsevo,
Smolensk reg. 1.87m 66kg. Luch Moskva.
At HJ: OG: '08- 14, '12- 3; WCh: '09- 6. '11- 5; EC:
'10- 4; WJ: '04- 2; WY: '03- 2=; EU23: '07- 1; EJ:
'05- 1; WI: '10- 4; EI: '09- 4=, '11- 4=; WUG: '05-4,
'07- 4; ECp: '10: 2. Russian champion 2010.
Progress at HJ: 2001- 1.75, 2002- 1.84, 2003- 1.88,
2004- 1.91, 2005- 1.92, 2006- 1.92, 2007- 1.96,
2008- 1.98, 2009- 1.98, 2010- 2.00i/1.98, 2011-
2.00i/1.99, 2012- 2.03.

Liliya SHOBUKHOVA b. 13 Nov 1977
Beloretsk, Bashkortostan 1.69m 50kg. née
Volkova. Beloretsk VS.
At 5000m: OG: '04- 13, '08- 6, '12- dnf; WCh:
'05- 9; EC: '02- 17, '06- 2; WCp: '06- 2; ECp: '04-
05-06: 2/1/1. At 10000m: WCh: '09- 19; EC: '10-
dnf. At Mar: OG: '12- dnf. At 3000m: WI: '06- 2;
EI: '02- 5, '05- 5. World 4km CC: '02- 23. Eur CC:
'02- 17, '04- 11. Won Russian 5000m 2002, 2005,
2008; 10,000m 2009.
Records: European 5000m 2008, World indoor
3000m 2006, world 30km road 2011; 3 Russian

marathon records 2010-11.
Progress at 5000m, 10000m, Mar: 1998- 16:50.64,
2001- 15:42.0, 2002- 15:25.00, 2004- 14:52.19, 2005-
14:47.07, 2006- 14:56.57, 2007- 15:51.53, 2008-
14:23.75, 2009- 30:29.36, 2:24:24; 2010- 2:20:25,
2011- 2:18:20, 2012- 2:22:59. pbs: 800m 2:03.18 '06,
1000m 2:39.81i '06, 1500m 4:03.78 '04, 1M 4:22.14
'04, 2000m 5:35.80 '07, 3000m 8:27.86i '06, 8:34.85
'04; Road: 10km 33:11 '01, HMar 69:25+ '11, 30k
1:38:23+ '11.
Marathons: London 3rd on marathon debut
2009, 1st 2010, 2nd 2011; won Chicago 2009-11
and the World Marathon Majors Series 2009/10
and 2010/11. Daughter Anna born in 2003,
expecting second child in 2013.

Tatyana SIBILEVA b. 17 May 1980 Chelyabinsk
1.59m 42kg. Chelyabinsk VS.
At 20kW: OG: '08- 11; WCh: '07- 9; EU23: '01- 4;
WUG: '03- 1, '05- 3; WCp: '08- 2; ECp: '07- 6.
Progress at 20kW: 1998- 1:29:53, 2000- 1:30:51,
2001- 1:27:33, 2002- 1:32:17, 2003- 1:27:54, 2004-
1:29:12, 2005- 1:31:18, 2006- 1:28:58, 2007- 1:28:51,
2008- 1:26:16, 2009- 1:31:59, 2010- 1:25:52, 2011-
1:30:37, 2012- 1:26:59. pbs: 10kW 42:15+ '08,
45:09.3t '06; 30000mW 2:24:56 '04 (world best).

Anzhelika SIDOROVA b. 28 Jun 1991. Moskva.
At PV: WJ: '10- 4; EI: '13- 3.
Progress at PV: 2007- 3.80, 2008- 4.00, 2009-
4.10i/4.00, 2010- 4.30, 2011- 4.40i/4.30, 2012- 4.50,
2013- 4.62i.

Yelena SLESARENKO b. 28 Feb 1982
Volgograd 1.78m 57kg. née Sivushenko.
Volgograd VS.
At HJ: OG: '04- 1, '08- 4; WCh: '07- 4, '09- 10,
'11- 4; EC: '06- 5; EU23: '03- 2; EJ: '01- 4; WUG:
'03- 3; WI: '04-06-08: 1/1/2; EI: '02- 5=; WCp:
'06- 1; ECp: '04- 1, '07- 1. Won WAF 2004,
Russian 2005.
Progress at HJ: 1999- 1.82, 2000- 1.88, 2001-
1.94i/1.88, 2002- 1.97, 2003- 1.98i/1.96, 2004- 2.06,
2005- 2.00, 2006- 2.02i/2.00, 2007- 2.02, 2008-
2.03, 2009- 1.96, 2010- 1.88i, 2011- 1.97.
Tied Russian indoor record to win gold at 2004
World Indoors and set a Russian record of 2.06
to win Olympic gold. Daughter Liza born on 20
July 2012.

Yelena SOBOLEVA b. 3 Oct 1982 Bryansk
1.76m 66kg. Lokomotiv Moskva.
At 1500m: WCh: '05- 4, '07- dq (2); EC: '06- 4;
EU23: '03- 6; WI: '06- 2, '08- dq (1); EI: '13- 6.
Won Russian 1500m 2006.
WIR 1500m 3:58.28 2006 (and two cancelled in
2008).
Progress at 800m, 1500m: 2002- 2:04.43, 2003-
2:01.65, 4:12.02; 2004- 4:11.98, 2005- 2:00.59,
4:01.14; 2006- 1:57.28, 3:56.43; 2007dq- 1:59.49,
3:57.30; 2008dq- 1:54.85, 3:56.59; 2011- 2:03.45.
4:06.64; 2012- 1:59.90, 4:00.09. pbs: 1000m 2:32.40i
'06, 2:36.50 '05; 1M 4:15.63dq '07, 2000m 5:36.43
'07, 3000m 8:55.89 '05.

Two-year drugs ban announced in 2008 and results cancelled from 26 Apr 2007. Son born in July 2010.

Vera SOKOLOVA b. 8 Jun 1987 Solianoy, Chuvashiya 1.51m 51kg. Mordovia VS.
At 20kmW: WCh: '09- 14, '11- 11; EC: '10- 3; WCp: '10- 4; ECp: '09- 10; Russian champion 2009. At 10000mW: WJ: '02-04-06: 9/3/4; EJ: '05- 1; WCp: '04/06- 1J; ECp: '03- 2J, '05- 1J. At 5000mW: WY: '03- 1.
Walks records: World 20km 2011, world junior 10,000m and 5000m indoors 2005.
Progress at 20kW: 2006- 1:40:03, 2007- 1:32:56, 2008- 1:30:11, 2009- 1:25:26, 2010- 1:25:35, 2011- 1:25:08, 2012- 1:28:06. 2013- 1:26:00. pbs: 3000m 12:51.96 '04, 5000mW 20:10.3i '10, 10kW 42:04+ '11, 43:11.34t '05.

Yelena SOKOLOVA b. 23 Jul 1986 Staryi Oskol, Belgorod reg. 1.70m 61kg. née Kremneva. Krasnodarsk krai.
At LJ: OG: '12- 2; WCh: '09- dnq 13; EU23: '07- 3; EI: '09- 2; WUG: '07- 2. Won DL 2012, Russian 2009, 2012.
Progress at LJ: 2002- 6.33, 2003- 6.39i?/6.31, 2006- 6.53, 2007- 6.71, 2008- 6.74, 2009- 6.92, 2010- 6.72/6.90w, 2011- 6.76, 2012- 7.07. pbs: 60m 7.34i '12, 100m 11.61 '12, TJ 13.15i/12.93 '03.

Irina TARASOVA b. 15 Apr 1987 Kovrov 1.79m 115kg.
At SP: OG: '12- 8; ECh: '12- 2; WI: '12- 8; WJ: '04- 9, '06- 3; WY: '03- 5; EU23: '07- 1; EJ: '05- 2; EI: '13- 5WUG: '07- 1.
Progress at SP: 2002- 14.01, 2003- 15.04, 2004- 16.16, 2005- 16.79i/16.53, 2006- 17.11, 2007- 18.27, 2008- 18.45, 2009- 18.21, 2010- 18.18, 2011- 18.72, 2012- 19.35.

Tatyana TOMASHOVA b. 1 Jul 1975 Perm 1.65m 52kg. Perm VS.
At 1500m: OG: '04- 2, '12- 4; WCh: '03- 1, '05- 1; EC: '02- 3, '06- 1; WCp: '02- 2, '06- 2; ECp: '02- 3.
At 5000m: OG: '00- 13; WCh: '01- 10; ECp: '00- 1.
Won GP 3000m 2001 (2nd 2002), RUS 1500m 2001-03, 5000m 2000.
Russian 5000m record 2000.
Progress at 1500m, 5000m: 1996- 4:17.97, 15:48.13; 1997- 4:16.39, 1998- 4:13.50, 1999- 4:08.5?, 15:26.67; 2000- 4:04.80, 14:53.00; 2001- 4:03.31, 14:39.22; 2002- 4:01.28, 14:47.85; 2003- 3:58.52, 2004- 3:58.12, 2005- 3:59.05, 2006- 3:56.91, 2007- 4:02.8dq, 2008- 3:59.42dq, 2011- 4:03.69, 2012- 3:59.71. pbs: 800m 2:02.09 '12, 1000m 2:34.91 '05, 1M 4:24.84 '07, 2000m 5:43.3 '01, 3000m 8:25.56 '01, road 10km 32:48 '99.
Two-year drugs ban announced in 2008 and results cancelled from 23 May 2007.

Kseniya USTALOVA b. 14 Jan 1988 Sverdlovsk 1.77m 65kg. Sverdlovsk. Engineering student.
At 400m/4x400m: EC: '10- 2/1R; EU23: '09- 1/1R; EJ: '07- 2/1R; WUG: '11- 1R; CCp: '10- 2R; WI: '12- 3R; ET: '10- 1/1R. Won RUS 2010.

Progress at 400m: 2005- 55.51, 2006- 54.00i. 2007- 52.90, 2008- 54.57, 2009- 51.45, 2010- 49.92, 2011- 52.03, 2012- 50.48. pbs: 200m 24.09 '10, 300m 36.76i '13.

Viktoriya VALYUKEVICH b. 22 May 1982 Sochi 1.78m 63kg. née Gurova. Krasnodar TU.
At TJ: OG: '04- dnq 21, '08- 7, '12- 8; WCh: '05- 10; EU23: '03- 1; EJ: '01- 3; WUG: '03- 2; EI: '05- 1; ECp: '06- 2, '07- 3.
Progress at TJ: 1998- 12.56, 1999- 13.02, 2000- 13.44, 2001- 13.75/13.92w, 2002- 14.22, 2003- 14.37, 2004- 14.65, 2005- 14.74i/14.38, 2006- 14.60, 2007- 14.46, 2008- 14.85, 2009- 14.40, 2012- 14.64. pb LJ 6.72 '07.
Married Dmitrij Valukevic (BLR/SVK triple jumper) in September 2008. Son Georgiy born in June 2010.

Olesya ZABARA b. 6 Oct 1982 Makhoshevskaya, Adygeya 1.65m 56kg. née Bufalova. Maikop TU.
At TJ: WCh: '07- 10; EC: '06- 5, "12- dnq 19; WI: 08- 7; EI: '07- 2, '11- 2. At 400mh: WY: '99- 5.
Progress at TJ: 2001- 13.09, 2005- 13.67, 2006- 14.50, 2007- 14.50i/14.49, 2008- 14.54i/14.48, 2011- 14.45i/14.19/14.36w, 2012- 14.41/14.48w. pbs: 100mh 14.07 '99, 400mh 59.96 '99.
Child born in 2009.

Kseniya ZADORINA b. 2 Mar 1987 Moskva 1.73m 59kg. Moskva Dyn.
At 400m/4x400m: WCh: '11- res (3)R; EC: '10- 1R, '12- 2; WJ: '06- 4; EU23: '07- 3/1R, 09- 2/1R; EJ: '05- 2/1R; WUG: '07- 3/2R; EI: '11- 3/1R, '13- 2R; ET: '10- 1R.
Progress at 400m: 2005- 52.64, 2006- 51.81, 2007- 51.06, 2008- 51.48, 2009- 51.41, 2010- 50.87, 2011- 50.92, 2012- 51.16. pbs: 200m 23.66i '11, 24.15 '08; 500m 1:08.94i '06 (WJR).

Yuliya ZARIPOVA b. 26 Apr 1986 Sbetlyi Yar, Volgograd reg. née Zarudneva. 1.72m 54kg. Volgograd Dyn.
At 3000mSt: OG: '12- 1; WCh: '09- 2, '11- 1; EC: '10- 1; CCp: '10- 1; ET: '10- 1. At 800m: EJ: '05- h.
At 3000m: EI: '09- 7. Eur CC: '05- 8J, '08- 3 U23.
Won Russian 3000mSt 2009, 2011-12.
Progress at 3000mSt: 2008- 9:54.9, 2009- 9:08.39, 2010- 9:17.57, 2011- 9:07.03, 2012- 9:05.02. pbs: 800m 2:05.44 '05, 1500m 4:01.70 '12, 3000m 8:54.50i '09, 5000m 16:02.81i '10.
Daughter Lenichke born 2007. Married Ildar Zaripov TJK in 2010.

Olga ZAYTSEVA b. 10 Nov 1984 Kaliningrad 1.76m 67kg. St Peterburg YR.
At 400m/4x400mR: EC: '06- 3/1R; EU23: '05- 1/1R. At 200m: WCh: '09- sf; ECp: '06- 1/1R. At LJ: WCh: '11- dnq 13. Won RUS 200m 2006, LJ 2011. World indoor 4x400m record 2006.
Progress at 400m. LJ: 2003- 6.36, 2004- 51.09, 2005- 50.06, 2006- 49.49, 2007- 52.93i, 2008- 51.42i/51.61; 2011- 7.01, 2012- 6.48. pbs: 100m 11.65 '08, 11.56w '09; 200m 22.67 '06, 600m 1:06.76i '06.
Switched from 400m back to long jump in 2011.

SAINT KITTS & NEVIS

Governing body: Saint Kitts Amateur Athletic Association, PO Box 932, Basseterre, St Kitts. Founded 1961.

Kim COLLINS b. 5 Apr 1976 Ogees, Saint-Peter 1.75m 64kg. Studied sociology at Texas Christian University, USA.
At 100m (/200m): OG: '96- qf, 00- 7/sf, '04- 6, '08- sf/6; WCh: '97- h, 99- h/h, '01- 5/3=, '03- 1, '05- 3, '07- sf, '09- qf/qf, '11- 3/sf/3R; CG: '02- 1; PAm: '07- 5, '11- 2; PAm-J: '95- 2; CAC: '99- 2, '01- 1/1, '03- 1; WCp: '02- 2/2R. At 60m: WI: '03- 2, '08- 2=. Won NCAA indoor 60m & 200m 2001. SKN records: 100m from 1996, 200m from 1998, 400m 2000.
Progress at 100m, 200m: 1995- 10.63, 21.85; 1996- 10.27, 21.06; 1998- 10.18/10.16w, 20.88/20.78w; 1999- 10.21, 20.43, 2000- 10.13A/10.15/10.02w, 20.31A/20.18w; 2001- 10.04A/10.00?/9.99w, 20.20/20.08w; 2002- 9.98, 20.49; 2003- 9.99/9.92w, 20.40w; 2004- 10.00, 20.98; 2005- 10.00, 2006- 10.33, 21.53; 2007- 10.14, 2008- 10.05, 20.25; 2009- 10.15/10.08w, 20.45; 2010- 10.20, 21.35/20.76w; 2011- 10.00A/10.01, 20.52; 2012- 10.01/9.96w. pbs: 60m 6.50i '11, 400m 46.93 '00.
The first athlete from his country to make Olympic and World finals and in 2003 the first to win a World Indoor medal and a World title; won a further medal in his 8th World Champs. There is a 'Kim Collins Highway' in St Kitts.

SENEGAL

Governing body: Fédération Sénégalaise d'Athlétisme, BP 1737, Stade Iba Mar DIOP, Dakar. Founded 1960.

Ndiss Kaba BADJI b. 21 Sep 1983 1.92m 79kg.
At LJ/(TJ): OG: '04- dnq 27, '08- 6/dnq nj; '12- dnq 24; WCh: '07- 7, '09- dnq 18; WJ: '02- dnq/9; AfG: '03- 2/4, '07- 5/1, '11- 3; AfCh: '02-04-08-10-12: 5/2/(1)/2/1; WI: '10- 6, '12- 5; WUG: '03- 5, '07- 2; CCp: '10- 6.
Senégal triple jump records 2007 & 2008.
Progress at LJ: 2001- 7.28, 2002- 7.83/7.90w, 2003- 7.92, 2004- 8.20A/8.03/8.30Aw, 2005- 7.88i/ (8.06/8.30w dq), 2007- 8.11, 2008- 8.16, 2009- 8.32, 2010- 8.27, 2011- 8.08, 2012- 8.17. pb TJ 17.07A '08, 16.80 '07, 17.15dq '05.
Drugs disqualification 2005-07.

SERBIA

Governing body: Athletic Federation of Serbia, Strahinjica Bana 73a, 11000 Beograd. Founded in 1921 (as Yugoslav Athletic Federation).
National Championships (Yugoslav) first held in 1920 (men) and 1923 (women). **2012 Champions: Men**: 100m/200m: Darko Sarovic 10.49w/21.52, 400m/400mh: Emir Bekric 46.91/49.87, 800m: Nemanja Kojic 1:51.20, 1500m: Uros Kutlesic 3:59.93, 5000m: Mirko Petrovic 14:55.86, 10000m/HMar: Kristjan Stosic 33:10.08/70:12, Mar: Ivan Miskeljin 2:38:55, 3000mSt: Goran Milicic 9:33.03, 110mh: Milan Ristic 13.91, HJ: Milos Todosijevic 2.05, PV: Mihail Dudas 4.80. LJ: Lazar Anic 7.50, TJ: Petar Djuric 15.16, SP: Asmir Kolasinac 20.48, DT: Milos Markovic 53.54, HT: Zoran Loncar 56.44, JT: Vedran Samac 76.72, Dec: Igor Sarcevic 7857, 10000mW: Predrag Filipovic 41:35.8, 20kW (440m short): Vladimir Savanovic 1:20:52. **Women**: 100m/200m: Tanja Mitic 11.64/24.22, 400m: Katarina Ilic 55.92, 800m: Marija Stambolic 2:09.50, 1500m: Sonja Stolic 4:26.22, 5000m: Milena Rmandic 16:39.99, 10000m/ HMar/3000mSt: Ana Subotic 35:47.76/1:24:34/ 10:38.61, Mar: *none*, 100mh: Mila Andric 13.95, 400mh: Maja Ciric 61.91, HJ: Zorana Bukvic 1.69, PV: Ksenija Marovic 3.60, LJ: Ivana Spanovic 6.50, TJ: Ivana Petrovic 12.58, SP: Dijana Sefcic 14.51, DT: Dragana Savanovic 35.80, HT: Sara Savatovic 59.03, JT: Tatjana Jelaca 54.52, Hep: *not held*, 10,000mW: Milica Stojanovic 59:24.8.

Mihail DUDAS b. 1 Nov 1989 Novi Sad 1.83m 84 kg. AV Crvena Zvezda.
At Dec: OG: '12- dnf; WCh: '11- 6; EC: '10- dnf, '12- 4; WJ: '08- 3; Eur23: '09- 3, '11- 3; EJ: '07- 15. At Hep: EI: '13- 3. Won SRB PV 2012. LJ & Dec 2011.
Two Serbian decathlon records 2011.
Progress at Dec: 2009- 7855, 2010- 7966, 2011- 8256, 2012- 8154. pbs: 60m 6.91i '13, 100m 10.71 '11, 400m 47.47 '11, 1000m 2:39.04i '13, 1500m 4:24.30 '09, 60mh 8.13i '13, 110mh 14.78 '12, HJ 2.04 '09, PV 4.90 '11, LJ 7.63 '10, SP 14.39i '12, 13.85 '11, DT 46.90 '12, JT 59.98 '12, Hep 6099i '13.

Asmir KOLASINAC b. 15 Oct 1984 Skopje, Macedonia 1.85m 130kg.
At SP: OG: '08- dnq 33, '12- 7; WCh: '09- dnq 22, '11- 11; EC: '10- 9, '12- 3; EU23: '05- dnq; EI: '13- 1; Won Balkan 2011; SRB 2008, 2010-12.
Progress at SP: 2004- 15.64, 2005- 17.88, 2006- 17.85, 2007- 19.30, 2008- 19.99, 2009- 20.41, 2010- 20.52i/20.38, 2011- 20.50, 2012- 20.85, 2013- 20.62i.

Women

Dragana TOMASEVIC b. 4 Jun 1982 Sremska Mitrovica 1.75m 80kg. AK Sirmijum, Sremska Mitrovica.
At DT: OG: '04/08/12- dnq 26/13/19; WCh: '05- 7, '07/09- dnq 19/19, '11- 7; EC: '06- 8, '10- 6, '12- 9; EU23: '03- 11; EJ: '01- 10; WUG: '05- 3, '07- 3; Won Balkan 2005, 2007, 2011; MedG 2005, SCG 2001-03, SRB 2006-07.
Four SCG/SRB discus records 2005-06.
Progress at DT: 1999- 34.93, 2000- 45.87/47.04dh, 2001-52.80/53.00dh, 2002- 54.41/55.33dh, 2003- 56.24/56.74dh, 2004- 59.52, 2005- 62.43, 2006- 63.63, 2007- 61.52, 2008- 62.70, 2009- 61.89, 2010- 62.55, 2011- 62.48, 2012- 61.92. pb SP 14.81 '04.

SLOVAKIA

Governing body: Slovak Athletic Federation, Junácka 6, 832 80 Bratislava. Founded 1939.
National Championships first held in 1939.
2012 Champions: Men: 100m: Adam Zavacky 10.61, 200m: Roman Turcáni 21.40, 400m: Dusan Páleník 48.19, 800m: Jozef Pelikán 1:49.34, 1500m/5000m: Jaroslav Szabo 3:58.42/15:11.34, 10000m: Ondrej Puskár 32:09.78, HMar: Imrich Pástor 71:45, Mar: Jozef Urban 2:25:34, 3000mSt: Jan Domény 9:49.17, 110mh: Matus Janecek 14.42, 400mh: Martin Kucera 50.73, HJ: Peter Horák 2.23, PV: Tomás Krajnák 4.80, LJ: Tomás Veszelka 7.02, TJ: Martin Koch 15.90, SP: Matus Olej 17.71, DT: Matej Gasaj 58.34, HT: Marcel Lomnicky 75.46, JT: Martin Benák 78.97, 20kW: Matej Tóth 1:27:54, 50kW: Dusan Majdan 3:59:05.
Women: 100m/200m: Alexandra Bezeková 11.97/24.28, 400m: Paula Habovstiaková 56.02, 800m: Lucia Klocová 2:05.05, 1500m/5000m/3000mSt: Lubomíra Maníková 4:44.14/18:41.22/11:32.60, 10000m: Petra Fasungová 37:12.19, HMar: Katerina Beresová 82:32, Mar: Ingrid Petnuchová 2:55:58, 100mh: Lucia Mokrásová 14.11, 400mh: Lucia Slanicková 62.27, HJ: Iveta Srnková 1.73, PV: Slovomíra Slúková 3.90, LJ: Jana Veldáková 6.64, TJ: Dana Veldáková 14.15, SP: Veronika Kanuchová 12.76, DT: Ivona Tomanová 44.45, HT: Martina Hrasnová 73.09, JT: Veronika Easová 46.80, 20kW: Mária Czaková 1:37:41.

Matej TÓTH b. 10 Feb 1983 Nitra 1.85m 73kg. Dukla Banská Bystrica.
At 20kW/(50kW): OG: '04- 32, '08- 26, '12- (8); WCh: '05- 21, 07- 14, '09- 9/10, '11- 13/dnf; EC: '06- 6, '10- 7, EU23: '03- 6; WCp: '10- (1); ECp: '09- 9, '11- 2. At 10000mW: WJ: '02- 16, WY: '99- 8; EJ: '01- 6. Won SVK 20kW 2005-08, 2010-12; 50kW 2011.
SVK 50k walk records 2009 & 2011.
Progress at 20kW, 50kW: 1999- 1:34:29, 2000- 1:30:28, 2001- 1:29:33, 2003- 1:13:17, 2004- 1:23:18, 2005- 1:21:38, 2006- 1:21:39, 2007- 1:25:10, 2008- 1:21:24, 2009- 1:20:53, 3:41:32; 2010- 1:22:04, 3:53:30; 2011- 1:20:16, 3:39:46; 2012- 1:20:25, 3:41:24. pbs: 3000mW 10:57.32i '11, 11:05.95 '12; 5000mW 18:34.56i '12, 18:54.39 '11; 10000W 39:45.03 '06, 39:07R '10; 30kW 2:12:46 '06.

Women

Martina HRASNOVÁ b. 21 Mar 1983 Bratislava 1.77m 88kg. née Danisová. Dukla Banská Bystrica.
At HT: OG: '08- 8, '12- dnq 20; WCh: '01/07: dnq 23/12, '09- 3; EC: '02 & '06- dnq 26, '12- 2; WJ: '00- 5, '02- 2; EJ: '99- 4, '01- 2; WUG: '07- 5, '09- 2. Won SVK SP 2003, 2006; HT 2000-01, 2006, 2008-09, 2011-12.
14 Slovakian hammer records 2001-09.
Progress at HT: 1999- 58.61, 2000- 61.62, 2001- 68.50, 2002- 68.22, 2003- 66.36, 2005- 69.24, 2006- 73.84, 2007- 69.22, 2008- 76.82, 2009- 76.90, 2011-

72.47, 2012- 73.34. pbs: 60m 7.96i '12, SP 15.02 '06, DT 43.15 '06, Wt 21.74i '11.
Two-year drugs ban (nandrolone) from July 2003. Daughter Rebeka born on 4 July 2010. Brother of Branislav Danis (HT 69.20 '06), who is now her coach.

Lucia KLOCOVÁ b. 20 Nov 1983 Martin, Zilina 1.71m 58kg. AK ZTS Martin.
At 800m: OG: '04/08- sf; WCh: '03/05/07/09/11- sf; EC: '06- sf, '10- 4, '12- 6; WJ: '00- 3, '02- 2; EU23: '03- 2, '05- 5; EJ: '01- 1. At 1500m: OG: '12- 8. Won SVK 400m 2007, 800m 2004, 2006, 2010-12; 1500m 2010-11.
SVK records: 1000m 2012, 1500m (4) 2010-12.
Progress at 800m, 1500m: 1998- 2:11.63, 2000- 2:04.00, 2001- 2:03.06, 2002- 2:01.59, 2003- 2:00.60, 2004- 2:00.79, 2005- 2:00.64, 2006- 2:00.28, 2007- 1:58.62, 2008- 1:58.51, 2009- 1:59.79, 4:30.65; 2010- 1:59.31, 4:08.86; 2011- 1:59.48, 4:30.95; 2012- 2:00.16, 4:02.99. pbs: 400m 52.98 '07, 600m 1:26.96 '08, 1000m 2:38.72 '12.
After seven successive 800m semi-finals at World and Olympics, made Olympic 1500m final at 1500m in 2012.
Baby due in June 2013.

Dana VELDÁKOVÁ b. 3 Jun 1981 Roznava 1.79m 60kg. AK Spartak Dubnica.
At (LJ/)TJ: OG: '08- dnq, '12- 12; WCh: '05- dnq 17, '07-09-11: 12/8/11; EC: '02/06- dnq 15/24, '10- 7, '12- 5; WJ: '98- 6, '00- 4/3; EU23: '01- 5, '03- 4; EJ: '99- 8; WI: '06-10-12: 8/6/8; EI: '07-09-11: 6/3/3; WUG: '03- 5, '07- 2. Won SVK 100mh 2003, TJ 2002-05, 2007-12, Hep 2001, 2004.
Two SVK triple jump records 2007-08.
Progress at TJ: 1998- 13.12, 1999- 13.13/13.19w, 2000- 13.92, 2001- 13.73, 2002- 13.99, 2003- 14.02, 2004- 13.96A, 2005- 14.16, 2006- 14.19, 2007- 14.41, 2008- 14.51, 2009- 14.43, 2010- 14.32/14.59w, 2011- 14.48, 2012- 14.36. pbs: 60m 7.73i '06, 60mh 8.82i '03, 100mh 14.38 '01, HJ 1.75 '01, LJ 6.56 '08, SP 11.56i '04, Hep 5191 '01, Pen 3746i '03.
Twin **Jana** LJ 6.72 '08, 6.88w '10; TJ 13.40 '04.

SLOVENIA

Governing body: Atletska Zveza Slovenije, Letaliska cesta 33c, 1122 Ljubljana. Current organisation founded 1948.
2012 National Champions: Men: 100m: Matic Osovnikar 10.49, 200m: Jan Zumer 21.15, 400m: Erik Voncina 47.84, 800m/1500m/HMar: Mitja Krevs 1:53.65/3:51.37/69:20, 3000m/5000m: Zid Zevnik 8:29.37/14:58.81, 10000m: Anton Kosmac 31:09.76, Mar: Mitja Kosovelj 2:22:09, 3000mSt: Bostjan Buc 9:06.77, 110mh: Damjan Zlatnar 14.43, 400mh: Marko Macuh 52.11, HJ: Rozle Prezelj 2.05, PV: Andrej Poljanec 5.00, LJ: Rok Viler 7.31, TJ: Andrej Batagelj 15.65, SP: Miroslav Vodovnik 17.40, DT: Tadej Hribar 50.91, HT: Nejc Plesko 62.10, JT: Matija Kranjc 73.36, Dec: Damjan Sitar 5468. **Women**: 100m: Sara Strajnar 11.76, 200m: Sabina Veit 24.00, 400m: Liona

Rebernik 54.40, 800m: Sonja Roman 2:07.11, 1500m: Sonja Neger 5:08.29, 3000m: Mojca Grandovec 10:39.44, 5000m/10000m: Zana Jereb 17:13.83/38:18.71, HMar: Lidija Cerkovnik 1:21:25, Mar: Barbara Clemenz Dimnik 3:14:35, 3000mSt: Klara Ljubi 11:46.44, 100mh: Marina Tomic 13.28, 400mh: Ursa Belaj 61.65, HJ: Marusa Novak 1.80, PV: Tina Sutej 4.40, LJ: Nina Kokot 6.22, TJ: Marija Sestak 14.17, SP: Spela Hus 13.52, DT: Veronika Domjan 44.01, HT: Barbara Spiler 67.65, JT: Martina Ratej 58.74, Hep: Brina Mljac 3471.

Primoz KOZMUS b. 30 Sep 1979 Novo mesto 1.88m 106kg. AK Brezice.
At HT: OG: '00- dnq 38, '04- 6, '08- 1, '12- 2; WCh: '03-07-09-11: 5/2/1/3; EC: '02- dnq 25, '06- 7; EU23: '99- 12, '01- 14; WJ: '98- dnq. SLO champion 1999-2004, 2006, 2008-09, 2011; WAF 2008-09.
Ten SLO hammer records 2000-09.
Progress at HT: 1995- 45.82, 1996- 54.10, 1997- 61.08, 1998- 66.28, 1999- 70.11, 2000- 76.84, 2001- 71.17, 2002- 75.87, 2003- 81.21, 2004- 79.34, 2006- 80.38, 2007- 82.30, 2008- 82.02, 2009- 82.58, 2011- 80.28, 2012- 79.36.
First Slovenian Olympic champion. Older sister Simona set Slovenian women's hammer record (58.60 '01).

Women

Martina RATEJ b. 2 Nov 1981 Celje 1.78m 69kg. AD Kladivar Celje.
At JT: OG: '08- dnq 37, '12- 7; WCh: '09- 11, '11- 7; EC: '06- dnq 21, '10- 7, '12- dnq 21; WJ: '00- dnq 15. SLO champion 2005-12.
Five SLO javelin records 2008-10.
Progress at JT: 1999- 48.74, 2000- 46.83, 2005- 50.86, 2006- 57.49, 2007- 58.49, 2008- 63.44, 2009- 63.42, 2010- 67.16, 2011- 65.89, 2012- 65.24.

SOUTH AFRICA

Governing body: Athletics South Africa, PO Box 2712, Houghton 2041. Original body founded 1894.
National Championships first held in 1894 (men), 1929 (women). **2012 Champions: Men**: 100m/200m: Simon Magakwe 10.11/20.59, 400m: Lebogang Moeng 45.75, 800m: Mbulueni Mulaudzi 1:45.78, 1500m: Johan Cronje 3:39.28, 5000m: Gladwin Mzazi 13:29.84, 10000m/HMar: Stephen Mokoka 27:40.73/60:57, Mar: Coolboy Ngamole 2:13:18, 3000mSt: Ruben Ramolefi 8:24.48, 110mh: Junior Mkhatini 13.96, 400mh: Cornel Fredericks 48.91, HJ: Ruan Claasen 2.13, PV: Heinrich Smit 4.90, LJ: Zarck Visser 8.21w, TJ: Tumelo Thagane 16.23w, SP: Orazio Cremona 19.68, DT: Victor Hogan 61.16, HT: Chris Harmse 70.41 (18th successive title), JT: Robert Oosthuizen 76.32, Dec: Willem Coertzen 8244, 20kW: Lebogang Shange 1:25:48.
Women: 100m: Tholofelo Thipe 11.56, 200m:

Sonja van der Merwe 23.60, 400m: Justine Palframan 52.33, 800m: Caster Semenya 2:02.68, 1500m: Mapaseka Makhanya 4:12.84, 5000m/ HMar: René Kalmer 15:55.05/74:40, 10000m: Mpho Mabuza 35:33.46, Mar: Charné Bosman 2:41:56, 3000mSt: Tebogo Masehla 10:12.12, 100mh: Claudia Viljoen 13.67, 400mh: Wenda Theron 55.79, HJ: Anika Smit 1.90, PV: Deoné Joubert 3.60, LJ/TJ: Patience Ntshinglia 6.60/13.55, SP: Sonia Smuts 15.09, DT: Elizna Naude 56.91, HT: Magdalene Louw 52.50, JT: Sunette Viljoen 61.15, Hep: Bianca Erwee 5432, 20kW: Jessica van Wyk 1:47:39.

Lehann FOURIE b. 16 Feb 1987 Mafikeng 1.96m 98kg. Reebok. Studied at University of Nebraska.
At 110mh: OG: '12- 7; WCh: '09-/11 h; WJ: '06- h; AfCh: '10-1R, '12- 1; WUG: '09- 2. Won RSA 2011. At 60mh: WI: '12- 7.
African 110mh record 2012.
Progress at 110mh: 2005- 14.23, 2006- 14.12/13.91w, 2008- 13.93/13.71w, 2009- 13.56, 2010- 13.44/13.41w/13.4w 2011- 13.56, 2012- 13.24. pbs: 200m 21.87 '08, 55mh 7.13+i '12, 60mh 7.64i '12, 400mh 51.22 '09.

Cornel FREDERICKS b. 3 Mar 1990 Caledon 1.78m 70kg.
At 400mh/4x400mR: OG: '12- h; WCh: '11- 5; WJ: '08- 4; WY: '07- 5; AfCh: '10- 2; Won RSA 2010, 2012; Af-J 110mh & 400mh 2009.
Progress at 400mh: 2008- 50.39, 2009- 49.92, 2010- 48.79A/48.99, 2011- 48.14, 2012- 48.91. pbs: 400m 46.95 '10, 300mh 35.15 '10.

Godfrey Khotso MOKOENA b. 6 Mar 1985 Heidelberg, Gauteng 1.90m 73kg. Tuks AC, Pretoria.
At LJ/(TJ): OG: '04- (dnq 29), '08- 2, '12- 8; WCh: '05-07-09-11: 7/5/2/dnq 15=; CG: '06- 4/2; WJ: '02- 12, '04- 2/1; AfG: '03- 3/2, '07- 3; AfCh: '06- 2/2, '10- 1; WI: '06-08-10: 5/1/2. At HJ: WY: '01- 5. Won RSA LJ 2005-07, 2009-11; TJ 2004-06.
Records: Three African LJ 2009, RSA LJ (5) 2005-09, TJ (2) 2004-05, African junior TJ 2004.
Progress at LJ, TJ: 2001- 7.17A, 2002- 7.82A, 16.03A; 2003- 7.84A/7.83, 16.28; 2004- 8.09, 16.96A/16.77; 2005- 8.37A/8.22, 17.25; 2006- 8.39/8.45w, 16.95; 2007- 8.34A/8.28/8.32w, 16.75; 2008- 8.25/8.35w, 2009- 8.50, 2010- 8.23A/8.15/8.22w, 2011- 8.25/8.31w, 2012- 8.29A/8.24. pbs: 100m 10.7A '09, HJ 2.10 '01.

Mbulaeni MULAUDZI b. 8 Sep 1980 Muduluni Village, Limpopo Province 1.71m 62kg. University of Johannesburg AC.
At 800m: OG: '04- 2, '08- sf; WCh: '01-03-05-07-09: 6/3/sf/7/1; CG: '02- 1; AfG: '03- 2, '07- 2; AfCh: '00-02-06: 2/3/6; WI: '04-06-08: 1/2/2; WCp: '06- 3; Won WAF 2006, AfrJ 1999, RSA 2001-03, 2005-09, 2012.
RSA 1000m record 2007.
Progress at 800m: 1998- 1:50.33A, 1999- 1:48.33A;

2000- 1:45.55, 2001- 1:44.01, 2002- 1:43.81, 2003-
1:42.89, 2004- 1:44.56, 2005- 1:44.08, 2006- 1:43.09,
2007- 1:43.74, 2008- 1:43.26, 2009- 1:42.86, 2010-
1:43.29, 2011- 1:45.50, 2012- 1:45.78. pbs: 400m
46.3 '07, 600m 1:17.25i '05, 1000m 2:15.86 '07,
1500m 3:38.55 '09.
Ten successive seasons, 2001-10, under 1:45.

Louis J. van ZYL b. 20 Jul 1985 Bloemfontein
1.86m 75kg. Tuks AC, Pretoria.
At 400mh/4x400mR: OG: '08- 5, '12- h; WCh:
'05- 6, '07- h, '09- sf, '11- 3/2R; CG: '06- 1/2R,
'10- 2; AfG: '07- 1; AfCh: '06- 1, '08- 1/1R, '10- 1;
WJ: '02- 1, '04- 4/2R; WY: '01- 3; WCp: '06- 2, '10-
5; RSA champion 2003, 2005-06, 2008, 2011.
Two RSA 400m hurdles records 2011.
Progress at 400mh: 2001- 51.14A, 2002- 48.89,
2003- 49.22, 2004- 49.06, 2005- 48.11, 2006- 48.05,
2007- 48.24, 2008- 48.22, 2009- 47.94, 2010-
48.51A/48.63, 2011- 47.66, 2012- 49,42A. pbs:
100m 10.62 '07, 10.3Aw '03, 10.5A '01; 200m
21.02A '09, 21.0A '03; 300m 32.32 '09, 400m
44.86A '11, 46.02 '08; 300mh 35.76 '04.
Ran world U18 record of 48.89 to win World
Junior title in 2002 after world age record at 15
in 2001. Commonwealth Games record to win
400mh gold and ran brilliant final leg in
4x400m to take RSA from fifth to second in
2006. Married Irvette van Blerk (pbs HMar
70:56 '11, Mar 2:33:41 '12) on 29 Sep 2012.

Women

Caster SEMENYA b. 7 Jan 1991 Polokwane,
Limpopo Province 1.70m 64kg. Tuks AC,
Pretoria. Student of sports science at University
of Pretoria.
At 800m: OG: '12- 2; WCh: ' 09- 1, '11- 2; WJ: '08-
h; Afr-J: '09- 1 (1 1500m), won RSA 800m 2011-
12, 1500m 2011, Southern Africa 800m 2009.
Two RSA 800m records 2009, 600m 2012.
Progress at 800m: 2007- 2:09.35, 2008- 2:04.23,
2009- 1:55.45, 2010- 1:58.16, 2011- 1:56.35, 2012-
1:57.23. pbs: 400m 52.54A, 53.16 '11, 600m 1:25.56
'12, 1500m 4:08.01 '09.
Questions over her gender arose at the African
Junior and World Champs in 2009, and she was
barred from competing by Athletics South
Africa until the IAAF determined whether she
was free to compete again. They did so in July
2010 but saying that the medical details of her
case remained confidential.

Sunette VILJOEN b. 6 Oct 1983 Johannesburg
1.68m 63kg. University of North West,
Potchefstroom.
At JT: OG: '04/08- dnq 35/33, '12- 4; WCh:
'03/09- dnq 16/18, '11- 3; CG: '06- 1, '10- 1; AfG:
'03- 3, '07- 3; AfCh: '04-06-08-10: 1/2/1/1; WUG:
'07- 5, '09- 1, '11- 1; CCp: '10- 2. Won Afro-Asian
Games 2003, RSA 2003-04, 2006, 2009-12.
Four African javelin records 2009-12, two
Commonwealth 2011-12.
Progress at JT: 1999- 43.89A, 2000- 45.50A, 2001-

50.70A, 2002- 58.33A, 2003- 61.59, 2004- 61.15A,
2005- 57.31, 2006- 60.72, 2007- 58.39, 2008-
62.24A, 2009- 65.43, 2010- 66.38, 2011- 68.38,
2012- 69.35.
Son Hervé born in 2005.

SPAIN

Governing body: Real Federación Española de
Atletismo, Avda. Valladolid, 81 - 1°, 28008
Madrid, Spain. Founded 1918.
National Championships first held in 1917
(men), 1931 (women). **2012 Champions**: **Men**:
100m/200m: Ángel David Rodríguez
10.35/20.98, 400m: Samuel García 46.77, 800m:
Luis Alberto Marco 1:47.77, 1500m: David
Bustos 3:45.93, 5000m/10000m: Manuel Ángel
Penas 13:57.92/28:17.69, HMar: Jaume Leiva
66:29, Mar (2011): Carles Castillejo 2:10:09,
3000mSt: Ángel Mullera 8:31.28, 110mh: Jackson
Quiñónez 13.72, 400mh: Diego Cabello 50.61,
HJ: Javier Bermejo 2.18, PV: Igor Bychkov 5.46,
LJ: Eusebio Cáceres 7.75, TJ: Vicente Docavo
16.62, SP: Borja Vivas 19.44, DT: Mario Pestano
63.28 (12th successive title), HT: Javier
Cienfuegos 74.44, JT: Jordi Sánchez 68.67, Dec:
David Gómez 7580, 10000mW/20kW: Miguel
Ángel López 40:25.31/1:20:59, 50kW: Jesús Ángel
García 3:51:29. **Women**: 100m: Concepción
Montaner 11.99, 200m: Sara María Santiago
24.16, 400m: Aauri Lorena Bokesa 53.94, 800m:
Khadija Rahmouni 2:06.77, 1500m: Natalia
Rodríguez 4:24.95, 5000m: Nuria Fernández
17:02.78, 10000m: Gema Barrachina 32:08.54,
HMar: Azucena Díaz 75:37, Mar (2011): Vanessa
Veiga 2:32:57, 3000mSt: Zulema Fuentes-Pila
10:09.40, 100mh: Desiree Valderrama 14.27,
400mh: Laura NatalíSotomayor 58.15, HJ: Ruth
Beitia 1.96, PV: Anna María Pinero 4.11, LJ:
María del Mar Jover 6.47, TJ: Patricia Sarrapio
13.74, SP: Úrsula Ruíz 16.95, DT: Sabina Asenjo
55.32, HT: Berta Castells 68.35 (10th successive
title), JT: Nora Aida Bicet 56.50, Hep: Laura
Ginés 5501, 10000mW: Beatriz Pascual 43:18.97,
20kW: María José Poves 1:28:15.

Frank Yennifer **CASAÑAS** b. 18 Oct 1978 La
Habana, Cuba 1.87m 115kg. Playas de Castellón.
At DT: OG: '00/04- dnq 24/17, '08- 5, '12- 7;
WCh: '03-05-09: dnq 21/21/16; EC: '10- 11, '12- 5;
WJ: '96- 3; PAm: '99- 4, '03- 2; CAG: '98- 2; PAm-
J: '97- 1; ET: '11- 2; won IbAm 2000, Cuban 2003-
05, MedG 2009.
Progress at DT: 1995- 50.08, 1996- 54.86, 1997-
57.36, 1998- 60.52, 1999- 63.90, 2000- 63.32, 2002-
64.04, 2003- 65.08, 2004- 64.20, 2005- 65.32, 2006-
67.14, 2007- 64.68, 2008- 67.91, 2009- 67.17, 2010-
66.95, 2010- 66.62, 2011- 67.18, 2012- 67.74. pb SP
17.68 '07.
Spanish citizen from 27 May 2008. Married to
Dolores Pedrares (HT pb 67.14 '04).

Jesús Ángel GARCÍA b. 17 Oct 1969 Madrid
1.72m 64kg. Canal de Isabel II.

At 50kW: OG: '92-96-00-04-08-12: 10/dnf/12 /5/4/20; WCh: '93-5-7-9-01-03-05-07-09-11:1/5/ 2/dnf/2/6/dq/dq/3/dq; EC: '94-98-02-06-10: 4/ dq/3/2/5; WCp: '93-5-7-9-02-04-06-08-10-12: 2/2/1/4/dq/6/6/14/5/7; ECp: '96-8-00-01-09: 1/2/1/1/2. At 20kW: WUG: '91- 5. Won Spanish 50kW 1997, 2000, 2007, 2012.
World M40 50km walk record 2010.
Progress at 50kW: 1991- 4:05:10, 1992- 3:48:24, 1993- 3:41:41, 1994- 3:41:28, 1995- 3:41:54, 1996- 3:46:59, 1997- 3:39.54, 1998- 3:43:17, 1999- 3:40:40, 2000- 3:42:51, 2001- 3:43:07, 2002- 3:44:33, 2003- 3:43:56, 2004- 3:44:42, 2005- 3:48:19, 2006- 3:42:48, 2007- 3:46:08, 2008- 3:44:08, 2009- 3:41:37, 2010- 3:47:56, 2011- 3:48:11, 2012- 3:48.15. pbs: 5000mW 19:33.3 '01, 10000mW 40:38.86 '09, road: 5kW 20:07 '04, 10kW 40:25 '99, 20kW 1:23:00 '09, 30kW 2:08:47 '01, 35km 2:31:06 '94; running Mar 2:47:43 '09.
Competed in all major champs 1992-2012, inc. tying men's record of six Olympic Games; has 53 races under 4 hours and 40 sub 3:50 for 50km and 21 years walking sub 3:50. In 1997 he married Carmen Acedo, who won a rhythmic gymnastics world title in 1993.

Miguel Ángel LÓPEZ b. 3 Jul 1988 Murcia 1.81m 70kg. UCAM Athleo Cieza.
At 20kW: OG: '12- 5; WCh: '11- 16; EC: '10- 14; EU23: '09- 1; WCp: '10- 12; ECp: '11- 7. At 10kW: WJ: '06- 14; WY: '05- 6; EJ: '05- 9, '07- 8; WCp: '06- 2J; ECp: '07- 2J. Won Spanish 10000mW & 20kW 2010, 2012.
Progress at 20kW: 2008- 1:23:44, 2009- 1:22:23, 2010- 1:23:08, 2011- 1:21:41, 2012- 1:19:49. pbs: 5000mW 19:33.19 '10, 10000mW 39:58.65 '11.

Manuel OLMEDO b. 17 May 1983 Sevilla 1.79m 60kg. FC Barcelona.
At 1500m: WCh: '11- 4; EC: '10- 3, '12- h; EI: '11- 1; ET: '11- 1. At 800m: OG: '04- h, '08- sf; WCh: '03-05-07-09: h/h/sf/h; EC: '06- sf; WJ: '00-h, '02- 8; EJ: '01-8: ECp: '08- 1, '11- 1; EU23: '03- 3, '05- 2; EI: '09- 5. Won Spanish 800m 2007-08, 1500m 2010-11.
Progress at 800m, 1500m: 1999- 1:52.63, 2000- 1:49.73, 2001- 1:49.01, 2002- 1:47.64/1:47.27i, 2003- 1:45.57, 2004- 1:45.30, 2005- 1:45.48, 2006- 1:45.74, 2007- 1:45.13, 3:42.29; 2008- 1:45.20, 2009- 1:45.91, 2010- 1:45.4, 3:36.98; 2011- 1:44.56, 3:34.44; 2012- 1:52.73, 3:36.50. pbs: 200m 22.70 '00, 300m 35.68 '99, 400m 48.49 '00, 600m 1:18.60 '06, 1000m 2:25.92 '01, 3000m 8:21.48 '09.

Mario PESTANO b. 8 Apr 1978 Santa Cruz de Tenerife 1.95m 120kg. Tenerife Cajacanarias.
At DT: OG: '04- dnq 12, '08- 9, '12- dnq 14; WCh: '99-01-03-05-07-09-11:   dnq   30/dnq 22/8/11/10/10/11; EC: '02-06-10-12: 4/4/6/4; EU23: '99- 3; EJ: '97- 11; WCp: '02- 3; ECp: '01-05-06-08-09: 2/1/3/1/3. Won WAF 2004, IbAm 2004, 2010; MedG 2005, Spanish 2001-12.
Eight Spanish discus records 2001-08.
Progress at DT: 1995- 49.36, 1996- 50.56, 1997- 53.68, 1998- 54.96, 1999- 61.73, 2000- 61.63, 2001-

67.92, 2002- 67.46, 2003- 64.99, 2004- 68.00, 2005- 66.57, 2006- 66.31, 2007- 68.26, 2008- 69.50, 2009- 66.63, 2010- 66.90, 2011- 67.97, 2012- 67.15. pb SP 18.75i '00, 18.64 '02.

Women

Ruth BEITIA b. 1 Apr 1979 Santander 1.92m 71kg. Piélagos Inelecma. Student of physical therapy at University of Santander.
At HJ: OG: '04- dnq 16=, '08- 7=, '12- 4; WCh: '03-05-07-09-11: 11=/dnq 19=/6/5/dnq 16; EC: '02-06-10-12: 11/9/6=; WJ: '96- dnq, '98- 8, EU23: '01- 1; EJ: '97- 9; WI: '01-03-06-08-10-12: 7/5=/3/4/2/6; EI: '05-07-09-11-13:/1 2/3/2/2/1; WCp: '02- 6=; ECp: '03-06-07-09-11: 2/2/2/2/3; Won IbAm 2010, Med G 2005, Spanish 2003, 2006-12 (and 11 indoors).
Nine Spanish HJ records 1998-2007 (and eight indoors 2001-07).
Progress at HJ: 1989- 1.29, 1990- 1.39, 1991- 1.50, 1992- 1.55, 1993- 1.66, 1994- 1.74, 1995- 1.80, 1996- 1.85, 1997- 1.87i/1.86, 1998- 1.89, 1999- 1.83, 2000- 1.86i/1.85, 2001- 1.94i/1.91, 2002- 1.94, 2003- 2.00, 2004- 2.00i/1.96, 2005- 1.99i/1.97, 2006- 1.98i/1.97, 2007- 2.02, 2008- 2.01, 2009- 2.01, 2010- 2.00, 2011- 1.96i/1.95, 2012- 2.00, 2013- 1.99i. pbs: 200m 25.26 '02, 100mh 14.95 '97, 14.93w '00; LJ 6.04 '03, TJ 12.43/12.73w '11.
Her sister Inmaculada (b. 8 Sep 1975) had TJ pb 13.43 '00.

Marta DOMÍNGUEZ b. 3 Nov 1975 Palencia 1.63m 52kg. Nike Running.
At 3000mSt: OG: '08- dnf, '12- 12; WCh: '09- 1; EC: '10- 2, '12- h. At 5000m: OG: '00- h; WCh: '99- 9, '01- 2, '03- 2, '05- 14; EC: '98- 3, '02- 1, '06- 1 (7 10000m); EU23: '97- 3 (1500m 5); WCp: '02- 2; ECp: '06- 2. At 3000m: WI: '95-7-01-03-04: 6/5/4/2/4; EI: '96-8-00-02-07: 3/3/3/1/2; ECp: '96- 3. At 1500m: OG: '96- h; WCh: '95- sf; WJ: '94- 2; EJ: '93- 1. World 4k CC: '00- 14; Eur CC: '07- 1. Won Spanish 1500m 1996, 5000m 1998-2003, 10000m 2006; CC 2006.
Spanish records 3000m 2000, 10000m 2006, 3000mSt (4) 2008-09.
Progress at 3000m, 5000m, 10000m: 1990- 10:15.0, 1991- 9:47.03, 1993- 9:35.16, 1994- 9:24.10, 1995- 9:01.79i, 1996- 8:53.34i/9:06.27, 1997- 8:52.74i/ 9:01.96, 15:41.91; 1998- 8:44.10, 14:59.49; 1999- 8:46.14, 15:16.93; 2000- 8:28.80, 15:26.00; 2001- 8:36.33, 14:58.12; 2002- 8:47.93, 15:10.67; 2003- 8:41.14i/8:50.6+, 14:48.33; 2004- 8:51.05i, 2005- 9:05.56, 14:54.98; 2006- 8:43.45, 14:56.18, 30:51.69; 2007- 8:44.40i, 2009- 8:36.53. At 3000mSt: 2008- 9:21.76, 2009- 9:07.32, 2010- 9:17.07, 2012- 9:24.26. pbs: 800m 2:06.1 '95, 1000m 2:50.1 '91, 1500m 4:04.27 '10, 2000m 5:46.64+i '03, HMar 70:54 '09.
Debut at 3000m steeplechase in 2008, set Spanish record in second race, but fell on last lap when in fourth place in Olympic final. Won all three steeplechases in 2009. Son Javier born in May 2011.

Beatriz PASCUAL b. 9 May 1982 Barcelona 1.63m 64kg. Valencia Terra i Mar.
At 20kW: OG: '08- 6, '12- 8; WCh: '07- 13, '09- 6, '11- 9; EC: '02- 12, '06- 20, '10- 5; EU23: '03- 4; WCp: '10- 11, '12- 5; ECp: '09- 6. At 10kW: WJ: '00- 6; EJ: '01- 3. Won Spanish 10000mW 2008, 2010, 2012; 20kW 2006, 2008-09, 2011.
Spanish walk records 5000m (3) 2008-12, 10000m 2010.
Progress at 20kW: 2002- 1:32:38, 2003- 1:31:31, 2004- 1:30:22, 2005- 1:32:49, 2006- 1:33:55, 2007- 1:30:37, 2008- 1:27:44, 2009- 1:29:54, 2010- 1:28:05, 2011- 1:28:51, 2012- 1:27:56. pbs: 3000mW 13:06.48 '04, 5000mW 20:45:11 '12, 10000mW 42:40.33 '10; HMar (run) 82:43 '08.

María José POVES b. 16 Mar 1978 Zaragoza 1.68m 52kg. Simply Scorpio 71.
At OG: '08- 17, '12- 12; WCh: '05- 28, '07- 12, '11- dq; EC: '06- 19, '10- 11; WCp: '08-10-12: 8/10/3; ECp: '11- 8. Won Spanish 10000mW 2006, 20kW 2005, 2007, 2010, 2012.
Progress at 20kW: 2000- 1:48:14, 2001- 1:45:33, 2002- 1:38:42, 2003- 1:35:32, 2004- 1:32:32, 2005- 1:31:55, 2006- 1:32:05, 2007- 1:30:48, 2008- 1:29:31, 2010- 1:31:15, 2011- 1:32:21, 2012- 1:28:15. pbs: 3000mW 12:43.27 '06, 5000mW 20:54.83 '12, 10kmW 43:56 '10, 44:22.59t '12.

Natalia RODRÍGUEZ b. 2 Jun 1979 Tarragona 1.64m 49kg. C.G.Tarragona.
At 1500m: OG: '00- h, '04- 10, '08- 6, '12- h; WCh: '01-03-05-09-11: 6/sf/6/dq/3, EC: '02- 6, '10- 3; EU23: '99- 4, '01- 2, WJ: '98- 6, EJ: '97- 5; WI: '10- 2; EI: '09- 2; ECp: '03- 1. At 800m: WJ: '96- h. At 3000m: ET: '11- 3. Won Spanish 1500m 2000-05, 2009-10, 2012.
Spanish 1500m record 2005.
Progress at 1500m: 1995- 4:42.4, 1996- 4:38.40, 1997- 4:17.28, 1998- 4:16.20, 1999- 4:10.65, 2000- 4:04.24, 2001- 4:06.32, 2002- 4:02.84, 2003- 4:01.30, 2004- 4:03.01, 2005- 3:59.51, 2008- 4:03.19, 2009- 4:03.73/4:03.36 dq, 2010- 4:01.30, 2011- 4:01.50, 2012- 4:09.25. pbs: 800m 2:01.35 '01, 1M 4:21.92 '08, 3000m 8:35.86 '09, 5000m 16:15.21 '11, 10km Rd 34:12 '09.
Finished first but disqualified for pushing through on inside and knocking Gelete Burka over in World 1500m 2009. Daughter Guadalupe born in November 2007.

María VASCO b. 26 Dec 1975 Barcelona 1.56m 45kg. AC.A.María Vasco.
At 20kW: OG: '00-04-08-12: 3/7/5/10; WCh: '99-01-03-05-07-09-11: 10/5/dnf/4/3/dnf/13; EC: '02- dnf, '06- 15, '10- dnf; WCp: '99-02-04-08-10: 23/8/3/5/1; ECp: '03-09-11: 3/1/4. At 10kW: OG: '96- 28; WCh: '95- 26; EC: '98- 5; EU23: '97- 2; WCp '95- 26, '97- 22. At 5000mW: WJ: '90- 15, '92- 6, '94- 4; EJ: '93- 4. Won Spanish 10kW 1996 10000mW (t) 1997-9, 2001-05; 20kW 1998, 2001-04.
Spanish records 5000m (3) 1997-2007, 10,000m track (5) 1996-2001, 10km 1998, 20km (7) 1998-2008.

Progress at 10kW, 20kW: 1993- 47:11, 1994- 47:05, 1995- 44:53, 1996- 44:51.60t, 1997- 43:54, 1998- 43:02, 1:34:11; 1999- 43:35, 1:32:38; 2000- 43:33.92t, 1:30:20; 2001- 43:02.04t, 1:30:09; 2002- 43:51, 1:28:47; 2003- 44:22, 1:28:10; 2004- 44:07+, 1:27:36; 2005- 43:59, 1:28:51; 2006- 44:43+, 1:32:50; 2007- 45:28+, 1:29:17; 2008- 43:21, 1:27:25; 2009- 43:27, 1:32:53; 2010- 44:43, 1:31:55A; 2011- 44:45.18t, 1:31:41; 2012- 43:43, 1:28:14. pbs: 3000mW 12:20.44 '04, 5000mW 20:57.11 '07, HMar (running) 85:48 '07.
Only Spanish female Olympic medallist. Married to José Antonio González (Spanish 50kW champion 2004 in pb 3:49:01).

SRI LANKA

Governing body: Athletic Association of Sri Lanka, n°33 Torrington Avenue, Colombo 7. Founded 1922.
National Champions 2012: Men: 100m: W.K. Himasha Eashan 10.50 drugs dq, 200m: A.R.M. Rajaskan 21.29, 400m: Y.M.W.G.Gunarathne 47.26, 800m: Prabath Kumara Mendis 1:52.37, 1500m: Punchi Hewage Chamal 3:52.02, 5000m: D. Lionel Samarajeewa 14:45.61, 10000m: N.M.C.C. Nawasinghe 31:12.14, 3000mSt: R.M.S. Pushpakumara 8:56.75, 110mh: K.W.Salinda Randeewa 14.95, 400mh: Jagath Gunathilake 51.66, HJ: Manjula Kumara Wijesekara 2.21, PV: Priyantha Senarathne 4.60, LJ: Lalith Ravindra Weerakkody 7.35, TJ: Eranda Dinesh Fernando 16.37, SP: Joy Danushka Perera 14.27, DT: E.P.D.Silva 43.86, HT: L.A.D.Alenson 44.16, JT: Aruna Dayarathne 73.27, Dec: W.K.D.S.Perera 5885, 20000mW: T.G.S.N.Appuhami 1:39:28.40.
Women: 100m: Jani Chathurangani Silva 11.85, 200m: Heela P.Sujani Buddika 23.92, 400m: Chandrika Subashini Rasnayake 54.63, 800m: Champika Dilrukshi 2:04.97, 1500m: D.A. Shanika Samanmali 4:21.97, 5000m: Geethani Rajasekara 16:43.09, 10000m: Chaturika Hemamali 35:24.3, 3000mSt: Eranga Rasika Dulakshi 10:11.72, 100mh: Amali Harshani Wijesinghe 14.26, 400mh: W.K.L.A. Nimali 62.56, HJ: Priyangika Madumanthi 1.81, PV: Anoma Karunawansa 3.20, LJ: N.C.D. Priyadharshani 5.95, TJ: L.D.D.E.Rathnasiri 12.26, SP: Nadeeka Muthunayake 14.50, DT: Sonali Weerasekara 42.56, HT: A.W.A.C.Amara–singhe 38.16, JT: Dilhani Lekamge 55.76, Hep: B.A.S.Ayesha 3731, 20000mW: Geetha Nandani 1:55:04.57.

SUDAN

Governing body: Sudan Athletic Association, PO Box 13274, 11 111 Khartoum. Founded 1959.

Abubaker KAKI Khamis b. 21 Jun 1989 Elmuglad 1.76m 63kg.
At 800m: OG: '08- sf, '12- 7; WCh: '07- h, '09- sf, '11- 2; WJ: '06- 6, '08- 1; WI: '08- 1, '10- 1; AfG: '07- 1. At 1500m: WY: '05- 3. At 4x400m: AfCh:

'08- 2R. Won Pan Arab G 800m & 1500m 2007. World junior records 800m & 1000m (& indoor 1000m) 2008. SUD records 800m (3), 1000m (2) 2008-10, 1500m 2011.
Progress at 800m, 1500m: 2005- 1:48.43, 3:45.06; 2006- 1:45.78, 3:47.58; 2007- 1:43.90, 3:47.92; 2008- 1:42.69, 3:39.71; 2009- 1:43.09, 3:39.89; 2010- 1:42.23, 2011- 1:43.13, 3:31.76; 2012- 1:43.32, 3:34.34. pbs: 1000m 2:13.62 '10, 10km Rd 30:18 '07.
Ran world's fastest 800m (WJR) for five years at Oslo 2008.

SWEDEN

Governing body: Svenska Friidrottsförbundet, Heliosgaten 3, 120 30 Stockholm. Founded 1895.
National Championships first held in 1896 (men), 1927 (women). **2012 Champions: Men**: 100m/200m: Nil de Oliveira 10.42/20.75, 400m: Johan Wissman 47.06, 800m: Johan Svensson 1:49.10, 1500m: Johan Walldén 3:54.19, 5000m: Nacerddine Hallil 14:02.90, 10000m: Mustafa Mohamed 29:10.77, HMar: Adil Bouafif 65:06, Mar: Fredrik Uhrbom 2:26:36, 3000mSt: Eric Senorski 8:39.97, 110mh: Alexander Brorsson 13.98, 400mh: Petter Olson 52.05, HJ: Jakob Thorvaldsson 2.13, PV: Alhaji Jeng 5.49, LJ/TJ: Michel Tornéus 7.80/15.90, SP: Leif Arrhenius 20.03, DT: Niklas Arrhenius 62.32, HT: Mattias Jons 70.90, JT: Kim Amb 80.73, Dec: Fabian Rosenquist 7368, 10,000mW: Ato Ibáñez 40:55.69, 20kW: Perseus Karlström 1:28:17, 50kW: Fredrik Svensson 4:43:43. **Women**: 100m/200m: Moa Hjelmer 11.66/23.50, 400m: Josefin Magnusson 54.73, 800m: Lovisa Lindh 2:08.28, 1500m: Viktoria Tegenfeldt 4:17.88, 5000m/10000m/HMar: Isabellah Andersson 16:25.14/ 33:16.67/ 70:30, Mar: Charlotte Karlsson 2:48:37, 3000mSt: Charlotta Fougberg 10:29.20, 100mh: Ellinore Hallin 13.62, 400mh: Frida Persson 59.19, HJ: Victoria Dronsfield 1.85, PV: Angelica Bengtsson 4.27, LJ: Erica Jarder 6.46, TJ: Angelica Ström 13.18, SP: Helena Engman 16.20, DT: Anna Söderberg (20th successive title) 52.37, HT: Tracey Andersson 66.89, JT: Sofi Flinck 55.22, Hep: Sara Söderberg 4760, 5000mW/10kW: Siw Karlsson 24:25.87/51:37, 20kW: Monica Månsson-Martinsson 1:55:18.

Michel TORNÉUS b. 26 May 1986 Norsborg, Botkyrka 1.84m 70kg. Hammarby IF.
At LJ: OG: '12- 4; WCh: '09-11: dnq 28/27; EC: '10- 9, '12- 3; EU23: '07- 10; EJ: '05- 4; EI: '13- 2; ET: '11- 2. Won Swedish LJ 2005, 2007-10, 2012; TJ 2012.   Swedish long jump record 2012.
Progress at LJ: 2001- 6.48, 2002- 6.74/6.86w, 2003- 7.07, 2004- 7.41, 2005- 7.94, 2006- 7.68, 2007- 7.85, 2008- 7.86, 2009- 8.11, 2010- 8.12/8.21w, 2011- 8.19, 2012- 8.22, 2013- 8.29i. pbs: 60m 6.93i '12, 100m 10.71/10.63w '11, 400mh 55.48 '04, HJ 1.99i '05, 1.92 '04; TJ 15.90 '12, Dec 6115 '04. Father came from DR of Congo.

Women

Isabellah ANDERSSON b. 12 Nov 1980 Manga, Kenya 1.67m 50kg. née Isabellah Moraa Amoro. Hässelby SK.
At Mar: OG: '12- 18; WCh: '11- 7; EC: '10- 4. Eur CC: '09- 18. Won Swedish 5000m 2009-10, 2012; 10,000m 2008-10, 2012; HMar 2009-12, Mar 2008-12.
Swedish records: 10km road 2009, HMar (3) 2008-12, marathon (3) 2010-11.
Progression at Mar: 2006- 2:51:40, 2008- 2:34:14, 2009- 2:33:52, 2010- 2:25:10, 2011- 2:23:41, 2012- 2:25:41, 2013- 2:26:05. Pbs: 1500m 4:30.27 '09, 3000m 9:21.8m+ '09, 5000m 15:45.08 '09, 10000m 33:16.67 '12; Road: 10km 32:24 '09, HMar 70:02 '10. Did not seriously pursue running at home in Kenya and first came to Sweden to learn about orienteering, met husband-to-be Lars Andersson (orienteering coach) and together they realised that her best option was to focus on running. Daughter Beyoncé was born on 25 Jan 2009. She became a Swedish citizen on 11 May 2009.

Abeba AREGAWI b. 5 Jul 1990 Adidrat, Tigray 1.70m 52kg.
At 1500m: '12- 5; EI: '13- 1; won DL 2012. At 800m: Af-J: '09- 3. Won ETH 800m 2009.
Ethiopian 1500m record 2012.
Progress at 1500m: 2010- 4:01.96, 2011- 4:01.47i/4:10.30, 2012- 3:56.54, 2013- 3:58.40i. pbs: 800m 1:59.39 '12.
Has lived in Stockholm since 2009; granted Swedish citizenship on 8 Jun 2012 and accepted by the IAAF to compete for Sweden from 10 Dec 2012.

Angelica BENGTSSON b. 8 July 1993 Väckelsång 1.64m 51kg. Hässelby SK.
At PV: OG: '12- dnq 19=, EC: '12- 10; WJ: '10- 1, '12- 1; WY: '09- 1; EJ: '11- 1; YthOG: '10- 1.
Pole vault records: Two world youth 2010; four world junior indoors 2011, two world junior outdoor bests, three Swedish 2011-12.
Progress at PV: 2005- 3.10, 2006- 3.40, 2007- 3.90, 2008- 4.12, 2009- 4.37, 2010- 4.47, 2011- 4.63i/4.57. 2012- 4.58.
Rising Star awards: IAAF 2010, European Athletics 2012. Her father Glenn had JT pb 67.08 '82, sister Victoria PV 4.00 '09.

Emma GREEN TREGARO b. 8 Dec 1984 Bergsjön Göteborg 1.80m 62kg. Örgryte IS.
At HJ: OG: '08- 9. '12- 8; WCh: '05-07-09-11: 3/7=/7=/11; EC: '06-10-12: 11/2/3=; WJ: '02- 9; EU23: '05- 2; EJ: '03- 3; WI: '10- 5=; EI: '05- 8, '13- 3; CCp: '10- 2; ECp: '09- 5, '11- 1. At 200m: ECp: '06- 5. Won Swedish HJ 2005, 2007-11 (& 7 indoors); LJ 2005.
Progress at HJ: 1998- 1.66i, 1999- 1.71, 2000- 1.75i/1.73, 2001- 1.82, 2002- 1.82, 2003- 1.86, 2004- 1.90, 2005- 1.97, 2006- 1.96i/1.92, 2007- 1.95, 2008- 1.98i/1.96, 2009- 1.96, 2010- 2.01, 2011- 1.95, 2012- 1.95i/1.93. pbs: 60m 7.42i '06, 100m 11.58

'06, 200m 23.02 '06, 400m 54.95 '06, LJ 6.41 '05, TJ 13.69i '06, 13.39 '07.
Her uncle Göte Green ran 47.9 for 400m in 1977. Married coach Yannick Tregaro in March 2011.

Ebba JUNGMARK b. 10 Mar 1987 Onsala 1.79m 57 kg. Mölndals AIK. Was at Washington State University, USA.
At HJ: OG: '12- dnq 20=; WCh: '07/11- dnq 23/17; EC: '10- dnq 17, '12- 10; WJ: '06- 5; EU23: '07- 3; EJ: '05- 12; WI: '12- 2=; EI: '11- 3, '13- 2. Won NCAA indoors 2008.
Progress at HJ: 2000- 1.50, 2001- 1.60, 2002- 1.73, 2003- 1.78, 2004- 1.77i/1.75, 2005- 1.80, 2006- 1.85i/1.84, 2007- 1.92, 2008- 1.89i/1.84, 2009- 1.86, 2010- 1.90, 2011- 1.96i/1.94, 2012- 1.95i/1.91, 2013- 1.96i. pbs: LJ 5.59i '09, TJ 12.98 '12, Pen 3642i '09.

SWITZERLAND

Governing body: Schweizerischer Leichtathletik–verband (SLV), Haus des Sports, Postfach 606, 3000 Bern 22. Formed 1905 as Athletischer Ausschuss des Schweizerischen Fussball-Verbandes.
National Championships first held in 1906 (men), 1934 (women). **2012 Champions: Men**: 100m: Rolf Fongué 10.49, 200m: Alex Wilson 20.66, 400m: Philipp Weissenberger 47.27, 800m: Jan Hochstrasser 1:51.28, 1500m: Mirco Zwahlen 4:09.06, 5000m: Rolf Rüfenacht 14:23.32, 10000m: Christoph Ryffel 29:31.85, HMar: Michael Ott 67:02, Mar: Christian Kreienbühl 2:19:38, 3000mSt: Marco Kern 8:57.76, 110mh: Andreas Kundert 14.22, 400mh: Kariem Hussein 49.61, HJ: Sven Tarnowski 2.09, PV: Patrick Schütz 5.20, LJ: Yves Zellweger 7.39, TJ: Alexandre Hochuli 16.15, SP: Yannis Croci 16.09, DT: Lukas Jost 53.64, HT: Martim Bingisser 66.40, JT: Nicola Müller 69.66, Dec: Jonas Fringeli 7494, 10000W/20kW: Paulo Ghirlanda 55:28/1:51:24. **Women**: 100m/200m: Mujinga Kambundji 11.26/23,26, 400m: Jessica Martins 54.08, 800m: Monika Augustin-Vogel 2:10.38, 1500m: Lisa Kurmann 4:18.01, 5000m: Nicola Spirig 16:14.33, 10000m: Mirja Jenni 34:00.67, HMar: Sabine Fischer 73:19, Mar: Maja Neuenschwander 2:31:56, 3000mSt: Fabienne Schlumpf 10:09.98, 100mh: Clélia Reuse 13.22, 400mh: Valentine Arrieta 58.33, HJ: Beatrice Lundmark 1.82, PV: Nicole Büchler 4.45, LJ/TJ: Barbara Leuthard 6.10/13.11, SP/DT: Elisabeth Graf 13.92/48.86, HT: Nicole Zihlmann 58.98, JT: Christa Wittwer 46.46, Hep: Valérie Reggel 5794, 5000kW/10kW/20kW: Laura Polli 22:59/47:36/1:38:11.

TADJIKISTAN

Governing body: Athletics Federation of Tadjikistan, Rudski Avenue 62, Dushanbe 734025. Founded 1932.

Dilshod NAZAROV b. 6 May 1982 Dushanbe 1.87m 115kg.
At HT: OG: '08- 11, '12- 10; WCh: '05-07-09-11: dnq 16/dnq 21/11/10; WJ: '98- dnq 15, '00- 5, AsiG: '98-02-06-10: 7/9/1/1; AsiC: '03-05-07-09: 3/2/2/1; CCp: '10- 2. Won Asi-J 1999, 2001, C. Asian 2003.
Progress at HT: 1998- 63.91, 1999- 63,56, 2000- 66.50, 2001- 68.08, 2002- 69.86, 2003- 75.56, 2004- 76.58, 2005- 77.63, 2006- 74.43, 2007- 78.89, 2008- 79.05, 2009- 79.28, 2010- 80.11, 2011- 80.30, 2012- 77.70. President of national federation.

TAIWAN

Governing body: Chinese Taipeh Track & Field Association.
National Champions 2012: Men: 100m: Pan Po-Yu 10.39, 200m: Yi Wei-Chen 21.05, 400m: Chen Chieh 47.39, 800m: Hung Yu-Chao 1:53.11, 1500m: Chang Chia-Hsing 3:57.51, 5000m/10000m: Ho Chin-Ping 14:48.42/30:32.18, 3000mSt: Chou Ting-Yin 9:18.46, 110mh: Szu Wei-Pin 14.10, 400mh: Chen Chieh 50.23, HJ: Hsiang Chun-Hsien 2.08, PV: Hsieh Chia-Han 5.22, LJ: Lin Hung-Min 7.86, TJ: Tsai Yi-Ta 15.55, SP/DT: Chang Ming-Huang 17.94/51.20, HT: Tseng Hao-Chan 58.79, JT: Huang Shih-Feng 73.29, Dec: Su Yi-Lun 6225, 10000mW: Luo Po-Ying 47:57.58. **Women**: 100m/200m: Hsu Yung-Chieh 11.76w/24.36, 400m: Pan Hsiu-Lien 57.80, 800m: Wang Chiu-Yen 2:16.42, 1500m: Yang Shu-Chun 4:44.50, 5000m: Chen Yu-Hsuan 17:48.08, 10000m: Yu Ya-Chun 36:44.78, 3000mSt: Li Ting-Yu 11:07.98, 100mh: Chuang Chih-Han 13.77, 400mh: Huang Chia-Lin 61.72, HJ: Cheng Yun-Huai 1.70, PV: Liu Yu-Yao 3.60, LJ: Chung Chiung-Hsuan 5.91, TJ: Chuang Chih-Han 12.45, SP: Lin Chia-Ying 16.82, DT: Li Wen-Hua 54.94, HT: Kuo Yu-hsuan 52.08, JT: Chang Ya-Ching 52.06, Hep: Chu Chia-Ling 4957, 10000mW: Chang Chia-Feng 49:00.52.

TRINIDAD & TOBAGO

Governing body: National Association of Athletics Admistrations of Trinidad & Tobago, PO Box 605, Port of Spain, Trinidad. Founded 1945, reformed 1971.
National Champions 2012: Men: 100m: Keston Bledman 9.86, 200m: Rondell Sorrillo 20.48, 400m: Lalonde Gordon 45.40, 800m: Jamaal James 1:47.25, 1500m: Gavyn Nero 3:55.16, 110mh: Wayne Davis II 13.62; 400mh Emmanuel Mayers 50.66, HJ: Rodney Liverpool 1.95, LJ: Kyron Blaise 7.63, TJ: Chris Hercules 16.17, SP: Akeem Stewart 16.95, DT: Quincy Wilson 56.25, HT: Sukraj Roodal 14.48, JT: Keshorn Walcott 75.00. **Women**: 100m: Kelly-Ann Baptiste 10.98, 200m: Kai Selvon 22.98, 400m: Sparkle McKnight 52.44, 800m: Melissa De Leon 2:07.35, 1500m: Pilar McShine 4:24.91, 100mh: Josanne Lucas 13.07, 400mh: Janeil Bellille 56.31, HJ: Jeanelle Ovid 1.65, LJ/TJ: Ayanna Alexander

6.28/14.04, SP: Cleopatra Borel 17.98, DT: Annie Alexander 56.54, HT: Ashlee Smith 45.48, JT: Geraldine George 40.62, Hep: Ayanna Glasgow 3814.

Keston BLEDMAN b. 8 Mar 1988 San Fernando 1.83m 75kg. Simplex.
At 100m/4x100mR: OG: '08- 2R, '12- sf/3R; WCh: '07- qf, '09- res(2)R, '11- sf; WJ: '06- 7 (h 200m); WY: '05- 3; PAm: '07- sf; CAG: '10- 7/1R. Won PAm-J 2007, CAC 2011, TRI 2012.
Progress at 100m: 2005- 10.48, 2006- 10.32, 2007- 10.14/10.05w, 2008- 10.18, 2009- 10.10/10.0, 2010- 10.01/9.93w, 2011- 9.93, 2012- 9.86. pbs: 60m 6.62i '12, 200m 20.73 '08.

Jehue GORDON b. 15 Dec 1991 Port of Spain 1.90m 80kg. adidas. Sports management student at University of West Indies, Trinidad.
At 400mh: OG: '12- 6; WCh: '09- 4, '11- sf; WJ: '08- sf, '10- 1; PAm-J: '09- 2. Won TRI 2008-11. Three TRI 400mh records 2009-12.
Progress at 400mh: 2008- 51.39, 2009- 48.26, 2010- 48.47, 2011- 48.66, 2012- 47.96. pbs: 400m 46.43 '10, 800m 1:53.32 '10, 110mh 13.82 '12. 200mhSt 23.00 '12.

Lalonde GORDON b. 25 Nov 1988 Lowlands, Tobago 1.79m 83kg. Tigers. Studied at Mohawk Valley CC.
At 400m/4x400mR: OG: '12- 3/3R; CG: '10- sf; CAG: '10- 3R; WI: '12- 3R. TRI champion 2012.
Progress at 400m: 2010- 46.33, 2011- 45.51, 2012- 44.52. pbs: 100m 10.45 '12, 200m 20.58i/20.62 '12, 300m 32.48i '13, 32.5+ '12.
Moved with his family to New York at the age of seven, and still lives there.

Rondell SORRILLO b. 21 Jan 1986 La Brea 1.78m 62kg. La Brea Athletics. Was at University of Kentucky, USA.
At 200m: OG: '08- qf, '12- h (sf 100m); WCh: '09- sf, '11- 7. Won NCAA 2010, TRI 2009, 2012; 2nd CAC 2008-09, 2011.
Progress at 200m: 2006- 20.97, 2007- 21.20, 2008- 20.43, 2009- 20.45, 2010- 20.29, 2011- 20.16, 2012- 20.40. pbs: 60m 6.60i '09, 100m 10.03 '12, 400m 48.06 '10.

Richard THOMPSON b. 7 Jun 1985 Cascade 1.87m 79kg. Memphis. Was at Louisiana State University.
At 100m: OG: '08- 2/2R, '12- 7/3R; WCh: '07- qf, '09- 5/2R, '11- sf; PAm: '07- h. Won TRI 100m 2009-11, 200m 2010; NCAC 100m 2007, NCAA 100m & 60m indoor 2008.
Progress at 100m, 200m: 2004- 10.65, 2005- 10.47, 21.73; 2006- 10.27/10.26w, 21.24; 2007- 10.09/9.95w, 20.90; 2008- 9.89, 20.18; 2009- 9.93, 20.65; 2010- 10.01/9.89w, 20.37; 2011- 9.85, 2012- 9.96, 20.80. pbs: 60m 6.45+ '09, 6.51i '08.

Keshorn WALCOTT b. 2 Apr 1993 Toco 1.83m 90kg. Toco tafac.
At JT: OG: '12- 1; WJ: '10- dnq, '12- 1; WY: '09- dnq 13; PAm: '11- 7. Won CAC-J 2010, 2012; TRI 2012.

Five Trinidad javelin records 2012, eight CAC junior 2011-12.
Progress at JT: 2009- 60.02, 2010- 67.01, 2011- 75.77A, 2012- 84.58. pb TJ 14.28 '10.
First Caribbean Olympic champion and also youngest ever Olympic champion in throwing events. Won IAAF Rising Star Award 2012. Elder brother Elton TJ pb 16.43/16.51w '11 & 4 WY '09, aunt Anna Lee Walcott Hep pb 5224 '00.

Women

Kelly-Ann BAPTISTE b. 14 Oct 1986 Plymouth, Tobago 1.60m 54kg. Zenith. Studied psychology at Louisiana State University.
At 100m/(200m): OG: '08- qf, '12- 6; WCh: '05- qf, '09: sf/sf, '11- 3; WJ: '02- sf, '04- (4); WY: '03- 3; PAm: '03- h; CCp: '10- 1/1R. Won NCAA 100m & indoor 60m 2008, TRI 100m 2005-06, 2008-10, 2012; 200m 2005.
TRI records: 100m (5) 2005-10, 200m (5) 2005-09.
Progress at 100m, 200m: 2002- 11.71, 24.03; 2003- 11.48, 23.22; 2004- 11.40, 23.41/22.99w; 2005- 11.17/11.04w, 22.93; 2006- 11.08, 22.73; 2007- 11.22, 22.90i/22.95; 2008- 11.06/10.97w, 22.67; 2009- 10.94/10.91w, 22.60; 2010- 10.84, 22.78/22.58w; 2011- 10.90, 2012- 10.86, 22.33w. pbs: 55m 6.73i '06, 60m 7.13i '08.

Cleopatra BOREL b. 3 Oct 1979 Port of Spain 1.68m 93kg. Was at University of Maryland; assistant coach at Virginia Tech University.
At SP: OG: '04- 10, '08- dnq 17, '12- 12; WCh: '05/07/09- dnq 19/18/13, '11- 13; CG: '02- 4, '06- 3, '10- 2; PAm: '03- 6, '07- 3, '11- 2; CAG: '06- 3, '10- 1; WI: '04-06-08: dnq 11/8/7. Won CAC 2008, 2011; TRI 2002, 2004, 2006-10, 2012.
Eight TRI records at shot 2004-11.
Progress at SP: 2000- 14.64i, 2001- 16.44, 2002- 17.50i/16.90, 2003- 17.95i/17.79, 2004- 19.48i/18.90, 2005- 18.44, 2006- 18.81, 2007- 18.91, 2008- 18.87, 2009- 18.52, 2010- 19.30, 2011- 19.42, 2012- 18.82. pb HT 51.28 '01.
Formerly competed under married name Borel-Brown.

TUNISIA

Governing body: Fédération Tunisienne d'Athlétisme, B.P. 264, Cité Mahrajane 1082, Tunis. Founded 1957.

Women

Habiba GHRIBI–Boudraa b. 9 Apr 1984 Kairouan 1.70m 57kg.
At 3000mSt: OG: '08- 13, '12- 2; WCh: '05- h, '09- 6, '11- 2; AfCh: '06- 2. At 5000m: AfCh: '02- 11.
Tunisian records: 3000m (2) 2008-11, 3000mSt (9) 2005-12.
Progress at 3000mSt: 2005- 9:51.49, 2006- 10:14.36, 2007- 9:50.04, 2008- 9:25.50, 2009- 9:12.52, 2011- 9:11.97, 2012- 9:08.37. pbs: 1500m: 4:12.37 '09, 3000m 8:56.22 '11, 5000m 16:12.9 '03, 10000m 35:03.83 '05, 10kmRd 33:30 '04.
Missed 2010 season after toe surgery. In 2012

she won the irst Olympic medal for a woman from Tunisia.

TURKEY

Governing body: Türkiye Atletizm Federasyonu, 19 Mayis Spor Kompleksi, Ulus-Ankara. Founded 1922.

National Champions 2012: **Men**: 100m: Ramil Guliyev 10.43, 200m: Hakan Karacaoglu 21.76, 400m: Mehmet Güzel 46.56, 800m: Levent Ates 1:48.92, 1500m: Cihat Ulus 3:41.54, 3000m: Resul Çevik 8:22.64, 5000m/1000m: Mert Girmalegese 13:45.28/29:58.61, Mar: Ali Haydar Tekgöz 2:26:01, 3000mSt: Sait Özdemir 9:26.95, 110mh: Batuhan Eruygun 14.27, 400mh: Furkan Hasan Can 53.64, HJ: Ümit Tan 2.19, PV: Mustafa Kivanç 4.30, LJ: Alper Kulaksiz 7.48, TJ: Mikail Yalçin 15.05, SP: Hüseyin Atici 19.65, DT: Kutay Kirmizi 46.63, HT: Esref Apak 78.28, JT: Aykut Tanriverdi 69.66, Dec: Hikmet Tugsuz 6727, 20kW: Kemal Gelecek 1:36:30. **Women**: 100m: Aksel Gürcan 12.14, 200m: Sema Apak 24.00, 400m: Özge Akin 54,18, 800m: Burcu Büyükbezgin 2:08.02, 1500m: Esma Aydemir 4:13.03, 3000m: Seyma Yildiz 9:44.75, 5000m/10000m: Dilek Bal 18:57.45/42:21.60, Mar: Sultan Haydar 2:29:41, 3000mSt: Cigdem Gezici 12:39.10, 100mh: Ilkay Avci 14.78, 400mh: Elif Yildirim 58.40, HJ: *none*, PV: Aysegul Yilmaz 3.40, LJ: Emel Güngör 6.33, TJ: Büsra Mutay 12.14, SP: Damla Karaoglu 10.26, DT: Dilek Esmer 53.72, JT: Gürcan Tezcan 41.07, Hep: Nuran Camur 3953, 20kW: Handan Koçyigit 1:45:03.

Tarik Langat AKDAG (ex Patrick Kipkurui LANGAT) b. 16 Jun 1988 Nandi, Kenya 1.76m 60kg. ENKA.
At 3000mSt: OG: '12- 9; EC: '12- 2.
Turkish 3000m steeplechase record 2012.
Progress at 3000mSt: 2004- 8:53.6A, 2005- 8:40.3A, 2006- 8:37.4A, 2007- 8:46.8A, 2008- 8:19.13, 2009- 8:21.38, 2010- 8:09.12, 2011- 8:08.59, 2012- 8:17.85. pbs: 3000m 7:47.68 '10, 2M 8:26.96 '10, 5000m 13:45.21A '06, 10000m 29:03.1 '06.
Switched from Kenya to Turkey 22 Jun 2011.

Polat Kemboi ARIKAN (ex Paul KEMBOI) b. 12 Dec 1990 Cheptirte, Kenya 1.73m 62kg.
At (5000m)/10000m: OG: '12- h/9; EC: '12- 3/1; ECp: '12- 1. At 3000m: EI: '13- 10. Eur CC: '12- 7.
Turkish records 3000m 2012, 5000m 2011.
Progress at 5000m, 10000m: 2006- 14:23.4A, 2009- 13:24.25, 2010- 13:18.12, 2011- 13:05.98, 2012- 13:12.55i/13:27.21, 27:38.81. pbs: 1500m 3:47.05 '12, 3000m 7:42.31 '12, HMar 63:50 '06.
Became a Turkish citizen 9 Jun 2011, originally with 2-year wait for international eligbility, but waiting period ended in February 2012.

Fatih AVAN b. 1 Jan 1989 Kahraman Maras 1.83m 90kg. Fenerbahçe Spor Kulubu.
At JT: OG: '12- dnq 20; WCh: '09: dnq 19, '11- 5; EC: '12- dnq 14; EU23: '09- 7, '11- 2; WUG: '11- 1.

Won Med G 2009, TUR 2008.
Eight Turkish javelin records 2009-12.
Progress at JT: 2005- 55.88, 2006- 61.40, 2007- 66.28, 2008- 71.73, 2009- 79.78, 2010- 79.13, 2011- 84.79, 2012- 85.60.

Ramil GULIYEV b. 29 May 1990 Baku 1.87m 73kg. Baku
At (100m/)200m: OG: '08- qf; WCh: '09- 7; WJ: '06- (h), '08- 5; WY: '07- 2; EJ: '09- 2/1; WUG: '09- 1. At 60m: EI: '09- 7. Won TUR 100m 2012.
Records: European Junior 200m 2009; AZE 100m (2) 2009, 200m (4) 2007-09; TUR 100m (2) & 200m 2011.
Progress at 200m: 2006- 21.74, 2007- 20.72, 2008- 20.66, 2009- 20.04, 2010- 20.73, 2011- 20.32, 2012- 20.53. pbs: 60m 6.58i '12, 100m 10.08 '09, 300m 33.62i '09.
Switched from Azerbaijan to Turkey on 26 Apr 2011, but not eligible to compete for Turkey until 1 Mar 2014.

Ilham Tanui ÖZBILEN (formerly William Biwott Tanui KEN) b. 5 Mar 1990 Kocholwo, Keiyo, Kenya 1.77m 61kg. ENKA.
At 1500m: OG: '12- 8; EC: '12- 6; WI: '12- 2; EI: '13- 2; won WAF 2009.
Records: World 4x1500m & world junior 1M 2009; Turkish 800m (3), 1500m (2) 2011-12.
Progress at 800m, 1500m: 2008- 3:42.5A, 2009- 3:31.70, 2010- 3:33.67, 2011- 1:44.25, 3:31.37; 2012- 3:33.32. pbs: 1000m 2:17.08 '11, 1M 3:49.29 '09, 3000m 7:50.61i '12.
Became a Turkish citizen on 9 Jun 2011.

Women

Elvan ABEYLEGESSE b. 11 Sep 1982 Addis Ababa, Ethiopia 1.59m 40kg. Enka.
At 5000m/(10000m): OG: '04- 12 (8 1500m), '08- 2/2; WCh: '01- h, '03- 5, '07- 5/2, '09- (dnf); EC: '02- 7, '06- 3/dnf, '10- 1/1; WJ: '00- 6 (6 1500m); WY: '99- (5 3000m); EU23: '03- 1; EJ: '99- 2, '01- 1 (1 3000m); CCp: '10- 4; ECp: '06-07-08: (1/1/1).
Won WAF 5000m 2003-04, Med G 10000m 2009.
World CC: '99- 9J; Eur CC: '00-01-02-03: 3J/1J/3/2.
Records: World 5000m 2004, European 10000m 2008. Turkish 2000m 2003, 3000m 2002, 5000m 2004, 10000m 2006 & 2008, HMar 2010.
Progress at 1500m, 5000m, 10000m: 1999- 4:24.1, 16:06.40; 2000- 4:18.7, 16:33.77; 2001- 4:11.31, 15:21.12, 33:29.20; 2002- 4:11.00, 15:00.49; 2003- 4:07.25, 14:53.56; 2004- 3:58.28, 14:24.68; 2005- 15:08.59; 2006- 4:11.61, 14:59.29, 30:21.67; 2007- 15:00.88, 31:25.15; 2008- 14:58.79, 29:56.34; 2009- 15:30.47, 31:51.98; 2010- 4:15.23, 14:31.52, 31:10.23. pbs: 800m 2:07.10 '04, 2000m 5:33.83 '03, 3000m 8:31.94 '02; Rd: 15km 49:29 '12, HMar 67:07 '10.
Known as Hewan Abeye ETH, then Elvan Can on move to Turkey. She became the first Turkish athlete to set a world record in 2004 and the first Turkish woman to win an Olympic medal in 2008. Married Semeneh Debelie ETH on 25

Feb 2011, their daughter Arsema was born on 28 July 2011.

Gamze BULUT b. 3 Aug 1992 Eskisehir 1,66m 48kg. Fenerbahçe Spor Kulubu, Student.
At 1500m: OG: '12- 2; EC: '12- 2. At 2000mSt: WY: '09- 5, EurY: '09- 3. Won Turkish 3000mSt 2010, 1500m 2011.
Progress at 1500m: 2006- 4:56.41, 2009- 4:31.82, 2010- 4:37.98, 2011- 4:18.23, 2012- 4:01.18. pbs: 800m 2:03.59 '12, 1M 4:42.18 '11, 5000m 15:49.21 '12, 3000mSt 9:34.88 '12.

Asli CAKIR Alptekin b. 20 Aug 1985 Antalya 1.68m 50kg. Üsküdar BSK.
At 1500m: OG: '12- 1; WCh: '11- sf; EC: '10- 5, '12- 1; WI: '12- 3; CCp: '10- 5; WUG: '11- 1. At 3000mSt: OG: '08- h; WCh: '09- h; WJ: '04- dq (6). Eur CC: '02-10-12: 6J/4/2.
Turkish 3000m steeplechase record 2008.
Progress at 1500m: 2002- 4:35.93, 2003- 4:34.33, 2004- 4:28.18, 2007- 4:37.26, 2008- 4:21.79, 2009- 4:08.07, 2010- 4:02.17, 2011- 4:05.53, 2012- 3:56.62. pbs: 800m 2:03.09 '10, 3000m 9:23.17 '08, 3000mSt 9:36.09 '09.
Two-years drugs ban after positive test at 2004 World Juniors. Won first Olympic gold medal for a Turkish athlete, but in March 2013 there were reports of "big abnormalities" in her biological passport. Married to Ihsan Alptekin (800m 1:50.31).

GülcanMINGIRb.21May1989Afyonkarahisar 1.65m 53kg. Istanbul Üsküdar SC.
At 3000mSt: WCh: '11- h; EC: '12- 1; WJ: '08- 12; EJ: '07- 9, EU23: '09- 5, '11- 1. Won TUR 3000mSt 2007. Turkish 3000m steeplechase record 2012.
Progress at 3000mSt: 2006- 10:57.87, 2007- 10:35.48, 2008- 10:15.55, 2009- 10:05.66, 2010- 10:02.19, 2011- 9:39.83, 2012- 9:13.53. pbs: 800m 2:09.50 '09, 1500m 4:23.14 '10, 3000m 9:11.94 '12, 2000mSt 6:35.72 '08.

Binnaz USLU b. 12 Mar 1985 Ankara 1.65m 55kg. ENKA Istanbul.
At 3000mSt: OG: '12- h; WCh: '11- 7; EC: '10- h (h 1500m), '12- h; WUG: '11- 1 (1 5000m). At 800m: OG: '04- h; WCh: '05- h; WJ: '04- dns; WUG: '05- 2. At 3000m: EJ: '03- 2. At 5000m: EU23: '05- 1. Eur CC: '03- 10J, '04- 1J, '06- 1 U23, '10- 2.
Turkish 3000m steeplechase record 2011.
Progress at 3000mSt: 2006- 10:17.48, 2007- 9:48.46, 2008- 9:31.58, 2009- 10:08.64, 2010- 10:00.88, 2011- 9:24.06. pbs: 400m 56.14 '05, 800m 2:00.94 '04, 1000m 2:41.79 '06, 1500m 4:11.36 '10, 1M 4:40.70 '06, 3000m 9:06.82 '10, 5000m 15:41.15 '11, 10000m 34:34.79 '06.
Two-year drugs ban 2007-09.

Nevin YANIT b. 16 Feb 1986 Mersin 1.69m 56kg. Fenerbahçe SK. Mersin University.
At 100mh: OG: '08- sf, '12- 5; WCh: '07/09/11- sf; EC: '06- h, '10- 1, '12- 1; WJ: '04- h; EU23: '07- 1; EJ: '05- sf; WUG: '07- 2, '09- 1; CCp: '10- 4. Won Med G 2009, TUR 2008-09, Balkan 2012. At

60mh: EI: '13- 1
Nine Turkish 100mh records 2006-12.
Progress at 100mh: 2003- 15.25, 2004- 13.75A/13.66w, 2005- 13.45A, 2006- 12.88, 2007- 12.76, 2008- 12.76/12.72w, 2009- 12.89, 2010- 12.63, 2011- 13.07, 2012- 12.58. pbs: 100m 11.71 '08, 200m 23.74 '08, 60mh 7.89i '13.

UGANDA

Governing body: Uganda Athletics Federation, PO Box 22726, Kampala. Founded 1925.

Jacob ARAPTANY b. 11 Feb 1992 Kaproron 1.68m 58kg.
At 3000mSt: OG: '12- h; WCh: '11- 6; WJ: '10- 3; AfG: '11- 5; AfCh: '12- 8; Af-J: '11- 5. World CC: '11- 9J.
Progress at 3000mSt: 2009- 8:26.4A, 2010- 8:28.14, 2011- 8:15.72A, 2012- 8:14.48. pbs: 800m 1:49.95A '11, 1500m 3:36.16A '11, 2000mSt 5:28.48 '11.

Benjamin KIPLAGAT b. 4 Mar 1989 Magoro 1.86m 61kg.
At 3000mSt: OG: '08- 9,'12- dq; WCh: '07- h, '09- 11, '11- 10; CG: '10- 4; WJ: '06- 6, '08- 2; AfG: '07- 7; AfCh: '10- 5, '12- 3; CCp: '10- 4. World CC: '07- 5J, '08- 4J.
Six Ugandan 3000mSt records 2007-10.
Progress at 3000mSt: 2005- 8:39.1A, 2006- 8:34.14, 2007- 8:21.73, 2008- 8:14.29, 2009- 8:12.98, 2010- 8:03.81, 2011- 8:08.43, 2012- 8:17.55. pbs: 1500m 3:38.86 '09, 3000m 7:46.50 '10, 5000m 13:22.67 '07, 10000m 29:03.1 '06.

Stephen KIPROTICH b. 18 Apr 1989 Kapchorwa 1.72m 56kg. Prison warden.
At Mar: OG: '12- 1; WCh: '11= 9. World CC: '09-12J, '11- 6.
Ugandan marathon record 2011.
Progress at Mar: 2011- 2:07:20, 2012- 2:07:50. Pbs: 5000m 13:23.70 '08, 10000m 27:58.03 '10, 3000mSt 8:26.66 '10.
Won Enschede marathon on debut 2011.

Moses KIPSIRO b. 2 Sep 1986 Chesimat 1.74m 59kg.
At 5000m(/10000m): OG: '08- 4, '12- 15/10; WCh: '05- h, '07- 3, '09- 4; CG: '06- 7, '10- 1/1; AfG: '07- 1, '11- 1; Af Ch: '06- 3/1, '10- 4/2; CCp: '10- 2 (2 3000m). At 3000m: WI: "12- 7. World CC: '03-05-08-09-10-11: 18J/20J/13/2/3/11.
Ugandan records: 3000m (4) 2005-09, 5000m 2007.
Progress at 5000m: 2005- 13:13.81, 2006- 13:01.88, 28:03.46; 2007- 12:50.72, 2008- 12:54.70, 2009- 12:59.27, 2010- 13:00.15, 27:33.37A; 2011- 13:09.17, 2012- 13:00.68, 27:04.48. pbs: 1500m 3:37.6 '08, 2000m 5:00.66+ '11, 3000m 7:30.95 '09, 2M 8:08.16i '12.
Sealed brilliant 5k/10k double at 2010 CG with last laps of 53.01 and 53.96.

UKRAINE

Governing body: Ukrainian Athletic

Federation, P.O. Box 607, Kiev 01019. Founded 1991. **National Champions 2012**: **Men**: 100m/200m: Sergiy Smelyk 10.38/20.63, 400m: Vitaliy Butrym 45.90, 800m: Igor Davydov 1:46.98, 1500m: Oleksandr Borysyuk 3:49.98, 5000m: Mykola Labovskyy 13:23.50, Mar: Igor Olefirenko 2:14:56, 3000mSt: Vadym Slobodenyuk 8:37.12, 110mh: Sergiy Kopanayko 13.77, 400mh: Stanislav Melnykov 49.53, HJ: Andriy Protsenko 2.31, PV: Vladyslav Revenko 5.55, LJ: Ivan Lihachov 7.90, TJ: Mykola Savolaynen 16.74w, SP: Andriy Semenov 20.05, DT: Mykyta Nesterenko 62.84, HT: Oleksandr Drygol 78.32, JT: Oleksandr Pyatnytsya 84.87, Dec: Sergiy Chemerys 7295, 20kW: Andriy Kovenko 1:20:51/1:21:36, 50kW: Oleksiy Shelest 3:53:46. **Women**: 100m: Olesya Povh 11.11, 200m: Yelizaveta Bryzgina 22.69, 400m: Alina Logvynenko 51.34, 800m: Nataliya Lupu 1:58.46, 1500m: Nataliya Batrak 4:21.64, 5000m: Anna Nosenko 15:41.29, Mar: Svitlana Stanko 2:39:47, 3000mSt: Svitlana Shmidt 9:31.16, 100mh: Yevgeniya Snigur 13.23, 400mh: Anna Titimets 54.98, HJ: Olena Holosha 1.93, PV: Natalya Mazuryk 4.30, LJ: Viktoriya Rybalko 6.95, TJ: Hanna Knyazheva 14.71, SP: Halyna Obleshchuk 17.78, DT: Natalya Semenova 62.90, HT: Hanna Skydan 74.21, JT: Vira Rebryk 62.61, Hep: Anna Melnychenko 6407, 20kW: Nadiya Borovska 1:33:10/Inna Kashyna 1:37:37.

Roman AVRAMENKO b. 23 Mar 1988 Kirovske 1.85m 90kg. Dynamo Krym.
At JT: OG: '08/12- dnq 29/14; WCh: '09- dnq 22, '11- 6; EC: '10- 8; WJ: '04 dnq, 06- 3; WY: '03- 5, '05- 2; EU23: '09- 4; EJ: '07- 2; WUG: '11- 2; ET: '09- 4. Won UKR 2006, 2008.
UKR javelin record 2011.
Progress at JT: 2003- 61.95, 2004- 72.68, 2005- 70.27, 2006- 76.01, 2007- 77.88, 2008- 80.08, 2009- 79.50, 2010- 81.12, 2011- 84.30, 2012- 81.87.

Ruslan DMYTRENKO b. 22 Mar 1986 Kyiv 1.80m 62kg. Donetsk.
At 20kW: WCh: '09- 33, '11- 7; EC: '10- 12; WCp: '12- 4; EU23: '07- 6; UKR champion 2009, 2011.
At 10000m/10kW: EJ: '05- 11; ECp: '05- 6J.
Progress at 20kW: 2006- 1:27:16, 2007- 1:23:31, 2008- 1:25:26, 2009- 1:21:21, 2010- 1:21:54, 2011- 1:21:31, 2012- 1:20:17. pbs: 5000mW 18:44.45i '12, 10000mW 39:26.90i '12, 39:33.91 '10.

Sheryf EL-SHERYF b. 2 Jan 1989 Simpheropol 1.83m 74kg. Dnipropetrovskaya. Student.
At TJ: OG: '12- dnq 13; WCh: '11- 12; EC: '12- 2; WJ: '06- 5, '08- 9; WY: '05- 5; EU23: '11- 1; EJ: '07- 6.
Progress at TJ: 2004- 15.53, 2005- 16.18, 2006- 16.30, 2007- 16.10, 2008- 16.60i/16.35, 2009- 15.90i/15.52, 2010- 16.56i/16.42, 2011- 17.72, 2012- 17.04/17.28w. pb LJ 8.05 '12.
Huge breakthrough at 2011 European U23s, improving pb from 16.92 to 16.99, 17.04 and then 17.72. His father, a gynaecologist, comes from Sudan.

Oleksiy KASYANOV b. 26 Aug 1985 Stakhanov, Lugansk 1.91m 84kg. Spartak Zaporozhye.
At Dec: OG: '08- 7, '12- 7; WCh: '09- 4, '11- 12; EC: '10- dnf, '12- 2; EU23: '07- 4; WUG: '07- 4; ECp: '09- 3. UKR champion 2008. At Hep: WI: '10- 6, '12- 2; EI: '09- 2.
Progress at Dec: 2006- 7599, 2007- 7964, 2008- 8238, 2009- 8479, 2010- 8381, 2011- 8251, 2012- 8312. pbs: 60m 6.83i '09, 100m 10.50 '11, 400m 47.46 '08, 1000m 2:42.41i '12, 1500m 4:22.27 '08, 60mh 7.85i '13, 110mh 14.01 '12, HJ 2.06i/2.05 '09, PV 4.82 '09, LJ 8.04i/7.97 '10, SP 15.72 '09, DT 51.95 '10, JT 55.84 '07, Hep 6254i '10.
Won Talence decathlon 2009.

Viktor KUZNETSOV b. 14 Jul 1986 Zaporozhye 1.90m 67kg. Kiev Dynamo.
At TJ (LJ): OG: '08- 8, '12- (dnq 31); WCh: '09- (dnq 17); EC: '06- (4), '10- 4; WJ: '04- 3; EI: '07- 7, '11- 4; WUG: '07- 2, '11- 2; ET: '10- 1, '11- 3.
World junior long jump best (indoors) 2005.
Progress at LJ, TJ: 2002- 6.89, 2003- 8.12i, 15.17; 2004- 16.84i/16.58, 2005- 8.22i, 16.51i; 2006- 7.96/8.25w, 16.35i/16.17; 2007- 7.74, 16.94; 2008- 17.16, 2009- 8.09, 2010- 8.11i, 17.29; 2011- 17.01, 2012- 8.10, 2013- 17.02i.

Oleksandr PYATNYTSYA b. 14 Jul 1985 Dnipropetrovsk 1.86m 90kg.
At JT: OG: '12- 2; WCh: '09/11- dnq 27/29; EC: '10- 4, '12- 5; EU23: '07- 3. UKR champion 2009, 2011.   UKR javelin records 2010 & 2012.
Progress at JT: 2005- 65.63, 2006- 72.20, 2007- 76.28, 2008- 78.54, 2009- 81.96, 2010- 84.11, 2011- 82.61, 2012- 86.12.

Oleksiy SOKYRSKYY b. 16 Mar 1985 Gorlivka 1.85m 108kg.
At HT: OG: '12- 4; WCh: '09-11: dnq 22/17; EC: '12- nt; WJ: '04- 8, EU23: '07- 6; WUG: '09- 3; ET: '11- 3. UKR champion 2010-11.
Progress at HT: 2005- 70.23, 2006- 71.95, 2007- 73.44, 2008- 75.54, 2009- 76.50, 2010- 76.62, 2011- 78.33, 2012- 78.91.

Women

Yelizaveta BRYZGINA b. 28 Nov 1989 Lugansk 1.72m 56kg. Student at Lugansk National teachers' training institute.
At (100m)/200m/4x100mR: OG: '12- sf/3R; WCh: '11- sf; EC: '10- 2/1R; WJ: '08- h/h; EJ: '07- 2/2R; WUG: '11- 1R; CCp: '10- 2/2R; ET: '10- 1. UKR champion 2012.
Progress at 200m: 2004- 24.13, 2005- 24.32, 2006- 24.24, 2007- 23.47, 2008- 23.37, 2009- 22.99, 2010- 22.44, 2011- 23.02, 2012- 22.64. pbs: 60m 7.37i '09, 100m 11.44 '07, 400m 52.67i '12.
Parents were Viktor Bryzgin (1 4x100m OG '80, EC '86, 2 WCh '07; 100m 10.03w?/10.11 '86) and Olga Vladykina (400m/400mR: OG '80: 1/1R, '92- 2/1R; WCh: '87- 1/2R, '91- 4/1R; EC: '86- 2, 48.27 '85, 200m 22.44 '85).

Nataliya DOBRYNSKA b. 29 May 1982

Khmelnitsky 1.80m 77kg. Vinnitsa K.
At Hep: OG: '04- 8, '08- 1, '12- dnf; WCh: '05- 9, '07- 8, '09- 4 (LJ dnq 20). '11- 5; EC: '06- 6, '10- 2; EU23: '03- 5; EJ: '01- 10. At Pen: WI: '04-08-10-12: 2/4/2/1; EI: '05- 3, '07- 5.
World indoor pentathlon record 2012.
Progress at Hep: 1999- 5226, 2000- 5322, 2001- 5742, 2002- 5936, 2003- 5877, 2004- 6387, 2005- 6299, 2006- 6356, 2007- 6327, 2008- 6733, 2009- 6558, 2010- 6778, 2011- 6539, 2012- 6311. pbs: 100m 11.60/11.2 '95, 200m 24.23 '10, 800m 2:11.15i '12, 2:11.34 '11; 60mh 8.33i '10, 100mh 13.43 '11, HJ 1.86 '06, LJ 6.63 '08, 6.73w '09; SP 17.29 '08, JT 49.25 '10, Pen 5013i '12.
Four pbs en route to UKR pentathlon record 4727 and WI silver medal 2004. Five pbs in Olympic gold performance 2008 including world heptathlon shot best and four pbs in EC 2nd 2010. Won Götzis and Talence and IAAF Combined Events Challenge 2009. Older sister Viktoriya (b. 18 Jan 1980) has pb 5787 '08.

Tetyana HAMERA-SHMYRKO b. 1 Jun 1983 Hrada, Ternopil 1.65m 52kg.
At Mar: OG: '12- 5; WCh: '11- 15.
Two UKR marathon records 2012.
Progression at marathon: 2011- 2:28:14, 2012- 2:24:32, 2013- 2:23:58. Pbs: 800m 2:08.81 '04, 1500m 4:26.61 '08, 3000m 9:32.06 '09, 5000m 16:16.55 '10, 10000m 32:50.13 '12, HMar 72:15 '12.
Won Kraków marathon on debut 2011, won Osaka 2013 (2nd 2012).

Hanna KNYAZYEVA b. 25 Sep 1989 Periaslav-Khmelnytskyi 1.78m 61kg. Kiev.
At TJ: OG: '12- 4; WJ: '08- 4; EJ: '07- 2; EU23: '11- 5. UKR champion 2012.
Progress at TJ: 2005- 12.87, 2006- 13.28, 2007- 13.85, 2009- 13.81, 2010- 13.65, 2011- 14.20, 2012- 14.71. pb LJ 6.40 '12.

Nataliya LUPU b. 4 nov 1987 1.70m 50kg. Cherniyevskaya.
At 800m: OG: '12- sf; WCh: '09- h; EC: '10- h; WI: '12- 2; EU23: '07- h, '09- 2; WJ: '06- 4; EJ: '05- 1/3R; EI: '13- 1; ET: '10- 1. Won UKR 2012.
Progress at 800m: 2002- 2:10.99, 2003- 2:07.75, 2004- 2:05.08, 2005- 2:02.66, 2006- 2:03.24, 2007- 2:04.62, 2008- 2:00.96, 2009- 2:00.32, 2010- 1:59.59, 2011- 1:59.12, 2012- 1:58.46. pbs: 400m 52.91 '11, 1000m 2:42.58i '13, 1500m 4:20.93 '03.

Anna MELNYCHENKO b. 24 Apr 1983 Tbilisi, Georgia 1.78m 59kg.
At Hep: OG: '08- 14, '12- 10; WCh: '07- dnf, '09- 6; EC: '06- 16, '10- dnf; EU23: '05- 13; WUG: '07- 3; ECp: '07-08-09-10: 3/1/1/1. UKR champion 2003, 2012. At Pen: '13- 3.
Progress at Hep: 2001- 4907, 2002- 5083, 2003- 5523, 2004- 5720, 2005- 5809, 2006- 6055w, 2007- 6143, 2008- 6306/6349u, 2009- 6445, 2010- 6098, 2012- 6407. pbs: 200m 24.09 '12, 24.08w '06; 800m 2:12.85 '09, 60mh 8.26i '13, 100mh 13.28 '08, HJ 1.86 '07, LJ 6.74 '12, TJ 13.21/13.40w '03, SP 14.05

'11, JT 45.11 '09, Pen 4748i '12.
Married to William Frullani ITA (Dec 7984 '02, Hep 5972 rec 6th EI '09).

Anna MISHCHENKO b. 25 Aug 1983 Sumy 1.66m 51kg. Kharkov Dyn.
At 1500m: OG: '08- 9, '12- h; WCh: '09/11- sf; EC: '10- 11, '12- 3; WUG: '11- 2; ET: '10- 1, '11- 3; UKR champion 2010.
Progress at 1500m: 2003- 4:21.41, 2004- 4:14.09, 2005- 4:19.74, 2006- 4:12.17, 2007- 4:14.57, 2008- 4:05.13, 2009- 4:06.45, 2010- 4:03.14, 2011- 4:01.73, 2012- 4:01.16. pbs: 800m 2:00.92 '12, 1000m 2:39.00 '08, 2000m 5:46.36 '09, 3000m 9:11.09i '11, 9:17.99 '07.

Anastasiya RABCHENYUK b. 14 Sep 1983 Ternovka 1.77m 64kg.
At 400mh: OG: '08- 4; WCh: '07- h, '09- 7, '11- 5; EC: '06- 8, '10- h; WY: '99- h; EJ: '01- 7; EU23: '06- 6; WUG: '03- 3. '07- 2; ECp: '08-09-10: 1/2/3&2R. UKR champion 2003-08.
Progress at 400mh: 1999- 60.88, 2000- 58.01, 2001- 59.31, 2002- 58.38, 2003- 56.30, 2004- 56.39, 2005- 56.14, 2006- 54.73, 2007- 55.48, 2008- 53.96, 2009- 54.49, 2010- 55.29, 2011- 54.18. pbs: 400m 52.64 '06, 800m 2:10.5i '09, 60mh 8.56i '07, 100mh 14.21 '07.
Married Sergiy Basenko (110mh 14.42 '04) in October 2008.

Vira REBRYK b. 25 Feb 1989 Yalta 1.76m 65kg.
At JT: OG: '08/12- dnq 16/19; WCh: '09- 9, '11- dnq 16; EC: '10- dnq 17; WJ: '06- 2, '08- 1; WY: '05- 2; EU23: '09- 2; EJ: '07- 1; WUG: '09- 2. '11- 4. Won UKR 2010-12.
World junior javelin record 2008; three UKR records 2012.
Progress at JT: 2003- 44.94, 2004- 52.47, 2005- 57.48, 2006- 59.64, 2007- 58.48, 2008- 63.01, 2009- 62.26, 2010- 63.36, 2011- 61.60, 2012- 66.86.

Viktoriya 'Vita' RYBALKO b. 26 Oct 1982 Dnepropetrovsk 1.77m 60kg. Zaporiziya. Was at Universities of Maine and Rochester, USA.
At LJ: OG: '08/12- dnq 23/20; WCh: '07- 11, '09/11- dnq 17/15; EC: '06- 4, '10- 4; WI: '10- 8; EI: '07- 7. UKR champion 2011-12.
Progress at LJ: 1999- 6.43, 2000- 6.17, 2002- 6.08, 2004- 6.30, 2005- 6.34, 2006- 6.82/6.87w, 2007- 6.41/6.70w, 2008- 6.87i/6.70, 2009- 6.70, 2010- 6.74/6.78w, 2011- 6.87, 2012- 6.95. pb TJ 13.95 '11.

Mariya RYEMYEN b. 28 Nov 1989 Lugansk 1.72m 56kg. Student at Lugansk National teachers' training institute.
At (100m)/200m/4x100mR: OG: '12- sf/3R; WCh: '11- sf/3R; EC: '10- (5)/1R, '12- 1; EU23: '07- h/5, '09- 7/8. At 60m: EI: '11- 2, '13- 2. Won UKR 200m 2009-10.
Progress at 200m: 2006- 24.35, 2007- 24.08, 2008- 24.02, 2009- 23.56, 2010- 23.16, 2011- 22.68, 2012- 22.58. pbs: 50m 6.19i '12, 60m 7.10i '13, 100m 11.20 '12, 11.18w '11.
Older brother Oleksiy has 100m pb 10.43 '11.

Olga SALADUHA b. 4 Jun 1983 Donetsk 1.75m 55kg.
At TJ: OG: '08- 9, '12- 3; WCh: '07- 7, '11- 1; EC: '06- 4, '10- 1, '12- 1; WJ: '02- 5; EU23: '05- 4; EJ: '01- 9; WI: '08- 6; WUG: '05- 2, '07- 1; WCp: '06- 6, '10- 2; ECp: '06-08-10-11: 1/1/1/1. Won DL 2011, UKR 2007-08.
Progress at TJ: 1998- 13.32, 1999- 12.86, 2000- 13.26, 2001- 13.48, 2002- 13.66i/13.63, 2003- 13.26i/13.03, 2004- 13.22, 2005- 14.04, 2006- 14.41/14.50w, 2007- 14.79, 2008- 14.84, 2010- 14.81, 2011- 14.98/15.06w, 2012- 14.99. pb LJ 6.37 '06. Married to pro road cyclist Denys Kostyuk.

Nataliya SEMENOVA b. 7 Jul 1982 Gorlivka, Donetsk 1.78m 85kg. née Fokina.
At DT: OG: '04-08-12: dnq 24/14/18; WCh: '05- 9, '07- 7, '11- dnq 16; EC: '06- 9, '12- 3; WJ: '00- 7; EU23: '03- 1; EJ: '01- 1; WUG: '03- 1; ECp: '04-07-08-09: 7/3/2/1. UKR champion 2008, 2011.
Progress at DT: 1997- 45.84, 1998- 48.21, 2000- 51.44, 2001- 59.88, 2002- 60.54, 2003- 63.11, 2004- 62.19, 2005- 62.80, 2006- 62.14, 2007- 62.44, 2008- 64.70, 2009- 63.11, 2011- 59.50, 2012- 63.56.

Anna YAROSHCHUK b. 24 Nov 1989 Dnipropetrovsk 1.76m 67kg.
At 400mh/4x400mR: OG: '12- sf; WCh: '11- sf; EC: '10- sf, '12- 3; WJ: '08- 6/2R; EU23: '09- 8, '11- 1/2R; WUG: '11- 1. At 200m: EJ: '07- h/2 4x100m.
Progress at 400mh: 2006- 57.52, 2007- 56.46, 2008- 56.09, 2009- 57.23, 2010- 55.60, 2011- 54.77, 2012- 54.35. pbs: 60m 7.74i '06, 200m 23.49 '10, 400m 53.31 '11, LJ 5.98 '10.

Lyudmyla YOSYPENKO b. 24 Sep 1984 Jahotyn, Kiev region 1.75m 63kg.
At Hep: OG: '12- 4; WCh: '09- 5, '11- 10; EC: '10- 6, '12- 2; ECp: '11- 2. UKR champion 2007-09, 2011.
Progress at Hep: 2002- 5026, 2003- 5327, 2004- 5563, 2005- 5782, 2006- 5708, 2007- 6025, 2008- 6262, 2009- 6423, 2010- 6260, 2011- 6318, 2012- 6618. pbs: 200m 23.68 '09, 800m 2:12.51 '11, 60mh 8.40i '08, 100mh 13.25 '12, HJ 1.88 '09, LJ 6.40 '09, SP 14.32 '12, JT 55.64 '12, Pen 4298i '07.

UNITED KINGDOM

Governing body: UK Athletics, Alexander Stadium, Walsall, Perry Barr, Birmingham B42 2LR. Founded 1999 (replacing British Athletics, founded 1991, which succeeded BAAB, founded 1932). The Amateur Athletic Association was founded in 1880 and the Women's Amateur Athletic Association in 1922.
National Championships (first were English Championships 1866-79, then AAA 1880-2006, WAAA from 1922). **2012 UK Champions: Men**: 100m: Dwain Chambers 10.25, 200m: James Ellington 20.56, 400m: Martyn Rooney 45.93, 800m: Andrew Osagie 1:46.89, 1500m: Andrew Baddeley 3:47.99, 5000m: Ross Millington

13:59.01, 10000m: James Walsh 28:37.30, Mar: Lee Merrien 2:13:41, 3000mSt: Luke Gunn 8:42.20, 110mh: Andrew Pozzi 13.41, 400mh: David Greene 49.47, HJ: Robbie Grabarz 2.28, PV: Steve Lewis 5.50, LJ: Greg Rutherford 8.12, TJ: Larry Achike 16.19, SP: Carl Myerscough 19.42, DT: Lawrence Okoye 63.46, HT: Alex Smith 74.79, JT Lee Doran 79.72, Dec: Edward Dunford 7443, 5000mW/10kW: Alex Wright 19:48.14/44:06, 20kW: Ben Wears 1:29:33, 50kW: Steve Allen 5:35:01. **Women**: 100m: Ashleigh Nelson 11.50, 200m: Margaret Adeoye 23.11, 400m: Christine Ohuruogu 51.89, 800m: Lynsey Sharp 2:01.72 1500m: Laura Weightman 4:18.83, 5000m: Jo Pavey 15:54.18, 10000m: Caryl Jones 32:52.53, Mar: Claire Hallissey 2:27:44, 3000mSt: Eilish McColgan 9:56.89, 100mh/HJ: Jessica Ennis 12.92/1.89, 400mh: Perri Shakes-Drayton 55.45, PV: Holly Bleasdale 4.71, LJ: Shara Proctor 6.95, TJ: Laura Samuel 13.73, SP/DT: Eden Francis 16.13/53.09, HT: Sophie Hitchon 69.79, JT: Goldie Sayers 58.45, Hep: Joanne Rowland 5381, 5000mW/10kW: Johanna Jackson 21:45.98/46:52, 20kW: Neringa Aidietyte LTU 1:38:21.

Lawrence CLARKE b. 13 Jan 1990 London 1.86m 75kg. Windsor, Slough, Eton & Hounslow. Bristol University.
At 110mh: OG: '12- 4; WCh: '11- h; CG: '10- 3; E23: '11- 3; EJ: '09- 1. UK champion 2011.
Progress at 110mh: 2008- 15.3, 2009- 13.91/13.82w, 2010- 13.69/13.51w, 2011- 13.58, 2012- 13.31/13.14w. Pbs: 100m 10.64 '12, 60mh 7.67i '12.

James DASAOLU b. 5 Sep 1987 Dulwich, London 1.80m 75kg. Croydon H. Graduate of Loughborough University.
At 100m: OG: '12- sf; EC: '10- sf. At 60m: EI: '13- 2.
Progress at 100m: 2006- 10.75/10.7/10.61w, 2007- 10.33, 2008- 10.26, 2009- 10.09, 2010- 10.23/10.06w, 2011- 10.11, 2012- 10.13. pbs: 60m 6.48i '12, 200m 21.9 '07.

Mohamed FARAH b. 23 March 1983 Mogadishu, Somalia 1.71m 65kg. Newham & Essex Beagles.
At 5000m (/10000m): OG: '08- h, '12- 1/1; WCh: '07- 6, '09- 7, '11- 1/2; EC: '06- 2, '10- 1/1, '12- 1; CG: '06- 9; WJ: '00- 10; WY: '99- 6; EJ: '01- 1; EU23: '03 & '05- 2; ECp: '08-09-10: 1/1/1 &(1). At 3000m: WI: '08- 6, '12- 4; EI: '05-07-09-11: 6/5/1/1; ECp: '05-06: 2/2. World CC: '07- 11, '10- 20; Eur CC: '99-00-01-04-05-06-08-09: 5J/7J/2J/15/21/1/2/2. Won UK 5000m 2007, 2011.
Records: European 10000m & indoor 5000m 2011, indoor 2M 2012; UK 5000m 2010 & 2011, half marathon 2011.
Progress at 5000m, 10000m: 2000- 14:05.72, 2001- 13:56.31, 2002- 14:00.5, 2003- 13:38.41, 2004- c.14:25, 2005- 13:30.53, 2006- 13:09.40, 2007- 13:07.00, 2008- 13:08.11, 27:44.54; 2009- 13:09.14, 2010- 12:57.94, 27:28.86; 2011- 12:53.11, 26:46.57; 2012- 12:56.98, 27:30.42. pbs: 800m 1:48.69 '03, 1500m 3:33.98 '09, 1M 3:56.49 '05, 2000m 5:06.34

'06, 3000m 7:34.47i '09, 7:38.15 '06; 2M 8:08.07i '12, 8:20.47 '07: 2000mSt 5:55.72 '00; road 15km 43:13 '09, 10M 46:25 '09, HMar 60:23 '11.
Sixth man in history to win Olympic 5000m/10,000m double at same Games; first British athlete to win either title. Joined his father in England in 1993. Won in New York on half marathon debut 2011.

Adam GEMILI b. 6 Oct 1993 London 1.78m 73kg. Blackheath & Bromley.
At 100m/4x100mR: OG: '12- sf; WJ: '12- 1; EJ: '11- 2/2R.
Progress at 100m: 2009- 11.2, 2010- 10.80/10.72w, 2011- 10.35/10.23w, 2012- 10.05. Pbs: 60m 6.68i '12, 200m 20.38 '12.
As a footballer he was a member of the youth academy at Chelsea before playing for Dagenham & Redbridge and then making a huge impact as a sprinter in 2011-12.

Robbie GRABARZ b. 3 Oct 1987 Enfield 1.92m 87kg. Newham & Essex Beagles.
At HJ: OG: '12- 3=; EC: '12- 1; WJ: '06- 12; EU23: '09- 11; WI: '12- 6=; EI: '13- 6; won DL 2012, UK 2012.   UK high jump record 2012.
Progress at HJ: 2002- 1.75, 2004- 2.00, 2005- 2.22, 2006- 2.20i/2.14, 2007- 2.21, 2008- 2.27, 2009- 2.23i/2.22, 2010- 2.28, 2011- 2.28, 2012- 2.37. pb TJ 14.40 '09.

David GREENE b. 11 Apr 1986 Llanelli 1.83m 75kg. Swansea Harriers.
At 400mh: OG: '12- 4; WCh: '09- 7 (res (2)R), '11- 1; EC: '06- h, '10- 1; CG: '10- 1; EU23: '07- 1; EJ: '05- 2; CCp: '10- 1; ET: '09-10-11: 1/1/1. UK champion 2009-10, 2012; won DL 2011.
Progress at 400mh: 2003- 55.0/55.06, 2004- 53.42, 2005- 51.14, 2006- 49.91, 2007- 49.58, 2008- 49.53, 2009- 48.27, 2010- 47.88, 2011- 48.20, 2012- 47.84. pbs: 100m 11.1 '06, 200m 22.1 '05, 21.73w '08, 400m 45.82 '11, 600m 1:16.22i '13.

Phillips IDOWU b. 30 Dec 1978 Hackney, London 1.92m 86kg. Belgrave H.
At TJ: OG: '00-04-08-12: 6/nj/2/dnq 14; WCh: '01-07-09-11: 9/6/1/2; EC: '02- 5, '06- 5, '10- 1; CG: '02- 2, '06- 1; EU23: '99-5; EJ: '97- 4; WI: '08- 1; EI: '07- 1; CCp: '10- 3; ECp: '04-07-08-09-10: 3/2/1/2/2. Won AAA 2000, 2002, 2006; UK 2008-10; DL 2011.
Progress at TJ: 1995- 13.90, 1996- 15.12/15.53w, 1997- 15.86/16.34w, 1998- 16.35, 1999- 16.41, 2000- 17.12, 2001- 17.33/17.38w, 2002- 17.68, 2004- 17.47, 2005- 17.30i/16.96; 2006- 17.50, 2007- 17.56i/17.35, 2008- 17.75i/17.62, 2009- 17.73, 2010- 17.81, 2011- 17.77, 2012- 17.31. pbs: 60m 6.81i '04, 100m 10.60 '06, LJ 7.83 '00.

Steve LEWIS b. 20 May 1986 Stoke-on-Trent 1.91m 83kg. Newham & Essex Beagles. Studied sports science at Loughborough University.
At PV: OG: '08- dnq, '12- 5=; WCh: '07- dnq, '09- 7=, '11- 9=; CG: '06- 3, '10- 2; WJ: '04- 9; WY: '03- 3; EU23: '07- 7; EJ: '05- 5; WI: '10- 6=, '12- 5=;

EI: '09- 4, '13- 6=. Won AAA 2006, UK 2007-08, 2011-12.
UK pole vault record 2012.
Progress at PV: 1999- 3.20, 2000- 3.70, 2001- 4.30i/4.20, 2002- 4.65, 2003- 5.05, 2004- 5.20, 2005- 5.35, 2006- 5.50, 2007- 5.61, 2008- 5.71, 2009- 5.75i/5.72, 2010- 5.72i/5.65, 2011- 5.65, 2012- 5.82, 2013- 5.71i.

Lawrence OKOYE b. 6 Oct 1991 London 1.98m 137kg. Croydon Harriers.
At DT: OG: '12- 12; EC: '12- 11; E23: '11- 1; WJ: '10- 6. UK champion 2012.
UK discus record 2012.
Progress at DT: 2011- 67.23, 2012- 68.24.

Andrew OSAGIE b. 19 Feb 1988 Harlow 1.89m 72kg. Harlow. St Mary's University College..
At 800m: OG: '12- 8; WCh: '11- sf; CG: '10- sf; EU23: '09- h; WI: '12- 3; EI: '11- 4. Won UK 2011-12.
Progress at 800m: 2004- 1:56.0, 2005- 1:52.90, 2006- 1:52.51, 2007- 1:47.34, 2008- 1:53.12, 2009- 1:47.15, 2010- 1:46.41, 2011- 1:45.36, 2012- 1:43.77. pbs: 400m 48.8 '09, 600m 1:16.45i '13, 1000m 2:18.56i '11, 1500m 3:48.99 '09.

Martyn ROONEY b. 3 Apr 1987 Croydon 1.98m 78kg. Croydon H. Was at Loughborough University.
At 400m/4x400mR: OG: '08- 6, '12- sf; WCh: '07- h, '09- sf/2R, '11- sf; EC: '10- 3/2R; CG: '06- 5; WJ: '06- 3/3R; EJ: '05- 2/1R; ECp: '07-08-10: 3/1&2R/1. Won UK 2008, 2010-12.
Progress at 400m: 2003- 49.4, 2004- 47.46, 2005- 46.44, 2006- 45.35, 2007- 45.47, 2008- 44.60, 2009- 45.35, 2010- 44.99, 2011- 45.30, 2012- 44.92. pbs: 60m 7.12i '09, 200m 21.33 '07, 20.87w '11; 600m 1:16.9 '05, 800m 1:50.55 '05.
Ran anchor leg in 43.73 on 4x400m at 2008 Olympics.

Greg RUTHERFORD b. 17 Nov 1986 Milton Keynes 1.88m 84kg. Marshall Milton Keynes.
At LJ: OG: '08- 10, '12- 1; WCh: '07- dnq 21, '09- 5, '11- dnq 15=; EC: '06- 2; CG: '06- 8, '10- 2; EJ: '05- 1; EI: '09- 6. Won AAA 2005-06, UK 2008, 2012. UK Long jump records 2009 and 2012.
Progress at LJ: 1999- 5.04, 2001- 6.16, 2003- 7.04, 2004- 7.28, 2005- 8.14, 2006- 8.26, 2007- 7.96, 2008- 8.20, 2009- 8.30, 2010- 8.22, 2011- 8.27/8.32w, 2012- 8.35. pbs: 60m 6.68i '09, 100m 10.26 '10.
Great-grandfather Jock Rutherford played 11 internationals for England at football 1904-08.

Chris TOMLINSON b. 15 Sep 1981 Middles–brough 1.97m 81kg. Newham & Essex Beagles.
At LJ: OG: '04- 5, '08- dnq 27, '12- 6; WCh: '03- 9, '05/07- dnq 14/16, '09- 8, '11- 11; EC: '02-06-10-12: 6/9/3/dnq 13; CG: '02-06-10: 6/6/nj; WJ: '00- 12; WI: '04- 6, '08- 2; EI: '07- 5, '13- 7; WCp: '02- 6; ECp: '01-02-04-10-11: 2/1/1/3/3; AAA champion 2004, UK 2009-10.
Three British long jump records 2002-2011.
Progress at LJ: 1996- 5.91/6.09w, 1997-

6.82w/6.44, 1998- 7.23i, 1999- 7.44i/7.40, 2000-
7.62, 2001- 7.75, 2002- 8.27, 2003- 8.16, 2004-
8.25/8.28w, 2005- 7.95i/7.82/7.83w, 2006- 8.09,
2007- 8.29, 2008- 8.18i/7.95/8.09w, 2009- 8.23.
2010- 8.23, 2011- 8.35, 2012- 8.26. pbs: 60m 6.84i
'09, 100m 10.69 '02, 10.61w/10.6 '01; 200m 21.73
'02, 21.43w '10; TJ 15.35 '01.

Jumped 8.27 at Tallahassee in April 2002, from
a previous best of 7.87 (and 8.19w), to break the
34-year-old British record set by Lynn Davies.

Women

Yamilé ALDAMA b. 14 Aug 1972 La Habana,
Cuba 1.73m 62kg. married name Dodds.
Shaftesbury Barnet Harriers, GBR.
At TJ: OG: '00- 4, '04- 5, '08- dnq, '12- 5; WCh:
'97-99-05-07-9-11: dnq 13/2/4/dnq 25/dnq 13/5;
PAm: '99- 1; AfG: '07- 1; AfCh: '04-06-08: 1/1/2;
CAG: '98- 1; WI: '97-9-04-06-08: 6/7/2/3/5; EI:
'13- 6; WCp: '98- 3, '06- 3. Won IbAm 1996, 1998;
Cuban 1997-2000, AAA 2003; Arab HJ, 2005, LJ
& TJ 2005, 2007, 2009.
Nine CAC triple jump records 1999-2003 (if still
eligible), CAC indoor (14.65 and 14.88) 2003,
three African and Sudan records 2004. SUD
records HJ (1.85) 2004, LJ 2005 & 2007; World
W35 2008 & 2012 indoors; world W40 indoors
2013.
Progress at TJ: 1994- 13.92, 1995- 13.84, 1996-
14.43, 1997- 14.46, 1998- 14.55, 1999- 14.77, 2000-
14.47, 2001- 13.85i, 2002- 14.40/14.54w, 2003-
15.29, 2004- 15.28, 2005- 14.82Julia, 2006-
14.86i/14.78, 2007- 14.58, 2008- 14.51, 2009-
14.48/14.68w, 2010- 12.41i, 2011- 14.50, 2012-
14.82i/14.65, 2013- 13.95i. pbs: 100mh 14.97/14.8
'92, HJ 1.88 '92, LJ 6.34 '07, Hep 5246 '93.
Aldama competed for Cuba to 2000, then for
Sudan from 2004 before gaining British eligi-
bility on 4 Aug 2011; uniquely she has competed and won medals at World Champs for three
nations. She had moved to London with
Scottish husband Andrew Dodds in 2001, in
which year her son Amil was born, and hoped
to be eligible for Britain but a three-year waiting period meant that she was unable to gain a
passport in sufficient time to compete at the
2003 Worlds (or 2004 Olympics).

Holly BLEASDALE b. 2 Nov 1991 Preston
1.75m 68kg. Blackburn Harriers.
At PV: OG: '12- 6=; WCh: '11- dnq; WI: '12- 3; WJ:
'10- 3; EU23: '11- 1; EI: '13- 1. UK champion 2011-12.
Three UK pole vault records 2011-12, five
indoors 2011-12.
Progress at PV: 2007- 2.30, 2008- 3.10i, 2009-
4.05, 2010- 4.35, 2011- 4.71i/4.70, 2012- 4.87i/4.71,
2013- 4.77i. pbs: SP 11.32 '11, JT 37.60 '11.
World age-19 best 2011, age-20 best 2012.
Engaged to 800m runner Paul Bradshaw
(1:47.37 '09).

Julia BLEASDALE b. 9 Sep 1981 Hilingdon,
London 1.67m 46kg.

At 5000m/(10000m): OG: '12- 8/8; EC: '12- 4; Eur
CC: '11- 13. Won UK 5000m 2011.
Progress at 5000m, 10000m: 2004- 16:34.07,
2005- 16:04.84, 2011- 15:44.00, 2012- 15:02.00,
30:55.63. pbs: 800m 2:09.4 '04, 1500m 4:16.56 '11,
3000m 8:46.38 '12, 15km Rd 50:01 '13.

Lisa DOBRISKEY b. 23 Dec 1983 New Romney.
Kent 1.71m 56kg. Ashford. Graduate of
Loughborough University.
At 1500m: OG: '08- 4, '12- 10; WCh: '07- sf, '09- 2,
'11- h; EC: '06- h, '10- 4; CG: '06- 1; WJ: '02- 4;
EU23: '03- 2; WUG: '05- 5. At 3000m: WI: '08- 10;
EI: '07- 5. Won UK 1500m 2008, 4km CC 2005.
Progress at 1500m: 1999- 4:31.7, 2000- 4:28.10,
2001- 4:25.25, 2002- 4:14.58, 2003- 4:12.95, 2004-
4:08.14, 2005- 4:05.42mx/4:07.47, 2006- 4:06.21,
2007- 4:06.22, 2008- 4:00.64mx/4:02.10, 2009-
3:59.50, 2010- 3:59.79, 2011- 4:04.76, 2012- 4:02.13.
pbs: 400m 56.0 '02, 800m 2:00.14 '10, 1000m
2:44.13i '05, 1M 4:20.35 '08, 3000m 8:47.25i/8:54.12
'07, 2M 9:33.78i '07.
Married Ricky Soos (b. 28 Jun 1983, 800m
1:45.70 '04) on 12 Dec 2009.

Hannah ENGLAND b. 6 Mar 1987 Oxford
1.77m 54kg. Oxford City, Graduate of Birming–
ham and Florida State Universities.
At 1500m (800m): WCh: '11- 2; EC: '10- 10; CG:
'10- 4 (5); WJ: '06- h; EU23: '07- 5; ECp: '09- 4 (4),
'10- 2. Won UK 2010-11, NCAA 2008.
Progress at 1500m: 2000- 4:46.81, 2001- 4:39.37,
2002- 4:33.05, 2003- 4:28.22, 2004- 4:25.86, 2005-
4:26.16, 2006- 4:17.31, 2007- 4:12.44, 2008- 4:06.19,
2009- 4:04.29, 2010- 4:04.33, 2011- 4:01.89, 2012-
4:04.05. pbs: 800m 1:59.66 '12, 1M 4:30.29i '09,
4:40.22 '08; 3000m 8:56.72i '10.
Married Luke Gunn (3000mSt 8:28.48 '08) in 2012.

Jessica ENNIS b. 28 Jan 1986 Sheffield 1.64m
57kg. Sheffield. Studied psychology at
University of Sheffield.
At Hep: OG: '12- 1; WCh: '07- 4, '09- 1, '11- 2; EC:
'06- 8, '10- 1; CG: '06- 3; WJ: '04- 8; WY: '03- 5; EJ:
'05- 1; WUG: '05- 3; ECp: '07- 1. At Pen: WI: '10-
1, '12- 2; EI: '07- 6. At 100mh: EU23: '07- 3. Won
UK 100mh 2007, 2009, 2012; HJ 2007, 2009, 2011-
12.
Records: Commonwealth heptathlon (2) 2012,
indoor pentathlon 2010 & 2012, UK high jump
2007, 100mh 2012, indoor 60mh 2010.
Progress at Hep: 2001- 4801, 2002- 5194, 2003-
5116, 2004- 5542, 2005- 5910, 2006- 6287, 2007-
6469, 2009- 6731, 2010- 6823, 2011- 6790, 2012-
6955. pbs: 60m 7.36i '10, 100m 11.39+ '10, 150mStr
16.99 '10, 200m 22.83 '12, 800m 2:07.81 '11, 60mh
7.87i '12, 100mh 12.54 '12, HJ 1.95 '07, LJ 6.51 '10,
6.54w '07; SP 14.79i '12, 14.67 '11; JT 47.49 '12, Pen
4965i '12.
Set four pbs in adding 359 points to best score
for third at 2006 Commonwealth Games. Stress
fracture ended 2008 season in May. Set SP pb
when winning 2009 World title and three
indoor bests when winning 2010 World Indoor

gold. Three pbs en route to Olympic gold 2012. Won Götzis heptathlon 2010-12. Laureus World Sportswoman of the Year 2013.

Katarina JOHNSON-THOMPSON b. 9 Jan 1993 Liverpool 1.83m 70kg. Liverpool H.
At Hep: OG: '12- 15; WY: '09- 1; EJ: '09- 8, '11- 6. At LJ: WJ: '12- 1 (sf 100mh).
Progress at Hep: 2008- 5343, 2009- 5481, 2011- 5787, 2012- 6267. pbs: 60m 7.70i '12, 100m 12.35 '08, 12.2 '09, 12.1w '10; 200m 23.73 '12, 300m 38.56i '08, 800m 2:10.76 '12, 60mh 8.48i '12, 100mh 13.48 '12, HJ 1.89 '12, LJ 6.51/6.81w '10, TJ 12.56i '12, 12.49 '10; SP 12.03i '13, 11.83 '12, JT 38.68 '12, Pen 4526i '12.

Jennifer MEADOWS b. 17 Apr 1981 Billinge, Wigan 1.56m 48kg. Wigan.
At 800m/4x400mR: OG: '08- sf; WCh: '03- 6R, '07- sf, '09- 3, '11- sf; EC: '10- 3; CG: '02- SR; WI: '08- 5, '10- 2; EI: '07-09-11-13: 5/4/1&2R/4; CCp: '10- 4; ECp: '07-08-09-11: 1R/1/3R/2. At 400m: WJ: '00- sf/1R; EU23: '01- 6/1R, '03- 7/2R; WUG: '01- 2R. Won DL 800m 2011, UK 800m 2011.
Progress at 800m: 1994- 2:16.80, 1995- 2:14.88, 1996- 2:16.4, 1997- 2:16.03, 1999- 2:11.5, 2000- 2:10.7, 2001- 2:05.8, 2002- 2:04.46/2:03.35i, 2003- 2:06.82mx/2:08.0, 2004- 2:06.84i, 2005- 2:02.05, 2006- 2:00.16, 2007- 1:59.39, 2008- 1:59.11, 2009- 1:57.93, 2010- 1:58.43i/1:58.88, 2011- 1:58.60. pbs: 100m 11.94/11.8w '01, 11.9 '02; 200m 24.32 '00, 24.0 '02, 23.90w '01; 400m 52.50mx '05, 52.67 '03; 600m 1:25.81i '07, 1000m 2:39.84 '07, 1500m 4:19.36 '06.

Christine OHURUOGU b. 17 May 1984 Forest Gate, London 1.75m 70kg. Newham & Essex Beagles. Studied linguistics at University College, London.
At 400m: OG: '04- sf/3R, '08- 1, '12- 2; WCh: '05- sf/3R, '07- 1/3R, '09- 5, '11- h; CG: '06- 1; EU23: '05- 2/2R; EJ: '03- 3; WI: '12- 1R; EI: '13- 1R. At 200m: ECp: '08- 2, '09- 3. Won AAA 400m 2004, UK 2009, 2012.
Progress at 400m: 2000- 59.0, 2001- 55.29, 2003- 54.21, 2004- 50.50, 2005- 50.73, 2006- 50.28, 2007- 49.61, 2008- 49.62, 2009- 50.21, 2010- 50.88, 2011- 50.85, 2012- 49.70. pbs: 60m 7.39i '06, 100m 11.35 '08, 150mStr 16.94 '09, 200m 22.85 '09, 300m 36.76+ '09.
Played for England U17 and U19 at netball. Withdrawn from GB European Champs team in 2006 after missing three drugs tests, receiving a one-year ban.

Joanne PAVEY b. 20 Sep 1973 Honiton 1.62m 51kg. née Davis. Bristol.
At 5000m/(10000m): OG: '00- 12, '04- 5 (h 1500m), '08- (12), '12- 7/7; WCh: '01- 11, 05- 15, '07- 9 (4); EC: '02- 5, '06- 4, '12- (2); CG: '02- 5, '06- 2; WCp: '02- 3; ECp: '02-03-10-12: 2/2/2/(2). At 3000m: WI: '04- 5; EI: '07- 6. At 1500m: WCh: '97- sf, '03- 10. Eur CC: '04- 3, '06- 8. Won UK 1500m 1997, AAA 5000m 2001, 2006; UK 5000m

2007-08, 2012; 10000m 2007-08, 2010.
2 Commonwealth indoor 3000m records 2004-07.
Progress at 1500m, 3000m, 5000m, 10000m: 1988- 4:27.9, 1989- 4:30.91, 1990- 4:26.7, 1993- 9:56.1, 1994- 4:23.36, 1995- 4:28.46, 1996- 4:21.14, 9:37.6; 1997- 4:07.28, 9:05.87; 1998- 8:58.2, 2000- 8:36.70, 14:58.27; 2001- 8:36.58, 15:00.56; 2002- 4:11.16, 8:31.27, 14:48.66; 2003- 4:01.79, 8:37.89, 15:09.04; 2004- 4:12.50, 8:34.55i/8:40.22, 14:49.11; 2005- 4:16.3i, 8:33.79, 14:40.71; 2006- 4:05.91, 8:38.80, 14:39.96; 2007- 8:31.50i/8:44.13, 15:04.77, 31:26.94; 2008- 14:58.62, 31:12.30; 2010- 15:02.31, 31:51.91; 2012- 15:02.84, 30:53.20. pbs: 800m 2:09.68 '90, 1M 4:30.77 '97, 2000m 5:41.2i '07, 5:41.6 '05; 2M 9:32.00i '07, Road: 15k 48:43 '08, 10M 52:46 '06, 20k 65:30 '08, HMar 68:53 '08, Mar 2:28:24 '11.
Set British under-15 record at 1500m with 4:27.9 in 1988 and won four national titles at U15/U17 level, but did not compete much in the early 1990s, also missing two years through injury 1998-2000. Married to middle-distance runner Gavin Pavey. Son Jacob born on 14 Sep 2009, expecting second child in September 2013. First non East-African at both 5000m and 10,000m at 2012 Olympics, taking 19.1 secs of 10,000m pb at age of 38.

Tiffany PORTER b. 13 Nov 1987 Ypsilanti, USA 1.72m 62kg. née Ofili. Doctorate in pharmacy from University of Michigan.
At 100mh: OG: '12- sf; WCh: '11- 4; WJ: '06- 3 (for USA). At 60mh: WI: '12- 2; EI: '11- 2. Won UK 100mh 2011, NCAA 100mh & 60mh indoors 2009.   Three British 100mh records 2011.
Progress at 100mh: 2005- 14.19, 2006- 13.37/13.15w, 2007- 12.80, 2008- 12.73, 2009- 12.77/12.57w, 2010- 12.85, 2011- 12.56, 2012- 12.65/12.47w. pbs: 60m 7.41i '11, 100m 11.70 '09, 11.63w '08; 200m 23.90 '08, 400mh 61.96 '06, LJ 6.48 '09; UK records: 50mh 6.83i '12, 55mh 7.38i '12, 60mh 7.80i '11.
Opted for British nationality in September 2010 through her mother being born in London (father born in Nigeria). Married US hurdler Jeff Porter (qv) in May 2011. Younger sister Cindy Ofili USA has pbs 60mh 8.22i & 100mh 13.34 '13.

Shara PROCTOR b. 16 Sep 1988 Anguilla 1.74m 56kg. Birchfield H. Was at University of Florida, USA.
At LJ: OG: '12- 9; WCh: '07-09-11: dnq 29/6/dnq 20; WI: '12- 3; CG: '06- dnq 13; WJ: '06- dnq 16; WY: '05- 6; EI: '13- 4. Won CAC 2009, UK 2011, 2012.
Records: Anguilla: LJ 2005-09, TJ 2007-09; UK LJ 2012.
Progress at LJ: 2003- 5.64, 2004- 5.99A. 2005- 6.24, 2006- 6.17, 2007- 6.17, 2008- 6.54A/6.52/6.61w, 2009- 6.71, 2010- 6.69, 2011- 6.81, 2012- 6.95. pbs: 60m 7.49i (2013), 100m 12.27 '08, 12.10w '10; TJ 13.88i '10, 13.74 '09.
Switched from Anguilla (a British Dependent

Territory without a National Olympic Committee) to Britain from 16 Nov 2010. Younger sister Shinelle (b. 27 Jun 91) set Anguillan high jump records at 1.70 in 2009 and 2010.

Goldie SAYERS b. 16 Jul 1982 Newmarket 1.71m 70kg. Belgrave H.
At OG: '04- dnq 20, '08- 4, '12- dnq; WCh: '05- 12, '07/09- dnq 18/13, '11- 10; EC: '06- 12, '12- 4; CG: '02- 6, '06- 5; WJ: '00- 6; WY: '99- 5; EJ: '01- 2; EU23: '03- 11; WUG: '03- 5, '05- 4; ECp: '10- 2, '11- 2. AAA champion 2003-06, UK 2007-12.
Three UK javelin records 2007-12.
Progress at JT: 1996- 41.56, 1997- 45.10, 1998- 51.92, new: 1999- 51.06, 2000- 54.48, 2001- 55.40, 2002- 58.20, 2003- 56.29, 2004- 60.85, 2005- 61.45, 2006- 60.41, 2007- 65.05, 2008- 65.75, 2009- 59.82, 2010- 63.15, 2011- 64.46, 2012- 66.17.

Perri SHAKES-DRAYTON b. 21 Dec 1988 London 1.70m 67kg. Victoria Park & Tower Hamlets, Brunel University.
At 400mh/4x400mR: WCh: '09- sf, '11- sf; EC: '10- 3/3R; WI: '12- 1R; WJ: '06- 8; EU23: '09-1; EJ: '07- 2/2R; ET: '11- 3. At 400m: EI: '13- 1/1R. Won UK 400m 2011, 400mh 2008, 2010-12.
Progress at 400mh: 2006- 57.52, 2007- 56.46, 2008- 56.09, 2009- 55.26, 2010- 54.18, 2011- 54.62, 2012- 53.77. pbs: 60m 7.44i '09, 100m 11.78 '09, 11.7w '07; 200m 23.71mx '10, 300m 36.9+i '13, 400m 50.85i '13, 51.26 '12, 800m 2:08.35mx/2:08.6 '11, 100mh 14.07 '08.

USA

Governing body: USA Track and Field, One RCA Dome, Suite #140, Indianapolis, IN 46225. Founded 1979 as The Athletics Congress, when it replaced the AAU (founded 1888) as the governing body.
National Championships first held in 1876 (men), 1923 (women). **2012 Champions: Men**: 100m: Justin Gatlin 9.80, 200m: Wallace Spearmon 19.82w, 400m: LaShawn Merritt 44.12, 800m: Nick Symmonds 1:43.92, 1500m: Leonel Manzano 3:35.75, 5000m/10000m: Galen Rupp 13:22.67/27:25.33, HMar: Abdi Abdirahman 62:46, Mar: Mebrahtom Keflezighi 2:09:08, 3000mSt: Evan Jager 8:17.40, 110mh: Aries Merritt 12.93, 400mh: Michael Tinsley 48.33, HJ: Jamie Nieto 2.28, PV: Brad Walker 5.67, LJ: Marquise Goodwin 8.33, TJ: Christian Taylor 17.63, SP: Reese Hoffa 22.00, DT: Lance Brooks 65.15, HT: Kibwé Johnson 74.97, JT: Sam Humphreys 81.86, Dec: Ashley Eaton 9039, 20000W: Trevor Barron 1:23:00.10, 50kW: John Nunn 4:04:41. **Women**: 100m: Carmelita Jeter 10.92, 200m: Allyson Felix 21.69, 400m: Sanya Richards-Ross 49.28, 800m: Alysia Montaño 1:59.08, 1500m: Morgan Uceny 4:04.59, 5000m: Julie Culley 15:13.77, 10000m: Amy Hastings 31:58.36, HMar: Kara Goucher 69:46, Mar: Shalane Flanagan 2:25:38, 3000mSt: Emma Coburn 9:32.78, 100mh: Dawn Harper 12.73,

400mh: Lashinda Demus 53.98, HJ: Chaunté Lowe 2.01, PV: Jenn Suhr 4.60, LJ: Brittney Reese 7.15, TJ: Amanda Smock 13.94, SP: Jill Camarena-Williams 19.16, DT: Stephanie Brown Trafton 65.18, HT: Amber Campbell 71.80, JT: Brittany Borman 61.51, Hep: Hyleas Fountain 6419, 20,000mW: Maria Michta 1:34:53.4.
NCAA Championships first held in 1921 (men), 1982 (women). **2012 Champions: Men**: 100m/110mh: Andrew Riley JAM 10.28/13.53, 200m: Maurice Mitchell 20.40, 400m: Tony McQuay 44.58, 800m: Charles Jock 1:45.59, 1500m: Andrew Bayer 3:43.82, 5000m/10000m: Cam Levins CAN 13:40.05/28:07.14, 3000mSt: Donn Cabral 8:35.44, 400mh: Amaechi Morton NGR 48.79, HJ: Erik Kynard 2.34, PV: Jack Whitt 5.65, LJ: Marquise Goodwin 8.23, TJ: Omar Craddock 16.92w, SP: Jordan Clarke 20.40, DT: Chad Wright JAM 62.79, JT: Tim Glover 81.69, Dec: Kurt Felix GRN 8062. **Women**: 100m: English Gardner 11.10, 200m: Kimberlyn Duncan 22.86, 400m: Ashley Spencer 50.95, 800m: Nachelle Mackie 2:01.06, 1500m: Katie Flood 4:13.79, 5000m: Abbey D'Agostino 16:11.34, 10000m: Natosha Rogers 32:41.63, 3000mSt: Shalaya Kipp 9:49.02, 100mh: Christina Manning 12.89, 400mh: Cassandra Tate 55.22, HJ: Brigetta Barrett 1.93, PV: Eketeríni Stefanídi GRE 4.45, LJ: Whitney Gipson 6.82w, TJ: Hanna Demydova UKR 14.20, SP: Tia Brooks 18.44, DT: Whitney Ashley 59.99, HT: Jeneva McCall 68.67, JT: Brittany Borman 56.27, Hep: Brianne Theisen CAN 6440.

Harry ADAMS b. 8 Jan 1990 1.82m 81kg. Dillard. Auburn University.
Progress at 100m, 200m: 2005- 10.57w, 2006- 10.33, 21.05; 2010- 10.17w, 2011- 10.19, 20.74; 2012- 9.96, 20.10. pbs: 60m 6.55i '12..
Returned from playing American Football to athletics in 2010.

Jeshua ANDERSON b. 22 Jun 1989 Mission Hills, California 1.88m 84kg. Was at Washington State University.
At 400mh/4x400mR: WCh: '11- sf; WJ: '08- 1/1R; WUG: '11- 1. Won US 2011; NCAA 2008-09, 2011.
Progress at 400mh: 2008- 48.68, 2009- 48.47, 2010- 48.63, 2011- 47.93, 2012- 48.88. pbs: 400m 46.08 '09, 500m 1:10.86i '12, 60mh 7.98i '11, 110mh 13.78 '11.
Broke 22 year-old US high school 300mh record with 35.28 in 2007. Played as wide receiver at American Football.

Ronnie ASH b. 2 Jul 1988 Raleigh NC 1.88m 86kg. Mike. Was at University of Oklahoma.
At 110mh: won NACAC 2010, NCAA 2009.
Progress at 110mh: 2008- 13.44, 2009- 13.27, 2010- 13.19/12.98w, 2011- 13.25/13.24w, 2012- 13.20/13.10w. pbs: 200m 22.08 '08, 60mh 7.55i '10.

Ryan BAILEY b. 13 Apr 1989 Portland, Oregon 1.93m 96kg. Nike.

At 100m/4x100mR: OG: '12- 5/2R. At 4x400m: WJ: '08- res (1)R.
Progress at 100m, 200m: 2007- 10.48/10.45w, 21.13/21.11w; 2008- 10.28, 20.69; 2009- 10.05, 20.45; 2010- 9.88, 20.10; 2012- 9.88, 20.43. pbs: 55m 6.20i '09, 60m 6.58A/6.61i '10, 300m 33.50 '07, 400m 47.05 '08, 60mh 7.97i '08, 110mh 14.13 '08.
His nephew Eric Bailey 400mh pb 50.04 '11.

Joel BROWN b. 31 Jan 1980 Baltimore 1.80m 75kg. adidas. Studied financial planning at Ohio State University.
At 110mh: WCh: '05- 6; won US indoor 60mh 2005.
Progress at 110mh: 2000- 14.49, 2001- 14.04, 2003- 13.74/13.58w, 2004- 13.35, 2005- 13.22, 2006- 13.30, 2007- 13.31, 2008- 13.33/13.2w, 2009- 13.27/13.18w, 2010- 13.24/13.1w, 2011- 13.20, 2012- 13.23. pbs: 55m 6.24i '06, 60m 6.74i '05, 100m 10.33 '04, 10.32w '05; 200m 20.54 '09, 20.36w '08; 50mh 6.48i '12, 55mh 7.18i '03, 60mh 7.48i '09, 400mh 51.94 '99.

Christian CANTWELL b. 30 Sep 1980 Jefferson City, Missouri 1.93m 154kg. Nike. Studied hotel and restaurant management at University of Missouri.
At SP: OG: '08- 2, '12- 4; WCh: '05- 5, '09- 1, '11- 4; WI: '04-08-10: 1/1/1; CCp: '10- 1; won DL 2010, WAF 2003, 2009; US 2005, 2009-10. At DT: PAm-J: '99- 2.
Progress at SP: 1999- 15.85, 2000- 19.67, 2001- 19.71, 2002- 21.45, 2003- 21.62, 2004- 22.54, 2005- 21.67, 2006- 22.45, 2007- 21.96, 2008- 22.18i/21.76, 2009- 22.16, 2010- 22.41, 2011- 22.07, 2012- 22.31. pbs: DT 59.32 '01, HT 57.18 '01, Wt 22.04i '03.
Three competitions over 22m in 2004, then 4th in US Olympic Trials. Married Teri Steer (b. 3 Oct 1975, SP pb 19.21 '01, 3 WI 1999) 29 Oct 2005.

Matthew CENTROWITZ b. 18 Nov 1989 Beltsville, Maryland 1.76m 61kg. Sociology student at the University of Oregon.
At 1500m: OG: '12- 4; WCh: '11- 3; WI: '12- 7. At 5000m WJ: '08- 11. Won US 2011, NCAA 2011, PAm-J 2007.
Progress at 1500m: 2007- 3:49.54, 2008- 3:44.98, 2009- 3:36.92, 2010- 3:40.14, 2011- 3:34.46, 2012- 3:31.96. pbs: 800m 1:47.77 '11, 1000m 2:19.56i '13, 1M 3:51.34i '13, 3:57.44 '12; 3000m 7:46.19i '12, 2M 8:40.55 '07, 5000m 13:47.73 '10.
Father Matt pbs: 1500m 3:36.60 '76, 3:54.94 '82, 5000m 13:12.91 '82, 10000m 28:32.7 '83; h OG 1500m 1976; 1 PAm 5000m 1979. Sister Lauren (b. 25 Sep 1986) has 1500m pb 4:10.23 '09. Their father Matt was 1979 Pan-American 5000m champion with pbs 1500m 3:36.70 '76, 1M 3:54.94 '82, 5000m US record 13:12.91 '82.

Bryan CLAY b. 3 Jan 1980 Austin, Texas 1.80m 83kg. Nike. Was at Azusa Pacific University.
At Dec: OG: '04- 2, '08- 1; WCh: '01/03/07- dnf, '05- 1; PAm-J: '99- 1. US champion 2004-05, 2008. At Hep: WI: '04-06-08-10: 2/2/1/1.

Progress at Dec: 1999- 7312, 2000- 7373, 2001- 8169, 2002- 8230, 2003- 8482, 2004- 8820, 2005- 8732, 2006- 8677, 2007- 8493, 2008- 8832, 2010- 8483, 2011- dnf. pbs: 60m 6.65i '04, 100m 10.35 '10, 200m 21.39 '08, 400m 47.78 '05, 1000m 2:49.41i '04, 1500m 4:38.93 '01, 60mh 7.71Ai '10, 7.74i '08; 110mh 13.64 '10, HJ 2.10i '06, 2.09 '07; PV 5.10 '04, LJ 7.96/8.06w '04, SP 16.27 '08, DT 55.87 '05, JT 72.00 '05, Hep 6371i '08.
Moved from Texas to Hawaii at age five. Brilliant breakthrough with four pbs in 2004 World Indoor heptathlon. Set decathlon discus WR with 55.87 during 2005 US Champs, and pbs at SP, 400m and JT when winning World gold in 2005. Won Götzis 2006 and 2010.

Will CLAYE b. 13 Jun 1991 Phoenix 1.80m 68kg. Student at University of Florida.
At LJ/TJ: OG: '12- 3/2; WCh: '11- 9/3; WI: '12- 4/1; won PAm-J and NCAA 2009.
Progress at LJ, TJ: 2007- 14.91/15.19w, 2008- 7.39/7.48w, 15.97; 2009- 7.89/8.00w, 17.19/17.24w; 2010- 7.30w, 16.30; 2011- 8.29, 17.50/17.62w; 2012- 8.25, 17.70i/17.62. pb 100m 10.64/10.53w '12.
Possibly youngest ever NCAA champion – he won 2009 title on his 18th birthday with 17.24w (and US junior record 17.19). First athlete to win Olympic medals at both LJ and TJ since 1936.

Kerron CLEMENT b. 31 Oct 1985 Port of Spain, Trinidad 1.88m 84kg. Nike. Was at University of Florida.
At 400mh/4x400mR: OG: '08- 2. '12- 8; WCh: '05- 4, '07- 1/res 1R, '09- 1/1R, '11- sf; WJ: '04- 1/1R; WI: '10- res 1R; WCp: '06- 1. Won WAF 2008-09, US 2005-06, NCAA 2004-05.
World junior 4x400m record 2004, world indoor records: 400m 2005, 4x400m 2006.
Progress at 400m, 400mh: 2002- 49.77H, 2003- 50.13H, 2004- 45.90, 48.51; 2005- 44.57i, 47.24; 2006- 44.71, 47.39; 2007- 44.48, 47.61; 2008- 45.10, 47.79; 2009- 45.08, 47.91; 2010- 46.01, 47.86; 2011- 45.42, 48.74; 2012- 46.49, 48.12. pbs: 60m 6.89i '10, 100m 10.23 '07, 200m 20.40i '05, 20.49 '07; 300m 31.94i '06, 55mh 7.28i '05, 60mh 7.80i '04, 110mh 13.78 '04.
Born in Trinidad, moved to Texas in 1998, US citizenship confirmed in 2005. Ran world-leading 47.24, the world's fastest time since 1998, to win 2005 US 400mh title.

Walter DIX b. 31 Jan 1986 Coral Springs, Florida 1.78m 84kg. Nike. Studied social science at Florida State University.
At 100m/200m: OG: '08- 3/3; WCh: '11- 2/2; won US 100m 2010-11, 200m 2008, 2011; NCAA 100m 2005, 2007; 200m 2006-08; DL 200m 2011.
World junior 200m indoor record (20.37) 2005.
Progress at 100m, 200m: 2002- 10.72/10.67w, 2003- 10.41/10.29w, 21.04/20.94w; 2004- 10.28, 20.62/20.54w; 2005- 10.06/9.96w, 20.18; 2006- 10.12, 20.25; 2007- 9.93, 19.69; 2008- 9.91/9.80w, 19.86; 2009- 10.00, 2010- 9.88, 19.72; 2011- 9.94, 19.53; 2012- 10.03/9.85w, 20.02. pbs: 55m 6.19i '07,

60m 6.59i '06, 150mSt 14.65 '11, 400m 46.75 '10, LJ 7.39 '04.

Johnny DUTCH b. 20 Jan 1989 Clayton NC 1.80m 82kg. Nike. Was at University of South Carolina.
At 400mh: WCh: '09- sf; WJ: '08- 2; PAm-J: '07- 1/2R. Won NCAA 2010.
Progress at 400mh: 2005- 52.06, 2006- 52.37, 2007- 50.07, 2008- 48.52, 2009- 48.18, 2010- 47.63, 2011- 48.47, 2012- 48.90. pbs: 400m 46.75 '13, 55mh 7.31i '10, 60mh 7.71i '09, 110mh 13.50/13.30w '10.

Ashton EATON b. 21 Jan 1988 Portland, Oregon 1.86m 86kg. Oregon TC. Graduate of University of Oregon.
At Dec: OG: '12- 1; WCh: '09- 18, '11- 2; won US 2012, NCAA 2008-10. At Hep: WI: '12- 1.
World decathlon record 2012, indoor heptathlon records 2010 (6499), 2011 (6568) and 2012.
Progress at Dec: 2007- 7123, 2008- 8122, 2009- 8241w/8091, 2010- 8457, 2011- 8729, 2012- 9039. pbs: 60m 6.66i '11, 100m 10.21 '12, 10.19w '10; 200m 21.03 '10, 400m 45.68 '12, 800m 1:55.90i '10, 1000m 2:32.67i '10, 1500m 4:14.48 '12, 60mh 7.60i '11, 110mh 13.35 '11, 13.34w '12; HJ 2.11i '10, 2.11 '12; PV 5.30 '12, LJ 8.23 '12, SP 15.40 '13, DT 47.36 '11, JT 66.64 '13, Hep 6645i '12.
Set best ever marks in decathlons with 100m 10.21 and LJ 8.23 in WR in Eugene 22/23 June 2012. Engaged to Brianne Theisen CAN (qv).

Dexter FAULK b. 14 Apr 1984 1.87m 75kg. Nike. Was at Barton County CC.
At 110mh: PAm-J: '03- 2; WY: '01- 6; won NACAC 2007.
Progress at 110mh: 2001- 14.23w, 2002- 13.97, 2003- 13.73/13.58w, 2004- 13.60/13.53w, 2005- 13.63, 2006- 13.68/13.58w, 2007- 13.34, 2008- 13.40, 2009- 13.13, 2010- 13.47, 2011- 13.35, 2012- 13.13/13.12w. pbs: 60m 6.72i '08, 100m 10.49 '09, 200m 21.34/21.18w '04, 50mh 6.50i '09, 60mh 7.40Ai '12, 7.50 '09; LJ 7.44 '00.

Justin GATLIN b. 10 Feb 1982 Brooklyn, NY 1.85m 79kg. Was at University of Tennessee.
At 100m/200m/4x100mR: OG: '04- 1/3/2R, '12- 3/2R; WCh: '05- 1/1, '11- sf. At 60m: WI: '03- 1, '12- 1. Won US 100m 2005-06, 2012; 200m 2005 (indoor 60m 2003), NCAA 100m & 200m 2001- 02 (& indoor 60m/200m 2002).
Progress at 100m, 200m: 2000- 10.36, 2001- 10.08, 20.29/19.86w; 2002: under international suspension 10.05/10.00w, 19.86; 2003- 9.97, 20.04; 2004- 9.85, 20.01; 2005- 9.88/9.84w, 20.00; 2006- 9.77dq, 2010- 10.09, 20.63; 2011- 9.95, 20.20; 2012- 9.79, 20.11. pbs: 60m 6.45i '03, 55mh 7.39i '02, 60mh 7.86i '01, 110mh 13.41dq '02, 13.78/13.74w '01; LJ 7.34i '01, 7.21 '00.
Top hurdler in high school (110mh 13.66 and 300mh 36.74 on junior hurdles). Retained NCAA sprint titles while ineligible for international competition in 2002 after failing a drugs test in 2001 (when he won 100m, 200m and 110mh at the US Juniors) for a prescribed medication to treat Attention Deficit Disorder. Reinstated by IAAF in July 2002. Won 2005 World 100m title by biggest ever winning margin of 0.17. Won all five 100m competitions in 2006, including tying the world record with 9.77 in Doha and taking the US title, but had tested positive for testosterone before these performances. He received a four-year drugs ban but returned to competition in August 2010.

Tyson GAY b. 9 Aug 1982 Lexington 1.83m 73kg. adidas. Studied marketing at University of Arkansas.
At 100m/(200m)/4x100mR: OG: '08- sf, '12- 4/2R; WCh: '05- (4), '07- 1/1/1R, '09- 2; WCp: '06- 1/1R, '10- 1R. Won DL 2010, WAF 100m 2009, 200m 2005-06, US 100m 2007-08, 200m 2007; NCAA 100m 2004.
Four N.American 100m records 2008-09.
Progress at 100m, 200m: 2000- 10.56, 21.27; 2001- 10.28, 21.23; 2002- 10.27/10.08w, 20.88/20.21w; 2003- 10.01w, 21.15/20.31w; 2004- 10.06/10.10w, 20.07; 2005- 10.08, 19.93; 2006- 9.84, 19.68; 2007- 9.84/9.76w, 19.62; 2008- 9.77/9.68w, 20.00; 2009- 9.69, 19.58; 2010- 9.78, 19.76; 2011- 9.79, 2012- 9.80, 20.21. pbs: 60m 6.39+ '09, 6.55i '05; 150mSt 14.51 '11, 200m/220ySt 19.41/19.54 '10, 400m 44.89 '10. Ran four 200m races in under 19.85 in 2006. Then greatest ever sprint double (9.84 and 19.62) at 2007 US Champs and ran fastest ever 100m 9.68w/+4.1 (after US record in qf) to win US Olympic Trials in 2008 but pulled hamstring in 200m qf and unable to compete again until Olympics, where he was not back to top form. IAAF Athlete of the Year 2006.

Justin GAYMON b. 13 Dec 1986 Stewartsville, New Jersey 1.75m 70kg. Nike, Was at University of Georgia.
At 400mh: won NACAC 2008.
Progress at 400mh: 2004- 52.87, 2005- 50.84, 2006- 50.20, 2007- 49.25, 2008- 48.46, 2009- 48.86, 2010- 48.65, 2011- 48.58, 2012- 48.97. pbs: 200m 21.28 '08, 400m 45.94i/46.17 '08, 55mh 7.47i '07, 60mh 7.86i '09, 110mh 13.90 '06, 13.85w '07.

Marquise GOODWIN b. 19 Nov 1990 Austin, Texas 1.78m 82kg. Studied kinesiology at University of Texas.
At LJ: OG: '12- 10; WCh: '11- dnq 13; WJ: '10- 1/1R; WUG: '11- 2; won NCAA 2010, 2012; US 2011-12.
Progress at LJ: 2007- 7.62, 2008- 7.74/7.96w, 2009- 8.18, 2010- 8.15, 2011- 8.17/8.33w, 2012- 8.33. pbs: 60m 6.69i '10, 100m 10.38 '08, 10.24w '09; 200m 21.57/21.24w '09, TJ 15.20/15.38w '09.
A wide receiver at American football.

Ryan HALL b. 14 Oct 1982 Big Bear Lake, California 1.80m 64kg. Asics. Graduate of Stanford University.
At 5000m: WCh: '05- h. At Mar: OG: '08- 10, '12- dnf. World 4k CC: '06- 19; 20k: '06- 11. Won US

HMar & Mar 2007, CC 2006; NCAA 5000m 2005. US records: 20km 2006, HMar 2007.
Progress at 5000m, Mar: 2004- 13:45.00, 2005- 13:16.03, 2006- 13:28.89, 2007- 2:08:24, 2008- 2:06:17, 2009- 2:09:40, 2010- 2:08:41dh, 2011- 2:04:58wdh/2:08:04, 2012- 2:09:30. pbs: 800m 1:51.07 '01, 1500m 3:42.70 '01, 1M 4:05.50 '05, 3000m 7:53.8+ '06, 2M 8:26.26 '06, 10000m 28:07.93 '07, Road: 15km 42:21 '07, 10M 45:33 '07, 20km 57:06e '07, HMar 59:43 '07, 30km 1:28:38 '08.
Marathon debut in 2007: 7th London 2:08:24, 1st US Trial 2:09:02; 5th London 2008, 3rd Boston 2009, 4th Boston 2010-11. Married to **Sara Bei-Hall** (b. 15 Apr 1983) pbs: 1500m 4:08.55 '08, 5000m 15:20.88 '06, WI 3000m: '06-12, '12- 8.

James Edward 'Trey' **HARDEE** b. 7 Feb 1984 Birmingham, Alabama 1.96m 95kg. Nike. Was at Mississippi State University and University of Texas.
At Dec: OG: '08- dnf, '12- 2; WCh: '09- 1, '11- 1; won NCAA 2005, US 2009. At Hep: WI: '10- 2.
Progress at Dec: 2003- 7544, 2004- 8041, 2005- 7881, 2006- 8465, 2008- 8534, 2009- 8790, 2011- 8689, 2012- 8671. pbs: 55m 6.30i '06, 60m 6.71i '06, 100m 10.39 '10, 10.28w '06; 200m 20.98 '06, 400m 47.51 '06, 1000m 2:45.67i '12, 1500m 4:40.94 '12, 60mh 7.70i '10, 110mh 13.54 '12; HJ 2.06i '10, 2.05 '08; PV 5.30Ai '06, 5.25 '08; LJ 7.88 '11, SP 15.94i '09, 15.72 '12; DT 52.68 '08, JT 68.99 '11, Hep 6208Ai '06.
Won IAAF Combined Events Challenge 2009.

Antwon HICKS b. 12 Mar 1983 1.87m 73kg. adidas. Sociology graduate of the University of Mississippi.
At 110mh: WJ: '02- 1; won NCAA indoor 60mh 2004-05.
Progress at 110mh: 2002- 13.59/13.42w, 2003- 13.49/13.46w, 2004- 13.45, 2005- 13.35, 2006- 13.49/13.37w, 2007- 13.36, 2008- 13.09, 2009- 13.24, 2010- 13.29, 2011- 13.35, 2012- 13.14. pbs: 60m 6.80i '08, 100m 10.94 '07, 200m 21.39 '05, 55mh 7.15i '04, 60mh 7.53i '08, HJ 2.08/2.16i '01.

Reese HOFFA b. 8 Oct 1977 Evans, Georgia 1.82m 133kg. New York AC. Was at University of Georgia.
At SP: OG: '04- dnq 22, '08- 7, '12- 3; WCh: '03-07-09-11: dnq/1/4/5; PAm: '03- 1; WI: '04-06-08-12: 2/1/2/4; WUG: '01- 9; WCp: '06- 2; won WAF 2006-07, DL 2012, USA 2007-08, 2012.
Progress at SP: 1998- 19.08, 1999- 19.35, 2000- 19.79, 2001- 20.22, 2002- 20.47, 2003- 20.95, 2004- 21.67, 2005- 21.74i/21.29, 2006- 22.11i/21.96, 2007- 22.43, 2008- 22.10, 2009- 21.89, 2010- 22.16, 2011- 22.09, 2012- 22.00. pbs: DT 58.46 '99, HT 60.05 '02.
Added 37cm to his best to win World Indoor gold 2006.

Bershawn JACKSON b. 8 May 1983 Miami 1.73m 69kg. Nike. Studied accountancy at St Augustine's University, Raleigh.

At 400mh/4x400mR: OG: '08- 3; WCh: '03- h (dq), '05- 1, '07- sf/res 1R, '09- 3/res 1R, '11- 6/1R; WJ: '02- 3/1R; CCp: '10- 3/1R; won DL 2010, WAF 2004-05, US 2003, 2008-10. At 400m: WI: '10- 5/1R; won US indoor 2005, 2010.
Progress at 400mh: 2000- 52.17, 2001- 50.86, 2002- 50.00, 2003- 48.23, 2004- 47.86, 2005- 47.30, 2006- 47.48, 2007- 48.13, 2008- 48.02, 2009- 47.98, 2010- 47.32, 2011- 47.93, 2012- 48.20. pbs: 200m 21.03/20.46w '04, 400m 45.06 '07, 600m 1:18.65i '06, 800m 1:53.40 '11, 200mhSt 22.26 '11.

Evan JAGER b. 8 Mar 1989 Algonquin, Illinois 1.88m 66kg. Oregon TC. Was at University of Wisconsin.
At 3000mSt: OG: '12- 6; US champion 2012. At 1500m: WJ: '08- 8. At 5000m: WCh: '09- h.
N.American 3000m steeplechase record 2012.
Progress at 3000mSt: 2012- 8:06.81. pbs: 800m 1:50.10i '10, 1:51.04 '08; 1500m 3:38.33 '09, 1M 3:54.35 '09, 3000m 7:35.16 '12, 2M 8:14.95i '13, 5000m 13:22.18 '09.
Set US record in only his fifth steeplechase race, improving pb by 10.59 secs. In 2009 he had come 3rd in the US Champs in only his second race at 5000m.

Kibwe JOHNSON b. 17 Jul 1981 San Francisco 1.89m 108kg. New York AC. Was at Ashland University.
At HT: OG: '12- 9; WCh: '07- nt, '11- dnq 14; PAm: '07- 2, '11- 1; US champion 2011-12.
Progress at HT: 2002- 64.26, 2003- 69.11, 2004- 69.49, 2005- 78.25, 2006- 75.32, 2007- 75.95, 2008- 75.53, 2009- 67.80, 2010- 77.07, 2011- 80.31, 2012- 77.17. pbs: SP 16.30i '05, DT 65.11 '05, Wt 25.12i '08.
Married to Crystal Smith (HT pb 68.60 '07, 11 CG '10 for Canada).

Dustin '**Dusty**' **JONAS** b. 19 Apr 1986 Floresville, Texas 1.98m 84kg. Nike. Was at University of Nebraska.
At HJ: OG: '08- dnq 26=; WCh: '11- dnq 30; WI: '10- 3; PAm-J: '05- 1; CCp: '10- 6. Won NCAA indoor 2008.
Progress at HJ: 2002- 2.16, 2003- 2.22, 2004- 2.13, 2005- 2.24, 2006- 2.28, 2007- 2.25i/2.24, 2008- 2.36A, 2009- 2.26i/2.24, 2010- 2.33, 2011- 2.31, 2012- 2.25i, 2013- 2.34i. pb LJ 7.47/7.76w '07; TJ 15.15i '12, 15.07 '07.

Trell KIMMONS b. 13 Jul 1985 Coldwater, Mississippi 1.78m 77kg. Was at Mississippi State University.
At 100m/4x100mR: OG: '12- 2R; WCh: '11- sf; WJ: '04- 1R. At 60m: WI: '10- 4, '12- 4.
Progress at 100m: 2003- 10.3w, 2004- 10.39/10.34w/10.0w, 2005- 10.22/10.16w, 2006- 10.17, 2007- 10.31/10.25w, 2008- 10.30, 2009- 10.16, 2010- 9.95/9.92w, 2011- 10.04/9.97w, 2012- 10.02/10.00w. pbs: 50m 5.68i '12, 60m 6.45Ai '12, 6.53i '06; 100y 9.37+ '10, 200m 20.37 '10, 20.3 '06, 20.32w '05; 400m 47.53 '10.

Erik KYNARD b. 3 Feb 1991 Toledo, Ohio 1.93m 86kg. Was at Kansas State University.
At HJ: OG: '12- 2; WCh: '11- dnq 14; WJ: '08- dnq 19=; NCAA champion 2011-12.
Progress at HJ: 2007- 2.13i, 2008- 2.23i/2.15, 2009- 2.24i/2.22, 2010- 2.25, 2011- 2.33i/2.31, 2012- 2.34, 2013- 2.33i. pb LJ 7.15i '09.

Bernard LAGAT b. 12 Dec 1974 Kapsabet, Kenya 1.75m 61kg. Nike. Studied business management at Washington State University, USA.
At 1500m (/5000m): OG: '00- 3, '04- 2, '08- sf/9, '12- (4); WCh: '01- 2, '05- sf, '07- 1/1, '09- 3/2, '11- (2); WI: '03- 2; AfCh: '02- 1; WUG: '99- 1; WCp: '02- 1; 2nd GP 1999-2000-02, WAF 2005-06. At 3000m: WI: '01-04-10-12: 6/1/1/1; CCp: '10- 1/(1). Won WAF 3000m 2005, 2008; KEN 1500m 2002, US 1500m 2006, 2008; 5000m 2006-08, 2010-11; NCAA 5000m 1999 (and indoor 1M/3000m).
Records: Commonwealth and KEN 1500m 2001, N.American 1500m 2005, 3000m 2010, 5000m 2010 & 2011, indoor 3000m 2007, 2M 2011 & 2013, 5000m 2010, 2012. World M35 3000m & 5000m 2010, 1M and 5000m 2011.
Progress at 1500m, 5000m: 1996- 3:37.7A, 1997- 3:41.19, 13:50.33; 1998- 3:34.48, 13:42.73; 1999- 3:30.56, 13:36.12; 2000- 3:28.51, 13:23.46; 2001- 3:26.34, 13:30.54; 2002- 3:27.91, 13:19.14; 2003- 3:30.55, 2004- 3:27.40, 2005- 3:29.30, 12:59.29; 2006- 3:29.68, 12:59.22; 2007- 3:33.85, 13:30.73; 2008- 3:32.75, 13:16.29; 2009- 3:32.56, 13:03.06; 2010- 3:32.51, 12:54.12; 2011- 3:33.11, 12:53.60; 2012- 3:34.63, 12:59.92. pbs: 800m 1:46.00 '03, 1000m 2:16.18 '08, 1M 3:47.28 '01, 2000m 4:55.49 '99, 3000m 7:29.00 '10, 2M 8:09.49i '13, 8:12.45 '08.
He was 2nd to Hicham El Guerrouj six times in 2001, including his 3:26.34 at Brussels for 2nd on the world all-time list, and six times in 2002. Withdrew from 2003 Worlds after testing positive for EPO, but this was later repudiated. Lives in Tucson, Arizona gained US citizenship 2005. First man ever to win 1500m/5000m double at the US Champs in 2006 and at World Champs in 2007. Oldest ever male World Indoor champion and medallist at 37y 89d in 2012.
From a large family: a sister **Mary Chepkemboi** competed at the 1982 Common-wealth Games and won African 3000m in 1984, and another **Evelyne Jerotich Langat** has 71:35 half marathon pb. Of his brothers **William Cheseret** has a marathon pb of 2:12:09 '04 and **Robert Cheseret** won NCAA 5000m in 2004 and 10000m in 2005, pbs 5000m 13:13.23 & 10000m 28:20.11 '05.

Tony McQUAY b. 16 Apr 1990 West Palm Beach, Florida 1.80m 70kg. Student at University of Florida.
At 400m: OG: '12- sf/2R; WCh: '11- h; US champion 2011, NCAA 2012.
Progress at 400m: 2008- 48.09, 2009- 46.84, 2010- 45.37, 2011- 44.68, 2012- 44.49. pbs: 100m 10.57 '10, 200m 20.60 '12.

Andra MANSON b. 30 Apr 1984 Brenham, Texas 1.96m 75kg. Nike. Kinesociology graduate of University of Texas.
At HJ: OG: '08- dnq 13; WCh: '09- 9; WJ: '02- 1; WI: '08- 3=; won NCAA 2004.
Progress at HJ: 2001- 2.13, 2002- 2.31, 2003- 2.22, 2004- 2.32, 2005- 2.26i/2.23, 2006- 2.28i/2.26, 2007- 2.33i/2.30, 2008- 2.33, 2009- 2.35, 2010- 2.23i/2.31, 2011- 2.25, 2012- 2.26i/2.20. pbs: 100m 10.81 '07, 10.73w '08; 200m 21.73 '08.
Won 2002 World Junior title with US junior record 2.31.

Leonel MANZANO b. 12 Sep 1984 Dolores Hidalgo, Guanajuato, Mexico 1.65m 57kg. Nike. Was at the University of Texas.
At 1500m: OG: '08- sf,'12- 2; WCh: '07- h, '09- 12, '11- sf; CCp: '10- 3. Won US 2012, NCAA 2005, 2008.
Progress at 1500m: 2003- 4:07.83M, 2005- 3:37.13, 2006- 3:39.49, 2007- 3:35.29, 2008- 3:36.67, 2009- 3:33.33, 2010- 3:32.37, 2011- 3:33.66, 2012- 3:34.08. pbs: 800m 1:44.56 '10, 1000m 2:19.73 '09, 1M 3:50.64 '10, 3000m 8:14.59i '06.
Has lived in the USA from the age of 4.

Cory MARTIN b. 22 May 1985 Bloomington, Indiana 1.96m 125kg. Nike. Was at Auburn University.
At SP: WJ: '04-11 (dnq 15 HT); Won NCAA SP & HT 2008.
Progress at SP: 2004- 17.95i/17.60, 2005- 18.85, 2006- 18.42i, 2007- 19.63, 2008- 20.35, 2009- 20.43, 2010- 22.10, 2011- 20.72, 2012- 21.31. pbs: DT 58.59 '08, HT 75.06 '09, 35lbWt 24.38i '10.

Aries MERRITT b. 24 Jul 1985 Marietta, Georgia 1.88m 75kg. Reebok. Studied sports management at University of Tennessee.
At 110mh: OG: '12- 1; WCh: '09- h, '11- 5=; WJ: '04- 1. At 60mh: WI: '12-1, Won DL 110mh 2012, NCAA 60mh indoors & 110mh 2006, US indoor 60mh & 110mh 2012.
World 110mh record 2012.
Progress at 110mh: 2004- 13.47, 2005- 13.38/13.34w, 2006- 13.12, 2007- 13.09, 2008- 13.24, 2009- 13.15, 2010- 13.61, 2011- 13.12, 2012- 12.80. pbs: 55m 6.43i '05, 60m 6.90i '10, 200m 21.31 '05, 50mh 6.54i '12, 55mh 7.02+i '12, 60mh 7.43Ai/7.44i '12, 400mh 51.94 '04.
Record 8 (and 2w) sub-13 second times in 2012.

LaShawn MERRITT b. 27 Jun 1986 Portsmouth, Virginia 1.88m 82kg. Nike. Studied sports management at Old Dominion University, Norfolk, Virginia.
At 400m/4x400mR: OG: '08- 1/1R; WCh: '05- res(1)R, '07- 2/1R, '09- 1/1R, '11- 2/1R; WJ: '04- 1/1R (1 at 4x100); WI: '06- 1R; WCp: '06- 1/1R; won WAF 2007-09, US 2008-09, 2012.
World junior records 4x100m and 4x400m 2004, World indoor 400m junior best (44.93) 2005.
Progress at 200m, 400m: 2002- 21.46, 2003- 21.33, 47.9?; 2004- 20.72/20.69w, 45.25; 2005- 20.38,

44.66; 2006- 20.10, 44.14; 2007- 19.98, 43.96; 2008-20.08/19.80w, 43.75; 2009- 20.07, 44.06; 2011-20.13, 44.63; 2012- 20.16, 44.12. pbs: 55m 6.33i '04, 60m 6.68i '06, 100m 10.47/10.38w '04, 300m 31.30 '09, 500m 1:01.39i '12.

World age-18 400m record with 44.66 in 2005 and world low-altitude 300m best 2006 and 2009. Spent a year at East Carolina University before signing for Nike and returning home to Portsmouth. Two-year drugs ban for three positive tests from October 2009, reduced by three months after US arbitration panel declared that he had taken the steroid accidentally in buying a product intended for sexual enhancement; successfully challenged IOC rule preventing anyone serving 6 months or more from a drugs offence from competing in the next Games. Injured, he had to pull up in 2012 Olympic heat.

Maurice MITCHELL b. 22 Dec 1989 Kansas City, Missouri 1.78m 73kg. Social sciences student at Florida State University.
At 200m: OG: '12- sf; Won NCAA 2011-12. At 4x100m: WCh: '11- h.
Progress at 200m: 2007- 20.77, 2008-21.40/21.23w/20.5w, 2009- 20.64, 2010- 20.24, 2011- 20.19/19.99w, 2012- 20.13/20.08w. pbs: 60m 6.55i '11, 100m 10.00 '11, 400m 47.60.

Bryshon NELLUM b. 1 May 1989 Los Angeles 1.83m 79kg. Was at University of Southern California.
At 400m/4x400mR: OG: '12- sf/2R; WJ: '06- 1R; WY: '05- 3.
Progress at 400m: 2004- 47.27, 2005- 46.81, 2006-46.20, 2007- 45.38, 2010- 45.94, 2011- 45.56, 2012-44.80. pb 200m 20.43 '07.
Career seriously threatened when he was shot three times in the leg by gang in 2009.

Adam NELSON b. 7 Jul 1975 Atlanta 1.83m 115kg. Saucony. Graduate of Dartmouth University. Training as a financial consultant.
At SP: OG: '00- 2, '04- 2, '08- nt; WCh: '01-03-05-07-09-11: 2/2/1/2/5/8; WI: '01- 2; WJ: '94- 1; WUG: '99- 2; WCp: '02- 1. GP 2002 (2nd 2000 and 3rd overall). Won WAF 2005, PAm-J 1993, GWG 2001, NCAA 1997, US 2000, 2002, 2004, 2006, 2011.
Progress at SP: 1993- 16.56, 1994- 18.34, 1995- 18.27, 1996- 19.14, 1997- 19.62, 1998- 20.61, 1999- 20.64, 2000- 22.12, 2001- 21.53, 2002- 22.51, 2003- 21.29, 2004- 21.68, 2005- 21.92, 2006- 22.04, 2007- 21.61, 2008- 22.40i/22.12, 2009- 21.11, 2010- 21.29i/21.16, 2011- 22.09, 2012- 21.54. pb DT 56.18 '96.
Had a great season in 2000, when he improved his best from 20.64 to 21.70 and then the world's longest throw for four years, 22.12 (to take the US title) in July. Further improvement as world number one in 2002. Small for a shot putter, but very fast and dynamic in the circle. Played American Football at high school and college.

James NIETO b. 2 Nov 1976 Seattle 1.93m 79kg. New York AC. Actor, business administration graduate of Eastern Michigan University.
At HJ: OG: '04- 4, '12- 6; WCh: '03- 7, '07- dnq 16=; PAm: '03- 2, '07- 7; WI: '03- 9; US champion 2003-04, 2012.
Equaled world age-35 high jump record 2012.
Progress at HJ: 1994- 1.93, 1995- 2.06, 1996- 2.14, 1997- 2.15, 1998- 2.25, 1999- 2.30, 2000- 2.23, 2001- 2.27, 2002- 2.30, 2003- 2.31, 2004- 2.34, 2005- 2.30, 2006- 2.28i/2.27, 2007- 2.27, 2008-2.30, 2009- 2.28, 2010- 2.28Ai/2.25, 2011- 2.28, 2012- 2.31.

David OLIVER b. 24 Apr 1982 Orlando 1.88m 93kg. Nike. Marketing graduate of Howard University.
At 110mh: OG: '08- 3; WCh: '07- sf, '11- 4; CCp: '10- 1. Won DL 2010, WAF 2008, US 2008, 2010-11. At 60mh: WI: '10- 3.
Two North American 110mh records 2010.
Progress at 110mh: 2001- 14.04, 2002-13.92/13.88w, 2003- 13.60, 2004- 13.55, 2005-13.29/13.23w, 2006- 13.20, 2007- 13.14, 2008-12.95/12.89w, 2009- 13.09, 2010- 12.89, 2011-12.94, 2012- 13.07. pbs: 60m 6.88i '04, 50mh 6.50i '12, 55mh 7.01+i '12, 60mh 7.37i '11.
Mother, Brenda Chambers, 400mh pb 58.54 '80.

Omo OSAGHAE b. 18 May 1988 1.84m 75kg. Was at Texas Tech University.
Progress at 110mh: 2007- 13.99, 2008- 13.65, 2009- 13.51/13.42w, 2011- 13.23/13.22w, 2012-13.24. pbs: 100m 10.62 '11, 60m 7.01i '08, 100m 10.64 '11, 200m 21.13 '09, 50mh 6.52i '12, 55mh 7.07i '11. 60mh 7.51i '11.

Travis PADGETT b. 13 Dec 1986 Shelby, North Carolina 1.74m 80kg. adidas. Studied sociology at Clemson University.
At 100m/4x100mR: OG: '08- dnf hR. Won NCAA indoor 60m 2007.
Progress at 100m: 2003- 10.54, 2004- 10.46, 2005-10.62/10.55w, 2006- 10.00, 2007- 10.09/10.05w, 2008- 9.89/9.85w, 2009- 10.00/9.93w, 2010-10.10/9.92w, 2011- 9.99/9.96w, 2012- 10.04/9.88w. pbs: 55m 6.17i '07, 60m 6.55i '10, 200m 20.32 '08.

Darvis PATTON b. 4 Dec 1977 Dallas 1.83m 75kg. Nike. Was at Texas Christian University.
At 200m/4x100m: OG: '04/12- res 2R; WCh: '03-2/1R, '07- 1R, '11- sf. At 100m: OG: '08- 8; WCh: '09- 8; PAm: '07- 2/3R. Won US 200m 2002-03. World over-35 60m record 2013.
Progress at 100m, 200m: 1998- 10.3, 20.49w; 2000- 10.22w/10.09w, 20.29; 2001- 10.16/10.14w, 20.31; 2002- 10.14, 20.12; 2003- 10.00/9.97w, 20.03, 2004- 10.12/9.89w, 20.17/20.07w; 2005- 10.27; 2006- 10.19, 20.50; 2007- 10.11, 20.49; 2008-9.89/9.84w; 2009- 9.89, 20.32; 2010- 10.19, 2011-9.94, 20.25/19.98w; 2012- 9.96, 20.32/20.24w; 2013- 9.75w. pbs: 60m 6.50i '13, LJ 8.12 '01, TJ 16.17i '98.
Concentrated on 100m from 2008. Turned to

athletics after dislocating his hip playing American football as a teenager.

David PAYNE b. 24 Jul 1982 Cincinnati 1.85m 81kg. Was at University of Cincinnati.
At 110mh: OG: '08- 2; WCh: '07- 3, '09- 3; PAm: '07- 2. US champion 2009.
Progress at 110mh: 2002- 13.92, 2003- 13.53, 2004- 13.48/13.42w, 2005- 13.33, 2006- 13.31, 2007- 13.02, 2008- 13.17/13.06w, 2009- 13.12, 2010- 13.22, 2011- 13.63, 2012- 13.32/13.22w. pbs: 100m 10.56 '07, 200m 21.15 '07, 60mh 7.51i '07, 400mh 51.16 '04.

Dwight PHILLIPS b. 1 Oct 1977 Decatur, Georgia 1.81m 78kg. Nike. Was at University of Kentucky, then Arizona State University.
At LJ: OG: '00- 8, '04- 1; WCh: '01-03-05-07-09-11: 8/1/1/3/1/1; WI: '03- 1; PAm: '99- 7; CCp: '10- 1. Won DL 2010, WAF 2003, 2005; US 2003-04, 2007, 2009-10.
Progress at LJ: 1996- 7.14, 1997- 7.26, 1999- 8.18, 2000- 8.21/8.30w, 2001- 8.13/8.23w, 2002- 8.38, 2003- 8.44, 2004- 8.60, 2005- 8.60, 2006- 8.32, 2007- 8.31/8.37w, 2008- 8.25/8.47w, 2009- 8.74, 2010- 8.46, 2011- 8.45. pbs: 50m 5.70i '05, 60m 6.47i '05, 100m 10.06 '09, 200m 20.68 '02, 400m 46.80 '97, TJ 16.41 '99.
World number one 2003-05, winning 34 of 42 competitions in those three years, and in 2009-10. Twelve consecutive years over 8m. Missed 2012 season through injury.

Jeff PORTER b. 27 Nov 1985 Summit, New Jersey 1.83m 84kg. Sports management degree from University of Michigan.
At 110mh: OG: '12- sf; PAm: '11- 4. Won NCAA indoor 60mh 2007.
Progress at 110mh: 2004- 14.08, 2005- 14.12, 2006- 13.93/13.92w, 2007- 13.57, 2008- 13.47, 2009- 13.37, 2010- 13.45, 2011- 13.26, 2012- 13.08. pbs: 60m 6.81i '12, 100m 10.56 '11, 50mh 6.50i '12, 7.54i '12.
Married to Tiffany Porter (see UK). His twin brother Joe played in the NFL.

Jason RICHARDSON b. 4 Apr 1986 Houston 1.86m 73kg. Nike. Was at University of South Carolina.
At 110mh: OG: '12- 2; WCh: '11- 1; WY: '03- 1 (1 400mh); won NCAA 2008.
Progress at 110mh: 2004- 13.76, 2005- 13.50, 2006- 13.43/13.36w, 2008- 13.21, 2009- 13.29, 2010- 13.34, 2011- 13.04, 2012- 12.98. pbs: 100m 10.90 '03, 200m 21.13 '03, 400m 46.96 '12, 60mh 7.53i '08, 400mh 49.79 '04.

Kurt ROBERTS b. 20 Feb 1988 1.91m 127kg. Was at Ashland University.
Progress at SP: 2007- 16.39, 2008- 17.81, 2009- 18.78, 2010- 19.80i/18.76, 2011- 19.55, 2012- 21.14, 2013- 20.89i.

Michael RODGERS b. 24 Apr 1985 Brenham, Texas 1.78m 73kg. Nike. Studied kinesiology at Oklahoma Baptist University.
At 100m: WCh: '09- sf; At 60m: WI: '08- 4, '10- 2. Won US 100m 2009, indoor 60m 2008.
Progress at 100m: 2004- 10.55/10.31w, 2005- 10.30/10.25w, 2006- 10.29/10.18w, 2007- 10.10, 10.07w, 2008- 10.06/10.01w, 2009- 9.94/9.9/9.85w, 2010- 10.00/9.99w, 2011- 9.85, 2012- 9.94, 2013- 9.93w. pbs: 60m 6.48Ai/6.50i '11, 200m 20.24 '09. Dropped out of US World Champs team after positive test for stimulant on 19 July 2011, for which he subsequently received a 9-month suspension. Younger sister Alishea Usery won US junior 400m 2009, pb 53.27 '09.

Galen RUPP b. 8 May 1986 Portland 1.80m 62kg. Nike. Studied business at University of Oregon.
At (5000/)10000m: OG: '08- 13, '12- 7/2; WCh: '07- 11, '09- 8, '11- 9/7. At 5000m: WJ: '04- 9; PAm-J: '03- 1. At 3000m: WI: '09- 5; WY: '03- 7. Won US 5000m 2012, 10000m 2009-12, NCAA 5000m & 10000m (& indoor 3000m & 5000m) 2009, CC 2008.
North American records: 10000m 2011, junior 5000m 2004, 10000m 2005; indoor 5000m (13:11.44) 2011, 3000m 2013, 2M 2012.
Progress at 5000m, 10000m: 2002- 14:34.05, 2003- 14:20.29, 2004- 13:37.91, 29:09.56; 2005- 13:44.72. 28:15.52; 2006- 13:47.04, 30:42.10; 2007- 13:30.49, 27:33.48; 2008- 13:59.14, 27:36.99; 2009- 13:18.12i/13:42.59+, 27:37.99; 2010- 13:07.35, 27:10.74; 2011- 13:06.86, 26:48.00; 2012- 12:58.90, 27:25.33. pbs: 800m 1:49.87i/1:50.00 '09, 1500m 3:34.75 '12, 1M 3:50.92i '13, 3:57.72 '10; 3000m 7:30.16i '13, 7:43.24 '10, 2M 8:09.72i '12, HMar 60:30 '11.

Duane SOLOMON b. 28 Dec 1984 Lompoc, California 1.91m 77kg. Sociology graduate of University of Southern California.
At 800m: OG: '12- 4; WCh: '07- h; PAm: '07- h. US indoor champion 2011.
Progress at 800m: 2002- 1:51.76, 2003- 1:49.79, 2005- 1:47.84, 2006- 1:47.45, 2007- 1:45.69, 2008- 1:45.71, 2009- 1:46.82, 2010- 1:45.23, 2011- 1:45.86, 2012- 1:42.82. pbs: 400m 45.98 '12, 600m 1:15.9+ '12, 1000m 2:17.84 '10, 1500m 3:48.29 '08, 1M 4:03.26 '10.

Wallace SPEARMON b. 24 Dec 1984 Chicago 1.90m 80kg. Saucony. Was at University of Arkansas.
At 200m/4x100mR: OG: '08- dq, '12- 4; WCh: '05- 2, '07- 3/1R, '09- 3; WCp: '06- 1/1R, '10- 1/1R. Won DL 2010, US 2006, 2010, 2012; NCAA 2004-05. At 4x400m: WI: '06- 1R.
WIR 4x400m and world indoor best 300m 2006. Two US indoor 200m records 2005.
Progress at 100m, 200m: 2003- 21.05, 2004- 10.38, 20.25/20.12w; 2005- 10.35/10.21w, 19.89; 2006- 10.11, 19.65; 2007- 9.96, 19.82; 2008- 10.07, 19.90; 2009- 10.18, 19.85; 2010- 10.15, 19.79/19.77w; 2011- 20.18; 2012- 10.26/10.06w, 19.90/19.82w; 2013- 9.92w. pbs: 60m 6.66i '12, 150mSt 14.87 '12, 300m 31.88i '06, 32.14 '09; 400m 45.22.

Disqualified for running out of his lane after crossing the line in 3rd place at the 2008 Olympics. His father (also Wallace, b. 3 Sep 1962) had pbs: of 100m 10.19 '87, 10.05w '86, 10.0w '81; 200m 20.27/20.20w '87; 1 WUG 200/4x100m, 3 PAm 200m 1987.

Nick SYMMONDS b. 30 Dec 1983 Blytheville, Arkansas 1.78m 73kg. Oregon TC. Biochemistry graduate of Willamette University.
At 800m: OG: '08- sf, '12- 5; WCh: '07- sf, '09- 6, '11- 5; WI: '08- 6; CCp: '10- 5. Won US 2008-12.
Progress at 800m: 2003- 1:49.51, 2004- 1:50.87, 2005- 1:48.82, 2006- 1:45.83, 2007- 1:44.54, 2008- 1:44.10, 2009- 1:43.83, 2010- 1:43.76, 2011- 1:43.83, 2012- 1:42.95. pbs: 400m 48.84 '04, 600m 1:14.47 '08, 1000m 2:16.35 '10, 1000m 2:20.52 '09, 1500m 3:36.04 '12, 1M 3:56.72i '07, 4:01.57 '12.

Angelo TAYLOR b. 29 Dec 1978 Albany, Georgia 1.88m 84kg. Nike. Was at Georgia Tech University.
At 400mh/4x400mR: OG: '00- 1/dq (res 1)R, '04- sf, '08- 1/1R, 12- 5/2R; WCh: '99- h/dq(1)R, '01- sf/dq(1)R, '07- (3 400m)/1R, '09- h/1R, '11- 7/1R; WJ: '96- 3; PAm-J: '97- 1/1R; won GP 2000 (and overall), NCAA 1998, US 400mh 1999-2001, 400m 2007, indoor 400m 1999
Progress at 400m, 400mh: 1995- -, 52.76, 1996- 46.7, 50.18; 1997- 46.19i/46.81, 48.72; 1998- 45.14, 47.90; 1999- 45.50i, 48.15; 2000- 44.89, 47.50; 2001- 44.68, 47.95; 2002- 44.85, 48.87; 2003- 46.32, 48.94; 2004- 45.85, 48.03; 2006- 45.24, 49.44; 2007- 44.05, 48.45; 2008- 44.38, 47.25; 2009- 45.15, 48.30; 2010- 44.72, 47.79; 2011- 44.82, 47.94; 2012- 44.93, 47.95. pbs: 100m 10.58 '08, 200m 20.23 '10, 300m 32.67 '02, TJ 14.76 '96.
Brilliant year in 1998, with fastest ever time by a 19 year-old and losing just twice (to Bryan Bronson) at 400mh. Went out in his heat (misjudging the finish) when favourite for 1999 World 400mh, but made amends with relay gold, and, after winning Olympic gold in 2000, stumbled off the last hurdle in 2001 World 400mh semi. Regained Olympic title in 2008.

Christian TAYLOR b. 18 Jun 1990 Fayetteville 1.90m 75kg. Student at University of Florida.
At (LJ/)TJ: OG: '12- 1; WCh: '11- 1; WI: '12- 2; WJ: '08- 7/8 (res 1 4x400m); WY: '07- 3/1. Won DL 2012, NACAC 2010-11, US 2011-12, NCAA indoor 2009-10.
Progress at TJ: 2007- 15.98, 2008- 16.05, 2009- 16.98i/16.65/16.91w, 2010- 17.18i/17.02/17.09w, 2011- 17.96, 2012- 17.81. pbs: 60m 6.79i '11, 200m 20.70 '13, 400m 45.34 '09, LJ 8.19 '10.

Dan TAYLOR b. 12 May 1982 Cleveland 1.98m 145kg. Nike. Construction management graduate of Ohio State University.
At SP: WCh: '07/09- dnq 34/26; PAm: '03- 4. Won NCAA indoor 2003-04.
Progress at SP: 2001- 18.31, 2002- 20.01i/19.15, 2003- 21.33i/20.44, 2004- 20.62, 2005- 20.75,

2006- 21.59, 2007- 21.57i/21.18, 2008- 20.85, 2009- 21.78, 2010- 20.89i/20.68, 2011- 20.90, 2012- 20.22. pbs: DT 59.00 '03, HT 69.35 '04, Wt 24.01i '04. Unique NCAA SP/Wt double 2004.

Matt TEGENKAMP b. 19 Jan 1982 Lee's Summit, Missouri 1.86m 66kg. Nike. Studied human ecology at University of Wisconsin.
At 5000m: OG: '08- 13; WCh: '07- 4, '09- 8; WCp: '06- 3. At 10000m: OG: '12- 19; WCh: '11- 10. World CC: '01- 5J. Won US 5000m 2009.
North American 2M record 2007.
Progress at 5000m, 10000m: 2001- 13:49.64, 2002- 13:44.77, 29:29.35; 2004- 13:30.90, 2005- 13:25.36, 2006- 13:04.90, 2007- 13:07.41, 2008- 13:25.71, 2009- 12:58.56, 2010- 13:25.09, 2011- 13:14.75, 27:28.22; 2012- 13:15.00, 27:33.94. pbs: 1500m 3:34.25 '07, 1M 3:56.38 '06, 2000m 5:01.3 '06, 3000m 7:34.98 '06, 2M 8:07.07 '07.

Michael TINSLEY b. 21 Apr 1984 Little Rock, Arkansas 1.85m 74kg. adidas. Studied criminal justice at Jackson State University.
At 400mh: OG: '12- 2; won NCAA 2008, US 2012.
Progress at 400mh: 2002- 52.5, 2004- 50.87, 2005- 48.55, 2006- 48.25, 2007- 48.02, 2008- 48.84, 2009- 48.53, 2010- 48.46, 2011- 48.45, 2012- 47.91. pbs: 60m 6.92i '05, 200m 20.66 '09, 400m 46.02i '06, 46.05 '07; 55mh 7.39i '04, 60mh 7.84i '06, 110mh 13.86 '04.

Terrence TRAMMELL b. 23 Nov 1978 Atlanta 1.88m 84kg. Trackstar Apparel. Studied retail management at University of South Carolina.
At 110mh/4x100m: OG: '00- 2, '04- 2, '08- h; WCh: '01-03-05-07-09: sf/2/5/2/2; WUG: '99- 1/1R; Won US 2004, 2007; NCAA 1999-2000. At 60mh: WI: '01- 1, '06- 1 (60m 3), '10- 2; won US 60mh 2000-01, 2006, 2009-10.
North American indoor 60mh record 2010.
Progress at 110mh: 1997- 13.87, 1998- 13.32, 1999- 13.28, 2000- 13.16, 2001- 13.23, 2002- 13.17, 2003- 13.17, 2004- 13.09, 2005- 13.02, 2006- 13.02, 2007- 12.95, 2008- 13.08/13.00w, 2009- 13.12, 2010- 13.39, 2011- 13.16, 2012- 13.36. pbs: 55m 6.12i '99, 60m 6.45Ai '00, 6.46i '03; 100m 10.04 '00, 200m 20.74 '98, 20.45w '99; 50mh 6.45i '12, 55mh 6.94i '99, 60mh 7.36i '10.

Brad WALKER b. 21 Jun 1981 Aberdeen, South Dakota 1.88m 86kg. Nike. Graduated in business administration from University of Washington
At PV: OG: '08- dnq nh, '12- nh; WCh: '05- 2, '07- 1; WI: '06-08-12: 1/2/3; Won WAF 2005, 2007; US 2005, 2007, 2009, 2012; indoors 2005-06, NCAA indoor 2003-04.
North American pole vault record 2008.
Progress at PV: 1999- 4.80, 2000- 5.12, 2001- 5.48i/5.36, 2002- 5.64, 2003- 5.80i/5.65, 2004- 5.82, 2005- 5.96, 2006- 6.00, 2007- 5.95, 2008- 6.04, 2009- 5.80, 2010- 5.61, 2011- 5.84, 2012- 5.90.

Jeremy WARINER b. 31 Jan 1984 Irving, Texas 1.83m 70kg. adidas. Studied outdoor recreation

at Baylor University.
At 400m/4x400mR: OG: '04- 1/1R, '08- 2/1R; WCh: '05- 1/1R, '07- 1/1R, '09- 2/1R; PAm-J: '03- 2/1R; CCp: '10- 1. Won DL 2010, US 2004-05, NCAA 2004, WAF 2006.
WIR 4x400m 2006.
Progress at 200m, 400m: 2001- 21.33/21.23w, 46.68; 2002- 21.17/20.8/20.41w, 45.57; 2003- 20.78, 45.13; 2004- 20.59, 44.00; 2005- 20.52w, 43.93; 2006- 20.19, 43.62; 2007- 20.35, 43.45; 2008- 20.37, 43.82; 2009- 20.30, 44.60; 2010- 44.13. 2011- 20.71, 44.88; 2012- 20.53, 44.96. pbs: 100m 10.52w '02, 300m 31.58+ '07.
His 43.93 to win 2005 World title was world's fastest 400m time for five years, his 43.62 to win Rome GP in 2006 the fastest for seven years and his 43.45 to win the 2007 World title took him to third on the world all-time list. He shared the Golden League jackpot and won all eleven 400m races in 2006 with three sub-44 times (a record seven sub-44.25s and 10 sub 44.50s) until he dropped out in Shanghai. Won all 10 races in 2007 apart from failure to start in Sheffield.

Andrew WHEATING b. 21 Nov 1987 Norwich, Vermont 1.96m 77kg. Oregon TC. Sociology graduate of University of Oregon.
At 800m: OG: '08- h. At 1500m: OG: '12- sf; WCh: '11- h. Won NCAA 800m 2009-10, 1500m 2010.
Progress at 800m, 1500m: 2006- 3:54.28. 2007- 1:50.17, 3:45.17; 2008- 1:45.03, 3:38.60; 2009- 1:46.21, 3:40.92; 2010- 1:44.56, 3:30.90; 2011- 1:45.95, 3:34.59; 2012- 1:46.33, 3:35.89. pbs: 1000m 2:17.44 '12, 1M 3:51.74 '10.

Ryan WHITING b. 24 Nov 1986 Harrisburg PA 1.90m 134kg. Nike. Studied civil engineering at Arizona State University.
At SP: OG: '12- 9; WCh: '11- 7; WI: '12- 1; PAm-J: '05- 1 (1 DT); Won NACAC 2009, NCAA 2009- 10, indoor 2008-10, DT 2010.
Progress at SP: 2006- 19.75, 2007- 20.35, 2008- 21.73i/20.60, 2009- 20.99, 2010- 21.97, 2011- 21.76, 2012- 22.00i/21.66, 2013- 21.80i. pb DT 61.11 '08, Wt 18.94i '10.

Jesse WILLIAMS b. 27 Dec 1983 Modesto 1.84m 75kg. Oregon TC. Graduate of University of Southern California, formerly at North Carolina State.
At HJ: OG: '08- dnq 19=, '12- 9=; WCh: '05/07- dnq 15/26, '11- 1; WJ: '02- 4=; WI: '08-10-12: 6=/5/6=; Won US 2008, 2010-11; NCAA indoors and out 2005-06; DL 2011.
Progress at HJ: 2001- 2.16, 2002- 2.21, 2003- 2.24, 2004- 2.24, 2005- 2.30, 2006- 2.32, 2007- 2.33, 2008- 2.32i/2.30, 2009- 2.36i/2.34, 2010- 2.34Ai/2.30, 2011- 2.37, 2012- 2.36. pb LJ 7.53 '06. Also a wrestler in high school.

Ryan WILSON b. 19 Dec 1980 Columbus, Ohio 1.88m 81kg. Nike. Graduate (art) of University of Southern California.
At 110mh: won NCAA 2003.

Progress at 110mh: 2000- 14.00/13.79w, 2001- 13.69, 2002- 13.55, 2003- 13.35, 2004- 13.65/13.58w, 2005- 13.99, 2006- 13.22, 2007- 13.02, 2008- 13.28, 2009- 13.21, 2010- 13.12, 2011- 13.36/13.35w, 2012- 13.18. pbs: 400m 48.52 '01, 50mh 6.78i '02, 55mh 7.18+i '12, 60mh 7.75i '12, 400mh 49.33 '03, LJ 7.29 '02.

Women

Nia ALI b. 23 Oct 1988 Philadelphia 1.70m 40kg. University of Southern California.
At 100mh: WUG: '11- 1. Won NCAA 2011.
Progress at 100mh: 2005- 14.20, 2006- 13.63/13.55w, 2007- 13.25, 2008- 13.14, 2009- 13.17, 2011- 12.73/12.63w, 2012- 12.78. pbs: 200m 23.90 '09, 800m 2:24.55 '07, 60mh 7.93A '13, 8.06i '11; HJ 1.86 '11, LJ 5.89 '09, SP 13.61 '09, JT 39.24 '09, Hep 5824 '09.

Alexandria ANDERSON b. 28 Jan 1987 Chicago 1.75m 60kg. Nike. Was at University of Texas.
At 100m/4x100mR: WCh: '11- res (1)R; WJ: '04- 1R, '06- 5/1R. At 200m: PAm-J: '05- 2. Won NCAA 100m 2009.
Progress at 100m, 200m: 2002- 11.81, 24.10w; 2003- 11.62, 23.48; 2004- 11.41, 23.45; 2005- 11.39/11.38w, 22.96; 2006- 11.12/11.10w, 23.16/23.14w; 2007- 11.21/11.11w, 22.67; 2008- 11.07/10.98w, 22.75; 2009- 11.02/10.92w, 22.60; 2010- 11.04, 22.83; 2011- 11.01/10.91w, 22.87; 2012- 11.12/10.88w, 22.98/22.84w. pbs: 50m 6.28i '12, 55m 6.88i '06, 60m 7.12Ai '11, 7.17i '08; 400m 52.63 '05, 60mh 8.83Ai '06, LJ 6.32 '05, TJ 11.68 '07.

Brigetta BARRETT b. 24 Dec 1990 Avondale, Arizona 1.83m 64kg. Student at University of Arizona.
At HJ: OG: '12- 2; WCh: '11- 10; WUG: '11- 1. Won US 2011, NCAA 2011-12.
Progress at HJ: 2007- 1.72, 2008- 1.83A, 2009- 1.83, 2010- 1.91, 2011- 1.96, 2012- 2.03.

Jessica BEARD b. 8 Jan 1989 Euclid, Ohio 1.68m 57kg. adidas. Psychology student at Texas A&M University.
At 400m/4x400mR: WCh: '09- sf/res (1)R, '11- sf/1R; WJ: '06- 5/1R, '08- 2/1R; PAm-J: '07- 3; won NCAA 2011.
Progress at 400m: 2004- 55.22, 2005- 52.39, 2006- 51.89, 2007- 51.63, 2008- 51.09A/51.47, 2009- 50.56, 2010- 51.02, 2011- 51.06, 2012- 51.19. pbs: 60m 7.52i '11, 100m 11.86 '09, 11.49w '11; 200m 22.95i, 23.02 '11.

Stephanie BROWN TRAFTON b. 1 Dec 1979 San Luis Obispo, California 1.93m 102kg. née Brown. Nike. Engineering graduate of Cal Poly San Luis Obispo.
At DT: OG: '04- dnq 24, '08- 1, "12- 8; WCh: '09- 12, '11- 5. US champion 2009, 2011-12.
US discus record 2012.
Progress at DT: 1997- 45.78, 1998- 55.24, 1999- 52.79, 2001- 51.46, 2002- 54.11, 2003- 57.78, 2004- 61.90, 2005- 55.35, 2006- 59.03, 2007- 61.40, 2008- 66.17, 2009- 66.21, 2010- 61.51, 2011- 64.13, 2012- 67.74. pbs: 400m 57.44 '08, SP 17.86 '04.

T'Erea BROWN b. 24 Oct 1989 Charleston, Missouri 1.78m 59kg. Studied advertising at University of Miami.
At 400mh: OG: '12- 6. Won US 2010, NCAA 2011.
Progress at 400mh: 2005- 60.60, 2006- 60.45, 2007- 62.60, 2008- 56.72, 2009- 55.98. 2010- 54.74, 2011- 55.59, 2012- 54.21. pbs: 200m 24.81 '08, 400m 53.25i '11, 60mh 8.00i '10, 100mh 12.84/12.70w '10.

Jillian CAMARENA-WILLIAMS b. 2 Aug 1982 Woodland, CA 1.80m 91kg. New York AC. Was at Stanford University.
At SP: OG: '08- 12, '12- dnq 15; WCh: '07/09: dnq 21/23, '11- 3; PAm: '07- 4; WI: '06-10-12: 7/6/4; WCp: '06- 6, '10- 5. Won PAm-J 2001, USA 2006, 2012 (indoor 2005-12).
N.American shot record 2011, indoors 2012.
Progress at SP: 1999- 15.53, 2000- 15.23, 2001- 16.38, 2002- 16.82i/16.79, 2003- 17.49, 2004- 18.15, 2005- 17.94, 2006- 19.26i/19.02, 2007- 18.92, 2008- 18.51, 2009- 18.59i/18.08, 2010- 19.50, 2011- 20.18, 2012- 19.89i/19.82. pb DT 52.52 '03.
Married to physiotherapist Dustin Williams.

Amber CAMPBELL b. 5 Jun 1981 Indianapolis 1.70m 91kg. Nike. Was at Coastal Carolina University.
At HT: OG: '08/12- dnq 21/13; WCh: '05: dnq 18, '09- 11, '11- dnq 14; PAm: '11- 3. Won US HT 2012, indoor Wt 2007-11.
Progress at HT: 2000- 49.16, 2001- 62.08, 2002- 63.76, 2003- 64.58, 2004- 67.23, 2005- 69.52, 2006- 67.52, 2007- 70.33, 2008- 70.19, 2009- 70.61, 2010- 71.94, 2011- 72.59, 2012- 71.80. pbs: SP 14.81i '02, 14.42 '04; 20lb Wt 24.70i '10.

Danielle CARRUTHERS b. 22 Dec 1979 Paducah, Kentucky 1.73m 62kg. Nike. Was at University of Indiana.
At 100mh: WCh: '11- 2; WUG: '01- 8. At 60mh: WI: '06- 4. Won US indoor 60mh 2005-06, DL 100mh 2011.
Progress at 100mh: 1998- 13.88/13.77w, 2000- 13.33, 2001- 12.96/12.79w, 2002- 12.68, 2003- 12.79, 2004- 12.56, 2005- 12.72/12.63w, 2006- 12.74, 2007- 12.89, 2008- 12.84, 2009- 12.73, 2010- 12.68, 2011- 12.47/12.37w, 2012- 12.73. pbs: 55m 6.79i '00, 60m 7.26i '02, 100m 11.43/11.42w '01, 200m 23.24 '01, 50mh 6.90i '09, 55mh 7.50i '09, 60mh 7.88i '06.

Michelle CARTER b. 12 Oct 1985 San Jose 1.75m 104kg. Nike. Liberal arts graduate from University of Texas.
At SP: OG: '08- 15, '12- 5; WCh: '09- 6, '11- 9; WI: '12- 3; WJ: '04- 1; WY: '01- 2; PAm: '11- 3; PAm-J: '03- 1. US champion 2008-09, 2011; NCAA indoor 2006.
Progress at SP: 2000- 14.76, 2001- 15.23, 2002- 16.25, 2003- 16.73, 2004- 17.55, 2005- 18.26, 2006- 17.98, 2007- 17.57, 2008- 18.85, 2009- 19.13, 2010- 18.80, 2011- 19.86, 2012- 19.60. pbs: DT 54.06 '07.
Her father Mike set a world junior shot record

in 1970 and won the Olympic silver in 1984, seven NCAA titles (4 in, 3 out) (for a unique father-daughter double) and WUG gold in 1981 and 1983, pb 21.76 '84. Her younger sister D'Andra (b. 17 Jun 1987) won the NCAA discus in 2009, pb 57.73 '08.

Kristi CASTLIN b. 7 Jul 1988 Douglasville, Georgia 1.70m 79kg. adidas. Graduate of political science from Virginia Tech University.
At 100mh: Won PAm-J 2007. At 60mh: WI: '12- dq/false start ht; won US indoors 2012.
Progress at 100mh: 2005- 13.85, 2006- 13.73, 2007- 12.91/12.82w, 2008- 12.81, 2009- 12.89, 2010- 12.83/12.59w, 2011- 12.83/12.68w, 2012- 12.56/12.48w. pbs: 55m 7.04i '08, 60m 7.47i '08, 100m 11.60 '12, 11.49w '11; 200m 23.46 '12, 50mh 6.81+i '12, 55mh 7.37i '12, 60mh 7.84Ai/7.91i '12. 400mh 60.44 '07.

Jessica COSBY b. 31 May 1982 Reseda, California 1.73m 77kg. Nike. Was at UCLA (now strength coach there).
At HT: OG: '08/12- dnq nt/14; WCh: '07: dnq 14, '09- 7, '11- 11; won NACAC 2007, US 2006, 2008-09, 2011. At SP: WJ: '00- 9, won NCAA 2002. US hammer record 2012,
Progress at HT: 2001- 55.73, 2002- 59.54, 2003- 61.15, 2005- 66.88, 2006- 70.78, 2007- 68.34, 2008- 70.72, 2009- 72.21, 2010- 71.24, 2011- 72.65, 2013- 74.19. pbs: SP 17.63 '05, 20lb Wt 20.40i '04.
4 months drugs ban from August 2009. Left-handed thrower.

Virginia CRAWFORD b. 7 Sep 1983 Seattle 1.78m 63kg. née Powell. Nike. Was at University of Southern California.
At 100mh: WCh: '05- sf, '07- 5, '09- 6; WY: '99- 8/2R; WCp: '06- 3. At 60mh: WI: '10- 5. Won US 100mh 2006-07, NCAA 100mh & indoor 60mh 2005-06.
Progress at 100mh: 2000- 14.07, 2001- 13.39, 2002- 13.62, 2003- 13.07, 2004- 13.07, 2005- 12.61, 2006- 12.48, 2007- 12.45, 2008- 12.75/12.74w, 2009- 12.64/12.47w, 2010- 12.63, 2011- 12.73/12.65w, 2012- 12.59. pbs: 60m 7.21i '06, 100m 11.10/10.93Aw '06, 200m 23.29 '06, 50mh 6.90i '12, 60mh 7.84i '06.
On 16 Apr 2010 married Shawn Crawford (Olympic champion at 200m 2004, 2nd 2008, World Indoor champion 2001; pbs: 60m 6.47i '04, 100m 9.88/9.86w '04, 200m.19.79 '04, 19.73w '09).

Cynthia 'Janay' DeLOACH b. 12 Oct 1985 Panama City, Florida 1.65m 59kg. Psychology graduate of Colorado State University.
At LJ: OG: '12- 3; WCh: '11- 6; WI: '12- 2; PAm: '07- 10. US indoor champion 2011-13.
Progress at LJ: 2004- 6.14Ai/6.05/6.14w, 2005- 6.27A/6.43w, 2006- 6.21Ai, 2007- 6.42Ai/6.41/6.45w, 2008- 6.48/6.51w, 2009- 6.33i/6.04, 2010- 6.61, 2011- 6.99Ai/6.97, 2012- 7.03/7.15w, 2013- 6.90i. pb 55m 6.85Ai '05, 60m 7.31Ai '06,

100m 11.45 '08, 200m 24.60 '07, 24.26Aw '08; 60mh 7.97i '13, 100mh 13.27 '12, 13.23w '10; HJ 1.73i '11, SP 12.67i '11, Pen 4289i '11.
Married Patrick Soukup in September 2012.

Lashinda DEMUS b. 10 Mar 1983 Palmdale, California 1.70m 62kg. Nike. Student at University of South Carolina.
At 400mh/4x400mR: OG: '04- sf, '12- 2; WCh: '05- 2, '09- 2/1R, '11- 1; WJ: '02- 1/1R; WCp: '06- 2/2R. Won WAF 2005-06, PAm-J 1999, US 2005-06, 2009, 2011; NCAA 2002.
Two world junior records 400mh 2002.
Progress at 400mh: 1998- 64.61, 1999- 57.04, 2001- 55.76, 2002- 54.70, 2003- 55.65, 2004- 53.43, 2005- 53.27, 2006- 53.02, 2008- 53.99, 2009- 52.63, 2010- 52.82, 2011- 52.47, 2012- 52.77. pbs: 50m 6.64i '01, 60m 7.73i '01, 100m 11.5 '01, 200m 24.0 '01, 23.50w '05; 400m 51.09 '10, 500y 1:05.8i '01, 800m 2:07.49 '12, 55mh 7.65i '04, 60mh 8.11i '04, 100mh 12.96 '11, 12.93w '05.
Twin sons Duane and Donte born 5 Jun 2007. Her mother, Yolanda Rich, had a 400m best of 52.19 in 1980.

Kimberlyn DUNCAN b. 2 Aug 1991 Katy, Texas 1.73m 59kg. Louisiana State University.
At 200m: won NCAA 2011-12.
Progress at 200m: 2007- 24.54, 2008- 24.33, 2009- 23.46, 2010- 23.08/22.96w, 2011- 22.24/22.18w, 2012- 22.22. pbs: 60m 7.16i '13, 100m 10.96, 10.94w '12.

Allyson FELIX b. 18 Nov 1985 Los Angeles 1.68m 57kg. Nike. Elementary education graduate of University of Southern California.
At 200m/4x400mR: OG: '04- 2, '08- 2/1R, '12- 1/1R (1 4x400m); WCh: '03- qf, '05- 1, '07- 1/1 4x100mR/1R, '09- 1/1R, '11- 3/1R (2 400m, 1 4x100m); WJ: '02- 5; PAm: '03- 3; WI: '10- 1R. At 100m: OG: '12- 5; WY: '01- 1 (1 Medley R). Won DL 200m & 400m 2010, WAF 200m 2005-06, 2009; US 100m 2010, 200m 2004-05, 2007-09, 2012; 400m 2011.
World junior record 200m 2004 after unratified (no doping test) at age 17 in 2003.
Progress at 100m, 200m, 400m: 2000- 12.19/11.99w, 23.90; 2001- 11.53, 23.31/23.27w; 2002- 11.40, 22.83/22.69w, 55.01; 2003- 11.29/11.12w, 22.11A/22.51, 52.26; 2004- 11.16, 22.18, 51.83A; 2005- 11.05, 22.13, 51.12; 2006- 11.04, 22.11; 2007- 11.01, 21.81, 49.70; 2008- 10.93, 21.93/21.82w, 49.83; 2009- 11.08, 21.88, 49.83; 2010- 11.27, 22.03, 50.15; 2011- 11.26+, 22.32, 49.59; 2012- 10.89, 21.69. pbs: 50m 6.43i '02, 60m 7.10i '12, 300m 36.33i '07.
First teenager to won a World sprint title. Unbeaten in ten 200m competitions 2005 and in five 2007. Has women's record eight world gold medals including three in 2007 when she had a record 0.53 winning margin at 200m and ran a 48.0 400m relay leg, and four Olympic gold medals. IAAF female Athlete of the Year 2012. Older brother Wes Felix won World Junior

bronze at 200m and gold in WJR at 4x100m in 2002, pbs: 100m 10.23 '05, 200m 20.43 '04.

Shalane FLANAGAN b. 8 Jul 1981 Boulder 1.65m 50kg. Nike. Was at University of North Carolina.
At 5000m/(10000m): OG: '04- h, '08- 10/3; WCh: '05- h, '07- 8, '09- (14), '11- (7). At Mar: OG: '10. World CC: '10- 12, '11-3; 4k: '04- 14, 05- 20. Won US 5000m 2005, 10000m 2008, 2011; HMar 2010, Mar 2012, CC 2008, 2010-11, 2013; 4km CC 2004-05, indoor 3000m 2007, NCAA CC 2002-03, indoor 3000m 2003.
North American records: 5000m and indoor 3000m 2007, 10000m (2) 2008.
Progress at 5000m, 10000m, Mar: 2001- 16:29.68, 2003- 15:20.54, 2004- 15:05.08, 2005- 15:10.96, 2007- 14:44.80, 2008- 14:59.69, 30:22.22; 2009- 14:47.62i/15:10.86, 31:23.43; 2010- 14:49.08, 2:28:40; 2011- 14:45.20, 30:39.57; 2012- 31:59.69, 2:25:38; 2013- 31:04.85. pbs: 800m 2:09.28 '02, 1500m 4:05.86 '07, 1M 4:33.81i '11, 4:48.47 '00; 3000m 8:33.25i/8:35.34 '07, Road: 10M 51:45 '10, HMar 68:37 '10.
2nd New York 2010 on marathon debut and won Olympic Trials 2012. Married to Steve Edwards. Mother, Cheryl Bridges, set marathon world best with 2:49:40 in 1971 and was 4th in 1969 International CC, father Steve ran in World Cross 1976-7, 1979.

Hyleas FOUNTAIN b. 14 Jan 1981 Columbus, Georgia 1.70m 64kg. Nike. University of Georgia.
At Hep: OG: '08- 2, '12- dnf; WCh: '05- 12, '07- dnf, '11- 25. At Pen: WI: '06- 8, '10- 4. Won NCAA Hep 2003, LJ 2004; US Hep 2005, 2007-08, 2010, 2012.
N.American indoor pentathlon record 2010.
Progress at Hep: 2001- 4905, 2002- 5673w, 2003- 5999, 2004- 6035, 2005- 6502, 2006- 6148, 2007- 6090, 2008- 6667, 2010- 6735w, 2012- 6419. pbs: 60m 7.47i '11, 200m 23.21 '08, 800m 2:15.32 '08, 55mh 7.61i '05, 60mh 7.98i '09, 100mh 12.70 '12, 12.65w '08; HJ 1.90 '10, LJ 6.89/6.95w '09; TJ 13.40 '04, SP 14.26i '10, 13.81 '09; JT 48.15 '08, Pen 4753i '10.
Won Talence and IAAF Combined Events Challenge 2008.

Kara GOUCHER b. 9 Jul 1978 Queens, New York 1.70m 58kg. née Grgas-Wheeler. Nike. Studied psychology at Colorado State University.
At (5000m)/10000m: OG: '08- 9/10; WCh: '07- 3, '11- 13. At Mar: OG: '12- 11; WCh: '09- 10. At 3000m: WCp: '06- 3. World 4k CC: '06- 21. Won US 5000m 2008-09, HMar 2012; NCAA 3000m, 5000m & CC 2000.
Progress at 5000m, 10000m: 1999- 16:57.31, 2000- 15:28.78, 2001- 15:31.77, 2003- 15:42.97, 33:44.86; 2004- 16:30.35, 2005- 15:17.55, 2006- 15:08.13, 31:17.12; 2007- 14:55.02, 32:02.05; 2008- 14:58.10, 30:55.16; 2009- 15:20.94, 2:27:48; 2011- 15:11.47, 31:16.65, 2:24:52wdh; 2012- 2:26:06, 2013- 31:46.64. pbs: 800m 2:06.79 '09, 1500m 4:05.14 '06, 1M

4:33.19i/4:37.58 '09, 2000m 5:41.28 '09, 3000m 8:34.99 '07, 2M 9:41.32 '07, Road: 15km 47:36 '07, 10M 50:59 '07, HMar 66:57 '07, 30km 1:43:33 '08, Mar 2:25:53 '08.

After surprise World 10000m bronze, made brilliant half marathon debut to win Great North Run 2007 with American best. Third New York Marathon 2008, with fastest ever US women's debut, and Boston 2009.

Married (2001) **Adam Goucher** (18 Feb 1975) (pbs: 1500m 3:36.64 '01, 1M 3:54.17 '99, 2000m 4:58.92 '99, 3000m 7:34.96 '01, 2M 8:12.73 '06, 5000m 13:10.00 '06, 10000m 27:59.41 '06). Their son Colton Mirko born on 24 Sep 2010.

Dawn HARPER b. 13 May 1984 Norman, Oklahoma 1.68m 61kg. Nike. Studied psychology at UCLA.
At 100mh: OG: '08- 1, '12- 2; WCh: '09- 7, '11- 3; won DL 2012, PAm-J 2003, US 2009.
Progress at 100mh: 2002- 13.63, 2003- 13.33/13.21w, 2004- 13.16/12.91w, 2005- 12.91, 2006- 12.80A/12.86, 2007- 12.67, 2008- 12.54, 2009- 12.48/12.36w, 2010- 12.77w, 2011- 12.47, 2012- 12.37. pbs: 60m 7.70i '05, 100m 11.66 '07, 200m 23.97 '06, 50mh 6.96i '12, 60mh 7.98i '06.
Married to Craig Everhart (b. 13 Sep 1983) 400m 44.89 '04.

Queen HARRISON b. 10 Sep 1988 Loch Sheldrake, New York 1.70m 60kg. Saucony. Student of business marketing at Virginia Tech.
At 400mh: OG: '08- sf; WCh: '11- sf; PAm-J: '07- 1 (2 100mh); won NCAA 100mh, 400mh & 60mh indoors 2010.
Progress at 100mh, 400mh: 2007- 12.98, 55.81; 2008- 12.70, 54.60; 2009- 13.14/12.98w, 56.03; 2010- 12.61/12.44w, 54.55; 2011- 12.88, 54.78; 2012- 12.62, 55.32. pbs: 400m 52.88 '08, 60mh 7.94i '10, LJ 5.82i '06.

Natasha HASTINGS b. 23 Jul 1986 Brooklyn, NY 1.73m 63kg. Nike. Student of exercise science at University of South Carolina.
At 400m/4x400m: OG: '08- res 1R; WCh: '07- sf/res 1R, '09/11- res 1R; WJ: '04- 1/1R; WY: '03- 1; WI: '10- 1R, '12- 3/2R; PAm-J: '03- 1R, '05- 1/1R. Won NCAA indoors and out 2007.
World junior 500m indoor best 2005.
Progress at 400m: 2000- 54.21, 2001- 55.06, 2002- 53.42, 2003- 52.09, 2004- 52.04, 2005- 51.34, 2006- 51.45, 2007- 49.84, 2008- 50.80, 2009- 50.89, 2010- 50.53, 2011- 50.83Ai/50.97, 2012- 50.72, 2013- 50.88i. pbs: 55m 7.08i '02, 60m 7.26i '13, 100m 11.40/11.39w '10, 200m 22.61 '07, 300m 35.9+ '07, 500m 1:10.05i '05.
Father from Jamaica, mother Joanne Gardner was British (ran 11.89 to win WAAA U15 100m at 14 in 1977).

Marshevet HOOKER b. 25 Sep 1984 Dallas 1.75m 67kg. Former married name Myers. adidas. Studied Liberal Arts at University of Texas.
At 100m/4x100m: WCh: '11- 8/1R; WJ: '02- 3/2R.

At 200m: OG: '08- 5; WCh: '09- sf. Won NCAA 100m, indoor 60m & LJ 2005.
Progress at 100m, 200m: 2000- 11.94, 24.26; 2001- 11.51, 23.59; 2002- 11.43/11.28w/11.1w, 23.25w; 2004- 11.14, 24.04w; 2005- 11.12/11.03w, 22.80/22.73w; 2006- 11.09, 22.75/22.70w; 2007- 11.06, 23.25/22.95w; 2008- 10.93/10.76w, 22.34/22.20w; 2009- 11.14/10.94w, 22.51/22.35w; 2010- 10.97, 22.90; 2011- 10.86/10.83w, 22.59. pbs: 55m 6.78i '06, 60m 7.18i '06, 400m 54.18 '10, LJ 6.83i '11, 6.65/6.89w '05.
Married Marcus Myers on 3 Oct 2009, but divorced in 2011. Her daughter Londyn was birn on 19 Oct 2012. Younger sister Destinee Hooker (b. 7 Sep 1987) won NCAA HJ 2006 & 2009, pb 1.98i/1.95 '09.

Kylie HUTSON b. 27 Nov 1987 Terre Haute 1.65m 57kg. Nike. Was at Indiana State University.
At PV: WCh: '11- dnq 15; won US 2011, NCAA 2009, 2011.
Progress at PV: 2006- 3.58, 2007- 4.10i/3.96, 2008- 4.30, 2009- 4.40, 2010- 4.51, 2011- 4.70i/4.65, 2012- 4.52Ai/4.40, 2013- 4.75Ai.

Lacy JANSON b. 20 Feb 1983 Norfolk, Virginia 1.78m 68kg. Nike. Was at Florida State University.
At PV: OG: '12- dnq 15=; WCh: '11- dnq 20; WI: '12- 5; WJ: '02- nh; Won PAm-J 2001, NCAA 2006, US indoor 2010.
Progress at PV: 2001- 4.01, 2002- 4.27, 2003- 4.45i/4.37, 2004- 4.25, 2005- 4.30i/4.11, 2006- 4.58, 2007- 4.60Ai/4.50, 2008- 4.64i/4.55, 2009- 4.50i/4.46, 2010- 4.66i/4.60A, 2011- 4.60i/4.50, 2012- 4.65i/4.50.

Carmelita JETER b. 24 Nov 1979 Los Angeles 1.63m 53kg. Nike. Was at California State University, Dominguez Hills.
At 100m/(200m)/4x100mR: OG: '12- 2/3/1R; WCh: '07- 3/res 1R, '09- 3, '11- 1/2/1R; won DL 100m 2010-11, 200m 2011; WAF 100m 2007, 2009; US 100m 2009, 2011-12. At 60m: WI: '10- 2.
Progress at 100m, 200m: 2000- 11.69, 23.65/23.99w; 2001- 11.82, 24.20; 2002- 11.77/11.46w, 24.10; 2003- 11.61/11.43w, 23.67; 2004- 11.56, 23.98; 2005- 12.00/11.72w, 2006- 11.48, 23.54; 2007- 11.02, 22.82; 2008- 10.97, 22.47/22.35w; 2009- 10.64, 22.59; 2010- 10.82, 22.54; 2011- 10.70, 22.20; 2012- 10.78, 22.11. pbs: 60m 7.02Ai/7.05i '10, 300m 37.52 '13, 400m 53.08 '09.
Second fastest woman of all-time at 100m.

Oluwafunmilayo '**Funmi**' **JIMOH** b. 29 May 1984 Seattle 1.73m 64kg. Was at Rice University.
At LJ: OG: '08- 12; WCh: '09- dnq 21, '11- nj; won US 2008-09, NCAA 2008.
Progress at LJ: 2004- 6.14, 2005- 6.31, 2006- 6.44, 2007- 6.46/6.62w, 2008- 6.91, 2009- 6.96, 2010- 6.81/6.87w, 2011- 6.88, 2012- 6.82. pbs: 60m 7.67i '04, 100m 12.03 '08, 11.65w '11; 200m 23.91A '11, 24.28 '08, 23.65w '06; 400m 59.57i '09, 60mh 8.32i '07, 100mh 13.51 '05, 13.39w '07; HJ 1.75i '05, 1.66 '07; SP 10.68i '06, Pen 3937i '06, Hep 5335 '07.

Lori 'Lolo' JONES b. 5 Aug 1982 Des Moines 1.75m 60kg. Nike. Spanish & economic graduate of Louisiana State University.
At 100mh: OG: '08- 7, '12- 4; WCh: '07- 6; CCp: '10- 2; Won US 2008, 2010; NACAC 2004. At 60mh: WI: '08- 1, '10- 1; won NCAA indoor 2003, US indoor 2007-09.
N.American indoor 60m hurdles record 2010.
Progress at 100mh: 2000- 14.04, 2001- 13.31/13.17w/12.7w, 2002- 12.84, 2003- 12.90, 2004- 12.77, 2005- 12.76, 2006- 12.56, 2007- 12.57, 2008- 12.43/12.29w, 2009- 12.47, 2010- 12.55, 2011- 12.67, 2012- 12.58. pbs: 55m 6.87i '03, 60m 7.27i '03, 100m 11.24 '06, 200m 23.76 '04, 23.50w '03; 50mh 6.78i '12, 55mh 7.57i '03, 60mh 7.72i '10, 400mh 59.95 '00.
Crashed into 9th hurdle when leading Olympic final after pb 12.43 in semi in 2008. Won gold in the 2-man bobsled as brakeman on the US team at the 2013 World Champiomships.

Bianca KNIGHT b. 2 Jan 1989 Ridgeland, Mississippi 1.63m 60kg. adidas. Psychology student at University of Texas.
At (100m)/200m: OG: '12- 1R; WCh: '11- 1R; WY: '05- 1/2/1 Med R; PAm-J: '07- 1. Won NCAA indoor 2008.
World junior indoor 200m record 2008.
Progress at 100m, 200m: 2002- 12.07, 24.37; 2003- 11.80, 23.81; 2004- 11.56, 23.06; 2005- 11.38, 23.33; 2006- 11.26, 22.94; 2007- 11.36/11.28w, 22.97Ai /23.17A/22.93w; 2008-11.07,22.40i/22.43/22.25w; 2009- 11.17/11.12w, 22.50; 2010- 11.40, 22.59; 2011- 11.22, 22.35; 2012- 11.13, 22.46/22.34w. pbs: 50m 6.28i '12, 55m 6.75+i '12, 60m 7.16i '08, 300m 36.41i '11, 400m 52.55 '11.

Yvette LEWIS b. 16 Mar 1985 Germany 1.73m 62kg. Norfolk Read Deal. Was at Hampton University, where now an assistant coach.
At 100mh(/TJ): PAm: '07- 8/6, '11- 1/7; WJ: '04- (dnq); won NCAA TJ 2007.
Progress at 100mh: 2005- 13.53, 2006- 13.14, 2007- 13.06, 2008- 12.85, 2009- 12.85, 2010- 13.19, 2011- 12.76/12.74w, 2012- 12.84/12.74w. pbs: 55m 6.96i '07, 60m 7.40i '06, 100m 11.56 '07, 200m 23.50 '06, 400m 56.63i '09, 50mh 7.06+i '09, 60mh 7.84i '13, HJ 1.78i '05, 1.78 '07; LJ 6.29i '09, 6.24 '07, 6.46w '12; TJ 13.84 '08, Hep 5378 '12, Pen 3852i '07.

Chaunté LOWE b. 12 Jan 1984 Templeton, California 1.75m 59kg. née Howard. Nike. Economics gradate of Georgia Tech University.
At HJ: OG: '04- dnq 26=, '08- 6, '12- 6; WCh: '05- 2, '09- 7=; PAm-J: '03- 3; WI: '06-10-12: 8/3/1; Won DL 2012, US 2006, 2008-10, 2012; NCAA 2004, indoors 2004-05.
Three N.American HJ records 2010, indoors 2012.
Progress at HJ: 2000- 1.75, 2001- 1.84, 2002- 1.87, 2003- 1.89, 2004- 1.98A, 2005- 2.00, 2006- 2.01, 2008- 2.00, 2009- 1.98, 2010- 2.05, 2011- 1.78, 2012- 2.02Ai/2.01. pbs: 100m 11.83 '05, 100mh 13.78 '04, LJ 6.90 '10, TJ 12.93 '04, 12.98w '05.
Married Mario Lowe (b. 20 Apr 1980, TJ pb 16.15 '02) in 2005, daughters Jasmine born 30 Jul 2007 and Aurora in 4 Apr 2011.

Francena McCORORY b. 20 Oct 1988 Hampton, VA 1.70m 60kg. adidas. Psychology graduate of Hampton University.
At 400m/4x400mR: OG: '12- 7/1R; WCh: '11- 4/1R; won NCAA indoors 2009-10, out 2010.
World junior indoor 300m best 2007.
Progress at 400m: 2004- 54.54, 2006- 51.93i, 2008- 51.54, 2009- 50.58, 2010- 50.52, 2011- 50.24, 2012- 50.06. pbs: 55m 6.86i '06, 60m 7.43i '07, 100m 11.68 '05, 11.56w '10; 200m 22.92 '10, 300m 36.67i '07, 500m 1:09.01i '12, 600m 1:29.07i '13, 800m 2:20.25i '07.

Tianna MADISON b. 30 Aug 1985 Elyria, Ohio 1.68m 60kg. Studied biology at University of Central Florida, formerly at University of Tennessee.
At 100m/4x100mR: OG: '12- 4/1R. At LJ: WCh: '05- 1, '07- 10; WI: '06- 2; PAm-J: '03- 4, NCAA champion indoors and out 2005. At 60m: WI: '12- 3; won US indoor 2012.
Progress at 100m, LJ: 2000- 5.73, 2001- 6.07, 2002- 11.98/11.91w, 6.20; 2003- 11.68, 6.28; 2004- 11.50/11.35w, 6.60; 2005- 11.41, 6.89/6.92w; 2006- 11.52/11.50w, 6.80i/6.60; 2007- 6.60/6.61w; 2008- 11.54, 6.53/6.58w; 2009- 11.05, 6.48; 2010- 11.20, 6.44; 2011- 11.29, 6.21/6.58w; 2012- 10.85, 6.48. pbs: 55m 6.69i '09, 60m 7.02i '12, 200m 22.37/22.33w '12. Set long jump pbs in qualifying and final of 2005 Worlds. Now concentrating on sprinting.

Georganne MOLINE b. 6 Mar 1990 Phoenix, Arizona 1.78m 59kg. Psychology and communication student at University of Arizona.
At 400mh: OG: '12- 5.
Progress at 400mh: 2010- 57.88, 2011- 57.41, 2012- 53.92. pbs: 200m 24.06 '11, 400m 52.92 '12.
53.92 in Olympic final was seventh 400mh pb of her 2012 season.

Alysia MONTAÑO b. 26 Apr 1986 Queens, New York 1.70m 61kg. née Johnson. Nike. Was at University of California.
At 800m: OG: '12- 5; WCh: '07- h, '11- 4; PAm: '07- 6; WI: '10- 3; CCp: '10- 8; won US 2007, 2010-12; NCAA 2007.
North American indoor 600m record 2013.
Progress at 800m: 2004- 2:08.97, 2005- 2:05.49, 2006- 2:01.80, 2007- 1:59.29, 2008- 2:00.57, 2009- 2:01.09, 2010- 1:57.34, 2011- 1:57.48, 2012- 1:57.37. pbs: 200m 24.41iA '13, 400m 52.09 '10, 600m 1:23.59i '13, 1:26.7+ '12; 1500m 4:28.43 '09.
Always runs with a flower in her hair.

LaShaunte'a MOORE b. 31 Jul 1983 Akron, Ohio 1.70m 56kg. adidas. Was at University of Arkansas. Training to be a nurse.
At 200m: OG: '04- sf, WCh: '07- 7; WY: '99- 4/1 MedR; won NCAA 2004.
Progress at 100m, 200m: 1997- 11.93, 1998- 11.67w, 23.86w; 1999- 11.66, 23.26; 2001- 11.64/11.57w, 23.59/23.40w; 2002- 11.47, 23.13/22.89w; 2003- 11.33/11.27w, 23.09/22.81w;

2004- 11.26, 22.63/22.37w; 2005- 11.39/11.25w, 22.93; 2006- 11.40, 22.89/22.64w; 2007- 11.26/11.10w, 22.46; 2008- 11.03, 22.70; 2009- 11.21, 22.57; 2010- 10.97, 22.46; 2011- 11.17/11.04w, 22.58; 2012- 11.11/10.93w, 22.71. pbs: 60m 7.36i '03, 400m 54.92 '07.

Anna PIERCE b. 31 Mar 1984 Portland, Maine 1.63m 54kg. née Willard. Nike. Sports management graduate of University of Michigan.
At 3000mSt: OG: '08- 10; WCh: '07- h; NACAC 2006, NCAA 2007. At 1500m: WCh: '09- 6. At 800m: WI: '10- 4; won WAF 2009. Won US 3000mSt 2008, 1500m 2010.
North American 3000m steeple record 2008.
Progress at 1500m, 3000mSt: 2005- 10:35.38, 2006- 2:07.12, 4:25.35, 10:06.83; 2007- 2:03.94, 4:15.93, 9:34.72; 2008- 2:02.72, 4:06.26, 9:22.76; 2009- 1:58.80, 3:59.38, 9:26.85; 2010- 1:58.89, 4:04.52; 2011- 2:00.19, 4:10.38; 2012- 1:59.16, 4:05.42. pbs: 1000m 2:38.76i '10, 1M 4:28.37 '08, 3000m 8:58.07 '08, 5000m 15:53.36 '07.
Married Jonathan Pierce (3000mSt 8:37.73 '08) in September 2009.

Barbara PIERRE b. 28 Apr 1987 Port-au-Prince, Haiti 1.75m 60kg. Was at St. Augustine's College.
At 100m/4x100mR: OG: '08- qf; PAm: '11- 2/2R. At 60m: WI: '12-4.
Haiti records at 100m 2009, 200m 2008-09.
Progress at 100m: 2003- 11.98, 2005- 11.78, 2006- 11.66, 2007- 11.30, 2008- 11.40A, 2009- 11.18, 2010- 11.35, 2011- 11.14, 2012- 11.34. pbs: 50m 6.22+i '12, 55m 6.89i '07, 60m 7.06Ai '12, 7.09 '13; 100y 10.38y '11, 200m 23.23 '10, 400m 57.04 '08.
Switched from US to Haiti 31 Dec 2007, and back to US 24 Mar 2010.

Brittney REESE b. 9 Sep 1986 Gulfport, Mississippi 1.73m 64kg. Nike. English graduate of University of Mississippi.
At LJ: OG: '08- 5, '12- 1; WCh: '07- 8, '09- 1, '11- 1; WI: '10- 1, '12- 1; won DL 2010-11, WAF 2009, US 2008-12, NCAA 2007-08.
North American indoor long jump record 2012.
Progress at LJ: 2004- 6.31, 2006- 5.94, 2007- 6.83, 2008- 6.95, 2009- 7.10, 2010- 6.94/7.05w, 2011- 7.19, 2012- 7.23i/7.15. pbs: 50m 6.23i '12, 60m 7.24i '11, 100m 11.63 '09, 11.20w '11; HJ 1.88i/1.84 '08, TJ 13.16 '08.
Concentrated on basketball at Gulf Coast Community College in 2005-06.

Sanya RICHARDS-ROSS b. 26 Feb 1985 Kingston, Jamaica 1.73m 61kg. Nike. University of Texas.
At (200m)/400m/4x400m: OG: '04- 6/dq1R, '08- 3/1R, '12- 5/1/1R; WCh: '03- sf/1R, '05- 2, '07- (5)/1R, '09- 1/1R, '11- 7/1R; WJ: '02- 3/2; WCp: '06- 1/1; WI: '12- 1/2R. Won WAF 200m 2008, 400m 2005-09, US 2003, 2005-06, 2008-09, 2012; NCAA 2003.
US & N.American 400m record 2006, world junior indoor bests 200m, 400m (2) 2004.

Progress at 200m, 400m: 1999- 23.84, 2000- 23.57, 54.34; 2001- 23.09, 53.49; 2002- 23.01, 50.69; 2003- 22.80i/22.86, 50.58; 2004- 22.49i/22.73, 49.89; 2005- 22.53, 48.92; 2006- 22.17, 48.70; 2007- 22.31, 49.27; 2008- 22.49, 49.74; 2009- 22.29, 48.83; 2010- 51.82; 2011- 22.63, 49.66; 2012- 22.09, 49.28. pbs: 60m 7.21i '04, 100m 10.97 '07, 10.89w '12; 300m 35.6 '05, 800m 2:10.74 '10, LJ 6.08 '01.
Left Jamaica at the age of 12 and gained US citizenship on 20 May 2002. Her 48.92 at Zürich in 2005 and then 48.70 at the World Cup in 2006 (to beat 22 year-old US record) were the world's fastest 400m times since 1996. Unbeaten in 13 finals outdoors at 400m in 2006 and after WAF win scored 200m/400m double at World Cup. Record 46 times sub-50 secs for 400m. Shared Golden League jackpot 2006, 2007 and 2009. IAAF female Athlete of the Year 2006 & 2009. Married New York Giants cornerback Aaron Ross on 26 Feb 2010.

Brianna ROLLINS b. 18 Aug 1991 1.64m 55kg. Student at Clemson University.
At 100mh: Won NACAC 2012. Won NCAA indoor 60mh 2011 & 2013.
Progress at 100mh: 2007- 14.48, 2008- 13.93, 2009- 13.83, 2011- 12.99/12.88w, 2012- 12.70/12.60Aw, 2013- 12.54w. pbs: 200m 23.22i '13, 24.13 '12; 300m 37.90i '10, 400m 53.93 '13, 60mh 7.78i '13, 400mh 60.58 '09.

Shannon ROWBURY b. 19 Sep 1984 San Francisco 1.65m 52kg. Nike. Was at Duke University.
At 1500m: OG: '08- 7, '12- 6; WCh: '09- 3, '11- sf; Won US 2008-09, NCAA indoor mile 2007. At 3000m: CCp: '10- 2.
Progress at 1500m: 2004- 4:17.41, 2005- 4:14.81, 2006- 4:12.31, 2008- 4:00.33, 2009- 4:00.81, 2010- 4:01.30, 2011- 4:05.73, 2012- 4:03.15. pbs: 800m 2:00.47 '10, 1M 4:20.34 '08, 3000m 8:31.38 '10, 5000m 15:00.51 '10, 3000mSt 9:59.4 '06.
Former ballet and Irish dancer.

Jennifer SIMPSON b. 23 Aug 1986 Webster City, Iowa 1.65m 50kg. née Barringer. New Balance/ Studied political science at University of Colorado.
At 1500m: OG: '12- sf; WCh: '11- 1. At 3000mSt: OG: '08- 9; WCh: '07- h, '09- 5; won NCAA 2006, 2008-09; US 2009.
Three N.American 3000mSt records 2008-09.
Progress at 1500m, 3000mSt: 2006- 9:53.04, 2007- 4:21.53, 9:33.95; 2008- 4:11.36, 9:22.26; 2009- 3:59.90, 9:12.50; 2010- 4:03.63, 2011- 4:03.54, 2012- 4:04.07. pbs: 800m 2:01.20 '11, 1M 4:25.91i '09, 3000m 8:42.03i '09, 8:48.72 '12; 5000m 15:01.70i/15:05.25 '09.
Married Jason Simpson on 8 Oct 2010. on 5th Avenue Mile 2011.

Shalonda SOLOMON b. 19 Dec 1985 Inglewood, California 1.69m 56kg. Reebok. Student at University of South Carolina.

At (100m)/200m/4x100m: WCh: '11- 4/res (1)R; WJ: '04- 1/1R; PAm-J: '03- 1/1/1R; CCp: '10- 2/1R. Won NCAA 200m 2006, NCAAC 100m & 200m 2006.
Progress at 100m, 200m: 2001- 11.57/11.37w, 23.65/23.22w; 2002- 11.51/11.46w, 23.31; 2003- 11.35/11.25w, 22.93; 2004- 11.41/11.32w, 22.82; 2005- 11.29, 22.74/22.72w; 2006- 11.09/11.07w, 22.36/22.30w; 2007- 11.33, 22.77; 2008- 11.16, 22.48/22.36w; 2009- 11.04/11.00w, 22.41; 2010- 10.90, 22.47; 2011- 11.08/10.90w, 22.15; 2012- 11.26, 22.82. pbs: 55m 6.72i '09, 60m 7.15Ai '11, 7.21i '06; 300m 36.45i '09, 400m 53.47 '08.

Ashley SPENCER b. 8 Jun 1993 1.68m 54kg. Student at University of Illinois
At 400m/4x400mR: WJ: '12- 1/1R.
Progress at 400m: 2012- 50.50. pbs: 60m 7.42i '13, 100m 11.46 '13, 200m 22.99 '12, 100mh 14.40/14.28w '11, 400mh 57.34 '13.

Jennifer SUHR b. 6 Feb 1982 Fredonia, New York 1.80m 64kg. adidas. née Stuczynski. Graduate of Roberts Wesleyan University, now studying child psychology.
At PV: OG: '08- 2, '12- 1; WCh: '07- 10, '11- 4; WI: '08- 2; WCp: '06- nh; US champion 2006-10, 2012; indoors 2005, 2007-09, 2011.
Records: world indoors 2013, four North American pole vault records 2007-08, four indoors 2009-13.
Progress at PV: 2002- 2.75, 2004- 3.49, 2005- 4.57i/4.26, 2006- 4.68i/4.66, 2007- 4.88, 2008- 4.92, 2009- 4.83i/4.81, 2010- 4.89, 2011- 4.91, 2012- 4.88i/4.81, 2013- 5.01A. pbs: 55mh 8.07i '05, JT 46.82 '05.
All-time top scorer at basketball at her university, then very rapid progress at vaulting.

Jeneba TARMOH b. 27 Sep 1989 San Jose CA 1.67m 59kg. Student at Texas A&M University.
At (100m)/200m/4x100m: OG: '12- res (1)R; WCh: '11- h; WJ: '06- 7/1R, '08- (1)/1R. Won NCAAC 100m 2010.
Progress at 100m, 200m: 2004- 12.07w, 2005- 11.81/11.61w, 24.04/23.56w; 2006- 11.24, 23.14; 2007- 11.27, 23.34/23.20w; 2008- 11.21, 22.94; 2009- 11.31, 23.31i/23.43/23.16w; 2010- 11.19/11.00w, 22.65; 2011- 11.23/10.94w, 22.28; 2012- 11.07, 22.35/22.30W. pbs: 50m 6.14+i '12. 55m 6.86Ai '06, 60m 7.22i '12.

Aretha THURMOND b. 14 Aug 1976 Seattle 1.81m 98kg. née Hill. Nike. Was at University of Washington.
At DT: OG: '96/04/12- dnq 34/19/25, '08- 10; WCh: '99/03/05/11: dnq 24/20/21/13; '09- 10; PAm: '99-03-07: 1/1/2; WUG: '97- 6; WCp: '06- 2. US champion 2003-04, 2006, 2008.
Progress at DT: 1992- 43.38, 1993- 47.48, 1994- 50.52, 1995- 54.84, 1996- 60.50, 1997- 59.92, 1998- 65.62dh/63.68, 1999- 62.15, 2000- 62.91, 2001- 61.64, 2002- 65.21, 2003- 65.10/66.23dh, 2004- 65.86, 2005- 64.56, 2006- 64.41, 2008- 65.20, 2009- 62.51, 2010- 62.47, 2011- 63.85, 2012- 63.44.

pb SP 15.91i/15.67 '98.
Reedus Thurmond (DT pb 62.06 '00) in May 2005, their son Theo born 4 Jun 2007 (she competed at US Champs 16 days later).

De'Hashia **'Deedee' TROTTER** b. 8 Dec 1982 Twentynine Palms, California 1.78m 60kg. Saucony. Degree in criminal justice from University of Tennessee.
At 400m/4x400mR: OG: '04- 5/dq 1R, '08- sf, '12- 3/1R; WCh: '03- sf/res (1)R, '05- 5, '07- 5/1R; WI: '10- 1R; PAm: '03- 1R; WCp: '06- 2R. Won US 2007, NCAA 2004.
Progress at 400m: 1998- 58.61, 1999- 59.12, 2000- 56.82, 2001- 56.02, 2002- 53.66, 2003- 50.66, 2004- 50.00, 2005- 49.88, 2006- 49.80, 2007- 49.64, 2008- 50.88, 2009- 52.00, 2010- 51.23Ai/51.52, 2011- 51.17, 2012- 49.72. pbs: 55m 6.93i '04, 60m 7.46i '05, 100m 11.65 '02, 200m 23.04 '06, 300m 35.8+ '07, LJ 6.00 '02.

Morgan UCENY b. 10 Mar 1985 Plymouth, Indiana 1.68m 57kg. adidas. Was at Cornell University.
At 800m: PAm: '07- h. At 1500m: OG: '12- dnf; WCh: '11- 10; won DL 2011, US 2011-12.
Progress at 800m, 1500m: 2002- 2:13.04, 2004- 2:19.73, 2005- 2:06.26, 2006- 2:04.32, 2007- 2:01.75, 4:17.18; 2008- 2:00.01, 4:06.93; 2009- 2:00.06, 4:09.95; 2010- 1:58.67, 4:02.40; 2011- 1:58.37, 4:00.06; 2012- 2:02.46, 4:01.59. pbs: 400m 55.50 '06, 600m 1:27.70i '07, 1000m 2:38.44i '12, 1M 4:38.87i '08.
Brought down at 950m in World 1500m in 2011, and fell at start of last lap in 2012 Olympics.

Maggie VESSEY b. 23 Dec 1981 Santa Cruz, California 1.70m 58kg. New Balance. Was at Cal Poly-San Luis Obispo.
At 800m: WCh: '09- sf, '11- 6.
Progress at 800m: 2002- 2:06.53, 2003- 2:05.78, 2005- 2:03.10, 2007- 2:11.57, 2008- 2:02.01, 2009- 1:57.84, 2010- 1:59.00, 2011- 1:58.50, 2012- 1:59.61. pbs: 400m 53.74 '10, 1500m 4:17.87 '11.

Kellie WELLS b. 16 Jul 1982 Richmond, Virginia 1.63m 57kg. Nike. Was at Hampton University.
At 100mh: OG: '12- 3; WCh: '11- dnf. US champion 2011.
Progress at 100mh: 2003- 13.96, 2004- 13.25, 2005- 13.57/13.29w, 2006- 13.25/13.17w, 2007- 12.93, 2008- 12.58, 2009- 13.01, 2010- 12.68, 2011- 12.50/12.35w, 2012- 12.48. pbs: 60m 7.33i '06, 100m 11.50 '08, 200m 23.53 '06, 50mh 6.84i '12, 55mh 7.37i '11, 60mh 7.79Ai/7.82i '11.
Suffered a serious hamstring injury after finishing the 2008 Olympic Trials semi in a pb 12.58 and struggled for two years until brilliant indoor season in 2011.

Charonda WILLIAMS b. 27 Mar 1987 Richmond, California 1.65m 54kg. adidas. Was at Arizona State University.
At 200m: WCh: '09- sf. Won DL 2012.

Progress at 200m: 2006- 24.19/24.08w, 2007- 23.53, 2008- 23.09, 2009- 22.55/22.39w, 2010- 22.97, 2011- 22.85/22.78w, 2012- 22.52. pbs: 55m 6.99Ai '08, 60m 7.29Ai '09, 7.36i '11; 100m 11.13 '12, 300m 37.04i '11, 400m 52.71 '11, LJ 5.91 '07, 6.03w '00.

Lauryn WILLIAMS b. 11 Sep 1983 Pittsburgh 1.57m 57kg. Saucony. Finance graduate of University of Miami.
At 100m/4x100mR: OG: '04- 2, '08- 4, '12- res (1) R;; WCh: '03- res (1)R, '05- 1/1R, '07- 2/1R, '09- 5; WJ: '02- 1/2R; PAm: '03- 1/1R. Won NCAA 2004. At 60m: WI: '06- 2.
Progress at 100m, 200m: 1999- 12.00/11.6, 24.2; 2000- 11.70, 24.31; 2001- 11.65/11.60w, 23.85; 2002- 11.33, 23.64/23.63w; 2003- 11.12, 23.25; 2004- 10.96/10.94w, 22.46; 2005- 10.88, 22.27; 2006- 11.09, 22.87; 2007- 11.01, 22.70; 2008- 10.90/10.86w, 22.59/22.21w; 2009- 11.01/10.94w, 22.34; 2010- 11.41, 2011- 11.15, 22.65; 2012- 11.13/10.96w, 22.8/22.96; 2013- 11.02w, 22.69w. pbs: 55m 6.70i '04, 60m 7.01i '06.

US VIRGIN ISLANDS

Tabarie HENRY b. 1 Dec 1987 Saint-Thomas 1.87m 79kg. Student at Texas A&M University (formerly Barton CC).
At 400m: OG: '08/12- sf; WCh: '09- 4, '11- 7; CAG: '10- 2; WI: '12- 4.
UVI records: 200m 2009, 400m (5) 2008-09.
Progress at 400m: 2005- 48.82, 2006- 46.51, 2007- 47.04, 2008- 45.19, 2009- 44.77, 2010- 45.07, 2011- 44.83, 2012- 45.19. pbs: 100m 11.05 '07, 200m 20.71 '09, 500m 1:01.28i '11, 600y 1:08.71i '09, 800m 1:53.33i '11. Moved to Miami at age 4.

Women

Laverne JONES-FERRETTE b. 16 Sep 1981 St Croix 1.73m 65kg. née Jones. Was at University of Oklahoma, USA.
At (100m)/200m: OG: '04/08- qf/qf, '12- sf/sf; WCh: '05- qf/sf, '07/09- sf; PAm: '07- (7) (7 400m), '11- 8; CAG: '06- 2/4. At 60m: WI: '10- dq2.
UVI records 60m (8), 100m (6), 200m (5), 400m 2004-12.
Progress at 100m, 200m: 2001- 11.77, 2002- 24.30, 2003- 11.37, 23.16i/23.26/22.93w; 2004- 11.25/11.23w, 22.81; 2005- 11.43/11.22w, 23.14; 2006- 11.30/11.29w, 22.92; 2007- 11.32/11.23w, 22.52; 2008- 11.24, 22.62; 2009- 11.13/11.03w, 22.46; 2011- 11.45A/11.45w, 2012- 11.07/10.91w, 22.62. pbs: 50m 6.14i '12, 60m 6.97i '10, 400m 51.47 '07.
Married to 400m runner Stephen Ferrette. After a positive test on 16 Feb 2010 she received a six-month ban and lost the 60m World Indoor silver medal. Daughter Asana born February 2011.

UZBEKISTAN

Governing body: Athletic Federation of Uzbekistan, Navoi str. 30, 100129 Tashkent.

Svetlana RADZIVIL b. 17 Jan 1987 Tashkent 1.84m 61kg
At HJ: OG: '08- dnq 18, '12- 7; WCh: '09- dnq 21=, '11- 8=; AsiG: '06- 7, '10- 1; AsiC: '11- 2; WJ: '02- dnq, '04- 13, '06- 1; WY: '03- dnq; WI: '12- 8.
Progress at HJ: 2002- 1.84, 2003- 1.78, 2004- 1.88, 2005- 1.85, 2006- 1.91, 2007- 1.91, 2008- 1.93, 2009- 1.91, 2010- 1.95, 2011- 1.95, 2012- 1.97.

VENEZUELA

Governing body: Federación Venezolana de Atletismo, Apartado Postal 29059, Caracas. Founded 1948.

National Champions 2012: **Men**: 100m: Jermaine Chirinos 10.91, 200m: Wilmer Valor 21.29, 400m: Albert Bravo 46.59, 800m: Wilfred Borotoche 1:50.86, 1500m: Diego Villanueva 3:51.23, 3000m: Nico José Herrera 8:47.46, 5000m: José Delgado 15:09.42, 10000m: Lervis Arias 30:29.74, 3000mSt: Alexis Peña 9:16.24, 110mh: Jonathan Davis 14.39, 400mh: Luccirio Garrido 50.65, HJ: Eure Yañez 2.23, PV: César González 4.90, LJ: Geormis Jaramillo 7.62, TJ: Peter Camacho 15.90w, SP/DT: Jesús Parejo 16.53/55.46, HT: Prinston Quailey 62.45, JT: Edwin Cuesta 62.94, Dec: Ricardo Herrada 7003, 20000mW: Yereman Salazar 1:31:33.0.
Women: 100m/200m: Nercely Soto 11.79/22.53, 400m: Amgela Alfonso 56.39, 800m: Magaly García 2:16.33, 1500m/5000m: Nubia Artegaga 4:39.56/17:45.54, 3000m: María Osorio 29:58.51, 10000m: Milagros Lugo 38:26.0, 3000mSt: Yoli Mendoza 11:24.54, 100mh: Ada Gabriela Hernández 14.36, 400mh: Estephany Balladares 62.84, HJ: Yolimar Rojas 1.66, PV: Isviansky Zerpa 3.50, LJ: Munich Tovar 6.36. TJ: Yudelis González 12.88, SP: Gioanny Rojas 14.13, DT: María Angélica Cubillán 50.91, HT: Diurkina Freytes 56.35, JT: Katherine Burlando 44.69, Hep: Thaimara Rivas 5553, 20000mW: Nayibet Rosales 1:44:28.7.

ZIMBABWE

Governing body: Amateur Athletic Association of Zimbabwe, PO Box MP 187, Mount Pleasant, Harare. Founded in 1912.

Ngonidzashe MAKUSHA b. 11 Mar 1987 Chitungwiza, Harare 1.78m 73kg. Student at Florida State University, USA.
At LJ (100m): OG: '08- 4; WCh: '11- 3 (sf); WJ: '06- 12 (sf); AfG: '07- 3R (sf). Won NCAA 100m 2011, LJ 2008-09, 2011; ZIM LJ 2006-07.
Zimbabwe records 100 (2) 2011, long jump (5) 2006-11.
Progress at 100m. LJ: 2005- 7.34?, 2006- 10.64Aw, 7.87A; 2007- 10.52, 7.69; 2008- 8.30, 2009- 8.21i/7.73/8.11w, 2010- 7.71i/7.54, 2011- 9.89, 8.40; 2012- 7.86. pbs: 55m 6.30i '08, 60m 6.60i '09, 200m 21.38A '06, TJ 14.90A '06.
Superb unique treble at 2011 NCAAs with 100m 9.89 and LJ 8.40 plus 4x100m leg. Suffered Achilles injury in May 2012.

INTRODUCTION TO WORLD LISTS AND INDEX

Records

World, World U20 and U18, Olympic, Area and Continental records are listed for standard events. In running events up to and including 400 metres, only fully automatic times are shown. Marks listed are those which are considered statistically acceptable by the ATFS, and thus may differ from official records. These are followed by road bests and bests by over 35/40 masters.

World All-time and Year Lists

Lists are presented in the following format: Mark, Wind reading (where appropriate), Name, Nationality (abbreviated), Date of birth, Position in competition, Meeting name (if significant), Venue, Date of performance.

In standard events the best 30 or so performances are listed followed by the best marks for other athletes. Position, meet and venue details have been omitted beyond 100th in year lists.

In the all-time lists performances which have been world records (or world bests, thus including some unratified marks) are shown with WR against them (or WIR for world indoor records).

Juniors (U20) are shown with-J after date of birth, and Youths (U18) with -Y.

Indexes

These contain the names of all athletes ranked with full details in the world year lists for standard events (and others such as half marathon). The format of the index is as follows: Family name, First name, Nationality, Birthdate, Height (cm) and Weight (kg), 2012 best mark, Lifetime best (with year) as at the end of 2011.

* indicates an athlete who is profiled in the Biographies section, and ^ one who has been profiled in previous editions.

General Notes

Altitude aid

Marks set at an altitude of 1000m or higher have been suffixed by the letter "A" in events where altitude may be of significance.

Although there are no separate world records for altitude assisted events, it is understood by experts that in all events up to 400m in length (with the possible exclusion of the 110m hurdles), and in the horizontal jumps, altitude gives a material benefit to performances. For events beyond 800m, however, the thinner air of high altitude has a detrimental effect.

Supplementary lists are included in relevant events for athletes with seasonal bests at altitude who have low altitude marks qualifying for the main list.

Some leading venues over 1000m

Addis Ababa ETH	2365m
Air Force Academy USA	2194
Albuquerque USA	1555
Antananarivo MAD	1350
Ávila ESP	1128
Bloemfontein RSA	1392
Bogotá COL	2644
Boulder USA	1655
Bozeman USA	1467
Calgary CAN	1045
Cali COL	1046
Ciudad de Guatemala GUA	1402
Ciudad de México MEX	2247
Cochabamba BOL	2558
Colorado Springs USA	1823
Cuenca ECU	2561
Denver USA	1609
El Paso USA	1187
Flagstaff USA	2107
Fort Collins USA	1521
Gabarone BOT	1006
Germiston RSA	1661
Guadalajara MEX	1567
Harare ZIM	1473
Irapuato MEX	1800
Johannesburg RSA	1748
Kampala UGA	1189
Krugersdorp RSA	1740
La Paz BOL	3630
Logan USA	1372
Medellín COL	1541
Monachil ESP	2302
Nairobi KEN	1675
Pietersburg RSA	1230
Pocatello USA	1361
Potchefstroom RSA	1351
Pretoria RSA	1400
Provo USA	1380
Reno USA	1369
Roodepoort RSA	1720
Rustenburg RSA	1157
Salt Lake City USA	1321
Secunda RSA	1628
Sestriere ITA	2050
Soría ESP	1056
South Lake Tahoe USA	1909
Sucre BOL	2750
Toluca MEX	2680
Tunja COL	2810
Windhoek NAM	1725
Xalapa MEX	1420

Some others over 500m

Albertville FRA	550
Almaty KZK	847
Ankara TUR	902
Bangalore, IND	949
Bern SUI	555
Blacksburg USA	634
Boise USA	818
Canberra AUS	581
La Chaux de Fonds SUI	997
Caracas VEN	922
Edmonton CAN	652

Jablonec CZE	598
Las Vegas USA	619
Lausanne SUI	597
Lubbock USA	988
Madrid ESP	640
Magglingen SUI	751
Malles ITA	980
Moscow, Idaho USA	787
München GER	520
Nampa, Idaho USA	760
Salamanca ESP	806
Santiago de Chile CHI	520
São Paulo BRA	725
Sofia BUL	564
Spokane USA	576
Trípoli GRE	655
Tucson USA	728
Uberlândia BRA	852
350m-500m	
Annecy FRA	448
Banská Bystrica SVK	362
Fayetteville USA	407
Genève SUI	385
Götzis AUS	448
Johnson City USA	499
Rieti ITA	402
Sindelfingen GER	440
Stuttgart GER	415
Tashkent UZB	477
Zürich SUI	410

Automatic timing

In the main lists for sprints and hurdles, only times recorded by fully automatic timing devices are included.

Hand timing

In the sprints and hurdles supplementary lists are included for races which are hand timed. Athletes with a hand timed best 0.01 seconds or more better than his or her automatically timed best has been included, but hand timed lists have been terminated close to the differential levels considered by the IAAF to be equivalent to automatic times, i.e. 0.24 sec. for 100m, 200m, 100mh, 110mh, and 0.14 sec. for 400m and 400mh. It should be noted that this effectively recognises bad hand timekeeping, for there should be no material difference between hand and auto times, but badly trained timekeepers anticipate the finish, having reacted to the flash at the start.

In events beyond 400m, auto times are integrated with hand timed marks, the latter identifiable by times being shown to tenths. All-time lists also include some auto times in tenths of a second, identified with '.

Indoor marks

Indoor marks are included in the main lists for field events and straightway track events, but not for other track events as track sizes vary in circumference (200m is the international standard) and banking, while outdoor tracks are standardised at 400m. Outdoor marks for athletes with indoor bests are shown in a supplemental list.

Mixed races

For record purposes athletes may not, except in road races, compete in mixed sex races. Statistically there would not appear to be any particular logic in this, and women's marks set in such races are shown in our lists – annotated with mx. In such cases the athlete's best mark in single sex competition is appended.

Field event series

Field event series are given (where known) for marks in the top 30 performances lists.

Tracks and Courses

As well as climatic conditions, the type and composition of tracks and runways will affect standards of performance, as will the variations in road race courses.

Wind assistance

Anemometer readings have been shown for sprints and horizontal jumps in metres per second to one decimal place. If the figure was given to two decimal places, it has been rounded to the next tenth upwards, e.g. a wind reading of +2.01m/s, beyond the IAAF legal limit of 2.0, is rounded to +2.1; or -1.22m/s is rounded up to -1.2.

For multi-events a wind-assisted mark is one in which the average of the three wind-measured events is > 2m/s.

Drugs bans

The IAAF Council may decertify an athlete's records, titles and results if he or she is found to have used a banned substance before those performances. Performances at or after such a positive finding are shown in footnotes. Such athletes are shown with ¶ after their name in year lists, and in all-time lists if at any stage of their career they have served a drugs suspension of a year or more (thus not including athletes receiving public warnings or 3 month bans for stimulants etc., which for that year only are indicated with a #). This should not be taken as implying that the athlete was using drugs at that time. Nor have those athletes who have subsequently unofficially admitted to using banned substances been indicated; the ¶ is used only for those who have been caught.

Venues

Place names occasionally change. Our policy is to use names in force at the time that the performance was set. Thus Leningrad prior to 1991, Sankt-Peterburg from its re-naming.

Amendments

Keen observers may spot errors in the lists. They are invited to send corrections as well as news and results for 2013.

Peter Matthews
Email p.matthews121@btinternet.com

WORLD & CONTINENTAL RECORDS

As at 1 April 2013. **Key:** W = World, Afr = Africa, Asi = Asia, CAC = Central America & Caribbean, Eur = Europe, NAm = North America, Oce = Oceania, SAm = South America, Com = Commonwealth, W20 = World Junior (U20), W18 = World Youth (U18, not officially ratified by IAAF). h hand timed.
Successive columns show: World or Continent, performance, name, nationality, venue, date.
A altitude over 1000m, + timing by photo-electric-cell, # awaiting ratification, § not officially ratified

100 METRES

W,CAC,Com	9.58	Usain BOLT	JAM	Berlin	16 Aug 2009
NAm	9.69	Tyson GAY	USA	Shanghai	20 Sep 2009
Afr	9.85	Olusoji FASUBA	NGR	Doha	12 May 2006
Eur	9.86	Francis OBIKWELU	POR	Athína	22 Aug 2004
Oce	9.93	Patrick JOHNSON	AUS	Mito	5 May 2003
Asi	9.99	Samuel FRANCIS	QAT	Amman	26 Jul 2007
SAm	10.00A	Róbson da SILVA	BRA	Ciudad de México	22 Jul 1988
W20	10.01	Darrel BROWN	TRI	Saint-Denis	24 Aug 2003
	10.01 §	Jeffery DEMPS	USA	Eugene	28 Jun 2008
W18	10.19	Yoshihide KIRYU	JPN	Fukuroi	3 Nov 2012

200 METRES

W,CAC,Com	19.19	Usain BOLT	JAM	Berlin	20 Aug 2009
NAm	19.32	Michael JOHNSON	USA	Atlanta	1 Aug 1996
Afr	19.68	Frank FREDERICKS	NAM	Atlanta	1 Aug 1996
Eur	19.72A	Pietro MENNEA	ITA	Ciudad de México	12 Sep 1979
SAm	19.81	Alonso EDWARD	PAN	Berlin	20 Aug 2009
Asi	20.03	Shingo SUETSUGU	JPN	Yokohama	7 Jun 2003
Oce	20.06A	Peter NORMAN	AUS	Ciudad de México	16 Oct 1968
W20	19.93	Usain BOLT	JAM	Hamilton, BER	11 Apr 2004
W18	20.13	Usain BOLT	JAM	Bridgetown	20 Jul 2003

400 METRES

W, NAm	43.18	Michael JOHNSON	USA	Sevilla	26 Aug 1999
Com	43.94	Kirani JAMES	GRN	London (OS)	6 Aug 2012
Afr	44.10	Gary KIKAYA	COD	Stuttgart	9 Sep 2006
CAC	44.14	Roberto HERNÁNDEZ	CUB	Sevilla	30 May 1990
SAm	44.29	Sanderlei PARRELA	BRA	Sevilla	26 Aug 1999
Eur	44.33	Thomas SCHÖNLEBE	GER	Roma	3 Sep 1987
Oce	44.38	Darren CLARK	AUS	Seoul	26 Sep 1988
Asi	44.56	Mohamed AL-MALKY	OMN	Budapest	12 Aug 1988
W20	43.87	Steve LEWIS	USA	Seoul	28 Sep 1988
W18	45.14	Obea MOORE	USA	Santiago de Chile	2 Sep 1995

800 METRES

W, Afr, Com	1:40.91	David RUDISHA	KEN	London (OS)	9 Aug 2012
Eur	1:41.11	Wilson KIPKETER	DEN	Köln	24 Aug 1997
SAm	1:41.77	Joaquim CRUZ	BRA	Köln	26 Aug 1984
NAm	1:42.60	Johnny GRAY	USA	Koblenz	28 Aug 1985
Asi	1:42.79	Youssef Saad KAMEL	BRN	Monaco	29 Jul 2008
CAC	1:42.85	Norberto TELLEZ	CUB	Atlanta	31 Jul 1996
Oce	1:44.3+ h	Peter SNELL	NZL	Christchurch	3 Feb 1962
W20	1:41.73	Nijel AMOS	BOT	London (OS)	9 Aug 2012
W18	1:43.37	Mohamed AMAN	ETH	Rieti	10 Sep 2011

1000 METRES

W, Afr, Com	2:11.96	Noah NGENY	KEN	Rieti	5 Sep 1999
Eur	2:12.18	Sebastian COE	GBR	Oslo	11 Jul 1981
NAm	2:13.9	Rick WOHLHUTER	USA	Oslo	30 Jul 1974
SAm	2:14.09	Joaquim CRUZ	BRA	Nice	20 Aug 1984
Asi	2:14.72	Youssef Saad KAMEL	BRN	Stockholm	22 Jul 2008
Oce	2:16.57	John WALKER	NZL	Oslo	1 Jul 1980
CAC	2:17.0	Byron DYCE	JAM	København	15 Aug 1973
W20	2:13.93 §	Abubaker KAKI	SUD	Stockholm	22 Jul 2008
W18	2:17.44	Hamza DRIOUCH	QAT	Sollentuna	9 Aug 2011

1500 METRES

W, Afr	3:26.00	Hicham EL GUERROUJ	MAR	Roma	14 Jul 1998
Com	3:26.34	Bernard LAGAT	KEN	Bruxelles	24 Aug 2001
Eur	3:28.95	Fermin CACHO	ESP	Zürich	13 Aug 1997
Asi	3:29.14	Rashid RAMZI	BRN	Roma	14 Jul 2006

NAm	3:29.30	Bernard LAGAT	USA	Rieti	28 Aug 2005
Oce	3:31.06	Ryan GREGSON	AUS	Monaco	22 Jul 2010
SAm	3:33.25	Hudson Santos de SOUZA	BRA	Rieti	28 Aug 2005
CAC	3:35.03	Maurys CASTILLO	CUB	Huelva	7 Jun 2012
W20	3:30.24	Cornelius CHIRCHIR	KEN	Monaco	19 Jul 2002
W18	3:33.72	Nicholas KEMBOI	KEN	Zürich	18 Aug 2006

1 MILE

W, Afr	3:43.13	Hicham El GUERROUJ	MAR	Roma	7 Jul 1999
Com	3:43.40	Noah NGENY	KEN	Roma	7 Jul 1999
Eur	3:46.32	Steve CRAM	GBR	Oslo	27 Jul 1985
NAm	3:46.91	Alan WEBB	USA	Brasschaat	21 Jul 2007
Asi	3:47.97	Daham Najim BASHIR	QAT	Oslo	29 Jul 2005
Oce	3:48.98	Craig MOTTRAM	AUS	Oslo	29 Jul 2005
SAm	3:51.05	Hudson de SOUZA	BRA	Oslo	29 Jul 2005
CAC	3:57.34	Byron DYCE	JAM	Stockholm	1 Jul 1974
W20	3:49.29	William BIWOTT TANUI	KEN	Oslo	3 Jul 2009
W18	3:54.56	Isaac SONGOK	KEN	Linz	20 Aug 2001

2000 METRES

W, Afr	4:44.79	Hicham EL GUERROUJ	MAR	Berlin	7 Sep 1999
Com	4:48.74	John KIBOWEN	KEN	Hechtel	1 Aug 1998
Oce	4:50.76	Craig MOTTRAM	AUS	Melbourne	9 Mar 2006
Eur	4:51.39	Steve CRAM	GBR	Budapest	4 Aug 1985
NAm	4:52.44	Jim SPIVEY	USA	Lausanne	15 Sep 1987
Asi	4:55.57	Mohammed SULEIMAN	QAT	Roma	8 Jun 1995
SAm	5:03.34	Hudson Santos de SOUZA	BRA	Manaus	6 Apr 2002
CAC	5:03.4	Arturo BARRIOS	MEX	Nice	10 Jul 1989
W20	4:56.25	Tesfaye CHERU	ETH	Reims	5 Jul 2011
W18	4:56.86	Isaac SONGOK	KEN	Berlin	31 Aug 2001

3000 METRES

W, Afr, Com	7:20.67	Daniel KOMEN	KEN	Rieti	1 Sep 1996
Eur	7:26.62	Mohammed MOURHIT	BEL	Monaco	18 Aug 2000
NAm	7:29.00	Bernard LAGAT	USA	Rieti	29 Aug 2010
Asi	7:30.76	Jamal Bilal SALEM	QAT	Doha	13 May 2005
Oce	7:32.19	Craig MOTTRAM	AUS	Athína	17 Sep 2006
CAC	7:35.71	Arturo BARRIOS	MEX	Nice	10 Jul 1989
SAm	7:39.70	Hudson Santos de SOUZA	BRA	Lausanne	2 Jul 2002
W20	7:28.78	Augustine CHOGE	KEN	Doha	13 May 2005
W18	7:32.37	Abreham CHERKOS Feleke	ETH	Lausanne	11 Jul 2006

5000 METRES

W, Afr	12:37.35	Kenenisa BEKELE	ETH	Hengelo	31 May 2004
Com	12:39.74	Daniel KOMEN	KEN	Bruxelles	22 Aug 1997
Eur	12:49.71	Mohammed MOURHIT	BEL	Bruxelles	25 Aug 2000
Asi	12:51.98	Saif Saaeed SHAHEEN	QAT	Roma	14 Jul 2006
NAm	12:53.60	Bernard LAGAT	USA	Monaco	22 Jul 2011
Oce	12:55.76	Craig MOTTRAM	AUS	London	30 Jul 2004
CAC	13:07.79	Arturo BARRIOS	MEX	London (CP)	14 Jul 1989
SAm	13:19.43	Marilson DOS SANTOS	BRA	Kassel	8 Jun 2006
W20	12:47.53	Hagos GEBRHIWET	ETH	Saint-Denis	6 Jul 2012
W18	12:54.19	Abreham CHERKOS Feleke	ETH	Roma	14 Jul 2006

10,000 METRES

W, Afr	26:17.53	Kenenisa BEKELE	ETH	Bruxelles	26 Aug 2005
Com	26:27.85	Paul TERGAT	KEN	Bruxelles	22 Aug 1997
Asi	26:38.76	Abdullah Ahmad HASSAN	QAT	Bruxelles	5 Sep 2003
Eur	26:46.57	Mohamed FARAH	GBR	Eugene	3 Jun 2011
NAm	26:48.00	Galen RUPP	USA	Bruxelles	16 Sep 2011
CAC	27:08.23	Arturo BARRIOS	MEX	Berlin	18 Aug 1989
Oce	27:24.95	Ben ST LAWRENCE	AUS	Stanford	1 May 2011
SAm	27:28.12	Marilson DOS SANTOS	BRA	Neerpelt	2 Jun 2007
W20	26:41.75	Samuel WANJIRU	KEN	Bruxelles	26 Aug 2005
W18	27:02.81	Ibrahim JAYLAN Gashu	ETH	Bruxelles	25 Aug 2006

HALF MARATHON

W, Afr	58:23	Zersenay TADESE	ERI	Lisboa	21 Mar 2010
Com	58:33	Samuel WANJIRU	KEN	Den Haag	17 Mar 2007
SAm	59:33	Marilson DOS SANTOS	BRA	Udine	14 Oct 2007
NAm	59:43	Ryan HALL	USA	Houston	14 Jan 2007

Eur	59:52	Fabian RONCERO	ESP	Berlin	1 Apr 2001
Oce	60:02	Darren WILSON	AUS	Tokyo	19 Jan 1997
Asi	60:25	Atsushi SATO	JPN	Udine	14 Oct 2007
CAC	60:14	Armando QUINTANILLA	MEX	Tokyo	21 Jan 1996
W20	59:16	Samuel WANJIRU	KEN	Rotterdam	11 Sep 2005
W18	60:38	Faustin BAHA Sulle	TAN	Lille	4 Sep 1999

MARATHON

W, Afr, Com	2:03:38	Patrick MAKAU	KEN	Berlin	25 Sep 2011
NAm	2:05:38	Khalid KHANNOUCHI (ex MAR)	USA	London	14 Apr 2002
SAm	2:06:05	Ronaldo da COSTA	BRA	Berlin	20 Sep 1998
Asi	2:06:16	Toshinari TAKAOKA	JPN	Chicago	13 Oct 2002
Eur	2:06:36 §	António PINTO	POR	London	16 Apr 2000
	2:06:36	Benoît ZWIERZCHIEWSKI	FRA	Paris	6 Apr 2003
Oce	2:08:16	Steve MONEGHETTI	AUS	Berlin	30 Sep 1990
CAC	2:08:30	Dionicio CERÓN	MEX	London	2 Apr 1995
W20	2:06:07	Edic NDIEMA	KEN	Amsterdam	16 Oct 2011
W18	2:11:43	LI He	CHN	Beijing	14 Oct 2001

3000 METRES STEEPLECHASE

W, Asi	7:53.63	Saïf Saaeed SHAHEEN	QAT	Bruxelles	3 Sep 2004
Afr	7:53.64	Brimin KIPRUTO	KEN	Monaco	22 Jul 2011
Com	7:55.72	Bernard BARMASAI	KEN	Köln	24 Aug 1997
Eur	8:01.18	Bouabdellah TAHRI	FRA	Berlin	18 Aug 2009
NAm	8:06.81	Evan JAGER	USA	Monaco	20 Jul 2012
Oce	8:14.05	Peter RENNER	NZL	Koblenz	29 Aug 1984
SAm	8:14.41	Wander MOURA	BRA	Mar del Plata	22 Mar 1995
CAC	8:25.69	Salvador MIRANDA	MEX	Barakaldo	9 Jul 2000
W20	7:58.66	Stephen CHERONO (now Shaheen)	KEN	Bruxelles	24 Aug 2001
W18	8:17.28 §	Jonathan NDIKU	KEN	Bydgoszcz	13 Jul 2008

110 METRES HURDLES

W, CAC	12.80	Aries MERRITT	USA	Bruxelles	7 Sep 2012
Asi	12.88	LIU Xiang	CHN	Lausanne	11 Jul 2006
NAm	12.89	David OLIVER	USA	Saint-Denis	16 Jul 2010
Eur, Com	12.91	Colin JACKSON	GBR/Wal	Stuttgart	20 Aug 1993
Afr	13.24	Lehann FOURIE	RSA	Bruxelles	7 Sep 2012
Oce	13.29	Kyle VANDER-KUYP	AUS	Göteborg	11 Aug 1995
SAm	13.27A	Paulo César VILLAR	COL	Guadalajara	28 Oct 2011
W20	13.12	LIU Xiang (with 3'6" hurdles)	CHN	Lausanne	2 Jul 2002
W20 99cm h	13.08 §	Wayne DAVIS	USA	Port of Spain	31 Jul 2009
W18	13.43	SHI Dongpeng	CHN	Shanghai	6 May 2001
W18 91cm h	13.18	Wayne DAVIS	USA	Ostrava	12 Jul 2007

400 METRES HURDLES

W, NAm	46.78	Kevin YOUNG	USA	Barcelona	6 Aug 1992
Afr, Com	47.10	Samuel MATETE	ZAM	Zürich	7 Aug 1991
CAC	47.25	Felix SÁNCHEZ	DOM	Saint-Denis	29 Aug 2003
Eur	47.37	Stéphane DIAGANA	FRA	Lausanne	5 Jul 1995
Asi	47.53	Hadi Sou'an AL-SOMAILY	KSA	Sydney	27 Sep 2000
SAm	47.84	Bayano KAMANI	PAN	Helsinki	7 Aug 2005
Oce	48.28	Rohan ROBINSON	AUS	Atlanta	31 Jul 1996
W20	48.02	Danny HARRIS	USA	Los Angeles	17 Jun 1984
W18	48.89	L.J. VAN ZYL	RSA	Kingston	19 Jul 2002

HIGH JUMP

W, CAC	2.45	Javier SOTOMAYOR	CUB	Salamanca	27 Jul 1993
Eur	2.42	Patrik SJÖBERG	SWE	Stockholm	30 Jun 1987
	2.42 i§	Carlo THRÄNHARDT	FRG	Berlin	26 Feb 1988
NAm	2.40 i§	Hollis CONWAY	USA	Sevilla	10 Mar 1991
		Charles AUSTIN	USA	Zürich	7 Aug 1991
Asi	2.39	ZHU Jianhua	CHN	Eberstadt	10 Jun 1984
	2.39	Mutaz Essa BARSHIM	QAT	Lausanne	23 Aug 2012
Com	2.38i	Steve SMITH	GBR/Eng	Wuppertal	4 Feb 1994
	2.38	Troy KEMP	BAH	Nice	12 Jul 1995
Afr, Com	2.38	Jacques FREITAG	RSA	Oudtshoorn	5 Mar 2005
Oce	2.36	Tim FORSYTH	AUS	Melbourne	2 Mar 1997
SAm	2.33	Gilmar MAYO	COL	Pereira	17 Oct 1994
W20	2.37	Dragutin TOPIC	YUG	Plovdiv	12 Aug 1990
		Steve SMITH	GBR	Seoul	20 Sep 1992
W18	2.33	Javier SOTOMAYOR	CUB	La Habana	19 May 1984

POLE VAULT

W, Eur	6.15 i§	Sergey BUBKA	UKR	Donetsk	21 Feb 1993
	6.14 A	Sergey BUBKA	UKR	Sestriere	31 Jul 1994
Oce, Com	6.05	Dmitriy MARKOV	AUS	Edmonton	9 Aug 2001
NAm	6.04	Brad WALKER	USA	Eugene	8 Jun 2008
Afr	6.03	Okkert BRITS	RSA	Köln	18 Aug 1995
Asi	5.92i	Igor POTAPOVICH	KAZ	Stockholm	19 Feb 1998
	5.90	Grigoriy YEGOROV	KAZ	Stuttgart 19 Aug 1993 & London (CP)	10 Sep 1993
	5.90	Igor POTAPOVICH	KAZ	Nice	10 Jul 1996
CAC	5.90	Lázaro BORGES	CUB	Daegu	29 Aug 2011
SAm	5.80	Fábio Gomes da SILVA	BRA	São Caetano do Sul	26 Feb 2011
W20	5.80	Maksim TARASOV	RUS	Bryansk	14 Jul 1989
	5.80	Raphael HOLZDEPPE	GER	Biberach	28 Jun 2008
W18	5.51	Germán CHIARAVIGLIO	ARG	Pôrto Alegre	1 May 2004

LONG JUMP

W, NAm	8.95	Mike POWELL	USA	Tokyo	30 Aug 1991
Eur	8.86 A	Robert EMMIYAN	ARM	Tsakhkadzor	22 May 1987
SAm	8.73	Irving SALADINO	PAN	Hengelo	24 May 2008
CAC	8.71	Iván PEDROSO	CUB	Salamanca	18 Jul 1995
Com	8.62	James BECKFORD	JAM	Orlando	5 Apr 1997
Oce	8.54	Mitchell WATT	AUS	Stockholm	29 Jul 2011
Afr	8.50	Khotso MOKOENA	RSA	Madrid	4 Jul 2009
Asi	8.48	Mohamed Salim AL-KHUWALIDI	KSA	Sotteville	2 Jul 2006
W20	8.35	Sergey MORGUNOV	RUS	Cheboksary	20 Jun 2012
W18	8.25	Luis Alberto BUENO	CUB	La Habana	28 Sep 1986

TRIPLE JUMP

W, Eur, Com	18.29	Jonathan EDWARDS	GBR/Eng	Göteborg	7 Aug 1995
NAm	18.09	Kenny HARRISON	USA	Atlanta	27 Jul 1996
CAC	17.92	James BECKFORD	JAM	Odessa, Texas	20 May 1995
SAm	17.90	Jadel GREGÓRIO	BRA	Belém	20 May 2007
Asi	17.59	LI Yanxi	CHN	Jinan	26 Oct 2009
Oce	17.46	Ken LORRAWAY	AUS	London (CP)	7 Aug 1982
Afr	17.37	Ndabezinhle MDHLONGWA	ZIM	Lafayette	28 Mar 1998
	17.37	Tareq BOUGTAÏB	MAR	Khémisset	14 Jul 2007
W20	17.50	Volker MAI	GDR	Erfurt	23 Jun 1985
W18	16.89	GU Junjie	CHN	Dalian	25 Aug 2000

SHOT

W, NAm	23.12	Randy BARNES	USA	Westwood	20 May 1990
Eur	23.06	Ulf TIMMERMANN	GER	Haniá	22 May 1988
Com	22.21	Dylan ARMSTRONG	CAN	Calgary	25 Jun 2011
Afr	21.97	Janus ROBBERTS	RSA	Eugene	2 Jun 2001
CAC	21.45	Dorian SCOTT	JAM	Tallahassee	28 Mar 2008
Oce	21.26	Scott MARTIN	AUS	Melbourne	21 Feb 2008
SAm	21.14	Marco Antonio VERNI	CHI	Santiago de Chile	29 Jul 2004
Asi	21.13	Sultan Abdulmajeed AL-HEBSHI	KSA	Doha	8 May 2009
W20	21.05 i§	Terry ALBRITTON	USA	New York	22 Feb 1974
	20.65 §	Mike CARTER	USA	Boston	4 Jul 1979
	20.43	David STORL	GER	Gerlingen	6 Jul 2009
W18	20.38	Jacko GILL	NZL	Auckland (North Shore)	5 Dec 2011
W20 6kg	22.73	David STORL	GER	Osterode	14 Jul 2009
W18 5kg	24.45	Jacko GILL	NZL	Auckland (North Shore)	19 Dec 2011

DISCUS

W, Eur	74.08	Jürgen SCHULT	GDR	Neubrandenburg	6 Jun 1986
NAm	72.34 ¶	Ben PLUCKNETT	USA	Stockholm	7 Jul 1981
	71.32 §	Ben PLUCKNETT	USA	Eugene	4 Jun 1983
CAC	71.06	Luis DELIS	CUB	La Habana	21 May 1983
Afr, Com	70.32	Frantz KRUGER	RSA	Salon-de-Provence	26 May 2002
Asi	69.32	Ehsan HADADI	IRI	Tallinn	3 Jun 2008
Oce	67.53	Benn HARRADINE	AUS	Townsville	5 May 2012
SAm	66.32	Jorge BALLIENGO	ARG	Rosario	15 Apr 2006
W20	65.62 §	Werner REITERER	AUS	Melbourne	15 Dec 1987
W18/20	65.31	Mykyta NESTERENKO	UKR	Tallinn	3 Jun 2008
W20 1.75kg	70.13	Mykyta NESTERENKO	UKR	Halle	24 May 2008
W18 1.5kg	77.50	Mykyta NESTERNKO	UKR	Koncha Zaspa	19 May 2008

¶ Disallowed by the IAAF following retrospective disqualification for drug abuse, but ratified by the AAU/TAC

HAMMER

W, Eur	86.74	Yuriy SEDYKH	UKR/RUS	Stuttgart	30 Aug 1986
Asi	84.86	Koji MUROFUSHI	JPN	Praha	29 Jun 2003
NAm	82.52	Lance DEAL	USA	Milano	7 Sep 1996
Afr, Com	80.63	Chris HARMSE	RSA	Durban	15 Apr 2005
Oce	79.29	Stuart RENDELL	AUS	Varazdin	6 Jul 2002
CAC	77.78	Alberto SANCHEZ	CUB	La Habana	15 May 1998
SAm	76.42	Juan CERRA	ARG	Trieste	25 Jul 2001
W20	78.33	Olli-Pekka KARJALAINEN	FIN	Seinäjoki	5 Aug 1999
W18	73.66	Vladislav PISKUNOV	UKR	Live	11 Jun 1994
W20 6kg	85.57	Ashraf Amgad EL-SEIFY	QAT	Barcelona	14 Jul 2012
W18 5kg	85.26	Ashraf Amgad EL-SEIFY	QAT	Rhede	20 Jul 2011

JAVELIN

W, Eur	98.48	Jan ZELEZNY	CZE	Jena	25 May 1996
Com	91.46	Steve BACKLEY	GBR/Eng	Auckland (NS)	25 Jan 1992
NAm	91.29	Breaux GREER	USA	Indianapolis	21 Jun 2007
Oce	89.02	Jarrod BANNISTER	AUS	Brisbane	29 Feb 2008
Afr	88.75	Marius CORBETT	RSA	Kuala Lumpur	21 Sep 1998
Asi	87.60	Kazuhiro MIZOGUCHI	JPN	San José	27 May 1989
CAC	87.20A	Guillermo MARTÍNEZ	CUB	Guadalajara	28 Oct 2011
SAm	84.70	Edgar BAUMANN	PAR	San Marcos	17 Oct 1999
W20	84.69	Zigismunds SIRMAIS	LAT	Bauska	22 Jun 2011
W18 700g	89.34	Braian Ezequiel TOLEDO	ARG	Mar del Plata	6 Mar 2010

DECATHLON

W, NAm	9039	Ashton EATON	USA	Eugene	23 Jun 2012
Eur	9026	Roman SEBRLE	CZE	Götzis	27 May 2001
Com	8847	Daley THOMPSON	GBR/Eng	Los Angeles	9 Aug 1984
Asi	8725	Dmitriy KARPOV	KAZ	Athína	24 Aug 2004
CAC	8654	Leonel SUÁREZ	CUB	La Habana	4 Jul 2009
Oce	8490	Jagan HAMES	AUS	Kuala Lumpur	18 Sep 1998
Afr	8302	Larbi BOURAADA	ALG	Ratingen	17 Jul 2011
SAm	8291A h	Tito STEINER	ARG	Provo	23 Jun 1983
	8276	Luiz Alberto de ARAÚJO	BRA	São Paulo	30 Jun 2012
W20	8397	Torsten VOSS (with 3'6" hurdles)	GDR	Erfurt	7 Jul 1982
W18	8104h	Valter KÜLVET	EST	Viimsi	23 Aug 1981
	7829	Valter KÜLVET	EST	Stockholm	13 Sep 1981

4 X 100 METRES RELAY

W, CAC, Com	36.84	JAM (Carter, Frater, Blake, Bolt)	London (OS)	11 Aug 2012
NAm	37.04	USA (Kimmons, Gatlin, Gay, R Bailey)	London (OS)	11 Aug 2012
Eur	37.73	GBR (Gardener, Campbell, Devonish, Chambers)	Sevilla	29 Aug 1999
SAm	37.90	BRA (V Lima, Ribeiro, A da Silva, Cl da Silva)	Sydney	30 Sep 2000
Afr	37.94	NGR (O Ezinwa, Adeniken, Obikwelu, D Ezinwa)	Athína	9 Aug 1997
Asi	38.03	JPN (Tsukahara, Suetsugu, Takahira, Asahara)	Osaka	1 Sep 2007
Oce	38.17	AUS (Henderson, Jackson, Brimacombe, Marsh)	Göteborg	12 Aug 1995
W20	38.66	USA (Kimmons, Omole, Williams, Merritt)	Grosseto	18 Jul 2004
W18	40.03	JAM (W Smith, M Frater, Spence, O Brown)	Bydgoszcz	18 Jul 1999

4 X 400 METRES RELAY

W, NAm	2:54.29	USA (Valmon, Watts, Reynolds, Johnson)	Stuttgart	22 Aug1993
Eur	2:56.60	GBR (Thomas, Baulch, Richardson, Black)	Atlanta	3 Aug 1996
CAC, Com	2:56.72	BAH (Brown, Pinder, Mathieu, Miller)	London (OS)	10 Aug 2012
SAm	2:58.56	BRA (C da Silva, A J dosSantos, de Araújo, Parrela)	Winnipeg	30 Jul 1999
Afr	2:58.68	NGR (Chukwu, Monye, Nada, Udo-Obong)	Sydney	30 Sep 2000
Oce	2:59.70	AUS (Frayne, Clark, Minihan, Mitchell)	Los Angeles	11 Aug 1984
Asi	3:00.76	JPN (Karube, K Ito, Osakada, Omori)	Atlanta	3 Aug 1996
W20	3:01.09	USA (Johnson, Merritt, Craig, Clement)	Grosseto	18 Jul 2004
W18	3:12.05	POL (Zrada, Kedzia, Grzegorczyk, Kowalski)	Kaunas	5 Aug 2001

20 KILOMETRES WALK

W, Eur	1:17:16	Vladimir KANAYKIN	RUS	Saransk	29 Sep 2007
	1:16:43 §	Sergey MOROZOV	RUS	Saransk	8 Jun 2008
SAm	1:17:21	Jefferson PÉREZ	ECU	Saint-Denis	23 Aug 2003
CAC	1:17:25.6 t	Bernardo SEGURA	MEX	Bergen (Fana)	7 May 1994
Oce, Com	1:17:33	Nathan DEAKES	AUS	Cixi	23 Apr 2005
Asi	1:17:36	WANG Zhen	CHN	Taicang	30 Mar 2012
Afr	1:19:02	Hatem GHOULA	TUN	Eisenhüttenstadt	10 May 1997
NAm	1:21:03	Arturo HUERTA	CAN	Etobicoke	7 Jul 2000

W20	1:18:06 §	Viktor BURAYEV	RUS	Adler	4 Mar 2001
W18	1:18:07	LI Gaobo	CHN	Cixi	23 Apr 2005

20,000 METRES TRACK WALK

W, CAC	1:17:25.6	Bernardo SEGURA	MEX	Bergen (Fana)	7 May 1994
Asi	1:18:03.3	BU Lingtang	CHN	Beijing	7 Apr 1994
Eur	1:18:35.2	Stefan JOHANSSON	SWE	Bergen (Fana)	15 May 1992
Oce, Com	1:19:48.1	Nathan DEAKES	AUS	Brisbane	4 Sep 2001
SAm	1:20:23.8	Andrés CHOCHO	ECU	Buenos Aires	5 Jun 2011
NAm	1:22:27.0	Tim BERRETT	CAN	Edmonds, WA	9 Jun 1996
Afr	1:22:51.84	Hatem GHOULA	TUN	Leutkirch	8 Sep 1994
W20	1:20:11.72	LI Gaobo	CHN	Wuhan	2 Nov 2007
W18	1:24:28.3	ZHU Hongjun	CHN	Xian	15 Sep 1999

50 KILOMETRES WALK

W, Eur	3:34:14	Denis NIZHEGORODOV	RUS	Cheboksary	11 May 2008
Oce, Com	3:35:47	Nathan DEAKES	AUS	Geelong	2 Dec 2006
Asi	3:36:06	YU Chaohong	CHN	Nanjing	22 Oct 2005
CAC	3:41:09	Erick BARRONDO	GUA	Dudince	23 Mar 2013
NAm	3:47:48	Marcel JOBIN	CAN	Québec	20 Jun 1981
SAm	3:49:26	Andrés CHOCHO	ECU	Valley Cottage	28 Oct 2012
Afr	3:55:32	Marc MUNDELL	RSA	London	11 Aug 2012
W20	3:41:10	ZHAO Jianguo	CHN	Wajima	16 Apr 2006
W18	3:45:46	YU Guoping	CHN	Guangzhou	23 Nov 2001

50,000 METRES TRACK WALK

W, Eur	3:35:27.2	Yoahnn DINIZ	FRA	Reims	12 Mar 2011
CAC	3:41:38.4	Raúl GONZÁLEZ	MEX	Bergen (Fana)	25 May 1979
Oce, Com	3:43:50.0	Simon BAKER	AUS	Melbourne	9 Sep 1990
Asi	3:48:13.7	ZHAO Yongshen	CHN	Bergen (Fana)	7 May 1994
NAm	3:56:13.0	Tim BERRETT	CAN	Saskatoon	21 Jul 1991
SAm	3:57:58.0	Claudio dos SANTOS	BRA	Blumenau	20 Sep 2008
Afr	4:21:44.5	Abdelwahab FERGUÈNE	ALG	Toulouse	25 Mar 1984

World Records at other men's events recognised by the IAAF

20,000m	56:25.98+	Haile GEBRSELASSIE	ETH	Ostrava	27 Jun 2007
1 Hour	21,285 m	Haile GEBRSELASSIE	ETH	Ostrava	27 Jun 2007
25,000m	1:12:25.4	Moses MOSOP	KEN	Eugene	3 Jun 2011
30,000m	1:26:47.4	Moses MOSOP	KEN	Eugene	3 Jun 2011
U18 Octathlon	6491	Jake STEIN	AUS	Villeneuve d'Ascq	7 Jul 2011
4 x 200m	1:18.68	Santa Monica Track Club	USA	Walnut	17 Apr 1994
		(Michael Marsh, Leroy Burrell, Floyd Heard, Carl Lewis)			
4 x 800m	7:02.43	Kenya Team	KEN	Bruxelles	25 Aug 2006
		(Joseph Mutua, William Yiampoy, Ismael Kombich, Wilfred Bungei)			
4 x l500m	14:36.23	W Biwott, Gathimba, G Rono, Choge	KEN	Bruxelles	4 Sep 2009

Walking

2 Hours track 29,572m+	Maurizio DAMILANO	ITA	Cuneo	3 Oct 1992
30km track 2:01:44.1	Maurizio DAMILANO	ITA	Cuneo	3 Oct 1992
U20 10,000m track: 38:46.4	Viktor BURAYEV	RUS	Moskva	20 May 2000
U20 10km road 37:44	WANG Zhen	CHN	Beijing	18 Sep 2010
W18 10km road 38:57	LI Tianlei	CHN	Beijing	18 Sep 2010

WOMEN

100 METRES

W, NAm	10.49	Florence GRIFFITH JOYNER	USA	Indianapolis	16 Jul 1988
CAC, Com	10.70	Shelly-Ann FRASER	JAM	Kingstobn	29 Jun 2012
Eur	10.73	Christine ARRON	FRA	Budapest	19 Aug 1998
Asi	10.79	LI Xuemei	CHN	Shanghai	18 Oct 1997
Afr	10.90	Glory ALOZIE	NGR	La Laguna	5 Jun 1999
	10.84 §	Chioma AJUNWA	NGR	Lagos	11 Apr 1992
Oce	11.12A	Melinda GAINSFORD/TAYLOR	AUS	Sestriere	31 Jul 1994
SAm	11.15	Ana Claudia SILVA	BRA	São Paulo	4 Sep 2010
W20	10.88	Marlies OELSNER/GÖHR	GDR	Dresden	1 Jul 1977
W18	11.13	Chandra CHEESEBOROUGH	USA	Eugene	21 Jun 1976

200 METRES

W, NAm	21.34	Florence GRIFFITH JOYNER	USA	Seoul	29 Sep 1988
CAC, Com	21.64	Merlene OTTEY	JAM	Bruxelles	13 Sep 1991
Eur	21.71	Marita KOCH	GDR	Chemnitz	10 Jun 1979
	21.71 §	Marita KOCH	GDR	Potsdam	21 Jul 1984

	21.71	Heike DRECHSLER	GDR	Jena	29 Jun 1986
	21.71 §	Heike DRECHSLER	GDR	Stuttgart	29 Aug 1986
Asi	22.01	LI Xuemei	CHN	Shanghai	22 Oct 1997
Afr	22.06 A§	Evette DE KLERK	RSA	Pietersburg	8 Apr 1989
	22.07	Mary ONYALI	NGR	Zürich	14 Aug 1996
Oce	22.23	Melinda GAINSFORD-TAYLOR	AUS	Stuttgart	13 Jul 1997
SAm	22.48	Ana Cláudia da SILVA	BRA	São Paulo	6 Aug 2011
W20	22.18	Allyson FELIX	USA	Athína	25 Aug 2004
	22.11A §	Allyson FELIX (no doping control)	USA	Ciudad de México	3 May 2003
W18	22.58	Marion JONES	USA	New Orleans	28 Jun 1992

400 METRES

W, Eur	47.60	Marita KOCH	GDR	Canberra	6 Oct 1985
Oce, Com	48.63	Cathy FREEMAN	AUS	Atlanta	29 Jul 1996
NAm	48.70	Sanya RICHARDS	USA	Athína	16 Sep 2006
Afr	49.10	Falilat OGUNKOYA	NGR	Atlanta	29 Jul 1996
CAC	48.89	Ana GUEVARA	MEX	Saint-Denis	27 Aug 2003
SAm	49.64	Ximena RESTREPO	COL	Barcelona	5 Aug 1992
Asi	49.81	MA Yuqin	CHN	Beijing	11 Sep 1993
W20	49.42	Grit BREUER	GER	Tokyo	27 Aug 1991
W18	50.01	LI Jing	CHN	Shanghai	18 Oct 1997

800 METRES

W, Eur	1:53.28	Jarmila KRATOCHVÍLOVÁ	CZE	München	26 Jul 1983
Afr,W20,Com	1:54.01	Pamela JELIMO	KEN	Zürich	29 Aug 2008
CAC	1:54.44	Ana Fidelia QUIROT	CUB	Barcelona	9 Sep 1989
Asi	1:55.54	LIU Dong	CHN	Beijing	9 Sep 1993
NAm	1:56.40	Jearl MILES CLARK	USA	Zürich	11 Aug 1999
SAm	1:56.68	Letitia VRIESDE	SUR	Göteborg	13 Aug 1995
Oce	1:58.25	Toni HODGKINSON	NZL	Atlanta	27 Jul 1996
W18	1:57.18	WANG Yuan	CHN	Beijing	8 Sep 1993

1000 METRES

W, Eur	2:28.98	Svetlana MASTERKOVA	RUS	Bruxelles	23 Aug 1996
Afr	2:29.34	Maria Lurdes MUTOLA	MOZ	Bruxelles	25 Aug 1995
Com	2:29.66	Maria Lurdes MUTOLA	MOZ	Bruxelles	23 Aug 1996
NAm	2:31.80	Regina JACOBS	USA	Brunswick	3 Jul 1999
SAm	2:32.25	Letitia VRIESDE	SUR	Berlin	10 Sep 1991
CAC	2:33.21	Ana Fidelia QUIROT	CUB	Jerez de la Frontera	13 Sep 1989
Asi	2:33.6 §	Svetlana ULMASOVA	UZB	Podolsk	5 Aug 1979
Oce	2:37.84	Zoe BUCKMAN	AUS	Oslo	24 May 2012
W20	2:35.4a	Irina NIKITINA	RUS	Podolsk	5 Aug 1979
	2:35.4	Katrin WÜHN	GDR	Potsdam	12 Jul 1984
W18	2:38.58	Jo WHITE	GBR	London (CP)	9 Sep 1977

1500 METRES

W, Asi	3:50.46	QU Yunxia	CHN	Beijing	11 Sep 1993
Eur	3:52.47	Tatyana KAZANKINA	RUS	Zürich	13 Aug 1980
Afr	3:55.30	Hassiba BOULMERKA	ALG	Barcelona	8 Aug 1992
NAm	3:57.12	Mary DECKER/SLANEY	USA	Stockholm	26 Jul 1983
Com	3:57.41	Jackline MARANGA	KEN	Monaco	8 Aug 1998
Oce	4:00.93	Sarah JAMIESON	AUS	Stockholm	25 Jul 2006
CAC	4:01.84	Yvonne GRAHAM	JAM	Monaco	25 Jul 1995
SAm	4:05.67	Letitia VRIESDE	SUR	Tokyo	31 Aug 1991
W20	3:51.34	LANG Yinglai	CHN	Shanghai	18 Oct 1997
W18	3:54.52	ZHANG Ling	CHN	Shanghai	18 Oct 1997

1 MILE

W, Eur	4:12.56	Svetlana MASTERKOVA	RUS	Zürich	14 Aug 1996
NAm	4:16.71	Mary SLANEY	USA	Zürich	21 Aug 1985
Com	4:17.57	Zola BUDD	GBR/Eng	Zürich	21 Aug 1985
Asi	4:17.75	Maryam Yusuf JAMAL	BRN	Bruxelles	14 Sep 2007
Afr	4:18.23	Gelete BURKA	ETH	Rieti	7 Sep 2008
Oce	4:22.66	Lisa CORRIGAN	AUS	Melbourne	2 Mar 2007
CAC	4:24.64	Yvonne GRAHAM	JAM	Zürich	17 Aug 1994
SAm	4:30.05	Soraya TELLES	BRA	Praha	9 Jun 1988
W20	4:17.57	Zola BUDD	GBR	Zürich	21 Aug 1985
W18	4:30.81	Gelete BURKA	ETH	Heusden	2 Aug 2003

2000 METRES

W, Eur	5:25.36	Sonia O'SULLIVAN	IRL	Edinburgh	8 Jul 1994

Com	5:26.93	Yvonne MURRAY	GBR/Sco	Edinburgh	8 Jul 1994
Asi	5:29.43+§	WANG Junxia	CHN	Beijing	12 Sep 1993
NAm	5:32.7	Mary SLANEY	USA	Eugene	3 Aug 1984
Afr	5:30.19	Gelete BURKA	ETH	Bruxelles	4 Sep 2009
Oce	5:37.71	Benita JOHNSON	AUS	Ostrava	12 Jun 2003
W20	5:33.15	Zola BUDD	GBR	London (CP)	13 Jul 1984
W18	5:46.5+	Sally BARSOSIO	KEN	Zürich	16 Aug 1995

3000 METRES

W, Asi	8:06.11	WANG Junxia	CHN	Beijing	13 Sep 1993
Eur	8:21.42	Gabriela SZABO	ROM	Monaco	19 Jul 2002
Com	8:22.20	Paula RADCLIFFE	Eng	Monaco	19 Jul 2002
Afr	8:23.23	Edith MASAI	KEN	Monaco	19 Jul 2002
NAm	8:25.83	Mary SLANEY	USA	Roma	7 Sep 1985
Oce	8:35.31	Kimberley SMITH	NZL	Monaco	25 Jul 2007
CAC	8:37.07	Yvonne GRAHAM	JAM	Zürich	16 Aug 1995
SAm	9:02.37	Delirde BERNARDI	BRA	Linz	4 Jul 1994
W20	8:28.83	Zola BUDD	GBR	Roma	7 Sep 1985
W18	8:36.45	MA Ningning	CHN	Jinan	6 Jun 1993

5000 METRES

W, Afr	14:11.15	Tirunesh DIBABA	ETH	Oslo	6 Jun 2008
Com	14:20.87	Vivian CHERUIYOT	KEN	Stockho;lm	29 Jul 2011
Eur	14:23.75	Liliya SHOBUKHOVA	RUS	Kazan	19 Jul 2008
Asi	14:28.09	JIANG Bo	CHN	Shanghai	23 Oct 1997
NAm	14:44.76	Molly HUDDLE	USA	Bruxelles	27 Aug 2010
Oce	14:45.93	Kimberley SMITH	NZL	Roma	11 Jul 2008
CAC	15:04.32	Adriana FERNÁNDEZ	MEX	Gresham	17 May 2003
SAm	15:18.85	Simone Alves da SILVA	BRA	São Paulo	20 May 2011
W20	14:30.88	Tirunesh DIBABA	ETH	Bergen (Fana)	11 Jun 2004
W18	14:45.71	SONG Liqing	CHN	Shanghai	21 Oct 1997

10,000 METRES

W, Asi	29:31.78	WANG Junxia	CHN	Beijing	8 Sep 1993
Afr	29:53.80	Meselech MELKAMU	ETH	Utrecht	14 Jun 2009
Eur	29:56.34	Elvan ABEYLEGESSE	TUR	Beijing	15 Aug 2008
Com	30:01.09	Paula RADCLIFFE	GBR/Eng	München	6 Aug 2002
NAm	30:22.22	Shalane FLANAGAN	USA	Beijing	15 Aug 2008
Oce	30:35.54	Kimberley SMITH	NZL	Stanford	4 May 2008
CAC	31:10.12	Adriana FERNANDEZ	MEX	Brunswick	1 Jul 2000
SAm	31:47.76	Carmen de OLIVEIRA	BRA	Stuttgart	21 Aug 1993
W20	30:26.50	Linet MASAI	KEN	Beijing	15 Aug 2008
W18	31:11.26	SONG Liqing	CHN	Shanghai	19 Oct 1997

HALF MARATHON

W, Afr, Com	65:50	Mary KEITANY	KEN	Ra's Al Khaymah	18 Feb 2011
Eur	66:25	Lornah KIPLAGAT	NED	Udine	14 Oct 2007
Oce	67:11	Kimberley SMITH	NZL	Philadelphia	18 Sep 2011
Asi	67:26	Kayoko FUKUSHI	JPN	Marugame	5 Feb 2006
NAm	67:34	Deena KASTOR	USA	Berrlin	2 Apr 2006
CAC	68:34 dh	Olga APPELL	MEX	Tokyo	24 Jan 1993
	69:28	Adrian FERNÁNDEZ	MEX	Kyoto	9 Mar 2003
SAm	70:30	Yolanda CABALLERO	COL	New York	17 Mar 2013
W20	67:57	Abebu GELAN	ETH	Ra's Al Khaymah	20 Feb 2009
W18	72:31	LIU Zhuang	CHN	Yangzhou	24 Apr 2011

MARATHON

W, Eur, Com	2:15:25	Paula RADCLIFFE	GBR/Eng	London	13 Apr 2003
Afr	2:18:37	Mary KEITANY	KEN	London	22 Apr 2012
Asi	2:19:12	Mizuki NOGUCHI	JPN	Berlin	25 Sep 2005
NAm	2:19:36	Deena KASTOR	USA	London	23 Apr 2006
Oce	2:22:36	Benita JOHNSON	AUS	Chicago	22 Oct 2006
CAC	2:22:59	Madai PÉREZ	MEX	Chicago	22 Oct 2006
SAm	2:29:17	Adriana da SILVA	BRA	Tokyo	26 Feb 2012
W20	2:22:38	ZHANG Yingying	CHN	Xiamen	5 Jan 2008

3000 METRES STEEPLECHASE

W, Eur	8:58.81	Gulnara GALKINA	RUS	Beijing	17 Aug 2008
Afr, Com	9:07.14	Milcah CHEMOS Cheywa	KEN	Oslo	7 Jun 2012
NAm	9:12.50	Jennifer BARRINGER	USA	Berlin	17 Aug 2009
Oce	9:18.35	Donna MacFARLANE	AUS	Oslo	6 Jun 2008

Asi	9:26.25	LIU Nian	CHN	Wuhan	2 Nov 2007
CAC	9:27.21	Mardrea HYMAN	JAM	Monaco	9 Sep 2005
SAm	9:41.22	Sabine HEITLING	BRA	London	25 Jul 2009
W20	9:20.37	Birtukan ADAMU	ETH	Roma	26 May 2011
W18	9:29.52	Korahubish ITA'A	ETH	Huelva	10 Jun 2009

100 METRES HURDLES

W, Eur	12.21	Yordanka DONKOVA	BUL	Stara Zagora	20 Aug 1988
Oce, Com	12.28	Sally PEARSON	AUS	Daegu	3 Sep 2011
NAm	12.33	Gail DEVERS	USA	Sacramento	23 Jul 2000
Asi	12.44	Olga SHISHIGINA	KAZ	Luzern	27 Jun 1995
Afr	12.44	Glory ALOZIE	NGR	Monaco	8 Aug 1998
	12.44	Glory ALOZIE	NGR	Bruxelles	28 Aug 1998
	12.44	Glory ALOZIE	NGR	Sevilla	28 Aug 1999
CAC	12.45	Brigitte FOSTER	JAM	Eugene	24 May 2003
SAm	12.71	Maurren MAGGI	BRA	Manaus	19 May 2001
W20	12.84	Aliuska LÓPEZ	CUB	Zagreb	16 Jul 1987
W18	12.95	Candy YOUNG	USA	Walnut	16 Jun 1979

400 METRES HURDLES

Eur, W	52.34	Yuliya PECHONKINA	RUS	Tula	8 Aug 2003
CAC, Com	52.42	Melaine WALKER	JAM	Berlin	20 Aug 2009
NAm	52.47	Lashinda DEMUS	USA	Daegu	1 Sep 2011
Afr	52.90	Nezha BIDOUANE	MAR	Sevilla	25 Aug 1999
Oce	53.17	Debbie FLINTOFF-KING	AUS	Seoul	28 Sep 1988
Asi	53.96	HAN Qing	CHN	Beijing	9 Sep 1993
	53.96	SONG Yinglan	CHN	Guangzhou	22 Nov 2001
SAm	55.84	Lucimar TEODORO	BRA	Belém	24 May 2009
W20	54.40	WANG Xing	CHN	Nanjing	21 Oct 2005
W18	55.20	Leslie MAXIE	USA	San Jose	9 Jun 1984

HIGH JUMP

W, Eur	2.09	Stefka KOSTADINOVA	BUL	Roma	30 Aug 1987
Afr, Com	2.06	Hestrie CLOETE	RSA	Saint-Denis	31 Aug 2003
NAm	2.05	Chaunté HOWARD-LOWE	USA	Des Moines	26 Jun 2010
CAC	2.04	Silvia COSTA	CUB	Barcelona	9 Sep 1989
Oce	1 98	Vanessa WARD	AUS	Perth	12 Feb 1989
	1.98	Alison INVERARITY	AUS	Ingolstadt	17 Jul 1994
Asi	1.99	Marina AITOVA	KAZ	Athína	13 Jul 2009
SAm	1.96	Solange WITTEVEEN	ARG	Oristano	8 Sep 1997
W20	2.01	Olga TURCHAK	KAZ	Moskva	7 Jul 1986
	2.01	Heike BALCK	GDR	Chemnitz	18 Jun 1989
W18	1.96A	Charmaine GALE	RSA	Bloemfontein	4 Apr 1981
	1.96	Olga TURCHAK	UKR	Donetsk	7 Sep 1984

POLE VAULT

W, Eur	5.06	Yelena ISINBAYEVA	RUS	Zürich	28 Aug 2009
NAm	4.92	Jennifer STUCZYNSKI	USA	Eugene	6 Jul 2008
Com	4.87i	Holly BLEASDALE	GBR	Villeurbanne	20 Jan 2012
SAm	4.85	Fabiana MURER	BRA	San Fernando	4 Jun 2010
	4.85	Fabiana MURER	BRA	Daegu	30 Aug 2011
Oce, Com	4.76	Alana BOYD	AUS	Perth	24 Feb 2012
Asi	4.64	GAO Shuying	CHN	New York	2 Jun 2007
CAC	4.75A	Yarisley SLVA	CUB	Guadalajara	24 Oct 2011
	4.75	Yarisley SLVA	CUB	London (OS)	6 Aug 2012
Afr	4.42	Elmarie GERRYTS	RSA	Wesel	12 Jun 2000
W20	4.63i	Angelica BENGTSSON	SWE	Stockholm	25 Feb 2011
	4.58	Angelica BENGTSSON	SWE	Sollentuna	5 Jul 2012
W18	4.47	Angelica BENGTSSON	SWE	Moskva	22 May 2010

LONG JUMP

W, Eur	7.52	Galina CHISTYAKOVA	RUS	Sankt-Peterburg	11 Jun 1988
NAm	7.49	Jackie JOYNER-KERSEE	USA	New York	22 May 1994
	7.49A §	Jackie JOYNER-KERSEE	USA	Sestriere	31 Jul 1994
SAm	7.26A	Maurren MAGGI	BRA	Bogotá	26 Jun 1999
CAC, Com	7.16A	Elva GOULBOURNE	JAM	Ciudad de México	22 May 2004
Afr	7.12	Chioma AJUNWA	NGR	Atlanta	1 Aug 1996
Asi	7.01	YAO Weili	CHN	Jinan	5 Jun 1993
Oce	7.00	Bronwyn THOMPSON	AUS	Melbourne	7 Mar 2002
W20	7.14	Heike DAUTE/Drechsler	GDR	Bratislava	4 Jun 1983
W18	6.91	Heike DAUTE/Drechsler	GDR	Jena	9 Aug 1981

TRIPLE JUMP

W, Eur	15.50	Inessa KRAVETS	UKR	Göteborg	10 Aug 1995
Afr, Com	15.39	Françoise MBANGO ETONE	CMR	Beijing	17 Aug 2008
CAC	15.29	Yamilé ALDAMA	CUB	Roma	11 Jul 2003
Asi	15.25	Olga RYPAKOVA	KAZ	Split	4 Sep 2010
SAm	14.99A	Caterine IBARGÜEN	COL	Bogotá	13 Aug 2011
NAm	14.45	Tiombé HURD	USA	Sacramento	11 Jul 2004
Oce	14.04	Nicole MLADENIS	AUS	Hobart	9 Mar 2002
	14.04	Nicole MLADENIS	AUS	Perth	7 Dec 2003
W20	14.62	Tereza MARINOVA	BUL	Sydney	25 Aug 1996
W18	14.57	HUANG Qiuyan	CHN	Shanghai	19 Oct 1997

SHOT

W, Eur	22.63	Natalya LISOVSKAYA	RUS	Moskva	7 Jun 1987
Asi	21.76	LI Meisu	CHN	Shijiazhuang	23 Apr 1988
Oce, Com	21.24	Valerie ADAMS	NZL	Daegu	29 Aug 2011
CAC	20.96	Belsy LAZA	CUB	Ciudad de México	2 May 1992
NAm	20.18	Ramona PAGEL	USA	San Diego	25 Jun 1988
	20.18	Jill CAMARENA-WILLIAMS	USA	Saint-Denis	8 Jul 2011
SAm	19.30	Elisângela ADRIANO	BRA	Tunja	14 Jul 2001
Afr	18.35	Vivian CHUKWUEMEKA	NGR	Ijebu Ode	17 Apr 2006
	18.43 §	Vivian CHUKWUEMEKA	NGR	Walnut	19 Apr 2003
W20	20.54	Astrid KUMBERNUSS	GDR	Orimattila	1 Jul 1989
W18	19.08	Ilke WYLUDDA	GDR	Karl-Marx-Stadt	9 Aug 1986

DISCUS

W, Eur	76.80	Gabriele REINSCH	GDR	Neubrandenburg	9 Jul 1988
Asi	71.68	XIAO Yanling	CHN	Beijing	14 Mar 1992
CAC	70.88	Hilda RAMOS	CUB	La Habana	8 May 1992
Oce, Com	68.72	Daniela COSTIAN	AUS	Auckland	22 Jan 1994
NAm	67.74	Stephanie TRAFTON-BROWN	USA	Wailuku	4 May 2012
Afr	64.87	Elizna NAUDE	RSA	Stellenbosch	2 Mar 2007
SAm	64.21	Andressa de MORAIS	BRA	Barquisimeto	10 Jun 2012
W20	74.40	Ilke WYLUDDA	GDR	Berlin	13 Sep 1988
W18	65.86	Ilke WYLUDDA	GDR	Neubrandenburg	1 Aug 1986

HAMMER

W, Eur	79.42	Betty HEIDLER	GER	Halle	21 May 2011
CAC	76.62	Yipsi MORENO	CUB	Zagreb	9 Sep 2008
Asi	76.99	ZHANG Wenxiu	CHN	Ostrava	24 May 2012
NAm, Com	75.04	Sultana FRIZELL	CAN	Tucson	16 May 2012
SAm	73.74	Jennifer DAHLGREN	ARG	Buenos Aires	10 Apr 2010
Oce	71.12	Bronwyn EAGLES	AUS	Adelaide	6 Feb 2003
Afr	69.10	Amy SÈNE	SEN	Angers	17 Jun 2012
W20	73.24	ZHANG Wenxiu	CHN	Changsha	24 Jun 2005
W18	70.60	ZHANG Wenxiu	CHN	Nanning	5 Apr 2003

JAVELIN

W, Eur	72.28	Barbora SPOTÁKOVÁ	CZE	Stuttgart	13 Sep 2008
CAC	71.70	Osleidys MENÉNDEZ	CUB	Helsinki	14 Aug 2005
Afr, Com	69.35	Sunette VILJOEN	RSA	New York	9 Jun 2012
Oce	66.80	Louise CURREY	AUS	Gold Coast	5 Aug 2000
NAm	66.67	Kara PATTERSON	USA	Des Moines	25 Jun 2010
Asi	65.11	LI Lingwei	CHN	Fuzhou	23 Jun 2012
SAm	62.62A	Sabina MOYA	COL	Ciudad de Guatemala	12 May 2002
W20	63.01	Vira REBRYK	UKR	Bydgoszcz	10 Jul 2008
W18	62.93	XUE Juan	CHN	Changsha	27 Oct 2003

HEPTATHLON

W, NAm	7291	Jackie JOYNER-KERSEE	USA	Seoul	24 Sep 1988
Eur	7032	Carolina KLÜFT	RUS	Osaka	26 Aug 2007
Com	6955	Jeccica ENNIS	GBR/Eng	London (OS)	4 Aug 2012
Asi	6942	Ghada SHOUAA	SYR	Götzis	26 May 1996
Oce	6695	Jane FLEMMING	AUS	Auckland	28 Jan 1990
CAC	6527	Diane GUTHRIE-GRESHAM	JAM	Knoxville	3 Jun 1995
Afr	6423	Margaret SIMPSON	GHA	Götzis	29 May 2005
SAm	6160	Lucimara DA SILVA	BRA	Barquisimeto	10 Jun 2012
W20	6542	Carolina KLÜFT	SWE	München	10 Aug 2002
W18	6185	SHEN Shengfei	CHN	Shanghai	18 Oct 1997

DECATHLON

W, Eur	8358	Austra SKUJYTE	LTU	Columbia, MO	15 Apr 2005
Asi	7798 §	Irina NAUMENKO	KAZ	Talence	26 Sep 2004
NAm	7577 §	Tiffany LOTT-HOGAN	USA	Lage	10 Sep 2000
CAC	7245 §	Magalys GARCÍA	CUB	Wien	29 Jun 2002
Afr, Com	6915	Margaret SIMPSON	GHA	Réduit	19 Apr 2007
SAm	6570	Andrea BORDALEJO	ARG	Rosario	28 Nov 2004
Oce	5740	Preya CAREY	AUS	Brisbane	6 Sep 2001

4 X 100 METRES RELAY

W, NAm	40.82	USA (Madison, Felix, Knight, Jeter)	London (OS)	10 Aug 2012
Eur	41.37	GDR (Gladisch, Rieger, Auerswald, Göhr)	Canberra	6 Oct 1985
CAC, Com	41.41	JAM (Fraser-Pryce, Simpson, Campbell-Brown, Stewart)	London (OS)	10 Aug 2012
Asi	42.23	Sichuan CHN (Xiao Lin, Li Yali, Liu Xiaomei, Li Xuemei)	Shanghai	23 Oct 1997
Afr	42.39	NGR (Utondu, Idehen, Opara-Thompson, Onyali)	Barcelona	7 Aug 1992
SAm	42.55	BRA (A C Silva, Krasucki, E dos Santos, R Santos)	London (OS)	10 Aug 2012
Oce	42.99A	AUS (Massey, Broadrick, Lambert, Gainsford-Taylor)	Pietersburg	18 Mar 2000
W20	43.29	USA (Knight, Tarmoh, Olear, Mayo)	Eugene	8 Aug 2006
W18	44.05	GDR (Koppetsch, Oelsner, Sinzel, Brehmer)	Athína	24 Aug 1975

4 X 400 METRES RELAY

W, Eur	3:15.17	URS (Ledovskaya, Nazarova, Pinigina, Bryzgina)	Seoul	1 Oct 1988
NAm	3:15.51	USA (D.Howard, Dixon, Brisco, Griffith Joyner)	Seoul	1 Oct 1988
CAC, Com	3:18.71	JAM (Whyte, Prendergast, N Williams-Mills, S Williams)	Daegu	3 Sep 2011
Afr	3:21.04	NGR (Bisi Afolabi, Yusuf, Opara, Ogunkoya)	Atlanta	3 Aug 1996
Oce	3:23.81	AUS (Peris, Lewis, Gainsford-Taylor, Freeman)	Sydney	30 Sep 2000
Asi	3:24.28	CHN / Hebei (An X, Bai X, Cao C, Ma Y)	Beijing	13 Sep 1993
SAm	3:26.68	BRA (Coutinho, de Oliveira, Souza, de Lima)	Helsinki	13 Aug 2005
W20	3:27.60	USA (Anderson, Kidd, Smith, Hastings)	Grosseto	18 Jul 2004
W18	3:36.98	GBR (Ravenscroft, E McMeekin, Kennedy, Pettett)	Duisburg	26 Aug 1973

10 KILOMETRES WALK

W, Eur	41:04	Yelena NIKOLAYEVA	RUS	Sochi	20 Apr 1996
Asi	41:16	WANG Yan	CHN	Eisenhüttenstadt	8 May 1999
Oce, Com	41:30	Kerry SAXBY-JUNNA	AUS	Canberra	27 Aug 1988
CAC	42:42	Graciela MENDOZA	MEX	Naumburg	25 May 1997
NAm	44:17	Michelle ROHL	USA	Göteborg	7 Aug 1995
SAm	45:03	Geovanna IRUSTA	BOL	Podebrady	19 Apr 1997
Afr	45:06A	Susan VERMEULEN	RSA	Bloemfontein	17 Apr 1999
W20	41:52 §	Tatyana MINEYEVA	RUS	Penza	5 Sep 2009
	41:57 §	GAO Hongmiao	CHN	Beijing	8 Sep 1993
W18	43:28	Aleksandra KUDRYASHOVA	RUS	Adler	19 Feb 2006

10,000 METRES TRACK WALK

W, Asi	41:37.9 §	GAO Hongmiao	CHN	Beijing	7 Apr 1994
W, Eur	41:56.23	Nadyezhda RYASHKINA	RUS	Seattle	24 Jul 1990
Oce, Com	41:57.22	Kerry SAXBY-JUNNA	AUS	Seattle	24 Jul 1990
NAm	44:30.1 m	Alison BAKER	CAN	Bergen (Fana)	15 May 1992
	44:06 no kerb	Michelle ROHL	USA	Kenosha	2 Jun 1996
CAC	44:16.21	Cristina LÓPEZ	ESA	San Salvador	13 Jul 2007
SAm	45:11.2A	Lorena ARENAS	COL	Medellín	15 Apr 2012
Afr	47:30.28	Chahinez AL-NASRI	TUN	Amman	16 May 2012
W20	42:49.7 §	GAO Hongmiao	CHN	Jinan	15 Mar 1992
	42:59.48	Yelena LASHMANOVA	RUS	Tallinn	21 Jul 2011
W18	42:56.09	GAO Hongmiao	CHN	Tangshan	27 Sep 1991

20,000 METRES TRACK WALK

W, Eur	1:26:52.3	Olimpiada IVANOVA	RUS	Brisbane	6 Sep 2001
Asi, W20	1:29:32.4 §	SONG Hongjuan	CHN	Changsha	24 Oct 2003
SAm	1:32:09.4	Ingrid HERNÁNDEZ	COL	Buenos Aires	5 Jun 2011
NAm	1:33:28.2	Teresa VAILL	USA	Carson	25 Jun 2005
Oce,Com	1:33:40.2	Kerry SAXBY-JUNNA	AUS	Brisbane	6 Sep 2001
CAC	1:34:56.7A	Maria del Rosario SÁNCHEZ	MEX	Xalapa	16 Jul 2000
Afr	1:36:43.43A	Nicolene CRONJE	RSA	Germiston	20 Mar 2004
W18	1:37:33.9	GAO Kelian	CHN	Xian	18 Sep 1999

20 KILOMETRES WALK

W, Eur	1:24:50 §	Olimpiada IVANOVA	RUS	Adler	4 Mar 2001
	1:25:02	Yeoena LASHMANOVA	RUS	London	11 Aug 2012
Asi	1:25:16	QIEYANG Shenjie	CHN	London	11 Aug 2012

Oce, Com	1:27:44		Jane SAVILLE	AUS	Naumburg	2 May 2004
CAC	1:28:54		Mima ORTIZ	GUA	Lugano	18 Mar 2012
SAm	1:31:25		Miriam RAMÓN	ECU	Lima	7 May 2005
NAm	1:31:51		Michelle ROHL	USA	Kenosha	13 May 2000
Afr	1:34:19	§	Grace WANJIRU-NJUE	KEN	Nairobi	1 Aug 2010
W20	1:25:30		Anisya KIRDYAPKINA	RUS	Adler	23 Feb 2008
W18	1:30:52		JIANG Kun	CHN	Dandong	13 Apr 2001

World Records at other track & field events recognised by the IAAF

1 Hour	18,517 m	Dire TUNE	ETH	Ostrava	12 Jun 2008
20,000m	1:05:26.6	Tegla LOROUPE	KEN	Borgholzhausen	3 Sep 2000
25,000m	1:27:05.84	Tegla LOROUPE	KEN	Mengerskirchen	21 Sep 2002
30,000m	1:45:50.0	Tegla LOROUPE	KEN	Warstein	6 Jun 2003
4x200m	1:27.46	USA (L Jenkins, L Colander, N Perry, M Jones)		Philadelphia	29 Apr 2000
4x800m	7:50.17	USSR (Olizarenko, Gurina, Borisova, Podyalovskaya)		Moskva	5 Aug 1984

WORLD BESTS AT NON-STANDARD EVENTS

Men

50m	5.47+e	Usain Bolt	JAM	Berlin (in 100m)	16 Aug 2009
60m	6.31+	Usain Bolt	JAM	Berlin (in 100m)	16 Aug 2009
100 yards	9.07	Asafa Powell	JAM	Ostrava	27 May 2010
150m turn	14.44+	Usain Bolt	JAM	Berlin (in 200m)	20 Aug 2009
150m straight	14.35	Usain Bolt	JAM	Manchester	17 May 2009
300m	30.85A	Michael Johnson	USA	Pretoria	24 Mar 2000
	30.97	Usain Bolt	JAM	Ostrava	27 May 2010
500m	59.32	Orestes Rodríguez	CUB	La Habana	15 Feb 2013
600m	1:12.81	Johnny Gray	USA	Santa Monica	24 May 1986
2 miles	7:58.61	Daniel Komen	KEN	Hechtel	19 Jul 1997
2000m Steeple	5:10.68	Mahiedine Mekhissi	FRA	Reims	30 Jun 2010
200mh	22.55	Laurent Ottoz	ITA	Milano	31 May 1995
(hand time)	22.5	Martin Lauer	FRG	Zürich	7 Jul 1959
200mh straight	22.10	Andrew Turner	GBR	Manchester	15 May 2011
220yh straight	21.9	Don Styron	USA	Baton Rouge	2 Apr 1960
300mh	34.48	Chris Rawlinson	GBR	Sheffield	30 Jun 2002
35lb weight	25.41	Lance Deal	USA	Azusa	20 Feb 1993
Pentathlon	4282 points	Bill Toomey	USA	London (CP)	16 Aug 1969
(1985 tables)		(7.58, 66.18, 21.3, 44.52, 4:20.3)			
Double decathlon	14,571 points	Joe Detmer	USA	Lynchburg	24/25 Sep 2010

10.93w, 7.30, 200mh 24.25w, 12.27, 5k 18:25.32, 2:02.23, 1.98, 400m 50.43, HT 31.82, 3kSt 11:22.47
15.01, DT 40.73, 200m 22.58, 4.85, 3k 10:25.99, 400mh 53.83, 51.95, 4:26.66, TJ 13.67, 10k 40:27.26

3000m track walk	10:47.11	Giovanni De Benedictis	ITA	San Giovanni Valdarno	19 May 1990
5000m track walk	18:05.49	Hatem Ghoula	TUN	Tunis	1 May 1997
10,000m track walk	37:53.09	Francisco Javier Fernández	ESP	Santa Cruz de Tenerife	27 Jul 2008
10 km road walk	37:11	Roman Rasskazov	RUS	Saransk	28 May 2000
30 km road walk	2:01:13+	Vladimir Kanaykin	RUS	Adler	19 Feb 2006
35 km road walk	2:21:31	Vladimir Kanaykin	RUS	Adler	19 Feb 2006
100 km road walk	8:38:07	Viktor Ginko	BLR	Scanzorosciate	27 Oct 2002

Women

50m	5.93+	Marion Jones	USA	Sevilla (in 100m)	22 Aug 1999
60m	6.85+	Marion Jones	USA	Sevilla (in 100m)	22 Aug 1999
100 yards	9.91	Veronica-Campbell-Brown	JAM	Ostrava	31 May 2011
150m	16.10+	Florence Griffith-Joyner	USA	Seoul (in 200m)	29 Sep 1988
300m	34.1+	Marita Koch	GDR	Canberra (in 400m)	6 Oct 1985
500m	1:05.9	Tatána Kocembová	CZE	Ostrava	2 Aug 1984
600m	1:22.63	Ana Fidelia Quirot	CUB	Guadalajara, ESP	25 Jul 1997
2 miles	8:58.58	Meseret Defar	ETH	Bruxelles	14 Sep 2007
2000m Steeple	6:03.38	Wioletta Janowska	POL	Gdansk	15 Jul 2006
200mh	25.6	Patricia Girard	FRA	Nantes	23 Aug 2001
	25.82	Patricia Girard	FRA	Nantes	22 Sep 1999
300mh	38.91	Zuzana Hejnová	CZE	Pardubice	13 Aug 2011
	38.6	Mame Tacko Diouf	SEN	Dakar	21 Feb 1999
4 x 1500m	17:08.34	Tennesse University	USA	Philadelphia	24 Apr 2009
		(Price, Wright, Bell, Bowman)			
Double heptathlon	10,798 pts	Milla Kelo	FIN	Turku	7/8 Sep 2002

100mh 14.89, HJ 1.51, 1500m 5:03.74, 400mh 62.18, SP 12.73, 200m 25.16, 100m 12.59
LJ 5.73w, 400m 56.10, JT 32.69, 800m 2:23.94, 200mh 28.72, DT 47.86, 3000m 11:48.68

3000m track walk	11:48.24	Ileana Salvador	ITA	Padova	29 Aug 1993
5000m track walk	20:02.60	Gillian O'Sullivan	IRL	Dublin	13 Jul 2002
50 km road walk	4:10:59	Monica Svensson	SWE	Scanzorosciate	21 Oct 2007
100km road walk	10:04:50	Jolanta Dukure	LAT	Scanzorosciate	21 Oct 2007

LONG DISTANCE WORLD BESTS – MEN TRACK

	hr:min:sec	Name	Nat	Venue	Date
15,000m	0:42:18.7+	Haile Gebrselassie	ETH	Ostrava	27 Jun 2007
10 miles	0:45:23.8+	Haile Gebrselassie	ETH	Ostrava	27 Jun 2007
15 miles	1:11:43.1	Bill Rodgers	USA	Saratoga, Cal.	21 Feb 1979
20 miles	1:39:14.4	Jack Foster	NZL	Hamilton, NZ	15 Aug 1971
30 miles	2:42:00+	Jeff Norman	GBR	Timperley, Cheshire	7 Jun 1980
50 km	2:48:06	Jeff Norman	GBR	Timperley, Cheshire	7 Jun 1980
40 miles	3:48:35	Don Ritchie	GBR	London (Hendon)	16 Oct 1982
50 miles	4:51:49	Don Ritchie	GBR	London (Hendon)	12 Mar 1983
100 km	6:10:20	Don Ritchie	GBR	London (CP)	28 Oct 1978
150 km	10:34:30	Denis Zhalybin	RUS	London (CP)	20 Oct 2002
100 miles	11:28:03	Oleg Kharitonov	RUS	London (CP)	20 Oct 2002
200 km	15:10:27+	Yiannis Kouros	AUS	Adelaide	4-5 Oct 1997
200 miles	27:48:35	Yiannis Kouros	GRE	Montauban	15-16 Mar 1985
500 km	60:23.00+ ??	Yiannis Kouros	GRE	Colac, Aus	26-29 Nov 1984
500 miles	105:42:09+	Yiannis Kouros	GRE	Colac, Aus	26-30 Nov 1984
1000 km	136:17:00	Yiannis Kouros	GRE	Colac, Aus	26-31 Nov 1984
1500 km	10d 17:28:26	Petrus Silkinas	LTU	Nanango, Qld	11-21 Mar 1998
1000 mile	11d 13:54:58+	Petrus Silkinas	LTU	Nanango, Qld	11-22 Mar 1998
2 hrs	37.994 km	Jim Alder	GBR	Walton-on-Thames	17 Oct 1964
12 hrs	162.400 km +	Yiannis Kouros	GRE	Montauban	15 Mar 1985
24 hrs	303.506 km	Yiannis Kouros	AUS	Adelaide	4-5 Oct 1997
48 hrs	473.797 km	Yiannis Kouros	AUS	Surgères	3-5 May 1996
6 days	1036.8 km	Yiannis Kouros	GRE	Colac, Aus	20-26 Nov 2005

LONG DISTANCE ROAD RECORDS & BESTS – MEN

Where superior to track bests (over 10km) and run on properly measured road courses. (I) IAAF recognition.

		Name	Nat	Venue	Date
10 km (I)	0:26:44	Leonard Patrick Komon	KEN	Utrecht	26 Sep 2010
15 km (I)	0:41:13	Leonard Patrick Komon	KEN	Nijmegen	21 Nov 2010
10 miles	0:44:24 §	Haile Gebrselassie	ETH	Tilburg	4 Sep 2005
	0:44:45	Paul Koech	KEN	Amsterdam-Zaandam	21 Sep 1997
20 km (I)	0:55:21+	Zersenay Tadese	ERI	Lisboa	21 Mar 2010
25 km (I)	1:11:18	Dennis Kimetto	KEN	Berlin	6 May 2012
30 km (I)	1:27:38	Patrick Makau	KEN	Berlin	25 Sep 2011
	1:27:37 §	Peter Kirui	KEN	Berlin (dnf Mar)	25 Sep 2011
20 miles	1:35:22+	Steve Jones	GBR	Chicago	10 Oct 1985
30 miles	2:37:31+	Thompson Magawana	RSA	Claremont-Kirstenbosch	12 Apr 1988
50km	2:43:38+	Thompson Magawana	RSA	Claremont-Kirstenbosch	12 Apr 1988
40 miles	3:45:39	Andy Jones	CAN	Houston	23 Feb 1991
50 miles	4:50:21	Bruce Fordyce	RSA	London-Brighton	25 Sep 1983
100 km (I)	6:13:33	Takahiro Sunada	JPN	Yubetsu	21 Jun 1998
1000 miles	10d:10:30:35	Yiannis Kouros	GRE	New York	21-30 May 1988
Ekiden (6) (I)	1:57:06 #	Kenya	KEN	Chiba	23 Nov 2005
5 stages	1:55:59	Ethiopia	ETH	Chiba	24 Nov 2003
10k Dejene Birhanu, 5k Hailu Mekonnen, 10k Gebr. Gebremariam, 5k Markos Geneti, 12.195k Sileshi Sihine					
12 hrs	162.543 km	Yiannis Kouros	GRE	Queen's, New York	7 Nov 1984

LONG DISTANCE WORLD BESTS – WOMEN TRACK

		Name	Nat	Venue	Date
15 km	0:48:54.91+	Dire Tune	ETH	Ostrava	12 Jun 2008
10 miles	0:54:21.8	Lorraine Moller	NZL	Auckland	9 Jan 1993
20 miles	1:59:09 !	Chantal Langlacé	FRA	Amiens	3 Sep 1983
30 miles	3:12:25+	Carolyn Hunter-Rowe	GBR	Barry, Wales	3 Mar 1996
50 km	3:18:52+	Carolyn Hunter-Rowe	GBR	Barry, Wales	3 Mar 1996
40 miles	4:26:43	Carolyn Hunter-Rowe	GBR	Barry, Wales	7 Mar 1993
50 miles	5:48:12.0+	Norimi Sakurai	JPN	San Giovanni Lupatoto	27 Sep 2003
100 km	7:14:05.8	Norimi Sakurai	JPN	San Giovanni Lupatoto	27 Sep 2003
150 km	13:45:54	Hilary Walker	GBR	Blackpool	5-6 Nov 1988
100 miles	13:52.02+	Mami Kudo	JPN	Soochow	10-11 Dec 2011
200 km	17:52.18+	Mami Kudo	JPN	Soochow	10-11 Dec 2011
200 miles	39:09:03	Hilary Walker	GBR	Blackpool	5-7 Nov 1988
500 km	77:53:46	Eleanor Adams	GBR	Colac, Aus.	13-16 Nov 1989
500 miles	130:59:58+	Sandra Barwick	NZL	Campbelltown, AUS	18-23 Nov 1990
1000 km	8d 00:27:06+	Eleanor Robinson	GBR	Nanango, Qld	11-19 Mar 1998
1500 km	12d 06:52:12+	Eleanor Robinson	GBR	Nanango, Qld	11-23 Mar 1998
1000 miles	13d 02:16:49	Eleanor Robinson	GBR	Nanango, Qld	11-24 Mar 1998
2 hrs	32.652 km	Chantal Langlacé	FRA	Amiens	3 Sep 1983
12 hrs	147.600 km	Ann Trason	USA	Hayward, Cal	3-4 Aug 1991
24 hours	255.303 km	Mami Kudo	JPN	Soochow	10-11 Dec 2011
48 hrs	385.130 km	Mami Kudo	JPN	Surgères	22-24 May 2010

| 6 days | 883.631 km | Sandra Barwick | NZL | Campbelltown, AUS | 18-24 Nov 1990 |

! Timed on one running watch only

LONG DISTANCE ROAD RECORDS & BESTS - WOMEN

	hr:min:sec	Name	Nat	Venue	Date
10 km (I)	0:30:21	Paula Radcliffe	GBR	San Juan	23 Feb 2003
15 km (I)	46:28	Tirunesh Dibaba	ETH	Nijmegen	15 Nov 2009
10 miles	0:50:05+	Mary Keitany	KEN	Ra's Al-Khaymah	18 Feb 2011
	0:50:01+ dh	Paula Radcliffe	GBR	Newcastle	21 Sep 2003
20 km (I)	1:02:36+	Mary Keitany	KEN	Ra's Al-Khaymah	18 Feb 2011
	1:02:21+ dh	Paula Radcliffe	GBR	Newcastle	21 Sep 2003
Half mar (I) qv +	1:05:50	Mary Keitany	KEN	Ra's Al-Khaymah	18 Feb 2011
	1:05:40 dh	Paula Radcliffe	GBR	South Shields	21 Sep 2003
25 km (I)	1:19:53	Mary Keitany	KEN	Berlin	9 May 2010
30 km (I)	1:38:23+ §	Liliya Shobukhova	RUS	Chicago	9 Oct 2011
	1:36:36+ dh	Paula Radcliffe	GBR	London	13 Apr 2003
20 miles	1:43:33+	Paula Radcliffe	GBR	London	13 Apr 2003
30 miles	3:01:16+	Frith van der Merwe	RSA	Claremont-Kirstenbosch	25 Mar 1989
50 km	3:08:39	Frith van der Merwe	RSA	Claremont-Kirstenbosch	25 Mar 1989
40 miles	4:26:13+	Ann Trason	USA	Houston	23 Feb 1991
50 miles	5:40:18	Ann Trason	USA	Houston	23 Feb 1991
100 km (I)	6:33:11	Tomoe Abe	JPN	Yubetsu	25 Jun 2000
100 miles	13:47:41	Ann Trason	USA	Queen's, New York	4 May 1991
200 km	19:00:31	Eleanor Adams	GBR	Milton Keynes (indoor)	3-4 Feb 1990
1000 km	7d 01:11:00+	Sandra Barwick	NZL	New York	16-23 Sep 1991
1000 miles	12d 14:38:40	Sandra Barwick	NZL	New York	16-29 Sep 1991
Ekiden (6 stages)	2:11:22	(I)	ETH	Chiba	24 Nov 2003

Berhane Adere, Tirunesh Dibaba, Eyerusalem Kuma, Ejegayou Dibaba, Meseret Defar, Werknesh Kidane

| 12 hours | 144.840 km | Ann Trason | USA | Queen's, New York | 4 May 1991 |
| 24 hours | 247.076 km | Lizzie Hawker | GBR | Llandudno | 23-24 Sep 2011 |

100 KILOMETRES CONTINENTAL RECORDS

Men

W, Asi	6:13:33	Takahiro SUNADA	JPN	Yubetsu	21 Jun 1998
Eur	6:16:41	Jean-Paul PRAET	BEL	Torhout	24 Jun 1989
SAm	6:18:09	Valmir NUNES	BRA	Winschoten	16 Sep 1995
Afr	6:25:07	Bruce FORDYCE	RSA	Stellenbosch	4 Feb 1989
Oce	6:29:23	Tim SLOAN	AUS	Ross-Richmond	23 Apr 1995
NAm	6:30:11	Tom JOHNSON	USA	Winschoten	16 Sep 1995

Women

W, Asi	6:33:11	Tomoe ABE	JPN	Yubetsu	25 Jun 2000
NAm	7:00:48	Ann TRASON	USA	Winschoten	16 Sep 1995
Eur	7:10:32	Tatyana ZHYRKOVA	RUS	Winschoten	11 Sep 2004
SAm	7:20:22	Maria VENÂNCIO	BRA	Cubatão	8 Aug 1998
Afr	7:31:47	Helena JOUBERT	RSA	Winschoten	16 Sep 1995
Oce	7:40:58	Linda MEADOWS	AUS	North Otago	18 Nov 1995

WORLD INDOOR RECORDS

Men
to March 2012

50 metres	5.56A	Donovan Bailey	CAN	Reno	9 Feb 1996
60 metres	6.39	Maurice Greene	USA	Madrid	3 Feb 1998
	6.39	Maurice Greene	USA	Atlanta	3 Mar 2001
200 metres	19.92	Frank Fredericks	NAM	Liévin	18 Feb 1996
400 metres	44.57	Kerron Clement	USA	Fayetteville	12 Mar 2005
800 metres	1:42.67	Wilson Kipketer	KEN	Paris (Bercy)	9 Mar 1997
1000 metres	2:14.96	Wilson Kipketer	KEN	Birmingham	20 Feb 2000
1500 metres	3:31.18	Hicham El Guerrouj	MAR	Stuttgart	2 Feb 1997
1 mile	3:48.45	Hicham El Guerrouj	MAR	Gent	12 Feb 1997
2000 metres #	4:49.99	Kenenisa Bekele	ETH	Birmingham	17 Feb 2007
3000 metres	7:24.90	Daniel Komen	KEN	Budapest	6 Feb 1998
2 miles #	8:04.35	Kenenisa Bekele	ETH	Birmingham	16 Feb 2008
5000 metres	12:49.60	Kenenisa Bekele	ETH	Birmingham	20 Feb 2004
10000 metres #	27:50.29	Mark Bett	KEN	Gent	10 Feb 2002
50 m hurdles	6.25	Mark McKoy	CAN	Kobe	5 Mar 1986
60 m hurdles	7.30	Colin Jackson	GBR	Sindelfingen	6 Mar 1994
High jump	2.43	Javier Sotomayor	CUB	Budapest	4 Mar 1989
Pole vault	6.15	Sergey Bubka	UKR	Donetsk	21 Feb 1993
Long jump	8.79	Carl Lewis	USA	New York	27 Jan 1984
Triple jump	17.92	Teddy Tamgho	FRA	Paris (Bercy)	6 Mar 2011

Event	Mark	Name	Nat	Place	Date
Shot	22.66	Randy Barnes	USA	Los Angeles	20 Jan 1989
Javelin #	85.78	Matti Närhi	FIN	Kajaani	3 Mar 1996
35 lb weight #	25.86	Lance Deal	USA	Atlanta	4 Mar 1995
3000m walk #	10:31.42	Andreas Erm	GER	Halle	4 Feb 2001
5000m walk	18:07.08	Mikhail Shchennikov	RUS	Moskva	14 Feb 1995
10000m walk #	38:31.4	Werner Heyer	GDR	Berlin	12 Jan 1980
4 x 200m	1:22.11	United Kingdom		Glasgow	3 Mar 1991

(Linford Christie, Darren Braithwaite, Ade Mafe, John Regis)

| 4 x 400m | 3:01.96 | USA (not ratified – no EPO analysis) | | Fayetteville | 11 Feb 2006 |

(Kerron Clement, Wallace Spearmon, Darold Williamson, Jeremy Wariner)

| 4 x 800m | 7:13.94 | USA/Global Athletics & Marketing | | Boston (Roxbury) | 6 Feb 2000 |

(Joey Woody, Karl Paranya, Rich Kenah, David Krummenacker)

| Heptathlon | 6645 points | Ashton Eaton | USA | Istanbul | 9/10 Mar 2012 |

(6.79 60m, 8.16 LJ, 14.56 SP, 2.03 HJ, 7.68 60mh, 5.20 PV, 2:32.77 1000m)

Women

Event	Mark	Name	Nat	Place	Date
50 metres	5.96+	Irina Privalova	RUS	Madrid	9 Feb 1995
60 metres	6.92	Irina Privalova	RUS	Madrid	11 Feb 1993 & 9 Feb 1995
200 metres	21.87	Merlene Ottey	JAM	Liévin	13 Feb 1993
400 metres	49.59	Jarmila Kratochvílová	CZE	Milano	7 Mar 1982
800 metres	1:55.82	Jolanda Ceplak	SLO	Wien	3 Mar 2002
1000 metres	2:30.94	Maria Lurdes Mutola	MOZ	Stockholm	25 Feb 1999
1500 metres	3:58.28	Yelena Soboleva	RUS	Moskva	18 Feb 2006
1 mile	4:17.14	Doina Melinte	ROM	East Rutherford	9 Feb 1990
2000 metres #	5:30.53	Gabriela Szabo	ROM	Sindelfingen	8 Mar 1998
3000 metres	8:23.72	Meseret Defar	ETH	Stuttgart	3 Feb 2007
2 miles #	9:06.26	Meseret Defar	ETH	Praha	26 Feb 2009
5000 metres	14:24.37	Meseret Defar	ETH	Stockholm	18 Feb 2009
50 m hurdles	6.58	Cornelia Oschkenat	GDR	Berlin	20 Feb 1988
60 m hurdles	7.68	Susanna Kallur	SWE	Karlsruhe	10 Feb 2008
High jump	2.08	Kajsa Bergqvist	SWE	Arnstadt	4 Feb 2006
Pole vault	5.02A	Jenn Suhr	USA	Albuquerque	2 Mar 2013
Long jump	7.37	Heike Drechsler	GDR	Wien	13 Feb 1988
Triple jump	15.36	Tatyana Lebedeva	RUS	Budapest	5 Mar 2004
Shot	22.50	Helena Fibingerová	CZE	Jablonec	19 Feb 1977
Javelin #	61.29	Taina Uppa/Kolkkala	FIN	Mustasaari	28 Feb 1999
20 lb weight #	25.56	Brittany Riley	USA	Fayetteville	10 Mar 2007
3000m walk	11:35.34 un	Gillian O'Sullivan	IRL	Belfast	15 Feb 2003
	11:40.33	Claudia Iovan/Stef	ROM	Bucuresti	30 Jan 1999
5000m walk #	20:37.77	Margarita Turova	BLR	Minsk	13 Feb 2005
10000m walk	43:54.63	Yelena Ginko	BLR	Mogilyov	22 Feb 2008
4 x 200m	1:32.41	Russia		Glasgow	29 Jan 2005

(Yekaterina Kondratyeva, Irina Khabarova, Yuliya Pechonkina, Yuliya Gushchina)

| 4 x 400m | 3:23.37 | Russia | | Glasgow | 28 Jan 2006 |

(Yuliya Gushchina, Olga Kotlyarova, Olga Zaytseva, Olesya Krasnomovets)

| 4 x 800m | 8:06.24 | Moskva | RUS | Moskva | 18 Feb 2011 |

(Aleksandra Bulanova, Yekaterina Martynova, Yelena Kofanova , Anna Balakshina)

| Pentathlon | 5013 points | Nataliya Dobrynska | UKR | Istanbul | 9 Mar 2012 |

(8.38 60mh, 1.84 HJ, 16.51 SP, 6.57 LJ, 2:11.15 800m)

events not officially recognised by the IAAF

WORLD INDOOR JUNIOR (U20) RECORDS

As approved by IAAF Council in 2011 and updated with 2012 marks. **Men**

Event	Mark	Name	Nat	Place	Date
60 metres	6.51	Mark Lewis-Francis	GBR	Lisboa	11 Mar 2001
200 metres	20.37	Walter Dix	USA	Fayetteville	11 Mar 2005
400 metres	44.80	Kirani James	GRN	Fayetteville	27 Feb 2011
800 metres	1:44.35	Yuriy Borzakovskiy	RUS	Dortmund	30 Jan 2000
1000 metres	2:15.77	Abubaker Kaki	SUD	Stockholm	21 Feb 2008
1500 metres	3:36.28	Belal Mansoor Ali (overage!)	BRN	Stockholm	20 Feb 2007
One mile	3:55.02	German Fernandez	USA	College Station	28 Feb 2009
3000 metres	7:32.87	Hagos Gebrhiwet	ETH	Boston (Roxbury)	2 Feb 2013
5000 metres	12:53.29	Isiah Koech	KEN	Düsseldorf	11 Feb 2011
60mh (99cm)	7.50	Konstadínos Douvalídis	GRE	Athína	11 Feb 2006
High jump	2.35	Volodymyr Yashchenko	URS	Milano	12 Mar 1978
Pole vault	5.68	Raphael Holzdeppe	GER	Halle	1 Mar 2008
Long jump	8.22	Viktor Kuznetsov	UKR	Brovary	22 Jan 2005
Triple jump	17.14	Volker Mai	GDR	Piréas	2 Mar 1985
Shot (6kg)	22.35	David Storl	GER	Rochlitz	20 Dec 2009
Heptathlon	6022	Gunnar Nixon	USA	Fayetteville	27/28 Jan 2012
(jnr imps)		(6.94, 7.96, 13.19, 1.96, 7.90, 4.60, 2:51.42)			

Women

60 metres	7.09	Joan Uduak Ekah	NGR	Maebashi	7 Mar 1999
200 metres	22.40	Bianca Knight	USA	Fayetteville	14 Mar 2008
400 metres	50.82	Sanya Richards	USA	Fayetteville	13 Mar 2004
800 metres	2:01.03	Meskerem Legesse	ETH	Fayetteville	14 Feb 2004
1000 metres	2:40.1m	Diana Richburg	USA	New London	7 Dec 1982
1500 metres	4:03.28	Kalkidan Gezahegne	ETH	Stockholm	10 Feb 2010
One mile	4:24.10	Kalkidan Gezahegne	ETH	Birmingham	20 Feb 2010
3000 metres	8:33.56	Tirunesh Dibaba	ETH	Birmingham	20 Feb 2004
5000 metres	14:53.99	Tirunesh Dibaba	ETH	Boston	31 Jan 2004
60m hurdles	8.06	Ulrike Denk	FRG	Dortmund	19 Feb 1983
	8.06	Monique Ewanje Épée	FRA	Madrid	22 Feb 1986
High jump	1.97	Mariya Kuchina	RUS	Trinec	26 Jan 2011
Pole vault	4.63	Angelica Bengtsson	SWE	Stockholm	22 Feb 2011
Long jump	6.88	Heike Daute	GDR	Berlin	1 Feb 1983
Triple jump	14.37	Ren Ruiping	CHN	Barcelona	11 Mar 1995
Shot	20.51	Heidi Krieger	GDR	Budapest	8 Feb 1984
Pentathlon	4558	Nafissatou Thiam	BLE	Gent	3 Feb 2013
		(8.65, 1.84, 14.00, 6.30, 2:21.18)			

WORLD VETERANS/MASTERS RECORDS

MEN – aged 35 or over

100 metres	9.97A	Linford Christie (2.4.60)	GBR	Johannesburg	23 Sep 1995
200 metres	20.11	Linford Christie (2.4.60)	GBR	Villeneuve d'Ascq	25 Jun 1995
400 metres	45.68	Alvin Harrison (20.1.74)	DOM	San Juan	5 Apr 2009
800 metres	1:43.36	Johnny Gray (19.6.60)	USA	Zürich	16 Aug 1995
1000 metres	2:18.8+	William Tanui (22.2.64)	KEN	Rome	7 Jul 1999
1500 metres	3:32.45	William Tanui (22.2.64)	KEN	Athína	16 Jun 1999
1 mile	3:51.38	Bernard Lagat (12.12.74)	USA	London (CP)	6 Aug 2011
2000 metres	4:58.3+ e	William Tanui (22.2.64	KEN	Monaco	4 Aug 1999
	4:57.31i	William Tanui		Sindelfingen	28 Feb 1999
3000 metres	7:29.00	Bernard Lagat (12.12.74)	USA	Rieti	29 Aug 2010
5000 metres	12:53.60	Bernard Lagat (12.12.74)	USA	Monaco	22 Jul 2011
10000 metres	26:51.20	Haile Gebrselassie (18.4.73)	ETH	Hengelo	24 May 2008
20000 metres	57:44.4+	Gaston Roelants (5.2.37)	BEL	Bruxelles	20 Sep 1972
1 Hour	20,822m	Haile Gebrselassie (18.4.73)	ETH	Hengelo	1 Jun 2009
Half Marathon	59:10 dh	Paul Tergat (17.6.69)	KEN	Lisboa	13 Mar 2005
	59:50	Haile Gebrselassie (18.4.73)	ETH	Den Haag	14 Mar 2009
Marathon	2:03:59	Haile Gebrselassie (18.4.73)	ETH	Berlin	28 Sep 2008
3000m steeple	8:04.95	Simon Vroemen (11.5.69)	NED	Bruxelles	26 Aug 2005
110m hurdles	12.96	Allen Johnson (1.3.71)	USA	Athína	17 Sep 2006
400m hurdles	48.13	Danny McFarlane (24.2.72)	JAM	Monaco	28 Jul 2009
High jump	2.31	Dragutin Topic (12.3.71)	SRB	Kragujevac	28 Jul 2009
	2.31	Jamie Nieto (2.11.76)	USA	New York	9 Jun 2012
Pole vault	5.90i	Björn Otto (16.10.77)	GER	Cottbus	30 Jan 2013
	5.90i	Björn Otto		Düsseldorf	8 Feb 2013
	5.85 sq	Derek miles (28.9.72)	USA	Berlin	7 Sep 2008
Long jump	8.50	Larry Myricks (10.3.56)	USA	New York	15 Jun 1991
	8.50	Carl Lewis (1.7.61)	USA	Atlanta	29 Jul 1996
Triple jump	17.92	Jonathan Edwards (10.5.66)	GBR	Edmonton	6 Aug 2001
Shot	22.67	Kevin Toth ¶ (29.12.67)	USA	Lawrence	19 Apr 2003
Discus	71.56	Virgilijus Alekna (13.2.72)	LTU	Kaunas	25 Jul 2007
Hammer	83.62	Igor Astapkovich (4.1.63)	BLR	Staiki	20 Jun 1998
Javelin	92.80	Jan Zelezny (16.6.66)	CZE	Edmonton	12 Aug 2001
Decathlon	8241	Kip Janvrin (8.7.65)	USA	Eugene	22 Jun 2001
		(10.98, 7.01, 14.21, 1.89, 48.41, 14.72, 45.59, 5.20, 60.41, 4:14.96)			
20 km walk	1:18:44	Vladimir Andreyev (7.9.66)	RUS	Cheboksary	12 Jun 2004
20000m t walk	1:20:55.4+	Maurizio Damilano (6.4.57)	ITA	Cuneo	3 Oct 1992
50 km walk	3:36:03	Robert Korzeniowski (30.7.68)	POL	Saint-Denis	27 Aug 2003
50000m t walk	3:49:29.7	Alain Lemercier (11.1.57)	FRA	Franconville	3 Apr 1994

MEN – aged 40 or over

100 metres	10.29	Troy Douglas (30.11.62)	NED	Leiden	7 Jun 2003
200 metres	20.64	Troy Douglas (30.11.62)	NED	Utrecht	9 Aug 2003
400 metres	47.82	Enrico Saraceni (19.5.64)	ITA	Århus	25 Jul 2004
	47.5u	Lee Evans (25.2.47)	USA		Apr 1989
800 metres	1:48.28	Anthony Whiteman (13.11.71)	GBR	Loughborough	20 May 2012
1000 metres	2:24.93i	Vyacheslav Shabunin (27.9.69)	RUS	Moskva	10 Jan 2010
1500 metres	3:42.02	Anthony Whiteman (13.11.71)	GBR	Manchester (Stretford)	7 Jul 2012
1 mile	3:58.79	Anthony Whiteman (13.11.71)	GBR	Nashville	2 Jun 2012
	3:58.15i	Eamonn Coghlan (21.11.52)	IRL	Boston	20 Feb 1994

Event	Mark	Athlete	Country	Venue	Date
3000 metres	8:02.54	Vyacheslav Shabunin (27.9.69)	RUS	Moskva	7 Jun 2010
	8:01.44i	Vyacheslav Shabunin (27.9.69)	RUS	Moskva	7 Feb 2010
5000 metres	13:43.15	Mohamed Ezzher (26.4.60)	FRA	Sotteville	3 Jul 2000
10000 metres	28:30.88	Martti Vainio (30.12.50)	FIN	Hengelo	25 Jun 1991
1 Hour	19.710k	Steve Moneghetti (26.9.62)	AUS	Geelong	17 Dec 2005
Half marathon	62:28	John Campbell (6.2.49)	NZL	Philadelphia	16 Sep 1990
Marathon	2:08:46	Andrés Espinosa (4.2.63)	MEX	Berlin	28 Sep 2003
3000m steeple	8:38.40	Angelo Carosi (20.1.64)	ITA	Firenze	11 Jul 2004
110m hurdles	13.97	David Ashford (24.1.63)	USA	Indianapolis	3 Jul 2004
	13.79 ?	Roger Kingdom (26.8.62)	USA	Slippery Rock	23 Jun 2004
400m hurdles	49.69	Danny McFarlane (14.6.72)	JAM	Kingston	29 Jun 2012
High jump	2.28	Dragutin Topic (12.3.71)	SRB	Beograd	20 May 2012
Pole vault	5.71i	Jeff Hartwig (25.9.67)	USA	Jonesboro	31 May 2008
	5.70	Jeff Hartwig		Eugene	29 Jun 2008
Long jump	7.68A	Aaron Sampson (20.9.61)	USA	Cedar City, UT	21 Jun 2002
	7.59i	Mattias Sunneborn (27.9.70)	SWE	Sätra	3 Feb 2013
	7.57	Hans Schicker (3.10.47)	FRG	Kitzingen	16 Jul 1989
Triple jump	16.58	Ray Kimble (19.4.53)	USA	Edinburgh	2 Jul 1993
Shot	21.41	Brian Oldfield (1.6.45)	USA	Innsbruch	22 Aug 1985
Discus	70.28	Virgilijus Alekna (13.2.72)	LTU	Klaipeda	23Jun 2012
Hammer	82.23	Igor Astapkovich (4.1.63)	BLR	Minsk	10 Jul 2004
Javelin	85.92	Jan Zelezny (16.6.66)	CZE	Göteborg	9 Aug 2006
Pentathlon	3510 pts	Werner Schallau (8.9.38)	FRG	Gelsenkirchen	24 Sep 1978
		6.74, 59.20, 23.0, 43.76, 5:05.7			
Decathlon	7525 pts	Kip Janvrin (8.7.65)	USA	San Sebastián	24 Aug 2005
		11.56, 6.78, 14.01, 1.80, 49.46, 15.40, 42.70, 4.70, 58.43, 4:25.87			
20 km walk	1:21:36	Willi Sawall (7.11.41)	AUS	Melbourne	4 Jul 1982
20000m t walk	1:24:58.8	Marcel Jobin (3.1.42)	CAN	Sept Isles	12 May 1984
50 km walk	3:40:46	Yuriy Andronov (6.11.71)	RUS	Moskva	11 Jun 2012
50000m t walk	3:51:54.5	José Marín (21.1.50)	ESP	Manresa	7 Apr 1990
4x100m	42.20	SpeedWest TC	USA	Irvine	2 May 2004
		(Frank Strong, Cornell Stephenson, Kettrell Berry, Willie Gault)			
4x400m	3:20.83	S Allah, K Morning, E Gonera, R Blackwell	USA	Philadelphia	27 Apr 2001

WOMEN – aged 35 or over

Event	Mark	Athlete	Country	Venue	Date
100 metres	10.74	Merlene Ottey (10.5.60)	JAM	Milano	7 Sep 1996
200 metres	21.93	Merlene Ottey (10.5.60)	JAM	Bruxelles	25 Aug 1995
400 metres	50.27	Jearl Miles Clark (4.9.66)	USA	Madrid	20 Sep 2002
800 metres	1:56.53	Lyubov Gurina (6.8.57)	RUS	Hechtel	30 Jul 1994
1000 metres	2:31.5	Maricica Puica (29.7.50)	ROM	Poiana Brasov	1 Jun 1986
1500 metres	3:57.73	Maricica Puica (29.7.50)	ROM	Bruxelles	30 Aug 1985
1 mile	4:17.33	Maricica Puica (29.7.50)	ROM	Zürich	21 Aug 1985
2000 metres	5:28.69	Maricica Puica (29.7.50)	ROM	London (CP)	11 Jul 1986
3000 metres	8:23.23	Edith Masai (4.4.67)	KEN	Monaco	19 Jul 2002
5000 metres	14:33.84	Edith Masai (4.4.67)	KEN	Oslo	2 Jun 2006
10000 metres	30:30.26	Edith Masai (4.4.67)	KEN	Helsinki	6 Aug 2005
Half Marathon	67:16	Edith Masai (4.4.67)	KEN	Berlin	2 Apr 2006
Marathon	2:19:19	Irina Mikitenko (23.8.72)	GER	Berlin	28 Sep 2008
3000m steeple	9:24.26	Marta Domínguez (3.11.75)	ESP	Huelva	7 Jun 2012
100m hurdles	12.40	Gail Devers (19.11.66)	USA	Lausanne	2 Jul 2002
400m hurdles	52.94	Marina Styepanova (1.5.50)	RUS	Tashkent	17 Sep 1986
High jump	2.01	Inga Babakova (27.6.67)	UKR	Oslo	27 Jun 2003
Pole vault	4.70	Stacy Dragila (25.3.71)	USA	Chula Vista	22 Jun 2008
Long jump	6.99	Heike Drechsler (16.12.64)	GER	Sydney	29 Sep 2000
Triple jump	14.68	Tatyana Lebedeva (21.7.76)	RUS	Cheboksary	3 Jul 2012
	14.82i	Yamilé Aldama (14.8.72)	GBR	Istanbul	19 Mar 2012
Shot	21.46	Larisa Peleshenko (29.2.64)	RUS	Moskva	26 Aug 2000
	21.47i	Helena Fibingerová (13.7.49)	CZE	Jablonec	9 Feb 1985
Discus	69.60	Faina Melnik (9.7.45)	RUS	Donetsk	9 Sep 1980
Hammer	72.42	Iryna Sekyachova (21.7.76)	UKR	Yalta	4 Jun 2012
Javelin	68.34	Steffi Nerius (1.7.72)	GER	Berlin (Elstal)	31 Aug 2008
Heptathlon	6533 pts	Jane Frederick (7.4.52)	USA	Talence	27 Sep 1987
		13.60, 1.82, 15.50, 24.73; 6.29, 49.70, 2:14.88			
5000m walk	20:12.41	Elisabetta Perrone (9.7.68)	ITA	Rieti	2 Aug 2003
10km walk	41:41	Kjersti Tysse Plätzer (18.1.72)	NOR	Kraków	30 May 2009
10000m t walk	43:26.5	Elisabetta Perrone (9.7.68)	ITA	Saluzzo	4 Aug 2004
20km walk	1:25:59	Tamara Kovalenko (5.6.64)	RUS	Moskva	19 May 2000
20000m t walk	1:27:49.3	Yelena Nikolayeva (1.2.66)	RUS	Brisbane	6 Sep 2001
4x100m	48.63	Desmier, Sulter, Andreas, Apavou	FRA	Eugene	8 Jun 1989
4x400m	3:50.80	Mitchell, Mathews, Beadnall, Gabriel	GBR	Gateshead	8 Aug 1999

WOMEN – aged 40 or over

Event	Mark	Athlete	Nat	Venue	Date
100 metres	10.99	Merlene Ottey (10.5.60)	JAM	Thessaloniki	30 Aug 2000
200 metres	22.72	Merlene Ottey (10.5.60)	SLO	Athína	23 Aug 2004
400 metres	53.05A	María Figueirêdo (11.11.63)	BRA	Bogotá	10 Jul 2004
	53.14	María Figueirêdo (11.11.63)	BRA	San Carlos, VEN	19 Jun 2004
800 metres	1:59.25	Yekaterina Podkopayeva (11.6.52)	RUS	Luxembourg	30 Jun 1994
1000 metres	2:36.16	Yekaterina Podkopayeva (11.6.52)	RUS	Nancy	14 Sep 1994
	2:36.08i	Yekaterina Podkopayeva	RUS	Liévin	13 Feb 1993
1500 metres	3:59.78	Yekaterina Podkopayeva (11.6.52)	RUS	Nice	18 Jul 1994
1 mile	4:23.78	Yekaterina Podkopayeva (11.6.52)	RUS	Roma	9 Jun 1993
3000 metres	9:11.2	Joyce Smith (26.10.37)	GBR	London	30 Apr 1978
	9:02.83i	Lyubov Kremlyova (21.12.61)	RUS	Moskva	22 Jan 2002
5000 metres	15:20.59	Elena Fidatov (24.7.60)	ROM	Bucuresti	7 Aug 2000
10000 metres	31:31.18	Edith Masai (4.4.67)	KEN	Alger	21 Jul 2007
1 hour	16.056k	Jackie Fairweather (10.11.67)	AUS	Canberra	24 Jan 2008
Half Marathon	69:56	Irina Permitina (3.2.68)	RUS	Novosibirsk	13 Sep 2008
Marathon	2:25:43	Lyudmila Petrova (7.10.68)	RUS	New York	2 Nov 2008
3000m steeple	10:26.27	Yamilka González (23.1.72)	ESP	Castellón	2 Jun 2012
100 m hurdles	13.20	Patricia Girard (8.4.68)	FRA	Paris	14 Jul 2008
400 m hurdles	58.35	Barbara Gähling (20.3.65)	GER	Erfurt	21 Jul 2007
	58.3 h	Gowry Retchakan (21.6.60)	GBR	Hoo	3 Sep 2000
High jump	1.87	Iryna Mikhalchenko (20.1.72)	UKR	Yalta	13 Jun 2012
Pole vault	4.10	Doris Auer (10.5.71)	AUT	Innsbruck	6 Aug 2011
	4.11 §	Doris Auer (10.5.71)	AUT	Wien	5 Jul 2011
Long jump	6.64	Tatyana Ter-Mesrobian (12.5.68)	RUS	Sankt-Peterburg	31 May 2008
	6.64i	Tatyana Ter-Mesrobian	RUS	Sankt-Peterburg	5 Jan 2010
Triple jump	13.95i twice	Yamilé Aldama (14.8.72)	GBR	Göteborg	3 Mar 2013
	13.51	Barbara Lah (24.3.72)	ITA	Chiari	23 Jun 2012
Shot	19.05	Antonina Ivanova (25.12.32)	RUS	Oryol	28 Aug 1973
	19.16i	Antonina Ivanova	RUS	Moskva	24 Feb 1974
Discus	67.89	Iryna Yatchenko (31.10.65)	BLR	Staiki	29 Jun 2008
Hammer	59.29	Oneithea Lewis (11.6.60)	USA	Princeton	10 May 2003
Javelin	61.96	Laverne Eve (16.6.65)	BAH	Monaco	9 Sep 2005
Heptathlon	5449 pts	Tatyana Alisevich (22.1.69)	BLR	Staiki	3 Jun 2010
	14.80, 1.62, 13.92, 26.18, 5.55, 45.44, 2:24.39				
5000m walk	22:19.91	Joanne Dow (19.3.64)	USA	Philadelphia	24 Apr 2010
10km walk	45:09+	Kerry Saxby-Junna (2.6.61)	AUS	Edmonton	9 Aug 2001
10000m t walk	46:43.94	Graciela Mendoza (23.3.63)	MEX	Iquique	14 Jun 2008
20km walk	1:33:04	Graciela Mendoza (23.3.63)	MEX	Lima	7 May 2005
20000m t walk	1:33:28.15t	Teresa Vaill (20.11.62)	USA	Carson	25 Jun 2005
4x100m	48.22	Cadinot, Barilly, Valouvin, Lapierre	FRA	Le Touquet	24 Jun 2006
4x400m	3:57.28	Loizou, Kay, Smithe, Cearns	AUS	Brisbane	14 Jul 2001

WORLD AND CONTINENTAL RECORDS SET IN 2012

OUTDOORS – MEN

Event	Cat	Mark	Athlete	Nat	Venue	Date
100	W18	10.21	Yoshihide KIRYU	JPN	Gifu	5 Oct 12
	W18	10.19	Yoshihide KIRYU	JPN	Fukuroi	3 Nov 12
400	CAC,Com	43.94	Kirani JAMES	GRN	London (OS)	6 Aug 12
800	W40	1:48.28	Anthony WHITEMAN	GBR	Loughborough	20 May 12
	W40	1:48.22	Anthony WHITEMAN	GBR	Indianapolis	6 Jun 12
	W, Afr	1:40.91	David RUDISHA	KEN	London (OS)	9 Aug 12
	W20	1:41.73	Nijel AMOS	BOT	London (OS)	9 Aug 12
1500	CAC	3:35.03	Maurys CASTILLO	CUB	Huelva	7 Jun 12
	W40	3:42.02	Anthony WHITEMAN	GBR	Manchester (Stretford)	7 Jul 12
	Oce	3:30.35	Nick WILLIS	NZL	Monaco	20 Jul 12
Mile	W40	3:58.79	Anthony WHITEMAN	GBR	Nashville	2 Jun 12
5000	W20	12:47.53	Hagos GEBRHIWET	ETH	Saint-Denis	6 Jul 12
25k	W	1:11:18	Dennis KIMETTO	KEN	Berlin	6 May 12
6 Hr	W	92.613k	Gábor MUHARI	HUN	Veszprém	31 Mar 12
24 Hr	NAm	277.543k	Mike MORTON	USA	Katowice	9 Sep 12
3000SC	NAm	8:06.81	Evan JAGER	USA	Monaco	20 Jul 12
110H/91	W18	13.12	Wilhen BELOCIAN	FRA	Lens	21 Jul 12
110H	W, NAm	12.80	Aries MERRITT	USA	Bruxelles	7 Sep 12
	Afr	13.24	Lehann FOURIE	RSA	Bruxelles	7 Sep 12
400H	W40	49.69	Danny McFARLANE	JAM	Kingston	29 Jun 12
HJ	W40	2.25	Dragutin TOPIC	SRB	Bar	1 May 12
	W40	2.28	Dragutin TOPIC	SRB	Beograd	20 May 12
	W35=	2.31	Jamie NIETO	USA	New York	9 Jun 12
	Asi=	2.39	Mutaz Essa BARSHIM	QAT	Lausanne	23 Aug 12
LJ	W20	8.35	Sergey MORGUNOV	RUS	Cheboksary	20 Jun 12

Event	Cat	Mark	Name	Nat	Place	Date
DT	Oce	67.53	Benn HARRADINE	AUS	Townsville	5 May 12
	W40	70.28	Virgilijus ALEKNA	LTU	Klaipeda	23 Jun 12
HT/6kg	W18,W20	85.57	Ashraf Amgad EL-SEIFY	QAT	Barcelona	14 Jul 12
Dec/100	W	10.21 (9039)	Ashton EATON	USA	Eugene	22 Jun 12
Dec/LJ	W	8.23 (9039)	Ashton EATON	USA	Eugene	22 Jun 12
Dec	W, NAm	9039	Ashton EATON	USA	Eugene	23 Jun 12

(10.21, 8.23, 14.20, 2.05, 46.70 / 13.70, 42.81, 5.30, 58.87, 4:14.48)

Event	Cat	Mark	Name	Nat	Place	Date
	SAm	8276	Luiz Alberto de ARAÚJO	BRA	São Paulo	30 Jun 12

(10.80, 7.39, 14.93, 1.98, 48.54 / 14.12, 46.15, 4.90, 52.11, 4:27.75)

Event	Cat	Mark	Name	Nat	Place	Date
4x100 R	NAm	37.38	Demps, Patton, Kimmons, Gatlin	USA	London (OS)	10 Aug 12
	Oce=	38.17	Alozie, Ntiamoah, McCabe, Ross	AUS	London (OS)	10 Aug 12
	W,CAC,Com	36.84	Carter, Frater, Blake, Bolt	JAM	London (OS)	11 Aug 12
	NAm	37.04	Kimmons, Gatlin, Gay, Bailey	USA	London (OS)	11 Aug 12
4x400 R	CAC,Com	2:56.72	Brown, Pinder, Mathieu, Miller	BAH	London (OS)	10 Aug 12
10000W	Asi	38:30.38t	WANG Zhen	CHN	Tianjin	16 Sep 12
20kW	Asi	1:17:36	WANG Zhen	CHN	Taicang	30 Mar 12
50kW	Afr	3:57:57	Marc MUNDELL	RSA	Saransk	13 May 12
	W40	3:40:46	Yuriy ANDRONOV	RUS	Moskva	11 Jun 12
	Afr	3:55:32	Marc MUNDELL	RSA	London	11 Aug 12
	SAm	3:49:26	Andrés CHOCHO	ECU	Valley Cottage	28 Oct 12

Drugs disqualification:

Event	Cat	Mark	Name	Nat	Place	Date
Dec	Afr	8332	Larbi BOURAADA	ALG	Ratingen	15 Jun 12

(10.58, 7.57, 13.64, 2.09, 47.40 / 14.78w, 34.80, 4.70, 67.68, 4:24.08)

OUTDOORS – WOMEN

Event	Cat	Mark	Name	Nat	Place	Date
100	CAC, Com	10.70	Shelly-Ann FRASER	JAM	Kingston	29 Jun 12
1000	Oce	2:37.84	Zoe BUCKMAN	AUS	Oslo	24 May 12
20k	Oce	1:05:06+	Kim SMITH	NZL	New York	18 Mar 12
30k	SAm	1:43:49+	Inés MELCHOR	PER	London	5 Aug 12
Mar	SAm	2:29:17	Adriana DA SILVA	BRA	Tokyo	26 Feb 12
	Afr	2:18:37	Mary KEITANY	KEN	London	22 Apr 12
24Hr	NAm	240.385k	Connie GARDNER	USA	Katowice	9 Sep 12
3000St	W40	10:26.27	Yamilka GONZÁLEZ	ESP	Castellón	2 Jun 12
	Afr, Com	9:07.14	Milcah CHEMOS CHEYWA	KEN	Oslo	7 Jun 12
	W35	9:24.26	Marta DOMÍNGUEZ	ESP	Huelva	7 Jun 12
HJ	W40	1.87	Iryna MIKHALCHENKO	UKR	Yalta	13 Jun 12
PV	Oce	4.66	Alana BOYD	AUS	Perth	11 Feb 12
	Oce	4.71, 4.76	Alana BOYD	AUS	Perth	24 Feb 12
	W20	4.58	Angelica BENGTSSON	SWE	Sollentuna	5 Jul 12
	CAC=	4.75	Yarisley SILVA	CUB	London (OS)	6 Aug 12
TJ	W40=	13.05	Barbara LAH	ITA	Lodi	19 May 12
	W40	13.51	Barbara LAH	ITA	Chiari	23 Jun 12
	W35	14.68	Tatyana LEBEDEVA	RUS	Cheboksary	3 Jul 12
DT	NAm	67.74	Stephanie TRAFTON-BROWN	USA	Wailuku	4 May 12
	SAm	62.36	Andressa de MORAIS	BRA	São Paulo	20 May 12
	SAm	64.21	Andressa de MORAIS	BRA	Barquisimeto	10 Jun 12
HT	Asi	75.72	ZHANG Wenxiu	CHN	Chengdu	12 Mar 12
	NAm, Com	75.04	Sultana FRIZELL	CAN	Tucson	16 Mar 12
	Asi	76.99	ZHANG Wenxiu	CHN	Ostrava	24 May 12
	W35	72.42	Iryna SEKACHYOVA	UKR	Yalta	4 Jun 12
	Afr	69.10	Amy SÈNE	SEN	Angers	17 Jun 12
JT	Asi	64.95	LU Huihui	CHN	Zhaoqing	14 Apr 12
	Afr, Com	69.35	Sunette VILJOEN	RSA	New York	9 Jun 12
	Asi	65.11	LI Lingwei	CHN	Fuzhou	23 Jun 12
Hep/100H	W	12.54 (6955)	Jessica ENNIS	GBR	London (OS)	3 Aug 12
Hep/SP	W	17.31 (6599)	Austra SKUJYTE	LTU	London (OS)	3 Aug 12
Hep/JT	W	56.96 (5947)	Sofia IFANTÍDOU	GRE	London (OS)	4 Aug 12
	W	60.90 (5880)	Barbora SPOTÁKOVÁ	CZE	Talence	16 Sep 12
Hep	Com	6906	Jessica ENNIS	GBR/Eng	Götzis	27 May 12

(12.81, 1.85, 14.51, 22.88 / 6.51, 47.11, 2:09.00)

Event	Cat	Mark	Name	Nat	Place	Date
	SAm	6160	Lucimara da SILVA	BRA	Barquisimeto	10 Jun 12

(13.78, 1.83, 12.63, 24.98 / 6.44, 42.22, 2:18.52)

Event	Cat	Mark	Name	Nat	Place	Date
	Com	6955	Jessica ENNIS	GBR/Eng	London (OS)	4 Aug 12

(12.54, 1.86, 14.28, 22.83 / 6.48, 47.49, 2:08.65)

Event	Cat	Mark	Name	Nat	Place	Date
4x100 R	SAm	42.55	Silva, Krasucki, E dos Santos, R Santos	BRA	London (OS)	9 Aug 12
	W, NAm	40.82	Madison, Felix, Knight, Jeter	USA	London (OS)	10 Aug 12
	CAC	41.41	Fraser-Pryce, Simpson, Campbell-Brown, Stewart	JAM	London (OS)	10 Aug 12
5000W	Asi	20:34.76t	LIU Hong	CHN	Tianjin	16 Sep 12
10000W	SAm	45:11.2tA	Lorena ARENAS	COL	Medellin	15 Apr 12
	Afr	47:30.28t	Chahinez AL-NASRI	TUN	Amman	16 May 12

20kW	CAC	1:28:54	Mirna ORTIZ	GUA	Lugano	18 Mar 12
	Asi	1:25:46	LIU Hong	CHN	Taicang	30 Mar 12
	W, Eur	1:25:02	Yelena LASHMANOVA	RUS	London	11 Aug 12
	Asi	1:25:16	QIEYANG Shenjie	CHN	London	11 Aug 12
50kW	NAm	4:33:23	Erin TAYLOR-TALCOTT	USA	Santee	22 Jan 12

Drugs disqualification:

SP	Afr	18.56, 18.86	Vivian CHUKWUEMEKA	NGR	Porto Novo	1 Jul 12

See ATHLETICS 2012 for Indoor Records set in January - March 2012 – and WOMEN

1000	W18	2:43.22	Anita HINRIKSDÓTTIR	ISL	Reykjavik	15 Dec 12
1M	W40	4:44.81	Sonja FRIEND-UHL	USA	Blacksburg	3 Mar 12
SP	Oce,Com	20.80 & 20.81	Valerie ADAMS	NZL	Zürich	29 Aug 12

WORLD AND CONTINENTAL RECORDS SET IN JAN – MAR 2013

INDOORS – MEN   # on oversized track

60	W35	6.50	Darvis PATTON	USA	New York (Armory)	16 Feb 13
600	NAm	1:15.70	Duane SOLOMON	USA	Glasgow	26 Jan 13
	W20, Asi	1:15.60	Mohamed AMAN	ETH	Moskva	3 Feb 13
	NAm	1:15.61	Erik SOWINSKI	USA	New York (Armory)	16 Feb 13
	CAC	1:16.19	Jarrin SOLOMON	TRI	New York (Armory)	16 Feb 13
	NAm	1:15.42#	Casimir LOXSOM	USA	Geneva, USA	23 Feb 13
3000	W35	7:34.71	Bernard LAGAT	USA	Karlsruhe	2 Feb 13
	W20	7:32.87	Hagos GEBRHIWET	ETH	Boston (Roxbury)	2 Feb 13
	NAm	7:30.16	Galen RUPP	USA	Stockholm	21 Feb 13
	CAC	7:46.95	Kemoy CAMPBELL	JAM	Fayetteville	9 Mar 13
2M	NAm,W35	8:09.49	Bernard LAGAT	USA	New York (Armory)	16 Feb 13
5000	NAm	13:07.00	Lopez LOMONG	USA	New York (Armory)	1 Mar 13
HJ	Asi=	2.37	Mutaz Essa BARSHIM	QAT	Moskva	3 Feb 13
PV	W35	5.90	Björn OTTO	GER	Cottbus	30 Jan 13
	W35=	5.90	Björn OTTO	GER	Düsseldorf	8 Feb 13
	SAm	5.66	Augusto Dutra de OLIVEIRA	BRA	São Caetano do Sul	16 Feb 13
	SAm	5.70	Fábio Gomes da SILVA	BRA	São Caetano do Sul	23 Feb 13
	SAm	5.71	Augusto Dutra de OLIVEIRA	BRA	São Caetano do Sul	2 Mar 13
LJ	W40	7.59	Mattias SUNNEBORN	SWE	Sätra	3 Feb 13
TJ	Asi	17.16	DONG Bin	CHN	Nanjing	7 Mar 13
SP/5kg	W18	21.44	Patrick M‹LLER	GER	Sassnitz	27 Jan 13
SP/6kg	W18	19.90, 20.12	Henning PRÜFER	GER	Ancona	2 Mar 13
Hep/HJ	W	2.25 (6156)	Jeremy TAIWO	USA	Nampa	8 Feb 13
	W	2.27, 2.30 (5817)	Derek DROUIN	CAN	Geneva, USA	22 Feb 13

INDOORS – WOMEN

60	Afr	7.00	Murielle AHOUR...	CIV	Houston	26 Jan 13
	Afr	6.99	Murielle AHOUR...	CIV	Birmingham	16 Feb 13
200	W18	23.15	Irene EKELUND	SWE	Norrköping	17 Feb 13
600	W20	1:27.30	Ajee' WILSON	USA	New York (Armory)	19 Jan 13
	NAm	1:23.59	Alysia MONTAÑO	USA	New York (Armory)	16 Feb 13
	W20	1:26.45	Ajee' WILSON	USA	New York (Armory)	16 Feb 13
1M	W18	4:32.78	Mary CAIN	USA	New York (Armory)	26 Jan 13
	W18	4:28.25	Mary CAIN	USA	New York (Armory)	16 Feb 13
5000	W35	15:41.42	Yelena ZADOROZHNAYA	RUS	Moskva	14 Feb 13
	Asi	15:54.18#	Yuriko KOBAYASHI	JPN	Seattle	1 Mar 13
	W18	16:42.99	Tessa BARRETT	USA	New York (Armory)	8 Mar 13
2000SC	W	6:05.29	Mariya BYKOVA	RUS	Belgorod	22 Jan 13
60H	W18	8.17A	Dior HALL	USA	Golden	9 Feb 13
PV	CAC	4.76	Yarisley SILVA	CUB	Donetsk	9 Feb 13
	CAC	4.78	Yarisley SILVA	CUB	Stockholm	21 Feb 13
	NAm	4.90A	Jenn SUHR	USA	Albuquerque	2 Mar 13
	W	5.02A	Jenn SUHR	USA	Albuquerque	2 Mar 13
TJ	W40	13.16	Yamilé ALDAMA	GBR	Glasgow	26 Jan 13
	W40	13.44	Yamilé ALDAMA	GBR	Sheffield	10 Feb 13
	W40	13.91	Yamilé ALDAMA	GBR	Birmingham	16 Feb 13
	W40	13.92	Yamilé ALDAMA	GBR	Göteborg	1 Mar 13
	W40	13.95 (twice)	Yamilé ALDAMA	GBR	Göteborg	3 Mar 13
	W18	13.89, 14.09	WANG Rong	CHN	Nanjing	7 Mar 13
Pen	CAC	4464	Makeba ALCIDE (8.45, 1.89, 12.05, 5.88, 2:16.94)	LCA	Fayetteville	25 Jan 13
	SAm	4261	Vanessa SPINOLA (8.92, 1.74, 12.62, 6.04, 2:16.82)	BRA	Tallinn	2 Feb 13
	W20	4558 §	Nafissatou THIAM (8.65, 1.84, 14.00, 6.30, 2:21.18)	BEL	Gent	3 Feb 13

| | CAC | 4569 | Makeba ALCIDE | LCA | Fayetteville | 22 Feb 13 |
| | | | (8.35, 1.87, 12.32, 6.15, 2:16.37) | | | |

OUTDOORS – MEN

500	W	59.32	Orestes RODRÍGUEZ	CUB	La Habana	5 Feb 13
HMar	Oce	60:56	Collis BIRMINGHAM	AUS	Marugame	3 Feb 13
50kmW	CAC	3:41:09	Erick BARRONDO	GUA	Dudince	23 Mar 13

OUTDOORS – WOMEN

HMar	SAm	70:30	Yolanda CABALLERO	COL	New York	17 Mar 13
2000SC	NAm	6:19.09	Bridget FRANEK	USA	Eugene	16 Mar 13
PV	CAC	4.81	Yarisley SILVA	CUB	La Habana	16 Mar 13
20kW	CAC=	1:28:54	Mirna ORTIZ	GUA	Lugano	17 Mar 13

SPLIT TIMES IN WORLD RECORDS

Men

			400m	800m	1200m	1600m	2000m	2400m	2800m
800m	1:41.01	Rudisha 2010	48.9	1:41.01		(600m 1:14.59)			
1000m	2:11.96	Ngeny 1999	49.66	1:44.62		(200m 24.12, 600m 1:17.14)			
1500m	3:26.00	El Guerrouj 1998	54.3	1:50.7	2:46.4	(1000m 2:18.8)			
1M	3:43.13	El Guerrouj 1999	55.2	1:51.2	2:47.0	(1000m 2:19.2)			
2000m	4:44.79	El Guerrouj 1999	57.1	1:55.4	2:52.4	3:49.60			
3000m	7:20.67	Komen 1996	57.6	1:57.0	2:54.9	3:53.6	4:53.4	5:51.3	6:51.2 (1500m 3:38.6)
2M	7:58.61	Komen 1997	58.6	2:00.4		3:58.4	4:58.2	5:56.7	6:57.5 (1M 3:59.2)

5000m 12:37.35 Bekele 2004 kms: 2:33.24, 5:05.47, 7:37.34, 10:07.93, last 400m 57.9
10,000m 26:17.53 Bekele 2005 kms: 2:40.6, 5:16.4, 7:53.3, 10:30.4, 13:09.4, 15:44.66, 18:23.98, 21:04.63, 23:45.09, 26:17.53, last 400m 57.1
3kmSt 7:53.63 Shaheen 2004 1000m 2:36.13, 2000m 5:18.09

Women

			400m	800m	1200m	1600m	2000m
800m	1:53.28	Kratochvílová 1983	56.1	1:53.28		(600m 1:25.0)	
1000m	2:28.98	Masterkova 1996	58.3	1:59.8		(200m 28.4, 600m 1:29.1)	
1500m	3:50.46	Qu Yunxia 1993	57.2	2:00.8	3:05.2		
1M	4:12.56	Masterkova 1996	62.0	2:06.7	3:12.2	(1000m 2:39.5, 1500m 3:56.77)	
2000m	5:25.36	O'Sullivan 1994	64.9	2:07.8	3:14.8	4:23.5	5:25.36

			1km	2km	3km	4km	5km	6km	7km	8km	9km
3000m	8:06.11	Wang J 1993	2:42.0	5:29.7	(last 400m 62.7)						
2M	8:58.58	Defar 2007	2:48.4	5:37.5	8:24.51 (1M 4:33.07, last 400m 62.6)						
5000m	14:11.15	Dibaba 2008	2:48.3	5:43.8	8:39.0	11:28.44	14:11.15				
10000m	29:31.78	Wang J 1993	2:54.7	5:56.6	8:59.2	12:02.8	15:05.7	18:10.1	21:14.4	23:59.9	26:44.8

3kmSt 8:58.81 Galkina 2008 1000m 2:58.63, 2000m 6:01.20

Most World Records: Sergey Bubka USR/UKR set a total of 35 at pole vault: 17 outdoors from 5.85 (1984) to 6.14 (1994) and 18 indoors (9 ratified by IAAF) from 5.81 (1844) to 6.15 (1993). Paavi Nurmi FIN set 22 official and 13 unofficial world records at distances from 1500m to 20,000m between 1921 and 1931.
The most world records by a woman at one event is 28 at pole vault (15 outdoors, 13 indoors) by Yelena Isinbayeva RUS 2003-09.

Oldest: 41y 238d Yekaterina Podkopayeva RUS women's 4x800m indoor 8:18.71 Moskva 4 Feb 1994.

Youngest: 14y 334d Wang Yan CHN 5000m walk 21:33.8 Jian 9 Mar 1986 (unratified).

Youngest male: 17y 198d Thomas Ray PV 3.42m Ulverston 19 Sep 1879 (prior to IAAF jurisdiction (from 1913).

Most world records set in one day: 6 Jesse Owens USA at Ann Arbor 23 May 1935: 100y 9.4, LJ 8.13m, 220y straight (& 200m) 20.3, 220y hurdles straight (& 220yh) 22.6.

Record span of setting world records: Men: 15 years Haile Gebrselassie ETH 1994-2009

Recent Marriages

Female	Male	
Mariya Abakumova RUS	Dmitriy Tarabin RUS	.9.12
Sarah Bowman USA	Darren Brown USA	2.9.12
Damu Cherry USA	Dennis Mitchell USA	
Hannah England GBR	Luke Gunn GBR	5.1.13
Aleksandra Fedoriva RUS	Aleksandr Shpayer RUS	.12
Sheree Francis JAM	Dwight Ruff USA	11.10.12
Øyunn Grindem NOR	Christian Settemsli Mogstad NOR	.6.12
Nikita Holder CAN	Justyn Warner CAN	12.10.12
Mona Holm NOR	Paul André Solberg NOR	29.4.12
Yekaterina Kostetskaya RUS	Steve Hooker AUS	.9.12
Jirina Ptácníková CZE	Petr Svoboda CZE	21.9.12
Stephanie Rothstein USA	Ben Bruce USA	26.10.12
Irvette van Blerk RSA	L.J. van Zyl RSA	29.9.12
Kseniya Vdovina RUS	Yevgeniy Ryzhov RUS	.1.13

Mark	Wind	Name		Nat	Born	Pos	Meet	Venue	Date

WORLD MEN'S ALL-TIME LISTS

100 METRES

Mark	Wind	Name		Nat	Born	Pos	Meet	Venue	Date
9.58 WR	0.9	Usain	Bolt	JAM	21.8.86	1	WCh	Berlin	16 Aug 09
9.63	1.5		Bolt			1	OG	London (OS)	5 Aug 12
9.69 WR	0.0		Bolt			1	OG	Beijing	16 Aug 08
9.69	2.0	Tyson	Gay	USA	9.8.82	1		Shanghai	20 Sep 09
9.69	-0.1	Yohan	Blake	JAM	26.12.89	1	Athl	Lausanne	23 Aug 12
9.71	0.9		Gay			2	WCh	Berlin	16 Aug 09
9.72 WR	1.7		Bolt			1	Reebok	New York (RI)	31 May 08
9.72	0.2	Asafa	Powell	JAM	23.11.82	1rA	Athl	Lausanne	2 Sep 08
9.74 WR	1.7		Powell			1h2	GP	Rieti	9 Sep 07
9.75	1.1		Blake			1	NC	Kingston	29 Jun 12
9.75	1.5		Blake			2	OG	London (OS)	5 Aug 12
9.76	1.8		Bolt			1		Kingston	3 May 08
9.76	1.3		Bolt			1	VD	Bruxelles	16 Sep 11
9.76	-0.1		Bolt			1	GGala	Roma	31 May 12
9.76	1.4		Blake			1	WK	Zürich	30 Aug 12
9.77 WR	1.6		Powell			1	Tsik	Athína	14 Jun 05
9.77 WR	1.5		Powell			1	BrGP	Gateshead	11 Jun 06
9.77 WR	1.0		Powell			1rA	WK	Zürich	18 Aug 06
9.77	1.6		Gay			1q1	NC/OT	Eugene	28 Jun 08
9.77	-1.3		Bolt			1	VD	Bruxelles	5 Sep 08
9.77	0.9		Powell			1h1	GP	Rieti	7 Sep 08
9.77	0.4		Gay			1	GGala	Roma	10 Jul 09
9.78	0.0		Powell			1	GP	Rieti	9 Sep 07
9.78	-0.4		Gay			1	LGP	London (CP)	13 Aug 10
9.78	0.9	Nesta	Carter	JAM	10.11.85	1		Rieti	29 Aug 10
9.78	1.0		Powell			1	Athl	Lausanne	30 Jun 11
9.79 WR	0.1	Maurice	Greene	USA	23.7.74	1rA	Tsik	Athína	16 Jun 99
9.79	-0.2		Bolt			1	GL	Saint-Denis	17 Jul 09
9.79	0.1		Gay			1	VD	Bruxelles	27 Aug 10
9.79	1.1		Gay			1h1		Clermont	4 Jun 11
9.79	0.6		Bolt			1	Bisl	Oslo	7 Jun 12
9.79	1.5	Justin	Gatlin ¶	USA	10.2.82	3	OG	London (OS)	5 Aug 12
		(32 performances by 7 athletes)							
9.80	0.4	Steve	Mullings ¶	JAM	29.11.82	1	Pre	Eugene	4 Jun 11
9.84 WR	0.7	Donovan	Bailey	CAN	16.12.67	1	OG	Atlanta	27 Jul 96
9.84	0.2	Bruny	Surin	CAN	12.7.67	2	WCh	Sevilla	22 Aug 99
		(10)							
9.85 WR	1.2	Leroy	Burrell	USA	21.2.67	1rA	Athl	Lausanne	6 Jul 94
9.85	1.7	Olusoji	Fasuba	NGR	9.7.84	2	SGP	Doha	12 May 06
9.85	1.3	Michael	Rodgers	USA	24.4.85	2	Pre	Eugene	4 Jun 11
9.85	1.0	Richard	Thompson	TRI	7.6.85	1	NC	Port of Spain	13 Aug 11
9.86 WR	1.2	Carl	Lewis	USA	1.7.61	1	WCh	Tokyo	25 Aug 91
9.86	-0.4	Frank	Fredericks	NAM	2.10.67	1rA	Athl	Lausanne	3 Jul 96
9.86	1.8	Ato	Boldon	TRI	30.12.73	1rA	MSR	Walnut	19 Apr 98
9.86	1.4	Keston	Bledman	TRI	8.3.88	1	NC	Port-of-Spain	23 Jun 12
9.86	0.6	Francis	Obikwelu	NGR/POR	22.11.78	2	OG	Athína	22 Aug 04
9.87	0.3	Linford	Christie ¶	GBR	2.4.60	1	WCh	Stuttgart	15 Aug 93
		(20)							
9.87A	-0.2	Obadele	Thompson	BAR	30.3.76	1	WCp	Johannesburg	11 Sep 98
9.88	1.8	Shawn	Crawford	USA	14.1.78	1	Pre	Eugene	19 Jun 04
9.88	0.6	Walter	Dix	USA	31.1.86	2		Nottwil	8 Aug 10
9.88	0.9	Ryan	Bailey	USA	13.4.89	2		Rieti	29 Aug 10
9.88	1.0	Michael	Frater	JAM	6.10.82	2	Athl	Lausanne	30 Jun 11
9.89	1.6	Travis	Padgett	USA	13.12.86	1q2	NC/OT	Eugene	28 Jun 08
9.89	1.6	Darvis	Patton	USA	4.12.77	1q3	NC/OT	Eugene	28 Jun 08
9.89	1.3	Ngonidzashe	Makusha	ZIM	11.3.87	1	NCAA	Des Moines	10 Jun 11
9.91	1.2	Dennis	Mitchell ¶	USA	20.2.66	3	WCh	Tokyo	25 Aug 91
9.91	0.9	Leonard	Scott	USA	19.1.80	2	WAF	Stuttgart	9 Sep 06
		(30)							
9.91	-0.5	Derrick	Atkins	BAH	5.1.84	2	WCh	Osaka	26 Aug 07
9.91	-0.2	Daniel	Bailey	ANT	9.9.86	2	GL	Saint-Denis	17 Jul 09
9.91	0.7	Churandy	Martina	NED	3.7.84	2s1	OG	London (OS)	5 Aug 12
9.92	0.3	Andre	Cason	USA	20.1.69	2	WCh	Stuttgart	15 Aug 93
9.92	0.8	Jon	Drummond	USA	9.9.68	1h3	NC	Indianapolis	12 Jun 97
9.92	0.2	Tim	Montgomery ¶	USA	28.1.75	2	NC	Indianapolis	13 Jun 97
9.92A	-0.2	Seun	Ogunkoya	NGR	28.12.77	2	WCp	Johannesburg	11 Sep 98

Mark	Wind	Name		Nat	Born	Pos	Meet	Venue	Date
9.92	1.0	Tim	Harden	USA	27.1.74	1	Spitzen	Luzern	5 Jul 99
9.92	2.0	Christophe	Lemaitre	FRA	11.6.90	1	NC	Albi	29 Jul 11
9.93A	WR1.4	Calvin	Smith	USA	8.1.61	1	USOF	USAF Academy	3 Jul 83
		(40)							
9.93	-0.6	Michael	Marsh	USA	4.8.67	1	MSR	Walnut	18 Apr 92
9.93	1.8	Patrick	Johnson	AUS	26.9.72	1		Mito	5 May 03
9.93	1.1	Ivory	Williams #	USA	2.5.85	1rA		Réthimno	20 Jul 09
9.93	1.3	Nickel	Ashmeade	JAM	4.7.90	2	Pre	Eugene	2 Jun 12
9.94	0.2	Davidson	Ezinwa ¶	NGR	22.11.71	1	Gugl	Linz	4 Jul 94
9.94	-0.2	Bernard	Williams	USA	19.1.78	2	WCh	Edmonton	5 Aug 01
9.95A	WR0.3	Jim	Hines	USA	10.9.46	1	OG	Ciudad de México	14 Oct 68
9.95A	1.9	Olapade	Adeniken	NGR	19.8.69	1A		El Paso	16 Apr 94
9.95	0.8	Vincent	Henderson	USA	20.10.72	1		Leverkusen	9 Aug 98
9.95	1.8	Joshua 'J.J.'	Johnson	USA	10.5.76	1r6	MSR	Walnut	21 Apr 02
		(50)							
9.95	0.6	Deji	Aliu	NGR	22.11.75	1	Afr G	Abuja	12 Oct 03
9.95	1.8	John	Capel ¶	USA	27.10.78	3	Pre	Eugene	19 Jun 04
9.95	1.6	Rodney	Martin	USA	22.12.82	2q2	NC/OT	Eugene	28 Jun 08
9.95	-0.8	Trell	Kimmons	USA	13.7.85	1	WK	Zürich	19 Aug 10
9.95	0.9	Mario	Forsythe	JAM	30.10.85	3		Rieti	29 Aug 10
9.95	1.8	Kemar	Hyman	CAY	11.10.89	1h2		Madrid	7 Jul 12
		(56)	100th man 10.02, 200th 10.08, 300th 10.12, 400th 10.16, 500th 10.19						

Doubtful wind reading

Mark	Wind	Name		Nat	Born	Pos	Meet	Venue	Date
9.91	-2.3	Davidson	Ezinwa ¶	NGR	22.11.71	1		Azusa	11 Apr 92

Low altitude best: 9.94 0.1 Ogunkoya 1 AfCh Dakar 19 Aug 98

Wind-assisted – performances to 9.78, performers listed to 9.92

Mark	Wind	Name		Nat	Born	Pos	Meet	Venue	Date
9.68	4.1	Tyson	Gay	USA	9.8.82	1	NC/OT	Eugene	29 Jun 08
9.69A	5+	Obadele	Thompson	BAR	30.3.76	1		El Paso	13 Apr 96
9.72	2.1		Powell			1	Bisl	Oslo	4 Jun 10
9.75	3.4		Gay			1h1	NC	Eugene	25 Jun 09
9.75	2.6		Powell			1h2	DL	Doha	14 May 10
9.76A	6.1	Churandy	Martina	AHO	3.7.84	1		El Paso	13 May 06
	9.92w		2.1			3	Bisl	Oslo	4 Jun 10
9.76	2.2		Gay			1	GP	New York	2 Jun 07
9.77	2.1		Bolt			1	GS	Ostrava	17 Jun 09
9.78	5.2	Carl	Lewis	USA	1.7.61	1	NC/OT	Indianpolis	16 Jul 88
9.78	3.7	Maurice	Greene	USA	23.7.74	1	GP II	Stanford	31 May 04
9.79	5.3	Andre	Cason	USA	20.1.69	1h4	NC	Eugene	16 Jun 93
9.80	4.1	Walter	Dix	USA	31.1.86	2	NC/OT	Eugene	29 Jun 08
9.80	2.2	Yohan	Blake	JAM	26.12.89	1		Kingston	7 May 11
9.83	7.1	Leonard	Scott	USA	19.1.80	1r1	Sea Ray	Knoxville	9 Apr 99
9.83	2.2	Derrick	Atkins	BAH	5.1.84	2	GP	New York	2 Jun 07
9.84	3.4	Justin	Gatlin ¶	USA	10.2.82	1	Pre	Eugene	4 Jun 05
9.84	5.4	Francis	Obikwelu	NGR/POR	22.11.78	1		Zaragoza	3 Jun 06
9.84	4.1	Darvis	Patton	USA	4.12.77	3	NC/OT	Eugene	29 Jun 08
9.85	4.8	Dennis	Mitchell ¶	USA	20.2.66	2	NC	Eugene	17 Jun 93
9.85A	3.0	Frank	Fredericks	NAM	2.10.67	1		Nairobi	18 May 02
9.85	4.1	Travis	Padgett	USA	13.12.86	4	NC/OT	Eugene	29 Jun 08
9.85w	3.6	Keston	Bledman	TRI	8.3.88	1rA		Clermont	2 Jun 12
9.86	2.6	Shawn	Crawford	USA	14.1.78	1	GP	Doha	14 May 04
9.86	3.6	Michael	Frater	JAM	6.10.82	2h4	NC	Kingston	23 Jun 11
9.87	11.2	William	Snoddy	USA	6.12.57	1		Dallas	1 Apr 78
9.87	4.9	Calvin	Smith	USA	8.1.61	1s2	NC/OT	Indianpolis	16 Jul 88
9.87	2.4	Michael	Marsh	USA	4.8.67	1rA	MSR	Walnut	20 Apr 97
9.88	2.3	James	Sanford	USA	27.12.57	1		Los Angeles (Ww)	3 May 80
9.88	5.2	Albert	Robinson	USA	28.11.64	4	NC/OT	Indianpolis	16 Jul 88
9.88	4.9	Tim	Harden	USA	27.1.74	1	NC	New Orleans	20 Jun 98
9.88	4.5	Coby	Miller	USA	19.10.76	1		Auburn	1 Apr 00
9.88	3.6	Patrick	Johnson	AUS	26.9.72	1		Perth	8 Feb 03
9.88	3.0	Darrel	Brown	TRI	11.10.84	1	NC	Port of Spain	23 Jun 07
9.88	3.7	Ivory	Williams #	USA	2.5.85	1	TexR	Austin	3 Apr 10
9.89	4.2	Ray	Stewart	JAM	18.3.65	1s1	PAm	Indianapolis	9 Aug 87
9.90	5.2	Joe	DeLoach	USA	5.6.67	5	NC/OT	Indianpolis	16 Jul 88
9.90	7.1	Kenny	Brokenburr	USA	29.10.68	2r1	Sea Ray	Knoxville	9 Apr 99
9.90A	7.8	Teddy	Williams	USA	3.7.88	1		El Paso	11 Apr 09
9.90	2.8	Lerone	Clarke	JAM	2.10.81	1		Clermont	11 Jun 11
9.91	5.3	Bob	Hayes	USA	20.12.42	1s1	OG	Tokyo	15 Oct 64
9.91	4.2	Mark	Witherspoon	USA	3.9.63	2s1	PAm	Indianapolis	9 Aug 87
9.91	3.7	Nicolas	Macrozonaris	CAN	22.8.80	1	NC	Edmonton	22 Jun 02
9.92A	4.4	Chidi	Imo ¶	NGR	27.8.63	1s1	AfG	Nairobi	8 Aug 87

Mark	Wind	Name		Nat	Born	Pos	Meet	Venue	Date
9.92A	2.8	Olapade	Adeniken	NGR	19.8.69	1rA		Sestriere	29 Jul 95
9.92	2.8	Kim	Collins	SKN	5.4.76	1rA	Tex R	Austin	5 Apr 03
9.92	3.7	Joshua 'J.J.'	Johnson	USA	10.5.76	2	Aragón	Zaragoza	28 Jul 07
9.92	3.7	Clement	Campbell	JAM	19.2.75	3	Aragón	Zaragoza	28 Jul 07
9.92	2.4	Trell	Kimmons	USA	13.7.85	4	DL	New York	12 Jun 10
Rolling start: 9.89w 3.7 Patrick Jarrett ¶				JAM	2.10.77	1	Pre	Eugene	27 May 01
Hand timing and three men at 9.7w									
9.7	1.9	Donovan	Powell ¶	JAM	31.10.71	1rA		Houston	19 May 95
9.7	1.9	Carl	Lewis	USA	1.7.61	2rA		Houston	19 May 95
9.7	1.9	Olapade	Adeniken	NGR	19.8.69	3rA		Houston	19 May 95
Drugs disqualification									
9.77	1.7	Justin	Gatlin ¶	USA	10.2.82	(1)	SGP	Doha	12 May 06
9.78	2.0	Tim	Montgomery ¶	USA	28.1.75	(1)	GPF	Paris (C)	14 Sep 02
9.79	1.1	Ben	Johnson ¶	CAN	30.12.61	(1)	OG	Seoul	24 Sep 88
9.87	2.0	Dwain	Chambers ¶	GBR	5.4.78	(2)	GPF	Paris (C)	14 Sep 02
9.7w ht	3.5		Johnson	CAN	30.12.61	(1)		Perth	24 Jan 87

200 METRES

Mark	Wind	Name		Nat	Born	Pos	Meet	Venue	Date
19.19	WR-0.3	Usain	Bolt	JAM	21.8.86	1	WCh	Berlin	20 Aug 09
19.26	0.7	Yohan	Blake	JAM	26.12.89	1	VD	Bruxelles	16 Sep 11
19.30	WR-0.9		Bolt			1	OG	Beijing	20 Aug 08
19.32	WR0.4	Michael	Johnson	USA	13.9.67	1	OG	Atlanta	1 Aug 96
19.32	0.4		Bolt			1	OG	London (OS)	9 Aug 12
19.40	0.8		Bolt			1	WCh	Daegu	3 Sep 11
19.44	0.4		Blake			2	OG	London (OS)	9 Aug 12
19.53	0.7	Walter	Dix	USA	31.1.86	2	VD	Bruxelles	16 Sep 11
19.54	0.0		Blake			1	VD	Bruxelles	7 Sep 12
19.56	-0.8		Bolt			1		Kingston	1 May 10
19.57	0.0		Bolt			1	VD	Bruxelles	4 Sep 09
19.58	1.3	Tyson	Gay	USA	9.8.82	1	Reebok	New York	30 May 09
19.58	1.4		Bolt			1	Athl	Lausanne	23 Aug 12
19.59	-0.9		Bolt			1	Athl	Lausanne	7 Jul 09
19.62	-0.3		Gay			1	NC	Indianapolis	24 Jun 07
19.63	0.4	Xavier	Carter	USA	8.12.85	1	Athl	Lausanne	11 Jul 06
19.63	-0.9		Bolt			1	Athl	Lausanne	2 Sep 08
19.65	0.0	Wallace	Spearmon	USA	24.12.84	1		Daegu	28 Sep 06
19.66	WR1.7		M Johnson			1	NC	Atlanta	23 Jun 96
19.66	0.0		Bolt			1	WK	Zürich	30 Aug 12
19.67	-0.5		Bolt			1	GP	Athína	13 Jul 08
19.68	0.4	Frank	Fredericks	NAM	2.10.67	2	OG	Atlanta	1 Aug 96
19.68	-0.1		Gay			1	WAF	Stuttgart	10 Sep 06
19.68	-0.1		Bolt			1	WAF	Thessaloníki	13 Sep 09
19.69	0.9		Dix			1	NCAA-r	Gainesville	26 May 07
19.70	0.4		Gay			2	Athl	Lausanne	11 Jul 06
19.70	0.8		Dix			2	WCh	Daegu	3 Sep 11
19.71A	1.8		M Johnson			1rA		Pietersburg	18 Mar 00
19.72A	WR 1.8	Pietro	Mennea	ITA	28.6.52	1	WUG	Ciudad de México	12 Sep 79
19.72	1.8		Dix			1	Pre	Eugene	3 Jul 10
19.72	0.1		Gay			1	Herc	Monaco	22 Jul 10
19.73	-0.2	Michael	Marsh	USA	4.8.67	1s1	OG	Barcelona	5 Aug 92
		(32/10)							
19.75	1.5	Carl	Lewis	USA	1.7.61	1	NC	Indianapolis	19 Jun 83
19.75	1.7	Joe	DeLoach	USA	5.6.67	1	OG	Seoul	28 Sep 88
19.75	0.2		Bolt			1	NC	Kingston	24 Jun 07
19.77	0.7	Ato	Boldon	TRI	30.12.73	1rA		Stuttgart	13 Jul 97
19.79	1.2	Shawn	Crawford	USA	14.1.78	1	OG	Athína	26 Aug 04
19.80	0.8	Christophe	Lemaitre	FRA	11.6.90	1	WCh	Daegu	3 Sep 11
19.81	-0.3	Alonso	Edward	PAN	8.12.89	2	WCh	Berlin	20 Aug 09
19.83A	WR 0.9	Tommie	Smith	USA	6.6.44	1	OG	Ciudad de México	16 Oct 68
19.84	1.7	Francis	Obikwelu	NGR/POR	22.11.78	1s2	WCh	Sevilla	25 Aug 99
19.84	0.4	Warren	Weir	JAM	31.10.89	3	OG	London (OS)	9 Aug 12
19.85	-0.3	John	Capel ¶	USA	27.10.78	1	NC	Sacramento	23 Jul 00
		(20)							
19.85	-0.5	Konstadínos	Kedéris ¶	GRE	11.7.73	1	EC	München	9 Aug 02
19.85	1.4	Churandy	Martina	NED	3.7.84	2	Athl	Lausanne	23 Aug 12
19.85	0.0	Nickel	Ashmeade	JAM	4.7.90	2	WK	Zürich	30 Aug 12
19.86A	1.0	Don	Quarrie	JAM	25.2.51	1	PAm	Cali	3 Aug 71
19.86	1.6	Maurice	Greene	USA	23.7.74	2rA	DNG	Stockholm	7 Jul 97
19.86	1.5	Jason	Young	JAM	21.3.91	1	Spitzen	Luzern	17 Jul 12

Mark	Wind	Name		Nat	Born	Pos	Meet	Venue	Date
19.87	0.8	Lorenzo	Daniel	USA	23.3.66	1	NCAA	Eugene	3 Jun 88
19.87A	1.8	John	Regis	GBR	13.10.66	1		Sestriere	31 Jul 94
19.87	1.2	Jeff	Williams	USA	31.12.65	1		Fresno	13 Apr 96
19.88	-0.3	Floyd	Heard	USA	24.3.66	2	NC	Sacramento	23 Jul 00
		(30)							
19.88	0.1	Joshua 'J.J'	Johnson	USA	10.5.76	1	VD	Bruxelles	24 Aug 01
19.89	-0.8	Claudinei	da Silva	BRA	19.11.70	1	GPF	München	11 Sep 99
19.89	1.3	Jaysuma	Saidy Ndure	NOR	1.1.84	1	WAF	Stuttgart	23 Sep 07
19.90	1.3	Asafa	Powell	JAM	23.11.82	1	NC	Kingston	25 Jun 06
19.92A	WR1.9	John	Carlos	USA	5.6.45	1	FOT	Echo Summit	12 Sep 68
19.96	-0.9	Kirk	Baptiste	USA	20.6.63	2	OG	Los Angeles	8 Aug 84
19.96	0.4	Robson	da Silva	BRA	4.9.64	1	VD	Bruxelles	25 Aug 89
19.96	-0.3	Coby	Miller	USA	19.10.76	3	NC	Sacramento	23 Jul 00
19.97	-0.9	Obadele	Thompson	BAR	30.3.76	1	Super	Yokohama	9 Sep 00
19.98	1.7	Marcin	Urbas	POL	17.9.76	2s2	WCh	Sevilla	25 Aug 99
19.98	0.3	Jordan	Vaden ¶	USA	15.9.78	2	NC	Indianapolis	25 Jun 06
19.98	1.4	LaShawn	Merritt ¶	USA	27.6.86	2	adidas	Carson	20 May 07
19.98	-0.3	Steve	Mullings ¶	JAM	29.11.82	5	WCh	Berlin	20 Aug 09
		(40)							
19.99	0.6	Calvin	Smith	USA	8.1.61	1	WK	Zürich	24 Aug 83
19.99	1.7	Rodney	Martin	USA	22.12.82	4	NC/OT	Eugene	6 Jul 08
19.99	2.0	Curtis	Mitchell	USA	11.3.89	1h1	NACAC	Miramar	10 Jul 10
20.00	0.0	Valeriy	Borzov	UKR	20.10.49	1	OG	München	4 Sep 72
20.00	0.0	Justin	Gatlin ¶	USA	10.2.82	1		Monterrey	11 Jun 05
20.01	-1.0	Michael	Bates	USA	19.12.69	3rA	WK	Zürich	19 Aug 92
20.01	0.1	Bernard	Williams	USA	19.1.78	2	VD	Bruxelles	24 Aug 01
20.02	1.7	Christopher	Williams ¶	JAM	15.3.72	1r5	MSR	Walnut	16 Apr 00
20.03	1.6	Clancy	Edwards	USA	9.8.55	1		Los Angeles (Ww)	29 Apr 78
20.03	1.5	Larry	Myricks ¶	USA	10.3.56	2	NC	Indianapolis	19 Jun 83
		(50)							
20.03	1.2	Jon	Drummond	USA	9.9.68	1	VD	Bruxelles	22 Aug 97
20.03	0.6	Shingo	Suetsugu	JPN	2.6.80	1	NC	Yokohama	7 Jun 03
20.03	0.6	Darvis	Patton	USA	4.12.77	1s1	WCh	Saint-Denis	28 Aug 03
		(53)	100th man 20.16, 200th 20.29, 300th 20.36, 400th 20.42, 500th 20.47						

Wind-assisted 2 performances to 19.73, performers listed to 19.99

Mark	Wind	Name		Nat	Born	Pos	Meet	Venue	Date
19.61	>4.0	Leroy	Burrell	USA	21.2.67	1	SWC	College Station	19 May 90
19.70	2.7		Johnson			1s1	NC	Atlanta	22 Jun 96
19.73	3.3	Shawn	Crawford	USA	14.1.78	1	NC	Eugene	28 Jun 09
19.80	3.2	LaShawn	Merritt ¶	USA	27.6.86	1		Greensboro	19 Apr 08
19.83	9.2	Bobby	Cruse	USA	20.3.78	1r2	Sea Ray	Knoxville	9 Apr 99
19.86	4.6	Roy	Martin	USA	25.12.66	1	SWC	Houston	18 May 86
19.86	4.0	Justin	Gatlin ¶	USA	10.2.82	1h2	NCAA	Eugene	30 May 01
19.90	3.8	Steve	Mullings ¶	JAM	29.11.82	1		Fort Worth	17 Apr 04
19.91		James	Jett	USA	28.12.70	1		Morgantown	18 Apr 92
19.93	2.4	Sebastián	Keitel	CHI	14.2.73	1		São Leopoldo	26 Apr 98
19.94	4.0	James	Sanford	USA	27.12.57	1s1	NCAA	Austin	7 Jun 80
19.94	3.7	Chris	Nelloms	USA	14.8.71	1	Big 10	Minneapolis	23 May 92
19.94	2.3	Kevin	Little	USA	3.4.68	1s3	NC	Sacramento	17 Jun 95
19.95	3.4	Mike	Roberson	USA	25.3.56	1h3	NCAA	Austin	5 Jun 80
19.96	2.2	Rohsaan	Griffin	USA	21.2.74	1s1	NC	Eugene	26 Jun 99
19.98	2.1	Aaron	Armstrong	TRI	14.10.77	1	NC	Port of Spain	26 Jun 05
19.98	2.1	Brendan	Christian	ANT	11.12.83	1		Austin	2 May 09
19.98	2.4	Darvis	Patton	USA	4.12.77	2	NC	Eugene	26 Jun 11
19.99	2.7	Ramon	Clay ¶	USA	29.6.75	2s1	NC	Atlanta	22 Jun 96
19.99	2.6	Maurice	Mitchell	USA	22.12.89	1	NCAA	Des Moines	11 Jun 11

Low altitude marks for athletes with lifetime bests at high altitude

19.94	0.3	Regis		2	WCh	Stuttgart	20 Aug 93	19.96	0.0	Mennea		1	Barletta	17 Aug 80

Suspended under IAAF rules

19.86	1.5	Justin	Gatlin ¶	USA	10.2.82	1	SEC	Starkville	12 May 02

Hand timing " during 220 yards race, * 220 yards less 0.1 seconds

19.7A		James	Sanford	USA	27.12.57	1		El Paso	19 Apr 80
19.7A	0.2	Robson C.	da Silva	BRA	4.9.64	1	AmCp	Bogotá	13 Aug 89

300 METRES

In 300m races only, not including intermediate times in 400m races

Mark		Name		Nat	Born	Pos	Meet	Venue	Date
30.85A		Michael	Johnson	USA	13.9.67	1		Pretoria	24 Mar 00
30.97		Usain	Bolt	JAM	21.8.86	1	GS	Ostrava	27 May 10
31.30		LaShawn	Merritt	USA	27.6.86	1	Pre	Eugene	7 Jun 09
31.31			Merritt			1		Eugene	8 Aug 06
31.48		Danny	Everett	USA	1.11.66	1		Jerez de la Frontera	3 Sep 90
31.48		Roberto	Hernández	CUB	6.3.67	2		Jerez de la Frontera	3 Sep 90
31.56		Doug	Walker ¶	GBR	28.7.73	1		Gateshead	19 Jul 98

Mark	Wind	Name		Nat	Born	Pos	Meet	Venue	Date

400 METRES

Mark	Wind	Name		Nat	Born	Pos	Meet	Venue	Date
43.18	WR	Michael	Johnson	USA	13.9.67	1	WCh	Sevilla	26 Aug 99
43.29	WR	Butch	Reynolds ¶	USA	8.6.64	1	WK	Zürich	17 Aug 88
43.39			Johnson			1	WCh	Göteborg	9 Aug 95
43.44			Johnson			1	NC	Atlanta	19 Jun 96
43.45		Jeremy	Wariner	USA	31.1.84	1	WCh	Osaka	31 Aug 07
43.49			Johnson			1	OG	Atlanta	29 Jul 96
43.50		Quincy	Watts	USA	19.6.70	1	OG	Barcelona	5 Aug 92
43.50			Wariner			1	DNG	Stockholm	7 Aug 07
43.62			Wariner			1rA	GGala	Roma	14 Jul 06
43.65			Johnson			1	WCh	Stuttgart	17 Aug 93
43.66			Johnson			1	NC	Sacramento	16 Jun 95
43.66			Johnson			1rA	Athl	Lausanne	3 Jul 96
43.68			Johnson			1	WK	Zürich	12 Aug 98
43.68			Johnson			1	NC	Sacramento	16 Jul 00
43.71			Watts			1s2	OG	Barcelona	3 Aug 92
43.74			Johnson			1	NC	Eugene	19 Jun 93
43.75			Johnson			1		Waco	19 Apr 97
43.75		LaShawn	Merritt	USA	27.6.86	1	OG	Beijing	21 Aug 08
43.76			Johnson			1	GWG	Uniondale, NY	22 Jul 98
43.81		Danny	Everett	USA	1.11.66	1	NC/OT	New Orleans	26 Jun 92
43.82			Wariner			1	WK	Zürich	29 Aug 08
43.83			Watts			1	WK	Zürich	19 Aug 92
43.84			Johnson			1	OG	Sydney	25 Sep 00
43.86A	WR	Lee	Evans	USA	25.2.47	1	OG	Ciudad de México	18 Oct 68
43.86			Johnson			1	Bisl	Oslo	21 Jul 95
43.86			Wariner			1	Gaz	Saint-Denis	18 Jul 08
43.87		Steve	Lewis	USA	16.5.69	1	OG	Seoul	28 Sep 88
43.88			Johnson			1	WK	Zürich	16 Aug 95
43.90			Johnson			1		Madrid	6 Sep 94
43.91			Reynolds			2	NC	Atlanta	19 Jun 96
43.91			Wariner			1	Gaz	Saint-Denis	8 Jul 06
		(31/8)							
43.94		Kirani	James	GRN	1.9.92	1	OG	London (OS)	6 Aug 12
43.97A		Larry	James	USA	6.11.47	2	OG	Ciudad de México	18 Oct 68
		(10)							
44.05		Angelo	Taylor	USA	29.12.78	1	NC	Indianapolis	23 Jun 07
44.09		Alvin	Harrison ¶	USA/DOM	20.1.74	3	NC	Atlanta	19 Jun 96
44.09		Jerome	Young ¶	USA	14.8.76	1	NC	New Orleans	21 Jun 98
44.10		Gary	Kikaya	COD	4.2.78	2	WAF	Stuttgart	9 Sep 06
44.13		Derek	Mills	USA	9.7.72	1	Pre	Eugene	4 Jun 95
44.14		Roberto	Hernández	CUB	6.3.67	2		Sevilla	30 May 90
44.15		Anthuan	Maybank	USA	30.12.69	1rB	Athl	Lausanne	3 Jul 96
44.16		Otis	Harris	USA	30.6.82	2	OG	Athína	23 Aug 04
44.17		Innocent	Egbunike	NGR	30.11.61	1rA	WK	Zürich	19 Aug 87
44.18		Samson	Kitur	KEN	25.2.66	2s2	OG	Barcelona	3 Aug 92
		(20)							
44.20A		Charles	Gitonga	KEN	5.10.71	1	NC	Nairobi	29 Jun 96
44.21		Ian	Morris	TRI	30.11.61	3s2	OG	Barcelona	3 Aug 92
44.26		Alberto	Juantorena	CUB	21.11.50	1	OG	Montreal	29 Jul 76
44.27		Alonzo	Babers	USA	31.10.61	1	OG	Los Angeles	8 Aug 84
44.27		Antonio	Pettigrew ¶	USA	3.11.67	1	NC	Houston	17 Jun 89
44.27		Darold	Williamson	USA	19.2.83	1s1	NCAA	Sacramento	10 Jun 05
44.28		Andrew	Valmon	USA	1.1.65	4	NC	Eugene	19 Jun 93
44.28		Tyree	Washington	USA	28.8.76	1		Los Angeles (ER)	12 May 01
44.29		Derrick	Brew	USA	28.12.77	1	SEC	Athens, GA	16 May 99
44.29		Sanderlei	Parrela	BRA	7.10.74	2	WCh	Sevilla	26 Aug 99
		(30)							
44.30		Gabriel	Tiacoh	CIV	10.9.63	1	NCAA	Indianapolis	7 Jun 86
44.30		Lamont	Smith	USA	11.12.72	4	NC	Atlanta	19 Jun 96
44.31		Alejandro	Cárdenas	MEX	4.10.74	3	WCh	Sevilla	26 Aug 99
44.33		Thomas	Schönlebe	GDR	6.8.65	1	WCh	Roma	3 Sep 87
44.34		Darnell	Hall	USA	26.9.71	1	Athl	Lausanne	5 Jul 95
44.35		Andrew	Rock	USA	23.1.82	2	WCh	Helsinki	12 Aug 05
44.36		Iwan	Thomas	GBR	5.1.74	1	NC	Birmingham	13 Jul 97
44.37		Roger	Black	GBR	31.3.66	2rA	Athl	Lausanne	3 Jul 96
44.37		Davis	Kamoga	UGA	17.7.68	2	WCh	Athína	5 Aug 97
44.37		Mark	Richardson	GBR	26.7.72	1	Bisl	Oslo	9 Jul 98
		(40)							
44.38		Darren	Clark	AUS	6.9.65	3s1	OG	Seoul	26 Sep 88

Mark	Wind	Name		Nat	Born	Pos	Meet	Venue	Date
44.40		Fred	Newhouse	USA	8.11.48	2	OG	Montreal	29 Jul 76
44.40		Chris	Brown	BAH	15.10.78	2	Bisl	Oslo	6 Jun 08
44.40		Jermaine	Gonzales	JAM	26.11.84	1	Herc	Monaco	22 Jul 10
44.41A		Ron	Freeman	USA	12.6.47	3	OG	Ciudad de México	18 Oct 68
44.43A		Ezra	Sambu	KEN	4.9.78	1	WCT	Nairobi	26 Jul 03
44.43		Jonathan	Borlée	BEL	22.2.88	1h3	OG	London (OS)	4 Aug 12
44.44		Tyler	Christopher	CAN	3.10.83	3	WCh	Helsinki	12 Aug 05
44.45A		Ronnie	Ray	USA	2.1.54	1	PAm	Ciudad de México	18 Oct 75
44.45		Darrell	Robinson	USA	23.12.63	2	Pepsi	Los Angeles (Ww)	17 May 86
44.45		Avard	Moncur	BAH	2.11.78	1		Madrid	7 Jul 01
44.45		Leonard	Byrd	USA	17.3.75	1	GP	Belém	5 May 02
44.45		Luguelin	Santos	DOM	12.11.93	1	FBK	Hengelo	27 May 12
(53)			100th man 44.65, 200th 44.90, 300th 45.11, 400th 45.29, 500th 45.42						
Drugs dq: 44.21 Antonio			Pettigrew ¶	USA	3.11.67	1		Nassau	26 May 99
Hand timing									
44.1		Wayne	Collett	USA	20.10.49	1	OT	Eugene	9 Jul 72
44.2*		John	Smith	USA	5.8.50	1	AAU	Eugene	26 Jun 71
44.2		Fred	Newhouse	USA	8.11.48	1s1	OT	Eugene	7 Jul 72

600 METRES

Mark	Wind	Name		Nat	Born	Pos	Meet	Venue	Date
1:12.81		Johnny	Gray	USA	19.6.60	1		Santa Monica	24 May 86
1:13.2 + ?		John	Kipkurgat	KEN	16.3.44	1		Pointe-à-Pierre	23 Mar 74
1:13.49		Joseph	Mutua	KEN	10.12.78	1		Liège (NX)	27 Aug 02
1:13.80		Earl	Jones	USA	17.7.64	2		Santa Monica	24 May 86

800 METRES

Mark	Wind	Name		Nat	Born	Pos	Meet	Venue	Date
1:40.91 WR		David	Rudisha	KEN	17.12.88	1	OG	London (OS)	9 Aug 12
1:41.01 WR			Rudisha			1rA		Rieti	29 Aug 10
1:41.09 WR			Rudisha			1	ISTAF	Berlin	22 Aug 10
1:41.11 WR		Wilson	Kipketer	DEN	12.12.70	1	ASV	Köln	24 Aug 97
1:41.24 WR			Kipketer			1rA	WK	Zürich	13 Aug 97
1:41.33			Rudisha			1		Rieti	10 Sep 11
1:41.51			Rudisha			1	NA	Heusden-Zolder	10 Jul 10
1:41.54			Rudisha			1	DL	Saint-Denis	6 Jul 12
1:41.73!WR		Sebastian	Coe	GBR	29.9.56	1		Firenze	10 Jun 81
1:41.73 WR			Kipketer			1rA	DNG	Stockholm	7 Jul 97
1:41.73		Nijel	Amos	BOT	15.3.94	2	OG	London (OS)	9 Aug 12
1:41.74			Rudisha			1	adidas	New York	9 Jun 12
1:41.77		Joaquim	Cruz	BRA	12.3.63	1	ASV	Köln	26 Aug 84
1:41.83			Kipketer			1	GP II	Rieti	1 Sep 96
1:42.01			Rudisha			1	GP	Rieti	6 Sep 09
1:42.04			Rudisha			1	Bisl	Oslo	4 Jun 10
1:42.12A			Rudisha			1	OT	Nairobi	23 Jun 12
1:42.17			Kipketer			1	TOTO	Tokyo	16 Sep 96
1:42.20			Kipketer			1	VD	Bruxelles	22 Aug 97
1:42.23		Abubaker	Kaki	SUD	21.6.89	2	Bisl	Oslo	4 Jun 10
1:42.27			Kipketer			1	VD	Bruxelles	3 Sep 99
1:42.28		Sammy	Koskei	KEN	14.5.61	2	ASV	Köln	26 Aug 84
1:42.32			Kipketer			1	GP II	Rieti	8 Sep 02
1:42.33 WR			Coe			1	Bisl	Oslo	5 Jul 79
1:42.34			Cruz			1r1	WK	Zürich	22 Aug 84
1:42.34		Wilfred	Bungei	KEN	24.7.80	2	GP II	Rieti	8 Sep 02
1:42.41			Cruz			1	VD	Bruxelles	24 Aug 84
1:42.47		Yuriy	Borzakovskiy	RUS	12.4.81	1	VD	Bruxelles	24 Aug 01
1:42.49			Cruz			1		Koblenz	28 Aug 85
1:42.51			Kipketer			1	Nik	Nice	10 Jul 96
(30/9)			*! photo-electric cell time*						
1:42.53		Timothy	Kitum (10)	KEN	20.11.94	3	OG	London (OS)	9 Aug 12
1:42.53		Mohammed	Aman	ETH	10.1.94	1	WK	Zürich	30 Aug 12
1:42.55		André	Bucher	SUI	19.10.76	1rA	WK	Zürich	17 Aug 01
1:42.58		Vebjørn	Rodal	NOR	16.9.72	1	OG	Atlanta	31 Jul 96
1:42.60		Johnny	Gray	USA	19.6.60	2r1		Koblenz	28 Aug 85
1:42.62		Patrick	Ndururi	KEN	12.1.69	2rA	WK	Zürich	13 Aug 97
1:42.67		Alfred	Kirwa Yego	KEN	28.11.86	2	GP	Rieti	6 Sep 09
1:42.69		Hezekiél	Sepeng ¶	RSA	30.6.74	2	VD	Bruxelles	3 Sep 99
1:42.69		Japheth	Kimutai	KEN	20.12.78	3	VD	Bruxelles	3 Sep 99
1:42.79		Fred	Onyancha	KEN	25.12.69	3	OG	Atlanta	31 Jul 96
1:42.79		Youssef Saad	Kamel	KEN/BRN	29.3.83	2	Herc	Monaco	29 Jul 08
(20)									
1:42.81		Jean-Patrick	Nduwimana	BDI	9.5.78	2rA	WK	Zürich	17 Aug 01

Mark	Wind	Name		Nat	Born	Pos	Meet	Venue	Date
1:42.82		Duane	Solomon	USA	28.12.84	4	OG	London (OS)	9 Aug 12
1:42.85		Norberto	Téllez	CUB	22.1.72	4	OG	Atlanta	31 Jul 96
1:42.86		Mbulaeni	Mulaudzi	RSA	8.9.80	3	GP	Rieti	6 Sep 09
1:42.88		Steve	Cram	GBR	14.10.60	1rA	WK	Zürich	21 Aug 85
1:42.91		William	Yiampoy	KEN	17.5.74	3	GP II	Rieti	8 Sep 02
1:42.95		Boaz	Lalang	KEN	8.2.89	2rA		Rieti	29 Aug 10
1:42.97		Peter	Elliott	GBR	9.10.62	1		Sevilla	30 May 90
1:42.95		Nick	Symmonds	USA	30.12.83	5	OG	London (OS)	9 Aug 12
1:42.98		Patrick	Konchellah	KEN	20.4.68	2	ASV	Köln	24 Aug 97
(30)									
1:43.03		Kennedy/Kenneth	Kimwetich	KEN	1.1.73	2		Stuttgart	19 Jul 98
1:43.06		Billy	Konchellah	KEN	20.10.62	1	WCh	Roma	1 Sep 87
1:43.07		Yeimer	López	CUB	20.8.82	1		Jerez de la Frontera	24 Jun 08
1:43.08		José Luiz	Barbosa	BRA	27.5.61	1		Rieti	6 Sep 91
1:43.09		Djabir	Saïd Guerni	ALG	29.3.77	5	VD	Bruxelles	3 Sep 99
1:43.13		Abraham Kipchirchir	Rotich	KEN	26.6.93	1	Herc	Monaco	20 Jul 12
1:43.15		Mehdi	Baala	FRA	17.8.78	5	GP II	Rieti	8 Sep 02
1:43.15		Asbel	Kiprop	KEN	30.6.89	2	Herc	Monaco	22 Jul 11
1:43.16		Paul	Ereng	KEN	22.8.67	1	WK	Zürich	16 Aug 89
1:43.17		Benson	Koech	KEN	10.11.74	1		Rieti	28 Aug 94
(40)									
1:43.20		Mark	Everett	USA	2.9.68	1rA	Gugl	Linz	9 Jul 97
1:43.22		Pawel	Czapiewski	POL	30.3.78	5rA	WK	Zürich	17 Aug 01
1:43.25		Amine	Laâlou	MAR	13.5.82	1	GGala	Roma	14 Jul 06
1:43.26		Sammy	Langat (Kibet)	KEN	24.1.70	1rB	WK	Zürich	14 Aug 96
1:43.30		William	Tanui	KEN	22.2.64	2		Rieti	6 Sep 91
1:43.30		Adam	Kszczot	POL	2.9.89	2		Rieti	10 Sep 11
1:43.31		Nixon	Kiprotich	KEN	4.12.62	1		Rieti	6 Sep 92
1:43.33		Robert	Chirchir	KEN	26.11.72	3		Stuttgart	19 Jul 98
1:43.33		William	Chirchir	KEN	6.2.79	6	VD	Bruxelles	3 Sep 99
1:43.33		Joseph Mwengi	Mutua	KEN	10.12.78	1rA	WK	Zürich	16 Aug 02
(50)		100th man 1:43.91, 200th 1:44.71, 300th 1:45.13, 400th 1:45.47, 500th 1:45.79							

1000 METRES

Mark	Wind	Name		Nat	Born	Pos	Meet	Venue	Date
2:11.96	WR	Noah	Ngeny	KEN	2.11.78	1	GP II	Rieti	5 Sep 99
2:12.18	WR	Sebastian	Coe	GBR	29.9.56	1	OsloG	Oslo	11 Jul 81
2:12.66			Ngeny			1	Nik	Nice	17 Jul 99
2:12.88		Steve	Cram	GBR	14.10.60	1		Gateshead	9 Aug 85
2:13.40	WR		Coe			1	Bisl	Oslo	1 Jul 80
2:13.56		Kennedy/Kenneth	Kimwetich	KEN	1.1.73	2	Nik	Nice	17 Jul 99
2:13.62		Abubaker	Kaki	SUD	21.6.89	1	Pre	Eugene	3 Jul 10
2:13.73		Noureddine	Morceli	ALG	28.2.70	1	BNP	Villeneuve d'Ascq	2 Jul 93
2:13.9	WR	Rick	Wohlhuter	USA	23.12.48	1	King	Oslo	30 Jul 74
2:13.96		Mehdi	Baala	FRA	17.8.78	1		Strasbourg	26 Jun 03

1500 METRES

Mark	Wind	Name		Nat	Born	Pos	Meet	Venue	Date
3:26.00	WR	Hicham	El Guerrouj	MAR	14.9.74	1	GGala	Roma	14 Jul 98
3:26.12			El Guerrouj			1	VD	Bruxelles	24 Aug 01
3:26.34		Bernard	Lagat	KEN/USA	12.12.74	2	VD	Bruxelles	24 Aug 01
3:26.45			El Guerrouj			1 rA	WK	Zürich	12 Aug 98
3:26.89			El Guerrouj			1	WK	Zürich	16 Aug 02
3:26.96			El Guerrouj			1	GP II	Rieti	8 Sep 02
3:27.21			El Guerrouj			1	WK	Zürich	11 Aug 00
3:27.34			El Guerrouj			1	Herc	Monaco	19 Jul 02
3:27.37	WR	Noureddine	Morceli	ALG	28.2.70	1	Nik	Nice	12 Jul 95
3:27.40			Lagat			1rA	WK	Zürich	6 Aug 04
3.27.52			Morceli			1	Herc	Monaco	25 Jul 95
3:27.64			El Guerrouj			2rA	WK	Zürich	6 Aug 04
3:27.65			El Guerrouj			1	WCh	Sevilla	24 Aug 99
3:27.91			Lagat			2	Herc	Monaco	19 Jul 02
3:28.12		Noah	Ngeny	KEN	2.11.78	2	WK	Zürich	11 Aug 00
3:28.21+			El Guerrouj			1	in 1M	Roma	7 Jul 99
3.28.37			Morceli			1	GPF	Monaco	9 Sep 95
3:28.37			El Guerrouj			1	Herc	Monaco	8 Aug 98
3:28.38			El Guerrouj			1	GP	Saint-Denis	6 Jul 01
3:28.40			El Guerrouj			1	VD	Bruxelles	5 Sep 03
3:28.51			Lagat			3	WK	Zürich	11 Aug 00
3:28.57			El Guerrouj			1rA	WK	Zürich	11 Aug 99
3:28.6+			Ngeny			2	in 1M	Roma	7 Jul 99
3:28.73			Ngeny			2	WCh	Sevilla	24 Aug 99

Mark	Wind	Name		Nat	Born	Pos	Meet	Venue	Date
3:28.84			Ngeny			1	GP	Paris (C)	21 Jul 99
3:28.86	WR		Morceli			1		Rieti	6 Sep 92
3:28.88		Asbel	Kiprop	KEN	30.6.89	1	Herc	Monaco	20 Jul 12
3:28.91			El Guerrouj			1rA	WK	Zürich	13 Aug 97
3:28.92			El Guerrouj			1	VD	Bruxelles	22 Aug 97
3:28.93			Ngeny			1	GPF	München	11 Sep 99
3:28.95		Fermín	Cacho	ESP	16.2.69	2rA	WK	Zürich	13 Aug 97
		(31/6))							
3:28.98		Mehdi	Baala	FRA	17.8.78	2	VD	Bruxelles	5 Sep 03
3:29.02		Daniel Kipchirchir	Komen	KEN	27.11.84	1	GGala	Roma	14 Jul 06
3:29.14		Rashid	Ramzi ¶	MAR/BRN	17.7.80	2	GGala	Roma	14 Jul 06
3:29.18		Vénuste	Niyongabo	BDI	9.12.73	2	VD	Bruxelles	22 Aug 97
		(10)							
3:29.27		Silas	Kiplagat	KEN	20.8.89	1	Herc	Monaco	22 Jul 10
3:29.29		William	Chirchir	KEN	6.2.79	3	VD	Bruxelles	24 Aug 01
3:29.46	WR	Saïd	Aouita	MAR	2.11.59	1	ISTAF	Berlin	23 Aug 85
3:29.46		Daniel	Komen	KEN	17.5.76	1	Herc	Monaco	16 Aug 97
3:29.47		Augustine	Choge	KEN	21.1.87	1	ISTAF	Berlin	14 Jun 09
3:29.51		Ali	Saïdi-Sief ¶	ALG	15.3.78	1	Athl	Lausanne	4 Jul 01
3:29.53		Amine	Laâlou	MAR	13.5.82	2	Herc	Monaco	22 Jul 10
3:29.67	WR	Steve	Cram	GBR	14.10.60	1	Nik	Nice	16 Jul 85
3:29.77		Sydney	Maree	USA	9.9.56	1	ASV	Köln	25 Aug 85
3:29.77		Sebastian	Coe	GBR	29.9.56	1		Rieti	7 Sep 86
		(20)							
3:29.77		Nixon	Chepseba	KEN	12.12.90	2	Herc	Monaco	20 Jul 12
3:29.91		Laban	Rotich	KEN	20.1.69	2rA	WK	Zürich	12 Aug 98
3:30.04		Timothy	Kiptanui	KEN	5.1.80	2	GP	Saint-Denis	23 Jul 04
3:30.07		Rui	Silva	POR	3.8.77	3	Herc	Monaco	19 Jul 02
3:30.18		John	Kibowen	KEN	21.4.69	3rA	WK	Zürich	12 Aug 98
3:30.20		Haron	Keitany	KEN	17.12.83	2	ISTAF	Berlin	14 Jun 09
3:30.24		Cornelius	Chirchir	KEN	5.6.83	4	Herc	Monaco	19 Jul 02
3:30.31		Ayanleh	Souleiman	DJI	3.12.92	2	FBK	Hengelo	27 May 12
3:30.33		Ivan	Heshko	UKR	19.8.79	2	VD	Bruxelles	3 Sep 04
3:30.35		Nick	Willis	NZL	25.4.83	3	Herc	Monaco	20 Jul 12
		(30)							
3:30.46		Alex	Kipchirchir	KEN	26.11.84	3	VD	Bruxelles	3 Sep 04
3:30.54		Alan	Webb	USA	13.1.83	1	Gaz	Saint-Denis	6 Jul 07
3:30.55		Abdi	Bile	SOM	28.12.62	1		Rieti	3 Sep 89
3:30.57		Reyes	Estévez	ESP	2.8.76	3	WCh	Sevilla	24 Aug 99
3:30.58		William	Tanui	KEN	22.2.64	3	Herc	Monaco	16 Aug 97
3:30.67		Benjamin	Kipkurui	KEN	28.12.80	2	Herc	Monaco	20 Jul 01
3:30.72		Paul	Korir	KEN	15.7.77	3	VD	Bruxelles	5 Sep 03
3:30.77	WR	Steve	Ovett	GBR	9.10.55	1		Rieti	4 Sep 83
3:30.80		Taoufik	Makhloufi	ALG	29.4.88	5	Herc	Monaco	20 Jul 12
3:30.83		Fouad	Chouki ¶	FRA	15.10.78	3	WK	Zürich	15 Aug 03
		(40)							
3:30.90		Andrew	Wheating	USA	21.11.87	4	Herc	Monaco	22 Jul 10
3:30.92		José Luis	González	ESP	8.12.57	3	Nik	Nice	16 Jul 85
3:30.92		Tarek	Boukensa	ALG	19.11.81	1	GGala	Roma	13 Jul 07
3:30.94		Isaac	Viciosa	ESP	26.12.69	5	Herc	Monaco	8 Aug 98
3:30.99		Robert	Rono	KEN	11.10.74	3	VD	Bruxelles	30 Aug 02
3:30.99		Isaac	Songok	KEN	25.4.84	3rA	WK	Zürich	6 Aug 04
3:31.00		Bethwell	Birgen	KEN	6.8.88	6	Herc	Monaco	20 Jul 12
3:31.01		Jim	Spivey	USA	7.3.60	1	R-W	Koblenz	28 Aug 88
3:31.04		Daham Najim	Bashir	KEN/QAT	8.11.78	2	SGP	Doha	13 May 05
3:31.06		Ryan	Gregson	AUS	26.4.90	5	Herc	Monaco	22 Jul 10
		(50)	100th man 3:32.18, 200th 3:34.01, 300th 3:35.20, 400th 3:36.11, 500th 3:36.50						

Drugs disqualification: 3:30.77 Adil Kaouch ¶   MAR   1.1.79   1   GGala   Roma   13 Jul 07

1 MILE

Mark	Wind	Name		Nat	Born	Pos	Meet	Venue	Date
3:43.13	WR	Hicham	El Guerrouj	MAR	14.9.74	1	GGala	Roma	7 Jul 99
3:43.40		Noah	Ngeny	KEN	2.11.78	2	GGala	Roma	7 Jul 99
3:44.39	WR	Noureddine	Morceli	ALG	28.2.70	1		Rieti	5 Sep 93
3:44.60			El Guerrouj			1	Nik	Nice	16 Jul 98
3:44.90			El Guerrouj			1	Bisl	Oslo	4 Jul 97
3:44.95			El Guerrouj			1	GGala	Roma	29 Jun 01
3:45.19			Morceli			1	WK	Zürich	16 Aug 95
3:45.64			El Guerrouj			1	ISTAF	Berlin	26 Aug 97
3:45.96			El Guerrouj			1	BrGP	London (CP)	5 Aug 00
3:46.24			El Guerrouj			1	Bisl	Oslo	28 Jul 00
3:46.32	WR	Steve	Cram	GBR	14.10.60	1	Bisl	Oslo	27 Jul 85
3:46.38		Daniel	Komen	KEN	17.5.76	2	ISTAF	Berlin	26 Aug 97

Mark	Wind	Name		Nat	Born	Pos	Meet	Venue	Date
3:46.70		Vénuste	Niyongabo	BUR	9.12.73	3	ISTAF	Berlin	26 Aug 97
3:46.76		Saïd	Aouita	MAR	2.11.59	1	WG	Helsinki	2 Jul 87
3:46.78			Morceli			1	ISTAF	Berlin	27 Aug 93
3:46.91		Alan	Webb	USA	13.1.83	1		Brasschaat	21 Jul 07
3:46.92			Aouita			1	WK	Zürich	21 Aug 85
3:47.10			El Guerrouj			1	BrGP	London (CP)	7 Aug 99
3:47.28		Bernard	Lagat	KEN/USA	12.12.74	2	GGala	Roma	29 Jun 01
3:47.30			Morceli			1	VD	Bruxelles	3 Sep 93
3:47.33	WR	Sebastian	Coe	GBR	29.9.56	1	VD	Bruxelles	28 Aug 81
		(21/10)							
3:47.65		Laban	Rotich	KEN	20.1.69	2	Bisl	Oslo	4 Jul 97
3:47.69		Steve	Scott	USA	5.5.56	1	OsloG	Oslo	7 Jul 82
3:47.79		José Luis	González	ESP	8.12.57	2	Bisl	Oslo	27 Jul 85
3:47.88		John	Kibowen	KEN	21.4.69	3	Bisl	Oslo	4 Jul 97
3:47.94		William	Chirchir	KEN	6.2.79	2	Bisl	Oslo	28 Jul 00
3:47.97		Daham Najim	Bashir	KEN/QAT	8.11.78	1	Bisl	Oslo	29 Jul 05
3:48.17		Paul	Korir	KEN	15.7.77	1	GP	London (CP)	8 Aug 03
3:48.23		Ali	Saïdi-Sief ¶	ALG	15.3.78	1	Bisl	Oslo	13 Jul 01
3:48.28		Daniel Kipchirchir	Komen	KEN	27.11.84	1	Pre	Eugene	10 Jun 07
3:48.38		Andrés Manuel	Díaz	ESP	12.7.69	3	GGala	Roma	29 Jun 01
		(20)							
3:48.40	WR	Steve	Ovett	GBR	9.10.55	1	R-W	Koblenz	26 Aug 81
3:48.50		Asbel	Kiprop	KEN	30.6.89	1	Pre	Eugene	7 Jun 09
3:48.78		Haron	Keitany	KEN	17.12.83	2	Pre	Eugene	7 Jun 09
3:48.80		William	Kemei	KEN	22.2.69	1	ISTAF	Berlin	21 Aug 92
3:48.83		Sydney	Maree	USA	9.9.56	1		Rieti	9 Sep 81
3:48.95		Deresse	Mekonnen	ETH	20.10.87	1	Bisl	Oslo	3 Jul 09
3:48.98		Craig	Mottram	AUS	18.6.80	5	Bisl	Oslo	29 Jul 05
3:49.08		John	Walker	NZL	12.1.52	2	OsloG	Oslo	7 Jul 82
3:49.20		Peter	Elliott	GBR	9.10.62	2	Bisl	Oslo	2 Jul 88
3:49.22		Jens-Peter	Herold	GDR	2.6.65	3	Bisl	Oslo	2 Jul 88
		(30)							
3:49.29		William	Biwott/Özbilen	KEN/TUR	5.3.90	2	Bisl	Oslo	3 Jul 09
3:49.31		Joe	Falcon	USA	23.6.66	1	Bisl	Oslo	14 Jul 90
3:49.34		David	Moorcroft	GBR	10.4.53	3	Bisl	Oslo	26 Jun 82
3:49.34		Benjamin	Kipkurui	KEN	28.12.80	3	VD	Bruxelles	25 Aug 00
3:49.38		Andrew	Baddeley	GBR	20.6.82	1	Bisl	Oslo	6 Jun 08
3:49.39		Silas	Kiplagat	KEN	20.8.89	2	Pre	Eugene	4 Jun 11
3:49.40		Abdi	Bile	SOM	28.12.62	4	Bisl	Oslo	2 Jul 88
3:49.45		Mike	Boit	KEN	6.1.49	2	VD	Bruxelles	28 Aug 81
3:49.50		Rui	Silva	POR	3.8.77	3	GGala	Roma	12 Jul 02
3:49.56		Fermín	Cacho	ESP	16.2.69	2	Bisl	Oslo	5 Jul 96
		(40)							
3:49.60		José Antonio	Redolat	ESP	17.2.76	4	GGala	Roma	29 Jun 01
3:49.70		Mekonnen	Gebremedhin	ETH	11.10.88	4	Pre	Eugene	4 Jun 11
3:49.75		Leonard	Mucheru	KEN/BRN	13.6.78	5	GGala	Roma	29 Jun 01
3:49.77		Ray	Flynn	IRL	22.1.57	3	OsloG	Oslo	7 Jul 82
3:49.77		Wilfred	Kirochi	KEN	12.12.69	2	Bisl	Oslo	6 Jul 91
3:49.77		Caleb	Ndiku	KEN	9.10.92	5	Pre	Eugene	4 Jun 11
3:49.80		Jim	Spivey	USA	7.3.60	3	Bisl	Oslo	5 Jul 86
3:49.83		Vyacheslav	Shabunin	RUS	27.9.69	6	GGala	Roma	29 Jun 01
3:49.91		Simon	Doyle	AUS	9.11.66	4	Bisl	Oslo	6 Jul 91
3:49.95		Tarek	Boukensa	ALG	19.11.81	6	Bisl	Oslo	29 Jul 05
3:49.98		Thomas	Wessinghage	FRG	22.2.52	3	ISTAF	Berlin	17 Aug 83
		(51)	100th 3:51.31, 200th 3:53.6, 300th 3:55.18						
Indoors: 3:49.78		Eamonn	Coghlan	IRL	24.11.52	1		East Rutherford	27 Feb 83

2000 METRES

Mark	Wind	Name		Nat	Born	Pos	Meet	Venue	Date
4:44.79	WR	Hicham	El Guerrouj	MAR	14.9.74	1	ISTAF	Berlin	7 Sep 99
4:46.88		Ali	Saïdi-Sief ¶	ALG	15.3.78	1		Strasbourg	19 Jun 01
4:47.88	WR	Noureddine	Morceli	ALG	28.2.70	1		Paris	3 Jul 95
4:48.36			El Guerrouj			1		Gateshead	19 Jul 98
4:48.69		Vénuste	Niyongabo	BUR	9.12.73	1	Nik	Nice	12 Jul 95
4:48.74		John	Kibowen	KEN	21.4.69	1		Hechtel	1 Aug 98
4:49.00			Niyongabo			1		Rieti	3 Sep 97
4:49.55			Morceli			1	Nik	Nice	10 Jul 96
4:50.08		Noah	Ngeny	KEN	2.11.78	1	DNG	Stockholm	30 Jul 99
4:50.76		Craig	Mottram	AUS	18.6.80	1		Melbourne (OP)	9 Mar 06
4:50.81	WR	Saïd	Aouita	MAR	2.11.59	1	BNP	Paris	16 Jul 87
4:51.30		Daniel	Komen	KEN	17.5.76	1		Milano	5 Jun 98
4:51.39	WR	Steve	Cram (10)	GBR	14.10.60	1	BGP	Budapest	4 Aug 85
4:49.99	ind	Kenenisa	Bekele	ETH	13.6.82	1		Birmingham	17 Feb 07

Mark	Wind	Name		Nat	Born	Pos	Meet	Venue	Date

3000 METRES

Mark	Wind	Name		Nat	Born	Pos	Meet	Venue	Date
7:20.67	WR	Daniel	Komen	KEN	17.5.76	1		Rieti	1 Sep 96
7:23.09		Hicham	El Guerrouj	MAR	14.9.74	1	VD	Bruxelles	3 Sep 99
7:25.02		Ali	Saïdi-Sief ¶	ALG	15.3.78	1	Herc	Monaco	18 Aug 00
7:25.09		Haile	Gebrselassie	ETH	18.4.73	1	VD	Bruxelles	28 Aug 98
7:25.11	WR	Noureddine	Morceli	ALG	28.2.70	1	Herc	Monaco	2 Aug 94
7:25.16			Komen			1	Herc	Monaco	10 Aug 96
7:25.54			Gebrselassie			1	Herc	Monaco	8 Aug 98
7:25.79		Kenenisa	Bekele	ETH	13.6.82	1	DNG	Stockholm	7 Aug 07
7:25.87			Komen			1	VD	Bruxelles	23 Aug 96
7:26.02			Gebrselassie			1	VD	Bruxelles	22 Aug 97
7:26.03			Gebrselassie			1	GP II	Helsinki	10 Jun 99
7:26.5 e			Komen			1	in 2M	Sydney	28 Feb 98
7:26.62		Mohammed	Mourhit ¶	BEL	10.10.70	2	Herc	Monaco	18 Aug 00
7:26.69			K Bekele			1	BrGP	Sheffield	15 Jul 07
7:27.18		Moses	Kiptanui	KEN	1.10.70	1	Herc	Monaco	25 Jul 95
7:27.26		Yenew	Alamirew	ETH	27.5.90	1	DL	Doha	6 May 11
7:27.3+			Komen			1	in 2M	Hechtel	19 Jul 97
7:27.42			Gebrselassie			1	Bisl	Oslo	9 Jul 98
7:27.50			Morceli			1	VD	Bruxelles	25 Aug 95
7:27.55		Edwin	Soi (10)	KEN	3.3.86	2	DL	Doha	6 May 11
7:27.59		Luke	Kipkosgei	KEN	27.11.75	2	Herc	Monaco	8 Aug 98
7:27.66		Eliud	Kipchoge	KEN	5.11.84	3	DL	Doha	6 May 11
7:27.67			Saïdi-Sief			1	Gaz	Saint-Denis	23 Jun 00
7:27.72			Kipchoge	KEN	5.11.84	1	VD	Bruxelles	3 Sep 04
7:27.75		Thomas	Nyariki	KEN	27.9.71	2	Herc	Monaco	10 Aug 96
7.28.04			Kiptanui			1	ASV	Köln	18 Aug 95
7:28.28			Kipkosgei			2	Bisl	Oslo	9 Jul 98
7:28.28		James	Kwalia	KEN/QAT	12.6.84	2	VD	Bruxelles	3 Sep 04
7:28.37			Kipchoge			1	SGP	Doha	8 May 09
7:28.41		Paul	Bitok	KEN	26.6.70	3	Herc	Monaco	10 Aug 96
		(30/15)							
7:28.45		Assefa	Mezegebu	ETH	19.6.78	3	Herc	Monaco	8 Aug 98
7:28.67		Benjamin	Limo	KEN	23.8.74	1	Herc	Monaco	4 Aug 99
7:28.70		Paul	Tergat	KEN	17.6.69	4	Herc	Monaco	10 Aug 96
7:28.70		Tariku	Bekele	ETH	21.1.87	1		Rieti	29 Aug 10
7:28.72		Isaac K.	Songok	KEN	25.4.84	1	GP	Rieti	27 Aug 06
		(20)							
7:28.76		Augustine	Choge	KEN	21.1.87	4	DL	Doha	6 May 11
7:28.93		Salah	Hissou	MAR	16.1.72	2	Herc	Monaco	4 Aug 99
7:28.94		Brahim	Lahlafi	FRA/MAR	15.4.68	3	Herc	Monaco	4 Aug 99
7:29.00		Bernard	Lagat	USA	12.12.74	2		Rieti	29 Aug 10
7:29.09		John	Kibowen	KEN	21.4.69	3	Bisl	Oslo	9 Jul 98
7:29.34		Isaac	Viciosa	ESP	26.12.69	4	Bisl	Oslo	9 Jul 98
7:29.45	WR	Saïd	Aouita	MAR	2.11.59	1	ASV	Köln	20 Aug 89
7:29.92		Sileshi	Sihine	ETH	29.1.83	1	GP	Rieti	28 Aug 05
7:30.09		Ismaïl	Sghyr	MAR/FRA	16.3.72	2	Herc	Monaco	25 Jul 95
7:30.09		Thomas	Longosiwa	KEN	14.1.82	2	SGP	Doha	8 May 09
		(30)							
7:30.15		Vincent	Chepkok	KEN	5.7.88	5	DL	Doha	6 May 11
7:30.36		Mark	Carroll	IRL	15.1.72	5	Herc	Monaco	4 Aug 99
7:30.43		Isiah	Koech	KEN	19.12.93	1	DNG	Stockholm	17 Aug 12
7:30.50		Dieter	Baumann ¶	GER	9.2.65	6	Herc	Monaco	8 Aug 98
7:30.53		El Hassan	Lahssini	MAR/FRA	1.1.75	6	Herc	Monaco	10 Aug 96
7:30.53		Hailu	Mekonnen	ETH	4.4.80	1	VD	Bruxelles	24 Aug 01
7:30.62		Boniface	Songok	KEN	25.12.80	3	VD	Bruxelles	3 Sep 04
7:30.76		Jamal Bilal	Salem	KEN/QAT	12.9.78	4	SGP	Doha	13 May 05
7:30.78		Mustapha	Essaïd	FRA	20.1.70	7	Herc	Monaco	8 Aug 98
7:30.84		Bob	Kennedy	USA	18.8.70	8	Herc	Monaco	8 Aug 98
		(40)							
7:30.95		Moses	Kipsiro	UGA	2.9.86	1	Herc	Monaco	28 Jul 09
7:30.99		Khalid	Boulami	MAR	7.8.69	1	Nik	Nice	16 Jul 97
7:30.99		Caleb	Ndiku	KEN	9.10.92	2	DNG	Stockholm	17 Aug 12
7:31.13		Julius	Gitahi	KEN	29.4.78	6	Bisl	Oslo	9 Jul 98
7:31.14		William	Kalya	KEN	4.8.74	3	Herc	Monaco	16 Aug 97
7:31.20		Joseph	Kiplimo	KEN	20.7.88	1	GP	Rieti	6 Sep 09
7:31.41		Sammy Alex	Mutahi	KEN	1.6.89	2	GP	Rieti	6 Sep 09
7:31.41		Daniel Kipchirchir	Komen	KEN	27.11.84	6	DL	Doha	6 May 11
7:31.59		Manuel	Pancorbo	ESP	7.7.66	7	Bisl	Oslo	9 Jul 98

Mark	Wind	Name		Nat	Born	Pos	Meet	Venue	Date
7:31.68		Yusuf	Biwott	KEN	12.11.86	1	GS	Ostrava	27 May 10
	(50)		100th man 7:35.35, 200th man 7:39.82, 300th 7:42.38, 400th 7:44.15, 500th 7:45.9						
Indoor									
7:24.90			Komen			1		Budapest	6 Feb 98
7:26.15			Gebrselassie			1		Karlsruhe	25 Jan 98
7:26.80			Gebrselassie			1		Karlsruhe	24 Jan 99
7:27.80			Alamirew			1	Spark	Stuttgart	5 Feb 11
7:27.93			Komen			1	Spark	Stuttgart	1 Feb 98
7:28.00		Augustine	Choge	KEN	21.1.87	2	Spark	Stuttgart	5 Feb 11

2 MILES

Mark	Wind	Name		Nat	Born	Pos	Meet	Venue	Date
7:58.61 WR		Daniel	Komen	KEN	17.5.76	1		Hechtel	19 Jul 97
7:58.91			Komen			1		Sydney	28 Feb 98
8:01.08 WR		Haile	Gebrselassie	ETH	18.4.73	1	APM	Hengelo	31 May 97
8:01.72			Gebrselassie			1	BrGP	London (CP)	7 Aug 99
8:01.86			Gebrselassie			1	APM	Hengelo	30 May 99
8:03.50		Craig	Mottram	AUS	18.6.80	1	Pre	Eugene	10 Jun 07
8:04.83		Tariku	Bekele	ETH	21.1.87	2	Pre	Eugene	10 Jun 07
Indoors									
8:04.35		Kenenisa	Bekele	ETH	13.6.82	1	GP	Birmingham	16 Feb 08
8:06.48		Paul Kipsiele	Koech	KEN	10.11.81	2	GP	Birmingham	16 Feb 08

5000 METRES

Mark	Wind	Name		Nat	Born	Pos	Meet	Venue	Date
12:37.35 WR		Kenenisa	Bekele	ETH	13.6.82	1	FBK	Hengelo	31 May 04
12:39.36 WR		Haile	Gebrselassie	ETH	18.4.73	1	GP II	Helsinki	13 Jun 98
12:39.74 WR		Daniel	Komen	KEN	17.5.76	1	VD	Bruxelles	22 Aug 97
12:40.18			K Bekele			1	Gaz	Saint-Denis	1 Jul 05
12:41.86 WR			Gebrselassie			1	WK	Zürich	13 Aug 97
12:44.39 WR			Gebrselassie			1	WK	Zürich	16 Aug 95
12:44.90			Komen			2	WK	Zürich	13 Aug 97
12:45.09			Komen			1	WK	Zürich	14 Aug 96
12:46.53		Eliud	Kipchoge	KEN	5.11.84	1	GGala	Roma	2 Jul 04
12:46.81		Dejen	Gebremeskel	ETH	24.11.89	1	DL	Saint-Denis	6 Jul 12
12:47.04		Sileshi	Sihine	ETH	29.9.83	2	GGala	Roma	2 Jul 04
12:47.53		Hagos	Gebrhiwet	ETH	11.5.94	2	DL	Saint-Denis	6 Jul 12
12:48.09			K Bekele			1	VD	Bruxelles	25 Aug 06
12:48.25			K Bekele			1	WK	Zürich	18 Aug 06
12:48.64		Isiah	Koech	KEN	19.12.93	3	DL	Saint-Denis	6 Jul 12
12:48.66		Isaac K.	Songok	KEN	25.4.84	2	WK	Zürich	18 Aug 06
12:48.77		Yenew	Alamirew (10)	ETH	27.5.90	4	DL	Saint-Denis	6 Jul 12
12:48.81		Stephen	Cherono/Shaheen	KEN/QAT	15.10.82	1	GS	Ostrava	12 Jun 03
12:48.98			Komen			1	GGala	Roma	5 Jun 97
12:49.04		Thomas	Longosiwa	KEN	14.1.82	5	DL	Saint-Denis	6 Jul 12
12:49.28		Brahim	Lahlafi	MAR	15.4.68	1	VD	Bruxelles	25 Aug 00
12:49.50		John	Kipkoech	KEN	29.12.91	6	DL	Saint-Denis	6 Jul 12
12:49.53			K Bekele			1	Aragón	Zaragoza	28 Jul 07
12:49.64			Gebrselassie			1	WK	Zürich	11 Aug 99
12:49.71		Mohammed	Mourhit ¶	BEL	10.10.70	2	VD	Bruxelles	25 Aug 00
12:49.87		Paul	Tergat	KEN	17.6.69	3	WK	Zürich	13 Aug 97
12:50.16			Sihine			1	VD	Bruxelles	14 Sep 07
12:50.18			K Bekele			1	WK	Zürich	29 Aug 08
12:50.22			Kipchoge			1	VD	Bruxelles	26 Aug 05
12:50.24		Hicham	El Guerrouj	MAR	14.9.74	2	GS	Ostrava	12 Jun 03
	(30/17)								
12:50.25		Abderrahim	Goumri ¶	MAR	21.5.76	2	VD	Bruxelles	26 Aug 05
12:50.55		Moses	Masai	KEN	1.6.86	1	ISTAF	Berlin	1 Jun 08
12:50.72		Moses	Kipsiro	UGA	2.9.86	3	VD	Bruxelles	14 Sep 07
	(20)								
12:50.80		Salah	Hissou	MAR	16.1.72	1	GGala	Roma	5 Jun 96
12:50.86		Ali	Saïdi-Sief ¶	ALG	15.3.78	1	GGala	Roma	30 Jun 00
12:51.00		Joseph	Ebuya	KEN	20.6.87	4	VD	Bruxelles	14 Sep 07
12:51.45		Vincent	Chepkok	KEN	5.7.88	2	DL	Doha	14 May 10
12:52.33		Sammy	Kipketer	KEN	29.9.81	2	Bisl	Oslo	27 Jun 03
12:52.40		Edwin	Soi	KEN	3.3.86	2	Gaz	Saint-Denis	8 Jul 06
12:52.45		Tariku	Bekele	ETH	21.1.87	2	ISTAF	Berlin	1 Jun 08
12:52.80		Gebre-egziabher	Gebremariam	ETH	10.9.84	3	GGala	Roma	8 Jul 05
12:52.99		Abraham	Chebii	KEN	23.12.79	4	Bisl	Oslo	27 Jun 03
12:53.11		Mohamed	Farah	GBR	23.3.83	1	Herc	Monaco	22 Jul 11
	(30)								
12:53.41		Khalid	Boulami	MAR	7.8.69	4	WK	Zürich	13 Aug 97

Mark	Wind	Name		Nat	Born	Pos	Meet	Venue	Date
12:53.46		Mark	Kiptoo	KEN	21.6.76	1	DNG	Stockholm	6 Aug 10
12:53.58		Imane	Merga	ETH	15.10.88	3	DNG	Stockholm	6 Aug 10
12:53.60		Bernard	Lagat	USA	12.12.74	2	Herc	Monaco	22 Jul 11
12:53.66		Augustine	Choge	KEN	21.1.87	4	GGala	Roma	8 Jul 05
12:53.72		Philip	Mosima	KEN	2.1.77	2	GGala	Roma	5 Jun 96
12:53.84		Assefa	Mezegebu	ETH	19.6.78	1	VD	Bruxelles	28 Aug 98
12:54.07		John	Kibowen	KEN	21.4.69	4	WCh	Saint-Denis	31 Aug 03
12:54.15		Dejene	Berhanu	ETH	12.12.80	3	GGala	Roma	2 Jul 04
12:54.19		Abreham	Cherkos	ETH	23.9.89	5	GGala	Roma	14 Jul 06
		(40)							
12:54.46		Moses	Mosop	KEN	17.7.85	3	Gaz	Saint-Denis	8 Jul 06
12:54.58		James	Kwalia	KEN/QAT	12.6.84	5	Bisl	Oslo	27 Jun 03
12:54.70		Dieter	Baumann ¶	GER	9.2.65	5	WK	Zürich	13 Aug 97
12:54.85		Moses	Kiptanui	KEN	1.10.70	3	GGala	Roma	5 Jun 96
12:54.99		Benjamin	Limo	KEN	23.8.74	3	Gaz	Saint-Denis	4 Jul 03
12:55.06		Lucas	Rotich	KEN	16.4.90	4	Bisl	Oslo	4 Jun 10
12:55.52		Hicham	Bellani	MAR	15.9.79	7	GGala	Roma	14 Jul 06
12:55.53		Chris	Solinsky	USA	5.12.84	5	DNG	Stockholm	6 Aug 10
12:55.58		Abebe	Dinkesa	ETH	6.3.84	2	Gaz	Saint-Denis	1 Jul 05
12:55.63		Mark	Bett	KEN	22.12.76	2	Bisl	Oslo	28 Jul 00
		(50)							

100th man 13:01.91, 200th 13:09.84, 300th 13:13.80, 400th 13:17.84, 500th 13:19.73

Indoors: 12:49.60 — K Bekele — 1 — Birmingham — 20 Feb 04

10,000 METRES

Mark	Wind	Name		Nat	Born	Pos	Meet	Venue	Date
26:17.53wr		Kenenisa	Bekele	ETH	13.6.82	1	VD	Bruxelles	26 Aug 05
26:20.31wr			K Bekele			1	GS	Ostrava	8 Jun 04
26:22.75wr		Haile	Gebrselassie	ETH	18.4.73	1	APM	Hengelo	1 Jun 98
26:25.97			K Bekele			1	Pre	Eugene	8 Jun 08
26:27.85wr		Paul	Tergat	KEN	17.6.69	1	VD	Bruxelles	22 Aug 97
26:28.72			K Bekele			1	FBK	Hengelo	29 May 05
26:29.22			Gebrselassie			1	VD	Bruxelles	5 Sep 03
26:30.03		Nicholas	Kemboi	KEN/QAT	25.11.83	2	VD	Bruxelles	5 Sep 03
26:30.74		Abebe	Dinkesa	ETH	6.3.84	2	FBK	Hengelo	29 May 05
26:31.32wr			Gebrselassie			1	Bisl	Oslo	4 Jul 97
26:35.63		Micah	Kogo	KEN	3.6.86	1	VD	Bruxelles	25 Aug 06
26:36.26		Paul	Koech	KEN	25.6.69	2	VD	Bruxelles	22 Aug 97
26:37.25		Zersenay	Tadese	ERI	8.2.82	2	VD	Bruxelles	25 Aug 06
26:38.08wr		Salah	Hissou	MAR	16.1.72	1	VD	Bruxelles	23 Aug 96
26:38.76		Abdullah Ahmad	Hassan (10)	QAT	4.4.81	3	VD	Bruxelles	5 Sep 03
		(Formerly Albert Chepkurui KEN)							
26:39.69		Sileshi	Sihine	ETH	29.9.83	1	FBK	Hengelo	31 May 04
26:39.77		Boniface	Kiprop	UGA	12.10.85	2	VD	Bruxelles	26 Aug 05
26:41.58			Gebrselassie			2	FBK	Hengelo	31 May 04
26:41.75		Samuel	Wanjiru	KEN	10.11.86	3	VD	Bruxelles	26 Aug 05
26:41.95			Kiprop			3	VD	Bruxelles	25 Aug 06
26:43.16			K Bekele			1	VD	Bruxelles	16 Sep 11
26:43.53wr			Gebrselassie			1	APM	Hengelo	5 Jun 95
26:43.98		Lucas	Rotich	KEN	16.4.90	2	VD	Bruxelles	16 Sep 11
26:46.19			K Bekele			1	VD	Bruxelles	14 Sep 07
26:46.31			K Bekele			1	WCh	Berlin	17 Aug 09
26:46.44			Tergat			1	VD	Bruxelles	28 Aug 98
26:46.57		Mohamed	Farah	GBR	23.3.83	1	Pre	Eugene	3 Jun 11
26:47.89			Koech			2	VD	Bruxelles	28 Aug 98
26:48.00		Galen	Rupp	USA	8.5.86	3	VD	Bruxelles	16 Sep 11
26:48.35		Imane	Merga	ETH	15.10.88	2	Pre	Eugene	3 Jun 11
		(30/17)							
26:48.99		Josphat	Bett	KEN	12.6.90	3	Pre	Eugene	3 Jun 11
26:49.02		Eliud	Kipchoge	KEN	5.11.84	2	FBK	Hengelo	26 May 07
26:49.20		Moses	Masai	KEN	1.6.86	2	VD	Bruxelles	14 Sep 07
		(20)							
26:49.38		Sammy	Kipketer	KEN	29.9.81	1	VD	Bruxelles	30 Aug 02
26:49.55		Moses	Mosop	KEN	17.7.85	3	FBK	Hengelo	26 May 07
26:49.90		Assefa	Mezegebu	ETH	19.6.78	2	VD	Bruxelles	30 Aug 02
26:50.20		Richard	Limo	KEN	18.11.80	3	VD	Bruxelles	30 Aug 02
26:50.63		Paul	Tanui	KEN	22.12.90	4	Pre	Eugene	3 Jun 11
26:51.16		Emmanuel	Bett	KEN	30.3.83	1	VD	Bruxelles	7 Sep 12
26:51.49		Charles	Kamathi	KEN	18.5.78	1	VD	Bruxelles	3 Sep 99
26:51.68		Vincent	Chepkok	KEN	5.7.88	2	VD	Bruxelles	7 Sep 12
26:52.23wr		William	Sigei	KEN	14.10.69	1	Bisl	Oslo	22 Jul 94
26:52.30		Mohammed	Mourhit ¶	BEL	10.10.70	2	VD	Bruxelles	3 Sep 99
		(30)							

Mark	Wind	Name		Nat	Born	Pos	Meet	Venue	Date
26:52.33		Gebre-egziabher	Gebremariam	ETH	10.9.84	4	FBK	Hengelo	26 May 07
26:52.65		Kenneth	Kipkemoi	KEN	2.8.84	3	VD	Bruxelles	7 Sep 12
26:52.87		John Cheruiyot	Korir	KEN	13.12.81	5	VD	Bruxelles	30 Aug 02
26:52.93		Mark	Bett	KEN	22.12.76	6	VD	Bruxelles	26 Aug 05
26:54.25		Mathew	Kisorio ¶	KEN	16.5.89	7	Pre	Eugene	3 Jun 11
26:54.64		Mark	Kiptoo	KEN	21.6.76	8	Pre	Eugene	3 Jun 11
26:55.29		Leonard Patrick	Komon	KEN	10.1.88	9	Pre	Eugene	3 Jun 11
26:55.73		Geoffrey	Kirui	KEN	16.2.93	6	VD	Bruxelles	16 Sep 11
26:56.74		Josphat	Menjo	KEN	20.8.79	1		Turku	29 Aug 10
26:57.36		Josphat	Muchiri Ndambiri	KEN	12.2.85	1		Fukuroi	3 May 09
		(40)							
26:57.56		Yigrem	Dimelash	ETH	28.1.94	4	VD	Bruxelles	7 Sep 12
26:58.38	WR	Yobes	Ondieki	KEN	21.2.61	1	Bisl	Oslo	10 Jul 93
26:59.51		Bernard	Kipyego	KEN	16.7.86	4	VD	Bruxelles	14 Sep 07
26:59.60		Chris	Solinsky	USA	5.12.84	1		Stanford	1 May 10
26:59.81		Titus	Mbishei	KEN	28.10.90	7	VD	Bruxelles	16 Sep 11
26:59.88		Martin Irungu	Mathathi	KEN	25.12.85	2		Fukuroi	3 May 09
27:01.83		Gideon	Ngatuny	KEN	10.10.86	2		Tendo	16 May 09
27:01.98		Wilson	Kiprop	KEN	14.4.87	1	OT	Eugene/USA	1 Jun 12
27:02.62		Abderrahim	Goumri ¶	MAR	21.5.76	3	FBK	Hengelo	29 May 05
27:02.62		Deriba	Merga	ETH	26.10.80	6	FBK	Hengelo	26 May 07
		(50)	100th man 27:17.03, 200th 27:31.46, 300th 27:40.69, 400th 27:46.87, 500th 27:54.28						

20,000 METRES & 1 HOUR

Mark		Name		Nat	Born	Pos	Meet	Venue	Date
56:25.98+	21 285m	Haile	Gebrselassie	ETH	18.4.73	1	GS	Ostrava	27 Jun 07
56:55.6+	21 101	Arturo	Barrios	MEX	12.12.63	1		La Flèche	30 Mar 91
57:24.19+	20 944	Jos	Hermens	NED	8.1.50	1		Papendal	1 May 76
57:18.4+	20 943	Dionísio	Castro	POR	22.11.63	1		La Flèche	31 Mar 90

HALF MARATHON

Included are the slightly downhill courses: Newcastle to South Shields 30.5m, Tokyo 33m, Lisboa (Spring to 2008) 69m

Mark		Name		Nat	Born	Pos	Meet	Venue	Date
58:23	WR	Zersenay	Tadese	ERI	8.2.82	1		Lisboa	21 Mar 10
58:30			Z Tadese			1		Lisboa	20 Mar 11
58:33	WR	Samuel	Wanjiru	KEN	10.11.86	1		Den Haag	17 Mar 07
58:46		Mathew	Kisorio ¶	KEN	16.5.89	1		Philadelphia	18 Sep 11
58:47		Atsedu	Tsegay	ETH	17.12.91	1		Praha	31 Mar 12
58:48		Sammy	Kitwara	KEN	26.11.86	2		Philadelphia	18 Sep 11
58:52		Patrick	Makau	KEN	2.3.85	1		Ra's Al Khaymah	20 Feb 09
58:53	WR		Wanjiru			1		Ra's Al Khaymah	9 Feb 07
58:54		Stephen	Kibet	KEN	9.11.86	1		Den Haag	11 Mar 12
58:55	WR	Haile	Gebrselassie	ETH	18.4.73	1		Tempe	15 Jan 06
58:56			Makau			1		Berlin	1 Apr 07
58:56	dh	Martin	Mathathi	KEN	25.12.85	1	GNR	South Shields	18 Sep 11
58:58			Kitwara			1		Rotterdam	13 Sep 09
58:59			Z Tadese			1	WCh	Udine	14 Oct 07
58:59		Wilson	Kipsang (10)	KEN	15.3.82	2		Ra's Al Khaymah	20 Feb 09
59:02			Makau			2	WCh	Udine	14 Oct 07
59:02		Jonathan	Maiyo	KEN	.88	2		Den Haag	11 Mar 12
59:05	dh		Tadese			1	GNR	South Shields	18 Sep 05
59:05		Evans	Cheruiyot	KEN	10.5.82	3	WCh	Udine	14 Oct 07
59:05		Ezekiel	Chebii	KEN	3.1.91	1		Lille	1 Sep 12
59:06	dh	Paul	Tergat	KEN	17.6.69	1		Lisboa	26 Mar 00
59:06	dh		Kipsang			1	GNR	South Shields	16 Sep 12
59:07		Paul	Kosgei	KEN	22.4.78	1		Berlin	2 Apr 06
59:07	dh	Micah	Kogo	KEN	3.6.86	2	GNR	South Shields	16 Sep 12
59:08			Maiyo			2		Rotterdam	13 Sep 09
59:09		James Kipsang	Kwambai	KEN	28.2.83	3		Rotterdam	13 Sep 09
59:10	dh		Tergat			1		Lisboa	13 Mar 05
59:10		Bernard	Kipyego	KEN	16.7.86	4		Rotterdam	13 Sep 09
59:10		Bernard	Koech	KEN	31.1.88	2		Lille	1 Sep 12
59:11		Kenneth	Kipkemoi	KEN	2.8.84	3		Den Haag	11 Mar 12
		(30/20)							
59:14		Dennis	Kimetto	KEN	22.4.84	1		Berlin	1 Apr 12
59:15		Deriba	Merga	ETH	26.10.80	1		New Delhi	9 Nov 08
59:15		Wilson	Chebet	KEN	12.7.85	5		Rotterdam	13 Sep 09
59:15		Wilson	Kiprop	KEN	14.4.87	2		Berlin	1 Apr 12
59:19		Tilahun	Regassa	ETH	18.1.90	1		Abu Dhabi	7 Jan 10
59:20	dh	Hendrick	Ramaala	RSA	2.2.72	2		Lisboa	26 Mar 00
59:20		Moses	Mosop	KEN	17.7.85	1	Stra	Milano	21 Mar 10

Mark	Wind	Name		Nat	Born	Pos	Meet	Venue	Date
59:21	dh	Robert Kipkoech	Cheruiyot	KEN	26.9.78	2		Lisboa	13 Mar 05
59:22		Feyisa	Lilesa	ETH	1.2.90	1		Houston	15 Jan 12
59:23		John	Kiprotich	KEN	.89	6		Rotterdam	13 Sep 09
		(30)							
59:25		Eliud	Kipchoge	KEN	5.11.84	3		Lille	1 Sep 12
59:26		Francis	Kibiwott	KEN	15.9.78	2		Berlin	1 Apr 07
59:26		Geoffrey	Kipsang	KEN	28.11.92	4		Den Haag	11 Mar 12
59:27	dh	Wilson	Kiprotich Kebenei	KEN	20.7.80	3		Lisboa	13 Mar 05
59:27		Patrick	Ivuti	KEN	30.6.78	4		Rotterdam	9 Sep 07
59:28		Robert	Kipchumba	KEN	24.2.84	2		Rotterdam	10 Sep 06
59:30	dh	Martin	Lel	KEN	29.10.78	1		Lisboa	26 Mar 06
59:30		Yonas	Kifle	ERI	24.3.77	5	WCh	Udine	14 Oct 07
59:30		Geoffrey	Mutai	KEN	7.10.81	1		Valencia	22 Nov 09
59:30		Philemon	Limo	KEN	2.8.85	1		Praha	2 Apr 11
		(40)							
59:30		Lelisa	Desisa	ETH	14.1.90	1		New Delhi	27 Nov 11
59:31		Victor	Kipchirchir	KEN	5.12.87	5		Den Haag	11 Mar 12
59:32		Dieudonné	Disi	RWA	24.4.78	6	WCh	Udine	14 Oct 07
59:33		Marílson	dos Santos	BRA	6.8.77	7	WCh	Udine	14 Oct 07
59:35		Tsegaye	Kebede	ETH	15.1.87	2		Ra's Al Khaymah	8 Feb 08
59:36		Sammy	Kosgei	KEN	20.1.86	2		Berlin	5 Apr 09
59:36		Joel	Kimurer	KEN	21.1.88	2		Valencia	21 Oct 12
59:37	dh	Dejene	Berhanu	ETH	12.12.80	1	GNR	South Shields	26 Sep 04
59:37		Stephen	Kibiwott	KEN	3.4.80	1		Lille	5 Sep 09
59:38	dh	Faustin	Baha	TAN	30.5.82	4		Lisboa	26 Mar 00
		(50)	100th man 60:00, 200th man 60:33, 300th 60:58, 400th 61:10, 500th 61:21						

Short course: 58:51 Paul Tergat KEN 17.6.69 1 Stra Milano 49m sh 30 Mar 96

MARATHON

In second column: L = loop course or start and finish within 30%, P = point-to-point or start and finish more than 30% apart, D = point-to-point and downhill over 1/1000

Mark	Wind	Name		Nat	Born	Pos	Meet	Venue	Date
2:03:38	WRL	Patrick	Makau	KEN	2.3.85	1		Berlin	25 Sep 11
2:03:42	L	Wilson	Kipsang Kiprotich	KEN	15.3.82	1		Frankfurt	30 Oct 11
2:03:59	WRL	Haile	Gebrselassie	ETH	18.4.73	1		Berlin	28 Sep 08
2:04:15	L	Geoffrey	Mutai	KEN	7.10.81	1		Berlin	30 Sep 12
2:04:16	L	Dennis	Kimetto	KEN	22.4.84	2		Berlin	30 Sep 12
2:04:23	L	Ayele	Abshero	ETH	28.12.90	1		Dubai	27 Jan 12
2:04:26	WRL		Gebrselassie			1		Berlin	30 Sep 07
2:04:27	L	Duncan	Kibet	KEN	25.4.78	1		Rotterdam	5 Apr 09
2:04:27	L	James Kipsang	Kwambai	KEN	28.2.83	2		Rotterdam	5 Apr 09
2:04:38	L	Tsegaye	Kebede	ETH	15.1.87	1		Chicago	7 Oct 12
2:04:40	L	Emmanuel	Mutai (10)	KEN	12.10.84	1		London	17 Apr 11
2:04:44	L		Kipsang Kiprotich			1		London	22 Apr 12
2:04:48	L		Makau			1		Rotterdam	11 Apr 10
2:04:48	L	Yemane	Tsegay	ETH	8.4.85	1		Rotterdam	15 Apr 12
2:04:50	L	Dino	Sefir	ETH	28.5.88	2		Dubai	27 Jan 12
2:04:50	L	Getu	Feleke	ETH	28.11.86	2		Rotterdam	15 Apr 12
2:04:52	L	Feyisa	Lilesa	ETH	1.2.90	2		Chicago	7 Oct 12
2:04:53	L		Gebrselassie			1		Dubai	18 Jan 08
2:04:54	L	Markos	Geneti	ETH	30.5.84	3		Dubai	27 Jan 12
2:04:55	WRL	Paul	Tergat	KEN	17.6.69	1		Berlin	28 Sep 03
2:04:55	L		G Mutai			2		Rotterdam	11 Apr 10
2:04:56	L	Sammy	Korir	KEN	12.12.71	2		Berlin	28 Sep 03
2:04:56	L	Jonathan	Maiyo	KEN	.88	4		Dubai	27 Jan 12
2:04:57	L		Kipsang			1		Frankfurt	31 Oct 10
2:05:03	L	Moses	Mosop	KEN	17.7.85	3		Rotterdam	15 Apr 12
2:05:04	L	Abel	Kirui (20)	KEN	4.6.82	3		Rotterdam	5 Apr 09
2:05:06	P		G Mutai			1		New York	6 Nov 11
2:05:08	L		Makau			1		Berlin	26 Sep 10
2:05:10	L	Samuel	Wanjiru	KEN	10.11.86	1		London	26 Apr 09
2:05:10	L		Mutai			2		Berlin	26 Sep 10
2:05:10	L	Tadesse	Tola	ETH	31.10.87	5		Dubai	27 Jan 12
		(31/22)							
2:05:12	L	Stanley	Biwott	KEN	21.4.86	1		Paris	15 Apr 12
2:05:13	L	Vincent	Kipruto	KEN	13.9.87	3		Rotterdam	11 Apr 10
2:05:15	L	Martin	Lel	KEN	29.10.78	1		London	13 Apr 08
2:05:16	L	Levi	Matebo Omari	KEN	3.11.89	2		Frankfurt	30 Oct 11
2:05:25	L	Bazu	Worku	ETH	15.9.90	3		Berlin	26 Sep 10
2:05:25	L	Albert	Matebor	KEN	20.12.80	3		Frankfurt	30 Oct 11
2:05:27	L	Jaouad	Gharib	MAR	22.5.72	3		London	26 Apr 09

Mark	Wind	Name		Nat	Born	Pos	Meet	Venue	Date
2:05:27	L	Wilson	Chebet	KEN	12.7.85	1		Rotterdam	10 Apr 11
		(30)							
2:05:27	L	Tilahun	Regassa	ETH	18.1.90	3		Chicago	7 Oct 12
2:05:30	L	Abderrahim	Goumri ¶	MAR	21.5.76	3		London	13 Apr 08
2:05:37	P	Wilson	Loyanei ¶	KEN	86	1		Seoul	18 Mar 12
2:05:38	WRL	Khalid	Khannouchi	MAR/USA	22.12.71	1		London	14 Apr 02
2:05:39	L	Eliud	Kiptanui	KEN	6.6.89	1		Praha	9 May 10
2:05:41	L	Yami	Dadi	ETH	82	6		Dubai	27 Jan 12
2:05:42	L	Abdullah Dawit	Shami	ETH	16.7.84	7		Dubai	27 Jan 12
2:05:42	L	Deresse	Chimsa	ETH	21.11.76	8		Dubai	27 Jan 12
2:05:44	L	Getu	Feleke	ETH	28.11.86	1		Amsterdam	17 Oct 10
2:05:48	L	Jafred	Kipchumba	KEN	8.8.83	1		Eindhoven	9 Oct 11
		(40)							
2:05:49	L	William	Kipsang	KEN	26.6.77	1		Rotterdam	13 Apr 08
2:05:50	L	Evans	Rutto	KEN	8.4.78	1		Chicago	12 Oct 03
2:05:54	L	Sammy	Kitwara	KEN	26.11.86	4		Chicago	7 Oct 12
2:06:05	WRL	Ronaldo da	Costa	BRA	7.6.70	1		Berlin	20 Sep 98
2:06:05	L	Laban	Korir	KEN	30.12.85	2		Amsterdam	16 Oct 11
2:06:05	L	Mariko	Kipchumba	KEN	.75	1		Reims	21 Oct 12
2:06:07	L	Eric	Ndiema	KEN	28.12.92	3		Amsterdam	16 Oct 11
2:06:07	L	Philip Sanga	Kimutai	KEN	10.9.83	4		Frankfurt	30 Oct 11
2:06:11	L	Franklin	Chepkwony	KEN	84	2		Eindhoven	14 Oct 12
2:06:12	L	Geoffrey	Kipsang	KEN	28.11.92	3		Berlin	30 Sep 12
		(50)	100th man 2:07:04, 200th 2:07:54, 300th 2:08:33, 400th 2:08:57, 500th 2:09:23						

Downhill point-to-point course – Boston marathon is downhill overall (139m) and sometimes strongly wind-aided.

Mark		Name		Nat	Born	Pos	Meet	Venue	Date
2:03:02		Geoffrey	Mutai	KEN	7.10.81	1		Boston	18 Apr 11
2:03:06		Moses	Mosop	KEN	17.7.85	2		Boston	18 Apr 11
2:04:53		Gebre-egziabher	Gebremariam	ETH	10.9.84	3		Boston	18 Apr 11
2:04:58		Ryan	Hall	USA	14.10.82	4		Boston	18 Apr 11
2:05:52		Robert Kiprono	Cheruiyot	KEN	10.8.88	1		Boston	19 Apr 10

2000 METRES STEEPLECHASE

Mark		Name		Nat	Born	Pos	Meet	Venue	Date
5:10.68		Mahiedine	Mekhissi	FRA	15.3.85	1		Reims	30 Jun 10
5:13.47		Bouabdellah	Tahri	FRA	20.12.78	1		Tomblaine	25 Jun 10
5:14.43		Julius	Kariuki	KEN	12.6.61	1		Rovereto	21 Aug 90
5:14.53		Saïf Saaeed	Shaheen	QAT	15.10.82	1	SGP	Doha	13 May 05
5:16.22		Phillip	Barkutwo	KEN	6.10.66	2		Rovereto	21 Aug 90
5:16.46		Wesley	Kiprotich	KEN	31.7.79	2	SGP	Doha	13 May 05
5:16.85		Eliud	Barngetuny	KEN	20.5.73	1		Parma	13 Jun 95

3000 METRES STEEPLECHASE

Mark		Name		Nat	Born	Pos	Meet	Venue	Date
7:53.63	WR	Saïf Saaeed	Shaheen	KEN/QAT	15.10.82	1	VD	Bruxelles	3 Sep 04
7:53.64		Brimin	Kipruto	KEN	31.7.85	1	Herc	Monaco	22 Jul 11
7:54.31		Paul Kipsiele	Koech	KEN	10.11.81	1	GGala	Roma	31 May 12
7:55.28	WR	Brahim	Boulami ¶	MAR	20.4.72	1	VD	Bruxelles	24 Aug 01
7:55.51			Shaheen			1	VD	Bruxelles	26 Aug 05
7:55.72	WR	Bernard	Barmasai	KEN	6.5.74	1	ASV	Köln	24 Aug 97
7:55.76		Ezekiel	Kemboi	KEN	25.5.82	2	Herc	Monaco	22 Jul 11
7:56.16		Moses	Kiptanui	KEN	1.10.70	2	ASV	Köln	24 Aug 97
7:56.32			Shaheen			1	Tsik	Athína	3 Jul 06
7:56.34			Shaheen			1	GGala	Roma	8 Jul 05
7:56.37			P K Koech			2	GGala	Roma	8 Jul 05
7:56.54			Shaheen			1	WK	Zürich	18 Aug 06
7:56.58			Koech			1	DL	Doha	11 May 12
7:56.81		Richard	Mateelong	KEN	14.10.83	2	DL	Doha	11 May 12
7:56.94			Shaheen			1	WAF	Monaco	19 Sep 04
7:57.28			Shaheen			1	Tsik	Athína	14 Jun 05
7:57.29		Reuben	Kosgei	KEN	2.8.79	2	VD	Bruxelles	24 Aug 01
7:57.32			P K Koech			3	Herc	Monaco	22 Jul 11
7:57.38			Shaheen			1	WAF	Monaco	14 Sep 03
7:57.42			P K Koech			2	WAF	Monaco	14 Sep 03
7:58.09			Boulami			1	Herc	Monaco	19 Jul 02
7:58.10			S Cherono			2	Herc	Monaco	19 Jul 02
7:58.50			Boulami			1	WK	Zürich	17 Aug 01
7:58.66			S Cherono			3	VD	Bruxelles	24 Aug 01
7:58.80			P K Koech			1	VD	Bruxelles	14 Sep 07
7:58.85			Kemboi			1	SGP	Doha	8 May 09
7:58.98			Barmasai			1	Herc	Monaco	4 Aug 99
7:59.08	WR	Wilson	Boit Kipketer	KEN	6.10.73	1	WK	Zürich	13 Aug 97
7:59.18	WR		Kiptanui			1	WK	Zürich	16 Aug 95

Mark	Wind	Name		Nat	Born	Pos	Meet	Venue	Date
7:59.42			P K Koech			1	DNG	Stockholm	7 Aug 07
		(3010)							
8:01.18		Bouabdellah	Tahri	FRA	20.12.78	3	WCh	Berlin	18 Aug 09
8:01.67		Abel	Mutai	KEN	2.10.88	2	GGala	Roma	31 May 12
8:01.69		Kipkirui	Misoi	KEN	23.12.78	4	VD	Bruxelles	24 Aug 01
8:02.09		Mahiédine	Mekhissi	FRA	15.3.85	1	DL	Saint-Denis	8 Jul 11
8:03.41		Patrick	Sang	KEN	11.4.64	3	ASV	Köln	24 Aug 97
8:03.57		Ali	Ezzine	MAR	3.9.78	1	Gaz	Saint-Denis	23 Jun 00
8:03.74		Raymond	Yator	KEN	7.4.81	3	Herc	Monaco	18 Aug 00
8:03.81		Benjamin	Kiplagat	UGA	4.3.89	2	Athl	Lausanne	8 Jul 10
8:03.89		John	Kosgei	KEN	13.7.73	3	Herc	Monaco	16 Aug 97
8:04.95		Simon	Vroemen ¶	NED	11.5.69	2	VD	Bruxelles	26 Aug 05
		(20)							
8:05.01		Eliud	Barngetuny	KEN	20.5.73	1	Herc	Monaco	25 Jul 95
8:05.35	WR	Peter	Koech	KEN	18.2.58	1	DNG	Stockholm	3 Jul 89
8:05.37		Philip	Barkutwo	KEN	6.10.66	2		Rieti	6 Sep 92
8:05.4	WR	Henry	Rono	KEN	12.2.52	1		Seattle	13 May 78
8:05.43		Christopher	Kosgei	KEN	14.8.74	2	WK	Zürich	11 Aug 99
8:05.51		Julius	Kariuki	KEN	12.6.61	1	OG	Seoul	30 Sep 88
8:05.68		Wesley	Kiprotich	KEN	1.8.79	4	VD	Bruxelles	3 Sep 04
8:05.75		Mustafa	Mohamed	SWE	1.3.79	1	NA	Heusden-Zolder	28 Jul 07
8:05.88		Bernard	Nganga (Mbugua)	KEN	.85	2	ISTAF	Berlin	11 Sep 11
8:05.99		Joseph	Keter	KEN	13.6.69	1	Herc	Monaco	10 Aug 96
		(30)							
8:06.13		Tareq Mubarak	Taher	BRN	24.3.84	3	Tsik	Athína	13 Jul 09
8:06.16		Roba	Gari	ETH	12.4.82	3	DL	Doha	11 May 12
8:06.81		Evan	Jager	USA	8.3.89	3	Herc	Monaco	20 Jul 12
8:06.77		Gideon	Chirchir	KEN	24.2.66	2	WK	Zürich	16 Aug 95
8:06.88		Richard	Kosgei	KEN	29.12.70	2	GPF	Monaco	9 Sep 95
8:07.02		Brahim	Taleb	MAR	16.2.85	2	NA	Heusden-Zolder	28 Jul 07
8:07.13		Paul	Kosgei	KEN	22.4.78	2	GP II	Saint-Denis	3 Jul 99
8:07.18		Obaid Moussa	Amer ¶	KEN/QAT	18.4.85	4	OG	Athína	24 Aug 04
8:07.44		Luis Miguel	Martín	ESP	11.1.72	2	VD	Bruxelles	30 Aug 02
8:07.59		Julius	Nyamu	KEN	1.12.77	5	VD	Bruxelles	24 Aug 01
		(40)							
8:07.62		Joseph	Mahmoud	FRA	13.12.55	1	VD	Bruxelles	24 Aug 84
8:07.71		Hillary	Yego	KEN	2.4.92	3	DL	Shanghai	15 May 11
8:07.75		Jonathan	Ndiku Muia	KEN	18.9.91	6	Herc	Monaco	22 Jul 11
8:07.96		Mark	Rowland	GBR	7.3.63	3	OG	Seoul	30 Sep 88
8:08.02	WR	Anders	Gärderud	SWE	28.8.46	1	OG	Montreal	28 Jul 76
8:08.12		Matthew	Birir	KEN	5.7.72	3	GGala	Roma	8 Jun 95
8:08.14		Sa'ad Shaddad	Al-Asmari	KSA	24.9.68	4	DNG	Stockholm	16 Jul 02
8:08.48		Michael	Kipyego	KEN	2.10.83	2	Herc	Monaco	28 Jul 09
8:08.57		Francesco	Panetta	ITA	10.1.63	1	WCh	Roma	5 Sep 87
8:08.59		Patrick	Langat	KEN/TUR	16.6.88	4	DL	Shanghai	15 May 11
		(50)							

100th man 8:12.58, 200th 8:18.57, 300th 8:22.24, 400th 8:24.59, 500th 8:26.66

Drugs disqualification: 7:53.17 Brahim Boulami ¶ MAR 20.4.72 1 WK Zürich 16 Aug 02

110 METRES HURDLES

Mark	Wind	Name		Nat	Born	Pos	Meet	Venue	Date
12.80	WR 0.3	Aries	Merritt	USA	24.7.85	1	VD	Bruxelles	7 Sep 12
12.87	WR 0.9	Dayron	Robles	CUB	19.11.86	1	GS	Ostrava	12 Jun 08
12.88	WR 1.1	Liu Xiang		CHN	13.7.83	1rA	Athl	Lausanne	11 Jul 06
12.88	0.5		Robles			1	Gaz	Saint-Denis	18 Jul 08
12.89	0.5	David	Oliver	USA	24.4.82	1	DL	Saint-Denis	16 Jul 10
12.90	1.1	Dominique	Arnold	USA	14.9.73	2rA	Athl	Lausanne	11 Jul 06
12.90	1.6		Oliver			1	Pre	Eugene	3 Jul 10
12.91	WR 0.5	Colin	Jackson	GBR	18.2.67	1	WCh	Stuttgart	20 Aug 93
12.91	WR 0.3		Liu Xiang			1	OG	Athína	27 Aug 04
12.91	0.2		Robles			1	DNG	Stockholm	22 Jul 08
12.92	WR -0.1	Roger	Kingdom	USA	26.8.62	1	WK	Zürich	16 Aug 89
12.92	0.9	Allen	Johnson	USA	1.3.71	1	NC	Atlanta	23 Jun 96
12.92	0.2		Johnson			1	VD	Bruxelles	23 Aug 96
12.92	1.5		Liu Xiang			1	GP	New York	2 Jun 07
12.92	0.0		Robles			1	WAF	Stuttgart	23 Sep 07
12.92	-0.3		Merritt			1	OG	London (OS)	8 Aug 12
12.93	WR -0.2	Renaldo	Nehemiah	USA	24.3.59	1	WK	Zürich	19 Aug 81
12.93	0.0		Johnson			1	WCh	Athína	7 Aug 97
12.93	-0.6		Liu Xiang			1	WAF	Stuttgart	9 Sep 06
12.93	0.1		Robles			1	OG	Beijing	21 Aug 08
12.93	1.7		Oliver			1	NC	Des Moines	27 Jun 10

Mark	Wind	Name		Nat	Born	Pos	Meet	Venue	Date
12.93	-0.3		Oliver			1	WK	Zürich	19 Aug 10
12.93	1.2		Merritt			1	NC/OT	Eugene	30 Jun 12
12.93	0.6		Merritt			1	LGP	London(CP)	13 Jul 12
12.93	0.0		Merritt			1	Herc	Monaco	20 Jul 12
12.94	1.6	Jack	Pierce (10)	USA	23.9.62	1s2	NC	Atlanta	22 Jun 96
12.94	1.8		Oliver			1	Pre	Eugene	4 Jun 11
12.94	0.1		Merritt			1s2	OG	London (OS)	8 Aug 12
12.95	0.6		Johnson			1	OG	Atlanta	29 Jul 96
12.95	1.5	Terrence	Trammell	USA	23.11.78	2	GP	New York	2 Jun 07
12.95	1.7		Liu Xiang			1	WCh	Osaka	31 Aug 07
12.95	2.0		Oliver			1	SGP	Doha	9 May 08
12.95	-1.7		Robles			1		Dubnica nad Váhom	7 Sep 08
12.95	-0.9		Merritt			1	DL	Birmingham	26 Aug 12
		(34/11)							
12.97	1.0	Ladji	Doucouré	FRA	28.3.83	1	NC	Angers	15 Jul 05
12.98	0.6	Mark	Crear	USA	2.10.68	1		Zagreb	5 Jul 99
12.98	1.5	Jason	Richardson	USA	4.4.86	1s3	NC/OT	Eugene	30 Jun 12
13.00	0.5	Anthony	Jarrett	GBR	13.8.68	2	WCh	Stuttgart	20 Aug 93
13.00	0.6	Anier	García	CUB	9.3.76	1	OG	Sydney	25 Sep 00
13.01	0.3	Larry	Wade ¶	USA	22.11.74	1rA	Athl	Lausanne	2 Jul 99
13.02	1.5	Ryan	Wilson	USA	19.12.80	3	GP	New York	2 Jun 07
13.02	1.7	David	Payne	USA	24.7.82	3	WCh	Osaka	31 Aug 07
13.03	-0.2	Greg	Foster	USA	4.8.58	2	WK	Zürich	19 Aug 81
		(20)							
13.03	1.0	Reggie	Torian	USA	22.4.75	1	NC	New Orleans	21 Jun 98
13.05	1.4	Tony	Dees ¶	USA	6.8.63	1		Vigo	23 Jul 91
13.05	-0.8	Florian	Schwarthoff	GER	7.5.68	1	NC	Bremen	2 Jul 95
13.08	1.2	Mark	McKoy	CAN	10.12.61	1	BNP	Villeneuve-d'Ascq	2 Jul 93
13.08	0.0	Stanislav	Olijar	LAT	22.3.79	2	Athl	Lausanne	1 Jul 03
13.08	1.2	Jeff	Porter	USA	27.11.85	3	NC/OT	Eugene	30 Jun 12
13.09	2.0	Antwon	Hicks	USA	12.3.83	2s2	NC/OT	Eugene	6 Jul 08
13.09	0.0	Orlando	Ortega	CUB	29.7.91	1		La Habana	27 May 12
13.09	-1.1	Sergey	Shubenkov	RUS	4.10.90	1s2	EC	Helsinki	1 Jul 12
13.12	1.5	Falk	Balzer ¶	GER	14.12.73	2	EC	Budapest	22 Aug 98
		(30)							
13.12	1.0	Duane	Ross ¶	USA	5.12.72	3	WCh	Sevilla	25 Aug 99
13.12	1.9	Anwar	Moore	USA	5.3.79	1	ModR	Modesto	5 May 07
13.13	1.6	Igor	Kovác	SVK	12.5.69	1	DNG	Stockholm	7 Jul 97
13.12	-0.3	Hansle	Parchment	JAM	17.6.90	3	OG	London (OS)	8 Aug 12
13.13	2.0	Dexter	Faulk	USA	14.4.84	2	GS	Ostrava	17 Jun 09
13.14	0.1	Ryan	Brathwaite	BAR	6.6.88	1	WCh	Berlin	20 Aug 09
13.15	0.3	Robin	Korving	NED	29.7.74	5rA	Athl	Lausanne	2 Jul 99
13.15	0.1	Dwight	Thomas	JAM	23.9.80	2	Bisl	Oslo	9 Jun 11
13.15	-0.3	Garfield	Darien	FRA	22.12.87	1s3	EC	Helsinki	1 Jul 12
13.17	-0.4	Sam	Turner	USA	17.6.57	2	Pepsi	Los Angeles (Ww)	15 May 83
		(40)							
13.17	0.0	Tonie	Campbell	USA	14.6.60	3	WK	Zürich	17 Aug 88
13.17	0.5	Courtney	Hawkins	USA	11.7.67	1		Ingolstadt	26 Jul 98
13.17	0.4	Mike	Fenner	GER	24.4.71	1		Leverkusen	9 Aug 98
13.17	-0.1	Maurice	Wignall	JAM	17.4.76	1s1	OG	Athína	26 Aug 04
13.18	0.5	Emilio	Valle	CUB	21.4.67	3s1	OG	Atlanta	29 Jul 96
13.19	1.9	Steve	Brown	USA/TRI	6.1.69	1h4	NC	Atlanta	21 Jun 96
13.19	1.7		Shi Dongpeng	CHN	6.1.84	5	WCh	Osaka	31 Aug 07
13.19	1.7	Ronnie	Ash	USA	2.7.88	3	NC	Des Moines	27 Jun 10
13.19	1.3	Andrew	Riley	JAM	9.6.88	2	NC/OT	Kingston	30 Jun 12
13.20	2.0	Stéphane	Caristan	FRA	31.5.64	1	EC	Stuttgart	30 Aug 86
13.20	1.8	Aleksandr	Markin ¶	RUS	8.9.62	1	Znam	Leningrad	11 Jun 88
13.20	1.7	Larry	Harrington	USA	24.11.70	2s1	NC	Atlanta	22 Jun 96
13.20	0.1	Joel	Brown	USA	31.1.80	3	Bisl	Oslo	9 Jun 11
		(53)	100th man 13.30, 200th 13.43, 300th 13.50, 400th 13.58, 500th 13.64						

Rolling start but accepted by race officials

Mark	Wind	Name		Nat	Born	Pos	Meet	Venue	Date
13.10A	2.0	Falk	Balzer ¶	GER	14.12.73	1	WCp	Johannesburg	13 Sep 98

Doubtful timing: Scheessel 4 Jun 95 +1.3 1. Mike Fenner GER 24.4.71 13.06, 2. Eric Kaiser ¶ GER 7.3.71 13.08

Wind-assisted marks   *Performances to 12.94, performers to 13.19*

Mark	Wind	Name		Nat	Born	Pos	Meet	Venue	Date
12.87	2.6	Roger	Kingdom	USA	26.8.62	1	WCp	Barcelona	10 Sep 89
12.87	2.4		Liu Xiang	CHN	13.7.83	1	Pre	Eugene	2 Jun 12
12.89	3.2	David	Oliver	USA	24.4.82	1s1	NC/OT	Eugene	6 Jul 08
12.91	3.5	Renaldo	Nehemiah	USA	24.3.59	1	NCAA	Champaign	1 Jun 79
12.94A	2.8		Jackson			1rA		Sestriere	31 Jul 94
12.98	3.1	Ronnie	Ash	USA	2.7.88	1	NACAC	Miramar	9 Jul 10

Mark	Wind	Name		Nat	Born	Pos	Meet	Venue	Date
13.00	2.6	Anwar	Moore	USA	5.3.79	1	DrakeR	Des Moines	28 Apr 07
13.05	3.6	Ryan	Brathwaite	BAR	6.6.88	1		Austin	2 May 09
13.06	2.1	Mark	McKoy	CAN	10.12.61	1	Gugl	Linz	13 Aug 92
13.14	2.9	Igor	Kazanov	LAT	24.9.63	1r1	Znam	Leningrad	8 Jun 86
13.15	2.1	Courtney	Hawkins	USA	11.7.67	1		Salamanca	10 Jul 98
13.18	4.7	Robert	Reading	USA	9.6.67	1		Azusa	23 Apr 94
13.18	2.3	Joel	Brown	USA	31.1.80	1	Tsik	Athína	13 Jul 09
13.18	3.8	Omo	Osaghae	USA	18.5.88	1		Lubbock	22 Apr 11
13.19	3.5	Barrett	Nugent	USA	29.1.90	1	TexR	Austin	9 Apr 11
Hand timing									
12.8	1.0	Renaldo	Nehemiah	USA	24.3.59	1		Kingston	11 May 79
Wind-assisted									
12.8	2.4	Colin	Jackson	GBR	18.2.67	1		Sydney	10 Jan 90
12.9	4.1	Mark	Crear	USA	2.10.68	1rA	S&W	Modesto	8 May 93
12.9	3.1	William	Sharman	GBR	12.9.84	1r2		Madrid	2 Jul 10

400 METRES HURDLES

Mark	Name		Nat	Born	Pos	Meet	Venue	Date
46.78 WR	Kevin	Young	USA	16.9.66	1	OG	Barcelona	6 Aug 92
47.02 WR	Edwin	Moses	USA	31.8.55	1		Koblenz	31 Aug 83
47.03	Bryan	Bronson	USA	9.9.72	1	NC	New Orleans	21 Jun 98
47.10	Samuel	Matete	ZAM	27.7.68	1rA	WK	Zürich	7 Aug 91
47.13 WR		Moses			1		Milano	3 Jul 80
47.14		Moses			1	Athl	Lausanne	14 Jul 81
47.17		Moses			1	ISTAF	Berlin	8 Aug 80
47.18		Young			1	WCh	Stuttgart	19 Aug 93
47.19	Andre	Phillips	USA	5.9.59	1	OG	Seoul	25 Sep 88
47.23	Amadou	Dia Bâ	SEN	22.9.58	2	OG	Seoul	25 Sep 88
47.24	Kerron	Clement	USA	31.10.85	1	NC	Carson	26 Jun 05
47.25	Félix	Sánchez	DOM	30.8.77	1	WCh	Saint-Denis	29 Aug 03
47.25	Angelo	Taylor	USA	29.12.78	1	OG	Beijing	18 Aug 08
47.27		Moses			1	ISTAF	Berlin	21 Aug 81
47.30	Bershawn	Jackson (10)	USA	8.5.83	1	WCh	Helsinki	9 Aug 05
47.32		Moses			1		Koblenz	29 Aug 84
47.32		Jackson			1	NC	Des Moines	26 Jun 10
47.35		Sánchez			1rA	WK	Zürich	16 Aug 02
47.37		Moses			1	WCp	Roma	4 Sep 81
47.37		Moses			1	WK	Zürich	24 Aug 83
47.37		Moses			1	NC/OT	Indianpolis	17 Jul 88
47.37		Young			1	Athl	Lausanne	7 Jul 93
47.37	Stéphane	Diagana	FRA	23.7.69	1	Athl	Lausanne	5 Jul 95
47.38		Moses			1	Athl	Lausanne	2 Sep 86
47.38	Danny	Harris ¶	USA	7.9.65	1	Athl	Lausanne	10 Jul 91
47.38		Sánchez			1rA	WK	Zürich	17 Aug 01
47.39		Clement			1	NC	Indianapolis	24 Jun 06
47.40		Young			1	WK	Zürich	19 Aug 92
47.42		Young			1	ASV	Köln	16 Aug 92
47.43		Moses			1	ASV	Köln	28 Aug 83
47.43	James	Carter	USA	7.5.78	2	WCh	Helsinki	9 Aug 05
	(31/13)							
47.48	Harald	Schmid	FRG	29.9.57	1	EC	Athína	8 Sep 82
47.53	Hadi Soua'an	Al-Somaily	KSA	21.8.76	2	OG	Sydney	27 Sep 00
47.54	Derrick	Adkins	USA	2.7.70	2	Athl	Lausanne	5 Jul 95
47.54	Fabrizio	Mori	ITA	28.6.69	2	WCh	Edmonton	10 Aug 01
47.60	Winthrop	Graham	JAM	17.11.65	1	WK	Zürich	4 Aug 93
47.63	Johnny	Dutch	USA	20.1.89	2	NC	Des Moines	26 Jun 10
47.66A	L.J. 'Louis'	van Zyl	RSA	20.7.85	1		Pretoria	25 Feb 11
	(20)							
47.67	Bennie	Brazell	USA	2.6.82	2	NCAA	Sacramento	11 Jun 05
47.72	Javier	Culson	PUR	25.7.84	1		Ponce	8 May 10
47.75	David	Patrick	USA	12.6.60	4	NC/OT	Indianpolis	17 Jul 88
47.81	Llewellyn	Herbert	RSA	21.7.77	3	OG	Sydney	27 Sep 00
47.82 WR	John	Akii-Bua	UGA	3.12.49	1	OG	München	2 Sep 72
47.82	Kriss	Akabusi	GBR	28.11.58	3	OG	Barcelona	6 Aug 92
47.82	Periklis	Iakovákis	GRE	24.3.79	2	GP	Osaka	6 May 06
47.84	Bayano	Kamani	PAN	17.4.80	2s1	WCh	Helsinki	7 Aug 05
47.84	David	Greene	GBR	11.4.86	2	DL	Saint Denis	6 Jul 12
47.89	Dai	Tamesue	JPN	3.5.78	3	WCh	Edmonton	10 Aug 01
	(30)							
47.91	Calvin	Davis	USA	2.4.72	1s2	OG	Atlanta	31 Jul 96

Mark	Wind	Name		Nat	Born	Pos	Meet	Venue	Date
47.91		Michael	Tinsley	USA	21.4.84	2	OG	London (OS)	6 Aug 12
47.92		Aleksandr	Vasilyev	BLR	26.7.61	2	ECp	Moskva	17 Aug 85
47.93		Kenji	Narisako	JPN	25.7.84	3	GP	Osaka	6 May 06
47.93		Jeshua	Anderson	USA	22.6.89	1	NC	Eugene	26 Jun 11
47.94		Eric	Thomas	USA	1.12.73	1	GGala	Roma	30 Jun 00
47.96		Jehue	Gordon	TRI	15.12.91	2s1	OG	London (OS)	4 Aug 12
47.97		Maurice	Mitchell	USA	14.5.71	2rA	WK	Zürich	14 Aug 96
47.97		Joey	Woody	USA	22.5.73	3	NC	New Orleans	21 Jun 98
47.98		Sven	Nylander	SWE	1.1.62	4	OG	Atlanta	1 Aug 96
		(40)							
47.99A		Omar	Cisneros	CUB	19.11.89	1	PAm	Guadalajara, MEX	25 Oct 11
48.00		Danny	McFarlane	JAM	14.2.72	1s2	OG	Athína	24 Aug 04
48.02A		Ockert	Cilliers	RSA	21.4.81	1		Pretoria	20 Feb 04
48.04		Eronilde	de Araújo	BRA	31.12.70	2	Nik	Nice	12 Jul 95
48.05		Ken	Harnden	ZIM	31.3.73	1	GP	Paris (C)	29 Jul 98
48.05		Kemel	Thompson	JAM	25.9.74	1	GP	London (CP)	8 Aug 03
48.05		Isa	Phillips	JAM	22.4.84	1	NC	Kingston	27 Jun 09
48.06		Oleg	Tverdokhleb	UKR	3.11.69	1	EC	Helsinki	10 Aug 94
48.06		Ruslan	Mashchenko	RUS	11.11.71	1	GP II	Helsinki	13 Jun 98
48.09		Alwyn	Myburgh	RSA	13.10.80	1	WUG	Beijing	31 Aug 01
		(50)							

100th man 48.51, 200th man 49.04, 300th man 49.31, 400th 49.51, 500th 49.68

Best at low altitude: 47.66   van Zyl   1   GS   Ostrava   31 May 11
Drugs Disqualification   47.15   Bronson ¶   1   GWG   Uniondale, NY   19 Jul 98

HIGH JUMP

Mark		Name		Nat	Born	Pos	Meet	Venue	Date
2.45 WR		Javier	Sotomayor ¶	CUB	13.10.67	1		Salamanca	27 Jul 93
2.44 WR			Sotomayor			1	CAC	San Juan	29 Jul 89
2.43 WR			Sotomayor			1		Salamanca	8 Sep 88
2.43i			Sotomayor			1	WI	Budapest	4 Mar 89
2.42 WR		Patrik	Sjöberg	SWE	5.1.65	1	DNG	Stockholm	30 Jun 87
2.42i WR		Carlo	Thränhardt	FRG	5.7.57	1		Berlin	26 Feb 88
2.42			Sotomayor			1		Sevilla	5 Jun 94
2.41 WR		Igor	Paklin	KGZ	15.6.63	1	WUG	Kobe	4 Sep 85
2.41i			Sjöberg			1		Pireás	1 Feb 87
2.41i			Sotomayor			1	WI	Toronto	14 Mar 93
2.41			Sotomayor			1	NC	La Habana	25 Jun 94
2.41			Sotomayor			1	TSB	London (CP)	15 Jul 94
2.40 WR		Rudolf	Povarnitsyn	UKR	13.6.62	1		Donetsk	11 Aug 85
2.40i			Thränhardt			1		Simmerath	16 Jan 87
2.40i			Sjöberg			1		Berlin	27 Feb 87
2.40			Sotomayor			1	NC	La Habana	12 Mar 89
2.40			Sjöberg			1	ECp-B	Bruxelles	5 Aug 89
2.40			Sotomayor			1	AmCp	Bogota	13 Aug 89
2.40		Sorin	Matei	ROU	6.7.63	1	PTS	Bratislava	20 Jun 90
2.40i		Hollis	Conway	USA	8.1.67	1	WI	Sevilla	10 Mar 91
2.40			Sotomayor			1		Saint Denis	19 Jul 91
2.40		Charles	Austin	USA	19.12.67	1	WK	Zürich	7 Aug 91
2.40			Sotomayor			1	Barr	La Habana	22 May 93
2.40			Sotomayor			1	TSB	London (CP)	23 Jul 93
2.40			Sotomayor			1	WCh	Stuttgart	22 Aug 93
2.40i			Sotomayor			1		Wuppertal	4 Feb 94
2.40i			Sotomayor			1	TSB	Birmingham	26 Feb 94
2.40			Sotomayor			1		Eberstadt	10 Jul 94
2.40			Sotomayor			1	Nik	Nice	18 Jul 94
2.40			Sotomayor			1	GWG	Sankt-Peterburg	29 Jul 94
2.40			Sotomayor			1	WCp	London (CP)	11 Sep 94
2.40			Sotomayor			1	PAm	Mar del Plata	25 Mar 95
2.40		Vyacheslav	Voronin	RUS	5.4.74	1	BrGP	London (CP)	5 Aug 00
2.40i		Stefan	Holm	SWE	25.5.76	1	EI	Madrid	6 Mar 05
2.40i		Ivan	Ukhov	RUS	29.3.86	1		Pireás	25 Feb 09
		(35/11)							
2.39 WR			Zhu Jianhua	CHN	29.5.63	1		Eberstadt	10 Jun 84
2.39i		Dietmar	Mögenburg	FRG	15.8.61	1		Köln	24 Feb 85
2.39i		Ralf	Sonn	GER	17.1.67	1		Berlin	1 Mar 91
2.39		Mutaz Essa	Barshim	QAT	24.6.91	1	Athl	Lausanne	23 Aug 12
2.38i		Gennadiy	Avdeyenko	UKR	4.11.63	2	WI	Indianapolis	7 Mar 87
2.38		Sergey	Malchenko	RUS	2.11.63	1		Banská Bystrica	4 Sep 88
2.38		Dragutin	Topic ¶	YUG	12.3.71	1		Beograd	1 Aug 93
2.38i		Steve	Smith	GBR	29.3.73	2		Wuppertal	4 Feb 94

Mark	Wind	Name		Nat	Born	Pos	Meet	Venue	Date
2.38i		Wolf-Hendrik	Beyer	GER	14.2.72	1		Weinheim	18 Mar 94
		(20)							
2.38		Troy	Kemp	BAH	18.6.66	1	Nik	Nice	12 Jul 95
2.38		Artur	Partyka	POL	25.7.69	1		Eberstadt	18 Aug 96
2.38i		Matt	Hemingway	USA	24.10.72	1	NC	Atlanta	4 Mar 00
2.38i		Yaroslav	Rybakov	RUS	22.11.80	1		Stockholm	15 Feb 05
2.38		Jacques	Freitag	RSA	11.6.82	1		Oudtshoorn	5 Mar 05
2.38		Andriy	Sokolovskyy	UKR	16.7.78	1	GGala	Roma	8 Jul 05
2.38i		Linus	Thörnblad	SWE	6.3.85	2	NC	Göteborg	25 Feb 07
2.38		Andrey	Silnov	RUS	9.9.84	1	LGP	London (CP)	25 Jul 08
2.37		Valeriy	Sereda	RUS	30.6.59	1		Rieti	2 Sep 84
2.37		Tom	McCants	USA	27.11.62	1	Owens	Columbus	8 May 88
		(30)							
2.37		Jerome	Carter	USA	25.3.63	2	Owens	Columbus	8 May 88
2.37		Sergey	Dymchenko	UKR	23.8.67	1		Kiyev	16 Sep 90
2.37i		Dalton	Grant	GBR	8.4.66	1	EI	Paris	13 Mar 94
2.37i		Jaroslav	Bába	CZE	2.9.84	2		Arnstadt	5 Feb 05
2.37		Jesse	Williams	USA	27.12.83	1	NC	Eugene	26 Jun 11
2.37		Robbie	Grabarz	GBR	3.10.87	3	Athl	Lausanne	23 Aug 12
2.36	WR	Gerd	Wessig	GDR	16.7.59	1	OG	Moskva	1 Aug 80
2.36		Sergey	Zasimovich	KZK	6.9.62	1		Tashkent	5 May 84
2.36		Eddy	Annys	BEL	15.12.58	1		Gent	26 May 85
2.36i		Jim	Howard	USA	11.9.59	1		Albuquerque	25 Jan 86
		(40)							
2.36i		Jan	Zvara	CZE	12.2.63	1	vGDR	Jablonec	14 Feb 87
2.36i		Gerd	Nagel	FRG	22.10.57	1		Sulingen	17 Mar 89
2.36		Nick	Saunders	BER	14.9.63	1	CG	Auckland	1 Feb 90
2.36		Doug	Nordquist	USA	20.12.58	2	NC	Norwalk	15 Jun 90
2.36		Georgi	Dakov	BUL	21.10.67	2	VD	Bruxelles	10 Aug 90
2.36		Lábros	Papakóstas	GRE	20.10.69	1	NC	Athína	21 Jun 92
2.36i		Steinar	Hoen	NOR	8.2.71	1		Balingen	12 Feb 94
2.36		Tim	Forsyth	AUS	17.8.73	1	NC	Melbourne	2 Mar 97
2.36		Sergey	Klyugin	RUS	24.3.74	1	WK	Zürich	12 Aug 98
2.36		Konstantin	Matusevich	ISR	25.2.71	1		Perth	5 Feb 00
		(50)							
2.36		Martin	Buss	GER	7.4.76	1	WCh	Edmonton	8 Aug 01
2.36		Aleksander	Walerianczyk	POL	1.9.82	1	EU23	Bydgoszcz	20 Jul 03
2.36		Michal	Bieniek	POL	17.5.84	1		Biala Podlaska	28 May 05
2.36i		Andrey	Tereshin	RUS	15.12.82	1	NC	Moskva	17 Feb 06
2.36A		Dusty	Jonas	USA	19.4.86	1	Big 12	Boulder	18 May 08
2.36		Aleksey	Dmitrik	RUS	12.4.84	1	NC	Cheboksary	23 Jul 11
2.36		Aleksandr	Shustov	RUS	29.6.84	2	NC	Cheboksary	23 Jul 11
		(55)	100th man 2.33, 200th 2.31, 300th 2.29, 400th 2.28, 500th 2.26						

Best outdoor marks for athletes with indoor bests

Mark	Name	Pos	Meet	Venue	Date		Mark	Name	Pos	Meet	Venue	Date
2.39	Conway	1	USOF	Norman	30 Jul 89		2.36	Mögenburg	3		Eberstadt	10 Jun 84
2.39	Ukhov	1	NC	Cheboksary	5 Jul 12		2.36	Howard	1		Rehlingen	8 Jun 87
2.38	Avdeyenko	2=	WCh	Roma	6 Sep 87		2.36	Zvara	1		Praha	23 Aug 87
2.37	Thränhardt	2		Rieti	2 Sep 84		2.36	Grant	4	WCh	Tokyo	1 Sep 91
2.37	Smith	1	WJ	Seoul	20 Sep 92		2.36	Hoen	1		Oslo	1 Jul 97
2.37	Holm	1		Athína	13 Jul 08		2.36	Bába	2=	GGala	Roma	8 Jul 05

Ancillary jumps – en route to final marks

Mark	Name	Date		Mark	Name	Date		Mark	Name	Date
2.40	Sotomayor	8 Sep 88		2.40	Sotomayor	29 Jul 89		2.40	Sotomayor	5 Jun 94

POLE VAULT

Mark	Wind	Name		Nat	Born	Pos	Meet	Venue	Date
6.15i		Sergey	Bubka	UKR	4.12.63	1		Donetsk	21 Feb 93
6.14i			Bubka			1		Liévin	13 Feb 93
6.14A	WR		Bubka			1		Sestriere	31 Jul 94
6.13i			Bubka			1		Berlin	21 Feb 92
6.13	WR		Bubka			1	TOTO	Tokyo	19 Sep 92
6.12i			Bubka			1	Mast	Grenoble	23 Mar 91
6.12	WR		Bubka			1		Padova	30 Aug 92
6.11i			Bubka			1		Donetsk	19 Mar 91
6.11	WR		Bubka			1		Dijon	13 Jun 92
6.10i			Bubka			1		San Sebastián	15 Mar 91
6.10	WR		Bubka			1	MAI	Malmö	5 Aug 91
6.09	WR		Bubka			1		Formia	8 Jul 91
6.08i			Bubka			1	NC	Volgograd	9 Feb 91
6.08	WR		Bubka			1	Znam	Moskva	9 Jun 91
6.07	WR		Bubka			1	Super	Shizuoka	6 May 91
6.06	WR		Bubka			1	Nik	Nice	10 Jul 88

Mark	Wind	Name		Nat	Born	Pos	Meet	Venue	Date
6.06i		Steve	Hooker	AUS	16.7.82	1		Boston (R)	7 Feb 09
6.05 WR			Bubka			1	PTS	Bratislava	9 Jun 88
6.05i			Bubka			1		Donetsk	17 Mar 90
6.05i			Bubka			1		Berlin	5 Mar 93
6.05			Bubka			1	GPF	London (CP)	10 Sep 93
6.05i			Bubka			1	Mast	Grenoble	6 Feb 94
6.05			Bubka			1	ISTAF	Berlin	30 Aug 94
6.05			Bubka			1	GPF	Fukuoka	13 Sep 97
6.05		Maksim	Tarasov	RUS	2.12.70	1	GP II	Athína	16 Jun 99
6.05		Dmitriy	Markov	BLR/AUS	14.3.75	1	WCh	Edmonton	9 Aug 01
6.04		Brad	Walker	USA	21.6.81	1	Pre	Eugene	8 Jun 08
6.03 WR			Bubka			1	Ros	Praha	23 Jun 87
6.03i			Bubka			1		Osaka	11 Feb 89
6.03		Okkert	Brits	RSA	22.8.73	1	ASV	Köln	18 Aug 95
6.03		Jeff	Hartwig	USA	25.9.67	1		Jonesboro	14 Jun 00
6.03i		Renaud	Lavillenie	FRA	18.9.86	1	EI	Paris (Bercy)	5 Mar 11
		(32/8)							
6.02i		Rodion	Gataullin	RUS	23.11.65	1	NC	Gomel	4 Feb 89
6.01		Igor	Trandenkov (10)	RUS	17.8.66	1	NC	Sankt Peterburg	4 Jul 96

Trandenkov hit bar hard, but kept it on with his had illegally. His next best

Mark	Wind	Name		Nat	Born	Pos	Meet	Venue	Date
		5.95				1		Dijon	26 May 96
6.01		Tim	Mack	USA	15.9.72	1	WAF	Monaco	18 Sep 04
6.01		Yevgeniy	Lukyanenko	RUS	23.1.85	1	EAF	Bydgoszcz	1 Jul 08
6.01	sq	Björn	Otto	GER	16.10.77	1		Aachen	5 Sep 12
6.00		Tim	Lobinger	GER	3.9.72	1	ASV	Köln	24 Aug 97
6.00i		Jean	Galfione	FRA	9.6.71	1	WI	Maebashi	6 Mar 99
6.00i		Danny	Ecker	GER	21.7.77	1		Dortmund	11 Feb 01
6.00		Toby	Stevenson	USA	19.11.76	1eA	CalR	Modesto	8 May 04
6.00		Paul	Burgess	AUS	14.8.79	1		Perth	25 Feb 05

Most competitions at 6 metres or more: S Bubka 44, Hartwig 8, Gataullin & Tarasov 7, Hooker 4, Brits & Walker 3

Mark	Wind	Name		Nat	Born	Pos	Meet	Venue	Date
5.98		Lawrence	Johnson	USA	7.5.74	1		Knoxville	25 May 96
5.97		Scott	Huffman	USA	30.11.64	1	NC	Knoxville	18 Jun 94
		(20)							
5.96		Joe	Dial	USA	26.10.62	1		Norman	18 Jun 87
5.95		Andrei	Tivontchik	GER	13.7.70	1	ASV	Köln	16 Aug 96
5.95		Michael	Stolle	GER	17.12.74	1	Herc	Monaco	18 Aug 00
5.95		Romain	Mesnil	FRA	13.6.77	1		Castres	6 Aug 03
5.94i		Philippe	Collet	FRA	13.12.63	1	Mast	Grenoble	10 Mar 90
5.93i WIR		Billy	Olson	USA	19.7.58	1		East Rutherford	8 Feb 86
5.93i		Tye	Harvey	USA	25.9.74	2	NC	Atlanta	3 Mar 01
5.93		Alex	Averbukh	ISR	1.10.74	1	GP	Madrid (C)	19 Jul 03
5.92		István	Bagyula	HUN	2.1.69	1	Gugl	Linz	5 Jul 91
5.92		Igor	Potapovich	KAZ	6.9.67	2		Dijon	13 Jun 92
		(30)							
5.92		Dean	Starkey	USA	27.3.67	1	Banes	São Paulo	21 May 94
5.91 WR		Thierry	Vigneron	FRA	9.3.60	2	GGala	Roma	31 Aug 84
5.91i		Viktor	Ryzhenkov	UZB	25.8.66	2		San Sebastián	15 Mar 91
5.91A		Riaan	Botha	RSA	8.11.70	1		Pretoria	2 Apr 97
5.91		Pawel	Wojciechowski	POL	6.6.89	1		Szczecin	15 Aug 11
5.91		Malte	Mohr	GER	24.7.86	1		Ingolstadt	22 Jun 12
5.91		Raphael	Holzdeppe	GER	28.9.89	3	OG	London (OS)	10 Aug 12
5.90		Pierre	Quinon	FRA	20.2.62	2	Nik	Nice	16 Jul 85
5.90i		Ferenc	Salbert	HUN/FRA	5.8.60	1	Mast	Grenoble	14 Mar 87
5.90		Miroslaw	Chmara	POL	9.5.64	1	BNP	Villeneuve d'Ascq	27 Jun 88
		(40)							
5.90i		Grigoriy	Yegorov	KAZ	12.1.67	1		Yokohama	11 Mar 90
5.90		Denis	Petushinskiy ¶	RUS	28.6.67	1	Znam	Moskva	13 Jun 93
5.90i		Pyotr	Bochkaryov	RUS	3.11.67	1	EI	Paris (B)	12 Mar 94
5.90		Jacob	Davis	USA	29.4.78	1	TexR	Austin	4 Apr 98
5.90		Viktor	Chistyakov	RUS/AUS	9.2.75	1		Salamanca	15 Jul 99
5.90		Pavel	Gerasimov	RUS	29.5.79	1		Rüdlingen	12 Aug 00
5.90		Nick	Hysong	USA	9.12.71	1	OG	Sydney	29 Sep 00
5.90		Giuseppe	Gibilisco	ITA	5.1.79	1	WCh	Saint-Denis	28 Aug 03
5.90i		Igor	Pavlov	RUS	18.7.79	1	EI	Madrid	5 Mar 05
5.90		Lázaro	Borges	CUB	19.6.86	2	WCh	Daegu	29 Aug 11
5.90i		Dmitriy	Starodubtsev	RUS	3.1.86	1		Chelyabinsk	18 Dec 11
		(51)	100th man 5.80, 200th 5.71, 300th 5.65, 400th 5.60, 500th 5.55						

Best outdoor marks for athletes with lifetime bests indoors

6.01	Lavillenie	1	ET	Leiria	21 Jun 09	5.98	Galfione	1		Amiens	23 Jul 99
6.00	Gataullin	1		Tokyo	16 Sep 89	5.93	Ecker	1		Ingolstadt	26 Jul 98
6.00	Hooker	1		Perth	27 Jan 08	5.90	Yegorov	2	WCh	Stuttgart	19 Aug 93

Mark	Wind	Name		Nat	Born	Pos	Meet	Venue	Date

Ancillary jump: 6.05i Bubka   13 Feb 93
Outdoors on built-up runway: 5.90 Pyotr Bochkaryov RUS 3.11.67 1 — Karlskrona — 28 Jun 96
Exhibition or Market Square competitions

Mark	Wind	Name		Nat	Born	Pos	Meet	Venue	Date
6.00		Jean	Galfione	FRA	9.6.71	1		Besançon	23 May 97
5.95		Viktor	Chistiakov	RUS/AUS	9.2.75	1		Chiari	8 Sep 99

LONG JUMP

Mark	Wind	Name		Nat	Born	Pos	Meet	Venue	Date
8.95 WR	0.3	Mike	Powell	USA	10.11.63	1	WCh	Tokyo	30 Aug 91
8.90A WR	2.0	Bob	Beamon	USA	29.8.46	1	OG	Ciudad de México	18 Oct 68
8.87	-0.2	Carl	Lewis	USA	1.7.61	*	WCh	Tokyo	30 Aug 91
8.86A	1.9	Robert	Emmiyan	ARM	16.2.65	1		Tsakhkadzor	22 May 87
8.79	1.9		Lewis			1	TAC	Indianapolis	19 Jun 83
8.79i	-		Lewis			1		New York	27 Jan 84
8.76	1.0		Lewis			1	USOF	Indianapolis	24 Jul 82
8.76	0.8		Lewis			1	NC/OT	Indianapolis	18 Jul 88
8.75	1.7		Lewis			1	PAm	Indianapolis	16 Aug 87
8.74	1.4	Larry	Myricks ¶	USA	10.3.56	2	NC/OT	Indianapolis	18 Jul 88
8.74A	2.0	Erick	Walder	USA	5.11.71	1		El Paso	2 Apr 94
8.74	1.2	Dwight	Phillips	USA	1.10.77	1	Pre	Eugene	7 Jun 09
8.73	1.2	Irving	Saladino	PAN	23.1.83	1	FBK	Hengelo	24 May 08
8.72	-0.2		Lewis			1	OG	Seoul	26 Sep 88
8.71	-0.4		Lewis			1	Pepsi	Los Angeles (Ww)	13 May 84
8.71	0.1		Lewis			1	OT	Los Angeles	19 Jun 84
8.71	1.9	Iván	Pedroso	CUB	17.12.72	1		Salamanca	18 Jul 95
8.71i		Sebastian	Bayer (10)	GER	11.6.86	1	EI	Torino	8 Mar 09
8.70	0.8		Myricks			1	NC	Houston	17 Jun 89
8.70	0.7		Powell			1		Salamanca	27 Jul 93
8.70	1.6		Pedroso			1	WCh	Göteborg	12 Aug 95
8.68	1.0		Lewis			Q	OG	Barcelona	5 Aug 92
8.68	1.6		Pedroso			1		Lisboa	17 Jun 95
8.67	0.4		Lewis			1	WCh	Roma	5 Sep 87
8.67	-0.7		Lewis			1	OG	Barcelona	6 Aug 92
8.66	0.8		Lewis			*	MSR	Walnut	26 Apr 87
8.66	1.0		Myricks			1		Tokyo	23 Sep 87
8.66	0.9		Powell			1	BNP	Villeneuve d'Ascq	29 Jun 90
8.66A	1.4		Lewis			*		Sestriere	31 Jul 94
8.66	0.3		Pedroso			1		Linz	22 Aug 95
8.66	1.6	Loúis	Tsátoumas	GRE	12.2.82	1		Kalamáta	2 Jun 07
		(31/11)							
8.63	0.5	Kareem	Streete-Thompson	CAY/USA	30.3.73	1	GP II	Linz	4 Jul 94
8.62	0.7	James	Beckford	JAM	9.1.75	1		Orlando	5 Apr 97
8.59i		Miguel	Pate	USA	13.6.79	1	NC	New York	1 Mar 02
8.56i	-	Yago	Lamela	ESP	24.7.77	2	WI	Maebashi	7 Mar 99
8.54	0.9	Lutz	Dombrowski	GDR	25.6.59	1	OG	Moskva	28 Jul 80
8.54	1.7	Mitchell	Watt	AUS	25.3.88	1	DNG	Stockholm	29 Jul 11
8.53	1.2	Jaime	Jefferson	CUB	17.1.62	1	Barr	La Habana	12 May 90
8.52	0.7	Savanté	Stringfellow	USA	6.11.78	1	NC	Stanford	21 Jun 02
8.51	1.7	Roland	McGhee	USA	15.10.71	2		São Paulo	14 May 95
		(20)							
8.50	0.2	Llewellyn	Starks	USA	10.2.67	2		Rhede	7 Jul 91
8.50	1.3	Godfrey Khotso	Mokoena	RSA	6.3.85	2	GP	Madrid	4 Jul 09
8.49	2.0	Melvin	Lister	USA	29.8.77	1	SEC	Baton Rouge	13 May 00
8.49	0.6	Jai	Taurima	AUS	26.6.72	2	OG	Sydney	28 Sep 00
8.48	0.8	Joe	Greene	USA	17.2.67	3		São Paulo	14 May 95
8.48	0.6	Mohamed Salim	Al-Khuwalidi	KSA	19.6.81	1		Sotteville-lès-Rouen	2 Jul 06
8.47	1.9	Kevin	Dilworth	USA	14.2.74	1		Abilene	9 May 96
8.47	0.9	John	Moffitt	USA	12.12.80	2	OG	Athína	26 Aug 04
8.47	-0.2	Andrew	Howe	ITA	12.5.85	2	WCh	Osaka	30 Aug 07
8.47	1.6	Christian	Reif	GER	24.10.84	1	EC	Barcelona	1 Aug 10
		(30)							
8.46	1.2	Leonid	Voloshin	RUS	30.3.66	1	NC	Tallinn	5 Jul 88
8.46	1.6	Mike	Conley	USA	5.10.62	2		Springfield	4 May 96
8.46	1.8	Cheikh Tidiane	Touré	SEN/FRA	25.1.70	1		Bad Langensalza	15 Jun 97
8.46	0.3	Ibrahin	Camejo	CUB	28.6.82	1		Bilbao	21 Jun 08
8.45	2.0	Nenad	Stekic	YUG	7.3.51	1	PO	Montreal	25 Jul 75
8.44	1.7	Eric	Metcalf	USA	23.1.68	1	NC	Tampa	17 Jun 88
8.43	0.8	Jason	Grimes	USA	10.9.59	*	NC	Indianapolis	16 Jun 85
8.43	1.8	Giovanni	Evangelisti	ITA	11.9.61	1		San Giovanni Valdarno	16 May 87
8.43i	-	Stanislav	Tarasenko	RUS	23.7.66	1		Moskva	26 Jan 94

Mark	Wind	Name		Nat	Born	Pos	Meet	Venue	Date
8.43	0.1	Luis Felipe	Méliz	CUB/ESP	11.8.79	2	OD	Jena	3 Jun 00
		(40)							
8.43	-0.2	Ignisious	Gaisah	GHA	20.6.83	2	GGala	Roma	14 Jul 06
8.42	0.4	Salim	Sdiri	FRA	26.10.78	1		Pierre-Bénite	12 Jun 09
8.41	1.5	Craig	Hepburn	BAH	10.12.69	1	NC	Nassau	17 Jun 93
8.41i	-	Kirill	Sosunov	RUS	1.11.75	2	WI	Paris (B)	8 Mar 97
8.40	1.4	Douglas de	Souza	BRA	6.8.72	1		São Paulo	15 Feb 95
8.40	0.4	Robert	Howard	USA	26.11.75	1	SEC	Auburn	17 May 97
8.40	2.0	Gregor	Cankar	SLO	25.1.75	1		Celje	18 May 97
8.40	0.0		Lao Jianfeng	CHN	24.5.75	1	NC	Zhaoqing	28 May 97
8.40	1.0	Yahya	Berrabah	MAR	13.10.81	1	Franc	Beirut	2 Oct 09
8.40	0.5	Fabrice	Lapierre	AUS	17.10.83	1		Nuoro	14 Jul 10
8.40	0.0	Ngonidzashe	Makusha	ZIM	11.3.87	1	NCAA	Des Moines	9 Jun 11
		(51)	100th man 8.31, 200th 8.22, 300th 8.17, 400th 8.11, 500th 8.08						

Best at low altitude: 8.61 1.3 Emmiyan 1 GWG Moskva 6 Jul 86   8.58 1.8 Walder 1 Springfield 4 May 86

Wind-assisted marks performances to 8.70, performers to 8.42

Mark	Wind	Name		Nat	Born	Pos	Meet	Venue	Date
8.99A	4.4	Mike	Powell	USA	10.11.63	1		Sestriere	21 Jul 92
8.96A	1.2+	Iván	Pedroso	CUB	17.12.72	1		Sestriere	29 Jul 95
8.95A	3.9		Powell			1		Sestriere	31 Jul 94
8.91	2.9	Carl	Lewis	USA	1.7.61	2	WCh	Tokyo	30 Aug 91
8.90	3.7		Powell			1	S&W	Modesto	16 May 92
8.79	3.0		Pedroso			1	Barr	La Habana	21 May 92
8.78	3.1	Fabrice	Lapierre	AUS	17.10.83	1	NC	Perth	18 Apr 10
8.77	3.9		Lewis			1	Pepsi	Los Angeles (Ww)	18 May 85
8.77	3.4		Lewis			1	MSR	Walnut	26 Apr 87
8.73	4.6		Lewis			Q	NC	Sacramento	19 Jun 81
8.73	3.2		Lewis			Q	NC	Indianapolis	17 Jun 83
8.73A	2.6		Powell			1		Sestriere	31 Jul 91
8.73	4.8		Pedroso			1		Madrid	20 Jun 95
8.72	2.2		Lewis			1	NYG	New York	24 May 92
8.72A	3.9		Lewis			2		Sestriere	31 Jul 94
8.70	2.5		Pedroso			1		Padova	16 Jul 95
8.68	4.9	James	Beckford	JAM	9.1.75	1	JUCO	Odessa, Tx	19 May 95
8.66A	4.0	Joe	Greene	USA	17.2.67	2		Sestriere	21 Jul 92
8.64	3.5	Kareem	Streete-Thompson	CAY/USA	30.3.73	2	NC	Knoxville	18 Jun 94
8.63	3.9	Mike	Conley	USA	5.10.62	2	NC	Eugene	20 Jun 86
8.57	5.2	Jason	Grimes	USA	10.9.59	1	vFRG,AFR	Durham	27 Jun 82
8.53	4.9	Kevin	Dilworth	USA	14.2.74	1		Fort-de-France	27 Apr 02
8.51	3.7	Ignisious	Gaisah	GHA	20.6.83	1	AfCh	Bambous	9 Aug 06
8.49	2.6	Ralph	Boston	USA	9.5.39	1	OT	Los Angeles	12 Sep 64
8.49	4.5	Stanislav	Tarasenko	RUS	23.7.66	2		Madrid	20 Jun 95
8.48	2.8	Kirill	Sosunov	RUS	1.11.75	1		Oristano	18 Sep 95
8.48	3.4	Peter	Burge	AUS	3.7.74	1		Gold Coast (RB)	10 Sep 00
8.48	2.1	Brian	Johnson	USA	25.3.80	1	Conseil	Fort-de-France	8 May 08
8.46	3.4	Randy	Williams	USA	23.8.53	1		Eugene	18 May 73
8.46		Vernon	George	USA	6.10.64	1		Houston	21 May 89
8.44		Keith	Talley	USA	28.1.64	Q		Odessa, Tx	16 May 85
8.42		Anthony	Bailous	USA	6.4.65	Q		Odessa, Tx	16 May 85
8.42A	4.5	Milan	Gombala	CZE	29.1.68	3		Sestriere	21 Jul 92

Exhibition: 8.46 Yuriy Naumkin RUS 4.11.68 1 Iglesias 6 Sep 96

Best outdoors

8.56 1.3 Lamela 1 Torino 24 Jun 99   8.49 1.6 Bayer 1 NC Ulm 4 Jul 09

8.46A 0.0 Pate 1 Cd. de México 3 May 03 and 8.45 1.5 2 NC Stanford 21 Jun 02, 8.48w 5.6 1 Fort Worth 21 Apr 01

Ancillary marks – other marks during series (to 8.67/8.70w)

8.84	1.7	Lewis	30 Aug 91	8.89Aw	2.4	Pedroso	29 Jul 95	8.75w	2.1	Lewis	16 Aug 87
8.71	0.6	Lewis	19 Jun 83	8.84Aw	3.8	Powell	21 Jul 92	8.75Aw	3.4	Powell	21 Jul 92
8.68	0.3	Lewis	18 Jul 88	8.83w	2.3	Lewis	30 Aug 91	8.73w	2.4	Lewis	18 May 85
8.68	0.0	Lewis	30 Aug 91	8.80Aw	4.0	Powell	21 Jul 92	8.73w		Powell	16 May 92
8.67	-0.2	Lewis	5 Sep 87	8.78Aw		Powell	21 Jul 92	8.71Aw		Powell	31 Jul 91

TRIPLE JUMP

Mark	Wind	Name		Nat	Born	Pos	Meet	Venue	Date
18.29	WR 1.3	Jonathan	Edwards	GBR	10.5.66	1	WCh	Göteborg	7 Aug 95
18.09	-0.4	Kenny	Harrison	USA	13.2.65	1	OG	Atlanta	27 Jul 96
18.01	0.4		Edwards			1	Bisl	Oslo	9 Jul 98
18.00	1.3		Edwards			1	McD	London (CP)	27 Aug 95
17.99	0.5		Edwards			1	EC	Budapest	23 Aug 98
17.98	WR 1.8		Edwards			1		Salamanca	18 Jul 95
17.98	1.2	Teddy	Tamgho	FRA	15.6.89	1	DL	New York	12 Jun 10
17.97	WR 1.5	Willie	Banks	USA	11.3.56	1	TAC	Indianapolis	16 Jun 85
17.96	0.1	Christian	Taylor	USA	18.6.90	1	WCh	Daegu	4 Sep 11

Mark	Wind		Name	Nat	Born	Pos	Meet	Venue	Date
17.93	1.6		Harrison			1	DNG	Stockholm	2 Jul 90
17.92	1.6	Khristo	Markov	BUL	27.1.65	1	WCh	Roma	31 Aug 87
17.92	1.9	James	Beckford	JAM	9.1.75	1	JUCO	Odessa, TX	20 May 95
17.92i	WIR -		Tamgho			1	EI	Paris (Bercy)	6 Mar 11
17.92	0.7		Edwards			1	WCh	Edmonton	6 Aug 01
17.91i	WIR -		Tamgho			1	NC	Aubière	20 Feb 11
17.91	1.4		Tamgho			1	Athl	Lausanne	30 Jun 11
17.90	1.0	Vladimir	Inozemtsev	UKR	25.5.64	1	PTS	Bratislava	20 Jun 90
17.90	0.4	Jadel	Gregório	BRA	16.9.80	1	GP	Belém	20 May 07
17.90i			Tamgho			1	WI	Doha	14 Mar 10
17.89A	WR 0.0	João Carlos	de Oliveira (10)	BRA	28.5.54	1	PAm	Ciudad de México	15 Oct 75
17.88	0.9		Edwards			2	OG	Atlanta	27 Jul 96
17.87	1.7	Mike	Conley	USA	5.10.62	1	NC	San José	27 Jun 87
17.86	1.3	Charles	Simpkins	USA	19.10.63	1	WUG	Kobe	2 Sep 85
17.86	0.3		Conley			1	WCh	Stuttgart	16 Aug 93
17.86	0.7		Edwards			1	CG	Manchester	28 Jul 02
17.85	0.9	Yoelbi	Quesada	CUB	4.8.73	1	WCh	Athína	8 Aug 97
17.84	0.7		Conley			1		Bad Cannstatt	4 Jul 93
17.83i	WIR -	Aliecer	Urrutia	CUB	22.9.74	1		Sindelfingen	1 Mar 97
17.83i	WIR -	Christian	Olsson	SWE	25.1.80	1	WI	Budapest	7 Mar 04
17.82	1.6		Edwards			1	WG	Helsinki	25 Jun 96
	(30/15)								
17.81	1.0	Marian	Oprea	ROU	6.6.82	1	Athl	Lausanne	5 Jul 05
17.81	0.1	Phillips	Idowu	GBR	30.12.78	1	EC	Barcelona	29 Jul 10
17.78	1.0	Nikolay	Musiyenko	UKR	16.12.59	1	Znam	Leningrad	7 Jun 86
17.78	0.6	Lázaro	Betancourt ¶	CUB	18.3.63	1	Barr	La Habana	15 Jun 86
17.78	0.8	Melvin	Lister	USA	29.8.77	1	NC/OT	Sacramento	17 Jul 04
	(20)								
17.77	1.0	Aleksandr	Kovalenko	RUS	8.5.63	1	NC	Bryansk	18 Jul 87
17.77i	-	Leonid	Voloshin	RUS	30.3.66	1		Grenoble	6 Feb 94
17.75	0.3	Oleg	Protsenko	RUS	11.8.63	1	Znam	Moskva	10 Jun 90
17.74	1.4	Nelson	Évora	POR	20.4.84	1	WCh	Osaka	27 Aug 07
17.73i		Walter	Davis	USA	2.7.79	1	WI	Moskva	12 Mar 06
17.73i	-	Fabrizio	Donato	ITA	14.8.76	2	EI	Paris (Bercy)	6 Mar 11
17.72i		Brian	Wellman	BER	8.9.67	1	WI	Barcelona	12 Mar 95
17.72	1.3	Sheryf	El-Sheryf	UKR	2.1.89	1	EU23	Ostrava	17 Jul 11
17.70i	-	Will	Claye	USA	13.6.91	1	WI	Istanbul	11 Mar 12
17.69	1.5	Igor	Lapshin	BLR	8.8.63	1		Stayki	31 Jul 88
	(30)								
17.69i		Yoandri	Betanzos	CUB	15.2.82	2	WI	Doha	14 Mar 10
17.68	0.4	Danil	Burkenya	RUS	20.7.78	1	NC	Tula	31 Jul 04
17.68A	1.6	Alexis	Copello	CUB	12.8.85	1		Ávila	17 Jul 11
17.66	1.7	Ralf	Jaros	GER	13.12.65	1	ECp	Frankfurt-am-Main	30 Jun 91
17.65	1.0	Aleksandr	Yakovlev	UKR	8.9.57	1	Znam	Moskva	6 Jun 87
17.65	0.8	Denis	Kapustin	RUS	5.10.70	2	Bisl	Oslo	9 Jul 98
17.64	1.4	Nathan	Douglas	GBR	4.12.82	1	NC	Manchester (SC)	10 Jul 05
17.63	0.9	Kenta	Bell	USA	16.3.77	1c2	MSR	Walnut	21 Apr 02
17.62i	-	Yoel	García	CUB	25.11.73	2		Sindelfingen	1 Mar 97
17.62	-0.2	Arne David	Girat	CUB	26.8.84	3	ALBA	La Habana	25 Apr 09
	(40)								
17.60	0.6	Vladimir	Plekhanov	RUS	11.4.58	2	NC	Leningrad	4 Aug 85
17.59i	-	Pierre	Camara	FRA	10.9.65	1	WI	Toronto	13 Mar 93
17.59	0.3	Vasiliy	Sokov	RUS	7.4.68	1	NC	Moskva	19 Jun 93
17.59	0.8	Charles	Friedek	GER	26.8.71	1		Hamburg	23 Jul 97
17.59	0.9	Leevan	Sands	BAH	16.8.81	3	OG	Beijing	21 Aug 08
17.59	0.0		Li Yanxi	CHN	26.6.84	1	NG	Jinan	26 Oct 09
17.58	1.5	Oleg	Sakirkin	KZK	23.1.66	2	NC	Gorkiy	23 Jul 89
17.58	1.6	Aarik	Wilson	USA	25.10.82	1	LGP	London (CP)	3 Aug 07
17.57A	0.0	Keith	Connor	GBR	16.9.57	1	NCAA	Provo	5 Jun 82
17.57	0.2	Dmitriy	Valyukevich/Valukevic	BLR/SVK	31.5.81	1	EU23	Bydgoszcz	19 Jul 03
	(50)		100th man 17.37, 200th 17.17, 300th 17.00, 400th 16.87, 500th 16.76						

Wind-assisted marks – performances to 17.86, performers to 17.58

Mark	Wind		Name	Nat	Born	Pos	Meet	Venue	Date
18.43	2.4	Jonathan	Edwards	GBR	10.5.66	1	ECp	Villeneuve d'Ascq	25 Jun 95
18.20	5.2	Willie	Banks	USA	11.3.56	1	NC/OT	Indianpolis	16 Jul 88
18.17	2.1	Mike	Conley	USA	5.10.62	1	OG	Barcelona	3 Aug 92
18.08	2.5		Edwards			1	BrGP	Sheffield	23 Jul 95
18.03	2.9		Edwards			1	GhG	Gateshead	2 Jul 95
18.01	3.7		Harrison			1	NC	Atlanta	15 Jun 96
17.97	7.5	Yoelbi	Quesada	CUB	4.8.73	1		Madrid	20 Jun 95
17.93	5.2	Charles	Simpkins	USA	19.10.63	2	NC/OT	Indianpolis	16 Jul 88

Mark	Wind		Name		Nat	Born	Pos	Meet	Venue	Date
17.92	3.4	Christian	Olsson		SWE	25.1.80	1	GP	Gateshead	13 Jul 03
17.91	3.2		Simpkins				1	NC	Eugene	21 Jun 86
17.86	3.9		Simpkins				1	NC/OT	New Orleans	21 Jun 92
17.86	5.7	Denis	Kapustin		RUS	5.10.70	1		Sevilla	5 Jun 94
17.82	2.5	Nelson	Évora		POR	20.4.84	1	NC	Seixal	26 Jul 09
17.81	4.6	Keith	Connor		GBR	16.9.57	1	CG	Brisbane	9 Oct 82
17.76A	2.2	Kenta	Bell		USA	16.3.77	1		El Paso	10 Apr 04
17.75		Gennadiy	Valyukevich		BLR	1.6.58	1		Uzhgorod	27 Apr 86
17.75	7.1	Brian	Wellman		BER	8.9.67	2		Madrid	20 Jun 95
17.73	4.1	Vasiliy	Sokov		RUS	7.4.68	1		Riga	3 Jun 89
17.69	3.9	Alexis	Copello		CUB	12.8.85	1	ALBA	La Habana	25 Apr 09
17.67	3.4	Daniele	Greco		ITA	1.3.89	1	NC	Bressanone	8 Jul 12
17.63	4.3	Robert	Cannon		USA	9.7.58	3	NC/OT	Indianpolis	16 Jul 88
17.59	2.1	Jerome	Romain		DMA/FRA	12.6.71	3	WCh	Göteborg	7 Aug 95
17.58	5.2	Al	Joyner		USA	19.1.60	5	NC/OT	Indianpolis	16 Jul 88

Best outdoor marks for athletes with indoor bests

17.79	1.4	Olsson	1	OG	Athína	22 Aug 04		17.65	1.4	Betanzos	2	ALBA	La Habana	25 Apr 09
17.75	1.0	Voloshin	2	WCh	Tokyo	26 Aug 91		17.67w	5.4		1		Bilbao	1 Jul 06
17.71	-0.7	Davis	1	NC	Indianapolis	25 Jun 06		17.62A	0.1	Wellman	1		El Paso	15 Apr 95
17.70	1.7	Urrutia	1	GP II	Sevilla	6 Jun 96		17.62	0.6	Claye	2	OG	London (OS)	9 Aug 12
								17.60	1.9	Donato	1		Milano	7 Jun 00
								17.63w	2.8		1	EC	Helsinki	30 Jun 12

Low altitude best: 17.65 0.1 Copello 1 Barr La Habana 30 May 09

Ancillary marks – other marks during series (to 17.78/17.84w)

18.16 WR	1.3	Edwards	7 Aug 95		17.84	1.7	Tamgho	12 Jun 10		18.06w	4.9	Banks	16 Jul 88
17.99	0.1	Harrison	27 Jul 96		18.39w	3.7	Edwards	25 Jun 95		17.90w	2.5	Edwards	25 Jun 95
										17.84w	2.1	Edwards	23 Aug 98

SHOT

Mark		Name		Nat	Born	Pos	Meet	Venue	Date
23.12 WR	Randy	Barnes ¶		USA	16.6.66	1		Los Angeles (Ww)	20 May 90
23.10		Barnes				1	Jenner	San José	26 May 90
23.06 WR	Ulf	Timmermann		GDR	1.11.62	1	Veniz	Haniá	22 May 88
22.91 WR	Alessandro	Andrei		ITA	3.1.59	1		Viareggio	12 Aug 87
22.86	Brian	Oldfield		USA	1.6.45	1	ITA	El Paso	10 May 75
22.75	Werner	Günthör		SUI	1.6.61	1		Bern	23 Aug 88
22.67	Kevin	Toth ¶		USA	29.12.67	1	KansR	Lawrence	19 Apr 03
22.66i		Barnes				1	Sunkist	Los Angeles	20 Jan 89
22.64 WR	Udo	Beyer		GDR	9.8.55	1		Berlin	20 Aug 86
22.62 WR		Timmermann				1		Berlin	22 Sep 85
22.61		Timmermann				1		Potsdam	8 Sep 88
22.60		Timmermann				1	vURS	Tallinn	21 Jun 86
22.56		Timmermann				1		Berlin	13 Sep 88
22.55i		Timmermann				1	NC	Senftenberg	11 Feb 89
22.54	Christian	Cantwell		USA	30.9.80	1	GP II	Gresham	5 Jun 04
22.52	John	Brenner		USA	4.1.61	1	MSR	Walnut	26 Apr 87
22.51		Timmermann				1		Erfurt	1 Jun 86
22.51	Adam	Nelson (10)		USA	7.7.75	1		Gresham	18 May 02
22.47		Timmermann				1		Dresden	17 Aug 86
22.47		Günthör				1	WG	Helsinki	2 Jul 87
22.47		Timmermann				1	OG	Seoul	23 Sep 88
22.45		Oldfield				1	ITA	El Paso	22 May 76
22.45		Cantwell				1	GP	Gateshead	11 Jun 06
22.43		Günthör				1	v3-N	Lüdenscheid	18 Jun 87
22.43	Reese	Hoffa		USA	8.10.77	1	LGP	London (CP)	3 Aug 07
22.42		Barnes				1	WK	Zürich	17 Aug 88
22.41		Cantwell				1	Pre	Eugene	3 Jul 10
22.40		Barnes				1		Rüdlingen	13 Jul 96
22.40i		Nelson				1		Fayetteville	15 Feb 08
22.39		Barnes				2	OG	Seoul	23 Sep 88
	(30/11)								
22.24	Sergey	Smirnov		RUS	17.9.60	2	vGDR	Tallinn	21 Jun 86
22.21	Dylan	Armstrong		CAN	15.1.81	1	NC	Calgary	25 Jun 11
22.20	John	Godina		USA	31.5.72	1		Carson	22 May 05
22.10	Sergey	Gavryushin		RUS	27.6.59	1		Tbilisi	31 Aug 86
22.10	Cory	Martin		USA	22.5.85	1		Tucson	22 May 10
22.10	Andrey	Mikhnevich ¶		BLR	12.7.76	1		Minsk	11 Aug 11
22.09	Sergey	Kasnauskas		BLR	20.4.61	1		Stayki	23 Aug 84
22.09i	Mika	Halvari		FIN	13.2.70	1		Tampere	7 Feb 00
22.02i	George	Woods		USA	11.2.43	1	LAT	Inglewood	8 Feb 74
	(20)								

Mark	Wind	Name		Nat	Born	Pos	Meet	Venue	Date
22.02		Dave	Laut	USA	21.12.56	1		Koblenz	25 Aug 82
22.00	WR	Aleksandr	Baryshnikov	RUS	11.11.48	1	vFRA	Colombes	10 Jul 76
22.00i		Ryan	Whiting	USA	24.11.86	1	WI	Istanbul	9 Mar 12
21.98		Gregg	Tafralis ¶	USA	9.4.58	1		Los Gatos	13 Jun 92
21.97		Janus	Robberts	RSA	10.3.79	1	NCAA	Eugene	2 Jun 01
21.96		Mikhail	Kostin	RUS	10.5.59	1		Vitebsk	20 Jul 86
21.95		Tomasz	Majewski	POL	30.8.81	1	DNG	Stockholm	30 Jul 09
21.93		Remigius	Machura ¶	CZE	3.7.60	1		Praha	23 Aug 87
21.92		Carl	Myerscough ¶	GBR	21.10.79	1	NCAA	Sacramento	13 Jun 03
21.88i		David	Storl	GER	27.7.90	2	WI	Istanbul	9 Mar 12
		(30)							
21.87		C.J.	Hunter ¶	USA	14.12.68	2	NC	Sacramento	15 Jul 00
21.85	WR	Terry	Albritton	USA	14.1.55	1		Honolulu	21 Feb 76
21.83i		Aleksandr	Bagach ¶	UKR	21.11.66	1		Brovary	21 Feb 99
21.82	WR	Al	Feuerbach	USA	14.1.48	1		San José	5 May 73
21.82		Andy	Bloom	USA	11.8.73	1	GPF	Doha	5 Oct 00
21.81		Yuriy	Bilonog ¶	UKR	9.3.74	1	NC	Kiev	3 Jul 03
21.78	WR	Randy	Matson	USA	5.3.45	1		College Station	22 Apr 67
21.78		Dan	Taylor	USA	12.5.82	1		Tucson	23 May 09
21.77i		Mike	Stulce ¶	USA	21.7.69	1	v GBR	Birmingham	13 Feb 93
21.77		Dragan	Peric	YUG	8.5.64	1		Bar	25 Apr 98
		(40)							
21.76		Michael	Carter	USA	29.10.60	2	NCAA	Eugene	2 Jun 84
21.74		Janis	Bojars	LAT	12.5.56	1		Riga	14 Jul 84
21.73		Augie	Wolf ¶	USA	3.9.61	1		Leverkusen	12 Apr 84
21.69		Reijo	Ståhlberg	FIN	21.9.52	1	WCR	Fresno	5 May 79
21.68		Geoff	Capes	GBR	23.8.49	1	4-N	Cwmbrân	18 May 80
21.68		Edward	Sarul	POL	16.11.58	1		Sopot	31 Jul 83
21.67		Hartmut	Briesenick	GDR	17.3.49	1		Potsdam	1 Sep 73
21.63i		Joachim	Olsen	DEN	31.5.77	1		Tallinn	25 Feb 04
21.63		Maris	Urtans	LAT	9.2.81	1	ET-2	Beograd	19 Jun 10
21.62		Rutger	Smith	NED	9.7.81	1		Leiden	10 Jun 06

(50)   100th man 21.10, 200th 20.68, 300th 20.32, 400th 20.04, 500th 19.77

Not recognised by GDR authorities

22.11		Rolf	Oesterreich	GDR	24.8.49	1		Zschopau	12 Sep 76

Drugs disqualification

22.84			Barnes			1		Malmö	7 Aug 90
21.82		Mike	Stulce ¶	USA	21.7.69	1		Brenham	9 May 90

Best outdoor marks for athletes with lifetime bests indoors

21.97	Whiting	1	NCAA	Eugene	12 Jun 10
21.63	Woods	2	CalR	Modesto	22 May 76
21.86	Storl	2	OG	London (OS)	3 Aug 12

21.61	Olsen	1		Köbenhavn	13 Jun 07
21.70	Stulce ¶	1	OG	Barcelona	31 Jul 92

Ancillary marks – other marks during series (to 22.45)

22.84	WR	Andrei	12 Aug 87	22.72	WR	Andrei	12 Aug 87	22.55	Barnes	20 May 90
22.76		Barnes	20 May 90	22.70		Günthör	23 Aug 88	22.49	Nelson	18 May 02
22.74		Andrei	12 Aug 87	22.58		Beyer	20 Aug 86	22.45	Timmermann	22 May 88

DISCUS

Mark	Wind	Name		Nat	Born	Pos	Meet	Venue	Date
74.08	WR	Jürgen	Schult	GDR	11.5.60	1		Neubrandenburg	6 Jun 86
73.88		Virgilijus	Alekna	LTU	13.2.72	1	NC	Kaunas	3 Aug 00
73.38		Gerd	Kanter	EST	6.5.79	1		Helsingborg	4 Sep 06
72.02			Kanter			1eA		Salinas	3 May 07
71.88			Kanter			1eA		Salinas	8 May 08
71.86	WR	Yuriy	Dumchev	RUS	5.8.58	1		Moskva	29 May 83
71.70		Róbert	Fazekas ¶	HUN	18.8.75	1		Szombathely	14 Jul 02
71.64			Kanter			1		Kohila	25 Jun 09
71.56			Alekna			1		Kaunas	25 Jul 07
71.50		Lars	Riedel	GER	28.6.67	1		Wiesbaden	3 May 97
71.45			Kanter			1		Chula Vista	29 Apr 10
71.32		Ben	Plucknett ¶	USA	13.4.54	1	Pre	Eugene	4 Jun 83
71.26		John	Powell	USA	25.6.47	1	NC	San José	9 Jun 84
71.26		Rickard	Bruch	SWE	2.7.46	1		Malmö	15 Nov 84
71.26		Imrich	Bugár (10)	CZE	14.4.55	1	Jenner	San José	25 May 85
71.25			Fazekas			1	WCp	Madrid (C)	21 Sep 02
71.25			Alekna			1	Danek	Turnov	20 May 08
71.18		Art	Burns	USA	19.7.54	1		San José	19 Jul 83
71.16	WR	Wolfgang	Schmidt	GDR	16.1.54	1		Berlin	9 Aug 78
71.14			Plucknett			1		Berkeley	12 Jun 83
71.14		Anthony	Washington	USA	16.1.66	1eA		Salinas	22 May 96
71.12			Alekna			1	WK	Zürich	11 Aug 00

Mark	Wind	Name		Nat	Born	Pos	Meet	Venue	Date
71.08			Alekna			1		Réthimno	21 Jul 06
71.06		Luis Mariano	Delís ¶	CUB	12.12.57	1	Barr	La Habana	21 May 83
71.06			Riedel			1	WK	Zürich	14 Aug 96
71.00			Bruch			1		Malmö	14 Oct 84
70.99			Alekna			1		Stellenbosch	30 Mar 01
70.98		Mac	Wilkins	USA	15.11.50	1	WG	Helsinki	9 Jul 80
70.98			Burns			1	Pre	Eugene	21 Jul 84
70.97			Alekna			1		Réthimno	23 Jun 04
		(30/15)							
70.82		Aleksander	Tammert	EST	2.2.73	1		Denton	15 Apr 06
70.66		Robert	Harting	GER	18.10.84	1	Danek	Turnov	22 May 12
70.54		Dmitriy	Shevchenko ¶	RUS	13.5.68	1		Krasnodar	7 May 02
70.38	WRu	Jay	Silvester	USA	27.8.37	1		Lancaster	16 May 71
70.32		Frantz	Kruger	RSA/FIN	22.5.75	1		Salon-de-Provence	26 May 02
		(20)							
70.06		Romas	Ubartas ¶	LTU	26.5.60	1		Smalininkay	8 May 88
70.00		Juan	Martínez ¶	CUB	17.5.58	2	Barr	La Habana	21 May 83
69.95		Zoltán	Kövágó	HUN	10.4.79	1		Salon-de-Provence	25 May 06
69.91		John	Godina	USA	31.5.72	1		Salinas	19 May 98
69.90		Jason	Young	USA	27.5.81	1		Lubbock	26 Mar 10
69.83		Piotr	Malachowski	POL	7.6.83	1		Gateshead	10 Jul 10
69.70		Géjza	Valent	CZE	3.10.53	2		Nitra	26 Aug 84
69.62		Knut	Hjeltnes ¶	NOR	8.12.51	2	Jen	San José	25 May 85
69.62		Timo	Tompuri	FIN	9.6.69	1		Helsingborg	8 Jul 01
69.50		Mario	Pestano	ESP	8.4.78	1	NC	Santa Cruz de Tenerife	27 Jul 08
		(30)							
69.46		Al	Oerter	USA	19.9.36	1	TFA	Wichita	31 May 80
69.44		Georgiy	Kolnootchenko	BLR	7.5.59	1	vUSA	Indianapolis	3 Jul 82
69.40		Art	Swarts ¶	USA	14.2.45	1		Scotch Plains	8 Dec 79
69.36		Mike	Buncic	USA	25.7.62	1		Fresno	6 Apr 91
69.32		Ehsan	Hadadi	IRI	21.1.85	1		Tallinn	3 Jun 08
69.28		Vladimir	Dubrovshchik	BLR	7.1.72	1	NC	Stayki	3 Jun 00
69.26		Ken	Stadel	USA	19.2.52	2	AAU	Walnut	16 Jun 79
68.94		Adam	Setliff	USA	15.12.69	1		Atascadero	25 Jul 01
68.91		Ian	Waltz	USA	15.4.77	1		Salinas	24 May 06
68.90		Jean-Claude	Retel	FRA	11.2.68	1		Salon-de-Provence	17 Jul 02
		(40)							
68.88		Vladimir	Zinchenko	UKR	25.7.59	1		Dnepropetrovsk	16 Jul 88
68.76		Jarred	Rome	USA	21.12.76	2cA		Chula Vista	6 Aug 11
68.64		Dmitriy	Kovtsun ¶	UKR	29.9.55	1		Riga	6 Jul 84
68.58		Attila	Horváth	HUN	28.7.67	1		Budapest	24 Jun 94
68.52		Igor	Duginyets	UKR	20.5.56	1	NC	Kyiv	21 Aug 82
68.50		Armin	Lemme	GDR	28.10.55	1	vUSA	Karl-Marx-Stadt	10 Jul 82
68.49A		Casey	Malone	USA	6.4.77	1		Fort Collins	20 Jun 09
68.48	WR	John	van Reenen	RSA	26.3.47	1		Stellenbosch	14 Mar 75
68.44		Vaclovas	Kidykas	LTU	17.10.61	1		Sochi	1 Jun 88
68.33		Martin	Wierig	GER	10.6.87	1		Schönebeck	26 Jul 12
		(50)	100th man 66.98, 200th 65.16, 300th 64.16, 400th 62.92, 500th 61.79						

Subsequent to or at drugs disqualification   ! recognised as US record

Mark	Wind	Name		Nat	Born	Pos	Meet	Venue	Date
72.34!		Ben	Plucknett ¶	USA	13.4.54	(1)	DNG	Stockholm	7 Jul 81
71.20			Plucknett			(1)	CalR	Modesto	16 May 81
70.84		Kamy	Keshmiri ¶	USA	23.1.69	(1)		Salinas	27 May 92

Sloping ground

Mark	Wind	Name		Nat	Born	Pos	Meet	Venue	Date
72.08		John	Powell	USA	25.6.47	1		Klagshamn	11 Sep 87
69.80		Stefan	Fernholm	SWE	2.7.59	1		Klagshamn	13 Aug 87
69.44		Adam	Setliff	USA	15.12.69	1		La Jolla	21 Jul 01
68.46		Andy	Bloom	USA	11.8.73	2cA		La Jolla	25 Mar 00

Ancillary marks – other marks during series (to 70.96)

72.35 Alekna 3 Aug 00   72.30 Kanter 4 Sep 06   71.08 Plucknett 4 Jun 83

HAMMER

Mark	Wind	Name		Nat	Born	Pos	Meet	Venue	Date
86.74	WR	Yuriy	Sedykh	RUS	11.6.55	1	EC	Stuttgart	30 Aug 86
86.73		Ivan	Tikhon ¶	BLR	24.7.76	1	NC	Brest	3 Jul 05
86.66	WR		Sedykh			1	vGDR	Tallinn	22 Jun 86
86.34	WR		Sedykh			1		Cork	3 Jul 84
86.04		Sergey	Litvinov	RUS	23.1.58	1	OD	Dresden	3 Jul 86
85.74			Litvinov			2	EC	Stuttgart	30 Aug 86
85.68			Sedykh			1	BGP	Budapest	11 Aug 86
85.60			Sedykh			1	PTG	London (CP)	13 Jul 84
85.60			Sedykh			1	Drz	Moskva	17 Aug 84
85.20			Litvinov			2		Cork	3 Jul 84

Mark	Wind	Name		Nat	Born	Pos	Meet	Venue	Date
85.14			Litvinov			1	PTG	London	11 Jul 86
85.14			Sedykh			1	Kuts	Moskva	4 Sep 88
85.02			Sedykh			1	BGP	Budapest	20 Aug 84
84.92			Sedykh			2	OD	Dresden	3 Jul 86
84.90		Vadim	Devyatovskiy ¶	BLR	20.3.77	1		Staiki	21 Jul 05
84.88			Litvinov			1	GP-GG	Roma	10 Sep 86
84.86		Koji	Murofushi	JPN	8.10.74	1	Odlozil	Praha	29 Jun 03
84.80			Litvinov			1	OG	Seoul	26 Sep 88
84.72			Sedykh			1	GWG	Moskva	9 Jul 86
84.64			Litvinov			2	GWG	Moskva	9 Jul 86
84.62		Igor	Astapkovich	BLR	4.1.63	1	Expo	Sevilla	6 Jun 92
84.60			Sedykh			1	8-N	Tokyo	14 Sep 84
84.58			Sedykh			1	Znam	Leningrad	8 Jun 86
84.51			Tikhon			1	NC	Grodno	9 Jul 08
84.48		Igor	Nikulin	RUS	14.8.60	1	Athl	Lausanne	12 Jul 90
84.46			Sedykh			1		Vladivostok	14 Sep 88
84.46			Tikhon			1		Minsk	7 May 04
84.40		Jüri	Tamm	EST	5.2.57	1		Banská Bystrica	9 Sep 84
84.36			Litvinov			2	vGDR	Tallinn	22 Jun 86
84.32			Tikhon			1		Staiki	8 Aug 03
		(30/8)							
84.19		Adrián	Annus ¶	HUN	28.6.73	1		Szombathely	10 Aug 03
83.68		Tibor	Gécsek ¶	HUN	22.9.64	1		Zalaegerszeg	19 Sep 98
		(10)							
83.46		Andrey	Abduvaliyev	TJK/UZB	30.6.66	1		Adler	26 May 90
83.43		Aleksey	Zagornyi	RUS	31.5.78	1		Adler	10 Feb 02
83.40 @		Ralf	Haber	GDR	18.8.62	1		Athína	16 May 88
82.54						1		Potsdam	9 Sep 88
83.38		Szymon	Ziólkowski	POL	1.7.76	1	WCh	Edmonton	5 Aug 01
83.30		Olli-Pekka	Karjalainen	FIN	7.3.80	1		Lahti	14 Jul 04
83.04		Heinz	Weis	GER	14.7.63	1	NC	Frankfurt	29 Jun 97
83.00		Balázs	Kiss	HUN	21.3.72	1	GP II	Saint-Denis	4 Jun 98
82.78		Karsten	Kobs	GER	16.9.71	1		Dortmund	26 Jun 99
82.64		Günther	Rodehau	GDR	6.7.59	1		Dresden	3 Aug 85
82.62		Sergey	Kirmasov ¶	RUS	25.3.70	1		Bryansk	30 May 98
		(20)	@ competitive meeting but unsanctioned by GDR federation						
82.62		Andrey	Skvaruk	UKR	9.3.67	1		Koncha-Zaspa	27 Apr 02
82.58		Primoz	Kozmus	SLO	30.9.79	1		Celje	2 Sep 09
82.54		Vasiliy	Sidorenko	RUS	1.5.61	1		Krasnodar	13 May 92
82.52		Lance	Deal	USA	21.8.61	1	GPF	Milano	7 Sep 96
82.45		Krisztián	Pars	HUN	18.2.82	1		Celje	13 Sep 06
82.40		Plamen	Minev	BUL	28.4.65	1	NM	Plovdiv	1 Jun 91
82.38		Gilles	Dupray	FRA	2.1.70	1		Chelles	21 Jun 00
82.28		Ilya	Konovalov ¶	RUS	4.3.71	1	NC	Tula	10 Aug 03
82.24		Benjaminas	Viluckis	LIT	20.3.61	1		Klaipeda	24 Aug 86
82.24		Vyacheslav	Korovin	RUS	8.9.62	1		Chelyabinsk	20 Jun 87
		(30)							
82.23		Vladislav	Piskunov ¶	UKR	7.6.78	2		Koncha-Zaspa	27 Apr 02
82.22		Holger	Klose	GER	5.12.72	1		Dortmund	2 May 98
82.16		Vitaliy	Alisevich	BLR	15.6.67	1		Parnu	13 Jul 88
82.08		Ivan	Tanev	BUL	1.5.57	1	NC	Sofia	3 Sep 88
82.00		Sergey	Alay	BLR	11.6.65	1		Stayki	12 May 92
81.88		Jud	Logan ¶	USA	19.7.59	1		State College	22 Apr 88
81.81		Libor	Charfreitag	SVK	11.9.77	3	Odlozil	Praha	29 Jun 03
81.79		Christophe	Épalle	FRA	23.1.69	1		Clermont-Ferrand	30 Jun 00
81.78		Christoph	Sahner	FRG	23.9.63	1		Wemmetsweiler	11 Sep 88
81.70		Aleksandr	Seleznyov	RUS	25.1.63	2		Sochi	22 May 93
		(40)							
81.66		Aleksandr	Krykun	UKR	1.3.68	1		Kiev	29 May 04
81.64		Enrico	Sgrulletti	ITA	24.4.65	1		Ostia	9 Mar 97
81.56		Sergey	Gavrilov	RUS	22.5.70	1	Army	Rostov	16 Jun 96
81.56		Zsolt	Németh	HUN	9.11.71	1		Veszprém	14 Aug 99
81.52		Juha	Tiainen	FIN	5.12.55	1		Tampere	11 Jun 84
81.49		Valeriy	Svyatokho	BLR	20.7.81	1	NCp	Brest	27 May 06
81.45		Esref	Apak	TUR	3.1.82	1	Cezmi	Istanbul	4 Jun 05
81.44		Yuriy	Tarasyuk	BLR	11.4.57	1		Minsk	10 Aug 84
81.39		Pawel	Fajdek	POL	4.6.89	1		Montreuil-sous-Bois	5 Jun 12
81.35		Wojciech	Kondratowicz	POL	18.4.80	1		Bydgoscscz	13 Jul 03
		(50)	100th man 80.00, 200th 77.34, 300th 75.50, 400th 74.16, 500th 72.80						

Mark	Wind	Name		Nat	Born	Pos	Meet	Venue	Date

Ancillary marks – other marks during series (to 84.85)

86.68 Sedykh 30 Aug 86	85.82 Sedykh 22 Jun 86	85.42 Litvinov 3 Jul 86	85.20 Sedykh 3 Jul 84
86.62 Sedykh 30 Aug 86	85.52 Sedykh 13 Jul 84	85.28 Sedykh 30 Aug 86	85.04 Sedykh 13 Jul 84
86.00 Sedykh 3 Jul 84	85.46 Sedykh 30 Aug 86	85.26 Sedykh 11 Aug 86	84.98 Sedykh 4 Sep 88
86.00 Sedykh 22 Jun 86	85.42 Sedykh 11 Aug 86	85.24 Sedykh 11 Aug 86	84.92 Litvinov 3 Jul 86

JAVELIN

Mark	Wind	Name		Nat	Born	Pos	Meet	Venue	Date
98.48 WR		Jan	Zelezny	CZE	16.6.66	1		Jena	25 May 96
95.66 WR			Zelezny			1	McD	Sheffield	29 Aug 93
95.54A WR			Zelezny			1		Pietersburg	6 Apr 93
94.64			Zelezny			1	GS	Ostrava	31 May 96
94.02			Zelezny			1		Stellenbosch	26 Mar 97
93.09		Aki	Parviainen	FIN	26.10.74	1		Kuortane	26 Jun 99
92.80			Zelezny			1	WCh	Edmonton	12 Aug 01
92.61		Sergey	Makarov	RUS	19.3.73	1		Sheffield	30 Jun 02
92.60		Raymond	Hecht	GER	11.11.68	1	Bisl	Oslo	21 Jul 95
92.42			Zelezny			1	GS	Ostrava	28 May 97
92.41			Parviainen			1	ECp-1A	Vaasa	24 Jun 01
92.28			Zelezny			1	GPF	Monaco	9 Sep 95
92.28			Hecht			1	WK	Zürich	14 Aug 96
92.12			Zelezny			1	McD	London (CP)	27 Aug 95
92.12			Zelezny			1	TOTO	Tokyo	15 Sep 95
91.82			Zelezny			1	McD	Sheffield	4 Sep 94
91.69		Kostadínos	Gatsioúdis	GRE	17.12.73	1		Kuortane	24 Jun 00
91.68			Zelezny			1	GP	Gateshead	1 Jul 94
91.59		Andreas	Thorkildsen	NOR	1.4.82	1	Bisl	Oslo	2 Jun 06
91.53		Tero	Pitkämäki	FIN	19.12.82	1		Kuortane	26 Jun 05
91.50			Zelezny			1	Kuso	Lublin	4 Jun 94
91.50A			Zelezny			1		Pretoria	8 Apr 96
91.50			Hecht			1		Gengenbach	1 Sep 96
91.46 WR		Steve	Backley	GBR	12.2.69	1		Auckland (NS)	25 Jan 92
91.40			Zelezny			1	BNP	Villeneuve d'Ascq	2 Jul 93
91.34			Zelezny			1		Cape Town	8 Apr 97
91.33			Pitkämäki			1	WAF	Monaco	10 Sep 05
91.31			Parviainen			2	WCh	Edmonton	12 Aug 01
91.30			Zelezny			1	ISTAF	Berlin	1 Sep 95
91.29		Breaux	Greer	USA	19.10.76	1	NC	Indianapolis	21 Jun 07

(30/9) 71 over 90m (most: Zelezny 35, Parviainen 8, Hecht, Pitkämäki & Thorkildsen 6, Makarov 5)

Mark	Wind	Name		Nat	Born	Pos	Meet	Venue	Date
90.73		Vadims	Vasilevskis	LAT	5.1.82	1		Tallinn	22 Jul 07
		(10)							
90.60		Seppo	Räty	FIN	27.4.62	1		Nurmijärvi	20 Jul 92
90.44		Boris	Henry	GER	14.12.73	1	Gugl	Linz	9 Jul 97
89.16A		Tom	Petranoff	USA	8.4.58	1		Potchefstroom	1 Mar 91
89.10 WR		Patrik	Bodén	SWE	30.6.67	1		Austin	24 Mar 90
89.02		Jarrod	Bannister	AUS	3.10.84	1	NC	Brisbane	29 Feb 08
88.90		Aleksandr	Ivanov	RUS	25.5.82	1	Znam	Tula	7 Jun 03
88.75		Marius	Corbett	RSA	26.9.75	1	CG	Kuala Lumpur	21 Sep 98
88.70		Peter	Blank	GER	10.4.62	1	NC	Stuttgart	30 Jun 01
88.36		Matthias	de Zordo	GER	21.2.88	1	VD	Bruxelles	16 Sep 11
88.34		Vitezslav	Vesely	CZE	27.2.83	Q	OG	London (OS)	8 Aug 12
		(20)							
88.24		Matti	Närhi	FIN	17.8.75	1		Soini	27 Jul 97
88.23		Petr	Frydrych	CZE	13.1.88	1	GS	Ostrava	27 May 10
88.22		Juha	Laukkanen	FIN	6.1.69	1		Kuortane	20 Jun 92
88.20		Gavin	Lovegrove	NZL	21.10.67	1	Bisl	Oslo	5 Jul 96
88.00		Vladimir	Ovchinnikov	RUS	2.8.70	1		Tolyatti	14 May 95
87.83		Andrus	Värnik	EST	27.9.77	1		Valga	19 Aug 03
87.82		Harri	Hakkarainen	FIN	16.10.69	1		Kuortane	24 Jun 95
87.79		Antti	Ruuskanen	FIN	21.2.84	1	NC	Lahti	26 Aug 12
87.60		Kazuhiro	Mizoguchi	JPN	18.3.62	1	Jenner	San José	27 May 89
87.40		Vladimir	Sasimovich ¶	BLR	14.9.68	2		Kuortane	24 Jun 95
		(30)							
87.34		Andrey	Moruyev	RUS	6.5.70	1	ECp	Birmingham	25 Jun 94
87.23		Teemu	Wirkkala	FIN	14.1.84	1		Joensuu	22 Jul 09
87.20		Viktor	Zaytsev	UZB	6.6.66	1	OT	Moskva	23 Jun 92
87.20		Peter	Esenwein	GER	7.12.67	1		Rehlingen	31 May 04
87.20A		Guillermo	Martínez	CUB	28.6.81	1	PAm	Guadalajara	28 Oct 11
87.17		Dariusz	Trafas	POL	16.5.72	1		Gold Coast (RB)	17 Sep 00
87.12		Tom	Pukstys	USA	28.5.68	2	OD	Jena	25 May 97
87.12		Emeterio	González	CUB	11.4.73	1	OD	Jena	3 Jun 00

Mark	Wind	Name		Nat	Born	Pos	Meet	Venue	Date
86.98		Yuriy	Rybin	RUS	5.3.63	1		Nitra	26 Aug 95
86.94		Mick	Hill	GBR	22.10.64	1	NC	London (CP)	13 Jun 93
		(40)							
86.80		Einar	Vihljálmsson	ISL	1.6.60	1		Reykjavik	29 Aug 92
86.80		Robert	Oosthuizen	RSA	23.1.87	1		Oudtshoorn	1 Mar 08
86.74		Pål Arne	Fagernes	NOR	8.6.74	Q	OG	Sydney	22 Sep 00
86.68		Tero	Järvenpää	FIN	2.10.84	1	NC	Tampere	27 Jul 08
86.67		Andrew	Currey	AUS	7.2.71	1		Wollongong	22 Jul 01
86.64		Klaus	Tafelmeier	FRG	12.4.58	1	NC	Gelsenkirchen	12 Jul 87
86.64		Ainars	Kovals	LAT	21.11.81	2	OG	Beijing	23 Aug 08
86.63		Harri	Haatainen	FIN	5.1.78	2	GP II	Gateshead	19 Aug 01
86.50		Tapio	Korjus	FIN	10.2.61	1		Lahti	25 Aug 88
86.47		Eriks	Rags	LAT	1.6.75	2	BrGP	London (CP)	22 Jul 01

(50)   100th man 84.26, 200th 81.50, 300th 79.89, 400th 78.74   new javelin introduced in 1986

Ancillary marks – other marks during series (to 91.40)

95.34	Zelezny	29 Aug 93	92.26	Zelezny	26 Mar 97	91.44	Zelezny	25 May 96
92.88	Zelezny	25 May 96	91.88	Zelezny	27 Aug 95	91.44	Zelezny	26 Mar 97
92.30	Zelezny	26 Mar 97	91.48	Zelezny	15 Sep 95			

Javelins with roughened tails, now banned by the IAAF

Mark	Wind	Name		Nat	Born	Pos	Meet	Venue	Date
96.96	WR	Seppo	Räty	FIN	27.4.62	1		Punkalaidun	2 Jun 91
94.74	Irreg		Zelezny			1	Bisl	Oslo	4 Jul 92
91.98	WR		Räty			1	Super	Shizuoka	6 May 91
90.82		Kimmo	Kinnunen	FIN	31.3.68	1	WCh	Tokyo	26 Aug 91
87.00		Peter	Borglund	SWE	29.1.64	1	vFIN	Stockholm	13 Aug 91
Downhill: 87.88	Antti		Ruuskanen	FIN	21.2.84	1		Savonlinna	16 Sep 07

DECATHLON

Mark		Name				Nat	Born	Pos	Meet	Venue			Date
9029 WR		Ashton	Eaton			USA	21.1.88	1	NC/OT	Eugene			23 Jun 12
	10.21/0.4	8.23/0.8	14.20	2.05	46.70		13.70/-0.8	42.81	5.30	58.87	4:14.48		
9026 WR			Roman Sebrle			CZE	26.11.74	1		Götzis	27 May 01		
	10.64/0.0	8.11/1.9	15.33	2.12	47.79		13.92/-0.2	47.92	4.80	70.16	4:21.98		
8994 WR		Tomás	Dvorák			CZE	11.5.72	1	ECp	Praha			4 Jul 99
	10.54/-0.1	7.90/1.1	16.78	2.04	48.08		13.73/0.0	48.33	4.90	72.32	4:37.20		
8902			Dvorák					1	WCh	Edmonton			7 Aug 01
	10.62/1.5	8.07/0.9	16.57	2.00	47.74		13.80/-0.4	45.51	5.00	68.53	4:35.13		
8900			Dvorák					1		Götzis			4 Jun 00
	10.54/1.3	8.03/0.0	16.68	2.09	48.36		13.89/-1.0	47.89	4.85	67.21	4:42.33		
8893			Sebrle					1	OG	Athína			24 Aug 04
	10.85/1.5	7.84/0.3	16.36	2.12	48.36		14.05/1.5	48.72	5.00	70.52	4:40.01		
8891 WR		Dan	O'Brien			USA	18.7.66	1		Talence			5 Sep 92
	10.43w/2.1	8.08/1.8	16.69	2.07	48.51		13.98/-0.5	48.56	5.00	62.58	4:42.10		
8869			Eaton					1	OG	London (OS)			9 Aug 12
	10.35/0.4	8.03/0.8	14.66	2.05	46.90		13.56/0.1	42.53	5.20	61.96	4:33.59		
8847 WR		Daley	Thompson			GBR	30.7.58	1	OG	Los Angeles			9 Aug 84
	10.44/-1.0	8.01/0.4	15.72	2.03	46.97		14.33/-1.1	46.56	5.00	65.24	4:35.00		
8844w			O'Brien					1	TAC	New York			13 Jun 91
	10.23	7.96	16.06	2.08	47.70		13.95W/4.2	48.08	5.10	57.40	4:45.54		
8842			Sebrle					1		Götzis			30 May 04
	10.92/0.5	7.86w/3.3	16.22	2.09	48.59		14.15/0.3	47.44	5.00	71.10	4:34.09		
8837			Dvorák					1	WCh	Athína			6 Aug 97
	10.60/0.8	7.64/-0.7	16.32	2.00	47.56		13.61/0.8	45.16	5.00	70.34	4:35.40		
8832 WR		Jürgen	Hingsen			FRG	25.1.58	1	OT	Mannheim			9 Jun 84
	10.70w/2.9	7.76/-1.6	16.42	2.07	48.05		14.07/0.2	49.36	4.90	59.86	4:19.75		
8832		Bryan	Clay			USA	3.1.80	1	NC/OT	Eugene			30 Jun 08
	10.39/-0.4	7.39/-1.6	15.17	2.08	48.41		13.75/1.9	52.74	5.00	70.55	4:50.97		
8825 WR			Hingsen					1		Bernhausen			5 Jun 83
	10.92/0.0	7.74	15.94	2.15	47.89		14.10	46.80	4.70	67.26	4:19.74		
8824			O'Brien					1	OG	Atlanta			1 Aug 96
	10.50/0.7	7.57/1.4	15.66	2.07	46.82		13.87/0.3	48.78	5.00	66.90	4:45.89		
8820			Clay					2	OG	Athína			24 Aug 04
	10.44w/2.2	7.96/0.2	15.23	2.06	49.19		14.13/1.5	50.11	4.90	69.71	4:41.65		
8817			O'Brien					1	WCh	Stuttgart			20 Aug 93
	10.57/0.9	7.99/0.4	15.41	2.03	47.46		14.08/0.0	47.92	5.20	62.56	4:40.08		
8815		Erki	Nool			EST	25.6.70	2	WCh	Edmonton			7 Aug 01
	10.60/1.5	7.63/2.0	14.90	2.03	46.23		14.40/0.0	43.40	5.40	67.01	4:29.58		
8812			O'Brien					1	WCh	Tokyo			30 Aug 91
	10.41/-1.6	7.90/0.8	16.24	1.91	46.53		13.94/-1.2	47.20	5.20	60.66	4:37.50		
8811			Thompson					1	EC	Stuttgart			28 Aug 86
	10.26/2.0	7.72/1.0	15.73	2.00	47.02		14.04/-0.3	43.38	5.10	62.78	4:26.16		

Mark	Wind	Name				Nat	Born	Pos	Meet	Venue			Date
8807			Sebrle					1		Götzis			1 Jun 03
	10.78/-0.2	7.86/1.2		15.41		2.12	47.83		13.96/0.0	43.42	4.90	69.22	4:28.63
8800			Sebrle					1		Götzis			2 Jun 02
	10.95/0.5	7.79/1.8		15.50		2.12	48.35		13.89/1.6	48.02	5.00	68.97	4:38.16
8800			Sebrle					1	EC	München			8 Aug 02
	10.83/1.3	7.92/0.8		15.41		2.12	48.48		14.04/0.0	46.88	5.10	68.51	4:42.94
8792	Uwe		Freimuth			GDR	10.9.61	1	OD	Potsdam			21 Jul 84
	11.06/	7.79/		16.30		2.03	48.43		14.66/	46.58	5.15	72.42	4:25.19
8791			Clay					1	OG	Beijing			22 Aug 08
	10.44/0.3	7.78/0.0		16.27		1.99	48.92		13.93/-0.5	53.79	5.00	70.97	5:06.59
8790	Trey		Hardee (10)			USA	7.2.84	1	WCh	Berlin			20 Aug 09
	10.45/0.2	7.83/1.9		15.33		1.99	48.13		13.86/0.3	48.08	5.20	68.00	4:48.91
8784	Tom		Pappas			USA	6.9.76	1	NC	Stanford			22 Jun 03
	10.78/0.2	7.96/1.4		16.28		2.17	48.22		14.13/1.7	45.84	5.20	60.77	4:48.12
8774 WR			Thompson					1	EC	Athína			8 Sep 82
	10.51/0.3	7.80/0.8		15.44		2.03	47.11		14.39/0.9	45.48	5.00	63.56	4:23.71
8762	Siegfried		Wentz			FRG	7.3.60	2		Bernhausen			5 Jun 83
	10.89	7.49/		15.35		2.09	47.38		14.00	46.90	4.80	70.68	4:24.90
	(30/12)												
8735	Eduard		Hämäläinen			FIN/BLR	21.1.69	1		Götzis			29 May 94
	10.50w/2.1	7.26/1.0		16.05		2.11	47.63		13.82/-3.0	49.70	4.90	60.32	4:35.09
8727	Dave		Johnson			USA	7.4.63	1		Azusa			24 Apr 92
	10.96/0.4	7.52w/4.5		14.61		2.04	48.19		14.17/0.3	49.88	5.28	66.96	4:29.38
8725	Dmitriy		Karpov			KAZ	23.7.81	3	OG	Athína			24 Aug 04
	10.50w/2.2	7.81/-0.9		15.93		2.09	46.81		13.97/1.5	51.65	4.60	55.54	4:38.11
8709	Aleksandr		Apaychev			UKR	6.5.61	1	vGDR	Neubrandenburg			3 Jun 84
	10.96/	7.57/		16.00		1.97	48.72		13.93/	48.00	4.90	72.24	4:26.51
8706	Frank		Busemann			GER	26.2.75	2	OG	Atlanta			1 Aug 96
	10.60/0.7	8.07/0.8		13.60		2.04	48.34		13.47/0.3	45.04	4.80	66.86	4:31.41
8698	Grigoriy		Degtyaryov			RUS	16.8.58	1	NC	Kiyev			22 Jun 84
	10.87/0.7	7.42/0.1		16.03		2.10	49.75		14.53/0.3	51.20	4.90	67.08	4:23.09
8694	Chris		Huffins			USA	15.4.70	1	NC	New Orleans			20 Jun 98
	10.31w/3.5	7.76w/2.5		15.43		2.18	49.02		14.02/1.0	53.22	4.60	61.59	4:59.43
8680	Torsten		Voss			GDR	24.3.63	1	WCh	Roma			4 Sep 87
	10.69/-0.3	7.88/1.2		14.98		2.10	47.96		14.13/0.1	43.96	5.10	58.02	4:25.93
	(20)												
8667 WR	Guido		Kratschmer			FRG	10.1.53	1		Bernhausen			14 Jun 80
	10.58w/2.4	7.80/		15.47		2.00	48.04		13.92/	45.52	4.60	66.50	4:24.15
8654	Leonel		Suárez			CUB	1.9.87	1	CAC	La Habana			4 Jul 09
	11.07/0.7	7.42/0.8		14.39		2.09	47.65		14.15/-0.6	46.07	4.70	77.47	4:27.29
8644	Steve		Fritz			USA	1.11.67	4	OG	Atlanta			1 Aug 96
	10.90/0.8	7.77/0.9		15.31		2.04	50.13		13.97/0.3	49.84	5.10	65.70	4:38.26
8644	Maurice		Smith			JAM	28.9.80	2	WCh	Osaka			1 Sep 07
	10.62/0.7	7.50/0.0		17.32		1.97	47.48		13.91/-0.2	52.36	4.80	53.61	4:33.52
8634 WR	Bruce		Jenner			USA	28.10.49	1	OG	Montreal			30 Jul 76
	10.94/0.0	7.22/0.0		15.35		2.03	47.51		14.84/0.0	50.04	4.80	68.52	4:12.61
8627	Robert		Zmelík			CZE	18.4.69	1		Götzis			31 May 92
	10.62w/2.1	8.02/0.2		13.93		2.05	48.73		13.84/1.2	44.44	4.90	61.26	4:24.83
8626	Michael		Smith			CAN	16.9.67	1		Götzis			26 May 96
	11.23/-0.6	7.72/0.6		16.94		1.97	48.69		14.77/-2.4	52.90	4.90	71.22	4:41.95
8617	Andrey		Kravchenko			BLR	4.1.86	1		Götzis			27 May 07
	10.86/0.2	7.90/0.9		13.89		2.15	47.46		14.05/-0.1	39.63	5.00	64.35	4:29.10
8603	Dean		Macey			GBR	12.12.77	3	WCh	Edmonton			7 Aug 01
	10.72/-0.7	7.59/0.4		15.41		2.15	46.21		14.34/0.0	46.96	4.70	54.61	4:29.05
8583w	Jón Arnar		Magnússon (30)			ISL	28.7.69	1	ECp-2	Reykjavik			5 Jul 98
	10.68/2.0	7.63/2.0		15.57		2.07	47.78		14.33W/5.2	44.53	5.00	64.16	4:41.60
	8573							3		Götzis			31 May 98
	10.74/0.5	7.60/-0.2		16.03		2.03	47.66		14.24/0.7	47.82	5.10	59.77	4:46.43
8574	Christian		Plaziat			FRA	28.10.63	1	EC	Split			29 Aug 90
	10.72/-0.6	7.77/1.1		14.19		2.10	47.10		13.98/0.7	44.36	5.00	54.72	4:27.83
8574	Aleksandr		Yurkov			UKR	21.7.75	4		Götzis			4 Jun 00
	10.69/0.9	7.93/1.8		15.26		2.03	49.74		14.56/-0.9	47.85	5.15	58.92	4:32.49
8571	Lev		Lobodin			RUS	1.4.69	3	EC	Budapest			20 Aug 98
	10.66w/2.2	7.42/0.2		15.67		2.03	48.65		13.97/0.9	46.55	5.20	56.55	4:30.27
8566	Sebastian		Chmara			POL	21.11.71	1		Alhama de Murcia			17 May 98
	10.97w/2.9	7.56/1.2		16.03		2.10	48.27		14.32/1.8	44.39	5.20	57.25	4:29.66
8558	Pascal		Behrenbruch			GER	19.1.85	1	EC	Helsinki			28 Jun 12
	10.93/0.8	7.15/-0.8		16.89		1.97	48.54		14.16/0.2	48.24	5.00	67.45	4:34.02
8554	Attila		Zsivoczky			HUN	29.4.77	5		Götzis			4 Jun 00
	10.64w/2.1	7.24/-1.0		15.72		2.18	48.13		14.87/-0.9	45.64	4.65	63.57	4:23.13

Mark	Wind	Name		Nat	Born	Pos	Meet	Venue			Date
8548		Paul	Meier	GER	27.7.71	3	WCh	Stuttgart			20 Aug 93
	10.57/0.9	7.57/1.1	15.45	2.15	47.73		14.63/0.0	45.72	4.60	61.22	4:32.05
8547		Igor	Sobolevskiy	UKR	4.5.62	2	NC	Kiyev			22 Jun 84
	10.64/0.7	7.71/0.2	15.93	2.01	48.24		14.82/0.3	50.54	4.40	67.40	4:32.84
8534		Siegfried	Stark	GDR	12.6.55	1	OT	Halle			4 May 80
	11.10w	7.64	15.81	2.03	49.53		14.86w	47.20	5.00	68.70	4:27.7
8534w/8478		Antonio	Peñalver	ESP	1.12.68	1		Alhama de Murcia			24 May 92
	10.76w/3.9	7.42W/6.2	16.50	2.12	49.50		14.32/0.8	47.38	5.00	59.32	4:39.94
	(40)	(7.19w/4.0)									
8528		Aleksandr	Pogorelov	RUS	10.1.80	3	WCh	Berlin			20 Aug 09
	10.95/-0.3	7.49/-0.4	16.65	2.08	50.27		14.19/0.3	48.46	5.10	63.95	4:48.70
8526		Francisco Javier	Benet	ESP	25.3.68	2		Alhama de Murcia			17 May 98
	10.72w/2.9	7.45/-1.2	14.57	1.92	48.10		13.83/1.8	46.12	5.00	65.37	4:26.81
8526		Kristjan	Rahnu	EST	29.8.79	1		Arles			5 Jun 05
	10.52w/2.2	7.58/1.6	15.51	1.99	48.60		14.04w/3.1	50.81	4.95	60.71	4:52.18
8524		Sébastien	Levicq	FRA	25.6.71	4	WCh	Sevilla			25 Aug 99
	11.05/0.2	7.52/-0.4	14.22	2.00	50.13		14.48/0.6	44.65	5.50	69.01	4:26.81
8522		Michael	Schrader	GER	1.7.87	1		Götzis			31 May 09
	10.64/0.8	8.05/1.9	14.33	1.94	49.71		14.21/1.6	43.09	5.00	64.04	4:22.26
8519		Yuriy	Kutsenko	RUS	5.3.52	3	NC	Kiyev			22 Jun 84
	11.07/0.5	7.54/-0.1	15.11	2.13	49.07		14.94/0.3	50.38	4.60	61.70	4:12.68
8506		Valter	Külvet	EST	19.2.64	1		Stayki			3 Jul 88
	11.05/-1.4	7.35/0.4	15.78	2.00	48.08		14.55/-0.8	52.04	4.60	61.72	4:15.93
8500		Christian	Schenk	GER	9.2.65	4	WCh	Stuttgart			20 Aug 93
	11.22/-0.9	7.63/0.0	15.72	2.15	48.78		15.29/0.0	46.94	4.80	65.32	4:24.44
8497		Aleksey	Sysoyev	RUS	8.3.85	2		Götzis			1 Jun 08
	10.86/-0.7	7.01/0.5	15.49	2.03	49.10		14.64/1.3	54.08	5.10	64.22	4:38.82
8496		Yordani	García	CUB	21.11.88	1		La Habana			30 May 09
	10.88/0.1	7.36/0.2	16.50	2.10	48.77		14.07/-0.5	43.97	4.80	68.10	4:46.80
8491		Aleksandr	Nevskiy	UKR	21.2.58	2		Götzis			20 May 84
	10.97/-1.6	7.24/1.2	15.04	2.08	48.44		14.67/1.0	46.06	4.70	69.56	4:19.62
	(50)		100th man 8322, 200th 8156, 300th 8055, 400th 7964, 500th 7889								

4 x 100 METRES RELAY

Mark		Nat	Team	Pos	Meet	Venue	Date
36.84	WR	JAM	N Carter 10.1, Frater 8.9, Blake 9.0, Bolt 8.8	1	OG	London (OS)	11 Aug 12
37.04	WR	JAM	N Carter, Frater, Blake, Bolt	1	WCh	Daegu	4 Sep 11
37.04		USA	Kimmons 10.1, Gatlin 8.9, Gay 9.0, Bailey 9.0	2	OG	London (OS)	11 Aug 12
37.10	WR	JAM	N Carter, Frater, Bolt, Powell	1	OG	Beijing	22 Aug 08
37.31		JAM	Mullings, Frater, Bolt, Powell	1	WCh	Berlin	22 Aug 09
37.38		USA	Demps, Patton, Kimmons, Gatlin	1h2	OG	London (OS)	10 Aug 12
37.39		JAM	Carter, Frater, Blake, Bailey-Cole	1h1	OG	London (OS)	10 Aug 12
37.40	WR	USA	Marsh, Burrell, Mitchell, C Lewis	1	OG	Barcelona	8 Aug 92
37.40	WR	USA	Drummond, Cason, D Mitchell, L Burrell	1s1	WCh	Stuttgart	21 Aug 93
37.45		USA	Kimmons, Spearmon, Gay, Rodgers	1	WK	Zürich	19 Aug 10
37.48		USA	Drummond, Cason, D Mitchell, L Burrell	1	WCh	Stuttgart	22 Aug 93
37.50	WR	USA	Cason, Burrell, Mitchell, C Lewis	1	WCh	Tokyo	1 Sep 91
37.59		USA	Drummond, Montgomery, B Lewis, Greene	1	WCh	Sevilla	29 Aug 99
37.59		USA	Conwright, Spearmon, Gay, Smoots	1	WCp	Athína	16 Sep 06
37.61		USA	Drummond, Williams, B Lewis, Greene	1	OG	Sydney	30 Sep 00
37.61		USA	Kimmons, Gatlin, Gay, Bailey	1	Herc	Monaco	20 Jul 12
37.62		TRI	Brown, Burns, Callander, Thompson	2	WCh	Berlin	22 Aug 09
37.65		USA	Drummond, Williams, C Johnson, Greene	1	ISTAF	Berlin	1 Sep 00
37.67	WR	USA	Marsh, Burrell, Mitchell, C Lewis	1	WK	Zürich	7 Aug 91
37.69		CAN	Esmie 10.47, Gilbert 9.02, Surin 9.25, Bailey 8.95	1	OG	Atlanta	3 Aug 96
37.70		JAM	Clarke, Frater, Mullins, Bolt	1	WK	Zürich	28 Aug 09
37.73		GBR	Gardener, Campbell, Devonish, Chambers	2	WCh	Sevilla	29 Aug 99
37.73		USA	Trammell, Rodgers, Patton, Spearmon	2	WK	Zürich	28 Aug 09
37.75		USA	Cason, Burrell, Mitchell, Marsh	1h2	WCh	Tokyo	31 Aug 91
37.76		JAM	Forsythe, Frater, S Mullings, Blake	2	WK	Zürich	19 Aug 10
37.77		GBR	Jackson, Jarrett, Regis, Christie	2	WCh	Stuttgart	22 Aug 93
37.77		USA	A Drummond, B Williams, Patton, Greene	1	ISTAF	Berlin (P)	10 Aug 03
37.78		USA	Patton 10.28, Spearmon 9.22, Gay 9.05, Dixon 9.23	1	WCh	Osaka	1 Sep 07
37.79	WR	FRA	Morinière, Sangouma, Trouabal, Marie-Rose	1	EC	Split	1 Sep 90
37.79	WR	Santa Monica TC/USA	Marsh, Burrell, Heard, C Lewis	1	Herc	Monaco	3 Aug 91
37.79		USA - Santa Monica TC	Marsh, Burrell, Heard, C Lewis	1	MSR	Walnut	17 Apr 94
37.79		USA	Kimmons, Gatlin, M.Mitchell, Padgett	1h1	WCh	Daegu	4 Sep 11
		(32 performances by teams from 6 nations) Further bests by nations:					
37.90		BRA	de Lima, Ribeiro, A da Silva, Cl da Silva	2	OG	Sydney	30 Sep 00
37.94		NGR	O Ezinwa, Adeniken, Obikwelu, D Ezinwa	1s2	WCh	Athína	9 Aug 97

Mark	Wind	Name	Nat	Born	Pos	Meet	Venue	Date
38.00		CUB Simón, Lamela, Isasi, Aguilera			3	OG	Barcelona	8 Aug 92
38.02		URS Yevgenyev, Bryzgin, Muravyov, Krylov			2	WCh	Roma	6 Sep 87
		(10)						
38.02		GER Reus, Unger, Kosenkow, Jakubczyk			1		Weinheim	27 Jul 12
38.03		JPN Tsukahara, Suetsugu 9.08, Takahira, Asahara			5	WCh	Osaka	1 Sep 07
38.12		GHA Duah, Nkansah, Zakari, Tuffour			1s1	WCh	Athína	9 Aug 97
38.17		AUS Henderson, Jackson, Brimacombe, Marsh			1s2	WCh	Göteborg	12 Aug 95
38.17		ITA Donati, Collio, Di Gregorio, Checcucci			2	EC	Barcelona	1 Aug 10
38.29		NED Mariano, Martina, Codrington, van Luijk			3h1	OG	London (OS)	10 Aug 12
38.31		POL Masztak, Kuc, Kubaczyk, Krynski			6h2	OG	London (OS)	10 Aug 12
38.38		CHN Guo Fan, Liang Jiahong, Su Bingtiang, Zhang Peimeng			5h1	OG	London (OS)	10 Aug 12
38.41		SKN Lestrod, Rogers, Adams, Lawrence			6h1	OG	London (OS)	10 Aug 12
38.45		AHO Goeloe, Raffaela, Duzant, Martina			6	WCh	Helsinki	13 Aug 05
		(20, with RUS and UKR for USSR)						
38.46		URS/RUS Zharov, Krylov, Fatun, Goremykin			4	EC	Split	1 Sep 90
38.47		RSA Nagel, du Plessis, Newton, Quinn			1	WCh	Edmonton	12 Aug 01
38.47		HKG Tang Yik Chun, Lai Chun Ho, Ng Ka Fung, Tsui Chi Ho			1		Taipei	26 May 12
38.53		UKR Rurak, Osovich, Kramarenko, Dologodin			1	ECp	Madrid	1 Jun 96
38.60		ESP Feo, José, Mayoral, Berlanga			3s1	WCh	Athína	9 Aug 97
38.60		CIV Meité, Douhou, Sonan, N'Dri			3s1	WCh	Edmonton	12 Aug 01
38.61		GRE Séggos, Alexópoulos, Panayiotópoulos, Hoídis			2	ECp	Paris (C)	19 Jun 99
38.62		SUI Mancini, Schenkel, Wilson, Schneeberger			3	WK	Zürich	8 Sep 11
38.63		SWE Karlsson, Mårtensson, Hedner, Strenius			3s2	OG	Atlanta	2 Aug 96
38.67		HUN Karaffa, Nagy, Tatár, Kovács			1	BGP	Budapest	11 Aug 86

Multi-nation team

Mark	Wind	Name	Nat	Born	Pos	Meet	Venue	Date
37.46		Racers TC Bailey/ANT, Blake JAM, Forsythe JAM, Bolt JAM			1	LGP	London (CP)	25 Jul 09
37.82		Drummond/USA, Jarrett/GBR, Regis/GBR, Mitchell/USA			2	MSR	Walnut	17 Apr 94

One man disqualified for drugs

Mark	Wind	Name	Nat	Born	Pos	Meet	Venue	Date
37.91		NGR Asonze ¶, Obikwelu, Effiong, Aliu			(3)	WCh	Sevilla	29 Aug 99

4 x 200 METRES RELAY

Mark	Wind	Name	Nat	Born	Pos	Meet	Venue	Date
1:18.68	WR	USA - Santa Monica Track Cluc						
		Marsh 20.0, Burrell 19.6, Heard 19.7, C Lewis 19.4			1	MSR	Walnut	17 Apr 94
1:19.10		World All-Stars			2	MSR	Walnut	17 Apr 94
		Drummond USA 20.4, Mitchell USA 19.3, Bridgewater USA 20.3, Regis GBR 19.1						
1:19.11	WR	Santa Monica TC/USA M.Marsh, L Burrell, Heard, C Lewis			1	Penn	Philadelphia	25 Apr 92
1:19.16		USA Red Team Crawford, Clay, Patton, Gatlin			1	PennR	Philadelphia	26 Apr 03
1:19.38	WR	Santa Monica TC/USA Everett, Burrell, Heard, C Lewis			1	R-W	Koblenz	23 Aug 89
1:19.39		USA Blue Drummond, Crawford, B Williams, Greene			1	PennR	Philadelphia	28 Apr 01
1:19.45		Santa Monica TC/USA DeLoach, Burrell, C.Lewis, Heard			1	Penn	Philadelphia	27 Apr 91
1:19.47		Nike Int./USA Brokenburr, A Harrison, Greene, M Johnson			1	Penn	Philadelphia	24 Apr 99

Best non-US nations

Mark	Wind	Name	Nat	Born	Pos	Meet	Venue	Date
1:20.79		Central Arizona DC/Jamaica			1	MSR	Walnut	24 Apr 88
		Bucknor, Campbell, O'Connor, Davis)						
1:21.10		ITA Tilli, Simionato, Bongiorno, Mennea			1		Cagliari	29 Sep 83
1:21.22		POL Tulin, Balcerzak, Pilarczyk, Urbas			2		Gdansk	14 Jul 01
1:21.29		GBR Adam, Mafe, Christie, Regis			1	vURS	Birmingham	23 Jun 89

4 x 400 METRES RELAY

Mark	Wind	Name	Nat	Born	Pos	Meet	Venue	Date
2:54.29	WR	USA Valmon 44.5, Watts 43.6, Reynolds 43.23, Johnson 42.94			1	WCh	Stuttgart	22 Aug 93
2:55.39		USA Merritt 44.4, Taylor 43.7, Neville 44.16, Wariner 43.18			1	OG	Beijing	23 Aug 08
2:55.56		USA Merritt 44.4, Taylor 43.7, Williamson 44.32, Wariner 43.10			1	WCh	Osaka	2 Sep 07
2:55.74	WR	USA Valmon 44.6, Watts 43.00, M.Johnson 44.73, S Lewis 43.41			1	OG	Barcelona	8 Aug 92
2:55.91		USA O Harris 44.5, Brew 43.6, Wariner 43.98, Williamson 43.83			1	OG	Athína	28 Aug 04
2:55.99		USA L Smith 44.62, A Harrison 43.84, Mills 43.66, Maybank 43.87			1	OG	Atlanta	3 Aug 96
2:56.16A	WR	USA Matthews 45.0, Freeman 43.2, James 43.9, Evans 44.1			1	OG	Ciu. México	20 Oct 68
2:56.16	WR	USA Everett 43.79, S Lewis 43.69, Robinzine 44.74, Reynolds 43.94			1	OG	Seoul	1 Oct 88
2:56.60		GBR I Thomas 44.92, Baulch 44.19, Richardson 43.62, Black 43.87			2	OG	Atlanta	3 Aug 96
2:56.65		GBR Thomas 44.8, Black 44.2, Baulch 44.08, Richardson 43.57			2	WCh	Athína	10 Aug 97
2:56.72		BAH Brown 44.9, Pinder 43.5, Mathieu 44.25, Miller 44.01			1	OG	London (OS)	10 Aug 12
2:56.75		JAM McDonald 44.5, Haughton 44.4, McFarlane 44.37, Clarke 43.51			3	WCh	Athína	10 Aug 97
2:56.91		USA Rock 44.7, Brew 44.3, Williamson 44.40, Wariner 43.49			1	WCh	Helsinki	14 Aug 05
2:57.05		USA Nellum 45.2, Mance 43.5, McQuay 43.41, Taylor 44.85			2	OG	London (OS)	10 Aug 12
2:57.29		USA Everett 45.1, Haley 44.0, McKay 44.20, Reynolds 44.00			1	WCh	Roma	6 Sep 87
2:57.32		USA Ramsey 44.9, Mills 44.6, Reynolds 43.74, Johnson 44.11			1	WCh	Göteborg	13 Aug 95
2:57.32		BAH McKinney 44.9, Moncur 44.6, A.Williams 44.43, Brown 43.42			2	WCh	Helsinki	14 Aug 05
2:57.53		GBR Black 44.7, Redmond 44.0, Regis 44.22, Akabusi 44.59			1	WCh	Tokyo	1 Sep 91
2:57.57		USA Valmon 44.9, Watts 43.4, D.Everett 44.31, Pettigrew 44.93			2	WCh	Tokyo	1 Sep 91
2:57.86		USA Taylor 45.4, Wariner 43.6, Clement 44.72, Merritt 44.16			1	WCh	Berlin	23 Aug 09

Mark	Wind	Name	Nat	Born	Pos	Meet	Venue	Date
2:57.87		USA L Smith 44.59, Rouser 44.33, Mills 44.32, Maybank 44.63			1s2	OG	Atlanta	2 Aug 96
2:57.91		USA Nix 45.59, Armstead 43.97, Babers 43.75, McKay 44.60			1	OG	Los Angeles	11 Aug 84
2:57.97		JAM McDonald , Haughton , McFarlane, D Clarke			1	PAm	Winnipeg	30 Jul 99
2:58.00		POL Rysiukiewicz 45.6, Czubak 44.2, Haczek 44.0, Mackowiak 44.2	2			GWG	Uniondale, NY	22 Jul 98
2:58.03		BAH Bain 45.9, Mathieu 44.1, A Williams 44.02, Brown 44.05	2			OG	Beijing	23 Aug 08
2:58.06		RUS Dyldin 45.5, Frolov 44.6, Kokorin 44.34, Alekseyev 43.56	3			OG	Beijing	23 Aug 08
2:58.07		JAM Ayre 44.9, Simpson 44.9, Spence 44.48, Clarke 43.81	3			WCh	Helsinki	14 Aug 05
2:58.19		BAH Moncur 45.1, C Brown 44.5, McIntosh 44.42, Munnings 44.13	2			WCh	Edmonton	12 Aug 01

(28/6) plus six times for teams that contained an athlete who was subsequently banned for drugs abuse

Mark	Wind	Name	Nat	Born	Pos	Meet	Venue	Date
2:58.56		BRA Cl. da Silva 44.6, A dos Santos 45.1, de Araújo 45.0, Parrela 43.9			2	PAm	Winnipeg	30 Jul 99
2:58.68		NGR Chukwu 45.18, Monye 44.49, Bada 44.70, Udo-Obong 44.31			1	OG	Sydney	30 Sep 00
2:58.96		FRA Djhone 45.4, Keita 44.7, Diagana 44.69, Raquil 44.15			2	WCh	Saint-Denis	31 Aug 03
2:59.13		CUB Martínez 45.6, Herrera 44.38, Tellez 44.81, Hernández 44.34			1h2	OG	Barcelona	7 Aug 92

(10)

Mark	Wind	Name	Nat	Born	Pos	Meet	Venue	Date
2:59.21		RSA Pistorius 45.58, Mogawane 43.97, de Beer 44.46, Victor 45.20			3h1	WCh	Daegu	1 Sep 11
2:59.37		BEL K Borlée 45.4, J Borlée 43.6, Van Branteghem 44.44, Ghislain 45.88			5	OG	Beijing	23 Aug 08
2:59.40		TRI L.Gordon 45.1, Solomon 43.9, Alleyne-Forte 45.51, Lendore 44.75			3	OG	London (OS)	10 Aug 12
2:59.63		KEN D Kitur 45.4, S Kitur 45.13, Kipkemboi 44.76, Kemboi 44.34			3h2	OG	Barcelona	7 Aug 92
2:59.70		AUS Frayne 45.38, Clark 43.86, Minihan 45.07, Mitchell 45.39			4	OG	Los Angeles	11 Aug 84
2:59.86		GDR Möller 45.8, Schersing 44.8, Carlowitz 45.3, Schönlebe 44.1			1	vURS	Erfurt	23 Jun 85
2:59.95		YUG Jovkovic, Djurovic, Macev, Brankovic 44.3			2h3	WCh	Tokyo	31 Aug 91
2:59.96		FRG Dobeleit 45.7, Henrich 44.3, Itt 45.12, Schmid 44.93			4	WCh	Roma	6 Sep 87
3:00.44A		DOM Cuesta 46.2, Peguero 44.6, Tapia 45.2, L Santos 44.5			2	PAm	Guadalajara	28 Oct 11
		3:02.02 Peguero, Santa, Vidal, Sánchez			3	PAm	Santo Domingo	9 Aug 03
3:00.64		SEN Diarra 46.53, Dia 44.94, Ndiaye 44.70, Faye 44.47			4	OG	Atlanta	3 Aug 96

(20)

Mark	Wind	Name	Nat	Born	Pos	Meet	Venue	Date
3:00.76		JPN Karube 45.88, Ito 44.86, Osakada 45.08, Omori 44.94			5	OG	Atlanta	3 Aug 96
3:00.79		ZIM Chiwira 46.2, Mukomana 44.6, Ngidhi 45.79, Harnden 44.20			2h3	WCh	Athína	9 Aug 97
3:00.82A		VEN A Ramírez 45.7, Aguilar 45.3, Acevedo 44.7, Longart 45.2			3	PAm	Guadalajara	28 Oct 11
		3:01.70 Ramírez, Bravo, Meléndez, Longart			2	IbAmC	Barquisimeto	10 Jun 12
3:01.12		FIN Lönnqvist 46.7, Salin 45.1, Karttunen 44.8, Kukkoaho 44.5			6	OG	München	10 Sep 72
3:01.37		ITA Bongiorni 46.2, Zuliani 45.0, Petrella 45.3, Ribaud 44.9			4	EC	Stuttgart	31 Aug 86
3:01.42		ESP I Rodríguez 46.0, Canal 44.1, Andrés 45.88, Reina 45.48			4h1	WCh	Edmonton	11 Aug 01
3:01.60		BAR Louis 46.67, Peltier 44.97, Edwards 45.04, Forde 44.92			6	OG	Los Angeles	11 Aug 84
3:01.61		BUL Georgiev 45.9, Stankulov 46.0, Raykov 45.07, Ivanov 44.66			2h1	WCh	Stuttgart	21 Aug 93
3:02.09		UGA Govile 46.72, Kyeswa 44.60, Rwamuhanda 46.40, Okot 44.37	7			OG	Los Angeles	11 Aug 84
3:02.11		MAR Kasbane, Dahane, Belcaid, Lahlou 44.5			1h2	WCh	Tokyo	31 Aug 91

Including subsequently banned athlete

Mark	Wind	Name	Nat	Born	Pos	Meet	Venue	Date
2:54.20(WR)		USA Young 44.3, Pettigrew ¶ 43.2, Washington 43.5, Johnson 43.2			(1)	GWG	Uniondale, NY	22 Jul 98
2:56.35		USA A Harrison 44.36, Pettigrew 44.17, C Harrison 43.53, Johnson 44.29			(1)	OG	Sydney	30 Sep 00
2:56.45		USA J Davis 45.2, Pettigrew 43.9, Taylor 43.92, M Johnson 43.49			(1)	WCh	Sevilla	29 Aug 99
2:56.47		USA Young 44.6, Pettigrew 43.1, Jones 44.80, Washington 44.80			(1)	WCh	Athína	10 Aug 97
2:56.60		USA Red Taylor 45.0, Pettigrew 44.2, Washington 43.7, Johnson 43.7			(1)	PennR	Philadelphia	29 Apr 00
2:57.54		USA Byrd 45.9, Pettigrew 43.9, Brew 44.03, Taylor 43.71			1	WCh	Edmonton	12 Aug 01

4 x 800 METRES RELAY

Mark	Wind	Name	Nat	Born	Pos	Meet	Venue	Date
7:02.43		KEN Mutua 1:46.73, Yiampoy 1:44.38, Kombich 1:45.92, Bungei 1:45.40			1	VD	Bruxelles	25 Aug 06
7:02.82		USA			2	VD	Bruxelles	25 Aug 06
		J Harris 1:47.05, Robinson 1:44.03, Burley 1:46.05, Krummenacker 1:45.69						
7:03.89 WR		GBR Elliott 1:49.14, Cook 1:46.20, Cram 1:44.54, Coe 1:44.01			1		London (CP)	30 Aug 82
7:04.70		RSA van Oudtshoorn 1:46.9, Sepeng 1:45.2, Kotze 1:48.3, J Botha 1:44.3			1		Stuttgart	6 Jun 99
7:06.66		QAT Sultan 1:45.81, Al-Badri 1:46.71, Suleiman 1:45.89, Ali Kamal 1:48.25			4	VD	Bruxelles	25 Aug 06

4 x 1500 METRES RELAY

Mark	Wind	Name	Nat	Born	Pos	Meet	Venue	Date
14:36.23 WR		KEN W Biwott 3:38.5, Gathimba 3:39.5, G Rono 3:41.4, Choge 3:36.9			1	VD	Bruxelles	4 Sep 09
14:38.8 WR		FRG Wessinghage 3:38.8, Hudak 3:39.1, Lederer 3:44.6, Fleschen 3:36.3			1		Köln	16 Aug 77
14:40.4 WR		NZL Polhill 3:42.9, Walker 3:40.4, Dixon 3:41.2, Quax 3:35.9			1		Oslo	22 Aug 73
14:45.63		URS Kalutskiy, Yakovlev, Legeda, Lotarev			1		Leningrad	4 Aug 85
14:46.16		Larios, ESP Jiménez 3:40.9, Pancorbo 3:41.2, A García 3:43.9, Viciosa 3:40.2			1		Madrid	5 Sep 97
14:46.3		USA Aldridge, Clifford, Harbour, Duits			1		Bourges	23 Jun 79
14:46.92		AUS Birmingham 3:39.2, Gregson 3:44.2, Kealey 3:43.3, Bromlet 3:40.3			3	VD	Bruxelles	4 Sep 09
14:48.2		FRA Bégouin 3:44.5, Lequement 3:44.3, Philippe 3:42.2, Dien 3:37.2			2		Bourges	23 Jun 79

Mixed Team

Mark	Wind	Name	Nat	Born	Pos	Meet	Venue	Date
14:44.31		Ali BRN 3:38.1, Birgen KEN 3:43.3, N Kemboi KEN 3:40.0, Campbell IRL 3:43.0			2	VD	Bruxelles	4 Sep 09

4 x 1 MILE RELAY

Mark	Wind	Name	Nat	Born	Pos	Meet	Venue	Date
15:49.08		IRL Coghlan 4:00.2, O'Sullivan 3:55.3, O'Mara 3:56.6, Flynn 3:56.98			1		Dublin	17 Aug 85
15:59.57		NZL Rogers 3:57.2, Bowden 4:02.5, Gilchrist 4:02.8, Walker 3:57.07			1		Auckland	2 Mar 83

Mark	Wind	Name		Nat	Born	Pos	Meet	Venue	Date

3000 METRES TRACK WALK

Mark	Wind	Name		Nat	Born	Pos	Meet	Venue	Date
10:47.11		Giovanni	De Benedictis	ITA	8.1.68	1		S.Giovanni Valdarno	19 May 90
10:52.44+		Yohann	Diniz	FRA	1.1.78	1	in 5k	Villeneuve d'Ascq	27 Jun 08
10:56.22		Andrew	Jachno	AUS	13.4.62	1		Melbourne	7 Feb 91
10:56.34+		Roman	Mrázek	SVK	21.1.62	1k	PTS	Bratislava	14 Jun 89
10:59.04		Luke	Adams	AUS	22.10.76	1		Cork	3 Jul 10
11:00.2+		Jozef	Pribilinec	SVK	6.7.60	1k		Banská Bystrica	30 Aug 85
11:00.50+		Francisco Javier	Fernández ¶	ESP	6.3.77	1	in 5k	Villeneuve d'Ascq	8 Jun 07
11:00.56		David	Smith	AUS	24.7.55	1		Perth	24 Jan 87
11:03.01		Vladimir	Andreyev	RUS	7.9.66	2		Formia	13 Jul 97

Indoors

Mark	Wind	Name		Nat	Born	Pos	Meet	Venue	Date
10:31.42		Andreas	Erm	GER	12.3.76	1		Halle	4 Feb 01
10:54.61		Carlo	Mattioli	ITA	23.10.54	1		Milano	6 Feb 80
10:56.77+		Ivano	Brugnetti	ITA	1.9.76	1	in 5k	Torino	21 Feb 09
10:56.88		Reima	Salonen	FIN	19.11.55	1		Turku	5 Feb 84
10:57.32		Matej	Tóth	SVK	10.2.83	1		Wien	12 Feb 11
11:00.86+		Frants	Kostyukevich	BLR	4.4.63	1k	EI	Genova	28 Feb 92

5000 METRES TRACK WALK

Mark	Wind	Name		Nat	Born	Pos	Meet	Venue	Date
18:05.49		Hatem	Ghoula	TUN	7.6.73	1		Tunis	1 May 97
18:17.22		Robert	Korzeniowski	POL	30.7.68	1		Reims	3 Jul 92
18:18.01		Yohann	Diniz	FRA	1.1.78	1		Villeneuve d'Ascq	27 Jun 08
18:27.34		Francisco Javier	Fernández ¶	ESP	6.3.77	1		Villeneuve d'Ascq	8 Jun 07
18:28.80		Roman	Mrázek	SVK	21.1.62	1	PTS	Bratislava	14 Jun 89
18:30.43		Maurizio	Damilano	ITA	6.4.57	1		Caserta	11 Jun 92

ndoors

Mark	Wind	Name		Nat	Born	Pos	Meet	Venue	Date
18:07.08		Mikhail	Shchennikov	RUS	24.12.67	1		Moskva	14 Feb 95
18:08.86		Ivano	Brugnetti	ITA	1.9.76	1	NC	Ancona	17 Feb 07
18:11.41		Ronald	Weigel	GDR	8.8.59	1mx		Wien	13 Feb 88
18:11.8		Valeriy	Borchin ¶	RUS	11.9.86	1		Saransk	30 Dec 10
18:15.25		Grigoriy	Kornev	RUS	14.3.61	1		Moskva	7 Feb 92
18:16.54 ?		Frants	Kostyukevich	BLR	4.4.63	2	NC	Gomel	4 Feb 89
18:17.13		Vladimir	Kanaykin ¶	RUS	21.3.85	2	Winter	Moskva	5 Feb 12
18:19.97		Giovanni	De Benedictis	ITA	8.1.68	1	EI	Genova	28 Feb 92
18:22.25		Andreas	Erm	GER	12.3.76	1	NC	Dortmund	25 Feb 01
18:23.18		Rishat	Shafikov	RUS	23.1.70	1		Samara	1 Mar 97
18:24.13		Francisco Javier	Fernández ¶	ESP	6.3.77	1		Belfast	17 Feb 07
18:26.82		Sergey	Bakulin	RUS	13.11.86	3	Winter	Moskva	5 Feb 12
18:27.15		Alessandro	Gandellini	ITA	30.4.73	1	NC	Genova	12 Feb 00
18:27.80		Jozef	Pribilinec	SVK	6.7.60	2	WI	Indianapolis	7 Mar 87
18:27.95		Stefan	Johansson	SWE	11.4.67	3	EI	Genova	28 Feb 92
18:30.91		Aleksandr	Yargunkin	RUS	6.1.81	1		Yekaterinburg	7 Jan 07

10,000 METRES TRACK WALK

Mark	Wind	Name		Nat	Born	Pos	Meet	Venue	Date
37:53.09		Francisco Javier	Fernández ¶	ESP	6.3.77	1	NC	Santa Cruz de Tenerife	27 Jul 08
37:58.6		Ivano	Brugnetti	ITA	1.9.76	1		Sesto San Gioavnni	23 Jul 05
38:02.60		Jozef	Pribilinec	SVK	6.7.60	1		Banská Bystrica	30 Aug 85
38:06.6		David	Smith	AUS	24.7.55	1		Sydney	25 Sep 86
38:12.13		Ronald	Weigel	GDR	8.8.59	1		Potsdam	10 May 86
38:18.0+		Valdas	Kazlauskas	LTU	23.2.58	1		Moskva	18 Sep 83
38:20.0		Moacir	Zimmermann	BRA	30.12.83	1		Blumenau	7 Jun 08
38:24 0+		Bernardo	Segura	MEX	11.2.70	1	SGP	Fana	7 May 94
38:24.31		Hatem	Ghoula	TUN	7.6.73	1		Tunis	30 May 98
38:26.4		Daniel	García	MEX	28.10.71	1		Sdr Omme	17 May 97
38:26.53		Robert	Korzeniowski	POL	30.7.68	1		Riga	31 May 02
38:27.57		Robert	Heffernan	IRL	20.2.78	1	NC	Dublin	20 Jul 08
38:30.38			Wang Zhen	CHN	24.8.91	1		Tianjin	16 Sep 12
38:32.0		Erik	Tysse	NOR	4.12.80	1	NC	Bergen (Fana)	13 Jun 08
38:37.6+		Jefferson	Pérez	ECU	1.7.74	1	in 20k	Fana	9 May 98
38:38.0		Walter	Arena	ITA	30.5.64	1		Catania	13 Apr 90

Indoors

Mark	Wind	Name		Nat	Born	Pos	Meet	Venue	Date
38:31.4		Werner	Heyer	GDR	14.11.56	1		Berlin	12 Jan 80

20 KILOMETRES WALK

Mark	Wind	Name		Nat	Born	Pos	Meet	Venue	Date
1:16:43		Sergey	Morozov ¶	RUS	21.3.88	1	NC	Saransk	8 Jun 08
1:17:16		Vladimir	Kanaykin ¶	RUS	21.3.85	1	RWC	Saransk	29 Sep 07
1:17:21 WR		Jefferson	Pérez	ECU	1.7.74	1	WCh	Saint-Denis	23 Aug 03
1:17:22 WR		Francisco Javier	Fernández ¶	ESP	6.3.77	1		Turku	28 Apr 02
1:17:23		Vladimir	Stankin	RUS	2.1.74	1	NC-w	Adler	8 Feb 04
1:17:25.6t		Bernardo	Segura	MEX	11.2.70	1	SGP	Bergen (Fana)	7 May 94

Mark	Wind	Name		Nat	Born	Pos	Meet	Venue	Date
1:17:30		Alex	Schwazer ¶	ITA	26.12.84	1		Lugano	18 Mar 12
1:17:33		Nathan	Deakes	AUS	17.8.77	1		Cixi	23 Apr 05
1:17:36			Kanaykin			1	NC	Cheboksary	17 Jun 07
1:17:36			Wang Zhen	CHN	24.8.91	1		Taicang	30 Mar 12
1:17:38		Valeriy	Borchin ¶ (10)	RUS	11.9.86	1	NC-w	Adler	28 Feb 09
1:17:40			Chen Ding	CHN	5.8.92	2		Taicang	30 Mar 12
1:17:41			Zhu Hongjun	CHN	18.8.83	2		Cixi	23 Apr 05
1:17:43		Yohann	Diniz	FRA	1.1.78	2		Lugano	18 Mar 12
1:17:46		Julio	Martínez	GUA	27.9.73	1		Eisenhüttenstadt	8 May 99
1:17:46		Roman	Rasskazov	RUS	28.4.79	1	NC	Moskva	19 May 00
1:17:47		Andrey	Ruzavin	RUS	28.3.86	1	NC-w	Sochi	18 Feb 12
1:17:52			Fernández			1		La Coruña	4 Jun 05
1:17:53			Cui Zhide	CHN	11.1.83	3		Cixi	23 Apr 05
1:17:55			Borchin			1	NC-w	Adler	23 Feb 08
1:17:56		Alejandro	López	MEX	9.2.75	2		Eisenhüttenstadt	8 May 99
1:18:00			Fernández			2	WCh	Saint-Denis	23 Aug 03
1:18:03.3twR			Bo Lingtang	CHN	12.8.70	1	NC	Beijing	7 Apr 94
1:18:05		Dmitriy	Yesipchuk (20)	RUS	17.11.74	1	NC-w	Adler	4 Mar 01
1:18:06		Viktor	Burayev ¶	RUS	23.8.82	2	NC-w	Adler	4 Mar 01
1:18:06		Vladimir	Parvatkin	RUS	10.10.84	1	NC-w	Adler	12 Mar 05
1:18:07			Rasskazov			1	NC-w	Adler	20 Feb 00
1:18:07			Rasskazov			3	WCh	Saint-Denis	23 Aug 03
1:18:07			Li Gaobo	CHN	4.5.89	4		Cixi	23 Apr 05
1:18:12		Artur	Meleshkevich	BLR	11.4.75	1		Brest	10 Mar 01
		(30/24)							
1:18:13 wR		Pavol	Blazek	SVK	9.7.58	1		Hildesheim	16 Sep 90
1:18:13			Wang Hao	CHN	16.8.89	1	NG	Jinan	22 Oct 09
1:18:14		Mikhail	Khmelnitskiy	BLR	24.7.69	1	NC	Soligorsk	13 May 00
1:18:14		Noé	Hernández	MEX	15.3.78	4	WCh	Saint-Denis	23 Aug 03
1:18:16		Vladimir	Andreyev	RUS	7.9.66	2	NC	Moskva	19 May 00
1:18:17		Ilya	Markov	RUS	19.6.72	2	NC-w	Adler	12 Mar 05
		(30)							
1:18:18		Yevgeniy	Misyulya	BLR	13.3.64	1		Eisenhüttenstadt	11 May 96
1:18:18		Sergey	Bakulin	RUS	13.11.86	2	NC-w	Adler	23 Feb 08
1:18:20 wR		Andrey	Perlov	RUS	12.12.61	1	NC	Moskva	26 May 90
1:18:20		Denis	Nizhegorodov	RUS	26.7.80	3	NC-w	Adler	4 Mar 01
1:18:22		Robert	Korzeniowski	POL	30.7.68	1		Hildesheim	9 Jul 00
1:18:23		Andrey	Makarov	BLR	2.1.71	2	NC	Soligorsk	13 May 00
1:18:25		Andrey	Krivov	RUS	14.11.85	3	NC-w	Sochi	18 Feb 12
1:18:25		Erick	Barrondo	GUA	14.6.91	3		Lugano	18 Mar 12
1:18:27		Daniel	García	MEX	28.10.71	2	WCp	Podebrady	19 Apr 97
1:18:27			Xing Shucai	CHN	4.8.84	5		Cixi	23 Apr 05
		(40)							
1:18:29		Stanislav	Yemelyanov	RUS	23.10.90	4	NC-w	Sochi	18 Feb 12
1:18:30			Yu Chaohong	CHN	12.12.76	6		Cixi	23 Apr 05
1:18:31			Han Yucheng	CHN	16.12.78	7		Cixi	23 Apr 05
1:18:32			Li Zewen	CHN	5.12.73	4	WCp	Podebrady	19 Apr 97
1:18:33			Liu Yunfeng ¶	CHN	3.8.79	8		Cixi	23 Apr 05
1:18:34		Eder	Sánchez	MEX	21.5.86	3	WCp	Cheboksary	10 May 08
1:18:35.2t		Stefan	Johansson	SWE	11.4.67	1	SGP	Bergen (Fana)	15 May 92
1:18:36		Mikhail	Shchennikov	RUS	24.12.67	1	NC	Sochi	20 Apr 96
1:18:37		Aleksandr	Pershin	RUS	4.9.68	2	NC	Moskva	26 May 90
1:18:37		Ruslan	Shafikov	RUS	27.6.75	1	NC-w23	Adler	11 Feb 95
		(50)	100th man 1:19:33, 200th 1:20:41, 300th 1:21:28, 400th 1:22:02, 500th 1:22:35						

Probable short course

Mark	Wind	Name		Nat	Born	Pos	Meet	Venue	Date
1:18:33		Mikhail	Shchennikov	RUS	24.12.67	1	4-N	Livorno	10 Jul 93

Drugs disqualification

Mark	Wind	Name		Nat	Born	Pos	Meet	Venue	Date
1:16:53dq		Vladimir	Kanaykin ¶	RUS	21.3.85	2	NC	Saransk	8 Jun 08
1:17:52			Morozov ¶			2	NC-w	Sochi	18 Feb 12

30 KILOMETRES WALK

Mark	Wind	Name		Nat	Born	Pos	Meet	Venue	Date
2:01:13+		Vladimir	Kanaykin ¶	RUS	21.3.85	1	in 35k	Adler	19 Feb 06
2:01:44.1t		Maurizio	Damilano	ITA	6.4.57	1		Cuneo	3 Oct 92
2:01:47+			Kanaykin			1	in 35k	Adler	13 Mar 05
2:02:27+			Kanaykin			1	in 35k	Adler	8 Feb 04
2:02:41		Andrey	Perlov	RUS	12.12.61	1	NC-w	Sochi	19 Feb 89
2:02:45		Yevgeniy	Misyulya	BLR	13.3.64	1		Mogilyov	28 Apr 91
2:03:06		Daniel	Bautista	MEX	4.8.52	1		Cherkassy	27 Apr 80
2:03:50+		Vladimir	Parvatkin	RUS	10.10.84	2	in 35k	Adler	19 Feb 06

Mark	Wind	Name		Nat	Born	Pos	Meet	Venue	Date
2:03:56.5t		Thierry	Toutain	FRA	14.2.62	1		Héricourt	24 Mar 91
2:04:00		Aleksandr	Potashov	BLR	12.3.62	1		Adler	14 Feb 93
2:04:24		Valeriy	Spitsyn	RUS	5.12.65	1	NC-w	Sochi	22 Feb 92
2:04:30		Vitaliy	Matsko (10)	RUS	8.6.60	2	NC-w	Sochi	19 Feb 89
2:04:49+		Semyon	Lovkin	RUS	14.7.77	1=	in 35k	Adler	1 Mar 03
2:04:49+		Stepan	Yudin	RUS	3.4.80	1=	in 35k	Adler	1 Mar 03
2:04:50+		Sergey	Kirdyapkin	RUS	16.1.80	2	in 35k	Adler	13 Mar 05
2:04:55.5t		Guillaume	Leblanc	CAN	14.4.62	1		Sept-Iles	16 Jun 90

35 KILOMETRES WALK

Mark	Wind	Name		Nat	Born	Pos	Meet	Venue	Date
2:21:31		Vladimir	Kanaykin ¶	RUS	21.3.85	1	NC-w	Adler	19 Feb 06
2:23:17			Kanaykin			1	NC-w	Adler	8 Feb 04
2:23:17			Kanaykin			1	NC-w	Adler	13 Mar 05
2:24:25		Semyon	Lovkin	RUS	14.7.77	1	NC-w	Adler	1 Mar 03
2:24:25		Sergey	Bakulin	RUS	13.11.86	1	NC-w	Adler	1 Mar 09
2:24:50		Denis	Nizhegorodov	RUS	26.7.80	2	NC-w	Adler	19 Feb 06
2:24:56			Nizhegorodov			2	NC-w	Adler	1 Mar 09
2:25:19		Andrey	Ruzavin	RUS	28.3.86	3	NC-w	Adler	1 Mar 09
2:25:38		Stepan	Yudin	RUS	3.4.80	2	NC-w	Adler	1 Mar 03
2:25:42		Sergey	Kirdyapkin	RUS	18.6.80	1	NC-w	Sochi	18 Feb 12
2:25:57			Kirdyapkin			2	NC-w	Adler	13 Mar 05
2:25:58		German	Skurygin ¶	RUS	15.9.63	1	NC-w	Adler	20 Feb 98
2:25:59			Kanaykin ¶			1	NC-w	Adler	23 Feb 08
2:25:59		Mikhail	Ryzhov	RUS	17.12.91	2	NC-w	Sochi	26 Feb 12
		(14/9)							
2:26:16		Alex	Schwazer ¶ (10)	ITA	26.12.84	1		Montalto Di Castro	24 Jan 10
2:26:25		Aleksey	Voyevodin ¶	RUS	9.8.70	2	NC-w	Adler	8 Feb 04
2:26:29		Yuriy	Andronov	RUS	6.11.71	4	NC-w	Adler	1 Mar 09
2:26:33		Ivan	Noskov	RUS	16.7.88	3	NC-w	Sochi	26 Feb 12
2:26:36		Igor	Yerokhin ¶	RUS	4.9.85	1	NC-w	Sochi	26 Feb 11
2:26:46		Oleg	Ishutkin	RUS	22.7.75	1	NC-w	Adler	9 Feb 97
2:27:02		Yevgeniy	Shmalyuk	RUS	14.1.76	1	NC-w	Adler	20 Feb 00
2:27:07		Dmitriy	Dolnikov	RUS	19.11.72	2	NC-w	Adler	20 Feb 98
2:27:21		Pavel	Nikolayev	RUS	18.12.77	3	NC-w	Adler	20 Feb 98
2:27:29		Nikolay	Matyukhin	RUS	13.12.68	2	NC-w	Adler	9 Feb 97

50 KILOMETRES WALK

Mark	Wind	Name		Nat	Born	Pos	Meet	Venue	Date
3:34:14 WR		Denis	Nizhegorodov	RUS	26.7.80	1	WCp	Cheboksary	11 May 08
3:35:27.2twR		Yohann	Diniz	FRA	1.1.78	1		Reims	12 Mar 11
3:35:29			Nizhegorodov			1	NC	Cheboksary	13 Jun 04
3:35:47		Nathan	Deakes	AUS	17.8.77	1	NC	Geelong	2 Dec 06
3:35:59		Sergey	Kirdyapkin	RUS	16.1.80	1	OG	London (OS)	11 Aug 12
3:36:03 WR		Robert	Korzeniowski	POL	30.7.68	1	WCh	Saint-Denis	27 Aug 03
3:36:04		Alex	Schwazer ¶	ITA	26.12.84	1	NC	Rosignano Solvay	11 Feb 07
3:36:06			Yu Chaohong	CHN	12.12.76	1	NG	Nanjing	22 Oct 05
3:36:13			Zhao Chengliang	CHN	1.6.84	2	NG	Nanjing	22 Oct 05
3:36:20			Han Yucheng	CHN	16.12.78	1	NC	Nanning	27 Feb 05
3:36:39 WR			Korzeniowski			1	EC	München	8 Aug 02
3:36:42		German	Skurygin ¶ (10)	RUS	15.9.63	2	WCh	Saint-Denis	27 Aug 03
3:36:53		Jared	Tallent	AUS	17.10.84	2	OG	London (OS)	11 Aug 12
3:37:04			Schwazer			2	WCp	Cheboksary	11 May 08
3:37:09			Schwazer			1	OG	Beijing	22 Aug 08
3:37:16			Si Tianfeng	CHN	17.6.84	3	OG	London (OS)	11 Aug 12
3:37:26 WR		Valeriy	Spitsyn	RUS	5.12.65	1	NC	Moskva	21 May 00
3:37:41 WR		Andrey	Perlov	RUS	12.12.61	1	NC	Leningrad	5 Aug 89
3:37:46		Andreas	Erm	GER	12.3.76	3	WCh	Saint-Denis	27 Aug 03
3:37:54		Robert	Heffernan	IRL	20.2.78	4	OG	London (OS)	11 Aug 12
3:37:54		Igor	Yerokhin ¶	RUS	4.9.85	5	OG	London (OS)	11 Aug 12
3:37:58			Xing Shucai	CHN	4.8.84	2	NC	Nanning	27 Feb 05
3:38:01		Aleksey	Voyevodin ¶	RUS	9.8.70	4	WCh	Saint-Denis	27 Aug 03
3:38:02			Nizhegorodov			1	WCp	La Coruña	14 May 06
3:38:08			Kirdyapkin			1	WCh	Helsinki	12 Aug 05
3:38:08			Yerokhin			1	NC	Saransk	8 Jun 08
3:38:08			Kirdyapkin			1	WCp	Saransk	13 May 12
3:38:10			Yerokhin			2	WCp	Saransk	13 May 12
3:38:17 WR		Ronald	Weigel	GDR	8.8.59	1	IM	Potsdam	25 May 86
3:38:23			Nizhegorodov			5	WCh	Saint-Denis	27 Aug 03
		(30/20)							
3:38:29		Vyacheslav	Ivanenko	RUS	3.3.61	1	OG	Seoul	30 Sep 88

Mark	Wind	Name		Nat	Born	Pos	Meet	Venue	Date
3:38:43		Valentí	Massana	ESP	5.7.70	1	NC	Orense	20 Mar 94
3:38:46		Sergey	Bakulin	RUS	13.11.86	1	NC	Saransk	12 Jun 11
3:39:01			Li Jianbo	CHN	14.11.86	7	OG	London (OS)	11 Aug 12
3:39:17			Dong Jimin	CHN	10.10.83	4	NC	Nanning	27 Feb 05
3:39:21		Vladimir	Potemin	RUS	15.1.80	2	NC	Moskva	21 May 00
3:39:22		Sergey	Korepanov	KAZ	9.5.64	1	WCp	Mézidon-Canon	2 May 99
3:39:34		Valentin	Kononen	FIN	7.3.69	1		Dudince	25 Mar 00
3:39:45		Hartwig	Gauder	GDR	10.11.54	3	OG	Seoul	30 Sep 88
3:39:46		Matej	Tóth	SVK	10.2.83	1	NC	Dudince	26 Mar 11
		(30)							
3:39:54		Jesús Angel	García	ESP	17.10.69	1	WCp	Podebrady	20 Apr 97
3:40:02		Aleksandr	Potashov	BLR	12.3.62	1	NC	Moskva	27 May 90
3:40:07		Andrey	Plotnikov	RUS	12.8.67	2	NC	Moskva	27 May 90
3:40:08		Tomasz	Lipiec ¶	POL	10.5.71	2	WCp	Mézidon-Canon	2 May 99
3:40:12		Oleg	Ishutkin	RUS	22.7.75	2	WCp	Podebrady	20 Apr 97
3:40:12		Yuki	Yamazaki	JPN	16.1.84	1		Wajima	12 Apr 09
3:40:13		Nikolay	Matyukhin	RUS	13.12.68	3	WCp	Mézidon-Canon	2 May 99
3:40:23			Gadasu Alatan	CHN	27.1.84	3	NG	Nanjing	22 Oct 05
3:40:40		Vladimir	Kanaykin ¶	RUS	21.3.85	1	NC	Saransk	12 Jun 05
3:40:46	WR	José	Marin	ESP	21.1.50	1	NC	Valencia	13 Mar 83
		(40)							
3:40:46		Yuriy	Andronov	RUS	6.11.71	1		Moskva	11 Jun 12
3:40:57.9t		Thierry	Toutain	FRA	14.2.62	1		Héricourt	29 Sep 96
3:41:02		Francisco Javier	Fernández ¶	ESP	6.3.77	1	NC	San Pedro del Pinatar	1 Mar 09
3:41:10			Zhao Jianguo	CHN	19.1.88	1	AsiC	Wajima	16 Apr 06
3:41:16		Trond	Nymark	NOR	28.12.76	2	WCh	Berlin	21 Aug 09
3:41:20	WR	Raúl	González	MEX	29.2.52	1		Podebrady	11 Jun 78
3:41:20			Zhao Yongsheng	CHN	16.4.70	1	WCp	Beijing	30 Apr 95
3:41:28.2t		René	Piller	FRA	23.4.65	1	SGP	Fana	7 May 94
3:41:30			Ni Liang	CHN	26.7.86	4	NG	Nanjing	22 Oct 05
3:41:47		Mikel	Odriozola	ESP	25.5.73	1	NC	El Prat de Llobregat	27 Feb 05
3:41:51		Venyamin	Nikolayev	RUS	7.10.58	2	NC	Leningrad	3 Aug 85
3:41:51		Oleg	Kistkin	RUS	13.5.83	3	ECp	Leamington	20 May 07
3:41:55			Wang Hao	CHN	16.8.89	2	NG	Jinan	26 Oct 09
		(50)	100th man 3:45:17, 200th 3:50:04, 300th 3:52:45, 400th 3:55:16. 500th 3:57:55						

Drugs disqualification

Mark	Wind	Name		Nat	Born	Pos	Meet	Venue	Date
3:36:55		Vladimir	Kanaykin ¶	RUS	21.3.85	(2)	WCp	Cheboksary	11 May 08

100 KILOMETRES WALK

Mark	Wind	Name		Nat	Born	Pos	Meet	Venue	Date
8:38.07		Viktor	Ginko	BLR	7.12.65	1		Scanzorosciate	27 Oct 02
8:43:30			Ginko			1		Scanzorosciate	29 Oct 00
8:44:28			Ginko			1		Scanzorosciate	19 Oct 03
8:48:28		Modris	Liepins	LAT	30.8.66	1		Scanzorosciate	28 Oct 01
8:54:35		Aleksey	Rodionov	RUS	5.3.57	1		Scanzorosciate	15 Nov 98
8:55:12		Pascal	Kieffer	FRA	6.5.61	1		Besançon	18 Oct 92
8:55:40		Vitaliy	Popovich	UKR	22.10.62	1		Scanzorosciate	31 Oct 99
8:58:12		Gérard	Lelièvre	FRA	13.11.49	1		Laval	7 Oct 84
8:58:47		Zóltan	Czukor	HUN	18.12.62	2		Scanzorosciate	27 Oct 02

Some notes on all-time lists at end of 2012

Deep all-time lists (generally 100 performances and 500 perfromers for all standard men's and women's events) have been compiled by Richard Hymans and Peter Matthews to be published next year by Jonas Hedman in a book that also includes the author's selections of the all-time top ten greats for each event.

Oldest mark in World Lists: Men: in wind assisted sections: LJ 8.49w Ralph Boston USA 2 Sep 1964, 100m 9.91w Bob Hayes USA 15 Oct 1964; in main lists: SP: 37= 21.78 Randy Matson USA 22 Apr 1967. Women: by an individual 100mh 48= 12.59 Anneliese Ehrhardt GDR 8 Sep 1972.

Changes in 2012: Most events had considerable changes to deep all-time lists, but those changing least were:
Men: LJ: 8.35 Rutherford & Morgunov to 68=, 8.33 Goodwin to 88= were the only top 100 changes.
Women
3000m: much less often run these days. Only one change to AT 100: Kipyego 8:35.89 to 88th.
But also 5000m: only three changes in top 100: first was 14:44.62 Nyaruai to 64th
SP: 20.48 Kolodko to 47th, 10.95 Li Ling 1cm better at 78th, Svirdova 19.72 to 98th.

Mark	Wind	Name		Nat	Born	Pos	Meet	Venue	Date

WOMEN'S ALL-TIME WORLD LISTS

100 METRES

Mark	Wind	Name		Nat	Born	Pos	Meet	Venue	Date
10.49wr	0.0	Florence	Griffith-Joyner	USA	21.12.59	1q1	NC/OT	Indianpolis	16 Jul 88
		@ Probably strongly wind-assisted, but recognised as a US and world record							
10.61	1.2		Griffith-Joyner			1	NC/OT	Indianpolis	17 Jul 88
10.62	1.0		Griffith-Joyner			1q3	OG	Seoul	24 Sep 88
10.64	1.2	Carmelita	Jeter	USA	24.11.79	1		Shanghai	20 Sep 09
10.65A	1.1	Marion	Jones ¶	USA	12.10.75	1	WCp	Johannesburg	12 Sep 98
10.67	-0.1		Jeter			1	WAF	Thessaloníki	13 Sep 09
10.70 (WR)	1.6		Griffith-Joyner			1s1	NC/OT	Indianapolis	17 Jul 88
10.70	-0.1		Jones			1	WCh	Sevilla	22 Aug 99
10.70	2.0		Jeter			1	Pre	Eugene	4 Jun 11
10.70	0.6	Shelly-Ann	Fraser-Pryce	JAM	27.12.86	1	NC	Kingston	29 Jun 12
10.71	0.1		Jones			1		Chengdu	12 May 98
10.71	2.0		Jones			1s2	NC	New Orleans	19 Jun 98
10.72	2.0		Jones			1	NC	New Orleans	20 Jun 98
10.72	0.0		Jones			1	Herc	Monaco	8 Aug 98
10.72	0.0		Jones			1	Athl	Lausanne	25 Aug 98
10.73	2.0	Christine	Arron	FRA	13.9.73	1	EC	Budapest	19 Aug 98
10.74	1.3	Merlene	Ottey	JAM/SLO	10.5.60	1	GPF	Milano	7 Sep 96
10.75	0.6		Jones			1	GGala	Roma	14 Jul 98
10.75	0.4	Kerron	Stewart	JAM	16.4.84	1	GGala	Roma	10 Jul 09
10.75	0.1		Stewart			2	WCh	Berlin	17 Aug 09
10.75	1.5		Fraser-Pryce			1	OG	London (OS)	4 Aug 12
10.76 WR	1.7	Evelyn	Ashford	USA	15.4.57	1	WK	Zürich	22 Aug 84
10.76	0.9		Jones			1	VD	Bruxelles	22 Aug 97
10.76	0.3		Jones			1q4	WCh	Sevilla	21 Aug 99
10.76	1.1	Veronica	Campbell-Brown	JAM	15.5.82	1	GS	Ostrava	31 May 11
10.77	0.9	Irina	Privalova (10)	RUS	22.11.68	1rA	Athl	Lausanne	6 Jul 94
10.77	-0.9		Jones			1rA	WK	Zürich	12 Aug 98
10.77	0.7	Ivet	Lalova	BUL	18.5.84	1	ECp-1A	Plovdiv	19 Jun 04
10.78A	1.0	Dawn	Sowell	USA	27.3.66	1	NCAA	Provo	3 Jun 89
10.78	1.7		Ottey			1	Expo	Sevilla	30 May 90
10.78	0.4		Ottey			1	GPF	Paris	3 Sep 94
10.78	1.1		Jones			1	BrGP	London (CP)	5 Aug 00
10.78	1.8	Torri	Edwards ¶	USA	31.1.77	1s2	OT	Eugene	28 Jun 08
10.78	0.0		Fraser			1	OG	Beijing	17 Aug 08
10.78	0.8		Campbell-Brown			1	Pre	Eugene	3 Jul 10
10.78	0.4		Jeter			1	VD	Bruxelles	16 Sep 11
10.78	1.5		Jeter			2	OG	London (OS)	4 Aug 12
		(37 performances by 13 athletes)							
10.79	0.0		Li Xuemei	CHN	5.1.77	1	NG	Shanghai	18 Oct 97
10.79	-0.1	Inger	Miller	USA	12.6.72	2	WCh	Sevilla	22 Aug 99
10.81 WR	1.7	Marlies	Göhr'	GDR	21.3.58	1	OD	Berlin	8 Jun 83
10.82	-1.0	Gail	Devers	USA	19.11.66	1	OG	Barcelona	1 Aug 92
10.82	0.4	Gwen	Torrence	USA	12.6.65	2	GPF	Paris	3 Sep 94
10.82	-0.3	Zhanna	Pintusevich-Block ¶	UKR	6.7.72	1	WCh	Edmonton	6 Aug 01
10.82	-0.7	Sherone	Simpson	JAM	12.8.84	1	NC	Kingston	24 Jun 06
		(20)							
10.83	1.7	Marita	Koch	GDR	18.2.57	2	OD	Berlin	8 Jun 83
10.83	-1.0	Juliet	Cuthbert	JAM	9.4.64	2	OG	Barcelona	1 Aug 92
10.83	0.1	Ekateríni	Thánou ¶	GRE	1.2.75	2s1	WCh	Sevilla	22 Aug 99
10.84	1.3	Chioma	Ajunwa ¶	NGR	25.12.70	1		Lagos	11 Apr 92
10.84	1.9	Chandra	Sturrup	BAH	12.9.71	1	Athl	Lausanne	5 Jul 05
10.84	1.8	Kelly-Ann	Baptiste	TRI	14.10.86	1		Clermont	5 Jun 10
10.85	2.0	Anelia	Nuneva	BUL	30.6.62	1h1	NC	Sofia	2 Sep 88
10.85	1.0	Muna	Lee	USA	30.10.81	1	OT	Eugene	28 Jun 08
10.85	1.5	Tianna	Madison	USA	30.8.85	4	OG	London (OS)	4 Aug 12
10.86	0.6	Silke	Gladisch'	GDR	20.6.64	1	NC	Potsdam	20 Aug 87
		(30)							
10.86	1.2	Chryste	Gaines ¶	USA	14.9.70	1	WAF	Monaco	14 Sep 03
10.86	2.0	Marshevet	Myers	USA	25.9.84	2	Pre	Eugene	4 Jun 11
10.88	0.4	Lauryn	Williams	USA	11.9.83	2	WK	Zürich	19 Aug 05
10.89	1.8	Katrin	Krabbe ¶	GDR	22.11.69	1		Berlin	20 Jul 88
10.89	0.0		Liu Xiaomei	CHN	11.1.72	2	NG	Shanghai	18 Oct 97
10.89	1.5	Allyson	Felix	USA	18.11.85	5	OG	London (OS)	4 Aug 12
10.90	1.4	Glory	Alozie	NGR/ESP	30.12.77	1		La Laguna	5 Jun 99
10.90	1.8	Shalonda	Solomon	USA	19.12.85	2		Clermont	5 Jun 10

Mark	Wind	Name		Nat	Born	Pos	Meet	Venue	Date
10.91	0.2	Heike	Drechsler'	GDR/GER	16.12.64	2	GWG	Moskva	6 Jul 86
10.91	1.1	Savatheda	Fynes	BAH	17.10.74	2	Athl	Lausanne	2 Jul 99
		(40)							
10.91	1.5	Debbie	Ferguson McKenzie	BAH	16.1.76	1	CG	Manchester	27 Jul 02
10.92	0.0	Alice	Brown	USA	20.9.60	2q2	NC/OT	Indianapolis	16 Jul 88
10.92	1.1	D'Andre	Hill	USA	19.4.73	3	NC	Atlanta	15 Jun 96
10.92	0.1	Yuliya	Nesterenko	BLR	15.6.79	1s1	OG	Athína	21 Aug 04
10.92	1.0	Blessing	Okagbare	NGR	9.10.88	1s3	OG	London (OS)	4 Aug 12
10.93	1.8	Ewa	Kasprzyk	POL	7.9.57	1	NC	Grudziadz	27 Jun 86
10.93	1.0	Tayna	Lawrence	JAM	17.9.75	3	VD	Bruxelles	30 Aug 02
10.94A	0.6	Diane	Williams	USA	14.12.60	2	USOF	USAF Academy	3 Jul 83
10.94	1.0	Carlette	Guidry	USA	4.9.68	1	NC	New York	14 Jun 91
10.95	1.0	Bärbel	Wöckel'	GDR	21.3.55	2	NC	Dresden	1 Jul 82
10.95	2.0	Me'Lisa	Barber	USA	4.10.80	2	adidas	Carson	20 May 07
10.95A	1.8	Simone	Facey	JAM	7.5.85	1	Big 12	Boulder	18 May 08
		(52)	100th women 11.04, 200th 11.14, 300th 11.20, 400th 11.26, 500th 11.30						

Doubtful wind reading

Mark	Wind	Name		Nat	Born	Pos	Meet	Venue	Date
10.83	0.0	Sheila	Echols	USA	2.10.64	1q2	NC/OT	Indianapolis	16 Jul 88
10.86	0.0	Diane	Williams	USA	14.12.60	2q1	NC/OT	Indianapolis	16 Jul 88

Probably semi-automatic timing

Mark	Wind	Name		Nat	Born	Pos	Meet	Venue	Date
10.87	1.9	Lyudmila	Kondratyeva	RUS	11.4.58	1		Leningrad	3 Jun 80

Low altitude best: 10.91 1.6 Sowell 1 NC Houston 16 Jun 89

Wind-assisted to 10.76 performances and 10.90 performers

Mark	Wind	Name		Nat	Born	Pos	Meet	Venue	Date
10.54	3.0		Griffith-Joyner			1	OG	Seoul	25 Sep 88
10.60	3.2		Griffith-Joyner			1h1	NC/OT	Indianpolis	16 Jul 88
10.68	2.2		Jones			1	DNG	Stockholm	1 Aug 00
10.70	2.6		Griffith-Joyner			1s2	OG	Seoul	25 Sep 88
10.72	3.0		Jeter			1s1	NC	Eugene	26 Jun 09
10.74	2.7		Jeter			1	NC	Eugene	24 Jun 11
10.75	4.1		Jones			1h3	NC	New Orleans	19 Jun 98
10.76	3.4	Marshevet	Hooker/Myers	USA	25.9.84	1q1	NC/OT	Eugene	27 Jun 08
10.77	2.3	Gail	Devers	USA	19.11.66	1	Jen	San José	28 May 94
10.77	2.3	Ekateríni	Thánou ¶	GRE	1.2.75	1		Rethymno	28 May 99
10.78	5.0	Gwen	Torrence	USA	12.6.65	1q3	NC/OT	Indianpolis	16 Jul 88
10.78	3.3	Muna	Lee	USA	30.10.81	2	NC	Eugene	26 Jun 09
10.79	3.3	Marlies	Göhr'	GDR	21.3.58	1	NC	Cottbus	16 Jul 80
10.80	2.9	Pam	Marshall	USA	16.8.60	1	NC	Eugene	20 Jun 86
10.80	2.8	Heike	Drechsler'	GDR	16.12.64	1	Bisl	Oslo	5 Jul 86
10.82	2.2	Silke	Gladisch/Möller	GDR	20.6.64	1s1	WCh	Roma	30 Aug 87
10.84	2.9	Alice	Brown	USA	20.9.60	2	NC	Eugene	20 Jun 86
10.86	3.4	Lauryn	Williams	USA	11.9.83	2q1	NC/OT	Eugene	27 Jun 08
10.86	2.9	Murielle	Ahouré	CIV	23.8.87	1		Clermont	4 Jun 11
10.87	3.0	Me'Lisa	Barber	USA	4.10.80	1s1	NC	Carson	25 Jun 05
10.88	5.9	Alexandria	Anderson	USA	28.1.87	1		Austin	14 Apr 12
10.89	3.1	Kerstin	Behrendt	GDR	2.9.67	2		Berlin	13 Sep 88
10.90	2.5	Damola	Osayomi ¶	NGR	26.6.86	1	AfrG	Maputo	12 Sep 11
10.89	2.9	Sanya	Richards-Ross	USA	26.2.85	1	TexR	Austin	31 Mar 12

Hand timing

Mark	Wind	Name		Nat	Born	Pos	Meet	Venue	Date
10.6	0.1	Zhanna	Pintusevich	UKR	6.7.72	1		Kiev	12 Jun 97
10.7		Merlene	Ottey	JAM	10.5.60	1h	NC	Kingston	15 Jul 88
10.7	1.1	Juliet	Cuthbert	JAM	9.4.64	1	NC	Kingston	4 Jul 92
10.7		Mary	Onyali	NGR	3.2.68	1	NC	Lagos	22 Jun 96
10.7	-0.2	Svetlana	Goncharenko	RUS	28.5.71	1		Rostov-na-Donu	30 May 98
10.7A	1.3	Blessing	Okagbare	NGR	9.10.86	1		El Paso	10 Apr 10
10.7w	2.6	Savatheda	Fynes	BAH	17.10.74	1	NC	Nassau	22 Jun 95

Drugs disqualification

Mark	Wind	Name		Nat	Born	Pos	Meet	Venue	Date
10.75	-0.4		Jones			1	OG	Sydney	23 Sep 00
10.78	0.1		Jones			1	ISTAF	Berlin	1 Sep 00
10.85	0.9	Kelli	White ¶	USA	1.4.77	1	WCh	Saint-Denis	24 Aug 03
10.79w	2.3	Kelli	White ¶	USA	1.4.77	1		Carson	1 Jun 03

200 METRES

Mark	Wind	Name		Nat	Born	Pos	Meet	Venue	Date
21.34WR	1.3	Florence	Griffith-Joyner	USA	21.12.59	1	OG	Seoul	29 Sep 88
21.56WR	1.7		Griffith-Joyner			1s1	OG	Seoul	29 Sep 88
21.62A	-0.6	Marion	Jones ¶	USA	12.10.75	1	WCp	Johannesburg	11 Sep 98
21.64	0.8	Merlene	Ottey	JAM	10.5.60	1	VD	Bruxelles	13 Sep 91
21.66	-1.0		Ottey			1	WK	Zürich	15 Aug 90
21.69	1.0	Allyson	Felix	USA	18.11.85	1	NC/OT	Eugene	30 Jun 12
21.71WR	0.7	Marita	Koch	GDR	18.2.57	1	v CAN	Karl-Marx-Stadt	10 Jun 79
21.71WR	0.3		Koch			1	OD	Potsdam	21 Jul 84
21.71WR	1.2	Heike	Drechsler'	GDR	16.12.64	1	NC	Jena	29 Jun 86

Mark	Wind	Name		Nat	Born	Pos	Meet	Venue	Date
21.71wr	-0.8		Drechsler			1	EC	Stuttgart	29 Aug 86
21.72	1.3	Grace	Jackson	JAM	14.6.61	2	OG	Seoul	29 Sep 88
21.72	-0.1	Gwen	Torrence	USA	12.6.65	1s2	OG	Barcelona	5 Aug 92
21.74	0.4	Marlies	Göhr'	GDR	21.3.58	1	NC	Erfurt	3 Jun 84
21.74	1.2	Silke	Gladisch'	GDR	20.6.64	1	WCh	Roma	3 Sep 87
21.74	0.6	Veronica (10)	Campbell-Brown	JAM	15.5.82	1	OG	Beijing	21 Aug 08
21.75	-0.1	Juliet	Cuthbert	JAM	9.4.64	2s2	OG	Barcelona	5 Aug 92
21.76	0.3		Koch			1	NC	Dresden	3 Jul 82
21.76	0.7		Griffith-Joyner			1q1	OG	Seoul	28 Sep 88
21.76	-0.8		Jones			1	WK	Zürich	13 Aug 97
21.77	-0.1		Griffith-Joyner			1q2	NC/OT	Indianapolis	22 Jul 88
21.77	1.0		Ottey			1	Herc	Monaco	7 Aug 93
21.77	-0.3		Torrence			1	ASV	Köln	18 Aug 95
21.77	0.6	Inger	Miller	USA	12.6.72	1	WCh	Sevilla	27 Aug 99
21.78	-1.3		Koch			1	NC	Leipzig	11 Aug 85
21.79	1.7		Gladisch			1	NC	Potsdam	22 Aug 87
21.80	-1.1		Ottey			1	Nik	Nice	10 Jul 90
21.80	0.4		Jones			1	GWG	Uniondale, NY	20 Jul 98
21.81	-0.1	Valerie	Brisco	USA	6.7.60	1	OG	Los Angeles	9 Aug 84
21.81	0.4		Ottey			1	ASV	Köln	19 Aug 90
21.81	-0.6		Torrence			1	OG	Barcelona	6 Aug 92
21.81	0.0		Torrence			1	Herc	Monaco	25 Jul 95
21.81	1.6		Jones			1	Pre	Eugene	30 May 99
21.81	1.7		Felix			1	WCh	Osaka	31 Aug 07
		(33/14)							
21.83	-0.2	Evelyn	Ashford	USA	15.4.57	1	WCp	Montreal	24 Aug 79
21.85	0.3	Bärbel	Wöckel'	GDR	21.3.55	2	OD	Potsdam	21 Jul 84
21.87	0.0	Irina	Privalova	RUS	22.11.68	2	Herc	Monaco	25 Jul 95
21.93	1.3	Pam	Marshall	USA	16.8.60	2	NC/OT	Indianapolis	23 Jul 88
21.95	0.3	Katrin	Krabbe ¶	GDR	22.11.69	1	EC	Split	30 Aug 90
21.97	1.9	Jarmila	Kratochvílová	CZE	26.1.51	1	PTS	Bratislava	6 Jun 81
		(20)							
21.99	0.9	Chandra	Cheeseborough	USA	10.1.59	2	NC	Indianapolis	19 Jun 83
21.99	1.1	Marie-José	Pérec	FRA	9.5.68	1	BNP	Villeneuve d'Ascq	2 Jul 93
21.99	1.1	Kerron	Stewart	JAM	16.4.84	2	NC	Kingston	29 Jun 08
22.00	1.3	Sherone	Simpson	JAM	12.8.84	1	NC	Kingston	25 Jun 06
22.01	-0.5	Anelia	Nuneva'	BUL	30.6.62	1	NC	Sofiya	16 Aug 87
22.01	0.0		Li Xuemei	CHN	5.1.77	1	NG	Shanghai	22 Oct 97
22.01	0.6	Muna	Lee	USA	30.10.81	4	OG	Beijing	21 Aug 08
22.04A	0.7	Dawn	Sowell	USA	27.3.66	1	NCAA	Provo	2 Jun 89
22.06A	0.7	Evette	de Klerk'	RSA	21.8.65	1		Pietersburg	8 Apr 89
22.07	-0.1	Mary	Onyali	NGR	3.2.68	1	WK	Zürich	14 Aug 96
		(30)							
22.09	-0.3	Sanya	Richards-Ross	USA	26.2.85	1	DL	New York	9 Jun 12
22.09	-0.2	Shelly-Ann	Fraser-Pryce	JAM	27.12.86	2	OG	London (OS)	8 Aug 12
22.10	-0.1	Kathy	Cook'	GBR	3.5.60	4	OG	Los Angeles	9 Aug 84
22.11	1.0	Carmelita	Jeter	USA	24.11.79	2	NC/OT	Eugene	30 Jun 12
22.13	1.2	Ewa	Kasprzyk	POL	7.9.57	2	GWG	Moskva	8 Jul 86
22.14	-0.6	Carlette	Guidry	USA	4.9.68	1	NC	Atlanta	23 Jun 96
22.15	1.0	Shalonda	Solomon	USA	19.12.85	1	NC	Eugene	26 Jun 11
22.17A	-2.3	Zhanna	Pintusevich-Block ¶	UKR	6.7.72	1		Monachil	9 Jul 97
	22.24		-0.3			2	VD	Bruxelles	30 Aug 02
22.18	-0.6	Dannette	Young-Stone	USA	6.10.64	2	NC	Atlanta	23 Jun 96
22.18	0.9	Galina	Malchugina	RUS	17.12.62	1s2	NC	Sankt Peterburg	4 Jul 96
		(40)							
22.18	0.5	Merlene	Frazer	JAM	27.12.73	1s2	WCh	Sevilla	25 Aug 99
22.19	1.5	Natalya	Bochina	RUS	4.1.62	2	OG	Moskva	30 Jul 80
22.19	0.0	Debbie	Ferguson McKenzie	BAH	16.1.76	1	GP II	Saint-Denis	3 Jul 99
22.19	1.9	Kimberlyn	Duncan	USA	2.8.91	1s2	NCAA	Des Moines	7 Jun 12
22.19	1.0	Aleksandra	Fedoriva	RUS	13.9.88	1	NC	Cheboksary	6 Jul 12
22.20	2.0	Kim	Gevaert	BEL	5.8.78	1	NC	Bruxelles	9 Jul 06
22.21 wr	1.9	Irena	Szewinska'	POL	24.5.46	1		Potsdam	13 Jun 74
22.22	-0.9	Falilat	Ogunkoya	NGR	12.5.68	1	AfCh	Dakar	22 Aug 98
22.22	0.6	Beverly	McDonald	JAM	15.2.70	2	WCh	Sevilla	27 Aug 99
22.22	0.3	Rachelle	Smith (Boone)	USA	30.6.81	2	NC	Carson	26 Jun 05
		(50)	100th woman 22.38, 200th 22.63, 300th 22.77, 4th 22.87, 500th 22.97						

Wind-assisted   *Performers listed to 22.20*

Mark	Wind	Name		Nat	Born	Pos	Meet	Venue	Date
21.82	3.1	Irina	Privalova	RUS	22.11.68	1	Athl	Lausanne	6 Jul 94
21.91	2.8	Muna	Lee	USA	30.10.81	1		Fort-de-France	10 May 08
22.10	2.4	Shelly-Ann	Fraser-Pryce	JAM	27.12.86	1		Kingston	7 May 11

Mark	Wind	Name		Nat	Born	Pos	Meet	Venue	Date
22.12	2.6	Kimberlyn	Duncan	USA	2.8.91	1	SEC	Baton Rouge	13 May 12
22.16	3.1	Dannette	Young-Stone	USA	6.10.64	2	Athl	Lausanne	6 Jul 94
22.16	3.2	Nanceen	Perry	USA	19.4.77	1		Austin	6 May 00
22.18A	2.8	Melinda	Gainsford-Taylor	AUS	1.10.71	1		Pietersburg	18 Mar 00
22.18	3.2	Kimberlyn	Duncan	USA	2.8.91	1		Baton Rouge	23 Apr 11
22.19A	3.1	Angella	Taylor'	CAN	28.9.58	1		Colorado Springs	21 Jul 82
22.20	5.6	Marshevet	Hooker/Myers	USA	25.9.84	3	NC/OT	Eugene	6 Jul 08

Hand timing

Mark	Wind	Name		Nat	Born	Pos	Meet	Venue	Date
21.9	-0.1	Svetlana	Goncharenko	RUS	28.5.71	1		Rostov-na-Donu	31 May 98
21.6w	2.5	Pam	Marshall	USA	16.8.60	1	NC	San José	26 Jun 87

Drugs disqualification

Mark	Wind	Name		Nat	Born	Pos	Meet	Venue	Date
22.05	-0.3	Kelli	White ¶	USA	1.4.77	1	WCh	Saint-Denis	28 Aug 03
22.18i		Michelle	Collins ¶	USA	12.2.71	1	WI	Birmingham	15 Mar 03

300 METRES

Times in 300m races only

Mark	Name		Nat	Born	Pos	Meet	Venue	Date
35.30A	Ana Gabriela	Guevara	MEX	4.3.77	1		Ciudad de México	3 May 03
35.46	Kathy	Cook'	GBR	3.5.60	1	Nike	London (CP)	18 Aug 84
35.46	Chandra	Cheeseborough	USA	10.1.59	2	Nike	London (CP)	18 Aug 84

Indoors

Mark		Name		Nat	Born	Pos	Meet	Venue	Date
35.45		Irina	Privalova	RUS	22.11.68	1		Moskva	17 Jan 93
35.48	#	Svetlana	Goncharenko	RUS	28.5.71	1		Tampere	4 Feb 98

400 METRES

Mark	Name		Nat	Born	Pos	Meet	Venue	Date
47.60 WR	Marita	Koch	GDR	18.2.57	1	WCp	Canberra	6 Oct 85
47.99 WR	Jarmila	Kratochvílová	CZE	26.1.51	1	WCh	Helsinki	10 Aug 83
48.16 WR		Koch			1	EC	Athína	8 Sep 82
48.16		Koch			1	Drz	Praha	16 Aug 84
48.22		Koch			1	EC	Stuttgart	28 Aug 86
48.25	Marie-José	Pérec	FRA	9.5.68	1	OG	Atlanta	29 Jul 96
48.26		Koch			1	GO	Dresden	27 Jul 84
48.27	Olga	Vladykina'	UKR	30.6.63	2	WCp	Canberra	6 Oct 85
48.45		Kratochvílová			1	NC	Praha	23 Jul 83
48.59	Tatána	Kocembová'	CZE	2.5.62	2	WCh	Helsinki	10 Aug 83
48.60 WR		Koch			1	ECp	Torino	4 Aug 79
48.60		Vladykina			1	ECp	Moskva	17 Aug 85
48.61		Kratochvílová			1	WCp	Roma	6 Sep 81
48.63	Cathy	Freeman	AUS	16.2.73	2	OG	Atlanta	29 Jul 96
48.65		Bryzgina'			1	OG	Seoul	26 Sep 88
48.70	Sanya	Richards	USA	26.2.85	1	WCp	Athína	16 Sep 06
48.73		Kocembová			2	Drz	Praha	16 Aug 84
48.77		Koch			1	v USA	Karl-Marx-Stadt	9 Jul 82
48.82		Kratochvílová			1	Ros	Praha	23 Jun 83
48.83	Valerie	Brisco	USA	6.7.60	1	OG	Los Angeles	6 Aug 84
48.83		Pérec			1	OG	Barcelona	5 Aug 92
48.83		Richards			1	VD	Bruxelles	4 Sep 09
48.85		Kratochvílová			2	EC	Athína	8 Sep 82
48.86		Kratochvílová			1	WK	Zürich	18 Aug 82
48.86		Koch			1	NC	Erfurt	2 Jun 84
48.87		Koch			1	VD	Bruxelles	27 Aug 82
48.88		Koch			1	OG	Moskva	28 Jul 80
48.89 WR		Koch			1		Potsdam	29 Jul 79
48.89		Koch			1		Berlin	15 Jul 84
48.89	Ana Gabriela	Guevara	MEX	4.3.77	1	WCh	Saint-Denis	27 Aug 03
	(30/9)							
49.05	Chandra (10)	Cheeseborough	USA	10.1.59	2	OG	Los Angeles	6 Aug 84
49.07	Tonique	Williams-Darling	BAH	17.1.76	1	ISTAF	Berlin	12 Sep 04
49.10	Falilat	Ogunkoya	NGR	12.5.68	3	OG	Atlanta	29 Jul 96
49.11	Olga	Nazarova ¶	RUS	1.6.65	1s1	OG	Seoul	25 Sep 88
49.16	Antonina	Krivoshapka	RUS	21.7.87	1	NC	Cheboksary	5 Jul 12
49.19	Mariya	Pinigina'	UKR	9.2.58	3	WCh	Helsinki	10 Aug 83
49.24	Sabine	Busch	GDR	21.11.62	2	NC	Erfurt	2 Jun 84
49.28 WR	Irena	Szewinska'	POL	24.5.46	1	OG	Montreal	29 Jul 76
49.28	Pauline	Davis-Thompson	BAH	9.7.66	4	OG	Atlanta	29 Jul 96
49.28	Yuliya	Gushchina	RUS	4.3.83	2	NC	Cheboksary	5 Jul 12
49.29	Charity	Opara ¶	NGR	20.5.72	1	GGala	Roma	14 Jul 98
	(20)							
49.30	Petra	Müller'	GDR	18.7.65	1		Jena	3 Jun 88
49.30	Lorraine	Fenton'	JAM	8.9.73	2	Herc	Monaco	19 Jul 02
49.32	Shericka	Williams	JAM	17.9.85	2	WCh	Berlin	18 Aug 09
49.35	Anastasiya	Kapachinskaya ¶	RUS	21.11.79	1	NC	Cheboksary	22 Jul 11

Mark	Wind	Name		Nat	Born	Pos	Meet	Venue	Date
49.40		Jearl	Miles-Clark	USA	4.9.66	1	NC	Indianapolis	14 Jun 97
49.42		Grit	Breuer ¶	GER	16.2.72	2	WCh	Tokyo	27 Aug 91
49.43		Kathy	Cook'	GBR	3.5.60	3	OG	Los Angeles	6 Aug 84
49.43A		Fatima	Yusuf	NGR	2.5.71	1	AfG	Harare	15 Sep 95
49.47		Aelita	Yurchenko	UKR	1.1.65	2	Kuts	Moskva	4 Sep 88
49.49		Olga	Zaytseva	RUS	10.11.84	1	NCp	Tula	16 Jul 06
		(30)							
49.53		Vanya	Stambolova ¶	BUL	28.11.83	1	GP	Rieti	27 Aug 06
49.54		Amantle	Montsho	BOT	4.7.83	1	AfrC	Porto Novo	28 Jun 12
49.56		Bärbel	Wöckel'	GDR	21.3.55	1		Erfurt	30 May 82
49.56		Monique	Hennagan	USA	26.5.76	1	NC/OT	Sacramento	17 Jul 04
49.57		Grace	Jackson	JAM	14.6.61	1	Nik	Nice	10 Jul 88
49.58		Dagmar	Rübsam'	GDR	3.6.62	3	NC	Erfurt	2 Jun 84
49.59		Marion	Jones ¶	USA	12.10.75	1r6	MSR	Walnut	16 Apr 00
49.59		Katharine	Merry	GBR	21.9.74	1	GP	Athína	11 Jun 01
49.59		Allyson	Felix	USA	18.11.85	2	WCh	Daegu	29 Aug 11
49.61		Ana Fidelia	Quirot	CUB	23.3.63	1	PAm	La Habana	5 Aug 91
		(40)							
49.61		Christine	Ohuruogu ¶	GBR	17.5.84	1	WCh	Osaka	29 Aug 07
49.63		Novlene	Williams-Mills	JAM	26.4.82	1		Shanghai	23 Sep 06
49.64		Gwen	Torrence	USA	12.6.65	2	Nik	Nice	15 Jul 92
49.64		Ximena	Restrepo	COL	10.3.69	3	OG	Barcelona	5 Aug 92
49.64		Deedee	Trotter	USA	8.12.82	1	NC	Indianapolis	23 Jun 07
49.64		Debbie	Dunn	USA	26.3.78	1	NC	Des Moines	26 Jun 10
49.65		Natalya	Nazarova	RUS	26.5.79	1	NC	Tula	31 Jul 04
49.65		Nicola	Sanders	GBR	23.6.82	2	WCh	Osaka	29 Aug 07
49.66		Christina	Brehmer/Lathan	GDR	28.2.58	3	OG	Moskva	28 Jul 80
49.66		Lillie	Leatherwood	USA	6.7.64	1	NC	New York	15 Jun 91
		(50)	100th woman 50.25, 200th 50.87, 300th 51.20, 400th 51.45, 500th 51.68						

Hand timing

Mark	Wind	Name		Nat	Born	Pos	Meet	Venue	Date
48.9		Olga	Nazarova ¶	RUS	1.6.65	1	NP	Vladivostok	13 Sep 88
49.2A		Ana Fidelia	Quirot	CUB	23.3.63	1	AmCp	Bogotá	13 Aug 89

600 METRES

Mark	Wind	Name		Nat	Born	Pos	Meet	Venue	Date
1:22.63		Ana Fidelia	Quirot	CUB	23.3.63	1		Guadalajara, ESP	25 Jul 97
1:22.87		Maria Lurdes	Mutola	MOZ	27.10.72	1		Liège (NX)	27 Aug 02
1:23.35		Pamela	Jelimo	KEN	5.12.89	1		Liège (NX)	5 Jul 12

800 METRES

Mark	Wind	Name		Nat	Born	Pos	Meet	Venue	Date
1:53.28 WR		Jarmila	Kratochvílová	CZE	26.1.51	1		München	26 Jul 83
1:53.43 WR		Nadezhda	Olizarenko'	UKR	28.11.53	1	OG	Moskva	27 Jul 80
1:54.01		Pamela	Jelimo	KEN	5.12.89	1	WK	Zürich	29 Aug 08
1:54.44		Ana Fidelia	Quirot	CUB	23.3.63	1	WCp	Barcelona	9 Sep 89
1:54.68			Kratochvílová			1	WCh	Helsinki	9 Aug 83
1:54.81		Olga	Mineyeva	RUS	1.9.52	2	OG	Moskva	27 Jul 80
1:54.82			Quirot			1	ASV	Köln	24 Aug 97
1:54.85 WR			Olizarenko			1	Prav	Moskva	12 Jun 80
1:54.87			Jelimo			1	OG	Beijing	18 Aug 08
1:54.94 WR		Tatyana	Kazankina ¶	RUS	17.12.51	1	OG	Montreal	26 Jul 76
1:54.97			Jelimo			1	Gaz	Saint-Denis	18 Jul 08
1:54.99			Jelimo			1	ISTAF	Berlin	1 Jun 08
1:55.04			Kratochvílová			1	OsloG	Oslo	23 Aug 83
1:55.05		Doina	Melinte	ROU	27.12.56	1	NC	Bucuresti	1 Aug 82
1:55.1 '			Mineyeva			1	Znam	Moskva	6 Jul 80
1:55.16			Jelimo			1	VD	Bruxelles	5 Sep 08
1:55.19		Maria Lurdes	Mutola	MOZ	27.10.72	1	WK	Zürich	17 Aug 94
1:55.19		Jolanda	Ceplak ¶	SLO	12.9.76	1rA	NA	Heusden	20 Jul 02
1:55.26		Sigrun	Wodars/Grau (10)	GDR	7.11.65	1	WCh	Roma	31 Aug 87
1:55.29			Mutola			2	ASV	Köln	24 Aug 97
1:55.32		Christine	Wachtel	GDR	6.1.65	2	WCh	Roma	31 Aug 87
1:55.41			Mineyeva			1	EC	Athína	8 Sep 82
1:55.41			Jelimo			1	Bisl	Oslo	6 Jun 08
1:55.42		Nikolina	Shtereva	BUL	25.1.55	2	OG	Montreal	26 Jul 76
1:55.43			Mutola			1	WCh	Stuttgart	17 Aug 93
1:55.45		Caster	Semenya	RSA	7.1.91	1	WCh	Berlin	19 Aug 09
1:55.46		Tatyana	Providokhina	RUS	26.3.53	3	OG	Moskva	27 Jul 80
1:55.5			Mineyeva			1	Kuts	Podolsk	21 Aug 82
1:55.54		Ellen	van Langen	NED	9.2.66	1	OG	Barcelona	3 Aug 92
1:55.54			Liu Dong	CHN	24.12.73	1	NG	Beijing	9 Sep 93
		(30/16)							

Mark	Wind	Name		Nat	Born	Pos	Meet	Venue	Date
1:55.56		Lyubov	Gurina	RUS	6.8.57	3	WCh	Roma	31 Aug 87
1:55.60		Elfi	Zinn	GDR	24.8.53	3	OG	Montreal	26 Jul 76
1:55.68		Ella	Kovacs	ROU	11.12.64	1	RomIC	Bucuresti	2 Jun 85
1:55.69		Irina	Podyalovskaya	RUS	19.10.59	1	Izv	Kyiv	22 Jun 84
		(20)							
1:55.74		Anita	Weiss'	GDR	16.7.55	4	OG	Montreal	26 Jul 76
1:55.87		Svetlana	Masterkova	RUS	17.1.68	1	Kuts	Moskva	18 Jun 99
1:55.87		Mariya	Savinova	RUS	13.8.85	1	WCh	Daegu	4 Sep 11
1:55.96		Lyudmila	Veselkova	RUS	25.10.50	2	EC	Athína	8 Sep 82
1:55.96		Yekaterina	Podkopayeva'	RUS	11.6.52	1		Leningrad	27 Jul 83
1:55.99		Liliya	Nurutdinova ¶	RUS	15.12.63	2	OG	Barcelona	3 Aug 92
1:56.00		Tatyana	Andrianova	RUS	10.12.79	1	NC	Kazan	18 Jul 08
1:56.0	WR	Valentina	Gerasimova	KAZ	15.5.48	1	NC	Kyiv	12 Jun 76
1:56.0		Inna	Yevseyeva	UKR	14.8.64	1		Kyiv	25 Jun 88
1:56.04		Janeth	Jepkosgei	KEN	13.12.83	1	WCh	Osaka	28 Aug 07
		(30)							
1:56.09		Zulia	Calatayud	CUB	9.11.79	1	Herc	Monaco	19 Jul 02
1:56.1		Ravilya	Agletdinova'	BLR	10.2.60	2	Kuts	Podolsk	21 Aug 82
1:56.2 '		Totka	Petrova ¶	BUL	17.12.56	1		Paris	6 Jul 79
1:56.2		Tatyana	Mishkel	UKR	10.6.52	3	Kuts	Podolsk	21 Aug 82
1:56.21		Martina	Kämpfert'	GDR	11.11.59	4	OG	Moskva	27 Jul 80
1:56.21		Zamira	Zaytseva	UZB	16.2.53	2		Leningrad	27 Jul 83
1:56.21		Kelly	Holmes	GBR	19.4.70	2	GPF	Monaco	9 Sep 95
1:56.24			Qu Yunxia	CHN	8.12.72	2	NG	Beijing	9 Sep 93
1:56.40		Jearl	Miles-Clark	USA	4.9.66	3	WK	Zürich	11 Aug 99
1:56.42		Paula	Ivan	ROU	20.7.63	1	Balk	Ankara	16 Jul 88
		(40)							
1:56.43		Hasna	Benhassi	MAR	1.6.78	2	OG	Athína	23 Aug 04
1:56.44		Svetlana	Styrkina	RUS	1.1.49	5	OG	Montreal	26 Jul 76
1:56.51		Slobodanka	Colovic	YUG	10.1.65	1		Beograd	17 Jun 87
1:56.53		Patricia	Djaté	FRA	3.1.71	3	GPF	Monaco	9 Sep 95
1:56.56		Ludmila	Formanová	CZE	2.1.74	4	WK	Zürich	11 Aug 99
1:56.57		Zoya	Rigel	RUS	15.10.52	3	EC	Praha	31 Aug 78
1:56.59		Natalya	Khrushchelyova	RUS	30.5.73	2	NC	Tula	31 Jul 04
1:56.59		Francine	Niyonsaba	BDI	5.5.93	1	VD	Bruxelles	7 Sep 12
1:56.60		Natalya	Tsyganova	RUS	7.2.71	1	NC	Tula	25 Jul 00
1:56.6		Tamara	Sorokina'	RUS	15.8.50	5	Kuts	Podolsk	21 Aug 82
		(50)							

100th woman 1:57.5, 200th 1:58.61, 300th 1:59.38, 400th 1:59.86, 500th 2:00.45

Mark	Wind	Name		Nat	Born	Pos	Meet	Venue	Date
Indoors: 1:55.85		Stephanie	Graf	AUT	26.4.73	2	EI	Wien	3 Mar 02

Drugs disqualification

Mark	Wind	Name		Nat	Born	Pos	Meet	Venue	Date
1:54.85		Yelena	Soboleva ¶	RUS	3.10.82	(1)	NC	Kazan	18 Jul 08

1000 METRES

Mark	Wind	Name		Nat	Born	Pos	Meet	Venue	Date
2:28.98	WR	Svetlana	Masterkova	RUS	17.1.68	1	VD	Bruxelles	23 Aug 96
2:29.34	WR	Maria Lurdes	Mutola	MOZ	27.10.72	1	VD	Bruxelles	25 Aug 95
2:30.6	WR	Tatyana	Providokhina	RUS	26.3.53	1		Podolsk	20 Aug 78
2:30.67	WR	Christine	Wachtel	GDR	6.1.65	1	ISTAF	Berlin	17 Aug 90
2:30.85		Martina	Kämpfert'	GDR	11.11.59	1		Berlin	9 Jul 80
2:31.50		Natalya	Artyomova ¶	RUS	5.1.63	1	ISTAF	Berlin	10 Sep 91
2:31.5		Maricica	Puica	ROU	29.7.50	1		Poiana Brasov	1 Jun 86
2:31.51		Sandra	Gasser ¶	SUI	27.7.62	1		Jerez de la Frontera	13 Sep 89

1500 METRES

Mark	Wind	Name		Nat	Born	Pos	Meet	Venue	Date
3:50.46	WR		Qu Yunxia	CHN	8.12.72	1	NG	Beijing	11 Sep 93
3:50.98			Jiang Bo	CHN	13.3.77	1	NG	Shanghai	18 Oct 97
3:51.34			Lang Yinglai	CHN	22.8.79	2	NG	Shanghai	18 Oct 97
3:51.92			Wang Junxia	CHN	9.1.73	2	NG	Beijing	11 Sep 93
3:52.47	WR	Tatyana	Kazankina ¶	RUS	17.12.51	1	WK	Zürich	13 Aug 80
3:53.91			Yin Lili ¶	CHN	11.11.79	3	NG	Shanghai	18 Oct 97
3:53.96		Paula	Ivan'	ROU	20.7.63	1	OG	Seoul	1 Oct 88
3:53.97			Lan Lixin	CHN	14.2.79	4	NG	Shanghai	18 Oct 97
3:54.23		Olga	Dvirna	RUS	11.2.53	1	NC	Kyiv	27 Jul 82
3:54.52			Zhang Ling (10)	CHN	13.4.80	5	NG	Shanghai	18 Oct 97
3:55.0 '	WR		Kazankina ¶			1	Znam	Moskva	6 Jul 80
3:55.01			Lan Lixin			1h2	NG	Shanghai	17 Oct 97
3:55.07			Dong Yanmei	CHN	16.2.77	6	NG	Shanghai	18 Oct 97
3:55.30		Hassiba	Boulmerka	ALG	10.7.68	1	OG	Barcelona	8 Aug 92
3:55.33		Süreyya	Ayhan ¶	TUR	6.9.78	1	VD	Bruxelles	5 Sep 03
3:55.38			Qu Yunxia			2h2	NG	Shanghai	17 Oct 97
3:55.47			Zhang Ling			3h2	NG	Shanghai	17 Oct 97
3:55.60			Ayhan			1	WK	Zürich	15 Aug 03

Mark Wind		Name	Nat	Born	Pos	Meet	Venue	Date
3:55.68	Yuliya	Chizhenko ¶	RUS	30.8.79	1	Gaz	Saint-Denis	8 Jul 06
3:55.82		Dong Yanmei			4h2	NG	Shanghai	17 Oct 97
3:56.0 WR		Kazankina ¶			1		Podolsk	28 Jun 76
3:56.14	Zamira	Zaytseva	UZB	16.2.53	2	NC	Kyiv	27 Jul 82
3:56.18	Maryam	Jamal	BRN	16.9.84	1	GP	Rieti	27 Aug 06
3:56.22		Ivan			1	WK	Zürich	17 Aug 88
3:56.31		Liu Dong	CHN	24.12.73	5h2	NG	Shanghai	17 Oct 97
3:56.43	Yelena	Soboleva ¶	RUS	3.10.82	2	Gaz	Saint-Denis	8 Jul 06
3:56.50	Tatyana	Pozdnyakova	RUS	4.3.56	3	NC	Kyiv	27 Jul 82
3:56.54	Abeba	Aregawi	ETH	5.7.90	1	GGala	Roma	31 May 12
3:56.55		Jamal			1	GGala	Roma	10 Jul 09
3:56.56		Kazankina ¶			1	OG	Moskva	1 Aug 80
	(30/20)							
3:56.62	Asli	Çakir Alptekin	TUR	20.8.85	1	DL	Saint-Denis	6 Jul 12
3:56.63	Nadezhda	Ralldugina	UKR	15.11.57	1	Drz	Praha	18 Aug 84
3:56.65	Yekaterina	Podkopayeva’	RUS	11.6.52	1		Rieti	2 Sep 84
3:56.7 ‘	Lyubov	Smolka	UKR	29.11.52	2	Znam	Moskva	6 Jul 80
3:56.7	Doina	Melinte	ROU	27.12.56	1		Bucuresti	12 Jul 86
3:56.77+	Svetlana	Masterkova	RUS	17.1.68	1	WK	Zürich	14 Aug 96
3:56.8 ‘	Nadezhda	Olizarenko’	UKR	28.11.53	3	Znam	Moskva	6 Jul 80
3:56.91	Lyudmila	Rogachova	RUS	30.10.66	2	OG	Barcelona	8 Aug 92
3:56.91	Tatyana	Tomashova ¶	RUS	1.7.75	1	EC	Göteborg	13 Aug 06
3:56.97	Gabriela	Szabo	ROU	14.11.75	1	Herc	Monaco	8 Aug 98
	(30)							
3:57.03		Liu Jing	CHN	3.2.71	6h2	NG	Shanghai	17 Oct 97
3:57.05	Svetlana	Guskova	MDA	19.8.59	4	NC	Kyiv	27 Jul 82
3:57.12	Mary	Decker/Slaney	USA	4.8.58	1	vNord	Stockholm	26 Jul 83
3:57.22	Maricica	Puica	ROU	29.7.50	1		Bucuresti	1 Jul 84
3:57.40	Suzy	Favor Hamilton	USA	8.8.68	1	Bisl	Oslo	28 Jul 00
3:57.4 ‘	Totka	Petrova ¶	BUL	17.12.56	1	Balk	Athína	11 Aug 79
3:57.41	Jackline	Maranga	KEN	16.12.77	3	Herc	Monaco	8 Aug 98
3:57.46		Zhang Linli	CHN	6.3.73	3	NG	Beijing	11 Sep 93
3:57.65	Anna	Alminova #	RUS	17.1.85	1	DL	Saint-Denis	16 Jul 10
3:57.71	Christiane	Wartenberg’	GDR	27.10.56	2	OG	Moskva	1 Aug 80
	(40)							
3:57.71	Carla	Sacramento	POR	10.12.71	4	Herc	Monaco	8 Aug 98
3:57.72	Galina	Zakharova	RUS	7.9.56	1	NP	Baku	14 Sep 84
3:57.73	Natalya	Yevdokimova	RUS	17.3.78	2	GP	Rieti	28 Aug 05
3:57.77	Genzebe	Dibaba	ETH	8.2.91	1	DL	Shanghai	19 May 12
3:57.90	Kelly	Holmes	GBR	19.4.70	1	OG	Athína	28 Aug 04
3:57.92	Tatyana	Samolenko/Dorovskikh	UKR	12.8.61	4	OG	Barcelona	8 Aug 92
3:58.12	Naomi	Mugo	KEN	2.1.77	5	Herc	Monaco	8 Aug 98
3:58.20	Anita	Weyermann	SUI	8.12.77	6	Herc	Monaco	8 Aug 98
3:58.2 ‘	Natalia	Marasescu’ ¶	ROU	3.10.52	1	NC	Bucuresti	13 Jul 79
3:58.28	Elvan	Abeylegesse	TUR	11.9.82	1	ECCp-A	Moskva	30 May 04
	(50)	100th woman 3:59.95, 200th 4:02.44, 300th 4:04.82, 400th 4:05.97, 500th 4:06.97						

Drugs disqualification: 3:56.15 Mariem Alaoui Selsouli ¶ MAR 8.4.84 1   DL   Saint-Denis   6 Jul 12

1 MILE

Mark Wind		Name	Nat	Born	Pos	Meet	Venue	Date
4:12.56 WR	Svetlana	Masterkova	RUS	17.1.68	1	WK	Zürich	14 Aug 96
4:15.61 WR	Paula	Ivan’	ROU	20.7.63	1	Nik	Nice	10 Jul 89
4:15.8	Natalya	Artyomova ¶	RUS	5.1.63	1		Leningrad	5 Aug 84
4:16.71 WR	Mary	Slaney (Decker)	USA	4.8.58	1	WK	Zürich	21 Aug 85
4:17.25	Sonia	O’Sullivan	IRL	28.11.69	1	Bisl	Oslo	22 Jul 94
4:17.33	Maricica	Puica	ROU	29.7.50	2	WK	Zürich	21 Aug 85
4:17.57	Zola	Budd’	GBR	26.5.66	3	WK	Zürich	21 Aug 85
4:17.14 indoor	Doina	Melinte	ROU	27.12.56	1		East Rutherford	9 Feb 90

Drugs dq: 4:15.63   Yelena   Soboleva ¶   RUS   3.10.82 1   Moskva   29 Jun 07

2000 METRES

Mark Wind		Name	Nat	Born	Pos	Meet	Venue	Date
5:25.36 WR	Sonia	O’Sullivan	IRL	28.11.69	1	TSB	Edinburgh	8 Jul 94
5:26.93	Yvonne	Murray	GBR	4.10.64	2	TSB	Edinburgh	8 Jul 94
5:28.69 WR	Maricica	Puica	ROU	29.7.50	1	PTG	London (CP)	11 Jul 86
5:28.72 WR	Tatyana	Kazankina ¶	RUS	17.12.51	1		Moskva	4 Aug 84
5:29.43+		Wang Junxia	CHN	9.1.73	1h2	NG	Beijing	12 Sep 93
5:29.64	Tatyana	Pozdnyakova	UKR	4.3.56	2		Moskva	4 Aug 84
5:30.19	Zola	Budd’	GBR	26.5.66	3	PTG	London (CP)	11 Jul 86
5:30.19	Gelete	Burka	ETH	15.2.86	1	VD	Bruxelles	4 Sep 09
5:30.92	Galina	Zakharova	RUS	7.9.56	3		Moskva	4 Aug 84
5:31.03	Gulnara	Samitova/Galkina	RUS	9.7.78	1		Sochi	27 May 07

Indoors: 5:30.53 Gabriela   Szabo   ROU   14.11.75 1   Sindelfingen   8 Mar 98

Mark	Wind	Name		Nat	Born	Pos	Meet	Venue	Date

3000 METRES

Mark	Wind	Name		Nat	Born	Pos	Meet	Venue	Date
8:06.11 WR			Wang Junxia	CHN	9.1.73	1	NG	Beijing	13 Sep 93
8:12.18			Qu Yunxia	CHN	8.12.72	2	NG	Beijing	13 Sep 93
8:12.19 WR			Wang Junxia			1h2	NG	Beijing	12 Sep 93
8:12.27			Qu Yunxia			2h2	NG	Beijing	12 Sep 93
8:16.50			Zhang Linli	CHN	6.3.73	3	NG	Beijing	13 Sep 93
8:19.78			Ma Liyan	CHN	6.9.68	3h2	NG	Beijing	12 Sep 93
8:21.26			Ma Liyan			4	NG	Beijing	13 Sep 93
8:21.42		Gabriela	Szabo	ROU	14.11.75	1	Herc	Monaco	19 Jul 02
8:21.64		Sonia	O'Sullivan	IRL	28.11.69	1	TSB	London (CP)	15 Jul 94
8:21.84			Zhang Lirong	CHN	3.3.73	5	NG	Beijing	13 Sep 93
8:22.06 WR			Zhang Linli			1h1	NG	Beijing	12 Sep 93
8:22.20		Paula	Radcliffe	GBR	17.12.73	2	Herc	Monaco	19 Jul 02
8:22.44			Zhang Lirong			2h1	NG	Beijing	12 Sep 93
8:22.62 WR		Tatyana	Kazankina ¶	RUS	17.12.51	1		Leningrad	26 Aug 84
8:23.23		Edith	Masai (10)	KEN	4.4.67	3	Herc	Monaco	19 Jul 02
8:23.26		Olga	Yegorova	RUS	28.3.72	1	WK	Zürich	17 Aug 01
8:23.75			Yegorova			1	GP	Saint-Denis	6 Jul 01
8:23.96			Yegorova			1	GGala	Roma	29 Jun 01
8:24.19			Szabo			2	WK	Zürich	17 Aug 01
8:24.31			Szabo			1	GP	Paris	29 Jul 98
8:24.51+		Meseret	Defar	ETH	19.11.83	1	in 2M	Bruxelles	14 Sep 07
8:24.66			Defar			1	DNG	Stockholm	25 Jul 06
8:25.03			Szabo			1	WK	Zürich	11 Aug 99
8:25.40		Yelena	Zadorozhnaya	RUS	3.12.77	2	GGala	Roma	29 Jun 01
8:25.56		Tatyana	Tomashova ¶	RUS	1.7.75	3	GGala	Roma	29 Jun 01
8:25.59			Szabo			1	GP	Paris (C)	21 Jul 99
8:25.62		Berhane	Adere	ETH	21.7.73	3	WK	Zürich	17 Aug 01
8:25.82			Szabo			1	VD	Bruxelles	3 Sep 99
8:25.83		Mary	Slaney	USA	4.8.58	1	GGala	Roma	7 Sep 85
8:25.92		Gelete	Burka	ETH	15.2.86	2	DNG	Stockholm	25 Jul 06
		(30/17)							
8:26.48		Zahra	Ouaziz	MAR	20.12.69	2	WK	Zürich	11 Aug 99
8:26.53		Tatyana	Samolenko' ¶	UKR	12.8.61	1	OG	Seoul	25 Sep 88
8:26.78 WR		Svetlana	Ulmasova	UZB	4.2.53	1	NC	Kyiv	25 Jul 82
		(20)							
8:27.12 WR		Lyudmila	Bragina	RUS	24.7.43	1	v USA	College Park	7 Aug 76
8:27.15		Paula	Ivan'	ROU	20.7.63	2	OG	Seoul	25 Sep 88
8:27.62		Getenesh	Wami	ETH	11.12.74	4	WK	Zürich	17 Aug 01
8:27.83		Maricica	Puica	ROU	29.7.50	2	GGala	Roma	7 Sep 85
8:28.41		Sentayehu	Ejigu	ETH	21.6.85	1	Herc	Monaco	22 Jul 10
8:28.66		Vivian	Cheruiyot	KEN	11.9.83	2	WAF	Stuttgart	23 Sep 07
8:28.80		Marta	Domínguez	ESP	3.11.75	3	WK	Zürich	11 Aug 00
8:28.83		Zola	Budd'	GBR	26.5.66	3	GGala	Roma	7 Sep 85
8:28.87		Maryam	Jamal	BRN	16.9.84	1	Bisl	Oslo	29 Jul 05
8:29.02		Yvonne	Murray	GBR	4.10.64	3	OG	Seoul	25 Sep 88
		(30)							
8:29.06		Priscah	Cherono	KEN	27.6.80	3	WAF	Stuttgart	23 Sep 07
8:29.14		Lydia	Cheromei	KEN	11.5.77	5	WK	Zürich	11 Aug 00
8:29.36		Svetlana	Guskova	MDA	19.8.59	2	NC	Kyiv	25 Jul 82
8:29.52		Mariem Alaoui	Selsouli ¶	MAR	8.4.84	1	Herc	Monaco	25 Jul 07
8:29.55		Tirunesh	Dibaba	ETH	1.10.85	1	LGP	London (CP)	28 Jul 06
8:30.18		Mariya	Pantyukhova	RUS	14.8.74	4	WK	Zürich	11 Aug 99
8:30.22		Carla	Sacramento	POR	10.12.71	2	Herc	Monaco	4 Aug 99
8:30.39		Irina	Mikitenko	GER	23.8.72	6	WK	Zürich	11 Aug 00
8:30.45		Yelena	Romanova	RUS	20.3.63	4	OG	Seoul	25 Sep 88
8:30.59		Daniela	Yordanova ¶	BUL	8.3.76	5	GP	Saint-Denis	6 Jul 01
		(40)							
8:30.66		Fernanda	Ribeiro	POR	23.6.69	3	Herc	Monaco	4 Aug 99
8:30.93		Wude	Ayalew	ETH	4.7.87	3	WAF	Thessaloníki	13 Sep 09
8:30.95		Tegla	Loroupe	KEN	9.5.73	2	Herc	Monaco	18 Aug 00
8:31.27		Joanne	Pavey	GBR	20.9.73	4	VD	Bruxelles	30 Aug 02
8:31.32		Isabella	Ochichi	KEN	28.10.79	1	Gaz	Saint-Denis	23 Jul 04
8:31.38		Shannon	Rowbury	USA	19.9.84	3	Herc	Monaco	22 Jul 10
8:31.67		Natalya	Artyomova ¶	RUS	5.1.63	5	OG	Seoul	25 Sep 88
8:31.69		Lidia	Chojecka	POL	25.1.77	5	VD	Bruxelles	30 Aug 02
8:31.75		Grete	Waitz'	NOR	1.10.53	1	OsloG	Oslo	17 Jul 79
8:31.94		Elvan	Abeylegesse	TUR	11.9.82	6	VD	Bruxelles	30 Aug 02
		(50)							

100th woman 8:37.30, 200th 8:43.95, 300th 8:48.16

Mark	Wind	Name		Nat	Born	Pos	Meet	Venue	Date
Indoors:									
8:23.72		Meseret	Defar	ETH	19.11.83	1	Spark	Stuttgart	3 Feb 07
8:23.74		Meselech	Melkamu	ETH	27.4.85	2	Spark	Stuttgart	3 Feb 07
8:25.27		Sentayehu	Ejigu	ETH	21.6.85	2	Spark	Stuttgart	6 Feb 10
8:27.86		Liliya	Shobukhova	RUS	13.11.77	1	NC	Moskva	17 Feb 06
8:28.49		Anna	Alminova	RUS	17.1.85	2	Spark	Stuttgart	7 Feb 09
8:29.00		Olesya	Syreva ¶	RUS	25.11.83	2	NC	Moskva	17 Feb 06

5000 METRES

Mark	Wind	Name		Nat	Born	Pos	Meet	Venue	Date
14:11.15 WR		Tirunesh	Dibaba	ETH	1.10.85	1	Bisl	Oslo	6 Jun 08
14:12.88		Meseret	Defar	ETH	19.11.83	1	DNG	Stockholm	22 Jul 08
14:16.63 WR			Defar			1	Bisl	Oslo	15 Jun 07
14:20.87		Vivian	Cheruiyot	KEN	11.9.83	1	DNG	Stockholm	29 Jul 11
14:22.51			Cheruiyot			2	Bisl	Oslo	15 Jun 07
14:23.46			T Dibaba			1	GP	Rieti	7 Sep 08
14:23.75		Liliya	Shobukhova	RUS	13.11.77	1	NC	Kazan	19 Jul 08
14:24.53 WR			Defar			1		New York (RI)	3 Jun 06
14:24.68 WR		Elvan	Abeylegesse	TUR	11.9.82	1	Bisl	Bergen (Fana)	11 Jun 04
14:25.43			Cheruiyot			1	VD	Bruxelles	5 Sep 08
14:25.52			Defar			2	VD	Bruxelles	5 Sep 08
14:27.41			Cheruiyot			1	DL	Saint-Denis	16 Jul 10
14:28.09 WR			Jiang Bo	CHN	13.3.77	1	NG	Shanghai	23 Oct 97
14:28.39		Sentayehu	Ejigu	ETH	21.6.85	2	DL	Saint-Denis	16 Jul 10
14:28.98			Defar			1	VD	Bruxelles	26 Aug 05
14:29.11		Paula	Radcliffe	GBR	17.12.73	1	ECpS	Bydgoszcz	20 Jun 04
14:29.32		Olga	Yegorova	RUS	28.3.72	1	ISTAF	Berlin	31 Aug 01
14:29.32		Berhane	Adere (10)	ETH	21.7.73	1	Bisl	Oslo	27 Jun 03
14:29.52			Defar			1	DL	Saint-Denis	8 Jul 11
14:29.82			Dong Yanmei	CHN	16.2.77	2	NG	Shanghai	23 Oct 97
14:30.10			Cheruiyot			1	WK	Zürich	8 Sep 11
14:30.18			Defar			1	GS	Ostrava	27 Jun 07
14:30.40			T Dibaba			1	Bisl	Oslo	2 Jun 06
14:30.42		Sally	Kipyego	KEN	19.12.85	2	WK	Zürich	8 Sep 11
14:30.63			T Dibaba			1	VD	Bruxelles	25 Aug 06
14:30.88		Getenesh	Wami	ETH	11.12.74	1	NA	Heusden-Zolder	5 Aug 00
14:30.88			T Dibaba			2	Bisl	Bergen (Fana)	11 Jun 04
14:30.96			Ejigu			1	DL	Shanghai	23 May 10
14:31.09			Adere			2	VD	Bruxelles	26 Aug 05
14:31.14		Linet	Masai	KEN	5.12.89	2	DL	Shanghai	23 May 10
		(30/14)							
14:31.20		Gelete	Burka	ETH	15.2.86	2	GS	Ostrava	27 Jun 07
14:31.48		Gabriela	Szabo	ROU	14.11.75	1	ISTAF	Berlin	1 Sep 98
14:31.91		Meselech	Melkamu	ETH	27.4.85	3	DL	Shanghai	23 May 10
14:31.91		Sylvia	Kibet	KEN	28.3.84	4	DL	Shanghai	23 May 10
14:32.08		Zahra	Ouaziz	MAR	20.12.69	2	ISTAF	Berlin	1 Sep 98
14:32.33			Liu Shixiang ¶	CHN	13.1.71	3h1	NG	Shanghai	21 Oct 97
		(20)							
14:32.74		Ejagayehu	Dibaba	ETH	25.6.82	3	Bisl	Bergen (Fana)	11 Jun 04
14:33.04		Werknesh	Kidane	ETH	21.11.81	2	Bisl	Oslo	27 Jun 03
14:33.13		Gulnara	Galkina	RUS	9.7.78	2	NC	Kazan	19 Jul 08
14:33.49		Lucy	Wangui Kabuu	KEN	24.3.84	2	Bisl	Oslo	6 Jun 08
14:33.84		Edith	Masai	KEN	4.4.67	3	Bisl	Oslo	2 Jun 06
14:34.86		Viola	Kibiwott	KEN	22.12.83	4	DL	Shanghai	15 May 11
14:35.13		Mercy	Cherono	KEN	7.5.91	3	DL	Saint-Denis	8 Jul 11
14:35.30		Priscah	Jepleting/Cherono	KEN	27.6.80	4	Bisl	Oslo	2 Jun 06
14:36.45 WR		Fernanda	Ribeiro	POR	23.6.69	1		Hechtel	22 Jul 95
14:36.52		Mariem Alaoui	Selsouli ¶	MAR	8.4.84	1	G Gala	Roma	13 Jul 07
		(30)							
14:37.07		Jéssica	Augusto	POR	8.11.81	5	DL	Saint-Denis	16 Jul 10
14:37.33 WR		Ingrid	Kristiansen'	NOR	21.3.56	1		Stockholm	5 Aug 86
14:37.56		Genzebe	Dibaba	ETH	8.2.91	3	Bisl	Oslo	9 Jun 11
14:38.09		Mariya	Konovalova	RUS	14.8.74	3	NC	Kazan	19 Jul 08
14:38.21		Isabella	Ochichi	KEN	28.10.79	4	VD	Bruxelles	26 Aug 05
14:38.44		Wude	Ayalew	ETH	4.7.87	5	Bisl	Oslo	3 Jul 09
14:39.19		Ines	Chenonge	KEN	1.2.82	6	DL	Saint-Denis	16 Jul 10
14:39.22		Tatyana	Tomashova ¶	RUS	1.7.75	4	ISTAF	Berlin	31 Aug 01
14:39.83		Leah	Malot	KEN	7.6.72	1	ISTAF	Berlin	1 Sep 00
14:39.96			Yin Lili ¶	CHN	11.11.79	4	NG	Shanghai	23 Oct 97
		(40)							
14:39.96		Jo	Pavey	GBR	20.9.73	3	VD	Bruxelles	25 Aug 06

Mark Wind	Name		Nat	Born	Pos	Meet	Venue	Date
14:40.14	Florence	Kiplagat	KEN	27.2.87	6	Bisl	Oslo	3 Jul 09
14:40.41		Sun Yingjie ¶	CHN	3.10.77	1	AsiG	Busan	12 Oct 02
14:40.47	Yelena	Zadorozhnaya	RUS	3.12.77	1	ECp-S	Bremen	24 Jun 01
14:41.02	Sonia	O'Sullivan	IRL	28.11.69	2	OG	Sydney	25 Sep 00
14:41.23	Ayelech	Worku	ETH	12.6.79	1	BrGP	London (CP)	5 Aug 00
14:41.28	Pauline	Korikwiang	KEN	1.3.88	7	DL	Shanghai	15 May 11
14:42.03	Irina	Mikitenko	GER	23.8.72	3	ISTAF	Berlin	7 Sep 99
14:42.53	Zhor	El Kamch	MAR	15.3.73	5	GGala	Roma	11 Jul 03
(50)		100th woman 14:53.06, 200th 15:06.04, 300th 15:14.08, 400th 15:19.47, 500th 15:25.13						
Indoors: 14:24.37		Defar			1		Stockholm	18 Feb 09
14:24.79		Defar			1	GE Galan	Stockholm	10 Feb 10
14:27.42		T Dibaba			1	BIG	Boston (R)	27 Jan 07
14:39.89	Kimberley	Smith	NZL	19.11.73	1		New York (Arm)	27 Feb 09
Drugs disqualification: 14:36.79	Alemitu	Bekele ¶	TUR	17.9.77	4	VD	Bruxelles	27 Aug 10

10,000 METRES

Mark Wind	Name		Nat	Born	Pos	Meet	Venue	Date
29:31.78 WR		Wang Junxia	CHN	9.1.73	1	NG	Beijing	8 Sep 93
29:53.80	Meselech	Melkamu	ETH	27.4.85	1		Utrecht	14 Jun 09
29:54.66	Tirunesh	Dibaba	ETH	1.10.85	1	OG	Beijing	15 Aug 08
29:56.34	Elvan	Abeylegesse	TUR	11.9.82	2	OG	Beijing	15 Aug 08
29:59.20	Meseret	Defar	ETH	19.11.83	1	NC	Birmingham	11 Jul 09
30:01.09	Paula	Radcliffe	GBR	17.12.73	1	EC	München	6 Aug 02
30:04.18	Berhane	Adere	ETH	21.7.73	1	WCh	Saint-Denis	23 Aug 03
30:07.15	Werknesh	Kidane	ETH	21.11.81	2	WCh	Saint-Denis	23 Aug 03
30:07.20		Sun Yingjie ¶	CHN	3.10.77	3	WCh	Saint-Denis	23 Aug 03
30:11.53	Florence	Kiplagat (10)	KEN	27.2.87	2		Utrecht	14 Jun 09
30:11.87	Wude	Ayalew	ETH	4.7.87	3		Utrecht	14 Jun 09
30:12.53	Lornah	Kiplagat (KEN)	NED	1.5.74	4	WCh	Saint-Denis	23 Aug 03
30:13.37		Zhong Huandi	CHN	28.6.67	2	NG	Beijing	8 Sep 93
30:13.74 WR	Ingrid	Kristiansen'	NOR	21.3.56	1	Bisl	Oslo	5 Jul 86
30:15.67		T Dibaba			1		Sollentuna	28 Jun 05
30:17.15		Radcliffe			1	GP	Gateshead	27 Jun 04
30:17.49	Derartu	Tulu	ETH	21.3.72	1	OG	Sydney	30 Sep 00
30:18.39	Ejegayehu	Dibaba	ETH	25.6.82	2		Sollentuna	28 Jun 05
30:19.39		Kidane			1	GP II	Stanford	29 May 05
30:20.75		T Dibaba			1	OG	London (OS)	3 Aug 12
30:21.67		Abeylegesse			1	ECp	Antalya	15 Apr 06
30:22.22	Shalane	Flanagan	USA	8.7.81	3	OG	Beijing	15 Aug 08
30:22.48	Getenesh	Wami	ETH	11.12.74	2	OG	Sydney	30 Sep 00
30:22.88	Fernanda	Ribeiro	POR	23.6.69	3	OG	Sydney	30 Sep 00
30:23.07	Alla	Zhilyayeva (20)	RUS	5.2.69	5	WCh	Saint-Denis	23 Aug 03
30:23.25		Kristiansen			1	EC	Stuttgart	30 Aug 86
30:24.02		T Dibaba			1	WCh	Helsinki	6 Aug 05
30:24.36		Xing Huina	CHN	25.2.84	1	OG	Athína	27 Aug 04
30:24.39		Dibaba			1	Pre	Eugene	1 Jun 12
30:24.56		Wami			1	WCh	Sevilla	26 Aug 99
	(30/21)							
30:26.20	Galina	Bogomolova	RUS	15.10.77	6	WCh	Saint-Denis	23 Aug 03
30:26.37	Sally	Kipyego	KEN	19.12.85	2	OG	London (OS)	3 Aug 12
30:26.50	Linet	Masai	KEN	5.12.89	4	OG	Beijing	15 Aug 08
30:26.70	Belaynesh	Oljira	ETH	26.6.90	3	Pre	Eugene	1 Jun 12
30:29.21mx	Philes	Ongori	KEN	19.7.86	1mx		Yokohama	23 Nov 08
30:29.36	Liliya	Shobukhova	RUS	13.11.77	1	NC	Cheboksary	23 Jul 09
30:30.26	Edith	Masai	KEN	4.4.67	5	WCh	Helsinki	6 Aug 05
30:30.44	Vivian	Cheruiyot	KEN	11.9.83	3	OG	London (OS)	3 Aug 12
30:31.03	Mariya	Konovalova	RUS	14.8.74	2	NC	Cheboksary	23 Jul 09
	(30)							
30:31.42	Inga	Abitova ¶	RUS	6.3.82	1	EC	Göteborg	7 Aug 06
30:32.03	Tegla	Loroupe	KEN	9.5.73	3	WCh	Sevilla	26 Aug 99
30:32.36	Susanne	Wigene	NOR	12.2.78	2	EC	Göteborg	7 Aug 06
30:32.72	Lidiya	Grigoryeva	RUS	21.1.74	3	EC	Göteborg	7 Aug 06
30:35.54	Kim	Smith	NZL	19.11.81	2		Stanford	4 May 08
30:37.68	Benita	Johnson	AUS	6.5.79	8	WCh	Saint-Denis	23 Aug 03
30:38.09		Dong Yanmei	CHN	16.2.77	1	NG	Shanghai	19 Oct 97
30:38.33	Mestawat	Tufa	ETH	14.9.83	1		Nijmegen	25 Jun 08
30:38.78	Jelena	Prokopcuka	LAT	21.9.76	6	EC	Göteborg	7 Aug 06
30:39.41		Lan Lixin	CHN	14.2.79	2	NG	Shanghai	19 Oct 97
	(40)							
30:39.96	Lucy	Wangui Kabuu	KEN	24.3.84	7	OG	Beijing	15 Aug 08
30:39.98		Yin Lili ¶	CHN	11.11.79	3	NG	Shanghai	19 Oct 97

Mark	Wind	Name		Nat	Born	Pos	Meet	Venue	Date
30:47.20		Sylvia	Kibet	KEN	28.3.84	4		Utrecht	14 Jun 09
30:47.22			Dong Zhaoxia	CHN	13.11.74	4	NG	Shanghai	19 Oct 97
30:47.25		Shitaye	Eshete	BRN	21.5.90	6	OG	London (OS)	3 Aug 12
30:47.59		Sonia	O'Sullivan	IRL	28.11.69	2	EC	München	6 Aug 02
30:47.72			Wang Dongmei	CHN	3.12.72	5	NG	Shanghai	19 Oct 97
30:48.26		Aberu	Kebede	ETH	12.9.89	5		Utrecht	14 Jun 09
30:48.89		Yoko	Shibui	JPN	14.3.79	1		Stanford	3 May 02
30:50.32		Deena	Drossin/Kastor	USA	14.2.73	2		Stanford	3 May 02
(50)			100th woman 31:13.21, 200th 31:34.37, 300th 31:51.44, 400th 32:02.89, 500th 32:16.50						

HALF MARATHON

Slightly downhill courses included: Newcastle-South Shields 30.5m, Tokyo 33m (to 1998), Lisboa (Spring to 2008) 69m

Mark	Wind	Name		Nat	Born	Pos	Meet	Venue	Date
65:40	dh	Paula	Radcliffe	GBR	17.12.73	1	GNR	South Shields	21 Sep 03
65:44	dh	Susan	Chepkemei	KEN	25.6.75	1		Lisboa	1 Apr 01
65:50	WR	Mary	Keitany	KEN	18.1.82	1		Ra's Al Khaymah	18 Feb 11
66:25		Lornah	Kiplagat	NED	1.5.74	1	WCh	Udine	14 Oct 07
66:34	dh		Kiplagat			2		Lisboa	1 Apr 01
66:36			Keitany			1	WCh	Birmingham	11 Oct 09
66:38		Florence	Kiplagat	KEN	27.2.87	1		Ostia	26 Feb 12
66:40*		Ingrid	Kristiansen	NOR	21.3.56	1	NC	Sandnes	5 Apr 87
66:43	dh	Masako	Chiba	JPN	18.7.76	1		Tokyo	19 Jan 97
66:44		Elana	Meyer	RSA	10.10.66	1		Tokyo	15 Jan 99
66:47			Radcliffe			1	WCh	Bristol	7 Oct 01
66:48			Keitany			2	WCh	Udine	14 Oct 07
66:49		Esther	Wanjiru	KEN	27.3.77	2		Tokyo	15 Jan 99
66:49			Keitany			1		Ra's Al-Khaymah	17 Feb 12
66:54			Keitany			1		New Delhi	1 Nov 09
66:56			L Kiplagat			1	City-Pier	Den Haag	25 Mar 00
66:57	dh	Kara	Goucher (10)	USA	9.7.78	1	GNR	South Shields	30 Sep 07
67:00			Keitany			1		Lille	5 Sep 09
67:03	dh	Derartu	Tulu	ETH	21.3.72	3		Lisboa	1 Apr 01
67:03		Joyce	Chepkirui	KEN	10.8.88	1		Praha	31 Mar 12
67:04		Lucy	Wangui Kabuu	KEN	24.3.84	1		New Delhi	27 Nov 11
67:06	dh		Wangui			1	GNR	South Shields	18 Sep 11
67:07	dh		Radcliffe			1	GNR	South Shields	22 Oct 00
67:07		Elvan	Abeylegesse	TUR	11.9.82	1		Ra's Al Khaymah	19 Feb 10
67:08	dh	Rita	Jeptoo	KEN	15.2.81	1		Lisboa	18 Mar 07
67:08		Sharon	Cherop	KEN	16.3.84	2		New Delhi	21 Nov 11
67:11	dh	Liz	McColgan	GBR	24.5.64	1		Tokyo	26 Jan 92
67:11		Kim	Smith	NZL	19.11.81	1		Philadelphia	18 Sep 11
67:12	dh	Tegla	Loroupe	KEN	9.5.73	1		Lisboa	10 Mar 96
67:13		Mare	Dibaba	ETH	20.10.89	2		Ra's Al Khaymah	19 Feb 10
(30/20)			* uncertain course measurement						
67:16		Edith	Masai	KEN	4.4.67	1		Berlin	2 Apr 06
67:17		Pasalia	Kipkoech	KEN	22.12.88	1		Rio de Janeiro	19 Aug 12
67:18		Dire	Tune	ETH	19.6.85	1		R'as Al Khaymah	20 Feb 09
67:19	dh	Sonia	O'Sullivan	IRL	28.11.69	1	GNR	South Shields	6 Oct 02
67:21		Aselefech	Mergia	ETH	23.1.85	3		New Delhi	21 Nov 11
67:22		Agnes	Kiprop	KEN	12.12.79	2		Ostia	26 Feb 12
67:23		Margaret	Okayo	KEN	30.5.76	1		Udine	28 Sep 03
67:26		Kayoko	Fukushi	JPN	25.3.82	1		Marugame	5 Feb 06
67:26		Lydia	Cheromei ¶	KEN	11.5.77	2		Praha	31 Mar 12
67:27		Belaynesh	Oljira	ETH	26.6.90	4		New Delhi	27 Nov 11
(30)									
67:28		Worknesh	Kidane	ETH	21.11.81	2		Philadelphia	18 Sep 11
67:32	dh	Berhane	Adere	ETH	21.7.73	2	GNR	South Shields	21 Sep 03
67:34		Deena	Kastor	USA	14.2.73	2		Berlin	2 Apr 06
67:35	dh	Tirunesh	Dibaba	ETH	1.6.85	1	GNR	South Shields	16 Sep 12
67:38		Philes	Ongori	KEN	19.7.86	2	WCh	Birmingham	11 Oct 09
67:39		Aberu	Kebede	ETH	12.9.89	3	WCh	Birmingham	11 Oct 09
67:41		Teyiba	Erkesso	ETH	30.10.82	4		Ra's Al Khaymah	19 Feb 10
67:41	dh	Edna	Kiplagat	KEN	15.9.79	2	GNR	South Shields	16 Sep 12
67:42		Tirfe	Tsegaye	ETH	25.11.84	3		Ostia	26 Feb 12
67:43		Mizuki	Noguchi	JPN	3.7.78	2		Marugame	5 Feb 06
(40)									
67:45		Meseret	Defar	ETH	19.11.83	1		Philadelphia	19 Sep 10
67:46		Valeria	Straneo	ITA	5.4.76	4		Ostia	26 Feb 12
67:47		Lineth	Chepkurui	KEN	23.2.88	2		Philadelphia	19 Sep 10
67:48		Kerryn	McCann	AUS	2.5.67	3		Tokyo	10 Jan 00
67:48		Peninah	Arusei	KEN	23.2.79	2		Lille	4 Sep 10

Mark	Wind	Name		Nat	Born	Pos	Meet	Venue	Date
67:48dh		Tiki	Gelana	ETH	22.10.87	3	GNR	South Shields	16 Sep 12
67:50	dh	Catherina	McKiernan	IRL	30.11.69	1		Lisboa	15 Mar 98
67:52	dh	Salina	Kosgei	KEN	16.11.76	1		Lisboa (dh 69m)	26 Mar 06
67:54		Catherine	Ndereba	KEN	21.7.72	1		Den Haag	24 Mar 01
67:55		Benita	Willis/Johnson	AUS	6.5.79	1	GNR	South Shields	26 Sep 04
		(50)							

100th woman 68:36, 200th 69:28, 300th 70:01, 400th 70:33, 500th 70:57

MARATHON

L = loop course or start and finish within 30%, P = point-to-point or start and finish more than 30% apart, D + point-to-point and downhil over 1/1000. 2nd column: M mixed marathon (men and women), W women only race

Mark	Wind	Name		Nat	Born	Pos	Meet	Venue	Date
2:15:25	LM	Paula	Radcliffe	GBR	17.12.73	1		London	13 Apr 03
2:17:18	LM		Radcliffe			1		Chicago	13 Oct 02
2:17:42	LW		Radcliffe			1		London	17 Apr 05
2:18:20	LM	Liliya	Shobukhova	RUS	13.11.77	1		Chicago	9 Oct 11
2:18:37	LW	Mary	Keitany	KEN	18.1.82	1		London	22 Apr 12
2:18:47	LM	Catherine	Ndereba	KEN	21.7.72	1		Chicago	7 Oct 01
2:18:56	LW		Radcliffe			1		London	14 Apr 02
2:18:58	LW	Tiki	Gelana	ETH	22.10.87	1		Rotterdam	15 Apr 12
2:19:12	LM	Mizuki	Noguchi	JPN	3.7.78	1		Berlin	25 Sep 05
2:19:19	LM	Irina	Mikitenko	GER	23.8.72	1		Berlin	28 Sep 08
2:19:19	LW		Keitany			1		London	17 Apr 11
2:19:26	LM		Ndereba			2		Chicago	13 Oct 02
2:19:31	LM	Aselefech	Mergia	ETH	23.1.85	1		Dubai	27 Jan 12
2:19:34	LM	Lucy	Wangui Kabuu	KEN	24.3.84	2		Dubai	27 Jan 12
2:19:36	LW	Deena	Kastor (10)	USA	14.2.73	1		London	23 Apr 06
2:19:39	LM		Sun Yingjie ¶	CHN	3.10.77	1		Beijing	19 Oct 03
2:19:41	LM	Yoko	Shibui	JPN	14.3.79	1		Berlin	26 Sep 04
2:19:44	LM	Florence	Kiplagat	KEN	27.2.87	1		Berlin	25 Sep 11
2:19:46	LM	Naoko	Takahashi	JPN	6.5.72	1		Berlin	30 Sep 01
2:19:50	LW	Edna	Kiplagat	KEN	15.9.79	2		London	22 Apr 12
2:19:51	PM		Zhou Chunxiu	CHN	15.11.78	1	Dong-A	Seoul	12 Mar 06
2:19:52	LM	Mare	Dibaba	ETH	20.10.89	3		Dubai	27 Jan 12
2:19:55	LM		Ndereba			2		London	13 Apr 03
2:20:14	LW	Priscah	Jeptoo	KEN	24.6.84	3		London	22 Apr 12
2:20:15	LW	Liliya	Shobukhova			2		London	17 Apr 11
2:20:25	LM		Shobukhova			1		Chicago	10 Oct 10
2:20:30	LM	Bezunesh	Bekele	ETH	18.9.83	4		Dubai	27 Jan 12
2:20:30	LM	Aberu	Kebede	ETH	12.9.89	1		Berlin	30 Sep 12
2:20:33	LM		Kebede			5		Dubai	27 Jan 12
2:20:38	LW		Zhou Chunxiu			1		London	22 Apr 07
		(30/20)							
2:20:42	LM	Berhane	Adere	ETH	21.7.73	1		Chicago	22 Oct 06
2:20:43	LM	Tegla	Loroupe	KEN	9.5.73	1		Berlin	26 Sep 99
2:20:47	LM	Galina	Bogomolova	RUS	15.10.77	2		Chicago	22 Oct 06
2:21:01		Meselech	Melkamu	ETH	27.4.85	1		Frankfurt	28 Oct 12
2:21:06	LM	Ingrid	Kristiansen	NOR	21.3.56	1		London	21 Apr 85
2:21:09		Meseret	Hailu	ETH	12.9.90	1		Amsterdam	21 Oct 12
2:21:19		Tirfe	Tsegaye	ETH	25.11.84	2		Berlin	30 Sep 12
2:21:21	LM	Joan	Benoit'	USA	16.5.57	1		Chicago	20 Oct 85
2:21:29	LW	Lyudmila	Petrova	RUS	7.10.68	2		London	23 Apr 06
2:21:30	LM	Constantina	Dita	ROU	23.1.70	2		Chicago	9 Oct 05
		(30)							
2:21:30		Lydia	Cheromei ¶	KEN	11.5.77	6		Dubai	27 Jan 12
2:21:31	LM	Svetlana	Zakharova	RUS	15.9.70	4		Chicago	13 Oct 02
2:21:31	LM	Askale	Tafa	ETH	27.9.84	2		Berlin	28 Sep 08
2:21:34	LM	Getenesh	Wami	ETH	11.12.74	1		Berlin	25 Sep 06
2:21:39		Georgina	Rono	KEN	19.5.84	2		Frankfurt	28 Oct 12
2:21:41		Eunice	Jepkirui	KEN	20.5.84	2		Amsterdam	21 Oct 12
2:21:45	LW	Masako	Chiba	JPN	18.7.76	2		Osaka	26 Jan 03
2:21:46	LW	Susan	Chepkemei ¶	KEN	25.6.75	3		London	23 Apr 06
2:21:51	LW	Naoko	Sakamoto	JPN	14.11.80	3		Osaka	26 Jan 03
2:21:59	LM	Mamitu	Daska	ETH	16.10.83	1		Frankfurt	30 Oct 11
		(40)							
2:22:03		Atsede	Baysa	ETH	16.4.87	1		Chicago	7 Oct 12
2:22:04		Rita	Jeptoo	KEN	15.2.81	2		Chicago	7 Oct 12
2:22:09	LM	Ejegayehu	Dibaba	ETH	25.6.82	2		Chicago	9 Oct 11
2:22:12	LW	Eri	Yamaguchi	JPN	14.1.73	1		Tokyo	21 Nov 99
2:22:22	LW	Lornah	Kiplagat	KEN/NED	1.5.74	4		Osaka	26 Jan 03
2:22:23	LM	Catherina	McKiernan	IRL	30.11.69	1		Amsterdam	1 Nov 98
2:22:35	LW	Margaret	Okayo	KEN	30.5.76	1		London	18 Apr 04

Mark	Wind	Name		Nat	Born	Pos	Meet	Venue	Date
2:22:36	LM	Benita	Willis/Johnson	AUS	6.5.79	3		Chicago	22 Oct 06
2:22:38	LM		Zhang Yingying	CHN	4.1.90	1	NC	Xiamen	5 Jan 08
2:22:39		Sharon	Cherop	KEN	16.3.84	7		Dubai	27 Jan 12
		(50)	100th woman 2:24:12, 200th 2:26:02, 300th 2:27:38, 400th 2:28:17, 500th 2:29:18						
Drugs dq: 2:20:23	LM	Wei Yanan ¶		CHN	6.12.81	1		Beijing	20 Oct 02
2:22:19	LW	Inga	Abitova ¶	RUS	6.3.82	2		London	25 Apr 10
Downhill point-to-point course – Boston marathon is downhill overall (139m) and sometimes strongly wind-aided.									
2:20:43	DM	Margaret	Okayo	KEN	30.5.76	1		Boston	15 Apr 02
2:21:45	DM	Uta	Pippig ¶	GER	7.9.65	1		Boston	18 Apr 94
2:22:36	DM	Caroline	Cheptonui Kilel	KEN	21.3.81	1		Boston	18 Apr 11
2:22:38	DM	Desiree	Davila	USA	26.7.83	2		Boston	18 Apr 11

2000 METRES STEEPLECHASE

Mark	Name		Nat	Born	Pos	Meet	Venue	Date
6:03.38	Wioletta	Janowska	POL	9.6.77	1		Gdansk	15 Jul 06
6:04.46	Dorcus	Inzikuru	UGA	2.2.82	1	GP II	Milano	1 Jun 05
6:11.63	Livia	Tóth	HUN	7.1.80	2		Gdansk	15 Jul 06
6:11.83	Korahubish	Itaa	KEN	28.2.92	1	WY	Bressanone	10 Jul 09
6:11.84	Marina	Pluzhnikova	RUS	25.2.63	1	GWG	Sankt-Peterburg	25 Jul 94

3000 METRES STEEPLECHASE

Mark		Name		Nat	Born	Pos	Meet	Venue	Date
8:58.81	WR	Gulnara	Samitova/Galkina	RUS	9.7.78	1	OG	Beijing	17 Aug 08
9:01.59	WR		Samitova/Galkina			1		Iráklio	4 Jul 04
9:05.02		Yuliya	Zaripova	RUS	26.4.86	1	DNG	Stockholm	17 Aug 12
9:06.57		Yekaterina	Volkova	RUS	16.2.78	1	WCh	Osaka	27 Aug 07
9:06.72			Zaripova			1	OG	London (OS)	6 Aug 12
9:07.03			Zaripova (Zarudneva)			1	WCh	Daegu	30 Aug 11
9:07.14		Milcah	Chemos Cheywa	KEN	24.2.86	1	Bisl	Oslo	7 Jun 12
9:07.32		Marta	Dominguez	ESP	3.11.75	1	WCh	Berlin	17 Aug 09
9:07.41		Eunice	Jepkorir	KEN	17.2.82	2	OG	Beijing	17 Aug 08
9:07.64			Volkova			3	OG	Beijing	17 Aug 08
9:08.21			Galkina			1	NC	Kazan	18 Jul 08
9:08.33	WR		Samitova			1	NC	Tula	10 Aug 03
9:08.37		Habiba	Ghribi	TUN	9.4.84	2	OG	London (OS)	6 Aug 12
9:08.39			Zarudneva			2	WCh	Berlin	17 Aug 09
9:08.57			Chemos			3	WCh	Berlin	17 Aug 09
9:09.00		Sofia	Assefa	ETH	14.11.87	2	Bisl	Oslo	7 Jun 12
9:09.19		Tatyana	Petrova	RUS	8.4.83	2	WCh	Osaka	27 Aug 07
9:09.39			Domínguez			1		Barcelona	25 Jul 09
9:09.61		Hiwot	Ayalew	ETH	6.3.90	3	Bisl	Oslo	7 Jun 12
9:09.84			Samitova			1		Réthimno	23 Jun 04
9:09.84			Assefa			3	OG	London (OS)	6 Aug 12
9:09.88			Chemos			4	OG	London (OS)	6 Aug 12
9:09.99			Zaripova			1	NC	Cheboksary	3 Jul 12
9:10.36			Ghribi			2	DNG	Stockholm	17 Aug 12
9:11.09			Galkina			4	WCh	Berlin	17 Aug 09
9:11.18			Jepkorir			1		Huelva	13 Jun 08
9:11.58			Galkina			1	GGala	Roma	10 Jul 09
9:11.68			Galkina			1	GP	Athína	2 Jul 07
9:11.71			Chemos			1	GGala	Roma	10 Jun 10
9:11.97			Ghribi			2	WCh	Daegu	30 Aug 11
		(30/10)							
9:12.50		Jennifer	Barringer/Simpson	USA	23.8.86	5	WCh	Berlin	17 Aug 09
9:13.16		Ruth	Bisibori	KEN	2.1.88	7	WCh	Berlin	17 Aug 09
9:13.22		Gladys	Kipkemboi	KEN	15.10.86	2	GGala	Roma	10 Jun 10
9:13.53		Gülcan	Mingir	TUR	21.5.89	1	Pavlov	Sofia	9 Jun 12
9:14.07		Etenesh	Diro	ETH	10.5.91	3	DNG	Stockholm	17 Aug 12
9:14.98		Lidya	Chepkurui	KEN	23.8.84	4	DNG	Stockholm	17 Aug 12
9:15.04		Dorcus	Inzikuru	UGA	2.2.82	1	SGP	Athína	14 Jun 05
9:16.51	WR	Alesya	Turova	BLR	6.12.79	1		Gdansk	27 Jul 02
9:16.85		Cristina	Casandra	ROU	21.10.77	5	OG	Beijing	17 Aug 08
9:16.94		Mercy	Njoroge	KEN	10.6.86	2	DL	Doha	6 May 11
		(20)							
9:17.15		Wioletta	Frankiewicz/Janowska	POL	9.6.77	1	SGP	Athína	3 Jul 06
9:17.85		Zemzem	Ahmed	ETH	27.12.84	7	OG	Beijing	17 Aug 08
9:18.03		Lydia	Rotich	KEN	8.8.88	3	Bisl	Oslo	4 Jun 10
9:18.35		Donna	MacFarlane	AUS	18.6.77	3	Bisl	Oslo	6 Jun 08
9:18.54		Antje	Möldner-Schmidt	GER	13.6.84	9	WCh	Berlin	17 Aug 09
9:18.54		Jéssica	Augusto	POR	8.11.81	2		Huelva	9 Jun 10
9:20.23		Mekdes	Bekele	ETH	20.1.87	2		Huelva	13 Jun 08
9:20.37		Birtukan	Adamu	ETH	29.4.92	4	GGala	Roma	26 May 11

Mark	Wind		Name	Nat	Born	Pos	Meet	Venue	Date
9:21.94		Lyubov	Ivanova' ¶	RUS	2.3.81	2	Tsik	Athína	3 Jul 06
9:22.12		Hanane	Ouhaddou	MAR	.82	1	NA	Heusden-Zolder	18 Jul 09
		(30)							
9:22.15		Yelena	Sidorchenkova	RUS	30.5.80	2	NC	Cheboksary	23 Jul 09
9:22.29	WR	Justyna	Bak	POL	1.8.74	1		Milano	5 Jun 02
9:22.51		Almaz	Ayana	ETH	21.11.91	3	VD	Bruxelles	27 Aug 10
9:22.76		Anna	Willard/Pierce	USA	31.3.84	2	NA	Heusden-Zolder	20 Jul 08
9:23.35		Jeruto	Kiptum	KEN	12.12.81	2	GP	Rieti	27 Aug 06
9:23.52		Gesa-Felicitas	Krause	GER	3.8.92	8	OG	London (OS)	6 Aug 12
9:23.53		Hyvin	Jepkemoi	KEN	13.1.92	2	Gugl	Linz	20 Aug 12
9:23.54		Emma	Coburn	USA	19.10.90	9	OG	London (OS)	6 Aug 12
9:24.06		Binnaz	Uslu ¶	TUR	12.3.85	1h1	WCh	Daegu	27 Aug 11
9:24.24		Barbara	Parker	GBR	8.11.82	4	Pre	Eugene	2 Jun 12
		(40)							
9:24.29		Melissa	Rollison	AUS	13.4.83	2	CG	Melbourne	22 Mar 06
9:24.84		Lisa	Aguilera	USA	30.11.79	5	VD	Bruxelles	27 Aug 10
9:25.14		Eva	Arias	ESP	8.10.80	5h1	WCh	Berlin	15 Aug 09
9:25.62		Sophie	Duarte	FRA	31.7.81	6	GGala	Roma	10 Jul 09
9:25.70		Ancuta	Bobocel	ROU	3.10.87	5	DNG	Stockholm	17 Aug 12
9:26.03		Lyudmila	Kuzmina	RUS	13.8.87	2	NC	Cheboksary	23 Jul 11
9:26.07		Salome	Chepchumba	KEN	29.9.82	3	GP	Rieti	27 Aug 06
9:26.23		Rosa María	Morató	ESP	19.6.79	2	NA	Heusden-Zolder	28 Jul 07
9:26.25			Liu Nian	CHN	26.4.88	1		Wuhan	2 Nov 07
9:26.93		Katarzyna	Kowalska	POL	7.4.85	4h2	WCh	Berlin	15 Aug 09
		(50)	100th woman 9:35.89, 200th 9:49.56, 300th 9:58.24						

100 METRES HURDLES

Mark	Wind		Name	Nat	Born	Pos	Meet	Venue	Date
12.21	WR 0.7	Yordanka	Donkova	BUL	28.9.61	1		Stara Zagora	20 Aug 88
12.24	0.9		Donkova			1h		Stara Zagora	28 Aug 88
12.25	WR 1.4	Ginka	Zagorcheva	BUL	12.4.58	1	v TCH,GRE	Drama	8 Aug 87
12.26	WR 1.5		Donkova			1	Balk	Ljubljana	7 Sep 86
12.26	1.7	Lyudmila	Narozhilenko ¶	RUS	21.4.64	1rB		Sevilla	6 Jun 92
		(now Ludmila Engquist SWE)							
12.27	-1.2		Donkova			1		Stara Zagora	28 Aug 88
12.28	1.8		Narozhilenko			1	NC	Kyiv	11 Jul 91
12.28	0.9		Narozhilenko			1rA		Sevilla	6 Jun 92
12.28	1.1	Sally	Pearson'	AUS	19.9.86	1	WCh	Daegu	3 Sep 11
12.29	WR-0.4		Donkova			1	ASV	Köln	17 Aug 86
12.32	1.6		Narozhilenko			1		Saint-Denis	4 Jun 92
12.33	1.4		Donkova			1		Fürth	14 Jun 87
12.33	-0.3	Gail	Devers	USA	19.11.66	1	NC	Sacramento	23 Jul 00
12.34	-0.5		Zagorcheva			1	WCh	Roma	4 Sep 87
12.35	WR 0.1		Donkova			1h2	ASV	Köln	17 Aug 86
12.35	-0.2		Pearson			1	OG	London (OS)	7 Aug 12
12.36	WR 1.9	Grazyna	Rabsztyn	POL	20.9.52	1	Kuso	Warszawa	13 Jun 80
12.36	WR-0.6		Donkova			1	NC	Sofiya	13 Aug 86
12.36	1.1		Donkova			1		Schwechat	15 Jun 88
12.36	0.3		Pearson			1s2	WCh	Daegu	3 Sep 11
12.37	1.4		Donkova			1	ISTAF	Berlin	15 Aug 86
12.37	0.7		Devers			1	WCh	Sevilla	28 Aug 99
12.37	1.5	Joanna	Hayes	USA	23.12.76	1	OG	Athína	24 Aug 04
12.37	-0.2	Dawn	Harper	USA	13.5.84	2	OG	London (OS)	7 Aug 12
12.38	0.0		Donkova			1	BGP	Budapest	11 Aug 86
12.38	-0.7		Donkova			1	EC	Stuttgart	29 Aug 86
12.38	0.2		Donkova			1	OG	Seoul	30 Sep 88
12.39	1.5	Vera	Komisova'	RUS	11.6.53	1	GGala	Roma	5 Aug 80
12.39	1.5		Zagorcheva			2	Balk	Ljubljana	7 Sep 86
12.39	1.8	Natalya	Grigoryeva ¶	UKR	3.12.62	2	NC	Kyiv	11 Jul 91
12.39	-0.7		Devers			1	WK	Zürich	11 Aug 00
12.39	1.3		Pearson			1s2	OG	London (OS)	7 Aug 12
		(32/10)							
12.42	1.8	Bettine	Jahn	GDR	3.8.58	1	OD	Berlin	8 Jun 83
12.42	2.0	Anjanette	Kirkland	USA	24.2.74	1	WCh	Edmonton	11 Aug 01
12.43	-0.9	Lucyna	Kalek (Langer)	POL	9.1.56	1		Hannover	19 Aug 84
12.43	-0.3	Michelle	Perry	USA	1.5.79	1s1	NC	Carson	26 Jun 05
12.43	0.2	Lolo	Jones	USA	5.8.82	1s1	OG	Beijing	18 Aug 08
12.44	-0.5	Gloria	Uibel (-Siebert)	GDR	13.1.64	2	WCh	Roma	4 Sep 87
12.44	-0.8	Olga	Shishigina ¶	KAZ	23.12.68	1	Spitzen	Luzern	27 Jun 95
12.44	0.4	Glory	Alozie	NGR/ESP	30.12.77	1	Herc	Monaco	8 Aug 98
12.44	0.6	Damu	Cherry ¶	USA	29.11.77	2rA	Athl	Lausanne	11 Jul 06

Mark	Wind	Name		Nat	Born	Pos	Meet	Venue	Date
12.45	1.3	Cornelia	Oschkenat'	GDR	29.10.61	1		Neubrandenburg	11 Jun 87
		(20)							
12.45	1.4	Brigitte	Foster-Hylton	JAM	7.11.74	1	Pre	Eugene	24 May 03
12.45	1.5	Olena	Krasovska	UKR	17.8.76	2	OG	Athína	24 Aug 04
12.45w	1.4	Virginia	Powell/Crawford	USA	7.9.83	1	GP	New York	2 Jun 07
12.46	0.7	Perdita	Felicien	CAN	29.8.80	1	Pre	Eugene	19 Jun 04
12.47	1.1	Marina	Azyabina	RUS	15.6.63	1s2	NC	Moskva	19 Jun 93
12.47	1.1	Danielle	Carruthers	USA	22.12.79	2	WCh	Daegu	3 Sep 11
12.49	0.9	Susanna	Kallur	SWE	16.2.81	1	ISTAF	Berlin	16 Sep 07
12.49	1.0	Priscilla	Lopes-Schliep	CAN	26.8.82	2	VD	Bruxelles	4 Sep 09
12.48	-0.2	Kellie	Wells	USA	16.7.82	3	OG	London (OS)	7 Aug 12
12.50	0.0	Vera	Akimova'	RUS	5.6.59	1		Sochi	19 May 84
		(30)							
12.50	-0.1	Delloreen	Ennis-London	JAM	5.3.75	3	WCh	Osaka	29 Aug 07
12.50	0.8	Josephine	Onyia ¶	NGR/ESP	15.7.86	1	ISTAF	Berlin	1 Jun 08
12.51	1.4	Miesha	McKelvy	USA	26.7.76	2	Pre	Eugene	24 May 03
12.52	-0.4	Michelle	Freeman	JAM	5.5.69	1s1	WCh	Athína	10 Aug 97
12.53	0.2	Tatyana	Reshetnikova	RUS	14.10.66	1rA	GP II	Linz	4 Jul 94
12.53	-0.4	Svetla	Dimitrova ¶	BUL	27.1.70	1	Herc	Stara Zagora	16 Jul 94
12.53	1.0	Melissa	Morrison	USA	9.7.71	1	DNG	Stockholm	5 Aug 98
12.54	0.4	Kerstin	Knabe	GDR	7.7.59	3	EC	Athína	9 Sep 82
12.54	0.9	Sabine	Paetz/John'	GDR	16.10.57	1		Berlin	15 Jul 84
12.54	1.7	Nichole	Denby	USA	10.10.82	2s2	OT	Eugene	6 Jul 08
		(40)							
12.54	1.3	Jessica	Ennis	GBR	28.1.86	1H5	OG	London (OS)	3 Aug 12
12.56	1.2	Johanna	Klier'	GDR	13.9.52	1r2		Cottbus	17 Jul 80
12.56	1.2	Monique	Ewanje-Epée	FRA	11.7.67	1	BNP	Villeneuve d'Ascq	29 Jun 90
12.56	0.7	Tiffany	Ofili/Porter	USA/GBR	13.11.87	1s3	WCh	Daegu	3 Sep 11
12.56	0.7	Kristi	Castlin	USA	7.7.88	2	Bisl	Oslo	7 Jun 12
12.57	0.3	Carolin	Nytra	GER	26.2.85	2	Athl	Lausanne	8 Jul 10
12.58	0.6	Nevin	Yanit	TUR	16.2.86	2s3	OG	London (OS)	7 Aug 12
12.59 WR	-0.6	Anneliese	Ehrhardt	GDR	18.6.50	1	OG	München	8 Sep 72
12.59	0.0	Natalya	Shekhodanova ¶	RUS	29.12.71	1	NC	Sankt Peterburg	3 Jul 96
12.59	1.0	Patricia	Girard ¶	FRA	8.4.68	2s2	OG	Atlanta	31 Jul 96
12.59	0.2	Brigita	Bukovec	SLO	21.5.70	2	OG	Atlanta	31 Jul 96
12.59	0.4	Kirsten	Bolm	GER	4.3.75	1	LGP	London (CP)	22 Jul 05
		(52)	100th woman 12.70, 200th 12.85, 300th 12.97, 400th 13.06, 500th 13.14						

Wind assisted performances to 12.37, performers to 12.59

Mark	Wind	Name		Nat	Born	Pos	Meet	Venue	Date
12.28	2.7	Cornelia	Oschkenat'	GDR	29.10.61	1		Berlin	25 Aug 87
12.29	3.5		Donkova			1	Athl	Lausanne	24 Jun 88
12.29	2.7	Gail	Devers	USA	19.11.66	1	Pre	Eugene	26 May 02
12.29	3.8	Lolo	Jones	USA	5.8.82	1	NC/OT	Eugene	6 Jul 08
12.35	2.4	Bettine	Jahn	GDR	3.8.58	1	WCh	Helsinki	13 Aug 83
12.35	3.7	Kellie	Wells	USA	16.7.82	1		Gainesville	16 Apr 11
12.36	2.2	Dawn	Harper	USA	13.5.84	1	NC	Eugene	28 Jun 09
12.37	2.7	Gloria	Uibel/Siebert'	GDR	13.1.64	2		Berlin	25 Aug 87
12.37	3.4	Danielle	Carruthers	USA	22.12.79	1s1	NC	Eugene	26 Jun 11
12.40	2.1	Michelle	Freeman	JAM	5.5.69	1	GPF	Fukuoka	13 Sep 97
12.41	2.2	Olga	Shishigina ¶	KAZ	23.12.68	1rA	Athl	Lausanne	5 Jul 95
12.42	2.4	Kerstin	Knabe	GDR	7.7.59	2	WCh	Helsinki	13 Aug 83
12.44	2.6	Melissa	Morrison	USA	9.7.71	1		Carson	22 May 04
12.44	5.3	Queen	Harrison	USA	10.9.88	1		Clemson	17 Apr 10
12.45	2.1	Perdita	Felicien	CAN	29.8.80	1	NC	Victoria	10 Jul 04
12.47	3.0	Tiffany	Ofili/Porter	USA/GBR	13.11.87	1		Gainesville	21 Apr 12
12.48	3.8	Kristi	Castlin	USA	7.7.88	1		Clermont	2 Jun 12
12.50	2.7	Svetla	Dimitrova ¶	BUL	27.1.70	1		Saint-Denis	10 Jun 94
12.51	3.2	Johanna	Klier'	GDR	13.9.52	1	NC	Cottbus	17 Jul 80
12.51	3.6	Sabine	Paetz/John'	GDR	16.10.57	1		Dresden	27 Jul 84
12.51A	3.3	Yuliya	Graudyn	RUS	13.11.70	1		Sestriere	31 Jul 94
12.53	2.2	Mihaela	Pogacian	ROU	27.1.58	1	IAC	Edinburgh	6 Jul 90
12.55	4.3	Angela	Whyte	CAN	22.5.80	2	NC	Windsor	14 Jul 07

Probably hand timed Officially 12.36, but subsequent investigations showed this unlikely to have been auto-timed

Mark	Wind	Name		Nat	Born	Pos	Meet	Venue	Date
12.4	0.7	Svetla	Dimitrova ¶	BUL	27.1.70	1		Stara Zagora	9 Jul 97

Hand timed

Mark	Wind	Name		Nat	Born	Pos	Meet	Venue	Date
12.3 WR	1.5	Anneliese	Ehrhardt	GDR	18.6.50	1	NC	Dresden	22 Jul 73
12.3		Marina	Azyabina	RUS	15.6.63	1		Yekaterinburg	30 May 93
12.0w	2.1	Yordanka	Donkova	BUL	28.9.61	1		Sofiya	3 Aug 86
12.1w	2.1	Ginka	Zagorcheva	BUL	12.4.58	2		Sofiya	3 Aug 86

Mark	Wind	Name		Nat	Born	Pos	Meet	Venue	Date

400 METRES HURDLES

Mark	Wind	Name		Nat	Born	Pos	Meet	Venue	Date
52.34	WR	Yuliya	Nosova-Pechonkina'	RUS	21.4.78	1	NC	Tula	8 Aug 03
52.42		Melaine	Walker	JAM	1.1.83	1	WCh	Berlin	20 Aug 09
52.47		Lashinda	Demus	USA	10.3.83	1	WCh	Daegu	1 Sep 11
52.61	WR	Kim	Batten	USA	29.3.69	1	WCh	Göteborg	11 Aug 95
52.62		Tonja	Buford-Bailey	USA	13.12.70	2	WCh	Göteborg	11 Aug 95
52.63			Demus			1	Herc	Monaco	28 Jul 09
52.64			Walker			1	OG	Beijing	20 Aug 08
52.70		Natalya	Antyukh	RUS	26.6.81	1	OG	London (OS)	8 Aug 12
52.73			Walker			2	WCh	Daegu	1 Sep 11
52.74	WR	Sally	Gunnell	GBR	29.7.66	1	WCh	Stuttgart	19 Aug 93
52.74			Batten			1	Herc	Monaco	8 Aug 98
52.77		Faní	Halkiá	GRE	2.2.79	1s2	OG	Athína	22 Aug 04
52.77			Demus			2	OG	London (OS)	8 Aug 12
52.79		Sandra	Farmer-Patrick	USA	18.8.62	2	WCh	Stuttgart	19 Aug 93
52.79		Kaliese	Spencer (10)	JAM	6.5.87	1	LGP	London (CP)	5 Aug 11
52.82		Deon	Hemmings	JAM	9.10.68	1	OG	Atlanta	31 Jul 96
52.82			Halkiá			1	OG	Athína	25 Aug 04
52.82			Demus			1	GGala	Roma	10 Jun 10
52.84			Batten			1	WK	Zürich	12 Aug 98
52.89		Daimí	Pernía	CUB	27.12.76	1	WCh	Sevilla	25 Aug 99
52.90			Buford			1	WK	Zürich	16 Aug 95
52.90		Nezha	Bidouane	MAR	18.9.69	2	WCh	Sevilla	25 Aug 99
52.90			Pechonkina			1	WCh	Helsinki	13 Aug 05
52.92			Antyukh			1	EC	Barcelona	30 Jul 10
52.94	WR	Marina	Styepanova'	RUS	1.5.50	1s	Spart	Tashkent	17 Sep 86
52.95		Sheena	Johnson/Tosta	USA	1.10.82	1	NC/OT	Sacramento	11 Jul 04
52.96A			Bidouane			1	WCp	Johannesburg	11 Sep 98
52.96			Demus			2	WCh	Berlin	20 Aug 09
52.97			Batten			1	NC	Indianapolis	14 Jun 97
52.97			Bidouane			1	WCh	Athína	8 Aug 97
		(30/14)							
53.02		Irina	Privalova	RUS	22.11.68	1	OG	Sydney	27 Sep 00
53.11		Tatyana	Ledovskaya	BLR	21.5.66	1	WCh	Tokyo	29 Aug 91
53.17		Debbie	Flintoff-King	AUS	20.4.60	1	OG	Seoul	28 Sep 88
53.20		Josanne	Lucas	TRI	14.5.84	3	WCh	Berlin	20 Aug 09
53.21		Marie-José	Pérec	FRA	9.5.68	2	WK	Zürich	16 Aug 95
		(20)							
53.22		Jana	Pittman/Rawlinson	AUS	9.11.82	1	WCh	Saint-Denis	28 Aug 03
53.24		Sabine	Busch	GDR	21.11.62	1	NC	Potsdam	21 Aug 87
53.25		Ionela	Târlea-Manolache	ROU	9.2.76	2	GGala	Roma	7 Jul 99
53.28		Tiffany	Ross-Williams	USA	5.2.83	1	NC	Indianapolis	24 Jun 07
53.29		Zuzana	Hejnová	CZE	19.12.86	1	DL	Saint-Denis	8 Jul 11
53.32		Sandra	Glover	USA	30.12.68	3	WCh	Helsinki	13 Aug 05
53.36		Andrea	Blackett	BAR	24.1.76	4	WCh	Sevilla	25 Aug 99
53.36		Brenda	Taylor	USA	9.2.79	2	NC/OT	Sacramento	11 Jul 04
53.37		Tetyana	Tereshchuk	UKR	11.10.69	3s2	OG	Athína	22 Aug 04
53.47		Janeene	Vickers	USA	3.10.68	3	WCh	Tokyo	29 Aug 91
		(30)							
53.48		Margarita	Ponomaryova'	RUS	19.6.63	3	WCh	Stuttgart	19 Aug 93
53.58		Cornelia	Ullrich'	GDR	26.4.63	2	NC	Potsdam	21 Aug 87
53.63		Ellen	Fiedler'	GDR	26.11.58	3	OG	Seoul	28 Sep 88
53.65A	mx	Myrtle	Bothma'	RSA	18.2.64	mx		Pretoria	12 Mar 90
53.74A						1		Johannesburg	18 Apr 86
53.68		Vania	Stambolova ¶	BUL	28.11.83	1		Rabat	5 Jun 11
53.72		Yekaterina	Bikert	RUS	13.5.80	2	NC	Tula	30 Jul 04
53.77		Irina	Davydova	RUS	27.5.88	1	EC	Helsinki	29 Jun 12
53.77		Perri	Shakes-Drayton	GBR	21.12.88	1	LGP	London (CP)	13 Jul 12
53.84		Natasha	Danvers	GBR	19.9.77	3	OG	Beijing	20 Aug 08
53.86		Anna	Jesien	POL	10.12.78	1s3	WCh	Osaka	28 Aug 07
		(40)							
53.88		Debbie-Ann	Parris	JAM	24.3.73	3s1	WCh	Edmonton	6 Aug 01
53.92		Georganne	Moline	USA	6.3.90	5	OG	London (OS)	8 Aug 12
53.93		Yevgeniya	Isakova	RUS	27.11.78	1	EC	Göteborg	9 Aug 06
53.95		Angela	Morosanu	ROU	26.7.86	1	NC	Bucuresti	2 Aug 09
53.96			Han Qing ¶	CHN	4.3.70	1	NG	Beijing	9 Sep 93
53.96			Song Yinglan	CHN	14.9.75	1	NG	Guangzhou	22 Nov 01
53.96		Anastasiya	Rabchenyuk	UKR	14.9.83	4	OG	Beijing	20 Aug 08
53.97		Nickiesha	Wilson	JAM	28.7.86	2s3	WCh	Osaka	28 Aug 07
54.00			Huang Xiaoxiao	CHN	3.3.83	2s2	WCh	Osaka	28 Aug 07

Mark	Wind	Name		Nat	Born	Pos	Meet	Venue	Date
54.02 WR		Anna	Ambraziené'	LTU	14.4.55	1	Znam	Moskva	11 Jun 83
54.02A		Judit	Szekeres ¶	HUN	18.11.66	1		Roodepoort	23 Jan 98
(51)			100th woman 54.74, 200th 55.49, 300th 55.92, 400th 56.31, 500th 56.68						
Drugs disqualification: 53.38		Jiang Limei ¶		CHN	.3.70	(1)	NG	Shanghai	22 Oct 97

HIGH JUMP

Mark	Wind	Name		Nat	Born	Pos	Meet	Venue	Date
2.09 WR		Stefka	Kostadinova	BUL	25.3.65	1	WCh	Roma	30 Aug 87
2.08 WR			Kostadinova			1	NM	Sofiya	31 May 86
2.08i		Kajsa	Bergqvist	SWE	12.10.76	1		Arnstadt	4 Feb 06
2.08		Blanka	Vlasic	CRO	8.11.83	1	Hanz	Zagreb	31 Aug 09
2.07 WR		Lyudmila	Andonova ¶	BUL	6.5.60	1	OD	Berlin	20 Jul 84
2.07 WR			Kostadinova			1		Sofiya	25 May 86
2.07			Kostadinova			1		Cagliari	16 Sep 87
2.07			Kostadinova			1	NC	Sofiya	3 Sep 88
2.07i		Heike	Henkel'	GER	5.5.64	1	NC	Karlsruhe	8 Feb 92
2.07			Vlasic			1	DNG	Stockholm	7 Aug 07
2.07		Anna	Chicherova	RUS	22.7.82	1	NC	Cheboksary	22 Jul 11
2.06			Kostadinova			1	ECp	Moskva	18 Aug 85
2.06			Kostadinova			1		Fürth	15 Jun 86
2.06			Kostadinova			1		Cagliari	14 Sep 86
2.06			Kostadinova			1		Wörrstadt	6 Jun 87
2.06			Kostadinova			1		Rieti	8 Sep 87
2.06i			Kostadinova			1		Pireás	20 Feb 88
2.06			Bergqvist			1		Eberstadt	26 Jul 03
2.06		Hestrie	Cloete	RSA	26.8.78	1	WCh	Saint-Denis	31 Aug 03
2.06		Yelena	Slesarenko	RUS	28.2.82	1	OG	Athína	28 Aug 04
2.06			Vlasic			1		Thessaloníki	30 Jul 07
2.06			Vlasic			1	ECp-1B	Istanbul	22 Jun 08
2.06			Vlasic			1	GP	Madrid	5 Jul 08
2.06		Ariane	Friedrich	GER	10.1.84	1	ISTAF	Berlin	14 Jun 09
2.06i			Vlasic			1		Arnstadt	6 Feb 10
2.06i			Chicherova			1		Arnstadt	4 Feb 12
2.05 WR		Tamara	Bykova (10)	RUS	21.12.58	1	Izv	Kyiv	22 Jun 84
2.05		Inga	Babakova	UKR	27.6.67	1		Tokyo	15 Sep 95
2.05i		Tia	Hellebaut	BEL	16.2.78	1	EI	Birmingham	3 Mar 07
2.05			Hellebaut			1	OG	Beijing	23 Aug 08
2.05		Chaunté	Lowe'	USA	12.1.84	1	NC	Des Moines	26 Jun 10
Further 2.05 performances: Kostadinova 10, Vlasic 10, Bergqvist, Chicherova 2, Henkel, Cloete, Freidrich 1									
(56/13)									
2.04		Silvia	Costa	CUB	4.5.64	1	WCp	Barcelona	9 Sep 89
2.04i		Alina	Astafei	GER	7.6.69	1		Berlin	3 Mar 95
2.04		Venelina	Veneva ¶	BUL	13.6.74	1		Kalamáta	2 Jun 01
2.04i		Antonietta	Di Martino	ITA	1.6.78	1		Banská Bystrica	9 Feb 11
2.04		Irina	Gordeyeva	RUS	9.10.86	1		Eberstadt	19 Aug 12
2.03 WR		Ulrike	Meyfarth	FRG	4.5.56	1	ECp	London (CP)	21 Aug 83
2.03		Louise	Ritter	USA	18.2.58	1		Austin	8 Jul 88
(20)									
2.03		Tatyana	Motkova	RUS	23.11.68	2		Bratislava	30 May 95
2.03		Níki	Bakoyiánni	GRE	9.6.68	2	OG	Atlanta	3 Aug 96
2.03i		Monica	Iagar/Dinescu	ROU	2.4.73	1		Bucuresti	23 Jan 99
2.03i		Marina	Kuptsova	RUS	22.12.81	1	EI	Wien	2 Mar 02
2.03		Brigetta	Barrett	USA	24.12.90	2	OG	London (OS)	11 Aug 12
2.03		Svetlana	Shkolina	RUS	9.3.86	3	OG	London (OS)	11 Aug 12
2.02i		Susanne	Beyer'	GDR	24.6.61	2	WI	Indianapolis	8 Mar 87
2.02		Yelena	Yelesina	RUS	4.4.70	1	GWG	Seattle	23 Jul 90
2.02		Viktoriya	Styopina	UKR	21.2.76	3	OG	Athína	28 Aug 04
2.02		Ruth	Beitia	ESP	1.4.79	1	NC	San Sebastián	4 Aug 07
(30)									
2.01 WR		Sara	Simeoni	ITA	19.4.53	1	v Pol	Brescia	4 Aug 78
2.01		Olga	Turchak	UKR	5.3.67	2	GWG	Moskva	7 Jul 86
2.01		Desiré	du Plessis	RSA	20.5.65	1		Johannesburg	16 Sep 86
2.01i		Gabriele	Günz	GDR	8.9.61	2		Stuttgart	31 Jan 88
2.01		Heike	Balck	GDR	19.8.70	1	vUSSR-j	Karl-Marx-Stadt	18 Jun 89
2.01i		Ioamnet	Quintero	CUB	8.9.72	1		Berlin	5 Mar 93
2.01		Hanne	Haugland	NOR	14.12.67	1	WK	Zürich	13 Aug 97
2.01i		Tisha	Waller	USA	1.12.70	1	NC	Atlanta	28 Feb 98
2.01		Yelena	Gulyayeva	RUS	14.8.67	2		Kalamata	23 May 98
2.01		Vita	Palamar	UKR	12.10.77	2=	WK	Zürich	15 Aug 03
(40)									
2.01		Amy	Acuff	USA	14.7.75	4	WK	Zürich	15 Aug 03

Mark	Wind	Name		Nat	Born	Pos	Meet	Venue	Date
2.01		Iryna	Myhalchenko	UKR	20.1.72	1		Eberstadt	18 Jul 04
2.01		Emma	Green Tregaro	SWE	8.12.84	2	EC	Barcelona	1 Aug 10
2.00 WR		Rosemarie	Ackermann'	GDR	4.4.52	1	ISTAF	Berlin	26 Aug 77
2.00i		Coleen	Sommer'	USA	6.6.60	1		Ottawa	14 Feb 82
2.00		Charmaine	Gale/Weavers	RSA	27.2.64	1		Pretoria	25 Mar 85
2.00i		Emilia	Dragieva'	BUL	11.1.65	3	WI	Indianapolis	8 Mar 87
2.00		Lyudmila	Avdyeyenko'	UKR	14.12.63	1	NC	Bryansk	17 Jul 87
2.00		Svetlana	Isaeva/Leseva	BUL	18.3.67	2	v TCH,GRE	Drama	8 Aug 87
2.00i		Larisa	Kositsyna	RUS	14.12.63	2	NC	Volgograd	11 Feb 88
		(50)							

2.00 also by Jan Wohlschlag' USA 1 Jul 89 Yolanda Henry USA 30 May 90, Biljana Petrovic ¶ 22 Jun 90, Tatyana Shevchik ¶ BLR Gomel 14 May 93, Britta Vörös/Bilac GDR/SLO 9 Feb 94 (i), Yuliya Lyakhova RUS 15 Feb 99 (i), Zuzana Hlavonová CZE 5 Jun 00, Dóra Györffy HUN 26 Jul 01, Viktoriya Seryogina RUS 11 Jun 02, Svetlana Lapina RUS/AZE 26 Feb 03 (i), Daniela Rath GER 22 Jun 03, Yekaterina Savchenko' 1 Jul 07, Viktoriya Klyugina RUS 7 Feb 09 (i), Meike Kröger GER 28 Feb 10 (i)

       (64)   100th woman 1.97, 200th 1.94, 300th 1.92, 400th 1.91, 500th 1.90

Best outdoor marks

2.03	Di Martino	1	ECp-1B	Milano	24 Jun 07	2.00	Quintero	1	Herc	Monaco	7 Aug 93
2.02	Iagar/Dinescu	1		Budapest	6 Jun 98	2.00	Kositsyna	1		Chelyabinsk	16 Jul 88
2.02	Kuptsova	1	FBK	Hengelo	1 Jun 03	2.00	Bilac	1	EC	Helsinki	14 Aug 94
2.01	Astafei	2		Wörrstadt	27 May 95	2.00	Waller	1	MSR	Walnut	18 Apr 99

Ancillary jumps: 2.06 Kostadinova 30 Aug 87, 2.05i Henkel 8 Feb 92, 2.05i Bergqvist 4 Feb 06, 2.05 Vlasic 31 Aug 09

POLE VAULT

Mark	Wind	Name		Nat	Born	Pos	Meet	Venue	Date
5.06 WR		Yelena	Isinbayeva	RUS	3.6.82	1	WK	Zürich	28 Aug 09
5.05 WR			Isinbayeva			1	OG	Beijing	18 Aug 08
5.04 WR			Isinbayeva			1	Herc	Monaco	29 Jul 08
5.03 WR			Isinbayeva			1	GGala	Roma	11 Jul 08
5.01 WR			Isinbayeva			2	WCh	Helsinki	12 Aug 05
5.01i			Isinbayeva			1	XL Galan	Stockholm	23 Feb 12
5.00 WR			Isinbayeva			1	LGP	London (CP)	22 Jul 05
5.00i			Isinbayeva			1		Donetsk	15 Feb 09
4.95 WR			Isinbayeva			1	GP	Madrid	16 Jul 05
4.95i			Isinbayeva			1		Donetsk	16 Feb 08
4.93 WR			Isinbayeva			1	Athl	Lausanne	5 Jul 05
4.93			Isinbayeva			1	VD	Bruxelles	26 Aug 05
4.93i			Isinbayeva			1		Donetsk	10 Feb 07
4.93			Isinbayeva			1	LGP	London (CP)	25 Jul 08
4.92 WR			Isinbayeva			1	VD	Bruxelles	3 Sep 04
4.92		Jennifer	Stuczynski/Suhr	USA	5.2.82	1	NC/OT	Eugene	6 Jul 08
4.91 WR			Isinbayeva (this jump on 25 Aug)			1	OG	Athína	25 Aug 04
4.91i			Isinbayeva			1		Donetsk	12 Feb 06
4.91			Isinbayeva			1	LGP	London (CP)	28 Jul 06
4.91			Isinbayeva			1	Gaz	Saint-Denis	6 Jul 07
4.91			Suhr			1		Rochester, NY	26 Jul 11
4.90 WR			Isinbayeva			1	GP	London (CP)	30 Jul 04
4.90i			Isinbayeva			1	EI	Madrid	6 Mar 05
4.90			Isinbayeva			1	Athl	Lausanne	11 Jul 06
4.90			Isinbayeva			1	GGala	Roma	13 Jul 07
4.90			Stuczynski			1	adidas	Carson	18 May 08
4.90i			Isinbayeva			1		Praha (O2)	26 Feb 09
4.89 WR			Isinbayeva			1		Birmingham	25 Jul 04
4.89i			Isinbayeva			1		Liévin	26 Feb 05
4.89			Suhr			1	NC	Des Moines	27 Jun 10
4.88 WR		Svetlana	Feofanova	RUS	16.7.80	1		Iráklio	4 Jul 04
		(30/3)							
4.87i		Holly	Bleasdale	GBR	2.11.91	1		Villeurbanne	20 Jan 12
4.85		Fabiana	Murer	BRA	16.3.81	1	IbAm	San Fernando	4 Jun 10
4.85i		Anna	Rogowska	POL	21.5.81	1	EI	Paris (Bercy)	6 Mar 11
4.83		Stacy	Dragila	USA	25.3.71	1	GS	Ostrava	8 Jun 04
4.82		Monika	Pyrek	POL	11.8.80	2	WAF	Stuttgart	22 Sep 07
4.82		Silke	Spiegelburg	GER	17.3.86	1	Herc	Monaco	20 Jul 12
4.80		Martina	Strutz	GER	4.11.81	2	WCh	Daegu	30 Aug 11
		(10)							
4.78		Tatyana	Polnova	RUS	20.4.79	2	WAF	Monaco	19 Sep 04
4.77		Annika	Becker	GER	12.11.81	1	NC	Wattenscheid	7 Jul 02
4.76		Alana	Boyd	AUS	10.5.84	1		Perth	24 Feb 12
4.75		Katerina	Badurová	CZE	18.12.82	2	WCh	Osaka	28 Aug 07
4.75i		Yuliya	Golubchikova	RUS	27.3.83	1		Athína (P)	13 Feb 08

Mark	Wind	Name		Nat	Born	Pos	Meet	Venue	Date
4.75A		Yarisley	Silva	CUB	1.6.87	1	PAm	Guadalajara, MEX	24 Oct 11
4.73		Chelsea	Johnson	USA	20.12.83	1		Los Gatos	26 Jun 08
4.72i		Kym	Howe	AUS	12.6.80	2		Donetsk	10 Feb 07
4.72i		Jillian	Schwartz	USA/ISR	19.9.79	1		Jonesboro	15 Jun 08
4.72		Carolin	Hingst	GER	18.9.80	1		Biberach	9 Jul 10
	(20)								
4.72		Jirina	Ptácníková	CZE	20.5.86	2	Odlozil	Praha	11 Jun 12
4.71		Nikolía	Kiriakopoúlou	GRE	21.3.86	4	LGP	London (CP)	5 Aug 11
4.70		Yvonne	Buschbaum	GER	14.7.80	1	NC	Ulm	29 Jun 03
4.70		Vanessa	Boslak	FRA	11.6.82	2	ECp-S	Málaga	28 Jun 06
4.70i		Kylie	Hutson	USA	27.11.87	1	DrakeR	Des Moines	27 Apr 11
4.68		Anna	Battke	GER	3.1.85	5	ISTAF	Berlin	14 Jun 09
4.67i		Kellie	Suttle	USA	9.5.73	1		Jonesboro	16 Jun 04
4.66i		Christine	Adams	GER	28.2.74	1	IHS	Sindelfingen	10 Mar 02
4.66i		Lacy	Janson	USA	20.2.83	1		Fayetteville	12 Feb 10
4.66i		Kristina	Gadschiew	GER	3.7.84	1		Potsdam	18 Feb 11
	(30)								
4.65		Mary	Sauer/Vincent	USA	31.10.75	2		Madrid (C)	3 Jul 02
4.65		Anastasiya	Ivanova/Shvedova	RUS/BLR	3.5.79	1	Odlozil	Praha	13 Jun 07
4.65		Aleksandra	Kiryashova	RUS	21.8.85	1	NCp	Tula	1 Aug 09
4.65		Lisa	Ryzih	GER	27.9.88	3	EC	Barcelona	30 Jul 10
4.64i		Pavla	Hamácková/Rybová	CZE	20.5.78	4		Bydgoszcz	14 Feb 07
4.64			Gao Shuying	CHN	28.10.79	2	GP	New York	2 Jun 07
4.63		Nastja	Ryshich	GER	19.9.77	1		Nürnberg	29 Jul 06
4.63		April	Steiner-Bennett	USA	22.4.80	1		Norman	12 Apr 08
4.63i		Angelica	Bengtsson	SWE	8.7.93	2		Stockholm	22 Feb 11
4.62b		Melissa	Mueller	USA	16.11.72	1		Clovis	4 Aug 01
		4.60Ai				1		Flagstaff	9 Feb 02
	(40)								
4.62Ai		Mary	Saxer	USA	21.6.87	2	NC	Albuquerque	25 Feb 12
4.61		Tina	Sutej	SLO	7.11.88	1	SEC	Athens, GA	14 May 11
4.61		Kate	Dennison	GBR	7.5.84	2		Barcelona	22 Jul 11
4.60	WR	Emma	George	AUS	1.11.74	1		Sydney	20 Feb 99
4.60		Yelena	Belyakova	RUS	7.4.76	1	NC	Tula	10 Aug 03
4.60A		Andrea	DuToit	USA	28.2.78	1		Albuquerque	1 May 04
4.60		Thórey Edda	Elisdóttír	ISL	30.6.77	2	SGP	Madrid	17 Jul 04
4.60		Tracy	O'Hara	USA	20.7.80	1	GP II	Stanford	30 May 05
4.60i		Julia	Hütter	GER	26.7.83	1	NC	Sindelfingen	24 Feb 08
4.60		Erin	Asay	USA	17.3.83	1		La Jolla	25 Apr 08
	(50)								
4.60		Anna	Giordano Bruno	ITA	13.12.80	1		Milano	2 Aug 09
4.60		Becky	Holliday	USA	12.3.80	2	NC	Des Moines	27 Jun 10
4.60i		Minna	Nikkanen	FIN	9.4.88	4=	EI	Paris (Bercy)	6 Mar 11
4.60i		Hanna	Sheleh	UKR-J	14.7.93	3		Donetsk	11 Feb 12
4.60Ai		Kelsie	Hendry	CAN	29.6.82	1		Flagstaff	16 Feb 12
4.60		Anastasiya	Savchenko	RUS	15.11.89	1	Colorful	Daegu	16 May 12
4.60		Nicole	Büchler	SUI	17.12.83	1		Riehen	17 Jun 12
	(57)	100th woman 4.46, 200th 4.35, 300th 4.25, 400th 4.20, 500th 4.14							

Outdoor bests

Mark	Name			Meet	Venue	Date
4.75	Golubchikova	4	OG		Beijing	18 Aug 08
4.65	Howe	1			Saulheim	30 Jun 07
4.65	Hutson	1	NC		Eugene	26 Jun 11
4.60	Suttle	1	ModR		Modesto	12 May 01
4.60	Hamácková	1	ECp-1B		Velenje	21 Jun 03
4.60	Mueller	1			Atascadero	9 Jul 03
4.60	Schwartz	1			Phoenix	14 May 04
4.60A	Janson	1			Missoula	5 Jun 10
4.60	Gadschiew	1			Reims	30 Jun 10
4.60	Saxer	1			Seattle	8 Jul 11

Ancillary jumps: Isinbayeva: 4.97 15 Feb 09, 4.96 WR 22 Jul 05, 4.95 18 Aug 08, 4.93 29 Jul 08, 4.92i 23 Feb 12

Exhibition: 4.72 Anastasiya Shvedova RUS 3.5.79 1 Aosta 5 Jul 08

LONG JUMP

Mark		Wind	Name		Nat	Born	Pos	Meet	Venue	Date
7.52	WR	1.4	Galina	Chistyakova	RUS	26.7.62	1	Znam	Leningrad	11 Jun 88
7.49		1.3	Jackie	Joyner-Kersee	USA	3.3.62	1	NYG	New York	22 May 94
7.49A		1.7		Joyner-Kersee			1		Sestriere	31 Jul 94
7.48		1.2	Heike	Drechsler	GER	16.12.64	1	v ITA	Neubrandenburg	9 Jul 88
7.48		0.4		Drechsler			1	Athl	Lausanne	8 Jul 92
7.45	WR	0.9		Drechsler'			1	v USSR	Tallinn	21 Jun 86
7.45	WR	1.1		Drechsler			1	OD	Dresden	3 Jul 86
7.45	WR	0.6		Joyner-Kersee			1	PAm	Indianapolis	13 Aug 87
7.45		1.6		Chistyakova			1	BGP	Budapest	12 Aug 88
7.44	WR	2.0		Drechsler			1		Berlin	22 Sep 85
7.43	WR	1.4	Anisoara	Cusmir/Stanciu	ROU	28.6.62	1	RomIC	Bucuresti	4 Jun 83
7.42		2.0	Tatyana	Kotova ¶	RUS	11.12.76	1	ECp-S	Annecy	23 Jun 02

Mark	Wind	Name		Nat	Born	Pos	Meet	Venue	Date
7.40	1.8		Daute' (Drechsler)			1		Dresden	26 Jul 84
7.40	0.7		Drechsler			1	NC	Potsdam	21 Aug 87
7.40	0.9		Joyner-Kersee			1	OG	Seoul	29 Sep 88
7.39	0.3		Drechsler			1	WK	Zürich	21 Aug 85
7.39	0.5	Yelena	Byelevskaya'	BLR	11.10.63	1	NC	Bryansk	18 Jul 87
7.39			Joyner-Kersee			1		San Diego	25 Jun 88
7.37i	-		Drechsler			1	v2N	Wien	13 Feb 88
7.37A	1.8		Drechsler			1		Sestriere	31 Jul 91
7.37		Inessa	Kravets ¶	UKR	5.10.66	1		Kyiv	13 Jun 92
7.36	0.4		Joyner			1	WCh	Roma	4 Sep 87
7.36	1.8		Byelevskaya			2	Znam	Leningrad	11 Jun 88
7.36	1.8		Drechsler			1		Jena	28 May 92
7.35	1.9		Chistyakova			1	GPB	Bratislava	20 Jun 90
7.34	1.6		Daute'			1		Dresden	19 May 84
7.34	1.4		Chistyakova			2	v GDR	Tallinn	21 Jun 86
7.34			Byelevskaya			1		Sukhumi	17 May 87
7.34	0.7		Drechsler			1	v USSR	Karl-Marx-Stadt	20 Jun 87
7.33	0.4		Drechsler			1	v USSR	Erfurt	22 Jun 85
7.33	2.0		Drechsler			1		Dresden	2 Aug 85
7.33	-0.3		Drechsler			1	Herc	Monaco	11 Aug 92
7.33	0.4	Tatyana	Lebedeva	RUS	21.7.76	1	NC	Tula	31 Jul 04
		(33/8)							
7.31	1.5	Yelena	Kokonova'	UKR	4.8.63	1	NP	Alma-Ata	12 Sep 85
7.31	1.9	Marion	Jones ¶	USA	12.10.75	1	Pre	Eugene	31 May 98
		(10)							
7.27	-0.4	Irina	Simagina/Meleshina	RUS	25.5.82	2	NC	Tula	31 Jul 04
7.26A	1.8	Maurren	Maggi ¶	BRA	25.6.76	1	SACh	Bogotá	26 Jun 99
7.24	1.0	Larisa	Berezhnaya	UKR	28.2.61	1		Granada	25 May 91
7.23i		Brittney	Reese	USA	9.9.86	1	WI	Istanbul	11 Mar 12
7.21	1.6	Helga	Radtke	GDR	16.5.62	2		Dresden	26 Jul 84
7.21	1.9	Lyudmila	Kolchanova	RUS	1.10.79	1		Sochi	27 May 07
7.20 WR	-0.5	Valy	Ionescu	ROU	31.8.60	1	NC	Bucuresti	1 Aug 82
7.20	2.0	Irena	Ozhenko'	LTU	13.11.62	1		Budapest	12 Sep 86
7.20	0.8	Yelena	Sinchukova'	RUS	23.1.61	1	BGP	Budapest	20 Jun 91
7.20	0.7	Irina	Mushayilova	RUS	6.1.67	1	NC	Sankt-Peterburg	14 Jul 94
7.19	1.8	Brittney	Reese	USA	9.9.86	1	NC	Eugene	26 Jun 11
		(20)							
7.17	1.8	Irina	Valyukevich	BLR	19.11.59	2	NC	Bryansk	18 Jul 87
7.16		Iolanda	Chen	RUS	26.7.61	1		Moskva	30 Jul 88
7.16A	-0.1	Elva	Goulbourne	JAM	21.1.80	1		Ciudad de México	22 May 04
7.14	1.8	Nijole	Medvedeva ¶	LTU	20.10.60	1		Riga	4 Jun 88
7.14	1.2	Mirela	Dulgheru	ROU	5.10.66	1	Balk G	Sofia	5 Jul 92
7.13	2.0	Olga	Kucherenko	RUS	5.11.85	1		Sochi	27 May 10
7.12	1.6	Sabine	Paetz/John'	GDR	16.10.57	2		Dresden	19 May 84
7.12	0.9	Chioma	Ajunwa ¶	NGR	25.12.70	1	OG	Atlanta	2 Aug 96
7.12	1.3	Naide	Gomes	CPV/POR	10.11.79	1	Herc	Monaco	29 Jul 08
7.11	0.8	Fiona	May	GBR/ITA	12.12.69	2	EC	Budapest	22 Aug 98
		(30)							
7.11	1.3	Anna	Nazarova	RUS	3.2.86	1	Mosc Ch	Moskva	20 Jun 12
7.10	1.6	Chelsea	Hayes	USA	9.2.88	2	NC/OT	Eugene	1 Jul 12
7.09 WR	0.0	Vilhelmina	Bardauskiené	LTU	15.6.53	Q	EC	Praha	29 Aug 78
7.09	1.5	Ljudmila	Ninova	AUT	25.6.60	1	GP II	Sevilla	5 Jun 94
7.08	0.5	Marieta	Ilcu ¶	ROU	16.10.62	1	RumIC	Pitesti	25 Jun 89
7.08	1.9	Anastasiya	Mironchik-Ivanova	BLR	13.4.89	1		Minsk	12 Jun 12
7.07	0.0	Svetlana	Zorina	RUS	2.2.60	1		Krasnodar	15 Aug 87
7.07	0.5	Yelena	Sokolova	RUS	23.7.86	2	OG	London (OS)	8 Aug 12
7.06	0.4	Tatyana	Kolpakova	KGZ	18.10.59	1	OG	Moskva	31 Jul 80
7.06	-0.1	Niurka	Montalvo	CUB/ESP	4.6.68	1	WCh	Sevilla	23 Aug 99
		(40)							
7.06		Tatyana	Ter-Mesrobyan	RUS	12.5.68	1		Sankt Peterburg	22 May 02
7.05	0.6	Lyudmila	Galkina	RUS	20.1.72	1	WCh	Athína	9 Aug 97
7.05	-0.4	Eunice	Barber	FRA	17.11.74	1	WAF	Monaco	14 Sep 03
7.05	1.1	Darya	Klishina	RUS	15.1.91	1	EU23	Ostrava	17 Jul 11
7.04	0.5	Brigitte	Wujak'	GDR	6.3.55	2	OG	Moskva	31 Jul 80
7.04	0.9	Tatyana	Proskuryakova'	RUS	13.1.56	1		Kyiv	25 Aug 83
7.04	2.0	Yelena	Yatsuk	UKR	16.3.61	1	Znam	Moskva	8 Jun 85
7.04	0.3	Carol	Lewis	USA	8.8.63	5	WK	Zürich	21 Aug 85
7.03	0.6	Níki	Xánthou	GRE	11.10.73	1		Bellinzona	18 Aug 97
7.03i	-	Dawn	Burrell	USA	1.11.73	1	WI	Lisboa	10 Mar 01
7.03	1.7	Janay	DeLoach	USA	12.10.85	*	NC/OT	Eugene	1 Jul 12
		(51)	100th woman 6.90, 200th 6.81, 300th 6.74, 400th 6.68, 500th 6.63						

Mark	Wind		Name	Nat	Born	Pos	Meet	Venue	Date
Drugs dq: 7.03	0.1		Xiong Qiying ¶	CHN	14.10.67	Q	NG	Shanghai	21 Oct 97
Wind assisted			*Performances to 7.35, performers to 7.05*						
7.63A	2.1	Heike	Drechsler	GER	16.12.64	1		Sestriere	21 Jul 92
7.45	2.6		Joyner-Kersee			1	NC/OT	Indianpolis	23 Jul 88
7.39	2.6		Drechsler			1		Padova	15 Sep 91
7.39	2.9		Drechsler			1	Expo	Sevilla	6 Jun 92
7.39A	3.3		Drechsler			2		Sestriere	31 Jul 94
7.36	2.2		Chistyakova			1	Znam	Volgograd	11 Jun 89
7.35	3.4		Drechsler			1	NC	Jena	29 Jun 86
7.23A	4.3	Fiona	May	ITA	12.12.69	1		Sestriere	29 Jul 95
7.22	4.3	Anastasiya	Mironchik-Ivanova	BLR	13.4.89	1	NC	Grodno	6 Jul 12
7.19A	3.7	Susen	Tiedtke ¶	GER	23.1.69	1		Sestriere	28 Jul 93
7.17	3.6	Eva	Murková	SVK	29.5.62	1		Nitra	26 Aug 84
7.15	2.8	Janay	DeLoach	USA	12.10.85	Q	NC/OT	Eugene	29 Jun 12
7.14A	4.5	Marieke	Veltman	USA	18.9.71	2		Sestriere	29 Jul 95
7.12A	5.8	Níki	Xánthou	GRE	11.10.73	3		Sestriere	29 Jul 95
7.12A	4.3	Nicole	Boegman	AUS	5.3.67	4		Sestriere	29 Jul 95
7.09	2.9	Renata	Nielsen	DEN	18.5.66	2		Sevilla	5 Jun 94
7.08	2.2	Lyudmila	Galkina	RUS	20.1.72	1		Thessaloniki	23 Jun 99
7.07A	5.6	Valentina	Uccheddu	ITA	26.10.66	5		Sestriere	29 Jul 95
7.07A	2.7	Sharon	Couch	USA	13.9.67	1		El Paso	12 Apr 97
7.07A	w	Erica	Johansson	SWE	5.2.74	1		Vygieskraal	15 Jan 00
7.06	3.4		Ma Miaolan	CHN	18.1.70	1	NG	Beijing	10 Sep 93

Best outdoor mark for athlete with all-time best indoors: 7.19 1.8 Reese 1 NC Eugene   16 Jun 11

Best at low altitude:
7.06   0.8   Maggi ¶   1   Milano   3 Jun 03   7.12w   3.4   May   1   NC   Bologna   25 May 96
7.17w   2.6   1   São Paulo   13 Apr 02

Ancillary marks – other marks during series (to 7.34/7.36w)
7.45   1.0   Chistyakova 11 Jun 88   7.47Aw   3.1 Drechsler   21 Jul 92   7.38w   2.2   Chistyakova 11 Jun 88
7.37   Drechsler   9 Jul 88   7.39Aw   3.1 Drechsler   21 Jul 92   7.36w   Joyner-Kersee 31 Jul 94

TRIPLE JUMP

Mark	Wind		Name	Nat	Born	Pos	Meet	Venue	Date
15.50 WR	0.9	Inessa	Kravets ¶	UKR	5.10.66	1	WCh	Göteborg	10 Aug 95
15.39	0.5	Françoise	Mbango	CMR	14.4.76	1	OG	Beijing	17 Aug 08
15.36i		Tatyana	Lebedeva	RUS	21.7.76	1	WI	Budapest	6 Mar 04
15.34	-0.5		Lebedeva			1		Iráklio	4 Jul 04
15.33	-0.1		Kravets			1	OG	Atlanta	31 Jul 96
15.33	1.2		Lebedeva			1	Athl	Lausanne	6 Jul 04
15.32	0.5		Lebedeva			1	Super	Yokohama	9 Sep 00
15.32	0.9	Hrisopiyi	Devetzí ¶	GRE	2.1.76	Q	OG	Athína	21 Aug 04
15.32	0.5		Lebedeva			2	OG	Beijing	17 Aug 08
15.30	0.6		Mbango			1	OG	Athína	23 Aug 04
15.29	0.3	Yamilé	Aldama	CUB/SUD/GBR	14.8.72	1		GGala	Roma 11 Jul 03
15.28	0.3		Aldama			1	GP	Linz	2 Aug 04
15.28	0.9	Yargelis	Savigne	CUB	13.11.84	1	WCh	Osaka	31 Aug 07
15.27	1.3		Aldama			1	GP	London (CP)	8 Aug 03
15.25	-0.8		Lebedeva			1	WCh	Edmonton	10 Aug 01
15.25	-0.1		Devetzí			2	OG	Athína	23 Aug 04
15.25	1.7	Olga	Rypakova	KAZ	30.11.84	1	C.Cup	Split	4 Sep 10
15.23	0.8		Lebedeva			1		Réthimno	23 Jun 04
15.23	0.6		Lebedeva			1	Tsik	Athína	3 Jul 06
15.23	1.6		Devetzí			3	OG	Beijing	17 Aug 08
15.22	1.5		Devetzí			1		Thessaloníki	9 Jul 08
15.21	1.2		Aldama			2		Réthimno	23 Jun 04
15.20	0.0	Sarka	Kaspárková	CZE	20.5.71	1	WCh	Athína	4 Aug 97
15.20	-0.3	Tereza	Marinova	BUL	5.9.77	1	OG	Sydney	24 Sep 00
15.20	1.3		Savigne			1	Vard	Réthimno	14 Jul 08
15.19	0.5		Lebedeva			1	Athl	Lausanne	11 Jul 06
15.18	0.3	Iva	Prandzheva ¶ (10)	BUL	15.2.72	2	WCh	Göteborg	10 Aug 95
15.18	-0.2		Lebedeva			1	WCh	Saint-Denis	26 Aug 03
15.16	0.1	Rodica	Mateescu ¶	ROU	13.3.71	2	WCh	Athína	4 Aug 97
15.16i WIR	-	Ashia	Hansen	GBR	5.12.71	1	EI	Valencia	28 Feb 98
15.16	0.7	Trecia	Smith	JAM	5.11.75	2	GP	Linz	2 Aug 04
			(31/13)						
15.14	1.9	Nadezhda	Alekhina	RUS	22.9.78	1	NC	Cheboksary	26 Jul 09
15.09 WR	0.5	Anna	Biryukova	RUS	27.9.67	1	WCh	Stuttgart	21 Aug 93
15.09	-0.5	Inna	Lasovskaya	RUS	17.12.69	1	ECCp-A	Valencia	31 May 97
15.08i		Marija	Sestak	SLO	17.4.79	1		Athína (P)	13 Feb 08

Mark	Wind	Name		Nat	Born	Pos	Meet	Venue	Date
15.07	-0.6	Paraskeví	Tsiamíta	GRE	10.3.72	Q	WCh	Sevilla	22 Aug 99
15.03i		Iolanda	Chen	RUS	26.7.61	1	WI	Barcelona	11 Mar 95
15.03	1.9	Magdelin	Martinez	ITA	10.2.76	1		Roma	26 Jun 04
(20)									
15.02	0.9	Anna	Pyatykh	RUS	4.4.81	3	EC	Göteborg	8 Sep 06
15.00	1.2	Kène	Ndoye	SEN	20.11.78	2		Iráklio	4 Jul 04
14.99A	1.7	Caterine	Ibargüen	COL	12.2.84	1		Bogotá	13 Aug 11
14.99	0.2	Olha	Saladuha	UKR	4.6.83	1	EC	Helsinki	29 Jun 12
14.98	1.8	Sofia	Bozhanova ¶	BUL	4.10.67	1		Stara Zagora	16 Jul 94
14.98	0.2	Baya	Rahouli	ALG	27.7.79	1	MedG	Almeria	1 Jul 05
14.96	0.7	Yelena	Govorova	UKR	18.9.73	4	OG	Sydney	24 Sep 00
14.94i	–	Cristina	Nicolau	ROU	9.8.77	1	NC	Bucuresti	5 Feb 00
14.94i		Oksana	Udmurtova	RUS	1.2.82	1		Tartu	20 Feb 08
14.90	1.0		Xie Limei	CHN	27.6.86	1		Urumqi	20 Sep 07
(30)									
14.85	1.2	Viktoriya	Gurova	RUS	22.5.82	3	NC	Kazan	19 Jul 08
14.83i	-	Yelena	Lebedenko	RUS	16.1.71	1		Samara	1 Feb 01
14.83	0.5	Yelena	Oleynikova	RUS	9.12.76	1	Odlozil	Praha	17 Jun 02
14.79	1.7	Irina	Mushayilova	RUS	6.1.67	1	DNG	Stockholm	5 Jul 93
14.78i		Adelina	Gavrila	ROU	26.11.78	1		Bucuresti	3 Feb 08
14.76	0.9	Galina	Chistyakova	RUS	26.7.62	1	Spitzen	Luzern	27 Jun 95
14.76	1.1	Gundega	Sproge ¶	LAT	12.12.72	3		Sheffield	29 Jun 97
14.76	0.4	Kseniya	Detsuk	BLR	23.4.86	*	NCp	Brest	26 May 12
14.72	1.8		Huang Qiuyan	CHN	25.1.80	1	NG	Guangzhou	22 Nov 01
14.72		Paraskeví	Papahrístou	GRE	17.4.89	1	Veniz	Haniá	11 Jun 11
(40)									
14.71	2.0	Hanna	Knyazyeva	UKR	25.9.89	1	NC	Yalta	15 Jun 12
14.71	1.4	Athanasía	Pérra	GRE	2.2.83	1	NC	Athína	16 Jun 12
14.70i		Oksana	Rogova	RUS	7.10.78	1		Volgograd	6 Feb 02
14.69	1.2	Anja	Valant	SLO	8.9.77	3		Kalamáta	4 Jun 00
14.69	1.2	Simona	La Mantia	ITA	14.4.83	1		Palermo	22 May 05
14.69	2.0	Teresa	N'zola Meso	ANG/FRA	30.11.83	1	ECp-S	München	23 Jun 07
14.68i		Anastasiya	Taranova-Potapova	RUS	6.9.85	1	EI	Torino	8 Mar 09
14.67	1.2	Ólga	Vasdéki	GRE	26.9.73	1	Veniz	Haniá	28 Jul 99
14.67	1.5	Natalya	Kutyakova	RUS	28.11.86	1		Huelva	2 Jun 11
14.67	0.4	Mabel	Gay	CUB	5.5.83	4	WCh	Daegu	1 Sep 11
(50)		100th woman 14.42, 200th 14.11, 300th 13.92, 400th 13.76, 500th 13.63							

Wind assisted   *Performances to 15.14, performers to 14.68*

Mark	Wind	Name		Nat	Born	Pos	Meet	Venue	Date
15.24A	4.2	Magdelin	Martinez	ITA	10.2.76	1		Sestriere	1 Aug 04
15.17	2.4	Anna	Pyatykh	RUS	4.4.81	2	SGP	Athína	3 Jul 06
15.10	2.7	Keila	Costa	BRA	6.2.83	1		Uberlandia	6 May 07
15.06	2.6	Olga	Saladuha	UKR	4.6.83	1	DNG	Stockholm	29 Jul 11
14.99	6.8	Yelena	Govorova	UKR	18.9.73	1	WUG	Palma de Mallorca	11 Jul 99
14.84	4.1	Galina	Chistyakova	RUS	26.7.62	1		Innsbruck	28 Jun 95
14.83	8.3		Ren Ruiping	CHN	1.2.76	1	NC	Taiyuan	21 May 95
14.83	2.2	Heli	Koivula-Kruger	FIN	27.6.75	2	EC	München	10 Aug 02
14.81	2.4	Kseniya	Detsuk	BLR	23.4.86	1	NCp	Brest	26 May 12
14.77	2.3	Paraskeví	Papahrístou	GRE	17.4.89	1		Ankara	5 Jun 12
14.75	4.2	Jelena	Blazevica	LAT	11.5.70	1	v2N	Kaunas	23 Aug 97
14.71	2.5	Simona	La Mantia	ITA	14.4.83	1		Roma	25 Jun 04

Best outdoor mark for athlete with all-time best indoors

15.15	1.7	Hansen	1	GPF	Fukuoka	13 Sep 97	14.85	1.4	Udmurtova	1		Padova	31 Aug 08
15.03	1.1	Sestak	6	OG	Beijing	17 Aug 08	14.75	1.1	Gavrila	3	GP II	Rieti	7 Sep 03
14.97wr	0.9	Chen	1	NC	Moskva	18 Jun 93	14.70	1.3	Nicolau	1	EU23	Göteborg	1 Aug 99

Ancillary marks – other marks during series (to 15.19)

15.30	0.5	Mbango	23 Aug 04	15.28	-0.3	Ledebeva	4 Jul 04	15.25i		Ledebeva	6 Mar 04
15.21	-0.2	Mbango	23 Aug 04	15.19	1.0	Lebedeva	3 Jul 06	15.19	1.3	Mbango	17 Aug 08

Best al low altitude: 14.85   -0.1   Ibargüen   1   Herc   Monaco   20 Jul 12

SHOT

Mark		Name		Nat	Born	Pos	Meet	Venue	Date
22.63	WR	Natalya	Lisovskaya	RUS	16.7.62	1	Znam	Moskva	7 Jun 87
22.55			Lisovskaya			1	NC	Tallinn	5 Jul 88
22.53	WR		Lisovskaya			1		Sochi	27 May 84
22.53			Lisovskaya			1		Kyiv	14 Aug 88
22.50i		Helena	Fibingerová	CZE	13.7.49	1		Jablonec	19 Feb 77
22.45	WR	Ilona	Slupianek' ¶	GDR	24.9.56	1		Potsdam	11 May 80
22.41			Slupianek			1	OG	Moskva	24 Jul 80
22.40			Slupianek			1		Berlin	3 Jun 83
22.38			Slupianek			1		Karl-Marx-Stadt	25 May 80
22.36	WR		Slupianek			1		Celje	2 May 80

Mark	Wind	Name		Nat	Born	Pos	Meet	Venue	Date
22.34			Slupianek			1		Berlin	7 May 80
22.34			Slupianek			1	NC	Cottbus	18 Jul 80
22.32 WR			Fibingerová			1		Nitra	20 Aug 77
22.24			Lisovskaya			1	OG	Seoul	1 Oct 88
22.22			Slupianek			1		Potsdam	13 Jul 80
22.19		Claudia	Losch	FRG	10.1.60	1		Hainfeld	23 Aug 87
22.14i			Lisovskaya			1	NC	Penza	7 Feb 87
22.13			Slupianek			1		Split	29 Apr 80
22.06			Slupianek			1		Berlin	15 Aug 78
22.06			Lisovskaya			1		Moskva	6 Aug 88
22.05			Slupianek			1	OD	Berlin	28 May 80
22.05			Slupianek			1		Potsdam	31 May 80
22.04			Slupianek			1		Potsdam	4 Jul 79
22.04			Slupianek			1		Potsdam	29 Jul 79
21.99 WR			Fibingerová			1		Opava	26 Sep 76
21.98			Slupianek			1		Berlin	17 Jul 79
21.96			Fibingerová			1	GS	Ostrava	8 Jun 77
21.96			Lisovskaya			1	Drz	Praha	16 Aug 84
21.96			Lisovskaya			1		Vilnius	28 Aug 88
21.95			Lisovskaya			1	IAC	Edinburgh	29 Jul 88
		(30/4)							
21.89 WR		Ivanka	Khristova	BUL	19.11.41	1		Belmeken	4 Jul 76
21.86		Marianne	Adam	GDR	19.9.51	1	v URS	Leipzig	23 Jun 79
21.76			Li Meisu	CHN	17.4.59	1		Shijiazhuang	23 Apr 88
21.73		Natalya	Akhrimenko	RUS	12.5.55	1		Leselidze	21 May 88
21.70i		Nadezhda	Ostapchuk ¶	BLR	12.10.80	1	NC	Mogilyov	12 Feb 10
21.69		Viktoriya	Pavlysh ¶	UKR	15.1.69	1	EC	Budapest	20 Aug 98
		(10)							
21.66			Sui Xinmei ¶	CHN	29.1.65	1		Beijing	9 Jun 90
21.61		Verzhinia	Veselinova	BUL	18.11.57	1		Sofiya	21 Aug 82
21.60i		Valentina	Fedyushina	UKR	18.2.65	1		Simferopol	28 Dec 91
21.58		Margitta	Droese/Pufe	GDR	10.9.52	1		Erfurt	28 May 78
21.57 @		Ines	Müller'	GDR	2.1.59	1		Athína	16 May 88
	21.45					1		Schwerin	4 Jun 86
21.53		Nunu	Abashidze ¶	UKR	27.3.55	2	Izv	Kyiv	20 Jun 84
21.52			Huang Zhihong	CHN	7.5.65	1	NC	Beijing	27 Jun 90
21.46		Larisa	Peleshenko ¶	RUS	29.2.64	1	Kuts	Moskva	26 Aug 00
21.45 WR		Nadezhda	Chizhova	RUS	29.9.45	1		Varna	29 Sep 73
21.43		Eva	Wilms	FRG	28.7.52	2	HB	München	17 Jun 77
		(20)	@ competitive meeting, but unsanctioned by GDR federation						
21.42		Svetlana	Krachevskaya'	RUS	23.11.44	2	OG	Moskva	24 Jul 80
21.31 @		Heike	Hartwig'	GDR	30.12.62	2		Athína	16 May 88
	21.27					1		Haniá	22 May 88
21.27		Liane	Schmuhl	GDR	29.6.61	1		Cottbus	26 Jun 82
21.24		Valerie	Adams	NZL	6.10.84	1	WCh	Daegu	29 Aug 11
21.22		Astrid	Kumbernuss	GDR/GER	5.2.70	1	WCh	Göteborg	5 Aug 95
21.21		Kathrin	Neimke	GDR	18.7.66	2	WCh	Roma	5 Sep 87
21.19		Helma	Knorscheidt	GDR	31.12.56	1		Berlin	24 May 84
21.15i		Irina	Korzhanenko ¶	RUS	16.5.74	1	NC	Moskva	18 Feb 99
21.10		Heidi	Krieger	GDR	20.7.65	1	EC	Stuttgart	26 Aug 86
21.06		Svetlana	Krivelyova ¶	RUS	13.6.69	1	OG	Barcelona	7 Aug 92
		(30)							
21.05		Zdenka	Silhavá' ¶	CZE	15.6.54	2	NC	Praha	23 Jul 83
21.01		Ivanka	Petrova-Stoycheva	BUL	3.2.51	1	NC	Sofiya	28 Jul 79
21.00		Mihaela	Loghin	ROU	1.6.52	1		Formia	30 Jun 84
21.00		Cordula	Schulze	GDR	11.9.59	4	OD	Potsdam	21 Jul 84
20.96		Belsy	Laza	CUB	5.6.67	1		Ciudad de México	2 May 92
20.95		Elena	Stoyanova ¶	BUL	23.1.52	2	Balk	Sofiya	14 Jun 80
20.91		Svetla	Mitkova	BUL	17.6.64	1		Sofiya	24 May 87
20.80		Sona	Vasícková	CZE	14.3.62	1		Praha	2 Jun 88
20.72		Grit	Haupt/Hammer	GDR	4.6.66	3		Neubrandenburg	11 Jun 87
20.70		Natalya	Mikhnevich	BLR	25.5.82	2	NC	Grodno	8 Jul 08
		(40)							
20.61		María Elena	Sarría	CUB	14.9.54	1		La Habana	22 Jul 82
20.61		Yanina	Korolchik ¶	BLR	26.12.76	1	WCh	Edmonton	5 Aug 01
20.60		Marina	Antonyuk	RUS	12.5.62	1		Chelyabinsk	10 Aug 86
20.54			Zhang Liuhong	CHN	16.1.69	1	NC	Beijing	5 Jun 94
20.53		Iris	Plotzitzka	FRG	7.1.66	1	ASV	Köln	21 Aug 88
20.50i		Christa	Wiese	GDR	25.12.67	2	NC	Senftenberg	12 Feb 89
20.48		Yevgeniya	Kolodko	RUS	2.7.90	2	OG	London (OS)	6 Aug 12

Mark	Wind	Name		Nat	Born	Pos	Meet	Venue	Date
20.47		Nina	Isayeva	RUS	6.7.50	1		Bryansk	28 Aug 82
20.47			Cong Yuzhen	CHN	22.1.63	2	IntC	Tianjin	3 Sep 88
20.44		Tatyana	Orlova	BLR	19.7.55	1		Staiki	28 May 83
	(50)		100th woman 19.68, 200th 18.804, 300th 18.13, 400th 17.67, 500th						

Best outdoor marks

21.58		Ostapchuk ¶	1		Minsk	18 Jul 12		20.82	Korzhanenko ¶ 1 Rostov na Donu 30 May 98
21.08		Fedyushina	1		Leselidze	15 May 88		21.06 drugs dq (1) OG Athína 18 Aug 04

Ancillary marks – other marks during series (to 22.09)

22.60	Lisovskaya (WR)	7 Jun 87	22.20	Slupianek	13 Jul 80	22.12	Slupianek	13 Jul 80
22.40	Lisovskaya	14 Aug 88	22.19	Lisovskaya	5 Jul 88	22.11	Slupianek	7 May 80
22.34	Slupianek	11 May 80	22.14	Slupianek	25 May 80	22.10	Slupianek	25 May 80
22.33	Slupianek	2 May 80	22.14	Slupianek	13 Jul 80	22.09	Slupianek	7 May 80

DISCUS

Mark	Wind	Name		Nat	Born	Pos	Meet	Venue	Date
76.80	WR	Gabriele	Reinsch	GDR	23.9.63	1	v ITA	Neubrandenburg	9 Jul 88
74.56	WR	Zdenka	Silhavá' ¶	CZE	15.6.54	1		Nitra	26 Aug 84
74.56		Ilke	Wyludda	GDR	28.3.69	1	NC	Neubrandenburg	23 Jul 89
74.44			Reinsch			1		Berlin	13 Sep 88
74.40			Wyludda			2		Berlin	13 Sep 88
74.08		Diana	Gansky'	GDR	14.12.63	1	v USSR	Karl-Marx-Stadt	20 Jun 87
73.90			Gansky			1	ECp	Praha	27 Jun 87
73.84		Daniela	Costian ¶	ROU	30.4.65	1		Bucuresti	30 Apr 88
73.78			Costian			1		Bucuresti	24 Apr 88
73.42			Reinsch			1		Karl-Marx-Stadt	12 Jun 88
73.36	WR	Irina	Meszynski	GDR	24.3.62	1	Drz	Praha	17 Aug 84
73.32			Gansky			1		Neubrandenburg	11 Jun 87
73.28		Galina	Savinkova'	RUS	15.7.53	1	NC	Donetsk	8 Sep 84
73.26	WR		Savinkova			1		Leselidze	21 May 83
73.26			Sachse/Gansky			1		Neubrandenburg	6 Jun 86
73.24			Gansky			1		Leipzig	29 May 87
73.22		Tsvetanka	Khristova ¶	BUL	14.3.62	1		Kazanlak	19 Apr 87
73.10		Gisela	Beyer	GDR	16.7.60	1	OD	Berlin	20 Jul 84
73.04			Gansky			1		Potsdam	6 Jun 87
73.04			Wyludda			1	ECp	Gateshead	5 Aug 89
72.96			Savinkova			1	v GDR	Erfurt	23 Jun 85
72.94			Gansky			2	v ITA	Neubrandenburg	9 Jul 88
72.92		Martina	Opitz/Hellmann	GDR	12.12.60	1	NC	Potsdam	20 Aug 87
72.90			Costian			1		Bucuresti	14 May 88
72.78			Hellmann			2		Neubrandenburg	11 Jun 87
72.78			Reinsch			1	OD	Berlin	29 Jun 88
72.72			Wyludda			1		Neubrandenburg	23 Jun 89
72.70			Wyludda			1	NC-j	Karl-Marx-Stadt	15 Jul 88
72.54			Gansky			1	NC	Rostock	25 Jun 88
72.52			Hellmann			1		Frohburg	15 Jun 86
72.52			Khristova			1	BGP	Budapest	11 Aug 86
	(31/10)								
72.14		Galina	Murashova	LTU	22.12.55	2	Drz	Praha	17 Aug 84
71.80	WR	Maria	Vergova/Petkova	BUL	3.11.50	1	NC	Sofiya	13 Jul 80
71.68			Xiao Yanling ¶	CHN	27.3.68	1		Beijing	14 Mar 92
71.58		Ellina	Zvereva' ¶	BLR	16.11.60	1	Znam	Leningrad	12 Jun 88
71.50	WR	Evelin	Schlaak/Jahl	GDR	28.3.56	1		Potsdam	10 May 80
71.30		Larisa	Korotkevich	RUS	3.1.67	1	RusCp	Sochi	29 May 92
71.22		Ria	Stalman	NED	11.12.51	1		Walnut	15 Jul 84
70.88		Hilda Elia	Ramos ¶	CUB	1.9.64	1		La Habana	8 May 92
70.80		Larisa	Mikhalchenko	UKR	16.5.63	1		Kharkov	18 Jun 88
70.68		Maritza	Martén	CUB	16.8.63	1	Ib Am	Sevilla	18 Jul 92
	(20)								
70.50	WR	Faina	Melnik	RUS	9.6.45	1	Znam	Sochi	24 Apr 76
70.34	@	Silvia	Madetzky	GDR	24.6.62	3		Athína	16 May 88
69.34						1		Halle	26 Jun 87
70.02		Natalya	Sadova ¶	RUS	15.7.72	1		Thessaloniki	23 Jun 99
69.86		Valentina	Kharchenko	RUS	.49	1		Feodosiya	16 May 81
69.72		Svetla	Mitkova	BUL	17.6.64	2	NC	Sofiya	15 Aug 87
69.68		Mette	Bergmann	NOR	9.11.62	1		Florø	27 May 95
69.51		Franka	Dietzsch	GER	22.1.68	1		Wiesbaden	8 May 99
69.50		Florenta	Craciunescu'	ROU	7.5.55	1	Balk	Stara Zagora	2 Aug 85
69.14		Irina	Yatchenko	BLR	31.10.65	1		Staiki	31 Jul 04
69.11		Sandra	Perkovic	CRO	21.6.90	1	OG	London (OS)	4 Aug 12
	(30)								
69.08		Carmen	Romero	CUB	6.10.50	1	NC	La Habana	17 Apr 76

Mark	Wind	Name		Nat	Born	Pos	Meet	Venue	Date
69.08		Mariana	Ionescu/Lengyel	ROU	14.4.53	1		Constanta	19 Apr 86
68.92		Sabine	Engel	GDR	21.4.54	1	v URS,POL	Karl-Marx-Stadt	25 Jun 77
68.89		Nadine	Müller	GER	21.11.85	1	ECp-w	Bar	18 Mar 12
68.80		Nicoleta	Grasu	ROU	11.9.71	1		Poiana Brasov	7 Aug 99
68.64		Margitta	Pufe'	GDR	10.9.52	1	ISTAF	Berlin	17 Aug 79
68.62			Yu Hourun	CHN	9.7.64	1		Beijing	6 May 88
68.62			Hou Xuemei	CHN	27.2.62	1	IntC	Tianjin	4 Sep 88
68.60		Nadezhda	Kugayevskikh	RUS	19.4.60	1		Oryol	30 Aug 83
68.58		Lyubov	Zverkova	RUS	14.6.55	1	Izv	Kyiv	22 Jun 84
	(40)								
68.52		Beatrice	Faumuiná	NZL	23.10.74	1	Bisl	Oslo	4 Jul 97
68.38		Olga	Burova'	RUS	17.9.63	2	RusCp	Sochi	29 May 92
68.18		Tatyana	Lesovaya	KAZ	24.4.56	1		Alma-Ata	23 Sep 82
68.18		Irina	Khval	RUS	17.5.62	1		Moskva	8 Jul 88
68.18		Barbara	Hechevarría	CUB	6.8.66	2		La Habana	17 Feb 89
68.03		Yarelis	Barrios	CUB	12.7.83	1	NC	La Habana	22 Mar 12
67.98			Li Yanfeng	CHN	15.5.79	1		Schönebeck	5 Jun 11
67.96		Argentina	Menis	ROU	19.7.48	1	RomIC	Bucuresti	15 May 76
67.90		Petra	Sziegaud	GDR	17.10.58	1		Berlin	19 May 82
67.82		Tatyana	Belova	RUS	12.2.62	1		Irkutsk	10 Aug 87
	(50)								

100th woman 65.68 200th 63.58, 300th 61.62, 400th 59.84, 500th 58.64

Unofficial meeting: Berlin 6 Sep 88: 1. Martina Hellmann 78.14, 2. Ilke Wyludda 75.36

Downhill: 69.44 Suzy Powell USA 3.9.76 1 La Jolla 27 Apr 02

Drugs disqualification:

Mark	Wind	Name		Nat	Born	Pos	Meet	Venue	Date
70.69		Darya	Pishchalnikova ¶	RUS	19.7.85	(1)	NC	Cheboksary	5 Jul 12
69.99		Sandra	Perkovic ¶	CRO	21.6.90	(1)		Varazdin	4 Jun 11

Ancillary marks – other marks during series (to 72.92)

73.32	Reinsch	13 Sep 88	73.28	Gansky	27 Jun 87	73.10	Reinsch	9 Jul 88
73.28	Gansky	11 Jun 87	73.16	Wyludda	13 Sep 88	73.06	Gansky	27 Jun 87
						72.92	Hellmann	20 Aug 87

HAMMER

Mark	Wind	Name		Nat	Born	Pos	Meet	Venue	Date
79.42 WR		Betty	Heidler	GER	14.10.83	1		Halle	21 May 11
78.69		Oksana	Menkova	BLR	28.3.82	1		Minsk	18 Jul 12
78.51		Tatyana	Lysenko ¶	RUS	9.10.83	1	NC	Cheboksary	5 Jul 12
78.30 WR		Anita	Wlodarczyk	POL	8.8.85	1	EAF	Bydgoszcz	6 Jun 10
78.19			Menkova			1		Brest	28 Apr 12
78.19			Menkova			1		Minsk	12 Jun 12
78.18			Lysenko			1	OG	London (OS)	10 Aug 12
78.07			Heidler			1	GS	Ostrava	24 May 12
77.96 WR			Wlodarczyk			1	WCh	Berlin	22 Aug 09
77.80 WR			Lysenko			1		Tallinn	15 Aug 06
77.53			Heidler			1		Fränkisch-Crumbach	12 Jun 11
77.60			Włodarczyk			2	OG	London (OS)	10 Aug 12
77.53			Heidler			1		Elstal	9 Sep 11
77.41 WR			Lysenko			1	Znam	Zhukovskiy	24 Jun 06
77.40			Heidler			1	ISTAF	Berlin	11 Sep 11
77.32			Menkova			1		Staiki	29 Jun 08
77.30			Lysenko			1		Adler	22 Apr 07
77.26 WR		Gulfiya	Khanafeyeva ¶	RUS	4.6.82	1	NC	Tula	12 Jun 06
77.24			Heidler			1	Colorful	Daegu	16 May 12
77.22			Heidler			1	GS	Ostrava	30 May 11
77.20			Wlodarczyk			1		Cottbus	8 Aug 09
77.20			Lysenko			1		Yerino	22 Jul 12
77.13			Lysenko			1	WCh	Daegu	4 Sep 11
77.12			Heidler			2	WCh	Berlin	22 Aug 09
77.12			Heidler			3	OG	London (OS)	10 Aug 12
77.08			Khanafeyeva			1		Zhukovskiy	23 Jun 12
77.06 WR			Lysenko			1	Kuts	Moskva	15 Jul 05
76.99			Zhang Wenxiu	CHN	22.3.86	2	GS	Ostrava	24 May 12
76.94			Khanafeyeva			1		Moskva	31 May 06
76.93			Khanafeyeva			1	RUSCp	Tula	15 Jul 06
	(30/6)								
76.90		Martina	Hrasnová' ¶	SVK	21.3.83	1		Trnava	16 May 09
76.83		Kamila	Skolimowska	POL	4.11.82	1	SGP	Doha	11 May 07
76.72		Mariya	Bespalova	RUS	21.5.86	2		Zhukovskiy	23 Jun 12
76.66		Olga	Tsander (10)	BLR	18.5.76	1		Staiki	21 Jul 05
76.63		Yekaterina	Khoroshikh ¶	RUS	21.1.83	2	Znam	Moskva	24 Jun 06
76.62		Yipsi	Moreno	CUB	19.11.80	1	GP	Zagreb	9 Sep 08
76.56		Alena	Matoshko	BLR	23.6.82	2		Minsk	12 Jun 12
76.33		Darya	Pchelnik	BLR	20.12.81	2		Staiki	29 Jun 08
76.21		Yelena	Konevtsova	RUS	11.3.81	3		Sochi	26 May 07

Mark	Wind	Name		Nat	Born	Pos	Meet	Venue	Date
76.07	WR	Mihaela	Melinte ¶	ROU	27.3.75	1		Rüdlingen	29 Aug 99
76.05		Kathrin	Klaas	GER	6.2.84	5	OG	London (OS)	10 Aug 12
75.68		Olga	Kuzenkova ¶	RUS	4.10.70	1	NCp	Tula	4 Jun 00
75.08		Ivana	Brkljacic	CRO	25.1.83	2	Kuso	Waszawa	17 Jun 07
75.04		Sultana	Frizell	CAN	24.10.84	1		Tucson	16 Mar 12
		(20)							
74.66		Manuèla	Montebrun	FRA	13.11.79	1	GP II	Zagreb	11 Jul 05
74.65		Mariya	Smolyachkova	BLR	10.2.85	2		Staiki	19 Jul 08
74.52		Iryna	Sekachova	UKR	21.7.76	1	NC	Kyiv	2 Jul 08
74.47		Zalina	Marghieva	MDA	5.2.88	1	Univ Ch	Chisinau	7 May 12
74.21		Hanna	Skydan	UKR	14.5.92	1	NC	Yalta	14 Jun 12
74.19		Jessica	Cosby	USA	31.5.82	4	Pre	Eugene	1 Jun 12
74.18		Joanna	Fiodorow	POL	4.3.89	1	EAF	Bydgoszcz	3 Jun 12
74.17		Tugçe	Sahutoglu	TUR	1.5.88	1		Izmir	19 May 12
74.10		Iryna	Novozhylova	UKR	7.1.86	1		Kyiv	19 May 12
74.02		Anna	Bulgakova	RUS	17.1.88	4	NC	Cheboksary	5 Jul 12
		(30)							
73.90		Arasay	Thondike	CUB	28.5.86	1		La Habana	18 Jun 09
73.87		Erin	Gilreath	USA	11.10.80	1	NC	Carson	25 Jun 05
73.74		Jennifer	Dahlgren	ARG	21.4.84	1		Buenos Aires	10 Apr 10
73.59		Ester	Balassini	ITA	20.10.77	1	NC	Bressanone	25 Jun 05
73.52		Bianca	Perie	ROU	1.6.90	1	NC	Bucuresti	16 Jul 10
73.40		Stéphanie	Falzon	FRA	7.1.83	1	NC	Albi	26 Jul 08
73.31		Oksana	Kondratyeva	RUS	22.11.85	1	Mosc Ch	Moskva	27 Jun 12
73.21		Eileen	O'Keeffe	IRL	31.5.81	1	NC	Dublin	21 Jul 07
73.16		Yunaika	Crawford	CUB	2.11.82	3	OG	Athína	25 Aug 04
72.83		Rosa	Rodríguez	VEN	2.7.86	1		Cakovec	5 May 12
		(40)							
72.74		Susanne	Keil	GER	18.5.78	1		Nikiti	15 Jul 05
72.59		Amber	Campbell	USA	5.6.81	1	MSR	Walnut	16 Apr 11
72.55		Kivilcim	Kaya	TUR	27.3.92	1	NC	Izmir	5 Jul 12
72.53		Marina	Marghieva ¶	MDA	28.6.86	1		Chisinau	5 May 09
72.51			Liu Yinghui	CHN	29.6.79	2	WUG	Izmir	16 Aug 05
72.51		Brittany	Riley	USA	26.8.86	1	DrakeR	Des Moines	28 Apr 07
72.46		Clarissa	Claretti	ITA	7.10.80	1	NC	Cagliari	19 Jul 08
72.36			Gu Yuan	CHN	9.5.82	2		Padova	3 Jul 04
72.22		Nataliya	Zolotuhina	UKR	4.1.85	1		Uman	21 May 11
72.16		Heather	Steacy	CAN	14.4.88	2	S.Angel	Tempe	6 Apr 12
		(50)							

100th woman 69.50, 200th 66.26, 300th 63.61, 400th 62.33, 500th 60.66

Downhill: 75.20 Manuéla Montebrun FRA 13.11.79 1 Vineuil 18 May 03

Ancillary marks – other marks during series to 77.19

77.67	Wlodarczyk	6 Jun 10	77.37	Lysenko	5 Jul 12	77.26	Lysenko	5 Jul 12
77.56	Lysenko	10 Aug 12	77.28	Lysenko	10 Aug 12	77.19	Heidler	21 May 11
						77.19	Lysenko	22 Jul 12

Drugs disqualification

Mark	Name		Nat	Born	Pos	Meet	Venue	Date
78.61	Tatyana	Lysenko ¶	RUS	9.10.83	(1)		Sochi	26 May 07
77.71		Lysenko			(1)	GS	Ostrava	27 Jun 07
77.36	Gulfiya	Khanafeyeva ¶	RUS	4.6.82	(2)		Sochi	26 May 07
77.01		Lysenko			(1)	Znam	Zhukovskiy	9 Jun 07

Ancillary mark: Lysenko: 77.32 27 Jun 07

JAVELIN

Mark	Wind	Name		Nat	Born	Pos	Meet	Venue	Date
72.28	WR	Barbora	Spotáková	CZE	30.6.81	1	WAF	Stuttgart	13 Sep 08
71.99		Mariya	Abakumova	RUS	15.1.86	1	WCh	Daegu	2 Sep 11
71.70	WR	Osleidys	Menéndez	CUB	14.11.79	1	WCh	Helsinki	14 Aug 05
71.58			Spotáková			2	WCh	Daegu	2 Sep 11
71.54	WR		Menéndez			1		Réthimno	1 Jul 01
71.53			Menéndez			1	OG	Athína	27 Aug 04
71.42			Spotáková			1	OG	Beijing	21 Aug 08
70.78			Abakumova			2	OG	Beijing	21 Aug 08
70.20		Christina	Obergföll	GER	22.8.81	1	ECp-S	München	23 Jun 07
70.03			Obergföll			2	WCh	Helsinki	14 Aug 05
69.82			Menéndez			1	WUG	Beijing	29 Aug 01
69.81			Obergföll			1		Berlin (Elstal)	31 Aug 08
69.57			Obergföll			1	WK	Zürich	8 Sep 11
69.55			Spotáková			1	OG	London (OS)	9 Aug 12
69.53			Menéndez			1	WCh	Edmonton	7 Aug 01
69.48	WR	Trine	Hattestad	NOR	18.4.66	1	Bisl	Oslo	28 Jul 00
69.45			Spotáková			1	Herc	Monaco	22 Jul 11
69.35		Sunette	Viljoen	RSA	6.1.83	1	DL	New York	9 Jun 12
69.15			Spotáková			1		Zaragoza	31 May 08

Mark	Wind		Name	Nat	Born	Pos	Meet	Venue	Date
68.92			Abakumova			Q	WCh	Berlin	16 Aug 09
68.91			Hattestad			1	OG	Sydney	30 Sep 00
68.89			Abakumova			1	DL	Doha	14 May 10
68.86			Obergföll			1	NC	Kassel	24 Jul 11
68.81			Spotáková			1	Odlozil	Praha	16 Jun 08
68.76			Obergföll			Q	WCh	Daegu	1 Sep 11
68.73			Spotáková			2	DL	New York	9 Jun 12
68.66			Spotáková			1	GGala	Roma	10 Jun 10
68.65			Spotáková			1	GGala	Roma	31 May 12
68.63			Obergföll			1		Elstal	12 Sep 10
68.59			Obergföll			1	ET	Leiria	20 Jun 09
	(30/6)								
68.34		Steffi	Nerius	GER	1.7.72	2		Berlin (Elstal)	31 Aug 08
67.67		Sonia	Bisset	CUB	1.4.71	1		Salamanca	6 Jul 05
67.51		Miréla	Manjani/Tzelíli	GRE	21.12.76	2	OG	Sydney	30 Sep 00
67.20		Tatyana	Shikolenko	RUS	10.5.68	1	Herc	Monaco	18 Aug 00
	(10)								
67.16		Martina	Ratej	SLO	2.11.81	3	DL	Doha	14 May 10
66.91		Tanja	Damaske	GER	16.11.71	1	NC	Erfurt	4 Jul 99
66.86		Vira	Rebryk	UKR	25.2.89	1	EC	Helsinki	29 Jun 12
66.81		Linda	Stahl	GER	2.10.85	1	EC	Barcelona	29 Jul 10
66.80		Louise	McPaul/Currey	AUS	24.1.69	1		Gold Coast (RB)	5 Aug 00
66.67		Kara	Patterson	USA	10.4.86	1	NC	Des Moines	25 Jun 10
66.17		Goldie	Sayers	GBR	16.7.82	1	LGP	London (CP)	14 Jul 12
65.91		Nikola	Brejchová'	CZE	25.6.74	1	GP	Linz	2 Aug 04
65.30		Claudia	Coslovich	ITA	26.4.72	1		Ljubljana	10 Jun 00
65.29		Xiomara	Rivero	CUB	22.11.68	1		Santiago de Cuba	17 Mar 01
	(20)								
65.17		Karen	Forkel	GER	24.9.70	2	NC	Erfurt	4 Jul 99
65.11			Li Lingwei	CHN	26.1.89	1		Fuzhou	23 Jun 1210
65.08		Ana Mirela	Termure ¶	ROU	13.1.75	1	NC	Bucuresti	10 Jun 01
64.95			Lu Huihui	CHN	26.6.89	1	NGP	Zhaoqing	14 Apr 12
64.90		Paula	Huhtaniemi'	FIN	17.2.73	1	NC	Helsinki	10 Aug 03
64.89		Yekaterina	Ivakina	RUS	4.12.64	4	Bisl	Oslo	28 Jul 00
64.87		Kelly	Morgan	GBR	17.6.80	1	NC	Birmingham	14 Jul 02
64.83		Christina	Scherwin	DEN	11.7.76	3	WAF	Stuttgart	9 Sep 06
64.67		Katharina	Molitor	GER	8.11.83	2	NC	Kassel	24 Jul 11
64.62		Joanna	Stone	AUS	4.10.72	2		Gold Coast (RB)	5 Aug 00
	(30)								
64.62		Nikolett	Szabó	HUN	3.3.80	1		Pátra	22 Jul 01
64.61		Oksana	Makarova	RUS	21.7.71	2	ECp	Paris (C)	19 Jun 99
64.51		Madara	Palameika	LAT	18.6.87	1	EU23	Kaunas	19 Jul 09
64.51		Monica	Stoian	ROU	25.8.82	4	WCh	Berlin	18 Aug 09
64.49		Valeriya	Zabruskova	RUS	29.7.75	1	Znam	Tula	7 Jun 03
64.46		Dörthe	Friedrich	GER	21.6.73	1	NC	Wattenscheid	7 Jul 02
64.34		Kathryn	Mitchell	AUS	10.7.82	3	GS	Ostrava	25 May 12
64.19		Kim	Kreiner	USA	26.7.77	1		Fortaleza	16 May 07
64.12		Kim	Mickle	AUS	28.12.84	1		Mannheim	23 Jun 12
64.08		Barbara	Madejczyk	POL	30.9.76	1	ECp-S	Málaga	28 Jun 06
	(40)								
64.07		Mercedes	Chilla	ESP	19.1.80	1		Valencia	12 Jun 10
64.06		Taina	Uppa/Kolkkala	FIN	24.10.76	1		Pihtipudas	23 Jul 00
64.03		Mikaela	Ingberg	FIN	29.7.74	6	ISTAF	Berlin	1 Sep 00
63.92			Wei Jianhua	CHN	23.3.79	1		Beijing	18 Aug 00
63.89		Felicia	Tilea-Moldovan ¶	ROU	29.9.67	2	WK	Zürich	16 Aug 02
63.82		Kimberley	Mickle	AUS	28.12.84	1		Sydney	19 Mar 11
63.73		Laverne	Eve	BAH	16.6.65	1		Nashville	22 Apr 00
63.69			Li Lei	CHN	4.5.74	1	OT	Jinzhou	8 Jun 00
63.65		Indre	Jakubaityté	LTU	24.1.76	1		Kaunas	14 Sep 07
63.53		Urszula	Piwnicka	POL	6.12.83	1		Kalamáta	30 May 09
	(50)	100th woman 61.24, 200th 57.77, 300th 55.98							

Ancillary marks – other marks during series (to 68.80)

71.25	Abakumova	2 Sep 11	69.32	Abakumova	21 Aug 08	
69.42	Menéndez	7 Aug 01	69.22	Spotáková	21 Aug 08	
			69.08	Abakumova	21 Aug 08	
			68.95	Obergföll	8 Sep 11	
			68.80	Spotáková	2 Sep 11	

Specification changed from 1 May 1999. See ATHLETICS 2000 for Old specification all-time list.

Mark	Wind	Name		Nat	Born	Pos		Venue	Date
80.00 WR		Petra	Felke	GDR	30.7.59	1		Potsdam	9 Sep 88

HEPTATHLON

Mark		Name		Nat	Born	Pos	Meet	Venue	Date
7291 WR		Jackie	Joyner-Kersee	USA	3.3.62	1	OG	Seoul	24 Sep 88
	12.69/0.5	1.86	15.80	22.56/1.6	7.27/0.7	45.66	2:08.51		

Mark	Wind	Name	Nat	Born	Pos	Meet	Venue	Date
7215 WR		Joyner-Kersee			1	NC/OT	Indianpolis	16 Jul 88
	12.71/-0.9	1.93 15.65		22.30/ 0.0	7.00/-1.3	50.08	2:20.70	
7158 WR		Joyner-Kersee			1	USOF	Houston	2 Aug 86
	13.18/-0.5	1.88 15.20		22.85/1.2	7.03w/2.9	50.12	2:09.69	
7148 WR		Joyner-Kersee			1	GWG	Moskva	7 Jul 86
	12.85/0.2	1.88 14.76		23.00/0.3	7.01/-0.5	49.86	2:10.02	
7128		Joyner-Kersee			1	WCh	Roma	1 Sep 87
	12.91/0.2	1.90 16.00		22.95/1.2	7.14/0.9	45.68	2:16.29	
7044		Joyner-Kersee			1	OG	Barcelona	2 Aug 92
	12.85/-0.9	1.91 14.13		23.12/0.7	7.10/1.3	44.98	2:11.78	
7032	Carolina	Klüft	SWE	2.2.83	1	WCh	Osaka	26 Aug 07
	13.15/0.1	1.95 14.81		23.38/0.3	6.85/1.0	47.98	2:12.56	
7007	Larisa	Nikitina ¶	RUS	29.4.65	1	NC	Bryansk	11 Jun 89
	13.40/1.4	1.89 16.45		23.97/1.1	6.73w/4.0	53.94	2:15.31	
7001		Klüft			1	WCh	Saint-Denis	24 Aug 03
	13.18/-0.4	1.94 14.19		22.98/1.1	6.68/1.0	49.90	2:12.12	
6985	Sabine	Braun	GER	19.6.65	1		Götzis	31 May 92
	13.11/-0.4	1.93 14.84		23.65/2.0	6.63w/2.9	51.62	2:12.67	
6979		Joyner-Kersee			1	NC	San José	24 Jun 87
	12.90/2.0	1.85 15.17		23.02/0.4	7.25/2.3	40.24	2:13.07	
6955	Jessica	Ennis	GBR	28.1.86	1	OG	London (OS)	4 Aug 12
	12.54/1.3	1.86 14.28		22.83/-0.3	6.48/-0.6	47.49	2:08.65	
6952		Klüft			1	OG	Athína	21 Aug 04
	13.21/0.2	1.91 14.77		23.27/-0.1	6.78/0.4	48.89	2:14.15	
6946 WR	Sabine	Paetz'	GDR	16.10.57	1	NC	Potsdam	6 May 84
	12.64/0.3	1.80 15.37		23.37/0.7	6.86/-0.2	44.62	2:08.93	
6942	Ghada	Shouaa	SYR	10.9.72	1		Götzis	26 May 96
	13.78/0.3	1.87 15.64		23.78/0.6	6.77/0.6	54.74	2:13.61	
6935 WR	Ramona	Neubert	GDR	26.7.58	1	v USSR	Moskva	19 Jun 83
	13.42/1.7	1.82 15.25		23.49/0.5	6.79/0.7	49.94	2:07.51	
6910		Joyner			1	MSR	Walnut	25 Apr 86
	12.9/0.0	1.86 14.75		23.24w/2.8	6.85/2.1	48.30	2:14.11	
6906		Ennis			1		Götzis	27 May 12
	12.81/0.0	1.85 14.51		22.88/1.9	6.51/0.8	47.11	2:09.00	
6897		John'			2	wOG	Seoul	24 Sep 88
	12.85/0.5	1.80 16.23		23.65/1.6	6.71/ 0.0	42.56	2:06.14	
6889	Eunice	Barber	FRA	17.11.74	1		Arles	5 Jun 05
	12.62w/2.9	1.91 12.61		24.12/1.2	6.78w/3.4	53.07	2:14.66	
6887		Klüft			1	WCh	Helsinki	7 Aug 05
	13.19/-0.4	1.82 15.02		23.70/-2.5	6.87/0.2	47.20	2:08.89	
6880	Tatyana	Chernova (10)	RUS	29.1.88	1	WCh	Daegu	30 Aug 11
	13.32/0.9	1.83 14.17		23.50/-1.5	6.61/-0.7	52.95	2:08.04	
6878		Joyner-Kersee			1	NC	New York	13 Jun 91
	12.77	1.89 15.62		23.42	6.97/0.4	43.28	2:22.12	
6875		Nikitina			1	ECp-A	Helmond	16 Jul 89
	13.55/-2.1	1.84 15.99		24.29/-2.1	6.75/-2.5	56.78	2:18.67	
6861		Barber			1	WCh	Sevilla	22 Aug 99
	12.89/-0.5	1.93 12.37		23.57/0.5	6.86/-0.3	49.88	2:15.65	
6859	Natalya	Shubenkova	RUS	25.9.57	1	NC	Kyiv	21 Jun 84
	12.93/1.0	1.83 13.66		23.57/-0.3	6.73/0.4	46.26	2:04.60	
6858	Anke	Vater/Behmer	GDR	5.6.61	3	OG	Seoul	24 Sep 88
	13.20/0.5	1.83 14.20		23.10/1.6	6.68/0.1	44.54	2:04.20	
6847		Nikitina			1	WUG	Duisburg	29 Aug 89
	13.47	1.81 16.12		24.12	6.66	59.28	2:22.07	
6845 WR		Neubert			1	v URS	Halle	20 Jun 82
	13.58/1.8	1.83 15.10		23.14/1.4	6.84w/2.3	42.54	2:06.16	
6845	Irina	Belova ¶	RUS	27.3.68	2	OG	Barcelona	2 Aug 92
	13.25/-0.1	1.88 13.77		23.34/0.2	6.82/0.0	41.90	2:05.08	
	(30/13)							
6832	Lyudmila	Blonska ¶	UKR	9.11.77	2	WCh	Osaka	26 Aug 07
	13.25/0.1	1.92 14.44		24.09/0.3	6.88/1.0	47.77	2:16.68	
6831	Denise	Lewis	GBR	27.8.72	1		Talence	30 Jul 00
	13.13/1.0	1.84 15.07		24.01w/3.6	6.69/-0.4	49.42	2:12.20	
6803	Jane	Frederick	USA	7.4.52	1		Talence	16 Sep 84
	13.27/1.2	1.87 15.49		24.15/1.6	6.43/0.2	51.74	2:13.55	
6778	Nataliya	Dobrynska	UKR	29.5.82	2	EC	Barcelona	31 Jul 10
	13.59/-1.6	1.86 15.88		24.23/-0.2	6.56/0.3	49.25	2:12.06	
6765	Yelena	Prokhorova	RUS	16.4.78	1	NC	Tula	23 Jul 00
	13.54/-2.8	1.82 14.30		23.37/-0.2	6.72/1.0	43.40	2:04.27	

Mark	Wind	Name		Nat	Born	Pos	Meet	Venue		Date
6750			Ma Miaolan	CHN	18.1.70	1	NG	Beijing		12 Sep 93
	13.28/1.5	1.89	14.98		23.86/		6.64/	45.82	2:15.33	
6741	Heike		Drechsler	GER	16.12.64	1		Talence		11 Sep 94
	13.34/-0.3	1.84	13.58		22.84/-1.1		6.95/1.0	40.64	2:11.53	
(20)										
6735(w)	Hyleas		Fountain	USA	14.1.81	1	NC	Des Moines		26 Jun 10
	12.93w/2.6	1.90	13.73		23.28w/3.3		6.79w/2.7	42.26	2:17.80	
6703	Tatyana		Blokhina	RUS	12.3.70	1		Talence		11 Sep 93
	13.69/-0.6	1.91	14.94		23.95/-0.4		5.99/-0.3	52.16	2:09.65	
6702	Chantal		Beaugeant ¶	FRA	16.2.61	2		Götzis		19 Jun 88
	13.10/1.6	1.78	13.74		23.96w/3.5		6.45/0.2	50.96	2:07.09	
6695	Jane		Flemming	AUS	14.4.65	1	CG	Auckland		28 Jan 90
	13.21/1.4	1.82	13.76		23.62w/2.4		6.57/1.6	49.28	2:12.53	
6683	Jennifer		Oeser	GER	29.11.83	3	EC	Barcelona		31 Jul 10
	13.37/-1.0	1.83	13.82		24.07/-0.3		6.68/-0.3	49.17	2:12.28	
6681	Kristina		Savitskaya	RUS	10.6.91	1	NC	Cheboksary		3 Jun 12
	13.52/0.0	1.88	15.27		24.61/0.0		6.65/0.0	46.83	2:14.73	
6660	Ines		Schulz	GDR	10.7.65	3		Götzis		19 Jun 88
	13.56/0.4	1.84	13.95		23.93w/2.8		6.70/0.7	42.82	2:06.31	
6658	Svetla		Dimitrova ¶	BUL	27.1.70	2		Götzis		31 May 92
	13.41/-0.7	1.75	14.72		23.06w/2.4		6.64/1.9	43.84	2:09.60	
6649	Lilli		Schwarzkopf	GER	28.8.83	2	OG	London (OS)		4 Aug 12
	13.26/0.9	1.83	14.77		24.77/0.9		6.30/-0.7	51.73	2:10.50	
6646	Natalya		Grachova	UKR	21.2.52	1	NC	Moskva		2 Aug 82
	13.80	1.80	16.18		23.86		6.65w/3.5	39.42	2:06.59	
(30)										
6635	Sibylle		Thiele	GDR	6.3.65	2	GWG	Moskva		7 Jul 86
	13.14/0.6	1.76	16.00		24.18		6.62/1.0	45.74	2:15.30	
6635	Svetlana		Buraga	BLR	4.9.65	3	WCh	Stuttgart		17 Aug 93
	12.95/0.1	1.84	14.55		23.69/0.0		6.58/-0.2	41.04	2:13.65	
6633	Natalya		Roshchupkina	RUS	13.1.78	2	NC	Tula		23 Jul 00
	14.05/-2.8	1.88	14.28		23.47/-0.2		6.45/0.4	44.34	2:07.93	
6623	Judy		Simpson’	GBR	14.11.60	3	EC	Stuttgart		30 Aug 86
	13.05/0.8	1.92	14.73		25.09/0.0		6.56w/2.5	40.92	2:11.70	
6619	Liliana		Nastase	ROU	1.8.62	4	OG	Barcelona		2 Aug 92
	12.86/-0.9	1.82	14.34		23.70/0.2		6.49/-0.3	41.30	2:11.22	
6618	Lyudmyla		Yosypenko	UKR	24.9.84	4	OG	London (OS)		4 Aug 12
	13.25/0.9	1.83	13.90		23.68/0.6		6.31/-0.6	49.63	2:13.28	
6616	Malgorzata		Nowak’	POL	9.2.59	1	WUG	Kobe		31 Aug 85
	13.27w/4.0	1.95	15.35		24.20/0.0		6.37w/3.9	43.36	2:20.39	
6604	Remigija		Nazaroviene’	LTU	2.6.67	2	URSCh	Bryansk		11 Jun 89
	13.26/1.4	1.86	14.27		24.12/0.7		6.58/0.9	40.94	2:09.98	
6604	Irina		Tyukhay	RUS	14.1.67	3		Götzis		28 May 95
	13.20/-0.7	1.84 14.97			24.33/1.7		6.71/0.5	43.84	2:17.64	
6599A	Jessica		Zelinka	CAN	3.9.81	1	NC	Calgary		28 Jun 12
	12.76/-0.6	1.77	14.74		23.42w/2.1		5.98w/2.9	46.60	2:08.95	
(40)										
6599	Austra		Skujyté	LTU	12.8.79	5	OG	London (OS)		4 Aug 12
	14.00/0.7	1.92	17.31		25.43/0.9		6.25/-0.6	51.13	2:20.59	
6598	Svetlana		Moskalets	RUS	22.1.69	1	NC	Vladimir		17 Jun 94
	13.20/0.8	1.82	13.78		23.56/0.1		6.74/0.8	42.48	2:14.54	
6591	Svetlana		Sokolova	RUS	9.1.81	1	NC	Tula		23 Jun 04
	13.56/1.1	1.82	15.09		24.02/0.6		6.26/0.3	45.07	2:07.23	
6577	DeDee		Nathan	USA	20.4.68	1		Götzis		30 May 99
	13.28/-0.1	1.76	14.74		24.23/0.2		6.59/1.6	50.08	2:16.92	
6576	Antoinette		Nana Djimou	FRA	2.8.85	6	OG	London (OS)		4 Aug 12
	12.96/1.3	1.80	14.26		24.72/0.3		6.13/-0.2	55.87	2:15.94	
6573	Rita		Ináncsi	HUN	6.1.71	3		Götzis		29 May 94
	13.66/2.0	1.84	13.94		24.20w/2.5		6.78/1.4	46.28	2:16.02	
6572	Heike		Tischler	GDR	4.2.64	2	EC	Split		31 Aug 90
	14.08/-0.9	1.82	13.73		24.29/0.9		6.22/-0.7	53.24	2:05.50	
6563	Natalya		Sazanovich	BLR	15.8.73	2	OG	Atlanta		28 Jul 96
	13.56/-1.6	1.80	14.52		23.72/-0.3		6.70/1.1	46.00	2:17.92	
6559	Olga		Kurban	RUS	16.12.87	1	NC	Chelyabinsk		16 Jun 08
	13.29/0.6	1.77	13.71		24.04/0.5		6.51/0.1	49.23	2:12.42	
6552	Nadezhda		Vinogradova’	RUS	1.5.58	2	NC	Kyiv		21 Jun 84
	13.92/1.0	1.80	15.19		23.84/0.2		6.67/0.1	38.60	2:06.80	

(50)   100th woman 6379, 200th 6192, 300th 6059, 400th 5966, 500th 5859

DECATHLON

Mark		Name		Nat	Born	Pos		Venue		Date
8358 WR	Austra		Skujyte	LTU	12.8.79	1		Columbia, MO		15 Apr 05
	12.49/1.6	46.19	3.10		48.78	57.19	14.22w/2.4 6.12/1.6	16.42	1.78	5:15.86

Mark	Wind	Name	Nat	Born	Pos	Meet	Venue	Date
8150 WR		Marie Collonvillé	FRA	23.11.73	1		Talence	26 Sep 04
	12.48/0.4	34.69 3.50		47.19	56.15	13.96/0.4 6.18/1.0 11.90 1.80		5:06.09
7885		Mona Steigauf	GER	17.1.70	1		Ahlen	21 Sep 97
	12.15/1.2	5.93 12.49		1.73	55.34	13.75/0.2 34.68 3.10 42.24		5:07.95

IAAF approved order: 100m, DT, PV, JT, 400m / 100mh, LJ, SP, HJ, 1500m, 1997/2000 events used men's order

4 x 100 METRES RELAY

Mark	Wind	Nat	Name	Pos	Meet	Venue	Date
40.82		USA	Madison, Felix, Knight, Jeter	1	OG	London (OS)	10 Aug 12
41.37 WR		GDR	Gladisch, Rieger, Auerswald, Göhr	1	WCp	Canberra	6 Oct 85
41.41		JAM	Fraser-Pryce, Simpson, Campbell-Brown, Stewart	2	OG	London (OS)	10 Aug 12
41.47		USA	Gaines, Jones, Miller, Devers	1	WCh	Athína	9 Aug 97
41.49		RUS	Bogoslovskaya, Malchugina, Voronova, Privalova	1	WCh	Stuttgart	22 Aug 93
41.49		USA	Finn, Torrence, Vereen, Devers	2	WCh	Stuttgart	22 Aug 93
41.52		USA	Gaines, Jones, Miller, Devers	1h1	WCh	Athína	8 Aug 97
41.53 WR		GDR	Gladisch, Koch, Auerswald, Göhr	1		Berlin	31 Jul 83
41.55		USA	Brown, Williams, Griffith, Marshall	1	ISTAF	Berlin	21 Aug 87
41.56		USA	B Knight, Felix, Myers, Jeter	1	WCh	Daegu	4 Sep 11
41.58		USA	Brown, Williams, Griffith, Marshall	1	WCh	Roma	6 Sep 87
41.58		USA	L.Williams, Felix, Lee, Jeter	1		Cottbus	8 Aug 09
41.60 WR		GDR	Müller, Wöckel, Auerswald, Göhr	1	OG	Moskva	1 Aug 80
41.61A		USA	Brown, Williams, Cheeseborough, Ashford	1	USOF	USAF Academy	3 Jul 83
41.63		USA	Brown, Williams, Cheeseborough, Ashford	1	v GDR	Los Angeles	25 Jun 83
41.64		USA	Madison, Tarmoh, Knight, L Williams	1h1	OG	London (OS)	9 Aug 12
41.65		USA	Brown, Bolden, Cheeseborough, Ashford	1	OG	Los Angeles	11 Aug 84
41.65		GDR	Gladisch, Koch, Auerswald, Göhr	1	ECp	Moskva	17 Aug 85
41.68		GDR	Möller, Krabbe, Behrendt, Günther	1	EC	Split	1 Sep 90
41.69		GDR	Gladisch, Koch, Auerswald, Göhr	1	OD	Potsdam	21 Jul 84
41.70		JAM	Fraser, Stewart, Simpson, Campbell-Brown	2	WCh	Daegu	4 Sep 11

(21 performances by 4 nations) from here just best by nation

Mark	Wind	Nat	Name	Pos	Meet	Venue	Date
41.78		FRA	Girard, Hurtis, Félix, Arron	1	WCh	Saint-Denis	30 Aug 03
41.92		BAH	Fynes, Sturrup, Davis-Thompson, Ferguson	1	WCh	Sevilla	29 Aug 99
42.04		UKR	Povh, Stuy, Ryemyen, Bryzgina	3	OG	London (OS)	10 Aug 12
42.08mx		BUL	Pavlova, Nuneva, Georgieva, Ivanova	mx		Sofiya	8 Aug 84
			42.29 Pencheva, Nuneva, Georgieva, Donkova	1		Sofiya	26 Jun 88
42.23		CHN	(Sichuan) Xiao Lin, Li Yali, Liu Xiaomei, Li Xuemei	1	NG	Shanghai	23 Oct 97
42.39		NGR	Utondu, Idehen, Opara-Thompson, Onyali (10)	2h2	OG	Barcelona	7 Aug 92
42.43		GBR	Hunte, Smallwood, Goddard, Lannaman	3	OG	Moskva	1 Aug 80
42.45		NED	Vassell, Schippers, Lubbers, Samuel	3h1	OG	London (OS)	9 Aug 12
42.54		BEL	Borlée, Mariën, Ouédraogo, Gevaert	2	OG	Beijing	22 Aug 08
42.55		BRA	Silva, Krasucki, E dos Santos, R Santos	4h1	OG	London (OS)	9 Aug 12
42.56		BLR	Nesterenko, Sologub, Nevmerzhitskaya, Dragun	3	WCh	Helsinki	13 Aug 05
42.59		FRG	Possekel, Helten, Richter, Kroniger	2	OG	Montreal	31 Jul 76
42.68		POL	Popowicz, Korczynska, Jeschke, Wedler	3	EC	Barcelona	1 Aug 10
42.77		CAN	Bailey, Payne, Taylor, Gareau	2	OG	Los Angeles	11 Aug 84
42.89		CUB	Ferrer, López, Duporty, Allen	6	WCh	Stuttgart	22 Aug 93
42.98		CZE/TCH	Sokolová, Soborová, Kocembová, Kratochvilová	1	WK	Zürich	18 Aug 82
			(20)				
42.99A		AUS	Massey, Broadrick, Lambert, Gainsford-Taylor	1		Pietersburg	18 Mar 00
43.03A		COL	M.Murillo, Palacios, Obregón, D Murillo	2	SAm-r	Bogotá	10 Jul 04
43.04		ITA	Pistone, Calí, Arcioni, Alloh	3	ECp-S	Annecy	21 Jun 08
43.07		GRE	Tsóni, Kóffa, Vasarmídou, Thánou	2	MedG	Bari	18 Jun 97
43.19		GHA	Akoto, Twum, Anim, Nsiah	5s1	OG	Sydney	29 Sep 00
43.22		TRI	Thomas, Baptiste, Hurtchinson, Hackett	3h1	WCh	Berlin	22 Aug 09
43.25A		RSA	Hartman, Moropane, Holtshausen, Seyerling	2		Pietersburg	18 Mar 00
43.35		KAZ	Aleksandrova, Kvast, Miljauskiene, Sevalnikova	2	SPART	Taskent	16 Sep 86
43.37		FIN	Pirtimaa, Hanhijoki, Hernesniemi, Salmela	7	WCh	Stuttgart	22 Aug 93
43.38		THA	Jaksunin, Saenrat, Klomdee, Thavoncharoen (30)	2		Nakhon R'sima	26 Jun 08

Best at low altitude

Mark	Wind	Nat	Name	Pos	Meet	Venue	Date
43.03		COL	M.Murillo, Palacios, Obregón, N.González	3h2	WCh	Helsinki	12 Aug 05
43.18		AUS	Wilson, Wells, Robertson, Boyle	5	OG	Montreal	31 Jul 76

One or more athlete susbsequently drugs dq

Mark	Wind	Nat	Name	Pos	Meet	Venue	Date
41.67		USA	A Williams, Jones ¶, L Williams, Colander	(1)	3-N	München	8 Aug 04
41.67		USA	A Williams, Jones ¶, L Williams, Colander	(1h1)	OG	Athína	26 Aug 04
41.71		USA	White ¶, Gaines, Miller, Jones ¶	(1)	WCh	Edmonton	11 Aug 01
42.31		TRI	Ahye, Baptiste, Selvon, Hackett #	2h1	OG	London (OS)	9 Aug 12

4 x 200 METRES RELAY

Mark	Wind	Nat	Name	Pos	Meet	Venue	Date
1:27.46 WR		USA Blue	Jenkins, Colander-Richardson, Perry, M Jones	1	PennR	Philadelphia	29 Apr 00
1:28.15 WR		GDR	Göhr, R.Müller, Wöckel, Koch	1		Jena	9 Aug 80
1:29.42		Texas A & M (USA)	Tarmoh, Mayo, Beard, Lucas	1	Penn R	Philadelphia	24 Apr 10
Drugs dq:	1:29.40	USA Red	Colander, Gaines, Miller, M Jones ¶	1	Penn	Philadelphia	24 Apr 04

Mark	Wind	Name	Nat	Born	Pos	Meet	Venue	Date

4 x 400 METRES RELAY

3:15.17 WR URS 1 OG Seoul 1 Oct 88
Ledovskaya 50.12, O.Nazarova 47.82, Pinigina 49.43, Bryzgina 47.80
3:15.51 USA 2 OG Seoul 1 Oct 88
D.Howard 49.82, Dixon 49.17, Brisco 48.44, Griffith-Joyner 48.08
3:15.92 WR GDR G.Walther 49.8, Busch 48.9, Rübsam 49.4, Koch 47.8 1 NC Erfurt 3 Jun 84
3:16.71 USA Torrence 49.0, Malone 49.4, Kaiser-Brown 49.48, Miles 48.78 1 WCh Stuttgart 22 Aug 93
3:16.87 GDR Emmelmann 50.9, Busch 48.8, Müller 48.9, Koch 48.21 1 EC Stuttgart 31 Aug 86
3:16.87 USA Trotter 50.3, Felix 48.1, McCorory 49.39, Richards-Ross 49.10 1 OG London (OS) 11 Aug 12
3:17.83 USA Dunn 50.5, Felix 48.8, Demus 50.14, Richards 48.44 1 WCh Berlin 23 Aug 09
3:18.09 USA Richards-Ross 49.3, Felix 49.4, Beard 49.84, McCorory 49.52 1 WCh Daegu 3 Sep 11
3:18.29 USA 1 OG Los Angeles 11 Aug 84
Leatherwood 50.50, S.Howard 48.83, Brisco-Hooks 49.23, Cheeseborough 49.73
3:18.29 GDR Neubauer 50.58, Emmelmann 49.89, Busch 48.81, Müller 48.99 3 OG Seoul 1 Oct 88
3:18.38 RUS 2 WCh Stuttgart 22 Aug 93
Ruzina 50.8, Alekseyeva 49.3, Ponomaryova 49.78, Privalova 48.47
3:18.43 URS 1 WCh Tokyo 1 Sep 91
Ledovskaya 51.7, Dzhigalova 49.2, Nazarova 48.87, Bryzgina 48.67
3:18.54 USA Wineberg 51.0, Felix 48.6, Henderson 50.06, Richards 48.93 1 OG Beijing 23 Aug 08

3:18.55 USA Trotter 51.2, Felix 48.0, Wineberg 50.24, Richards 49.07 1 WCh Osaka 2 Sep 07
3:18.58 URS I.Nazarova, Olizarenko, Pinigina, Vladykina 1 ECp Moskva 18 Aug 85
3:18.63 GDR Neubauer 51.4, Emmelmann 49.1, Müller 48.64, Busch 49.48 1 WCh Roma 6 Sep 87
3:18.71 JAM Whyte 50.0, Prendergast 49.6, Williams-Mills 49.84, Williams 49.22 2 WCh Daegu 3 Sep 11
3:18.82 RUS Gushchina 50.6, Litvinova 49.2, Firova 49.20, Kapachinskaya 49.82 2 OG Beijing 23 Aug 08
3:19.01 USA Trotter 49.8, Henderson 49.7, Richards 49.81, Hennagan 49.73 (1) OG Athína 28 Aug 04
Note team was disqualified as Crystal Cox (subject of retrospective drugs ban) ran for them in the heat
3:19.04 WR GDR Siemon' 51.0, Busch 50.0, Rübsam 50.2, Koch 47.9 1 EC Athína 11 Sep 82
3:19.12 URS Baskakova, I.Nazarova, Pinigina, Vladykina 1 Drz Praha 18 Aug 84
3:19.23 WR GDR Maletzki 50.05, Rohde 49.00, Streidt 49.51, Brehmer 49.79 1 OG Montreal 31 Jul 76
3:19.36 RUS 3 WCh Daegu 3 Sep 11
Krivoshapka 50.3, Antyukh 50.0, Litvinova 49.96, Kapachinskaya 49.22
3:19.49 GDR Emmelmann, Busch, Neubauer, Koch 47.9 1 WCp Canberra 4 Oct 85
3:19.50 URS Yurchenko 51.2, O.Nazarova 50.2, Pinigina 49.09, Bryzgina 49.03 2 WCh Roma 6 Sep 87
3:19.60 USA Leatherwood, S.Howard, Brisco-Hooks, Cheeseborough 1 Walnut 25 Jul 84
3:19.62 GDR Kotte, Brehmer, Köhn, Koch 48.3 1 ECp Torino 5 Aug 79
(26/4 with USSR and Russia counted separately)
3:19.73 JAM S Williams 50.5, Lloyd 50.1, Prendergast 50.18, NWilliams 48.93 2 WCh Osaka 2 Sep 07
3:20.04 GBR Ohuruogu 50.6, Okoro 50.9, McConnell 49.79, Sanders 48.76 3 WCh Osaka 2 Sep 07
3:20.32 CZE/TCH 2 WCh Helsinki 14 Aug 83
Kocembová 48.93, Matejkovicová 52.13, Moravcíková 51.51, Kratochvílová 47.75
3:21.04 NGR Afolabi 51.13, Yusuf 49.72, Opara 51.29, Ogunkoya 48.90 2 OG Atlanta 3 Aug 96
3:21.21 CAN Crooks 50.30, Richardson 50.22, Killingbeck ¶ 50.62, Payne 50.07 2 OG Los Angeles 11 Aug 84
3:21.85 BLR Kozak 52.0, Khlyustova 50.3, I Usovich 49.85, S Usovich 49.69 4 OG Beijing 23 Aug 08
(10)
3:21.94 UKR Dzhigalova, Olizarenko, Pinigina, Vladykina 1 URSCh Kyiv 17 Jul 86
3:22.34 FRA Landre 51.3, Dorsile 51.1, Elien 50.54, Pérec 49.36 1 EC Helsinki 14 Aug 94
3:22.49 FRG Thimm 50.81, Arendt 49.95, Thomas 51.50, Abt 50.23 4 OG Seoul 1 Oct 88
3:23.21 CUB Díaz 51.1, Calatayud 51.2, Clement 50.47, Terrero 50.46 6 OG Beijing 23 Aug 08
3:23.81 AUS Peris-K 51.71, Lewis 51.69, Gainsford-T 51.06, Freeman 49.35 4 OG Sydney 30 Sep 00
3:24.28 CHN (Hebei) An X, Bai X, Cao C, Ma Y 1 NG Beijing 13 Sep 93
3:24.49 POL Guzowska 52.2, Bejnar 50.2, Prokopek 50.47, Jesien 51.59 4 WCh Helsinki 14 Aug 05
3:25.68 ROU Ruicu 52.69, Rîpanu 51.09, Barbu 52.64, Tîrlea 49.26 2 ECp Paris (C) 20 Jun 99
3:25.7a FIN Eklund 53.6, Pursiainen 50.6, Wilmi 51.6, Salin 49.9 2 EC Roma 8 Sep 74
3:25.71 ITA Bazzoni 53.7, Milani 50.8, Spacca 51.64, Grenot 49.61 4 EC Barcelona 1 Aug 10
(20)
3:25.81 BUL Ilieva, Stamenova, Penkova, Damyanova 1 v Hun,Pol Sofiya 24 Jul 83
3:26.33 GRE Kaidantzi 53.2, Goudenoúdi 51.6, Boudá 51.76, Halkiá 49.75 3 ECpS Bydgoszcz 20 Jun 04
3:26.68 BRA (Bovespa) Coutinho, de Oliveira, Sousa, de Lima 1 NC São Paulo 7 Aug 11
3:26.89 IND R Kaur 53.1, Beenamol 51.4, Soman 52.51, M Kaur 49.85 3h2 OG Athína 27 Aug 04
3:27.08 CMR Nguimgo 51.7, Kaboud 52.1, Atangana 51.98, Béwouda 51.35 7 WCh Saint-Denis 31 Aug 03
3:27.14 MEX Rodríguez 53.3, Medina 51.2, Vela 52.94, Guevara 49.70 4h2 WCh Osaka 1 Sep 07
3:27.48 IRL Andrews 53.4, Cuddihy 49.9, Bergin 52.60, Carey 51.54 4h3 WCh Daegu 2 Sep 11
3:27.54 LTU Navickaite, Valiuliene, Mendzoryte, Ambraziene 3 SPART Moskva 22 Jun 83
3:27.57 ESP Merino 52.2, Lacambra 52.0, Myers 50.85, Ferrer 52.56 7 WCh Tokyo 1 Sep 91
3:27.86 HUN Orosz, Forgács, Tóth, Pál 5 OG Moskva 1 Aug 80

5000 METRES WALK (TRACK)

20:02.60 WR Gillian O'Sullivan IRL 21.8.76 1 NC Dublin (S) 13 Jul 02
20:03.0 WR Kerry Saxby-Junna AUS 2.6.61 1 Sydney 11 Feb 96
20:07.52 WR Beate Anders/Gummelt GDR 4.2.68 1 vURS Rostock 23 Jun 90

Mark	Wind	Name		Nat	Born	Pos	Meet	Venue	Date
20:11.45		Sabine	Zimmer	GER	6.2.81	1	NC	Wattenscheid	2 Jul 05
20:12.41		Elisabetta	Perrone	ITA	9.7.68	1	NC	Rieti	2 Aug 03
20:18.87		Melanie	Seeger	GER	8.1.77	1	NC	Braunschweig	10 Jul 04
20:21.69		Annarita	Sidoti	ITA	25.7.69	1	NC	Cesenatico	1 Jul 95
20:27.59	wr	Ileana	Salvador	ITA	16.1.62	1		Trento	3 Jun 89
20:28.05		Tatyana	Kalmykova	RUS	10.1.90	1	WY	Ostrava	12 Jul 07

10 KILOMETRES WALK

Mark	Wind	Name		Nat	Born	Pos	Meet	Venue	Date
41:04	wr	Yelena	Nikolayeva	RUS	1.2.66	1	NC	Sochi	20 Apr 96
41:16			Wang Yan	CHN	3.5.71	1		Eisenhüttenstadt	8 May 99
41:16		Kjersti	Plätzer (Tysse)	NOR	18.1.72	1	NC	Os	11 May 02
41:17		Irina	Stankina	RUS	25.3.77	1	NC-w	Adler	9 Feb 97
41:24		Olimpiada	Ivanova ¶	RUS	26.8.70	2	NC-w	Adler	9 Feb 97
41:29	wr	Larisa	Ramazanova	RUS	23.9.71	1	NC	Izhevsk	4 Jun 95
41:30	wr	Kerry	Saxby-Junna	AUS	2.6.61	1	NC	Canberra	27 Aug 88
41:30			O Ivanova			2	NC	Izhevsk	4 Jun 95
41:31		Yelena	Gruzinova	RUS	24.12.67	2	NC	Sochi	20 Apr 96
41:37.9t			Gao Hongmiao	CHN	17.3.74	1	NC	Beijing	7 Apr 94
41:38		Rossella	Giordano (10)	ITA	1.12.72	1		Naumburg	25 May 97
41:41			Nikolayeva			2		Naumburg	25 May 97
41:41			Tysse Plätzer			1		Kraków	30 May 09
41:42		Olga	Kaniskina	RUS	19.1.85	2		Kraków	30 May 09
41:45			Liu Hongyu	CHN	11.1.75	2		Eisenhüttenstadt	8 May 99
41:46		Annarita	Sidoti	ITA	25.7.69	1		Livorno	12 Jun 94
41:46			O Ivanova			1	NC/w	Adler	11 Feb 96
41:47			Saxby-Junna			1		Eisenhüttenstadt	11 May 96
41:48			Li Chunxiu	CHN	13.8.69	1	NG	Beijing	8 Sep 93
41:49			Ramazanova			3	NC	Sochi	20 Apr 96
41:49			Nikolayeva			1	OG	Atlanta	29 Jul 96
41:50		Yelena	Arshintseva	RUS	5.4.71	1	NC-w	Adler	11 Feb 95
		(22/15)							
41:51		Beate	Anders/Gummelt	GER	4.2.68	2		Eisenhüttenstadt	11 May 96
41:52		Tatyana	Mineyeva ¶	RUS	10.8.90	1	NCp-j	Penza	5 Sep 09
41:52		Tatyana	Korotkova	RUS	24.4.80	1		Buy	19 Sep 10
41:53		Tatyana	Sibileva	RUS	17.5.80	1	RWC-F	Beijing	18 Sep 10
41:56		Yelena	Sayko	RUS	24.12.67	2	NC/w	Adler	11 Feb 96
		(20)							
41:56.23t		Nadezhda	Ryashkina	RUS	22.1.67	1	GWG	Seattle	24 Jul 90
42:01		Tamara	Kovalenko	RUS	5.6.64	3	NC-w	Adler	11 Feb 95
42:01		Olga	Panfyorova	RUS	21.8.77	1	NC-23	Izhevsk	16 May 98
42:04+		Vera	Sokolova	RUS	8.6.87	1=	in 20k	Sochi	26 Feb 11
42:04+		Anisya	Kirdyapkina	RUS	23.10.89	1=	in 20k	Sochi	26 Feb 11
42:04+		Tatyana	Shemyakina	RUS	3.9.87	1=	in 20k	Sochi	26 Feb 11
42:05+		Margarita	Turova	BLR	28.12.80	1+	in 20k	Adler	12 Mar 05
42:06		Valentina	Tsybulskaya	BLR	19.2.68	4		Eisenhüttenstadt	8 May 99
42:07		Ileana	Salvador	ITA	16.1.62	1		Sesto San Giovanni	1 May 92
42:09		Elisabetta	Perrone	ITA	9.7.68	4		Eisenhüttenstadt	11 May 96
		(30)							
42:11		Nina	Alyushenko	RUS	29.5.68	3	NC	Izhevsk	4 Jun 95
42:13		Natalya	Misyulya	BLR	16.4.66	5		Eisenhüttenstadt	8 May 99
42:13.7t		Madelein	Svensson	SWE	20.7.69	2	SGP	Fana	15 May 92
42:15			Gu Yan	CHN	17.3.74	3	WCp	Podebrady	19 Apr 97
42:15		Erica	Alfridi	ITA	22.2.68	5		Naumburg	25 May 97
42:15		Jane	Saville	AUS	5.11.74	6		Eisenhüttenstadt	8 May 99
42:16		Alina	Ivanova	RUS	16.3.69	1		Novopolotsk	27 May 89
42:16		Norica	Cîmpean	ROU	22.3.72	1		Calella	9 May 99
42:17		Katarzyna	Radtke	POL	31.8.69	5		Eisenhüttenstadt	11 May 96
42:19+		Iraida	Pudovkina	RUS	2.11.80	2	in 20k	Adler	12 Mar 05
		(40)	50th woman 42:35, 100th 43:13, 200th 44:12, 300th 44:52						

Probable short course: Livorno 10 Jul 93: 1. Ileana Salvador ITA 16.1.62 41:30, 2. Elisabeta Perrone 9.7.68 41:56

Best track times

Mark	Wind	Name		Nat	Born	Pos	Meet	Venue	Date
41:57.22		Kerry	Saxby-Junna	AUS	2.6.61	2	GWG	Seattle	24 Jul 90
42:11.5		Beate	Anders/Gummelt	GER	4.2.68	1	SGP	Fana	15 May 92

20 KILOMETRES WALK

Mark	Wind	Name		Nat	Born	Pos	Meet	Venue	Date
1:24:50		Olimpiada	Ivanova ¶	RUS	26.8.70	1	NC-w	Adler	4 Mar 01
1:24:56		Olga	Kaniskina	RUS	19.1.85	1	NC-w	Adler	28 Feb 09
1:25:02		Yelena	Lashmanova	RUS	9.4.92	1	OG	London	11 Aug 12
1:25:08	wr	Vera	Sokolova	RUS	8.6.87	1	NC-w	Sochi	26 Feb 11
1:25:09		Anisya	Kirdyapkina	RUS	23.10.89	2	NC-w	Sochi	26 Feb 11

Mark	Wind	Name		Nat	Born	Pos	Meet	Venue	Date
1:25:09			Kaniskina			2	OG	London	11 Aug 12
1:25:11			Kaniskina			1	NC-w	Adler	23 Feb 08
1:25:11			Kirdyapkina			1	NC-w	Sochi	20 Feb 10
1:25:16			Qieyang Shenjie	CHN	11.11.90	3	OG	London	11 Aug 12
1:25:18		Tatyana	Gudkova	RUS	23.1.78	1	NC	Moskva	19 May 00
1:25:20		Olga	Polyakova	RUS	23.9.80	2	NC	Moskva	19 May 00
1:25:26			Sokolova			2	NC-w	Adler	28 Feb 09
1:25:26			Kirdyapkina			3	NC-w	Adler	28 Feb 09
1:25:27		Elmira	Alembekova	RUS	30.6.90	1	NC-w	Sochi	18 Feb 12
1:25:29		Irina	Stankina (10)	RUS	25.3.77	3	NC	Moskva	19 May 00
1:25:30			Kirdyapkina			2	NC-w	Adler	23 Feb 08
1:25:32		Yelena	Shumkina	RUS	24.1.88	4	NC-w	Adler	28 Feb 09
1:25:35			Sokolova			2	NC-w	Sochi	20 Feb 10
1:25:41	WR		O Ivanova			1	WCh	Helsinki	7 Aug 05
1:25:42			Kaniskina			1	WCp	Cheboksary	11 May 08
1:25:46		Tatyana	Shemyakina	RUS	3.9.87	3	NC-w	Adler	23 Feb 08
1:25:46			Liu Hong	CHN	12.5.87	1		Taicang	30 Mar 12
1:25:52		Larisa	Yemelyanova	RUS	6.1.80	5	NC-w	Adler	28 Feb 09
1:25:52		Tatyana	Sibileva	RUS	17.5.80	3	NC-w	Sochi	20 Feb 10
1:25:59		Tamara	Kovalenko	RUS	5.6.64	4	NC	Moskva	19 May 00
1:26:00			Liu Hong			4	OG	London	11 Aug 12
1:26:02			Kaniskina			1	NC-w	Adler	19 Feb 06
1:26:08			Ivanova			5	NC	Moskva	19 May 00
1:26:11		Margarita	Turova	BLR	28.12.80	1	NC	Nesvizh	15 Apr 06
1:26:14		Irina	Petrova	RUS	26.5.85	2	NC-w	Adler	19 Feb 06
		(30/18)							
1:26:16		Lyudmila	Arkhipova	RUS	25.11.78	5	NC-w	Adler	23 Feb 08
1:26:22	WR		Wang Yan (20)	CHN	3.5.71	1	NG	Guangzhou	19 Nov 01
1:26:22	WR	Yelena	Nikolayeva	RUS	1.2.66	1	ECp	Cheboksary	18 May 03
1:26:23			Wang Liping	CHN	8.7.76	2	NG	Guangzhou	19 Nov 01
1:26:28		Iraida	Pudovkina	RUS	2.11.80	1	NC-w	Adler	12 Mar 05
1:26:34		Tatyana	Kalmykova	RUS	10.1.90	1	NC	Saransk	8 Jun 08
1:26:35			Liu Hongyu	CHN	11.1.75	3	NG	Guangzhou	19 Nov 01
1:26:46			Song Hongjuan	CHN	4.7.84	1	NC	Guangzhou	20 Mar 04
1:26:50		Natalya	Fedoskina	RUS	25.6.80	2	ECp	Dudince	19 May 01
1:26:57		Lyudmila	Yefimkina	RUS	22.8.81	3	NC-w	Adler	19 Feb 06
1:27:01			Lu Xiuzhi	CHN	26.10.93	2		Taicang	30 Mar 12
1:27:07		Kjersti	Tysse Plätzer	NOR	18.1.72	2	OG	Beijing	21 Aug 08
		(30)							
1:27:08		Anna	Lukyanova	RUS	23.4.91	5	NC-w	Sochi	18 Feb 12
1:27:09		Elisabetta	Perrone	ITA	9.7.68	3	ECp	Dudince	19 May 01
1:27:12		Elisa	Rigaudo	ITA	17.6.80	3	OG	Beijing	21 Aug 08
1:27:14		Antonina	Petrova	RUS	1.5.77	1	NC-w	Adler	1 Mar 03
1:27:18		Alena	Nartova	RUS	1.1.82	6	NC-w	Adler	23 Feb 08
1:27:19			Jiang Jing	CHN	23.10.85	1	NC	Nanning	25 Feb 05
1:27:22		Gillian	O'Sullivan	IRL	21.8.76	1		Sesto San Giovanni	1 May 03
1:27:25		María	Vasco	ESP	26.12.75	5	OG	Beijing	21 Aug 08
1:27:27		Vira	Zozulya	UKR	31.8.70	1	NC	Sumy	7 Jun 08
1:27:29		Erica	Alfridi	ITA	22.2.68	4	ECp	Dudince	19 May 01
		(40)							
1:27:30	WB	Nadezhda	Ryashkina	RUS	22.1.67	1	NC-w	Adler	7 Feb 99
1:27:30		Tatyana	Kozlova	RUS	2.9.83	2	NC-w	Adler	12 Mar 05
1:27:35		Tatyana	Korotkova	RUS	24.4.80	2	NC	Cheboksary	12 Jun 04
1:27:37			Bo Yanmin	CHN	29.6.87	1	NG	Nanjing	20 Oct 05
1:27:41		Claudia	Iovan/Stef ¶	ROU	25.2.78	1		La Coruña	5 Jun 04
1:27:43		Yekaterina	Yezhova	RUS	3.7.82	7	NC-w	Adler	23 Feb 08
1:27:44		Jane	Saville	AUS	5.11.74	4	WCp	Naumburg	2 May 04
1:27:44		Beatriz	Pascual	ESP	9.5.82	6	OG	Beijing	21 Aug 08
1:27:45		Olive	Loughnane	IRL	14.1.76	7	OG	Beijing	21 Aug 08
1:27:46		Norica	Cîmpean	ROU	22.3.72	1		Békéscsaba	28 Mar 99
1:27:46		Ana	Cabecinha	POR	29.4.84	8	OG	Beijing	21 Aug 08
		(50)	100th best woman 1:29:30, 200th 1:31:34, 300th 1:33:15						

50 KILOMETRES WALK

Mark	Wind	Name		Nat	Born	Pos	Meet	Venue	Date
4:10:59		Monica	Svensson	SWE	26.12.78	1		Scanzorosciate	21 Oct 07
4:12:16		Yelena	Ginko	BLR	30.7.76	1		Scanzorosciate	17 Oct 04
4:16:27		Jolanta	Dukure	LAT	20.9.79	1		Paralepa	9 Sep 06
4:25:22		Brigita	Virbalyte	LTU	1.2.85	1		Villa di Serio	17 Oct 10
4:28:13		Evaggelía	Xinoú	GRE	22.11.81	2		Scanzorosciate	17 Oct 04
4:28:53		Neringa	Aidietité	LTU	5.6.83	1		Ivano-Frankivsk	1 Oct 06

Mark	Wind	Name		Nat	Born	Pos	Meet	Venue	Date

JUNIOR MEN'S ALL-TIME LISTS

100 METRES

Mark	Wind	Name		Nat	Born	Pos	Meet	Venue	Date
10.01	0.0	Darrel	Brown	TRI	11.10.84	1q3	WCh	Saint-Denis	24 Aug 03
10.01	1.6	Jeffery	Demps	USA	8.1.90	2q1	NC/OT	Eugene	28 Jun 08
10.03	0.7	Marcus	Rowland	USA	11.3.90	1	PAm-J	Port of Spain	31 Jul 09
10.04	1.7	DeAngelo	Cherry	USA	1.8.90	1h4	NCAA	Fayetteville	10 Jun 09
10.04	0.2	Christoph	Lemaitre	FRA	11.6.90	1	EJ	Novi Sad	24 Jul 09
10.05		Davidson	Ezinwa	NGR	22.11.71	1		Bauchi	4 Jan 90
10.05	0.1	Adam	Gemili	GBR	6.10.93	1	WJ	Barcelona	11 Jul 12
10.06	2.0	Dwain	Chambers	GBR	5.4.78	1	EJ	Ljubljana	25 Jul 97
10.06	1.5	Walter	Dix	USA	31.1.86	1h1	NCAA-r	New York	27 May 05
10.07	2.0	Stanley	Floyd	USA	23.6.61			Austin	24 May 80
10.07	1.1	DaBryan	Blanton	USA	3.7.84	1h2	NCAA-r	Lincoln, NE	30 May 03
10.07	0.2	Tamunosiki	Atorudibo	NGR	21.3.85	1s2	NC	Abuja	9 Jul 04
10.07	0.3	Jimmy	Vicaut	FRA	27.2.92	1	EJ	Tallinn	22 Jul 11

Wind assisted to 10.05

Mark	Wind	Name		Nat	Born	Pos	Meet	Venue	Date
9.83	7.1	Leonard	Scott	USA	19.1.80	1		Knoxville	9 Apr 99
9.96	4.5	Walter	Dix	USA	31.1.86	1rA	TexR	Austin	9 Apr 05
9.97	??	Mark	Lewis-Francis	GBR	4.9.82	1q3	WCh	Edmonton	4 Aug 01
10.02	2.8	DeAngelo	Cherry	USA	1.8.90	1h2	NC-j	Eugene	26 Jun 09
10.02	2.4	Marcus	Rowland	USA	11.3.90	1	NC-j	Eugene	26 Jun 09
10.03	4.9	Christoph	Lemaitre	FRA-	11.6.90	1		Forbach	31 May 09
10.05	2.1	J-Mee	Samuels	USA	20.5.87	1s2		Greensboro	23 Jul 05
10.05	3.0	Keston	Bledman	TRI	8.3.88	3	NC	Port of Spain	23 Jun 07
10.05	2.2	Marvin	Bracy	USA	15.12.93	1	NC-j	Eugene	24 Jun 11

200 METRES

Mark	Wind	Name		Nat	Born	Pos	Meet	Venue	Date
19.93	1.4	Usain	Bolt	JAM	21.8.86	1		Hamilton, BER	11 Apr 04
20.04	0.1	Ramil	Guliyev	AZE	29.5.90	1	WUG	Beograd	10 Jul 09
20.07	1.5	Lorenzo	Daniel	USA	23.3.66	1	SEC	Starkville	18 May 85
20.13	1.7	Roy	Martin	USA	25.12.66	1		Austin	11 May 85
20.14	1.8	Tyreek	Hill	USA	1.3.94	1		Orlando	26 May 12
20.16A	-0.2	Riaan	Dempers	RSA	4.3.77	1	NC-j	Germiston	7 Apr 95
20.18	1.0	Walter	Dix	USA	31.1.86	1s2	NCAA	Sacramento	9 Jun 05
20.22	1.7	Dwayne	Evans	USA	13.10.58	2	OT	Eugene	22 Jun 76
20.23	0.5	Michael	Timpson	USA	6.6.67	1		State College	16 May 86
20.24	0.2	Joe	DeLoach	USA	5.6.67	3		Los Angeles	8 Jun 85
20.24	0.2	Francis	Obikwelu	NGR	22.11.78	2rB		Granada	29 May 96
20.24	1.4	Roberto	Skyers	CUB	12.11.91	1h5		Camagüey	14 Mar 09

Wind assisted

Mark	Wind	Name		Nat	Born	Pos	Meet	Venue	Date
19.86	4.0	Justin	Gatlin	USA	10.2.82	1h2	NCAA	Eugene	30 May 01
20.01	2.5	Derald	Harris	USA	5.4.58	1		San José	9 Apr 77
20.08	9.2	Leonard	Scott	USA	19.1.80	2r2		Knoxville	9 Apr 99
20.10	4.6	Stanley	Kerr	USA	19.6.67	2r2	SWC	Houston	18 May 86
20.16	5.2	Nickel	Ashmeade	JAM	4.7.90	1	Carifta	Basseterre	24 Mar 08

Hand timing: 19.9 Davidson Ezinwa NGR 22.11.71 1 Bauchi 18 Mar 89

400 METRES

Mark	Wind	Name		Nat	Born	Pos	Meet	Venue	Date
43.87		Steve	Lewis	USA	16.5.69	1	OG	Seoul	28 Sep 88
44.36		Kirani	James	GRN	1.9.92	1	WK	Zürich	8 Sep 11
44.45		Luguelín	Santos	DOM	12.11.93	1	FBK	Hengelo	27 May 12
44.66		Hamdam Odha	Al-Bishi	KSA	5.5.81	1	WJ	Santiago de Chile	20 Oct 00
44.66		LaShawn	Merritt	USA	27.6.86	1		Kingston	7 May 05
44.69		Darrell	Robinson	USA	23.12.63	2	USOF	Indianapolis	24 Jul 82
44.73A		James	Rolle	USA	2.2.64	1	USOF	USAF Academy	2 Jul 83
44.75		Darren	Clark	AUS	6.9.65	4	OG	Los Angeles	8 Aug 84
44.75		Deon	Minor	USA	22.1.73	1s1	NCAA	Austin	5 Jun 92
44.93		Nagmeldin	El Abubakr	SUD	22.2.86	1	Is.Sol	Makkah	14 Apr 05

800 METRES

Mark	Wind	Name		Nat	Born	Pos	Meet	Venue	Date
1:41.73		Nijel	Amos	BOT	15.3.94	2	OG	London (OS)	9 Aug 12
1:42.53		Timothy	Kitum	KEN	20.11.94	3	OG	London (OS)	9 Aug 12
1:42.53		Mohammed	Aman	ETH	10.1.94	1	WK	Zürich	30 Aug 12
1:42.69		Abubaker	Kaki	SUD	21.6.89	1	Bisl	Oslo	6 Jun 08
1:43.13		Abraham Kipchirchir	Rotich	KEN	26.6.93	1	Herc	Monaco	20 Jul 12
1:43.64		Japheth	Kimutai	KEN	20.12.78	3rB	WK	Zürich	13 Aug 97
1:43.81		Edwin	Melly	KEN	6.7.95	2		Rieti	9 Sep 12
1:43.99		David	Mutua	KEN	20.4.92	4	Herc	Monaco	22 Jul 11
1:43.40		Leonard	Kosencha	KEN	21.8.94	2	Herc	Monaco	20 Jul 12
1:44.15		David	Rudisha	KEN	17.12.88	1	VD	Bruxelles	14 Sep 07

Mark	Wind	Name		Nat	Born	Pos	Meet	Venue	Date
1:44.27		Majid Saeed	Sultan	QAT	3.11.86	1	AsiC	Inchon	4 Sep 05

1000 METRES
2:13.93		Abubaker	Kaki	SUD	21.6.89	1	DNG	Stockholm	22 Jul 08
2:15.00		Benjamin	Kipkurui	KEN	28.12.80	5	Nik	Nice	17 Jul 99

1500 METRES
3:30.24		Cornelius	Chirchir	KEN	5.6.83	4	Herc	Monaco	19 Jul 02
3:31.13		Mulugueta	Wondimu	ETH	28.2.85	2rA	NA	Heusden	31 Jul 04
3:31.42		Alex	Kipchirchir	KEN	26.11.84	5	VD	Bruxelles	5 Sep 03
3:31.54		Isaac	Songok	KEN	25.4.84	1	NA	Heusden	2 Aug 03
3:31.64		Asbel	Kiprop	KEN	30.6.89	1	GGala	Roma	11 Jul 08
3:31.70		William	Biwott	KEN	5.3.90	3	GGala	Roma	10 Jul 09
3:32.02		Caleb	Ndiku	KEN	9.10.92	4	FBK	Hengelo	29 May 11
3:32.48		Augustine	Choge	KEN	21.1.87	1	ISTAF	Berlin	3 Sep 06
3:32.68		Abdelaati	Iguider	MAR	25.3.87	5	VD	Bruxelles	25 Aug 06
3:32.91		Noah	Ngeny	KEN	2.11.78	9	Herc	Monaco	16 Aug 97
3:33.16		Benjamin	Kipkurui	KEN	28.12.80	1rB	WK	Zürich	11 Aug 99

1 MILE
3:49.29		William	Biwott	KEN	5.3.90	2	Bisl	Oslo	3 Jul 09
3:49.77		Caleb	Ndiku	KEN	9.10.92	5	Pre	Eugene	4 Jun 11
3:50.25		Alex	Kipchirchir	KEN	26.11.84	2	GP II	Rieti	7 Sep 03
3:50.39		James	Kwalia	KEN	12.6.84	1	FBK	Hengelo	1 Jun 03
3:50.41		Noah	Ngeny	KEN	2.11.78	2	Nik	Nice	16 Jul 97
3:50.69		Cornelius	Chirchir	KEN	5.6.83	5	GGala	Roma	12 Jul 02
3:50.83		Nicholas	Kemboi	KEN	18.12.89	6	Bisl	Oslo	6 Jun 08

2000 METRES
4:56.25		Tesfaye	Cheru	ETH	2.3.93	1		Reims	5 Jul 11
4:56.86		Isaac	Songok	KEN	25.4.84	6	ISTAF	Berlin	31 Aug 01
4:58.18		Soresa	Fida	ETH	27.5.93	4		Reims	5 Jul 11
4:58.76		Jairus	Kipchoge	KEN	15.12.92	7		Reims	5 Jul 11

3000 METRES
7:28.78		Augustine	Choge	KEN	21.1.87	2	SGP	Doha	13 May 05
7:29.11		Tariku	Bekele	ETH	21.1.87	2	GP	Rieti	27 Aug 06
7:30.43		Isiah	Koech	KEN	19.12.93	1	DNG	Stockholm	17 Aug 12
7:30.67		Kenenisa	Bekele	ETH	13.6.82	2	VD	Bruxelles	24 Aug 01
7:30.91		Eliud	Kipchoge	KEN	5.11.84	2	VD	Bruxelles	5 Sep 03
7:32.37		Abreham	Cherkos	ETH	23.9.89	2	Athl	Lausanne	11 Jul 06
7:32.72		John	Kipkoech	KEN	29.12.91	4		Rieti	29 Aug 10
7:33.00		Hailu	Mekonnen	ETH	4.4.80	2		Stuttgart	6 Jun 99
7:33.01		Levy	Matebo	KEN	3.11.89	2	GP	Rieti	7 Sep 08
7:34.32		Richard	Limo	KEN	18.11.80	4	VD	Bruxelles	3 Sep 99

5000 METRES
12:47.53		Hagos	Gebrhiwet	ETH	11.5.94	2	DL	Saint-Denis	6 Jul 12
12:48.64		Isiah	Koech	KEN	19.12.93	3	DL	Saint-Denis	6 Jul 12
12:52.61		Eliud	Kipchoge	KEN	5.11.84	3	Bisl	Oslo	27 Jun 03
12:53.66		Augustine	Choge	KEN	21.1.87	4	GGala	Roma	8 Jul 05
12:53.72		Philip	Mosima	KEN	2.1.77	2	GGala	Roma	5 Jun 96
12:53.81		Tariku	Bekele	ETH	21.1.87	4	GGala	Roma	14 Jul 06
12:54.07		Sammy	Kipketer	KEN	29.9.81	2	GGala	Roma	30 Jun 00
12:54.19		Abreham	Cherkos	ETH	23.9.89	5	GGala	Roma	14 Jul 06
12:54.58		James	Kwalia	KEN	12.6.84	5	Bisl	Oslo	27 Jun 03
12:56.15		Daniel	Komen	KEN	17.5.76	2	GG	Roma	8 Jun 95
12:57.05		Mulugueta	Wondimu	ETH	28.2.85	2	ISTAF	Berlin	12 Sep 04

10,000 METRES
26:41.75		Samuel	Wanjiru	KEN	10.11.86	3	VD	Bruxelles	26 Aug 05
26:55.73		Geoffrey	Kirui	KEN	16.2.93	6	VD	Bruxelles	16 Sep 11
26:57.56		Yigrem	Demelash	ETH	28.1.94	4	VD	Bruxelles	7 Sep 12
27:02.81		Ibrahim	Jeylan	ETH	12.6.89	4	VD	Bruxelles	25 Aug 06
27:04.00		Boniface	Kiprop	UGA	12.10.85	5	VD	Bruxelles	3 Sep 04
27:04.45		Bernard Kipyego	Kiprop	KEN	16.7.86	4	FBK	Hengelo	29 May 05
27:06.35		Geoffrey	Kipsang	KEN	28.11.92	10	Pre	Eugene	3 Jun 11
27:06.47		Habtanu	Fikadu	ETH	13.3.88	8	FBK	Hengelo	26 May 07
27:07.29		Moses	Masai	KEN	1.6.86	7	VD	Bruxelles	3 Sep 04
27:11.18		Richard	Chelimo	KEN	21.4.72	1	APM	Hengelo	25 Jun 91
27:12.42		Sammy Alex	Mutahi	KEN	1.6.89	1		Tokamchi	29 Sep 07

Mark	Wind	Name		Nat	Born	Pos	Meet	Venue	Date

3000 METRES STEEPLECHASE

Mark	Wind	Name		Nat	Born	Pos	Meet	Venue	Date
7:58.66		Stephen	Cherono	KEN	15.10.82	3	VD	Bruxelles	24 Aug 01
8:03.49		Conseslus	Kipruto	KEN	8.12.94	1	Herc	Monaco	20 Jul 12
8:03.74		Raymond	Yator	KEN	7.4.81	3	Herc	Monaco	18 Aug 00
8:05.52		Brimin	Kipruto	KEN	31.7.85	1	FBK	Hengelo	31 May 04
8:07.18		Moussa	Omar Obaid	QAT	18.4.85	4	OG	Athína	24 Aug 04
8:07.69		Paul	Kosgei	KEN	22.4.78	5	DNG	Stockholm	7 Jul 97
8:07.71		Hillary	Yego	KEN	2.4.92	3	DL	Shanghai	15 May 11
8:09.37		Abel	Cheruiyot/Yugut	KEN	26.12.84	2	NA	Heusden	2 Aug 03
8:11.27		Gilbert	Kirui	KEN	22.1.94	7	DL	Doha	11 May 12
8:11.31		Jairus	Birech	KEN	15.12.92	5	DL	Saint Denis	8 Jul 11
8:12.91		Thomas	Kiplitan	KEN	15.6.83	7	GP	Doha	15 May 02

110 METRES HURDLES (106cm)

Mark	Wind	Name		Nat	Born	Pos	Meet	Venue	Date
13.12	1.6		Liu Xiang	CHN	13.7.83	1rB	Athl	Lausanne	2 Jul 02
13.23	0.0	Renaldo	Nehemiah	USA	24.3.59	1r2	WK	Zürich	16 Aug 78
13.40	-1.0		Shi Dongpeng	CHN	6.1.84	1	NC	Shanghai	14 Sep 03
13.44	-0.8	Colin	Jackson	GBR	18.2.67	1	WJ	Athína	19 Jul 86
13.46	1.8	Jon	Ridgeon	GBR	14.2.67	1	EJ	Cottbus	23 Aug 85
13.46	-1.6	Dayron	Robles	CUB	19.11.86	1	PAm-J	Windsor	29 Jul 05
13.47	1.9	Holger	Pohland	GDR	5.4.63	2	vUSA	Karl-Marx-Stadt	10 Jul 82
13.47	1.2	Aries	Merritt	USA	24.7.85	4	NCAA	Austin	12 Jun 04
13.47	0.2		Xie Wenjun	CHN	11.7.90	2	GP	Shanghai	20 Sep 08
13.49	0.6	Stanislav	Olijar	LAT	22.3.79	1		Valmiera	11 Jul 98
13.49	1.2	Booker	Nunley	USA	2.7.90	2	SEC	Gainesville	17 May 09

Wind assisted

Mark	Wind	Name		Nat	Born	Pos	Meet	Venue	Date
13.41	2.6	Dayron	Robles	CUB	19.11.86	2	CAC	Nassau	10 Jul 05
13.42	4.5	Colin	Jackson	GBR	18.2.67	2	CG	Edinburgh	27 Jul 86
13.42	2.6	Antwon	Hicks	USA	12.3.83	1	WJ	Kingston	21 Jul 02
13.47	2.1	Frank	Busemann	GER	26.2.75	1	WJ	Lisboa	22 Jul 94

99 cm Hurdles

Mark	Wind	Name		Nat	Born	Pos	Meet	Venue	Date
13.08	2.0	Wayne	Davis	USA	2.7.90	1	PAm-J	Port of Spain	31 Jul 09
13.14	1.6	Eddie	Lovett	USA	25.6.92	1	PAm-J	Miramar	23 Jul 11
13.18	1.0	Yordan	O'Farrill	CUB	9.2.93	1	WJ	Barcelona	12 Jul 12
13.23	1.5	Artur	Noga	POL	2.5.88	1	WJ	Beijing	20 Aug 06
13.24	1.6	Roy	Smith	USA	12.4.92	2	PAm-J	Miramar	23 Jul 11

Wind assisted

Mark	Wind	Name		Nat	Born	Pos	Meet	Venue	Date
13.03	2.9	Eddie	Lovett	USA	25.6.92	1h1	PAm-J	Miramar	23 Jul 11
13.15	2.7	Brendan	Ames	USA	6.10.88	1	NC-j	Indianapolis	21 Jun 07
13.18		Arthur	Blake	USA	19.8.66	1	GWest	Sacramento	9 Jun 84
13.23	2.3	William	Wynne	USA	30.1.90	1h1	NC-j	Eugene	26 Jun 09
Hand timed: 12.9y		Renaldo	Nehemiah	USA	24.3.59	1		Jamaica, NY	30 May 77

400 METRES HURDLES

Mark	Wind	Name		Nat	Born	Pos	Meet	Venue	Date
48.02		Danny	Harris	USA	7.9.65	2s1	OT	Los Angeles	17 Jun 84
48.26		Jehue	Gordon	TRI	15.12.91	4	WCh	Berlin	18 Aug 09
48.51		Kerron	Clement	USA	31.10.85	1	WJ	Grosseto	16 Jul 04
48.52		Johnny	Dutch	USA	20.1.89	5	NC/OT	Eugene	29 Jun 08
48.62		Brandon	Johnson	USA	6.3.85	2	WJ	Grosseto	16 Jul 04
48.68		Bayano	Kamani	USA	17.4.80	1	NCAA	Boise	4 Jun 99
48.68		Jeshua	Anderson	USA	22.6.89	1	WJ	Bydgoszcz	11 Jul 08
48.72		Angelo	Taylor	USA	29.12.78	2	NCAA	Bloomington	6 Jun 97
48.74		Vladimir	Budko	BLR	4.2.65	2	DRZ	Moskva	18 Aug 84
48.76A		Llewellyn	Herbert	RSA	21.7.77	1		Pretoria	7 Apr 96

HIGH JUMP

Mark	Wind	Name		Nat	Born	Pos	Meet	Venue	Date
2.37		Dragutin	Topic	YUG	12.3.71	1	WJ	Plovdiv	12 Aug 90
2.37		Steve	Smith	GBR	29.3.73	1	WJ	Seoul	20 Sep 92
2.36		Javier	Sotomayor	CUB	13.10.67	1		Santiago de Cuba	23 Feb 86
2.35i		Vladimir	Yashchenko	UKR	12.1.59	1	EI	Milano	12 Mar 78
2.34						1	Prv	Tbilisi	16 Jun 78
2.35		Dietmar	Mögenburg	FRG	15.8.61	1		Rehlingen	26 May 80
2.34		Tim	Forsyth	AUS	17.8.73	1	Bisl	Oslo	4 Jul 92
2.33			Zhu Jianhua	CHN	29.5.63	1	AsiG	New Delhi	1 Dec 82
2.33		Patrik	Sjöberg	SWE	5.1.65	1	OsloG	Oslo	9 Jul 83
2.32i		Jaroslav	Bába	CZE	2.9.84	3		Arnstadt	8 Feb 03
2.32			Huang Haiqiang	CHN	8.2.88	1	WJ	Beijing	17 Aug 06

POLE VAULT

Mark	Wind	Name		Nat	Born	Pos	Meet	Venue	Date
5.80		Maksim	Tarasov	RUS	2.12.70	1	vGDR-j	Bryansk	14 Jul 89

Mark	Wind	Name		Nat	Born	Pos	Meet	Venue	Date
5.80		Raphael	Holzdeppe	GER	28.9.89	2		Biberach	28 Jun 08
5.75		Konstadínos	Filippídis	GRE	26.11.86	2	WUG	Izmir	18 Aug 05
5.72		Andrew	Irwin	USA	23.1.93	1	SEC	Baton Rouge	13 May 12
5.71		Lawrence	Johnson	USA	7.5.74	1		Knoxville	12 Jun 93
5.71		Germán	Chiaraviglio	ARG	16.4.87	1	WJ	Beijing	19 Aug 06
5.70		Viktor	Chistyakov	RUS	9.2.75	1		Leppävirta	7 Jun 94
5.70		Artyom	Kuptsov	RUS	22.4.84	1	Znam	Tula	7 Jun 03
5.67i		Leonid	Kivalov	RUS	1.4.88	1	NC-j	Penza	1 Feb 07
5.65		Rodion	Gataullin	UZB	23.11.65	2	NC	Donetsk	8 Sep 84
5.65		István	Bagyula	HUN	2.1.69	1	WJ	Sudbury	28 Jul 88
5.65i		Jacob	Davis	USA	29.4.78	1	Big 12	Lincoln	21 Feb 97

LONG JUMP

Mark	Wind	Name		Nat	Born	Pos	Meet	Venue	Date
8.35	1.1	Sergey	Morgunov	RUS	9.2.93	1	NC-j	Cheboksary	19 Jun 12
8.34	0.0	Randy	Williams	USA	23.8.53	Q	OG	München	8 Sep 72
8.28	0.8	Luis Alberto	Bueno	CUB	22.5.69	1		La Habana	16 Jul 88
8.27	1.7	Eusebio	Cáceres	ESP	10.9.91	Q	EC	Barcelona	30 Jul 10
8.24	0.2	Eric	Metcalf	USA	23.1.68	1	NCAA	Indianapolis	6 Jun 86
8.24	1.8	Vladimir	Ochkan	UKR	13.1.68	1	vGDR-j	Leningrad	21 Jun 87
8.22		Larry	Doubley	USA	15.3.58	1	NCAA	Champaign	3 Jun 77
8.22		Iván	Pedroso	CUB	17.12.72	1		Santiago de Cuba	3 May 91
8.22i		Viktor	Kuznetsov	UKR	14.7.86	1		Brovary	22 Jan 05
8.21A	2.0	Vance	Johnson	USA	13.3.63	1	NCAA	Provo	4 Jun 82
8.20	1.5	James	Stallworth	USA	29.4.71	Q	WJ	Plovdiv	9 Aug 90

Wind assisted

Mark	Wind	Name		Nat	Born	Pos	Meet	Venue	Date
8.40	3.2	Kareem	Streete-Thompson	CAY	30.3.73	1		Houston	5 May 91
8.35	2.2	Carl	Lewis	USA	1.7.61	1	NCAA	Austin	6 Jun 80
8.29	2.3	James	Beckford	JAM	9.1.75	1		Tempe	2 Apr 94
8.23	4.4	Peller	Phillips	USA	23.6.70	1		Sacramento	11 Jun 88
8.21	2.8	Masaki	Morinaga	JPN	27.3.72	1		Hamamatsu	7 Sep 91

TRIPLE JUMP

Mark	Wind	Name		Nat	Born	Pos	Meet	Venue	Date
17.50	0.4	Volker	Mai	GDR	3.5.66	1	vURS	Erfurt	23 Jun 85
17.42	1.3	Khristo	Markov	BUL	27.1.65	1	Nar	Sofiya	19 May 84
17.40A	0.4	Pedro	Pérez	CUB	23.2.52	1	PAm	Cali	5 Aug 71
17.40	0.8	Ernesto	Revé	CUB	26.2.92	1		La Habana	10 Jun 11
17.31	-0.2	David	Girat Jr.	CUB	26.8.84	Q	WCh	Saint-Denis	23 Aug 03
17.29	1.3	James	Beckford	JAM	9.1.75	1		Tempe	2 Apr 94
17.27		Aliecer	Urrutia	CUB	22.9.74	1		Artemisa	23 Apr 93
17.23	0.2	Yoelbi	Quesada	CUB	4.8.73	1	NC	La Habana	13 May 92
17.19	-0.4	Teddy	Tamgho	FRA	15.6.89	4	Herc	Monaco	29 Jul 08
17.19	2.0	Will	Claye	USA	13.6.91	*	NCAA	Fayetteville	13 Jun 09

Wind assisted to 17.15

Mark	Wind	Name		Nat	Born	Pos	Meet	Venue	Date
17.33	2.1	Teddy	Tamgho	FRA	15.6.89	1	WJ	Bydgoszcz	11 Jul 08
17.24	2.5	Will	Claye	USA	13.6.91	1	NCAA	Fayetteville	13 Jun 09

SHOT

Mark		Name		Nat	Born	Pos	Meet	Venue	Date
21.05i		Terry	Albritton	USA	14.1.55	1	AAU	New York	22 Feb 74
20.38						2	MSR	Walnut	27 Apr 74
20.65		Mike	Carter	USA	29.10.60	1	vSU-j	Boston	4 Jul 79
20.43		David	Storl	GER	27.7.90	2		Gerlingen	6 Jul 09
20.39		Janus	Robberts	RSA	10.3.79	1	NC	Germiston	7 Mar 98
20.38		Jacko	Gill	NZL	10.12.94	1		Auckland (NS)	5 Dec 11
20.20		Randy	Matson	USA	5.3.45	2	OG	Tokyo	17 Oct 64
20.20		Udo	Beyer	GDR	9.8.55	2	NC	Leipzig	6 Jul 74
20.13		Jeff	Chakouian	USA	20.4.82	2		Atlanta	18 May 01
19.99		Karl	Salb	USA	19.5.49	4	OT	Echo Summit	10 Sep 68
19.95		Edis	Elkasevic	CRO	18.2.83	1		Velenje	15 Jun 02

6 kg Shot (* 6.25kg shot)

Mark		Name		Nat	Born	Pos	Meet	Venue	Date
22.73		David	Storl	GER	27.7.90	1		Osterode	14 Jul 09
22.31		Jacko	Gill	NZL	10.12.94	1		Auckland (NS)	5 Dec 11
21.96		Edis	Elkasevic	CRO	18.2.83	1	NC-j	Zagreb	29 Jun 02
21.78		Krzysztof	Brzozowski	POL	15.7.93	2	WJ	Barcelona	11 Jul 12
21.68		Marin	Premeru	CRO	29.8.90	1		Rijeka	19 May 09
21.24		Georgi	Ivanov	BUL	13.3.85	1	NC-j	Sofia	12 Jun 04
21.14		Damien	Birkinhead	AUS	8.4.93	3	WJ	Barcelona	11 Jul 12

DISCUS

Mark		Name		Nat	Born	Pos	Meet	Venue	Date
65.62		Werner	Reiterer	AUS	27.1.68	1		Melbourne	15 Dec 87
65.31		Mykyta	Nesterenko	UKR	15.4.91	3		Tallinn	3 Jun 08
63.64		Werner	Hartmann	FRG	20.4.59	1	vFRA	Strasbourg	25 Jun 78

Mark	Wind	Name		Nat	Born	Pos	Meet	Venue	Date
63.26		Sergey	Pachin	UKR	24.5.68	2		Moskva	25 Jul 87
63.22		Brian	Milne	USA	7.1.73	1		State College	28 Mar 92
62.52		John	Nichols	USA	23.8.69	1		Baton Rouge	23 Apr 88
62.36		Nuermaimaiti	Tulake	CHN	8.3.82	2	NG	Guangzhou	21 Nov 01
62.16		Zoltán	Kövágó	HUN	10.4.79	1		Budapest	9 May 97
62.04		Kenth	Gardenkrans	SWE	2.10.55	2		Helsingborg	11 Aug 74
62.04			Wu Tao	CHN	3.10.83	1	NGP	Shanghai	18 May 02

1.75kg Discus

Mark	Wind	Name		Nat	Born	Pos	Meet	Venue	Date
70.13		Mykyta	Nesterenko	UKR	15.4.91	1		Halle	24 May 08
67.32		Margus	Hunt	EST	14.7.87	1	WJ	Beijing	16 Aug 06
66.88		Traves	Smikle	JAM	7.5.92	1		Kingston	31 Mar 11
66.45		Gordon	Wolf	GER	17.1.90	1		Halle	23 May 09
65.88		Omar	El-Ghazaly	EGY	9.2.84	1		Cairo	7 Nov 03
65.55		Mihai	Grasu	ROM	21.4.87	1	NC	Bucuresti	23 Jul 06
65.52A		Victor	Hogan	RSA	25.7.89	1		Potchefstroom	3 Jul 08
65.71		Marin	Premeru	CRO	29.8.90	1		Split	31 May 09
65.51		Andrius	Gudzius	LTU	14.2.91	1		Siauliai	30 Jun 10

HAMMER

Mark	Wind	Name		Nat	Born	Pos	Meet	Venue	Date
78.33		Olli-Pekka	Karjalainen	FIN	7.3.80	1	NC	Seinäjoki	5 Aug 99
78.14		Roland	Steuk	GDR	5.3.59	1	NC	Leipzig	30 Jun 78
78.00		Sergey	Dorozhon	UKR	17.2.64	1		Moskva	7 Aug 83
76.54		Valeriy	Gubkin	BLR	3.9.67	2		Minsk	27 Jun 86
76.42		Ruslan	Dikiy	TJK	18.1.72	1		Togliatti	7 Sep 91
75.52		Sergey	Kirmasov	RUS	25.3.70	1		Kharkov	4 Jun 89
75.42		Szymon	Ziolkowski	POL	1.7.76	1	EJ	Nyíregyhazá	30 Jul 95
75.24		Christoph	Sahner	FRG	23.9.63	1	vPOL-j	Göttingen	26 Jun 82

6kg Hammer (* 6.25kg hammer)

Mark	Wind	Name		Nat	Born	Pos	Meet	Venue	Date
85.57		Ashraf Amgad	El-Seify	QAT-Y	20.2.95	1	WJ	Barcelona	14 Jul 12
82.97		Javier	Cienfuegos	ESP	15.7.90	1		Madrid	17 Jun 09
82.84		Quentin	Bigot	FRA	1.12.92	1		Bondoufle	16 Oct 11
82.62		Yevgeniy	Aydamirov	RUS	11.5.87	1	NC-j	Tula	22 Jul 06
81.34		Krisztián	Pars	HUN	18.2.82	1		Szombathely	2 Sep 01
81.15		Ákos	Hudi	HUN	10.8.91	1		Veszprém	7 Jul 10
81.04		Werner	Smit	RSA	14.9.84	1		Bellville	29 Mar 03
80.79		Conor	McCullough	USA	31.1.91	1	WJ	Moncton	25 Jul 10

JAVELIN

Mark	Wind	Name		Nat	Born	Pos	Meet	Venue	Date
84.69		Zigismunds	Sirmais	LAT	6.5.92	2		Bauska	22 Jun 11
84.58		Keshorn	Walcott	TRI	2.4.93	1	OG	London (OS)	11 Aug 12
83.87		Andreas	Thorkildsen	NOR	1.4.82	1		Fana	7 Jun 01
83.55		Aleksandr	Ivanov	RUS	25.5.82	2	NC	Tula	14 Jul 01
83.07		Robert	Oosthuizen	RSA	23.1.87	1	WJ	Beijing	19 Aug 06
82.52		Harri	Haatainen	FIN	5.1.78	4		Leppävirta	25 May 96
82.52		Till	Wöschler	GER	9.6.91	1	WJ	Moncton	23 Jul 10
81.95		Jakub	Vadlejch	CZE	10.10.90	1		Domazlice	26 Sep 09
81.80		Sergey	Voynov	UZB	26.2.77	1		Tashkent	6 Jun 96
80.94		Aki	Parviainen	FIN	26.10.74	4	NC	Jyväskylä	5 Jul 92
80.57		Teemu	Wirkkala	FIN	14.1.84	1		Espoo	14 Sep 03

DECATHLON

Mark				Nat	Born	Pos	Meet	Venue			Date
8397	Torsten	Voss		GDR	24.3.63	1	NC	Erfurt			7 Jul 82
	10.76	7.66	14.41	2.09	48.37		14.37	41.76	4.80	62.90	4:34.04
8257	Yordani	Garcia		CUB	21.11.88	8	WCh	Osaka			1 Sep 07
	10.73/0.7	7.15/0.2	14.94	2.09	49.25		14.08/-0.2	42.91	4.70	68.74	4:55.42
8114	Michael	Kohnle		FRG	3.5.70	1	EJ	Varazdin			26 Aug 89
	10.95	7.09/0.1	15.27	2.02	49.91		14.40	45.82	4.90	60.82	4:49.43
8104	Valter	Külvet		EST	19.2.64	1		Viimsi			23 Aug 81
	10.7	7.26	13.86	2.09	48.5		14.8	47.92	4.50	60.34	4:37.8
8082	Daley	Thompson		GBR	30.7.58	1	ECp/s	Sittard			31 Jul 77
	10.70/0.8	7.54/0.7	13.84	2.01	47.31		15.26/2.0	41.70	4.70	54.48	4:30.4
8041		Qi Haifeng		CHN	7.8.83	1	AsiG	Busan			10 Oct 02
	11.09/0.2	7.22/0.0	13.05	2.06	49.09		14.54/0.0	43.16	4.80	61.04	4:35.17
8036	Christian	Schenk		GDR	9.2.65	5		Potsdam			21 Jul 84
	11.54	7.18	14.26	2.16	49.23		15.06	44.74	4.20	65.98	4:24.11
8018	Gunnar	Nixon		USA	13.1.93	1	WJ	Barcelona			11 Jul 12
	11.23/-0.1	7.12/-0.2	14.54	2.10	49.13		14.54/-0.7	42.23	4.50	56.25	4:22.36
7992	Kevin	Mayer		FRA	10.2.92	8		Kladno			16 Jun 11
	11.23/0.1	7.34/0.2	12.44	2.01	48.66		14.74/-2.0	38.64	4.90	60.96	4:19.79
7938	Frank	Busemann		GER	26.2.75	1		Zeven			2 Oct 94
	10.68/1.6	7.37/1.1	13.08	2.03	50.41		14.34/-1.1	39.84	4.40	63.00	4:37.31)

Mark	Wind	Name		Nat	Born	Pos	Meet	Venue				Date

IAAF Junior specification with 99cm 110mh, 6kg shot, 1.75kg Discus

Mark	Wind	Name		Nat	Born	Pos	Meet	Venue	Date
8131		Arkadiy	Vasilyev	RUS	19.1.87	1		Sochi	27 May 06
	11.28/-0.8	7.70/2.0	14.59	2.00	49.17		14.67/0.6	46.30 4.70 56.96	4:32.10
8126		Andrey	Kravchenko	BLR	4.1.86	1	WJ	Grosseto	15 Jul 04
	11.09/-0.5	7.46-0.2	14.51	2.16	48.98		14.55*/0.4	43.41 4.50 52.84	4:28.46
8124		Kévin	Mayer	FRA	10.2.92	1	EJ	Tallin	24 Jul 11
	11.40/-1.7	7.52/1.5	14.65	2.04	49.41		14.09/0.7	41.00 4.80 56.60	4:25.23

10,000 METRES WALK

Mark	Name		Nat	Born	Pos	Meet	Venue	Date
38:46.4	Viktor	Burayev	RUS	23.8.82	1	NC-j	Moskva	20 May 00
38:54.75	Ralf	Kowalsky	GDR	22.3.62	1		Cottbus	24 Jun 81
39:28.45	Andrey	Ruzavin	RUS	28.3.86	1	EJ	Kaunas	23 Jul 05
39:35.01	Stanislav	Yemelyanov	RUS	23.10.90	1	WJ	Bydgoszcz	11 Jul 08
39:44.71	Giovanni	De Benedictis	ITA	8.1.68	1	EJ	Birmingham	7 Aug 87
39:47.20		Chen Ding	CHN	5.8.92	2	WJ	Bydgoszcz	11 Jul 08
39:49.22		Pei Chuang	CHN	5.12.81	2	NSG	Chengdu	8 Sep 00
39:49.44		Li Tianlei	CHN	13.1.95	4		Tianjin	16 Sep 12
39:50.32		Cui Jin	CHN	1.12.87	2		Jinzhou	30 Aug 06
39:50.73	Jefferson	Pérez	ECU	1.7.74	1	PAmJ	Winnipeg	15 Jul 93

20 KILOMETRES WALK

Mark	Name		Nat	Born	Pos	Meet	Venue	Date
1:18:06	Viktor	Burayev	RUS	23.8.82	2	NC-w	Adler	4 Mar 01
1:18:07		Li Gaobo	CHN	23.7.89	4		Cixi	23 Apr 05
1:18:44		Chu Yafei	CHN	5.9.88	5		Yangzhou	22 Apr 06
1:18:52		Chen Ding	CHN	5.8.92	3		Taicang	22 Apr 11
1:18:57		Bai Xuejin	CHN	6.6.87	7		Yangzhou	22 Apr 06
1:19:02	Éder	Sánchez	MEX	21.5.86	11		Cixi	23 Apr 05
1:19:14		Xu Xingde	CHN	12.6.84	3	NC	Yangzhou	12 Apr 03
1:19:34		Li Jianbo	CHN	14.11.86	16		Cixi	23 Apr 05
1:19:38		Yu Guohui	CHN	30.4.77	2	NC	Zhuhai	10 Mar 96
1:19:47		Wang Hao	CHN	16.8.89	4	OG	Beijing	16 Aug 08

4 x 100 METRES RELAY

Mark	Nat	Name	Pos	Meet	Venue	Date
38.66	USA	Kimmons, Omole, I Williams, L Merritt	1	WJ	Grosseto	18 Jun 04
38.97	JAM	Tracey, Skeen, Minzie, Murphy	2	WJ	Barcelona	14 Jul 12
39.01	JPN	Oseto, Hashimoto, Cambridge, Kanamori	1h1	WJ	Barcelona	13 Jul 12
39.05	GBR	Edgar, Grant, Benjamin, Lewis-Francis	1	WJ	Santiago de Chile	22 Oct 00
39.17	TRI	Simpson, Burns, Holder, Brown	3	WJ	Kingston	21 Jul 02
39.25	FRG	Dobeleit, Klameth, Evers, Lübke	1	EJ	Schwechat	28 Aug 83
39.29	BRA	de Araújo, Monteiro, R dos Santos Jnr, Rocha	2h1	WJ	Barcelona	13 Jul 12
39.33	FRA	Pognon, Calligny, Doucoure, Djhone	2	WJ	Santiago de Chile	22 Oct 00

4 x 400 METRES RELAY

Mark	Nat	Name	Pos	Meet	Venue	Date
3:01.09	USA	B Johnson, L Merritt, Craig, Clement	1	WJ	Grosseto	18 Jul 04
3:03.80	GBR	Grindley, Patrick, Winrow, Richardson	2	WJ	Plovdiv	12 Aug 90
3:04.06	JAM	S Clarke, Bolt, Myers, Gonzales	2	WJ	Kingston	21 Jul 02
3:04.22	CUB	Cadogan, Mordoche, González, Hernández	2	WJ	Athína	20 Jul 86
3:04.50	RSA	le Roux, Gebhardt, Julius, van Zyl	2	WJ	Grosseto	18 Jul 04
3:04.58	GDR	Preusche, Löper, Trylus, Carlowitz	1	EJ	Utrecht	23 Aug 81
3:04.74	AUS	McFarlane, Batman, Thom, Vincent	1	WJ	Annecy	2 Aug 98
3:05.05	POL	Zalewski, Smoleń, Kuśnierz, Dobek	2	WJ	Barcelona	15 Jul 12

JUNIOR WOMEN'S ALL-TIME LISTS

100 METRES

Mark	Wind	Name		Nat	Born	Pos	Meet	Venue	Date
10.88	2.0	Marlies	Oelsner	GDR	21.3.58	1	NC	Dresden	1 Jul 77
10.89	1.8	Katrin	Krabbe	GDR	22.11.69	1rB		Berlin	20 Jul 88
11.03	1.7	Silke	Gladisch	GDR	20.6.64	3	OD	Berlin	8 Jun 83
11.03	0.6	English	Gardner	USA	22.4.92	1	Pac10	Tucson	14 May 11
11.04	1.4	Angela	Williams	USA	30.1.80	1	NCAA	Boise	5 Jun 99
11.07	0.7	Bianca	Knight	USA	2.1.89	4q2	NC/OT	Eugene	27 Jun 08
11.08	2.0	Brenda	Morehead	USA	5.10.57	1	OT	Eugene	21 Jun 76
11.11	0.2	Shakedia	Jones	USA	15.3.79	1		Los Angeles (Ww)	2 May 98
11.11	1.1	Joan Uduak	Ekah	NGR	16.12.80	5	Athl	Lausanne	2 Jul 99
11.12	2.0	Veronica	Campbell	JAM	15.5.82	1	WJ	Santiago de Chile	18 Oct 00
11.12	1.2	Alexandria	Anderson	USA	28.1.87	1	NC-j	Indianapolis	22 Jun 06
11.12	1.1	Aurieyall	Scott	USA	18.5.92	1	NC-j	Eugene	24 Jun 11

Uncertain timing: 10.99 1.9 Natalya Bochina RUS 4.1.62 2 Leningrad 3 Jun 80
Wind assisted to 11.11

Mark	Wind	Name		Nat	Born	Pos	Meet	Venue	Date
10.96	3.7	Angela	Williams	USA	30.1.80	1		Las Vegas	3 Apr 99
10.97	3.3	Gesine	Walther	GDR	6.10.62	4	NC	Cottbus	16 Jul 80

Mark	Wind	Name		Nat	Born	Pos	Meet	Venue	Date
11.02	2.1	Nikole	Mitchell	JAM	5.6.74	1	Mutual	Kingston	1 May 93
11.04	5.6	Kelly-Ann	Baptiste	TRI	14.10.86	1rB	TexR	Austin	9 Apr 05
11.06	2.2	Brenda	Morehead	USA	5.10.57	1s2	OT	Eugene	21 Jun 76
11.09		Angela	Williams	TRI	15.5.65	1		Nashville	14 Apr 84

200 METRES

Mark	Wind	Name		Nat	Born	Pos	Meet	Venue	Date
22.11A	-0.5	Allyson	Felix	USA	18.11.85	1		Ciudad de México	3 May 03
	22.18		0.8			2	OG	Athína	25 Aug 04
22.19	1.5	Natalya	Bochina	RUS	4.1.62	2	OG	Moskva	30 Jul 80
22.37	1.3	Sabine	Rieger	GDR	6.11.63	2	vURS	Cottbus	26 Jun 82
22.42	0.4	Gesine	Walther	GDR	6.10.62	1		Potsdam	29 Aug 81
22.43	0.8	Bianca	Knight	USA	2.1.89	1	Reebok	New York (RI)	31 May 08
22.45	0.5	Grit	Breuer	GER	16.2.72	2	ASV	Köln	8 Sep 91
22.51	2.0	Katrin	Krabbe	GDR	22.11.69	3		Berlin	13 Sep 88
22.52	1.2	Mary	Onyali	NGR	3.2.68	6	WCh	Roma	3 Sep 87
22.53	0.2	Anthonique	Strachan	BAH	22.8.93	1	WJ	Barcelona	13 Jul 12
22.58	0.8	Marion	Jones	USA	12.10.75	4	TAC	New Orleans	28 Jun 92
22.69	-0.3	Dafne	Schippers	NED	15.6.92	1h3	WCh	Daegu	1 Sep 11

Indoors

Mark	Wind	Name		Nat	Born	Pos	Meet	Venue	Date
22.40		Bianca	Knight	USA	2.1.89	1r2	NCAA	Fayetteville	15 Mar 08
22.49		Sanya	Richards	USA	26.2.85	2rA	NCAA	Fayetteville	12 Mar 04

Wind assisted to 22.65

Mark	Wind	Name		Nat	Born	Pos	Meet	Venue	Date
22.25	5.6	Bianca	Knight	USA	2.1.89	5	NC/OT	Eugene	6 Jul 08
22.34	2.3	Katrin	Krabbe	GDR	22.11.69	1	WJ	Sudbury	30 Jul 88
22.49	2.3	Brenda	Morehead	USA	5.10.57	1	OT	Eugene	24 Jun 76
22.53	2.5	Valerie	Brisco	USA	6.7.60	2	AAU	Walnut	17 Jun 79
22.64	2.3	Chandra	Cheeseborough	USA	10.1.59	2	OT	Eugene	24 Jun 76
22.65	3.5	Shakedia	Jones	USA	15.3.79	1	NC-j	Edwardsville IL	27 Jun 98

400 METRES

Mark	Wind	Name		Nat	Born	Pos	Meet	Venue	Date
49.42		Grit	Breuer	GER	16.2.72	2	WCh	Tokyo	27 Aug 91
49.77		Christina	Brehmer	GDR	28.2.58	1		Dresden	9 May 76
49.89		Sanya	Richards	USA	26.2.85	2	NC/OT	Sacramento	17 Jul 04
50.01			Li Jing	CHN	14.2.80	1	NG	Shanghai	18 Oct 97
50.19		Marita	Koch	GDR	18.2.57	3	OD	Berlin	10 Jul 76
50.50		Ashley	Spencer	USA	8.6.93	1	WJ	Barcelona	13 Jul 12
50.59		Fatima	Yusuf	NGR	2.5.71	1	HGP	Budapest	5 Aug 90
50.74		Monique	Henderson	USA	18.2.83	1		Norwalk	3 Jun 00
50.78		Danijela	Grgic	CRO	28.9.88	1	WJ	Beijing	17 Aug 06
50.86		Charity	Opara	NGR	20.5.72	2		Bologna	7 Sep 91
50.87		Denean	Howard	USA	5.10.64	1	TAC	Knoxville	20 Jun 82
50.87		Magdalena	Nedelcu	ROM	12.5.74	1	NC-j	Bucuresti	31 Jul 92

800 METRES

Mark	Wind	Name		Nat	Born	Pos	Meet	Venue	Date
1:54.01		Pamela	Jelimo	KEN	5.12.89	1	WK	Zürich	29 Aug 08
1:55.45		Caster	Semenya	RSA	7.1.91	1	WCh	Berlin	19 Aug 09
1:56.59		Francine	Niyonsaba	BDI	5.5.93	1	VD	Bruxelles	7 Sep 12
1:57.18			Wang Yuan	CHN	8.4.76	2h2	NG	Beijing	8 Sep 93
1:57.45		Hildegard	Ullrich	GDR	20.12.59	5	EC	Praha	31 Aug 78
1:57.62			Lang Yinglai	CHN	22.8.79	1	NG	Shanghai	22 Oct 97
1:57.63		Maria	Mutola	MOZ	27.10.72	4	WCh	Tokyo	26 Aug 91
1:57.77			Lu Yi	CHN	10.4.74	4	NG	Beijing	9 Sep 93
1:57.86		Katrin	Wühn	GDR	19.11.65	1		Celje	5 May 84
1:58.16			Lin Nuo	CHN	18.1.80	3	NG	Shanghai	22 Oct 97
1:58.18		Marion	Hübner	GDR	29.9.62	2		Erfurt	2 Aug 81

1500 METRES

Mark	Wind	Name		Nat	Born	Pos	Meet	Venue	Date
3:51.34			Lang Yinglai	CHN	22.8.79	2	NG	Shanghai	18 Oct 97
3:53.91			Yin Lili	CHN	11.11.79	3	NG	Shanghai	18 Oct 97
3:53.97			Lan Lixin	CHN	14.2.79	4	NG	Shanghai	18 Oct 97
3:54.52			Zhang Ling	CHN	13.4.80	5	NG	Shanghai	18 Oct 97
3:59.60		Gelete	Burka	ETH	15.2.86	5	GP	Rieti	28 Aug 05
3:59.81			Wang Yuan	CHN	8.4.76	7	NG	Beijing	11 Sep 93
3:59.96		Zola	Budd	GBR	26.5.66	3	VD	Bruxelles	30 Aug 85
4:00.05			Lu Yi	CHN	10.4.74	8	NG	Beijing	11 Sep 93
4:01.71			Li Ying	CHN	24.6.75	4h2	NG	Beijing	10 Sep 93
4:02.98		Kalkedan	Gezahegn	ETH	8.5.91	3	Tsik	Athína	13 Jul 09
4:03.45		Anita	Weyermann	SUI	8.12.77	1	Athl	Lausanne	3 Jul 96

1 MILE: 4:17.57 Zola Budd GBR 26.5.66 3 WK Zürich 21 Aug 85

2000 METRES: 5:33.15 Zola Budd GBR 26.5.66 1 London 13 Jul 84

Mark	Wind	Name		Nat	Born	Pos	Meet	Venue	Date

3000 METRES

Mark	Wind	Name		Nat	Born	Pos	Meet	Venue	Date
8:28.83		Zola	Budd	GBR	26.5.66	3	GG	Roma	7 Sep 85
8:35.89		Sally	Barsosio	KEN	21.3.78	2	Herc	Monaco	16 Aug 97
8:36.45			Ma Ningning	CHN	1.6.76	4	NC	Jinan	6 Jun 93
8:38.61		Kalkedan	Gezahegn	ETH	8.5.91	5	WAF	Thessaloníki	13 Sep 09
8:38.97		Linet	Masai	KEN	5.12.89	5	GP	Rieti	9 Sep 07
8:39.65		Buze	Diriba	ETH-	9.2.94	3	Herc	Monaco	20 Jul 12
8:39.90		Gelete	Burka	ETH	15.2.86	3	SGP	Doha	13 May 05
8:40.08		Gabriela	Szabo	ROM	14.11.75	3	EC	Helsinki	10 Aug 94
8:40.28		Meseret	Defar	ETH	19.11.83	10	VD	Bruxelles	30 Aug 02
8:41.86		Tirunesh	Dibaba	ETH	2.6.85	11	VD	Bruxelles	30 Aug 02

5000 METRES

Mark	Wind	Name		Nat	Born	Pos	Meet	Venue	Date
14:30.88		Tirunesh	Dibaba	ETH	1.10.85	2	Bisl	Bergen (Fana)	11 Jun 04
14:35.18		Sentayehu	Ejigu	ETH	21.6.85	4	Bisl	Bergen (Fana)	11 Jun 04
14:39.96			Yin Lili	CHN	11.11.79	4	NG	Shanghai	23 Oct 97
14:43.29		Emebet	Anteneh	ETH	13.1.92	5	Bisl	Oslo	9 Jun 11
14:45.33			Lan Lixin	CHN	14.2.79	2h2	NG	Shanghai	21 Oct 97
14:45.71			Song Liqing	CHN	20.1.80	3h2	NG	Shanghai	21 Oct 97
14:45.90			Jiang Bo	CHN	13.3.77	1		Nanjing	24 Oct 95
14:45.98		Pauline	Korikwiang	KEN	1.3.88	7	Bisl	Oslo	2 Jun 06
14:46.71		Sally	Barsosio	KEN	21.3.78	3	VD	Bruxelles	22 Aug 97
14:47.13		Mercy	Cherono	KEN	7.5.91	7	DL	Shanghai	23 May 10
14:47.14		Linet	Masai	KEN	5.12.89	4	FBK	Hengelo	24 May 08

10,000 METRES

Mark	Wind	Name		Nat	Born	Pos	Meet	Venue	Date
30:26.50		Linet	Masai	KEN	5.12.89	4	OG	Beijing	15 Aug 08
30:31.55			Xing Huina	CHN	25.2.84	7	WCh	Saint-Denis	23 Aug 03
30:39.41			Lan Lixin	CHN	14.2.79	2	NG	Shanghai	19 Oct 97
30:39.98			Yin Lili	CHN	11.11.79	3	NG	Shanghai	19 Oct 97
30:59.92		Merima	Hashim	ETH	.81	3	NA	Heusden-Zolder	5 Aug 00
31:06.20		Lucy	Wangui	KEN	24.3.84	1rA		Okayama	27 Sep 03
31:11.26			Song Liqing	CHN	20.1.80	7	NG	Shanghai	19 Oct 97
31:15.38		Sally	Barsosio	KEN	21.3.78	3	WCh	Stuttgart	21 Aug 93
31:16.50		Evelyne	Kimwei	KEN	25.8.87	1		Kobe	21 Oct 06
31:17.30			Zhang Yingying	CHN	4.1.90	1		Wuhan	2 Nov 07
31:20.38		Tigist	Kiros	ETH	8.6.92	4	GS	Ostrava	31 May 11

MARATHON

Mark	Wind	Name		Nat	Born	Pos	Meet	Venue	Date
2:22:38			Zhang Yingying	CHN	4.1.90	1	NC	Xiamen	5 Jan 08
2:23:06		Merima	Mohamed	ETH	10.6.92	3		Toronto	26 Sep 10
2:23:37			Liu Min	CHN	29.11.83	1		Beijing	14 Oct 01
2:23:57			Zhu Xiaolin	CHN	20.4.84	4		Beijing	20 Oct 02
2:25:48			Jin Li	CHN	29.5.83	6		Beijing	14 Oct 01
2:26:34			Wei Yanan	CHN	6.12.81	1		Beijing	15 Oct 00
2:27:05			Chen Rong	CHN	18.5.88	1		Beijing	21 Oct 07
2:27:30			Ai Dongmei	CHN	15.10.79	3	NG	Beijing	4 Oct 97

3000 METRES STEEPLECHASE

Mark	Wind	Name		Nat	Born	Pos	Meet	Venue	Date
9:20.37		Birtukan	Adamu	ETH	29.4.92	4	GGala	Roma	26 May 11
9:22.51		Almaz	Ayana	ETH	21.11.91	3	VD	Bruxelles	27 Aug 10
9:24.51		Ruth	Bisibori	KEN	2.1.88	1		Daegu	3 Oct 07
9:26.25			Liu Nian	CHN	26.4.88	1		Wuhan	2 Nov 07
9:29.52		Korahubish	Itaa	ETH	28.2.92	1		Huelva	10 Jun 09
9:30.70		Melissa	Rollison	AUS	13.4.83	1	GWG	Brisbane	4 Sep 01
9:31.35		Christine	Muyanga	KEN	21.3.91	1	WJ	Bydgoszcz	10 Jul 08
9:32.74		Gesa-Felicitas	Krause	GER	3.8.92	9	WCh	Daegu	30 Aug 11
9:33.19		Karoline Bjerkeli	Grøvdal	NOR	14.6.90	4		Neerpelt	2 Jun 07
9:33.49		Elizabeth	Mueni	KEN	28.12.91	5	Bisl	Oslo	3 Jul 09

100 METRES HURDLES

Mark	Wind	Name		Nat	Born	Pos	Meet	Venue	Date
12.84	1.5	Aliuska	López	CUB	29.8.69	2	WUG	Zagreb	16 Jul 87
12.88	1.5	Yelena	Ovcharova	UKR	17.6.76	2	ECp	Villeneuve d'Ascq	25 Jun 95
12.89	1.3	Anay	Tejeda	CUB	3.4.83	1		Padova	1 Sep 02
12.91	1.8	Kristina	Castlin	USA	7.7.88	1	NCAA-r	Gainesville	26 May 07
12.92	0.0		Sun Hongwei	CHN	24.11.79	6	NG	Shanghai	18 Oct 97
12.95	1.5	Candy	Young	USA	21.5.62	2	AAU	Walnut	16 Jun 79
12.95A	1.5	Cinnamon	Sheffield	USA	8.3.70	2	NCAA	Provo	3 Jun 89
12.98	1.8	Queen	Harrison	USA	10.9.88	5	NCAA	Sacramento	8 Jun 07
13.00	0.7	Gloria	Kovarik	GDR	13.1.64	3h2	NC	Karl-Marx-Stadt	16 Jun 83
13.00	2.0	Lyudmila	Khristosenko	UKR	14.10.66	1	NC-j	Krasnodar	16 Jul 85

Mark	Wind	Name		Nat	Born	Pos	Meet	Venue	Date
13.01	0.4	Sally	McLellan	AUS	19.9.86	1		Brisbane	27 Nov 05
Wind assisted to 12.99									
12.81	3.4	Anay	Tejeda	CUB	3.4.83	1	WJ	Kingston	21 Jul 02
12.82	2.1	Kristina	Castlin	USA	7.7.88	1		College Park	21 Apr 07
12.90	3.0	Adrianna	Lamalle	FRA	27.9.82	1		Fort-de-France	28 Apr 01
12.95	2.4	Shermaine	Williams	JAM	4.2.90	1	NCAA II	San Angelo	23 May 09

400 METRES HURDLES

Mark	Wind	Name		Nat	Born	Pos	Meet	Venue	Date
54.40			Wang Xing	CHN	30.11.86	2	NG	Nanjing	21 Oct 05
54.58		Ristananna	Tracey	JAM	5.9.92	2	NC	Kingston	24 Jun 11
54.70		Lashinda	Demus	USA	10.3.83	1	WJ	Kingston	19 Jul 02
54.93			Li Rui	CHN	22.11.79	1	NG	Shanghai	22 Oct 97
55.11		Kaliese	Spencer	JAM	6.4.87	1	WJ	Beijing	17 Aug 06
55.15			Huang Xiaoxiao	CHN	3.3.83	2	NG	Guangzhou	22 Nov 01
55.20		Lesley	Maxie	USA	4.1.67	2	TAC	San Jose	9 Jun 84
55.20A		Jana	Pittman	AUS	9.11.82	1		Pietersburg	18 Mar 00
55.22		Tiffany	Ross	USA	5.2.83	2	NCAA	Baton Rouge	31 May 02
55.26		Ionela	Tîrlea	ROM	9.2.76	1	Nik	Nice	12 Jul 95
Drugs disqualification: 54.54		Peng Yinghua ¶		CHN	21.2.79	(2)	NG	Shanghai	22 Oct 97

HIGH JUMP

Mark	Wind	Name		Nat	Born	Pos	Meet	Venue	Date
2.01		Olga	Turchak	UKR	5.3.67	2	GWG	Moskva	7 Jul 86
2.01		Heike	Balck	GDR	19.8.70	1	vURS-j	Karl-Marx-Stadt	18 Jun 89
2.00		Stefka	Kostadinova	BUL	25.3.65	1		Sofiya	25 Aug 84
2.00		Alina	Astafei	ROM	7.6.69	1	WJ	Sudbury	29 Jul 88
1.98		Silvia	Costa	CUB	4.5.64	2	WUG	Edmonton	11 Jul 83
1.98		Yelena	Yelesina	RUS	5.4.70	1	Druzh	Nyiregyháza	13 Aug 88
1.97		Svetlana	Isaeva	BUL	18.3.67	2		Sofiya	25 May 86
1.97i		Mariya	Kuchina	RUS	14.1.93	1		Trinec	26 Jan 11
1.96A		Charmaine	Gale	RSA	27.2.64	1	NC-j	Bloemfontein	4 Apr 81
1.96i		Desislava	Aleksandrova	BUL	27.10.75	2	EI	Paris	12 Mar 94
1.96		Marina	Kuptsova	RUS	22.12.81	1	NC	Tula	26 Jul 00
1.96		Blanka	Vlasic	CRO	8.11.83	1	WJ	Kingston	20 Jul 02
1.96		Airine	Palsyte	LTU	13.7.92	2	WUG	Shenzhen	21 Aug 11

POLE VAULT

Mark	Wind	Name		Nat	Born	Pos	Meet	Venue	Date
4.63i		Angelica	Bengtsson	SWE	8.7.93	2		Stockholm	22 Feb 11
4.58						1		Sollentuna	5 Jul 12
4.60i		Hanna	Sheleh	UKR	14.7.93	3		Donetsk	11 Feb 12
4.52i		Katie	Byres	GBR	11.9.93	2		Nevers	18 Feb 12
4.50		Valeriya	Volik	RUS	11.5.89	1		Krasnodar	4 Jun 08
4.50		Liz	Parnov	AUS	9.5.94	1		Perth	17 Feb 12
4.48i		Silke	Spiegelburg	GER	17.3.86	2		Münster	25 Aug 05
4.47i		Yelena	Isinbayeva	RUS	3.6.82	1		Budapest	10 Feb 01
4.46						2	ISTAF	Berlin	31 Aug 01
4.46i			Zhang Yingning	CHN	6.1.90	1		Shanghai	15 Mar 07
4.45						1		Changsha	29 Oct 06
4.45i			Zhao Yingying	CHN	15.2.86	3		Madrid	24 Feb 05
4.45i			Li Ling	CHN	6.7.89	1		Beijing	26 Feb 08
4.45						1		Hangzhou	12 Apr 08
4.45		Marianna	Zachariadi	CYP	25.2.90	2	MedG	Pescara	30 Jun 09
4.45i		Joana	Kraft	GER	27.7.91	4	NC	Karlsruhe	28 Feb 10
Exhibition: 4.45		Yvonne	Buschbaum	GER	14.7.80	1		Zeiskam	17 Jul 99

LONG JUMP

Mark	Wind	Name		Nat	Born	Pos	Meet	Venue	Date
7.14	1.1	Heike	Daute	GDR	16.12.64	1	PTS	Bratislava	4 Jun 83
7.03	1.3	Darya	Klishina	RUS	15.1.91	1	Znam	Zhukovskiy	26 Jun 10
7.00	-0.2	Birgit	Grosshennig	GDR	21.2.65	2		Berlin	9 Jun 84
6.94	-0.5	Magdalena	Khristova	BUL	25.2.77	2		Kalamáta	22 Jun 96
6.91	0.0	Anisoara	Cusmir	ROM	28.6.62	1		Bucuresti	23 May 81
6.90	1.4	Beverly	Kinch	GBR	14.1.64	*	WCh	Helsinki	14 Aug 83
6.88	0.6	Natalya	Shevchenko	RUS	28.12.66	2		Sochi	26 May 84
6.84		Larisa	Baluta	UKR	13.8.65	2		Krasnodar	6 Aug 83
6.82	1.8	Fiona	May	GBR	12.12.69	*	WJ	Sudbury	30 Jul 88
6.81	1.6	Carol	Lewis	USA	8.8.63	1	TAC	Knoxville	20 Jun 82
6.81	1.4	Yelena	Davydova	KZK	16.11.67	1	NC-j	Krasnodar	17 Jul 85
Wind assisted									
7.27	2.2	Heike	Daute	GDR	16.12.64	1	WCh	Helsinki	14 Aug 83
6.93	4.6	Beverly	Kinch	GBR	14.1.64	5	WCh	Helsinki	14 Aug 83
6.88	2.1	Fiona	May	GBR	12.12.69	1	WJ	Sudbury	30 Jul 88
6.84	2.8	Anu	Kaljurand	EST	16.4.69	2		Riga	4 Jun 88

Mark	Wind	Name		Nat	Born	Pos	Meet	Venue	Date
TRIPLE JUMP									
14.62	1.0	Tereza	Marinova	BUL	5.9.77	1	WC	Sydney	25 Aug 96
14.57	0.2		Huang Qiuyan	CHN	25.1.80	1	NG	Shanghai	19 Oct 97
14.52	0.6	Anastasiya	Ilyina	RUS	16.1.82	q	WJ	Santiago de Chile	20 Oct 00
14.46	1.0		Peng Fengmei	CHN	2.7.79	1		Chengdu	18 Apr 98
14.43	0.6	Kaire	Leibak	EST	21.5.88	1	WJ	Beijing	17 Aug 06
14.38	-0.7		Xie Limei	CHN	27.6.86	1	AsiC	Inchon	1 Sep 05
14.37i	-		Ren Ruiping	CHN	1.2.76	3	WI	Barcelona	11 Mar 95
	14.36		0.0			1	NC	Beijing	1 Jun 94
14.36	0.0	Dailenys	Alcántara	CUB	10.8.91	3	Barr/NC	La Habana	29 May 09
14.35		Yana	Borodina	RUS	21.4.92	1J	Mosc Ch	Moskva	15 Jun 11
14.32	-0.1	Yelena	Lysak ¶	RUS	19.10.75	1		Voronezh	18 Jun 94
14.29	1.2	Mabel	Gay	CUB	5.5.83	1		La Habana	5 Apr 02
Wind assisted									
14.83	8.3		Ren Ruiping	CHN	1.2.76	1	NC	Taiyuan	21 May 95
14.43	2.7	Yelena	Lysak ¶	RUS	19.10.75	1	WJ	Lisboa	21 Jul 94
SHOT									
20.54		Astrid	Kumbernuss	GDR	5.2.70	1	vFIN-j	Orimattila	1 Jul 89
20.51i		Heidi	Krieger	GDR	20.7.65	2		Budapest	8 Feb 84
	20.24					5		Split	30 Apr 84
20.23		Ilke	Wyludda	GDR	28.3.69	1	NC-j	Karl-Marx-Stadt	16 Jul 88
20.12		Ilona	Schoknecht	GDR	24.9.56	2	NC	Erfurt	23 Aug 75
20.02			Cheng Xiaoyan	CHN	30.11.75	3	NC	Beijing	5 Jun 94
19.90		Stephanie	Storp	FRG	28.11.68	1		Hamburg	16 Aug 87
19.63			Wang Yawen	CHN	23.8.73	1		Shijiazhuang	25 Apr 92
19.57		Grit	Haupt	GDR	4.6.66	1		Gera	7 Jul 84
19.48		Ines	Wittich	GDR	14.11.69	5		Leipzig	29 Jul 87
19.46			Gong Lijiao	CHN	24.1.89	Q	OG	Beijing	16 Aug 08
19.42		Simone	Michel	GDR	18.12.60	3	vSU	Leipzig	23 Jun 79
DISCUS									
74.40		Ilke	Wyludda	GDR	28.3.69	2		Berlin	13 Sep 88
	75.36	unofficial meeting				2		Berlin	6 Sep 88
67.38		Irina	Meszynski	GDR	24.3.62	1		Berlin	14 Aug 81
67.00		Jana	Günther	GDR	7.1.68	6	NC	Potsdam	20 Aug 87
66.80		Svetla	Mitkova	BUL	17.6.64	1		Sofiya	2 Aug 83
66.60		Astrid	Kumbernuss	GDR	5.2.70	1		Berlin	20 Jul 88
66.34		Franka	Dietzsch	GDR	22.1.68	2		Saint-Denis	11 Jun 87
66.30		Jana	Lauren	GDR	28.6.70	1	vURS-j	Karl-Marx-Stadt	18 Jun 89
66.08			Cao Qi	CHN	15.1.74	1	NG	Beijing	12 Sep 93
65.96		Grit	Haupt	GDR	4.6.66	3		Leipzig	13 Jul 84
65.22		Daniela	Costian	ROM	30.4.65	3		Nitra	26 Aug 84
HAMMER									
73.24			Zhang Wenxiu	CHN	22.3.86	1	NC	Changsha	24 Jun 05
71.71		Kamila	Skolimowska	POL	4.11.82	1	GPF	Melbourne	9 Sep 01
70.39		Mariya	Smolyachkova	BLR	10.2.85	1		Staiki	26 Jun 04
70.62		Alexandra	Tavernier	FRA	13.12.93	1	WJ	Barcelona	14 Jul 12
69.73		Natalya	Zolotukhina	UKR	4.1.85	1		Kiev	24 Jul 04
69.63		Bianca	Perie	ROU	1.6.90	1	NC-j	Bucuresti	14 Aug 09
68.74		Arasay	Thondike	CUB	28.5.86	2	Barr	La Habana	2 May 05
68.50		Martina	Danisová	SVK	21.3.83	1		Kladno	16 Jun 01
68.49		Anna	Bulgakova	RUS	17.1.88	6		Sochi	26 May 07
68.40		Bianca	Achilles	GER	17.4.81	1		Dortmund	25 Sep 99
68.26		Katerina	Safránková	CZE	8.6.89	1		Pardubice	7 May 08
JAVELIN									
63.01		Vira	Rebryk	UKR	25.2.89	1	WJ	Bydgoszcz	10 Jul 08
62.93			Xue Juan	CHN	10.2.86	1	NG	Changsha	27 Oct 03
62.09			Zhang Li	CHN	17.1.89	1		Beijing	25 May 08
61.99			Wang Yaning	CHN	4.1.80	1	NC	Huizhou	14 Oct 99
61.79		Nikolett	Szabó	HUN	3.3.80	1		Schwechat	23 May 99
61.61			Chang Chunfeng	CHN	4.5.88	1	NC-j	Chengdu	4 Jun 07
61.49			Liang Lili	CHN	16.11.83	1	NC	Benxi	1 Jun 02
61.40		Sofi	Flinck	SWE	8.7.95	1	WJ	Barcelona	11 Jul 12
61.38		Annika	Suthe	GER	15.10.85	1-j		Halle	23 May 04
Pre 1999 specification									
71.88		Antoaneta	Todorova	BUL	8.6.63	1	ECp	Zagreb	15 Aug 81
71.82		Ivonne	Leal	CUB	27.2.66	1	WUG	Kobe	30 Aug 85

Mark	Wind	Name		Nat	Born	Pos	Meet	Venue		Date
70.12		Karen	Forkel	GDR	24.9.70	1	EJ	Varazdin		26 Aug 89
68.94		Trine	Solberg	NOR	18.4.66	1	vURS	Oslo		16 Jul 85

HEPTATHLON

Mark	Wind	Name		Nat	Born	Pos	Meet	Venue		Date
6768w		Tatyana	Chernova	RUS	29.1.88	1		Arles		3 Jun 07
	13.04w/6.1	1.82	13.57	23.59w/5.2	6.61/1.2	53.43	2:15.05			
	6227				1	WJ	Beijing			19 Aug 06
	13.70/1.6	1.80	12.18	24.05/0.3	6.35/-0.4	50.51	2:25.49			
6542		Carolina	Klüft	SWE	2.2.83	1	EC	München		10 Aug 02
	13.33/-0.3	1.89	13.16	23.71/-0.3	6.36/1.1	47.61	2:17.99			
6465		Sibylle	Thiele	GDR	6.3.65	1	EJ	Schwechat		28 Aug 83
	13.49	1.90	14.63	24.07	6.65	36.22	2:18.36			
6436		Sabine	Braun	FRG	19.6.65	1	vBUL	Mannheim		9 Jun 84
	13.68	1.78	13.09	23.88	6.03	52.14	2:09.41			
6428		Svetla	Dimitrova ¶	BUL	27.1.70	1	NC	Sofiya		18 Jun 89
	13.49/-0.7	1.77	13.98	23.59/-0.2	6.49/0.7	40.10	2:11.10			
6403		Emilia	Dimitrova	BUL	13.11.67	6	GWG	Moskva		7 Jul 86
	13.73	1.76	13.46	23.17	6.29	43.30	2:09.85			
6276		Larisa	Nikitina	RUS	29.4.65	8	URS Ch	Kiyev		21 Jun 84
	13.87/1.6	1.86	14.04	25.26/-0.7	6.31/0.1	48.62	2:22.76			
6267		Katarina	Johnson-Thompson	GBR	9.1.93	15	OG	London (OS)		4 Aug 12
	13.48/0.9	1.89	11.32	23.73/-0.3	6.19/-0.4	38.37	2:10.76			
6218		Jana	Sobotka	GDR	3.10.65	6	OD	Potsdam		21 Jul 84
	14.40	1.74	13.28	24.19	6.27	43.64	2:06.83			
6198		Anke	Schmidt	GDR	5.2.68	7		Götzis		24 May 87
	13.80/0.9	1.72	13.32	23.82/0.3	6.63/2.0	35.78	2:12.44			

Drugs disqualification: 6534 Svetla Dimitrova   BUL   27.1.70   (3)   ECp   Helmond   16 Jul 89
13.30/1.0   1.84   14.35   23.33/-2.2   6.47/-1.4   39.20   2:13.56

10 KILOMETRES WALK

Mark	Wind	Name		Nat	Born	Pos	Meet	Venue	Date
41:52		Tatyana	Mineyeva	RUS	10.8.90	1	NCp-j	Penza	5 Sep 09
41:55		Irina	Stankina	RUS	25.3.77	1	NC-wj	Adler	11 Feb 95
41:57			Gao Hongmiao	CHN	17.3.74	2	NG	Beijing	8 Sep 93
42:15+		Anisya	Kirdyapkina	RUS	23.10.89	1=	in 20k	Adler	23 Feb 08
42:29		Tatyana	Kalmykova	RUS	10.1.90	1	NC-wj	Adler	23 Feb 08
42:31		Irina	Yumanova	RUS	17.6.90	2	NC-wj	Adler	23 Feb 08
42:43.0	t	Svetlana	Vasilyeva	RUS	24.7.92	1	NC-wj	Sochi	27 Feb 11
42:44			Long Yuwen	CHN	1.8.75	3	NC	Shenzen	18 Feb 93
42:45			Li Yuxin	CHN	4.12.74	4		Shenzhen	18 Feb 93
42:45		Kseniya	Trifonova	RUS	7.5.90	2	NC-wj	Adler	28 Feb 09

20 KILOMETRES WALK

Mark	Wind	Name		Nat	Born	Pos	Meet	Venue	Date
1:25:30		Anisya	Kirdyapkina	RUS	23.10.89	2	NC-w	Adler	23 Feb 08
1:26:36		Tatyana	Kalmykova	RUS	10.1.90	1	NC	Saransk	8 Jun 08
1:27:01			Lu Xiuzhi	CHN	26.10.93	2		Taicang	30 Mar 12
1:27:16			Song Hongjuan	CHN	4.7.84	1	NC	Yangzhou	14 Apr 03
1:27:34			Jiang Jing	CHN	23.10.85	2	WCp	Naumburg	2 May 04
1:27:35		Natalya	Fedoskina	RUS	25.6.80	2	WCp	Mézidon-Canon	2 May 99

4 X 100 METRES RELAY

Mark	Nat	Names	Pos	Meet	Venue	Date
43.29	USA (Blue)	Knight, Tarmoh, Olear, Mayo	1		Eugene	8 Aug 06
43.40	JAM	Simpson, Stewart, McLaughlin, Facey	1	WJ	Kingston	20 Jul 02
43.42	GER	Burghardt, Grompe, Pinto, Frese	1	EJ	Tallinn	24 Jul 11
43.44A	NGR	Utondu, Iheagwam, Onyali, Ogunkoya	1	AfrG	Nairobi	9 Aug 87
43.48	GDR	Breuer, Krabbe, Dietz, Henke	1	WJ	Sudbury	31 Jul 88
		Unsanctioned race 43.33 Breuer, Krabbe, Dietz, Henke	1		Berlin	20 Jul 88
43.68	FRA	Vouaux, Jacques-Sebastien, Kamga, Banco	3	WJ	Grosseto	18 Jul 04
43.87	URS	Lapshina, Doronina, Bulatova, Kovalyova	1	vGDR-j	Leningrad	20 Jun 87
43.98	BRA	Silva, Leoncio, Krasucki, Santos	2	PAm-J	São Paulo	7 Jul 07
44.04	CUB	Riquelme, Allen, López, Valdivia	2	WJ	Sudbury	31 Jul 88
44.09	NED	Schippers, Kuhurima, Lubbers, Samuel	3	WJ	Moncton	24 Jul 10

4 X 400 METRES RELAY

Mark	Nat	Names	Pos	Meet	Venue	Date
3:27.60	USA	Anderson, Kidd, Smith, Hastings	1	WJ	Grosseto	18 Jul 04
3:28.39	GDR	Derr, Fabert, Wöhlk, Breuer	1	WJ	Sudbury	31 Jul 88
3:29.66	JAM	Stewart, Morgan, Walker, Hall	1	PennR	Philadelphia	28 Apr 01
3:30.03	RUS	Talko, Shapayeva, Soldatova, Kostetskaya	2	WJ	Grosseto	18 Jul 04
3:30.38	AUS	Scamps, R Poetschka, Hanigan, Andrews	1	WJ	Plovdiv	12 Aug 90
3:30.46	GBR	Wall, Spencer, James,. Miller	2	WJ	Kingston	21 Jul 02
3:30.72	BUL	Kireva, Angelova, Rashova, Dimitrova	3	v2N	Sofiya	24 Jul 83
3:30.84	NGR	Abugan, Odumosu, Eze, Adesanya	2	WJ	Beijing	20 Aug 06

Mark	Name		Nat	Born	Pos	Meet	Venue	Date

MEN'S WORLD LISTS 2012

60 METRES INDOORS

Mark	Name		Nat	Born	Pos	Meet	Venue	Date
6.45A	Trell	Kimmons	USA	13.7.85	1	NC	Albuquerque	26 Feb
6.56					3h1	GP	Birmingham	18 Feb
6.46	Justin	Gatlin	USA	10.2.82	1	WI	Istanbul	10 Mar
6.47	Lerone	Clarke	JAM	2.10.81	1	GP	Birmingham	18 Feb
6.47A		Gatlin			2	NC	Albuquerque	26 Feb
6.49	Nesta	Carter	JAM	10.11.85	2	GP	Birmingham	18 Feb
6.50		Clarke			1		Liévin	14 Feb
6.50	Asafa	Powell	JAM	23.11.82	1h1	GP	Birmingham	18 Feb
6.50		Powell			3	GP	Birmingham	18 Feb
6.50		Gatlin			1s1	WI	Istanbul	10 Mar
6.51		Carter			1h2	GP	Birmingham	18 Feb
6.51A		Gatlin			1h1	NC	Albuquerque	25 Feb
	(11/5)							
6.52	Jeffery	Demps	USA	8.1.90	1h1	NCAA	Nampa	9 Mar
6.53	Jimmy	Vicaut	FRA	27.2.92	1		Düsseldorf	10 Feb
6.55	Harry	Adams	USA	27.11.89	1		Birmingham, AL	21 Jan
6.55	Yunier	Pérez	CUB	16.2.85	1		Gent	18 Feb
6.55A	Phil	DeRosier	USA	11.4.84	1s1	NC	Albuquerque	26 Feb
	(10)							
6.56	Kemar	Hyman	CAY	11.10.89	2		Birmingham, AL	21 Jan
6.56	Richard	Thompson	TRI	7.6.85	1h1		Fayetteville	11 Feb
6.56	Kim	Collins	SKN	5.4.76	2h1	GP	Birmingham	18 Feb
6.57	Christophe	Lemaitre	FRA	11.6.90	2		Liévin	14 Feb
6.57	Andrew	Riley	JAM	6.9.88	2	NCAA	Nampa	10 Mar
6.58	Ramil	Guliyev	TUR	29.5.90	1		Sumy	13 Jan
6.58A	Ryan	Milus	USA	19.9.90	2		Albuquerque	10 Feb
6.58	Dwain	Chambers	GBR	5.4.78	1	NC	Sheffield	12 Feb
6.58A	Rakieem	Salaam	USA	5.4.90	1h2	NC	Albuquerque	25 Feb
6.58A	DeAngelo	Cherry	USA	1.8.90	3	NC	Albuquerque	26 Feb
	(20)							
6.59	Julian	Reus	GER	29.4.88	1		Chemnitz	27 Jan
6.59	Justyn	Warner	CAN	28.6.87	1		Toronto	29 Jan
6.59	Gerald	Phiri	ZAM	6.10.88	4		Fayetteville	11 Feb
6.59	Hasan	Heidarpoor	IRI	31.1.88	1s1	AsiC	Hangzhou	18 Feb
6.59	Terrell	Wilks	USA	20.12.89	6	GP	Birmingham	18 Feb
6.59A	Joshua	Norman	USA	26.7.80	3s2	NC	Albuquerque	26 Feb
6.59	Maurice	Mitchell	USA	22.12.89	2h1	NCAA	Nampa	9 Mar
6.60	Reginald	Dixon	USA	7.6.88	1h4		University Park	27 Jan
6.60	Peter	Emelieze	NGR	19.4.88	2rA		Val-de-Reuil	18 Feb
6.60	Christian	Blum	GER	10.3.87	1s2	NC	Karlsruhe	25 Feb
	(30)							
6.60	Emmanuel	Biron	FRA	29.7.88	2	NC	Aubière	25 Feb
6.61	Keith	Ricks	USA	9.10.90	2		Blacksburg	3 Feb
6.61	Richard	Kilty	GBR	2.9.89	1s1		Birmingham	4 Feb
6.61	Andrew	Robertson	GBR	17.12.90	2	NC	Sheffield	12 Feb
6.61	Michael	LeBlanc	CAN	25.2.87	1		Toronto	19 Feb
6.61A	Calesio	Newman	USA	20.8.86	2s1	NC	Albuquerque	26 Feb
6.61A	Cordero	Gray	USA	9.5.89	3s1	NC	Albuquerque	26 Feb
6.61	Marc	Burns	TRI	7.1.83	1		Birmingham, AL	3 Mar
6.61	Ángel David	Rodriguez	ESP	25.4.80	1		Madrid	3 Mar
6.61	Keenan	Brock	USA	1.6.92	2h2	NCAA	Nampa	9 Mar
	(40)							
6.61	Clayton	Vaughn	USA	15.5.92	3h1	NCAA	Nampa	9 Mar
6.61	Isiah	Young	USA	5.1.90	3h3	NCAA	Nampa	9 Mar
6.61	Michael	Granger	USA	17.3.91	4h1	NCAA	Nampa	9 Mar
6.62	Reza	Ghasemi	IRI	24.7.87	1		Tehran	19 Jan
6.62	Simone	Collio	ITA	27.12.79	1h1		Mondeville	4 Feb
6.62	Keston	Bledman	TRI	8.3.88	1	Mill	New York (Armory)	11 Feb
6.62	Michael	Frater	JAM	6.10.82	3		Liévin	14 Feb

Mark	Name		Nat	Born	Date		Mark	Name		Nat	Born	Date
6.63	Evander	Wells	USA	7.12.87	27 Jan		6.64		Egwero Ogho-Oghene	NGR	26.11.88	2 Feb
6.63	Samuel	Effah	CAN	29.12.88	3 Feb		6.64	Ivory	Williams	USA	2.5.85	11 Feb
6.63A	Daniel	Auberry (50)	USA	13.9.89	4 Feb		6.64		Liang Jiahong	CHN	6.3.88	18 Feb
6.63	Darvis	Patton	USA	4.12.77	11 Feb		6.64	Jaysuma	Saidy Ndure	NOR	1.7.84	18 Feb
6.63	Marcus	Rowland	USA	11.3.90	3 Mar		6.64	Antoine	Adams	SKN	31.8.88	18 Feb
6.64	Rytis	Sakalauskas	LTU	27.6.87	21 Jan		6.64	Michael	Tumi	ITA	12.2.90	26 Feb
6.64	Simeon	Williamson	GBR	16.1.86	22 Jan		6.64	Joe	Morris	USA	4.10.89	2 Mar
6.64	Tim	Abeyie	GHA	7.11.82	27 Jan							

Mark	Wind	Name		Nat	Born	Pos	Meet	Venue	Date

100 METRES

Mark	Wind	Name		Nat	Born	Pos	Meet	Venue	Date
9.63	1.5	Usain	Bolt	JAM	21.8.86	1	OG	London (OS)	5 Aug
9.69	-0.1	Yohan	Blake	JAM	26.12.89	1	Athl	Lausanne	23 Aug
9.75	1.1		Blake			1	NC	Kingston	29 Jun
9.75	1.5		Blake			2	OG	London (OS)	5 Aug
9.76	-0.1		Bolt			1	GGala	Roma	31 May
9.76	1.4		Blake			1	WK	Zürich	30 Aug
9.79	0.6		Bolt			1	Bisl	Oslo	7 Jun
9.79	1.5	Justin	Gatlin	USA	10.2.82	3	OG	London (OS)	5 Aug
9.80	1.8		Gatlin			1	NC/OT	Eugene	24 Jun
9.80	1.5	Tyson	Gay	USA	9.8.82	4	OG	London (OS)	5 Aug
9.82	1.8		Bolt			1		Kingston	5 May
9.82	0.7		Gatlin			1s1	OG	London (OS)	5 Aug
9.83	-0.1		Gay			2	Athl	Lausanne	23 Aug
9.84	0.5		Blake			1		Georgetown, CAY	9 May
9.85	0.6	Asafa	Powell	JAM	23.11.82	2	Bisl	Oslo	7 Jun
9.85	1.6		Blake			1rA	Spitzen	Luzern	17 Jul
9.85	1.7		Blake			1s3	OG	London (OS)	5 Aug
9.86	1.4	Keston	Bledman	TRI	8.3.88	1	NC	Port of Spain	23 Jun
9.86	1.8		Gay			2	NC/OT	Eugene	24 Jun
9.86	1.1		Bolt			2	NC	Kingston	29 Jun
9.86	0.3		Bolt			1	VD	Bruxelles	7 Sep
9.87	0.4		Gatlin			1	DL	Doha	11 May
9.87	1.0		Bolt			1s2	OG	London (OS)	5 Aug
9.88	0.4		Powell			2	DL	Doha	11 May
9.88	1.1		Powell			3	NC	Kingston	29 Jun
9.88	1.5	Ryan	Bailey	USA	13.4.89	1h3	OG	London (OS)	4 Aug
9.88	1.5		Bailey			5	OG	London (OS)	5 Aug
9.89	0.9		Bledman			1h2		Orlando	26 May
9.90	1.6		Blake			1		Kingston	14 Apr
9.90	1.3		Gatlin			1	Pre	Eugene	2 Jun
9.90	0.7		Blake			1	adidas	New York	9 Jun
9.90	1.7		Gatlin			1h5	NC/OT	Eugene	23 Jun
9.90	1.7		Gay			2s3	OG	London (OS)	5 Aug
		(33/7)							
9.91	0.7	Churandy	Martina	NED	3.7.84	2s1	OG	London (OS)	5 Aug
9.93	1.3	Nickel	Ashmeade	JAM	4.7.90	2	Pre	Eugene	2 Jun
9.94	1.8	Michael	Rodgers	USA	24.4.85	4	NC/OT	Eugene	24 Jun
		(10)							
9.94	1.1	Michael	Frater	JAM	6.10.82	4	NC	Kingston	29 Jun
9.95	1.5	Nesta	Carter	JAM	10.11.85	2s1	NC	Kingston	29 Jun
9.95	1.8	Kemar	Hyman	CAY	11.10.89	1h2		Madrid	7 Jul
9.96	1.4	Harry	Adams	USA	27.11.89	1s2	NCAA	Des Moines	6 Jun
9.96	1.4	Richard	Thompson	TRI	7.6.85	2	NC	Port of Spain	23 Jun
9.96	1.8	Darvis	Patton	USA	4.12.77	5	OT	Eugene	24 Jun
9.97	0.3	Kemar	Bailey-Cole	JAM	10.1.92	3	VD	Bruxelles	7 Sep
9.98	1.0	Rakieem Mookie	Salaam	USA	5.4.90	1		Auburn	21 Apr
9.99	0.4	Lerone	Clarke	JAM	2.10.81	3	DL	Doha	11 May
10.00	1.6	Marc	Burns	TRI	7.1.83	3rA	Spitzen	Luzern	17 Jul
		(20)							
10.01	1.4	Kim	Collins	SKN	5.4.76	4	WK	Zürich	30 Aug
10.02	1.4	Andrew	Riley	JAM	9.9.88	2s2	NCAA	Des Moines	6 Jun
10.02	1.8	Trell	Kimmons	USA	13.7.85	6	NC/OT	Eugene	24 Jun
10.02	2.0	Dwain	Chambers	GBR	5.4.78	1h7	OG	London (OS)	4 Aug
10.02	-0.1	Jimmy	Vicaut	FRA	27.2.92	5	Athl	Lausanne	23 Aug
10.03	1.3	Maurice	Mitchell	USA	22.12.89	1s3	NCAA	Des Moines	6 Jun
10.03	1.4	Rondell	Sorrillo	TRI	21.1.86	3	NC	Port of Spain	23 Jun
10.03	0.7	Walter	Dix	USA	31.1.86	1h1	NC/OT	Eugene	23 Jun
10.04	0.5	Travis	Padgett	USA	13.12.86	2		Orlando	26 May
10.04	-0.1	Christophe	Lemaitre	FRA	11.6.90	3	GGala	Roma	31 May
		(30)							
10.05	1.4	Charles	Silmon	USA	4.7.91	3h2	NCAA	Des Moines	6 Jun
10.05	0.1	Adam	Gemili	GBR-J	6.10.93	1	WJ	Barcelona	11 Jul
10.06A	1.8	Simon	Magakwe	RSA	25.5.85	1s3		Johannesburg	27 Apr
10.06A	0.9	Jason	Rogers	SKN	31.8.91	1	NACAC	Irapuato	6 Jul
10.06	1.0	Jason	Young	JAM	21.3.91	1rB	Spitzen	Luzern	17 Jul
10.06	1.5	Ben Youssef	Meité	CIV	11.11.86	2h3	OG	London (OS)	4 Aug
10.07	0.4	Calesio	Newman	USA	20.8.86	1		Port of Spain	19 May
10.07	1.5	Emmanuel	Callender	TRI	10.5.84	1		Rio de Janeiro	20 May
10.07	1.3	Ryota	Yamagata	JPN	10.6.92	2h6	OG	London (OS)	4 Aug

Mark	Wind	Name		Nat	Born	Pos	Meet	Venue	Date
10.08	1.0	Jacques	Harvey	JAM	5.4.89	4s2	NC	Kingston	29 Jun
		(40)							
10.08	0.7	Derrick	Atkins	BAH	5.1.84	4s3	OG	London (OS)	5 Aug
10.09	1.0	Keenan	Brock	USA	1.6.92	3		Auburn	21 Apr
10.09	1.3	Marcus	Rowland	USA	11.3.90	3s3	NCAA	Des Moines	6 Jun
10.09	1.4	Isiah	Young	USA	5.1.90	4s2	NCAA	Des Moines	6 Jun
10.09	0.7	Julian	Reus	GER	29.4.88	1r1		Weinheim	27 Jul
10.09	1.5	Justyn	Warner	CAN	28.6.87	3h3	OG	London (OS)	4 Aug
10.10	1.8	Daniel	Bailey	ANT	9.9.86	5		Kingston	5 May
10.10	1.5	Ramone	McKenzie	JAM	15.11.90	1		Clermont	19 May
10.10	1.0	Antoine	Adams	SKN	31.8.88	1	NC	Basseterre	3 Jun
10.10	1.4	Aziz	Ouhadi	MAR	24.7.84	1		Brazzaville	10 Jun
		(50)							
10.10	1.4	Jeffrey	Demps	USA	8.1.90	2s1	NC/OT	Eugene	24 Jun
10.11	1.5	Cordero	Gray	USA	9.5.89	2		Clermont	19 May
10.11	1.3	Prezel	Hardy	USA	1.6.92	4s3	NCAA	Des Moines	6 Jun
10.11	0.8	Obinna	Metu	NGR	12.7.88	1	NC	Calabar	20 Jun
10.11	1.9	Mario	Forsythe	JAM	30.10.85	3	Kuso	Szczecin	21 Jul
10.11	1.0	Gerald	Phiri	ZAM	6.10.88	5s2	OG	London (OS)	5 Aug
10.12	1.2	Brijesh BJ	Lawrence	SKN	27.12.89	1		Crete, NE	21 Apr
10.12	1.5	Oshane	Bailey	JAM	9.8.89	3		Clermont	19 May
10.13	1.1	Jaysuma	Saidy Ndure	NOR	1.7.84	1s1	EC	Helsinki	27 Jun
10.13	0.4	James	Dasaolu	GBR	5.9.87	3h4	OG	London (OS)	4 Aug
		(60)							
10.14	1.0	Sheldon	Mitchell	JAM	.90	2rB		Kingston	5 May
10.14	1.3	Gavin	Smellie	CAN	26.6.86	1r4		Weinheim	27 Jul
10.15	1.8	Dexter	Lee	JAM	18.1.91	8		Kingston	5 May
10.15	1.5	Zye	Boey	USA	8.5.89	1q3	NCAA-W	Austin	25 May
10.15	1.2	Darrell	Wesh	USA	21.1.92	1s1	NCAA	Des Moines	6 Jun
10.15	0.8	Rytis	Sakalauskas	LTU	27.6.87	1		Valmiera	8 Jun
10.17	0.2	Mike	Granger	USA	17.3.91	1		Oxford, MS	14 Apr
10.17	1.9	Mickey	Grimes	USA	10.10.76	1		Azusa	20 Apr
10.17	-0.6	Nicholas	Watson	JAM	.90	1h1		Kingston	19 May
10.17	1.7	Ameer	Webb	USA	19.3.91	1h6	NCAA-W	Austin	24 May
		(70)							
10.17	1.2	Aaron	Ernest	USA-J	8.11.93	2s1	NCAA	Des Moines	6 Jun
10.17A	1.8	Ángel David	Rodríguez	ESP	25.4.80	1		Monachil	9 Jun
10.17	1.4	Jamol	James	TRI	16.7.92	6	NC	Port of Spain	23 Jun
10.17	1.6	Phil	DeRosier	USA	11.4.84	3h4	NC/OT	Eugene	23 Jun
10.18	1.3	Masashi	Eriguchi	JPN	17.12.88	1h1	Oda	Hiroshima	29 Apr
10.18	2.0	Aaron	Brown	CAN	27.5.92	1	PAC-12	Eugene	13 May
10.18	1.5	Dentarius	Locke	USA	12.12.89	4=		Clermont	19 May
10.18	1.2	Warren	Fraser	BAH	8.7.91	3s1	NCAA	Des Moines	6 Jun
10.18	1.3	Everett	Walker	USA	3.10.90	5s3	NCAA	Des Moines	6 Jun
10.18	0.7	Su'Waibou	Sanneh	GAM	30.10.90	8s1	OG	London (OS)	5 Aug
		(80)							
10.19	1.5	Marek	Niit	EST	9.8.87	1		Fayetteville	31 Mar
10.19	1.3	Abraham	Hall	USA-J	12.9.93	1		Austin	12 May
10.19	0.1	Julian	Forte	JAM-J	1.7.93	1		Kingston	26 May
10.19	1.7	Tyreek	Hill	USA-J	1.3.94	1h2		Orlando	26 May
10.19	-0.1	Aleksandr	Brednev	RUS	12.2.88	1h2	Znam	Zhukovskiy	17 Jun
10.19	0.8	Egweru	Ogho-Oghene	NGR	26.11.88	2	NC	Calabar	20 Jun
10.19	0.0	Jeremy	Bascom	GUY	15.10.83	1		Omaha	6 Jul
10.19	1.0	Jared	Connaughton	CAN	20.7.85	2		Ottawa	14 Jul
10.19	1.3		Su Bingtian	CHN	29.8.89	3h6	OG	London (OS)	4 Aug
10.19	0.5	Yoshihide	Kiryu	JPN-Y	15.12.95	1		Fukuroi	3 Nov
		(90)							
10.19A	1.3	Akani	Simbine	RSA-J	21.9.93	1		Lusaka	11 Dec
10.20	0.9	Roscoe	Engel	RSA	6.3.89	2	NC	Port Elizabeth	14 Apr
10.20	1.0	Kimmari	Roach	JAM	21.9.90	5r2		Kingston	5 May
10.20	0.4	Ivory	Williams	USA	2.5.85	2		Port of Spain	19 May
10.20	0.8	Patrick	Chinedu	NGR	26.4.84	1		Tres Cantos	2 Jun
10.20	0.3	Dariusz	Kuc	POL	24.4.86	1	NC	Bielsko-Biala	15 Jun
10.20	1.5	Lucas	Jakubczyk	GER	28.4.85	1h3	NC	Wattenscheid	16 Jun
10.20	0.1	Rodney	Green	BAH	8.12.85	1h4	NC	Nassau	22 Jun
10.20A	1.0	Ian	Warner	CAN	15.5.90	2	NC/OT	Calgary	29 Jun
10.20	0.0	Kenroy	Anderson	JAM	27.6.87	1		La Roche-sur-Yon	18 Jul
		(100)							
10.20	0.7	Tobias	Unger	GER	10.7.79	2r2		Weinheim	27 Jul
10.20	1.0	Harry	Aikines-Aryeetey	GBR	29.8.88	4		Rovereto	4 Sep
10.20	1.2	Aldemir Gomes	da Silva	BRA	8.6.92	1	NC-23	Maringá	8 Sep

Mark	Wind	Name	Nat	Born	Date
10.21	0.1	Ryan Milus	USA	19.9.90	24 Mar
10.21	1.2	Keith Ricks	USA	9.10.90	20 Apr
10.21		Mark Lewis-Francis	GBR	4.9.82	28 Apr
10.21	1.3	Yusuke Kotani	JPN	23.9.89	29 Apr
10.21	1.9	Ramon Gittens	BAR	20.7.87	13 May
10.21A	1.4	Miguel López	PUR	9.4.90	27 May
10.21	0.4	Ashton Eaton	USA	21.1.88	22 Jun
10.21	-0.2	Aaron Armstrong	TRI	14.10.77	23 Jun
10.21	1.7	Jacques Riparelli	ITA	27.3.83	10 Jul
10.22	1.8	Omar Douglas	JAM	30.10.83	5 May
10.22	2.0	James Alaka	GBR	8.9.89	13 May
10.22	1.7	Moriba Morain	TRI	8.10.92	27 May
10.22A	1.0	Oluseyi Smith	CAN	21.2.87	29 Jun
10.22	1.3	Reto Amaru Schenkel	SUI	28.4.88	27 Jul
10.22	0.4	Amr Ibrahim Seoud	EGY	10.6.86	4 Aug
10.22	1.3	Peter Emelieze	NGR	19.4.88	4 Aug
10.23	0.3	Richard Kilty	GBR	2.9.89	7 Apr
10.23	-0.4	Joshua Ross	AUS	9.2.81	14 Apr
10.23	1.3	Keneil Lee	JAM	12.6.88	14 Apr
10.23A	0.4	Hannes Dreyer	RSA	13.1.85	27 Apr
10.23	1.3	Kazuma Oseto	JPN-J	5.8.94	29 Apr
10.23	1.3	Takumi Kuki	JPN	18.5.92	8 Jun
10.23A	0.9	Akeem Haynes	CAN	3.11.92	6 Jul
10.23	0.7	Carlos Rafael Jorge	DOM	24.9.86	21 Jul
10.24	0.0	Yasser Al-Nashiri	KSA	10.2.87	29 Feb
10.24	1.1	Carlin Isles	USA	21.11.89	24 Mar
10.24	1.1	Isidro Montoya	COL	3.11.90	14 Apr
10.24	1.1	Bruno de Barros	BRA	7.1.87	28 Apr
10.24	2.0	Arthur Delaney	USA-J	23.6.93	13 May
10.24	1.9	Jonathan Hancock	USA	31.3.87	13 May
10.24	1.5	Jason Smyth	IRL	4.7.87	19 May
10.24	0.1	Danny Talbot	GBR	1.5.91	14 Jun
10.24	0.3	Fabio Cerutti	ITA	26.9.85	17 Jun
10.24	0.6	Reza Ghasemi	IRI	24.7.87	30 Jun
10.24	0.7	Rasheed Dwyer	JAM	29.1.89	2 Sep
10.25	1.2	Marvin Bracy	USA-J	15.12.93	26 Apr
10.25	1.3	Naoki Tsukahara	JPN	10.5.85	29 Apr
10.25	1.5	Sam Effah	CAN	29.12.88	19 May
10.25	-0.6	Andrew Hinds	BAR	25.4.84	19 May
10.25	0.1	Ainsley Waugh	JAM	17.9.81	27 May
10.25	1.5	Rolf Fongué	SUI	25.11.87	17 Jun
10.25	0.3	Abdourahim Haroun	CHA	12.4.92	17 Jun
10.25	-0.2	Darrel Brown	TRI	11.10.84	23 Jun
10.25	-1.2	Jazeel Murphy	JAM-J	27.2.94	11 Jul
10.25	-0.1	Joel Fearon	GBR	11.10.88	21 Jul
10.26	0.9	Sandro Viana	BRA	26.3.77	3 Mar
10.26	2.0	Reginald Dixon	USA	7.6.88	17 Mar
10.26	0.7	Horatio Williams	USA	28.8.89	11 May
10.26	-0.1	Wallace Spearmon	USA	24.12.84	20 May
10.26	0.3	Jermaine Brown	JAM	4.7.91	26 May
10.26	2.0	Samuel Francis	QAT	27.3.87	15 Jun
10.26	1.5	Alex Wilson	SUI	19.9.90	17 Jun
10.26	0.7	Jon Juin	HAI	17.12.89	21 Jul
10.26	0.7	Nilson André	BRA	30.1.86	4 Aug
10.26	1.5	Chijindu Ujah	GBR-J	5.3.94	25 Aug
10.27	1.9	DionDre Batson	USA	13.7.92	6 Apr
10.27A	1.9	Ray Bozmans	USA-J	16.12.94	21 Apr
10.27		Christian Malcolm	GBR	3.6.79	28 Apr
10.27	0.2	Jordan Taylor	USA	12.12.91	12 May
10.27	0.9	Simone Collio	ITA	27.12.79	2 Jun
10.27	1.3	Stanley Azie	NGR	13.3.89	6 Jun
10.27	0.8	Patrick van Luijk	NED	17.9.84	9 Jun
10.27	-0.7	Adetoyi Durotoye	NGR	9.5.86	14 Jun
10.27	-0.3	Allah Laryes-Alrong	GHA	27.5.83	14 Jun
10.27A	1.7	Alex Quiñónez	ECU	11.8.89	30 Jun
10.27	1.3	Michael LeBlanc	CAN	25.2.87	14 Jul
10.27A	1.9	Bruno Hortelano	ESP	18.9.91	28 Jul
10.28	1.1	Carlos de Moräes	BRA	27.2.90	28 Apr
10.28	1.7	Shavez Hart	BAH	9.6.92	5 May
10.28	1.2	Yi Wei-Chen	TPE	28.8.88	26 May
10.28	1.9	Alexander Kosenkow	GER	14.3.77	26 May
10.28	1.3	Beejay Lee	USA-J	5.3.93	6 Jun
10.28	1.1	Jevaughn Minzie	JAM-Y	20.7.95	16 Jun
10.28	0.3	Idrissa Adam	CMR	28.12.84	17 Jun
10.28	1.0	Ronalds Arajs	LAT	29.11.87	27 Jun
10.28	0.8	Sergiy Smelyk	UKR	19.4.87	27 Jun
10.28	1.7	Emmanuel Biron	FRA	29.7.88	27 Jun
10.28	1.3	Winston Barnes	JAM	7.11.88	28 Jun
10.28	0.1	Odean Skeen	JAM-J	28.8.94	11 Jul
10.28	0.4	Zhang Peimeng	CHN	13.3.87	13 Sep
10.29A	2.0	Gideon Trotter	RSA	3.3.92	25 Feb
10.29	1.5	Woodrow Randall	USA	9.11.89	30 Mar
10.29	1.6	Tyrone Edgar	GBR	29.3.82	7 Apr
10.29	0.0	Xu Jun	CHN	24.6.90	14 Apr
10.29	1.9	Brian Barnett	CAN	10.2.87	20 Apr
10.29	1.3	Shinji Takahira	JPN	18.7.84	29 Apr
10.29	1.3	Shintaro Kimura	JPN	30.6.87	29 Apr
10.29	2.0	Ravel Gray	JAM	11.3.87	6 May
10.29	0.9	Christian Blum	GER	10.3.87	26 May
10.29	1.6	Deji Tobais	GBR	31.10.91	11 Jun
10.29A		Ibrahim Muya	KEN	22.8.84	14 Jun
10.29	0.8	Simeon Williamson	GBR	16.1.86	23 Jun
10.29	0.2	Shermund Allsop	TRI	21.3.91	23 Jun
10.29	1.8	Yunier Pérez	CUB	16.2.85	7 Jul
10.29	0.3	Martin Keller	GER	26.9.86	27 Jul

(198)

Wind assisted

Mark	Wind	Name	Nat	Born	Pos	Meet	Venue	Date
9.81	4.1	Gatlin			1	Déca	Albi	15 Aug
9.85	2.4	Walter Dix	USA	31.1.86	1rA	MSR	Walnut	21 Apr
9.85	3.6	Keston Bledman	TRI	8.3.88	1rA		Clermont	2 Jun
9.88	3.6	Travis Padgett	USA	13.12.86	2rA		Clermont	2 Jun
9.94	2.6	Christophe Lemaitre	FRA	11.6.90	1	NC	Angers	16 Jun
9.96	2.4	Kim Collins	SKN	5.4.76	2		Tomblaine	8 Jul
10.00	5.0	Trell Kimmons	USA	13.7.85	1		Baton Rouge	21 Apr
10.01	2.9	Jeffrey Demps	USA	8.1.90	1rA	TexR	Austin	31 Mar
10.03	3.4	Prezel Hardy	USA	1.6.92	1	Big 12	Manhattan	13 May
10.04	2.9	Su Bingtian	CHN	29.8.89	1	GGP	Kawasaki	6 May
10.04	4.3	Charles Silmon	USA	4.7.91	2q2	NCAA-W	Austin	25 May
10.05	4.9	Ameer Webb	USA	19.3.91	1		Tempe	17 Mar
10.05	3.6	Ramone McKenzie	JAM	15.11.90	3		Clermont	2 Jun
10.06	2.8	Wallace Spearmon	USA	24.12.84	1		Fort Worth	16 Mar
10.06	2.4	Marvin Bracy	USA-J	15.12.93	1	TexR-HS	Austin	31 Mar
10.06	3.6	Oshane Bailey	JAM	9.8.89	1h3		Clermont	19 May
10.06	3.6	Aaron Armstrong	TRI	14.10.77	4rA		Clermont	2 Jun
10.07	3.6	Tyrone Edgar	GBR	29.3.82	5		Clermont	2 Jun
10.07	2.4	Mario Forsythe	JAM	30.10.85	4		Tomblaine	8 Jul
10.08	2.4	Peter Emelieze	NGR	19.4.88	3rA	MSR	Walnut	21 Apr
10.08	2.2	Isiah Young	USA	5.1.90	1	Drake	Des Moines	28 Apr
10.08	2.3	Rytis Sakalauskas	LTU	27.6.87	1	Znam	Zhukovskiy	17 Jun
10.09	3.1	Aaron Brown	CAN	27.5.92	1rB	TexR	Austin	31 Mar
10.09	3.1	Cordero Gray	USA	9.5.89	2rB	TexR	Austin	31 Mar
10.10	2.4	DionDre Batson	USA	13.7.92	1		San Mateo	11 May
10.10	2.6	Emmanuel Biron	FRA	29.7.88	3	NC	Angers	16 Jun

Mark	Wind	Name		Nat	Born	Pos	Meet	Venue	Date
10.12	3.4	Mickey	Grimes	USA	10.10.76	1rB	MSR	Walnut	21 Apr
10.12	3.4	Everett	Walker	USA	3.10.90	2	Big 12	Manhattan	13 May
10.12A	5.7	Romel	Lewis	JAM	28.1.88	1	NCAA-2	Pueblo, CO	26 May
10.12A	5.7	Rushane	Scott	USA	7.7.88	2	NCAA-2	Pueblo, CO	26 May
10.12A	5.7	Tommy	Curry	USA	8.4.89	3	NCAA-2	Pueblo, CO	26 May
10.13	3.2	Carlin	Isles	USA	21.11.89	1rB	TexR	Austin	31 Mar
10.13	2.4	Egweru	Ogho-Oghene	NGR	26.11.88	4rA	MSR	Walnut	21 Apr
10.13	3.4	Ian	Warner	CAN	15.5.90	4	Big 12	Manhattan	13 May
10.15	2.9	Aaron	Ernest	USA-J	8.11.93	2	TexR-HS	Austin	31 Mar
10.15	2.5	Richard	Kilty	GBR	2.9.89	2rC	MSR	Walnut	21 Apr
10.15	3.6	Willie	Perry	USA	16.5.87	6rA		Clermont	2 Jun
10.15	2.3	Ramil	Guliyev	TUR	29.5.90	2	Znam	Zhukovskiy	17 Jun
10.16	4.9	Dominique	Hubert	USA	4.11.90	3		Tempe	17 Mar
10.16	3.1	Jared	Connaughton	CAN	20.7.85	4rB	TexR	Austin	31 Mar
10.16	5.6	Shavez	Hart	BAH	9.6.92	1		Lubbock	14 Apr
10.16	4.1	Gabriel	Mvumuvre	ZIM	23.4.88	1rB		Baton Rouge	21 Apr
10.16	2.4	Christian	Malcolm	GBR	3.6.79	5rA	MSR	Walnut	21 Apr
10.16	2.9	Joshua	Ross	AUS	9.2.81	5		Kawasaki	6 May
10.16A	5.7	Tim	Price	USA	26.12.87	4	NCAA-2	Pueblo, CO	26 May
10.16	3.2	Ivory	Williams	USA	2.5.85	1h1		Atlanta	3 Jun
10.16	2.5	Remontay	McClain	USA	21.9.92	1		Chula Vista	9 Jun
10.16	2.7	Lucas	Jakubczyk	GER	28.4.85	1	NC	Wattenscheid	16 Jun
10.16	2.7	Aleixo-Platini	Menga	GER	29.9.87	2	NC	Wattenscheid	16 Jun
10.16	3.8	Kimmari	Roach	JAM	21.9.90	5		Madrid	7 Jul
10.17	3.6	Jason	Smyth	IRL	4.7.87	7rA		Clermont	2 Jun
10.17	4.1	Ronald	Pognon	FRA	16.11.82	5		Albi	15 Aug
10.18	3.2	Philip	Redrick	USA	2.8.88	2rB	TexR	Austin	31 Mar
10.18	3.3	Stanley	Azie	NGR	13.3.89	1q2	NCAA-W	Austin	25 May
10.18	3.0	Akeem	Haynes	CAN	3.11.92	1rB		Edmonton	16 Jun
10.19	4.0		Lai Chun Ho	HKG	5.2.89	1		Hong Kong	1 Apr
10.19	3.4	Chris	Hargrett	USA	2.8.84	1rB	FlaR	Gainesville	6 Apr
10.19	3.1	Horatio	Williams	USA	28.8.89	3		Clemson	5 May
10.19	3.0	Carlos	Nascimento	POR-J	12.10.94	1	NC	Lisboa (Un)	7 Jul
10.19	2.7	Sean	Safo-Antwi	GBR	31.10.90	1		Gent	18 Jul
10.20	2.6	Ben	Bassaw	FRA	9.7.89	4	NC	Angers	16 Jun
10.20	3.6	Yazaldes	Nascimento	POR	17.4.86	1h1	NC	Lisboa (Un)	7 Jul

Mark	Wind	Name		Nat	Born	Date
10.21	2.3	Levonte	Whitfield	USA-J	8.10.93	6 Apr
10.21	5.6	Greg	Turner	USA	27.9.89	14 Apr
10.21		Aldrich	Bailey	USA-J	6.2.94	20 Apr
10.21	3.3	Rubin	Williams	USA	9.7.83	12 May
10.21	3.4	Michael	Bryan	USA	9.6.91	13 May
10.21A	5.7	Mandela	Clifford	LCA	.86	26 May
10.21A	2.1	Oluseyi	Smith	CAN	21.2.87	29 Jun
10.21	2.5	Deji	Tobais	GBR	31.10.91	7 Jul
10.22	2.7	Michael	Mathieu	BAH	24.6.83	16 Mar
10.22A	3.4	Gideon	Trotter	RSA	3.3.92	30 Mar
10.22	3.0	Anson	Henry	CAN	9.3.79	16 Jun
10.22	2.6	Joel	Fearon	GBR	11.10.88	18 Aug
10.23	3.4	Patrick	van Luijk	NED	17.9.84	14 May
10.24	2.1	Anaso	Jobodwana	RSA	30.7.92	14 Apr
10.24	2.2	Albert	Huntley	USA	3.1.90	14 Apr
10.24	3.4	Marquise	Goodwin	USA	19.11.90	13 May
10.24	2.8	Dominique	Kone	USA	.91	26 May
10.24	3.4	Andrew	Robertson	GBR	17.12.90	26 May
10.24	2.2	Odean	Skeen	JAM-J	28.8.94	16 Jun
10.24	4.1	Sergiy	Smelyk	UKR	19.4.87	15 Aug
10.25	3.4	Brent	Lee	USA	14.6.90	6 Apr
10.25	5.6	Trevorvano	Mackey	BAH	5.1.92	14 Apr
10.25	3.4	Simone	Collio	ITA	27.12.79	26 May
10.25	3.1	Marvin	Bonde	ZIM	23.7.84	2 Jun
10.25	2.3	Sven	Knipphals	GER	20.9.85	9 Jun
10.25		Alfred	Higgs	BAH	31.12.91	16 Jun
10.26	2.8	Otis	McDaniel	USA	30.6.86	16 Mar
10.26	2.8	Mychal	Dungey	USA	13.10.88	16 Mar
10.26	3.1	Michael	LeBlanc	CAN	25.2.87	5 May
10.26	3.2	Tim	Young	USA	24.8.91	12 May
10.26	2.6	Martin	Keller	GER	26.9.86	19 May
10.26	2.2	Gustavo	dos Santos	BRA	12.2.91	19 May
10.26	4.3	Beejay	Lee	USA-J	5.3.93	25 May
10.26	5.7	Ravel	Gray	JAM	11.3.87	26 May
10.26A	2.4	Tremayne	Acy	USA-Y	21.1.95	2 Jun
10.26A	2.4	Trae	Armstrong	USA-J	26.2.94	2 Jun
10.26	2.8	Jamial	Rolle	BAH	16.4.80	2 Jun
10.26	2.3	Vitaliy	Korzh	UKR	5.10.87	17 Jun
10.26	3.8	Yunier	Pérez	CUB	16.2.85	7 Jul
10.26	4.6	Yoshihiro	Suzuki	JPN	26.9.86	15 Jul
10.27A	5.6	Martynas	Jurgilas	LTU	5.9.88	14 Apr
10.27	6.0	Lamar	Hicks	USA	1.1.87	14 Apr
10.27	4.8	Jermaine	Authorlee	USA-J	24.9.93	9 Jun
10.27	4.4	Michael	Tumi	ITA	12.2.90	15 Jun
10.27	2.7	Ryo	Onabuta	JPN	13.7.91	28 Jul
10.28A	4.6	Siphelo	Ngqabaza	RSA-J	4.2.93	31 Mar
10.28	4.9	Daniel	Auberry	USA	13.9.89	17 Mar
10.28	3.1	Keyth	Talley	USA	3.3.90	24 Mar
10.28	4.0		Ng Ka Fung	HKG	27.10.92	1 Apr
10.28	3.4	Evan	Emery	USA	22.12.91	6 Apr
10.28	2.4	Leroy	Dixon	USA	20.6.83	21 Apr
10.28	3.3	Jerome	Avery	USA	22.12.78	12 May
10.28		Dennis	Bain	BAH	15.12.90	16 Jun
10.28	2.7	David	Walters	ISV	5.4.89	17 Jun
10.28	2.3	Mikhail	Idrisov	RUS	21.6.88	17 Jun
10.28	7.7	Yuya	Yamazaki	JPN	23.6.92	24 Jun
10.28	3.9	Jonathan	Åstrand	FIN	9.9.85	28 Jul
10.29	2.8	Jacob	Norman	USA	7.11.85	16 Mar
10.29A	4.0	Anthony	Wright	USA	3.4.89	14 Apr
10.29	2.5	Babatunde	Ridley	USA	12.3.78	21 Apr
10.29	2.8	Greg	Bolden	USA	30.6.84	28 Apr
10.29	3.1	Kyle	Stevenson	USA	18.7.88	5 May
10.29	3.4	Johnathan	Farquharson	BAH-J	3.2.93	2 Jun

Doubtful timing

10.23	0.2	Aziz	Zakari	GHA	2.9.76	16 Jun
10.18	nwi	Gilbert	Haimata	NAM-J		31 Mar

Drugs disqualification

10.27A	2.0	Kagiso	Kumbane ¶	RSA	21.11.88	-25 Feb

Low altitude bests

10.11 0.9 Magakwe 1 NC Port Eizabeth 27 Apr

10.24	-0.2	Rogers	23 Jun	10.27	1.0	Haynes	21 Apr	10.29	0.2	López	12 May
10.26	0.5	Rodríguez	31 May	10.27	0.7	O Smith	11 Jul	10.27w	3.4	Jurgilas	13 May
	10.24w	4.2	19 May					10.29w	2.5	Lewis	5 May

Mark	Wind	Name		Nat	Born	Pos	Meet	Venue	Date

Hand timing

Mark	Wind		Name	Nat	Born	Pos	Meet	Venue	Date
10.0		Roberto	Skyers	CUB	12.11.91	1		La Habana	22 Jun
10.0		David	Lescay	CUB	19.2.89	2		La Habana	22 Jun
10.0	0.8	Phil	DeRosier	USA	11.4.84	1		Holmdel	16 Jun
9.8w?		Abraham	Hall	USA-J	12.9.93	1		Duncanville	12 Apr
9.9w?		Mateo	Edward	PAN-J	1.5.93	1		Ciudad de Panamá	25 Feb
10.0	dt?	Kyle	Redwine	USA-J	28.3.94	1		Auburn Hulls	11 Apr

JUNIORS

See main list for top 7 juniors. 14 performances by 8 men to 10.19. Additional marks and further juniors:

Name	Mark	Wind	Pos	Meet	Venue	Date	Mark	Wind	Pos	Meet	Venue	Date
Gemili	10.06	1.7	3s3	OG	London (OS)	5 Aug	10.11	0.0	3h5	OG	London (OS)	4 Aug
	10.08	0.8	1		Regensburg	2 Jun	10.15	-0.7	2rB	WK	Zürich	30 Aug
	10.11	1.2	1h4		Regensburg	2 Jun	10.18	-0.5	1s2	WJ	Barcelona	11 Jul
Ernest	10.17	0.1	2	WJ	Barcelona	11 Jul	10.16w	5.0	5		Baton Rouge	21 Apr

Mark	Wind	Name		Nat	Born	Pos	Meet	Venue	Date
10.23	1.3	Kazuma	Oseto	JPN	5.8.94	3h1	Oda	Hiroshima	29 Apr
10.24	2.0	Arthur	Delaney	USA	23.6.93	3	PAC-12	Eugene	13 May
10.25	1.2	Marvin	Bracy (10)	USA	15.12.93	1		Bunnell, FL	26 Apr
10.25	-1.2	Jazeel	Murphy	JAM	27.2.94	2s1	WJ	Barcelona	11 Jul
10.26	1.5	Chijindu	Ujah	GBR	5.3.94	1		Bedford	25 Aug
10.27A	1.9	Ray	Bozmans	USA	16.12.94	1		Lakewood	21 Apr
10.28	1.3	Beejay	Lee	USA	5.3.93	7s3	NCAA	Des Moines	6 Jun
10.28	1.1	Jevaughn	Minzie	JAM-Y	20.7.95	1	NC-y	Kingston	16 Jun
10.28	0.1	Odean	Skeen	JAM	28.8.94	3	WJ	Barcelona	11 Jul
10.33	1.2	David	Bolarinwa	GBR	20.10.93	1rC		Gainesville	21 Apr
10.33A	1.3	Siphello	Ngqabaza	RSA	4.2.93	2		Lusaka	11 Dec
10.34	1.8	Delano	Williams	TKS	23.12.93	1		Montego Bay	18 Feb
10.35	1.2	Levonte	Whitfield (20)	USA	8.10.93	1		Orlando	26 May

Wind assisted to 10.29w. See main lists for 3 juniors to 10.19w (& 4 performances by 3 men)

Mark	Wind	Name		Nat	Born	Pos	Meet	Venue	Date
10.21	2.3	Levonte	Whitfield	USA	8.10.93	1	FlaR	Gainesville	6 Apr
10.21		Aldrich	Bailey	USA	6.2.94	1		Lancaster, TX	20 Apr
10.24	2.2	Odean	Skeen	JAM	28.8.94	1	NC-j	Kingston	16 Jun
10.26	4.3	Beejay	Lee	USA	5.3.93	4r2	NCAA-W	Austin	25 May
10.26A	2.4	Tremayne	Acy	USA-Y	21.1.95	2		Albuquerque	2 Jun
10.26A	2.4	Trae	Armstrong	USA	26.2.94	3		Albuquerque	2 Jun
10.27	4.8	Jermaine	Authorlee	USA	24.9.93	1	G.West	Folsom	9 Jun
10.28A	4.6	Siphelo	Ngqabaza	RSA	4.2.93	1	NC-j	Germiston	31 Mar
10.29w	3.4	Johnathan	Farquharson	BAH	3.2.93	4rB		Clermont	2 Jun

150 Metres Straight: 14.87 -0.1 Wallace Spearmon USA 24.12.84 1 Manchester 20 May

200 METRES

Mark	Wind	Name		Nat	Born	Pos	Meet	Venue	Date
19.32	0.4	Usain	Bolt	JAM	21.8.86	1	OG	London (OS)	9 Aug
19.44	0.4	Yohan	Blake	JAM	26.12.89	2	OG	London (OS)	9 Aug
19.54	0.0		Blake			1	VD	Bruxelles	7 Sep
19.58	1.4		Bolt			1	Athl	Lausanne	23 Aug
19.66	0.0		Bolt			1	WK	Zürich	30 Aug
19.80	-0.5		Blake			1	NC	Kingston	1 Jul
19.83	-0.5		Bolt			2	NC	Kingston	1 Jul
19.84	0.4	Warren	Weir	JAM	31.10.89	3	OG	London (OS)	9 Aug
19.85	1.4	Churandy	Martina	NED	3.7.84	2	Athl	Lausanne	23 Aug
19.85	0.0	Nickel	Ashmeade	JAM	4.7.90	2	WK	Zürich	30 Aug
19.86	1.5	Jason	Young	JAM	21.3.91	1rA	Spitzen	Luzern	17 Jul
19.90	0.4	Wallace	Spearmon	USA	24.12.84	4	OG	London (OS)	9 Aug
19.91	1.1		Blake			1		Kingston	5 May
19.91	1.1	Christophe	Lemaitre	FRA	11.6.90	1	LGP	London (CP)	14 Jul
19.92	0.0		Young			2	VD	Bruxelles	7 Sep
19.93	1.7		Blake			1s2	NC	Kingston	30 Jun
19.94	0.1		Martina			1	adidas	New York	9 Jun
19.94	0.1		Ashmeade			2	adidas	New York	9 Jun
19.94	1.4		Ashmeade			3	Athl	Lausanne	23 Aug
19.95	1.8		Spearmon			1		Arlington	24 Mar
19.95	1.1		Martina			2	LGP	London (CP)	14 Jul
19.99	1.7		Weir			2s2	NC	Kingston	30 Jun
20.00	0.4		Martina			5	OG	London (OS)	9 Aug
20.00	1.4		Young			4	Athl	Lausanne	23 Aug
20.01	-0.5		Blake			1s1	OG	London (OS)	8 Aug
20.02	1.7		Spearmon			1	Drake	Des Moines	28 Apr
20.02	-0.5	Walter	Dix	USA	31.1.86	1	DL	Doha	11 May
20.02	0.0		Ashmeade			1	Herc	Monaco	20 Jul
20.02	-0.5		Spearmon			2s1	OG	London (OS)	8 Aug

Mark	Wind	Name		Nat	Born	Pos	Meet	Venue	Date
20.03	-0.5		Weir			3	NC	Kingston	1 Jul
20.03	-0.5		Lemaitre			3s1	OG	London (OS)	8 Aug
20.03	1.4		Weir			5	Athl	Lausanne	23 Aug
		(32/9)							
20.10	-1.1	Harry	Adams	USA	27.11.89	1		Coral Gables	14 Apr
		(10)							
20.11	1.0	Justin	Gatlin	USA	10.2.82	1		Gainesville	21 Apr
20.13	0.2	Maurice	Mitchell	USA	22.12.89	1q1	NCAA-E	Jacksonville	26 May
20.14	1.8	Tyreek	Hill	USA-J	1.3.94	1		Orlando	26 May
20.16	0.9	LaShawn	Merritt	USA	27.6.86	1		Saint-Martin	5 May
20.16	0.8	Michael	Mathieu	BAH	24.6.83	1	GP	Belém	6 May
20.21	0.1	Marvin	Anderson	JAM	12.5.82	4	adidas	New York	9 Jun
20.21	0.0	Tyson	Gay	USA	9.8.82	2	DL	Birmingham	26 Aug
20.22A	-0.5	Tremaine	Harris	CAN	10.2.92	1	NACAC	Irapuato	8 Jul
20.23	-1.1	Demetrius	Pinder	BAH	13.2.89	2		Coral Gables	14 Apr
20.27	-0.6	Anaso	Jobodwana	RSA	30.7.92	2s2	OG	London (OS)	8 Aug
		(20)							
20.28	1.5	Calesio	Newman	USA	20.8.86	1h3	NC/OT	Eugene	29 Jun
20.28	0.7	Alex	Quiñónez	ECU	11.8.89	1h7	OG	London (OS)	7 Aug
20.30	0.3	Jared	Connaughton	CAN	20.7.85	1		Fortaleza	9 May
20.31	0.7	Jonathan	Borlée	BEL	22.2.88	1		Lubbock	5 May
20.32	-0.2	Darvis	Patton	USA	4.12.77	1rB	Athl	Lausanne	23 Aug
20.33	1.9	Isiah	Young	USA	5.1.90	2		Oxford, MS	14 Apr
20.33	1.5	Prezel	Hardy	USA	1.6.92	1	Big 12	Manhattan	13 May
20.33	1.9	Aleixo Platini	Menga	GER	29.9.87	1r2		Mannheim	9 Jun
20.33	-0.7	Mario	Forsythe	JAM	30.10.85	1	Gyulai	Budapest	20 Aug
20.34	-0.5	Jaysuma	Saidy Ndure	NOR	1.7.84	3	DL	Doha	11 May
		(30)							
20.36	0.2	Kind	Butler	USA	8.4.89	2q1	NCAA-E	Jacksonville	26 May
20.37	1.2	Nesta	Carter	JAM	10.11.85	2h1	NC	Kingston	30 Jun
20.37	0.8	Bruno	de Barros	BRA	7.1.87	1	NC	São Paulo	1 Jul
20.38A	-1.3	Simon	Magakwe	RSA	25.5.85	1		Potchefstroom	24 Mar
20.38	1.0	Julian	Forte	JAM-J	1.7.93	1	NC-J	Kingston	17 Jun
20.38	0.8	Aldemir Gomes	da Silva	BRA	8.6.92	2	NC	São Paulo	1 Jul
20.38	1.1	Adam	Gemili	GBR-J	6.10.93	1		Derby	9 Sep
20.39	1.8	Jeremy	Dodson	USA	30.8.87	1	MSR	Walnut	21 Apr
20.40	0.3	Diego Henrique	Cavalcanti	BRA	18.3.91	2		Fortaleza	9 May
20.40	1.5	Rondell	Sorrillo	TRI	21.1.86	3rA	Spitzen	Luzern	17 Jul
		(40)							
20.42	0.0	Kei	Takase	JPN	25.11.88	1	NC	Osaka	10 Jun
20.42	-0.6	Aaron	Brown	CAN	27.5.92	4s2	OG	London (OS)	8 Aug
20.43	0.5	Sandro	Viana	BRA	26.3.77	2		São Paulo	28 Apr
20.43	0.6	Antoine	Adams	SKN	31.8.88	1	NC	Basseterre	3 Jun
20.43	0.0	Ryan	Bailey	USA	13.4.89	5	DL	Birmingham	26 Aug
20.44A	-0.4	Thuso	Mpuang	RSA	1.3.84	1		Pretoria	5 May
20.45	1.3	Akheem	Gauntlett	JAM	26.8.90	1		Fayetteville	4 May
20.45	1.7	James	Alaka	GBR	8.9.89	1	PAC-12	Eugene	13 May
20.45	1.0	Keith	Ricks	USA	9.10.90	1q2	NCAA-E	Jacksonville	26 May
20.45	0.0	Shota	Iizuka	JPN	25.6.91	2	NC	Osaka	10 Jun
		(50)							
20.46	1.3	Ameer	Webb	USA	19.3.91	1		Los Angeles	24 Mar
20.46	1.2	Christian	Malcolm	GBR	3.6.79	1r1		Regensburg	2 Jun
20.47	0.5	Keenan	Brock	USA	1.6.92	1		Auburn	21 Apr
20.47	0.5	Dedric	Dukes	USA	4.2.92	2q2	NCAA-E	Jacksonville	26 May
20.47	1.0	Horatio	Williams	USA	28.8.89	2q3	NCAA-E	Jacksonville	26 May
20.47	0.7	Patrick	van Luijk	NED	17.9.84	1		Leiden	9 Jun
20.47	1.6	Manteo	Mitchell	USA	6.7.87	2h5	OT	Eugene	29 Jun
20.48A	0.0	Terrel	Cotton	USA	19.7.88	1h1	NCAA-2	Pueblo, CO	25 May
20.48	1.3	Reto Amaru	Schenkel	SUI	28.4.88	1		Weinheim	26 May
20.48	-0.8	Shawn	Crawford	USA	14.1.78	1s3	OT	Eugene	30 Jun
		(60)							
20.48	-0.4	Delano	Williams	TKS-J	23.12.93	1	WJ	Barcelona	13 Jul
20.48A	0.0	Bernardo	Baloyes	COL-J	6.1.94	1	NC-j	Medellin	18 Aug
20.49	0.4	Troy	Faulkner	USA	24.4.89	1		San Angelo	5 Apr
20.50	0.0	Richard	Kilty	GBR	2.9.89	1	Sun A	Tempe	7 Apr
20.50	1.8	DionDre	Batson	USA	13.7.92	2	MSR	Walnut	21 Apr
20.50	-0.9	Ramon	Miller	BAH	17.2.87	1		Tampa	27 May
20.50	0.2	Aziz	Ouhadi	MAR	24.7.84	1		Brazzaville	10 Jun
20.51A	-1.3	Lebogang	Moeng	RSA	10.10.89	3		Potchefstroom	24 Mar
20.51	1.3	Zye	Boey	USA	8.5.89	1		Nashville	20 Apr
20.51	1.5	Marcus	Rowland	USA	11.3.90	2h3	OT	Eugene	29 Jun
		(70)							

Mark	Wind	Name	Nat	Born	Pos	Meet	Venue	Date
20.52	0.3	Likoúrgos-Stéfanos Tsákonas	GRE	8.3.90	1r1		Genève	2 Jun
20.52A	-0.5	Trevorvano Mackey	BAH	5.1.92	4	NACAC	Irapuato	8 Jul
20.52	0.4	Danny Talbot	GBR	1.5.91	1rB	Spitzen	Luzern	17 Jul
20.52	0.7	Alex Wilson	SUI	19.9.90	1r2		Weinheim	27 Jul
20.53	1.8	Jeremy Wariner	USA	31.1.84	2		Arlington	24 Mar
20.53	0.7	Sven Knipphals	GER	20.9.85	1r3		Mannheim	9 Jun
20.53	-0.4	Aaron Ernest	USA-J	8.11.93	2	WJ	Barcelona	13 Jul
20.53	0.0	Ramil Guliyev	TUR	29.5.90	1		Lappeenranta	18 Jul
20.54A	-0.6	Gil Roberts	USA	15.3.89	1		El Paso	24 Mar
20.54	1.8	Everett Walker	USA	3.10.90	2q2	NCAA-W	Austin	26 May
		(80)						
20.54	0.5	Xie Zhenye	CHN-J	17.8.93	1		Zibo	27 May
20.54	1.0	Obinna Metu	NGR	12.7.88	1h2	NC	Calabar	21 Jun
20.54	1.7	Ramone McKenzie	JAM	15.11.90	4s2	NC	Kingston	30 Jun
20.54	0.6	Noah Akwu	NGR	23.9.90	1		Kumasi	6 Jul
20.54	-0.4	Karol Zalewski	POL-J	7.8.93	4	WJ	Barcelona	13 Jul
20.54	0.4	Paul Hession	IRL	27.1.83	2rB	Spitzen	Luzern	17 Jul
20.54	-1.4	Kenroy Anderson	JAM	27.6.87	1		La Roche-sur-Yon	18 Jul
20.55	1.2	Fernada Blakely	USA	28.9.81	1		Fayetteville	31 Mar
20.55	1.7	Devonte Stewart	USA-J	11.6.93	3	PAC-12	Eugene	13 May
20.55	0.3	James Ellington	GBR	6.9.85	2r1		Genève	2 Jun
		(90)						
20.55	0.2	Michael Coleman	USA	26.1.87	1		Houston	16 Jun
20.55	1.5	Justin Austin	USA	8.10.89	4h3	OT	Eugene	29 Jun
20.56	0.9	Ainsley Waugh	JAM	17.9.81	2		Saint-Martin	5 May
20.56	0.0	Shinji Takahira	JPN	18.7.84	3	NC	Osaka	10 Jun
20.56	1.3	Kamil Krynski	POL	12.5.87	1h1	NC	Bielsko-Biala	16 Jun
20.57	0.3	Johan Wissman	SWE	2.11.82	1		Los Angeles	12 May
20.57	0.2	Reginald Dixon	USA	7.6.88	3q1	NCAA-E	Jacksonville	26 May
20.57	-0.8	Remontay McClain	USA	21.9.92	1		Los Angeles (Ww)	2 Jun
20.57	0.0	Hitoshi Saito	JPN	9.10.86	4	NC	Osaka	10 Jun
20.57	-0.7	Steven Colvert	IRL	24.8.90	2		Velenje	14 Jun
		(100)						
20.57A	1.5	José Carlos Herrera	MEX	5.2.86	1		Toluca	23 Jun

Mark	Wind	Name	Nat	Born	Date
20.58	1.1	Abraham Hall	USA-J	12.9.93	12 May
20.58		Edino Steele	JAM	6.1.87	12 May
20.58	-0.3	Aleksandr Brednev	RUS	12.2.88	11 Jun
20.58	1.1	Julian Reus	GER	29.4.88	17 Jun
20.58	0.5	Ben Bassaw	FRA	9.7.89	17 Jun
20.58	0.5	Jimmy Vicaut	FRA	27.2.92	17 Jun
20.58	0.1	Roberto Skyers	CUB	12.11.91	29 Jun
20.58	-0.4	Brendan Christian	ANT	11.12.83	8 Aug
20.59	-0.5	Dentarius Locke	USA	12.12.89	14 Apr
20.59	1.0	Dane Hyatt	JAM	2.1.84	14 Apr
20.59	0.3	Rubin Williams	USA	9.7.83	12 May
20.59	1.2	Sebastian Ernst	GER	11.10.84	2 Jun
20.59	-0.1	Dariusz Kuc	POL	24.4.86	17 Jun
20.59	1.2	Rasheed Dwyer	JAM	29.1.89	30 Jun
20.59	2.0	Pavel Maslák	CZE	21.2.91	8 Sep
20.60		Daniel Bailey	ANT	9.9.86	14 Apr
20.60	0.5	Tony McQuay	USA	16.4.90	21 Apr
20.60	1.2	Luke Fagan	GBR	31.7.88	18 Aug
20.61	1.6	James Johnson	USA	31.7.91	13 May
20.61	-1.2	Ben Youssef Meité	CIV	11.11.86	30 Jun
20.61	0.7	Deji Tobais	GBR	31.10.91	7 Jul
20.62	1.0	Josh Edmonds	USA	23.7.91	14 Apr
20.62	1.9	Trell Kimmons	USA	13.7.85	14 Apr
20.62	0.8	Brijesh BJ Lawrence	SKN	27.12.89	21 Apr
20.62	0.7	Nery Brenes	CRC	25.9.85	6 May
20.62	1.1	Lalonde Gordon	TRI	25.11.88	12 May
20.62	1.7	Ailson da Silva	BRA	13.8.88	12 May
20.62	0.8	Brady Gehret	USA	9.5.92	13 May
20.62	1.6	LaShawn Butler	USA	3.2.87	29 Jun
20.62	-1.0	Amr Ibrahim Seoud	EGY	10.6.86	30 Jun
20.62	0.3	Nil de Oliveira	SWE	3.9.86	19 Jul
20.63	0.8	Carlos Rafael Jorge	DOM	24.9.86	5 May
20.63	1.5	Vyacheslav Muravyev	KAZ	14.7.82	5 May
20.63	0.0	Kenji Fujimutsu	JPN	1.5.86	9 Jun
20.63	-0.2	Sergiy Smelyk	UKR	19.4.87	14 Jun
20.63	-0.2	Mosito Lehata	LES	8.4.89	30 Jun
20.64A	-0.4	Roscoe Engel	RSA	6.3.89	5 May
20.64	-0.2	Roland Palacios	HON	3.5.87	28 Jun
20.64	0.1	Michael Herrera	CUB	5.6.85	29 Jun
20.64	0.1	Marlon Devonish	GBR	1.6.76	30 Jun
20.64A	0.2	Bruno Hortelano	ESP	18.9.91	28 Jul
20.65	1.0	Chris Burrows	USA	15.3.90	14 Apr
20.65	0.3	Charles Silmon	USA	4.7.91	21 Apr
20.65	0.2	Chris Clarke	GBR	25.1.90	29 Apr
20.65		Lansford Spence	JAM	15.12.82	9 May
20.66	-0.3	Ryota Yamagata	JPN	10.6.92	3 May
20.66	-1.2	Blake Heriot	USA	26.9.91	12 May
20.66	1.2	Ashhad Agyapong	GHA	23.9.85	17 May
20.66	1.6	Gavin Smellie	CAN	26.6.86	19 May
20.67	1.0	Ryan Milus	USA	19.9.90	14 Apr
20.67	0.8	Stanley Azie	NGR	13.3.89	13 May
20.67	0.6	Roland Lestrod	SKN	5.9.92	3 Jun
20.67	0.2	Jamil Ahmad Hubbard	USA	12.5.86	16 Jun
20.67	0.8	Nilson André	BRA	30.1.86	1 Jul
20.67	1.7	Nicholas Hough	AUS-J	20.10.93	22 Dec
20.68	1.0	Akeem Williams	JAM	.91	26 May
20.68	1.2	Tobias Unger	GER	10.7.79	2 Jun
20.68	-0.5	Nicholas Watson	JAM	.90	8 Jul
20.68A	-1.9	Akani Simbine	RSA-J	21.9.93	12 Dec
20.69	0.3	Javon Young	USA	21.8.90	20 Apr
20.69A	0.3	Diego Palomeque ¶	COL-J	5.12.93	29 Apr
20.69		Abdourahim Haroun	CHA	12.4.92	5 May
20.69	1.9	David Bolarinwa	GBR-J	20.10.93	2 Jun
20.69	1.2	Andrew McCabe	AUS	29.8.90	7 Jul
20.70	2.0	Brian Barnett	CAN	10.2.87	20 Apr
20.70	0.1	Miguel López	PUR	9.4.90	12 May
20.70	1.0	Keyth Talley	USA	3.3.90	26 May
20.70A	0.9	Cristián Reyes	CHI	5.8.86	27 May
20.70	-0.4	Yoshihide Kiryu	JPN-Y	15.12.95	21 Oct
20.71	1.9	Darryl Brown	USA-J	5.3.93	15 Mar
20.71	1.7	Jordan Boase	USA	10.10.85	28 Apr
20.71	1.7	Greg Nixon	USA	12.9.81	28 Apr
20.71	-0.1	James Taylor	USA	30.6.90	3 May
20.71	0.8	Tim Faust	USA	11.8.92	13 May
20.71	0.2	Shermund Allsop	TRI	21.3.91	26 May
20.71A	-1.0	Oluwasegun Makinde	CAN	6.7.91	30 Jun
20.72	1.6	Jeffrey John	FRA	6.6.92	2 Jun
20.72	-0.2	José Acevedo	VEN	30.3.86	24 Jun
20.72	1.8	Jermaine Brown	JAM	4.7.91	7 Jul
20.72	1.8	David Lima	POR	6.9.90	8 Jul
20.72	0.4	Arnaldo Abrantes	POR	27.11.86	17 Jul
20.72	0.3	David Winter	USA-J	19.2.94	22 Jul

Mark	Wind	Name		Nat	Born	Pos	Meet	Venue	Date
20.72	1.0	Jonathan	Åstrand	FIN	9.9.85				26 Aug
20.73	0.3	Whitney	Prevost	USA	18.9.88				21 Apr
20.73	0.8	Luguelin	Santos	DOM-J	12.11.93				5 May
20.73	1.3	Arthur	Delaney	USA-J	23.6.93				12 May
20.73	0.1	Pierre-Alexis	Pessoneaux	FRA	16.5.87				2 Jun
20.73	1.3	Jon	Juin	HAI	17.12.89				21 Jul
20.74	0.9	Dontae	Richards-Kwok	CAN	1.3.89				7 Apr
20.74	0.0	David	Alerte	FRA	18.9.84				1 May
20.74A	-0.5	Trae	Armstrong	USA-J	26.2.94				12 May
20.74	-0.8	Igor	Bodrov	UKR	9.7.87				4 Jun
20.74	0.7	Emmanuel	Callender	TRI	10.5.84				24 Jun
20.74A	1.7	Daniel	Grueso	COL	30.7.85				30 Jun
20.74	1.5	Yuichi	Kobayashi	JPN	25.8.89				7 Jul
20.75	1.0	Mike	Mitchell	USA	16.5.81				20 Apr
20.75	1.8	Michael	Rodgers	USA	24.4.85				21 Apr
20.75	1.5	Jamial	Rolle	BAH	16.4.80				5 May
20.75	-0.5	Devon	Allen	USA-J	12.12.94				12 May
20.75	0.0	Brandon	Byram	USA	11.9.88				12 May

(201, 227 to 20.79)

Wind assisted

Mark	Wind	Name		Nat	Born	Pos	Meet	Venue	Date
19.82	2.3	Wallace	Spearmon	USA	24.12.84	1	OT	Eugene	1 Jul
20.08	3.4	Maurice	Mitchell	USA	22.12.89	1r1	FlaR	Gainesville	6 Apr
20.16	2.3	Isiah	Young	USA	5.1.90	3	OT	Eugene	1 Jul
20.17	2.3	Calesio	Newman	USA	20.8.86	4	OT	Eugene	1 Jul
20.20	2.4	Ameer	Webb	USA	19.3.91	1h5	NCAA-W	Austin	25 May
20.24	2.2	Shavez	Hart	BAH	9.6.92	1		Lubbock	14 Apr
20.24	2.9	Curtis	Mitchell	USA	11.3.89	1		Clermont	2 Jun
20.24	2.3	Darvis	Patton	USA	4.12.77	5	OT	Eugene	1 Jul
20.25	2.3	Jeremy	Dodson	USA	30.8.87	6	OT	Eugene	1 Jul
20.26	2.2	Greg	Turner	USA	27.9.89	2		Lubbock	14 Apr
20.28A	4.2	Josh	Edmonds	USA	23.7.91	1	NCAA-2	Pueblo, CO	26 May
20.29	3.3	Ramon	Miller	BAH	17.2.87	1r3	FlaR	Gainesville	6 Apr
20.32	3.1	Shawn	Crawford	USA	14.1.78	3h1	OT	Eugene	29 Jun
20.33	2.4	Remontay	McClain	USA	21.9.92	1		Chula Vista	9 Jun
20.33	3.2	Aldemir Gomes	da Silva	BRA	8.6.92	1	NC-23	Maringá	9 Sep
20.37	2.6	Zye	Boey	USA	8.5.89	1q3	NCAA-W	Austin	26 May
20.38	2.9	Charles	Clark	USA	10.8.87	2rA		Clermont	2 Jun
20.38	2.9	Brandon	Byram	USA	11.9.88	3rA		Clermont	2 Jun
20.38	3.3	Ashhad	Agyapong	GHA	23.9.85	1rB		Clermont	2 Jun
20.39	3.7	Aaron	Ernest	USA-J	8.11.93	2	SEC	Baton Rouge	13 May
20.39A	4.2	Terrel	Cotton	USA	19.7.88	2	NCAA-2	Pueblo, CO	26 May
20.40	3.0	Steven	Colvert	IRL	- 24.8.90	1h1	NC	Dublin	7 Jul
20.41	3.9	Antoine	Adams	SKN	31.8.88	1		San Marcos	28 Mar
20.42	2.1	Sebastian	Ernst	GER	11.10.84	1		Weinheim	26 May
20.43	2.8	Alex	Wilson	SUI	19.9.90	1h1		Bulle	17 Jun
20.46A	4.2	Tim	Price	USA	26.12.87	3	NCAA-2	Pueblo, CO	26 May
20.49	5.5	Aldrich	Bailey	USA-J	6.2.94	1	G.West	Folsom	9 Jun
20.50	2.3	Marcus	Rowland	USA	11.3.90	8	OT	Eugene	1 Jul
20.51	2.8	Torrin	Lawrence	USA	11.4.89	3r2	FlaR	Gainesville	6 Apr
20.51A	4.2	Tommy	Curry	USA	8.4.89	4	NCAA-2	Pueblo, CO	26 May
20.53	2.3	Everett	Walker	USA	3.10.90	1		Orlando	24 Mar
20.54	2.4	Chris	Burrows	USA	15.3.90	2q1	NCAA-W	Austin	26 May
20.55	2.3	Blake	Heriot	USA	26.9.91	2		Orlando	24 Mar
20.56	4.2	Marcus	Boyd	USA	3.3.89	1		Austin	14 Apr
20.57	3.0	James	Johnson	USA	31.7.91	1		San Marcos	7 Apr
20.57	2.5	Tobias	Unger	GER	10.7.79	1rC		Weinheim	26 May
20.58	3.4	Gavin	Smellie	CAN	26.6.86				6 Apr
20.59	2.2	Justin	Allen	USA	15.11.91				14 Apr
20.59A	4.2	Jonathan	Woodson	USA	8.6.90				26 May
20.60	3.7	Waymon	Storey	USA	10.5.92				13 May
20.60	2.2	David	Lima	POR	6.9.90				17 Jun
20.60	3.6	Chris	Clarke	GBR	25.1.90				24 Jun
20.62	5.0	Oluwasegun	Makinde	CAN	6.7.91				21 Apr
20.62	2.5	Sheldon	Mitchell	JAM	.90				22 Apr
20.63A	3.0	Sibusiso	Sishi	RSA	22.6.85				22 Apr
20.63	2.4	Akeem	Williams	JAM	.91				7 Jun
20.63	3.5	Reynier	Mena	CUB-Y	21.11.96				18 Jul
20.64	3.3	Jeffrey	Demps	USA	8.1.90				6 Apr
20.64	5.0	Michael	Bryan	USA	9.6.91				21 Apr
20.67	3.1	Philip	Osei	CAN	30.10.90				29 Apr
20.67	2.6	David	Alerte	FRA	18.9.84				27 May
20.68	2.4	Arthur	Delaney	USA-J	23.6.93				26 May
20.68	2.9	Jamial	Rolle	BAH	16.4.80				2 Jun
20.69	2.2	Whitney	Prevost	USA	18.9.88				14 Apr
20.70	2.2	Markus	Henderson	USA	13.9.89				14 Apr
20.70	4.0	Brandon	O'Connor	USA	2.9.89				2 Jun
20.71	3.3	Leonardo	Seymore	USA	.90				6 Apr
20.73	3.4	Calvin	Smith	USA	10.12.87				6 Apr
20.73	2.3	Konstantin	Petryashov	RUS	16.12.84				6 Jul
20.74	4.0	Aaron	Anderson	USA	18.12.88				2 Jun
20.75	2.7	Raymond	Miller	USA	28.10.88				20 Apr

Indoors

Mark	Wind	Name		Nat	Born	Pos	Meet	Venue	Date
20.39		Ameer	Webb	USA	19.3.91	1h2	NCAA	Nampa	9 Mar
20.58		Lalonde	Gordon	TRI	25.11.88	1		Boston (Allston)	28 Jan

Low altitude bests

20.59 0.7 Magakwe 1 NC Port Elizabeth 14 Apr | 20.60 0.7 Mpuang 2 NC Port Elizabeth 14 Apr
20.63 0.6 T Harris 19 May | 20.66 0.0 Cotton 29 Jun | 20.68 0.9 Mackey 23 Jun
20.42w 2.4 16 Jun | 20.62w 2.4 16 Jun

Hand timing

Mark	Wind	Name		Nat	Born	Pos	Venue	Date
20.1A	0.0	Thuso	Mpuang	RSA	1.3.84	1	Johannesburg	28 Apr
20.3A	0.0	Simon	Magakwe	RSA	25.5.85	2	Johannesburg	28 Apr

+ intermediate time in longer race, A made at an altitude of 1000m or higher, D made in a decathlon, h made in a heat, qf quarter-final, sf semi-final, i indoors, Q qualifying round, r race number, -J juniors, -Y youths (b. 1995 or later)

Mark		Name	Nat	Born	Pos	Meet	Venue	Date

JUNIORS

See main list for top 9 juniors. 14 performances by 8 men to 20.54. Additional marks and further juniors:

Hill 20.49 1.0 1 Orlando 26 May   20.54 -0.43 WJ Barcelona   13 Jul
Forte 20.40 1.7 3s2 NC Kingston 30 Jun
Gemili 20.53 0.0 6 BrGP Birmingham 26 Aug
Williams 20.53 0.6 1 Montego Bay 18 Feb
Ernest 20.54 0.5 4q2 NCAA-E Jacksonville 26 May

Mark		Name		Nat	Born	Pos	Meet	Venue	Date
20.58	1.1	Abraham	Hall (10)	USA	12.9.93	1		Austin	12 May
20.67	1.7	Nicholas	Hough	AUS	20.10.93	1		Sydney	22 Dec
20.68A	-1.9	Akani	Simbine	RSA	21.9.93	1		Lusaka	12 Dec
20.69A	0.3	Diego	Palomeque ¶	COL	5.12.93	1		Medellín	29 Apr
20.69	1.9	David	Bolarinwa	GBR	20.10.93	1r3		Regensburg	2 Jun
20.70	-0.4	Yoshihide	Kiryu	JPN-Y	15.12.95	1	NC-y	Nagoya	21 Oct
20.71	1.9	Darryl	Brown	USA	5.3.93	1		Winfield, KS	15 Mar
20.72	0.3	David	Winter	USA	19.2.94	1		Durham	22 Jul
20.73	0.8	Luguelin	Santos	DOM	12.11.93	2		Mayagüez	5 May
20.73	1.3	Arthur	Delaney	USA	23.6.93	3h3	PAC-12	Eugene	12 May
20.74A	-0.5	Trae	Armstrong (20)	USA	26.2.94	1		Mesa	12 May

Wind assisted. See main list for top 2 juniors (top 2 performances to 20.53)

Mark		Name		Nat	Born	Pos	Meet	Venue	Date
20.63	3.5	Reynier	Mena	CUB-Y	21.11.96	1	NC-y	Las Tunas	18 Jul
20.68	2.4	Arthur	Delaney	USA-J	23.6.93	3q1	NCAA-W	Austin	26 May

300 METRES

Mark	Name		Nat	Born	Pos	Meet	Venue	Date
31.87	Jonathan	Borlée	BEL	22.2.88	1		Liège (NX)	5 Jul
32.35	Pavel	Maslák	CZE	21.2.91	1		Susice	15 May
32.52	Obakeng	Ngwigwa	BOT	9.7.85	2		Liège (NX)	5 Jul
32.56	Luguelin	Santos	DOM-J	12.11.93	1		Uppsala	28 Jul

32.67 Kei Takase JPN 25.11.88 22 Apr | 32.74 Marek Niit EST 9.8.87 29 Aug
32.69 Yuzo Kanemaru JPN 18.9.87 22 Apr | 32.84 Javere Bell JAM 20.9.92 28 Jul

In Olympic 400m London (OS) 6 Aug: James 32.0, Pinder 32.3, Santos, Brown 32.4, Gordon 32.5

400 METRES

Mark	Name		Nat	Born	Pos	Meet	Venue	Date
43.94	Kirani	James	GRN	1.9.92	1	OG	London (OS)	6 Aug
44.12	LaShawn	Merritt	USA	27.6.86	1	NC/OT	Eugene	24 Jun
44.19		Merritt			1	DL	Doha	11 May
44.37		James			1	Athl	Lausanne	23 Aug
44.43	Jonathan	Borlée	BEL	22.2.88	1h3	OG	London (OS)	4 Aug
44.45	Luguelín	Santos	DOM-J	12.11.93	1	FBK	Hengelo	27 May
44.46		Santos			2	OG	London (OS)	6 Aug
44.46		James			1	Gugl	Linz	20 Aug
44.49	Tony	McQuay	USA	16.4.90	2	NC/OT	Eugene	24 Jun
44.52	Lalonde	Gordon	TRI	25.11.88	3	OG	London (OS)	6 Aug
44.56	Kévin	Borlée	BEL	22.2.88	1h1	NC	Bruxelles	16 Jun
44.58		McQuay			1	NCAA	Des Moines	8 Jun
44.58		Gordon			1s1	OG	London (OS)	5 Aug
44.59		James			1s2	OG	London (OS)	5 Aug
44.63		K Borlée			1	NC	Bruxelles	17 Jun
44.67		McQuay			1s3	NCAA	Des Moines	6 Jun
44.67	Chris	Brown	BAH	15.10.78	2s2	OG	London (OS)	5 Aug
44.72		James			1		Daegu	16 May
44.73		Merritt			1		Baie Mahault	1 May
44.74		J Borlée			1	Herc	Monaco	20 Jul
44.75	Michael	Berry	USA	10.12.91	2	NCAA	Des Moines	8 Jun
44.75		K Borlée			1	VD	Bruxelles	7 Sep
44.76		James			2	Herc	Monaco	20 Jul
44.77	Demetrius	Pinder (10)	BAH	13.2.89	1	NC	Nassau	23 Jun
44.78		Merritt			1s2	NC/OT	Eugene	23 Jun
44.78		Santos			1s3	OG	London (OS)	5 Aug
44.79		Brown			4	OG	London (OS)	6 Aug
44.80	Bryshon	Nellum	USA	1.5.89	3	NC/OT	Eugene	24 Jun
44.81		K Borlée			5	OG	London (OS)	6 Aug
44.83	Josh	Mance	USA	21.3.92	2s3	NCAA	Des Moines	6 Jun
44.83	Dane	Hyatt	JAM	22.1.84	1	NC	Kingston	1 Jul
44.83		J Borlée			6	OG	London (OS)	6 Aug
	(32/13)							
44.84	Gil	Roberts	USA	15.3.89	3s3	NCAA	Des Moines	6 Jun
44.87	Ramon	Miller	BAH	17.2.87	2	NC	Nassau	23 Jun
44.91	Pavel	Maslák	CZE	21.2.91	2h3	OG	London (OS)	4 Aug
44.92	Martyn	Rooney	GBR	3.4.87	1	MSR	Walnut	21 Apr

Mark	Name		Nat	Born	Pos	Meet	Venue	Date
44.93	Angelo	Taylor	USA	29.12.78	1	DL	Birmingham	26 Aug
44.96	Jeremy	Wariner	USA	31.1.84	2	MSR	Walnut	21 Apr
44.96	Manteo	Mitchell	USA	6.7.87	5	NC/OT	Eugene	24 Jun
	(20)							
44.97	Steven	Solomon	AUS-J	16.5.93	3s1	OG	London (OS)	5 Aug
45.00	Pavel	Trenikhin	RUS	24.3.86	3h3	OG	London (OS)	4 Aug
45.01	Maksim	Dyldin	RUS	19.5.87	1	NC	Cheboksary	5 Jul
45.06	David	Verburg	USA	14.5.91	1		Fairfax	5 May
45.06	Michael	Mathieu	BAH	24.6.83	1		Uberlândia	13 May
45.08	Conrad	Williams	GBR	20.3.82	1r1		Genève	2 Jun
45.10	Rusheen	McDonald	JAM	17.8.92	2	NC	Kingston	1 Jul
45.11	Nigel	Levine	GBR	30.4.89	1	Bisl	Oslo	7 Jun
45.12	Calvin	Smith	USA	10.12.87	1		Rieti	9 Sep
45.13	Deon	Lendore	TRI	28.10.92	1	Big 12	Manhattan	13 May
	(30)							
45.13	Akheem	Gauntlett	JAM	26.8.90	2s2	NCAA	Des Moines	6 Jun
45.13	Rabah	Yousif	SUD	11.12.86	4s1	OG	London (OS)	5 Aug
45.18	Jermaine	Gonzales	JAM	26.11.84	3	NC	Kingston	1 Jul
45.19	Aldrich	Bailey	USA-J	6.2.94	1		Lubbock	28 Apr
45.19	Tabarie	Henry	ISV	1.12.87	6s1	OG	London (OS)	5 Aug
45.20	Nery	Brenes	CRC	25.9.85	3	FBK	Hengelo	27 May
45.22	Brady	Gehret	USA	9.5.92	1	Big 10	Madison	13 May
45.23	Luke	Lennon-Ford	GBR	5.5.89	2r1		Genève	2 Jun
45.25	Isaac	Makwala	BOT	29.9.86	1	AfrC	Porto Novo	28 Jun
45.25	Hederson	Estefani	BRA	11.9.91	1	NC	São Paulo	29 Jun
	(40)							
45.25	Errol	Nolan	USA/JAM	18.8.91	4	NC	Kingston	1 Jul
45.30	Yannick	Fonsat	FRA	16.6.88	1		Villeneuve d'Ascq	9 Jun
45.31	Jarrin	Solomon	TRI	11.1.86	2		Bottrop	7 Jul
45.34	Félix	Sánchez	DOM	30.8.77	1		Los Angeles (ER)	5 May
45.36	Bralon	Taplin	USA	8.5.92	3		Lubbock	5 May
45.36	Riker	Hylton	JAM	13.12.88	3s1	NC	Kingston	30 Jun
45.36	Vladimir	Krasnov	RUS	19.8.90	3	NC	Cheboksary	5 Jul
45.38	Edino	Steele	JAM	6.1.87	5	NC	Kingston	1 Jul
45.39	Arman	Hall	USA-J	14.2.94	2	WJ	Barcelona	12 Jul
45.40	Torrin	Lawrence	USA	11.4.89	5s2	NC/OT	Eugene	23 Jun
	(50)							
45.41	Joey	Hughes	USA	26.10.90	4s3	NCAA	Des Moines	6 Jun
45.43	Kind	Butler	USA	8.4.89	1		Indianapolis	16 Jun
45.43	Denis	Alekseyev	RUS	26.12.87	4	NC	Cheboksary	5 Jul
45.43	Youssef	Al-Masrahi	KSA	31.12.87	3h4	OG	London (OS)	4 Aug
45.44	Kyle	Clemons	USA	27.8.90	3s1	NCAA	Des Moines	6 Jun
45.45	Tavaris	Tate	USA	21.12.90	1		Baton Rouge	7 Apr
45.46	Piotr	Wiaderek	POL	5.2.84	1	NC	Bielsko-Biala	16 Jun
45.47	Yuzo	Kanemaru	JPN	18.9.87	1		Fukuroi	3 May
45.47	Robert	Tobin	GBR	20.12.83	1r2		Genève	2 Jun
45.47	Omar	Cisneros	CUB	19.11.89	1		Padova	2 Sep
	(60)							
45.48	Renny	Quow	TRI	25.8.87	2		Kingston	5 May
45.48	Chris	Vaughn	USA	1.2.90	2	Big 10	Madison	13 May
45.51A	Philip	Osei	CAN	30.10.90	2	NACAC	Irapuato	7 Jul
45.51	Allodin	Fothergill	JAM	2.7.87	5	Gugl	Linz	20 Aug
45.52	Miles	Smith	USA	24.9.84	1		Clermont	2 Jun
45.52	Marcell	Deák Nagy	HUN	28.1.92	2	EC	Helsinki	29 Jun
45.52	Pedro	de Oliveira	BRA	17.2.92	1	SAm-23	São Paulo	22 Sep
45.54A	Ofentse	Mogawane	RSA	20.2.82	1		Pretoria	5 May
45.57	Teddy	Atine-Venel	FRA	16.3.85	3		Villeneuve d'Ascq	9 Jun
45.58	James	Harris	USA	18.9.91	2		Baton Rouge	7 Apr
	(70)							
45.59	Ânderson	Henriques	BRA	3.3.92	1	IbAmC	Barquisimeto	8 Jun
45.60	Daniel	Harper	CAN	28.8.89	5		Lubbock	5 May
45.60	Jermaine	Gayle	JAM	23.7.91	1rB		Kingston	5 May
45.60	Liemarvin	Bonevacia	CUR	5.4.89	3h2	OG	London (OS)	4 Aug
45.61	John	Steffensen	AUS	30.8.82	1		Sydney	18 Feb
45.61	Jordan	Boase	USA	10.10.85	4		Baie Mahault	1 May
45.61	Richard	Buck	GBR	14.11.86	4r1		Genève	2 Jun
45.61	Brian	Gregan	IRL	31.12.89	1		Dublin	25 Jul
45.61	Albert	Bravo	VEN	29.8.87	5h4	OG	London (OS)	4 Aug
45.62A	Diego	Palomeque ¶	COL-J	5.12.93	1		Medellin	28 Apr
	(80)							
45.63	Marcin	Marciniszyn	POL	7.9.82	2	NC	Bielsko-Biala	16 Jun

Mark	Name	Nat	Born	Pos	Meet	Venue	Date
45.64A	Alphas Kishoyan	KEN-J	12.10.94	1		Nairobi	9 Jun
45.67	Daundre Barnaby	CAN	9.12.90	4s1	NCAA	Des Moines	6 Jun
45.67	Sergey Zaykov	KAZ	23.9.87	1	NC	Almaty	18 Jun
45.67	Willie de Beer	RSA	14.3.88	3	AfrC	Porto Novo	28 Jun
45.68	Ashton Eaton	USA	21.1.88	1D		Santa Barbara	2 Apr
45.68	Marcus Boyd	USA	3.3.89	2rA		Moskva	11 Jun
45.70	Troy Faulkner	USA	24.4.89	2r2		Waco	21 Apr
45.70	Marco Vistali	ITA	3.10.87	1		Velenje	14 Jun
45.71	Ricardo Chambers (90)	JAM	7.10.84	4		Kingston	5 May
45.71	Donald Sanford	ISR	2 .2.87	5h3	OG	London (OS)	4 Aug
45.72A	Vernon Norwood	USA	10.4.92	1		El Paso	24 Mar
45.74	Toumane Coulibaly	FRA	6.1.88	1		Castres	7 Jul
45.75	Lebogang Moeng	RSA	10.10.89	1	NC	Port Elizabeth	14 Apr
45.75	Josh Scott	USA	9.3.85	1		Greensboro	21 Apr
45.77	Greg Nixon	USA	12.9.81	3		Uberlândia	13 May
45.77	Louis Persent	GBR	18.7.90	2r2		Genève	2 Jun
45.78	Andrae Williams	BAH	11.7.83	4	NC	Nassau	23 Jun
45.78	Javere Bell	JAM	20.9.92	2s3	NC	Kingston	30 Jun
45.79	Caleb Williams (100)	USA	14.12.90	3		Baton Rouge	7 Apr
45.79	Gustavo Cuesta	DOM	14.11.88	1		Santo Domingo	30 May

Mark	Name	Nat	Born	Date
45.80	Williams Collazo	CUB	31.8.86	8 Jun
45.81	Akino Ming	JAM	29.11.90	7 Apr
45.81	Hiroyuki Nakano	JPN	9.12.88	3 May
45.82	David Rudisha	KEN	17.12.88	18 Feb
45.82	Mathieu Gnaligo	BEN	13.12.86	28 Jun
45.83	Andrew Steele	GBR	19.9.84	30 Jun
45.84	Arturo Ramírez	VEN	19.4.91	8 Jun
45.85	Valentin Kruglyakov	RUS	22.8.85	5 Jul
45.86	Avard Moncur	BAH	2.11.78	7 Apr
45.87	Jarrell Elliott	USA	15.2.90	20 Apr
45.87	Michael Bingham	GBR	13.4.86	12 May
45.88	Janis Leitis	LAT	13.4.89	28 Jun
45.89A	Josh Edmonds	USA	23.7.91	24 May
45.89	Kacper Kozlowski	POL	7.12.86	16 Jun
45.90	Vitaliy Butrym	UKR	10.1.91	13 Jun
45.91	Marek Niit	EST	9.8.87	21 Apr
45.93	Fernada Blakely	USA	28.9.81	4 May
45.93	Clayton Gravesande	USA	9.6.92	12 May
45.93	Brycen Spratling	USA	10.3.92	1 Jun
45.94	Jamaal Torrance	USA	20.7.83	13 May
45.94	Brandon Bennett-Green	USA	28.8.92	13 May
45.94	Nijel Amos	BOT-J	15.3.94	20 Jun
45.95	Oral Thompson	JAM	11.12.82	14 Apr
45.95	Randall Dameron	USA	10.10.90	26 May
45.96	Ben Offereins	AUS	12.3.86	3 Mar
45.96	Thomas Murdaugh	USA	25.9.89	31 Mar
45.97A	Shaun de Jager	RSA	28.6.91	5 Apr
45.97	Quentin Iglehart-Summers	USA	15.6.87	31 May
45.97	Eric Krüger	GER	21.3.88	9 Jun
45.98	Duane Solomon	USA	28.12.84	5 May
45.99	Javier Culson	PUR	25.7.84	31 Mar
45.99A	Takeshi Fujiwara	ESA	5.8.85	28 Apr
45.99	Robert Simmons	USA	18.7.89	12 May
45.99	David Neville	USA	1.6.84	9 Jun
45.99	Abiola Onakoya	NGR	10.10.90	6 Jul
45.99	Jack Green	GBR	6.10.91	14 Jul
46.00A	Boniface Mweresa	KEN-J	13.11.93	9 Jun
46.00	Jarryd Dunn	GBR	30.1.92	23 Jun
46.01	Marquis Holston	PUR	10.7.89	5 May
46.01	Kamil Budziejewski	POL	14.9.88	16 Jun
46.02	Chris Clarke	GBR	25.1.90	21 Apr
46.02	Machel Cedenio	TRI-Y	6.9.95	23 Jun
46.03	Neal Braddy	USA	18.10.91	4 May
46.03	Chris Giesting	USA	10.12.92	6 May
46.03	Antoine Gillet	BEL	22.3.88	17 Jun
46.05	Armanti Hayes	USA	23.9.87	19 May
46.05	Erison Hurtault	DMA	29.12.84	4 Aug
46.06A	Jacob Ramokoka	RSA	20.9.84	18 Feb
46.06	Naman Keïta	FRA	9.4.78	29 May
46.06	Jacques de Swardt	RSA	12.8.92	7 Jun
46.06	Javon Francis	JAM-J	14.12.94	11 Jul
46.07	Nicholas Maitland	JAM	.89	24 Mar
46.07	Alex Beck	AUS	7.2.92	14 Apr
46.07	Volodomyr Burakov	UKR	6.5.85	27 May
46.07	Jamil Hubbard	USA	12.5.86	16 Jun
46.07A	Bernardo Baloyes	COL-J	6.1.94	17 Aug
46.08	Richard Strachan	GBR	18.11.86	26 Jun
46.09	Drew Morano	USA	28.3.85	21 Apr
46.10A	Vincent Mumo	KEN	3.8.82	15 Jun
46.10	Sergey Petukhov	RUS	22.12.83	5 Jul
46.11	Chidi Okezie	USA-J	8.8.93	12 May
46.12	Amaechi Morton	NGR	30.10.89	29 Apr
46.13	Ade Alleyne-Forte	TRI	11.10.88	23 Jun
46.14A	O'Jay Ferguson	BAH-J	17.10.93	24 Mar
46.14	Yusuke Ishitsuka	JPN	19.6.87	3 May
46.14	P.P.Kunhu Muhammed	IND	5.3.87	11 May
46.14	David Dickens	USA	19.3.85	9 Jun
46.15	LeJerald Betters	USA	6.2.88	21 Apr
46.15	Graham Hedman	GBR	6.2.79	2 Jun
46.15	Claudio Licciardello	ITA	11.1.86	8 Jul
46.16	Reggie Witherspoon	USA	31.5.85	9 Jun
46.16	Joel Milburn	AUS	17.3.86	7 Jul
46.17	Cass Brown	USA	2.8.92	21 Apr
46.17	Segun Ogunkole	NGR	11.6.84	6 Jun
46.17	Yoandys Lescay	CUB-J	5.1.94	1 Jul
46.18	Brandon O'Connor	USA	2.9.89	23 Mar
46.18	Kavarha Holmes	USA-J	25.2.94	5 May
46.18	Quincy Downing	USA-J	16.1.93	25 May
46.18	Wesley Neymour	BAH	1.9.88	23 Jun
46.18	Marcus Chambers	USA-J	3.11.94	29 Jul
46.19	Thomas Schneider	GER	7.11.88	26 May
46.19	Sandro Viana	BRA	26.3.77	2 Jun
46.19	Hakim Ibrahimov (184)	AZE	2.10.90	15 Jun

Hand timed

Mark	Name	Nat	Born	Date
45.6A	Thapelo Ketlogetswe	BOT	12.4.91	21 Apr
45.8A	David Rudisha	KEN	17.12.88	20 Apr
45.9A	Rafith Rodriguez	COL	1.6.89	15 Apr
46.0A	Mark Mutai	KEN	23.3.78	17 Apr

Indoors

Mark	Name	Nat	Born	Pos	Meet	Venue	Date
45.11	Nery Brenes	CRC	25.9.85	1	WI	Istanbul	10 Mar
45.72	Frankie Wright	USA	1 .2.85	1		Fayetteville	10 Feb
45.82	Brycen Spratling	USA	10.3.92				9 Mar
46.06	Najee Glass	USA-J	12.6.94				26 Feb
46.18	Hugh Graham	USA	10.10.92				25 Feb

Low altitude bests

Mark	Name	Date	Mark	Name	Date	Mark	Name	Date	Mark	Name	Date
45.80	Mogawane	28 May	46.01	de Jager	7 Jun	46.13	Mumo	28 Jun	46.16	Osei	14 Jul
45.98	Norwood	21 Apr	46.05	Edmonds	24 Mar	46.16	Mweresa	10 Jul	46.19	Kishoyan	12 Jul

With prosthetics

Mark	Name	Nat	Born	Pos	Meet	Venue	Date
45.20A	Oscar Pistorius	RSA	22.11.86	1h4		Pretoria	17 Mar
best low altitude 45.44				2h1	OG	London (OS)	4 Aug

Mark	Name	Nat	Born	Pos	Meet	Venue	Date

JUNIORS

See main list for top 6 juniors. 15 performances by 3 men to 45.24. Additional marks and further juniors:

Mark	Pos	Meet	Venue	Date	Mark	Pos	Meet	Venue	Date
Santos 3+ 44.85	1	WJ	Barcelona	12 Jul	45.04	1h1	OG	London (OS)	4 Aug
44.88	2	DL	Doha	11 May	45.10	4	Herc	Monaco	20 Jul
44.96	2	BrGP	Birmingham	26 Aug	45.15	1		Bottrop	7 Ju
45.03	2	Athl	Lausanne	23 Aug	45.24	1	DL	New York	9 Jun
Solomon 45.14	8	OG	London (OS)	6 Aug	45.18	1h6	OG	London (OS)	4 Aug

Mark	Name		Nat	Born	Pos	Meet	Venue	Date
45.94	Nijel	Amos	BOT	15.3.94	1		Oedt	20 Jun
46.00A	Boniface	Mweresa	KEN	13.11.93	2		Nairobi	9 Jun
46.16					1h1	WJ	Barcelona	10 Jul
46.02	Machel	Cedenio	TRI-Y	6.9.95	5	NC	Port of Spain	23 Jun
46.06	Javon	Francis (10)	JAM	14.12.94	2s3	WJ	Barcelona	11 Jul
46.07A	Bernardo	Baloyes	COL	6.1.94	1	NC-j	Medellin	17 Aug
46.11	Chidi	Okezie	USA	8.8.93	1h2	IC4A	Princeton	12 May
46.14A	O'Jay	Ferguson	BAH	17.10.93	2		El Paso	24 Mar
46.17	Yoandys	Lescay	CUB	5.1.94	1		San Salvador	1 Jul
46.18	Kavarha	Holmes	USA	25.2.94	1		Baton Rouge	5 May
46.18	Quincy	Downing	USA	16.1.93	3q1	NCAA-E	Jacksonville	25 May
46.18	Marcus	Chambers	USA	3.11.94	1	Jnr Oly	Baltimore	29 Jul
46.20A	Michael	Newton	USA	19.10.93	2		Albuquerque	2 Jun
46.25	Patryk	Dobek	POL	13.2.94	1	NC-j	Bialystok	23 Jun
46.25	Brandon	McBride (20)	CAN	15.6.94	1	NC-j	Winnipeg	28 Jul
Best la: 46.19 Alphas		Kishoyan	KEN	12.10.94	6	WJ	Barcelona	12 Jul

600 METRES

Mark	Name		Nat	Born	Pos	Meet	Venue	Date
1:14.30+	David	Rudisha	KEN	17.12.88	1	in 800m	London (OS)	9 Aug
1:14.4A	Timothy	Kitum	KEN-J	20.11.94	1rA		Nairobi	1 Mar
1:15.4+					5	in 800m	London (OS)	9 Aug
1:14.79+		Rudisha			1	in 800m	Saint-Denis	6 Jul
1:14.79A	Antonio Manuel	Reina	ESP	13.6.81	1		Ávila	28 Jul
1:15.0+	Nijel	Amos	BOT-J	15.3.94	2	in 800m	London (OS)	9 Aug
1:15.0+	Mohammed	Aman	ETH-J	10.1.94	3	in 800m	London (OS)	9 Aug
1:15.2+	Abubaker	Kaki	SUD	21.6.89	4	in 800m	London (OS)	9 Aug

Mark	Name		Nat	Born	Date
1:15.8A	Anthony	Chemut	KEN	17.12.92	23 Jun
1:15.90	Robert	Lathouwers	NED	8.7.83	6 May
1:15.9+	Duane	Solomon	USA	28.12.84	9 Aug
1:16.14	Patryk	Dobek	POL-J	13.2.94	6 May

Mark	Name		Nat	Born	Date
1:16.35+	Leonard	Kosencha	KEN-J	21.8.94	20 Jul

Indoors

Mark	Name		Nat	Born	Date
1:15.26	Adam	Kszczot	POL	2.9.89	5 Feb
1:15.86	Harun	Abda	USA	1.1.90	25 Feb
1:16.08	Yuriy	Borzakovskiy	RUS	12.4.81	5 Feb

800 METRES

Mark	Name		Nat	Born	Pos	Meet	Venue	Date
1:40.91	David	Rudisha	KEN	17.12.88	1	OG	London (OS)	9 Aug
1:41.54		Rudisha			1	DL	Saint-Denis	6 Jul
1:41.73	Nijel	Amos	BOT-J	15.3.94	2	OG	London (OS)	9 Aug
1:41.74		Rudisha			1	adidas	New York	9 Jun
1:42.12A		Rudisha			1	OT	Nairobi	23 Jun
1:42.53	Timothy	Kitum	KEN-J	20.11.94	3	OG	London (OS)	9 Aug
1:42.53	Mohammed	Aman	ETH-J	10.1.94	1	WK	Zürich	30 Aug
1:42.81		Rudisha			2	WK	Zürich	30 Aug
1:42.82	Duane	Solomon	USA	28.12.84	4	OG	London (OS)	9 Aug
1:42.95	Nick	Symmonds	USA	30.12.83	5	OG	London (OS)	9 Aug
1:43.10		Rudisha			1	DL	Doha	11 May
1:43.11		Amos			1		Mannheim	9 Jun
1:43.13	Abraham Kipchirchir	Rotich	KEN-J	26.6.93	1	Herc	Monaco	20 Jul
1:43.15		Rotich			1	NA	Heusden-Zolder	7 Jul
1:43.20		Aman			6	OG	London (OS)	9 Aug
1:43.32	Abubaker	Kaki	SUD	21.6.89	7	OG	London (OS)	9 Aug
1:43.40	Leonard	Kosencha	KEN-J	21.8.94	2	Herc	Monaco	20 Jul
1:43.44		Solomon			3	Herc	Monaco	20 Jul
1:43.51		Aman			1		Daegu	16 May
1:43.56		Aman			1rA	DNG	Stockholm	17 Aug
1:43.58		Aman			1		Rabat	27 May
1:43.60		Kosencha			2		Rabat	27 May
1:43.62		Rotich			1		Liège (NX)	5 Jul
1:43.62		Aman			1	ISTAF	Berlin	2 Sep
1:43.69		Kaki			1		Sollentuna	5 Jul
1:43.71		Kaki			1	Pre	Eugene	2 Jun
1:43.71	Taoufik	Makhloufi (10)	ALG	29.4.88	2rA	DNG	Stockholm	17 Aug
1:43.74		Aman			2	Pre	Eugene	2 Jun
1:43.74	Kevin	López	ESP	12.6.90	4	Herc	Monaco	20 Jul
1:43.74		Makhloufi			1		Rieti	9 Sep

(30/11)

Mark	Name		Nat	Born	Pos	Meet	Venue	Date
1:43.76	Job	Kinyor	KEN	2.9.90	2	DL	Doha	11 May
1:43.77	Andrew	Osagie	GBR	19.2.88	8	OG	London (OS)	9 Aug
1:43.81	Edwin	Melly	KEN-Y	6.7.95	2		Rieti	9 Sep
1:43.83	Adam	Kszczot	POL	2.9.89	1	FBK	Hengelo	27 May
1:43.96A	Anthony	Chemut	KEN	17.12.92	3	OT	Nairobi	23 Jun
1:44.29	André	Olivier	RSA	29.12.89	6	Herc	Monaco	20 Jul
1:44.34	Marcin	Lewandowski	POL	13.6.87	4	FBK	Hengelo	27 May
1:44.48	Jeff	Riseley	AUS	11.11.86	2		Lignano	17 Jul
1:44.49	Alfred	Kirwa Yego	KEN	28.11.86	2	adidas	New York	9 Jun
	(20)							
1:44.54	Khadevis	Robinson	USA	19.7.76	4	Pre	Eugene	2 Jun
1:44.61	Robert	Lathouwers	NED	8.7.83	5	FBK	Hengelo	27 May
1:44.65	Antonio Manuel	Reina	ESP	13.6.81	4	DL	Doha	11 May
1:44.66	David	Mutua	KEN	20.4.92	5	DL	Doha	11 May
1:44.75	Charles	Jock	USA	23.11.89	1		Irvine	12 May
1:44.75	Tyler	Mulder	USA	15.2.87	3		Lignano	17 Jul
1:44.77	Ryan	Martin	USA	23.3.89	2		Irvine	12 May
1:44.80	Sören	Ludolph	GER	25.2.88	6	FBK	Hengelo	27 May
1:44.8 A	Silas	Kiplagat	KEN	20.8.89	1		Nairobi	4 May
1:44.83	Boaz	Lalang	KEN	8.2.89	4	adidas	New York	9 Jun
	(30)							
1:44.86	Michael	Rimmer	GBR	3.2.86	6	DL	Doha	11 May
1:44.89	Mauris Surel	Castillo	CUB	19.10.84	1		Huelva	22 Jun
1:44.89	Andreas	Bube	DEN	13.7.87	10	Herc	Monaco	20 Jul
1:44.97	Pierre-Ambroise	Bosse	FRA	11.5.92	2		Villeneuve d'Ascq	9 Jun
1:44.98	Gareth	Warburton	GBR	23.4.83	1	Bisl	Oslo	7 Jun
1:44.98	Mohamed Ahmed	Hamada	EGY	22.10.92	1	Nebiolo	Torino	8 Jun
1:45.00	Amine	El Manaoui	MAR	20.11.91	3		Rabat	27 May
1:45.01	Nicholas	Kipkoech	KEN	22.10.92	3		Villeneuve d'Ascq	9 Jun
1:45.06	Robby	Andrews	USA	29.3.91	5	adidas	New York	9 Jun
1:45.09	Yuriy	Borzakovskiy	RUS	12.4.81	5s2	OG	London (OS)	7 Aug
	(40)							
1:45.12	Jakub	Holusa	CZE	20.2.88	8	DL	Doha	11 May
1:45.14	Luis Alberto	Marco	ESP	20.8.86	2		Huelva	22 Jun
1:45.19	Abdulrahman Musaeb	Balla	QAT	19.3.89	9	DL	Doha	11 May
1:45.20	Michael	Rutt	USA	28.10.87	6	adidas	New York	9 Jun
1:45.28	Amine	Laâlou	MAR	13.5.82	4		Rabat	27 May
1:45.29	Wesley	Vázquez	PUR-J	27.3.94	4	WJ	Barcelona	15 Jul
1:45.31	Fabiano	Peçanha	BRA	5.6.82	1		Porto Alegre	25 May
1:45.32	Kléberson	Davide	BRA	20.7.85	1		São Paulo	2 Jun
1:45.34	Giordano	Benedetti	ITA	22.5.89	4		Lignano	17 Jul
1:45.40	Elijah	Greer	USA	24.10.90	6	NC/OT	Eugene	25 Jun
	(50)							
1:45.41	Rafith	Rodriguez	COL	1.6.89	1		Ponce	12 May
1:45.44	Reuben	Bett	KEN	6.11.84	2		Liège (NX)	5 Jul
1:45.52	Abdelaziz	Ladan Mohammed	KSA	7.1.91	6		Rabat	27 May
1:45.6 A	Nixon	Chepseba	KEN	12.12.90	1		Nairobi	18 May
1:45.62	Diomar	de Souza	BRA	24.8.89	1		Porto Alegre	22 Apr
1:45.62	Diego	Gomes	BRA	19.4.85	2		Rio de Janeiro	20 May
1:45.62	Mark	Wieczorek	USA	25.12.84	7	NC/OT	Eugene	25 Jun
1:45.67	Benson	Seurei	KEN	27.3.88	1		Bottrop	7 Jul
1:45.70	Mouhcine	El Amine	MAR	8.1.82	7		Rabat	27 May
1:45.71	Jackson	Kivuva	KEN	11.8.88	8	FBK	Hengelo	27 May
	(60)							
1:45.75	Lachlan	Renshaw	AUS	4.2.87	7		Lignano	17 Jul
1:45.77	Mark	English	IRL-J	18.3.93	1		Oordegem	26 May
1:45.78	Mbulaeni	Mulaudzi	RSA	8.9.80	1	NC	Port Elizabeth	14 Apr
1:45.78	Bilal Ali	Mansour	BRN	17.10.83	2		Stockholm	9 Jun
1:45.79A	Richard	Kiplagat	KEN	3.7.84	7	OT	Nairobi	23 Jun
1:45.85	Paul	Renaudie	FRA	2.4.90	8		Villeneuve d'Ascq	9 Jun
1:45.89	Yeimer	López	CUB	20.8.82	4		Daegu	16 May
1:45.90	Erik	Sowinski	USA	21.12.89	2	NCAA	Des Moines	8 Jun
1:45.91	Asbel	Kiprop	KEN	30.6.89	1		Sydney	18 Feb
1:45.91	Evans	Kipkorir	KEN	.85	2	NA	Heusden-Zolder	7 Jul
	(70)							
1:45.94	Álvaro	Rodríguez	ESP	25.5.87	1rB		Madrid	7 Jul
1:45.96	Hamid	Oualich	FRA	26.4.88	4	GS	Ostrava	25 May
1:45.97	Geoffrey	Harris	CAN	30.1.87	2h4	OG	London (OS)	6 Aug
1:45.98	Sadjad	Moradi	IRI	30.3.83	3rB	DL	Doha	11 May
1:46.02	Tevan	Everett	USA	27.7.87	1		West Chester, PA	9 Jun
1:46.02	Stepan	Poistogov	RUS	14.12.86	1	Kuts	Moskva	13 Jun

Mark	Name		Nat	Born	Pos	Meet	Venue	Date
1:46.07	Brandon	McBride	CAN-J	15.6.94	6	WJ	Barcelona	15 Jul
1:46.10	Mukhtar	Mohammed	GBR	1.12.90	3rB	DNG	Stockholm	17 Aug
1:46.12	Casimir	Loxsom	USA	17.3.91	1	Big 10	Madison	13 May
1:46.18	Nick	Willis	NZL	25.4.83	3	NA	Heusden-Zolder	7 Jul
	(80)							
1:46.19	Masato	Yokota	JPN	19.11.87	8		Daegu	16 May
1:46.2	Andrew	Kiptoo	KEN	.87	1s1		Nairobi	11 May
1:46.20	Edward	Kemboi	KEN	12.12.91	2s3	NCAA	Des Moines	6 Jun
1:46.21	Lopez	Lomong	USA	1.1.85	3		Los Angeles (ER)	18 May
1:46.22	Andy	González	CUB	17.10.87	1		La Habana	27 May
1:46.23	Brandon	Johnson	USA	6.3.85	3	Jerome	Burnaby	10 Jun
1:46.33	Sebastian	Keiner	GER	22.8.89	2		Mannheim	9 Jun
1:46.33	Andrew	Wheating	USA	21.11.87	4rB	DNG	Stockholm	17 Aug
1:46.36	Rynhardt	van Rensburg	RSA	23.3.92	3	NC	Port Elizabeth	14 Apr
1:46.37	Lutimar	Paes	BRA	14.12.88	2		São Paulo	2 Jun
	(90)							
1:46.40	Brian	Gagnon	USA	8.5.87	2		West Chester, PA	9 Jun
1:46.4 A	Ismael	Kombich	KEN	16.10.85	2		Nairobi	18 May
1:46.4 A	Cornelius	Kiplangat	KEN	21.12.92	2	NC	Nairobi	14 Jun
1:46.41	Richard	West	CAN	11.9.90	4s3	NCAA	Des Moines	6 Jun
1:46.43	Michael	Preble	USA	15.4.90	1		Los Angeles	24 Mar
1:46.45	James	Gurr	AUS	20.12.83	4		Melbourne	3 Mar
1:46.46	Thijmen	Kupers	NED	4.10.91	9	FBK	Hengelo	27 May
1:46.48	Mohamed	Al-Azimi	KUW	16.6.82	dq(3)h1	OG	London (OS)	6 Aug
	1:47.13				4		Sollentuna	5 Jul
1:46.5A	Esrael	Awoke	ETH-J	5.4.94	1	NC	Addis Ababa	10 May
1:46.56		Teng Haining	CHN-J	25.6.93	1		Colombo	12 Jun
	(100)							
1:46.56	Ioan	Zaizan	ROU	21.7.83	1		Bottrop	6 Jul

Mark	Name		Nat	Born	Date
1:46.58	Patrick	Roach	USA	19.12.86	9 Jun
1:46.58	Mor	Seck	SEN	24.9.85	20 Jun
1:46.59	Rob	Novak	USA	20.3.86	12 May
1:46.59	Khaled	Benmehdi	ALG	22.10.88	22 Jun
1:46.60	Pierre Antoine	Balhan	BEL	21.10.92	5 Jul
1:46.61	Prince	Mumba	ZAM	28.8.84	21 Apr
1:46.61	Samir	Jamaa	MAR	9.2.90	27 May
1:46.62	David	Pachuta	USA	21.6.89	6 Jun
1:46.62	Jozef	Repcik	SVK	3.8.86	28 Jun
1:46.63	Mekonnen	Gebremedhin	ETH	11.10.88	7 Jul
1:46.63	Mohamed	Al-Garni	QAT	2.7.92	2 Sep
1:46.65	Harun	Abda	USA	1.1.90	6 Jun
1:46.66	Andrew	Ellerton	CAN	18.11.83	18 May
1:46.66	Aaron	Evans	BER	31.1.90	8 Jun
1:46.66	Liam	Boylan-Pett	USA	11.9.85	9 Jun
1:46.67	Raphael	Pallitsch	AUT	18.12.89	6 Jul
1:46.68	Geoffrey	Rono	KEN	21.4.87	16 May
1:46.68	Raidel	Acea	CUB	31.10.90	27 May
1:46.7 A	Shiferaw	Wole	ETH	23.2.89	10 May
1:46.70	Mohamed	Belbachir	ALG-J	11.1.94	15 Jul
1:46.72	Hamza	Driouch	QAT-J	16.11.94	12 Jun
1:46.74A	Nathan	Brannen	CAN	8.9.82	30 Jun
1:46.74	Ahmed	Mainy	MAR	20.8.86	21 Jul
1:46.76	Miguel	Quesada	ESP	18.9.79	7 Jun
1:46.79	Zan	Rudolf	SLO-J	9.5.93	14 Jun
1:46.79	Leonel	Manzano	USA	12.9.84	10 Jul
1:46.8 A	Timothy	Sein	KEN	.88	18 May
1:46.83	Kyle	Smith	CAN	25.1.85	16 Jun
1:46.85	Emad Hamed	Mohamed Nour	KSA	21.4.90	7 Jul
1:46.86	Brice	Panel	FRA	13.6.83	27 May
1:46.87	Johan	Cronje	RSA	13.4.82	14 Jun
1:46.87	Oleksandr	Osmolovych	UKR	8.10.85	17 Jun
1:46.88	Jamaal	James	TRI	4.9.88	9 Jun
1:46.88	Ivan	Nesterov	RUS	10.2.85	13 Jun
1:46.88	Thomas	Roth	NOR	11.2.91	28 Jun
1:46.88	Soresa	Fida	ETH-J	27.5.93	7 Jul
1:46.89	Sho	Kawamoto	JPN-J	1.3.93	26 May
1:46.90	David	Torrence	USA	26.11.85	21 Jul
1:46.92A	Thapelo	Madiba	RSA-J	8.9.93	24 Mar
1:46.92A	Isaac	Seoke	BOT	19.3.91	5 May
1:46.92	Dustin	Emrani	ISR	6.1.85	14 Jun
1:46.92	Dennis	Krüger	GER-J	24.4.93	15 Jul
1:46.95	Mario	Scapini	ITA	2.2.89	31 May
1:46.95	Tetlo	Emmen	USA	24.1.84	9 Jun
1:46.95	Alex	Kibet	KEN-J	20.10.94	28 Jul
1:46.96	Andrew	Dawson	USA	24.9.85	16 Jun
1:46.98	Igor	Davydov	UKR	12.11.88	14 Jun

Mark	Name		Nat	Born	Date
1:47.01		Xia Xiudong	CHN	19.1.88	23 May
1:47.02	Paul	Robinson	IRL	24.5.91	2 Sep
1:47.03	Martin	Conrad	GER	8.1.86	28 May
1:47.04	Julius	Mutekanga	UGA	1.12.87	21 May
1:47.04	Sharif	Webb	USA	9.6.89	16 Jun
1:47.05	Ignacio	Laguna	ESP	18.5.87	18 Jul
1:47.07	Lance	Roller	USA	24.5.90	6 Jun
1:47.08	Niall	Brooks	GBR	8.7.91	21 Aug
1:47.09	Jackson	Langat	USA	15.12.80	16 Jun
1:47.10	Tamás	Kazi	HUN	16.5.85	6 Aug
1:47.1A	Jema	Umar	ETH-Y	24.12.95	10 May
1:47.11	Radouane	Baaziri	MAR-J	23.7.93	5 May
1:47.13	James	Kaan	AUS	17.9.90	18 Feb
1:47.13	Brandon	Shaw	USA	11.9.81	21 May
1:47.14	Guy	Learmonth	GBR	24.4.92	7 Jun
1:47.14	Takeshi	Kuchino	JPN	7.4.86	21 Jul
1:47.16	Szymon	Krawczyk	POL	29.12.88	16 Jun
1:47.17	Patrick	Schoenball	GER	26.6.89	6 Jul
1:47.2 A	Isaac	Kipketer	KEN	29.9.83	4 May
1:47.23	Francisco	Roldán	ESP	26.5.90	18 Jul
1:47.24	Martin	Bischoff	GER	18.7.90	20 May
1:47.25	Jan	Van Den Broeck	BEL	11.3.89	26 May
1:47.26	Rabie	Doukkana	MAR	6.12.87	27 Jun
1:47.26	Anis	Ananenko	BLR	29.11.85	3 Jun
1:47.27	Ehsan	Mohajershojaei	IRI	21.3.83	11 May
1:47.27	Johannes	Ghirmai	ERI	5.10.84	7 Jun
1:47.28	Andreas	Vojta	AUT	9.6.89	14 Jun
1:47.29	John	Bolas	USA	1.11.87	21 Jul
1:47.31	Johan	Svensson	SWE	16.5.89	7 Jun
1:47.33	Ivan	Tukhtachev	RUS	12.7.89	13 Jun
1:47.33	Charlie	Grice	GBR-J	7.11.93	21 Jul
1:47.34	Nabil	Madi	ALG	9.6.81	8 Jul
1:47.34	Moise	Joseph	HAI	27.12.81	21 Jul
1:47.35	Andréas	Dimitrákis	GRE	8.9.90	25 Jul
1:47.36	Azzeddine	Boudjémaa	FRA	17.9.82	26 May
1:47.37	Tlou	Seloba	RSA	8.5.85	14 Apr
1:47.38	Andreas	Rapatz	AUT	5.9.86	2 Jun
1:47.39	Eliud	Rutto	KEN	4.6.88	16 May
1:47.40	Bartosz	Nowicki	POL	26.2.84	3 Jun
1:47.40	Jeff	See	USA	6.6.86	9 Jun
1:47.40	Yevgeniy	Sharmin	RUS	25.3.86	21 Jun
1:47.40	Tesfaye	Homiyu	ETH-J	23.6.93	4 Jul
1:47.4A	Dawit	Wolde	ETH	19.5.91	10 May
1:47.4 A	Moses	Kipkemboi	KEN-Y	16.6.95	9 Jun
1:47.41	Pablo	Solares	MEX	22.12.84	8 Jul
1:47.42	Omar	Kenani	ALG	19.9.87	8 Jul
1:47.43	Richard	Jones	USA	15.7.88	18 May

Mark	Name		Nat	Born		Pos	Meet	Venue		Date	
1:47.43	Oleg	Kayafa	UKR	4.4.89	28 May	1:47.44	Vladimir	Obnosov	RUS	24.9.87	21 Jun
1:47.43	Mamadou	Guèye	SEN	1.4.86	4 Jul	1:47.45	Sajeesh	Joseph	IND	14.1.87	11 May
1:47.44	Christian	Smith	USA	31.10.83	16 Jun	1:47.45	Ayanleh Suleiman (201)		DJI	3.12.92	18 Jul

Indoors

Mark	Name		Nat	Born		Pos	Meet	Venue		Date	
1:45.71	Ahmed	Ismail	SUD	10.9.84		1		Mustasaari			7 Feb
1:46.33	Joe	Thomas	GBR	29.1.88		4		Stockholm			23 Feb
1:46.65	Andreas	Rapatz	AUT	5.9.86	11 Feb	1:47.22	Sean	Obinwa	USA	4.1.91	28 Jan
1:47.14	Joey	Roberts	USA	17.4.90	28 Jan	1:47.34	Selasi	Lumax	GHA	1.8.90	25 Feb
1:47.19	Jan	Van Den Broeck	BEL	11.3.89	7 Jan	1:47.43	Benjamin	Scheetz	USA	1.10.88	25 Feb

JUNIORS

See main list for top 11 juniors. 15 performances by 5 men to 1:43.74 in main list. Further performances to 1:44.20

Mark	Name		Pos	Meet	Venue		Born		Pos	Meet	Venue	Date
Amos	1:43.79		1	WJ	Barcelona		15 Jul					
Kitum	1:43.94A		2	OT	Nairobi		23 Jun	1:44.00	2	FBK	Hengelo	27 May
1:46.70	Mohamed	Belbachir	ALG	11.1.94	7	WJ	Barcelona					15 Jul
1:46.72	Hamza	Driouch	QAT	16.11.94	2		Colombo					12 Jun
1:46.79	Zan	Rudolf	SLO	9.5.93	1		Velenje					14 Jun
1:46.88	Soresa	Fida	ETH	27.5.93	5		Bottrop					7 Jul
1:46.89	Sho	Kawamoto	JPN	1.3.93	2		Yokohama					26 May
1:46.92A	Thapelo	Madiba	RSA	8.9.93	2		Potchefstroom					24 Mar
1:46.92	Dennis	Krüger	GER	24.4.93	8	WJ	Barcelona					15 Jul
1:46.95	Alex	Kibet	KEN	20.10.94	1		Huizingen					28 Jul
1:47.1A	Jema	Umar (20)	ETH-Y	24.12.95	3	NC	Addis Ababa					10 May

1000 METRES

Mark	Name		Nat	Born		Pos	Meet	Venue		Date	
2:16.39	Benson	Seurei	KEN	27.3.88		1	Gugl	Linz			20 Aug
2:16.52	Nathan	Brannen	CAN	8.9.82		2	Gugl	Linz			20 Aug
2:16.58	Nick	Willis	NZL	25.4.83		3	Gugl	Linz			20 Aug
2:16.63	Jeff	Riseley	AUS	11.11.86		4	Gugl	Linz			20 Aug
2:17.08	Abraham Kipchirchir Rotich		KEN-J	26.6.93		1		Dubnica nad Váhom			26 Aug
2:17.13	Michael	Rimmer	GBR	3.2.86	20 Aug	2:17.46	David	Torrence	USA	26.11.85	20 Aug
2:17.16	Nicholas	Kipkoech	KEN	22.10.92	20 Aug	2:17.60	Timothy	Sein	KEN	.88	20 Aug
2:17.21	Yassine	Bensghir	MAR	3.1.83	20 Aug	2:17.96	Timothy	Kitum	KEN-J	20.11.94	26 Aug
2:17.32	Mohamed	Al-Garni	QAT	1.7.92	20 Aug	2:18.34	Andreas	Vojta	AUT	9.6.89	20 Aug
2:17.44	Andrew	Wheating	USA	21.11.87	20 Aug	2:18.96	Cornelius	Kiplangat	KEN	21.12.92	18 Aug

1500 METRES

Mark	Name		Nat	Born	Pos	Meet	Venue	Date	
3:28.88	Asbel	Kiprop	KEN	30.6.89	1	Herc	Monaco	20	Jul
3:29.63	Silas	Kiplagat	KEN	20.8.89	1	DL	Doha	11	May
3:29.77	Nixon	Chepseba	KEN	12.12.90	2	Herc	Monaco	20	Jul
3:29.78		Kiprop			2	DL	Doha	11	May
3:29.90		Chepseba			1	FBK	Hengelo	27	May
3:30.31	Ayanleh	Souleiman	DJI	3.12.92	2	FBK	Hengelo	27	May
3:30.35	Nick	Willis	NZL	25.4.83	3	Herc	Monaco	20	Jul
3:30.54	Amine	Laâlou	MAR	13.5.82	4	Herc	Monaco	20	Jul
3:30.80	Taoufik	Makhloufi	ALG	29.4.88	5	Herc	Monaco	20	Jul
3:31.00	Bethwel	Birgen	KEN	6.8.88	6	Herc	Monaco	20	Jul
3:31.17		Birgen			3	DL	Doha	11	May
3:31.32		Chepseba			4	DL	Doha	11	May
3:31.45	Mekonnen	Gebremedhin	ETH	11.10.88	3	FBK	Hengelo	27	May
3:31.61	Benson	Seurei (10)	KEN	27.3.88	7	Herc	Monaco	20	Jul
3:31.78		Kiplagat			1	Athl	Lausanne	23	Aug
3:31.86		Gebremedhin			2	Athl	Lausanne	23	Aug
3:31.86		Kiplagat			1		Rieti	9	Sep
3:31.96	Matthew	Centrowitz	USA	18.10.89	3	Athl	Lausanne	23	Aug
3:31.98		Kiplagat			1	VD	Bruxelles	7	Sep
3:32.08	Collins	Cheboi	KEN	25.9.87	8	Herc	Monaco	20	Jul
3:32.10		Gebremedhin			2	VD	Bruxelles	7	Sep
3:32.24		Birgen			3	VD	Bruxelles	7	Sep
3:32.31		Chepseba			4	Athl	Lausanne	23	Aug
3:32.39	Caleb	Ndiku	KEN	9.10.92	5	Athl	Lausanne	23	Aug
3:32.47		Centrowitz			4	VD	Bruxelles	7	Sep
3:32.58		Makhloufi			1	Hanz	Zagreb	4	Sep
3:32.64		Cheboi			5	DL	Doha	11	May
3:32.88		Kiprop			5	VD	Bruxelles	7	Sep
3:32.98	Daniel Kipchirchir	Komen	KEN	27.11.84	6	VD	Bruxelles	7	Sep
3:33.11		Chepseba			1	ISTAF	Berlin	2	Sep
	(30/14)								
3:33.31	James	Magut	KEN	20.7.90	2	NC	Zagreb	4	Sep
3:33.32	Ilham Tanui	Özbilen	TUR	5.3.90	6	DL	Doha	11	May
3:33.39	Geoffrey	Barusei	KEN-J	.94	4	FBK	Hengelo	27	May

Mark	Name		Nat	Born	Pos	Meet	Venue	Date	
3:33.64	Carsten	Schlangen	GER	31.12.80	2		Bottrop	6	Jul
3:33.69	Hamza	Driouch	QAT-J	16.11.94	9	DL	Doha	11	May
3:33.81	Eliah	Kiptoo	KEN	9.6.86	10	DL	Doha	11	May
(20)									
3:33.82	Dawit	Wolde	ETH	19.5.91	5	FBK	Hengelo	27	May
3:33.83	Gideon	Gathimba	KEN	9.3.80	9	Athl	Lausanne	23	Aug
3:33.92	Ryan	Gregson	AUS	26.4.90	11	DL	Doha	11	May
3:33.99	Abdelati	Iguider	MAR	25.3.87	1s2	OG	London (OS)	5	Aug
3:34.08	Leonel	Manzano	USA	12.9.84	10	Athl	Lausanne	23	Aug
3:34.10	Álvaro	Rodríguez	ESP	25.5.87	6	FBK	Hengelo	27	May
3:34.11	Russell	Brown	USA	3.3.85	12	DL	Doha	11	May
3:34.19	Emad Hamed Mohamed	Nour	KSA	21.4.90	3		Bottrop	6	Jul
3:34.22	Nathan	Brannen	CAN	8.9.82	8	FBK	Hengelo	27	May
3:34.34	Abubaker	Kaki	SUD	21.6.89	13	DL	Doha	11	May
(30)									
3:34.50	Yassine	Bensghir	MAR	3.1.83	1		Sollentuna	5	Jul
3:34.52	Ayoub	Tiouali	MAR	26.5.91	4		Bottrop	6	Jul
3:34.55	Teshome	Diressa	ETH-J	25.4.94	1	Odlozil	Praha	11	Jun
3:34.55	Bader	Rassioui	MAR	8.6.85	5		Bottrop	6	Jul
3:34.56	Florian	Orth	GER	24.7.89	5	ISTAF	Berlin	2	Sep
3:34.60	German	Fernandez	USA	2.11.90	7	ISTAF	Berlin	2	Sep
3:34.63	Bernard	Lagat	USA	12.12.74	1	adidas	New York	9	Jun
3:34.66	Mo	Farah	GBR	23.3.83	1r1		Los Angeles (ER)	18	May
3:34.75	Galen	Rupp	USA	8.5.86	2r1		Los Angeles (ER)	18	May
3:34.76	Ross	Murray	GBR	8.10.90	9	FBK	Hengelo	27	May
(40)									
3:34.77	David	Bustos	ESP	25.8.90	2		Huelva	7	Jun
3:34.78	Robby	Andrews	USA	29.3.91	3r1		Los Angeles (ER)	18	May
3:34.85	Jamel	Aarass	FRA	15.11.81	1r3		Los Angeles (ER)	18	May
3:35.02A	Abednego	Chesebe	KEN	.82	3	NC	Nairobi	15	Jun
3:35.03	Mauris Surel	Castillo	CUB	19.10.84	3		Huelva	7	Jun
3:35.03	Yoann	Kowal	FRA	28.5.87	10	Herc	Monaco	20	Jul
3:35.11	Zebene	Alemayehu	ETH	4.9.92	6		Bottrop	6	Jul
3:35.16	Diego	Ruíz	ESP	5.2.82	4		Huelva	7	Jun
3:35.19	Andrew	Baddeley	GBR	20.6.82	1	Jordan	Stanford	29	Apr
3:35.20	Benjamin	Kipkurui	KEN	28.12.80	7		Bottrop	6	Jul
(50)									
3:35.21	Jeff	See	USA	6.6.86	1		Indianapolis	16	Jun
3:35.22	Soresa	Fida	ETH-J	27.5.93	8		Bottrop	6	Jul
3:35.25	James	Kangogo	KEN	22.11.85	2		Dessau	25	May
3:35.33	Johan	Cronje	RSA	13.4.82	3		Dessau	25	May
3:35.38	Aman	Wote	ETH	18.4.84	5		Rabat	27	May
3:35.40	Bilal Ali	Mansour	BRN	17.10.83	7s2	OG	London (OS)	5	Aug
3:35.41	David	Torrence	USA	26.11.85	2r3		Los Angeles (ER)	18	May
3:35.43	Henrik	Ingebrigtsen	NOR	24.2.91	5	OG	London (OS)	1	Jul
3:35.45	Vincent	Mutai	KEN-J	3.11.94	4		Dessau	25	May
3:35.46	Mohammed	Moustaoui	MAR	2.4.85	3		Reims	4	Jul
(60)									
3:35.52	Juan	van Deventer	RSA	26.3.83	3	Odlozil	Praha	11	Jun
3:35.59	Kyle	Merber	USA	19.11.90	1		Philadelphia (Sw)	14	May
3:35.62	Abderrahmane	Anou	ALG	29.1.91	1		Amiens	30	Jun
3:35.63	Jordan	McNamara	USA	7.3.87	1		Eugene	16	Jun
3:35.71	Fouad	El Kaam	MAR	27.5.88	7		Rabat	27	May
3:35.72	Cornelius	Kangogo	KEN-J	31.12.93	1		Rehlingen	28	May
3:35.74	Collis	Birmingham	AUS	27.12.84	2		Sydney	18	Feb
3:35.82	Imad	Touil	ALG	11.2.89	10		Rabat	27	May
3:35.82	Juan Carlos	Higuero	ESP	3.8.78	12	FBK	Hengelo	27	May
3:35.87	Tarek	Boukensa	ALG	19.11.81	1	NC	Alger	8	Jul
(70)									
3:35.87	Anter	Zerguelaine	ALG	4.1.85	2	NC	Alger	8	Jul
3:35.89	Andrew	Wheating	USA	21.11.87	1	Jerome	Burnaby	10	Jun
3:36.03	Garrett	Heath	USA	3.11.85	2		Eugene	16	Jun
3:36.04	Nick	Symmonds	USA	30.12.83	2r2		Los Angeles (ER)	18	May
3:36.06	Ismael	Kombich	KEN	16.10.85	5	Odlozil	Praha	11	Jun
3:36.08	Jamal	Hitrane	MAR	1.9.89	3	NC	Fes	17	Jun
3:36.10	Jeff	Riseley	AUS	11.11.86	1		Lapinlahti	8	Jul
3:36.15	Mateusz	Demczyszak	POL	18.1.86	6		Huelva	7	Jun
3:36.15	Hillary	Ngetich	KEN-Y	15.9.95	7	Hanz	Zagreb	4	Sep
3:36.29	Cornelius	Ndiwa	KEN	17.12.88	8	Hanz	Zagreb	4	Sep
(80)									
3:36.33	John	Bolas	USA	1.11.87	2		Indianapolis	16	Jun

Mark	Name		Nat	Born	Pos	Meet	Venue	Date
3:36.33	Will	Leer	USA	15.4.85	3		Indianapolis	16 Jun
3:36.35	Craig	Miller	USA	3.8.87	4		Indianapolis	16 Jun
3:36.41	Andrew AJ	Acosta	USA	13.4.88	5r1		Los Angeles (ER)	18 May
3:36.45A	Bernard	Kaptingei	KEN	.86	4	NC	Nairobi	15 Jun
3:36.46	Grégory	Beugnet	FRA	14.9.87	13	FBK	Hengelo	27 May
3:36.50	Teklit	Teweldebrhan	ERI-J	1.10.93	7		Huelva	7 Jun
3:36.50	Manuel	Olmedo	ESP	17.5.83	8		Huelva	7 Jun
3:36.53	Zane	Robertson	NZL	14.11.89	3	Jordan	Stanford	29 Apr
3:36.56	Peter	van der Westhuizen	RSA	21.12.84	2		Kingston	5 May
(90)								
3:36.60	Linus	Kiplagat	KEN-J	23.12.94	1rA	NA	Heusden-Zolder	7 Jul
3:36.61A	Vincent	Letting	KEN-J	.93	5	NC	Nairobi	15 Jun
3:36.63	Marouane	Habti	MAR	13.10.87	1		Radès	9 Jun
3:36.63	Mohamed	Al-Garni	QAT	2.7.92	5	adidas	New York	9 Jun
3:36.65	Majdubi	Kamali	MAR-J	1.5.93	10		Bottrop	6 Jul
3:36.72	Abiyot	Abinet	ETH	10.5.89	1		Marseille	31 May
3:36.74	Jordan	Williamsz	AUS	21.8.92	2		Philadelphia (Sw)	14 May
3:36.77	Lawi	Lalang	KEN	15.6.91	4	Jordan	Stanford	29 Apr
3:36.81	Sam	McEntee	AUS	3.2.92	4		Philadelphia (Sw)	14 May
3:36.84	Necerddine	Hallil	ALG	10.4.88	2	Bisl	Oslo	7 Jun
(100)								

Mark	Name		Nat	Born	Date
3:36.88	Niclas	Sandells	FIN	14.3.84	8 Jul
3:37.0 A	Elijah	Kipchirchir	KEN		24 Mar
3:37.05	Liam	Boylan-Pett	USA	11.9.85	14 May
3:37.05	Florian	Carvalho	FRA	9.3.89	3 Aug
3:37.1	Othmane	Belharbazi	FRA	3.11.88	19 Jul
3:37.17	Taylor	Milne	CAN	14.6.81	18 May
3:37.19	Riley	Masters	USA	5.4.90	18 May
3:37.2 A	Nicholas	Kipchumba	KEN	.89	24 Mar
3:37.24	Andrew	Bayer	USA	3.2.90	1 Jul
3:37.24	Bryan	Cantero	FRA	28.4.91	6 Jul
3:37.26	Alan	Webb	USA	13.1.83	18 May
3:37.28	Yegor	Nikolayev	RUS	12.2.88	5 Aug
3:37.43	Bartosz	Nowicki	POL	26.2.84	7 Jul
3:37.47	Augustine	Choge	KEN	21.1.87	9 Jun
3:37.50	Miles	Batty	USA	1.6.87	18 May
3:37.51	David	Bishop	GBR	9.5.87	29 Apr
3:37.53	Dan	Huling	USA	16.7.83	14 May
3:37.55	Bayisa	Moleta	ETH	.88	27 Apr
3:37.59	Abdelhadi	Labäli	MAR-J	26.4.93	12 May
3:37.60	Samuel	Vázquez	PUR	3.5.84	16 Jun
3:37.61	Shiferaw	Wole	ETH	23.2.89	27 Apr
3:37.63	Haïs	Welday	ERI	24.10.89	28 May
3:37.68	Matt	Maldonado	USA	18.9.90	18 May
3:37.69	Dorian	Ulrey	USA	11.7.87	18 May
3:37.91	Paul	Robinson	IRL	24.5.91	8 Jul
3:37.95	Chris	O'Hare	GBR	23.11.90	29 Apr
3:37.96A	Hosea	Chirchir	KEN	.84	9 Jun
3:37.96	Evanson	Kosgei	KEN	.92	15 Jul
3:38.00	Tom	Lancashire	GBR	2.7.85	27 May
3:38.03 A	Solomon	Barngetuny	KEN	.84	15 Jun
3:38.04	Hamish	Carson	NZL	1.11.88	14 May
3:38.04	James	Kaan	AUS	17.9.90	6 Jun
3:38.06	Erik	van Ingen	USA	25.8.89	12 May
3:38.09	Andreas	Vojta	AUT	9.6.89	7 Jun
3:38.36	Brian	Gagnon	USA	8.5.87	14 May
3:38.36	Ryan	Hill	USA	31.1.90	7 Jul
3:38.39	Mohammed	Abid	MAR-Y	18.3.95	27 May
3:38.39	John	Mickowski	USA	24.4.86	16 Jun
3:38.40	Nabil	Madi	ALG	9.6.81	6 Jul
3:38.41	Hicham	Sigueni	MAR-J	30.1.93	28 Apr
3:38.46	Tesfaye	Cheru	ETH-J	2.3.93	10 Jun
3:38.49	Hélio	Gomes	POR	27.12.84	8 Jul
3:38.53	Mohamed	Bensghir	MAR	16.11.91	12 May
3:38.56	Homiyu	Tesfaye	ETH-J	23.6.93	2 Jun
3:38.56	Juan Luis	Barrios	MEX	24.6.83	7 Jul
3:38.60	Soufiane	Bouqantar	MAR-J	30.8.93	1 Jun
3:38.60	Rob	Finnerty	USA	4.2.90	17 Jun
3:38.61	Stephen	Pifer	USA	7.12.84	16 Jun
3:38.62	Francisco Javier	Abad	ESP	18.8.81	7 Jun
3:38.64+	Lopez	Lomong	USA	1.1.85	6 Jun
3:38.68	Brenton	Rowe	AUT	17.8.87	18 Feb
3:38.68	Dmitrijs	Jurkevics	LAT	7.1.87	7 Jun
3:38.7 A	Isiah	Koech	KEN-J	19.12.93	18 May
3:38.82	Jerry	Motsau	RSA	12.3.90	20 Mar
3:38.84	Remmy Ndiwa	Limo	KEN	3.2.88	17 Jul
3:38.89	Younès	Essalhi	MAR-J	24.8.94	27 May
3:38.94	Brett	Robinson	AUS	8.5.91	18 Feb
3:38.96	Alberto	Imedio	ESP	24.5.91	8 Jul
3:39.00	Cory	Leslie	USA	24.10.89	29 Apr
3:39.06	Duncan	Phillips	USA	7.6.89	16 Jun
3:39.08	Kris	Gauson	GBR	29.1.88	18 May
3:39.1 A	Paul Kipsiele	Koech	KEN	10.11.81	18 May
3:39.11	Abdellah	Haidane	ITA	28.3.89	19 May
3:39.11	Dan	Clark	USA	6.9.86	13 Jun
3:39.14	Amor	Ben Yahia	TUN	1 .7.85	9 Jun
3:39.22	Michael	Hammond	USA	7.11.89	29 Apr
3:39.22	Pavel	Khvorostukhin	RUS	26.10.86	13 Jun
3:39.27	Luke	Rucks	USA	14.6.88	14 May
3:39.27	Geoffrey	Martinson	CAN	26.3.86	18 May
3:39.28	Omar	Kenani	ALG	19.9.87	27 May
3:39.32	Matthew	Lincoln	CAN	30.7.82	10 Jun
3:39.38	Oleksandr	Borysyuk	UKR	9.12.85	30 Jun
3:39.40	Dmitriy	Nizelskiy	RUS	6.11.86	13 Jun
3:39.4	Lyès	Belkheir	ALG	5.10.87	8 Jun
3:39.42	Joe	Stilin	USA	5.12.89	14 May
3:39.42	Mohamed Othman	Shahween	KSA	15.2.86	3 Aug
3:39.47	Jeremy	Roff	AUS	22.11.83	9 Jun
3:39.47	Krzysztof	Zebrowski	POL	9.7.90	9 Jun
3:39.50	Roman	Maleyev	RUS	23.8.86	13 Jun
3:39.51	Simon	Denissel	FRA	22.5.90	20 May
3:39.53	Mohamed	Abdikadar	ITA-J	12.6.93	9 Sep
3:39.55	Jeremy	Rae	CAN	19.5.91	13 Jun
3:39.55	Pieter-Jan	Hannes	BEL	30.10.92	7 Jul
3:39.59	James	Brewer	GBR	18.6.88	26 Aug
3:39.63	Yilma	Gurara	ETH	11.9.90	27 Apr
3:39.64	Victor José	Corrales	ESP	12.3.89	8 Jul
3:39.65	Abdelghani	Bensaadi	ALG	31.7.87	27 May
3:39.67	Silas	Kisorio	KEN	8.1.83	21 Jul
3:39.68	Oleg	Sidorov	RUS	7.6.90	13 Jun
3:39.7 A	Elkana	Yego	KEN-J	7.12.94	24 Mar
3:39.7 A	Nicholas	Kemboi	KEN	18.12.89	18 May
3:39.73	Brandon	Bethke	USA	19.1.87	9 Jun
3:39.74	Mikael	Bergdahl	FIN	15.8.83	8 Jul
3:39.82	Reuben	Bett	KEN	6.11.84	4 Sep
3:39.88	Fabiano	Peçanha	BRA	5.6.82	9 May
3:39.90	Trevor	van Ackeren	USA	1.8.89	14 May
3:39.92	Lander	Tijtgat	BEL	6.4.83	7 Jul
3:39.93	Otmane	Laaroussi	MAR	20.3.92	27 May
3:39.94	Damian	Roszko	POL	11.11.91	17 Jun
3:39.95	Christian	Gonzalez	USA	17.5.89	18 May
3:39.96	Sebastian	Keiner	GER	22.8.89	5 Aug
(201					

Indoors

Mark	Name		Nat	Born	Pos	Meet	Venue	Date
3:35.49	Ismael	Kombich	KEN	16.10.85	4		Liévin	14 Feb

Mark	Name		Nat	Born	Date
3:37.76	Marcin	Lewandowski	POL	13.6.87	14 Feb
3:38.03	James	Brewer	GBR	18.6.88	18 Feb
3:39.42	Mehdi	Baala	FRA	17.8.78	14 Feb
3:39.42	Yohan	Durand	FRA	14.5.85	29 Feb

Mark	Name		Nat	Born	Pos	Meet	Venue	Date
3:39.54+	Silas	Kisorio	KEN	8.1.83	11 Feb			
3:39.73	Valentin	Smirnov	RUS	13.2.86	5 Feb			

JUNIORS

See main list for top 11 juniors. 11 performances by 7 men to 3:36.41. Additional marks and further juniors:

Mark	Name		Nat	Born	Pos	Meet	Venue	Date
Driouch	3:34.80+				3	in 1M	Oslo	7 Jun
Dirissa	3:35.46				10	FBK	Hengelo	27 May
Fida	3:35.59				5		Dessau	25 May
	3:36.41				3		Rehlingen	28 May
3:37.59	Abdelhadi	Labäli	MAR	26.4.93	2		Rabat	12 May
3:38.39	Mohammed	Abid	MAR-Y	18.3.95	1rB		Rabat	27 May
3:38.41	Hicham	Sigueni	MAR	30.1.93	3		Marrakech	28 Apr
3:38.46	Tesfaye	Cheru	ETH-	2.3.93	3		Brazzaville	10 Jun
3:38.56	Homiyu	Tesfaye	ETH-	23.6.93	2		Regensburg	2 Jun
3:38.60	Soufiane	Bouqantar	MAR	30.8.93	1		Montbéliard	1 Jun
3:38.7 A	Isiah	Koech	KEN	19.12.93	1		Nairobi	18 May
3:38.89	Younès	Essalhi	MAR	24.8.94	3rB		Rabat	27 May
3:39.2 A	Elkana	Yego (20)	KEN	7.12.94			Thika	24 Mar

1 MILE

Mark	Name		Nat	Born	Pos	Meet	Venue	Date
3:49.22	Asbel	Kiprop	KEN	30.6.89	1	Bisl	Oslo	7 Jun
3:49.40		Kiprop			1	Pre	Eugene	2 Jun
3:50.00	Caleb	Ndiku	KEN	9.10.92	2	Bisl	Oslo	7 Jun
3:50.02	Mekonnen	Gebremedhin	ETH	11.10.88	3	Bisl	Oslo	7 Jun
3:50.17		Gebremedhin			2	Pre	Eugene	2 Jun
3:50.21	Ayanleh	Souleiman	DJI	3.12.92	3	Pre	Eugene	2 Jun
3:50.24	Gideon	Gathimba	KEN	9.3.80	4	Bisl	Oslo	7 Jun
3:50.43	Bethwel	Birgen	KEN	6.8.88	4	Pre	Eugene	2 Jun
3:50.43	Amine	Laâlou	MAR	13.5.82	5	Bisl	Oslo	7 Jun
3:50.68	James	Magut	KEN	20.7.90	6	Bisl	Oslo	7 Jun
3:50.73		Birgen			7	Bisl	Oslo	7 Jun
3:50.79		Ndiku			5	Pre	Eugene	2 Jun
3:50.90	Hamza	Driouch	QAT-J	16.11.94	8	Bisl	Oslo	7 Jun
3:51.44	Collins	Cheboi	KEN	25.9.87	6	Pre	Eugene	2 Jun
3:51.77	Nick	Willis	NZL	25.4.83	7	Pre	Eugene	2 Jun
3:51.78	Abdelati	Iguider	MAR	25.3.87	8	Pre	Eugene	2 Jun
3:52.01	David	Torrence	USA	26.11.85	9	Pre	Eugene	2 Jun
3:52.12		Laâlou			10	Pre	Eugene	2 Jun
3:52.21	Jamel	Aarass	FRA	15.11.81	1	MSR	Walnut	20 Apr
3:52.44	Silas	Kiplagat	KEN	20.8.89	1	LGP	London (CP)	14 Jul
	(20/15)							
3:52.77	Ross	Murray	GBR	8.10.90	2	LGP	London (CP)	14 Jul
3:53.02	Aman	Wote	ETH	18.4.84	9	Bisl	Oslo	7 Jun
3:53.04	Daniel Kipchirchir	Komen	KEN	27.11.84	11	Pre	Eugene	2 Jun
3:53.07	Leonel	Manzano	USA	12.9.84	12	Pre	Eugene	2 Jun
3:53.62	Ryan	Gregson	AUS	26.4.90	10	Bisl	Oslo	7 Jun
	(20)							
3:54.17	Bernard	Lagat	USA	12.12.74	6	LGP	London (CP)	14 Jul
3:54.28	Henrik	Ingebrigtsen	NOR	24.2.91	7	LGP	London (CP)	14 Jul
3:54.29	Taylor	Milne	CAN	14.6.81	2	MSR	Walnut	20 Apr
3:54.48	Russell	Brown	USA	3.3.85	2	Pre	Eugene	1 Jun
3:54.81	Nathan	Brannen	CAN	8.9.82	3	MSR	Walnut	20 Apr

Mark	Name		Nat	Born	Date
3:55.14	Lopez	Lomong	USA	1.1.85	2 Jun
3:55.51	Jeff	See	USA	6.6.86	1 Jun
3:55.62	Dorian	Ulrey	USA	11.7.87	1 Jun
3:55.86	Jeff	Riseley	AUS	11.11.86	14 Jul
3:56.07	Jordan	McNamara	USA	7.3.87	11 Aug
3:56.13	Zane	Robertson	NZL	14.11.89	20 Apr
3:56.21	Garrett	Heath	USA	3.11.85	11 Aug
3:56.39	Will	Leer	USA	15.4.85	25 Jul
3:56.41	Craig	Miller	USA	3.8.87	20 Apr
3:56.50	Tesfaye	Cheru	ETH-J	2.3.93	1 Jun
3:56.56	James	Brewer	GBR	18.6.88	18 Aug
3:56.77	Andrew	Wheating	USA	21.11.87	2 Jun
3:56.78	Ryan	Hill	USA	31.1.90	25 Jul
3:56.90	Peter	van der Westhuizen	RSA	21.12.84	21 Apr
3:57.02	Ciarán	O'Lionáird	IRL	11.4.88	25 Jul
3:57.08	Andrew AJ	Acosta	USA	13.4.88	21 Apr
3:57.44	Matthew	Centrowitz	USA	18.10.89	1 Jun
3:57.48	Dawit	Wolde	ETH	19.5.91	1 Jun

Indoors

Mark	Name		Nat	Born	Pos	Meet	Venue	Date
3:53.92	Matthew	Centrowitz	USA	18.10.89	1	Mill	New York (Arm)	11 Feb
3:54.08	Russell	Brown	USA	3.3.85	4		Fayetteville	11 Feb
3:54.54	Miles	Batty	USA	1.6.87	2	Mill	New York (Arm)	11 Feb
3:54.76	Ciarán	O'Lionáird	IRL	11.4.88	6		Fayetteville	11 Feb

Mark	Name		Nat	Born	Date
3:55.09	Lawi	Lalang	KEN	15.6.91	28 Jan
3:55.24	Garrett	Heath	USA	3.11.85	11 Feb
3:55.47	Jeff	See	USA	6.6.86	11 Feb
3:55.75	David	McCarthy	IRL	3.8.88	28 Jan
3:55.84	Silas	Kisorio	KEN	8.1.83	11 Feb
3:56.37	Erik	van Ingen	USA	25.8.89	11 Feb
3:56.63	Chris	O'Hare	GBR	23.11.90	11 Feb
3:56.85	Cory	Leslie	USA	24.10.89	28 Jan
3:57.10	Galen	Rupp	USA	8.5.86	4 Feb
3:57.16	Cameron	Levins	CAN	28.3.89	11 Feb
3:57.22	Andrew	Baddeley	GBR	20.6.82	21 Jan

JUNIORS

Mark	Name		Nat	Born	Pos	Meet	Venue	Date
3:50.90	Hamza	Driouch	QAT	16.11.94	8	Bisl	Oslo	7 Jun
3:56.50	Tesfaye	Cheru	ETH	2.3.93	7	Pre	Eugene	1 Jun

Mark	Name		Nat	Born	Pos	Meet	Venue	Date
3:57.90	Charlie	Grice	GBR-J	7.11.93	10	LGP	London (CP)	14 Jul

2000 METRES

Mark	Name		Nat	Born	Pos	Meet	Venue	Date
5:00.30+	Collins	Cheboi	KEN	25.9.87	1	DNG	Stockholm	17 Aug

3000 METRES

Mark	Name		Nat	Born	Pos	Meet	Venue	Date
7:30.42	Augustine	Choge	KEN	21.1.87	1	DL	Doha	11 May
7:30.43	Isiah	Koech	KEN-J	19.12.93	1	DNG	Stockholm	17 Aug
7:30.99	Caleb	Ndiku	KEN	9.10.92	2	DNG	Stockholm	17 Aug
7:31.40	Eliud	Kipchoge	KEN	5.11.84	2	DL	Doha	11 May
7:31.88	Moses	Kipsiro	UGA	2.9.86	3	DL	Doha	11 May
7:32.43		I Koech			4	DL	Doha	11 May
7:33.68	Thomas	Longosiwa	KEN	14.1.82	5	DL	Doha	11 May
7:34.03	John	Kipkoech	KEN	29.12.91	3	DNG	Stockholm	17 Aug
7:34.75	Edwin	Soi	KEN	3.3.86	4	DNG	Stockholm	17 Aug
7:35.04	Vincent	Chepkok	KEN	5.7.88	5	DNG	Stockholm	17 Aug
7:35.16	Evan	Jager	USA	8.3.89	6	DNG	Stockholm	17 Aug
7:35.41		Ndiku			1	Gyulai	Budapest	20 Aug
7:35.43	Arne	Gabius	GER	22.3.81	7	DNG	Stockholm	17 Aug
7:35.45	Collis	Birmingham	AUS	27.12.84	8	DNG	Stockholm	17 Aug
(14/12)								
7:39.73	Cornelius	Kangogo	KEN-J	31.12.93	2	GS	Ostrava	25 May
7:39.86	Andrew	Baddeley	GBR	20.6.82	3	GS	Ostrava	25 May
7:40.00	Kenenisa	Bekele	ETH	13.6.82	7	DL	Doha	11 May
7:40.37	Japheth	Korir	KEN-J	30.6.93	4	GS	Ostrava	25 May
7:40.85	Abera	Kuma	ETH	31.8.90	8	DL	Doha	11 May
7:41.02	Tigabu	Gebremariam	ETH	.90	5	GS	Ostrava	25 May
7:41.38	Elroy	Gelant	RSA	25.8.86	6	GS	Ostrava	25 May
7:41.74	Daniele	Meucci	ITA	8.4.85	10	DNG	Stockholm	17 Aug
(20)								
7:42.22	Ayanleh	Souleiman	DJI	3.12.92	9	DL	Doha	11 May
7:42.31	Polat Kemboi	Arikan	TUR	12.12.90	10	DL	Doha	11 May
7:42.52	Joseph	Kiplimo	KEN	20.7.88	7	GS	Ostrava	25 May
7:43.50	Albert	Rop	KEN-J	20.12.94	4	Gyulai	Budapest	20 Aug
7:43.53+	Gideon	Gathimba	KEN	9.3.80	1	DL	Saint-Denis	6 Jul
7:43.65	Bobby	Curtis	USA	28.11.84	2		Rieti	9 Sep
7:44.07	Josephat	Menjo	KEN	20.8.79	1		Lappeenranta	18 Jul
7:44.09	Conseslus	Kipruto	KEN-J	8.12.94	3		Rieti	9 Sep
7:44.23	Jamal	Hitrane	MAR	1.9.89	4		Rieti	9 Sep
7:44.24	Ezekiel	Kemboi	KEN	25.5.82	5		Rieti	9 Sep
(30)								
7:44.40	Ben	True	USA	29.12.85	1		Dublin	25 Jul
7:44.61	James	Kangogo	KEN	22.11.85	1		Rehlingen	28 May
7:44.71	Andrew	Bumbalough	USA	14.3.87	11	DNG	Stockholm	17 Aug
7:44.80	Daniel Kipchirchir	Komen	KEN	27.11.84	5	Gyulai	Budapest	20 Aug
7:45.08	Elliott	Heath	USA	4.2.89	6		Rieti	9 Sep
7:45.92	Hayle	Ibrahimov	AZE	18.1.90	8	GS	Ostrava	25 May

Mark	Name		Nat	Born	Date		Mark	Name		Nat	Born	Date
7:47.00	Vincent	Mutai	KEN-J	3.11.94	13 May		7:51.17	Ben	Kipkurui	KEN	18.12.80	13 May
7:47.80	David	Torrence	USA	26.11.85	17 Aug		7:51.34	Garrett	Heath	USA	3.11.85	21 Jul
7:48.30	Mateusz	Demczyszak	POL	18.1.86	25 May		7:51.36	James	Kwalia Kurui	QAT	12.6.84	11 May
7:49.28+	Kenneth	Kipkemoi	KEN	2.8.84	2 Jun		7:51.37	Simon	Denissel	FRA	22.5.90	2 Jun
7:49.48	Lucas	Rotich	KEN	16.4.90	11 May		7:51.70	Juan Luis	Barrios	MEX	24.6.83	17 Aug
7:49.48	Abrar	Osman	ERI-J	1.1.94	25 May		7:51.90	Elkana	Yego	KEN-J	7.12.94	6 May
7:50.50	Abiyot	Abinet	ETH	10.5.89	10 Jul		7:51.90	Tsegat	Tuemay	ETH-Y	20.12.95	2 Jun
7:50.60	Faisa Dame	Tasama	ETH	12.10.87	18 Aug		7:52.02	Geofrey	Barusei	KEN-J	.94	10 Jul
							7:52.03	Fikadu	Haftu	ETH-J	21.2.94	25 May

Indoors

Mark	Name		Nat	Born	Pos	Venue	Date
7:29.94	Augustine	Choge	KEN	21.1.87	1	Karlsruhe	12 Feb
7:29.94	Edwin	Soi	KEN	3.3.86	2	Karlsruhe	12 Feb
7:31.23	Yenew	Alamirew	ETH	27.5.90	3	Karlsruhe	12 Feb
7:32.03		Kipchoge			4	Karlsruhe	12 Feb
7:32.56		Soi			1	Liévin	14 Feb
7:32.89		I Koech			2	Liévin	14 Feb
7:33.30		Alamirew			3	Liévin	14 Feb
7:33.55		I Koech			1	Stockholm	23 Feb
7:34.14	Dejen	Gebremeskel	ETH	24.11.89	2	Stockholm	23 Feb
7:34.74		Choge			3	Stockholm	23 Feb
7:34.81		Longosiwa			4	Liévin	14 Feb
7:35.42		Ndiku			4	Stockholm	23 Feb
7:37.0+	Tariku	Bekele	ETH	21.1.87	1	Birmingham	18 Feb
7:37.4+	Mo	Farah	GBR	23.3.83	3	Birmingham	18 Feb

Mark	Name		Nat	Born	Pos	Meet	Venue	Date
7:39.07	Brimin	Kipruto	KEN	31.7.85	5		Liévin	14 Feb
7:39.09	Abera	Kuma	ETH	31.8.90	7		Stockholm	23 Feb
7:39.70	Gideon	Gathimba	KEN	9.3.80	8		Stockholm	23 Feb
7:39.78	Yitayal	Atnafu	ETH-J	20.1.93	6		Karlsruhe	12 Feb
7:41.02	Silas	Kiplagat	KEN	20.8.89	3		Boston (R)	4 Feb
7:41.44	Bernard	Lagat	USA	12.12.74	1	WI	Istanbul	11 Mar
7:41.48	Hayle	Ibrahimov	AZE	18.1.90	8		Karlsruhe	12 Feb
7:43.08	Ryan	Hill	USA	31.1.90	1		Seattle	11 Feb
7:43.35	Abiyot	Abinet	ETH	10.5.89	9		Stockholm	23 Feb
7:43.88	Bilisuma	Shugi	BRN	19.7.89	1	AsiC	Hangzhou	19 Feb
7:44.08	Hagos	Gebrhiwet	ETH-J	11.5.94	4		Boston (R)	4 Feb
7:44.16	Lopez	Lomong	USA	1.1.85	6	WI	Istanbul	11 Mar
7:44.26	Yoann	Kowal	FRA	28.5.87	7		Liévin	14 Feb
7:44.45	Andrew	Bumbalough	USA	14.3.87	1		Seattle	3 Mar
7:44.46	Yohan	Durand	FRA	14.5.85	2		Bordeaux	28 Jan
7:44.48	Lawi	Lalang	KEN	15.6.91	1		Seattle	25 Feb
7:44.63	Diego	Estrada	USA/MEX	12.12.89	2		Seattle	11 Feb
7:45.75	Cameron	Levins	CAN	28.3.89	5		Boston (R)	4 Feb
7:45.80	Garrett	Heath	USA	3.11.85	6		Boston (R)	4 Feb

Mark	Name		Nat	Born	Date		Mark	Name		Nat	Born	Date
7:46.17	Mohamed	Al-Garni	QAT	1.7.92	19 Feb		7:49.24	Aziz	Lahbabi	MAR	3.2.91	28 Jan
7:46.19	Matthew	Centrowitz	USA	18.10.89	4 Feb		7:49.58	Miles	Batty	USA	1.6.87	28 Jan
7:46.81	Chris	Derrick	USA	17.10.90	10 Mar		7:49.87	Paul	Chelimo	KEN	27.10.90	4 Feb
7:46.89	Mekonnen	Gebremedhin	ETH	11.10.88	23 Feb		7:50.23	Andrew	Bayer	USA	3.2.90	4 Feb
7:46.95	Paul Kipsiele	Koech	KEN	10.11.81	14 Feb		7:50.52	Samuel	Chelanga	KEN	23.2.85	28 Jan
7:47.88	Mourad	Amdouni	FRA	21.1.88	28 Jan		7:50.61	Ilham	Özbilen	TUR	5.3.90	18 Feb
7:48.04	Alemu	Bekele	BRN	23.3.90	19 Feb		7:50.86	Kevin	Chelimo	KEN	14.2.83	28 Jan
7:48.23	Craig	Mottram	AUS	18.6.80	11 Mar		7:51.55	Trevor	Dunbar	USA	29.4.91	25 Feb
7:48.62	Florian	Carvalho	FRA	9.3.89	14 Feb		7:51.59	Stephen	Sambu	KEN	7.7.88	28 Jan
7:48.96	Benson	Seurei	KEN	27.3.88	2 Feb		7:51.75	Mitch	Goose	GBR	16.3.89	11 Feb
7:48.96	Dawit	Wolde	ETH	19.5.91	14 Feb		7:51.76	Teshome	Diressa	ETH-J	25.4.94	23 Feb
7:49.11	Ross	Millington	GBR	19.9.89	11 Feb		7:51.83	Leonard	Korir	KEN	10.12.86	17 Feb
7:49.14	Chris	Thompson	GBR	17.4.81	28 Jan		7:52.02	Ben	Hubers	CAN	22.12.88	11 Feb

JUNIORS

See main list for top 5 juniors (and 2 indoors). Additional marks and further juniors:

Mark	Name		Nat	Born	Pos	Meet	Venue	Date
I Koech 4+	7:37.14				1	GS	Ostrava	25 May
12 performances (2 indoors) by 6 to 7:48.00.								
Korir	7:46.15				1		Montgeron	13 May
7:47.31					2		Rehlingen	28 May
7:47.00	Vincent	Mutai	KEN	3.11.94	2		Montgeron	13 May
7:49.48	Abrar	Osman	ERI	1.1.94	11	GS	Ostrava	25 May
7:51.76i	Teshome	Diressa	ETH	25.4.94	11		Stockholm	23 Feb
7:51.90	Elkana	Yego	KEN	7.12.94	1		Pliezhausen	6 May
7:51.90	Tsegat	Tuemay	ETH-Y	20.12.95	2		Oordegem	2 Jun
7:52.02	Geofrey	Barusei	KEN	.94	5		Sotteville-lès-Rouen	10 Jul
7:52.03	Fikadu	Haftu	ETH	21.2.94	12	GS	Ostrava	25 May
7:54.45	Weynay	Gebrselassie	ERI	24.3.94	3		Oordegem	2 Jun
7:54.76i	Tesfaye	Cheru	ETH-J	2.3.93	6		Bordeaux	28 Jan

2 MILES INDOORS

Mark	Name		Nat	Born	Pos	Meet	Venue	Date
8:07.39	Eliud	Kipchoge	KEN	5.11.84	1	GP	Birmingham	18 Feb
8:08.08	Mo	Farah	GBR	23.3.83	2	GP	Birmingham	18 Feb
8:08.16	Moses	Kipsiro	UGA	2.9.86	3	GP	Birmingham	18 Feb
8:08.27	Tariku	Bekele	ETH	21.1.87	4	GP	Birmingham	18 Feb
8:09.72	Galen	Rupp	USA	8.5.86	5	GP	Birmingham	18 Feb
8:10.78	Arne	Gabius	GER	22.3.81	6	GP	Birmingham	18 Feb

5000 METRES

Mark	Name		Nat	Born	Pos	Meet	Venue	Date
12:46.81	Dejen	Gebremeskel	ETH	24.11.89	1	DL	Saint-Denis	6 Jul
12:47.53	Hagos	Gebrhiwet	ETH-J	11.5.94	2	DL	Saint-Denis	6 Jul
12:48.64	Isiah	Koech	KEN-J	19.12.93	3	DL	Saint-Denis	6 Jul
12:48.77	Yenew	Alamirew	ETH	27.5.90	4	DL	Saint-Denis	6 Jul
12:49.04	Thomas	Longosiwa	KEN	14.1.82	5	DL	Saint-Denis	6 Jul
12:49.50	John	Kipkoech	KEN	29.12.91	6	DL	Saint-Denis	6 Jul
12:54.13	Tariku	Bekele	ETH	21.1.87	7	DL	Saint-Denis	6 Jul
12:55.34	Eliud	Kipchoge	KEN	5.11.84	8	DL	Saint-Denis	6 Jul
12:55.79	Kenenisa	Bekele	ETH	13.6.82	9	DL	Saint-Denis	6 Jul
12:55.99	Edwin	Soi (10)	KEN	3.3.86	10	DL	Saint-Denis	6 Jul
12:56.98	Mo	Farah	GBR	23.3.83	1	Pre	Eugene	2 Jun
12:57.63		I Koech			2	Pre	Eugene	2 Jun
12:58.90	Galen	Rupp	USA	8.5.86	3	Pre	Eugene	2 Jun
12:58.92		Gebremeskel			1	Bisl	Oslo	7 Jun
12:58.98		I Koech			1	WK	Zürich	30 Aug
12:58.99		Gebrhiwet			2	Bisl	Oslo	7 Jun

Mark	Name		Nat	Born	Pos	Meet	Venue	Date	
12:59.21	Moses	Masai	KEN	1.6.86	11	DL	Saint-Denis	6	Jul
12:59.24		Longosiwa			2	WK	Zürich	30	Aug
12:59.28	Vincent	Chepkok	KEN	5.7.88	1		Rabat	27	May
12:59.77	Imane	Merga	ETH	15.10.88	3	Bisl	Oslo	7	Jun
12:59.92	Bernard	Lagat	USA	12.12.74	3	WK	Zürich	30	Aug
13:00.41		T Bekele			4	Bisl	Oslo	7	Jun
13:00.54		K Bekele			5	Bisl	Oslo	7	Jun
13:00.68	Moses	Kipsiro	UGA	2.9.86	6	Bisl	Oslo	7	Jun
13:00.83		Gebremeskel			4	WK	Zürich	30	Aug
13:01.39	Sileshi	Sihine	ETH	29.1.83	7	Bisl	Oslo	7	Jun
13:01.48		K Bekele			4	Pre	Eugene	2	Jun
13:01.91	Albert	Rop	KEN-J	20.12.94	1rA	NA	Heusden-Zolder	7	Jul
13:02.11		Kipkoech			5	WK	Zürich	30	Aug
13:02.62		T Bekele			6	WK	Zürich	30	Aug
13:02.69	Moukhled	Al Outaibi	KSA	20.6.76	2rA	NA	Heusden-Zolder	7	Jul
	(31/20)								
13:02.94	Jacob	Chesari	KEN	6.4.84	2		Rabat	27	May
13:03.30	Yigrem	Demelash	ETH-J	28.1.94	8	Bisl	Oslo	7	Jun
13:03.37	Kenneth	Kipkemoi	KEN	2.8.84	3rA	NA	Heusden-Zolder	7	Jul
13:04.06	Aziz	Lahbabi	MAR	3.2.91	4		Rabat	27	May
13:04.34	Muktar	Edris	ETH-J	14.1.94	12	DL	Saint-Denis	6	Jul
13:06.23	Mark	Kiptoo	KEN	21.6.76	13	DL	Saint-Denis	6	Jul
13:08.13	Yitayal	Atnafu	ETH-J	20.1.93	10	Bisl	Oslo	7	Jun
13:08.35	Emmanuel	Bett	KEN	30.3.83	11	Bisl	Oslo	7	Jun
13:08.59	Alex	Oleitiptip	KEN	22.9.82	1		Huelva	7	Jun
13:09.17	Abdelati	Iguider	MAR	25.3.87	2		Villeneuve d'Ascq	9	Jun
	(30)								
13:09.32	Abera	Kuma	ETH	31.8.90	12	Bisl	Oslo	7	Jun
13:09.57	Collis	Birmingham	AUS	27.12.84	2	LGP	London (CP)	13	Jul
13:09.58	Lucas	Rotich	KEN	16.4.90	13	Bisl	Oslo	7	Jun
13:09.67	Samuel	Chelanga	KEN	23.2.85	8	Pre	Eugene	2	Jun
13:09.84	David	Bett	KEN	18.10.92	5		Rabat	27	May
13:09.90	Daniel Kipchirchir	Komen	KEN	27.11.84	5rA	NA	Heusden-Zolder	7	Jul
13:10.55	Josephat Kiprono	Menjo	KEN	20.8.79	2		Huelva	7	Jun
13:10.68	Hassan	Hirt	FRA	16.1.80	14	DL	Saint-Denis	6	Jul
13:11.34	Hayle	Ibrahimov	AZE	18.1.90	1		Rovereto	4	Sep
13:11.61	Abdullah Abdulaziz	Al-Joud	KSA	10.7.75	7		Rabat	27	May
	(40)								
13:11.63	Lopez	Lomong	USA	1.1.85	1	Jordan	Stanford	29	Apr
13:12.15	Abdennacer	Fathi	MAR	20.5.87	8		Rabat	27	May
13:12.67	Victor	Chumo	KEN	19.3.87	9		Rabat	27	May
13:13.43	Arne	Gabius	GER	22.3.81	14	Bisl	Oslo	7	Jun
13:13.54	Juan Luis	Barrios	MEX	24.6.83	2		Los Angeles (ER)	18	May
13:14.57	Kevin	Chelimo	KEN	14.2.83	2	Jordan	Stanford	29	Apr
13:14.72	Dathan	Ritzenhein	USA	30.12.82	4		Los Angeles (ER)	18	May
13:15.00	Matt	Tegenkamp	USA	19.1.82	3	Jordan	Stanford	29	Apr
13:15.21	Chris	Thompson	GBR	17.4.81	4	Jordan	Stanford	29	Apr
13:15.31	Thomas	Farrell	GBR	23.3.91	5	Jordan	Stanford	29	Apr
	(50)								
13:15.50	Augustine	Choge	KEN	21.1.87	7	DL	Shanghai	19	May
13:16.08	Craig	Mottram	AUS	18.6.80	6rA	NA	Heusden-Zolder	7	Jul
13:16.21	Sammy Alex	Mutahi	KEN	1.6.89	8	DL	Shanghai	19	May
13:16.26	Andrew	Bumbalough	USA	14.3.87	6	Jordan	Stanford	29	Apr
13:16.53	David	Torrence	USA	26.11.85	7	Jordan	Stanford	29	Apr
13:17.03	Hussein Jamaan	Al-Hamdah	KSA	4.8.83	10		Rabat	27	May
13:17.25	Teklemariam	Medhin	ERI	24.6.89	15	Bisl	Oslo	7	Jun
13:17.32	Abrar	Osman	ERI-J	.94	9	DL	Shanghai	19	May
13:17.41	Mosinet	Geremew	ETH	12.2.92	10	DL	Shanghai	19	May
13:17.66	Othmane	El Goumri	MAR	28.5.92	11		Rabat	27	May
	(60)								
13:17.90	Yohan	Durand	FRA	14.5.85	4		Villeneuve d'Ascq	9	Jun
13:18.29	Cameron	Levins	CAN	28.3.89	8h2	OG	London (OS)	8	Aug
13:18.54	Vincent	Yator	KEN	11.7.89	11	DL	Shanghai	19	May
13:18.60	David	McNeill	AUS	6.10.86	7rA	NA	Heusden-Zolder	7	Jul
13:18.81	Nick	McCormick	GBR	11.9.81	3		Huelva	7	Jun
13:18.88	Lawi	Lalang	KEN	15.6.91	2	MSR	Walnut	20	Apr
13:19.00	Daniele	Meucci	ITA	8.4.85	8rA	NA	Heusden-Zolder	7	Jul
13:19.18	Paul	Tanui	KEN	22.12.90	1		Fukuroi	3	May
13:19.59	Soufiyan	Bouqantar	MAR-J	30.8.93	12		Rabat	27	May
13:20.25	Aaron	Braun	USA	28.5.87	2		Portland	9	Jun
	(70)								

Mark	Name		Nat	Born	Pos	Meet	Venue	Date	
13:20.43	Dejene	Regassa	BRN	18.4.89	1		Ninove	21	Jul
13:20.53	Ben	True	USA	29.12.85	2		Ninove	21	Jul
13:20.88	Japheth	Korir	KEN-J	30.6.93	1		Carquefou	1	Jun
13:20.94	Bilisuma	Shugi	BRN	19.7.89	10rA	NA	Heusden-Zolder	7	Jul
13:20.99	Rabah	Aboud	ALG	.81	11rA	NA	Heusden-Zolder	7	Jul
13:21.01	Tilahun	Regassa	ETH	18.1.90	8		Villeneuve d'Ascq	9	Jun
13:21.02	Bidan	Karoki	KEN	21.8.90	1		Fukuoka	22	Sep
13:21.12	Sergio	Sánchez	ESP	1.10.82	12rA	NA	Heusden-Zolder	7	Jul
13:21.21	Mumin	Gala	SOM	6.9.86	10h2	OG	London (OS)	8	Aug
13:21.22	Patrick	Mutunga	KEN-J	20.11.94	2		Fukuroi	3	May
	(80)								
13:21.27	Daniel	Salel	KEN	11.12.90	14	DL	Shanghai	19	May
13:21.38	Chakir	Boujattaoui	MAR	16.1.83	13		Rabat	27	May
13:21.54	Alemu	Bekele	BRN	23.3.90	3		Ninove	21	Jul
13:21.55A	Mike	Kigen	KEN	15.1.86	6	OT	Nairobi	23	Jun
13:21.57	Abraham	Kiplimo	UGA	14.4.89	4		Huelva	7	Jun
13:21.66	Nassir	Dawud	ERI	.91	2		Carquefou	1	Jun
13:21.89	Paul	Chelimo	KEN	27.10.90	8	Jordan	Stanford	29	Apr
13:22.63	Jamal	Hitrane	MAR	1.9.89	14		Rabat	27	May
13:22.89	Jonathan	Maiyo	KEN	5.5.88	2	AfrC	Porto Novo	1	Jul
13:22.90	Ezekiel	Meli	KEN	21.4.84	1	Nebiolo	Torino	8	Jun
	(90)								
13:22.91	Lelisa	Desisa	ETH	14.1.90	9		Villeneuve d'Ascq	9	Jun
13:22.92	Goltom	Kifle	ERI-J	3.12.93	14		Rabat	27	May
13:23.09	Mohammed	Moustaoui	MAR	2.4.85	13rA	NA	Heusden-Zolder	7	Jul
13:23.20	Andrew	Vernon	GBR	7.1.86	4	MSR	Walnut	20	Apr
13:23.25	Thomas	Ayeko	UGA	10.2.92	2	Nebiolo	Torino	8	Jun
13:23.40	Charles	Ndirangu	KEN-J	8.2.93	2		Fukuoka	22	Sep
13:23.41	John	Thuo	KEN	27.11.85	3		Fukuroi	3	May
13:23.50	Mykola	Labovskyy	UKR	4.5.83	1	NC	Yalta	14	Jun
13:23.52	Aron	Rono	KEN	1.11.82	5	MSR	Walnut	20	Apr
13:23.58	Stefano	La Rosa	ITA	22.9.85	6	MSR	Walnut	20	Apr
	(100)								

Mark	Name		Nat	Born	Date	
13:23.72	Bayron	Piedra	ECU	19.8.82	21	Jul
13:23.73	Adrian	Blincoe	NZL	4.11.79	18	May
13:23.88	Moses	Kibet	UGA	23.3.91	7	Jun
13:24.22	Clement	Langat	KEN	18.12.91	15	Apr
13:24.30	Ben	St. Lawrence	AUS	7.11.81	4	Feb
13:24.42	Abdelghani	Bensaadi	ALG	31.7.87	9	Jun
13:24.50	Gladwin	Mzazi	RSA	28.8.88	20	Mar
13:24.67	Timothy	Kiptoo	KEN	2.8.84	1	Jul
13:25.54	Daisuke	Shimizu	JPN	2.8.82	7	Jul
13:25.75	Amanuel	Mesel	ERI	29.12.90	1	Jun
13:25.82	William	Malel Sitonik	KEN-J	1.3.94	20	May
13:25.98	Elroy	Gelant	RSA	25.8.86	20	Mar
13:26.01	Sergiy	Lebid	UKR	15.7.75	9	Jun
13:26.09	Tonny	Wamulwa	ZAM	6.8.89	8	Jun
13:26.34	Ryan	Hill	USA	31.1.90	21	Jul
13:26.65	Joseph	Kiplimo	KEN	20.7.88	8	Jun
13:26.66	Jake	Robertson	NZL	14.11.89	7	Jul
13:26.84	Leonard	Barsoton	KEN-J	21.10.94	23	Sep
13:26.88	Nicholas	Chepseba	KEN-J	12.10.94	7	Jul
13:26.94	Brian	Olinger	USA	2.6.83	20	Apr
13:27.06	Martin	Mathathi	KEN	25.12.85	3	May
13:27.07	Garrett	Heath	USA	3.11.85	29	Apr
13:27.15	Maksym	Obrubanskyy	ITA	21.6.88	8	Jun
13:27.21	Polat Kemboi	Arikan	TUR	12.12.90	8	Aug
13:27.40	Kidane	Tadese	ERI	31.8.87	7	Jul
13:27.41	Zeray	Kibrom	ERI	12.1.86	1	Jun
13:27.61	Edward	Waweru	KEN	3.10.90	23	Jun
13:27.70	Rory	Fraser	GBR	25.4.87	20	Apr
13:28.20	Elliott	Heath	USA	4.2.89	28	Jun
13:28.40	Scott	Bauhs	USA	11.5.86	18	May
13:28.61	Kennedy	Kithuka	KEN	4.6.89	20	Apr
13:28.70	Kensuke	Takezawa	JPN	11.10.86	7	Apr
13:28.79	Yuki	Sato	JPN	26.11.86	5	Jul
13:28.8 A	Geoffrey	Kipsang	KEN	28.11.92	14	Jun
13:28.97	Daniel	Gitau	KEN	1.10.87	7	Apr
13:29.02	Jesper	van der Wielen	NED	2.8.91	26	May
13:29.08	Stephen	Mokoka	RSA	31.1.85	3	Mar
13:29.09	Bashir	Abdi	BEL	10.2.89	26	May
13:29.26	Brandon	Bethke	USA	19.1.87	18	May
13:29.36	Tsegay	Tuemay	ERI-Y	20.12.95	26	May
13:29.50	Tsuyoshi	Ugachi	JPN	27.4.87	7	Apr
13:29.56	Nick	Willis	NZL	25.4.83	29	Apr
13:29.62	Robert	Cheseret	USA	8.10.83	20	Apr
13:29.83	Dennis	Licht	NED	30.5.84	26	May
13:30.07	Paul	Kuira	KEN	25.1.90	7	Apr
13:30.21	Hassan	Mead	USA	28.8.89	28	Jun
13:30.30	Andrey	Safronov	RUS	16.12.85	4	Jul
13:30.33	Bolota	Asmerom	USA	12.10.78	18	May
13:30.43	Anatoliy	Rybakov	RUS	27.2.85	13	Jun
13:30.69	Nicholas	Togom	KEN	25.11.86	8	Jun
13:30.70	Ian	Dobson	USA	6.2.82	18	May
13:30.89	Illias	Fifa	MAR	16.5.89	7	Jun
13:31.20	Manuel Ángel	Penas	ESP	9.11.77	7	Jun
13:31.24	Philipp	Pflieger	GER	16.7.87	26	May
13:31.36	Yevgeniy	Rybakov	RUS	27.2.85	13	Jun
13:31.51	Stephen	Sambu	KEN	7.7.88	6	Apr
13:31.52	Leul	Gebrselassie	ETH-J	20.9.93	15	Apr
13:31.63	James Kwalia	Chepkurui	QAT	12.6.84	7	Jun
13:31.85	Brent	Vaughn	USA	4.12.84	6	Apr
13:32.01	Gideon	Ngatuny	KEN	10.10.86	27	Jun
13:32.15	Kyle	Alcorn	USA	18.3.85	6	Apr
13:32.55	Philimon	Maritim	KEN		4	Sep
13:32.61	Benjamin	Gando	KEN	21.5.90	15	Apr
13:32.71	Joílson	da Silva	BRA	29.8.87	26	May
13:32.76	Alistair	Cragg	IRL	13.6.80	6	Apr
13:32.82	Jake	Riley	USA	11.2.88	18	May
13:32.99	Mohamed	Trafeh	USA	1.5.85	16	Jun
13:33.09	Soufiane	Bouchikhi	BEL	22.3.90	7	Jul
13:33.19	Tony	Okello	UGA	26.12.83	18	May
13:33.2+e	Gebre-egziabher	Gebremariam	ETH	10.9.84	27	May
13:33.25	Andrew	Bayer	USA	3.2.90	6	Apr
13:33.34	Takuya	Fukatsu	JPN	10.11.87	7	Apr
13:33.47	Adil	Bouafif	SWE	31.12.78	14	Jun
13:33.58	Jonathan	Ndiku	KEN	18.9.91	20	May
13:33.6+e	Haile	Gebrselassie	ETH	18.4.73	27	May
13:33.62	Daniel	Kitonyi	KEN-Y	12.1.94	15	Apr
13:33.64	Haron	Lagat	KEN	15.8.83	20	Apr
13:33.84	Suguru	Osako	JPN	23.5.91	7	Jul
13:33.96	Tolossa	Gedefa	ETH	.92	1	Jul
13:34.10	Agato	Yashin Hasen	ETH	19.1.86	23	Jun
13:34.34	Yosef	Ghebray	USA	18.5.87	6	Apr
13:34.41	Mitch	Goose	GBR	16.3.89	29	Apr
13:34.48	Francisco Javie	Alves	ESP	3.9.80	7	Jun
13:34.49	Dan	Lowry	USA	30.10.89	6	Apr

Mark	Name		Nat	Born	Pos	Meet	Venue	Date
13:34.58	Harry	Summers	AUS	19.5.90				4 Feb
13:34.64	Jordan	McNamara	USA	7.3.87				29 Apr
13:34.72	Sindre	Buraas	NOR	8.5.89				29 Apr
13:34.83	Girma	Mecheso	USA	16.1.88				6 Apr
13:34.91	Anis	Selmouni	MAR	15.3.79				12 May
13:35.27	George	Alex	USA	20.1.90				6 Apr
13:35.33	Monder	Rizki	BEL	16.8.79				16 Jun
13:35.33	Yegor	Nikolayev	RUS	12.2.88				27 May
13:35.38	Zewdie	Million	ETH	24.1.89				23 Jun
13:35.5A	Josphat	Bett	KEN	12.6.90				18 May
13:35.54	Charles	Ndungu	KEN-Y	20.2.96				27 Jun
13:35.76	Stepan	Kiselev	RUS	3.11.86				13 Jun
13:36.09	Jeremiah	Thuku	KEN-J	7.7.94				23 Jun
13:36.15	Will	Leer	USA	15.4.85				3 Mar
13:36.2 A	Johnstone	Chepkwony	KEN	5.5.84				12 May
13:36.62	Brenton	Rowe (200)	AUT	17.8.87				26 May

Indoors

Mark	Name		Nat	Born	Pos	Meet	Venue	Date
12:58.67		Longosiwa			1		Düsseldorf	10 Feb
13:02.36		I Koech			2		Düsseldorf	10 Feb
13:02.69	Paul Kipsiele	Koech	KEN	10.11.81	3		Düsseldorf	10 Feb
13:04.18	Yitayal	Atnafu	ETH-J	20.1.93	4		Düsseldorf	10 Feb
13:08.28	Lawi	Lalang	KEN	15.6.91	2	Mill	New York (Arm)	11 Feb
13:11.44	Japheth	Korir	KEN-J	30.6.93	6		Düsseldorf	10 Feb
13:12.55	Polat Kemboi	Arikan	TUR	12.12.90	7		Düsseldorf	10 Feb
13:13.74	Stephen	Sambu	KEN	7.7.88	3	Mill	New York (Arm)	11 Feb
13:19.54	Leonard	Korir	KEN	10.12.86	4	Mill	New York (Arm)	11 Feb
13:19.58	Chris	Derrick	USA	17.10.90	5	Mill	New York (Arm)	11 Feb
13:22.44	Andrew	Baddeley	GBR	20.6.82	6	Mill	New York (Arm)	11 Feb
13:32.20	Josphat	Bett	KEN	12.6.90	8		Düsseldorf	10 Feb

Drugs disqualification

Mark	Name		Nat	Born	Pos	Meet	Venue	Date
13:22.46	Mohammed	El Hachimi ¶	MAR	5.9.80	3		Carquefou	1 Jun

JUNIORS

See main list for top 12 juniors (2 indoors). 17 + 4 indoor perfs by 9 men to 13:20.0. Additional marks & further juniors:

	Mark		Pos	Meet	Venue		Date				
Gebrhiwet 2+	13:11.00	1		DL	Shanghai		18 May				
I Koech 4+	13:09.80A	1		OT	Nairobi		23 Jun				
Rop	13:12.47	10		Pre	Eugene		2 Jun	13:10.96i	5	Düsseldorf	10 Feb
Demelash	13:04.14	7		WK	Zürich		30 Aug				
Edris	13:06.92	1			Villeneuve d'Ascq		9 Jun				
Bouqantar	13:19.93	6			Villeneuve d'Ascq		9 Jun				

Mark	Name		Nat	Born	Pos	Meet	Venue	Date
13:25.82	William	Malel Sitonik	KEN	1.3.94	1		Tokyo	20 May
13:26.84	Leonard	Barsoton	KEN	21.10.94	2		Yokohama	23 Sep
13:26.88	Nicholas	Chepseba	KEN	12.10.94	4rB	NA	Heusden-Zolder	7 Jul
13:29.36	Tsegay	Tuemay	ERI-Y	20.12.95	3		Oordegem	26 May
13:31.52	Leul	Gebrselassie	ETH	20.9.93	2		Yokohama	15 Apr
13:33.62	Daniel	Kitonyi	KEN-Y	12.1.94	4		Yokohama	15 Apr
13:35.54	Charles	Ndungu	KEN-Y	20.2.96	2		Fukagawa	27 Jun
13:36.09	Jeremiah	Thuku (20)	KEN	7.7.94	3		Fukuroi	23 Jun

10,000 METRES

Mark	Name		Nat	Born	Pos	Meet	Venue	Date
26:51.16	Emmanuel	Bett	KEN	30.3.83	1	VD	Bruxelles	7 Sep
26:51.68	Vincent	Chepkok	KEN	5.7.88	2	VD	Bruxelles	7 Sep
26:52.65	Kenneth	Kipkemoi	KEN	2.8.84	3	VD	Bruxelles	7 Sep
26:57.56	Yigrem	Demelash	ETH-J	28.1.94	4	VD	Bruxelles	7 Sep
27:01.58	Leonard Patrick	Komon	KEN	10.1.88	5	VD	Bruxelles	7 Sep
27:01.98	Wilson	Kiprop	KEN	14.4.87	1	OT	Eugene	1 Jun
27:02.25	Moses	Masai	KEN	1.6.86	2	OT	Eugene	1 Jun
27:02.59	Kenenisa	Bekele	ETH	13.6.82	1		Birmingham	22 Jun
27:03.24	Tariku	Bekele	ETH	21.1.87	2		Birmingham	22 Jun
27:03.49	Mike	Kigen (10)	KEN	15.1.86	6	VD	Bruxelles	7 Sep
27:03.58	Gebre-egziabher	Gebremariam	ETH	10.9.84	3		Birmingham	22 Jun
27:03.65	Sileshi	Sihine	ETH	29.1.83	4		Birmingham	22 Jun
27:04.48	Moses	Kipsiro	UGA	2.9.86	5		Birmingham	22 Jun
27:05.50	Bidan	Karoki	KEN	21.8.90	3	OT	Eugene	1 Jun
27:07.90		E Bett			4	OT	Eugene	1 Jun
27:08.44	Geoffrey	Kirui	KEN-J	16.2.93	5	OT	Eugene	1 Jun
27:09.38	Lucas	Rotich	KEN	16.4.90	6	OT	Eugene	1 Jun
27:11.70		T Bekele			1	FBK	Hengelo	27 May
27:11.93	Eliud	Kipchoge	KEN	5.11.84	7	OT	Eugene	1 Jun
27:11.98	Lelisa	Desisa	ETH	14.1.90	2	FBK	Hengelo	27 May
27:12.60		Sihine			3	FBK	Hengelo	27 May
27:13.66		Gebremariam			4	FBK	Hengelo	27 May
27:14.02	Imane	Merga	ETH	15.10.88	7	VD	Bruxelles	7 Sep
27:16.69	Teklemariam	Medhin (20)	ERI	24.6.89	5	FBK	Hengelo	27 May
27:17.03	Isiah	Koech	KEN-J	19.12.93	8	VD	Bruxelles	7 Sep
27:18.17		Desisa			1		Liège (NX)	5 Jul
27:18.22	Mark	Kiptoo	KEN	21.6.76	8	OT	Eugene	1 Jun
27:18.39	Abera	Kuma	ETH	31.8.90	2		Liège (NX)	5 Jul

Mark	Name		Nat	Born	Pos	Meet	Venue	Date
27:18.90	Tilahun	Regassa	ETH	18.1.90	6	FBK	Hengelo	27 May
27:19.70	Jacob	Chesari	KEN	6.4.84	9	VD	Bruxelles	7 Sep
27:19.74		Kipkemoi			1	AfrC	Porto Novo	28 Jun
	(31/25)							
27:20.39	Haile	Gebrselassie	ETH	18.4.73	7	FBK	Hengelo	27 May
27:21.40	Ali Hasan	Mahboob	BRN	31.12.81	1		Wageningen	30 May
27:22.54	Lewis	Mosoti	KEN	.88	3	AfrC	Porto Novo	28 Jun
27:23.04	Micah	Kogo	KEN	3.6.86	9	OT	Eugene	1 Jun
27:25.33	Galen	Rupp	USA	8.5.86	1	OT	Eugene	22 Jun
	(30)							
27:27.56	Paul	Tanui	KEN	22.12.90	11	OT	Eugene	1 Jun
27:27.96	Cameron	Levins	CAN	28.3.89	1rA	Jordan	Stanford	29 Apr
27:28.10	Nguse	Tesfaldet	ERI	10.11.86	2		Wageningen	30 May
27:28.82	Juan Luis	Barrios	MEX	24.6.83	3		Wageningen	30 May
27:29.10	Edward	Waweru	KEN	3.10.90	1		Fukagawa	27 Jun
27:29.82	Samuel	Chelanga	KEN	23.2.85	2rA	Jordan	Stanford	29 Apr
27:30.32	Patrick	Mutunga	KEN-J	20.11.94	2		Fukagawa	27 Jun
27:30.42	Mo	Farah	GBR	23.3.83	1	OG	London (OS)	4 Aug
27:31.38	Chris	Derrick	USA	17.10.90	3rA	Jordan	Stanford	29 Apr
27:31.61	Moukhled	Al Outaibi	KSA	20.6.76	1		Radès	9 Jun
	(40)							
27:32.72	John	Thuo	KEN	27.11.85	3		Fukagawa	27 Jun
27:32.79	Dennis	Masai	KEN	1.12.91	12	OT	Eugene	1 Jun
27:32.86	Daniele	Meucci	ITA	8.4.85	4rA	Jordan	Stanford	29 Apr
27:32.90	Diego	Estrada	USA/MEX	12.12.89	5rA	Jordan	Stanford	29 Apr
27:33.51	Zersenay	Tadese	ERI	8.2.82	6	OG	London (OS)	4 Aug
27:33.94	Matt	Tegenkamp	USA	19.1.82	2	NC/OT	Eugene	22 Jun
27:34.64	Mohammed	Ahmed	CAN	5.1.91	6rA	Jordan	Stanford	29 Apr
27:35.16	Martin	Mathathi	KEN	25.12.85	1		Kobe	21 Apr
27:36.09	Dathan	Ritzenhein	USA	30.12.82	3	NC/OT	Eugene	22 Jun
27:38.81	Polat Kemboi	Arikan	TUR	12.12.90	9	OG	London (OS)	4 Aug
	(50)							
27:39.65	Josphat	Bett	KEN	12.6.90	13	OT	Eugene	1 Jun
27:40.21	Brent	Vaughn	USA	4.12.84	7rA	Jordan	Stanford	29 Apr
27:40.73	Stephen	Mokoka	RSA	31.1.85	1	NC	Port Elizabeth	13 Apr
27:41.17	Ben	True	USA	29.12.85	8rA	Jordan	Stanford	29 Apr
27:41.39	Patrick	Mwaka	KEN	2.11.92	3rA		Fukuoka	21 Sep
27:41.54	Aaron	Braun	USA	28.5.87	5	NC/OT	Eugene	22 Jun
27:41.57	Chihiro	Miyawaki	JPN	28.8.91	4rA		Fukuoka	21 Sep
27:42.91	Daniel	Gitau	KEN	1.10.87	4		Fukagawa	27 Jun
27:43.22	Thomas	Ayeko	UGA	10.2.92	6		Birmingham	22 Jun
27:43.96	Joseph	Chirlee	USA	14.2.80	4		Wageningen	30 May
	(60)							
27:45.93	Daniel	Salel	KEN	11.12.90	12	VD	Bruxelles	7 Sep
27:46.10	Kevin	Chelimo	KEN	14.2.83	14	OT	Eugene	1 Jun
27:49.16	Azmeraw	Bekele	ETH	22.1.86	10	FBK	Hengelo	27 May
27:49.76	Abraham	Kiplimo	UGA	14.4.89	11	FBK	Hengelo	27 May
27:50.50	Daisuke	Shimizu	JPN	2.8.82	3		Kobe	21 Apr
27:50.58	Brian	Olinger	USA	2.6.83	9rA	Jordan	Stanford	29 Apr
27:50.59	Akinobu	Murasawa	JPN	28.3.91	10rA	Jordan	Stanford	29 Apr
27:50.64	Yusuke	Hasegawa	JPN	8.6.88	1		Machida	24 Nov
27:51.07	Ryan	Vail	USA	19.3.86	12rA	Jordan	Stanford	29 Apr
27:51.71	Agato	Yashin Hasen	ETH	19.1.86	1		Toyota	13 Oct
	(70)							
27:52.79	Tsuyoshi	Ugachi	JPN	27.4.87	13rA	Jordan	Stanford	29 Apr
27:53.52	Bobby	Mack	USA	30.12.84	14rA	Jordan	Stanford	29 Apr
27:53.65	Andrew	Vernon	GBR	7.1.86	15rA	Jordan	Stanford	29 Apr
27:54.52	Zewdie	Million	ETH	24.1.89	1		Abashiri	7 Jul
27:54.86	Alex	Mwangi	KEN	14.6.90	2		Machida	24 Nov
27:56.20	Alemu	Bekele	BRN	23.3.90	13	FBK	Hengelo	27 May
27:56.62	Luke	Puskedra	USA	8.2.90	8	NC/OT	Eugene	22 Jun
27:56.67	Micah	Njeru	KEN	5.8.88	2		Abashiri	7 Jul
27:56.67	Robert	Kajuga	RWA	1.1.85	14	OG	London (OS)	4 Aug
27:56.94	Suguru	Osako	JPN	23.5.91	2		Nobeoka	12 May
	(80)							
27:57.07	Yuki	Sato	JPN	26.11.86	16rA	Jordan	Stanford	29 Apr
27:57.07	Lewis	Korir	KEN	11.6.86	1		Keuruu	5 Aug
27:58.02	Charles	Ndirangu	KEN-J	8.2.93	1rB		Kobe	21 Apr
27:58.05	Simon	Bairu	CAN	8.8.83	17rA	Jordan	Stanford	29 Apr
27:58.48	Bobby	Curtis	USA	28.11.84	10	NC/OT	Eugene	22 Jun
27:59.04	Hassan	Mead	USA	28.8.89	11	NC/OT	Eugene	22 Jun

Mark	Name		Nat	Born	Pos	Meet	Venue	Date
27:59.15	Titus	Mbishei	KEN	28.10.90	15	OT	Eugene	1 Jun
27:59.78	Yuki	Matsuoka	JPN	14.1.86	5rA		Fukuoka	21 Sep
28:01.98	Jacob	Wanjuki	KEN	16.1.86	2rB		Kobe	21 Apr
28:02.26	Johnson	Kiumbani	KEN-J	27.1.93	3		Abashiri	7 Jul
(90)								
28:03.16	Tebalu	Zawude	ETH	2.11.87	4	AfrC	Porto Novo	28 Jun
28:03.21	Mulue	Andon	ERI	12.10.91	5		Wageningen	30 May
28:04.22	Ayad	Lamdassem	ESP	11.10.81	2	ECp	Bilbao	3 Jun
28:04.25	Johana	Maina	KEN	24.12.90	6		Fukagawa	27 Jun
28:04.90	Mykola	Labovskyy	UKR	4.5.83	1	NCp	Yalta	27 May
28:06.06	Alemu	Desta	ETH	18.2.92	7rA		Fukuoka	21 Sep
28:06.16	Stephen	Sambu	KEN	7.7.88	1	MSR	Walnut	19 Apr
28:06.28	Takuya	Fukatsu	JPN	10.11.87	8rA		Fukuoka	21 Sep
28:06.63	Collis	Birmingham	AUS	27.12.84	18rA	Jordan	Stanford	29 Apr
28:06.74	Aron	Rono	KEN	1.11.82	19rA	Jordan	Stanford	29 Apr
(100)								

Mark	Name		Nat	Born	Date
28:07.01	Shinobu	Kubota	JPN	12.12.91	12 May
28:07.50	Carles	Castillejo	ESP	18.8.78	3 Jun
28:08.36	Jake	Riley	USA	2.11.88	22 Jun
28:09.49	Takuya	Ishikawa	JPN	29.10.87	12 May
28:09.58	David	McNeill	AUS	6.10.86	29 Apr
28:10.49	Leul	Gebrselassie	ETH-J	20.9.93	7 Jul
28:10.74	Gideon	Ngatuny	KEN	10.10.86	21 Sep
28:10.81	Tomoya	Onishi	JPN	28.3.87	7 Jul
28:11.22	Naoki	Okamoto	JPN	26.5.84	12 May
28:11.75	Josphat	Boit	KEN	26.11.83	29 Apr
28:11.76	Liam	Adams	AUS	4.9.86	29 Apr
28:12.03	James	Strang	USA	7.12.84	29 Apr
28:12.37	Yuichiro	Ueno	JPN	29.7.85	7 Jul
28:12.40	El Hassan	Elabassi	MAR	15.7.79	17 Jun
28:12.42	Mike	Sayenko	USA	12.7.84	29 Apr
28:12.65	Josh	Simpson	USA	17.3.84	29 Apr
28:12.82	Yuta	Shitara	JPN	18.12.91	27 Jun
28:12.87	Tasama	Moogas	ISR	2.2.88	16 Jan
28:12.95	Tony	Okello	UGA	26.12.83	29 Apr
28:13.23	Harry	Summers	AUS	19.5.90	29 Apr
28:13.62	Stefano	La Rosa	ITA	22.9.85	29 Apr
28:14.27	Kenta	Murayama	JPN-J	23.2.93	13 Oct
28:14.34A	Stephen	Tum	KEN	12.6.86	14 Jun
28:14.36A	Nicholas	Murei	KEN	25.12.86	14 Jun
28:14.49	Shuhei	Yamamoto	JPN	24.5.91	27 Jun
28:14.56	David	Jankowski	USA	23.10.84	29 Apr
28:14.80	Paul	Kuira	KEN	25.1.90	27 Jun
28:15.02	Yusuke	Mita	JPN	24.10.89	24 Nov
28:15.11	Tim	Nelson	USA	27.2.84	22 Jun
28:15.79	Kensuke	Takezawa	JPN	11.10.86	29 Apr
28:15.90	Keita	Shitara	JPN	18.12.91	21 Apr
28:15.94	Carlos	Trujillo	USA	17.7.85	29 Apr
28:16.92	Naohiro	Domoto	JPN	23.7.89	24 Nov
28:16.97	Girma	Mecheso	USA	16.1.88	29 Apr
28:17.69	Manuel Angel	Penas	ESP	9.11.77	24 Mar
28:17.77	Olivier	Irabaruta	BDI	25.8.90	28 Jun
28:18.50	Bashir	Abdi	BEL	10.2.89	30 May
28:18.62	Christopher	Landry	USA	29.4.86	29 Apr
28:18.93	Enoch	Omwamba	KEN-J	4.4.93	13 May
28:18.97	Kennedy	Kithuka	KEN	4.6.89	19 Apr
28:19.22	Tomohiro	Shiya	JPN	27.9.86	13 Oct
28:19.40	Azmeraw	Mengistu	ETH	15.9.92	22 Sep
28:20.18	Gladwin	Mzazi	RSA	28.8.88	13 Apr
28:20.22	Jeff	Schirmer	USA	8.11.86	29 Apr
28:21.43	Brett	Gotcher	USA	1.9.84	29 Apr
28:21.47	Masato	Kihara	JPN	13.7.86	21 Apr
28:21.58	Ryuji	Kashiwabara	JPN	13.7.89	21 Sep
28:22.59	Shogo	Nakamura	JPN	16.9.92	27 Jun
28:22.72A	Charles	Toroitich	KEN	.88	14 Jun
28:22.95	Yevgeniy	Rybakov	RUS	27.2.85	30 Jun
28:23.0 A	Geoffrey	Mutai	KEN	7.10.81	17 May
28:23.1 A	Mathew	Kisorio ¶	KEN	16.5.89	17 May
28:23.17	Ian	Burrell	USA	15.2.85	29 Apr
28:23.46	Mumin	Gala	DJI	6.9.86	27 May
28:23.54	Tyler	Pennel	USA	21.12.87	6 Apr
28:23.98	Philemon	Cheboi	KEN-J	8.11.93	10 Jul
28:24.17	Kazuhiro	Maeda	JPN	19.4.81	2 Dec
28:24.62	Ryo	Matsumoto	JPN	19.10.90	24 Nov
28:24.68	Sota	Hoshi	JPN	6.1.88	24 Nov
28:24.79	Abdi	Nageeye	NED	2.3.89	30 May
28:25.14	Keiji	Akutsu	JPN	20.3.87	27 Jun
28:25.19		Baek Seung-ho	KOR	16.12.90	7 Jul
28:25.19	Kenta	Murozuka	JPN	12.2.86	24 Nov
28:25.2 A	Isaac	Korir	KEN	26.8.90	3 May
28:25.32	Tsubasa	Hayakawa	JPN	2.7.90	27 Jun
28:25.57	Vianney	Ndiho	BDI	25.12.92	28 Jun
28:25.82	Benjamin	Gandu	KEN	21.5.90	9 Jun
28:26.27	Jesús	España	ESP	21.8.78	24 Mar
28:26.27	Takayuki	Matsumiya	JPN	21.2.80	7 Jul
28:26.44	Jonathan	Grey	USA	13.2.88	29 Apr
28:26.82	Khalid	Choukoud	NED	23.3.86	30 Jun
28:27.1A	Nicholas	Togom	KEN	25.12.86	18 May
28:28.05	Samson	Gebreyohannes	ERI	7.2.92	27 May
28:28.42	Daniel	Mwiba	KEN-J	12.1.94	9 Jun
28:28.50	Belete	Assefa	ETH	3.3.91	27 May
28:28.54	Roman	Romanenko	UKR	30.1.88	27 May
28:29.20	Xolisa	Tyali	RSA	2.12.89	13 Apr
28:29.29	Masato	Imai	JPN	2.4.84	21 Sep
28:29.3 A	William	Malel Sitonik	KEN-J	1.3.94	8 Ju
28:29.46	Bodan	Semenovych	UKR	18.7.86	27 May
28:29.76	Daisuke	Matsufuji	JPN	12.1.86	1 Dec
28:30.55	Sean	Houseworth	USA	13.5.87	6 Apr
28:30.84	Kazuhiro	Kuga	JPN	7.3.91	1 Dec
28:31.13	Tatsonori	Hamasaki	JPN	4.7.88	1 Dec
28:31.16	Rui Pedro	Silva	POR	6.5.81	30 Jun
28:31.48	Yusuke	Takabayashi	JPN	19.7.87	13 Oct
28:31.97	Hisanori	Kitajima	JPN	16.10.84	9 Jun
28:32.29	Koen	Naert	BEL	3.9.89	29 Apr
28:32.61	Ronald	Schröer	NED	28.9.84	29 Apr
28:32.67	Ben	St. Lawrence	AUS	7.11.81	4 Aug
28:33.12	Mark	Kenneally	IRL	18.4.81	30 May
28:33.15	Ryuji	Ono	JPN	27.1.85	27 Jun
28:33.35	Dustin	Emerick	USA	.90	29 Apr
28:33.36	Jun	Shinoto	JPN	2.4.85	24 Nov
28:33.37	Ghirmay	Gebrselassie	ERI-J	14.11.95	27 May
28:33.94	Scott	Smith	USA	13.7.86	29 Apr
28:34.36	Dmytro	Siruk	UKR	12.4.91	27 May
28:34.43	James	Carney (200)	USA	24.5.78	

Drugs disqualification: 28:05.60A Mathew Kisorio ¶ KEN 16.5.89 3 NC Nairobi 14 Jun

JUNIORS

See main list for top 6 juniors. 14 performances by 10 men to 28:24.1. Additional marks and further juniors:

Name	Mark	Pos	Meet	Venue	Date			
Demelash	28:16.07	1	WJ	Barcelona	10 Jul			
G Kirui	27:21.12	10	VD	Bruxelles	7 Sep			
Kiumbani	28:16.88	3		Yokohama	1 Dec	28:24.03	14 Fukagawa	27 Jun

Mark	Name		Nat	Born	Pos	Meet	Venue	Date
28:10.49	Leul	Gebrselassie	ETH	20.9.93	5		Abashiri	7 Jul
28:14.27	Kenta	Murayama	JPN-	23.2.93	4		Toyota	13 Oct
28:18.93	Enoch	Omwamba	KEN	4.4.93	1		Tokyo	13 May
28:23.98	Philemon	Cheboi (10)	KEN	8.11.93	2	WJ	Barcelona	10 Jul
28:28.42	Daniel	Mwiba	KEN	12.1.94	2		Yokohama	9 Jun

Mark	Name		Nat	Born	Pos	Meet	Venue	Date
28:29.3 A	William	Malel Sitonik	KEN	1.3.94	1	NC-j	Nairobi	8 Jun
28:33.37	Ghirmay	Gebrselassie	ERI	14.11.95	17	FBK	Hengelo	27 May
28:38.52	Jeremiah	Thuku	KEN	7.7.94	1		Toyohashi	3 Jun
28:43.69	Kazuto	Nishiike	JPN	17.2.93	1rD		Machida	24 Nov
28:44.60	Hironori	Tsuetaki	JPN	8.5.93	5		Tokyop	24 Nov
28:45.66	Kota	Murayama	JPN	23.2.93	3		Yokohama	17 Nov
28:46.91A	Moses	Kurong	UGA	7.7.94	2		Kampala	7 Apr
28:48.6 A	Kinde	Atanaw	ETH	15.4.93	2	NC-j	Addis Ababa	31 May
28:50.78	Kaleb	Basore (20)	ETH	13.1.93	7		Yokohama	17 Nov
Best European: 29:41.20 Dino		Bosnjak	CRO	21.1.94	1		Postojna	6 May

10 KILOMETRES ROAD

Mark	Name		Nat	Born	Pos	Meet	Venue	Date
27:29	Geoffrey	Mutai	KEN	7.10.81	1		Boston	24 Jun
27:34+	Philemon	Limo	KEN	2.8.85	1	in HMar	Ostia	26 Feb

Where superior to track best

Mark		Name		Nat	Born	Pos	Meet	Venue	Date
27:35+		Daniel	Chebii	KEN	28.5.85		in 10M	Zaandam	23 Sep
27:36		Mosinet	Geremew	ETH	12.2.92	1		Hyderabad	25 Nov
27:37	dh	Peter	Kirui	KEN	2.1.88	1	Peach	Atlanta (24m dh)	4 Jul
27:37		Nicholas	Kipkemboi	KEN	.86	2		Hyderabad	25 Nov
27:40+		Daniel Kiprop	Limo	KEN	10.12.83		in HMar	Ostia	26 Feb
27:42+		Shumi	Dechasa	ETH	28.5.89		in HMar	Ostia	26 Feb
27:45+		Hillary	Kipchumba	KEN	25.11.92		in 10M	Zaandam	23 Sep
27:48+		Timothy	Kiptoo	KEN	2.8.84		in 10M	Zaandam	23 Sep
27:49		Edwin	Kipyego	KEN	.91	1		London	8 Jul
27:50		Philip	Yego	KEN	.79	1		Brunssum	1 Apr
27:51		Henry	Kiplagat	KEN	16.12.82	1		Praha	8 Sep
27:51+		Joel	Kimurer	KEN	21.1.88		in HMar	Valencia	21 Oct
27:52+		John	Mwangangi	KEN	1.11.90		in HMar	Valencia	21 Oct
27:53+		Jonathan	Maiyo	KEN	5.5.88	1	in HMar	Den Haag	11 Mar
27:53+		Stephen	Kibet	KEN	9.11.86		in HMar	Den Haag	11 Mar
27:53+		Geoffrey	Kipsang	KEN	28.11.92		in HMar	Den Haag	11 Mar
27:53		Philip	Langat	KEN	23.4.90	2		Boston	24 Jun
27:54+		Victor	Kipchirchir	KEN	5.12.87		in HMar	Den Haag	11 Mar
27:54+		Merkebu	Birke	ETH	.88		in HMar	Den Haag	11 Mar
27:54+		Bernard	Koech	KEN	31.1.88		in HMar	Den Haag	11 Mar
27:54+		Jacob	Chesire	KEN	.82		in HMar	Den Haag	11 Mar
27:54+		Andualem	Belay	ETH	5.4.92		in HMar	Den Haag	11 Mar
27:56		Ahmed	Baday	MAR	12.1.74	1		Taroudant	11 Mar
27:56		Ayele	Abshero	ETH	28.12.90	2		Manchester	20 May
27:56		Tsegaye	Kebede	ETH	15.1.87	3		Manchester	20 May
27:56		Richard	Mengich	KEN	.89	2		Berlin	14 Oct
27:56		David	Kosgei	KEN	.85	3		Berlin	14 Oct
27:57		Simon	Cheprot	KEN-J	2.7.93	2		Taroudant	11 Mar
27:59		Alfred	Cherop	KEN	2.3.86	2		Brunssum	1 Apr
27:59		Birhan	Nebebew	ETH		2		Rennes	14 Oct
27:59+		Bernard	Kitur	KEN	10.1.90		in HMar	Valencia	21 Oct
28:00		Stanley	Biwott	KEN	21.4.86	1		Cape Elizabeth	4 Aug
28:01+		Mathew	Kisorio ¶	KEN	16.5.89	1	in HMar	Marugame	5 Feb
28:01		Richard	Sigei	KEN	11.5.84	3		Brunssum	1 Apr
28:01		Mark	Korir	KEN	10.1.85	1		Santos	20 May
28:01	dh	Paul	Lonyangat	KEN	12.12.92	4	Peach	Atlanta	4 Jul
28:02		Sammy	Kitwara	KEN	26.11.86	1		San Juan	26 Feb
28:02+		Deriba	Merga	ETH	26.10.80		in HMar	New York	18 Mar
28:02		Peter	Wanjiru	KEN	.82	4		Brunssum	1 Apr
28:02		Abdullah Ahmad	Hassan	QAT	29.7.81	5		Brunssum	1 Apr
28:02+		Wilson	Kipsang	KEN	15.3.82		in HMar	Newcastle	16 Sep
28:02+		Kennedy	Kimutai	KEN	18.6.90		in 15k	Nijmegen	18 Nov
28:03+		Feyisa	Lilesa	ETH	1.2.90	1	in HMar	Houston	15 Jan
28:03+		Atsedu	Tsegay	ETH	17.12.91		in HMar	Praha	31 Mar
28:03+		Sentayehu	Merga	ETH	18.3.85		in HMar	Praha	31 Mar
28:04		Mohamed	El Hachimi #	MAR	5.9.80	2		Santos	20 May
28:05		Leonard	Langat	KEN	7.8.90	1		Oelde	8 Jun

Mark		Name		Nat	Born	Date	Mark		Name		Nat	Born	Date
28:08		Isaac	Mwangi	KEN	.88	14 Oct	28:14		Solomon	Deksisa	ETH	.82	7 Apr
28:09+		John	Kiprotich	KEN	5.6.83	26 Feb	28:14		Patrick	Ereng	KEN	87	16 Sep
28:09+		Laban	Korir	KEN	30.12.85	26 Feb	28:15		Alex	Oleititip	KEN	22.9.82	14 Oct
28:09		Alex	Korir	KEN	22.9.82	27 May	28:16		Stanley	Koech	KEN		20 May
28:09		Hafid	Chani	MAR	12.2.86	7 Oct	28:16	dh	Silas	Sang	KEN	21.8.78	4 Jul
28:09		Stephen	Kiplagat	KEN		14 Oct	28:16		Kadengoi	Loitareng	KEN	17.7.83	16 Sep
28:10		Abraham	Cheroben	KEN	10.11.92	14 Oct	28:16+		Pius	Kirop	KEN	8.1.90	7 Oct
28:13		Kiplimo	Kimutai	KEN	10.12.81	4 Aug	28:16		Tolossa	Gedefa	ETH	.92	7 Oct
28:13		Fredrick	Ngeny	KEN		2 Sep	28:16		Jackson	Kiprop	UGA	20.10.86	25 Nov
28:14		Charles	Maina	KEN	11.10.82	1 Apr	28:17+		Geoffrey	Ngugi	KEN	11.9.84	31 Mar

Mark	Name		Nat	Born	Date
28:17	Ismail	Juma	TAN		20 May
28:17	James	Barmasai	KEN	.84	8 Jun
28:17	Fikadu	Haftu	ETH-J	21.2.94	23 Jun
28:18+	Edeo	Mamo	ETH		11 Mar
28:18	Wilfred	Murgor	KEN	12.12.88	3 Jun
28:18	Reuben	Limaa	KEN	.87	23 Jun
28:18	Edward	Muge	KEN	26.6.83	4 Aug
28:19	Shadrack	Kosgei	KEN	24.11.84	24 Mar
28:19	Stephen	Kiprotich	UGA	18.4.89	20 May
28:19	Adugna	Tekele	ETH	26.2.89	8 Sep
28:19	Julius	Koskei	KEN	6.4.82	7 Oct
28:19	Silas	Ngetich	KEN		14 Oct
28:20	Titus	Masai	KEN	9.10.89	1 May
28:20	Najim	El Gady	MAR	31.12.80	7 Oct
28:21	Allan	Kiprono	KEN	15.2.90	7 Apr
28:21	Jacob	Kendagor	KEN	19.9.84	29 Apr
28:21	Fredrick	Musyoki	KEN	14.9.90	13 May
28:21	Patrick	Makau	KEN	2.3.85	20 May
28:21	Ali	Abdosh	ETH	28.8.87	24 Jun
28:22+	Benjamin	Gando	KEN	21.5.90	5 Feb
28:22+	Dennis	Kimetto	KEN	22.1.84	6 May
28:22+	Wilfred	Kigen	KEN	23.2.76	6 May
28:22+	Edwin	Kiptoo	KEN	28.12.87	6 May
28:22+	Aschealew	Meketa	ETH		6 May
28:22+	Nguse	Tesfaldet	ERI	10.11.86	23 Sep
28:22	Charles	Toroitich	KEN	.88	30 Sep

Mark	Name		Nat	Born	Date
28:23+	Matthew	Koech	KEN	1.1.83	23 Sep
28:23	Berhanu	Legesse	ETH		30 Dec
28:24	Julius	Kogo	KEN	12.8.85	25 Mar
28:24+	Dawit	Wolde	ETH	19.5.91	31 Mar
28:24	Gilbert	Kirwa	KEN	20.12.85	3 Jun
28:24	Edwin	Korir	KEN	2.8.87	9 Sep
28:24	Baisa	Moleta	ETH		30 Dec
28:25+	Deressa	Chimsa	ETH	21.11.86	6 Oct
28:25	Silas	Kipruto	KEN	26.9.84	14 Oct
28:25	Kinde	Atanaw	ETH-J	15.4.93	30 Dec
28:26+	Ezekiel	Chebii	KEN	3.1.91	1 Apr
28:26+	Gideon	Kipketer	KEN	10.11.92	1 Apr
28:26+	Joseph	Kiptum	KEN	25.9.87	1 Apr
28:26	Tigabu	Gebremariam	ETH	.90	23 Jun
28:27	Abrar	Osman	ETH-J	1.1.94	30 Dec
28:28+	Elisha	Rotich	KEN	.90	12 May
28:28+	Milton	Rotich	KEN	.84	21 Oct
28:29+	Vincent	Kipruto	KEN	13.9.87	26 Feb
28:29	Gebretsadik	Adhana	ETH	16.7.92	4 Aug
28:29+	Robert	Chomesin	KEN	.89	23 Sep
28:30+	Eric	Ndiema	KEN	28.12.92	26 Feb
28:30	Leonard	Korir	KEN	10.12.86	12 May
28:30	Kiprop	Mutai	KEN		20 May
28:30	Abdelhadid	El Mouaziz	MAR	1.1.77	23 Jun
28:30	Dominic	Ondoro	KEN	.88	23 Sep
28:30	Alex	Oleitiptip	KEN	22.9.82	31 Dec

Excessively downhill: Apr 29, Rockville (60mdh): 1, Julius Kogo KEN 12.8.85 28:12, 2. Abiyote Endale ETH 3.5.86 28:16, 3. Zenbaba Yegezu ETH 26.9.83 28:20; Nov 4, Taule-Morlaix (86mdh): Ezechiel Nizigiyimana BDI 30.3.90 28:24

See also Half Marathon lists

15/20 KILOMETRES ROAD

20k	15k	Name		Nat	Born	Pos	Meet	Venue	Date
56:53	41:48+	Philemon Kimeli	Limo	KEN	2.8.85	2	in HMar	Praha	31 Mar
	42:01	Nicholas	Kipkemboi	KEN	.86	1		Nijmegen	18 Nov
	42:14+	John	Mwangangi	KEN	1.11.90		in HMar	Lisboa	25 Mar
57:09	42:32+	Bernard	Koech	KEN	31.1.88		in HMar	Den Haag	11 Mar
57:11	42:16+	Zersenay	Tadese	ERI	8.2.82	1	in HMar	Kavarna	7 Oct
	42:18		L Komon			2		Nijmegen	18 Nov
	42:25	Geoffrey	Mutai	KEN	7.10.81	1		's-Heerenberg	2 Dec
	42:26	Philip	Langat	KEN	23.4.90	2		's-Heerenberg	2 Dec
	42:28	Nguse	Tesfaldet	ERI	10.11.86	3		Nijmegen	18 Nov
	42:29	Kennedy	Kimutai	KEN	18.6.90	4		Nijmegen	18 Nov
	42:33+	Lucas	Rotich	KEN	16.4.90		in HMar	Lisboa	25 Mar
57:13	42:37+	Andualem	Belay	ETH	5.4.92		in HMar	Den Haag	11 Mar
	42:40+		B Koech				in HMar	Paris	4 Mar
57:02	42:48+	Dennis	Kimetto	KEN	22.1.84		in 25k	Berlin	6 May
57:33	42:47+	Feyisa	Lilesa	ETH	1.2.90		in HMar	New York	18 Mar
57:47		Benjamin	Gando	KEN	21.5.91	1		Tachikawa	20 Oxt
57:50	42:51+	Jacob	Wanjuki	KEN	16.1.86		in HMar	Marugame	5 Feb
57:53	42:45	Pius	Kirop	KEN	8.1.90		in HMar	Kavarna	7 Oct
57:55+		Henry	Kiplagat	KEN	16.12.82		in HMar	Göteborg	12 May
58:00	42:15+	Kenneth	Kipkemoi	KEN	2.8.84		in HMar	Praha	31 Mar
58:00	43:17+	Bernard	Kipyego	KEN	16.7.86	in HMar		Ra's Al-Khaymah	17 Feb
	42:48+	Jacob	Kendagor	KEN	.84		in 25k	Berlin	6 May
58:02	42:53+	John	Mwangangi	KEN	1.11.90		in HMar	Kavarna	7 Oct
	42:53	Getu	Feleke	ETH	28.11.86	3		's-Heerenberg	2 Dec
	42:56+	Wilfred	Kigen	KEN	23.2.66		in 25k	Berlin	6 May
	43:01	Tilahun	Regassa	ETH	18.1.90	1		Utica	8 Jul
	43:06++	Gideon	Kipketer	KEN	10.11.92		in HMar	Egmond Aan Zee	8 Jan
	43:06++	Belete	Assefa	ETH	3.3.91		in HMar	Egmond Aan Zee	8 Jan
	43:10	Fikadu	Haftu	ETH-J	21.2.94	1		Puy-en-Velay	1 May
	43:14	Robert	Chomesin	KEN	.89	2		Puy-en-Velay	1 May
	43:15+	Jonathan	Kibet	KEN	.82		in HMar	Kavarna	6 Oct
58:07	43:17+	Gilbert	Maina	KEN	.91		in HMar	Barcelona	26 Feb
58:15	43:18	Elicky	Mase	KEN	.84		in HMar	Barcelona	26 Feb
	43:21+	Gilbert	Masai	KEN	20.5.81		in HMar	Lisboa	25 Mar
58:11		Ezechiel	Nizigiyimana	BDI	30.3.90	1		Paris	14 Oct
58:15		Evans	Kiplagat	KEN	5.3.88	2		Paris	14 Oct

10 MILES ROAD

10M	15k	Name		Nat	Born	Pos	Meet	Venue	Date
44:48	41:46	Leonard	Komon	KEN	10.1.88	1		Zaandam	23 Sep
44:49dh		Wilson	Kipsang	KEN	15.3.82	1=	in HMar	South Shields	16 Sep
44:49dh		Micah	Kogo	KEN	3.6.86	1=	in HMar	South Shields	16 Sep

Mark		Name		Nat	Born	Pos	Meet	Venue	Date
45:02	41:58	Daniel	Chebii	KEN	28.5.85	2		Zaandam	23 Sep
45:15		Allan	Kiprono	KEN	15.2.90	1		Washington	1 Apr
45:28	42:19	Abera	Kuma	ETH	31.8.90	3		Zaandam	23 Sep
45:37	42:21	Hillary	Kipchumba	KEN	25.11.92	4		Zaandam	23 Sep
45:38	42:45	Pius	Kirop	KEN	8.1.90	1		Tilburg	2 Sep
45:40	42:45	John	Mwangangi	KEN	1.11.90	2		Tilburg	2 Sep
45:41	42:46	Patrick	Makau	KEN	2.3.85	3		Tilburg	2 Sep
45:43+		Stanley	Biwott	KEN	21.4.86		in HMar	Philadelphia	16 Sep
45:47	42:45	Philip	Langat	KEN	23.4.90	4		Tilburg	2 Sep
45:55	42:47	Charles	Torotiich	KEN	.88	5		Tilburg	2 Sep
45:57	42:52	Philemon	Rono	KEN	8.2.91	6		Tilburg	2 Sep
46:05+		Paul	Lonyangat	KEN	12.12.92		in HMar	Philadelphia	16 Sep
46:07	42:57	Tsegay	Tuemay	ERI	20.12.95	7		Tilburg	2 Sep
46:10	42:48	Timothy	Kiptoo	KEN	2.8.84	5		Zaandam	23 Sep
46:13	43:10	Nguse	Tesfaldet	ERI	10.11.86	6		Zaandam	23 Sep
46:15	43:11?	Kadengoi	Loitareng	KEN	17.7.83	7		Zaandam	23 Sep
46:19	43:12	Hais	Welday	ERI	24.10.89	8		Zaandam	23 Sep
46:24+		Dathan	Ritzenhein	USA	30.12.82		in HMar	Philadelphia	16 Sep
46:24+		Hassan	El Abbassi	MAR	15.7.79	in HMar		Philadelphia	16 Sep
46:25		Enoch	Omwamba	KEN-J	4.4.93	1r1		Kosa	2 Dec
46:26		Tomohiro	Shiya	JPN	27.9.86	1r2		Kosa	2 Dec
46:28		Lani	Kiplagat	KEN		2		Washington	1 Apr
46:29	43:17	Ghirmay	Ghebreslassie	ERI-Y	14.11.95	8		Tilburg	2 Sep
46:31	43:13	Matthew	Koech	KEN	1.1.83	9		Zaandam	23 Sep
46:31		Yusuke	Hasegawa	JPN	8.6.88	2r2		Kosa	2 Dec
46:38		Alex	Mwangi	KEN	14.6.90	2r1		Kosa	2 Dec
46:40	43:28	Stephen	Mokoka	RSA	31.1.85	1	Gt South	Portsmouth	28 Oct
46:40		Ryo	Matsumoto	JPN	19.10.90	3r2		Kosa	2 Dec
46:43		Yuya	Konishi	JPN	22.8.90	4r2		Kosa	2 Dec
46:44	43:29	Ayad	Lamdassem	ESP	11.10.81	2	Gt South	Portsmouth	28 Oct
46:45		Julius	Kogo	KEN	12.8.85	1		Flint	25 Aug
46:45	43:29	Tariku	Bekele	ETH	21.1.87	3	Gt South	Portsmouth	28 Oct
46:46		Kyohei	Nishi	JPN	3.9.91	5r2		Kosa	2 Dec
46:50	43:30	Daniele	Meucci	ITA	7.10.85	4	Gt South	Portsmouth	28 Oct

HALF MARATHON

HMar	20k	15k	Name		Nat	Born	Pos	Meet	Venue	Date
58:47	55:52	41:46	Atsedu	Tsegay	ETH	17.12.91	1		Praha	31 Mar
58:54	55:58	42:03	Stephen	Kibet	KEN	9.11.86	1		Den Haag	11 Mar
59:02	55:58	42:03	Jonathan	Maiyo	KEN	5.5.88	2		Den Haag	11 Mar
59:05			Ezekiel	Chebii	KEN	3.1.91	1		Lille	1 Sep
59:06dh	56:10	41:51	Wilson	Kipsang	KEN	15.3.82	1	GNR	South Shields	16 Sep
59:07dh	56:10	41:51	Micah	Kogo	KEN	3.6.86	2	GNR	South Shields	16 Sep
59:10			Bernard	Koech	KEN	31.1.88	2		Lille	1 Sep
59:11	56:52	42:03	Kenneth	Kipkemoi	KEN	2.8.84	3		Den Haag	11 Mar
59:14			Dennis	Kimetto	KEN	22.1.84	1		Berlin	1 Apr
59:15			Wilson	Kiprop (10)	KEN	14.4.87	2		Berlin	1 Apr
59:22	56:19		Feyisa	Lilesa	ETH	1.2.90	1		Houston	15 Jan
59:22				Chebii			3		Berlin	1 Apr
59:25			Pius	Kirop	KEN	8.1.90	4		Berlin	1 Apr
59:25			Eliud	Kipchoge	KEN	5.11.84	3		Lille	1 Sep
59:26	56:20	42:06	Geoffrey	Kipsang	KEN	28.11.92	4		Den Haag	11 Mar
59:31	56:21	42:04	Victor	Kipchirchir	KEN	5.12.87	5		Den Haag	11 Mar
59:32		41:47	Philemon Kimeli	Limo	KEN	2.8.85	1		Ostia	26 Feb
59:34		42:09	Zersenay	Tadese	ERI	8.2.82	1		Lisboa	25 Mar
59:36	56:37	42:16	Joel	Kimurer	KEN	21.1.88	1		Valencia	21 Oct
59:39	56:34	42:08	Peter	Kirui	KEN	2.1.88	1		New York	18 Mar
59:44		42:39	Stanley	Biwott (20)	KEN	21.4.86	1		Paris	4 Mar
59:46				Kipkemoi			2		Valencia	21 Oct
59:48	56:35	42:08	Deriba	Merga	ETH	26.10.80	2		New York	18 Mar
59:49			Daniel	Chebii	KEN	28.5.85	1		České Budějovice	9 Jun
59:51		42:08	Shumi	Dechasa	ETH	28.5.89	2		Ostia	26 Feb
59:53			Paul Kipchumba	Lonyangat	KEN	12.12.92	5		Berlin	1 Apr
59:53			Gideon	Kipketer	KEN	10.11.92	4		Lille	1 Sep
59:55		42:11	Daniel Kiprop	Limo	KEN	10.12.83	3		Ostia	26 Feb
59:56dh			Imane	Merga	ETH	15.10.88	3	GNR	South Shields	16 Sep
59:57				Koech			1		Nice	28 Apr
59:57			Gilbert	Masai	KEN	20.5.81	5		Lille	1 Sep
			(31/28)							

Mark			Name		Nat	Born	Pos	Meet	Venue	Date	
59:58	56:46		John	Mwangangi	KEN	1.11.90	3		Valencia	21	Oct
60:01	56:53	41:49	Henry	Kiplagat	KEN	16.12.82	2		Praha	31	Mar
			(30)								
60:02	56:57	42:18	Mathew	Kisorio ¶	KEN	16.5.89	1		Marugame	5	Feb
60:02		42:35	John	Kiprotich	KEN	5.6.83	4		Ostia	26	Feb
60:05			Leonard	Langat	KEN	7.8.90	6		Berlin	1	Apr
60:10			Andualem	Belay	ETH	5.4.92	6		Lille	1	Sep
60:14	57:14	42:34	Merkebu	Birke	ETH	.88	6		Den Haag	11	Mar
60:15			Nicholas	Kipkemboi	KEN	.86	7		Berlin	1	Apr
60:18dh			Mike	Kigen	KEN	15.1.86	4	GNR	South Shields	16	Sep
60:19			Abera	Kuma	ETH	31.8.90	2		Birmingham	21	Oct
60:23			Robert	Chomesin	KEN	.89	1		Udine	23	Sep
60:26			Joseph	Kiptum	KEN	25.9.87	8		Berlin	1	Apr
			(40)								
60:28	57:18	43:11	Abel	Kirui	KEN	4.6.82	1		Barcelona	26	Feb
60:29			Titus	Masai	KEN	9.10.89	2		Nice	29	Apr
60:32			Tesfaye	Abera	ETH	31.3.92	3		Nice	29	Apr
60:32			Lucas	Rotich	KEN	16.4.90	7		Lille	1	Sep
60:34			Abraham	Gebretsadik	ETH	16.7.92	4		Nice	29	Apr
60:38		42:43	Laban	Korir	KEN	30.12.85	5		Ostia	26	Feb
60:43	57:35	42:48	Milton	Rotich	KEN	.84	2		Göteborg	12	May
60:46		43:06	Dawit	Wolde	ETH	19.5.91	1		Egmond Aan Zee	8	Jan
60:46	57:29	43:12	Jairus	Chanchaima	KEN	5.12.84	2		Barcelona	26	Feb
60:46		43:09	Vincent	Kipruto	KEN	13.9.87	6		Ostia	26	Feb
			(40)								
60:48			Richard	Mengich	KEN	.89	1		Remich	30	Sep
60:49	57:35	43:24	Azmeraw	Bekele	ETH	22.1.86	2		Ra's Al-Khaymah	17	Feb
60:51	57:44	43:01	Deressa	Chimsa	ETH	21.11.86	2	WCh	Kavarna	6	Oct
60:52			Haile	Gebrselassie	ETH	18.4.73	1		Wien	15	Apr
60:53	57:50	43:23	Chihiro	Miyawaki	JPN	28.8.91	1		Yamaguchi	18	Mar
60:55			Edwin	Kipyego	KEN	.90	1		Delhi	30	Sep
60:56dh			Emmanuel	Bett	KEN	29.3.85	5	GNR	South Shields	16	Sep
60:57		42:44	Reuben	Limaa	KEN	.87	3		Paris	4	Mar
60:57			Stephen	Mokoka	RSA	31.1.85	1		Cape Town	26	Aug
60:57			Dathan	Ritzenhein	USA	30.12.82	3		Philadelphia	16	Sep
			(50)								
60:58			Philemon	Rono	KEN	8.2.91	1		Paderborn	7	Apr
60:59			Belaye	Assefa	ETH	17.6.92	1		Verbania	11	Mar
60:59	57:50	43:23	Jacob	Wanjuki	KEN	16.1.86	2		Yamaguchi	18	Mar
60:59	57:47	42:37	Bernard	Kitur	KEN	10.1.90	4		Valencia	21	Oct
61:00dh			Chris	Thompson	GBR	17.4.81	6	GNR	South Shields	16	Sep
61:01	57:50	42:58	Daniel	Gitau	KEN	1.10.87	2		Marugame	5	Feb
61:01	57:48	42:05	Josphat	Bett	KEN	12.6.90	4		Praha	31	Mar
61:02	57:44	43:12	Wilfred K.	Murgor	KEN	12.12.88	3		Barcelona	26	Feb
61:02	57:50	42:15	Sentayehu	Merga	ETH	18.3.85	5		Praha	31	Mar
61:02			Vincent	Yator	KEN	11.7.89	2		Remich	30	Sep
			(60)								
61:05			Robert	Langat	KEN	17.9.88	1		Krems	16	Sep
61:05	58:00		Philip	Langat	KEN	23.4.90	1		Breda	7	Oct
61:06	57:51	42:58	Benjamin	Gando	KEN	21.5.91	4		Marugame	5	Feb
61:07			Yakob	Jarso	ETH	5.2.88	1		Milano	25	Mar
61:07			Julius	Lamerinyang	KEN	15.7.83	1		Rabat	1	Apr
61:07			Justus	Moranga	KEN	.87	1		Ivry-Vitry	8	Apr
61:07			Benson	Oloisunga	KEN	.86	2		Krems	16	Sep
61:07			Simon	Cheprot	KEN-J	2.7.93	3		Remich	30	Sep
61:07			Tesfaalem	Mehari	ETH-J	.93	1		Boulogne Billancourt	18	Nov
61:08?			Pkumun	Loritenyang Meke?	KEN		2		Rabat	1	Apr
			(70)								
61:08			Lucky Mohale	Modike	RSA	21.8.85	2		Cape Town	26	Aug
61:08	57:59		Kennedy	Kimutai	KEN	18.6.90	2		Breda	7	Oct
61:09		43:06	Samuel	Tsegay	ERI	24.2.88	3		Egmond Aan Zee	8	Jan
61:09			Habtamu	Assefa	ETH	29.3.85	1		Azkoitia	31	Mar
61:11			Andrea	Lalli	ITA	20.5.87	2		Milano	25	Mar
61:11			Ayele	Abshero	ETH	28.12.90	1		Yangzhou	29	Apr
61:11			Abera	Chane	ETH	10.5.85	1		Arezzo	28	Oct
61:12	57:59		Charles	Toroitich	KEN	.88	3		Breda	7	Oct
61:13		42:52	Raji	Assefa	ETH	18.2.86	4		Paris	4	Mar
61:14			Geoffrey	Kenesi	KEN	.90	9		Lille	1	Sep
			(80)								
61:15	57:59	43:12	Peter	Kamais	KEN	7.11.76	4		Barcelona	26	Feb
61:15			Eric	Ndiema	KEN	28.12.92	7		Ostia	26	Feb

Mark			Name		Nat	Born	Pos	Meet	Venue	Date
61:15			Hillary	Kiprono	KEN	21.7.85	8		Ostia	26 Feb
61:15	57:58	43:23	Masato	Kihara	JPN	13.7.86	3		Yamaguchi	18 Mar
61:15			Peter	Wanjiru	KEN	28.11.82	2		Ivry-Vitry	8 Apr
61:15			El Hassan	Elabassi	MAR	15.7.79	4		Philadelphia	16 Sep
61:15			Jacob	Kendagor	KEN	.84	1		Uster	22 Sep
61:17			Hosea	Nailel	KEN	.88	2		Paderborn	7 Apr
61:19	57"58	43:14	Bernard	Waweru	KEN-J	5.1.94	5		Barcelona	26 Feb
61:19	58:19	43:45	Wesley	Korir (100)	KEN	15.11.82	4		New York	18 Mar
61:19	58:19	43:46	Samuel	Chelanga	KEN	23.2.85	5		New York	18 Mar
61:19			Mark	Korir	KEN	10.1.85	2		Azkoitia	31 Mar
61:19			Daniel	Wanjiru	KEN	26.5.92	3		Krems	16 Sep

Mark	Name		Nat	Born	Date
61:21	Kevin	Chelimo	KEN	14.2.83	18 Mar
61:21	Alfred	Cherop	KEN	2.3.86	8 Apr
61:22A	Nathan	Ayeko	UGA-J	10.10.93	2 Sep
61:23	Gebre	Gebremedhin	ETH		1 Apr
61:23	Julius	Koech	KEN	.86	7 Apr
61:25	Takuya	Fukatsu	JPN	10.11.87	4 Mar
61:25	Scott	Overall	GBR	9.2.83	18 Mar
61:25	Bernard	Kipyego	KEN	16.7.86	1 Sep
61:25dh	Collis	Birmingham	AUS	27.12.84	16 Sep
61:26	Marílson	dos Santos	BRA	6.8.77	18 Mar
61:26	Laban	Wanjiku	KEN	.85	8 Apr
61:26A	Solomon	Mutai	UGA	.92	2 Sep
61:27	Michael	Shelley	AUS	10.10.83	18 Mar
61:27A	Jackson	Kiprop	UGA	20.10.86	2 Sep
61:28	Tilahun	Regassa	ETH	18.1.90	15 Jan
61:28	Gilbert	Maina	KEN	.91	26 Feb
61:28	Mulue	Andom	ERI	12.10.91	1 Sep
61:28	Martin	Lel	KEN	29.10.78	30 Sep
61:29	Martin	Mathathi	KEN	25.12.85	20 May
61:30	Scott	Bauhs	USA	11.5.86	15 Jan
61:31	Yusuke	Takabayashi	JPN	19.7.87	5 Feb
61:31	Mengistu	Tabor	ETH	3.11.77	18 Mar
61:31	Adil	Annani	MAR	30.6.80	18 Mar
61:34	Arata	Fujiwara	JPN	12.9.81	5 Feb
61:34	Dickson	Chumba	KEN	27.10.86	11 Mar
61:34	Johana Manyim	Maina	KEN	24.12.90	13 May
61:34	Solomon	Yego	KEN	.87	14 Oct
61:36	Luke	Puskedra	USA	8.2.90	15 Jan
61:36	Elicky	Mase	KEN	.84	26 Feb
61:36	Philemon	Yator	KEN	2.4.92	11 Mar
61:36A	Isaak	Ayeko	UGA	31.12.89	2 Sep
61:37	Lahcen	Mokraji	MAR	12.3.79	26 Feb
61:37	Nicholas	Togom	KEN	25.12.86	23 Sep
61:38	Shinobu	Kubota	JPN	12.12.91	5 Feb
61:38	Jospeh	Aperumoi	KEN	.90	5 Mar
61:38+	Yemane Tsegay	Adhane	ETH	8.4.85	15 Apr
61:38	Abebe	Dinkesa	ETH	6.3.84	12 May
61:38	Gladwin	Mzazi	RSA	28.8.88	26 Aug
61:38	Albert	Matebor	KEN	20.12.80	30 Sep
61:39+	Getu	Feleke	ETH	28.11.86	15 Apr
61:39	Nguse	Tesfaldet	ERI	10.11.86	30 May
61:40A	Daniel	Rotich	UGA	1.1.92	2 Sep
61:41	Mebrahtom	Keflezighi	USA	5.5.75	18 Mar
61:41+	Stephen	Chemlany	KEN	9.8.82	15 Apr
61:41+	Moses	Mosop	KEN	17.7.85	15 Apr
61:41	Elisha	Rotich	KEN	.90	12 May
61:41	Gebreyesus	Girmay	ETH-J	.93	18 Nov
61:42	Shota	Yamaguchi	JPN	19.12.85	5 Feb
61:42	Evans	Kosgei	KEN	.89	1 Sep
61:42A	Alex	Chiesakit	UGA		2 Sep
61:44	Daisuke	Shimizu	JPN	2.8.82	5 Feb
61:44	Mekubo	Mogusu	KEN	25.12.86	5 Feb
61:44	Yuya	Konishi	JPN	22.8.90	5 Feb
61:44	Benson	Barus	KEN	4.7.80	16 Sep
61:44	Allan	Kiprono	KEN	15.2.90	7 Oct
61:45	Tatsunori	Hamasaki	JPN	4.7.88	5 Feb
61:45	Ryotaro	Nitta	JPN	14.12.89	5 Feb
61:45	Keita	Shitara	JPN	18.12.91	5 Feb
61:45	Gilbert	Kipruto Kirwa	KEN	20.12.85	10 Jun
61:46	Yuta	Igarashi	JPN	2.11.88	5 Feb
61:46	Daisuke	Matsufuji	JPN	12.1.86	5 Feb
61:46A	Peter	Some	KEN	5.6.90	8 Jul
61:46	Wilson	Loyanae ¶	KEN	.86	19 Aug
61:47	Silas	Kipruto	KEN	26.9.84	29 Apr
61:48	Yuta	Shitara	JPN	18.12.91	18 Mar
61:48	William	Chebor	KEN	22.12.82	23 Sep
61:48	Hosea	Kiplagat	KEN		30 Sep
61:49	Mamoru	Hirano	JPN	24.9.85	5 Feb
61:50	John Kipsang	Lotiang	KEN	.91	10 Jun
61:50	Afewerk	Mesfin	ETH	12.10.92	18 Nov
61:51	Robert	Kajuga	RWA	.85	1 Apr
61:51+	Richard	Limo	KEN	18.11.80	15 Apr
61:52	Geoffrey	Ngugi (42:36)	KEN	11.9.84	31 Mar
61:52+	Sisay	Jisa	ETH	29.11.82	15 Apr
61:52	Fekadu	Lemma	ETH	19.2.84	9 Sep
61:53+	Tariku	Jifar	ETH	18.7.84	15 Apr
61:53+	Eshetu	Wondimu	ETH	26.1.82	15 Apr
61:53+	Joseph Kimeli	Lagat	KEN	.86	15 Apr
61:53	Tujuba	Megersa	ETH	15.10.87	23 Jun
61:54	Ryo	Yamamoto	JPN	18.5.84	5 Feb
61:54	Birhanu	Girma	ETH	22.11.86	26 Feb
61:54	Allan	Masai Ndiwa	KEN	19.9.84	31 Mar
61:54+	Debebe	Tolossa	ETH	7.7.91	15 Apr
61:54	David	Kosgei	KEN	.85	1 Sep
61:55	Tomoyuki	Morita	JPN	8.7.84	5 Feb
61:55	Lani	Rutto	KEN		7 Oct
61:56	Hiromitsu	Kakuage	JPN	14.9.90	5 Feb
61:57	Takahiro	Yamanaka	JPN	12.7.86	5 Feb
61:57	Samuel	Ndungu	KEN	4.4.88	20 May
61:57	Isaac	Kemboi Kimaiyo	KEN	28.11.78	15 Jul
61:58	Yuki	Iwai	JPN	30.12.82	5 Feb
61:58	Shuji	Yoshikawa	JPN	6.12.85	5 Feb
61:58	Masamichi	Shinozaki	JPN	5.9.88	5 Feb
61:59	Evans Lagat	Chebet (194)	KEN		16 Sep

Dec 2, Pune: (distance?): 1, M Belachew ETH 61:19; 2, G Getahun ETH 61:24; 3, G Wabi ETH 61:24; 4, D Yegon KEN 61:52

See main list for top 3 juniors.

JUNIORS

Mark	Name		Nat	Born	Pos	Meet	Venue	Date
61:22	Nathan	Ayeko	UGA	10.10.93	1	NC	Kampala	2 Sep
61:41	Gebreyesus	Girmay	ETH	.93	4		Boulogne Billancourt	18 Nov
62:44	Kenta	Murayama	JPN	23.2.93	7		Tachikawa	4 Mar
62:55	Gereme	Wnedem	ETH	.93	9		Boulogne Billancourt	18 Nov
62:58	Hiroto	Inoue	JPN	6.1.93	45		Marugame	5 Feb
63:19	Keita	Shioya	JPN	3.8.93	5		Ageo	18 Nov
63:37	Mitsunori	Asaoka (10)	JPN	11.1.93	27		Tachikawa	4 Mar
63:42A	Mike	Rotich	KEN	11.12.93	7		Nairobi	28 Oct
63:46	Fikadu	Haftu	ETH	21.2.94	15		Lille	1 Sep
63:50	Kazuki	Matsumara	JPN	14.1.93	73		Marugame	5 Feb

25 – 30 KILOMETRES ROAD

In addition to those shown in Marathon listing

25k	30k	Name		Nat	Born	Pos		Venue	Date
1:11:18		Dennis	Kimetto	KEN	22.1.84	1		Berlin	6 May

Mark			Name		Nat	Born	Pos	Meet	Venue	Date
1:11:29			Wilfred	Kigen	KEN	23.2.76	2		Berlin	6 May
1:11:59			Jacob	Kendagor	KEN	.84	3		Berlin	6 May
1:12:39			Edwin	Kiptoo	KEN	28.12.87	4		Berlin	6 May
1:13:22	1:28:05		Feyisa	Lilesa	ETH	1.2.90		in Mar	London	22 Apr
1:13:39	1:28:12		Jonathan	Maiyo	KEN	5.5.88		in Mar	Berlin	30 Sep
1:13:41	1:28:22		Eshetu	Wondimu	ETH	26.1.82		in Mar	Paris	15 Apr
1:13:40	1:28:26		Joseph	Kimeli	KEN	8.10.86		in Mar	Paris	15 Apr
1:13:41	1:28:44		Tariku	Jifar	ETH	18.7.84		in Mar	Paris	15 Apr
1:13:42	1:28:27		Eric	Ndiema	KEN	28.12.92		in Mar	Paris	15 Apr
1:13:42	1:28:45		Debebe	Tolossa	ETH	7.7.91		in Mar	Paris	15 Apr
1:14:12	1:28:40		Tadesse	Tola	ETH	31.10.87		in Mar	Eindhoven	14 Oct
1:14:35	1:29:04		Samuel	Ndungu	KEN	4.4.88		in Mar	Chicago	7 Oct
1:14:36	1:29:05		Yami	Dadi	ETH	.82		in Mar	Chicago	7 Oct
	1:29:06		Bazu	Worku	ETH	15.9.90		in Mar	London	22 Apr
1:14:15	1:29:07		Hailu	Mekonnen	ETH	4.4.80		in Mar	Tokyo	26 Feb
1:14:37	1:29:08		Abdullah Dawit	Shami	ETH	16.7.74		in Mar	Chicago	7 Oct
1:13:49	1:29:14		Tsegaye	Kebede	ETH	15.1.87		in Mar	London	22 Apr
1:14:13	1:29:20		Stephen	Tum	KEN	12.7.86		in Mar	Eindhoven	14 Oct
1:13:28	1:29:25		Stephen	Chemlany	KEN	9.8.82		in Mar	Rotterdam	15 Apr
1:14:01	1:29:25		Abreham	Cherkos	ETH	23.9.89		in Mar	London	22 Apr
1:14:17	1:29:28		Tefere	Kebede	ETH	10.4.86		in Mar	Paris	15 Apr
1:14:32	1:29:26		Deressa	Chimsa	ETH	21.11.86		in Mar	Frankfurt	28 Oct
1:14:32	1:29:29		Bazu	Worku	ETH	15.9.90		in Mar	Frankfurt	28 Oct
1:13:49	1:29:36		Vincent	Kipruto	KEN	13.9.87		in Mar	London	22 Apr

MARATHON

Mark	25k	30k	Name		Nat	Born	Pos	Venue	Date
2:04:15	1:13:38	1:28:11	Geoffrey	Mutai	KEN	7.10.81	1	Berlin	30 Sep
2:04:16	1:13:39	1:28:11	Dennis	Kimetto	KEN	22.1.84	2	Berlin	30 Sep
2:04:23			Ayele	Abshero	ETH	28.12.90	1	Dubai	27 Jan
2:04:38	1:14:34	1:29:03	Tsegaye	Kebede	ETH	15.1.87	1	Chicago	7 Oct
2:04:44	1:13:22	1:28:05	Wilson	Kipsang	KEN	15.3.82	1	London	22 Apr
2:04:48	1:13:01	1:27:41	Yemane Tsegay	Adhane	ETH	8.4.85	1	Rotterdam	15 Apr
2:04:50			Dino	Sefir	ETH	28.5.88	2	Dubai	27 Jan
2:04:50	1:13:02	1:27:42	Getu	Feleke	ETH	28.11.86	2	Rotterdam	15 Apr
2:04:52	1:14:37	1:29:04	Feyisa	Lilesa	ETH	1.2.90	2	Chicago	7 Oct
2:04:54			Markos	Geneti (10)	ETH	30.5.84	3	Dubai	27 Jan
2:04:56			Jonathan	Maiyo	KEN	5.5.88	4	Dubai	27 Jan
2:05:03	1:13:06	1:28:01	Moses	Mosop	KEN	17.7.85	3	Rotterdam	15 Apr
2:05:10			Tadesse	Tola	ETH	31.10.87	5	Dubai	27 Jan
2:05:12	1:13:41	1:28:05	Stanley	Biwott	KEN	21.4.86	1	Paris	15 Apr
2:05:27	1:14:36	1:29:03	Tilahun	Regassa	ETH	18.1.90	3	Chicago	7 Oct
2:05:37	1:14:46	1:29:43	Wilson	Loyanai ¶	KEN	.86	1	Seoul	18 Mar
2:05:41			Yami	Dadi	ETH	.82	6	Dubai	27 Jan
2:05:41	1:14:40	1:29:51	Wilson	Chebet	KEN	12.7.85	1	Amsterdam	21 Oct
2:05:42			Abdullah Dawit	Shami	ETH	16.7.74	7	Dubai	27 Jan
2:05:42			Deressa	Chimsa (20)	ETH	21.11.86	8	Dubai	27 Jan
2:05:46	1:14:12	1:28:36	Dickson	Chumba	KEN	27.10.86	1	Eindhoven	14 Oct
2:05:50		1:30:00	James Kipsang	Kwambai	KEN	28.2.83	1	Seoul	4 Nov
2:05:54	1:14:35	1:29:04	Sammy	Kitwara	KEN	26.11.86	4	Chicago	7 Oct
2:05:58		1:30:02		Shami			1	Hamburg	29 Apr
2:06:03	1:14:46	1:29:43		Kwambai			2	Seoul	18 Mar
2:06:05		1:29:39	Mariko	Kipchumba	KEN	.75	1	Reims	21 Oct
2:06:08	1:14:32	1:29:29	Patrick	Makau	KEN	2.3.85	1	Frankfurt	28 Oct
2:06:11	1:14:12	1:28:39	Frankline	Chepkwony	KEN	15.6.84	2	Eindhoven	14 Oct
2:06:12	1:13:38	1:28:11	Geoffrey	Kipsang	KEN	28.11.92	3	Berlin	30 Sep
2:06:13	1:14:36	1:29:04	Wesley	Korir	KEN	15.11.82	5	Chicago	7 Oct
2:06:17			Seboka	Tola	ETH	10.11.87	9	Dubai	27 Jan
2:06:17	1:14:12	1:28:45	Eric	Ndiema (32/30)	KEN	28.12.92	3	Eindhoven	14 Oct
2:06:21			Abraham	Gebretsadik	ETH	16.7.92	2	Amsterdam	21 Oct
2:06:22	1:14:40		Bentayehu	Assefa	ETH		3	Amsterdam	21 Oct
2:06:24	1:13:41	1:28:17	Raji	Assefa	ETH	18.2.86	2	Paris	15 Apr
2:06:26	1:14:39	1:29:50	Feyisa	Bekele	ETH	.83	4	Amsterdam	21 Oct
2:06:27	1:13:40	1:28:09	Sisay	Jisa	ETH	29.11.82	3	Paris	15 Apr
2:06:40	1:14:36	1:29:05	Bernard	Kipyego	KEN	16.7.86	6	Chicago	7 Oct
2:06:44	1:14:46	1:29:43	Eliud	Kiptanui	KEN	6.6.89	3	Seoul	18 Mar
2:06:48	1:14:40	1:29:51	Abraham	Girma	ETH	.86	5	Amsterdam	21 Oct
2:06:51		1:30:06	Tariku	Jifar	ETH	18.7.84	1	Houston	15 Jan

Mark			Name		Nat	Born	Pos	Meet	Venue	Date	
2:06:51	1:14:46	1:29:43	Philip Sanga	Kimutai	KEN	10.9.83	4		Seoul	18	Mar
			(40)								
2:06:51	1:13:38	1:29:06	Martin	Lel	KEN	29.10.78	2		London	22	Apr
2:06:58			Henry	Sugut	KEN	4.5.85	1		Wien	15	Apr
2:06:58		1:30:38	Joseph	Gitau	KEN	3.1.88	1		Fukuoka	2	Dec
2:07:01			Lawrence	Kimaiyo	KEN	.90	1		Kosice	7	Oct
2:07:04			Samuel	Ndungu	KEN	4.4.88	1		Otsu	4	Mar
2:07:11	1:14:40	1:29:51	Mulugueta	Wami	ETH	17.7.82	6		Amsterdam	21	Oct
2:07:17		1:29:46	Stephen	Tum	KEN	12.7.86	2		Praha	13	May
2:07:23			Augustine	Rono	KEN	.81	3		Hamburg	29	Apr
2:07:28			Eshetu	Wondimu	ETH	26.1.82	11		Dubai	27	Jan
2:07:30			Patrick	Tambwé	COD	5.5.75	1		Tiberias	12	Jan
			(50)								
2:07:31			Felix	Keny	KEN	25.12.85	5		Seoul	18	Mar
2:07:32			Francis	Kibiwott	KEN	15.9.78	2		Tiberias	12	Jan
2:07:35			Tefere	Kebede	ETH	10.4.86	3		Tiberias	12	Jan
2:07:35	1:14:34	1:29:30	Gilbert	Kirwa	KEN	28.12.85	3		Frankfurt	28	Oct
2:07:37			Peter	Kamais	KEN	7.11.76	1		Xiamen	7	Jan
2:07:37	1:14:17	1:29:27	Mike	Kipyego	KEN	2.10.83	1		Tokyo	26	Feb
2:07:37			Alfred	Kering	KEN	.80	1		Köln	14	Oct
2:07:38			Gilbert	Koech	KEN	.81	2		Wien	15	Apr
2:07:39			Henryk	Szost	POL	20.1.82	2		Otsu	4	Mar
2:07:39			Limenih	Getachew	ETH	.91	2		Köln	14	Oct
			(60)								
2:07:41		1:30:06	Debebe	Tolossa	ETH	7.7.91	2		Houston	15	Jan
2:07:41			Charles	Munyeki Kiama	KEN	2.11.86	6		Seoul	18	Mar
2:07:43			Gemechu	Worku	ETH	.85	4		Tiberias	12	Jan
2:07:43			Jairus	Chanchaima	KEN	5.12.84	7		Seoul	18	Mar
2:07:43		1:30:02	Adil	Annani	MAR	30.6.80	4		London	22	Apr
2:07:44			John	Kiprotich	KEN	5.6.83	3		Wien	15	Apr
2:07:44		1:30:02	Jaouad	Gharib	MAR	22.5.72	5		London	22	Apr
2:07:45			Moses	Kigen	KEN	10.1.83	12		Dubai	27	Jan
2:07:47		1:30:05	Dathan	Ritzenhein	USA	30.12.82	9		Chicago	7	Oct
2:07:48			Bazu	Worku	ETH	15.9.90	13		Dubai	27	Jan
			(70)								
2:07:48		1:30:19	Arata	Fujiwara	JPN	12.9.81	2		Tokyo	26	Feb
2:07:49			Philemon	Baaru	KEN	20.5.81	2		Kosice	7	Oct
2:07:49			Evans	Ruto	KEN	14.1.84	3		Kosice	7	Oct
2:07:50	1:14:20	1:29:51	Stephen	Kiprotich	UGA	27.2.89	3		Tokyo	26	Feb
2:07:51			Elijah	Kemboi	KEN	10.9.84	4		Kosice	7	Oct
2:07:53			Duncan	Koech	KEN	28.12.81	3		Köln	14	Oct
2:07:56	1:13:23	1:28:04	Abel	Kirui	KEN	4.6.82	6		London	22	Apr
2:07:56			Shumi	Dechase	ETH	28.5.89	4		Hamburg	29	Apr
2:07:57			David	Kiyeng	KEN	.83	1		Daegu	8	Apr
2:08:01			Julius	Nderitu	KEN	.76	14		Dubai	27	Jan
			(80)								
2:08:01	1:13:38	1:29:06	Emmanuel	Mutai	KEN	12.10.84	7		London	22	Apr
2:08:01			Laban	Mutai	KEN	.85	4		Köln	14	Oct
2:08:03		1:30:03	Marílson	dos Santos	BRA	6.8.77	8		London	22	Apr
2:08:04	1:14:57	1:29:57	Lukas	Kanda	KEN	1.1.87	1		Roma	18	Mar
2:08:05	1:13:07	1:28:22	Stephen	Kibet	KEN	9.11.86	4		Rotterdam	15	Apr
2:08:06	1:13:39	1:29:06	Samuel	Tsegay	ERI	24.2.88	9		London	22	Apr
2:08:07			Hailu	Mekonnen	ETH	4.4.80	1		Hengshui	22	Sep
2:08:11			Stephen	Kibiwott	KEN	3.4.80	15		Dubai	27	Jan
2:08:13			Julius	Maisei	KEN		2		Hengshui	22	Sep
2:08:14		1:29:50	Gideon	Kipketer	KEN	10.11.92	7		Amsterdam	21	Oct
			(90)								
2:08:16			Gilbert	Chepkwony	KEN	28.8.85	2		Daegu	8	Apr
2:08:17	1:14:15	1:29:07	Haile	Gebrselassie	ETH	18.4.73	4		Tokyo	26	Feb
2:08:18			Joel	Kimurer	KEN	21.1.88	2		Valencia	18	Nov
2:08:21	1:14:12	1:28:45	Francis	Bowen	KEN	12.10.73	5		Eindhoven	14	Oct
2:08:24			Hiroyuki	Horibata	JPN	28.10.86	2		Fukuoka	2	Dec
2:08:28			Gidena	Gebremedhin	ETH	.82	5		Tiberias	12	Jan
2:08:28	1:14:12	1:29:51	Nicholas Manza	Kamakya	KEN	2.3.85	4		Berlin	30	Sep
2:08:29	1:14:34	1:29:29	Peter	Some	KEN	5.6.90	4		Frankfurt	28	Oct
2:08:30	1:14:11	1:28:40	Solomon	Kiptoo	KEN	.87	6		Eindhoven	14	Oct
2:08:32			Viktor	Röthlin	SUI	14.10.74	5		Tokyo	26	Feb
			(100)								
2:08:32			William	Kibor	KEN	.80	5		Wien	15	Apr

Mark	Name		Nat	Born	Date		Mark	Name		Nat	Born	Date	
2:08:35	Abraham	Kiprotich	KEN	17.8.85	29	Apr	2:08:36	Abdullah Ahmad Hassan		QAT	29.7.81	29	Apr
2:08:36	Benson	Barus	KEN	4.7.80	8	Apr	2:08:37	Abdellah	Taghrafet	MAR	.85	4	Mar

Mark	Name		Nat	Born	Pos	Meet	Venue	Date
2:08:38	Kazuhiro	Maeda	JPN	9.4.81				26 Feb
2:08:38	Joseph	Kimeli	KEN	8.10.86				15 Apr
2:08:39	Daniel Kiprugut	Too	KEN	21.11.76				15 Apr
2:08:39	Bellor	Yator	KEN	.84				7 Oct
2:08:39	Boniface Muema	Mbuvi	KEN	20.12.86				21 Oct
2:08:41 -	Josphat	Keiyo	KEN	.80				30 Sep
2:08:43	Nixson	Kurgat	KEN	7.11.87				15 Apr
2:08:44	Ryo	Yamamoto	JPN	18.5.84				4 Mar
2:08:44	Jepkopol	Kamzee	KEN	11.2.84				30 Sep
2:08:49	Ennaji	El Idrissi	MAR	8.12.86				8 Apr
2:08:51	Yonas	Kifle	ERI	24.3.77				18 Mar
2:08:51	Berhanu	Shiferaw	ETH-J	31.5.93				2 Sep
2:08:51	Elias	Chelimo Kemboi	KEN	10.3.84				21 Oct
2:08:52	Samson	Barmao	KEN	17.4.82				18 Mar
2:08:52	Daniel	Abera	ETH	15.9.88				22 Sep
2:08:53	Kentaro	Nakamoto	JPN	7.12.82				4 Mar
2:08:53	Albert	Matebor	KEN	20.12.80				28 Oct
2:09:01	Solomon	Tsege	ETH	24.10.87				7 Jan
2:09:01	Beraki	Beyene	ERI	6.2.80				22 Sep
2:09:01	Sylvester	Teimet	KEN	4.6.84				2 Dec
2:09:06	Weldon	Kirui (1:14:12)	KEN	2.12.88				14 Oct
2:09:08	Mebrahtom	Keflezighi	USA	5.5.75				14 Jan
2:09:08	Yusuf	Songoka	KEN	5.2.79				8 Apr
2:09:08	Elijah	Keitany	KEN	18.10.83				21 Oct
2:09:09	Alemayehu	Shumye	ETH	6.4.88				15 Apr
2:09:09	Ismael	Chemtan	KEN	7.7.91				22 Apr
2:09:09 -	Julius	Chepkwony	KEN					14 Oct
2:09:10	Silas	Sang	KEN	21.8.78				15 Apr
2:09:12	Tomoyuki	Morita	JPN	8.7.84				4 Mar
2:09:13	Juius Kiplagat	Korir	KEN	10.1.82				22 Apr
2:09:13	Laban	Moiben	KEN	30.10.83				27 May
2:09:13	Victor	Lagat	KEN	.85				14 Oct
2:09:13	Victor	Kipchirchir (1:29:28)	KEN	5.12.87				28 Oct
2:09:14	Robert	Kwambai	KEN	22.11.85				22 Apr
2:09:15	Peter	Kirui	KEN	2.1.88				21 Oct
2:09:16	Takashi	Horiguchi	JPN	26.9.79				4 Mar
2:09:16	Ahmed Ibrahim	Baday	MAR	12.1.74				8 Apr
2:09:16	Jason	Mbote	KEN	5.1.77				21 Oct
2:09:18	Mike	Mutai	KEN	.87				27 Jan
2:09:21	Isaiah	Kosgei	KEN	12.2.89				22 Sep
2:09:22	Chala	Dechase	ETH	13.6.84				27 Jan
2:09:22	Essa Ismail	Rasheed	QAT	14.12.86				21 Oct
2:09:24	John Kipkorir	Komen	KEN	28.8.77				15 Apr
2:09:24	Henry	Chirchir	KEN	14.5.85				14 Oct
2:09:25	Philemon	Limo	KEN	2.8.85				13 May
2:09:28	Takayuki	Matsumiya	JPN	21.2.80				26 Feb
2:09:29	Gezahagn	Girma	ETH	28.11.83				29 Jan
2:09:30	Vincent	Kiplagat	KEN	10.8.84				7 Jan
2:09:30	Ryan	Hall	USA	14.10.82				14 Jan
2:09:38	Harun	Njoroge	KEN	11.6.88				5 Feb
2:09:40	Mohamed	El Hachimi	MAR	5.9.80				8 Apr
2:09:43	Stephen	Mokoka	RSA	31.1.85				2 Dec
2:09:45	Mike	Tiony	KEN	27.8.85				7 Jan
2:09:46	Robert	Kipchumba	KEN	24.2.84				7 Jan
2:09:47	Abdi	Abdirahman	USA	1.1.77				14 Jan
2:09:47	Lemma	Feyisa	ETH	23.1.85				4 Nov
2:09:47	Gashaw	Melese	ETH	25.9.78				4 Nov
2:09:50	Joel	Kositany	KEN	.88				12 Jan
2:09:50	Dereje	Yadete	ETH	5.2.83				12 Jan
2:09:50	Daniel	Rono	KEN	13.7.78				29 Jan
2:09:50	Fikadu	Lemma	ETH	19.2.84				29 Apr
2:09:52	Laban	Korir (1:29:19)	KEN	.85				7 Oct
2:09:55	Isaiah	Kosgei	KEN	.80				12 Jan
2:09:55	Masashi	Hayashi	JPN	17.7.79				4 Mar
2:09:56	Joseph	Kiptum	KEN	25.9.87				5 May
2:09:56	Megersa	Bacha	ETH	18.1.85				5 May
2:09:58	Michele	Butter	NED	5.11.85				21 Oct
2:09:59	Moses	Kurgat ¶	KEN	.77				22 Apr
2:09:59	Endeshaw	Negesse	ETH					25 Nov
2:10:00	Geoffrey	Ndungu	KEN	11.3.87				15 Apr
2:10:01	Shume	Hailu	ETH	27.10.87				28 Oct
2:10:02	Takehiro	Deki	JPN	12.4.90				4 Mar
2:10:02	Benjamin	Kipruto	KEN	22.2.82				22 Apr
2:10:02	Levy	Matebo (1:29:06)	KEN	3.11.89				7 Oct
2:10:03dh	Nixon	Machichin	KEN	.83				3 Jun
2:10:04	Ernest	Kebenei	KEN	20.11.84				4 Mar
2:10:06	Ruggero	Pertile	ITA	8.8.74				4 Mar
2:10:06	Yigzawe	Debas	ETH	21.12.80				22 Apr
2:10:07	Marcin	Chabowski	POL	28.5.86				29 Apr
2:10:08	Stephen	Chemlany	KEN	9.8.82				15 Apr
2:10:08	Bunta	Kuroki	JPN	28.1.85				2 Dec
2:10:09	Peter	Kurui	KEN	2.1.88				5 May
2:10:13	Takeshi	Kumamoto	JPN	6.1.84				26 Feb
2:10:13	Abderrahim	Bouramdane	MAR	1.1.78				22 Apr
2:10:14	Paul	Biwott	KEN	18.4.78				29 Apr
2:10:14dh	Deats	Gebrehiwet	ETH	15.1.89				3 Jun
2:10:15	Teshome	Gelana	ETH	31.10.83				29 Jan
2:10:15	Abdisa	Sori	ETH	.80				5 May
2:10:20	Solomon	Molla	ETH	20.1.87				25 Nov
2:10:23	Paulo Roberto	Paula	BRA	8.7.79				22 Apr
2:10:26	Abraham	Tadesse	ERI	12.8.82				8 Apr
2:10:27	William	Chebor	KEN	22.12.82				4 Nov
2:10:28	Nahashon	Kimaiyo	KEN	4.5.83				29 Apr
2:10:29	Edwin	Kimaiyo	KEN	.86				18 Mar
2:10:29	Yuki	Kawauchi	JPN	5.3.87				2 Dec
(200)								

Drugs disqualification: 2:08:40 Moses Kurgat ¶   KEN   .77   3   Gyeongju   21 Oct

JUNIORS

Mark	Name		Nat	Born	Pos	Venue	Date
2:08:51	Berhanu	Shiferaw	ETH	31.5.93	1	Taiyuan	2 Sep
	2:09:40	1				Ljubljana	28 Oct
	2:11:54	5				Milano	15 Apr
2:15:11	Peter	Limo	KEN	.94	6	Dalian	12 May

100 KILOMETRES

Mark	Name		Nat	Born	Pos	Meet	Venue	Date
6:23:22	Giorgio	Calcaterra	ITA	11.2.72	1	WCh/EC	Seregno	22 Apr
6:28:58	Jonas	Buud	SWE	28.3.74	2	WCh/EC	Seregno	22 Apr
6:33:32	Yoshikazu	Hara	JPN	13.8.72	1		Yubetsu	24 Jun
6:35:52	Hideo	Nojo	JPN	24.12.76	2		Yubetsu	24 Jun
6:40:32	Alberico	Di Cecco	ITA	19.4.74	3	WCh/EC	Seregno	22 Apr
6:43:55	Takayoshi	Shigemi	JPN	8.6.82	3		Yubetsu	24 Jun
6:44:51		Calcaterra			1		Faenza	27 May
6:44:54	Asier	Cuevas	ESP	16.1.73	4	WCh/EC	Seregno	22 Apr
6:45:19	David	Riddle	USA	25.9.81	5	WCh	Seregno	22 Apr
6:45:45		Hara			1		Nakamura	21 Oct
(10/8)								
6:45:49	André	Collet	GER	21.9.71	6	WCh/EC	Seregno	22 Apr
6:48:22	Oleksandr	Holovnytsky (10)	UKR	29.6.75	1		Torhout	23 Jun
6:48:51	Jonathan	Olsen	USA	18.8.74	7	WCh	Seregno	22 Apr
6:48:59	Michael	Wardian	USA	12.4.74	8	WCh	Seregno	22 Apr
6:49:15	Takahiro	Shimamoto	JPN	.80	4		Yubetsu	24 Jun
6:51:59	Pietro	Colnaghi	ITA	30.10.74	2		Faenza	27 May

Mark	Name		Nat	Born	Date		Mark	Name		Nat	Born	Date
6:53:22	Dominique	Bordet	FRA	2.12.68	22 Apr		6:56:58	Jan-Albert	Lantink	GER	12.5.58	6 Oct
6:54:29	Joseph	Binder	USA	16.8.83	22 Apr		6:58:19	Masakazu	Takahashi	JPN	23.12.73	24 Jun
6:55:26	Brendan	Davies	AUS	3.1.77	22 Apr		6:59:28	Kouji	Kayama	JPN	.73	24 Jun

Mark	Name		Nat	Born	Pos	Meet	Venue	Date
24 HOURS								
277.543	Michael	Morton	USA	20.10.71	1	WCh	Katowice	9 Sep
261.718	Florian	Reus	GER	2.3.84	2	WCh/EC	Katowice	9 Sep
261.365	Ryoichi	Sekiya	JPN	12.2.67	1		Taipei	9 Dec
257.819	Ludovic	Dilmi	FRA	11.4.65	3	WCh/EC	Katowice	9 Sep
257.634	Masahiko	Honda	JPN	15.5.63	1		Tokyo	8 Oct
256.861	Shuhei	Odani	JPN	25.8.88	2		Tokyo	8 Oct
255.487	Ryo	Abiko	JPN	16.1.75	4	WCh	Katowice	9 Sep
255.369		Reus			1		Stadtoldendorf	3 Jun
255.129	Jonathan	Olsen	USA	18.8.74	1	NC	Cleveland	7 May
254.093	Piotr Pawel	Sawicki	POL	17.9.74	5	WCh/EC	Katowice	9 Sep
252.498	Geert	Stynen	BEL	23.12.69	2		Steenbergen	13 May
	(11/10)							
252.387	Toshiro	Naraki	JPN	10.8.76	3		Tokyo	8 Oct
252.250	Jari	Tomppo	FIN	16.2.66	6	WCh/EC	Katowice	9 Sep
252.058t	Jo	Fejes	USA	14.12.65	1		Phoenix	15 Dec
251.799	Michael	Vanicek	GER	25.4.68	7	WCh/EC	Katowice	9 Sep
251.411	Christian	Dilmi	FRA	15.6.66	1		Ville-de-Vierzon	7 Oct
251.128	Emmanuel	Fontaine	FRA	6.12.68	8	WCh/EC	Katowice	9 Sep
250.459	Andrey	Zemtsov	RUS	22.6.64	9	WCh/EC	Katowice	9 Sep
250.234 t	Vladimir	Bychkov	RUS	13.5.67	1		Moscow	13 May

Mark	Name		Nat	Born	Date		Mark	Name		Nat	Born	Date
249.809	Andrzej	Radzikowski	POL	1.4.81	9 Sep		245.939	Patrick	Hösl	GER	18.7.73	9 Sep
248.235	Takahisa	Furukita	JPN	28.6.80	8 Oct		245.710	Yasuhiro	Hiura	JPN	29.4.62	8 Oct
247.787	Gjermund	Sørstad	NOR	17.2.79	9 Sep		245.280	Oliver	Leu	ESP	5.8.74	16 Dec
247.762	Jean-Francois	Harruis	FRA	3.5.59	9 Sep		244.271	Michael	Hilzinger	GER	19.4.60	3 Jun
247.590	Martin	Fryer	AUS	10.9.61	9 Dec		243.064	Shukai	Akaba	JPN	3.6.70	8 Oct
247.023	MarcinMarek	Sieja	POL	11.11.62	10 Jun		**Best track**					
246.921	Serge	Arbona	USA	13.3.65	7 May		247.163 t	Andrey	Zemtsov	RUS	22.6.64	13 May
246.190	Tiziano	Marchesi	ITA	2.3.69	25 Nov		**Indoors**					
246.071	Patrick	Robbins	GBR	12.3.72	9 Sep		245.360	Bjørn Tore Kronen Taranger		NOR	23.4.79	2 Dec
							243.467	Juha	Hietanen	FIN	30.1.71	26 Feb

Mark	Name		Nat	Born	Pos	Meet	Venue	Date
3000 METRES STEEPLECHASE								
7:54.31	Paul Kipsiele	Koech	KEN	10.11.81	1	GGala	Roma	31 May
7:56.58		Koech			1	DL	Doha	11 May
7:56.81	Richard	Mateelong	KEN	14.10.83	2	DL	Doha	11 May
8:00.57		Koech			1	DL	Saint-Denis	6 Jul
8:01.67	Abel	Mutai	KEN	2.10.88	2	GGala	Roma	31 May
8:01.73	Brimin	Kipruto	KEN	31.7.85	2	DL	Saint-Denis	6 Jul
8:03.11		B Kipruto			1	VD	Bruxelles	7 Sep
8:03.15		Mutai			3	DL	Saint-Denis	6 Jul
8:03.43	Jairus	Birech	KEN	14.12.92	4	DL	Saint-Denis	6 Jul
8:03.49	Conseslus	Kipruto	KEN-J	8.12.94	1	Herc	Monaco	20 Jul
8:03.70		C Kipruto			2	VD	Bruxelles	7 Sep
8:03.90		Koech			2	Herc	Monaco	20 Jul
8:04.01		Koech			3	VD	Bruxelles	7 Sep
8:05.71		Birech			4	VD	Bruxelles	7 Sep
8:05.80		Koech			1	Athl	Lausanne	23 Aug
8:06.10		C Kipruto			1	WJ	Barcelona	15 Jul
8:06.16	Roba	Gari	ETH	12.4.82	3	DL	Doha	11 May
8:06.38		Birech			2	Athl	Lausanne	23 Aug
8:06.71		Koech			1		Villeneuve d'Ascq	9 Jun
8:06.72		Birech			4	DL	Doha	11 May
8:06.81	Evan	Jager	USA	8.3.89	3	Herc	Monaco	20 Jul
8:08.33	Bernard	Mbugua	KEN	17.1.85	3	Athl	Lausanne	23 Aug
8:08.36		Mutai			4	Athl	Lausanne	23 Aug
8:08.44		Mutai			1		Brazzaville	10 Jun
8:08.79		Birech			3	GGala	Roma	31 May
8:08.85		Gari			2		Brazzaville	10 Jun
8:08.92		C Kipruto			5	DL	Doha	11 May
8:09.23		Mbugua			4	Herc	Monaco	20 Jul
8:09.34		Birech			3		Brazzaville	10 Jun
8:10.04		Gari			1		Rabat	27 May
	(30/9)							
8:10.20	Brahim	Taleb (10)	MAR	16.2.85	2		Rabat	27 May
8:10.55	Ezekiel	Kemboi	KEN	25.5.82	4	GGala	Roma	31 May
8:10.90	Mahiedine	Mekhissi-Benabbad	FRA	15.3.85	2		Villeneuve d'Ascq	9 Jun
8:11.27	Gilbert	Kirui	KEN-J	22.1.94	7	DL	Doha	11 May
8:11.83	Hillary	Yego	KEN	2.4.92	6	GGala	Roma	31 May
8:12.84	Elijah	Chelimo	KEN	10.3.84	8	DL	Doha	11 May
8:13.71	Ángel	Mullera	ESP	20.4.84	7	VD	Bruxelles	7 Sep

Mark	Name		Nat	Born	Pos	Meet	Venue	Date
8:14.48	Jacob	Araptany	UGA	11.2.92	7	GGala	Roma	31 May
8:15.20	Víctor	García	ESP	13.3.85	1		Huelva	7 Jun
8:16.48	Silas	Kitum	KEN	25.5.90	8	VD	Bruxelles	7 Sep
8:16.93	Hamid	Ezzine	MAR	5.10.83	2		Huelva	7 Jun
	(20)							
8:16.96	Wilson	Maraba	KEN	.87	2	AfrC	Porto Novo	29 Jun
8:17.55	Benjamin	Kiplagat	UGA	4.3.89	8	GGala	Roma	31 May
8:17.85	Tarik Langat	Akdag	TUR	22.4.89	4h1	OG	London (OS)	3 Aug
8:17.88	Jonathan	Ndiku	KEN	18.9.91	8	DL	Saint-Denis	6 Jul
8:18.03	Abdelaziz	Merzougui	ESP	30.8.91	3		Huelva	7 Jun
8:18.16	Nahom	Mesfin	ETH	3.6.89	5h1	OG	London (OS)	3 Aug
8:18.63	Birhan	Getahun	ETH	5.9.91	9	DL	Saint-Denis	6 Jul
8:18.89	Nour-eddine	Gezzar ¶	FRA	17.2.80	3		Villeneuve d'Ascq	9 Jun
8:19.14	Donn	Cabral	USA	12.12.89	1		Los Angeles (ER)	18 May
8:20.81	Dan	Huling	USA	16.7.83	2		Los Angeles (ER)	18 May
	(30)							
8:20.86	Kyle	Alcorn	USA	18.3.85	3		Los Angeles (ER)	18 May
8:21.42	Billy	Nelson	USA	11.9.84	9	GGala	Roma	31 May
8:21.66	Yoann	Kowal	FRA	28.5.87	9	VD	Bruxelles	7 Sep
8:21.78	Hicham	Sigueni	MAR-J	30.1.93	1		Liège (NX)	5 Jul
8:21.80	Lukasz	Parszczynski	POL	4.5.85	10	GGala	Roma	31 May
8:21.98	Youcef	Abdi	AUS	7.12.77	2		Istanbul	9 Jun
8:22.09	Ion	Luchianov	MDA	31.1.81	5h3	OG	London (OS)	3 Aug
8:22.19	Vadym	Slobodenyuk	UKR	17.3.81	1	NCp	Yalta	28 May
8:22.24	Nelson	Kipkosgei	KEN-J	9.3.93	2		Liège (NX)	5 Jul
8:22.32	Mohamed-Khaled	Belabbas	ALG	4.7.81	6h3	OG	London (OS)	3 Aug
	(40)							
8:22.62	Yuri	Floriani	ITA	25.12.81	11	GGala	Roma	31 May
8:22.62	Alexandre	Genest	CAN	30.6.86	7h3	OG	London (OS)	3 Aug
8:22.70	Amor	Benyahia	TUN	1.7.85	7h1	OG	London (OS)	3 Aug
8:22.81	Nikolay	Chavkin	RUS	22.4.84	10	VD	Bruxelles	7 Sep
8:22.93	Steffen	Uliczka	GER	17.7.84	3		Liège (NX)	5 Jul
8:23.07	Ildar	Minshin	RUS	5.2.85	3		Moskva	11 Jun
8:23.22	Hakan	Duvar	TUR	21.8.90	3		Istanbul	9 Jun
8:23.31	Andrey	Farnosov	RUS	9.7.80	4		Moskva	11 Jun
8:23.61	Timothy	Toroitich	UGA	10.10.91	4		Brazzaville	10 Jun
8:23.62	Simon	Ayeko	UGA	10.5.87	2		Mataró	8 Jul
	(50)							
8:24.06	José Gregorio	Peña	VEN	12.1.87	8h1	OG	London (OS)	3 Aug
8:24.13	Artyom	Kosinov	KAZ	31.7.86	5		Moskva	11 Jun
8:24.19	Antonio David	Jiménez	ESP	18.2.77	4		Huelva	7 Jun
8:24.28	Sisay	Korme	ETH	9.1.85	1		Fortaleza	9 May
8:24.28	Ruben	Ramolefi	RSA	17.7.78	11	DL	Doha	11 May
8:24.53	Roberto	Alaiz	ESP	20.7.90	6		Huelva	7 Jun
8:24.76	Tumelo	Motlagale	RSA	26.11.86	2	NC	Port Elizabeth	14 Apr
8:25.12	Haron	Lagat	KEN	15.8.83	1		Dessau	25 May
8:25.50	Krystian	Zalewski	POL	11.4.89	2		Dessau	25 May
8:25.66	Dejene	Regassa	BRN	18.4.89	3	Spitzen	Luzern	17 Jul
	(60)							
8:25.67	Clement	Kemboi	KEN	1.2.92	4	Spitzen	Luzern	17 Jul
8:25.98	Jaouad	Chemlal	MAR-J	11.4.94	8		Rabat	27 May
8:26.00	Sebastián	Martos	ESP	20.6.89	4		Mataró	8 Jul
8:26.08	Benjamin	Bruce	USA	10.9.82	1		Nashville	2 Jun
8:26.12	Abraham	Chirchir	KEN	1.8.80	9		Rabat	27 May
8:26.22	Ali Ahmed	Al-Amri	KSA	28.12.87	9h1	OG	London (OS)	3 Aug
8:26.33	Tafese	Soboka	ETH-J	.93	5	AfrC	Porto Novo	29 Jun
8:26.51	Donnie	Cowart	USA	24.10.85	1		Indianapolis	13 Jun
8:27.24	Patrick	Terer	KEN	6.7.89	7		Moskva	11 Jun
8:27.61	Lukasz	Oslizlo	POL	14.5.89	2		Bottrop	7 Jul
	(70)							
8:27.65	Eliseo	Martín	ESP	5.11.73	6		Mataró	8 Jul
8:27.77	David	Adams	USA	4.1.89	5		Los Angeles (ER)	18 May
8:27.96	Jukka	Keskisalo	FIN	27.3.81	8	Herc	Monaco	20 Jul
8:28.46	Chris	Winter	CAN	22.7.86	6	Spitzen	Luzern	17 Jul
8:28.52	Diego	Tamayo	ESP	6.12.83	7		Mataró	8 Jul
8:28.77	Abdellah	Dacha	MAR	26.1.92	1		Oordegem	26 May
8:28.90	Craig	Forys	USA	13.7.89	1	Big 10	Madison	12 May
8:28.97	Weynay	Ghebreselassie	ERI-J	24.3.94	2		Oordegem	26 May
8:29.03	Habtamu	Jaleta	ETH-J	19.4.93	6	AfrC	Porto Novo	29 Jun
8:29.08	Patrick	Nasti	ITA	30.8.89	7		Huelva	7 Jun
	(80)							

Mark	Name		Nat	Born	Pos	Meet	Venue	Date	
8:29.17	Dmitriy	Balashov	RUS	19.1.89	2	NC	Cheboksary	3	Jul
8:29.22	Luke	Gunn	GBR	22.3.85	3		Ooredegem	26	May
8:29.29	Augustus	Maiyo	USA	10.5.83	4h2	NC/OT	Eugene	25	Jun
8:29.32	Stuart	Stokes	GBR	5.12.76	4		Oordegem	26	May
8:29.39	Enrique	Sánchez	ESP	14.10.83	8		Mataró	8	Jul
8:29.59	Ilgizar	Safiulin	RUS	9.12.92	4	NC	Cheboksary	3	Jul
8:29.7 A	Peter	Mateelong	KEN	26.11.89	4	NC	Nairobi	15	Jun
8:29.78	Mounatcer	Zaghou	MAR	.89	2		Fes	5	May
8:29.8 A	Hillary	Kemboi	KEN	.86	3		Nairobi	12	May
8:29.98	Dean (90)	Brummer	RSA	15.9.88	4		Oordegem	26	May
8:30.08	Brian	Olinger	USA	2.6.83	5h2	NC/OT	Eugene	25	Jun
8:30.34	Halil	Akkas	TUR	1.7.83	1		Izmir	20	May
8:30.54	Max	King	USA	24.2.80	6	NC/OT	Eugene	28	Jun
8:30.80	Nelson	Kosgei	KEN-J	.93	6		Dessau	25	May
8:30.83	Lyle	Weese	USA	26.10.79	7		Los Angeles (ER)	18	May
8:31.01	Abdelmadjed	Touil	ALG	11.2.89	3		Bottrop	7	Jul
8:31.02	Tomasz	Szymkowiak	POL	5.7.83	11	DL	Saint-Denis	6	Jul
8:31.08	Cory	Leslie	USA	24.10.89	4h1	NC/OT	Eugene	25	Jun
8:31.15	Josh	McAdams	USA	26.3.80	5h1	NC/OT	Eugene	25	Jun
8:31.2 A	Lawrence (100)	Kemboi	KEN-J	.93	1h1	NC	Nairobi	14	Jun

Mark	Name		Nat	Born	Date	
8:31.4 A	Alex	Kibet	KEN-J	20.10.94	8	Jun
8:31.58	Yevgeniy	Cherepanov	RUS	28.4.91	27	May
8:31.62	Rob	Mullett	GBR	31.7.87	18	May
8:31.63	Rabie	Makhloufi	ALG	11.11.86	9	Jun
8:31.77	Matthew	Hughes	CAN	3.8.89	29	Apr
8:31.77	Younes	Essalhi	MAR-J	20.2.93	9	Jun
8:32.08	Bilal	Tabti	ALG-J	7.6.93	15	Jul
8:32.15	Tareq Mubarak Taher		BRN	24.3.84	7	Jul
8:32.2 A	Michael	Kimutai	KEN		14	Jun
8:32.55	Stanislav	Anishchenkov	RUS	21.8.82	3	Jul
8:32.63	Saeed Abbas	Al-Thomali	KSA	20.6.85	7	Jul
8:32.73	Radoslaw	Kleczek	POL	12.4.85	3	Jun
8:32.75	Vincent Zouaoui Dandrieux		FRA	12.10.80	31	May
8:32.76	Dawid	Zebrowski	POL	6.1.91	15	Jun
8:32.82	Noureddine	Smaïl	FRA	6.2.87	17	Jun
8:33.09	Alberto	Paulo	POR	3.10.85	5	Jul
8:33.21	Mohammed	Boulama	MAR-J	32.12.93	9	Jun
8:33.23	Romain	Collenot-Spriet	FRA	9.1.92	5	Jul
8:33.40	Tomás	Tajadura	ESP	25.6.85	13	Jun
8:33.42	Tanguy	Pepiot	FRA	6.7.91	7	Jul
8:33.5 A	Kennedy	Njiru	KEN	,87	14	Jun
8:33.89	Jordan	Fife	USA	18.8.83	29	Apr
8:33.98	Justin	Tyner	USA	20.7.89	18	May
8:34.00	James	Wilkinson	GBR	13.7.90	7	Jun
8:34.03	Itai	Magidi	ISR	9.1.81	26	May
8:34.1 A	Hillary	Kemboi	KEN	.86	14	Jun
8:34.25A	Ben	Siwa	UGA	27.5.89	23	Jul
8:34.27	Marvin	Blanco	VEN	16.5.88	26	May
8:34.28	Matthew	Brunsting	CAN	1.1.89	13	Jun
8:34.4A	Pholip	Yego	KEN	.79	18	May
8:34.8 A	Edwin	Kirwa	KEN		14	Jun
8:34.95	Minato	Yamashita	JPN	15.11.88	8	Jun
8:35.00	Ryan	Haebe	USA	14.11.90	9	Jun
8:35.07	Yuriy	Kloptsov	RUS	22.12.89	26	May
8:35.27	Tsuyoshi	Takeda	JPN	22.1.87	8	Jun
8:35.28	Ahmed Mohammed Burhan		KSA-J	21.6.93	27	May
8:35.51	Fernando	Carro	ESP	1.4.92	16	Jun
8:35.69	Hichem	Bouchicha	ALG	19.5.89	27	May
8:35.76	Peter	Nowill	AUS	15.6.79	3	Mar
8:35.77	Andrew	Poore	USA	3.12.88	12	May
8:35.79	Corey	Nowitzke	USA	26.4.84	19	Apr
8:36.06	Aoi	Matsumoto	JPN	7.9.87	5	Oct
8:36.10	Kaur	Kivistik	EST	29.4.91	27	Jun
8:36.13	Meresa	Kassaye	ETH-Y	23.5.96	13	Jul
8:36.13	Jun	Shinoto	JPN	2.4.85	23	Sep
8:36.3 A	Geoffrey	Tanui	KEN-J		8	Jun
8:36.35	Gladson	Barbosa	BRA	16.8.79	9	May
8:36.39	Hudson	de Souza	BRA	25.2.77	9	May
8:36.39	De'Sean	Turner	USA	16.9.88	12	May
8:36.44	Hillary	Bor	KEN	22.11.89	18	May
8:36.6 A	Linus	Chumba	KEN	9.2.80	12	May
8:36.75	Mariano	Mastromarino	ARG	15.9.82	2	Jun
8:37.03	Ben	Toroitoich	KEN		25	May
8:37.17	Steve	Slattery	USA	14.8.80	25	Jun
8:37.28	Cameron	Bean	USA	17.12.86	13	Jun
8:37.32	Luis Miguel	Ibarra	MEX	4.7.80	6	Apr
8:37.38	Anthony	Famiglietti	USA	8.11.78	2	Jun
8:37.45	Carlos	Alonso	ESP	15.9.89	9	Jun
8:37.45	Aric	Van Halen	USA	6.10.89	13	Jun
8:37.57	Francisco Javier Lara		ESP	24.6.76	26	May
8:37.62	Alex	Brill	USA	23.9.90	12	May
8:37.79	James	Nipperess	AUS	21.5.90	18	May
8:37.84	Benedikt	Karus	GER	22.1.90	25	May
8:37.95		Lin Xiangqian	CHN	27.1.87	13	Sep
8:38.05	Jonathan	Taylor	GBR	10.10.87	9	Jun
8:38.07	Zak	Seddon	GBR-J	28.6.94	9	Jun
8:38.52	Brett	Hales	USA	18.11.86	9	Jun
8:38.55	Derek	Scott	USA	7.11.85	25	Jun
8:38.60	JT	Sullivan	USA	17.9.88	18	May
8:38.87	Jared	Bassett	USA	6.5.90	18	May
8:38.90	Henry	Lelei	KEN	31.12.88	13	May
8:39.19	José Luis	Blanco	ESP	3.6.75	30	May
8:39.22		Wang Yashuan	CHN	26.6.88	25	Sep
8:39.27	Gervais	Hakizimana	RWA	5.9.87	26	May
8:39.29	Hiroyoshi	Umegae	JPN	5.1.84	5	Oct
8:39.32	Ilya	Slavinskiy	BLR	2.8.84	3	Jun
8:39.37	Ibrahim	Ezzaydouny	MAR	28.4.91	18	Jul
8:39.4 A	Charles	Sigei	KEN		18	May
8:39.52	Abdelhamid	Zerrifi	ALG	20.6.86	9	Jun
8:39.56	Lukasz	Kujawski	POL	2.3.88	25	May
8:39.70	Vladislav	Nikolayev	BLR	2.10.92	25	May
8:39.70	Carl	Stones	USA	1.11.89	7	Jun
8:39.71	Henry	Kiplagat	KEN	.90	18	Apr
8:39.97	Eric	Senorski (184)	SWE	25.7.89	25	Aug

JUNIORS

See main list for top 10 juniors. 13 performances by 4 men to 8:23.0. Additional marks and further juniors:

Name		Mark	Pos	Meet	Venue	Date		Mark	Pos	Meet	Venue	Date	
C Kipruto 4+		8:15.79	5	Athl	Lausanne	23	Aug	8:19.49	2		Kawasaki	6	May
		8:19.46	1h2	WJ	Barcelona	13	Jul	8:21.3A	1	NC-j	Nairobi	8	Jun
Kirui		8:19.94	2	WJ	Barcelona	15	Jul	8:21.16	4		Kawasaki	6	May

Mark	Name		Nat	Born	Pos	Meet	Venue	Date	
8:31.4 A	Alex	Kibet	KEN	20.10.94	3	NC-j	Nairobi	8	Jun
8:31.77	Younes	Essalhi	MAR	20.2.93	3		Casablanca	9	Jun
8:32.08	Bilal	Tabti	ALG	7.6.93	5	WJ	Barcelona	15	Jul
8:33.21	Mohammed	Boulama	MAR	32.12.93	4		Casablanca	9	Jun
8:35.28	Ahmed Mohammed	Burhan	KSA	21.6.93	12		Rabat	27	May
8:36.13	Meresa	Kassaye	ETH-Y	23.5.96	7	WJ	Barcelona	13	Jul

Mark	Name		Nat	Born	Pos	Meet	Venue	Date
8:36.3 A	Geoffrey	Tanui	KEN		3	NC-j	Nairobi	8 Jun
8:38.07	Zak	Seddon	GBR	28.6.94	5		Watford	9 Jun
8:40.1A	Festus	Rono	KEN	28.12.93	8	NC-j	Nairobi	8 Jun
8:40.2A	Peter	Mutuku (20)	KEN	12.1.94	5h1	NC	Nairobi	14 Jun

60 METRES HURDLES INDOORS

Mark	Name		Nat	Born	Pos	Meet	Venue	Date
7.40A	Dexter	Faulk	USA	14.4.84	1h3	NC	Albuquerque	25 Feb
7.54					3	GP	Birmingham	18 Feb
7.41		Liu Xiang	CHN	13.7.83	1	GP	Birmingham	18 Feb
7.43A	Aries	Merritt	USA	24.7.85	1	NC	Albuquerque	26 Feb
7.44		Merritt			1	WI	Istanbul	11 Mar
7.46A	Kevin	Craddock	USA	25.6.87	2	NC	Albuquerque	26 Feb
7.53					1		Düsseldorf	10 Feb
7.49	Jarret	Eaton	USA	24.6.89	1		University Park	27 Jan
7.49		Liu			1h1	GP	Birmingham	18 Feb
7.49		Liu			2	WI	Istanbul	11 Mar
7.50	Dayron	Robles	CUB	19.11.86	2	GP	Birmingham	18 Feb
7.51	David	Oliver	USA	24.4.82	1	Mill	New York (Armory)	11 Feb
7.51A	Terrence	Trammell	USA	23.11.78	3	NC	Albuquerque	26 Feb
7.52		Trammell			2	Mill	New York (Armory)	11 Feb
7.52	Konstantin (13/9)	Shabanov	RUS	17.11.89	1h1		Karlsruhe	12 Feb
7.53	Andrew	Riley (10)	JAM	6.9.88	1		Fayetteville	11 Feb
7.53A	Omo	Osaghae	USA	18.5.88	1h1	NC	Albuquerque	25 Feb
7.53	Pascal	Martinot-Lagarde	FRA	22.9.91	3	WI	Istanbul	11 Mar
7.54	Jeff	Porter	USA	27.11.85	1		Karlsruhe	12 Feb
7.54	Fred	Townsend	USA	19.2.82	1		Val-de-Reuil	18 Feb
7.55	Devon	Hill	USA	26.10.89	2	NCAA	Nampa	10 Mar
7.55	Barrett	Nugent	USA	29.1.90	3	NCAA	Nampa	10 Mar
7.56	Joel	Brown	USA	31.1.80	2		Liévin	14 Feb
7.56	Sergey	Shubenkov	RUS	4.10.90	1	NC-23	Saransk	2 Mar
7.56	Andrew	Pozzi	GBR	15.5.92	2s1	WI	Istanbul	11 Mar
7.57	Emanuele (20)	Abate	ITA	8.7.85	1		Magglingen	4 Feb
7.57	Orlando	Ortega	CUB	29.7.91	1r2		Metz	29 Feb
7.58	Helge	Schwarzer	GER	26.11.85	1		Kirchberg	4 Feb
7.59	Ronald	Ash	USA	2.7.88	1		Birmingham, AL	21 Jan
7.59	Gregor	Traber	GER	2.12.92	1	NC	Karlsruhe	25 Feb
7.60	Spencer	Adams	USA	10.9.89	5	NCAA	Nampa	10 Mar
7.61	Cédric	Lavanne	FRA	13.11.80	2r2		Metz	29 Feb
7.63	Maksim	Lynsha	BLR	6.4.85	3	Winter	Moskva	5 Feb
7.63	Konstadínos	Douvalídis	GRE	10.3.87	1	NC	Athina (P)	22 Feb
7.64	Lehann	Fourie	RSA	16.2.87	3		Boston (Roxbury)	4 Feb
7.64	Yevgeniy (30)	Borisov	RUS	7.3.84	2=	NC	Moskva	22 Feb
7.65	Thomas	Delmestre	FRA	31.3.91	2		Val-de-Reuil	18 Feb
7.65	Artur	Noga	POL	2.5.88	1	NC	Spala	26 Feb
7.66A	Ashton	Eaton	USA	21.1.88	3h2	NC	Albuquerque	25 Feb
7.66	Edward	Lovett	USA	25.6.92	2h1	NCAA	Nampa	9 Mar
7.67 OUT	David	Payne	USA	24.7.82	1		Daytona Beach	28 Jan
7.67	Lawrence	Clarke	GBR	12.3.90	3	v4N	Glasgow	28 Jan
7.67	Balázs	Baji	HUN	9.6.89	2		Kirchberg	4 Feb
7.67A	Andrew	Brunson	USA	4.4.86	4h1	NC	Albuquerque	25 Feb
7.67	Richard	Phillips	JAM	26.1.83	1		Fairfax	26 Feb
7.67	Caleb (40)	Cross	USA	31.5.91	3h1	NCAA	Nampa	9 Mar
7.68A	Dominic	Berger	USA	19.5.86	4h3	NC	Albuquerque	25 Feb
7.68	Dominik	Bochenek	POL	14.5.87	2	NC	Spala	26 Feb
7.69	Mantas	Silkauskas	LTU	10.4.88	1		Manhattan KS	21 Jan
7.69	Dimitri	Bascou	FRA	20.7.87	4		Liévin	14 Feb
7.69	Alexander	John	GER	3.5.86	2	NC	Karlsruhe	25 Feb
7.70	Gianni	Frankis	GBR	16.4.88	2		Wien	31 Jan
7.70	Paolo	Dal Molin	ITA	31.7.87	1h2		Gent	18 Feb
7.70	Matthias	Bühler	GER	2.9.86	3	NC	Karlsruhe	25 Feb
7.70	Wayne	Davis	TRI	22.8.91	7	NCAA	Nampa	10 Mar
7.71	Jackson (50)	Quiñónez	ESP	12.6.80	1		Zaragoza	4 Feb
7.71	Samuel	Coco-Viloin	FRA	19.10.87	5h1		Karlsruhe	12 Feb
7.71	Julian	Adeniran	GBR	28.9.88	7h2	GP	Birmingham	18 Feb
7.71	Ladji	Doucouré	FRA	28.3.83	3	NC	Aubière	25 Feb

Mark		Name		Nat	Born	Pos	Meet	Venue	Date	

110 METRES HURDLES

Mark		Name		Nat	Born	Pos	Meet	Venue	Date	
12.80	0.3	Aries	Merritt	USA	24.7.85	1	VD	Bruxelles	7	Sep
12.92	-0.3		Merritt			1	OG	London (OS)	8	Aug
12.93	1.2		Merritt			1	NC/OT	Eugene	30	Jun
12.93	0.6		Merritt			1	LGP	London(CP)	13	Jul
12.93	0.0		Merritt			1	Herc	Monaco	20	Jul
12.94	0.1		Merritt			1s2	OG	London (OS)	8	Aug
12.95	-0.9		Merritt			1	DL	Birmingham	26	Aug
12.97	0.4		Liu Xiang	CHN	13.7.83	1	DL	Shanghai	19	May
12.97	1.2		Merritt			1	ISTAF	Berlin	2	Sep
12.98	1.5	Jason	Richardson	USA	4.4.86	1s3	NC/OT	Eugene	30	Jun
12.98	1.2		Richardson			2	NC/OT	Eugene	30	Jun
12.98	-0.9		Richardson			2	DL	Birmingham	26	Aug
13.01	1.2		Merritt			1s2	NC/OT	Eugene	30	Jun
13.03	1.0		Merritt			1		Fayetteville	4	May
13.04	-0.3		Richardson			2	OG	London (OS)	8	Aug
13.05	0.3		Richardson			2	VD	Bruxelles	7	Sep
13.06	0.6		Richardson			2	LGP	London(CP)	13	Jul
13.07	0.0		Richardson			2	Herc	Monaco	20	Jul
13.07	0.7		Merritt			1h5	OG	London (OS)	7	Aug
13.07	0.3	David	Oliver	USA	24.4.82	1		Albi	15	Aug
13.07	-0.4		Richardson			1	Hanz	Zagreb	4	Sep
13.08	1.2	Jeff	Porter	USA	27.11.85	3	NC/OT	Eugene	30	Jun
13.08	-0.6		Richardson			1	Athl	Lausanne	23	Aug
13.09	0.2		Liu Xiang			1		Kawasaki	6	May
13.09	0.0	Orlando	Ortega	CUB	29.7.91	1		La Habana	27	May
13.09	-1.1	Sergey	Shubenkov	RUS	4.10.90	1s2	EC	Helsinki	1	Jul
13.09	0.0		Shubenkov			3	Herc	Monaco	20	Jul
13.09	0.0		Shubenkov			1	Gugl	Linz	20	Aug
13.10	0.1	Dayron	Robles	CUB	19.11.86	1s3	OG	London (OS)	8	Aug
13.12	-0.3	Hansle	Parchment	JAM	17.6.90	3	OG	London (OS)	8	Aug
13.12	0.3		Shubenkov			2		Albi	15	Aug
		(31/9)								
13.13	1.4	Dexter	Faulk (10)	USA	14.4.84	1	GS	Ostrava	25	May
13.14	1.2	Antwon	Hicks	USA	12.3.83	4	NC/OT	Eugene	30	Jun
13.15	-0.3	Garfield	Darien	FRA	22.12.87	1s3	EC	Helsinki	1	Jul
13.18	0.6	Ryan	Wilson	USA	19.12.80	3	LGP	London (CP)	13	Jul
13.19	1.3	Andrew	Riley	JAM	9.9.88	2	NC	Kingston	30	Jun
13.20	1.0	Ronnie	Ash	USA	2.7.88	2		Kingston	5	May
13.23	1.6	Joel	Brown	USA	31.1.80	1		Tomblaine	8	Jul
13.23	0.7	Ryan	Brathwaite	BAR	6.6.88	2h5	OG	London (OS)	7	Aug
13.24	1.0	Omo	Osaghae	USA	18.5.88	2	Drake	Des Moines	28	Apr
13.24	0.3	Lehann	Fourie	RSA	16.2.87	6	VD	Bruxelles	7	Sep
13.27	0.5	Artur	Noga	POL	2.5.88	3	EC	Helsinki	1	Jul
		(20)								
13.28	0.7	Emanuele	Abate	ITA	8.7.85	3	Nebiolo	Torino	8	Jun
13.30	0.1	Tyrone	Akins	USA	6.1.86	1rB	Spitzen	Luzern	17	Jul
13.31A	1.8	Shane	Brathwaite	BAR	8.2.90	1	NACAC	Irapuato	7	Jul
13.31	-0.5	Lawrence	Clarke	GBR	12.3.90	3s1	OG	London (OS)	8	Aug
13.32	1.2	David	Payne	USA	24.7.82	2h3	NC/OT	Eugene	29	Jun
13.32A	1.8	Barrett	Nugent	USA	29.1.90	2	NACAC	Irapuato	7	Jul
13.34	1.6	Dimitri	Bascou	FRA	20.7.87	3		Tomblaine	8	Jul
13.34	-0.9	Andrew	Pozzi	GBR	15.5.92	4h2	LGP	London (CP)	13	Jul
13.34	1.3	Matthias	Bühler	GER	2.9.86	1r4		Weinheim	27	Jul
13.34	0.1		Xie Wenjun	CHN	11.7.90	3s2	OG	London (OS)	8	Aug
		(30)								
13.35	1.9	Devon	Hill	USA	26.10.89	1	ACC	Charlottesville	21	Apr
13.35	0.7	Alexander	John	GER	3.5.86	1r3		Weinheim	27	Jul
13.36	1.0	Terrence	Trammell	USA	23.11.78	3	Drake	Des Moines	28	Apr
13.36	0.9	Dwight	Thomas	JAM	23.9.80	1h2		Clermont	2	Jun
13.36	0.3	Maksim	Lynsha	BLR	6.4.85	3	Déca	Albi	15	Aug
13.37	1.5	Ladji	Doucouré	FRA	28.3.83	5		Gainesville	21	Apr
13.37	1.8	Wayne	Davis II	USA/TRI	22.8.91	1	Big 12	Manhattan	13	May
13.37	-0.3	Konstadínos	Douvalídis	GRE	10.3.87	2s3	EC	Helsinki	1	Jul
13.39	1.9	Spencer	Adams	USA	10.9.89	2	ACC	Charlottesville	21	Apr
13.39	1.1	Fred	Townsend	USA	19.2.82	1		Sundsvall	17	Jun
		(40)								
13.41	1.9	Andrew	Turner	GBR	19.9.80	1	ECCp	Vila Real de Santo António	27	May
13.41	1.3	Pascal	Martinot-Lagarde	FRA	22.9.91	1		Castres	24	Jun
13.42	1.5	Kevin	Craddock	USA	25.6.87	3s3	NC/OT	Eugene	30	Jun

Mark	Wind	Name		Nat	Born	Pos	Meet	Venue	Date
13.42	-0.5	Adrian	Deghelt	BEL	10.5.85	4s1	OG	London (OS)	8 Aug
13.43	-0.7	Richard	Phillips	JAM	26.1.83	2		Clermont	9 Jun
13.44	1.3	Jarret	Eaton	USA	24.6.89	1q1	NCAA-E	Jacksonville	26 May
13.44	1.2	Dominic	Berger	USA	19.5.86	4h3	NC/OT	Eugene	29 Jun
13.45	1.7	Chris	Thomas	USA	9.2.81	1rA	TexR	Austin	31 Mar
13.45	1.3	Johnathan	Cabral	CAN/USA	31.12.92	1q2	NCAA-W	Austin	26 May
13.45	0.5	Gregory	Sedoc	NED	16.10.81	6	EC	Helsinki	1 Jul
		(50)							
13.46	-0.5	Erik	Balnuweit	GER	21.9.88	2		Nottwil	30 Jun
13.46	1.3	Keiron	Stewart	JAM	21.11.89	4	NC	Kingston	30 Jun
13.47	-0.5	Gregor	Traber	GER	2.12.92	4		Genève	2 Jun
13.47	0.8	Cédric	Lavanne	FRA	13.11.80	2		Elancourt	27 Jun
13.47	0.0	Philip	Nossmy	SWE	6.12.82	2s1	EC	Helsinki	1 Jul
13.47	1.3	João	Almeida	POR	5.4.88	1	NC	Lisboa (Un)	8 Jul
13.48	1.9	Mikel	Thomas	TRI	23.11.87	1rB	TexR	Austin	31 Mar
13.48	1.8	Fawez Dahesh	Al-Shammari	KUW	3.4.77	1	BUL Ch	Sliven	15 Jun
13.49	1.8	Ryan	Fontenot	USA	4.5.86	1		Lafayette, LA	28 Apr
13.49	0.1		Shi Dongpeng	CHN	6.1.84	2		Zibo	27 May
		(60)							
13.49	1.2	Eddie	Lovett	USA	25.6.92	5h3	NC/OT	Eugene	29 Jun
13.50	0.0		Ji Wei	CHN	5.2.84	1		Zhaoqing	15 Apr
13.50	1.1	Balázs	Baji	HUN	9.6.89	2h5	EC	Heksinki	30 Jun
13.50	0.1	Rouhollah	Ashgari	IRI	8.1.82	1		Almaty	1 Jul
13.50	-1.1	Samuel	Coco-Viloin	FRA	19.10.87	3s2	EC	Helsinki	1 Jul
13.50	1.1	William	Sharman	GBR	12.9.84	1rA2		Loughborough	7 Jul
13.51	0.4	Selim	Nurudeen	NGR	1.2.83	2h6	OG	London (OS)	7 Aug
13.52	-0.8	Greggmar	Swift	BAR	16.2.91	2	NC	Nassau	24 Jun
13.53	0.0	Dániel	Kiss	HUN	12.2.82	1		Moskva	11 Jun
13.53	-0.5	Jeffrey	Julmis	HAI	6.1.87	1	BAH Ch	Nassau	23 Jun
		(70)							
13.54	-0.7		Jiang Fan	CHN	16.9.89	1		Kanchanaburi	11 May
13.54	1.0	Ignacio	Morales	CUB	28.1.87	1	IbAmC	Barquisimeto	9 Jun
13.54	2.0	Hideki	Omuro	JPN	25.7.90	1		Hiratsuka	23 Jun
13.54	0.1	Trey	Hardee	USA	7.2.84	1D	OG	London (OS)	9 Aug
13.55	1.3	Vladimir	Vukicevic	NOR	6.5.91	2r2		Weinheim	27 Jul
13.55	0.6	Paulo César	Villar	COL	28.7.78	5h1	OG	London (OS)	7 Aug
13.56		Shamar	Sands	BAH	30.4.85	6		Georgetown, CAY	9 May
13.56	0.1	Ashton	Eaton	USA	21.1.88	2D	OG	London (OS)	9 Aug
13.57	1.1	Konstandin	Shabanov	RUS	17.11.89	1h2	NC	Cheboksary	5 Jul
13.58	-0.3	Abdulaziz	Al-Mandeel	KUW	22.5.89	1		Bangkok	8 May
		(80)							
13.58	1.8	David	Ilariani	GEO	20.1.81	2	BUL Ch	Sliven	15 Jun
13.59	1.5	Dominik	Bochenek	POL	14.5.87	1h3	NC	Bielsko-Biala	17 Jun
13.59	-0.5	Marlon	Odom	GER	4.12.82	3		Nottwil	30 Jun
13.59	0.1	Denis	Semenov	KAZ	10.10.90	2		Almaty	1 Jul
13.61	0.5	Damian	Warner	CAN	4.10.89	1D		Tucson	30 Mar
13.61	1.8	Helge	Schwarzer	GER	26.11.85	2r3		Mannheim	9 Jun
13.62	2.0	Hiroyuki	Sato	JPN	6.8.90	1		Tokyo	13 May
13.62	1.5	Eric	Keddo	JAM	1.7.84	1rB		Clermont	9 Jun
13.63	1.3	Lawson	Montgomery	USA	9.7.90	3q2	NCAA-W	Austin	26 May
13.64	1.5	Aramis	Massenberg	USA	6.8.89	2h1		Raleigh	30 Mar
		(90)							
13.64	1.6	Andrew	Brunson	USA	4.4.86	1		Clemson	5 May
13.64	0.0	Paolo	Dal Molin	ITA	31.7.87	1rB		Mannheim	12 May
13.64	1.9	Rasul	Dabo	POR	14.2.89	2	ECCp	Vila Real de Santo António	27 May
13.64	0.2	Richard	Alleyne	GBR	7.5.83	1		Oordegem	2 Jun
13.64	1.2	Joseph	Hylton	GBR	17.11.89	2h4	NC	Birmingham	24 Jun
13.64	-0.1	Lyès	Mokdel	ALG	20.6.90	1	NC	Alger	8 Jul
13.65	1.0	Malcolm	Anderson	USA	18.9.89	2		Fayetteville	4 May
13.65	1.8	Tre	Lathan	USA	15.7.92	3	Big 12	Manhattan	13 May
13.65	0.4	Thingalaya	Siddhanth	IND	1.3.91	2	BEL Ch	Bruxelles	17 Jun
13.66	-0.2		Park Tae-kyong	KOR	30.7.80	1h1	Oda	Hiroshima	29 Apr
		(100)							
13.66	1.2	Logan	Taylor	USA	3.4.86	1		Chula Vista	9 Jun

Mark	Wind	Name		Nat	Born	Date		Mark	Wind	Name		Nat	Born	Date
13.67	1.1	Johnny	Dutch	USA	20.1.89	24 Mar		13.69	1.9	Dayron	Capetillo	CUB	11.9.87	22 Mar
13.67	1.3	Durell	Busby	TRI	23.12.89	26 May		13.69	0.5	Todd	McKown	USA	19.1.90	21 Apr
13.67	0.9	Jhoanis	Portilla	CUB	24.7.90	15 Jun		13.69	0.2	Ronald	Brookins	USA	5.7.89	3 May
13.67	-0.1	Alex	Al-Ameen	GBR	2.3.89	24 Jun		13.69	1.0	Damien	Broothaerts	BEL	12.11.84	26 May
13.68	-1.6	Keith	Nkrumah	GHA	28.11.90	5 May		13.69	1.0	Héctor	Cotto	PUR	8.8.84	9 Jun
13.68	1.4	Adams	Abdulrazaaq	USA	27.4.88	12 May		13.69	1.6	Paul	Dittmer	GER	1.1.87	16 Jun
13.68	1.8	Martin	Arnaudov	BUL	5.4.90	15 Jun		13.70	0.0	Ronnie	McGirt	USA	19.2.88	12 May
13.68	-0.1	Gianni	Frankis	GBR	16.4.88	24 Jun		13.70		Yevgeniy	Borisov	RUS	7.3.84	23 Jun

Mark	Wind	Name	Nat	Born	Date
13.71	1.1	Yutaro Furukawa	JPN	3.6.85	29 Apr
13.71	1.0	Caleb Cross	USA	31.5.91	4 May
13.71	0.2	Tatsuya Wado	JPN	4.10.90	6 May
13.71	0.6	Andreas Kundert	SUI	1.10.84	19 May
13.72	-0.8	Deuce Carter	JAM	28.9.90	26 May
13.72	-0.6	Kenji Yahata	JPN	4.11.80	10 Jun
13.72	1.2	Jackson Quiñónez	ESP	12.6.80	26 Aug
13.73	0.0	Tasuku Tanonaka	JPN	23.9.78	9 Jun
13.73A	1.5	Matthew Brisson	CAN	21.9.88	29 Jun
13.73	1.2	Brendan Ames	USA	6.10.88	29 Jun
13.74	0.0	Ethan Holmes	USA	16.3.91	13 May
13.74		Mohsin Ali	PAK	19.3.88	19 May
13.74	0.8	Marcus Maxey	USA	9.10.90	26 May
13.74	0.1	Zhang Jianxin	CHN	29.10.87	27 May
13.74	0.6	Ronald Forbes	CAY	5.4.85	9 Jun
13.74	0.4	Matheus Inocêncio	BRA	17.5.81	1 Jul
13.75	0.5	Trevor Brown	USA	24.3.92	21 Apr
13.75	0.7	Bryan Clay	USA	3.1.80	12 May
13.75	1.3	Kendall Parks	USA	.89	26 May
13.75	0.3	Othman Hadj Lazib	ALG	10.5.83	9 Jun
13.75	0.5	Wataru Yazawa	JPN	2.7.91	10 Jun
13.75	-0.7	Nick Gayle	GBR	4.1.85	24 Jun
13.75	0.7	Aleksey Dryomin	RUS	10.5.89	7 Aug
13.76	1.0	Jamele Mason	PUR	19.10.89	7 Apr
13.76	1.1	Stefano Tedesco	ITA	4.7.88	10 Jul
13.77		Muhammad Sajjad Ahmad	PAK	2.2.86	19 May
13.77	1.8	Thomas Martinot-Lagarde	FRA	7.2.88	25 May
13.77	1.0	Francisco Javier López	ESP	29.12.89	9 Jun
13.77	0.3	Mariusz Kubaszewski	POL	11.7.82	9 Jun
13.77	0.0	Sergiy Kopanayko	UKR	5.11.88	12 Jun
13.78	0.3	Bano Traoré	FRA	25.4.85	27 May
13.79	-1.6	Akeem Smith	JAM	15.10.87	5 May
13.79	0.2	Kim Byung-jun	KOR	15.8.91	9 May
13.79	0.9	Justin Johnson	USA-J	.93	26 May
13.79	0.7	Rico Freimuth	GER	14.3.88	27 May
13.79	0.1	Sekou Kaba	CAN	25.8.90	28 May
13.79	1.8	Dario Seghers/De Borger	BEL	20.3.92	9 Jun
13.79	1.8	Thomas Ravon	FRA	1.5.84	27 Jun
13.80	1.6	Kemar Clarke	USA	20.5.88	5 May
13.80A	0.0	Dennis Bain	BAH	15.12.90	25 May
13.80	2.0	Josh Thompson	USA-J	16.1.93	25 May
13.80	0.5	Yuto Aoki	JPN	11.7.84	10 Jun
13.80	0.4	Thiago Castelo Branco	BRA	6.11.79	1 Jul
13.81	0.2	Rayzam Shah Wan Sofian	MAS	11.1.88	15 Apr
13.81	1.6	Demoye Bogle	USA	8.11.91	28 Apr
13.81	1.6	Gonzalo Barroilhet	CHI	19.8.86	5 May
13.81	1.4	Gerkenz Senesca	USA	6.4.90	12 May
13.81	1.0	Ben Reynolds	IRL	26.9.90	26 May
13.81	0.3	Koen Smet	NED	9.8.92	9 Jun
13.81	0.5	Jermaine Morris	JAM	15.7.86	30 Jun
13.81	0.4	João de Oliveira	BRA	15.5.92	1 Jul
13.82	0.9	Jehue Gordon	TRI	15.12.91	1 Apr
13.82	1.2	Ronald Bennett	HON	11.10.86	16 Jun
13.82	1.5	Damian Czykier	POL	10.8.92	17 Jun
13.82	0.1	Filipp Shabanov	RUS	29.1.91	5 Jul
13.82	2.0	Liu Yu	CHN	5.2.91	25 Sep
13.83	-1.5	Carlos Rafael Jorge	DOM	24.9.86	20 Apr
13.83	-0.7	Jumrus Rittidet	THA	1.2.89	11 May
13.83	1.1	Luis Fernando Ferreira	BRA	8.4.89	20 May
13.83	2.0	Kyohei Mita	JPN	16.8.91	23 Jun
13.83A	1.5	Nathan Arnett	BAH	15.12.90	7 Jul
13.83	1.8	Yuki Eguchi	JPN-J	.94	26 Aug
13.83	1.1	Petr Penáz	CZE	27.8.91	1 Sep
13.84	0.3	Ruan de Vries	RSA	1.2.86	17 May
13.84		Gilbert Okon	NGR	6.6.86	21 Apr
13.84		Carrington Queen	USA	21.9.87	1 Jun
13.84	-0.7	Stanislav Olijar	LAT	22.3.79	9 Jun
13.84	1.1	Samuele Devarti	ITA	8.7.90	10 Jul
13.85	-0.1	Mantas Silkauskas	LTU	10.4.88	12 May
13.85	2.0	Kyohei Hayakawa	JPN	20.11.91	23 Jun
13.85A	1.5	Ingvar Moseley	CAN	24.11.91	29 Jun
13.85	0.9	Aydar Gilyazov	RUS	11.6.87	5 Jul
13.86	-0.4	Masayuki Ida	JPN	11.8.87	29 Apr
13.86	-0.7	Keyunta Hayes	USA	15.2.92	13 May
13.86	1.7	Chu Pengfei	CHN-J	28.12.93	13 May
13.86	0.6	De'Lon Isom	USA	1.5.88	31 May
13.86	0.8	Yoichi Iwafune	JPN	12.6.85	8 Oct
13.87	0.0	Charlton Rolle	USA	18.5.89	31 Mar
13.87	0.6	Tobias Furer	SUI	13.8.87	26 May
13.87	1.0	Moussa Dembélé	SEN	30.10.88	1 Jun
13.87	-0.6	Masanori Nishizawa	JPN	16.7.87	10 Jun
13.87	1.2	Terence Somerville	USA	5.11.89	29 Jun

(199), 13.88 by 9 men, 13.89 by 6 men

Wind assisted

Mark	Wind	Name	Nat	Born	Pos	Meet	Venue	Date
12.87	2.4	Liu Xiang	CHN	13.7.83	1	Pre	Eugene	2 Jun
12.96	2.4	Merritt			2	Pre	Eugene	2 Jun
12.99	2.9	Merritt			1h3		Fayetteville	4 May
13.10	3.0	Ronnie Ash	USA	2.7.88	1r1	FlaR	Gainesville	6 Apr
13.11	2.4	Richardson			3	Pre	Eugene	2 Jun
13.12	2.4	Dexter Faulk	USA	14.4.84	4	Pre	Eugene	2 Jun
13.14	4.7	Lawrence Clarke	GBR	12.3.90	1h1		Madrid	7 Jul
13.17	4.3	Dwight Thomas	JAM	23.9.80	1		Clermont	2 Jun
13.20	7.3	Omo Osaghae	USA	18.5.88	1		Lubbock	14 Apr
13.22	2.4	David Payne	USA	24.7.82	1		Madrid	7 Jul
13.26	2.2	Wayne Davis II	USA/TRI	22.8.91	1s2	NCAA	Des Moines	7 Jun
13.30	2.1	Pascal Martinot-Lagarde	FRA	22.9.91	1		Montgeron	13 May
13.31	2.6	Mikel Thomas	TRI	23.11.87	2		Port of Spain	19 May
13.34	2.4	Ashton Eaton	USA	21.1.88	7	Pre	Eugene	2 Jun
13.36	2.2	Keiron Stewart	JAM	21.11.89	2s2	NCAA	Des Moines	7 Jun
13.38	2.2	Spencer Adams	USA	10.9.89	3s2	NCAA	Des Moines	7 Jun
13.39	3.8	Ryan Fontenot	USA	4.5.86	1		Baton Rouge	21 Apr
13.42	2.2	Todd McKown	USA	19.1.90	2q1	NCAA-W	Austin	26 May
13.49	3.1	Greggmar Swift	BAR	16.2.91	1		Wichita	13 May
13.50	3.0	Abdulaziz Al-Mandeel	KUW	22.5.89	1		Al-Kuwait	5 Mar
13.50	4.3	Héctor Cotto	PUR	8.8.84	6		Clermont	2 Jun
13.51	4.3	Ronald Forbes	CAY	5.4.85	7		Clermont	2 Jun
13.56	3.7	Bano Traoré	FRA	25.4.85	5	MSR	Walnut	21 Apr
13.56	2.7	Helge Schwarzer	GER	26.11.85	2		Regensburg	2 Jun
13.57	2.1	Park Tae-kyong	KOR	30.7.80	1	Oda	Hiroshima	29 Apr
13.59	2.1	Hiroyuki Sato	JPN	6.8.90	2	Oda	Hiroshima	29 Apr
13.59	2.6	Tre Lathan	USA	15.7.92	1h4	NCAA-W	Austin	25 May
13.60	3.7	Logan Taylor	USA	3.4.86	6	MSR	Walnut	21 Apr
13.60A	7.6	Ty'reak Murray	USA	.92	1	NCAA-2	Pueblo, CO	26 May
13.62	2.5	Rasul Dabo	POR	14.2.89	1		Lisboa (Un)	10 Jun
13.63	3.7	Ronald Brookins	USA	5.7.89	7	MSR	Walnut	21 Apr
13.64	2.3	De'Lon Isom	USA	1.5.88	1		Austin	21 Apr
13.64	2.4	Damien Broothaerts	BEL	12.11.84	2h1		Élancourt	8 Jun

Mark	Wind	Name	Nat	Born	Pos	Meet	Venue	Date
13.65	2.1	Kemar Clarke	USA	20.5.88	2h1	NCAA-E	Jacksonville	25 May
13.66	3.0	Kendall Parks	USA	.89				25 May
13.67	?	Brandon Priebe	USA					6 Apr
13.67	3.0	Keyunta Hayes	USA	15.2.92				12 May
13.68A	7.6	Dennis Bain	BAH	15.12.90				26 May
13.68	4.1	Caleb Cross	USA	31.5.91				26 May
13.69	2.1	Wataru Yazawa	JPN	2.7.91				29 Apr
13.69A	2.1	Francisco Javier López	ESP	29.12.89				28 Jul
13.70	2.1	Tatsuya Wado	JPN	4.10.90				29 Apr
13.71A	7.6	Darius Reed	USA	2.1.88				26 May
13.71A	7.6	Brice Myers	USA	7.8.89				26 May
13.72	2.4	Demetrius Lindo	USA	28.3.92				31 Mar
13.72	2.1	Tasuku Tanonaka	JPN	23.9.78				29 Apr
13.72	3.5	Ramón Sosa	DOM	11.1.86				2 Jun
13.72	3.0	Matthew Brisson	CAN	21.9.88				16 Jun
13.75	2.9	Jamele Mason	PUR	19.10.89				31 Mar
13.75	2.4	Masanori Nishizawa	JPN	16.7.87				10 Jun
13.76A	7.6	Aaron Wilmore	BAH	1.3.92				26 May
13.76	4.3	Thomas Martinot-Lagarde	FRA	7.2.88				7 Jul
13.77	2.7	Nathan Arnett	BAH	15.12.90				13 May
13.78	3.7	Cedrique Smith	USA	18.9.90				21 Apr
13.78	2.3	Soloman Williams	USA	1.6.91				25 May
13.78	2.8	Samuel Okon	NGR	6.6.86				20 Jun
13.79	2.4	Kyohei Mita	JPN	16.8.91				10 Jun
13.79	4.3	Mohamed Koné	MLI	22.10.88				7 Jul
13.80	3.8	Sheldon Wilkinson	JAM	21.12.86				14 Apr
13.80	2.7	Rayzam Shah Wan Sofian	MAS	11.1.88				2 Jun
13.81	3.0	Alexander Brorsson	SWE	29.5.90				28 Jul
13.83	2.3	Jon McDowell	USA	28.10.84				24 Mar
13.83	3.5	Jeffrey Artis	USA	13.8.90				25 May
13.83	3.1	Andreas Dengler	GER	22.12.80				16 Jun
13.83	3.8	Joona-Ville Heinä	FIN	11.5.89				8 Aug
13.84	3.1	Bertony Jean-Louis	USA	19.8.90				25 May
13.84	4.1	Andrew Blaser	USA	5.8.89				26 May
13.85	3.0	Robert Jackson	USA	23.1.90				25 May

Low altitude bests

Mark	Wind	Name	Pos	Meet	Venue	Date
13.36	1.8	Nugent	2s3	NCAA	Des Moines	7 Jun
13.85	0.7	Brisson				14 Jul
13.46	1.8	S Brathwaite	2	Big 12	Manhattan	13 May
13.43w	2.9		2	TexR	Austin	31 Mar
13.75w	2.4	López				7 Jul

Hand timing

Mark	Wind	Name	Nat	Born	Pos	Meet	Venue	Date
13.2	1.6	Dayron Capetillo	CUB	11.9.87	1h2	NC	La Habana	22 Mar
13.4		Jhoanis Portilla	CUB	24.7.90	1		La Habana	22 Jun
13.5	1.6	Ignacio Morales	CUB	28.1.87				22 Mar
13.6		Carrington Queen	USA	21.9.87				16 Jun
13.6		Moussa Dembélé	SEN	30.10.88				16 Jun

JUNIORS

Mark	Wind	Name	Nat	Born	Pos	Meet	Venue	Date
13.79	0.9	Justin Johnson	USA	.93	1	NCAA-3	Claremont	26 May
13.80	2.0	Josh Thompson	USA	16.1.93	2h2	NCAA-E	Jacksonville	25 May
13.83	1.8	Yuki Eguchi	JPN	.94	1		Gwangju	26 Aug
13.86	1.7	Chu Pengfei	CHN	28.12.93	2		Tianjin	13 May
13.88	1.8	Kenneth Minkah	USA	28.8.93	5	Big 12	Manhattan	13 May
13.91	-2.9	Yordan O'Farrill	CUB	9.2.93	1h1		La Habana	2 Mar
13.92	0.8	Genta Masuno	JPN	24.5.93	4		Gifu	8 Oct
13.94	0.1	Jussi Kanervo	FIN	1.2.93	1	NC	`Lahti	25 Aug
13.99	1.7	(10) Chen Shuyan	CHN	26.1.93	3		Tianjin	13 May
13.99	1.3	Calvin Arsenault	CAN	29.9.93	7q1	NCAA-E	Jacksonville	26 May
14.01	2.0	Shin-ya Tanaka	JPN	23.6.93	7		Hiratsuka	23 Jun
14.02	0.7	Václav Sedlák	CZE	6.2.93	2	NC	Vyskov	16 Jun
14.03	1.0	Masaki Okazaki	JPN	12.7.94	1		Gifu	8 Oct
14.04	0.7	Lorenzo Perini	ITA	22.7.94	8	Nebiolo	Torino	8 Jun
14.05	1.0	Gen Yada	JPN	2.4.94	2		Gifu	8 Oct

110 Metres Hurdles – 99 cm hurdles

Mark	Wind	Name	Nat	Born	Pos	Meet	Venue	Date
13.18	1.0	Yordan O'Farrill	CUB	9.2.93	1	WJ	Barcelona	12 Jul
13.27	0.0				1	CAC-J	San Salvador	1 Jul
13.28	0.8				1s2	WJ	Barcelona	11 Jul
13.27	1.0	Nicholas Hough	AUS	20.10.93	2	WJ	Barcelona	12 Jul
13.38	1.1				1h2		Mannheim	23 Jun
13.29	1.0	Wilhem Belocian	FRA	22.6.95	3	WJ	Barcelona	12 Jul
13.30	-0.5				1s3	WJ	Barcelona	11 Jul
13.30	1.2	James Gladman	GBR	3.6.93	1		Mannheim	23 Jun
13.36	0.8				1h4		Mannheim	23 Jun
13.37	1.0				4	WJ	Barcelona	12 Jul
13.37	-0.5				2s2	WJ	Barcelona	11 Jul
13.35	-1.4	Artie Burns	USA-Y	1.5.95	1		Jacksonville	17 Mar
13.43	0.8	Jordan Moore	USA	13.12.93	1		Powder Springs	28 Apr
13.49	-2.5	Donovan Robertson	USA	8.11.93	1		Amherst	18 May
13.52	1.0	Devon Allen	USA	12.12.94	1		Arcadia	7 Apr
13.56	1.3	Dapo Akinmolagdun	USA	28.2.93	1		Jefferson City	26 May
13.56	-1.8	Dondre Echols (10)	USA	6.7.93	1	NC-j	Bloomington IN	15 Jun
13.57		Chu Pengfei	CHN	28.12.93	1	NC-j	Changzhou	21 Apr
13.59	-1.8	Josh Thompson	USA	16.1.93	2	NC-j	Bloomington IN	15 Jun
13.61	0.8	Shin-ya Tanaka	JPN	23.6.93	2s2	WJ	Barcelona	11 Jul
13.61	-0.5	Jussi Kanervo	FIN	1.2.93	3s3	WJ	Barcelona	11 Jul
13.62	0.0	Stefan Fennell	JAM	5.11.93	2	CAC-J	San Salvador	1 Jul
13.63	-1.2	Cheng Yun-yin	TPE	28.4.94	1s1		Taipei	21 Apr
13.64	1.2	Jonas Christen	GER	16.8.93	4		Mannheim	23 Jun
13.65	1.2	Máté Gönnczöl	HUN	29.9.93	5		Mannheim	23 Jun
13.66	1.3	Lorenzo Perini	ITA	22.7.94	1		Genève	2 Jun
13.69		Lei Yiwen (20)	CHN	11.12.93	2	NC-j	Changzhou	21 Apr
13.69	-1.3	Jonathan Jones	USA	20.9.93	1		Jefferson	12 May
13.69	1.5	Elmo Lakka	FIN	10.4.93	1r2		Jämsä	14 Jun

Mark	Wind	Name		Nat	Born	Pos	Meet	Venue	Date	
Wind assisted										
13.32	4.5	Devon	Allen	USA	12.12.94	1	G.West	Folsom	9	Jun
13.39		Jordan	Moore	USA	13.12.93	1		Fairbirn	21	Apr
13.57	2.1	Jussi	Kanervo	FIN	1.2.93	1		Mannheim	24	Jun
13.61	2.1	Máté	Gönnczöl	HUN	29.9.93	2		Mannheim	24	Jun
13.67	2.3	Jermaine	Collier	USA	5.7.93	1		Old Bridge	11	Jun

200 METRES HURDLES

Mark	Wind	Name		Nat	Born	Pos	Meet	Venue	Date	
23.08w	2.8	Yasuhiro	Fueki	JPN	20.12.85	1r2		Kaysuura	27	Oct

400 METRES HURDLES

Mark	Wind	Name		Nat	Born	Pos	Meet	Venue	Date	
47.63		Félix	Sánchez	DOM	30.8.77	1	OG	London (OS)	6	Aug
47.76			Sánchez			1s1	OG	London (OS)	4	Aug
47.78		Javier	Culson	PUR	25.7.84	1	DL	Saint-Denis	6	Jul
47.78			Culson			1	LGP	London (CP)	13	Jul
47.84		David	Greene	GBR	11.4.86	2	DL	Saint-Denis	6	Jul
47.91		Michael	Tinsley	USA	21.4.84	2	OG	London (OS)	6	Aug
47.92			Culson			1	Bisl	Oslo	7	Jun
47.93			Culson			1s2	OG	London (OS)	4	Aug
47.95		Angelo	Taylor	USA	29.12.78	2s2	OG	London (OS)	4	Aug
47.96		Jehue	Gordon	TRI	15.12.91	2s1	OG	London (OS)	4	Aug
48.00			Culson			1		Ponce	12	May
48.10			Greene			2	LGP	London (CP)	13	Jul
48.10			Culson			3	OG	London (OS)	6	Aug
48.12		Kerron	Clement	USA	31.10.85	3s1	OG	London (OS)	4	Aug
48.13			Sánchez			1	Gugl	Linz	20	Aug
48.14			Culson			1	GGala	Roma	31	May
48.18			Tinsley			1s3	OG	London (OS)	4	Aug
48.19			Greene			4s1	OG	London (OS)	4	Aug
48.20		Bershawn	Jackson	USA	8.5.83	1	KansR	Lawrence	21	Apr
48.23		Omar	Cisneros	CUB	19.11.89	3s2	OG	London (OS)	4	Aug
48.24			Greene			4	OG	London (OS)	6	Aug
48.25			Jackson			2	GGala	Roma	31	May
48.25			Taylor			5	OG	London (OS)	6	Aug
48.29			Taylor			1	WK	Zürich	30	Aug
48.33			Tinsley			1	NC/OT	Eugene	1	Jul
48.33			Culson			1h4	OG	London (OS)	3	Aug
48.34			Cisneros			2	WK	Zürich	30	Aug
48.40			Gordon			3	WK	Zürich	30	Aug
48.41		Takayuki	Kishimoto	JPN	6.5.90	1	NC	Osaka	9	Jun
48.42			Sánchez			4	WK	Zürich	30	Aug
(30/10)										
48.60		Jack	Green	GBR	6.10.91	4	LGP	London (CP)	13	Jul
48.61		Leford	Green	JAM	14.11.86	2s3	OG	London (OS)	4	Aug
48.79		Amaechi	Morton	NGR	30.10.89	1	NCAA	Des Moines	8	Jun
48.80		Mamadou	Kassé Hann	SEN	10.10.86	5s1	OG	London (OS)	4	Aug
48.88		Jeshua	Anderson	USA	22.6.89	1	Sun A	Tempe	7	Apr
48.89		Jamele	Mason	PUR	19.10.89	2	NCAA	Des Moines	8	Jun
48.90		Johnny	Dutch	USA	20.1.89	1		Clermont	9	Jun
48.91		Cornel	Fredericks	RSA	3.3.90	1	NC	Port Elizabeth	14	Apr
48.97		Justin	Gaymon	USA	13.12.86	3	Bisl	Oslo	7	Jun
49.02		Kurt	Couto	MOZ	14.5.85	1	Odlozil	Praha	11	Jun
(20)										
49.03		Roxroy	Cato	JAM	1.5.88	1		Port of Spain	19	May
49.04		Periklís	Iakovákis	GRE	24.3.79	1h1	NC	Athína	16	Jun
49.10		Michaël	Bultheel	BEL	30.6.86	6s1	OG	London (OS)	4	Aug
49.10		Mahau	Suguimati	BRA	13.11.84	1		Odawara	14	Oct
49.11		Reggie	Wyatt	USA	17.9.90	3	NCAA	Des Moines	8	Jun
49.13		Tristan	Thomas	AUS	23.5.86	4h4	OG	London (OS)	3	Aug
49.15		Eric	Alejandro	PUR	15.4.86	7s1	OG	London (OS)	4	Aug
49.15		Keisuke	Nozawa	JPN	7.6.91	2		Odawara	14	Oct
49.16		Josef	Robertson	JAM	14.5.87	4		Kingston	5	May
49.17		Rhys	Williams	GBR	27.2.84	5h4	OG	London (OS)	3	Aug
(30)										
49.19		Amaurys	Valle	CUB	18.1.90	1h1	OG	London (OS)	3	Aug
49.21		Silvio	Schirrmeister	GER	7.12.88	1		Regensburg	2	Jun
49.21		Emir	Bekric	SRB	14.3.91	2h3	OG	London (OS)	3	Aug
49.23		Miles	Ukaoma	USA	21.7.92	1	Big 10	Madison	13	May
49.24		Brendan	Cole	AUS	29.5.81	2h1	OG	London (OS)	3	Aug
49.33		José	Bencosme de Leon	ITA	16.5.92	1	NC	Bressanone	8	Jul

Mark	Wind	Name		Nat	Born	Pos	Meet	Venue	Date	
49.36		Nathan	Woodward	GBR	17.10.89	1		London (OS)	1	Aug
49.37		Georg	Fleischauer	GER	21.10.88	4	ISTAF	Berlin	2	Sep
49.38		Keyunta	Hayes	USA	15.2.92	4	NCAA	Des Moines	8	Jun
49.38		Akihiko	Nakamura	JPN	23.10.90	2	NC	Osaka	9	Jun
		(40)								
49.38		Brent	LaRue	SLO	26.4.87	4h3	OG	London (OS)	3	Aug
49.39		Richard	Yates	GBR	26.1.86	1		Oordegem	26	May
49.42A		Louis 'L.J.'	van Zyl	RSA	20.7.85	1		Pretoria	5	Apr
49.43		Ali	Arastu	USA	18.6.92	2	Big 10	Madison	13	May
49.45		Michael	Stigler	USA	5.4.92	1	Big 12	Manhattan	13	May
49.45		Boniface	Mucheru	KEN	2.5.92	3	AfrC	Porto Novo	28	Jun
49.47		Takatoshi	Abe	JPN	12.12.91	2s1	NC	Osaka	9	Jun
49.49		Tetsuya	Tateno	JPN	5.8.91	2s2	NC	Osaka	9	Jun
49.49		Yuta	Imazeki	JPN	6.11.87	3s2	NC	Osaka	9	Jun
49.53		Stanislav	Melnykov	UKR	26.2.87	1	NC	Yalta	14	Jun
		(50)								
49.54		Kenneth	Medwood	BIZ	14.12.87	3	MSR	Walnut	21	Apr
49.54		David	Aristil	USA	12.12.88	5	NCAA	Des Moines	8	Jun
49.54		Rasmus	Mägi	EST	4.5.92	3s1	EC	Helsinki	28	Jun
49.54		Varg	Königsmark	GER	28.4.92	1		Nottwil	30	Jun
49.57		Ben	Sumner	GBR	16.8.83	3		Oordegem	26	May
49.59			Cheng Wen	CHN	18.3.92	3	DL	Shanghai	19	May
49.59		Vyacheslav	Sakayev	RUS	12.1.88	1	NC	Cheboksary	4	Jul
49.61		Kaiem	Hussein	SUI	1.4.89	1	NC	Bern	7	Jul
49.63		Yuta	Konishi	JPN	31.7.90	1		Osaka	13	May
49.66		Marek	Plawgo	POL	25.2.81	1h2	NC	Bielsko-Biala	15	Jun
		(60)								
49.68			Chen Chieh	TPE	8.5.92	1		Taipei	8	May
49.69		David	Gollnow	GER	8.4.89	1		München	26	May
49.69		Danny	McFarlane	JAM	14.6.72	4	NC	Kingston	29	Jun
49.70		Adrien	Clémenceau	FRA	25.5.88	4	EC	Helsinki	29	Jun
49.71		Hederson	Estefani	BRA	11.9.91	3	IbAmC	Barquisimeto	8	Jun
49.71		Vladimir	Antmanis	RUS	12.3.84	1h1	NC	Cheboksary	3	Jul
49.71		Yasuhiro	Fueki	JPN	20.12.85	1		Chiba	11	Aug
49.74		Josef	Prorok	CZE	16.11.87	4	Odlozil	Praha	11	Jun
49.75		Tobias	Giehl	GER	25.7.91	2		München	26	May
49.77		Ludovic	Dubois	FRA	13.4.86	1		La Chaux-de-Fonds	27	Jun
		(70)								
49.78		Andrés	Silva	URU	27.3.86	2		Rio de Janeiro	20	May
49.78		Artyom	Dyatlov	UZB	22.5.89	1	KAZ Ch	Almaty	19	Jun
49.79		Viktor	Leptikov	KAZ	2.7.87	1		Bishkek	10	Jun
49.81		Adrian	Findlay	JAM	1.10.82	2		Port of Spain	19	May
49.83		Reuben	McCoy	USA	16.3.86	3		Clermont	9	Jun
49.86		Isa	Phillips	JAM	22.4.84	1		Houston	14	Jun
49.86			Li Zhilong	CHN	9.3.88	1		Tianjin	15	Sep
49.88		Tomoharu	Kino	JPN	4.8.89	4s1	NC	Osaka	9	Jun
49.88		Kotaro	Miyao	JPN	12.7.91	1s2		Tokyo	11	Sep
49.91		Heni	Kéchi	FRA	31.8.80	2	NC	Angers	17	Jun
		(80)								
49.93		Richard	Davenport	GBR	12.9.85	2		Moskva	11	Jun
49.94		Aleksandr	Derevyagin	RUS	24.3.79	1h3	NC	Cheboksary	3	Jul
49.98		Joseph	Abraham	IND	11.9.81	1		Patiala	23	Apr
49.98		Naohiro	Kawakita	JPN	10.7.80	5s2	NC	Osaka	9	Jun
49.99		Tatsuhiko	Mizuno	JPN	25.10.90	4		Tokyo	20	May
49.99		Satinder	Singh	IND	7.2.87	1		Hyderabad	25	Jun
50.00		Emanuel	Mayers	TRI	9.3.89	1h3	JAM OT	Kingston	28	Jun
50.02		Nikita	Yakovlev	BLR	6.1.89	4s2	EC	Helsinki	28	Jun
50.04A		Christopher	Ngetich	KEN	25.12.92	2	NC	Nairobi	15	Jun
50.04		Václav	Barák	CZE	22.10.90	1	NC	Vyskov	17	Jun
		(90)								
50.07		Steven	White	USA	27.7.91	1		Denton	7	Apr
50.08		Chris	Carter	USA	10.4.87	3s3	NCAA	Des Moines	6	Jun
50.09		Yoan	Décimus	FRA	30.11.87	4	NC	Angers	17	Jun
50.10		Joe	Greene	USA	20.11.87	3		Port of Spain	19	May
50.10		Thomas	Kortbeek	NED	2.4.81	1		Assen	20	May
50.10		Jibri	Victorian	USA	26.6.91	2q2	NCAA-E	Jacksonville	25	May
50.10		Aramis	Díaz	CUB	22.11.74	1		Kessel-Lo	18	Aug
50.14		Adam	Kunkel	CAN	24.2.81	1		Windsor	26	May
50.14		Bryan	Steele	JAM	23.3.84	2h3	NC	Kingston	28	Jun
50.15		Winder	Cuevas	DOM	1.8.88	6h2	OG	London (OS)	3	Aug
		(100)								

Mark	Name	Nat	Born	Pos	Meet	Venue	Date
50.19	Noriuki Ideura	JPN	29.10.87				25 May
50.19	Antonio Blanks	USA	17.10.92				25 May
50.22	Adam Durham	USA	30.8.85				19 May
50.22A	Vincent Kosgei	KEN	11.11.85				14 Jun
50.22	Thomas Barr	IRL	24.7.92				28 Jun
50.22	Artur Langowski	BRA	8.5.91				30 Jun
50.24	Eric Futch	USA-J	25.4.93				13 Jul
50.25	Jermaine Lowery	USA	13.1.90				6 May
50.25	Hugo Grillas	FRA	28.2.89				7 Jul
50.26	Sabiel Anderson	JAM	21.6.88				28 Jun
50.27A	Jeffrey Gibson	BAH	15.8.90				8 Jul
50.28	Yasmany Copello	CUB	15.4.87				14 Jul
50.29	Naman Keïta	FRA	9.4.78				11 Apr
50.29	Nathan Arnett	BAH	15.12.90				25 May
50.30A	PC Beneke	RSA	18.7.90				4 May
50.30	Caleb Cross	USA	31.5.91				13 May
50.30	Carson Blanks	USA	19.9.89				13 May
50.30	Dmitriy Koblov	KAZ	28.11.92				19 Jun
50.31	Alex Wilright	USA	12.6.88				28 Jun
50.36	Kim Dae-hong	KOR	17.10.90				7 Jun
50.37	Naoki Ihara	JPN	22.4.82				9 Jun
50.37	Mohamed Sghaier	TUN	18.7.88				29 Jun
50.38	Austin Hollimon	USA	12.1.90				3 Jun
50.39	LaRon Bennett	USA	25.11.82				3 Jun
50.39	El Hadji Seth Mbow	SEN	2.4.85				10 Jun
50.39	Silvestras Guogis	LTU	2.3.90				21 Jul
50.40	Keith Nkrumah	GHA	28.11.90				5 May
50.41	Takahiro Matsumoto	JPN-J	19.9.94				13 Jul
50.42	Takayuki Koike	JPN	12.10.84				20 May
50.43	Nikita Andriyanov	RUS	7.2.90				11 Jun
50.43	Mickaël François	FRA	12.3.88				17 Jun
50.43	Quentin Seigel	GER	7.4.88				17 Jun
50.43	Jorge Paula	POR	8.10.84				8 Jul
50.44	Jithin Paul	IND	13.3.90				12 Apr
50.45	Thomas Phillips	GBR	23.4.89				9 Jun
50.45	Denys Teslenko	UKR	18.4.89				14 Jun
50.45	Javan Gallimore	JAM-J	7.8.93				12 Jul
50.46	Eric Cray	USA	6.11.88				13 May
50.46	Andre Walsh	JAM	14.9.89				25 May
50.46	Jun-ya Imai	JPN	23.6.87				9 Jun
50.46	Chen Ke	CHN	14.9.89				15 Sep
50.47	Fawaz Dahesh Al-Shammari	KUW	3.4.77				9 Jun
50.47	Ibrahim Mohamed Saleh	KSA-Y	30.5.95				13 Jul
50.48	Felix Franz	GER-J	6.5.93				2 Jun
50.48	Mirko Schmidt	GER	16.9.88				16 Jun
50.48A	Leslie Murray	ISV	24.1.91				8 Jul
50.48A	Diego Cabello	ESP	14.1.88				28 Jul
50.50	Sebastian Rodger	GBR	29.6.91				18 Aug
50.51	Denys Nechyporenko	UKR	7.1.90				14 Jun
50.52	Ricardo Lima	POR	2.1.85				8 Jul
50.52A	Paulo César Villar	COL	28.7.78				16 Nov
50.54	James Forman	GBR	12.12.91				3 Jun
50.55	Hiroaki Masuoka	JPN	18.2.88				14 Jul
50.57	Mowen Boino	PNG	16.12.79				7 Jul
50.59	Niall Flannery	GBR	26.4.91				3 Jun
50.60	Leonardo Capotosti	ITA	24.7.88				2 Jun
50.61	Takaoki Hashimoto	JPN	18.7.92				9 Jun
50.61	Chen Dayu	CHN	11.1.88				15 Sep
50.62A	Javier Sagredo	ESP	27.3.87				9 Jun
50.62	Shota Madokoro	JPN-J	22.5.94				16 Jun
50.62	Yegor Kuznetsov	RUS-J	29.11.94				3 Jul
50.62	Hideki Yano	JPN	13.12.85				22 Sep
50.63A	Romel Lewis	JAM	28.1.88				26 May
50.64	Tim Rummens	BEL	16.12.87				13 May
50.65	Lucirio Garrido	VEN	4.10.88				12 May
50.66	Chris Lawson	USA	.89				12 May
50.66	Yuta Amano	JPN	29.5.90				8 Jun
50.67	Javonte Lipsey	USA	17.10.92				21 Apr
50.67	Robert Brylinski	POL	2.4.91				16 Jun
50.68	Cory Beebe	USA	8.7.87				20 Apr
50.68	Chen Yu-Teh	TPE	17.6.89				27 Oct
50.69	Mohamed Amine Gouniber	ALG	25.2.88				8 Jul
50.70	Tim Gbunblee	USA	1.10.91				16 Jun
50.71	Atsushi Yamada	JPN	3.7.91				7 Apr
50.71	Juan Enrique Vallés	ESP	25.3.86				7 Jun
50.71	Yuichi Nagano	JPN-J	11.1.93				15 Sep
50.72	Marcus Pope	USA	1.2.89				13 May
50.72	Spiridon-Ioánnis Papadópoulos	GRE	25.9.87				16 Jun
50.73	Kei Maeno	JPN	10.5.91				3 May
50.73	Martin Kucera	SVK	10.5.90				17 Jun
50.73	Kenta Takeda	JPN	27.4.86				11 Aug
50.74	Konstantin Andreyev	RUS	10.8.90				27 May
50.74	Ivan Babich	RUS	19.11.90				21 Jul
50.76	Roscoe Payne	USA	27.9.89				13 May
50.77A	Sergio Rios	MEX	30.8.91				26 May
50.78	Raphael Fernandes (186)	BRA	8.11.84				5 May

Hand timing

Mark	Name	Nat	Born	Pos	Meet	Venue	Date
50.7	João Ferreira	POR	20.10.86				13 May

Low altitude bests

Mark	Name	Date		Mark	Name	Date		Mark	Name	Date
50.31	Kosgei	29 Jun		50.46	Ngetich	29 Jun		50.69	Gibson	21 Apr
50.31	van Zyl	3 Aug		50.49	Cabello	12 Jun		50.77	Sagredo	7 Jun

JUNIORS

Mark	Name		Nat	Born	Pos	Meet	Venue	Date
50.24	Eric	Futch	USA	25.4.93	1	WJ	Barcelona	13 Jul
50.41	Takahiro	Matsumoto	JPN	19.9.94	2	WJ	Barcelona	13 Jul
50.45	Javan	Gallimore	JAM	7.8.93	1s2	WJ	Barcelona	12 Jul
	50.49	4 WJ	Barcelona	13 Jul			8 performances by 7 men to 50.62	
50.47	Ibrahim Mohamed	Saleh	KSA-Y	30.5.95	3	WJ	Barcelona	13 Jul
50.48	Felix	Franz	GER	6.5.93	1rC		Regensburg	2 Jun
50.62	Shota	Madokoro	JPN	22.5.94	1		Otsu	16 Jun
50.62	Yegor	Kuznetsov	RUS	29.11.94	2h2	NC	Cheboksary	3 Jul
50.71	Yuichi	Nagano	JPN	11.1.93	1		Tokyo	15 Sep
50.80	Durgesh	Kumar Pal	IND	20.4.94	3		Hyderabad	25 Jun
50.80	Timofey	Chalyy (10)	RUS	7.4.94	2s2	WJ	Barcelona	12 Jul
50.80	Oskai	Mörö	FIN	31.1.93	6	WJ	Barcelona	13 Jul
50.81	Shavon	Barnes	JAM	1.1.93	1	NC-j	Kingston	16 Jun
50.81	Mitja	Lindic	SLO	5.2.93	2s3	WJ	Barcelona	12 Jul
50.83A	Taariq	Solomons	RSA	22.8.93	2		Pretoria	5 Apr
50.87	Yuichi	Nagano	JPN	11.1.93	1	NC-j	Nagano	21 Oct
50.95A	William	Mutunga	KEN	17.9.93	1	NC-j	Nairobi	8 Jun
50.95	Greg	Coleman	USA	24.7.93	1h7	WJ	Barcelona	11 Jul
50.98	Naoto	Noguchi	JPN	27.5.94	2		Niigata	31 Jul
51.15		Xu Xiangchao	CHN	26.10.93	1		Wuhan	29 Apr
51.16	Omar	McLeod (20)	JAM	25.4.94	3	NC-j	Kingston	16 Jun

Mark	Name			Nat	Born	Pos	Meet	Venue	Date

HIGH JUMP

Mark	Name			Nat	Born	Pos	Meet	Venue	Date
2.39	Ivan		Ukhov	RUS	29.3.86	1	NC	Cheboksary	5 Jul
	2.15/1 2.20/1 2.24/1 2.28/3 2.31/2 2.33/1 2.35/1 2.37/x 2.39/1 2.41/xx								
2.38	1	OG	London (OS)		7 Aug	2.20/1 2.25/1 2.29/2 2.33/1 2.36/1 2.38/1 2.40/x			
2.37	1		Opole		6 Jun	2.16/1 2.20/1 2.24/1 2.28/1 2.34/1 2.37/1 2.41/xxx			
2.37	2	Athl	Lausanne		23 Aug	2.20/1 2.24/1 2.27/1 2.30/1 2.33/1 2.35/1 2.37/1 2.39/xx2.41/x			
2.34i	1	NC	Moskva		23 Feb	2.15/1 2.20/1 2.24/1 2.27/1 2.30/1 2.32/2 2.34/2 2.36/x			
2.33i	1		Banská Bystrica		8 Feb	2.15/1 2.25/1 2.31/3 2.33/3 2.37/xxx			
2.39	Mutaz Essa		Barshim	QAT	24.6.91	1	Athl	Lausanne	23 Aug
	2.20/1 2.24/1 2.27/1 2.30/1 2.33/3 2.35/3 2.37/2 2.39/2								
2.37i	1	AsiC	Hangzhou		19 Feb	2.10, 2.15, 2.20, 2.24/all 1 2.28/2 2.31/1 2.34/1 2.37/1 2.40/xxx			
2.35	1		Eberstadt		18 Aug	2.20/1 2.24/1 2.27/2 2.30/3 2.33/1 2.35/3 2.38/x			
2.33i	1		Spala		11 Feb	2.10/1 2.17/1 2.23/1 2.26/1 2.30/2 2.33/1			
2.33	1		Warszawa		14 Jul				
2.37	Andrey		Silnov	RUS	9.9.84	2	NC	Cheboksary	5 Jul
	2.15/1 2.20/1 2.24/1 2.28/1 2.31/2 2.33/2 2.35/2 2.37/1 2.39/xx2.41/x								
2.36i	1		Moskva		5 Feb	2.20/1 2.24/1 2.27/1 2.30/2 2.32/1 2.34/2 2.36/1 2.41/x			
2.35i	1		Moskva		1 Feb	2.20/1 2.24/1 2.27/2 2.30/1 2.33/3 2.35/1			
2.34i	2	NC	Moskva		23 Feb	2.15/1 2.20/1 2.24/1 2.27/2 2.30/2 2.32/1 2.34/3 2.36/xxx			
2.33i	2	WI	Istanbul		11 Mar	2.20/1 2.24/1 2.28/1 2.31/2 2.33/2 2.35/xxx			
2.37	Robbie		Grabarz	GBR	3.10.87	3	Athl	Lausanne	23 Aug
	2.24/1 2.30/2 2.33/1 2.35/x 2.37/1 2.39/xxx								
2.36	2	adidas	New York		9 Jun	2.25/2 2.28/1 2.31/1 2.34/1 2.36/1 2.38/xxx			
2.34i	1		Wuppertal		21 Jan	2.19/3 2.23/3 2.26/1 2.28/2 2.30/1 2.32/x 2.34/2			
2.33	1	GGala	Roma		31 May	2.25/1 2.28/1 2.31/1 2.33/1 2.35/xxx			
2.33	2	Herc	Monaco		20 Jul	2.22/1 2.26/3 2.30/1 2.33/3 2.36/xxx			
2.33	2		Eberstadt		18 Aug	2.24/1 2.30/2 2.33/1 2.35/xxx			
2.36	Jesse		Williams	USA	27.12.83	1	adidas	New York	9 Jun
	2.20/1 2.25/1 2.28/1 2.31/1 2.34/1 2.36/1 2.38/xpp								
2.33	1	Herc	Monaco		20 Jul	2.17/1 2.22/1 2.26/1 2.30/1 2.33/3 2.36/xxx			
2.35i	Aleksey		Dmitrik	RUS	12.4.84	1		Hustopece	28 Jan
	2.15/1 2.20/1 2.24/1 2.28/1 2.31/1 2.33/2 2.35/3 2.41/xxx								
2.33	4	NC	Cheboksary		5 Jul	2.15/1 2.20/2 2.24/1 2.28/1 2.31/1 2.33/2 2.35/xxx			
2.35	Aleksandr		Shustov	RUS	29.6.84	3	NC	Cheboksary	5 Jul
	2.20/1 2.24/1 2.28/1 2.31/2 2.33/1 2.35/3 2.37/xxx								
2.34	Erik		Kynard	USA	3.2.91	1	NCAA	Des Moines	7 Jun
	2.10/1 2.15/1 2.20/2 2.25/1 2.28/3 2.31/1 2.34/1 2.37/xx2.38/x								
2.33	2	OG	London (OS)		7 Aug	2.20/1 2.25/2 2.29/1 2.33/1 2.36/x 2.38/x 2.40/x			
2.33i	Dimitrios		Hondrokoúkis ¶	GRE	26.1.88	1	WI	Istanbul	11 Mar
	(30/9)					2.20/1 2.24/1 2.28/2 2.31/2 2.33/1 2.35/xx			
2.32i	Raúl		Spank (10)	GER	13.7.88	1	NC	Karlsruhe	26 Feb
2.32	Ricky		Robertson	USA	19.9.90	1	FlaR	Gainesville	7 Apr
2.32	Rozle		Prezelj	SLO	26.9.79	1		Maribor	17 Jun
2.31i	Andriy		Protsenko	UKR	20.5.88	1		Lvov	20 Jan
2.31i	Samson		Oni	GBR	25.6.81	3=		Hustopece	28 Jan
2.31i	Jaroslav		Bába	CZE	2.9.84	5		Hustopece	28 Jan
2.31i	Konstadínos		Baniótis	GRE	6.11.86	3=		Banská Bystrica	8 Feb
2.31i	Michal		Kabelka	SVK	4.2.85	3=		Banská Bystrica	8 Feb
2.31i	Silvano		Chesani	ITA	17.7.88	1	NC	Ancona	26 Feb
2.31i	Trevor		Barry	BAH	14.6.83	8	WI	Istanbul	11 Mar
2.31i			Zhang Guowei	CHN	4.6.91	4=	WI	Istanbul	11 Mar
	(20)								
2.31A	Mickaël		Hanany	FRA	25.3.83	1		El Paso	31 Mar
2.31	Michael		Mason	CAN	30.9.86	1		Baie Mahault	1 May
2.31	Derek		Drouin	CAN	6.3.90	1	Big 10	Madison	12 May
2.31	James		Nieto	USA	2.11.76	3=	adidas	New York	9 Jun
2.31	Bogdan		Bondarenko	UKR	30.8.89	1		Mykolaiv	17 Jun
2.31	Raivydas		Stanys	LTU	3.2.87	2	EC	Helsinki	29 Jun
2.31	Sergey		Mudrov	RUS	8.9.90	5	NC	Cheboksary	5 Jul
2.31	Daniyil		Tsyplakov	RUS	12.7.92	6	NC	Cheboksary	5 Jul
2.31	Gianmarco		Tamberi	ITA	1.6.92	1	NC	Bressanone	8 Jul
2.31	Oleksandr		Nartov	UKR	21.5.88	1		Berdychiv	7 Sep
	(30)								
2.30i	Andrey		Patrakov	RUS	7.11.89	2		Moskva	1 Feb
2.30	Kyriakos		Ioannou	CYP	26.7.84	1	NC	Lemessos	9 Jun
2.28i	Peter		Horák	SVK	7.12.83	6		Hustopece	28 Jan
2.28	Ryan		Ingraham	BAH-J	2.11.93	1		Nassau	12 May
2.28			Pai Long	CHN	8.10.89	1		Tianjin	12 May
2.28	Martyn		Bernard	GBR	15.12.84	1		Garbsen	20 May
2.28	Dragutin		Topic	SRB	12.3.71	1		Beograd	20 May
2.28	Wanner		Miller	COL	22.7.87	1		La Habana	27 May

Mark	Name		Nat	Born	Pos	Meet	Venue	Date	
2.28	Andrey	Churyla	BLR-J	19.5.93	1		Brest	30	May
2.28	Guilherme	Cobbo	BRA	1.10.87	1		São Paulo	2	Jun
	(40)								
2.28	Fabrice	Saint-Jean	FRA	21.11.80	1		Genève	2	Jun
2.28	Dwight	Barbiasz	USA	16.7.90	3	NCAA	Des Moines	7	Jun
2.28	Szymon	Kiecana	POL	26.3.89	1	NC	Bielsko-Biala	17	Jun
2.28	Osku	Torro	FIN	21.8.79	1		Jyväskylä	20	Jun
2.28	Nick	Ross	USA	8.8.91	3	OT	Eugene	25	Jun
2.28	Viktor	Shapoval	UKR	17.10.79	2		Berdychiv	7	Sep
2.28		Wang Yu	CHN	18.8.91	2	NC	Kunshan	23	Sep
2.27i	Filippo	Campioli	ITA	21.2.82	1		Hirson	21	Jan
2.27i	James	Harris	USA	18.9.91	1		New York (Arm)	4	Feb
2.27i	Viktor	Ninov	BUL	19.6.88	1		Praha	16	Feb
	(50)								
2.27i	Piotr	Sleboda	POL	22.1.87	2		Praha	16	Feb
2.27i	Marius	Dumitrache	ROU	15.6.89	1	NC	Bucuresti	24	Feb
2.27	Donald	Thomas	BAH	1.7.84	1		Kingston	5	May
2.27	Mihai	Donisan	ROU	24.7.88	1	NC	Bucuresti	5	Jul
2.26i	Andra	Manson	USA	30.4.84	2		Glasgow	28	Jan
2.26Ai	Olivér	Harsányi	HUN	20.3.87	1		Air Force Academy	10	Feb
2.26Ai	Bryan	McBride	USA	10.12.91	1		Albuquerque	10	Feb
2.26i	Abdoulaye	Diarra	FRA	27.5.88	1		Mayenne	11	Feb
2.26i	Keith	Moffatt	USA	20.6.84	2		New York (Arm)	11	Feb
2.26i	Major	Clay	USA	24.12.88	1		Charleston	17	Feb
	(60)								
2.26	Simón	Siverio	ESP	2.8.88	1		Santa Cruz de Tenerife	18	Feb
2.26i	Marco	Fassinotti	ITA	29.4.89	2	NC	Ancona	26	Feb
2.26i	Matthias	Haverney	GER	21.7.85	2	NC	Karlsruhe	26	Feb
2.26i	James	White	USA	22.1.92	1	JUCO	Charleston	3	Mar
2.26i	Majed El Dein	Ghazal	SYR	21.4.87	12q	WI	Istanbul	10	Mar
2.26	Keyvan	Ghanbarzadeh	IRI	26.5.90	1	NC	Shiraz	21	Apr
2.26	Pramote	Poom-urai	THA	24.9.89	2	As GP	Kanchanaburi	11	May
2.26	Dmytro	Demyanyuk	UKR	30.6.83	1	NCp	Yalta	27	May
2.26	Eike	Onnen	GER	3.8.82	1		Regensburg	2	Jun
2.26	Zurab	Gogochuri	GEO	22.3.90	1		Tbilisi	16	Jun
	(70)								
2.26	Dmitriy	Semyonov	RUS	2.8.92	2	NC-23	Yerino	22	Jul
2.26	Dmitriy	Pokidov	RUS	20.12.90	1	NC-23	Irkutsk	3	Aug
2.25i	Sergey	Milokumov	RUS	13.11.87	2		Volgograd	21	Jan
2.25i	Yuriy	Krymarenko	UKR	11.8.83	1		Zaporizhzhya	28	Jan
2.25i	Dusty	Jonas	USA	19.4.86	2		NewYork	28	Jan
2.25i	Janick	Klausen	DEN-J	3.4.93	1		Malmö	29	Jan
2.25i	Matús	Bubenik	SVK	14.11.89	9		Banská Bystrica	8	Feb
2.25	Edward	Dudley	USA	21.6.92	1		Winston-Salem	16	Mar
2.25	Diego	Ferrín	ECU	21.3.88	1		La Habana	17	Mar
2.25	Sergio	Mestre	CUB	30.8.91	2		La Habana	17	Mar
	(80)								
2.25	Brandon	Williams	DMA	14.12.87	3		La Habana	17	Mar
2.25	Edgar	Rivera	MEX	13.2.91	1		Tucson	31	Mar
2.25	Ed	Wright	USA	3.3.86	3	MSR	Walnut	21	Apr
2.25	Tom	Parsons	GBR	5.5.84	1		Loughborough	20	May
2.25	Ali Mohamed Younes	Idriss	SUD	15.9.89	1		Montreuil-sous-Bois	5	Jun
2.25	Artyom	Zaytsev	BLR	7.12.84	2		Minsk	12	Jun
2.25	Justin	Frick	USA	3.8.88	5=	NC/OT	Eugene	25	Jun
2.25A	Luis Joel	Castro	PUR	28.1.91	1		Bogotá	30	Jun
2.25	Kabelo Mmono	Kgosimang	BOT	7.1.86	1	AfrC	Porto Novo	1	Jul
2.25	Adónios	Mástoras	GRE	6.1.91	2	Balk C	Eskisehir	21	Jul
	(90)								
2.25	Wojciech	Theiner	POL	25.6.86	2	Kuso	Szczecin	21	Jul
2.25	Andriy	Rubel	UKR	24.5.89	4		Berdychiv	7	Sep
2.25		Sun Chao	CHN	8.2.90	2		Tianjin	17	Sep
2.25		Lee Sung	KOR	6.5.88	1	NG	Daegu	16	Oct
2.24i	Zack	Riley	USA	20.5.92	1		Carbondale	14	Jan
2.24i	Donte	Nall	USA	27.1.88	1		Chapel Hill	28	Jan
2.24i	Ivan	Ilyichev	RUS	14.10.86	6		Moskva	1	Feb
2.24i		Jin Qichao	CHN	24.11.91	1		Hangzhou	17	Feb
2.24	Jeff	Herron	USA	22.4.90	1		Baton Rouge	7	Apr
2.24	Anthony	May	USA	19.9.90	1		Fayetteville	4	May
	(100)								
2.24	Maalik	Reynolds	USA	26.4.92	1		Philadelphia	6	May
2.24		Bi Xiaoliang	CHN	26.12.92	2=		Tianjin	12	May

Mark	Name		Nat	Born	Pos	Meet	Venue	Date
2.24		Guo Jinqi	CHN	21.9.92	2=		Tianjin	12 May
2.24	Marcus	Jackson	USA	8.7.91	5	NCAA	Des Moines	7 Jun
2.24	Sergey	Zasimovich	KAZ	11.3.86	1		Bishkek	10 Jun
2.24	James	Grayman	ANT	11.10.85	1		Cagnes-sur-Mer	24 Jun
2.24	Eduard	Malchenko	RUS	24.10.86	7	NC	Cheboksary	5 Jul
2.24	Falk	Wendrich	GER-Y	12.6.95	2	WJ	Barcelona	13 Jul
2.24	Nikita	Anishchenkov	RUS	25.7.92	4	NC-23	Yerino	22 Jul
2.24	Yaroslav	Rybakov	RUS	22.11.80	3=	Gyulai	Budapest	20 Aug
2.24	Carlos	Layoy	ARG	26.2.91	1		Buenos Aires	24 Nov
2.24i	Kris	Kornegay-Gober	USA	6.10.91	1		Winston-Salem	1 Dec

Mark		Name	Nat	Born	Date
2.23i	Mark	Dillon	CAN	6.10.84	3 Mar
2.23i	Geoffrey	Davis	USA	8.8.90	3 Mar
2.23i	Darius	King	USA	16.8.91	10 Mar
2.23	Michael	Krone	USA	24.9.91	21 Apr
2.23	David	Smith	USA	2.5.92	21 Apr
2.23	Manjula Kumara	Wijesekara	SRI	30.1.84	8 May
2.23	Eure	Yáñez	VEN-J	20.5.93	12 May
2.23	Dmitriy	Kroyter	ISR-J	18.2.93	31 May
2.23	Alexandru	Tufa	ROU	28.5.89	15 Jun
2.23	Takuya	Tomiyama	JPN	7.4.85	9 Sep
2.23i	Ilya	Ivanyuk	RUS-J	9.3.93	22 Dec
2.22i	Ronnie	Black	USA	2.8.90	14 Jan
2.22i	Sven	Tarnowski	GER	4.3.90	15 Jan
2.22i	Miguel Ángel	Sancho	ESP	24.4.90	28 Jan
2.22i	Javier	Bermejo	ESP	23.12.78	28 Jan
2.22i	Douwe	Amels	NED	16.9.91	5 Feb
2.22i	Keith	Benford	USA	16.1.91	24 Feb
2.22i	Frankie	Hammond	USA	17.2.90	25 Feb
2.22i	Noah	Kittelson	USA	3.12.91	2 Mar
2.22i	Karl	Lumi	EST	4.4.85	4 Mar
2.22	Darius	Purcell	USA	10.1.89	16 Mar
2.22	Montez	Blair	USA	23.10.90	27 Apr
2.22	Martin	Günther	GER	8.10.86	19 May
2.22	Hiromi	Takahari	JPN	13.11.87	20 May
2.22	Victor	Moya	CUB	24.10.82	22 Jun
2.22	Rashid	Al-Mannai	QAT	18.7.88	30 Jun
2.22	Vitaliy	Tsykunov	KAZ	22.1.87	1 Jul
2.22	Lukás	Beer	SVK	23.8.89	1 Sep
2.22	Naoto	Tobe	JPN	31.3.92	10 Sep
2.22	Jithin	Thomas	IND	1.6.90	12 Sep
2.21i	Vitaliy	Samoylenko	UKR	22.5.84	20 Jan
2.21i	Matt	Fisher	USA	3.3.88	21 Jan
2.21i	Andrea	Lemmi	ITA	12.5.84	21 Jan
2.21i	Yuriy	Dergachev	KAZ-J	8.11.94	28 Jan
2.21i	Martin	Heindl	CZE	2.6.92	1 Feb
2.21i	Lev	Missirov	RUS	4.8.90	3 Feb
2.21i	Noel	James	USA	.91	4 Feb
2.21i	Brede Raa	Ellingsen	NOR	13.12.88	11 Feb
2.21i	Mihai	Anastasiu	ROU-J	11.3.93	17 Feb
2.21i	Chris	Copeland	USA	1.5.90	9 Mar
2.21	Tanner	Anderson	USA	4.5.92	6 Apr
2.21	Talles	Silva	BRA	20.8.91	13 May
2.21	Rafael	dos Santos	BRA	10.10.91	13 May
2.21	Artyom	Naumovich	BLR	18.2.91	29 May
2.21		Lee Hup Wei	MAS	5.5.87	24 Jun
2.21	Mathias	Cianci	FRA	25.10.82	24 Jun
2.21	Anpalagan Kavee	Alagan	MAS	2.6.92	11 Jul
2.21	Semen	Pozdnyakov	RUS	28.11.92	22 Jul
2.21	Arseniy	Rasov	RUS	23.6.92	22 Jul
2.21	Leonid	Biryukov	RUS	16.11.91	22 Jul
2.21	Dakarai	Hightower	USA-J	.94	28 Jul
2.21i	Yevgeniy	Korshunov	RUS	11.4.86	23 Dec
2.20i	Mike	Edwards	GBR	11.7.90	7 Jan
2.20i	Chris	Baker	GBR	2.2.91	7 Jan
2.20i	Vadim	Vrublevskiy	RUS-J	18.7.93	7 Jan
2.20i	Mikhail	Andreyev	RUS	4.4.91	9 Jan
2.20i	Darvin	Edwards	LCA	11.9.86	15 Jan
2.20i	Milos	Todosijevic	SRB	8.3.86	21 Jan
2.20i	Briar	Ploude	USA	9.3.91	27 Jan
2.20i	Péter	Bakosi	HUN-J	23.6.93	28 Jan
2.20i	Jim	Dilling	USA	23.4.85	28 Jan
2.20	Andrei	Mîticov	MDA	15.11.86	3 Feb
2.20	Chris	Bryan	JAM-Y	26.4.96	11 Feb
2.20	Robert	Wolski	POL	8.12.82	12 Feb
2.20i		Su Shiwen	CHN	14.5.90	14 Feb
2.20i		Li Peng	CHN	1.8.90	17 Feb
2.20i		Feng Xiaoming	CHN	12.5.90	17 Feb
2.20i		Yi Shisuo	CHN	20.2.90	17 Feb
2.20i	Matthew	Jeune	USA	.92	18 Feb
2.20i	Ray	Bobrownicki	USA	3.3.84	19 Feb
2.20i	Michael	Salomon	FRA	1.6.89	26 Feb
2.20	Raudelys	Rodríguez	CUB	27.9.92	17 Mar
2.20	Jacorian	Duffield	USA	2.9.92	14 Apr
2.20	Tora	Harris	USA	21.9.78	21 Apr
2.20	Cameron	Ostrowski	USA	.92	21 Apr
2.20		Chen Ji	CHN	27.1.90	28 Apr
2.20	Henderson	Dottin	BAR	4.1.80	28 Apr
2.20	Leander	Toney	USA	29.10.87	6 May
2.20	Muamer Aissa	Barshim	QAT-J	3.1.94	11 May
2.20		He Ziqi	CHN-J	6.7.93	12 May
2.20		Chen Hangqi	CHN	23.10.90	12 May
2.20		Huang Haiqiang	CHN	8.2.88	12 May
2.20		Gao Wenbo	CHN	16.6.88	12 May
2.20		Zhu Xusheng	CHN	4.2.91	12 May
2.20		Zhao Kuansong	CHN	11.2.86	26 May
2.20	AJ	Maricich	USA	17.10.91	26 May
2.20		Wu Xiaowei	CHN	28.1.89	26 May
2.20	Dmytro	Yakovenko	UKR	17.9.92	4 Jun
2.20	Andriy	Kovalyov	UKR	11.6.92	4 Jun
2.20	Sylwester	Bednarek	POL	28.4.89	6 Jun
2.20	Harrison	Steed	USA	6.9.91	7 Jun
2.20	Jon	Hill	USA	11.12.91	7 Jun
2.20	Takashi	Eto	JPN	5.2.91	10 Jun
2.20	Andrey	Chubsa	BLR	29.11.82	12 Jun
2.20	Angel	Kararadev	BUL	18.4.79	13 Jun
2.20	Marco	Gelati	ITA	14.2.90	15 Jun
2.20	Mickaël	Diaz	FRA	28.10.86	26 Jun
2.20	Roman	Yevgenyev	RUS	4.2.88	5 Jul
2.20		Yoon Sung-hyun	KOR-J	1.6.94	3 Aug
2.20	Domanique	Missick	TKS	9.1.92	6 Aug
2.20	Mateusz	Przybylko	GER	9.3.92	17 Aug
2.20	Kou	Iwamoto	JPN	11.12.91	25 Aug
2.20	Giuseppe	Carollo	ITA	7.5.91	7 Oct
2.20	Hiroaki	Akai (216)	JPN	12.9.83	8 Oct

Best outdoors

Mark	Name	Pos	Meet	Venue	Date
2.32	Hondrokoúkis ¶	1	DL	Doha	11 May
2.31	Barry	2=	GGala	Roma	31 May
2.31	Protsenko	1	NC	Yalta	14 Jun
2.31	Zhang Guowei	1	NC	Kunshan	23 Sep
2.28	Oni	1		Rehlingen	28 May
2.28	Bába	1	Odlozil	Praha	11 Jun
2.27	Dumitrache	1		Bucuresti	15 Jun
2.27	J Ninov	3		Bucuresti	5 Jul
2.26	White	1		Fayetteville	31 Mar
2.26	Ghazal	1	As GP	Kanchanaburi	11 May
2.25	Spank	2		Garbsen	20 May
2.25	Haverney	3		Garbsen	20 May
2.25	Baniótis	2	Odlozil	Praha	11 Jun
2.25	Diarra	1		Niort	1 Jul
2.25	Campioli	2	NC	Bressanone	8 Jul
2.24	Jin Qichao	1		Wuhan	28 Apr
2.24	Fassinotti	1		Orvieto	3 Jun
2.24	Sleboda	3		Opole	6 Jun
2.24	Kabelka	6=	EC	Helsinki	29 Jun
2.24	Ilyichev	3	NCp	Yerino	14 Jul

Mark	Name	Date		Mark	Name	Date
2.23	Riley	7 Apr		2.22	Chesani	8 Jul
2.23	Horák	16 Jun		2.21	Kornegay-Gober	30 Mar
2.22A	Harsányi	25 May		2.21	Nall	6 Apr
2.22	Bermejo	22 Jun		2.21	King	14 Apr
2.21	Black	13 May		2.21	Missirov	3 Jun
2.21	Amels	17 May		2.20	Siverio	11 Feb
2.21	Krymarenko	17 May		2.20	McBride	24 Mar
2.21	Ivanyuk	20 May		2.20	Davis	31 Mar

MEN 2012

Mark	Name			Nat	Born	Pos	Meet	Venue	Date

2.20	Moffatt	21 Apr	2.20 Sancho 13 May	2.20 Lemmi 3 Jun	2.20 Samoylenko 17 Jun
2.20	Manson	28 Apr	2.20 Feng Xiaoming 26 May	2.20 Edwards 10 Jun	2.20 Dergachev 19 Jun
2.20	Li Peng	12 May	2.20 Yi Shisuo 26 May	2.20 Bubeník 12 Jun	2.20 Korshunov 5 Jul
2.20	Su Shiwen	12 May	2.20 Bobrownicki 28 May	2.20 Mîtîcov 13 Jun	2.20 Vrublevskiy 14 Jul

JUNIORS

See main list for top 4 juniors. 12 performances (3 indoors) by 7 men to 2.23. Additional marks and further juniors:

Mark		Name		Nat	Born	Pos	Meet	Venue	Date
Ingraham	2.24	3	WJ	Barcelona					13 Jul
Churyla	2.25	1		Minsk		12 Jun	2.24 1 WJ Barcelona		13 Jul
	2.23i	1		Gomel		27 Jan			
Wendrich	2.24	7		Eberstadt		18 Aug			
2.23	Eure		Yáñez	VEN	20.5.93	1		Caracas	12 May
2.23	Dmitriy		Kroyter	ISR	18.2.93	2		Hérouville	31 May
2.23i	Ilya		Ivanyuk	RUS	9.3.93	1		Moskva	22 Dec
	2.21					1		Krasnodar	20 May
2.21i	Yuriy		Dergachev	KAZ	8.11.94	1	NC	Karaganda	28 Jan
2.21i	Mihai		Anastasiu	ROU	11.3.93	1	NC-j	Bucuresti	17 Feb
2.21	Dakarai		Hightower (10)	USA	.94	1	Jnr Oly	Baltimore	28 Jul
2.20i	Vadim		Vrublevskiy	RUS	18.7.93	5		Yekaterinburg	7 Jan
	2.20					5	NCp	Yerino	14 Jul
2.20i	Péter		Bakosi	HUN	23.6.93	1		Nyiregyháza	28 Jan
2.20	Chris		Bryan	JAM-Y	26.4.96	1		Montego Bay	11 Feb
2.20			He Ziqi	CHN	6.7.93	7		Tianjin	12 May
2.20			Chen Hangqi	CHN	23.10.90	8		Tianjin	12 May
2.20			Yoon Sung-hyun	KOR	1.6.94	1		Daegu	3 Aug
2.19Ai	Deante		Kemper	USA	27.3.93	1		Flagstaff	28 Jan
	2.18					1c2	MSR	Walnut	20 Apr
2.19 best out	Janick		Klausen	DEN	3.4.93	2		Mannheim	24 Jun
2.19	Mariusz		Baszczynski	POL	19.5.93	3		Ilawa	29 Jun
2.19	Naviraj		Subramaniam (19)	MAS	14.2.93	2		Kuantan	11 Jul

POLE VAULT

Mark	Name		Nat	Born	Pos	Meet	Venue	Date
6.01	Björn	Otto	GER	16.10.77	1		Aachen	5 Sep

5.71/3 5.91/3 6.01/2

5.92i	1		Potsdam	18 Feb	5.52/1 5.72/2 5.82/1 5.92/2 6.01/xxx
5.92i	1	NC	Karlsruhe	26 Feb	5.52/1 5.72/1 5.82/xx 5.87/1 5.92/1 6.01/xxx
5.92	2	EC	Helsinki	1 Jul	5.50/1 5.66/1 5.77/3 5.82/3 5.92/2 6.02/xxx
5.91	2	OG	London (OS)	10 Aug	5.50/1 5.65/1 5.75/2 5.85/2 5.91/1 5.97/xx 6.02/x
5.84i	1		Dessau	2 Mar	6.01/xxx
5.83	1sq		Recklinghausen	23 May	5.43/1 5.63/1 5.83/3
5.82i	2		Donetsk	11 Feb	5.52/1 5.72/2 5.82/3 5.92/xxx
5.82	1		Chula Vista	5 Apr	5.42/1 5.62/2 5.72/2 5.82/1 5.92/xxx
5.81	1=		Jockgrim	25 Jul	5.61/1 5.81/1 6.01/xxx
5.81	1		Landau	16 Aug	5.51/1 5.71/2 5.81/1 5.93/x

| 5.97 | Renaud | Lavillenie | FRA | 18.9.86 | 1 | EC | Helsinki | 1 Jul |

5.60/2 5.77/1 5.82/3 5.87/1 5.92/1 5.97/1 6.02/xxx

5.97	1	OG	London (OS)	10 Aug	5.65/1 5.75/1 5.85/1 5.91/x 5.97/2 6.02/x 6.07/xx
5.95i	1	WI	Istanbul	10 Mar	5.75/1 5.80/2 5.85/1 5.90/2 5.95/1 6.00/x 6.02/xx
5.93i	1		Nevers	18 Feb	5.66/1 5.72/2 5.82/1 5.93/1 6.05/xXX
5.90	1	GS	Ostrava	25 May	5.42/1 5.62/1 5.78/2 5.83/1 5.90/3 6.00/xXX
5.85	1	NC	Angers	17 Jun	5.62/2 5.77/2 5.85/1 5.95/xxx
5.83	1	Déca	Albi	15 Aug	5.33/1 5.53/1 5.63/2 5.73/1 5.83/2 5.90/xxx
5.82i	1		Donetsk	11 Feb	5.52/1 5.72/1 5.82/1 5.92/xxx
5.82	1	GGala	Roma	31 May	5.60/1 5.82/1
5.82	1	Bisl	Oslo	7 Jun	5.52/2 5.72/3 5.82/1 5.92/xxx
5.82	1		Villeneuve d'Ascq	9 Jun	5.52/1 5.72/3 5.82/2 5.92/xxx

| 5.91 | Malte | Mohr | GER | 24.7.86 | 1 | | Ingolstadt | 22 Jun |

5.43/2 5.63/2 5.73/1 5.91/2 6.01/xxx

5.87i	2	NC	Karlsruhe	26 Feb	5.62/3 5.77/1 5.87/1 5.97/xxx
5.82	1	NC	Wattenscheid	17 Jun	5.52/1 5.72/1 5.77/1 5.82/2
5.81	4		Jockgrim	25 Jul	5.61/3 5.81/2 6.01/xxx

| 5.91 | Raphael | Holzdeppe | GER | 28.9.89 | 3 | OG | London (OS) | 10 Aug |

5.65/2 5.75/2 5.85/3 5.91/1 5.97/xxx

| 5.82i | 3 | NC | Karlsruhe | 26 Feb | 5.52/1 5.72/1 5.77/1 5.82/2 5.87/x 5.92/xX |
| 5.81 | 1= | | Jockgrim | 25 Jul | 5.61/1 5.81/1 5.91/xxx |

| 5.90 | Brad | Walker | USA | 21.6.81 | 1 | | Chula Vista | 12 Jul |

5.50/1 5.70/2 5.90/3 6.00/xxx

| 5.86Ai | 1 | NC | Albuquerque | 26 Feb | 5.54/1 5.72/1 5.86/1 6.00/xxx |
| 5.81 | 1= | | Jockgrim | 25 Jul | 5.61/1 5.81/1 6.01/xxx |

| 5.82 | Steve | Lewis | GBR | 20.5.86 | 1 | Kuso | Szczecin | 21 Jul |

(33/6)
5.52/1 5.72/1 5.82/2 5.92/xxx

Mark	Name		Nat	Born	Pos	Meet	Venue	Date	
5.80i	Dmitriy	Starodubtsev	RUS	3.1.86	1		Chelyabinsk	14	Jan
5.80	Konstadínos	Filippídis	GRE	26.11.86	4	Athl	Lausanne	23	Aug
5.75	Yevgeniy	Lukyanenko	RUS	23.1.85	5=	OG	London (OS)	10	Aug
5.73i	Karsten	Dilla	GER	17.7.89	1		Bad Oeynhausen	3	Mar
	(10)								
5.73	Jan	Kudlicka	CZE	29.4.88	1		Kladno	30	May
5.72i	Lukasz	Michalski	POL	2.8.88	1		Bordeaux	28	Jan
5.72i	Lázaro	Borges	CUB	19.6.86	4		Donetsk	11	Feb
5.72i	Romain	Mesnil	FRA	13.6.77	2		Liévin	14	Feb
5.72i	Maksym	Mazuryk	UKR	2.4.83	2		Potsdam	18	Feb
5.72	Daichi	Sawano	JPN	16.9.80	2	MSR	Walnut	21	Apr
5.72i	Steve	Hooker	AUS	16.7.82	1		Perth	11	May
5.72	Andrew	Irwin	USA-J	23.1.93	1	SEC	Baton Rouge	13	May
5.72	Jere	Bergius	FIN	4.4.87	1		Haapajärvi	26	May
5.72i	Jack	Whitt	USA	12.4.90	1		Tulsa	2	Jun
	(20)								
5.72	Denys	Yurchenko	UKR	27.1.78	1		Yalta	4	Jun
5.72	Jordan	Scott	USA	22.2.88	1		Wichita	9	Jun
5.72	Sergey	Kucheryanu	RUS	30.6.85	1		Moskva	21	Jun
5.72	Alhaji	Jeng	SWE	13.12.81	1	NA	Heusden-Zolder	7	Jul
5.70i	Hendrik	Gruber	GER	28.9.86	1		Metz	29	Feb
5.70	Fábio G	da Silva	BRA	4.8.83	1		Fortaleza	9	May
5.70	Vladislav	Revenko	UKR	15.11.84	1		Kharkiv	18	Jul
5.70		Yang Yansheng	CHN	5.1.88	1	NC	Kunshan	24	Sep
5.65	Hiroki	Ogita	JPN	30.12.87	1	Oda	Hiroshima	29	Apr
5.65	Dmitry	Zhelyabin	RUS	20.5.90	4	NC	Cheboksary	5	Jul
	(30)								
5.65	Seito	Yamamoto	JPN	11.3.92	1		Odawara	14	Oct
5.64i	Edi	Maia	POR	10.11.87	1		Pombal	26	Feb
5.63	Mark	Hollis	USA	1.12.84	2		Chula Vista	14	Jun
5.62		Kim Yoo-suk	KOR	19.1.82	1		La Jolla	28	Apr
5.62	Przemyslaw	Czerwinski	POL	28.7.83	5	GS	Ostrava	25	May
5.62	Pawel	Wojciechowski	POL	6.6.89	3	EAF	Bydgoszcz	3	Jun
5.62	Robbert Jan	Jansen	NED	22.7.83	1		Thionville	6	Jun
5.62	Vincent	Favretto	FRA	5.4.84	1		Bron	5	Jul
5.61	Tobias	Scherbarth	GER	17.8.85	2		Leverkusen	25	Aug
5.60i	Derek	Miles	USA	28.9.72	1		Vermillion, SD	2	Feb
	(40)								
5.60i	Claudio Michel	Stecchi	ITA	23.11.91	1	NC	Ancona	25	Feb
5.60Ai	Scott	Roth	USA	25.6.88	2	NC	Albuquerque	26	Feb
5.60i	Marco	Boni	ITA	21.5.84	1		Fermo	4	Mar
5.60	Nikita	Filippov	KAZ	7.10.91	1		Almaty	14	May
5.60	Eemeli	Salomäki	FIN	11.10.87	2		Haapajärvi	26	May
5.60	Igor	Pavlov	RUS	18.7.79	2		München	5	Jun
5.60A	Rory	Quiller	USA	17.4.84	1		Fort Collins	9	Jun
5.60	Stanislav	Tivonchik	BLR	5.3.85	1		Minsk	12	Jun
5.60	Chris	Swanson	USA	6.6.82	1		Walnut	12	Jun
5.60	Ivan	Horvat	CRO-J	17.8.93	1		Varazdin	17	Jun
	(50)								
5.60	Mareks	Arents	LAT	6.6.86	1		Valmiera	20	Jun
5.60	Giorgio	Piantella	ITA	6.7.81	1		Nembro	22	Jun
5.60	Jeremy	Scott	USA	21.5.81	2	NC/OT	Eugene	28	Jun
5.60	Artem	Burya	RUS	11.4.86	1	NCp	Yerino	14	Jul
5.60	Anton	Ivakin	RUS	3.2.91	1	NC-23	Yerino	21	Jul
5.60		Xue Changrui	CHN	31.5.91	2	NC	Kunshan	24	Sep
5.58i	Shawn	Barber	CAN-J	27.5.94	1		Denton	29	Dec
5.56i	Igor	Bychkov	ESP	7.3.87	3		Nevers	17	Feb
5.56	Tom	Konrad	GER	30.3.91	1-U23		Leverkusen	25	Aug
5.55i	Andrew	Sutcliffe	GBR	10.7.91	1	NC	Sheffield	11	Feb
	(60)								
5.55	Michael	Woepse	USA	29.5.91	1		Los Angeles (Ww)	24	Mar
5.55	Matti	Mononen	FIN	25.11.83	1		Lappeenranta	19	May
5.55	Ivan	Gertleyn	RUS	25.9.87	3=		Sochi	26	May
5.55i	Jérôme	Clavier	FRA	3.5.83	1		Aulnay-sus-Bois	2	Jun
5.55	Ivan	Yeryomin	UKR	30.5.89	2=	NC	Yalta	14	Jun
5.55	Paul	Litchfield	USA	27.11.80	1		Livermore, CA	16	Jun
	Note this was made with US HS (75m pegs), Next 5.52Ai 1 Pocatello 17 Feb, 5.50 8 MSR Walnut 21 Apr								
5.55	Dídac	Salas	ESP-J	19.5.93	1=		Barcelona	16	Jun
5.55	Alexandre	Feger	FRA	22.1.90	3	NC	Angers	17	Jun
5.55	Anatoliy	Bednyuk	RUS	30.1.89	5	NC	Cheboksary	5	Jul
5.55	Stanley	Joseph	FRA	24.10.91	1		Castres	7	Jul
	(70)								

Mark	Name		Nat	Born	Pos	Meet	Venue	Date
5.55	Thiago	da Silva	BRA-J	16.12.93	1	WJ	Barcelona	12 Jul
5.54i	Damiel	Dossévi	FRA	3.2.83	4		Villeurbanne	20 Jan
5.54	Nikita	Kirillov	USA-J	5.6.93	1	NC-j	Bloomington	15 Jun
5.53i	Jason	Colwick	USA	25.1.88	1		Seattle	11 Feb
5.53i	Tim	Lobinger	GER	3.9.72	3		Bad Oeynhausen	3 Mar
5.53i	Michel	Frauen	GER	19.1.86	4=		Bad Oeynhausen	3 Mar
5.53i	Rasmus	Jørgensen	DEN	23.1.89	4=		Bad Oeynhausen	3 Mar
5.53A	Cale	Simmons	USA	5.2.91	1		Air Force Academy	12 May
5.53	Logan	Cunningham	USA	30.5.91	1		San Marcos	13 May
5.53A	Mike	Arnold	USA	13.8.90	1		Pocatello	1 Jun
	(80)							
5.53	Nicholas	Frawley	USA	21.6.88	2		Chula Vista	7 Jun
5.53	Maston	Wallace	USA	2.7.89	5		Chula Vista	7 Jun
5.53	Dustin	DeLeo	USA	3.1.86	3		Chula Vista	14 Jun
5.53	Jake	Pauli	USA	15.6.79	1		Cedar Falls	15 Jun
5.52i	Fabian	Schulze	GER	7.3.84	2		Linz	2 Feb
5.52i	Giuseppe	Gibilisco	ITA	5.1.79	7=		Liévin	14 Feb
5.52	Emile	Denecker	FRA	28.3.92	1		Besancon	29 May
5.52	Valentin	Lavillenie	FRA	16.7.91	2		Besancon	29 May
5.52	Levi	Keller	USA	30.1.86	1		Chula Vista	31 May
5.52	Marvin Rene	Reitze	GER	24.8.88	7	NC	Wattenscheid	17 Jun
	(90)							
5.52	Xavier	Tromp	FRA	3.3.84	1		Bourgoin Jallie	27 Jun
5.51	Seth	Arnold	USA	29.7.92	1		Austin	19 May
5.51	Jason	Wurster	CAN	23.9.84	1		London, ON	19 May
5.51		Jin Min-sup	KOR	2.9.92	1		Taipei	25 May
5.51 solo	Darren	Niedermeyer	USA	2.4.82	1		Rolling Meadows	12 Jun
	5.50				2		Adrian	27 May
5.51	Alexander	Straub	GER	14.10.83	4		Landau	16 Aug
5.51	Oleksandr	Korchmid	UKR	22.1.82	1	Slus M	Miedzyzroje	17 Aug
5.50i	Victor	Weirich	USA	25.10.87	1		Nampa	14 Jan
5.50i	Viktor	Chistyakov	RUS	9.2.75	2		Moskva	18 Feb
5.50i	Matteo	Rubbiani	ITA	31.8.78	2	NC	Ancona	25 Feb
	(100)							
5.50	Derick	Hinch	USA	2.2.91	1		Tempe	24 Mar
5.50	Baptiste	Boirie	FRA	26.12.92	1		Aix-les-Bains	6 May
5.50	Sam	Kendricks	USA	7.9.92	2	SEC	Baton Rouge	13 May
5.50		Zhang Wei	CHN-J	22.3.94	1		Zibo	26 May
5.50	Pauls	Pujats	LAT	6.8.91	1		Jogeva	31 May
5.50	Robert	Renner	SLO-J	8.3.94	3		Innsbruck	1 Jun
5.50	Nico	Weiler	GER	5.4.90	4	NCAA	Des Moines	8 Jun
5.50	Lukás	Bechyne	CZE	4.10.83	1		Praha	7 Jul
5.50	Ilya	Mudrov	RUS	17.11.91	2	NC-23	Yerino	21 Jul
5.50	Germán	Chiaraviglio	ARG	16.4.87	1		Buenos Aires	8 Sep

Mark		Name	Nat	Born	Date		Mark		Name	Nat	Born	Date
5.48	Cyriel	Verberne	NED	4.12.84	27 May		5.42 sq	Robert	Sobera	POL	19.1.91	27 May
5.48	Melker	Svärd-Jacobsson	SWE-J	8.1.94	2 Sep		5.42	Chase	Brannon	USA	8.2.91	1 Jun
5.47i	Aleksandr	Gripich	RUS	21.9.86	24 Feb		5.42	Dimítrios	Patsoukákis	GRE	18.3.87	7 Jul
5.46i	Arnaud	Art	BEL-J	28.1.93	18 Feb		5.41i	Ryan	Vu	CAN	16.5.88	28 Jan
5.46	Sean	Young	USA	27.12.85	19 May		5.41	Kyal	Meyers	USA	5.9.91	14 Apr
5.45i	Max	Eaves	GBR	31.5.88	11 Feb		5.41	Diego	Ferreira	POR	30.7.90	31 May
5.45i	Luke	Cutts	GBR	13.2.88	11 Feb		5.41	Mickaël	Guillaume	FRA	8.9.89	24 Jun
5.45i	Michael	Seaman	USA	29.9.87	23 Feb		5.41	João Gabriel	Sousa	BRA	6.11.84	7 Jul
5.45i	Stevy	Dume	FRA	8.4.88	25 Feb		5.41	Danny	Ecker	GER	21.7.77	25 Aug
5.45i	Adam	Pasiak	CZE	18.7.90	26 Feb		5.40i	Craig	Van Leeuwen	USA	17.7.87	20 Jan
5.45	Yankier	Lara	CUB	1.1.89	2 Mar		5.40Ai	Joe	Berry	USA	17.2.89	20 Jan
5.45i	Kevin	Schipper	USA	5.8.89	9 Mar		5.40i	Andrej	Poljanec	SLO	10.11.84	28 Jan
5.45	Augusto	de Oliveira	BRA	16.7.90	21 Apr		5.40i	Takafumi	Suzuki	JPN	25.5.87	4 Feb
5.45	Gonzalo	Barroilhet	CHI	19.8.86	11 May		5.40i	Spas	Bukhalov	BUL	14.11.80	10 Feb
5.45	Robbie	Haynie	USA	18.3.84	25 May		5.40i	Chip	Heuser	USA	9.2.85	10 Feb
5.45	Mitch	Greeley	USA	5.5.86	28 May		5.40Ai	Nick	Mossberg	USA	5.4.86	11 Feb
5.45	Daniel	Clemens	GER	28.4.92	2 Jun		5.40i	Nikolay	Lavrinenko	RUS	16.5.84	11 Feb
5.45	Michal	Balner	CZE	12.9.82	2 Jun		5.40i	Parker	Smith	USA	25.7.88	9 Mar
5.44i	Nate	Polacek	USA	22.6.90	17 Feb		5.40	Jeff	Rodriguez	USA	3.10.90	24 Mar
5.44	Jonathon	Juilfs	USA-J	7.2.93	12 May		5.40	Chris	Roy	USA	10.5.89	31 Mar
5.44i	Daniel	Ryland	USA	6.8.79	12 May		5.40	Mick	Viken	USA	21.9.90	14 Apr
5.43i	Kevin	Ménaldo	FRA	12.7.92	14 Jan		5.40	Hunter	Hall	USA	3.11.88	20 Apr
5.43i	Eelco	Sintnicolaas	NED	7.4.87	4 Feb		5.40	Jeff	Coover	USA	1.12.87	21 Apr
5.43i	Jeremy	Klas	USA	5.9.89	11 Feb		5.40	Kyle	Inks	USA	25.5.89	28 Apr
5.43i	Jared	Jodon	USA	10.12.87	18 Feb		5.40	Carlo	Paech	GER	18.12.92	19 May
5.43	Mikkel	Nielsen	DEN	13.9.88	22 Jun		5.40	Peter	Geraghty	USA	11.6.91	26 May
5.43	Florian	Gaul	GER	21.9.91	22 Jun		5.40	Daniel	Gooris	USA	28.9.89	26 May
5.42i	Bryant	Wilson	USA	27.3.87	17 Feb		5.40	Alexandre	Marchand	FRA	23.2.90	6 Jun
5.42i	Stephan	Munz	GER	19.10.88	26 Feb		5.40	Samuel	Lauret	FRA	19.6.88	6 Jun
5.42	Giovanni	Lanaro	MEX	27.9.81	28 Apr		5.40	Kolby	Shephard	USA	9.4.89	8 Jun

Mark	Name		Nat	Born	Pos Meet	Venue	Date

Mark	Name	Nat	Born	Date
5.40	Joe Davis	USA	1.12.88	8 Jun
5.40	Andrew LaHaye	USA	11.3.90	8 Jun
5.40	Nikandros Stylianou	CYP	22.8.89	10 Jun
5.40	Manel Concepción	ESP	27.3.90	20 Jun
5.40	Mikhail Gelmanov	RUS	18.3.90	21 Jul
5.40	Georgiy Gorokhov	RUS-J	20.4.93	21 Jul
5.40	Jun-ya Nagata	JPN	15.4.88	23 Sep
5.38	Olli Rannikko	FIN	18.9.84	02 Sep
5.37	Thomas Skipper	USA	14.4.84	31 May
5.36i	Flavien Basson	FRA	15.5.88	7 Jan
5.36i	Wout van Wengeren	NED	16.2.87	7 Jan
5.36i	Reese Watson	USA-J	8.10.93	4 Feb
5.36i	Nicolas Guigon	FRA	10.10.80	17 Feb
5.36i	Pierre-Charles Peuf	FRA	27.4.79	17 Feb
5.36	Albert Vélez	ESP	26.10.88	26 Aug

Best outdoors

Mark	Name	Pos	Meet	Venue	Date
5.75	Starodubtsev	4	OG	London (OS)	10 Aug
5.72	Dilla	2	GS	Ostrava	25 May
5.72	Mazuryk	1	NCp	Yalta	27 May
5.72	Mesnil	2	GGala	Roma	31 May
5.72	Michalski	1	EAF	Bydgoszcz	3 Jun
5.72	Hooker	3	Kuso	Szczecin	21 Jul
5.65	Whitt	1	NCAA	Des Moines	8 Jun
5.60	Borges	1		Ponce	12 May
5.60	Roth	3	NC/OT	Eugene	28 Jun
5.60	Miles	4	NC/OT	Eugene	28 Jun
5.60	Stecchi	1	NC	Bressanone	7 Jul
5.57	Barber	1		Humble	4 Aug
5.56	Bychkov	1		Zaragoza	9 Jun
5.55	Maia	1		Lisboa (Un)	9 Jun
5.55	Gruber	1		Leverkusen	30 Jun
5.52	Frauen	6	NC	Wattenscheid	17 Jun
5.50	Weirich	2	TexR	Austin	31 Mar
5.50	Jørgensen	2		Soest	19 May

Mark	Name	Date	Mark	Name	Date	Mark	Name	Date	Mark	Name	Date
5.46	Sutcliffe	11 Aug	5.40	Schipper	21 Apr	5.40	Boni	9 Jun	5.37	Dossévi	11 Apr
5.43	Cutts	7 Jul	5.40	Pasiak	19 May	5.40	Bukhalov	13 Jun	5.37	Vu	31 May
5.42	Rubbiani	25 Apr	5.40	Lobinger	20 May	5.40	Lavrinenko	21 Jun	5.36	Sintnicolaas	27 Mar
5.40	Ménaldo	14 Apr	5.40	Mossberg	2 Jun	5.40	Suzuki	4 Aug	5.36	Munz	28 May

Extra trial: 5.75 Jan Kudlicka CZE 29.4.88 * Opava 16 Aug

Exhibition: Jun 2, Praha: 1. Michal Balner CZE 5.66, 2. Adam Pasiak CZE 5.46

JUNIORS

See main lists for top 8 juniors. 13 performances (1 indoors) by 6 men to 5.52. Additional marks and further juniors:

Mark	Name	Nat	Born	Pos	Meet	Venue	Date
5.60	Irwin			1		Fayetteville	31 Mar
5.53i				1	SEC	Lexington	26 Feb
5.55i				1	NCAA	Nampa	9 Mar
5.55	Horvat			2	WJ	Barcelona	12 Jul
5.52				1		Split	20 May
5.55	Barber 2+			3	WJ	Barcelona	12 Jul
5.48	Melker Svärd-Jacobsson	SWE	8.1.94	3	vFIN	Göteborg	2 Sep
5.46i	Arnaud Art (10)	BEL	28.1.93	2eB		Nevers	18 Feb
5.35				1		Nivelles	19 May
5.44	Jonathon Juilfs	USA	7.2.93	1	Pac-12	Eugene	12 May
5.40	Georgiy Gorokhov	RUS	20.4.93	3=		Yerino	21 Jul
5.36i	Reese Watson	USA	8.10.93	1		Joshua	4 Feb
5.35i	Jacob Blankenship	USA	15.3.94	1		Oberlin	26 Feb
5,23				1		Columbus	2 Jun
5.32	Andreas Duplantis	SWE	2.5.93	8=q	NCAA-E	Jacksonville	26 May
5.30	Thibault Boisseau	FRA	10.10.93	7	WJ	Barcelona	12 Jul
5.30	Shota Enoki	JPN	7.2.94	1c2		Toyota	13 Oct
5.25	Dylan Bell	USA	21.7.93	2		Austin	30 Mar
5.25	Jonas Efferoth (19)	GER	3.2.93	3	NC-j	Kandel	29 Jul
5.20	11 juniors						

LONG JUMP

Mark	Wind	Name	Nat	Born	Pos	Meet	Venue	Date
8.35	2.0	Greg Rutherford	GBR	17.11.86	1		Chula Vista	3 May
		7.89w 8.02 x 8.35 p p						
8.32	0.0				1	GGala	Roma	31 May
		8.04 7.98 8.07 8.11 8.15 8.32						
8.31	-0.1				1	OG	London (OS)	4 Aug
		6.28 8.21/-0.6 8.14 8.31 x 6.33						
8.35	1.1	Sergey Morgunov	RUS-J	9.2.93	1	NC-j	Cheboksary	19 Jun
		8.00 6.31 8.06 7.93 8.12 8.35						
8.34	0.3	Sebastian Bayer	GER	11.6.86	1	EC	Helsinki	1 Jul
		x x 8.03 8.09 8.33/0.7 8.34						
8.25	0.1				1		Wesel	28 May
		8.25 8.17 p 8.01 p p						
8.34w	2.4				Q	EC	Helsinki	29 Jun
		8.34w p p						
8.33	1.4	Marquise Goodwin	USA	19.11.90	1	NC/OT	Eugene	24 Jun
		8.07 x 8.23 8.21w 7.72 8.33						
8.23	0.5				1	NCAA	Des Moines	6 Jun
		8.19 7.87 7.99 8.15 8.11 8.23						
8.29A	0.0	Khotso Mokoena	RSA	6.3.85	1		Pretoria	20 Apr
		8.29 x p p x p						
8.24	1.7				3	LGP	London (CP)	13 Jul
		5.95 7.73 8.24 7.90 7.90 8.03						
8.29	-0.5	Aleksandr Menkov	RUS	7.12.90	1	VD	Bruxelles	7 Sep
		x x x 8.03 8.29 x						
8.24i					1		Moskva	5 Feb
		x x 7.83 8.04 8.24						
8.24	0.2				1	NC	Cheboksary	5 Jul
		8.10 8.24 x 6.52 P P						
8.22i					3	WI	Istanbul	10 Mar
		8.12 8.22 x x 8.10 x						
8.22	1.6				1	DL	Doha	11 May
		x x x 8.22						
8.28i		Mauro Vinícius da Silva	BRA	26.12.86	Q	WI	Istanbul	9 Mar
		7.93 x 8.28						
8.23i					1	WI	Istanbul	10 Mar
		7.73 x x 7.77 8.23 8.23						

Mark	Wind	Name		Nat	Born	Pos	Meet	Venue		Date
8.28	1.0	Mitchell	Watt	AUS	25.3.88	1	LGP	London (CP)		13 Jul
					8.06	x	8.28	6.58	8.25/1.3	8.03
8.26w	3.7				1			Madrid		7 Jul
					x	8.23w/2.1	8.26w	p	p	p
8.27	1.4	Henry	Frayne	AUS	14.4.90	1		Sydney		18 Feb
					8.06	x	x	x	8.27	8.13
8.23i					2	WI		Istanbul		10 Mar
					8.17	x	x	x	7.89	8.23
8.26	1.4	Christian	Reif (10)	GER	24.10.84	1		Weinheim		26 May
					8.26	p	p	p	p	p
8.26	0.2	Chris	Tomlinson	GBR	15.9.81	2	LGP	London (CP)		13 Jul
					7.98	8.06	8.02	8.12w	8.09	8.26
8.25	1.6	Will	Claye	USA	13.6.91	1		Gainesville		21 Apr
					7.77w	7.64	7.89w	x	8.00w	8.25
8.24i					1			Fayetteville		10 Feb
					7.80	7.94	8.17	8.24		
8.22	0.9				*	NC/OT		Eugene		22 Jun
					x	7.77	8.23w	x	x	8.22
8.25	1.0		Li Jinzhe	CHN	1.9.89	1		Wuhan		28 Apr
8.25	1.6	Yeóryios	Tsákonas	GRE	22.1.88	1		Thíva		25 Jul
					x	x	8.25	8.02	p	8.23
8.23	0.8	Ashton	Eaton	USA	21.1.88	1D	NC/OT	Eugene		22 Jun
					8.23	p	p			
8.22	-2.2	Luis	Rivera	MEX	21.6.87	1	MSR	Walnut		21 Apr
					7.94	8.14	x	7.70	7.96	8.22
8.22	1.4	Roman	Novotny	CZE	5.1.86	2		Brno		4 Jul
8.22	2.0	Michel	Tornéus	SWE	26.5.86	1		Kuortane		22 Jul
			(32/18)		8.14w	8.06w	p	7.63	p	8.22
8.21	0.9	Tyron	Stewart	USA	8.7.89	1		Chula Vista		14 Jun
8.21	0.6	George	Kitchens	USA	16.1.83	3	NC/OT	Eugene		24 Jun
			(20)							
8.21	1.7	Luis Felipe	Méliz	ESP	11.8.79	2	EC	Helsinki		1 Jul
8.21	1.9	Stepán	Wagner	CZE	5.10.81	*		Brno		4 Jul
8.20i			Zhang Xiaoyi	CHN	25.5.89	1		Nanjing		13 Feb
8.20	-0.1	Alyn	Camara	GER	31.3.89	2		Wesel		28 May
8.20A	1.8	Arsen	Sargsyan	ARM	20.11.76	1		Artashat		8 Jun
8.20	1.6	Stanley	Gbabeke	NGR	24.7.89	1	NC	Calabar		21 Jun
8.20A ?	1.9	Vartan	Pahlevanyan	ARM	27.2.88	1		Artashat		6 Jul
8.17i			Yun Zhiming	CHN	9.10.88	2		Nanjing		13 Feb
8.17	1.5	Ndiss Kaba	Badji	SEN	21.9.83	1		Aix-les-Bains		20 May
8.17	1.3	Mohammad	Arzandeh	IRI	30.10.87	1		Tehran		7 Jul
			(30)							
8.16A	0.9	Kendall	Spencer	USA	24.7.91	1		Albuquerque		7 Apr
8.16	0.2	Irving	Saladino	PAN	23.1.83	1	Herc	Monaco		20 Jul
8.15A	0.8	Zarck	Visser	RSA	15.9.89	1		Pretoria		4 May
8.13	1.2	Damar	Forbes	JAM	18.9.90	2	SEC	Baton Rouge		12 May
8.12	1.4	Marcin	Starzak	POL	20.10.85	1		Bilbao		3 Jun
8.12	1.1	Christian	Taylor	USA	18.6.90	4	OT	Eugene		24 Jun
8.11	0.3	Jeremy	Hicks	USA	19.9.86	1		Baton Rouge		16 Jun
8.11	1.8	Dimítrios	Diamantáras	GRE	18.7.84	1	Veniz	Haniá		4 Jul
8.11	1.5	J.J.	Jegede	GBR	3.10.85	5	LGP	London (CP)		13 Jul
8.11A	1.4	Darius	Aucyna	LTU	7.5.89	1		Artashat		15 Sep
			(40)							
8.10	0.0	Viktor	Kuznetsov	UKR	14.7.86	1	NCp	Yalta		28 May
8.10		Levance	Williams	USA		1		Lancaster		2 Jun
8.10	2.0	Fabrice	Lapierre	AUS	17.10.83	*	adidas	New York		9 Jun
8.09i		Alexandr	Cuharenco	MDA	7.3.87	1	NC	Chisinau		3 Feb
8.09	0.0	Yohei	Sugai	JPN	30.8.85	2	MSR	Walnut		21 Apr
8.09A		Elijah	Kimitei	KEN	.86	1	NC	Nairobi		14 Jun
8.08	1.9	Daniel	Pineda	CHI	19.9.85	1	NC	Santiago		21 Apr
8.08	nwi	Nicolas	Gomont	FRA	15.9.86	1		Bonneuil-sur-Marne		25 May
8.00	-0.4					1		Amiens		30 Jun
8.08	1.5	Pavel	Shalin	RUS	15.3.87	2	NC	Cheboksary		5 Jul
8.08	2.0	Shin-ichiro	Shimono	JPN	10.10.90	1		Fukuoka		14 Jul
			(50)							
8.07	1.9	Raymond	Higgs	BAH	24.1.91	1		Fayetteville		21 Apr
8.06i		Marquis	Dendy	USA	17.11.92	1	SEC	Lexington		25 Feb
8.06	0.3	Morten	Jensen	DEN	2.12.82	Q	EC	Helsinki		29 Jun
8.06	0.4	Eusebio	Cáceres	ESP	10.9.91	5	EC	Helsinki		1 Jul
8.05	-0.3	Rogério	Bispo	BRA	16.11.85	1		São Paulo		11 Feb
8.05i		Loúis	Tsátoumas	GRE	12.2.82	1	NC	Pireás		21 Feb
8.05	-0.8	Norris	Frederick	USA	17.2.86	5	MSR	Walnut		21 Apr
8.05	nwi	Kafétien	Gomis	FRA	23.3.80	2		Bonneuil-sur-Marne		25 May
7.89	1.1					Q	EC	Helsinki		29 Jun
8.05	0.0	Sheryf	El-Sheryf	UKR	2.1.89	2	NCp	Yalta		28 May

Mark	Wind	Name		Nat	Born	Pos	Meet	Venue	Date
8.05	0.1	Tomasz	Jaszczuk	POL	9.3.92	1	NC	Bielsko-Biala	15 Jun
		(60)							
8.05	-0.5	Ronni	Ollikainen	FIN	27.8.90	*		Jämsä	16 Jun
8.05	0.1		Su Xiongfeng	CHN	21.3.87	1		Tianjin	18 Sep
8.04	0.7	Ignisious	Gaisah	GHA	20.6.83	1		Kumasi	6 Jul
8.04	-0.2		Wang Jianan	CHN-Y	27.8.96	1	NC	Kunshan	22 Sep
8.03i			Tang Gongchen	CHN	24.4.89	3		Nanjing	13 Feb
8.03	0.6	Nils	Winter	GER	27.3.77	3		Wesel	28 May
8.03	1.3	Andreas	Otterling	SWE	25.5.86	1		Lerum	12 Jun
8.02	1.2	Carl	Morgan	CAY	25.8.86	2		Athens, GA	24 Mar
8.02	1.4	Mikko	Kivinen	FIN	16.1.88	2		Jämsä	16 Jun
8.01		Salah	Al-Haddad	KUW	27.5.86	1		Al-Kuwait	3 Jan
		(70)							
8.01	0.3	Tommy	Evilä	FIN	6.4.80	2		Bad Langensalza	3 Jun
8.01	1.2	Sergey	Polyanskiy	RUS	29.10.89	1	NCp	Yerino	14 Jul
8.00i		Elvijs	Misans	LAT	8.4.89	1		Riga	3 Feb
8.00i		Marcos	Chuva	POR	8.8.89	1	NC	Espinho	18 Feb
8.00i		Sergey	Nikolayev	RUS	1.9.87	1	NC	Moskva	24 Feb
8.00	-0.5	Rikiya	Saruyama	JPN	15.2.84	6	MSR	Walnut	21 Apr
8.00	1.6	Marko	Prugovecki	CRO	1.1.87	1		Slovenska Bistrica	26 May
8.00	-0.4		Zhao Xiaoxi	CHN	19.3.89	*		Fuzhou	23 Jun
8.00	0.2	Konstantin	Safronov	KAZ	2.9.87	1		Almaty	1 Jul
7.98	1.1	Salim	Sdiri	FRA	26.10.78	3	NC	Angers	17 Jun
		(80)							
7.98	0.7	Samson	Idiata	NGR	28.2.82	*		Vitoria	21 Jul
7.97	0.9	Andrly	Makarchev	UKR	15.11.85	1		Yalta	4 Jun
7.97	-0.3	Tyrone	Smith	BER	7.8.86	Q	OG	London (OS)	3 Aug
7.96i			Xu Jianping	CHN	1.1.90	2		Chengdu	10 Mar
7.96	0.4	Michael	Hartfield	USA	29.3.90	1	Big 10	Madison	12 May
7.96	2.0		Lin Qing	CHN-Y	5.4.95	1		Colombo	10 Jun
7.95i		Fabrizio	Donato	ITA	14.8.76	1	NC	Ancona	25 Feb
7.95	2.0	Joe	Allen	USA	7.7.78	1		Norwalk	21 Apr
7.95	0.6	Denis	Eradiri	BUL	24.10.83	1		Sofia	24 May
7.95	2.0	Marius	Rudys	LTU	15.11.85	1		Jurbakas	30 Jun
		(90)							
7.94i		Bryce	Lamb	USA	9.11.90	1		Lubbock	20 Jan
7.94i			Zhuang Haitao	CHN	6.1.89	4		Nanjing	13 Feb
7.94i		Andrey	Khaylov	RUS	3.7.89	2	NC	Moskva	24 Feb
7.94A	0.8	Rushwal	Samaai	RSA	25.9.91	1	NC-23	Germiston	31 Mar
7.94	0.1	Vitaliy	Shkurlatov	RUS	25.5.79	1		Krasnodar	8 Jun
7.94	1.5	Jean Marie	Okutu	ESP	4.8.88	*		Vigo	1 Jul
7.94	1.0	Kumaravel	Prem Kumar	IND-J	2.6.93	1		Pune	22 Sep
7.93i		Pavel	Karavayev ¶	RUS	27.8.88	1		Moskva	14 Jan
7.93	1.8	Ronnie	Taylor	USA	13.8.90	1		Lincoln	5 May
7.93		Nafee	Harris	USA	29.5.86	2		Georgetown/CAY	9 May
		(100)							
7.93	0.1		Zhang Yu	CHN	17.7.92	2		Zibo	26 May
7.93			Kim Sang-su	KOR	5.6.84	1		Goseong	26 Jun
7.93	0.7	Sumito	Minagawa	JPN	26.9.90	2		Tokyo	15 Jul

Mark	Wind	Name		Nat	Born	Date
7.92	2.0	George	Fields	USA	29.12.86	5 May
7.92	0.0	Konrad	Podgórski	POL	1.6.89	9 Jun
7.92	-0.5	Aleksandr	Petrov	RUS	9.8.86	17 Jun
7.92	1.2		Ge Xiaodong	CHN	1.9.92	23 Jun
7.91i		Valentin	Toboc	ROU	17.3.92	25 Feb
7.91	1.9	Kyron	Blaise	TRI	3.10.89	12 May
7.90i		Valeriy	Kupreyev	RUS	13.4.88	14 Jan
7.90	0.0	Ivan	Lyhachov	UKR	27.4.89	13 Jun
7.90	1.0	Stefano	Tremigliozzi	ITA	7.5.85	13 Jun
7.90			Kim Duk-hyun	KOR	8.12.85	26 Jun
7.89i		Yan	Chaginov	RUS	8.9.90	13 Jan
7.89	1.8	Gaspar	Araújo	POR	17.12.81	26 May
7.89	1.9	Hussein	Al-Sabee	KSA	14.11.79	9 Jun
7.88i		Julian	Howard	GER	3.4.89	25 Feb
7.88A		Jamal	Bowen	PAN	5.1.91	19 Apr
7.88	0.0	Frédéric	Erin	FRA	23.4.80	28 May
7.88	0.9	Artyom	Primak	RUS-J	14.1.93	9 Jun
7.88	0.6		Jiang Zhaodan	CHN	19.2.89	18 Sep
7.87i		Mychael	Stewart	USA	9.6.86	27 Jan
7.87	1.8	Ryo	Nishiumi	JPN	5.12.92	19 May
7.87		Behrouz	Sistanipour	IRI	11.4.86	25 May
7.87	0.5	Adrian	Vasile	ROU	9.4.86	16 Jun
7.87	1.1	Aleksandr	Zolotoglaviy	RUS	22.10.89	20 Jun
7.87	0.3	Kirill	Sukharev	RUS	24.5.92	21 Jul
7.87	1.9	Michal	Lukasiak	POL	7.3.84	18 Aug
7.87	0.3	Eero	Haapala	FIN	10.7.89	25 Aug
7.87	2.0	Benjamin	Compaoré	FRA	5.8.87	15 Sep
7.86	0.2	Robert	Crowther	AUS	2.8.87	3 Mar
7.86	1.5	Ngonidzashe	Makusha	ZIM	11.3.87	23 Mar
7.86	-0.5	Daniel	Dobrev	BUL	7.4.92	3 Jun
7.86A		Tera	Langat	KEN	26.12.85	14 Jun
7.86	1.6	Dmitriy	Plotnikov	RUS	30.1.87	4 Jul
7.86	0.0		Lin Hung-Min	TPE	7.9.90	27 Oct
7.85i		Nick	Gordon	JAM	17.9.88	2 Mar
7.85i			Gu Junjie	CHN	5.5.85	10 Mar
7.85	1.3	Lavell	Handy	USA	17.8.90	4 May
7.85	0.0	Maksym	Moskalenko	UKR	20.10.87	4 Jun
7.85	2.0	Reindell	Cole	USA	16.2.88	9 Jun
7.85	0.6	Bashir	Ramzy	USA	4.5.79	16 Jun
7.85	1.0	Povilas	Mykolaitis	LTU	23.2.83	7 Jul
7.85	1.5	Adrian	Strzalkowski	POL	28.3.90	1 Sep
7.84i		Emanuele	Catania	ITA	3.10.88	25 Feb
7.84	-1.0		Lin Ching-Hsuan	TPE	14.5.92	8 May
7.84	1.7	Jamal	Peden	USA	22.6.92	12 May
7.84	2.0	Mikese	Morse	USA	30.10.87	19 May
7.84	-1.6	Nyles	Stuart	BAH	10.2.80	3 Jun
7.84		Jeff	Henderson	USA	19.2.89	16 Jun
7.84	0.9	Juho-Matti	Pimiä	FIN	28.12.84	16 Jun
7.84	1.0	Arttu	Halmela	FIN	25.9.91	22 Jun
7.83Ai		Jarod	Tobler	USA	30.9.82	26 Feb

Mark	Wind	Name		Nat	Born	Pos	Meet	Venue	Date
7.83	1.7	Jarrett	Samuels	USA-J	12.2.93				12 May
7.83	0.3	Jerome	Wilson	JAM	10.9.91				17 May
7.83	0.7	Alessio	Guarini	ITA	5.4.85				27 May
7.83	1.9	Toros	Pilikoglu	TUR-J	21.3.93				5 Jun
7.83	1.7	Marcos	Caldeira	POR	27.2.88				7 Jul
7.83	0.6	Matthew	Burton	GBR	18.12.87				14 Jul
7.83	0.3		Jie Lei	CHN	8.5.89				18 Sep
7.82i			Yu Zhenwei	CHN	18.3.86				13 Feb
7.82i		Chris	Phipps	USA	14.9.90				9 Mar
7.82	1.8	Jorge	McFarlane	PER	20.2.88				23 Mar
7.82	0.8	Jarrion	Lawson	USA-J	6.5.94				11 May
7.82	0.0	Malcolm	Pennix	USA	30.10.89				12 May
7.82	1.9	Mamoru	Nimura	JPN	18.4.86				13 May
7.82	1.2	Jharyl	Bowry	CAN	28.1.90				17 May
7.82	0.3	Stephan	Hartmann	GER-J	13.1.94				28 May
7.82	1.0	Clive	Chafausipo	ZIM	2.6.88				6 Jun
7.82	1.6	Vladimir	Kabets	BLR	30.7.85				7 Jul
7.82	-0.4	Andreas	Trajkovski	DEN-J	18.3.93				11 Jul
7.81	1.1	Julian	Kellerer	AUT	22.8.89				28 May
7.81	-0.6	Kazunaka	Saeki	JPN	29.1.80				5 Oct
7.80	1.0	Nick	Newman	GBR	12.10.83				4 Feb
7.80i		Mario	Kral	GER	15.2.89				5 Feb
7.80i			Zhang Xin	CHN	24.4.83				13 Feb
7.80i			Fu Zhihu	CHN	4.9.91				10 Mar
7.80	2.0	Mandhla	Mgijima	ZIM	2.5.87				14 Apr
7.80	0.4	David	Registe	DMA	2.5.88				20 Apr
7.80	1.7	Daisuke	Arakawa	JPN	19.9.81				29 Apr
7.80	1.3		Wang Qicheng	CHN	20.9.92				26 May
7.80	0.9	Olivier	Huet	FRA	26.5.90				30 Jun
7.80	0.8	Seiji	Hiura (183)	JPN	15.1.91				15 Jul

Doubtful performance: 8.12 1.7 Boleslav Shkirtladze GEO 14.6.87 1 Tel Aviv 30 May

Wind assisted

Mark	Wind	Name		Nat	Born	Pos	Meet	Venue	Date
8.36	3.4	Raymond	Higgs	BAH	24.1.91	1	SEC	Baton Rouge	12 May

  7.89 7.99 x 8.19w 8.20w 8.36w
  8.23 3.6 1 NCAA-w Austin 24 May 8.23w p p p p p

Mark	Wind	Name		Nat	Born	Pos	Meet	Venue	Date
8.32	2.2	Ronni	Ollikainen	FIN	27.8.90	1		Jämsä	16 Jun

  x 8.01 x x 8.32w 8.05

Mark	Wind	Name		Nat	Born	Pos	Meet	Venue	Date
8.31	2.1	Eusebio	Cáceres	ESP	10.9.91	1	NC-23	Toledo	21 Jul

  p 7.73 p 7.75 7.99 8.31w

Mark	Wind	Name		Nat	Born	Pos	Meet	Venue	Date
8.27	2.7	George	Kitchens	USA	16.1.83	1		Athens, GA	24 Mar

  8.11w 8.14 8.27w 7.82 p p

Mark	Wind	Name		Nat	Born	Pos	Meet	Venue	Date
8.26	2.5	Stepán	Wagner	CZE	5.10.81	1		Brno	4 Jul
8.21	2.2	Zarck	Visser	RSA	15.9.89	1	NC	Port Elizabeth	13 Apr
8.14	2.5	Fabrice	Lapierre	AUS	17.10.83	2	adidas	New York	9 Jun
8.13	3.5	Kafétien	Gomis	FRA	23.3.80	2		Gainesville	21 Apr
8.11	2.2	Rogério	Bispo	BRA	16.11.85	1		São Paulo	18 Feb
8.09	3.5		Zhao Xiaoxi	CHN	19.3.89	1		Fuzhou	23 Jun
8.07	4.3		Jiang Zhaodan	CHN	19.2.89	2		Fuzhou	23 Jun
8.06	4.9	Clive	Chafausipo	ZIM	2.6.88	4	NCAA-W	Austin	24 May
8.05	3.4	Jean Marie	Okutu	ESP	4.8.88	3		Madrid	7 Jul
8.03	3.2	Jonathan	Silva	BRA	21.7.91	Q		São Paulo	7 Apr
8.02	2.9	Jerome	Wilson	JAM	10.9.91	1		Lubbock	5 May
8.02	2.8	Geormis	Jaramillo	VEN	6.3.89	1	IbAmC	Barquisimeto	8 Jun
8.02	4.5	Samson	Idiata	NGR	28.2.82	5		Madrid	7 Jul
8.01	2.4	Frédéric	Erin	FRA	23.4.80	2	NC	Angers	17 Jun
8.00	2.3	Rudon	Bastian	BAH	13.1.87	2		Fayetteville	4 May
8.00	2.2	Larona	Koosimile	BOT	14.10.85	1		La Habana	8 Jun
7.98	3.2	Jarrett	Samuels	USA-J	12.2.93	1	TexR	Austin	31 Mar
7.97	2.3	Pedro Enrique	Díaz	CUB	19.1.89	1		La Habana	9 Mar
7.97	3.4	Jarrod	Hutchen	USA	6.2.89	1		Clemson	5 May
7.97	2.1	Denis	Eradiri	BUL	24.10.83	1	NC	Sliven	16 Jun
7.97	3.8	Yasamuchi	Konishi	JPN	13.4.90	1		Tokyo	15 Jul
7.96	3.8	Higor	Alves	BRA-J	23.2.94	1	NC-j	Maringá	17 Jun
7.96	3.0	Robert Braz	Firmiano	BRA	28.7.92	1	SAm-23	São Paulo	22 Sep
7.95		Barrett	Saunders	USA	27.3.85	1		Miramar, FL	12 May
7.92	2.3	Neamen	Wise	USA	25.4.91				5 May
7.91	2.4	Jeff	Henderson	USA	19.2.89				19 May
7.91	3.0	Nick	Gordon	JAM	17.9.88				2 Jun
7.90	2.2	Taylor	Stewart	CAN	11.4.91				10 Jun
7.89	2.1	Jarrion	Lawson	USA-J	6.5.94				28 Apr
7.89	2.3	Chris	Phipps	USA	14.9.90				24 May
7.89	2.2	Eero	Haapala	FIN	10.7.89				22 Jul
7.88	2.5	Akira	Ota	JPN	14.12..90				21 Apr
7.88	2.1	Ivan	Pucelj	CRO	11.7.81				26 May
7.88	2.5		Kim Sang-su	KOR	5.6.84				8 Jul
7.87	2.9	Semen	Popov	RUS-J	26.5.94				19 May
7.87	4.1	Reindell	Cole	USA	16.2.88				24 May
7.87	3.1	Stefano	Dacastello	ITA	17.2.80				26 May
7.86	2.9	Futa	Hayashi	JPN	13.1.92				19 May
7.86?	(1.6)	Mikese	Morse	USA	30.10.87				25 May
7.86	2.6	Jeroen	Vanmulder	BEL	26.4.91				8 Sep
7.85	3.9	Stephan	Scott-Ellis	USA	19.6.90				12 May
7.85	2.2	Dmitriy	Astrovskiy	BLR	5.6.89				25 May
7.84	3.1	Mantas	Silkauskas	LTU	10.4.88				12 May
7.84	2.1	Kamal	Fuller	JAM	20.1.91				12 May
7.84	3.6	Tyler	Williamson	USA	22.9.90				24 May
7.83	4.1	Keenan	Soles	USA	16.4.92				5 May
7.83		Jerel	Morrow	USA-J					18 May
7.83	3.0	Yuhi	Oiwa	JPN	17.2.91				19 May
7.83	2.6	Yves	Renaux	FRA	12.6.86				17 Jun
7.83	3.4	Kyosuke	Ogawa	JPN	7.3.87				13 Jul
7.82A	6.5	Eetu	Viitala	FIN	27.3.87				14 Apr
7.82	2.1	Julian	Howard	GER	3.4.89				16 Jun
7.82	3.4	István	Virovecz	HUN	1.12.89				23 Jun

Low altitude bests

Mark	Wind	Name	Pos	Meet	Venue	Date
8.12	0.0	Pahlevanyan	1	GEO Ch	Tbilisi	20 May
8.07	1.0	Visser	*	NC	Port Elizabeth	13 Apr
8.01i	0.9	Spencer	1	NCAA	Nampa	9 Mar
7.85	0.7	Aucyna	1		Molndal	4 Aug
8.01w	2.9		1		Uppsala	28 Jul

Drugs disqualification: 8.00 1.1 Luvo Maniyonga ¶ RSA 18.11.91 1 Stellenbosch 20 Mar

Best outdoors

Mark	Wind	Name	Pos	Meet	Venue	Date
8.11	-0.6	M da Silva	1		München	5 Jun
8.10	0.7	Yun Zhiming	1		Regensburg	2 Jun
7.98	2.0	Tsátoumas	2	Veniz	Haniâ	4 Jul
7.96	0.8	Misans	2		Daegu	16 May
7.96	0.6	Cuharenco	1		Bucuresti	26 May
7.96	0.3	Chuva	Q	EC	Helsinki	29 Jun
7.94w	2.6	Lamb	2	TexR	Austin	31 Mar
7.94	-0.2	Zhuang Haitao	1		Zibo	26 May

Mark	Wind	Name	Nat	Born	Pos	Meet	Venue	Date
7.91	-1.3	Karavayev ¶						13 May
7.91	1.0	Nikolayev						20 Jun
7.91	1.2	Tang Gongchen						23 Jun
7.87	1.0	Khaylov						4 Jul

Mark	Wind	Name		Pos	Meet	Venue	Date
7.86	1.6	Xu Jianping	26 May	7.81	-0.8	Tobler	21 Apr
7.85	-0.2	Zhang Xiaoyi	14 Apr	7.81	0.5	Dendy	24 May
7.83	0.8	Gordon	7 Apr	7.81	0.4	Howard	16 Jun

JUNIORS

See main list for top 4 juniors (+ 3w). 12 (+3w) performances by 4 men to 7.94. Additional marks and further juniors:

Morgunov 8.09 0.4 1 WJ Barcelona 11 Jul   8.01 -0.4 Q WJ Barcelona 11 Jul
           8.08 1.2 Q NC-j Cheboksary 19 Jun   7.96 1.7 1   Krasnodar 19 May
           8.04 -0.2 2 VD Bruxelles 7 Sep   7.96 0.0 1 Gugl Linz 20 Aug
           8.02 0.0 1   Rovereto 4 Sep   7.94i   1 NC Volgograd 11 Feb

Mark	Wind	Name		Nat	Born	Pos	Meet	Venue	Date
7.88	0.9	Artyom	Primak	RUS-J	14.1.93	1		Khabarovsk	9 Jun
7.83	1.7	Jarrett	Samuels	USA	12.2.93	5	SEC	Baton Rouge	12 May
7.83	1.9	Toros	Pilikoglu	TUR	21.3.93	1		Ankara	5 Jun
7.82	0.8	Jarrion	Lawson	USA	6.5.94	1		Austin	11 May
7.82	0.3	Stephan	Hartmann	GER	13.1.94	1j		Wesel	28 May
7.82	-0.4	Andreas	Trajkovski (10)	DEN	18.3.93	2	WJ	Barcelona	11 Jul
7.79	+1.6		Huang Changzhou	CHN	20.8.94	1		Shanghai	10 Aug
7.78	0.2	Johnny	Carter	USA	15.9.93	1	Jnr Oly	Humble	31 Jul
7.76i		Devin	Field	USA	9.10.93	1		Fayetteville	14 Jan
7.76	0.1		Zhang Yaoguang	CHN	21.6.93	4		Zhaoqing	14 Apr
7.76	-1.6		Huang Haibing	CHN	23.2.93	1	NC-j	Changzhou	21 Apr
7.71	1.9	Radek	Juska	CZE	8.3.93	3	NC	Vyskov	16 Jun
7.70i			Zhou Liangjun	CHN	16.2.93	9		Nanjing	13 Feb
7.70	1.1	Oliver	Newport (18)	GBR-Y	7.1.95	1§	ENG Ch	Birmingham	3 Jun
7.68		five juniors							

Wind assisted

Mark	Wind	Name		Nat	Born	Pos	Meet	Venue	Date
			Morgunov	8.20	3.8	Q		Krasnodar	18 May
7.89	2.1	Jarrion	Lawson	USA-J	6.5.94	1		Commerce	28 Apr
7.87	2.9	Semen	Popov	RUS-J	26.5.94	2		Krasnodar	19 May
7.83		Jerel	Morrow	USA-J		1		Emproia	18 May
7.76	2.6	Guy-Elphège	Aniouman	FRA	13.6.94	2		Aix-les-Bains	20 May
7.70	2.7	José	Despagne	CUB-Y	.96	2		La Habana	22 Jun

TRIPLE JUMP

17.81 0.6 Christian Taylor USA 18.6.90 1 OG London (OS) 9 Aug
     x   x   17.15 17.81 17.55/-0.2 x
  17.63i   2 WI Istanbul 11 Mar 17.63 x 17.02 17.29 17.05 17.20
  17.63 0.0 1 NC/OT Eugene 30 Jun 17.63 x p p p p
  17.62 1.9 1 Pre Eugene 1 Jun 17.38/1.0 17.62 x p 17.43/1.0 p
  17.41 -0.2 1 LGP London (CP) 14 Jul 16.96 17.12 16.78 17.24/0.6 x
  17.39i   Q WI Istanbul 9 Mar 17.39 p p
  17.30 0.4 1 Gyulai Budapest 20 Aug x 16.91 17.30 p 16.64 x
  17.27 1.5 Q NC/OT Eugene 28 Jun 17.27 p p
17.70i Will Claye USA 13.6.91 1 WI Istanbul 11 Mar
    16.89 x x 17.70 17.63 17.53
  17.63Ai   1 NC Albuquerque 25 Feb 17.25 17.40 17.44 17.63 p p
  17.62 0.6 2 OG London (OS) 9 Aug x 17.54/0.0 17.43/0.1 17.62 17.25/-0.3 16.66
  17.55 0.0 2 NC/OT Eugene 30 Jun 17.55 17.28/-1.1 17.29/-1.1 p p p
  17.48 1.2 2 Pre Eugene 1 Jun 17.03 17.14 17.48 p x x
  17.39i   1 Fayetteville 11 Feb x 17.39 x p
17.53 1.8 Lyukman Adams RUS 24.9.88 1 Sochi 27 May
    x 17.53 x x
  17.36i   3 WI Istanbul 11 Mar 16.98 x x x 17.36 x
17.53 0.8 Fabrizio Donato ITA 14.8.76 * EC Helsinki 30 Jun
    17.63w 17.53 17.49/1.5 17.17 p 16.08
  17.52 1.4 2 NC Bressanone 8 Jul x 17.52 17.02 17.50w/2.6 x 17.45/1.6
  17.48 0.6 3 OG London (OS) 9 Aug 17.38/0.4 17.44.0.1 17.45/-0.2 17.48 p x
  17.29 1.6 1 WK Zürich 30 Aug 16.43 16.62 16.60 16.96 16.98 17.29
  17.28i   4 WI Istanbul 11 Mar 16.99 17.28 x p p p
17.49 1.7 Osviel Hernández CUB 31.5.89 1 La Habana 3 Feb
    16.83w 17.08w 17.01 17.49
17.47 1.7 Daniele Greco ITA 1.3.89 1 Potenza 9 Jun
    x x x 17.25/1.5 p 17.47
  17.39 1.1 * NC Bressanone 8 Jul 16.75w 17.39 14.11 17.67w3.4 x p
  17.34 0.9 4 OG London (OS) 9 Aug 16.90 17.34 x x p 16.92
  17.28i   5 WI Istanbul 11 Mar 16.55 16.93 x 16.93 x 17.28
17.39 1.8 Jonathan Silva BRA 21.7.91 1 São Paulo 31 Mar
    x 17.39 p p p p
17.38 0.5 Dong Bin CHN 22.11.88 1 Zhaoqing 14 Apr
    17.08 17.01 17.38 p x x
17.35 0.3 Cao Shuo CHN 8.10.91 2 Zhaoqing 14 Apr
    x x 16.81 x 17.35 x

Mark	Wind	Name		Nat	Born	Pos	Meet	Venue	Date
17.31	1.0	Phillips	Idowu	GBR	30.12.78	1	FBK	Hengelo	27 May
		(30/10)			16.79	17.12	17.31	x x	p
17.25	1.9	Ruslan	Samitov	RUS	11.2.91	1		Penza	6 Jun
17.23	0.6	Henry	Frayne	AUS	14.4.90	*		Melbourne	2 Mar
17.23	0.8	Tosin	Oke	NGR	1.10.80	1	NC	Calabar	20 Jun
17.23	0.0	Leevan	Sands	BAH	16.8.81	1	DL	Saint Denis	6 Jul
17.22	-0.3	Yevgeniy	Ektov	KAZ	1.9.86	1		Almaty	30 Jun
17.20	0.2	Roman	Valiyev	KAZ	27.3.84	1	NC	Almaty	18 Jun
17.19	1.8	Aleksey	Fyodorov	RUS	25.5.91	1	NC-23	Yerino	22 Jul
17.17	1.0	Arne David	Girat	CUB	26.8.84	3		La Habana	3 Mar
17.17	0.2	Alexis	Copello	CUB	12.8.85	1		Rio de Janeiro	20 May
17.17	0.7	Benjamin	Compaoré	FRA	5.8.87	1		Rieti	9 Sep
		(20)							
17.13	1.3	Ernesto	Revé	CUB	26.2.92	1	NC	La Habana	24 Mar
17.09	0.7	Karol	Hoffmann	POL	1.6.89	Q	EC	Helsinki	28 Jun
17.07	-1.1	Aarik	Wilson	USA	25.10.82	1	MSR	Walnut	21 Apr
17.04i		Yuriy	Kovalyov	RUS	18.6.91	1	NC-23	Saransk	2 Mar
17.04	1.1	Sheryf	El-Sheryf	UKR	2.1.89	2	DNG	Stockholm	17 Aug
16.99	1.5	Jadel	Gregório	BRA	16.9.80	1	NC	São Paulo	1 Jul
16.97i		Marian	Oprea	ROU	6.6.82	1	NC	Bucuresti	24 Feb
16.97	-1.0	Fabrizio	Schembri	ITA	27.1.81	1		Busto Arsizio	19 May
16.95	0.1	Viktor	Yastrebov	UKR	13.1.82	1	NCp	Yalta	29 May
16.93	0.0	Osniel	Tosca	CUB	30.6.84	2		Baie Mahault	1 May
		(30)							
16.90A	-1.3	Jefferson	Dias Sabino	BRA	4.11.82	1		Cali	24 Jun
16.89	-0.9	Issam	Nima	ALG	8.4.79	1	Odlozil	Praha	11 Jun
16.89A	0.4	José Adrián	Sornoza	ECU	5.8.92	1		Quito	17 Jun
16.88	1.4	Samyr	Laine	HAI	17.7.84	1		New York	10 Jun
16.87	0.3	Yoandris	Betanzos	CUB	15.2.82	3	NC	La Habana	24 Mar
16.87	0.9	Igor	Spasovkhodskiy	RUS	1.8.79	2		Moskva	21 Jun
16.87	1.3	Gaëtan	Saku Bafuanga	FRA	22.7.91	1	NC-23	Reims	14 Jul
16.85i		Andrea	Chiari	ITA	12.2.91	1	NC	Ancona	26 Feb
16.85	0.6	Renjith	Maheswary	IND	30.1.86	1		Patiala	21 Apr
16.85	1.3	Walter	Davis	USA	2.7.79	1		Ponce	12 May
		(40)							
16.85	1.6	Dmitriy	Platnitskiy	BLR	26.8.88	1		Kalamáta	2 Jun
16.84	0.6		Li Yanxi	CHN	26.6.83	1		Wuhan	28 Apr
16.84	0.0	Karl	Taillepierre	FRA	13.8.76	2	DL	Saint Dens	6 Jul
16.84	1.3	Darius	Aucyna	LTU	7.5.89	1	NC	Kaunas	8 Jul
16.82	0.4	Aleksey	Tsapik	BLR	4.8.88	1	NCp	Brest	26 May
16.81	0.2	Yochai	Halevi	ISR	10.5.82	1		Sofia	9 Jun
16.80	0.0	Vladimir	Letnicov	MDA	7.10.81	2	NCp	Brest	26 May
16.80	1.9	Julien	Kapek	FRA	12.1.79	1		Nivelles	23 Jun
16.80A	1.0	José Emilio	Bellido	ESP	25.5.87	1		Monachil	14 Jul
16.79	1.8	Momchil	Karailiev	BUL	21.5.82	*	NC	Sliven	15 Jun
		(50)							
16.79	-0.6	Pedro Pablo	Pichardo	CUB-J	30.6.93	1	WJ	Barcelona	15 Jul
16.78	-0.3	Mohammed Abbas	Darwish	UAE	28.3.86	1		Plovdiv	23 Jun
16.76	0.0	Yoann	Rapinier	FRA	29.9.89	4		Baie Mahault	1 May
16.76	1.2	Artyom	Primak	RUS-J	14.1.93	1	NC-j	Cheboksary	21 Jun
16.76	0.2	Harold	Correa	FRA	26.6.88	3	DL	Saint-Denis	6 Jul
16.75i		Fabien	Florant	NED	1.2.83	1		Kenosha, WI	27 Jan
16.75i		Omar	Craddock	USA	26.4.91	1	NCAA	Nampa	10 Mar
16.75	-0.6	Dimítrios	Tsiámis	GRE	12.1.82	2	Odlozil	Praha	11 Jun
16.74	-1.1	Chris	Benard	USA	4.4.90	2	MSR	Walnut	21 Apr
16.73	0.7	Zlatozar	Atanasov	BUL	12.12.89	2		Sofia	9 Jun
		(60)							
16.73	0.0	Yevgen	Semenenko	UKR	17.7.84	2	NC	Yalta	15 Jun
16.73	1.1	Peder	Nielsen	DEN	13.9.88	1		Göteborg	8 Jul
16.72	0.8	Alphonso	Jordan	USA	1.11.87	*		Atlanta	12 May
16.72	0.9	Vicente	Docavo	ESP	13.2.92	1		Huelva	7 Jun
16.72	2.0	Zacharias	Arnos	CYP	24.11.86	*	Veniz	Haniá	4 Jul
16.71A	1.2	Tumelo	Thagane	RSA	3.7.84	1		Potchefstroom	24 Mar
16.71	0.4	Brandon	Roulhac	USA	13.12.83	1		Tallahassee	14 Apr
16.67	1.9	Igor	Syunin	EST	4.12.90	1		Viljandi	3 Jul
16.67	0.0	Sergey	Yarmak	RUS	21.3.86	4	NC	Cheboksary	5 Jul
16.66	-1.2	Troy	Doris	USA	12.4.89	1	Big 10	Madison	13 May
		(70)							
16.66A		Elijah	Kimitei	KEN	.86	1		Nairobi	15 Jun
16.65	1.6	Lawrence	Willis	USA	12.7.81	1		Baton Rouge	24 Mar
16.64	1.1	Dmitriy	Detsuk	BLR	9.4.85	1		Minsk	12 Jun

Mark	Wind	Name		Nat	Born	Pos	Meet	Venue	Date	
16.64	0.9	Andreas	Pohle	GER	6.4.81	1	NC	Wattenscheid	16	Jun
16.64	-0.2	Latario	Collie-Minns	BAH-J	10.3.94	3	NC	Nassau	22	Jun
16.63i		Marcus	Robinson	USA	18.12.88	1eB		Fayetteville	11	Feb
16.62	0.3	Mykola	Savolaynen	UKR	25.3.80	2	NCp	Yalta	29	May
16.61	-2.5	Chris	Carter	USA	11.3.89	3	MSR	Walnut	21	Apr
16.61	-0.2	Roumen	Dimitrov	BUL	19.9.86	1		Plovdiv	26	May
16.61	1.8	Floyd	Ross	USA	7.3.90	2	NCAA	Des Moines	8	Jun
		(80)								
16.60i		Ryan	Grinnell	USA	4.2.87	1		Blacksburg	4	Feb
16.60	0.9	Anton	Boltenkov	RUS	29.6.85	1	Kuts	Moskva	13	Jun
16.59	1.0	Murad	Ibadullayev	AZE	6.4.92	1	NC	Baku	16	Jun
16.58	-0.2		Wu Bo	CHN	17.6.84	3		Fuzhou	23	Jun
16.57i		Colomba	Fofana	FRA	11.4.77	3	NC	Aubière	25	Feb
16.57	0.0	Arpinder	Singh	IND	30.12.92	2		Kanchanaburi	11	May
16.56	0.2	Bryce	Lamb	USA	9.11.90	1		Lubbock	5	May
16.56	0.0	Alexandru George	Baciu	ROU	25.2.91	1		Bucuresti	8	Jun
16.56	1.7		Jia Lingli	CHN	16.2.84	4		Fuzhou	23	Jun
16.56	0.7	Aleksandr	Yurchenko	RUS	30.7.92	Q	NC	Cheboksary	3	Jul
		(90)								
16.55	1.0	Aleksandr	Sergeyev	RUS	29.7.83	6	NC	Cheboksary	5	Jul
16.54i		Raúl	Spank	GER	13.7.88	1		Chemnitz	22	Jan
16.54	0.7	Yuma	Okabe	JPN	13.7.90	1	NC	Osaka	10	Jun
16.53	1.1	Jean	Cassimiro Rosa	BRA	1.2.90	2	NC	São Paulo	1	Jul
16.52	1.6	Tyron	Stewart	USA	8.7.89	1		Tucson	19	May
16.51	1.0	Adrian	Swiderski	POL	27.9.86	1		Kielce	30	Jun
16.50	1.8	Jonathan	Clark	USA	15.12.88	1		Azusa	20	Apr
16.49Ai		Nkosinza	Balumbu	USA	16.3.87	4	NC	Albuquerque	25	Feb
16.49	0.8	Kyron	Blaise	TRI	3.10.89	2	SEC	Baton Rouge	13	May
16.49	0.8	Adrian	Daianu	ROU	27.11.87	1		Bucuresti	15	Jun
		(100)								

Mark		Name		Nat	Born	Date	
16.47i		Vladimir	Chicherov	RUS	2.4.85	22	Feb
16.46	-0.6	Nathan	Douglas	GBR	4.12.82	27	May
16.46	1.0	Dmytro	Tyden	UKR	17.1.85	4	Jun
16.45	1.7	Lysvanys	Pérez	ESP	24.1.82	3	Jun
16.44i		Aleksandr	Lebedko	BLR	24.5.87	10	Feb
16.44	1.8	Marcos	Caldeira	POR	27.2.88	10	Jun
16.44	1.3	Jaanus	Uudmäe	EST	24.12.80	3	Jul
16.44	1.0	Aleksi	Tammentie	FIN	6.8.86	22	Jul
16.43	-2.4	Aboubacar	Bamba	FRA	20.6.91	20	May
16.43	0.7	Randy	Lewis	GRN	14.10.80	28	May
16.41	0.5	Rafeeq	Curry	USA	19.8.83	28	Jun
16.40	0.8		Kim Duk-hyun	KOR	8.12.85	16	Oct
16.39		José Ernesto	Martínez	CUB	1.1.91	16	Jun
16.39	-0.6	Muhammad	Halim	ISV	26.10.86	7	Aug
16.38i		Maksim	Shakko	RUS	14.5.84	14	Jan
16.38	1.0	Hilton	da Silva	BRA	13.4.87	31	Mar
16.38	1.1		Fu Haitao	CHN-J	1.11.93	9	Jun
16.37		Eranda Dinesh	Fernando	SRI	8.7.90	10	Nov
16.37A	0.1	Jhon Fredy	Murillo	COL	13.7.84	14	Nov
16.36i		Taras	Moiseyenko	RUS	5.5.86	23	Feb
16.36	1.2		Kim Dong-hyun	KOR	5.6.89	11	May
16.35Ai		Josh	Como	USA	25.5.88	4	Feb
16.35i		Julian	Reid	GBR	23.9.88	11	Feb
16.35i		Anders	Møller	DEN	5.9.77	26	Feb
16.34i		Myhaylo	Vlasov	UKR	13.6.90	18	Feb
16.34i		Hugo	Mamba-Schlick	CMR	1.2.82	25	Feb
16.34A		Charles	le Roux	RSA	5.5.85	17	Mar
16.34	1.5	Devon	Bond	GUY	4.4.88	5	May
16.33	1.8	Alwyn	Jones	AUS	28.2.85	22	Jan

Mark		Name		Nat	Born	Date	
16.33i		Dmitriy	Kolosov	RUS	19.5.86	25	Jan
16.33		Wilbert	Walker	JAM	7.1.85	28	Jan
16.33A	0.6	Levon	Aghasyan	ARM-Y	19.1.95	27	May
16.32Ai		Kenta	Bell	USA	16.3.77	25	Feb
16.32i		Hasheem	Halim	ISV	12.2.90	10	Mar
16.32	2.0	Atsushi	Nagayama	JPN	22.8.83	17	Jun
16.32	0.7	Michal	Lewandowski	POL	28.8.88	14	Jul
16.31	0.0	Maximiliano	Díaz	ARG	15.11.88	11	Feb
16.31	2.0	Lasha	Gulelauri	GEO-J	26.5.94	5	May
16.31	2.0	Yevgeniy	Zhukov	RUS	3.1.89	2	Jun
16.30	1.3	Alberto	Alvarez	MEX	8.3.91	7	Apr
16.30	0.0		Li Cong	CHN	5.12.89	14	Apr
16.30	1.5	Phillip	Young	USA	9.10.92	21	Apr
16.30	1.5	Larry	Achike	GBR	31.1.75	3	Jun
16.29	-0.6	Andrius	Gricevius	LTU	14.12.83	21	May
16.29	1.3	Nathan	Fox	GBR	21.10.90	16	Jun
16.29	1.0	Tarik	Bougtaïb	MAR	30.4.81	30	Jun
16.27	1.6	Ethan	DeJongh	USA	.90	20	Apr
16.27	0.4		Xu Xiaolong	CHN	20.12.92	26	May
16.27	0.2	Pávlos	Galaktiádis	GRE	15.5.84	15	Jun
16.26	0.6	Yordanis	Durañona	DMA	16.6.88	17	Mar
16.26	1.2	Manuel	Ziegler	GER	28.7.90	16	Jun
16.26	1.6	Yevgeniy	Plotnir	RUS	26.6.77	21	Jun
16.26	0.9	Kevin	Luron	FRA	8.11.91	5	Jul
16.25	1.9	Pratchaya	Thepparak	THA-J	1.9.93	9	Jun
16.25	-4.0	Kola	Adedoyin	GBR	8.4.91	16	Jun
16.25	1.6	Shoichi	Matsushita	JPN	18.4.89	9	Sep
16.25	0.2		Yan Qiang	CHN	4.10.90	14	Sep
16.25	-0.7		Kong Guanyong	CHN	18.3.88	14	Sep
16.25		I.D.S.S.	Jayasinghe (159)	SRI		10	Nov

Wind assisted

Mark	Wind	Name		Nat	Born	Pos	Meet	Venue	Date	
17.67	3.4	Daniele	Greco	ITA	1.3.89	1	NC	Bressanone	8	Jul
17.63	2.8	Fabrizio	Donato	ITA	14.8.76	1	EC	Helsinki	30	Jun
17.34	2.4	Henry	Frayne	AUS	14.4.90	1		Melbourne	2	Mar
17.34	2.2	Arne David	Girat	CUB	26.8.84	1		La Habana	22	Jun
17.28	2.2	Sheryf	El-Sheryf	UKR	2.1.89	2	EC	Helsinki	30	Jun
			17.28w	16.99	16.94	16.57	p	p		
17.23	2.5	Fabrizio	Schembri	ITA	27.1.81	3	NC	Bressanone	8	Jul
17.22	2.3	Osniel	Tosca	CUB	30.6.84	2		La Habana	3	Feb
16.97	3.8	Aleksey	Tsapik	BLR	4.8.88	3	EC	Helsinki	30	Jun
16.93	2.4	Momchil	Karailiev	BUL	21.5.82	1	NC	Sliven	15	Jun
16.92	2.9	Omar	Craddock	USA	26.4.91	1	NCAA	Des Moines	8	Jun
16.88	2.8	Alphonso	Jordan	USA	1.11.87	1		Atlanta	12	May
16.88	2.2	Peder	Nielsen	DEN	13.9.88	5	Bisl	Oslo	7	Jun
16.87	3.3	Dmitriy	Platnitskiy	BLR	26.8.88	1	NC	Grodno	6	Jul

Mark	Wind	Name		Nat	Born	Pos	Meet	Venue	Date
16.86	2.2	Nkosinza	Balumbu	USA	16.3.87	1		Stanford	7 Apr
16.86	2.1	Yochai	Halevi	ISR	10.5.82	1	NC	Tel Aviv	13 Jun
16.84	3.7	Marcos	Caldeira	POR	27.2.88	1		Lisboa (Un)	10 Jun
16.76	2.6	Julian	Reid	GBR	23.9.88	1	TexR	Austin	30 Mar
16.74	3.3	Brandon	Roulhac	USA	13.12.83	1		Port of Spain	19 May
16.74	3.0	Mykola	Savolaynen	UKR	25.3.80	1	NC	Yalta	15 Jun
16.74	3.3	Roumen	Dimitrov	BUL	19.9.86	2	NC	Sliven	15 Jun
16.73	2.5	Zacharias	Arnos	CYP	24.11.86	1	Veniz	Haniá	4 Jul
16.70	2.5	José Ernesto	Martinez	CUB	1.1.91	2		La Habana	22 Jun
16.66	3.1	Latario	Collie-Minns	BAH-J	10.3.94	1		Nassau	17 Mar
16.59	2.1	Michael	Puplampu	GBR	11.1.90	1		Bedford	10 Jun
16.53	3.6	Alwyn	Jones	AUS	28.2.85	1		Melbourne	22 Jan
16.53	5.4	Kyron	Blaise	TRI	3.10.89	2		Baton Rouge	24 Mar
16.53	2.1	Yuriy	Opatskyy	UKR	5.11.79	3	NC	Yalta	15 Jun
16.52	3.2	Alberto	Alvarez	MEX	8.3.91	2		Stanford	7 Apr

Mark	Wind	Name		Nat	Born	Date			
16.49	2.9	Hasheem	Halim	ISV	12.2.90	8 Jun	16.46	2.5 Aleksi Tammentie FIN 6.8.86	2 Sep
16.48	2.4	Colomba	Fofana	FRA	11.4.77	13 May	16.33A	2.3 Roger Haitengi NAM 12.9.83	28 Apr
16.47	3.6	Pablo	Torrijos	ESP	12.5.92	13 May	16.30	Tydree Lewis USA 26.11.85	31 May

Low altitude bests

16.67i   Dias Sabino 10q WI   Istanbul   10 Mar
   16.70w 3.3, 16.66 1.1   2 IbAmC   Barquisimeto   9 Jun

16.65   1.9   Bellido   1   Mataró   8 Jul
16.32   0.3   Murillo   27 May
16.28   1.2   Kimitei   30 Jun

Best outdoors

16.83   2.0   Chiari   1 NC-23   Mis. Adriatico   16 Jun
16.71   0.9   Craddock   2 FlaR   Gainesville   7 Apr
16.68   -0.3   Kovalyov   3 NC   Cheboksary   5 Jul

16.56   -1.7   Grinnell   1   Athens, GA   13 Apr
16.56   1.1   Oprea   2 ROU IC   Bucuresti   8 Jun
  16.68w 2.2   1 ECCp   VRI de S.Antóniio   17 May
16.49   1.0   Balumbu   *   Stanford   7 Apr

16.47   0.0   Fofana   29 May   16.35   0.4   Florant   28 Jun   16.30   0.8   Vlasov   29 May
16.46   1.7   Robinson   8 Jun   16.34   0.5   Mamba-Schlick   30 Jun   16.29   1.0   Halim   8 Jun
16.44   2.0   Spank   12 May   16.28   0.5   Lebedko   12 Jun

JUNIORS

See main list for top 3 juniors. 11 performances by 3 men to 16.40 (& 2 wa by 2 men). Additional marks, further juniors:

Pichardo   16.66   0.9 2   La Habana   9 Jun   16.56   -1.0 5   La Habana   27 May
           16.64   0.3 Q   WJ   Barcelona   13 Jul   16.40   0.6 1   CAC-J   San Salvador   1 Jul
Primak   16.60   -0.2 2   WJ   Barcelona   15 Jul
Collie-Minns   16.51   1.7 Q   WJ   Barcelona   13 Jul   16.47   -0.5 1   Nassau   24 Mar
           16.46   1.6 1   NC-j   Nassau   9 Jun

Mark	Wind	Name		Nat	Born	Pos	Meet	Venue	Date
16.38	1.1		Fu Haitao	CHN	1.11.93	1		Colombo	9 Jun
16.33A	0.6	Levon	Aghasyan	ARM-Y	19.1.95	1		Artashat	27 May
16.31	2.0	Lasha	Gulelauri	GEO	26.5.94	1		Almaty	5 May
16.25	1.9	Pratchaya	Thepparak	THA	1.9.93	2		Colombo	9 Jun
16.24	0.2	Divie	Murillo	COL	3.6.93	2	NG	Santander de Quilichao	14 Nov
16.17	-0.2		Fang Yaoqing	CHN-Y	20.4.96	4	NC	Kunshan	25 Sep
16.14		Paulo	Oliveira (10)	BRA	1.6.93	2		São Paulo	23 Nov
16.10	1.6	Nikólaos	Tsiókos	GRE	4.5.93	3	NC	Athína	15 Jun
16.06	0.5	Lathona	Collie-Minns	BAH	10.3.94	2	CAC-J	San Salvador	1 Jul
16.04	0.3	Georgi	Tsonov	BUL	2.5.93	7	Pavlov	Sofia	9 Jun
16.04	1.2	Henrique	da Silva	BRA	6.2.93	5	WJ	Barcelona	15 Jul
16.00	1.0	Ilya	Potapchev	RUS	19.4.93	*		Krasnodar	18 May
15.98	1.3	José Luis	Despaigne	CUB-Y	1,2,95	1	NC-j	Las Tunas	19 Jul
15.95	1.5	Simon	Karlén	SWE	2.6.94	Q	WJ	Barcelona	13 Jul
15.95	0.2	Daniel	Pacheco	ESP	15.3.93	1		Granollers	17 Jul

Wind assisted

Mark	Wind	Name		Nat	Born	Pos	Meet	Venue	Date
			Pichardo		16.52	2.8	3	La Habana	24 Feb
16.23	5.1	Ilya	Potapchev	RUS	19.4.93	1		Krasnodar	18 May
16.10	2.9	Georgi	Tsonov	BUL	2.5.93	4	WJ	Barcelona	15 Jul
16.00	2.1	Daniel	Pacheco	ESP	15.3.93	Q	WJ	Barcelona	13 Jul

SHOT

22.31   Christian   Cantwell   USA   30.9.80   1   Champaign   7 Jul
                                  21.10   x   21.28   21.73   21.60   22.31
   21.71   2 KansR   Lawrence   18 Apr   21.30   x   21.19   x   21.70   21.71
   21.53i   3 NC   Albuquerque   26 Feb   20.95   21.43   21.53   x   21.51   x
22.00i   Ryan   Whiting   USA   24.11.86   1   WI   Istanbul   9 Mar
                                  21.59   x   21.06   21.16   22.00   21.98
   21.66   2 NC/OT   Eugene   24 Jun   21.66   x   21.07   21.28   21.12   21.46
   21.60i   2 NC   Albuquerque   26 Feb   21.44   x   21.60   21.21   21.07   21.27
   21.50   1   University Park   4 May   21.13   21.47   21.50   x   ?   ?
   21.49i   2 WK   Zürich   29 Aug   20.89   20.74   20.72   21.01   21.49   21.05
   21.43i   1   Fayetteville   11 Feb   x   21.32   21.43   x
22.00   Reese   Hoffa   USA   8.10.77   1   NC/OT   Eugene   24 Jun
                                  21.46   21.28   22.00   x   21.46   21.93
   21.87i   1   Chemnitz   27 Jan   20.81   20.73   x   x   21.08   21.87
   21.81   1 Pre   Eugene   2 Jun   21.40   21.81   21.37   21.72   21.69   x

Mark	Name	Nat	Born	Pos	Meet	Venue	Date	Series
21.80	1 Hanz					Zagreb	4 Sep	21.34 21.76 21.56 21.80 x 21.70
21.75i	1 NC					Albuquerque	26 Feb	20.96 20.70 21.08 21.38 21.75 21.66
21.73	1 KansR					Lawrence	18 Apr	20.84 21.12 21.25 x 21.65 21.73
21.72	1 SkM					Warszawa	19 Aug	21.03 21.47 21.65 x x 21.72
21.64i	1 WK					Zürich	29 Aug	20.53 21.12 21.64 x 21.01 21.04
21.55i	4 WI					Istanbul	9 Mar	20.41 21.55 20.86 x x x
21.49	2					Athens, GA	14 Apr	20.94 20.92 21.48 21.17 x 21.49
21.89	Tomasz Majewski	POL	30.8.81	1	OG	London (OS)	3 Aug	21.19 21.72 21.87 x 21.72 21.89
21.72i	3 WI					Istanbul	9 Mar	21.28 21.65 x 20.94 21.72 x
21.60	2 Pre					Eugene	2 Jun	20.96 21.60 20.94 21.06 x x
21.88i	David Storl	GER	27.7.90	2	WI	Istanbul	9 Mar	21.88 x 21.86 x x x
21.86	2 OG					London (OS)	3 Aug	21.84 21.86 21.46 x x x
21.58	1 EC					Helsinki	29 Jun	21.19 x 21.58 x x p
21.43i	Q WI					Istanbul	9 Mar	21.43 p p
21.54	Adam Nelson	USA	7.7.75	1		Athens, GA	14 Apr	x 21.54 x x x x
21.51	Maksim Sidorov	RUS	13.5.86	1	NC	Cheboksary	4 Jul	21.44 x x 21.06 x 21.51
21.50	Dylan Armstrong	CAN	15.1.81	3	Pre	Eugene	2 Jun	21.18 21.08 21.49 21.35 21.24 21.50
21.44	1 FBK					Hengelo	26 May	x 21.11 21.44 20.66 20.85 21.01
	(30/8)							
21.31	Cory Martin	USA	22.5.85	1		Linz	19 Aug	
21.14	Kurtis Roberts	USA	20.2.88	1		Tucson	19 May	
	(10)							
21.11	Justin Rodhe	CAN	17.10.84	3	KansR	Lawrence	18 Apr	
21.08	Joe Kovacs	USA	28.6.89	4	NC/OT	Eugene	24 Jun	
21.02	Marco Fortes	POR	26.9.82	1		Bar	18 Mar	
21.00	Ivan Yushkov	RUS	15.1.81	1		Adler	27 May	
20.95	Zack Lloyd	USA	10.10.84	1		Orem, UT	30 Mar	
20.90	Andrey Mikhnevich	BLR	12.7.76	1		Minsk	18 Jul	
20.86i	Jordan Clarke	USA	10.7.90	1	NCAA	Nampa	9 Mar	
20.85	Asmir Kolasinac	SRB	15.10.84	1	CRO Ch	Rijeka	21 Jul	
20.84	Germán Lauro	ARG	2.4.84	6	OG	London (OS)	3 Aug	
20.78	Anton Lyuboslavskiy	RUS	26.6.84	1		Irkutsk	8 May	
	(20)							
20.72	Dorian Scott	JAM	1.2.82	1	NC	Kingston	1 Jul	
20.71	Kemal Mesic	BIH	4.8.85	2		Tucson	19 May	
20.69	Om Prakash Singh	IND	4.1.87	1		Szombathely	12 May	
20.69	Pavel Lyzhin	BLR	24.3.81	8	OG	London (OS)	3 Aug	
20.66	Nedzad Mulabegovic	CRO	4.2.81	2		Kingston	5 May	
20.63	Dale Stevenson	AUS	1.1.88	1		Clemson	12 May	
20.56i	Rutger Smith	NED	9.7.81	1	NC	Apeldoorn	25 Feb	
20.55	Andriy Semenov	UKR	4.7.84	1	NCp	Yalta	29 May	
20.51	Russ Winger	USA	2.8.84	1		Sydney	18 Feb	
20.51i	Tim Nedow	CAN	16.10.90	1		New York (Arm)	19 Feb	
	(30)							
20.50i	Jacob Thormaehlen	USA	13.2.90	2	NCAA	Nampa	9 Mar	
20.50	Carlos Véliz	CUB	12.8.87	1	NC	La Habana	23 Mar	
20.48	Darlan Romani	BRA	9.4.91	1	NC-23	Maringá	9 Sep	
20.45	Damian Kusiak ¶	POL	14.4.88	1		Biala Podlaska	5 May	
20.45	Marin Premeru	CRO	29.8.90	2	1 NC	Rijeka	21 Jul	
20.42	Hüseyin Atici	TUR	3.5.86	1		Ankara	5 Jun	
20.41i	Soslan Tsirikhov	RUS	24.11.84	2		Volgograd	21 Jan	
20.40	Ralf Bartels	GER	21.2.78	2		Sondershausen	15 Aug	
20.38	Dmytro Savytskyy	UKR	14.12.90	1		Kyiv	19 May	
20.38	Antonin Zalsky	CZE	7.8.80	1	Odlozil	Praha	11 Jun	
	(40)							
20.33	Georgi Ivanov	BUL	13.3.85	1	NC	Sliven	16 Jun	
20.31	O'Dayne Richards	JAM	14.12.88	3		Champaign	7 Jul	
20.29i	Ryan Crouser	USA	18.12.92	1		Fayetteville	27 Jan	
20.25	Chang Ming-Huang	TPE	7.8.82	2		Toronto	11 Jul	
20.22i	Odinn Björn Thorsteinsson	ISL	3.12.81	1		Hafnafjördur	31 Mar	
20.22	Dan Taylor	USA	12.5.82	6	KansR	Lawrence	18 Apr	
20.20	Kevin Bookout	USA	16.3.83	1		Shawnee	31 Mar	
20.20	Wang Guangfu	CHN	15.11.87	1	NC	Kunshan	22 Sep	
20.17	Lajos Kürthy	HUN	22.10.86	1		Budapest	9 Jun	
20.16i	Zhang Jun	CHN	11.4.83	1		Nanjing	13 Feb	
	(50)							

Mark	Name		Nat	Born	Pos	Meet	Venue	Date	
20.14	Denis	Kurtsev	RUS	20.8.88	2		Moskva	11	Jun
20.14	Marco	Schmidt	GER	5.9.83	2	NC	Wattenscheid	17	Jul
20.14	Ladislav	Prásil	CZE	17.5.90	2		Tábor	8	Sep
20.13	Carl	Myerscough	GBR	21.10.79	1		Maidla	1	Jul
20.12	Burger	Lambrechts	RSA	3.4.73	1		Germiston	25	Feb
20.10i	Candy	Bauer	GER	31.7.86	2		Rochlitz	5	Feb
20.08i	Stephen	Saenz	MEX	23.8.90	4	NCAA	Nampa	9	Mar
20.08	Chris	Figures	USA	8.10.81	3		Los Angeles (Ww)	2	Jun
20.06	Borja	Vivas	ESP	26.5.84	3	ECp-w	Bar	18	Mar
20.05i	Valeriy	Kokoyev	RUS	25.7.88	4	NC	Moskva	23	Feb
	(60)								
20.05	Aleksandr	Lesnoy	RUS	28.7.88	3		Adler	22	Apr
20.05	Jacko	Gill	NZL-J	20.12.94	1		Waitakere	24	Nov
20.04	Raigo	Toompuu	EST	17.7.81	1		Sillamäe	18	Jun
20.03	Leif	Arrhenius	SWE	15.7.86	1	NC	Stockholm	25	Aug
20.02	Luke	Pinkelman	USA	5.5.88	2	Big 12	Manhattan	13	May
20.02	Kim	Christensen	DEN	1.4.84	3	DL	Saint-Denis	6	Jul
19.99	Hamza	Alic	BIH	20.1.79	1		Senta	19	May
19.92	Hayden	Baillio	USA	22.7.91	1	NCAA-W	Austin	24	May
19.89	Mason	Finley	USA	7.10.90	1	KansR	Lawrence	20	Apr
19.86i	Jakub	Giza	POL	26.9.85	1		Gdánsk	18	Feb
	(70)								
19.86	Andriy	Borodkin	UKR	18.4.78	3		Kyiv	19	May
19.85	Bozidar	Antunovic	SRB	24.7.91	4		Tucson	19	May
19.84	Maris	Urtans	LAT	9.2.81	1		Riga	5	Jun
19.83	Milan	Jotanovic	SRB	11.1.84	2		Dra_evina	28	Apr
19.83	Derrick	Vicars	USA	8.5.89	1		Toledo, OH	15	Jun
19.82	Blake	Eaton	USA	2.5.89	2		University Park	4	May
19.81	Sultan	Al-Hebshi	KSA	31.1.85	1		Bialogard	7	Jul
19.79	Yasser Fathi	Ibrahim	EGY	2.5.84	1		Boulder	31	May
19.77	Eric	van Vreumingen	NED	15.6.78	1		Leiden	9	Jun
19.76	Orazio	Cremona	RSA	1.7.89	2		Germiston	18	Feb
	(80)								
19.75i	Konstantin	Lyadusov	RUS	2.3.88	5	NC	Moskva	23	Feb
19.75	Jaco	Engelbrecht	RSA	8.3.87	1		Pretoria	20	Apr
19.75	Robert	Golabek	USA	27.4.89	2		Toledo, OH	15	Jun
19.74i	Niklas	Arrhenius	SWE	10.9.82	1		Provo	20	Jan
19.71	Nikita	Zhidkov	RUS	29.2.88	1	Kuts	Moskva	13	Jun
19.70i	Mihaíl	Stamatóyiannis	GRE	20.5.82	1	NC	Pireás	21	Feb
19.70	Aleksandr	Lobynya	RUS	31.5.84	4	NC	Cheboksary	4	Jul
19.61	Jan	Marcell	CZE	4.6.85	2		Kladno	2	Jun
19.59	Jakub	Szyszkowski	POL	21.8.91	1	NC-23	Radom	1	Sep
19.57	Nick	Jones	USA	22.6.89	1		Commerce, TX	5	May
	(90)								
19.57	Matt	DeChant	USA	31.5.89	5	NCAA	Des Moines	9	Jun
19.57	Eric	Werskey	USA	17.7.87	1		Marietta, GA	10	Jun
19.56i	Anton	Tikhomirov	RUS	29.4.88	1		Sankt-Peterburg	5	Feb
19.56i	Artur	Hoppe	GER	3.5.88	3	NC	Karlsruhe	25	Feb
19.56	Tobias	Dahm	GER	23.5.87	3	NC	Wattenscheid	17	Jun
19.54	Caleb	Whitener	USA	29.5.92	3	NCAA-E	Jacksonville	26	May
19.53	Eder César	Moreno	COL	4.2.89	1	NG	Santander de Quilichao	16	Nov
19.52	Noah	Bryant	USA	11.5.84	5	Drake	Des Moines	28	Apr
19.51	Nick	Vena	USA-J	16.4.93	1		Charlottesville	20	Apr
19.51	Vladislav	Tulácek	CZE	9.7.88	2		Olomouc	8	May
	(100)								
19.51	Amin	Nikfar	IRI	2.1.81	1	MSR	Walnut	20	Apr

Mark	Name		Nat	Born	Date	
19.47	Ivan	Ivanov	KAZ	3.1.92	18	Jun
19.46	Emanuele	Fuamatu	SAM	27.10.89	3	Mar
19.42	John	Ybarra	USA	5.6.84	21	Apr
19.41	Raymond	Brown	JAM	15.1.88	17	Mar
19.40	Mateusz	Mikos	POL	10.4.87	15	Jun
19.39	Albert	Fournette	USA	21.10.91	31	Mar
19.39	Dennis	Aliotta	USA	16.5.89	12	May
19.37	Scott	Barnas	USA	9.10.86	14	Apr
19.35	Brandon	Mitchell	USA	19.6.75	28	Apr
19.34i	Kamil	Zbroszczyk	POL	24.1.87	8	Feb
19.34		Wang Like	CHN	2.4.89	23	Jun
19.33	Tumatai	Dauphin	FRA	12.1.88	13	Jun
19.33	Tom	Walsh	NZL	1.3.92	30	Jun
19.32	Cody	Hunt	USA	8.2.88	8	May
19.31	Alex	Adams	USA	6.8.89	7	Apr

Mark	Name		Nat	Born	Date	
19.31	Timothy	Hendry-Gallagher	CAN	3.2.90	11	Jul
19.30	Maksim	Afonin	RUS	6.1.92	20	Jul
19.26i	Yoiser	Toledo	CUB	24.4.83	28	Jan
19.26	Michal	Bosko	POL	25.7.88	7	Jul
19.25i	Zack	Hill	USA	3.3.91	9	Mar
19.25	Rafal	Kownatke	POL	24.3.85	11	Jul
19.24	Aleksandr	Bulanov	RUS	26.12.89	11	Jun
19.23	Robert	Dippl	GER	21.10.83	17	Jun
19.23	Martin	Stasek	CZE	8.4.89	21	Jun
19.22	Lukas	Weißhaidinger	AUT	20.2.92	18	Aug
19.21i	Markus	Bandekow	GER	22.5.87	5	Feb
19.20i	Michael	Putman	PER	7.3.89	25	Feb
19.20	Jon	Kalnas	USA	18.4.80	16	Jun
19.18	Georgios	Arestis	CYP	27.12.81	8	Jul
19.17		Guo Yanxiang	CHN	29.1.87	22	Sep

Mark	Name		Nat	Born	Pos	Meet	Venue	Date
19.16	Grigoriy	Kamulya	UZB	31.1.89				17 Apr
19.15i	Mihai-Liviu	Grasu	ROU	21.4.87				24 Feb
19.15		Fu Qingnan	CHN	22.2.89				13 Sep
19.14		Ding Weiye	CHN	13.4.90				23 Jun
19.13	Denis	Ananiyev	RUS	13.2.79				9 Jun
19.11	Paul	Davis	USA	.91				13 May
19.10i	Stephen	Mozia	USA-J	16.8.93				18 Feb
19.10	Mehdi	Shahrokhi	IRI	23.5.85				10 May
19.10	Paolo	Dal Soglio	ITA	29.7.70				10 Jun
19.09i	Daniel	Vanek	SVK	18.1.83				20 Jan
19.09	Carlos	Tobalina	ESP	2.8.85				11 Aug
19.08i	Ahmed Hassan	Gholoum	KUW	31.5.80				19 Feb
19.08	Reinaldo	Proenza	CUB	20.11.84				23 Mar
19.06	Laurentiu	Popa	ROU	19.1.84				15 Jun
19.01	Justin	Anlezark	AUS	14.8.77				1 Apr
19.01	Justin	Romero	USA	27.9.89				24 May
18.99		Li Meng	CHN-J	22.7.93				22 Sep
18.98i	Matt	Hoty	USA	21.10.91				26 Feb
18.97i	Viktor	Samolyuk	UKR	5.9.86				16 Feb
18.96	Richard	Garrett	USA	.90				24 May
18.94	Yves	Niaré	FRA	20.7.77				2 Jun
18.93	Michal	Rozporski	POL	20.12.88				15 Jun
18.93	Thomas	Schmitt	GER	23.1.89				8 Jul
18.91i	Viktor	Levchenko	UKR	10.8.88				11 Feb
18.91i	Dan	Block	USA	8.1.91				24 Feb
18.91	Chris	Reed	USA	22.7.92				26 May
18.91	Sergey	Bakhar	BLR	27.6.89				18 Jul
18.90i	Krzysztof	Brzozowski	POL-J	15.7.93				25 Feb
18.90		Feng Jie	CHN	18.1.86				28 Apr
18.89	Logan	Caldwell	USA	18.4.90				13 May
18.89	Andy	Dittmar	GER	5.7.74				23 Jun
18.88	Christopher	Adams	USA					16 Mar
18.88	Ross	Jordaan	RSA	29.3.85				13 Apr
18.87		Liu Yang	CHN	29.10.86				28 Apr
18.87	Nick	Price	USA	15.10.80				12 May
18.87	Andrey	Sinyakov	BLR	6.1.82				25 May
18.87	Damian	Birkinhead	AUS-J	8.4.93				20 Oct
18.85	William	Braido	BRA	18.3.92				9 Jun
18.84i	Bobby	Grace	USA	10.10.90				3 Mar
18.84		Li Jun	CHN-J	2.1.93				22 Sep
18.80	Tomasz	Söderlund	FIN	14.5.89				7 Jun
18.78	Milos	Markovic	SRB	22.11.89				19 May
18.77	Stian	Andersen	NOR	1.2.88				24 Aug
18.76	Daniel	Ståhl	SWE	27.8.92				28 Jul
18.74	Curtis	Jensen	USA	1.11.90				12 May
18.74	Sylwester	Zielinski	POL	13.8.89				26 May
18.73	Terron	Armstead	USA	.91				24 May
18.72i	Mohamed Hossein	Eskandari	IRI					19 Jan
18.71i	Daniele	Secci	ITA	9.3.92				21 Jan
18.70i	Martin	Gratzer	AUT	23.1.82				25 Feb
18.69	Ali Reza	Mehrsafooti	IRI	21.2.91				22 Jun
18.66	Marco	Di Maggio	ITA	22.5.83				20 May
18.65i	Max	Bedewitz	GER	18.10.90				12 Feb
18.65i	Hendrik	Müller	GER	28.8.90				12 Feb
18.64i	Francisco	Belo	POR	27.3.91				19 Feb
18.63i	Andrew	Smith	CAN	19.11.88				17 Mar
18.63	Tyler	Blatchley	USA	12.3.86				21 Apr
18.63	Robert	Gire	USA	.88				21 Apr
18.63	Chad	Wright	JAM	25.3.91				13 May
18.62	Mikhal	Abramchuk	BLR	15.11.92				28 Apr
18.59i	Joaquin	Millán	ESP	2.12.83				25 Feb
18.59	Robert	Häggblom	FIN	9.8.82				15 Sep
18.57i	Josh	Uchtman	USA	18.12.88				17 Feb
18.56	Vincent	Elardo	USA	18.12.88				13 May
18.55	Jon	Arthur	USA					24 Mar
18.54i	Tyler	Hitchler	USA	16.11.88				21 Jan
18.53	Nicolás	Martina	ARG	15.8.89				28 Sep
18.52	Tomás	Stanek	CZE	13.6.91				5 Jun
18.51	Nate	Hunter	USA	4.10.86				19 May
18.51	Willy	Irwin	USA	.91				27 May
18.51	Rimantas	Martisauskas	LTU	18.9.86				14 Jul
18.50	Luka	Rujevic (203)	SRB	14.10.85				15 Jul

Best outdoors

Mark	Name	Pos	Meet	Venue	Date
20.55	Smith	Q	ECp-w	Helsinki	27 Jun
20.40	Clarke	1	NCAA	Des Moines	9 Jun
20.31	Thormaehlen	1	Big 12	Manhattan	12 May
20.21	Nedow	3	NC	Calgary	30 Jun
20.17	Tsirikhov	13q	OG	London (OS)	3 Aug
19.91	Saenz	2	NCAA-E	Jacksonville	26 May
19.77	Bauer	4		Gotha	27 May
19.67	Zhang Jun	5		Tucson	19 May
19.65	Stamatóyiannis	1	NC	Athína	15 Jun

Mark	Name	Date		Mark	Name	Date
19.49	Kokoyev	4 Jul		19.31	Zbroszczyk	19 May
19.48	Giza	26 May		19.30	Thorsteinsson	12 Jun
19.48	Lyadusov	2 Jun		19.29	Hoppe	17 May
19.43	Arrhenius	4 Aug		19.12	Toledo	14 Jul
19.40	Tikhomirov	1 Jun		18.97	Gholoum	12 Dec
19.32	Crouser	24 May		18.95	Bandekow	17 Jun
18.87	Hill	26 May		18.61	Bedewitz	28 Jul
18.81	Mozia	6 May		18.54	Hoty	13 May
18.81	Brzozowski	19 May		18.51	Putman	26 May
18.64	Müller	18 Mar		18.50	Samolyuk	19 May
18.61	Smith	30 Jun				

Drugs disqualification: 19.80 Saurabh Vij ¶ IND 14.6.87 1 Patiala 8 Apr

JUNIORS

See main list for top 2 juniors. 11 performances by 7 men to 18.84. Additional marks and further juniors:

Mark	Name		Nat	Born	Pos	Meet	Venue	Date
Vena	19.27				1		Fairfax	14 Apr
	19.08				4		PennR Philadelphia	27 Apr
	19.07				1		Jacksonville	30 Mar
	18.92i				1		Blacksburg	3 Mar
19.10i	Stephen	Mozia	USA	16.8.93	1		Ithaca	18 Feb
	18.81				1		Philadelpjhia	6 May
18.99		Li Meng	CHN	22.7.93	5	NC	Kunshan	22 Sep
18.90i	Krzysztof	Brzozowski	POL	15.7.93	3	NC	Spala	25 Feb
	18.81				2		Katowice	19 May
18.87	Damian	Birkinhead	AUS	8.4.93	1		Melbourne (Doncaster)	20 Oct
18.84		Li Jun	CHN	2.1.93	7	NC	Kunshan	22 Sep
18.07i	Ben	Glauser	USA	12.8.93	2		New York (Arm)	28 Jan
	17.97				2		Philadelphia	6 May
18.01	Boris	Vain	FRA	11.3.93	3	NC	Angers	16 Jun
17.85	Arttu	Kangas (10)	FIN	13.7.93	4		Hämeenkyrö	16 Jun
17.82	Jordan	Young	CAN	21.6.93	6		Tucson	17 May
17.75i	Jaromír	Mazgal	CZE	20.1.93	3	NC	Praha	25 Feb
17.73	Kevin	Farley	USA	18.7.93	2		Louisville	20 Apr
17.73	Kyle	Strawn	USA	28.4.93	6		Los Angeles (Ww)	2 Jun
17.72	Bodo	Göder	GER	27.6.93	2		Karlsruhe	30 Jun
17.72	Joaquín	Ballivián	CHI	22.4.93	1		Puerto Montt	11 Nov
17.70	Bob	Bertemes	LUX	24.5.93	1		Metz	7 Jun
17.63i	Denis	Lewke	GER	23.7.93	4		Rochlitz	5 Feb
17.62i	Darrell	Hill	USA	17.8.93	8		New York (Arm)	3 Feb
	17.53				3		Houston	24 Mar
17.55	Ashinia	Miller (20)	JAM	6.6.93	2		Spanish Town	10 Mar

Mark	Name	Nat	Born	Pos	Meet	Venue	Date

6 KG SHOT

Mark	Name	Nat	Born	Pos	Meet	Venue	Date
22.30	Jacko Gill	NZL-Y	10.12.94	1	NC-J	Waitakere	24 Mar
22.20				1	WJ	Barcelona	11 Jul
21.50				Q	WJ	Barcelona	11 Jul
22.06				1		Christchurch	4 Feb
21.78	Krzysztof Brzozowski	POL	15.7.93	2	WJ	Barcelona	11 Jul
21.14				1	NC-j	Bialystok	22 Jun
21.14	Damien Birkinhead	AUS	8.4.93	3	WJ	Barcelona	11 Jul
21.12				1		Melbourne	26 May
20.35				1	NC-j	Sydney	16 Mar
20.53				1		Mannheim	23 Jun
20.31				1		Brisbane	2 Jun
20.51				1		Melbourne	19 May
20.31	Arttu Kangas	FIN	13.7.93	1		Hämeenkyrö	14 Jun
20.20	Stephen Mozia	USA-J	16.8.93	1	NC-j	Bloomington IN	16 Jun
20.19	Joaquín Ballivián	CHI	22.4.93	1		Santiago de Chile	9 Oct
20.15	Ashinia Miller	JAM	6.6.93	1		Kingston	25 Jan
20.06	Li Meng	CHN	22.7.93	1	NC-j	Changzhou	21 Apr
19.96	Mesud Pezer	BIH	27.8.94	Q	WJ	Barcelona	11 Jul
19.95i	Denis Lewke (10)	GER	23.7.93	1	v2N	Val-de-Reuil	3 Mar
19.95	Li Jun	CHN	2.1.93	2	NC-j	Changzhou	21 Apr
19.89i	Vladyslav Chernikov	UKR	8.3.94	1	v2N	Mogilyov	26 Feb
19.72i	Boris Vain	FRA	11.3.93	1		Mayenne	23 Dec
19.70	Bodo Göder	GER	27.6.93	7	WJ	Barcelona	11 Jul
19.61	Dawid Krzyzan	POL	20.4.94	1		Bydgoszcz	27 May
19.55	Alejandro Noguera	ESP	11.3.93	8	WJ	Barcelona	11 Jul
19.37	Nick Scarvelis	USA	2.2.93	2	NC-j	Bloomington IN	16 Jul
19.36	Bradley Szypka	USA	13.2.93	1		Ashland	9 Jun
19.33	Han Fei	CHN	7.9.93	3	NC-j	Changzhou	21 Apr
19.33	Bob Bertemes (20)	LUX	24.5.93	3		Mannheim	23 Jun

12LB (5.44KG) SHOT

Mark	Name	Nat	Born	Pos	Meet	Venue	Date
21.49	Tyler Schultz	USA	29.3.94	1		Custer	17 May
20.94	Braheme Days	USA-Y	18.1.95	1	PennR	Phladelphia	28 Apr

DISCUS

Mark	Name	Nat	Born	Pos	Meet	Venue	Date	1	2	3	4	5	6
70.66	Robert Harting	GER	18.10.84	1	Danek	Turnov	22 May	69.18	x	70.66	x	x	66.33
70.31				1		Halle	19 May	x	66.41	70.31	x	x	x
68.52				1		Wiesbaden	12 May	x	67.35	x	x	68.52	x
68.30				1	EC	Helsinki	30 Jun	63.02	65.80	x	68.30	p	67.07
68.27				1	OG	London (OS)	7 Aug	67.79	x	67.27	66.45	68.27	67.08
68.13				1	FBK	Hengelo	27 May	65.94	67.34	x	68.13	66.98	x
68.00				1		Neubrandenburg	19 Aug	68.00	x	66.02	64.21	66.91	x
67.79				1	NC	Wattenscheid	17 Jun	64.74	67.79	x	x	x	x
67.40				1	ISTAF	Berlin	2 Sep	61.12	67.40	64.81	66.92	66.54	65.93
70.28	Virgilijus Alekna	LTU	13.2.72	1		Klaipeda	23 Jun	x	68.03	70.28	66.64	x	66.43
69.04				1		Villeneuve d'Ascq	9 Jun	68.05	69.04	68.47	68.91	66.12	68.40
68.79				1		Bellinzona	5 Jun	67.71	68.79	x	x	65.37	66.83
68.50				1	Kuso	Szczecin	21 Jul	63.61	65.61	68.50	x	x	67.45
67.93				1	NC	Kaunas	7 Jul	62.91	63.97	x	67.93	65.62	65.02
67.38				4	OG	London (OS)	7 Aug	67.38	x	x	66.07	x	x
68.94	Piotr Malachowski	POL	7.6.83	2		Halle	19 May	68.31	66.02	66.93	68.37	68.94	68.46
67.53				1	DL	Doha	11 May	67.53	x	66.44	64.18		
67.37				2	Danek	Turnov	22 May	67.37	x	66.41	67.37	x	x
68.33	Martin Wierig	GER	10.6.87	1		Schönebeck	26 Jul	67.66	68.33	x	66.84	x	67.12
68.24	Lawrence Okoye	GBR	6.10.91	3		Halle	19 May	66.24	x	x	68.24	66.95	64.04
68.20	Ehsan Hadadi	IRI	21.1.85	4		Halle	19 May	67.45	67.83	64.22	67.36	68.20	66.12
68.18				2	OG	London (OS)	7 Aug	68.18	64.09	67.28	66.98	x	x
67.92				1		Bergsheim	25 Jul	67.92	64.08	65.26	65.60	64.15	65.62
68.03	Gerd Kanter	EST	6.5.79	3	OG	London (OS)	7 Aug	65.07	65.79	66.02	65.96	68.03	66.99
67.71				1		Bottnaryd	16 Jun	60.75	x	66.20	65.36	x	67.71
67.36				1		London (He)	28 Jul	?					
67.74	Frank Casañas	ESP	18.10.78	1	ECCp	Vila Real de Santo António	27 May	60.45	62.53	67.74	x		
67.53	Benn Harradine	AUS	14.10.82	1		Townsville	5 May	35.01	61.40	67.53	x	65.39	63.03
67.50	Ercüment Olgundeniz (10)	TUR	7.7.76	2	ECCp	Vila Real de Santo António	27 May	65.18	67.50	x	x		

Mark	Name		Nat	Born	Pos	Meet	Venue	Date
67.30	Erik (30/11)	Cadée	NED	15.2.84	1		Hoorn	12 May
67.15	Jason	Morgan	JAM	6.10.82	1		Monroe, LA	12 May
67.15	Mario	Pestano	ESP	8.4.78	1		Las Palmas de Gran Canaria	21 Jul
67.12	Traves	Smikle	JAM	7.5.92	1	NC	Kingston	30 Jun
66.97	Rutger	Smith	NED	9.7.81	1		La Jolla	28 Apr
66.93	Robert	Urbanek	POL	29.4.87	5		Halle	19 May
66.58	Aleksander	Tammert	EST	2.2.73	2		Klaipeda	23 Jun
66.53	Martin	Maric	CRO	19.4.84	1		Chula Vista	19 Apr
66.28	Vikas	Gowda	IND	5.7.83	1		Norman	12 Apr
66.28	Markus (20)	Münch	GER	13.6.86	6		Halle	19 May
66.05	Jorge	Fernández	CUB	2.10.87	1		La Habana	9 Mar
65.96	Bogdan	Pishchalnikov	RUS	26.8.82	1		Adler	26 May
65.96	Oleksiy	Semenov	UKR	27.6.82	1		Kyiv	15 Jul
65.63	Scott	Martin	AUS	12.10.82	1		Wailuku	4 May
65.61	Przemyslaw	Czajkowski	POL	26.10.88	1		Lódz	12 May
65.46	Russ	Winger	USA	2.8.84	1		Perth	11 Feb
65.41	Ronald	Julião	BRA	16.6.85	1		Rio de Janeiro	20 May
65.36	Apostolos	Parellis	CYP	24.7.85	1		Haniá	3 Jun
65.28	Jason	Young	USA	27.5.81	1		Lubbock	14 Apr
65.24	Carl (30)	Myerscough	GBR	21.10.79	1		Claremont	9 Jun
65.24	Abdul	Buhari	GBR	26.6.82	1		London (He)	30 Jun
65.17	Yunio	Lastre	CUB	26.10.81	1		La Habana	29 Jun
65.15	Lance	Brooks	USA	1.1.84	1	NC/OT	Eugene	28 Jun
65.14	Róbert	Fazekas ¶	HUN	18.8.75	3		La Jolla	26 Apr
65.08	Sultan Mubarak	Al-Dawoodi	KSA	16.6.77	1		Kielce	30 Jun
65.02	Märt	Israel	EST	23.9.83	2		London (He)	28 Jul
64.84	Julian	Wruck	AUS	6.7.91	1		Los Angeles (Ww)	14 Apr
64.77	Mohammed	Samimi	IRI	29.3.87	1	BLR Ch	Grodno	6 Jul
64.76	Jarred	Rome	USA	21.12.76	1		San Diego	20 Jun
64.69	Niklas (40)	Arrhenius	SWE	10.9.82	2		Helsingborg	17 Jun
64.37	Daniel	Jasinski	GER	5.8.89	1		Osterode	5 Jun
64.36	Mahmoud	Samimi	IRI	18.9.88	1		Tehran	24 May
64.35	Brett	Morse	GBR	11.2.89	2		London (He)	30 Jun
64.24	Irfan	Yildirum	TUR	26.7.88	1		Bursa	6 May
64.24	Giovanni	Faloci	ITA	13.10.85	1		Tarquinia	27 May
64.20	Mykyta	Nesterenko	UKR	15.4.91	1		Kyiv	20 May
64.08	Gaute	Myklebust	NOR	29.4.79	3		Helsingborg	17 Jun
63.79	Danijel	Furtula	MNE	31.7.92	1		Sremska Mitrovica	2 Jun
63.74	Adam	Kuehl	USA	19.1.84	4		Wailuku	4 May
63.69	Lois Maikel (50)	Martínez	ex-CUB	3.6.81	2		Castellón	3 Apr
63.55	Germán	Lauro	ARG	2.4.84	1	IbAmC	Barquisimeto	8 Jun
63.46	Zane	Duquemin	GBR	23.9.91	3		London (He)	30 Jun
63.40	Konrad	Szuster	POL	21.1.84	1		Aleksandrów	31 Aug
63.39	Andrius	Gudzius	LTU	14.2.91	2		Viljandi	3 Jul
63.37	Will	Conwell	USA	12.9.82	1		Marietta	27 May
63.33	Gerhard	Mayer	AUT	20.5.80	4		Helsingborg	17 Jun
63.30	Jorge	Balliengo	ARG	5.1.78	1		Rosario	28 Mar
63.17	Jan	Marcell	CZE	4.6.85	3	ECCp	Vila Real de Santo António	27 May
63.01	Nikolay	Sedyuk	RUS	29.4.88	2	Kuts	Moskva	13 Jun
62.92	Yeóryios (60)	Trémos	GRE	21.3.89	1		Lárisa	9 Jun
62.88	Chad	Wright	JAM	25.3.91	1		Lincoln	17 Jun
62.84	Mikko	Kyyrö	FIN	12.7.80	1		Kokemäki	15 Jun
62.80	Eduardo	Albertazzi	ITA	14.9.91	1		Tarquinia	7 Jun
62.78	Leif	Arrhenius	SWE	15.7.86	4		Sollentuna	5 Jul
62.76	Victor	Hogan	RSA	25.7.89	3		Bilbao	3 Jun
62.70	Luke	Bryant	USA	5.12.88	2		Norman	31 May
62.64	Musaeb	Al-Momani	JOR	28.8.86	1		Amman	11 Oct
62.46A	Casey	Malone	USA	6.4.77	1		Fort Collins	28 Apr
62.44	Roland	Varga	CRO	22.10.77	2		Zagreb	5 Jun
62.40	Ian (70)	Waltz	USA	15.4.77	2		Norman	14 Apr
62.32	Martin	Kupper	EST	31.5.89	2		Kohila	29 Aug
62.28	Dmitriy	Sivakov	BLR	15.2.83	1		Minsk	18 Jul
62.25	Fredrik	Amundgård	NOR	12.1.89	2eB		Chula Vista	19 Apr

Mark	Name		Nat	Born	Pos	Meet	Venue	Date
62.18	Ahmad Mohamed	Dheeb	QAT	29.9.85	2	W.Asian	Dubai	15 Dec
62.16	Daniel	Ståhl	SWE	27.8.92	1	NC	Stockholm	25 Aug
62.05	Omar	El-Ghazaly	EGY	9.2.84	6		Sollentuna	5 Jul
62.04	Hannes	Kirchler	ITA	22.12.78	10		La Jolla	28 Apr
62.00	Stanislav	Nesterovskyy	UKR	31.7.80	3	NC	Yalta	12 Jun
61.95A	Nick	Jones	USA	22.6.89	1		El Paso	14 Apr
61.91	Emeka	Udechuku	GBR	10.7.79	1		London (He)	16 Jun
(80)								
61.74	Tomás	Vonavka	CZE	4.6.90	1		Domazlice	14 Sep
61.73		Wu Jian	CHN	25.5.86	1		Zibo	26 May
61.68	Gleb	Sidorchenko	RUS	15.5.86	2		Adler	26 May
61.67	Wes	Stockbarger	USA	5.6.85	1		Tucson	19 May
61.57	Axel	Härstedt	SWE	28.2.87	1		Vellinge	10 Jun
61.54	Dan	Hytinen	USA	18.10.85	1		Madison	5 May
61.51	Chase	Madison	USA	13.9.85	1		Cedar Falls	10 Jun
61.40	Mason	Finley	USA	7.10.90	1		Baldwin City, KS	24 Mar
61.26	Jared	Thomas	USA	17.2.90	1		Louisville	11 May
61.26	Matej	Gasaj	SVK	27.12.81	1		Ceske Budejovice	2 Jun
(90)								
61.24	Sergiu	Ursu	ROU	26.4.80	1	BUL Ch	Sliven	15 Jun
61.22	Christopher	Harting	GER	4.10.90	4		Schönebeck	26 Jul
61.20	Brian	Bishop	USA	16.4.89	1		Whitewater	10 Jun
61.17	Mihai-Liviu	Grasu	ROU	21.4.87	7	ECp-w	Bar	17 Mar
61.17	Pedro José	Cuesta	ESP	22.8.83	1		León	7 Jul
61.15	Jared	Schuurmans	USA	20.8.87	1		Modesto	10 Jun
61.10	Oskars	Vaisjuns	LAT	21.8.83	6		Viljandi	3 Jul
61.09	Bryan	Powlen	USA	3.12.87	1eB		Tucson	19 May
61.06	Vadim	Hranovschi	MDA	14.2.83	1		Chisinau	26 May
60.95	Jean-François	Aurokium	FRA	14.4.81	1		Le Tampon	14 Apr
(100)								

Mark	Name		Nat	Born	Date
60.89	Jorge	Grave	POR	1.9.82	21 Jul
60.72	Ulf	Ankarling	SWE	12.4.88	7 Aug
60.67	Gordon	Wolf	GER	17.1.90	4 Feb
60.65	Mikhail	Dvornikov	RUS	15.8.89	26 May
60.65	Igor	Gondor	CZE	10.3.79	27 Jun
60.45	Mario	Cota	MEX	11.9.90	20 Apr
60.42	Sergey	Roganov	BLR	18.4.86	24 Feb
60.42	Yasser Fathi	Ibrahim	EGY	2.5.84	31 May
60.36	Sergey	Dementyev	UZB	1.6.90	10 Jun
60.31	Jouni	Waldén	FIN	9.1.82	25 Jul
60.30	Jason	Dixon	USA	16.8.84	5 Jun
60.23	Maarten	Persoon	NED	15.3.87	1 Jul
60.22	Maximilian	Alonso	CHI	10.10.86	17 May
60.20	Orestis	Antoniades	CYP	10.7.85	20 Jun
60.17	Nathaniel	Moses	USA	1.4.90	25 May
60.05	Lolassonn	Djouhan	FRA	18.5.91	6 Jul
60.03	Sergiy	Pruglo	UKR	18.11.83	27 May
59.97	Petr	Vuklisevic	CZE	25.2.82	30 Jun
59.92	Kole	Weldon	USA	25.3.92	14 Apr
59.91	Ryan	Crouser	USA	18.12.92	18 Jun
59.90	Ruslan	Khlybov	BLR	15.2.83	6 Jul
59.64	Dan	Block	USA	8.1.91	12 May
59.60	Gerhard	de Beer	RSA-J	5.7.94	6 Jul
59.58	Jamie	Williamson	GBR	16.7.87	30 Jun
59.52	Fabian	Pudenz	GER	26.6.91	20 May
59.40	Michael	Salzer	GER	25.10.91	30 Jun
59.37	Tom	Norman	GBR	15.9.82	30 Jun
59.27	Carter	Comito	USA	26.10.90	9 May
59.25	Brian	Trainor	USA	14.3.80	14 Apr
59.25	Federico	Apolloni	ITA	14.3.87	23 May
59.24	Tim	Nedow	CAN	16.10.90	11 May
59.18	Priidu	Niit	EST	27.1.90	18 Jun
59.15	Mike	Torie	USA	12.3.86	17 May
59.13	Tyler	Hitchler	USA	16.11.88	24 Mar
59.06	Servell	Dandridge	USA	.90	28 Apr
59.05	James	Plummer	USA	.90	10 Jun
59.03	Matthew	Kosecki	USA	1.7.91	13 May
58.98	Marek	Bárta	CZE	8.12.92	16 Sep
58.91	Andrew	Evans	USA	25.1.91	6 Jun
58.85	Sean	Pruitt	USA	19.12.86	17 Mar
58.85	Dalton	Rowan	USA-J	6.4.93	6 Jun
58.84	Russel	Tucker	RSA	4.11.90	20 Mar
58.84	Simon	Cooke	GBR	3.10.85	16 Jun
58.83	András	Seres	HUN	31.1.89	1 Sep
58.80	Aleksandr	Lesnoy	RUS	4.7.88	26 May
58.74	Essa Mohamed	Al-Zankawi	KUW	17.10.92	7 Mar
58.70	Gabe	Hull	USA-J	1.12.93	21 Apr
58.69	Aleksas	Abromavicius	LTU	6.12.84	9 Jun
58.67	Geoffrey	Tabor	USA	8.3.89	6 Jun
58.67	Filipe Vital	e Silva	POR	27.1.83	18 Jul
58.57	Jordan	Williams	USA	22.5.90	4 May
58.52	Greg	Garza	USA	6.1.85	24 May
58.49	Wojciech	Praczyk	POL-J	10.1.93	16 Jun
58.43	Ville	Kivioja	FIN	9.7.90	5 Sep
58.39	Lonnie	Pugh	USA	23.2.90	24 May
58.37		Xin Jia	CHN	1.3.88	26 May
58.34	Stéphane	Marthély	FRA	9.9.79	25 Feb
58.32	Benedikt	Stienen	GER	12.1.92	17 Jun
58.31	O'Dayne	Richards	JAM	14.12.88	30 Jun
58.30	Randy	Noa	CUB	18.11.87	29 Jun
58.29	Martin	Premeru	CRO	29.8.90	22 Jul
58.27	Quincy	Wilson	TRI	3.4.91	19 May
58.21	John	Bowman	USA	29.8.86	7 Jun
58.20	Pavlo	Karsak	UKR	11.11.87	27 May
58.19	Joni	Mattila	FIN	30.11.88	20 May
58.18	Willy	Irwin	USA	.91	28 Apr
58.18	Brady	Maska	USA	1.3.86	28 Apr
58.16	Ali Khalifa	Maaloul	LBA	11.5.83	7 Apr
58.16	Michal	Hodun	POL	17.2.83	12 May
58.13ii	Chris	Scott	GBR	21.3.88	10 Mar
58.12	Rodney	Brown	USA-J	21.5.93	17 Mar
58.12	John	Talbert	USA	3.7.89	14 Apr
58.10	Stéphane	Nativel	FRA	4.4.75	9 Jun
58.09	Drew	Ulrick	USA	13.1.85	24 Mar
58.09	Nazzareno	Di Marco	ITA	30.4.85	28 Apr
58.06	Alex	Thompson	USA	3.8.92	5 May
58.00	Lukas	Weißhaidinger	AUT	20.2.92	20 Aug
(177)					

Drugs disqualification

Mark	Name		Nat	Born	Pos	Meet	Venue	Date
68.21	Zoltán	Kővágó	HUN	10.4.79	(1)		Budapest	4 May

5th throw, only the best measured

| 67.91 | | Kővágó | | | (1) | NC | Szekszád | 17 Jun |

61.42   x   67.91   x   x   x

| 58.59 | Kirpal | Singh ¶ | IND | 19.5.92 | (1) | | Patiala | 21 Apr |

Mark	Name		Nat	Born	Pos	Meet	Venue	Date

JUNIORS

Mark	Name		Nat	Born	Pos	Meet	Venue	Date
59.60	Gerhard	de Beer	RSA	5.7.94	3		Bottrop	6 Jul
58.85	Dalton	Rowan	USA	6.4.93	8	NCAA	Des Moines	6 Jun
	58.62	3q NCAAW	Austin	26	May			
58.70	Gabe	Hull	USA	1.12.93	2		Iowa City	21 Apr
	57.52	1	Columbia MO	14	Apr			
58.49	Wojciech	Praczyk	POL	10.1.93	4	NC	Bielsko-Biala	16 Jun
	57.80	1	Szprotawa	12	May			
58.12	Rodney	Brown	USA	21.5.93	2		Lafayette	17 Mar
	57.98	5 TexR	Austin	31	Mar	11 performances by 5 men to 57.32		
57.32	Viktor	Butenko	RUS	10.3.93	8		Moskva	11 Jun
56.74	Jordan	Young	CAN	21.6.93	2cB		Tucson	19 May
55.72	Darian	Brown	USA	.93	2		San Marcos	13 May
55.45	Fedric	Dacres	JAM	28.2.94	2		Mona	9 Jun
55.29	Thiago Adtiano	Negreiros (10)	BRA	12.10.94	1		São Paulo	12 May
55.00	Mauricio	Ortega	COL	4.8.94	1	NG	Santander de Quilichao	13 Nov
54.84	Nick	Vena	USA	16.4.93	1		Charlottesville	21 Apr
54.83	Damian	Kaminski	POL	15.12.93	1		Warszawa	10 Jun
54.72		Mo Ke	CHN	10.10.93	7		Zibo	26 May
54.33	Sam	Mattis	USA	19.3.94	3		New York	10 Jun
54.17	Felipe	Lorenzon	BRA	11.11.93	3	NC	São Paulo	30 Jun

1.75KG DISCUS

Mark	Name		Nat	Born	Pos	Meet	Venue	Date
64.22	Wojciech	Praczyk	POL	10.1.93	1	NC-j	Bialystok	24 Jun
	63.22	1	Zielona Góra	23 May	62.67	1	Siedlce	10 Jun
	62.75	2 WJ	Barcelona	12 Jul	61.58	1	Szprotawa	12 May
63.01	Rodney	Brown	USA	21.5.93	1	NC-j	Bloomington	17 Jun
62.80	Fedric	Dacres	JAM	28.2.94	1	WJ	Barcelona	12 Jul
	61.55	1 NC-j	Kingston	16	Jun			
62.09	Viktor	Butenko	RUS	10.3.93	1		Moskva	9 Jun
61.64A	Gerhard	de Beer	RSA	5.7.94	1		Windhoek	28 Apr
	61.57	3 WJ	Barcelona	12	Jul	10 performances by 4 men to 62.90		
61.44	Sebastien	Scheffel	GER	17.11.93	1		Neubrandenburg	8 Jun
61.32	Dalton	Rowan	USA	6.4.93	2	NC-j	Bloomington	17 Jun
61.18	Felipe	Lorenzon	BRA	11.11.93	5	WJ	Barcelona	12 Jul
61.01	Damian	Kaminski	POL	15.12.93	1		Warszawa	10 Jun
60.72A	Jordan	Young (10)	CAN	21.6.93	1		Boulder	7 Jun
60.65A	Jan-Louw	Kotze	RSA	18.3.94	2		Windhoek	28 Apr
60.20	Stephen	Mozia	USA	16.8.93	3	NC-j	Bloomington	17 Jun
59.84	Mauricio	Ortega	COL	4.8.94	Q	WJ	Barcelona	10 Jul
59.73	Gabe	Hull	USA	1.12.93	1		Iowa City	21 Apr
59.59	Phillip	van Dijck	GER	23.8.93	2		Halle	19 May
59.57	Behnam	Shiri	IRI	21.5.93	1	NC-j	Mashad	16 May
59.53	Nicholas	Percy	GBR	6,12.94	1	NC-j	Bedford	17 Jun
59.28	Mojtaba	Shabaneh	IRI	27.8.93	2	NC-j	Mashad	16 May
59.93	Stefano	Petrei	ITA	27.12.93	1		Gorizia	25 Apr
58.71	Matthias	Fischer (20)	GER	9.3.93	2		Neubrandenburg	8 Jun

HAMMER

Mark	Name		Nat	Born	Pos	Meet	Venue	Date
82.81	Ivan	Tikhon ¶	BLR	24.7.76	1	NCp	Brest	25 May
	78.09	79.58	80.88	x	81.02	82.81		
82.28	Krisztián	Pars	HUN	18.2.82	1	GS	Ostrava	24 May
	81.37	82.28	p	p	p	p		
81.48	1	Velenje	14 Jun	77.37	80.01	80.16	81.48 p p	
81.28	1	Tapolca	25 Aug	79.41	79.41	81.28	x x 81.14	
81.16	1	Veszprém	28 Apr	x	80.05	79.10	x 81.16 p	
80.85	1	Madrid	7 Jul	76.59	79.42	x	79.16 80.85 p	
80.59	1 OG	London (OS)	5 Aug	79.14	78.33	80.59	79.70 79.28 78.88	
80.28	1 NC	Szekszárd	17 Jun	x	80.12	x	x 80.28 x	
80.22	2	Montreuil-sous-Bois	5 Jun	x	79.18	78.81	80.22 x 80.06	
79.84	1	Dubnica nad Váhom	26 Aug	74.62	79.69	79.84	x 78.63 79.19	
79.74	1 Gyulai	Budapest	20 Aug	x	79.15	78.09	79.74 x x	
79.72	1 EC	Helsinki	28 Jun	78.57	79.40	x	79.72 79.46 77.47	
79.37	Q OG	London (OS)	3 Aug	77.11	79.37	p		
81.39	Pawel	Fajdek	POL	4.6.89	1		Montreuil-sous-Bois	5 Jun
	77.66	78.54	79.76	x	78.11	81.39		
80.36	2 GS	Ostrava	24 May	77.46	80.06	80.36	79.23 x 79.43	
80.32	1 NC	Bielsko-Biala	16 Jun	77.93	x	80.32	75.33 x 80.24	
79.82	1	Lódz	13 May	x	74.15	x	79.82 78.02 x	
80.98	Sergey	Litvinov	RUS	27.1.86	1	Kuts	Moskva	13 Jun
	77.79	80.57	80.63	79.76	80.98	78.40		

Mark	Name	Nat	Born	Pos	Meet	Venue		Date
80.33	1 Zhukovskiy 23 Jun		78.17	80.33	78.67	x	x	77.24
79.55	1 Moskva 21 Jun		79.06	78.05	79.55	64.41	x	78.57
80.71	Kirill Ikonnikov	RUS	5.3.84	1	NC	Cheboksary		5 Jul
			x	76.72	78.82	78.24	79.86	80.71
79.46	2 Kuts Moskva 13 Jun		x	x	79.46	77.20	76.77	x
79.37	2 Zhukovskiy 23 Jun		78.30	x	75.56	x	78.30	79.37
80.25	Pavel Krivitskiy	BLR	17.4.84	1	Klim	Minsk (Staiki)		12 Jun
			80.25	79.43	x	77.62	x	80.16
79.37	1 NC-w Minsk (Staiki) 24 Feb		75.80	76.45	75.80	79.37	x	77.41
80.25	Andrey Vorontsov	BLR	24.7.75	2	Klim	Minsk (Staiki)		12 Jun
			x	77.12	x	80.25	x	78.86
79.75	Nicolas Figère	FRA	19.5.79	1		Bobigny		23 May
79.60	Vadim Devyatovskiy	BLR	20.3.77	3	Klim	Minsk (Staiki)		12 Jun
			79.60	x	x	x	x	x
79.56	Dmitriy Marshin (10)	AZE	24.2.72	4	Klim	Minsk (Staiki)		12 Jun
			70.90	x	76.08	78.85	79.08	79.56
79.44	Lukás Melich	CZE	16.9.80	1		Lovosice		12 May
79.42	Oleksandr Drygol (31/12)	UKR	25.4.66	1		Jablonec nad Nisou		29 Apr
79.36	Primoz Kozmus	SLO	30.9.79	2	OG	London (OS)		5 Aug
79.20	A.G. Kruger	USA	18.2.79	1		Ashland		9 Jun
79.18	Yuriy Shayunov	BLR	22.10.87	5	Klim	Minsk (Staiki)		12 Jun
79.08	Lorenzo Povegliano	ITA	11.11.84	1		Codroipo		12 May
78.91	Oleksiy Sokyrskyy	UKR	16.3.85	2		Madrid		7 Jul
78.71	Koji Murofushi	JPN	8.10.74	3	OG	London (OS)		5 Aug
78.51	Szymon Ziólkowski	POL	1.7.76	1		Forbach		27 May
78.44	Valeriy Svyatokho (20)	BLR	20.7.81	2	NCp	Brest		25 May
78.40	Aleksey Zagornyi	RUS	31.5.78	3	GS	Ostrava		24 May
78.28	Quentin Bigot	FRA	1.12.92	1		Thaon-les-Vosges		24 Jun
78.28	Esref Apak	TUR	3.1.82	1	NC	Izmir		6 Jul
78.26	Jérôme Bortoluzzi	FRA	20.5.82	1		Metz		7 Jun
78.22	Igor Vinichenko	RUS	11.4.84	1		Adler		21 Apr
78.21	Igors Sokolovs	LAT	17.8.74	1		Valmiera		8 Jun
78.18	Artem Rubanko	UKR	21.3.74	1		Kyiv		19 May
77.93	Markus Esser	GER	3.2.80	2		Metz		7 Jun
77.70	Dilshod Nazarov	TJK	6.5.82	3		Montreuil-sous-Bois		5 Jun
77.70	Andriy Martynyuk (30)	UKR	25.9.90	2	NC	Kyiv		14 Jun
77.53	David Söderberg	FIN	11.8.79	1		Mänttä-Vilppula		11 Jul
77.43	Marcel Lomnicky	SVK	6.7.87	1	FlaR	Gainesville		6 Apr
77.22	Chris Harmse	RSA	31.5.73	1	AfrC	Porto Novo		30 Jun
77.17	Kibwé Johnson	USA	17.7.81	Q	OG	London (OS)		3 Aug
77.14	Mostafa Hicham Al-Gamal	EGY	1.10.88	1		Boulder		13 Jun
77.08	Roberto Janet	CUB	29.8.86	1	NC	La Habana		23 Mar
77.06	Sergey Kolomoyets	BLR	11.8.89	4		Brest		28 Apr
77.05	Frédérick Pouzy	FRA	18.2.83	3		Forbach		27 May
76.69	Hassan Mohamed Mahmoud	EGY	10.2.84	4		Forbach		27 May
76.42	Nicola Vizzoni (40)	ITA	4.11.73	Q	EC	Helsinki		28 Jun
76.21	Javier Cienfuegos	ESP	15.7.90	1		Salamanca		5 May
76.19	Aleksandr Pozdnyakov	RUS	1.2.87	1		Sankt-Peterburg		1 Jun
76.15	Dmitriy Velikopolskiy	RUS	27.11.84	2		Adler		21 Apr
76.14	Ali Mohamed Al-Zankawi	KUW	27.2.84	1	W.Asian	Dubai		13 Dec
76.12	Mattias Jons	SWE	19.11.82	5		Madrid		7 Jul
76.11	Drew Loftin	USA	15.9.80	2		Fort Collins		13 Jun
76.10	Marco Lingua	ITA	4.6.78	3		Metz		7 Jun
75.97	Michael Mai	USA	27.7.77	1		San Jose		19 Apr
75.97	Mohsen Anani	EGY	25.5.85	1		Cairo		15 Jun
75.78	Alexander Ziegler (50)	GER	7.7.87	1	NCAA	Des Moines		8 Jun
75.67	Kristóf Németh	HUN	17.9.87	2	NC-w	Szombathely		3 Mar
75.63	Alex Smith	GBR	6.3.88	1		Loughborough		3 Mar
75.57	Eivind Henriksen	NOR	14.9.90	2		Florø		2 Jun
75.50	Aleksey Korolyov	RUS	5.4.82	3		Zhukovskiy		23 Jun
75.20	Sergey Marghiev	MDA	7.11.92	1		Chisinau		26 May
75.16	Olli-Pekka Karjalainen	FIN	7.3.80	2		Kuortane		22 Jul
75.09	Conor McCullough	IRL	31.1.91	3	Spitzen	Luzern		17 Jul
75.01	Libor Charfreitag	SVK	11.9.77	1	MSR	Walnut		21 Apr
74.96	Jim Steacy	CAN	29.5.84	2		Tucson		17 May
74.96	Dmitriy Shako (60)	BLR	25.3.79	3	NC	Grodno		6 Jul

Mark	Name		Nat	Born	Pos	Meet	Venue	Date	
74.84	Denis	Lukyanov	RUS	11.7.89	4		Zhukovskiy	23	Jun
74.82	Mark	Dry	GBR	11.10.87	1		Loughborough	20	May
74.75	Juan Ignacio	Cerra	ARG	16.10.76	1		Santa Fé	8	May
74.38	Noleysis	Vicet	CUB	6.2.81	2		La Habana	28	Jun
74.37	Fatih	Eryildirim	TUR	1.3.79	2	NC	Izmir	6	Jul
74.36	Chris	Cralle	USA	13.6.88	2	NC/OT	Beaverton	21	Jun
74.20	Sukhrob	Khodjayev	UZB-J	21.5.93	1	KAZ Ch	Almaty	18	Jun
73.95	András	Haklits	CRO	23.9.77	1		Varazdin	17	Jun
73.86	Reinier	Mejias	CUB	22.9.90	3		La Habana	28	Jun
73.86	Constantinos	Stathelakos	CYP	30.12.87	1		Nikítí	7	Jul
(70)									
73.67	Tuomas	Seppänen	FIN	16.5.86	6		Halle	19	May
73.62	Oleg	Dubitskiy	BLR	14.10.90	2		Brest	28	Apr
73.55	Ákos	Hudi	HUN	10.8.91	2		Zalaegerszeg	26	May
73.52	Wojciech	Nowicki	POL	22.2.89	1		Warszawa	2	Jun
73.33	Markus	Johansson	SWE	8.5.90	2		Uppsala	28	Jul
73.24	Sven	Möhsner	GER	30.1.86	2		Rhede	7	Jun
73.23	Andy	Fryman	USA	3.2.85	1		Rome, GA	8	Jun
73.16	Kaveh	Mousavi	IRI	27.5.85	6		Zhukovskiy	23	Jun
73.02	Zakhar	Makhrosenko	BLR	10.10.91	5	NC-w	Minsk (Staiki)	24	Feb
72.96	Dmytro	Mykolaychuk	UKR	30.1.87	4	NC-w	Yalta	23	Feb
(80)									
72.96	Steffen	Nerdal	NOR	22.2.85	1		Nadderud	17	Jun
72.90	Yevgen	Vynogradov	UKR	30.4.84	1		Yalta	4	Jun
72.78	Wágner	Domingos	BRA	23.6.83	1		Varazdin	29	Apr
72.74	Roberto	Sawyers	CRC	17.10.86	1		West Point	7	May
72.72	Juha	Kauppinen	FIN	16.8.86	4		Kaustinen	16	Jun
72.66	Benjamin	Boruschewski	GER	23.4.80	9		Halle	19	May
72.55	Arkadiusz	Milkiewicz	POL	13.8.87	1		Torun	9	Jun
72.30	Aleksey	Kochnev	RUS	6.4.90	1	NC-w23	Minsk (Staiki)	24	Feb
72.25	Pavel	Boreysho	BLR	16.2.91	6	NC-w	Minsk (Staiki)	24	Feb
71.95	Alaa El-Din M.	El-Ashry	EGY	6.1.91	2		Cairo	15	Jun
(90)									
71.81	Dário	Manso	POR	1.7.82	1		Lovelhe	13	Jul
71.80	Aléxandros	Papadimitríou	GRE	18.6.73	1		Trípoli	19	May
71.75	Peter	Smith	GBR	20.7.90	1		Hull	15	Apr
71.72	Garland	Porter	USA	10.2.82	2		Tucson	19	May
71.69	Jacob	Freeman	USA	5.11.80	1		Monmouth	3	Jun
71.54		Lee Yun-chul	KOR	28.3.82	1		Mokpo	6	Sep
71.48	Simone	Falloni	ITA	26.9.91	3		Lucca	29	Jan
71.36	Andrew	Frost	GBR	17.4.81	2		Hull	22	Apr
71.29	Michal	Fiala	CZE	22.6.85	1		Pardubice	4	Jul
71.22	Hiroshi	Noguchi	JPN	3.5.83	2	NC	Osaka	8	Jun
(100)									

Mark	Name		Nat	Born	Date	
71.21	Sergey	Aydamirov	RUS	11.5.87	28	Feb
71.12		Qi Dakai	CHN	23.5.87	18	Sep
70.77	Yevgeniy	Shaytar	BLR	28.1.88	6	Jul
70.76	Tim	Driesen	AUS	27.3.84	2	Mar
70.74	Ryan	Loughney	USA	21.8.89	24	May
70.73	Jeremy	Postin	USA	7.3.90	28	Apr
70.72	Andreas	Sahner	GER	27.1.85	17	Jun
70.70	Mergen	Mamedov	TKM	24.12.90	5	May
70.68	James	Bedford	GBR	29.12.88	20	May
70.56	Anton	Krykun	UKR	22.1.90	28	May
70.43	Ainars	Vaiculens	LAT	21.3.83	25	May
70.39	Tibor	Petrovszki	HUN	8.11.89	4	May
70.38	Johannes	Bichler	GER	3.7.90	7	Jul
70.32	Mats	Granö	FIN	6.9.81	17	Mar
70.28	Oleksandr	Myahkyh	UKR	7.5.86	19	May
70.28	Chris	Bryce	USA	20.5.78	19	May
70.27	Mirko	Micuda	CRO	22.12.89	17	Jun
70.22	Aurélien	Boisrond	FRA	17.2.85	1	Apr
70.16	Pellegrino	Delli Carri	ITA	4.8.76	1	Jul
70.15	Henrik	Rittweg	GER	19.4.88	23	Jun
70.12	Driss	Barid	MAR	12.12.86	3	Jun
70.09	Jerrit	Lipske	GER	1.2.87	27	May
70.01	Jens	Rautenkrantz	GER	11.4.82	17	Jun
70.00	Yevgeniy	Korotovskiy	RUS	1.6.92	27	Jun
69.90	Travis	Nutter	USA	9.2.75	19	May
69.89	Kevin	Becker	USA	1.5.84	14	Apr
69.89	Alec	Faldermeyer	USA	9.7.92	21	Apr
69.85	Isaac	Vicente	ESP	30.4.87	2	Jun
69.80	Hiroaki	Doi	JPN	2.12.78	8	Jun
69.75	Reza	Moghaddam	IRI	17.11.88	1	Jun
69.71	Pavel	Sedlácek	CZE	5.4.68	26	Aug
69.70	Bruno	Boccalatte	FRA	10.11.88	24	Jun
69.62		Wang Shizhu	CHN	20.2.89	18	Sep
69.54	Giovanni	Sanguin	ITA	14.5.69	19	May
69.48	Collin	Post	USA	13.2.82	3	Jun
69.40	Zach	Hazen	USA	12.1.84	27	Apr
69.37	Markus	Kahlmeyer	GER	20.1.82	21	Apr
69.31	Lucais	MacKay	USA	13.4.81	9	Jun
69.30	Colin	Dunbar	USA	27.6.88	18	Jun
69.19		Park Young-sik	KOR	1.8.89	13	Oct
69.18	Trey	Henderson	CAN	10.10.89	23	Mar
69.17	Andrei	Alestar ¶	ROU	6.8.87	8	Jun
69.12	Kai	Räsänen	FIN	29.6.90	24	Mar
68.97	Marc	Felice	ITA	10.10.79	10	Jun
68.93	Brian	Richotte	USA	17.4.84	9	Jun
68.91		Wan Yong	CHN	22.7.87	23	Jun
68.90		Dan Zhangcheng	CHN	14.12.88	28	Apr
68.77	Justin	Welch	USA	29.9.91	15	Jun
68.74	Michael	Bomba	GBR	10.10.86	7	Apr
68.72	Arno	Laitinen	FIN	9.3.88	7	Mar
68.65	Nick	Welihozkiy	USA	12.2.81	30	May
68.55	Özkan	Baltaci	TUR-J	13.2.94	5	Jun
68.44	Fabaán	Di Paolo	ARG	25.11.83	31	Mar
68.35	Joachim	Koivu	FIN	5.9.88	24	Mar
68.30	Simon	Wardhaugh	AUS	14.1.86	26	Feb
68.08	Chris	Bennett	GBR	17.12.89	10	Jun
68.07	Kevin	Nabialek	FRA	16.12.86	27	Jun
68.06	Nikolay	Bashan	BLR	18.11.92	21	Apr
(158)						

JUNIORS

Mark	Name	Nat	Born	Pos	Meet	Venue	Date
74.20	Sukhrob Khodyayev	UZB	21.5.93	1	KAZ Ch	Almaty	18 Jun
72.06				1		Tashkent	1 Jun
68.45				1		Bishkek	10 Jun
70.26				1		Tashkent	18 Apr
68.55	Özkan Baltaci	TUR	13.2.94	3		Anakara	5 Jun
67.89	Ilmari Lahtinen	FIN	12.10.93	2		Kuortane	7 Mar
67.74	Jesse Lehto	FIN	12.2.93	4		Lapinlahti	8 Jul
67.56	Nick Miller	GBR	1.5.93	1		Wigan	1 Jul
67.44	Sergiy Reheda	UKR	6.2.94	3	NC-w23	Yalta	24 Mar
67.04	Alexandros Pousanides	CYP	23.1.93	3	NC	Lemesos	10 Jun
65.81	Juho Saarikoski	FIN	19.5.93	1		Helsinki	3 Sep
65.77	Bence Pásztor	HUN-Y	5.2.95	6	NC	Szekszárd	17 Jun
65.65	Bastian Abend (10)	GER	22.4.93	1		Halle	28 Jan
64.78	Valeriy Pronkin	RUS	15.6.94	3	u23	Adler	17 Feb

6KG HAMMER

Mark	Name	Nat	Born	Pos	Meet	Venue	Date
85.57	Ashraf Amgad El-Seify	QAT-Y	20.2.95	1	WJ	Barcelona	14 Jul
82.22				1		Doha	25 Apr
79.67				1	Gulf-j	Al Kuwait	4 Apr
80.85				1	Asi-J	Colombo	11 Jun
78.62				1	Arab-j	Amman	17 May
79.98				Q	WJ	Barcelona	13 Jul
79.39	Valeriy Pronkin	RUS	15.6.94	1		Adler	21 Apr
77.51				1		Adler	17 Feb
	12 performances by 6 men under 77m						
77.86	Alexandros Pousanides	CYP	23.1.93	1		Nicosia	22 Jun
77.70	Özkan Baltaci	TUR	13.2.94	1		Anakara	16 Jun
77.02	Bence Pásztor	HUN	5.2.95	1		Veszprém	20 May
77.02	Sergiy Reheda	UKR	6.2.94	1	NC-j	Yalta	31 May
76.16	Sukhrob Khodyayev	UZB	21.5.93	3	WJ	Barcelona	14 Jul
75.83	Igor Buryi	RUS	8.4.93	5	WJ	Barcelona	14 Jul
75.26	Ilmari Lahtinen	FIN	12.10.93	6	WJ	Barcelona	14 Jul
74.89	Juho Saarikoski (10)	FIN	19.5.93	7	WJ	Barcelona	14 Jul
74.37	Diego del Real	MEX	6.3.94	1	NC-j	Ciudad de México	13 May
74.11	Adam Kennan	CAN	26.3.93	1		Kamloops	22 Sep
73.76	Nick Miller	GBR	1.5.93	1		Livingston	30 Jun
73.73	Marco Bortolato	ITA	11.2.94	1		Lucca	25 Feb
73.34	Michael Painter	GBR	9.10.94	1		Norwich	1 Sep
73.27	Islam Ahmed Taha	EGY	23.7.93	1		Al Qahira	1 May
73.18	Rudy Winkler	USA	6.12.94	Q	WJ	Barcelona	13 Jul
73.09	Callum Brown	GBR	20.7.94	1		Mannheim	23 Jun
73.08	Oskar Vestlund	SWE	27.4.93	1		Trosa	27 May
72.66	Krisztián Árvai (20)	HUN	27.4.93	1		Veszprém	7 Jul
12lb (5.44kg) hammer: 76.53	Rudy Winkler	USA	6.12.94	1		West Point	7 May

JAVELIN

Mark	Name	Nat	Born	Pos	Meet	Venue	Date						
88.34	Vitezslav Vesely	CZE	27.2.83	Q	OG	London (OS)	8 Aug	88.34	p	p			
88.11				1	Bisl	Oslo	7 Jun	83.07	81.70	88.11	79.96	p	p
85.67				1	GS	Ostrava	25 May	84.91	80.69	84.16	85.67	84.51	x
85.66				1		Rovereto	4 Sep	78.47	x	77.58	77.96	x	85.66
85.40				1	DL	Shanghai	19 May	78.40	85.40	79.84	p	p	p
87.79	Antti Ruuskanen	FIN	21.2.84	1	NC	Lahti	26 Aug	74.69	78.90	79.83	79.60	83.71	87.79
85.67				2	vSWE	Göteborg	2 Sep	85.28	85.67	85.04	79.08	P	84.08
84.95				1		Tampere	10 Jun	x	73.40	x	75.97	81.36	84.95
84.12				3	OG	London (OS)	11 Aug	79.60	81.09	81.60	81.97	84.12	79.88
86.98	Tero Pitkämäki	FIN	19.12.82	1	DNG	Stockholm	17 Aug	x	79.79	76.31	77.69	86.98	p
86.86				1	vSWE	Göteborg	2 Sep	x	83.16	86.86	85.42	p	p
85.27				1	WK	Zürich	30 Aug	75.67	78.80	81.47	80.38	82.68	85.27
84.90				1		Kuortane	22 Jul	x	82.50	x	x	79.92	84.90
86.50	Vadims Vasilevskis	LAT	5.1.82	1		Valmiera	8 Jun	77.53	x	80.18	86.50	p	82.34
84.65				1	Pre	Eugene	2 Jun	77.27	83.44	81.87	x	80.31	84.65
86.31	Stuart Farquhar	NZL	15.3.82	1	Oda	Hiroshima	29 Apr	77.00	x	79.27	x	86.31	x
86.12	Oleksandr Pyatnytsya	UKR	14.7.85	1		Kyiv	20 May	81.90	81.74	83.60	79.60	86.12	x
85.67				1	DL	Saint-Denis	6 Jul	78.66	80.91	78.68	79.74	85.67	78.78
84.87				1	NC	Yalta	14 Jun	83.03	82.91	79.67	84.58	84.87	x
84.51				2	OG	London (OS)	11 Aug	77.47	81.61	84.51	81.53	81.01	83.53
84.32				Q	NC	Yalta	13 Jun	84.32	p	p			
85.60	Fatih Avan	TUR	1.1.89	1		Izmir	20 May	80.26	85.60	p	80.39	p	p

Mark	Name		Nat	Born	Pos	Meet	Venue		Date
85.03	Ivan	Zaytsev	UZB	11.11.88	1	Znam	Zhukovskiy		17 Jun
				80.59	83.92	82.36	85.03		
84.99	Pawel	Rakoczy	POL	15.5.87	1		Lódz		13 May
				79.40	80.39	80.10	84.99	x	x
84.72	Andreas	Thorkildsen (10)	NOR	1.4.82	2	GS	Ostrava		25 May
				x	78.03	84.14	77.56	84.72	p
84.47	Q OG	London (OS)		8 Aug	76.20	84.47	p		
84.62	Ari	Mannio	FIN	23.7.87	2	NC	Lahti		26 Aug
				77.51	x	78.94	82.23	x	84.62
84.31	Q EC	Helsinki		27 Jun	77.81	84.31	p		
84.58	Keshorn	Walcott	TRI-J	2.4.93	1	OG	London (OS)		11 Aug
				83.51	84.58	x	80.64	x	p
84.28	Genki	Dean	JPN	30.12.91	2	Oda	Hiroshima		29 Apr
	(30/13)			84.28	p	p	p	p	73.85
84.06	Zigismunds	Sirmais	LAT	6.5.92	1		Tartu		29 May
84.06	Lassi	Etelätalo	FIN	30.4.88	2		Kuortane		22 Jul
83.95	Yukifumi	Murakami	JPN	23.12.79	2	NC	Osaka		9 Jun
83.89	Bartosz	Osewski	POL	20.3.91	2		Lódz		13 May
83.89	Ainars	Kovals	LAT	21.11.81	1		Bauska		14 Jun
83.73	Teemu	Wirkkala	FIN	14.1.84	1		Raasepori		7 Jun
83.70	Jarrod	Bannister	AUS	3.10.84	3	DL	Saint Denis		6 Jul
	(20)								
83.39	Sergey	Makarov	RUS	19.3.73	1		Adler		18 Feb
83.23	Valeriy	Iordan	RUS	14.2.92	2	EC	Helsinki		28 Jun
83.02	Spirídon	Lebésis	GRE	30.5.87	1		Nicosia		19 May
82.86	Vladimir	Kozlov	BLR	20.4.85	1	NC	Grodno		6 Jul
82.75	Dmitriy	Tarabin	RUS	29.10.91	1		Daegu		16 May
82.73	Sean	Furey	USA	31.8.82	1		Lisle, IL		9 Jun
82.72	Guillermo	Martínez	CUB	28.6.81	1	NC	La Habana		23 Mar
82.58	Marcin	Krukowski	POL	14.6.92	1	NC-23	Pastek		15 Sep
82.37	Igor	Janik	POL	18.1.83	Q	EC	Helsinki		27 Jun
82.31	Craig	Kinsley	USA	19.1.89	2		Lisle, IL		9 Jun
	(30)								
82.25	Ihab Abdelrahman	Sayed	EGY	1.5.89	1		El Maadi		29 Nov
82.15	Mervyn	Luckwell	GBR	27.11.84	1		Loughborough		20 May
82.10	Tino	Häber	GER	6.10.82	2		St Wendel		10 Jun
82.10	Risto	Mätas	EST	30.4.84	1		Tallinn		8 Jul
82.05		Jung Sang-jin	KOR	16.4.84	1	NC	Daejeon		7 Jun
81.87	Roman	Avramenko	UKR	23.3.88	2	NC	Yalta		14 Jun
81.86	Sam	Humphreys	USA	12.9.90	1	NC/OT	Eugene		25 Jun
81.84	Kim	Amb	SWE	18.1.90	1		Växjö		25 May
81.81	Julius	Yego	KEN	4.1.89	Q	OG	London (OS)		8 Aug
81.74		Zhao Qinggang	CHN	24.7.85	1	NC	Kunshan		23 Sep
	(40)								
81.69	Tim	Glover	USA	1.11.90	1	NCAA	Des Moines		7 Jun
81.65	Oleksandr	Nychyporchuk	UKR	14.4.92	2		Kyiv		20 May
81.62	Matthias	de Zordo	GER	21.2.88	2		Shanghai		19 May
81.50	Mark	Frank	GER	21.6.77	1		Dessau		25 May
81.45	Gabriel	Wallin	SWE	14.10.81	1		Göteborg		14 Jun
81.35	Tom	Goyvaerts	BEL	20.3.84	1		Amsterdam		21 Jul
81.21	Curtis	Moss	CAN	12.4.87	1		Victoria		13 Jun
81.20	Rolands	Strobinders	LAT	14.4.92	1		Bauska		11 Aug
81.14	Petr	Frydrych	CZE	13.1.88	1		Tábor		8 Sep
81.02	Cyrus	Hostetler	USA	8.8.86	4	Pre	Eugene		2 Jun
	(50)								
80.95	Corey	White	USA	31.1.86	1		Tucson		19 May
80.81	Andreas	Hofmann	GER	16.12.91	1		Schutterwald		24 Jun
80.80	Sam	Crouser	USA	31.12.91	2	NC/OT	Eugene		25 Jun
80.79	Thomas	Röhler	GER	30.9.91	3		St Wendel		10 Jun
80.77		Qin Qiang	CHN	18.4.83	1		Zhaoqing		15 Apr
80.75	Tanel	Laanmäe	EST	29.9.89	1		Tallinn		3 Sep
80.61A	Dayron	Márquez	COL	19.11.83	1		Bogotá		30 Jun
80.60	Scott	Russell	CAN	16.1.79	1	KansR	Lawrence		20 Apr
80.60A	Arley	Ibargüen	COL	4.12.82	2		Bogotá		30 Jun
80.40	Jakub	Vadlejch	CZE	10.10.90	2		Potchefstroom		24 Mar
	(60)								
80.19	Leslie	Copeland	FIJ	23.4.88	13q	OG	London (OS)		8 Aug
80.14	Rajesh	Kumar Bind	IND-J	20.7.94	1	NC-j	Lucknow		27 Oct
79.90	Ken	Arai	JPN	22.12.81	4	Oda	Hiroshima		29 Apr
79.87	Braian	Toledo	ARG-J	8.9.93	1		Manresa		24 Jul
79.82	Yervásios	Filippídis ¶	GRE	24.7.87	1		Thessaloníki		19 May

Mark	Name		Nat	Born	Pos	Meet	Venue	Date
79.72	Lee	Doran	GBR	5.3.85	1	NC	Birmingham	23 Jun
79.71	Melik	Janoyan	ARM	24.3.85	2		Adler	18 Feb
79.61	Ilya	Korotkov	RUS	6.12.83	1	NC	Cheboksary	4 Jul
79.55	Lars	Hamann	GER	4.4.89	5		St Wendel	10 Jun
79.52	Sampo	Lehtola	FIN	10.5.89	3		Saarijärvi	23 Jun
	(70)							
79.41	Till	Wöschler	GER	9.6.91	1		Eisenberg	12 May
79.40	Lukasz	Grzeszczuk	POL	3.3.90	3		Lódz	13 May
79.33	Hamish	Peacock	AUS	15.10.90	1		Launceston	27 May
79.23		Jiang Xingyu	CHN	16.3.87	1		Wuhan	29 Apr
79.22	Norbert	Bonvecchio	ITA	14.8.85	1		Andorf	18 Aug
79.14	Harri	Haatainen	FIN	5.1.78	1		Urjala	6 Aug
79.11	Aleksey	Tovarnov	RUS	21.1.85	2	NC	Cheboksary	4 Jul
78.98	Timothy	Herman	BEL	19.10.90	1		Gentbrugge	4 Aug
78.97	Josh	Robinson	AUS	4.10.85	3		Melbourne	3 Mar
78.97	Martin	Benák	SVK	27.5.88	1	NC	Banská Bystrica	17 Jun
	(80)							
78.95	Marcin	Plener	POL	22.8.90	3	NC-23	Paslek	15 Sep
78.92		Wang Qingbo	CHN	24.5.88	1	NC	Kunshan	23 Sep
78.89	Patrik	Zenúch	SVK	30.12.90	1		Nitra	19 Sep
78.88	Jonas	Lohse	SWE	15.5.87	1		Mölndal	12 May
78.85	Ioánnis-Yeóryios	Smaliós	GRE	17.2.87	1		Helsingborg	30 Jun
78.82	Ahti	Peder	EST	29.8.76	1		Rakvere	22 Jul
78.80	Pawel	Rozinski	POL	11.7.87	1		Bialogard	28 Jul
78.60	Mihkel	Kukk	EST	8.10.83	2		Rakvere	22 Jul
78.60		Park Jae-myong	KOR	15.12.81	1		Daegu	15 Oct
78.53	Björn	Lange	GER	15.6.79	2		Dessau	25 May
	(90)							
78.45	Hubert	Chmielak	POL	19.6.89	2		Sopot	9 Jun
78.35	Jérôme	Haeffler	FRA	12.5.82	1		Saint-Denis, Réunion	11 Apr
78.17	Kazuki	Yamamoto	JPN	8.10.83	1		Kumagaya	19 May
78.16	Matthew	Outzen	AUS	12.10.87	1		Newcastle	21 Jan
78.00	Ryohei	Arai	JPN	23.6.91	1		Odawara	14 Oct
77.99	Joonas	Verronen	FIN	24.4.90	1		Haapajärvi	26 May
77.99	Barry	Krammes	USA	1.9.81	Q	NC/OT	Eugene	23 Jun
77.89	Stipe	Zunic	CRO	13.12.90	1	TexR	Austin	30 Mar
77.80	Sachith	Maduranga	SRI	15.6.90	1		Colombo	6 Jul
77.78		Chen Qi	CHN	10.3.82	4		Wuhan	29 Apr
	(100)							

Mark	Name		Nat	Born	Date		Mark	Name		Nat	Born	Date
77.76	Vedran	Samac	SRB	22.1.90	30 Jun		75.94	Jaka	Muhar	SLO-J	15.3.93	18 Mar
77.65	Bobur	Shokirjanov	UZB	5.12.90	24 Apr		75.91A	Ruan	Erasmus	RSA-J	9.2.93	25 Jan
77.59	Matija	Kranjc	SLO	12.6.84	18 Aug		75.84	Bernhard	Seifert	GER-J	15.2.93	13 Jul
77.52	Krisztián	Török	HUN	4.5.87	7 Jul		75.83	Matthias	Treff	GER	27.2.88	7 Jun
77.45	Dejan	Mileusnic	BIH	16.11.91	6 Jun		75.81	Dawid	Kosciów	POL	5.6.90	26 May
77.33	David	Golling	GER	13.3.90	15 Aug		75.75	Peter	Esenwein	GER	7.12.67	6 Jul
77.24	Giacomo	Puccini	ITA	4.4.89	22 Sep		75.73	Joe	Dunderdale	GBR	4.9.92	17 Jun
77.18	Robert	Oosthuizen	RSA	23.1.87	14 Jun		75.72	Karol	Jakimowicz	POL	15.6.87	16 Jun
77.17	Kyle	Nielsen	CAN	22.4.89	17 May		75.69	Leonardo	Gottardo	ITA	21.3.88	31 Mar
77.17	Nikolay	Vasilyachov	BLR	24.5.82	18 Jul		75.67	Daan	Meijer	NED	17.2.83	8 Sep
77.14	Juan José	Méndez	MEX	27.4.88	10 Mar		75.66	Júlio César	de Oliveira	BRA	4.2.86	3 May
77.12	Sean	Keller	USA-J	13.10.93	23 Jun		75.66	Bence	Papp	HUN	5.9.85	16 Jun
77.10		Cheng Chao-Tsun	TPE-J	17.10.93	16 Nov		75.60	Martins	Pildavs	LAT	6.7.88	14 Apr
77.08	Jayson	Henning	RSA	13.8.90	20 Apr		75.55	Tiago	Aperta	POR	15.1.92	18 Mar
77.01	Igor	Sukhomlinov	RUS	13.2.77	17 Jun		75.52	Daniel	Pembroke	GBR	16.7.91	13 May
76.98	Mika	Aalto	FIN	11.3.82	22 Jul		75.41	Raymond	Dykstra	CAN	18.6.92	30 Mar
76.97	Magnus	Kirt	EST	10.4.90	19 Aug		75.41	Manuel	Nau	GER	2.7.77	15 Jul
76.94	Leonel	Suárez	CUB	1.9.87	9 Aug		75.35		Song Bin	CHN	30.9.90	24 Jun
76.73	Diego	Moraga	CHI	6.10.76	1 Apr		75.24	Bjorn	Blommerde	NED	6.7.87	19 May
76.71	Sami	Peltomäki	FIN	11.1.91	6 Jul		75.21	Luke	Cann	AUS-J	17.7.94	24 Feb
76.70	Aleksandr	Ashomko	BLR	18.2.84	24 Feb		75.21	Billy	Stanley	USA-J	6.2.94	26 May
76.57	Rinat	Tarzumanov	UZB	26.3.84	14 May		75.19	Andy	Fahringer	USA	30.5.89	12 May
76.54		Huang Shih-Feng	TPE	2.3.92	16 Nov		75.15	Víctor	Fatecha	PAR	10.3.88	9 Jun
76.49A	Noraldo	Palacios	COL	8.7.80	28 Apr		75.14	Aris	Borjas	USA	28.9.84	9 Jun
76.49	Eriks	Rags	LAT	1.6.75	7 Jul		75.09	Davinder	Singh	IND	.91	13 Sep
76.40	Mustafa	Tan	TUR	10.4.90	6 May		75.06	Killian	Duréchou	FRA	15.8.92	15 Jun
76.29	Morné	Moolman	RSA-J	1.9.94	13 Jul		75.05	Yuriy	Kushniruk	UKR-J	6.12.94	14 Jun
76.18	Yoshihiro	Nakajima	JPN-J	12.3.93	12 May		75.00	Ansis	Bruns	LAT	30.3.89	10 Mar
76.16	Mike	Hazle	USA	22.3.79	21 Jan		74.97	Levente	Bartha	ROU	8.3.77	21 Jul
76.13		Zhao Pengju	CHN	6.2.88	23 Sep		74.92	Jens	Merseburg	GER	1.1.88	21 Apr
76.12	Rajender	Singh Dalvir	IND	5.4.89	23 Apr		74.92		Dai Li	CHN	20.5.91	13 May
76.03	Brian	Chaput	USA	9.4.81	7 Apr		74.90	Timo	Moorast	EST	26.3.86	24 May
76.02	Shuya	Inui	JPN	29.7.91	13 May		74.86	Naoya	Imada	JPN	22.5.90	12 May
76.02	Yuya	Koriki	JPN	19.10.89	8 Oct		74.84	Ignacio	Guerra	CHI	15.9.87	7 Jun
75.96	Örn	Davídssn	ISL	17.3.90	24 Jun		74.83	Intars	Isejevs	LAT-J	15.2.93	14 Jun

Mark	Name		Nat	Born	Pos	Meet	Venue	Date
74.82	Yasuo	Ikeda	JPN	28.7.77				8 Oct
74.78	Anil	Singh Kumar	IND	4.3.85				23 Apr
74.78	Ben	Chretien	USA	9.5.89				7 Jun
74.74	Marko	Jänes	EST	29.8.76				27 Jun
74.66	Ben	Baker	AUS	19.1.83				15 Apr
74.64		Park Won-kil	KOR	24.2.90				15 Oct
74.62	Sergiy	Dyachok	UKR	12.6.90				24 Feb
74.59	Thomas	Smet	BEL	12.7.88				12 May
74.57	Jitender	Singh	IND	5.12.92				13 Sep
74.54	Toni	Sirviö	FIN	8.1.92				17 Jun
74.51	Johannes	Swanepoel	RSA	12.9.91				20 Apr
74.47	Kohei	Hasegawa	JPN	1.1.90				7 Jul
74.38	Mykola	Shama	UKR	5.4.91				13 Jun
74.36A	José	Lagunes	MEX	30.6.85				24 Mar
74.35	Roberto	Bertolini	ITA	10.9.85				22 Sep
74.34	Jarkko	Koski-Vähälä	FIN	21.11.78				1 Sep
74.34		Hu Hailong	CHN	26.8.88				23 Sep
74.30	Brian	Moore	USA	5.9.88				31 Mar
74.28		Sun Jianjun	CHN	9.6.91				24 Jun
74.26		Yan Zekun	CHN	5.5.89				27 May
74.20	Sho	Tanaka	JPN-J	28.2.94				13 May
74.18	Ranno	Koorep	EST	24.1.90				3 Jun
74.12	Benjamin	Woodruff	USA	9.5.89				13 Apr
74.12	Peerachet	Janthra	THA	9.9.90				17 Dec
74.12	Yutaro	Tanemoto	JPN	30.11.84				3 Nov
74.11	Pasi	Kuusinen	FIN	8.5.81				30 May
74.09	Gudmundur	Hólmar Sverrisson	ISL	24.5.90				22 Jul
74.07	Viktor	Goncharov	RUS	9.5.91				21 Jul
74.05	Povilas	Dabasinskas	LTU-J	16.6.94				22 May
(199)								

Drugs disqualification

76.73	Rohit	Kumar ¶	IND-J	15.7.94				23 Apr

JUNIORS

See main list for top 3 juniors. 12 performances by 3 men to 77.83. Additional marks and further juniors:

Name	Mark	Pos	Meet	Venue	Date
Walcott	82.83	1	CAC-J	San Salvador	1 Jul
	81.75	Q	OG	London (OS)	8 Aug
	80.11	1		La Habana	27 May
	78.94	1		Port of Spain	19 May
	78.64	1	WJ	Barcelona	13 Jul
Toledo	79.73	1		Buenos Aires	3 May
	78.57	1		Mar del Plata	29 Apr
	78.49	1	SAm23	São Paulo	23 Sep
	77.83	1		Buenos Aires	19 May

Mark	Name	Nat	Born	Pos	Meet	Venue	Date
77.12	Sean Keller	USA-J	13.10.93	Q	NC/OT	Eugene	23 Jun
77.10	Cheng Chao-Tsun	TPE	17.10.93	1		Kinmen	16 Nov
76.29	Morné Moolman	RSA	1.9.94	3	WJ	Barcelona	13 Jul
76.18	Yoshihiro Nakajima	JPN	12.3.93	2		Tokyo	12 May
75.94	Jaka Muhar	SLO	15.3.93	2	ECp-w23	Bar	18 Mar
75.91A	Ruan Erasmus	RSA	9.2.93	1		Potchefstroom	25 Jan
75.84	Bernhard Seifert (10)	GER	15.2.93	4	WJ	Barcelona	13 Jul
75.21	Luke Cann	AUS	17.7.94	1		Melbourne	24 Feb
75.21	Billy Stanley	USA	6.2.94	1		Shippensburg	26 May
75.05	Yuriy Kushniruk	UKR	6.12.94	4	NC	Yalta	14 Jun
74.83	Intars Isejevs	LAT	15.2.93	1	Lusis-j	Bauska	14 Jun
74.20	Sho Tanaka	JPN	28.2.94	2		Osaka	13 May
74.05	Povilas Dabasinskas	LTU	16.6.94	1		Kaunas	22 May
73.87	Joni Karvinen	FIN	7.2.94	1		Virrat	5 Sep
73.57	William White	AUS	6.6.94	2		Melbourne	25 Feb
73.38	Håkon Løvenskiold Kveseth	NOR	19.4.93	1	NC-j	Sigdla	29 Jul
73.05	Paulo da Silva (20)	BRA	28.9.93	1	NC-23	Maringá	9 Sep

Drugs disqualification: 76.73   Rohit Kumar ¶   IND-J   15.7.94   (1)   Patiala   23 Apr

DECATHLON

9039   Ashton Eaton   USA   21.1.88   1   NC/OT   Eugene   23 Jun
10.21/0.4   8.23/0.8   14.20   2.05   46.70   13.70/-0.8   42.81   5.30   58.87   4:14.48

8869   Eaton   1   OG   London (OS)   9 Aug
10.35/0.4   8.03/0.8   14.66   2.05   46.90   13.56/0.1   42.53   5.20   61.96   4:33.59

8671   Trey Hardee   USA   7.2.84   2   OG   London (OS)   9 Aug
10.42/0.4   7.53/1.1   15.28   1.99   48.11   13.54/0.1   48.26   4.80   66.65   4:40.94

8558   Pascal Behrenbruch   GER   19.1.85   1   EC   Helsinki   28 Jun
10.93/0.8   7.15/-0.8   16.89   1.97   48.54   14.16/0.2   48.24   5.00   67.45   4:34.02

8523   Leonel Suárez   CUB   1.9.87   3   OG   London (OS)   9 Aug
11.27/0.7   7.52/0.5   14.50   2.11   49.04   14.45/1.0   45.75   4.70   76.94   4:30.08

8519   Hans Van Alphen   BEL   12.1.82   1   Götzis   27 May
10.96/1.0   7.62/1.1   15.23   2.06   49.54   14.55/0.4   45.45   4.96   64.15   4:20.87

8506   Eelco Sintnicolaas   NED   7.4.87   2   Götzis   27 May
10.77/-0.7   7.27/-1.6   14.20   2.00   48.02   14.10/0.8   42.81   5.36   63.59   4:26.98

8447w/8415   Kevin Mayer   FRA   10.2.92   1   Bruxelles   1 Jul
11.19/1.1   7.63w/5.7 & 7.50/1.3   13.23   2.09   48.75   14.21/1.6   43.13   5.15   61.58   4:18.04

8447   Van Alphen   4   OG   London (OS)   9 Aug
11.05/-0.7   7.64/1.5   15.48   2.05   49.18   14.89/1.0   48.28   4.80   61.69   4:22.50

8442   Damian Warner   CAN   4.10.89   5   OG   London (OS)   9 Aug
10.48/0.4   7.54/0.9   13.73   2.05   48.20   14.38/0.1   45.90   4.70   62.77   4:29.85

8433   Behrenbruch   3   Götzis   27 May
11.11/-0.6   7.09/-0.2   16.26   2.03   48.64   14.19/0.7   47.99   4.86   66.72   4:36.88

8383   Hardee   2   NC/OT   Eugene   23 Jun
10.50/0.4   7.55/1.0   15.72   1.99   49.11   13.71/-0.8   49.05   5.00   57.00   5:08.67

8365   Sergey Sviridov   RUS   20.10.90   1   NCp   Adler   8 May
10.88/1.2   7.52/1.2   15.03   1.94   48.28   14.83/0.5   49.01   4.40   68.89   4:25.15

8322   Rico Freimuth (10)   GER   14.3.88   4   Götzis   27 May
10.62/-0.7   7.16/-0.7   15.14   1.91   47.51   13.79/0.7   47.26   4.86   58.05   4:40.55

Mark	Name		Nat	Born	Pos	Meet	Venue			Date
8321	Oleksiy	Kasyanov	UKR	26.8.85	2	EC	Helsinki			28 Jun
	10.57/0.8	7.49/1.9 14.38	2.00	48.07		14.23/0.2	47.75	4.80	52.37	4:32.66
8320		Freimuth			6	OG	London (OS)			9 Aug
	10.65/0.4	7.21/-0.1 14.87	1.90	48.06		13.89/0.1	49.11	4.90	57.37	4:37.62
8293		Van Alphen			1		Talence			16 Sep
	11.09/0.9	7.27/0.1 15.29	2.01	49.06		14.96/-0.8	48.92	4.72	65.76	4:30.22
8289		Suárez			5		Götzis			27 May
	11.35/-0.6	6.85/0.2 13.95	2.09	49.33		14.34/0.7	44.71	4.86	71.99	4:23.26
8283		Kasyanov			7	OG	London (OS)			9 Aug
	10.56/0.4	7.55/-0.4 14.45	1.99	48.44		14.09/-0.4	46.72	4.60	54.87	4:33.68
8276	Luiz Alberto	de Araújo	BRA	27.9.87	1	NC	São Paulo			30 Jun
	10.80	7.39 14.93	1.98	48.54		14.12	46.15	4.90	52.11	4.27.75
8244	Willem	Coertzen	RSA	30.12.82	1	NC	Port Elizabeth			14 Apr
	11.18/0.1	7.47/0.0 13.85	2.04	49.39		14.34/0.1	43.47	4.63	66.95	4:23.75
8228	Jan Felix	Knobel	GER	16.1.89	2		Ratingen			15 Jun
	11.04/0.6	7.21/-0.5 15.89	1.94	48.89		14.61w/2.4	43.56	4.90	71.38	4:48.24
8224	Ingmar	Vos	NED	28.5.86	6		Götzis			27 May
	10.92/-1.5	7.36/0.8 14.14	2.06	49.50		14.35/1.4	43.31	4.76	63.89	4:34.47
8219	Ilya	Shkurenov	RUS	11.1.91	3	EC	Helsinki			28 Jun
	10.98/0.8	7.32/0.7 13.16	2.06	49.92		14.24/0.2	44.82	5.20	56.70	4:30.41
8219		Sviridov			8	OG	London (OS)			9 Aug
	10.78/-0.7	7.45/-2.1 14.42	1.99	48.91		15.42/-0.9	47.43	4.60	68.42	4:36.63
8218		Kasyanov			2		Talence			16 Sep
	10.66/0.9	7.54/0.3 14.95	1.95	48.76		14.41/-0.5	47.51	4.82	52.59	4:38.03
8173	Dmitriy	Karpov	KAZ	23.7.81	1		Kladno			10 Jun
	11.12/-1.2	7.14w/4.0 16.12	2.04	48.86		14.26/0.0	51.58	4.77	50.45	4:45.52
8173		Coertzen			9	OG	London (OS)			9 Aug
	11.09/0.7	7.17/0.7 13.79	2.05	48.56		14.15/1.0	43.58	4.50	64.79	4:26.52
8172		Karpov		(30/17)	1		Desenzano			6 May
	11.04/0.4	7.26/-0.9 16.22	2.01	49.30		14.41/0.6	50.75	5.15	50.48	5:00.22
8154	Mihail	Dudas	SRB	1.11.89	4	EC	Helsinki			28 Jun
	10.81/0.8	7.36/-1.3 13.64	1.97	48.02		14.78/-0.5	43.55	4.80	59.98	4:27.54
8130	Kai	Kazmirek	GER	28.1.91	1	vUSA	Marburg			22 Jul
	10.86/1.4	740/1.1 1342	2.07	47.53		14.94/0.4	39.47	5.05	56.52	4:35.09
8118	Florian	Geffrouais	FRA	5.12.88	1	NC	Angers			16 Jun
	11.18/0.2	7.04/-0.3 15.15	1.93	49.43		14.97/0.6	47.65	4.90	58.44	4:17.97
(20)										
8102	Daniel	Awde	GBR	22.6.88	1		Arona			27 May
	10.87/-1.1	7.47/-0.1 13.67	1.91	47.14		14.44/0.5	42.88	4.70	54.55	4:23.66
8098	Gaël	Quérin	FRA	26.6.87	5	EC	Helsinki			28 Jun
	11.17/0.7	7.56/0.4 13.05	1.97	48.20		14.37/-0.5	40.32	5.00	53.60	4:17.29
8097	Roman	Sebrle	CZE	26.11.74	2		Kladno			10 Jun
	11.38/-1.1	7.49w/2.8 15.47	2.01	51.14		14.61/0.0	44.78	4.77	66.93	4:44.86
8080	Artem	Lukyanenko	RUS	30.1.90	2	NCp	Adler			8 May
	10.97/1.2	7.40/1.2 14.34	2.03	49.50		14.15/0.5	39.83	4.70	62.37	4:40.63
8073	Pelle	Rietveld	NED	4.2.85	3		Kladno			10 Jun
	10.98/-1.2	7.19/1.6 14.35	1.86	47.78		14.09/0.0	41.51	4.97	60.65	4:37.93
8070	Aleksandr	Tabala	RUS	23.5.86	3	NCp	Adler			8 May
	11.73/1.2	7.02/0.8 15.29	2.06	51.87		14.78/0.5	47.37	5.00	64.16	4:29.65
8067	Isaac	Murphy	USA	5.10.90	1	TexR	Austin			29 Mar
	10.47/1.5	7.53/1.3 13.07	1.87	48.01		14.42/1.3	41.71	4.90	52.12	4:28.44
8065	Gonzalo	Barroilhet	CHI	19.8.86	1		Charlottesville			20 Apr
	10.99/0.8	6.96/0.0 14.34	2.06	50.84		14.14/0.2	45.22	5.30	54.70	4:49.19
8064	Adam Sebastian	Helcelet	CZE	27.10.91	3		Talence			16 Sep
	11.10/0.8	7.26/0.3 14.28	2.07	49.09		14.48/-0.8	41.33	4.82	60.46	4:40.98
8062	Kurt	Felix	GRN	4.7.88	1	NCAA	Des Moines			7 Jun
	10.90w/3.0	7.40/-2.4 13.08	2.05	48.77		15.01/1.4	41.51	4.60	69.36	4:42.93
(30)										
8061	Yordani	García	CUB	21.11.88	7		Götzis			27 May
	10.94/-0.7	6.56/0.9 14.99	2.06	49.30		14.37/0.7	41.96	4.66	65.36	4:33.10
8059	Vasiliy	Kharlamov	RUS	8.10.86	2	NC	Cheboksary			3 Jun
	11.38/0.0	7.37/0.0 15.49	1.94	49.55		14.83/0.8	47.45	4.60	65.00	4:39.37
8057	Brent	Newdick	NZL	31.1.85	1	AUS Ch	Melbourne			14 Apr
	11.02/-0.7	7.56/1.6 14.48	1.95	49.22		14.55/0.0	48.25	4.70	56.43	4:46.21
8055	Nikolay	Shubyanok	BLR	4.5.85	1		Asikkala			5 Aug
	11.48/0.2	7.14/0.2 14.97	2.07	50.59		14.58/-0.4	43.50	4.80	63.65	4:32.59
8037	Keisuke	Ushiro	JPN	24.7.86	1	NC	Nagano			3 Jun
	11.29/1.2	7.45/1.6 13.89	2.03	50.58		15.01/-1.7	47.25	4.70	66.27	4:42.63
8034	Norman	Müller	GER	7.8.85	8		Götzis			27 May
	10.90/1.0	7.29/0.8 14.55	2.00	49.55		14.94/0.4	40.38	5.06	56.90	4:33.86

Mark		Name			Nat	Born	Pos	Meet	Venue			Date
8008		Bastien	Auzeil		FRA	22.10.89	3		Cannes			13 May
		11.19/0.9	7.21/1.8	15.65	2.01	50.51		14.81w/2.4 46.93	5.10	55.96		4:54.35
8003		Attila	Szabó		HUN	16.7.84	1		Budapest			3 Jul
		11.25/-2.7	7.28/1.5	15.22	1.92	49.83		14.87/1.0 45.32	4.55	68.87		4:40.77
7981		Darius	Draudvila		LTU	29.3.83	1	BLR Ch	Grodno			7 Jul
		10.98/0.1	7.24w/3.2	15.40	1.91	48.78		14.07/-0.7 49.03	4.50	53.54		4:49.84
7977		Romain	Martin		FRA	12.7.88	2	TexR	Austin			29 Mar
		10.98/1.5	7.22/1.1	12.92	2.05	49.12		14.51/0.6 37.77	5.00	61.37		4:39.90
	(40)											
7956		Yunior	Díaz		CUB	28.4.87	1	NC	La Habana			23 Mar
		11.27/-1.2	7.74/0.9	14.10	1.95	47.59		15.06/0.0 44.00	4.50	57.84		4:39.04
7955		Kevin	Lazas		USA	25.1.92	3	NCAA	Des Moines			7 Jun
		11.05/0.4	7.33/-0.4	14.09	1.99	51.34		15.12/0.9 40.71	5.10	60.09		4:31.33
7954		Gray	Horn		USA	18.2.90	3	NC/OT	Eugene			23 Jun
		10.93/0.4	7.60/0.0	13.49	1.96	50.66		14.41/0.8 38.34	5.00	56.31		4:33.02
7942		Mathias	Brugger		GER	6.8.92	1		Ulm			25 May
		10.99/0.0	7.29/1.3	13.91	2.03	48.64		14.65/-0.5 43.51	4.70	49.65		4:31.67
7932	(w)	Wesley	Bray		USA	11.4.88	3	TexR	Austin			29 Mar
		10.94w/2.2	7.43w/2.2	13.99	1.87	49.90		14.71/1.8 41.75	4.70	61.70		4:30.88
7931		Joe	Detmer		USA	3.9.83	4	NC/OT	Eugene			23 Jun
		10.97/0.1	7.38/0.0	13.18	1.90	49.14		14.92/-1.1 40.30	4.90	54.39		4:14.77
7928		Eduard	Mikhon		BLR	7.6.89	17	OG	London (OS)			9 Aug
		10.74/0.4	6.94/-0.1	14.75	1.93	48.42		14.15/-0.4 44.42	4.40	55.69		4:38.06
7911		Jérémy	Lelièvre		FRA	8.2.91	1	NC-23	Aubagne			8 Jul
		10.83/2.7	7.26/1.6	14.39	1.87	48.77		15.21/1.1 43.03	4.65	58.43		4:28.07
7898		Einar Dadi	Lárusson		ISL	10.5.90	5		Kladno			10 Jun
		11.23/-1.1	7.35/1.6	13.99	2.04	49.16		14.49/0.0 38.74	4.77	56.03		4:37.12
7897		Björn	Barrefors		SWE	27.10.87	1	Big 10	Madison			12 May
		11.04/3.5	7.57/1.7	13.49	2.02	50.22		14.46/0.3 46.27	5.06	46.29		4:53.41
	(50)											
7892		Gunnar	Nixon		USA-J	13.1.93	5	NCAA	Des Moines			7 Jun
		10.93w/3.0	7.25/-1.4	13.73	2.05	48.92		14.51/1.0 36.48	4.60	56.12		4:30.41
7884		Johannes	Hock		GER	24.3.92	2	NC	Hannover			26 Aug
		10.98/-0.4)	7.08/1.2	15.49	1.85	49.61		15.02/0.4 49.42	4.60	61.40		4:51.54
7879		Simon	Hechler		GER	15.6.88	10		Götzis			27 May
		10.89/-0.7	7.41/-0.8	13.13	1.91	50.61		14.74/1.4 41.99	4.76	61.58		4:35.20
7877		Steffen	Kahlert		GER	30.5.87	2		Ulm			25 May
		11.20/0.0	7.17/-0.4	14.48	1.91	50.00		14.82/-0.5 42.87	5.20	53.19		4:35.64
7872		David	Gómez		ESP	13.2.81	1		Vigo			7 Jul
		11.08/1.0	7.34/0.5	13.43	1.97	49.98		14.50/1.4 38.25	4.62	60.50		4:26.66
7870		Mikhail	Logvinenko		RUS	19.4.84	4	NC	Cheboksary			3 Jun
		11.06/1.6	7.21/0.8	14.41	1.97	49.07		14.47/0.0 44.63	5.00	43.78		4:43.78
7863		Mathias	Prey		GER	9.8.88	3		Ulm			25 May
		11.22/0.0	7.66/0.5	15.59	1.85	49.89		15.06/-0.5 47.79	4.20	58.50		4:35.96
7862		Jack	Szmanda		USA	15.3.90	2	Big 10	Madison			12 May
		11.14/0.4	6.93w/2.4	13.81	1.96	50.01		14.99/1.3 42.40	5.16	54.44		4:27.93
7861		Yevgeniy	Sarantsev		RUS	5.8.88	4	NCp	Adler			8 May
		11.16/1.2	6.94/1.2	14.91	2.00	50.25		14.89/0.5 44.76	4.50	63.47		4:41.28
7857		Petter	Olson		SWE	14.2.91	5	TexR	Austin			29 Mar
		10.90/1.5	7.12w/2.8	13.60	1.90	48.40		14.49/0.6 37.16	4.80	57.13		4:27.57
	(60)											
7857		Igor	Sarcevic		SRB	25.8.84	1	NC	Novi Sad			7 May
		11.03/-0.2	7.21/+1.4	14.55	2.01	50.14		14.38/-3.4 40.50	5.10	52.60		4:55.34
7844		Stephen	Cain		AUS	23.7.84	1		Melbourne			26 Feb
		11.23w/2.1	6.69/0.0	13.90	1.97	50.50		14.80/0.8 43.99	4.80	64.10		4:31.5
7840		Chris	Randolph		USA	25.4.84	1		Santa Barbara			3 Apr
		11.41/0.0	6.98	14.44	1.93	49.34		15.13/-1.0 43.34	4.60	64.32		4:27.61
7840		Jake	Arnold		USA	3.1.84	1		Dallas			3 Jun
		10.93/1.8	6.36/1.2	13.78	1.90	49.96		14.32w/2.2 44.59	5.15	59.79		4:41.81
7837		Ashley	Bryant		GBR	17.5.91	12		Götzis			27 May
		11.02/1.0	7.38/1.1	13.42	1.82	48.87		14.69/1.4 39.70	4.56	69.26		4:41.47
7833		José Angel	Mendieta		CUB	16.10.91	1		La Habana			5 May
		10.50/0.3	7.01/1.0	15.28	1.96	50.88		14.41/0.9 41.03	4.40	62.65		4:47.68
7832		Dave	Grzesiak		USA	28.7.88	3	Big 10	Madison			12 May
		11.36w/3.5	6.92/1.6	13.40	2.11	49.47		14.78/0.3 36.37	4.96	56.35		4:26.10
7829		Jonas	Fringeli		SUI	12.1.88	1		Ibach			17 Jun
		11.08w/2.2	6.80/-0.4	12.69	2.01	48.68		14.45/0.0 39.90	4.80	53.39		4:19.59
7828		Ivan	Grigoryev		RUS	27.10.89	5	NC	Cheboksary			3 Jun
		10.84/1.6	7.12/0.2	12.96	1.97	49.52		15.18/0.6 41.12	4.70	59.54		4:29.74

Mark	Name		Nat	Born	Pos	Meet	Venue	Date
7823	Marcus	Nilsson	SWE	3.5.91	6	NCAA	Des Moines	7 Jun
	11.12w/3.2 6.91/-0.4 12.76	2.02 49.69	15.24/-0.6 42.40 4.80 56.45					4:18.01
	(70)							
7797	André	Niklaus	GER	30.8.81	4		Ulm	25 May
	11.47/0.0 6.94/0.3 14.02	1.97 51.41	14.70/-0.4 45.84 4.90 62.30					4:43.45
7793	Dakotah	Keys	USA	27.9.91	1	Pac-12	Eugene	6 May
	11.16/1.4 7.20/1.6 12.86	2.06 51.11	14.88/1.1 36.92 4.80 63.38					4:33.84
7789	Aleksandr	Parkhomenko	BLR	22.3.81	2	NC	Minsk (Staiki)	31 May
	11.44/0.3 6.89/0.3 14.65	1.91 50.99	15.59/1.5 46.32 4.70 67.48					4:32.02
7769		Kim Kun-woo	KOR	29.2.80	1		Changwon	21 Jun
	11.27/ -0.2 7.33/+1.3 13.27	1.91 49.49	15.27/-1.4 40.70 5.00 53.03					4:22.30
7764	Curtis	Beach	USA	22.7.90	2		Charlottesville	20 Apr
	10.90/0.8 7.56w/2.5 11.41	1.88 46.96	14.59/0.2 37.66 4.60 47.88					4:15.81
7750w/7736	Eric	Broadbent	USA	5.8.85	2	MSR	Azusa	19 Apr
	10.87w/2.3 7.38w/3.8 & 7.32/2.9 13.39	2.18 49.15	14.64/0.1 38.07 4.20 46.56					4:35.82
7744		Chris Helwick	USA	18.3.85	5	NC/OT	Eugene	23 Jun
	11.49/-0.2 6.78/-0.6 14.25	1.93 51.97	15.30/0.8 43.61 4.90 68.37					4:33.85
7739	Derek	Steinbach	USA	18.11.88	4	Big 10	Madison	12 May
	11.15/0.4 6.97w/2.5 14.44	1.87 50.93	14.94/1.3 41.62 4.76 64.21					4:37.23
7733	Scott	McLaren	NZL	22.2.82	14		Götzis	27 May
	11.18/-0.1 6.87/1.0 14.45	1.88 50.03	15.14/0.4 43.43 4.76 60.45					4:34.63
7729	Hadi	Sepehrzad	IRI	19.1.83	1		Tehran	25 May
	10.82 6.94 16.24	1.94 49.82	14.80 49.11 4.40 52.66					5:09.59
	(80)							
7725	Anatoliy	Koshar	BLR	11.6.89	2		Asikkala	5 Aug
	11.51/0.2 6.97/-0.3 14.35	2.07 50.64	15.10/-0.4 43.81 4.50 60.94					4:41.01
7721(w)	Matthew	Johnson	USA	4.10.89	2		Dallas	3 Jun
	10.63/1.8 7.52w/2.7 12.69	1.96 50.33	14.60w/2.2 35.29 4.65 58.91					4:48.25
7720	Aleksandr	Korzun	BLR	17.3.85	3	NC	Minsk (Staiki)	31 May
	10.88/0.3 6.71/-0.5 13.05	2.00 48.96	14.41/1.5 40.85 4.90 55.40					4:53.67
7720	Maximilian	Gilde	GER	5.1.90	5		Ratingen	15 Jun
	11.32/0.1 7.31/0.1 13.28	1.91 50.14	14.76w/2.2 40.53 4.50 66.72					4:41.20
7715	Ryan	Harlan	USA	25.4.81	6	NC/OT	Eugene	23 Jun
	11.26/-0.2 6.74/-1.0 15.48	2.02 50.78	14.43/0.8 44.70 4.80 60.73					5:18.20
7712	Miller	Moss	USA	14.3.88	7	NC/OT	Eugene	23 Jun
	10.85/0.4 6.91/-1.4 14.03	1.87 49.62	14.91/-0.8 44.76 4.70 53.22					4:36.84
7710	Akihiko	Nakamura	JPN	23.10.90	2	NC	Nagano	3 Jun
	10.81/0.6 7.08/0.0 11.94	2.03 47.17	14.11/1.7 32.61 4.20 50.05					4:14.09
7708	Patrick	Spinner	GER	28.11.85	6		Ratingen	15 Jun
	11.11/0.6 7.22/0.1 14.27	1.91 50.57	15.09w/2.2 39.71 4.40 67.70					4:42.31
7706	Jamie	Adjetey-Nelson	CAN	20.5.84	2		Tucson	30 Mar
	10.86/0.0 7.26/0.0 15.47	2.02 50.53	14.96/0.5 43.19 4.20 57.80					5:02.60
7705	Corbin	Duer	USA	29.11.88	1		Walnut	27 May
	11.27 6.99w/2.1 12.73	1.99 50.30	15.06/0.9 43.15 4.95 56.82					4:38.36
	(90)							
7703	Attila	Zsivoczky-Pandel	HUN	29.4.77	1		Budapest	16 Sep
	11.33/1.9 7.12w/3.6 15.34	2.02 51.71	15.26/-0.4 43.45 4.20 60.81					4:32.91
7692		Guo Qi	CHN	28.12.90	1		Fuzhou	24 Jun
	11.33/-0.4 7.14w/2.9 13.60	2.03 49.71	14.64/-0.3 40.99 4.70 53.26					4:43.57
7684	Matthew	Clark	USA	31.5.87	3		Dallas	3 Jun
	10.97/1.8 6.90/0.6 13.06	1.96 50.55	16.07w/2.4 42.36 4.75 63.91					4:32.06
7670	Rudy	Bourguignon	FRA	16.7.79	4		Cannes	13 May
	11.11/2.0 6.69/0.6 14.33	1.89 50.57	15.47/2.4 45.21 4.90 58.85					4:39.37
7664	Dominik	Distelberger	AUT	16.3.90	1		Nieuwpoort	8 Jul
	10.92/-1.7 7.30/0.1 12.38	1.89 48.60	14.91/0.4 40.51 4.90 52.63					4:46.13
7662	Ben	Hazell	GBR	1.10.84	1		Barcelona	6 May
	11.29/0.7 6.90/1.1 13.71	1.98 50.81	15.42/0.4 46.09 4.40 58.91					4:27.49
7662	Hendrik	Lepik	EST	18.4.90	1	NC	Rakvere	29 Jul
	11.30/0.9 7.58/2.0 13.89	2.09 51.97	15.06w/2.8 35.70 5.05 52.97					4:53.51
7655	Franck	Logel	FRA	8.1.85	2	AUS Ch	Melbourne	14 Apr
	11.30/-0.7 7.19/1.3 13.10	2.01 50.91	14.56/0.0 43.08 4.80 50.66					4:42.45
7649	Edgars	Erins	LAT	18.6.86	22	OG	London (OS)	9 Aug
	10.99/0.7 6.98/0.6 13.45	1.93 50.62	15.22/-0.9 45.10 4.50 57.35					4:35.88
7648	Lars-Niklas	Heinke	GER	7.11.89	9		Ratingen	15 Jun
	11.11/0.6 7.13/-0.4 12.49	1.79 49.81	14.84w/2.2 41.77 5.00 58.22					4:37.21
	(100)							

Mark	Name		Nat	Born	Date		Mark	Name		Nat	Born	Date
7644	Tarmo	Riitmuru	EST	31.1.86	28 Jun		7635	Heath	Nickles	USA	10.3.89	12 May
7642	Ánderson	Venâncio	BRA	6.1.87	20 May		7632	Nick	Huber	USA	7.6.89	6 May
7638	Cedric	Nolf	BEL	18.6.89	27 May		7630A	Jeff	Mohl	USA	28.3.91	10 May
7636	Timothy	Wunderlich	USA	2.4.87	3 Jun		7629	Daniel	Gooris	USA	28.9.89	7 Jun
7636	Sami	Itani	FIN	24.3.87	24 Aug		7620	Moritz	Cleve	GER	18.2.87	15 Jun

Mark	Name		Nat	Born	Pos Meet		Venue		Date
7620	Ivan	Rudnev	RUS	26.12.92	8 Sep				
7619	Fabian	Rosenquist	SWE	1.4.91	3 Jun				
7616	Japeth	Cato	USA	25.12.90	19 Apr				
7606		Qi Haifeng	CHN	7.8.83	24 Jun				
7600	Ryota	Tsuji	JPN	6.7.86	3 Jun				
7598	Robbie	Haynie	USA	.90	25 May				
7597	Jake	Waruch	USA	29.8.89	11 Apr				
7597	Niels	Pittomvils	BEL	18.7.92	5 Aug				
7596	Felix	Hepperle	GER	23.11.89	26 Aug				
7592	Danilo	Batista	CUB	5.4.92	2 Jun				
7590		Yu Bin	CHN	26.11.85	24 Jun				
7589	Aleksandr	Frolov	RUS	5.3.87	3 Jun				
7586	Jangy	Addy	LBR	2.3.85	9 Aug				
7585	Terry	Prentice	USA	7.1.89	11 May				
7570	Kevin	Dwyer	USA	26.12.85	17 May				
7567	Hans Olav	Uldal	NOR	16.12.82	6 May				
7564	Alexandre	Folacci	FRA	26.3.91	8 Jul				
7560	Lars	Albert	GER	9.2.82	17 Jun				
7558	Derek	Masterson	USA	30.1.90	3 Apr				
7554	Quentin	Jammier	FRA	24.7.88	13 May				
7554w	Ben	Gregory	GBR	21.11.90	9 Jun				
7548	Maicel	Uibo	EST	27.12.92	29 Jul				
7547	Tom	FitzSimons	USA	8.3.89	7 Jun				
7543	Jonay	Jordán	ESP	12.5.91	3 Jul				
7538	Renato	da Câmara	BRA	16.9.85	20 May				
7538	Dominik	Alberto	SUI	28.4.92	17 Jun				
7537	Mourad	Souissi	ALG	7.7.84	18 May				
7536	Aleksey	Spirin	BLR	3.6.92	7 Jul				
7534	Rene	Stauß	GER	17.9.87	3 Jun				
7534	John	Lane	GBR	29.1.89	10 Jun				
7530	Daniel	Kinsey	USA	25.7.86	3 Jun				
7519(w)	Brent	Vogel	USA	2.5.90	3 Jun				
7513	Nick	Armstrong	USA	15.12.87	19 Apr				
7513A	Richard	York	USA	13.12.90	10 May				
7512	Nick	Adcock	USA	2.4.88	17 May				
7509	Mattias	Cerlati	FRA	25.10.83	7 Jul				
7508	Thomas	Barrineau	FIN	28.8.88	13 Apr				
7508	Tomas	Kirielius	LTU	10.6.89	12 May				
7493	Martin	Brockman	GBR	13.11.87	8 Jan				
7492	Steffen	Fricke	GER	25.3.83	26 Aug				
7488	Marek	Lukás	CZE	16.7.91	20 May				
7485		Liu Haibo	CHN	17.3.87	15 Apr				
7475	Clayton	Chaney	USA	16.9.89	12 May				
7471	Lukas	Tächl	GER	27.6.89	20 May				
7465	Clement	Buisson	FRA	13.9.90	7 Jul				
7459	Maksim	Fayzulin	RUS	18.1.92	8 May				
7456	Jarrod	Sims	AUS	11.6.84	14 Apr				
7451	Lars Vikan	Rise	NOR	23.11.88	16 Sep				
7448	Marek	Lukás	CZE	16.7.91	20 May				
7445	Yevgeniy	Teptin	RUS	16.3.90	3 Jun				
7445	Maxime	Maugein	FRA	27.9.92	8 Jul				
7443	Edward	Dunford	GBR	15.9.84	27 May				
7443	Ali	Kamé	MAD	21.5.84	10 Jun				
7440	Lassi	Raunio	FIN	11.10.83	24 Aug				
7439	Ivan	da Silva	BRA	30.7.82	30 Jun				
7432wA	Zavion	Kotze	RSA	6.11.88	28 Apr				
7425	Devin	Dick	USA	12.1.90	12 May				
7422	Tom	Bechert	GER	2.7.87	5 Aug				
7418	Harold	Bust	NED	3.6.92	18 May				
7416	Michael	Ayers	USA	7.11.88	11 May				
7410	Garrett	Scantling	USA-J	19.5.93	13 Apr				
7407	Patrick	Woods	USA	4.10.85	3 Jun				
7401	Kenny	Greaves	USA	13.10.88	29 Mar				

(173)

Drugs disqualification

8332	Larbi	Bouraada ¶	ALG	10.5.88	(1)	Ratingen	15 Jun
	10.58/0.6	7.57/-0.4	13.64	2.09	47.40	14.78w/2.4 34.80 4.70 67.68	4:24.08

JUNIORS

7892 Gunnar Nixon USA 13.1.93 5 NCAA Des Moines 7 Jun
    7660   4   MSR Azusa   19 Apr   7544   3   SEC Baton Rouge   11 May

7410 Garrett Scantling USA 19.5.93 3 Athens, GA 13 Apr
    11.34/-1.3 6.99/0.0 13.59 2.07 52.38 14.93/2.0 36.89 4.55 58.23 4:55.08

7171 Li Mingyang CHN 15.3.93 5 Fuzhou 24 Jun
    11.15/-0.4 6.98/0.2 11.84 1.91 48.86 15.20/-0.3 36.20 4.30 48.07 4:41.34

7163 Wang Qunhao CHN-Y 3.2.95 5 NC Kunshan 25 Sep
    11.47 6.97/-0.2 10.56 2.00 48.78 15.30 36.45 4.00 56.02 4:36.78

7161 Manuel A. González CUB 23.3.93 2 NC La Habana 23 Mar
    11.70/-1.2 7.29w/2.7 14.40 1.98 52.56 15.65/0.0 38.32 3.90 55.27 4:41.73

7104 Hu Yufei CHN 9.11.93 8 Fuzhou 24 Jun
    11.37/-0.4 7.06w/2.6 12.52 1.97 51.09 15.15/-0.3 39.90 4.20 48.66 4:56.30

7097 Li Dalin CHN 1.12.93 9 Fuzhou 24 Jun
    11.36/-0.1 7.21/-0.5 10.86 1.94 50.55 15.29/-0.6 36.85 4.40 49.08 4:44.28

7063 Wang Jianan CHN-Y 27.8.96 5 Zhaoqing 15 Apr
    10.88/-0.1 7.80/-0.2 8.53 1.94 51.17 16.30/-0.1 34.57 5.00 44.99 4:56.80

IAAF junior specification – with 99cm 110mh, 6kg SP, 1.75kg DT

8018 Gunnar Nixon USA 13.1.93 1 WJ Barcelona 11 Jul
    11.23/-0.1 7.12/-0.2 14.54 2.10 49.13 14.54/-0.7 42.23 4.50 56.25 4:22.36
    7760   1   NC-j Bloomington IN   16 Jun

7955 Jake Stein AUS 17.1.94 2 WJ Barcelona 11 Jul
    11.31/-0.8 7.41/1.1 16.39 1.95 51.15 14.90/-0.7 51.43 3.80 69.61 4:45.34
    7886   1   NC-j Sydney   1 Apr   7637   1   Melbourne   11 Mar

7953 Pieter Braun NED 21.1.93 1 NC-j Emmeloord 18 May
    11.30/0.7 7.28/1.7 14.74 1.98 49.58 14.42/-1.0 44.23 4.40 60.27 4:31.20

7815 Tim Dekker NED 29.9.93 3 WJ Barcelona 11 Jul
    11.06/-0.8 7.23/0.4 14.69 2.04 49.70 14.02/-0.7 43.69 4.20 48.04 4:34.34

7631h Abdel-Kader Larrigana CUB 13.7.94 1 La Habana 2 Jun
    10.7/0.1 7.00/0.7 15.92 2.05 51.5 14.1/-0.4 40.71 3.90 57.00 4:50.9

7584 Cedric Dubler AUS-Y 13.1.95 4 WJ Barcelona 11 Jul
    11.05/-0.8 7.47/0.5 12.35 2.07 49.70 14.62/-0.7 36.15 4.50 50.59 4:46.04

7583 Karl-Robert Saluri EST 6.8.93 5 WJ Barcelona 11 Jul
    11.04/0.3 7.21/0.2 14.20 1.83 49.60 15.51/-0.4 39.30 4.50 55.80 4:26.69

7517h Manuel A. González CUB 23.3.93 2 La Habana 2 Jun
    11.5/0.1 6.93/0.0 16.57 1.96 52.5 15.5/-0.4 45.94 4.50 58.42 4:45.7

7498 Riben Gado FRA 13.12.93 7 WJ Barcelona 11 Jul
    11.10/-0.8 7.31/0.5 12.42 1.74 49.21 14.92/-0.4 39.54 4.70 50.40 4:24.00

Mark	Name		Nat	Born	Pos	Meet	Venue	Date
7444	Lukas	Schmitz (10)	GER	3.1.93	8	WJ	Barcelona	11 Jul
	11.00/-0.8	7.34/-0.7 12.75	1.86	47.73		14.96/-0.1	36.93 4.40 46.53	4:35.38
7434	Garrett	Scantling	USA-J	19.5.93	2	NC-j	Bloomington IN	16 Jun
	11.47/-1.0	6.73/1.3 14.30	2.08	52.08		14.98/0.9	42.24 4.70 57.96	5:12.31
7406	Václav	Sedlák	CZE	6.2.93	1	NC-j	Stará Boleslav	20 May
	11.15/0.2	6.62/-1.4 13.83	1.99	48.98		14.18/-1.7	38.89 4.50 43.07	4:46.52
7368		Li Mingyang	CHN	15.3.93	1	NC-j	Changzhou	21 Apr
	11.00/0.7	7.17/-0.9 13.35	1.88	49.23		14.80	38.49 4.00 50.97	4:38.53
7356	Tim	Nowak	GER-Y	13.8.95	9	WJ	Barcelona	11 Jul
	11.31/-0.1	6.70/-0.7 14.89	1.98	50.81		14.87/-0.1	42.57 3.80 53.85	4:39.36
7302	Luca	Di Tizio	SUI	31.8.93	10	WJ	Barcelona	11 Jul
	11.42/0.3	7.02/0.7 11.88	1.95	51.03		15.00/-0.1	36.58 4.50 54.11	4:31.47
7288	Marvin	Gregor	GER	3.10.93	1	NC-j	Hannover	26 Aug
	11.41/0.5	6.65/0.0 13.40	1.90	53.35		14.74/-1.6	41.64 4.70 58.48	4:53.24
7280	Felipe V.	dos Santos	BRA	30.7.94	11	WJ	Barcelona	11 Jul
	11.07/0.3	7.06/1.0 14.44	1.86	50.38		14.70/-0.4	41.37 3.80 49.52	4:43.75
7277	Máté	Hódosi	HUN	28.5.93	1	NC-j	Budapest	16 Sep
	11.12/1.9	6.97w/3.6 14.16	2.02	51.01		15.28/0.2	36.88 3.90 52.34	4:40.54
7275	Kevin	Nielsen	USA	12.1.93	3	NC-j	Bloomington IN	16 Jun
	11.55/-0.4	7.03w/2.8 12.41	1.99	49.82		15.21/-0.3	36.52 4.40 47.76	4:27.81
7264	Arne	Broeders (20)	BEL	5.11.93	12	WJ	Barcelona	11 Jul
	11.58/-0.1	6.96w/2.2 13.37	1.83	51.37		15.48/-0.4	40.02 4.50 57.62	4:35.45

4 X 100 METRES RELAY

Mark	Nat	Team	Pos	Meet	Venue	Date
36.84	JAM	N.Carter 10.1, Frater 8.9, Blake 9.0, Bolt 8.8	1	OG	London (OS)	11 Aug
37.04	USA	Kimmons 10.1, Gatlin 8.8, Gay 9.1, Bailey 9.0	2	OG	London (OS)	11 Aug
37.38	USA	Demps, Patton, Kimmons, Gatlin	1h2	OG	London (OS)	10 Aug
37.39	JAM	Carter, Frater, Blake, Bailey-Cole	1h1	OG	London (OS)	10 Aug
37.61	USA	Kimmons, Gatlin, Gay, Bailey	1	Herc	Monaco	20 Jul
37.82	Racers TC/JAM	Forsythe, Blake, Roach, Bolt	1		Kingston	14 Apr
37.83	USA	B Rodgers, Mitchell, Patton, Demps	2	Herc	Monaco	20 Jul
38.02	GER	Reus, Unger, Kosenkow, Jakubczyk	1		Weinheim	27 Jul
38.02	USA	Patton, Spearmon, Gay, Bailey	1	WK	Zürich	30 Aug
38.05	CAN	Smellie, S.Smith, Connaughton, Warner	2h1	OG	London (OS)	10 Aug
38.07	JPN	Yamagata, Eriguchi, Takahira, Iizuka	2h2	OG	London (OS)	10 Aug
38.10	TRI	Thompson, Burns, Callender, Bledman	3h2	OG	London (OS)	10 Aug
38.12	TRI	Thompson, Burns, Callender, Bledman	3	OG	London (OS)	11 Aug
38.15	FRA	Vicaut, Lemaitre, Pessoneaux, Pognon	4h2	OG	London (OS)	10 Aug
38.16	FRA	Vicaut, Lemaitre, Pessoneaux, Pognon	4	OG	London (OS)	11 Aug
38.17	AUS	Alozie, Ntiamoah, McCabe, Ross	5h2	OG	London (OS)	10 Aug
38.19	JAM	Forsythe, Young, Weir, Bailey-Cole	2	WK	Zürich	30 Aug
38.23	TRI	Sorrillo, Burns, Callender, Thompson	3	OG	London (OS)	11 Aug
38.29	NED	Mariano, Martina, Codrington, van Luijk	3h1	OG	London (OS)	10 Aug
38.30	Auburn University USA	Rowland, Adams, DeHaven, Brock	1	TexR	Austin	31 Mar
38.30	GBR	Malcolm, Chambers, Talbot, Gemili (10)	3	WK	Zürich	30 Aug
38.31	POL	Masztak, Kuc, Kubaczyk, Krynski	6h2	OG	London (OS)	10 Aug
38.34	NED	Mariano, Martina, Codrington, van Luijk	1	EC	Helsinki	1 Jul
38.35	BRA	A. da Silva, Viana, André, de Barros	4h1	OG	London (OS)	10 Aug
38.35	JPN	Yamagata, Eriguchi, Takahira, Iizuka	5	OG	London (OS)	11 Aug
38.37	GER	Reus, Unger, Kosenkow, Jakubczyk	7h2	OG	London (OS)	10 Aug
38.38	CHN	Guo Fan, Liang Jiahong, Su Bingtiang, Zhang Peimeng	5h1	OG	London (OS)	10 Aug
38.39	NED	Mariano, Martina, Codrington, van Luijk	6	OG	London (OS)	10 Aug
		(27 performances by teams from 13 nations)				
38.41	SKN	Lestrod, Rogers, Adams, Lawrence	6h1	OG	London (OS)	10 Aug
38.47	HKG	Tang Yik Chun, Lai Chun Ho, Ng Ka Fung, Tsui Chi Ho	1		Taipei	26 May
38.58	ITA	Collio, Riparelli, Mananeti, Cerutti	7h1	OG	London (OS)	10 Aug
38.67	RUS	Idrisov, Petryashkov, Kolesnichenko, Karavay	4	EC	Helsinki	1 Jul
38.78	TPE	Wang, Liu, Liang, Yi	2		Taipei	26 May
38.83	SUI	Wilson, Schneeberger, Schenkel, Fongué	5	EC	Helsinki	1 Jul
39.06	VEN	Chirinos, Ramírez, Rivas, Acevedo	2	IbAmC	Barquisimeto	10 Jun
		(20)				
39.08A	RSA	Dreyer, Magakwe, Mpuang, Engel	1		Pretoria	6 May
Best at low altitude: 39.26		Dreyer, Magakwe, Engel, Mpuang	1	AfrC	Porto Novo	29 Jun
39.28	KOR	Yeo, Jeon, Cho, Oh	6		Fukuroi	3 May
39.30	NGR	Emelieze, Ogho-Oghene, Metu, Adukwu	2		Atlanta	12 May
39.31	Interamericana/PUR		1		Ponce	22 Apr
39.36	BAH	Atkins, Rolle, Farquharson, Fenn	3		Rio de Janeiro	20 May

Mark	Nat	Date		Mark	Nat	Date		Mark	Nat	Date		Mark	Nat	Date		Mark	Nat	Date
39.38	GHA	28 Jun		39.58	SIN	11 May		39.66	POR	30 Jun		39.71	FIN	1 Sep		39.94	LAT	8 Jun
39.41	CZE	25 May		39.60	ESP	31 May		39.68	THA-J	13 Jul		39.76	ZIM	23 Mar				
39.51	IND	8 May		39.64	SWE	1 Sep		39.69A	COL	13 Nov		39.94	LTU	8 Jun				

Mark	Name	Nat	Born	Pos	Meet	Venue	Date

Mixed nationality teams

38.27	Maximising Velocity/JAM-GBR			2		Kingston	14 Apr
	Chambers/GBR, Frater, Carter, Powell						
38.38	Louisiana St Un USA Nugent, Ernest, Talley, Allsop TRI			1	NCAA	Des Momies	9 Jun

JUNIORS

38.67	USA	T Hill, A Bailey, Delaney, Ernest		1	WJ	Barcelona	14 Jul
38.97	JAM	Tracey, Skeen, Minzie, Murphy		2	WJ	Barcelona	14 Jul
39.01	JPN	Oseto, Hashimoto, Cambridge, Kanamori		1h1	WJ	Barcelona	13 Jul
39.02	JPN	Oseto, Hashimoto, Cambridge, Kanamori		3	WJ	Barcelona	14 Jul
39.09	GBR	Stephens, Ujah, Holligan, Gemili		1h3	WJ	Barcelona	13 Jul
39.29	BRA	de Araújo, Monteiro, R dos Santos Jnr, Rocha		2h1	WJ	Barcelona	13 Jul
39.31	POL	Bijowski, Slowikowski, Zalewski, Jabłoński		3h1	WJ	Barcelona	13 Jul
39.34	AUS	Jaworski, Donovan, Hough, Bertacco		4h1	WJ	Barcelona	13 Jul
39.48	BAH	Farrington, Bartlett, S Jones, Newbold		2h2	WJ	Barcelona	13 Jul
39.68	THA	Ruttanapon, Namsuwan, Jaran, Meenapra		5h1	WJ	Barcelona	13 Jul
39.86	NGR	Chukwudike, Nmaju, Mamus, Martins		6h1	WJ	Barcelona	13 Jul
39.87	RSA	Julies, Ngqabaza, Conradie, Mofokeng		7h1	WJ	Barcelona	13 Jul
39.99	TRI	Richards, Berkley, Sobers, Holder		3	CAC-J	San Salvador	30 Jun

4 x 200m Relay: 1:21.21 Texas A&M University 1 — TexR Austin 31 Mar

4 X 400 METRES RELAY

2:56.72	BAH	Brown 44.9, Pinder 43.5, Mathieu 44.25, Miller 44.01	1	OG	London (OS)	10 Aug
2:57.05	USA	Nellum 45.2, Mance 43.5, McQuay 43.41, Taylor 44.85	2	OG	London (OS)	10 Aug
2:58.87	BAH	Miller 45.7, Pinder 43.7, Mathieu 44.78, Brown 44.58	1h2	OG	London (OS)	9 Aug
2:58.87	USA	Mitchell 46.1, Mance 44.6, McQuay 43.65, Nellum 44.37	2h2	OG	London (OS)	9 Aug
2:59.40	TRI	L.Gordon 45.1, Solomon 43.9, Alleyne-Forte 45.51, Lendore 44.75	3	OG	London (OS)	10 Aug
2:59.53	GBR	C Williams 45.2, J Green 44.6, Greene 45.53, Rooney 44.09	4	OG	London (OS)	10 Aug
3:00.02	Florida/USA	Dukes 46.6, Graham 44.3, Seymore 45.31, McQuay 44.00	1	NCAA	Des Moines	9 Ju
3:00.09	RUS	Dyldin 45.4, Alekseyev 45.1, Krasnov 44.69, Trenikhin 44.83	5	OG	London (OS)	10 Aug
3:00.15	USA	C.Smith 46.4, Taylor 44.7, Jackson 44.2, Merritt 44.8	1	Penn R	Philadelphia	28 Apr
3:00.38	TRI	L.Gordon 44.9, Solomon 44.8, Alleyne-Forte 46.12, Lendore 44.49	1h1	OG	London (OS)	9 Aug
3:00.38	GBR	Levine 45.9, C Williams 45.1, J Green 44.42, Rooney 44.84	2h1	OG	London (OS)	9 Aug
3:00.43	CUB	Ruíz, Acea, Rodríguez, Collazo	1	IbAmC	Barquisimeto	10 Jun
3:00.45	TRI	Quow, Gordon, Solomon, Lendore	1	NC	Port of Spain	24 Jun
3:00.55	CUB	Collazo 45.9, Acea 44.5, Rodríguez 45.19, Cisneros 44.89	3h1	OG	London (OS)	9 Aug
3:00.56	BAH	Pinder 45.4, Miller 45.1, Mathieu 44.5, Brown 45.6	2	Penn R	Philadelphia	28 Apr
3:00.64	U. of S.California/USA	Hughes 45.6, Mance 44.9, Wyatt 45.30, Nellum 44.82	2	NCAA	Des Moines	9 Jun
3:01.04	JPN	Takase, Kanemaru, Ishizuka, Nakano	1		Daegu	16 May
3:01.09	BEL	Gillet 46.5, J.Borlée 44.3, Bouckaert 45.96, K.Borlée 44.22	1	EC	Helsinki	1 Jul
3:01.52	Penn State USA	Nadolsky 46.9, Bennett-Green 44.8, Loxsom 45.55, Gehret 44.22	1h2	NCAA DM		7 Jun
3:01.56	GBR	Levine 45.4, C Williams 44.8, Tobin 45.88, Buck 45.31	2	EC	Helsinki	1 Jul
3:01.58	AUS	Solomon, Offereins, Cole, Thomas	2		Daegu	16 May
		(21/9)				
3:01.70	VEN	Ramírez, Bravo, Meléndez, Longart (10)	2	IbAmC	Barquisimeto	10 Jun
3:01.77	GER	Plass 46.0, Gaba 45.3, Krüger 45.66, Schneider 44.73	3	EC	Helsinki	1 Jul
3:02.37	POL	Wiaderek 46.1, Ciepiela 45.2, Marciniiszyn 45.69, Kozlowski 45.32	4	EC	Helsinki	1 Jul
3:02.39	NGR	Salihu, Morton, Onakoya, Weigopwa	1	AfrC	Porto Novo	1 Jul
3:02.72	CZE	Nemecek 46.4, Maslák 44.5, Prorok 45.97, Holusa 45.81	5	EC	Helsinki	1 Jul
3:03.02	DOM	Cuesta, Soriano, W Cuevas, L Santos	3	IbAmC	Barquisimeto	10 Jun
3:03.04	FRA	Venel 46.0, Coulibaby 45.9, Macedot 45.64, Fonsat 45.48	6	EC	Helsinki	1 Jul
3:03.05	BRA	P de Oliveira, Estefani, J da Silva, Henriques	4	IbAmC	Barquisimeto	10 Jun
3:03.28	JAM	Hyatt 45.9, Gonzales 45.4, Fothergill 45.7, Barrett 46.3	3	Penn R	Philadelphia	28 Apr
3:03.46	RSA	de Jager 46.2, de Beer 45.2, van Zyl 46.27, Pistorius 45.69	8	OG	London (OS)	10 Aug
3:03.84	BOT	Makwala, Ngwigwa, Amos, Mokgadi	1		Warri	14 Jun
		(20)				
3:03.89	ESP	Briones, Ujakpor, Testa, García	3	GGala	Roma	31 May
3.04.05	VEN	Mezones, Aguilar, Melendez, Longart	2		Port of Spain	24 Jun
3:04.56	UKR	Ryemyen 46.9, Melnykov 45.9, Hutsol 46.17, Burakov 45.50	7	EC	Helsinki	1 Jul
3:05.04	ITA	Valentini, Juarez, Barberi, Tricaa	4	GGala	Roma	31 May
3:05.68	NED	Moerman 46.2, Peters 45.9, Spillekom 47.15, El Rhalfioui 46.35	8	EC	Helsinki	1 Jul
3:06.16	Liaoning CHN	Su Pengfei, Sun Yi, Huo Gang, Zhang Yunpeng	1		Kunshan	25 Sep

3:07.01 COL	20 May	3:07.58 HUN	3 Jun	3:07.82 IND	11 May	3:08.78 ISR	3 Jun	3:08.88 NZL	18 Jul
3:07.34 KSA	12 May	3:07.68 KOR	16 May	3:08.10 TUR	24 Jun	3:08.85 GRE	28 Apr		

Hand timing: 3:03.5A Defense Forces KEN M Mutai, J Kibet, Z Kosgei, Mumo 1 — NC Nairobi 15 Jun

Mixed nationaliy teams

3:01.21	Louisiana State Un	3	NCAA	Des Moines	9 Jun
	Simmons 46.0, Downing 46.1, Alleyne-Forte TRI 44.84, Hylton JAM 44.29				
3:01.32	South Plains JC, USA Moona CAN, Harper CAN, Norwood, Taplin	1		Lubbock	5 May
3:01.54	Central Texas All-Stars B Miller, Henry ISV, Boyd, Wariner 44.58	1	TexR	Austin	31 Mar

Mark	Name	Nat	Born	Pos	Meet	Venue	Date

JUNIORS

Mark	Name	Nat		Pos	Meet	Venue	Date
3:03.99	USA	Downing, A Bailey, Okezie, A Hall		1	WJ	Barcelona	15 Jul
3:05.05	POL	Zalewski, Smolen, Kusnierz, Dobek		2	WJ	Barcelona	15 Jul
3:05.95	TRI	Guevara, Benjamin, Lewis, Cedenio		3		Port of Spain	24 Jun
3:06.58	AUS	Buchan, Meaney, Waldron, Solomon		4	WJ	Barcelona	15 Jul
3:07.31	JAM	Barnes, J Francis, L Williams, Fyffe		5	WJ	Barcelona	15 Jul
3:07.88	KSA	Saleh, Abkar, Al-Kaabi, Al Barakati		4h2	WJ	Barcelona	14 Jul
3:08.16	JPN	Yokoyama, Kenta Kimura, Kozuma, Kazushi Kimura		1h3	WJ	Barcelona	14 Jul
3:08.58	RUS	Chalyy, Semakin, Kashefrazov, Vesnin		3h3	WJ	Barcelona	14 Jul
3:08.82	GER	Lange, Schmitz, Steudel, Brücher		4h3	WJ	Barcelona	14 Jul
3:08.87	ITA	Incantalupo, Rontini, Re, Tricca		2h1	WJ	Barcelona	14 Jul
3:08.96	BAH	Munroe, Newbold, McBride, Ferguson		3h1	WJ	Barcelona	14 Jul

4 x 110m Hurdles: 54.30 Star Athletics Faulk USA, Brathwaite BAR, Brown USA, Dutch USA 1 FlaR Gainesville 6Apr

3000 METRES WALK

Mark	Name		Nat	Born	Pos	Meet	Venue	Date
11:05.95	Matej	Tóth	SVK	10.2.83	1		Dubnica nad Váhom	26 Aug
11:14.29	Robert	Heffernan	IRL	20.2.78	1		Cork	17 Jul
11:15.32	Anton	Kucmin	SVK	7.6.84	2		Dubnica nad Váhom	26 Aug
11:21.90	Grzegorz	Sudol	POL	28.8.78	3		Dubnica nad Váhom	26 Aug
11:23.05	Dane	Bird-Smith	AUS	15.7.92	1		Brisbane (St Lucia	6 Jun
11:23.12+	Jared	Tallent	AUS	17.10.84	1	in 5k	Sydney	18 Feb
11:23.30+	Iñaki	Gómez	CAN	16.1.88	2	in 5k	Sydney	18 Feb
11:24.02	Pierre-Louis	de Villiers	RSA	18.8.85	1		Stellenbosch	20 Mar
11:27.01+	Adam	Rutter	AUS	24.12.86	4	in 5k	Sydney	18 Feb

11:28.83+	Chris	Erickson (10)	AUS	1.12.81	18 Feb	11:39.8	Rhydian	Cowley	AUS	4.1.91	3 Nov
11:30.67+	Evans	Dunfee	CAN	28.9.90	18 Feb	11:32.25i	Dawid	Tomala	POL	27.8.89	15 Jan
						11:36.27iA	Trevor	Barron	USA	30.9.92	25 Feb

5000 METRES WALK

Mark	Name		Nat	Born	Pos	Meet	Venue	Date
18:45.64	Iñaki	Gómez	CAN	16.1.88	1		Sydney	18 Feb
18:47.45	Yohann	Diniz	FRA	1.1.78	1		Reims	4 Jul
18:47.77	Jared	Tallent	AUS	17.10.84	2		Sydney	18 Feb
19:02.59	Dane	Bird-Smith	AUS	15.7.92	3		Sydney	18 Feb
19:05.18	Kevin	Campion	FRA	23.5.88	2		Reims	4 Jul
19:06.07	Grzegorz	Sudol	POL	28.8.78	3		Reims	4 Jul
19:08.83		Tallent			1	NC	Melborune	14 Apr
19:08.87	Evans	Dunfee	CAN	28.9.90	4		Sydney	18 Feb
19:08.89	Erik	Tysse	NOR	4.12.80	1	NC	Kristiansand	24 Aug
19:10.97	Adam	Rutter	AUS	24.12.86	5		Sydney	18 Feb
19:17.49	Antonin	Boyez (10)	FRA	9.11.84	4		Reims	4 Jul
19:17.82	Dawid	Tomala	POL	27.8.89	1		Gdansk	26 May
19:19.10	Takuya	Yoshida	JPN	10.8.90	1		Morioka	20 Oct
19:21.81	Bertrand	Moulinet	FRA	6.1.87	1		Amiens	30 Jun

19:26.76	Chris	Erickson	AUS	1.12.81	18 Feb	19:30.6	João	Vieira	POR	20.2.76	14 Jan
19:27.30	Hichem	Medjber	ALG	10.2.82	17 Mar	19:30.80	Jakub	Jelonek	POL	7.7.85	8 Sep
19:29.90	Hassanine	Sbaï	TUN	21.1.84	9 Jun	19:32.14	Mohamed	Ameur	ALG	1.11.84	17 Mar
19:30.58	Rafal	Fedaczynski	POL	3.12.80	26 May	19:34.30	Lukasz	Nowak	POL	18.12.88	15 Sep

Indoors

Mark	Name		Nat	Born	Pos	Meet	Venue	Date
18:16.54	Valeriy	Borchin	RUS	11.9.86	1	Winter	Moskva	5 Feb
18:17.13	Vladimir	Kanaykin	RUS	21.3.85	2	Winter	Moskva	5 Feb
18:26.82	Sergey	Bakulin	RUS	13.11.86	3	Winter	Moskva	5 Feb
18:34.56	Matej	Tóth	SVK	10.2.83	1		Wien	11 Feb
18:44.45	Ruslan	Dmytrenko	UKR	22.3.86	4	Winter	Moskva	5 Feb
18:47.80		Diniz			5	Winter	Moskva	5 Feb
18:58.81	Denis	Nizhegorodov	RUS	26.7.80	6	Winter	Moskva	5 Feb
19:06.58	Robert	Heffernan	IRL	20.2.78	1	NC	Belfast	11 Feb
19:08.84	João	Vieira	POR	20.2.76	1		Pombal	28 Jan
19:14.86	Anton	Kucmin	SVK	7.6.84	2		Wien	11 Feb
19:21.33	Bertrand	Moulinet	FRA	6.1.87	1		Bompas	19 Feb
19:22.15	Rafal	Sikora	POL	17.2.87	2	NC	Spala	26 Feb
19:22.80	Giorgio	Rubino	ITA	15.4.86	1	NC	Ancona	25 Feb

19:30.43	Veli-Matti	Partanen	FIN	28.10.91	18 Feb	19:35.0	Aleksandr	Ivanov	RUS-J	25.4.93	6 Jan
19:30.63	Rafal	Augustyn	POL	14.5.84	26 Feb	19:35.06	Jamie	Costin	IRL	1.6.77	11 Feb
19:34.12	Kirill	Frolov	RUS-J	29.9.93	22 Dec	19:35.67	Rafal	Fedaczynski	POL	3.12.80	26 Feb

JUNIORS

Mark		Name		Nat	Born	Pos	Meet	Venue	Date
19:34.12	i	Kirill	Frolov	RUS	29.9.93	1		Moskva	22 Dec
19:35.0	i	Aleksandr	Ivanov	RUS	25.4.93	1		Chelyabinsk	6 Jan

10,000 METRES TRACK WALK

Mark	Name	Nat	Born	Pos	Meet	Venue	Date
38:30.38	Wang Zhen	CHN	24.8.91	1		Tianjin	16 Sep
38:59.98	Cai Zelin	CHN	11.4.91	2		Tianjin	16 Sep

Mark	Name		Nat	Born	Pos	Meet	Venue	Date
39:14.6	Andriy	Kovenko	UKR	25.11.73	1		Mukachevo	2 Nov
39:22.47		Chu Yafei	CHN	5.9.88	3		Tianjin	16 Sep
39:46.74	Yohann	Diniz	FRA	1.1.78	1	NC	Angers	16 Jun
39:48.8	Ivan	Trotskiy	BLR	27.5.76	1		Minsk	18 Jul
39:49.44		Li Tianlei	CHN-Y	13.1.95	4		Tianjin	16 Sep
39:50.17	Giorgio	Rubino	ITA	15.4.86	1		Saluzzo	18 Jul
39:50.53		Wang Zhen			2		Saluzzo	18 Jul
39:51.34	Yasuke	Suzuki	JPN	1.2.88	1		Fukuoka	22 Sep
39:55.09	Jarkko	Kinnunen	FIN	19.1.84	1		Kauhava	8 Jul
	(10/11)							
39:55.52	Evans	Dunfee	CAN	28.9.90	1		Coquitlam	15 Jul
39:56.21	Benjamín	Sánchez	ESP	10.3.85	1		Águilas	2 Jun
39:58.65	Miguel Ángel	López	ESP	3.7.88	2		Águilas	2 Jun
40:04.04		Chen Ding	CHN	5.8.92	5		Tianjin	16 Sep
40:04.92	Koichiro	Morioka	JPN	2.4.85	2		Fukuoka	22 Sep
40:05.0	Alekandr	Lyakhovich	BLR	4.7.89	2		Minsk	18 Jul
40:07.71	Hiroki	Arai	JPN	18.5.88	3		Fukuoka	22 Sep
40:08.74	Hayato	Katsuki	JPN	28.11.90	1		Tokyo	13 May
40:08.98	Takuya	Yoshida	JPN	10.8.90	1		Tama	16 Dec
40:09.74	Eider	Arévalo	COL-J	9.3.93	1	WJ	Barcelona	13 Jul
	(20)							
40:10.47	André	Höhne	GER	10.3.78	1	NC	Diez	24 Jun
40:11.71	Takumi	Saito	JPN-J	23.3.93	2		Gifu	7 Oct
40:12.90	Aleksandr	Ivanov	RUS-J	26.6.94	2	WJ	Barcelona	13 Jul
40:16.87		Su Gianyu	CHN-J	26.6.94	3	WJ	Barcelona	13 Jul

40:17.71	Hagen	Pohle	GER	5.3.92	24 Jun	40:27.31		Zhao Fujian	CHN-J		16 Sep
40:19.19	Carsten	Schmidt	GER	28.5.86	24 Jun	40:29.84	Veli-Matti	Partanen	FIN	28.10.91	1 Sep
40:19.59	Yuki	Sasagawa	JPN	18.11.91	13 May	40:30.50		Yu Wei	CHN	11.9.87	16 Sep
40:26.0A	Benjamin	Thorne	CAN-J	19.3.93	30 Jun	40:34.6	Vitaliy	Talankov	BLR	29.4.82	18 Jul
						40:35.52	Alvaro	Martín	ESP-J	18.6.94	13 Jul

Indoors

Mark	Name		Nat	Born	Pos	Meet	Venue	Date
39:26.90	Ruslan	Dmytrenko	UKR	22.3.86	1	NC	Sumy	16 Feb
39:43.81	Ivan	Losev	UKR	26.1.86	2	NC	Sumy	16 Feb
39:49.55	Nazar	Kovalenko	UKR	9.2.89	3	NC	Sumy	16 Feb
40:12.2	Sergiy	Budza	UKR	6.12.84	1		Sumy	24 Dec

40:25.98	Vitaliy	Talankov	BLR	29.4.82	10 Feb	40:39.8	Oleksandr	Venglovskyy	UKR	5.8.85	24 Dec

JUNIORS

See main list for top 5 juniors. 10 performances by 8 men to 40:40.0. Additional marks and further juniors:

Saito		40:19.10	4	WJ	Barcelona		13 Jul	40:32.74	3		Tokyo	13 May

40:26.0A	Benjamin	Thorne	CAN	19.3.93	1	NC-j	Calgary	30 Jun
40:27.31		Zhao Fujian	CHN		1		Tianjin	16 Sep
40:35.52	Alvaro	Martín	ESP-J	18.6.94	5	WJ	Barcelona	13 Jul
40:54.53	Daisuke	Matsunaga	JPN-Y	24.3.95	2		Sasebo	9 Dec
41:05.59	Jesús	Vega	MEX-Y	23.5.94	6	WJ	Barcelona	13 Jul
41:11.7	Edgars	Gjacs (10)	LAT	27.8.93	1		Ogre	6 Oct
41:14.73	Pavel	Parshin	RUS-Y	2.1.94	1	NC-j	Moskva	10 Jun
41:17.72	Nils	Brembach	GER	23.2.93	5	NC	Diez	24 Jun
41:21.60	Igor	Lyashchenko	UKR	24.8.93	8	WJ	Barcelona	13 Jul
41:26.37	Aleksandr	Pichkalov	RUS	16.6.93	2	NC-j	Moskva	10 Jun
41:36.02 i	Boris	Shargar	BLR	31.3.93	5	NC	Mogilyov	10 Feb

10 KILOMETRES ROAD WALK

See also 20km list for many intermediate times

Mark	Name		Nat	Born	Pos	Meet	Venue	Date
38:59	Veli-Matti	Partanen	FIN	28.10.91	1		Tuusula	14 Apr
39:11	Mikhail	Ryzhov	RUS	17.12.91	1		Voronovo	16 Sep
39:16	Sergey	Sergachev	RUS	10.7.87	1		Podolsk	9 May
39:16	Sergey	Korepanov	RUS	15.7.84	2		Podolsk	9 May
39:17	Giorgio	Rubino	ITA	15.4.86	1	NC	Bressanone	6 Jul
39:24	Pyotr	Trofimov	RUS	28.11.83	1	NGP	Buy	2 Sep
39:27		Wang Zhen	CHN	24.8.91	1	RWC-F	Ordos	14 Sep
39:31	Aleksey	Bartsaykin	RUS	22.3.89	2		Voronovo	16 Sep
39:33	Pyotr	Bogatyrev	RUS	11.3.91	3		Voronovo	16 Sep
39:37		Trofimov			4		Voronovo	16 Sep
39:44	Moacir	Zimmermann	BRA	30.12.83	1		Gaspar	19 May
39:44		Cai Zelin	CHN	11.4.91	2	RWC-F	Ordos	14 Sep

Where better than track best

39:49	Jakub	Jelonek	POL	7.7.85	5		Voronovo	16 Sep
39:51		Chen Ding	CHN	5.8.92	3	RWC-F	Ordos	14 Sep
39:54	Aleksandr	Yargunkin	RUS	6.1.81	2	NGP	Buy	2 Sep
39:54	Aleksey	Golovin	RUS	24.12.88	6		Voronovo	16 Sep
39:56+	Jared	Tallent	AUS	17.10.84	1=	in 20k	Taicang	30 Mar
39:56		Li Jianbo	CHN	14.11.86	4	RWC-F	Ordos	14 Sep

Mark	Name		Nat	Born	Pos	Meet	Venue	Date	
39:57	Matteo	Giupponi	ITA	8.10.88	2	NC	Bressanone	3	Jul
39:59+	Robert	Heffernan	IRL	20.2.78	6	in 20k	Lugano	18	Mar
39:59	Aleksandr	Pichkalov	RUS-J	16.6.93	3	NGP	Buy	2	Sep
40:07+	Rafal	Augustyn	POL	14.5.84	8	in 20k	Lugano	18	Mar
40:08+	Valeriy	Borchin	RUS	11.9.86	1=	in 20k	London	4	Aug
40:08+	Vladimir	Kanaykin	RUS	21.3.85	1=	in 20k	London	4	Aug

40:13+	Gurmeet	Singh	IND	1.7.85	11 Mar
40:20+	Omar	Zepeda	MEX	8.6.77	14 Apr
40:21	Dane	Bird-Smith	AUS	15.7.92	29 Jun
40:21+	Erik	Tysse	NOR	4.12.80	4 Aug

40:24	Jean-Jacques	Nkouloukidi	ITA	15.4.82	6	Jul
40:25+	Grzegorz	Sudol	POL	28.8.78	4	Aug
40:25+	Eider	Arévalo	COL-J	9.3.93	4	Aug

JUNIORS WHERE INFERIOR TO TRACK BEST

Mark	Name		Nat	Born	Pos	Meet	Venue	Date	
39:59	Aleksandr	Pichkalov	RUS	16.6.93	3	NGP	Buy	2	Sep
40:14+	Takumi	Saito	JPN	23.3.93	2	in 20k	Kobe	19	Feb
40:25+	Eider	Arévalo	COL	9.3.93	21	in 20k	London	4	Aug
40:35	Igor	Lyashchenko	UKR	24.8.93	9	in 20k	Lugano	18	Mar
40:48	Aleksandr	Ivanov	RUS	26.6.94	1	NC-wj	Sochi	19	Feb
40:49	Kirill	Frolov	RUS	29.9.93	1		Grodno	6	Oct
40:53	Damir	Babykov	RUS	5.5.94	2	NC-wj	Sochi	19	Feb
40:59	Pavel	Parshin	RUS-Y	2.1.94	4	NC-wj	Sochi	19	Feb
41:01	Yevgeniy	Zaleskiy	BLR	18.7.93	2		Grodno	6	Oct
41;02+		Qi Zhao	CHN	14.1.93		in 20k	Saransk	12	May
41:21		Jiang Shan	CHN-Y	14.7.95	1		Taicang	31	Mar
41:27	Daisuke	Matsunaga	JPN-Y	24.3.95	1	NC-j	Kobe	18	Feb
41:27	Artyom	Turkov	BLR	5.1.94	2	NCp-j	Nesvizh	7	Apr

20 KILOMETRES WALK

20k	10k	Name		Nat	Born	Pos	Meet	Venue	Date	
1:17:30	39:06	Alex	Schwazer ¶	ITA	26.12.84	1		Lugano	18	Mar
1:17:36	39:56		Wang Zhen	CHN	24.8.91	1		Taicang	30	Mar
1:17:40	39:56		Chen Ding	CHN	5.8.92	2		Taicang	30	Mar
1:17:43	39:15	Yohann	Diniz	FRA	1.1.78	2		Lugano	18	Mar
1:17:47	38:35	Andrey	Ruzavin	RUS	28.3.86	1	NC-w	Sochi	18	Feb
1:18:25	38:45	Andrey	Krivov	RUS	14.11.85	2	NC-w	Sochi	18	Feb
1:18:25	39:06	Erick	Barrondo	GUA	14.6.91	3		Lugano	18	Mar
1:18:29	38:47	Stanislav	Yemelyanov	RUS	23.10.90	3	NC-w	Sochi	18	Feb
1:18:46	40:08		Chen Ding			1	OG	London	4	Aug
1:18:47	39:57		Cai Zelin	CHN	11.4.91	3		Taicang	30	Mar
1:18:57	40:09		Barrondo			2	OG	London	4	Aug
1:19:13	40:11		Wang Zhen			1	WCp	Saransk	12	May
1:19:20	38:52	Pyotr	Trofimov (10)	RUS	28.11.83	4	NC-w	Sochi	18	Feb
1:19:25	40:08		Wang Zhen			3	OG	London	4	Aug
1:19:27	40:16		Krivov			2	WCp	Saransk	12	May
1:19:42			Cai Zelin			1	OT	Huaian	12	Feb
1:19:43	40:16	Vladimir	Kanaykin	RUS	21.3.85	3	WCp	Saransk	12	May
1:19:44	40:15		Cai Zelin			4	OG	London	4	Aug
1:19:49	40:08	Miguel Ángel	López	ESP	3.7.88	5	OG	London	4	Aug
1:19:52	40:08	Eder	Sánchez	MEX	21.5.86	6	OG	London	4	Aug
1:19:55	39:57	Nazar	Kovalenko	UKR	9.2.89	4		Lugano	18	Mar
1:19:58			Zhao Qi	CHN-J	14.1.93	1-j		Taicang	30	Mar
1:20:02	40:08	Jared	Tallent	AUS	17.10.84	7	OG	London	4	Aug
1:20:06			Yu Wei	CHN	11.9.87	1e2		Taicang	30	Mar
1:20:10	40:04	Giorgio	Rubino	ITA	15.4.86	4		Taicang	30	Mar
1:20:12	40:11	Bertrand	Moulinet	FRA	6.1.87	8	OG	London	4	Aug
1:20:17	40:40	Ruslan	Dmytrenko (20)	UKR	22.3.86	4	WCp	Saransk	12	May
1:20:18	40:13	Robert	Heffernan	IRL	20.2.78	9	OG	London	4	Aug
1:20:19	40:37		Dmytrenko			5		Lugano	18	Mar
1:20:21	40:10	Kolothum Thodi Irfan (30/22)		IND	8.2.90	10	OG	London	4	Aug
1:20:22.52t		Gurmeet	Singh	IND	1.7.85	1		Bhubaneswar	3	Feb
1:20:25	40:20	Matej	Tóth	SVK	10.2.83	1		Rio Maior	14	Apr
1:20:31	39:45	Denis	Strelkov	RUS	26.10.90	5	NC-w	Sochi	18	Feb
1:20:38	40:15	Isamu	Fujisawa	JPN	12.10.87	1	NC-w	Kobe	19	Feb
1:20:39		Erik	Tysse	NOR	4.12.80	1	Nordic	Eskilstuna	15	Sep
1:20:41	40:51	Christopher	Linke	GER	24.10.88	6		Taicang	30	Mar
1:20:41	40:27	João	Vieira	POR	20.2.76	11	OG	London	4	Aug
1:20:42	40:17	Denis (30)	Simanovich	BLR	20.4.87	12	OG	London	4	Aug
1:20:48	40:37	Ivan	Losev	UKR	26.1.86	7		Lugano	18	Mar

Mark		Name		Nat	Born	Pos	Meet	Venue	Date	
1:20:50	40:42	Dawid	Tomala	POL	27.8.89	1		Zaniemysl	21	Apr
1:20:51	39:37	Pyotr	Bogatyrev	RUS	11.3.91	6	NC-w	Sochi	18	Feb
1:20:51		Andriy	Kovenko	UKR	25.11.73	1	NC-w	Yevpatoriya	6	Mar
1:20:53		Rafal	Augustyn	POL	14.5.84	2		Zaniemysl	21	Apr
1:20:55	40:37		Li Jianbo	CHN	14.11.86	1		La Coruña	9	Jun
1:20:58	39:58	Matteo	Giupponi	ITA	8.10.88	9		Lugano	18	Mar
1:20:58		Grzegorz	Sudol	POL	28.8.78	3		Zaniemysl	21	Apr
1:20:58	40:24	Iñaki	Gómez	CAN	16.1.88	13	OG	London	4	Aug
1:21:01	40:14	Takumi	Saito	JPN-J	23.3.93	2	NC	Kobe	19	Feb
		(40)								
1:21:01			Li Tianlei	CHN-Y	13.1.95	2e2		Taicang	30	Mar
1:21:05		Jakub	Jelonek	POL	7.7.85	4		Zaniemysl	21	Apr
1:21:06	40:43	Aleksandr	Prokhorov	RUS	22.1.86	7	NC-w	Sochi	18	Feb
1:21:07		Igor	Lyashchenko	UKR-J	24.8.93	3	NC-w	Yevpatoriya	6	Mar
1:21:07			Yin Jiaxing	CHN-J	16.3.94	2-j		Taicang	30	Mar
1:21:10	40:33	Hiroki	Arai	JPN	18.5.88	3	NC	Kobe	19	Feb
1:21:12		Lukasz	Nowak	POL	18.12.88	5		Zaniemysl	21	Apr
1:21:12	40:44	Aléxandros	Papamihaíl	GRE	18.9.88	15	OG	London	4	Aug
1:21:14	40:43	Hayato	Katsuki	JPN	28.11.90	4	NC	Kobe	19	Feb
1:21:14	40:20	Isaac	Palma	MEX	26.10.90	3		Rio Maior	14	Apr
		(50)								
1:21:21		Rafal	Fedaczynski	POL	3.12.80	6		Zaniemysl	21	Apr
1:21:22	40:32		Zhu Chundong	CHN	1.1.90	1	AsiC	Nomi	11	Mar
1:21:23	40:51	Adam	Rutter	AUS	24.12.86	9		Taicang	30	Mar
1:21:23	40:21	Ivan	Trotskiy	BLR	27.5.76	16	OG	London	4	Aug
1:21:24	40:34	André	Höhne	GER	10.3.78	2		Naumburg	22	Apr
1:21:29	40:16	Valeriy	Borchin	RUS	11.9.86	9	WCp	Saransk	12	May
1:21:30	40:19	Anatoliy	Kukushkin	RUS	12.2.86	8	NC-w	Sochi	18	Feb
1:21:31	40:13	Takayuki	Tanii	JPN	14.2.83	5	NC	Kobe	19	Feb
1:21:36		Caio	Bonfim	BRA	19.3.91	1	NC	São Paulo	29	Jun
1:21:36	40:28		Kim Hyun-sub	KOR	31.5.85	17	OG	London	4	Aug
		(60)								
1:21:42	40:17		Byun Young-jun	KOR	20.3.84	3	AsiC	Nomi	11	Mar
1:21:49		Eider	Arévalo	COL-J	9.3.93	1		Eugene	1	Apr
1:21:52	40:16	Koichiro	Morioka	JPN	2.4.85	6	NC	Kobe	19	Feb
1:21:55		Benjamin	Thorne	CAN-J	19.3.93	1	NC	Edmonton	15	Sep
1:21:56		Mauricio	Arteaga	ECU	8.8.88	2		Eugene	1	Apr
1:21:59			Wang Zhendong	CHN	11.1.91	4	OT	Huaian	12	Feb
1:22:00		Federico	Tontodonati	ITA	30.10.89	14		Lugano	18	Mar
1:22:00.86	t	Baljinder	Singh	IND	18.9.86	1		Patiala	15	Feb
1:22:04	40:25	Horacio	Nava	MEX	20.1.82	5		Rio Maior	14	Apr
1:22:09		Rafal	Sikora	POL	17.2.87	7		Zaniemysl	21	Apr
		(70)								
1:22:09.56	t	Surender	Singh	IND	4.7.88	2		Patiala	15	Feb
1:22:10	40:35	Juan Manuel	Cano	ARG	12.12.87	22	OG	London	4	Aug
1:22:12		Alvaro	Martín	ESP-J	18.6.94	16		Lugano	18	Mar
1:22:13		Trevor	Barron	USA	30.9.92	3		Eugene	1	Apr
1:22:13			Niu Wenbin	CHN	20.1.91	2		Ordos	13	Sep
1:22:15			Li Shijia	CHN	14.1.92	6	OT	Huaian	12	Feb
1:22:15	40:21	Ever	Palma	MEX	18.3.92	6		Rio Maior	14	Apr
1:22:17		Dawid	Wolski	POL	15.6.89	8		Zaniemysl	21	Apr
1:22:19.35	t	Abbal Singh	Rana	IND	14.3.90	3		Patiala	15	Feb
1:22:20	40:55	Chris	Erickson	AUS	1.12.81	20	WCp	Saransk	12	May
		(80)								
1:22:25		Marius	Ziukas	LTU	29.6.85	17		Lugano	18	Mar
1:22:25			Sun Chengang	CHN	11.3.91	4e2		Taicang	30	Mar
1:22:25		Antón	Kucmín	SVK	7.6.84	23	OG	London	4	Aug
1:22:30			Chen Zongliang	CHN	9.1.92	5e2		Taicang	30	Mar
1:22:30		Yusuke	Suzuki	JPN	2.1.88	1		Takahata	28	Oct
1:22:33		Eiki	Takahashi	JPN	19.11.92	2		Takahata	28	Oct
1:22:34			Xie Sichao	CHN-J	28.2.93	2-j		Huaian	12	Feb
1:22:36		Ato	Ibañez	SWE	14.11.85	2	Nordic	Eskilstuna	15	Sep
1:22:37.26	t	Mani Ram	Patel	IND	16.9.91	4		Patiala	15	Feb
1:22:41			Liu Jianmin	CHN	9.3.88	8	OT	Huaian	12	Feb
		(90)								
1:22:42		Takuya	Yoshida	JPN	10.8.90	3		Takahata	28	Oct
1:22:48			Su Guanyu	CHN-J	26.6.94	1-j		Xintai	15	Jun
1:22:50		Luke	Adams	AUS	22.10.76	10		Taicang	30	Mar
1:22:53			Bian Fongda	CHN	1.4.91	9	OT	Huaian	12	Feb
1:22:54		James	Rendón	COL	7.4.85	28	OG	London	4	Aug
1:22:55		Aleksandr	Lyakhovich	BLR	4.7.89	1		Grodno	6	Oct

Mark	Name	Nat	Born	Pos	Meet	Venue	Date
1:22:56 40:45	Babu Bhai Panocha	IND	10.8.78	23	WCp	Saransk	12 May
1:23:02	Ma Haijun	CHN	24.11.92	10	OT	Huaian	12 Feb
1:23:06.83t	Xu Faguang	CHN	17.5.87	1		Tianjin	18 Sep
1:23:10 40:11	Recep Celik	TUR	10.8.83	18		Lugano	18 Mar
	(100)						

Mark	Name		Nat	Born	Date
1:23:12	Artur	Brzozowski	POL	29.3.85	21 Apr
1:23:13	Jarkko	Kinnunen	FIN	19.1.84	21 Apr
1:23:14		Si Tianfeng	CHN	17.6.84	9 Jun
1:23:15	Dane	Bird-Smith	AUS	15.7.92	30 Mar
1:23:18	Hagen	Pohle	GER	5.3.92	30 Mar
1:23:19A	Fredy	Hernández	COL	25.4.78	3 Mar
1:23:19	Yuki	Yamazaki	JPN	16.1.84	12 May
1:23:20	Edikt	Khaybullin	RUS	29.5.89	18 Feb
1:23:20	Andreas	Gustafsson	SWE	10.8.81	15 Sep
1:23:21	Georgiy	Sheyko	KAZ	24.8.89	18 Feb
1:23:21	Pedro	Gómez	MEX	31.12.90	9 Jun
1:23:23	Patryk	Rogowski	POL	11.4.89	21 Apr
1:23:27	Jonathan	Rieckmann	BRA	20.8.87	24 Mar
1:23:28		He Yongqiang	CHN-J	27.11.93	12 Feb
1:23:29	Kevin	Campion	FRA	23.5.88	9 Jun
1:23:32	Vitaliy	Anichkin	KAZ	26.8.89	18 Feb
1:23:32	Máté	Helebrandt	HUN	12.1.89	4 Aug
1:23:34	Marco	De Luca	ITA	12.5.81	18 Mar
1:23:34	Gustavo	Restrepo	COL	27.7.82	12 May
1:23:35	Hassane	Sbaï	TUN	21.4.84	7 Jul
1:23:36A	David	Kimutai	KEN	19.8.69	15 Jun
1:23:39	Oleksandr	Verbytskyy	UKR	28.7.92	24 Mar
1:23:40		Wang Hao	CHN	16.8.89	12 May
1:23:40	Andrés	Chocho	ECU	4.11.83	29 Jun
1:23:41	Luis Fernando	López	COL	3.6.79	9 Jun
1:23:41.57t	José	Montaña	COL	21.3.92	22 Sep
1:23:43	Maksim	Kovalenko	UKR	9.1.89	9 Jun
1:23:43	Perseus	Karlström	SWE	2.5.90	15 Sep
1:23:45		Choi Byung-kwang	KOR	7.4.91	30 Mar
1:23:47	Takaki	Matsuzaki	JPN	12.8..92	28 Oct
1:23:52		Zhang Hang	CHN	28.10.91	30 Mar
1:23:52		Ding Xianyu	CHN-J	27.11.93	30 Mar
1:23:52		Kim Dae-ro	KOR	30.4.88	15 Oct
1:23:53		Wang Gang	CHN	2.4.91	12 Feb
1:23:53	Luis Manuel	Corchete	ESP	14.5.84	9 Jun
1:23:54	Sándor	Rácz	HUN	14.9.86	21 Apr
1:23:54	Valeriy	Filipchuk	RUS	30.6.91	10 Jun
1:23:55	Cédric	Houssaye	FRA	13.12.79	18 Mar
1:23:56	Pavel	Samoylenko	RUS	13.3.88	18 Feb
1:23:58	Hatem	Ghoula	TUN	7.6.73	7 Jul
1:23:59	Takafumi	Higuma	JPN	3.9.82	19 Feb
1:24:00		Ji Chunlong	CHN	25.2.88	13 Sep
1:24:00.2t	Jai	Bhagwan	IND		13 Mar
1:24:01	Ebrahim	Rahimian	IRI	29.6.81	11 Mar
1:24:01	Aleksey	Golovin	RUS	24.12.88	10 Jun
1:24:06	Oleksandr	Venglovskyy	UKR	5.8.85	9 Jun
1:24:09	Aleksandr	Yargunkin	RUS	6.1.81	18 Mar
1:24:10	Luis Alberto	Amezcua	ESP	1.5.82	18 Mar
1:24:10	Benjamín	Sánchez	ESP	10.3.85	12 May
1:24:18	Arnis	Rumbenieks	LAT	4.4.88	1 Jun
1:24:19		Han Jijang	CHN-J	20.7.93	12 Feb
1:24:19	Predrag	Filipovic	SRB	5.10.78	18 Mar
1:24:21	Evans	Dunfee	CAN	28.9.90	9 Jun
1:24:23	Ken	Akashi	JPN	6.11.76	19 Feb
1:24:28.57t		Chu Yafei	CHN	5.9.88	18 Sep
1:24:29		Hu Enxi	CHN-J	26.3.94	12 Feb
1:24:30	Francisco	Arcilla	ESP	14.1.84	14 Apr
1:24:31	Hichem	Medjber	ALG	10.2.82	21 Apr
1:24:33		Jiang Jie	CHN-J	25.10.94	30 Mar
1:24:34	Moacir	Zimmermann	BRA	30.12.83	17 Mar
1:24:34	Rhydian	Cowley	AUS	4.1.91	26 Aug
1:24:41		Zhao Fujie	CHN-J	11.11.93	30 Mar
1:24:45	Colin	Griffin	IRL	3.8.82	22 Apr
1:24:47		Hu Wanli	CHN	27.5.92	13 Sep
1:24:48		Rong Yufei	CHN	8.4.92	12 Feb
1:24:48	Vitaliy	Talankov	BLR	29.4.82	7 Apr
1:24:49		Zhao Yinliang	CHN-J	6.1.93	30 Mar
1:24:49	Carsten	Schmidt	GER	29.5.86	22 Apr
1:24:49	Thomas	Bosworth	GBR	17.1.90	9 Jun
1:24:51		Han Yucheng	CHN	16.12.78	12 Feb
1:24:52	Yuki	Sasagawa	JPN	18.11.91	11 Mar
1:24:54	Takataru	Kutsuna	JPN-J	17.2.94	28 Oct
1:24:57	Daniele	Paris	ITA	18.10.84	22 Apr
1:24:58	Tomofumi	Kanno	JPN-J	25.4.93	28 Oct
1:24:59	(175)	Wang Yue	CHN	7.4.92	12 Feb

Best track times

Mark	Name		Nat	Born	Pos	Meet	Venue	Date
1:23:00.10	Trevor	Barron	USA	30.9.92	1	NC/OT	Eugene	30 Jun
1:23:22.83	Caio	Bonfim	BRA	19.3.91				22 Sep
1:23:37.21		Li Tianlei	CHN-Y	13.1.95				18 Sep
1:24:44.22	Babu Bhai	Panocha	IND	10.8.78				15 Feb

Drugs disqualification

Mark	Name	Nat	Born	Pos	Meet	Venue	Date
1:17:52 38:35	Sergey Morozov ¶	RUS	21.3.88	(2)	NC-w	Sochi	18 Feb
1:19:51 39:08	Morozov ¶			(1)	NC	Moskva	10 Jun

JUNIORS

See main list for top 10 juniors. 10 performances by 6 men to 1:21:50. Additional marks and further juniors:

Name	Mark	Pos	Venue	Date					
Zhao Qi	1:21:06	1J	Huaian	12 Feb	1:21:46	10	WCp	Saransk	12 May
Saito	1:21:44	2	Nomi	11 Mar					
Lyashchenko	1:21:40	12	Lugano	18 Mar					

Mark	Name	Nat	Born	Pos	Meet	Venue	Date
1:23:28	He Yongqiang	CHN	27.11.93	3-j	OT	Huaian	12 Feb
1:23:52	Ding Xianyu	CHN	27.11.93	4-j		Taicang	30 Mar
1:24:19	Han Jijang	CHN	20.7.93	5-j	OT	Huaian	12 Feb
1:24:29	Hu Enxi	CHN	26.3.94	6-j	OT	Huaian	12 Feb
1:24:33	Jiang Jie	CHN	25.10.94	5-j		Taicang	30 Mar
1:24:41	Zhao Fujie	CHN	11.11.93	6-j		Taicang	30 Mar
1:24:49	Zhao Yinliang	CHN	6.1.93	7-j		Taicang	30 Mar
1:24:54	Takataru Kutsuna	JPN	17.2.94	6		Takahata	28 Oct
1:24:58	Tomofumi Kanno	JPN	25.4.93	7		Takahata	28 Oct
1:25:09	Liu Xu	CHN	11.12.94	2j		Ordos	13 Sep
1:25:53	Hiu Ying (20)	CHN	28.2.94	7j		Taicang	30 Mar

30 & 35 KILOMETRES WALK

Mark		Name	Nat	Born	Pos	Meet	Venue	Date
2:05:46	2:25:42	Sergey Kirdyapkin	RUS	18.6.80	1	NC-w	Sochi	18 Feb
2:05:39	2:25:59	Mikhail Ryzhov	RUS	17.12.91	2	NC-w	Sochi	26 Feb
2:06:01	2:26:27	Ryzhov			1	NCp	Cheboksary	9 Sep
2:05:56	2:26:33	Ivan Noskov	RUS	16.7.88	3	NC-w	Sochi	26 Feb
2:06:17	2:27:50	Aleksey Bartsaykin	RUS	22.3.89	4	NC-w	Sochi	18 Feb
2:06:52	2:28:10	Alex Schwazer ¶	ITA	26.12.84	1		Latina	29 Jan

Mark			Name		Nat	Born	Pos	Meet	Venue	Date
2:06:57	2:28:11		Yuriy	Andronov	RUS	6.11.71	5	NC-w	Sochi	26 Feb
2:07:13	2:29:15			Bartsaykin			2	NCp	Cheboksary	9 Sep
2:08:36	2:31:07			Noskov			3	NCp	Cheboksary	9 Sep
	2:31:29			Wang Zhen	CHN	24.8.91	2		Latina	29 Jan

and see **further lists on page 527** as well as intermediate times in 50km list that follows.

50 KILOMETRES WALK

Mark			Name		Nat	Born	Pos	Meet	Venue	Date
3:35:59	2:10:56	2:32:37	Sergey	Kirdyapkin	RUS	18.6.80	1	OG	London	11 Aug
3:36:53	2:10:57	2:32:37	Jared	Tallent	AUS	17.10.84	2	OG	London	11 Aug
3:37:16	2:11:07	2:32:16		Si Tianfeng	CHN	17.6.84	3	OG	London	11 Aug
3:37:54	2:12:09	2:33:31	Robert	Heffernan	IRL	20.2.78	4	OG	London	11 Aug
3:37:54	2:10:54	2:32:24	Igor	Yerokhin	RUS	4.9.85	5	OG	London	11 Aug
3:38:08				Kirdyapkin			1	WCp	Saransk	13 May
3:38:10				Yerokhin			2	WCp	Saransk	13 May
3:38:55	2:10:49	2:32:22	Sergey	Bakulin	RUS	13.11.86	6	OG	London	11 Aug
3:39:01	2:12:10	2:33:31		Li Jianbo	CHN	14.11.86	7	OG	London	11 Aug
3:40:32				Tallent			3	WCp	Saransk	13 May
3:40:46			Yuriy	Andronov	RUS	6.11.71	1	NC	Moskva	11 Jun
3:40:58			Alex	Schwazer ¶	ITA	26.12.84	1		Dudince	24 Mar
3:41:24	2:12:41	2:34:49	Matej	Tóth (10)	SVK	10.2.83	8	OG	London	11 Aug
3:41:47	2:11:31	2:33:06	Yuki	Yamazaki	JPN	16.1.84	1	NC	Wajima	15 Apr
3:42:47	2:13:51	2:35:55	Lukasz	Nowak	POL	18.12.88	9	OG	London	11 Aug
3:43:05				Si Tianfeng			4	WCp	Saransk	13 May
3:43:14	2:13:16	2:35:20	Koichiro	Morioka	JPN	2.4.85	10	OG	London	11 Aug
3:43:56	2:12:07	2:34:43	Takayuki	Tanii	JPN	14.2.83	2	NC	Wajima	15 Apr
3:44:24				Nowak			2		Dudince	24 Mar
3:44:26	2:14:20	2:36:12	André	Höhne	GER	10.3.78	11	OG	London	11 Aug
3:44:59			Erick	Barrondo	GUA	14.6.91	1	ESP Ch	Pontevedra	4 Mar
3:45:17			João	Vieira	POR	20.2.76	2	1 NC	Pontevedra	4 Mar
3:45:22				Morioka			3	NC	Wajima	15 Apr
3:45:35			Bertrand	Moulinet	FRA	6.1.87	12	OG	London	11 Aug
3:45:55				Park Chil-sung	KOR	8.7.82	13	OG	London	11 Aug
3:46:01			Grzegorz	Sudol (20)	POL	28.8.78	1		Gleina	14 Oct
3:46:09			Ivan	Trotskiy	BLR	27.5.76	14	OG	London	11 Aug
3:46:14				Bakulin			5	WCp	Saransk	13 May
3:46:25			Jarkko	Kinnunen	FIN	19.1.84	15	OG	London	11 Aug
3:46:52	2:14:29	2:37:01	Rafal	Sikora (30/23)	POL	17.2.87	3		Dudince	24 Mar
3:46:59			Horacio	Nava	MEX	20.1.82	16	OG	London	11 Aug
3:47:08			Hiroki	Arai	JPN	18.5.88	1		Takahata	28 Oct
3:47:19			Marco	De Luca	ITA	12.5.81	17	OG	London	11 Aug
3:47:33			Christopher	Linke	GER	24.10.88	6	WCp	Saransk	13 May
3:48:07			Igor	Hlavan	UKR	25.9.90	19	OG	London	11 Aug
3:48:15			Jesús Ángel	García	ESP	17.10.69	7	WCp	Saransk	13 May
3:48:18			Konstantin	Maksimov (30)	RUS	17.6.82	2	NC	Moskva	11 Jun
3:48:37	2:13:07	2:34:04	Trond	Nymark	NOR	28.12.76	21	OG	London	11 Aug
3:48:38A			Omar	Zepeda	MEX	8.6.77	1		Chihuahua	3 Mar
3:48:45	2:10:54	3:32:24	Nathan	Deakes	AUS	17.8.77	22	OG	London	11 Aug
3:48:47				Xu Faguang	CHN	17.5.87	8	WCp	Saransk	13 May
3:49:26			Andrés	Chocho	CAN	28.9.90	1		Valley Cottage	28 Oct
3:49:53			Rafal	Augustyn	POL	14.5.84	10	WCp	Saransk	13 May
3:49:56			Aléxandros	Papamihaíl	GRE	18.9.88	25	OG	London	11 Aug
3:50:17			Oleksiy	Kazanin	UKR	22.5.82	11	WCp	Saransk	13 May
3:50:47			Andreas	Gustafsson	SWE	10.8.81	2		Valley Cottage	28 Oct
3:50:53			Aleksandr	Yargunkin (40)	RUS	6.1.81	3	NC	Moskva	11 Jun
3:50:57A			Clemente	García	MEX	21.8.89	2		Chihuahua	3 Mar
3:51:17			Ken	Akashi	JPN	6.11.76	4	NC	Wajima	15 Apr
3:51:31A			José	Leyver	MEX	12.11.85	3		Chihuahua	3 Mar
3:51:37			Federico	Tontodonati	ITA	30.10.89	1	NC	Villa Di Serio	14 Oct
3:52:04				Zhao Jianguo	CHN	19.1.88	2	OT	Huaian	11 Feb
3:52:18A			Cristian D.	Berdeja	MEX	21.6.81	4		Chihuahua	3 Mar
3:52:45			Michal	Stasiewicz	POL	28.9.88	2		Gleina	14 Oct
3:52:47A			Horacio	Olivares	MEX	18.4.91	5		Chihuahua	3 Mar
3:52:53			Takafumi	Higuma	JPN	3.9.82	5	NC	Wajima	15 Apr
3:52:55			Colin	Griffin (50)	IRL	3.8.82	15	WCp	Saransk	13 May

Mark		Name		Nat	Born	Pos	Meet	Venue	Date
3:53:02		Sergiy	Budza	UKR	6.12.84	16	WCp	Saransk	13 May
3:53:41	2:11:09 2:34:03	Luke	Adams	AUS	22.10.76	26	OG	London	11 Aug
3:53:46		Oleksiy	Shelest	UKR	27.3.73	1	NC	Ivano-Frankivsk	21 Oct
3:53:49		Mikhail	Ryzhov	RUS	17.12.91	18	WCp	Saransk	13 May
3:53:57		Emerson	Hernández	ESA	20.1.89	27	OG	London	11 Aug
3:54:32		Aleksey	Khimin	RUS	26.2.89	4	NC	Moskva	11 Jun
3:54:40		Igor	Saharuk	UKR	3.6.88	2	NC	Ivano-Frankivsk	21 Oct
3:54:41		Adrian	Blocki	POL	11.4.90	1		København	6 Oct
3:54:42			Cui Zhide	CHN	11.1.83	3	OT	Huaian	11 Feb
3:55:01		Brendan	Boyce	IRL	15.10.86	29	OG	London	11 Aug
(60)									
3:55:03		Quentin	Rew	NZL	16.7.84	30	OG	London	11 Aug
3:55:16		Ivan	Noskov	RUS	16.7.88	20	WCp	Saransk	13 May
3:55:16		Cédric	Houssaye	FRA	13.12.79	31	OG	London	11 Aug
3:55:32		Marc	Mundell	RSA	7.7.83	32	OG	London	11 Aug
3:55:51		Damian	Blocki	POL	28.4.89	2		København	6 Oct
3:56:00		Fredy	Hernández	COL	25.4.78	33	OG	London	11 Aug
3:56:12			Kim Dong-young	KOR	6.3.80	22	WCp	Saransk	13 May
3:56:20		Ivan	Banzeruk	UKR	9.2.90	3	NC	Ivano-Frankivsk	21 Oct
3:56:34			Lim Jung-hyun	KOR	8.9.87	34	OG	London	11 Aug
3:56:38		Håvard	Haukenes	NOR	22.4.90	3	1 NC	København	6 Oct
(70)									
3:56:39A		Juan Emilio	Toscano	MEX	3.7.81	7		Chihuahua	3 Mar
3:56:47			Geng Zhiyao	CHN	15.8.87	1	OT	Ordos	15 Sep
3:56:48		Basant Bahadur	Rana	IND	18.1.84	36	OG	London	11 Aug
3:57:34		Semyon	Lovkin	RUS	14.7.77	5	NC	Moskva	11 Jun
3:57:47			Wang Zhendong	CHN	11.1.91	2		Ordos	15 Sep
3:57:52		Marius	Cocioran	ROU	10.7.83	39	OG	London	11 Aug
3:58:00		Pedro	Isidro	POR	17.7.85	27	WCp	Saransk	13 May
3:58:22			Wu Qianlong	CHN	30.1.90	3		Ordos	15 Sep
3:58:31		Oleksandr	Romanenko	UKR	26.6.81	8		Dudince	24 Mar
3:58:51		Benjamín	Sánchez	ESP	10.3.85	4	2 NC	Pontevedra	4 Mar
(80)									
3:58:57		Xavier	Moreno	ECU	15.11.79	10	OG	London	11 Aug
3:59:02		Igors	Kazakevics	LAT	19.4.80	11		Dudince	24 Mar
3:59:05		Dusan	Majdan	SVK	8.9.87	12	1 NC	Dudince	24 Mar
3:59:10		Maik	Berger	GER	17.2.79	13		Dudince	24 Mar
3:59:17A		Luis	Bustamante	MEX	10.6.84	8		Chihuahua	3 Mar
3:59:19		Teodorico	Caporaso	ITA	14.9.87	28	WCp	Saransk	13 May
3:59:58		Luis Manuel	Corchete	ESP	14.5.84	5	3 NC	Pontevedra	4 Mar
3:59:58		Evan	Dunfee	CAN	28.9.90	3		Valley Cottage	28 Oct
4:00:39		Ian	Rayson	AUS	4.2.88	2	NC	Melbourne	8 Dec
4:00:55		Oleksandr	Venglovskyy	UKR	5.8.85	30	WCp	Saransk	13 May
(90)									
4:00:58			Liu Jianmin	CHN	9.3.88	4		Ordos	15 Sep
4:01:13		Juan Manuel	Molina	ESP	15.3.79	6	4 NC	Pontevedra	4 Mar
4:01:24		Miguel Ángel	Prieto	ESP	20.9.64	7	5 NC	Pontevedra	4 Mar
4:01:32			Li Lei	CHN	29.11.87	1		Taicang	31 Mar
4:01:50		Antti	Kempas	FIN	3.10.80	41	OG	London	11 Aug
4:02:03A		Edward	Araya	CHI	14.2.86	9		Chihuahua	3 Mar
4:02:07		Pavel	Yerokhov	BLR	21.7.82	14		Dudince	24 Mar
4:02:09		Mário José	dos Santos	BRA	10.9.79	31	WCp	Saransk	13 May
4:02:48		Mikel	Odriozola	ESP	25.5.73	42	OG	London	11 Aug
4:03:04			Xu Dexing	CHN	20.8.88	5		Ordos	15 Sep
(100)									

Mark			Nat	Born	Date		Mark			Nat	Born	Date
4:03:20	Anatole	Ibáñez	SWE	14.11.85	24 Mar		4:06:37	Pedro	Martins	POR	12.1.68	4 Mar
4:03:28	John	Nunn	USA	3.2.78	11 Aug		4:06:48	Tomasz	Gaidamavcius	LTU	7.11.87	24 Mar
4:03:38	Rodrigo	Moreno	COL	29.4.66	13 May		4:06:55	Johan	Augeron	FRA	29.7.83	30 Sep
4:03:40		Zhang Hang	CHN	28.10.91	15 Sep		4:06:57		Hu Wanli	CHN	27.5.92	15 Sep
4:03:45	Sandeep	Kumar	IND	16.12.86	13 May		4:07:36	Alex	Florez	SUI	11.5.71	13 May
4:03:53	Dmitriy	Dzyubin	BLR	12.7.90	13 May		4:07:46	Luís	Gil	POR	6.4.75	4 Mar
4:04:02	Andrey	Stepanchuk	BLR	12.6.79	13 May		4:07:51		Niu Wenbin	CHN	20.1.91	25 Sep
4:04:16	Sergey	Korepanov	RUS	15.7.84	11 Jun		4:07:58	Ricardas	Rekst	LTU	10.10.87	24 Mar
4:04:17	Nenad	Filipovic	SRB	5.10.78	24 Mar		4:08:02		Zhang Kuo	CHN	12.12.89	31 Mar
4:05:06	Xavier	Le Coz	FRA	30.12.79	13 May		4:08:41	Matias	Korpela	FIN	16.11.89	24 Mar
4:05:20	Maciej	Rosiewicz	GEO	31.7.77	11 Aug		4:08:45	Aleksey	Bartsaykin	RUS	22.3.89	11 Jun
4:05:50	Tim	Seaman	USA	14.5.72	22 Jan		4:08:48		Du Yunpeng	CHN	6.9.88	11 Feb
4:06:24A	Ferney	Rojas	COL	30.9.87	15 Nov		4:08:51	Vitaliy	Anichkin	KAZ	11.11.88	11 Jun
4:06:27		Oh Se-hyun	KOR	17.11.88	13 May		4:09:22	Hidehito	Kusaka	JPN	22.6.86	15 Apr
4:06:29	Tadas	Suskevicius	LTU	22.5.85	13 May		4:09:32	Milos	Bátovsky	SVK	26.5.79	11 Aug
4:06:34	Dominic	King	GBR	30.5.83	24 Mar		4:09:56		Zhao Ziyang	CHN	29.7.91	25 Sep
							(132)					

WOMEN'S WORLD LISTS 2012

60 METRES INDOORS

Mark	Name		Nat	Born	Pos	Meet	Venue	Date
7.01	Veronica	Campbell-Brown	JAM	15.5.82	1	WI	Istanbul	11 Mar
7.02	Tianna	Madison	USA	30.8.85	1		Fayetteville	11 Feb
7.02A		Madison			1	NC	Albuquerque	26 Feb
7.04	Murielle	Ahouré	CIV	23.8.87	2	WI	Istanbul	11 Mar
7.05		Madison			1h1		Fayetteville	11 Feb
7.05	Laverne	Jones-Ferrette	ISV	16.9.81	1		Eaubonne	16 Feb
7.06A		Madison			1s1	NC	Albuquerque	26 Feb
7.06A	Barbara	Pierre	USA	28.4.87	2	NC	Albuquerque	26 Feb
7.07		Madison			1	GP	Birmingham	18 Feb
7.07	Gloria	Asumnu	NGR	22.5.85	1		Birmingham, AL	3 Mar
7.08		Jones-Ferrette			1		Houston	28 Jan
7.08		Ahouré			1h2		Fayetteville	11 Feb
7.08		Campbell-Brown			2		Fayetteville	11 Feb
7.08A		Pierre			1s2	NC	Albuquerque	26 Feb
	(14/6)							
7.10	Allyson	Felix	USA	18.11.85	2h2		Fayetteville	11 Feb
7.12	English	Gardner	USA	22.4.92	1	NCAA	Nampa	10 Mar
7.13	Olesya	Povh	UKR	18.10.87	1		Düsseldorf	10 Feb
7.13A	Kya	Brookins	USA	28.7.89	1h2	NC	Albuquerque	25 Feb
	(10)							
7.14	Ivet	Lalova	BUL	18.5.84	2	GP	Birmingham	18 Feb
7.15	Verena	Sailer	GER	16.10.85	1	NC	Karlsruhe	25 Feb
7.15	Octavious	Freeman	USA	20.4.92	2	NCAA	Nampa	10 Mar
7.17	Mariya	Ryemyen	UKR	2.8.87	1	NCp	Zaporizhzhya	27 Jan
7.17	Ezinne	Okparaebo	NOR	3.3.88	3	GP	Birmingham	18 Feb
7.18	Aleen	Bailey	JAM	25.11.80	2		Karlsruhe	12 Feb
7.18A	Alex	Anderson	USA	28.1.87	2s1	NC	Albuquerque	26 Feb
7.18A	Bianca	Knight	USA	2.1.89	3s1	NC	Albuquerque	26 Feb
7.18	Aurieyall	Scott	USA	18.5.92	2h2	NCAA	Nampa	9 Mar
7.19	Asha	Philip	GBR	25.10.90	4	GP	Birmingham	18 Feb
	(20)							
7.19	Dafne	Schippers	NED	15.6.92	1	NC	Apeldoorn	26 Feb
7.19	Chandra	Sturrup	BAH	12.9.71	5	WI	Istanbul	11 Mar
7.20	Jeanette	Kwakye	GBR	20.3.83	1	NC	Sheffield	12 Feb
7.20	Kai	Selvon	TRI	13.4.92	1	SEC	Lexington	26 Feb
7.21	Shayla	Sanders	USA-J	6.1.94	1		Seattle	26 Feb
7.21A	Candyce	McGrone	USA	24.3.89	3s2	NC	Albuquerque	26 Feb
7.22	Stormy	Kendrick	USA	6.1.91	1		New York (Armory)	3 Feb
7.22	Jeneba	Tarmoh	USA	27.9.89	4h2		Fayetteville	11 Feb
7.22A	Me'Lisa	Barber	USA	4.10.80	3h3	NC	Albuquerque	25 Feb
7.22A	Leslie	Cole	USA	16.2.87	4s1	NC	Albuquerque	26 Feb
	(30)							
7.23	Lauryn	Williams	USA	11.9.83	2h1		Birmingham	26 Jan
7.23	Christina	Manning	USA	29.5.90	1	Big 10	Lincoln NE	25 Feb
7.24	Yuliya	Balykina	BLR	12.4.84	1h		Minsk	18 Jan
7.24	Brittney	Reese	USA	9.9.86	1		Saskatoon	3 Feb
7.24	Tameka	Williams	SKN	31.8.89	3		Karlsruhe	12 Feb
7.24	Chelsea	Hayes	USA	9.2.88	1h2	WAC	Nampa	24 Feb
7.24	Ashley	Collier	USA	4.2.92	4	NCAA	Nampa	10 Mar
7.25	Dezerea	Bryant	USA-J	27.4.93	3		Birmingham AL	21 Jan
7.25	Ruddy	Zang Milama	GAB	6.6.87	1h1		Bordeaux	28 Jan
7.25	Natalya	Murinovich	RUS	27.5.85	3	Winter	Moskva	5 Feb
	(40)							
7.25	Yekaterina	Filatova	RUS	11.8.89	1s2	NC	Moskva	22 Feb
7.25	Guzel	Khubbieva	UZB	2.5.76	4s3	WI	Istanbul	11 Mar
7.26	Kimberlyn	Duncan	USA	2.8.91	2	Tyson	Fayetteville	10 Feb
7.26	Jessica	Young	USA	6.4.87	2	Mill	New York (Arm)	11 Feb
7.26A	Shayla	Mahan	USA	18.1.89	5s1	NC	Albuquerque	26 Feb
7.26	Lina	Grincikaite	LTU	3.5.87	5s1	WI	Istanbul	11 Mar
7.27A	Lekeisha	Lawson	USA	3.6.87	1		Flagstaff	4 Feb
7.27	Yuliya	Nesterenko	BLR	15.6.79	1h2	NC	Mogilyov	10 Feb
7.27	Trisha-Ann	Hawthorne	JAM	8.11.89	3	Mill	New York (Arm)	11 Feb
7.27	Vida	Anim	GHA	7.12.83	4		Karlsruhe	12 Feb
	(50)							
7.27	Myriam	Soumaré	FRA	29.10.86	1h2	NC	Aubière	25 Feb
7.27	Jasmine	Edgerson	USA	6.6.91	2		Boston (Allston)	25 Feb

Mark	Wind	Name		Nat	Born	Pos	Meet	Venue	Date	

100 METRES

Mark	Wind	Name		Nat	Born	Pos	Meet	Venue	Date	
10.70	0.6	Shelly-Ann	Fraser-Pryce	JAM	27.12.86	1	NC	Kingston	29	Jun
10.75	1.5		Fraser-Pryce			1	OG	London (OS)	4	Aug
10.78	1.5	Carmelita	Jeter	USA	24.11.79	2	OG	London (OS)	4	Aug
10.81	1.0		Jeter			1		Kingston	5	May
10.81	1.5	Veronica	Campbell-Brown	JAM	15.5.82	3	OG	London (OS)	4	Aug
10.81	0.7		Jeter			1	DL	Birmingham	26	Aug
10.82	0.6		Campbell-Brown			2	NC	Kingston	29	Jun
10.83	1.5		Jeter			1h2	OG	London (OS)	3	Aug
10.83	0.0		Jeter			1s1	OG	London (OS)	4	Aug
10.83	-0.4		Fraser-Pryce			1	WK	Zürich	30	Aug
10.85	1.2		Fraser-Pryce			1s2	OG	London (OS)	4	Aug
10.85	1.5	Tianna	Madison	USA	30.8.85	4	OG	London (OS)	4	Aug
10.86	1.0	Kelly-Ann	Baptiste	TRI	14.10.86	2		Kingston	5	May
10.86	-0.1		Jeter			1	Athl	Lausanne	23	Aug
10.86	-0.1		Fraser-Pryce			2	Athl	Lausanne	23	Aug
10.89	0.0		Campbell-Brown			2s1	OG	London (OS)	4	Aug
10.89	1.5	Allyson	Felix	USA	18.11.85	5	OG	London (OS)	4	Aug
10.90	0.7		Fraser-Pryce			2	DL	Birmingham	26	Aug
10.92	0.7		Felix			1	DL	Doha	11	May
10.92	-0.1		Fraser-Pryce			1	DL	New York	9	Jun
10.92	0.9		Jeter			1	NC/OT	Eugene	23	Jun
10.92	1.0	Blessing	Okagbare	NGR	9.10.88	1s3	OG	London (OS)	4	Aug
10.92	1.0		Madison			2s3	OG	London (OS)	4	Aug
10.93	1.4		Fraser-Pryce			1h1	LGP	London (CP)	14	Jul
10.93	0.7		Okagbare			1h4	OG	London (OS)	3	Aug
10.93	-0.1		Baptiste			3	Athl	Lausanne	23	Aug
10.94	0.7		Campbell-Brown			2	DL	Doha	11	May
10.94	0.6	Kerron	Stewart	JAM	16.4.84	3	NC	Kingston	29	Jun
10.94	1.5		Campbell-Brown			1h3	OG	London (OS)	3	Aug
10.94	1.2		Felix			2s2	OG	London (OS)	4	Aug
10.94	1.5		Baptiste			6	OG	London (OS)	4	Aug
		(31/8)								
10.96	1.9	Kimberlyn	Duncan	USA	2.8.91	1	SEC	Baton Rouge	13	May
10.99	1.3	Murielle	Ahouré (10)	CIV	23.8.87	1h7	OG	London (OS)	3	Aug
11.01	1.9	Ashley	Collier	USA	4.2.92	1	Big 12	Manhattan KS	13	May
11.01	0.6	Sherone	Simpson	JAM	12.8.84	4	NC	Kingston	29	Jun
11.03	1.1	Ruddy	Zang Milama	GAB	6.6.87	1		Port of Spain	19	May
11.04	1.5	Aleen	Bailey	JAM	25.11.80	2h3	NC	Kingston	29	Jun
11.05	1.3	Sheri-Ann	Brooks	JAM	11.2.83	1	Bailey	Edmonton	16	Jun
11.05	1.5	Schillonie	Calvert	JAM	27.7.88	3h3	NC	Kingston	29	Jun
11.05	1.4	Verena	Sailer	GER	16.10.85	1r1		Weinheim	27	Jul
11.06	1.7	Ivet	Lalova	BUL	18.5.84	1h2	EC	Helsinki	27	Jun
11.07	0.9	Sheniqua	Ferguson	BAH	24.11.89	1		Auburn	21	Apr
11.07	0.9	Jeneba	Tarmoh	USA	27.9.89	3=	NC/OT	Eugene	23	Jun
		(20)								
11.07	0.4	Myriam	Soumaré	FRA	29.10.86	2h1	OG	London (OS)	3	Aug
11.07	1.3	Laverne	Jones-Ferrette	ISV	16.9.81	2h7	OG	London (OS)	3	Aug
11.08	1.2	Olesya	Povh	UKR	18.10.87	1r2		Yalta	4	Jun
11.09	1.5	Octavious	Freeman	USA	20.4.92	1	Conf USA	New Orleans	13	May
11.10	1.9	Semoy	Hackett # ?	TRI	27.11.88	2	SEC	Baton Rouge	13	May
11.10	1.8	English	Gardner	USA	22.4.92	1s3	NCAA	Des Moines	6	Jun
11.10	1.2	Ezinne	Okparaebo	NOR	3.3.88	4s2	OG	London (OS)	4	Aug
11.11	0.2	LaShauntea	Moore	USA	31.7.83	1		Baie Mahault	1	May
11.11	0.6	Samantha	Henry-Robinson	JAM	25.9.88	6	NC	Kingston	29	Jun
11.12	0.7	Olga	Bludova	KAZ	5.11.91	1		Tashkent	1	Jun
		(30)								
11.12	1.4	Alex	Anderson	USA	28.1.87	1s2	NC/OT	Eugene	23	Jun
11.13	0.7	Mikele	Barber	USA	4.10.80	6	DL	Doha	11	May
11.13	-0.3	Gloria	Asumnu	NGR	22.5.85	2	NC	Calabar	19	Jun
11.13	1.4	Bianca	Knight	USA	2.1.89	2s2	NC/OT	Eugene	23	Jun
11.13	0.1	Charonda	Williams	USA	27.3.87	3	Spitzen	Luzern	17	Jul
11.15	1.8	Chelsea	Hayes	USA	9.2.88	2s3	NCAA	Des Moines	6	Jun
11.15	1.4	Lauryn	Williams	USA	11.9.83	3s2	NC/OT	Eugene	23	Jun
11.17	1.9	Allison	Peter	ISV	14.7.92	2	Big 12	Manhattan KS	13	May
11.17	1.4	Anne	Cibis	GER	27.9.85	2r1		Weinheim	27	Jul
11.17	0.0	Rosângela	Santos	BRA	20.12.90	3s1	OG	London (OS)	4	Aug
		(40)								

Mark	Wind	Name		Nat	Born	Pos	Meet	Venue	Date
11.18	2.0	Tameka	Williams dq?	SKN	31.8.89	1		San Marcos	28 Apr
11.19	1.5	Michelle-Lee	Ahye	TRI	10.4.92	2	MSR	Walnut	21 Apr
11.19	1.7	Tatjana	Pinto	GER	2.7.92	1h5		Weinheim	26 May
11.19	-0.3	Lauretta	Ozoh ¶	NGR	5.9.90	3	NC	Calabar	19 Jun
11.19A	1.6	Aurieyall	Scott	USA	18.5.92	1	NACAC	Irapuato	6 Jul
11.19	1.5	Lina	Grincikaité	LTU	3.5.87	4h3	OG	London (OS)	3 Aug
11.20	1.5	Me'Lisa	Barber	USA	4.10.80	3	MSR	Walnut	21 Apr
11.20	1.5	Chastity	Riggien	USA	5.7.89	1		Hattiesburg	28 Apr
11.20	2.0	Nataliya	Pogrebnyak	UKR	19.2.88	1s3	NC	Yalta	12 Jun
11.20	-1.2	Sally	Pearson	AUS	19.9.86	1		Nivelles	23 Jun
		(50)							
11.20	1.5	Jura	Levy	JAM	4.11.90	4h3	NC	Kingston	29 Jun
11.20	1.7	Anthonique	Strachan	BAH-J	22.8.93	1	WJ	Barcelona	11 Jul
11.20	0.6	Mariya	Ryemyen	UKR	2.8.87	1	Quercia	Rovereto	4 Sep
11.21	1.2	Abi	Oyepitan	GBR	30.12.79	1h1		Orlando	26 May
11.21	1.8	Kai	Selvon	TRI	13.4.92	3s3	NCAA	Des Moines	6 Jun
11.22	1.2	Tiffany	Townsend	USA	14.6.89	2	FlaR	Gainesville	6 Apr
11.22	0.6	Trisha-Ann	Hawthorne	JAM	8.11.89	1r2		New York	30 May
11.22	1.4	Leslie	Cole	USA	16.2.87	1		Los Angeles (Ww)	2 Jun
11.22	1.5	Guzel	Khubbieva	UZB	2.5.76	4h6	OG	London (OS)	3 Aug
11.24	1.5	Anneisha	McLaughlin	JAM	6.1.86	1		Kingston	26 May
		(60)							
11.24	1.4	Carrie	Russell	JAM	18.10.90	5h1	LGP	London (CP)	14 Jul
11.25	1.1	Phylicia	George	CAN	16.11.87	4		Port of Spain	19 May
11.26	-1.8	Shalonda	Solomon	USA	19.12.85	1		Coral Gables	14 Apr
11.26	1.0	Debbie	Ferguson McKenzie	BAH	16.1.76	7		Kingston	5 May
11.26	1.7	Olga	Belkina	RUS	23.8.90	2h2	EC	Helsinki	27 Jun
11.26	1.0	Tezdzhan	Naimova	BUL	1.5.87	3		Rieti	9 Sep
11.27	nwi	Laura	Turner	GBR	12.8.82	1		Mesa AZ	28 Apr
11.27	1.0	Christine	Arron	FRA	13.9.73	1h2	NC	Angers	16 Jun
11.27	2.0	Melissa	Breen	AUS	17.9.90	2rB	Spitzen	Luzern	17 Jul
11.28	1.0	Tori	Bowie	USA	27.8.90	2		Baton Rouge	21 Apr
		(70)							
11.28	0.4	Alexis	Love	USA	24.4.91	1	OVC	Cape Girardeau	5 May
11.28	1.9	Paris	Daniels	USA	25.1.90	3	Big 12	Manhattan KS	13 May
11.29	1.0	Dezerea	Bryant	USA-J	27.4.93	1		Charlottesville	21 Apr
11.29	1.2	Cleo	VanBuren	USA	1.5.86	1rB		Clermont	2 Jun
11.30	0.6	Ana Cláudia	da Silva	BRA	6.11.88	1h1		São Paulo	3 Mar
11.30	2.0	Dominique	Duncan	USA	7.5.90	1h3	TexR	Austin	30 Mar
11.30	0.9	Ashton	Purvis	USA	12.7.92	1		SanMateo	11 May
11.30	1.9	Darshay	Davis	USA	23.9.91	3	SEC	Baton Rouge	13 May
11.30	0.4	Reyare	Thomas	TRI	23.11.87	1	JUCO	Levelland	17 May
11.30	0.4	Cathleen	Tschirch	GER	23.7.79	1h2		Jena	19 May
		(80)							
11.30	0.3	Yuliya	Chermoshanskaya	RUS	6.1.86	1	NCp	Yerino	14 Jul
11.30	0.5	Viktoriya	Pyatachenko	UKR	7.5.89	1	Déca	Albi	15 Aug
11.31	1.5	Damola	Osayomi	NGR	26.6.86	5	MSR	Walnut	21 Apr
11.31	1.4	Lekeisha	Lawson	USA	3.6.87	2		Los Angeles (Ww)	2 Jun
11.31	1.1	Anyika	Onuora	GBR	28.10.84	3		Regensburg	2 Jun
11.32	2.0	Simone	Facey	JAM	7.5.85	1		Orlando	24 Mar
11.32	1.2	Véronique	Mang	FRA	15.12.84	1		Montgeron	13 May
11.32	0.3	Katerina	Cechová	CZE	21.3.88	1	NC	Vyskov	16 Jun
11.32	0.6	Kerri Ann	Mitchell	CAN	29.3.83	1		Toronto	23 Jun
11.32	-1.0	Natalya	Rusakova	RUS	12.12.79	1s1	NC	Cheboksary	4 Jul
		(90)							
11.32	0.4	Andreea	Ogrâzeanu	ROU	24.3.90	1h1	NC	Bucuresti	5 Jul
11.33	-0.1	Shayla	Sanders	USA-J	6.1.94	1		Fort Lauderdale	24 Mar
11.33	2.0	Tawanna	Meadows	USA	4.8.86	2		San Marcos	28 Apr
11.33	1.7	Cambrya	Jones	USA	20.9.90	4s2	NCAA	Des Moines	6 Jun
11.33	0.9	Nimet	Karakus	TUR-J	23.1.93	1	Balk-J	Eskisehir	23 Jun
11.34	1.5	Agnes	Osazuwa	NGR	21.6.90	6	MSR	Walnut	21 Apr
11.34	0.3	Chisato	Fukushima	JPN	27.6.88	1	Oda	Hiroshima	29 Apr
11.34	1.3	Terra	Evans	USA	7.10.89	1		Lubbock	5 May
11.34	0.6	Melinda	Smedley	USA	11.2.81	1		Los Angeles (ER)	5 May
11.34	1.9	Chalonda	Goodman	USA	29.9.90	5	Big 12	Manhattan KS	13 May
		(100)							
11.34	-0.1	Yelizaveta	Savlinis	RUS	14.8.87	2	Mosc C	Moskva	11 Jun
11.34	nwi	María	Belibasáki	GRE	19.6.91	1	NC	Athína	15 Jun
11.34	1.3	Crystal	Emmanuel	CAN	27.11.91	4	Bailey	Edmonton	16 Jun
11.34	0.9	Barbara	Pierre	USA	28.4.87	3s1	NC/OT	Eugene	23 Jun
11.34	0.8	Miana	Griffiths	CAN	17.1.90	1		Toronto	11 Jul

Mark	Wind	Name		Nat	Born	Date
11.35	1.2	Shayla	Mahan	USA	18.1.89	6 Apr
11.35	1.9	Ariana	Wright	USA-J	20.6.93	7 Apr
11.35	1.6	Franciela	Krasucki	BRA	26.4.88	7 Apr
11.35	1.8	Takeia	Pinckney	USA	24.7.91	12 May
11.35	1.2	Tangela	Neal	USA	7.4.79	26 May
11.35	0.8	Yekaterina	Voronenkova	RUS	8.9.88	7 Jun
11.36	1.6	Sharika	Nelvis	USA	10.5.90	12 May
11.36	0.6	Evelyn	dos Santos	BRA	11.4.85	20 May
11.36	1.7	Grecia	Bolton	USA	2.10.89	6 Jun
11.36	1.2	Dafne	Schippers	NED	15.6.92	9 Jun
11.37	0.4	Kandace	Thomas	USA-J	6.2.93	17 May
11.37	-0.9	Yuliya	Katsura	RUS	28.5.83	26 May
11.37	2.0	Phobay	Kutu-Akoi	LBR	3.12.87	28 Apr
11.37	0.4	Tasha	Allen	USA	8.5.90	17 May
11.37	1.4	Kenyanna	Wilson	USA	27.10.88	2 Jun
11.38	1.8	Shataya	Hendricks	USA	15.8.89	6 Jun
11.38	1.2	Jamile	Samuel	NED	24.4.92	9 Jun
11.38	0.1	Natasha	Hastings	USA	23.7.86	9 Jun
11.38	0.3	Yuliya	Balykina	BLR	12.4.84	11 Jun
11.38	-0.1	Yevgeniya	Polyakova	RUS	29.5.83	11 Jun
11.38	1.1	Candyce	McGrone	USA	24.3.89	22 Jun
11.39	1.0	Jasmine	Edgerson	USA	6.6.91	21 Apr
11.39	0.4	Shai-Anne	Davis	CAN-J	4.12.93	22 Apr
11.39	1.1	Virgil	Hodge	SKN	17.11.83	3 Jun
11.39	0.2	Daria	Korczynska	POL	30.7.81	15 Jun
11.39	1.7	Sheila	Paul	USA	30.9.89	6 Jun
11.39	1.8	Johanna	Danois	FRA	4.4.87	16 Jun
11.39	-0.3	Peace	Uko	NGR-Y	26.12.95	19 Jun
11.39	-0.3	Carima	Louami	FRA	12.5.79	5 Jul
11.40	-1.5	Scottesha	Miller	USA	14.1.88	21 Apr
11.40	1.3	Taylor	Evans	USA	7.10.89	5 May
11.40	1.6	Ayodelé	Ikuesan	FRA	15.5.85	16 Jun
11.40	2.0	Jessica	Young	USA	6.4.87	17 Jul
11.41	1.4	Shaunae	Miller	BAH-J	15.4.94	23 Mar
11.41	0.1		Wei Yongli	CHN	11.10.91	6 May
11.41	1.7	Morolake	Akinosun	USA-J	17.5.94	19 May
11.41	0.3	Porscha	Lucas	USA	18.6.88	9 Jun
11.41	0.8	Émilie	Gaydu	FRA	5.2.89	22 Jun
11.41	1.5	Leena	Günther	GER	16.4.91	27 Jul
11.42	2.0	Tiffani	McReynolds	USA	4.12.91	24 Mar
11.42	2.0	Chesna	Sykes	USA	28.8.92	24 Mar
11.42	1.0	Tarika	Williams	JAM	26.9.89	21 Apr
11.42	1.7	Chaniqua	Corinealdi	USA	5.2.92	6 Jun
11.42	0.5	Martina	Amidei	ITA	8.4.91	8 Jun
11.42	0.3	Shakera	Reece	BAR	31.8.88	14 Jun
11.42	0.2	Marta	Jeschke	POL	2.6.86	15 Jun
11.42	0.2	Anne	Zagré	BEL	13.3.90	17 Jun
11.42	1.0	Hayley	Jones	GBR	14.9.88	17 Jun
11.42	1.7	Tamiris	Liz	BRA-Y	18.11.95	11 Jul
11.42	1.5	Yasmin	Kwadwo	GER	9.11.90	27 Jul
11.43	0.0	Christina	Manning	USA	29.5.90	31 Mar
11.43	1.8	Anna	Doi	JPN-Y	24.8.95	13 May
11.43	1.1	Ayanna	Hutchinson	TRI	18.2.78	19 May
11.43	1.7	Jasmine	Gibbs	USA-J	15.1.94	1 Jun
11.43	1.8	Audrey	Alloh	ITA	21.7.87	10 Jun
11.43	0.2	Marika	Popowicz	POL	28.4.88	15 Jun
11.43	1.0	Ashleigh	Nelson	GBR	20.2.91	27 Jun
11.44	2.0	Dominique	Booker	USA	10.2.92	24 Mar
11.44A	1.5	Janae	Gennette	USA		26 Apr
11.44	0.8	Anastasiya	Pilipenko	KAZ	13.9.86	4 May
11.44	1.2	Mandy	White	USA	23.10.88	2 Jun
11.44	0.5	Gabriela	Laleva	BUL	14.4.90	9 Jun
11.44	1.2	Aaliyah	Brown	USA-Y	6.1.95	9 Jun
11.44	1.8	Jennifer	Galais	FRA	7.3.92	16 Jun
11.44	1.7	Martina	Giovanetti	ITA	10.8.87	14 Jul
11.44	1.0	Esther	Cremer	GER	29.3.88	27 Jul
11.45	0.0	Muna	Lee	USA	30.10.81	24 Mar
11.45	1.7		Ha Xianping	CHN	15.10.90	14 Apr
11.45	1.6	Kana	Ichikawa	JPN	14.1.91	29 Apr
11.45	0.4	LaKeidra	Stewart	USA	8.10.89	12 May
11.45	1.9	Kia	Jackson	USA	15.1.92	13 May
11.45	1.6	Ariana	Washington	USA-Y	4.9.96	19 May
11.45	0.6	Gabrielle	Houston	USA	12.6.90	24 May
11.45	1.8	Katie	Nelms	USA	25.9.92	6 Jun
11.45	1.2	Kali	Davis-White	USA-J	27.10.94	9 Jun
11.45	0.7	Chandra	Sturrup	BAH	12.9.71	22 Jun
11.45	0.5	Vanusa	dos Santos	BRA	22.1.90	8 Sep
11.46	1.4	Endurance	Abinuwa	NGR	31.7.87	30 Mar
11.46	nwi	Margaret	Adeoye	GBR	27.4.85	28 Apr
11.46	2.0	Folake	Akinyemi	NOR	31.3.90	2 Jun
11.46	1.7	Inna	Weit	GER	5.8.88	16 Jun
11.46	2.0	Monique	Spencer	JAM-J	20.10.94	16 Jun
11.46	1.7	Khamica	Bingham	CAN-J	15.6.94	11 Jul
11.47	0.0	Brittany	Jones	USA	6.3.89	31 Mar
11.47	1.2	Bianca	Williams	GBR-J	18.12.93	20 Apr
11.47	1.9	Christy	Udoh	NGR	30.9.91	13 May
11.47	0.0	Connie	Moore	USA	29.8.81	26 May
11.47	0.0	Yelizaveta	Bryzgina	UKR	28.11.89	12 Jun
11.47	0.4	Sophie	Papps	GBR-J	6.10.94	16 Jun
11.47	0.9	Montell	Douglas	GBR	24.1.86	7 Jul
11.47	1.7	Ida	Mayer (196)	GER-J	9.3.93	11 Jul

Doubtful timing

Mark	Wind	Name		Nat	Born	Date
11.41	-0.9	Jinthara	Seangdee	THA	18.5.90	28 Apr

Wind assisted

Mark	Wind	Name		Nat	Born	Pos	Meet	Venue	Date
10.88	5.9	Alex	Anderson	USA	28.1.87	1		Austin	14 Apr
10.89	2.9	Sanya	Richards-Ross	USA	26.2.85	1	TexR	Austin	31 Mar
10.91	4.5	Laverne	Jones-Ferrette	ISV	16.9.81	1		Tomblaine	8 Jul
10.92	2.5		Anderson			1		Clermont	2 Jun
10.93	5.9	LaShauntea	Moore	USA	31.7.83	2		Austin	14 Apr
10.94	3.0	Kimberlyn	Duncan	USA	2.8.91	1	TexR	Austin	31 Mar
10.94	2.5	Samantha	Henry-Robinson	JAM	25.9.88	2		Clermont	2 Jun
10.95	4.5	Charonda	Williams	USA	27.3.87	2		Tomblaine	8 Jul
10.96	2.5	Lauryn	Williams	USA	11.9.83	3		Clermont	2 Jun
11.00	2.5	English	Gardner	USA	22.4.92	1	Pac-12	Eugene	13 May
11.01	4.5	Ivet	Lalova	BUL	18.5.84	3		Tomblaine	8 Jul
11.02	5.9	Porscha	Lucas	USA	18.6.88	3		Austin	14 Apr
11.07	2.2	Rosângela	Santos	BRA	20.12.90	2h5	OG	London (OS)	3 Aug
11.09	3.0	Chelsea	Hayes	USA	9.2.88	2	TexR	Austin	31 Mar
11.09	5.9	Tameka	Williams	SKN	31.8.89	4		Austin	14 Apr
11.09	3.7	Chastity	Riggien	USA	5.7.89	1		Clemson	5 May
11.14	2.2	Me'Lisa	Barber	USA	4.10.80	1		Chula Vista	9 Jun
11.15	3.0	Dominique	Duncan	USA	7.5.90	3	TexR	Austin	31 Mar
11.16	5.9	Allison	Peter	ISV	14.7.92	5		Austin	14 Apr
11.17	5.9	Tasha	Allen	USA	8.5.90	1		Lubbock	14 Apr
11.19	5.9	Terra	Evans	USA	7.10.89	2		Lubbock	14 Apr
11.19	2.5	Cathleen	Tschirch	GER	23.7.79	1		Jena	19 May
11.20	2.3	Toyin	Olupona	CAN	29.1.83	2h2		Clermont	19 May
11.20	2.7	Miana	Griffiths	CAN	17.1.90	1		Windsor	16 Jun
11.21	2.4	Yuliya	Nesterenko	BLR	15.6.79	1h3	NCp	Brest	25 May
11.21	4.5	Carima	Louami	FRA	12.5.79	4		Tomblaine	8 Jul
11.22	5.9	Tiffani	McReynolds	USA	4.12.91	3		Lubbock	14 Apr
11.22	2.6	Grecia	Bolton	USA	2.10.89	1q1	NCAA-W	Austin	25 May

Mark	Wind	Name		Nat	Born	Pos	Meet	Venue	Date
11.23	3.4	Chalonda	Goodman	USA	29.9.90	1rB		Fort Worth	16 Mar
11.23	5.9	Taylor	Evans	USA	7.10.89	2		Lubbock	14 Apr
11.23	4.2	Paris	Daniels	USA	25.1.90	1h5	NCAA-W	Austin	24 May
11.23	4.4	Latoya	King	JAM	25.4.89	1	NCAA-II	Pueblo	26 May
11.26	2.3	Adella	King	USA	.90	1h1		Raleigh	30 Mar
11.27	4.2	Sharika	Nelvis	USA	10.5.90	2h5	NCAA-W	Austin	24 May
11.27	2.2	Toea	Wisil	PNG	1.1.88	2.2	OG	London (OS)	3 Aug
11.28	2.3	Cleo	VanBuren	USA	1.5.86	1rB	TexR	Austin	31 Mar
11.28	2.5	Cambrya	Jones	USA	20.9.90	1	Big East	Tampa	6 May
11.28	3.3	Tristie	Johnson	USA-J	20.11.93	1		Orlando	26 May
11.29	2.3	Andreea	Ogrâzeanu	ROU	24.3.90	1	NC	Bucuresti	5 Jul
11.30	4.8	Dominique	Kimpel	USA-J	6.2.93	1		Wichita	14 Apr
11.30	2.6	Marion	Wagner	GER	1.2.78	2r4		Mannheim	9 Jun
11.30	2.6	Leena	Günther	GER	16.4.91	2		Mannheim	9 Jun
11.30	3.6	Virgil	Hodge	SKN	17.11.83	1	Robinson	Nassau	16 Jun
11.30A	2.5	Crystal	Emmanuel	CAN	27.11.91	2	NC	Calgary	29 Jun
11.31	2.6	Shataya	Hendricks	USA	15.8.89	3q1	NCAA-W	Austin	25 May
11.32	2.9	Tawanna	Meadows	USA	4.8.86	6	TexR	Austin	31 Mar
11.32	nwi	Shayla	Sanders	USA-J	6.1.94	1		Lake Worth	26 Apr
11.32	2.4	Yuliya	Balykina	BLR	12.4.84	2	NCp	Brest	25 May
11.32	2.5	Amy	Foster	IRL	2.10.88	5		Clermont	2 Jun
11.32	2.3	Daria	Korczynska	POL	30.7.81	3	Kuso	Szczecin	21 Jul
11.33	2.5	Connie	Moore	USA	29.8.81	6		Clermont	2 Jun

Mark	Wind	Name		Nat	Born	Date		Mark	Wind	Name		Nat	Born	Date
11.34	5.9	Tara	Thomas	USA	2.5.89	14 Apr		11.40	2.3	Katie	Nelms	USA	25.9.92	25 May
11.34	5.9	Cierra	White	USA-J	29.4.93	14 Apr		11.41	5.9	Kia	Jackson	USA	15.1.92	23 Mar
11.34	5.9	Christy	Udoh	NGR	30.9.91	14 Apr		11.41	3.0	Endurance	Abinuwa	NGR	31.7.87	31 Mar
11.34	5.1	Diamond	Dixon	USA	29.6.92	27 Apr		11.41	2.3	Chaniqua	Corinealdi	USA	5.2.92	25 May
11.34	2.3	Lorraine	Ugen	GBR	22.8.91	25 May		11.41	3.6	Mariely	Sánchez	DOM	30.12.88	16 Jun
11.34	3.5	Khamica	Bingham	CAN-J	15.6.94	9 Jun		11.42	2.3	Brianna	Glenn	USA	18.4.80	14 Apr
11.34	4.5	Natasha	Hastings	USA	23.7.86	8 Jul		11.42	3.4	Ky	Westbrook	USA-Y	25.2.96	12 May
11.36	2.3	Émilie	Gaydu	FRA	5.2.89	22 Jun		11.42	2.2	Antonette	Carter	USA	16.2.84	9 Jun
11.37	4.4	Shavine	Hodges	JAM	22.10.91	26 May		11.43	2.6	Nelkys	Casabona	CUB	12.5.84	22 Mar
11.38	2.9	Shakera	Reece	BAR	31.8.88	31 Mar		11.43	2.2	Lakadron	Ivery	USA	23.6.83	14 Apr
11.38	2.5	Lauryn	Newson	USA	6.8.90	13 May		11.43	3.0	Inna	Weit	GER	5.8.88	16 Jun
11.38	2.7	Esther	Cremer	GER	29.3.88	26 May		11.44	3.3	Margarita	Manzueta	DOM	17.11.89	3 Mar
11.38	2.3	Jessica	Young	USA	6.4.87	14 Jul		11.44	2.3	Brooklyn	Morris	USA	27.3.86	30 Mar
11.39	3.5	Patricia	Hall	JAM	16.10.82	16 Mar		11.44	2.9	LaKeidra	Stewart	USA	8.10.89	21 Apr
11.39	3.3	Brittany	Jones	USA	6.3.89	12 May		11.44	4.2	Erica	Alexander	USA	24.6.90	24 May
11.39	4.2	Gerrone	Black	USA	26.10.89	24 May		11.45	4.3	Akeyla	Mitchell	USA-Y	11.11.95	27 Apr
11.39	4.2	Shawna	Anderson	JAM	3.5.89	24 May		11.45	3.3	Natasha	Joe-Mayers	VIN	10.3.79	9 Jun
11.40	2.3	Chauntae	Bayne/Watson	USA	4.4.84	31 Mar		11.46		Jennifer	Madu	USA-J	23.9.94	28 Apr
11.40	3.5	Griffin	Matthew	USA	19.7.88	5 May		11.46	2.5	Aareon	Payne	USA	3.9.90	13 May
								11.46	3.5	Irene	Siragusa	ITA-J	23.6.93	15 Jun

Hand timed

Mark		Name		Nat	Born	Pos	Meet	Venue	Date
11.0		Tezdzhan	Naimova	BUL	1.5.87	1		Stara Zagora	11 May
11.2A		Erika	Chávez	ECU	4.6.90	1		Cuenca	31 May

Best at low altitude: 11.21   1.5   A Scott   1   Conf USA   New Orleans   13 May
Drugs disqualification: 11.04   1.5 Semoy Hackett #   TRI   27.11.88   2h6   OG   London (OS)   3 Aug

JUNIORS

See main list for top 4 juniors (& 2 wa). 8 performances by 4 women to 11.35. Additional marks and further juniors:

Strachan   11.22   1.4   1   Nassau   23 Mar   11.35   1.5   1   Atlanta   12 May
Bryant   11.34   0.2   1   Charlottesville   21 Apr
Sanders   11.34   1.2   1J   DL   New York   9 Jun   11.33w?   1   Sunrise   21 Mar

Mark	Wind	Name		Nat	Born	Pos	Meet	Venue	Date
11.35	1.9	Ariana	Wright	USA	20.6.93	1		Los Angeles	7 Apr
11.37	0.4	Kandace	Thomas	USA	6.2.93	2	JUCO	Levelland	17 May
11.39	0.4	Shai-Anne	Davis	CAN	4.12.93	3		Port of Spain	22 Apr
11.39	-0.3	Peace	Uko	NGR-Y	26.12.95	5	NC	Calabar	19 Jun
11.41	1.4	Shaunae	Miller	BAH	15.4.94	2-19		Nassau	23 Mar
11.41	1.7	Morolake	Akinosun (10)	USA	17.5.94	1		Charleston	19 May
11.42	1.7	Tamiris	Liz	BRA-Y	18.11.95	1s3	WJ	Barcelona	11 Jul
11.43	1.8	Anna	Doi	JPN-Y	24.8.95	1s3		Kumagaya	13 May
11.43	1.7	Jasmine	Gibbs	USA	15.1.94	1h2		Clovis	1 Jun
11.44	1.2	Aaliyah	Brown	USA-Y	6.1.95	2J		New York	9 Jun
11.45	1.6	Ariana	Washington	USA-Y	4.9.96	1		Walnut	19 May
11.45	1.2	Kali	Davis-White	USA	27.10.94	3j		New York	9 Jun
11.46	2.0	Monique	Spencer	JAM	20.10.94	1	NC-j	Kingston	16 Jun
11.46	1.7	Khamica	Bingham	CAN	15.6.94	4	WJ	Barcelona	11 Jul
11.47	1.2	Bianca	Williams	GBR	18.12.93	1		Azusa	20 Apr
11.47	0.4	Sophie	Papps (20)	GBR	6.10.94	1	NC-j	Bedford	16 Jun
11.47	1.7	Ida	Mayer	GER	9.3.93	2s3	WJ	Barcelona	11 Jul

Wind assisted: 4 performances by 4 women to 11.33w. Nire to 11.46w

Strachan   11.22   4.4   1   Carifta Devonshire   7 Apr

Mark	Wind	Name		Nat	Born	Pos	Venue	Date
11.34	5.9	Cierra	White	USA	29.4.93	6	Lubbock	14 Apr

Mark	Wind	Name		Nat	Born	Pos	Meet	Venue	Date	
11.34	3.5	Khamica	Bingham	CAN	15.6.94	1		Brockville	9	Jun
11.42	3.4	Ky	Westbrook	USA-Y	25.2.96	1s3		Mesa	12	May
11.45	4.3	Akeyla	Mitchell	USA-Y	11.11.95	1h1		Corpus Christi	27	Apr
11.46		Jennifer	Madu	USA	23.9.94	1		Lubbock	28	Apr
11.46	3.5	Irene	Siragusa	ITA	23.6.93	1h1	NC-J	Misano Adriatico	15	Jun

150m Straight: Gateshead Q 15 Aug: (1.0) 1. Anyika Onuora GBR 16.70, 2. Shayla Mahan USA 16.99

200 METRES

Mark	Wind	Name		Nat	Born	Pos	Meet	Venue	Date	
21.69	1.0	Allyson	Felix	USA	18.11.85	1	NC/OT	Eugene	30	Jun
21.88	-0.2		Felix			1	OG	London (OS)	8	Aug
22.09	-0.3	Sanya	Richards-Ross	USA	26.2.85	1	DL	New York	9	Jun
22.09	-0.2	Shelly-Ann	Fraser-Pryce	JAM	27.12.86	2	OG	London (OS)	8	Aug
22.10	0.6		Fraser-Pryce			1	NC	Kingston	1	Jul
22.11	1.0	Carmelita	Jeter	USA	24.11.79	2	NC/OT	Eugene	30	Jun
22.14	-0.2		Jeter			3	OG	London (OS)	8	Aug
22.15	0.6		Richards-Ross			1s2	NC/OT	Eugene	29	Jun
22.19	1.9	Kimberlyn	Duncan	USA	2.8.91	1s2	NCAA	Des Moines	7	Jun
22.19	1.0	Aleksandra	Fedoriva	RUS	13.9.88	1	NC	Cheboksary	6	Jul
22.22	0.1		Duncan			1q1	NCAA-E	Jacksonville	26	May
22.22	1.0		Richards-Ross			3	NC/OT	Eugene	30	Jun
22.23	0.8		Felix			1	Pre	Eugene	2	Jun
22.30	0.8		Felix			1s3	NC/OT	Eugene	29	Jun
22.30	0.8		Richards-Ross			1s3	OG	London (OS)	7	Aug
22.31	1.5		Jeter			1		Los Angeles (Ww)	14	Apr
22.31	1.0		Felix			1s2	OG	London (OS)	7	Aug
22.32	1.0	Veronica	Campbell-Brown	JAM	15.5.82	1s1	OG	London (OS)	7	Aug
22.34	1.0		Duncan			4	NC/OT	Eugene	30	Jun
22.34	0.8		Fraser-Pryce			2s3	OG	London (OS)	7	Aug
22.35	1.0	Jeneba	Tarmoh	USA	27.9.89	5	NC/OT	Eugene	30	Jun
22.35	-0.2		Felix			1	Hanz	Zagreb	4	Sep
22.37	0.3	Tianna	Madison	USA	30.8.85	1		Ponce	12	May
22.37	0.6		Duncan			2s2	NC/OT	Eugene	29	Jun
22.37	0.6	Sherone	Simpson (10)	JAM	12.8.84	2	NC	Kingston	1	Jul
22.38	-0.3		Campbell-Brown			1	GS	Ostrava	25	May
22.38	-0.2		Campbell-Brown			4	OG	London (OS)	8	Aug
22.39	1.0		Jeter			2s1	OG	London (OS)	7	Aug
22.39	-0.2		Richards-Ross			5	OG	London (OS)	8	Aug
22.42	1.5	Murielle	Ahouré	CIV	23.8.87	1	Bisl	Oslo	7	Jun
22.42	0.6		Campbell-Brown			3	NC	Kingston	1	Jul
22.42	1.2	Natalya	Rusakova	RUS	12.12.79	1h3	NC	Cheboksary	6	Jul
		(32/12)								
22.45	1.4	Tameka	Williams	SKN	31.8.89	1	NC	Basseterre	3	Jun
22.46	-0.3	Bianca	Knight	USA	2.1.89	2	DL	New York	9	Jun
22.52	1.0	Charonda	Williams	USA	27.3.87	1	Spitzen	Luzern	17	Jul
22.53	0.1	Nercely	Soto	VEN	23.8.90	1	NC	Caracas	12	May
22.53	0.2	Anthonique	Strachan	BAH-J	22.8.93	1	WJ	Barcelona	13	Jul
22.55	0.2	Semoy	Hackett #	TRI	27.11.88	1q2	NCAA-E	Jacksonville	26	May
22.56	1.0	Myriam	Soumaré	FRA	29.10.86	3s1	OG	London (OS)	7	Aug
22.58	1.5	Mariya	Ryemyen	UKR	2.8.87	1h5	OG	London (OS)	6	Aug
		(20)								
22.61	0.6	Anneisha	McLaughlin	JAM	6.1.86	4	NC	Kingston	1	Jul
22.62	0.4	Yelizaveta	Savlinis	RUS	14.8.87	1h2	NC	Cheboksary	6	Jul
22.62	1.0	Laverne	Jones-Ferrette	ISV	16.9.81	4s2	OG	London (OS)	7	Aug
22.63	0.9	Leslie	Cole	USA	16.2.87	1	MSR	Walnut	21	Apr
22.63	0.8	Blessing	Okagbare	NGR	9.10.88	3	Pre	Eugene	2	Jun
22.64	1.9	Sheniqua	Ferguson	BAH	24.11.89	1		Auburn	7	Apr
22.64	1.0	Yelizaveta	Bryzgina	UKR	28.11.89	5s2	OG	London (OS)	7	Aug
22.65	0.9	Porscha	Lucas	USA	18.6.88	1		Port of Spain	19	May
22.66	0.3	Hrystyna	Stuy	UKR	3.2.88	3h4	OG	London (OS)	6	Aug
22.68	1.0	Aurieyall	Scott	USA	18.5.92	8	NC/OT	Eugene	30	Jun
		(30)								
22.68	1.7	Schillonie	Calvert	JAM	27.7.88	1		Madrid	7	Jul
22.70	0.4	Shaunae	Miller	BAH-J	15.4.94	1		Nassau	1	Mar
22.70	0.0	Dafne	Schippers	NED	15.6.92	1s1	EC	Helsinki	29	Jun
22.70	0.6	Kerron	Stewart	JAM	16.4.84	5	NC	Kingston	1	Jul
22.71	-0.3	LaShaunte'a	Moore	USA	31.7.83	1	Colorful	Daegu	16	May
22.71	1.5	Abi	Oyepitan	GBR	30.12.79	2	Bisl	Oslo	7	Jun
22.71	-0.5	Viktoriya	Pyatachenko	UKR	7.5.89	2	NC	Yalta	14	Jun
22.72	0.2	Cambrya	Jones	USA	20.9.90	2q2	NCAA-E	Jacksonville	26	May

Mark	Wind	Name		Nat	Born	Pos	Meet	Venue	Date
22.72	1.9	Christy	Udoh	NGR	30.9.91	2s2	NCAA	Des Moines	7 Jun
22.73	0.1	Lauretta	Ozoh ¶	NGR	5.9.90	1	NC	Calabar	21 Jun
(40)									
22.73	1.0	Olga	Belkina	RUS	23.8.90	4	NC	Cheboksary	6 Jul
22.73	0.6	Natalya	Antyukh	RUS	26.6.81	1h3	NC-23	Yerino	21 Jul
22.74	1.9	Octavious	Freeman	USA	20.4.92	3s2	NCAA	Des Moines	7 Jun
22.77	0.2	Allison	Peter	ISV	14.7.92	1h3	Big 12	Manhattan KS	12 May
22.77	0.6	Samantha	Henry-Robinson	JAM	25.9.88	6	NC	Kingston	1 Jul
22.82	1.7	Shalonda	Solomon	USA	19.12.85	3		Kingston	5 May
22.82	1.3	English	Gardner	USA	22.4.92	1	Pac-12	Eugene	13 May
22.82	1.0	Yuliya	Chermoshanskaya	RUS	6.1.86	5	NC	Cheboksary	6 Jul
22.82	1.0	Evelyn	dos Santos	BRA	11.4.85	7s2	OG	London (OS)	7 Aug
22.83	-0.3	Jessica	Ennis	GBR	28.1.86	2H5	OG	London (OS)	3 Aug
(50)									
22.84	0.6	Aleen	Bailey	JAM	25.11.80	7	NC	Kingston	1 Jul
22.85	0.5	Chalonda	Goodman	USA	29.9.90	2r1	FlaR	Gainesville	6 Apr
22.85	0.3	Kai	Selvon	TRI	13.4.92	4h4	OG	London (OS)	6 Aug
22.85	-0.7	Libania	Grenot	ITA	12.7.83	3		Padova	2 Sep
22.86	0.9	Ashton	Purvis	USA	12.7.92	1		Norwalk	19 May
22.86	0.5	Johanna	Danois	FRA	4.4.87	2	NC	Angers	17 Jun
22.89A	0.0	Tsholofelo	Thipe ¶	RSA	9.12.86	1		Potchefstroom	24 Mar
22.89	0.0	Amantle	Montsho	BOT	4.7.83	1		Fukuroi	3 May
22.89	0.6	Paris	Daniels	USA	25.1.90	1h2	Big 12	Manhattan KS	12 May
22.89	0.6	Ashley	Collier	USA	4.2.92	2h2	Big 12	Manhattan KS	12 May
(60)									
22.89	0.1	Gloria	Asumnu	NGR	22.5.85	2	NC	Calabar	21 Jun
22.91	0.7	Shayla	Mahan	USA	18.1.89	1		Brazzaville	10 Jun
22.92	1.4	Viktoriya	Zyabkina	KAZ	4.9.92	1		Bishkek	10 Jun
22.92	0.0	Rosângela	Santos	BRA	20.12.90	1	NC	São Paulo	1 Jul
22.92	1.0	Eleni	Artymata	CYP	16.5.86	8s2	OG	London (OS)	7 Aug
22.93	-0.9	Jamile	Samuel	NED	24.4.92	2	FBK	Hengelo	27 May
22.93	0.6	Anyika	Onuora	GBR	28.10.84	1		Regensburg	2 Jun
22.93	0.6	Natasha	Hastings	USA	23.7.86	4s2	NC/OT	Eugene	29 Jun
22.94	0.2	Dominique	Duncan	USA	7.5.90	2h3	Big 12	Manhattan KS	12 May
22.94	0.5	Margaret	Adeoye	GBR	27.4.85	3h1	OG	London (OS)	6 Aug
(70)									
22.95	-0.3	Yuliya	Gushchina	RUS	4.3.83	1	Znam	Zhukovskiy	17 Jun
22.95	0.7	Gloria	Hooper	ITA	3.3.92	2h4	EC	Helsinki	29 Jun
22.96	-0.3	Mikele	Barber	USA	4.10.80	3	DL	New York	9 Jun
22.96	0.8	Tiffany	Townsend	USA	14.6.89	3s3	NC/OT	Eugene	29 Jun
22.96	0.7	Lauryn	Williams	USA	11.9.83	1	WK	Zürich	30 Aug
22.97	0.1	Dezerea	Bryant	USA-J	27.4.93	2q1	NCAA-E	Jacksonville	26 May
22.98	1.5	Cathleen	Tschirch	GER	23.7.79	1		Jena	19 May
22.98	1.2	Alex	Anderson	USA	28.1.87	2h6	NC/OT	Eugene	28 Jun
22.98	0.9	Nelly	Banco	FRA	17.2.86	3		Sotteville-lès-Rouen	10 Jul
22.98	1.0	Ivet	Lalova	BUL	18.5.84	6s1	OG	London (OS)	7 Aug
(80)									
22.99	1.2	Ashley	Spencer	USA-J	8.6.93	1	Big 10	Madison	13 May
23.00	0.5	Lina	Jacques-Sébastien	FRA	10.4.85	3	NC	Angers	17 Jun
23.01	-0.7	Ana Claúdia	da Silva	BRA	6.11.88	2h1	NC	São Paulo	30 Jun
23.02	1.0	Sally	Pearson	AUS	19.9.86	1		Melbourne	3 Mar
23.02	1.5	Yekaterina	Voronenkova	RUS	8.9.88	1h1	NC	Cheboksary	6 Jul
23.03	0.5	Darshay	Davis	USA	23.9.91	3	FlaR	Gainesville	6 Apr
23.03	1.3	Phyllis	Francis	USA	4.5.92	2	Pac-12	Eugene	13 May
23.03	0.9	Alexis	Love	USA	24.4.91	3s3	NCAA	Des Moines	7 Jun
23.03	-0.7	Antonina	Krivoshapka	RUS	21.7.87	5		Padova	2 Sep
23.04	1.0	Marina	Panteleyeva	RUS	16.5.89	6	NC	Cheboksary	6 Jul
(90)									
23.05		Yelena	Migunova	RUS	4.1.84	1	Tatar Ch	Kazan	15 Jun
23.06	-0.3	Marlena	Wesh	HAI	16.2.91	2	ACC	Charlottesville	21 Apr
23.08	1.5	Inna	Weit	GER	5.8.88	1r1		Mannheim	9 Jun
23.08	0.0	Léa	Sprunger	SUI	5.3.90	2h2	EC	Helsinki	29 Jun
23.08	1.2	Janelle	Redhead	GRN	27.12.89	3h2	OG	London (OS)	6 Aug
23.09A	0.6	Erika	Chávez	ECU	4.6.90	1		Ciudad de México	13 May
23.09	1.3	Lauryn	Newson	USA	6.8.90	3	Pac-12	Eugene	13 May
23.09	1.8	Yuliya	Katsura	RUS	28.5.83	2rB	Znam	Zhukovskiy	17 Jun
23.10	1.0	Joanna	Atkins	USA	31.1.89	4h3	NC/OT	Eugene	28 Jun
23.10	0.8	Crystal	Emmanuel	CAN	27.11.91	5h6	OG	London (OS)	6 Aug
(100)									

Mark	Wind	Name		Nat	Born	Date		Mark	Wind	Name		Nat	Born	Date
23.11	0.8	Candace	Jackson	USA	13.2.91	5 May		23.12	0.0	Chisato	Fukushima	JPN	27.6.88	3 May
23.11	1.7	Evelyn	de Santana	BRA	8.7.84	9 Jun		23.12	1.7	Simone	Facey	JAM	7.5.85	5 May
23.12		Shericka	Williams	JAM	17.9.85	28 Jan		23.13	0.8	Michelle-Lee	Ahye	TRI	10.4.92	27 May

Mark	Wind	Name	Nat	Born	Date
23.14	1.1	Tasha Allen	USA	8.5.90	28 Apr
23.15A	1.1	Darlenis Obregón	COL	21.2.86	28 Apr
23.15	0.7	Kelly Fogarty	USA	7.3.89	12 May
23.15A	0.0	Latoya King	JAM	25.4.89	25 May
23.15	0.2	Anne Cibis	GER	27.9.85	28 May
23.15	1.9	Aareon Payne	USA	3.9.90	7 Jun
23.15	0.2	Olivia Ekponé	USA-J	5.1.93	13 Jul
23.16	1.5	Sheri-Ann Brooks	JAM	11.2.83	7 Jun
23.17	-0.9	Alena Kievich	BLR	6.10.87	18 Jul
23.18	1.3	Krisztina Khorosheva	RUS-J	5.4.93	7 Jun
23.19	1.4	Bukola Abogunloko	NGR-J	18.8.94	12 May
23.20	0.1	Brittany Jones	USA	6.3.89	26 May
23.20	0.9	Alejandra Idrobo	COL	8.4.88	9 Jun
23.20	0.8	Mariely Sánchez	DOM	30.12.88	6 Aug
23.21	1.0	Angela Morosanu	ROU	26.7.86	6 Jul
23.21	0.3	Yelena Kozlova	RUS	19.9.88	6 Jul
23.22A	0.0	Justine Palframan	RSA-J	4.11.93	24 Mar
23.22	0.5	Chelsea Hayes	USA	9.2.88	11 May
23.22	0.5	Jennifer Galais	FRA	7.3.92	17 Jun
23.23	0.8	Geisa Coutinho	BRA	1.6.80	6 May
23.23	0.2	Taylor Evans	USA	7.10.89	12 May
23.24	-0.1	Shai-Anne Davis	CAN-J	4.12.93	29 Apr
23.24	0.8	Olivia Borlée	BEL	10.4.86	5 May
23.24	0.3	Patricia Hall	JAM	16.10.82	12 May
23.24	0.5	Alina Logvynenko	UKR	18.7.90	28 May
23.25	-1.1	Shayla Sanders	USA-J	6.1.94	3 Mar
23.25	1.8	Francena McCorory	USA	20.10.88	14 Apr
23.25	-0.1	Joice Maduaka	GBR	30.9.73	5 May
23.25	0.1	Sheila Paul	USA	30.9.89	26 May
23.25	0.0	Ebonie Floyd	USA	21.10.83	31 May
23.25	-0.2	Debbie Ferguson McKenzie	BAH	16.1.76	21 Jul
23.26	0.4	Keshia Baker	USA	30.1.88	7 Apr
23.26	1.4	Jasmine Edgerson	USA	6.6.91	5 May
23.26	-3.3	Jura Levy	JAM	4.11.90	26 May
23.26	0.7	Hanne Claes	BEL	4.8.91	29 Jun
23.26	-0.9	Marie Josée Lou Gonerie	CIV	18.11.88	30 Jun
23.26	-0.4	Mujinga Kambundji	SUI	17.6.92	7 Jul
23.27	1.0	Christina Manning	USA	29.5.90	12 May
23.27	0.3	Lekeisha Lawson	USA	3.6.87	2 Jun
23.28	1.0	Amara Jones	BAH	18.9.91	5 May
23.28	0.8	Erica Alexander	USA	24.6.90	5 May
23.28	-0.5	Nataliya Strohova	UKR	26.12.92	14 Jun
23.28	-0.1	María Belibasáki	GRE	19.6.91	16 Jun
23.28	-0.8	Desiree Henry	GBR-Y	26.8.95	12 Jul
23.29	1.9	Sparkle McKnight	TRI	21.12.91	5 May
23.29	1.0	Andreea Ogrâzeanu	ROU	24.3.90	6 Jul
23.30	-0.3	Melissa Breen	AUS	17.9.90	15 Apr
23.30	0.4	Ezinne Okparaebo	NOR	3.3.88	2 Jun
23.30	1.1	Moa Hjelmer	SWE	19.6.90	11 Aug
23.31	0.0	Jessica Beard	USA	8.1.89	31 May
23.32	2.0	Nivea Smith	BAH	18.2.90	21 Apr
23.32	1.4	Amonn Nelson	CAN	23.12.88	12 May
23.32	1.4	Marika Popowicz	POL	28.4.88	16 Jun
23.32	1.2	Sabina Veit	SLO	2.12.85	17 Jun
23.32	-0.3	Jessica Zelinka	CAN	3.9.81	3 Aug
23.32		Vu Thi Huong	VIE	7.10.86	9 Oct
23.33	-3.3	Adella King	USA	.90	26 May
23.33	1.0	Shareese Woods	USA	20.2.85	28 Jun
23.34	0.6	Anna Golovina	RUS	28.6.89	6 Jul
23.35	0.3	Sharika Nelvis	USA	10.5.90	20 Apr
23.35	1.4	Virgil Hodge	SKN	17.11.83	3 Jun
23.35		Kerri Ann Mitchell	CAN	29.3.83	8 Jul
23.35	-1.5	Shericka Jackson	JAM-J	15.7.94	12 Jul
23.35	0.9	Esther Cremer	GER	29.3.88	27 Jul
23.36	-1.9	Reyare Thomas	TRI	23.11.87	24 Jun
23.36	1.3	Katie Nelms	USA	25.9.92	13 May
23.36	1.1	Louise Bloor	GBR	21.9.85	24 Jun
23.36	0.4	Kseniya Vdovina	RUS	19.4.87	13 Jun
23.37	0.5	Hanna Mariën	BEL	16.5.82	17 Jun
23.37	0.6	Peace Uko	NGR-Y	26.12.95	20 Jun
23.37	-0.7	Wei Yongli	CHN	11.10.91	24 Jun
23.37	1.3	Muna Lee	USA	30.10.81	7 Jul
23.38	2.0	Shana Cox	GBR	22.1.85	20 Apr
23.38	0.1	Natalya Rakacheva	RUS	16.4.88	9 Jun
23.38	0.6	Anastasiya Tulapina	KAZ	5.3.90	1 Jul
23.38	0.1	Hanna-Maari Latvala	FIN	30.10.87	26 Aug
23.39A	0.4	Globine Mayova	NAM	29.2.88	5 May
23.39	1.7	Maike Dix	GER	2.7.86	26 May
23.39	1.5	Connie Moore	USA	29.8.81	9 Jun
23.40	0.7	Tiffani McReynolds	USA	4.12.91	24 Mar
23.40A	0.4	Tjipekapor Herunga	NAM	1.1.88	5 May
23.40	1.7	Jacqueline Gasser	SUI	23.2.90	26 May
23.40	1.4	Nataliya Pogrebnyak	UKR	19.2.88	28 May
23.40	1.5	Yelena Bolsun	RUS	25.6.82	6 Jul
23.41	1.9	Amoy Blake	JAM	21.9.90	5 May
23.41	1.4	Ariana Washington	USA-Y	4.9.96	2 Jun
23.41	-0.5	Mariya Shmidova	UKR	3.4.92	14 Jun
23.41	0.2	Janet Amponsah	GHA-J	12.4.93	13 Jul
23.41	0.5	Kaylin Whitney	USA-Y	9.3.98	28 Jul
23.42	0.0	Gabrielle Houston	USA	12.6.90	26 May
23.42	0.5	Hayley Jones	GBR	14.9.88	24 Jun
23.42	1.3	Me'Lisa Barber	USA	4.10.80	7 Jul
23.42	-1.5	Isidora Jiménez	CHI-J	10.8.93	12 Jul

(199, 39 women 23.43 to 23.49(

Doubtful performance

Mark	Wind	Name	Nat	Born	Date
23.27	0.7	Klodiana Shala	ALB	22.8.79	17 Jun

Hand timed

Mark	Wind	Name	Nat	Born	Pos	Meet	Venue	Date
22.8	1.2	Lauryn Williams	USA	11.9.83	1	GP	Uberlândia	13 May
23.0	1.2	Geisa Coutinho	BRA	1.6.80	2	GP	Uberlândia	13 May

Indoors

Mark	Wind	Name	Nat	Born	Pos	Meet	Venue	Date
22.86		Kamaria Brown	USA	21.12.92	1	Big 12	College Station	25 Feb
22.88		Patricia Hall	JAM	16.10.82	1		Eaubonne	16 Feb
23.03		Jura Levy	JAM	4.11.90	1	NAIA	Geneva OH	3 Mar
23.23		Muriel Hurtis	FRA	25.3.79				29 Feb
23.42		Yekaterina Vukolova	RUS	10.8.87				12 Feb
23.49		Rebecca Alexander	USA	2.5.90				28 Jan

Wind assisted

Mark	Wind	Name	Nat	Born	Pos	Meet	Venue	Date
22.12	2.6	Kimberlyn Duncan	USA	2.8.91	1	SEC	Baton Rouge	13 May
22.23	3.8	Kelly-Ann Baptiste	TRI	14.10.86	1		Clermont	2 Jun
22.30	3.4	Jeneba Tarmoh	USA	27.9.89	1s1	NC/OT	Eugene	29 Jun
22.33	3.4	Tianna Madison	USA	30.8.85	2s1	NC/OT	Eugene	29 Jun
22.34	3.4	Bianca Knight	USA	2.1.89	3s1	NC/OT	Eugene	29 Jun
22.45	3.8	Libania Grenot	ITA	12.7.83	2		Clermont	2 Jun
22.50	3.6	Samantha Henry-Robinson	JAM	25.9.88	1rB		Clermont	2 Jun
22.56	3.4	Aurieyall Scott	USA	18.5.92	4s1	NC/OT	Eugene	29 Jun
22.57	2.1	Abi Oyepitan	GBR	30.12.79	2		Clermont	19 May
22.65	2.2	Paris Daniels	USA	25.1.90	1s1	NCAA	Des Moines	7 Jun
22.66	2.2	Kai Selvon	TRI	13.4.92	2s1	NCAA	Des Moines	7 Jun
22.69	2.7	Patricia Hall	JAM	16.10.82	1		Austin	14 Apr
22.70	2.2	Dominique Duncan	USA	7.5.90	3s1	NCAA	Des Moines	7 Jun
22.79	3.8	Aleen Bailey	JAM	25.11.80	3		Clermont	2 Jun
22.80A	4.7	Latoya King	JAM	25.4.89	1	NCAA II	Pueblo	26 May
22.83	2.2	Joanna Atkins	USA	31.1.89	1		Clermont	9 Jun
22.84	2.7	Alex Anderson	USA	28.1.87	2		Austin	14 Apr
22.86	3.6	Connie Moore	USA	29.8.81	2rB		Clermont	2 Jun

Mark	Wind	Name		Nat	Born	Pos	Meet	Venue	Date
22.92	3.0	Sheri-Ann	Brooks	JAM	11.2.83	1	Bailey	Edmonton	16 Jun
22.93	2.8	Tiffany	Townsend	USA	14.6.89	6	DL	Shanghai	19 May
23.02	4.6	Taylor	Evans	USA	7.10.89	1		Lubbock	14 Apr
23.02	4.6	Candace	Jackson	USA	13.2.91	2		Lubbock	14 Apr
23.04A	4.7	Shavine	Hodges	JAM	22.10.91	2	NCAA-II	Pueblo	26 May
23.08	3.5	Adella	King	USA	.90	1		Allendale	11 May
23.08	3.0	Crystal	Emmanuel	CAN	27.11.91	2	Bailey	Edmonton	16 Jun

Mark	Wind	Name		Nat	Born	Date
23.10	4.9	Chelsea	Hayes	USA	9.2.88	21 Apr
23.13	2.8	Deedee	Trotter	USA	8.12.82	24 Mar
23.13	3.3	Diamond	Dixon	USA	29.6.92	27 Apr
23.15	2.6	Brittany	Jones	USA	6.3.89	13 May
23.15	3.0	Amonn	Nelson	CAN	23.12.88	16 Jun
23.15	2.5	Joanne	Cuddihy	IRL	11.5.84	7 Jul
23.18	4.2	Jasmine	Chaney	USA	25.8.88	17 Mar
23.18	4.6	Tiffani	McReynolds	USA	4.12.91	14 Apr
23.18	3.1	Marika	Popowicz	POL	28.4.88	17 Jun
23.19	2.3	Lekeisha	Lawson	USA	3.6.87	9 Jun
23.19	2.3	Antonette	Carter	USA	16.2.84	9 Jun
23.20	2.2	Regina	George	USA/NGR	17.2.91	4 May
23.20A	4.7	Jillisa	Grant	JAM	21.10.89	26 May
23.20	3.0	Jessica	Zelinka	CAN	3.9.81	16 Jun
23.22	2.2	Hayley	Jones	GBR	14.9.88	17 Jun
23.24	3.7	Joice	Maduaka	GBR	30.9.73	30 Jun
23.26	4.6	Erica	Alexander	USA	24.6.90	14 Apr
23.26	2.3	Ashton	Purvis	USA	12.7.92	11 May
23.26	3.5	Kadecia	Baird	GUY-Y	24.2.95	16 Jun
23.26	3.1	Ewelina	Ptak	POL	20.3.87	17 Jun
23.27	2.1	Karene	King	IVB	24.10.87	20 Apr
23.28	2.1	Amanda	Kimbers	USA	13.9.90	6 May
23.29	3.8	Shareese	Woods	USA	20.2.85	2 Jun
23.29	3.1	Anna	Kielbasinska	POL	26.6.90	17 Jun
23.29	5.4	Hanna	Mariën	BEL	16.5.82	18 Jul
23.30	2.5	Jonnique	Lawrence	USA	5.1.91	6 May
23.30	3.3	Yekaterina	Vukolova	RUS	10.8.87	27 May
23.32	3.1	Marta	Jeschke	POL	2.6.86	17 Jun
23.33	2.1	Martina	Giovanetti	ITA	10.8.87	14 Jul
23.38A	4.7	Shelisia	Crawford	USA	16.6.88	26 May
23.39	3.0	Kimberley	Hyacinthe	CAN	28.3.89	16 Jun
23.40	6.8	Natasha	Gay	USA	18.5.90	14 Apr
23.41	2.4	Shataya	Hendricks	USA	15.8.89	26 May

Best at low altitude

Mark	Wind	Name		Date
23.21	-1.4	Thipe ¶		30 Jun
23.36	0.9	Chávez		9 Jun

JUNIORS

See main list for top 4 juniors. 11 performances by 4 women to 23.05. Additional marks and further juniors:

Name	Mark	Wind	Pos	Meet	Venue	Date
Strachan	22.75	1.4	1		Atlanta	12 May
	22.82	1.0	5s1	OG	London (OS)	7 Aug
	22.75	0.8	2h6	OG	London (OS)	6 Aug
	22.85	-0.7	1	Carifta	Devonshire	9 Apr
Miller	22.95	-0.2	1		Nassau	17 Feb
Bryant	23.05	-0.3	1		Charlottesville	21 Apr
	23.05	1.5	1		Clemson	12 May

Mark	Wind	Name		Nat	Born	Pos	Meet	Venue	Date
23.15	0.2	Olivia	Ekponé	USA	5.1.93	2	WJ	Barcelona	13 Jul
23.18	1.3	Krisztina	Khorosheva	RUS	5.4.93	1		Penza	7 Jun
23.19	1.4	Bukola	Abogunloko	NGR	18.8.94	2		Atlanta GA	12 May
23.22A	0.0	Justine	Palframan	RSA	4.11.93	2		Potchefstroom	24 Mar
23.24	-0.1	Shai-Anne	Davis	CAN	4.12.93	1		Basseterre	29 Apr
23.25	-1.1	Shayla	Sanders (10)	USA	6.1.94	1		Miami	3 Mar
23.28	-0.8	Desiree	Henry	GBR-Y	26.8.95	2s3	WJ	Barcelona	12 Jul
23.35	-1.5	Shericka	Jackson	JAM	15.7.94	1h7	WJ	Barcelona	12 Jul
23.37	0.6	Peace	Uko	NGR-Y	26.12.95	1h2	NC	Calabar	20 Jun
23.41	1.4	Ariana	Washington	USA-Y	4.9.96	1		Clovis	2 Jun
23.41	0.2	Janet	Amponsah	GHA	12.4.93	5	WJ	Barcelona	13 Jul
23.41	0.5	Kaylin	Whitney	USA-Y	9.3.98	1	Jnr Oly	Baltimore	28 Jul
23.42	-1.5	Isidora	Jiménez	CHI	10.8.93	2h7	WJ	Barcelona	12 Jul
23.43	1.1	Carmiesha	Cox	BAH-Y	16.5.95	3	NC	Nassau	23 Jun
23.44	1.9	Cierra	White	USA	29.4.93	3rB		Lubbock	5 May
23.47	-0.5	Tristie	Johnson (20)	USA	20.11.93	4	NC-j	Bloomington IN	17 Jun
23.47	1.0	Marcquita	Stalbert	USA-Y	5.3.95	1	NC-y	Arlington	30 Jun
23.47	0.2	Imke	Vervaet	BEL	11.4.93	6	WJ	Barcelona	13 Jul
23.26w	3.5	Kadecia	Baird	GUY-Y	24.2.95	1h3		Greensboro	16 Jun
23.45w	4.3	Robin	Reynolds	USA-J	22.2.94	1		Miramar	18 Apr

300 METRES

Mark	Name		Nat	Born	Pos	Meet	Venue	Date
36.50	Leslie	Cole	USA	16.2.87	1		Pasadena	24 Mar
37.11	Patricia	Hall	JAM	16.10.82				29 Aug
37.36	Tiffany	Williams	USA	5.2.83				2 Jun
37.30	Ciara	Short	USA	11.3.89				24 Mar
37.38	Léa	Sprunger	SUI	5.3.90				5 May

In Olympic 400m London (OS) 5 Aug: Krivoshapka, McCorory 35.8, Trotter 35.9, Richards-Ross 36.0, Ohurogu 36.2, Montsho 36.3, Wlliams-Mills 36.6, Whyte 36.9

Indoors

Mark	Name		Nat	Born	Pos	Venue	Date
35.69	Patricia	Hall	JAM	16.10.82	1	Liévin	14 Feb
36.42	Antonina	Krivoshapka	RUS	21.7.87	2	Liévin	14 Feb
36.54	Aleksandra	Fedoriva	RUS	13.9.88	1	Moskva	14 Jan
36.81	Vania	Stambolova	BUL	28.11.83	1rB	Liévin	14 Feb
36.94	Kseniya	Ustalova	RUS	14.1.88	1	Yekaterinburg	6 Jan

400 METRES

Mark	Name		Nat	Born	Pos	Meet	Venue	Date
49.16	Antonina	Krivoshapka	RUS	21.7.87	1	NC	Cheboksary	5 Jul
49.28	Sanya	Richards-Ross	USA	26.2.85	1	NC/OT	Eugene	24 Jun
49.28	Yuliya	Gushchina	RUS	4.3.83	2	NC	Cheboksary	5 Jul
49.39		Richards-Ross			1	Pre	Eugene	2 Jun
49.43		Krivoshapka			1		Krasnodar	8 Jun
49.54	Amantle	Montsho	BOT	4.7.83	1	AfrC	Porto Novo	28 Jun

Mark	Name		Nat	Born	Pos	Meet	Venue	Date
49.55		Richards-Ross			1	OG	London (OS)	5 Aug
49.56		Gushchina			1s3	NC	Cheboksary	4 Jul
49.62		Montsho			2	Pre	Eugene	2 Jun
49.68		Montsho			1	Bisl	Oslo	7 Jun
49.70	Christine	Ohuruogu	GBR	17.5.84	2	OG	London (OS)	5 Aug
49.72	Tatyana	Firova	RUS	10.10.82	3	NC	Cheboksary	5 Jul
49.72	Deedee	Trotter	USA	8.12.82	3	OG	London (OS)	5 Aug
49.75		Montsho			4	OG	London (OS)	5 Aug
49.76		Firova			1s2	NC	Cheboksary	4 Jul
49.77		Montsho			1	DL	Saint-Denis	6 Jul
49.78	Novlene	Williams-Mills	JAM	26.4.82	3	Pre	Eugene	2 Jun
49.81		Krivoshapka			1s3	OG	London (OS)	4 Aug
49.87		Trotter			2s3	OG	London (OS)	4 Aug
49.89		Richards-Ross			1	DNG	Stockholm	17 Aug
49.91		Williams-Mills			3s3	OG	London (OS)	4 Aug
49.94		Krivoshapka			1	Quercia	Rovereto	4 Sep
49.95		Williams-Mills			2	DL	Saint-Denis	6 Jul
49.99		Williams-Mills			1		Kingston	5 May
50.00		Williams-Mills			1	DL	Shanghai	19 May
50.00	Natalya	Nazarova	RUS	26.5.79	2s3	NC	Cheboksary	4 Jul
50.02		Trotter			2	NC/OT	Eugene	24 Jun
50.03		Montsho			2	DNG	Stockholm	17 Aug
50.05		Krivoshapka			1s1	NC	Cheboksary	4 Jul
50.06	Francena	McCorory	USA	20.10.88	1	DL	New York	9 Jun
	(30/10)							
50.08	Rosemarie	Whyte	JAM	8.9.86	1	Hanz	Zagreb	4 Sep
50.34	Shericka	Williams	JAM	17.9.85	1	Gyulai	Budapest	20 Aug
50.37	Anastasiya	Kapachinskaya	RUS	21.11.79	5	NC	Cheboksary	5 Jul
50.43	Kseniya	Vdovina	RUS	19.4.87	2s2	NC	Cheboksary	4 Jul
50.48	Kseniya	Ustalova	RUS	14.1.88	2		Sochi	26 May
50.50	Ashley	Spencer	USA-J	8.6.93	1	WJ	Barcelona	13 Jul
50.55	Libania	Grenot	ITA	12.7.83	2	Gyulai	Budapest	20 Aug
50.61	Lyudmila	Litvinova	RUS	8.6.85	3s3	NC	Cheboksary	4 Jul
50.63	Kaliese	Spencer	JAM	6.5.87	1		Rieti	9 Sep
50.71	Patricia	Hall	JAM	16.10.82	2	Bisl	Oslo	7 Jun
	(20)							
50.72	Natasha	Hastings	USA	23.7.86	1		Ponce	12 May
50.85	Christine	Day	JAM	23.8.86	2s1	NC	Kingston	30 Jun
50.87	Vania	Stambolova	BUL	28.11.83	1		Izmir	19 May
50.88	Diamond	Dixon	USA	29.6.92	4	NC/OT	Eugene	24 Jun
50.91	Yelena	Migunova	RUS	4.1.84	3s2	NC	Cheboksary	4 Jul
51.00	Svetlana	Usovich	BLR	14.10.80	1		Minsk	12 Jun
51.04	Kadecia	Baird	GUY-Y	24.2.95	2	WJ	Barcelona	13 Jul
51.09	Nataliya	Pygyda	UKR	30.1.81	2h6	OG	London (OS)	3 Aug
51.10	Erika	Rucker	USA-J	29.9.93	3	WJ	Barcelona	13 Jul
51.11	Regina	George	USA/NGR	17.2.91	2	AfrC	Porto Novo	28 Jun
	(30)							
51.12	Joanna	Atkins	USA	31.1.89	1		Atlanta GA	12 May
51.13	Moa	Hjelmer	SWE	19.6.90	1	EC	Helsinki	29 Jun
51.13A	Rebecca	Alexander	USA	2.5.90	1	NACAC	Irapuato	7 Jul
51.19	Jessica	Beard	USA	8.1.89	6	DL	New York	9 Jun
51.19	Alina	Logvynenko	UKR	18.7.90	1h5	NC	Yalta	12 Jun
51.22	Phyllis	Francis	USA	4.5.92	1s1	NCAA	Des Moines	6 Jun
51.22	Debbie	Dunn ¶	USA	26.3.78	3	Bisl	Oslo	7 Jun
51.23	Keshia	Baker	USA	30.1.88	5	NC/OT	Eugene	24 Jun
51.23A	Marlena	Wesh	HAI	16.2.91	2	NACAC	Irapuato	7 Jul
51.24A	Tjipekapora	Herunga	NAM	1.1.88	1		Pretoria	4 May
	(40)							
51.25	Shaunae	Miller	BAH-J	15.4.94	1		Freeport	27 May
51.26	Perri	Shakes-Drayton	GBR	21.12.88	1	BIG	Bedford	10 Jun
51.26	Kseniya	Zadorina	RUS	2.3.87	2	EC	Helsinki	29 Jun
51.27	Natalya	Antyukh	RUS	26.6.81	6	WK	Zürich	30 Aug
51.28	Omolara	Omotosho	NGR-J	25.5.93	2	NC	Calabar	21 Jun
51.31	Ilona	Usovich	BLR	14.11.82	4	Gyulai	Budapest	20 Aug
51.42	Sherone	Simpson	JAM	12.8.84	1		Kingston	28 Jan
51.43	Joanne	Cuddihy	IRL	11.5.84	1		Fukuroi	3 May
51.43	Anna	Tashpulatova	BLR	21.10.87	2		Minsk	12 Jun
51.43	Mariya	Savinova	RUS	13.8.85	3h4	NC	Cheboksary	3 Jul
	(50)							
51.46	Leslie	Cole	USA	16.2.87	1		Los Angeles (ER)	5 May

Mark	Name		Nat	Born	Pos	Meet	Venue	Date
51.46	Geisa	Coutinho	BRA	1.6.80	1	NC	São Paulo	29 Jun
51.47A	Tsholofelo	Thipe ¶	RSA	9.12.86	2		Pretoria	4 May
51.53A	Jenna	Martin	CAN	31.3.88	1	NC	Calgary	30 Jun
51.54	Joelma	Sousa	BRA	13.7.84	2	NC	São Paulo	29 Jun
51.54	Shana	Cox	GBR	22.1.85	7	DL	New York	9 Jun
51.57	Bukola	Abogunloko	NGR-J	18.8.94	2		Atlanta	12 May
51.60	Marie	Gayot	FRA	18.12.89	1		Forbach	27 May
51.60	Pinar	Saka	TUR	5.11.85	1	Pavlov	Sofia	9 Jun
51.61A	Rorisang	Rammonye	RSA	31.12.90	1		Potchefstroom	24 Mar
	(60)							
51.67	Margaret	Etim	NGR	28.11.92	1		Warri	6 Jun
51.67	Viktoriya	Zyabkina	KAZ	4.9.92	1		Almaty	30 Jun
51.68	Yuliya	Olishevska	UKR	2.2.89	3	NC	Yalta	13 Jun
51.68	Ami Mbacké	Thiam	SEN	10.11.76	3	AfrC	Porto Novo	28 Jun
51.70	Darya	Prystupa	UKR	26.11.87	4	NC	Yalta	13 Jun
51.70	Shereefa	Lloyd	JAM	2.9.82	5	NC	Kingston	1 Jul
51.71	Indira	Terrero	CUB	29.11.85	2		Pergine Valsugana	21 Jul
51.72	Kanika	Beckles	GRN	3.10.91	1h1	Big 12	Manhattan KS	12 May
51.72	Dominique	Blake	JAM	15.2.87	3s1	NC	Kingston	30 Jun
51.73	Alena	Kyevich	BLR	6.10.87	1	NC	Grodno	6 Jul
	(70)							
51.76	Esther	Cremer	GER	29.3.88	1		Rehlingen	28 May
51.82	Olga	Zemlyak	UKR	16.1.90	2h2	NC	Yalta	12 Jun
51.85	Tatyana	Veshkurova	RUS	23.9.81	4		Sochi	26 May
51.85	Joyce	Zakari	KEN	6.6.86	3h1	OG	London (OS)	3 Aug
51.87	Justine	Palframan	RSA-J	4.11.93	5	WJ	Barcelona	13 Jul
51.88	Joke	Odumosu	NGR	27.10.87	2h1	NC	Calabar	19 Jun
51.89	Anneisha	McLaughlin	JAM	6.1.86	2		Kingston	28 Jan
51.93	Mary	Wineberg	USA	3.1.80	2h4	NC/OT	Eugene	22 Jun
51.96	Floria	Guei	FRA	2.5.90	1		Liège (NX)	5 Jul
51.97	Kristina	Malvinova	RUS	16.7.89	4h4	NC	Cheboksary	3 Jul
	(80)							
51.98	Lee	McConnell	GBR	9.10.78	3s1	EC	Helsinki	28 Jun
52.00	Olesea	Cojuhari	MDA	29.3.90	1		Bucuresti	15 Jun
52.00	Jody Ann	Muir	JAM	1.1.91	2q3	NCAA-E	Jacksonville	25 May
52.02	Carol	Rodriguez	PUR	16.12.85	1		Moncton	5 Jul
52.02	Phara	Anacharsis	FRA	17.12.83	2		Liège (NX)	5 Jul
52.06	Lanie	Whittaker	USA	21.5.91	1rB	FlaR	Gainesville	6 Apr
52.07	Denisa	Rosolová	CZE	21.8.86	2	Hanz	Zagreb	4 Sep
52.07	Ebony	Eutsey	USA	3.5.92	2rB	FlaR	Gainesville	6 Apr
52.09	Florence	Nwankwe	NGR-J	28.7.94	3		Warri	6 Jun
52.10	Aliann	Pompey	GUY	9.3.78	1		Omaha NE	6 Jul
	(90)							
52.11	Mirela	Lavric	ROU	17.2.91	1	NC	Bucuresti	5 Jul
52.11	Muriel	Hurtis	FRA	25.3.79	2h4	EC	Helsinki	27 Jun
52.11	Jonique	Day	JAM	13.11.88	2q1	NCAA-E	Jacksonville	25 May
52.11	Davita	Prendergast	JAM	16.12.84	4s2	NC	Kingston	30 Jun
52.12	Daysurami	Bonne	CUB	9.3.88	1		La Habana	29 Jun
52.12	Yulianna	Yushchenko	BLR	14.8.84	3	NC	Grodno	6 Jul
52.14	Moushaumi	Robinson	USA	13.4.81	1	CAA	Brazzaville	10 Jun
52.14A	Pamela	Jelimo	KEN	5.12.89	1h1	NC	Nairobi	14 Jun
52.15	Samantha	Edwards	USA	14.1.90	1	CIAA	Petersburg	20 Apr
52.16	Alysia	Montaño	USA	26.4.86	1		Berkeley	28 Apr
	(100)							

Mark	Name		Nat	Born	Date	Mark	Name		Nat	Born	Date
52.19	Robin	Reynolds	USA-J	22.2.94	18 Apr	52.37	Catherine	Eke	USA	8.12.88	2 Jun
52.20	Lenora	Guion Firmin	FRA	7.8.91	13 May	52.37	Liliya	Molgacheva	RUS	2.3.90	11 Jun
52.20	Bianca	Râzor	ROU-J	8.8.94	13 Jul	52.38	Sophia	Smellie	JAM	6.11.79	21 Apr
52.22	Marilyn	Okoro	GBR	23.9.84	20 Aug	52.38	Kelly	Massey	GBR	11.1.85	26 May
52.23	Aauri Lorena	Bokesa	ESP	14.12.88	7 Jul	52.38	Idara	Otu	NGR	5.7.87	22 Apr
52.25	Brianna	Frazier	USA	19.2.92	6 Apr	52.39	Yuliya	Terekhova	RUS	20.2.90	21 Jul
52.26	Marina	Maslenko	KAZ	3.7.82	18 Jun	52.40	Kseniya	Karandyuk	UKR	21.6.86	27 May
52.28	Verone	Chambers	JAM	16.12.88	26 May	52.40	Courtney	Okolo	USA-J	15.3.94	11 May
52.29	Janin	Lindenberg	GER	20.1.87	28 May	52.41	Agata	Bednarek	POL	28.6.88	16 Jun
52.30	Yelena	Voynova	RUS	10.3.85	3 Jul	52.41	Rashan	Brown	BAH-J	27.11.93	23 Jun
52.31	Endurance	Abinuwa	NGR	31.7.87	21 Jun	52.41	Monica	Hargrove	USA	30.12.82	5 May
52.31	Chris-Ann	Gordon	JAM-J	18.9.94	13 Jul	52.43	Amara	Jones	BAH	18.9.91	5 May
52.32	Mikele	Barber	USA	4.10.80	21 Apr	52.44	Sparkle	McKnight	TRI	21.12.91	23 Jun
52.33A	Raysa	Sánchez	DOM	6.5.88	28 Apr	52.46	Agné	Serksniené	LTU	18.2.88	2 Jun
52.33	Nicola	Sanders	GBR	23.6.82	3 Jun	52.47	Ashley	Liverpool	USA	11.2.92	13 May
52.34	Josphine	Ehigwe	NGR	12.6.85	21 Apr	52.47	Sanda	Belgyan	ROU	17.12.92	5 Jul
52.36	Irina	Khlyustova	BLR	14.6.78	12 Jun	52.48	Chantel	Malone	IVB	2.12.91	9 May
52.36	CeCe	Williams	USA	21.11.89	12 May	52.49	Alina Andreea	Panainte	ROU	7.11.88	8 Jun

Mark	Name		Nat	Born	Pos	Meet	Venue	Date
52.49	Patience	Okon	NGR	25.11.91			21 Apr	
52.49	Yaneisi	Borlot	CUB	18.2.91			29 Jun	
52.49	Briana	Nelson	USA	18.7.92			6 Apr	
52.50	Ndèye Fatou	Soumah	SEN	6.4.86			29 Apr	
52.53A	Kayan	Robinson	JAM	27.3.89			26 May	
52.53	Maria Enrica	Spacca	ITA	20.3.86			8 Jul	
52.54	Tiffany	Williams	USA	5.2.83			19 May	
52.55	Yekaterina	Vukolova	RUS	10.8.87			4 Jul	
52.57	Kineke	Alexander	VIN	21.2.86			17 May	
52.58	Marina	Konovalova	RUS	17.9.90			3 Aug	
52.58	Eléa Mariama	Diarra	FRA	8.3.90			17 Jun	
52.59	Shaniqua	McGinnis	USA	24.4.90			13 May	
52.60	Kendall	Baisden	USA-Y	5.3.95			17 Jun	
52.61	Elena	Bonfanti	ITA	9.7.88			8 Jul	
52.61	Estie	Wittstock	RSA	15.9.80			28 Jun	
52.62	Chiara	Bazzoni	ITA	5.7.84			8 Jul	
52.63	Raasin	McIntosh	LBR	29.4.82			27 Jun	
52.64	Tosin	Adeloye	NGR-Y	2.7.96			5 May	
52.64	Olga	Tovarnova	RUS	11.4.85			17 Jun	
52.65	Lydia	Mashila	BOT	22.6.90			27 Jun	
52.65	Kristin	Bridges	USA	2.3.90			25 May	
52.66	Shawna	Fermin	TRI	17.8.91			13 May	
52.67A	Gabriela	Medina	MEX	3.3.85			27 Apr	
52.67	Precious	Holmes	USA-Y	27.11.95			12 May	
52.68	Caitlin	Pincott	AUS	18.12.82			1 Apr	
52.68	Ristananna	Tracey	JAM	5.9.92			2 Jun	
52.68	Olivia	James	JAM-J	1.6.94			13 Jul	
52.69	Christian	Brennan	CAN-Y	27.3.95			26 May	
52.69	Emily	Diamond	GBR	11.6.91			2 Jun	
52.70	Pirrenee	Steinert	AUS	20.2.85			28 Jan	
52.70	Whitney	Jones	USA	24.1.90			4 May	
52.71	Eilidh	Child	GBR	20.2.87			6 May	
52.71	Yekaterina	Shestakova	RUS	3.4.85			26 May	
52.71	Laniece	Clarke	BAH	4.11.87			27 May	
52.72	Jitka	Bartonicková	CZE	22.12.85			17 Jun	
52.73	Turquoise	Thompson	USA	31.7.91			14 Apr	
52.73	Hanna	Titimets	UKR	5.3.89			18 May	
52.73	Diamond	Richardson	USA	6.4.90			25 May	
52.74	Jailma	de Lima	BRA	31.12.86			29 Jun	
52.75A	Sonja	van der Merwe	RSA	19.5.92			5 Apr	
52.75	Iga	Baumgart	POL	11.4.89			16 Jun	
52.75	Carline	Muir	CAN	1.10.87			12 May	
52.76	Patrycja	Wyciszkiewicz	POL-J	8.1.94			11 Jul	
52.77	Kseniya	Prytkova	RUS	29.3.89			14 Jul	
52.77	Tamsyn	Manou	AUS	20.7.78			3 Mar	
52.77	Ashley	Kelly	IVB	25.3.91			12 May	
52.79	Aymée	Martínez	CUB	17.11.88			15 Jun	
52.80		Chen Jingwen	CHN	8.2.90			23 Sep	
52.80	Cierra	McGee	USA	30.7.90			25 May	
52.81	Marina	Arzamasova	BLR	17.12.87			16 May	
52.81	Justyna	Swiety	POL	3.12.92			16 Jun	
52.82	Lauren	Boden	AUS	3.8.88			1 Jul	
52.82	Nicole	Leach	USA	18.7.87			21 Apr	
52.83	Olga	Bibik	UKR	5.2.90			18 May	
52.85	Jessica	Cousins	USA	10.4.85			4 May	
52.85	Blessing	Mayungbe	NGR	15.4.92			6 Jun	
52.87A	Zuley Melisa	Torres	COL-Y	29.4.95			30 Jun	
52.88	Marina	Karnaushchenko	RUS	2.10.88			11 Jun	
52.90	Lucimar	Teodoro	BRA	1.5.81			29 Jun	
52.91		Zhao Yanmin	CHN	26.1.91			23 Sep	
52.91	Ciara	Short (197)	USA	11.3.89			2 Jun	

Indoors

Mark	Name		Nat	Born	Pos	Meet	Venue	Date
51.18	Aleksandra	Fedoriva	RUS	13.9.88	1	NC	Moskva	23 Feb
51.94	Irina	Davydova	RUS	27.5.88	1h8	NC	Moskva	22 Feb
52.46	Marina	Karnaushchenko	RUS	2.10.88	11			Feb
52.60	Kamaria	Brown	USA	21.12.92	25			Feb
52.63	Svetlana	Pospelova	RUS	24.12.79	22			Feb
52.67	Yelizaveta	Bryzgina	UKR	28.11.89	16			Feb
52.71A	Jernail	Hayes	USA	8.7.88	26			Feb
52.75	Erica	Moore	USA	25.3.88	14			Jan
52.75	Taylor	Ellis-Watson	USA-J	6.5.93	4			Feb

Best at low altitude

Mark	Name		Pos	Meet	Venue	Date
51.20	Alexander		2	NCAA	Des Moines	8 Jun
51.43	Wesh		1		Charlottesville	21 Apr
51.69	Martin		2		Georgetown	9 May
51.79	Thipe ¶		1		Marseille	31 May
51.86	Herunga		3		Madrid	7 Jul
51.98	Rammonye		1		Stellenbosch	20 Mar
52.47	Sánchez		5h3	OG	London (OS)	3 Aug

Hand timed

Mark	Name		Nat	Born	Pos	Venue	Date
50.1	Kseniya	Ustalova	RUS	14.1.88	1	Bishkek	21 Apr
51.5	Lorraine	King	USA		1	Norwalk	3 Mar
51.8	Tatyana	Veshkurova	RUS	23.9.81		Bishkek	21 Apr

Drugs disqualification

Mark	Name		Nat	Born	Pos	Meet	Venue	Date
50.78	Debbie	Dunn ¶	USA	26.3.78	(4)	NC/OT	Eugene	24 Jun
51.86	Antonina	Yefremova ¶	UKR	19.7.81	(2)r3		Yalta	27 May

JUNIORS

See main list for top 8 juniors. 12 performances by 6 women to 51.70. Additional marks and further juniors:

	Mark		Pos	Meet	Venue		Date		Mark2		Pos2	Meet2	Venue2		Date2
Spencer	50.95		1	NCAA	Des Moines		8 Jun		51.33		1s3	NCAA	Des Moines		6 Jun
	51.02		1		Big 10 Madison		13 May		51.68		1	NC-j	Bloomogton		17 Jun
Omotosho	51.41		4s3	OG	London (OS)		4 Aug								
Miller	51.44		1		Nassau		12 May								

Mark	Name		Nat	Born	Pos	Meet	Venue	Date
52.19	Robin	Reynolds	USA	22.2.94	1		Miramar	18 Apr
52.20	Bianca	Râzor (10)	ROU	8.8.94	6	WJ	Barcelona	13 Jul
52.31	Chris-Ann	Gordon	JAM	18.9.94	7	WJ	Barcelona	13 Jul
52.40	Courtney	Okolo	USA	15.3.94	1		Austin	11 May
52.41	Rashan	Brown	BAH	27.11.93	1	NC	Nassau	23 Jun
52.60	Kendall	Baisden	USA-Y	5.3.95	3	NC-j	Bloomington IN	17 Jun
52.64	Tosin	Adeloye	NGR-Y	2.7.96	1		Akure	5 May
52.67	Precious	Holmes	USA-Y	27.11.95	2		White Plains	12 May
52.68	Olivia	James	JAM	1.6.94	8	WJ	Barcelona	13 Jul
52.69	Christian	Brennan	CAN-Y	27.3.95	1		Windsor	26 May
52.76	Patrycja	Wyciszkiewicz	POL	8.1.94	2h4	WJ	Barcelona	11 Jul
52.87A	Zuley Melisa	Torres	COL-Y	29.4.95	1		Bogotá	30 Jun

600 METRES

Mark	Name		Nat	Born	Pos	Meet	Venue	Date
1:23.35	Pamela	Jelimo	KEN	5.12.89	1		Liège (NX)	5 Jul
1:24.36	Marilyn	Okoro	GBR	23.9.84	2		Liège (NX)	5 Jul
1:25.56	Caster	Semenya	RSA	7.1.91	1	PNG	Turku	13 Jun
1:25.79	Tamsyn	Manou	AUS	20.7.78	3		Liège (NX)	5 Jul
1:25.89+		Jelimo			1	in 800m	London (OS)	11 Aug
1:26.37+	Fantu	Magiso	ETH	9.6.92	1	in 800m	Doha	11 May

Mark	Name		Nat	Born	Pos	Meet	Venue	Date
1:26.6+	Mariya	Savinova	RUS	13.8.85	11 Aug			
1:26.6+	Yekaterina	Poistogova	RUS	1.3.91	11 Aug			
1:26.6+	Janeth	Jepkosgei	KEN	13.12.83	11 Aug			
1:26.7+	Alysia	Montaño	USA	26.4.86	11 Aug			
1:26.72	Angela	Smit	NZL	16.8.91	5 Jul			
1:26.9+	Yelena	Arzhakova	RUS	8.9.89	11 Aug			
1:27.34	Patrycja	Wyciszkiewicz	POL-J	8.1.94	8 Sep			
1:27.60	Carolin	Walter	GER	29.2.88	6 May			
1:27.76	Justyna	Swiety	POL	3.12.92	3 May			

800 METRES

Mark	Name		Nat	Born	Pos	Meet	Venue	Date
1:56.19	Mariya	Savinova	RUS	13.8.85	1	OG	London (OS)	11 Aug
1:56.59	Francine	Niyonsaba	BDI-J	5.5.93	1	VD	Bruxelles	7 Sep
1:56.76	Pamela	Jelimo	KEN	5.12.89	1	NA	Heusden	7 Jul
1:56.94		Jelimo			1	DL	Doha	11 May
1:57.23	Caster	Semenya	RSA	7.1.91	2	OG	London (OS)	11 Aug
1:57.24		Jelimo			2	VD	Bruxelles	7 Sep
1:57.37	Alysia	Montaño	USA	26.4.86	1	Pre	Eugene	1 Jun
1:57.42		Savinova			1h6	NC	Cheboksary	3 Jul
1:57.46	Yekaterina	Kostetskaya	RUS	31.12.86	1h1	NC	Cheboksary	3 Jul
1:57.48	Fantu	Magiso	ETH	9.6.92	1	DL	New York	9 Jun
1:57.53	Yekaterina	Poistogova	RUS	1.3.91	3	OG	London (OS)	11 Aug
1:57.56		Magiso			1	GGala	Roma	31 May
1:57.59		Jelimo			4	OG	London (OS)	11 Aug
1:57.59		Jelimo			1	Athl	Lausanne	23 Aug
1:57.65		Niyonsaba			1		Rieti	9 Sep
1:57.67	Yelena	Arzhakova	RUS	8.9.89	1h4	NC	Cheboksary	3 Jul
1:57.67		Semenya			1s2	OG	London (OS)	9 Aug
1:57.77	Yelena	Kofanova (10)	RUS	8.8.88	1h3	NC	Cheboksary	3 Jul
1:57.79	Janeth	Jepkosgei	KEN	13.12.83	1	FBK	Hengelo	27 May
1:57.82	Irina	Maracheva	RUS	29.9.84	1		Sochi	27 May
1:57.90		Magiso			2	DL	Doha	11 May
1:57.93		Savinova			1	Mosc C	Moskva	11 Jun
1:57.93		Poistogova			1	Kuts	Moskva	13 Jun
1:57.93		Montaño			5	OG	London (OS)	11 Aug
1:58.10		Savinova			2	Athl	Lausanne	23 Aug
1:58.13		Arzhakova			2s2	OG	London (OS)	9 Aug
1:58.15		Poistogova			1	NC	Cheboksary	4 Jul
1:58.26		Jepkosgei			3s2	OG	London (OS)	9 Aug
1:58.28		Arzhakova			2	Mosc C	Moskva	11 Jun
1:58.33		Jelimo			2	GGala	Roma	31 May
	(30/12)							
1:58.46	Nataliya	Lupu	UKR	4.11.87	1	NC	Yalta	14 Jun
1:58.53	Yusneisis	Santiusti	CUB	24.12.84	2	FBK	Hengelo	27 May
1:58.55	Tatyana	Markelova	RUS	19.12.88	2h4	NC	Cheboksary	3 Jul
1:58.72	Svetlana	Usovich	BLR	14.10.80	1	NCp	Brest	26 May
1:58.84	Halima	Hachlaf	MAR	6.9.88	5s2	OG	London (OS)	9 Aug
1:59.03	Svetlana	Cherkasova	RUS	20.5.78	4	Mosc C	Moskva	11 Jun
1:59.08	Annet	Negesa	UGA	24.4.92	3	FBK	Hengelo	27 May
1:59.13	Eunice	Sum	KEN	2.9.88	2	AfrC	Porto Novo	1 Jul
	(20)							
1:59.14	Brenda	Martinez	USA	8.9.87	4	VD	Bruxelles	7 Sep
1:59.16	Anna	Pierce	USA	31.3.84	5	VD	Bruxelles	7 Sep
1:59.18	Molly	Beckwith	USA	4.8.87	2	DL	New York	9 Jun
1:59.20	Margarita	Mukasheva	KAZ	4.1.86	3s3	OG	London (OS)	9 Aug
1:59.24	Geena	Gall	USA	18.1.87	2	NC/OT	Eugene	25 Jun
1:59.25	Yuliya	Krevsun	UKR	8.12.80	2	NC	Yalta	14 Jun
1:59.32	Olena	Zhushman	UKR	30.12.85	3	NC	Yalta	14 Jun
1:59.33	Marilyn	Okoro	GBR	23.9.84	4	FBK	Hengelo	27 May
1:59.37	Emma	Jackson	GBR	7.6.88	5	DL	Doha	11 May
1:59.37	Winny	Chebet	KEN	20.12.90	3		Rieti	9 Sep
	(30)							
1:59.39	Abeba	Aregawi	ETH	5.7.90	3	ISTAF	Berlin	2 Sep
1:59.40	Yuliya	Tutayeva ¶	RUS	7.12.88	3	Kuts	Moskva	13 Jun
1:59.46	Alice	Schmidt	USA	3.10.81	3	NC/OT	Eugene	25 Jun
1:59.54	Malika	Akkaoui	MAR	25.12.87	7	Mosc C	Moskva	11 Jun
1:59.55	Rose M.	Almanza	CUB	13.7.92	1		La Habana	29 Jun
1:59.62	Liliya	Lobanova	UKR	14.10.85	4	NC	Yalta	14 Jun
1:59.63	Marina	Arzamasova	BLR	17.12.87	2		Montreuil-sous-Bois	5 Jun
1:59.66	Hannah	England	GBR	6.3.87	1	Gugl	Linz	20 Aug
1:59.69	Tintu	Luka	IND	26.4.89	6s2	OG	London (OS)	9 Aug
1:59.70	Marina	Pospelova	RUS	23.7.90	1	NC-23	Yerino	21 Jul
	(40)							
1:59.72	Phoebe	Wright	USA	30.8.88	5	NC/OT	Eugene	25 Jun
1:59.74	Mirela	Lavric	ROU	17.2.91	5	FBK	Hengelo	27 May

Mark	Name		Nat	Born	Pos	Meet	Venue	Date	
1:59.82	Melissa	Bishop	CAN	5.8.88	3	Pre	Eugene	1	Jun
1:59.85	Yekaterina	Kupina	RUS	2.2.86	5	Kuts	Moskva	13	Jun
1:59.86	Jessica	Smith	CAN	11.10.89	1	Jerome	Burnaby	10	Jun
1:59.90	Yelena	Soboleva	RUS	3.10.82	9	Mosc C	Moskva	11	Jun
1:59.98	Maggie	Vessey #	USA	23.12.81	1		Ninove	21	Jul
2:00.05	Erica	Moore	USA	25.3.88	2		Ninove	21	Jul
2:00.06	Oksana	Dyomina	RUS	4.8.90	2h3	NC	Cheboksary	3	Jul
2:00.15	Chanelle	Price	USA	22.8.90	3		Ninove	21	Jul
	(50)								
2:00.16	Lucia	Klocová	SVK	20.11.83	9	GGala	Roma	31	May
2:00.16	Rosibel	García	COL	13.2.81	3s1	OG	London (OS)	9	Aug
2:00.22	Btissam	Lakhouad	MAR	7.12.80	1		Rabat	27	May
2:00.23	Tatyana	Paliyenko	RUS	18.11.83	4		Sochi	27	May
2:00.23	Merve	Aydin	TUR	17.3.90	1		Minsk	12	Jun
2:00.24	Yekaterina	Martynova	RUS	6.8.86	10	Mosc C	Moskva	11	Jun
2:00.27	Lydia	Wafula	KEN	15.2.88	2		Bottrop	6	Jul
2:00.33	Natalya	Peryakova	RUS	4.3.83	2h7	NC	Cheboksary	3	Jul
2:00.34	Corinna	Harrer	GER	19.1.91	3	Déca	Albi	15	Aug
2:00.38	Kristina	Khaleyeva	RUS	22.10.87	2rB	Mosc Ch	Moskva	21	Jun
	(60)								
2:00.39	Alena	Glazkova	RUS	6.5.88	3rB	Mosc Ch	Moskva	21	Jun
2:00.44	Eléni	Filándra	GRE	12.1.84	1	NC	Athína	16	Jun
2:00.44	Maryam	Jamal	BRN	16.9.84	1		Nottwil	30	Jun
2:00.52	Lynsey	Sharp	GBR	11.7.90	2	EC	Helsinki	29	Jun
2:00.53	Cherono	Koech	KEN	8.12.92	5s3	OG	London (OS)	9	Aug
2:00.55	Olga	Lyakhovaya	UKR	18.3.92	6	NC	Yalta	14	Jun
2:00.55	Diane	Cummins	CAN	19.1.74	5	Hanz	Zagreb	4	Sep
2:00.59mx	Yvonne	Hak	NED	30.6.86	1		Gouda	25	Aug
2:02.33					7		Reims	4	Jul
2:00.64	Elena	Popescu	MDA	6.9.89	1rB	NCp	Yalta	28	May
	(70)								
2:00.67	Angela	Smit	NZL	16.8.91	2	NA	Heusden	7	Jul
2:00.68	Adriana	Muñoz	CUB	16.3.82	2		La Habana	29	Jun
2:00.68	Neisha	Bernard-Thomas	GRN	21.1.81	8s2	OG	London (OS)	9	Aug
2:00.69	Svetlana	Podosyonova	RUS	24.5.88	2	Mosc Ch	Moskva	21	Jun
2:00.72	Jemma	Simpson	GBR	10.2.84	4		Lignano	17	Jul
2:00.78	Anastasiya	Tkachuk	UKR-J	20.4.93	1	NCp	Yalta	28	May
2:00.79	Yevgeniya	Zolotova	RUS	28.4.83	3rB	Mosc C	Moskva	11	Jun
2:00.82	Lemlem	Ogbasilassie	CAN	10.12.87	4	Jerome	Burnaby	10	Jun
2:00.90A	Jane	Jelagat	KEN	25.11.83	2	NC	Nairobi	15	Jun
2:00.9	Sahily	Diago	CUB-Y	26.8.95	1		La Habana	22	Jun
	(80)								
2:00.91	Ajee'	Wilson	USA-J	8.5.94	1	WJ	Barcelona	12	Jul
2:00.92	Anna	Mishchenko	UKR	25.8.83	2	NCp	Yalta	28	May
2:00.93	Yuliya	Chizhenko	RUS	30.8.79	1		Sankt-Peterburg	26	Jun
2:00.96	Jessica	Judd	GBR-Y	7.1.95	2	WJ	Barcelona	12	Jul
2:01.06	Nachelle	Mackie	USA	15.3.90	1	NCAA	Des Moines	8	Jun
2:01.13mx	Ingvill	Måkestad Bovim	NOR	7.8.81	1		Oslo	24	Jul
2:03.61					2		Karlstad	19	Jul
2:01.18	Genzebe	Shumi	BRN	29.1.91	2		Nottwil	30	Jun
2:01.21A	Sylvia	Chesebe	KEN	16.4.89	3	NC	Nairobi	15	Jun
2:01.22	Hilary	Stellingwerff	CAN	7.8.81	6	Athl	Lausanne	23	Aug
2:01.25	Natalya	Yevdokimova	RUS	17.3.78	2		Sankt-Peterburg	26	Jun
	(90)								
2:01.27	LaTavia	Thomas	USA	17.12.88	6	Pre	Eugene	1	Jun
2:01.30	Nicole	Sifuentes	CAN	30.6.86	5		Lignano	17	Jul
2:01.32	Angelika	Cichocka	POL	15.3.88	6	Hanz	Zagreb	4	Sep
2:01.33	Lea	Wallace	USA	19.12.88	2		Victoria	13	Jun
2:01.35	Marta	Milani	ITA	9.3.87	6		Lignano	17	Jul
2:01.38	Lenka	Masná	CZE	22.4.85	1		Huelva	7	Jun
2:01.40	Charlene	Lipsey	USA	16.7.91	2	NCAA	Des Moines	8	Jun
2:01.40	Katie	Palmer-Cox	USA	1.12.84	6	Jerome	Burnaby	10	Jun
2:01.46	Teodora	Kolarova	BUL	29.5.81	5		Madrid	7	Jul
2:01.46		Zhao Jing	CHN	9.7.88	1	NC	Kunshan	24	Sep
2:01.48		Wang Chunyu	CHN-Y	17.1.95	2	NC	Kunshan	24	Sep
	(100)								

Mark	Name		Nat	Born	Date		Mark	Name		Nat	Born	Date	
2:01.53	Tamsyn	Manou	AUS	20.7.78	18	Feb	2:01.63	Kate	Grace	USA	24.10.88	18	May
2:01.54	Heather	Kampf	USA	19.1.87	22	Jun	2:01.64	Aleksandra	Bulanova	RUS	10.6.89	21	Jun
2:01.55	Kenia	Sinclair	JAM	14.7.80	30	Jun	2:01.65	Shannon	Leinert	USA	30.6.87	9	Jun
2:01.58	Ewelina	Setowska-Dryk	POL	5.3.80	3	Jun	2:01.70		Truong Thanh Hang	VIE	1.5.86	30	Jun
2:01.61	Olga	Soldatova	RUS	8.9.85	27	May	2:01.74	Élodie	Guégan	FRA	19.12.85	4	Jul
2:01.63	Andrea	Ferris	PAN	21.9.87	12	May	2:01.87	Olga	Nitsina	RUS	11.2.89	3	Jul

Mark	Name	Nat	Born	Pos	Meet	Venue	Date
2:01.87	Anna Konovalova	RUS	4.7.88				4 Aug
2:01.89	Yelena Kobeleva	RUS	12.6.88				3 Jul
2:01.91	Oksana Zbrozhek	RUS	12.1.78				3 Jul
2:01.93	Treniere Moser	USA	27.10.81				21 Apr
2:01.97	Linda Marguet	FRA	11.9.83				6 Jul
2:01.99	Svetlana Rogozina	RUS	26.12.92				21 Jun
2:02.04	Karine Belleau-Béliveau	CAN	29.12.83				7 Jun
2:02.09	Laura Roesler	USA	19.12.91				6 Jun
2:02.09	Tatyana Tomashova	RUS	1.7.75				11 Jun
2:02.12	Olga Lvova	RUS	21.9.89				3 Jun
2:02.12	Natalija Piliusina	LTU	22.10.90				28 Jun
2:02.12mx	Denise Krebs	GER	27.6.87				1 Aug
2:02.14	Clarisse Moh	FRA	6.12.86				15 Aug
2:02.16	Fotiní Dagglí-Pagotto	GRE	13.8.85				16 Jun
2:02.17	Sanne Verstegen	NED	10.11.85				27 May
2:02.19	Zoe Buckman	AUS	21.12.88				2 Sep
2:02.20	Kimarra McDonald	USA	14.8.87				2 Jun
2:02.22	Anna Sidorova	UZB	9.9.84				8 May
2:02.23	Katie Mackey	USA	12.11.87				21 Jul
2:02.25	Maggie Infeld	USA	10.4.86				1 Jun
2:02.26	Althea Chambers	JAM	14.3.83				1 Jun
2:02.29	Diana Sujew	GER	2.11.90				17 Jul
2:02.30	Jana Hartmann	GER	23.5.81				7 Jun
2:02.32	Emily Dudgeon	GBR-J	3.3.93				11 Jul
2:02.35	Ruriko Kubo	JPN	23.1.89				21 Jul
2:02.37	Mantegbosh Melese	ETH	.88				15 Jul
2:02.38	Winnie Nanyondo	UGA-J	23.8.93				11 Jul
2:02.43	Nuria Fernández	ESP	16.8.76				7 Jul
2:02.46	Kelly Hetherington	AUS	10.3.89				28 Jan
2:02.46	Morgan Uceny	USA	10.3.85				29 Apr
2:02.49	Laura Januszewski	USA	28.2.86				18 May
2:02.52	Laura Weightman	GBR	1.7.91				9 Jun
2:02.54	Tara Bird	GBR	22.7.87				26 Aug
2:02.57A	Monique Stander	RSA-Y	10.3.95				20 Apr
2:02.62	Rose-Anne Galligan	IRL	9.12.87				6 Jul
2:02.63drugs dq	Anzhela Shevchenko	UKR	29.10.87				28 May
2:02.64	Tatyana Gudkova	RUS	26.3.85				3 Jul
2:02.64	Elisa Cusma	ITA	24.7.81				21 Jul
2:02.66	Anne Maria Kesselring	GER	4.12.89				6 Jun
2:02.68	Gerezine Gebremariam	ETH-Y	15.4.95				1 Jul
2:02.77	Tereza Capková	CZE	24.7.87				21 Aug
2:02.78	Sinimole Paulose	IND	24.6.83				11 May
2:02.78	Nelly Jepkosgei	KEN	14.7.91				25 May
2:02.78	María Kládou	GRE	19.3.85				16 Jun
2:02.82	Sonja Mosler	GER-J	23.8.93				11 Jul
2:02.83	Gabriele Anderson	USA	25.6.86				14 Jul
2:02.86	Nicole Schappert	USA	30.10.86				21 Jul
2:02.88	Rowena Cole	GBR	13.1.92				21 Jul
2:02.90	Christina Rodgers	USA	4.8.88				7 Apr
2:02.91	Sianne Toemoe	AUS	17.6.89				23 Feb
2:02.91	Charlotte Best	GBR	7.3.85				9 Jun
2:02.93	Monika Merl	GER	21.9.79				15 Jul
2:02.99A	Jepleting Busienei	KEN	.88				15 Jun
2:03.01	Elina Sujew	GER	2.11.90				15 Jul
2:03.03	Manal Bahraoui	MAR-J	6.1.94				27 May
2:03.03	Caroline King	USA	21.9.88				6 Jun
2:03.03	Anna Shchagina	RUS	7,12.91				11 Jun
2:03.06	Svetlana Uloga	RUS	23.11.86				3 Jul
2:03.07	Simoya Campbell	JAM-J	1.3.94				3 Mar
2:03.07	Phillippa Aukett	GBR	9.9.84				21 Jul
2:03.09	Rebekka Simko	USA	31.8.91				16 Jun
2:03.11	Tatyana Suprun	BLR	16.2.86				7 Jul
2:03.13	Renata Plis	POL	5.2.85				25 May
2:03.15	Aníta Hinriksdóttir	ISL-Y	13.1.96				11 Jul
2:03.16	Lyndsay Harper	USA	26.10.88				9 Jun
2:03.18	Desreen Montague	JAM-J	2.1.93				3 Mar
2:03.18	Adele Tracey	GBR-J	27.5.93				21 Jul
2:03.22	Agatha Kimaswai	KEN-J	2.4.94				10 Jul
2:03.24	Tatyana Myazina	RUS	18.3.88				3 Jul
2:03.26	Yuliya Pavlenko	RUS	11.4.88				3 Jul
2:03.26	Claire Gibson	GBR	25.12.82				21 Jul
2:03.33	Ashley Miller	USA	16.3.89				7 Apr
2:03.34	Mary Cain	USA-Y	3.5.96				12 May
2:03.35	Kathy Klump	USA	26.12.89				6 Jun
2:03.35	Diana Mezuliáníková	CZE	10.4.92				7 Jun
2:03.37	Alison Leonard	GBR	17.3.90				18 Aug
2:03.39mx	Isabel Macías	ESP	11.8.84				25 Jul
2:03.40	Eglé Balciunaité	LTU	31.10.88				11 Jun
2:03.41	Annie Leblanc	CAN	29.4.92				11 Jul
2:03.43	Dorina Korozsi	ROU	22.5.82				6 Jul
2:03.44	Anastasiya Grigoryeva	RUS	23.11.88				3 Jun
2:03.45	Christiane dos Santos	BRA	6.10.81				9 May
2:03.46	Claire Tarplee	IRL	22.9.88				21 Jul
2:03.49	Jenny Simpson (196)	USA	23.8.86				18 May

Indoors

Mark	Name	Nat	Born	Pos	Meet	Venue	Date
1:58.83	Jelimo			1	WI	Istanbul	11 Mar
1:59.01	Malika Akkaoui	MAR	25.12.87	1		Liévin	14 Feb
1:59.45	Marina Pospelova	RUS	23.7.90	1h6	NC	Moskva	22 Feb
1:59.97	Erica Moore	USA	25.3.88	3	WI	Istanbul	11 Mar
2:01.29	Carolin Walter	GER	29.2.88	1	NC	Karlsruhe	26 Feb
2:01.53	Elisa Cusma	ITA	24.7.81				14 Feb
2:02.03	Vania Stambolova	BUL	28.11.83				21 Jan
2:02.06	Anna Luchkina	RUS	13.1.86				22 Feb
2:02.67	Natalya Koreyvo	BLR	14.11.85				11 Feb
2:03.33	Fanjanteino Félix	FRA	26.1.80				28 Jan
2:03.37	Stephanie Charnigo	USA	25.7.88				21 Jan
2:03.45	Svetlana Lebedeva	RUS	5.9.84				22 Feb

Drugs disqualification

Mark	Name	Nat	Born	Pos	Meet	Venue	Date
1:58.78	Zahra Bouras ¶	ALG	13.1.87	1		Montreuil-sous-Bois	5 Jun
1:59.61	Maggie Vessey #	USA	23.12.81	(1)	Hanz	Zagreb	4 Sep
2:00.26i	Yuliya Rusanova ¶	RUS	3.7.86	(1h1)	WI	Istanbul	9 Mar
2:00.47	Tetyana Petlyuk &	UKR	22.2.82	(5)	NC	Yalta	14 Jun

JUNIORS

See main list for top 5 juniors. 12 performances by 5 women to 2:00.96. Additional mark and further juniors:

Mark	Name	Nat	Born	Pos	Meet	Venue	Date
Niyonsaba 2+ 1:58.67				2s3	OG	London (OS)	9 Aug
1:58.58				2	Herc	Monaco	20 Jul
1:58.78				2	ISTAF	Berlin	2 Sep
1:59.11				1	AfrC	Porto Novo	1 Jul
1:59.63				7	OG	London (OS)	11 Aug
2:01.48	Wang Chunyu	CHN-Y	17.1.95	2	NC	Kunshan	24 Sep
2:02.32	Emily Dudgeon	GBR	3.3.93	1s2	WJ	Barcelona	11 Jul
2:02.38	Winnie Nanyondo	UGA	23.8.93	2s3	WJ	Barcelona	11 Jul
2:02.57A	Monique Stander	RSA-Y	10.3.95	2		Pretoria	20 Apr
2:02.68	Gerezine Gebremariam (10)	ETH-Y	15.4.95	5	AfrC	Porto Novo	1 Jul
2:02.82	Sonja Mosler	GER	23.8.93	3s2	WJ	Barcelona	11 Jul
2:03.03	Manal Bahraoui	MAR	6.1.94	7		Rabat	27 May
2:03.07	Simoya Campbell	JAM	1.3.94	1		Kingston	3 Mar
2:03.15	Aníta Hinriksdóttir	ISL-Y	13.1.96	2s1	WJ	Barcelona	11 Jul
2:03.18	Desreen Montague	JAM	2.1.93	2		Kingston	3 Mar
2:03.18	Adele Tracey	GBR	27.5.93	6		Solihull	21 Jul
2:03.22	Agatha Kimaswai	KEN	2.4.94	3h1	WJ	Barcelona	10 Jul
2:03.34	Mary Cain	USA-Y	3.5.96	1		White Plains	12 May
2:03.69	Olena Sidorska	UKR	30.7.94	7	NCp	Yalta	28 May
2:03.85	Shelby Houlihan (20)	USA	8.2.93	6		Sun Angel Tempe	7 Apr

Mark	Name		Nat	Born	Pos	Meet	Venue	Date

1000 METRES

Mark	Name		Nat	Born	Pos	Meet	Venue	Date
2:37.84	Zoe	Buckman	AUS	21.12.88	1		Oslo	24 May
2:38.48	Brenda	Martinez	USA	8.9.87				26 Aug
2:38.48	Marina	Arzamasova	BLR	17.12.87				26 Aug
2:38.72	Lucia	Klocová	SVK	20.11.83				26 Aug
2:38.78	Angelika	Cichocka	POL	15.3.88				26 Aug
2:38.89	Ciara	Mageean	IRL	12.3.92				24 May
2:39.65	Ingvill	Måkestad Bovim	NOR	7.8.81				24 May
2:39.68	Charlotte	Best	GBR	7.3.85				24 May
2:39.79	Amela	Terzic	SRB-J	2.4.93				26 Aug
2:39.80	Annett	Horna	GER	4.2.87				6 May
2:40.09	Diana	Sujew	GER	2.11.90				6 May

Indoors

Mark	Name		Nat	Born	Pos	Meet	Venue	Date
2:36.69	Yelena	Arzhakova	RUS	8.9.89	1	Winter	Moskva	5 Feb
2:37.36	Natalya	Koreyvo	BLR	14.11.85	2	Winter	Moskva	5 Feb
2:37.58	Yelena	Kofanova	RUS	8.8.88	3	Winter	Moskva	5 Feb
2:38.14	Btissam	Lakhouad	MAR	7.12.80				4 Feb
2:38.16	Yekaterina	Martynova	RUS	6.8.86				5 Feb
2:38.44	Morgan	Uceny	USA	10.3.85				4 Feb
2:38.91	Anna	Pierce	USA	31.3.84				4 Feb
2:38.92	Yevgeniya	Zolotova	RUS	28.4.83				14 Jan
2:38.94	Yekaterina	Poistogova	RUS	1.3.91				5 Feb
2:38.97	Yekaterina	Kupina	RUS	2.2.86				5 Feb
2:39.55	Olga	Soldatova	RUS	8.9.85				5 Feb
2:39.99	Maggie	Infeld	USA	10.4.86				4 Feb
2:40.01	Anzhela	Shevchenko	UKR	29.10.87				29 Dec
2:40.03	Charlene	Thomas	GBR	6.5.82				4 Feb
2:40.22	Yuliya	Tutayeva ¶	RUS	7.12.88				27 Jan
2:40.30	Anna	Luchkina	RUS	13.1.86				14 Jan
2:40.32	Phoebe	Wright	USA	30.8.88				4 Feb
2:40.38	Natalya	Yevdokimova	RUS	17.3.78				10 Feb
2:40.43	Malika	Akkaoui	MAR	25.12.87				16 Feb
2:40.51	Tizita	Bogale	ETH-J	13.7.93				16 Feb

1500 METRES

Mark	Name		Nat	Born	Pos	Meet	Venue	Date
3:56.54	Abeba	Aregawi	ETH	5.7.90	1	GGala	Roma	31 May
3:56.62	Asli	Çakir Alptekin	TUR	20.8.85	1	DL	Saint-Denis	6 Jul
3:57.77	Genzebe	Dibaba	ETH	8.2.91	1	DL	Shanghai	19 May
3:58.59		Aregawi			2	DL	Saint-Denis	6 Jul
3:59.23		Aregawi			2	DL	Shanghai	19 May
3:59.25	Viola	Kibiwott	KEN	22.12.83	3	DL	Saint-Denis	6 Jul
3:59.28	Yekaterina	Kostetskaya	RUS	31.12.86	1	NC	Cheboksary	6 Jul
3:59.49	Yekaterina	Martynova	RUS	6.8.86	2	NC	Cheboksary	6 Jul
3:59.61	Svetlana	Podosyonova	RUS	24.5.88	1	Kuts	Moskva	13 Jun
3:59.65	Btissam	Lakhouad	MAR	7.12.80	4	DL	Saint-Denis	6 Jul
3:59.68	Hellen	Obiri	KEN	13.12.89	2	GGala	Roma	31 May
3:59.71	Tatyana	Tomashova (10)	RUS	1.7.75	3	NC	Cheboksary	6 Jul
3:59.89	Yekaterina	Gorbunova	RUS	17.1.89	2	Kuts	Moskva	13 Jun
4:00.09	Yelena	Soboleva	RUS	3.10.82	4	NC	Cheboksary	6 Jul
4:00.11	Yekaterina	Poistogova	RUS	1.3.91	1	Znam	Zhukovskiy	17 Jun
4:00.33		Soboleva			3	Kuts	Moskva	13 Jun
4:00.53	Kristina	Khaleyeva	RUS	22.10.87	4	Kuts	Moskva	13 Jun
4:00.82	Yelena	Arzhakova	RUS	8.9.89	5	Kuts	Moskva	13 Jun
4:00.85		Dibaba			3	GGala	Roma	31 May
4:01.03		Aregawi			1s2	OG	London (OS)	8 Aug
4:01.14		Soboleva			2	Znam	Zhukovskiy	17 Jun
4:01.16	Anna	Mishchenko	UKR	25.8.83	5	DL	Saint-Denis	6 Jul
4:01.18	Gamze	Bulut	TUR	3.8.92	2s2	OG	London (OS)	8 Aug
4:01.19	Maryam	Jamal	BRN	16.9.84	1	DNG	Stockholm	17 Aug
4:01.43		Obiri			6	DL	Saint-Denis	6 Jul
4:01.59	Morgan	Uceny	USA	10.3.85	4	GGala	Roma	31 May
4:01.62		Martynova			1h2	NC	Cheboksary	5 Jul
4:01.69		Lakhouad			3	DL	Shanghai	19 May
4:01.70	Yuliya	Zaripova	RUS	26.4.86	2h2	NC	Cheboksary	5 Jul
4:01.72	Mimi	Belete	BRN	9.6.88	2	DNG	Stockholm	17 Aug
(30/20)								
4:01.85	Natalya	Yevdokimova	RUS	17.3.78	5	NC	Cheboksary	6 Jul
4:02.13	Lisa	Dobriskey	GBR	23.12.83	7	DL	Saint-Denis	6 Jul
4:02.33	Yuliya	Chizhenko	RUS	30.8.79	1		Sankt-Peterburg	19 Jun
4:02.37	Natalya	Koreyvo	BLR	14.11.85	6s2	OG	London (OS)	8 Aug
4:02.59	Siham	Hilali	MAR	2.5.86	8	DL	Saint-Denis	6 Jul
4:02.99	Laura	Weightman	GBR	1.7.91	7s2	OG	London (OS)	8 Aug
4:02.99	Lucia	Klocová	SVK	20.11.83	8s2	OG	London (OS)	8 Aug
4:03.15	Shannon	Rowbury	USA	19.9.84	4	DNG	Stockholm	17 Aug
4:03.18	Mary	Kuria	KEN	29.11.87	1	Quercia	Rovereto	4 Sep
(30)								
4:03.71	Ingvill	Måkestad Bovim	NOR	7.8.81	10	DL	Saint-Denis	6 Jul
4:03.82	Faith	Kipyegon	KEN-J	10.1.94	5	DL	Shanghai	19 May
4:04.05	Hannah	England	GBR	6.3.87	1	FBK	Hengelo	27 May
4:04.07	Jenny	Simpson	USA	23.8.86	2	Quercia	Rovereto	4 Sep
4:04.26	Eunice	Sum	KEN	2.9.88	11	DL	Saint-Denis	6 Jul
4:04.30	Corinna	Harrer	GER	19.1.91	5	GGala	Roma	31 May
4:04.48	Renata	Plis	POL	5.2.85	7	GGala	Roma	31 May
4:04.76	Nicole	Sifuentes	CAN	30.6.86	1		San Diego	20 Jun

Mark	Name		Nat	Born	Pos	Meet	Venue	Date
4:04.84	Isabel	Macías	ESP	11.8.84	12	DL	Saint-Denis	6 Jul
4:04.84	Gabriele	Anderson	USA	25.6.86	1		Lignano	17 Jul
(40)								
4:05.03	Zoe	Buckman	AUS	21.12.88	10s2	OG	London (OS)	8 Aug
4:05.08	Hilary	Stellingwerff	CAN	7.8.81	8	GGala	Roma	31 May
4:05.16	Genzebe	Shumi	BRN	29.1.91	4	FBK	Hengelo	27 May
4:05.42	Anna	Pierce	USA	31.3.84	2		San Diego	20 Jun
4:05.52	Janet	Achola	UGA	26.6.88	5	FBK	Hengelo	27 May
4:05.61	Kaila	McKnight	AUS	5.5.86	6	DL	Shanghai	19 May
4:05.64	Alice	Schmidt	USA	3.10.81	1	Pre	Eugene	1 Jun
4:05.71	Diana	Sujew	GER	2.11.90	6	FBK	Hengelo	27 May
4:05.76	Lucy	Van Dalen	NZL	18.11.88	3		San Diego	20 Jun
4:05.80	Rabab	Arrafi	MAR	12.1.91	1	AfrC	Porto Novo	29 Jun
(50)								
4:06.01	Denise	Krebs	GER	27.6.87	2	Anhalt	Dessau	25 May
4:06.06	Senbera	Teferi	ETH-Y	3.5.95	4	Quercia	Rovereto	4 Sep
4:06.42	Mercy	Cherono	KEN	7.5.91	2	WK	Zürich	30 Aug
4:06.48	Marina	Muncan	SRB	6.11.82	3		Lignano	17 Jul
4:06.50	Yuliya	Krevsun	UKR	8.12.80	1h1	NC	Yalta	12 Jun
4:06.50	Margaret	Muriuki	KEN	21.3.86	3	AfrC	Porto Novo	29 Jun
4:06.52	Meskerem	Assefa	ETH	20.9.85	2	Colorful	Daegu	16 May
4:06.57	Nuria	Fernández	ESP	16.8.76	10s1	OG	London (OS)	8 Aug
4:06.6A	Vivian	Cheruiyot	KEN	11.9.83	1		Nairobi	18 May
4:06.66	Gemeda	Feyne	ETH	28.6.92	1	CAA	Brazzaville	10 Jun
(60)								
4:06.67	Katie	Mackey	USA	12.11.87	3rB		Los Angeles (ER)	18 May
4:06.73	Yelena	Korobkina	RUS	25.11.90	1		Joensuu	18 Aug
4:06.79	Angelika	Cichocka	POL	15.3.88	2	EAF	Bydgoszcz	3 Jun
4:06.87	Nicole	Schappert	USA	30.10.86	4		Lignano	17 Jul
4:06.96	Brenda	Martinez	USA	8.9.87	3		Los Angeles (ER)	18 May
4:07.06	Charlene	Thomas	GBR	6.5.82	7	FBK	Hengelo	27 May
4:07.07	Sheila	Reid	CAN	2.8.89	5		Lignano	17 Jul
4:07.23	Julia	Lucas	USA	4.3.84	4		Los Angeles (ER)	18 May
4:07.34	Janeth	Jepkosgei	KEN	13.12.83	8	DL	Shanghai	19 May
4:07.36	Elina	Sujew	GER	2.11.90	4		Bottrop	6 Jul
(70)								
4:07.49	Stephanie	Twell	GBR	17.8.89	9	Bisl	Oslo	7 Jun
4:07.55	Elisa	Cusma	ITA	24.7.81	6		Lignano	17 Jul
4:07.59	Feyna	Gudato	ETH		5	Colorful	Daegu	16 May
4:07.59	Amela	Terzic	SRB-J	2.4.93	2	WJ	Barcelona	15 Jul
4:07.63	Halima	Hachlaf	MAR	6.9.88	1		Rabat	27 May
4:07.67	Sonja	Roman	SLO	11.3.79	10	FBK	Hengelo	27 May
4:07.77	Emily	Infeld	USA	21.3.90	7		Lignano	17 Jul
4:07.86	Lidia	Chojecka	POL	25.1.77	2	NC	Bielsko-Biala	17 Jun
4:07.90	Malindi	Elmore	CAN	13.3.80	6	Colorful	Daegu	16 May
4:08.12	Liz	Maloy	USA	10.8.85	9		Lignano	17 Jul
(80)								
4:08.24	Sifan	Hassan	ETH-J	.93	5		Bottrop	6 Jul
4:08.25	Sarah	Bowman	USA	15.10.86	6	NC/OT	Eugene	1 Jul
4:08.27	Tereza	Capková	CZE	24.7.87	4		Dessau	25 May
4:08.30	Svetlana	Kireyeva	RUS	12.6.87	3	NCp	Yerino	14 Jul
4:08.31	Maggie	Infeld	USA	10.4.86	7	NC/OT	Eugene	1 Jul
4:08.32	Danuta	Urbanik	POL	24.12.89	3	NC	Bielsko-Biala	17 Jun
4:08.34	Sara	Vaughn	USA	16.5.86	5		Los Angeles (ER)	18 May
4:08.36	Anna	Konovalova	RUS	4.7.88	1		Irkutsk	3 Aug
4:08.38	Olesya	Mikheyeva	RUS	23.7.81	10	NC	Cheboksary	6 Jul
4:08.39	Azemra	Gebru	ETH	5.5.92	3		Tomblaine	8 Jul
(90)								
4:08.48	Tizita	Bogale	ETH-J	13.7.93	3	CAA	Brazzaville	10 Jun
4:08.59	Sally	Kipyego	KEN	19.12.85	1		Eugene	20 Apr
4:08.6A	Lucy Wangui	Kabuu	KEN	24.3.84	2		Nairobi	18 May
4:08.65mx	Luiza	Gega	ALB	5.11.88	1		Ohrid	17 Jun
4:09.76					1	NC	Tirane	7 Jun
4:08.72	Phoebe	Wright	USA	30.8.88	6		Los Angeles (ER)	18 May
4:08.80	Brie	Felnagle	USA	9.12.86	6rB		Los Angeles (ER)	18 May
4:08.87	Betlhem	Desalegn	UAE	13.11.91	1		Casablanca	9 Jun
4:08.91	Alfiya	Muryasova	RUS	3.10.88	4	Znam	Zhukovskiy	17 Jun
4:08.94	Margherita	Magnani	ITA	26.2.87	10		Lignano	17 Jul
4:09.06	Esma	Aydemir	TUR	1.1.92	1		Izmir	19 May
(100)								

4:09.09 Hind Dehiba FRA 17.3.79 6 Jul | 4:09.10 Nancy Langat KEN 22.8.81 17 Aug

Mark	Name		Nat	Born	Pos	Meet	Venue	Date
4:09.19	Ioana	Doagâ	ROU	5.4.92				5 Jul
4:09.25	Natalia	Rodríguez	ESP	2.6.79				17 Aug
4:09.34	Nazeret	Weldu	ERI	.90				8 Jul
4:09.34	Treniere	Moser	USA	27.10.81				17 Jul
4:09.36	Rkia	Elmoukim	MAR	22.2.88				10 Jun
4:09.41	Nancy	Chepkwemoi	KEN-J	8.10.93				27 May
4:09.42	Emma	Coburn	USA	19.10.90				18 May
4:09.51	Natalija	Piliusina	LTU	22.10.90				29 Apr
4:09.53	Fadime	Suna	TUR	25.10.86				9 Jun
4:09.93	Jessica	Judd	GBR-Y	7.1.95				15 Jul
4:09.95	Orla	Drumm	IRL	6.4.84				25 May
4:09.96	Perine	Nengampi	KEN	1.1.89				18 Jul
4:10.03	Gete	Dima	ETH	10.3.92				16 May
4:10.03	Olga	Golovkina	RUS	17.12.86				5 Jul
4:10.07	Jemma	Simpson	GBR	10.2.84				21 Jul
4:10.21	Amy	Mortimer-Garman	USA	16.8.81				10 Jun
4:10.22	Katarzyna	Broniatowska	POL	22.2.90				25 May
4:10.24	Roxana	Bârcâ	ROU	22.6.88				5 Jul
4:10.33	Yekaterina	Nikiforova	RUS	25.3.89				5 Jul
4:10.37	Irina	Maracheva	RUS	29.9.84				5 Jul
4:10.57	Kate	Grace	USA	24.10.88				1 Jun
4:10.72	Sinimole	Paulose	IND	24.6.83				8 Jul
4:10.74	Ciara	Mageean	IRL	12.3.92				5 Jul
4:10.74	Yevgeniya	Zolotova	RUS	28.4.83				13 Jun
4:10.84	Susan	Kuijken	NED	8.7.86				19 May
4:10.91	Stephanie	Charnigo	USA	25.7.88				1 Jun
4:10.96	Buze	Diriba	ETH-J	9.2.94				27 Apr
4:11.01	Mary	Cain	USA-Y	3.5.96				15 Jul
4:11.20	Carmen	Douma-Hussar	CAN	12.3.77				16 Jun
4:11.22	Lauren	Johnson	USA	4.5.87				29 Apr
4:11.30	Ayako	Jinnouchi	JPN	21.1.87				21 Jul
4:11.31	Renee	Tomlin	USA	21.11.88				1 Jun
4:11.33	Georgie	Clarke	AUS	17.6.84				21 Jan
4:11.35	Annett	Horna	GER	4.2.87				25 May
4:11.38	Katie	Flood	USA	29.2.92				29 Jun
4:11.40	Marina	Pospelova	RUS	23.7.90				22 Jul
4:11.45	Kate	Van Buskirk	CAN	9.6.87				11 Jul
4:11.46	Lyubov	Pulyayeva	RUS	26.4.82				5 Jul
4:11.49	Ashley	Miller	USA	16.3.89				29 Jun
4:11.52	Barbara	Parker	GBR	8.11.82				21 Jul
4:11.54	Emma	Jackson	GBR	7.6.88				20 May
4:11.58 drugs dq	Tetyana	Petlyuk	UKR	22.2.82				17 Jun
4:11.70	Delilah	DiCrescenzo	USA	28.2.83				9 Jun
4:11.72mx	Maren	Kock	GER	22.6.90				22 Aug
4:11,78mx	Eilish	McColgan	GBR	25.11.90				21 Aug
4:13.19								21 Jul
4:11.83	Johanna	Lehtinen	FIN	21.2.79				18 Aug
4:11.91		Xue Fei	CHN	8.8.89				19 May
4:11.93	Lauren	Bonds	USA	9.6.88				29 Apr
4:11.94	Gesa-Felicitas	Krause	GER	3.8.92				17 Jun
4:11.95	Iris María	Fuentes-Pila	ESP	10.8.80				8 Jul
4:11.98	Alem	Gereziher	ETH-Y	15.4.95				27 Apr
4:12.01	Mapaseka	Makhanya	RSA	9.4.85				28 May
4:12.16		Sun Lu	CHN	19.2.88				23 Sep
4:12.25	Salima	Alami	MAR	29.12.83				17 Jun
4:12.26	Oksana	Zbrozhek	RUS	12.1.78				5 Jul
4:12.27	Hannah	Brooks	GBR	25.6.88				21 Jul
4:12.29	Greta	Feldman	USA	30.3.91				29 Jun
4:12.34	Mason	Cathey	USA	29.4.82				6 Jun
4:12.36	Natalya	Aristarkhova	RUS	31.10.89				3 Aug
4:12.48	Genevieve	LaCaze	AUS	4.8.89				16 Jun
4:12.52	Karly	Hamric	USA	13.10.87				29 Jun
4:12.53	Kim	Conley	USA	14.3.86				9 Jun
4:12.61	Cory	McGee	USA	29.5.92				29 Apr
4:12.61	Julie	Culley	USA	10.9.81				9 Jun
4:12.67	Elena	García	ESP	19.6.86				25 Jul
4:12.67	Geena	Gall	USA	18.1.87				29 Apr
4:12.68	Jordan	Hasay	USA	12.9.91				7 Jun
4:12.71	Beverly	Ramos	PUR	24.8.87				10 Jun
4:12.80	Ashley	Higginson	USA	17.3.89				9 Jun
4:12.81	Larisa	Arcip	ROU	19.2.86				27 May
4:12.82	Gulnara	Galkina	RUS	9.7.78				13 May
4:12.82	Melissa	Salerno	USA	22.11.86				29 Apr
4:12.83	Julia	Kawamoto	CAN	8.11.83				11 Jul
4:12.87	Lea	Wallace	USA	19.12.88				18 May
4:12.88		Liu Fang	CHN	25.2.90				23 Sep
4:12.92	Bridey	Delaney	AUS	16.7.89				18 Feb
4:12.92	Alem	Embaye	ETH-J					15 Jul
4:12.95	Lydia	Wafula	KEN	15.2.88				4 Sep
4:12.96	Bridget	Franek	USA	8.11.87				21 Jul
4:12.96	Jennifer	Walsh	GBR-J	22.2.93				15 Jul
4:13.0A	Stacy	Ndiwa	KEN	6.12.92				15 Jun
4:13.01	Sara	Moreira	POR	17.10.85				7 Jul
4:13.06	Becca	Friday	USA	7.5.91				7 Jun
4:13.08	Amanda	Winslow	USA	13.8.90				7 Jun
4:13.10	Saïda	El Mehdi	MAR	21.9.81				8 Jul
4:13.20	Morgane	Gay	USA	19.8.90				7 Jun
4:13.30	Violah	Lagat	KEN	1.3.89				7 Jun
4:13.31	Morag	MacLarty	GBR	10.2.86				21 Jul
4:13.33	Kristen	Gillespie	USA	1.6.89				29 Apr
4:13.34	Melissa	Duncan	AUS	30.1.90				21 Jan
4:13.34	Rose-Anne	Galligan	IRL	9.12.87				21 Jul
4:13.34	Viktoriya	Polyudina	KGZ	29.6.89				5 Jul
4:13.39	Yelena	Orlova	RUS	30.5.80				23 Jun
4:13.43	Eleonora	Berlanda	ITA	6.4.76				17 Jul
4:13.48	Rebecca	Tracy	USA	20.2.91				7 Jun
4:13.48	Maureen	Koster	NED	3.7.92				29 Jun
4:13.54	Gemma	Kersey (198)	GBR	6.2.92				21 Jul

Indoors

Mark	Name		Nat	Born	Pos	Meet	Venue	Date
4:00.13		G Dibaba			1		Karlsruhe	12 Feb
4:01.33		G Dibaba			1	GP	Birmingham	18 Feb
4:03.67	Mariem	Alaoui Selsouli ¶	MAR	8.4.84	1		Liévin	14 Feb
4:06.01	Tizita	Bogale	ETH-J	13.7.93	3		Liévin	14 Feb
4:08.55	Hind	Dehiba	FRA	17.3.79	6		Liévin	14 Feb
4:08.93	Svitlana	Shmidt	UKR	20.3.90	2	NCp	Zaporizhzhya	27 Jan
4:09.04	Fanjanteino	Félix	FRA	26.1.80				14 Feb
4:09.70	Helen	Clitheroe	GBR	2.1.74				23 Feb
4:09.71		Xue Fei	CHN	8.8.89				13 Feb
4:11.97	Lauren	Centrowitz	USA	25.9.86				11 Feb
4:12.22	Wioletta	Frankiewicz	POL	9.6.77				18 Feb
4:12.41	Liliana	Popescu	ROU	5.2.82				31 Jan
4:12.81	Sylvia	Kibet	KEN	28.3.84				14 Feb

Drugs disqualification

Mark	Name		Nat	Born	Pos	Meet	Venue	Date
3:56.15	Mariem	Alaoui Selsouli ¶	MAR	8.4.84	1	DL	Saint-Denis	6 Jul
4:05.96	Anzhela	Shevchenko	UKR	29.10.87	9	GGala	Roma	31 May

JUNIORS

See main list for top 5 juniors. 11 performances (& 4 indoors) by 5 women to 4:09.3. Additional marks and further juniors:

Name	Mark	Pos	Meet	Venue	Date	Mark	Pos	Meet	Venue	Date
Kipyegon	4:04.96	1	WJ	Barcelona	15 Jul	4:08.78	9h3	OG	London (OS)	6 Aug
	4:08.53A	3	OT	Nairobi	23 Jun	4:09.1A	1	NC-j	Nairobi	8 Jun
Teferi	4:08.28	3	WJ	Barcelona	15 Jul					
Bogale 1i+	4:09.29	12	FBK	Hengelo	27 May	4:08.86i	1		Val-De-Reuil	18 Feb
	4:07.88i	2	XL G	Stockholm	23 Feb	4:08.91i	3h2	WI	Istanbul	9 Mar

Mark	Name		Nat	Born	Pos	Meet	Venue	Date
4:09.41	Nancy	Chepkwemoi	KEN	8.10.93	4		Rabat	27 May
4:09.93	Jessica	Judd	GBR-Y	7.1.95	5	WJ	Barcelona	15 Jul
4:10.96	Buze	Diriba	ETH	9.2.94	2		Dubai	27 Apr
4:11.01	Mary	Cain	USA-Y	3.5.96	6	WJ	Barcelona	15 Jul
4:11.98	Alem	Gereziher (10)	ETH-Y	15.4.95	3		Dubai	27 Apr
4:12.92	Alem	Embaye	ETH		7	WJ	Barcelona	15 Jul
4:12.96	Jennifer	Walsh	GBR	22.2.93	8	WJ	Barcelona	15 Jul

Mark	Name		Nat	Born	Pos	Meet	Venue	Date
4:13.68	Sofia	Ennaoui	POL-Y	30.8.95	3h2	WJ	Barcelona	13 Jul
4:13.90	Selam	Abrhaley	ETH	9.11.94	4		Dubai	27 Apr
4:13.91	Mary	Waithera	KEN	12.12.94	1	JPN Sch	Niigata	30 Jul
4:14.11	Luula	Berhane	ERI-J	5.3.94	2		Oordegem	26 May
4:14.22mx	Emelia	Gorecka	GBR	29.1.94	1		Watford	27 Jun
4:14.52mx	Laura	Muir	GBR-J	9.5.93	2		Glasgow	3 Aug
4:14.96	Marusa	Mismas	SLO-J	24.10.94	9	WJ	Barcelona	15 Jul
4:15.98	Saki	Yoshimizu	JPN-Y	31.7.95	2	N.Sch	Niigata	30 Jul

1 MILE

Mark	Name		Nat	Born	Pos	Meet	Venue	Date
4:26.76	Brenda	Martinez	USA	8.9.87	1		Falmouth	11 Aug
4:27.23	Kim	Conley	USA	14.3.86	1		Kessel-Lo	18 Aug
4:27.94	Gabriele	Anderson	USA	25.6.86	2		Falmouth	11 Aug
4:28.11	Almensch	Belete	ETH/BEL	26.7.89	2		Kessel-Lo	18 Aug
4:28.83	Janet	Achola	UGA	26.6.88	3		Kessel-Lo	18 Aug
4:29.85	Sifan	Hassan	ETH-J	.93	4		Kessel-Lo	18 Aug
4:30.18	Chelsea	Reilly	USA	9.5.89				11 Aug
4:30.65	Nicole	Schappert	USA	30.10.86				25 Jul
4:30.86	Zoe	Buckman	AUS	21.12.88				25 Jul
4:31.04	Hilary	Stellingwerff	CAN	7.8.81				20 Apr
4:31.28	Esma	Aydemir	TUR	1.1.92				2 Jun
4:31.40	Sarah	Bowman	USA	15.10.86				11 Aug
4:31.52	Marina	Muncan	SRB	6.11.82				20 Apr
4:31.78	Lucy	Van Dalen	NZL	18.11.88				17 Jul
4:32.11	Delilah	DiCrescenzo	USA	28.2.83				20 Apr
4:32.19	Genevieve	LaCaze	AUS	4.8.89				25 Jul
4:32.20	Dudu	Karakaya	TUR	11.11.85				2 Jun
4:32.69	Tereza	Capková	CZE	24.7.87				25 Jul
4:33.21	Lauren	Bonds	USA	9.6.88				20 Apr
4:33.24	Emma	Coburn	USA	19.10.90				25 Jul
4:33.33	Kaila	McKnight	AUS	5.5.86				17 Jul

Indoors

Mark	Name		Nat	Born	Pos	Meet	Venue	Date
4:28.41	Sally	Kipyego	KEN	19.12.85	1		Seattle	11 Feb
4:28.48	Katie	Flood	USA	29.2.92	2		Seattle	11 Feb
4:29.37	Hilary	Stellingwerff	CAN	7.8.81	3		Seattle	11 Feb
4:29.73	Kristina	Khaleyeva	RUS	22.10.87	1		Orenburg	3 Feb
4:31.52	Yuliya	Vasilyeva	RUS	23.3.87				3 Feb
4:31.98	Oksana	Suntsova	RUS	25.2.81				3 Feb
4:32.61	Anne Maria	Kesselring	GER	4.12.89				11 Feb
4:32.71	Malindi	Elmore	CAN	13.3.80				11 Feb

2000 METRES

Indoors

Mark	Name		Nat	Born	Pos	Meet	Venue	Date
5:44.54+i	Meseret	Defar	ETH	19.11.83	1	in 3000	Birmingham	18 Feb
5:44.8+	Hellen	Obiri	KEN	13.12.89				18 Feb
5:45.0+	Meselech	Melkamu	ETH	27.4.85				18 Feb
5:45.?+	Gelete	Burka	ETH	15.2.86				18 Feb
5:46.5+	Svitlana	Shmidt	UKR	20.3.90				12 Feb
5:48.85	Yelena	Arzhakova	RUS	8.9.89				14 Jan
5:49.0+	Helen	Clitheroe	GBR	2.1.74				18 Feb
5:49.30	Yevgeniya	Zolotova	RUS	28.4.83				6 Jan

Drugs disqualification

Mark	Name		Nat	Born	Pos	Meet	Venue	Date
5:41.24+	Mariem	Alaoui Selsouli ¶	MAR	8.4.84	1	in 3000	Eugene	2 Jun

3000 METRES

Mark	Name		Nat	Born	Pos	Meet	Venue	Date
8:35.89	Sally	Kipyego	KEN	19.12.85	2	Pre	Eugene	2 Jun
8:38.51	Mercy	Cherono	KEN	7.5.91	1	Herc	Monaco	20 Jul
8:39.14	Sylvia	Kibet	KEN	28.3.84	2	Herc	Monaco	20 Jul
8:39.65	Buze	Diriba	ETH-J	9.2.94	3	Herc	Monaco	20 Jul
8:39.83	Shannon	Rowbury	USA	19.9.84	4	Herc	Monaco	20 Jul
8:40.01	Azemra	Gebru	ETH	5.5.92	5	Herc	Monaco	20 Jul
8:40.59		Cherono			1	Athl	Lausanne	23 Aug
8:40.81	Veronica	Nyaruai	KEN	29.10.89	6	Herc	Monaco	20 Jul
8:41.21		Cherono			1	DL	Birmingham	26 Aug
8:41.22	Vivian	Cheruiyot	KEN	11.9.83	2	DL	Birmingham	26 Aug
(10/8)								
8:43.20	Emebet	Anteneh	ETH	13.1.92	7	Herc	Monaco	20 Jul
8:43.52	Gabriele	Anderson	USA	25.6.86	8	Herc	Monaco	20 Jul
(10)								
8:43.64	Mimi	Belete	BRN	9.6.88	9	Herc	Monaco	20 Jul
8:43.75	Viola	Kibiwott	KEN	22.12.83	4	DL	Birmingham	26 Aug
8:44.60	Yuliya	Chizhenko	RUS	30.8.79	1		Sankt-Peterburg	25 Jul
8:45.09	Gelete	Burka	ETH	15.2.86	4	Athl	Lausanne	23 Aug
8:45.57	Julie	Culley	USA	10.9.81	10	Herc	Monaco	20 Jul
8:46.38	Julia	Bleasdale	GBR	9.9.81	6	DL	Birmingham	26 Aug
8:46.49	Meseret	Defar	ETH	19.11.83	2	DL	Doha	11 May
8:48.16	Mary	Waithera	KEN-J	12.12.94	1		Gifu	9 Oct
8:48.72	Jenny	Simpson	USA	23.8.86	11	Herc	Monaco	20 Jul
8:49.64	Almaz	Ayana	ETH	21.11.91	3		Haldensleben	15 Jul
(20)								
8:50.04	Priscah	Cherono	KEN	27.6.80	5	DL	Doha	11 May
8:50.95	Liz	Maloy	USA	10.8.85	3	Pre	Eugene	2 Jun
c.8:51+	Genet	Ayalew	ETH	31.12.92		in 5000m	Roma	31 May
8:51.38	Brie	Felnagle	USA	9.12.86	4	Pre	Eugene	2 Jun
8:51.62	Yuliya	Vasilyeva	RUS	23.3.87	12	Herc	Monaco	20 Jul
8:51.63	Janet	Kisa	KEN	5.3.92	7	DL	Doha	11 May

Mark	Name		Nat	Born	Pos	Meet	Venue	Date
8:51.97	Rosemary	Wanjiru	KEN-J	9.12.94	1		Niigata	2 Aug
8:52.02	Almensch	Belete	ETH/BEL	26.7.89	8	Athl	Lausanne	23 Aug
8:52.04	Pauline	Korikwiang	KEN	1.3.88	8	DL	Doha	11 May
8:52.43	Delilah	DiCrescenzo	USA	28.2.83	2		New York	1 Jun
(30)								
8:52.94	Yelena	Korobkina	RUS	25.11.90	1	Mosc Ch	Moskva	21 Jun
8:52.95	Lisa	Uhl	USA	31.8.87	5	Pre	Eugene	2 Jun
8:53.12	Eunice	Sum	KEN	2.9.88	6	Pre	Eugene	2 Jun
8:53.26	Perine	Nengampi	KEN	1.1.89	1		Kuortane	22 Jul
8:54.51	Maryam	Jamal	BRN	16.9.84	9	DL	Doha	11 May
8:55.01mx	Fionnuala	Britton	IRL	24.9.84	1		Dublin	20 May
8:55.11	Emelia	Gorecka	GBR-J	29.1.94	9	DL	Birmingham	26 Aug
8:55.47	Corinna	Harrer	GER	19.1.91	1		Lichtenfels	28 Apr
8:55.60mx	Maren	Kock	GER	22.6.90	1		Dortmund	16 May
8:55.95mx	Karoline Bjerkeli	Grøvdal	NOR	14.6.90	1		Oslo	24 Jul
(40)								

Mark	Name		Nat	Born	Date
8:56.01mx	Silvia	Weissteiner	ITA	13.7.79	24 Jul
8:56.38	Kim	Conley	USA	14.3.86	23 Aug
8:56.52	Nancy	Chepkwemoi	KEN-J	8.10.93	11 May
8:56.99	Sara	Hall	USA	15.4.83	17 Jul
8:57.06	Mercy	Njoroge	KEN	10.6.86	26 Aug
8:57.43	Margaret	Muriuki	KEN	21.3.86	11 May
8:57.86	Molly	Huddle	USA	31.8.84	2 Jun
8:58.21	Amy	Hastings	USA	21.1.84	2 Jun
8:58.23	Jackie	Areson	USA	31.3.88	2 Jun
8:58.37	Elena	Romagnolo	ITA	5.10.82	17 Jul
8:58.62	Barbara	Parker	GBR	8.11.82	26 Aug
8:58.83mx	Eilish	McColgan	GBR	25.11.90	4 Sep
8:59.06	Purity	Rionoripo	KEN-J	10.6.93	28 Jul
8:59.24	Ashley	Higginson	USA	17.3.89	17 Jul
8:59.27	Gulnara	Galkina	RUS	9.7.78	14 May
8:59.39	Renee	Metivier-Baillie	USA	25.12.81	2 Jun
9:00.97	Goytetom	Gebresilasie	ETH-Y	15.1.95	11 May
9:01.63	Magdalene	Masai	KEN-J	4.4.93	17 Jul
9:01.64	Stephanie	Twell	GBR	17.8.89	11 May
9:01.93	Waganesh	Mekasha	ETH	16.1.92	9 Sep
9:01.96	Natalya	Popkova	RUS	21.9.88	15 Jul
9:02.04mx	Katrina	Wootton	GBR	2.9.85	30 May
9:02.22	Phanencer	Chemion	KEN	8.4.89	17 Jul
9:02.29mx	Johanna	Lehtinen	FIN	21.2.79	22 Jun
9:02.62	Laura	Weightman	GBR	1.7.91	6 May
9:02.91	Stephanie	Reilly	IRL	23.2.78	17 Jul
9:03.00	Ruti	Aga	ETH-J	16.1.94	23 Aug
9:03.72	Mika	Yoshikawa	JPN	16.9.84	29 Apr
9:03.76	Beatrice	Wainaina	KEN-J	23.11.93	7 Jul
9:03.82	Eloise	Wellings	AUS	9.11.82	17 Jul

Drugs disqualification – ? date

8:34.47	Mariem	Alaoui Selsouli ¶	MAR	8.4.84	1	Pre	Eugene	2 Jun

Indoors

Mark	Name		Nat	Born	Pos	Meet	Venue	Date
8:31.56	Meseret	Defar	ETH	19.11.83	1	GP	Birmingham	18 Feb
8:33.57		Defar			1		Boston (R)	4 Feb
8:35.35	Hellen	Obiri	KEN	13.12.89	2	GP	Birmingham	18 Feb
8:36.59	Gelete	Burka	ETH	15.2.86	3	GP	Birmingham	18 Feb
8:36.87	Mariem	Alaoui Selsouli ¶	MAR	8.4.84	1		Karlsruhe	12 Feb
8:37.16		Obiri			1	WI	Istanbul	11 Mar
8:38.26		Defar			2	WI	Istanbul	11 Mar
8:40.18		Burka			3	WI	Istanbul	11 Mar
8:40.50		Kibet			4	WI	Istanbul	11 Mar
8:41.01	Svitlana	Shmidt	UKR	20.3.90	1	NC	Sumy	18 Feb
8:43.93	Meselech	Melkamu	ETH	27.4.85	3		Karlsruhe	12 Feb
8:45.59	Helen	Clitheroe	GBR	2.1.74	2	v4N	Glasgow	28 Jan
8:46.01	Goytetom	Gebresilasie	ETH-Y	15.1.95	2		Boston (R)	4 Feb
8:46.17	Siham	Hilali	MAR	2.5.86	3		Boston (R)	4 Feb
8:49.27	Shitaye	Eshete	BRN	21.5.90	1	AsiC	Hangzhou	19 Feb
8:49.50	Mekdes	Bekele	ETH	20.1.87	4		Karlsruhe	12 Feb
8:53.18	Meskerem	Assefa	ETH	20.9.85	1		Eaubonne	16 Feb
8:53.56	Betlhem	Desalegn	UAE	13.11.91	2	AsiC	Hangzhou	19 Feb
8:53.75	Tejitu	Daba	BRN	20.8.91	3	AsiC	Hangzhou	19 Feb
8:54.40	Mestawat	Tadesse	ETH	19.7.85	2		Eaubonne	16 Feb
8:54.75	Sara	Hall	USA	15.4.83	4		Boston (R)	4 Feb
8:55.05	Lidia	Chojecka	POL	25.1.77	3		Eaubonne	16 Feb
8:55.31	Katie	Flood	USA	29.2.92	2		Seattle	28 Jan

Mark	Name		Nat	Born	Date
8:56.80	Nicole	Sifuentes	CAN	30.6.86	3 Mar
8:57.37	Kristina	Khaleyeva	RUS	22.10.87	22 Feb
8:57.52	Olga	Golovkina	RUS	17.12.86	22 Feb
8:58.73	Birtukan	Adamu	ETH	29.4.92	12 Feb
8:59.65	Sandra	Eriksson	FIN	4.6.89	7 Feb
8:59.95	Malindi	Elmore	CAN	13.3.80	28 Jan
9:00.13	Emily	Infeld	USA	21.3.90	10 Feb
9:00.27	Wioletta	Frankiewicz	POL	9.6.77	12 Feb
9:00.86	Chelsea	Reilly	USA	9.5.89	11 Feb
9:00.98	Alfiya	Muryasova	RUS	3.10.88	22 Feb
9:01.03	Alia Mohamed	Saeed	UAE	18.5.91	19 Feb
9:01.16	Julia	Lucas	USA	4.3.84	28 Jan
9:01.16	Gesa-Felicitas	Krause	GER	3.8.92	12 Feb
9:01.35	Silvia	Weissteiner (non mx)	ITA	13.7.79	26 Feb
9:01.37	Paula	González	ESP	2.5.85	12 Feb
9:01.83	Sheila	Reid	CAN	2.8.89	3 Mar
9:01.86	Gemma	Steel	GBR	12.11.85	18 Feb
9:02.15	Abbey	D'Agostino	USA	25.5.92	10 Feb
9:02.35	Deborah	Maier	USA	17.8.90	25 Feb
9:02.58	Yelena	Orlova	RUS	30.5.80	22 Feb
9:03.95	Jordan	Hasay	USA	12.9.91	25 Feb

JUNIORS

See main list for top 4 juniors. 10 perfs (& 1 indoors) by 5 women to 8:58.0. Additional marks and further juniors:

Diriba	8:44.62	2		Haldensleben	15 Jul	8:46.85	2	Spitz	Luzern	17 Jul
	8:45.38	6	Athl	Lausanne	23 Aug	8:50.94	3		Rieti	9 Sep
Waithera	8:52.59	2		Niigata	2 Aug					

Mark	Name		Nat	Born	Pos	Meet	Venue	Date
8:56.52	Nancy	Chepkwemoi	KEN	8.10.93	10	DL	Doha	11 May
8:59.06	Purity	Rionoripo	KEN	10.6.93	1		Uppsala	28 Jul
9:00.97	Goytetom	Gebresilasie	ETH-Y	15.1.95	12	DL	Doha	11 May
9:01.63	Magdalene	Masai	KEN	4.4.93	7	Spitzen	Luzern	17 Jul
9:03.00	Ruti	Aga	ETH	16.1.94	11	Athl	Lausanne	23 Aug
9:03.76	Beatrice	Wainaina (10)	KEN	20.11.93	1		Abashiri	7 Jul
9:06.91	Miyuki	Uehara	JPN-Y	22.11.95	1		Kagoshima	3 Jun
9:08.10	Sifan	Hassan	ETH	.93	5		Haldensleben	15 Jul
9:08.32	Alemitu	Haroye	ETH-Y	9.5.95	4		Cork	17 Jul
9:07.79i	Aisling	Cuffe	USA	12.9.93	1		Seattle	3 Mar
2 Miles Indoord 9:21.60i Tirunesh Dibaba			ETH	1.10.85	1		Boston (R)	4 Feb

5000 METRES

Mark	Name		Nat	Born	Pos	Meet	Venue	Date
14:35.62	Vivian	Cheruiyot	KEN	11.9.83	1	GGala	Roma	31 May
14:35.65	Meseret	Defar	ETH	19.11.83	2	GGala	Roma	31 May
14:39.53	Viola	Kibiwott	KEN	22.12.83	3	GGala	Roma	31 May
14:41.43	Gelete	Burka	ETH	15.2.86	4	GGala	Roma	31 May
14:43.11	Sally	Kipyego	KEN	19.12.85	1	Jordan	Stanford	29 Apr
14:44.82	Veronica	Nyaruai	KEN	29.10.89	5	GGala	Roma	31 May
14:46.01		Cheruiyot			1	VD	Bruxelles	7 Sep
14:46.73	Sylvia	Kibet	KEN	28.3.84	6	GGala	Roma	31 May
14:47.18	Mercy	Cherono	KEN	7.5.91	2	VD	Bruxelles	7 Sep
14:47.88		Kibiwott			3	VD	Bruxelles	7 Sep
14:48.43	Genet	Ayalew	ETH	31.12.92	7	GGala	Roma	31 May
14:48.86		Cheruiyot			1	LGP	London (CP)	13 Jul
14:49.26		M Cherono			2	LGP	London (CP)	13 Jul
14:50.80	Tirunesh	Dibaba (10)	ETH	1.10.85	1	DL	New York	9 Jun
14:51.66		Burka			4	VD	Bruxelles	7 Sep
14:53.04		Kibet			5	VD	Bruxelles	7 Sep
14:53.06	Buze	Diriba	ETH-J	9.2.94	6	VD	Bruxelles	7 Sep
14:53.93	Linet	Masai	KEN	5.12.89	3	LGP	London (CP)	13 Jul
14:56.04		Kipyego			7	VD	Bruxelles	7 Sep
14:57,02		Defar			2	DL	New York	9 Jun
14:57.68	Janet	Kisa	KEN	5.3.92	2		Rabat	27 May
14:57.75		Nyaruai			4	LGP	London (CP)	13 Jul
14:57.97	Almaz	Ayana	ETH	21.11.91	8	VD	Bruxelles	7 Sep
14:58.23	Azemra	Gebru	ETH	5.5.92	8	GGala	Roma	31 May
14:58.48		T Dibaba			1h1	OG	London (OS)	7 Aug
14:58.70		Defar			2h1	OG	London (OS)	7 Aug
14:59.31		Kibiwott			3h1	OG	London (OS)	7 Aug
14:59.53	Priscah	Cherono	KEN	27.6.80	3		Rabat	27 May
15:00.88		Nyaruai			9	VD	Bruxelles	7 Sep
15:01.20	Afera (30/17)	Godfay	ETH	25.9.91	4		Rabat	27 May
15:01.32	Molly	Huddle	USA	31.8.84	10	VD	Bruxelles	7 Sep
15:02.00	Julia	Bleasdale	GBR	9.9.81	4h2	OG	London (OS)	7 Aug
15:02.51	Emebet (20)	Anteneh	ETH	13.1.92	5	LGP	London (CP)	13 Jul
15:02.80	Yelena	Nagovitsyna	RUS	7.12.82	6h2	OG	London (OS)	7 Aug
15:02.84	Jo	Pavey	GBR	20.9.73	7h2	OG	London (OS)	7 Aug
15:04.12mx	Almensch	Belete	ETH/BEL	26.7.89	1		Oordegem	2 Jun
15:10.24					11h2	OG	London (OS)	7 Aug
15:04.65	Worknesh	Kidane	ETH	21.11.81	4	DL	New York	9 Jun
15:05.26	Olga	Golovkina	RUS	17.12.86	4h1	OG	London (OS)	7 Aug
15:05.38	Julie	Culley	USA	10.9.81	5h1	OG	London (OS)	7 Aug
15:05.48	Shitaye	Eshete	BRN	21.5.90	8h2	OG	London (OS)	7 Aug
15:05.59	Tejitu	Daba	BRN	20.8.91	6h1	OG	London (OS)	7 Aug
15:06.38	Elena	Romagnolo	ITA	5.10.82	9h2	OG	London (OS)	7 Aug
15:06.81	Silvia (30)	Weissteiner	ITA	13.7.79	7h1	OG	London (OS)	7 Aug
15:07.35	Waganesh	Mekasha	ETH	16.1.92	9	GGala	Roma	31 May
15:08.33	Sara	Moreira	POR	17.10.85	1		Watford	9 Jun
15:08.36	Svetlana	Kireyeva	RUS	12.6.87	1		Sochi	27 May
15:08.52	Julia	Lucas	USA	4.3.84	2	Jordan	Stanford	29 Apr
15:09.31	Kayoko	Fukushi	JPN	25.3.82	8h1	OG	London (OS)	7 Aug
15:10.20	Hitomi	Niiya	JPN	26.2.88	10h2	OG	London (OS)	7 Aug
15:10.28	Lyudmyla	Kovalenko	UKR	26.6.89	1	NCp	Yalta	28 May
15:12.81	Barbara	Parker	GBR	8.11.82	9h1	OG	London (OS)	7 Aug
15:12.97	Fionnuala	Britton	IRL	24.9.84	10h1	OG	London (OS)	7 Aug

Mark	Name		Nat	Born	Pos	Meet	Venue	Date	
15:13.40	Roxana	Bârcâ	ROU	22.6.88	5	EC	Helsinki	28	Jun
	(40)								
15:14.31	Jackie	Areson	USA	31.3.88	1		Los Angeles (ER)	18	May
15:14.48	Kim	Conley	USA	14.3.86	12h2	OG	London (OS)	7	Aug
15:15.22	Lisa	Uhl	USA	31.8.87	2		Los Angeles (ER)	18	May
15:15.24	Stephanie	Twell	GBR	17.8.89	5	Jordan	Stanford	29	Apr
15:16.50	Nadia	Noujani	MAR	3.9.81	7		Rabat	27	May
15:16.54	Nadia	Ejjafini	ITA	8.11.77	6	EC	Helsinki	28	Jun
15:16.77	Mika	Yoshikawa	JPN	16.9.84	13h2	OG	London (OS)	7	Aug
15:16.89mx	Sabrina	Mockenhaupt	GER	6.12.80	1rB		Bottrop	6	Jul
15:17.05	Yeshaneh	Ababel	ETH	10.6.90	2		Lillestrøm	3	Jul
15:17.75	Magdalene	Masai	KEN-J	4.4.93	4		Reims	4	Jul
	(50)								
15:18.01	Sally	Chepyego	KEN	3.10.85	1		Nobeoka	12	May
15:18.73	Yelena	Zadorozhnaya	RUS	3.12.77	3		Sochi	27	May
15:19.43	Jessica	Tebo	USA	8.4.88	6	Jordan	Stanford	29	Apr
15:19.77	Etenesh	Diro	ETH	10.5.91	1		Carquefou	1	Jun
15:19.98	Abbey	D'Agostino	USA	25.5.92	5	NC/OT	Eugene	28	Jun
15:20.00	Dudu	Karakaya	TUR	11.11.85	2		Istanbul	9	Jun
15:20.17	Olesya	Shuklina	RUS	27.6.84	4		Sochi	27	May
15:20.28	Eloise	Wellings	AUS	9.11.82	7	Jordan	Stanford	29	Apr
15:20.39	Judith	Plá	ESP	2.5.78	12h1	OG	London (OS)	7	Aug
15:20.41	Yuliya	Vasilyeva	RUS	23.3.87	1	NC	Cheboksary	4	Jul
	(60)								
15:20.84	Christine	Bardelle	FRA	16.8.74	1		Bagnols-sur-Cèze	18	May
15:21.36	Ruti	Aga	ETH-J	16.1.94	1		Kessel-Lo	18	Aug
15:21.75	Megan	Metcalfe Wright	CAN	27.1.82	8	Jordan	Stanford	29	Apr
15:21.77	Beatrice	Wainaina	KEN-J	20.11.93	2		Kumamoto	7	Apr
15:21.88	Rkia	Elmoukim	MAR	22.2.88	8		Rabat	27	May
15:22.39	Brie	Felnagle	USA	9.12.86	3		Stanford	6	Apr
15:22.82	Mary	Waithera	KEN-J	12.12.94	1		Yokohama	23	Sep
15:23.38mx	Yuriko	Kobayashi	JPN	12.12.88	1mx		Yokohama	27	May
	15:30.95				1		Fukuroi	3	May
15:23.51	Deena	Kastor	USA	14.2.73	3		Los Angeles (ER)	18	May
15:23.54	Lucy	Van Dalen	NZL	18.11.88	4	MSR	Walnut	20	Apr
	(70)								
15:23.64	Sheila	Reid	CAN	2.8.89	5	MSR	Walnut	20	Apr
15:24.00	Natalya	Puchkova	RUS	28.1.87	3	NC	Cheboksary	4	Jul
15:24.74	Natalya	Popkova	RUS	21.9.88	4	NC	Cheboksary	4	Jul
15:24.82	Alisha	Williams	USA	5.2.82	4		Stanford	6	Apr
15:24.85	Liz	Maloy	USA	10.8.85	7	NC/OT	Eugene	28	Jun
15:24.86	Karoline Bjerkeli	Grøvdal	NOR	14.6.90	13h1	OG	London (OS)	7	Aug
15:24.96	Alina	Prokopeva	RUS	16.8.85	5	NC	Cheboksary	4	Jul
15:25.73	Yelena	Korobkina	RUS	25.11.90	3	Kuts	Moskva	13	Jun
15:26.07	Aliphine	Tuliamuk	KEN	5.4.89	7	MSR	Walnut	20	Apr
15:27.54	Mariya	Konovalova	RUS	14.8.74	6	NC	Cheboksary	4	Jul
	(80)								
15:27.65	Maren	Kock	GER	22.6.90	1		Koblenz	23	May
15:27.97	Barbara	Maveau	BEL	16.2.87	1		Herentals	1	May
15:28.27	Tadelech	Bekele	ETH	11.4.91	2		Dubai	27	Apr
15:28.56	Renee	Metivier-Baillie	USA	25.12.81	1		Portland	9	Jun
15:28.60	Emily	Infeld	USA	21.3.90	8	NC/OT	Eugene	28	Jun
15:29.62	Tiblet	Hayu	ETH		3		Dubai	27	Apr
15:29.97	Gulnara	Galkina	RUS	9.7.78	8	NC	Cheboksary	4	Jul
15:30.00	Emily	Brichacek	AUS	7.7.90	10	Jordan	Stanford	29	Apr
15:31.29	Georgie	Clarke	AUS	17.6.84	11	Jordan	Stanford	29	Apr
15:31.59	Katie	Mackey	USA	12.11.87	9	MSR	Walnut	20	Apr
	(90)								
15:31.65	Kumiko	Otani	JPN-Y	23.3.95	1		Yokohama	1	Dec
15:31.66	Kellyn	Johnson	USA	22.7.86	2		Portland	9	Jun
15:31.72	Ai	Igarashi	JPN	25.10.88	2		Fukuroi	3	May
15:31.74	Susan	Wairimu	KEN	11.10.92	3		Fukuroi	3	May
15:31.98	Lyudmila	Stepanova	RUS	15.8.83	9	NC	Cheboksary	4	Jul
15:32.22	Sairi	Maeda	JPN	7.11.91	2		Yokohama	1	Dec
15:32.23	Grace	Kimanzi	KEN	1.3.92	4		Fukuroi	3	May
15:32.48	Natalya	Leontyeva	RUS	5.7.87	10	NC	Cheboksary	4	Jul
15:32.64	Amanda	Dunne	USA	5.12.82	3		Portland	9	Jun
15:32.88	Misaki	Onishi	JPN	24.2.85	2		Fukuoka	22	Sep
	(100)								

+ intermediate time in longer race, A made at altitude of 1000m or higher, H made in a heptathlon, h made in a heat, qf quarter-final, sf semi-final, i indoors, Q qualifying round, r race number, -J juniors, -Y youths (born 1995 or later)

Mark	Name	Nat	Born	Date
15:32.89	Bouchra Benthami	FRA	19.5.79	27 May
15:33.38	Katrina Wootton	GBR	2.9.85	9 Jun
15:33.4+	Amy Hastings	USA	21.1.84	3 Aug
15:33.42	Megan Brown	CAN	30.4.85	29 Apr
15:33.72	Yuka Ando	JPN-J	16.3.94	1 Dec
15:33.76	Kathy Kroeger	USA	20.6.91	29 Apr
15:33.88	Layes Abdullayeva	AZE	29.5.91	28 Jun
15:33.92	Tara Erdmann	USA	14.6.89	9 Jun
15:33.95	Nicole Aish	USA	18.3.76	29 Apr
15:34.15	Ayuko Suzuki	JPN	8.10.91	5 Oct
15:34.21	Hanae Tanaka	JPN	12.2.90	22 Sep
15:34.21	Emelia Gorecka	GBR-J	29.1.94	9 Jun
15:34.31	Magdalena Lewy Boulet	USA	1.8.73	28 Jun
15:34.5+	Janet Cherobon-Bawcom	USA	22.8.78	3 Aug
15:34.54	Emily Sisson	USA	12.10.91	20 Apr
15:34.69	Riko Matsuzaki	JPN	24.12.92	29 Apr
15:35.12	Kate Avery	GBR	10.10.91	9 Jun
15:35.13	Lidia Rodríguez	ESP	26.5.86	9 Jun
15:35.26	Yelena Sokolova	RUS	27.12.79	4 Jul
15:35.27	Emma Pallant	GBR	4.6.89	9 Jun
15:35.35	Caroline Nyakagwa	KEN	12.12.86	18 Nov
15:35.46	Tomoka Inadomi	JPN	16.1.86	12 May
15:35.49	Mai Ishibashi	JPN	2.7.89	18 Nov
15:35.75	Iwona Lewandowska	POL	19.2.85	9 Jun
15:35.90	Kumi Ogura	JPN	24.6.85	18 Nov
15:35.96	Kaila McKnight	AUS	5.5.86	3 Jul
15:36.55	Sabine Fischer	SUI	29.6.73	9 Jun
15:36.57	Cruz Nonata da Silva	BRA	18.8.74	29 Jun
15:36.74	Agnes Chebet	KEN-Y	12.12.95	11 Jul
15:36.90	Alex Kosinski	USA	29.3.89	7 Apr
15:37.00	Sandra Lopez	MEX	16.4.84	20 Apr
15:37.09	Joyce Mwangi	KEN	29.9.88	27 May
15:37.21	Johanna Lehtinen	FIN	21.2.79	9 Jun
15:37.27	Eina Yokosawa	JPN	29.10.92	4 Jul
15:37.28	Doricah Obare	KEN	10.1.90	22 Sep
15:37.3	Caryl Jones	GBR	4.4.87	21 Jul
15:37.32	Yurie Doi	JPN	8.12.88	3 May
15:37.34	Xue Fei	CHN	8.8.89	15 Sep
15:37.49	Sarah Waldron	GBR	11.2.88	29 Apr
15:37.56	Deborah Maier	USA	17.8.90	28 Jun
15:37.61	Hao Xiaofan	CHN	9.12.89	15 Sep
15:37.78	Yuko Shimizu	JPN	13.7.85	5 Oct
15:38.15	Xiao Huimin	CHN	1.3.92	15 Sep
15:38.22	Marta Tigabea	ETH	4.10.90	8 Jul
15:38.39	Misaki Katsumata	JPN	26.12.85	10 Jun
15:38.76	Felista Wanjugu	KEN	18.2.90	4 Jul
15:38.88	Ryoko Kizaki	JPN	21.6.85	10 Jun
15:38.90	Faridah Chelanga	UGA	8.10.89	5 Jun
15:39.01	Trihas Gebre	ETH	29.4.90	8 Jul
15:39.35	Karima Saleh Jassem	BRN	18.2.88	7 Jul
15:39.5A	Gladys Cherono	KEN	12.5.83	14 Jun
15:39.58	Zakya Mrisho	TAN	19.2.84	7 Aug
15:39.76	Cao Mojie	CHN	10.4.92	15 Sep
15:39.84	Toshika Tamura	JPN	6.6.90	12 May
15:39.84	Risa Kikuchi	JPN	5.2.90	22 Sep
15:39.87	Haruka Kyuma	JPN-J	20.12.93	13 Oct
15:40.0A	Lucy Wangui Kabuu	KEN	24.3.84	24 Mar
15:40.22	Miki Sakakibara	JPN-J	5.4.93	22 Dec
15:40.35	Rosemary Wanjiru	KEN-J	9.12.94	1 Dec
15:40.53	Natalya Novichkova	RUS	9.10.88	4 Jul
15:40.55	Rui Aoyama	JPN	15.4.89	22 Dec
15:40.64	Beatrice Mutai	KEN-J	.94	5 Jun
15:40.73	Megumi Kinukawa	JPN	7.8.89	3 May
15:40.81	Alia Mohamed Saeed	UAE	18.5.91	27 May
15:40.94	Nanaka Izawa	JPN	13.5.91	1 Dec
15:41.02	Miho Shimizu	JPN	.90	1 Dec
15:41.29	Hanna Nosenko	UKR	1.10.88	14 Jun
15:41.31	Jen Rhines	USA	1.7.74	29 Apr
15:41.36	Risa Takenaka	JPN	6.1.90	10 Jun
15:41.49	Mutsumi Ikeda	JPN	30.9.92	1 Dec
15:41.50	Madaí Pérez	MEX	2.2.80	20 Apr
15:41.60	Rie Kawauchi	JPN-Y	15.3.95	2 Dec
15:41.70	Hiroko Shoi	JPN	18.6.80	4 Jul
15:41.78	Lauren Bonds	USA	9.6.88	6 Apr
15:41.94	Jiang Xiaoli	CHN	6.4.89	15 Sep
15:42.00	Lyudmila Lebedeva	RUS	23.5.90	4 Jul
15:42.23	Ding Changqin	CHN	27.11.91	15 Sep
15:42.67	Amy Van Alstine	USA	11.11.87	29 Apr
15:42.90	Adriënne Herzog	NED	30.9.85	20 Apr
15:43.0A	Joyce Wanjiku	KEN		24 Mar
15:43.01	Melissa Cook	USA	22.11.79	6 Apr
15:43.23	Isabel Checa	ESP	27.12.82	8 Jul
15:43.32	Laura Thweatt	USA	17.12.88	29 Apr
15:43.51	Yuka Takashima	JPN	12.5.88	23 Jun
15:43.58	Gulshat Fazlitdinova	RUS	28.8.92	27 May
15:43.85	Yoko Aizu	JPN	28.4.86	23 Jun
15:43.89	Maya Iino	JPN	5.2.88	13 Oct
15:44.0A	Edith Chelimo	KEN	16.7.86	14 Jun
15:44.01	Charlotte Purdue	GBR	10.6.91	6 May
15:44.07	Yuki Mitsunobu	JPN	9.11.92	23 Jun
15:44.09	Gemma Turtle	GBR	15.5.86	19 May
15:44.15	Bogdana Mimic	SRB	9.1.89	20 Apr
15:44.17	Honoka Yuzawa	JPN-J	11.4.94	13 Oct
15:44.53	Akari Ota	JPN-J	26.1.94	8 Dec
15:44.62	Yuka Miyazaki	JPN	.92	22 Sep
15:44.62	Eilish McColgan	GBR	25.11.90	13 Jul
15:44.68	Shiori Yano	JPN-Y	11.2.95	7 Apr
15:44.75	Paula González	ESP	2.5.85	8 Jul
15:44.85	Shiho Yahagi	JPN-Y	6.7.95	13 Oct
15:44.87	Jordan Hasay (200)	USA	12.9.91	29 Apr

Unsanctioned meeting: 15:22 mx Janet Cherobon-Bawcom USA 22.8.78 mx Atlanta 12 Jun

Indoors

Mark	Name	Nat	Born	Pos	Venue	Date
15:29.24	Deborah Maier	USA	17.8.90	2	Seattle	10 Feb
15:36.09	Betsy Saina	KEN	30.6.88			11 Feb

Drugs disqualification - ? date for Selsouli

Mark	Name	Nat	Born	Pos	Meet	Venue	Date
14:45.91	Mariem Alaoui Selsouli ¶	MAR	8.4.84	1		Rabat	27 May
15:26.19	Inga Abitova ¶	RUS	6.3.82	6	NC	Cheboksary	4 Jul
15:28.71	Simret Restle-Apel ¶	GER	4.5.84	2		Koblenz	23 May

JUNIORS

See main list for top 6 juniors. 10 performances by 5 women to 15:33.0. Additional marks and further juniors:

Diriba 15:11.53 1 Montreuil-sous-Bois 5 Jun 15:32.94 1 WJ Barcelona 11 Jul
M Masai 15:28.48 9 Rabat 27 May 15:28,64 7 LGP London (CP) 13 Jul
Aga 15:32.95 2 WJ Barcelona 11 Jul

Mark	Name	Nat	Born	Pos	Meet	Venue	Date
15:33.72	Yuka Ando	JPN	16.3.94	3		Yokohama	1 Dec
15:34.21	Emelia Gorecka	GBR	29.1.94	4		Watford	9 Jun
15:36.74	Agnes Chebet	KEN-Y	12.12.95	3	WJ	Barcelona	11 Jul
15:39.87	Haruka Kyuma (10)	JPN	20.12.93	1		Fukuroi	13 Oct
15:40.22	Miki Sakakibara	JPN	5.4.93	1		Yokohama	22 Dec
15:40.35	Rosemary Wanjiru	KEN	1.1.94	4		Yokohama	1 Dec
15:40.64	Beatrice Mutai	KEN	.94	6		Montreuil-sous-Bois	5 Jun
15:41.60	Rie Kawauchi	JPN-Y	15.3.95	1		Isahaya	2 Dec
15:44.17	Honoka Yuzawa	JPN	11.4.94	3		Fukuroi	13 Oct
15:44.53	Akari Ota	JPN	26.1.94	1		Haruno	8 Dec
15:44.68	Shiori Yano	JPN-Y	11.2.95	4		Kumamoto	7 Apr
15:44.85	Shiho Yahagi	JPN-Y	6.7.95	4		Fukuroi	13 Oct
15:45.39	Megumi Aoba	JPN-Y	1.8.95	6		Fukuroi	13 Oct
15:45.57	Eri Makikawa (20)	JPN	22.4.93	7		Fukuroi	13 Oct

Mark	Name		Nat	Born	Pos	Meet	Venue	Date	

10,000 METRES

Mark	Name		Nat	Born	Pos	Meet	Venue	Date	
30:20.75	Tirunesh	Dibaba	ETH	1.10.85	1	OG	London (OS)	3	Aug
30:24.39		Dibaba			1	Pre	Eugene	1	Jun
30:24.85	Florence	Kiplagat	KEN	27.2.87	2	Pre	Eugene	1	Jun
30:26.37	Sally	Kipyego	KEN	19.12.85	2	OG	London (OS)	3	Aug
30:26.70	Belaynesh	Oljira	ETH	26.6.90	3	Pre	Eugene	1	Jun
30:30.44	Vivian	Cheruiyot	KEN	11.9.83	3	OG	London (OS)	3	Aug
30:39.38	Worknesh	Kidane	ETH	21.11.81	4	OG	London (OS)	3	Aug
30:45.56		Oljira			5	OG	London (OS)	3	Aug
30:47.25	Shitaye	Eshete	BRN	21.5.90	6	OG	London (OS)	3	Aug
30:50.16		Kidane			4	Pre	Eugene	1	Jun
30:53.20	Jo	Pavey	GBR	20.9.73	7	OG	London (OS)	3	Aug
30:55.63	Julia	Bleasdale	GBR	9.9.81	8	OG	London (OS)	3	Aug
30:59.19	Hitomi	Niiya (10)	JPN	26.2.88	9	OG	London (OS)	3	Aug
31:07.88	Yelizaveta	Grechishnikova	RUS	12.12.83	1	Mosc C	Moskva	11	Jun
31:09.28	Aberu	Kebede	ETH	12.9.89	5	Pre	Eugene	1	Jun
31:10.35	Kayoko	Fukushi	JPN	25.3.82	10	OG	London (OS)	3	Aug
31:10.69	Amy	Hastings	USA	21.1.84	11	OG	London (OS)	3	Aug
31:12.68	Janet	Cherobon-Bawcom	USA	22.8.78	12	OG	London (OS)	3	Aug
31:12.80	Lisa	Uhl	USA	31.8.87	13	OG	London (OS)	3	Aug
31:15.97	Betsy	Saina	KEN	30.6.88	1	Jordan	Stanford	29	Apr
31:16.44	Sara	Moreira	POR	17.10.85	14	OG	London (OS)	3	Aug
31:19.87		Hastings			2	Jordan	Stanford	29	Apr
31:23.51		Moreira			1	ECp	Bilbao	3	Jun
31:28.19		Kidane			1	NC	Birmingham	23	Jun
31:28.26		Niiya			1		Kobe	22	Apr
31:28.71	Mika	Yoshikawa	JPN	16.9.84	1	NC	Osaka	8	Jun
31:29.22	Fionnuala	Britton	IRL	24.9.84	3	Jordan	Stanford	29	Apr
31:29.57		Bleasdale			4	Jordan	Stanford	29	Apr
31:32.22		Pavey			2	ECp	Bilbao	3	Jun
31:33.50		Cherobon-Bawcom			5	Jordan	Stanford	29	Apr
	(30/20)								
31:33.76	Sally	Chepyego	KEN	3.10.85	1		Fukuoka	21	Sep
31:35.81	Christelle	Daunay	FRA	5.12.74	3	ECp	Bilbao	3	Jun
31:36.76	Sabrina	Mockenhaupt	GER	6.12.80	4	ECp	Bilbao	3	Jun
31:41.54	Sule	Utura	ETH	8.2.90	6	Pre	Eugene	1	Jun
31:42.25	Caroline	Nyakogwa	KEN		7	Pre	Eugene	1	Jun
31:44.75	Dulce	Félix	POR	23.10.82	1	EC	Helsinki	1	Jul
31:45.14	Nadia	Ejjafini	ITA	8.11.77	5	ECp	Bilbao	3	Jun
31:48.53	Abebech	Afework	ETH	11.12.90	8	Pre	Eugene	1	Jun
31:49.23	Deena	Kastor	USA	14.2.73	7	Jordan	Stanford	29	Apr
31:51.32	Olga	Skrypak	UKR	2.12.90	3	EC	Helsinki	1	Jul
	(30)								
31:51.91	Yuriko	Kobayashi	JPN	12.12.88	2		Fukuoka	21	Sep
31:55.83	Natalya	Popkova	RUS	21.9.88	2	Mosc C	Moskva	11	Jun
31:57.38	Alina	Prokopeva	RUS	16.8.85	3	Mosc C	Moskva	11	Jun
31:59.21	Natosha	Rogers	USA	7.5.91	2	NC/OT	Eugene	22	Jun
31:59.69	Shalane	Flanagan	USA	8.7.81	3	NC/OT	Eugene	22	Jun
32:00.73	Ayumi	Hagiwara	JPN	1.6.92	4		Fukuoka	21	Sep
32:00.94	Kim	Conley	USA	14.3.86	8	Jordan	Stanford	29	Apr
32:01.60	Lara	Tamsett	AUS	12.10.88	9	Jordan	Stanford	29	Apr
32:03.07	Alisha	Williams	USA	5.2.82	10	Jordan	Stanford	29	Apr
32:03.55	Charlotte	Purdue	GBR	10.6.91	11	Jordan	Stanford	29	Apr
	(40)								
32:03.85	Aheza	Kiros	ETH	26.3.82	9	Pre	Eugene	1	Jun
32:07.82	Valentina	Galimova	RUS	11.5.86	4	Mosc C	Moskva	11	Jun
32:08.54	Gema	Barrachina	ESP	10.4.86	1		Lisboa (I)	24	Mar
32:09.15	Tara	Erdmann	USA	14.6.89	6	NC/OT	Eugene	22	Jun
32:10.43	Tetyana	Holovchenko	UKR	13.2.80	1	NCp	Yalta	27	May
32:10.57	Alevtina	Ivanova	RUS	22.5.75	5	Mosc C	Moskva	11	Jun
32:12.47	Deborah	Maier	USA	17.8.90	12	Jordan	Stanford	29	Apr
32:13.62	Ana	Dias	POR	15.1.74	2	1 NC	Lisboa (I)	24	Mar
32:14.27	Meaghan	Nelson	USA	12.2.90	13	Jordan	Stanford	29	Apr
32:15.72	Cruz Nonata	da Silva	BRA	18.8.74	1	NC	São Paulo	27	Jun
	(50)								
32:15.87	Valeria	Straneo	ITA	5.4.76	6	ECp	Bilbao	3	Jun
32:16.51	Neely	Spence	USA	16.4.90	1	Zát	Melbourne	8	Dec
32:17.28	Doricah	Obare	KEN	10.1.90	1		Kumagaya	19	May
32:17.58	Ai	Igarashi	JPN	25.10.88	1		Abashiri	7	Jul

Mark	Name		Nat	Born	Pos	Meet	Venue	Date
32:18.40	Yoko	Aizu	JPN	28.4.86	1		Fukagawa	27 Jun
32:19.32	Pauline	Korikwiang	KEN	1.3.88	10	Pre	Eugene	1 Jun
32:20.34	Megumi	Kinukawa	JPN	7.8.89	3	NC	Osaka	8 Jun
32:20.98	Mari	Ozaki	JPN	16.7.75	2		Fukagawa	27 Jun
32:21.80	Miho	Ihara	JPN	4.2.88	3		Fukagawa	27 Jun
32:23.98	Hiroko	Shoi	JPN	18.6.80	3		Abashiri	7 Jul
	(60)							
32:24.25	Stephanie	Rothstein-Bruce	USA	14.1.84	8	NC/OT	Eugene	22 Jun
32:24.26	Hitomi	Nakamura	JPN	23.6.87	4		Abashiri	7 Jul
32:24.43mx	Ayame	Takaki	JPN	15.7.92	1mx		Yokohama	5 May
32:24.71A	Joyce	Chepkirui	KEN	20.8.88	2	NC	Nairobi	15 Jun
32:25.43	Eloise	Wellings	AUS	9.11.82	21	OG	London (OS)	3 Aug
32:25.69	Allie	Kieffer	USA	16.9.87	14	Jordan	Stanford	29 Apr
32:26.55	Misaki	Katsumata	JPN	26.12.85	1rB		Fukuoka	21 Sep
32:27.23	Akiko	Matsuyama	JPN	24.7.89	6		Abashiri	7 Jul
32:27.70	Tomomi	Tanaka	JPN	25.1.88	6		Fukuoka	21 Sep
32:27.91	Madaí	Pérez	MEX	2.2.80	15	Jordan	Stanford	29 Apr
	(70)							
32:29.28	Ayumi	Sakaida	JPN	7.11.85	7		Abashiri	7 Jul
32:29.94	Susan	Wairimu	KEN	11.10.92	8		Abashiri	7 Jul
32:30.33	Yuko	Mizuguchi	JPN	24.5.85	2rB		Fukuoka	21 Sep
32:30.40	Kellyn	Johnson	USA	22.7.86	10	NC/OT	Eugene	22 Jun
32:30.45	Rei	Ohara	JPN	10.8.90	4		Kobe	22 Apr
32:31.33	Yuki	Mitsunobu	JPN	9.11.92	10		Abashiri	7 Jul
32:31.66	Alissa	McKaig	USA	21.2.86	11	NC/OT	Eugene	22 Jun
32:31.76	Hiroko	Miyauchi	JPN	19.6.83	5		Kobe	22 Apr
32:31.97	Kate	DiCamillo	USA	14.12.86	2		Stanford	6 Apr
32:32.06	Yelena	Nagovitsyna	RUS	7.12.82	6	Mosc C	Moskva	11 Jun
	(80)							
32:32.89	Kayo	Sugihara	JPN	24.2.83	4	NC	Osaka	8 Jun
32:33.61	Yuko	Shimizu	JPN	13.7.85	5	NC	Osaka	8 Jun
32:33.83	Yoko	Miyauchi	JPN	19.6.83	6	NC	Osaka	8 Jun
32:34.49	Yuka	Takashima	JPN	12.5.88	12		Abashiri	7 Jul
32:34.51	Eri	Sato	JPN	5.4.86	3rB		Fukuoka	21 Sep
32:34.53	Olesya	Shuklina	RUS	27.6.84	7	Mosc C	Moskva	11 Jun
32:34.76	Alvina	Begay	USA	9.9.80	1rB	Jordan	Stanford	29 Apr
32:34.81	Gemma	Steel	GBR	12.11.85	9	ECp	Bilbao	3 Jun
32:36.05	Rebecca	Donaghue	USA	24.2.76	1		Portland	8 Jun
32:36.07	Sarah	Waldron	GBR	11.2.88	4		Stanford	6 Apr
	(90)							
32:36.25	Edith	Chelimo	KEN	16.7.86	1		Ponzano Veneto	29 Jun
32:37.04	Perine	Nengampi	KEN	1.1.89	1		Keuruu	5 Aug
32:37.22	Sarah	Porter	USA	22.8.89	2		Portland	8 Jun
32:37.66	Addie	Bracy	USA	4.8.86	3		Portland	8 Jun
32:37.83	Katie	McGregor	USA	2.9.77	16	Jordan	Stanford	29 Apr
32:37.90	Kumi	Ogura	JPN	24.6.85	1		Kure	24 Nov
32:38.29A	Priscah	Cherono	KEN	27.6.80	5	NC	Nairobi	15 Jun
32:38.41	Preeja	Sreedharan	IND	13.3.82	2		Ponzano Veneto	29 Jun
32:38.59	Megumi	Hirai	JPN	14.2.90	7		Kobe	22 Apr
32:38.95	Adriana	Nelson	USA	31.1.80	14	NC/OT	Eugene	22 Jun
	(100)							

Mark	Name		Nat	Born	Date
32:39.12	Elena	Romagnolo	ITA	5.10.82	3 Jun
32:39.31	Nanaka	Izawa	JPN	13.5.91	7 Jul
32:39.35	Aliphine	Tuliamuk	KEN	5.4.89	6 Apr
32:39.53	Rachel	Ward	USA	11.10.89	22 Jun
32:40.55	Liz	Costello	USA	23.2.88	6 Apr
32:40.82	Rebecca	Wade	USA	9.2.89	6 Apr
32:40.86	Carla Salomé	Rocha	POR	25.4.90	24 Mar
32:40.89	Natalya	Novichkova	RUS	9.10.88	11 Jun
32:41.40	Gladys	Cherono	KEN	12.5.83	30 Jun
32:42.23	Shino	Saito	JPN	7.9.88	22 Apr
32:42.68	Aya	Nagata	JPN	31.3.90	21 Sep
32:44.58	Katie	Matthews	USA	19.11.90	6 Apr
32:45.86	Michi	Numata	JPN	6.5.89	21 Sep
32:45.96	Madoka	Ogi	JPN	26.10.83	21 Sep
32:45.96	Diane	Nukuri-Johnson	BDI	1.12.84	29 Apr
32:47.20	Rika	Shintaku	JPN	19.10.85	21 Sep
32:47.67A	Margaret	Agai	KEN	.81	15 Jun
32:48.45	Wendy	Thomas	USA	19.1.79	8 Jun
32:49.92	Lauren	Kleppin	USA	22.11.88	6 Apr
32:50.13	Tetyana	Hamera-Shmyrko	UKR	1.6.83	1 Jun
32:50.30	Teresa	McWalters	USA	15.11.84	6 Apr
32:50.74	Chinami	Mori	JPN	5.5.90	22 Apr
32:51.02	Remi	Nakazato	JPN	24.6.88	7 Jul
32:51.12	Asami	Kato	JPN	12.10.90	22 Apr
32:51.17	Sarah	Callister	USA	10.7.91	6 Apr
32:51.28	Dani	Stack	USA	5.3.90	29 Apr
32:52.11	Yuka	Hakoyama	JPN	9.3.90	7 Jul
32:52.11A	Doris	Changeiywo	KEN	12.12.84	15 Jun
32:52.53	Caryl	Jones	GBR	4.4.87	23 Jun
32:52.84	Chihiro	Takato	JPN	20.7.91	21 Sep
32:52.91	Yuko	Watanabe	JPN	3.11.87	27 Jun
32:53.08	Mai	Ito	JPN	23.5.84	18 May
32:53.61	Yoko	Nishimi	JPN	17.7.87	21 Sep
32:54.01	Sayaka	Inoue	JPN	19.6.91	21 Sep
32:54.9 A	Mamitu	Daska	ETH	16.10.83	10 May
32:55.82	Hikari	Yoshimoto	JPN	14.1.90	22 Apr
32:56.25	Iwona	Lewandowska	POL	19.2.85	23 Jun
32:56.28	Rina	Yamazaki	JPN	6.5.88	7 Jul
32:56.60	Erin	Nehus-Vergara	USA	16.3.81	6 Apr
32:56.94	Allie	Woodward	USA-J	14.1.93	7 Jun
32:57.26	Kavita	Raut	IND	5.5.85	29 Jun
32:57.33	Kara	Millhouse	USA	20.2.90	8 Jun
32:57.69		Xue Fei	CHN	8.8.89	15 Apr
32:58.16	Marisol	Romero	MEX	26.11.83	29 Apr

Mark	Name		Nat	Born	Pos	Meet	Venue	Date
32:58.73	Katie	Kellner	USA					6 Apr
32:59.1A	Sharon	Cherop	KEN	16.3.84				15 Jun
32:59.37	Yoko	Shibui	JPN	14.3.79				21 Sep
32:59.51	Lidia	Rodríguez	ESP	26.5.86				24 Mar
32:59.58	Tomoka	Inadomi	JPN	16.1.86				18 May
32:59.59	Misato	Horie	JPN	10.3.87				27 Jun
32:59.64	Haruka	Kyuma	JPN-J	20.12.93				9 Sep
33:00.10	Aleksandra	Zhavoronkova	RUS	15.4.90				11 Jun
33:00.32		Xiao Huimin	CHN	1.3.92				22 Sep
33:00.69mx	Ayako	Mitsui	JPN	17.1.92				21 Dec
33:01.03	Kaitlin	Gregg	USA					8 Jun
33:01.42		Jiang Xiaoli	CHN	6.4.89				22 Sep
33:02.04	Elvin	Kibet	KEN	4.2.90				7 Jun
33:02.37	Claudia	Pinna	ITA	4.12.77				3 Jun
33:02.61mx	Mutsumi	Ikeda	JPN	30.9.92				21 Dec
33:03.33		Jia Chaofeng	CHN	16.11.88				22 Sep
33:03.82	Chika	Horie	JPN	15.2.81				21 Sep
33:04.49	Ai	Furukobo	JPN-J	23.2.93				9 Sep
33:04.90	Kathy	Newberry	USA	31.8.78				8 Jun
33:05.92	Leonor	Carneiro	POR	18.5.78				1 Jul
33:06.18	Maiko	Murayama	JPN	19.5.82				22 Dec
33:06.96	Gulshat	Fazlitdinova	RUS	28.8.92				22 Jul
33:07.72	Mai	Tsuda	JPN-J	21.2.93				9 Sep
33:07.93	Clara	Peterson	USA	26.1.84				29 Apr
33:08.30	Chizuru	Ideta	JPN	15.11.86				7 Jul
33:08.30	Linda	Spencer	GBR/AUS	16.1.82				8 Dec
33:08.59	Yukiko	Akaba	JPN	18.10.79				7 Jul
33:08.70	Rose	Tanui	KEN	22.12.88				6 Apr
33:08.99	Hollie	Knight	IRL	25.11.88				6 Apr
33:09.25	Tone Ilstad	Hjalmarsen	NOR	19.6.85				24 Aug
33:09.25	Merima	Hasen	ETH	10.6.92				30 Jun
33:09.47	Getenesh	Tamirat	GBR	11.7.77				23 Jun
33:09.57	Mai	Shoji	JPN-J	9.12.93				22 Dec
33:09.59	Diana	Martín (178)	ESP	1.4.81				24 Mar

Drugs disqualification

Mark	Name		Nat	Born	Pos	Meet	Venue	Date
31:55.97	Inga	Abitova ¶	RUS	6.3.82	3	Mosc C	Moskva	11 Jun
32:41.50	Simret	Restle-Apel ¶	GER	4.5.84	2	NC	Marburg	5 May

JUNIORS

Mark	Name		Nat	Born	Pos	Meet	Venue	Date
32:56.94	Allie	Woodward	USA	14.1.93	5	NCAA	Des Moines	7 Jun
32:59.64	Haruka	Kyuma	JPN	20.12.93	1	Univ Ch	Tokyo	9 Sep
33:04.49	Ai	Furukobo	JPN	23.2.93	2	Univ Ch	Tokyo	9 Sep
33:07.72	Mai	Tsuda	JPN	.93	3	Univ Ch	Tokyo	9 Sep
33:09.57	Mai	Shoji	JPN	9.12.93	2		Yokohama	22 Dec
33:17.28mx	Cayla	Hatton	USA	14.5.94	1mx		Medford	31 Mar
33:24.04	Kumiko	Otani	JPN-Y	23.3.95	5		Yokohama	22 Dec
33:33.85	Sakurako	Fukuuchi	JPN	31.8.93	2		Tokyo	24 Nov
33:36.18	Moe	Kyuma	JPN	20.12.93	5	Univ Ch	Tokyo	9 Sep
33:37.21	Rika	Saito	JPN	16.9.93	3		Tokyo	24 Nov
33:39.69		Wu Xufeng (10)	CHN	10.1.93	9	NC	Kunshan	22 Sep
33:44.00		Liu Zhuang	CHN-Y	18.1.95	11	NC	Kunshan	22 Sep
33:44.79		Gong Lihua	CHN	10.5.93	1	NSG	Tiuanjin	14 Sep
33:46.36	Mai	Shinozuka	JPN	1.4.93	6	Univ Ch	Tokyo	9 Sep
33:53.53	Rina	Nabeshina	JPN	16.12.93	1		Fukuoka	20 May
33:56.86	Gabriella	Gonzalez	USA	26.1.93	7r2		Stanford	6 Apr

10 KILOMETRES ROAD

Mark	Name		Nat	Born	Pos	Meet	Venue	Date
30:47	Vivian	Cheruiyot	KEN	11.9.83	1		San Juan	26 Feb
30:57	Pasalia	Chepkorir	KEN	22.12.88	1		Santos	20 May
30:57	Gladys	Cherono	KEN	12.5.83	1		Tilburg	2 Sep
30:58	Emily	Chebet	KEN	18.2.86	2		Tilburg	2 Sep
31:09+	Mary	Keitany	KEN	18.1.82	1	in HMar	Ra's Al-Khaymah	17 Feb
31:09	Joyce	Chepkirui	KEN	20.8.88	2		San Juan	26 Feb
31:10		Chepkirui			3		Tilburg	2 Sep
31:15	Linet	Masai	KEN	5.12.89	3		San Juan	26 Feb
31:19		Masai			4		Tilburg	2 Sep
31:25+	Sarah	Chepchirchir	KEN	27.7.84	1=	in HMar	Paris	4 Mar
31:25+	Pauline	Njeri	KEN	28.7.85	1=	in HMar	Paris	4 Mar
31:25+	Peninah	Arusei	KEN	23.2.79	1=	in HMar	Paris	4 Mar
31:28	Mary Wacera	Ngugi	KEN	17.12.88	1		Montereau	28 Oct
31:31	Goreti	Chepkoech	KEN-J	7.3.94	2		Montereau	28 Oct
31:33	Esther	Chemtai	KEN	4.6.88	1		Brunssum	1 Apr
31:35+	Lydia	Cheromei	KEN	11.5.77		in HMar	Praha	31 Mar
31:35	Ruti	Aga	ETH-J	16.1.94	5		Tilburg	2 Sep
31:36	Kim	Smith	NZL	19.11.81	1		Boston	24 Jun

Where better than 10,000m track times

Mark	Name		Nat	Born	Pos	Meet	Venue	Date
31:43	Hilda	Kibet	NED	27.3.81	2		Brunssum	1 Apr
31:44	Irina	Mikitenko	GER	23.8.72	2		Paderborn	7 Apr
31:44	Helah	Kiprop	KEN	7.4.85	1		Groesbeek	3 Jun
31:46	Karoline Bjerkeli	Grøvdal	NOR	14.6.90	1		Hole	20 Oct
31:47+	Netsanet	Achamo	ETH	14.12.87		in HMar	Paris	4 Mar
31:47	Marta	Domínguez	ESP	3.11.75	1		Laredo	10 Mar
31:47	Waganesh	Mekasha	ETH	16.1.92	1		Taroudant	11 Mar
31:49+	Sharon	Cherop	KEN	16.3.84		in HMar	Philadelphia	16 Mar
31:50	Belaynesh	Fikadu	ETH	28.3.87	3		Paderborn	7 Apr
31:50+	Jemima	Jelagat	KEN	21.12.84		in HMar	Philadelphia	16 Sep
31:51	Agnes	Barsosio	KEN	.83	2		Taroudant	11 Mar
31:52	Margaret	Muriuki	KEN	21.3.86	1		Cape Elizabeth	4 Aug
31:52	Afera	Godfay	ETH	25.9.91	2		Houilles	30 Dec
31:53	Debele	Degefa	ETH		3		Houilles	30 Dec
31:54	Lineth	Chepkurui	KEN	23.2.88	3		Cape Elizabeth	4 Aug

Mark	Name		Nat	Born	Pos	Meet	Venue	Date
31:54+	Georgina	Rono	KEN	19.5.84	1	in HMar	Udine	23 Sep
31:55	Vicoty	Chepkemok	KEN	.86	4		Paderborn	7 Apr
31:57+	Agnes	Kiprop	KEN	12.12.79	2=	in HMar	Ostia	26 Feb
31:57+	Tirfe	Tsegaye	ETH	25.11.84	2=	in HMar	Ostia	26 Feb
31:57+	Shone	Imana	ETH	17.11.91	2=	in HMar	Ostia	26 Feb
31:57	Eunice	Jepkirui	KEN	20.5.84	2		Santos	20 May
31:57	Aheza	Kiros	ETH	26.3.82	2		Boston	24 Jun
31:58	Rita	Jeptoo	KEN	15.2.81	4		Cape Elizabeth	4 Aug
32:00+	Firehiwot	Dado	ETH	9.1.84	1	in HMar	New York	18 Mar
32:02	Winnie	Jepkemoi	KEN-J	9.10.93	3		Taroudant	11 Mar
32:03	Fate	Tola	ETH	22.10.87	1		Oelde	8 Jun
32:04	Doris	Changeiywo	KEN	12.12.84	3		Manchester	20 May
32:06	Gemma	Steel	GBR	12.11.85	1		Dublin	15 Apr
32:08+	Valeria	Straneo	ITA	5.4.76		in HMar	Ostia	26 Feb
32:08+	Anna	Incerti	ITA	19.1.80		in HMar	Ostia	26 Feb
32:08	Edna	Kiplagat	KEN	15.11.79	1		New York	9 Jun
32:09+	Tiki	Gelana	ETH	22.10.87		in 15k	Njimegen	18 Nov
32:12	Lucy	Macharia	KEN	7.12.87	1		Stadskanaal	9 Apr
32:12	Susanne	Hahn	GER	23.4.78	1		Tessenderlo	9 Jul
32:16	Valentine	Kibet	KEN	.89	3		Brunssum	1 Apr
32:16	Felista	Wanjugu	KEN	18.2.90	1		Okayama	23 Dec
32:16	Marisa	Barros	POR	25.2.80	4		Houilles	30 Dec
32:17	Jelliah	Kerubo	KEN	10.10.85	4		Boston	24 Jun
32:17	Lisa	Weightman	AUS	16.1.79	1		Gold Coast	30 Jun
32:19	Genoveva	Jelagat	KEN	9.8.80	1		New Orleans	7 Apr

Mark	Name		Nat	Born	Date
32:21+	Emebet	Etea	ETH	11.1.90	6 Oct
32:21+	Feyse	Tadese	ETH	19.11.88	6 Oct
32:22 dh	Mamitu	Daska	ETH	16.10.83	4 Jul
32:22+	Meseret	Hailu	ETH	12.9.90	6 Oct
32:23 dh	Risper	Gesabwa	KEN	10.2.89	4 Jul
32:24	Agnes	Cheserek	KEN	.87	22 Apr
32:24	Leonida	Mosop	KEN	.91	28 Oct
32:25	Filomena	Cheyech	KEN	5.7.82	5 Aug
32:26	Alessandra	Aguilar	ESP	1.7.78	16 Jun
32:27	Lornah	Kiplagat	NED	1.5.74	12 Feb
32:28	Mara	Yamauchi	GBR	13.8.73	20 May
32:28	Cynthia	Kosgei	KEN-J	.93	9 Sep
32:28+	Beatrice	Mutai	KEN-J	.94	18 Nov
32:29	Magdaline	Mukunzi	KEN	22.10.83	1 Apr
32:29+	Bezunesh	Bekele	ETH	29.1.83	23 Sep
32:29+	Sylvia	Kibet	KEN	28.3.84	23 Sep
32:30+	Josehine	Chepkoech	KEN	,89	23 Sep
32:30	Hellen	Jemutai	KEN	.81	8 Oct
32:30	Grace	Kimanzi	KEN	1.3.92	23 Dec
32:31+	Caroline	Kilel	KEN	21.3.81	15 Jan
32:31	Renee	Baillie	USA	25.12.81	4 Aug
32:31	Caryl	Jones	GBR	4.4.87	9 Sep
32:31	Worknesh	Alemu	ETH		28 Oct
32:31	Priscah	Jeptoo	KEN	26.6.84	31 Dec
32:32+	Belaynesh	Zemedkun	ETH	23.12.87	15 Jan
32:32+	Caroline	Chepkwony	KEN	18.4.84	1 Apr
32:32+	Philes	Ongori	KEN	19.7.86	1 Apr
32:32	Consalater	Yadaa	KEN	12.3.83	22 Apr
32:33+	Kara	Goucher	USA	9.7.78	18 Mar
32:33	Adero	Nyakisi	UGA	2.7.86	2 Sep
32:34	Mary	Wangeci	KEN-J	.93	2 Sep
32:36+	Alice	Mogire	KEN	27.11.81	21 Oct
32:37	Yuka	Ando	JPN-J	16.3.94	23 Dec
32:37	Waka	Chaltu	ETH		30 Dec
32:38	Diane	Nukuri-Johnson	BDI	1.12.84	9 Jun
32:38	Yebrgual	Melese	ETH	18.4.90	30 Jun
32:38+	Gelete	Burka	ETH	15.2.86	18 Nov
32:40	Julia	Lucas	USA	4.3.84	4 Aug
32:41+	Bekele	Alemu	ETH	11.4.91	12 May
32:41	Chelsea	Reilly	USA	9.5.89	8 Oct
32:42	Lucy	Liavoga	KEN	.89	2 Sep
32:43+	Bekelech	Bedada	ETH	.92	18 Mar
32:43+	Caroline	Rotich	KEN	13.5.84	18 Mar
32:43	Judith	Plá	ESP	2.5.78	22 Apr
32:43	Gulnara	Galkina	RUS	9.7.78	29 Apr
32:44	Elleanor	Baker	GBR	11.12.83	11 Mar
32:45	Rose	Chelimo	KEN	12.7.89	7 Apr
32:45	Maryanne	Wanjiru	KEN	.86	29 Apr
32:46	Eunice	Kales	KEN	6.12.84	23 Sep
32:46	Laurane	Picoche	FRA	17.7.85	30 Dec
32:47	Irene	Jerotich	KEN	8.9.74	20 May
32:48	Dorcas	Talam	KEN	.82	1 Apr
32:49+	Tsegereda	Girma	ETH-Y	.95	23 Sep
32:50	Lizzie	Adams	GBR	19.5.86	6 Apr
32:50	Renè	Kalmer	RSA	3.11.80	15 Apr

Excessively downhill: Dec 31. Madrid (50m): 1. Gelete Burka ETH 30:53, 3. Diane Martín ESP 32:32

JUNIORS

Mark	Name		Nat	Born	Pos	Venue	Date
32:59	Akari	Ota	JPN	26.1.94	6	Okayama	23 Dec
33:12	Kotomi	Takayama	JPN	18.2.93	2	Karatsu	12 Feb
33:14	Risper	Chebet	KEN	.94	6	Düsseldorf	2 Sep
33:17	Eunice	Chbebichii	KEN	23.5.93	2	Jakarta	20 May
33:24	Misuza	Nakahara	JPN	29.11.94	3	Tamana	4 Mar
33:38	Nozomi	Nishiyama	JPN	.94	10	Tamana	4 Mar

15 KILOMETRES ROAD

See also intermediate times in 10km, 10 miles, 20km and half marathon lists

Mark	Name		Nat	Born	Pos	Meet	Venue	Date
47:08	Tirunesh	Dibaba	ETH	1.10.85	1		Nijmegen	18 Nov
48:09	Tiki	Gelana	ETH	22.10.87	1		Nijmegen	18 Nov
48:38	Mulu	Seboka	ETH	25.9.84	1		Istanbul	11 Nov
48:40+	Diane	Chepkemoi	KEN	.87		in HMar	Lisboa	25 Mar
48:52	Beatrice	Mutai	KEN-J	.94	3		Nijmegen	18 Nov
49:00	Lucy	Macharia	KEN	.91	4		Nijmegen	18 Nov
49:15	Atsede	Baysa	ETH	16.4.87	1		's-Heerenberg	2 Dec
49:26	Mamitu	Daska	ETH	16.10.83	1		Utica	8 Jul
49:26	Gelete	Burka	ETH	23.1.86	5		Nijmegen	18 Nov

Mark	Name		Nat	Born	Pos	Meet	Venue	Date
49:29	Elvan	Abeylegesse	TUR	11.9.82	2		Istanbul	11 Nov
49:43	Caroline	Chepkwony	KEN	18.4.84	1		Kerzers	17 Mar
49:44	Risper	Gesabwa	KEN	10.2.89	2		Utica	8 Jul
49:48	Tigist	Kiros	ETH	8.6.92	2		Puy-en-Velay	1 May
49:53+	Rose	Chelimo	KEN	12.7.89		in HMar	Göteborg	12 May
49:55	Helen	Jemutai	KEN	.81	3		Utica	8 Jul
49:56+	Magdaline	Mukunzi	KEN	22.10.83		in HMar	Verbania	11 Mar
49:57	Molly	Huddle	USA	31.8.84	2	NC	Jacksonville	11 Mar

10 MILES ROAD

10M	15k	Name		Nat	Born	Pos	Meet	Venue	Date
51:28+		Sharon	Cherop	KEN	16.3.84	1	in HMar	Philadelphia	16 Sep
51:30+		Mare	Dibaba	ETH	20.10.89	2	in HMar	Philadelphia	16 Sep
51:42	48:24	Sylvia	Kibet	KEN	28.3.84	1		Zaandam	23 Sep
51:43+		Jemima	Jelagat	KEN	21.12.84	3	in HMar	Philadelphia	16 Sep
51:45	48:23	Bezunesh	Bekele	ETH	29.1.83	2		Zaandam	23 Sep
51:45	48:23	Esther	Chemtai	KEN	4.6.88	3		Zaandam	23 Sep
52:04+ dh		Jelena	Prokopcuka	LAT	21.9.76		in HMar	South Shields	16 Sep
52:45	49:07	Hilda	Kibet	NED	27.3.81	4		Zaandam	23 Sep
53:00	49:17	Jo	Pavey	GBR	20.9.73	1	Gt South	Portsmouth	28 Oct
53:17	49:35	Josephine	Jepkoech	KEN	.89	5		Zaandam	23 Sep
53:43		Caroline	Rotich	KEN	13.5.84	1		Flint	25 Aug
53:43		Janet	Cherobon-Bawcom	USA	22.8.78	1		Saint Paul	7 Oct
53:43		Jessica	Coulson	GBR	18.4.90	2	Gt South	Portsmouth	28 Oct

20 KILOMETRES ROAD

20k	15k	Name		Nat	Born	Pos	Meet	Venue	Date
65:25	49:10	Tiki	Gelana	ETH	22.10.87	1	in HMar	Marugame	5 Feb
65:34		Cynthia	Jerotich	KEN	18.12.89	1		Paris	14 Oct
65:41		Elvan	Abeylegesse	TUR	11.9.82	2		Paris	14 Oct
65:41+	48:51+	Pasalia	Kipkoech	KEN	22.12.88		in HMar	Kavarna	7 Oct
65:44+	49:12	Georgina	Rono	KEN	19.5.84		in HMar	Ra's Al-Khaymah	17 Feb
66:20+	49:08+	Helah	Kiprop	KEN	7.4.85		in HMar	Göteborg	12 May
66:38+	49:53	Monica	Jepkoech	KEN	.85		in HMar	Breda	7 Oct
67:00		Gladys	Kipsoi	KEN	.86	3		Paris	14 Oct
67:06+	49:42	Bekelech	Bedada	ETH	.92		in HMar	New York	18 Mar
67:08		Renee	Baillie	USA	25.12.81	1	NC	New Haven	3 Sep

HALF MARATHON

HMar	20k	15k	Name		Nat	Born	Pos	Meet	Venue	Date
66:38		47:43	Florence	Kiplagat	KEN	27.2.87	1		Ostia	26 Feb
66:49	63:12	47:12	Mary	Keitany	KEN	18.1.82	1		Ra's Al-Khaymah	17 Feb
67:03	63:39	47:20	Joyce	Chepkirui	KEN	20.8.88	1		Praha	31 Mar
67:17			Pasalia	Kipkoech	KEN	22.12.88	1		Rio de Janeiro	19 Aug
67:21			Sharon	Cherop	KEN	16.3.84	1		Philadelphia	16 Sep
67:22		47:50	Agnes	Kiprop	KEN	12.12.79	2		Ostia	26 Feb
67:26	63:56	47:20	Lydia	Cheromei	KEN	11.5.77	2		Praha	31 Mar
67:35dh	64:34		Tirunesh	Dibaba	ETH	1.10.85	1	GNR	South Shields	16 Sep
67:41dh	64:34		Edna	Kiplagat	KEN	15.11.79	2	GNR	South Shields	16 Sep
67:42		47:56	Tirfe	Tsegaye (10)	ETH	25.11.84	3		Ostia	26 Feb
67:44			Mare	Dibaba	ETH	20.10.89	2		Philadelphia	16 Sep
67:46		48:24	Valeria	Straneo	ITA	5.4.76	4		Ostia	26 Feb
67:48dh			Tiki	Gelana	ETH	22.10.87	3	GNR	South Shields	16 Sep
67:55		47:37	Pauline	Njeri	KEN	28.7.85	1		Paris	4 Mar
67:58			Georgina	Rono	KEN	19.5.84	1		Udine	23 Sep
68:06			Filomena	Chepchirchir	KEN	1.12.81	1		Lille	1 Sep
68:08			Diane	Chepkemoi	KEN	.87	2		Lille	1 Sep
68:09dh		48:33	Jelena	Prokopcuka	LAT	21.9.76	4	GNR	South Shields	16 Sep
68:11A				Kipkoech			1		Nairobi	28 Oct
68:12		47:56	Peninah	Arusei	KEN	23.2.79	2		Paris	4 Mar
68:18		48:24	Anna	Incerti (20)	ITA	19.1.80	5		Ostia	26 Feb
68:18	64:40	47:20	Gladys	Cherono	KEN	12.5.83	3		Praha	31 Mar
68:20				Kipkoech			1		Iguazu	8 Jul
68:25			Philes	Ongori	KEN	19.7.86	1		Berlin	1 Apr
68:26	65:00		Belaynesh	Oljira	ETH	26.6.90	1		Houston	15 Jan
68:26			Helah	Kiprop	KEN	7.4.85	2		Berlin	1 Apr
68:28	65:00		Caroline	Kilel	KEN	21.3.81	2		Houston	15 Jan
68:34		47:42	Sarah	Chepchirchir	KEN	27.7.84	3		Paris	4 Mar
68:35		48:45	Jemima	Jelagat	KEN	21.12.84	1		Verbania	11 Mar

Mark			Name		Nat	Born	Pos	Meet	Venue	Date
68:35	65:06	48:32	Firehiwot	Dado	ETH	9.1.84	1		New York	18 Mar
68:35			Priscah	Cherono	KEN	27.6.80	3		Lille	1 Sep
68:36			Caroline	Chepkwony	KEN	18.4.84	3		Berlin	1 Apr
			(32/30							
68:39			Eunice	Jepkirui	KEN	20.5.84	1		Azkoitia	31 Mar
68:43	65:06	48:31	Kim	Smith	NZL	19.11.81	2		New York	18 Mar
68:51	65:18		Belaynesh	Zemedkun	ETH	23.12.87	3		Houston	15 Jan
68:52		48:30	Shalane	Flanagan	USA	8.7.81	1		Lisboa	25 Mar
68:55	65:41	48:51	Meseret	Hailu	ETH	12.9.90	1	WCh	Kavarna	6 Oct
68:56	65:41	48:51	Feyse	Tadese	ETH	19.11.88	2	WCh	Kavarna	6 Oct
69:09			Bezunesh	Bekele	ETH	29.1.83	1	GSR	Glasgow	2 Sep
69:10		48:26	Netsanet	Achamo	ETH	14.12.87	4		Paris	4 Mar
69:12	65:40	49:02	Kara	Goucher	USA	9.7.78	3		New York	18 Mar
69:12			Monica	Jepkoech	KEN	.85	6		Lille	1 Sep
			(40)							
69:20	dh		Jo	Pavey	GBR	20.9.73	5	GNR	South Shields	16 Sep
69:21		48:49	Margaret	Muriuki	KEN	21.3.86	3		Lisboa	25 Mar
69:22			Gladys	Kipsoi	KEN	.86	7		Lille	1 Sep
69:27	65:55	49:07	Hilda	Kibet	NED	27.3.81	1		Göteborg	12 May
69:31	65:55	49:07	Bekele	Alemu	ETH	11.4.91	2		Göteborg	12 May
69:39			Atsede	Baysa	ETH	16.4.87	1		Tarsus	25 Mar
69:41			Karoline Bjerkeli	Grøvdal	NOR	14.6.90	1		Oslo	22 Sep
69:42+			Aselefech	Mergia	ETH	23.1.85	1=	in Mar	Dubai	27 Jan
69:42+			Aberu	Kebede	ETH	12.9.89	1=	in Mar	Dubai	27 Jan
69:42+			Mamitu	Daska	ETH	16.10.83	1=	in Mar	Dubai	27 Jan
			(50)							
69:45			Yebrgual	Melese	ETH	18.4.90	8		Lille	1 Sep
69:46+			Lucy Wangui	Kabuu	KEN	24.3.84		in Mar	Dubai	27 Jan
69:47	66:11	49:39	Tomomi	Tanaka	JPN	25.1.88	1		Yamaguchi	18 Mar
69:50	66:16	49:23	Dulce	Félix	POR	23.10.82	3		Göteborg	12 May
69:53+			Mulu	Seboka	ETH	25.9.84		in Mar	Dubai	27 Jan
69:53 +			Shetaye	Bedaso	ETH	85	-		Dubai	27 Jan
69:55	66:17	49:25	Janet	Cherobon-Bawcom	USA	22.8.78	5		New York	18 Mar
69:56			Mariya	Konovalova	RUS	14.8.74	1		Novosibirsk	8 Sep
69:56	66:18	49:47	Yukiko	Akaba	JPN	18.10.79	1		Okayama	23 Dec
69:57	66:30	49:27	Alice	Mogire	KEN	27.11.81	1		Valencia	21 Oct
			(60)							
70:01			Filomena	Cheyech	KEN	5.7.82	2		Iguazu	8 Jul
70:01	66:23	48:56	Emebet	Etea	ETH	11.1.90	5	WCh	Kavarna	6 Oct
70:05	66:23	49:24	Madaí	Pérez	MEX	2.2.80	6		New York	18 Mar
70:06			Cynthia	Limo	KEN	18.12.89	1		Ivry-Vitry	8 Apr
70:06	66:29	49:48	Yuko	Watanabe	JPN	3.11.87	2		Okayama	23 Dec
70:07		48:55	Shone	Imana	ETH	17.11.91	6		Ostia	26 Feb
70:10	66:35	49:42	Lisa	Weightman	AUS	16.1.79	7		New York	18 Mar
70:13	dh		Renè	Kalmer	RSA	3.11.80	6	GNR	South Shields	16 Sep
70:17	66:34	49:39	Caroline	Rotich	KEN	13.5.84	8		New York	18 Mar
70:17	66:30	49:48	Beatrice	Wainaina	KEN-J	20.11.93	3		Okayama	23 Dec
			(70)							
70:24+			Valentine	Kipketer	KEN-J	5.1.93		in Mar	Hamburg	29 Apr
70:25+			Meselech	Melkamu	ETH	27.4.85	1=	in Mar	Frankfurt	28 Oct
70:25+			Agnes	Barsosio	KEN	.83	1=	in Mar	Frankfurt	28 Oct
70:26			Marisa	Barros	POR	25.2.80	1		Viana do Castelo	22 Jan
70:26			Lucy	Macharia	KEN	7.12.87	1		Poznan	1 Apr
70:26			Magdaline	Mukunzi	KEN	22.10.83	1		Krems	16 Sep
70:27			Kejeta	Melat	ETH	.92	3		Ivry-Vitry	8 Apr
70:29+	66:32	49:20	Merima	Hasen	ETH	10.6.92	2	in Mar	Rotterdam	15 Apr
70:30		49:39	Isabellah	Andersson	SWE	12.11.80	5		Göteborg	12 May
70:31			Goitetom	Haftu	ETH	.87	9		Lille	1 Sep
			(80)							
70:31	distance?		Lisa	Stublic	CRO	18.5.84	1		Zagreb	11 Nov
70:32	66:59	49:58	Kaoru	Nagao	JPN	26.9.89	2		Marugame	5 Feb
70:32			Priscah	Jeptoo	KEN	26.6.84	1		Lisboa	30 Sep
70:34	66:59	49:58	Sayo	Nomura	JPN	18.4.89	3		Marugame	5 Feb
70:36			Farida	Chelagat	KEN	21.8.86	1		Remich	30 Sep
70:36			Edinah	Kwambai	KEN	22.3.86	2		Remich	30 Sep
70:37	66:59	49:58	Misato	Horie	JPN	10.3.87	4		Marugame	5 Feb
70:37			Malika	Asahssah	MAR	24.9.82	1		Albacete	13 May
70:39	66:59	49:58	Mai	Ito	JPN	23.5.84	5		Marugame	5 Feb
70:40	67:02	49:53	Yuka	Tokuda	JPN	1.6.88	2		Yamaguchi	18 Mar
			(90)							
70:42	67:05		Josephine	Jepkoech	KEN	.89	2		Breda	7 Oct

Mark	Name		Nat	Born	Pos	Meet	Venue	Date
70:46+	Sultan	Haydar	TUR	23.5.87		in Mar	Paris	15 Apr
70:45+	Meseret	Legesse	ETH	28.8.87		in Mar	Paris	15 Apr
70:45+	Makda	Harun	ETH	.88		in Mar	Paris	15 Apr
70:45	Molly	Pritz	USA	7.4.88	1		San Francisco	29 Jul
70:45 67:02 49:53	Rebecca	Chesire	KEN		3		Breda	7 Oct
70:44 67:08	Desiree	Davila	USA	26.7.83	9		New York	18 Mar
70:46 dh	Gemma	Steel	GBR	12.11.85	7	GNR	South Shields	16 Sep
70:48 67:04 49:58	Hiroko	Miyauchi	JPN	19.6.83	6		Marugame	5 Feb
70:48 67:05 49:58	Ai	Igarashi	JPN	25.10.88	3		Yamaguchi	18 Mar
(100)								
70:48+	Etalemahu	Kidane	ETH	14.2.83	2		Hamburg	29 Apr
70:48 67:05	Elizeba	Cherono	KEN	6.6.88	4		Breda	7 Oct

Mark	Name		Nat	Born	Date
70:50	Rita	Jeptoo	KEN	15.2.81	25 Mar
70:50	Rose	Chelimo	KEN	12.7.89	10 Jun
70:54	Bekelech	Bedada	ETH	.92	18 Mar
70:54+	Korene	Jelela	ETH	18.1.87	22 Apr
70:54	Mercy Wacera	Ngugi	KEN	17.12.88	21 Oct
70:55	Diane	Nukuri-Johnson	BDI	1.12.84	18 Mar
70:55+	Dinknesh	Mekasha (67:08)	ETH	.85	29 Apr
70:55	Sara	Moreira	POR	17.10.85	20 May
70:56	Karolina	Jarzynska	POL	6.9.81	1 Apr
70:56	Maegan	Krifchin	USA	8.4.88	16 Jun
70:58+	Risa	Shigetomo	JPN	29.8.87	29 Jan
70:58+	Yuko	Shimizu	JPN	13.7.85	29 Jan
70:59+	Aheza	Kiros	ETH	26.3.82	27 Jan
70:59+	Kayoko	Fukushi	JPN	25.3.82	29 Jan
71:00	Leonida	Mosop	KEN	.91	7 Oct
71:01	Tsegereda	Girma	ETH-Y	.95	11 Mar
71:02	Rei	Ohara	JPN	10.8.90	18 Mar
71:03+	Azusa	Nojiri	JPN	6.6.82	29 Jan
71:04	Jackline	Nytepi	KEN	.84	7 Apr
71:04	Yoko	Miyauchi	JPN	19.6.83	1 Jul
71:05+	Yeshimebet	Tadesse	ETH	.88	27 Jan
71:05	Kumi	Ogura	JPN	24.6.85	23 Dec
71:10	Ayame	Takaki	JPN	15.7.92	18 Mar
71:10	Shino	Saito	JPN	7.9.88	18 Mar
71:10	Doris	Changeiywo	KEN	12.12.84	31 Mar
71:10	Wude	Ayalew	ETH	4.7.87	30 Sep
71:10	Susan	Partridge	GBR	4.1.80	14 Oct
71:11	Waganesh	Mekasha	ETH	16.1.92	1 Apr
71:11	Dorcas	Talam	KEN	.82	7 Apr
71:11	Tigist	Kiros	ETH	8.6.92	18 Nov
71:12	Vicoty	Chepkemok	KEN		1 Apr
71:13+	Alemitu	Abera	ETH	.86	15 Jan
71:13	Woynishet	Girma	ETH	28.7.86	21 Oct
71:14	Krisztina	Papp	HUN	17.12.82	26 Feb
71:15	Aziza	Aliyu	ETH	20.10.85	18 Mar
71:16	Kaori	Yoshida	JPN	4.8.81	8 Jan
71:16	Lineth	Chepkurui	KEN	23.2.88	16 Sep
71:16+	Fatuma	Sado	ETH	11.10.91	7 Oct
71:16	Helen	Jepkurgat	KEN	21.2.89	21 Oct
71:16+	Genet	Getaneh	ETH	6.1.86	21 Oct
71:16	Chihiro	Takato	JPN	20.7.91	23 Dec
71:18	Nikki	Chapple	AUS	9.2.81	2 Sep
71:18 dh	Caryl	Jones	GBR	4.4.87	16 Sep
71:19	Jane	Muia	KEN	20.12.86	11 Mar
71:19	Mercy	Tanui	KEN	.84	1 Apr
71:19	Abebech	Afework	ETH	11.12.90	1 Sep
71:21	Asami	Kato	JPN	12.10.90	13 May
71:21	Miriam	Wangari	KEN	22.2.79	29 Apr
71:22	Edith	Chelimo	KEN	16.7.86	31 Mar
71:22	Emily	Biwott	KEN	.84	30 Sep
71:23	Rosaria	Console	ITA	17.12.79	6 May
71:24	Eunice	Kales	KEN	6.12.84	1 Apr
71:25	Sharon	Tavengwa	ZIM	9.12.83	25 Mar
71:27	Hellen	Jemutai	KEN	.81	18 Mar
71:30+	Yoshimi	Ozaki	JPN	1.7.81	11 Mar
71:30+	Remi	Nakazato	JPN	24.6.88	11 Mar
71:31+	Yoko	Shibui	JPN	14.3.79	11 Mar
71:31+	Misaki	Katsumata	JPN	26.12.85	11 Mar
71:32	Ecler	Loywapet	KEN	.85	29 Apr
71:32	Yuka	Hakoyama	JPN	9.3.90	23 Dec
71:33	Malika	Mejdoub	MAR	10.5.82	18 Mar
71:36	Mari	Ozaki	JPN	16.7.75	23 Dec
71:38	Chieko	Kido	JPN	14.3.90	23 Dec
71:39+	Zemzem	Ahmed	ETH	27.12.84	28 Oct
71:40	Megumi	Seike	JPN	26.2.87	5 Feb
71:40+	Eri	Okubo	JPN	2.6.83	26 Feb
71:40	Fridah	Domongole	KEN	15.1.84	31 Mar
71:40+	Robe	Guta	ETH	12.10.86	29 Apr
71:40+	Beatrice	Toroitich	KEN	15.12.81	29 Apr
71:42A	Grace	Momanyi	KEN	3.3.82	8 Jul
71:43+	Mizuki	Noguchi	JPN	3.7.78	11 Mar
71:43	Helaria	Johannes	NAM	13.8.80	30 Sep
71:45	Yoshiko	Fujinaga	JPN	15.8.81	5 Feb
71:45	Lindsey	Scherf	USA	18.9.86	18 Mar
71:45	Michelle	Frey	USA	15.4.82	16 Jun
71:49	Andrea	Mayr	AUT	15.10.79	1 Apr
71:50	Hiroko	Shoi	JPN	18.6.80	18 Mar
71:50	Mary	Davies	NZL	27.8.82	19 Aug
71:50	Hannah	Walker	GBR	9.8.91	30 Sep
71:51	Noriko	Higuchi	JPN	23.5.85	5 Feb
71:51	Meriyem	Lamachi	MAR	20.12.87	26 Feb
71:51	Lemlem	Berhe	ETH	.92	1 Sep
71:51	Bethlehem	Moges	ETH	3.5.91	16 Sep
71:52	Rika	Shintaku	JPN	19.10.85	5 Feb
71:52	Emily	Samoei	KEN	11.11.80	26 Feb
71:55?	Edna	Kimaiyo	KEN	.88	16 Sep
71:56A	Pamela	Cheyech	KEN	.82	7 Oct
71:56	Misiker	Mekonnin	ETH	23.7.86	18 Nov
71:56+	Mizuho	Nasukawa	JPN	22.11.79	18 Nov
71:57+	Mayumi	Fujita	JPN	26.5.83	18 Nov
71:58	Beatrice	Jepchumba	KEN	25.11.83	26 Feb
71:58+	Ferhiwot	Goshu	ETH	28.6.90	15 Apr
71:58	Ehitu	Kiros	ETH	.88	12 May
71:58+	Olena	Shurhno	UKR	8.1.78	30 Sep
71:58+	Fate	Tola	ETH	22.10.87	30 Sep
71:59	Kayo	Sugihara	JPN	24.2.83	26 Feb
71:59	Claudette	Mukasakindi	RWA	12.10.80	26 Feb
72:01+	Irina	Mikitenko (200)	GER	23.8.72	22 Apr

Pune 2 Dec: ? Pauline Kaveke Kamulu KEN 68:37; Agnes Mutune Katunge KEN 20.6.86 69:04; Hellen Musyoka Nzembi KEN 3.1.87 71:07; Gladys Jepkechei KEN 71:36

Excessively downhill: 68:37 Kim Smith NZL 19.11.81 1 San Diego (84m) 3 Jun

See Main list for top 2 juniors. More: **JUNIORS**

Mark	Name		Nat	Born	Pos	Meet	Venue	Date
71:01	Tsegereda	Girma	ETH-Y	.95	1		Orvault	11 Mar
72:28	Eriko	Kushima	JPN	9.2.93	3		Matsue	18 Mar
72:49	Mary	Wangeci	KEN	.93	5	RduVin	Remich	30 Sep
73:13	Mulit	Mewcha	ETH	.93	3		Boulogne-Billancourt	18 Nov
73:25	Aya	Goto	JPN	8.2.93	19		Marugame	5 Feb

25 – 30 KILOMETRES ROAD

20k	25k	30k	Name		Nat	Born	Pos	Meet	Venue	Date
	1:22:56		Caroline	Chepkwony	KEN	18.4.84	1		Berlin	6 May
1:23:37	1:39:53+		Joyce	Chepkirui	KEN	20.8.88		in Mar	London	22 Apr

Mark			Name		Nat	Born	Pos	Meet	Venue	Date
69:21		1:40:19+	Lydia	Cheromei	KEN	11.5.77	1	in Mar	Praha	13 May
	1:23:39	1:40:39+	Atsede	Baysa	ETH	16.4.87		in Mar	London	22 Apr
	1:23:29	1:40:41	Shetaye	Bedaso	ETH	.85		in Mar	Paris	15 Apr
	1:24:27	1:41:15+	Fatuma	Sado	ETH	11.10.91		in Mar	Chicago	7 Oct
	1:24:28	1:41:22+	Merima	Hasen	ETH	10.6.92		in Mar	Chicago	7 Oct
	1:24:03	1:41:49+	Kayoko	Fukushi	JPN	25.3.82		in Mar	Osaka	29 Jan
	1:24:08	1:41:51+		Hasen				in Mar	Rotterdam	15 Apr
	1:24:15	1:42:01+	Ashu	Kasim	ETH	20.10.84		in Mar	Berlin	30 Sep
	1:24:04	1:42:09+	Meseret	Legesse	ETH	28.8.87		in Mar	Paris	15 Apr
	1:24:36		Janet	Cherobon-Bawcom	USA	22.8.78	1	NC	Grand Rapids	12 May
	1:24:32	1:42:41	Korene	Jelela	ETH	18.1.87		in Mar	London	22 Apr
	1:25:12		Lindsey	Scherf	USA	18.9.86	2	NC	Grand Rapids	12 May
	1:25:15	1:42:32+	Eshetu	Degefa	ETH	.82		in Mar	Berlin	30 Sep
	1:25:21		Taemo	Weldegebril	ETH	11.9.86	2		Berlin	6 May
	1:25:27		Christelle	Daunay	FRA	5.12.74	3		Berlin	6 May
	1:26:23	1:42:44+	Mare	Dibaba	ETH	20.10.89		in Mar	London	5 Aug
		1:42:55	Shalane	Flanagan	USA	8.7.81		in Mar	London	5 Aug
		1:43:01+	Albina	Mayorova	RUS	16.5.77		in Mar	London	5 Aug
	1:25:29	1:43:03+	Kim	Smith	NZL	19.11.81		in Mar	Yokohama	18 Nov
		1:43:05	Dinknesh	Mekasha	ETH	.85		in Mar	Hamburg	29 Apr

MARATHON

Mark	25k	30k	Name		Nat	Born	Pos	Meet	Venue	Date
2:18:37	1:23:37	1:39:53	Mary	Keitany	KEN	18.1.82	1		London	22 Apr
2:18:58	1:22:33	1:39:07	Tiki	Gelana	ETH	22.10.87	1		Rotterdam	15 Apr
2:19:31			Aselefech	Mergia	ETH	23.1.85	1		Dubai	27 Jan
2:19:34			Lucy Wangui	Kabuu	KEN	24.3.84	2		Dubai	27 Jan
2:19:50	1:23:39	1:39:53	Edna	Kiplagat	KEN	15.11.79	2		London	22 Apr
2:19:52			Mare	Dibaba	ETH	20.10.89	3		Dubai	27 Jan
2:20:14	1:23:38	1:39:53	Priscah	Jeptoo	KEN	26.6.84	3		London	22 Apr
2:20:30			Bezunesh	Bekele	ETH	29.1.83	4		Dubai	27 Jan
2:20:30	1:23:32	1:40:01	Aberu	Kebede	ETH	12.9.89	1		Berlin	30 Sep
2:20:33				Kebede			5		Dubai	27 Jan
2:20:57	1:23:39	1:39:53	Florence	Kiplagat (10)	KEN	27.2.87	4		London	22 Apr
2:21:01	1:23:23	1:39:58	Meselech	Melkamu	ETH	27.4.85	1		Frankfurt	28 Oct
2:21:09	1:24:20	1:41:07	Meseret	Hailu	ETH	12.9.90	1		Amsterdam	21 Oct
2:21:19	1:23:32	1:40:01	Tirfe	Tsegaye	ETH	25.11.84	2		Berlin	30 Sep
2:21:30			Lydia	Cheromei	KEN	11.5.77	6		Dubai	27 Jan
2:21:39	1:23:23	1:39:58	Georgina	Rono	KEN	19.5.84	2		Frankfurt	28 Oct
2:21:40	1:23:27	1:39:54		Tsegaye			1		Paris	15 Apr
2:21:41	1:24:21	1:41:08	Eunice	Jepkirui	KEN	20.5.84	2		Amsterdam	21 Oct
2:22:03	1:24:27	1:41:20	Atsede	Baysa	ETH	16.4.87	1		Chicago	7 Oct
2:22:04	1:24:29	1:41:16	Rita	Jeptoo	KEN	15.2.81	2		Chicago	7 Oct
2:22:39			Sharon	Cherop	KEN	16.3.84	7		Dubai	27 Jan
2:22:41			Wang Jiali (20)		CHN	1.2.86	1	NC	Chongqing	17 Mar
2:22:41	1:24:26	1:41:15		Kabuu			3		Chicago	7 Oct
2:22:59	1:24:28	1:41:20	Liliya	Shobukhova	RUS	13.11.77	4		Chicago	7 Oct
2:23:07	1:26:23	1:42:44		Gelana			1	OG	London	5 Aug
2:23:07	1:24:23	1:41:19		Cheromei			1		Yokohama	18 Nov
2:23:07			Feyse	Tadese	ETH	19.11.88	1		Shanghai	2 Dec
2:23:09			Ashu	Kasim	ETH	20.10.84	1		Xiamen	7 Jan
2:23:12	1:26:23	1:42:44		P Jeptoo			2	OG	London	5 Aug
2:23:12	1:23:38	1:39:53		Kabuu			5		London	22 Apr
2:23:13				Baysa			8		Dubai	27 Jan
2:23:14	1:24:22	1:41:34	Alemitu	Abera	ETH	.86	1		Houston	15 Jan
2:23:22	1:24:28	1:41:16	Caroline	Rotich	KEN	13.5.84	5		Chicago	7 Oct
2:23:23	1:24:03	1:40:52	Risa	Shigetomo	JPN	29.8.87	1		Osaka	29 Jan
2:23:26				Tadese			1	Dong-A	Seoul	18 Mar
2:23:29	1:26:28	1:42:53	Tatyana	Arkhipova	RUS	8.4.83	3	OG	London	5 Aug
2:23:32	1:25:16	1:42:18	Olena	Shurhno	UKR	8.1.78	3		Berlin	30 Sep
2:23:42				Zhou Chunxiu	CHN	15.11.78	2	NC	Chongqing	17 Mar
2:23:44	1:25:13	1:42:30	Valeria	Straneo (30)	ITA	5.4.76	2		Rotterdam	15 Apr
2:23:52	1:26:20	1:43:06	Albina	Mayorova	RUS	16.5.77	1		Nagoya	11 Mar
2:23:52	1:23:23	1:39:58	Mamitu	Daska	ETH	16.10.83	3		Frankfurt	28 Oct
2:23:56	1:26:23	1:42:44		Keitany			4	OG	London	5 Aug
2:23:57				Cherop			1		Torino	18 Nov
2:23:58	1:23:23	1:40:16		Bekele			4		Frankfurt	28 Oct
2:24:04	1:23:38	1:40:24		Kebede			6		London	22 Apr

(45/32)

Mark			Name		Nat	Born	Pos	Meet	Venue	Date
2:24:12		1:41:08	Netsanet	Achamo	ETH	14.12.87	1		Hamburg	29 Apr
2:24:14	1:24:57	1:42:31	Yoshimi	Ozaki	JPN	1.7.81	2		Nagoya	11 Mar
2:24:17			Margaret	Agai	KEN	.81	3		Shanghai	2 Dec
2:24:19				Zhu Xiaolin	CHN	20.2.84	3	NC	Chongqing	17 Mar
2:24:27	1:23:23	1:39:58	Agnes	Barsosio	KEN	.83	5		Frankfurt	28 Oct
2:24:28	1:24:57	1:42:31	Remi	Nakazato	JPN	24.6.88	3		Nagoya	11 Mar
2:24:32	1:26:40	1:43:45	Tetyana	Hamera-Shmyrko	UKR	1.6.83	5	OG	London	5 Aug
2:24:53	1:25:19	1:42:40	Irina	Mikitenko	GER	23.8.72	7		London	22 Apr
			(40)							
2:24:56	1:23:32	1:40:16	Filomena	Chepchirchir	KEN	1.12.81	4		Berlin	30 Sep
2:24:57	1:24:25	1:41:54	Azusa	Nojiri	JPN	6.6.82	3		Osaka	29 Jan
2:24:59	1:25:38	1:42:41	Jéssica	Augusto	POR	8.11.81	8		London	22 Apr
2:25:02	1:24:58	1:42:32	Yoko	Shibui	JPN	14.3.79	4		Nagoya	11 Mar
2:25:09	1:23:30		Sultan	Haydar	TUR	23.5.87	2		Paris	15 Apr
2:25:14	1:25:15	1:42:07	Fate	Tola	ETH	22.10.87	5		Berlin	30 Sep
2:25:21			Merima	Hasen	ETH	10.6.92	4		Shanghai	2 Dec
2:25:26	1:24:58	1:42:31	Mai	Ito	JPN	23.5.84	5		Nagoya	11 Mar
2:25:28	1:26:52	1:44.02	Atsede	Habtamu	ETH	26.10.87	1		Tokyo	26 Feb
2:25:29			Askale	Tafa Magarsa	ETH	27.9.84	2	Dong-A	Seoul	18 Mar
			(50)							
2:25:33	1:25:21	1:42:31	Mizuki	Noguchi	JPN	3.7.78	6		Nagoya	11 Mar
2:25:34		1:43:39	Helena	Kirop	KEN	9.9.76	1		Köln	14 Oct
2:25:38			Shalane	Flanagan	USA	8.7.81	1	OT	Houston	14 Jan
2:25:38	1:24:27	1:41:36	Mariya	Konovalova	RUS	14.8.74	6		Chicago	7 Oct
2:25:38	1:24:20	1:41:08	Genet	Getaneh	ETH	6.1.86	3		Amsterdam	21 Oct
2:25:39 D			Fatuma	Sado	ETH	11.10.91	1	122m dh	Los Angeles	18 Mar
2:25:41			Isabellah	Andersson	SWE	12.11.80	10		Dubai	27 Jan
2:25:41		1:41:32	Agnes	Kiprop	KEN	12.12.79	1		Praha	13 May
2:25:45			Mulu	Seboka	ETH	25.9.84	11		Dubai	27 Jan
2:25:46			Hilda	Kibet	NED	27.3.81	2		Torino	18 Nov
			(60)							
2:25:49		1:42:21	Etalemahu	Kidane	ETH	14.2.83	2		Hamburg	29 Apr
2:25:53				Wang Xueqin	CHN	1.1.91	4	NC	Chongqing	17 Mar
2:25:55			Desiree	Davila	USA	26.7.83	2	OT	Houston	14 Jan
2:26:00			Yeshi	Esayias	ETH	28.12.85	2		Tokyo	26 Feb
2:26:06			Kara	Goucher	USA	9.7.78	3	OT	Houston	14 Jan
2:26:08	1:25:19	1:42:48	Eri	Okubo	JPN	2.6.83	4		Tokyo	26 Feb
2:26:08	1:24:57	1:42:31	Yukiko	Akaba	JPN	18.10.79	8		Nagoya	11 Mar
2:26:09	1:26:30	1:43:30	Helaria	Johannes	NAM	13.8.80	12	OG	London	5 Aug
2:26:13	1:26:30	1:43:30	Marisa	Barros	POR	25.2.80	13	OG	London	5 Aug
2:26:23	1:24:58	1:42:32	Yoko	Miyauchi	JPN	19.6.83	9		Nagoya	11 Mar
			(70)							
2:26:27			Sechale	Delasa	ETH		5		Shanghai	2 Dec
2:26:41A			Salome	Biwott	KEN	.83	1		Nairobi	28 Oct
2:26:42	1:25:30	1:43:04	Mizuho	Nasukawa	JPN	22.11.79	2		Yokohama	18 Nov
2:26:46	1:23:41		Makda	Harun	ETH	.88	3		Paris	15 Apr
2:26:52			Emily	Samoei	KEN	11.11.80	1		Barcelona	25 Mar
2:26:55	1:26:10	1:43:56	Jelena	Prokopcuka	LAT	21.9.76	4		Yokohama	18 Nov
2:26:59	1:26:31	1:43:29	Kim	Smith	NZL	19.11.81	15	OG	London	5 Aug
2:27:12	1:25:13	1:42:58	Zemzem	Ahmed	ETH	27.12.84	6		Frankfurt	28 Oct
2:27:14			Shetaye	Bedaso	ETH	.85	12		Dubai	27 Jan
2:27:16	1:26:38	1:44:13	Ryoko	Kizaki	JPN	21.6.85	16	OG	London	5 Aug
			(80)							
2:27:17			Amy	Hastings	USA	21.1.84	4	OT	Houston	14 Jan
2:27:17	1:26:34	1:43:42	Renee	Metivier-Baillie	USA	25.12.81	8		Chicago	7 Oct
2:27:18			Olga	Glok	RUS	16.12.82	2		Wien	15 Apr
2:27:20			Mekuria	Aberume	ETH		1		Eindhoven	14 Oct
2:27:21			Souad	Aït Salem	ALG	6.1.79	4		Praha	13 May
2:27:24		1:44:43	Anastasiya	Starovoytova	BLR	4.11.82	2		Düsseldorf	29 Apr
2:27:28	1:23:29		Goitetom	Haftu	ETH	.87	4		Paris	15 Apr
2:27:32		1:44:47	Miranda	Boonstra	NED	29.8.72	4		Rotterdam	15 Apr
2:27:32			Lisa	Weightman	AUS	16.1.79	17	OG	London (OS)	5 Aug
2:27:32	1:24:20	1:41:14	Diane	Chepkemoi	KEN	.87	4		Amsterdam	21 Oct
			(90)							
2:27:32			Deribe	Godana	ETH	13.3.88	4		Torino	18 Nov
2:27:40				Jia Chaofeng	CHN	16.11.88	1		Beijing	25 Nov
2:27:41		1:43:34	Beatrice	Toroitich	KEN	15.12.81	3		Hamburg	29 Apr
2:27:44 D			Alevtina	Ivanova	RUS	22.5.75	1		San Diego (86.5m)	3 Jun
2:27:44		1:44:31	Claire	Hallissey	GBR	17.3.83	11		London	22 Apr
2:27:50			Yeshimebet	Tadesse	ETH	.88	13		Dubai	27 Jan
2:27:50		1:42:44	Melkam	Gisaw	ETH	17.9.90	3		Düsseldorf	29 Apr
2:27:55				Sun Lamei	CHN	4.1.91	2		Beijing	25 Nov

Mark			Name		Nat	Born	Pos	Meet	Venue	Date
2:28:01	1:24:58	1:42:31	Misaki	Katsumata	JPN	26.12.85	10		Nagoya	11 Mar
2:28:01	D		Meseret	Legesse (100)	ETH	28.8.87	2		San Diego (86.5m)	3 Jun
2:28:02		1:41:07	Valentine	Kipketer	KEN-J	5.1.93	4		Hamburg	29 Apr

Mark	Name		Nat	Born	Date
2:28:03		Sun Weiwei	CHN	13.1.85	25 Nov
2:28:04A	Alice	Chelagat	KEN	27.12.76	28 Oct
2:28:05	Korene	Jelela	ETH	18.1.87	22 Apr
2:28:08	Olga	Dubovskaya	BLR	2.10.83	29 Apr
2:28:09dh	Misiker	Mekonnin	ETH	23.7.86	18 Mar
2:28:10	Freya	Murray-Ross	GBR	20.9.83	22 Apr
2:28:12	Dulce	Félix	POR	23.10.82	5 Aug
2:28:15	Emma	Quaglia	ITA	15.8.80	18 Nov
2:28:19	Eri	Hayakawa	JPN	15.11.81	11 Mar
2:28:22	Lishan	Dula	BRN	17.2.87	26 Feb
2:28:24	Benita	Willis	AUS	6.5.79	15 Jan
2:28:27	Serena	Burla	USA	29.7.82	18 Mar
2:28:31		He Yinli	CHN	1.2.88	25 Nov
2:28:32	Iwona	Lewandowska	POL	19.2.85	28 Oct
2:28:35	Chika	Horie	JPN	15.2.81	29 Jan
2:28:36	Eyerusalem	Kuma	ETH	4.11.81	26 Feb
2:28:38	Kateryna	Stetsenko	UKR	22.1.82	26 Feb
2:28:38	Amane	Gobena	ETH	11.9.82	11 Nov
2:28:39		Sun Juan	CHN	20.11.85	25 Nov
2:28:45	Alevtina	Biktimirova	RUS	10.9.82	30 Sep
2:28:54	Inés	Melchor	PER	30.8.86	5 Aug
2:28:57	Mary	Davies	NZL	27.8.82	14 Oct
2:29:00	Radiya	Adlo	ETH	22.9.89	17 Mar
2:29:02	Haile	Kebebush	ETH	13.4.86	29 Apr
2:29:02	Mayumi	Fujita	JPN	26.5.83	18 Nov
2:29:17	Adriana	da Silva	BRA	22.7.81	26 Feb
2:29:19	Alessandra	Aguilar	ESP	1.7.78	5 Aug
2:29:20	Beata	Naigambo	NAM	11.3.80	27 Jan
2:29:20	Yuko	Watanabe	JPN	3.11.87	11 Mar
2:29:22	Robe	Guta	ETH	12.10.86	29 Apr
2:29:22	Birhane	Dibaba	ETH-J	11.9.93	18 Nov
2:29:26	Sumiko	Suzuki	JPN	10.3.86	26 Feb
2:29:29	Rasa	Drazdauskaité	LTU	20.3.81	5 Aug
2:29:32	Diana	Lobacevske	LTU	7.8.80	5 Aug
2:29:33	Milka	Cherotich	KEN	24.2.78	18 Nov
2:29:37	Svetlana	Kovgan	BLR	10.8.80	15 Apr
2:29:38	Anna	Incerti	ITA	19.1.80	5 Aug
2:29:45	Janet	Cherobon-Bawcom	USA	22.8.78	14 Jan
2:29:46		Wei Xiaojie	CHN	20.11.89	12 May
2:29:51	Kiyoko	Shimahara	JPN	22.12.76	29 Jan
2:29:52	Biruktawit	Eshetu	ETH	.82	25 Mar
2:29:53		Kim Seong-eun	KOR	24.2.89	18 Mar
2:29:56	Dinknesh	Mekasha	ETH	.85	29 Apr
2:29:59	Hellen	Mugo	KEN	12.12.85	7 Oct
2:30:06		Yin Yuanyuan	CHN	31.5.91	22 Sep
2:30:08	Shuru	Diriba	ETH	.85	25 Nov
2:30:09	Emmah	Muthoni	KEN	4.1.81	13 May
2:30:09	Rosaria	Console	ITA	17.12.79	5 Aug
2:30:10	Natalya	Sokolova	RUS	12.3.82	9 Sep
2:30:11	Tetyana	Filonyuk	UKR	5.4.84	18 Mar
2:30:13	Diane	Nukuri-Johnson	BDI	1.12.84	5 Aug
2:30:14	Anna	Hahner	GER	20.11.89	29 Apr
2:30:17	Natalya	Puchkova	RUS	28.1.87	6 May
2:30:18		Yue Chao	CHN	5.1.91	25 Nov
2:30:19		Cao Mojie	CHN	10.4.92	17 Mar
2:30:19	Caroline	Kilel	KEN	21.3.81	16 Dec
2:30:22	Susanne	Hahn	GER	23.4.78	5 Aug
2:30:23	Malika	Asahssah	MAR	24.9.82	29 Apr
2:30:26	Halima	Hassen	ETH	10.11.92	6 May
2:30:27	Zeyneba	Hasso	ETH	26.6.85	6 May
2:30:27	Silviya	Skvortsova	RUS	16.11.74	13 May
2:30:34		Chung Yun-hee	KOR	3.1.83	18 Mar
2:30:34	Caroline	Chepkwony	KEN	18.4.84	30 Sep
2:30:36	Kaori	Yoshida	JPN	4.8.81	1 Jul
2:30:38	Ferhiwot	Goshu	ETH	28.6.90	15 Apr
2:30:40	Deena	Kastor	USA	14.2.73	14 Jan
2:30:41		Kim Mi-gyong	PRK	17.10.90	8 Apr
2:30:45	Worknesh	Tola	ETH	3.6.77	28 Oct
2:30:46	Clara	Grandt	USA	24.3.87	14 Jan
2:30:46	Magdaline	Mukunzi	KEN	22.10.83	29 Oct
2:30:51	Renè	Kalmer	RSA	3.11.80	5 Aug
2:30:52	Elena María	Espeso	ESP	10.10.72	25 Mar
2:30:53	Fantu	Jimma	ETH	.91	29 Apr
2:30:56	Sonia	Samuels	GBR	16.5.79	30 Sep
2:30:57	Karolina	Jarzynska	POL	6.9.81	5 Aug
2:30:58	Yuliya	Andreyeva	KGZ	7.3.84	13 May
2:31:02	Jessica	Trengove	AUS	15.8.87	11 Mar
2:31:06	Jane	Rotich	KEN	11.12.80	29 Apr
2:31:07	Irene	Jerotich	KEN	8.9.74	15 Apr
2:31:07	Jacqueline	Kiplimo	KEN	.85	18 Nov
2:31:10	Faith	Chemaoi	KEN	.87	29 Oct
2:31:11	Hellen	Kimutai	KEN	28.12.77	18 Mar
2:31:13	Korei	Omata	JPN	15.7.87	11 Mar
2:31:15A	Marisol	Romero	MEX	26.1.83	4 Mar
2:31:19	Delelecha	Yihunlish	ETH	22.10.81	15 Jan
2:31:20dh	Tetyana	Mezentseva	UKR	17.1.72	18 Mar
2:31:23	Ashete	Dido	ETH	.88	18 Mar
2:31:23	Valentina	Galimova	RUS	11.5.86	9 Dec
2:31:28	Lisa	Hahner	GER	20.11.89	28 Oct
2:31:29		Kim Hye-song	PRK-J	9.3.93	8 Apr
2:31:29	Marina	Damantsevich	BLR	6.6.85	7 Oct
2:31:30	Miriam	Wangari	KEN	22.2.79	7 Jan
2:31:30	Karina	Pérez	MEX	4.10.82	4 Mar
2:31:30A	Mercy	Tanui	KEN	.84	28 Oct
2:31:31	Elizabeth	Rumokol	KEN	26.3.83	17 Jun
2:31:33	Olga	Ochal	POL	15.7.85	15 Apr
2:31:37	Genoveva	Jelagat	KEN	9.8.80	4 Mar
2:31:37	Louise	Damen	GBR	12.10.82	22 Apr
2:31:39	Misato	Horie	JPN	10.3.87	11 Mar
2:31:40	(200)	Jon Gyong-hui	PRK	12.12.86	8 Apr

Drugs disqualification

Mark			Name		Nat	Born	Pos	Venue	Date
2:23:47		1:42:04	Rael	Kiyara	KEN	4.4.84	(1)	Hamburg	29 Apr

JUNIORS

Mark	Name		Nat	Born	Pos	Venue	Date
2:28:02	Valentine	Kipketer	KEN	5.1.93	4	Hamburg	29 Apr
2:29:22	Birhane	Dibaba	ETH	11.9.93	1	Valencia	18 Nov
2:33:07			4	Barcelona	25 Mar	2:34:58 2	São Paulo 17 Jun
2:31:29		Kim Hye-song	PRK	9.3.93	2	Pyongyang	8 Apr
2:33:28		Gong Lihua	CHN	10.5.93	6	Shanghai	2 Dec
2:38:58A	Eunice	Chebichii	KEN	23.5.93	9	Nairobi	28 Oct
Uncertain distance: 2:31:44A	Caroline Kipkirui		KEN	26.5.94	2	Kisumu	16 Dec

100 KILOMETRES

Mark	Name		Nat	Born	Pos	Meet	Venue	Date
7:33:38	Shiho	Katayama	JPN	18.12.77	1		Yubetsu	24 Jun
7:34:07	Amy	Sproston	USA	5.2.74	1	WCh	Seregno	22 Apr
7:35:07	Monica	Carlin	ITA	20.6.71	1		Faenza	27 May
7:35:21	Kajsa	Berg	SWE	16.1.79	2	WCh/EC	Seregno	22 Apr
7:35:57	Irina	Vishnevskaya	RUS	2.6.82	3	WCh/EC	Seregno	22 Apr
7:41:52	Megan	Arbogast	USA	16.4.61	4	WCh	Seregno	22 Apr
7:43:03	Pam	Smith	USA	22.9.74	5	WCh	Seregno	22 Apr
7:43:52	Judit	Földing Nagy	HUN	9.12.65	6	WCh/EC	Seregno	22 Apr
7:48:05	Mami	Kudo	JPN	17.7.64	7	WCh	Seregno	22 Apr
7:52:07		Vishnevskaya			1		Torhout	23 Jun
7:53:31	Mai	Fujisawa (10/	JPN	21.9.74	2		Yubetsu	24 Jun

Mark	Name		Nat	Born	Pos	Meet	Venue	Date
7:54:24	Akiko	Odagiri	JPN	31.1.74	3		Yubetsu	24 Jun
7:56:42	Naomi	Ochiai	JPN	13.5.80	4		Yubetsu	24 Jun
7:57:18	Yuko	Ito	JPN	3.8.72	8	WCh	Seregno	22 Apr
7:58:05	Marina	Zanardi	ITA	7.1.72	9	WCh/EC	Seregno	22 Apr
7:59:39	Mariya	Aksenova	RUS	25.10.88	11	WCh/EC	Seregno	22 Apr
8:02:54	Irina	Pankovskaya	RUS	10.1.86	2		Faenza	27 May
8:03:54	Francesca	Marin	ITA	23.2.77	12	WCh/EC	Seregno	22 Apr
8:04:02	Yuka	Ezaki	JPN	20.10.81	5		Yubetsu	24 Jun
8:04:05	Paola	Sanna	ITA	19.3.77	3		Faenza	27 May
8:05:07	Emily	Gelder	GBR	1.4.75	1	NC	Redwick	22 Jul
	(20)							

8:08:53	Tomoko	Hara	JPN	.73	21 Oct		8:12:29	Branka	Hajek	GER	16.6.84	6 Oct
8:12:16	Tanja	Hooß	GER	25.9.67	6 Oct		8:14:39	Nadezhda	Shikhanova	RUS	14.5.84	2 Sep

Thes here and in the men's list in the Seregno race are gun times and not the incorrect net times generally published.

24 HOURS

Mark	Name		Nat	Born	Pos	Meet	Venue	Date
244.232	Michaela	Dimitriadu	CZE	23.12.73	1	WCh/EC	Katowice	9 Sep
243.381	Mikie	Sakane	JPN	31.7.75	1		Tokyo	8 Oct
240.385	Constance	Gardner	USA	6.11.63	2	WCh	Katowice	9 Sep
238.875	Emily	Gelder	GBR	1.4.75	3	WCh/EC	Katowice	9 Sep
238.021	Sabrina	Moran	USA	12.7.86	1	NC	Cleveland	7 May
235.129	Mami	Kudo	JPN	17.7.64	1		Taipei	9 Dec
234.524	Cécile	Nissen	FRA	21.3.72	4	WCh/EC	Katowice	9 Sep
232.454	Szilvia	Lubics	HUN	27.5.74	1	NC	Sárvár	29 Apr
231.074	Suzanna	Bon	USA	28.7.64	5	WCh	Katowice	9 Sep
229.890	Anna	Grundahl (10)	SWE	6.4.76	6	WCh/EC	Katowice	9 Sep
229.346	Ruthann	Sheahan	IRL	30.4.75	7	WCh/EC	Katowice	9 Sep
229.041		Gardner			2	NC	Cleveland	7 May
228.595	Melanie	Straß	GER	16.5.75	1		Stadtoldendorf	3 Jun
226.518	Cristina	González	ESP	19.2.84	8	WCh/EC	Katowice	9 Sep
225.720	Anne	Riddle-Lundblad	USA	21.6.66	1		Morganton	1 Jan
	(15/14)							
223.026	Anne-Marie	Vernet	FRA	15.12.67	10	WCh/EC	Katowice	9 Sep
222.982	Sayuri	Oka	JPN	6.8.70	2		Tokyo	8 Oct
222.962	Kiyoko	Shirakawa	JPN	22.6.66	2		Taipei	9 Dec
221.555	Sumie	Inagaki	JPN	6.4.66	3		Taipei	9 Dec
218.227	Sabrina	Moran	USA	12.7.86	1		Grapevine	18 Nov
218.172	Eva Esnaola	Agesta (20)	ESP	23.11.60	12	WCh/EC	Katowice	9 Sep

217.592	Antje	Krause	GER	1.5.72	9 Sep		211.141	Torill	Fonn	SWE	1.11.67	9 Sep
217.180	Debbie	Martin-Consani	GBR	4.4.75	9 Sep		211.006	Debra	Horn	USA	11.3.59	15 Dec
216.643	Wilma	Dierx	NED	11.5.66	3 Jun		210.854	Marika	Heinlein	GER	1.9.62	9 Sep
215.793	Yuko	Ito	JPN	3.8.72	9 Sep		210.640	Monica	Barchetti	ITA	28.11.68	9 Sep
214.037	Aleksandra	Niwinska	POL	23.1.86	9 Sep		210.567	Regina	Strasser	AUT	17.1.72	8 Jul
213.005	Christine	Tamnga	FRA	3.8.74	7 Oct		210.404	Sharon	Law	GBR	9.3.75	9 Sep
211.224	Sylvie	Peuch	FRA	22.11.61	11 Nov		**Best track**					
							212.794	Constance	Gardner	USA	6.11.63	15 Dec

Indoors

Mark	Name		Nat	Born	Pos	Meet	Venue	Date
228.222	Sumie	Inagaki	JPN	6.4.66	1		Espoo	26 Feb
214.282	Frida	Södermark	SWE	5.8.78	1		Oslo	2 Dec

2000 METRES STEEPLECHASE

Mark	Name		Nat	Born	Pos	Meet	Venue	Date
6:20.80	Sanaa	Koubaa	GER	6.1.85	1		Pliezhausen	6 May
6:22.06	Maya	Rehberg	GER-J	28.4.94	1	NC-j	Mönchengladbach	21 Jul
6:26.66	Bridget	Franek	USA	8.11.87	1		Eugene	18 Mar

More Juniors

Mark	Name		Nat	Born	Pos	Meet	Venue	Date
6:30.73	Brianna	Nerud	USA-J	16.9.94	1		South Huntington	4 May
6:32.61	Oona	Kettunen	FIN-J	10.2.94	1	Nordic-J	Växjö	19 Aug
6:34.80	Aníta	Hinriksdóttir	ISL-Y	13.1.96	2	Nordic-J	Växjö	19 Aug
6:36.60	Pippa	Woolven	GBR	26.7.93	1	Univ Ch	London (OS)	5 May

3000 METRES STEEPLECHASE

Mark	Name		Nat	Born	Pos	Meet	Venue	Date
9:05.02	Yuliya	Zaripova	RUS	26.4.86	1	DNG	Stockholm	17 Aug
9:06.72		Zaripova			1	OG	London (OS)	6 Aug
9:07.14	Milcah	Chemos Cheywa	KEN	24.2.86	1	Bisl	Oslo	7 Jun
9:08.37	Habiba	Ghribi	TUN	9.4.84	2	OG	London (OS)	6 Aug
9:09.00	Sofia	Assefa	ETH	14.11.87	2	Bisl	Oslo	7 Jun
9:09.61	Hiwot	Ayalew	ETH	6.3.90	3	Bisl	Oslo	7 Jun
9:09.84		Assefa			3	OG	London (OS)	6 Aug
9:09.88		Chemos			4	OG	London (OS)	6 Aug
9:09.99		Zaripova			1	NC	Cheboksary	3 Jul
9:10.36		Ghribi			2	DNG	Stockholm	17 Aug

Mark	Name		Nat	Born	Pos	Meet	Venue	Date	
9:12.98		Ayalew			5	OG	London (OS)	6	Aug
9:13.53	Gülcan	Mingir	TUR	21.5.89	1	Pavlov	Sofia	9	Jun
9:13.69		Chemos			1	Pre	Eugene	2	Jun
9:14.07	Etenesh	Diro	ETH	10.5.91	3	DNG	Stockholm	17	Aug
9:14.98	Lidya	Chepkurui	KEN	23.8.84	4	DNG	Stockholm	17	Aug
9:15.45		Assefa			2	Pre	Eugene	2	Jun
9:15.81		Chemos			1	DL	Shanghai	19	May
9:15.84		Ayalew			3	Pre	Eugene	2	Jun
9:16.14		Ayalew			1		Rabat	27	May
9:16.83		Assefa			2	DL	Shanghai	19	May
9:19.89		Diro			6	OG	London (OS)	6	Aug
9:21.54		Diro			1		Huelva	7	Jun
9:21.64		Assefa			1	ISTAF	Berlin	2	Sep
9:21.78	Antje	Möldner-Schmidt	GER	13.6.84	7	OG	London (OS)	6	Aug
9:22.27		Chepkurui			2	ISTAF	Berlin	2	Sep
9:22.66		Chepkurui			3	DL	Shanghai	19	May
9:23.52		Chepkurui			1	Gugl	Linz	20	Aug
9:23.52	Gesa-Felicitas	Krause (10)	GER	3.8.92	8	OG	London (OS)	6	Aug
9:23.53	Hyvin	Jepkemoi	KEN	13.1.92	2	Gugl	Linz	20	Aug
9:23.54	Emma	Coburn	USA	19.10.90	9	OG	London (OS)	6	Aug
	(20/12)								
9:24.24	Barbara	Parker	GBR	8.11.82	4	Pre	Eugene	2	Jun
9:24.26	Marta	Domínguez	ESP	3.11.75	2		Huelva	7	Jun
9:24.60	Gulnara	Galkina	RUS	9.7.78	1	Mosc Ch	Moskva	21	Jun
9:25.21	Mercy	Njoroge	KEN	10.6.86	4	Bisl	Oslo	7	Jun
9:25.70	Ancuta	Bobocel	ROU	3.10.87	5	DNG	Stockholm	17	Aug
9:25.85	Zemzem	Ahmed	ETH	27.12.84	1		Sotteville-lès-Rouen	10	Jul
9:27.21	Polina	Jelizarova	LAT	1.5.89	4h1	OG	London (OS)	4	Aug
9:29.53	Bridget	Franek	USA	8.11.87	4	LGP	London (CP)	14	Jul
	(20)								
9:30.06	Clarisse	Cruz	POR	9.7.78	5h2	OG	London (OS)	4	Aug
9:30.42	Eunice	Jepkorir	KEN	17.2.82	5	ISTAF	Berlin	2	Sep
9:30.95	Dorcus	Inzikuru	UGA	2.2.82	1		Bottrop	6	Jul
9:31.03	Salima	Alami	MAR	29.12.83	1	GP	Rio de Janeiro	20	May
9:31.09	Lydia	Rotich	KEN	8.8.88	6	Pre	Eugene	2	Jun
9:31.16	Svitlana	Shmidt	UKR	20.3.90	1	NC	Yalta	13	Jun
9:31.37	Yelena	Orlova	RUS	30.5.80	3	NC	Cheboksary	3	Jul
9:31.93	Natalya	Aristarkhova	RUS	31.10.89	1		Sochi	26	May
9:32.81	Ruth	Bisibori	KEN	2.1.88	7	ISTAF	Berlin	2	Sep
9:34.14	Katarzyna	Kowalska	POL	7.4.85	5	LGP	London (CP)	14	Jul
	(30)								
9:34.29		Li Zhenzhu	CHN	13.12.85	7h1	OG	London (OS)	4	Aug
9:34.49	Ashley	Higginson	USA	17.3.89	6	LGP	London (CP)	14	Jul
9:34.88	Gamze	Bulut	TUR	3.8.92	1		Izmir	19	May
9:35.03	Fancy	Cherotich	KEN	10.8.90	2		Dubnica nad Váhom	26	Aug
9:35.31	Phanencer	Chemion	KEN	8.4.89	4		Rabat	27	May
9:35.41	Lyudmila	Kuzmina	RUS	13.8.87	8	Pre	Eugene	2	Jun
9:35.55	Natalya	Gorchakova	RUS	17.4.83	4	NC	Cheboksary	3	Jul
9:35.61	Purity	Kirui	KEN	13.8.91	3		Huelva	7	Jun
9:35.73	Shalaya	Kipp	USA	19.8.90	3	NC/OT	Eugene	29	Jun
9:35.77	Diana	Martín	ESP	1.4.81	8h1	OG	London (OS)	4	Aug
	(40)								
9:36.40	Birtukan	Adamu	ETH	29.4.92	8	Bisl	Oslo	7	Jun
9:36.81	Lyubov	Kharlamova	RUS	2.3.81	2	Mosc C	Moskva	11	Jun
9:37.02	Valentyna	Zhudina	UKR	12.3.83	2	NCp	Yalta	28	May
9:37.18	Mekdes	Bekele	ETH	20.1.87	6		Rabat	27	May
9:37.41	Natalya	Vlasova	RUS	19.7.88	3	Mosc C	Moskva	11	Jun
9:37.90	Genevieve	LaCaze	AUS	4.8.89	9h1	OG	London (OS)	4	Aug
9:37.95	Korine	Hinds	JAM	18.1.76	10h1	OG	London (OS)	4	Aug
9:38.32	Özlem	Kaya	TUR	20.4.90	2		Izmir	19	May
9:38.45	Eilish	McColgan	GBR	25.11.90	9	Bisl	Oslo	7	Jun
9:38.62	Almaz	Ayana	ETH	21.11.91	2		Bottrop	6	Jul
	(50)								
9:39.33	Beverly	Ramos	PUR	24.8.87	5		Sotteville-lès-Rouen	10	Jul
9:39.43	Svetlana	Kudzelich	BLR	7.5.87	3		Bottrop	6	Jul
9:39.87	Matylda	Szlezak	POL	11.1.89	6		Huelva	7	Jun
9:40.69	Kaltoum	Bouaasayriya	MAR	23.8.82	7		Rabat	27	May
9:41.44		Yin Annuo	CHN	23.3.92	1	NGP	Tianjin	12	May
9:41.69	Regina	Nguria	KEN	.84	6	Gugl	Linz	20	Aug
9:41.95	Lisa	Aguilera	USA	30.11.79	5	NC/OT	Eugene	29	Jun

Mark	Name		Nat	Born	Pos	Meet	Venue	Date
9:42.58	Lyudmila	Lebedeva	RUS	23.5.90	5	Mosc C	Moskva	11 Jun
9:42.71	Ángela	Figueroa	COL	28.6.84	3	GP	Rio de Janeiro	20 May
9:42.72	Silvia	Danekova	BUL	7.2.83	6h1	EC	Helsinki	28 Jun
(60)								
9:42.96	Sara	Hall	USA	15.4.83	12	Pre	Eugene	2 Jun
9:43.08	Sanaa	Koubaa	GER	6.1.85	7h1	EC	Helsinki	28 Jun
9:43.28	Delilah	DiCrescenzo	USA	28.2.83	2	Jordan	Stanford	29 Apr
9:43.38	Sandra	Eriksson	FIN	4.6.89	1		Lapinlahti	8 Jul
9:43.95	Türkan	Özata-Erismis	TUR	5.1.84	2		Bucuresti	15 Jun
9:44.04	Zulema	Fuentes-Pila	ESP	25.5.77	8		Huelva	7 Jun
9:44.11	Claire	Navez	FRA	6.10.87	9		Huelva	7 Jun
9:44.15	Stephanie	Reilly	IRL	23.2.78	6h2	EC	Helsinki	28 Jun
9:44.71	Christine	Muyanga	KEN	21.3.91	4	GP	Rio de Janeiro	20 May
9:44.91	Mariya	Shatalova	UKR	3.3.89	3	NC	Yalta	13 Jun
(70)								
9:45.01	Carrie	Dimoff	USA	31.5.83	6	NC/OT	Eugene	29 Jun
9:45.92		Jin Yuan	CHN	11.2.88	1	NGP	Zhaoqing	14 Apr
9:46.60	Sophie	Duarte	FRA	31.7.81	10		Huelva	7 Jun
9:47.22	Daisy	Jepkemei	KEN-Y	25.10.96	1	WJ	Barcelona	12 Jul
9:47.32	Mason	Cathey	USA	29.4.82	3h1	NC/OT	Eugene	25 Jun
9:47.45	Valeriya	Mara	UKR	22.2.83	3	NCp	Yalta	28 May
9:47.57	Eliane	Sahalinirina	MAD	20.3.82	6		Sotteville-lès-Rouen	10 Jul
9:47.70	Sudha	Singh	IND	25.6.86	11		Huelva	7 Jun
9:47.76	Stephanie	Garcia	USA	3.5.88	2		Indianapolis	13 Jun
9:48.01	Giulia	Martinelli	ITA	16.6.91	12		Huelva	7 Jun
(80)								
9:48.04	Rebecca	Wade	USA	9.2.89	1		Houston	16 Jun
9:48.35	Lennie	Waite	GBR	4.5.86	1		Stanford	6 Apr
9:49.03	María Teresa	Urbina	ESP	20.3.85	13		Huelva	7 Jun
9:49.11	Élodie	Olivarès	FRA	22.5.76	7		Sotteville-lès-Rouen	10 Jul
9:50.51	Tejinesh	Gebisa	ETH-Y	3.3.95	2	WJ	Barcelona	12 Jul
9:50.58	Stella	Ruto	KEN-Y	.96	3	WJ	Barcelona	12 Jul
9:50.8A	Tabitha	Chelangat	KEN	.89	1		Mumias	21 Apr
9:51.30	Aisha	Praught	USA	14.12.89	1rB	MSR	Walnut	19 Apr
9:51.42	Jamie	Cheever	USA	28.2.87	6h2	NC/OT	Eugene	25 Jun
9:51.51	Victoria	Mitchell	AUS	25.4.82	1		Gold Coast	7 Jul
(90)								
9:51.91	Carla Salomé	Rocha	POR	25.4.90	2		Lisboa (Un)	12 May
9:52.43	Sarah	Pease	USA	9.11.87	7h2	NC/OT	Eugene	25 Jun
9:52.65	Veerle	Dejaeghere	BEL	1.8.73	2		Oordegem	26 May
9:52.82	Rebeka	Stowe	USA	9.3.90	5	Jordan	Stanford	29 Apr
9:52.90	Alyssa	Kulik	USA	2.2.90	1		Charlottesville	20 Apr
9:52.92	Natalya	Tarantinova	RUS	28.11.87	2	Mosc Ch	Moskva	21 Jun
9:53.15	Astrid	Leutert	SUI	12.9.87	1h1	NCAA-E	Jacksonville	25 May
9:53.47	Emily	Stewart	GBR	24.12.91	10	LGP	London (CP)	14 Jul
9:53.7A	Agnes	Chesang	KEN	.86	5	NC	Nairobi	15 Jun
9:53.79	Collier	Lawrence	USA	4.10.86	2rB	Jordan	Stanford	29 Apr
(100)								

Mark	Name		Nat	Born	Date		Mark	Name		Nat	Born	Date
9:53.85	Betsy	Graney	USA	23.10.89	29 Apr		9:58.41	Kara	June Thorne	USA	10.8.82	19 Apr
9:53.94	Amber	Henry	USA	27.12.90	29 Apr		9:58.48	Widad	Mendil	ALG	12.5.83	1 Jun
9:54.04	Sabine	Heitling	BRA	2.7.87	20 May		9:58.83	Cristina	Casandra	ROU	21.10.77	4 Aug
9:54.36	Vaida	Zusinaité	LTU	13.1.88	6 Jul		9:59.29	Bethany	Nickless	USA	4.10.85	9 Jun
9:54.42	Nolene	Conrad	RSA	26.7.85	26 May		9:59.29	Irina	Titova	RUS	26.3.92	21 Jul
9:54.70	Chantelle	Groenewoud	CAN	3.3.89	29 Apr		9:59.32	Dana	Buchanan	CAN	6.5.84	29 Apr
9:54.84	Birtukan	Fente	ETH	18.6.89	10 Jul		9:59.38	Oona	Kettunen	FIN-J	10.2.94	24 Aug
9:54.90	Mary	Goldkamp	USA	4.10.88	2 Jun		9:59.60	Lindsey	Sundell	USA	.86	9 Jun
9:55.27	Minna-Maria	Kangas	FIN	5.2.83	26 May		9:59.90	Melanie	Thompson	USA	18.4.91	6 Jun
9:55.39	Iryna	Ananenko	BLR	9.1.86	29 May		9:59.96	Athiná	Koíni	GRE	17.12.92	15 Jun
9:55.44	Helen	Hofstede	NED	31.12.80	29 Apr		9:59.99	Rena	Chesser	USA	17.5.83	2 Jun
9:55.50	Fabienne	Schlumpf	SUI	17.11.90	2 Jun		10:00.72	Brianna	Nerud	USA-J	16.9.94	12 Jul
9:55.89	Alexi	Pappas	USA	28.3.90	25 May		10:01.05	Yelena	Petrova	RUS	1.6.87	3 Jul
9:55.93	Yoshika	Arai	JPN	26.2.82	10 Jun		10:01.38	Wioletta	Frankiewicz	POL	9.6.77	6 Jul
9:56.13	Minori	Hayakari	JPN	29.11.72	21 Apr		10:01.43	Milly	Clark	AUS	1.3.89	31 Mar
9:56.32	Shayla	Houlihan	USA	26.2.85	29 Apr		10:01.48	Johanna	Lehtinen	FIN	21.2.79	2 Sep
9:56.46	Yevdokiya	Bukina	RUS-J	10.2.93	12 Jul		10:01.57	Valentina	Costanza	ITA	27.2.87	9 Jun
9:56.66	Lois	Ricardi Keller	USA	29.9.84	9 Jun		10:01.77	Rini	Budiarti	INA	22.1.83	15 Sep
9:56.73	Kerry	Harty	IRL	15.7.81	19 Apr		10:01.97	Renata	Krasnova	RUS	21.12.90	3 Jul
9:56.92		Fu Tinglian	CHN	5.7.87	14 Apr		10:02.15	Eva	Krchová	CZE	10.9.89	29 Apr
9:57.00	Hatti	Archer	GBR	2.2.82	28 Jun		10:02.17		Fang Xiaoyu	CHN	6.3.87	12 May
9:57.46	Amina	Bettiche	ALG	14.12.87	7 Jul		10:02.53	Colleen	Quigley	USA	20.11.92	20 Apr
9:57.55	Hitomi	Nakamura	JPN	23.6.87	10 Jun		10:02.62	Allix	Potratz-Lee	USA	3.5.86	5 May
9:58.15	Aleksandra	Pavlyutenkova	RUS	21.3.90	21 Jul		10:02.67	Asmarework	Bekele	ETH	11.8.91	1 Jun
9:58.29	Mardrea	Hyman	JAM	22.12.72	13 Jun		10:02.68	Nadia	Noujani	MAR	3.9.81	11 Jun
9:58.33	Natalya	Izmodenova	RUS	1.1.81	3 Jul		10:02.69	Eliane	Pereira	BRA	5.1.83	20 May

Mark	Name		Nat	Born	Date
10:03.09	Maya	Rehberg	GER-J	28.4.94	12 Jul
10:03.37	Samantha	Dow	USA	9.11.90	25 May
10:03.40	Leah	O'Connor	USA	30.8.92	25 May
10:03.70	Jessica	Furlan	CAN	15.3.90	13 Jun
10:03.72	Kirsten	Weberg	USA	3.6.91	25 May
10:03.92	Nicole	Bush	USA	4.4.86	29 Apr
10:04.04	Oksana	Juravel	MDA	23.2.86	15 Jun
10:04.20	Nicol	Traynor	USA	6.5.89	6 May
10:04.25	Breanne	Ehrman	USA	26.7.89	21 Apr
10:04.26	Yekaterina	Sokolenko	RUS	13.9.92	26 May
10:04.31	Verena	Dreier	GER	15.1.85	17 Jun
10:04.49	Lauren	Johnson	USA	4.5.87	21 Apr
10:04.51	Fiona	Crombie	NZL	15.8.82	18 May
10:04.59	Mariya	Bykova	RUS	7.11.89	3 Jul
10:04.89		Sun Ran	CHN	10.5.91	12 May
10:05.03	Justyna	Korytkowska	POL	12.3.86	7 Jun
10:05.07	Jekaterina	Patjuk	EST	6.4.83	8 Jul
10:05.35	Shelby	Greany	USA	1.4.91	6 Jun
10:05.40	Misato	Horie	JPN	10.3.87	10 Jun
10:05.73	Erika	Lima	BRA-J	13.8.93	27 May
10:06.18	Lívia	Tóth	HUN	7.1.80	6 Jul
10:06.30	Marta	Tigabea	ETH	4.10.90	2 Jun
10:06.58	Kimber	Mattox	USA		21 Apr
10:07.77	Olga	Dereveva	RUS	5.4.85	26 May
10:07.77	Rolanda	Bell	PAN	27.10.87	2 Jun
10:07.98	Maggie	Callahan	USA	28.9.88	29 Apr
10:08.01	Olga	Tarantinova	RUS	28.11.87	21 Jun
10:08.25	Antonina	Behnke	POL	13.6.89	3 Jun
10:08.28	Meredith	McGregor	CAN	10.3.85	29 Apr
10:08.35	Azusa	Saito	JPN	9.6.86	4 May
10:08.77	Friederike	Feil	GER	23.5.86	21 Jul
10:08.99	Kristen	Hemphill	USA	30.6.87	6 Apr
10:09.08	Yekaterina	Rogozina	RUS	21.12.89	26 May
10:09.10	Geneviève	Lalonde	CAN	5.9.91	18 May
10:09.36	Lucie	Sekanová	CZE	5.8.89	11 Jun
10:09.53	Lemlem	Berhe	ETH	.92	1 Jul
10:09.70	Hannah	Davidson	USA	15.4.90	4 May
10:10.55	Genna	Hartung	USA	5.8.91	25 May
10:10.69	Natalya	Tsitsoryna ¶	BLR	26.10.79	6 Jul
10:10.81	Eva	Arias	ESP	5.10.80	25 Aug
10:10.89	Alicia	Nelson	USA	20.10.90	19 Apr
10:11.13	Korahubish	Itaa	ETH	28.2.92	1 Jun
10:11.44	Tugba	Malakçi	TUR	4.11.91	19 May
10:11.51	Heather	Stephens	USA	16.1.90	6 Apr
10:11.72	Eranga Rasika	Dulakshi	SRI	21.3.91	9 Nov
10:11.85	Alexandra	Leptich	USA	3.2.92	6 Apr
10:11.86	Pippa	Woolven	GBR-J	26.7.93	9 Jun
10:12.12	Tebogo	Masehla (200)	RSA	6.1.79	14 Apr

JUNIORS

See main list for top 3 juniors. 10 performances by 7 women to 10:04.0. Additional marks and further juniors:

Mark	Name		Nat	Born	Pos	Meet	Venue	Date
Jepkemei	9:56.33				1h2	WJ	Barcelona	10 Jul
Gebosa	10:01.48				1h1	WJ	Barcelona	10 Jul
Kettunen	10:03.15				7	WJ	Barcelona	12 Jul
9:56.46	Yevdokiya	Bukina	RUS	10.2.93	4	WJ	Barcelona	12 Jul
9:59.38	Oona	Kettunen	FIN	10.2.94	2	NC	Lahti	24 Aug
10:00.72	Brianna	Nerud	USA	16.9.94	5	WJ	Barcelona	12 Jul
10:03.09	Maya	Rehberg	GER	28.4.94	6	WJ	Barcelona	12 Jul
10:05.73	Erika	Lima	BRA	13.8.93	1-j		São Paulo	27 May
10:11.86	Pippa	Woolven	GBR	26.7.93	4		Watford	9 Jun
10:14.52	Zulema	Arenas (10)	PER-Y	15.11.95	1	SAm-23	São Paulo	22 Sep
10:14.8A	Yabsera	Betaw	ETH		1	NC-j	Addis Ababa	3 Jun
10:15.16	Mary Kate	Anselmini	USA	22.4.93	4	Pac-12	Eugene	12 May
10:16.79	Kseniya	Levina	RUS	29.11.93	2	NC-j	Cheboksary	20 Jun
10:17.57		Zhang Xinyan	CHN	9.2.94	6	NGP	Tianjin	12 May
10:19.34	Elena	Panaet	ROU	5.6.93	8	WJ	Barcelona	12 Jul
10:19.73	Nanami	Niwa	JPN-Y	27.5.95	1		Maebashi	26 Aug
10:19.78		Li Jiayi	CHN	26.12.93	1	NC-j	Changzhou	22 Apr
10:20.57	Mizuki	Sato	JPN	.94	2		Maebashi	26 Aug
10:20.58		Yang Chunlei	CHN	11.8.93	6	NC	Kunshan	25 Sep
10:21.17	Belén	Cassetta (20)	ARG	26.9.94	1		Mar del Plata	10 Mar

60 METRES HURDLES INDOORS

Mark	Name		Nat	Born	Pos	Meet	Venue	Date
7.73	Sally	Pearson	AUS	19.9.86	1	WI	Istanbul	10 Mar
7.84A	Kristi	Castlin	USA	7.7.88	1	NC	Albuquerque	26 Feb
7.85		Pearson			1h1	WI	Istanbul	9 Mar
7.87	Jessica	Ennis	GBR	28.1.86	1	GP	Birmingham	18 Feb
7.89	Lolo	Jones	USA	5.8.82	1	Winter	Moskva	5 Feb
7.90A		Castlin			1h2	NC	Albuquerque	26 Feb
7.91		Castlin			1	Mill	New York (Arm)	11 Feb
7.91	Christina	Manning	USA	29.5.90	1	NCAA	Nampa	10 Mar
7.91	Danielle	Carruthers	USA	22.12.79	2	GP	Birmingham	18 Feb
7.91		Ennis			1P	WI	Istanbul	9 Mar
	(10/6)							
7.93	Tiffany	Porter	GBR	13.11.87	2	Mill	New York (Arm)	11 Feb
7.93A	Vanneisha	Ivy	USA	26.10.87	2	NC	Albuquerque	26 Feb
7.93	Brianna	Rollins	USA	18.8.91	1h2	NCAA	Nampa	9 Mar
7.95Ai	Yvette	Lewis	USA	16.3.85	1h1	NC	Albuquerque	26 Feb
	(10)							
7.95	Bridgette	Owens	USA	14.3.92	2h2	NCAA	Nampa	9 Mar
7.96	Cindy	Roleder	GER	21.8.89	1	NC	Karlsruhe	25 Feb
7.97	Ginnie	Crawford	USA	7.9.83	1		Fayetteville	11 Feb
7.97	Carolin	Nytra	GER	26.2.85	1h2		Karlsruhe	12 Feb
7.97	Alina	Talay	BLR	14.5.89	3	WI	Istanbul	10 Mar
7.98A	Janay	DeLoach	USA	12.10.85	2h1	NC	Albuquerque	26 Feb
7.99	Yekaterina	Poplavskaya	BLR	7.5.87	1	Univ Ch	Gomel	18 Feb
8.00	Nikkita	Holder	CAN	7.5.87	2		Liévin	14 Feb
8.02	Angela	Whyte	CAN	22.5.80	1		Moscow ID	3 Feb

Mark		Name		Nat	Born	Pos	Meet	Venue	Date
8.02		Tatyana (20)	Dektyareva	RUS	8.5.81	2		Karlsruhe	12 Feb
8.02		Beate	Schrott	AUT	15.4.88	1r1		Wien	18 Feb
8.02		Tatyana	Chernova	RUS	29.1.88	1s2	NC	Moskva	22 Feb
8.02		Jackie	Coward	USA	5.11.89	2h1	NCAA	Nampa	9 Mar
8.03		Dawn	Harper	USA	13.5.84	2		Fayetteville	11 Feb
8.03		Sharona	Bakker	NED	12.4.90	2h1		Karlsruhe	12 Feb
8.03		Phylicia	George	CAN	16.11.87	3		Liévin	14 Feb
8.03		Jasmin	Stowers	USA	23.9.91	1	SEC	Lexington	26 Feb
8.03A		Michaylin	Golladay	USA	10.4.88	2h2	NC	Albuquerque	26 Feb
8.03		Eline	Berings	BEL	28.5.86	2s1	WI	Istanbul	10 Mar
8.03		Sonata (30)	Tamosaityté	LTU	26.6.87	3s2	WI	Istanbul	10 Mar
8.04		Yekaterina	Galitskaya	RUS	24.2.87	1	NC	Moskva	22 Feb
8.04A		Gabby	Mayo	USA	26.1.89	3	NC	Albuquerque	26 Feb
8.04		Tiffani	McReynolds	USA	4.12.91	4	NCAA	Nampa	10 Mar
8.05		Loreal	Smith	USA	12.10.85	2h2	Gugl	Linz	2 Feb
8.05		Lucie	Skrobáková	CZE	4.1.82	4		Düsseldorf	10 Feb
8.05		Queen	Harrison	USA	10.9.88	1h1		Birmingham	3 Mar
8.06		Marzia	Caravelli	ITA	23.10.81	1		Pordenone	28 Jan
8.06		Natasha	Ruddock	JAM	25.12.89	3	Mill	New York (Arm)	11 Feb
8.07		Reina-Flor	Okori	FRA	2.5.80	1	NC	Aubière	25 Feb
8.07		Seun (40)	Adigun	NGR	3.1.87	4s1	WI	Istanbul	10 Mar
8.08		Svetlana	Topylina	RUS	6.1.85	2	NC	Moskva	22 Feb
8.08		Anne-Kathrin	Elbe	GER	24.2.87	1h2	NC	Karlsruhe	25 Feb
8.09		Adrianna	Lamalle	FRA	27.9.82	1h2	NC	Aubière	25 Feb
8.09A		Korey	Hardiway	USA	21.8.86	5	NC	Albuquerque	26 Feb
8.10		Sandra	Gomis	FRA	21.11.83	2	NC	Aubière	25 Feb
8.10A		Tamika	Robinson	USA	24.8.89	4h1	NC	Albuquerque	26 Feb
8.11		Vonette	Dixon	JAM	26.11.75	1		Clemson	27 Jan
8.11		Elisabeth	Davin	BEL	3.6.81	1		Metz	11 Feb
8.11		Angela	Morosanu	ROU	26.7.86	1	NC	Bucuresti	25 Feb
8.11		Anne (50)	Zagré	BEL	13.3.90	2	NC	Gent	26 Feb
8.11		Kierre	Beckles	BAR	21.5.90	2	SEC	Lexington	26 Feb
8.13		Marina	Tomic	SLO	30.4.83	1h1		Val-de-Reuil	18 Feb
8.13		Ivanique	Kemp	BAH	11.6.91	1		Fayetteville	2 Mar
8.13		Derval	O'Rourke	IRL	28.5.81	6s1	WI	Istanbul	10 Mar

100 METRES HURDLES

Mark		Name		Nat	Born	Pos	Meet	Venue	Date
12.35	-0.2	Sally	Pearson	AUS	19.9.86	1	OG	London (OS)	7 Aug
12.37	-0.2	Dawn	Harper	USA	13.5.84	2	OG	London (OS)	7 Aug
12.39	1.3		Pearson			1s2	OG	London (OS)	7 Aug
12.40	0.0		Pearson			1	DL	Saint-Denis	6 Jul
12.43	0.5		Harper			1	Athl	Lausanne	23 Aug
12.46	0.9		Harper			1s1	OG	London (OS)	7 Aug
12.48	-0.2	Kellie	Wells	USA	16.7.82	3	OG	London (OS)	7 Aug
12.49	0.8		Pearson			1		Melbourne	3 Mar
12.49	0.7		Pearson			1	Bisl	Oslo	7 Jun
12.51	1.5	Brigitte	Foster-Hylton	JAM	7.11.74	1		Kingston	5 May
12.51	0.6		Wells			1s3	OG	London (OS)	7 Aug
12.52	0.4		Pearson			1		Nivelles	23 Jun
12.53	0.5		Pearson			1h2	LGP	London (CP)	14 Jul
12.54	0.5		Wells			2h2	LGP	London (CP)	14 Jul
12.54	1.3	Jessica	Ennis	GBR	28.1.86	1H5	OG	London (OS)	3 Aug
12.55	1.0		Wells			1		Saint-Martin	5 May
12.56	0.7	Kristi	Castlin	USA	7.7.88	2	Bisl	Oslo	7 Jun
12.57	0.6		Wells			1	LGP	London (CP)	14 Jul
12.57	-0.1		Pearson			1h5	OG	London (OS)	6 Aug
12.58	0.6	Nevin	Yanit	TUR	16.2.86	2s3	OG	London (OS)	7 Aug
12.58	-0.2	Lolo	Jones	USA	5.8.82	4	OG	London (OS)	7 Aug
12.58	-0.2		Yanit			5	OG	London (OS)	7 Aug
12.59	0.4		Pearson			1h1	Bisl	Oslo	7 Jun
12.59	0.0	Virginia	Crawford	USA	7.9.83	2	DL	Saint-Denis	6 Jul
12.59	0.6		Pearson			2	LGP	London (CP)	14 Jul
12.59	0.3		Harper			1	WK	Zürich	30 Aug
12.60	0.1		Foster-Hylton			1	DL	Doha	11 May
12.61	0.7		Crawford			1	Spitzen	Luzern	17 Jul
12.61	-0.2		Yanit	-		1	BalkC	Eskisehir	22 Jul

Mark		Name		Nat	Born	Pos	Meet	Venue	Date
12.62	1.1		Crawford			1h1	LGP	London (CP)	14 Jul
12.62	0.5	Queen	Harrison	USA	10.9.88	2	Athl	Lausanne	23 Aug
		(31/10)							
12.64	1.5	Priscilla	Lopes-Schliep	CAN	26.8.82	2		Kingston	5 May
12.65	1.5	Tiffany	Porter	GBR	13.11.87	3		Kingston	5 May
12.65	1.3	Jessica	Zelinka	CAN	3.9.81	2H5	OG	London (OS)	3 Aug
12.65	0.6	Phylicia	George	CAN	16.11.87	3s3	OG	London (OS)	7 Aug
12.68	0.4	Christina	Manning	USA	29.5.90	1		Tucson	31 Mar
12.68	0.9	Natalya	Ivoninskaya	KAZ	22.2.85	1	NC	Almaty	19 Jun
12.69	1.3	Anastasiya	Pilipenko	KAZ	13.9.86	1		Bishkek	9 Jun
12.70	0.5	Brianna	Rollins	USA	18.8.91	2s3	NC/OT	Eugene	23 Jun
12.70	1.3	Hyleas	Fountain	USA	14.1.81	3H5	OG	London (OS)	3 Aug
12.71	1.7	Bridgette	Owens	USA	14.3.92	1s1	NCAA	Des Moines	7 Jun
		(20)							
12.71	0.6	Alina	Talay	BLR	14.5.89	1h1	OG	London (OS)	6 Aug
12.72	0.1	Reina-Flor	Okori	FRA	2.5.80	1		Nottwil	30 Jun
12.73	1.1	Danielle	Carruthers	USA	22.12.79	3h1	LGP	London (CP)	14 Jul
12.74	1.5	Carolin	Nytra	GER	26.2.85	1r1		Mannheim	9 Jun
12.75	1.2	Michelle	Perry	USA	1.5.79	1		Los Angeles (Ww)	14 Apr
12.75	0.6	Tatyana	Dektyareva	RUS	8.5.81	4s3	OG	London (OS)	7 Aug
12.77	1.3	Latoya	Greaves	JAM	31.5.86	2	NC	Kingston	1 Jul
12.78	1.7	Chelsea	Carrier-Eades	USA	21.8.89	2s1	NCAA	Des Moines	7 Jun
12.78	1.0	Nia	Ali	USA	23.10.88	2	Bailey	Edmonton	16 Jun
12.78	1.3	Shermaine	Williams	JAM	4.2.90	3	NC	Kingston	1 Jul
		(30)							
12.78	1.1	Yekaterina	Galitskaya	RUS	24.2.87	1h2	NC	Cheboksary	5 Jul
12.79	1.4	Anne	Zagré	BEL	13.3.90	1rB	Spitzen	Luzern	17 Jul
12.80A	0.7	Nikkita	Holder	CAN	7.5.87	3	NC	Calgary	30 Jun
12.81	1.7	Jackie	Coward	USA	5.11.89	3s1	NCAA	Des Moines	7 Jun
12.81	0.6	Lucie	Skrobáková	CZE	4.1.82	5s3	OG	London (OS)	7 Aug
12.82	0.6	Olga	Samylova	RUS	4.1.86	2	Znam	Zhukovskiy	17 Jun
12.82	1.4	Beate	Schrott	AUT	15.4.88	2rB	Spitzen	Luzern	17 Jul
12.83	1.0	Angela	Whyte	CAN	22.5.80	3	Bailey	Edmonton	16 Jun
12.84	2.0	Tiki	James	USA	21.10.86	1rB		Clermont	2 Jun
12.84	0.9	Yvette	Lewis	USA	16.3.85	1H	NC/OT	Eugene	29 Jun
		(40)							
12.85	1.8	Marzia	Caravelli	ITA	23.10.81	1h1		Montgeron	13 May
12.85	0.5	Candice	Price	USA	26.10.85	3s3	NC/OT	Eugene	23 Jun
12.87	1.0	Joanna	Hayes	USA	23.12.76	1	Scott	Irvine	29 Apr
12.88	1.3	Alice	Decaux	FRA	10.4.85	1	NC	Angers	16 Jun
12.88	1.3	Aïsseta	Diawara	FRA	29.6.89	2	NC	Angers	16 Jun
12.89	1.8	Sandra	Gomis	FRA	21.11.83	1		Elancourt	4 Jul
12.90	1.3	Vonette	Dixon	JAM	26.11.75	4	NC	Kingston	1 Jul
12.91	0.2	Yekaterina	Poplavskaya	BLR	7.5.87	1		Riga	5 Jun
12.91	1.7	Cindy	Roleder	GER	21.8.89	2	NC	Wattenscheid	16 Jun
12.91	-0.7	Derval	O'Rourke	IRL	28.5.81	4h4	OG	London (OS)	6 Aug
		(50)							
12.92	0.9	Jasmin	Stowers	USA	23.9.91	1		Baton Rouge	21 Apr
12.92	1.3	Indira	Spence	JAM	8.9.86	5	NC	Kingston	1 Jul
12.93	1.1	Yuliya	Kondakova	RUS	4.12.81	3	NC	Cheboksary	5 Jul
12.93A	-1.5	Perdita	Felicien	CAN	29.8.80	2h2	NC	Calgary	30 Jun
12.94	1.5	Nadine	Hildebrand	GER	20.9.87	2r1		Mannheim	9 Jun
12.94	1.3	Sara	Aerts	BEL	25.1.84	4H5	OG	London (OS)	3 Aug
12.94	-0.1	Loreal	Smith	USA	12.10.85	4	Gugl	Linz	20 Aug
12.95	1.0	Eline	Berings	BEL	28.5.86	2	NC	Bruxelles	17 Jun
12.95	0.9	Anastasiya	Soprunova	KAZ	14.1.86	3	NC	Almaty	19 Jun
12.95	1.2	LaTisha	Holden	USA	29.8.89	3h1	NC/OT	Eugene	22 Jun
		(60)							
12.95A	0.4	Lina	Flórez	COL	1.11.84	1	NG	Santander de Quilichao	13 Nov
12.96	-0.6	Vanneisha	Ivy	USA	26.10.87	1		Greensboro	21 Apr
12.96	1.0	Adrianna	Lamalle	FRA	27.9.82	1h1		Forbach	27 May
12.96	1.3	Antoinette	Nana Djimou	FRA	2.8.85	5H5	OG	London (OS)	3 Aug
12.97	0.0	April	Garner	USA	25.12.83	1r1		New York	1 Jun
12.97	1.3	Cindy	Billaud	FRA	11.3.86	5	NC	Angers	16 Jun
12.97	0.6	Kimberley	Laing	JAM	8.1.89	3h2	NC	Kingston	1 Jul
12.98	1.0		Wu Shujiao	CHN	19.6.92	1	NC	Kunshan	24 Sep
12.99	1.9	Kori	Carter	USA	6.3.92	1	Pac-12	Eugene	13 May
13.00	0.9	Donique	Flemings	USA	1.11.91	2		Baton Rouge	21 Apr
		(70)							
13.00		Nickiesha	Wilson	JAM	28.7.86	4		George Town	9 May
13.00	1.4	Monique	Gracia	USA	20.4.90	1h2		Clemson	11 May

Mark	Wind	Name		Nat	Born	Pos	Meet	Venue	Date
13.00	0.5	Katie	Nelms	USA	25.9.92	2s3	NCAA	Des Moines	7 Jun
13.00	1.3	Delloreen	Ennis	JAM	5.3.75	6	NC	Kingston	1 Jul
13.01	1.3	Andrea	Bliss	JAM	5.10.80	7	NC	Kingston	1 Jul
13.03	1.3	Kendra	Harrison	USA	18.9.92	1		Clemson	12 May
13.03	0.0	Michaylin	Golladay	USA	10.4.88	2r1		New York	1 Jun
13.04	1.9	Tiffani	McReynolds	USA	4.12.91	1		Orlando	24 Mar
13.04	1.7	Ayako	Kimura	JPN	11.6.88	1	Oda	Hiroshima	29 Apr
13.04	1.9	Marina	Tomic	SLO	30.4.83	1		Slovenska Bistrica	26 May
		(80)							
13.05	0.6	Veronica	Borsi	ITA	13.6.87	1h2		Montgeron	13 May
13.05A	-0.2	Raven	Clay	USA	5.10.90	1h1	NCAA-II	Pueblo	25 May
13.06	1.7		Chung Hye-rim	KOR	1.7.87	2	Oda	Hiroshima	29 Apr
13.06	0.6	Giulia	Pennella	ITA	27.10.89	1		Orvieto	3 Jun
13.07	-0.4	Micol	Cattaneo	ITA	14.5.82	3		Genève	2 Jun
13.07	1.1	Josanne	Lucas	TRI	14.5.84	1	NC	Port of Spain	23 Jun
13.07	1.0		Zhang Rong	CHN	5.1.83	2	NC	Kunshan	24 Sep
13.07A	0.4	Brigith	Merlano	COL	29.4.82	2	NG	Santander de Quilichao	13 Nov
13.08	1.2	Shalina	Clarke	USA	8.8.88	4		Los Angeles (Ww)	14 Apr
13.08	-0.7	Lisa	Urech	SUI	27.7.89	2		Bellinzona	5 Jun
		(90)							
13.08	1.1	Nina	Argunova	RUS	15.9.89	2h2	NC	Cheboksary	5 Jul
13.08	1.4	Aleksandra	Antonova	RUS	24.3.80	2h3	NC	Cheboksary	5 Jul
13.09	1.1	Jasmine	Edgerson	USA	6.6.91	2h1		Clemson	11 May
13.09	0.5	Shericka	Ward	USA	30.3.90	4s3	NCAA	Des Moines	7 Jun
13.09	2.0	Crystal	Bardge	USA	25.9.88	3rB		Clermont	9 Jun
13.09A	-0.6	Brianne	Theisen	CAN	18.12.88	2H	NC	Calgary	27 Jun
13.09	0.3	Maíla Paula	Machado	BRA	22.1.81	1		São Paulo	25 Aug
13.10		Yvana	Hepburn-Bailey	USA	9.11.87	1r2		Miramar FL	12 May
13.10	-0.9	Nooralotta	Neziri	FIN	9.11.92	1	NC-23	Mikkeli	12 Aug
13.11	0.6	Shanekia	Hall	JAM	27.11.88	4q1	NCAA-E	Jacksonville	26 May
		(100)							
13.11	1.0	Yekaterina	Bleskina	RUS	29.1.93	1	NC-j	Cheboksary	19 Jun

Mark	Wind	Name		Nat	Born	Date
13.13	1.7	Morgan	Snow	USA-J	26.7.93	7 Jun
13.13	1.1	Ivanique	Kemp	BAH	11.6.91	7 Jun
13.14	0.2	Sharona	Bakker	NED	12.4.90	12 May
13.15	1.7	Hitomi	Shimura	JPN	8.11.90	29 Apr
13.15	2.0	Aleesha	Barber	TRI	16.5.87	2 Jun
13.15	0.4	Eliecet	Palacios	COL	15.8.87	9 Jun
13.15	0.5	Noemi	Zbären	SUI-J	12.3.94	6 Jul
13.16	0.0	Keisha	Wallace	JAM	25.1.90	21 Apr
13.16	0.6	Sarah	Claxton	GBR	23.9.79	28 May
13.16	-0.2	Pamela	Spindler	GER	16.3.82	2 Jun
13.16	2.0	Kierre	Beckles	BAR	21.5.90	2 Jun
13.17	0.5	Cassandra	Lloyd	USA	27.1.90	26 May
13.17	-1.5	Sonata	Tamosaityté	LTU	26.6.87	3 Jun
13.17	1.3	Gnima	Faye	SEN	17.11.84	16 Jun
13.17	-0.1	Christina	Vukicevic	NOR	18.6.87	29 Jun
13.17	1.1	Anastasiya	Solovyova	RUS	18.2.85	5 Jul
13.17	0.0	Svetlana	Topylina	RUS	6.1.85	14 Jul
13.18	1.5	Lavonne	Idlette	DOM	31.10.85	13 May
13.18	0.7	Dedeh	Erawati	INA	25.5.79	26 May
13.18	1.0	Yariatou	Touré	FRA	27.12.90	27 May
13.19A	-0.2	Ladonna	Richardson	JAM	.92	25 May
13.19	2.0	Natasha	Ruddock	JAM	25.12.89	9 Jun
13.19	0.2	Clélia	Reuse	SUI	1.8.88	21 Jul
13.20	0.5	Katie	Grimes	USA	22.12.90	7 Jun
13.20	0.6	Yevgeniya	Snigur	UKR	7.3.84	8 Jun
13.20	1.7	Franziska	Hofmann	GER-J	27.3.94	16 Jun
13.20	1.0		Sun Yawei	CHN	17.10.87	24 Sep
13.21	0.4	Belkis	Milanés	CUB	16.1.90	9 Jun
13.22	1.3	Sharika	Nelvis	USA	10.5.90	12 May
13.22	0.8	Breeana	Coleman	USA	19.6.92	13 May
13.22	1.3	Valentina	Kibalnikova	UZB	16.10.90	9 Jun
13.22	0.0	Mariya	Aglitskaya	RUS	20.6.91	5 Jul
13.22	0.7	Karolina	Tyminska	POL	4.10.84	3 Aug
13.23	1.9	Lauren	Blackburn	USA	18.11.91	13 May
13.23	-0.2	Andrea	Miller	NZL	13.3.82	2 Jun
13.23	-0.2	Aurore	Ruet	FRA	14.2.84	6 Jun
13.23	0.0	Ilona	Dudko	UKR	26.6.91	12 Jun
13.24	-0.1	Louise	Wood	GBR	13.5.83	5 May
13.24	-0.1	Nichole	Denby	USA	10.10.82	20 May
13.24	1.9	Janice	Jackson	USA	30.10.91	26 May
13.25	1.3	Falesha	Ankton	USA	8.6.87	2 Jun
13.25	1.8	Irina	Shevchenko	RUS	2.9.75	14 Jul
13.25	0.9	Lyudmyla	Yosypenko	UKR	24.9.84	3 Aug
13.26	1.1	Tenaya	Jones	USA	22.3.89	21 Apr
13.26	0.0	Yekaterina	Gubina	RUS	27.11.85	14 Jul
13.26	0.9	Lilli	Schwarzkopf	GER	28.8.83	3 Aug
13.27	1.3	Janay	DeLoach	USA	12.10.85	21 Apr
13.27	0.0	Hanna	Platitsyna	UKR	1.1.87	12 Jun
13.28	1.8	Celriece	Law	USA	2.9.86	13 Apr
13.28	1.4	Uhunoma	Osazuwa	NGR	23.11.87	26 May
13.28	1.1	Victoria	Schreibeis	AUT	9.1.79	7 Jun
13.28	1.7	Serita	Solomon	GBR	1.3.90	17 Jun
13.28	0.1	Lucimara	da Silva	BRA	10.7.85	28 Jun
13.29	0.2	Jesica	Ejesieme	USA	20.5.92	12 May
13.29	1.7	Ashley	Helsby	GBR	1.7.90	17 Jun
13.29	0.3	Elisa	Leinonen	FIN	27.1.87	29 Jun
13.30	-0.1	Giselle	de Albuquerque	BRA	11.7.88	20 May
13.31	1.2	Vashti	Thomas	USA	21.4.90	27 Apr
13.31	0.3	Stefanie	Saumweber	GER	5.3.88	24 May
13.31	1.6	Antonia	Werner	GER	18.1.88	9 Jun
13.32A	0.0	Samantha	Elliott	JAM	3.2.92	25 May
13.32	1.6	Kendra	Newton	USA	3.8.87	8 Jul
13.32	2.0	Anna	Melnychenko	UKR	24.4.83	3 Aug
13.33		Tamika	Robinson	USA	24.8.89	31 Mar
13.33	0.0	Marlen	Affentranger	SUI	28.3.87	5 May
13.33	1.9	Dalilah	Muhammad	USA	7.2.90	26 May
13.33	1.5	Sasha	Wallace	USA-Y	21.9.95	2 Jun
13.33	1.6	Anne-Kathrin	Elbe	GER	24.2.87	9 Jun
13.34	0.0	Jasmine	Chaney	USA	25.8.88	24 Mar
13.34	1.1	Karessa	Farley	BAR	8.12.88	13 May
13.34	1.9	Keia	Pinnick	USA	23.1.91	13 May
13.34	1.4	Francesca	Doveri	ITA	21.12.82	19 May
13.34	0.0	Tatyana	Chernova	RUS	29.1.88	26 May
13.34	1.3	Urszula	Bhebhe	POL	27.2.92	17 Jun
13.35	2.0	Ellen	Sprunger	SUI	5.8.86	3 Jun
13.36	0.0	Brittany	Hyter	USA	24.10.89	21 Apr
13.36	2.0	Solène	Hamelin	FRA	9.12.88	20 May
13.36	1.3	Elisabeth	Davin	BEL	3.6.81	28 May
13.36	0.7	Chantae	McMillan	USA	1.5.88	29 Jun
13.36	0.3	Grit	Sadeiko	EST	29.7.89	29 Jun
13.36	0.0	Matilda	Bogdanoff	FIN	8.10.90	1 Sep
13.37	0.0	Racquel	Farquharson	JAM	9.7.90	21 Apr
13.37	1.8	Ugonna	Ndu	USA	27.6.91	13 May
13.37	1.1	Demeeka	Jones	USA	4.10.88	13 May
13.37	0.4	Ivana	Loncarek	CRO	8.4.91	5 Jun
13.37	0.9	Kristina	Savitskaya	RUS	10.6.91	3 Aug
13.38A	-0.2	Korey	Hardiway	USA	21.8.86	14 Apr
13.38	-1.2	Gabby	Mayo	USA	26.1.89	12 May

Mark	Wind	Name	Nat	Born	Pos	Meet	Venue	Date
13.38	1.1	Sade-Mariah Greenidge	BAR-J	14.10.93				13 May
13.38	-0.9	Rosina Hodde	NED	10.2.83				27 May
13.38	1.0	Christie Gordon	CAN	5.10.86				16 Jun
13.38	-0.4	Isabelle Pedersen	NOR	27.1.92				29 Jun
13.38	0.1	Seun Adigun	NGR	3.1.87				6 Jul
13.39	1.2	Kendell Williams	USA-Y	14.6.95				4 May
13.39	1.4	Michelle Jenneke	AUS-J	23.6.93				23 Jun
13.39	1.3	Airi Ito	JPN	5.7.89				24 Jun
13.39	0.0	Caroline Lundahl	SWE	16.10.91				1 Sep

(198)

Doubtful Timing: 12.97 Shericka Ward USA 30.3.90 1 Holmdel 16 Jun

Wind assisted

Mark	Wind	Name	Nat	Born	Pos	Meet	Venue	Date
12.47	3.0	Tiffany Porter	GBR	13.11.87	1		Gainesville	21 Apr
12.48	3.8	Kristi Castlin	USA	7.7.88	1		Clermont	2 Jun
12.57	3.0	Christina Manning	USA	29.5.90	2		Gainesville	21 Apr
12.60A	4.5	Brianna Rollins	USA	18.8.91	1	NACAC	Irapuato	7 Jul
12.61	2.5	Porter			1h1		Gainesville	21 Apr
12.61	3.0	Wells			3		Gainesville	21 Apr
12.65	3.8	Shermaine Williams	JAM	4.2.90	2		Clermont	2 Jun
12.70	2.5	Michelle Perry	USA	1.5.79	1	MSR	Walnut	21 Apr
12.72	2.5	Joanna Hayes	USA	23.12.76	2	MSR	Walnut	21 Apr
12.74	2.5	Yvette Lewis	USA	16.3.85	3	MSR	Walnut	21 Apr
12.74	3.4	Nikkita Holder	CAN	7.5.87	1		Port of Spain	19 May
12.75	2.5	Angela Whyte	CAN	22.5.80	4	MSR	Walnut	21 Apr
12.78	3.3	Nichole Denby	USA	10.10.82	1	TexR	Austin	31 Mar
12.79	3.4	Candice Price	USA	26.10.85	2		Port of Spain	19 May
12.80A	5.5	Indira Spence	JAM	8.9.86	1	NCAA II	Pueblo	26 May
12.80	3.8	Vonette Dixon	JAM	26.11.75	4		Clermont	2 Jun
12.80	3.8	Perdita Felicien	CAN	29.8.80	5		Clermont	2 Jun
12.81	2.5	Shalina Clarke	USA	8.8.88	1rB	MSR	Walnut	21 Apr
12.82	4.3	Yuliya Kondakova	RUS	4.12.81	3		Madrid	7 Jul
12.84	2.6	Josanne Lucas	TRI	14.5.84	2h1		Clermont	2 Jun
12.85	2.4	Yekaterina Poplavskaya	BLR	7.5.87	1h2	PNG	Turku	13 Jun
12.86	3.0	Michaylin Golladay	USA	10.4.88	1		Clemson	5 May
12.87	2.3	Donique Flemings	USA	1.11.91	1	Big 12	Manhattan, KS	13 May
12.97	2.2	Tiffani McReynolds	USA	4.12.91	2	TexR	Austin	31 Mar
12.97	2.2	Keisha Wallace	JAM	25.1.90	3	TexR	Austin	31 Mar
12.97	3.4	Kierre Beckles	BAR	21.5.90	3		Port of Spain	19 May
12.98	3.4	Natasha Ruddock	JAM	25.12.89	4		Port of Spain	19 May
12.99	2.2	Katie Grimes	USA	22.12.90	1		Lubbock	14 Apr
12.99	2.5	Sharika Nelvis	USA	10.5.90	1q3	NCAA-W	Austin	26 May
13.02	2.5	Vashti Thomas	USA	21.4.90	2rB	MSR	Walnut	21 Apr
13.02	3.2	Kendra Harrison	USA	18.9.92	1h1	NCAA-E	Jacksonville	25 May
13.03	2.1	Veronica Borsi	ITA	13.6.87	3		Montgeron	13 May
13.04	4.0	Morgan Snow	USA-J	26.7.93	2q2	NCAA-W	Austin	26 May
13.09	3.3	Tenaya Jones	USA	22.3.89	4	TexR	Austin	31 Mar
13.09	4.0	Demeeka Jones	USA	4.10.88	3q2	NCAA-W	Austin	26 May
13.12A	5.5	Samantha Elliott	JAM	3.2.92				26 May
13.13A	5.5	Ladonna Richardson	JAM	.92				26 May
13.13	2.2	Seun Adigun	NGR	3.1.87				20 Jun
13.16	3.1	Precious Nwokey	USA	27.4.89				5 May
13.16	2.2	Uhunoma Osazuwa	NGR	23.11.87				20 Jun
13.21	3.3	Kim Francis	USA	6.1.92				25 May
13.21A	4.5	Ashlea Maddex	CAN	16.12.92				7 Jul
13.22	2.1	Traci Hicks	USA-J	29.1.94				21 Apr
13.22	2.1	Yekaterina Gubina	RUS	27.11.85				26 Jun
13.25	2.5	Brittany Hyter	USA	24.10.89				26 May
13.25	2.4	Antonia Werner	GER	18.1.88				9 Jun
13.26	2.3	Serita Solomon	GBR	1.3.90				17 Jun
13.27	3.1	Karessa Farley	BAR	8.12.88				25 May
13.27	4.1	Solène Hamelin	FRA	9.12.88				7 Jul
13.28	3.3	Christie Gordon	CAN	5.10.86				31 Mar
13.29	2.9	Racquel Farquharson	JAM	9.7.90				25 May
13.30	6.6	Trinity Wilson	USA-J	4.9.94				9 Jun
13.30	2.2	Jessica Ohanaja	NGR	6.12.85				20 Jun
13.31A	2.3	Dior Hall	USA-Y	2.1.96				17 May
13.32	3.6	Krystal Bodie	BAH	3.1.90				25 May
13.33	3.8	Ladonna Richardson	USA-J					5 May
13.34	2.4	Jade Barber	USA-J	4.4.93				6 May
13.34	2.9	Mariah Georgetown	USA	14.3.92				25 May
13.34A	4.5	Marissa Smith	USA	2.4.87				7 Jul
13.35	3.2	Christienne Linton	USA	27.7.91				25 May
13.36	4.1	Mathilde Raibaut	FRA	18.4.92				7 Jul
13.37	3.1	Gabby Mayo	USA	26.1.89				28 Apr
13.37	3.4	Richelle Farley	USA	19.8.91				25 May
13.37	3.1	Leslie Aririguzo	USA	19.8.90				25 May
13.37A	5.5	Rosemarie Carty	JAM	26.2.90				26 May
13.37	3.9	Ellinore Hallin	SWE	12.8.87				28 Jul
13.38A	3.2	Jessica Flax	USA	4.9.90				6 Jul
13.39	2.9	Breana Norman	USA	14.9.92				25 May
13.39A	5.5	Lexus Williams	USA	26.12.91				26 May
13.40	2.9	Clémence Vifquin	FRA	9.6.86				5 Jul
13.40	2.6	Andreia Felisberto	POR	22.6.86				8 Jul
13.40mx	2.4	Shannon McCann	AUS	20.12.88				7 Dec
13.41	2.9	Alexandria Johnson	USA-J	19.12.92				21 Apr
13.41	2.5	Lauren Smith	USA	27.8.81				21 Apr
13.43	3.7	Suzuka Akai	JPN	25.9.90				12 May
13.43	3.2	Layne Baggett	USA	1.10.90				25 May
13.43	2.5	Shaquana Logan	USA	4.1.91				26 May
13.44	2.9	Chene Townsend	JAM	12.12.90				6 May
13.45	2.9	Kaila Barber	USA	4.4.93				6 May
13.46	2.8	Yilian Durruthy	CUB	30.1.90				23 Mar
13.46	2.4	Keenan Davis	JAM-J	5.2.93				30 Mar
13.47	2.9	Madalayne Smith	USA	4.4.92				6 May
13.47	2.2	Chelsea Stephen	USA	25.11.91				25 May
13.47	2.8	Mónica Lopes	POR	18.1.86				10 Jun
13.47A	4.5	Kenrisha Brathwaite	BAR	28.4.92				7 Jul
13.48	3.1	Jessie Gaines	USA	12.8.90				7 Jul
13.49	2.2	Jana Koresová	CZE	8.4.81				27 May

Best at low altitude

12.83 1.1 Holder 1 Toronto 11 Jul
12.93 0.0 Felicien 6 DL Saint-Denis 6 Jul
12.80w 3.8 Spence 3 Clermont 2 Jun
13.17 -0.3 Flórez 6 Aug | 13.21 -0.7 Merlano 6 Aug
13.19 1.6 R Clay 8 Jul | 13.30 -0.4 Theisen 7 Jun | 13.29w 3.4 Maddex 19 May
13.16w 4.6 3 May | 13.21w 2.4 7 Apr | 13.39w 4.0 M Smith 26 May

Hand timing: 13.2 Belkis Milanés CUB 16.1.90 1 La Habana 10 Feb and 13.1w 1h2 NC La Hanaba 22 Mar

Mark	Wind	Name		Nat	Born	Pos	Meet	Venue	Date
		JUNIORS							
13.11	1.0	Yekaterina	Bleskina	RUS	29.1.93	1	NC-j	Cheboksary	19 Jun
		13.24	0.3 1s1 WJ	Barcelona	14 Jul				
13.13	1.7	Morgan	Snow	USA	26.7.93	5s1	NCAA	Des Moines	7 Jun
		13.26	-1.8 1 NC-j	Bloomington	16 Jun				
13.15	0.5	Noemi	Zbären	SUI	12.3.94	1s2	NC	Bern	6 Jul
		13.25	-0.6 1h3 NC	Bern	6 Jul	13.29	0.1 2	Nottwil	30 Jun
		13.27	-0.3 2 NC	Bern	7 Jul				
13.20	1.7	Franziska	Hofmann	GER	27.3.94	5	NC	Wattenscheid	16 Jun
		13.28	1.4 1h1	Mannheim	23 Jun	10 performances by 4 women to 13.29.			
13.33	1.5	Sasha	Wallace	USA-Y	21.9.95	1		Clovis	2 Jun
13.38	1.1	Sade-Mariah	Greenidge	BAR	14.10.93	5	Conf USA	New Orleans	13 May
13.39	1.2	Kendell	Williams	USA-Y	14.6.95	1h1		Albany GA	4 May
13.39	1.4	Michelle	Jenneke	AUS-J	23.6.93	2		Mannheim	23 Jun
13.40	-1.1		Wang Dou	CHN	18.5.93	1s2	WJ	Barcelona	14 Jul
13.41	1.5	Trinity	Wilson (10)	USA	4.9.94	1h1		Stanford	7 Apr
13.41	0.4	Alexandra	Burghardt	GER	28.4.94	1J	WK	Zürich	30 Aug
13.43	1.3	Karolina	Koleczek	POL	15.1.93	2	NC	Bielsko-Biala	17 Jun
13.45	0.0	Brea	Buchanan	USA	8.1.93	1h4	NC-j	Bloomington IN	16 Jun
13.45	-1.8	Dior	Hall	USA-Y	2.1.96	2	NC-j	Bloomington IN	16 Jun
13.48	-0.7	Katarina	Johnson-Thompson	GBR	9.1.93	2h3	WJ	Barcelona	13 Jul
13.49	1.9	Melia	Cox	USA	23.11.93	7	Pac-12	Eugene	13 May
13.50	-0.1	Nadine	Visser	NED-Y	9.2.95	1	NC-j	Breda	3 Jun
13.53	1.3	Alicia	Perkins	USA	19.8.93	2rB		Fort Worth	16 Mar
13.55	-1.8	Jade	Barber	USA	4.4.93	4	NC-j	Bloomington	16 Jun
13.56	0.1	Chrisdale	McCarthy (20)	JAM	12.4.94	5		Kingston	14 Apr
13.56	-2.4	Jonna	Berghem	FIN	25.2.93	6	WJ	Barcelona	15 Jul

Wind assisted 5 performances by 2 women to 13.28

Mark	Wind	Name		Nat	Born	Pos	Meet	Venue	Date
13.04	4.0	Morgan	Snow	USA-J	26.7.93	2q2	NCAA-W	Austin	26 May
		13.14	2.3 3 Big 12	Manhattan	13 May	13.20	5.3 2h3 NCAA-W	Austin	25 May
		13.16	3.8 2h2 Big 12	Manhattan	12 May				
13.22	2.1	Traci	Hicks	USA	29.1.94	1	MSR-HS	Walnut	21 Apr
13.30	6.6	Trinity	Wilson	USA	4.9.94	1	G.West	Folsom	9 Jun
13.31A	2.3	Dior	Hall	USA-Y	2.1.96	1h2		Lakewood	17 May
13.33	3.8	Ladonna	Richardson	USA		1h2		Emporia	5 May
13.34	2.4	Jade	Barber	USA	4.4.93	2		Tampa	6 May
13.41	2.9	Alexandria	Johnson	USA	19.12.92	1		Gainesville	21 Apr
13.46	2.4	Keenan	Davis	JAM	5.2.93	1h2		Kingston	30 Mar
13.53	2.4	Megan	Simmonds	JAM	18.3.94	2h2		Kingston	30 Mar
13.53	2.2	Mako	Fukube	JPN-Y	28.10.95	1		Hiroshima	17 Jun

400 METRES HURDLES

Mark	Name		Nat	Born	Pos	Meet	Venue	Date
52.70	Natalya	Antyukh	RUS	26.6.81	1	OG	London (OS)	8 Aug
52.77	Lashinda	Demus	USA	10.3.83	2	OG	London (OS)	8 Aug
53.33		Antyukh			1s1	OG	London (OS)	6 Aug
53.38	Zuzana	Hejnová	CZE	19.12.86	3	OG	London (OS)	8 Aug
53.40		Antyukh			1	NC	Cheboksary	4 Jul
53.49	Kaliese	Spencer	JAM	6.5.87	1	Athl	Lausanne	23 Aug
53.62		Hejnová			2s1	OG	London (OS)	6 Aug
53.66		Spencer			4	OG	London (OS)	8 Aug
53.69		Spencer			1	VD	Bruxelles	7 Sep
53.74	Melaine	Walker	JAM	1.1.83	2	Athl	Lausanne	23 Aug
53.77	Irina	Davydova	RUS	27.5.88	1	EC	Helsinki	29 Jun
53.77	Perri	Shakes-Drayton	GBR	21.12.88	1	LGP	London (CP)	13 Jul
53.78		Spencer			1	DL	Birmingham	26 Aug
53.83		Shakes-Drayton			3	Athl	Lausanne	23 Aug
53.87		Davydova			1		Sochi	27 May
53.89		Shakes-Drayton			2	VD	Bruxelles	7 Sep
53.90		Antyukh			1h2	OG	London (OS)	5 Aug
53.92	Georganne	Moline	USA	6.3.90	5	OG	London (OS)	8 Aug
53.96		Hejnová			4	Athl	Lausanne	23 Aug
53.96		Hejnová			1h1	OG	London (OS)	5 Aug
53.98		Demus			1	NC/OT	Eugene	1 Jul
54.02		Spencer			2h2	OG	London (OS)	5 Aug
54.04	Vania	Stambolova	BUL	28.11.83	1		Izmir	20 May
54.08		Stambolova			1	EAF	Bydgoszcz	3 Jun
54.08		Shakes-Drayton			2	DL	Birmingham	26 Aug
54.08		Demus			1s2	OG	London (OS)	6 Aug
54.09		Hejnová			3	VD	Bruxelles	7 Sep
54.12		Hejnová			1	Herc	Monaco	20 Jul

Mark	Wind	Name		Nat	Born	Pos	Meet	Venue	Date
54.14			Hejnová			3	DL	Birmingham	26 Aug
54.15			Stambolova			1	GS	Ostrava	25 May
	(30/9)								
54.21		T'Erea	Brown (10)	USA	24.10.89	3s1	OG	London (OS)	6 Aug
54.24		Denisa	Rosolová	CZE	21.8.86	2	EC	Helsinki	29 Jun
54.35		Anna	Yaroshchuk	UKR	24.11.89	3	EC	Helsinki	29 Jun
54.40		Joke	Odumosu	NGR	27.10.87	1s3	OG	London (OS)	6 Aug
54.78		Yelena	Churakova ¶	RUS	16.12.86	5	EC	Helsinki	29 Jun
54.81		Angela	Morosanu	ROU	26.7.86	1	IntC	Bucuresti	8 Jun
54.89		Yadisleidy	Pedroso	CUB	28.1.87	1	CAA	Brazzaville	10 Jun
54.96		Eilidh	Child	GBR	20.2.87	1		Genève	2 Jun
54.98		Hanna	Titimets	UKR	5.3.89	1	NC	Yalta	14 Jun
55.01		Tiffany	Williams	USA	5.2.83	2		Istanbul	9 Jun
55.18		Latosha	Wallace	USA	25.3.85	1	GP	Belém	6 May
	(20)								
55.20		Elodie	Ouédraogo	BEL	27.2.81	4s1	OG	London (OS)	6 Aug
55.22		Cassandra	Tate	USA	11.9.90	1	NCAA	Des Moines	8 Jun
55.22		Vera	Barbosa	POR	13.1.89	3h3	OG	London (OS)	5 Aug
55.28		Turquoise	Thompson	USA	31.7.91	2	NCAA	Des Moines	8 Jun
55.32		Queen	Harrison	USA	10.9.88	3	DL	New York	9 Jun
55.36A		Wanda	Theron	RSA	30.7.88	1		Pretoria	5 May
55.37		Nicole	Leach	USA	18.7.87	4	DL	New York	9 Jun
55.41		Hayat	Lambarki	MAR	18.5.88	2	AfrC	Porto Novo	1 Jul
55.44		Anna	Jesien	POL	10.12.78	4h2	OG	London (OS)	5 Aug
55.45		Lauren	Boden	AUS	3.8.88	1		Sydney	18 Feb
	(30)								
55.47			Huang Xiaoxiao	CHN	3.3.83	1h2	NGP	Zhaoqing	14 Apr
55.48		Anastasiya	Ott	RUS	7.9.88	2		Sochi	27 May
55.50		Nickiesha	Wilson	JAM	28.7.86	3	NC	Kingston	29 Jun
55.54		Manuela	Gentili	ITA	7.2.78	1rB	Spitzen	Luzern	17 Jul
55.55		Ellen	Wortham	USA	5.1.90	1	SEC	Baton Rouge	13 May
55.58		Christine	Spence	USA	25.11.81	1		Los Angeles (Ww)	2 Jun
55.64		Ristananna	Tracey	JAM	5.9.92	4	NC	Kingston	29 Jun
55.68		Sara	Petersen	DEN	9.4.87	1	Kuso	Szczecin	21 Jul
55.70		Dominique	Darden	USA	9.12.83	3s2	NC/OT	Eugene	29 Jun
55.71A		Sarah	Wells	CAN	10.11.89	1	NC	Calgary	30 Jun
	(40)								
55.71		Tatyana	Azarova	KAZ	2.12.85	1		Almaty	30 Jun
55.78		Zuzana	Bergrová	CZE	24.11.84	4s2	EC	Helsinki	28 Jun
55.85		Satomi	Kubokura	JPN	27.4.82	5h5	OG	London (OS)	5 Aug
55.87		Tina	Matusinska	POL	12.7.88	2	NC	Bielsko-Biala	16 Jun
55.91		Janeil	Bellille	TRI	18.6.89	1	TexR	Austin	31 Mar
55.92		Josanne	Lucas	TRI	14.5.84	1		Clermont	9 Jun
55.93		Jessie	Barr	IRL	24.7.89	4s1	EC	Helsinki	28 Jun
55.97		Phara	Anacharsis	FRA	17.12.83	1	NC	Angers	17 Jun
55.99		Raasin	McIntosh	LBR	29.4.82	3	AfrC	Porto Novo	1 Jul
56.03		Jasmine	Chaney	USA	25.8.88	1	Sun Angel	Tempe	7 Apr
	(50)								
56.09		Shevon	Stoddart	JAM	21.11.82	2h2	NC	Kingston	28 Jun
56.10		Danielle	Dowie	JAM	5.5.92	1	Big 12	Manhattan KS	13 May
56.13		Natalya	Asanova	UZB	29.11.89	1	NCp	Tashkent	18 Apr
56.16		Jailma	de Lima	BRA	31.12.86	1	NC	São Paulo	1 Jul
56.16		Janet	Lawless	RSA	15.5.85	6		Genève	2 Jun
56.18		Jennifer	Grossarth	USA	18.5.83	6s1	NC/OT	Eugene	29 Jun
56.19		Dalilah	Muhammad	USA	7.2.90	2s1	NCAA	Des Moines	6 Jun
56.19		Sharolyn	Scott	CRC	27.10.84	1rB		Rehlingen	28 May
56.21		Tomomi	Yoneda	JPN	11.8.90	1s1	NC	Osaka	9 Jun
56.24		Lucimar	Teodoro	BRA	1.5.81	2	NC	São Paulo	1 Jul
	(60)								
56.26		Aleksandra	Kuzina	KAZ	26.12.90	2		Almaty	30 Jun
56.27		Tina	Kron	GER	3.4.81	3		Oordegem	26 May
56.30		Jernail	Hayes	USA	8.7.88	1		Salem	10 May
56.34		Thandi	Stewart	USA	19.12.91	4h1	NC/OT	Eugene	28 Jun
56.37		Mame Fatou	Faye	SEN	19.8.86	1	NC	Dakar	15 Jul
56.38		Svetlana	Gogoleva	RUS	11.12.86	3		Sochi	27 May
56.40		Kou	Luogon	LBR	11.6.84	4	AfrC	Porto Novo	1 Jul
56.41		Kianna	Elahi	USA	24.8.90	2	Big 12	Manhattan KS	13 May
56.47		Vera	Rudakova	RUS	20.3.92	1		Lapinlahti	8 Jul
56.50A		Lucy	Jaramillo	ECU	23.2.83	1		Calí	24 Jun
	(70)								
56.50A		Fawn	Dorr	CAN	19.4.87	2	NC	Calgary	30 Jun

Mark	Name		Nat	Born	Pos	Meet	Venue	Date
56.54	Meghan	Beesley	GBR	15.11.89	1		Los Angeles (Ww)	14 Apr
56.55	Lamia	Lhabz	MAR	19.5.84	6		Rabat	27 May
56.57	Miyabi	Tago	JPN	15.7.88	3		Fukuroi	3 May
56.58	Egle	Staisiunaite	LTU	30.9.88	4h2	EC	Helsinki	27 Jun
56.60	Axelle	Dauwens	BEL	1.12.90	5		Oordegem	26 May
56.62	Sema	Apak	TUR	17.8.85	2		Ankara	6 Jun
56.62	Janeive	Russell	JAM-J	14.11.93	1	WJ	Barcelona	14 Jul
56.63	Anastasiya	Korshunova	RUS	17.5.92	6	NC	Cheboksary	4 Jul
56.65		Yang Qi	CHN	13.4.91	1		Fuzhou	24 Jun
	(80)							
56.67	London	Finley	USA	1.2.90	1		Tampa	6 May
56.68	Sayaka	Aoki	JPN	15.12.86	1		Fukuoka	22 Sep
56.70	Ayla	Smith	USA	16.5.88	6s2	NC/OT	Eugene	29 Jun
56.72	Kendra	Harrison	USA	18.9.92	1q2	NCAA-E	Jacksonville	25 May
56.74	Joanna	Currie	USA	9.10.87	1		Winston-Salem	17 Mar
56.76	Olesya	Tsaranok	RUS	3.7.89	3h3	NC	Cheboksary	3 Jul
56.78	Asia	Washington	USA	25.2.88	2		Princeton	21 Apr
56.79	Maureen	Maiyo	KEN	28.5.85	6	AfrC	Porto Novo	1 Jul
56.81	Darya	Korableva	RUS	23.5.88	4		Sochi	27 May
56.82		Deng Xiaoqing	CHN	13.6.89	2	NC	Kunshan	23 Sep
	(90)							
56.87	Christina	Holland	USA	5.8.91	3	Big 12	Manhattan KS	13 May
56.87A	Noelle	Montcalm	CAN	3.4.88	3	NC	Calgary	30 Jun
56.99	Polina	Bordyugova	RUS	18.8.91	8	NC	Cheboksary	4 Jul
57.04	Déborah	Rodríguez	URU	2.12.92	7h5	OG	London (OS)	5 Aug
57.05A	Princesa	Oliveros	COL	10.8.75	2		Calí	24 Jun
57.11	Shiori	Miki	JPN	25.12.91	1		Osaka	13 May
57.11A	Annerie	Ebersohn	RSA	9.8.90	2	Univ Ch	Johannesburg	28 Apr
57.12	Latoya	Griffith	BAR	7.2.90	1	Big 10	Madison	13 May
57.14	Nikolina	Horvat	CRO	18.9.86	1		Ljubljana	7 Jun
57.14	Aurélie	Chaboudez	FRA-J	9.5.93	2	WJ	Barcelona	14 Jul
	(100)							

Mark	Name		Nat	Born	Date	Mark	Name		Nat	Born	Date
57.15	Leslie	Njoku	NGR	30.5.89	12 May	57.67	Rushell	Clayton	JAM	18.10.92	14 Apr
57.15	Christine	Merrill	SRI	20.8.87	5 Aug	57.68	Haruka	Shibata	JPN	13.1.91	10 Jun
57.15	Yolanda	Osana	DOM	11.8.87	8 Jun	57.69	Kiani	Profit	USA	18.2.90	6 Apr
57.16	Kemi	Adekoya	NGR-Y	6.1.96	14 Jun	57.70	Irina	Reshetkina	RUS	30.1.89	3 Jul
57.19	Fernanda	Tavares	BRA	2.4.84	1 Jul	57.71		Xiao Xia	CHN	6.6.91	23 Sep
57.20	Aneta	Jakóbczak	POL	3.7.85	16 Jun	57.71	Ryann	Krais	USA	21.3.90	13 May
57.24	Nusrat	Ceesay	GAM	18.3.81	20 Apr	57.72	Joanna	Linkiewicz	POL	2.5.90	2 Sep
57.25A	Michelle	Cumberbatch	BAH	20.9.88	26 May	57.73	Manami	Kira	JPN	23.10.91	9 Jun
57.29	Chante'sean	White	USA	14.10.90	12 May	57.74	Frederike	Hogrebe	GER	19.2.91	7 Jun
57.29	Kaila	Barber	USA-J	4.4.93	13 Jul	57.76	Donique	Flemings	USA	1.11.91	7 Apr
57.30	Jesica	Ejesieme	USA	20.5.92	13 May	57.78	Stine	Tomb	NOR	27.8.86	7 Jun
57.31	Justine	Kinney	IRL	6.4.88	2 Jun	57.79	Liliane Cristina	Barbosa	BRA	8.10.87	12 May
57.32A	Yanique	Haye	JAM	22.3.90	26 May	57.80	Leslie	Farmer	USA	18.4.90	12 May
57.33	Nikita	Tracey	JAM	18.9.90	26 May	57.81	Anastasiya	Buldakova	BLR	29.4.88	6 Jul
57.33	Elif	Yildirim	TUR	11.2.90	27 May	57.81	MacKenzie	Hill	USA	5.1.86	5 May
57.33	Jaelynn	Pryor	USA	6.6.92	13 May	57.82	Valeriya	Khramova	RUS	13.8.92	3 Jul
57.34	Keia	Pinnick	USA	23.1.91	20 Apr	57.82	Taylor	Farquhar	CAN-J	2.9.94	13 Jul
57.34	Vilde	Svortevik	NOR-J	18.5.94	13 Jul	57.83	Chelsea	Carrier-Eades	USA	21.8.89	6 May
57.35	Nyjah	Cousar	USA	23.5.91	13 May	57.83	Frida	Persson	SWE	14.12.89	27 Jun
57.35	Olena	Kolesnychenko	UKR-J	3.6.93	13 Jul	57.85	Ghofrane	Mohammad #	SYR	6.6.89	11 May
57.36		Quach Thi Lan	VIE-Y	18.10.95	4 Oct	57.85	Angelica	Weaver	USA	11.7.92	13 May
57.36	Claudia	Wehrsen	GER	18.10.84	28 May	57.89	Marina	Reznikova	RUS	10.6.91	21 Jul
57.39	Francesca	Doveri	ITA	21.12.82	8 Jul	57.90	Anastasiya	Sinkevich	RUS	4.3.90	21 Jul
57.40	Alexa	Duling	USA	11.7.90	25 May	57.91	Crystal	Bardge	USA	25.9.88	26 May
57.41	Christiane	Klopsch	GER	21.8.90	19 May	57.91		Ruan Zhuofen	CHN	21.1.85	24 Jun
57.41	Lyndsay	Pekin	AUS	13.6.86	18 Feb	57.92	Jenea	McCammon	USA	9.6.91	5 May
57.41	Marzena	Koscielniak	POL	28.12.89	15 Jun	57.92	Stacia	Weatherford	USA	28.5.91	13 May
57.42	Megan	Duncan	USA	28.12.88	21 Apr	57.93	Dotrine	Jacobs	USA	16.8.92	5 May
57.42	Sparkle	McKnight	TRI	21.12.91	31 Mar	57.93	Zalika	Dixon	USA		26 May
57.43	Elaine	Paixão	BRA	15.6.88	12 May	57.95	Özge	Akin	TUR	17.6.85	6 Jun
57.44	Shamier	Little	USA-Y	20.3.95	16 Jun	57.95	Caryl	Granville	GBR	24.9.89	28 Jul
57.45	Kübra	Sesli	TUR-J	1.11.93	13 Jul	57.96	Jess	Gulli	AUS	19.3.88	15 Apr
57.46	Stephanie	McPherson	JAM	25.11.88	17 Mar	57.97	Miki	Sawada	JPN	20.6.86	3 May
57.46	LaToya	James	USA	18.1.89	9 May	57.98	Kaymarie	Jones	JAM	3.3.90	26 Apr
57.48	Natalie	Morerod	USA	6.10.91	13 May	57.98	Ilona	Punkkinen	FIN	28.10.82	2 Sep
57.49	Valeriya	Znamenskaya	RUS	25.3.90	15 Jul	57.99	Andrea	Sutherland	JAM	26.5.88	31 May
57.56	Yevgeniya	Isakova	RUS	27.11.78	21 Jun	58.00	Fabienne	Kohlmann	GER	6.11.89	7 Jun
57.59	Ugonna	Ndu	USA	27.6.91	6 Apr	58.00	Marina	Boika	BLR	2.11.88	2 Jun
57.60	Kori	Carter	USA	6.3.92	29 Apr	58.02	Sara	Klein	AUS-J	19.5.94	17 Mar
57.60	Ese	Okoro	GBR	4.7.90	24 Jun	58.03	Kendra	Harrison	USA	18.9.92	6 Jun
57.61	Emma	Millard	FIN	10.8.90	27 Jun	58.04	Sage	Watson	CAN-J	20.6.94	13 Jul
57.65	Christine	Salterberg	GER-J	9.6.94	24 Jun	58.07	Laura Natalí	Sotomayor	ESP	22.4.86	8 Jul
57.66	Angele	Cooper	USA/LBR	3.11.90	25 May	58.07	Amaliya	Sharoyan	ARM	19.6.88	27 May

Mark	Name		Nat	Born	Pos	Meet	Venue	Date
58.07	Tessa	Consedine	AUS-Y	15.8.95				17 Mar
58.09	Nicole	Dumpson	USA	26.10.82				6 May
58.09	Magdalena	Mendoza	VEN	20.10.90				23 Sep
58.09	Iris	Campbell	USA	16.7.91				25 May
58.11	Lorraine	King	USA	28.2.87				5 May
58.11	Emel	Sanli	TUR-J	7.7.93				10 Jun
58.12	Airi	Nishino	JPN	26.3.92				9 Jun
58.13	Anastasiya	Lebid	UKR-J	30.10.93				13 Jul
58.14	Kayla	Sanchez	USA	29.1.90				25 May
58.15A	Anisia	Castro	MEX	5.3.86				11 May
58.16	Lucie	Slanícková	SVK	8.11.88				19 May
58.18	Sarah	Carli	AUS-J	5.9.94				17 Mar
58.19	Cassandra	Blake	JAM					14 Apr
58.19	Jill	Richards (200)	GER	14.1.87				19 May

Hand timed: 56.3A Princesa Oliveros COL 10.8.75 1 Medellín 18 Apr

Best at low altitude

55.79	Theron	1	NC	Port Elizabeth	14 Apr		56.7	Dorr	1	Holmdel	16 Jun
55.97	Wells	4		Genève	2 Jun			57.27	1	Clemson	12 May
57.21	Montcalm	15 Jul	57.74 Jaramillo	5 Aug			57.14	Oliveros	5 GP	Belém	6 May
57.70	Haye	6 May	58.11 Ebersohn	14 Apr							

JUNIORS

See main list for top 2 juniors. 12 performances by 9 women to 57.45. Additional marks and further juniors:

Mark	First	Last	Nat	Born	Pos	Meet	Venue	Date
Russell	57.04				4h2	NC	Kingston	26 Jun
	57.23				1s3	WJ	Barcelona	13 Jul
57.16	Kemi	Adekoya	NGR-Y	6.1.96	2		Warri	14 Jun
	57.22				2	NC	Calabar	21 Jun
57.29	Kaila	Barber	USA	4.4.93	1s2	WJ	Barcelona	13 Jul
57.34	Vilde	Svortevik	NOR	18.5.94	2s2	WJ	Barcelona	13 Jul
57.35	Olena	Kolesnychenko	UKR	3.6.93	1s1	WJ	Barcelona	13 Jul
57.36		Quach Thi Lan	VIE-Y	18.10.95	1	NC	Hanoi	4 Oct
57.44	Shamier	Little	USA-Y	20.3.95	1	NC-J	Bloomington	16 Jun
57.45	Kübra	Sesli	TUR	1.11.93	3s2	WJ	Barcelona	13 Jul
57.65	Christine	Salterberg (10)	GER	9.6.94	1		Mannheim	24 Jun
57.82	Taylor	Farquhar	CAN	2.9.94	3s1	WJ	Barcelona	13 Jul
58.02	Sara	Klein	AUS	19.5.94	1	NC-j	Sydney	17 Mar
58.04	Sage	Watson	CAN	20.6.94	4s2	WJ	Barcelona	13 Jul
58.07	Tessa	Consedine	AUS-Y	15.8.95	2	NC-j	Sydney	17 Mar
58.11	Emel	Sanli	TUR	7.7.93	2	NC-j	Eskisehir	10 Jun
58.13	Anastasiya	Lebid	UKR	30.10.93	3s3	WJ	Barcelona	13 Jul
58.18	Sarah	Carli	AUS	5.9.94	3	NC-j	Sydney	17 Mar
58.23	Ann	Nwaogu	NGR	1.10.93	2		Warri	6 Jun
58.27	Aya	Takizawa	JPN-	16.8.94	1		Niigata	31 Jul
58.39	Kateryna	Slyusarenko (20)	UKR	15.3.93	3	NC-j	Yalta	1 Jun

HIGH JUMP

2.06i Anna Chicherova RUS 22.7.82 1 Arnstadt 4 Feb
 1.85/1 1.91/1 1.97/1 2.00/2 2.03/1 2.06/3
 2.05 1 OG London (OS) 11 Aug 1.89/1 1.93/1 1.97/1 2.00/1 2.03/1 2.05/2
 2.03 1 NC Cheboksary 4 Jul 1.85/1 1.89/1 1.92/1 1.95/1 1.99/1 2.01/2 2.03/1 2.08/xxx
 2.02 1 Pre Eugene 2 Jun 1.86/1 1.91/1 1.94/1 1.97/1 2.00/2 2.02/2
 2.00i 1 Chelyabinsk 9 Jan 1.83/1 1.86/1 1.89/1 1.95/1 2.00/1 2.05/xxx
 2.00i 1 Antwerpen 28 Jan 1.89/1 1.95/1 2.00/2 2.02/xxx
 2.00i 1 Banská Bystrica 8 Feb 1.85/1 1.90/1 1.96/1 1.98/1 2.00/2 2.04/xxx
 2.00i 1 Stockholm 23 Feb 1.84/1 1.91/1 1.94/1 2.00/1 2.04/xxx
 2.00 1 DNG Stockholm 17 Aug 1.84/1 1.91/1 1.94/1 2.00/1 2.05/xx 2.08/x

2.04 Irina Gordeyeva RUS 9.10.86 1 Eberstadt 19 Aug
 1.80/1 1.88/1 1.91/1 1.94/1 1.97/1 2.00/1 2.04/3 2.08/xxx
 1.99 3 NC Cheboksary 4 Jul 1.89/1 1.93/1 1.97/1 2.00/1 2.03/1 2.05/2

2.03 Brigetta Barrett USA 24.12.90 2 OG London (OS) 11 Aug
 1.89/1 1.93/1 1.97/2 2.00/2 2.03/2 2.05/xxx
 2.01 2 NC/OT Eugene 30 Jun 1.79/1 1.84/1 1.89/1 1.92/1 1.95/2 1.98/1 2.01/1 2.04/xxx

2.03 Svetlana Shkolina RUS 9.3.86 3 OG London (OS) 11 Aug
 1.89/1 1.93/1 1.97/1 2.00/1 2.03/3 2.05/xxx
 2.01 2 NC Cheboksary 4 Jul 1.85/1 1.89/1 1.95/1 1.97/1 1.99/x 2.01/2 2.03/xxx
 2.01 1 Rieti 9 Sep 1.89/1 1.93/1 1.97/1 2.01/1 2.05/xxx
 2.00 2 Pre Eugene 2 Jun 1.86/1 1.91/1 1.94/1 1.97/1 2.00/1 2.02/xxx
 2.00 2 Eberstadt 19 Aug 1.88/1 1.91/1 1.94/1 1.97/1 2.00/1 2.02/xxx
 2.00 1 VD Bruxelles 7 Sep 1.89/1 1.92/1 1.95/2 1.98/1 2.00/1 2.03/xxx
 1.98 1 Mosc C Moskva 11 Jun 1.86/1 1.89/1 1.92/1 1.95/1 1.98/2 2.01/xxx

2.02Ai Chaunté Lowe USA 12.1.84 1 NC Albuquerque 26 Feb
 1.77/1 1.82/1 1.87/1 1.93/2 1.96/1 1.99/2 2.02/3 2.04/xxx
 2.01 1 NC/OT Eugene 30 Jun 1.79/1 1.84/1 1.89/1 1.92/1 1.95/1 1.98/1 2.01/1 2.04/xxx
 2.00 1 Auburn 21 Apr 1.80/1 1.83/1 1.86/1 1.92/1 1.96/3 1.98/1 2.00/1 2.02/xxx
 2.00 1 LGP London (CP) 13 Jul 1.83/1 1.87/1 1.91/1 1.94/1 1.97/1 2.00/3 2.02/xxx
 1.98i 1 WI Istanbul 10 Mar 1.84/1 1.88/1 1.92/2 1.95/2 1.98/1 2.01/xxx
 1.98 1 DrakeR Des Moines 28 Apr 1.80/1 1.85/1 1.90/1 1.96/1 1.98/1 2.01/xxx

2.00 Ruth Beitia ESP 1.4.79 1 Santander 25 Jul
 1.85/1 1.90/1 1.95/1 1.98/2 2.00/1 2.03/xxx
 2.00 4 OG London (OS) 11 Aug 1.89/1 1.93/1 1.97/2 2.00/1 2.03/xxx
 (28/6)

Mark	Name		Nat	Born	Pos	Meet	Venue	Date
1.97i	Tia	Hellebaut	BEL	16.2.78	3		Arnstadt	4 Feb
1.97	Tonje	Angelsen	NOR	17.1.90	2	EC	Helsinki	28 Jun
1.97	Svetlana	Radzivil	UZB	17.1.87	7	OG	London (OS)	11 Aug
1.96i	Mariya	Kuchina	RUS-J	14.1.93	1		Vendryne	30 Jan
	(10)							
1.96	Olena	Holosha	UKR	26.1.82	1		Mykolaiv	17 Jun
1.95i	Ebba	Jungmark	SWE	10.3.87	1	NC	Örebro	19 Feb
1.95i	Emma	Green Tregaro	SWE	8.12.84	2	NC	Örebro	19 Feb
1.95i	Antonietta	Di Martino	ITA	1.6.78	Q	WI	Istanbul	9 Mar
1.95	Amy	Acuff	USA	14.7.75	1	TexR	Austin	31 Mar
1.95	Inika	McPherson	USA	29.9.86	1=	MSR	Walnut	21 Apr
1.95	Venelina	Veneva-Mateeva	BUL	13.6.74	1		Izmir	20 May
1.95	Nadezhda	Dusanova	UZB	17.11.87	1	NC	Tashkent	22 Jun
1.95	Marina	Aitova	KAZ	13.9.82	1		Almaty	30 Jun
1.95	Airiné	Palsyté	LTU	13.7.92	1	NC	Kaunas	7 Jul
	(20)							
1.95	Mirela	Demireva	BUL	28.9.89	1	Spitzen	Luzern	17 Jul
1.95	Marie-Laurence	Jungfleisch	GER	7.10.90	2	Spitzen	Luzern	17 Jul
1.94i	Esthera	Petre	ROU	13.5.90	1		Bucuresti	15 Jan
1.93i	Viktoriya	Styopina	UKR	21.2.76	1	NC	Sumy	17 Feb
1.93i	Oksana	Okuneva	UKR	14.3.90	2	NC	Sumy	17 Feb
1.93i	Anna	Iljustsenko	EST	12.10.85	1	NC	Tartu	19 Feb
1.93i	Mélanie	Melfort	FRA	8.11.82	1	NC	Aubière	25 Feb
1.93	Burcu	Ayhan	TUR	3.5.90	Q	OG	London (OS)	9 Aug
1.93	Adonía	Steryíou	GRE	7.7.85	13q	OG	London (OS)	9 Aug
1.93	Ariane	Friedrich	GER	10.1.84	14q	OG	London (OS)	9 Aug
	(30)							
1.93	Viktoriya	Dobrynska	UKR	18.1.80	1=		Berdychiv	7 Sep
1.93	Nataliya	Hapchuk	UKR	15.11.88	1=		Berdychiv	7 Sep
1.92i	Yekaterina	Bolshova	RUS	4.2.88	1P	NC	Moskva	7 Feb
1.92i		Zheng Xingjuan	CHN	20.3.89	1	AsiC	Hangzhou	18 Feb
1.92	Becky	Christensen	USA	24.2.87	3	MSR	Walnut	21 Apr
1.92	Oldriska	Maresová	CZE	14.10.86	1		Olomouc	8 May
1.92	Alessia	Trost	ITA-J	8.3.93	1		Gorizia	19 May
1.92	Izabela	Mikolajczyk	POL	4.9.90	1	OFS	Opole	6 Jun
1.92	Yevgeniya	Kononova	RUS	28.9.89	1		Sankt-Peterburg	10 Jun
1.92	Lesyaní	Mayor	CUB	8.7.89	1		La Habana	22 Jun
	(40)							
1.92	Sahana	Kumari	IND	6.3.81	1		Hyderabad	23 Jun
1.92		Duong Thi Viet Anh	VIE	30.12.90	2		Almaty	30 Jun
1.92	Shanay	Briscoe	USA	7.8.92	4	NC/OT	Eugene	30 Jun
1.92	Oksana	Starostina	RUS	1.4.88	1	NCp	Yerino	15 Jul
1.92	Austra	Skujyté	LTU	12.8.79	1H	OG	London (OS)	3 Aug
1.92	Eleriin	Haas	EST	4.7.92	3	VD	Bruxelles	7 Sep
1.92		Wang Yang	CHN	14.2.89	2	NC	Kunshan	25 Sep
1.91i	Nadja	Kampschulte	GER	5.9.92	1		Leverkusen	5 Feb
1.91i	Jessica	Ennis	GBR	28.1.86	1	NC	Sheffield	11 Feb
1.91i	Ana	Simic	CRO	5.5.90	3	BalkC	Istanbul	18 Feb
	(50)							
1.91	Yana	Maksimova	BLR	9.1.89	1=H		Götzis	26 May
1.91	Sarah	Cowley	NZL	3.2.84	1=H		Götzis	26 May
1.91	Levern	Spencer	LCA	23.6.84	1		Regensburg	2 Jun
1.91	Tatyana	Mnatsakanova	RUS	25.5.83	3	NA	Heusden	7 Jul
1.91	Valentyna	Lyashenko	UKR	30.1.81	3		Berdychiv	7 Sep
1.90i	Yuliya	Kostrova	RUS	20.8.91	3		Bordeaux	28 Jan
1.90i	Ma'ayan	Furman	ISR	9.11.86	1	NC	Chisinau	3 Feb
1.90	Elizabeth	Lamb	NZL	12.5.91	1	Porritt	Hamilton	11 Feb
1.90	Anika	Smit	RSA	26.5.86	1	NC	Port Elizabeth	14 Apr
1.90A	Romary	Rifka	MEX	8.4.73	1	NC	Ciudad de México	11 May
	(60)							
1.90	Vita	Palamar	UKR	12.10.77	2	NCp	Yalta	27 May
1.90	Isobel	Pooley	GBR	21.12.92	1	BIG	Bedford	10 Jun
1.90	Iryna	Herashchenko	UKR-Y	10.3.95	3	NC	Yalta	13 Jun
1.90	Deirdre	Ryan	IRL	1.6.82	1		Bottrop	6 Jul
1.90	Monika	Gollner	AUT	23.10.74	1		Bratislava	7 Jul
1.90	Miyuki	Fukumoto	JPN	4.1.77	1		Osaka	9 Aug
1.90	Doreen	Amata	NGR	6.5.88	17q	OG	London (OS)	9 Aug
1.89i	Tamara	Biryuk	UKR-Y	11.4.95	1		Lviv	20 Jan
1.89i	Gema	Martín-Pozuelo	ESP	21.6.87	1		Madrid	21 Jan
1.89i	Øyunn	Grindem Mogstad	NOR	11.11.87	1		Oslo	21 Jan
	(70)							

Mark	Name		Nat	Born	Pos	Meet	Venue	Date
1.89i	Iryna	Kovalenko	UKR	17.6.86	1	NCp	Zaporizhzhya	28 Jan
1.89i	Emma	Perkins	GBR	4.9.85	2	NC	Sheffield	11 Feb
1.89i	Raffaella	Lamera	ITA	13.4.83	1	NC	Ancona	25 Feb
1.89	Urszula	Domel	POL	21.7.88	2		Rehlingen	28 May
1.89	Kamila	Stepaniuk	POL	22.3.86	2		Opole	6 Jun
1.89	Karolina	Gronau	POL	12.7.84	2	NC	Bielsko-Biala	16 Jun
1.89	Wanida	Boonwan	THA	30.8.86	3		Almaty	30 Jun
1.89	Gabrielle	Williams	USA-Y	6.9.96	5	NC/OT	Eugene	30 Jun
1.89	Saniel	Atkinson	BAH	2.7.91	1	NC	Kingston	1 Jul
1.89	Chiara	Vitobello	ITA	21.10.91	1	NC	Bressanone	7 Jul
(80)								
1.89	Alesya	Paklina	KGZ	22.6.88	2	NCp	Yerino	15 Jul
1.89	Katarina	Johnson-Thompson	GBR-J	9.1.93	2H	OG	London (OS)	3 Aug
1.88i	Brianne	Theisen	CAN	18.12.88	1P		College Station	27 Jan
1.88Ai	Barbara	Szabó	HUN	17.2.90	1		Albuquerque	3 Feb
1.88i	Melina	Brenner	GER-J	28.6.93	1j		Leverkusen	5 Feb
1.88i	Yekaterina	Kuntsevich	RUS	13.7.84	1		Wien	18 Feb
1.88i	Krystle	Schade	USA	2.7.90	1	SEC	Lexington	26 Feb
1.88i		Chen Yanjun	CHN	13.1.88	1	NGP	Chengdu	11 Mar
1.88A	Julia	du Plessis	RSA-Y	27.5.96	1	NC-y	Germiston	1 Apr
1.88		Ye Jiaying	CHN-J	7.1.93	1	NC-j	Changzhou	22 Apr
(90)								
1.88	Kristina	Savitskaya	RUS	10.6.91	2H	NC	Cheboksary	2 Jun
1.88	Georgiana	Zârcan	ROU	30.5.88	1	IntC	Bucuresti	8 Jun
1.88	Daniela	Stanciu	ROU	15.10.87	2	IntC	Bucuresti	8 Jun
1.88		Pham Thi Diem	VIE	24.1.90	1		Ho Chi Minh	12 Jul
1.88	Lissa	Labiche	SEY-J	18.2.93	2	WJ	Barcelona	15 Jul
1.88	Alexandra	Plaza	GER-J	10.6.94	4	WJ	Barcelona	15 Jul
1.88	Victoria	Dronsfield	SWE	6.6.91	1-22	Nord/Balt	Jessheim	22 Jul
1.88	Nafissatou	Thiam	BEL-J	19.8.94	1H	NC	Verviers	25 Aug

Mark	Name		Nat	Born	Date
1.87	Trudy	Thompson	AUS	13.1.90	21 Jan
1.87i	Gintaré	Nesteckyté	LTU-Y	30.12.95	26 Feb
(100)					
1.87i	Hanne	Van Hessche	BEL	5.7.91	3 Mar
1.87	Tynita	Butts	USA	10.6.90	6 Apr
1.87	Megan	Seidl	USA	4.11.86	21 Apr
1.87	Allison	Barwise	USA	21.7.91	13 May
1.87	Karolina	Blazej	POL	21.11.86	19 May
1.87	Kateryna	Tabashnyk	UKR-J	15.6.94	31 May
1.87	Sibel	Çinar-Yasa	TUR	16.1.87	6 Jun
1.87	Toni	Young	USA	11.1.91	8 Jun
1.87	Jillian	Drouin	CAN	30.9.86	10 Jun
1.87	Oksana	Krasnokutskaya	RUS-J	24.9.93	10 Jun
1.87	Iryna	Myhalchenko	UKR	20.1.72	13 Jun
1.87	Beatrice	Lundmark	SUI	26.4.80	17 Jun
1.87	Sietske	Noorman	NED	16.7.91	17 Jun
1.87	Daniellys	Dutil	CUB-Y	12.2.95	22 Jun
1.87	Hyleas	Fountain	USA	14.1.81	29 Jun
1.87	Sharon	Day	USA	9.6.85	29 Jun
1.87	Barbara	Nwaba	USA	18.1.89	29 Jun
1.87	Julia	Straub	GER	10.4.86	2 Sep
1.87	Hannelore	Desmet	BEL	25.2.89	9 Sep
1.87	Eleanor	Patterson	AUS-Y	22.5.96	1 Dec
1.86i	Katarina	Mögenburg	NOR	16.6.91	21 Jan
1.86i	Magdalena	Ogrodnik	POL	25.7.89	30 Jan
1.86i	Olga	Kurban	RUS	16.12.87	7 Feb
1.86i	Yekaterina	Stepanova	RUS-J	24.7.94	12 Feb
1.86i	Natasha	McLaren	USA	21.8.92	3 Mar
1.86	Liz	Patterson	USA	9.6.88	17 Mar
1.86	Chanice	Porter	JAM-J	25.5.94	30 Mar
1.86	Michelle	Theophille	CAN	27.2.91	6 May
1.86	Aline Fernanda	Santos	BRA	16.4.89	6 May
1.86	Anna	Ustinova	KAZ	8.12.85	11 May
1.86	Stephanie	Pywell	GBR	12.6.87	20 May
1.86	Valeryia	Bogdanovich	BLR	1.5.92	25 May
1.86	Mariya	Nestserchuk	BLR	14.8.89	29 May
1.86	Dior	Delophont	FRA-J	19.10.94	8 Jun
1.86	Emma	Nuttall	GBR	23.4.92	16 Jun
1.86	Elena	Vallortigara	ITA	21.9.91	16 Jun
1.86A	Nicole	Forrester	CAN	17.11.76	29 Jun
1.86	Sheree	Ruff	JAM	20.10.83	1 Jul
1.86	Nadine	Broersen	NED	29.4.90	3 Aug
1.86	Elina	Smolander	FIN	11.10.89	25 Aug
1.85i	Yuliya	Babayeva	RUS	22.5.88	21 Jan
1.85i	Laura	Voß	GER-J	29.1.94	29 Jan
1.85	Ashleigh	Reid	AUS	25.2.88	18 Feb
1.85i	Alina	Rotaru	ROU-J	5.6.93	18 Feb
1.85i	Enrica	Cipolloni	ITA	19.10.90	25 Feb
1.85i	Laura	Ikauniece	LAT	31.5.92	25 Feb
1.85	Shanice	Hall	JAM-J	21.7.93	25 Feb
1.85	Yilian	Durruthy	CUB	30.1.90	2 Mar
1.85	Lauren	Collins	USA	2.8.87	3 Mar
1.85	Catherine	Nina	DOM-J	25.10.93	31 Mar
1.85A	Fabiola Elizabeth	Ayala	MEX	31.12.86	11 May
1.85	Stine	Kufaas	NOR	7.4.86	12 May
1.85	Laura	Rautanen	FIN	13.2.88	19 May
1.85	Kimberly	Williamson	JAM-J	2.10.93	26 May
1.85	Eliska	Klucinová	CZE	14.4.88	26 May
1.85	Alina	Fyodorova	UKR	31.7.89	27 May
1.85A	Kendell	Williams	USA-Y	14.6.95	31 May
1.85	Giovanna	Demo	SUI	29.6.87	9 Jun
1.85	Uhunoma	Osazuwa	NGR	23.11.87	29 Jun
1.85	Jeannelle	Scheper	LCA-J	21.11.94	29 Jun
1.85	Marina	Smolyakova	RUS	20.6.89	4 Jul
1.85	Svetlana	Linkevich	RUS	26.9.91	15 Jul
1.85	My	Nordström	SWE	21.4.90	25 Aug
1.85i	Irina	Iliyeva	RUS-Y	2.12.95	17 Dec
1.84i	Ida	Virdebrant	SWE-J	4.4.94	21 Jan
1.84i	Elena	Meuti #	ITA	26.6.83	22 Jan
1.84i	Remona	Fransen	NED	25.11.85	29 Jan
1.84i		Gu Xuan	CHN	19.11.87	14 Feb
1.84i		Qiao Yanrui	CHN	29.9.88	14 Feb
1.84i	Ulyana	Aleksandrova	RUS	1.1.91	16 Feb
1.84i	Anna	Melnychenko	UKR	24.4.83	16 Feb
1.84i	Nataliya	Dobrynska	UKR	29.5.82	16 Feb
1.84i	Viktorija	Zemaityté	LTU	11.3.85	18 Feb
1.84i	Tatyana	Chernova	RUS	29.1.88	9 Mar
1.84i	Dorcas	Akinniyi	USA	23.1.90	10 Mar
1.84	Alyx	Treasure	CAN	15.5.92	31 Mar
1.84	Jane	Doolittle	AUS/USA	28.10.86	13 Apr
1.84		Liu Xiaoyun	CHN-J	12.6.93	22 Apr
1.84	Peaches	Roach	JAM	21.12.84	25 Apr
1.84	Ann	Dudley	USA	28.5.91	27 Apr
1.84	Lucimara	da Silva	BRA	10.7.85	5 May
1.84	Blandine	Maisonnier	FRA	3.1.86	5 May
1.84	Mónica	de Freitas	BRA	21.6.84	9 May
1.84	Charlotte	Brauch	GER	25.6.91	20 May
1.84	Justyna	Kasprzycka	POL	20.8.87	28 May
1.84	Agnieszka	Borowska	POL	21.10.91	9 Jun
1.84A	Kashani	Ríos	PAN	7.2.91	16 Jun
1.84	Priscilla	Frederick	USA	14.2.89	16 Jun
1.84	Valdiléia	Martins	BRA	19.9.89	30 Jun

Mark	Name		Nat	Born	Pos	Meet	Venue	Date
1.84	Tatiána	Goúsin	GRE-J	26.1.94				22 Jul

Best outdoor marks

Mark	Name	Pos	Meet	Venue	Date
1.97	Hellebaut	2	LGP	London (CP)	13 Jul
1.93	Melfort	Q	OG	London (OS)	9 Aug
1.93	Green Tregaro	Q	OG	London (OS)	9 Aug
1.92	Zheng Xingjuan	1	NGP	Zhaoqing	14 Apr
1.92	Iljustsenko	1		Sillamäe	26 Aug
1.91	Jungmark	7	Pre	Eugene	2 Jun
1.87	Y Kuntsevich				7 Jun
1.87	Schade				8 Jun
1.87	Brenner				24 Jun
1.87	Okuneva				7 Jul
1.86	Kostrova				2 Jun
1.86	Szabó				17 Jun
1.86	Lamera				7 Jul
1.86	Kovalenko				19 Jul
1.86	Martín-Pozuelo				26 Aug
1.85	Furman				27 May

Mark	Name	Nat	Born	Pos	Meet	Venue	Date
1.84	Shen Xin	CHN	5.11.92				25 Sep
1.84	Wang Lin (192)	CHN-Y	8.1.95				25 Sep
1.91	Bolshova			1H	NC	Cheboksary	2 Jun
1.90	Styopina			2	NC	Yalta	13 Jun
1.89	Kuchina			1	NC-j	Cheboksary	20 Jun
1.89	Ennis			1	NC	Birmingham	23 Jun
1.88	Simic			1	GP	Belém	6 May
1.88	Mogstad			1		Lillestrøm	3 Jul
1.85	Babayeva						10 Jun
1.85	Nesteckyté						30 Jun
1.85	Petre						9 Aug
1.84	Chen Yanjun						14 Apr
1.84	Kampschulte						19 May
1.84	Theisen						7 Jun
1.84	Cipolloni						16 Jun
1.84	Qiao Yanrui						23 Jun
1.84	Van Hessche						7 Jul

JUNIORS

See main list for top 12 juniors. 12 performances by 3 women to 1.90. Additional marks and further juniors:

Name	Mark	Pos	Meet	Venue	Date
Kuchina 2+	1.93i	4		Hustopece	28 Jan
	1.91i	3	NC	Moskva	23 Feb
Trost	1.91i	1		Pordenone	29 Jan
	1.91	1	WJ	Barcelona	15 Jul
	1.90i	5		Banská Bystrica	8 Feb
	1.91i	3		Tallinn	23 Feb
	1.90i	2		Volgograd	21 Jan
	1.90	1	NC-j	Misano Adriatico	15 Jun
	1.90	1		Spilimbergo	15 Sep

Mark	Name		Nat	Born	Pos	Meet	Venue	Date
1.87i	Gintaré	Nesteckyté	LTU-Y	30.12.95	1	v2N-y	Võru	26 Feb
1.85					1		Jurbarkas	30 Jun
1.87	Kateryna	Tabashnyk	UKR	15.6.94	1H	NC-j	Yalta	31 May
1.87	Oksana	Krasnokutskaya	RUS	24.9.93	1		Tampere	10 Jun
1.87	Daniellys	Dutil	CUB-Y	12.2.95	2		La Habana	22 Jun
1.87	Eleanor	Patterson	AUS-Y	22.5.96	1		Hobart	1 Dec
1.86i	Yekaterina	Stepanova	RUS	24.7.94	2	NC-j	Volgograd	12 Feb
1.86	Chanice	Porter	JAM	25.5.94	1-19		Kingston	30 Mar
1.86	Dior	Delophont (20)	FRA	19.10.94	1		Pierre-Benite	8 Jun
1.87 best out	Melina	Brenner	GER	28.6.93	2		Mannheim	24 Jun

POLE VAULT

Mark		Name		Nat	Born	Pos	Meet	Venue	Date
5.01i		Yelena	Isinbayeva	RUS	3.6.82	1	XL Galan	Stockholm	23 Feb

    4.72/2　4.82/1　4.92/3　5.01/2

	4.81i	1		Liévin	14 Feb
	4.80i	1	WI	Istanbul	11 Mar
	4.75	1		Sotteville-lès-Rouen	10 Jul
	4.70i	1		Volgograd	21 Jan
	4.70	3	OG	London (OS)	6 Aug

    4.71/2　4.81/1　4.91/xxx
    4.70/1　4.80/1　5.02/xxx
    4.70/x　4.75/1　4.85/xxx
    4.70/1　4.80/xxx
    4.55/x　4.65/1　4.70/1　4.75/xx　4.80/x

4.88i	Jenn	Suhr	USA	5.2.82	1		Boston (R)	4 Feb

    4.52/1　4.63/1　4.72/3　4.88/1　5.01/x

	4.83	1		Fredonia NY	22 Sep
	4.81	1		Champaign	7 Jul
	4.75i	1	DrakeR-M	Des Moines	25 Apr
	4.75	1	OG	London (OS)	6 Aug
	4.70i	1		Buffalo NY	30 Sep

    4.50/1　4.66/1　4.83/1　5.00/xxx
    4.63/1　4.81/2　4.93/xxx
    4.60/2　4.75/1　4.90/xxx
    4.55/1　4.70/1　4.75/2　4.80/xxx
    4.50/1　4.70/3　4.85/xxx

4.87i	Holly	Bleasdale	GBR	2.11.91	1		Villeurbanne	20 Jan

    4.44/1　4.60/1　4.72/1　4.80/1　4.87/3　5.01/xxx

	4.72i	2	XL Galan	Stockholm	23 Feb
	4.71	1	NC	Birmingham	24 Jun
	4.70i	1	NC	Sheffield	12 Feb
	4.70i	1	GP	Birmingham	18 Feb
	4.70i	3	WI	Istanbul	11 Mar
	4.70	2		Sotteville-lès-Rouen	10 Jul

    4.52/1　4.72/1　4.82/xxx
    4.40/3　4.50/3　4.60/1　4.71/2　4.80/xxx
    4.52/1　4.70/2　4.89/xxx
    4.52/3　4.70/1　4.78/xxx
    4.45/2　4.65/1　4.70/2　4.75/xxx
    4.45/1　4.60/2　4.70/1　4.75/xxx

4.82	Silke	Spiegelburg	GER	17.3.86	1	Herc	Monaco	20 Jul

    4.54/1　4.70/2　4.82/2

	4.77i	1		Leverkusen	15 Jan
	4.76	1	Odlozil	Praha	11 Jun
	4.75	1	VD	Bruxelles	7 Sep
	4.70	1	NC	Wattenscheid	16 Jun

    4.40/2　4.55/1　4.65/3　4.77/1
    4.40/1　4.56/2　4.68/2　4.76/2　4.81/xxx
    4.45/1　4.55/1　4.65/2　4.70/xx　4.75/1　4.83/xxx
    4.40/1　4.50/2　4.60/1　4.70/2　4.81/xxx

4.77	Fabiana	Murer	BRA	16.3.81	1	DL	New York	9 Jun

    4.50/1　4.60/1　4.70/1　4.77/2　4.86/xxx

4.76	Alana	Boyd	AUS	10.5.84	1		Perth	24 Feb

    4.40/1　4.50/3　4.60/3　4.71/1　4.76.3　4.81/xx

4.75	Yarisley	Silva	CUB	1.6.87	2	OG	London (OS)	6 Aug

    4.45/2　4.55/1　4.65/1　4.70/1　4.75/2　4.80/xxx

	4.72i	3	XL Galan	Stockholm	23 Feb
	4.71i	2		Liévin	14 Feb
	4.70i	1		Potsdam	17 Feb
	4.70	2	DL	New York	9 Jun
	4.70	1	DNG	Stockholm	17 Aug

    4.42/3　4.52/2　4.62/3　4.72/3　4.82/xxx
    4.40/1　4.52/3　4.60/1　4.71/3　4.82/xxx
    4.42/1　4.52/1　4.70/1　4.80/xxx
    4.50/3　4.60/3　4.70/1　4.77/xxx
    4.46/2　4.64/2　4.70/1　4.76/xxx

Mark	Name		Nat	Born	Pos	Meet	Venue		Date
4.72	Jirina	Ptácníková	CZE	20.5.86	2	Odlozil	Praha	11	Jun
		4.30/1	4.50/1	4.62/1	4.72/2	4.76/xxx			
	4.70i	1	Donetsk	11 Feb	4.30/2	4.50/2	4.60/1	4.70/3	4.76/xxx
4.71i	Anna	Rogowska	POL	21.5.81	1	NC	Spala	26	Feb
		4.46/1	4.58/1	4.71/2	4.80/xxx				
	4.70i	2 GP	Birmingham	18 Feb	4.52/2	4.62/1	4.70/2	4.78/xxx	
	4.70	3	Sotteville-lès-Rouen	10 Jul	4.45/1	4.60/3	4.70/3	4.75/xxx	
4.70i	Vanessa	Boslak	FRA	11.6.82	2	WI	Istanbul	11	Mar
	(38/10)	4.30/1	4.45/1	4.55/1	4.65/1	4.70/1	4.75/xxx		
4.65	Lisa	Ryzih	GER	27.9.88	2	NC	Wattenscheid	16	Jun
4.65	Svetlana	Feofanova	RUS	16.7.80	1	NC	Cheboksary	4	Jul
4.65i	Lacy	Janson	USA	20.2.83	5	WI	Istanbul	11	Mar
4.62Ai	Mary	Saxer	USA	21.6.87	2	NC	Albuquerque	25	Feb
4.60i	Hanna	Sheleh	UKR-J	14.7.93	3		Donetsk	11	Feb
4.60Ai	Kelsie	Hendry	CAN	29.6.82	1		Flagstaff	16	Feb
4.60	Anastasiya	Savchenko	RUS	15.11.89	1	Colorful	Daegu	16	May
4.60	Nikoléta	Kiriakopoúlou	GRE	21.3.86	3	DL	New York	9	Jun
4.60	Nicole	Büchler	SUI	17.12.83	1		Riehen	17	Jun
4.60	Martina	Strutz	GER	4.11.81	2	EC	Helsinki	30	Jun
	(20)								
4.60	Kristina	Gadschiew	GER	3.7.84	2		Rottach-Egern	7	Jul
4.58	Angelica	Bengtsson	SWE-J	8.7.93	1		Sollentuna	5	Jul
4.57i	Becky	Holliday	USA	12.3.80	1		Jonesboro	12	May
4.56	Kate	Dennison	GBR	7.5.84	1	Spitzen	Luzern	17	Jul
4.55i	Tina	Sutej	SLO	7.11.88	1	SEC	Lexington	25	Feb
4.55	Aleksandra	Kiryashova	RUS	21.8.85	3	NC	Cheboksary	4	Jul
4.55	Anastasiya	Shvedova	BLR	3.5.79	1		Padova	2	Sep
4.52i	Anna	Battke	GER	3.1.85	1		Ludwigshafen	21	Jan
4.52i	Jillian	Schwartz	ISR	19.9.79	1	US Open	New York	28	Jan
4.52i	Katie	Byres	GBR-J	11.9.93	2		Nevers	18	Feb
	(30)								
4.52	Tori	Pena	IRL	30.7.87	2		La Jolla	28	Apr
4.52	Carolin	Hingst	GER	18.9.80	1		Wipperfürth	23	May
4.52Ai	Kylie	Hutson	USA	27.11.87	4	NC	Albuquerque	25	Feb
4.51	Ekateríni	Stefanídi	GRE	4.2.90	1c1		Livermore	16	Jun
4.50	Liz	Parnov	AUS-J	9.5.94	1		Perth	17	Feb
4.50i		Li Ling	CHN	6.7.89	1	AsiC	Hangzhou	19	Feb
4.50	Daylis	Caballero	CUB	6.3.88	2	Viloria	Barquisimeto	4	May
4.50	Shade	Weygandt	USA	24.1.91	1		Lubbock	5	May
4.50	Katy	Viuf	USA	23.5.87	1		Chula Vista	10	May
4.50	April	Steiner Bennett	USA	22.4.80	2		Chula Vista	17	May
	(40)								
4.50	Nataliya	Mazuryk	UKR	5.3.83	1		Yalta	4	Jun
4.50	Monika	Pyrek	POL	11.8.80	4	DL	New York	9	Jun
4.50	Stélla-Iró	Ledáki	GRE	18.7.88	2	NC	Athína	15	Jun
4.50	Anzhelika	Sidorova	RUS	28.6.91	4	NC	Cheboksary	4	Jul
4.50	Malin	Dahlström	SWE	26.8.89	3		Rottach-Egern	7	Jul
4.46	Melissa	Gergel	USA	24.4.89	1		Walnut	2	Jun
4.44	Morgann	LeLeux	USA	14.11.92	1	SEC	Baton Rouge	12	May
4.42i	Janice	Keppler	USA	22.3.87	2	US Open	New York	28	Jan
4.42i	Anna Katharina	Schmid	SUI	2.12.89	1		Magglingen	4	Feb
4.42i	Annika	Roloff	GER	10.3.91	5		Karlsruhe	12	Feb
	(50)								
4.42i	Caroline Bonde	Holm	DEN	19.7.90	2		Potsdam	17	Feb
4.42i	Marion	Fiack	FRA	13.10.92	4		Nevers	18	Feb
4.42i	Sally	Peake	GBR	8.2.86	5		Nevers	18	Feb
4.42i	Maria Eleonor	Tavares	POR	24.9.85	3	NC	Aubière	26	Feb
4.42	Katharina	Bauer	GER	12.6.90	1		Wipperfürth	7	Jun
4.41i	Cathrine	Larsåsen	NOR	5.12.86	1	v2N	Steinkjer	11	Feb
4.41i	Joanna	Piwowarska	POL	4.11.83	6	GP	Birmingham	18	Feb
4.41		Choi Yun-hee	KOR	28.5.86	1		Gimcheon	8	May
4.40i	Anna	Giordano Bruno	ITA	13.12.80	1		Udine	22	Jan
4.40i	Julia	Hütter	GER	26.7.83	2		Sindelfingen	28	Jan
	(60)								
4.40i	Lyudmila	Yeremina	RUS	8.8.91	1		Moskva	15	Feb
4.40	Samantha	Sonnenberg	USA	10.2.88	1		St. Paul	25	Apr
4.40	Romana	Malácová	CZE	15.5.87	1	ECCp-B	Dubnica nad Váhom	27	May
4.40	Bethany	Buell	USA	4.12.91	3	NCAA	Des Moines	6	Jun
4.40	Angie	Rummans	USA	23.3.92	1		Knoxville	8	Jun
4.40	Minna	Nikkanen	FIN	9.4.88	1		Stockholm	9	Jun
4.40	Tomomi	Abiko	JPN	17.3.88	1	NC	Osaka	9	Jun

Mark	Name		Nat	Born	Pos	Meet	Venue	Date
4.40	Mélanie	Blouin	CAN	14.7.90	1	Jerome	Burnaby	10 Jun
4.40	Angelina	Zhuk	RUS	7.2.91	1	Kuts	Moskva	13 Jun
4.40	April	Kubishta	USA	5.7.85	5		Chula Vista	14 Jun
	(70)							
4.40	Kat	Majester	USA	22.5.87	5	NC/OT	Eugene	24 Jun
4.40	Tatyana	Polnova	RUS	20.4.79	5	NC	Cheboksary	4 Jul
4.40	Marion	Lotout	FRA	19.11.89	1		Vénissieux	6 Jul
4.40	Bryson	Stately	USA	22.11.86	1		Seattle	7 Jul
4.40	Loréla	Mánou	GRE	20.12.90	1	BalkC	Eskisehir	21 Jul
4.38	Logan	Miller	USA	21.5.91	2	Pac-12	Eugene	13 May
4.37i	Keisa	Monterola	VEN	26.2.88	1		Seattle	28 Jan
4.37i	Victoria	von Eynatten	GER	6.10.91	1		Blacksburg	18 Feb
4.37i	Tara	Diebold	USA	28.11.88	2	SEC	Lexington	25 Feb
4.37	Vera	Neuenswander	USA	3.12.87	1		Knoxville	19 May
	(80)							
4.37	Melinda	Owen	USA	30.10.84	3		Chula Vista	9 Jun
4.36i	Katie	Tannehill	USA	9.9.87	2		Jonesboro	17 Jun
4.35i	Joanna	Wright	USA	3.5.89	1		Birmingham	11 Feb
4.35	Vicky	Parnov	AUS	24.10.90	2		Perth	11 Feb
4.35i	Naroa	Agirre	ESP	15.5.79	1	NC	Sabadell	25 Feb
4.35i	Leslie	Brost	USA	28.9.89	4	NCAA	Nampa	10 Mar
4.35	Télie	Mathiot	FRA	25.5.87	1		Pézenas	26 May
4.35	Alex	Acker	USA	12.9.88	5	NCAA	Des Moines	6 Jun
4.35	Anna María	Pinero	ESP	15.1.86	1		Barcelona	16 Jun
4.35	Marion	Buisson	FRA	19.2.88	2	NC	Angers	16 Jun
	(90)							
4.35	Roberta	Bruni	ITA-J	8.3.94	1	NC-j	Misano Adriatico	16 Jun
4.35	Giorgia	Benecchi	ITA	9.7.89	1		Modena	29 Jun
4.34	Stephanie	Richartz	USA	21.1.92	1	Big 10	Madison	13 May
4.33i	Rianna	Galiart	NED	22.11.85	1		Gent	18 Feb
4.32i	Natalya	Demidenko	RUS-J	7.8.93	5	NC	Moskva	22 Feb
4.32	Karla	da Silva	BRA	12.11.84	1		São Paulo	2 Jun
4.32	Emily	Grove	USA-J	22.5.93	1		Yankton	2 Jun
4.31i	Martina	Schultze	GER	12.9.90	2		Boston (Allston)	24 Feb
4.31	Jade	Reibold	USA	14.4.91	1		Charleston	24 Apr
4.31	Katelin	Rains	USA	20.8.87	1		Jonesboro	28 Apr
	(100)							
4.31	Anjuli	Knäsche	GER-J	18.10.93	1		Hamburg	3 Jul

Mark	Name		Nat	Born	Date
4.30i	Yekaterina	Kazeka	RUS	7.10.90	14 Jan
4.30i	Agnieszka	Kolasa	POL	20.5.92	29 Jan
4.30i	Kaitlin	Petrillose	USA	12.10.92	2 Feb
4.30i	Christen	Botteron-Gunther	USA	14.9.89	3 Feb
4.30i		Wu Sha	CHN	21.10.87	17 Feb
4.30i	Rachel	Laurent	USA	21.9.89	10 Mar
4.30	Mandissa	Marshall	USA	2.4.91	24 Mar
4.30A	Jenny	Soceka	USA	1.3.87	24 Mar
4.30	Carly	Dockendorf	CAN	31.12.83	20 Apr
4.30	Shaylah	Simpson	USA	16.3.92	20 Apr
4.30		Xu Huiqin	CHN-J	4.9.93	28 Apr
4.30	Yuliya	Golubchikova	RUS	27.3.83	11 May
4.30 sq	Fanny	Smets	BEL	21.4.86	23 May
4.25					10 Jun
4.30	Daniela	Inchausti	ARG	3.4.78	2 Jun
4.30	Alice	Ost	FRA	25.10.87	16 Jun
4.30	Lillian	Schnitzerling	GER-J	5.12.93	23 Jun
4.30A	Vicky	Dressler	CAN	9.4.85	30 Jun
4.30	Zoë	Brown	IRL	15.9.83	22 Jul
4.30	Allison	Stokke	USA	22.3.89	24 Jul
4.29	Chloé	Henry	BEL	5.3.87	7 Jul
4.28i	Aurélie	De Ryck	BEL	17.12.92	18 Feb
4.27Ai	Kelsey	Hintz	USA	21.9.90	24 Feb
4.27	Heather	Hamilton	CAN	31.3.88	4 May
4.26i	Alixe	Guigon	FRA	24.1.85	18 Feb
4.26	Henrietta	Paxton	GBR	19.9.83	24 Jun
4.26	Catherine	Street	USA	9.5.90	7 Jul
4.25i	Laura	Asimakis	USA	26.11.88	24 Feb
4.25	Kelsie	Ahbe	USA	6.7.91	31 Mar
4.25	Caroline	Hasse	GER	8.3.91	28 Jul
4.25	Joana	Kraft	GER	27.7.91	1 Aug
4.24i	Nicole	Hope	USA	4.4.90	26 Feb
4.24i	Neal	Tisher	USA	3.7.91	3 Mar
4.24	Kiley	Tobel	USA	7.7.91	13 May
4.23i	Natalya	Bartnovskaya	RUS	7.1.89	17 Feb
4.23i	Sandi	Morris	USA	8.7.92	18 Feb
4.23i	Breanna	Bussel	USA	8.8.89	24 Feb

Mark	Name		Nat	Born	Date
4.23i	Lembi	Vaher	EST	11.2.87	25 Feb
4.23i	Denise	Groot	NED	26.5.90	2 Mar
4.23	Megan	Jamerson	USA	4.5.86	31 May
4.22i	Demi	Payne	USA	30.9.91	10 Feb
4.22Ai	Tori	Anthony	USA	19.4.89	10 Feb
4.22i	Robin	Wingbermühle	NED	20.5.92	17 Feb
4.22i	Sarah	Rasnick	USA	5.5.92	19 Feb
4.22	Abby	Schaffer	USA	26.3.90	21 Apr
4.21	Alissa	Söderberg	SWE-J	12.4.94	10 Jun
4.20i	Olga	Chigirintseva	RUS	29.6.87	15 Feb
4.20	Amy	Fryt	USA	27.3.89	30 Mar
4.20	Sara	Pereira	BRA	3.8.90	7 Apr
4.20	Valeria	Chiaraviglio	ARG	9.4.89	7 Apr
4.20	Jade	Vigneron	FRA	6.9.91	11 Apr
4.20	Katrine	Haarklau	NOR	21.2.91	25 Apr
4.20	Alexis	Paine	USA	12.10.90	6 Jun
4.20	Anna	Chkhaidze	RUS-Y	6.1.96	8 Jun
4.20	Elizabeth	Norvell	USA	23.9.88	9 Jun
4.20	Roslinda	Samsu	MAS	9.6.82	16 Jun
4.20	Alayna	Lutkovskaya	RUS-Y	15.3.96	29 Jun
4.20	Tatyana	Stetsuk	RUS	27.8.92	4 Jul
4.20	Valeriya	Snegova	RUS	25.8.87	4 Jul
4.20	Krista	Obizhajeva	LAT-Y	30.4.96	7 Jul
4.20	Olga	Mullina	RUS	1.8.92	20 Jul
4.20i	Alina	Kakoshinskaya	RUS	16.11.86	24 Jul
4.18	Michelle	Eby	USA	5.10.89	17 Mar
4.17	Georgia	Reynolds	USA		25 May
4.16i	Iben	Høgh-Pedersen	DEN	14.8.90	12 Feb
4.16i	Leah	Vause	CAN	4.5.87	18 Feb
4.16		Gao Shuying	CHN	28.10.79	3 May
4.16	Kristen	Hixson	USA	1.7.92	11 May
4.16	Anaïs	Poumarat	FRA	25.2.89	23 May
4.16	Fanny	Berglund	SWE	8.2.88	1 Sep
4.15i	Reena	Koll	EST-Y	15.11.96	14 Jan
4.15i		Shi Qiaowen	CHN	25.12.90	17 Feb
4.15i	Megumi	Nakada	JPN	6.12.88	19 Feb
4.15	Paris	McCathrion	AUS-Y	29.4.95	25 Feb

Mark	Name	Nat	Born	Pos	Meet	Venue	Date
4.15i	Ren Mengqian	CHN-J	4.10.93				10 Mar
4.15A	Caitlin Maulin	USA	28.1.92				2 May
4.15	Angie Aguilar	USA	3.10.83				9 May
4.15	Kayla Coffee	USA					11 May
4.15A	Robin Taylor	USA					12 May
4.15	Elena Horn	GER	17.9.87				13 May
4.15	Li Caixia	CHN	23.8.87				26 May
4.15	Leonie Schilder	NED	15.9.90				27 May
4.15	Alevtina Ruyeva	UKR	13.3.88				28 May
4.15	Petra Olsen	SWE	2.10.90				6 Jun
4.15	Kira Grünberg	AUT-J	13.8.93				14 Jul
4.15	Rosbelys Peinado	VEN-Y	26.11.97				11 Sep
4.15	Wang Hui	CHN	17.6.93				25 Sep
4.14i	Bryony Raine	GBR	30.8.86				20 Jan
4.14i	Michaela Meijer	SWE-J	30.7.93				25 Feb
4.14	Emily Brigham	USA-Y	14.4.95				21 Jul
4.13i	Valeriya Snegova	RUS	25.8.87				25 Feb
4.13	Natasha Masterson	USA	1.8.91				12 May
4.12i	Sally Scott	GBR	12.4.91				29 Jan
4.12i	Ariane Beaumont-Courteau	CAN	11.1.90				11 Feb
4.12i	Alicia Rue	USA	4.8.88				11 Feb
4.12i	Yekaterina Kolesova	RUS	4.9.90				22 Feb
4.12i	Daniela Höllwarth	AUT	24.8.87				25 Feb
4.12i	Tory Worthen	USA	19.9.90				26 Feb
4.12A	Sonia Grabowska	POL	15.12.88				21 Apr
4.12	Arlette Brülhart	SUI	13.8.87				28 May
4.12	Patrícia dos Santos	BRA	13.6.84				2 Jun
(201)							

Best outdoor marks

Mark	Name	Pos	Meet	Venue	Date
4.70	Rogowska	3		Sotteville-lès-Rouen	10 Jul
4.55	Sutej	1	TexR	Austin	31 Mar
4.55	Holliday	2	NC/OT	Eugene	24 Jun
4.55	Boslak	Q	OG	London (OS)	4 Aug
4.53	Saxer	2		Champaign	7 Jul
4.52	Hendry	1		La Jolla	28 Apr
4.50	Janson	2	Colorful	Daegu	16 May
4.41	Schwartz	1		Gent	18 Jul
4.40	Hutson	2	MSR	Walnut	21 Apr
4.40	Roloff	4		Landau	19 May
4.40	Schmid	5		Landau	19 May
4.40	Keppler	1		Knoxville	15 Jun
4.40	Giordano Bruno	1		Gorizia	28 Jul
4.40	Li Ling	1	NC	Kunshan	25 Sep
4.36	Byres	1	NC-j	Bedford	17 Jun
4.36	Holm	1	W.Int	Cardiff	18 Jul
4.35	Tavares	1		Marseille	31 May
4.32	Galiart	1		Thionville	6 Jun

Mark	Name	Date	Mark	Name	Date	Mark	Name	Date	Mark	Name	Date
4.30	Schultze	20 Apr	4.26	Laurent	7 Apr	4.20	Payne	27 Apr	4.15	Ren Mengqian	26 May
4.30	Tannehill	4 May	4.26	Agirre	23 Jun	4.20	Piwowarska	12 May	4.15	Shi Qiaowen	26 May
4.30 sq	Larsåsen	23 May	4.25	Botteron-Gunther	31 Mar	4.20	Sheleh	1 Jun	4.15	Høgh-Pedersen	3 Jun
4.30	Peake	2 Jun	4.25	Brost	24 Jun	4.20	Kazeka	2 Jun	4.15	Morris	6 Jun
4.30	Kolasa	9 Jun	4.22	Hintz	28 Apr	4.17	von Eynatten	11 May	4.15	De Ryck	17 Jun
4.30	Demidenko	19 Jun	4.21	Bartnovskaya	16 May	4.15	Diebold	31 Mar	4.14	Tisher	24 Mar
4.30	Wu Sha	25 Sep	4.21	Yeremina	3 Aug	4.15	Asimakis	31 Mar	4.12	Vause	28 Apr
4.27	Monterola	7 Jul	4.20	Wright	6 Apr	4.15	Bussel	14 Apr			

Technical irregularities: Jun 16, Livermore: 2c1. Megan Jamerson USA 4.5.86, 1c2. Allison Stokke USA 22.3.89 4.36

JUNIORS

See main list for top 7 juniors. 11 performances by 4 women to 4.45. Additional marks and further juniors:

Sheleh	4.52i	4		Liévin	14 Feb				
Bengtsson	4.50	1		Karlskrona	17 Jun	4.46	1	vFIN	Göteborg	1 Sep
	4.50	1	WJ	Barcelona	14 Jul	4.45	5	VD	Bruxelles	7 Sep
	4.46	6	DNG	Stockholm	17 Aug				
Parnov	4.45	1		Melbourne	3 Mar				

Mark	Name	Nat	Born	Pos	Meet	Venue	Date
4.30	Xu Huiqin	CHN	4.9.93	1	NGP	Wuhan	28 Apr
4.30	Lillian Schnitzerling	GER	5.12.93	2		Mannheim	23 Jun
4.25	Kristina Bondarenko (10)	RUS-Y	10.8.95	2		Sochi	26 May
4.25	Michaela Donie	GER-	27.1.93	3		Mannheim	23 Jun
4.21	Alissa Söderberg	SWE	12.4.94	1		Sollentuna	10 Jun
4.20	Anna Chkhaidze	RUS-Y	6.1.96	1J	Mosc Ch	Moskva	8 Jun
4.20	Alayna Lutkovskaya	RUS-Y	15.3.96	1	NC-y	Penza	29 Jun
4.20	Krista Obizhajeva	LAT-Y	30.4.96	1		Liepaja	7 Jul
4.15i	Reena Koll	EST-Y	15.11.96	1		Tartu	14 Jan
4.15	Paris McCathrion	AUS-Y	29.4.95	1		Melbourne	25 Feb
4.15i	Ren Mengqian	CHN	4.10.93	3	NGP	Chengdu	10 Mar
4.15				4	NGP	Zibo	26 May
4.15	Kira Grünberg	AUT	13.8.93	4=	WJ	Barcelona	14 Jul
4.15	Rosbelys Peinado (20)	VEN-Y	26.11.97	1		Barquisimeto	11 Sep
Best out: 4.30	Natalya Demidenko	RUS-J	7.8.93	1	NC-j	Cheboksary	19 Jun
4.20	Hanna Sheleh	UKR-J	14.7.93	1	NC-j	Yalta	1 Jun

LONG JUMP

Mark		Name	Nat	Born	Pos	Meet	Venue	Date
7.23i		Brittney Reese	USA	9.9.86	1	WI	Istanbul	11 Mar

    x   x   6.82   6.92   6.73   7.23
    7.15   1.0 1 NC/OT Eugene   1 Jul   x   7.06/1.9   x   6.87w/2.3   p   7.15
    7.12   -0.9 1 MSR Walnut   21 Apr   6.75   6.72   x   7.12   x   p
    7.12   0.8 1 OG London (OS)   8 Aug   7.12   x   x   6.69   x
    7.04   -0.1 1 Oxford MS   14 Apr   x   x   6.35   x   6.90/1.8   7.04

| 7.11 | 1.3 | Anna Nazarova | RUS | 3.2.86 | 1 | Mosc Ch | Moskva | 20 Jun |

    6.84/-0.1   x   7.00/2.0   x   6.97/1.6   7.11
    6.90   0.7 Q NC Cheboksary   3 Jul   x   6.90   p

| 7.10 | 1.6 | Chelsea Hayes | USA | 9.2.88 | 2 | NC/OT | Eugene | 1 Jul |

    6.76   x   x   x   x   7.10

| 7.08 | 1.9 | Anastasiya Mironchik-Ivanova | BLR | 13.4.89 | 1 | | Minsk | 12 Jun |

    x   6.93/1.4   6.86/0.7   6.65   6.97w/3.0   7.08
    7.01   2.0 * NC Grodno   6 Jul   7.01/2.0   7.22w/4.3   x   x   6.77w/2.2   x

Mark	Wind	Name		Nat	Born	Pos	Meet	Venue	Date
7.07	0.5	Yelena	Sokolova	RUS	23.7.86	2	OG	London (OS)	8 Aug
					6.80/1.3	7.07	6.84/0.4	6.93/0.5 6.78	6.79
	7.06	0.0 1 NC	Cheboksary		4 Jul	7.06	x	6.94/0.1 p 6.76	p
	6.92	0.5 1 WK	Zürich		30 Aug	x	6.62	6.92 p 6.89/0.6	x
	6.89	-0.1 1 Athl	Lausanne		23 Aug	6.89/-0.1	6.68	x 6.70 6.89/-0.1	p
7.03	1.3	Olga	Kucherenko	RUS	5.11.85	1		Sochi	26 May
					6.86/1.1	6.91/1.1	6.84/0.5	7.03	
	6.91i	1	Krasnodar		29 Jan	6.65	6.90	6.84 6.75 x	6.91
	6.90	0.5 1	Velenje		14 Jun	6.58	6.77	6.90 6.78 6.85/0.1	6.71
7.03	1.7	Janay	DeLoach	USA	12.10.85	*	NC/OT	Eugene	1 Jul
					x	6.82/1.7	7.03/1.7	6.60 7.08w	6.90w/2.3
	6.98i	2	WIIstanbul		11 Mar	x	6.74	6.78 6.67 6.73	6.98
	6.90i	Q	WIIstanbul		10 Mar	6.52	6.55	6.90	
	6.89Ai	1 NC	Albuquerque		26 Feb	6.89	6.86	6.89 6.69 p	6.57
	6.89	0.2 3 OG	London (OS)		8 Aug	6.77	x	6.71 6.74 6.89	x
7.01	1.1	Veronika	Shutkova	BLR	26.5.86	2		Minsk	12 Jun
					x	6.93/1.4	6.86/0.7	6.65 6.97w/3.0	7.08
6.97	0.3	Blessing	Okagbare	NGR	9.10.88	1	NC	Calabar	21 Jun
	6.96	1.7 1 AfrC	Porto Novo		29 Jun	6.26	6.96	6.43 6.29 p	p
6.97	1.0	Vashti	Thomas (10)	USA	21.4.90	Q	NC/OT	Eugene	29 Jun
					x	6.97			
6.97	1.2	Whitney	Gipson	USA	20.9.90	4	NC/OT	Eugene	1 Jul
					6.73	x	6.78	6.87/0.6 x	6.97
	6.91i	1 NCAA	Nampa		9 Mar	6.64	6.30	x x 6.91	6.22
6.95	1.9	Viktoriya	Rybalko	UKR	26.10.82	1	NC	Yalta	13 Jun
					6.69	6.95	p	x 6.88/1.9	x
6.95	0.1	Shara	Proctor	GBR	16.9.88	1	NC	Birmingham	24 Jun
					6.77	6.85/0.6	6.95	p p	p
	6.89i	3	WIIstanbul		11 Mar	x	x	6.86 6.55 6.74	6.89
6.93	1.8	Darya	Klishina	RUS	15.1.91	1	NCp	Yerino	15 Jul
	(32/14)				x	6.85w/2.3	6.90w/2.1	6.93 x	6.91/1.6
6.88	0.1	Sosthene	Moguenara	GER	17.10.89	1		Wesel	28 May
6.88	1.2	Ineta	Radevica	LAT	13.7.81	4	OG	London (OS)	8 Aug
6.87	0.4	Lyudmila	Kolchanova	RUS	1.10.79	3	NC	Cheboksary	4 Jul
6.85	0.5	Maurren Higa	Maggi	BRA	25.6.76	1	GP	São Paulo	16 May
6.85	-0.1	Olga	Sudarova	BLR	22.2.84	3		Minsk	12 Jun
6.85	1.4	Brianna	Glenn	USA	18.4.80	5	NC/OT	Eugene	1 Jul
	(20)								
6.82		Funmi	Jimoh	USA	29.5.84	1		Chula Vista	24 May
6.81	0.5	Éloyse	Lesueur	FRA	15.7.88	1	EC	Helsinki	28 Jun
6.80	0.7	Abigail	Irozuru	GBR	3.1.90	1	Pavlov	Sofia	9 Jun
6.80	0.8	Margaryta	Tverdohlib	UKR	2.6.91	2	NC	Yalta	13 Jun
6.79i		Bianca	Stuart	BAH	17.5.88	2		Fayetteville	11 Feb
6.78	0.0	Tori	Bowie	USA	27.8.90	1	Conf USA	New Orleans	12 May
6.76	1.3	Viorica	Tigâu	ROU	12.8.79	1		Bucuresti	16 Jun
6.75	1.8	Hyleas	Fountain	USA	14.1.81	1		Tucson	17 May
6.74	1.7	Anna	Melnychenko	UKR	24.4.83	Q	NC	Yalta	12 Jun
6.74	0.5	Lorraine	Ugen	GBR	22.8.91	2	NC	Birmingham	24 Jun
	(30)								
6.73	1.7	Viktoriya	Molchanova	UKR	26.5.82	1		Yalta	4 Jun
6.73A	1.8	Caterine	Ibargüen	COL	12.2.84	*	SAmGP	Bogotá	30 Jun
6.72i		Oksana	Zhukovskaya	RUS	12.9.84	1		Sankt-Peterburg	4 Jan
6.72	2.0	Svetlana	Denyayeva	RUS	12.5.91	1		Moskva	13 May
6.72	0.0	Lena	Malkus	GER-J	6.8.93	1	NC-23	Kandel	28 Jul
6.71	0.9	Ola	Sesay	SLE	30.5.79	1		Houston	31 May
6.71i		Veronika	Mosina	RUS	17.10.90	1		Sankt-Peterburg	28 Dec
6.70i		Yekaterina	Poplavskaya	BLR	7.5.87	1	Univ Ch	Gomel	20 Feb
6.69A	1.1	María del Mar	Jover	ESP	21.4.88	1		Monachil	28 Jul
6.69	1.7	Shameka	Marshall	USA	9.9.83	Q	NC/OT	Eugene	29 Jun
	(40)								
6.68	1.4	Keila	Costa	BRA	6.2.83	2	GP	São Paulo	16 May
6.68	1.1	Melanie	Bauschke	GER	14.7.88	2		Garbsen	20 May
6.68	1.9	Yekaterina	Levichkaya	RUS	2.1.87	2	NCp	Yerino	15 Jul
6.67i		Cornelia	Deiac	ROU	20.3.88	1		Bucuresti	28 Jan
6.67 ?	1.7	Maiko	Gogoladze	GEO	9.9.91	1		Sofia	2 May
6.67		Yana	Gubar	RUS	2.7.90	1		Khabarovsk	9 Jun
6.67	1.2	Margrethe	Renstrøm	NOR	21.3.85	3	EC	Helsinki	28 Jun
6.67	0.6	Lauma	Griva	LAT	27.10.84	1		Viljandi	3 Jul
6.67	1.2	Jazmin	Sawyers	GBR-J	21.5.94	3	WJ	Barcelona	13 Jul
6.66i		Nadja	Käther	GER	29.9.88	1		Bielefeld	12 Feb
	(50)								

Mark	Wind	Name		Nat	Born	Pos	Meet	Venue	Date
6.66i		Karin Melis	Mey ¶	TUR	31.5.84	2	GP	Birmingham	18 Feb
6.66	0.6	Irène	Pusterla	SUI	21.6.88	1		Chiasso	20 Jun
6.66	0.2	Tatyana	Kotova	RUS	11.12.76	6	NC	Cheboksary	4 Jul
6.65	0.0	Kristina	Savitskaya	RUS	10.6.91	1H	NC	Cheboksary	3 Jun
6.65	1.4	Krystyna	Hryshutyna	UKR	21.3.92	4	NC	Yalta	13 Jun
6.65	0.4	Teresa	Dobija	POL	19.10.82	1	NC	Bielsko-Biala	17 Jun
6.65	0.0	Jana	Veldáková	SVK	3.6.81	1		Brno	4 Jul
6.64	0.0		Lu Minjia	CHN	29.12.92	1	AsiGP	Kanchanaburi	11 May
6.64	0.1	Sinje	Florczak	GER	28.11.86	3		Wesel	28 May
6.64	1.1	Ivana	Spanovic	SRB	10.5.90	1	NCp	Sremska Mitrovica	3 Jun
		(60)							
6.63	1.1	Kerrie	Perkins	AUS	2.4.79	1		Gold Coast	26 May
6.63	-0.4	Aiga	Grabuste	LAT	24.3.88	1		Valmiera	9 Jun
6.63	0.7		Xu Xiaoling	CHN	13.5.92	1		Fuzhou	24 Jun
6.63	1.7	Tatyana	Ter-Mesrobyan	RUS	12.5.68	1		Sankt-Peterburg	26 Jun
6.62	1.4	Marestella	Torres	PHI	20.2.81	1	AsiGP	Chonburi	14 May
6.61i		Tatyana	Chernova	RUS	29.1.88	Q	NC	Moskva	22 Feb
6.61	0.9	Eliane	Martins	BRA	26.5.86	2		Santiago de Chile	14 Apr
6.61	1.8	Amber	Bledsoe	USA	18.8.85	1		Clermont	16 Apr
6.61	1.9	Akiba	McKinney	USA	9.3.79	1		Chula Vista	10 May
6.61	0.4	Anna	Jagaciak	POL	10.2.90	2	NC	Bielsko-Biala	17 Jun
		(70)							
6.60i		Yuliya	Pidluzhnaya	RUS	1.10.88	1		Chelyabinsk	13 Jan
6.60	0.8	Patience	Ntshingila	RSA	26.8.89	1	NC	Port Elizabeth	13 Apr
6.60	0.1	Jovanee	Jarrett	JAM	15.1.83	1		Auburn	21 Apr
6.60	1.8	Darya	Reznichenko	UZB	3.4.91	1	NCp	Tashkent	24 Apr
6.60	-0.6	Patricia	Sylvester	GRN	3.2.83	1		Toronto	22 May
6.60	0.1	Bianca	Kappler	GER	8.8.77	4		Wesel	28 May
6.60	0.9	Macarena	Reyes	CHI	30.3.84	1	NC-j	Santiago de Chile	3 Jun
6.60	1.1	Concepción	Montaner	ESP	14.1.81	1		Barcelona (SE)	6 Jun
6.60	-0.7	Mayookha	Johny	IND	9.4.88	1		Rhede	7 Jun
6.60	2.0	Paraskeví	Papahrístou	GRE	17.4.89	1	NC	Athína	15 Jun
		(80)							
6.60	0.0	Chinazor	Amadi	NGR	12.9.87	2	NC	Calabar	21 Jun
6.60	-0.9	Oksana	Zubkovska	UKR	15.7.81	1	Paral F12	London (OS)	7 Sep
6.59	-1.3	Yilian	Durruthy	CUB	30.1.90	1H		La Habana	5 May
6.59	0.7	Sonnisha	Williams	USA	20.4.91	2	Conf USA	New Orleans	12 May
6.58	1.9	Christabel	Nettey	CAN	2.6.91	1		Tempe	17 Mar
6.58	1.3	Lakadron	Ivery	USA	23.6.83	2		Houston	16 Jun
6.58	1.5	Jéssica Carolina	dos Reis	BRA-J	17.3.93	1	NC-j	Maringá	16 Jun
6.58	0.7	Chanice	Porter	JAM-J	25.5.94	4	WJ	Barcelona	13 Jul
6.57i		Nataliya	Dobrynska	UKR	29.5.82	1P	WI	Istanbul	9 Mar
6.57	1.4	Francine	Simpson	JAM	1.11.89	4	NCAA	Des Moines	7 Jun
		(90)							
6.57	0.0	Alina	Rotaru	ROU-J	5.6.93	1	IntC	Bucuresti	8 Jun
6.57	1.9	Cristina	Sandu	ROU	4.3.90	*		Bucuresti	16 Jun
6.57	0.6	Tania	Vicenzino	ITA	1.4.86	2		Chiasso	20 Jun
6.56i		Xenia	Atschkinadze	GER	14.1.89	1	NC	Karlsruhe	26 Feb
6.56	0.8	Brooke	Stratton	AUS-J	12.7.93	2	NC	Melbourne	15 Apr
6.56	0.4	Yekaterina	Koneva	RUS	25.9.88	3		Sochi	26 May
6.56	0.6	Anastasiya	Kadicheva	RUS-J	23.2.94	1	NC-j	Cheboksary	19 Jun
6.56	0;9	Renata	Medgyesová	SVK	28.1.83	1		Brno	20 Jun
6.56	0.5	Nectaria	Panayi	CYP	20.3.90	1	Veniz	Haniá	4 Jul
6.55A	0.4	Janice	Josephs	RSA	31.3.82	1		Pretoria	4 May
		(100)							
6.55	0.3	Maria Natalia	Londa	INA	29.10.90	1		Taipei	25 May
6.55	1.7	Karynn	Dunn	USA	14.8.91	5	NCAA	Des Moines	7 Jun
6.55	0.0	Saeko	Okayama	JPN	12.4.82	1	NC	Osaka	8 Jun

Mark	Wind	Name		Nat	Born	Date		Mark	Wind	Name		Nat	Born	Date
6.54i		Jamesha	Youngblood	USA	24.4.89	11 Feb		6.50	2.0	Arantxa	King	BER	27.11.89	31 Mar
6.54i		Karolina	Tyminska	POL	4.10.84	18 Feb		6.50	1.3	Andrea	Geubelle	USA	21.6.91	21 Apr
6.54	1.1	Dafne	Schippers	NED	15.6.92	17 Jun		6.50	-0.3	Sophie	Krauel	GER	2.3.85	9 Jun
6.54	0.1	Tori	Polk	USA	21.9.83	29 Jun		6.50	1.4	Andriana	Bânova	BUL	1.5.87	9 Jun
6.53i		Inna	Ahkozova	UKR	16.9.84	18 Feb		6.49	1.2	Skye	Morrison	USA		11 May
6.53	1.1	Anika	Leipold	GER	13.4.87	28 May		6.49	0.2	Brittni	Dixon-Smith	USA	20.1.89	19 May
6.52i		Yekaterina	Bolshova	RUS	4.2.88	9 Mar		6.49	0.7	Stefanie	Voss	GER	9.9.89	28 May
6.52	0.1	Uhunoma	Osazuwa	NGR	23.11.87	21 Jun		6.49	0.6	Beatrice	Marscheck	GER	23.9.85	9 Jun
6.52	1.6	Anastasiya	Mokhnyuk	UKR	1.1.91	18 Jul		6.49	2.0	Stephanie	LeFever	USA	25.7.89	14 Jun
6.52	2.0	Sachiko	Masumi	JPN	20.12.84	11 Nov		6.49	1.5	Julia	Mächtig	GER	1.1.86	15 Jun
6.51i		Haoua	Kessely	FRA	2.2.88	25 Feb		6.49	0.7	Anastassia	Angioi	ITA-Y	28.4.95	17 Jun
6.51	0.8	Jessica	Ennis	GBR	28.1.86	27 May		6.48	1.9	Michelle	Weitzel	GER	18.6.87	26 May
6.51	1.3	Katarina	Johnson-Thompson	GBR-J	9.1.93	12 Jul		6.48	1.8	Hanako	Kotake	JPN	13.9.90	7 Apr
6.51	1.9	Marina	Kasatkina	RUS	19.11.91	15 Jul		6.48	0.9	Tianna	Madison	USA	30.8.85	12 May

Mark	Wind	Name	Nat	Born	Date
6.48	1.3	Tamaka Shimizu	JPN	22.6.91	19 May
6.48	1.6	Erica Jarder	SWE	2.4.86	27 May
6.48	2.0	Jessie Gaines	USA	12.8.90	10 Jun
6.48	0.8	Efthimía Kolokithá	GRE	9.7.87	20 Jun
6.48	0.0	Olga Zaytseva	RUS	10.11.84	3 Jul
6.48	2.0	Juliet Itoya	ESP	17.8.86	21 Jul
6.47i		Leah Eber	USA	22.11.88	3 Feb
6.47	2.0	Jade Nimmo	GBR	23.3.91	14 Apr
6.47	0.0	Yuliya Tarasova	UZB	13.3.86	11 May
6.47	1.9	Jana Koresová	CZE	8.4.81	7 Jul
6.47	1.5	Polina Yurchenko	RUS-J	20.8.93	19 Jun
6.46	0.5	Wang Wupin	CHN	18.1.91	15 Apr
6.46	1.9	Emel Güngör	TUR	29.11.88	14 May
6.46	0.8	Olga Kurban	RUS	16.12.87	3 Jun
6.46	1.8	Yvette Lewis	USA	16.3.85	9 Jun
6.45i		Malaika Mihambo	GER-J	3.2.94	19 Feb
6.45	1.7	Constance Ezugha	USA	15.5.91	12 May
6.45	0.0	Paula Beatriz Álvarez	CUB-Y	11.9.95	27 May
6.45	-0.5	Dominique Blaize	GBR	3.10.87	16 Jun
6.45i		Florentina Marincu	ROU-Y	8.4.06	7 Dec
6.44	1.3	Maren Schwerdtner	GER	3.10.85	27 May
6.44		Yamina Hajjaji	MAR	6.11.88	3 Jun
6.44	0.5	Lucimara da Silva	BRA	10.7.85	10 Jun
6.44	1.0	Evaggelía Galéni	GRE	29.12.88	20 Jun
6.44	0.0	Comfort Onyali	NGR	25.4.83	21 Jun
6.44	2.0	Claudia Rath	GER	25.4.86	14 Jul
6.43i		Yelena Klimina	RUS	20.1.89	21 Jan
6.43i		Anastasiya Kudinova	KAZ	27.2.88	28 Jan
6.43	1.6	Jessica Penney	AUS	21.12.87	15 Apr
6.43	1.5	Janae Gennette	USA		20 Apr
6.43	0.3	Amy Harris	GBR	14.9.87	20 Apr
6.43	0.0	Naide Gomes	POR	20.11.79	13 May
6.43	0.0	Anna Kornuta	UKR	10.11.88	28 May
6.43	1.8	Kseniya Kurnavina	UKR	25.4.87	4 Jun
6.43	1.2	Kylie Price	USA-J	10.11.93	7 Jun
6,42A		Monja Goosen	RSA	2.10.91	25 Feb
6.42	0.6	Xu Yue	CHN	12.3.90	13 May
6.42	1.8	Nataliya Snigur	UKR	20.6.88	13 Jun
6.42	0.9	Rose Richmond	USA	29.1.81	29 Jun
6.42	1.2	Antoinette Nana Djimou	FRA	2.8.85	30 Jun
6.41i		Mariya Shumilova	RUS	10.1.90	7 Feb
6.41i		Yao Jiajia	CHN	7.4.88	13 Feb
6.41i		Kristin Gierisch	GER	20.8.90	26 Feb
6.41Ai		Marshevet Hooker	USA	25.9.84	26 Feb
6.41	1.9	Zhang Lan	CHN	27.2.88	15 Apr
6.40i		Ruslana Tsyhotska	UKR	23.3.86	17 Feb
6.40	0.6	Hanna Knyazyeva	UKR	25.9.89	28 May
6.39Ai		Chaunté Lowe	USA	12.1.84	26 Feb
6.39	1.4	Jade Johnson	GBR	7.6.80	21 Apr
6.39A	0.0	Daniela Pávez	CHI	6.3.82	29 Apr
6.39	-0.5	Vanessa Seles	BRA	26.10.81	16 May
6.39	1.1	Anna Yermakova	UKR	1.10.91	17 May
6.39	0.9	Malgorzata Reszka	POL	23.8.89	17 Jun
6.39	-0.2	Wang Rong	CHN-Y	1.7.96	23 Sep
6.38i		Anastasiya Potapova	RUS	6.9.85	29 Jan
6.38	1.5	Nickiesha Beaumont	JAM	13.1.91	5 May
6.38	0.5	Lynique Prinsloo	RSA	30.3.91	10 Jun
6.38	1.2	Yekaterina Poplavskaya	BLR	7.5.87	13 Jun
6.38	-0.3	Agnieszka Cichowlas	POL	17.8.88	17 Jun
6.38	1.0	Lisa Steinkamp	GER	17.8.90	28 Jul
6.37i		Sarah Nambawa	UGA	23.9.85	7 Jan
6.37i		Oksana Klovska	UKR	15.7.84	13 Jan
6.37A	1.2	Alesha Walker	USA	9.4.88	7 Apr
6.37	0.9	Andressa Fidelis	BRA-J	20.1.94	7 Apr
6.37	0.6	Blandine Maisonnier	FRA	3.1.86	6 May
6.37	-1.2	Todea-Kay Willis (197)	JAM	23.11.88	29 Jun

Wind assisted

Mark	Wind	Name	Nat	Born	Pos	Meet	Venue	Date
7.22	4.3	Anastasiya Mironchik-Ivanova	BLR	13.4.89	1	NC	Grodno	6 Jul
7.15	2.8	Janay DeLoach	USA	12.10.85	Q	NC/OT	Eugene	29 Jun
7.15w								
7.08	2.4	DeLoach			3	NC/OT	Eugene	1 Jul
7.04	3.6	Éloyse Lesueur	FRA	15.7.88	1		Coral Gables	14 Apr
7.04w	x	x	x	6.59	x			
6.96	2.6	Kucherenko			1	Bisl	Oslo	7 Jun
6.96w	6.53w	6.85w/3.0	6.40	p	x			
6.95	2.7	Sokolova			1	ECCp	Vila Real de Santo António	27 May
6.95w	x	6.78	x					
6.87A	4.1	Caterine Ibargüen	COL	12.2.84	1	SAmGP	Bogotá	30 Jun
6.85	2.2	Svetlana Denyayeva	RUS	12.5.91	1		Yerino	2 Jun
6.83	2.8	Lorraine Ugen	GBR	22.8.91	1		Fort Worth	16 Mar
6.81	2.5	Katarina Johnson-Thompson	GBR-J	9.1.93	1	WJ	Barcelona	13 Jul
6.80	2.7	Lena Malkus	GER-J	6.8.93	2	WJ	Barcelona	13 Jul
6.78	4.3	Chanice Porter	JAM-J	25.5.94	1	NC-j	Kingston	16 Jun
6.72	3.1	Alexis Tanner	USA	24.8.87	1		San Marcos	28 Apr
6.72	3.1	Xenia Atschkinadze	GER	14.1.89	2		Wesel	28 May
6.70	3.1	Kerrie Perkins	AUS	2.4.79	1	NC	Melbourne	15 Apr
6.70	2.7	Cristina Sandu	ROU	4.3.90	2		Bucuresti	16 Jun
6.67	4.1	Saeko Okayama	JPN	12.4.82	1		Kawasaki	6 May
6.67	2.4	Francine Simpson	JAM	1.11.89	1	Big 12	Manhattan, KS	12 May
6.66	3.4	Chantel Malone	IVB	2.12.91	4	TexR	Austin	31 Mar
6.65	3.6	Anna Jagaciak	POL	10.2.90	1		Lódz	9 Jun
6.65	2.1	Tania Vicenzino	ITA	1.4.86	1		Bressanone	8 Jul
6.62	2.6	Jana Koresová	CZE	8.4.81	2		Brno	4 Jul
6.60	3.2	Michelle Weitzel	GER	18.6.87	1		Weinheim	26 May
6.58	2.1	Alina Rotaru	ROU-J	5.6.93	Q	WJ	Barcelona	12 Jul
6.58	3.1	Yelena Sitnikova	RUS	12.11.89	3	NCp	Yerino	15 Jul

Mark	Wind	Name	Nat	Born	Date
6.56	2.4	Malaina Payton	USA	16.10.91	14 Apr
6.56A	8.5	Janae Gennette	USA		14 Apr
6.56	2.7	Sachiko Masumi	JPN	20.12.84	21 Oct
6.55	2.6	Ti'Anca Mock	USA	5.6.88	31 Mar
6.55	3.1	Arantxa King	BER	27.11.89	24 May
6.54	5.6	Rose Richmond	USA	29.1.81	27 Apr
6.52	2.6	Andrea Geubelle	USA	21.6.91	24 May
6.52	2.5	Tatyana Akmukhamedova	RUS-J	14.1.93	19 Jun
6.50	3.6	Malaika Mihambo	GER-J	3.2.94	24 Jun
6.49	2.1	Wang Wupin	CHN	18.1.91	2 Jun
6.48A	2.1	Daniela Pávez	CHI	6.3.82	29 Apr
6.47A	3.4	Krysha Bayley	CAN	21.1.84	29 Jun
6.46	4.2	Mara Griva	LAT	4.8.89	24 May
6.45	2.2	Leah Eber	USA	22.11.88	14 Apr
6.45	2.2	Yanique Levy	JAM	10.3.83	20 Apr
6.45A	3.9	Sydney Conley	USA-J	11.12.93	2 Jun
6.43	2.2	Austra Skujyte	LTU	12.8.79	7 Jul
6.41	2.5	Asha Ruth	USA		5 May
6.40	2.5	Carla Marais	RSA	10.12.87	13 Apr
6.39	4.2	Elisa Zanei	ITA	18.6.84	8 Jul
6.39	2.8	Heather Miller	USA	30.3.87	22 Jul
6.38	2.4	Daria Derkach	UKR-J	27.3.93	15 Jun
6.38	3.2	Irina Bolshakova	RUS	27.12.92	26 Jun
6.38	3.0	Teresa Di Loreto	ITA	26.12.89	8 Jul

Mark	Wind	Name	Nat	Born	Pos	Meet	Venue	Date

Best outdoors
```
6.66  0.5  Stuart      4 Pre  Eugene       2 Jun | 6.64  0.6  Zhukovskaya  2        Sochi         26 May
6.54 -1.1  Mey ¶      20 May | 6.52  0.4  Atschkinadze 28 May | 6.46  0.8  Mosina         20 Jun
6.54  0.0  Deiac       6 Jul | 6.50  2.0  Youngblood   17 May | 6.45  0.9  Bolshova        3 Jun
           6.58w 2.3  16 Jun |           6.54w 2.3    19 May | 6.39  1.0  Kudinova       19 Jun
6.54  0.5  Chernova    4 Aug | 6.47  0.5  Käther        3 Jun | 6.45w 2.2  Eber           14 Apr
```
Best at low altitude
```
6.63  1.5  Ibargüen   *   Ponce    12 May | 6.57  0.4  Jover    2       Barcelona         16 Jun
           6.66w 2.2  1   Ponce    12 May |           6.65w 5.6  2 ECCp  VR de S.António   27 May
                                          | 6.43  -2.5  Josephs         10 Mar
```

Drugs disqualification: 6.80 0.2 Karin Melis Mey ¶ TUR 31.5.84 Q OG London (OS) 7 Aug

JUNIORS

See main list for top 7 juniors. 10 perfs by 7 women & 4 wa by 4 women to 6.55. Additional marks and further juniors:

```
Malkus    6.57  1.5 1      Mannheim    24 Jun
Sawyers   6.64  0.8 3  NC  Birmimgham  24 Jun
dos Reis  6.55  1.1 1      São Paulo   28 Apr
```

Mark	Wind	Name		Nat	Born	Pos	Meet	Venue	Date
6.51	1.3	Katarina	Johnson-Thompson	GBR	9.1.93	Q	WJ	Barcelona	12 Jul
6.49	0.7	Anastassia	Angioi	ITA-Y	28.4.95	1		Sassari	17 Jun
6.47	1.5	Polina	Yurchenko (10)	RUS	20.8.93	Q	NC-j	Cheboksary	19 Jun
6.45i		Malaika	Mihambo	GER	3.2.94	1	NC-j	Sindelfingen	19 Feb
6.45	0.0	Paula Beatriz	Álvarez	CUB-Y	11.9.95	1		La Habana	27 May
6.45i		Florentina	Marincu	ROU-Y	8.4.06	1		Bucuresti	7 Dec
6.43	1.2	Kylie	Price	USA	10.11.93	7	NCAA	Des Moines	7 Jun
6.39	-0.2		Wang Rong	CHN-Y	1.7.96	2	NC	Kunshan	23 Sep
6.37	0.9	Andressa	Fidelis	BRA	20.1.94	3		São Paulo	7 Apr
6.36	0.8	Marina	Bekh	UKR-Y	18.7.95	1	NC-j	Yalta	31 May
6.36	0.1	Akela	Jones	BAR-Y	31.12.95	1	CAC-y	San Salvador	29 Jun
6.35	1.4	Julia	Gerter	GER-J	13.7.94	1cB		Mannheim	24 Jun
6.32i		Maryse	Luzolo (20)	GER-Y	13.3.95	1		Frankfurt	22 Jan
6.32	1.9	Malaika	Mihambo	GER	3.2.94	*		Mannheim	24 Jun

Wind assisted to 6.37

Mark	Wind	Name		Nat	Born	Pos	Meet	Venue	Date
6.52	2.5	Tatyana	Akmukhamedova	RUS	14.1.93	2	NC-j	Cheboksary	19 Jun
6.50	3.6	Malaika	Mihambo	GER	3.2.94	2		Mannheim	24 Jun
6.45A	3.9	Sydney	Conley	USA	11.12.93	1		Albuquerque	2 Jun
6.38	2.4	Daria	Derkach	UKR	27.3.93	1	NC-j	Misano Adriatico	15 Jun
6.37 nwi		Jasmine	Gibbs	USA	15.1.94	1		Oceanside	11 May

TRIPLE JUMP

```
14.99   0.2  Olha            Saladuha       UKR   4.6.83   1    EC       Helsinki                 29 Jun
             14.99  14.84/1.0 x     14.65/0.9   x        14.89/1.0
        14.79i       1 XL Galan     Stockholm  23 Feb   14.16   14.62   x       x       x   14.70
        14.79  0.5 3 OG   London (OS)      5 Aug   13.92   14.48   x       14.53   14.51   14.79
        14.77  0.0 Q EC   Helsinki        27 Jun   14.77   p       p
        14.75  1.1 1      Rabat           27 May   14.48   14.72/0.8 x   14.64/0.9 14.67/0.3 14.75
        14.75  0.1 1 GGala Roma          31 May   x       14.75   x       14.18   14.72/1.1 14.63/-0.3
14.98  -0.4  Olga            Rypakova       KAZ  30.11.84  1    OG       London (OS)               5 Aug
             14.54/-1.6 x       14.98   x       14.89/0.7 14.40
        14.84i       1 NC   Karaganda       27 Jan  13.99   14.50   x       14.84   x       x
        14.79  0.5 Q OG   London (OS)      3 Aug   x       13.99   14.79
        14.73 -1.2 2 GGala Roma          31 May   14.46   14.13   14.47   14.63/1.2 14.52/-0.8 14.73
        14.72  0.4 1 VD   Bruxelles        7 Sep   14.27   14.62/0.2 14.72  p       14.62/0.5 14.55/0.2
        14.71 -0.9 1 DL   New York         9 Jun   14.71   x       x       p       13.93   14.49
        14.68 -0.6 1 Athl Lausanne        23 Aug   x       14.45   14.68   14.56/-1.3 p     p
        14.63i       2 WI   Istanbul        10 Mar  x       x       x       14.45   14.63   x
14.95A  0.9  Caterine        Ibargüen       COL  12.2.84   1             Medellin                 28 Apr
             14.93/-0.7 14.95   14.70/0.1 x     x       x
        14.85 -0.1 1 Herc  Monaco          20 Jul  14.72/0.0 14.85  x    14.74/-0.2 14.79/0.2 14.80/0.1
        14.80  0.4 2 OG   London (OS)      5 Aug   14.45   13.99   14.67/-0.4 14.37 14.35   14.80
        14.73  0.2 1      Baie Mahault     1 May   13.90   14.71/-0.2 14.61/-0.1 14.73 x    p
        14.71  0.1 3 GGala Roma          31 May   14.17   14.65/0.7 x   14.58/-0.2 14.56/1.3 14.71
        14.66 -0.8 1 LGP  London (CP)     14 Jul   14.13   14.28   14.61/-0.1 14.41 14.27   14.66
14.82i       Yamilé          Aldama         GBR  14.8.72   1    WI       Istanbul                 10 Mar
             14.10   14.82   x       p       p       p
        14.65 -0.3 4 GGala Roma          31 May   14.10   14.65   p       p       p       p
        14.62i       Q WI   Istanbul         9 Mar  14.62   p       p
14.76   0.4  Kseniya         Detsuk         BLR  23.4.86   *    NCp      Brest                    26 May
             14.49   x       p       14.76   14.81w/2.4 14.44
14.71   2.0  Hanna           Knyazyeva      UKR  25.9.89   1    NC       Yalta                    15 Jun
             14.71   p       x       x       p       x
14.71   1.4  Athanasía       Pérra          GRE   2.2.83   1    NC       Athína                   16 Jun
             x       x       14.51/0.9 x     x       14.71
```

Mark	Wind	Name		Nat	Born	Pos	Meet	Venue			Date
14.68		Tatyana	Lebedeva	RUS	21.7.76	1	NC	Cheboksary			4 Jul
			14.54/0.9	x		14.47	14.51	14.68			14.37
14.64		Viktoriya	Valyukevich	RUS	22.5.82	2	NC	Cheboksary			4 Jul
			x		14.11	x	14.59	x			14.64
14.60i		Yekaterina	Koneva (10)	RUS	25.9.88	1		Krasnodar			29 Jan
			14.30		14.41	14.45	14.60	p			x
14.58	-1.4	Dailenis	Alcántara	CUB	10.8.91	1		La Habana			27 May
			14.43	x		14.52/0.1		x			14.58 x
14.58	0.9	Paraskeví	Papahrístou	GRE	17.4.89	2	NC	Athína			16 Jun
			x	x		13.80w	13.98w	13.96			14.58
14.58	0.0		Ibargüen			1		Reims			4 Jul
		(32/12)			14.08	14.46	14.58	14.56/-0.1	14.38		p
14.55i		Yargeris	Savigne	CUB	13.11.84	1		Metz			29 Feb
14.53	1.0	Ruslana	Tsyhotska	UKR	23.3.86	1	NCp	Yalta			29 May
14.53	0.0	Kimberly	Williams	JAM	3.11.88	Q	OG	London (OS)			3 Aug
14.52	1.8	Patrícia	Mamona	POR	21.11.88	2	EC	Helsinki			29 Jun
14.50	1.9	Hanna	Demydova	UKR	8.4.87	2	NC	Yalta			15 Jun
14.50	1.7	Níki	Panétta	GRE	21.4.86	3	NC	Athína			16 Jun
14.50		Veronika	Mosina	RUS	17.10.90	3	NC	Cheboksary			4 Jul
14.43	0.3	Yekaterina	Kayukova	RUS	9.10.86	2	Mosc Ch	Moskva			21 Jun
		(20)									
14.41	1.8	Yana	Borodina	RUS	21.4.92	1		Sochi			27 May
14.41		Olesya	Zabara	RUS	6.10.82	4	NC	Cheboksary			4 Jul
14.40	0.7	Mabel	Gay	CUB	5.5.83	1	GP	Belém			6 May
14.40		Anna	Krylova	RUS	3.10.85	5	NC	Cheboksary			4 Jul
14.37	0.1	Valeriya	Zavyalova	RUS	16.1.88	1		Krasnodar			9 Jun
14.36	0.5	Dana	Veldáková	SVK	3.6.81	Q	EC	Helsinki			27 Jun
14.35	1.8	Viktoriya	Dolgacheva	RUS	17.4.91	1	NC-23	Yerino			22 Jul
14.35	-0.2	Trecia	Smith	JAM	5.11.75	7	OG	London (OS)			5 Aug
14.34	0.2	Anastasiya	Juravlyeva	UZB	9.10.81	1	NCp	Tashkent			24 Apr
14.31	0.5	Keila	Costa	BRA	6.2.83	2	DL	Doha			11 May
		(30)									
14.30	1.6	Josleidy	Ribalta	CUB	2.5.90	1		La Habana			17 Feb
14.29	0.5	Simona	La Mantia	ITA	14.4.83	1	Nebiolo	Torino			8 Jun
14.29	0.3	Irina	Ektova	KAZ	8.1.87	2		Almaty			30 Jun
14.28	1.5	Yarianna	Martínez	CUB	20.9.84	3		La Habana			3 Feb
14.28	0.4	Svetlana	Bolshakova	BEL	14.10.84	1		Lokeren			28 May
14.27	0.9	Françoise	Mbango	FRA	14.4.76	1	NC	Angers			17 Jun
14.26	-0.4	Marija	Sestak	SLO	17.4.79	1		Velenje			14 Jun
14.24i		Adelina	Gavrilâ	ROU	26.11.78	1	NC	Bucuresti			24 Feb
14.24i		Irina	Gumenyuk	RUS	6.1.88	1		Sankt-Peterburg			29 Dec
14.23i		Anastasiya	Potapova	RUS	6.9.85	3		Krasnodar			29 Jan
		(40)									
14.23i			Li Yanmei	CHN	6.2.90	Q	WI	Istanbul			9 Mar
14.21i			Xie Limei	CHN	27.6.86	1	NGP	Nanjing			14 Feb
14.21	1.0	Katja	Demut	GER	21.12.83	1		Wesel			28 May
14.20	0.7	Snezana	Rodic	SLO	19.8.82	2		Ljubljana			7 Jun
14.19i		Kristin	Gierisch	GER	20.8.90	1	NC	Karlsruhe			25 Feb
14.19	1.1	Susana	Costa	POR	22.9.84	2	NC	Lisboa (Un)			8 Jul
14.18	0.8	Nataliya	Yastrebova	UKR	12.10.84	3	NCp	Yalta			29 May
14.18	1.9		Hu Qian	CHN	14.1.89	1		Fuzhou			24 Jun
14.17	-1.0	Ana	Peleteiro	ESP-Y	2.12.95	1	WJ	Barcelona			12 Jul
14.17	1.6	Dovilé	Dzindzalietaité	LTU-J	14.7.93	2	WJ	Barcelona			12 Jul
		(50)									
14.16	-0.6		Wang Huiqin	CHN	7.2.90	1	NGP	Wuhan			29 Apr
14.15	1.0	Ayanna	Alexander	TRI	20.7.82	1		Port of Spain			19 May
14.14i		Cristina	Bujin	ROU	12.4.88	1		Bucuresti			27 Jan
14.14i		Andriana	Bânova	BUL	1.5.87	1	NC	Dobrich			12 Feb
14.11	0.1	Yelena	Sidorkina	RUS	27.9.88	2		Krasnodar			9 Jun
14.08	1.7	Alsu	Murtazina	RUS	12.12.87	1	NCp	Yerino			14 Jul
14.06	0.5	Jenny	Elbe	GER	18.4.90	1	NC	Wattenscheid			17 Jun
14.05	1.5	Gisele	de Oliveira	BRA	1.8.80	1		São Paulo			20 May
14.04i		Nadezhda	Alekhina	RUS	22.9.78	6	NC	Moskva			24 Feb
14.03	-0.3	Nina	Serbezova	CYP	6.5.81	2		Athína (Filothéi)			30 May
		(60)									
14.03	0.4	Nathalie	Marie-Nelly	FRA	24.11.86	2		Montreuil-sous-Bois			5 Jun
14.02	2.0	Teresa	Nzola Meso Ba	FRA	30.11.83	3		Montreuil-sous-Bois			5 Jun
14.02	2.0	Amy	Zongo-Filet	FRA	4.10.80	1		Saint-Denis			22 Jun
14.01i		Aleksandra	Kotlyarova	UZB	10.10.88	4		Krasnodar			29 Jan
14.00i		Valeriya	Kanatova	UZB	29.8.92	5		Krasnodar			29 Jan
14.00	-0.8	Svitlana	Mamyeyeva	UKR	19.4.82	4	NCp	Yalta			29 May

Mark	Wind	Name		Nat	Born	Pos	Meet	Venue	Date
13.97	0.3		Chen Yufei	CHN	26.1.89	2	NC	Kunshan	24 Sep
13.96	1.5	Erica	McLain	USA	24.1.86	1		Stanford	7 Apr
13.96	1.1	Petia	Dacheva	BUL	10.3.85	2	NC	Sliven	16 Jun
13.95i		Mayookha	Johny	IND	9.4.88	12q	WI	Istanbul	9 Mar
(70)									
13.94	1.2	Amanda	Smock	USA	27.7.82	1	NC/OT	Eugene	25 Jun
13.92	0.1	Sarah	Nambawa	UGA	23.9.85	1		Kumasi	6 Jul
13.91	0.0	Liuba M.	Zaldívar	CUB-J	5.4.93	4		La Habana	27 May
13.90	-0.7	Patricia	Sarrapio	ESP	16.11.82	16q	EC	Helsinki	27 Jun
13.90	0.1	Noor Amira Mohd	Nafiah	MAS	16.7.89	1	NC	Kuala Lumpur	6 Oct
13.89A	0.6	Patience	Ntshingila	RSA	26.8.89	1		Potchefstroom	24 Mar
13.89	1.4	Olesya	Tikhonova	RUS	22.1.90	4	NC-23	Yerino	22 Jul
13.88	0.9	Malgorzata	Trybanska	POL	21.6.81	1	NC	Bielsko-Biala	15 Jun
13.87	1.2	Toni	Smith	USA	13.10.84	2	MSR	Walnut	21 Apr
13.87	1.7	Anna	Jagaciak	POL	10.2.90	1	NC-23	Radom	2 Sep
(80)									
13.85i		Biljana	Topic	SRB	17.10.77	1		Chemnitz	27 Jan
13.85	0.9		Li Xiaohong	CHN-Y	8.1.95	3	NC	Kunshan	24 Sep
13.84i		Natalya	Vyatkina	BLR	10.2.87	1	NC	Kaunas	18 Feb
13.84	1.7	Andrea	Geubelle	USA	21.6.91	3	NCAA	Des Moines	9 Jun
13.83i		Baya	Rahouli	ALG	27.7.79	14q	WI	Istanbul	9 Mar
13.83	-0.5	Sheena	Gordon	USA	26.9.83	2	NC/OT	Eugene	25 Jun
13.82	1.0	Blessing	Ibrahim	NGR	4.4.90	2		Kumasi	6 Jul
13.81Ai		Crystal	Manning	USA	15.4.86	1		Albuquerque	21 Jan
13.80	1.1	Charlene	Potgieter	RSA	22.9.85	1		Tampere	10 Jun
13.79	0.1		Xu Tingting	CHN	12.7.89	3	NGP	Zhaoqing	15 Apr
(90)									
13.78	1.4		Sun Yan	CHN	30.3.91	4	NGP	Zhaoqing	15 Apr
13.77i			Chen Mudan	CHN-J	4.10.93	1	NGP	Chengdu	11 Mar
13.77	-0.2		Liu Yanan	CHN	18.1.87	2		Fuzhou	24 Jun
13.76	0.4		Wang Rong	CHN-Y	1.7.96	3		Fuzhou	24 Jun
13.75	0.7	Maja	Bratkic	SLO	14.5.91	2		Nova Gorica	2 Jun
13.75	1.7	Laura	Samuel	GBR	19.2.91	1	ENG-23	Bedford	17 Jun
13.75	2.0	Jamaa	Chnaïk	MAR	28.7.84	3	AfrC	Porto Novo	1 Jul
13.72	1.1	Santa	Matule	LAT	13.12.92	1		Valmiera	8 Jun
13.71	0.7	Nadia	Williams	GBR	17.11.81	1	ENG Ch	Birmingham	2 Jun
13.71	0.0	Inger Anne	Frøysedal	NOR	25.4.89	1	NC	Kristiansand	24 Aug
(100)									

Mark	Wind	Name		Nat	Born	Date
13.69i			Hu Guanlian	CHN	18.7.90	11 Mar
13.66		Maliakkal	Prajusha	IND	20.5.87	26 Jun
13.65	1.1	Ciarra	Brewer	USA-J	12.3.93	9 Jun
13.65	2.0	Violetta	Maksimchuk	RUS	1.12.90	27 Jun
13.64	1.9	Blessing	Ufodiama	USA	28.11.81	5 May
13.64	-0.4	Shanieka	Thomas	JAM	2.2.92	1 Jul
13.64A	-0.1	Giselly Andrea	Landazuri	COL	8.8.92	17 Nov
13.63	0.4	Lyudmila	Grankovskaya	KAZ	13.2.89	30 Jun
13.63	-1.4	Suslaidy	Girat	CUB	19.8.87	16 Jul
13.62	2.0	Stephanie	Warren	USA	22.8.80	21 Apr
13.62	-1.2	Eleonora	D'Elicio	ITA	28.5.89	14 Jun
13.62	0.5	Jolanta	Verseckaité	LTU	9.2.88	30 Jun
13.62			Tran Hue Hoa	VIE	8.8.91	11 Jul
13.61i		Tiombé	Hurd	USA	17.8.73	18 Feb
13.60	1.9	Anna	Kornuta	UKR	10.11.88	28 May
13.60	1.0	Lucie	Májková	CZE	9.7.88	16 Jun
13.60	-0.5		Yan Xianting	CHN	16.5.90	24 Jun
13.60	-0.1		Xu Xiaoling	CHN	13.5.92	24 Sep
13.59	1.8	Michelle	Jenije	USA	17.8.90	26 May
13.59	2.0	Anna	Zych	POL	15.5.88	9 Jun
13.59	1.6	Francesca	Lanciano	ITA-J	3.4.94	11 Jul
13.59	1.9	Nadezhda	Korytkina	RUS	7.2.91	22 Jul
13.59	1.2		Zhang Guihua	CHN	15.10.85	24 Sep
13.58i		Natalya	Kutyakova	RUS	28.11.86	12 Feb
13.57i		Khaddi	Sagnia	SWE-J	20.4.94	11 Feb
13.56	0.7	Gita	Dodova	BUL	2.5.82	5 Jul
13.55	0.2	Linda	Allen	AUS	22.3.87	21 Jan
13.55	0.7	Nataliya	Snigur	UKR	20.6.88	19 Jul
13.54i		Lynn	Johnson	SWE-J	16.3.94	11 Feb
13.54i		Patricia	Sylvester	GRN	3.2.83	19 Feb
13.53i		Sevim	Sinmez	TUR	20.4.87	25 Feb
13.53i		Maitane	Azpeitia	ESP	1.3.89	25 Feb
13.53	0.8	Martyna	Bielawska	POL	15.11.90	27 May
13.53	-1.5	Haoua	Kessely	FRA	2.2.88	17 Jun
13.52	0.1	Irina	Kosko	RUS	1.3.90	9 Jun
13.52	1.1	Kristiina	Mäkelä	FIN	20.11.92	10 Jun
13.52	1.9	Hanna	Aleksandrova	UKR-J	11.7.93	15 Jun
13.52	1.5	Lauryn	Newson	USA	6.8.90	23 Jun
13.51	1.9	April	Sinkler	USA	1.9.89	9 Jun
13.51	0.1	Viktoriya	Leonova	RUS-J	2.12.94	9 Jun
13.51	0.8	Barbara	Lah	ITA	24.3.72	23 Jun
13.51	0.4		Xu Yue	CHN	12.3.90	15 Sep
13.50i		Yasmine	Regis	GBR	12.12.86	11 Feb
13.50	0.5		Qu Nuo	CHN	27.9.91	24 Sep
13.48	0.6		Yao Jiajia	CHN	7.4.88	15 Apr
13.48	1.9	Darya	Shushenkova	KAZ	4.9.90	1 Jun
13.48	1.7	Darya	Nelovko	RUS-J	9.2.94	21 Jun
13.48	0.4	Elina	Torro	FIN	22.7.86	26 Aug
13.47	-0.3	Brenda	Baar	NED	19.7.87	20 May
13.46	0.0	Verónica	Davis	VEN	22.5.87	24 Mar
13.46	0.4		Bae Chan-mi	KOR	24.3.91	7 May
13.46	1.2	Maria Natalia	Londa	INA	29.10.90	15 Sep
13.46	-0.2	Daria	Derkach	UKR-J	27.3.93	22 Sep
13.45i		Oksana	Udmurtova	RUS	1.2.82	24 Feb
13.45	0.1	Gabriela	Petrova	BUL	29.6.92	26 May
13.44		Tatyana	Nagornaya	BLR	14.12.89	12 Jun
13.43i			Lai Mengqin	CHN	21.1.91	11 Mar
13.43	0.7	Tatiana	Cicanci	MDA	16.8.92	8 Jun
13.42i		Jana	Nosova	LTU	25.8.90	18 Feb
13.42	0.0	Mariya	Kostusyeva	UKR	14.11.90	29 May
13.41i			Liu Jiaqi	CHN	3.8.87	14 Feb
13.41i		Olga	Salomatina	RUS	15.8.92	4 Mar
13.41	0.8	Anastasiya	Sayenko	RUS	11.11.92	11 Jun
13.41	1.8	Essi	Lindgren	FIN	10.4.90	16 Jun
13.41		Yekaterina	Lutsenko	RUS	9.1.89	3 Aug
13.40	0.2	Kristina	Marukhlenko	RUS	8.9.89	9 Jun
13.40	1.1	Jihad	Bakhchi	MAR	22.8.91	17 Jun
13.39	0.3	Ruth Marie	Ndoumbe	ESP	1.1.87	30 May
13.39	1.2	Anja	Valant Velepec	SLO	8.9.77	2 Jun
13.38i		Katarzyna	Plonka	POL	28.6.88	26 Feb
13.37	0.0	Whitney	Liehr	USA	9.6.88	19 May
13.37	-0.2	Maria	Dimitrova	BUL	7.8.76	23 Jun
13.37	1.7	Georgiana	Michnea	ROU	16.8.92	5 Jul
13.37	1.0	Yekaterina	Sariyeva	AZE-Y	18.12.95	11 Jul

Mark	Wind	Name	Nat	Born	Pos	Meet	Venue	Date
13.36	1.7	Keri Emanuel	USA	30.6.92				30 Mar
13.36	0.0	Viktoriya Rybalko	UKR	26.10.82				14 Jun
13.36	1.9	Iryna Yanchenko	UKR	22.3.88				15 Jun
13.35	2.0	Çagdas Arslan	TUR	10.3.86				5 Jun
13.34i		Fu Bingling	CHN-J	15.9.93				14 Feb
13.34	0.7	Tânia da Silva	BRA	17.12.86				18 Feb
13.34i		Tori Franklin	USA	7.10.92				10 Mar
13.34	-0.7	Brooke Stratton	AUS-J	12.7.93				15 Mar
13.34	0.9	Asta Dauksaité	LTU	3.4.88				8 Jun
13.34	1.7	Samantha Williams	JAM					9 Jun
13.34	-0.6	Sachiko Masumi	JPN	20.12.84				18 Aug
13.33	0.9	Ellen Pettitt	AUS	13.5.86				14 Apr
13.33	1.0	Hannah Frankson	GBR	11.1.89				10 Jun
13.32	1.5	Alitta Boyd	USA	7.12.91				26 May
13.32	1.4	Ottavia Cestonaro	ITA-Y	12.1.95				23 Jun
13.31i		Débora Calveras	ESP	26.12.88				25 Feb
13.31i		Jasmine Manuel	USA	7.8.90				10 Mar
13.31	0.2	Theresa Greb	GER	13.2.90				20 May
13.31	1.1	Sanna Nygård	FIN	22.3.88				1 Sep
13.30i		Kristina Damyanova	BUL	13.10.86				12 Feb
13.30	1.2	Jacqueline Triana	MEX	18.6.87				21 Apr
13.30	0.2	Lin Yan	CHN-J	26.1.93				27 May
13.30	0.6	Shakira Whight	GBR	17.10.89				24 Jun
13.30	1.0	Sineade Gutzmore	GBR	9.10.86				24 Jun
13.30	1.2	Eleftheria Christofi (199)	CYP	29.10.86				14 Jul

Wind assisted

Mark	Wind	Name	Nat	Born	Pos	Meet	Venue	Date
14.81	2.4	Kseniya Detsuk	BLR	23.4.86	1	NCp	Brest	26 May
14.77	2.3	Paraskeví Papahrístou	GRE	17.4.89	1		Ankara	5 Jun
14.77w	14.72w/2.2				p	p	p	p
14.48	2.6	Olesya Zabara	RUS	6.10.82	1	Kuso	Szczecin	21 Jul
14.39	2.1	Josleidy Ribalta	CUB	2.5.90	1		La Habana	22 Jun
14.38	2.4	Françoise Mbango	FRA	14.4.76	Q	EC	Helsinki	27 Jun
14.31	3.0	Marija Sestak	SLO	17.4.79	1	NCp	Maribor	16 Jun
14.30	4.6	Patricia Sarrapio	ESP	16.11.82	1	ECCp	V.R .e Santo António	26 May
14.25	2.4	Cristina Bujin	ROU	12.4.88	1	NC	Bucuresti	5 Jul
14.18	2.8	Liuba M. Zaldívar	CUB-J	5.4.93	1		La Habana	8 Jun
14.17	2.9	Andrea Geubelle	USA	21.6.91	1q	NCAA-W	Austin	26 May
14.16	5.7	Amy Zongo-Filet	FRA	4.10.80	1		Nemours	1 Jul
14.08	3.0	Cecilia Pacchetti	ITA	18.5.89	2	NC	Bressanone	7 Jul
14.06	3.5	Anna Jagaciak	POL	10.2.90	1		Lódz	9 Jun
14.00	2.4	Svetlana Denyayeva	RUS	12.5.91	2	NC-23	Yerino	22 Jul
13.96	5.6	Shanieka Thomas	JAM	2.2.92	2	NCAA	Des Moines	9 Jun
13.94	2.1	Violetta Maksimchuk	RUS	1.12.90	3	NC-23	Yerino	22 Jul
13.93	2.2	Crystal Manning	USA	15.4.86	1	MSR	Walnut	21 Apr
13.93	4.2	Inger Anne Frøysedal	NOR	25.4.89	1		Nadderud	4 Sep
13.90	3.1	Charlene Potgieter	RSA	22.9.85	2	AfCh	Porto Novo	1 Jul
13.87	2.5	Viktoriya Rybalko	UKR	26.10.82	4	NC	Yalta	15 Jun
13.80	3.1	Martyna Bielawska	POL	15.11.90	1	Univ Ch	Lódz	13 May

Mark	Wind	Name	Nat	Born	Date
13.72	3.3	Barbara Lah	ITA	24.3.72	7 Jul
13.70	4.1	Linda Allen	AUS	22.3.87	2 Mar
13.69	2.5	Hu Guanlian	CHN	18.7.90	24 Jun
13.68	2.7	Sachiko Masumi	JPN	20.12.84	7 Oct
13.67	2.7	Eleonora D'Elicio	ITA	28.5.89	7 Jul
13.66	2.4	Ellen Pettitt	AUS	13.5.86	14 Apr
13.64	2.7	Daria Derkach	UKR-J	27.3.93	16 Jun
13.60	3.0	Nataliya Snigur	UKR	20.6.88	15 Jun
13.59	2.3	Gita Dodova	BUL	2.5.82	5 Jul
13.56	2.9	Hanna Aleksandrova	UKR-J	11.7.93	15 Jun
13.53	2.6	Ruth Marie Ndoumbe	ESP	1.1.87	9 Jun
13.52	4.9	Sevim Sinmez	TUR	20.4.87	16 Jun
13.48	2.7	Anastasiya Sayenko	RUS	11.11.92	22 Jul
13.44	2.9	Sanna Nygård	FIN	22.3.88	26 Aug
13.43	2.9	Samantha Williams	JAM		26 May
13.42	2.6	Georgiana Michnea	ROU	16.8.92	25 May
13.42	3.6	Irina Vaskovskaya	BLR	2.4.91	29 May
13.41	?	Tânia da Silva	BRA	17.12.86	23 Nov
13.40	2.5	Irina Yanchenko	UKR	22.3.88	15 Jun
13.38	3.2	Liane Pintsaar	EST	17.3.90	17 Jun
13.35	2.4	Dilyara Abuova	KAZ-J	6.1.94	12 Jun
13.33	3.9	Sineade Gutzmore	GBR	9.10.86	30 Jun
13.32	3.8	Nadia Eke	USA-J	11.1.93	26 May
13.31	2.2	Allison Nankivell	AUS	26.6.90	29 Jun
13.30	3.3	Mara Griva	LAT	4.8.89	26 May

Best outdoors

Mark	Wind	Name	Pos	Meet	Venue	Date
14.36	0.6	Koneva	1	MoscC	Moskva	11 Jun
14.35	-1.1	Savigne	2		La Habana	3 Feb
14.20	0.5	Potapova	4	MoscC	Moskva	11 Jun
14.13		Bujin	1		Constanta	12 May
14.07	0.9	Gavrilâ	1	IntC	Bucuresti	8 Jun
14.03	1.6	Bânova	1	NC	Sliven	16 Jun
14.03		Gumenyuk	9	NC	Cheboksary	4 Jul
Gumenyuk 14.18w	2.6		2	ECCp	VR S.António	26 May
13.97	0.0	Li Yanmei	1		Zeven	27 May
13.94	0.2	Gierisch	1		Garbsen	20 May
13.91	1.2	Johny	1		Dillingen	22 Jul
13.82	-0.5	Kotlyarova	1	NCp	Tashkent	18 Apr
13.82	0.4	Xie Limei	2		Zeven	27 May
13.72	-0.2	Chen Mudan	4		Fuzhou	24 Jun

Mark	Wind	Name	Date
13.67	1.7	Hu Guanlian	24 Sep
13.66	0.0	Topic	3 Aug
13.65	0.6	Manning	21 Apr
13.57	0.7	Kutyakova	13 Jun
13.50	1.4	Rahouli	1 Jul
13.46	0.0	Alekhina	30 May
13.46	2.0	Johnson	20 Jun
13.44	1.3	Sinmez	27 May
13.42	1.3	Azpeitia	30 May
13.41A	1.8	Sylvester	30 Jun
13.41	0.9	Lai Mengqin	24 Sep
13.38	1.1	Liu Jiaqi	15 Apr
13.36	0.9	Vyatkina	7 Jul
13.33		Hurd	28 Apr
13.30	1.3	Fu Bingling	15 Apr

Best at low altitude

Mark	Wind	Name	Date
13.31	1.5	Landazuri	22 Sep

JUNIORS

See main list for top 5 juniors (& 1w). 13 perfs (1 Indoors) by 6 women to 13.72. Additional marks and further juniors:

Mark	Wind	Name	Nat	Born	Pos	Meet	Venue	Date
Dzindzalietaité 13.73	1.4				1		Jurbarkas	30 Jun
13.72	1.1				1		Mannheim	23 Jun
Zaldívar 13.90	0.3				3	WJ	Barcelona	12 Jul
13.79	0.9				4	NC	La Habana	24 Mar
13.80	0.5				Q	WJ	Barcelona	11 Jul
13.78	-0.4				1	CAC-J	San Salvador	1 Jul
13.65	1.1	Ciarra Brewer	USA	12.3.93	4	NCAA	Des Moines	9 Jun
13.59	1.6	Francesca Lanciano	ITA	3.4.94	Q	WJ	Barcelona	11 Jul
13.57i		Khaddi Sagnia	SWE	20.4.94	1	v2N	Steinkjer	11 Feb
13.54i		Lynn Johnson	SWE	16.3.94	2	v2N	Steinkjer	11 Feb
13.52	1.9	Hanna Aleksandrova (10)	UKR	11.7.93	*	NC	Yalta	15 Jun
13.56w	2.9				7	NC	Yalta	15 Jun
13.51	0.1	Viktoriya Leonova	RUS	2.12.94	6		Krasnodar	9 Jun

Mark		Name		Nat	Born	Pos	Meet	Venue	Date
13.48	1.7	Darya	Nelovko	RUS	9.2.94	1	NC-j	Cheboksary	21 Jun
13.46	-0.2	Daria	Derkach	UKR	27.3.93	1		Modena	22 Sep
13.64w	2.7					1	ITA-j	Misano Adriatico	16 Jun
13.37	1.0	Yekaterina	Sariyeva	AZE-Y	18.12.95	Q	WJ	Barcelona	11 Jul
13.34i			Fu Bingling	CHN	15.9.93	6	NGP	Nanjing	14 Feb
13.32	1.4	Ottavia	Cestonaro	ITA-Y	12.1.95	1		Milano	23 Jun
13.30	0.2		Lin Yan	CHN	26.1.93	7	NGP	Zibo	27 May
13.29	-0.7	Liselis	Moracén	CUB	20.6.94	6	NC	La Habana	24 Mar
13.26	0.4	Dilyara	Abuova	KAZ	6.1.94	9	WJ	Barcelona	12 Jul
13.35w	2.4					2	Asi-J	Colombo	12 Jun
13.25	1.8	Josie	Nichol (20)	AUS-Y	15.7.95	1	NC-j	Sydney	18 Mar

Wind assisted. 2 marks by 2 women to 13.72

Dzindzalietaité	13.85w	2.7	Q	WJ	Barcelona	11 Jul	
13.32	3.8	Nadia	Eke	USA-J	11.1.93	4q	NCAA-E Jacksonville	26 May

SHOT

Mark	First	Last	Nat	Born	Pos	Meet	Venue	Date	Series
21.58	Nadezhda	Ostapchuk ¶	BLR	12.10.80	1		Minsk	18 Jul	21.47 21.58 x p p p
21.39					1	NC	Grodno	6 Jul	19.91 21.32 21.05 x x 21.39
21.13					1		Minsk	12 Jun	20.66 20.65 21.13 x 20.31 x
20.70i					1	NC	Mogilyov	10 Feb	19.65 20.37 20.70 x x 20.20
20.53					1	DL	Doha	11 May	20.53 x x x
20.42i					2	WI	Istanbul	10 Mar	20.20 x 20.12 x 20.42 x
20.29					1	ECp-w	Bar	17 Mar	x 18.93 19.52 19.97 20.28 20.29
21.11	Valerie	Adams	NZL	6.10.84	1	Spitzen	Luzern	17 Jul	20.72 20.91 21.01 21.11 x 20.86
21.03					1	GGala	Roma	31 May	19.61 19.85 20.04 21.03 20.14 20.89
20.97					1		Tomblaine	8 Jul	20.41 20.62 20.26 20.29 20.97 20.54
20.95					1	Athl	Lausanne	23 Aug	20.73 20.28 x x x 20.95
20.81i					1	WK	Zürich	29 Aug	20.52 20.80 20.81 20.41 20.36 20.48
20.77					1		Rieti	9 Sep	19.86 20.37 20.77 19.79 20.16 20.54
20.70					1	OG	London (OS)	6 Aug	20.61 x 20.70 x x 20.24
20.67					1		Sydney	18 Feb	20.09 x 20.38 20.61 x 20.67
20.60					1	DL	New York	9 Jun	19.13 20.09 20.60 x 20.07 x
20.54i					1	WI	Istanbul	10 Mar	x 20.48 x 20.41 20.29 20.54
20.52					1	DL	Birmingham	26 Aug	20.52 20.18 20.25 x 20.21 20.49
20.40					Q	OG	London (OS)	6 Aug	20.40 p
20.35					1		Christchurch	4 Feb	19.54 x 20.11 19.79 20.35 x
20.26					1	DNG	Stockholm	17 Aug	20.05 20.26 x x 20.06 20.17
20.19					1	Porritt	Hamilton	11 Feb	x 19.69 19.75 20.19 20.13 20.09
20.48	Yevgeniya	Kolodko	RUS	2.7.90	2	OG	London (OS)	6 Aug	19.45 19.52 x x x 20.48
20.22					1		Adler	27 May	20.07 20.22 19.83 19.42
20.15					1	NC	Cheboksary	4 Jul	19.90 x 19.89 20.15 20.05 x
20.22		Gong Lijiao	CHN	24.1.89	3	OG	London (OS)	6 Aug	20.13 19.67 19.91 19.76 20.22 20.00
20.21					1	Anhalt	Dessau	25 May	19.59 19.87 20.21 19.64 19.23 19.64
20.13					1		Wiesbaden	25 Jul	19.27 19.74 20.13 20.11 19.89 19.87
19.95		Li Ling	CHN	7.2.85	2		Wiesbaden	25 Jul	x 19.90 19.60 19.90 19.95 19.75
19.89i	Jill	Camarena-Williams	USA	2.8.82	1		Fayetteville	11 Feb	x 19.67 19.89 19.15

(30/6)

Mark	First	Last	Nat	Born	Pos	Meet	Venue	Date
19.77	Natalya	Mikhnevich	BLR	25.5.82	2	NC	Grodno	6 Jul
19.72	Olesya	Sviridova	RUS	28.10.89	2		Adler	27 May
19.67	Nadine	Kleinert	GER	20.10.75	3	DL	Doha	11 May
19.60	Michelle	Carter	USA	12.10.85	2	Athl	Lausanne	23 Aug

(10)

Mark	First	Last	Nat	Born	Pos	Meet	Venue	Date
19.54	Anna	Avdeyeva	RUS	6.4.85	1	Znam	Zhukovskiy	17 Jun
19.35	Irina	Tarasova	RUS	15.4.87	3		Adler	27 May
19.24		Liu Xiangrong	CHN	6.6.88	3		Wiesbaden	25 Jul
19.23	Halyna	Obleshchuk	UKR	23.2.89	1		Kyiv	19 May
19.15i	Christina	Schwanitz	GER	24.12.85	1		Leipzig	12 Feb
19.10i	Jeneva	McCall	USA	28.10.89	1		Carbondale	8 Dec
19.02	Geisa	Arcanjo	BRA	19.9.91	7	OG	London (OS)	6 Aug
19.00i	Tia	Brooks	USA	2.8.90	1	NCAA	Nampa	10 Mar
18.90i	Alena	Kopets	BLR	14.2.88	3	NC	Mogilyov	10 Feb
18.87	Josephine	Terlecki	GER	17.2.86	2	NC	Wattenscheid	16 Jun

(20)

Mark	First	Last	Nat	Born	Pos	Meet	Venue	Date
18.82	Cleopatra	Borel	TRI	3.10.79	1	Quercia	Rovereto	4 Sep
18.80	Anna	Omarova	RUS	3.10.81	2	Kuts	Moskva	13 Jun
18.80	Natalia	Ducó	CHI	31.1.89	9	OG	London (OS)	6 Aug

Mark	Name		Nat	Born	Pos	Meet	Venue	Date
18.79	Sarah	Walker	USA	2.4.86	3		Tucson	19 May
18.71i	Yevgeniya	Solovyova	RUS	28.6.86	2	Winter	Moskva	5 Feb
18.63	Chiara	Rosa	ITA	28.1.83	6	GGala	Roma	31 May
18.63	Yanina	Provalinskaya	BLR	26.12.76	3		Minsk	12 Jun
18.62	Misleydis	González	CUB	19.6.78	1		La Habana	27 May
18.48	Anita	Márton	HUN	15.1.89	1		Drazevina	28 Apr
18.36	Denise	Hinrichs	GER	7.6.87	3	NC	Wattenscheid	16 Jun
	(30)							
18.35	Alyssa	Hasslen	USA	13.5.91	2	MSR	Walnut	21 Apr
18.22	Kearsten	Peoples	USA	20.12.91	4	NC/OT	Eugene	29 Jun
18.21	Mailín	Vargas	CUB	24.3.83	1		La Habana	15 Jun
18.20	Radoslava	Mavrodieva	BUL	13.3.87	1	Pavlov	Sofia	9 Jun
18.19	Julie	Labonté	CAN	12.1.90	3		Tucson	17 May
17.99	Úrsula	Ruiz	ESP	11.8.83	16q	OG	London (OS)	6 Aug
17.98	Leyla	Rajabi	IRI	18.4.83	4	NC	Grodno	6 Jul
17.92	Brittany	Smith	USA	25.3.91	1	Sea Ray	Knoxville	14 Apr
17.90	Tiffany	Howard	USA	28.12.86	1		Louisville KY	11 May
17.89i	Lyudmila	Morunova	RUS	27.1.85	3	Mosc Ch	Moskva	11 Feb
	(40)							
17.79i	Paulina	Guba	POL	14.5.91	1	NC	Spala	26 Feb
17.70i	Annie	Alexander	TRI	28.8.87	1		Birmingham	21 Jan
17.68	Yelena	Smolyanova	UZB	16.2.86	1	NC	Almaty	18 Jun
17.64	Vivian	Chukwuemeka ¶	NGR	4.3.75	1		Los Angeles (Ww)	2 Jun
17.64	Helena	Engman	SWE	16.6.76	8	EC	Helsinki	29 Jun
17.59	Rebecca	O'Brien	USA	30.4.90	1		Lewisburg	15 Apr
17.57i	Ashley	Duncan	USA	16.9.86	1		Bloomington IN	10 Feb
17.56	Sandra	Lemus	COL	1.1.89	4		Uberlândia	13 May
17.53	Angela	Rivas	COL	13.8.89	2	NCp	Bogotá	24 Mar
17.53	Vera	Yepimashko	BLR	10.7.76	3	NCp	Brest	25 May
	(50)							
17.52i	Melissa	Boekelman	NED	11.5.89	1		Gammertingen	22 Jan
17.47i	Danielle	Frere	USA	27.4.90	1		Ames	11 Feb
17.47	Olga	Holodnaya	UKR	14.11.91	1	NC-w23	Yalta	23 Mar
17.47i	Felisha	Johnson	USA	24.7.89	1		Charleston	7 Dec
17.44	Sofia	Burkhanova	UZB	1.12.89	2	NC	Almaty	18 Jun
17.43i	Sophie	Kleeberg	GER	30.5.90	5	NC	Karlsruhe	25 Feb
17.43		Lin Chia-Ying	TPE	5.11.82	25q	OG	London (OS)	6 Aug
17.42i	Skylar	White	USA	15.9.91	4	NCAA	Nampa	10 Mar
17.41	Aleksandra	Fisher	KAZ	3.6.88	3	NC	Almaty	18 Jun
17.40	Trecey	Hoover	USA	11.1.88	3		La Jolla	28 Apr
	(60)							
17.40	Adriane	Blewitt-Wilson	USA	24.5.80	1		Seneca	16 Jun
17.39	Chinwe	Okoro	NGR	20.6.89	1		Tampa	5 May
17.39		Li Meiju	CHN	3.10.81	4	NGP	Tianjin	12 May
17.38	Anca	Heltne	ROU	1.1.78	1		Thessaloniki	26 May
17.36i	Christina	Hillman	USA-J	6.10.93	1		Ames	7 Dec
17.35	Baillie	Gibson	USA	18.11.91	5		Tucson	17 May
17.31	Jessica	Cérival	FRA	20.1.82	3	Nebiolo	Torino	8 Jun
17.31	Austra	Skujyté	LTU	12.8.79	1H	OG	London (OS)	3 Aug
17.27	Anna	Jelmini	USA	15.7.90	5		Tucson	19 May
17.25		Meng Qianqian	CHN	6.1.91	5	NGP	Tianjin	12 May
	(70)							
17.24	Eden	Francis	GBR	19.10.88	1		Loughborough	20 May
17.22	Annastasia	Muchkaev	ISR	18.7.91	1		Tel Aviv	28 Apr
17.21i	Lena	Urbaniak	GER	31.10.92	6		Nordhausen	20 Jan
17.18	Keely	Medeiros	BRA	30.4.87	1		Tallahassee	14 Apr
17.18	Michelle	Anumba	USA	18.9.91	1	ACC	Charlottesville	20 Apr
17.15	Shanice	Craft	GER-J	15.5.93	1	WJ	Barcelona	10 Jul
17.13i	Julaika	Nicoletti	ITA	20.3.88	1		Firenxe	16 Feb
17.12	Khadija	Abdullah	USA	24.7.90	1q	NCAA-E	Jacksonville	24 May
17.10		Guo Tianqian	CHN-Y	1.6.95	4	NGP	Zhaoqing	14 Apr
17.07		Gao Yang	CHN-J	1.3.93	4	NGP	Wuhan	28 Apr
	(80)							
17.07	Ahymará	Espinoza	VEN	28.5.85	1		Rijeka	22 Jul
17.03	Yekaterina	Zyuganova	RUS	18.1.91	1	Mosc Ch	Moskva	26 Jun
17.02i	Samira	Burkhardt	GER	9.8.90	6	NC	Karlsruhe	25 Feb
17.01i	Catarina	Andersson	SWE	17.11.77	1		Malmö	29 Jan
17.01		Yang Yanbo	CHN	9.3.90	4	NSG	Tianjin	17 Sep
17.00	Agnieszka	Dudzinska	POL	16.3.88	2	NC	Bielsko-Biala	15 Jun
16.98i	Kelsey	Card	USA	20.8.92	6	NCAA	Nampa	10 Mar
16.98		Lee Mi-young	KOR	19.8.79	1		Andong	24 Apr

Mark	Name	Nat	Born	Pos	Meet	Venue	Date
16.98	Ifeatu Okafor	USA	20.8.90	1		Lubbock	5 May
16.98	Kyla Buckley	USA	22.3.91	9	NCAA	Des Moines	8 Jun
(90)							
16.97	Bian Ka	CHN-J	5.1.93	5	NGP	Zibo	26 May
16.96	Ma Qiao	CHN	28.9.89	5	NC	Kunshan	25 Sep
16.95i	Whitney Ashley	USA	18.2.89	1		Albuquerque	10 Feb
16.91i	Abby Ruston	USA	3.4.83	1		Houston	13 Jan
16.88	Nia Henderson	USA	21.10.86	1		Mount Pleasant	16 Jun
16.87	Emel Dereli	TUR-Y	25.2.96	3-22	ECp-w	Bar	17 Mar
16.87	Chandra Brewer	USA	26.7.81	1		Tuscaloosa	24 Mar
16.86i	Denise Kemkers	NED	11.4.85	1	NC	Apeldoorn	26 Feb
16.83i	Kelly Closse	FRA	8.8.88	2		College Station	28 Jan
16.82	Valentina Muzaric	CRO	23.7.92	1	FlaR	Gainesville	7 Apr
(100)							

Mark	Name	Nat	Born	Date
16.79i	Karen Shump	USA	14.8.89	25 Feb
16.78i	Zara Northover	JAM	6.3.84	18 Feb
16.77	Tremanisha Taylor	USA	10.3.92	24 May
16.76i	Natalya Troneva	RUS-J	24.3.93	23 Feb
16.76	Nieves B. Berroa	CUB	16.3.90	24 Mar
16.74	Assunta Legnante	ITA	14.5.78	5 Sep
16.68	Hanna Samolyuk	UKR	13.1.88	19 May
16.67i	Filiz Kadogan	TUR	12.2.82	4 Feb
16.65i	Dani Bunch	USA	16.5.91	2 Mar
16.65	Dani Samuels	AUS	26.5.88	13 Apr
16.65	Jana Kárníková	CZE	14.2.81	21 Jun
16.63	Aliona Dubitskaya	BLR	25.1.90	6 Jul
16.60i	Sam Lockhart	USA	25.8.91	25 Feb
16.58	Nilgün Öztürk	TUR	30.1.82	12 May
16.55	Yevgeniya Smirnova	RUS	16.3.91	20 Jul
16.54	Hilenn James	TRI	16.3.90	8 Jun
16.53i	Anna Rüh	GER-J	17.6.93	5 Feb
16.51i	Nataliya Dobrynska	UKR	29.5.82	9 Mar
16.50i	Vanessa Henry	DMA	11.9.90	20 Jan
16.46i	Monique Riddick	USA	8.11.89	24 Feb
16.43i	Amanda Van Dyke	USA	27.2.90	2 Mar
16.43i	Amashi-Ali Kendall	USA	11.3.91	3 Mar
16.43	Ana Po'uhila-Kisina	TGA	12.10.79	24 Mar
16.43	Xu Yang	CHN	22.4.91	25 Sep
16.34i	Gu Siyu	CHN-J	11.2.93	13 Feb
16.31	Shaunagh Brown	GBR	15.3.90	17 Jun
16.30i	Taylor Smith	USA	20.7.91	4 Feb
16.30	Veronica Grizzle	USA	8.8.91	7 Apr
16.29i	Rong Jun	CHN	7.4.89	17 Feb
16.29	Kristin Zaumsegel	GER	9.6.92	31 May
16.28	Cui Shuang	CHN	9.8.91	25 Sep
16.28	Yekaterina Burmistrova	RUS	18.8.90	20 Jul
16.28i	Kim Fortney	USA	15.8.91	8 Dec
16.24i	Anna Wloka	POL-J	14.3.93	14 Jan
16.24	Taryn Suttie	CAN	7.12.90	6 Jun
16.23i	Mary Theisen	USA	3.11.90	26 Feb
16.23	Sophie McKinna	GBR-J	31.8.94	30 Jun
16.23i	Jill Rushin	USA	18.7.91	7 Dec
16.21	Myriam Lixfé	FRA	29.4.89	2 Jun
16.18	Meagan McKee	USA	6.12.91	14 Apr
16.18	Brittany Cox	USA	18.4.88	28 Apr
16.18	Victoria Flowers	USA	17.1.90	5 May
16.17	Lawanda Henry	USA	11.7.89	14 Apr
16.16	Jacquelyne Leffler	USA	10.2.90	12 May
16.16	Irache Quintanal	ESP	18.9.78	16 Jun
16.15i	Bailey Wagner	USA	26.1.90	10 Feb
16.15	Olga Sidorina	RUS	23.8.92	20 Jul
16.15	Trine Mulbjerg	DEN	23.4.90	21 Aug
16.15	Geng Shuang	CHN-J	9.7.93	25 Sep
16.13i	Jasmine Boyer	USA	5.3.91	17 Feb
16.13	Rachel Wallader	GBR	1.9.89	20 May
16.12	Joh'vonnie Mosley	USA	24.5.92	5 May
16.12	Omotayo Talabi	NGR	11.8.92	17 May
16.12	Andréa Maria Pereira	BRA	8.12.73	1 Jul
16.11i	Lauren Buresh	USA		10 Mar
16.11	Yuliya Sahan	UKR	19.2.90	19 May
16.09i	Magdalena Zebrowska	POL	11.1.91	26 Feb
16.08	Hayli Bozarth	USA	10.6.91	24 May
16.03i	Markéta Cervenková	CZE	20.8.91	25 Feb
16.03	Kelsey Samuels	USA	28.6.91	26 Apr
16.01i	Kayla Kovar	USA	11.8.91	11 Feb
16.01	Margaret Satupai	SAM	9.7.92	24 Mar
16.01	Kayla Muyskens	USA	17.12.88	26 May
16.00	Tina DeLakis	USA		12 May
16.00	Torie Owers	USA-J	6.3.94	27 May
16.00	Yukiko Shirai	JPN	16.4.79	1 Sep
15.98	Renata Severiano	BRA	2.6.90	6 May
15.98	Julia Mächtig	GER	1.1.86	14 Jun
15.96i	Li Fengfeng	CHN	9.1.79	13 Feb
15.96	Dong Yangzi	CHN	22.10.92	12 May
15.95i	Jasmine Mosley	USA	8.10.88	17 Feb
15.94i	Taylor Freeman	USA	28.1.90	27 Jan
15.93	Laura Ruíz	MEX	30.9.88	2 Mar
15.91	Ify Agwuenu	USA	9.6.89	24 May
15.90	Annie Jackson	USA	11.3.90	24 May
15.89	Carlie Pinkelman	USA	21.11.91	5 May
15.87	Sun Yuting	CHN-J	6.5.94	26 May
15.87	Ashlie Blake	USA-Y	7.6.96	2 Aug
15.86i	Wang Ping	CHN	28.7.90	17 Feb
15.85	Atasha Warren (180)	USA	4.3.90	24 Mar

Best outdoors

Mark	Name	Pos	Meet	Venue	Date
19.05	Schwanitz	1		Bottrop	6 Jul
18.47	Brooks	1	DrakeR	Des Moines	27 Apr
18.03	Solovyova	3		Yerino	2 Jun
17.89	McCall	1		Wichita KS	12 May
17.83	Kopets	5	ECp-w	Bar	17 Mar
17.75	Morunova	4	Kuts	Moskva	13 Jun
17.47	Guba	1	NC	Bielsko-Biala	15 Jun
17.42	Kleeberg	1-22	ECp-w	Bar	17 Mar
17.36	Alexander	4	NCAA	Des Moines	8 Jun
17.35	F Johnson	5	NCAA	Des Moines	8 Jun
17.14	Boekelman	1		Lisse	5 May
17.09	Nicoletti	1		Rieti	19 May
16.91	S White	1	TexR	Austin	31 Mar
16.89	Ashley	5q	NCAA-W	Austin	24 May

Mark	Name	Date	Mark	Name	Date
16.65	Frere	8 Jun	16.48	Duncan	20 Apr
16.62	Urbaniak	20 May	16.46	Bunch	12 May
16.58	Northover	5 May	16.43	Kendall	20 Apr
16.52	Closse	31 Mar	16.41	Hillman	25 Jul
16.48	Henry	14 Apr	16.39	Burkhardt	16 Jun
16.32	Troneva	17 Mar	16.07	Rushin	31 Mar
16.25	T Smith	23 Mar	15.96	Theisen	12 May
16.25	Riddick	12 May	15.95	Cervenková	15 Sep
16.21	Rong Jun	28 Apr	15.94	Card	12 May
16.20	Fortney	8 Jun	15.89	Wagner	27 Apr
16.09	Gu Siyu	12 May	15.88	Lockhart	26 May

Drugs disqualification

Mark	Name	Nat	Born	Pos	Meet	Venue	Date
21.36	Ostapchuk			(1)	OG	London (OS)	6 Aug
20.76	Ostapchuk			(Q)	OG	London (OS)	6 Aug
18.86	Vivian Chukwuemeka ¶	NGR	4.3.75	(1)	AfrC	Porto Novo	1 Jul

JUNIORS

See main list for top 6 juniors. 1 performances by 6 women to 16.80. Additional marks and further juniors:

Name	Mark	Pos	Meet	Venue	Date	Mark	Pos	Meet	Venue	Date
Guo Tianqian	16.93	6	NC	Kunshan	25 Sep					
Gao Yang	17.06	3		Zibo	26 May	16.81	1	NC-j	Changzhao	20 Apr

Mark	Name	Nat	Born	Pos	Meet	Venue	Date
16.86	Gao Yang			6		Tianjin	12 May
16.76i	Natalya Troneva	RUS	24.3.93	5	NC	Moskva	23 Feb
16.32				5	ECp-w-23	Bar	17 Mar
16.53i	Anna Rüh	GER	17.6.93	6		Rochlitz	5 Feb
16.34i	Gu Siyu	CHN	11.2.93	6	NGP	Nanjing	13 Feb
16.09				9	NGP	Tianjin	12 May
16.24i	Anna Wloka (10)	POL	14.3.93	1		Brzeszcze	14 Jan
16.23	Sophie McKinna	GBR	31.8.94	2		Eton	30 Jun
16.15	Geng Shuang	CHN	9.7.93	1cB	NC	Kunshan	25 Sep
16.00	Torie Owers	USA	6.3.94	1	=	Marietta	27 May
15.87	Sun Yuting	CHN	6.5.94	9	NGP	Zibo	26 May
15.87	Ashlie Blake	USA-Y	7.6.96	1y	Jun Oly	Humble	2 Aug
15.82	Sarah Howard	USA	11.10.93	1		Macon	21 Mar
15.82	Wang Xiaoyun	CHN	7.12.93	11	NC	Kunshan	25 Sep
15.71	Margo Britton	USA	21.9.93	2cB	PennR	Philadelphia	26 Apr
15.69	Yiliena Otamendi	CUB-Y	12.4.96	2		La Habana	20 Ded
15.64	Izabela Rodrigues da Silva (20)	BRA-Y	2.8.95	1		São Paulo	31 Mar
Best outdoors: 16.41	Christina Hillman	USA-J	6.10.93	1		Baltimore	25 Jul

DISCUS

Mark	Pos	Meet	Name / Venue	Nat	Born	Pos	Meet	Venue	Date	Series
69.11			Sandra Perkovic	CRO	21.6.90	1	OG	London (OS)	4 Aug	64.58 68.11 69.11 x 66.96 64.03
68.77	1	DNG	Stockholm						17 Aug	57.29 x 66.26 63.09 x 68.77
68.24	1	DL	Shanghai						19 May	x 62.53 64.89 x 62.39 68.24
67.64	1	NCp	Varazdin						16 Jun	59.06 63.19 x 63.97 x 67.64
67.62	1	EC	Helsinki						1 Jul	x x 67.62 62.93 x 62.53
67.19	1	ECp-w23	Bar						18 Mar	x 66.02 62.83 62.75 67.19 66.28
66.94	1	NC	Rijeka						21 Jul	++
66.92	1	Pre	Eugene						1 Jun	59.19 63.70 66.92 65.13 x 63.92
66.85	1	NC-w	Split						3 Mar	++
65.79	1	Hanz	Zagreb						4 Sep	65.40 65.79 x x 65.08 62.65
65.74	Q	OG	London (OS)						3 Aug	65.74 p p
68.89			Nadine Müller	GER	21.11.85	1	ECp-w	Bar	18 Mar	66.34 65.00 68.81 67.70 67.07 68.89
66.68	1	Werfer	Halle						19 May	66.51 65.32 66.15 66.68 66.40 64.06
66.47	1	NC	Wattenscheid						16 Jun	66.47 63.20 x 62.16 63.84 64.88
66.19	1		Halle						21 Jan	63.53 x 65.57 61.61 63,31 66.19
66.07	1		Kienbaum						4 Feb	61.22 64.32 66.07 x p p
65.94	4	OG	London (OS)						4 Aug	65.71 65.06 x 64.16 64.35 65.94
65.89	Q	OG	London (OS)						3 Aug	65.89 p p
68.03			Yarelys Barrios	CUB	12.7.83	1	NC	La Habana	22 Mar	68.03 60.70 x 60.45 x x
66.59	1	ISTAF	Berlin						1 Sep	59.36 64.78 66.59 x x 65.76
66.38	3	OG	London (OS)						4 Aug	63.97 66.38 64.84 64.06 x 65.21
65.94	Q	OG	London (OS)						3 Aug	x 65.94 p
65.77	1	DKB	Neubrandenburg						19 Aug	60.11 x 62.62 65.45 65.77 64.28 65.68
67.84			Li Yanfeng	CHN	15.5.79	1	Werfer	Wiesbaden	12 May	x 67.84 x 66.10 63.29 64.64
67.22	2	OG	London (OS)						4 Aug	x 67.22 x x 63.64 x
66.28	1		Fränkisch-Crumbach						27 May	x 66.28 63.75 63,98 x 63.78
66.01	1c1		Wiesbaden						25 Jul	x x x 61.02 64.87 66.01
65.85	1	NGP	Wuhan						28 Apr	
65.61	1		Fuzhou						24 Jun	62.80 62.31 x x x 65.61
67.74			Stephanie Brown Trafton	USA	1.12.79	1		Wailuku	4 May	65.63 65.21 67.74 x 62.79 62.92
66.86	1		Wailuku						5 May	65.68 x 66.86 65.94 66.07 62.86
(30/6)										
65.60			Denia Caballero	CUB	13.1.90	1		La Habana	9 Mar	
65.34			Zaneta Glanc	POL	11.3.83	2	Werfer	Halle	19 May	
64.76			Krishna Poonia	IND	5.5.82	2		Wailuku	5 May	
64.56			Darya Pishchalnikova ¶	RUS	19.7.85	1		Adler	22 Apr	
(10)										
64.22			Julia Fischer	GER	1.4.90	3	Werfer	Wiesbaden	12 May	
64.21			Andressa de Morais	BRA	21.12.90	1	IbAmC	Barquisimeto	10 Jun	
64.20			Vera Ganeyeva	RUS	6.11.88	1	NC	Cheboksary	5 Jul	
64.03			Zinaida Sendriuté	LTU	10.6.84	1		Valmiera	9 Jun	
63.98			Mélina Robert-Michon	FRA	18.7.79	6	OG	London (OS)	4 Aug	
63.97			Gia Lewis-Smallwood	USA	1.4.79	3		Wailuku	5 May	
63.97			Dani Samuels	AUS	26.5.88	Q	OG	London (OS)	3 Aug	
63.91			Ma Xuejun	CHN	26.3.85	1cB	Werfer	Wiesbaden	12 May	
63.56			Nataliya Semenova	UKR	7.7.82	1	NCp	Yalta	27 May	

Mark	Name		Nat	Born	Pos	Meet	Venue	Date
63.52	Yekaterina	Strokova	RUS	17.12.89	1		Adler	26 May
	(20)							
63.44	Aretha	Thurmond	USA	14.8.76	2		La Jolla	28 Apr
63.38	Anna	Rüh	GER-J	17.6.93	1		Schönebeck	26 Jul
63.32		Yang Yanbo	CHN	9.3.90	3		La Jolla	28 Apr
63.25	Svetlana	Saykina	RUS	10.7.85	2		Adler	26 May
62.92	Shanice	Craft	GER-J	15.5.93	4	NC	Wattenscheid	16 Jun
62.91	Irina	Rodrigues	POR	5.2.91	1	Werf-23	Halle	20 May
62.60	Seema	Antil	IND	27.7.83	1		Irvine	24 Mar
62.50	Yaimé	Pérez	CUB	29.5.91	3		La Habana	9 Mar
62.32		Sun Taifeng	CHN	26.8.82	2cB	Werfer	Wiesbaden	12 May
62.13	Natalia	Artîc ¶	MDA	24.7.87	1		Vila Real de Santo António	4 Mar
	(30)							
61.92	Dragana	Tomasevic	SRB	4.6.82	1	NCp	Sremska Mitrovica	2 Jun
61.92	Joanna	Wisniewska	POL	24.5.72	1	NC	Bielsko-Biala	17 Jun
61.86	Nicoleta	Grasu	ROU	11.9.71	14q	OG	London (OS)	3 Aug
61.26	Suzy	Powell	USA	3.9.76	2		Modesto	10 Jun
61.21	Allison	Randall	JAM	25.5.88	1		Coral Gables	17 Mar
61.18	Heike	Koderisch	GER	27.5.85	2		Leipzig	28 May
61.16	Sabine	Rumpf	GER	18.3.83	1		Lindschied	1 Jun
60.96	Liz	Podominick	USA	5.12.84	2		Tucson	17 May
60.94	Vera	Cechlová	CZE	19.11.78	1	Danek	Turnov	22 May
60.90	Svetlana	Serova	BLR	28.8.86	1	NC	Grodno	7 Jul
	(40)							
60.77	Summer	Pierson	USA	3.9.78	4		Wailuku	5 May
60.59		Gu Siyu	CHN-J	11.2.93	1	NC-j	Changzhou	21 Apr
60.59	Shelbi	Vaughan	USA-J	24.8.94	1	NC-j	Bloomington IN	15 Jun
60.51	Jade	Nicholls	GBR	30.3.87	1		Chula Vista	19 Apr
60.50		Liang Yan	CHN-Y	2.1.95	1cB	NC	Kunshan	25 Sep
60.47		Jiang Fengjing	CHN	28.8.87	1	NSG	Tianjin	13 Sep
60.43		Yang Fei	CHN	20.7.87	1	NGP	Zibo	27 May
60.32		Su Xinyue	CHN	8.11.91	4	NGP	Zhaoqing	15 Apr
60.23		Li Wen-Hua	TPE	3.12.89	1		Taipei	25 May
60.09	Karen	Gallardo	CHI	6.3.84	21q	OG	London (OS)	3 Aug
	(50)							
60.03	Kateryna	Karsak	UKR	26.12.85	2	NCp	Yalta	27 May
59.99	Rocío	Comba	ARG	14.7.87	1		Santa Fé	24 Mar
59.99	Whitney	Ashley	USA	18.2.89	1	NCAA	Des Moines	6 Jun
59.96	Monique	Jansen	NED	3.10.78	1		Leiden	9 Jun
59.77	Anna	Jelmini	USA	15.7.90	3		Tucson	17 May
59.70	Julia	Bremser	GER	27.4.82	2		Lindschied	1 Jun
59.70	Natalya	Sadova	RUS	15.7.72	3	NC	Cheboksary	5 Jul
59.65	Ulrike	Giesa	GER	16.8.84	4		Fränkisch-Crumbach	27 May
59.64		Lu Xiaoxin	CHN	22.2.89	3	NC	Kunshan	25 Sep
59.59	Jeré	Summers	USA	21.5.87	1	Hamilton	Berkeley	28 Apr
	(60)							
59.56	Wioletta	Potepa	POL	14.12.80	3	NC	Bielsko-Biala	17 Jun
59.52		Song Aimin	CHN	15.3.78	4	NC	Kunshan	25 Sep
59.50	Tamara	Apostolico	ITA	28.4.89	1		Split	12 May
59.45	Jeneva	McCall	USA	28.10.89	1		Auburn	21 Apr
59.05	Yuliya	Kurylo	UKR	3.7.91	1-22		Kyiv	20 May
58.97A	Elizna	Naude	RSA	14.9.78	1		Potchefstroom	24 Mar
58.92	Fernanda Raquel	Borges	BRA	26.7.88	2		São Paulo	20 May
58.90	Salome	Rigishvili	GEO	26.1.90	1		Tbilisi	13 May
58.87	Laura	Bordignon	ITA	26.3.81	1		Viterbo	7 Jun
58.76	Trecey	Hoover	USA	11.1.88	1		Natchitoches	6 Apr
	(70)							
58.74	Alla	Denisenko	RUS	12.10.83	1	Mosc Ch	Moskva	27 Jun
58.70	Eliska	Stanková	CZE	11.11.84	2	Danek	Turnov	22 May
58.64		Weng Chunxia	CHN	29.8.92	5	NGP	Wuhan	28 Apr
58.49	Jessica	Kolotzei	GER	6.4.85	1		Neubrandenburg	8 Jun
58.42	Agnieszka	Jarmuzek	POL	3.2.84	2	Univ Ch	Lódz	12 May
58.32	Harwant	Kaur	IND	5.7.80	2	Mosc Ch	Moskva	20 Jun
58.25	Chinwe	Okoro	NGR	20.6.89	1		Louisville	11 May
58.24		Xu Shaoyang	CHN	9.2.83	7	NGP	Wuhan	28 Apr
58.22	Elisângela	Adriano	BRA	27.7.72	2		Porto Alegre	23 Jun
58.16	Yuliya	Maltseva	RUS	30.11.90	1-22		Adler	17 Feb
	(80)							
58.05	Rachel	Longfors	USA	6.6.83	1		Mesa	5 Jun
58.03	Suzanne	Kragbé	CIV	22.12.81	1		Savona	23 May
57.97	Yelena	Panova	RUS	2.3.87	5	NC	Cheboksary	5 Jul

Mark	Name	Nat	Born	Pos	Meet	Venue	Date
57.94	Ashley Hearn	USA	14.4.89	3	NCAA	Des Moines	6 Jun
57.87	Anastasiya Kashtonova	BLR	14.1.89	2		Brest	28 Apr
57.82	Beth Rohl	USA	7.11.90	7	NC/OT	Eugene	24 Jun
57.79	Kirsty Law	GBR	11.10.86	1	CAU	Bedford	26 Aug
57.75	Rachel Varner	USA	20.7.83	1		Claremont	9 Jun
57.74	Kristin Pudenz	GER-J	9.2.93	3j		Wiesbaden	12 May
57.68	Kelechi Anyanwu	USA	27.12.85	4		Modesto	10 Jun
(90)							
57.67	Skylar White	USA	15.9.91	1		Lubbock	14 Apr
57.66	Irène Donzelot	FRA	8.12.88	1		Salon-de-Provence	16 May
57.61	Eden Francis	GBR	19.10.88	1		Eton	30 Jun
57.57	Jitka Kubelová	CZE	2.10.91	1		Olomouc	8 May
57.56	Dilek Esmer	TUR	15.1.88	1		Mersin	4 Mar
57.20	Sanna Kämäräinen	FIN	8.2.86	1		Helsingborg	9 Jun
57.15	Yanisley Collado	CUB	30.4.85	2		La Habana	25 Feb
57.11	Sam Lockhart	USA	25.8.91	1		Ashland	7 Jun
57.10	Hristoúla Anagnostopoúlou	GRE	27.8.91	1		Thíva	25 Jul
56.94	Mary Angell	USA	29.8.89	1		Allendale	11 May
(100)							

Mark	Name	Nat	Born	Date
56.86	Marie-Josée LeJour	CAN	13.1.79	26 Apr
56.86	Calista Lyon	AUS	2.1.86	28 Apr
56.79	Cecilia Barnes	USA	24.7.80	7 Apr
56.78	Annie Alexander	TRI	28.8.87	13 May
56.74	Sabina Asenjo	ESP	3.8.86	19 May
56.73	Jessica Maroszek	USA	26.2.92	10 Jun
56.69	Rachel Andres	USA	21.4.87	14 Apr
56.62	Siositina Hakeai	NZL-J	1.3.94	16 Dec
56.46	Luz Montaño	COL	20.12.88	7 Apr
56.45	Te Rina Keenan	NZL	29.9.90	15 Dec
56.44	Tanja Komulainen	FIN	2.3.80	18 Mar
56.34	Kimberley Mulhall	AUS	9.1.91	5 May
56.26	Li Shanshan	CHN	6.1.92	27 May
56.10	Veronika Watzek	AUT	13.8.85	5 May
55.95	Morgan Wilken	USA	15.4.90	27 Apr
55.92	Hilenn James	TRI	16.3.90	13 May
55.83	Baillie Gibson	USA	18.11.91	17 May
55.77	Brittany Borman	USA	1.7.89	14 Apr
55.75	Marike Steinacker	GER	4.3.92	16 Jun
55.72	Wang Lan	CHN-J	8.7.93	21 Apr
55.67	Grete Etholm	NOR	25.1.76	9 Jun
55.67	Viktoriya Klochko	UKR	2.9.92	12 Jun
55.66	Sarah Thornton	USA	29.8.86	6 Apr
55.62	Feng Bin	CHN-J	3.4.94	21 Apr
55.60	Kearsten Peoples	USA	20.12.91	6 Jun
55.48	Taylor Smith	USA	20.7.91	10 Jun
55.43	Ifeatu Okafor	USA	20.8.90	28 Apr
55.42	Erin Pendleton	USA	13.3.91	13 May
55.39	Sarah Morris	USA	14.9.88	11 May
55.24	Ashley Duncan	USA	16.9.86	21 Apr
55.18	Samia Stokes	USA	22.7.89	13 May
55.17	Natalya Shirobokova	RUS-J	18.1.94	20 Jun
55.15	Brittany Smith	USA	25.3.91	14 Apr
55.09	Maryke Oberholzer	RSA	27.11.89	14 Apr
55.09	Alyssa Hasslen	USA	13.5.91	13 May
55.08	Emily Pendleton	USA	16.4.89	25 May
55.06	Katerina Klausová	CZE	28.2.89	29 May
55.03	Felisha Johnson	USA	24.7.89	25 May
55.01	Rosalía Vázquez	CUB-Y	11.10.95	9 Mar
54.98	Annastasia Muchkaev	ISR	18.7.91	14 Jun
54.95	Pauline Pousse	FRA	17.9.87	1 Jul
54.88	Subenrat Insaeng	THA-J	10.2.94	5 Mar
54.86	Androniki Lada	CYP	19.4.91	4 Jul
54.82	Alexis Cooks	USA-J	11.9.93	12 May
54.75	Khadija Abdullah	USA	24.7.90	7 Apr
54.64	Katri Hirvonen	FIN	25.6.90	30 May
54.59	Gabriella Dixson	USA	24.8.81	20 Apr
54.48	Lindsey Spencer	USA	7.1.89	14 Apr
54.44	Rebecca O'Brien	USA	30.4.90	9 Jun
54.38	Alix Kennedy	AUS	22.1.92	25 May
54.36	Marie-Christine Lehm	GER	19.6.83	16 Jun
54.28	Liu Jing	CHN	1.1.91	15 Apr
54.28	Erica Chaney	USA	13.8.88	27 Apr
54.24A	Alex Collatz	USA-J	25.5.93	7 Apr
54.22	Ayumi Takahashi	JPN	31.8.89	12 Sep
54.16	Yekaterina Burmistrova	RUS	18.8.90	26 May
54.09	Mélanie Pingeon	FRA	4.11.86	26 Jun
54.08	Lin Xiaojing	CHN	8.1.86	15 Jul
54.04	Jasmine Burrell	USA	27.2.92	21 Apr
54.02A	Julie Labonté	CAN	12.1.90	29 Jun
53.97	Irache Quintanal	ESP	18.9.78	30 May
53.95	Wang Bin	CHN	7.1.87	15 Apr
53.93	Gökçe Çelenk	TUR	22.7.88	4 Mar
53.90	Liliana Cá	POR	5.11.86	28 Jul
53.90	Olha Abramchuk	UKR	12.4.91	12 Jun
53.86	Ashlee Smith	TRI	17.5.91	6 Jun
53.85	Anita Márton	HUN	15.1.89	3 Mar
53.78	Erin Wykoff	USA	6.7.90	12 May
53.78i	Kelsey Card	USA	20.8.92	20 Jan
53.63				21 Apr
53.76	Viktoriya Isayeva	RUS	25.2.92	9 Jun
53.67	Sonka Kielmann	GER	17.1.92	28 May
53.66	Heidi Schmidt	SWE-J	13.11.93	12 Aug
53.61	Erica Brand	USA	1.8.92	25 May
53.56	Valentina Aniballi	ITA	19.4.84	15 Sep
53.55	Tetyana Yuryeva	UKR-Y	21.1.95	31 May
53.51	Yuka Murofushi (176)	JPN	11.2.77	29 Apr

Drugs suspension (pending)

Mark	Name	Nat	Born	Pos	Meet	Venue	Date
70.69	Darya Pishchalnikova ¶	RUS	19.7.85	(1)	NC	Cheboksary	5 Jul

68.80   66.20   70.69   p   67.20   x

| 69.34 | Pishchalnikova | | | (1) | | Yerino | 21 Jul |

x   66.11   69.34   68.64   69.13   x

| 68.18 | Pishchalnikova | | | (1) | Mosc Ch | Moskva | 20 Jun |

65.54   66.36   x   65.00   65.38   68.18

| 67.56 | Pishchalnikova | | | (2) | OG | London (OS) | 4 Aug |

65.19   62.07   65.06   66.42   67.56   59.13

| 67.00 | Pishchalnikova | | | (1) | | Adler | 26 May |

66.06   59.82   67.00   66.06

| 66.85 | Pishchalnikova | | | (2) | DNG | Stockholm | 17 Aug |

64.69   x   63.03   64.09   66.85   65.39

| 66.38 | Pishchalnikova | | | (1) | | Portland | 3 Jun |
| 65.47 | Pishchalnikova | | | (2) | ISTAF | Berlin | 1 Sep |

63.90   65.47   x   65.05   x   60.77

| 65.02 | Pishchalnikova | | | (Q) | OG | London (OS) | 3 Aug |

65.02   p   p

Mark	Name	Nat	Born	Pos	Meet	Venue	Date

JUNIORS

See main list for top 6 juniors. 10 performances by 2 women to 61.60. Additional marks and further juniors:

Name	Mark	Pos	Meet	Venue	Date	Mark	Pos	Meet	Venue	Date
Rüh	63.14	3	NC	Wattenscheid	16 Jun	62.38	1	WJ	Barcelona	15 Jul
	63.04	1J		Halle	19 May	62.32	6	Werfer	Halle	19 May
	62.98	Q	OG	London (OS)	3 Aug	62.12	1		Leipzig	28 May
	62.65	4	EC	Helsinki	1 Jul	61.89	4		Dessau	25 May
Craft	62.84	2		Schönebeck	26 Jul					

Mark	Name	Nat	Born	Pos	Meet	Venue	Date
56.62	Siositina Hakeai	NZL	1.3.94	1		Auckland (NS)	16 Dec
55.72	Wang Lan	CHN	8.7.93	2	NC-j	Changzhou	21 Apr
55.62	Feng Bin	CHN	3.4.94	3	NC-j	Changzhou	21 Apr
55.17	Natalya Shirobokova (10)	RUS	18.1.94	1	NC-j	Cheboksary	20 Jun
55.01	Rosalía Vázquez	CUB-Y	11.10.95	4		La Habana	9 Mar
54.88	Subenrat Insaeng	THA	10.2.94	1	NG	Khon Kaen	5 Mar
54.82	Alexis Cooks	USA	11.9.93	1		Mount Pleasant	12 May
54.24A	Alex Collatz	USA	25.5.93	1		Provo	7 Apr
53.66	Heidi Schmidt	SWE	13.11.93	1	NC-j	Sollentuna	12 Aug
53.55	Tetyana Yuryeva	UKR-Y	21.1.95	1	NC-j	Yalta	31 May
53.41	Ling Shan	CHN-Y	8.3.95	11		Wuhan	28 Apr
53.15	Taylah Sengul	AUS-Y	3.11.95	1	NC-j	Sydney	15 Mar
53.02	Kätlin Töllasson	EST	4.6.93	2		Valmiera	9 Jun
52.80	Taryn Gollshewsky (20)	AUS	18.5.93	1		Melbourne	25 Feb

HAMMER

Mark	Name	Nat	Born	Pos	Meet	Venue	Date	1	2	3	4	5	6
78.69	Oksana Menkova	BLR	28.3.82	1		Minsk	18 Jul						
								x	73.70	78.69	62.43	74.00	
78.19				1		Brest	28 Apr	76.50	78.19	x	70.34	71.94	75.04
78.19				1		Minsk	12 Jun	76.76	78.19	x	74.41	x	x
78.51	Tatyana Lysenko	RUS	9.10.83	1	NC	Cheboksary	5 Jul						
								77.37	76.81	76.24	X	78.51	77.26
78.18				1	OG	London (OS)	10 Aug	77.56	75.86	74.39	77.12	78.18	77.28
77.20				1		Yerino	22 Jul	76.50	77.20	76.47	74.96	74.57	77.19
76.14				2	Colorful	Daegu	16 May	73.41	76.14	75.92	75.63		
75.48				1	Znam	Zhukovskiy	17 Jun	73.17	72.92	72.74	75.48		
78.07	Betty Heidler	GER	14.10.83	1	GS	Ostrava	24 May						
								75.32	76.07	76.06	75.83	78.07	74.29
77.24				1	Colorful	Daegu	16 May	75.18	77.24	74.55	73.60		
77.12				3	OG	London (OS)	10 Aug	73.90	71.52	72.77	x	77.12	72.77
76.66				1		Pretoria	4 May	72.56	73.92	75.07	70.85	75.35	76.66
75.93				1	Pre	Eugene	1 Jun	74.89	73.82	71.78	75.93	72.86	74.47
75.78				1		Fränkisch-Crumbach	27 May	75.25	x	75.78	x	x	x
75.35				1	DKB	Neubrandenburg	19 Aug	73.23	72.90	70.04	75.35	73.42	70.83
77.60	Anita Wlodarczyk	POL	8.8.85	2	OG	London (OS)	10 Aug						
								75.01	76.02	75.72	x	77.10	77.60
76.81				1	Kuso	Szczecin	21 Jul	x	76.81	x	74.89	75.59	74.53
76.70				1	Skolim	Warszawa	19 Aug	72.59	75.38	75.88	75.95	76.70	74.26
75.68				Q	OG	London (OS)	8 Aug	75.68	p	p			
75.60				2	Pre	Eugene	1 Jun	73.05	75.60	75.49	x	x	75.10
77.08	Gulfiya Khanafeyeva	RUS	4.6.82	1		Zhukovskiy	23 Jun						
								x	69.61	71.69	72.75	75.17	77.08
76.04				2	NC	Cheboksary	5 Jul	66.74	x	70.39	70.86	72.90	76.04
76.99	Zhang Wenxiu	CHN	22.3.86	2	GS	Ostrava	24 May						
								75.46	74.95	74.19	72.75	76.99	76.52
76.34				4	OG	London (OS)	10 Aug	72.96	76.34	73.81	68.20	75.56	x
75.72				1	NGP	Chengdu	12 Mar						
75.68				3	Colorful	Daegu	16 May	75.68	73.78	68.38	72.17		
76.72	Mariya Bespalova	RUS	21.5.86	2		Zhukovskiy	23 Jun						
								73.11	x	75.04	76.39	74.45	76.72
76.56	Alena Matoshko	BLR	23.6.82	2		Minsk	12 Jun						
								76.05	76.56	x	73.85	74.23	75.90
76.05	Kathrin Klaas	GER	6.2.84	5	OG	London (OS)	10 Aug						
								x	72.79	76.05	74.66	72.88	x
75.59	Yipsi Moreno	CUB	19.11.80	1		Reims	4 Jul						
	(30/10)							73.99	x	x	71.15	x	75.59
75.04	Sultana Frizell	CAN	24.10.84	1		Tucson	16 Mar						
74.47	Zalina Marghieva	MDA	5.2.88	1	Univ Ch	Chisinau	7 May						
74.21	Hanna Skydan	UKR	14.5.92	1	NC	Yalta	14 Jun						
74.19	Jessica Cosby	USA	31.5.82	4	Pre	Eugene	1 Jun						
74.18	Joanna Fiodorow	POL	4.3.89	1	EAF	Bydgoszcz	3 Jun						
74.17	Tuğçe Sahutoglu	TUR	1.5.88	1		Izmir	19 May						
74.10	Iryna Novozhylova	UKR	7.1.86	1		Kyiv	19 May						

Mark	Name		Nat	Born	Pos	Meet	Venue	Date	
74.02	Anna	Bulgakova	RUS	17.1.88	4	NC	Cheboksary	5	Jul
73.34	Martina	Hrasnová	SVK	21.3.83	2	EC	Helsinki	1	Jul
73.31	Oksana	Kondratyeva	RUS	22.11.85	1	Mosc Ch	Moskva	27	Jun
(20)									
73.06	Stéphanie	Falzon	FRA	7.1.83	9	OG	London (OS)	10	Aug
72.83	Rosa	Rodríguez	VEN	2.7.86	1		Cakovec	5	May
72.79	Jenny	Dahlgren	ARG	27.8.84	1	NC	Santa Fe	22	Apr
72.55	Kivilcim	Kaya	TUR	27.3.92	1	NC	Izmir	5	Jul
72.42	Iryna	Sekachyova	UKR	21.7.76	1		Yalta	4	Jun
72.16	Heather	Steacy	CAN	14.4.88	2	Sun Angel	Tempe	6	Apr
71.98	Sophie	Hitchon	GBR	11.7.91	Q	OG	London (OS)	8	Aug
71.95	Gwen	Berry	USA	29.6.89	1		Bowling Green	14	Apr
71.81	Marina	Marghieva ¶	MDA	28.6.86	2	NC	Chisinau	26	May
71.80	Amber	Campbell	USA	5.6.81	1	NC/OT	Beaverton	21	Jun
(30)									
71.78	Amanda	Bingson	USA	20.2.90	2	NC/OT	Beaverton	21	Jun
71.70	Yelena	Konevtsova	RUS	11.9.81	3	Kuts	Moskva	13	Jun
71.50	Ariannis	Vichy	CUB	18.5.89	1		La Habana	28	Jun
71.25	Barbara	Spiler	SLO	2.1.92	2		Cakovec	5	May
71.16	Katerina	Safránková	CZE	8.6.89	4	ECp-w	Bar	18	Mar
70.90	Aubrey	Baxter	USA	7.11.85	1		San Jose	26	May
70.73	Britney	Henry	USA	17.10.84	1		Eugene	18	Mar
70.63	Amy	Haapanen	USA	23.3.84	4	NC/OT	Beaverton	21	Jun
70.62	Alexandra	Tavernier	FRA-J	13.12.93	1	WJ	Barcelona	14	Jul
70.48	Keelin	Godsey	USA	2.1.84	5	NC/OT	Beaverton	21	Jun
(40)									
70.44	Jessika	Guehaseim	FRA	23.8.89	1		Aix-lès-Bains	6	Jul
70.40	Olga	Tsander	BLR	18.5.76	1	NC-w	Stayki	24	Feb
70.33	Tracey	Andersson	SWE	5.12.84	1		Jablonec	15	Apr
70.31	Alina	Kastrova	BLR	2.3.90	2	NC-w	Stayki	24	Feb
70.20	Silvia	Salis	ITA	17.9.85	1	NC-w	Lucca	26	Feb
70.14	Yelena	Rigert	RUS	2.12.83	2		Cheboksary	19	May
70.05	Bianca	Perie	ROU	1.6.90	1		Bucuresti	15	Jun
69.69	Mona	Holm Solberg	NOR	5.8.83	1		Oslo	24	May
69.66	Yunaika	Crawford	CUB	2.11.82	1		La Habana	15	Jun
69.59	Berta	Castells	ESP	24.1.84	1		Manresa	24	Jul
(50)									
69.56	Arasay	Thondike	CUB	28.5.86	2	NC	La Habana	24	Mar
69.39	Jeneva	McCall	USA	28.10.89	1		Nashville	24	Mar
69.35	Daryia	Pchelnik	BLR	20.12.81	2	Univ Ch	Brest	16	May
69.29	Johana	Moreno	COL	15.4.85	2	GP	São Paulo	16	May
69.29	Brittany	Riley	USA	26.8.86	6	NC/OT	Beaverton	21	Jun
69.20	Tereza	Králová	CZE	22.10.89	1		Kladno	2	Jun
69.15	Malgorzata	Zadura	POL	3.10.82	1		Kielce	28	Apr
69.15	Laura	Redondo	ESP	3.7.88	1		Barcelona (SE)	21	Jul
69.14		Wang Zheng	CHN	14.12.87	2	NGP	Chengdu	12	Mar
69.10	Amy	Sène	SEN	6.4.85	3	NC	Angers	17	Jun
(60)									
69.03	Éva	Orbán	HUN	29.11.84	6	Werfer	Halle	19	May
69.02	Alena	Krechyk	BLR	20.7.87	1	Big 12	Manhattan KS	11	May
68.94	Laura	Igaune	LAT	2.10.88	1		Nashville	21	Apr
68.86	Loree	Smith	USA	6.11.82	1		Los Angeles (Ww)	2	Jun
68.72		Liu Tingting	CHN	29.10.90	3	NGP	Chengdu	12	Mar
68.50	Sarah	Holt	GBR	17.4.87	1	ENG Ch	Birmingham	2	Jun
68.45	Yirisleyidi	Ford	CUB	18.8.91	1		La Habana	2	Mar
68.45	Brittany	Smith	USA	25.3.91	2	NCAA	Des Moines	7	Jun
68.27		Hao Shuai	CHN	19.7.87	2	NGP	Zhaoqing	14	Apr
68.25	Kristin	Smith	USA	23.12.87	1		Marietta	10	Jun
(70)									
68.13	Manuéla	Montebrun	FRA	13.11.79	1		Chelles	11	Apr
68.12	Shelby	Ashe	USA-J	13.3.93	1	NC-j	Bloomington IN	16	Jun
68.08	Jenny	Ozorai	HUN	3.12.90	1		Fullerton	10	Mar
68.08	Aleksandra	Lushcheko	RUS	1.3.87	1		Bryansk	8	Jun
67.98	Alexia	Sedykh	FRA-J	13.9.93	1		Kessel-Lo	18	Aug
67.96	Alena	Lysenko	RUS	3.2.88	Q	NC	Cheboksary	3	Jul
67.82	Nina	Volkova	RUS	26.8.84	3		Cheboksary	19	May
67.67	Yana	Kleshchevnikova	RUS	24.7.88	2		Bryansk	8	Jun
67.63	Zlata	Tarasova	RUS	2.12.86	4		Adler	21	Apr
67.53	Gabrielle	Neighbour	AUS	22.11.83	1		Melbourne	1	Apr
(80)									
67.43	Merja	Korpela	FIN	15.5.81	1	NC	Lahti	25	Aug

Mark	Name		Nat	Born	Pos	Meet	Venue	Date
67.39	Zoë	Derham	GBR	24.11.80	1	ECCp-B	Dubnica nad Váhom	27 May
67.35	Marissa	Minderler	USA	7.5.89	1	Pac-12	Eugene	12 May
67.16	Elisa	Palmieri	ITA	18.9.83	2	NC-w	Lucca	26 Feb
67.13	Alena	Novogrodskaya	BLR-J	11.5.93	3	WJ	Barcelona	14 Jul
67.08	Natalya	Polyakova	RUS	9.12.90	1	U23	Bryansk	8 Jun
67.04	Vânia	Silva	POR	8.6.80	7	ECp-w	Bar	18 Mar
67.00	Julia	Ratcliffe	NZL-J	14.7.93	4	WJ	Barcelona	14 Jul
66.93	Aysegül	Alniaçik	TUR	15.4.87	2		Eskisehir	15 May
66.72	Chandra	Andrews	USA	4.9.83	1		Warrensburg	20 Apr
(90)								
66.71	Amélie	Perrin	FRA	30.3.80	4	NC	Angers	17 Jun
66.61	Karina	Frolova	RUS	2.3.90	2	Mosc Ch	Moskva	27 Jun
66.58	Laëtitia	Bambara	BUR	30.3.84	5	NC	Angers	17 Jun
66.50	Chelsea	Cassulo	USA	10.6.90	1		Mesa	5 Jun
66.48	Ida	Storm	SWE	11.10.91	4		Los Angeles (Ww)	2 Jun
66.19	Eleni	Larsson	SWE-J	4.4.93	1	Nordic-J	Växjö	19 Aug
66.11	Lidiya	Provozina	UKR	13.2.86	3		Kyiv	19 May
65.93	Olivia	Waldet	FRA	23.5.84	7		Forbach	27 May
65.80		Wang Lu	CHN	22.12.91	2	NGP	Zibo	26 May
65.78	Emma	Johannesson	SWE	16.1.84	2		Jablonec	15 Apr
(100)								

Mark	Name		Nat	Born	Date
65.74	Jenni	Penttilä	FIN	9.3.91	16 Jun
65.52	Fruzsina	Fertig	HUN-J	2.9.93	26 May
65.18	Carolin	Paesler	GER	16.12.90	4 Feb
65.10	Kimery	Hern	USA	24.2.87	17 May
65.09		Zhang Li	CHN-J	13.3.93	12 Mar
65.07	Gabi	Wolfarth	GER	6.9.89	17 Mar
64.96	Carys	Parry	GBR	24.7.81	23 Jun
64.91	Masumi	Aya	JPN	1.1.80	10 Jun
64.88	Jessica	Rowland	USA	25.2.90	15 Jun
64.88	Malwina	Kopron	POL-J	16.11.94	23 Jun
64.85	Cecilia	Nilsson	SWE	22.6.79	26 Aug
64.83	Cintia	Gergelics	HUN	16.11.91	16 Jun
64.66	Karolina	Pedersen	SWE	16.4.87	15 Apr
64.65	Susan	McKelvie	GBR	15.6.85	18 Aug
64.63	Josefin	Berg	SWE	27.12.85	20 Jun
64.62	Alexis	Thomas	USA	25.12.90	11 May
64.55	Nikola	Lomnická	SVK	16.9.88	7 Jun
64.53	Ashley	Harbin	USA	15.2.86	17 May
64.36	Megann	Rodhe	CAN	27.8.85	29 Apr
64.26	Zeliha	Uzunbilek	TUR	10.6.91	5 Jun
64.23	Trude	Raad	NOR	27.4.90	24 May
64.20		Wang Yingying	CHN-J	16.5.93	28 Apr
64.13	Odette	Palma	CHI	7.8.82	9 Jun
64.10	Johanna	Salmela	FIN	6.11.90	25 Aug
63.97	Yekaterina	Ryabtseva	RUS	29.1.92	21 Jun
63.96	Magdalena	Szewa	POL	20.9.90	27 Apr
63.83	Brittany	Hinchcliffe	USA	24.7.82	21 Apr
63.80		Kang Na-ru	KOR	25.4.83	16 May
63.79	Sini	Latvala	FIN	3.2.80	2 Sep
63.78	Taylor	Bush	USA	26.11.89	20 Apr
63.77	Valerie	Fraizer	USA	4.10.86	9 Jun
63.70	Lena	Solvin	FIN	4.7.86	16 Jun
63.61		Luo Na	CHN-J	8.10.93	12 Mar
63.54	Hanna	Zinchuk	BLR-J	4.2.94	16 May
63.53	Alicja	Filipkowska	POL	15.4.87	27 May
63.53	Tatyana	Tsimafeichyk	BLR	6.3.86	6 Jul
63.51	Sara	Savatovic	SRB-J	5.10.93	13 May
63.50	Elisa	Magni	ITA	22.6.91	18 Jul
63.47	Zsófia	Bácskay	HUN-Y	18.3.97	13 Oct
63.45	Tatiana	Massamba	FRA	17.8.89	22 May
63.42	Sandra	Malinowska	POL-J	31.7.93	19 May
63.40	Jade	Niemeyer	USA	22.9.88	26 May
63.40	Mélanie	Fromentin	FRA	10.10.81	17 Jul
63.38	Sarah	Bensaad	TUN	27.1.87	6 Jun
63.36		Xia Youlian	CHN-J	4.8.93	21 Jul
63.35	Melissa	Kurzdorfer	USA	30.12.91	26 May
63.33	Eva	Reinders	NED-J	12.5.93	9 Jun
63.32	Iliána	Korosídou	GRE-Y	14.1.95	14 Jul
63.24	Victoria	Flowers	USA	17.1.90	21 Apr
63.16	Paraskevi	Theodorou	CYP	15.3.86	10 Jun
63.13	Hanna	Lutska	UKR	6.5.88	19 May
62.96	Samantha	Hynes	GBR	20.1.86	19 May
62.93	Favian	Cowards	USA	11.5.90	26 May
62.89	Sharon	Ayala	MEX	28.9.86	27 May
62.89	Delphine	Ramothe	FRA	17.7.91	18 Jul
62.87	Beth	Rohl	USA	7.11.90	11 May
62.81	Jennifer	Joyce	CAN	25.9.80	30 Jun
62.78	Zuleima	Mina	ECU	5.6.90	2 Sep
62.68	Josiane	Soares	BRA	21.6.76	19 May
62.66	Annabelle	Rolnin	FRA	28.12.87	3 Jun
62.65	Dóra	Lévai	HUN	20.6.88	7 Jul
62.62	Liz	Murphy	USA	23.4.90	3 May
62.62	Deanna	Price	USA-J	8.6.93	26 May
62.56	Brieanna	Kennedy	USA	24.2.90	21 Apr
62.52	Natalya	Shayunova	BLR	11.9.89	24 Feb
62.42	Maggie	Mullen	CAN	2.3.89	21 Apr
62.38	Kearsten	Peoples	USA	20.12.91	26 May
62.38	Micaela	Mariani	ITA	11.2.88	22 Sep
62.35	Alyona	Shamotina	UKR-Y	27.12.95	1 Jun
62.30	Daniela	Manz	GER	19.9.86	17 Jun
62.28	Mareike	Nannen	GER	2.1.90	20 May
62.20	Erin	Atkinson	USA	30.1.92	11 May
62.20	Amanda	Murphy	USA	.90	26 May
62.14	Caressa	Sims	USA	7.3.86	17 May
62.06	Irina	Sarvilova	RUS	11.11.91	21 Apr
62.03	Réka	Gyurátz	HUN-Y	31.5.96	16 Jun
62.01	Kristýna	Krouzková	CZE	5.3.90	16 Jun
61.99	Lindsey	Spencer	USA	7.1.89	11 May
61.98	Marylou	Bontemps	FRA	23.10.91	2 Jun
61.96	Yuka	Murofushi	JPN	11.2.77	26 May
61.93	Galina	Mityayeva	TJK	29.4.91	12 May
61.92		Li Juan	CHN	6.2.88	21 Jul
61.88	Lisa	Wilson	USA	29.3.88	12 May
61.88	Romana	Grómanová	CZE	11.10.84	27 May
61.76	Melinda	Bendik	USA	3.3.89	26 May
61.66	Mariana	Grasielly Marcelino	BRA	16.7.92	23 Sep
61.61	Shant'e	White	USA	1.5.90	15 Apr
61.61	Crystal	Bourque	USA	7.1.89	28 Apr
61.57	Dagmara	Stala	POL	9.12.91	2 Sep
61.56	Agápi	Proskinitopoúlou	GRE-J	3.9.93	1 Jul
61.41	Mele	Vaisima	USA	.89	21 Apr
61.38	Rachel	Gair	GBR	12.9.86	30 Jun
61.37	Heli	Rinnekari	FIN-J	30.9.94	19 Jun
61.33	Katerina	Chlupová	CZE	22.10.86	8 Sep
61.32	Shannon	Popp	USA	23.10.84	7 Apr
61.32	Latifah	Johnson	USA	23.1.90	26 May
61.29	Liz	Dubourt	CAN	.86	30 Jun
61.22	Brooke	Pleger	USA	21.6.92	7 Apr
61.20	Amy	Thayer	USA	26.7.81	7 Apr
61.19	Monteka	Flowers (200)	USA	1.11.89	13 May

JUNIORS

See main list for top 6 juniors. 11 performances by 4 women to 67.13. Additional marks and further juniors:

Tavernier	68.46	1	Aix-les-Bains	7 Oct	67.89	1	Aix-les-Bains	29 Sep
	68.44	2	Forbach	27 May	67.59	1	Montceau-les-Mines	21 Oct
Sedykh	67.57	5	Villeneuve d'Ascq	9 Jun	67.34	2 WJ	Barcelona	14 Jul

Mark			Name		Nat	Born	Pos	Meet	Venue			Date
Sedykh	67.48	2		Uppsala		28	Jul					
65.52			Fruzsina	Fertig	HUN	2.9.93	1		Zalaegerszeg			26 May
65.09				Zhang Li	CHN	13.3.93	5	NGP	Chengdu			12 Mar
64.88			Malwina	Kopron	POL	16.11.94	1	NC-j	Bialystok			23 Jun
64.20	(10)			Wang Yingying	CHN	16.5.93	5	NGP	Wuhan			28 Apr
63.61				Luo Na	CHN	8.10.93	6	NGP	Chengdu			12 Mar
63.54			Hanna	Zinchuk	BLR-	4.2.94	5		Brest			16 May
63.51			Sara	Savatovic	SRB	5.10.93	1		Sremska Mitrovica			13 May
63.47			Zsófia	Bácskay	HUN-Y	18.3.97	1		Veszprém			13 Oct
63.42			Sandra	Malinowska	POL	31.7.93	1		Szczecin			19 May
63.36				Xia Youlian	CHN	4.8.93	3		Dalian			21 Jul
63.33			Eva	Reinders	NED	12.5.93	1		Fränkisch-Crumbach			9 Jun
63.32			Iliána	Korosídou	GRE-Y	14.1.95	5	WJ	Barcelona			14 Jul
62.62			Deanna	Price	USA-J	8.6.93	10q	NCAA-W	Austin			26 May
62.35			Alyona	Shamotina (20)	UKR-Y	27.12.95	1	NC-j	Yalta			1 Jun

JAVELIN

Mark				Name		Nat	Born	Pos	Meet	Venue			Date
69.55				Barbora	Spotáková	CZE	30.6.81	1	OG	London (OS)			9 Aug
					66.90	66.88	66.24	69.55	x	x			
	68.73	2	DL	New York		9 Jun	68.72	65.24	61.70	65.49	65.63	68.73	
	68.65	1	GGala	Roma		31 May	61.22	x	62.66	60.33	65.54	68.65	
	67.78	1	GS	Ostrava		25 May	66.84	60.98	67.78	66.15	x	61.03	
	67.19	1	Athl	Lausanne		23 Aug	67.19	61.41	67.19	x	63.55	64.80	
	66.91	1	VD	Bruxelles		7 Sep	61.56	61.84	62.78	61.68	66.91	65.69	
	66.83	2	ISTAF	Berlin		2 Sep	60.84	62.47	x	61.48	x	66.83	
	66.19	Q	OG	London (OS)		7 Aug	66.19	p	p				
	66.17	2	DL	Doha		11 May	66.17	65.88	64.87	62.22			
	66.08	1	DL	Birmingham		26 Aug	66.08	64.37	p	63.89	61.93	p	
	65.88	1	Odlozil	Praha		11 Jun	54.38	61.80	p	x	65.88	65.40	
69.35				Sunette	Viljoen	RSA	6.1.83	1	DL	New York			9 Jun
					60.48	64.51	65.34	66.60	69.35	x			
	67.95	2	GGala	Roma		31 May	61.35	57.78	61.29	63.64	64.13	67.95	
	67.52	1	ISTAF	Berlin		2 Sep	64.07	62.20	63.78	63.46	62.93	67.52	
	65.92	Q	OG	London (OS)		7 Aug	65.92	p	p				
	65.33	2	VD	Bruxelles		7 Sep	61.82	60.63	61.71	60.89	63.19	65.33	
67.04				Christina	Obergföll	GER	22.8.81	1		St. Wendel			10 Jun
					63.01	x	67.04	x	x	x			
	66.14	Q	OG	London (OS)		7 Aug	66.14	p	p				
	65.86	1	NC	Wattenscheid		17 Jun	63.94	65.86	x	x	65.05	x	
	65.16	2	OG	London (OS)		9 Aug	65.16	x	x	x	x	x	
	65.12	2	EC	Helsinki		29 Jun	65.12	x	63.53	64.55	x	63.17	
66.86				Mariya	Abakumova	RUS	15.1.86	1	DL	Doha			11 May
					x	58.52	66.86	62.22					
	65.80	2	Athl	Lausanne		23 Aug	62.65	65.80	x	62.30	x	65.40	
66.86				Vira	Rebryk	UKR	25.2.89	1	EC	Helsinki			29 Jun
					57.04	63.44	x	62.83	66.86	64.77			
	66.53	1	NCp	Yalta		28 May	60.77	60.06	64.42	x	66.53	x	
66.17				Goldie	Sayers	GBR	16.7.82	1	LGP	London (CP)			14 Jul
					66.17	64.44	65.74	59.92	p	x			
65.24				Martina	Ratej	SLO	2.11.81	1	NC-w	Domzale			25 Feb
					++								
65.11					Li Lingwei	CHN	26.1.89	1		Fuzhou			23 Jun
					58.24	61.91	65.11	57.71	57.76	58.17			
64.95					Lu Huihui	CHN	26.6.89	1	NGP	Zhaoqing			14 Apr
64.91				Linda	Stahl	GER	2.10.85	3	OG	London (OS)			9 Aug
	(30/10)				59.49	63.24	62.67	64.91	x	x			
64.74					Zhang Li	CHN	17.1.89	1	NGP	Wuhan			28 Apr
64.34				Kathryn	Mitchell	AUS	10.7.82	3	GS	Ostrava			25 May
64.12				Kim	Mickle	AUS	28.12.84	1		Mannheim			23 Jun
63.20				Katharina	Molitor	GER	8.11.83	3	NC	Wattenscheid			17 Jun
62.81					Liu Chunhua	CHN	1.10.86	1	NGP	Tianjin			12 May
62.77				Ásdís	Hjálmsdóttir	ISL	28.10.85	Q	OG	London (OS)			7 Aug
62.75				Yanet	Cruz	CUB	8.2.88	1	NC	La Habana			24 Mar
62.74				Madara	Palameika	LAT	18.6.87	5	Athl	Lausanne			23 Aug
62.53				Sinta	Ozolina-Kovala	LAT	26.2.88	1		Liepaja			7 Jul
62.36				Yuki	Ebihara	JPN	28.10.85	1	NC	Osaka			10 Jun
	(20)												
61.89					Du Xiaowei	CHN	11.8.87	2	NGP	Chengdu			12 Mar
61.84				Margaryta	Dorozhon	UKR	4.9.87	2	NCp	Yalta			28 May
61.51				Brittany	Borman	USA	1.7.89	1	NC/OT	Eugene			1 Jul
61.46				Hanna	Hatsko	UKR	3.10.90	1	NC-w	Yalta			23 Feb

Mark	Name		Nat	Born	Pos	Meet	Venue	Date	
61.40	Sofi	Flinck	SWE-Y	8.7.95	1	WJ	Barcelona	11	Jul
61.17	Anastasiya	Svechnikova	UZB	20.9.92	1	NCp	Tashkent	24	Apr
61.15	Liz	Gleadle	CAN	5.12.88	1	Jerome	Burnaby	10	Jun
61.06	Rachel	Yurkovich	USA	10.10.86	1		Baie Mahault	1	May
61.04	Lina	Muze	LAT	4.12.92	1	NC	Kaunas	8	Jul
60.96A	Jarmila	Klimesová	CZE	9.2.81	1		Potchefstroom	24	Mar
(30)									
60.89	Tatjana	Jelaca	SRB	10.8.90	1		Sremska Mitrovica	15	Jul
60.70	Yainelis	Ribiaux	CUB	30.12.87	2	NC	La Habana	24	Mar
60.59	Viktoriya	Sudarushkina	RUS	2.9.90	1		Sotteville-lès-Rouen	10	Jul
60.56		Chang Chunfeng	CHN	4.5.88	3	NGP	Chengdu	12	Mar
60.49	Kara	Patterson	USA	10.4.86	Q	NC/OT	Eugene	29	Jun
60.33	Marina	Maksimova	RUS	20.5.85	3	ECp-w	Bar	17	Mar
60.21	Laila	e Silva	BRA	30.7.82	1	GP	Rio de Janeiro	20	May
60.08	Oksana	Gromova	RUS	23.9.80	1	Kuts	Moskva	13	Jun
59.96	Sávva	Líka	GRE	27.6.70	1		Athína (E)	9	Jun
59.95		Xue Juan	CHN	10.2.86	5	NGP	Wuhan	28	Apr
(40)									
59.88		Yang Xinli	CHN	7.2.88	6	NGP	Wuhan	28	Apr
59.85	Mareike	Rittweg	GER	1.6.84	4	Werfer	Halle	19	May
59.83	Marina	Novik	BLR	19.1.84	1		Brest	28	Apr
59.43	Zahra	Bani	ITA	31.12.79	5	Werfer	Halle	19	May
59.34	Krista	Woodward	CAN	22.11.84	1		Surrey BC	20	Jun
59.33	Yusbelys	Parra	VEN	31.7.86	2		La Habana	22	Jun
59.32A	Flor Denis	Ruíz	COL	24.1.91	1		Medellin	28	Apr
59.31	Sanni	Utriainen	FIN	5.2.91	1	U23	Leverkusen	1	Jun
59.31	Vanda	Juhász	HUN	6.6.89	1	NC	Szekszárd	16	Jun
59.22	Yuka	Sato	JPN	21.7.92	1		Osaka	13	May
(50)									
59.20		Liu Shiying	CHN-J	24.9.93	2	WJ	Barcelona	11	Jul
59.15	Tatyana	Khaladovich	BLR	21.6.91	1	NC	Grodno	6	Jul
59.14		Wang Ping	CHN	28.7.90	4	NGP	Tianjin	12	May
59.14	Oona	Sormunen	FIN	2.8.89	1	NC	Lahti	25	Aug
59.12	Kristine	Harutyunyan	ARM	18.5.91	2	U23	Adler	21	Apr
59.05	Indré	Jakubaityté	LTU	24.1.76	18q	OG	London (OS)	7	Aug
58.93	Haruka	Matoba	JPN	24.4.87	2	NC	Osaka	10	Jun
58.82	Nora Aida	Bicet	ESP	29.10.77	1		Los Corrales de Buelna	18	Jul
58.52	Lyubov	Zhatkina	RUS	30.3.90	1	NC-23	Yerino	21	Jul
58.51	Melissa	Dupré	BEL	5.11.86	1		Sint-Niklaas	17	May
(60)									
58.42	Esther	Eisenlauer	GER	29.10.77	5	ECp-w	Bar	17	Mar
58.27	Risa	Miyashita	JPN	26.4.84	3	NC	Osaka	10	Jun
58.07		Kim Kyung-ae	KOR	5.3.88	1		Gimcheon	9	May
58.04	Kim	Hamilton	USA	28.11.85	3	NC/OT	Eugene	1	Jul
57.97	Alicia	DeShasier	USA	15.4.84	3		Tucson	19	May
57.90		Liu Beibei	CHN	5.10.90	8	NGP	Wuhan	28	Apr
57.85	Jucilene	de Lima	BRA	14.9.90	1	NC	São Paulo	30	Jun
57.77	Leryn	Franco	PAR	1.3.82	2	IbAmC	Barquisimeto	8	Jun
57.77	Hanna	Habina	UKR	26.10.92	3	NC	Yalta	14	Jun
57.75i	Anna	Wessman	SWE	9.10.89	1		Växjö	10	Mar
	54.68A				1		Potchefstroom	1	Mar
(70)									
57.68	Susanne	Rosenbauer	GER	2.8.84	2		Wetzlar	18	Aug
57.52		Chen Ping	CHN	8.9.89	7	NGP	Chengdu	12	Mar
57.42	Xénia	Nagy	HUN	29.3.86	3		Leverkusen	1	Jun
57.41	Irena	Sedivá	CZE	19.1.92	8	GS	Ostrava	25	May
57.40	Mercedes	Chilla	ESP	19.1.80	1		Durango	19	May
57.27	Antoinette	Nana Djimou	FRA	2.8.85	2H	Décastar	Talence	16	Sep
57.23	Prescilla	Lecurieux	FRA	1.12.92	1		Aix-lès-Bains	20	May
57.22	Magdalena	Czenska	POL	14.6.81	1	NC	Bielsko-Biala	15	Jun
57.22	Séphora	Bissoly	FRA	6.11.81	3		Sotteville-lès-Rouen	10	Jul
57.12	Marija	Vucenovic	SRB-J	3.4.93	3	WJ	Barcelona	11	Jul
(80)									
56.96	Sofía	Ifantídou	GRE	10.1.85	1H	OG	London (OS)	4	Aug
56.93	Desirée	Schwarz	GER	24.4.92	1		Heilbronn	8	Jul
56.89A	Abigail	Gómez	MEX	30.6.91	1	NACAC	Irapuato	8	Jul
56.84	Kiho	Kuze	JPN-Y	28.3.95	5	NC	Osaka	10	Jun
56.76	Nadeeka	Lakmali	SRI	18.9.81	1		Colombo	14	Nov
56.72	Barbara	Madejczyk	POL	30.9.76	1	Kuso	Szczecin	21	Jul
56.67	Maria	Negoitâ	ROU	6.12.86	1	IntC	Bucuresti	8	Jun
56.61	Eliza	Toader	ROU	12.5.90	1	Univ Ch	Cluj-Napolca	20	May

Mark	Name		Nat	Born	Pos	Meet	Venue	Date
56.56		Song Xiaodan	CHN-J	23.1.93	5	NC	Kunshan	24 Sep
56.52	Matilde	Andraud	FRA	28.4.89	2		Aix-lès-Bains	20 May
(90)								
56.49	Charlotte	Müller	GER-J	14.9.93	1	NC-j	Mönchengladbach	21 Jul
56.36		Suh Hae-an	KOR	1.7.85			Goseong	27 Jun
56.34	Ismaray	Armentero	CUB-J	13.10.94	1		La Habana	2 Jun
56.33	Lismania	Muñoz	CUB-J	28.2.93	2		La Habana	2 Jun
56.20A	Tiffany	Perkins	CAN	1.1.91	2	NACAC	Irapuato	8 Jul
56.20	Sarah	Mayer	GER	20.5.91	1	NC-23	Kandel	29 Jul
56.17	Raine	Kuningas	EST	20.10.88	1		Tallinn	24 May
56.11	Suman	Devi	IND	15.7.85	1		Patiala	21 Apr
56.10	Liveta	Jasiunaité	LTU-J	25.7.94	1		Kaunas	3 Jun
55.97	Franziska	Krebs	GER	11.10.85	2	Kuso	Szczecin	21 Jul
(100)								

Mark	Name		Nat	Born	Date
55.95	Aggelikí	Tsiolakoúdi	GRE	10.5.76	8 Jul
55.90	Margaret	Simpson	GHA	2.8.82	27 May
55.86	Bregje	Crolla	NED	31.1.86	12 May
55.80	Elisabeth	Eberl	AUT	25.3.88	23 May
55.79	Isabelle	Jeffs	GBR	3.2.92	30 Jun
55.76	Dilhani	Lekamge	SRI	14.1.87	10 Nov
55.74	Christin	Hussong	GER-J	17.4.94	19 Feb
55.73	Karlee	McQuillen	USA	31.5.89	29 Jun
55.71		Sui Liping	CHN	1.5.91	28 Apr
55.67	Kateryna	Derun	UKR-J	24.9.93	17 Mar
55.64	Lyudmyla	Yosypenko	UKR	24.9.84	16 Sep
55.44		Zhu Dandan	CHN-J		10 Aug
55.38	Sílvia	Cruz	POR	29.12.80	10 Jun
55.37A	Gerlize	de Klerk	RSA	23.3.89	20 Apr
55.36	Karolina	Boldysz	POL-J	21.4.93	5 May
55.22	Haley	Crouser	USA-J	11.2.94	13 Apr
55.18	Urszula	Jakimowicz	POL	11.6.88	2 Jun
55.18		Ma Ning	CHN	4.11.83	15 Jul
55.16	Dana	Lyon	USA	5.6.84	1 Jul
54.99	Kateema	Riettie	JAM	12.5.73	6 Jul
54.97	Nadine	Broersen	NED	29.4.90	27 May
54.93	Brianna	Bain	USA-J	23.6.93	6 Jun
54.92	Agnieszka	Lewandowska	POL	10.9.88	9 Jun
54.83	Caroline	Schlör	GER	29.12.87	10 Jun
54.77	Yu	Kawanobe	JPN	22.11.91	19 May
54.72	Niina	Kelo	FIN	26.3.80	26 Aug
54.62	Coralys	Ortiz	PUR	16.4.85	15 Mar
54.60	Jen	Austin	USA	14.8.82	24 Mar
54.59	Laura	Henkel	GER	29.2.92	3 Mar
54.59	Janice	Waldvogel	GER-J	7.4.93	19 May
54.55	Alessandra	Resende	BRA	5.3.75	25 Feb
54.54	María	Murillo	COL	5.5.91	28 Jan
54.40	Evelien	Dekkers	NED	28.4.88	12 May
54.39	Silvia	Carli	ITA	17.9.85	6 Jun
54.37	Hiroko	Takigawa	JPN-J	25.7.94	25 May
54.33	Hitomi	Sukenaga	JPN	4.5.88	22 Sep
54.32	Nicoleta	Anghelescu	ROU	3.1.92	16 Jun
54.26		Song Dan	CHN	5.7.90	24 Sep
54.25	Laura	Whittingham	GBR	6.6.86	10 Jun
54.24	Melissa	Fraser	CAN	.89	14 Apr
54.17	Nikolett	Szabó	HUN	3.3.80	10 Jun
54.16		Xing Xinxin	CHN		28 Apr
54.09		Zhang Ying	CHN	5.1.88	28 Apr
54.07	Nikol	Ogrodníková	CZE	18.8.90	8 Jul
54.06	Amy	Backel	USA	27.9.87	19 May
54.05	Sabine	Kopplin	GER	23.11.90	29 Jul
54.04	Nuttha	Nacharn	THA	4.6.90	4 Nov
53.98	Sara	Kolak	CRO-Y	22.6.95	24 Jun
53.95		Fu Lin	CHN	21.2.89	26 May
53.95	Annu	Rani	IND	29.8.92	23 Jun
53.91	Yevgeniya	Ananchenko	RUS	7.11.92	29 Feb
53.91	Marta	Kakol	POL	25.2.92	15 Jun
53.90	Osleidys	Menéndez	CUB	14.11.79	27 May
53.81	Xénia	Frajka	HUN	24.1.82	16 Jun
53.76A	Justine	Robbeson	RSA	15.5.85	20 Apr
53.73	Laura	Ikauniece	LAT	31.5.92	19 May
53.66	Lisanne	Schol	NED	22.6.91	28 May
53.61	Gundega	Griva	LAT	8.4.91	15 Sep
53.59	Leigh	Petranoff	USA	16.5.89	1 Jul
53.52	Svetlana	Zaytseva	BLR	30.10.87	18 Jul
53.51		Wu You	CHN	18.12.92	24 Sep
53.50	Gwendolyn	Weber	GER	16.10.90	17 Jun
53.48	Ariana	Ince	USA	14.3.89	21 Apr
53.47	Marina	Saito	JPN-Y	15.10.95	30 Jul
53.42		Lee Hye-rim	KOR	6.3.89	25 Apr
53.38	Ingeborg Sverdrup	Rønningen	NOR-J	11.1.94	20 Jun
53.37	Linda	Treiel	EST	8.5.91	25 Aug
53.36	Tetyana	Fetiskina	UKR-J	11.9.94	17 May
53.24	Tiziana	Rocco	ITA	2.12.78	25 Feb
53.21	Tatyana	Chernova	RUS	29.1.88	27 May
53.21	Ieva	Sciukauskaité	LTU	3.2.90	14 Jun
53.18	Lilli	Schwarzkopf	GER	28.8.83	27 May
53.15	Maddalena	Purgato	ITA	6.7.89	25 Feb
53.15	Felicia	Moldovan	ROU	29.9.67	19 May
53.15	Aleksandra	Spikina	RUS	16.1.89	4 Jul
53.13	Chika	Shimada (176)	JPN	28.2.91	11 Dec

Drugs disqualification: 59.47 Lada Chernova ¶ RUS 1.1.70 (2) NC-w Adler 29 Feb

JUNIOR

See main list for top 9 juniors. 10 performances by 6 women to 56.40. Additional marks and further juniors:

Mark	Name		Nat	Born	Pos	Meet	Venue	Date
Flinck	58.16	Q	WJ	Barcelona	10 Jul	56.87 1 vFIN	Göteborg	1 Sep
Liu Shiying	58.47	Q	WJ	Barcelona	10 Jul	57.52 1 NC-j	Changzhou	20 Apr
55.74	Christin	Hussong (10)	GER	17.4.94	1	NC-j	Sindelfingen	19 Feb
55.67	Kateryna	Derun	UKR	24.9.93	3	ECp-w	Bar23	17 Mar
55.36	Karolina	Boldysz	POL	21.4.93	1		Gdansk	5 May
55.22	Haley	Crouser	USA	11.2.94	1		Aloha	13 Apr
54.93	Brianna	Bain	USA	23.6.93	2	NCAA	Des Moines	6 Jun
54.59	Janice	Waldvogel	GER	7.4.93	1-19	Werfer	Halle	19 May
54.37	Hiroko	Takigawa	JPN	25.7.94	1		Osaka	25 May
53.98	Sara	Kolak	CRO-Y	22.6.95	1	NC-j	Zagreb	24 Jun
53.47	Marina	Saito	JPN-Y	15.10.95	Q		Niigata	30 Jul
53.38	Ingeborg Sverdrup	Rønningen	NOR	11.1.94	1		Ski	20 Jun
53.36	Tetyana	Fetiskina (20)	UKR	11.9.94	1	Univ Ch	Yalta	17 May

HEPTATHLON

Mark	Name		Nat	Born	Pos	Meet	Venue	Date
6955	Jessica	Ennis	GBR	28.1.86	1	OG	London (OS)	4 Aug
	12.54/1.3	1.86	14.28	22.83/-0.3	6.48/-0.6	47.49	2:08.65	
6906		Ennis			1		Götzis	27 May
	12.81/0.0	1.85	14.51	22.88/1.9	6.51/0.8	47.11	2:09.00	

Mark	Name		Nat	Born	Pos	Meet	Venue	Date
6774	Tatyana	Chernova	RUS	29.1.88	2		Götzis	27 May
	13.34/0.0	1.82 13.75 23.49/1.9		6.44/1.0		53.21	2:08.94	
6681	Kristina	Savitskaya	RUS	10.6.91	1	NC	Cheboksary	3 Jun
	13.52/0.0	1.88 15.27 24.61/0.0		6.65/0.0		46.83	2:14.73	
6649	Lilli	Schwarzkopf	GER	28.8.83	2	OG	London (OS)	4 Aug
	13.26/0.9	1.83 14.77 24.77/0.9		6.30/-0.7		51.73	2:10.50	
6628		Chernova			3	OG	London (OS)	4 Aug
	13.48/1.3	1.80 14.17 23.67/-0.3		6.54/0.5		46.29	2:09.56	
6618	Lyudmyla	Yosypenko	UKR	24.9.84	4	OG	London (OS)	4 Aug
	13.25/0.9	1.83 13.90 23.68/0.6		6.31/-0.6		49.63	2:13.28	
6599A	Jessica	Zelinka	CAN	3.9.81	1	NC	Calgary	28 Jun
	12.76/-0.6	1.77 14.74 23.42w/2.1		5.98w/2.9		46.60	2:08.95	
6599	Austra	Skujyté	LTU	12.8.79	5	OG	London (OS)	4 Aug
	14.00/0.7	1.92 17.31 25.43/0.9		6.25/-0.6		51.13	2:20.59	
6576	Antoinette	Nana Djimou	FRA	2.8.85	6	OG	London (OS)	4 Aug
	12.96/1.3	1.80 14.26 24.72/0.3		6.13/-0.2		55.87	2:15.94	
6544		Nana Djimou			1	EC	Helsinki	30 Jun
	13.11/0.4	1.77 13.48 24.52/-0.5		6.42/1.2		55.82	2:17.99	
6528	Olga	Kurban	RUS	16.12.87	2	NC	Cheboksary	3 Jun
	13.40/0.0	1.82 14.11 23.67/0.0		6.46/0.8		42.07	2:11.38	
6501		Yosypenko			3		Götzis	27 May
	13.42/0.2	1.82 13.92 24.03/1.9		6.30/1.3		48.79	2:15.28	
6493		Skujyté			4		Götzis	27 May
	14.18/-1.5	1.91 16.49 25.31/0.4		6.31/0.5		49.18	2:20.94	
6480		Zelinka			7	OG	London (OS)	4 Aug
	12.65/1.3	1.68 14.81 23.32/-0.3		5.91/-1.3		45.75	2:09.15	
6466	Yekaterina	Bolshova (10)	RUS	4.2.88	3	NC	Cheboksary	3 Jun
	13.53/0.0	1.91 13.58 24.17/0.0		6.45/0.9		37.62	2:10.42	
6461		Schwarzkopf			5		Götzis	27 May
	13.51/0.0	1.82 14.13 24.86/1.6		6.07/-1.5		53.18	2:13.57	
6452		Savitskaya			8	OG	London (OS)	4 Aug
	13.37/0.9	1.83 14.77 24.46/0.3		6.21/-0.3		43.70	2:12.27	
6440	Brianne	Theisen	CAN	18.12.88	1	NCAA	Des Moines	8 Jun
	13.30/-0.4	1.84 12.92 24.09/1.1		6.28/1.7		46.38	2:13.81	
6419	Hyleas	Fountain	USA	14.1.81	1	NC/OT	Eugene	30 Jun
	12.86/0.9	1.87 13.17 23.84/1.0		6.30/1.3		40.43	2:17.90	
6414	Laura	Ikauniece	LAT	31.5.92	9	OG	London (OS)	4 Aug
	13.71/2.0	1.83 12.64 24.16/0.3		6.13/-0.4		51.27	2:12.13	
6407	Anna	Melnychenko	UKR	24.4.83	1	NCp	Yalta	28 May
	13.60/-1.6	1.82 14.05 24.14/-0.7		6.56/0.0		39.47	2:13.07	
6401		Yosypenko			1	Décastar	Talence	16 Sep
	13.60/0.9	1.82 12.71 24.32/-1.3		6.23/0.6		55.64	2:20.74	
6393		Zelinka			6		Götzis	27 May
	13.02/0.0	1.73 14.56 23.46/1.9		5.86/0.5		43.43	2:09.19	
6393A		Theisen			2	NC	Calgary	28 Jun
	13.09/-0.6	1.83 13.21 24.11w/2.1		6.32/1.7		43.14	2:16.07	
6392		Melnychenko			10	OG	London (OS)	4 Aug
	13.32/2.0	1.80 12.96 24.09/0.6		6.40/-0.5		43.86	2:12.90	
6390		Nana Djimou			2	Décastar	Talence	16 Sep
	13.43/0.9	1.76 13.76 25.07/-1.3		6.21/0.5		57.27	2:19.67	
6387		Yosypenko			2	EC	Helsinki	30 Jun
	13.42/0.4	1.77 14.32 24.14/-0.4		6.14/1.0		49.61	2:17.63	
6383		Theisen			11	OG	London (OS)	4 Aug
	13.30/1.3	1.83 12.89 24.35/-0.3		6.01/-1.2		46.47	2:09.27	
6360	Dafne	Schippers	NED	15.6.92	7		Götzis	27 May
	13.43/0.0 (30/15)	1.73 13.82 22.73/1.9		6.49/-0.3		40.41	2:18.66	
6345	Jennifer	Oeser	GER	29.11.83	8		Götzis	27 May
	13.54/0.2	1.82 13.56 24.55/0.7		6.19/0.3		47.83	2:16.05	
6345	Julia	Mächtig	GER	1.1.86	1		Ratingen	15 Jun
	14.28/0.9	1.75 15.98 25.07/-0.2		6.49/1.5		47.54	2:16.92	
6343	Sharon	Day	USA	9.6.85	2	NC/OT	Eugene	30 Jun
	13.71/1.6	1.87 13.40 24.26/1.0		6.11/1.3		45.03	2:14.55	
6325	Aiga	Grabuste	LAT	24.3.88	4	EC	Helsinki	30 Jun
	13.66/0.3	1.74 13.52 24.47/0.0		6.46/2.6		45.85	2:12.90	
6319	Nadine	Broersen	NED	29.4.90	13	OG	London (OS)	4 Aug
	13.64/-0.2 (20)	1.86 13.57 25.13/0.8		5.94/0.5		51.98	2:16.98	
6311	Nataliya	Dobrynska	UKR	29.5.82	9		Götzis	27 May
	13.97/0.2	1.82 15.61 25.14/1.9		6.31/1.6		44.40	2:17.98	

Mark	Name		Nat	Born	Pos	Meet	Venue	Date
6300	Jessica	Samuelsson	SWE	14.3.85	14	OG	London (OS)	4 Aug
	13.58/2.0	1.77 14.18 24.25/0.6		6.18/-0.7		42.02	2:11.31	
6283	Eliska	Klucinová	CZE	14.4.88	1		Kladno	10 Jun
	14.11/-2.6	1.83 14.17 24.77/-1.9		6.25/-0.4		46.33	2:16.28	
6267	Katarina	Johnson-Thompson	GBR-J	9.1.93	15	OG	London (OS)	4 Aug
	13.48/0.9	1.89 11.32 23.73/-0.3		6.19/-0.4		38.37	2:10.76	
6245	Margaret	Simpson	GHA	2.8.82	13		Götzis	27 May
	13.85/0.2	1.79 12.43 24.96/2.9		6.07/0.9		55.90	2:17.88	
6210	Claudia	Rath	GER	25.4.86	7	EC	Helsinki	30 Jun
	13.68/0.3	1.77 12.88 24.54/-0.4		6.42/1.2		39.99	2:11.09	
6198	Yana	Maksimova	BLR	9.1.89	17	OG	London (OS)	4 Aug
	13.97/0.7	1.89 14.09 25.43/0.8		5.99/-1.2		42.33	2:13.37	
6192	Yana	Panteleyeva	RUS	16.6.88	4	NC	Cheboksary	3 Jun
	13.50/0.0	1.82 13.61 24.79/0.0		6.32/1.0		40.77	2:19.26	
6188	Chantae	McMillan	USA	1.5.88	3	NC/OT	Eugene	30 Jun
	13.36/0.7	1.72 15.02 24.32w/3.0		5.52/1.6		50.24	2:17.71	
6182	Marisa	De Aniceto	FRA	11.11.86	1		Arona	27 May
	13.81/-0.3	1.80 12.91 25.24/0.0		6.10/0.0		51.92	2:19.10	
	(30)							
6160	Lucimara	da Silva	BRA	10.7.85	1	IbAmC	Barquisimeto	10 Jun
	13.78/-2.0	1.83 12.63 24.98/-0.4		6.44/0.5		42.22	2:18.52	
6154	Maren	Schwerdtner	GER	3.10.85	17		Götzis	27 May
	13.62/0.2	1.73 13.77 24.46/1.9		6.44/1.3		44.56	2:23.89	
6143	Bettie	Wade	USA	11.9.86	1		Tucson	30 Mar
	13.42/0.0	1.81 13.20 24.41w/2.2		6.22/-1.9		39.40	2:19.29	
6135	Sarah	Cowley	NZL	3.2.84	18		Götzis	27 May
	14.02/-0.3	1.91 13.22 25.48/2.9		6.12/1.4		40.66	2:15.37	
6126	Alina	Fyodorova	UKR	31.7.89	2	NCp	Yalta	28 May
	14.29/-1.6	1.85 14.43 25.12/-0.7		6.33/1.1		37.18	2:15.78	
6124	Ellen	Sprunger	SUI	5.8.86	1		Landquart	20 May
	13.54/0.6	1.72 12.91 24.52/-3.3		6.13/2.1		46.83	2:17.31	
6110	Aleksandra	Butvina	RUS	14.2.86	5	NC	Cheboksary	3 Jun
	14.20/0.0	1.79 14.52 25.04/0.0		6.03/1.0		41.87	2:13.08	
6109	Sofía	Ifantídou	GRE	10.1.85	1		Desenzano del Garda	6 May
	13.76/-0.1	1.72 12.49 25.75/0.8		6.05/0.3		55.72	2:16.75	
6082	Blandine	Maisonnier	FRA	3.1.86	2		Desenzano del Garda	6 May
	14.03/-0.1	1.84 12.59 25.16/-0.2		6.37/0.6		40.32	2:16.67	
6077	Sara	Aerts	BEL	25.1.84	20		Götzis	27 May
	13.06/0.0	1.64 13.61 23.47/1.9		6.08/1.4		36.49	2:14.12	
	(40)							
6073	Ida	Marcussen	NOR	1.11.87	9	EC	Helsinki	30 Jun
	14.08/-1.1	1.71 13.29 25.14/-0.5		6.18/1.3		46.03	2:12.36	
6072	Carolin	Schäfer	GER	5.12.91	1		Ulm	25 May
	13.77/0.3	1.75 13.50 24.31/0.0		5.83/1.6		49.50	2:22.88	
6049	Uhunoma	Osazuwa	NGR	23.11.87	1	PAmCp	Ottawa	27 May
	13.28/1.4	1.81 13.12 23.85/-1.3		6.16/0.9		33.87	2:22.07	
6042	Marina	Goncharova	RUS	26.4.86	6	NC	Cheboksary	3 Jun
	14.11/0.0	1.82 13.57 25.56/0.0		6.14/1.0		43.30	2:18.01	
6030	Györgyi	Farkas	HUN	13.2.85	22		Götzis	27 May
	14.27/0.8	1.82 13.30 25.70/0.4		5.99/0.6		45.61	2:14.93	
6015	Vanessa	Spínola	BRA	5.3.90	1	NC-23	Maringá	9 Sep
	14.25w/2.2	1.72 13.61 23.91/0.2		6.08w/2.8		44.11	2:20.54	
6013	Grit	Sadeiko	EST	29.7.89	23	OG	London (OS)	4 Aug
	13.50/0.9	1.74 12.43 24.25/0.6		6.11/-0.6		44.12	2:23.01	
5995	Irina	Karpova	KAZ	13.2.80	1		Almaty	6 May
	13.99/0.3	1.75 13.90 24.99/0.7		5.95/0.7		43.19	2:17.30	
5994	Yorgelis	Rodríguez	CUB-Y	25.1.95	1		La Habana	5 May
	14.09/0.1	1.78 13.44 24.44/1.8		6.16/0.7		38.97	2:19.40	
5986	Barbara	Nwaba	USA	18.1.89	2		Santa Barbara	3 Apr
	13.98/0.0	1.84 13.49 24.37/0.3		5.46/0.5		43.17	2:17.70	
	(50)							
5973	Judith	Nagy	ROU	14.9.89	1	NC	Bucuresti	8 Jul
	13.74/0.8	1.71 12.14 24.54		5.97/0.0		46.20	2:16.99	
5968	Izabela	Mikolajczyk	POL	4.9.90	1	NC	Bialogard	27 May
	14.07/1.4	1.87 11.00 24.63/0.3		6.14/0.2		42.02	2:20.44	
5966	Yilian	Durruthy	CUB	30.1.90	2		La Habana	5 May
	13.52/0.1	1.78 12.92 24.08/1.8		6.59/-1.3		33.76	2:30.46	
5964	Remona	Fransen	NED	25.11.85	12	EC	Helsinki	30 Jun
	13.88/-1.1	1.80 13.16 24.59/0.0		6.03/0.9		34.78	2:14.37	
5959	Stefanie	Saumweber	GER	5.3.88	2		Ulm	25 May
	13.31/0.3	1.78 12.68 25.14/0.0		5.83/-0.9		42.90	2:19.72	

Mark	Name		Nat	Born	Pos	Meet	Venue	Date
5959	Ivona	Dadic	AUT-J	29.12.93	23		Götzis	27 May
	14.63/0.8	1.76 12.45 24.11/0.7		6.14/0.7		38.12	2:10.67	
5957	Xénia	Krizsán	HUN-J	13.1.93	2	WJ	Barcelona	13 Jul
	14.25/-1.1	1.78 12.76 25.83/-1.5		5.94/0.3		48.40	2:16.08	
5940	Yekaterina	Netsvetayeva	BLR	26.6.89	1	NC	Grodno	7 Jul
	13.74/0.0	1.62 14.20 24.58/-1.7		5.64/1.3		44.90	2:12.42	
5935	Yasmina	Omrani	ALG	1.1.88	1	FRA Ch	Angers	16 Jun
	13.61/0.7	1.78 12.72 24.84/-0.5		5.80/1.4		41.34	2:17.68	
5916w	Martina	Salander	SWE	11.2.92	1	v2N	Viljandi	3 Jun
	13.79w/2.7	1.68 12.72 23.99w/5.3		6.03/-0.3		39.21	2:16.22	
	(60)							
5916	Nafissatou	Thiam	BEL-J	19.8.94	1	NC-j	Verviers	26 Aug
	14.56	1.88 13.83 26.04		5.99/1.3		45.68	2:26.65	
5900	Tamara	de Souza	BRA-J	8.9.93	3	WJ	Barcelona	13 Jul
	14.13/-1.0	1.75 13.89 24.06/-0.9		6.06w/4.4		42.51	2:31.23	
5891	Yasmiany	Pedroso	CUB	5.8.84	3		La Habana	5 May
	14.09/0.1	1.75 15.61 25.91/1.8		5.94/1.6		45.39	2:29.41	
5885	Mariya	Shumilova	RUS	10.1.90	2	NCp	Adler	8 May
	13.56/1.2	1.71 13.27 24.24/0.2		5.92/0.4		37.21	2:19.15	
5880	Barbora	Spotáková	CZE	30.6.81	6	Décastar	Talence	16 Sep
	14.66/1.5	1.76 13.42 25.50/-1.0		5.44/1.4		60.90	2:28.31	
5878	Kira	Biesenbach	GER	7.10.92	1	vUSA	Marburg	22 Jul
	13.96/1.7	1.71 13.21 24.18w/2.5		5.98/0.6		37.84	2:17.77	
5872	Sofia	Linde	SWE-Y	12.1.95	4	WJ	Barcelona	13 Jul
	13.86/-1.0	1.72 13.29 25.31/-2.3		6.12/-0.2		39.40	2:18.36	
5861	Aisha	Adams	USA	24.9.87	1		San Angelo	4 Apr
	13.99/-0.4	1.70 11.62 24.33/0.0		6.21/1.1		37.72	2:14.32	
5860	Laura	Ginés	ESP	11.6.86	1		Barcelona (SE)	3 Jul
	13.97/0.9	1.77 13.18 24.54/1.0		5.70/1.5		43.76	2:24.05	
5856	Louise	Hazel	GBR	6.10.85	27	OG	London (OS)	4 Aug
	13.48/2.0	1.59 12.81 24.48/0.9		5.77/0.1		47.38	2:18.78	
	(70)							
5855	Abbie	Stechschulte/Norton	USA	28.4.85	6	NC/OT	Eugene	30 Jun
	13.76/0.7	1.72 13.45 24.88/3.0		6.02/1.3		35.66	2:16.78	
5851	Annett	Fleming	GER	4.5.84	1	MSR	Azusa	19 Apr
	14.35/0.9	1.76 13.42 26.13/1.4		5.72/1.1		45.92	2:14.00	
5850	Linda	Züblin	SUI	21.3.86	5		Ratingen	15 Jun
	13.66/0.1	1.66 12.74 25.39/-0.2		5.84/1.0		49.06	2:20.81	
5840w	Niina	Kelo	FIN	26.3.80	2	v2N	Viljandi	3 Jun
	14.06w/2.7	1.65 14.80 25.80w/5.3		5.58/-1.0		52.60	2:23.43	
5839	Chelsea	Carrier-Eades	USA	21.8.89	3	NCAA	Des Moines	8 Jun
	13.15/-0.4	1.69 11.46 23.73/1.1		6.05/-0.4		32.93	2:16.92	
5838	Brittany	Harrell	USA	5.12.91	1	SEC	Baton Rouge	11 May
	13.83w/2.4	1.73 11.49 24.98/-0.7		5.88/0.0		42.40	2:14.37	
5837	Veronica	Torr	NZL	17.5.87	2		Melbourne	26 Feb
	13.78w/2.2	1.77 13.08 24.89/0.1		6.16w/2.7		36.30	2:24.7	
5832	Megan	Wheatley	AUS	10.3.88	1	NC	Melbourne	15 Apr
	13.80/1.4	1.66 13.27 25.00/1.8		6.02/0.6		39.12	2:15.87	
5830	Anastasiya	Mokhnyuk	UKR	1.1.91	3	NCp	Yalta	28 May
	13.91/-1.6	1.79 12.42 25.78/-0.7		6.39/1.9		35.56	2:20.75	
5826	Jessica	Flax	USA	4.9.90	4	NCAA	Des Moines	8 Jun
	13.72/-0.3	1.69 13.10 25.09/1.0		5.68/-1.5		43.12	2:16.43	
	(80)							
5817(w)	Ryann	Krais	USA	21.3.90	7	NC/OT	Eugene	30 Jun
	13.84/1.6	1.75 12.00 24.91w/3.0		5.61/1.5		40.50	2:12.03	
5807	Lindsay	Lettow	USA	6.6.90	8	NC/OT	Eugene	30 Jun
	13.96/1.3	1.75 12.13 24.51/3.0		5.85/1.3		36.83	2:14.91	
5801	Ellinore	Hallin	SWE	12.8.87	5		Kladno	10 Jun
	13.95/-2.6	1.74 14.02 25.38/-3.4		5.81/0.0		37.95	2:18.39	
5794	Valérie	Reggel	SUI	3.1.87	1	NC	Hochdorf	23 Sep
	14.07/0.0	1.66 13.50 24.59/0.4		5.91/-0.3		41.36	2:20.30	
5793A	Jennifer	Cotten	CAN	14.10.87	3	NC	Calgary	28 Jun
	13.69/-0.6	1.65 11.53 24.72w/2.1		6.34w/3.5		32.00	2:10.22	
5783	Nadja	Casadei	SWE	3.4.83	1		Sandnes	17 Jun
	14.14/-1.3	1.64 13.18 25.06/-1.6		6.13/1.5		37.60	2:13.75	
5780	Lucie	Slaníčková	SVK	8.11.88	1		Hexham	1 Jul
	14.25/1.5	1.75 11.05 25.14/0.7		6.10		41.35	2:16.18	
5779	Heather	Miller	USA	30.3.87	9	NC/OT	Eugene	30 Jun
	14.18/0.5	1.69 11.68 24.22/2.8		5.99/1.8		39.29	2:15.59	
5766	Gabriela	Kouassi	CIV	18.11.79	3	AfrC	Bambous	14 Apr
	13.96/1.8	1.68 13.45 25.77/-0.5		5.83/1.7		47.57	2:24.25	

Mark	Name		Nat	Born	Pos	Meet	Venue	Date
5764	Anouk	Vetter	NED-J	4.2.93	1	NC-j	Emmeloord	18 May
	14.34/0.5	1.72 12.29 24.92/-0.3		5.62/1.5		51.95	2:25.75	
	(90)							
5761	Keia	Pinnick	USA	23.1.91	5	NCAA	Des Moines	8 Jun
	13.48/-0.4	1.63 11.37 24.00/1.1		5.91/-0.5		33.33	2:09.29	
5757	Yelena	Molodchinina	RUS	16.4.91	2		Adler	9 Sep
	14.28/0.4	1.70 11.40 25.28/0.1		5.95/-0.5		44.20	2:14.53	
5755	Grace	Clements	GBR	2.5.84	1		Barcelona	6 May
	14.61/-0.1	1.74 12.74 25.99/0.2		5.94/1.8		43.80	2:16.00	
5753	Allison	Reaser	USA	9.9.92	6	NCAA	Des Moines	8 Jun
	13.77/-0.8	1.63 11.71 24.20/1.1		5.96/-0.5		40.25	2:17.45	
5752	Helga Margrét	Thorsteinsdóttir	ISL	15.11.91	1		Aubagne	8 Jul
	14.77/0.3	1.65 14.31 25.64/-0.2		5.58/-0.4		49.82	2:17.24	
5734	Precious	Nwokey	USA	27.4.89	7	NCAA	Des Moines	8 Jun
	13.50/-0.4	1.75 11.03 23.96/1.1		6.15/-2.1		25.36	2:14.42	
5733	Dorcas	Akinniyi	USA	23.1.90	8	NCAA	Des Moines	8 Jun
	13.80/-0.2	1.75 13.82 25.02/1.4		5.88/-0.4		36.33	2:26.85	
5713	Liane	Weber	GER	24.2.86	7		Desenzano del Garda	6 May
	13.90/0.6	1.69 12.56 25.78/-0.2		5.57/0.3		45.05	2:15.97	
5709	Peaches	Roach	JAM	21.12.84	1	DrakeR	Des Moines	26 Apr
	13.89/1.8	1.84 11.58 24.27/-1.5		5.52w/4.2		32.92	2:17.34	
5702h	Yusleidys	Mendieta	CUB-J	17.2.94	1		La Habana	2 Jun
	15.3/0.5	1.77 14.12 24.3/0.9		6.17/0.4		45.93	2:39.8	
	(100)							

Mark	First	Last	Nat	Born	Date
5696	Yana	Cherepanova	RUS	1.2.84	8 May
5696	Anna	Maiwald	GER	21.7.90	22 Jul
5695	Kiani	Profit	USA	18.2.90	20 Apr
5693	Ulyana	Aleksandrova	RUS	1.1.91	3 Jun
5686	Olimpia	Nowak	POL	21.4.88	26 Apr
5680	Miia	Kurppa	FIN	30.1.88	20 May
5679	Kristina	Poltavets	RUS	6.11.90	8 May
5677	Alina	Biesenbach	GER	27.4.92	22 Jul
5668		Wang Qingling	CHN-J	14.1.93	22 Apr
5666(w)	Crystal	Ruiz	MEX	1.1.88	15 Mar
5664	Kasey	Hill	USA	10.10.85	17 May
5659	Yvonne	van Langen	NED	6.6.82	10 Jun
5658	Mari	Klaup	EST	27.2.90	29 Jul
5653	Portia	Bing	NZL-J	17.4.93	13 Jul
5651	Sushmita	Singha Roy	IND	26.3.84	26 Jun
5635	Mariya	Yefremova	RUS	4.10.87	9 Sep
5622	Thaimara	Rivas	VEN	23.7.82	10 Jun
5621	Makeba	Alcide	LCA	24.2.90	26 Apr
5614	Pinar	Aday	TUR-J	7.10.93	10 Jun
5614	Lindsay	Schwartz	USA	23.4.90	30 Jun
5610	Lucia	Mokrásová	SVK-J	27.3.94	13 Jul
5606	Deanna	Latham	USA	23.2.92	8 Jun
5606	Niemi	Zbären	SUI-J	12.3.94	25 Aug
5600	Katerina	Cachová	CZE	26.2.90	27 May
5593	Sami	Spenner	USA	21.3.91	26 Apr
5586	Liz	Roehrig	USA	19.11.85	17 May
5578	Kendell	Williams	USA-Y	14.6.95	13 Jul
5578		Wang Yunhan	CHN-J	20.2.93	23 Sep
5574	Elisa	Trevisan	ITA	5.3.80	8 Jul
5573	Anna	Blank	RUS	12.1.90	9 Sep
5563	Fabia	McDonald	USA	18.4.92	11 May
5560	Kaylon	Eppinger	USA	17.9.89	11 May
5551	Svetlana	Nedospasova	RUS	31.1.89	3 Jun
5549	Beatrice	Puiu	ROU	22.3.86	8 Jul
5547	Erica	Bougard	USA-J	26.7.93	17 Jun
5535	Yunna	Dmitriyeva	RUS	7.7.88	9 Sep
5533	Frida	Thorsås	NOR-J	31.1.94	27 May
5531	Francia	Manzanillo	DOM	3.6.80	27 May
5524w	Grete	Sadeiko	EST-J	29.5.93	3 Jun
5517	Lindsay	Vollmer	USA	10.9.92	12 May
5507	Tine Bach	Ejlersen	DEN	25.7.85	12 Aug
5506		Sun Lu	CHN	19.2.88	23 Sep
5505	Agnieszka	Borowska	POL	21.10.91	27 May
5504	Krystsina	Alekseyenko	BLR	2.8.91	31 May
5503	Myrte	Goor	NED	3.4.89	10 Jun
5500	Rokhaya	Mbaye	FRA	12.3.92	8 Jul
5490	Karolina	Kedzia	POL	8.7.90	1 Jul
5487	Emily	Pearson	USA	8.8.85	27 May
5486	Lucija	Cvitanovic	CRO	17.9.91	20 May
5479	Camila	Pirelli	PAR	10.1.89	10 Jun
5477	Charlene	Charles	FRA	1.10.90	8 Jun
5477A	Rachael	McIntosh	CAN	17.1.91	28 Jun
5475	Susan	Coltman	CAN	10.4.81	19 Apr
5475	Nadine	Visser	NED-Y	9.2.95	18 May
5472	Tanya	Friesen	USA	23.6.91	12 May
5472	Lauren	Foote	AUS	27.4.84	26 Feb
5451	Suzuka	Akai	JPN	25.9.90	3 Jun
5443	Louise	Wood	GBR	13.5.83	6 May
5443	Lucie	Ondraschková	CZE	12.10.89	11 May
5437	Alicja	Sakowicz	POL	1.2.88	27 May
5432	Bianca	Erwee	RSA	4.3.90	14 Apr
5432	Maureen	Rots	NED-J	25.2.93	18 May
5430	Chie	Kiriyama	JPN	2.8.91	3 Jun
5427	Gemma	Weetman	GBR	4.10.87	27 May
5425	Sveinbjörg	Zophaniasdóttir	ISL	27.4.92	8 Jul
5422	Jasmine	Cotten	USA	13.7.88	5 May
5418	Estefanía	Fortes	ESP	25.4.87	6 May
5409	Sara	Gambetta	GER-J	18.2.93	13 May
5409	Darya	Khramtsova	RUS	7.1.90	3 Jun
5404	Mélanie	Cellier (170)	FRA	2.1.88	16 Jun

Best at low altitude: 5707 Jen Cotton   3   Tucson   30 Mar
13.69/0.0   1.69   11.14 24.59w/2.2   6.18/0.0   29.79   2:12.01

Best without wind assistance
5694 Krais   30 Mar | 5692 Kelo   30 Jun | 5517 Grete Sadeiko 13 Jul | 5469 Ruiz   4 Apr

JUNIORS

See main list for top 8 juniors. 11 performances by 6 women to 5900. Additional marks and further juniors:

	Mark	Pos	Meet	Venue	Date	Mark	Pos	Venue	Date
J-Thompson	6248	2		Kladno	10 Jun	6007	3	Desenzano del G	6 May
Rodríguez	5966	1	WJ	Barcelona	13 Jul				
Dadic	5935	23		Götzis	27 May				
Thiam	5906	2	AfrC	Bambous	14 Apr				

Mark	Name		Nat	Born	Pos	Meet	Venue	Date
5668		Wang Qingling	CHN	14.1.93	1	NC-j	Changzhou	22 Apr
	14.05	1.72 12.00 24.99/-0.3		6.19/2.0		37.44	2:26.04	
5653	Portia	Bing (10)	NZL	17.4.93	5	WJ	Barcelona	13 Jul
	14.14/-1.1	1.75 11.24 24.65/-0.9		5.91/1.6		36.88	2:20.42	
5614	Pinar	Aday	TUR	7.10.93	1		Eskisehir	10 Jun
	13.74w/2.3	1.80 11.03 25.95/-1.0		6.20/0.1		33.99	2:24.90	

Mark	Name		Nat	Born	Pos	Meet	Venue	Date
5610	Lucia	Mokrásová	SVK	27.3.94	6	WJ	Barcelona	13 Jul
	13.99/-1.1	1.75 10.86 24.33/-0.9		6.03w/3.0	31.36		2:20.44	
5606	Niemi	Zbären	SUI	12.3.94	3		Hannover	25 Aug
	13.33/0.0	1.78 11.33 24.91/0.0		5.89/0.2	33.79		2:29.35	
5578	Kendell	Williams	USA-Y	14.6.95	8	WJ	Barcelona	13 Jul
	13.74/-1.0	1.81 10.70 24.94/-1.5		6.11/2.9	30.48		2:26.60	
5578		Wang Yunhan	CHN	20.2.93	1	NC	Kunshan	23 Sep
	14.29	1.75 11.11 25.346.22/0.8		35.62			2:24.37	
5547	Erica	Bougard	USA	26.7.93	1	NC-j	Bloomington IN	17 Jun
	13.79/-1.6	1.75 9.46 24.61/-0.6		6.03/-0.3	28.37		2:14.39	
5533	Frida	Thorsås	NOR	31.1.94	1	NC-j	Bergen	27 May
	15.02/-0.9	1.68 12.09 26.03/0.3		5.73/1.3	41.85		2:12.31	
5524w	Grete	Sadeiko	EST	29.5.93	6	v2N	Viljandi	3 Jun
	14.48w/2.7	1.74 11.33 25.21w/5.3		5.61/0.2	46.42		2:29.36	
5475	Nadine	Visser	NED-Y	9.2.95	2	NC-j	Emmeloord	18 May
	13.76/0.5	1.66 12.22 24.99/-0.3		5.72/0.9	35.02		2:25.11	
5432	Maureen	Rots (20)	NED	25.2.93	3	NC-j	Emmeloord	18 May
	14.33/0.5	1.69 11.45 25.49/-0.3		5.80/0.7	35.88		2:20.68	

4 X 100 METRES RELAY

Mark	Nat	Name	Pos	Meet	Venue	Date
40.82	USA	Madison, Felix, Knight, Jeter	1	OG	London (OS)	10 Aug
41.41	JAM	Fraser-Pryce, Simpson, Campbell-Brown, Stewart	2	OG	London (OS)	10 Aug
41.64	USA	Madison, Tarmoh, Knight, L Williams	1h1	OG	London (OS)	9 Aug
42.04	UKR	Povh, Stuy, Ryemyen, Bryzgina	3	OG	London (OS)	10 Aug
42.19	USA Red	Madison, Felix, Knight, Jeter	1	PennR	Philadelphia	28 Apr
42.24	USA 'B'	L Williams, Anderson, Gardner, K Duncan	1	Herc	Monaco	20 Jul
42.36	UKR	Povh, Stuy, Ryemyen, Bryzgina	1h2	OG	London (OS)	19 Aug
42.37	JAM	Henry-Robinson, Simpson, Calvert, Stewart	2h2	OG	London (OS)	9 Aug
42.45	NED	Vassell, Schippers, Lubbers, Samuel	3h1	OG	London (OS)	9 Aug
42.51	GER	Gunther, Cibis, Pinto, Sailer	1	EC	Helsinki	1 Jul
42.55	BRA	Silva, Krasucki, E dos Santos, R Santos	4h1	OG	London (OS)	9 Aug
42.56	UKR	Povh, Stuy, Ryemyen, Bryzgina	2	Athl	Lausanne	23 Aug
42.60	UKR	Pogrebnyak, Ryemyen, Povh, Pyatachenko	1	NCp	Yalta	29 May
42.64	NGR	Osayomi, Asumnu, Abinuwa, Okagbare	4	OG	London (OS)	10 Aug
42.65	USA	Bobby Kersee All-Stars Crawford, Tarmoh, Harper, Felix	1		Los Angeles (Ww)	14 Apr
42.67	GER	Gunther, Cibis, Pinto, Sailer	5	OG	London (OS)	10 Aug
42.69	GER	Gunther, Cibis, Pinto, Sailer	3h2	OG	London (OS)	9 Aug
42.70	UKR	Povh, Pogrebnyak, Ryemyen, Pyatachenko	1h1	EC	Helsinki	30 Jun
42.70	NED	Vassell, Schippers, Lubbers, Samuel	6	OG	London (OS)	10 Aug
42.74	NGR	Udoh, Asumnu, Osayomi, Okagbare	5h1	OG	London (OS)	9 Aug
42.80	NED	Vassell, Schippers, Lubbers, Samuel	2	EC	Helsinki	1 Jul
42.82	USA	Texas A & M Un L Stewart, Ekponé, D Duncan, Collier	2	NCAA	Des Moines	9 Jun
42.87	USA	Kersey All-Stars Crawford, Tarmoh, Harper, Felix	1	MSR	Walnut	21 Apr
42.90	NED	Babel, Vassell, Lubbers, Samuel	1		Genève	2 Jun
42.90	USA	Texas A & M Un L Stewart, Ekponé, D Duncan, Collier	1h2	NCAA	Des Moines	6 Jun
		(25 performances by teams from 7 nations)				
43.06	POL	Popowicz, Korczynska, Jeschke, Ptak	3	EC	Helsinki	1 Jul
43.07	BAH	S.Ferguson, Sturrup, Amertil, Strachan	6h1	OG	London (OS)	9 Aug
43.12	FRA	Louami, Ikuesan, Galais, Arron	2h1	EC	Helsinki	30 Jun
		(10)				
43.21	COL	Hinestroza, González, Obregón, Palacios	5h2	OG	London (OS)	9 Aug
43.24	RUS	Polyakova, Rusakova-Kresova, Savlinis, Fedoriva	6h2	OG	London (OS)	9 Aug
43.51	SUI	Cueni, Gasser, E Sprunger, L Sprunger	4h1	EC	Helsinki	30 Jun
43.54	BLR	Astoshko, Hanchar, Nevmerzhitskaya, Balykina	1	EAF	Bydgoszcz	3 Jun
43.79	JPN	Doi, Takahashi, Fukushima, Ichikawa	1		Fukuroi	3 May
43.81	BEL	Borlée, Mariën, Claes, Zagré	4h2	EC	Helsinki	30 Jun
43.90	ITA	Hooper, Alloh, Amidei, Draisci	5h2	EC	Helsinki	30 Jun
43.96	CHN	Huang Qiuju, Liang Qiuping, Wei Yongli, Tao Yujia	1		Kanchanaburi	11 May
44.01	AUS	Butler, Breen, van Veenendaal, Pearson	1		Brisbane	14 Jan
44.04	DOM	Sánchez, Chalas, Mejía, Manzueta	2	IbAm	Barquisimeto	10 Jun
		(20)				
44.07	TRI	Selvon, Ahye, Thomas, Hackett	4	PennR	Philadelphia	28 Apr
44.28	SLO	Sitar, Strajnar, Zumer, Ottey	6h1	E	Helsinki	30 Jun
44.35	THA	Seangdee, Jaksunin, Wannakit, Klomdee	2		Kanchanaburi	11 May
44.35	GHA	Amenebede, Owusu-Agyapong, Gyaman, Amponsah	2	AfCh	Porto Novo	29 Jun
44.37	GBR	Bloor, B Williams, H Jones, Onuora	5	Athl	Lausanne	23 Aug

44.62	LTU	2 Jun	44.65	PUR	22 Apr	44.78A	RSA	5 May	44.90	SKN	10 Jun
44.64	CAN	19 May	44.71	HUN	28 May	44.81	VEN	10 Jun	44.92	SWE	1 Sep
44.64	FIN	1 Sep	44.72	GRN	24 Jun	44.87	IVB	28 Apr	44.96	BUL	3 Jun

44.99	ESP	12 May
45.04	POR	3 Jun
45.0hA	ECU	29 Sep

Mark	Name	Nat	Born	Pos	Meet	Venue	Date

Mixed nationality teams

| 42.51 | JAM/USA Henry-Robinson, Stewart, Bailey all JAM, Barber USA | | | 1 | Athl | Lausanne | 23 Aug |
| 42.81 | USA Auburn Elite Atkins USA, Stewart JAM, Ferguson BAH, Strachan BAH | | | 1 | | Auburn | 21 Apr |

Drugs disqualification for one athlete

42.31	TRI Ahye, Baptiste, Selvon, Hackett #			2h1	OG	London (OS)	9 Aug
42.68	LSU USA Pinckney, Hackett TRI #, R Alexander, K Duncan			1h1	NCAA	Des Moines	6 Jun
42.75	LSU USA Pinckney, Hackett TRI #, R Alexander, K Duncan			1	NCAA	Des Moines	9 Jun

JUNIORS

43.89	USA Snow, Bryant, Madu, Sanders			1	WJ	Barcelona	14 Jul
43.95	USA Snow, Davis-White, Madu, Sanders			1h1	WJ	Barcelona	13 Jul
44.24	GER Burghardt, Mayer, Grompe, Maduka			2	WJ	Barcelona	14 Jul
44.29	BRA de Souza, Luz, da Rosa, dos Reis			3	WJ	Barcelona	14 Jul
44.47	GBR Tagoe, Thomas, Johncock, Papps			1h2	WJ	Barcelona	13 Jul
44.51	JAM M Spencer, C Williams, Whitehorne, Lewin			1	CAC-J	San Salvador	30 Jun
44.58	NGR Omaka, Isoken, Thomas, Kalu			2h3	WJ	Barcelona	13 Jul
44.68	NED Lobo, van Schagen, Sedney, Duijn			2h1	WJ	Barcelona	13 Jul
44.88	BEL Depuydt, Laus, Vervaet, Grillet			3h2	WJ	Barcelona	13 Jul
44.95	POL Kalinowska, Sokólska, Stepien, Ciba			4	WJ	Barcelona	14 Jul
45.02	BAH Charlton, C Cox, R Brown, Strachan			1	Carifta	Devonshire	8 Apr
45.15	ITA Paiero, Siragusa, Bongiorni, Ekeh Udochi			4h3	WJ	Barcelona	13 Jul
45.32	SUI Frey, Atcho, Keller, Mayer			7		Genève	2 Jun
45.52	AUS C Williams, Gayen, Pires-Parenzee, Whittaker			2		Brisbane	14 Jan

4 X 200 METRES RELAY

| 1:30.01 | LSU Univ USA Tate, Hackett TRI, R.Alexander, K.Duncan | | | 1 | TexR | Austin | 31 Mar |
| 1:30.98 | Un of Texas USA Nelson, Udoh, Goodman, Peter ISV | | | 2 | TexR | Austin | 31 Mar |

4 X 400 METRES RELAY

3:16.87	USA Trotter 50.3, Felix 48.1, McCorory 49.39, Richards-Ross 49.10			1	OG	London (OS)	11 Aug
3:20.23	RUS Gushchina 50.9, Krivoshapka 49.8, Firova 49.88, Antyukh 49.67			2	OG	London (OS)	11 Aug
3:20.95	JAM Day 51.1, Whyte 50.1, S Williams 50.29, N Williams-Mills 49.46			1h1	OG	London (OS)	10 Aug
3:21.18	USA Red McCorory 51.3, Felix 50.1, Hastings 50.3, Richards-Ross 49.5			1	PennR	Philadelphia	28 Apr
3:22.09	USA Baker 51.7, McCorory 50.4, Dixon 50.26, Trotter 49.78			1h2	OG	London (OS)	10 Aug
3:23.11	RUS Gushchina 50.9, Firova 50.7, Nazarova 50.69, Kapachinskaya 50.87			2h2	OG	London (OS)	10 Aug
3:23.57	UKR Logvynenko 51.0, Zemlyak 50.4, Yaroshchuk 51.56, Pygyda 50.63			4	OG	London (OS)	11 Aug
3:24.76	GBR Cox 52.8, McConnell 51.1, Shakes-Drayton 50.28, Ohuruogu 50.65			5	OG	London (OS)	11 Aug
3:25.05	GBR Cox 51.7, McConnell 51.2, Child 51.54, Ohuruogu 50.61			3h2	OG	London (OS)	10 Aug
3:25.07	UKR Olishevska 52.6, Zemlyak 50.4, Pygyda 50.52, Logvynenko 51.49			1	EC	Helsinki	1 Jul
3:25.13	JAM Day 50.6, Lloyd 52.7, S Williams 51.07, Whyte 50.78			1h3	OG	London (OS)	10 Aug
3:25.49	FRA Anacharsis 51.7, Guion Firmin 51.4, Gayot 51.35, Guei 50.91			2	EC	Helsinki	1 Jul
3:25.90	UKR Zemlyak 51.3, Logvynenko 52.0, Yaroshchuk 51.61, Pygyda 50.99			2h1	OG	London (OS)	10 Aug
3:25.92	FRA Anacharsis 52.1, Hurtis 51.8, Gayot 51.15, Guei 50.93			6	OG	London (OS)	11 Aug
3:25.94	FRA Anacharsis 51.5, Hurtis 52.4, Gayot 51.46, Guei 50.67			3h1	OG	London (OS)	10 Aug
3:26.02	CZE Hejnová 52.2, Bergrová 52.0, Bartoníčková 51.12, Rosolová 50.59			3	EC	Helsinki	1 Jul
3:26.20	GBR Cox 52.4, Sanders 51.5, McConnell 51.42, Child 50.86			4	EC	Helsinki	1 Jul
3:26.20	CZE Rosolová 51.4, Bergrová 52.2, Bartoníčková 51.66, Hejnová 51.03			4h2	OG	London (OS)	10 Aug
3:26.29	NGR Omotosho 52.2, Otu 51.8, Abogunloko 51.70, George 50.61			4h1	OG	London (OS)	10 Aug
3:26.36	UKR Yefremova, Logvinenko, Pygyda, Olshevska			1	NCp	Yalta	29 May
3:26.52	BLR Kievich 51.0, Khlyustova 53.1, I Usovich 51.90, S Usovich 50.59			5h1	OG	London (OS)	10 Aug
3:26.55	JAM S Williams, N Williams-Mills, Smellie 52.1, Spencer 52.5			2	PennR	Philadelphia	28 Apr
	(22/9)						
3:27.41	CUB A Martínez 51.7, Peña 52.7, Borlot 52.03, Bonne 51.01			6h1	OG	London (OS)	11 Aug
3:27.81	GER Cremer 52.0, Lindenberg 51.1, Klopsch 52.21, Kohlmann 52.44			5	EC	Helsinki	1 Jul
3:28.56	BRA Sousa, J de Lima, Coutinho, Teodoro			1	IbAm	Barquisimeto	10 Jun
3:29.01	ITA Bazzoni 52.5, Spacca 52.3, Bonfanti 52.17, Grenot 52.13			7h1	OG	London (OS)	10 Aug
3:29.33	POL Wyciszkiewicz, Jesien, Bednarek, Baumgart			1	EAF	Bydgoszcz	3 Jun
3:29.80	ROU Belgyan 53.1, Lavric 51.3, Razor 53.47, Morosanu 51.79			7	EC	Helsinki	1 Jul
3:30.55	IRL Heffernan 53.5, Cuddihy 50.8, Barr 53.37, Carey 52.93			6h2	OG	London (OS)	10 Aug
3:31.27	BOT Seleka, Mashila, Babolayi, Montsho			2	AfCh	Porto Novo	1 Jul
3:31.64	SEN Faye, Thiam, Diabaye, Fall			3	AfCh	Port oNovo	1 Jul
3:31.88	CAN Brennan, Martin, Nelson, Muir			6	PennR	Philadelphia	28 Apr
3:33.03A	TRI Fermin, Brooks, James, McKnight			2	NACAC	Irapuato	8 Jul
	(20)						
3:33.21	RSA Rammonye, Wittstock, Thipe, Theron			4	AfCh	Porto Novo	1 Jul
3:33.24	LBR Kutu-Akoi, McIntosh, Cooper, Luogon			5	AfCh	Porto Novo	1 Jul
3:33.28	Guangdong CHN Zhou Yanling, Tang Xiaoyin, Chen Yanmei, Chen Jingwen			1	NC	Kunshan	25 Sep
3:33.60A	Police KEN C Koech, P Chelimo, Shikanda. Zakari			1	NC	Nairobi	15 Jun

+ intermediate time in longer race, A made at an altitude of 1000m or higher, D made in a decathlon, h made in a heat, qf quarter-final, sf semi-final, i indoors, Q qualifying round, r race number, -J juniors, =Y youths (b. 1995 or later)

Mark	Name	Nat	Born	Pos	Meet	Venue	Date

3:33.64 JPN 13 May | 3:34.70 TUR 1 Jul | 3:36.40 FIN 2 Sep | 3:37.74 NOR 1 Jul | 3:38.99 VEN 10 Jun
3:34.12 AUS 14 Jan | 3:36.29 BEL 3 Jun | 3:36.78 COL-J 20 May | 3:38.00 ESP 1 Jul | Best at low altitude
3:34.36 LBR 14 Jun | 3:36.29 SWE 2 Sep | 3:36.82 IND 11 May | 3:38.48 DOM 10 Jun | 3:35.06 KEN 1 Jul

Mixed nationality teams

Mark	Name		Pos	Meet	Venue	Date
3:24.14	One Goal Athletics USA Robinson, Williams-Mills JAM, J Martin, Hastings		1	FlaR	Gainesville	7 Apr
3:24.54	Un of Oregon USA		1	NCAA	Des Moines	9 Jun
	Gardner 51.1, Okodogbe NGR 51.4, Roesler 51.80, Francis 50.15					
3:24.59	Louisiana State Un USA		2	NCAA	Des Moines	9 Jun
	McDermott JAM 52.5, Alexander 49.5, Tate 50.90, J Day JAM 51.67					

<h2 style="text-align:center">JUNIORS</h2>

Mark	Nat	Name	Pos	Meet	Venue	Date
3:30.01	USA	Rucker, Ekponé, Baisden, Spencer	1	WJ	Barcelona	15 Jul
3:32.97	JAM	Farquharson, James, Jackson, Russell	2	WJ	Barcelona	15 Jul
3:35.56	CAN	Courtnall, Wiebe, Zrinyi, Watson	2h2	WJ	Barcelona	14 Jul
3:35.83	RUS	Glotova, Galitskaya, Koltachikhina, Renzhina	3h2	WJ	Barcelona	14 Jul
3:35.97	UKR	Ralko, Slyusarenko, Shevchenko, Tkachuk	4h2	WJ	Barcelona	14 Jul
3:36.78	COL	Largacha, Torres, Escobar, Aguilar	2		Rio de Janeiro	20 May
3:37.23	GER	Schachtschneider, Meyer, Bellerich, Mosler	5	WJ	Barcelona	15 Jul
3:37.90	POL	Karczmarczyk, Wyciszkiewicz, Curylo, Dąbrowska	7	WJ	Barcelona	15 Jul
3:38.17	NGR		1		Accra	19 Jun
3:38.84	AUS	de la Motte, Solin, Consedine, Mitchell	8	WJ	Barcelona	15 Jul
3:39.44	COL	Largacha, Aguilar, Escobar, Torres	6h2	WJ	Barcelona	14 Jul
3:40.00	RSA	Neuhoff, Seeliger, Wicksell, Palframan	2h1	WJ	Barcelona	14 Jul
3:40.28	JPN	Hamamatsu city: Sugiura, Matsumoto, Nagura, Tatebe	1		Niigata	2 Aug
3:40.44	BAH	R Brown, K Seymour, R Johnson, Miller	2	Carifta	Devonshire	9 Apr

4 X 100 METRES HURDLES

Mark	Name		Pos	Meet	Venue	Date
52.38	Star Athletics USA D Mitchell, Smith, James, Wells		1r1	FlaR	Gainesville	7 Apr
52.59	Boogiefast TC Q Harrison, Castlin, Golladay all USA, Schrott AUT		2r1	FlaR	Gainesville	7 Apr
52.87	Clemson Un USA Rollins, Owens, K Harrison, Gracia		1r2	FlaR	Gainesville	7 Apr

3000 METRES WALK

Mark	Name		Nat	Born	Pos	Meet	Venue	Date
12:31.86	Ana	Cabecinha	POR	29.4.84	1		Faro	23 May
12:31.89	Kate	Veale	IRL-J	5.1.94	1		Cork	19 May
12:31.89	Agnieszka	Dygacz	POL	18.7.85	1		Kraków	8 Sep
12:36.27	Olive	Loughnane	IRL	14.1.76	1		Cork	17 Jul

Indoors

Mark	Name		Nat	Born	Pos	Meet	Venue	Date
11:44.10	Anisya	Kirdyapkina	RUS	23.10.89	1	Winter	Moskva	5 Feb
12:18.70	Sabine	Krantz	GER	6.2.81	1	NC	Dortmund	29 Jan
12:27.50	Claudia	Stef	ROU	25.2.78	2	Winter	Moskva	5 Feb
12:28.00	Tatyana	Korotkova	RUS	24.4.80	3	Winter	Moskva	5 Feb
12:35.00	Olena	Shumkina	UKR	24.1.88	4	Winter	Moskva	5 Feb
12:35.12	Vera	Santos	POR	3.12.81	1		Pombal	28 Jan

12:38.84 Paulina Buziak POL 16.12.86 26 Feb | 12:44.29 Melanie Seeger GER 8.1.77 29 Jan

5000 METRES WALK

Mark	Name		Nat	Born	Pos	Meet	Venue	Date
20:34.76		Liu Hong	CHN	12.5.87	1		Tianjin	16 Sep
20:42.67		Qieyang Shenjie	CHN	11.11.90	2		Tianjin	16 Sep
20:43.95mx	Kumi	Otoshi	JPN	29.7.85	1		Chiba	21 Apr
20:45.11	Beatriz	Pascual	ESP	9.5.82	1		Granollers	18 Jul
20:51.89		Wang Shanshan	CHN	16.6.87	3		Tianjin	16 Sep
20:54.83	María José	Poves	ESP	16.3.78	1		Barcelona	16 Jun
21:01.73	Sabine	Krantz	GER	6.2.81	1	NC	Diez	24 Jun
21:05.84		Nie Jingjing	CHN	1.3.88	4		Tianjin	16 Sep
21:12.91		Mao Yanxue	CHN-J	15.2.94	5		Tianjin	16 Sep
21:15.57	María	Vasco	ESP	26.12.75	2		Granollers	18 Jul
21:17.76	Julia	Takács	ESP	29.6.89	2		Barcelona	16 Jun
21:21.25	Tanya	Holliday	AUS	21.9.88	1		Sydney	18 Feb
21:23.60	Bekki	Lee	AUS	25.11.86	2		Sydney	18 Feb
21:29.12	Claire	Tallent	AUS	7.6.81	3		Sydney	18 Feb

21:34.33 Lucie Pelantová CZE 7.5.86 2 Jun | 21:51.07 Zhang Xin CHN 17.8.89 16 Sep
21:40.65 Mayumi Kawasaki JPN 10.5.80 19 May | 21:53.88 KumikoOkada JPN 17.10.91 16 Dec
21:45.98 Jo Jackson GBR 17.1.85 24 Jun | 21:56.99 Anastasiya Yatsevich BLR 18.1.85 18 May
21:47.61 Gao Ni CHN 14.9.91 16 Sep | 21:56.99 Ainhoa Pinedo ESP 17.2.83 2 Jun
21:50.41 Eleonora Giorgi ITA 14.9.89 27 May

10 KILOMETRES WALK

See also 20km list for many intermediate times

Mark	Name		Nat	Born	Pos	Meet	Venue	Date
43:16.68 t	mx	Liu Hong	CHN	12.5.87	1		Saluzzo	18 Jul
43:18		Liu Hong			1		Ordos	14 Sep
43:18.97 t	Beatriz	Pascual	ESP	9.5.82	1	NC	Pamplona	25 Aug-
43:24	Tatyana	Korotkova	RUS	31.5.82	1		Voronovo	16 Sep

Mark	Name		Nat	Born	Pos	Meet	Venue	Date
43:29	Marina	Pandakova	RUS	1.3.89	2		Voronovo	16 Sep
43:31	Ana	Cabecinha	POR	29.4.84	2		Ordos	14 Sep-
43:35	Anna	Yermina	RUS-J	24.6.93	3		Voronovo	16 Sep
43:43+	Claire	Tallent	AUS	7.6.81	10	in 20k	London	11 Aug
43:58	Tanya	Holliday	AUS	21.9.88	1		Adelaide	28 Jul
43:59	Irina	Shushina	RUS	30.10.86	2	NGP	Buy	2 Sep
44:11.26 t		Nie Jingjing	CHN	1.3.88	1		Tianjin	18 Sep
44:12.15 t		Wang Shanshan	CHN	16.6.87	2		Tianjin	18 Sep
44:17	Brigita	Virbalyté	LTU	1.2.85	1	NC	Druskininkai	9 Sep
44:22+	Olena	Shumkina	UKR	24.1.88	18	in 20k	London	11 Aug
44:22.59 t	María José	Poves	ESP	16.3.78	2	NC	Pamplona	25 Aug
44:29+	Anna	Lukyanova	RUS	23.4.91	7	in 20k	Moskva	10 Jun
44:30.49 t	Yekaterina	Medvedyeva	RUS-J	29.3.94	1	NC-j	Moskva	10 Jun
44:31	Anezka	Drahotová	CZE-Y	22.7.95	1		Chiasso	14 Oct
44:31	Chiaki	Asada	JPN	21.1.91	2		Wajima	14 Apr
44:31	Hanna	Drabenya	BLR	15.8.87	2		Grodno	6 Oct
44:31.32 t		Mao Yanxue	CHN-J	15.2.94	3		Tianjin	18 Sep
44:31.53t mx		Ni Yuanyuan	CHN-Y	6.4.95	3		Saluzzo	18 Jul
44:32	Nadezhda	Leontyeva	RUS-J	6.11.94	1	NC-wj	Sochi	19 Feb
44:32.22 t		Jeon Yong-eun	KOR	24.5.88	1		Changwon	20 Jun-
44:42.28 t	Olga	Dubrovina	RUS-J	11.6.93	1	NC-j	Moskva	10 Jun
45:00	Vera	Santos	POR	3.12.81	1		Lisboa	7 Jan
45:01	Sibilla	Di Vincenzo	ITA	22.1.83	2		Andria	11 Mar
45:01	Yevdokiya	Korotkova	RUS	28.2.79	5		Voronovo	16 Sep
45:08.24 t	Eleonora	Giorgi	ITA	14.9.89	1		Firenze	25 Mar
45:11.2A t	Lorena	Arenas	COL-J	17.9.93	1		Medellín	15 Apr
45:11.54 t	Agnese	Pastare	LAT	27.10.88	1		Liepaja	8 Jul
45:17.60 t	Anita	Kazemaka	LAT	30.5.90	2		Liepaja	8 Jul
45:24+	Claudia	Stef	ROU	25.2.78	30	in 20k	London	11 Aug
45:26	Federica	Ferraro	ITA	18.8.88	2		Bacuch	23 Sep
45:26,3 t	Lyudmyla	Olyanovska	UKR	20.2.93	1	NCp	Muchachevo	2 Nov
45:31.5 t	Alina	Halchenko	UKR-J	18.9.94	1	NC-j	Yevpatoriya	6 Mar

Mark	Name		Nat	Born	Date
45:35	Agnieszka	Szwarnóg	POL	28.12.86	16 Sep
45:37+	Susana	Feitor	POR	28.1.75	13 May
45:41+	Katarzyna	Kwoka	POL	29.6.85	8 Jul
45:42.4 t	Gaurav	Kumari	IND	5.9.88	13 Mar
45:45	Rossella	Giordano	ITA	1.12.72	6 Jul
45:45+	Annabel	Orjuela	COL	24.7.88	11 Aug
45:47+	Mayra Carolina	Herrera	GUA	20.12.88	11 Aug
45:49+	Ayman	Kozhakhmetova	KAZ	23.4.91	11 Aug
45:52	Alena	Azyrkina	RUS-J	10.6.94	19 Feb
45:57+	Jamy	Franco	GUA	1.7.91	11 Aug
45:58+	Lina	Bikulova	RUS	1.10.88	10 Jun
46:00	Alejandra	Ortega	MEX-J	8.7.94	12 May
46:00.46t	Julia	Takács	ESP	29.6.89	25 Aug
46:01	Kristina	Gracheva	RUS-J	19.1.94	19 Feb
46:02	Ai	Michiguchi	JPN	3.6.88	1 Jan
46:03.38t		Zhang Xin	CHN	17.8.89	18 Sep
46:10.56t	Ainhoa	Pinedo	ESP	17.2.83	25 Aug
46:14	Antonella	Palmisano	ITA	6.8.91	26 Oct
46:17+	Sandra	Galvis	COL	28.6.86	14 Apr
46:17	Natalya	Serezhkina	RUS	7.5.92	9 May
46:19+	Galina	Kichigina	KAZ	14.7.88	10 Jun
46:20+	Sholpan	Kozakhmetova	KAZ	23.4.91	10 Jun
46:23.07t		Wang Min	CHN	2.12.91	18 Sep
46:28.9 t	Natlya	Kopliyenko	RUS-J	30.6.94	6 Mar
46:30.50t	Eva María	Iglesias	ESP	10.6.85	25 Aug
46:33+	Viktória	Madarász	HUN	12.5.85	11 Aug
46:35+		Li Yanfei	CHN	12.1.90	29 Jan
46:35	Anne	Halkivaha	FIN	9.2.86	14 Apr

Best track times where better road times above or in 20k list below

Mark	Name		Nat	Born	Pos	Meet	Venue	Date
43:37.91 t	Ana	Cabecinha	POR	29.4.84	1		Lisboa	7 Jul
43:57.28t mx	Elisa	Rigaudo	ITA	17.6.80	2		Saluzzo	18 Jul
44:22.97	Mayumi	Kawasaki	JPN	10.5.80	1		Gifu	8 Oct
44:45.52	Kumi	Otoshi	JPN	29.7.85	2		Gifu	8 Oct
44:57.69	Inês	Henriques	POR	1.5.80	1		Leiria	31 Mar
45:04.72	Vera	Santos	POR	3.12.81	3	NC	Lisboa (Un)	7 Jul
45:09.31	Anastasiya	Yatsevich	BLR	18.1.85	1		Brest	16 May
45:18.05	Kristina	Saltanovic	LTU	20.2.75	1		Lisboa	30 Jun

Mark	Name		Nat	Born	Date
45:43.64	Nadezhda	Leontyeva	RUS-J	6.11.94	11 Jul
45:44.3	Tanya	Holliday	AUS	21.9.88	5 Feb
45:53.9	Natalya	Kholodilina	RUS	21.7.89	2 Jun
46:00.96mx	Rei	Inoue	JPN	23.7.91	23 Jun
46:11.46	Anna	Yermina	RUS-J	24.6.93	10 Jun
46:21.88	Annabel	Orjuela	COL	24.7.88	9 Jun
46:23.14mx	Chiaki	Asada	JPN	21.1.91	25 Nov
46:29.95	Anezka	Drahotová	CZE-Y	22.7.95	11 Jul
46:38.38t	Ai	Michiguchi	JPN	3.6.88	22 Sep

Drugs disqualification

Mark	Name		Nat	Born	Pos	Meet	Venue	Date
44:13	Tatyana	Mineyeva	RUS	10.8.90	2		Podolsk	9 May

JUNIORS

See main list for top 19 juniors. 10 performances by 7 women to 44:45. Additional marks and further juniors:

Name	Mark		Nat	Born	Pos	Meet	Venue	Date
Lu Xiuzhi	43:37				3		Ordos	14 Sep
Yermina	44:43				1		Cheboksary	9 Sep

Mark	Name		Nat	Born	Pos	Meet	Venue	Date
45:52	Alena	Azyrkina	RUS	10.6.94	3	NC-wj	Sochi	19 Feb
46:00	Alejandra	Ortega	MEX	8.7.94	2	WCp-j	Saransk	12 May
46:01	Kristina	Gracheva	RUS	19.1.94	4	NC-wj	Sochi	19 Feb
46:28.9 t	Natlya	Kopliyenko	RUS	30.6.94	2		Yevpatoriya	6 Mar

Track bests

Mark	Name		Nat	Born	Pos	Meet	Venue	Date
46:11.46	Anna	Yermina	RUS	24.6.93	3	NC-j	Mpskva	10 Jun
46:29.95	Anezka	Drahotová	CZE-Y	22.7.95	6	WJ	Barcelona	11 Jul

Mark		Name		Nat	Born	Pos	Meet	Venue	Date

20 KILOMETRES WALK

Mark		Name		Nat	Born	Pos	Meet	Venue	Date
1:25:02	43:16	Yelena	Lashmanova	RUS	9.4.92	1	OG	London	11 Aug
1:25:09	42:33	Olga	Kaniskina	RUS	19.1.85	2	OG	London	11 Aug
1:25:16	43:16		Qieyang Shenjie	CHN	11.11.90	3	OG	London	11 Aug
1:25:27		Elmira	Alembekova	RUS	30.6.90	1	NC-w	Sochi	18 Feb
1:25:46	43:55		Liu Hong	CHN	12.5.87	1		Taicang	30 Mar
1:26:00	42:50		Liu Hong			4	OG	London	11 Aug
1:26:26	43:16	Anisya	Kirdyapkina	RUS	23.10.89	5	OG	London	11 Aug
1:26:30			Lashmanova			2	NC-w	Sochi	18 Feb
1:26:47	44:xx	Irina	Yumanova	RUS	6.11.90	3	NC-w	Sochi	18 Feb
1:26:59	44:17?	Tatyana	Sibileva	RUS	17.5.80	4	NC-w	Sochi	18 Feb
1:27:01	43:56		Lu Xiuzhi	CHN-J	26.10.93	2		Taicang	30 Mar
1:27:04	43:55		Qieyang Shenjie			3		Taicang	30 Mar
1:27:08		Anna	Lukyanova (10)	RUS	23.4.91	5	NC-w	Sochi	18 Feb
1:27:10	43:16		Lu Xiuzhi			6	OG	London	11 Aug
1:27:32	44:27		Liu Hong			1		La Coruña	9 Jun
1:27:36	43:29	Elisa	Rigaudo	ITA	17.6.80	7	OG	London	11 Aug
1:27:38	44:33		Lashmanova			1	WCp	Saransk	13 May
1:27:43	44:27		Kirdyapkina			1	NC	Moskva	10 Jun
1:27:56	43:58	Beatriz	Pascual	ESP	9.5.82	8	OG	London	11 Aug
1:28:03	44:17		Sibileva			1		Lugano	18 Mar
1:28:03	43:43	Ana	Cabecinha	POR	29.4.84	9	OG	London	11 Aug
1:28:06	44:27	Vera	Sokolova	RUS	8.6.87	2	NC	Moskva	10 Jun
1:28:06	44:20		Gao Ni	CHN	14.9.91	4		Taicang	30 Mar
1:28:14	43:43	María	Vasco	ESP	26.12.75	10	OG	London	11 Aug
1:28:15	44:11	María José	Poves	ESP	16.3.78	1	NC	Pontevedra	4 Mar
1:28:16		Nina	Okhotnikova	RUS	11.3.91	6	NC-w	Sochi	18 Feb
1:28:26			Nie Jingjing	CHN	1.3.88	1	NGP	Taicang	30 Mar
1:28:29		Lyudmila	Arkhipova	RUS	25.11.78	7	NC-w	Sochi	18 Feb
1:28:29		Marina	Pandakova (30/21)	RUS	1.3.89	8	NC-w	Sochi	18 Feb
1:28:30	43:20	Svetlana	Vasilyeva	RUS	24.7.92	1	NCp	Cheboksary	9 Sep
1:28:41	44:10	Masami	Fuchise	JPN	2.9.86	11	OG	London	11 Aug
1:28:53	44:37	Claire	Tallent	AUS	7.6.81	5		Taicang	30 Mar
1:28:54	44:15	Mirna	Ortiz	GUA	28.2.87	2		Lugano	18 Mar
1:29:01			He Qin	CHN	23.3.92	2	NGP	Taicang	30 Mar
1:29:39	44:14	Olive	Loughnane	IRL	14.1.76	13	OG	London	11 Aug
1:29:43			Wang Shanshan	CHN	16.6.87	3	NGP	Taicang	30 Mar
1:29:44	45:11	Paulina	Buziak	POL	16.12.86	1		Zaniemysl	21 Apr
1:29:48	44:25	Kumi	Otoshi (30)	JPN	29.7.85	1	NC	Kobe	19 Feb
1:29:48	45:21	Eleonora	Giorgi	ITA	14.9.89	14	OG	London	11 Aug
1:29:54	44:18	Inês	Henriques	POR	1.5.80	15	OG	London	11 Aug
1:30:03	44:22	Nadiya	Borovska	UKR	25.2.81	16	OG	London	11 Aug
1:30:08	44:22	Regan	Lamble	AUS	14.10.91	17	OG	London	11 Aug
1:30:14	44:42		Ding Huiqin	CHN	5.2.90	1	AsiC	Nomi	11 Mar
1:30:20	44:22	Mayumi	Kawasaki	JPN	10.5.80	18	OG	London	11 Aug
1:30:21	43:55		Sun Huanhuan	CHN	15.3.90	6		Taicang	30 Mar
1:30:25			Mao Yanxue	CHN-J	15.2.94	1J		Huaian	11 Feb
1:30:27			Li Li	CHN	18.6.87	3	OT	Huaian	11 Feb
1:30:37	45:05	Julia	Takács (40)	ESP	29.6.89	4		La Coruña	9 Jun
1:30:44	44:32	Melanie	Seeger	GER	8.1.77	19	OG	London	11 Aug
1:30:56		Agnieszka	Szwarnóg	POL	28.12.86	2		Zaniemysl	21 Apr
1:30:57	45:46	Jamy	Franco	GUA	1.7.91	4		Lugano	18 Mar
1:30:57	45:08	Sabine	Krantz	GER	6.2.81	5		La Coruña	9 Jun
1:31:01		Lina	Bikulova	RUS	1.10.88	9	NC-w	Sochi	18 Feb
1:31:02	46:02	Laura	Reynolds	IRL	20.1.89	20	OG	London	11 Aug
1:31:03	45:04	Mayra Carolina	Herrera	GUA	20.12.88	5		Lugano	18 Mar
1:31:04	44:56	Kristina	Saltanovic	LTU	20.2.75	21	OG	London	11 Aug
1:31:08	45:23	Brigita	Virbalyté	LTU	1.2.85	6		Lugano	18 Mar
1:31:08	45:34	Déspina	Zapounídou (50)	GRE	5.10.85	7		Lugano	18 Mar
1:31:22			Bo Yanmin	CHN	29.6.87	4	NGP	Taicang	30 Mar
1:31:22			Shi Tianshu	CHN	7.6.88	5	NGP	Taicang	30 Mar
1:31:25		Tatyana	Korotkova	RUS	31.5.82	10	NC-w	Sochi	18 Feb
1:31:25	45:47	Katarzyna	Kwoka	POL	29.6.85	8		Lugano	18 Mar
1:31:28		Tanya	Holliday	AUS	21.9.88	1		Adelaide	19 May
1:31:28	45:03	Agnieszka	Dygacz	POL	18.7.85	23	OG	London	11 Aug

Mark		Name		Nat	Born	Pos	Meet	Venue	Date	
1:31:32			Tong Lingling	CHN	25.1.92	6	NGP	Taicang	30	Mar
1:31:45		Federica	Ferraro	ITA	18.8.88	1		Chiasso	14	Oct
1:31:46	45:49	Claudia	Stef	ROU	25.2.78	4		Rio Maior	14	Apr
1:31:49			Luo Xingcai	CHN-J	18.7.94	1j	NGP	Taicang	30	Mar
		(60)								
1:31:50	45:03	Lorena	Luaces	ESP	29.2.84	4	NC	Pontevedra	4	Mar
1:31:53	45:50	Erica	de Sena	BRA	3.5.85	5		Rio Maior	14	Apr
1:31:54	45:20	Agnese	Pastare	LAT	27.10.88	24	OG	London	11	Aug
1:31:55	44:47	Olena	Shumkina	UKR	24.1.88	9		Lugano	18	Mar
1:31:55		Ayman	Kozhakhmetova	KAZ	23.4.91	11	RUS-w	Sochi	18	Feb
1:31:57			Li Yanfei	CHN	12.1.90	1	NGP	Ordos	14	Sep
1:31:58	45:13	Hanna	Drabenya	BLR	15.8.87	25	OG	London	11	Aug
1:32:01		Paola	Pérez	ECU	21.12.89	4		Zaniemysl	21	Apr
1:32:03	45:32	Irina	Shushina	RUS	30.10.86	3	NCp	Cheboksary	9	Sep
1:32:07	44:22	Olga	Yakovenko	UKR	1.6.87	27	OG	London	11	Aug
		(70)								
1:32:08			Song Xiaoling	CHN	21.12.87	6	OT	Huaian	11	Feb
1:32:14	45:39	Beki	Lee	AUS	25.11.86	28	OG	London	11	Aug
1:32:16	44:52	Anastasiya	Yatsevich	BLR	18.1.85	8	NC	Moskva	10	Jun
1:32:23			Pei Mowen	CHN-Y	17.9.95	2J		Huaian	11	Feb
1:32:27	46:02	Maria	Michta	USA	23.6.86	29	OG	London	11	Aug
1:32:28	46:03	Monica	Equihua	MEX	23.9.82	30	OG	London	11	Aug
1:32:30	46:35	Sibilla	Di Vincenzo	ITA	22.1.83	4		Latina	29	Jan
1:32:36			Chen Shuangyan	CHN	14.8.91	8	OT	Huaian	11	Feb
1:32:36	45:59	Susana	Feitor	POR	28.1.75	7		Rio Maior	14	Apr
1:32:36	46:09	Lorena	Arenas	COL-J	17.9.93	8		La Coruña	9	Jun
		(80)								
1:32:43	45:15	Rei	Inoue	JPN	23.7.91	2	NC	Kobe	19	Feb
1:32:46			Sun Xueping	CHN	10.12.88	9	OT	Huaian	11	Feb
1:32:48	46:20	Vera	Santos	POR	3.12.81	3	NC	Quarteira	18	Mar
1:32:53	46:14	Lucie	Pelantová	CZE	7.5.86	11		Lugano	18	Mar
1:33:01			He Dan	CHN	22.7.84	10	OT	Huaian	11	Feb
1:33:05	46:17	Neringa	Aidietyté	LTU	5.6.83	12		Lugano	18	Mar
1:33:05	46:07	Rachel	Lavallée Seaman	CAN	14.1.86	2		Naumburg	22	Apr
1:33:12			Yang Yawei	CHN	16.10.83	8	NGP	Taicang	30	Mar
1:33:15		Ainhoa	Pinedo	ESP	17.2.83	8	NC	Pontevedra	4	Mar
1:33:20	45:48	Natalya	Kholodilina	RUS	21.7.89	11	NC	Moskva	10	Jun
		(90)								
1:33:20			Kim Mi-jung	KOR	10.6.79	1	NG	Daegu	15	Oct
1:33:21	46:20	Sholpan	Kozhakhmetova	KAZ	23.4.91	12	NC	Moskva	10	Jun
1:33:24	46:13	Sandra	Galvis	COL	28.6.86	9		La Coruña	9	Jun
1:33:25			Xie Lijuan	CHN-J	14.5.93	2j	NGP	Taicang	30	Mar
1:33:28			Kang Jinzi	CHN	25.1.90	9	NGP	Taicang	30	Mar
1:33:28	45:47	Claudia	Balderrama	BOL	13.11.83	33	OG	London	11	Aug
1:33:34	46:42	Viktória	Madarász	HUN	12.5.85	13		Lugano	18	Mar
1:33:34	45:45	Ingrid	Hernández	COL	29.11.88	34	OG	London	11	Aug
1:33:36	46:09	Nguyen Thi Thanh	Phuc	VIE	12.8.90	36	OG	London	11	Aug
1:33:43			Liu Shuyu	CHN-J	13.12.93	3J		Huaian	11	Feb
		(100)								

Mark		Name	Nat	Born	Date	
1:33:52		Wang Yingliu	CHN	1.3.92	30	Mar
1:33:56	Mariya	Tyureva	RUS	24.7.91	9	Sep
1:33:59		Jeon Yong-eun	KOR	24.5.88	15	Oct
1:34:00		Li Hua	CHN	15.1.91	30	Mar
1:34:02	Natalya	Makarova (46:01)	RUS	17.4.87	10	Jun
1:34:07	Edina	Füsti	HUN	24.6.82	15	Apr
1:34:08		Yang Mingxia	CHN	13.1.90	14	Sep
1:34:11	Sylwia	Korzeniowska	FRA	25.4.80	15	Apr
1:34:13	Tatyana	Shemyakina	RUS	3.9.87	18	Feb
1:34:27	Kumiko	Okada (45:52)	JPN	17.10.91	19	Feb
1:34:27	Antonella	Palmisano	ITA	6.8.91	21	Apr
1:34:29	Anita	Kazemaka	LAT	30.5.90	1	Jun
1:34:30		Weon Aseas-byeol	KOR	8.4.90	15	Oct
1:34:40	Natalya	Serezhkina	RUS	7.5.92	18	Feb
1:34:41	Annabel	Orjuela	COL	24.7.88	17	Mar
1:34:47	Yadira	Guamán	ECU	8.6.86	11	Aug
1:34:53	Ana Veronica	Rodean	ROU	23.6.84	11	Mar
1:34:56.92t	Miranda	Melville	USA	20.3.89	1	Jul
1:35:00	Galina	Kireyeva	RUS	11.10.91	18	Feb
1:35:01	Hiroi	Maeda	JPN	1.6.91	11	Mar
1:35:09	Galina	Kichigina	KAZ	14.7.88	18	Feb
1:35:10		Liu Huan	CHN-J	24.2.93	11	Feb
1:35:21		Zhou Kang	CHN	24.12.89	14	Sep
1:35:24	Olena	Shevchuk	UKR	23.3.86	6	Mar
1:35:25	Jo	Jackson (46:27)	GBR	17.1.85	9	Jun
1:35:33	Semiha	Mutlu	TUR	15.3.87	11	Aug
1:35:40.05t	Erin	Gray	USA	15.5.87	1	Jul
1:35:47	Chiaki	Asada	JPN	21.1.91	19	Feb
1:35:51	Ai	Michiguchi	JPN	3.6.88	11	Mar
1:35:56		Xu Liqin	CHN	6.2.90	14	Sep
1:35:57		Chen Zhen	CHN-J	3.11.94	11	Feb
1:36:02	Olga	Suranova	RUS	7.12.86	9	Sep
1:36:05		Wang Min	CHN	2.12.91	14	Sep
1:36:11	Mami	Urabe	JPN	18.1.88	19	Feb
1:36:11	Zuzana	Schindlerová	CZE	25.4.87	21	Apr
1:36:20	Katarzyna	Golba	POL	21.12.89	8	Jul
1:36:21	Snezhana	Yurchenko	BLR	1.8.84	7	Apr
1:36:32	Raquel	González	ESP	16.11.89	9	Jun
1:36:33	Fumiko	Okabe	JPN	8.7.90	11	Mar
1:36:37		Hou Yongbo	CHN-J	15.9.94	30	Mar
1:36:45	Milángela	Rosales	VEN	21.2.87	17	Mar
1:36:45		Ni Yuanyuan	CHN-Y	6.4.95	14	Sep
1:36:47		Duan Dandan	CHN-Y	23.5.95	14	Sep
1:36:48	Marie	Polli	SUI	28.10.80	18	Mar
1:36:59	Alina	Matveyuk	BLR	29.7.90	7	Apr
1:36:59		Xu Yaozhi	CHN	20.5.90	14	Sep
1:37:00.07t	Jill	Cobb	USA	13.2.75	1	Jul
1:37:01		Zhou Tongmei	CHN	4.4.88	30	Mar

Mark	Name	Nat	Born	Pos	Meet	Venue	Date
1:37:05	Anne Halkivaha	FIN	9.2.86				22 Apr
1:37:08	Zhao Jing	CHN	18.2.92				30 Mar
1:37:12	Laura Polli	SUI	7.9.83				18 Mar
1:37:15	Mu Juan	CHN	20.6.89				30 Mar
1:37:15	Eva María Iglesias	ESP	10.6.85				18 Mar
1:37:16	Myriam Fernández	ESP	31.1.90				18 Mar
1:37:17	Ana Maria Groza	ROU	1.6.76				7 Apr
1:37:19	Anastasiya Pavlenko	RUS	28.9.89				18 Feb
1:37:20	Monika Kapera	POL	15.2.90				21 Apr
1:37:20A	Grace Wanjiru Njue	KEN	10.1.79				12 May
1:37:21	Liang Rui	CHN-J	18.6.94				30 Mar
1:37:23	Serena Pruner	ITA	21.5.86				25 Jan
1:37:26	Shi Yang	CHN	24.1.83				14 Sep
1:37:28	Khushbir Kaur	IND-J	9.7.93				23 Apr
1:37:28	Liu Ke	CHN	2.10.90				11 Feb
1:37:32	Nicola Evangelista	CAN	14.6.88				15 Sep
1:37:36	Huang Jing	CHN	28.2.88				30 Mar
1:37:37	Inna Kashyna	UKR	27.9.91				9 Jun
1:37:41	Mária Czaková	SVK	2.10.88				24 Mar
1:37:49	Inès Pastorino	FRA	20.10.92				15 Apr
1:37:51	Wang Jiaojiao	CHN-J	11.12.93				11 Feb
1:37:56	Xiao Junying	CHN	16.6.92				11 Feb
1:37:56	Emilie Menuet	FRA	27.11.91				15 Apr
1:37:57.58t	Gaurav Kumari	IND	5.9.88				15 Feb
1:38:04	Lauren Forgues	USA	16.4.88				22 Apr
1:38:04	Antigóni Drisbióti	GRE	21.3.84				1 Jun
1:38:07	Georgiana Enache	ROU	19.2.91				7 Apr
1:38:07	Esther Sánchez	MEX	9.1.83				14 Apr
1:38:10	Karoliina Kaasalainen	FIN	1.4.88				10 Jun
1:38:13	Li Maocuo	CHN	20.10.92				15 Jun
1:38:16	Natsuki Hosaka	JPN	15.9.88				19 Feb
1:38:20.20t	Joanne Dow	USA	19.3.64				1 Jul
1:38:23	Lizbeth Silva	MEX	30.9.89				14 Apr
1:38:25	Ma Faying	CHN-J	30.8.93				30 Mar
1:38:25	Justyna Swierczynska	POL	26.2.87				6 Oct
1:38:29.6t	Yesenia Carrillo	COL-J	22.10.93				23 Sep
1:38:32	Yorimi Inaba	JPN	31.1.91				11 Mar
1:38:32	Nadezhda Darazhuk	BLR	23.1.90				18 Mar
1:38:32	Kelly Ruddick	AUS	19.4.73				9 Dec
1:38:33	Valentina Trapletti	ITA	12.7.85				14 Oct
1:38:41	Cheryl Webb	AUS	3.10.76				26 Aug
1:38:42	Anna Krakhmaleva	RUS	1.5.92				18 Feb
1:38:44	Zhang Shasha	CHN	4.12.92				11 Feb
1:38:45A	Emily Ngii	KEN	13.8.86				14 Jun
1:38:46	Zhao Huimin	CHN-J	12.10.93				30 Mar
1:38:46	Yelena Zubakina	RUS	20.6.88				10 Jun
1:38:48	Nataliya Zhornyak	UKR	26.5.89				6 Mar
1:38:51	Anne-Gaëlle Retout	FRA	15.8.80				15 Apr
1:38:56	Wang Yalan	CHN-J	19.2.93				11 Feb
1:38:57	Janeth Guamán	ECU	15.1.88				29 Jun
1:38:58.0t	Florida Miniyanova (200)	KAZ	1.7.92				28 Mar

Track bests

Mark	Name	Nat	Born	Pos	Meet	Venue	Date
1:34:53.33	Michta	USA	23.6.86				1 Jul
1:37:40.59	Zapounídou	GRE	5.10.85				22 Jan
1:37:46.79	K Kaur	IND-J	9.7.93				15 Feb

Drugs disqualification

Mark	Name	Nat	Born	Pos	Meet	Venue	Date
1:30:56	Tatyana Mineyeva ¶	RUS	10.8.90	9	NC-w	Sochi	18 Feb

JUNIORS

See main list for top 7 juniors. 10 performances by 7 women to 1:34:00. Additional marks and further juniors:

Mark	Name	Nat	Born	Pos	Meet	Venue	Date
Lu Xiuzhi 2+	1:29:55	4	WCp			Saransk	13 May
Arenas	1:33:2132	OG				London	11 Aug
1:35:10	Liu Huan	CHN	24.2.93	5J		Huaian	11 Feb
1:35:57	Chen Zhen	CHN	3.11.94	6J		Huaian	11 Feb
1:36:37 (10)	Hou Yongbo	CHN	15.9.94	6	NGP-j	Taicang	30 Mar
1:36:45	Ni Yuanyuan	CHN-Y	6.4.95	4j	NGP	Ordos	14 Sep
1:36:47	Duan Dandan	CHN-Y	23.5.95	5j	NGP	Ordos	14 Sep
1:37:21	Liang Rui	CHN	18.6.94	7	NGP-j	Taicang	30 Mar
1:37:28	Khushbir Kaur	IND	9.7.93	1		Patiala	23 Apr
1:37:51	Wang Jiaojiao	CHN	11.12.93	8J		Huaian	11 Feb
1:38:25	Ma Faying	CHN	30.8.93	9j	NGP	Taicang	30 Mar
1:38:29.6 t	Yesenia Carrillo	COL	22.10.93	1	SA-23	São Paulo	23 Sep
1:38:46	Zhao Huimin	CHN	12.10.93	10	NGP-j	Taicang	30 Mar
1:38:56	Wang Yalan	CHN	19.2.93	10J		Huaian	11 Feb
1:39:47	Zhu Dan (20)	CHN	27.1.93	12J		Huaian	11 Feb

50 Kilomettes Walk: 4:33:23 Erin Talcott USA 21.5.78 1 Santee 22 Jan

Contnuation lists for Men's 30 and 35 Kilometres Walk from page 445

30k	35k	Name	Nat	Born	Pos	Meet	Venue	Date
2:08:19	2:32:24	Igor Yerokhin	RUS	4.9.85	6	NC-w	Sochi	18 Feb
2:10:54	2:32:24+	Yohann Diniz	FRA	1.1.78	3	in 50k	London	11 Aug
2:10:49	2:32:26+	Erick Barrondo	GUA	14.6.91	6	in 50k	London	11 Aug
2:08:30		Jared Tallent	AUS	17.10.84	1		Canberra	10 Jun
2:08:19	2:32:40	Aleksandr Yargunkin	RUS	6.1.81	7	NC-w	Sochi	18 Feb
2:08:49		Jarkko Kinnunen	FIN	19.1.84	1	NC	Vantaa	10 Jun
	2:33:52	Giorgio Rubino	ITA	15.4.86	3		Latina	29 Jan
	2:34:43	Matteo Giupponi	ITA	8.10.88	4		Latina	29 Jan
2:12:33		Su Guanyu	CHN-J	26.6.94	1		Taicang	31 Mar
2:12:41		Zhao Qi	CHN-J	14.1.93	1		Ordos	15 Sep
2:13:07		Yin Jiaxing	CHN-J	16.3.94	2		Ordos	15 Sep
	2:35:20	Oleksiy Kazanin	UKR	22.5.82	1	NC-w	Yevpatoriya	6 Mar
	2:35:31	Ivan Trotskiy	BLR	27.5.76	1	NCp	Nesvizh	7 Apr
	2:35:46	Jean-Jacques Nkouloukidi	ITA	15.4.82	5		Latina	29 Jan
	2:36:09	Dmitriy Dzyubin	BLR	12.7.90	2	NCp	Nesvizh	7 Apr
2:14:03	2:36:10+	Christopher Linke	GER	24.10.88	17	in 50k	London	11 Aug
2:14:21		He Yongqiang	CHN-J	27.11.93	3		Ordos	15 Sep
	2:36:20	Semyon Lovkin	RUS	14.7.77	8	NC-w	Sochi	18 Feb
	2:36:20	Oleksiy Shelest	UKR	27.3.73	2	NC-w	Yevpatoriya	6 Mar
2:14:28	2:36:22	Edikt Khaybullin	RUS	29.5.89	4	NCp	Cheboksary	9 Sep
	2:36:33	Federico Tontodonati	ITA	30.10.89	6		Latina	29 Jan
2:14:29	2:37:01+	Grzegorz Sudol	POL	28.8.78	4	in 50k	Dudince	24 Mar
	2:37:03	Andrey Talashko	BLR	31.5.82	3	NCp	Nesvizh	7 Apr
2:13:21	2:37:25	Anton Sivakov	RUS	19.1.89	9	NC-w	Sochi	18 Feb
2:14:25	(2:38:33)	Hiroki Arai	JPN	18.5.88	4	in 50k	Wajima	15 Apr

WORLD LIST TRENDS – MEN

This table shows the 10th and 100th bests in the year lists for the last seven years and 2004, with previous bests.

Men 10th Bests

	Pre 2004	2004	2006	2007	2008	2009	2010	2011	2012
100m	9.98- 97	10.01	10.02	10.02	9.95	9.97	9.95	**9.89**	9.94
200m	**20.03**- 00	20.17	20.19	20.06	20.17	20.17	20.11	20.16	20.10
400m	**44.51**- 96	44.72	44.73	44.62	44.70	44.81	44.81	44.78	44.77
800m	**1:43.66**- 96	1:44.09	1:43.93	1:44.27	1:44.10	1:43.82	1:43.89	1:44.07	1:43.71
1500m	3:31.49- 01	**3:31.10**	3:31.85	3:32.13	3:32.16	3:31.90	3:32.20	3:31.84	3:31.61
5000m	**12:54.99**- 03	12:59.04	12:56.41	13:02.89	13:03.04	12:58.16	12:55.95	12:59.15	12:55.99
10000m	27:14.61- 03	27:05.14	27:14.84	**27:00.30**	27:08.06	27:15.94	27:17.61	26:52.84	27:03.49
Half Mar	60:20- 02	60:22	60:12	59:32	59:37	59:30	59:40	59:39	**59:15**
Marathon	2:06:48- 03	2:07:43	2:07:14	2:07:19	2:06:25	2:06:14	2:05:52	2:05:45!	**2:04:54**
3000mSt	**8:08.14**- 02	8:11.44	8:11.36	8:09.72	8:12.72	8:10.63	8:09.87	8:08.43	8:10.20
110mh	13.20- 98	13.22	13.22	13.19	13.24	13.21	13.28	13.23	13.13
400mh	48.25- 02	**48.16**	48.57	48.26	48.52	48.30	48.47	48.47	48.41
HJ	**2.36**- 88	2.32	2.33	2.34	2.34	2.33	2.32	2.33	2.32
PV	**5.90**- 98	5.81	5.81	5.83	5.81	5.80	5.80	5.80	5.73
LJ	**8.35**- 97	8.28	8.32	8.26	8.25	8.30	8.25	8.27	8.26
TJ	**17.48**- 85	17.41	17.38	17.39	17.43	17.41	17.29	17.35	17.31
SP	**21.63**- 84	21.14	20.85	20.87	21.19	20.99	21.29	21.16	21.14
DT	**68.20**- 82	66.73	66.50	66.61	67.91	66.19	66.90	67.21	67.50
HT	**81.88**- 88	80.90	80.54	80.00	80.58	79.48	78.73	79.27	79.56
JT	**87.12**- 96/97	85.83	85.30	84.35	85.05	84.24	85.12	84.81	84.72
Decathlon	**8526**- 98	8285	8310	8298	8372	8406	8253	8288	8322
20kmW	**1:18:30**- 05	1:19:30	1:19:12	1:19:34	1:19:15	1:19:55	1:20:36	1:19:57	1:19:20
50kmW	3:41:30- 05	3:44:42	3:43:58	3:44:26	3:45:21	3:41:55	3:47:54	3:44:03	**3:41:24**

Peak years shown in bold.

Men 100th Bests

	Pre 2004	2004	2006	2007	2008	2009	2010	2011	2012
100m	10.24- 00	10.26	10.27	10.25	10.23	10.22	10.26	10.21	**10.20**
200m	20.66- 99/00	20.67	20.70	20.66	20.67	20.68	20.71	20.63	**20.57**
400m	**45.78**- 00	45.86	45.90	45.91	45.89	45.86	45.92	45.91	45.79
800m	**1:46.54**- 99	1:46.67	1:46.80	1:46.99	1:46.70	1:46.88	1:46.76	1:46.50	1:46.56
1500m	3:38.42- 97	3:38.50	3:39.26	3:38.66	3:38.57	3:38.60	3:38.47	3:37.77	**3:36.84**
5000m	13:28.62- 00	13:25.52	13:27.46	13:27.48	13:25.05	13:26.90	13:25.88	13:26.29	**13:23.58**
10000m	28:15.98- 00	28:21.4	28:21.98	28:10.73	**28:04.47**	28:18.00	28:21.00	28:15.79	28:06.74
Half Mar	62:00- 00	62:06	62:07	61:54	61:50	**61:28**	61:38	61:31	**61:19**
Marathon	2:10:38- 03	2:11:13	2:10:54	2:10:43	2:10:22	2:09:53	2:09:31	2:09:19!	**2:08:32**
3000mSt	8:33.58- 03	**8:31.06**	8:34.10	8:32.94	8:32.12	8:35.21	8:35.29	8:35.45	8:31.2
110mh	13.72- 96	13.70	13.77	13.72	13.67	13.71	13.68	13.67	**13.66**
400mh	**50.06**- 00	50.14	50.37	50.28	50.33	50.35	50.41	50.28	50.15
HJ	**2.24**- 84/88/89/92/96	2.23	2.23	2.23	2.23	2.23	2.23	**2.24**	**2.24**
PV	**5.55**- 00	5.50	5.50	5.50	5.50	5.46	5.42	5.45	5.50
LJ	7.94- 96	**7.96**	7.90	7.90	7.93	7.94	7.91	7.94	7.93
TJ	**16.60**- 88	16.55	16.43	16.44	16.53	16.46	16.46	16.53	16.40
SP	19.48- 84	19.28	19.12	19.22	19.21	19.15	19.08	19.18	**19.51**
DT	**60.96**- 84	60.05	59.63	59.75	60.77	60.00	59.77	59.98	60.95
HT	**73.06**- 84	71.12	70.19	70.58	70.89	70.66	70.78	70.44	71.22
JT	77.14- 91	76.31	75.98	75.66	76.28	77.03	76.71	77.38	**77.78**
Decathlon	**7702**- 88	7572	7496	7545	7594	7623	7526	7678	7648
20kmW	**1:22:48**- 05	1:23:25	1:23:47	1:23:55	1:23:32	1:23:57	1:24:24	1:23:40	1:23:10
50kmW	4:03:49- 99	4:05:13	4:13:16	4:04:52	4:05:05	4:09:24	4:08:08	4:06:15	**4:03:04**

! From 2011 main marathon lists no longer include Boston or other such excessively downhill races.

Number of athletes achieving base level standards for world lists:

Men		2007	2008	2009	2010	2011	2012
100m	10.29	147	154	161	133	166	198
200m	20.79	143	165	174	140	175	227
400m	46.29	150	150	163	154	151	184
800m	1:47.70	156	173	154	169	198	219
1500m	3:39.99	149	139	141	152	170	201
5000m	13:40.0	197	202	211	203	213	233
10000m	28:40.0	218	247	180	198	196	225
HMar	61:59	105	112	158	145	147	197
Mar	2:10:59	111	129	160	175	215	233
3000St	8:39.99	155	166	140	135	147	184
110mh	13.89	164	172	171	196	194	214
400mh	50.79	148	165	152	155	171	186

		2007	2008	2009	2010	2011	2012
HJ	2.20	197	180	184	194	192	216
PV	5.35	178	179	172	172	176	200
LJ	7.80	179	191	182	173	186	183
TJ	16.30	137	167	123	139	142	145
SP	18.50	166	170	171	168	163	203
DT	58.00	150	172	164	156	155	179
HT	68.00	135	155	149	158	149	158
JT	74.00	145	152	166	168	173	199
Dec	7400	137	155	150	136	165	173
20kmW	1:25:00	144	147	136	124	154	175
50kmW	4:10:00	115	123	105	103	110	132
TOTAL		3526	3765	3667	3646	3908	4464

The 2012 numbers compared to those of 2011: for 10th best 14-9, 100th best 18-4 (1 tie), base level 22-1

WORLD LIST TRENDS – WOMEN

This table shows the 10th and 100th bests in the year lists for the last seven years and 2004, with previous bests.

10th Bests	Pre 2004	2004	2006	2007	2008	2009	2010	2011	2012
100m	**10.92**- 88	11.04	11.08	11.04	10.95	11.04	11.08	11.01	10.99
200m	**22.24**- 88	22.46	22.51	22.49	22.43	22.45	22.49	22.55	22.37
400m	**49.74**- 84	50.19	50.14	50.16	50.11	50.27	50.43	50.67	50.06
800m	**1:56.91**- 88	1:57.96	1:57.88	1:58.61	1:57.9	1:58.80	1:58.67	1:58.21	1:57.77
1500m	**3:58.07**- 97	4:01.29	4:01.31	4:02.8	4:02.44	4:00.86	4:00.25	4:01.73	3:59.71
5000m	14:45.35- 00	14:44.81	14:46.99	14:45.22	14:43.89	14:41.62	**14:38.64**	14:39.44	14:50.80
10000m	31:01.07- 03	31:04.34	31:14.80	31:22.80	**30:39.96**	30:51.92	31:29:03	31:10.02	30:59.19
Half Mar	68:23- 00	68:52	69:17	68:28	68:51	68:14	67:52	68:07	**67:42**
Marathon	2:23:33- 02	2:24:27	2:23:22	2:24:23	2:24:14	2:25:06	2:23:44	2:22:43!	**2:20:57**
3000mSt	9:44.95- 03	9:39.84	9:27.35	9:26.63	9:21.76	**9:18.54**	9:24.84	9:25.96	9:23.52
100mh	12.67- 98	12.60	12.66	12.67	**12.58**	12.67	12.65	12.73	12.62
400mh	54.15- 99	**53.99**	54.47	54.14	54.45	54.49	54.58	54.69	54.21
HJ	**2.01**- 03	2.00	1.98	1.97	1.98	1.98	1.97	1.96	1.96
PV	4.60- 02/03	4.60	4.62	4.70	4.70	4.65	4.66	**4.71**	4.70
LJ	**7.07**- 88	6.83	6.83	6.89	6.89	6.87	6.89	6.88	6.97
TJ	14.76- 03	14.78	14.54	14.69	**14.84**	14.62	14.48	14.57	14.60
SP	**20.85**- 87	19.29	19.10	19.13	19.29	19.38	19.47	19.26	19.60
DT	**70.34**- 88	65.25	64.20	64.87	64.10	63.89	64.04	63.91	64.45
HT	71.12- 03	72.57	74.31	73.94	74.40	73.07	73.40	72.65	**75.59**
JT	64.89- 00	63.07	63.20	63.58	63.24	63.89	63.36	63.50	**64.91**
Heptathlon	**6540**- 88	6287	6356	6327	6465	6323	6204	6338	6466
20kmW	1:27:55- 01	1:27:52	1:28:26	1:28:51	1:27:18	1:28:50	1:29:20	1:28:41	**1:27:08**

100th Bests	Pre 2004	2004	2006	2007	2008	2009	2010	2011	2012
100m	11.36- 00	11.38	11.41	11.37	11.36	11.41	11.40	11.36	**11.34**
200m	23.21- 00	23.20	23.28	23.27	**23.17**	23.26	23.27	23.21	**23.10**
400m	52.25- 00	52.14	52.24	52.14	**52.08**	52.44	52.52	52.33	52.16
800m	2:01.50- 84	2:01.98	2:02.31	2:02.25	2:02.50	2:02.13	2:02.14	2:01.86	**2:01.48**
1500m	4:10.22- 84	4:10.34	4:11.61	4:11.67	4:11.64	4:11.06	4:10.50	4:09.88	**4:09.06**
5000m	15:29.36- 00	**15:27.20**	15:31.57	15:33.90	15:27.50	15:37.31	15:37.45	15:31.67	15:32.88
10000m	32:32.47- 00	32:37.88	32:42.44	32:46.28	**32:30.10**	32:54.64	32:57.59	32:53.44	32:38.95
Half Mar	71:29- 01	71:44	71:37	71:15	71:19	70:57	70:59	71:06	**70:48**
Marathon	2:31:05- 01	2:31:53	2:31:08	2:31:25	2:29:53	2:30:08	2:29:36	2:28:32	**2:28:01**
3000mSt	10:23.76- 03	10:18.55	10:06.30	10:03.2	9:56.48	10:02.94	10:03.50	9:59.44	**9:53.79**
100mh	13.22- 00	13.26	13.30	13.25	13.22	13.28	13.23	13.16	**13.11**
400mh	57.48- 00	57.33	57.35	57.21	57.46	57.45	57.22	57.26	**57.14**
HJ	**1.88**- 86/87/88/92/93	1.87	1.86	1.87	1.86	1.86	1.87	1.86	1.87
PV	4.15- 03	4.20	4.20	4.22	4.25	4.21	4.25	4.30	**4.31**
LJ	6.53- 88	6.50	6.51	6.49	6.52	6.49	6.51	6.50	**6.55**
TJ	13.68- 00	13.70	13.66	13.64	**13.75**	13.65	13.67	13.70	13.71
SP	**17.19**- 87	16.76	16.60	16.54	16.49	16.43	16.46	16.60	16.82
DT	**58.50**- 92	55.15	55.93	55.92	55.43	56.06	55.05	56.12	56.94
HT	63.23- 03	63.73	63.72	64.34	64.81	63.77	64.12	64.79	**65.78**
JT	55.55- 00	55.09	55.00	55.07	54.81	55.16	54.98	55.34	**55.97**
Heptathlon	**5741**- 88	5631	5633	5674	5687	5586	5568	5591	5702
20kmW	1:34:11- 05	1:34:32	1:36:01	1:35:57	1:34:30	1:35:54	1:36:32	1:34:52	**1:33:43**

All-time record levels indicated in bold.
! From 2011 main marathon lists no longer include Boston or other such excessively downhill races.

Number of athletes achieving base level standards for world lists:

Women		2007	2008	2009	2010	2011	2012
100m	11.50	183	202	185	171	195	217
200m	23.39	135	166	140	135	146	185
400m	52.99	193	199	169	167	187	210
800m	2:03.5	143	147	153	153	176	196
1500m	4:13.5	131	124	154	163	176	196
5000m	15:45.0	171	178	136	139	163	201
10000m	33:15.0	150	160	144	133	146	200
HMar	72:00	143	143	173	156	174	199
Mar	2:32:00	138	137	143	152	165	212
3000mSt	10:12.0	153	150	147	144	177	199
100mh	13.39	140	156	140	154	177	198

Women		2007	2008	2009	2010	2011	2012
400mh	58.44	178	177	179	169	181	228
HJ	1.85	149	144	136	142	172	164
PV	4.15	147	163	153	156	176	189
LJ	6.35	180	205	181	180	185	212
TJ	13.30	181	189	183	182	191	199
SP	15.85	159	160	159	159	163	180
DT	53.65	146	154	139	144	153	172
HT	61.00	161	179	163	167	181	205
JT	53.00	149	158	154	151	160	177
Hep	5450	157	155	137	126	146	157
20kmW	1:40:00	168	189	163	155	207	214
TOTAL		3455	3688	3431	3387	3782	4311

The 2012 marks compared to those of 2011: for 10th best 19-2 (1 tie), 100th best 21-1, base level 22-0.

	Name		Nat	Born	Ht/Wt	Event	2012 Mark	Pre-2012 Best

MEN'S INDEX 2012

Athletes included are those ranked in the top 100s at standard (World Championships) events (plus shorter lists for 1000m, 1M, 2000m and 3000m). Those with detailed biographical profiles are indicated in first column by:
* in this year's Annual, ^ featured in a previous year's Annual.

	Name		Nat	Born	Ht/Wt	Event	2012 Mark	Pre-2012 Best
	Aarass	Jamel	FRA	15.11.81	187/75	1500	3:34.85	3:37.49- 10
						1M	3:52.21	-0-
	Abate	Emanuele	ITA	8.7.85	190/78	110h	13.28	13.54- 11
	Abdi	Youcef	AUS	7.12.77	178/66	3kSt	8:21.98	8:16.36- 08
	Abe	Takatoshi	JPN	12.11.91	189/82	400h	49.47	49.46- 10
	Abera	Tesfaye	ETH	31.3.92		HMar	60:32	-0-
	Abinet	Abiyot	ETH	10.5.89		1500	3:36.72	3:36.07- 10
						3000	7:43.35i, 7:50.50	7:47.94i- 11
	Aboud	Rabah	ALG	.81	169/54	5000	13:20.99	13:19.00- 11
	Abraham	Joseph	IND	11.9.81	166/66	400h	49.98	49.51- 07
*	Abshero	Ayele	ETH	28.12.90	167/52	HMar	61:11	59:42- 11
						Mar	2:04:23	-0-
	Acosta	Andrew AJ	USA	13.4.88	188/73	1500	3:36.41	3:36.48- 10
	Adams	Antoine	SKN	31.8.88	180/79	100	10.10	10.34, 10.19w- 11
						200	20.43, 20.41w	20.76A- 11, 20.80- 10
	Adams	David	USA	4.1.89	184/70	3kSt	8:27.77	8:40.31- 11
*	Adams	Harry	USA	27.11.89	182/81	100	9.96	10.19- 11, 10.17w- 10
						200	20.10	20.74- 11
^	Adams	Luke	AUS	22.10.76	189/70	20kW	1:22:50	1:19:15- 08
						50kW	3:53:41	3:43:39- 09
*	Adams	Lyukman	RUS	24.9.88	194/87	TJ	17.53	17.32i- 11, 17.17, 17.21w- 10
	Adams	Spencer	USA	10.9.89	188/84	110h	13.39, 13.38w	13.55, 13.48w- 11
*	Adhane	Yemane Tsegay	ETH	8.4.85		Mar	2:04:48	2:06:30- 09
	Adjetey-Nelson	Jamie	CAN	20.5.84	190/86	Dec	7706	8239- 10
	Agyapong	Ashhad	GHA	23.9.85	175/73	200	20.66, 20.38w	20.45- 08
	Ahmed	Mohammed	CAN	5.1.91	180/61	10k	27:34.64	28:57.44- 10
	Aikines-Aryeetey	Harry	GBR	29.8.88	176/86	100	10.20	10.10- 08, 10.09w- 11
	Akashi	Ken	JPN	6.11.76	169/59	50kW	3:51:17	3:50:11- 08
*	Akdag	Tarik Langat	TUR	22.4.89	176/60	3kSt	8:17.85	8:08.59- 11
	Akins	Tyrone	USA	6.1.86	180/79	110h	13.30	13.25- 08, 13.2w- 10
^	Akkas	Halil	TUR	1.7.83	175/60	3kSt	8:30.34	8:18.43- 07
	Akwu	Noah	NGR	23.9.90	181/73	200	20.54	20.91- 10, 20.86i- 11
	Al Outaibi	Moukhled	KSA	20.6.76	174/67	5000	13:02.69	12:58.58- 05
						10k	27:31.61	28:22.13- 10
	Alaiz	Roberto	ESP	20.7.90		3kSt	8:24.53	8:40.82- 11
	Alaka	James	GBR	8.9.89	180/73	200	20.45	20.59- 11
*	Alamirew	Yenew	ETH	27.5.90	175/57	3000	7:31.23i	7:27.26- 11
						5000	12:48.77	13:00.46- 11
	Al-Amri	Ali Ahmed	KSA	28.12.87	186/70	3kSt	8:26.22	8:21.87- 06
^	Al-Azimi	Mohamed	KUW	16.6.82	176/70	800	1:46.48 dq obstruction, 1:47.13	1:44.13- 06
	Albertazzi	Eduardo	ITA	14.9.91	201/98	DT	62.80	57.62- 11
	Alcorn	Kyle	USA	18.3.85	193/80	3kSt	8:20.86	8:21.46- 08
	Al-Dawoodi	Sultan Mubarak	KSA	16.6.77	180/110	DT	65.08	64.55- 06
	Alejandro	Eric	PUR	15.4.86	180/70	400h	49.15	50.16- 11
*	Alekna	Virgilijus	LTU	13.2.72	200/130	DT	70.28	73.88- 00
	Alekseyev	Denis	RUS	26.12.87	185/73	400	45.43	45.35- 08
	Alemayehu	Zebene	ETH	4.9.92	175/57	1500	3:35.11	3:34.59- 11
	Al-Gamal	Mostafa Hicham	EGY	1.10.88	191/96	HT	77.14	74.76- 11
	Al-Garni	Mohamed	QAT	1.7.92	168/57	1000	2:17.32	2:22.32- 09
						1500	3:36.63	3:34.61- 11
	Al-Haddad	Salah	KUW	27.5.86	179/65	LJ	8.01	8.02- 09, 8.05w- 07
	Al-Hamdah	Hussein Jamaan	KSA	4.8.83	170/55	5000	13:17.03	13:11.64- 09
	Al-Hebshi	Sultan	KSA	31.1.85	180/103	SP	19.81	21.13- 09
	Alic	Hamza	BIH	20.1.79	192/108	SP	19.99	20.56- 08
	Al-Joud	Abdullah Abdulaziz	KSA	10.7.75	178/60	5000	13:11.61	13:24.54- 11
	Allen	Joe	USA	7.7.78	196/90	LJ	7.95	8.06- 04
	Alleyne	Richard	GBR	7.5.83	183/80	110h	13.64	13.71- 07, 13.65w- 08
	Al-Mandeel	Abdulaziz	KUW	22.5.89	175/66	110h	13.58, 13.50w	13.78- 10
	Al-Masrahi	Youssef	KSA	31.12.87	176/76	400	45.43	45.44- 11
	Almeida	João	POR	5.4.88	188/79	110h	13.47	13.78, 13.49w- 11
	Al-Momani	Musaeb	JOR	28.8.86	184/110	DT	62.64	62.36- 09
	Al-Shammari	Fawez Dahesh	KUW	3.4.77	185/65	110h	13.48	13.62- 10
	Alvarez	Alberto	MEX	8.3.91	189/72	TJ	16.30, 16.52w	16.20A- 11
	Alves	Higor	BRA-J	23.2.94		LJ	7.96w	7.28, 7.33w- 11
*	Al-Zankawi	Ali Mohamed	KUW	27.2.84	179/100	HT	76.14	79.74- 09
*	Aman	Mohammed	ETH-J	10.1.94	169/55	800	1:42.53	1:43.37- 11

Name		Nat	Born	Ht/Wt	Event	2012 Mark	Pre-2012 Best
Amb	Kim	SWE	18.1.90	180/86	JT	81.84	80.09- 11
* Amos	Nijel	BOT-J	15.3.94	179/60	800	1:41.73	1:47.28- 11
Amundgård	Fredrik	NOR	12.1.89	210/140	DT	62.25	63.72- 10
Anani	Mohsen	EGY	25.5.85	187/117	HT	75.97	77.36- 10
* Anderson	Jeshua	USA	22.6.89	187/84	400h	48.88	47.93- 11
Anderson	Kenroy	JAM	27.6.87	172/64	100	10.20	10.18, 10.15w- 11
					110h	13.65	13.79- 10
* Anderson	Marvin	JAM	12.5.82	175/69	200	20.21	20.06- 07
Andom	Mulue	ERI	12.10.91		10k	28:03.21	29:48.3- 09
Andrews	Robby	USA	29.3.91	177/68	800	1:45.06	1:44.71- 11
					1500	3:34.78	3:40.77- 11
* Andronov	Yuriy	RUS	6.11.71	180/68	50kW	3:40:46	3:42:06- 02
Annani	Adil	MAR	30.6.80		Mar	2:07:43	2:10:15- 09
Anou	Abderrahmane	ALG	29.1.91	172/60	1500	3:35.62	3:35.2- 11
Antmanis	Vladimir	RUS	12.3.84	188/77	400h	49.71	49.74- 07
Antunovic	Bozidar	SRB	24.7.91	198/114	SP	19.85	18.86- 11
Apak	Esref	TUR	3.1.82	185/115	HT	78.28	81.45- 05
Arai	Hiroki	JPN	18.5.88	179/61	20kW	1:21:10	1:22:47- 11
					50kW	3:47:08	3:48:40- 11
Arai	Ken	JPN	22.12.81	172/73	JT	79.90	78.87- 11
Arai	Ryohei	JPN	23.6.91	182/86	JT	78.00	78.21- 11
* Araptany	Jacob	UGA	11.2.92	168/58	3kSt	8:14.48	8:15.72A- 11
Arastu	Ali	USA	18.6.92	188/77	400h	49.43	50.90- 11
de Araújo	Luiz Alberto	BRA	27.9.87	190/90	Dec	8276	8115- 11
Araya	Edward	CHI	14.2.86	177/58	50kW	4:02:03A	4:03:02- 11
Arents	Mareks	LAT	6.6.86	190/85	PV	5.60	5.46- 11
Arévalo	Eider	COL-J	9.3.93	165/58	20kW	1:21:49	-0-
* Arikan	Polat Kembpi	TUR	12.12.90	173/62	3000	7:42.31	7:48.74- 09
5000	13:12.55i		13:05.98- 11		10k	27:38.81	-0-
Aristil	David	USA	12.12.88	183/73	400h	49.54	49.94- 11
Armstrong	Aaron	TRI	14.10.77	173/70	100	10.21,10.06w	10.03- 09,10.00w- 05, 9.8w- 99
* Armstrong	Dylan	CAN	15.1.81	190/125	SP	21.50	22.21- 11
^ Arnold	Jake	USA	3.1.84	191/91	Dec	7840	8253- 10
Arnold	Mike	USA	13.8.90	190/84	PV	5.53A	5.38i, 5.25- 10
Arnold	Seth	USA	29.7.92	186/80	PV	5.51	5.11- 11
Arnos	Zacharias	CYP	24.11.86	186/77	TJ	16.72, 16.73w	16.40- 10
Arrhenius	Leif	SWE	15.7.86	192/120	SP	20.03	19.92i, 19.37- 11
					DT	62.78	64.46- 11
Arrhenius	Niklas	SWE	10.9.82	192/125	SP	19.74i, 19.43	19.91i- 04, 19.79- 11
					DT	64.69	66.22- 11
Arteaga	Mauricio	ECU	8.8.88	178/62	20kW	1:21:56	1:23:46.5t- 11
Arzandeh	Mohammad	IRI	30.10.87	180/76	LJ	8.17	7.95- 09
* Ash	Ronnie	USA	2.7.88	188/86	110h	13.20, 13.10w	13.19, 12.98w- 10
Ashgari	Rouhollah	IRI	8.1.82	183/79	110h	13.50	13.68- 10
* Ashmeade	Nickel	JAM	4.7.90	184/84	100	9.93	9.96- 11
					200	19.85	19.91- 11
Assefa	Belaye	ETH	17.6.92		HMar	60:59	-0-
Assefa	Bentayehu	ETH		167/52	Mar	2:06:22	-0-
Assefa	Habtamu	ETH	29.3.85		HMar	61:09	-0-
Assefa	Raji	ETH	18.2.86		HMar	61:13	60:07- 08
					Mar	2:06:24	2:12:12- 11
Atanasov	Zlatozar	BUL	12.12.89		TJ	16.73	16.39- 11
Atici	Hüseyin	TUR	3.5.86	188/118	SP	20.42	18.96- 11
Atine-Venel	Teddy	FRA	16.3.85	184/77	400	45.57	45.54- 08
^ Atkins	Derrick	BAH	5.1.84	185/84	100	10.08	9.91, 9.83w- 07
Atnafu	Yitayal	ETH-J	20.1.93	172/55	3000	7:39.78i	8:01.22- 10
					5000	13:08.13, 13:04.18i	13:16.30- 11
Aucyna	Darius	LTU	7.5.89	193/80	LJ	8.11A	7.92, 7.96w- 11
					TJ	16.84	16.23, 16.25w- 11
Augustyn	Rafal	POL	14.5.84	177/71	20kW	1:20:53	1:20:57- 11
					50kW	3:49:53	3:46:56- 11
Aurokium	Jean-François	FRA	14.4.81	192/92	DT	60.95	62.38- 10
Austin	Justin	USA	8.10.89	186/80	200	20.55	20.46, 20.31w- 11
Auzeil	Bastien	FRA	22.10.89	190/82	Dec	8008	7683- 11
* Avan	Fatih	TUR	1.1.89	183/90	JT	85.60	84.79- 11
* Avramenko	Roman	UKR	23.3.88	185/90	JT	81.87	84.30- 11
Awde	Daniel	GBR	22.6.88	182/75	Dec	8102	7889- 11
Awoke	Esrael	ETH-J	5.4.94		800	1:46.5A	1:47.3A- 11
Ayeko	Simon	UGA	10.5.87	178/62	3kSt	8:23.62	8:18.04- 09
Ayeko	Thomas	UGA	10.2.92	168/58	5000	13:23.25	13:31.32- 11
					10k	27:43.22	28:27.54A- 11

	Name		Nat	Born	Ht/Wt	Event	2012 Mark	Pre-2012 Best
	Azie	Stanley	NGR	13.3.89	170/66	100	10.27, 10.18w	10.20- 11
	Baaru	Philemon	KEN	20.5.81		Mar	2:07:49	2:09:51- 11
*	Bába	Jaroslav	CZE	2.9.84	196/82	HJ	2.31i, 2.28	2.37i, 2.36- 05
	Baciu	Alexandru George	ROU	25.2.91	186/65	TJ	16.56	16.44- 11
^	Baddeley	Andrew	GBR	20.6.82	186/70	1500	3:35.19	3:34.36- 08
	3000	7:39.86			7:42.75- 10	5000	13:22.44i	13:20.85- 10
*	Badji	Ndiss Kaba	SEN	21.9.83	192/79	LJ	8.17	8.32- 09
	Bailey	Aldrich	USA-J	6.2.94	183/70	200	20.78, 20.49w	21.09- 11
						400	45.19	46.53- 11
^	Bailey	Daniel	ANT	9.9.86	173/70	100	10.10	9.91- 09
	Bailey	Oshane	JAM	9.8.89	168/64	100	10.12, 10.06w	10.11- 10
*	Bailey	Ryan	USA	13.4.89	193/98	100	9.88	9.88- 10
						200	20.43	20.10- 10
*	Bailey-Cole	Kemar	JAM	10.1.92	193/83	100	9.97	10.28- 11
	Baillio	Hayden	USA	22.7.91	186/141	SP	19.92	19.51- 11
	Bairu	Simon	CAN	8.8.83	173/57	10k	27:58.05	27:23.63- 10
	Baji	Balázs	HUN	9.6.89	192/84	110h	13.50	13.58- 11
*	Bakulin	Sergey	RUS	13.11.86	169/58	50kW	3:38:55	3:38:46- 11
	Balashov	Dmitriy	RUS	19.1.89		3kSt	8:29.17	8:41.26- 11
	Balla	Abdulrahman Musaeb	QAT	19.3.89	175/60	800	1:45.19	1:45.92- 11
	Balliengo	Jorge	ARG	5.1.78	194/110	DT	63.30	66.32- 06
	Balner	Michal	CZE	12.9.82	193/78	PV	5.45, 5.66ex	5.76i, 5.73- 10
	Balnuweit	Erik	GER	21.9.88	189/80	110h	13.46	13.49- 11
	Baloyes	Bernardo	COL-J	6.1.94	177/66	200	20.48A	21.17A, 21.11Aw- 11
	Balumbu	Nkosinza	USA	16.3.87	175/64	TJ	16.49Ai, 16.49, 16.86w	16.59- 10, 16.77w- 11
*	Baniótis	KonstadÌnos	GRE	6.11.86	202/80	HJ	2.31i, 2.25	2.32i, 2.28- 11
*	Bannister	Jarrod	AUS	3.10.84	190/100	JT	83.70	89.02- 08
	Banzeruk	Ivan	UKR	9.2.90		50kW	3:56:20	4:06:52- 11
	Barák	Václav	CZE	22.10.90		400h	50.04	51.85- 11
	Barber	Shawn	CAN-J	27.5.94	190/82	PV	5.58i, 5.57	5.03- 11
	Barbiasz	Dwight	USA	16.7.90	186/77	HJ	2.28	2.23- 11
	Barnaby	Daundre	CAN	9.12.90	189/75	400	45.67	46.35- 09
	Barrefors	Björn	SWE	27.10.87	183/82	Dec	7897	7689- 09
	Barrios	Juan Luis	MEX	24.6.83	175/63	5000	13:13.54	13:09.81- 11
						10k	27:28.82	27:30.68- 11
	Barroilhet	Gonzalo	CHI	19.8.86	196/96	Dec	8065	7986A- 11, 7907- 08
	Barron	Trevor	USA	30.9.92	191/73	20kW	1:22:13, 1:23:00.10t	1:24:51- 11
*	Barrondo	Erick	GUA	14.6.91	172/60	20kW	1:18:25	1:20:58- 11
						50kW	3:44:59	-0-
*	de Barros	Bruno	BRA	7.1.87	178/70	200	20.37	20.16- 11
*	Barry	Trevor	BAH	14.6.83	190/77	HJ	2.31i, 2.31	2.32- 11
*	Barshim	Mutaz Essa	QAT	24.6.91	192/70	HJ	2.39	2.35- 11
*	Bartels	Ralf	GER	21.2.78	186/138	SP	20.40	21.44i- 10, 21.37- 09
	Barusei	Geoffrey	KEN-J	.94	164/53	1500	3:33.39	3:35.54- 11
	Bascom	Jeremy	GUY	15.10.83	170/73	100	10.19	10.47A- 08
	Bascou	Dimitri	FRA	20.7.87	182/81	110h	13.34	13.37, 13.26w- 11
	Bassaw	Ben	FRA	9.7.89	183/77	100	10.20w	10.53, 10.46w- 11
	Bastian	Rudon	BAH	13.1.87	183/73	LJ	8.00w	7.87i, 7.80, 7.98w- 10
	Batson	DionDre	USA	13.7.92	188/75	100	10.27, 10.10w	10.55, 10.40w- 11
						200	20.50	21.16- 11
	Bauer	Candy	GER	31.7.86	190/110	SP	20.10i, 19.77	19.98- 11
*	Bayer	Sebastian	GER	11.6.86	189/79	LJ	8.34	8.71i, 8.49- 09
	Beach	Curtis	USA	22.7.90	183/76	Dec	7764	8083- 11
	Bednyuk	Anatoliy	RUS	30.1.89		PV	5.55	5.50i- 11, 5.30- 09
*	Behrenbruch	Pascal	GER	19.1.85	196/94	Dec	8558	8439- 09
	Bekele	Alemu	BRN	23.3.90	163/50	5000	13:21.54	13:38.10- 10
						10k	27:56.20	28:41.23- 11
	Bekele	Azmeraw	ETH	22.1.86	171/55	10k	27:49.16	28:20.61- 11
						HMar	60:49	59:39- 11
	Bekele	Feyisa	ETH	.83	170/55	Mar	2:06:26	-0-
*	Bekele	Kenenisa	ETH	13.6.82	162/54	3000	7:40.00	7:25.79- 07
	5000	12:55.79			12:37.35- 04	10k	27:02.59	26:17.53- 05
*	Bekele	Tariku	ETH	21.1.87	168/62	3000	7:37.0+i	7:28.70- 10
	2M	8:08.27i		5000	12:54.13	12:52.45- 08	10k	27:03.24	-0-
	Bekric	Emir	SRB	14.3.91	196/87	400h	49.21	49.55- 11
	Belabbas	Mohamed-Khaled	ALG	4.7.81	178/65	3kSt	8:22.32	8:17.37- 08
	Belay	Andualem	ETH	5.4.92		HMar	60:10	-0-
	Bell	Javere	JAM	20.9.92	184/73	400	45.78	46.54- 11
	Bellido	José Emilio	ESP	25.5.87	180/68	TJ	16.80A, 16.65	16.55- 11
	Benák	Martin	SVK	27.5.88	193/98	JT	78.97	79.90- 10
	Benard	Chris	USA	4.4.90	190/79	TJ	16.74	15.75- 11

Name		Nat	Born	Ht/Wt	Event	2012 Mark	Pre-2012 Best
Bencosme de Leon	José	ITA	16.5.92	187/73	400h	49.33	49.94- 11
Benedetti	Giordano	ITA	22.5.89	189/67	800	1:45.34	1:46.32- 11
Bensghir	Yassine	MAR	3.1.83	170/68	1000	2:17.21	2:16.27- 07
					1500	3:34.50	3:33.04- 07
Benyahia	Amor	TUN	1.7.85	176/54	3kSt	8:22.70	8:30.02- 11
Berdeja	Cristian David	MEX	21.6.81	169/58	50kW	3:52:18A	3:56:26A- 10
Berger	Dominic	USA	19.5.86	181/79	110h	13.44	13.32- 11
Berger	Maik	GER	17.2.79	190/74	50kW	3:59:10	3:54:24- 07
Bergius	Jere	FIN	4.4.87	182/72	PV	5.72	5.60- 11
Bernard	Martyn	GBR	15.12.84	196/83	HJ	2.28	2.30i- 07, 2.30- 08
Berry	Michael	USA	10.12.91	184/73	400	44.75	44.91- 11
* Betanzos	Yoandris	CUB	15.2.82	179/71	TJ	16.87	17.69i- 10, 17.65- 09, 17.67w- 06
Bett	David	KEN	18.10.92	169/54	5000	13:09.84	13:06.06- 10
* Bett	Emmanuel	KEN	30.3.83	170/55	5000	13:08.35	13:27e- 11
*	10k				10k	26:51.16	26:51.95- 11
					HMar	60:56dh	62:10- 11
Bett	Josphat	KEN	12.6.90	173/60	10k	27:39.65	26:48.99- 11
	5000				5000	13:35.5A	12:57.43- 09
					HMar	61:01	-0-
Bett	Reuben	KEN	6.11.84	180/70	800	1:45.44	1:44.79- 09
Beugnet	Grégory	FRA	14.9.87	173/64	1500	3:36.46	3:36.71- 11
Bian Fongda		CHN	1.4.91		20kW	1:22:53	1:22:42- 11
Bigot	Quentin	FRA	1.12.92	179/95	HT	78.28	72.71- 11
* Birech	Jairus	KEN	14.12.92	165/54	3kSt	8:03.43	8:11.31- 11
* Birgen	Bethwel	KEN	6.8.88	178/64	1500	3:31.00	3:34.59- 11
					1M	3:50.43	3:56.22- 11
Birke	Merkebu	ETH	.88		HMar	60:14	-0-
Birmingham	Collis	AUS	27.12.84	189/71	1500	3:35.74	3:35.50- 10
	3000				3000	7:35.45	7:38.77- 10
					5000	13:09.57	13:10.97- 10
	10k				10k	28:06.63	27:29.73- 09
					HMar	61:25dh	65:46- 08
Biron	Emmanuel	FRA	29.7.88	178/65	100	10.28, 10.10w	10.29- 11
Bishop	Brian	USA	16.4.89	188/110	DT	61.20	59.35- 11
Bispo	Rogério	BRA	16.11.85	180/75	LJ	8.05, 8.11w	8.21, 8.32Aw- 06
* Biwott	Stanley	KEN	21.4.86		HMar	59:44	60:23- 11
					Mar	2:05:12	2:07:03- 11
Blaise	Kyron	TRI	3.10.89	180/73	TJ	16.49, 16.53w	16.36i- 11, 16.11- 10
* Blake	Yohan	JAM	26.12.89	181/79	100	9.69	9.82, 9.80w- 11
					200	19.44	19.26- 11
Blakely	Fernada	USA	28.9.81	185/79	200	20.55	20.52- 05
* Bledman	Keston	TRI	8.3.88	183/75	100	9.86, 9.85w	9.93- 11
Blocki	Adrian	POL	11.4.90	173/63	50kW	3:54:41	3:56:27- 10
Blocki	Damian	POL	28.4.89	180/65	50kW	3:55:51	-0-
Boase	Jordan	USA	10.10.85	181/75	400	45.61	44.82- 08
Bochenek	Dominik	POL	14.5.87	182/70	110h	13.59	13.44- 11, 13.3w- 10
Boey	Zye	USA	8.5.89	178/82	100	10.15	10.20- 09, 10.15w- 11
					200	20.51, 20.37w	20.67- 11
Bogatyrev	Pyotr	RUS	11.3.91		20kW	1:20:51	1:20:18- 11
Bolas	John	USA	1.11.87	183/72	1500	3:36.33	3:37.64- 09
* Bolt	Usain	JAM	21.8.86	196/93	100	9.63	9.58- 09
					200	19.32	19.19- 09
Boltenkov	Anton	RUS	29.6.85		TJ	16.60	16.63- 07
Bondarenko	Bogdan	UKR	30.8.89	197/80	HJ	2.31	2.30- 11
Bonevacia	Liemarvin	CUR	5.4.89	190/79	400	45.60	46.58- 11
Bonfim	Caio	BRA	19.3.91	170/58	20kW	1:21:36, 1:23:22.83t	1:20:58.5t- 11
Boni	Marco	ITA	21.5.84	182/80	PV	5.60i	5.40- 09
Bonvecchio	Norbert	ITA	14.8.85	181/75	JT	79.22	75.52- 11
Bookout	Kevin	USA	16.3.83	203/118	SP	20.20	20.13- 11
* Borchin	Valeriy	RUS	11.9.86	178/63	20kW	1:21:29	1:17:38- 09
Boreysho	Pavel	BLR	16.2.91	193/105	HT	72.25	69.62- 11
* Borges	Lázaro	CUB	19.6.86	173/70	PV	5.72i, 5.60	5.90- 11
* Borlée	Jonathan	BEL	22.2.88	180/70	200	20.31	20.42- 11
					400	44.43	44.71- 10
* Borlée	Kévin	BEL	22.2.88	180/71	400	44.56	44.74- 11
Borodkin	Andriy	UKR	18.4.78	202/135	SP	19.86	20.38- 04
Bortoluzzi	Jérôme	FRA	20.5.82	180/111	HT	78.26	77.33- 08
Boruschewski	Benjamin	GER	23.4.80	190/130	HT	72.66	76.19- 09
* Borzakovskiy	Yuriy	RUS	12.4.81	182/72	800	1:45.09	1:42.47- 01
Bosse	Pierre-Ambroise	FRA	11.5.92	185/68	800	1:44.97	1:46.18- 11
Boujattaoui	Chakir	MAR	16.1.83	180/66	5000	13:21.38	13:05.65- 10
^ Boukensa	Tarek	ALG	19.11.81	178/62	1500	3:35.87	3:30.92- 07
Bouqantar	Soufiyan	MAR-J	30.8.93	173/54	5000	13:19.59	13:38.73- 11
Bourguignon	Rudy	FRA	16.7.79	185/82	Dec	7670	8025- 05
Bowen	Francis	KEN	12.10.73		Mar	2:08:21	2:10:41- 07

Name		Nat	Born	Ht/Wt	Event	2012 Mark	Pre-2012 Best
Boyce	Brendan	IRL	15.10.86	183/76	50kW	3:55:01	3:57:58- 11
Boyd	Marcus	USA	3.3.89	185/75	200	20.56w	21.24- 07, 20.47w- 11
					400	45.68	45.42- 11
Bracy	Marvin	USA-J	15.12.93	178/74	100	10.25, 10.06w	10.28, 10.05w- 11
Brannen	Nathan	CAN	8.9.82	175/59	1000	2:16.52	2:17.34- 08
800	1:46.74A		1:46.00- 02		1500	3:34.22	3:34.65- 08
* Brathwaite	Ryan	BAR	6.6.88	186/75	110h	13.23	13.14, 13.05w- 09
Brathwaite	Shane	BAR	8.2.90	185/75	110h	13.31A, 13.46, 13.43w	13.58- 11
Braun	Aaron	USA	28.5.87	183/65	5000	13:20.25	13:27.01- 11
					10k	27:41.54	27:57.88- 11
Bravo	Albert	VEN	29.8.87	198/85	400	45.61	46.04- 11
Bray	Wesley	USA	11.4.88	180/80	Dec	7932(w)	7571(w)- 11
Brednev	Aleksandr	RUS	12.2.88	184/73	100	10.19	10.38- 10
* Brenes	Nery	CRC	25.9.85	174/62	400	45.20, 45.11i	44.65A- 11, 44.84- 10
Broadbent	Eric	USA	5.8.85	190/77	Dec	7750w/7730	7558- 11
Brock	Keenan	USA	1.6.92	172/64	100	10.09	10.21, 10.12w- 11
					200	20.47	20.77- 11
Brookins	Ronald	USA	5.7.89	185/75	110h	13.69, 13.63w	13.42- 11
Brooks	Lance	USA	1.1.84	198/123	DT	65.15	64.79A- 10
Broothaerts	Damien	BEL	12.11.84	180/74	110h	13.69, 13.64w	13.62- 09, 13.53w- 11
Brown	Aaron	CAN	27.5.92	185/79	100	10.18, 10.09w	10.38, 10.25w- 11
					200	20.42	21.00- 11
* Brown	Chris	BAH	15.10.78	178/68	400	44.67	44.40- 08
* Brown	Joel	USA	31.1.80	180/73	110h	13.23 13.20- 11, 13.18w- 09, 13.1w- 10	
Brown	Russell	USA	3.3.85	188/77	1500	3:34.11	3:35.70- 11
					1M	3:54.08i, 3:54.48	3:51.45- 11
Bruce	Benjamin	USA	10.9.82	185/68	3kSt	8:26.08	8:19.10- 11
Brugger	Mathias	GER	6.8.92	192/93	Dec	7942	-0-
Brummer	Dean	RSA	15.9.88	180/66	3kSt	8:29.98	8:35.86- 11
Brunson	Andrew	USA	4.4.86	182/75	110h	13.64	13.33- 08
Bryant	Ashley	GBR	17.5.91	178/75	Dec	7837	7789- 11
Bryant	Luke	USA	5.12.88	188/110	DT	62.70	59.39- 10
Bryant	Noah	USA	11.5.84	185/120	SP	19.52	20.80- 11
Bube	Andreas	DEN	13.7.87	178/65	800	1:44.89	1:45.04- 11
Bubenik	Matús	SVK	14.11.89	196/77	HJ	2.25i, 2.20	2.21i- 10, 2.15- 09
Buck	Richard	GBR	14.11.86	191/92	400	45.61	45.99- 11
Budza	Sergiy	UKR	6.12.84	180/72	50kW	3:53:02	3:53:33- 09
Buhari	Abdul	GBR	26.6.82	192/125	DT	65.24	65.44- 11
Bühler	Matthias	GER	2.9.86	189/78	110h	13.34	13.36- 09, 13.2w- 10
Bultheel	Michaïl	BEL	30.6.86	186/76	400h	49.10	49.38- 10
Bumbalough	Andrew	USA	14.3.87	173/64	3000	7:44.71, 7:44.45i	7:51.87- 10
					5000	13:16.26	13:16.77- 11
^ Burns	Marc	TRI	7.1.83	183/88	100	10,00	9.96- 05
Burrows	Chris	USA	15.3.90	173/73	200	20.65, 20.54w	20.90- 11
Burya	Artem	RUS	11.4.86	183/77	PV	5.60	5.50- 08
Bustamante	Luis	MEX	10.6.84		50kW	3:59:17A	4:17:11- 10
Bustos	David	ESP	25.8.90	182/65	1500	3:34.77	3:39.09- 11
Butler	Kind	USA	8.4.89	183/75	200	20.36	20.76- 11
					400	45.43	46.37- 11
Bychkov	Igor	ESP	7.3.87	188/77	PV	5.56	5.60- 11
Byram	Brandon	USA	11.9.88	188/82	200	20.75, 20.38w	20.31- 10
Byun Young-jun		KOR	20.3.84	175/57	20kW	1:21:42	1:22:07- 10
Cabral	Donn	USA	12.12.89	175/60	3kSt	8:19.14	8:32.14- 11
Cabral	Johnathan	CAN/USA	31.12.92	193/82	110h	13.45	-0-
^ Cáceres	Eusebio	ESP	10.9.91	176/69	LJ	8.06, 8.31w	8.27- 10
* Cadée	Erik	NED	15.2.84	201/120	DT	67.30	66.95- 11
* Cai Zelin		CHN	11.4.91	172/55	20kW	1:18:47	1:21:07- 11
Cain	Stephen	AUS	23.7.84	180/75	Dec	7844	7734- 11
Caldeira	Marcos	POR	27.2.88	175/70	TJ	16.44, 16.84w	16.23- 11, 16.41w- 09
Callender	Emmanuel	TRI	10.5.84	184/79	100	10.07	10.05- 09
Camara	Alyn	GER	31.3.89	195/85	LJ	8.20	8.08- 11
Campioli	Filippo	ITA	21.2.82	192/82	HJ	2.27i, 2.25	2.30i- 08, 2.30- 09
Cano	Juan Manuel	ARG	12.12.87	168/57	20kW	1:22:10	1:23.09.0t- 11
* Cantwell	Christian	USA	30.9.80	193/154	SP	22.31	22.54- 04
Cao Shuo		CHN	8.10.91	183/69	TJ	17.35	17.13- 09
Capetillo	Dayron	CUB	11.9.87	185/77	110h	13.69, 13.2	13.46, 13.39w- 09, 13.2- 08
Caporaso	Teodorico	ITA	14.9.87	166/60	50kW	3:59:19	4:01:00- 11
Carter	Chris	USA	10.4.87	188/75	400h	50.08	49.19- 06
Carter	Chris	USA	11.3.89	186/80	TJ	16.61	16.86- 11
* Carter	Nesta	JAM	10.11.85	178/70	100	9.95	9.78- 10
					200	20.37	20.25- 11

Name		Nat	Born	Ht/Wt	Event	2012 Mark	Pre-2012 Best
* Casañas	Frank	ESP	18.10.78	187/115	DT	67.74	67.91- 08
Cassimiro Rosa	Jean	BRA	1.2.90		TJ	16.53	16.34- 11
Castillo	Mauris Surel	CUB	19.10.84	182/60	800	1:44.89	1:45.11- 11
					1500	3:35.03	3:38.88- 09
Castro	Luis Joel	PUR	28.1.91		HJ	2.25A	2.15- 11
Cato	Roxroy	JAM	1.5.88	175/66	400h	49.03	49.45- 10
Cavalcanti	Diego Henrique	BRA	18.3.91	175/68	200	20.40	20.57- 11
Celik	Recep	TUR	10.8.83	175/65	20kW	1:23:10	1:22:31- 11
* Centrowitz	Matthew	USA	18.10.89	176/61	1500	3:31.96	3:34.46- 11
1M	3:53.92i, 3:57.44		3:57.92i- 09		3K	7:46.19i	7:50.59i- 11
Cerra	Juan Ignacio	ARG	16.10.76	180/95	HT	74.75	76.42- 01
Chafausipo	Clive	ZIM	2.6.88	178/75	LJ	7.82, 8.06w	7.83, 8.09w- 11
^ Chambers	Dwain	GBR	5.4.78	180/83	100	10.02	9.97- 99, 9.87dq- 02
^ Chambers	Ricardo	JAM	7.10.84	177/73	400	45.71	44.54- 10
Chanchaima	Jairus	KEN	5.12.84	180/67	HMar	60:46	59:43- 09
					Mar	2:07:43	2:13:53- 11
Chane	Abera	ETH	10.5.85		HMar	61:11	61:56- 10
Chang Ming-Huang		TPE	7.8.82	194/130	SP	20.25	20.58- 11
^ Charfreitag	Libor	SVK	11.9.77	191/117	HT	75.01	81.81- 03
Chavkin	Nikolay	RUS	22.4.84	183/70	3kSt	8:22.81	8:26.03- 11
* Chebet	Wilson	KEN	12.7.85	174/59	Mar	2:05:41	2:05:27- 11
Chebii	Daniel	KEN	28.5.85		HMar	59:49	60:56- 11
Chebii	Ezekiel	KEN	3.1.91		HMar	59:05	61:40- 11
* Cheboi	Collins	KEN	25.9.87	175/64	1500	3:32.08	3:32.45- 11
1M	3:51.44				2k	5:00.30+	-0-
Chelanga	Samuel	KEN	23.2.85	168/57	5000	13:09.67	13:24.73- 08, 13:19.79i- 09
10k	27:29.82		27:08.39- 10		HMar	61:19	-0-
* Chelimo	Elijah	KEN	10.3.84	175/57	3kSt	8:12.84	8:10.63- 09
Chelimo	Kevin	KEN	14.2.83	168/55	5000	13:14.57	13:30.55- 10
					10k	27:46.10	27:30.50- 11
Chelimo	Paul	KEN	27.10.90	170/57	5000	13:21.89	13:53.02- 11
Chemlal	Jaouad	MAR-J	11.4.94		3kSt	8:25.98	8:36.68- 11
Chemut	Anthony	KEN	17.12.92	170/57	800	1:43.96A	1:45.74- 11
Chen Chieh		TPE	8.5.92	174/55	400h	49.68	50.14- 11
* Chen Ding		CHN	5.8.92	180/62	20kW	1:17:40	1:18:52- 11
Chen Qi		CHN	10.3.82	189/92	JT	77.78	81.38- 04
Chen Zongliang		CHN	9.1.92		20kW	1:22:30	1:24:00- 11
Cheng Wen		CHN	18.3.92	187/77	400h	49.59	49.28- 11
* Chepkok	Vincent	KEN	5.7.88	174/60	3000	7:35.04	7:30.15- 11
5000	12:59.28		12:51.45- 10		10k	26:51.68	28:23.46- 06
Chepkwony	Frankline	KEN	15.6.84		Mar	2:06:11	2:11:00A- 11
Chepkwony	Gilbert	KEN	28.8.85		Mar	2:08:16	2:08:33- 10
Cheprot	Simon	KEN-J	2.7.93		HMar	61:07	64:08- 12
* Chepseba	Nixon	KEN	12.12.90	185/66	800	1:45.6A	1:46.82- 11
					1500	3:29.77	3:30.94- 11
Chesani	Silvano	ITA	17.7.88	190/75	HJ	2.31i, 2.22	2.28- 11
Chesari	Jacob	KEN	6.4.84	178/64	5000	13:02.94	12:59.72- 10
					10k	27:19.70	27:32.43- 10
Chesebe	Abednego	KEN	.82		1500	3:35.02A	3:43.1A- 09
Chiari	Andrea	ITA	12.2.91	186/70	TJ	16.85i, 16.83	16.39- 10
* Chimsa	Deressa	ETH	21.11.86	175/62	HMar	60:51	61:44- 11
					Mar	2:05:42	2:07:39wdh- 11. 2:07:54- 09
Chinedu	Patrick	NGR	26.4.84	170/64	100	10.20	10.34- 11
Chirchir	Abraham	KEN	1.8.80	173/59	3kSt	8:26.12	8:19.81- 08
Chirlee	Joseph	USA	14.2.80	165/55	10k	27:43.96	29:06.4A- 05
Chmielak	Hubert	POL	19.6.89	188/88	JT	78.45	77.48- 10
Chocho	Andrés	CAN	28.9.90	167/57	50kW	3:49:26	3:49:32- 11
* Choge	Augustine	KEN	21.1.87	162/53	3000	7:30.42, 7:29.94i	7:28.00i, 7:28.76- 11
1500	3:37.47		3:29.47- 09		5000	13:15.50	12:53.66- 05
Chomesin	Robert	KEN	.89		HMar	60:23	-0-
Christensen	Kim	DEN	1.4.84	187/115	SP	20.02	20.39i, 20.06- 11
Chumba	Dickson	KEN	27.10.86	167/50	Mar	2:05:46	2:07:23- 11
Chumo	Victor	KEN	19.3.87		5000	13:12.67	-0-
Churyla	Andrey	BLR-J	19.5.93	190/72	HJ	2.28	2.18- 11
Chuva	Marcos	POR	8.8.89	182/75	LJ	8.00i, 7.96	8.34- 11
Cienfuegos	Javier	ESP	15.7.90	188/120	HT	76.21	75.31- 11
* Cisneros	Omar	CUB	19.11.89	186/80	400	45.47	45.76- 09, 45.7- 08, 44.8dt- 07
					400h	48.23	47.99A- 11, 48.21- 10
^ Clark	Charles	USA	10.8.87	178/74	200	20.78, 20.38w	20.22- 08, 20.00w- 09
Clark	Jonathan	USA	15.12.88	190/77	TJ	16.50	16.17- 11
Clark	Matthew	USA	31.5.87	181/78	Dec	7684	7785- 09

Name		Nat	Born	Ht/Wt	Event	2012 Mark	Pre-2012 Best
Clarke	Jordan	USA	10.7.90	193/125	SP	20.86i, 20.40	19.75- 11
Clarke	Kemar	USA	20.5.88	178/70	110h	13.80, 13.65w	13.78- 11
* Clarke	Lawrence	GBR	12.3.90	187/78	110h	13.31, 13.14w	13.58- 11, 13.51w- 10
* Clarke	Lerone	JAM	2.10.81	174/66	100	9.99	9.99- 09, 9.90w- 11
^ Clavier	Jérôme	FRA	3.5.83	185/73	PV	5.55	5.81i- 11, 5.75- 08
Clay	Major	USA	24.12.88	181/76	HJ	2.26i	2.25i, 2.22- 11
* Claye	Will	USA	13.6.91	180/68	LJ	8.25	8.29- 11
					TJ	17.70i, 17.62	17.50, 17.62w- 11
Clémenceau	Adrien	FRA	25.5.88	186/76	400h	49.70	49.72- 11
* Clement	Kerron	USA	31.10.85	188/84	400h	48.12	47.24- 05
Clemons	Kyle	USA	27.8.90	181/73	400	45.44	45.98- 10
Cobbo	Guilherme	BRA	1.10.87	185/65	HJ	2.28	2.22- 11
Cocioran	Marius	ROU	10.7.83	178/76	50kW	3:57:52	4:14:07- 08
Coco-Viloin	Samuel	FRA	19.10.87	186/76	110h	13.50	13.46- 08
Coertzen	Willem	RSA	30.12.82	186/80	Dec	8244	8146- 09
Cole	Brendan	AUS	29.5.81	187/81	400h	49.24	49.35- 09
Coleman	Michael	USA	26.1.87	183/75	200	20.55	20.68- 08
Collie-Minns	Latario	BAH-J	10.3.94		TJ	16.64, 16.66w	16.55- 11
* Collins	Kim	SKN	5.4.76	173/66	100	10.01, 9.96w	9.98- 02, 9.92w- 03
Colvert	Steven	IRL	24.8.90	187/77	200	20.57, 20.40w	20.76, 20.73w- 11
Colwick	Jason	USA	25.1.88	182/77	PV	5.53i	5.72- 09
* Compaoré	Benjamin	FRA	5.8.87	189/86	TJ	17.17	17.31- 11
Connaughton	Jared	CAN	20.7.85	175/77	100	10.19, 10.16w	10.15- 08, 10.04w- 11
					200	20.30	20.34- 08
Conwell	Will	USA	12.9.82	196/111	DT	63.37	63.61- 07
Copeland	Leslie	FIJ	23.4.88	186/94	JT	80.19	80.45- 11
* Copello	Alexis	CUB	12.8.85	185/80	TJ	17.17	17.68A- 11, 17.65, 17.69w- 09
Corchete	Luis Manuel	ESP	14.5.84	185/74	50kW	3:59:58	4:05:25- 11
Correa	Harold	FRA	26.6.88	190/78	TJ	16.76	16.54i- 11, 16.43- 10
Cotto	Héctor	PUR	8.8.84	190/81	110h	13.69, 13.50w 13.49A, 13.45w- 11, 13.54- 10
Cotton	Terrel	USA	19.7.88	182/73	200	20.48A, 20.39Aw, 20.66, 20.62w	20.80- 09
Coulibaly	Toumane	FRA	6.1.88	190/80	400	45.74	46.64- 11
Couto	Kurt	MOZ	14.5.85	180/71	400h	49.02	49.12- 07
Cowart	Donnie	USA	24.10.85	170/60	3kSt	8:26.51	8:26.38- 11
Craddock	Kevin	USA	25.6.87	193/84	110h	13.42	13.46, 13.41w- 08
Craddock	Omar	USA	26.4.91	178/79	TJ	16.75i, 16.71, 16.92w	16.57i- 11, 16.56- 10
Cralle	Chris	USA	13.6.88	183/109	HT	74.36	71.09- 10
^ Crawford	Shawn	USA	14.1.78	181/86	200	20.48, 20.32w	19.79- 04, 19.73w- 09
Cremona	Orazio	RSA	1.7.89		SP	19.76	19.29- 10
Cronje	Johan	RSA	13.4.82	180/65	1500	3:35.33	3:33.63- 09
Crouser	Ryan	USA	18.12.92	201/109	SP	20.29i, 19.32	19.48i- 11
Crouser	Sam	USA	31.12.91	196/102	JT	80.80	77.84- 10
Cuesta	Pedro José	ESP	22.8.83	187/108	DT	61.17	61.95- 11
Cuevas	Winder	DOM	1.8.88	170/65	400h	50.15	49.20A- 11, 49.71- 10
Cuharenco	Alexandr	MDA	7.3.87	183/77	LJ	8.09i, 7.96	7.97- 11
^ Cui Zhide		CHN	11.1.83	182/73	50kW	3:54:42	3:44:20- 05
* Culson	Javier	PUR	25.7.84	198/79	400h	47.78	47.72- 10
Cunningham	Logan	USA	30.5.91	183/80	PV	5.53	5.25- 11
Curry	Tommy	USA	8.4.89	183/75	100	10.12wA	10.71- 09, 10.50w- 08
					200	20.51wA	21.33- 08
Curtis	Bobby	USA	28.11.84	182/68	3000	7:43.65	7:50.17i- 08, 7:57.28- 10
					10k	27:58.48	27:24.67- 11
Czajkowski	Przemyslaw	POL	26.10.88	190/100	DT	65.61	64.42- 10
^ Czerwinski	Przemyslaw	POL	28.7.83	185/80	PV	5.62	5.82i- 10, 5.80- 06
Dabo	Rasul	POR	14.2.89	183/73	110h	13.64, 13.62w	13.86, 13.60w- 11
Dacha	Abdellah	MAR	26.1.92		3kSt	8:28.77	8:34.48- 10
Dadi	Yami	ETH	.82		Mar	2:05:41	2:11:04- 11
Dahm	Tobias	GER	23.5.87	203/117	SP	19.56	18.63- 10
Daianu	Adrian	ROU	27.11.87	175/64	TJ	16.49	16.42- 07
Dal Molin	Paolo	ITA	31.7.87	179/76	110h	13.64	13.67- 11
* Darien	Garfield	FRA	22.12.87	187/76	110h	13.15	13.34- 10
Darwish	Mohammed Abbas	UAE	28.3.86	176/64	TJ	16.78	16.80- 10
* Dasaolu	James	GBR	5.9.87	180/75	100	10.13	10.09- 09, 10.06w- 10
Davenport	Richard	GBR	12.9.85	180/78	400h	49.93	49.76- 11
Davide	Kléberson	BRA	20.7.85	175/67	800	1:45.32	1:44.21- 11
^ Davis	Walter	USA	2.7.79	188/83	TJ	16.85	17.73i, 17.71- 06
Davis II	Wayne	USA/TRI	22.8.91	178/72	110h	13.37, 13.26w	13.54- 11
Dawud	Nassir	ERI	.91	170/55	5000	13:21.66	13:29.54- 10
de Beer	Willie	RSA	14.3.88	188/73	400	45.67	45.68A, 45.87- 11
De Luca	Marco	ITA	12.5.81	189/72	50kW	3:47:19	3:46:31- 09
de Oliveira	Pedro	BRA	17.2.92	180/80	400	45.52	46.33- 11

	Name		Nat	Born	Ht/Wt	Event	2012 Mark	Pre-2012 Best
*	de Zordo	Matthias	GER	21.2.88	190/97	JT	81.62	88.36- 11
	Deák Nagy	Marcell	HUN	28.1.92	188/79	400	45.52	45.42- 11
^	Deakes	Nathan	AUS	17.8.77	183/66	50kW	3:48:45	3:35:47- 06
	Dean	Genki	JPN	30.12.91	182/88	JT	84.28	79.20- 11
	DeChant	Matt	USA	31.5.89	195/115	SP	19.57	19.82i- 11, 18.54- 10
	Dechasa	Shumi	ETH	28.5.89		HMar	59:51	60:03- 11
						Mar	2:07:56	2:11:36- 09
	Décimus	Yoan	FRA	30.11.87	182/62	400h	50.09	50.67- 11
	Deghelt	Adrian	BEL	10.5.85	180/68	110h	13.42	13.55- 09
	DeLeo	Dustin	USA	3.1.86	185/82	PV	5.53	5.51- 08
	Demczyszak	Mateusz	POL	18.1.86	176/62	1500	3:36.15	3:38.72- 10
*	Demelash	Yigrem	ETH-J	28.1.94	167/52	5000	13:03.30 & 10k 26:57.56	-0-
^	Demps	Jeffrey	USA	8.1.90	175/77	100	10.10, 10.01w	10.01- 08, 9.96w- 10
	Demyanyuk	Dmytro	UKR	30.6.83	200/84	HJ	2.26	2.35- 11
	Dendy	Marquis	USA	17.11.92	190/75	LJ	8.06i	7.86. 7.65wi- 11
	Denecker	Emile	FRA	28.3.92	198/87	PV	5.52	5.63- 11
	Derevyagin	Aleksandr	RUS	24.3.79	178/80	400h	49.94	49.00- 08
	DeRosier	Phil	USA	11.4.84	179/73	100	10.17, 10.0	10.20A- 08, 10.23- 09
	Derrick	Chris	USA	17.10.90	180/64	3000	7:46.81i	7:56.31i- 09
		5000	13:19.58i, 13:37.55		13:29.74- 11	10k	27:31.38	28:26.65- 11
*	Desisa	Lelisa	ETH	14.1.90	170/55	5000	13:22.91	-0-
						10k	27:11.98	28:46.74- 09
	Desta	Alemu	ETH	18.2.92	171/53	10k	28:06.06	27:51.17- 11
	Detmer	Joe	USA	3.9.83	180/73	Dec	7931	8090- 10
	Detsuk	Dmitriy	BLR	9.4.85	196/78	TJ	16.64	17.02- 11
^	Devyatovskiy	Vadim	BLR	20.3.77	194/120	HT	79.60	84.90- 05
	Dheeb	Ahmad Mohamed	QAT	29.9.85	195/113	DT	62.18	63.70, 64.56dq- 10
	Diamantáras	Dimítrios	GRE	18.7.84	180/65	LJ	8.11	8.12- 05
	Diarra	Abdoulaye	FRA	27.5.88	184/82	HJ	2.26i, 2.25	2.27i- 09, 2.24- 10
	Dias Sabino	Jefferson	BRA	4.11.82	192/94	TJ	16.90A, 16.67i, 16.66, 16.70w	17.28- 08
	Dìaz	Aramis	CUB	22.11.74	182/79	400h	50.10	50.53- 10
	Dìaz	Pedro Enrique	CUB	19.1.89	177/74	LJ	7.97w	7.60- 09
^	Dìaz	Yunior	CUB	28.4.87	193/80	Dec	7956	8357- 09
	Dilla	Karsten	GER	17.7.89	188/74	PV	5.73i, 5.72	5.72- 11
	Dimitrov	Roumen	BUL	19.9.86		TJ	16.61, 16.74w	16.40- 09
*	Diniz	Yohann	FRA	1.1.78	185/69	20kW	1:17:43	1:18:58- 07
	Diressa	Teshome	ETH-J	25.4.94	175/56	1500	3:34.55	3:38.76- 11
	Distelberger	Dominik	AUT	16.3.90	182/77	Dec	7664	7840- 11
*	Dix	Walter	USA	31.1.86	178/84	100	10.03, 9.85w	9.88- 10, 9.80w- 08
						200	20.02	19.53- 11
	Dixon	Reginald	USA	7.6.88	170/73	200	20.57	20.71- 09
*	Dmitrik	Aleksey	RUS	12.4.84	191/69	HJ	2.35i, 2.33	2.36- 11
*	Dmytrenko	Ruslan	UKR	22.3.86	180/62	20kW	1:20:17	1:21:21- 09
	Docavo	Vicente	ESP	13.2.92	181/69	TJ	16.72	16.61i, 16.21- 11
	Dodson	Jeremy	USA	30.8.87	184/75	200	20.39, 20.25w	20.33, 20.07w- 11
	Domingos	Wágner	BRA	23.6.83	183/126	HT	72.78	71.84- 10
*	Donato	Fabrizio	ITA	14.8.76	189/82	LJ	7.95i	8.03i- 11, 8.00- 06
						TJ	17.53, 17.63w	17.73i- 11, 17.60- 00
	Dong Bin		CHN	22.11.88	179/67	TJ	17.38	17.01i, 17.05w- 11, 16.86- 10
	Donisan	Mihai	ROU	24.7.88	193/74	HJ	2.27	2.30- 11
	Doran	Lee	GBR	5.3.85	178/85	JT	79.72	78.63- 11
	Doris	Troy	USA	12.4.89	174/73	TJ	16.66	16.46- 11
^	Dossévi	Damiel	FRA	3.2.83	182/82	PV	5.54i, 5.37	5.75- 05
^	Doucouré	Ladji	FRA	28.3.83	183/75	110h	13.37	12.97- 05
	Douvalìdis	Konstadìnos	GRE	10.3.87	184/78	110h	13.37	13.46- 08
	Draudvila	Darius	LTU	29.3.83	188/87	Dec	7981	8032- 10
	Driouch	Hamza	QAT-J	16.11.94	180/67	1500	3:33.69	3:34.43- 11
		800	1:46.72		1:46.39- 11	1M	3:50.90	
*	Drouin	Derek	CAN	6.3.90	195/80	HJ	2.31	2.33i- 11, 2.27- 09
	Dry	Mark	GBR	11.10.87	184/110	HT	74.82	72.49- 11
	Drygol	Oleksandr	UKR	25.4.66	183/104	HT	79.42	77.96- 90
	Dubitskiy	Oleg	BLR	14.10.90	184/100	HT	73.62	73.60- 11
	Dubois	Ludovic	FRA	13.4.86	186/72	400h	49.77	50.03- 11
*	Dudas	Mihail	SRB	1.11.89	183/82	Dec	8154	8256- 11
	Dudley	Edward	USA	21.6.92	194/80	HJ	2.25	2.22- 11
	Duer	Corbin	USA	29.11.88	183/77	Dec	7705	7350- 11
	Dukes	Dedric	USA	4.2.92	180/70	200	20.47	20.94- 09, 20.88w- 11
	Dumitrache	Marius	ROU	15.6.89		HJ	2.27i, 2.27	2.17i- 11, 2.14- 08
	Dunfee	Evan	CAN	28.9.90	182/70	50kW	3:59:58	-0-
	Duquemin	Zane	GBR	23.9.91	185/110	DT	63.46	57.35- 11
	Durand	Yohan	FRA	14.5.85	174/58	3000	7:44.46i	7:46.46- 11
						5000	13:17.90	13:36.33- 09

Name		Nat	Born	Ht/Wt	Event	2012 Mark	Pre-2012 Best
* Dutch	Johnny	USA	20.1.89	180/82	400h	48.90	47.63- 10
Duvar	Hakan	TUR	21.8.90		3kSt	8:23.22	8:37.21- 11
Dyatlov	Artyom	UZB	22.5.89	182/75	400h	49.78	51.51- 11
Dyldin	Maksim	RUS	19.5.87	185/78	400	45.01	45.42- 08
* Eaton	Ashton	USA	21.1.88	186/86	100	10.21	10.26-11, 10.19w- 10
400	45.68			46.28- 10	110h	13.56, 13.34w	13.35- 11
LJ	8.23			8.04- 10	Dec	9039	8729- 11
Eaton	Blake	USA	2.5.89	188/136	SP	19.82	19.57- 10
Eaton	Jarret	USA	24.6.89	183/82	110h	13.44	13.63- 11
Edgar	Tyrone	GBR	29.3.82	183/83	100	10.29, 10.07w	10.06- 08, 10,04w- 03
Edmonds	Josh	USA	23.7.91	184/75	200	20.62, 20.28wA	20.95- 11
Edris	Muktar	ETH-J	14.1.94	172/57	5000	13:04.34	-0-
Edward	Mateo	PAN-J	1.5.93	180/66	100	9.9w?	10.47A- 11
Ektov	Yevgeniy	KAZ	1.9.86	186/73	TJ	17.22	17.07- 08
Elabassi	El Hassan	MAR	15.7.79		HMar	61:15	61:13- 11
El Amine	Mouhcine	MAR	8.1.82	175/64	800	1:45.70	1:45.62- 11
El-Ashry	Alaa El-Din M.	EGY	6.1.91		HT	71.95	71.00- 11
^ El-Ghazaly	Omar	EGY	9.2.84	196/120	DT	62.05	66.58- 07
El Goumri	Othmane	MAR	28.5.92	171/57	5000	13:17.66	13:48.09- 11
El Hachimi ¶	Mohammed	MAR	5.9.80	169/55	5000	13:22.46dq	13:36.94- 08
El Kaam	Fouad	MAR	27.5.88	177/62	1500	3:35.71	3:34.01- 11
El Manaoui	Amine	MAR	20.11.91	186/66	800	1:45.00	1:45.46- 11
* El-Sheryf	Sheryf	UKR	2.1.89	183/74	LJ	8.05	7.99- 11
					TJ	17.04, 17.28w	17.72- 11
Ellington	James	GBR	6.9.85	180/75	200	20.55	20.52- 11
Emelieze	Peter	NGR	19.4.88	167/68	100	10.22, 10.08w	10.18- 08
Engel	Roscoe	RSA	6.3.89	178/72	100	10.20	10.19- 11
Engelbrecht	Jaco	RSA	8.3.87	200/125	SP	19.75	19.42- 11
English	Mark	IRL-J	18.3.93	184/73	800	1:45.77	1:47.09- 11
Eradiri	Denis	BUL	24.10.83	183/93	LJ	7.95, 7.97w	7.73- 10
Erickson	Chris	AUS	1.12.81	175/60	20kW	1:22:20	1:22:53- 09
Eriguchi	Masashi	JPN	17.12.88	170/62	100	10.18	10.07- 09
Erin	Frédéric	FRA	23.4.80	189/83	LJ	7.88, 8.01w	8.12- 11
Erins	Edgars	LAT	18.6.86	191/87	Dec	7649	8312- 11
Ernest	Aaron	USA-J	8.11.93	183/75	100	10.17, 10.15w	10.33, 10.17w- 11
					200	20.53, 20.39w	20.86, 20.72w- 11
Ernst	Sebastian	GER	11.10.84	183/72	200	20.59, 20.42w	20.36- 04
Eryildirim	Fatih	TUR	1.3.79	183/89	HT	74.37	75.90- 08
* Esser	Markus	GER	3.2.80	180/105	HT	77.93	81.10- 06
Estefani	Hederson	BRA	11.9.91	184/75	400	45.25	46.14- 10
					400h	49.71	50.44- 10
Estrada	Diego	USA/MEX	12.12.89	180/61	3000	7:44.63i	7:52.18i- 11
					10k	27:32.90	28:40.19- 11
Etelätalo	Lassi	FIN	30.4.88	193/80	JT	84.06	84.41- 11
Everett	Tevan	USA	27.7.87	188/77	800	1:46.02	1:46.27- 09
^ Evilä	Tommy	FIN	6.4.80	194/83	LJ	8.01	8.22- 08, 8.41w- 07
* Ezzine	Hamid	MAR	5.10.83	174/60	3kSt	8:16.93	8:09.72- 07
* Fajdek	Pawel	POL	4.6.89	186/120	HT	81.39	78.54- 11
Falloni	Simone	ITA	26.9.91		HT	71.48	66.73- 11
Faloci	Giovanni	ITA	13.10.85	192/115	DT	64.24	63.89- 11
* Farah	Mo	GBR	23.3.83	171/60	1500	3:34.66	3:33.98- 09
3000	7:37.4+i	7:34.47i- 09, 7:38.15- 06			2M	8:08.08i	8:29.27- 07
5000	12:56.98		12:53.11- 11		10k	27:30.42	26:46.57- 11
Farnosov	Andrey	RUS	9.7.80	182/66	3kSt	8:23.31	8:21.95- 11
* Farquhar	Stuart	NZL	15.3.82	187/98	JT	86.31	85.35- 10
Farrell	Thomas	GBR	23.3.91	173/66	5000	13:15.31	13:26.59- 11
Fassinotti	Marco	ITA	29.4.89	188/70	HJ	2.26i, 2.24	2.29i- 11, 2.28- 10
Fathi	Abdennacer	MAR	20.5.87		5000	13:12.15	13:58.8- 10
* Faulk	Dexter	USA	14.4.84	187/75	110h	13.13, 13.12w	13.13- 09
Faulkner	Troy	USA	24.4.89	180/68	200	20.49	21.51A, 21.28A w- 10
					400	45.70	46.65- 11
Favretto	Vincent	FRA	5.4.84	188/73	PV	5.62	5.65- 06
^ Fazekas ¶	Róbert	HUN	18.8.75	193/110	DT	65.14	71.70- 02
Fedaczynski	Rafal	POL	3.12.80	160/50	20kW	1:21:21	1:22:07- 11
Feger	Alexandre	FRA	22.1.90	178/75	PV	5.55	5.35- 11
Feleke	Getu	ETH	28.11.86		Mar	2:04:50	2:05:44- 10
Felix	Kurt	GRN	4.7.88	190/88	Dec	8062	7412- 10
Fernandez	German	USA	2.11.90	173/61	1500	3:34.60	3:39.00- 09
* Fernández	Jorge	CUB	2.10.87	190/100	DT	66.05	66.00- 10
Ferrìn	Diego	ECU	21.3.88	180/68	HJ	2.25	2.30A- 11
Fiala	Michal	CZE	22.6.85	191/108	HT	71.29	70.51- 11

Name		Nat	Born	Ht/Wt	Event	2012 Mark	Pre-2012 Best
Fida	Soresa	ETH-J	27.5.93	168/55	1500	3:35.22	3:34.72- 11
^ Figère	Nicolas	FRA	19.5.79	177/100	HT	79.75	80.88- 01
Figures	Chris	USA	8.10.81	180/116	SP	20.08	20.38- 08
* Filippìdis	Konstadìnos	GRE	26.11.86	190/78	PV	5.80	5.75- 05
Filippìdis ¶	Yervásios	GRE	24.7.87	186/90	JT	79.82	82.38- 11
Filippov	Nikita	KAZ	7.10.91	191/84	PV	5.60	5.50i, 5.40- 11
Findlay	Adrian	JAM	1.10.82	179/70	400h	49.81	48.93- 08
Finley	Mason	USA	7.10.90	203/150	SP	19.89	20.71i, 19.84- 11
					DT	61.40	60.65- 11
Firmiano	Robert Braz	BRA	28.7.92		LJ	7.96w	7.16- 11
Fleischauer	Georg	GER	21.10.88	192/82	400h	49.37	48.72- 11
Florant	Fabien	NED	1.2.83	176/73	TJ	16.75i	16.65- 09
Floriani	Yuri	ITA	25.12.81	180/64	3kSt	8:22.62	8:28.64- 11
Fofana	Colomba	FRA	11.4.77	187/81	TJ	16.57i, 16.47	17.34- 08
Fonsat	Yannick	FRA	16.6.88	190/75	400	45.30	45.68- 09
Fontenot	Ryan	USA	4.5.86	188/75	110h	13.49, 13.39w	13.48- 10
Forbes	Damar	JAM	18.9.90	185/77	LJ	8.13	8.23- 11
Forbes	Ronald	CAY	5.4.85	186/79	110h	13.51w	13.50, 13.24w- 11
Forsythe	Mario	JAM	30.10.85	173/68	100	10.11, 10.07w	9.95- 10
					200	20.33	20.29- 11
Forte	Julian	JAM-J	1.7.93	186/73	100	10.19	10.49- 10
					200	20.38	21.04- 10
* Fortes	Marco	POR	26.9.82	189/139	SP	21.02	20.89- 11
Forys	Craig	USA	13.7.89	176/64	3kSt	8:28.90	8:41.59- 11
Fothergill	Allodin	JAM	2.7.87	183/75	400	45.51	45.24- 10
* Fourie	Lehann	RSA	16.2.87	196/99	110h	13.24	13.44, 13.41w, 13.4w- 10
^ Frank	Mark	GER	21.6.77	187/97	JT	81.50	84.88- 05
Fraser	Warren	BAH	8.7.91	172/73	100	10.18	10.28- 11, 10.26w- 09
* Frater	Michael	JAM	6.10.82	170/67	100	9.94	9.88, 9.86w- 11
Frauen	Michel	GER	19.1.86	179/76	PV	5.53i, 5.52	5.53- 09
Frawley	Nicholas	USA	21.6.88	178/70	PV	5.53	5.51i- 09, 5.50- 11
* Frayne	Henry	AUS	14.4.90	187/72	LJ	8.27	7.99- 09
					TJ	17.23, 17.34w	17.04- 11
Frederick	Norris	USA	17.2.86	183/79	LJ	8.05	8.12i- 08, 8.10- 11
Fredericks	Cornel	RSA	3.3.90	178/70	400h	48.91	48.14- 11
* Freeman	Jacob	USA	5.11.80	193/129	HT	71.69	76.86- 09
* Freimuth	Rico	GER	14.3.88	196/92	Dec	8322	8287- 11
Frick	Justin	USA	3.8.88	195/82	HJ	2.25	2,23- 11
Fringeli	Jonas	SUI	12.1.88	187/85	Dec	7829	7489- 11
Frost	Andrew	GBR	17.4.81	189/115	HT	71.36	72.79- 11
Frydrych	Petr	CZE	13.1.88	198/99	JT	81.14	88.23- 10
Fryman	Andy	USA	3.2.85	188/130	HT	73.23	72.00- 11
Fueki	Yasuhiro	JPN	20.12.85	181/73	400h	49.71	50.07- 07
Fujisawa	Isamu	JPN	12.10.87	164/56	20kW	1:20:38	1:20:12- 10
Fujiwara	Arata	JPN	12.9.81	167/54	Mar	2:07:48	2:08:40- 08
Fukatsu	Takuya	JPN	10.11.87	168/54	10k	28:06.28	27:56.29- 10
Furey	Sean	USA	31.8.82	190/95	JT	82.73	81.62- 11
Furtula	Danijel	MNE	31.7.92	195/115	DT	63.79	60.19- 11
Fyodorov	Aleksey	RUS	25.5.91	184/73	TJ	17.19	17.12, 17.18w- 10
Gabius	Arne	GER	22.3.81	188/68	3000	7:35.43	7:46.05- 09
2M	8:10.78i				5000	13:13.43	13:26.69- 08
Gagnon	Brian	USA	8.5.87	185/70	800	1:46.40	1:46.56- 09
^ Gaisah	Ignisious	GHA	20.6.83	186/70	LJ	8.04	8.43, 8.51w- 06
Gala	Mumin	SOM	6.9.86	178/62	5000	13:21.21	13:17.77- 11
Gando	Benjamin	KEN	21.5.91	169/57	HMar	61:06	-0-
Garcìa	Clemente	MEX	21.8.89		50kW	3:50:57A	4:01:00- 11
* Garcìa	Jesús Ángel	ESP	17.10.69	172/64	50kW	3:48:15	3:39:54- 97
Garcìa	Vìctor	ESP	13.3.85	173/56	3kSt	8:15.20	8:22.61- 11
* Garcìa	Yordani	CUB	21.11.88	193/88	Dec	8061	8496- 09
Gari	Roba	ETH	12.4.82	181/60	3kSt	8:06.16	8:09.87- 10
Gasaj	Matej	SVK	27.12.81	205/130	DT	61.26	57.89- 09
* Gathimba	Gideon	KEN	9.3.80	179/64	1500	3:33.83	3:33.53- 11
1M	3:50.24		3:50.53- 10		3000	7:43.53+, 7:39.70i	7:40.10- 11
* Gatlin	Justin	USA	10.2.82	185/83	100	9.79	9.85- 04, 9.84w- 05, 9.77dq- 06
					200	20.11	20.00- 05, 19.86w- 01, 19.86dq- 02
Gauntlett	Akheem	JAM	26.8.90	184/70	200	20.45	20.58- 11
					400	45.13	46.38- 11
* Gay	Tyson	USA	9.8.82	183/73	100	9.80	9.69- 09, 9.68w- 08
					200	20.21	19.58- 09
Gayle	Jermaine	JAM	23.7.91	177/68	400	45.60	46.34- 11
* Gaymon	Justin	USA	13.12.86	175/70	400h	48.97	48.46- 08

Name		Nat	Born	Ht/Wt	Event	2012 Mark	Pre-2012 Best
Gbabeke	Stanley	NGR	24.7.89	190/74	LJ	8.20	8.15- 11
* Gebremariam	Gebre-egziabher	ETH	10.9.84	178/56	10k	27:03.58	26:52.33- 07
Gebremariam	Tigabu	ETH	.9	165/52	3000	7:41.02	-0-
Gebremedhin	Gidena	ETH	.82	174/60	Mar	2:08:28	2:10:15- 11
* Gebremedhin	Mekonnen	ETH	11.10.88	180/64	1500	3:31.45	3:31.57- 10
					1M	3:50.02	3:49.70- 11
* Gebremeskel	Dejen	ETH	24.11.89	178/57	3000	7:34.14i	7:35.37i- 11, 7:45.9- 10
					5000	12:46.81	12:53.56- 10
Gebretsadik	Abraham	ETH	16.7.92		HMar	60:34	63:52- 11
					Mar	2:06:21	-0-
* Gebrhiwet	Hagos	ETH-J	11.5.94	167/65	3000	7:44.08i	7:45.11- 11
					5000	12:47.53	14:10.0A- 11
* Gebrselassie	Haile	ETH	18.4.73	164/53	10k	27:20.39	26:22.75- 98
HMar	60:52			58:55- 06	Mar	2:08:17	2:03:59- 08
Geffrouais	Florian	FRA	5.12.88	183/78	Dec	8118	8057- 10
Gehret	Brady	USA	9.5.92	188/77	400	45.22	46.22i, 46.69- 11
Gelant	Elroy	RSA	25.8.86	174/55	3000	7:41.38	7:41.59- 11
* Gemili	Adam	GBR-J	6.10.93	178/73	100	10.05	10.35, 10.23w- 11
					200	20.38	20.98- 11
Genest	Alexandre	CAN	30.6.86	175/57	3kSt	8:22.62	8:19.33- 11
* Geneti	Markos	ETH	30.5.84	175/55	Mar	2:04:54	2:06:35- 11
Geng Zhiyao		CHN	15.8.87	182/67	50kW	3:56:47	3:53:26- 11
Geremew	Mosinet	ETH	12.2.92		5000	13:17.41	13:57.1A- 11
Gertleyn	Ivan	RUS	25.9.87	184/75	PV	5.55	5.55- 10
Getachew	Limenih	ETH	.91		Mar	2:07:39	-0-
Getahun	Birhan	ETH	5.9.91	181/64	3kSt	8:18.63	8:17.36- 11
Gezzar ¶	Nour-eddine	FRA	17.2.80	184/60	3kSt	8:18.89	8:12.25- 11
Ghanbarzadeh	Keyvan	IRI	26.5.90	193/78	HJ	2.26	2.20- 10
* Gharib	Jaouad	MAR	22.5.72	176/60	Mar	2:07:44	2:05:27- 09
Ghazal	Majed El Dein	SYR	21.4.87	193/70	HJ	2.26i, 2.26	2.28- 11
Ghebreselassie	Weynay	ERI-J	24.3.94	182/62	3kSt	8:28.97	8:33.59- 11
^ Gibilisco	Giuseppe	ITA	5.1.79	183/79	PV	5.52i	5.90- 03
Giehl	Tobias	GER	25.7.91	193/77	400h	49.75	49.81- 11
Gilde	Maximilian	GER	5.1.90	180/75	Dec	7720	7717- 11
* Gill	Jacko	NZL-J	20.12.94	190/115	SP	20.05	20.38- 11
* Girat	Arne David	CUB	26.8.84	182/72	TJ	17.17, 17.34w	17.62- 09
Girma	Abraham	ETH	.86		Mar	2:06:48	-0-
Gitau	Daniel	KEN	1.10.87	175/57	10k	27:42.91	27:57.63- 11
					HMar	61:01	61:08- 10
Gitau	Joseph	KEN	3.1.88	167/49	Mar	2:06:58	2:21:54- 10
Giupponi	Matteo	ITA	8.10.88	190/65	20kW	1:20:58	1:22:36- 11
Giza	Jakub	POL	26.9.85	188/140	SP	19.86i, 19.48	20.06- 10
Glover	Tim	USA	1.11.90	185/86	JT	81.69	80.33- 11
Gogochuri	Zurab	GEO	22.3.90		HJ	2.26	2.10- 11
Golabek	Robert	USA	27.4.89	178/116	SP	19.75	19.44- 11
Gollnow	David	GER	8.4.89	180/69	400h	49.69	49.56- 11
Gomes	Diego	BRA	19.4.85	184/73	800	1:45.62	1:46.02- 11
Gómez	David	ESP	13.2.81	186/96	Dec	7872	7940- 04
Gómez	Iñaki	CAN	16.1.88	172/60	20kW	1:20:58	1:22:06- 11
^ Gomis	Kafétien	FRA	23.3.80	183/67	LJ	8.05nwi, 7.89, 8.13w	8.24- 10
Gomont	Nicolas	FRA	15.9.86	193/89	LJ	8.08nwi, 8.00	7.92- 10, 8.07w- 11
* Gonzales	Jermaine	JAM	26.11.84	190/79	400	45.18	44.40- 10
González	Andy	CUB	17.10.87	183/70	800	1:46.22	1:45.3- 08, 1:45.40- 10
* Goodwin	Marquise	USA	19.11.90	173/70	LJ	8.33	8.18- 09, 8.33w- 11
* Gordon	Jehue	TRI	15.12.91	190/80	400h	47.96	48.26- 09
* Gordon	Lalonde	TRI	25.11.88	179/83	400	44.52	45.51- 11
* Gowda	Vikas	IND	5.7.83	206/115	DT	66.28	64.91- 11
Goyvaerts	Tom	BEL	20.3.84	200/91	JT	81.35	82.25- 09
* Grabarz	Robbie	GBR	3.10.87	192/87	HJ	2.37	2.28- 10
Granger	Mike	USA	17.3.91	168/68	100	10.17	10.24, 10.16w- 11
Grasu	Mihai-Liviu	ROU	21.4.87	190/110	DT	61.17	62.20- 11
Gray	Cordero	USA	9.5.89	173/68	100	10.11, 10.09w	10.20, 10.12w- 11
* Greco	Daniele	ITA	1.3.89	184/75	TJ	17.47, 17.67w	17.20- 09
Green	Jack	GBR	6.10.91	187/82	400h	48.60	48.98- 11
* Green	Leford	JAM	14.11.86	186/79	400h	48.61	48.47- 10
Green	Rodney	BAH	8.12.85	168/66	100	10.20	10.28- 08, 10.15w- 11
* Greene	David	GBR	11.4.86	183/75	400h	47.84	47.88- 10
Greene	Joe	USA	20.11.87	188/77	400h	50.10	49.67- 09
Greer	Elijah	USA	24.10.90	185/66	800	1:45.40	1:45.06- 11
Gregan	Brian	IRL	31.12.89	190/85	400	45.61	45.96- 11
^ Gregório	Jadel	BRA	16.9.80	202/102	TJ	16.99	17.90- 07

Name		Nat	Born	Ht/Wt	Event	2012 Mark	Pre-2012 Best
^ Gregson	Ryan	AUS	26.4.90	184/68	1500	3:33.92	3:31.06- 10
					1M	3:53.62	3:52.24- 10
Griffin	Colin	IRL	3.8.82	185/70	50kW	3:52:55	3:51:32- 07
Grigoryev	Ivan	RUS	27.10.89		Dec	7828	7554- 11
Grimes	Mickey	USA	10.10.76	185/84	100	10.17, 10.12w	9.99- 03
Grinnell	Ryan	USA	4.2.87	188/82	TJ	16.60i, 16.56	16.58- 11
Gruber	Hendrik	GER	28.9.86	192/82	PV	5.70i, 5.55	5.70- 10
Grzesiak	Dave	USA	28.7.88	193/91	Dec	7832	7364- 10
Grzeszczuk	Lukasz	POL	3.3.90	189/95	JT	79.40	80.58- 11
Gudzius	Andrius	LTU	14.2.91	198/125	DT	63.39	61.85- 10
* Guliyev	Ramil	TUR	29.5.90	187/73	100	10.15w	10.08- 09
					200	20.53	20.04- 09
Gunn	Luke	GBR	22.3.85	182/63	3kSt	8:29.22	8:28.48- 08
Guo Qi		CHN	28.12.90		Dec	7692	7126- 11
Gurr	James	AUS	20.12.83	180/68	800	1:46.45	1:46.52- 11
Gustafsson	Andreas	SWE	10.8.81	180/67	50kW	3:50:47	3:54:08- 11
^ Haatainen	Harri	FIN	5.1.78	186/85	JT	79.14	86.63- 01
Häber	Tino	GER	6.10.82	185/76	JT	82.10	83.46- 09
Habti	Marouane	MAR	13.10.87		1500	3:36.63	
* Hadadi	Ehsan	IRI	21.1.85	193/125	DT	68.20	69.32- 08
Haeffler	Jérôme	FRA	12.5.82	182/69	JT	78.35	80.37- 10
^ Haklits	András	CRO	23.9.77	189/103	HT	73.95	80.41- 05
Halevi	Yochai	ISR	10.5.82	184/78	TJ	16.81, 16.86w	16.77- 11
Halim	Hasheem	ISV	12.2.90	180/82	TJ	16.39, 16.49w	16.70i,16.53- 10, 16.66w- 08
Hall	Abraham	USA-J	12.9.93	179/77	100	10.19, 9.8	10.42w- 11
Hall	Arman	USA-J	14.2.94	188/77	400	45.39	46.01- 11
Hallil	Necerddine	ALG	10.4.88		1500	3:36.84	3:40.55- 10
Hamada	Mohamed Ahmed	EGY	22.10.92	176/64	800	1:44.98	1:46.44- 11
Hamann	Lars	GER	4.4.89	185/83	JT	79.55	77.24- 10
Hanany	MickaÎl	FRA	25.3.83	198/84	HJ	2.31A	2.32- 08
* Hardee	Trey	USA	7.2.84	196/95	110h	13.54	13.69, 13.61w- 11
					Dec	8671	8790- 09
Hardy	Prezel	USA	1.6.92	168/64	100	10.11, 10.03w	10.13- 11, 10.08w- 09
					200	20.33	20.65- 11
Hargrett	Chris	USA	2.8.84	170/76	100	10.19w	10.12- 08
Harlan	Ryan	USA	25.4.81	190/93	Dec	7715	8171- 04
Harmse	Chris	RSA	31.5.73	184/118	HT	77.22	80.63- 05
Harper	Daniel	CAN	28.8.89	178/75	400	45.60	46.22- 09
* Harradine	Benn	AUS	14.10.82	198/115	DT	67.53	66.45- 10
Harris	Geoffrey	CAN	30.1.87	170/64	800	1:45.97	1:47.9 - 09
Harris	James	USA	18.9.91	188/80	400	45.58	46.19- 11
Harris	James	USA	18.9.91	196/88	HJ	2.27i	2.25i, 2.23- 11
Harris	Nafee	USA	29.5.86	188/83	LJ	7.93	7.96- 10, 7.97w- 09
Harris	Tremaine	CAN	10.2.92	181/79	200	20.22A, 20.63, 20.42w	21.04- 11
Harsányi	Olivér	HUN	20.3.87	198/82	HJ	2.26Ai, 2.22A	2.25- 09
Härstedt	Axel	SWE	28.2.87	196/115	DT	61.57	61.14- 11
Hart	Shavez	BAH	9.6.92	176/70	100	10.28, 10.16w	10.51, 10.42w- 11
					200	20.24w	21.12- 11
Hartfield	Michael	USA	29.3.90	190/77	LJ	7.96	7.91, 7.95w- 11
Harting	Christopher	GER	4.10.90	205/117	DT	61.22	62.12- 11
* Harting	Robert	GER	18.10.84	201/126	DT	70.66	69.43- 09
Harvey	Jacques	JAM	5.4.89	182/73	100	10.08	10.09, 10.03w- 11
Hasegawa	Yusuke	JPN	8.6.88	173/56	10k	27:50.64	28:07.47- 10
Haukenes	Håvard	NOR	22.4.90	180/68	50kW	3:56:38	4:04:48- 11
Haverney	Matthias	GER	21.7.85	200/84	HJ	2.26i, 2.25	2.28- 11
Hayes	Keyunta	USA	15.2.92	183/73	400h	49.38	51.86- 11
Haynes	Akeem	CAN	3.11.92	170/66	100	10.23A, 10.27, 10.18w	10.47- 09, 10.30w- 11
Hazell	Ben	GBR	1.10.84	186/87	Dec	7662	7726- 09
Heath	Elliott	USA	4.2.89		3000	7:45.08	7:52.27- 11
Heath	Garrett	USA	3.11.85	178/65	1500	3:36.03	3:37.12- 10
	1M	3:56.21, 3:55.24i	3:55.87i, 3:58.71- 08		3000	7:45.80i, 7:51.34	7:50.28i- 11, 7:52.91- 11
Hechler	Simon	GER	15.6.88	189/79	Dec	7879	8058- 11
* Heffernan	Robert	IRL	20.2.78	173/55	20kW	1:20:18	1:19:22- 08
					50kW	3:37:54	3:45:30- 10
Heinke	Lars-Niklas	GER	7.11.89	191/80	Dec	7648	7593- 11
Helcelet	Adam Sebastian	CZE	27.10.91	187/86	Dec	8064	7969- 11
Helwick	Chris	USA	18.3.85	193/92	Dec	7744	8143- 08
Henriksen	Eivind	NOR	14.9.90	191/116	HT	75.57	74.59- 11
Henriques	Ånderson	BRA	3.3.92	187/80	400	45.59	45.71A, 45.81- 11
* Henry	Tabarie	ISV	1.12.87	187/79	400	45.19	44.77- 09
Heriot	Blake	USA	26.9.91	178/70	200	20.66, 20.55w	20.99, 20.92w- 09

Name		Nat	Born	Ht/Wt	Event	2012 Mark	Pre-2012 Best
Herman	Timothy	BEL	19.10.90	179/71	JT	78.98	72.58- 11
Hernández	Emerson	ESA	20.1.89	167/61	50kW	3:53:57	3:56:09- 11
Hernández	Fredy	COL	25.4.78	173/60	50kW	3:56:00	3:59:40A- 11
Hernández	Osviel	CUB	31.5.89	179/76	TJ	17.49	17.08- 09
Herrera	José Carlos	MEX	5.2.86	186/74	200	20.57A	20.71A- 10
Hession	Paul	IRL	27.1.83	184/76	200	20.54	20.30- 07, 20.26w- 08
* Hicks	Antwon	USA	12.3.83	187/79	110h	13.14	13.09- 08
Hicks	Jeremy	USA	19.9.86	178/75	LJ	8.11	8.06, 8.20Aw- 10
Higgs	Raymond	BAH	24.1.91	188/75	LJ	8.07, 8.36w	8.15- 11
^ Higuero	Juan Carlos	ESP	3.8.78	180/60	1500	3:35.82	3:31.57- 06
Higuma	Takafumi	JPN	3.9.82		50kW	3:52:53	3:56:35- 11
Hill	Devon	USA	26.10.89	185/75	110h	13.35	13.54, 13.52w- 11
Hill	Ryan	USA	31.1.90		3000	7:43.08i	7:50.78i- 11
Hill	Tyreek	USA-J	1.3.94	178/79	100	10.19	10.74- 11
					200	20.14	-0-
Hirt	Hassan	FRA	16.1.80	179/65	5000	13:10.68	13:25.42- 11
Hitrane	Jamal	MAR	1.9.89	175/57	1500	3:36.08	3:43.11- 11
3000	7:44.23		7:54.2- 11		5000	13:22.63	13:48.23- 11
Hlavan	Igor	UKR	25.9.90	172/62	50kW	3:48:07	4:03:18- 11
Hock	Johannes	GER	24.3.92	185/86	Dec	7884	-0-
* Hoffa	Reese	USA	8.10.77	182/133	SP	22.00	22.43- 07
Hoffmann	Karol	POL	1.6.89	196/78	TJ	17.09	16.50, 16.87w- 11
Hofmann	Andreas	GER	16.12.91	192/89	JT	80.81	77.84- 10
Hogan	Victor	RSA	25.7.89	198/108	DT	62.76	62.60- 11
^ Höhne	André	GER	10.3.78	185/72	20kW	1:21:24	1:20:00- 05
					50kW	3:44:26	3:43:19- 09
Hollis	Mark	USA	1.12.84	190/84	PV	5.63	5.75- 08
Holusa	Jakub	CZE	20.2.88	183/72	800	1:45.12	1:45.56- 10
* Holzdeppe	Raphael	GER	28.9.89	178/69	PV	5.91	5.80- 08^
^ Hondrokoúkis ¶	Dimitrios	GRE	26.1.88	193/73	HJ	2.33i, 2.32	2.32- 11
* Hooker	Steve	AUS	16.7.82	187/85	PV	5.72i, 5.72	6.06i- 09, 6.00- 08
Hoppe	Artur	GER	3.5.88	187/115	SP	19.56i, 19.29	19.64i- 10, 19.32- 11
Horák	Peter	SVK	7.12.83	197/83	HJ	2.28i	2.30i- 07, 2.28- 09
Horibata	Hiroyuki	JPN	28.10.86	189/68	Mar	2:08:24	2:09:25- 11
Horn	Gray	USA	18.2.90	191/91	Dec	7954	7914- 11
Horvat	Ivan	CRO-J	17.8.93	183/70	PV	5.60	5.51- 11
Hostetler	Cyrus	USA	8.8.86	190/95	JT	81.02	83.16- 09
Houssaye	Cédric	FRA	13.12.79	178/65	50kW	3:55:16	3:53:24- 11
Hranovschi	Vadim	MDA	14.2.83	198/110	DT	61.06	64.43- 10
Hubert	Dominique	USA	4.11.90	173/73	100	10.16w	10.57, 10.52w- 11
Hudi	Ákos	HUN	10.8.91	185/95	HT	73.55	72.60- 10
Hughes	Joey	USA	26.10.90	178/70	400	45.41	45.05- 11
Huling	Dan	USA	16.7.83	185/70	3kSt	8:20.81	8:13.29- 10
Humphreys	Sam	USA	12.9.90	201/115	JT	81.86	76.73- 11
Hussein	Kaiem	SUI	1.4.89	190/77	400h	49.61	51.09- 11
Hutchen	Jarrod	USA	6.2.89	175/73	LJ	7.97w	7.94- 09
Hyatt	Dane	JAM	22.1.84	182/77	400	44.83	45.56- 09
Hylton	Joseph	GBR	17.11.89	184/90	110h	13.64	14.05- 11
Hylton	Riker	JAM	13.12.88	190/73	400	45.36	45.30- 11
Hyman	Kemar	CAY	11.10.89	178/74	100	9.95	10.26- 09
Hytinen	Dan	USA	18.10.85	188/101	DT	61.54	61.26- 11
^ Iakovákis	PeriklÌs	GRE	24.3.79	185/76	400h	49.04	47.82- 06
Ibadullayev	Murad	AZE	6.4.92		TJ	16.59	16.25- 11
Ibañez	Ato	SWE	14.11.85	175/64	20kW	1:22:36	1:23:30- 10
Ibargüen	Arley	COL	4.12.82	183/84	JT	80.60A	81.07- 09
Ibrahim	Yasser Fathi	EGY	2.5.84	185/127	SP	19.79	19.97- 09
* Ibrahimov	Hayle	AZE	18.1.90	168/58	3000	7:45.92, 7:41.48i	7:42.54i- 11, 7:51.68- 09
					5000	13:11.34	13:32.98- 10
Idiata	Samson	NGR	28.2.82	186/75	LJ	7.98, 8.02w	7.90, 7.95w- 11
* Idowu	Phillips	GBR	30.12.78	192/86	TJ	17.31	17.81- 10
Idriss	Ali Mohamed Younes	SUD	15.9.89	191/75	HJ	2.25	2.25- 11
* Iguider	Abdelati	MAR	25.3.87	170/52	1500	3:33.99	3:31.47- 09
1M	3:51.78		3:59.79- 09		5000	13:09.17	-0-
Iizuka	Shota	JPN	25.6.91	185/80	200	20.45	20.58- 10
* Ikonnikov	Kirill	RUS	5.3.84	187/115	HT	80.71	79.20- 08
Ilariani	David	GEO	20.1.81	195/84	110h	13.58	13.67- 08
Ilyichev	Ivan	RUS	14.10.86		HJ	2.24i, 2.24	2.28i- 06, 2.26- 08
Imazeki	Yuta	JPN	6.11.87	177/62	400h	49.49	49.27- 11
* Ingebrigtsen	Henrik	NOR	24.2.91	180/69	1500	3:35.43	3:38.61- 10
					1M	3:54.28	4:02.18- 11
Ingraham	Ryan	BAH-J	2.11.93	194/73	HJ	2.28	2.23- 11

Name		Nat	Born	Ht/Wt	Event	2012 Mark	Pre-2012 Best
* Ioannou	Kyriakos	CYP	26.7.84	193/66	HJ	2.30	2.35- 07
Iordan	Valeriy	RUS	14.2.92	192/95	JT	83.23	80.15- 11
Irfan	Kolothum Thodi	IND	8.2.90		20kW	1:20:21	1:28:09- 11
Irwin	Andrew	USA-J	23.1.93	190/84	PV	5.72	5.41i, 5.34- 11
Isidro	Pedro	POR	17.7.85	175/58	50kW	3:58:00	4:10:45- 11
Isles	Carlin	USA	21.11.89	175/75	100	10.24, 10.13w	10.46- 10, 10.19w- 11
^ Ismail	Ahmed	SUD	10.9.84	191/71	800	1:45.71i	1:43.82- 09
Isom	De'Lon	USA	1.5.88	185/79	110h	13.86, 13.64w	13.73- 08, 13.62w- 10
^ Israel	Märt	EST	23.9.83	190/119	DT	65.02	66.98- 11
Ivakin	Anton	RUS	3.2.91	178/73	PV	5.60	5.52- 11
Ivanov	Georgi	BUL	13.3.85	187/130	SP	20.33	20.02- 08
* Jackson	Bershawn	USA	8.5.83	170/68	400h	48.20	47.30- 05
* Jager	Evan	USA	8.3.89	180/66	3000	7:35.16	7:41.78- 09
					3kSt	8:06.81	-0-
Jakubczyk	Lucas	GER	28.4.85	183/73	100	10.20, 10.16w	10.49- 11
Jaleta	Habtamu	ETH-J	19.4.93		3kSt	8:29.03	8:31.06- 11
James	Jamol	TRI	16.7.92	175/70	100	10.17	10.38- 11
* James	Kirani	GRN	1.9.92	185/74	400	43.94	44.36- 11
Janet	Roberto	CUB	29.8.86	187/95	HT	77.08	76.50- 10
* Janik	Igor	POL	18.1.83	200/112	JT	82.37	84.76- 08
Janoyan	Melik	ARM	24.3.85	180/80	JT	79.71	78.03- 08
Jansen	Robbert Jan	NED	22.7.83	175/67	PV	5.62	5.60- 10
Jaramillo	Geormis	VEN	6.3.89	185/80	LJ	8.02w	
Jarso	Yakob	ETH	5.2.88	173/54	HMar	61:07	60:07- 10
Jasinski	Daniel	GER	5.8.89	207/125	DT	64.37	61.28- 11
Jaszczuk	Tomasz	POL	9.3.92	197/86	LJ	8.05	8.11- 11
Jegede	J.J.	GBR	3.10.85	179/73	LJ	8.11	8.04- 11
Jelonek	Jakub	POL	7.7.85	182/60	20kW	1:21:05	1:22:17- 09
Jeng	Alhaji	SWE	13.12.81	185/77	PV	5.72	5.81i- 09, 5.80- 06
Jensen	Morten	DEN	2.12.82	189/81	LJ	8.06	8.25- 05
Ji Wei		CHN	5.2.84	194/83	110h	13.50	13.40- 07
Jia Lingli		CHN	16.2.84	184/72	TJ	16.56	16.69- 09
Jiang Fan		CHN	16.9.89	188/75	110h	13.54	13.47- 11
Jiang Xingyu		CHN	16.3.87	182/78	JT	79.23	79.55- 11
Jiang Zhaodan		CHN	19.2.89		LJ	7.88, 8.07w	8.12- 11
Jifar	Tariku	ETH	18.7.84	173/55	Mar	2:06:51	2:08:10- 08
^ Jiménez	Antonio David	ESP	18.2.77	178/63	3kSt	8:24.19	8:11.52- 01
Jin Min-sup		KOR	2.9.92	185/75	PV	5.51	5.35- 11
Jisa	Sisay	ETH	29.11.82		Mar	2:06:27	-0-
Jobodwana	Anaso	RSA	30.7.92	188/71	200	20.27	21.32A- 10
Jock	Charles	USA	23.11.89	188/73	800	1:44.75	1:44.67- 11
Johansson	Markus	SWE	8.5.90	183/110	HT	73.33	72.40- 11
John	Alexander	GER	3.5.86	185/77	110h	13.35	13.35- 09
Johnson	Brandon	USA	6.3.85	175/68	800	1:46.23	1:50.85- 07
Johnson	James	USA	31.7.91	183/73	200	20.61, 20.57w	21.52- 11
* Johnson	Kibwé	USA	17.7.81	189/108	HT	77.17	80.31- 11
Johnson	Matthew	USA	4.10.89	188/84	Dec	7721(w)	7686w, 7685- 11
* Jonas	Dusty	USA	19.4.86	198/84	HJ	2.25i	2.36A- 08, 2.33- 10
Jones	Alwyn	AUS	28.2.85	189/72	TJ	16.33, 16.53w	16.83- 09
Jones	Nick	USA	22.6.89	188/109	SP	19.57	18.90- 11
					DT	61.95A	60.92- 10
Jons	Mattias	SWE	19.11.82	182/108	HT	76.12	74.76- 10
Jordan	Alphonso	USA	1.11.87	190/75	TJ	16.72, 16.88w	16.74- 11
Jørgensen	Rasmus	DEN	23.1.89	180/75	PV	5.53i, 5.50	5.50- 10
Joseph	Stanley	FRA	24.10.91	181/66	PV	5.55	5.10- 11
Jotanovic	Milan	SRB	11.1.84	184/123	SP	19.83	20.17- 11
Julião	Ronald	BRA	16.6.85	194/113	DT	65.41	63.30- 11
Julmis	Jeffrey	HAI	6.1.87	183/80	110h	13.53	13.50, 13.38w- 11
Jung Sang-jin		KOR	16.4.84	188/95	JT	82.05	80.89- 10
Kabelka	Michal	SVK	4.2.85	192/77	HJ	2.31i, 2.24	2.24i- 09, 2.21- 07
Kahlert	Steffen	GER	30.5.87	189/75	Dec	7877	7740- 09
Kajuga	Robert	RWA	1.1.85	158/61	10k	27:56.67	
* Kaki	Abubaker	SUD	21.6.89	176/63	800	1:43.32	1:42.23- 10
					1500	3:34.34	3:31.76- 11
Kamais	Peter	KEN	7.11.76	173/57	HMar	61:15	59:53- 10
					Mar	2:07:37	2:09:50wdh, 2:12:58- 11
Kamakya	Nicholas Manza	KEN	2.3.85	170/55	Mar	2:08:28	2:06:34- 11
Kamali	Majdubi	MAR-J	1.5.93		1500	3:36.65	3:48.45- 11
* Kanaykin	Vladimir	RUS	21.3.85	170/65	20kW	1:19:43	1:17:16- 07, 1:16:53dq- 08
Kanda	Lukas	KEN	1.1.87		Mar	2:08:04	2:08:40- 11
Kanemaru	Yuzo	JPN	18.9.87	177/75	400	45.47	45.16- 09

Name		Nat	Born	Ht/Wt	Event	2012 Mark	Pre-2012 Best
Kangogo	Cornelius	KEN-J	31.12.93	178/64	1500	3:35.72 & 3000 7:39.73	- 0-
Kangogo	James	KEN	22.11.85	176/60	1500	3:35.25	3:36.36- 10
					3000	7:44.61	7:55.27i- 11
* Kanter	Gerd	EST	6.5.79	196/125	DT	68.03	73.38- 06
Kapek	Julien	FRA	12.1.79	178/70	TJ	16.80	17.38- 06
Kaptingei	Bernard	KEN	.86		1500	3:36.45A	3:42.05A- 09
Karailiev	Momchil	BUL	21.5.82	188/75	TJ	16.79, 16.93w	17.41- 09
Karavayev ¶	Pavel	RUS	27.8.88	185/74	LJ	7.91, 7.93i	8.08- 11
* Karjalainen	Olli-Pekka	FIN	7.3.80	194/118	HT	75.16	83.30- 04
* Karoki	Bidan	KEN	21.8.90	169/53	5000	13:21.02	13:15.76- 11
					10k	27:05.50	27:13.67- 11
* Karpov	Dmitriy	KAZ	23.7.81	198/98	Dec	8173	8725- 04
Kassé Hann	Mamadou	SEN	10.10.86	190/73	400h	48.80	48.89- 10
* Kasyanov	Oleksiy	UKR	26.8.85	191/82	Dec	8321	8479- 09
Katsuki	Hayato	JPN	28.11.90	168/58	20kW	1:21:14	1:23:57- 11
Kauppinen	Juha	FIN	16.8.86	182/103	HT	72.72	74.38- 09
Kawakita	Naohiro	JPN	10.7.80	181/74	400h	49.98	49.04- 09
Kazakevics	Igors	LAT	19.4.80	176/67	50kW	3:59:02	3:52:38- 08
Kazanin	Oleksiy	UKR	22.5.82	170/58	50kW	3:50:17	3:50:30- 08
Kazmirek	Kai	GER	28.1.91	190/85	Dec	8130	7802- 11
Kebede	Tefere	ETH	10.4.86		Mar	2:07:35	2:11:35- 10
* Kebede	Tsegaye	ETH	15.1.87	158/50	Mar	2:04:38	2:05:18- 09
Kéchi	Heni	FRA	31.8.80	186/75	400h	49.91	49.34- 10
Keddo	Eric	JAM	1.7.84	186/77	110h	13.62	13.49- 11, 13.0- 10
Keiner	Sebastian	GER	22.8.89	183/65	800	1:46.33	1:45.98- 08
Keller	Levi	USA	30.1.86	183/82	PV	5.52	5.35- 10
Kemboi	Clement	KEN	1.2.92		3kSt	8:25.67	8:28.13- 11
Kemboi	Edward	KEN	12.12.91	170/57	800	1:46.20	1:46.06- 11
Kemboi	Elijah	KEN	10.9.84		Mar	2:07:51	2:11:15- 11
* Kemboi	Ezekiel	KEN	25.5.82	175/62	3000	7:44.24	7:49.95- 11
					3kSt	8:10.55	7:55.76- 11
Kemboi	Hillary	KEN	.86		3kSt	8:29.8 A	8:36.7A- 10
Kemboi	Lawrence	KEN-J	.93		3kSt	8:31.2 A	
Kempas	Antti	FIN	3.10.80	191/70	50kW	4:01:50	3:55:19- 08
Kendagor	Jacob	KEN	.84		HMar	61:15	61:43- 04
Kenesi	Geoffrey	KEN	.90		HMar	61:14	62:20- 11
Keny	Felix	KEN	25.12.85		Mar	2:07:31	2:07:36- 10
Kering	Alfred	KEN	.80	172/57	Mar	2:07:37	2:07:11- 10
^ Keskisalo	Jukka	FIN	27.3.81	184/66	3kSt	8:27.96	8:10.67- 09
Ketlogetswe	Thapelo	BOT	12.4.91	174/64	400	45.58A	46.29A- 10
Keys	Dakotah	USA	27.9.91	188/79	Dec	7793	-0-
Kgosimang	Kabelo Mmono	BOT	7.1.86	184/70	HJ	2.25	2.34A- 08, 2.30- 06
Kharlamov	Vasiliy	RUS	8.10.86	182/77	Dec	8059	8166- 11
Khaylov	Andrey	RUS	3.7.89		LJ	7.94i, 7.87	7.66- 09
Khimin	Aleksey	RUS	26.2.89		50kW	3:54:32	4:06:37- 09
Khodjayev	Sukhrob	UZB-J	21.5.93	186/105	HT	74.20	66.27- 11
* Kibet	Stephen	KEN	9.11.86	172/55	HMar	58:54	60:09- 10
					Mar	2:08:05	2:09:27- 11
Kibiwott	Francis	KEN	15.9.78		Mar	2:07:32	2:09:00- 09
Kibiwott	Stephen	KEN	3.4.80		Mar	2:08:11	2:07:54 09
Kibor	William	KEN	.80		Mar	2:08:32	2:10:21- 11
Kiecana	Szymon	POL	26.3.89	193/67	HJ	2.28	2.21- 11
Kifle	Goltom	ERI-J	3.12.93	178/60	5000	13:22.92	13:23.07- 11
* Kigen	Mike	KEN	15.1.86	170/54	5000	13:21.55A	12:58.58- 06
	10k 27:03.49			27:30.53- 11	HMar	60:18dh	59:58- 11
Kigen	Moses	KEN	10.1.83		Mar	2:07:45	2:10:21- 11
Kihara	Masato	JPN	13.7.86	167/50	HMar	61:15	61:50- 06
Kilty	Richard	GBR	2.9.89	184/79	100	10.23, 10.15w	10.32- 11
					200	20.50	20.53- 11
Kim Dong-young		KOR	6.3.80	176/62	50kW	3:56:12	3:51:12- 11
* Kim Hyun-sub		KOR	31.5.85	175/53	20kW	1:21:36	1:19:31- 11
Kim Kun-woo		KOR	29.2.80	185/84	Dec	7769	7860- 11
Kim Sang-su		KOR	5.6.84	186/75	LJ	7.93	7.88- 10
Kim Yoo-suk		KOR	19.1.82	191/84	PV	5.62	5.66- 07
Kimaiyo	Lawrence	KEN	.90		Mar	2:07:01	2:11:46- 10
* Kimetto	Dennis	KEN	22.1.84		HMar	59:14	61:30A- 11
					Mar	2:04:16	-0-
Kimitei	Elijah	KEN	.86		LJ	8.09A	7.67A- 11
					TJ	16.66A, 16.28	16.28A- 11
* Kimmons	Trell	USA	13.7.85	178/77	100	10.02, 10.00w	9.95, 9.92w- 10
Kimurer	Joel	KEN	21.1.88		HMar	59:36	60:05- 11
					Mar	2:08:18	2:15:48- 11

Name		Nat	Born	Ht/Wt	Event	2012 Mark		Pre-2012 Best
Kimutai	Kennedy	KEN	18.6.90	173/59	HMar	61:08		61:30- 11
Kimutai	Philip Sanga	KEN	10.9.83	175/59	Mar	2:06:51		2:06:07- 11
King	Max	USA	24.2.80	168/60	3kSt	8:30.54		8:31.26- 07
Kinnunen	Jarkko	FIN	19.1.84	187/69	50kW	3:46:25		3:47:36- 09
Kino	Tomoharu	JPN	4.8.89	177/69	400h	49.88		49.57- 10
Kinsley	Craig	USA	19.1.89	186/82	JT	82.31		78.10- 10
Kinyor	Job	KEN	2.9.90	176/68	800	1:43.76		1:45.07A- 11
Kipchirchir	Victor	KEN	5.12.87		HMar	59:31		61:21- 11
* Kipchoge	Eliud	KEN	5.11.84	167/52	3000	7:31.40		7:27.66- 11
2M	8:07.39i				5000	12:55.34		12:46.53- 04
10k	27:11.93		26:49.02- 07		HMar	59:25		-0-
Kipchumba	Mariko	KEN	.75	183/64	Mar	2:06:05		2:09:03- 08
Kipkemboi	Nicholas	KEN	.86		HMar	60:15		-0-
* Kipkemoi	Kenneth	KEN	2.8.84	165/52	5000	13:03.37		-0-
10k	26:52.65		27:48.5A- 11		HMar	59:11		59:47- 11
Kipketer	Gideon	KEN	10.11.92		HMar	59:53		-0-
					Mar	2:08:14		-0-
Kipkoech	John	KEN	29.12.91	160/52	3000	7:34.03		7:32.72- 10
*					5000	12:49.50		13:26.03- 10
Kipkoech	Nicholas	KEN	22.10.92	168/57	800	1:45.01		1:45.47- 11
					1000	2:17.16		2:18.70- 06
Kipkorir	Evans	KEN	.85	174/61	800	1:45.91		
Kipkosgei	Nelson	KEN-J	9.3.93		3kSt	8:22.24		
Kipkurui	Benjamin	KEN	28.12.80	174/57	1500	3:35.20		3:30.67- 01
* Kiplagat	Benjamin	KEN	4.3.89	186/61	3kSt	8:17.55		8:03.81- 10
Kiplagat	Henry	KEN	16.12.82		HMar	60:01		62:31- 07
Kiplagat	Linus	KEN-J	23.12.94	170/57	1500	3:36.60		3:40.54- 11
Kiplagat	Richard	KEN	3.7.84	178/64	800	1:45.79A		1:44.77- 10
* Kiplagat	Silas	KEN	20.8.89	170/57	800	1:44.8 A		
1500	3:29.63	3:29.27- 10	1M	3:52.44	3:49.39- 11	3000	7:41.02i	7:39.94- 10
Kiplangat	Cornelius	KEN	21.12.92	168/55	800	1:46.4 A		1:49.2A- 09
Kiplimo	Abraham	UGA	14.4.89	165/52	5000	13:21.57		13:10.40- 11
					10k	27:49.76		-0-
Kiplimo	Joseph	KEN	20.7.88	173/57	3000	7:42.52		7:31.20- 09
Kiprono	Hillary	KEN	21.7.85		HMar	61:15		61:29- 08
* Kiprop	Asbel	KEN	30.6.89	186/70	800	1:45.91		1:43.15- 11
1500	3:28.88		3:30.46- 11		1M	3:49.22		3:48.50- 09
* Kiprop	Wilson	KEN	14.4.87	179/62	10k	27:01.98		27:26.93- 10
					HMar	59:15		59:39- 10
Kiprotich	John	KEN	5.6.83	165/55	HMar	60:02		59:23- 09
					Mar	2:07:44		2:07:08- 11
* Kiprotich	Stephen	UGA	27.2.89	172/56	Mar	2:07:50		2:07:20- 11
* Kipruto	Brimin	KEN	31.7.85	176/54	3000	7:39.07i		7:47.33- 06, 7:42.99i- 10
					3kSt	8:01.73		7:53.64- 11
Kipruto	Conseslus	KEN-J	8.12.94	174/55	3000	7:44.09		-0-
*					3kSt	8:03.49		8:27.30- 11
^ Kipruto	Vincent	KEN	13.9.87		HMar	60:46		61:43- 10
* Kipsang	Geoffrey	KEN	28.11.92		HMar	59:26		59:31- 11
					Mar	2:06:12		-0-
* Kipsang	Wilson	KEN	15.3.82	178/59	HMar	59:06dh		58:59- 09
					Mar	2:04:44		2:03:42- 11
* Kipsiro	Moses	UGA	2.9.86	174/59	3000	7:31.88		7:30.95- 09
2M	8:08.16i	5000	13:00.68	12:50.72- 07	10k	27:04.48	27:33.37- 10	
* Kiptanui	Eliud	KEN	6.6.89	169/55	Mar	2:06:44		2:05:39- 10
Kiptoo	Andrew	KEN	.87	188/73	800	1:46.2		1:46.84- 10
Kiptoo	Eliah	KEN	9.6.86	186/68	1500	3:33.81		
* Kiptoo	Mark	KEN	21.6.76	175/64	5000	13:06.23		12:53.46- 10
					10k	27:18.22		26:54.64- 11
Kiptoo	Solomon	KEN	.87		Mar	2:08:30		-0-
Kiptum	Joseph	KEN	25.9.87		HMar	60:26		61:08- 11
* Kipyego	Bernard	KEN	16.7.86	160/50	Mar	2:06:40		2:06:29- 11
Kipyego	Edwin	KEN	.9		HMar	60:55		61:23- 11
* Kipyego	Mike	KEN	2.10.83	168/59	Mar	2:07:37		2:06:48- 11
Kirchler	Hannes	ITA	22.12.78	194/110	DT	62.04		65.01- 07
* Kirdyapkin	Sergey	RUS	18.6.80	178/67	50kW	3:35:59		3:38:08- 05
Kirillov	Nikita	USA-J	5.6.93	188/85	PV	5.54		5.23- 11
Kirop	Pius	KEN	8.1.90		HMar	59:25		61:16- 10
* Kirui	Abel	KEN	4.6.82	177/62	HMar	60:28		60:11- 07
					Mar	2:07:56		2:05:04- 09
Kirui	Geoffrey	KEN-J	16.2.93	158/50	10k	27:08.44		26:55.73- 11
Kirui	Gilbert	KEN-J	22.1.94	172/55	3kSt	8:11.27		8:25.03A- 11
* Kirui	Peter	KEN	2.1.88	182/66	HMar	59:39		59:40- 11

Name		Nat	Born	Ht/Wt	Event	2012 Mark	Pre-2012 Best
	Kirwa	Gilbert	KEN	28.12.85	174/64	Mar	2:07:35	2:06:14- 09
*	Kirwa Yego	Alfred	KEN	28.11.86	175/56	800	1:44.49	1:42.67- 09
	Kiryu	Yoshihide	JPN-Y	15.12.95	175/66	100	10.19	10.58- 11
	Kishimoto	Takayuki	JPN	6.5.90	171/61	400h	48.41	49.27- 11
	Kishoyan	Alphas	KEN-J	12.10.94	162/56	400	45.64A	46.34A, 46.52- 11
	Kisorio ¶	Mathew	KEN	16.5.89	178/62	HMar	60:02	58:46- 11
	Kiss	Dániel	HUN	12.2.82	195/73	110h	13.53	13.32, 13.20w- 10
^	Kitchens	George	USA	16.1.83	183/77	LJ	8.21, 8.27w	7.98, 8.23w- 09
	Kitum	Silas	KEN	25.5.90	167/52	3kSt	8:16.48	8:12.17- 11
*	Kitum	Timothy	KEN-J	20.11.94	172/60	800	1:42.53	1:44.98- 11
	Kitur	Bernard	KEN	10.1.90		HMar	60:59	62:04- 11
*	Kitwara	Sammy	KEN	26.11.86		Mar	2:05:54	-0-
	Kiumbani	Johnson	KEN-J	27.1.93	168/56	10k	28:02.26	-0-
	Kivinen	Mikko	FIN	16.1.88	183/70	LJ	8.02	7.89, 7.91w- 09
	Kivuva	Jackson	KEN	11.8.88	172/59	800	1:45.71	1:43.72- 10
	Kiyeng	David	KEN	.83		Mar	2:07:57	2:06:26- 09
	Klausen	Janick	DEN-J	3.4.93	175/68	HJ	2.25i, 2.19	2.27i, 2.25- 11
	Knipphals	Sven	GER	20.9.85	190/85	200	20.53	20.93- 09
*	Knobel	Jan Felix	GER	16.1.89	192/91	Dec	8228	8288- 11
	Kochnev	Aleksey	RUS	6.4.90	185/110	HT	72.30	73.93- 10
	Koech	Bernard	KEN	31.1.88		HMar	59:10	-0-
	Koech	Duncan	KEN	28.12.81		Mar	2:07:53	2:08:38- 11
	Koech	Gilbert	KEN	.81		Mar	2:07:38	2:06:18- 09
*	Koech	Isiah	KEN-J	19.12.93	178/60	3000	7:30.43	7:37.50i, 7:47.6- 11
	5000	12:48.64	12:54.18, 12:53.29i- 11			10k	27:17.03	-0-
*	Koech	Paul Kipsiele	KEN	10.11.81	168/57	3kSt	7:54.31	7:56.37- 05
						5000	13:02.69i	13:05.18, 13:02.95i- 10
*	Kogo	Micah	KEN	3.6.86	170/60	10k	27:23.04	26:35.63- 06
						HMar	59:07dh	61:30- 10, 60:03dh- 11
	Kokoyev	Valeriy	RUS	25.7.88	197/118	SP	20.05i, 19.49	20.42i- 11, 20.20- 09
*	Kolasinac	Asmir	SRB	15.10.84	185/130	SP	20.85	20.52i- 10, 20.50- 11
	Kolomoyets	Sergey	BLR	11.8.89	190/102	HT	77.06	77.52- 11
^	Kombich	Ismael	KEN	16.10.85	183/73	800	1:46.4 A	1:44.24- 06
						1500	3:36.06	3:33.31- 10
*	Komen	Daniel Kipchirchir	KEN	27.11.84	175/60	1500	3:32.98	3:29.02- 06
	1M	3:53.04	3:48.28- 07	3000	7:44.80	7:31.41- 11	5000 13:09.90	13:04.02- 10
*	Komon	Leonard Patrick	KEN	10.1.88	175/52	10k	27:01.58	26:55.29- 11
	Königsmark	Varg	GER	28.4.92	193/84	400h	49.54	49.70- 11
	Konishi	Yasamuchi	JPN	13.4.90	170/56	LJ	7.97w	7.95- 11
	Konishi	Yuta	JPN	31.7.90	182/70	400h	49.63	49.41- 11
	Konrad	Tom	GER	30.3.91	183/79	PV	5.56	5.35- 10
	Koosimile	Larona	BOT	14.10.85		LJ	8.00w	7.70- 10
	Korchmid	Oleksandr	UKR	22.1.82	188/89	PV	5.51	5.81- 05
*	Korir	Japheth	KEN-J	30.6.93	168/55	3000	7:40.37	7:40.93- 11
	5000	13:20.88	13:17.18- 11			5000	13:11.44i	
	Korir	Laban	KEN	30.12.85		HMar	60:38	61:03- 10
	Korir	Leonard	KEN	10.12.86	173/61	5000	13:19.54i	13:26.01i, 13:35.71- 11
	Korir	Lewis	KEN	11.6.86	168/52	10k	27:57.07	27:41.33- 11
	Korir	Mark	KEN	10.1.85		HMar	61:19	61:33- 11
	Korir	Wesley	KEN	15.11.82		HMar	61:19	62:40- 10
						Mar	2:06:13	2:06:15- 11
	Korme	Sisay	ETH	9.1.85	170/62	3kSt	8:24.28	8:20.72- 11
	Korolyov	Aleksey	RUS	5.4.82		HT	75.50	79.36- 08
	Korotkov	Ilya	RUS	6.12.83	192/101	JT	79.61	85.47- 10
	Kortbeek	Thomas	NED	2.4.81	191/78	400h	50.10	48.95- 03
	Korzun	Aleksandr	BLR	17.3.85	194/76	Dec	7720	7777- 07
*	Kosencha	Leonard	KEN-J	21.8.94	175/64	800	1:43.40	1:44.08- 11
	Kosgei	Nelson	KEN-J	.93		3kSt	8:30.80	8:56.6A- 11
	Koshar	Anatoliy	BLR	11.6.89		Dec	7725	7599- 11
	Kosinov	Artyom	KAZ	31.7.86	182/67	3kSt	8:24.13	8:35.11- 11
	Kovacs	Joe	USA	28.6.89	188/114	SP	21.08	19.84i, 19.15- 11
^	Kövágó ¶	Zoltán	HUN	10.4.79	204/127	DT	68.21dq	69.95- 06
	Kovalenko	Nazar	UKR	9.2.89	177/65	20kW	1:19:55	1:21:34- 11
	Kovals	Ainars	LAT	21.11.81	192/105	JT	83.89	86.64- 08
	Kovalyov	Yuriy	RUS	18.6.91		TJ	17.04i, 16.58	17.06- 11
	Kovenko	Andriy	UKR	25.11.73	174/64	20kW	1:20:51	1:21:44- 11
	Kowal	Yoann	FRA	28.5.87	172/58	1500	3:35.03	3:33.75- 11
	3000	7:44.26i	7:46.19i- 11, 8:01.04- 08			3kSt	8:21.66	8:34.66- 08
	Kozlov	Vladimir	BLR	20.4.85	183/87	JT	82.86	82.06- 08
*	Kozmus	Primoz	SLO	30.9.79	188/106	HT	79.36	82.58- 09
	Krammes	Barry	USA	1.9.81	190/102	JT	77.99	78.97- 08

Name		Nat	Born	Ht/Wt	Event	2012 Mark	Pre-2012 Best
Krasnov	Vladimir	RUS	19.8.90	190/70	400	45.36	45.12- 10
* Krivitskiy	Pavel	BLR	17.4.84	184/115	HT	80.25	80.67- 11
* Krivov	Andrey	RUS	14.11.85	185/72	20kW	1:18:25	1:19:06- 08
Kruger	A.G.	USA	18.2.79	193/118	HT	79.20	79.26- 04
Krukowski	Marcin	POL	14.6.92	182/92	JT	82.58	79.19- 11
^ Krymarenko	Yuriy	UKR	11.8.83	187/65	HJ	2.25i, 2.12	2.34i- 07, 2.33- 05
Krynski	Kamil	POL	12.5.87	187/88	200	20.56	20.81- 10
* Kszczot	Adam	POL	2.9.89	178/68	800	1:43.83	1:43.30- 11
Kuc	Dariusz	POL	24.4.86	178/64	100	10.20	10.15- 11
Kucheryanu	Sergey	RUS	30.6.85	185/75	PV	5.72	5.81- 08
Kucmìn	Antón	SVK	7.6.84	180/64	20kW	1:22:25	1:23:21- 11
* Kudlicka	Jan	CZE	29.4.88	184/76	PV	5.73, 5.75 extra trial	5.70- 08, 5.81ex- 11
Kuehl	Adam	USA	19.1.84	188/116	DT	63.74	64.98- 07
Kukk	Mihkel	EST	8.10.83	187/98	JT	78.60	81.77- 08
Kukushkin	Anatoliy	RUS	12.2.86	179/67	20kW	1:21:30	1:21:19- 11
* Kuma	Abera	ETH	31.8.90	160/50	3000	7:40.85, 7:39.09i	7:47.9- 11
5000 13:09.32 13:00.15- 11					10k 27:18.39 27:22.54- 11 HMar 60:19		-0-
Kumar Bind	Rajesh	IND-J	20.7.94		JT	80.14	- 0-
Kunkel	Adam	CAN	24.2.81	180/77	400h	50.14	48.24- 07
Kupers	Thijmen	NED	4.10.91	180/65	800	1:46.46	1:50.3- 11, 1:50.37- 10
Kupper	Martin	EST	31.5.89	195/108	DT	62.32	60.18- 11
Kürthy	Lajos	HUN	22.10.86	190/125	SP	20.17	20.78- 08
Kurtsev	Denis	RUS	20.8.88	188/130	SP	20.14	19.02- 11
Kusiak ¶	Damian	POL	14.4.88	190/105	SP	20.45	20.10- 11
* Kuznetsov	Viktor	UKR	14.7.86	190/67	LJ	8.10	8.22i- 05, 8.09- 09, 8.25w- 06
* Kwambai	James Kipsang	KEN	28.2.83	162/52	Mar	2:05:50	2:05:36- 08
* Kynard	Erik	USA	3.2.91	193/86	HJ	2.34	2.33i, 2.31- 11
Kyyrö	Mikko	FIN	12.7.80	191/106	DT	62.84	64.14- 07
La Rosa	Stefano	ITA	22.9.85	166/55	5000	13:23.58	13:32.66- 10
* Laâlou	Amine	MAR	13.5.82	178/57	800	1:45.28	1:43.25- 06
1500 3:30.54			3:29.53- 10		1M	3:50.43	3:50.22- 10
Laanmäe	Tanel	EST	29.9.89	184/89	JT	80.75	81.96- 09
Labovskyy	Mykola	UKR	4.5.83	172/62	5000	13:23.50	13:49.89- 11
					10k	28:04.90	-0-
Ladan Mohammed Abdelaziz		KSA	7.1.91	184/68	800	1:45.52	1:47.78- 11
* Lagat	Bernard	USA	12.12.74	174/61	1500	3:34.63	3:26.34- 01
1M 3:54.17 3:47.28- 01					3000 7:41.44i 7:29.00- 10 5000 12:59.92		12:53.60- 11
Lagat	Haron	KEN	15.8.83	174/57	3kSt	8:25.12	8:15.80- 11
Lahbabi	Aziz	MAR	3.2.91	178/62	5000	13:04.06	13:13.68- 11
Lai Chun Ho		HKG	5.2.89	170/64	100	10.19w	10.32- 10
Laine	Samyr	HAI	17.7.84	188/82	TJ	16.88	17.39A, 17.45w- 09, 17.09- 11
Lalang	Boaz	KEN	8.2.89	174/62	800	1:44.83	1:42.95- 10
* Lalang	Lawi	KEN	15.6.91	168/58	1500	3:36.77	3:42.15- 11
3000 7:44.48i			7:54.32i- 11		5000	13:18.88, 13:08.28	13:30.64- 11
Lalli	Andrea	ITA	20.5.87	169/56	HMar	61:11	62:32- 11
Lamb	Bryce	USA	9.11.90	183/80	LJ	7.94i, 7.94w	8.15- 11
					TJ	16.56	16.47i- 10, 16.01- 09, 16.10w- 10
^ Lambrechts	Burger	RSA	3.4.73	200/145	SP	20.12	20.56- 00
Lamdassem	Ayad	ESP	11.10.81	173/50	10k	28:04.22	27:45.58- 08
Lamerinyang	Julius	KEN	15.7.83		HMar	61:07	60:31- 10
Langat	Leonard	KEN	7.8.90		HMar	60:05	59:52- 11
Langat	Philip	KEN	23.4.90		HMar	61:05	61:56- 11
Langat	Robert	KEN	17.9.88	174/	HMar	61:05	64:35A- 08
Lange	Björn	GER	15.6.79	194/110	JT	78.53	85.21- 01
^ Lapierre	Fabrice	AUS	17.10.83	179/66	LJ	8.10, 8.14w	8.40, 8.78w- 10
LaRue	Brent	SLO	26.4.87	188/84	400h	49.38	49.77- 11
Lárusson	Einar Dadi	ISL	10.5.90	185/83	Dec	7898	7587- 11
Lastre	Yunio	CUB	26.10.81	189/104	DT	65.17	64.58- 10
Lathan	Tre	USA	15.7.92	180/68	110h	13.65, 13.59w	13.90, 13.80w- 11
Lathouwers	Robert	NED	8.7.83	189/78	800	1:44.61	1:44.75- 08
* Lauro	Germán	ARG	2.4.84	185/127	SP	20.84	20.43- 10
					DT	63.55	62.77- 11
Lavanne	Cédric	FRA	13.11.80	183/72	110h	13.47	13.44- 06
* Lavillenie	Renaud	FRA	18.9.86	177/69	PV	5.97	6.03i- 11, 6.01- 09
Lavillenie	Valentin	FRA	16.7.91	170/65	PV	5.52	5.31- 11
Lawrence	Brijesh BJ	SKN	27.12.89	180/93	100	10.12	10.28- 11
^ Lawrence	Torrin	USA	11.4.89	186/77	200	20.51w	20.55- 11
					400	45.40	45.61- 11
Lazas	Kevin	USA	25.1.92	178/84	Dec	7955	7802- 11
Lebésis	Spirìdon	GRE	30.5.87	190/91	JT	83.02	82.90- 10
Lee	Dexter	JAM	18.1.91	186/77	100	10.15	10.06- 11

	Name		Nat	Born	Ht/Wt	Event	2012 Mark	Pre-2012 Best
	Lee Sung		KOR	6.5.88	184/70	HJ	2.25	2.20- 09
	Lee Yun-chul		KOR	28.3.82	188/110	HT	71.54	71.79- 08
	Leer	Will	USA	15.4.85	184/70	1500	3:36.33	3:36.33- 11
	Lehtola	Sampo	FIN	10.5.89	188/82	JT	79.52	83.77- 11
*	Lel	Martin	KEN	29.10.78	171/54	Mar	2:06:51	2:05:15- 08
	Lelièvre	Jérémy	FRA	8.2.91	193/82	Dec	7911	7468- 11
*	Lemaitre	Christophe	FRA	11.6.90	189/74	100	10.04, 9.94w	9.92- 11
						200	19.91	19.80- 11
	Lendore	Deon	TRI	28.10.92	179/75	400	45.13	46.50- 11
	Lennon-Ford	Luke	GBR	5.5.89	183/75	400	45.23	45.56- 11
	Lepik	Hendrik	EST	18.4.90	186/79	Dec	7662	7410- 10
	Leptikov	Viktor	KAZ	2.7.87	195/81	400h	49.79	50.35- 09
	Lescay	David	CUB	19.2.89	175/68	100	10.0	10.20- 09, 9.8- 10
	Leslie	Cory	USA	24.10.89	175/60	3kSt	8:31.08	8:40.42- 11
	Lesnoy	Aleksandr	RUS	28.7.88	194/116	SP	20.05	19.60- 11
	Letnicov	Vladimir	MDA	7.10.81	174/68	TJ	16.80	17.06- 02
	Letting	Vincent	KEN-J	.93		1500	3:36.61A	3:48.15A- 90
	Levine	Nigel	GBR	30.4.89	178/68	400	45.11	45.78- 09
	Levins	Cameron	CAN	28.3.89	181/68	3000	7:45.75i	-0-
	5000	13:18.29		13:40.30- 11		10k	27:27.96	-0-
*	Lewandowski	Marcin	POL	13.6.87	180/64	800	1:44.34	1:43.84- 09
	Lewis	Romel	JAM	28.1.88	178/75	100	10.12wA	10.52, 10.44w- 09
*	Lewis	Steve	GBR	20.5.86	191/83	PV	5.82	5.75i, 5.72- 09
	Leyver	José	MEX	12.11.85	178/65	50kW	3:51:31A	3:49.16- 11
*	Li Jianbo		CHN	14.11.86	176/57	20kW	1:20:55	1:19:10- 09
						50kW	3:39:01	3:43:02- 06
	Li Jinzhe		CHN	1.9.89	188/64	LJ	8.25	8.18- 09, 8.29w- 10
	Li Lei		CHN	29.11.87	168/53	50kW	4:01:32	3:47:34- 10
	Li Shijia		CHN	14.1.92		20kW	1:22:15	1:26:13- 11
	Li Tianlei		CHN-Y	13.1.95		20kW	1:21:01, 1:23:37.21t	1:22:23- 11
^	Li Yanxi		CHN	26.6.83	182/72	TJ	16.84	17.59- 09
	Li Zhilong		CHN	9.3.88	185/75	400h	49.86	49.47- 11
*	Lilesa	Feyisa	ETH	1.2.90	158/50	HMar	59:22	60:33- 10
						Mar	2:04:52	2:05:23- 10
	Lim Jung-hyun		KOR	8.9.87	182/66	50kW	3:56:34	3:53:05- 11
	Limaa	Reuben	KEN	.87		HMar	60:57	
	Limo	Daniel Kiprop	KEN	10.12.83		HMar	59:55	61:31- 09
	Limo	Philemon Kimeli	KEN	2.8.85	180/62	HMar	59:32	59:30- 11
	Lin Qing		CHN-Y	5.4.95		LJ	7.96	7.95- 11
^	Lingua	Marco	ITA	4.6.78	178/118	HT	76.10	79.97- 08
	Linke	Christopher	GER	24.10.88	190/65	20kW	1:20:41	1:20:51- 11
						50kW	3:47:33	3:52:56- 11
	Litchfield	Paul	USA	27.11.80	185/80	PV	5.55 HS, 5.52A, 5.50	5.60A- 05, 5.50- 08
*	Litvinov	Sergey	RUS	27.1.86	185/105	HT	80.98	78.98- 10
*	Liu Xiang		CHN	13.7.83	189/74	110h	12.97, 12.87w	12.88- 06
	Liu Jianmin		CHN	9.3.88		20kW	1:22:41	1:23:06- 11
						50kW	4:00:58	4:12:48- 11
	Lloyd	Zack	USA	10.10.84	191/141	SP	20.95	21.03- 08
^	Lobinger	Tim	GER	3.9.72	193/86	PV	5.53i, 5.40	6.00- 97
	Lobynya	Aleksandr	RUS	31.5.84	193/115	SP	19.70	21.00- 11
	Locke	Dentarius	USA	12.12.89	170/68	100	10.18	10.25, 10.12w- 11
	Loftin	Drew	USA	15.9.80	190/102	HT	76.11	75.42- 10
	Logel	Franck	FRA	8.1.85	182/73	Dec	7655	7947w- 08, 7831- 10
	Logvinenko	Mikhail	RUS	19.4.84	186/83	Dec	7870	8004- 11
	Lohse	Jonas	SWE	15.5.87	202/110	JT	78.88	81.40- 08
	Lomnicky	Marcel	SVK	6.7.87	180/90	HT	77.43	75.84- 11
	Lomong	Lopez	USA	1.1.85	178/67	800	1:46.21	1:45.58- 08
	3000	7:44.16i	7:49.74i- 07, 7:50.36- 11			5000	13:11.63	15:07.06- 07
*	Longosiwa	Thomas	KEN	14.1.82	175/57	3000	7:33.68	7:30.09- 09
						5000	12:49.04	12:51.95- 07
	Lonyangat	Paul Kipchumba	KEN	12.12.92		HMar	59:53	-0-
	López	Kevin	ESP	12.6.90	172/60	800	1:43.74	1:44.49- 11
*	López	Miguel Ángel	ESP	3.7.88	181/70	20kW	1:19:49	1:21:41- 11
^	López	Yeimer	CUB	20.8.82	184/73	800	1:45.89	1:43.07- 08
	Losev	Ivan	UKR	26.1.86	176/65	20kW	1:20:48	1:21:31- 10
	Lovett	Eddie	USA	25.6.92	181/73	110h	13.49	13.64- 11
	Lovkin	Semyon	RUS	14.7.77	180/67	50kW	3:57:34	3:51:36- 03
	Loxsom	Casimir	USA	17.3.91	183/64	800	1:46.12	1:45.28- 11
	Loyanai ¶	Wilson	KEN	.86		Mar	2:05:37	2:09:23- 11
	Luchianov	Ion	MDA	31.1.81	178/67	3kSt	8:22.09	8:18.97- 08
	Luckwell	Mervyn	GBR	27.11.84	192/108	JT	82.15	83.52- 11

	Name	Nat	Born	Ht/Wt	Event	2012 Mark	Pre-2012 Best
	Ludolph Sören	GER	25.2.88	180/68	800	1:44.80	1:45.04- 11
	Lukyanenko Artem	RUS	30.1.90	193/84	Dec	8080	7869- 11
^	Lukyanenko Yevgeniy	RUS	23.1.85	190/80	PV	5.75	6.01- 08
	Lukyanov Denis	RUS	11.7.89	190/115	HT	74.84	74.24- 11
	Lyadusov Konstantin	RUS	2.3.88	190/125	SP	19.75i, 19.48	18.93i, 18.89- 11
	Lyakhovich Aleksandr	BLR	4.7.89		20kW	1:22:55	1:23:16- 10
	Lyashchenko Igor	UKR-J	24.8.93		20kW	1:21:07	-0-
	Lynsha Maksim	BLR	6.4.85	190/72	110h	13.36	13.46- 08
	Lyuboslavskiy Anton	RUS	26.6.84	190/137	SP	20.78	20.77- 07
*	Lyzhin Pavel	BLR	24.3.81	189/110	SP	20.69	21.21- 10
	Ma Haijun	CHN	24.11.92		20kW	1:23:02	-0-
	Mack Bobby	USA	30.12.84	170/57	10k	27:53.52	28:11.00- 11
	Mackey Trevorvano	BAH	5.1.92		200	20.52A	21.13- 11, 20.95w- 10
	Madison Chase	USA	13.9.85	192/130	DT	61.51	62.85- 08
	Maduranga Sachith	SRI	15.6.90		JT	77.80	77.29- 11
	Magakwe Simon	RSA	25.5.85	177/73	100	10.06A, 10.11	10.14A- 10, 10.18- 11
					200	20.38A, 20.59, 20.3A	20.23A, 20.44- 10
	Mägi Rasmus	EST	4.5.92	186/75	400h	49.54	50.14- 11
	Magut James	KEN	20.7.90	180/64	1500	3:33.31	3:36.8A- 09
					1M	3:50.68	
	Mahboob Ali Hasan	BRN	31.12.81	178/69	10k	27:21.40	27:24.46- 08
	Maheswary Renjith	IND	30.1.86	177/72	TJ	16.85	17.07- 10, 17.19w- 07
	Mahmoud Hassan Mohamed	EGY	10.2.84	188/123	HT	76.69	74.30- 11
	Mai Michael	USA	27.7.77	188/123	HT	75.97	76.28- 08
	Maia Edi	POR	10.11.87	176/75	PV	5.64i, 5.55	5.60- 11
	Maina Johana	KEN	24.12.90	170/54	10k	28:04.25	29:33.1A- 10
	Maisei Julius	KEN			Mar	2:08:13	2:11:12- 11
	Maiyo Augustus	USA	10.5.83	174/60	3kSt	8:29.29	8:34.28- 07
	Maiyo Jonathan	KEN	5.5.88	175/52	5000	13:22.89	13:46.3A- 10
	HMar 59:02				59:08- 09	Mar	2:04:56	2:12:45- 10
	Majdan Dusan	SVK	8.9.87		50kW	3:59:05	4:00:51- 10
*	Majewski Tomasz	POL	30.8.81	204/142	SP	21.89	21.95- 09
	Makarchev Andrly	UKR	15.11.85	192/76	LJ	7.97	8.15- 09
^	Makarov Sergey	RUS	19.3.73	192/100	JT	83.39	92.61- 02
*	Makau Patrick	KEN	2.3.85	173/57	Mar	2:06:08	2:03:38- 11
*	Makhloufi Taoufik	ALG	29.4.88	181/66	800	1:43.71	1:46.32- 11
					1500	3:30.80	3:32.94- 10
	Makhrosenko Zakhar	BLR	10.10.91		HT	73.02	68.10- 11
	Maksimov Konstantin	RUS	17.6.82	178/67	50kW	3:48:18	4:09:34- 02
	Makwala Isaac	BOT	29.9.86	183/73	400	45.25	45.56- 09
*	Malachowski Piotr	POL	7.6.83	193/130	DT	68.94	69.83- 10
^	Malcolm Christian	GBR	3.6.79	174/67	100	10.27, 10.16w	10.11, 10.09w?- 01
					200	20.46	20.08- 01
^	Malone Casey	USA	6.4.77	203/109	DT	62.46A	68.49A- 09
	Mance Josh	USA	21.3.92	190/77	400	44.83	45.29- 11
^	Maniyonga ¶ Luvo	RSA	18.11.91	185/65	LJ	8.00dq	8.26- 11
*	Mannio Ari	FIN	23.7.87	185/104	JT	84.62	85.70- 09
	Manso Dário	POR	1.7.82	183/117	HT	71.81	74.98- 07
*	Manson Andra	USA	30.4.84	196/75	HJ	2.26i, 2.20	2.35- 09
*	Mansour Bilal Ali	BRN	17.10.83	170/61	800	1:45.78	1:44.02- 07
					1500	3:35.40	3:31.49- 07
*	Manzano Leonel	USA	12.9.84	165/57	1500	3:34.08	3:32.37- 10
					1M	3:53.07	3:50.64- 10
	Maraba Wilson	KEN	.87		3kSt	8:16.96	8:37.6A- 09
	Marcell Jan	CZE	4.6.85	197/111	SP	19.61	20.76- 11
					DT	63.17	66.00- 11
	Marciniszyn Marcin	POL	7.9.82	185/72	400	45.63	45.27- 11
	Marco Luis Alberto	ESP	20.8.86	183/70	800	1:45.14	1:45.26- 10
	Marghiev Sergey	MDA	7.11.92	195/93	HT	75.20	67.54- 11
	Maric Martin	CRO	19.4.84	196/115	DT	66.53	65.81- 11
	Márquez Dayron	COL	19.11.83	181/93	JT	80.61A	79.35A- 11, 82.20Au- 08
	Marshin Dmitriy	AZE	24.2.72	180/100	HT	79.56	77.01- 10
*	Martin Cory	USA	22.5.85	196/125	SP	21.31	22.10- 10
	Martin Romain	FRA	12.7.88	198/86	Dec	7977	7867(w), 7727- 11
	Martin Ryan	USA	23.3.89	185/68	800	1:44.77	1:45.34- 11
^	Martin Scott	AUS	12.10.82	190/130	DT	65.63	64.00- 06
	Martìn Alvaro	ESP-J	18.6.94	181/65	20kW	1:22:12	-0-
^	Martìn Eliseo	ESP	5.11.73	172/61	3kSt	8:27.65	8:09.09- 03
*	Martina Churandy	NED	3.7.84	180/68	100	9.91	9.93- 08, 9.76Aw- 06, 9.92w- 10
					200	19.85	20.08- 10
	Martinez José Ernesto	CUB	1.1.91	175/73	TJ	16.39, 16.70w	61.31- 09

Name		Nat	Born	Ht/Wt	Event	2012 Mark	Pre-2012 Best
* Martìnez	Guillermo	CUB	28.6.81	185/100	JT	82.72	87.20A- 11
Martìnez	Lois Maikel	ex-CUB	3.6.81	185/90	DT	63.69	67.45- 05
Martinot-Lagarde	Pascal	FRA	22.9.91	190/80	110h	13.41, 13.30w	13.74- 10
Martos	Sebastián	ESP	20.6.89	177/60	3kSt	8:26.00	8:23.02- 11
Martynyuk	Andriy	UKR	25.9.90	179/86	HT	77.70	73.10- 11
Masai	Dennis	KEN	1.12.91	168/52	10k	27:32.79	27:32.97- 11
Masai	Gilbert	KEN	20.5.81		HMar	59:57	60:28- 10
* Masai	Moses	KEN	1.6.86	172/57	5000	12:59.21	12:50.55- 08
					10k	27:02.25	26:49.20- 07
Masai	Titus	KEN	9.10.89		HMar	60:29	59:51- 10
* Maslák	Pavel	CZE	21.2.91	176/67	400	44.91	46.89- 10
Mason	Jamele	PUR	19.10.89	190/85	400h	48.89	49.30- 11
Mason	Michael	CAN	30.9.86	186/67	HJ	2.31	2.30i, 2.30- 08
Massenberg	Aramis	USA	6.8.89	186/79	110h	13.64	13.71, 13.63 w- 11
Mástoras	Adónios	GRE	6.1.91	198/77	HJ	2.25	2.24i-10, 2.21- 08
Mätas	Risto	EST	30.4.84	190/87	JT	82.10	81.56- 11
Mateelong	Peter	KEN	26.11.89		3kSt	8:29.7A	8:37.7A- 10
* Mateelong	Richard	KEN	14.10.83	179/65	3kSt	7:56.81	8:00.89- 09
* Mathathi	Martin	KEN	25.12.85	167/52	10k	27:35.16	26:59.88- 09
Mathieu	Michael	BAH	24.6.83	180/78	200	20.16	20.38- 11
100	10.22w		10.27- 11		400	45.06	45.17- 08
Matsuoka	Yuki	JPN	14.1.86	176/59	10k	27:59.78	28:03.46- 11
Mayer	Gerhard	AUT	20.5.80	191/100	DT	63.33	65.24- 10
* Mayer	Kevin	FRA	10.2.92	186/77	Dec	8447w/8415	7992- 11
Mayers	Emanuel	TRI	9.3.89	178/70	400h	50.00	49.65- 10
Mazuryk	Maksym	UKR	2.4.83	190/85	PV	5.72i, 5.72	5.88i- 11, 5.82- 08
^ Mbishei	Titus	KEN	28.10.90	178/59	10k	27:59.15	26:59.81- 11
* Mbugua	Bernard	KEN	17.1.85	170/55	3kSt	8:08.33	8:05.88- 11
McAdams	Josh	USA	26.3.80	175/68	3kSt	8:31.15	8:21.36- 07
McBride	Brandon	CAN-J	15.6.94	186/75	800	1:46.07	1:48.41- 11
McBride	Bryan	USA	10.12.91	188/77	HJ	2.26Ai, 2.20	2.14- 11
McClain	Remontay	USA	21.9.92	188/85	100	10.16w	10.31, 10.28w- 11
					200	20.57, 20.33w	20.68- 11
McCormick	Nick	GBR	11.9.81	188/72	5000	13:18.81	13:25.34- 06
McCoy	Reuben	USA	16.3.86	186/75	400h	49.83	48.37- 08
McCullough	Conor	IRL	31.1.91	186/102	HT	75.09	72.67- 11
McDonald	Rusheen	JAM	17.8.92	175/73	400	45.10	47.32- 11
McEntee	Sam	AUS	3.2.92	183/64	1500	3:36.81	3:43.34- 11
^ McFarlane	Danny	JAM	14.6.72	185/81	400h	49.69	48.00- 04
McKenzie	Ramone	JAM	15.11.90	184/82	100	10.10, 10.05w	10.35- 09
					200	20.54	20.56- 09, 20.33w- 08
McKown	Todd	USA	19.1.90	190/80	110h	13.69, 13.42w	13.93, 13.76w- 11
McLaren	Scott	NZL	22.2.82	190/89	Dec	7733	7542- 07
McNamara	Jordan	USA	7.3.87	178/64	1500	3:35.63	3:37.19- 11
McNeill	David	AUS	6.10.86	175/59	5000	13:18.60	13:25.63- 10
* McQuay	Tony	USA	16.4.90	178/64	400	44.49	44.68- 11
Mead	Hassan	USA	28.8.89	174/61	10k	27:59.04	29:04.79- 11
* Medhin	Teklemariam	ERI	24.6.89	178/57	5000	13:17.25	13:04.55- 10
					10k	27:16.69	27:37.21- 11
Medwood	Kenneth	BIZ	14.12.87	180/73	400h	49.54	49.66- 10
Mehari	Tesfaalem	ETH-J	.93		HMar	61:07	
Meité	Ben Youssef	CIV	11.11.86	179/70	100	10.06	10.08A- 10, 10.21- 09, 10.14w- 11
Mejias	Reinier	CUB	22.9.90	180/96	HT	73.86	73.39- 11
* Mekhissi-Benabbad	Mahiedine	FRA	15.3.85	190/75	3kSt	8:10.90	8:02.09- 11
Mekonnen	Hailu	ETH	4.4.80	172/61	Mar	2:08:07	2:07:35- 11
Meli	Ezekiel	KEN	21.4.84		5000	13:22.90	13:29.85- 11
* Melich	Lukás	CZE	16.9.80	186/110	HT	79.44	79.36- 05
^ Méliz	Luis Felipe	ESP	11.8.79	182/80	LJ	8.21	8.43- 00
Melly	Edwin	KEN-Y	6.7.95	173/59	800	1:43.81	1:49.1- 11
Melnykov	Stanislav	UKR	26.2.87	184/70	400h	49.53	49.09- 10
Mendieta	José Angel	CUB	16.10.91	187/84	Dec	7833	7682- 11
Menga	Aleixo-Platini	GER	29.9.87	179/76	100	10.16w	10.27- 08
					200	20.33	20.52- 09
Mengich	Richard	KEN	.89		HMar	60:48	-0-
* Menjo	Josephat Kiprono	KEN	20.8.79	168/50	3000	7:44.07	7:42.6- 10
					5000	13:10.55	12:55.95- 10
* Menkov	Aleksandr	RUS	7.12.90	178/74	LJ	8.29	8.28- 11
Merber	Kyle	USA	19.11.90	180/64	1500	3:35.59	3:45.00- 10
Merga	Deriba	ETH	26.10.80	168/52	HMar	59:48	59:15- 08
* Merga	Imane	ETH	15.10.88	172/55	5000	12:59.77	I have 174/61 12:53.58- 10
*	10k	27:14.02		26:48.35- 11	HMar	59:56dh	-0-

Name		Nat	Born	Ht/Wt	Event	2012 Mark	Pre-2012 Best
Merga	Sentayehu	ETH	18.3.85		HMar	61:02	61:38- 11
* Merritt	Aries	USA	24.7.85	188/77	110h	12.80	13.09- 07
* Merritt	LaShawn	USA	27.6.86	188/82	200	20.16	19.98- 07, 19.80w- 08
					400	44.12	43.75- 08
Merzougui	Abdelaziz	ESP	30.8.91	179/64	3kSt	8:18.03	8:22.00- 11
Mesfin	Nahom	ETH	3.6.89	180/62	3kSt	8:18.16	8:12.04- 11
Mesic	Kemal	BIH	4.8.85	196/110	SP	20.71	19.68- 09
* Mesnil	Romain	FRA	13.6.77	188/80	PV	5.72i, 5.72	5.95- 03
Mestre	Sergio	CUB	30.8.91	194/85	HJ	2.25	2.20- 11
Metu	Obinna	NGR	12.7.88	185/75	100	10.11	10.16, 10.0- 08, 10.12w- 11
					200	20.54	20.55- 08, 20.5- 07
Meucci	Daniele	ITA	8.4.85	178/62	3000	7:41.74	7:43.85- 10
5000	13:19.00		13:24.38- 10		10k	27:32.86	27:44.50- 11
* Michalski	Lukasz	POL	2.8.88	190/85	PV	5.72i, 5.72	5.85- 11
* Mikhnevich	Andrey	BLR	12.7.76	202/140	SP	20.90	22.10- 11
Mikhon	Eduard	BLR	7.6.89	194/85	Dec	7928	8152- 11
^ Miles	Derek	USA	28.9.72	190/88	PV	5.60i, 5.60	5.85i- 05, 5.85sq- 08
Milkiewicz	Arkadiusz	POL	13.8.87	185/85	HT	72.55	67.79- 11
Miller	Craig	USA	3.8.87	185/72	1500	3:36.35	3:37.56- 11
Miller	Ramon	BAH	17.2.87	180/73	200	20.50, 20.29w	21.29- 08, 21.06w- 11
					400	44.87	44.99- 09
Miller	Wanner	COL	22.7.87	190/78	HJ	2.28	2.22- 09
Million	Zewdie	ETH	24.1.89	166/53	10k	27:54.52	
Milne	Taylor	CAN	14.6.81	180/66	1M	3:54.29	3:56.54- 09
Milokumov	Sergey	RUS	13.11.87		HJ	2.25i	2.24- 10
Minagawa	Sumito	JPN	26.9.90	182/67	LJ	7.93	7.83- 09
Minshin	Ildar	RUS	5.2.85	172/63	3kSt	8:23.07	8:17.74- 11
Misans	Elvijs	LAT	8.4.89	190/77	LJ	8.00i, 7.96	8.00i, 7.88- 11
Mitchell	Curtis	USA	11.3.89	188/79	200	20.24w	19.99- 10
Mitchell	Manteo	USA	6.7.87	178/73	200	20.47	20.78- 11, 20.73w- 09
					400	44.96	45.95- 11
* Mitchell	Maurice	USA	22.12.89	181/73	100	10.03	10.00- 11
					200	20.13, 20.08w	20.19, 19.99w- 11
Mitchell	Sheldon	JAM	.90	181/75	100	10.14	10.22- 11
Miyao	Kotaro	JPN	12.7.91	172/72	400h	49.88	50.85- 11
Miyawaki	Chihiro	JPN	28.8.91	174/55	10k	27:41.57	27:41.57- 11
					HMar	60:53	-0-
Mizuno	Tatsuhiko	JPN	25.10.90	176/67	400h	49.99	50.36- 11
Modike	Lucky Mohale	RSA	21.8.85		HMar	61:08	61:58- 10
Moeng	Lebogang	RSA	10.10.89	173/67	200	20.51A	20.58- 11
					400	45.75	45.47- 11
Moffatt	Keith	USA	20.6.84	203/84	HJ	2.26i	2.30- 06
Mogawane	Ofentse	RSA	20.2.82	179/63	400	45.54A, 45.80	45.11- 06
Mohammed	Mukhtar	GBR	1.12.90	175/59	800	1:46.10	1:45.90- 11
* Mohr	Malte	GER	24.7.86	192/84	PV	5.91	5.90- 10
Möhsner	Sven	GER	30.1.86	190/115	HT	73.24	73.82- 09
Mokdel	Lyès	ALG	20.6.90	195/84	110h	13.64	13.80- 11, 13.5- 10
* Mokoena	Khotso	RSA	6.3.85	190/73	LJ	8.29A	8.50- 09
Mokoka	Stephen	RSA	31.1.85	156/50	10k	27:40.73	27:56.18- 11
HMar	60:57		61:26- 09		Mar	2:09:43	2:08:33- 10
Molina	Juan Manuel	ESP	15.3.79	173/67	50kW	4:01:13	3:55:12- 06
Mononen	Matti	FIN	25.11.83	176/75	PV	5.55	5.70- 06
Montgomery	Lawson	USA	9.7.90	186/80	110h	13.63	14.03, 13.70w- 11
Moradi	Sadjad	IRI	30.3.83	182/67	800	1:45.98	1:44.74- 05
Morales	Ignacio	CUB	28.1.87	183/69	110h	13.54, 13.5	13.51- 09, 13.1- 08
Moranga	Justus	KEN	.87		HMar	61:07	62:03- 09
Moreno	Eder César	COL	4.2.89	185/120	SP	19.53	19.48- 11
Moreno	Xavier	ECU	15.11.79	168/60	50kW	3:58:57	3:52:07- 07
Morgan	Carl	CAY	25.8.86	183/82	LJ	8.02	7.82- 08
Morgan	Jason	JAM	6.10.82	186/114	DT	67.15	64.11- 11
* Morgunov	Sergey	RUS-J	9.2.93	178/70	LJ	8.35	8.10, 8.18w- 11
* Morioka	Koichiro	JPN	2.4.85	184/65	20kW	1:21:52	1:20:43- 10
					50kW	3:43:14	3:44:45- 11
^ Morozov ¶	Sergey	RUS	21.3.88	170/60	20kW	1:17:52dq	1:16:43- 08
Morse	Brett	GBR	11.2.89	191/114	DT	64.35	66.06- 11
Morton	Amaechi	NGR	30.10.89	186/79	400h	48.79	48.94- 10
* Mosop	Moses	KEN	17.7.85	172/57	Mar	2:05:03	2:05:36, 2:03:06wdh- 11
Mosoti	Lewis	KEN	.88	167/54	10k	27:22.54	28:55.2A- 09
Moss	Curtis	CAN	12.4.87	175/82	JT	81.21	78.32- 09
Moss	Miller	USA	14.3.88	193/86	Dec	7712	7996- 11
Motlagale	Tumelo	RSA	26.11.86		3kSt	8:24.76	8:30.24- 11

Name		Nat	Born	Ht/Wt	Event	2012 Mark	Pre-2012 Best
^ Mottram	Craig	AUS	18.6.80	188/72	5000	13:16.08	12:55.76- 04
Moulinet	Bertrand	FRA	6.1.87	178/63	20kW	1:20:12	1:21:50- 11
					50kW	3:45:35	3:50:49- 11
Mousavi	Kaveh	IRI	27.5.85	196/105	HT	73.16	75.26- 11
* Moustaoui	Mohammed	MAR	2.4.85	174/60	1500	3:35.46	3:32.06- 08
					5000	13:23.09	13:22.61- 05
Mpuang	Thuso	RSA	1.3.84	177/75	200	20.44A,20.60,20.1A 20.53A- 08	20.55,20.40w- 11
Mucheru	Boniface	KEN	2.5.92	185/75	400h	49.45	50.35A- 11
* Mudrov	Sergey	RUS	8.9.90	188/79	HJ	2.31	2.30i- 09, 2.30- 11
Mulabegovic	Nedzad	CRO	4.2.81	190/120	SP	20.66	20.56- 10
Mulaudzi	Mbulaeni	RSA	8.9.80	171/62	800	1:45.78	1:42.86- 09
* Mulder	Tyler	USA	15.2.87	189/77	800	1:44.75	1:44.83- 11
Müller	Norman	GER	7.8.85	195/84	Dec	8034	8295- 09
Mullera	Ángel	ESP	20.4.84	175/62	3kSt	8:13.71	8:16.47- 11
Münch	Markus	GER	13.6.86	207/117	DT	66.28	64.96- 07
Mundell	Marc	RSA	7.7.83	189/86	50kW	3:55:32	4:04:42- 09
Munyeki Kiama	Charles	KEN	2.11.86		Mar	2:07:41	2:07:06- 09
* Murakami	Yukifumi	JPN	23.12.79	186/102	JT	83.95	83.53- 11
Murasawa	Akinobu	JPN	28.3.91	166/53	10k	27:50.59	28:00.78- 11
Murgor	Wilfred K.	KEN	12.12.88	178/65	HMar	61:02	-0-
* Murofushi	Koji	JPN	8.10.74	187/103	HT	78.71	84.86- 03
Murphy	Isaac	USA	5.10.90	188/83	Dec	8067	7806- 11
Murray	Ross	GBR	8.10.90	180/70	1500	3:34.76	3:43.51- 10
					1M	3:52.77	-0-
Murray	Ty'reak	USA	.92		110h	13.60wA	14.08- 00, 13.5- 02
Mutahi	Sammy Alex	KEN	1.6.89	177/58	5000	13:16.21	13:00.12- 10
* Mutai	Abel	KEN	2.10.88	187/73	3kSt	8:01.67	8:11.40- 09
* Mutai	Emmanuel	KEN	12.10.84	168/54	Mar	2:08:01	2:04:40- 11
* Mutai	Geoffrey	KEN	7.10.81	170/54	Mar	2:04:15	2:04:55- 10, 2:03:02wdh- 11
Mutai	Laban	KEN	.85		Mar	2:08:01	-0-
Mutai	Vincent	KEN-J	3.11.94	174/61	1500	3:35.45	3:39.17- 11
Mutua	David	KEN	20.4.92	184/68	800	1:44.66	1:43.99- 11
Mutunga	Patrick	KEN-J	20.11.94	172/54	5000	13:21.22	13:19.13- 11
					10k	27:30.32	-0-
Mvumuvre	Gabriel	ZIM	23.4.88	172/75	100	10.16w	10.23, 10.10w- 11
Mwaka	Patrick	KEN	2.11.92	165/45	10k	27:41.39	27:33.14- 11
Mwangangi	John	KEN	1.11.90		HMar	59:58	59:45- 11
Mwangi	Alex	KEN	14.6.90	158/50	10k	27:54.86	27:42.20- 10
^ Myerscough	Carl	GBR	21.10.79	209/149	SP	20.13	21.92- 03
					DT	65.24	65.10- 04
Myklebust	Gaute	NOR	29.4.79	195/120	DT	64.08	63.32- 05
Mykolaychuk	Dmytro	UKR	30.1.87	192/89	HT	72.96	75.24- 11
Nailel	Hosea	KEN	.88		HMar	61:17	63:16A- 11
Nakamura	Akihiko	JPN	23.10.90	180/73	400h	49.38	50.04- 11
					Dec	7710	7675- 11
Nartov	Oleksandr	UKR	21.5.88	182/67	HJ	2.31	2.30i- 07, 2.30- 08
Nascimento	Carlos	POR-J	12.10.94	179/70	100	10.19w	10.58- 11
Nascimento	Yazaldes	POR	17.4.86	181/75	100	10.20w	10.39, 10.15w- 11
Nasti	Patrick	ITA	30.8.89	193/75	3kSt	8:29.08	8:40.30- 11
* Nava	Horacio	MEX	20.1.82	175/62	20kW	1:22:04	1:22:15- 11
					50kW	3:46:59	3:45:21- 08
* Nazarov	Dilshod	TJK	6.5.82	187/115	HT	77.70	80.30- 11
Nderitu	Julius	KEN	.76		Mar	2:08:01	2:10:25- 11
Ndiema	Eric	KEN	28.12.92	174/58	HMar	61:15	59:57- 09
					Mar	2:06:17	2:06:07- 11
* Ndiku	Caleb	KEN	9.10.92	183/68	1500	3:32.39	3:32.02- 11
1M	3:50.00		3:49.77- 11		3000	7:30.99	7:52.89- 09
* Ndiku	Jonathan	KEN	18.9.91	173/60	3kSt	8:17.88	8:07.75- 11
Ndirangu	Charles	KEN-J	8.2.93	170/50	5000	13:23.40	13:15.44- 11
					10k	27:58.02	-0-
Ndiwa	Cornelius	KEN	17.12.88	183/64	1500	3:36.29	3:36.09- 10
Ndungu	Samuel	KEN	4.4.88	166/53	Mar	2:07:04	-0-
Nedow	Tim	CAN	16.10.90	198/125	SP	20.51i, 20.21	19.51i, 18.84- 11
* Nellum	Bryshon	USA	1.5.89	183/79	400	44.80	45.38- 07
* Nelson	Adam	USA	7.7.75	183/115	SP	21.54	22.51- 02
Nelson	Billy	USA	11.9.84	167/55	3kSt	8:21.42	8:17.27- 11
Németh	Kristóf	HUN	17.9.87	190/97	HT	75.67	76.45- 10
Nerdal	Steffen	NOR	22.2.85	197/130	HT	72.96	72.60- 10
Nesterenko	Mykyta	UKR	15.4.91	202/97	DT	64.20	65.31- 08
Nesterovskyy	Stanislav	UKR	31.7.80	198/110	DT	62.00	64.94- 07
Newdick	Brent	NZL	31.1.85	189/89	Dec	8057	8114- 11

Name		Nat	Born	Ht/Wt	Event	2012 Mark	Pre-2012 Best
Newman	Calesio	USA	20.8.86	172/66	100	10.07	10.14- 11, 10.08w- 08
					200	20.28, 20.17w	20.53- 11
Ngetich	Christopher	KEN	25.12.92		400h	50.04A, 50.46	51.10A- 11
Ngetich	Hillary	KEN-Y	15.9.95		1500	3:36.15	
Niedermeyer	Darren	USA	2.4.82	193/84	PV	5.51	5.71i- 10. 5.70- 09
Nielsen	Peder	DEN	13.9.88	184/75	TJ	16.73, 16.88w	16.49- 11
* Nieto	James	USA	2.11.76	193/79	HJ	2.31	2.34- 04
Niit	Marek	EST	9.8.87	188/79	100	10.19	10.21, 10.17w- 11
Nikfar	Amin	IRI	2.1.81	198/130	SP	19.51	20.05- 11
Niklaus	André	GER	30.8.81	190/82	Dec	7797	8371- 07
Nikolayev	Sergey	RUS	1.9.87		LJ	8.00i, 7.91	8.07- 10, 8.20w- 11
Nilsson	Marcus	SWE	3.5.91	185/90	Dec	7823	7400- 11
Nima	Issam	ALG	8.4.79	186/74	TJ	16.89	16.80- 11
Ninov	Viktor	BUL	19.6.88	197/82	HJ	2.27i, 2.27	2.29- 11
Niu Wenbin		CHN	20.1.91		20kW	1:22:13	1:24:23- 10
^ Nixon	Greg	USA	12.9.81	183/75	400	45.77	44.61- 10
Nixon	Gunnar	USA-J	13.1.93	190/77	Dec	7892	7577w, 7524- 11
Njeru	Micah	KEN	5.8.88	166/53	10k	27:56.67	27:48.40- 07
^ Noga	Artur	POL	2.5.88	195/82	110h	13.27	13.29, 13.20w- 10
Noguchi	Hiroshi	JPN	3.5.83	176/115	HT	71.22	71.58- 10
Nolan	Errol	USA/JAM	18.8.91	178/73	400	45.25	45.30- 11
Norwood	Vernon	USA	10.4.92	187/77	400	45.72A, 45.98	47.47, 46.61dq- 11
Noskov	Ivan	RUS	16.7.88		50kW	3:55:16	-0-
Nossmy	Philip	SWE	6.12.82	189/87	110h	13.47	13.50- 03
Nour Emad Hamed Mohamed		KSA	21.4.90	171/55	1500	3:34.19	3:37.21- 10
Novotny	Roman	CZE	5.1.86	180/73	LJ	8.22	8.21- 08
* Nowak	Lukasz	POL	18.12.88	194/77	20kW	1:21:12	1:23:34- 10, 1:21:30sh- 11
					50kW	3:42:47	3:46:40- 11
Nowicki	Wojciech	POL	22.2.89	190/90	HT	73.52	72.72- 11
Nozawa	Keisuke	JPN	7.6.91	175/63	400h	49.15	50.32- 11
Nugent	Barrett	USA	29.1.90	186/77	110h	13.32A, 13.36	13.35- 10, 13.19w- 11
Nurudeen	Selim	NGR	1.2.83	183/75	110h	13.51	13.55- 10
Nychyporchuk	Oleksandr	UKR	14.4.92	185/84	JT	81.65	75.28- 11
^ Nymark	Trond	NOR	28.12.76	180/66	50kW	3:48:37	3:41:16- 09
Odom	Marlon	GER	4.12.82	189/75	110h	13.59	13.50- 10, 13.45w- 06
Odriozola	Mikel	ESP	25.5.73	180/62	50kW	4:02:48	3:41:47- 05
Ogho-Oghene	Egweru	NGR	26.11.88	171/66	100	10.19, 10.13w	10.06- 11, 10.0- 08
Ogita	Hiroki	JPN	30.12.87	185/78	PV	5.65	5.56- 08
Okabe	Yuma	JPN	13.7.90	170/62	TJ	16.54	16.30- 11
* Oke	Tosin	NGR	1.10.80	178/77	TJ	17.23	17.22A- 10, 17.21- 11
* Okoye	Lawrence	GBR	6.10.91	198/137	DT	68.24	67.63- 11
Okutu	Jean Marie	ESP	4.8.88	179/70	LJ	7.94, 8.05w	7.94- 09
Oleitiptip	Alex	KEN	22.9.82	176/58	5000	13:08.59	13:12.76- 11
Olgundeniz	Ercüment	TUR	7.7.76	203/120	DT	67.50	66.89- 11
Olinger	Brian	USA	2.6.83	178/62	10k	27:50.58	28:07.52- 11
					3kSt	8:30.08	8:19.29- 07
Olivares	Horacio	MEX	18.4.91		50kW	3:52:47A	-0-
* Oliver	David	USA	24.4.82	188/93	110h	13.07	12.89- 10
Olivier	André	RSA	29.12.89	192/72	800	1:44.29	1:45.41- 09
Ollikainen	Ronni	FIN	27.8.90	188/76	LJ	8.05, 8.32w	8.04- 11
* Olmedo	Manuel	ESP	17.5.83	179/60	1500	3:36.50	3:34.44- 11
Oloisunga	Benson	KEN	.86		HMar	61:07	-0-
Olson	Petter	SWE	14.2.91	183/81	Dec	7857	7724- 11
Omuro	Hideki	JPN	25.7.90	180/67	110h	13.54	13.76- 10, 13.66w- 11
Oni	Samson	GBR	25.6.81	183/74	HJ	2.31i, 2.28	2.31i- 10, 2.30- 08
^ Onnen	Eike	GER	3.8.82	194/83	HJ	2.26	2.34- 07
Opatskyy	Yuriy	UKR	5.11.79	180/75	TJ	16.53w	16.48- 01
* Oprea	Marian	ROU	6.6.82	190/80	TJ	16.97i, 16.56, 16.68w	17.81- 05
Ortega	Orlando	CUB	29.7.91	185/70	110h	13.09	13.29, 13.1w- 11
Orth	Florian	GER	24.7.89	181/64	1500	3:34.56	3:40.60- 10
* Osaghae	Omo	USA	18.5.88	188/82	110h	13.24, 13.20w	13.23, 13.18w- 11
* Osagie	Andrew	GBR	19.2.88	189/72	800	1:43.77	1:45.36- 11
Osako	Suguru	JPN	23.5.91	170/53	10k	27:56.94	28:35.75- 10
Osei	Philip	CAN	30.10.90	176/64	400	45.51A	46.83- 11
Osewski	Bartosz	POL	20.3.91	191/100	JT	83.89	72.30- 11
Oslizlo	Lukasz	POL	14.5.89	178/60	3kSt	8:27.61	8:38.28- 11
Osman	Abrar	ERI-J	1.1.94	173/55	5000	13:17.32	13:43.02- 11
Otterling	Andreas	SWE	25.5.86	183/80	LJ	8.03	7.89i, 7.72, 7.97w- 11
* Otto	Björn	GER	16.10.77	191/90	PV	6.01	5.90- 07
Oualich	Hamid	FRA	26.4.88	184/68	800	1:45.96	1:46.06- 10
Ouhadi	Aziz	MAR	24.7.84	175/73	100	10.10	10.09- 11, 9.9- 09
					200	20.50	20.51A- 10, 20.62- 11

Name		Nat	Born	Ht/Wt	Event	2012 Mark	Pre-2012 Best
Outzen	Matthew	AUS	12.10.87	185/100	JT	78.16	79.41- 10
* Özbilen	Ilham Tanui	TUR	5.3.90	177/62	1500	3:33.32	3:31.37- 11
* Padgett	Travis	USA	13.12.86	174/80	100	10.04, 9.88w	9.89, 9.85w- 08
Paes	Lutimar	BRA	14.12.88	179/70	800	1:46.37	1:45.32- 11
Pahlevanyan	Vartan	ARM	27.2.88	192/82	LJ	8.20A ?, 8.12	8.00A, 7.90w- 11, 7.82- 10
Pai Long		CHN	8.10.89		HJ	2.28	2.20- 10
Palma	Ever	MEX	18.3.92	176/66	20kW	1:22:15	1:21:02- 11
Palma	Isaac	MEX	26.10.90	174/59	20kW	1:21:14	1:24:04- 11
Palomeque ¶	Diego	COL-J	5.12.93	176/68	400	45.62A	46.74A- 11
Panocha	Babu Bhai	IND	10.8.78		20kW	1:22:56	1:23:04- 11
^ Papadimitrìou	Aléxandros	GRE	18.6.73	185/115	HT	71.80	80.45- 00
PapamihaÌl	Aléxandros	GRE	18.9.88	178/63	20kW	1:21:12	1:23:21- 11
					50kW	3:49:56	4:11:21- 08
* Parchment	Hansle	JAM	17.6.90	196/90	110h	13.12	13.24- 11
Parellis	Apostolos	CYP	24.7.85	186/110	DT	65.36	61.92- 10
Park Chil-sung		KOR	8.7.82	174/64	50kW	3:45:55	3:47:13- 11
Park Jae-myong		KOR	15.12.81	180/95	JT	78.60	83.99- 04
Park Tae-kyong		KOR	30.7.80	181/75	110h	13.66, 13.57w	13.48- 10
Parkhomenko	Aleksandr	BLR	22.3.81	182/82	Dec	7789	8136- 06
* Pars	Krisztián	HUN	18.2.82	188/113	HT	82.28	82.45- 06
Parsons	Tom	GBR	5.5.84	192/80	HJ	2.25	2.31i- 11, 2.30- 08
Parszczynski	Lukasz	POL	4.5.85	180/64	3kSt	8:21.80	8:15.47- 11
Patel	Mani Ram	IND	16.9.91		20kW	1:22:37.26t	1:24:51.0t- 11
Patrakov	Andrey	RUS	7.11.89	196/80	HJ	2.30i	2.25i , 2.21- 11
* Patton	Darvis	USA	4.12.77	183/75	100	9.96	9.89, 9.84w- 08
					200	20.32, 20.24w	20.03- 03, 19.98w- 11
Pauli	Jake	USA	15.6.79	191/86	PV	5.53	5.82- 07
^ Pavlov	Igor	RUS	18.7.79	187/83	PV	5.60	5.90i- 05, 5.81- 07
* Payne	David	USA	24.7.82	185/81	110h	13.32, 13.22w	13.02- 07
Peacock	Hamish	AUS	15.10.90	186/96	JT	79.33	77.58- 11
Peçanha	Fabiano	BRA	5.6.82	186/73	800	1:45.31	1:44.60- 07
Peder	Ahti	EST	29.8.76	178/82	JT	78.82	75.33- 11
Peña	José Gregorio	VEN	12.1.87	163/60	3kSt	8:24.06	8:34.90- 11
Perry	Willie	USA	16.5.87	178/73	100	10.15w	10.12- 06
Persent	Louis	GBR	18.7.90	183/75	400	45.77	46.56- 10
* Pestano	Mario	ESP	8.4.78	195/120	DT	67.15	69.50- 08
^ Phillips	Isa	JAM	22.4.84	193/84	400h	49.86	48.05- 09
Phillips	Richard	JAM	26.1.83	188/75	110h	13.43	13.39- 04, 13.33w- 08
Phiri	Gerald	ZAM	6.10.88	184/80	100	10.11	10.06- 11, 10.03Aw- 08
Piantella	Giorgio	ITA	6.7.81	183/81	PV	5.60	5.60- 10
Pichardo	Pedro Pablo	CUB-J	30.6.93	184/71	TJ	16.79	16.09- 11
* Pinder	Demetrius	BAH	13.2.89	178/70	200	20.23	20.54- 11
					400	44.77	44.78- 11
Pineda	Daniel	CHI	19.9.85	178/72	LJ	8.08	8.00A- 11, 7.97- 10
Pinkelman	Luke	USA	5.5.88	190/114	SP	20.02	20.07i, 19.17- 11
* Pishchalnikov	Bogdan	RUS	26.8.82	196/120	DT	65.96	67.23- 10
Pistorius	Oscar	RSA	22.11.86	181/77	400	45.20A, 45.44 with prosthetics	45.07- 11
* Pitkämäki	Tero	FIN	19.12.82	195/92	JT	86.98	91.53- 05
Platnitskiy	Dmitriy	BLR	26.8.88	189/80	TJ	16.85, 16.87w	16.91- 10
^ Plawgo	Marek	POL	25.2.81	183/72	400h	49.66	48.12- 07
Plener	Marcin	POL	22.8.90	184/84	JT	78.95	75.00- 10
^ Pognon	Ronald	FRA	16.11.82	185/75	100	10.17w	9.99- 05
Pohle	Andreas	GER	6.4.81	178/65	TJ	16.64	16.99- 04
Poistogov	Stepan	RUS	14.12.86	182/68	800	1:46.02	1:46.59- 11
Pokidov	Dmitriy	RUS	20.12.90		HJ	2.26	2.18- 10
Polyanskiy	Sergey	RUS	29.10.89		LJ	8.01	8.00, 8.18w- 11
Poom-urai	Pramote	THA	24.9.89		HJ	2.26	2.14- 09
Porter	Garland	USA	10.2.82	193/118	HT	71.72	72.99- 11
* Porter	Jeff	USA	27.11.85	183/84	110h	13.08	13.26- 11
Portilla	Jhoanis	CUB	24.7.90	181/70	110h	13.67, 13.41	13.62, 13.4, 13.3dt- 10, 13.1w- 11
Pouzy	Frédérick	FRA	18.2.83	184/88	HT	77.05	76.95- 07
Povegliano	Lorenzo	ITA	11.11.84	187/102	HT	79.08	76.96- 11
* Powell	Asafa	JAM	23.11.82	190/88	100	9.85	9.72- 08
Powlen	Bryan	USA	3.12.87	193/120	DT	61.09	57.01- 11
Pozdnyakov	Aleksandr	RUS	1.2.87	187/100	HT	76.19	76.59- 11
Pozzi	Andrew	GBR	15.5.92	186/79	110h	13.34	13.73, 13.66w- 11
Prásil	Ladislav	CZE	17.5.90	198/125	SP	20.14	18.41- 11
Preble	Michael	USA	15.4.90	181/68	800	1:46.43	1:47.27i, 1:47.71- 11
Prem Kumar	Kumaravel	IND-J	2.6.93		LJ	7.94	7.86- 10
Premeru	Marin	CRO	29.8.90	186/115	SP	20.45	19.80-09
Prey	Mathias	GER	9.8.88	192/89	Dec	7863	7923(w), 7827- 11

Name		Nat	Born	Ht/Wt	Event	2012 Mark		Pre-2012 Best
Prezelj	Rozle	SLO	26.9.79	193/73	HJ	2.32		2.31i- 04, 2.30- 06
Price	Tim	USA	26.12.87	183/84	100	10.16wA		10.42, 10.27w- 11
					200	20.46wA		21.23, 20.92w- 11
Prieto	Miguel Ángel	ESP	20.9.64	187/81	50kW	4:01:24		4:03:35- 11
Primak	Artyom	RUS-J	14.1.93	190/77	TJ	16.76		15.60- 11
Prokhorov	Aleksandr	RUS	22.1.86	176/62	20kW	1:21:06		1:20:51- 06
Prorok	Josef	CZE	16.11.87	190/78	400h	49.74		49.68- 10
Protsenko	Andriy	UKR	20.5.88	190/65	HJ	2.31i, 2.31		2.31- 11
Prugovecki	Marko	CRO	1.1.87	180/75	LJ	8.00		7.77- 10
Puplampu	Michael	GBR	11.1.90	176/73	TJ	16.59w		15.44- 09
Puskedra	Luke	USA	8.2.90	193/75	10k	27:56.62		28:33.47- 11
* Pyatnytsya	Oleksandr	UKR	14.7.85	186/90	JT	86.12		84.11- 10
Qin Qiang		CHN	18.4.83	184/105	JT	80.77		81.48- 09
Quérin	Gaîl	FRA	26.6.87	182/76	Dec	8098		7939- 11
Quiller	Rory	USA	17.4.84	190/82	PV	5.60A		5.65i- 08, 5.51- 07
^ Quiñónez	Alex	ECU	11.8.89	176/65	200	20.28	20.49A,	21.05, 20.95w- 11
^ Quow	Renny	TRI	25.8.87	170/66	400	45.48		44.53- 09
Rakoczy	Pawel	POL	15.5.87	187/90	JT	84.99		82.53- 11
Ramolefi	Ruben	RSA	17.7.78	174/56	3kSt	8:24.28		8:11.50- 11
Rana	Abbal Singh	IND	14.3.90		20kW	1:22:19.35t		-0-
Rana	Basant Bahadur	IND	18.1.84		50kW	3:56:48		4:10:42- 08
Randolph	Chris	USA	25.4.84	190/89	Dec	7840		8066- 08
Rapinier	Yoann	FRA	29.9.89	182/70	TJ	16.76	17.23i- 11,	16.58, 16.73w- 10
Rassioui	Bader	MAR	8.6.85	179/66	1500	3:34.55		3:35.00- 10
Rayson	Ian	AUS	4.2.88	185/75	50kW	4:00:39		3:57:55- 11
Redrick	Philip	USA	2.8.88	183/79	100	10.18w		10.27, 10.23w- 11
Regassa	Dejene	BRN	18.4.89	173/55	5000	13:20.43		13:24.27- 11
					3kSt	8:25.66		8:39.53- 11
Regassa	Tilahun	ETH	18.1.90	170/54	5000	13:21.01		13:12.40- 08
10k	27:18.90		27:32.60- 08		Mar	2:05:27		-0-
Reid	Julian	GBR	23.9.88	186/77	TJ	16.35i, 16.76w		16.98, 17.10w- 09
* Reif	Christian	GER	24.10.84	195/84	LJ	8.26		8.47- 10
^ Reina	Antonio Manuel	ESP	13.6.81	186/71	800	1:44.65		1:43.83- 02
Reitze	Marvin Rene	GER	24.8.88	180/77	PV	5.52		5.46- 06
Renaudie	Paul	FRA	2.4.90	192/78	800	1:45.85		1:46.99- 11
Rendón	James	COL	7.4.85	170/60	20kW	1:22:54		1:21:13.6t- 11
Renshaw	Lachlan	AUS	4.2.87	180/70	800	1:45.75		1:45.66- 11
Reus	Julian	GER	29.4.88	176/75	100	10.09		10.28- 07
* Revé	Ernesto	CUB	26.2.92	181/65	TJ	17.13		17.40- 11
Revenko	Vladislav	UKR	15.11.84	181/71	PV	5.70		5.80- 05
Rew	Quentin	NZL	16.7.84		50kW	3:55:03		4:06:57- 11
Richards	O'Dayne	JAM	14.12.88	180/114	SP	20.31		19.93- 11
* Richardson	Jason	USA	4.4.86	186/73	110h	12.98		13.04- 11
Ricks	Keith	USA	9.10.90	183/75	200	20.45		20.80- 11
Rietveld	Pelle	NED	4.2.85	184/75	Dec	8073		7955- 07
* Riley	Andrew	JAM	9.9.88	188/80	100	10.02		10.40- 11
					110h	13.19		13.32- 11
^ Rimmer	Michael	GBR	3.2.86	180/71	800	1:44.86		1:43.89- 10
					1000	2:17.13		2:19.77- 08
Riseley	Jeff	AUS	11.11.86	192/75	800	1:44.48		1:44.64- 11
1000	2:16.63		2:16.75- 11		1500	3:36.10		3:32.93- 09
^ Ritzenhein	Dathan	USA	30.12.82	170/52	5000	13:14.72		12:56.27- 09
10k	27:36.09	27:22.28- 09		HMar	60:57		60:00- 09	Mar 2:07:47	2:10:00- 09
Rivera	Edgar	MEX	13.2.91	191/80	HJ	2.25		2.28- 11
Rivera	Luis	MEX	21.6.87	183/82	LJ	8.22	7.99i- 10, 7.95- 09,	7.99w- 10
Roach	Kimmari	JAM	21.9.90	175/73	100	10.20, 10.16w		10.13- 10
Roberts	Gil	USA	15.3.89	183/75	200	20.54A		20.65- 11
					400	44.84		44.86- 09
* Roberts	Kurtis	USA	20.2.88	191/127	SP	21.14		19.80i- 10, 19.55- 11
Robertson	Josef	JAM	14.5.87	176/63	400h	49.16		49.22- 09
Robertson	Ricky	USA	19.9.90	178/70	HJ	2.32		2.29- 11
Robertson	Zane	NZL	14.11.89	180/65	1500	3:36.53		3:41.77- 11
Robinson	Josh	AUS	4.10.85	187/95	JT	78.97		80.73- 07
Robinson	Khadevis	USA	19.7.76	183/74	800	1:44.54		1:43.68-06
Robinson	Marcus	USA	18.12.88	188/79	TJ	16.63i, 16.46		16.06- 11
* Robles	Dayron	CUB	19.11.86	191/91	110h	13.10		12.87- 08
* Rodgers	Michael	USA	24.4.85	178/73	100	9.94		9.85- 11
Rodhe	Justin	CAN	17.10.84	188/125	SP	21.11		20.77i, 20.06- 11
Rodriguez	Rafith	COL	1.6.89	187/73	800	1:45.41		1:44.31- 11
Rodríguez	Álvaro	ESP	25.5.87	185/66	800	1:45.94		1:45.8- 10
					1500	3:34.10		3:35.76- 09

Name		Nat	Born	Ht/Wt	Event	2012 Mark	Pre-2012 Best
Rodrìguez	Ángel David	ESP	25.4.80	178/66	100	10.17A, 10.26, 10.24w	10.14- 08
Rogers	Jason	SKN	31.8.91	173/66	100	10.06A, 10.24	10.35A- 11
Röhler	Thomas	GER	30.9.91	191/82	JT	80.79	78.20- 11
Romanenko	Oleksandr	UKR	26.6.81	168/60	50kW	3:58:31	4:01:05- 11
Romani	Darlan	BRA	9.4.91		SP	20.48	18.46- 11
Rome	Jarred	USA	21.12.76	194/140	DT	64.76	68.76- 11
Rono	Aron	KEN	1.11.82	173/57	5000	13:23.52	13:30.58- 11
					10k	28:06.74	27:31.15- 11
Rono	Augustine	KEN	.81		Mar	2:07:23	2:08:05- 11
Rono	Philemon	KEN	8.2.91		HMar	60:58	0
* Rooney	Martyn	GBR	3.4.87	198/78	400	44.92	44.60- 08
Rop	Albert	KEN-J	20.12.94	176/55	3000	7:43.50	7:35.66- 11
					5000	13:01.91	13:03.70- 11
Ross	Floyd	USA	7.3.90	185/73	TJ	16.61	15.66i, 15.53- 10
Ross	Joshua	AUS	9.2.81	185/81	100	10.23, 10.16w	10.08- 07
Ross	Nick	USA	8.8.91	188/75	HJ	2.28	2.25i- 11, 2.22- 09
Roth	Scott	USA	25.6.88	180/73	PV	5.60Ai, 5.60	5.72i- 10, 5.72- 11
^ Röthlin	Viktor	SUI	14.10.74	172/60	Mar	2:08:32	2:07:23- 08
* Rotich	Abraham Kipchirchir	KEN-J	26.6.93	181/62	800	1:43.13	1:46.4A- 11
					1000	2:17.08	-0-
* Rotich	Lucas	KEN	16.4.90	171/57	5000	13:09.58	12:55.06- 10
10k	27:09.38		26:43.98- 11		HMar	60:32	59:44- 11
Rotich	Milton	KEN	.84		HMar	60:43	61:12- 11
^ Roulhac	Brandon	USA	13.12.83	188/73	TJ	16.71, 16.74w	17.26, 17.44w- 09
Rowland	Marcus	USA	11.3.90	176/73	100	10.09	10.03, 10.02w- 09
					200	20.51, 20.50w	20.49, 20.48w- 11
Rozinski	Pawel	POL	11.7.87	198/91	JT	78.80	78.83- 11
Rubanko	Artem	UKR	21.3.74	191/110	HT	78.18	80.44- 04
Rubel	Andriy	UKR	24.5.89		HJ	2.25	2.23i- 10, 2.20- 09
* Rubino	Giorgio	ITA	15.4.86	176/55	20kW	1:20:10	1:19:37- 09
* Rudisha	David	KEN	17.12.88	189/73	800	1:40.91	1:41.01- 10
Rudys	Marius	LTU	15.11.85		LJ	7.95	7.79- 11
Rulz	Diego	ESP	5.2.82	178/68	1500	3:35.16	3:33.18- 11
* Rupp	Galen	USA	8.5.86	180/62	1500	3:34.75	3:39.14- 09
1M	3:57.10i		3:56.22i, 3:57.72- 10		2M	8:09.72i	8:57.75i- 03
5000	12:58.90		13:06.86- 11		10k	27:25.33	26:48.00- 11
Russell	Scott	CAN	16.1.79	206/122	JT	80.60	84.81- 11
* Rutherford	Greg	GBR	17.11.86	188/84	LJ	8.35	8.30- 09, 8.32w- 11
Ruto	Evans	KEN	14.1.84		Mar	2:07:49	2:08:36- 09
Rutt	Michael	USA	28.10.87	175/64	800	1:45.20	1:46.47- 09
Rutter	Adam	AUS	24.12.86	168/54	20kW	1:21:23	1:21:49- 08
* Ruuskanen	Antti	FIN	21.2.84	189/86	JT	87.79	87.33- 08, 87.88dh- 07
* Ruzavin	Andrey	RUS	28.3.86	175/70	20kW	1:17:47	1:20:07- 07
Ryzhov	Mikhail	RUS	17.12.91	176/64	50kW	3:53:49	-0-
Saenz	Stephen	MEX	23.8.90	183/116	SP	20.08i, 19.81	19.82- 11
Safiulin	Ilgizar	RUS	9.12.92		3kSt	8:29.59	8:37.94- 11
Safo-Antwi	Sean	GBR	31.10.90	173/68	100	10.19w	10.72, 10.53w- 11
Safronov	Konstantin	KAZ	2.9.87	184/68	LJ	8.00	8.06- 10
Saharuk	Igor	UKR	3.6.88		50kW	3:54:40	4:10:39- 11
* Saidy Ndure	Jaysuma	NOR	1.7.84	192/72	100	10.13	9.99- 11, 9.98w- 10
					200	20.34	19.89- 07
Saint-Jean	Fabrice	FRA	21.11.80	190/84	HJ	2.28	2.25- 10
Saito	Hitoshi	JPN	9.10.86	180/70	200	20.57	20.42- 09
Saito	Takumi	JPN-J	23.3.93	178/61	20kW	1:21:01	1:23:45- 11
Sakalauskas	Rytis	LTU	27.6.87	185/83	100	10.15, 10.08w 10.14, 10.10w- 11, 10.0dt- 09	
Sakayev	Vyacheslav	RUS	12.1.88	185/79	400h	49.59	49.79- 11
Saku Bafuanga	Gaîtan	FRA	22.7.91	181/75	TJ	16.87	16.82- 11
Salaam	Rakieem Mookie	USA	5.4.90	180/73	100	9.98	9.97- 11
* Saladino	Irving	PAN	23.1.83	183/70	LJ	8.16	8.73- 08
Salas	Dìdac	ESP-J	19.5.93	187/75	PV	5.55	5.42- 11
^ Salel	Daniel	KEN	11.12.90	173/57	5000	13:21.27	13:08.23- 10
					10k	27:45.93	27:07.85- 10
Salomäki	Eemeli	FIN	11.10.87	182/71	PV	5.60	5.60- 09
Samaai	Rushwal	RSA	25.9.91		LJ	7.94A	7.75, 7.80w- 11
Sambu	Stephen	KEN	7.7.88	169/55	5000	13:13.74i	13:28.48i, 13:34.19- 11
					10k	28:06.16	27:28.64- 11
Samimi	Mahmoud	IRI	18.9.88	190/105	DT	64.36	64.67- 09
Samimi	Mohammed	IRI	29.3.87	188/104	DT	64.77	65.41- 10
* Samitov	Ruslan	RUS	11.2.91	187/77	TJ	17.25	16.90- 11
Samuels	Jarrett	USA-J	12.2.93		LJ	7,83, 7.98w	7.23, 7.46w- 11
Sánchez	Benjamìn	ESP	10.3.85	185/72	50kW	3:58:51	-0-

Name		Nat	Born	Ht/Wt	Event	2012 Mark	Pre-2012 Best
* Sánchez	Eder	MEX	21.5.86	176/67	20kW	1:19:52	1:18:34- 08
Sánchez	Enrique	ESP	14.10.83	178/62	3kSt	8:29.39	8:29.12- 09
* Sánchez	Félix	DOM	30.8.77	178/73	400	45.34	44.90- 01
					400h	47.63	47.25- 03
^ Sánchez	Sergio	ESP	1.10.82	179/64	5000	13:21.12	13:19.21- 10
* Sands	Leevan	BAH	16.8.81	190/75	TJ	17.23	17.59- 08
Sands	Shamar	BAH	30.4.85	178/73	110h	13.56	13.38- 09, 13.32Aw- 08
Sanford	Donald	ISR	2 .2.87	193/84	400	45.71	45.21- 10
Sanneh	Su'Waibou	GAM	30.10.90	178/77	100	10.18	10.25- 11
* Santos	Luguelìn	DOM-J	12.11.93	173/61	400	44.45	44.71A- 11, 46.19- 10
* dos Santos	Marìlson	BRA	6.8.77	174/58	Mar	2:08:03	2:06:34- 11
dos Santos	Mário José	BRA	10.9.79	172/59	50kW	4:02:09	3:58:30- 08
Sarantsev	Yevgeniy	RUS	5.8.88		Dec	7861	7822- 11
Sarcevic	Igor	SRB	25.8.84	191/85	Dec	7857	7995- 10
Sargsyan	Arsen	ARM	20.11.76	189/76	LJ	8.20A	8.02- 08
Saruyama	Rikiya	JPN	15.2.84	175/68	LJ	8.00	8.05- 11
Sato	Hiroyuki	JPN	6.8.90	182/72	110h	13.62, 13.59w	13.67- 11
Sato	Yuki	JPN	26.11.86	178/59	10k	27:57.07	27:38.25- 09
Saunders	Barrett	USA	27.3.85	188/80	LJ	7.95w	7.85, 7.87w- 07
Savolaynen	Mykola	UKR	25.3.80	189/76	TJ	16.62, 16.74w	17.17- 07
Savytskyy	Dmytro	UKR	14.12.90	196/125	SP	20.38	19.18- 11
^ Sawano	Daichi	JPN	16.9.80	183/75	PV	5.72	5.83- 05
Sawyers	Roberto	CRC	17.10.86		HT	72.74	67.76- 11
Sayed	Ihab Abdelrahman	EGY	1.5.89	194/96	JT	82.25	81.84- 10
Schembri	Fabrizio	ITA	27.1.81	183/74	TJ	16.97, 17.23w	17.27- 09
Schenkel	Reto Amaru	SUI	28.4.88	173/66	200	20.48	20.51- 11
Scherbarth	Tobias	GER	17.8.85	195/81	PV	5.61	5.76i, 5.70- 09
Schirrmeister	Silvio	GER	7.12.88	193/82	400h	49.21	49.86- 10
Schlangen	Carsten	GER	31.12.80	189/68	1500	3:33.64	3:34.19- 10
Schmidt	Marco	GER	5.9.83	201/130	SP	20.14	20.58i- 10, 20.28- 09
^ Schulze	Fabian	GER	7.3.84	192/79	PV	5.52i	5.83i- 07 , 5.81- 06
Schuurmans	Jared	USA	20.8.87	198/118	DT	61.15	60.19- 11
Schwarzer	Helge	GER	26.11.85	185/76	110h	13.61, 13.56w	13.39- 09
^ Schwazer ¶	Alex	ITA	26.12.84	185/73	20kW	1:17:30	1:18:24- 10
					50kW	3:40:58	3:36:04- 07
Scott	Dorian	JAM	1.2.82	185/136	SP	20.72	21.45- 08
^ Scott	Jeremy	USA	21.5.81	206/91	PV	5.60	5.82i, 5.75- 09
Scott	Jordan	USA	22.2.88	188/84	PV	5.72	5.71- 10
Scott	Josh	USA	9.3.85	193/84	400	45.75	45.01- 10
Scott	Rushane	USA	7.7.88	178/79	100	10.12wA	10.53- 09
^ Sdiri	Salim	FRA	26.10.78	185/80	LJ	7.98	8.42- 09
* Sebrle	Roman	CZE	26.11.74	186/88	Dec	8097	9026- 01
Sedoc	Gregory	NED	16.10.81	179/74	110H	13.45	13.37- 07, 13.1w- 10
Sedyuk	Nikolay	RUS	29.4.88	198/115	DT	63.01	64.72- 08
See	Jeff	USA	6.6.86	186/72	1500	3:35.21	3:40.06- 10
^ Sefir	Dino	ETH	28.5.88	172/59	Mar	2:04:50	2:10:33- 11
Sein	Timothy	KEN	.88		1000	2:17.60	-0-
Semenenko	Yevgen	UKR	17.7.84	178/67	TJ	16.73	17.16- 09
Semenov	Andriy	UKR	4.7.84	204/117	SP	20.55	20.63- 11
Semenov	Denis	KAZ	10.10.90	189/76	110h	13.59	14.39, 14.31w- 09
Semenov	Oleksiy	UKR	27.6.82	204/115	DT	65.96	65.40- 08
Semyonov	Dmitriy	RUS	2.8.92		HJ	2.26	2.20- 11
Sepehrzad	Hadi	IRI	19.1.83	186/100	Dec	7729	7711- 08
Seppänen	Tuomas	FIN	16.5.86	180/107	HT	73.67	75.31- 11
Sergeyev	Aleksandr	RUS	29.7.83	191/78	TJ	16.55	17.23i, 17.11- 04
Seurei	Benson	KEN	27.3.88	172/62	800	1:45.67	1:45.79- 11
	1000	2:16.39			2:19.18- 11	1500	3:31.61	3:34.67- 11
Shabanov	Konstandin	RUS	17.11.89	184/75	110h	13.57	13.35- 11
Shako	Dmitriy	BLR	25.3.79	192/101	HT	74.96	78.54- 08
Shalin	Pavel	RUS	15.3.87	175/73	LJ	8.08	8.25- 10, 8.33w- 11
Shami	Abdullah Dawit	ETH	16.7.74	176/53	Mar	2:05:42	2:09:42- 11
Shapoval	Viktor	UKR	17.10.79	198/75	HJ	2.28	2.34- 09
^ Sharman	William	GBR	12.9.84	188/82	110h	13.50	13.30- 09, 12.9w- 10
Shayunov	Yuriy	BLR	22.10.87	193/105	HT	79.18	80.72- 09
* Shelest	Oleksiy	UKR	27.3.73	173/64	50kW	3:53:46	3:54:03- 09
Shi Dongpeng		CHN	6.1.84	192/85	110h	13.49	13.19- 07
Shimizu	Daisuke	JPN	2.8.82	182/64	10k	27:50.50	28:10.68- 07
Shimono	Shin-ichiro	JPN	10.10.90	177/64	LJ	8.08	7.82- 11
Shkurenov	Ilya	RUS	11.1.91	191/82	Dec	8219	7894- 11
Shkurlatov	Vitaliy	RUS	25.5.79	182/76	LJ	7.94	8.38i- 00, 8.23- 03
* Shubenkov	Sergey	RUS	4.10.90	190/75	110h	13.09	13.46- 11

Name		Nat	Born	Ht/Wt	Event	2012 Mark	Pre-2012 Best
Shubyanok	Nikolay	BLR	4.5.85	190/75	Dec	8055	8028- 07
Shugi	Bilisuma	BRN	19.7.89	178/60	3000	7:43.88i	7:42.71- 11
					5000	13:20.94	13:06.73- 11
* Shustov	Aleksandr	RUS	29.6.84	199/85	HJ	2.35	2.36- 11
* Si Tianfeng		CHN	17.6.84	181/67	50kW	3:37:16	3:38:48- 11
Siddhanth	Thingalaya	IND	1.3.91	191/82	110h	13.65	13.77- 11
Sidorchenko	Gleb	RUS	15.5.86	197/110	DT	61.68	59.38- 10
* Sidorov	Maksim	RUS	13.5.86	190/126	SP	21.51	21.45- 11
Sigueni	Hicham	MAR-J	30.1.93		3kSt	8:21.78	
* Sihine	Sileshi	ETH	29.1.83	168/58	5000	13:01.39	12:47.04- 04
					10k	27:03.65	26:39.69- 04
Sikora	Rafal	POL	17.2.87	187/76	20kW	1:22:09	1:21:04- 11
					50kW	3:46:52	3:46:16- 11
Silmon	Charles	USA	4.7.91	175/72	100	10.05, 10.04w	10.20A, 10.19w, 10.23- 10
* Silnov	Andrey	RUS	9.9.84	198/83	HJ	2.37	2.38- 08
da Silva	Aldemir Gomes	BRA	8.6.92	186/73	100	10.20	10.36A- 11
					200	20.38, 20.33w	20.94A, 20.98- 11
Silva	Andrés	URU	27.3.86	180/76	400h	49.78	49.16- 11
* da Silva	Fábio Gomes	BRA	4.8.83	178/74	PV	5.70	5.80- 11
Silva	Jonathan	BRA	21.7.91	185/75	LJ	8.03w	7.72- 11
					TJ	17.39	16.70- 11
* da Silva	Mauro Vinìcius	BRA	26.12.86	183/69	LJ	8.28i, 8.11	8.27- 11
da Silva	Thiago	BRA-J	16.12.93	193/84	PV	5.55	5.31- 11
Simanovich	Denis	BLR	20.4.87	179/58	20kW	1:20:42	1:21:01- 11
Simbine	Akani	RSA-J	21.9.93		100	10.19A	10.57A- 11
Simmons	Cale	USA	5.2.91	178/70	PV	5.53A	5.38A- 11
Singh	Arpinder	IND	30.12.92	186/77	TJ	16.57	16.63- 11
Singh	Baljinder	IND	18.9.86		20kW	1:22:00.86t	1:24:51- 11
Singh	Gurmeet	IND	1.7.85		20kW	1:20:22.52	1:20:35- 11
Singh	Om Prakash	IND	4.1.87	196/125	SP	20.69	20.07- 11
Singh	Satinder	IND	7.2.87	178/68	400h	49.99	50.39- 11
Singh	Surender	IND	4.7.88		20kW	1:22:09.56t	1:27:49- 11
* Sintnicolaas	Eelco	NED	7.4.87	186/81	Dec	8506	8436- 10
* Sirmais	Zigismunds	LAT	6.5.92	191/90	JT	84.06	84.69- 11
Sivakov	Dmitriy	BLR	15.2.83	190/120	DT	62.28	64.83- 08
Siverio	Simón	ESP	2.8.88	190/80	HJ	2.26	2.25- 10
Skyers	Roberto	CUB	12.11.91	187/75	100	10.0	10.29, 9.9dt- 10
Sleboda	Piotr	POL	22.1.87	185/62	HJ	2.27i, 2.24	2.27- 11
Slobodenyuk	Vadym	UKR	17.3.81	189/74	3kSt	8:22.19	8:24.15- 06
Smaliós	Ioánnis-Yeóryios	GRE	17.2.87	192/90	JT	78.85	80.77- 10
Smellie	Gavin	CAN	26.6.86	180/75	100	10.14	10.20, 10.11w- 11
Smikle	Traves	JAM	7.5.92	201/95	DT	67.12	59.83- 11
Smith	Alex	GBR	6.3.88	184/105	HT	75.63	74.62- 11
Smith	Calvin	USA	10.12.87	180/75	400	45.12	44.81- 10
Smith	Miles	USA	24.9.84	190/77	400	45.52	45.16- 05
Smith	Peter	GBR	20.7.90	186/105	HT	71.75	69.92- 10
* Smith	Rutger	NED	9.7.81	197/129	SP	20.56i, 20.55	21.62- 06
					DT	66.97	67.77- 11
Smith	Tyrone	BER	7.8.86	183/70	LJ	7.97	8.22- 10
Smyth	Jason	IRL	4.7.87	170/64	100	10.24, 10.17w	10.22- 11
Soboka	Tafese	ETH-J	.93		3kSt	8:26.33	
Söderberg	David	FIN	11.8.79	185/100	HT	77.53	78.83- 03
* Soi	Edwin	KEN	3.3.86	168/53	3000	7:34.75, 7:29.94i	7:27.55- 11
					5000	12:55.99	12:52.40- 06
^ Sokolovs	Igors	LAT	17.8.74	187/110	HT	78.21	80.14- 09
* Sokyrskyy	Oleksiy	UKR	16.3.85	185/108	HT	78.91	78.33- 11
* Solomon	Duane	USA	28.12.84	191/73	800	1:42.82	1:45.23- 10
Solomon	Jarrin	TRI	11.1.86	173/73	400	45.31	45.68- 09
* Solomon	Steven	AUS-J	16.5.93	186/73	400	44.97	45.58- 11
Some	Peter	KEN	5.6.90		Mar	2:08:29	2:10:16- 11
Sornoza	José Adrián	ECU	5.8.92	176/66	TJ	16.89A	16.03A- 09
* Sorrillo	Rondell	TRI	21.1.86	178/62	100	10.03	10.17- 11, 10.05w- 10
					200	20.40	20.16- 11
Souleiman	Ayanleh	DJI	3.12.92	172/60	1500	3:30.31	3:34.32- 11
1M	3:50.21			-0-	3000	7:42.22	8:31.83- 09
de Souza	Diomar	BRA	24.8.89	184/73	800	1:45.62	1:47.79- 08
Sowinski	Erik	USA	21.12.89	186/70	800	1:45.90	1:47.71- 11
* Spank	Raúl	GER	13.7.88	190/75	HJ	2.32i, 2.25	2.33- 09
					TJ	16.54i, 16.44	15.82i- 11
^ Spasovkhodskiy	Igor	RUS	1.8.79	191/91	TJ	16.87	17.44- 01
* Spearmon	Wallace	USA	24.12.84	190/80	100	10.26, 10.06w	9.96- 07
					200	19.90, 19.82w	19.65- 06

Name		Nat	Born	Ht/Wt	Event	2012 Mark	Pre-2012 Best
Spencer	Kendall	USA	24.7.91	178/73	LJ	8.16A, 8.01i, 7.81	7.52w- 11
Spinner	Patrick	GER	28.11.85	180/75	Dec	7708	7818- 11
Ståhl	Daniel	SWE	27.8.92	200/155	DT	62.16	55.60- 11
Stamatóyiannis	Mihàll	GRE	20.5.82	188/112	SP	19.70i, 19.65	20.36i- 10, 20.17- 11
Stanys	Raivydas	LTU	3.2.87	184/77	HJ	2.31	2.28- 11
* Starodubtsev	Dmitriy	RUS	3.1.86	188/82	PV	5.80i, 5.75	5.90i- 11, 5.75- 08
Starzak	Marcin	POL	20.10.85	178/63	LJ	8.12	8.21- 07
Stasiewicz	Michal	POL	28.9.88	181/63	50kW	3:52:45	3:57:52- 10
Stathelakos	Constantinos	CYP	30.12.87	181/105	HT	73.86	74.38- 11
Steacy	Jim	CAN	29.5.84	189/115	HT	74.96	79.13- 08
Stecchi	Claudio Michel	ITA	23.11.91	187/75	PV	5.60i, 5.60	5.55- 11
Steele	Bryan	JAM	23.3.84	179/73	400h	50.14	49.02- 06
Steele	Edino	JAM	6.1.87	175/68	400	45.38	45.77- 07
^ Steffensen	John	AUS	30.8.82	180/71	400	45.61	44.73- 06
Steinbach	Derek	USA	18.11.88	188/88	Dec	7739	7310- 11
Stevenson	Dale	AUS	1.1.88	183/114	SP	20.63	19.99- 10
Stewart	Devonte	USA-J	11.6.93	185/77	200	20.55	20.84- 11
Stewart	Keiron	JAM	21.11.89	180/73	110h	13.46, 13.36w	13.44, 13.38w- 11
Stewart	Tyron	USA	8.7.89	180/70	LJ	8.21	7.94- 11
					TJ	16.52	16.60- 10
Stigler	Michael	USA	5.4.92	178/70	400h	49.45	52.07- 11
Stockbarger	Wes	USA	5.6.85	190/120	DT	61.67	64.38- 11
Stokes	Stuart	GBR	5.12.76	180/70	3kSt	8:29.32	8:23.66- 08
* Storl	David	GER	27.7.90	199/122	SP	21.88i, 21.86	21.78- 11
^ Straub	Alexander	GER	14.10.83	180/78	PV	5.51	5.81- 08
Strelkov	Denis	RUS	26.10.90		20kW	1:20:31	1:20:19- 10
Strobinders	Rolands	LAT	14.4.92	193/90	JT	81.20	75.71- 11
Su Bingtian		CHN	29.8.89	185/65	100	10.19, 10.04w	10.16- 11
Su Guanyu		CHN-J	26.6.94		20kW	1:22:48	1:23:45- 11
Su Xiongfeng		CHN	21.3.87	183/70	LJ	8.05	8.27i- 11, 8.19- 11
* Suárez	Leonel	CUB	1.9.87	181/76	Dec	8523	8654- 09
* Sudol	Grzegorz	POL	28.8.78	174/60	20kW	1:20:58	1:20:50- 10
					50kW	3:46:01	3:42:24- 10
Sugai	Yohei	JPN	30.8.85	179/75	LJ	8.09	8.10- 10, 8.13w- 08
Suguimati	Mahau	BRA	13.11.84	184/78	400h	49.10	48.67- 09
Sugut	Henry	KEN	4.5.85		Mar	2:06:58	2:08:22- 11
Sumner	Ben	GBR	16.8.83	188/80	400h	49.57	50.29- 11
Sun Chao		CHN	8.2.90		HJ	2.25	2.20- 10
Sun Chengang		CHN	11.3.91		20kW	1:22:25	1:24:35- 11
Sutcliffe	Andrew	GBR	10.7.91	193/82	PV	5.55i, 5.46	5.36i, 5.35- 10
Suzuki	Yusuke	JPN	2.1.88	169/56	20kW	1:22:30	1:20:06- 10
* Sviridov	Sergey	RUS	20.10.90	192/85	Dec	8365	8102A, 7832- 11
* Svyatokho	Valeriy	BLR	20.7.81	186/112	HT	78.44	81.49- 06
Swanson	Chris	USA	6.6.82	188/77	PV	5.60	5.40- 11
Swiderski	Adrian	POL	27.9.86	188/74	TJ	16.51	16.69- 10, 16.72w- 11
Swift	Greggmar	BAR	16.2.91	183/68	110h	13.52, 13.49w	13.84- 11
* Symmonds	Nick	USA	30.12.83	178/73	800	1:42.95	1:43.76- 10
					1500	3:36.04	3:38.18- 11
Syunin	Igor	EST	4.12.90	173/70	TJ	16.67	16.86- 10
Szabó	Attila	HUN	16.7.84	194/94	Dec	8003	7748- 09
Szmanda	Jack	USA	15.3.90	193/94	Dec	7862	7286- 11
Szost	Henryk	POL	20.1.82	188/69	Mar	2:07:39	2:09:39- 11
Szuster	Konrad	POL	21.1.84	192/115	DT	63.40	62.70- 10
Szymkowiak	Tomasz	POL	5.7.83	176/58	3kSt	8:31.02	8:18.23- 10
Szyszkowski	Jakub	POL	21.8.91	187/105	SP	19.59	17.62- 10
Tabala	Aleksandr	RUS	23.5.86	186/87	Dec	8070	7979- 10
* Tadese	Zersenay	ERI	8.2.82	160/56	10k	27:33.51	26:37.25- 06
					HMar	59:34	58:23- 10
^ Taillepierre	Karl	FRA	13.8.76	176/67	TJ	16.84	17.45- 05
Takahashi	Eiki	JPN	19.11.92		20kW	1:22:33	1:26:16- 11
Takahira	Shinji	JPN	18.7.84	180/62	200	20.56	20.22- 09
Takase	Kei	JPN	25.11.88	179/62	200	20.42	20.53- 11
Talbot	Danny	GBR	1.5.91	184/73	200	20.52	20.54- 11
Taleb	Brahim	MAR	16.2.85	182/70	3kSt	8:10.20	8:07.02- 07
* Tallent	Jared	AUS	17.10.84	178/60	20kW	1:20:02	1:19:15- 10
					50kW	3:36:53	3:38:56- 09
Tamayo	Diego	ESP	6.12.83	175/60	3kSt	8:28.52	8:35.32- 10
Tamberi	Gianmarco	ITA	1.6.92	189/71	HJ	2.31	2.25- 11
Tambwé	Patrick	COD	5.5.75	182/65	Mar	2:07:30	2:08:55- 04
^ Tammert	Aleksander	EST	2.2.73	196/126	DT	66.58	70.82- 06
Tang Gongchen		CHN	24.4.89	185/71	LJ	8.03i, 7.91	7.97- 08

Name		Nat	Born	Ht/Wt	Event	2012 Mark	Pre-2012 Best
Tanii	Takayuki	JPN	14.2.83	167/57	20kW	1:21:31	1:20:39- 04
					50kW	3:43:56	3:47:23- 06
* Tanui	Paul	KEN	22.12.90	172/54	5000	13:19.18	13:04.65- 11
					10k	27:27.56	26:50.63- 11
Taplin	Bralon	USA	8.5.92	180/73	400	45.36	46.79- 11
* Tarabin	Dmitriy	RUS	29.10.91	176/85	JT	82.75	85.10- 11
Tate	Tavaris	USA	21.12.90	170/64	400	45.45	44.84- 10
Tateno	Tetsuya	JPN	5.8.91	177/73	400h	49.49	50.06- 11
* Taylor	Angelo	USA	29.12.78	188/84	400	44.93	44.05- 07
					400h	47.95	47.25- 08
* Taylor	Christian	USA	18.6.90	190/75	LJ	8.12	8.19- 10
					TJ	17.81	17.96- 11
* Taylor	Dan	USA	12.5.82	198/145	SP	20.22	21.78- 09
Taylor	Logan	USA	3.4.86	183/70	110h	13.66, 13.60w	13.69- 08
Taylor	Ronnie	USA	13.8.90		LJ	7.93	7.74- 11
Tegenkamp	Matt	USA	19.1.82	186/66	5000	13:15.00	12:58.56- 09
*					10k	27:33.94	27:28.22- 11
Teng Haining		CHN-J	25.6.93	183/65	800	1:46.56	1:46.62- 11
Terer	Patrick	KEN	6.7.89	178/60	3kSt	8:27.24	8:13.96- 09
Tesfaldet	Nguse	ERI	10.11.86	180/56	10k	27:28.10	29:05.26- 11
Teweldebrhan	Teklit	ERI-J	1.10.93	172/65	1500	3:36.50	3:41.76- 11
Thagane	Tumelo	RSA	3.7.84	180/70	TJ	16.71A	17.09- 10
Theiner	Wojciech	POL	25.6.86	187/74	HJ	2.25	2.30- 10
Thomas	Chris	USA	9.2.81	178/76	110h	13.45	13.54- 08
* Thomas	Donald	BAH	1.7.84	190/75	HJ	2.27	2.35- 07
* Thomas	Dwight	JAM	23.9.80	185/82	110h	13.36, 13.17w	13.15- 11, 13.1w- 10
Thomas	Jared	USA	17.2.90	190/122	DT	61.26	58.98- 10
Thomas	Joe	GBR	29.1.88	180/72	800	1:46.33i	1:46.20- 08
Thomas	Mikel	TRI	23.11.87	182/77	110h	13.48, 13.31w	13.62, 13.57w-08
Thomas	Tristan	AUS	23.5.86	184/70	400h	49.13	48.68- 09
Thompson	Chris	GBR	17.4.81	176/70	5000	13:15.21	13:11.51- 10
3000	7:49.14i		7:43.34- 10		HMar	61:00dh	62:13- 11
* Thompson	Richard	TRI	7.6.85	187/79	100	9.96	9.85- 11
* Thorkildsen	Andreas	NOR	1.4.82	188/90	JT	84.72	91.59- 06
Thormaehlen	Jacob	USA	13.2.90	193/118	SP	20.50i, 20.13	19.16- 11
Thorne	Benjamin	CAN-J	19.3.93		20kW	1:21:55	-0-
Thorsteinsson	Odinn Björn	ISL	3.12.81	200/128	SP	20.22i, 19.30	19.83- 11
* Thuo	John	KEN	27.11.85	168/55	5000	13:23.41	13:15.53- 11
					10k	27:32.72	27:11.88- 09
Tikhomirov	Anton	RUS	29.4.88		SP	19.56i	17.39- 11
^ Tikhon ¶	Ivan	BLR	24.7.76	186/110	HT	82.81	86.73- 05
* Tinsley	Michael	USA	21.4.84	185/74	400h	47.91	48.02- 07
Tiouali	Ayoub	MAR	26.5.91		1500	3:34.52	
Tivonchik	Stanislav	BLR	5.3.85	183/79	PV	5.60	5.40- 11
Tobin	Robert	GBR	20.12.83	190/75	400	45.47	45.01- 05
* Tola	Seboka	ETH	10.11.87	172/53	Mar	2:06:17	2:13:49- 11
Tola	Tadesse	ETH	31.10.87	178/60	Mar	2:05:10	2:06:31- 10
Toledo	Braian	ARG-J	8.9.93	182/86	JT	79.87	79.53A- 11
Tolossa	Debebe	ETH	7.7.91		Mar	2:07:41	2:09:57- 11
Tomala	Dawid	POL	27.8.89	182/65	20kW	1:20:50	1:22:31- 10
* Tomlinson	Chris	GBR	15.9.81	197/81	LJ	8.26	8.35- 11
Tontodonati	Federico	ITA	30.10.89	169/55	20kW	1:22:00	1:26:01- 11
					50kW	3:51:37	3:55:04- 11
Toompuu	Raigo	EST	17.7.81	188/118	SP	20.04	20.20- 10
^ Topic	Dragutin	SRB	12.3.71	197/77	HJ	2.28	2.38- 93
* Tornéus	Michel	SWE	26.5.86	184/70	LJ	8.22	8.19- 11, 8.21w- 10
Toroitich	Charles	KEN	.88		HMar	61:12	-0-
Toroitich	Timothy	UGA	10.10.91		3kSt	8:23.61	8:46.42A- 11
Torrence	David	USA	26.11.85	175/61	1000	2:17.46	-0-
1500	3:35.41		3:34.25- 10		1M	3:52.01	3:54.01- 12
3000	7:47.80		7:51.52i- 09		5000	13:16.53	-0-
Torro	Osku	FIN	21.8.79	183/68	HJ	2.28	2.33i- 11, 2.27- 07
^ Tosca	Osniel	CUB	30.6.84	182/78	TJ	16.93, 17.22w	17.52- 07
Toscano	Juan Emilio	MEX	3.7.81		50kW	3:56:39A	4:04:31A- 02
* Tóth	Matej	SVK	10.2.83	185/72	20kW	1:20:25	1:20:16- 11
					50kW	3:41:24	3:39:46- 11
Touil	Abdelmadjed	ALG	11.2.89	172/62	3kSt	8:31.01	-0-
Touil	Imad	ALG	11.2.89	172/62	1500	3:35.82	3:36.05- 11
Tovarnov	Aleksey	RUS	21.1.85	184/82	JT	79.11	81.21- 09
Townsend	Fred	USA	19.2.82	188/82	110h	13.39	13.42, 13.40w- 11
Traber	Gregor	GER	2.12.92	190/80	110h	13.47	13.55- 11

Name		Nat	Born	Ht/Wt	Event	2012 Mark	Pre-2012 Best
* Trammell	Terrence	USA	23.11.78	188/84	110h	13.36	12.95- 07
Traoré	Bano	FRA	25.4.85	180/65	110h	13.78, 13.56w 13.49A, 13.54- 08, 13.51w- 11	
Trémos	Yeóryios	GRE	21.3.89	196/103	DT	62.92	60.33- 11
Trenikhin	Pavel	RUS	24.3.86	187/77	400	45.00	45.55- 11
Trofimov	Pyotr	RUS	28.11.83	174/63	20kW	1:19:20	1:19:02- 09
Tromp	Xavier	FRA	3.3.84	191/86	PV	5.52	5.55i, 5.50- 06
^ Trotskiy	Ivan	BLR	27.5.76	171/64	20kW	1:21:23	1:19:40- 03
					50kW	3:46:09	3:54.48- 09
True	Ben	USA	29.12.85	183/70	3000	7:44.40	7:59.29i- 10
5000	13:20.53		13:24.11- 11		10k	27:41.17	28:16.65- 11
Tsákonas	Likoúrgos-Stéfanos	GRE	8.3.90	184/67	200	20.52	20.56- 11
Tsákonas	Yeóryios	GRE	22.1.88	190/78	LJ	8.25	8.03- 11, 8.04w- 08
Tsapik	Aleksey	BLR	4.8.88		TJ	16.82, 16.97w	16.46- 10, 16.69w- 11
* Tsátoumas	Loúis	GRE	12.2.82	187/76	LJ	8.05i, 7.98	8.66- 07
Tsegay	Atsedu	ETH	17.12.91		HMar	58:47	61:12- 11
Tsegay	Samuel	ERI	24.2.88	176/55	HMar	61:09	60:17- 09
					Mar	2:08:06	2:07:28- 11
Tsiámis	Dimìtrios	GRE	12.1.82	178/67	TJ	16.75	17.55- 06
Tsirikhov	Soslan	RUS	24.11.84	195/125	SP	20.41i, 20.17	20.76- 11
Tsyplakov	Daniyil	RUS	12.7.92	190/75	HJ	2.31	2.26- 11
Tulácek	Vladislav	CZE	9.7.88	193/115	SP	19.51	18.68- 11
Tum	Stephen	KEN	12.7.86		Mar	2:07:17	-0-
^ Turner	Andrew	GBR	19.9.80	184/77	110h	13.41	13.22- 11, 13.2u- 09
Turner	Greg	USA	27.9.89	168/68	200	20.26w	21.37- 11
^ Tysse	Erik	NOR	4.12.80	184/59	20kW	1:20:39	1:19:11- 08
Udechuku	Emeka	GBR	10.7.79	176/125	DT	61.91	64.93- 04
Ugachi	Tsuyoshi	JPN	27.4.87	163/49	10k	27:52.79	27:40.69- 11
Ukaoma	Miles	USA	21.7.92	183/75	400h	49.23	50.70- 11
* Ukhov	Ivan	RUS	29.3.86	192/67	HJ	2.39	2.40i- 09, 2.36- 10
Uliczka	Steffen	GER	17.7.84	179/65	3kSt	8:22.93	8:25.39- 10
Unger	Tobias	GER	10.7.79	180/72	100	10.20	10.14- 10, 10.11w- 05
^					200	20.68, 20.57w	20.20- 05
Urbanek	Robert	POL	29.4.87	196/115	DT	66.93	64.37- 11
Ursu	Sergiu	ROU	26.4.80	202/127	DT	61.24	64.74- 10
^ Urtans	Maris	LAT	9.2.81	188/123	SP	19.84	21.63- 10
Ushiro	Keisuke	JPN	24.7.86	196/95	Dec	8037	8076w, 8073- 11
Vadlejch	Jakub	CZE	10.10.90	190/93	JT	80.40	84.47- 10
Vail	Ryan	USA	19.3.86	173/59	10k	27:51.07	27:57.42- 11
Vaisjuns	Oskars	LAT	21.8.83	196/115	DT	61.10	59.31- 10
Valiyev	Roman	KAZ	27.3.84	190/73	TJ	17.20	16.98- 06
Valle	Amaurys	CUB	18.1.90	186/80	400h	49.19	49.56- 08
* Van Alphen	Hans	BEL	12.1.82	191/91	Dec	8519	8200- 11
van der Westhuizen	Peter	RSA	21.12.84	186/73	1500	3:36.56	3:35.33- 09
van Deventer	Juan	RSA	26.3.83	184/70	1500	3:35.52	3:34.30- 09
van Luijk	Patrick	NED	17.9.84	188/89	200	20.47	20.52- 09
van Rensburg	Rynhardt	RSA	23.3.92		800	1:46.36	1:48.87- 11
van Vreumingen	Eric	NED	15.6.78	193/119	SP	19.77	19.04- 08
* van Zyl	Louis 'L.J.'	RSA	20.7.85	186/75	400h	49.42A, 50.31	47.66- 11
^ Varga	Roland	CRO	22.10.77	196/125	DT	62.44	67.38- 02
* Vasilevskis	Vadims	LAT	5.1.82	188/101	JT	86.50	90.73- 07
Vaughn	Brent	USA	4.12.84	185/66	10k	27:40.21	28:05.33- 10
Vaughn	Chris	USA	1.2.90	186/77	400	45.48	47.14- 11
Vázquez	Wesley	PUR-J	27.3.94	184/73	800	1:45.29	1:47.38- 11
Velikopolskiy	Dmitriy	RUS	27.11.84	188/110	HT	76.15	78.76- 08
Véliz	Carlos	CUB	12.8.87	185/120	SP	20.50	20.76- 11
Vena	Nick	USA-J	16.4.93	194/120	SP	19.51	-0-
Venhlovskyy	Oleksandr	UKR	5.8.85	184/66	50kW	4:00:55	4:15:28- 07
Verburg	David	USA	14.5.91	168/64	400	45.06	46.09- 11
Vernon	Andrew	GBR	7.1.86	178/65	5000	13:23.20	13:27.85- 11
					10k	27:53.65	28:11.43- 10
Verronen	Joonas	FIN	24.4.90	187/85	JT	77.99	78.14- 10
Vesely	Vitezslav	CZE	27.2.83	186/94	JT	88.34	86.45- 10
* Viana	Sandro	BRA	26.3.77	188/77	200	20.43	20.32- 08
Vicars	Derrick	USA	8.5.89	188/114	SP	19.83	19.39i, 18.35- 11
Vicaut	Jimmy	FRA	27.2.92	188/83	100	10.02	10.07- 11
* Vicet	Noleysis	CUB	6.2.81	193/103	HT	74.38	75.40- 11
Victorian	Jibri	USA	26.6.91	186/86	400h	50.10	51.12- 11
^ Vieira	João	POR	20.2.76	174/58	20kW	1:20:41	1:20:09- 06
					50kW	3:45:17	3:52:00- 04
Vij ¶	Saurabh	IND	14.6.87	180/105	SP	19.80dq	19.81, 20.65dq- 10
Villar	Paulo César	COL	28.7.78	175/64	110h	13.55	13.27A- 11, 13.29- 06

Name		Nat	Born	Ht/Wt	Event	2012 Mark	Pre-2012 Best
Vinichenko	Igor	RUS	11.4.84	196/119	HT	78.22	80.00- 07
Visser	Zarck	RSA	15.9.89	178/70	LJ	8.15A, 8.07, 8.21w	7.85- 11
Vistali	Marco	ITA	3.10.87	184/70	400	45.70	45.38- 10
Vivas	Borja	ESP	26.5.84	203/140	SP	20.06	20.18i- 11, 20.01- 09
* Vizzoni	Nicola	ITA	4.11.73	193/126	HT	76.42	80.50- 01
Vonavka	Tomás	CZE	4.6.90		DT	61.74	59.14- 11
Vorontsov	Andrey	BLR	24.7.75	191/105	HT	80.25	81.31- 08
Vos	Ingmar	NED	28.5.86	186/80	Dec	8224	8105- 11
Vukicevic	Vladimir	NOR	6.5.91	193/83	110h	13.55	13.89- 11
Vynogradov	Yevgen	UKR	30.4.84	195/98	HT	72.90	80.58- 08
Wagner	Stepán	CZE	5.10.81	187/74	LJ	8.21, 8.26w	8.15, 8.18w- 09
* Walcott	Keshorn	TRI-J	2.4.93	184/90	JT	84.58	75.77A- 11
* Walker	Brad	USA	21.6.81	188/86	PV	5.90	6.04- 08
Walker	Everett	USA	3.10.90	180/75	100	10.18, 10.12w	10.27, 10.05w-ui- 11
					200	20.54, 20.53w	20.79, 20.47w- 11
Wallace	Maston	USA	2.7.89	185/81	PV	5.53	5.56- 09
Wallin	Gabriel	SWE	14.10.81	193/94	JT	81.45	80.88- 11
^ Waltz	Ian	USA	15.4.77	186/122	DT	62.40	68.91- 06
Wami	Mulugueta	ETH	17.7.82		Mar	2:07:11	2:08:32- 10
Wang Guangfu		CHN	15.11.87	192/110	SP	20.20	19.07- 11
Wang Jianan		CHN-Y	27.8.96		LJ	8.04	
Wang Qingbo		CHN	24.5.88	182/78	JT	78.92	80.25- 09
Wang Yu		CHN	18.8.91	189/64	HJ	2.28	2.28- 11
* Wang Zhen		CHN	24.8.91	180/62	20kW	1:17:36	1:18:30- 11
Wang Zhendong		CHN	11.1.91		20kW	1:21:59	1:23:13- 10
					50kW	3:57:47	4:16:44- 11
Wanjiru	Daniel	KEN	26.5.92		HMar	61:19	
Wanjiru	Peter	KEN	28.11.82		HMar	61:15	62:17- 11
Wanjuki	Jacob	KEN	16.1.86	178/52	10k	28:01.98	27:48.74- 11
					HMar	60:59	60:32- 10
Warburton	Gareth	GBR	23.4.83	185/72	800	1:44.98	1:46.47- 10
* Wariner	Jeremy	USA	31.1.84	183/70	200	20.53	20.19- 06
					400	44.96	43.45- 07
* Warner	Damian	CAN	4.10.89	185/83	110h	13.61	13.87A, 13.89- 11
					Dec	8442	8102A, 7832- 11
Warner	Ian	CAN	15.5.90	170/69	100	10.20A, 10.13w	10.44- 11
Warner	Justyn	CAN	28.6.87	174/70	100	10.09	10.15- 11
Watson	Nicholas	JAM	.9	183/75	100	10.17	10.23- 11
* Watt	Mitchell	AUS	25.3.88	184/83	LJ	8.28	8.54- 11
Waugh	Ainsley	JAM	17.9.81	186/84	200	20.56	20.22- 09
Waweru	Bernard	KEN-J	5.1.94		HMar	61:19	
Waweru	Edward	KEN	3.10.90	178/60	10k	27:29.10	27:13.94- 10
Webb	Ameer	USA	19.3.91	175/75	100	10.17, 10.05w	10.37- 10
					200	20.46, 20.20w	20.49- 11
Weese	Lyle	USA	26.10.79	188/68	3kSt	8:30.83	8:33.14- 05
* Weir	Warren	JAM	31.10.89	178/75	200	19.84	20.43- 11
Weirich	Victor	USA	25.10.87		PV	5.50i, 5.50	5.50Ai, 5.35- 11
Werskey	Eric	USA	17.7.87	188/120	SP	19.57	19.83- 11
Wesh	Darrell	USA	21.1.92	173/70	100	10.15	10.42- 10
West	Richard	CAN	11.9.90	182/66	800	1:46.41	1:50.18- 10
* Wheating	Andrew	USA	21.11.87	195/77	800	1:46.33	1:44.56- 10
1000	2:17.44			-0-	1500	3:35.89	3:30.90- 10
White	Corey	USA	31.1.86	185/91	JT	80.95	81.70- 11
White	James	USA	22.1.92	179/61	HJ	2.26i, 2.26	2.28- 09
White	Steven	USA	27.7.91	165/61	400h	50.07	51.19- 10
Whitener	Caleb	USA	29.5.92	190/129	SP	19.54	17.74- 11
* Whiting	Ryan	USA	24.11.86	190/134	SP	22.00i, 21.66	21.97- 10
Whitt	Jack	USA	12.4.90	193/84	PV	5.72i, 5.65	5.65- 11
Wiaderek	Piotr	POL	5.2.84	186/76	400	45.46	45.78- 11
Wieczorek	Mark	USA	25.12.84	178/68	800	1:45.62	1:46.00- 11
* Wierig	Martin	GER	10.6.87	202/108	DT	68.33	67.21- 11
Williams	Andrae	BAH	11.7.83	185/82	400	45.78	44.90- 05
Williams	Brandon	DMA	14.12.87	180/75	HJ	2.25	2.21A- 11
Williams	Conrad	GBR	20.3.82	182/76	400	45.08	45.45- 10
Williams	Delano	TKS-J	23.12.93	183/72	200	20.48	20.73- 11
Williams	Horatio	USA	28.8.89	188/79	100	10.26, 10.19w	10.25- 11
					200	20.47	20.44, 20.32w- 11
^ Williams	Ivory	USA	2.5.85	174/77	100	10.20, 10.16w	9.93- 09, 9.88w- 10
* Williams	Jesse	USA	27.12.83	184/75	HJ	2.36	2.37- 11
Williams	Levance	USA			LJ	8.10	7.53i- 09
Williams	Rhys	GBR	27.2.84	183/73	400h	49.17	48.96- 10

Name		Nat	Born	Ht/Wt	Event	2012 Mark	Pre-2012 Best
Williamsz	Jordan	AUS	21.8.92	174/61	1500	3:36.74	3:40.96- 11
Willis	Lawrence	USA	12.7.81	188/78	TJ	16.65	16.97- 07, 17.05w- 10
Willis	Nick	NZL	25.4.83	183/68	800	1:46.18	1:45.54- 04
* 1000	2:16.58		2:16.93- 08		1500	3:30.35	3:31.79- 11
1M	3:51.77		3:50.66- 08		5000	13:29.56	13:27.54- 05
^ Wilson	Aarik	USA	25.10.82	190/88	TJ	17.07	17.58- 07
Wilson	Alex	SUI	19.9.90	179/77	200	20.52, 20.43w	20.51- 11
Wilson	Jerome	JAM	10.9.91	183/70	LJ	7,83, 8.02w	7.56- 11
* Wilson	Ryan	USA	19.12.80	188/81	110h	13.18	13.02- 07
Winger	Russ	USA	2.8.84	191/120	SP	20.51	21.29i- 08, 21.25- 10
					DT	65.46	66.04- 11
Winter	Chris	CAN	22.7.86	185/66	3kSt	8:28.46	8:39.91- 10
Winter	Nils	GER	27.3.77	187/84	LJ	8.03	8.22i- 09, 8.21- 05
* Wirkkala	Teemu	FIN	14.1.84	187/85	JT	83.73	87.23- 09
^ Wissman	Johan	SWE	2.11.82	180/75	200	20.57	20.30- 07, 20.26w- 05
Woepse	Michael	USA	29.5.91	185/79	PV	5.55	5.33- 10
* Wojciechowski	Pawel	POL	6.6.89	186/77	PV	5.62	5.91- 11
Wolde	Dawit	ETH	19.5.91	175/62	1500	3:33.82	3:34.13- 11
3000	7:48.96i		7:42.65- 11		HMar	60:46	-0-
Wolski	Dawid	POL	15.6.89	175/62	20kW	1:22:17	1:23:20- 11
Wondimu	Eshetu	ETH	26.1.82	165/52	Mar	2:07:28	2:06:46- 10
Woodward	Nathan	GBR	17.10.89	193/79	400h	49.36	48.71- 11
Worku	Bazu	ETH	15.9.90	170/52	Mar	2:07:48	2:05:25- 10
Worku	Gemechu	ETH	.85		Mar	2:07:43	2:12:03- 11
^ Wöschler	Till	GER	9.6.91	196/110	JT	79.41	84.38- 11
Wote	Aman	ETH	18.4.84	178/62	1500	3:35.38	3:35.61- 11
					1M	3:53.02	
Wright	Chad	JAM	25.3.91		DT	62.88	57.88- 11
Wright	Ed	USA	3.3.86	188/79	HJ	2.25	2.25- 10
Wright	Frankie	USA	1 .2.85	180/73	400	45.72i	46.24- 07
Wruck	Julian	AUS	6.7.91	198/125	DT	64.84	65.74- 11
Wu Bo		CHN	17.6.84	174/60	TJ	16.58	17.10- 08
Wu Jian		CHN	25.5.86	189/95	DT	61.73	63.54- 11
Wu Qianlong		CHN	30.1.90	176/62	50kW	3:58:22	3:57:56- 09
Wurster	Jason	CAN	23.9.84	185/82	PV	5.51	5.50- 09
Wyatt	Reggie	USA	17.9.90	188/73	400h	49.11	49.41- 11
Xie Sichao		CHN-J	28.2.93		20kW	1:22:34	1:27:30- 11
Xie Wenjun		CHN	11.7.90	186/74	110h	13.34	13.45- 11
Xie Zhenye		CHN-J	17.8.93	183/72	200	20.54	20.79- 11
Xu Dexing		CHN	20.8.88	183/60	50kW	4:03:04	4:08:53- 11
Xu Faguang		CHN	17.5.87	178/69	20kW	1:23:06.83t	1:20:26- 08
					50kW	3:48:47	3:42:20- 11
Xu Jianping		CHN	1.1.90		LJ	7.96i, 7.86	7.70i- 11, 7.55- 10
Xue Changrui		CHN	31.5.91	183/60	PV	5.60	5.30- 11
Yakovlev	Nikita	BLR	6.1.89		400h	50.02	51.15- 11
Yamagata	Ryota	JPN	10.6.92	176/70	100	10.07	10.23- 11
Yamamoto	Kazuki	JPN	8.10.83	192/96	JT	78.17	77.47- 04
Yamamoto	Seito	JPN	11.3.92	178/67	PV	5.65	5.35- 11
* Yamazaki	Yuki	JPN	16.1.84	179/63	50kW	3:41:47	3:40:12- 09
Yang Yansheng		CHN	5.1.88	189/75	PV	5.70	5.75- 10
Yargunkin	Aleksandr	RUS	6.1.81	182/68	50kW	3:50:53	3:56:56- 02
Yarmak	Sergey	RUS	21.3.86		TJ	16.67	16.71- 08
Yashin Hasen	Agato	ETH	19.1.86	175/58	10k	27:51.71	
Yastrebov	Viktor	UKR	13.1.82	185/73	TJ	16.95	17.32- 04
Yates	Richard	GBR	26.1.86	185/77	400h	49.39	49.06- 08
Yator	Vincent	KEN	11.7.89	170/55	5000	13:18.54	13:04.50- 10
					HMar	61:02	60:43- 09
* Yego	Hillary	KEN	2.4.92	178/60	3kSt	8:11.83	8:07.71- 11
Yego	Julius	KEN	4.1.89	175/85	JT	81.81	78.34- 11
* Yemelyanov	Stanislav	RUS	23.10.90	175/62	20kW	1:18:29	1:19:33- 11
* Yerokhin	Igor	RUS	4.9.85	166/56	50kW	3:37:54	3:38:08- 08
Yerokhov	Pavel	BLR	21.7.82		50kW	4:02:07	4:05:52- 11
Yeryomin	Ivan	UKR	30.5.89		PV	5.55	5.40- 10
Yildirum	Irfan	TUR	26.7.88	202/100	DT	64.24	64.96- 11
Yin Jiaxing		CHN-J	16.3.94		20kW	1:21:07	1:25:59- 11
Yokota	Masato	JPN	19.11.87	177/62	800	1:46.19	1:46.16- 09
Yoshida	Takuya	JPN	10.8.90		20kW	1:22:42	1:25:33- 11
Young	Isiah	USA	5.1.90	183/75	100	10.09, 10.08w	10.31- 11
					200	20.33, 20.16w	20.81- 11
* Young	Jason	JAM	21.3.91	180/68	100	10.06	10.63- 11
					200	19.86	20.53- 11

Name		Nat	Born	Ht/Wt	Event	2012 Mark	Pre-2012 Best
* Young	Jason	USA	27.5.81	185/116	DT	65.28	69.90- 10
Yousif	Rabah	SUD	11.12.86	183/73	400	45.13	45.13- 11
Yu Wei		CHN	11.9.87	180/60	20kW	1:20:06	1:20:41- 09
Yun Zhiming		CHN	9.10.88	184/60	LJ	8.17i, 8.10	8.05- 11
Yurchenko	Aleksandr	RUS	30.7.92		TJ	16.56	16.35- 11
Yurchenko	Denys	UKR	27.1.78	175/76	PV	5.72	5.85i- 05, 5.83-08
Yushkov	Ivan	RUS	15.1.81	193/115	SP	21.00	21.01- 08
Zaghou	Mounatcer	MAR	.89		3kSt	8:29.78	8:47.80- 11
* Zagornyi	Aleksey	RUS	31.5.78	197/135	HT	78.40	83.43- 02
Zaizan	Ioan	ROU	21.7.83	178/55	800	1:46.56	1:46.99- 07
Zalewski	Karol	POL-J	7.8.93	185/73	200	20.54	21.35, 20.92w- 11
Zalewski	Krystian	POL	11.4.89	184/67	3kSt	8:25.50	8:27.55- 11
Zalsky	Antonin	CZE	7.8.80	200/128	SP	20.38	20.71- 04
Zawude	Tebalu	ETH	2.11.87		10k	28:03.16	-0-
Zaykov	Sergey	KAZ	23.9.87	190/76	400	45.67	46.93- 08
Zaytsev	Artyom	BLR	7.12.84	202/75	HJ	2.25	2.28i- 07, 2.28- 09
Zaytsev	Ivan	UZB	11.11.88	190/98	JT	85.03	79.39- 11
Zenúch	Patrik	SVK	30.12.90		JT	78.89	70.35- 11
Zepeda	Omar	MEX	8.6.77	177/68	50kW	3:48:38A	3:49:01- 05
Zerguelaine	Anter	ALG	4.1.85	177/60	1500	3:35.87	3:31.21- 09
Zhang Guowei		CHN	4.6.91	200/77	HJ	2.31i, 2.31	2.31- 11
Zhang Jun		CHN	11.4.83	186/125	SP	20.16i, 19.67	20.41- 09
Zhang Xiaoyi		CHN	25.5.89	186/65	LJ	8.20i, 7.85	8.27- 09
Zhang Yu		CHN	17.7.92		LJ	7.93	7.92- 11
Zhao Jianguo		CHN	19.1.88	175/55	50kW	3:52:04	3:50:18- 11
Zhao Qi		CHN-J	14.1.93		20kW	1:19:58	1:22:05- 11
Zhao Qinggang		CHN	24.7.85	184/75	JT	81.74	79.80- 10
Zhao Xiaoxi		CHN	19.3.89	173/75	LJ	8.00, 8.09w	7.97- 10
Zhelyabin	Dmitry	RUS	20.5.90	187/75	PV	5.65	5.55- 11
Zhidkov	Nikita	RUS	29.2.88		SP	19.71	17.60i- 10, 17.27- 11
Zhu Chundong		CHN	1.1.90	168/50	20kW	1:21:22	1:28:12- 10
Zhuang Haitao		CHN	6.1.89	170/60	LJ	7.94i, 7.94	8.00- 09
Ziegler	Alexander	GER	7.7.87	180/89	HT	75.78	73.68- 10
* Ziólkowski	Szymon	POL	1.7.76	192/120	HT	78.51	83.38- 01
Ziukas	Marius	LTU	29.6.85	185/70	20kW	1:22:25	1:22:31, 1:21:40sh- 11
^ Zsivoczky-Pandel	Attila	HUN	29.4.77	193/82	Dec	7703	8554- 00
Zunic	Stipe	CRO	13.12.90	188/95	JT	77.89	75.01- 11

WOMEN'S INDEX 2012

Name		Nat	Born	Ht/Wt	Event	2012 Mark	Pre-2012 Best
Ababel	Yeshaneh	ETH	10.6.90		5000	15:17.05	
* Abakumova	Mariya	RUS	15.1.86	180/80	JT	66.86	71.99- 11
Abdullah	Khadija	USA	24.7.90		SP	17.12	16.96i- 10, 16.58- 11
Abera	Alemitu	ETH	.86		Mar	2:23:14	2:26:33- 11
Aberume	Mekuria	ETH			Mar	2:27:20	2:32:24- 11
Abiko	Tomomi	JPN	17.3.88	175/53	PV	4.40	4.25- 10
^ Abitova ¶	Inga	RUS	6.3.82	153/47	5000	15:26.19dq	15:11.6+- 08
					10k	31:55.97dq	30:31.42- 06
Abogunloko	Bukola	NGR-J	18.8.94	170/53	400	51.57	52.35- 11
Achamo	Netsanet	ETH	14.12.87	167/53	HMar	69:10	70:41- 11
					Mar	2:24:12	2:28:28- 11
Achola	Janet	UGA	26.6.88	161/63	1500	4:05.52	4:09.51- 10
					1M	4:28.83	
Acker	Alex	USA	12.9.88		PV	4.35	4.23- 11
^ Acuff	Amy	USA	14.7.75	188/66	HJ	1.95	2.01- 03
Adams	Aisha	USA	24.9.87	168/64	Hep	5861	5795(w), 5698- 10
* Adams	Valerie	NZL	6.10.84	193/123	SP	21.11	21.24- 11
* Adamu	Birtukan	ETH	29.4.92		3kSt	9:36.40	9:20.37- 11
Adeoye	Margaret	GBR	27.4.85	175/64	200	22.94	23.30, 23.14w- 11
^ Adriano	Elisângela	BRA	27.7.72	180/95	DT	58.22	61.96- 98, 62.23dq- 99
Aerts	Sara	BEL	25.1.84	182/64	100h	12.94	13.31- 10
					Hep	6077	6084- 10
Afework	Abebech	ETH	11.12.90		10k	31:48.53	32:05.06- 11
Aga	Ruti	ETH-J	16.1.94		5000	15:21.36	
Agai	Margaret	KEN	.81			2:24:17	
^ Agirre	Naroa	ESP	15.5.79	177/64	PV	4.35i, 4.26	4.56i- 07, 4.50- 06
Aguilera	Lisa	USA	30.11.79	160/46	3kSt	9:41.95	9:24.84- 10
* Ahmed	Zemzem	ETH	27.12.84	164/48	Mar	2:27:12	-0-
					3kSt	9:25.85	9:17.85- 08
* Ahouré	Murielle	CIV	23.8.87	167/57	100	10.99	11.06, 10.86w- 11
					200	22.42	22.78- 09

Name		Nat	Born	Ht/Wt	Event	2012 Mark	Pre-2012 Best
Ahye	Michelle-Lee	TRI	10.4.92	160/64	100	11.19	11.20, 11.15w- 11
Aidietyté	Neringa	LTU	5.6.83	177/64	20kW	1:33:05	1:33:54- 07
Aït Salem	Souad	ALG	6.1.79	167/51	Mar	2:27:21	2:25:08- 07
* Aitova	Marina	KAZ	13.9.82	180/60	HJ	1.95	1.99- 09
Aizu	Yoko	JPN	28.4.86	156/42	10k	32:18.40	33:02.11- 11
^ Akaba	Yukiko	JPN	18.10.79	158/44	HMar	69:56	68:11- 08
					Mar	2:26:08	2:24:09- 11
Akinniyi	Dorcas	USA	23.1.90	170/	Hep	5733	5584- 10
Akkaoui	Malika	MAR	25.12.87	160/46	800	1:59.54, 1:59.01i	1:59.75- 11
Alami	Salima	MAR	29.12.83	175/53	3kSt	9:31.03	9:42.51- 11
^ Alaoui Selsouli ¶	Mariem	MAR	8.4.84	165/49	1500	4:03.67i, 3:56.15dq	4:00.77- 11
2000 5:41.24+dq 5:40.0+i- 08			3000 8:34.47dq, 8:36.87i			8:29.52- 07 5000 14:45.91dq	14:36.52- 07
Alcántara	Dailenis	CUB	10.8.91	163/56	TJ	14.58	14.56- 11
* Aldama	Yamilé	GBR	14.8.72	173/62	TJ	14.82i, 14.65	15.29- 03
^ Alekhina	Nadezhda	RUS	22.9.78	176/62	TJ	14.04i	15.14- 09
* Alembekova	Elmira	RUS	30.6.90		20kW	1:25:27	1:27:35- 11
Alemu	Bekele	ETH	11.4.91		HMar	69:31	71:44- 11
Alexander	Annie	TRI	28.8.87	175/91	SP	17.70i, 17.36	17.66- 11
Alexander	Ayanna	TRI	20.7.82	172/65	TJ	14.15	13.99i- 10, 13.98- 11
Alexander	Rebecca	USA	2.5.90	168/55	400	51.13A, 51.20	53.17- 09
* Ali	Nia	USA	23.10.88	170/64	100h	12.78	12.73, 12.63w- 11
Allen	Tasha	USA	8.5.90		100	11.37, 11.17w	11.62- 09, 11.47w- 11
Almanza	Rose M.	CUB	13.7.92	166/53	800	1:59.55	2:00.56- 11
Alniaçik	Aysegül	TUR	15.4.87		HT	66.93	61.65- 11
Amadi	Chinazor	NGR	12.9.87		LJ	6.60	6.43- 07
* Amata	Doreen	NGR	6.5.88	185/55	HJ	1.90	1.95- 08
Anacharsis	Phara	FRA	17.12.83	177/60	400	52.02	51.87- 08
					400h	55.97	56.53- 11
Anagnostopoúlou	Hristoúla	GRE	27.8.91	176/79	DT	57.10	55.68- 11
* Anderson	Alexandria	USA	28.1.87	175/60	100	11.12, 10.88w	11.01, 10.91w- 11
					200	22.98, 22.84w	22.60- 09
Anderson	Gabriele	USA	25.6.86	168/55	1500	4:04.84	4:06.77- 11
1M 4:27.94			4:33.57- 11		3000	8:43.52	9:31.62i- 09
Andersson	Catarina	SWE	17.11.77	172/88	SP	17.01i	16.48- 11
* Andersson	Isabellah	SWE	12.11.80	167/51	HMar	70:30	70:02- 10
					Mar	2:25:41	2:23:41- 11
Andersson	Tracey	SWE	5.12.84	167/80	HT	70.33	69.28- 10
Andraud	Matilde	FRA	28.4.89	172/68	JT	56.52	56.80- 09
Andrews	Chandra	USA	4.9.83		HT	66.72	63.71- 08
Angell	Mary	USA	29.8.89		DT	56.94	56.26- 11
* Angelsen	Tonje	NOR	17.1.90	179/62	HJ	1.97	1.92- 11
Anteneh	Emebet	ETH	13.1.92		3000	8:43.20	8:55.24- 10
					5000	15:02.51	14:43.29- 11
Antil	Seema	IND	27.7.83	183/85	DT	62.60	64.84- 04
^ Antonova	Aleksandra	RUS	24.3.80	162/59	100h	13.08	12.78- 06
* Antyukh	Natalya	RUS	26.6.81	182/73	200	22.73	22.75- 04
400 51.27			49.85- 04		400h	52.70	52.92- 10
Anumba	Michelle	USA	18.9.91	165/77	SP	17.18	16.41- 11
Anyanwu	Kelechi	USA	27.12.85	173/82	DT	57.68	58.01- 08
Aoki	Sayaka	JPN	15.12.86	163/51	400h	56.68	55.94- 08
Apak	Sema	TUR	17.8.85	169/59	400h	56.62	57.09A, 57.22- 11
Apostolico	Tamara	ITA	28.4.89	178/77	DT	59.50	55.16- 11
Arcanjo	Geisa	BRA	19.9.91	180/92	SP	19.02	17.11- 10
* Aregawi	Abeba	ETH	5.7.90	170/52	800	1:59.39	2:01.98- 09
		(now SWE)			1500	3:56.54	4:01.47i- 11, 4:01.96- 10
Arenas	Lorena	COL-J	17.9.93		20kW	1:32:36	-0-
Areson	Jackie	USA	31.3.88	150/50	5000	15:14.31	15:39.81i- 11, 15:51.56- 10
Argunova	Nina	RUS	15.9.89		100h	13.08	13.02- 11
Aristarkhova	Natalya	RUS	31.10.89		3kSt	9:31.93	9:56.04- 11
Arkhipova	Lyudmila	RUS	25.11.78	167/55	20kW	1:28:29	1:26:16- 08
* Arkhipova	Tatyana	RUS	8.4.83	160/53	Mar	2:23:29	2:25:01- 11
Armentero	Ismaray	CUB-J	13.10.94	171/68	JT	56.34	54.49- 11
Arrafi	Rabab	MAR	12.1.91	155/47	1500	4:05.80	4:21.59- 06
^ Arron	Christine	FRA	13.9.73	177/64	100	11.27	10.73- 98
Artîc ¶	Natalia	MDA	24.7.87		DT	62.13	56.62- 11
Artymata	Eleni	CYP	16.5.86	178/58	200	22.92	22.61- 10
Arusei	Peninah	KEN	23.2.79	165/51	HMar	68:12	67:48- 10
Arzamasova	Marina	BLR	17.12.87	173/57	800	1:59.63	1:59.30- 11
* Arzhakova	Yelena	RUS	8.9.89	170/56	800	1:57.67	1:58.77- 11
1000 2:36.69i			2:35.21i- 11		1500	4:00.82	4:07.69- 11

Name		Nat	Born	Ht/Wt	Event	2012 Mark	Pre-2012 Best
Asahssah	Malika	MAR	24.9.82		HMar	70:37	69:54- 09
Asanova	Natalya	UZB	29.11.89	165/68	400h	56.13	57.16- 10
Aselefech	Mergia	ETH	23.1.85	168/45	Mar	2:19:31	2:22:38- 10
Ashe	Shelby	USA-J	13.3.93	173/88	HT	68.12	65.32- 10
Ashley	Whitney	USA	18.2.89	178/80	SP	16.95i, 16.89	15.82- 11
					DT	59.99	54.75- 11
Assefa	Meskerem	ETH	20.9.85	155/43	1500	4:06.52	4:02.12- 11
					3000	8:53.18i	8:46.37- 09
* Assefa	Sofia	ETH	14.11.87	171/58	3kSt	9:09.00	9:15.04- 11
Asumnu	Gloria	NGR	22.5.85	163/52	100	11.13	11.03- 08
					200	22.89	22.70- 07
Atkins	Joanna	USA	31.1.89	175/61	200	23.10, 22.83w	22.68- 11
					400	51.12	50.39- 09
Atkinson	Saniel	BAH	2.7.91		HJ	1.89	1.83- 11
Atschkinadze	Xenia	GER	14.1.89	174/58	LJ	6.56i, 6.52, 6.72w	6.44- 11
* Augusto	Jéssica	POR	8.11.81	165/46	Mar	2:24:59	2:24:33- 11
* Avdeyeva	Anna	RUS	6.4.85	170/90	SP	19.54	20.07- 09
* Ayalew	Genet	ETH	31.12.92		3000	c.8:51+	9:01.75- 10
					5000	14:48.43	15:03.52- 10
* Ayalew	Hiwot	ETH	6.3.90	173/51	3kSt	9:09.61	9:23.88- 11
Ayana	Almaz	ETH	21.11.91		3000	8:49.64	8:53.49- 11
5000	14:57.97		15:12.24- 11		3kSt	9:38.62	9:22.51- 10
Aydemir	Esma	TUR	1.1.92		1500	4:09.06	4:22.34- 11
Aydin	Merve	TUR	17.3.90	180/58	800	2:00.23	2:00.33- 08
Ayhan	Burcu	TUR	3.5.90	182/58	HJ	1.93	1.94- 11
Azarova	Tatyana	KAZ	2.12.85	166/54	400h	55.71	54.78- 07
* Bailey	Aleen	JAM	25.11.80	170/64	100	11.04	11.04- 04
					200	22.84, 22.79w	22.33- 04
Baird	Kadecia	GUY-Y	24.2.95	167/52	400	51.04	-0-
Baker	Keshia	USA	30.1.88	170/61	400	51.23	50.76- 10
Balderrama	Claudia	BOL	13.11.83	168/49	20kW	1:33:28	1:37:32A- 11
Balykina	Yuliya	BLR	12.4.84	165/60	100	11.38, 11.32w	11.42- 11
Bambara	Laëtitia	BUR	30.3.84	180/75	HT	66.58	68.53- 11
Banco	Nelly	FRA	17.2.86	161/52	200	22.98	23.14- 08, 23.12w- 07
Bani	Zahra	ITA	31.12.79	173/73	JT	59.43	62.75- 05
Bânova	Andiana	BUL	1.5.87		TJ	14.03, 14.14i	14.34- 11
* Baptiste	Kelly-Ann	TRI	14.10.86	160/54	100	10.86	10.84- 10
					200	22.23w	22.60- 09, 22.58w- 10
^ Barber	Me'Lisa	USA	4.10.80	160/52	100	11.20, 11.14w	10.95- 07, 10.87w- 05
Barber	Mikele	USA	4.10.80	159/50	100	11.13	11.02- 07, 10.96w- 11
					200	22.96	22.73- 07, 22.71w- 01
Barbosa	Vera	POR	13.1.89	168/58	400h	55.22	55.81- 11
Bârcâ	Roxana	ROU	22.6.88	165/44	5000	15:13.40	15:33.12- 10
Bardelle	Christine	FRA	16.8.74	160/48	5000	15:20.84	15:38.85- 07
Bardge	Crystal	USA	25.9.88	158/50	100h	13.09	13.64- 11
Barr	Jessie	IRL	24.7.89	178/59	400h	55.93	56.62- 11
Barrachina	Gema	ESP	10.4.86	162/49	10k	32:08.54	31:54.64- 10
* Barrett	Brigetta	USA	24.12.90	183/64	HJ	2.03	1.96- 11
* Barrios	Yarelys	CUB	12.7.83	172/98	DT	68.03	66.40A- 11, 66.68ex- 07
Barros	Marisa	POR	25.2.80	160/50	HMar	70:26	69:09- 10
					Mar	2:26:13	2:25:04- 11
Barsosio	Agnes	KEN	.83		HMar	70:25+	72:03- 08
					Mar	2:24:27	2:53:38- 07
* Battke	Anna	GER	3.1.85	173/58	PV	4.52i	4.68- 09
Bauer	Katharina	GER	12.6.90	178/66	PV	4.42	4.31i, 4.25- 11
Bauschke	Melanie	GER	14.7.88	179/63	LJ	6.68	6.83- 09
Baxter	Aubrey	USA	7.11.85	173/84	HT	70.90	65.53- 11
Baysa	Atsede	ETH	16.4.87		HMar	69:39	68:42- 10
					Mar	2:22:03	2:22:04- 10
* Beard	Jessica	USA	8.1.89	168/57	400	51.19	50.56- 09
Beckles	Kanika	GRN	3.10.91	170/57	400	51.72	53.24- 11
Beckles	Kierre	BAR	21.5.90	169/54	100h	13.16, 12.97w	13.01- 11
Beckwith	Molly	USA	4.8.87	173/59	800	1:59.18	1:59.12- 11
Bedaso	Shetaye	ETH	.85		Mar	2:27:14 (HMar 69:53+)	2:25:09- 11
Beesley	Meghan	GBR	15.11.89	165/63	400h	56.54	55.69- 11
Begay	Alvina	USA	9.9.80	165/48	10k	32:34.76	34:55.45- 09
* Beitia	Ruth	ESP	1.4.79	192/71	HJ	2.00	2.02- 07
* Bekele	Bezunesh	ETH	29.1.83	145/38	HMar	69:09	68:07- 07
					Mar	2:20:30	2:23:09- 08
Bekele	Mekdes	ETH	20.1.87	180/58	3000	8:49.50i	8:44.25i- 11, 9:01.17- 10
					3kSt	9:37.18	9:20.23- 08

Name		Nat	Born	Ht/Wt	Event	2012 Mark	Pre-2012 Best
Bekele	Tadelech	ETH	11.4.91		5000	15:28.27	
Belete	Almensch	ETH/BEL	26.7.89	156/44	1M	4:28.11	4:42.14- 11
					3000	8:52.02	8:51.76- 09
					5000	15:04.12	15:03.63- 11
* Belete	Mimi	BRN	9.6.88	164/62	1500	4:01.72	4:00.25- 10
					3000	8:43.64	8:32.18- 10
Belibasáki	María	GRE	19.6.91	174/54	100	11.34	11.98, 11.85w- 10
Belkina	Olga	RUS	23.8.90	173/58	100	11.26	11.40- 11
					200	22.73	24.00- 10
Bellille	Janeil	TRI	18.6.89	172/60	400h	55.91	55.80- 11
Benecchi	Giorgia	ITA	9.7.89	164/55	PV	4.35	4.36i- 10, 4.40ex- 11, 4.20- 10
* Bengtsson	Angelica	SWE-J	8.7.93	164/51	PV	4.58	4.63i, 4.57- 11
Benthami	Bouchra	FRA	19.5.79	175/47	5000	15:32.89	15:12.17- 06
Bergrová	Zuzana	CZE	24.11.84	174/62	400h	55.78	55.96- 10
Berings	Eline	BEL	28.5.86	162/53	100h	12.95	12.94- 09
Bernard-Thomas	Neisha	GRN	21.1.81	165/56	800	2:00.68	1:59.60- 10
Berry	Gwen	USA	29.6.89	165/68	HT	71.95	70.52- 11
* Bespalova	Mariya	RUS	21.5.86	183/80	HT	76.72	71.93- 11
Bian Ka		CHN-J	5.1.93		SP	16.97	16.34- 11
Bicet	Nora Aida	ESP	29.10.77	178/78	JT	58.82	63.32- 04
Bielawska	Martyna	POL	15.11.90	175/58	TJ	13.53, 13.80w	13.97- 11
Biesenbach	Kira	GER	7.10.92	186/70	Hep	5878	5480- 09
Bikulova	Lina	RUS	1.10.88		20kW	1:31:01	1:32:39- 09
Billaud	Cindy	FRA	11.3.86	167/59	100h	12.97	12.93- 11
Bingson	Amanda	USA	20.2.90	170/89	HT	71.78	69.79- 11
Biryuk	Tamara	UKR-Y	11.4.95		HJ	1.89i	1.80- 10
Bishop	Melissa	CAN	5.8.88	173/58	800	1:59.82	2:02.69- 11
^ Bisibori	Ruth	KEN	2.1.88	170/55	3kSt	9:32.81	9:13.16- 09
Bissoly	Séphora	FRA	6.11.81	168/66	JT	57.22	59.52- 06
Biwott	Salome	KEN	.83		Mar	2:26:41A	2:39:02- 11
Blake	Dominique	JAM	15.2.87	178/64	400	51.72	52.15- 08
* Bleasdale	Holly	GBR	2.11.91	175/68	PV	4.87i, 4.71	4.71i, 4.70- 11
* Bleasdale	Julia	GBR	9.9.81	167/46	3000	8:46.38	9:09.1+- 11
					5000	15:02.00	15:44.00- 11
					10k	30:55.63	34:20.77- 05
Bledsoe	Amber	USA	18.8.85		LJ	6.61	6.32- 10
Bleskina	Yekaterina	RUS-J	29.1.93		100h	13.11	13.38- 10
Blewitt-Wilson	Adriane	USA	24.5.80	178/79	SP	17.40	18.29- 05
Bliss	Andrea	JAM	5.10.80	173/63	100h	13.01	12.83- 05
Blouin	Mélanie	CAN	14.7.90	175/64	PV	4.40	4.30- 11
Bludova	Olga	KAZ	5.11.91	171/62	100	11.12	11.37- 11
Bo Yanmin		CHN	29.6.87	170/51	20kW	1:31:22	1:27:37- 05
Bobocel	Ancuta	ROU	3.10.87	163/52	3kSt	9:25.70	9:30.07- 08
Boden	Lauren	AUS	3.8.88	179/66	400h	55.45	55.25- 10
Boekelman	Melissa	NED	11.5.89	177/66	SP	17.52i, 17.14	18.17- 10
Bogale	Tizita	ETH-J	13.7.93		1500	4:08.48, 4:06.01i	4:03.94- 11
* Bolshakova	Svetlana	BEL	14.10.84	178/68	TJ	14.28	14.55- 10
* Bolshova	Yekaterina	RUS	4.2.88	178/66	HJ	1.92i, 1.91	1.87- 10
					Hep	6466	5738- 10
Bolton	Grecia	USA	2.10.89	169/57	100	11.36, 11.22w	11.35, 11.30w- 11
Bonne	Daysurami	CUB	9.3.88	173/56	400	52.12	51.69A- 11, 51.81- 09
Boonstra	Miranda	NED	29.8.72	174/52	Mar	2:27:32	2:29:23- 11
Boonwan	Wanida	THA	30.8.86	185/52	HJ	1.89	1.92- 11
Bordignon	Laura	ITA	26.3.81	180/78	DT	58.87	59.21- 08
Bordyugova	Polina	RUS	18.8.91		400h	56.99	59.57- 11
* Borel	Cleopatra	TRI	3.10.79	168/93	SP	18.82	19.48i- 04. 19.42- 11
Borges	Fernanda Raquel	BRA	26.7.88	165/65	DT	58.92	60.91- 11
Borman	Brittany	USA	1.7.89	180/77	JT	61.51	54.32- 11
Borodina	Yana	RUS	21.4.92		TJ	14.41	14.35- 11
Borovska	Nadiya	UKR	25.2.81	165/50	20kW	1:30:03	1:32:30- 11
Borsi	Veronica	ITA	13.6.87	168/51	100h	13.05, 13.03w	13.08- 11
* Boslak	Vanessa	FRA	11.6.82	170/57	PV	4.70i, 4.55	4.70- 06
Bouaasayriya	Kaltoum	MAR	23.8.82	157/46	3kSt	9:40.69	
Bouras ¶	Zahra	ALG	13.1.87	170/52	800	1:58.78dq	1:59.21- 11
Bowie	Tori	USA	27.8.90	175/61	100	11.28	11.76, 11.72w- 10
					LJ	6.78	6.64- 11
Bowman	Sarah	USA	15.10.86	170/52	1500	4:08.25	4:05.67- 09
Bracy	Addie	USA	4.8.86	158/47	10k	32:37.66	33:08.39- 11
Bratkic	Maja	SLO	14.5.91		TJ	13.75	13.71- 10
Breen	Melissa	AUS	17.9.90	174/66	100	11.27	11.33- 08, 11.22w- 09
Bremser	Julia	GER	27.4.82	176/78	DT	59.70	59.84- 11
Brenner	Melina	GER-J	28.6.93	181/63	HJ	1.88i, 1.87	1.85- 11
Brewer	Chandra	USA	26.7.81		SP	16.87	18.03- 08

Name		Nat	Born	Ht/Wt	Event	2012 Mark	Pre-2012 Best
Brichacek	Emily	AUS	7.7.90		5000	15:30.00	16:17.06- 10
Briscoe	Shanay	USA	7.8.92		HJ	1.92	1.88- 11
* Britton	Fionnuala	IRL	24.9.84	158/45	5000	15:12.97	15:21.45mx, 15:31.26- 11
3000	8:55.01mx		9:02.11- 11		10k	31:29.22	-0-
Broersen	Nadine	NED	29.4.90	171/62	Hep	6319	5932(w), 5854- 11
Brooks	Sheri-Ann	JAM	11.2.83	170/64	100	11.05	11.05- 07
					200	23.16, 22.92w	22.70- 08
Brooks	Tia	USA	2.8.90	183/109	SP	19.00i, 18.47	18.00- 11
Brost	Leslie	USA	28.9.89	163/57	PV	4.35i	4.30- 10
Brown	Kamaria	USA	21.12.92		200	22.86i	23.53- 10
* Brown	T'Erea	USA	24.10.89	178/59	400h	54.21	54.74- 10
* Brown Trafton	Stephanie	USA	1.12.79	193/102	DT	67.74	66.21- 09
Bruni	Roberta	ITA-J	8.3.94	170/54	PV	4.35	4.20- 11
Bryant	Dezerea	USA-J	27.4.93	157/50	100	11.29	11.59- 10
					200	22.97	23.51- 10
* Bryzgina	Yelizaveta	UKR	28.11.89	172/56	200	22.64	22.44- 10
Büchler	Nicole	SUI	17.12.83	161/56	PV	4.60	4.50- 09
Buckley	Kyla	USA	22.3.91		SP	16.98	15.63- 11
Buckman	Zoe	AUS	21.12.88	167/50	800	2:02.19	2:02.50-08
1000	2:37.84				1500	4:05.03	4:05.06- 11
Buell	Bethany	USA	4.12.91	163/59	PV	4.40	4.20- 11
Buisson	Marion	FRA	19.2.88	176/61	PV	4.35	4.50- 08
* Bujin	Cristina	ROU	12.4.88	171/52	TJ	14.14i, 14.13, 14.25w	14.42- 09
* Bulgakova	Anna	RUS	17.1.88	173/90	HT	74.02	73.79- 08
* Bulut	Gamze	TUR	3.8.92	165/48	1500	4:01.18	4:18.23- 11
					3kSt	9:34.88	10:13.73- 11
* Burka	Gelete	ETH	15.2.86	165/45	3000	8:45.09, 8:36.59i	8:25.92- 06
					5000	14:41.43	14:31.20- 07
Burkhanova	Sofia	UZB	1.12.89	170/60	SP	17.44	17.19- 10
Burkhardt	Samira	GER	9.8.90	182/82	SP	17.02i	17.09- 11
Butvina	Aleksandra	RUS	14.2.86	181/71	Hep	6110	6079- 10
Buziak	Paulina	POL	16.12.86	170/52	20kW	1:29:44	1:32:44- 10
Byres	Katie	GBR-J	11.9.93	171/63	PV	4.52i, 4.36	4.20- 11
Caballero	Daylis	CUB	6.3.88	166/59	PV	4.50	4.51- 11
Caballero	Denia	CUB	13.1.90	175/73	DT	65.60	62.94- 11
* Cabecinha	Ana	POR	29.4.84	168/52	20kW	1:28:03	1:27:46- 08
* Çakir Alptekin	Asli	TUR	20.8.85	168/50	1500	3:56.62	4:02.17- 10
Calvert	Schillonie	JAM	27.7.88	166/57	100	11.05	11.05- 11
					200	22.68	22.55- 11
* Camarena-Williams	Jill	USA	2.8.82	180/91	SP	19.89i	20.18- 11
* Campbell	Amber	USA	5.6.81	170/91	HT	71.80	72.59- 11
* Campbell-Brown	Veronica	JAM	15.5.82	163/61	100	10.81	10.76- 11
					200	22.32	21.74- 08
Capková	Tereza	CZE	24.7.87	162/53	1500	4:08.27	4:08.89- 11
Caravelli	Marzia	ITA	23.10.81	176/64	100h	12.85	13.01- 11
Card	Kelsey	USA	20.8.92		SP	16.98i, 15.94	15.46- 11
Carrier-Eades	Chelsea	USA	21.8.89	168/59	100h	12.78	13.06, 12.96w- 11
					Hep	5839	5927w, 5761- 11
* Carruthers	Danielle	USA	22.12.79	173/62	100h	12.73	12.47, 12.37w- 11
Carter	Kori	USA	6.3.92	165/52	100h	12.99	13.12- 11
* Carter	Michelle	USA	12.10.85	175/104	SP	19.60	19.86- 11
Casadei	Nadja	SWE	3.4.83	174/66	Hep	5783	5905- 09
Cassulo	Chelsea	USA	10.6.90	173/77	HT	66.50	64.26- 11
Castells	Berta	ESP	24.1.84	174/79	HT	69.59	69.53- 11
* Castlin	Kristi	USA	7.7.88	170/57	100h	12.56, 12.48w	12.81- 08, 12.59w- 10
Cathey	Mason	USA	29.4.82	168/52	3kSt	9:47.32	9:53.66- 11
Cattaneo	Micol	ITA	14.5.82	178/68	100h	13.07	12.98- 08
^ Cechlová	Vera	CZE	19.11.78	178/78	DT	60.94	67.71- 03
Cechová	Katerina	CZE	21.3.88	170/52	100	11.32	11.40- 11, 11.35w- 10
Cérival	Jessica	FRA	20.1.82	185/120	SP	17.31	17.99i- 11, 17.87- 09
Chaboudez	Aurélie	FRA-J	9.5.93	173/60	400h	57.14	57.35- 11
Chaney	Jasmine	USA	25.8.88	160/52	400h	56.03	55.22- 11
Chang Chunfeng		CHN	4.5.88	179/75	JT	60.56	61.61- 07
Chávez	Erika	ECU	4.6.90	174/58	200	23.09A	23.40A- 11, 23.49- 10
Chebet	Winny	KEN	20.12.90	165/50	800	1:59.37	2:00.88A- 10
Cheever	Jamie	USA	28.2.87	173/57	3kSt	9:51.42	10:02.18- 11
Chelagat	Farida	KEN	21.8.86		HMar	70:36	
Chelangat	Tabitha	KEN	.89		3kSt	9:50.8A	10:17.3- 06
Chelimo	Edith	KEN	16.7.86		10k	32:36.25	
Chemion	Phanencer	KEN	8.4.89		3kSt	9:35.31	
* Chemos Cheywa	Milcah	KEN	24.2.86	163/48	3kSt	9:07.14	9:08.57- 09

Name		Nat	Born	Ht/Wt	Event	2012 Mark	Pre-2012 Best
Chen Mudan		CHN-J	4.10.93		TJ	13.77i, 13.72	13.67- 11
Chen Ping		CHN	8.9.89	170/67	JT	57.52	56.42- 11
Chen Shuangyan		CHN	14.8.91		20kW	1:32:36	1:35:33- 11
Chen Yanjun		CHN	13.1.88	180/58	HJ	1.88i, 1.84	1.88- 10
Chen Yufei		CHN	26.1.89	170/63	TJ	13.97	14.11- 09
Chepchirchir	Filomena	KEN	1.12.81	165/43	HMar	68:06	68:22- 11
					Mar	2:24:56	2:24:21- 11
Chepchirchir	Sarah	KEN	27.7.84		HMar	68:34	68:07- 11
Chepkemoi	Diane	KEN	.87		HMar	68:08	70:40- 11
					Mar	2:27:32	2:26:53- 11
* Chepkirui	Joyce	KEN	20.8.88		10k	32:24.71A	31:26.10- 11
					HMar	67:03	69:04- 11
* Chepkurui	Lidya	KEN	23.8.84		3kSt	9:14.98	9:30.73- 11
Chepkwony	Caroline	KEN	18.4.84		HMar	68:36	70:05- 10
Chepyego	Sally	KEN	3.10.85	160/42	5000	15:18.01	15:06.26- 06
					10k	31:33.76	31:27.98- 11
^ Cherkasova	Svetlana	RUS	20.5.78	171/55	800	1:59.03	1:56.93- 05
^ Chermoshanskaya	Yuliya	RUS	6.1.86	176/65	100	11.30	11.33- 08
					200	22.82	22.57- 08
* Chernova	Tatyana	RUS	29.1.88	189/63	LJ	6.61i, 6.54	6.82- 11
100h	13.34		13,32-11, 13.07w- 07		Hep	6774	6880- 11
Cherobon-Bawcom	Janet	USA	22.8.78	170/52	10k	31:12.68	34:21.80- 05
5000	15:34.5+, 15:22u mx		16:19.59i- 05		HMar	69:55	70:59- 10
* Cheromei	Lydia	KEN	11.5.77	162/47	HMar	67:26	67:33- 11
					Mar	2:21:30	2:22:34- 11
Cherono	Elizeba	KEN	6.6.88		HMar	70:48	71:26- 11
Cherono	Gladys	KEN	12.5.83		HMar	68:18	69:26- 09
* Cherono	Mercy	KEN	7.5.91	178/59	1500	4:06.42	4:02.31- 11
3000	8:38.51		8:42.09- 10		5000	14:47.18	14:35.13- 11
* Cherono	Priscah	KEN	27.6.80	160/47	3000	8:50.04	8:29.06- 07
5000	14:59.53		14:35.30- 06		10k	32:38.29A	30:56.43- 11
					HMar	68:35	
* Cherop	Sharon	KEN	16.3.84	158/44	HMar	67:21	67:08- 11
					Mar	2:22:39	2:22:42- 11
Cherotich	Fancy	KEN	10.8.90		3kSt	9:35.03	10:08.73- 09
* Cheruiyot	Vivian	KEN	11.9.83	155/38	1500	4:06.6A	4:06.65- 07
3000	8:41.22 8:28.66- 07		5000 14:35.62 14:20.87- 11		10k	30:30.44	30:48.98- 11
Chesang	Agnes	KEN	.86		3kSt	9:53.7A	
Chesebe	Sylvia	KEN	16.4.89		800	2:01.21A	2:01.61A- 11
Chesire	Rebecca	KEN			HMar	70:45	78:00- 06
Cheyech	Filomena	KEN	5.7.82		HMar	70:01	68:44- 09
* Chicherova	Anna	RUS	22.7.82	180/57	HJ	2.06i	2.07- 11
Child	Eilidh	GBR	20.2.87	172/59	400h	54.96	55.16- 10
Chilla	Mercedes	ESP	19.1.80	170/60	JT	57.40	64.07- 10
^ Chizhenko	Yuliya	RUS	30.8.79	173/63	800	2:00.93	1:57.07- 06
1500	4:02.33		3:55.68- 06		3000	8:44.60	8:59.67- 06
Chnaïk	Jamaa	MAR	28.7.84	177/60	TJ	13.75	13.63- 09, 14.02w- 10
Choi Yun-hee		KOR	28.5.86	171/58	PV	4.41	4.40- 11
^ Chojecka	Lidia	POL	25.1.77	163/47	1500	4:07.86	3:59.22- 00
Christensen	Becky	USA	24.2.87	183/59	HJ	1.92	1.91i- 09, 1.85- 11
Chukwuemeka ¶	Vivian	NGR	4.3.75	175/98	SP	17.64, 18.86dq	18.43- 03
Chung Hye-rim		KOR	1.7.87	169/51	100h	13.06	13.11- 11
Churakova	Yelena	RUS	16.12.86	175/56	400h	54.78	54.79- 11
Cibis	Anne	GER	27.9.85	173/68	100	11.17	11.33- 10
Cichocka	Angelika	POL	15.3.88	169/54	800	2:01.32	2:00.20- 11
1000	2:38.78		2:37.01- 09		1500	4:06.79	4:06.50- 11
Clarke	Georgie	AUS	17.6.84	162/38	5000	15:31.29	15:24.03- 08
Clarke	Shalina	USA	8.8.88		100h	13.08, 12.18w	13.09- 10
Clay	Raven	USA	5.10.90		100h	13.05A, 13.19, 13.16w	13.26- 11
Clements	Grace	GBR	2.5.84	170/64	Hep	5755	5819- 10
Clitheroe	Helen	GBR	2.1.74	168/57	3000	8:45.59i	8:39.81i- 11, 8:51.82- 10
Closse	Kelly	FRA	8.8.88	178/84	SP	16.83i	16.60- 11
Coburn	Emma	USA	19.10.90	173/54	3kSt	9:23.54	9:37.16- 11
Cojuhari	Olesea	MDA	29.3.90	170/58	400	52.00	53.30- 10
Cole	Leslie	USA	16.2.87	164/54	100	11.22	11.43- 11
	22.63		22.91- 11		400	51.46	51.20- 09
^ Collado	Yanisley	CUB	30.4.85	178/74	DT	57.15	64.10- 09
Collier	Ashley	USA	4.2.92	172/60	100	11.01	11.42- 11, 11.37w- 10
					200	22.89	23.15- 11
Comba	Rocío	ARG	14.7.87	175/78	DT	59.99	59.86- 08

Name		Nat	Born	Ht/Wt	Event	2012 Mark	Pre-2012 Best
Conley	Kim	USA	14.3.86	160/49	1M	4:27.23	
5000	15:14.48		15:38.13- 11		10k	32:00.94	33:22.28- 10
* Cosby	Jessica	USA	31.5.82	173/77	HT	74.19	72.65- 11
^ Costa	Keila	BRA	6.2.83	170/62	LJ	6.68	6.88- 07
					TJ	14.31	14.57, 15.10w- 07
Costa	Susana	POR	22.9.84	176/65	TJ	14.19	13.77i- 08, 13.70- 11
Cotten	Jennifer	CAN	14.10.87	175/	Hep	5793A, 5707	5685- 11
Coutinho	Geisa	BRA	1.6.80	160/53	400	51.46	51.08- 11
Coward	Jackie	USA	5.11.89	167/55	100h	12.81	12.87, 12.79w- 11
Cowley	Sarah	NZL	3.2.84	176/66	HJ	1.91	1.84- 11
					Hep	6135	5752- 11
Cox	Shana	GBR	22.1.85	171/57	400	51.54	50.84- 08
Craft	Shanice	GER-J	15.5.93	184/94	SP	17.15	15.74i- 11, 15.63- 10
					DT	62.92	58.65- 11
* Crawford	Virginia	USA	7.9.83	178/63	100h	12.59	12.45- 07
^ Crawford	Yunaika	CUB	2.11.82	164/78	HT	69.66	73.16- 04
Cremer	Esther	GER	29.3.88	170/55	400	51.76	52.08- 11
Cruz	Clarisse	POR	9.7.78	170/54	3kSt	9:30.06	9:44.94- 08
Cruz	Yanet	CUB	8.2.88	170/70	JT	62.75	63.50- 11
Cuddihy	Joanne	IRL	11.5.84	184/64	400	51.43	50.73- 07
Culley	Julie	USA	10.9.81	172/57	3000	8:45.57	8:55.62i- 09, 9:32.69- 10
					5000	15:05.38	15:21.18- 11
^ Cummins	Diane	CAN	19.1.74	165/48	800	2:00.55	1:58.39- 01
Currie	Joanna	USA	9.10.87		400h	56.74	56.82- 10
Cusma	Elisa	ITA	24.7.81	167/49	1500	4:07.55	4:04.98- 09
Czenska	Magdalena	POL	14.6.81	171/68	JT	57.22	56.92- 04
Daba	Tejitu	BRN	20.8.91	162/44	3000	8:53.75i	9:01.22- 10
					5000	15:05.59	15:14.62- 11
Dacheva	Petia	BUL	10.3.85	168/52	TJ	13.96	14.45- 10
Dadic	Ivona	AUT-J	29.12.93	183/60	Hep	5959	5455- 11
* Dado	Firehiwot	ETH	9.1.84	165/	HMar	68:35	69:26- 09
D'Agostino	Abbey	USA	25.5.92	158/48	5000	15:19.98	15:40.69- 11
Dahlgren	Jenny	ARG	27.8.84	180/115	HT	72.79	73.74- 10
* Dahlström	Malin	SWE	26.8.89	171/60	PV	4.50	4.50i. 4.36- 11
Danekova	Silvia	BUL	7.2.83	165/50	3kSt	9:42.72	10:10.98- 11
Daniels	Paris	USA	25.1.90	163/52	100	11.28, 11.23w	11.88- 10
					200	22.89, 22.65w	24.21, 23.91w- 10
Danois	Johanna	FRA	4.4.87	169/53	200	22.86	23.03- 09, 23.00w- 11
Darden	Dominique	USA	9.12.83	165/54	400h	55.70	54.88- 06
* Daska	Mamitu	ETH	16.10.83	165/	HMar	69:42+	68:07- 09
					Mar	2:23:52	2:21:59- 11
Daunay	Christelle	FRA	5.12.74	163/43	10k	31:35.81	31:44.84- 11
Dauwens	Axelle	BEL	1.12.90	171/62	400h	56.60	57.68- 11
Davila	Desiree	USA	26.7.83	157/45	HMar	70:44	70:34- 11
					Mar	2:25:55	2:22:38dh- 11, 2:26:20- 10
Davis	Darshay	USA	23.9.91	173/62	100	11.30	11.53, 11.32w- 11
					200	23.03	23.59- 11
* Davydova	Irina	RUS	27.5.88	170/65	400	51.94i	53.12- 11
					400h	53.77	55.48- 11
Day	Christine	JAM	23.8.86	168/51	400	50.85	51.54- 09
Day	Jonique	JAM	13.11.88	176/	400	52.11	53.91- 11
Day	Sharon	USA	9.6.85	173/66	Hep	6343	6177- 09
De Aniceto	Marisa	FRA	11.11.86	162/57	Hep	6182	6080- 09
Decaux	Alice	FRA	10.4.85	165/61	100h	12.88	12.95- 11
* Defar	Meseret	ETH	19.11.83	155/42	3000	8:46.49, 8:31.56i	8:23.72i, 8:24.51- 07
2000	5:44.54i		5:34.74i, 5:38.0- 06		5000	14:35.65	14:12.88- 08
^ Dehiba	Hind	FRA	17.3.79	162/44	1500	4:08.55i	3:59.76- 10
Deiac	Cornelia	ROU	20.3.88	171/55	LJ	6.67i, 6.54, 6.58w	6.70- 10
Dejaeghere	Veerle	BEL	1.8.73	159/46	3kSt	9:52.65	9:28.47- 07
* Dektyareva	Tatyana	RUS	8.5.81	174/60	100h	12.75	12.68- 10
Delasa	Sechale	ETH			Mar	2:26:27	
* DeLoach	Janay	USA	12.10.85	165/59	LJ	7.03, 7.15w	6.99Ai, 6.97- 11
Demidenko	Natalya	RUS-J	7.8.93		PV	4.32i, 4.30	4.40- 11
Demireva	Mirela	BUL	28.9.89	180/50	HJ	1.95	1.88- 07
* Demus	Lashinda	USA	10.3.83	170/62	400h	52.77	52.47- 11
Demut	Katja	GER	21.12.83	175/55	TJ	14.21	14.57- 11
Demydova	Hanna	UKR	8.4.87	178/50	TJ	14.50	13.88- 10, 13.91w- 11
^ Denby	Nichole	USA	10.10.82	163/52	100h	13.24, 12.78w	12.54- 08
Deng Xiaoqing		CHN	13.6.89	165/58	400h	56.82	57.04- 06
Denisenko	Alla	RUS	12.10.83		DT	58.74	58.26- 06
^ Dennison	Kate	GBR	7.5.84	171/59	PV	4.56	4.61- 11

	Name		Nat	Born	Ht/Wt	Event	2012 Mark	Pre-2012 Best
	Denyayeva	Svetlana	RUS	12.5.91		LJ	6.72, 6.85w	6.48- 11
						TJ	14.00w	13.68- 11
	Dereli	Emel	TUR-Y	25.2.96		SP	16.87	16.26i, 15.95- 11
	Derham	Zoë	GBR	24.11.80	180/118	HT	67.39	68.63- 08
	Desalegn	Betlhem	UAE	13.11.91		1500	4:08.87	4:12.36- 11
						3000	8:53.56i	
	DeShasier	Alicia	USA	15.4.84	180/75	JT	57.97	58.01A- 11
	Detsuk	Kseniya	BLR	23.4.86	177/56	TJ	14.76, 14.81w	14.39,14.54w- 10
	Devi	Suman	IND	15.7.85		JT	56.11	54.36- 05
*	Di Martino	Antonietta	ITA	1.6.78	169/57	HJ	1.95i	2.04i- 11, 2.03- 07
	Di Vincenzo	Sibilla	ITA	22.1.83	174/51	20kW	1:32:30	1:32:10- 10
	Diago	Sahily	CUB-Y	26.8.95	168/49	800	2:00.9	2:04.09- 11
	Dias	Ana	POR	15.1.74		10k	32:13.62	31:38.48- 03
	Diawara	Aïsseta	FRA	29.6.89	169/54	100h	12.88	13.07, 13.06w- 11
*	Dibaba	Genzebe	ETH	8.2.91	168/52	1500	3:57.77	4:04.80i- 10, 4:05.90- 11
*	Dibaba	Mare	ETH	20.10.89	160/42	HMar	67:44	67:13- 10
						Mar	2:19:52	2:23:25- 11
*	Dibaba	Tirunesh	ETH	1.10.85	160/47	2M	9:21.60i	9:12.23i- 10
	5000	14:50.80	14:11.15- 08	10k	30:20.75	29:54.66- 08	HMar	67:35dh	-0-
	DiCamillo	Kate	USA	14.12.86		10k	32:31.97	
	DiCrescenzo	Delilah	USA	28.2.83	168/53	3000	8:52.43	9:18.35- 09
						3kSt	9:43.28	9:40.63- 11
	Diebold	Tara	USA	28.11.88	167/	PV	4.37i, 4.15	4.30i, 4.20- 11
	Dimoff	Carrie	USA	31.5.83	155/45	3kSt	9:45.01	9:53.43- 08
	Ding Huiqin		CHN	5.2.90		20kW	1:30:14	1:31:23- 11
	Diriba	Buze	ETH-J	9.2.94		3000	8:39.65 and 5000 14:53.06	-0-
*	Diro	Etenesh	ETH	10.5.91	169/47	5000	15:19.77	15:21.51- 11
						3kSt	9:14.07	9:49.18- 11
	Dixon	Diamond	USA	29.6.92	168/55	400	50.88	51.55- 11
^	Dixon	Vonette	JAM	26.11.75	170/62	100h	12.90, 12.80w	12.64- 07
	Dobija	Teresa	POL	19.10.82	175/62	LJ	6.65	6.78- 11
*	Dobriskey	Lisa	GBR	23.12.83	171/56	1500	4:02.13	3:59.50- 09
*	Dobrynska	Nataliya	UKR	29.5.82	180/77	LJ	6.57i	6.63- 08, 6.73w- 09
						Hep	6311	6778- 10
	Dobrynska	Viktoriya	UKR	18.1.80	176/65	HJ	1.93	1.90- 07
	Dolgacheva	Viktoriya	RUS	17.4.91		TJ	14.35	
	Domel	Urszula	POL	21.7.88	178/55	HJ	1.89	1.88- 11
*	Domínguez	Marta	ESP	3.11.75	163/52	3kSt	9:24.26	9:07.32- 09
	Donaghue	Rebecca	USA	24.2.76	163/50	10k	32:36.05	32:50.32- 10
	Donzelot	Irène	FRA	8.12.88	170/68	DT	57.66	53.89- 11
	Dorozhon	Margaryta	UKR	4.9.87	180/75	JT	61.84	60.60- 09
	Dorr	Fawn	CAN	19.4.87		400h	56.50A, 56.7, 57.27	55.57- 10
	Dowie	Danielle	JAM	5.5.92		400h	56.10	57.33- 11
	Drabenya	Hanna	BLR	15.8.87	153/46	20kW	1:31:58	1:33:35- 09
	Dronsfield	Victoria	SWE	6.6.91	170/52	HJ	1.88	1.84- 11
	du Plessis	Julia	RSA-Y	27.5.96		HJ	1.88A	1.80- 11
	Du Xiaowei		CHN	11.8.87	180/72	JT	61.89	60.26- 11
^	Duarte	Sophie	FRA	31.7.81	170/54	3kSt	9:46.60	9:25.62- 09
	Ducó	Natalia	CHI	31.1.89	177/95	SP	18.80	18.65- 08
	Dudzinska	Agnieszka	POL	16.3.88	178/86	SP	17.00	16.44i- 08, 16.30- 09
	Duncan	Ashley	USA	16.9.86		SP	17.57i, 16.48	17.46i- 10, 16.80- 08
	Duncan	Dominique	USA	7.5.90	169/59	100	11.30, 11.15w	11.32, 11.05w- 11
						200	22.94, 22.70w	23.03, 22.79w- 11
*	Duncan	Kimberlyn	USA	2.8.91	173/59	100	10.96, 10.94w	11.09, 11.02w- 11
						200	22.19, 22.12w	22.24, 22.18w- 11
	Dunn	Karynn	USA	14.8.91	168/61	LJ	6.55	6.21- 10
^	Dunn ¶	Debbie	USA	26.3.78	168/57	400	51.22, 50.78dq	49.64- 10
	Dunne	Amanda	USA	5.12.82		5000	15:32.64	
	Duong Thi Viet Anh		VIE	30.12.90	160/52	HJ	1.92	1.90- 11
	Dupré	Melissa	BEL	5.11.86	170/61	JT	58.51	58.25- 11
	Durruthy	Yilian	CUB	30.1.90	177/77	LJ	6.59	6.18- 11
						Hep	5966	5752- 11
	Dusanova	Nadezhda	UZB	17.11.87	174/56	HJ	1.95	1.96i, 1.95- 09
	Dygacz	Agnieszka	POL	18.7.85	160/51	20kW	1:31:28	1:30:56- 11
	Dyomina	Oksana	RUS	4.8.90		800	2:00.06	2:01.73- 11
	Dzindzalietaité	Dovilé	LTU-J	14.7.93	167/58	TJ	14.17	13.35, 13.43w- 11
	Ebersohn	Annerie	RSA	9.8.90		400h	57.11A, 58.11	59.66- 08
	Ebihara	Yuki	JPN	28.10.85	164/66	JT	62.36	61.56- 10
	Edgerson	Jasmine	USA	6.6.91	163/52	100h	13.09	13.37- 11
	Edwards	Samantha	USA	14.1.90		400	52.15	53.18- 11
	Eisenlauer	Esther	GER	29.10.77	180/75	JT	58.42	61.04- 10

Name		Nat	Born	Ht/Wt	Event	2012 Mark	Pre-2012 Best
Ejjafini	Nadia	ITA	8.11.77	168/51	5000	15:16.54	15:22.39- 06
					10k	31:45.14	32:14.63- 11
Ektova	Irina	KAZ	8.1.87	173/61	TJ	14.29	14.48- 11
Elahi	Kianna	USA	24.8.90	168/61	400h	56.41	56.73- 11
Elbe	Jenny	GER	18.4.90	180/60	TJ	14.06	13.92i, 13.89- 11
Elmore	Malindi	CAN	13.3.80	168/53	1500	4:07.90	4:02.64- 04
Elmoukim	Rkia	MAR	22.2.88		5000	15:21.88	15:34.75- 11
Emmanuel	Crystal	CAN	27.11.91	170/50	100	11.34, 11.30Aw	11.50, 11.45Aw- 11
					200	23.10, 23.08w	22.90- 11
* England	Hannah	GBR	6.3.87	177/54	800	1:59.66	1:59.94- 09
					1500	4:04.05	4:01.89- 11
Engman	Helena	SWE	16.6.76	171/94	SP	17.64	18.17- 10
Ennis	Delloreen	JAM	5.3.75	178/67	100h	13.00	12.50- 07
* Ennis	Jessica	GBR	28.1.86	164/57	200	22.83	23.11- 11
100h	12.54	12.79- 11		HJ	1.91i, 1.89	1.95- 07 Hep 6955	6823- 10
Equihua	Monica	MEX	23.9.82	167/53	20kW	1:32:28	1:34:50A- 11
Erdmann	Tara	USA	14.6.89	155/45	10k	32:09.15	33:10.15- 11
Eriksson	Sandra	FIN	4.6.89	163/48	3kSt	9:43.38	9:45.50- 09
Esayias	Yeshi	ETH	28.12.85		Mar	2:26:00	2:26:04- 11
* Eshete	Shitaye	BRN	21.5.90	159/56	3000	8:49.27i	
5000	15:05.48		15:15.79- 10		10k	30:47.25	31:21.57- 11
Esmer	Dilek	TUR	15.1.88		DT	57.56	53.10- 09
Espinoza	Ahymará	VEN	28.5.85		SP	17.07	16.32- 09
Etea	Emebet	ETH	11.1.90		HMar	70:01	70:54- 10
Etim	Margaret	NGR	28.11.92	150/52	400	51.67	51.24- 10
Eutsey	Ebony	USA	3.5.92	166/55	400	52.07	52.07- 09
Evans	Taylor	USA	7.10.89		100	11.40, 11.23w	11.87, 11.80Aw- 05
					200	23.23, 23.02w	23.53, 23.30Aw- 11
Evans	Terra	USA	7.10.89	172/64	100	11.34, 11.19w	11.28, 11.19w- 10
Facey	Simone	JAM	7.5.85	162/53	100	11.32	10.95A, 11.11- 08, 11.0- 04
* Falzon	Stéphanie	FRA	7.1.83	170/75	HT	73.06	73.40- 08
Farkas	Györgyi	HUN	13.2.85	170/58	Hep	6030	6068- 11
Faye	Mame Fatou	SEN	19.8.86	170/	400h	56.37	57.46- 09
* Fedoriva	Aleksandra	RUS	13.9.88	172/61	200	22.19	22.41- 10
					400	51.18i	54.64i- 11
^ Feitor	Susana	POR	28.1.75	160/52	20kW	1:32:36	1:27:55- 01
* Felicien	Perdita	CAN	29.8.80	165/57	100h	12.93A, 12.93, 12.80w	12.46, 12.45w- 04
* Felix	Allyson	USA	18.11.85	168/57	100	10.89	10.93- 08
					200	21.69	21.81- 07
Félix	Dulce	POR	23.10.82	165/53	10k	31:44.75	31:30.90*- 09, 31:33.42- 11
HMar	69:50		68:33- 11		Mar	2:28:12	2:25:40- 11
Felnagle	Brie	USA	9.12.86	170/57	1500	4:08.80	4:08.54- 08
3000	8:51.38				5000	15:22.39	15:43.87- 11
* Feofanova	Svetlana	RUS	16.7.80	164/53	PV	4.65	4.88- 04
Ferguson	Sheniqua	BAH	24.11.89	170/57	100	11.07	11.17- 11
					200	22.64	22.85- 08
^ Ferguson McKenzie	Debbie	BAH	16.1.76	170/57	100	11.26	10.91- 02
^ Fernández	Nuria	ESP	16.8.76	170/57	1500	4:06.57	4:00.20- 10
Ferraro	Federica	ITA	18.8.88	168/51	20kW	1:31:45	1:33:36- 11
Feyne	Gemeda	ETH	28.6.92		1500	4:06.66	4:10.63- 11
Fiack	Marion	FRA	13.10.92	170/60	PV	4.42i	4.36i, 4.15- 11
Figueroa	Ángela	COL	28.6.84	167/60	3kSt	9:42.71	9:53.44- 10
Filándra	Eléni	GRE	12.1.84	174/60	800	2:00.44	2:00.88- 10
Finley	London	USA	1.2.90	168/55	400h	56.67	58.10- 10
* Fiodorow	Joanna	POL	4.3.89	168/77	HT	74.18	70.06- 11
* Firova	Tatyana	RUS	10.10.82	174/59	400	49.72	49.89- 10
Fischer	Julia	GER	1.4.90	190/84	DT	64.22	59.60- 11
Fisher	Aleksandra	KAZ	3.6.88	172/75	SP	17.41	17.21i- 10, 15.81- 11
* Flanagan	Shalane	USA	8.7.81	165/50	10k	31:59.69	30:22.22- 08
HMar	68:52		68:37- 10		Mar	2:25:38	2:28:40- 10
Flax	Jessica	USA	4.9.90	173/64	Hep	5826	5440- 11
Fleming	Annett	GER	4.5.84	178/66	Hep	5851	5760(w)- 11, 5675- 09
Flemings	Donique	USA	1.11.91	163/55	100h	13.00, 12.87w	13.33- 10
Flinck	Sofi	SWE-Y	8.7.95	168/69	JT	61.40	54.83- 11
Flood	Katie	USA	29.2.92	168/55	1M	4:28.48i	4:47.45i- 11
Florczak	Sinje	GER	28.11.86		LJ	6.64	6.46, 6.53w- 11
Flórez	Lina	COL	1.11.84	170/58	100h	12.95A, 13.17	12.94- 11
Ford	Yirisleyidi	CUB	18.8.91	168/69	HT	68.45	67.93- 09
Foster	Amy	IRL	2.10.88		100	11.50, 11.32w	11.49- 11, 11.32w- 10
^ Foster-Hylton	Brigitte	JAM	7.11.74	170/62	100h	12.51	12.45- 03

Name		Nat	Born	Ht/Wt	Event	2012 Mark	Pre-2012 Best
* Fountain	Hyleas	USA	14.1.81	170/64	100h	12.70	12.78, 12.65w- 08
LJ	6.75		6.89- 10, 6.95w- 09		Hep	6419	6735w- 10, 6667- 08
Francis	Eden	GBR	19.10.88	178/85	SP	17.24	16.73- 11
					DT	57.61	59.78- 11
Francis	Phyllis	USA	4.5.92	178/61	200	23.03	
					400	51.22	52.93- 11
Franco	Jamy	GUA	1.7.91	170/48	20kW	1:30:57	1:32:38A- 11
Franco	Leryn	PAR	1.3.82	174/54	JT	57.77	56.17- 11
Franek	Bridget	USA	8.11.87	160/50	3kSt	9:29.53	9:32.35- 10
Fransen	Remona	NED	25.11.85	189/71	Hep	5964	6198- 11
* Fraser-Pryce	Shelly-Ann	JAM	27.12.86	160/52	100	10.70	10.73- 09
					200	22.09	22.15- 08
Freeman	Octavious	USA	20.4.92	169/57	100	11.09	11.16, 11.11Aw- 10
					200	22.74	22.96- 11
Frere	Danielle	USA	27.4.90		SP	17.47i, 16.65	16.79- 11
* Friedrich	Ariane	GER	10.1.84	179/57	HJ	1.93	2.06- 09
* Frizell	Sultana	CAN	24.10.84	183/110	HT	75.04	72.24- 10
Frolova	Karina	RUS	2.3.90		HT	66.61	65.06- 11
Frøysedal	Inger Anne	NOR	25.4.89	173/58	TJ	13.71, 13.93w	13.63, 13.88w- 10
* Fuchise	Masami	JPN	2.9.86	161/51	20kW	1:28:41	1:28:03- 09
Fuentes-Pila	Zulema	ESP	25.5.77	166/52	3kSt	9:44.04	9:29.40- 08
Fukumoto	Miyuki	JPN	4.1.77	172/53	HJ	1.90	1.92- 04
* Fukushi	Kayoko	JPN	25.3.82	161/45	5000	15:09.31	14:53.22- 05
					10k	31:10.35	30:51.81- 02
Fukushima	Chisato	JPN	27.6.88	165/51	100	11.34	11.21- 10, 11.16w- 11
Furman	Ma'ayan	ISR	9.11.86	184/62	HJ	1.90i	1.92- 11
Fyodorova	Alina	UKR	31.7.89		Hep	6126	6008- 11
* Gadschiew	Kristina	GER	3.7.84	170/62	PV	4.60	4.66i- 11, 4.60- 10
Galiart	Rianna	NED	22.11.85	168/56	PV	4.33i, 4.32	4.31i- 08, 4.31- 11
Galimova	Valentina	RUS	11.5.86		10k	32:07.82	32:24.47- 09
Galitskaya	Yekaterina	RUS	24.2.87	174/63	100h	12.78	12.95- 11
* Galkina	Gulnara	RUS	9.7.78	174/56	5000	15:29.97	14:33.13- 08
					3kSt	9:24.60	8:58.81- 08
Gall	Geena	USA	18.1.87	168/52	800	1:59.24	1:59.62- 11
Gallardo	Karen	CHI	6.3.84	175/95	DT	60.09	60.48- 11
Galvis	Sandra	COL	28.6.86		20kW	1:33:24	1:36:36- 11
Ganeyeva	Vera	RUS	6.11.88	172/87	DT	64.20	63.61- 11
Gao Ni		CHN	14.9.91	163/51	20kW	1:28:06	1:29:38- 11
Gao Yang		CHN-J	1.3.93		SP	17.07	
Garcia	Stephanie	USA	3.5.88	168/52	3kSt	9:47.76	9:41.12- 11
García	Rosibel	COL	13.2.81	171/62	800	2:00.16	1:59.38- 08
Gardner	English	USA	22.4.92	162/50	100	11.10, 11.00w	11.03- 11
					200	22.82	23.02- 11
Garner	April	USA	25.12.83	173/60	100h	12.97	13.20- 08
^ Gavrilâ	Adelina	ROU	26.11.78	174/59	TJ	14.24i, 14.07	14.78i- 08, 14.75- 03
* Gay	Mabel	CUB	5.5.83	185/69	TJ	14.40	14.67- 11
Gayot	Marie	FRA	18.12.89	171/58	400	51.60	53.04- 11
Gebisa	Tejinesh	ETH-Y	3.3.95		3kSt	9:50.51	10:57.73- 11
Gebresilasie	Goytetom	ETH-Y	15.1.95		3000	8:46.01i	8:56.36- 11
Gebru	Azemra	ETH	5.5.92		1500	4:08.39	
3000	8:40.01		8:48.63- 11		5000	14:58.23	14:58.34- 11
Gega	Luiza	ALB	5.11.88	166/56	1500	4:08.65mx, 4:09.76	4:14.22- 11
* Gelana	Tiki	ETH	22.10.87	165/48	HMar	67:48dh	70:22- 08
					Mar	2:18:58	2:22:08- 11
Gennette	Janae	USA				6.43, 6.56wA	
Gentili	Manuela	ITA	7.2.78	163/52	400h	55.54	55.78- 10
* George	Phylicia	CAN	16.11.87	178/65	100	11.25	11.38- 11
					100h	12.65	12.73- 11
George	Regina	USA/NGR	17.2.91	176/61	400	51.11	52.30i, 52.31- 11
Gergel	Melissa	USA	24.4.89	168/57	PV	4.46	4.45i- 10, 4.45- 11
Getaneh	Genet	ETH	6.1.86		Mar	2:25:38	2:25:57- 11
Geubelle	Andrea	USA	21.6.91	165/57	TJ	13.84, 14.17w	13.29- 10
* Ghribi	Habiba	TUN	9.4.84	173/52	3kSt	9:08.37	9:11.97- 11
Gibson	Baillie	USA	18.11.91		SP	17.35	17.07- 11
Gierisch	Kristin	GER	20.8.90	177/57	TJ	14.19i, 13.94	14.10i- 11, 14.02- 09
Giesa	Ulrike	GER	16.8.84	183/93	DT	59.65	60.63- 05
Ginés	Laura	ESP	11.6.86	176/66	Hep	5860	5583- 11
Giordano Bruno	Anna	ITA	13.12.80	171/63	PV	4.40i, 4.40	4.60- 09
Giorgi	Eleonora	ITA	14.9.89	162/52	20kW	1:29:48	1:33:46- 11
Gipson	Whitney	USA	20.9.90	168/57	LJ	6.97	6.63, 6.69w- 11
Gisaw	Melkam	ETH	17.9.90		Mar	2:27:50	2:26:52- 11

	Name		Nat	Born	Ht/Wt	Event	2012 Mark	Pre-2012 Best
*	Glanc	Zaneta	POL	11.3.83	187/86	DT	65.34	63.99- 11
	Glazkova	Alena	RUS	6.5.88		800	2:00.39	2:02.97- 10
	Gleadle	Liz	CAN	5.12.88	183/95	JT	61.15	58.40- 11
	Glenn	Brianna	USA	18.4.80	168/55	LJ	6.85	6.78. 7.00w- 11
	Glok	Olga	RUS	16.12.82		Mar	2:27:18	2:28:27- 09
	Godana	Deribe	ETH	13.3.88		Mar	2:27:32	2:31:31- 09
	Godfay	Afera	ETH	25.9.91		5000	15:01.20	16:14.28- 10
	Godsey	Keelin	USA	2.1.84		HT	70.48	68.90- 11
	Gogoladze	Maiko	GEO	9.9.91		LJ	6.67 ?	5.43- 11
	Gogoleva	Svetlana	RUS	11.12.86		400h	56.38	56.56- 07
	Golladay	Michaylin	USA	10.4.88	170/64	100h	13.03, 12.86w	13.01, 12.82w- 11
	Gollner	Monika	AUT	23.10.74	180/61	HJ	1.90	1.92- 96
	Golovkina	Olga	RUS	17.12.86	170/50	5000	15:05.26	15:16.95- 10
	Gómez	Abigail	MEX	30.6.91	164/69	JT	56.89A	53.13- 11
	Gomis	Sandra	FRA	21.11.83	165/53	100h	12.89	12.93- 11
	Goncharova	Marina	RUS	26.4.86	173/64	Hep	6042	6319- 08
*	Gong Lijiao		CHN	24.1.89	174/110	SP	20.22	20.35- 09
*	González	Misleydis	CUB	19.6.78	178/85	SP	18.62	19.50- 08
	Goodman	Chalonda	USA	29.9.90	175/59	100	11.34, 11.23w	11.22- 09
						200	22.85	22.94- 09
	Gorbunova	Yekaterina	RUS	17.1.89	164/52	1500	3:59.89	4:01.02- 11
	Gorchakova	Natalya	RUS	17.4.83		3kSt	9:35.55	9:42.05- 09
*	Gordeyeva	Irina	RUS	9.10.86	183/52	HJ	2.04	2.02- 09
	Gordon	Sheena	USA	26.9.83	178/55	TJ	13.83	13.76- 08
*	Goucher	Kara	USA	9.7.78	170/58	HMar	69:12	66:57- 07
						Mar	2:26:06	2:24:52wdh- 11, 2:25:53- 08
*	Grabuste	Aiga	LAT	24.3.88	178/67	LJ	6.63	6.65- 11
						Hep	6325	6507(w), 6414- 11
	Gracia	Monique	USA	20.4.90	170/59	100h	13.00	13.44, 13.26w- 11
*	Grasu	Nicoleta	ROU	11.9.71	176/88	DT	61.86	68.80- 99
	Greaves	Latoya	JAM	31.5.86		100h	12.77	12.99A- 08, 13.05- 10
	Grechishnikova	Yelizaveta	RUS	12.12.83	168/50	10k	31:07.88	-0-
*	Green Tregaro	Emma	SWE	8.12.84	180/62	HJ	1.95i, 1.93	2.01- 10
*	Grenot	Libania	ITA	12.7.83	175/61	200	22.85, 22.45w	22.93- 09
						400	50.55	50.30- 09
	Griffith	Latoya	BAR	7.2.90		400h	57.12	57.87- 09
	Griffiths	Miana	CAN	17.1.90		100	11.34, 11.20w	11.63- 09. 11.61Aw- 11
	Grimes	Katie	USA	22.12.90		100h	13.20, 12.99w	13.21- 11
	Grincikaité	Lina	LTU	3.5.87	167/62	100	11.19	11.31- 09
	Grindem Mogstad	Øyunn	NOR	11.11.87	180/64	HJ	1.89i, 1,88	1.90- 11
	Griva	Lauma	LAT	27.10.84	180/64	LJ	6.67	6.86- 11
	Gromova	Oksana	RUS	23.9.80	178/75	JT	60.08	61.12- 03
	Gronau	Karolina	POL	12.7.84	180/60	HJ	1.89	1.92- 07
	Grossarth	Jennifer	USA	18.5.83	175/61	400h	56.18	55.51- 10
	Grøvdal	Karoline Bjerkeli	NOR	14.6.90	167/52	5000	15:24.86	15:25.40- 10
	3000	8:55.95mx		9:05.83- 11		HMar	69:41	
	Grove	Emily	USA-J	22.5.93	168/59	PV	4.32	3.86i- 11, 3.81- 10
	Gu Siyu		CHN-J	11.2.93		DT	60.59	56.12- 11
	Guba	Paulina	POL	14.5.91	184/90	SP	17.79i, 17.47	17.17- 11
	Gubar	Yana	RUS	2.7.90		LJ	6.67	6.55- 11
	Gudato	Feyna	ETH			1500	4:07.59	4:17.2- 11
	Guehaseim	Jessika	FRA	23.8.89	176/79	HT	70.44	68.93- 11
	Guei	Floria	FRA	2.5.90	166/53	400	51.96	52.77- 11
*	Gumenyuk	Irina	RUS	6.1.88		TJ	14.24i, 14.03, 14.18w	14.14- 11
	Günther	Leena	GER	16.4.91	164/50	100	11.30w	11.33- 11
	Guo Tianqian		CHN-Y	1.6.95		SP	17.10	16.98- 11
*	Gushchina	Yuliya	RUS	4.3.83	174/63	200	22.95	22.53- 05
						400	49.28	50.01- 08
	Haapanen	Amy	USA	23.3.84	172/79	HT	70.63	67.66- 11
	Haas	Eleriin	EST	4.7.92	180/	HJ	1.92	1.84i- 09, 1.82- 11
	Habina	Hanna	UKR	26.10.92		JT	57.77	57.40- 11
*	Habtamu	Atsede	ETH	26.10.87	162/50	Mar	2:25:28	2:24:25- 11
*	Hachlaf	Halima	MAR	6.9.88	167/56	800	1:58.84	1:58.27- 11
						1500	4:07.63	4:16.48- 07
	Hackett #	Semoy	TRI	27.11.88	173/70	100	11.10, 11.04dq	11.17, 10.98w- 11
						200	22.55	22.75- 10, 22.41w- 11
	Haftu	Goitetom	ETH		.87	HMar	70:31	70:57- 11
						Mar	2:27:28	2:26:21- 11
	Hagiwara	Ayumi	JPN	1.6.92	155/41	10k	32:00.73	
*	Hailu	Meseret	ETH	12.9.90		HMar	68:55	74:29- 09
						Mar	2:21:09	2:30:42- 10

Name		Nat	Born	Ht/Wt	Event	2012 Mark	Pre-2012 Best
^ Hak	Yvonne	NED	30.6.86	177/57	800	2:00.59mx, 2:02.23	1:58.85- 10
Hall	Patricia	JAM	16.10.82	165/58	200	23.24, 22.88i, 22.69w	23.07, 22.84w- 11
					400	50.71	51.40- 11
Hall	Sara	USA	15.4.83	163/48	3000	8:54.75i, 8:56.99	8:52.35- 10
					3kSt	9:42.96	9:39.48- 11
Hall	Shanekia	JAM	27.11.88		100h	13.11	13.80- 11
Hallin	Ellinore	SWE	12.8.87	173/70	Hep	5801	5635- 09
Hallissey	Claire	GBR	17.3.83	164/48	Mar	2:27:44	2:29:27- 11
* Hamera-Shmyrko	Tetyana	UKR	1.6.83	165/52	Mar	2:24:32	2:28:14- 11
Hamilton	Kim	USA	28.11.85	170/70	JT	58.04	54.76- 11
Hao Shuai		CHN	19.7.87	178/65	HT	68.27	69.37- 11
Hapchuk	Nataliya	UKR	15.11.88	182/62	HJ	1.93	1.92- 09
* Harper	Dawn	USA	13.5.84	168/61	100h	12.37	12.47- 11, 12.36w- 09
Harrell	Brittany	USA	5.12.91	173/	Hep	5838	5452- 11
Harrer	Corinna	GER	19.1.91	166/54	800	2:00.34	2:01.85mx, 2:02.27- 11
1500	4:04.30			4:08.63- 11	3000	8:55.47	9:01.29- 11
Harrison	Kendra	USA	18.9.92		100h	13.03, 13.02w	13.49- 11
					400h	56.72	59.13- 11
* Harrison	Queen	USA	10.9.88	170/60	100h	12.62	12.61, 12.44w- 10
					400h	55.32	54.55- 10
Harun	Makda	ETH	.88		Mar	2:26:46 (& HMar 70:45+)	2:27:30- 11
Harutyunyan	Kristine	ARM	18.5.91	168/62	JT	59.12	48.02- 11
Hasen	Merima	ETH	10.6.92	154/41	HMar	70:29+	68:36- 10
					Mar	2:25:21	2:23:06- 10
Hassan	Sifan	ETH-J	.93	163/50	1500	4:08.24	4:20.13- 11
Hasslen	Alyssa	USA	13.5.91	180/91	SP	18.35	17.56- 11
Hastings	Amy	USA	21.1.84	163/46	10k	31:10.69	32:18.72- 08
					Mar	2:27:17	2:27:03- 11
* Hastings	Natasha	USA	23.7.86	173/63	200	22.93	22.61- 07
					400	50.72	49.84- 07
Hatsko	Hanna	UKR	3.10.90	175/70	JT	61.46	60.10- 11
Hawthorne	Trisha-Ann	JAM	8.11.89	165/57	100	11.22	11.31- 11
Haydar	Sultan	TUR	23.5.87	170/55	Mar	2:25:09 (& HMar 70:46+)	2:35:06- 11
Hayes	Chelsea	USA	9.2.88	168/55	100	11.15, 11.09w	11.34, 11.18w- 11
200	23.22, 23.10w			23.55- 11	LJ	7.10	6.50, 6.53w- 11
Hayes	Jernail	USA	8.7.88		400h	56.30	56.53- 10
Hayes	Joanna	USA	23.12.76	167/58	100h	12.87, 12.72w	12.37- 04
Hayu	Tiblet	ETH			5000	15:29.62	
Hazel	Louise	GBR	6.10.85	167/57	Hep	5856	6166(w)- 11, 6156- 10
He Dan		CHN	22.7.84	167/58	20kW	1:33:01	1:28:20- 06
He Qin		CHN	23.3.92		20kW	1:29:01	1:30:13- 11
Hearn	Ashley	USA	14.4.89	173/77	DT	57.94	56.16- 11
* Heidler	Betty	GER	14.10.83	174/80	HT	78.07	79.42- 11
* Hejnová	Zuzana	CZE	19.12.86	170/54	400h	53.38	53.29- 11
* Hellebaut	Tia	BEL	16.2.78	182/62	HJ	1.97i, 1.97	2.05i- 07, 2.05- 08
Heltne	Anca	ROU	1.1.78	175/80	SP	17.38	19.90i- 10, 19.08- 09
Henderson	Nia	USA	21.10.86		SP	16.88	16.20- 08
Hendricks	Shataya	USA	15.8.89		100	11.38, 11.31w	11.30- 07
Hendry	Kelsie	CAN	29.6.82	170/59	PV	4.60Ai, 4.52	4.55- 08
* Henriques	Inês	POR	1.5.80	158/46	20kW	1:29:54	1:29:36- 10
Henry	Britney	USA	17.10.84	178/84	HT	70.73	71.27- 10
Henry-Robinson	Samantha	JAM	25.9.88	160/52	100	11.11, 10.94w	11.14- 09, 11.04w- 08
					200	22.77, 22.50w	22.80- 09
Hepburn-Bailey	Yvana	USA	9.11.87		100h	13.10	13.33- 11
Herashchenko	Iryna	UKR-Y	10.3.95		HJ	1.90	1.87- 11
Hernández	Ingrid	COL	29.11.88	169/61	20kW	1:33:34	1:32:09.4t- 11
Herrera	Mayra Carolina	GUA	20.12.88	158/55	20kW	1:31:03	1:34:39- 11
Herunga	Tjipekapora	NAM	1.1.88	167/51	400	51.24A, 51.86	51.84- 11
Higginson	Ashley	USA	17.3.89	165/52	3kSt	9:34.49	9:52.73- 10
Hilali	Siham	MAR	2.5.86	157/47	1500	4:02.59	4:01.33- 11
					3000	8:46.17i	8:59.60i- 11
Hildebrand	Nadine	GER	20.9.87	158/51	100h	12.94	12.96- 10, 12.91w- 11
Hillman	Christina	USA-J	6.10.93	178/84	SP	17.36i, 156.41	15.24- 11
^ Hinds	Korine	JAM	18.1.76	163/54	3kSt	9:37.95	9:28.86- 07
* Hingst	Carolin	GER	18.9.80	174/60	PV	4.52	4.72- 10
Hinrichs	Denise	GER	7.6.87	181/81	SP	18.36	19.63i, 19.47- 09
Hirai	Megumi	JPN	14.2.90	156/42	10k	32:38.59	33:52.62- 10
Hitchon	Sophie	GBR	11.7.91	167/74	HT	71.98	69.59- 11
Hjálmsdóttir	Ásdís	ISL	28.10.85	175/65	JT	62.77	61.37- 09
Hjelmer	Moa	SWE	19.6.90	172/60	400	51.13	51.58- 11
Hodge	Virgil	SKN	17.11.83	165/56	100	11.39, 11.30w	11.21- 08

Name		Nat	Born	Ht/Wt	Event	2012 Mark	Pre-2012 Best
Hodges	Shavine	JAM	22.10.91		200	23.04wA	23.94, 23.82w- 11
Holden	LaTisha	USA	29.8.89	170/61	100h	12.95	13.07, 12.89w- 11
Holder	Nikkita	CAN	7.5.87	170/57	100h	12.80A, 12.83, 12.74w	12.84- 11
Holland	Christina	USA	5.8.91	165/55	400h	56.87	57.82- 11
Holliday	Becky	USA	12.3.80	180/52	PV	4.57i, 4.55	4.60- 10, 4.61dh- 11
Holliday	Tanya	AUS	21.9.88		20kW	1:31:28	1:37:54- 11
Holm	Caroline Bonde	DEN	19.7.90	178/68	PV	4.42i, 4.36	4.40i, 4.30- 11
Holm Solberg	Mona	NOR	5.8.83	169/78	HT	69.69	70.43- 11
Holodnaya	Olga	UKR	14.11.91		SP	17.47	16.83- 11
Holosha	Olena	UKR	26.1.82	162/56	HJ	1.96	1.92- 07
Holovchenko	Tetyana	UKR	13.2.80	164/44	10k	32:10.43	31:59.98- 07
Holt	Sarah	GBR	17.4.87	183/76	HT	68.50	66.46- 11
Hooper	Gloria	ITA	3.3.92	175/63	200	22.95	23.61- 11
Hoover	Trecey	USA	11.1.88		SP	17.40	16.74- 10
					DT	58.76	58.64- 11
Horie	Misato	JPN	10.3.87	168/49	HMar	70:37	72:16- 11
Horvat	Nikolina	CRO	18.9.86	160/52	400h	57.14	56.28- 08
Howard	Tiffany	USA	28.12.86		SP	17.90	16.87- 09
* Hrasnová	Martina	SVK	21.3.83	180/100	HT	73.34	76.90- 09
Hryshutyna	Krystyna	UKR	21.3.92		LJ	6.65	6.39- 11
Hu Qian		CHN	14.1.89	177/59	TJ	14.18	13.62- 07
Huang Xiaoxiao		CHN	3.3.83	175/65	400h	55.47	54.00- 07
^ Huddle	Molly	USA	31.8.84	163/48	5000	15:01.32	14:44.76- 10
Hurtis	Muriel	FRA	25.3.79	180/68	400	52.11	51.41- 10
* Hutson	Kylie	USA	27.11.87	165/57	PV	4.52A, 4.40i	4.70i, 4.65- 11
Hütter	Julia	GER	26.7.83	169/57	PV	4.40i	4.60i- 08, 4.57- 07
* Ibargüen	Caterine	COL	12.2.84	181/65	LJ	6.73A,6.87wA, 6.63,6.66w	6.63A, 6.58- 11
					TJ	14.95A, 14.80	14.99A, 14.84- 11
Ibrahim	Blessing	NGR	4.4.90		TJ	13.82	13.51- 11
Ifantídou	Sofía	GRE	10.1.85	164/53	JT	56.96	54.04- 11
					Hep	6109	6004- 10
Igarashi	Ai	JPN	25.10.88	147/38	5000	15:31.72	15:34.60- 09
10k	32:17.58				HMar	70:48	73:20- 09
Igaune	Laura	LAT	2.10.88	170/70	HT	68.94	64.44- 11
Ihara	Miho	JPN	4.2.88	154/40	10k	32:21.80	32:18.00mx- 11
* Ikauniece	Laura	LAT	31.5.92	179/60	Hep	6414	6063- 11
* Iljustsenko	Anna	EST	12.10.85	168/49	HJ	1.93i, 1.92	1.96- 11
Imana	Shone	ETH	17.11.91		HMar	70:07	
Incerti	Anna	ITA	19.1.80	168/45	HMar	68:18	69:06- 11
Infeld	Emily	USA	21.3.90	162/48	1500	4:07.77	4:08.96- 11
					5000	15:28.60	15:38.23- 11
Infeld	Maggie	USA	10.4.86	170/55	1500	4:08.31	4:10.57- 10
Inoue	Rei	JPN	23.7.91	155/41	20kW	1:32:43	1:34:22- 11
^ Inzikuru	Dorcus	UGA	2.2.82	158/49	3kSt	9:30.95	9:15.04- 05
* Isinbayeva	Yelena	RUS	3.6.82	174/66	PV	5.01i, 4.75	5.06- 09
Ito	Mai	JPN	23.5.84	156/41	HMar	70:39	70:03- 11
					Mar	2:25:26	2:26:55- 11
Ivanova	Alevtina	RUS	22.5.75	160/53	10k	32:10.57	32:26.21- 02
					Mar	2:27:44dh	2:26:39- 08
Ivery	Lakadron	USA	23.6.83	170/57	LJ	6.58	6.32- 04
Ivoninskaya	Natalya	KAZ	22.2.85	176/54	100h	12.68	12.82- 08
Ivy	Vanneisha	USA	26.10.87	165/62	100h	12.96	12.99- 11
Jackson	Candace	USA	13.2.91		200	23.11, 23.02w	23.35, 22.89w- 11
Jackson	Emma	GBR	7.6.88	173/63	800	1:59.37	1:59.77- 11
Jacques-Sébastien	Lina	FRA	10.4.85	176/63	200	23.00	22.59- 10
Jagaciak	Anna	POL	10.2.90	177/59	LJ	6.61, 6.65w	6.74- 10
					TJ	13.87, 14.06w	14.25- 11
Jakubaityté	Indré	LTU	24.1.76	177/70	JT	59.05	63.65- 07
* Jamal	Maryam	BRN	16.9.84	155/44	800	2:00.44	1:57.80- 08
1500	4:01.19		3:56.18- 06		3000	8:54.51	8:28.87- 05
James	Tiki	USA	21.10.86	168/59	100h	12.84	12.91, 12.70w- 11
Jansen	Monique	NED	3.10.78	186/95	DT	59.96	62.22- 11
* Janson	Lacy	USA	20.2.83	178/68	PV	4.65i, 4.50	4.66i, 4.60A- 10
Jaramillo	Lucy	ECU	23.2.83	168/65	400h	56.50A, 57.74	56.95A- 11, 58.81- 07
Jarmuzek	Agnieszka	POL	3.2.84	190/97	DT	58.42	59.74- 09
Jarrett	Jovanee	JAM	15.1.83	172/64	LJ	6.60	6.75- 09, 6.85w- 08
Jasiunaité	Liveta	LTU-J	25.7.94		JT	56.10	52.00- 11
Jelaca	Tatjana	SRB	10.8.90	178/76	JT	60.89	60.35- 09
Jelagat	Jane	KEN	25.11.83		800	2:00.90A	2:02.55A- 11
Jelagat	Jemima	KEN	21.12.84		HMar	68:35	71:25- 10

Name		Nat	Born	Ht/Wt	Event	2012 Mark	Pre-2012 Best
* Jelimo	Pamela	KEN	5.12.89	175/60	400	52.14A	52.78- 08
					800	1:56.76	1:54.01- 08
Jelizarova	Polina	LAT	1.5.89	155/47	3kSt	9:27.21	9:54.94- 08
Jelmini	Anna	USA	15.7.90	176/	SP	17.27	17.63- 10
					DT	59.77	60.80- 10
Jepkemei	Daisy	KEN-Y	25.10.96		3kSt	9:47.22	
Jepkemoi	Hyvin	KEN	13.1.92		3kSt	9:23.53	10:00.50- 11
Jepkirui	Eunice	KEN	20.5.84	158/45	HMar	68:39	70:29- 11
					Mar	2:21:41	-0-
Jepkoech	Josephine	KEN	.89		HMar	70:42	
Jepkoech	Monica	KEN	.85		HMar	69:12	
Jepkorir	Eunice	KEN	17.2.82	164/48	3kSt	9:30.42	9:07.41- 08
* Jepkosgei	Janeth	KEN	13.12.83	167/47	800	1:57.79	1:56.04- 07
					1500	4:07.34	4:02.32- 11
* Jeptoo	Priscah	KEN	26.6.84	165/49	HMar	70:32	70:26- 11
					Mar	2:20:14	2:22:55- 11
* Jeptoo	Rita	KEN	15.2.81	165/48	Mar	2:22:04	2:23:38dh- 06, 2:24:02- 05
^ Jesien	Anna	POL	10.12.78	168/56	400h	55.44	53.86- 07
* Jeter	Carmelita	USA	24.11.79	163/63	100	10.78	10.64- 09
					200	22.11	22.20- 11
Jia Chaofeng		CHN	16.11.88	164/47	Mar	2:27:40	2:29:40- 11
Jiang Fengjing		CHN	28.8.87	180/75	DT	60.47	62.56- 11
* Jimoh	Funmi	USA	29.5.84	173/64	LJ	6.82	6.96- 09
Jin Yuan		CHN	11.2.88	168/49	3kSt	9:45.92	9:41.60- 08
Johannes	Helaria	NAM	13.8.80	164/50	Mar	2:26:09	2:30:37- 11
Johannesson	Emma	SWE	16.1.84		HT	65.78	65.29- 11
Johnson	Felisha	USA	24.7.89	185/105	SP	17.47i, 17.35	16.55- 11
Johnson	Kellyn	USA	22.7.86	13/50	5000	15:31.66	15:45.38- 11
					10k	32:30.40	
Johnson	Tristie	USA-J	20.11.93		100	11.28w	12.03- 11
* Johnson-Thompson	Katarina	GBR-J	9.1.93	183/70	HJ	1.89	1.84- 11
LJ 6.51, 6.81w			6.44- 11		Hep	6267	5787- 11
Johny	Mayookha	IND	9.4.88		LJ	6.60	6.64- 10
					TJ	13.95i, 13.91	14.11- 11
Jones	Cambrya	USA	20.9.90	171/64	100	11.33, 11.28w	11.67- 11
					200	22.72	23.51- 11
Jones	Demeeka	USA	4.10.88		100h	13.09w	13.39, 13.25w- 11
* Jones	Lolo	USA	5.8.82	175/60	100h	12.58	12.43, 12.29w- 08
Jones	Tenaya	USA	22.3.89		100h	13.26, 13.09w	13.20- 10, 13.05w- 11
* Jones-Ferrette	Laverne	ISV	16.9.81	173/66	100	11.07, 10.91w	11.13- 09
					200	22.62	22.46- 09
Josephs	Janice	RSA	31.3.82	160/60	LJ	6.55A, 6.43	6.79- 07
Jover	María del Mar	ESP	21.4.88	161/51	LJ	6.69A, 6.57, 6.65w	6.36- 11
Judd	Jessica	GBR-Y	7.1.95	180/	800	2:00.96	2:02.70- 11
Juhász	Vanda	HUN	6.6.89	172/71	JT	59.31	58.03- 11
Jungfleisch	Marie-Laurence	GER	7.10.90	181/68	HJ	1.95	1.93- 11
* Jungmark	Ebba	SWE	10.3.87	179/57	HJ	1.95i, 1.91	1.96i, 1.94- 11
Juravlyeva	Anastasiya	UZB	9.10.81	172/57	TJ	14.34	14.55- 05
* Kabuu	Lucy Wangui	KEN	24.3.84	155/41	1500	4:08.6A	4:09.60- 02
HMar 69:46+			67:04- 11		Mar	2:19:34	-0-
Kadicheva	Anastasiya	RUS-J	23.2.94		LJ	6.56	6.15- 10
Kalmer	Renè	RSA	3.11.80	167/55	HMar	70:13	70:37- 09
Kämäräinen	Sanna	FIN	8.2.86	182/72	DT	57.20	57.30- 11
Kampschulte	Nadja	GER	5.9.92	186/66	HJ	1.91i, 1.84	1.88- 11
Kanatova	Valeriya	UZB	29.8.92	180/70	TJ	14.00i	14.28- 11
Kang Jinzi		CHN	25.1.90		20kW	1:33:28	1:35:12- 10
* Kaniskina	Olga	RUS	19.1.85	161/45	20kW	1:25:09	1:24:56- 09
* Kapachinskaya	Anastasiya	RUS	21.11.79	176/65	400	50.37	49.35- 11
^ Kappler	Bianca	GER	8.8.77	180/62	LJ	6.60	6.90- 07, 6.97w- 06
Karakaya	Dudu	TUR	11.11.85	170/55	5000	15:20.00	15:24.86- 09
Karakus	Nimet	TUR-J	23.1.93	168/64	100	11.33	11.53- 11
Karpova	Irina	KAZ	13.2.80	180/63	Hep	5995	6140- 03
Karsak	Kateryna	UKR	26.12.85	183/88	DT	60.03	64.40- 07
Kashtonova	Anastasiya	BLR	14.1.89	163/50	DT	57.87	57.38- 11
Kasim	Ashu	ETH	20.10.84		Mar	2:23:09	2:25:49- 09
Kastor	Deena	USA	14.2.73	163/48	5000	15:23.51	14:51.62- 00
^ 10k 31:49.23			30:50.32- 02		Mar	2:30:40	2:19:36- 06
Kastrova	Alina	BLR	2.3.90		HT	70.31	67.30- 11
Käther	Nadja	GER	29.9.88	178/62	LJ	6.66i, 6.47	6.66- 10
Katsumata	Misaki	JPN	26.12.85	164/47	10k	32:26.55	32:51.92- 11
					Mar	2:28:01	2:31:10- 11

Name		Nat	Born	Ht/Wt	Event	2012 Mark	Pre-2012 Best
Katsura	Yuliya	RUS	28.5.83	170/61	200	23.09	23.15i- 10, 23.27, 23.14w- 09
Kaur	Harwant	IND	5.7.80	166/72	DT	58.32	63.05- 04
Kawasaki	Mayumi	JPN	10.5.80	167/52	20kW	1:30:20	1:28:49- 09
Kaya	Kivilcim	TUR	27.3.92	166/85	HT	72.55	66.74- 11
Kaya	Özlem	TUR	20.4.90	165/49	3kSt	9:38.32	10:12.05- 11
Kayukova	Yekaterina	RUS	9.10.86		TJ	14.43	14.64- 09
* Kebede	Aberu	ETH	12.9.89	163/50	10k	31:09.28	30:48.26- 09
HMar	69:42+		67:39- 09		Mar	2:20:30	2:23:58- 10
* Keitany	Mary	KEN	18.1.82	168/53	HMar	66:49	65:50- 11
					Mar	2:18:37	2:19:19- 11
Kelo	Niina	FIN	26.3.80	178/69	Hep	5840w, 5692	5956- 06
Kemkers	Denise	NED	11.4.85	182/81	SP	16.86i	17.66i, 17.30- 09
Keppler	Janice	USA	22.3.87	178/68	PV	4.42i, 4.40	4.42- 11
Khaladovich	Tatyana	BLR	21.6.91		JT	59.15	55.94- 11
Khaleyeva	Kristina	RUS	22.10.87		800	2:00.38	2:04.19- 11
1500	4:00.53		4:08.79- 09		1M	4:29.73i	
* Khanafeyeva	Gulfiya	RUS	4.6.82	170/84	HT	77.08	77.26- 06, 77.36dq- 07
Kharlamova	Lyubov	RUS	2.3.81	169/57	3kSt	9:36.81	9:21.94- 06
Kholodilina	Natalya	RUS	21.7.89		20kW	1:33:20	1:36:28- 11
Khubbieva	Guzel	UZB	2.5.76	173/65	100	11.22	11.20- 07
^ Kibet	Hilda	NED	27.3.81	168/46	HMar	69:27	68:39- 10
					Mar	2:25:46	2:24:27- 11
* Kibet	Sylvia	KEN	28.3.84	157/44	3000	8:39.14	8:37.48- 10
					5000	14:46.73	14:31.91- 10
* Kibiwott	Viola	KEN	22.12.83	157/45	1500	3:59.25	4:02.10- 07
3000	8:43.75		8:40.14- 03		5000	14:39.53	14:34.86- 11
Kidane	Etalemahu	ETH	14.2.83		Mar	2:25:49 (& HMar 70:48+)	2:31:11- 09
* Kidane	Worknesh	ETH	21.11.81	158/41	5000	15:04.65	14:33.04- 03
					10k	30:39.38	30:07.15- 03
Kieffer	Allie	USA	16.9.87		10k	32:25.69	
Kilel	Caroline	KEN	21.3.81	172/54	HMar	68:28	68:16- 09
Kim Kyung-ae		KOR	5.3.88	163/62	JT	58.07	58.76- 08
Kim Mi-jung		KOR	10.6.79	165/55	20kW	1:33:20	1:29:38- 08
Kimanzi	Grace	KEN	1.3.92	162/46	5000	15:32.23	15:38.80- 11
Kimpel	Dominique	USA-J	6.2.93		100	11.48, 11.30w	11.76- 10
Kimura	Ayako	JPN	11.6.88	167/52	100h	13.04	13.19- 11
King	Adella	USA	.90		100	11.26w	11.82- 11
					200	23.33, 23.08w	23.63- 11
King	Latoya	JAM	25.4.89		100	11.50A, 11.23w	11.60- 05, 11.51w- 11
					200	23.15A, 22.80wA	23.57- 05
King	Lorraine	USA			400	51.5	
Kinukawa	Megumi	JPN	7.8.89	153/38	10k	32:20.34	31:10.02mx- 11, 31:23.21- 08
Kipketer	Valentine	KEN-J	5.1.93		HMar	70:24+	68:31- 11
Kipkoech	Pasalia	KEN	22.12.88		HMar	67:17	69:43- 10
* Kiplagat	Edna	KEN	15.11.79	171/54	HMar	67:41dh	69:00- 11
					Mar	2:19:50	2:20:46- 11
* Kiplagat	Florence	KEN	27.2.87	155/42	10k	30:24.85	30:11.53- 09
HMar	66:38		67:40- 10		Mar	2:20:57	2:19:44- 11
Kipp	Shalaya	USA	19.8.90	170/58	3kSt	9:35.73	9:56.37- 11
Kiprop	Agnes	KEN	12.12.79	171/51	HMar	67:22	68:48- 10
					Mar	2:25:41	2:23:54- 11
Kiprop	Helah	KEN	7.4.85	164/48	HMar	68:26	69:29- 09
Kipsoi	Gladys	KEN	.86		HMar	69:22	
* Kipyego	Sally	KEN	19.12.85	168/52	1500	4:08.59	4:06.23- 11
1M	4:28.41i		4:27.19i- 09		3000	8:35.89	8:48.77i- 09, 8:51.07- 11
5000	14:43.11		14:30.42- 11		10k	30:26.37	30:38.35- 11
* Kipyegon	Faith	KEN-J	10.1.94	157/42	1500	4:03.82	4:09.48- 11
* Kirdyapkina	Anisya	RUS	23.10.89	165/51	20kW	1:26:26	1:25:09- 11
Kireyeva	Svetlana	RUS	12.6.87		1500	4:08.30	4:07.20- 11
					5000	15:08.36	15:27.33- 11
* Kiriakopoúlou	Nikoléta	GRE	21.3.86	167/54	PV	4.60	4.71- 11
Kirop	Helena	KEN	9.9.76	165/48	Mar	2:25:34	2:23:37- 11
Kiros	Aheza	ETH	26.3.82	152/42	10k	32:03.85	31:06.93- 08
Kirui	Purity	KEN	13.8.91		3kSt	9:35.61	9:36.34- 10
* Kiryashova	Aleksandra	RUS	21.8.85	166/53	PV	4.55	4.65i- 10, 4.65- 11
Kisa	Janet	KEN	5.3.92		3000	8:51.63	
					5000	14:57.68	15:24.75A- 11
Kizaki	Ryoko	JPN	21.6.85	157/44	Mar	2:27:16	2:26:32- 11
* Klaas	Kathrin	GER	6.2.84	168/72	HT	76.05	75.48- 11
Kleeberg	Sophie	GER	30.5.90	182/82	SP	17.43i, 17.42	17.92- 11
* Kleinert	Nadine	GER	20.10.75	190/90	SP	19.67	20.20- 09

Name		Nat	Born	Ht/Wt	Event	2012 Mark	Pre-2012 Best
Kleshchevnikova	Yana	RUS	24.7.88		HT	67.67	66.33- 10
Klimesová	Jarmila	CZE	9.2.81	172/78	JT	60.96A	62.60- 06
* Klishina	Darya	RUS	15.1.91	180/57	LJ	6.93	7.05- 11
* Klocová	Lucia	SVK	20.11.83	176/53	800	2:00.16	1:58.51- 08
1000	2:38.72		2:39.04i- 03		1500	4:02.99	4:08.86- 10
* Klucinová	Eliska	CZE	14.4.88	177/68	Hep	6283	6268- 10
Knäsche	Anjuli	GER-J	18.10.93	169/61	PV	4.31	4.21- 11
* Knight	Bianca	USA	2.1.89	163/60	100	11.13	11.07- 08
					200	22.46, 22.34w	22.35- 11, 22.25w- 08
* Knyazyeva	Hanna	UKR	25.9.89	178/61	TJ	14.71	14.20- 11
Kobayashi	Yuriko	JPN	12.12.88	163/46	5000	15:23.38	15:05.37mx, 15:07.37- 08
					10k	31:51.91	
Kock	Maren	GER	22.6.90	173/55	5000	15:27.65	15:54.00- 11
Koderisch	Heike	GER	27.5.85	188/87	DT	61.18	58.62- 10
Koech	Cherono	KEN	8.12.92	158/53	800	2:00.53	1:59.68A- 11
* Kofanova	Yelena	RUS	8.8.88	174/61	800	1:57.77	1:58.04- 11
-Kotulskaya					1000	2:37.58i	2:41.19i- 11
Kolarova	Teodora	BUL	29.5.81	172/52	800	2:01.46	2:00.00- 06
* Kolchanova	Lyudmila	RUS	1.10.79	175/60	LJ	6.87	7.21- 07
* Kolodko	Yevgeniya	RUS	2.7.90	188/85	SP	20.48	19.78- 11
Kolotzei	Jessica	GER	6.4.85	186/86	DT	58.49	60.31- 08
Kondakova	Yuliya	RUS	4.12.81	170/57	100h	12.93, 12.82w	12.79- 08
Kondratyeva	Oksana	RUS	22.11.85	180/80	HT	73.31	71.90- 10
Koneva	Yekaterina	RUS	25.9.88	169/55	LJ	6.56	6.70, 6.80w- 11
					TJ	14.60i, 14.36	14.46- 11
Konevtsova	Yelena	RUS	11.9.81	183/80	HT	71.70	76.21- 07
Kononova	Yevgeniya	RUS	28.9.89		HJ	1.92	1.85i- 11, 1.84- 09
Konovalova	Anna	RUS	4.7.88		1500	4:08.36	4:03.92- 11
* Konovalova	Mariya	RUS	14.8.74	179/58	5000	15:27.54	14:38.09- 08
HMar	69:56		70:30- 11		Mar	2:25:38	2:23:50- 10
Kopets	Alena	BLR	14.2.88	178/72	SP	18.90i, 17.83	18.82i- 11, 17.99- 10
Korableva	Darya	RUS	23.5.88		400h	56.81	56.01- 09
Korczynska	Daria	POL	30.7.81	172/68	100	11.39, 11.32w	11.22- 08
Koresová	Jana	CZE	8.4.81		LJ	6.47, 6.62w	6.65- 09
Koreyvo	Natalya	BLR	14.11.85	172/49	1000	2:37.36i	2:37.33i- 11
					1500	4:02.37	4:06.40- 11
* Korikwiang	Pauline	KEN	1.3.88	163/39	3000	8:52.04	8:41.11- 10
					10k	32:19.32	31:06.29- 10
Korobkina	Yelena	RUS	25.11.90		1500	4:06.73	4:07.82- 10
3000	8:52.94		8:51.41- 10		5000	15:25.73	15:22.14- 11
Korotkova	Tatyana	RUS	31.5.82	165/58	20kW	1:31:25	1:27:35- 04
Korpela	Merja	FIN	15.5.81	170/75	HT	67.43	69.56- 09
Korshunova	Anastasiya	RUS	17.5.92		400h	56.63	57.97- 11
* Kostetskaya	Yekaterina	RUS	31.12.86	168/59	800	1:57.46	1:56.67- 08
					1500	3:59.28	4:01.77- 11
Kostrova	Yuliya	RUS	20.8.91	174/59	HJ	1.90i, 1.86	1.92- 11
Kotlyarova	Aleksandra	UZB	10.10.88	170/64	TJ	14.01i, 13.82	14.35- 11
Kotova ¶	Tatyana	RUS	11.12.76	182/60	LJ	6.66	7.42- 02
^ Kouassi	Gabriela	CIV	18.11.79	170/65	Hep	5766	5775- 08
Koubaa	Sanaa	GER	6.1.85	168/58	3kSt	9:43.08	10:01.89- 11
Kovalenko	Iryna	UKR	17.6.86		HJ	1.89i, 1.86	1.95i- 03, 1.93- 04
Kovalenko	Lyudmyla	UKR	26.6.89		5000	15:10.28	
Kowalska	Katarzyna	POL	7.4.85	177/55	3kSt	9:34.14	9:26.93- 09
Kozhakhmetova	Ayman	KAZ	23.4.91	165/60	20kW	1:31:55	1:38:02- 11
Kozhakhmetova	Sholpan	KAZ	23.4.91	170/50	20kW	1:33:21	1:39:24- 11
Kragbé	Suzanne	CIV	22.12.81	179/92	DT	58.03	59.32- 11
Krais	Ryann	USA	21.3.90	173/61	Hep	5817(w), 5692	6030- 11
Králová	Tereza	CZE	22.10.89		HT	69.20	66.63- 11
Krantz	Sabine	GER	6.2.81	167/51	20kW	1:30:57	1:27:56- 04
* Krause	Gesa-Felicitas	GER	3.8.92	167/49	3kSt	9:23.52	9:32.74- 11
Krebs	Denise	GER	27.6.87	157/48	1500	4:06.01	4:07.70- 11
Krebs	Franziska	GER	11.10.85	166/65	JT	55.97	57.36- 09
Krechyk	Alena	BLR	20.7.87		HT	69.02	68.61- 09
Krevsun	Yuliya	UKR	8.12.80	178/66	800	1:59.25	1:57.32- 08
					1500	4:06.50	4:25.90- 10
* Krivoshapka	Antonina	RUS	21.7.87	168/60	200	23.03	24.28- 07
					400	49.16	49.29- 09
Krizsán	Xénia	HUN-J	13.1.93		Hep	5957	5794- 11
Kron	Tina	GER	3.4.81	173/55	400h	56.27	55.58- 07
* Krylova	Anna	RUS	3.10.85		TJ	14.40	14.35- 11
Kubelová	Jitka	CZE	2.10.91		DT	57.57	57.37- 11

Name		Nat	Born	Ht/Wt	Event	2012 Mark	Pre-2012 Best
Kubishta	April	USA	5.7.85	165/57	PV	4.40	4.33i- 10, 4.32- 08
Kubokura	Satomi	JPN	27.4.82	161/52	400h	55.85	55.34- 11
* Kucherenko	Olga	RUS	5.11.85	172/59	LJ	7.03	7.13- 10
* Kuchina	Mariya	RUS-J	14.1.93	182/60	HJ	1.96i, 1,89	1.97i, 1.95- 11
Kudzelich	Svetlana	BLR	7.5.87		3kSt	9:39.43	
Kulik	Alyssa	USA	2.2.90		3kSt	9:52.90	9:57.51- 11
Kumari	Sahana	IND	6.3.81		HJ	1.92	1.86- 08
Kuningas	Raine	EST	20.10.88		JT	56.17	58.24- 09
Kuntsevich	Yekaterina	RUS	13.7.84		HJ	1.88i, 1.87	1.94- 06
Kupina	Yekaterina	RUS	2.2.86		800	1:59.85	2:01.44- 11
Kurban	Olga	RUS	16.12.87	178/66	Hep	6528	6559- 08
* Kuria	Mary	KEN	29.11.87		1500	4:03.18	4:09.24- 10
Kurylo	Yuliya	UKR	3.7.91		DT	59.05	54.82- 10
Kuze	Kiho	JPN-Y	28.3.95	165/58	JT	56.84	49.53- 11
Kuzina	Aleksandra	KAZ	26.12.90	168/58	400h	56.26	56.92- 11
Kuzmina	Lyudmila	RUS	13.8.87	158/49	3kSt	9:35.41	9:26.03- 11
Kwambai	Edinah	KEN	22.3.86		HMar	70:36	70:52- 10
Kwoka	Katarzyna	POL	29.6.85	168/55	20kW	1:31:25	1:34:21- 10
Kyevich	Alena	BLR	6.10.87		400	51.73	53.60- 08
* La Mantia	Simona	ITA	14.4.83	177/65	TJ	14.29	14.69- 05, 14.71w- 04
Labiche	Lissa	SEY-J	18.2.93	172/52	HJ	1.88	1.80- 11
Labonté	Julie	CAN	12.1.90	183/91	SP	18.19	18.31- 11
LaCaze	Genevieve	AUS	4.8.89	164/53	3kSt	9:37.90	9:59.44- 11
Lah	Barbara	ITA	24.3.72	180/61	TJ	13.51, 13.72w	14.38- 03
Laing	Kimberley	JAM	8.1.89		100h	12.97	13.15, 12.92w- 10
* Lakhouad	Btissam	MAR	7.12.80	172/55	800	2:00.22	2:01.66- 07
1000	2:38.14i				1500	3:59.65	3:59.35- 10
Lakmali	Nadeeka	SRI	18.9.81	165/60	JT	56.76	58.48- 07
* Lalova	Ivet	BUL	18.5.84	166/52	100	11.06, 11.01w	10.77- 04
					200	22.98	22.51- 04
Lamalle	Adrianna	FRA	27.9.82	168/63	100h	12.96	12.67- 06
Lamb	Elizabeth	NZL	12.5.91	174/53	HJ	1.90	1.86- 11
Lambarki	Hayat	MAR	18.5.88	168/62	400h	55.41	55.96A- 10, 56.72- 11
Lamble	Regan	AUS	14.10.91	173/55	20kW	1:30:08	1:31:39- 11
Lamera	Raffaella	ITA	13.4.83	175/56	HJ	1.89i, 1.86	1.95- 10
Larsåsen	Cathrine	NOR	5.12.86	172/59	PV	4.41i, 4.30	4.40- 11
Larsson	Eleni	SWE-J	4.4.93	186/100	HT	66.19	59.42- 11
* Lashmanova	Yelena	RUS	9.4.92	170/48	20kW	1:25:02	-0-
Lavallée Seaman	Rachel	CAN	14.1.86	173/60	20kW	1:33:05	1:33:33- 11
Lavric	Mirela	ROU	17.2.91	162/45	400	52.11	52.56- 11
					800	1:59.74	2:00.06- 08
Law	Kirsty	GBR	11.10.86		DT	57.79	55.17- 11, 55.52dh- 07
Lawless	Janet	RSA	15.5.85	173/63	400h	56.16	55.82A- 06
Lawrence	Collier	USA	4.10.86		3kSt	9:53.79	10:25.27- 08
Lawson	Lekeisha	USA	3.6.87	168/57	100	11.31	11.39. 11.26w- 10
Leach	Nicole	USA	18.7.87	170/60	400h	55.37	54.32- 07
Lebedeva	Lyudmila	RUS	23.5.90		3kSt	9:42.58	9:53.15- 10
^ Lebedeva	Tatyana	RUS	21.7.76	171/61	TJ	14.68	15.34- 04
Lecurieux	Prescilla	FRA	1.12.92	180/82	JT	57.23	57.18- 11
Ledáki	Stélla-Iró	GRE	18.7.88	170/58	PV	4.50	4.45- 11
Lee	Beki	AUS	25.11.86	165/46	20kW	1:32:14	1:33:09- 11
Lee Mi-young		KOR	19.8.79	174/97	SP	16.98	17.62- 05
Legesse	Meseret	ETH	28.8.87		HMar	70:45+	
					Mar	2:28:01dh	2:29:05- 11
LeLeux	Morgann	USA	14.11.92	170/61	PV	4.44	4.34- 11
Lemus	Sandra	COL	1.1.89	170/102	SP	17.56	16.31- 11
Leontyeva	Natalya	RUS	5.7.87		5000	15:32.48	15:57.50- 11
* Lesueur	Éloyse	FRA	15.7.88	179/65	LJ	6.81, 7.04w	6.91- 11
Lettow	Lindsay	USA	6.6.90	175/62	Hep	5807	5610w, 5547- 11
Leutert	Astrid	SUI	12.9.87		3kSt	9:53.15	10:23.95- 11
Levichkaya	Yekaterina	RUS	2.1.87		LJ	6.68	6.49- 11
Levy	Jura	JAM	4.11.90	157/50	100	11.20	11.10, 11.07w- 11
					200	23.26, 23.03i	22.76- 11
* Lewis	Yvette	USA	16.3.85	173/62	100h	12.84, 12.74w	12.76, 12.74w- 11
Lewis-Smallwood	Gia	USA	1.4.79	183/93	DT	63.97	65.58- 10
Lhabz	Lamia	MAR	19.5.84	178/59	400h	56.55	56.07- 08
Li Li		CHN	18.6.87	164/50	20kW	1:30:27	1:31:33- 10
Li Ling		CHN	6.7.89	185/70	PV	4.50i, 4.40	4.45- 08
* Li Ling		CHN	7.2.85	183/84	SP	19.95	19.94- 10
Li Lingwei		CHN	26.1.89	172/75	JT	65.11	60.60- 10
^ Li Meiju		CHN	3.10.81	172/100	SP	17.39	19.38- 09

Name		Nat	Born	Ht/Wt	Event	2012 Mark	Pre-2012 Best
Li Wen-Hua		TPE	3.12.89	180/130	DT	60.23	58.07- 11
Li Xiaohong		CHN-Y	8.1.95		TJ	13.85	13.38- 11
Li Yanfei		CHN	12.1.90	168/55	20kW	1:31:57	1:28:43- 11
* Li Yanfeng		CHN	15.5.79	179/90	DT	67.84	67.98- 11
Li Yanmei		CHN	6.2.90	171/56	TJ	14.23i, 13.97	14.35- 11
Li Zhenzhu		CHN	13.12.85	168/45	3kSt	9:34.29	9:32.35- 07
Liang Yan		CHN-Y	2.1.95		DT	60.50	54.42- 11
Líka	Sávva	GRE	27.6.70	173/68	JT	59.96	63.13- 07
de Lima	Jailma	BRA	31.12.86	174/65	400h	56.16	56.00- 11
de Lima	Jucilene	BRA	14.9.90	172/63	JT	57.85	56.75- 09
Limo	Cynthia	KEN	18.12.89		HMar	70:06	70:39- 11
Lin Chia-Ying		TPE	5.11.82	168/82	SP	17.43	17.06- 10
Linde	Sofia	SWE-Y	12.1.95	174/66	Hep	5872	-0-
Lipsey	Charlene	USA	16.7.91	168/57	800	2:01.40	2:03.73- 11
* Litvinova	Lyudmila	RUS	8.6.85	177/60	400	50.61	50.27- 09
Liu Beibei		CHN	5.10.90		JT	57.90	56.21- 08
Liu Chunhua		CHN	1.10.86	164/65	JT	62.81	60.65- 11
* Liu Hong		CHN	12.5.87	161/48	20kW	1:25:46	1:27:17- 11
Liu Shiying		CHN-J	24.9.93		JT	59.20	55.10- 11
Liu Shuyu		CHN-J	13.12.93		20kW	1:33:43	1:38:48- 11
Liu Tingting		CHN	29.10.90		HT	68.72	69.46- 11
* Liu Xiangrong		CHN	6.6.88	182/84	SP	19.24	18.74- 11
Liu Yanan		CHN	18.1.87		TJ	13.77	14.09- 09
Lloyd	Shereefa	JAM	2.9.82	164/53	400	51.70	50.62- 08
Lobanova	Liliya	UKR	14.10.85	168/54	800	1:59.62	1:58.30- 11
Lockhart	Sam	USA	25.8.91		DT	57.11	52.42- 11
Logvynenko	Alina	UKR	18.7.90	180/68	400	51.19	53.04- 11
Londa	Maria Natalia	INA	29.10.90		LJ	6.55	6.47- 11
Longfors	Rachel	USA	6.6.83	183/82	DT	58.05	57.48- 04
^ Lopes-Schliep	Priscilla	CAN	26.8.82	163/67	100h	12.64	12.49- 09
Lotout	Marion	FRA	19.11.89	165/54	PV	4.40	4.50- 11
Louami	Carima	FRA	12.5.79	165/50	100	11.39, 11.21w	11.28, 11.25w- 11
Loughnane	Olive	IRL	14.1.76	160/49	20kW	1:29:39	1:27:45- 08
Love	Alexis	USA	24.4.91	163/52	100	11.28	11.97- 11
					200	23.03	25.34- 08
* Lowe	Chaunté	USA	12.1.84	175/59	HJ	2.02Ai, 2.01	2.05- 10
* Lu Huihui		CHN	26.6.89	168/60	JT	64.95	58.72- 11
Lu Minjia		CHN	29.12.92	172/58	LJ	6.64	6.74- 09
Lu Xiaoxin		CHN	22.2.89		DT	59.64	57.61- 11
* Lu Xiuzhi		CHN-J	26.10.93	167/52	20kW	1:27:01	1:29:50- 11
Luaces	Lorena	ESP	29.2.84	161/48	20kW	1:31:50	1:32:42- 10
^ Lucas	Josanne	TRI	14.5.84	170/55	100h	13.07, 12.84w	12.99- 09, 12.98w- 06
					400h	55.92	53.20- 09
Lucas	Julia	USA	4.3.84	174/60	1500	4:07.23	4:15.47- 08
3000	9:01.16i		9:03.47i- 07.	9:26.78- 04	5000	15:08.52	15:33.05- 08
Lucas	Porscha	USA	18.6.88	170/56	100	11.41, 11.02w	11.12- 09, 11.07w- 10
					200	22.65	22.29A- 08, 22.38- 09
Luka	Tintu	IND	26.4.89	157/50	800	1:59.69	1:59.17- 10
Lukyanova	Anna	RUS	23.4.91		20kW	1:27:08	1:27:49- 11
Luo Xingcai		CHN-J	18.7.94		20kW	1:31:49	1:32:03- 11
Luogon	Kou	LBR	11.6.84		400h	56.40	55.55- 09
* Lupu	Nataliya	UKR	4.11.87	170/50	800	1:58.46	1:59.12- 11
Lushcheko	Aleksandra	RUS	1.3.87		HT	68.08	68.09- 11
Lyakhovaya	Olga	UKR	18.3.92		800	2:00.55	2:03.30- 09
Lyashenko	Valentyna	UKR	30.1.81		HJ	1.91	1.86- 05
Lysenko	Alena	RUS	3.2.88		HT	67.96	64.10- 11
* Lysenko	Tatyana	RUS	9.10.83	180/84	HT	78.51	77.80- 06, 78.61dq- 07
Ma Qiao		CHN	28.9.89	185/150	SP	16.96	17.50- 10
* Ma Xuejun		CHN	26.3.85	185/96	DT	63.91	65.00- 06
Machado	Maíla Paula	BRA	22.1.81	167/62	100h	13.09	12.86- 04
Macharia	Lucy	KEN	7.12.87		HMar	70:26	70:04- 11
Mächtig	Julia	GER	1.1.86	187/80	Hep	6345	6320- 09
Macías	Isabel	ESP	11.8.84	165/52	1500	4:04.84	4:06.50- 11
Mackey	Katie	USA	12.11.87	165/52	1500	4:06.67	4:07.44- 11
800	2:02.23		2:02.63- 11		5000	15:31.59	15:37.84- 11
Mackie	Nachelle	USA	15.3.90		800	2:01.06	2:04.26- 10
Madarász	Viktória	HUN	12.5.85	153/46	20kW	1:33:34	1:34:37- 11
Madejczyk	Barbara	POL	30.9.76	180/81	JT	56.72	64.08- 06
* Madison	Tianna	USA	30.8.85	168/60	100	10.85	11.05- 09
200	22.37, 22,33w		23.27- 10		LJ	6.48	6.89, 6.92w- 05
Maeda	Sairi	JPN	7.11.91	158/45	5000	15:32.22	

Name		Nat	Born	Ht/Wt	Event	2012 Mark	Pre-2012 Best
* Maggi	Maurren Higa	BRA	25.6.76	178/66	LJ	6.85	7.26A- 99, 7.06- 03, 7.17w- 02
* Magiso	Fantu	ETH	9.6.92	178/60	800	1:57.48	1:59.17- 11
Magnani	Margherita	ITA	26.2.87	161/45	1500	4:08.94	4:12.54- 10
Mahan	Shayla	USA	18.1.89	160/50	200	22.91	23.38- 06
Maier	Deborah	USA	17.8.90	166.54	5000	15:37.56,15:29.24i	15:58.49i- 10,16:07.20- 10
					10k	32:12.47	
Maisonnier	Blandine	FRA	3.1.86	179/65	Hep	6082	6157- 08
Maiyo	Maureen	KEN	28.5.85	157/58	400h	56.79	56.65A, 57.72- 11
Majester	Kat	USA	22.5.87	173/59	PV	4.40	4.29- 11
Måkestad Bovim	Ingvill	NOR	7.8.81	172/58	800	2:01.13mx, 2:03.61	1:59.82- 10
					1500	4:03.71	4:02.20- 10
Maksimchuk	Violetta	RUS	1.12.90		TJ	23.65, 13.94w	13.31, 13.60w- 11
Maksimova	Marina	RUS	20.5.85	177/80	JT	60.33	60.73- 11
Maksimova	Yana	BLR	9.1.89	182/70	HJ	1.91	1.88- 10
					Hep	6198	6094- 11
Malácová	Romana	CZE	15.5.87	164/57	PV	4.40	4.41sq- 10
Malkus	Lena	GER-J	6.8.93	180/74	LJ	6.72, 6.80w	6.70- 11
Malone	Chantel	IVB	2.12.91		LJ	6.66w	6.65i- 11, 6.56- 10
Maloy	Liz	USA	10.8.85	172/56	1500	4:08.12	4:09.24- 10
3000	8:50.95		8:56.89- 10		5000	15:24.85	15:15.34- 11
Maltseva	Yuliya	RUS	30.11.90		DT	58.16	55.56- 10
Malvinova	Kristina	RUS	16.7.89		400	51.97	54.55- 11
Mamona	Patrícia	POR	21.11.88	168/53	TJ	14.52	14.42- 11
Mamyeyeva	Svitlana	UKR	19.4.82	175/65	TJ	14.00	14.38- 09
Mang	Véronique	FRA	15.12.84	173/63	100	11.32	11.11, 11.06w- 10
Manning	Christina	USA	29.5.90	163/54	100h	12.68, 12.57w	12.86, 12.72w- 11
Manning	Crystal	USA	15.4.86	173/64	TJ	13.81Ai, 13.93w	13.96- 10
Mánou	Loréla	GRE	20.12.90	167/52	PV	4.40	4.20- 11
Mao Yanxue		CHN-J	15.2.94	162/44	20kW	1:30:25	1:31:03- 11
Mara	Valeriya	UKR	22.2.83	163/50	3kSt	9:47.45	9:38.91- 10
Maracheva	Irina	RUS	29.9.84	165/50	800	1:57.82	1:58.71- 11
Marcussen	Ida	NOR	1.11.87	173/67	Hep	6073	6226- 07
Maresová	Oldriska	CZE	14.10.86	187/67	HJ	1.92	1.90i, 1.89- 10
* Marghieva	Zalina	MDA	5.2.88	174/90	HT	74.47	72.93- 11
Marghieva ¶	Marina	MDA	28.6.86	185/85	HT	71.81	72.53- 09
Marie-Nelly	Nathalie	FRA	24.11.86	175/66	TJ	14.03	14.01, 14.18w- 11
Markelova	Tatyana	RUS	19.12.88	166/59	800	1:58.55	2:00.92- 11
Marshall	Shameka	USA	9.9.83	163/54	LJ	6.69	6.73, 6.74w- 10
Martin	Jenna	CAN	31.3.88	173/65	400	51.53A, 51.69	51.91- 07
Martín	Diana	ESP	1.4.81	162/50	3kSt	9:35.77	9:40.28- 11
Martinelli	Giulia	ITA	16.6.91	167/43	3kSt	9:48.01	9:39.21- 11
Martinez	Brenda	USA	8.9.87	163/52	800	1:59.14	2:00.85- 09
1500	4:06.96		4:09.52- 09		1M	4:26.76	4:32.29- 11
Martínez	Yarianna	CUB	20.9.84	167/56	TJ	14.28	14.42- 11
Martín-Pozuelo	Gema	ESP	21.6.87	187/71	HJ	1.89i, 1.86	1.89i- 10, 1.87- 07
Martins	Eliane	BRA	26.5.86		LJ	6.61	6.66- 07
Márton	Anita	HUN	15.1.89	171/84	SP	18.48	18.20- 10
* Martynova	Yekaterina	RUS	6.8.86	169/55	800	2:00.24	1:59.17- 11
1000	2:38.16i		2:37.63i- 08		1500	3:59.49	4:01.68- 11
* Masai	Linet	KEN	5.12.89	170/55	5000	14:53.93	14:31.14- 10
Masai	Magdalene	KEN-J	4.4.93		5000	15:17.75	16:12.4- 11
Masná	Lenka	CZE	22.4.85	170/55	800	2:01.38	1:59.71- 10
Masumi	Sachiko	JPN	20.12.84	176/62	LJ	6.52, 6.56w	6.65- 09
Mathiot	Télie	FRA	25.5.87	168/55	PV	4.35	4.41- 11
Matoba	Haruka	JPN	24.4.87	163/60	JT	58.93	55.70- 11
Matoshko	Alena	BLR	23.6.82	177/	HT	76.56	73.83- 08
Matsuyama	Akiko	JPN	24.7.89	156/41	10k	32:27.23	
Matule	Santa	LAT	13.12.92		TJ	13.72	13.40- 11
Matusinska	Tina	POL	12.7.88	161/52	400h	55.87	55.90- 11
Maveau	Barbara	BEL	16.2.87	175/60	5000	15:27.97	
Mavrodieva	Radoslava	BUL	13.3.87	178/86	SP	18.20	17.54i- 11, 17.42- 10
Mayer	Sarah	GER	20.5.91	170/60	JT	56.20	59.29- 11
Mayor	Lesyaní	CUB	8.7.89	176/58	HJ	1.92	1.93- 10
Mayorova	Albina	RUS	16.5.77	153/42	Mar	2:23:52	2:28:06- 10
Mazuryk	Nataliya	UKR	5.3.83	172/63	PV	4.50	4.52- 08
* Mbango	Françoise	FRA	14.4.76	169/63	TJ	14.27, 14.38w	15.39- 08
McCall	Jeneva	USA	28.10.89	178/102	SP	19.10i, 17.89	17.38i, 16.96- 11
DT	59.45		58.44- 10		HT	69.39	69.55- 11
McColgan	Eilish	GBR	25.11.90	154/53	3kSt	9:38.45	9:44.80- 11
^ McConnell	Lee	GBR	9.10.78	178/64	400	51.98	50.82- 02
* McCorory	Francena	USA	20.10.88	170/60	400	50.06	50.24- 11

Name		Nat	Born	Ht/Wt	Event	2012 Mark	Pre-2012 Best
McGregor	Katie	USA	2.9.77	168/55	10k	32:37.83	31:21.20- 05
McIntosh	Raasin	LBR	29.4.82	170/59	400h	55.99	54.16- 04
McKaig	Alissa	USA	21.2.86	165/53	10k	32:31.66	32:14.51- 11
McKinney	Akiba	USA	9.3.79	160/57	LJ	6.61	6.83- 06
McKnight	Kaila	AUS	5.5.86	172/52	1500	4:05.61	4:05.65- 11
McLain	Erica	USA	24.1.86	170/62	TJ	13.96	14.33- 10
* McLaughlin	Anneisha	JAM	6.1.86	163/54	100	11.24	11.35- 09
200	22.61		22.54- 10		400	51.89	52.31- 01
McMillan	Chantae	USA	1.5.88	170/62	Hep	6188	6003- 11
McPherson	Inika	USA	29.9.86	168/55	HJ	1.95	1.93A- 11
McReynolds	Tiffani	USA	4.12.91	153/50	100	11.42, 11.22w	11.53, 11.37w- 11
					100h	13.04, 12.97w	13.05, 12.74w- 11
Meadows	Tawanna	USA	4.8.86	168/55	100	11.33, 11.32w	11.27, 11.13w- 08, 11.1w- 10
Medeiros	Keely	BRA	30.4.87		SP	17.18	17.26- 11
Medgyesová	Renata	SVK	28.1.83	172/53	LJ	6.56	6.79- 10
Mekasha	Waganesh	ETH	16.1.92		5000	15:07.35	15:11.50- 11
Melat	Kejeta	ETH	.92		HMar	70:27	70:43- 11
Melese	Yebrgual	ETH	18.4.90		HMar	69:45	
* Melfort	Mélanie	FRA	8.11.82	182/61	HJ	1.93i, 1.93	1.97i, 1.96- 07
* Melkamu	Meselech	ETH	27.4.85	158/48	3000	8:43.93i	8:23.74i- 07, 8:34.73- 05
HMar	70:25+		-0-		Mar	2:21:01	-0-
* Melnychenko	Anna	UKR	24.4.83	178/59	LJ	6.74	6.43- 09
					Hep	6407	6445- 09
Mendieta	Yusleidys	CUB-J	17.2.94	180/66	Hep	5702h	5544- 11
Meng Qianqian		CHN	6.1.91	178/65	SP	17.25	18.31- 11
* Menkova	Oksana	BLR	28.3.82	183/91	HT	78.69	77.32- 08
* Mergia	Aselefech	ETH	23.1.85	168/45	HMar	69:42+	67:21- 11
Merlano	Brigith	COL	29.4.82	174/64	100h	13.07A, 13.21	12.89- 11
Metcalfe Wright	Megan	CAN	27.1.82	157/51	5000	15:21.75	15:11.23- 08
Metivier-Baillie	Renee	USA	25.12.81	160/50	5000	15:28.56	15:15.78- 05
					Mar	2:27:17	
^ Mey ¶	Karin Melis	TUR	31.5.84	173/57	LJ	6.66i, 6.54, 6.80dq	6.93- 07
Michta	Maria	USA	23.6.86	165/51	20kW	1:32:27	1:34:52- 11
* Mickle	Kim	AUS	28.12.84	169/69	JT	64.12	63.82- 11
Migunova	Yelena	RUS	4.1.84	173/65	200	23.05	23.44- 09, 23.34w- 11
					400	50.91	50.59- 08
Mikheyeva	Olesya	RUS	23.7.81		1500	4:08.38	4:02.55- 05
* Mikhnevich	Natalya	BLR	25.5.82	180/85	SP	19.77	20.70- 08
Miki	Shiori	JPN	25.12.91	164/50	400h	57.11	56.92- 11
* Mikitenko	Irina	GER	23.8.72	158/49	Mar	2:24:53	2:19:19- 08
Mikolajczyk	Izabela	POL	4.9.90	177.60	HJ	1.92	1.81- 11
					Hep	5968	5779- 11
Milani	Marta	ITA	9.3.87	172/60	800	2:01.35	2:01.50- 11
Miller	Heather	USA	30.3.87	173/63	Hep	5779	5239- 10
Miller	Logan	USA	21.5.91		PV	4.38	4.10- 11
Miller	Shaunae	BAH-J	15.4.94	185/69	200	22.70	23.70- 11
					400	51.25	51.84- 11
Minderler	Marissa	USA	7.5.89	178/77	HT	67.35	64.09- 11
* Mingir	Gülcan	TUR	21.5.89	165/52	3kSt	9:13.53	9:39.83- 11
* Mironchik-Ivanova	Anastasiya	BLR	13.4.89	171/54	LJ	7.08, 7.22w	6.85, 6.92w- 11
* Mishchenko	Anna	UKR	25.8.83	166/51	800	2:00.92	2:02.44- 11
					1500	4:01.16	4:01.73- 11
Mitchell	Kathryn	AUS	10.7.82	168/75	JT	64.34	59.68- 10
Mitchell	Kerri Ann	CAN	29.3.83	163/57	100	11.32	11.41- 11
Mitchell	Victoria	AUS	25.4.82	164/48	3kSt	9:51.51	9:30.84- 06
Mitsunobu	Yuki	JPN	9.11.92	161/47	10k	32:31.33	
Miyashita	Risa	JPN	26.4.84	171/71	JT	58.27	60.08- 11
Miyauchi	Hiroko	JPN	19.6.83	154/40	10k	32:31.76	31:42.86mx- 08, 32:18.57- 07
					HMar	70:48	69:54- 08
Miyauchi	Yoko	JPN	19.6.83	154/42	10k	32:33.83	31:50.45- 07
					Mar	2:26:23	2:33:36- 10
Mizuguchi	Yuko	JPN	24.5.85	164/43	10k	32:30.33	33:40.29- 08
Mnatsakanova	Tatyana	RUS	25.5.83		HJ	1.91	1.95- 11
^ Mockenhaupt	Sabrina	GER	6.12.80	156/45	5000	15:16.89mx	14:59.88mx- 09, 15:03.47- 04
					10k	31:36.76	31:14.21- 08
Mogire	Alice	KEN	27.11.81		HMar	69:57	71:07- 07
Moguenara	Sosthene	GER	17.10.89	182/68	LJ	6.88	6.83- 11
Mokhnyuk	Anastasiya	UKR	1.1.91		Hep	5830	5497- 11
Molchanova	Viktoriya	UKR	26.5.82	171/55	LJ	6.73	6.82- 09
* Möldner-Schmidt	Antje	GER	13.6.84	174/55	3kSt	9:21.78	9:18.54- 09
* Moline	Georganne	USA	6.3.90	178/59	400h	53.92	57.41- 11

Name		Nat	Born	Ht/Wt	Event	2012 Mark	Pre-2012 Best
* Molitor	Katharina	GER	8.11.83	182/76	JT	63.20	64.67- 11
Molodchinina	Yelena	RUS	16.4.91		Hep	5757	5686- 10
^ Montaner	Concepción	ESP	14.1.81	170/56	LJ	6.60	6.92- 05
* Montaño	Alysia	USA	26.4.86	170/61	400	52.16	52.09- 10
					800	1:57.37	1:57.34- 10
Montcalm	Noelle	CAN	3.4.88	167/	400h	56.87A, 57.21	
^ Montebrun	Manuéla	FRA	13.11.79	176/84	HT	68.13	74.66- 05
Monterola	Keisa	VEN	26.2.88	173/60	PV	4.37i, 4.27	4.33- 11
* Montsho	Amantle	BOT	4.7.83	173/57	200	22.89	22.94, 22.88w- 11
					400	49.54	49.56- 11
Moore	Connie	USA	29.8.81	165/63	100	11.47, 11.33w	11.21- 03
					200	23.39, 22.86w	22.40- 10
Moore	Erica	USA	25.3.88	178/64	800	2:00.05, 1:59.97i	2:00.17- 11
* Moore	LaShauntea	USA	31.7.83	165/59	100	11.11, 10.93w	10.97- 10
					200	22.71	22.46- 07
de Morais	Andressa	BRA	21.12.90	178/100	DT	64.21	59.56- 11
* Moreira	Sara	POR	17.10.85	168/51	5000	15:08.33	14:54.71- 10
10k	31:16.44		31:26.55- 10		HMar	70:55	70:08- 10
Moreno	Johana	COL	15.4.85	175/78	HT	69.29	69.80- 09
* Moreno	Yipsi	CUB	19.11.80	171/81	HT	75.59	76.62- 08
Morosanu	Angela	ROU	26.7.86	178/57	400h	54.81	53.95- 09
Morunova	Lyudmila	RUS	27.1.85		SP	17.89i, 17.75	17.89- 08
Mosina	Veronika	RUS	17.10.90	172/57	LJ	6.71i, 6.46	5.92- 09
					TJ	14.50	13.20i- 11, 13.14- 08
Muchkaev	Annastasia	ISR	18.7.91	185/93	SP	17.22	15.52- 11
Muhammad	Dalilah	USA	7.2.90	170/62	400h	56.19	56.04- 11
Muir	Jody Ann	JAM	1.1.91	163/52	400	52.00	52.64- 11
Mukasheva	Margarita	KAZ	4.1.86	166/50	800	1:59.20	2:00.29- 10
Mukunzi	Magdaline	KEN	22.10.83		HMar	70:26	68:52- 08
Müller	Charlotte	GER-J	14.9.93	175/78	JT	56.49	51.09- 11
* Müller	Nadine	GER	21.11.85	192/95	DT	68.89	67.78- 10
Muncan	Marina	SRB	6.11.82	165/49	1500	4:06.48	4:08.02- 07
Muñoz	Adriana	CUB	16.3.82	165/54	800	2:00.68	2:00.10- 04
Muñoz	Lismania	CUB-J	28.2.93	171/63	JT	56.33	55.82- 11
* Murer	Fabiana	BRA	16.3.81	172/64	PV	4.77	4.85- 10
Muriuki	Margaret	KEN	21.3.86	158/45	1500	4:06.50	4:11.10- 08
3000	8:57.43		8:37.97- 10		HMar	69:21	
Murtazina	Alsu	RUS	12.12.87		TJ	14.08	14.55- 11 14.63w- 10
Muryasova	Alfiya	RUS	3.10.88		1500	4:08.91	4:07.86- 11
Muyanga	Christine	KEN	21.3.91		3kSt	9:44.71	9:31.35- 08
Muzaric	Valentina	CRO	23.7.92		SP	16.82	15.74- 11
Muze	Lina	LAT	4.12.92	181/75	JT	61.04	60.64- 11
Nafiah	Noor Amira Mohd	MAS	16.7.89		TJ	13.90	13.33- 11
Nagao	Kaoru	JPN	26.9.89	160/46	HMar	70:32	70:45- 10
Nagovitsyna	Yelena	RUS	7.12.82	165/55	5000	15:02.80	15:28.06- 11
					10k	32:32.06	32:08.00- 11
Nagy	Judith	ROU	14.9.89	171/58	Hep	5973	5772- 11
Nagy	Xénia	HUN	29.3.86		JT	57.42	56.46- 11
* Naimova	Tezdzhan	BUL	1.5.87	166/58	100	11.26, 11.0	11.04- 07
Nakamura	Hitomi	JPN	23.6.87	157/43	10k	32:24.26	32:23.49- 11
Nakazato	Remi	JPN	24.6.88	152/35	Mar	2:24:28	2:24:29- 11
Nambawa	Sarah	UGA	23.9.85	165.64	TJ	13.92	14.06- 11
* Nana Djimou	Antoinette	FRA	2.8.85	174/69	100h	12.96	13.15- 11
JT	57.27		55.79- 11		Hep	6576	6409- 11
Nasukawa	Mizuho	JPN	22.11.79	164/45	Mar	2:26:42	2:25:38- 09
Naude	Elizna	RSA	14.9.78	180/105	DT	58.97A	64.87- 07
Navez	Claire	FRA	6.10.87	170/50	3kSt	9:44.11	10:08.67- 11
* Nazarova	Anna	RUS	3.2.86	175/58	LJ	7.11	6.89i, 6.88- 11
Nazarova	Natalya	RUS	26.5.79	166/57	400	50.00	49.65- 04
Negesa	Annet	UGA	24.4.92	172/58	800	1:59.08	2:00.40- 11
Negoitâ	Maria	ROU	6.12.86	171/74	JT	56.67	62.20- 09
Neighbour	Gabrielle	AUS	22.11.83	167/75	HT	67.53	66.31- 10
Nelms	Katie	USA	25.9.92		100h	13.00	13.57- 11
Nelson	Adriana	USA	31.1.80	162/47	10k	32:38.95	34:02.79- 04
Nelson	Meaghan	USA	12.2.90	163/52	10k	32:14.27	
Nelvis	Sharika	USA	10.5.90	176/	100	11.36, 11.27w	11.78. 11.54w- 11
					100h	13.22, 12.99w	13.45- 11
Nengampi	Perine	KEN	1.1.89		1500	4:09.96	
3000	8:53.26				10k	32:37.04	
^ Nesterenko	Yuliya	BLR	15.6.79	173/61	100	11.21w	10.92- 04
Netsvetayeva	Yekaterina	BLR	26.6.89		Hep	5940	5702- 11

	Name		Nat	Born	Ht/Wt	Event	2012 Mark	Pre-2012 Best
	Nettey	Christabel	CAN	2.6.91	163/	LJ	6.58	6.49, 6.54w- 11
	Neuenswander	Vera	USA	3.12.87	168/57	PV	4.37	4.36- 11
	Newson	Lauryn	USA	6.8.90	168/59	200	23.09	23.65- 10
	Neziri	Nooralotta	FIN	9.11.92	171/55	100h	13.10	13.30- 11
	Nguria	Regina	KEN	.84		3kSt	9:41.69	10:05.94- 08
	Nicholls /Lally	Jade	GBR	30.3.87	183/81	DT	60.51	60.76- 11
	Nicoletti	Julaika	ITA	20.3.88	178/90	SP	17.13i, 17.09	16.47- 11
	Nie Jingjing		CHN	1.3.88	168/45	20kW	1:28:26	1:29:50- 06
*	Niiya	Hitomi	JPN	26.2.88	166/44	5000	15:10.20	15:13.12- 11
						10k	30:59.19	-0-
	Nikkanen	Minna	FIN	9.4.88	169/53	PV	4.40	4.60i- 11, 4.46- 09
*	Niyonsaba	Francine	BDI-J	5.5.93	161/56	800	1:56.59	
	Njeri	Pauline	KEN	28.7.85		HMar	67:55	68:55- 11
*	Njoroge	Mercy	KEN	10.6.86	158/46	3kSt	9:25.21	9:16.94- 11
*	Noguchi	Mizuki	JPN	3.7.78	150/41	Mar	2:25:33	2:19:12- 05
	Nojiri	Azusa	JPN	6.6.82	156/43	Mar	2:24:57	2:25:29- 11
	Nomura	Sayo	JPN	18.4.89	157/48	HMar	70:34	71:54- 09
	Noujani	Nadia	MAR	3.9.81	164/46	5000	15:16.50	
	Novik	Marina	BLR	19.1.84	168/60	JT	59.83	63.25- 09
	Novogrodskaya	Alena	BLR-J	11.5.93	180/96	HT	67.13	62.24- 11
	Novozhylova	Iryna	UKR	7.1.86	175/71	HT	74.10	71.82- 08
	Ntshingila	Patience	RSA	26.8.89	175/61	LJ	6.60	6.37- 09, 6.39Aw- 11
						TJ	13.89A	13.31- 09
	Nwaba	Barbara	USA	18.1.89	175/64	Hep	5986	5733- 11
	Nwankwe	Florence	NGR-J	28.7.94		400	52.09	53.18- 11
	Nwokey	Precious	USA	27.4.89	170/	Hep	5734	5543- 10
	Nyakogwa	Caroline	KEN			10k	31:42.25	
*	Nyaruai	Veronica	KEN	29.10.89	165/43	3000	8:40.81	9:01.3- 05
						5000	14:44.82	15:05.38- 08
*	Nytra	Carolin	GER	26.2.85	175/63	100h	12.74	12.57- 10
	Nzola Meso Ba	Teresa	FRA	30.11.83	169/53	TJ	14.02	14.69- 07
	Obare	Doricah	KEN	10.1.90	162/48	10k	32:17.28	31:37.07- 10
*	Obergföll	Christina	GER	22.8.81	175/79	JT	67.04	70.20- 07
*	Obiri	Hellen	KEN	13.12.89	155/45	1500	3:59.68	4:02.42- 11
	2000	5:44.8+i				3000	8:35.35i	
	Obleshchuk	Halyna	UKR	23.2.89		SP	19.23	17.27- 11
	O'Brien	Rebecca	USA	30.4.90		SP	17.59	17.22- 11
*	Odumosu	Joke	NGR	27.10.87	168/59	400	51.88	51.39- 08, 50.46dt- 07
						400h	54.40	54.59- 10
*	Oeser	Jennifer	GER	29.11.83	176/65	Hep	6345	6683- 10
	Ogbasilassie	Lemlem	CAN	10.12.87		800	2:00.82	2:00.85- 11
	Ogrâzeanu	Andreea	ROU	24.3.90	179/62	100	11.32, 11.29w	11.34, 11.29w- 11
	Ogura	Kumi	JPN	24.6.85	159/48	10k	32:37.90	32:43.66- 11
	Ohara	Rei	JPN	10.8.90	165/47	10k	32:30.45	32:50.50- 11
*	Ohuruogu	Christine	GBR	17.5.84	173/70	400	49.70	49.61- 07
	Okafor	Ifeatu	USA	20.8.90		SP	16.98	17.77- 11
*	Okagbare	Blessing	NGR	9.10.88	180/60	100	10.92	11.00, 10.7A, 10.98w- 10
	200	22.63			22.71- 10	LJ	6.97	6.91- 08
	Okayama	Saeko	JPN	12.4.82	180/63	LJ	6.55, 6.67w	6.56, 6.61w- 11
	Okhotnikova	Nina	RUS	11.3.91	162/46	20kW	1:28:16	1:28:41- 11
	Okori	Reina-Flor	FRA	2.5.80	163/56	100h	12.72	12.65- 08
	Okoro	Chinwe	NGR	20.6.89		SP	17.39	16.79- 11
						DT	58.25	54.24- 11
	Okoro	Marilyn	GBR	23.9.84	167/60	800	1:59.33	1:58.45- 08
	Okparaebo	Ezinne	NOR	3.3.88	164/56	100	11.10	11.21- 11, 11.12w- 09
	Okubo	Eri	JPN	2.6.83	164/47	Mar	2:26:08	2:28:49- 11
	Okuneva	Oksana	UKR	14.3.90	165/55	HJ	1.93i, 1.87	1.94- 11
	Olishevska	Yuliya	UKR	2.2.89	167/56	400	51.68	52.90- 09
	Olivarès	Élodie	FRA	22.5.76	170/51	3kSt	9:49.11	9:33.12- 02
	de Oliveira	Gisele	BRA	1.8.80	160/57	TJ	14.05	14.28, 14.31w- 08
	Oliveros	Princesa	COL	10.8.75	168/53	400h	57.05A, 56.3A, 57.14	56.26A- 11,57.19- 01
*	Oljira	Belaynesh	ETH	26.6.90	165/49	10k	30:26.70	31:17.80- 11
						HMar	68:26	67:27- 11
	Olupona	Toyin	CAN	29.1.83	177/63	100	11.20w	11.29, 11.24w- 08
*	Omarova	Anna	RUS	3.10.81	180/103	SP	18.80	19.69- 07
	Omotosho	Omolara	NGR-J	25.5.93	152/50	400	51.28	52.74- 11
	Omrani	Yasmina	ALG	1.1.88	183/67	Hep	5935	5979- 10
	Ongori	Philes	KEN	19.7.86	158/47	HMar	68:25	67:38- 09
*	Onishi	Misaki	JPN	24.2.85	164/47	5000	15:32.88	15:34.47- 11
	Onuora	Anyika	GBR	28.10.84	175/69	100	11.31	11.18- 11
						200	22.93	22.93- 11

Name		Nat	Born	Ht/Wt	Event	2012 Mark	Pre-2012 Best
^ Orbán	Éva	HUN	29.11.84	173/75	HT	69.03	71.33- 11
Orlova	Yelena	RUS	30.5.80	168/55	3kSt	9:31.37	9:22.15- 09
* O'Rourke	Derval	IRL	28.5.81	168/57	100h	12.91	12.65- 10
Ortiz	Mirna	GUA	28.2.87	158/44	20kW	1:28:54	1:32:30- 11
^ Osayomi	Damola	NGR	26.6.86	163/63	100	11.31	10.99, 10.90w- 11, 10.8- 08
Osazuwa	Agnes	NGR	21.6.90	150/60	100	11.34	11.33A- 10, 11.35- 08
Osazuwa	Uhunoma	NGR	23.11.87	178/65	Hep	6049	5668- 11
^ Ostapchuk ¶	Nadezhda	BLR	12.10.80	180/90	SP	21.58	21.70i- 10, 21.09- 05
Otani	Kumiko	JPN-Y	23.3.95	150/37	5000	15:31.65	
Otoshi	Kumi	JPN	29.7.85	161/46	20kW	1:29:48	1:29:11- 11
Ott	Anastasiya	RUS	7.9.88	175/61	400h	55.48	54.74- 08
Ouédraogo	Elodie	BEL	27.2.81	175/62	400h	55.20	55.29- 11
Owen	Melinda	USA	30.10.84		PV	4.37	4.55Ai- 11, 4.52- 10
Owens	Bridgette	USA	14.3.92	163/52	100h	12.71	13.08, 13.05w- 11
^ Oyepitan	Abi	GBR	30.12.79	165/55	100	11.21	11.17- 04
					200	22.71, 22.57w	22.50- 04
Ozaki	Mari	JPN	16.7.75	162/46	10k	32:20.98	31:34.15- 05
* Ozaki	Yoshimi	JPN	1.7.81	155/41	Mar	2:24:14	2:23:30- 08
Özata-Erismis	Türkan	TUR	5.1.84		3kSt	9:43.95	9:28.84- 09
Ozoh ¶	Lauretta	NGR	5.9.90	165/55	100	11.19	11.42- 11
					200	22.73	23.36- 11
Ozolina-Kovala	Sinta	LAT	26.2.88	185/72	JT	62.53	60.13- 08
Ozorai	Jenny	HUN	3.12.90	164/70	HT	68.08	66.12- 10
Pacchetti	Cecilia	ITA	18.5.89	172/57	TJ	14.08w	13.34- 10
Paklina	Alesya	KGZ	22.6.88		HJ	1.89	1.80- 11
^ Palamar	Vita	UKR	12.10.77	187/66	HJ	1.90	2.01- 03
* Palameika	Madara	LAT	18.6.87	185/76	JT	62.74	64.51- 09
Palframan	Justine	RSA-J	4.11.93	169/52	400	51.87	52.93A, 53.35- 11
Paliyenko	Tatyana	RUS	18.11.83		800	2:00.23	1:59.76- 11
Palmer-Cox	Katie	USA	1.12.84	170/60	800	2:01.40	2:03.26- 09
Palmieri	Elisa	ITA	18.9.83	169/85	HT	67.16	67.33- 11
Palsyté	Airiné	LTU	13.7.92	186/62	HJ	1.95	1.96- 11
Panayi	Nectaria	CYP	20.3.90		LJ	6.56	6.35- 11
Pandakova	Marina	RUS	1.3.89		20kW	1:28:29	1:33:00- 11
Panétta	Níki	GRE	21.4.86	171/54	TJ	14.50	14.55- 11
Panova	Yelena	RUS	2.3.87		DT	57.97	56.83- 10
Panteleyeva	Marina	RUS	16.5.89	175/65	200	23.04	23.52- 11
Panteleyeva	Yana	RUS	16.6.88	170/63	Hep	6192	6430- 08
* Papahrístou	Paraskeví	GRE	17.4.89	170/53	LJ	6.60	6.55- 11
					TJ	14.58, 14.77w	14.72- 11
Parker	Barbara	GBR	8.11.82	170/54	5000	15:12.81	15:27.03- 11
3000	8:56.62		8:52.90i- 10, 9:02.92- 09		3kSt	9:24.24	9:35.17- 10
Parnov	Liz	AUS-J	9.5.94	176/57	PV	4.50	4.40- 10
Parnov	Vicky	AUS	24.10.90		PV	4.35	4.40- 07
Parra	Yusbelys	VEN	31.7.86	170/65	JT	59.33	57.58- 11
* Pascual	Beatriz	ESP	9.5.82	163/53	20kW	1:27:56	1:27:44- 08
Pastare	Agnese	LAT	27.10.88	178/70	20kW	1:31:54	1:31:25- 10
Patterson	Kara	USA	10.4.86	175/76	JT	60.49	66.67- 10
* Pavey	Jo	GBR	20.9.73	162/51	5000	15:02.84	14:39.96- 06
10k	30:53.20		31:12.30- 08		HMar	69:20	68:53- 08
Payton	Malaina	USA	16.10.91			6.56w	6.40- 11
Pchelnik	Daryia	BLR	20.12.81	185/97	HT	69.35	76.33- 08
Peake	Sally	GBR	8.2.86	164/57	PV	4.42i, 4.30	4.35- 11
* Pearson	Sally	AUS	19.9.86	166/60	100	11.20	11.14- 07
200	23.02		23.02- 09		100h	12.35	12.28- 11
Pease	Sarah	USA	9.11.87	158/48	3kSt	9:52.43	9:56.91- 10
Pedroso	Yadisleidy	CUB	28.1.87	168/51	400h	54.89	56.14- 11, 56.1- 10
Pedroso	Yasmiany	CUB	5.8.84	179/75	Hep	5891	5942- 07
Pei Mowen		CHN-Y	17.9.95		20kW	1:32:23	1:35:14- 11
Pelantová	Lucie	CZE	7.5.86	168/60	20kW	1:32:53	1:32:57- 10
Peleteiro	Ana	ESP-Y	2.12.95	160/40	TJ	14.17	13.17- 11
Pena	Tori	IRL	30.7.87	167/57	PV	4.52	4.40- 11
Pennella	Giulia	ITA	27.10.89	169/53	100h	13.06	13.29- 11
Peoples	Kearsten	USA	20.12.91		SP	18.22	16.30- 11
^ Pérez	Madaí	MEX	2.2.80	158/44	10k	32:27.91	31:30.23- 08
					HMar	70:05	69:45- 10
Pérez	Paola	ECU	21.12.89	148/55	20kW	1:32:01	1:39:35- 11
Pérez	Yaimé	CUB	29.5.91	174/78	DT	62.50	59.30- 10
* Perie	Bianca	ROU	1.6.90	170/70	HT	70.05	73.52- 10
Perkins	Emma	GBR	4.9.85		HJ	1.89i	1.83- 11
Perkins	Kerrie	AUS	2.4.79	174/59	LJ	6.63, 6.70w	6.66- 06

Name		Nat	Born	Ht/Wt	Event	2012 Mark	Pre-2012 Best
Perkins	Tiffany	CAN	1.1.91		JT	56.20A	50.24- 11
* Perkovic	Sandra	CRO	21.6.90	183/80	DT	69.11	67.96- 11
Pérra	Athanasía	GRE	2.2.83	167/55	TJ	14.71	14.62- 09
Perrin	Amélie	FRA	30.3.80	172/90	HT	66.71	71.38- 06
Perry	Michelle	USA	1.5.79	173/64	100h	12.75, 12.70w	12.43- 05
Peryakova	Natalya	RUS	4.3.83		800	2:00.33	2:01.33- 07
Peter	Allison	ISV	14.7.92	173/59	100	11.17, 11.16w	11.47- 09, 11.46w- 11
					200	22.77	23.08- 09
Petersen	Sara	DEN	9.4.87	171/57	400h	55.68	55.97- 11
^ Petlyuk ¶	Tetyana	UKR	22.2.82	174/60	800	2:00.47dq	1:57.34- 06
* Petre	Esthera	ROU	13.5.90	175/60	HJ	1.94i, 1.85	1.98- 11
Pham Thi Diem		VIE	24.1.90		HJ	1.88	1.87- 11
Phuc	Nguyen Thi Thanh	VIE	12.8.90	154/45	20kW	1:33:36	1:41:41- 11
Pidluzhnaya	Yuliya	RUS	1.10.88	180/63	LJ	6.60i	6.84- 10,6.85w- 11
* Pierce	Anna	USA	31.3.84	163/54	800	1:59.16	1:58.80- 09
1000	2:38.91i		2:38.76i- 10		1500	4:05.42	3:59.38- 09
* Pierre	Barbara	USA	28.4.87	160.64	100	11.34	11.14- 11
Pierson	Summer	USA	3.9.78	180/84	DT	60.77	61.19, 61.25dh- 09
Pilipenko	Anastasiya	KAZ	13.9.86	175/56	100h	12.69	12.81- 08
Pinedo	Ainhoa	ESP	17.2.83	171/60	20kW	1:33:15	1:34:05- 10
Pinero	Anna María	ESP	15.1.86	168/60	PV	4.35	4.41- 11
Pinnick	Keia	USA	23.1.91	165/55	Hep	5761	5455- 11
Pinto	Tatjana	GER	2.7.92	170/56	100	11.19	11.46- 10
* Pishchalnikova ¶	Darya	RUS	19.7.85	190/103	DT	64.56, 70.69dq?	65.55- 06, 67.28dq- 08
Piwowarska	Joanna	POL	4.11.83	172/56	PV	4.41i	4.53- 06
Plá	Judith	ESP	2.5.78	168/53	5000	15:20.39	15:20.87- 08
Plaza	Alexandra	GER-J	10.6.94	176/58	HJ	1.88	1.82- 10
Plis	Renata	POL	5.2.85	165/51	1500	4:04.48	4:03.50- 11
Podominick	Liz	USA	5.12.84	188/86	DT	60.96	57.82A- 11
Podosyonova	Svetlana	RUS	24.5.88		800	2:00.69	2:06.20- 11
					1500	3:59.61	4:12.03i, 4:13.04- 11
Pogrebnyak	Nataliya	UKR	19.2.88	171/62	100	11.20	11.17- 11
* Poistogova	Yekaterina	RUS	1.3.91	175/65	800	1:57.53	2:02.11- 09
1000	2:38.94i		2:46.19i- 08		1500	4:00.11	4:17.9- 11
^ Polnova	Tatyana	RUS	20.4.79	173/64	PV	4.40	4.78- 04
Polyakova	Natalya	RUS	9.12.90		HT	67.08	63.22- 11
^ Pompey	Aliann	GUY	9.3.78	168/55	400	52.10	50.71- 09
Pooley	Isobel	GBR	21.12.92	191/	HJ	1.90	1.86i- 11, 1.83- 10
* Poonia	Krishna	IND	5.5.82	180/86	DT	64.76	63.69- 10
Popescu	Elena	MDA	6.9.89	167/52	800	2:00.64	2:06.61- 11
Popkova	Natalya	RUS	21.9.88	165/50	5000	15:24.74	15:05.95- 09
					10k	31:55.83	32:21.17- 11
Poplavskaya	Yekaterina	BLR	7.5.87	172/60	100h	12.91, 12.85w	13.10- 11
					LJ	6.70i, 6.38	6.15- 11
Porter	Chanice	JAM-J	25.5.94		LJ	6.58, 6.78w	6.43- 10
Porter	Sarah	USA	22.8.89	163/48	10k	32:37.22	32:57.15- 11
* Porter	Tiffany	GBR	13.11.87	172/62	100h	12.65, 12.47w	12.56- 11
Pospelova	Marina	RUS	23.7.90		800	1:59.70, 1:59.45i	2:00.76- 11
* Potapova	Anastasiya	RUS	6.9.85	178/61	TJ	14.23i, 14.20	14.68i, 14.40- 09
^ Potepa	Wioletta	POL	14.12.80	189/86	DT	59.56	66.01- 06
Potgieter	Charlene	RSA	22.9.85		TJ	13.80, 13.90w	13.45- 11
* Poves	María José	ESP	16.3.78	168/52	20kW	1:28:15	1:29:31- 08
Povh	Olesya	UKR	18.10.87	169/58	100	11.08	11.24, 11.14w- 11
Powell	Suzy	USA	3.9.76	180/80	DT	61.26	67.67- 07, 69.44dh- 02
Praught	Aisha	USA	14.12.89	163/54	3kSt	9:51.30	10:23.56- 11
Prendergast	Davita	JAM	16.12.84	169/58	400	52.11	50.86- 11
Price	Candice	USA	26.10.85		100h	12.85, 12.79w	12.71- 08
Price	Chanelle	USA	22.8.90	166/53	800	2:00.15	2:01.61- 08
Pritz	Molly	USA	7.4.88		HMar	70:45	71:05- 11
* Proctor	Shara	GBR	16.9.88	174/56	LJ	6.95	6.81- 11
^ Prokopcuka	Jelena	LAT	21.9.76	168/48	HMar	68:09dh	68:11- 05
					Mar	2:26:55	2:22:56- 05
Prokopeva	Alina	RUS	16.8.85		5000	15:24.96	15:23.78- 08
					10k	31:57.38	32:01.57- 09
Provalinskaya	Yanina	BLR	26.12.76	186/85	SP	18.63	20.61- 01
Provozina	Lidiya	UKR	13.2.86	176/75	HT	66.11	66.70- 11
Prystupa	Darya	UKR	26.11.87	162/55	400	51.70	52.06- 10
* Ptácníková (-Svodobová)	Jirina	CZE	20.5.86	175/69	PV	4.72	4.66- 10
Puchkova	Natalya	RUS	28.1.87		5000	15:24.00	15:27.57- 10
Pudenz	Kristin	GER-J	9.2.93	190/92	DT	57.74	54.15- 11
Purdue	Charlotte	GBR	10.6.91	155/47	10k	32:03.55	32:36.75- 10

Name		Nat	Born	Ht/Wt	Event	2012 Mark	Pre-2012 Best
Purvis	Ashton	USA	12.7.92	173/60	100	11.30	11.17- 10
Purvis	Ashton	USA	12.7.92	173/60	200	22.86	22.90- 10
Pusterla	Irène	SUI	21.6.88	176/64	LJ	6.66	6.84- 11
Pyatachenko	Viktoriya	UKR	7.5.89	170/57	100	11.30	11.64- 09
					200	22.71	23.76- 11
Pygyda	Nataliya	UKR	30.1.81	167/54	400	51.09	51.38, 51.28dq- 09
Pyrek	Monika	POL	11.8.80	170/54	PV	4.50	4.82- 07
* Qieyang Shenjie		CHN	11.11.90	160/50	20kW	1:25:16	1:28:04- 11
* Radevica	Ineta	LAT	13.7.81	174/57	LJ	6.88	6.92- 10
* Radzivil	Svetlana	UZB	17.1.87	184/61	HJ	1.97	1.95- 10
^ Rahouli	Baya	ALG	27.7.79	179/64	TJ	13.83i, 13.50	14.98- 05
Rains	Katelin	USA	20.8.87	168/59	PV	4.31	4.40i, 4.24- 09
Rajabi	Leyla	IRI	18.4.83	185/95	SP	17.98	18.06- 06
Rammonye	Rorisang	RSA	31.12.90	175/70	400	51.61A, 51.98	53.28- 11
Ramos	Beverly	PUR	24.8.87	163/51	3kSt	9:39.33	9:41.87- 11
Randall	Allison	JAM	25.5.88	180/95	DT	61.21	57.14- 11
Ratcliffe	Julia	NZL-J	14.7.93	171/66	HT	67.00	62.28- 11
* Ratej	Martina	SLO	2.11.81	178/69	JT	65.24	67.16- 10
Rath	Claudia	GER	25.4.86	175/58	Hep	6210	6107- 10
Reaser	Allison	USA	9.9.92	171/61	Hep	5753	5408A(w)- 11
* Rebryk	Vira	UKR	25.2.89	176/65	JT	66.86	63.36- 10
Redhead	Janelle	GRN	27.12.89	162/56	200	23.08	22.91A, 23.11- 11, 23.04w- 10
Redondo	Laura	ESP	3.7.88	165/80	HT	69.15	67.12- 11
* Reese	Brittney	USA	9.9.86	173/64	LJ	7.23i, 7.15	7.19- 11
Reggel	Valérie	SUI	3.1.87		Hep	5794	5513- 11
Reibold	Jade	USA	14.4.91		PV	4.31	4.17- 10
Reid	Sheila	CAN	2.8.89	166/52	1500	4:07.07	4:11.85- 11
					5000	15:23.64	15:37.57- 11
Reilly	Stephanie	IRL	23.2.78	155/46	3kSt	9:44.15	9:42.91- 11
dos Reis	Jéssica Carolina	BRA-J	17.3.93		LJ	6.58	6.42- 11
Renstrøm	Margrethe	NOR	21.3.85	179/60	LJ	6.67	6.68- 10
Restle-Apel ¶	Simret	GER	4.5.84	170/45	5000	15:28.71	15:45.55- 11
Reyes	Macarena	CHI	30.3.84	165/58	LJ	6.60	6.37, 6.49w- 11
Reynolds	Laura	IRL	20.1.89	173/57	20kW	1:31:02	1:35:34- 11
Reznichenko	Darya	UZB	3.4.91		LJ	6.60	6.55- 11
Ribalta	Josleidy	CUB	2.5.90	183/74	TJ	14.30, 14.39w	14.61- 11
Ribiaux	Yainelis	CUB	30.12.87	163/57	JT	60.70	63.18- 09
* Richards-Ross	Sanya	USA	26.2.85	172/63	100	10.89w	10.97- 07
200	22.09		22.17- 06		400	49.28	48.70- 06
Richartz	Stephanie	USA	21.1.92	175/64	PV	4.34	4.06- 11
Rifka	Romary	MEX	8.4.73	180/64	HJ	1.90A	1.97- 04
* Rigaudo	Elisa	ITA	17.6.80	168/56	20kW	1:27:36	1:27:12- 08
Rigert	Yelena	RUS	2.12.83	167/73	HT	70.14	71.92- 08
Riggien	Chastity	USA	5.7.89	157/52	100	11.20, 11.09w	11.34, 11.13w- 11
Rigishvili	Salome	GEO	26.1.90		DT	58.90	49.36- 11
Riley	Brittany	USA	26.8.86	173/110	HT	69.29	72.51- 07
Rittweg	Mareike	GER	1.6.84	173/78	JT	59.85	60.63- 07
Rivas	Angela	COL	13.8.89	180/82	SP	17.53	17.12- 11
Roach	Peaches	JAM	21.12.84	170/53	Hep	5709	5780- 10
* Robert-Michon	Mélina	FRA	18.7.79	180/85	DT	63.98	65.78- 02
Robinson	Moushaumi	USA	13.4.81	170/59	400	52.14	50.38- 05
Rocha	Carla Salomé	POR	25.4.90		3kSt	9:51.91	9:57.30- 11
Rodic	Snezana	SLO	19.8.82	180/66	TJ	14.20	14.47, 14.52w- 10
Rodrigues	Irina	POR	5.2.91	182/81	DT	62.91	58.35- 11
Rodriguez	Carol	PUR	16.12.85	175/65	400	52.02	51.39- 08
Rodríguez	Déborah	URU	2.12.92	174/63	400h	57.04	58.63- 11
Rodríguez	Rosa	VEN	2.7.86	179/78	HT	72.83	69.46- 09
Rodríguez	Yorgelis	CUB-Y	25.1.95	173/60	Hep	5994	
Rogers	Natosha	USA	7.5.91	160/50	10k	31:59.21	
* Rogowska	Anna	POL	21.5.81	171/53	PV	4.71i, 4.70	4.85i- 11, 4.83- 05
Rohl	Beth	USA	7.11.90		DT	57.82	55.94- 11
Roleder	Cindy	GER	21.8.89	175/62	100h	12.91	12.91- 11
* Rollins	Brianna	USA	18.8.91	164/55	100h	12.70, 12.60wA	12.99, 12.88w- 11
Roloff	Annika	GER	10.3.91	166/54	PV	4.42i, 4.40	4.40- 11
Romagnolo	Elena	ITA	5.10.82	163/47	5000	15:06.38	15:13.19- 09
Roman	Sonja	SLO	11.3.79	165/54	1500	4:07.67	4:02.13- 09
Rono	Georgina	KEN	19.5.84		HMar	67:58	69:08- 11
					Mar	2:21:39	2:24:33- 11
Rosa	Chiara	ITA	28.1.83	178/112	SP	18.63	19.15- 07
Rosenbauer	Susanne	GER	2.8.84	173/69	JT	57.68	58.83- 09
* Rosolová	Denisa	CZE	21.8.86	175/63	400	52.07	50.84- 11
					400h	54.24	60.09- 04

Name		Nat	Born	Ht/Wt	Event	2012 Mark	Pre-2012 Best
Rotaru	Alina	ROU-J	5.6.93	175/54	LJ	6.57, 6.58w	6.46- 11
Rothstein-Bruce	Stephanie	USA	14.1.84	167/52	10k	32:24.25	33:08.37- 08
Rotich	Caroline	KEN	13.5.84		HMar	70:17	68:52- 11
					Mar	2:23:22	2:24:26dh, 2:27:06- 11
* Rotich	Lydia	KEN	8.8.88	163/42	3kSt	9:31.09	9:18.03- 10
* Rowbury	Shannon	USA	19.9.84	166/52	1500	4:03.15	4:00.33- 08
					3000	8:39.83	8:31.38- 10
Rucker	Erika	USA-J	29.9.93	168/57	400	51.10	54.59- 11
Rudakova	Vera	RUS	20.3.92		400h	56.47	57.10- 11
Ruddock	Natasha	JAM	25.12.89		100h	13.19, 12.98w	12.87- 10
Rüh	Anna	GER-J	17.6.93	186/78	DT	63.38	59.97- 11
Ruiz	Úrsula	ESP	11.8.83	170/84	SP	17.99	17.02- 11
Ruíz	Flor Denis	COL	24.1.91	171/67	JT	59.32A	57.26- 11
Rummans	Angie	USA	23.3.92	168/57	PV	4.40	4.00- 11
Rumpf	Sabine	GER	18.3.83	176/95	DT	61.16	62.21- 10
Rusakova	Natalya	RUS	12.12.79	177/70	100	11.32	11.18- 06
					200	22.42	22.53- 06
^ Rusanova ¶	Yuliya	RUS	3.7.86		800	2:00.26idq	1:56.99- 11
^ Russell	Carrie	JAM	18.10.90	171/68	100	11.24	11.05- 11
Russell	Janeive	JAM-J	14.11.93		400h	56.62	57.71- 11
Ruston	Abby	USA	3.4.83		SP	16.91i	18.13- 08
Ruto	Stella	KEN-Y	.96		3kSt	9:50.58	
Ryan	Deirdre	IRL	1.6.82	183/62	HJ	1.90	1.95- 11
* Rybalko	Viktoriya	UKR	26.10.82	177/60	LJ	6.95	6.87i- 08, 6.87- 11
					TJ	13.36, 13.87w	13.95- 11
* Ryemyen	Mariya	UKR	2.8.87	171/62	100	11.20	11.21, 11.18w- 11
					200	22.58	22.68- 11
* Rypakova	Olga	KAZ	30.11.84	183/62	TJ	14.98	15.25- 10
* Ryzih	Lisa	GER	27.9.88	179/59	PV	4.65	4.65- 10
Sadeiko	Grit	EST	29.7.89	172/62	Hep	6013	6134- 11
Sado	Fatuma	ETH	11.10.91		Mar	2:25:39dh	2:28:01- 11
^ Sadova	Natalya	RUS	15.7.72	180/90	DT	59.70	70.02- 99
Safránková	Katerina	CZE	8.6.89	191/105	HT	71.16	69.39- 11
Sahalinirina	Eliane	MAD	20.3.82		3kSt	9:47.57	10:02.24- 10
Sahutoglu	Tugçe	TUR	1.5.88	180/115	HT	74.17	70.09- 11
* Sailer	Verena	GER	16.10.85	166/50	100	11.05	11.10, 11.06w- 10
Saina	Betsy	KEN	30.6.88		10k	31:15.97	33:13.13- 10
Saka	Pinar	TUR	5.11.85	165/54	400	51.60	51.53- 11
Sakaida	Ayumi	JPN	7.11.85	157/44	10k	32:29.28	32:37.03- 11
* Saladuha	Olha	UKR	4.6.83	175/55	TJ	14.99	14.98, 15.06w- 11
Salander	Martina	SWE	11.2.92		Hep	5916w	5446- 10
Salis	Silvia	ITA	17.9.85	179/74	HT	70.20	71.93- 11
Saltanovic	Kristina	LTU	20.2.75	163/54	20kW	1:31:04	1:30:44- 02
Samoei	Emily	KEN	11.11.80		Mar	2:26:52	2:34:29- 11
Samuel	Jamile	NED	24.4.92	168/54	200	22.93	23.21- 10
Samuel	Laura	GBR	19.2.91	165/65	TJ	13.75	13.75- 10
* Samuels	Dani	AUS	26.5.88	182/82	DT	63.97	65.84- 10
Samuelsson	Jessica	SWE	14.3.85	176/65	Hep	6300	6182- 11
Samylova	Olga	RUS	4.1.86	163/50	100h	12.82	13.06- 10
Sanders	Shayla	USA-J	6.1.94	168/55	100	11.33, 11.32w	11.45- 11
Sandu	Cristina	ROU	4.3.90	172/58	LJ	6.57, 6.70w	6.54i- 11, 6.53- 09
Santiusti	Yusneisis	CUB	24.12.84	166/60	800	1:58.53	1:58.70- 11
dos Santos	Evelyn	BRA	11.4.85	172/52	200	22.82	23.08- 08
Santos	Rosângela	BRA	20.12.90	165/55	100	11.17, 11.07w	11.22A, 11.36- 11
					200	22.92	23.70- 11
* Santos	Vera	POR	3.12.81	164/57	20kW	1:32:48	1:28:14- 08
Sarrapio	Patricia	ESP	16.11.82	168/58	TJ	13.90, 14.30w	14.10- 10
Sato	Eri	JPN	5.4.86	154/40	10k	32:34.51	32:48.89- 10
Sato	Yuka	JPN	21.7.92	161/68	JT	59.22	57.31- 10
Saumweber	Stefanie	GER	5.3.88	176/62	Hep	5959	5462- 11
* Savchenko	Anastasiya	RUS	15.11.89	175/65	PV	4.60	4.40- 11
* Savigne	Yargeris	CUB	13.11.84	165/55	TJ	14.55i, 14.35	15.28- 07
* Savinova	Mariya	RUS	13.8.85	169/55	400	51.43	52.05i- 10, 52.71- 11
					800	1:56.19	1:55.87- 11
* Savitskaya	Kristina	RUS	10.6.91	180/72	HJ	1.88	1.78- 11
LJ	6.65		6.18- 11		Hep	6681	5989- 11
Savlinis	Yelizaveta	RUS	14.8.87	178/65	100	11.34	11.30, 11.17w- 11
					200	22.62	22.62- 11
Sawyers	Jazmin	GBR-J	21.5.94		LJ	6.67	6.23, 6.27w- 11
Saxer	Mary	USA	21.6.87	166/57	PV	4.62Ai, 4.53	4.60- 11

Name		Nat	Born	Ht/Wt	Event	2012 Mark	Pre-2012 Best
* Sayers	Goldie	GBR	16.7.82	171/70	JT	66.17	65.75- 08
Saykina	Svetlana	RUS	10.7.85	177/82	DT	63.25	63.42- 08
Schade	Krystle	USA	2.7.90		HJ	1.88i, 1.87	1.85i- 11, 1.83- 10
Schäfer	Carolin	GER	5.12.91	176/66	Hep	6072	5941- 11
Schappert	Nicole	USA	30.10.86	158/50	1500	4:06.87	4:10.02- 11
* Schippers	Dafne	NED	15.6.92	179/68	200	22.70	22.69- 11
LJ	6.54			6.47-11	Hep	6360	6172- 11
Schmid	Anna Katharina	SUI	2.12.89	166/56	PV	4.42i, 4.40	4.45- 11
Schmidt	Alice	USA	3.10.81	180/64	800	1:59.46	1:58.61- 11
					1500	4:05.64	4:08.09- 11
Schrott	Beate	AUT	15.4.88	177/68	100h	12.82	12.95- 11
* Schultze	Martina	GER	12.9.90	172/59	PV	4.31i, 4.30	4.40- 10
Schwanitz	Christina	GER	24.12.85	180/103	SP	19.15i, 19.05	19.68i, 19.31- 08
* Schwartz	Jillian	ISR	19.9.79	173/63	PV	4.52i, 4.41	4.72i- 08, 4.60- 04
^ Schwarz	Desirée	GER	24.4.92	171/70	JT	56.93	51.78- 10
* Schwarzkopf	Lilli	GER	28.8.83	174/65	Hep	6649	6536- 08
Schwerdtner	Maren	GER	3.10.85	182/72	Hep	6154	6167- 10
Scott	Aurieyall	USA	18.5.92	170/60	100	11.19A, 11.21	11.12- 11
					200	22.68, 22.56w	22.83, 22.82w- 11
Scott	Sharolyn	CRC	27.10.84	167/64	400h	56.19	57.23A, 57.66- 11
Seboka	Mulu	ETH	25.9.84		Mar	2:25:45 (& HMar 69:53+)	2:29:06- 08
Sedivá	Irena	CZE	19.1.92		JT	57.41	56.38- 11
Sedykh	Alexia	FRA-J	13.9.93	173/69	HT	67.98	65.02- 11
^ Seeger	Melanie	GER	8.1.77	169/55	20kW	1:30:44	1:28:17- 04
Sekachyova	Iryna	UKR	21.7.76	165/72	HT	72.42	74.52- 08
Selvon	Kai	TRI	13.4.92	165/59	100	11.21	11.41- 10, 11.19w- 11
					200	22.85, 22.66w	22.89- 11
* Semenova	Nataliya	UKR	7.7.82	178/65	DT	63.56	64.70- 08
* Semenya	Caster	RSA	7.1.91	170/64	800	1:57.23	1:55.45- 09
de Sena	Erica	BRA	3.5.85	152/52	20kW	1:31:53	1:35:29.6t- 11
Sendriuté	Zinaida	LTU	10.6.84	188/89	DT	64.03	62.49- 11
Sène	Amy	SEN	6.4.85	174/70	HT	69.10	68.45- 11
Serbezova	Nina	CYP	6.5.81		TJ	14.03	13.98- 04
Serova	Svetlana	BLR	28.8.86	178/92	DT	60.90	59.45- 10
Sesay	Ola	SLE	30.5.79	173/64	LJ	6.71	6.73- 09
^ Sestak	Marija	SLO	17.4.79	178/56	TJ	14.26, 14.31w	15.08i, 15.03- 08
* Shakes-Drayton	Perri	GBR	21.12.88	170/67	400	51.26	51.47- 11
					400h	53.77	54.18- 10
Sharp	Lynsey	GBR	11.7.90	175/60	800	2:00.52	2:00.65- 11
Shatalova	Mariya	UKR	3.3.89		3kSt	9:44.91	9:47.21- 10
Sheleh	Hanna	UKR-J	14.7.93	166/54	PV	4.60i, 4.20	4.30- 10
Shevchenko ¶	Anzhela	UKR	29.10.87	177/55	1500	4:05.96dq	4:07.24- 11
Shi Tianshu		CHN	7.6.88	174/55	20kW	1:31:22	1:31:53- 11
^ Shibui	Yoko	JPN	14.3.79	165/50	Mar	2:25:02	2:19:41- 04
Shigetomo	Risa	JPN	29.8.87	168/50	Mar	2:23:23	2:31:28- 11
Shimizu	Yuko	JPN	13.7.85	158/43	10k	32:33.61	31:43.25mx- 11
* Shkolina	Svetlana	RUS	9.3.86	188/80	HJ	2.03	2.00i, 1.99- 11
Shmidt	Svitlana	UKR	20.3.90	167.52	1500	4:08.93i	4:17.83- 10
3000	8:41.01i		9:06.13i- 11		3kSt	9:31.16	9:46.91- 11
* Shobukhova	Liliya	RUS	13.11.77	169/50	Mar	2:22:59	2:18:20- 11
Shoi	Hiroko	JPN	18.6.80	152/40	10k	32:23.98	32:17.39mx- 11
Shuklina	Olesya	RUS	27.6.84		5000	15:20.17	
					10k	32:34.53	
Shumi	Genzebe	BRN	29.1.91	166/45	800	2:01.18	2:03.13- 11
					1500	4:05.16	4:11.27- 11
Shumilova	Mariya	RUS	10.1.90		Hep	5885	5362- 11
Shumkina	Olena	UKR	24.1.88	153/47	20kW	1:31:55	1:25:32- 09
Shurhno	Olena	UKR	8.1.78	171/56	Mar	2:23:32	2:28:34- 11
Shushina	Irina	RUS	30.10.86		20kW	1:32:03	1:37:14- 11
Shutkova	Veronika	BLR	26.5.86	171/51	LJ	7.01	6.95- 11
* Shvedova	Anastasiya	BLR	3.5.79	174/63	PV	4.55	4.65- 07, 4.72ex- 08
Sibileva	Tatyana	RUS	17.5.80	164/51	20kW	1:26:59	1:25:52- 10
Sidorkina	Yelena	RUS	27.9.88		TJ	14.11	14.02- 10
* Sidorova	Anzhelika	RUS	28.6.91		PV	4.50	4.40i- 11, 4.30- 10
Sifuentes	Nicole	CAN	30.6.86	173/57	800	2:01.30	2:02.63- 09
1500	4:04.76		4:06.34- 10		3000	8:56.80i	9:09.32i- 10
da Silva	Ana Cláudia	BRA	6.11.88	158/55	100	11.30	11.15- 10
					200	23.01	22.48- 11
da Silva	Cruz Nonata	BRA	18.8.74		10k	32:15.72	32:53.72- 11
da Silva	Karla	BRA	12.11.84	168/58	PV	4.32	4.35- 11
da Silva	Lucimara	BRA	10.7.85	172/63	Hep	6160	6133A- 11

Name		Nat	Born	Ht/Wt	Event	2012 Mark	Pre-2012 Best
e Silva	Laila	BRA	30.7.82	180/80	JT	60.21	57.81- 11
Silva	Vânia	POR	8.6.80	174/78	HT	67.04	69.55- 11
* Silva	Yarisley	CUB	1.6.87	169/68	PV	4.75	4.75A- 11
Simic	Ana	CRO	5.5.90	177/58	HJ	1.91i, 1.88	1.92- 10
Simpson	Francine	JAM	1.11.89		LJ	6.57, 6.67w	6.51- 07
Simpson	Jemma	GBR	10.2.84	168/58	800	2:00.72	1:58.74- 10
* Simpson	Jennifer	USA	23.8.86	165/54	1500	4:04.07	3:59.90- 09
					3000	8:48.72	8:42.03i- 09, 9:12.50- 09
* Simpson	Margaret	GHA	2.8.82	162/53	Hep	6245	6423- 05
* Simpson	Sherone	JAM	12.8.84	163/59	100	11.01	10.82- 06
200	22.37			22.00- 06	400	51.42	51.25- 08
Singh	Sudha	IND	25.6.86		3kSt	9:47.70	9:55.67- 10
Sitnikova	Yelena	RUS	12.11.89		LJ	6.36, 6.58w	6.35- 11
Skrobáková	Lucie	CZE	4.1.82	170/62	100h	12.81	12.73- 09
Skrypak	Olga	UKR	2.12.90	160/43	10k	31:51.32	34:26.46- 09
* Skujyté	Austra	LTU	12.8.79	188/80	HJ	1.92	1.89i- 07, 1.87- 11
SP	17.31			17.86- 09	Hep	6599	6435- 04
Skydan	Hanna	UKR	14.5.92	183/114	HT	74.21	67.56- 11
Slanícková	Lucie	SVK	8.11.88	179/65	Hep	5780	5684- 10
Smedley	Melinda	USA	11.2.81	163/58	100	11.34	11.27. 11.24w- 06
Smit	Angela	NZL	16.8.91		800	2:00.67	2:03.87- 10
Smit	Anika	RSA	26.5.86	182/56	HJ	1.90	1.93- 07
Smith	Ayla	USA	16.5.88	160/55	400h	56.70	56.54- 11
Smith	Brittany	USA	25.3.91	178/	SP	17.92	17.19i- 11, 15.98- 10
					HT	68.45	62.88- 11
Smith	Jessica	CAN	11.10.89	175/52	800	1:59.86	2:01.54- 11
* Smith	Kimberly	NZL	19.11.81	166/48	HMar	68:43, 68:27dh	67:11- 11
					Mar	2:26:59	2:25:21- 10
Smith	Kristin	USA	23.12.87		HT	68.25	66.87- 11
Smith	Loreal	USA	12.10.85	162/57	100h	12.94	12.81- 11
Smith	Loree	USA	6.11.82	168/89	HT	68.86	70.64- 09
Smith	Toni	USA	13.10.84		TJ	13.87	13.99- 08, 14.02w- 10
^ Smith	Trecia	JAM	5.11.75	185/76	TJ	14.35	15.16- 04
Smock	Amanda	USA	27.7.82	170/57	TJ	13.94	14.18- 11
Smolyanova	Yelena	UZB	16.2.86		SP	17.68	15.60- 11
Snow	Morgan	USA-J	26.7.93		100h	13.13, 13.04w	13.51- 11
* Soboleva	Yelena	RUS	3.10.82	176/66	800	1:59.90	1:57.28- 06
					1500	4:00.09	3:56.43- 06
* Sokolova	Vera	RUS	8.6.87	151/51	20kW	1:28:06	1:25:08- 11
* Sokolova	Yelena	RUS	23.7.86	173/66	LJ	7.07	6.92- 09
* Solomon	Shalonda	USA	19.12.85	169/56	100	11.26	10.90- 10
					200	22.82	22.15- 11
Solovyova	Yevgeniya	RUS	28.6.86	185/90	SP	18.71i, 18.03	17.55- 11
^ Song Aimin		CHN	15.3.78	178/95	DT	59.52	65.44- 09
Song Xiaodan		CHN-J	23.1.93		JT	56.56	55.35- 11
Song Xiaoling		CHN	21.12.87	167/49	20kW	1:32:08	1:28:23- 06
Sonnenberg	Samantha	USA	10.2.88	167/57	PV	4.40	4.35- 11
Soprunova	Anastasiya	KAZ	14.1.86	165/52	100h	12.95	12.99- 11
Sormunen	Oona	FIN	2.8.89		JT	59.14	58.72- 11
Soto	Nercely	VEN	23.8.90	169/55	200	22.53	24.22- 10, 22.8- 11
* Soumaré	Myriam	FRA	29.10.86	167/57	100	11.07	11.17, 11.12w- 11
					200	22.56	22.32- 10
Sousa	Joelma	BRA	13.7.84	174/51	400	51.54	52.23- 11
de Souza	Tamara	BRA-J	8.9.93	185/76	Hep	5900	5545- 11
Spanovic	Ivana	SRB	10.5.90	176/67	LJ	6.64	6.78- 10
Spence	Christine	USA	25.11.81	174/64	400h	55.58	54.21- 08
Spence	Indira	JAM	8.9.86	/61	100h	12.92, 12.80w	12.93- 11
Spence	Neely	USA	16.4.90		10k	32:16.51	-0-
* Spencer	Ashley	USA-J	8.6.93	168/54	200	22.99 & 400 50.50	-0-
* Spencer	Kaliese	JAM	6.5.87	173/59	400	50.63	50.55- 08
					400h	53.49	52.79- 11
Spencer	Levern	LCA	23.6.84	180/54	HJ	1.91	1.98- 10
* Spiegelburg	Silke	GER	17.3.86	173/64	PV	4.82	4.76i, 4.75- 11
Spiler	Barbara	SLO	2.1.92	184/79	HT	71.25	67.06- 11
Spínola	Vanessa	BRA	5.3.90	178/68	Hep	6015	5763- 09
* Spotáková	Barbora	CZE	30.6.81	182/80	JT	69.55	72.28- 08
					Hep	5880	5873- 00
Sprunger	Ellen	SUI	5.8.86	172/56	Hep	6124	5844- 11
Sprunger	Léa	SUI	5.3.90	183/67	200	23.08	23.81- 11
Sreedharan	Preeja	IND	13.3.82	155/52	10k	32:38.41	31:50.47- 10
* Stahl	Linda	GER	2.10.85	174/72	JT	64.91	66.81- 10

Name		Nat	Born	Ht/Wt	Event	2012 Mark	Pre-2012 Best
Staisiunaite	Egle	LTU	30.9.88	174/59	400h	56.58	58.37- 11
* Stambolova	Vania	BUL	28.11.83	173/63	400	50.87	49.53- 06
					400h	54.04	53.68- 11
Stanciu	Daniela	ROU	15.10.87	175/57	HJ	1.88	1.88- 11
Stanková	Eliska	CZE	11.11.84		DT	58.70	57.82- 11
Starostina	Oksana	RUS	1.4.88		HJ	1.92	1.88- 11
Starovoytova	Anastasiya	BLR	4.11.82	162/50	Mar	2:27:24	2:34:08- 11
Stately	Bryson	USA	22.11.86	165/57	PV	4.40	4.35- 07
Steacy	Heather	CAN	14.4.88	175/73	HT	72.16	70.98- 11
Stechschulte/Norton	Abbie	USA	28.4.85	173/60	Hep	5855	5927- 11
Steel	Gemma	GBR	12.11.85		10k	32:34.81	-0-
					HMar	70:46	72:21- 11
Stef	Claudia	ROU	25.2.78	160/48	20kW	1:31:46	1:27:41- 04
Stefanídi	Ekateríni	GRE	4.2.90	172/60	PV	4.51	4.45- 11
Steiner Bennett	April	USA	22.4.80	175/58	PV	4.50	4.63- 08
Stellingwerff	Hilary	CAN	7.8.81	160/48	800	2:01.22	2:02.20- 07
					1500	4:05.08	4:05.69- 07
					1M	4:29.37i, 4:31.04	4:28.62- 07
Stepaniuk	Kamila	POL	22.3.86	184/65	HJ	1.89	1.93- 09
Stepanova	Lyudmila	RUS	15.8.83		5000	15:31.98	
Steryíou	Adonía	GRE	7.7.85	180/58	HJ	1.93	1.97- 08
Stewart	Emily	GBR	24.12.91		3kSt	9:53.47	-0-
* Stewart	Kerron	JAM	16.4.84	175/61	100	10.94	10.75- 09
					200	22.70	21.99- 08
Stewart	Thandi	USA	19.12.91	162/52	400h	56.34	57.71- 11
Stoddart	Shevon	JAM	21.11.82	165/52	400h	56.09	54.47- 05
Storm	Ida	SWE	11.10.91	188/	HT	66.48	63.72- 11
Stowe	Rebeka	USA	9.3.90		3kSt	9:52.82	9:53.12- 11
Stowers	Jasmin	USA	23.9.91	175/64	100h	12.92	12.88, 12.86w- 11
* Strachan	Anthonique	BAH-J	22.8.93	168/57	100	11.20	11.38- 11
					200	22.53	22.70- 11
Straneo	Valeria	ITA	5.4.76	168/44	10k	32:15.87	32:35.11- 11
					HMar	67:46	69:42- 11
					Mar	2:23:44	2:26:33- 11
Stratton	Brooke	AUS-J	12.7.93		LJ	6.56	6.60- 11
Strokova	Yekaterina	RUS	17.12.89		DT	63.52	59.61- 11
* Strutz	Martina	GER	4.11.81	160/57	PV	4.60	4.80- 11
Stuart	Bianca	BAH	17.5.88		LJ	6.79i, 6.66	6.81, 6.91w- 11
Stublic	Lisa	CRO	18.5.84	158/44	HMar	70:31 distance?	74:15- 11
Stuy	Hrystyna	UKR	3.2.88	168/57	200	22.66	22.79- 11
^ Styopina	Viktoriya	UKR	21.2.76	175/56	HJ	1.93i, 1.90	2.02- 04
Su Xinyue		CHN	8.11.91	179/70	DT	60.32	57.57- 11
Sudarova	Olga	BLR	22.2.84	176/63	LJ	6.85	6.72- 08
Sudarushkina	Viktoriya	RUS	2.9.90		JT	60.59	58.46- 11
Sugihara	Kayo	JPN	24.2.83	161/43	10k	32:32.89	31:34.35mx- 11, 31:47.60- 06
Suh Hae-an		KOR	1.7.85	181/93	JT	56.36	57.61- 10
* Suhr	Jenn	USA	5.2.82	180/64	PV	4.88i, 4.83	4.92- 08
Sujew	Diana	GER	2.11.90	166/52	1500	4:05.71	4:09.13- 11
Sujew	Elina	GER	2.11.90	164/51	1500	4:07.36	4:10.80- 11
Sum	Eunice	KEN	2.9.88	159/53	800	1:59.13	1:59.66A- 11
					1500	4:04.26	4:12.41- 11
					3000	8:53.12	
Summers	Jeré	USA	21.5.87		DT	59.59	57.68- 08
Sun Huanhuan		CHN	15.3.90	161/50	20kW	1:30:21	1:29:46- 11
Sun Lamei		CHN	4.1.91		Mar	2:27:55	2:41:16- 09
Sun Taifeng		CHN	26.8.82	185/105	DT	62.32	64.98- 07
Sun Xueping		CHN	10.12.88	160/48	20kW	1:32:46	1:33:19- 09
Sun Yan		CHN	30.3.91		TJ	13.78	14.00- 10
Sutej	Tina	SLO	7.11.88	173/58	PV	4.55i, 4.55	4.61- 11
Svechnikova	Anastasiya	UZB	20.9.92	165/60	JT	61.17	60.06- 11
Sviridova	Olesya	RUS	28.10.89		SP	19.72	18.34- 11
Sylvester	Patricia	GRN	3.2.83	175/59	LJ	6.60	6.71- 08
Szabó	Barbara	HUN	17.2.90		HJ	1.88Ai, 1.86	1.85- 09
Szlezak	Matylda	POL	11.1.89	165/54	3kSt	9:39.87	9:48.77- 11
Szwarnóg	Agnieszka	POL	28.12.86	167/59	20kW	1:30:56	1:33:50- 11
Tadese	Feyse	ETH	19.11.88	167/53	HMar	68:56	68:44- 11
					Mar	2:23:07	2:25:20- 11
Tadesse	Mestawat	ETH	19.7.85		3000	8:54.40i	8:56.62i- 04, 9:01.86- 05
Tadesse	Yeshimebet	ETH	.88		Mar	2:27:50	2:27:45- 10
* Tafa Magarsa	Askale	ETH	27.9.84		Mar	2:25:29	2:21:31- 08
Tago	Miyabi	JPN	15.7.88	170/50	400h	56.57	55.99- 10
Takács	Julia	ESP	29.6.89	171/55	20kW	1:30:37	1:30:14- 10
Takaki	Ayame	JPN	15.7.92	162/41	10k	32:24.43	
Takashima	Yuka	JPN	12.5.88	153/42	10k	32:34.49	32:22.93- 10

Name		Nat	Born	Ht/Wt	Event	2012 Mark	Pre-2012 Best
* Talay	Alina	BLR	14.5.89	164/54	100h	12.71	12.87- 10
Tallent	Claire	AUS	7.6.81	163/52	20kW	1:28:53	1:32:02- 10
Tamsett	Lara	AUS	12.10.88	161/47	10k	32:01.60	32:20.39- 09
* Tan Jian		CHN	20.1.88	179/80	DT	64.45	63.72- 11
Tanaka	Tomomi	JPN	25.1.88	154/40	10k	32:27.70	
					HMar	69:47	74:57- 08
Tannehill	Katie	USA	9.9.87	175/	PV	4.36i, 4.30	4.41- 10
Tanner	Alexis	USA	24.8.87		LJ	6.72w	6.12- 11
Tarantinova	Natalya	RUS	28.11.87		3kSt	9:52.92	9:44.60- 11
* Tarasova	Irina	RUS	15.4.87		SP	19.35	18.72- 11
Tarasova	Zlata	RUS	2.12.86		HT	67.63	66.36- 11
* Tarmoh	Jeneba	USA	27.9.89	165/59	100	11.07	11.19- 10, 10.94w- 11
					200	22.35, 22,30w	22.28- 11
Tashpulatova	Anna	BLR	21.10.87	169/61	400	51.43	51.79- 11
Tate	Cassandra	USA	11.9.90	174/64	400h	55.22	55.99- 11
Tavares	Maria Eleonor	POR	24.9.85	164/55	PV	4.42i, 4.35	4.50- 11
Tavernier	Alexandra	FRA-J	13.12.93	170/75	HT	70.62	62.13- 11
Tebo	Jessica	USA	8.4.88		5000	15:19.43	15:25.58- 11
Teferi	Senbera	ETH-Y	3.5.95	159/45	1500	4:06.06	4:09.80- 11
Teodoro	Lucimar	BRA	1.5.81	178/67	400h	56.24	55.84- 09
Terlecki	Josephine	GER	17.2.86	183/84	SP	18.87	18.29- 11
Ter-Mesrobyan	Tatyana	RUS	12.5.68	178/59	LJ	6.63	7.06- 02
Terrero	Indira	CUB	29.11.85	161/52	400	51.71	50.98A, 50.5- 08, 51.00- 07
Terzic	Amela	SRB-J	2.4.93	169/50	1500	4:07.59	4:13.46- 10
* Theisen	Brianne	CAN	18.12.88	180/64	100h	13.09A, 13.30, 13.21w	13.39- 10
HJ	1.88i		1.86- 10		Hep	6440	6094- 10
Theron	Wanda	RSA	30.7.88	165/60	400h	55.36A, 55.79	56.13- 11
^ Thiam	Ami Mbacké	SEN	10.11.76	183/70	400	51.68	49.86- 01
Thiam	Nafissatou	BEL-J	19.8.94		HJ	1.88	1.81- 11
					Hep	5916	-0-
Thipe ¶	Tsholofelo	RSA	9.12.86	168/53	200	22.89A, 23.21	23.28A- 08, 23.25Aw- 09
					400	51.47A, 51.79	
Thomas	Charlene	GBR	6.5.82	166/52	1500	4:07.06	4:05.06- 09
Thomas	LaTavia	USA	17.12.88	173/	800	2:01.27	1:59.67- 11
Thomas	Reyare	TRI	23.11.87	168/60	100	11.30	11.43- 09, 11.36w- 11
Thomas	Shanieka	JAM	2.2.92		TJ	13.64, 13.96w	12.98i, 12.90- 11
Thomas	Vashti	USA	21.4.90	175/60	100h	13.31, 13.02w	13.03- 07
					LJ	6.97	6.45- 10
Thompson	Turquoise	USA	31.7.91	178/66	400h	55.28	55.53- 11
^ Thondike	Arasay	CUB	28.5.86	165/83	HT	69.56	73.90- 09
Thorsteinsdóttir	Helga Margrét	ISL	15.11.91		Hep	5752	5878- 09
* Thurmond	Aretha	USA	14.8.76	181/98	DT	63.44	65.86- 04, 66.23dh- 03
Tigâu	Viorica	ROU	12.8.79	171/60	LJ	6.76	6.85, 6.87w- 00
Tikhonova	Olesya	RUS	22.1.90		TJ	13.89	13.55- 11
Titimets	Hanna	UKR	5.3.89	173/62	400h	54.98	54.69- 11
Tkachuk	Anastasiya	UKR-J	20.4.93	168/56	800	2:00.78	2:00.37- 11
Toader	Eliza	ROU	12.5.90	170/54	JT	56.61	53.82- 11
Tokuda	Yuka	JPN	1.6.88	164/47	HMar	70:40	
Tola	Fate	ETH	22.10.87		Mar	2:25:14	
* Tomasevic	Dragana	SRB	4.6.82	175/80	DT	61.92	63.63- 06
* Tomashova	Tatyana	RUS	1.7.75	165/52	1500	3:59.71	3:56.91- 06
Tomic	Marina	SLO	30.4.83	167/55	100h	13.04	13.10- 11
Tong Lingling		CHN	25.1.92		20kW	1:31:32	1:33:14- 11
^ Topic	Biljana	SRB	17.10.77	180/60	TJ	13.85i, 13.66	14.56- 09
Toroitich	Beatrice	KEN	15.12.81		Mar	2:27:41	2:32:58- 11
Torr	Veronica	NZL	17.5.87	175/61	Hep	5837	5520- 10
Torres	Marestella	PHI	20.2.81	174/63	LJ	6.62	6.71- 11
Townsend	Tiffany	USA	14.6.89	163/50	100	11.22	11.13- 09, 11.09w- 11
					200	22.96, 22.93w	22.58- 11
Tracey	Ristananna	JAM	5.9.92		400h	55.64	54.58- 11
* Trost	Alessia	ITA-J	8.3.93	188/68	HJ	1.92	1.90- 10
* Trotter	Deedee	USA	8.12.82	180/63	400	49.72	49.64- 07
Trybanska	Malgorzata	POL	21.6.81	177/59	TJ	13.88	14.44- 10
^ Tsander	Olga	BLR	18.5.76	174/83	HT	70.40	76.66- 05
Tsaranok	Olesya	RUS	3.7.89		400h	56.76	56.75- 10
Tschirch	Cathleen	GER	23.7.79	167/54	100	11.30, 1.19w	11.35- 09, 11.17w- 11
					200	22.98	22.97- 07, 22.87w- 11
* Tsegaye	Tirfe	ETH	25.11.84	165/54	HMar	67:42	69:24- 09
					Mar	2:21:19	2:22:44- 10
Tsyhotska	Ruslana	UKR	23.3.86	166/49	TJ	14.53	14.45- 11
Tuliamuk	Aliphine	KEN	5.4.89		5000	15:26.07	15:51.37- 11

Name		Nat	Born	Ht/Wt	Event	2012 Mark	Pre-2012 Best
Turner	Laura	GBR	12.8.82	168/57	100	11.27	11.11- 10, 11.09w- 07
Tutayeva ¶	Yuliya	RUS	7.12.88		800	1:59.40	1:59.83- 11
Tverdohlib	Margaryta	UKR	2.6.91	179/70	LJ	6.80	6.37- 11
^ Twell	Stephanie	GBR	17.8.89	168/54	1500	4:07.49	4:02.54- 10
					5000	15:15.24	14:54.08- 10
* Uceny	Morgan	USA	10.3.85	168/55	1500	4:01.59	4:00.06- 11
Udoh	Christy	NGR	30.9.91	173/58	200	22.72	23.03- 11
Ugen	Lorraine	GBR	22.8.91		LJ	6.74, 6.83w	6.54- 11
Uhl	Lisa	USA	31.8.87		3000	8:52.95	8:53.14i- 11, 9:05.62- 10
5000 15:15.22			14:55.74- 10		10k	31:12.80	31:18.07- 10
Urbaniak	Lena	GER	31.10.92	175/	SP	17.21i, 16.62	16.65- 11
Urbanik	Danuta	POL	24.12.89	167/58	1500	4:08.32	4:09.04- 11
Urbina	María Teresa	ESP	20.3.85	177/53	3kSt	9:49.03	9:41.95- 09
Urech	Lisa	SUI	27.7.89	168/53	100h	13.08	12.62- 11
^ Usovich	Ilona	BLR	14.11.82	170/60	400	51.31	50.31- 07
^ Usovich	Svetlana	BLR	14.10.80	165/52	400	51.00	50.55i- 05, 50.79- 04
					800	1:58.72	1:58.11- 07
* Ustalova	Kseniya	RUS	14.1.88	177/65	400	50.48, 50.1	49.92- 10
Utriainen	Sanni	FIN	5.2.91	170/64	JT	59.31	58.24- 11
Utura	Sule	ETH	8.2.90	169/50	10k	31:41.54	32:06.89- 11
* Valyukevich	Viktoriya	RUS	22.5.82	178/63	TJ	14.64	14.85- 08
Van Dalen	Lucy	NZL	18.11.88	168/53	1500	4:05.76	4:11.59- 11
					5000	15:23.54	
VanBuren	Cleo	USA	1.5.86	175/60	100	11.29, 11.28w	11.10- 06
Vargas	Mailín	CUB	24.3.83	175/77	SP	18.21	19.13- 11
Varner	Rachel	USA	20.7.83	175/86	DT	57.75	57.93- 04
* Vasco	María	ESP	26.12.75	156/45	20kW	1:28:14	1:27:25- 08
Vasilyeva	Svetlana	RUS	24.7.92		20kW	1:28:30	-0-
Vasilyeva	Yuliya	RUS	23.3.87		3000	8:51.62	
1M 4:31.52i					5000	15:20.41	15:40.00i- 11, 15:40.23- 09
Vaughan	Shelbi	USA-J	24.8.94	188/91	DT	60.59	53.78- 11
Vaughn	Sara	USA	16.5.86		1500	4:08.34	4:08.74- 11
Vdovina	Kseniya	RUS	19.4.87	172/62	400	50.43	50.67- 11
* Veldáková	Dana	SVK	3.6.81	178/59	TJ	14.36	14.51- 08, 14.59w- 10
Veldáková	Jana	SVK	3.6.81	177/59	LJ	6.65	6.72- 08, 6.88w- 10
* Veneva-Mateeva	Venelina	BUL	13.6.74	179/61	HJ	1.95	2.04- 01
^ Veshkurova	Tatyana	RUS	23.9.81	180/70	400	51.85, 51.8	49.99- 06
* Vessey #	Maggie	USA	23.12.81	172/53	800	1:59.98, 1:59.61dq	1:57.84- 09
Vetter	Anouk	NED-J	4.2.93		Hep	5764	5549- 11
Vicenzino	Tania	ITA	1.4.86	168/59	LJ	6.57, 6.65w	6.54- 09
Vichy	Ariannis	CUB	18.5.89	170/70	HT	71.50	69.02- 11
* Viljoen	Sunette	RSA	6.1.83	168/63	JT	69.35	68.38- 11
Virbalyté	Brigita	LTU	1.2.85	165/50	20kW	1:31:08	1:32:08- 09
Vitobello	Chiara	ITA	21.10.91	173/59	HJ	1.89	1.88i, 1.86- 10
Viuf	Katy	USA	23.5.87	175/61	PV	4.50	4.32- 10
Vlasova	Natalya	RUS	19.7.88		3kSt	9:37.41	9:55.05- 11
Volkova	Nina	RUS	26.8.84		HT	67.82	64.87- 11
von Eynatten	Victoria	GER	6.10.91	174/54	PV	4.37i, 4.17	4.35i- 10, 4.30- 11
Voronenkova	Yekaterina	RUS	8.9.88	169/57	200	23.02	23.37i, 23.42, 23.10w- 11
Vucenovic	Marija	SRB-J	3.4.93	172/70	JT	57.12	54.73- 11
Vyatkina	Natalya	BLR	10.2.87	176/50	TJ	13.84i, 13.36	14.32- 11
Wade	Bettie	USA	11.9.86	178/64	Hep	6143	6052(w)- 11, 6000- 10
Wade	Rebecca	USA	9.2.89	160/48	3kSt	9:48.04	10:12.16- 09
Wafula	Lydia	KEN	15.2.88		800	2:00.27	2:02.84- 05
Wagner	Marion	GER	1.2.78	178/60	100	11.48, 11.30w	11.24- 09
Wainaina	Beatrice	KEN-J	20.11.93	161/45	5000	15:21.77	15:36.74- 09
					HMar	70:17	-0-
Wairimu	Susan	KEN	11.10.92	160/40	5000	15:31.74	15:40.30- 11
					10k	32:29.94	
Waite	Lennie	GBR	4.5.86	173/60	3kSt	9:48.35	9:49.67- 11
Waithera	Mary	KEN-J	12.12.94	169/49	3000	8:48.16	8:58.07- 11
					5000	15:22.82	15:36.86mx- 11
Waldet	Olivia	FRA	23.5.84	177/85	HT	65.93	67.20- 08
Waldron	Sarah	GBR	11.2.88		10k	32:36.07	33:51.08- 11
Walker	Melaine	JAM	1.1.83	173/55	400h	53.74	52.42- 09
* Walker	Sarah	USA	2.4.86	178/83	SP	18.79	18.40- 07
Wallace	Keisha	JAM	25.1.90		100h	13.16, 12.97w	13.33, 13.24w- 11
Wallace	Latosha	USA	25.3.85	173/60	400h	55.18	55.85- 08
Wallace	Lea	USA	19.12.88	163/52	800	2:01.33	2:02.15- 11
Walter	Carolin	GER	29.2.88	168/55	800	2:01.29i	2:04.22- 09
Wang Chunyu		CHN-Y	17.1.95		800	2:01.48	2:01.34- 11

Name		Nat	Born	Ht/Wt	Event	2012 Mark	Pre-2012 Best
Wang Huiqin		CHN	7.2.90	168/52	TJ	14.16	14.03- 11
Wang Jiali		CHN	1.2.86	164/47	Mar	2:22:41	2:26:12- 11
Wang Lu		CHN	22.12.91		HT	65.80	63.82- 11
Wang Ping		CHN	28.7.90		JT	59.14	58.42- 11
Wang Rong		CHN-Y	1.7.96		TJ	13.76	
Wang Shanshan		CHN	16.6.87	168/50	20kW	1:29:43	1:29:54- 09
Wang Xueqin		CHN	1.1.91	162/50	Mar	2:25:53	2:28:17- 10
Wang Yang		CHN	14.2.89	185/65	HJ	1.92	1.88- 10
Wang Zheng		CHN	14.12.87	174/87	HT	69.14	71.19- 10
Wanjiru	Rosemary	KEN-J	9.12.94	158/45	3000	8:51.97	9:09.42- 11
Ward	Shericka	USA	30.3.90	168/57	100h	13.09	13.12- 10
Washington	Asia	USA	25.2.88		400h	56.78	56.90- 09
Watanabe	Yuko	JPN	3.11.87	151/41	HMar	70:06	71:40- 11
Weber	Liane	GER	24.2.86	179/60	Hep	5713	5928- 10
Weightman	Laura	GBR	1.7.91	172/56	1500	4:02.99	4:07.94mx- 11, 4:12.82- 10
Weightman	Lisa	AUS	16.1.79	157/44	HMar	70:10	69:00- 10
					Mar	2:27:32	2:28:48- 10
Weissteiner	Silvia	ITA	13.7.79	163/46	5000	15:06.81	15:02.65- 07
Weit	Inna	GER	5.8.88	166/56	200	23.08	24.08- 11
Weitzel	Michelle	GER	18.6.87	181/63	LJ	6.48, 6.60w	6.64- 11
Wellings	Eloise	AUS	9.11.82	172/53	5000	15:20.28	14:54.11- 06
					10k	32:25.43	31:41.31- 11
* Wells	Kellie	USA	16.7.82	163/57	100h	12.48	12.50, 12.35w- 11
Wells	Sarah	CAN	10.11.89	167/56	400h	55.71A, 55.97	56.85- 10
Weng Chunxia		CHN	29.8.92		DT	58.64	56.85- 11
Wesh	Marlena	HAI	16.2.91	167/55	200	23.06	23.26- 11
					400	51.23A, 51.43	52.28- 11
Wessman	Anna	SWE	9.10.89	164/70	JT	57.75i, 54.68A	57.09- 11
Weygandt	Shade	USA	24.1.91	168/54	PV	4.50	4.45- 11
Wheatley	Megan	AUS	10.3.88		Hep	5832	5800- 09
White	Skylar	USA	15.9.91		SP	17.42i, 16.91	17.16- 11
					DT	57.67	54.34- 11
Whittaker	Lanie	USA	21.5.91	170/57	400	52.06	53.25- 08
^ Whyte	Angela	CAN	22.5.80	170/56	100h	12.83, 12.75w	12.63, 12.55w- 07
* Whyte	Rosemarie	JAM	8.9.86	175/66	400	50.08	49.84- 11
Williams	Alisha	USA	5.2.82		5000	15:24.82	15:45.75- 10
					10k	32:03.07	33:17.46- 11
* Williams	Charonda	USA	27.3.87	167/55	100	11.13, 10.95w	11.14- 09
					200	22.52	22.55, 22.39w- 09
Williams	Gabrielle	USA-Y	6.9.96		HJ	1.89	1.78- 11
* Williams	Kimberly	JAM	3.11.88	169/66	TJ	14.53	14.25- 11, 14.38w- 09
Williams	Lauryn	USA	11.9.83	157/57	100	11.15, 10.96w	10.88- 05, 10.86w- 08
					200	22.96, 22.8	22.27- 05
Williams	Nadia	GBR	17.11.81	170/66	TJ	13.71	13.77, 13.94w- 11
* Williams	Shericka	JAM	17.9.85	170/54	400	50.34	49.32- 09
Williams	Shermaine	JAM	4.2.90	174/62	100h	12.78, 12.65w	13.03, 12.95w- 11
Williams	Sonnisha	USA	20.4.91	168/59	LJ	6.59	6.50- 11
Williams	Tameka	SKN	31.8.89	165/52	100	11.09w, 11.18 dq?	11.42- 10, 11.33w- 11
					200	22.45	23.06A, 22.89w- 11, 23.19- 08
Williams	Tiffany	USA	5.2.83	158/57	400h	55.01	53.28- 07
* Williams-Mills	Novlene	JAM	26.4.82	170/57	400	49.78	49.63- 06
Wilson	Ajee'	USA-J	8.5.94	168/52	800	2:00.91	2:02.64- 11
* Wilson	Nickiesha	JAM	28.7.86	173/64	100h	13.00	12.79. 12.72w- 09
					400h	55.50	53.97- 07
^ Wineberg	Mary	USA	3.1.80	178/61	400	51.93	50.24- 07
Wisil	Toea	PNG	1.1.88	168/63	100	11.49, 11.27w	11.49- 10
Wisniewska	Joanna	POL	24.5.72	178/84	DT	61.92	63.97- 99
* Wlodarczyk	Anita	POL	8.8.85	178/94	HT	77.60	78.30- 10
Woodward	Krista	CAN	22.11.84	163/59	JT	59.34	58.64- 11
Wortham	Ellen	USA	5.1.90	174/61	400h	55.55	55.70- 11
Wright	Joanna	USA	3.5.89	165/	PV	4.35i	4.31- 11
Wright	Phoebe	USA	30.8.88	170/57	800	1:59.72	1:58.22- 10
					1500	4:08.72	4:08.60- 11
Wu Shujiao		CHN	19.6.92	143/43	100h	12.98	13.19- 11
Xie Lijuan		CHN-J	14.5.93		20kW	1:33:25	1:36:03- 11
^ Xie Limei		CHN	27.6.86	173/57	TJ	14.21i, 13.82	14.90- 07
Xu Shaoyang		CHN	9.2.83	173/70	DT	58.24	63.29- 08
Xu Tingting		CHN	12.7.89		TJ	13.79	14.15- 08
Xu Xiaoling		CHN	13.5.92		LJ	6.63	6.52- 10
Xue Juan		CHN	10.2.86	174/65	JT	59.95	62.93- 03
Yakovenko	Olga	UKR	1.6.87	159/46	20kW	1:32:07	1:32:08- 11

Name		Nat	Born	Ht/Wt	Event	2012 Mark	Pre-2012 Best
Yang Fei		CHN	20.7.87	186/90	DT	60.43	59.45- 11
Yang Qi		CHN	13.4.91	171/58	400h	56.65	56.69- 11
Yang Xinli		CHN	7.2.88		JT	59.88	54.99- 11
Yang Yanbo		CHN	9.3.90		SP	17.01	17.41- 11
					DT	63.32	62.26- 11
Yang Yawei		CHN	16.10.83	168/51	20kW	1:33:12	1:27:58- 05
* Yanit	Nevin	TUR	16.2.86	168/60	100h	12.58	12.63- 10
* Yaroshchuk	Anna	UKR	24.11.89	176/67	400h	54.35	54.77- 11
Yastrebova	Nataliya	UKR	12.10.84	175/57	TJ	14.18	14.50- 11
Yatsevich	Anastasiya	BLR	18.1.85		20kW	1:32:16	1:29:30- 11
Ye Jiaying		CHN-J	7.1.93		HJ	1.88	1.84- 09
^ Yefremova ¶	Antonina	UKR	19.7.81		400	51.86dq	50.69- 11
Yepimashko	Vera	BLR	10.7.76	181/74	SP	17.53	18.95- 10
Yeremina	Lyudmila	RUS	8.8.91		PV	4.40i, 4.21	4.30i- 10, 4.30- 11
^ Yevdokimova	Natalya	RUS	17.3.78	178/65	800	2:01.25	1:58.75- 03
					1500	4:01.85	3:57.73- 05
Yin Annuo		CHN	23.3.92		3kSt	9:41.44	9:49.55- 11
Yoneda	Tomomi	JPN	11.8.90	166/52	400h	56.21	57.10- 11
Yoshikawa	Mika	JPN	16.9.84	155/39	5000	15:16.77	15:15.33mx- 11, 15:28.44- 10
					10k	31:28.71	31:55.06- 11
* Yosypenko	Lyudmyla	UKR	24.9.84	175/63	Hep	6618	6423- 09
Youngblood	Jamesha	USA	24.4.89		LJ	6.50, 6.54w	6.63- 10
Yumanova	Irina	RUS	6.11.90		20kW	1:26:47	1:29:26- 11
Yurkovich	Rachel	USA	10.10.86	180/77	JT	61.06	60.40- 11
Yushchenko	Yulianna	BLR	14.8.84	173/56	400	52.12	51.01- 07
* Zabara	Olesya	RUS	6.10.82	165/56	TJ	14.41, 14.48w	14.54i- 08, 14.50- 06
* Zadorina	Kseniya	RUS	2.3.87	173/59	400	51.26	50.87- 10
^ Zadorozhnaya	Yelena	RUS	3.12.77	157/42	5000	15:18.73	14:40.47- 01
Zadura	Malgorzata	POL	3.10.82	171/85	HT	69.15	70.36- 10
Zagré	Anne	BEL	13.3.90	178/69	100h	12.79	13.09- 11
Zakari	Joyce	KEN	6.6.86	170/60	400	51.85	51.56- 09
Zaldívar	Liuba M.	CUB-J	5.4.93	163/53	TJ	13.91, 14.18w	13.70- 11
Zang Milama	Ruddy	GAB	6.6.87	156/46	100	11.03	11.09- 11
Zapounídou	Déspina	GRE	5.10.85	166/55	20kW	1:31:08	1:32:47- 11
Zârcan	Georgiana	ROU	30.5.88	174/54	HJ	1.88	1.89- 10
* Zaripova	Yuliya	RUS	26.4.86	172/54	1500	4:01.70	4:04.59- 09
					3kSt	9:05.02	9:07.03- 11
Zavyalova	Valeriya	RUS	16.1.88		TJ	14.37	14.21- 11
* Zelinka	Jessica	CAN	3.9.81	172/62	100h	12.65	12.97- 08
200	23.32, 23.20w		23.64- 08		Hep	6599A, 6480	6490- 08
Zemedkun	Belaynesh	ETH	23.12.87		HMar	68:51	69:17- 11
Zemlyak	Olga	UKR	16.1.90	165/55	400	51.82	53.40- 09
Zhang Li		CHN	17.1.89	174/65	JT	64.74	62.09- 08
Zhang Rong		CHN	5.1.83	174/65	100h	13.07	13.06- 11
* Zhang Wenxiu		CHN	22.3.86	182/108	HT	76.99	75.65- 11
Zhao Jing		CHN	9.7.88	168/55	800	2:01.46	2:02.10- 11
Zhatkina	Lyubov	RUS	30.3.90		JT	58.52	54.80- 10
Zheng Xingjuan		CHN	20.3.89	184/60	HJ	1.92i, 1.92	1.95- 09, 1.94i- 10
* Zhou Chunxiu		CHN	15.11.78	162/51	Mar	2:23:42	2:19:51- 06
* Zhu Xiaolin		CHN	20.2.84	166/50	Mar	2:24:19	2:23:57- 02
Zhudina	Valentyna	UKR	12.3.83	160/49	3kSt	9:37.02	9:27.26- 08
Zhuk	Angelina	RUS	7.2.91		PV	4.40	4.30i, 4.25- 11
Zhukovskaya	Oksana	RUS	12.9.84		LJ	6.72i, 6.64	6.77- 07, 6.95w- 11
Zhushman	Olena	UKR	30.12.85	172/58	800	1:59.32	2:04.20- 11
Zolotova	Yevgeniya	RUS	28.4.83		800	2:00.79	1:59.85- 09
Zongo-Filet	Amy	FRA	4.10.80	165/52	TJ	14.02, 14.16w	14.08i- 09, 14.03- 08
Zubkovska	Oksana	UKR	15.7.81		LJ	6.60	6.71- 07
Züblin	Linda	SUI	21.3.86	171/58	Hep	5850	6018- 08
Zyabkina	Viktoriya	KAZ	4.9.92	170/55	200	22.92	23.26- 11
					400	51.67	
Zyuganova	Yekaterina	RUS	18.1.91		SP	17.03	15.97- 11

WORLD INDOOR LISTS 2013 – MEN

60 METRES

! In late 2012, # Oversized track (over 200m)

Time	First	Last	Nat	DOB	Pos	Meet	Venue	Date
6.48	Jimmy	Vicaut	FRA	27.2.92	1	EI	Göteborg	2 Mar
6.48	James	Dasaolu	GBR	5.9.87	2	EI	Göteborg	2 Mar
6.49A	DeAngelo	Cherry	USA	1.8.90	1	NC	Albuquerque	3 Mar
6.53					1h1	NCAA	Fayetteville	8 Mar
6.50	Darvis	Patton	USA	4.12.77	1	Mill	New York (Armory)	16 Feb
6.51	Yunier	Pérez	CUB	16.2.85	1		Mondeville	2 Feb
6.51	Michael	Tumi	ITA	12.2.90	1	NC	Ancona	17 Feb
6.52	Lerone	Clarke	JAM	2.10.81	1		Düsseldorf	8 Feb
6.53	Michael	Rodgers	USA	24.4.85	1	GP	Birmingham	16 Feb
6.53	Kim	Collins	SKN	5.4.76	1		Metz	24 Feb
6.54	Marvin	Bracy	USA	15.12.93	1	Tyson	Fayetteville	8 Feb
6.54A	Reginald	Dixon	USA	7.6.88	2	NC	Albuquerque	3 Mar
6.55	Ángel David	Rodríguez	ESP	25.4.80	3		Düsseldorf	8 Feb
6.55		Su Bingtian	CHN	29.8.89	1rA		Nanjing	6 Mar
6.55	Marcus	Rowland	USA	11.3.90	2	NCAA	Fayetteville	9 Mar
6.56	Dentarius	Locke	USA	12.12.89	2	Tyson	Fayetteville	8 Feb
6.56	Nesta	Carter	JAM	10.11.85	2	GP	Birmingham	16 Feb
6.56	Julian	Reus	GER	29.4.88	1	NC	Dortmund	23 Feb
6.57A	Joe	Morris	USA	4.10.89	1		Air Force Academy	12 Jan
6.57	Darrell	Wesh	USA	21.1.92	2h1	NCAA	Fayetteville	8 Mar
6.58	Dwain	Chambers	GBR	5.4.78	1	v4N	Glasgow	26 Jan
6.58A	Jeremy	Dodson	USA	30.8.87	3	NC	Albuquerque	3 Mar
6.58		Zhang Peimeng	CHN	13.3.87	1		Beijing	29 Mar
6.59	Jaysuma	Saidy Ndure	NOR	1.7.84	2s1	EI	Göteborg	2 Mar

Time	First	Last	Nat	DOB	Date		Time	First	Last	Nat	DOB	Date
6.60	Yevgeniy	Ustavshchikov	RUS	20.7.88	1 Feb		6.61	Harry	Adams	USA	27.11.89	9 Mar
6.60	Catalin	Cîmpeanu	ROU	10.3.85	9 Feb		6.62	Mark	Jelks	USA	10.4.84	25 Jan
6.60	Antoine	Adams	SKN	31.8.88	16 Feb		6.62	Patrick	Chinedu	NGR	26.4.84	1 Feb
6.60	Marquesh	Woodson	USA	6.9.93	24 Feb		6.62	Egwero	Ogho-Oghene	NGR	26.11.88	10 Feb
6.60	Charles	Silmon	USA	4.7.91	8 Mar		6.62	Reza	Ghasemi	IRI	24.7.87	14 Feb
6.61	Sean	Safo-Antwi	GBR	31.10.90	23 Jan		6.62	Richard	Kilty	GBR	2.9.89	17 Feb
6.61	Bryce	Robinson	USA		1 Feb		6.62	Odain	Rose	SWE	19.7.92	2 Mar
6.61	Cameron	Burrell	USA-J	11.9.94	24 Feb		6.62A	Cordero	Gray	USA	9.5.89	3 Mar
							6.62A	Keith	Ricks	USA	9.10.90	3 Mar

200 METRES

Time	First	Last	Nat	DOB	Pos	Meet	Venue	Date
20.37	Ameer	Webb	USA	19.3.91	1h1	NCAA	Fayetteville	8 Mar
20.47	Anaso	Jobodwana	RSA	30.7.92	1r2	NCAA	Fayetteville	8 Mar
20.48	Trey	Hadnot	USA	7.3.92	2r2	NCAA	Fayetteville	8 Mar
20.53	Aaron	Ernest	USA	8.11.93	1r2	SEC	Fayetteville	24 Feb
20.60	Lalonde	Gordon	TRI	25.11.88	1		Boston (Allston)	26 Jan
20.67	Akheem	Gauntlett	JAM	26.8.90	2r1	NCAA	Fayetteville	8 Mar

Time	First	Last	Nat	DOB	Date		Time	First	Last	Nat	DOB	Date
20.70	Dedric	Dukes	USA	4.2..92	24 Feb		20.76	Marek	Niit	EST	9.8.87	1 Mar
20.71	Wallace	Spearmon	USA	24.12.84	9 Feb		20.78	Prezel	Hardy	USA	1.6.92	12 Jan
20.72	Jonathan	Åstrand	FIN	9.9.85	9 Feb		**Oversized track**					
20.75		Zhang Peimeng	CHN	13,3,87	30 Mar		20.73	Omar	Johnson	JAM	25.11.88	2 Mar
							20.77	Blake	Heriot	USA	26.9.91	23 Feb

300 METRES

Time	First	Last	Nat	DOB	Pos	Venue	Date
32.48	Lalonde	Gordon	TRI	25.11.88	1	New York (Armory)	11 Jan
32.58	Pavel	Maslák	CZE	21.2.91	1	Gent	10 Feb
32.72	Kevin	Borlée	BEL	22.2.88	2	Gent	10 Feb
32.84	Jonathan	Borlée	BEL	22.2.88	1	Gent	2 Feb

400 METRES

Time	First	Last	Nat	DOB	Pos	Meet	Venue	Date
45.15	Deon	Lendore	TRI	28.10.92	1h1	SEC	Fayetteville	23 Feb
45.64	Michael	Berry	USA	10.12.91	2h1	NCAA	Fayetteville	8 Mar
45.66	Pavel	Maslák	CZE	21.2.91	1	EI	Göteborg	3 Mar
45.67	Hugh	Graham	USA	10.10.92	2r2	SEC	Fayetteville	24 Feb
45.72	Errol	Nolan	JAM	18.8.91	1h2	NCAA	Fayetteville	8 Mar
45.82A	Jeremy	Wariner	USA	31.1.84	1	NC	Albuquerque	3 Mar
45.92	Patrick	Feeney	USA	29.12.91	3h1	NCAA	Fayetteville	8 Mar

Time	First	Last	Nat	DOB	Date		Time	First	Last	Nat	DOB	Date
45.97	Najee	Glass	USA-J	12.6.94	8 Mar		46.09	Anton	Kokorin	RUS	5.4.87	9 Mar
46.00	Pavel	Trenikhin	RUS	24.3.86	2 Mar		46.14	Akheem	Gauntlett	JAM	26.8.90	1 Mar
46.02	Vernon	Norwood	USA	10.4.92	8 Feb		46.21	Nigel	Levine	GBR	30.4.89	3 Mar
46.07	Brian	Gregan	IRL	31.12.89	27 Jan		46.22	Richard	Strachan	GBR	18.11.86	2 Feb

Oversized track

Time	First	Last	Nat	DOB	Date	Pos		Venue	Date
45.83	David	Verburg	USA	14.5.91		1rA		Geneva	9 Feb
45.92	Brycen	Spratling	USA	10.3.92		1r1		Notre Dame	1 Mar
46.05	Christopher	Giesting	USA	10.12.92	1 Mar		46.07	Stephon Pamilton	USA	19.9.91	23 Feb

600 METRES

Time	First	Last	Nat	DOB	Pos	Meet	Venue	Date
1:15.60	Muhammad	Aman	ETH-J	10.1.94	1rA		Moskva	3 Feb
1:15.61	Erik	Sowinski	USA	21.12.89	1	Mill	New York (Armory)	16 Feb

1:15.63 Pierre-Ambroise Bosse   FRA   11.5.92   1rB   Moskva   3 Feb
1:15.70 Duane   Solomon   USA   28.12.84   1   v4N   Glasgow   26 Jan
1:15.79 Casimir   Loxsom   USA   17.3.91   1   University Park   26 Jan
1:16.08 Abdulrahman Musaeb Bala QAT 19.3.89 3 Feb | 1:16.22 David   Greene   GBR 11.4.86 26 Jan
1:16.19 Jarrin   Solomon   TRI 11.1.86 16 Feb | 1:16.27 Yuriy   Borzakovskiy RUS 12.4.81 3 Feb
Oversized track
1:15.42 Casimir   Loxsom   USA   17.3.91   1r1 Big 10 Geneva   23 Feb
1:15.80 Harun   Abda   SOM   1.1.90   1r2 Big 10 Geneva   23 Feb

800 METRES

1:45.05 Muhammad   Aman   ETH-J 10.1.94   1   Stockholm   21 Feb
1:46.07 Leoman   Momoh   USA   30.3.91   1   Fayetteville   1 Mar
1:46.53# Lopez   Lomong   USA   1.1.85   1   Seattle   9 Feb
1:46.55 Michael   Rimmer   GBR   3.2.86   1   GP   Birmingham   16 Feb
1:46.57 Abubaker   Kaki   SUD   21.6.89   2   GP   Birmingham   16 Feb
1:46.58 Mukhtar   Mohammed   GBR   1.12.90   3   GP   Birmingham   16 Feb
1:46.62 Adam   Kszczot   POL   2.9.89   2   Stockholm   21 Feb
1:46.72 Kevin   López   ESP   12.6.90   1   Karlsruhe   2 Feb

1:46.73# Elijah   Greer   USA 24.10.90 23 Feb | 1:47.06 Anthony   Chemut   KEN 17.12.92 10 Feb
         1:47.13   9 Mar | 1:47.09# Mark   Wieczorek USA 25.12.84 9 Feb
1:46.75 Abraham   Rotich   KEN 26.6.93 10 Feb | 1:47.09A Erik   Sowinski   USA 21.12.89 3 Mar
1:46.76 Tomas   Squella CHI 18.10.91 1 Mar | 1:47.13A Robby   Andrews   USA 29.3.91   3 Mar
1:46.80# Tyler   Mulder   USA 15.2.87 9 Feb | 1:47.14 Andreas   Vojta   AUT 9.6.89   31 Jan
         1:47.18A   2 Mar | 1:47.19 Francisco Roldán   ESP 26.5.90   27 Jan
1:46.96 Luis Alberto Marco ESP 20.8.86 27 Jan | 1:47.24# Joe   Abbott   USA 3.3.90   2 Feb
1:46.96 Zan   Rudolf   SLO 9.5.93   31 Jan | 1:47.39# Felix   Kitur   KEN 17.4.87   9 Feb
1:46.97 Andrew   Osagie   GBR 19.2.88 16 Feb | 1:47.41 Guy   Learmonth GBR 24.4.92   16 Feb
1:46.98 Casimir   Loxsom   USA 17.3.91 12 Jan | 1:47.42# Boru   Guyota   ETH 1.1.90   23 Feb
                                                   | 1:47.43# Edward   Kemboi   KEN 12.12.91 26 Jan

1000 METRES

2:17.05 Ayanleh   Souleiman   DJI   3.12.92   1   Stockholm   21 Feb
2:17.77 Marcin   Lewandowski POL   13.6.87   2   Stockholm   21 Feb

2:17.90 Robby Andrews USA 29.3.91 2 Feb | 2:18.27 Michael Rutt   USA 28.10.87 1 Mar
2:18.26 Brian Gagnon   USA 8.5.87   1 Mar | 2:18.78 Andrew   Osagie GBR 19.2.88   21 Feb

1500 METRES

3:34.78+ Galen   Rupp   USA   8.5.86   1   in 1M Boston (Allston)   26 Jan
3:35.25 Bethwell   Birgen   KEN   6.8.88   1   Moskva   3 Feb
3:35.31 Aman   Wote   ETH   18.4.84   2   Moskva   3 Feb
3:36.13 Ayanleh   Souleiman   DJI   3.12.92   1rA   Düsseldorf   8 Feb
3:36.52+ Lopez   Lomong   USA   1.1.85   1   in 1M New York (Armory)   16 Feb
3:36.65+ Matthew   Centrowitz   USA   18.10.89   2   in 1M New York (Armory)   16 Feb
3:36.69 Collins   Cheboi   KEN   25.9.87   3   Moskva   3 Feb
3:36.85+ Ciarán   O'Lionáird   IRL   11.4.88   3   in 1M New York (Armory)   16 Feb
3:36.95 Mahiedine   Mekhissi-Benabbad FRA 15.3.85 1   Karlsruhe   2 Feb
3:37.22 Ilham   Özbilen   TUR   5.3.90   2   EI   Göteborg   3 Mar
3:37.25+ Chris   O'Hare   GBR   23.11.90   4   in 1M New York (Armory)   16 Feb
3:37.32 Abdelaati   Iguider   MAR   25.3.87   3   Metz   24 Feb

3:37.55 Valentin Smirnov   RUS   13.2.86   3 Feb | 3:39.20+ Ryan   Gregson   AUS 26.4.90   16 Feb
3:37.64 Teshome   Diressa   ETH-J 25.4.94   2 Feb | 3:39.30 Mekonnen   Gebremedhin   ETH 11.10.88 16 Feb
3:37.70 Simon   Denissel   FRA   22.5.90   3 Mar | 3:39.36 Arturo   Casado   ESP 26.1.83   3 Mar
3:37.99 Daniel Kipchirchir Komen KEN 27.11.84 3 Feb | 3:39.38 Tesfaye Homiyu   ETH 23.6.93   8 Feb
3:38.34 Marcin   Lewandowski POL   13.6.87   16 Feb | 3:39.46 Hélio   Gomes   POR 27.12.84 3 Mar
3:38.36 Yegor   Nikolayev   RUS   12.2.88   3 Feb | 3:39.50+ Ryan   Hill   USA 31.1.90   16 Feb
3:38.41 David   Bustos   ESP   25.8.90   8 Feb | 3:39.65 Bartosz   Nowicki   POL 26.2.84   2 Feb
3:38.58 Benson   Seurei   KEN   27.3.88   8 Feb | 3:39.97 Florian   Orth   GER 24.7.89   2 Feb
3:38.60+ Lawi   Lalang   KEN   15.6.91   16 Feb | 3:40.02 Cornelius Ndiwa   KEN 17.12.88 29 Jan
3:38.61+ Garrett Heath   USA   3.11.85   16 Feb | 3:40.10 Álvaro   Rodríguez   ESP 25.5.87   2 Feb
3:38.73 Bouabdellah Tahri   FRA   20.12.78   16 Feb | 3:40.24 Bryan   Cantero   FRA 28.4.91   2 Feb
3:39.15 Andreas   Vojta   AUT   9.6.89   16 Feb | 3:40.41 Florian   Carvalho   FRA 9.3.89   8 Feb

1 MILE

3:50.92 Galen   Rupp   USA   8.5.86   1   Boston (Allston)   26 Jan
3:51.21 Lopez   Lomong   USA   1.1.85   1   Mill   New York (Armory)   16 Feb
3:51.34 Matthew   Centrowitz   USA   18.10.89   2   Mill   New York (Armory)   16 Feb
3:52.10 Ciarán   O'Lionáird   IRL   11.4.88   3   Mill   New York (Armory)   16 Feb
3:52.98 Chris   O'Hare   GBR   23.11.90   4   Mill   New York (Armory)   16 Feb
3:54.56 Lawi   Lalang   KEN   15.6.91   5   Mill   New York (Armory)   16 Feb

3:54.89 Ryan   Hill   USA 31.1.90   16 Feb | 3:56.35 William   Leer   USA 15.4.85   2 Feb
3:55.55 Garrett Heath   USA 3.11.85   16 Feb | 3:56.41# Donn   Cabral   USA 12.12.89 9 Feb
3:55.97 Ryan   Gregson   AUS 26.4.90   16 Feb | 3:56.85 Craig   Miller   USA 3.8.87   2 Feb
3:56.04 Richard Peters   GBR 18.2.90   14 Feb | 3:57.11# Robert   Creese   USA 30.8.93   9 Feb
3:56.12# Andrew Bumbalough   USA 14.3.87   9 Feb | 3:57.14# Michael Atchoo   USA 16.8.91   23 Feb
3:56.14# Evan   Jager   USA 8.3.89   9 Feb | 3:57.22 David   McCarthy IRL 3.8.88   26 Jan
3:56.25 Riley   Masters   USA 5.4.90   8 Feb | 3:57.43 Jeff   See   USA 6.6.86   2 Feb
3:56.28 Patrick Casey   USA 23.5.90   26 Jan | 3:57.79# Raul   Botezan   ROU 22.4.88   9 Feb

| 3:57.81 | Cory | Leslie | USA | 24.10.89 | 2 Feb | 3:57.85 | Chris | Gowell | GBR | 26.9.85 | 8 Feb |
| 3:57.81 | Craig | Huffer | AUS | 27.10.89 | 2 Feb | 3:57.93 | Austin | Mudd | USA | 13.5.93 | 9 Mar |

2000 METRES

| 5:00.59 | Soresa | Fida | ETH | 27.5.93 | 1 | | Metz | 24 Feb |
| 5:00.69 | Bouabdellah | Tahri | FRA | 20.12.78 | 2 | | Metz | 24 Feb |

| 5:02.13 | Abiyot | Abinet | ETH | 10.5.89 | 26 Jan | 5:02.16 | Bernard | Kiptum | KEN | 8.10.86 | 26 Jan |

3000 METRES

7:30.16	Galen	Rupp	USA	8.5.86	1		Stockholm	21 Feb
7:31.66	Caleb	Ndiku	KEN	9.10.92	2		Stockholm	21 Feb
7:32.87	Hagos	Gebrhiwet	ETH-J	11.5.94	1	BIG	Boston (Roxbury)	2 Feb
7:34.71	Bernard	Lagat	USA	12.12.74	1		Karlsruhe	2 Feb
7:34.92	Abdelaati	Iguider	MAR	25.3.87	3		Stockholm	21 Feb
7:38.35	Paul Kipsiele	Koech	KEN	10.11.81	4		Stockholm	21 Feb
7:38.57	Yenew	Alamirew	ETH	27.5.90	2		Karlsruhe	2 Feb
7:39.59	Albert	Rop	KEN-J	20.12.94	1		Gent	10 Feb
7:39.59	Hayle	Ibrahimov	AZE	18.1.90	5		Stockholm	21 Feb
7:39.81	Ayanleh	Souleiman	DJI	3.12.92	3		Gent	10 Feb
7:39.98+	Evan	Jager	USA	8.3.89	2	in 2M	New York (Armory)	16 Feb
7:40.41+	Andrew	Bumbalough	USA	14.3.87	3	in 2M	New York (Armory)	16 Feb
7:41.16	Daniel Kipchirchir	Komen	KEN	27.11.84	4		Gent	10 Feb
7:41.59	Mekonnen	Gebremedhin	ETH	11.10.88	5		Gent	10 Feb
7:41.74+	Cameron	Levins	CAN	28.3.89	4	in 2M	New York (Armory)	16 Feb
7:42.00	KaravMohammed	Farah	GBR	23.3.83	1	GP	Birmingham	16 Feb
7:42.79	Lawi	Lalang	KEN	15.6.91	1		Fayetteville	26 Jan
7:43.32	Dejen	Gebremeskel	ETH	24.11.89	3	BIG	Boston (Roxbury)	2 Feb
7:43.47	Tesfaye	Cheru	ETH	2.3.93	7		Stockholm	21 Feb
7:43.72	Mahiedine	Mekhissi-Benabbad	FRA	15.3.85	3		Düsseldorf	8 Feb
7:43.99	Aman	Wote	ETH	18.4.84	8		Stockholm	21 Feb
7:44.18	Bouabdellah	Tahri	FRA	20.12.78	9		Stockholm	21 Feb

7:45.77	Florian	Carvalho	FRA	9.3.89	16 Feb	7:48.49	Andrey	Safronov	RUS	16.12.85	12 Feb
7:46.72	Yoann	Kowal	FRA	28.5.87	2 Feb	7:48.64	Augustine	Choge	KEN	21.1.87	2 Feb
7:46.95	Kemoy	Campbell	JAM	14.1.91	9 Mar	7:49.17	Kirubel	Erassa	USA	17.6.93	9 Mar
7:47.01	Valentin	Smirnov	RUS	13.2.86	12 Feb	7:49.20#	Ryan	Hill	USA	31.1.90	9 Feb
7:47.16	Simon	Denissel	FRA	22.5.90	10 Feb	7:49.53	Diego	Estrada	MEX	12.12.89	9 Mar
7:47.57	Yegor	Nikolayev	RUS	12.2.88	12 Feb	7:49.55	Juan Carlos	Higuero	ESP	3.8.78	2 Feb
7:47.91#	Henry	Lelei	KEN	31.12.88	1 Mar	7:49.98+	Leonard	Korir	KEN	10.12.86	16 Feb
7:48.20	Stephen	Kiprotich	KEN	25.11.90	23 Feb	7:50.23+	Will	Leer	USA	15.4.85	16 Feb

Disqualified for impeding: 7:46.21 Eric Jenkins USA 24.11.91 (2) NCAA Fayetteville 9 Mar

TWO MILES

New York (Armory) 16 Feb: (Mill) 1. Bernard Lagat USA 12.12.74 8:09.49, 3. Andrew Bumbalough USA 8:13.02, 3. Cameron Levins CAN 8:14.69, 4. Evan Jager USA 8:14.95 8.3.89; 5. Will Leer USA 8:21.53, 6. Leonad Korir 8:22.44

5000 METRES

13:07.00	Lopez	Lomong	USA	1.1.85	1		New York (Armory)	1 Mar
13:12.00	Chris	Derrick	USA	17.10.90	2		New York (Armory)	1 Mar
13:23.68	Andrew	Bumbalough	USA	14.3.87	3		New York (Armory)	1 Mar
13:25.38	Kennedy	Kithuka	KEN	4.6.89	1	NCAA	Fayetteville	8 Mar

| 13:30.24 | Diego | Estrada | MEX | 12.12.89 | 8 Mar | 13:33.47 | Evan | Jager | USA | 8.3.89 | 1 Mar |
| 13:33.22 | Elliott | Heath | USA | 4.2.89 | 1 Mar | 13:35.46 | Matt | Tegenkamp | USA | 19.1.82 | 1 Mar |

60 METRES HURDLES

7.49	Sergey	Shubenkov	RUS	4.10.90	1	EI	Göteborg	1 Mar
7.50	Kevin	Craddock	USA	25.6.87	1		Düsseldorf	8 Feb
7.50	Edward	Lovett	USA	25.6.92	1	NCAA	Fayetteville	9 Mar
7.51	Omo	Osaghae	USA	18.5.88	1	GP	Birmingham	16 Feb
7.51	Paolo	Dal Molin	ITA	31.7.87	2	EI	Göteborg	1 Mar
7.53	Pascal	Martinot-Lagarde	FRA	22.9.91	1	NC	Aubière	16 Feb
7.54	Orlando	Ortega	CUB	29.7.91	1h2		Karlsruhe	2 Feb
7.56	Dimitri	Bascou	FRA	20.7.87	2	NC	Aubière	16 Feb
7.56	Balázs	Baji	HUN	9.6.89	4	EI	Göteborg	1 Mar
7.58	Andrew	Pozzi	GBR	15.5.92	1h2		Birmingham	3 Feb
7.58	Erik	Balnuweit	GER	21.9.88	5	EI	Göteborg	1 Mar
7.58	Maksim	Lynsha	BLR	6.4.85	6	EI	Göteborg	1 Mar
7.59	Spencer	Adams	USA	10.9.89	1r1		New York (Armory)	1 Feb
7.59	Konstantin	Shabanov	RUS	17.11.89	1		Moskva	3 Feb
7.59	Jeff	Porter	USA	27.11.85	1	Mill	New York (Armory)	16 Feb
7.59	Wayne	Davis II	TRI	22.8.91	2	NCAA	Fayetteville	9 Mar

7.60		Xie Wenjun	CHN	11.7.90	16 Feb	7.63	Keiron	Stewart	JAM	21.11.89	8 Mar
7.60	Andrew	Riley	JAM	9.9.88	16 Feb	7.64	Konstadíinos	Douvalídis	GRE	10.3.87	1 Mar
7.62A	Brendan	Ames	USA	6.10.88	1 Feb	7.65	Caleb	Cross	USA	31.5.91	8 Feb
7.63	Aries	Merritt	USA	24.7.85	26 Jan	7.65	Yordan	O'Farrill	CUB-J	9.2.93	8 Feb
7.63	Jarret	Eaton	USA	24.6.89	16 Feb	7.66	Barrett	Nugent	USA	29.1.90	8 Feb

7.67	Gianni	Frankis	GBR	16.4.88	29 Jan
7.68	Greggmar	Swift	BAR	16.2.91	8 Feb
7.68	Ray	Stewart	USA	5.4.89	22 Feb
7.68	Gregor	Traber	GER	2.12.92	23 Feb
7.68	Rasul	Dabó	POR	14.2.89	1 Mar
7.69	Koen	Smet	NED	9.8.92	13 Jan
7.69	Terence	Somerville	USA	5.11.89	15 Feb
7.69	Matthias	Bühler	GER	2.9.86	23 Feb
7.69	Vladimir	Vukicevic	NOR	6.5.91	1 Mar
7.69	Keith	Hayes	USA	16.2.90	8 Mar

Hand timing

7.5	Maksim	Lynsha	BLR	6.4.85	17 Jan

HIGH JUMP

Mark	First	Last	Nat	DOB	Pos		Venue	Date
2.37	Moataz Essa	Barshim	QAT	24.6.91	1		Moskva	3 Feb
2.36	Aleksey	Dmitrik	RUS	12.4.84	1		Arnstadt	2 Feb
2.35	Sergey	Mudrov	RUS	8.9.90	1	El	Göteborg	2 Mar
2.35	Derek	Drouin	CAN	6.3.90	1	NCAA	Fayetteville	9 Mar
2.34	Dusty	Jonas	USA	19.4.86	1		Lincoln	2 Feb
2.33	Erik	Kynard	USA	3.2.91	1		Manhattan, KS	16 Feb
2.33	Silvano	Chesani	ITA	17.7.88	1	NC	Ancona	17 Feb
2.32		Zhang Guowei	CHN	4.6.91	1		Nanjing	7 Mar
2.31	Robert	Grabarz	GBR	3.10.87	1	NC	Sheffield	10 Feb
2.31	Jaroslav	Bábá	CZE	2.9.84	3	El	Göteborg	2 Mar
2.30	Mihai	Donisan	ROU	24.7.88	1		Bucuresti	18 Jan
2.30	Ivan	Ukhov	RUS	29.3.86	1		Hustopece	26 Jan
2.30	Gianmarco	Tamberi	ITA	1.6.92	3		Banská Bystrica	6 Feb
2.30	Konstadínos	Baniótis	GRE	6.11.86	5		Banská Bystrica	6 Feb
2.30		Wang Yu	CHN	18.8.91	1		Brno	12 Feb
2.30	Dmitriy	Semyonov	RUS	2.8.92	2	NC	Moskva	13 Feb
2.30	Daniyil	Tsyplakov	RUS	12.7.92	3	NC	Moskva	13 Feb
2.30	Viktor	Ninov	BUL	19.6.88	1		Praha	14 Feb
2.29	Richard	Robertson	USA	19.9.90	1		Jonesboro	25 Jan
2.29	Donald	Thomas	BAH	1.7.84	4	GP	Birmingham	16 Feb
2.29	Adonios	Mástoras	GRE	6.1.91	4	El	Göteborg	2 Mar
2.29	Marcus	Jackson	USA	8.7.91	2	NCAA	Fayetteville	9 Mar
2.28	Mickaël	Hanany	FRA	25.3.83	Q	El	Göteborg	1 Mar

Mark	First	Last	Nat	DOB	Date
2.27	James	White	USA	22.1.92	12 Jan
2.27	Montez	Blair	USA	23.10.90	19 Jan
2.27	Alexandru	Tufa	ROU	28.5.89	25 Jan
2.27	Marco	Fassinotti	ITA	29.4.89	26 Jan
2.27	Ilya	Ivanyuk	RUS	9.3.93	31 Jan
2.27	Ivan	Ilyichev	RUS	14.10.86	3 Feb
2.27	Andrey	Patrakov	RUS	7.11.89	13 Feb
2.26	Edward	Wright	USA	3.3.86	11 Jan
2.26	Torian	Ware	USA	17.12.92	11 Jan
2.26	Matus	Bubeník	SVK	14.11.89	22 Jan
2.26	Edgar	Rivera-Morales	MEX	13.2.91	25 Jan
2.26	Matthias	Haverney	GER	21.7.85	25 Jan
2.26	Osku	Torro	FIN	21.8.79	26 Jan
2.26	Michal	Kabelka	SVK	4.2.85	26 Jan
2.26	Geoffrey	Davis	USA	8.8.90	16 Feb
2.26	James	Harris	USA	18.9.91	1 Mar
2.26	Ronnie	Black	USA	2.8.90	9 Mar
2.25	Nikita	Anishchenkov	RUS	25.7.92	26 Jan
2.25	Jeremy	Taiwo	USA	15.1.90	8 Feb
2.25	Yuriy	Krymarenko	UKR	11.8.83	14 Feb
2.25	Dmytro	Demyanyuk	UKR	30.6.83	14 Feb
2.25	Vitaliy	Samoylenko	UKR	22.5.84	14 Feb

POLE VAULT

Mark	First	Last	Nat	DOB	Pos		Venue	Date
6.01	Renaud	Lavillenie	FRA	18.9.86	1	El	Göteborg	3 Mar
5.90	Björn	Otto	GER	16.10.77	1		Cottbus	30 Jan
5.83	Konstadínos	Filippídis	GRE	26.11.86	1		Linz	31 Jan
5.82	Raphael	Holzdeppe	GER	28.9.89	2		Rouen	26 Jan
5.81	Malte	Mohr	GER	24.7.86	1		Zweibrucken	9 Mar
5.80		Yang Yansheng	CHN	5.1.88	2		Düsseldorf	8 Feb
5.77	Jan	Kudlická	CZE	29.4.88	1	NC	Praha (Strom)	17 Feb
5.75		Xue Changrui	CHN	31.5.91	2		Nevers	23 Feb
5.75	Hendrik	Gruber	GER	28.9.86	3	NC	Dortmund	24 Feb
5.75	Tobias	Scherbarth	GER	17.8.85	4	NC	Dortmund	24 Feb
5.71	Seito	Yamamoto	JPN	11.3.92	1		Osaka	3 Feb
5.71	Augusto	de Oliveira	BRA	16.7.90	1		São Caetano do Sul	2 Mar
5.71	Steven	Lewis	GBR	20.5.86	6=	El	Göteborg	3 Mar
5.71	Robert	Sobera	POL	19.1.91	6=	El	Göteborg	3 Mar
5.70	Sergey	Kucheryanu	RUS	30.6.85	3	Mast	Donetsk	9 Feb
5.70	Fábio Gomes	da Silva	BRA	4.8.83	1		São Caetano do Sul	23 Feb
5.70	Valentin	Lavillenie	FRA	16.7.91	3		Metz	24 Feb
5.70	Andrew	Irwin	USA	23.1.93	1	NCAA	Fayetteville	8 Mar
5.65	Karsten	Dilla	GER	17.7.89	1		Leverkusen	19 Jan
5.65	Anton	Ivakin	RUS	3.2.91	1	NC	Moskva	14 Feb
5.63	Rasmus	Jørgensen	DEN	23.1.89	3		Potsdam	16 Feb
5.62	Jérôme	Clavier	FRA	3.5.83	2		Orleans	12 Jan
5.62	Emile	Denecker	FRA	28.3.92	3		Rouen	26 Jan
5.62	Alhaji	Jeng	SWE	13.12.81	6		Rouen	26 Jan
5.62		Zhang Wei	CHN-J	22.3.94	1		Lyon	7 Feb
5.62	Stanley	Joseph	FRA	24.10.91	2		Villeurbanne	10 Feb
5.62	Romain	Mesnil	FRA	13.6.77	3		Villeurbanne	10 Feb
5.62	Robert	Renner	SLO-J	8.3.94	4		Villeurbanne	10 Feb
5.61	Jack	Whitt	USA	12.4.90	1		Norman	22 Feb

Mark	First	Last	Nat	DOB	Date
5.60	Shawn	Barber	CAN-J	27.5.94	11 Jan
5.60A	Michael	Woepse	USA	29.5.91	8 Feb
5.60	Ivan	Horvat	CRO	17.8.93	23 Feb
5.60	Marek	Arents	LAT	6.6.86	23 Feb

Mark	First	Last	Nat	DOB	Date
5.60	Ivan	Yeryomin	UKR	30.5.89	2 Mar
5.60	Jason	Wurster	CAN	23.9.84	2 Mar
5.60A	Jordan	Scott	USA	22.2.88	3 Mar
5.60	Sam	Kendricks	USA	7.9.92	8 Mar
5.60	Jake	Blankenship	USA-J	15.3.94	8 Mar
5.60	Daichi	Sawano	JPN	16.9.80	15 Mar
5.55	Eemeli	Salomäki	FIN	11.10.87	26 Jan
5.55	Maksym	Mazuryk	UKR	2.4.83	5 Feb
5.55	Giuseppe	Gibilisco	ITA	5.1.79	5 Feb
5.55	Artem	Burya	RUS	11.4.86	14 Feb
5.55	Aleksandr	Gripich	RUS	21.9.86	14 Feb
5.55	Kevin	Menalso	FRA	12.7.92	17 Feb
5.55A	Jake	Winder	USA	12.11.87	3 Mar
5.55A	Jeff	Coover	USA	1.12.87	3 Mar
5.54A	Victor	Weirich	USA	25.10.87	9 Feb
5.54A	Cale	Simmons	USA	5.2.91	9 Feb
5.53	Carlo	Paech	GER	18.12.92	16 Feb
5.53A	Logan	Cunningham	USA	30.5.91	23 Feb
5.51	Shawn	Francis	USA	16.12.85	1 Feb
5.51	Thiago	da Silva	BRA	16.12.93	16 Feb
5.51	João Gabriel	Sousa	BRA	6.11.84	2 Mar
5.50	14 men				

LONG JUMP

Mark	First	Last	Nat	DOB	Pos	Meet	Venue	Date
8.31	Aleksandr	Menkov	RUS	7.12.90	1	EI	Göteborg	3 Mar
8.29	Michel	Tornéus	SWE	26.5.86	2	EI	Göteborg	3 Mar
8.28	Marquis	Dendy	USA	17.11.92	1	NCAA	Fayetteville	8 Mar
8.21	Damar	Forbes	JAM	18.9.90	2	NCAA	Fayetteville	8 Mar
8.15	Yeóryios	Tsákonas	GRE	22.1.88	1	NC	Athína (Pireás)	16 Feb
8.15	Khotso	Mokoena	RSA	6.3.85	2		Stockholm	21 Feb
8.15	Christian	Reif	GER	24.10.84	Q	EI	Göteborg	2 Mar
8.11	Eero	Haapala	FIN	10.7.89	1		Pori	26 Jan
8.11		Li Jinzhe	CHN	1.9.89	3		Stockholm	21 Feb
8.08	Loúis	Tsátoumas	GRE	12.2.82	2	NC	Athína (Pireás)	16 Feb
8.04	Jeremy	Hicks	USA	19.9.86	1		Baton Rouge	15 Feb
8.04	Daniel	Dobrev	BUL	7.4.92	1	NC	Dobrich	16 Feb
8.03	Tomas	Vitonis	LTU	19.9.91	1		Kuldiga	19 Jan
8.02		Gao Xinglong	CHN-J	12.3.94	1		Nanjing	6 Mar
8.00		Zhao Xiaoxi	CHN	19.3.89	2		Nanjing	6 Mar

Mark	First	Last	Nat	DOB	Date
7.98	Michael	Hartfield	USA	29.3.90	11 Jan
7.98	Valentin	Toboc	ROU	17.3.92	10 Feb
7.98	Christopher	Tomlinson	GBR	15.9.81	2 Mar
7.97	Sebastian	Bayer	GER	11.6.86	23 Feb
7.97		Zhang Yaoguang	CHN	21.6.93	6 Mar
7.96	Adrian	Vasile	ROU	9.4.86	26 Jan
7.96	Emanuele	Catania	ITA	3.10.88	3 Feb
7.96	Jarvis	Gotch	USA	25.3.92	16 Feb
7.96	Tommi	Evilä	FIN	6.4.80	3 Mar
7.95	Pavel	Karavayev ¶	RUS	27.8.88	11 Jan
7.95	Raymond	Higgs	BAH	24.1.91	11 Jan
7.95	Stefano	Tremigliozzi	ITA	7.5.85	16 Feb
7.94	Maksim	Kolesnikov	RUS	28.2.91	5 Jan
7.94	Matthew	Burton	GBR	18.12.87	9 Feb
7.93		Li Chengbin	CHN	22.2.90	6 Mar
7.93		Wang Jianan	CHN-Y	27.8.96	23 Mar
7.92	Elvijs	Misans	LAT	4.8.89	2 Mar
7.92	Jarrion	Lawson	USA-J	6.5.94	8 Mar

TRIPLE JUMP

Mark	First	Last	Nat	DOB	Pos	Meet	Venue	Date
17.70	Daniele	Greco	ITA	1.3.89	1	EI	Göteborg	2 Mar
17.30	Ruslan	Samitov	RUS	11.2.91	2	EI	Göteborg	2 Mar
17.17	Marian	Oprea	ROU	6.6.82	1		Bucuresti	25 Jan
17.16		Dong Bin	CHN	22.11.88	1		Nanjing	7 Mar
17.12	Aleksey	Fyodorov	RUS	25.5.91	3	EI	Göteborg	2 Mar
17.02	Viktor	Kuznetsov	UKR	14.7.86	4	EI	Göteborg	2 Mar
16.98	Dimitríos	Tsiámis	GRE	12.1.82	1		Athína (Pireás)	10 Feb
16.96	Bryce	Lamb	USA	9.11.90	1	NCAA	Fayetteville	9 Mar
16.94	Harold	Correa	FRA	26.6.88	1	NC	Aubière	16 Feb
16.94	Gaëtan	Saku Bafuanga	FRA	22.7.91	1		Metz	24 Feb
16.87	Tosin	Oke	NGR	1.10.80	1	NC	Sheffield	9 Feb
16.86	Benjamin	Compaoré	FRA	5.8.87	1		Val-de-Reuil	3 Feb
16.84	Yuriy	Kovalyov	RUS	18.6.91	1	NC-23	Volgograd	24 Feb
16.83	Karl	Taillepierre	FRA	13.8.76	2	NC	Aubière	16 Feb
16.80	Omar	Craddock	USA	26.4.91	2	NCAA	Fayetteville	9 Mar
16.73	Fabian	Florant	NED	1.2.83	1	Tyson	Fayetteville	9 Feb

Mark	First	Last	Nat	DOB	Date
16.70	Zlatozar	Atanasov	BUL	12.12.89	15 Feb
16.67	Yevgen	Semenenko	UKR	17.7.84	14 Feb
16.67	Aleksey	Tsapik	BLR	4.8.88	17 Feb
16.65	Michele	Boni	ITA	2.4.81	19 Jan
16.61	Viktor	Yastrebov	UKR	13.1.82	14 Feb
16.60	Vicente	Docavo	ESP	13.2.92	16 Feb
16.60	Samyr	Laine	HAI	17.7.84	24 Feb
16.59	Vladimir	Letnicov	MDA	7.10.81	23 Feb
16.59A	Josh	Honeycutt	USA	7.3.89	3 Mar
16.58	Georgi	Tsonov	BUL	2.5.93	1 Mar
16.54	Hugo	Mamba-Schlick	CMR	1.2.82	24 Feb
16.53	Tarik	Batchelor	JAM	22.3.90	24 Feb

SHOT

Mark	First	Last	Nat	DOB	Pos	Meet	Venue	Date
21.80	Ryan	Whiting	USA	24.11.86	1	NC	Albuquerque	3 Mar
20.98	Cory	Martin	USA	22.5.85	2		Bydgoszcz	12 Feb
20.89	Kurt	Roberts	USA	20.2.88	3	NC	Albuquerque	3 Mar
20.73	Martin	Stasek	CZE	8.4.89	1	NC	Praha (Strom)	17 Feb
20.62	Asmir	Kolasinac	SRB	15.10.84	1	EI	Göteborg	1 Mar
20.59	Jordan	Clarke	USA	10.7.90	1		Flagstaff	12 Jan
20.59	Georgi	Ivanov	BUL	13.3.85	1		Dobrich	12 Feb
20.51	Ladislav	Prásil	CZE	17.5.90	1		Praha (Strom)	22 Jan
20.34	Hamza	Alic	BIH	20.1.79	2	EI	Göteborg	1 Mar
20.29	Leif	Arrhenius	SWE	15.7.86	1		København	13 Feb
20.27	Dmytro	Savytskyy	UKR	14.12.90	1	NC	Sumy	13 Feb
20.25	Reese	Hoffa	USA	8.10.77	3		Nordhausen	18 Jan
20.18	Zach	Lloyd	USA	10.10.84	1		Provo	17 Jan
20.16	Ralf	Bartels	GER	21.2.78	4	EI	Göteborg	1 Mar

Mark	First	Last	Nat	DOB	Pos	Meet	Venue	Date
20.12	Derrick	Vicars	USA	8.5.89	1		Kent	12 Jan
20.10	Maksim	Sidorov	RUS	13.5.86	1	NC	Moskva	13 Feb
20.08	Nedsad	Mulabegovic	CRO	4.2.81	1		Rijeka	16 Feb
20.06	Mason	Finley	USA	7.10.90	1		Air Force Academy	26 Jan
20.05	Richard	Garrett	USA	.90	1	WAC	Albuquerque	22 Feb
20.02	Bozidar	Antunovic	SRB	24.7.91	2	WAC	Albuquerque	22 Feb
20.02	Marco	Fortes	POR	26.9.82	5	EI	Göteborg	1 Mar
20.02	Kole	Weldon	USA	25.3.92	2	NCAA	Fayetteville	8 Mar

Mark	First	Last	Nat	DOB	Date		Mark	First	Last	Nat	DOB	Date
20.00	Dan	Block	USA	8.1.91	8 Mar		19.71	Mihaíl	Stamatóyiannis	GRE	20.5.82	16 Feb
19.97	Valeriy	Kokoyev	RUS	25.7.88	13 Feb		19.70	Stephen	Saenz	MEX	23.8.90	24 Feb
19.92	Aleksandr	Bulanov	RUS	26.12.89	28 Feb		19.67	Kim	Christensen	DEN	1.4.84	12 Jan
19.89	Stephen	Mozia	USA	16.8.93	19 Jan		19.64	Martin	Premeru	CRO	29.8.90	16 Feb
19.86	Luke	Pinkelman	USA	5.5.88	2 Feb		19.63	Robert	Golabek	USA	27.4.89	15 Dec
19.81	Borja	Vivas	ESP	26.5.84	12 Jan		19.63	Hayden	Baillio	USA	22.7.91	24 Feb
19.81	Marco	Schmidt	GER	5.9.83	26 Jan		19.60	Andriy	Semenov	UKR	4.7.84	13 Feb
19.77	Niklas	Arrhenius	SWE	10.9.82	17 Feb		19.59	Jonathan	Jones	USA	23.4.91	22 Feb
19.76	Kemal	Mesic	BIH	4.8.85	17 Jan		19.59	Huseyin	Atici	TUR	3.5.86	28 Feb
19.76	Lajos	Kürthy	HUN	22.10.86	8 Feb		19.52	Jacob	Thormaehlen	USA	13.2.90	3 Mar
19.76		Wang Guangfu	CHN	15.11.87	29 Mar		19.52		Wang Like	CHN	2.4.89	29 Mar
19.72	Rafal	Kownatke	POL	24.3.85	2 Feb		19.50		Liu Yang	CHN	29.10.86	6 Mar

WEIGHT

Mark	First	Last	Nat	DOB	Pos	Meet	Venue	Date
23.69	Alexander	Ziegler	GER	7.7.87	1	ACC	Blacksburg	22 Feb
23.51	Jacob	Freeman	USA	5.11.80	1	NC	Albuquerque	2 Mar
23.37	A.G.	Kruger	USA	18.2.79	2	NC	Albuquerque	2 Mar
23.18	Mattias	Jons	SWE	19.11.82	1	NC	Norrköping	15 Feb
22.55	Brandon	Pounds	USA	24.9.89	1		Notre Dame	1 Feb
22.25	Antonio	James	USA	7.4.92	2	NCAA	Fayetteville	9 Mar

Mark	First	Last	Nat	DOB	Date		Mark	First	Last	Nat	DOB	Date
22.21	Lonnie	Pugh	USA	23.2.90	23 Feb		21.90	Chukwuebuka	Enekwechi	USA	28.1.93	23 Feb
22.20	Colin	Dunbar	USA	27.6.88	2 Mar		21.85	Justin	Welch	USA	29.9.91	7 Dec
22.00	Joe	Frye	USA	20.7.88	26 Jan		21.84	Micah	Hegerle	USA	2.10.89	15 Feb

HEPTATHLON

Points	First	Last	Nat	DOB	Pos	Meet	Venue	Date
6372	Eelco	Sintnicolaas	NED	7.7.87	1	EI	Göteborg	3 Mar
	6.88	7.61	14.11	2.02		7.91	5.40	2:38.73
6297	Kevin	Mayer	FRA	10.2.92	2	EI	Göteborg	3 Mar
	7.10	7.54	15.16	2.05		8.01	5.20	2:37.30
6232A	Gunnar	Nixon	USA	13.1.93	1	NC	Albuquerque	2 Mar
	6.86	7.42	14.27	2.14		7.93	4.80	2:41.49
6175	Kevin	Lazas	USA	25.1.92	1	NCAA	Fayetteville	9 Mar
	6.90	7.55	15.00	1.99		8.27	5.40	2:49.00
6165	Japheth	Cato	USA	25.12.90	2	NCAA	Fayetteville	9 Mar
	7.08	7.67	12.13	2.11		7.95	5.30	2:45.26
6156	Jeremy	Taiwo	USA	15.1.90	1		Nampa	9 Feb
	7.02	7.42	14.18	2.25		8.08	4.25	2:33.44
6145	Eduard	Mikhon	BLR	7.6.89	1	NC	Gomel	24 Jan
	6.93	7.56	14.81	2.04		8.06	4.70	2:39.06
6099	Mihail	Dudas	SRB	1.11.89	3	EI	Göteborg	3 Mar
	6.91	7.55	14.12	2.08		8.13	4.60	2:39.04
6095	Adam Sebastian	Helcelet	CZE	27.10.91	4	EI	Göteborg	3 Mar
	7.07	7.49	14.48	2.02		8.06	5.00	2:42.26
6038	Mikhail	Logvinenko	RUS	19.4.84	1		Irkutsk	26 Jan
	7.19	7.32	15.43	2.05		8.10	4.90	2:44.11
6024	Mikk	Pahapill	EST	18.7.83	1		Tallinn	2 Feb
	7.18	7.36	15.29	2.10		8.33	4.94	2:45.92
6018	Ilya	Shkurenyov	RUS	11.1.91	5	EI	Göteborg	3 Mar
	7.05	7.36	13.54	2.05		8.22	5.20	2:46.36
6017	Garrett	Scantling	USA	19.5.93	3	NCAA	Fayetteville	9 Mar
	7.07	7.04	14.12	2.11		8.10	5.10	2:47.07
6008	Artyom	Lukyanenko	RUS	30.1.90	1	NC	Volgograd	9 Feb
	7.04	7.23	15.23	2.00		8.04	4.90	2:45.62
5997	Jérémy	Lelièvre	FRA	8.2.91	1	NC	Aubière	17 Feb
	6.87	7.36	15.07	1.97		8.32	4.55	2:35.89
5979	Fabian	Rosenquist	SWE	1.4.91	6	EI	Göteborg	3 Mar
	7.00	7.53	13.24	2.02		8.30	4.80	2:38.14
5975	Maicel	Uibo	EST	27.12.92	4	NCAA	Fayetteville	9 Mar
	7.19	7.36	13.64	2.02		8.28	5.10	2:39.72
5973	Gaël	Quérin	FRA	26.6.87	3	NC	Aubière	17 Feb
	7.23	7.41	13.20	1.97		8.13	4.95	2:32.50
5937	Zach	Ziemek	USA		5	NCAA	Fayetteville	9 Mar
	7.01	7.22	12.73	2.05		8.37	5.40	2:50.06
5916	Luiz Alberto	de Araújo	BRA	27.9.87	2		Tallinn	2 Feb
	6.95	7.29	15.20	1.92		8.06	4.84	2:49.45
5906	Pelle	Rietveld	NED	4.2.85	8	EI	Göteborg	3 Mar
	6.95	7.22	13.79	1.90		7.93	4.80	2:40.98

5899	Kaarel	Jõeväli	EST	8.1.90	2 Feb		5817#	Derek	Drouin	CAN	6.3.90	23 Feb
5895A	Curtis	Beach	USA	22.7.90	2 Mar		5815	Matthias	Prey	GER	9.8.88	27 Jan
5873	Johannes	Hock	GER	24.3.92	9 Mar		5805	Tiago	Marto	POR	5.4.86	17 Feb
5847	Dominik	Distelberger	AUT	16.3.90	17 Feb		5803	Bastien	Auzeil	FRA	22.10.89	17 Feb
5826	Terry	Prentice	USA	7.1.89	9 Feb		5793	Andy	Lillejord	USA	30.5.90	9 Mar
5819	Tom	Bechert	GER	2.7.87	15 Dec		5783	Petter	Olson	SWE	14.2.91	10 Feb

3000m Walk: Athlone 27 Jan: 1. Robert Heffernan IRL 20.2.78 11:13.92, 2. Alex Weight GBR 19.12.90 11:23.99

5000 METRES WALK

18:28.54	Igor	Yerokhin	RUS	4.9.85	1		Samara	31 Jan
18:43.33	Valeriy	Borchin	RUS	11.9.86	2		Samara	31 Jan
18:55.65	Yohann	Diniz	FRA	1.1.78	1		Reims	3 Feb
19:03.48	Grzegorz	Sudol	POL	28.8.78	1	NC	Spala	17 Feb
19:06.16	Antonin	Boyez	FRA	9.11.84	1	NC	Aubière	17 Feb

19:13.03	Robert	Heffernan	IRL	20.2.78	16 Feb		19:19.08	Alsksandr	Lyakovich	BLR	4.7.89	17 Feb
19:13.16	Dawid	Tomala	POL	27.8.89	17 Feb		19:20.89	Oleksandr	Venglovskyy	UKR	5.8.85	29 Jan
19:18.66	Lukasz	Nowak	POL	18.12.88	17 Feb		19:22.98	Rafal	Augustyn	POL	14.5.84	17 Feb

10,000m Walk: 40:01.51   Oleksandr Venglovskyy UKR 5.8.85   1   NC   Sumi   13 Feb

WORLD INDOOR LISTS 2013 – WOMEN

60 METRES

6.99	Murielle	Ahouré	CIV	23.8.87	1	GP	Birmingham		16 Feb
7.04	Shelly-Ann	Fraser-Pryce	JAM	27.12.86	1		Stockholm		21 Feb
7.07	Myriam	Soumaré	FRA	29.10.86	1s2	EI	Göteborg		3 Mar
7.08A	Barbara	Pierre	USA	28.4.87	1	NC	Albuquerque		3 Mar
7.10	Mariya	Ryemyen	UKR	2.8.87	1s1	EI	Göteborg		3 Mar
7.10	Tezdzhan	Naimova	BUL	1.5.87	1	EI	Göteborg		3 Mar
7.10A	Lekeisha	Lawson	USA	3.6.87	2	NC	Albuquerque		3 Mar
7.12	Ruddy	Zang Milama	GAB	6.6.87	2		Moskva		3 Feb
7.12	Verena	Sailer	GER	16.10.85	1h1	EI	Göteborg		1 Mar
7.12	Ivet	Lalova	BUL	18.5.84	4	EI	Göteborg		3 Mar
7.13	Laverne	Jones-Ferrette	ISV	16.9.81	2		Houston		26 Jan
7.13	Aurieyall	Scott	USA	18.5.92	1		Birmingham, AL		24 Feb
7.13	Ezinne	Okparaebo	NOR	3.3.88	1h2	EI	Göteborg		1 Mar
7.14	Dafne	Schippers	NED	15.6.92	5	EI	Göteborg		3 Mar
7.15	Asha	Philip	GBR	25.10.90	1	NC	Sheffield		9 Feb
7.15	English	Gardner	USA	22.4.92	1h1	NCAA	Fayetteville		8 Mar
7.16	Kimberlyn	Duncan	USA	2.8.91	1r1		New York (Armory)		1 Feb
7.16	Octavious	Freeman	USA	20.4.92	3	NCAA	Fayetteville		9 Mar
7.18A	Carmelita	Jeter	USA	24.11.79	1		Albuquerque		2 Feb
7.18					4	GP	Birmingham		16 Feb
7.19	Dezerea	Bryant	USA	27.4.93	1		Clemson		11 Jan
7.19	Sheri-Ann	Brooks	JAM	11.2.83	3h1	GP	Birmingham		16 Feb
7.19A	Shayla	Mahan	USA	18.1.89	2h2	NC	Albuquerque		3 Mar

7.21A	Kya	Brookins	USA	28.7.89	3 Mar		7.24	Lauryn	Williams	USA	11.9.83	16 Feb
7.22	Jeneba	Tarmoh	USA	27.9.89	16 Feb		7.24	Trisha-Ann	Hawthorne	JAM	8.11.89	16 Feb
7.23	Tatjana	Pinto	GER	2.7.92	26 Jan		7.24	Jura	Levy	JAM	4.11.90	2 Mar
7.24	Katerina	Cechová	CZE	21.3.88	16 Feb		7.25	Montell	Douglas	GBR	14.1.86	13 Feb
							7.25	Hanni-Mari	Latvala	FIN	30.10.87	1 Mar

200 METRES

22.54	Kimberlyn	Duncan	USA	2.8.91	1	SEC	Fayetteville	24 Feb
22.68	Aurieyall	Scott	USA	18.5.92	1r1	Tyson	Fayetteville	9 Feb
22.70	Ashton	Purvis	USA	12.7.92	2	SEC	Fayetteville	24 Feb
22.72	Octavious	Freeman	USA	20.4.92	2h3	NCAA	Fayetteville	8 Mar
22.73	Kamaria	Brown	JAM	21.12.92	1rB	SEC	Fayetteville	24 Feb
22.81	Johanna	Danois	FRA	4.4.87	1	NC	Aubière	16 Feb
22.87	Myriam	Soumaré	FRA	29.10.86	1		Eaubonne	7 Feb
22.98	Margaret	Adeoye	GBR	27.4.85	1s1		Birmingham	3 Feb
23.00	Regina	George	NGR	17.2.91	1h1	SEC	Fayetteville	23 Feb
23.00	Dezerea	Bryant	USA	27.4.93	2r2	NCAA	Fayetteville	8 Mar

23.11	Trisha-Ann	Hawthorne	JAM	8.11.89	25 Jan		23.22	Brianna	Rollins	USA	18.8.91	2 Feb
23.13	Christy	Udoh	USA	30.9.91	8 Mar		23.23	Paris	Daniels	USA	25.1.90	8 Mar
23.14	Ashley	Collier	USA	4.2.92	23 Feb		23.26	Shaunae	Miller	BAH-J	15.4.94	9 Feb
23.15	Irene	Ekelund	SWE-Y	8.3.97	17 Feb		**Oversized track**					
23.20	Patricia	Hall	JAM	16.10.82	7 Feb		23.15	Paris	Daniels	USA	25.1.90	23 Feb
23.21	Yuliya	Katsura	RUS	28.5.83	16 Jan		23.20	Jura	Levy	JAM	4.11.90	2 Mar

300 METRES

36.76	Kseniya	Ustalova	RUS	14.1.88	1rA		Yekaterinburg	7 Jan
36.9+	Perri	Shakes-Drayton	GBR	21.12.88	1	in 400m	Göteborg	3 Mar
37.1+	Eilidh	Child	GBR	20.2.87	2/3	in 400m	Birmingham	16 Feb

400 METRES

50.85	Perri	Shakes-Drayton	GBR	21.12.88	1	EI	Göteborg	3 Mar

50.88	Natasha	Hastings	USA	23.7.86	1	GP	Birmingham	16 Feb
50.88	Shaunae	Miller	BAH-J	15.4.94	1r1	NCAA	Fayetteville	9 Mar
51.05	Regina	George	NGR	17.2.91	2r1	NCAA	Fayetteville	9 Mar
51.27	Zuzana	Hejnová	CZE	19.12.86	2s2	EI	Göteborg	1 Mar
51.27	Ashley	Spencer	USA	8.6.93	1r2	NCAA	Fayetteville	9 Mar
51.31	Kseniya	Ustalova	RUS	14.1.88	1	NC	Moskva	13 Feb
51.45	Eilidh	Child	GBR	20.2.87	2	EI	Göteborg	3 Mar
51.76	Kineke	Alexander	VIN	21.2.86	1r1		College Station	9 Feb
51.82	Ebonie	Floyd	USA	21.10.83	1r2		College Station	26 Jan
51.98	Marie	Gayot	FRA	18.12.89	1rA	NC	Aubière	17 Feb
52.01	Phyllis	Francis	USA	4.5.92	2r2	NCAA	Fayetteville	9 Mar
52.02	Indira	Terrero	CUB	29.11.85	1		Metz	24 Feb
52.04	Moa	Hjelmer	SWE	19.6.90	3	EI	Göteborg	3 Mar
52.07	Angela	Morosanu	ROU	26.7.86	1h2	EI	Göteborg	1 Mar

52.09	Georganne	Moline	USA	6.3.90	9 Mar		52.35	Margaret	Adeoye	GBR	22.4.85	24 Feb
52.12	Mary	Wineberg	USA	3.1.80	26 Jan		52.37	Ella	Räsänen	FIN-J	27.1.94	1 Mar
52.12	Denisa	Rosolová	CZE	21.8.86	1 Mar		52.38	Nadezhda	Kotlyarova	RUS	12.6.89	25 Jan
52.16	Kamaria	Brown	JAM	21.12.92	24 Feb		52.38	Diamond	Dixon	USA	29.6.92	9 Mar
52.18	Patricia	Hall	JAM	16.10.82	3 Feb		52.44	Jessica	Beard	USA	8.1.89	9 Feb
52.20	Francena	McCorory	USA	20.10.88	16 Feb		52.46	Olga	Tovarnova	RUS	11.4.85	13 Feb
52.22	Erika	Rucker	USA	29.9.93	24 Feb		52.48	Ebony	Eutsey	USA	3.5.92	23 Feb
52.24	Kseniya	Zadorina	RUS	2.3.87	25 Jan		52.52	Sparkle	McKnight	TRI	21.12.91	9 Mar

600 METRES

1:23.59	Alysia	Montaño	USA	26.4.86	1	Mill	New York (Armory)	16 Feb
1:26.45	Ajee'	Wilson	USA-J	8.5.94	2	Mill	New York (Armory)	16 Feb
1:26.48	Erica	Moore	USA	25.3.88	3	Mill	New York (Armory)	16 Feb

800 METRES

1:59.58	Yekaterina	Kupina	RUS	2.2.86	1		Belgorod	3 Feb
2:00.26	Nataliya	Lupu	UKR	4.11.87	1	EI	Göteborg	3 Mar
2:00.31	Alena	Glazkova	RUS	6.5.88	1h3	NC	Moskva	12 Feb
2:00.32	Svetlana	Podosyonova	RUS	24.5.88	2h3	NC	Moskva	12 Feb
2:00.90	Yelena	Kotulskaya	RUS	8.8.88	1h4	NC	Moskva	12 Feb
2:00.97	Marina	Pospelova	RUS	23.7.90	1h1	NC	Moskva	12 Feb
2:01.02	Jennifer	Meadows	GBR	17.4.81	1s1	EI	Göteborg	2 Mar
2:01.21	Marina	Arzamasova	BLR	17.1.87	3	EI	Göteborg	3 Mar
2:01.32	Ayvika	Malanova	RUS	28.11.92	2h1	NC	Moskva	12 Feb
2:01.32	Olha	Lyakhova	UKR	18.3.92	3s1	EI	Göteborg	2 Mar
2:01.43	Yekaterina	Poistogova	RUS	1.3.91	1		Novocheboksarsk	12 Jan

2:01.56	Olga	Lvova	RUS	21.9.89	12 Feb		2:02.18	Svetlana	Rogozina	RUS	26.12.92	12 Feb
2:01.64	Selina	Büchel	SUI	26.7.91	2 Mar		2:02.22	Irina	Maracheva	RUS	24.9.84	12 Feb
2:01.66	Svetlana	Cherkasova	RUS	20.5.78	12 Feb		2:02.27	Luiza	Gega	ALB	5.11.88	10 Feb
2:01.93	Malika	Akkaoui	MAR	25.12.87	12 Feb		2:02.32	Laura	Roesler	USA	19.12.91	9 Mar
2:01.93	Yelena	Soboleva	RUS	3.10.82	12 Feb		2:02.42	Anastasiya	Grigoryeva	RUS	23.11.88	12 Feb
2:02.00	Natoya	Goule	JAM	30.3.91	9 Mar		2:02.47	Charlene	Lipsey	USA	16.7.91	9 Mar

1000 METRES

drugs dq	4:07.65	Anzhela	Shevchenko ¶	UKR	29.10.87	(1)		Moskva	3 Feb
	2:36.97	Yekaterina	Poistogova	RUS	1.3.91	1		Moskva	3 Feb
	2:37.01	Yelena	Kotulskaya	RUS	8.8.88	2		Moskva	3 Feb

2:38.20	Marina	Pospelova	RUS	23.7.90	3 Feb		2:38.73	Svetlana	Podosyonova	RUS	24.5.88	3 Feb
2:38.38	Anna	Shchagina	RUS	7.12.91	11 Jan		2:38.95	Ayvika	Malanova	RUS	28.11.92	11 Jan

1500 METRES

3:58.40	Abeba	Aregawi	SWE	5.7.90	1		Stockholm	21 Feb
4:00.83	Genzebe	Dibaba	ETH	8.2.91	1	GP	Birmingham	16 Feb
drugs dq 4:07.65	Anzhela	Shevchenko ¶	UKR	29.10.87	(1)		Sankt Peterburg	24 Jan
4:07.99	Siham	Hilali	MAR	2.5.86	2	GP	Birmingham	16 Feb
4:09.11	Axumawit	Embaye	ETH-J	18.10.94	2		Stockholm	21 Feb
4:09.36	Rabab	Arrafi	MAR	12.1.91	3		Stockholm	21 Feb
4:09.86	Natalia	Rodríguez	ESP	2.6.79	2		Düsseldorf	8 Feb

4:09.90	Luiza	Gega	ALB	5.11.88	16 Feb		4:10.80+	Sheila	Reid	CAN	2.8.89	16 Feb
4:09.95	Anna	Shchagina	RUS	7.12.91	25 Jan		4:10.94	Isabel	Macías	ESP	11.8.84	10 Feb
4:10.28	Yelena	Korobkina	RUS	25.11.90	14 Feb		4:10.96	Elina	Sujew	GER	2.11.90	16 Feb
4:10.47	Svetlana	Podosyonova	RUS	24.5.88	14 Feb		4:11.02	Yelena	Soboleva	RUS	3.10.82	14 Feb
4:10.76	Danuta	Urbanik	POL	24.12.89	17 Feb		4:11.26	Diana	Sujew	GER	2.11.90	16 Feb

1 MILE

4:27.02	Sheila	Reid	CAN	2.8.89	1	Mill	New York (Armory)	16 Feb
4:28.25	Mary	Cain	USA-Y	3.5.96	2	Mill	New York (Armory)	16 Feb
4:28.79	Kate	Grace	USA	24.10.88	3	Mill	New York (Armory)	16 Feb

4:29.86	Emma	Coburn	USA	19.10.90	16 Feb		4:30.50	Hilary	Edmondson	CAN	7.8.81	16 Feb
4:30.03	Abbey	D'Agostino	USA	25.5.92	16 Feb		4:31.08	Amanda	Winslow	USA	13.8.90	9 Mar

2000m: 5:37.2+ Genzebe   Dibaba   ETH   8.2.91   1   in 3000   Stockholm   21 Feb

3000 METRES

8:26.95	Genzebe	Dibaba	ETH	8.2.91	1		Stockholm	21 Feb
8:35.28	Meseret	Defar	ETH	19.11.83	1		Karlsruhe	2 Feb
8:38.44+	Tirunesh	Dibaba	ETH	1.10.85	1	in 2M	Boston (Roxbury)	2 Feb
8:48.27	Svetlana	Kireyeva	RUS	12.6.87	1	NC	Moskva	12 Feb
8:49.31	Eilish	McColgan	GBR	25.11.90	2		Stockholm	21 Feb
8:50.10	Almaz	Ayana	ETH	21.10.91	3		Stockholm	21 Feb
8:50.16	Helen	Clitheroe	GBR	2.1.74	1	GP	Birmingham	16 Feb

8:50.42	Yelena	Korobkina	RUS	25.11.90	12 Feb	8:54.14	Almensch	Belete	BEL	26.7.89	7 Feb
8:50.76	Natalya	Aristarkhova	RUS	31.10.89	12 Feb	8:54.37	Fionnuala	Britton	IRL	24.9.84	21 Feb
8:51.04	Corinna	Harrer	GER	19.1.91	2 Feb	8:54.74#	Brianna	Felnagle	USA	9.12.86	26 Jan
8:52.00	Lauren	Howarth	GBR	21.4.90	16 Feb	8:55.06#	Kate	Grace	USA	24.10.88	26 Jan
8:52.48	Sara	Moreira	POR	17.10.85	7 Feb	8:55.41#	Abbey	D'Agostino	USA	25.5.92	26 Jan
8:52.86	Ancuta	Bobocel	ROU	3.10.87	16 Feb	8:56.06	Polina	Jelizarova	LAT	1.5.89	21 Feb
8:53.12	Siham	Hilali	MAR	2.5.86	21 Feb	8:57.01	Christine	Bardelle	FRA	16.8.74	7 Feb
8:53.89	Chelsea	Reilly	USA	9.5.89	16 Feb	8:57.17	Layes	Abdullayeva	AZE	29.5.91	2 Feb

2 MILES

9:13.17	Tirunesh	Dibaba	ETH	1.10.85	1	BIG	Boston (Roxbury)	2 Feb
9:37.97	Sheila	Reid	CAN	2.8.89	2	BIG	Boston (Roxbury)	2 Feb
9:38.68	Mary	Cain	USA-Y	3.5.96	3	BIG	Boston (Roxbury)	2 Feb

5000 METRES

15:21.66#	Betsy	Saina	KEN	30.6.88	1		Ames	9 Feb
15:33.66					2	NCAA	Fayetteville	8 Mar
15:25.47#	Aliphine	Tuliamok-Bolton	KEN	5.4.89	2		Ames	9 Feb
15:28.11	Abbey	D'Agostino	USA	25.5.92	1	NCAA	Fayetteville	8 Mar

2000 METRES STEEPLECHASE

6:05.29	Mariya	Bykova	RUS	7.11.89	1		Belgorod	22 Jan
6:09.13	Rimma	Rodko	RUS	4.11.87	1	NC	Moskva	13 Feb
6:11.29	Olga	Tarantinova	RUS	28.11.87	2		Belgorod	22 Jan
6:12.76	Yevdokiya	Bukina	RUS	10.2.93	2	NC	Moskva	13 Feb

3000mSt: 9:30.99 Valentyna Zhudina   UKR   12.3.83   1   Zaporizhzhya   29 Jan

60 METRES HURDLES

7.78	Brianna	Rollins	USA	18.8.91	1		Clemson	11 Jan
7.84	Yvette	Lewis	USA	16.3.85	1	Mill	New York (Armory)	16 Feb
7.89	Nevin	Yanit	TUR	16.2.86	1	EI	Göteborg	1 Mar
7.89	Alina	Talay	BLR	14.5.89	2	EI	Göteborg	1 Mar
7.93	Yuliya	Kondakova	RUS	4.12.81	1		Moskva	3 Feb
7.93A	Nia	Ali	USA	23.10.88	1	NC	Albuquerque	3 Mar
8.08					5	Mill	New York (Armory)	16 Feb
7.94	Veronica	Borsi	ITA	13.6.87	3	EI	Göteborg	1 Mar
7.95	Eline	Berings	BEL	28.5.86	1r2		Gent	2 Feb
7.95	Derval	O'Rourke	IRL	28.5.81	4	EI	Göteborg	1 Mar
7.96	Beate	Schrott	AUT	15.4.88	1r2		Wien	23 Feb
7.96	Tiffany	McReynolds	USA	4.12.91	2	NCAA	Fayetteville	9 Mar
7.97	Janay	DeLoach	USA	12.10.85	1		Boston (Allston)	26 Jan
7.97	Virginia	Crawford	USA	7.9.83	2	Mill	New York (Armory)	16 Feb
7.97A	Kristi	Castlin	USA	7.7.88	2	NC	Albuquerque	3 Mar
8.03					3	Mill	New York (Armory)	16 Feb
7.99	Tiffany	Porter	GBR	13.11.87	2		Boston (Allston)	26 Jan
8.00	Olga	Samylova	RUS	4.1.86	1h		Sankt Peterburg	20 Jan
8.00A	Queen	Harrison	USA	10.9.88	4	NC	Albuquerque	3 Mar
8.03					4	Mill	New York (Armory)	16 Feb
8.01	Sara	Aerts	BEL	25.1.84	1	NC	Gent	17 Feb

8.03	Lucie	Skrobáková	CZE	4.1.82	2 Feb	8.07	Aleksandra	Antonova	RUS	24.3.80	31 Jan
8.03	Marzia	Caravelli	ITA	23.10.81	2 Feb	8.07	Nadine	Hildebrand	GER	20.9.87	2 Feb
8.03	Reina-Flor	Okori	FRA	2.5.80	16 Feb	8.07	Loreal	Smith	USA	12.10.85	8 Feb
8.04	Svetlana	Topylina	RUS	6.1.85	31 Jan	8.07	Cindy	Billaud	FRA	11.3.86	16 Feb
8.04	Christina	Manning	USA	29.5.90	12 Feb	8.07	Nooralotta	Neziri	FIN	9.11.92	17 Feb
8.04	Alice	Decaux	FRA	10.4.85	16 Feb	8.08	Cassandra	Lloyd	USA	27.1.90	25 Jan
8.05	Sharona	Bakker	NED	12.4.90	1 Mar	8.08	Angela	Whyte	CAN	22.5.80	1 Feb
8.05A	LaTisha	Holden	USA	29.8.89	3 Mar	8.08	Micol	Cattaneo	ITA	14.5.82	1 Mar
8.06	Danielle	Carruthers	USA	22.12.79	8 Feb	8.08	Danielle	Williams	USA	10.10.89	9 Mar
8.06	Jasmin	Stowers	USA	23.9.91	24 Feb	8.09	Tatyana	Filatova	RUS	22.1.87	12 Feb

HIGH JUMP

2.00	Alessia	Trost	ITA	8.3.93	1		Trinec	29 Jan
1.99	Ruth	Beitia	ESP	1.4.79	1	EI	Göteborg	3 Mar
1.97	Tia	Hellebaut	BEL	16.2.78	1		Eaubonne	7 Feb
1.96	Ebba	Jungmark	SWE	10.3.87	2	EI	Göteborg	3 Mar

1.96	Emma	Green-Tregaro	SWE	8.12.84	3	EI	Göteborg	3 Mar
1.95	Mariya	Kuchina	RUS	14.1.93	1		Samara	16 Dec
1.95	Olena	Holosha	UKR	26.1.82	2		Eaubonne	7 Feb
1.95	Brigetta	Barrett	USA	24.12.90	1	NCAA	Fayetteville	8 Mar
1.94	Anja	Iljustsenko	EST	12.10.85	3		Arnstadt	2 Feb
1.93	Venelina	Veneva-Mateeva	BUL	13.6.74	2		Hustopece	26 Jan
1.93	Mélanie	Melfort	FRA	8.11.82	1	NC	Aubière	17 Feb
1.93	Ana	Simic	CRO	5.5.90	1	Balk	Istanbul	23 Feb
1.92	Kamila	Stepaniuk	POL	22.3.86	1		Spala	9 Feb
1.92A	Barbara	Szabó	HUN	17.2.90	1		Golden	8 Feb
1.92	Iryna	Herashchenko	UKR-J	10.3.95	2	NC	Sumy	15 Feb
1.92	My	Nordström	SWE	21.4.90	3	NC	Norrköping	17 Feb
1.92	Mirela	Demireva	BUL	28.9.89	Q	EI	Göteborg	2 Mar

1.91	Oksana	Starostina	RUS	1.4.88	9 Jan		1.90	Marina	Aitova	KAZ	13.9.82	26 Jan
1.91	Yuliya	Kostrova	RUS	20.8.91	13 Jan		1.90	Nadezhda	Dusanova	UZB	17.11.87	2 Feb
1.91	Esthera	Petre	ROU	13.5.90	26 Jan		1.90	Marie-Laurence	Jungfleisch	GER	7.10.90	2 Feb
1.91	Jeannelle	Scheper	LCA-J	21.11.94	9 Feb		1.90	Kateryna	Tabashnyk	UKR-J	15.6.94	6 Feb
1.91	Tatyana	Kivimyagi	RUS	23.6.84	13 Feb		1.90	Justyna	Kasprzycka	POL	20.8.87	6 Mar
1.91	Irina	Gordeyeva	RUS	9.10.86	13 Feb		1.89	Irina	Iliyeva	RUS-J	22.12.95	9 Jan
1.91	Daniela	Stanciu	ROU	15.10.87	23 Feb		1.89	Makeba	Alcide	LCA	24.2.90	25 Jan
1.90	Yekaterina	Kuntsevich	RUS	13.7.84	19 Jan		1.89	Viktoriya	Dobrynska	UKR	18.1.80	30 Jan
1.90	Yana	Maksimova	BLR	9.1.89	23 Jan		1.89	Nataliya	Hapchuk	UKR	15.11.88	30 Jan
1.90	Tynita	Butts	USA	10.690	25 Jan		1.89	Yekaterina	Bolshova	RUS	4.2.88	8 Feb
1.90	Alesya	Paklina	KGZ	22.6.88	26 Jan		1.89	Valeriya	Bogdanovich	BLR	1.5.92	2 Mar
1.90	Eleriin	Haas	EST	4.7.92	26 Jan		1.89A	Inika	McPherson	USA	29.9.86	3 Mar

POLE VAULT

5.02A	Jennifer	Suhr	USA	5.2.82	1	NC	Albuquerque	2 Mar
4.78	Yarisley	Silva	CUB	1.6.87	1		Stockholm	21 Feb
4.77	Holly	Bleasdale	GBR	2.11.91	1	NC	Sheffield	9 Feb
4.75A	Kylie	Hutson	USA	27.11.87	2	NC	Albuquerque	2 Mar
4.71	Anastasiya	Savchenko	RUS	15.11.89	2		Stockholm	21 Feb
4.67	Anna	Rogowska	POL	21.5.81	2	EI	Göteborg	2 Mar
4.65	Fabiana	Murer	BRA	16.3.81	2		Moskva	3 Feb
4.64	Jirina	Svobodová	CZE	20.5.86	3		Stockholm	21 Feb
4.62	Anzhelika	Sidorova	RUS	28.6.91	3	EI	Göteborg	2 Mar
4.60	Nikoléta	Kiriakopoúlou	GRE	21.3.86	3	Mast	Donetsk	9 Feb
4.60	Roberta	Bruni	ITA-J	8.3.94	1	NC	Ancona	17 Feb
4.60A	Mary	Saxer	USA	21.6.87	3	NC	Albuquerque	2 Mar
4.60A	Janice	Keppler	USA	22.3.87	4	NC	Albuquerque	2 Mar
4.56	Aleksandra	Kiryashova	RUS	21.8.85	1		Sankt Peterburg	17 Feb
4.55	Angelina	Zhuk	RUS	7.2.91	1		Moskva	25 Jan
4.55	Kristina	Gadschiew	GER	3.7.84	5	Mast	Donetsk	9 Feb
4.50	Morgann	LeLeux	USA	14.11.92	1		Fayetteville	25 Jan
4.50	Lyudmila	Yeremina	RUS	8.8.91	1		Irkutsk	26 Jan
4.50	Elizaveta	Ryzih	GER	27.9.88	3	v4N	Glasgow	26 Jan
4.50A	Becky	Holliday	USA	12.3.80	5	NC	Albuquerque	2 Mar
4.46	Katharina	Bauer	GER	12.6.90	Q	EI	Göteborg	1 Mar
4.46	Angelica	Bengtsson	SWE	8.7.93	9q	EI	Göteborg	1 Mar
4.45	April	Steiner-Bennett	USA	22.4.80	4		Boston (Allston)	26 Jan
4.45A	Ekateríni	Stefanídi	GRE	4.2.90	1		Flagstaff	1 Feb
4.45A	Tori	Pena	IRL	30.7.87	1		Flagstaff	14 Feb
4.45A	April	Kubishta	USA	5.7.85	2		Flagstaff	14 Feb
4.45	Minna	Nikkanen	FIN	9.4.88	4=		Stockholm	21 Feb
4.45	Martina	Schultze	GER	12.9.90	1	ACC	Blacksburg	22 Feb
4.45	Stélla-Iró	Ledáki	GRE	18.7.88	1	Balk	Istanbul	23 Feb
4.45	Natalya	Bartnovskaya	RUS	7.1.89	1	NCAA	Fayetteville	9 Mar
4.45	Jade	Reibold	USA	14.4.91	2	NCAA	Fayetteville	9 Mar
4.43	Sandy	Morris	USA	8.7.92	1		Fayetteville	1 Mar
4.42	Romana	Malacová	CZE	15.5.87	2		Praha	3 Feb
4.41	Bethany	Buell	USA	4.12.91	1		Vermillion	25 Feb

4.40	Yekaterina	Kazeka	RUS	7.10.90	9 Jan		4.40	Karla Rosa	da Silva	BRA	12.11.84	16 Feb
4.40A	Katy	Viuf	USA	23.5.87	18 Jan		4.40	Marion	Lotout	FRA	19.11.89	16 Feb
4.40	Martina	Strutz	GER	4.11.81	20 Jan		4.40	Giorgia	Benecchi	ITA	9.7.89	17 Feb
4.40	Sally	Peake	GBR	8.2.86	26 Jan		4.40		Ren Mengqian	CHN	4.10.93	29 Mar
4.40	Victoria	von Eynatten	GER	6.10.91	26 Jan		4.36	Melissa	Gergel	USA	24.4.89	13 Mar

LONG JUMP

7.01	Darya	Klishina	RUS	15.1.91	1	EI	Göteborg	2 Mar
7.00	Olga	Kucherenko	RUS	5.11.85	1		Krasnodar	20 Jan
6.90	Janay	DeLoach	USA	12.10.85	1	Mill	New York (Armory)	16 Feb
6.90	Eloyse	Lesueur	FRA	15.7.88	2	EI	Göteborg	2 Mar
6.85	Brittney	Reese	USA	9.9.86	2	Mill	New York (Armory)	16 Feb
6.78	Shara	Proctor	GBR	16.9.88	1	GP	Birmingham	16 Feb
6.76	Svetlana	Denyayeva	RUS	12.5.91	3	NC	Moskva	13 Feb
6.73	Ivana	Spanovic	SRB	10.5.90	1	Balk	Istanbul	23 Feb

Mark	First name	Surname	Nation	DOB	Pl	Meet	Venue	Date
6.71	Veronika	Mosina	RUS	17.10.90	1		Sankt Peterburg	28 Dec
6.71	Erica	Jarder	SWE	2.4.86	3	EI	Göteborg	2 Mar
6.69	Andrea	Geubelle	USA	21.6.91	1		New York (Armory)	1 Feb
6.68	Oksana	Zhukovskaya	RUS	12.9.84	1		Moskva	25 Jan
6.68	Melanie	Bauschke	GER	14.7.88	2		Karlsruhe	2 Feb
6.67	Margaryta	Tverdohlib	UKR	2.6.91	1		Donetsk	23 Feb
6.65A	Whitney	Gipson	USA	20.9.90	2	NC	Albuquerque	2 Mar
6.62	Anastasiya	Mokhnyuk	UKR	1.1.91	1		Kyiv	11 Jan
6.62	Cornelia	Deiac	ROU	20.3.88	1	NC	Bucuresti	10 Feb
6.60	Olga	Sudareva	BLR	22.2.84	1	NC	Mogilyov	6 Feb

Mark	First name	Surname	Nation	DOB	Date	Mark	First name	Surname	Nation	DOB	Date
6.59	Alina	Rotaru	ROU	5.6.93	10 Feb	6.55	Christabel	Nettey	CAN	2.6.91	8 Mar
6.59	Francine	Simpson	JAM	1.11.89	23 Feb	6.54	Stefanie	Voss	GER	9.9.89	3 Feb
6.58	Anastasiya	Mironchik-Ivanova	BLR	13.4.89	19 Jan	6.51	Evaggelía	Galéni	GRE	29.12.88	26 Jan
6.58	Bianca	Stuart	BAH	17.5.88	8 Feb	6.50	Florentina	Marincu	ROU-Y	8.4.96	10 Feb
6.57	Yekaterina	Bolshova	RUS	4.2.88	8 Feb	6.50	Iryna	Ilyina	RUS	25.5.85	12 Feb
6.57A	Alesha	Walker	USA	9.4.88	2 Mar	6.50A	Jessie	Gaines	USA	12.8.90	2 Mar

TRIPLE JUMP

Mark	First name	Surname	Nation	DOB	Pl	Meet	Venue	Date
14.88	Olga	Saladuha	UKR	4.6.83	1	EI	Göteborg	3 Mar
14.50	Natalya	Kutyakova	RUS	28.11.86	Q	NC	Moskva	13 Feb
14.48	Irina	Gumenyuk	RUS	6.1.88	1		Sankt Peterburg	6 Jan
14.42	Yekaterina	Koneva	RUS	25.9.88	1		Samara	31 Jan
14.41	Viktoriya	Dolgacheva	RUS	17.4.91	2	NC	Moskva	14 Feb
14.30	Veronika	Mosina	RUS	17.10.90	2		Sankt Peterburg	26 Jan
14.26	Simona	La Mantia	ITA	14.4.83	3	EI	Göteborg	3 Mar
14.24	Cristina	Bujin	ROU	12.4.88	1		Bucuresti	25 Jan
14.20	Trecia-Kaye	Smith	JAM	5.11.75	2	GP	Birmingham	16 Feb
14.19	Yekaterina	Chernenko	RUS	9.10.86	5	NC	Moskva	14 Feb
14.18	Andrea	Geubelle	USA	21.6.91	1	NCAA	Fayetteville	9 Mar
14.14	Gabriela	Petrova	BUL	29.6.92	1	NC	Dobrich	16 Feb
14.11	Valeriya	Zavyalova	RUS	16.1.88	6	NC	Moskva	14 Feb
14.09	Anna	Krylova	RUS	3.10.85	7	NC	Moskva	14 Feb
14.09		Wang Rong	CHN-Y	1.7.96	7		Nanjing	7 Mar
14.08A	Shanieka	Thomas	JAM	2.2.92	1		Albuquerque	8 Feb
14.07	Patricia	Sarrapio	ESP	16.11.82	5	EI	Göteborg	3 Mar
14.06		Li Xiaohong	CHN-J	8.1.95	2		Nanjing	7 Mar
14.04	Dana	Veldáková	SVK	3.6.81	1		Gent	10 Feb
14.02	Alsu	Murtazina	RUS	12.12.87	8	NC	Moskva	14 Feb

Mark	First name	Surname	Nation	DOB	Date	Mark	First name	Surname	Nation	DOB	Date
13.99	Gita	Dodova	BUL	2.5.82	12 Feb	13.86	Anastasiya	Juravlyeva	UZB	9.10.81	26 Feb
13.99	Patricia	Mamona	POR	21.11.88	1 Mar	13.84	Svetlana	Bolshakova	BEL	14.10.84	10 Feb
13.96	Svetlana	Denyayeva	RUS	12.5.91	19 Jan	13.82	Nathalie	Marie-Nelly	FRA	24.11.86	17 Feb
13.96	Jenny	Elbe	GER	18.4.90	20 Jan	13.82		Sun Yan	CHN	30.3.91	7 Mar
13.96	Kseniya	Detsuk	BLR	23.4.86	16 Feb	13.81	Níki	Panétta	GRE	21.4.86	26 Jan
13.95	Yamilé	Aldama	GBR	14.8.72	3 Mar	13.81		Hu Qian	CHN	14.1.89	7 Mar
13.94	Susana	Costa	POR	22.9.84	24 Feb	13.79	Ruslana	Tsyhotska	UKR	23.3.86	15 Feb
13.91	Kristin	Gierisch	GER	20.8.90	8 Feb	13.78		Xie Limei	CHN	27.6.86	7 Mar
13.89	Tatyana	Lebedeva	RUS	21.7.76	8 Feb	13.75	Ana	Peleteiro	ESP-J	2.12.95	17 Feb
13.88	Carmen	Toma	ROU	28.3.89	25 Jan	13.69	Ciarra	Brewer	USA	12.3.93	9 Mar

SHOT

Mark	First name	Surname	Nation	DOB	Pl	Meet	Venue	Date
20.75	Valerie	Adams	NZL	6.10.84	1		Auckland	2 Mar
19.88		Gong Lijiao	CHN	24.1.89	1		Beijing	29 Mar
19.79	Christina	Schwanitz	GER	24.12.85	1	NC	Dortmund	23 Feb
19.41	Michelle	Carter	USA	12.10.85	1	NC	Albuquerque	3 Mar
19.24	Yevgeniya	Kolodko	RUS	2.7.90	1	NC	Moskva	13 Feb
19.22	Tia	Brooks	USA	2.8.90	1	NCAA	Fayetteville	9 Mar
19.10	Jeneva	McCall	USA	28.10.89	1		Carbondale	8 Dec
19.06	Alena	Kopets	BLR	14.2.88	1		Mogilyov	19 Jan
18.81		Liu Xiangrong	CHN	6.6.88	1		Nanjing	6 Mar
18.67	Anca	Heltne	ROU	1.1.78	1		Bollnas	19 Feb
18.37	Chiara	Rosa	ITA	28.1.83	4	EI	Göteborg	3 Mar
18.31	Irina	Tarasova	RUS	15.4.87	5	EI	Göteborg	3 Mar
18.25	Nadine	Kleinert	GER	20.10.75	2		Sassnitz	27 Jan
18.24	Halyna	Obleshchuk	UKR	23.2.89	1		Ivano-Frankivsk	13 Jan
18.24	Olha	Holodnaya	UKR	14.11.91	1		Zaporizhzhya	29 Jan
18.16	Josephine	Terlecki	GER	17.2.86	6	EI	Göteborg	3 Mar
18.10	Vera	Yepimashko	BLR	10.7.76	2		Mogilyov	19 Jan

Mark	First name	Surname	Nation	DOB	Date	Mark	First name	Surname	Nation	DOB	Date
17.87	Alyona	Dubitskaya	BLR	25.1.90	5 Feb	17.48	Alyssa	Hasslen	USA	13.5.91	9 Feb
17.80	Felisha	Johnson	USA	24.7.89	26 Jan	17.46		Meng Qianqian	CHN	6.1.91	6 Mar
17.69	Christina	Hillman	USA	6.10.93	9 Mar	17.40		Ma Qiao	CHN	28.9.89	6 Mar
17.66	Shanice	Craft	GER	15.5.93	23 Feb	17.35	Anna	Jelmini	USA	15.7.90	14 Feb
17.55	Anna	Omarova	RUS	3.10.81	13 Feb	17.34	Anita	Márton	HUN	15.1.89	23 Feb
17.52	Julie	Labonté	CAN	12.1.90	9 Mar	17.34	Helena	Engman	SWE	16.6.76	2 Mar
17.49	Úrsula	Ruíz	ESP	11.8.83	2 Feb	17.32	Radoslava	Mavrodieva	BUL	13.3.87	2 Mar

Drugs disqualification: 18.66 Yevgeniya Solovyova RUS 28.6.86 (2) NC Moskva 13 Feb

20 LB WEIGHT

24.70	Gwendolyn	Berry	USA	29.6.89	1	NC	Albuquerque	2 Mar
23.94	Jeneva	McCall	USA	28.10.89	1		Carbondale	11 Jan
23.68	Amber	Campbell	USA	5.6.81	2	NC	Albuquerque	2 Mar
23.52	Felisha	Johnson	USA	24.7.89	1	NCAA	Fayetteville	8 Mar
22.31	Beth	Rohl	USA	7.11.90	2	NCAA	Fayetteville	8 Mar
22.30	Britney	Waller	USA	31.8.91	3		Blacksburg	8 Feb

21.76	Alena	Krechyk	BLR	20.7.87	2 Feb		21.51	Brittany	Smith	USA	25.3.91	8 Dec
21.61	Dani	Bunch	USA	16.5.91	23 Feb		21.50	Sam	Lockhart	USA	25.8.91	23 Feb
21.61	Brittany	Funk	USA	13.5.92	2 Mar		21.50	Taylor	Smith	USA	20.7.91	23 Feb
21.57	Denise	Hinton	USA	17.12.91	15 Feb		21.34	Victoria	Flowers	USA	17.1.90	16 Feb

PENTATHLON

4851	Yekaterina	Bolshova	RUS	4.2.88	1	NC	Volgograd	9 Feb
	8.50	1.89	13.40	6.57		2:10.53		
4666	Antoinette	Nana Djimou	FRA	2.8.85	1	EI	Göteborg	1 Mar
	8.12	1.75	15.35	6.32		2:20.62		
4658	Yana	Maksimova	BLR	9.1.89	2	EI	Göteborg	1 Mar
	8.63	1.90	14.65	5.94		2:14.84		
4623	Anna	Melnychenko	UKR	24.4.83	1	NC	Zaporizhzhya	29 Jan
	8.30	1.80	13.30	6.39		2:17.01		
4622	Alina	Fyodorova	UKR	31.7.89	1	NC	Sumy	13 Feb
	8.75	1.85	14.94	6.16		2:17.20		
4615	Aleksandra	Butvina	RUS	14.2.86	1		Sankt Peterburg	6 Jan
	8.34	1.82	12.83	6.24		2:20.86		
4571	Remona	Fransen	NED	25.11.85	4	EI	Göteborg	1 Mar
	8.43	1.81	13.42	6.29		2:17.88		
4569	Makeba	Alcide	LCA	24.2.90	1	SEC	Fayetteville	22 Feb
	8.35	1.87	12.32	6.15		2:16.37		
4558	Nafissatou	Thiam	BEL-J	19.8.94	1	NC	Gent	3 Feb
	8.65	1.84	14.00	56.30		2:21.18		
4531	Sofia	Linde	SWE-J	12.1.95	5	EI	Göteborg	1 Mar
	8.36	1.78	14.14	6.12		2:18.77		
4507	Anastasiya	Mokhnyuk	UKR	1.1.91	2	NC	Sumy	13 Feb
	8.34	1.82	12.83	6.24		2:20.86		
4478A	Sharon	Day	USA	9.6.85	1	NC	Albuquerque	1 Mar
	8.57	1.82	15.07	5.82		2:20.86		
4470	Ulyana	Aleksandrova	RUS	1.1.91	1	NCp	Belgorod	27 Feb
	8.76	1.86	12.67	6.42		2:24.14		
4463	Julia	Mächtig	GER	1.1.86	7	EI	Göteborg	1 Mar
	8.95	1.75	15.97	5.98		2:17.47		
4454	Yekaterina	Netsvetayeva	BLR	26.6.89	1		Gomel	17 Feb
	8.55	1.73	14.49	5.94		2:14.57		
4436	Nadine	Broersen	NED	29.4.90	2	v4N	Valencia	26 Jan
	8.44	1.83	13.02	5.81		2:16.68		
4399	Erica	Bougard	USA	26.7.93	1	NCAA	Fayetteville	8 Mar
	8.34	1.75	11.00	6.11		2:10.80		
4395	Beatrice	Puiu	ROU	1.1.86	1	NC	Bucuresti	18 Feb
	8.48	1.81	13.51	6.14		2:27.16		
4372	Ellinore	Hallin	SWE	12.8.87	9	EI	Göteborg	1 Mar
	8.43	1.72	13.71	5.97	2:18.37			

4349	Yunna	Dmitriyeva	RUS	7.7.88	6 Jan		4271A	Sami	Spenner	USA	21.3.91	1 Mar
4333A	Bettie	Wade	USA	11.9.86	1 Mar		4261	Vanessa	Spínola	BRA	5.3.90	2 Feb
4327	Shakeia	Pinnick	USA	23.1.91	8 Mar		4256	Eliska	Klucinová	CZE	14.4.88	9 Feb
4320	Yelena	Molodchinina	RUS	16.4.91	27 Feb		4240	Ivana	Spanovic	SRB	10.5.90	19 Jan
4301A	Lindsay	Lettow	USA	6.6.90	1 Mar		4228	Lucie	Ondraschková	CZE	12.10.89	8 Mar
4296	Laura	Ikauniece	LAT	31.5.92	2 Feb		4209	Tatyana	Tarasova	RUS	2.10.90	9 Feb
4274	Ellen	Sprunger	SUI	5.8.86	10 Feb		4209	Martina	Salander	SWE	11.2.92	8 Mar

3000 METRES WALK

11:57.86	Olga	Kaniskina	RUS	19.1.85	1		Samara	31 Jan
12:21.40	Katarzyna	Kwoka	POL	29.6.85	1	NC	Spala	17 Feb
12:21.56	Ana	Cabecinha	POR	29.4.84	1		Pombal	16 Feb
12:24.41	Brigita	Virbalyte	LTU	1.2.85	1		Kaunas	2 Feb
12:25.36	Ines	Henriques	POR	1.5.80	2		Pombal	16 Feb

| 12:31.62 | Paulina | Buziak | POL | 16.12.86 | 17 Feb | | 12:38.0 | Olga | Shargina | RUS-Y | 96 | 6 Jan |
| | | | | | | | 12:38.43 | Lyudmila | Olyanovska | UKR | 20.2.93 | 11 Jan |

5000 METRES WALK

21:12.00	Irina	Yumanova	RUS	6.11.90	1		Novocheboksarsk	12 Jan
21:48.28	Inna	Kashyna	UKR	27.9.91	1	NC	Sumy	13 Feb
21:52.0	Natalya	Makarova	RUS	17.4.87	1		Chelyabinsk	6 Jan